THE KOVELS'
COMPLETE
ANTIQUES PRICE LIST

BOOKS BY RALPH AND TERRY KOVEL

Dictionary of Marks—Pottery and Porcelain

A Directory of American Silver, Pewter and Silver
    Plate

American Country Furniture, 1780–1875

Know Your Antiques,® Revised

The Kovels' Complete Antiques Price List

The Kovels' Complete Bottle Price List

The Kovels' Collector's Guide to American Art
    Pottery

Kovels' Organizer for Collectors

The Kovels' Price Guide for Collector Plates, Figurines,
    Paperweights, and Other Limited Editions

TWELFTH EDITION

THE KOVELS'
COMPLETE
ANTIQUES PRICE LIST

A guide to the 1979–1980 market for professionals,
dealers, and collectors

by Ralph and Terry Kovel

ILLUSTRATED

Crown Publishers, Inc., New York

To Vickie
who isn't an antique but a welcome addition
to the collection anyhow
and of course
to
Kim and Lee

Inquiries should be addressed to Crown Publishers, Inc., One Park Avenue, New York, N.Y. 10016

Printed in the United States of America

Published simultaneously in Canada by General Publishing Company Limited
Library of Congress Catalog Card Number: 72-84290
ISBN: 0-517-538792

INTRODUCTION

The pressures of inflation, the movement of the American dollar, and a greater interest in antiques and collectibles as an investment have again pushed up the prices for the entire antiques market. Worldwide, the prices for fine paintings, top-quality Chinese porcelains, Lalique, Gallé, and Art Nouveau furniture have been among the most popular items. The political situation in Iran caused prices to drop in the Oriental rug market, but by June of 1979 prices bounced back to the earlier levels. Top-quality American furniture, photographs, Victorian jewelry, Tiffany, toys, dolls, quality folk art, and art pottery seem to be advancing in price faster than inflation or the other areas of collecting.

A few prices are lower if the inflated dollar is not considered. Collector plates, pewter, bottles, and some types of art glass remain at the same or lower levels. Plated American silver, Royal Doulton, Hummel Goebel, Fiesta ware and related twentieth-century pieces, advertising art, eighteenth-century English porcelain, and Victorian furniture increased in price.

Record auction prices were set for many antiques, but prices are confusing because most of the announced auction prices do not include the extra 10 percent charged as a buyer's premium.

An American folk art sale brought over $1,300,000, which was a record for an auction of that type. A wood carving of Captain M. Starbuck sold for $30,000; a molded copper weathervane of an Indian at $25,000; a Canadian goose decoy for $12,500; a mourning picture for $9,500; a theorem painting for $3,250. There is no doubt that the extra dollars were paid because the pieces were from a famous collection, often exhibited in museums and pictured in books.

English porcelain, a collecting field that has seen little movement in the past ten years, has begun to interest the collectors. A Derby porcelain mug commemorating Nelson's Nile Victory sold in London for $10,500; a pair of Worcester bough pots brought $8,500, while a Worcester coffeepot sold for $7,900.

Rookwood prices surprised many buyers. A decorated vase with a full-length portrait of an Indian sold in Ohio for a record $3,600, while a Rookwood vase with thistles brought $3,200 at a sale in Massachusetts. Other records for porcelain included $22,000 for a KPM plaque of the Sabine women that was made about 1874 and $2,500 for a Goss china piece called "St. Iltyd's Font." A stoneware inkwell marked "C. Crolius Manufacturer, Manhattan-Wells, New York," sold for $1,600.

American furniture has continued to set records: an amazing $140,000 was realized for a Goddard-Townsend Chippendale mahogany block-front desk c. 1765; a John Hurd Chippendale carved mahogany serpentine front desk and bookcase, c. 1770, brought $65,000; while a Chippendale 5-legged mahogany card table was sold for $55,000. The record high was $176,000 (buyer's premium included) for a pair of Philadelphia Queen Anne walnut side chairs c. 1750.

Other interesting furniture records include $1,760,000 for a Louis XV cabinet; $196,000 for a table attributed to Thomas Chippendale; $13,000 for a Charles Mackintosh chair; $16,000 for a set of 6 painted American fancy chairs; $8,000 for a Belter table; $42,000 for a three-piece Belter parlor set; $990 for a set of 6 pressed-back oak chairs; and $14,750 for a mission oak Gustav Stickley desk and chair sold in Maine.

Photographs have been popular and the interest is still growing. Records for the year range from $3,960 for a portrait of Richard Wagner to $15,000 for an albumen print of a steamship launching. Other prices: $13,000 for 14 Brady prints; $6,250 for a photograph by Ansel Adams, a living photographer. Cameras are still in demand, and a Lewis-style bellows camera sold for $7,250.

Glass records included $2,650 for a blue inkwell made at the Mount Vernon Glass Works, New York, c. 1820–40. A triple overlay Gallé lamp sold for $42,000; a Lalique vase sold for $26,000; and at a reported private sale a Henry Clay flask sold for $30,000.

Tiffany records are made each year. A jack-in-the-pulpit vase sold for $17,000; a lava glass vase for $19,000; a spiderweb lamp sold for $150,000; a dragonfly lamp for $28,000; and a wisteria lamp for $120,000.

Toys keep rising and continue to sell well in all parts of the country. A cast-iron mechanical bank more than doubled the previous record with $18,500 for a "Jonah and the Whale" that was sold in Pennsylvania. A Dinky toy Pickford's van of 1934 sold in London for $707; an 1890 Pratt and Letchworth cast-iron artillery toy sold for $9,500 in Connecticut. Dolls are still popular. A set of

5 Dionne Quintuplet dolls went for $800 in Pennsylvania; a bisque-headed BeBe brought $10,890 in England. A Kammer and Reinhardt googly doll was $6,000 in Pennsylvania, and a Kammer and Reinhardt character doll sold in England for $7,638.

Record prices have appeared in all areas. A Lalique necklace sold for $41,000; a lace maker's bobbin dated 1871 sold at $223; a Chinese snuff bottle for $17,000; an Indian basket for $16,000; and a violin bow for $21,000.

Collectible records include a "Perils of Pauline" movie poster for $2,100; $5,367 for a Charles Evans Hughes political button; $1,300 for a silk handkerchief commemorating a cricket match; $3,750 for a barn louvre; $800 for an AJS-type 64-valve radio receiver; and $417 for Queen Victoria's bloomers. What next?

HENRY FRANCIS DU PONT WINTERTHUR MUSEUM COLOR PICTURES

Imagine over 100 rooms built with period walls and woodwork, furnished with period furniture, rugs, draperies, porcelains, and silver, and placed in one building so the collector can view it with ease. The Henry Francis du Pont Winterthur Museum in Winterthur, Delaware, is this type of building. Henry Francis du Pont started collecting American decorative and fine arts and rebuilding the family home at Winterthur in 1927. The original three-story house had been built in 1839, and many additions from that time have created the present large building.

Visitors may see several different views of the Winterthur collection. A one-hour chronological sample tour of the collection is available each day the museum is open. Just walk in. Tours of the main building can be easily arranged on a reservation basis. Telephone 302-656-9581 or write ahead to Winterthur Museum, Winterthur, Delaware 19735 for reservations. If you have a very special interest in one type of object, tell the museum when you make the reservations and they will try to furnish the proper guide. Both half-day and full-day tours are planned with a special guide for each small group. Lunch is available in the museum cafeteria. Visitors can also visit the 963 acres of woodlands and gardens.

The richness of the Winterthur collection makes it difficult to describe. Visitors are taken directly into the rooms, as if it were a visit to a friend's home. No glass walls or ropes distract from the interiors.

The color pictures in this book reflect the range of the collection. Six style periods are included: seventeenth century, William and Mary, Queen Anne, Chippendale, Federal, and Empire. Special collections include folk art, Shaker materials, exterior architecture, and miniatures. Collectors of ceramics, metal, textiles, rugs, needlework, and, of course, furniture and paintings will be delighted. Those who wish to view the rooms as examples of interior design will be equally pleased.

The museum is open to the public year round from 10 A.M. to 4 P.M. Tuesday through Saturday, and noon to 4 P.M. Sundays except for major holidays. Winterthur is on Route 52, six miles northwest of Wilmington, Delaware, in the heart of Brandywine Valley. The reserved tours are not advised for those with trouble walking; the sampler tour is suitable for such visitors. Children under 12 are not admitted.

SPECIAL THANKS

Our special thanks to Dr. James Morton Smith, Director of Winterthur Museum, who has become a special "antique" friend and has survived the snow and travel problems with us. The staff at Winterthur made our job so easy, and to them another special thanks: Susan Swan, Registrar's office; Alberta Brandt, Registrar's office; and Katherine Wheeler, Public Relations office. To the guides, curators, and others who have helped us through the years to appreciate the collections at Winterthur, we add a special word of gratitude.

GUIDE TO USE

There are just a few simple rules to follow in using this book. Each listing is arranged in the following manner: CATEGORY (such as pressed glass, silver, or furniture); OBJECT (such as vase, spoon, table); DESCRIPTION (which includes as much information as possible about size, age, color, and pattern). Pressed glass is the only exception to this rule, and it is listed CATEGORY, PATTERN, OBJECT, DESCRIPTION. All items are presumed to be in good condition, undamaged, unless otherwise noted. Leaf through the book and examine the various category headings. Most of them are exactly as one would expect.

Several special categories were formed to make a more sensible listing of items possible. "Fire" includes fire-fighting equipment, fireplace equipment, and related pieces. "Kitchen" and "tool" include special equipment. As it would be unreasonable to expect the casual collector to know the proper name for each variety of tool, such as an "adze" or a "trephine," we have lumped them together in the special categories. Other special categories are "commemorative," "store," "nautical," "weapon," and "railroad."

This book has several idiosyncrasies of style that must be noted before it can be used properly. The prices are compiled by computer, and the machine has dictated several strange rules. Everything in the book is listed alphabetically according to the IBM alphabetic system. This means that words such as "mt." are alphabetized as "M-T," not as "M-O-U-N-T." Another peculiarity of the machine alphabetizing is that all numerals come after all letters, thus 2 comes after z. A quick glance at a listing will make this clear, as the alphabetizing is consistent throughout the book.

No price over $9,999 can be listed.

We have made several editorial decisions that affect the use of the book. A bowl is a bowl and not a dish unless it is a special type of dish, such as a pickle dish. A butter dish is a "butter" and a celery dish is a "celery." A salt dish is called a "salt" to differentiate it from a saltshaker. A toothpick holder is called a "toothpick." It is always a "sugar and creamer," never a "creamer and sugar." Where one dimension is given, it is the height of the piece, or if the object is round, the dimension is the diameter. Height of a picture is listed before width. Glass is clear unless a color is indicated.

This book does not include price listings of fine-art paintings, books, comic books, stamps, coins, and a few other categories that are covered in specialized books. Prices for collector's editions and bottles are included, although both are more completely reported in *Kovels' Price Guide for Collector Plates, Figurines, Paperweights, and Other Limited Editions* and *Kovels' Complete Bottle Price List.*

Several categories such as "milk glass" and "bottles" include special reference numbers. These numbers refer the reader to the most widely known books about the category. When these numbers appear, the name of the special book is given in the paragraph heading. All of these numbers take the form "B-22," "McK-G-11," and so forth. The letter is the author's initial; the number refers to a picture in the author's book.

All black-and-white pictures in *Kovels' Complete Antiques Price List* are of antiques sold during the past year. The prices are as reported by the seller. Each piece pictured is listed with the word "illus." as part of the description. Pictures are placed as close to the price listing as is possible. Color pictures are all from the collections of the Henry Francis du Pont Winterthur Museum, and no prices are given for these antiques.

All prices included in this book are reports, not estimates. This means that at some sales in the United States between June 1978 and June 1979 the antiques described were offered for sale at the prices we have listed. A few prices are from auctions, but most are from shops and shows. The prices have been taken from sales in all parts of the country, and the variations are due to the geographic differences in pricing. We feel this is as accurate a method of reporting as is possible. Every price has been checked for accuracy, but we cannot be responsible for any errors that may have occurred. We welcome any suggestions for future editions of this book but cannot answer letters asking for advice or appraisals.

Ralph M. Kovel, American Society of Appraisers, Senior Member
Terry H. Kovel, American Society of Appraisers, Senior Member

AN IMPORTANT ANNOUNCEMENT TO COLLECTORS AND DEALERS

Each year *The Kovels' Complete Antiques Price List* is completely rewritten. Every entry is new because of the rapidly changing antiques market. The only way so complete a revision can be accomplished is by using a computer, making it possible to publish the bound book two months after the last price is received.

Yet many price changes occur between editions of *The Kovels' Complete Antiques Price List.* Important sales produce new record prices each day. Inflation, the changing price of silver and gold, and the international demand for some types of antiques influence sales in the United States.

The collector will want to keep up with developments from month to month. Therefore, we call your attention to a new service to provide price information almost instantaneously: *Kovels on Antiques and Collectables,* a nationally distributed illustrated newsletter, published monthly.

This new monthly newsletter covers prices, special interest antiques, what to buy, how to buy or sell antiques, forums and classes to attend, refinishing and first aid for your possessions, marks, book reviews, and other pertinent antiques news.

Information about the newsletter is available from the authors at P.O. Box 22200, Beachwood, Ohio 44122.

PICTURE ACKNOWLEDGMENTS

Americana Mail Auction; Jay Anderson Antiques; James Bayman; Richard A. Bourne Co.; C. B. Charles Galleries; Christie's; Robert C. Eldred Co., Inc.; Fleetville Auctions; O. Rundle Gilbert; Donald Hall; Gene Harris; Hog Eye Antiques; Julia's Auction Service; Kinzle Auction Service; Kruse Auction Co.; The Magnificent Doll; Manor House Galleries; Milwaukee Auction Gallery; Morton's Auction Exchange; Nostalgia Co.; Phillips; Nicholas Pine; Plaza Auction Galleries; Richard's Antiques; Bob, Chuck & Rich Roan Inc.; Robert W. Skinner Gallery; Sotheby Parke Bernet; Auctions by Theriault; Woody Auctions.

THE KOVELS'
COMPLETE
ANTIQUES PRICE LIST

A WALTER NANCY.

Almaric Walter made pate-de-verre glass under contract at the Daum glassworks, 1908 to 1914. He started his own firm in Nancy, France, in 1919. Pieces made before 1914 are signed "Daum, Nancy" with a cross. After 1919 the signature is "A. Walter Nancy."

A.Walter, Bowl, Head Of Bacchus, Nancy, Signed, Pate De Verre, 6 In.Diam.	2250.00
A.Walter, Pendant, Beetle, Pate De Verre, Impressed A.W.	475.00
A.Walter, Pendant, Pate De Verre	750.00
A.Walter, Plaque, Locust With Shafts Of Wheat, Pate De Verre, Signed, 3 In.	495.00
A.Walter, Tray, Pin, Red Beetles, Pate De Verre, Signed, Nancy, 6 1/2 In.	150.00

ABC plates, or children's alphabet plates, were popular from 1780 to 1860. The letters on the plate were meant as teaching aids for the children who were learning to read. The plates were made of pottery, porcelain, metal, or glass.

ABC, Book, Linen	9.00
ABC, Pitcher, Animals, German, 3 1/4 In.	22.00
ABC, Plate, Baby, Alphabet Around Rim, Jack & Jill In Center, Germany	25.00
ABC, Plate, Boy & Trio Of Dogs Raiding Banquet Table	52.00
ABC, Plate, Boy Fishing	40.00
ABC, Plate, Brown Transfer Of Sheep, Thoroughbreds, Porcelain, 6 1/4 In.	39.00
ABC, Plate, Brownie, Tin, Patent 1896, 9 In.	67.50
ABC, Plate, Busy Bee, Staffordshire, 6 In.	65.00
ABC, Plate, Child's Feeding Dish, 3 Bears Roller Skating	26.00
ABC, Plate, Child's Head In Center, Satin Finish, 8 In.	15.00
ABC, Plate, Child's, Staffordshire, Small	30.00
ABC, Plate, Children & Cat, Playing At Lovers, 6 In.	13.00
ABC, Plate, Children & Dogs	45.00
ABC, Plate, Children Playing Marbles	34.50
ABC, Plate, Civil War General Winfred Scott	100.00
ABC, Plate, Clock In Center, Numbers, Alphabet	30.00
ABC, Plate, Clowns & Performing Dog	55.00
ABC, Plate, Cock Robin, Tin, 8 In.	38.00
ABC, Plate, Cow, Adams, England	35.00
ABC, Plate, Crusoe At Work, Sepia Transfer, Signed, 7 1/4 In.	50.00
ABC, Plate, Crusoe, Tunstall, England, 8 1/4 In.	39.00
ABC, Plate, Daisy Center, Clear, 6 In.	30.00
ABC, Plate, Dog Head Center, Clear, 6 In., Higbee	25.00
ABC, Plate, Dutch Windmill, Cottage Scene, Staffordshire	27.50
ABC, Plate, Elephant Center, Clear, 6 In.	25.00
ABC, Plate, Farm Scene, Haywagon & Oxen, 4 In.	35.00
ABC, Plate, Feeding, Stork Center, Green Glass, 7 1/2 In.	55.00
ABC, Plate, Fishing Scene, 7 1/2 In.	35.00
ABC, Plate, Floral Center, 6 1/2 In.	16.00
ABC, Plate, Franklin's Proverb, Put Out The Kitchen Fire	35.00
ABC, Plate, Frosted Child's Head Center, Vaseline	32.00
ABC, Plate, Hand-Painted Chickens, Porcelain, Germany, 6 1/4 In.	39.00
ABC, Plate, Horse, Rider, Brown Transfer, C.1845, Staffordshire, 7 1/4 In.	35.00
ABC, Plate, Hunters & Dogs	28.50
ABC, Plate, Hunting Scene	45.00
ABC, Plate, International Exhibition, 1881, Scene, 3 In.	75.00
ABC, Plate, Kangaroo, English Registry Mark, 6 1/2 In.	20.00
ABC, Plate, Mary Had A Little Lamb, Tin	40.00
ABC, Plate, Miss Muffet, China, 6 1/2 In.	35.00
ABC, Plate, Months, Days Of Week Border, Clock Face Center, 7 In.	40.00
ABC, Plate, Mother With Child In Cradle, 7 In.	35.00
ABC, Plate, Nursery Rhyme, Marked McNicol	37.00
ABC, Plate, Octagonal, Joseph's Two Dreams, Luster Border, 7 In.	45.00
ABC, Plate, Old Mother Hubbard	46.00
ABC, Plate, Peacock, Alphabet, 7 In.	35.00
ABC, Plate, Proverb, There Are No Gains Without Pains	35.00
ABC, Plate, Punch & Judy, 6 1/2 In.	35.00
ABC, Plate, Puss & Boots	35.00
ABC, Plate, Red Riding Hood	29.50
ABC, Plate, Sancho & Dapple Center, Clear, 6 In.	35.00
ABC, Plate, Silver Plated	25.00
ABC, Plate, Stag & Fawn, 7 In.	35.00
ABC, Plate, Sunbonnet, I Love You	58.00

ABC, Plate, The Blind Girl, Ironstone, 6 In. 45.00
ABC, Plate, The First Nibble, Hard Paste 65.00
ABC, Plate, Tom & Dick Playing At Horses, Staffordshire, 5 1/8 In. 38.00
ABC, Plate, Who Killed Cock Robin, Tin, 8 In. 45.00
ABC, Plate, Wild Animals, The Lion, Marked Tunstall, England 45.00
ABC, Plate, Willie & His Rabbit 45.00
ABC, Plate, 3 Boys Reading Letter, Staffordshire, Impressed Mark, 5 In. 30.00
ABC, Table Set, Knife, Fork, Spoon, Steel 12.00
Abingdon, Bowl, Centerpiece, White, 7 X 18 In. 8.00

Adams china was made by William Adams and Sons of Staffordshire,
England. The firm was founded in 1769 and is still working.
Adams, see also Flow Blue
Adams, Barrel, Biscuit, Signed, 6 1/2 In. 145.00
Adams, Chocolate Pot, Calyx Ware, Floral Design, C.1895, Bud Finial 80.00
Adams, Plate, Audubon Baltimore Oriole, 10 1/4 In. 20.00
Adams, Plate, Grecian Font, Pink, 9 1/2 In. 25.00
Adams, Plate, Rose, Rabbit & Frog Border, 9 In. 35.00
Advertising, see Store

Agata glass was made by Joseph Locke of the New England Glass
Company of Cambridge, Massachusetts, after 1885. A metallic stain was
applied to New England Peachblow and the mottled design characteristic of
agata appeared.
Agata, Bottle, Snuff, Hollowed Inside, Polished Exterior 175.00
Agata, Bowl, Ruffled Top, 2 1/2 X 5 1/4 In.Diameter 950.00
Agata, Box, Oval, 19th Century, 1 1/2 In. 90.00
Agata, Toothpick 600.00

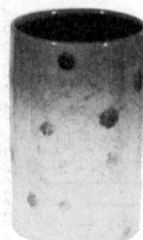

Agata, Tumbler

Agata, Tumbler .... *Illus* 550.00
Agata, Tumbler, Raspberry, Blue Black Oil Spots, Gold Staining 995.00
Agata, Vase, Lily, Gold Mottling, Rose Shading To White, 9 In. 2250.00
Agata, Vase, Lily, Wild Rose Color, 6 In. 700.00
Agata, Vase, Lily, 8 In. 1275.00
Agate, Bowl, Striated, Signed George Wild, 7 1/4 X 4 1/2 X 2 In. 900.00
Agate, Epergne, Circular Razzas, Square Pedestal, 19th Century, 14 7/8 In. 150.00
Agate, Figurine, Anteater, Diamond Eyes, Striated Agate, 2 X 3 1/4 In. 565.00
Agate, Figurine, Chimpanzee With Diamond Eyes, Striated, 2 1/2 In. 515.00
Agate, Figurine, Drunken Monkey With Bottle, Signed, L.Freres, 1900s, 3 In. 600.00
Agate, Figurine, Horse, Running In Oriental Manner, Carved Mineral, 5 In. 90.00
Agate, Figurine, Kangaroo, Diamond Eyes, Juchem, Oberstein, German, 3 In. 475.00
Airplane, Propeller, Miller, Iowa, 6 Feet 160.00

Akro agate glass was made in Clarksburg, West Virginia, from 1932 to
1951. Before that time the firm made children's glass marbles. Most of the
glass is marked with a crow flying through the letter A.
Akro Agate, Ashtray, Blue & White Shell 2.25
Akro Agate, Ashtray, Blue & White Veined, Leaf Shape 4.00
Akro Agate, Ashtray, Ellipsoid, Red & White Marbleized 7.00
Akro Agate, Ashtray, Iron Bunny 12.50
Akro Agate, Cornucopia, Miniature, Blue & White 8.00
Akro Agate, Cup & Saucer, Child's 4.00
Akro Agate, Cup, Pumpkin, Concentric Ring 7.00

Akro Agate, Jar, Covered, Blue	48.00
Akro Agate, Jar, Covered, Colonial Lady	48.00
Akro Agate, Jar, Mexicali, Sombrero Lid, 4 1/2 In.	30.00
Akro Agate, Jar, Powder, Covered, Colonial Girl, Blue	60.00
Akro Agate, Jar, Powder, Pink Lady	36.00
Akro Agate, Jar, Powder, Scottie Dog, White	38.00
Akro Agate, Match Holder, Cobalt, 8 Sided, 2 3/4 In.	12.00
Akro Agate, Planter, Orange & White Swirl, Signed	15.00
Akro Agate, Shaving Mug, Lid, White	3.50
Akro Agate, Sugar & Creamer, Child's, Yellow, Panels, Darts	10.00
Akro Agate, Sugar & Creamer, Concentric Circle	9.00
Akro Agate, Tea Set, Green & White, Original Box, 17 Pieces	45.00
Akro Agate, Vase, Lily Pattern, White With Orange, 4 1/4 In.	12.00 To 16.00
Akro Agate, Vase, Orange, Marked, 6 1/4 In.	18.00
Akro Agate, Vase, Pink, Orange & White Lily, 4 1/2 In.	18.00
Alabaster, Box, Jewlery, Pewter Lady Sitting On Top	135.00
Alabaster, Vase, Campana Form, C.1900, 16 In., Pair	125.00

Album, Photograph, see Photography, Album

Alexandrite glass was first made by Thomas Webb & Sons at the beginning of the 20th century. It is a transparent glass shading from pale yellow to rose to blue. Stevens & Williams later produced alexandrite glassware by plating a transparent yellow body with rose and blue glass.

Alexandrite, see also Moser

Alexandrite, Match Holder, Honeycomb, 6-Sided Top, 2 5/8 X 2 1/2 In.Diam.	595.00
Alexandrite, Rose Bowl, Hexagonal Top, Amber To Fuchsia, 3 X 2 In.	1100.00
Alexandrite, Toothpick Holder, Inverted Thumbprint, Ruffled Top, Amber	1200.00

Amber glass is the name of any glassware with the proper yellow-brown shade. It was a popular color after the Civil War.

Amber Glass, Bowl, Covered, Owl, Blown Glass Eyes	250.00
Amber Glass, Box, Cavalier Heads, Openwork, Metal Feet, 3 5/8 In.	47.00
Amber Glass, Box, Enameled Ormolu, 4 X 3 1/2 In.	95.00
Amber Glass, Box, Footed, Side Brass Rings, Enameled Foliage, 3 1/4 In.Diam.	85.00
Amber Glass, Cruet, Fluted Trefoil Lip, Ribbed Applied Handle, Stopper, 7 In.	35.00
Amber Glass, Decanter, Wine, Doughnut Shape, Etched, Original Stopper	35.00
Amber Glass, Dish, Butter, Cover, Sadiron Shape, 8 X 5 In.	65.00
Amber Glass, Dish, Butter, Covered, Daisy & Button	65.00
Amber Glass, Goblet, Vintage Design, Signed Sinclaire	27.50
Amber Glass, Perfume, Petticoat, Cathedral Stopper, Gold Flowers & Trim	175.00
Amber Glass, Pitcher, Blown, Applied Strap Handle, 19th Century, 7 7/8 In.	200.00
Amber Glass, Pitcher, Gold Banding, 15 In.	5.00
Amber Glass, Pitcher, Water, Bulbous, Ruffled, Enameled, Lacy Gold, 8 In.	118.00
Amber Glass, Pitcher, Water, Tankard Shape, Reeded Applied Handle, 13 In.	245.00
Amber Glass, Plate, Jersey Swirl	30.00
Amber Glass, Rolling Pin	45.00
Amber Glass, Rose Bowl, Concentric Swirls & Iridescence, 4 1/2 X 4 In.	59.00
Amber Glass, Slipper, Oxford, Daisy & Button, October 19, '86	20.00
Amber Glass, Sugar & Creamer, Sahara, Amber, Octagon	20.00
Amber Glass, Toothpick, Boot, 2 3/4 In.	22.50
Amber Glass, Vase, Applied Fish, Enamel Decoration, 5 1/4 In.	40.00
Amber Glass, Vase, Swirled Diamond Pattern, Frilled Ruffled Neck, 7 In.	29.50
Amber, Holder, Cigar, Case	12.50
Amber, Vase, Applied Feet, Leaves, Vines & Pears, 12 Green Leaves, 12 In.	975.00

Amberette, see Pressed Glass, Klondike

Amberina is a two-toned glassware made from 1883 to about 1900. It was patented by Joseph Locke of the New England Glass Company. The glass shades from red to amber.

Amberina, see also Bluerina, Plated Amberina

Amberina, Basket, Swirl, Applied Feet, Rope Handle, 8 X 5 In.Diameter	175.00
Amberina, Bowl, Center, Footed, Grotesque Flute	35.00
Amberina, Bowl, Diamond-Quilted, J.Locke, 19th Century, 3 1/2 X 9 1/2 In.	385.00
Amberina, Bowl, Finger, Inverted Thumbprint, 3 X 4 1/2 In.Diameter	85.00
Amberina, Bowl, Finger, Reverse, Diamond Pattern, 2 3/4 X 4 3/4 In.	100.00
Amberina, Bowl, Finger, Square, 5 In.	48.50
Amberina, Bowl, Finger, Swirl, Red Shading, Amber, 3 X 4 3/8 In.Diameter	145.00

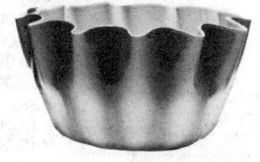

Amberina, Bowl, New England Glass Co., C.1870

Amberina, **Bowl,** Fruit, Diamond-Quilted, Amber Rigaree Trim, 9 1/2 In.	385.00
Amberina, **Bowl,** Fuchsia Top, 12 1/2 In.Diameter	330.00
Amberina, **Bowl,** Fuchsia Top, 13 1/2 In.Diameter	270.00
Amberina, **Bowl,** New England Glass Co., C.1870 *Illus*	550.00
Amberina, **Bowl,** Oval, Footed, Ruffled Applied Top Edge, 6 3/8 In.	375.00
Amberina, **Bowl,** Rolled Rim, Iridescent, 9 1/2 In.	100.00
Amberina, **Bowl,** Rose, Diamond Quilted, 6 1.'¹ X 22 1/2 In.	95.00
Amberina, **Bowl,** Swirl Footed, Ruffled Top, Oval, Cranberry Shading, 6 5/8 In.	325.00
Amberina, **Bowl,** Swirl, Fan Shaped, Applied Amber Wishbone Feet, 8 1/4 In.	395.00
Amberina, **Bowl,** 4 3/4 X 4 1/4 X 2 1/4 In.	80.00
Amberina, **Carafe,** Reverse, Diamond	175.00
Amberina, **Celery,** Square Crimped Top, Deep Color	190.00
Amberina, **Compote,** Diamond-Quilted, Footed, 4 1/2 X 8 In.	725.00
Amberina, **Compote,** 1920s, 4 In.High X 7 1/4 In.Wide	25.00
Amberina, **Creamer,** Square Mouth, Bulbous, Crystal Rope Handle, 3 3/8 In.	225.00
Amberina, **Creamer,** Thumbprint, Top Color	150.00
Amberina, **Cruet,** Amber Applied Handle, Ball Stopper, 5 3/4 In.	165.00
Amberina, **Cruet,** Applied Handle, Coin Spot Design	70.00
Amberina, **Cruet,** Baby Thumbprint, Reeded Handle, Faceted Top	145.00
Amberina, **Cruet,** Clear Handle & Stopper	200.00
Amberina, **Cruet,** Draped, Faceted Amber Stopper, Pontil	250.00
Amberina, **Cruet,** Inverted Thumbprint, Amber Handle & Stopper 150.00 To	250.00
Amberina, **Cruet,** Inverted Thumbprint, Clear Reeded Handle, Faceted Stopper	235.00
Amberina, **Cruet,** Inverted Thumbprint, Rose Amber, Applied Amber Handle	295.00
Amberina, **Cruet,** Inverted Thumbprint, Teardrop Shape	450.00
Amberina, **Cruet,** Long Ribs, Bulbous, Amber Trim	250.00
Amberina, **Cup,** Punch, Flared & Ribbed Body, Applied Amber Handle	1525.00
Amberina, **Cup,** Punch, Fuchsia, Diaper Pattern, Amber Handle, 2 1/4 In.	125.00
Amberina, **Cup,** Punch, Fuchsia, Shading To Yellow, Diamond Pattern, 2 1/4 In.	135.00
Amberina, **Cup,** Punch, Reeded Handle	90.00
Amberina, **Cup,** Punch, Ribbed	115.00
Amberina, **Decanter,** Six Glasses, Baby Thumbprint, Amber & Fuchsia	190.00
Amberina, **Decanter,** Swirl, Gold Decorated, Bubble Stopper, 8 1/2 In.	225.00
Amberina, **Dish,** Butter, Covered, Inverted Thumbprint, Snail Finial	595.00
Amberina, **Dish,** Cheese, Coin Dot	200.00
Amberina, **Dish,** Cheese, Covered, Inverted Thumbprint, 6 1/4 X 6 3/8 In.Diam.	295.00
Amberina, **Dish,** Daisy & Button, Amber To Fuchsia, 5 In.Square	105.00
Amberina, **Dish,** Ice Cream, Daisy & Button, Square, Flint, 5 1/2 In.	125.00
Amberina, **Dish,** Ice Cream, Daisy & Button, 5 1/2 In.Diameter	98.00
Amberina, **Dish,** Pickle, Poppy	60.00
Amberina, **Dish,** Sauce, Daisy & Button, Flint, 5 In.Square	95.00
Amberina, **Figurine,** Horse, Rearing, Smith	40.00
Amberina, **Glass,** Whiskey, Underplate, 2 In., Plate 4 In.Diameter	175.00
Amberina, **Goblet,** Diamond-Quilted	30.00
Amberina, **Jar,** Mustard, Sterling Top, Handle & Spoon, Enamel Design	250.00
Amberina, **Lemonade Set,** Thumbprint, Pitcher, 11 In., 8 Handles Mugs, 9 Piece	1200.00
Amberina, **Pitcher,** Applied Handle, 8 1/4 In.	250.00
Amberina, **Pitcher,** Inverted Thumbprint, Amber Handle, Square Rim, 7 1/2 In.	190.00
Amberina, **Pitcher,** Inverted Thumbprint, Square Mouth, 4 1/2 In.	175.00
Amberina, **Pitcher,** Inverted Thumbprint, Triangular Top, 8 3/4 In.	300.00
Amberina, **Pitcher,** Lemonade, 2 Tumblers, Enameled White & Pink, 9 3/4 In.	375.00
Amberina, **Pitcher,** Melon Ribbed, Herringbone, Applied Amber Handle	100.00
Amberina, **Pitcher,** Miniature, Tricorner Top, Amber Reeded Handle, 2 1/4 In.	155.00
Amberina, **Pitcher,** Puffed Melon Shaped, Ruffled Top, Clear Reeded Handle	275.00
Amberina, **Pitcher,** Spherical Body, Applied Reeded Handle, C.1900, 8 3/4 In.	150.00
Amberina, **Pitcher,** Thumbprint, 6 In.	145.00
Amberina, **Pitcher,** Water, Honeycomb, Pleated Mouth	110.00

Amberina, **Pitcher,** 12 Tumblers, Shaded Cranberry, Amber, Optic, 12 In.	975.00
Amberina, **Rose Bowl,** Hobnail	235.00
Amberina, **Rose Bowl,** Quilted Satin, 6 1/2 In.	270.00
Amberina, **Salt & Pepper,** Baby Inverted Thumbprint, Original Tops, 4 In.	175.00
Amberina, **Saltshaker,** Pewter Top, 4 In.	120.00
Amberina, **Sauce,** Daisy & Button, Flint, 5 In.	95.00
Amberina, **Sauce,** Daisy & Button, 4 3/4 In.Square	75.00
Amberina, **Sauce,** Diamond-Quilted, Fuchsia, 4 1/2 X 1 1/2 In., Pair	175.00
Amberina, **Sconce,** Diamond-Quilted, Opalescent Center, 1887, 5 1/4 In., Pair	385.00
Amberina, **Spooner,** Scalloped Rim	95.00
Amberina, **Spoonholder,** Swirled, Deep Color, 6 In.	120.00
Amberina, **Sugar & Creamer,** Miniature, Bull's-Eye Pattern	35.00
Amberina, **Sugar & Creamer,** Texas	40.00
Amberina, **Sugar Shaker,** Inverted Thumbprint	150.00
Amberina, **Sugar Shaker,** Reverse Thumbprint, Enameled Flowers, 4 3/4 In.	245.00
Amberina, **Sugar Shaker,** Thumbprint, 5 1/4 In.	195.00
Amberina, **Toothpick Holder,** Venetian Diamond, Fuchsia	165.00
Amberina, **Toothpick,** Baby Thumbprint, Flared, Fuchsia Rim	115.00
Amberina, **Toothpick,** Daisy & Button, Footed, 3 In.	185.00
Amberina, **Toothpick,** Fuchsia Crown, Inverted Diamonds, Square Top	187.00
Amberina, **Toothpick,** Inverted Thumbprint, Hat Shape, Piecrust Rim	375.00
Amberina, **Tumbler,** Baby Inverted Thumbprint	30.00
Amberina, **Tumbler,** Covered With Coin Gold, Enameled Butterflies, 3 1/4 In.	265.00
Amberina, **Tumbler,** Diamond-Quilted, Fuchsia Top	79.00
Amberina, **Tumbler,** Diamond-Quilted, Ruby To Golden Amber, 3 3/4 In.	90.00
Amberina, **Tumbler,** Inverted Baby Thumbprint, Enameling, Gold	75.00
Amberina, **Tumbler,** Inverted Baby Thumbprint, Rose To Amber	54.00
Amberina, **Tumbler,** Reverse, Venetian Diamond, 4 X 2 3/4 In.Diameter	80.00
Amberina, **Tumbler,** Swirl, Pontil	80.00
Amberina, **Tumbler,** Swirl, Red To Golden Amber, 3 3/4 In.	95.00
Amberina, **Tumbler,** Thumbprint, Pontil	80.00
Amberina, **Tumbler,** Whiskey, Amber To Fuchsia, Pontil, 2 1/2 In.	138.00
Amberina, **Vase,** Amber Rigaree, Enameled Flower Sprays, 9 1/4 In., Pair	445.00
Amberina, **Vase,** Basket Weave, Fuchsia, Scalloped Rim, 9 3/4 In.	175.00
Amberina, **Vase,** Bulbous, Blown Ribbed, 11 In.	350.00
Amberina, **Vase,** Bulbous, Thin Neck, Ruffled Top, White Lining, 12 1/2 In.	385.00
Amberina, **Vase,** Celery, Diamond-Quilted, Square Ruffled Top, 6 In.	265.00
Amberina, **Vase,** Cylindrical, Enameled Flowers, 9 1/2 In.	89.00
Amberina, **Vase,** Diamond-Quilted, Clear Shell Feet, Reverse, 6 In.	95.00
Amberina, **Vase,** Diamond-Quilted, Footed, Gold, Blue & White Enamel, 8 In.	245.00
Amberina, **Vase,** Dimpled Body, Rigaree At Neck, 9 X 4 1/2 In.Diameter	250.00
Amberina, **Vase,** Enameled Flowers, Amber Applied Rosettes, Handle, 5 In.	95.00
Amberina, **Vase,** Fan Shaped, Enamel Decoration, 7 X 11 1/2 In.	325.00
Amberina, **Vase,** Figural, Bird Wings Open, Tree Branches, Fluted, Signed	155.00
Amberina, **Vase,** Fluted & Crimped Rim, Red Base, 14 In.	249.00
Amberina, **Vase,** Fluted Top, Fuchsia, 7 In.	180.00
Amberina, **Vase,** Fuchsia To Amber, Ground Pontil, New England, 7 In., Pair	325.00
Amberina, **Vase,** Inverted Thumbprint, Jack-In-The-Pulpit Top, 12 1/2 In.	245.00
Amberina, **Vase,** Jack-In-The-Pulpit, Applied Foot & Rim, 12 1/2 In.	195.00
Amberina, **Vase,** Jack-In-The-Pulpit, Cranberry To Amber, Enameled, 11 In.	235.00
Amberina, **Vase,** Jack-In-The-Pulpit, Crystal Spiral Applique, 14 1/8 In.	195.00
Amberina, **Vase,** Libbey, Paneled, Teardrop Shape, Elongated, Signed, 11 1/8 In.	475.00
Amberina, **Vase,** Lily, N.E.G. Co., 9 3/4 In.	275.00
Amberina, **Vase,** Lily, Trefoil, 10 1/2 In.	325.00
Amberina, **Vase,** Ruffled, Crimpled, Pontil, Red Collar, 13 1/2 In.	259.00
Amberina, **Vase,** Swirl, Applied Feet & Ruffle, Paisley Design, 11 1/2 In.	225.00
Amberina, **Vase,** Thumbprint, 14 In.	30.00
Amberina, **Water Set,** Pitcher, 4 Barrel Tumblers, Pitcher, 11 1/2 In.	425.00
Amberina, **Water Set,** 4 Tumblers, Inverted Thumbprint, Reeded Handle, 7 In.	375.00
Amberina, **Wine,** Stemmed, Inverted Thumbprint	75.00

*American Encaustic Tiling Co. of Zanesville, Ohio, worked from 1879
to 1935. Decorative glazed, embossed, and faience tiles were made.*

American Encaustic Tiling Co., Tile, Bryan & McKinley, 3 In.Square, Pair ... 40.00

*Amethyst glass is any of the many glasswares made in the proper dark purple
shade. It was a color popular after the Civil War.*

Amethyst Glass, Bowl, Footed, 13 In.Diameter	25.00
Amethyst Glass, Box, White Flowers, Cover, 2 3/8 In.	15.00
Amethyst Glass, Butter, Covered, Enameled Flowers, Scalloped Skirt	95.00
Amethyst Glass, Candlestick, 3 Mold, Blown, Domed Foot, 9 In., Pair	48.00
Amethyst Glass, Compote, Knob Stems, 8 Rims, Folded Rim, 7 X 5 3/4 In.	95.00
Amethyst Glass, Console Set, Bowl, 2 Candlesticks, 9 In.	45.00
Amethyst Glass, Cruet, Original Stopper, 6 1/4 In.	28.00
Amethyst Glass, Cup, 2 Handled	10.00
Amethyst Glass, Decanter, Gothic Arch, 13 In.	30.00
Amethyst Glass, Decanter, Liqueur, Cut Bands & Ovals, Gold Trim, 9 5/8 In.	150.00
Amethyst Glass, Decanter, 4 Tumblers, Pinch Type, Crystal Stopper, 36 Oz.	53.00
Amethyst Glass, Finger Bowl, Ground Pontil	35.00
Amethyst Glass, Lemonade Set, Bulbous Bottom, Applied Handle, 5 Tumblers	175.00
Amethyst Glass, Pitcher, Oval Shape, Silver Overlay, Marked, 8 X 7 3/4 In.	145.00
Amethyst Glass, Pitcher, Water, Enameled Flowers, Gold Bands	95.00
Amethyst Glass, Plate, 8 In.	11.00
Amethyst Glass, Rolling Pin, 14 1/2 In.	175.00
Amethyst Glass, Rose Bowl, Crimped Top, Enameling, 4 X 4 1/4 In.Diameter	95.00
Amethyst Glass, Salt & Pepper, Agitator, Christmas, Original Tops	135.00
Amethyst Glass, Salt & Pepper, Flowers, Square	16.00
Amethyst Glass, Saltshaker, Swag With Brackets, Original Top	25.00
Amethyst Glass, Sherbet & Underplate, Dark	42.00
Amethyst Glass, Tieback, Gold Floral Center, 2 3/4 In.Round, Pair	32.00
Amethyst Glass, Tray, Condiment, S-Repeat	38.00
Amethyst Glass, Vase, Crystal Base, 14 In.	25.00
Amethyst Glass, Vase, Double Handled, 8 In.	25.00
Amethyst Glass, Vase, Enameled Design, 10 1/2 In.	35.00
Amethyst Glass, Vase, Galleried Rim, Applied Funnel Base, 7 In.	185.00
Amethyst Glass, Vase, Hand Blown, Cut Overlay, Clear Optic Circles, 12 In.	95.00
Amethyst Glass, Vase, Overshot, Serpent Around Neck, Bulbous, 7 In.	150.00
Amethyst Glass, Vase, Portrait, Full Figure Of Girl Of The 1890s	75.00
Amethyst Glass, Vase, Ruffled Edging, Diamond-Quilted, 4 1/2 X 6 In.Diam.	50.00
Amethyst Glass, Vase, White & Gold Enameled, Polished Pontil, 7 In.	27.50
Amethyst Glass, Witches' Ball	40.00
Amphora, see Teplitz	
Andiron, many related fireplace items, see, Fire	
Animal Trophy, Grizzly Bear, Front Half Mount *Illus*	800.00
Animal Trophy, Horned Owl, Stuffed & Mounted, 24 In.	110.00
Animal Trophy, Kudu Head, Spiral Horns, Shield Mount *Illus*	1000.00
Animal Trophy, Lion, Leaping	1300.00
Animal Trophy, Rhinoceros Head	525.00
Apothecary jar, see Bottle, Apothecary	
Apple Peeler, see Kitchen, Peeler, Apple	
Arequipa, Bowl, 11 In.Diameter	75.00
Argy-Rousseau, see G. Argy-Rousseau	
Arita, Vase, Fish, Birds, Geometric Patterns, Square, Tapering, 7 In.	170.00

Art Deco, or Art Moderne, is a style started at the Paris Exposition of 1925, characterized by linear, geometric designs.All types of furniture and decorative arts, jewelry, bookbindings, and even games, were designed in this style.

Art Deco, Ashtray, Flapper Girl Lying Down, Knees Up	9.00
Art Deco, Ashtray, Girl Lying In The Edge	7.50
Art Deco, Ashtray, Nude, Green Malachite Glass	30.00
Art Deco, Ashtray, Tan Onyx, Brass Finish, Kneeling Nude, 8 In.	55.00
Art Deco, Basket, Multicolored Baccarat Glass Fruit, Brass Footed Bed	175.00
Art Deco, Bell, Dinner, Striker, Nude Holds Crossbar, Brass, 7 X 7 In.	45.00
Art Deco, Blotter, Rocking, Brass, 4 1/2 In.	6.00
Art Deco, Bookends, Antelope, Crescent Metal Works, C.1932, 7 In.	20.00
Art Deco, Bookends, Egyptian Design, Cast Iron	10.00
Art Deco, Bookends, Nude With 2 Russian Wolfhounds	25.00
Art Deco, Bookends, Woman, White Metal	15.00
Art Deco, Bottle, Perfume, Amber, Nude Girl, Signed Ingrid, Czechoslovakia	40.00
Art Deco, Bowl, Cased Pink Inside, Controlled Bubbles, Narrow End	25.00
Art Deco, Box, Cigarette, Brass, White Roll Top, Park Sherman	12.00
Art Deco, Box, Cigarette, Glass Cover, Inverted Diamond Design	12.00
Art Deco, Box, Jewelry, Bird's-Eye Maple, Etched Mirror	20.00

Animal Trophy, Grizzly Bear,
Front Half Mount

Art Glass, Vase, Peachblow Color,
Ruffled Rim, 16 3/4 In., Pair
(See Page 9)

Animal Trophy, Kudu Head,
Spiral Horns, Shield Mount

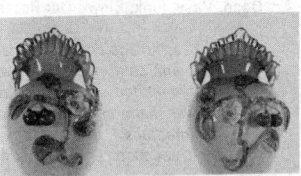

Art Glass, Vase, Amber, Blue, Cased
Victorian, 8 3/4 In., Pair
(See Page 9)

Art Deco, Lighter, Table, Chrome &
Plastic, Bar Shape, 7 In.
(See Page 8)

Art Deco, Box, Lady Sitting On Lid, Bavaria 15.00
Art Deco, Box, Nude, Exposed Breast, 12 Nude Children, 7 1/4 X 5 1/4 In. 58.00
Art Deco, Case, Cigarette, With Lighter, Nude On Front 15.00
Art Deco, Clock Set, China, Design In Gold, Brass Finials, 30 Hour, 19 In. 240.00
Art Deco, Compact, Black Enamel Woman, Enamel Chain 30.00
Art Deco, Compote, Sterling, Hand Hammered, 8 In., Pair 150.00
Art Deco, Dish, Candy, Border Brown & Gold, 7 In. 10.00
Art Deco, Dresser Set, Green Celluloid & Silver, Pieces Fit Into Case 35.00
Art Deco, Figurine, Girl, Blue Dress, Germany, No.8183, 9 1/2 In. 45.00
Art Deco, Figurine, Trojan, Signed, 1930, Bronze Finish, 6 1/2 In. 18.00
Art Deco, Flask, Scent, Silver Gilt, Enamel, Glass, French, C.1930, 2 7/8 In. 275.00
Art Deco, Flower Frog, Draped Lady In Dance, White Glazed, 8 In. 25.00
Art Deco, Flower Frog, Nude, White Porcelain, Germany 30.00
Art Deco, Flower Frog, Semi-Nude Girl In Hoop, Marked, Germany, 7 In. 25.00
Art Deco, Flower Frog, Two Nudes, Shawls, White, Germany, 3 1/2 X 7 In. 22.00
Art Deco, Inkstand, Silvered Metal, Marble Base, Delannoys, C.1925, 7 In. 100.00
Art Deco, Jar, Powder, Pink Frosted, Pair 35.00
Art Deco, Lamp, Dancing Soldier, Geometric 42.50
Art Deco, Lamp, Desk, Adjustable, Brass 165.00
Art Deco, Lamp, Floor, Chrome, 3 Inverted Cones, Fluted Column, 67 In. 900.00
Art Deco, Lamp, Multi-Colored Glass, 7 X 7 In. 35.00
Art Deco, Lamp, Pink Frosted Glass, Nude Lady, Square Shade, 9 In., Pair 50.00
Art Deco, Light, Night, Flapper Girl, Bobbed Hair, Bavarian, 7 1/2 In. 75.00
Art Deco, Lighter, Cigar, Advertising, Mirror & Clock 125.00
Art Deco, Lighter, Giraffe Shape 7.50
Art Deco, Lighter, Table, Chrome & Plastic, Bar Shape, 7 In. ....Illus   450.00
Art Deco, Lighter, Table, Figural Nude Woman, Battery Operated 21.00
Art Deco, Liquor Set, Prismatic, 7 Piece 125.00
Art Deco, Mirror, Hand, Celluloid 10.00
Art Deco, Mirror, Pocket, Hidden Erotic Scene, Turn Upside Down To See 10.00
Art Deco, Nude Dancer, Marble Base, Bronze, Signed Fiedler, 13 In. 250.00
Art Deco, Porringer, Carnelian Stone In Handle, Sterling, Grief, 5 1/4 In. 165.00
Art Deco, Pot, Hot Water, Lid Raises In Pouring, Silver Plate, 8 In. 32.00
Art Deco, Salt & Pepper, Gold Top, Iridescent Body, Butterflies At Top 5.25
Art Deco, Screen, Mirrored, 3 Paneled Side Pointed, Arched, 6 Feet 250.00
Art Deco, Screen, 3 Panel, Oil, Janet Laura Scott, 68 X 60 In. 250.00
Art Deco, Tobacco Jar, Bronze & Silver, Lid 35.00
Art Deco, Tray, Etched Dogs, Flowers, Trees, Chrome Handles 22.00
Art Deco, Vase, Bulbous, Geometric Design, Brass Cover, Signed, 5 X 6 In. 50.00
Art Deco, Vase, Clear Base, Cranberry Prunts & Stems, Signed, 10 In. 165.00
Art Deco, Vase, Pink, Blown Out Roses, Czechoslovakia, 9 In. 89.00

Art glass means any of the many forms of glassware made during the late
nineteenth century or early twentieth century. These wares were expensive and
made in limited production. Art glass is not the typical commercial glass
that was made in large quantities, and most of the art glass was produced by
hand methods.

Art Glass, see also separate headings such as Burmese, Nash,
Schneider, etc.

Art Glass, Basket, Bushel, Basket Weave, Applied Floral, White Opaque, 5 In. 60.00
Art Glass, Basket, Green, Bubble Pattern, Leaves & Cherries, 9 1/2 In. 120.00
Art Glass, Basket, Green, Gold Highlights, Applied Clear Handle, 13 In. 175.00
Art Glass, Basket, Opalescent, Applied Leaves & Flowers, Amber Handle, 8 In. ... 125.00
Art Glass, Basket, Pink, White, Swirled Ribs, Notched Applied Handle, 11 In. 135.00
Art Glass, Basket, Spatter, Twisted Handle, Blue 75.00
Art Glass, Biscuit Jar, French, Hand-Painted Winter Scene, Signed, 6 In. 60.00
Art Glass, Bowl, Crimped, Turned-Out Rim, Iridescence, Ground Pontil, 7 In. 80.00
Art Glass, Cookie Jar, Underplate, Gold Designs & White Enamel 225.00
Art Glass, Flask, Perfume, Ovoid, Swirls, Gold Stone, Gold Stopper, 3 X 1 In. 38.00
Art Glass, Lamp, Gas, Brass Frame, Caramel, 11 X 23 In.Diameter 395.00
Art Glass, Pitcher, Opalescent, Victorian, Pontil Mark, 8 1/2 In. 225.00
Art Glass, Rolling Pin, Nailsea Type, Pink & White Loopings 65.00
Art Glass, Rose Bowl, Acid Finish, Ribbed Body, Camphor Glass Feet 80.00
Art Glass, Rose Bowl, Satin Finish, Loopings, Blue Ground, Verre De Moire 125.00
Art Glass, Shade Set, Spatter, Purple, Red, Yellow, Set Of 5 .... 32.00
Art Glass, Shade, Cased, Ruffled Opening, Dark Pink, 2 1/4 In.Rim 65.00

Art Glass, Shade, Diamond-Quilted, Gold Aurene, Signed Steuben	185.00
Art Glass, Shade, Gold Spider Webbing & Leaves, Opalescent Glass, 6 In.	165.00
Art Glass, Shade, Green Feather, Luster, Set Of 4	440.00
Art Glass, Shade, Hanging, 252 Pieces, 102 Buttons, 12 X 24 In.Diameter	1375.00
Art Glass, Shade, Lamp, Cameo, 2 In.Neck, Frosted Ground	125.00
Art Glass, Sugar Shaker, Quilted Phlox, Bulbous, Cased, 4 1/4 In.	135.00
Art Glass, Toothpick, Applied Twisted Rigaree To Form 3 Seats, 4 In.	75.00
Art Glass, Tray & Box, Covered, Round, Square Tray	145.00
Art Glass, Tumbler, Diamond-Quilted, Satin Shading, Pink To Raspberry	110.00
Art Glass, Vase, Amber, Blue, Cased Victorian, 8 3/4 In., Pair .... Illus	700.00
Art Glass, Vase, Apricot, Signed De Lucie, Original French Label, 4 In.	75.00
Art Glass, Vase, Art Nouveau, Enameled Scenes, Frosted Ground, 16 In.	79.00
Art Glass, Vase, Blown, Floral, Scroll, Fluted Top, Green, Orange, 11 In.	57.50
Art Glass, Vase, Blue, Yellow Hearts, 5 In.	100.00
Art Glass, Vase, Cameo, Cranberry Florentine, Butterfly, 7 In.	49.00
Art Glass, Vase, Cut Velvet, Green, Diamond-Quilted Pattern, 6 1/2 In.	190.00
Art Glass, Vase, Fish, Green, Edvard Hald	300.00
Art Glass, Vase, Green, Silver Overlay, 11 In.	110.00
Art Glass, Vase, Iridescent Swirl, In Ormolu, 15 X 7 In.	195.00
Art Glass, Vase, Mixed Coloring, Faure, 4 1/2 X 1 1/2 In.Diameter	150.00
Art Glass, Vase, Peachblow Color, Ruffled Rim, 16 3/4 In., Pair .... Illus	350.00

Art Nouveau, a style characterized by free-flowing organic design, reached
its zenith between 1895 and 1905. The style encompassed all decorative and
functional arts from architecture to furniture and posters.

Art Nouveau, see also Furniture, Various Glass Categories, etc.

Art Nouveau, Ashtray, Running Bronze Nude In Center, 8 In.Round	125.00
Art Nouveau, Book Rack, Lady's Head In Relief, Brass Patina Over Copper	150.00
Art Nouveau, Bookends, Dancing Lady, Draped	32.00
Art Nouveau, Bookends, Expanding, Full Figure Girl, Brass	25.00
Art Nouveau, Bookends, Full Head, Tusk & Trunk Of Elephant, Extends 21 In.	39.00
Art Nouveau, Bookends, Girl, Short Skirt, White Alabaster Base, Metal	75.00
Art Nouveau, Bookends, Iron & Brass, Extends To 14 In.Full Body Owl	39.00
Art Nouveau, Bookends, Nude Male Against Rock, Signed J.A.Meliodon, C.1915	67.50
Art Nouveau, Bookmark, Heart Shape, Female Heads, Sterling	30.00
Art Nouveau, Bottle, Wine, Silver Overlay, Melon Shape Base, 11 In.	165.00
Art Nouveau, Box, Covered, Entwined Nudes, Malachite Glass, 3 1/2 In.Diam.	65.00
Art Nouveau, Box, Hinged, Lady Holding Rose, Cobalt, Glass, 6 X 5 In.	165.00
Art Nouveau, Box, Jewel, Footed, Gilt, 2 1/2 X 3 3/4 In.	17.50
Art Nouveau, Box, Letter, Brass, 9 X 6 In.	70.00
Art Nouveau, Box, Match Holder, Brass, 4 1/2 X 4 In.	26.00
Art Nouveau, Box, Powder, Brass Bridal Wreath Holder, Celluloid Lid	12.00
Art Nouveau, Box, Ring, Gold Metal, 2 X 2 1/2 In.	45.00
Art Nouveau, Brush, Ladies With Flowing Hair, 1902, Sterling, 7 In.	32.00
Art Nouveau, Buckle, Saint, Lady's Head	20.00
Art Nouveau, Candleholder, Brass Tri-Leaf, Twig Handles, Pair	35.00
Art Nouveau, Candleholder, Brass, Lady With Outstretched Arms, 10 In.	149.00
Art Nouveau, Candleholder, Figural Lady Stem, 8 1/2 In., Pair	35.00
Art Nouveau, Candleholder, Nude Youth On Ball Footed Base, Signed, 8 1/2 In	27.50
Art Nouveau, Candleholder, White Metal, Figural Lady Stem, Pair	35.00
Art Nouveau, Candlestick, Flowers, Bisque, 8 In., Pair	135.00
Art Nouveau, Centerpiece, 4 Supports With Bowls, Stellmacher, Teplitz, 7 In.	250.00
Art Nouveau, Chandelier, Gold Leaf, 5 Rosette Connectors, From Theater	25.00
Art Nouveau, Compote, Woman's Head In Relief On Base, Silver Plate	95.00
Art Nouveau, Decanter, Peacock, Head Lifts, Wings Are Handle, 18 1/2 In.	600.00
Art Nouveau, Figurine, Kneeling Nude Woman, Stellmacher, C.1900, 32 In.	1550.00
Art Nouveau, Figurine, Nude, Marble Base, Bronze, Signed Queste	395.00
Art Nouveau, Figurine, Woman, Bronze, Gerome, 14 In.	690.00
Art Nouveau, Flower Frog, Girl Standing In Center Of Flowers, German	20.00
Art Nouveau, Frame, Easel, Draped Figure, Brass Plated Iron, 10 X 13 In.	67.50
Art Nouveau, Jar, Sweetmeat, Applique Fruit, Covered, 4 1/2 X 7 1/2 In.	265.00
Art Nouveau, Lamp, Art Glass Globe, 21 In.	250.00
Art Nouveau, Lamp, Base Is Brass Rose, 2 Handled, Filigree On Shade	300.00
Art Nouveau, Lamp, Figural, Les Marquerites, White Metal	275.00
Art Nouveau, Lamp, Raised Painted Flowers, Green, Japanese, 16 In.Tall	55.00
Art Nouveau, Lamp, 3 Brass Lions, Signed Quezal, Shades, Orange Drape	450.00
Art Nouveau, Lamp, 3 Nude Ladies On Base, Satin Shade	125.00

Art Nouveau, Mirror, Hand, Beveled Edge, Silver Plate, Derby Silver, Co., 1891 .... 50.00
Art Nouveau, Mirror, Hand, Cherub, Fish & Waves, 1905, Silver, 5 In. 50.00
Art Nouveau, Mirror, Shaving, Lady Holding Horseshoe, Beveled, Gilded, 7 In. 55.00
Art Nouveau, Table Set, Butter, Sugar, Creamer & Spooner, Clear, Gold Trim 155.00
Art Nouveau, Travel Case, Ebony & Sterling, Fitted, Nouveau Lady On Lid 175.00
Art Nouveau, Tray, Held By Slave Girl, 6 3/4 In.High, 6 In.Across 45.00
Art Nouveau, Vase, Bronze Girl, Flowing Hair, Handle Looking At Swan, 6 In. 35.00
Art Nouveau, Vase, Bronze, Foliage, Dragonflies, H.Elmquist, C.1900, 10 In. 250.00
Art Nouveau, Vase, Corset Shape, Handled, Flowers In Relief, Signed, Pair 95.00
Art Nouveau, Vase, Dancing Figures, Pan Playing Pipes, Black Amethyst 32.50
Art Nouveau, Vase, Geometric Shapes Of Flowers, Signed, 9 X 4 1/2 In. 225.00
Art Nouveau, Vase, Reptile Rigaree, Iridescent Green, 10 In. 195.00
    Art Pottery, see under factory name
Art Pottery, Vase, Green Glaze, Handles At Neck, 16 In. 18.00
    Arthur Osborne, see Ivorex
Ashburton, Decanter, Long Neck, Wide Ring Lip, Straw Marks 90.00

AURENE   *Aurene glass was made by Frederick Carder of New York about 1904.*
                  It is an iridescent gold glass, usually marked Aurene or Steuben.
    Aurene, see also Steuben
Aurene, Basket, Gold & Blue, Signed 450.00
Aurene, Bonbon, Gold Iridescence, Signed, 4 1/2 In.Diameter 140.00
Aurene, Bottle, Cologne, Melon Ribbed, 3 Curled Shell Feet, Signed 775.00
Aurene, Bowl, Blue Iridescent, Urn-Shape, Signed, 10 X 5 1/2 In. 595.00
Aurene, Bowl, Blue, Signed, 3 1/4 X 6 In.Diameter 395.00
Aurene, Bowl, Melon Ribbing, Turned In Scalloped Top, Signed, 5 In. 325.00
Aurene, Bowl, Triangular, Iridized Opal, Green Feathering, Signed & No. 650.00
Aurene, Box, Blue Iridescent, Covered, Signed, 4 In. 475.00
Aurene, Candlestick, Blue Iridescent, Twisted Stem, No.686, 10 In., Pair 825.00
Aurene, Cup & Saucer, Gold Iridescent, Signed 375.00
Aurene, Cup, Loving, 4 Handles, Flared At Top, Signed, 4 1/2 X 8 In.Diameter 750.00
Aurene, Dish, Ruffled, Blue, Signed, 2 X 6 In.Diameter 235.00
Aurene, Dish, Salt, Gold, 2 1/2 X 3/4 In. 100.00
Aurene, Epergne, Gold Iridescence, Signed, 7 In. 250.00
Aurene, Goblet, Gold Iridescent, Blown In 3 Pieces, Signed, 8 In. 95.00
Aurene, Rose Bowl, Gold 195.00
Aurene, Salt, Master, Shape Of Rose Bowl, Blue, Signed, 3 In.Diameter 395.00
Aurene, Salt, Pedestal, Calcite & Gold, Pair 120.00
Aurene, Salt, Pedestal, Gold Iridescence 135.00
Aurene, Salt, Steuben, Blue, Ruffled Turned Out Edge, Signed, 3 1/2 In. 425.00
Aurene, Shade, Gold Hearts & Threading, Gold Lining, Signed, Set Of 4 .... 400.00
Aurene, Shade, Ribbed, Twisted, Flared Bottom, Steuben, 2 1/4 In.Fitting 120.00
Aurene, Vase, Blue Iridescence, Signed, 5 In. 450.00
Aurene, Vase, Blue Iridescent, Signed, 8 In. 425.00
Aurene, Vase, Blue Iridescent, Stick Body, Signed, 8 X 3 In. 250.00
Aurene, Vase, Blue Iridescent, Tree Stump, Signed, 6 1/4 In. 335.00
Aurene, Vase, Blue, No.2647, Signed Steuben, 2 3/4 In. 325.00
Aurene, Vase, Bud, Gold, Wafer Base, Flared At Top, Signed, 12 In. 195.00
Aurene, Vase, Bud, Pedestaled Foot, Gold, Signed Aurene, 5 1/2 In. 225.00
Aurene, Vase, Bud, Tree Stump, Thorny Base, Blue Iridescent, Signed, 6 1/4 In. 335.00
Aurene, Vase, Bulbous, Flared Top, Signed, 10 3/4 X 2 1/4 In. 225.00
Aurene, Vase, Golden, Blue Iridescent, Signed, 6 In. 250.00
Aurene, Vase, Green Iridescent, Gold Leaf & Vine, No.257, 7 1/2 In. 2250.00
Aurene, Vase, Pedestal Foot, Flared, Ruffled Rim, Iridescent, 6 1/4 In. 235.00
Aurene, Vase, Ruffled Shape, Gold Iridescence, Signed, 4 In. 185.00
Aurene, Vase, Scalloped Edge, Signed, 4 In. 165.00
Aurene, Vase, Steuben, Blue, Jar Shape, Turned In Top, No.6299, 6 1/4 In. 1300.00
Aurene, Vase, Stick, Blue, Signed, 10 In. 295.00
Aurene, Vase, Three-Prong Tree Trunk, Blue, Signed, 6 1/4 In. 675.00
    Austria, see Royal Dux, Kauffmann, Porcelain
    Auto, Ornament, Hood, see also Lalique
        Auto parts and accessories are collectors' items today.
Auto, Ashtray, Chevrolet Insignia, Plastic 3.50
Auto, Balloon Tire Tester, 1920, Schrader 60.00
Auto, Book, Instruction, De Soto, 1955 .... 5.00
Auto, Cap, Radiator, Pontiac Indian Head, 1930s 35.00
Auto, Car Light, Lucas, King Of The Road, 2 Side, 1 Tail, Brass, Signed 420.00

Auto, Clock, 8 Day, Cowell & Hubbard Co., 2 5/8 In.Diameter	50.00
Auto, Coupe, Ford, 1938, 5 Passenger	2850.00
Auto, Defroster, Windshield, Casco, 1930	8.00
Auto, Dodge, Car Emblem, Orange & Black	9.50
Auto, Emblem, Essex Super Six, Black & White	10.50
Auto, Emblem, Nash	22.00
Auto, Emblem, Radiator, Ford, Oval, Script	6.50
Auto, Emblem, Reo	30.00
Auto, G. & E. Motor Meter, 1930s, Nickel Over Brass	12.50
Auto, Gas Pump Globe, Amoco Gas	100.00
Auto, Gas Pump Globe, Atlantic Premium, Milk Glass	90.00
Auto, Gas Pump Globe, Dino Gasoline	45.00
Auto, Gas Pump Globe, Energee True	60.00
Auto, Gas Pump Globe, Gold Star, Texaco, Frosted Glass, 18 In.Diameter	650.00
Auto, Gas Pump Globe, Gulf, Milk Glass	100.00
Auto, Gas Pump Globe, Mobil Red Horse Insert, 16 In.	100.00
Auto, Gas Pump Globe, Red Star	150.00
Auto, Gas Pump Globe, Shamrock	50.00
Auto, Gas Pump Globe, Shell	135.00
Auto, Gas Pump Globe, Sky Chief	150.00
Auto, Gas Pump Globe, Standard Gold Crown	135.00
Auto, Gas Pump Globe, Standard Oil	135.00
Auto, Gas Pump Globe, Texaco Ethyl Gas, Milk Glass, Pair	90.00
Auto, Gas Pump Globe, Texaco, Milk Glass	125.00
Auto, Gas Pump Globe, Tydol	60.00
Auto, Gas Pump Globe, White Crown	125.00
Auto, Gauge, Brass, Dial-Type, U.S.Gauge Company	12.00
Auto, Gauge, Gasoline, Ford, Wooden, 15 In.	8.50
Auto, Gauge, Tire, Balloon, Schrader	5.00
Auto, Gauge, Tire, Brass, Clip-On	5.00
Auto, Gauge, Tire, Buick, Case	18.00
Auto, Gauge, Tire, Fisk Tires, Chicopee, Mass.	15.00
Auto, Gauge, Tire, Model A Ford, Leather Case	7.50
Auto, Gauge, Tire, Schrader Balloon Tire	4.00
Auto, Globe, Free Air & Water, 12 In.	300.00
Auto, Glove, Driving, High Gauntlet	8.00
Auto, Goggles, Leather, 1910, Pair	8.50
Auto, Headlight, Cadillac, Solid Brass	70.00
Auto, Headlight, Ford, Carbide Lighted, Separate Hangers, Brass & Steel	150.00
Auto, Hood Ornament, Bulldog, Mack Truck	20.00
Auto, Hood Ornament, Eagle	50.00
Auto, Hood Ornament, Eagle, Chevrolet, 1931	25.00
Auto, Hood Ornament, Flying Lady, Chrome, Walnut Base	35.00
Auto, Hood Ornament, Ford, Model T, Brass	5.00
Auto, Hood Ornament, Horizontal Nude Lady, Chrome	15.00
Auto, Hood Ornament, Indian Head, Illuminated	12.50
Auto, Hood Ornament, Nash, Deco Girl, Signed Petty	25.00
Auto, Hood Ornament, Pontiac, 1950	30.00
Auto, Hood Ornament, Ram, Dodge, 1938	25.00
Auto, Hood Ornament, Reo, Carved Bulldog, 25 In.	195.00
Auto, Hood Ornament, Swan	5.00
Auto, Horn, Brass & Copper, Coach, 4 Feet	26.00
Auto, Horn, Ford, Model A	5.00
Auto, Hubcap, Dodge Bros.	7.50
Auto, Hubcap, Essex, Set Of 4	27.50
Auto, Hubcap, Ford, Set Of 4	3.00
Auto, Keycase, Leather, Dodge	5.00
Auto, Knob, Clutch, Mottled Orange	8.00
Auto, Knob, Gearshift, Cobalt Blue, White Swirls	12.00
Auto, Knob, Gearshift, Large Red Dice, White Dots	8.00
Auto, Knob, Gearshift, Swirl	18.00
Auto, Knob, Gearshift, Threaded Brass Insert	20.00
Auto, Knob, Gearshift, 1940s, Studebaker, Blue	2.00
Auto, Knob, Marble Swirl, Stick-Shift, C.1920	15.00
Auto, Lamp, Kerosene, 1908-11, Dietz Eureka, Bail, 11 1/2 In.	45.00
Auto, Lamp, Westinghouse, Mazda, Tin, 2 1/2 X 3 1/2 In.	12.00

Auto, Lamp, 2 Side Lamps, 1 Rear, Beveled Glass, C.1910-12, Set 295.00
Auto, Lantern, Dietz Roadster Wagon, Red Reflector 25.00
Auto, License Plate, California, 1939, Commercial, World's Fair 15.00
Auto, License Plate, Connecticut, 1917 & 1918 .... 35.00
Auto, License Plate, Idaho, 1918 .... 8.00
Auto, License Plate, Iowa, Pair, 1920-23 .... 4.00
Auto, License Plate, Iowa, Pair, 1927-29 .... 4.00
Auto, License Plate, Iowa, 1933, Truck 7.00
Auto, License Plate, Iowa, 1937 .... 3.00
Auto, License Plate, Kansas City, Missouri, 1920 .... 15.00
Auto, License Plate, Kentucky, 1947 .... 3.00
Auto, License Plate, Louisiana, 1939 .... 4.50
Auto, License Plate, Massachusetts, 1926 .... 4.00
Auto, License Plate, Massachusetts, 1966 .... 2.00
Auto, License Plate, Michigan, 1939, Pair 13.75
Auto, License Plate, Mississippi, 1932 .... 5.00
Auto, License Plate, Mississippi, 1932, Dealer 10.00
Auto, License Plate, North West Territory, 1974, Polar Bear 5.00
Auto, License Plate, Oregon, 1918 .... 10.00
Auto, License Plate, Oregon, 1920 .... 7.00
Auto, License Plate, Pennsylvania, 1907 .... 85.00
Auto, License Plate, Pennsylvania, 1917 .... 12.50
Auto, License Plate, Pennsylvania, 1918 .... 12.50
Auto, License Plate, South Carolina, 1919 .... 15.00
Auto, License Plate, South Carolina, 1920 .... 15.00
Auto, License Plate, South Carolina, 1921 .... 15.00
Auto, License Plate, South Dakota, 1916, 1917, Pair 16.00
Auto, License Plate, Tennessee, 1941 .... 3.00
Auto, License Plate, Texas, 1939 .... 3.50
Auto, License Plate, Texas, 1942 .... 3.50
Auto, License Plate, Vermont, 1911, Porcelain 17.50
Auto, License Plate, Vermont, 1912 .... 17.50
Auto, License Plate, Vermont, 1912, Enameled 7.50
Auto, License Plate, Vermont, 1914, Blue On White 25.50
Auto, License Plate, Vermont, 1921 .... 3.50 To 4.00
Auto, License Plate, Vermont, 1925 .... 4.00
Auto, License Plate, Vermont, 1940 .... 2.00
Auto, License Plate, Vermont, 1952 .... 1.50
Auto, License Plate, Washington, 1916 .... 10.00
Auto, Manual, 1931, Franklin, Operation Maintenance Repair 35.00
Auto, Medallion, Studebaker, Bronze 15.00
Auto, Motometer, Boyce, 1918, Oakland, Radiator Cap 40.00
Auto, Motometer, Ford, C.1920, Nickel Over Brass 15.00
Auto, Pinback, 1934, Ford Motors 5.00
Auto, Points, Model T, Set Of 3 .... 5.00
Auto, Prestone, Gallon Tin, Early Car Pictured, Dated 1929 .... 12.00
Auto, Pump, Tire, Brass 8.00
Auto, Pump, Tire, Built In Trunk Of Pierce Arrow 50.00
Auto, Pump, Tire, Model T Ford, Mounts On Running Board 18.00
Auto, Rack, Luggage, Running Board 8.00
Auto, Radiator, Chevrolet, Honeycomb, Filler Hole, 1 3/4 In.Diameter 135.00
Auto, Sign, Ford, Dealer, Both Sides, Porcelain, Oval 50.00
Auto, Sign, Peerless Motor Car Co., Cleveland, Ohio, Dated 1910, Framed 45.00
Auto, Spotlight, Buick, 1926 .... 10.00
Auto, Vase, Cornucopia Shape, 12 In. 18.00
Auto, Vase, Etched, Silver Rim 20.00
Auto, Vase, Holder, Carnival Glass 22.50
Auto, Vase, Smoke Glass, Jack-In-The-Pulpit Top, 9 In. 20.00
Auto, Veil, Lady's, In Original Package 10.00
Auto, Visor, Sun, Fits Cars Of 40s 6.50
Auto, Whistle, Exhaust, 4 Tube, Model T Ford, Brass 28.00
Auto, Wrench, Connecting Rod, Model T Ford 3.00
Auto, Wrench, Ford, Spark Plug 3.00
Auto, Wrench, Monkey, Ford 5.50
Auto, Wrench, Nash 4.50
Auto, Wrench, 3 Way, 2 Socket, Cast Iron, Ford 7.50

Autumn Leaf pattern china was made for the Jewel Tea Company from 1936. Hall China Company of East Liverpool, Ohio, Crooksville China Company of Crooksville, Ohio, Harker Potteries of Chester, West Virginia, and Paden City Pottery, Paden City, West Virginia, made dishes with this design. Autumn Leaf dishes have been made in the 1970s.

Autumn Leaf, Bowl, Jewel Tea, Red Poppy, Set Of 3	37.50
Autumn Leaf, Bowl, Mixing, Hall	9.00
Autumn Leaf, Bowl, Mixing, Jewel Tea, Set	23.50
Autumn Leaf, Canister, Jewel Tea	5.00
Autumn Leaf, Casserole, Covered, Jewel Tea	18.00
Autumn Leaf, Casserole, Hall	9.50
Autumn Leaf, Coffeepot, Jewel Tea	18.50
Autumn Leaf, Coffeepot, Jewel Tea, Insert	20.00
Autumn Leaf, Cookie Jar, Jewel Tea	35.00
Autumn Leaf, Cup & Saucer, Jewel Tea, Set Of 4	75.00
Autumn Leaf, Goblet, Jewel Tea	75.00
Autumn Leaf, Gravy Boat, Jewel Tea	12.00
Autumn Leaf, Hot Pad, Jewel Tea, Oval, 10 3/4 In., Pair	11.00
Autumn Leaf, Mustard, Open, Underplate, Jewel Tea	18.00
Autumn Leaf, Pitcher, Milk, Jewel Tea	8.50
Autumn Leaf, Pitcher, Tilt, Hall	12.00
Autumn Leaf, Pitcher, Water, Jewel Tea	15.00
Autumn Leaf, Plate, Jewel Tea, 9 In.	3.00
Autumn Leaf, Plate, Jewel Tea, 10 In.	4.00
Autumn Leaf, Teapot, Aladdin, Insert	22.00
Autumn Leaf, Teapot, Jewel Tea, Aladdin, Oval Warmer	35.00
Autumn Leaf, Teapot, Jewel Tea, 8 In.	25.00
Autumn Leaf, Tray, Jewel Tea, 2 Tiered	25.00
Aventurine, Vase, Enamel Flowers, Green, 3 3/4 In., Pair	370.00
Avon, see Bottle, Avon	
Avon Pottery, Chamber Set, Tooth Brush Holder, Mug, Soap Dish, C.1902	55.00
Avon Pottery, Jardiniere, Japanese Birdimal, Signed F.H.Rhead	800.00
Avon Pottery, Pitcher, Hound Handled, Hounds Attacking Stag, Green Matte	185.00
Aynsley, see also Chelsea Grape	
Aynsley, Tea Set, White, Cobalt Blue, Gilt, 3 Piece	175.00
Baby Carriage, Adjustable Canopy, Wicker, Early 1900s	500.00
Baby Carriage, Diaper Storage Area, Adjustable Hood	300.00
Baby Carriage, Perambulator, Parasol Cover, 1877	550.00
Baby Carriage, Stroller, Wicker, Cleveland, Ohio, 1902	495.00
Baby Carriage, The Kinley Manufacturing Company, 1860	185.00
Baby Carriage, Victorian, Rattan, 50 In.	650.00
Baby Carriage, Whitney Reed	1000.00
Baby Carriage, Wood Wheels, Wicker	125.00

Baccarat glass was made in France by La Compagnie des Cristalleries de Baccarat, located about 150 miles from Paris. The factory was started in 1765. The firm went bankrupt and began operating again about 1822. Famous cane and millefiori paperweights were made there during the 1860-1880 period. The firm is still working near Paris making paperweights and glasswares.

Baccarat, Atomizer, Rubena Swirl	24.00 To 27.50
Baccarat, Bell, Clear Cut	34.50
Baccarat, Bottle, Atomizer, Signed, Original Green Leather Case	95.00
Baccarat, Bottle, Perfume, Amberina Swirl	75.00
Baccarat, Bottle, Perfume, Cranberry To Clear, Faceted Stopper, 4 1/4 In.	65.00
Baccarat, Bottle, Perfume, Frosted, Gold Swags, Signed	38.00
Baccarat, Bottle, Perfume, Mushroom Stopper, Signed, 4 1/4 In.	20.00
Baccarat, Bottle, Perfume, Pink Swirl, Stopper	25.00
Baccarat, Bottle, Perfume, Powder Box, In Beveled Glass Box, 2 Bottles	115.00
Baccarat, Bottle, Perfume, Stopper, 4 In.	22.50
Baccarat, Bowl, Engraved Border, Crystal, 9 In.Diameter	35.00
Baccarat, Bowl, Etched, Marked, 9 In.	85.00
Baccarat, Bowl, Pedestal, Cranberry, Signed	55.00
Baccarat, Carafe, Water, Matching Plate & Tumbler 7 3/4 In.	145.00
Baccarat, Carafe, Water, Tumbler, Cranberry To Clear, Signed	75.00
Baccarat, Cologne, Amberina, Swirl, Stopper & Bases Numbered, Pair	55.00

Baccarat, Vase, Cameo, Green Flowers
& Border, Square, 10 In.

Baccarat, Compote, Cut, Signed, 11 X 10 In.Diameter	600.00
Baccarat, Compote, Swirl Pattern, Clear, 6 1/2 X 8 In.Diameter	65.00
Baccarat, Decanter, Etched, Pumpkin Seed Shape, Signed, 9 1/2 In.	28.00
Baccarat, Decanter, Six Liquors, Seaweed Design	125.00
Baccarat, Dish, Pin, Stippled Ground, Cut Pink Flowers, 9 1/2 X 3 1/2 In.	52.00
Baccarat, Dresser Set, Matching Stoppers, 5 Piece	995.00
Baccarat, Ice Bucket, Harvard, Amberina, Signed	135.00
Baccarat, Inkwell, Hinged Cover	32.00
Baccarat, Lamp, Fairy, Peacock Blue, Candle Cup, Signed, 6 X 5 In.	275.00
Baccarat, Lamp, Hurricane, Clear Holder, Acid Cut, 15 1/2 X 5 In., Pair	650.00
Baccarat, Lamp, Perfume, Clear To Blue, Brass Screw Top, 6 1/2 In.	42.00
Baccarat, Lamp, Whale Oil, Amberina Swirl, Glass, 13 In.	100.00
Baccarat, Obelisk, Crystal, Signed, 10 In.	85.00
Baccarat, Paperweight, Bergstrom, Evangeline, Sulfide	90.00
Baccarat, Paperweight, Bonaparte, Napoleon, Original Box	70.00
Baccarat, Paperweight, Frog, Lead Crystal, 4 1/4 X 2 1/2 In.	50.00
Baccarat, Paperweight, Hoover, Herbert	70.00
Baccarat, Paperweight, Hoover, Herbert, Blue Overlay, Sulfide	250.00
Baccarat, Paperweight, Jackson, Andrew	70.00
Baccarat, Paperweight, Kennedy, J.F.	250.00
Baccarat, Paperweight, Kennedy, J.F., White Overlay, Sulfide	700.00
Baccarat, Paperweight, Millefiori With Zodiac Silhouettes, 1969	175.00
Baccarat, Paperweight, Monroe, James	70.00
Baccarat, Paperweight, Pope John XX111, Sulfide, Red Ground	90.00 To 120.00
Baccarat, Paperweight, Pope Pius, Overlay	400.00
Baccarat, Paperweight, Rayburn, Sam, Sulfide On Blue Ground	350.00
Baccarat, Paperweight, Red Mark, Wigstand, 13 In.	450.00
Baccarat, Paperweight, Rogers, Will, Sulfide	80.00
Baccarat, Paperweight, Roosevelt, Eleanor	70.00
Baccarat, Paperweight, Roosevelt, Eleanor, Purple Overlay, Sulfide	275.00
Baccarat, Paperweight, Roosevelt, Theodore	85.00 To 90.00
Baccarat, Paperweight, Roosevelt, Theodore, Gray Overlay, Sulfide	325.00
Baccarat, Paperweight, Squirrel, Lead Crystal, 4 1/2 X 1 3/4 In.	50.00
Baccarat, Paperweight, Stevenson, Adlai	65.00 To 70.00
Baccarat, Paperweight, Stevenson, Adlai, Overlay	200.00 To 225.00
Baccarat, Paperweight, Turtle, Lead Crystal, 4 X 1 1/4 In.	60.00
Baccarat, Paperweight, Wilson, Woodrow	65.00 To 70.00
Baccarat, Paperweight, 8 Pointed Yellow Flower On Blue Ground, 1971	190.00
Baccarat, Perfume, Cobalt Stopper, Signed Shalimare	45.00
Baccarat, Pitcher, Water, 6 Glasses, Amberina, Marked	420.00
Baccarat, Tumble-Up, Signed, 3 Pieces	165.00
Baccarat, Turtle, Crystal, Signed, 2 1/2 X 4 X 1 1/2 In.	50.00
Baccarat, Vase, Blanc De Chine, Paper Label, 12 In.	175.00
Baccarat, Vase, Bronze Trim, Crystal, Signed, 14 In.	295.00
Baccarat, Vase, Cameo, Green Flowers & Border, Square, 10 In. ....Illus	200.00
Baccarat, Vase, Cameo, 3 Color, Flowers, Leaves, 10 1/2 In. ....Illus	650.00
Baccarat, Vase, Enameled Gold Snake Winding Around Body, Signed, 8 In.	475.00
Baccarat, Vase, Linear Geometric Motif, Bearing Stamp, 10 In.	150.00
Baccarat, Vase, Red Iris, Stippled Ground, Wheel Cut, 8 Ix 3 1/8 In.Diam.	195.00
Baccarat, Vase, Stick, Sapphire Blue, Cameo, Bamboo Stump, 8 In.	275.00
Baccarat, Vase, Trumpet Shape, Crystal, Late 19th Century, 11 1/4 In.	200.00
Baccarat, Vase, Trumpet, Scalloped Edge, Bronze Base, Signed, 11 1/2 In.	195.00

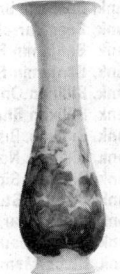

Baccarat, Vase, Cameo, 3 Color,
Flowers, Leaves, 10 1/2 In.

Baccarat, Wine, Crystal, 6 In., 6 Piece	70.00
Badge, Civil Defense Deputy, Douglas County, Nebraska	26.00
Badge, Correction Officer, Camden County Prison, Hallmarked	37.50
Badge, Deputy Sheriff, Greene County, Missouri, Porcelain, Seal, Hallmarked	52.50
Badge, Deputy Sheriff, Seven Point, Platte County, Missouri, Porcelain	50.00
Badge, Deputy Sheriff, Winnebago County, Illinois Seal, 6 Point Star	60.00
Badge, Deputy, Game Protector, Ft.Lewis, Shield Type, Hallmarked	30.00
Badge, Employee's, John Deere Plow Works	25.00
Badge, Employee's, Railway Express Agency, Porcelain	25.00
Badge, Park Ranger, Jackson County, Missouri, Sunburst	65.00
Badge, Police, City Of Miami, Seal, Round, Eagle Top	42.50
Badge, Police, Marshall, Missouri, Eagle Top	45.00
Badge, Police, Northwestern Pacific R.R., 7 Point	25.00
Badge, S.W.A.T. Squad, California Stare, Enameled	22.00
Bag, Beaded, see Beaded Bag	
Bakalowitz, Vase, Salmon Iridescent, Bronze Nouveau Holder, 10 In.	325.00

Metal banks have been made since 1868. There are still banks, mechanical banks, and registering banks (those which total money deposited on the face of the bank). Many old banks have been reproduced since the 1950s in iron or plastic.

Bank, A. & P. Eight O'Clock Coffee Can, Red, Coffee Grinder On Front	5.00
Bank, Acrobats, Iron	35.00
Bank, Add-O-Bank, Blue, Citizens' & Southern Bank, Key, 4 In.	30.00
Bank, Alphabet, English, Cast Iron	15.00
Bank, American Can Co., Thomas Jefferson, John Hancock, Tin	16.50
Bank, Antlered Deer	50.00
Bank, Arabian Safe, Cast Iron	30.00 To 50.00
Bank, Armored Car, Rubber Tires, Die Cast, 5 1/4 In.	35.00
Bank, Astronauts, Cast Iron	20.00
Bank, Atlas, Strong Shoulder Midget, Slot In Lid	20.00
Bank, Auto, Cast Iron	375.00
Bank, Babbit Can, 3 In.	3.00
Bank, Babo	8.00
Bank, Bank Building, Cast Iron	22.50 To 45.00
Bank, Banthrico Automobile, Cast Iron	8.50
Bank, Barrel Shape, Lebanon Bank, Cast Iron	6.50
Bank, Barrel, Ceramic, Austria, 3 In.	10.00
Bank, Barrel, Dodge Car, Tin	8.00
Bank, Barrel, Happy Days, Tin	8.00
Bank, Barrel, Red Ware, Red, Gold Bands	28.00
Bank, Barrel, Wood, Brass Hoops, Key	15.00
Bank, Baseball Player, Cast Iron	75.00 To 100.00
Bank, Baseball, Glass	7.00 To 10.00
Bank, Baseball, 1839-1939	10.00
Bank, Basket Of Scotties	25.00 To 45.00
Bank, Basket, 2 Handles, Cast Iron	50.00
Bank, Batman's Robin, Ceramic	15.00
Bank, Bear Begging, Iron	33.00
Bank, Bear Standing, Iron	55.00
Bank, Bear Standing, Pig In Arms, Brass, 5 1/2 In.	45.00
Bank, Bear, Glass, 8 1/2 In.	6.50

Bank, Beehive, Brown Flip Stoneware, A.Stough Incised On Front, Dated 1886 .... 250.00
Bank, Beer Barrel, Metz Premium Beer, Porcelain, 8 In. 65.00
Bank, Benjamin Franklin Book 24.00
Bank, Benjamin Franklin Thrift Bank, Register 34.00
Bank, Billiken On Throne 65.00
Bank, Billiken Shoes Bring Luck, Cast Iron 45.00
Bank, Billiken, Bisque, 5 3/4 In. 12.75
Bank, Billiken, No.48, Iron 95.00
Bank, Billiken, Signed Good Luck, Cast Iron, 4 1/2 In. 65.00
Bank, Bird On Stump, Cast Iron 175.00
Bank, Black Bear, Cast Iron, C.1940, 6 1/2 In. 15.00
Bank, Black Beauty, Cast Iron 38.00
Bank, Black Mammy, Hands On Hips, Large, Cast Iron 45.00
Bank, Black Man, Original Paint, Cast Iron, 5 1/2 In. 50.00
Bank, Blue Sunoco, Tin 5.00
Bank, Bokar Coffee Can, Black 3.50
Bank, Book Style, Celluloid Cover, Day & Month Change As Coins Inserted 200.00
Bank, Book, Irving Savings Bank, N.Y.C., Pair 17.00
Bank, Book, New York Life Insurance Company 12.00
Bank, Boot, Roy Rogers, Pot Metal, 6 In. 27.00
Bank, Boscul Coffee 8.00
Bank, Boston Bull Dog, Standing 49.50
Bank, Boston Terrier, Standing, Cast Iron, 5 1/4 In. 45.00
Bank, Bottle, Snow Crest, Bear 5.00
Bank, Bottle, Snow Crest, Elephant 5.00
Bank, Bottle, Snow Crest, Pig 5.00
Bank, Boxer, Iron 12.50
Bank, Boy Scout, Cast Iron .... 40.00 To 80.00
Bank, Broadway Savings, Cast Iron 11.00
Bank, Buffalo, Cast Iron 100.00
Bank, Building, 12 Stories High, Iron, 5 1/2 In. 30.00
Bank, Building, 16 Front Windows, Cast Iron, 3 In. 20.00
Bank, Bull, Angus, Cast Iron, 11 X 5 1/2 In. 25.00
Bank, Bulldog, Black & White, Blue Bow, Fly On Back, Iron 34.00
Bank, Bulldog, Brown & White, Cast Iron 10.00
Bank, Bulldog, Seated, Cast Iron 28.00
Bank, Bulldog, Standing, Cast Iron, 5 1/2 In. 65.00
Bank, Burglar House Safe, Cast Iron 45.00
Bank, Burma Shave, Glass 10.00
Bank, Buster Brown & Tige, Good Luck, Cast Iron 100.00
Bank, Cabin, Chein 12.00
Bank, Calendar Advertising, Tin & Plastic, 1942 .... 15.00
Bank, Camel, Small, Cast Iron 75.00
Bank, Campbell Kids 97.50
Bank, Capitalist, Cast Iron 55.00
Bank, Captain Kidd Mystery Bank, Tin 14.00
Bank, Car, Buick, 1950s, Cast Iron 68.00
Bank, Casey Jones, Cast Iron 21.00
Bank, Cash Register, Dime, Chein 17.00
Bank, Cash Register, Happy Days, Tin, Chein 20.00
Bank, Cash Register, Uncle Sam's, Tin 27.50
Bank, Cat On Tub, Cast Iron 20.00
Bank, Cat Rolling Ball, Gold Gilt 80.00
Bank, Cat With Ball, Iron 37.00
Bank, Cat With Bow Tie, Iron 31.00
Bank, Cat, Seated, Cast Iron 95.00
Bank, Church, Chein, Tin 8.00
Bank, Clock, Hands Move, Cast Iron 18.00
Bank, Clown, Battery Operated 27.00
Bank, Clown, Cast Iron .... 25.00 To 40.00
Bank, Clown, Daily Dime 15.00
Bank, Clown, Do You Know Me, Tin, Gold & Red Paint, 6 1/4 In. 255.00
Bank, Clown, Glass, 7 In. 8.50
Bank, Coffin, Tin, Japanese 12.00
Bank, Columbia, Eagle & Uncle Sam Carrying Satchel, Cast Iron 148.50
Bank, Cook Stove, Tin Sides, Cast Iron, Cook With Cash 40.00
Bank, Copper Boot, 5 In. 45.00

Bank, Covered Wagon, 1940, Pot Metal	50.00
Bank, Cow, Small, Cast Iron	150.00
Bank, Cowardly Lion, 8 In.	15.00
Bank, Cowboy, Cast Iron	15.00
Bank, Cylinder Shape, Coin Slot, Tin	12.00
Bank, Cylinder Shape, 2 Cent To 25 Cent Slots, Sun With 5 Cent In Mouth	25.00
Bank, Decker's Iowana Pig, Cast Iron	70.00
Bank, Deer, Cast Iron	20.00 To 65.00
Bank, Devil, Cast Iron	35.00
Bank, Dime Register, Dwarfs	25.00
Bank, Dime Register, Flat, Jackie Robinson	25.00
Bank, Dime Register, Picture Of Clown & Monkey, Tin, 1930s	27.00
Bank, Dime Savings, 1907, Metal	15.00
Bank, Dime Savings, 1915, Metal	15.00
Bank, Dirigible, Gray China, 9 In.	20.00
Bank, Dog Head, Staffordshire	32.00
Bank, Dog House, Brass	40.00
Bank, Dog On Tub	60.00
Bank, Dog With Pack, Brass	15.00
Bank, Dog With Pack, Iron	35.00 To 42.00
Bank, Dog, Sitting, Cast Iron	18.00
Bank, Donkey, Cast Iron	26.00 To 115.00
Bank, Donkey, Original Paint, Cast Iron	40.00
Bank, Double Face, Cast Iron, 4 In.	65.00
Bank, Drum, Ohio Art	10.00
Bank, Drum, Remember Pearl Harbor, Tin	7.50
Bank, Duck On Tub, Save For A Rainy Day, Iron	55.00
Bank, Electrolux Refrigerator, Cast Iron, 4 X 2 In.	20.00
Bank, Elephant On Drum, Cast Iron, 4 3/4 In.	100.00
Bank, Elephant On Wheels	100.00
Bank, Elephant With Howdah, Cast Iron, 3 In.	35.00
Bank, Elephant, Blue, Chein	40.00
Bank, Elephant, Cast Iron	30.00 To 47.50
Bank, Elephant, Standing On Tub, Cast Iron	65.00
Bank, Fat Chicken, Cast Iron	35.00
Bank, Fat Hen & Chicks, Chalkware, 9 In.	16.00
Bank, Feed The Kitty, Pot Metal	35.00 To 45.00
Bank, Fido, Cast Iron	40.00
Bank, Fireman, Cast Iron	150.00
Bank, First National Bank Of Greenville, Dated 1925, Chrome Plated	20.00
Bank, Flat Iron Building, Cast Iron	35.00
Bank, Floor Safe, Key, Cast Iron	22.00
Bank, Football Player, Cast Iron	75.00
Bank, Ford, Akron Dime Bank, Key, Cast Iron	12.50
Bank, Gas Pump, Cast Iron	325.00
Bank, General Lee	200.00
Bank, General MacArthur, Bust, Cast Iron	6.00
Bank, General Pershing, Cast Iron	95.00
Bank, George Washington	300.00
Bank, Give Me A Penny, Iron	75.00
Bank, Give Me A Penny, Original Glossy Paint	120.00
Bank, Globe On Half Arc, Cast Iron	116.00
Bank, Globe, Chein, Tin	15.00
Bank, Golden Spaniel, Cast Iron	10.00
Bank, Good Luck, Cast Iron	25.00
Bank, Good Luck, Dime, Ottumwa Courier Home Paper	8.00
Bank, Goose, Cast Iron	75.00
Bank, Goose, Gilded, Cast Iron, 5 In.	55.00
Bank, Graf Zeppelin, 1929, Lead, 6 3/4 In.	30.00
Bank, Gulf-Pride Oil Can	3.50
Bank, Hat, World War I, Cast Iron	115.00
Bank, Hershey Bank, Plastic & Tin	20.00
Bank, Hole-In-One, Battery Operated	45.00
Bank, Home Savings	50.00
Bank, Horse On Tub, Cast Iron	50.00
Bank, Horse, Gold Colored, Cast Iron, 10 In.	6.00
Bank, Horse, Prancing, Cast Iron	28.00

Bank, Horseshoe	115.00
Bank, Horseshoe, Opens With 10 Dimes, 1 In.	100.00
Bank, House, Cast Iron	10.00 To 55.00
Bank, House, Pittsburgh Paints, Glass	21.50
Bank, House, Two Story, Iron	30.00
Bank, Humpty Dumpty, Iron	35.00
Bank, Independence Hall, Cast Iron	175.00
Bank, Indian Head National Bank, Cast Iron	55.00 To 65.00
Bank, Indian Head, China	15.00
Bank, Indian, Cast Iron, 6 In.	65.00
Bank, Indian, Standing, Iron, 6 In.	70.00
Bank, Iowa Bank, Oval, Cast Iron	6.50
Bank, J.F.Kennedy, Cast Iron	9.00
Bank, John Deere, Tin	10.00
Bank, Jug, Red Ware	20.00
Bank, Kewpie, Glass	65.00
Bank, Kitten With Ribbon, Iron	31.00
Bank, Lady, Colonial Dress, Pot Metal	15.00
Bank, Lamb	27.50
Bank, Liberty Bell	25.00 To 55.00
Bank, Liberty Bell 1926, Sesquicentennial, Cast Iron, 4 In.	75.00
Bank, Liberty Bell, 1926 Exposition, Peerless Silver Co., New York	25.00
Bank, Lighthouse, Iron, Coins Deposited In Tower, Red, Bronze, 10 1/2 In.	165.00
Bank, Lincoln High Hat, Iron	60.00
Bank, Lincoln Log Cabin, VanDyke Tea, Ceramic	18.00
Bank, Lincoln, Glass	5.00
Bank, Lindbergh Bust, Cast Iron	45.00
Bank, Lion On Wheels	100.00
Bank, Lion Standing, Brass, 4 X 5 In.	40.00
Bank, Lion, Cast Iron, 4 In.	20.00
Bank, Lion, Cast Iron, 5 In.	22.00
Bank, Lion, Standing, Cast Iron	29.00
Bank, Lion, Standing, Open Mouth, Head Slot, Cast Iron, 3 3/4 X 4 1/4 In.	40.00
Bank, Little Millionaire Savings	9.00
Bank, Little Red Riding Hood	500.00
Bank, Log Cabin Syrup, Tin	22.00
Bank, Log Cabin, Cast Iron, Large	55.00
Bank, Log Cabin, Glass	18.50
Bank, Log Cabin, Milk Glass	19.50
Bank, Log Cabin, Pottery, Brown Glaze	22.00
Bank, Long Horn Steer, Iron	42.00
Bank, Mailbox With Eagle, Cast Iron	45.00
Bank, Mailbox, Cast Iron	28.00 To 100.00
Bank, Mailbox, Moveable Letter Slot	30.00
Bank, Mailbox, On Post, Cast Iron, 6 1/2 In.	45.00
Bank, Mailbox, Original Green Paint, Gold Lettering, Cast Iron	32.50
Bank, Mailbox, 4 Legs, Pot Metal	15.00
Bank, Mammy With Spoon	75.00
Bank, Mammy, Blue Kerchief, Red & White Dress, Cast Iron	55.00
Bank, Mammy, Coconut Head, Cast Iron	15.00
Bank, Man, McCoy	8.50

Mechanical banks were first made about 1870. Any bank with moving parts is considered mechanical, although those most collected are the metal banks made before World War I. Reproductions are being made.

Bank, Mechanical, Baseball Player	60.00
Bank, Mechanical, Bear, Ive's, Dated 1872	550.00
Bank, Mechanical, Book Of Knowledge, Leap Frog, Cast Iron, 7 X 5 In.	200.00
Bank, Mechanical, Cabin	235.00
Bank, Mechanical, Calumet II	150.00
Bank, Mechanical, Church, Chein	50.00
Bank, Mechanical, Clown, Tongue Sticks Out, Tin	12.50
Bank, Mechanical, Coin Activates Top To Rotate & Show Pictures, Tin	350.00
Bank, Mechanical, Creedmoor	150.00 To 250.00
Bank, Mechanical, Dog, I Hear A Call	175.00
Bank, Mechanical, Dog, Tray	3000.00
Bank, Mechanical, Donkey, Cast Iron	225.00

Bank, Mechanical, Duck, Tin, Disney, 1940s 45.00
Bank, Mechanical, Eagle & Eaglets, 1883 .... 175.00 To 250.00
Bank, Mechanical, Elephant With Howdah 65.00
Bank, Mechanical, Elephant, Swings Trunk, Small 100.00
Bank, Mechanical, Elephant, Trunk Puts Coin In, Metal 19.50
Bank, Mechanical, Frog On Rock 250.00
Bank, Mechanical, Giant In Tower 7000.00
Bank, Mechanical, Globe On Arc 150.00
Bank, Mechanical, Hippo, Wind Up, Tin, C.1950 .... 10.00
Bank, Mechanical, Humpty Dumpty, Iron 185.00
Bank, Mechanical, Jolly Nigger, Large 90.00
Bank, Mechanical, Jolly Nigger, Patented March 14th, 1892 .... 95.00
Bank, Mechanical, Jolly Nigger, Small 115.00
Bank, Mechanical, Jonah & The Whale, 10 X 3 1/2 X 5 1/2 In. 650.00
Bank, Mechanical, Kiltie 675.00
Bank, Mechanical, Lion & Monkeys, Glass Eyes, Dated July 17, 1883, Key 375.00
Bank, Mechanical, Magician 450.00
Bank, Mechanical, Mason And Hod Carrier 600.00
Bank, Mechanical, Mason, Cast Iron 295.00
Bank, Mechanical, Merry-Go-Round 195.00
Bank, Mechanical, Monkey & Parrot, Tin, German 350.00
Bank, Mechanical, Monkey, Tips Hat, Chein, Tin 15.00
Bank, Mechanical, Negro In Cabin .... 120.00 To 135.00
Bank, Mechanical, Old Cabin, 3/4 X 1/4 In. 100.00
Bank, Mechanical, Organ Cat & Dog 265.00
Bank, Mechanical, Organ, 1882 .... 150.00
Bank, Mechanical, Owl, Turns Head 150.00
Bank, Mechanical, Parking Meter, Metal, 1940s 22.00
Bank, Mechanical, Patronize The Blind Man 2500.00
Bank, Mechanical, Popeye, Knock Out .... 525.00 To 550.00
Bank, Mechanical, Pump & Bucket 750.00
Bank, Mechanical, Punch & Judy .... 350.00 To 380.00
Bank, Mechanical, Rabbit In Cabbage Patch 225.00
Bank, Mechanical, Rocket 15.00
Bank, Mechanical, Soldier Shoots Coin Into Bottle 35.00
Bank, Mechanical, Southern Comfort, Concealed Lock 49.00
Bank, Mechanical, Speaking Dog 350.00
Bank, Mechanical, Sweet Thrift, Vending, 1920s, Glass Front, Tin, 6 In. 195.00
Bank, Mechanical, Tammany .... 95.00 To 150.00
Bank, Mechanical, Teddy And The Bear, Original Paint 125.00
Bank, Mechanical, Trick Dog, Solid Base 225.00
Bank, Mechanical, Uncle Remus 2500.00
Bank, Mechanical, Uncle Wiggley, Chein 105.00
Bank, Mechanical, Walking Elephant, Cast Iron, Ive's 125.00
Bank, Mechanical, William Tell .... 200.00 To 225.00
Bank, Mechanical, Windmill, Tin 120.00
Bank, Mechanical, Wise Owl, Glass Eyes, Original 115.00
Bank, Merry-Go-Round, Semi-Mechanical, Dated 50.00
Bank, Mickey Mouse, Sitting On Drum, Playing Mandolin, 1920s, Pot Metal 600.00
Bank, Middy, Cast Iron 75.00
Bank, Monkey, Tin, Chein 20.00
Bank, Mother Hubbard 300.00
Bank, Mr.Peanut, 8 1/2 In. 4.00
Bank, Mulligan The Cop 85.00
Bank, Mutt & Jeff, Cast Iron .... 27.50 To 85.00
Bank, Old Auto, China 5.00
Bank, Old Lady In Shoe, Cast Iron 5.00
Bank, Owl On Stump, Cast Iron .... 65.00 To 125.00
Bank, Owl, Carnival Glass, Marigold 32.00
Bank, Owl, Cast Iron, Original Paint, 4 1/4 In. 90.00
Bank, Owl, Royal Ruby 145.00
Bank, Panda 17.50
Bank, Peaked Roof House, Tole 16.00
Bank, Pennies Make Pounds, War Bank, Cast Iron 15.00
Bank, Pig In Pocketbook, China 35.00
Bank, Pig With Bow Tie 50.00

Bank, Pig, Black & White, Pink Mouth & Nostrils	45.00
Bank, Pig, Cast Iron	10.00 To 50.00
Bank, Pig, Glass	3.00
Bank, Pig, Iron, 3 X 7 In.	60.00
Bank, Pig, Ohio Pottery, Crown Mottled, 4 1/2 In.	45.00
Bank, Pig, Red Bow & Flowers On White, Roseville, Ceramic, Silver Sticker	65.00
Bank, Pig, Seated	39.50
Bank, Pig, Signed Banthrico	20.00
Bank, Pig, Sitting, Cast Iron	25.00 To 29.00
Bank, Poll Parrot Shoes, Tin	37.50
Bank, Pony, Cast Iron, 2 3/4 X 3 1/4 In.	55.00
Bank, Pony, Cast Iron, 3 1/4 In.	20.00
Bank, Popeye & Cage	90.00
Bank, Possum, Cast Iron	275.00
Bank, Post Box, Cast Iron	24.00
Bank, Presto	42.50
Bank, Prince Albert, Padlock, Silver Plated Brass, 3 3/4 In.	20.00
Bank, Prosperity Pail, Cast Iron	14.50
Bank, Prudential Rock, Cast Iron	39.00
Bank, Puppy Dog, Cast Iron	35.00
Bank, Rabbit, Iron, 4 3/4 In.	37.00
Bank, Radio, Cast Iron, 3 X 4 1/2 In.	75.00
Bank, Radio, Glass	12.00
Bank, Radio, Majestic, Cast Iron	35.00 To 53.00
Bank, Radio, 3 Knobs, Original Paint, Cast Iron	65.00
Bank, Red Circle Coffee, Yellow	8.00
Bank, Red Goose Shoes, Cast Iron	95.00 To 110.00
Bank, Refrigerator, Servel, Die Cast	25.00
Bank, Register, 10 Cent, Flat, Girl & Boy	10.50
Bank, Rhino, Cast Iron	275.00
Bank, Robin's Nest, 3 Eggs In Nest	300.00
Bank, Roly Poly Clown, Chrome Plated, Tin, 6 1/2 In.	35.00
Bank, Rooster, Cast Iron	35.00
Bank, Rudolph The Reindeer, Cast Iron	22.00
Bank, Safe Deposit, Dated May 12, 1885, 5 X 4 X 4 1/4 In.	75.00
Bank, Safe, Centerpost, Key, Cast Iron	25.00
Bank, Safe, Combination, Lucky Deposit, Cast Iron	10.00
Bank, Safe, I-Deal Safe Deposit, Footed	25.00
Bank, Safe, Key, Cast Iron	28.00
Bank, Safe, Odd Shape, Leopolis, Wisconsin, Cast Iron	20.00
Bank, Safe, Penny Trust Co., Tin Top	12.00
Bank, Safe, Siegel Co., Boston, Cast Iron	22.00
Bank, Safe, Signed, 1897	28.00
Bank, Safe, Union Bank, Cast Iron	28.00
Bank, Sailor, Cast Iron, 5 1/4 In.	85.00 To 115.00
Bank, Santa Claus, Back Pack, Hat Opens, Cast Iron, 4 In.	35.00
Bank, Santa Claus, The Pennsylvania Trust Co., Reading, Pa.	80.00
Bank, Santa In Chair, Chalkware	15.00
Bank, Santa With Child, Cast Iron	20.00
Bank, Santa With Phone, Cast Iron	18.00
Bank, Santa, Sleeping In Chair, Attleboro, Mass., Cast Iron, 6 X 7 In.	20.00
Bank, Schenley Whiskey, Bottle Center, Ashtray, Cast Iron, 3 In.	12.50
Bank, Schoolhouse, Cast Iron	20.00
Bank, Scottie, Cast Iron	20.00
Bank, Scottie, 1940s, Cast Iron	12.00
Bank, Seal, Glass, 7 1/2 In.	8.50
Bank, Security Safe Deposit, Dated March I, 1877, Cast Iron, 4 In.	45.00
Bank, Security Safe Deposit, Wooden Drawers Inside, Iron	37.50
Bank, Share Cropper, Cast Iron	70.00 To 97.50
Bank, Sheep, Cast Iron	32.00 To 65.00
Bank, Shoe House, Cast Iron	8.00
Bank, Shriner's Hat, Red & Black, Al Menah Emblem, Cast Iron	6.50
Bank, Simple Simon, Tin	15.00
Bank, Sitting Pig, Metal, Bronzed	20.00
Bank, St.Bernard, Cast Iron	75.00
Bank, State Bank, Cast Iron, 7 1/2 X 5 1/2 In.	60.00 To 95.00
Bank, Statue Of Liberty, Cast Iron	47.00 To 50.00

Bank, Stein, Pewter	25.00
Bank, Strato, Key, Cast Iron	22.50
Bank, Structo 66	15.00
Bank, Suitcase Type, W.R. Burns, 1901, Cast Iron	25.00
Bank, Supermarket, Early 1930s, Lithograph, Child's, Tin	12.50
Bank, Sweet Thrift, Glass & Vending Drawer, Tin, Key	295.00
Bank, Syrup Bottle, Log Cabin, Original Lid	20.00
Bank, Teddy Bear, Cast Iron	65.00
Bank, Teddy Bear, Pushing Cart, Cast Iron	10.00
Bank, Thrifty Pig, Upright	55.00
Bank, Tiny Mite, Combination Safe	15.00
Bank, Top Hat, Pass Around The Hat	75.00
Bank, Tractor, Cast Iron	30.00
Bank, Train Engine, Cast Iron, Japan	25.00
Bank, Train, Casey Jones, Pot Metal	10.00
Bank, Traveling Teller, Slots For Various Coins, 2 1/2 X 4 In.	20.00
Bank, Treasure Chest, Iron	9.00
Bank, Troll, Cast Iron	7.00
Bank, Trunk, Tin, May 29, 1888, 3 In.	32.00
Bank, Turkey, Small, Cast Iron	55.00
Bank, Two Bears & Beehive, Cast Iron	37.00
Bank, Two Faced Women, Small	67.50
Bank, Typewriter, Underwood, 1939 World's Fair, Cast Iron	18.00
Bank, U.S. Tank, W.W.I, Iron	50.00
Bank, U.S.Mail, Lift Top, Cast Iron, 3 1/2 X 2 1/2 In.	35.00
Bank, U.S.Savings Bank, Wooden, Patented 1877, 14 1/2 In.	25.00
Bank, Uncle Sam Head, Bennington Green Flint, Enamel, 4 1/2 In.	95.00
Bank, Uncle Sam Register, Cast Iron, 1930s	10.00
Bank, Uncle Sam, Bust, Glazed Bisque, Signed, 1814, 4 1/2 In.	22.50
Bank, Uncle Sam, China	20.00
Bank, Uncle Sam, Globe, Plastic	18.00
Bank, Uncle Sam, Hat, Chein	28.00
Bank, Uncle Sam's 3-Coin Register	25.00 To 35.00
Bank, Uncle Scrooge, China	5.00
Bank, Union Safe, Cast Iron	26.00
Bank, Veedol Can, Blue	3.50
Bank, Watch Me Grow Tall, Tin	30.00
Bank, White City Puzzle, Cast Iron	55.00
Bank, Windmill, Cast Iron	75.00
Bank, Windmill, Music Box, Wood, 7 1/2 X 4 1/2 In.	25.00
Bank, Wishing Well, Cast Iron	5.00
Bank, Woolworth Building, Large	72.50
Bank, Woolworth Building, Pot Metal, 4 In.	30.00
Bank, Zeppelin, Iron	85.00
Banko, Vase, Tapestry Effect, Signed, Small, 3 1/4 In.	65.00
Barber Chair, Cast Iron, Porcelain, Upholstered, Koch	350.00
Barber Chair, White Porcelain	250.00
Barber Chair, Wooden	450.00
Barber, Chair, Wooden, Brass Feet, 1800s	1500.00
Barometer, Carved, Fitzsimons Barometer, Thermometer, Atmosphere, 11 X 47 In.	450.00
Barometer, George III, Mahogany, Mid-19th Century, 38 3/4 In.	425.00
Barometer, Hand Carved, Oak, Aneroid, 35 In.	245.00
Barometer, Stick, English, Queen Anne	385.00
Barometer, Thermometer, Mahogany, Negretti & Zambra, London, 1800s, 41 In.	525.00

Basalt is a black stoneware made by mixing iron and oxides into a basic clay.
It is very hard and can be finished on a lathe. Wedgwood developed his
famous black basalt in 1769, which was an improvement on a similar ware made in
Staffordshire, England, as early as 1740. Basalt is still being made in
England and on the Continent.

Basalt, see also Wedgwood

Basalt, Cup & Saucer	16.00
Basalt, Figurine, Halloween Cat, 4 X 3 In.	50.00
Basalt, Tea Set, Pot, Covered Sugar, Pitcher, Black Widow Pattern	68.00
Basalt, Tray, Bronze Mounted, 4 Paw Feet, Classical Figures, 1800s, 25 In.	325.00
Basket, Apache, Single Coil, Stem, Early 1900s	60.00
Basket, Apple Drying, 46 X 23 In.	275.00

Basket, Bicycle, Wicker, 15 In. 18.00
Basket, Cheese, 19th Century 195.00
Basket, Drying, Herb, Coiled Rye, Round, 15 In. 55.00
Basket, Eel, Oak Splint, Cone Shaped, 16 In. 60.00
Basket, Egg, Nantucket 85.00
Basket, Grocery, Reinforced With Metal, 1890 .... 35.00
Basket, Indian Loom, Pyramid Diagonal Top, 8 In. 55.00
Basket, Indian, Brown & Natural Woven Design, Hopi, 4 1/2 X 3 1/4 In. 15.00
Basket, Indian, Decorated, Double Handled 40.00
Basket, Indian, Maine, Red & Yellow, Covered, Rectangular, 23 X 13 X 11 In. .. 145.00
Basket, Indian, Mohawk, Covered, 19th Century, 14 1/2 In. 75.00
Basket, Indian, Turban Shape, Coiled Rye Bottom, Plaited Top, 11 In.Diam. .. 185.00
Basket, Ivory & Wood, Carved, Procession Of Animals, African, 16 1/4 In. ... 100.00
Basket, Market, Oak Splint, 17 In. 30.00
Basket, Nantucket, Brass Ears, 7 In. 290.00
Basket, Nantucket, 25 X 14 In. 435.00
Basket, Oval, Handle, 1/2 Bushel 30.00
Basket, Papago Indian, Coiled Construction, 2 Handles, 12 In. 35.00
Basket, Pennsylvania, Rye Straw, Beehive Shape, C.1820, 11 In. 35.00
Basket, Pennsylvania, Rye Straw, 13 In.Diameter 33.00
Basket, Picnic, Wicker 19.00
Basket, Reed, Woven, Handle, 18 X 9 In. 30.00
Basket, Round, Handles, Plaited Colors, C.1800, 16 1/2 X 13 In. 70.00
Basket, Sewing, Peking Beads & Coins, Chinese, 11 1/2 In.Diameter 22.50
Basket, Side Handle, Round Top & Square Bottom, Shaker, 16 X 6 In. 90.00
Basket, Splint, Grid Design, Carved Ash Handle, 7 1/4 X 10 X 7 1/4 In. 65.00
Basket, Splint, Mellow Color, 19 In. 65.00
Basket, Split Wood, Round, Handle, Gold & Black, 14 1/2 In. 22.50
Basket, Split Wood, Woven, Covered, Handle, 14 X 9 In. 30.00
Basket, Swing Handle, Round, Splint, 15 In.Diameter 150.00
Basket, Tea, Woven, Brass Hinges & Clasp, Tea Cozy, Cup & Teapot Inside ... 50.00
Basket, Tole & Wicker 10.00
Basket, Tulare Type, Storage, 8 X 16 In.Diameter 225.00
Basket, Turtle Shape, Branch Handle, Reed, 21 X 15 X 14 In. 65.00
Basket, Wicker, Handled, 9 X 16 In. 22.00
Basket, Wicker, Lift Up Lid, 2 Colors, 4 Quart 50.00
Basket, Woven Split Wood, Round, Handled, 15 X 7 In. 55.00
Batchelder, Vase, Blue & Copper Color, 1926, 4 In. 50.00
Batman, Lunch Box 5.00
Batman, Scope, Black Plastic, 1966, 22 In.Extended 15.00

Battersea enamels are enamels painted on copper and made in the Battersea District of London from about 1750 to 1756. Many similar enamels are mistakenly called Battersea.

Battersea, Box, A Pinch Of This Deserves A Kiss, Swimming Fish 140.00
Battersea, Box, Cover, Oval, Flowers 190.00
Battersea, Box, Lid Has Man On Horse, Green 265.00
Battersea, Box, Scalloped, Lid, Esteem The Giver, Black On White 120.00
Battersea, Plate, Birds & Flowers, 8 1/2 In. Diameter 118.00

Bavaria was a district where many types of pottery and porcelain were made for centuries. The words "Bavaria, Germany," appeared after 1871.

Bavarian, Berry Set, Bowl & 6 Dishes, All Signed Pasteur 175.00
Bavarian, Celery, Green, Pink & White Roses, Gold Trim 24.50
Bavarian, Creamer, Gray & Tan Roses, Gold Trim, 5 In. 10.00
Bavarian, Cup & Saucer, Demitasse, Crown Mark, Set Of 6 .... 59.00
Bavarian, Dish, Rolled Top, Flowers Inside & Out, Crown Mark, 7 1/2 In. ... 36.00
Bavarian, Humidor, Figural, Bust Of Man In Tri-Cornered Hat, Holding Pipe .. 45.00
Bavarian, Marmalade Set, Blue Border, Tiny Fruits, Ladle, Saucer, Signed .. 20.00
Bavarian, Mayonnaise Set, Footed Bowl, Ladle, Plate 65.00
Bavarian, Mug, Head Portrait Of Elk, Lizard Handle 60.00
Bavarian, Mush Set, Gibson Girl & Child, Signed 57.50
Bavarian, Perfume Atomizer, King Tut Art Design, Black & Gold 35.00
Bavarian, Pitcher, Cider, Gold Handle & Trim, Blue Ground, Signed, 6 1/2 In. .. 75.00
Bavarian, Plate, Allegorical Scene, Crown Over Double Circle Mark, Germany .. 5.00
Bavarian, Plate, Bird, Gold Rim, 8 In., 6 Piece 65.00
Bavarian, Plate, Boy With Lamb, Gold Trimmed, Signed Schuman, 8 1/4 In. .. 25.00

Bavarian, Plate, Heinrich, Marcella, Silver Raised Leaves, Marked, 13 In.	75.00
Bavarian, Plate, Pheasants, Gold Trimmed, Signed Schuman, 6 1/2 In.	20.00
Bavarian, Plate, Portrait, Cobalt, 6 In.	35.00
Bavarian, Plate, Portrait, Dark Haired Beauty, Gold Border, Marked, 9 In.	40.00
Bavarian, Plate, Scalloped Pierced Corners, Gold Trim, 8 In. Square	45.00
Bavarian, Plate, Violets, Leaves, 2 Gold Handles, Signed W.Wilson	35.00
Bavarian, Plate, Yellow Daffodils, Gold Border, Signed, 8 X 4 In.	15.00
Bavarian, Portrait Plate, Irregular Edge, Signed, R.C.Crown, 6 In.	17.50
Bavarian, Sugar & Creamer, Cobalt & Gold Trim	10.00
Bavarian, Sugar, Pink Roses, Gold Trim, Lid, Green	10.00
Bavarian, Syrup, Underplate, Bulbous, Iris & Gold	65.00
Bavarian, Teapot & Sugar, Floral, Pink, Green, White, Gold, C.S. & Co.	45.00
Bavarian, Vase, White Ground, Applied Flowers, C.1876, 5 3/4 In.	50.00
Bayonet, see Weapon, Bayonet	
Beaded Bag, Amber Color Rim, Fringe, France	25.00
Beaded Bag, Art Nouveau, Marked Sterling Frame, Raised Flowers	45.00
Beaded Bag, Black, Embroidered Pink & Red Tulips, Belgian	15.00
Beaded Bag, Blue Carnival Beads, Pouch Style	39.00
Beaded Bag, Drawstring, Draped Beading, Blue & Black, 8 3/4 X 5 In.	20.00
Beaded Bag, Drawstring, Turquoise Beads On Gray Silk, 10 1/4 X 5 1/4 In.	20.00
Beaded Bag, Envelope Style, Blue	15.00
Beaded Bag, Floral Frame, Silver Plate Chain, Chamois Lining, C.1805	15.00
Beaded Bag, Gold & Silver Beads, Brass Chain & Frame, 5 1/4 X 5 1/2 In.	25.00
Beaded Bag, Gun Metal Beads On Leather, Silver Plate Frame, Round, 1901	22.00
Beaded Bag, Iridescent Beads, Fringe, Filigree Clasp, 7 X 6 In.	40.00
Beaded Bag, Seed Pearls & Satin Embroidery, Brass Frame & Chain	35.00
Beaded Bag, Stylized Design, Champleve Enamel Top & Clasp, 6 X 8 In.	47.50
Beatles, Clock, Sheffield, Yellow Submarine, 1969	75.00
Beatles, Doll, Ringo	10.00
Beatles, Doll, 1964	8.50
Beatles, Game, Flip Your Wig	20.00
Beatles, Key Chain	4.50
Beatles, Magazine, 1964	8.00
Beatles, Nodder, 4 In.	20.00
Beatles, Paperweight, Picture Of Four Beatles	4.50
Beatles, Paul McCARTNEY, PLASTIC, 3 IN.	5.00
Beatles, Tour Program, 1964, 1965	8.00
Beck, see also Buffalo Pottery	
Beck, Plate, Flying Bird, 9 1/4 In.	57.00
Beck, Plate, Hand-Painted, Ear Of Corn, Signed, 9 In.	15.00
Beck, Plate, Peafowl & Hen, 8 In.	18.00
Beck, Plate, Spaniel, Bird In Mouth, 9 1/2 In.	65.00
Beck, Plate, 3 Cows, Full Background, Signed, 12 1/2 In.	75.00
Beck, Platter, Corn, 4 Plates	110.00
Beck, Platter, Grazing Cows, 13 In.	30.00

Beehive, Austria, or Beehive, Vienna, china includes all the many types of decorated porcelain marked with the famous beehive mark. The mark has been used since the eighteenth century.

Beehive, see also Royal Vienna

Beehive, Bowl, Portrait, Cobalt Blue Rim, Signed Kauffmann, 6 1/4 In.	35.00
Beehive, Chocolate Pot, Portrait, Woman, Turquoise, Gold Trim, Marked	75.00
Beehive, Cup & Saucer, Demitasse, Blue, Green & Gold, Signed	95.00
Beehive, Cup & Saucer, Panels Of Roosters & Ducks, C.1810	145.00
Beehive, Cup & Saucer, 2-Handled Cup, Pedestal, Signed A.Kauffmann, 4 In.	70.00
Beehive, Egg Cup & Underplate, Floral & Gold Decoration, Marked	30.00
Beehive, Jar, Honey, Covered, Glass	12.50
Beehive, Mustache Cup Saucer, Portrait, Lady, Austria	48.00
Beehive, Plate, Girl With Daisies, Cobalt Rim, Marked, 9 1/2 In.	250.00
Beehive, Plate, Green, Red & Gold, 2 Ladies, Marked, 8 In.	50.00
Beehive, Plate, Maroon Border, Medallions, Signed, 7 In.	25.00
Beehive, Plate, Portrait, Brunette. Lilacs In Hair, Beehive Mark, 10 In.	75.00
Beehive, Plate, Portrait, Green Border, Dutch Scene, Beehive Mark, 9 3/4 In.	48.00
Beehive, Plate, Portrait, Lady, Marked, 10 In.	125.00
Beehive, Plate, Portrait, Raised Figure, Girl With Lilacs In Hair, 9 7/8 In.	150.00
Beehive, Plate, Service, German, Gold Center Of Nymphs, Turquoise, Marked	55.00
Beehive, Plate, Thrushes, Signed W.Hein, 13 In.	325.00
Beehive, Plate, 2 Girls On Rock, 1 Placing Wreath On Head, Signed, 10 In.	100.00

Beehive, Plate, 3 Girls Pulling Chariot With Cupid, Signed, 10 In. 100.00
Beehive, Vase, Painted Figures All Around, 11 In. 150.00
Beehive, Vase, Portrait, Marked, 12 In., Pair 195.00

Beer cans have been made since the 1930s. Collectors search for old or new
cans. The number T-xx refers to the book "American Beer Can
Encyclopedia" by Thomas Toepfer. The number M-xx refers to two books
by Jack Martells, "Cone Top Collector's Bible" or "Beer Can
Collector's Bible."

Beer Can, Amana, 1975 .... 15.00
Beer Can, Andy's Beer, Map Can 12.00
Beer Can, Andy's Grecian Brew, Six Pack 13.00
Beer Can, Augsburger, Huber, Monroe, Wisconsin .... .60
Beer Can, Ballantine Ale XXX, Green, Black, Gold, Flat Top 25.00
Beer Can, Barrel, 5 Liter, Metal, German, 10 X 6 1/2 In.Diameter, Set Of 4 .... 49.00
Beer Can, Bavarian's, Red, White, Gold, Covington, Kentucky, M-21 .... 45.00
Beer Can, Bicentennial, Grafton, Iowa 3.00
Beer Can, Bismark Premium, Bismark, Chicago, T-140, M-222 .... 12.50
Beer Can, Black Label, Silver 2.50
Beer Can, Bub's B.C.C.S., Commemorative 12.00
Beer Can, Bub's Special, Red, Yellow, White, Schell, New Ulm, Minnesota 1.00
Beer Can, Budweiser, Bottle, Red, Gold, T-227, M-372 .... 5.00
Beer Can, Budweiser, 10 Oz. 10.00
Beer Can, Burgie, 1974 .... .75
Beer Can, Canadian Ace Beer, Cone Top 30.00
Beer Can, Canadian Ace, Extra Pale, Brown Woodgrain, Chicago, T-285, M-457 .... 8.00
Beer Can, Cone Top, Goetz Country Club Pilsener Beer, Red & White 30.00
Beer Can, Cone Top, Gold Medal, Old Topper 25.00
Beer Can, Cone Top, Kessler Beer, Helena, Montana, Blue 150.00
Beer Can, Cone Top, Wagner's Gambrinus, Quality Pale Beer 50.00
Beer Can, Country Club, Red Can, Goetz, St.Joesph, Montana, M-138 .... 40.00
Beer Can, Drewry's Beer, Green, Brown, White, Flat Top 20.00
Beer Can, Drewry's Beer, Horoscope Gemini, Copper, Brown, White, Flat Top 20.00
Beer Can, Drewry's Extra Dry, Silver & Red, South Bend, Indiana, T-400 .... 12.50
Beer Can, Eulberg, Blue, Red, Silver, White, Crown Logo, Wisconsin, M-823 .... 15.00
Beer Can, Falstaff Bicentennial 1.00
Beer Can, Friars Ale, Monk's Head Above Friar, Indiana, T-561, M-956 .... 35.00
Beer Can, Genesee, 12 Horse, Copper 18.00
Beer Can, Gluek Stite, Rampant Lion Shield Emblem, Minneapolis, M-3063 .... 3.50
Beer Can, Goebel Block, Brown, White, Bubbled, Detroit, M-1073 .... 15.00
Beer Can, Great Lakes, Red, Silver, White Shield Logo, Indiana, M-1162 .... 9.00
Beer Can, Grossvater Beer, Akron, Ohio, Silver, Red & Blue Crown 40.00
Beer Can, Grossvater, Regular Cone 75.00
Beer Can, Haas, Houghton, Michigan, M-318 .... 15.00
Beer Can, Hi Brau, Huber, Monroe, Wisconsin, T-783, M-1317 .... 1.00
Beer Can, Hull's Cream Ale, New Haven, Connecticut, T-826, M-1386 .... 40.00
Beer Can, India, 25th Anniversary, Puerto Rico, 10 Ounce 6.00
Beer Can, Iron City Beer, Red, White & Black 40.00
Beer Can, King Snedley's, Bicentennial, San Francisco 3.00
Beer Can, Land Of Lakes, Pilsen, Chicago, T-964, M-1614 .... 10.00
Beer Can, Metz, Red, White, Black, Silver Ends & Seam, Nebraska, T-1053 .... 3.00
Beer Can, Narragansett, Hi Neighbor 9.00
Beer Can, National Lager, Fischbach, Montana, T-1117, M-1923 .... 5.00
Beer Can, Northern, Green, Brown, Yellow, Superior, Wisconsin, M-469 .... 12.50
Beer Can, Nova Scotia, Alpine 1.00
Beer Can, Nova Scotia, Keith's 1.00
Beer Can, Nova Scotia, Moosehead 1.00
Beer Can, Nova Scotia, Schooner 1.00
Beer Can, Pabst Blue Ribbon, Blue Slogan On Gold, T-1259, M-2159 .... 6.00
Beer Can, Pabst, Blue & Pink Box, Announces Their New Label, T-1257, M-2158 .... 15.00
Beer Can, Paul Bunyan Beer, Flat Top 25.00
Beer Can, Peerless, Red, Black, Gold, Wisconsin, M-2208 .... 20.00
Beer Can, Red Top Ale, Red, White, Silver, Atlantic, Chicago, Spokane, M-2395 .... 22.50
Beer Can, Reisch, Springfield, Illinois, M-595 .... 35.00
Beer Can, Rheingold Scotch Ale, A.Liebmann, New York 20.00
Beer Can, Rogue, South African Breweries 1.00
Beer Can, San Miguel, B.Muehlebach, Kansas City, Mo. 1.50

Beer Can, **Schaefer,** Wood Grain, Brooklyn, T-1457, M-2552 .... 15.00
Beer Can, **Scheel's Export Light,** New Ulm, Mn. 10.00
Beer Can, **Scheel's Halloween Beer,** New Ulm, Mn. 12.00
Beer Can, **Schoenling,** Red Lager, Gold, White, Cincinnati, T-1511, M-2635 .... 18.00
Beer Can, **Shell's 1978 Christmas Brew** 12.00
Beer Can, **Simon Pure Bank,** Flat Top 40.00
Beer Can, **Star Model,** Silver Bands, Star Union, Chicago, T-1577, M-2732 .... 12.50
Beer Can, **Wana Beer** 18.00
Beer Can, **White Utica Club** 18.00
Beer Can, **Wooden Shoe,** Minster, Ohio, Lager Beer 60.00
Beer, Can, Old Crown, Lazy Aged Sleeping Elf, Centlivre, Ft.Wayne, T-1168 .... 10.00

Bells have been made of china, glass, or metal. All types are collected.

Bell, **Barn,** Iron Horseshoe Attached, C.1900, 6 In.Diameter 22.50
Bell, **Black Mammy,** Feet Are Clappers, Brass 50.00
Bell, **Brass,** Carousel, 1908, Herchell Spillman Merry-Go-Round 150.00
Bell, **Brass,** Crane Standing On Turtle Base, Holding A Bell, Gong, 8 X 5 In. 30.00
Bell, **Bronze,** School, Liberty Bell, Cleveland, Ohio, 6-2-1917 .... 63.00
Bell, **Bronze,** School, Wooden Handle, Brass Knob, 9 1/2 In. 25.00
Bell, **Calf,** Wrought Iron 7.50
Bell, **Camel,** 1870s, Jerusalem, 5 1/2 In., Pair 20.00
Bell, **Chanticleer Handle,** Cast Iron, 5 In. 12.00
Bell, **Chime,** Dinner, Brass & Oak, Victorian 24.00
Bell, **Church,** Bronze, Troy, New York, 22 In.Diameter 1450.00
Bell, **Church,** Engraved Gift From Pope Leo XII, C.1829 .... 750.00
Bell, **Conestoga,** Graduated, Original Strap, Large 225.00
Bell, **Cow,** Round, Wooden Gong, 5 In. 18.00
Bell, **Cow,** 7 1/2 In. 22.50
Bell, **Crystal,** Columbian Exposition 1893, Frosted Swirl Handle, Etched 85.00
Bell, **Desk,** New Departure Bell Company, Nickel Plated 18.00
Bell, **Ding Dong Bell,** Pussy's Not In The Well, Cast Iron 100.00
Bell, **Dinner,** Aunt Jemima, Bisque 8.50
Bell, **Dinner,** Fan Handle, Teardrop Edging, 3 3/4 X 2 1/4 In.Diameter 15.00
Bell, **Dinner,** Indian Girl 7.00
Bell, **Dinner,** Mammy, Calico Dress 9.00
Bell, **Dinner,** Sterling Handle, 5 In. 14.00
Bell, **Glass,** Cased With Cranberry Swirl, Clear Handle, 6 1/2 In. 85.00
Bell, **Goat,** 1890s, Jerusalem, 2 In., Pair 12.50
Bell, **Hame,** Hand Forged, 2 Tier Bracket, Brass, 5 Bells 145.00
Bell, **Hand,** Double-Chiming, Bronze 145.00
Bell, **Hotel Desk,** Clockwork Mechanism, Iron 35.00
Bell, **Hotel,** Ornate Frame, Cast Iron 9.00
Bell, **Indian Mission,** Iron, 33 In.Diameter 400.00
Bell, **Lacy,** Skirt Forms Bell, Brass, 4 In. 18.00
Bell, **Lady,** Ruffled Cap, Full Skirt Curved At Sides, Brass, 3 1/4 In. 35.00
Bell, **Lily-Of-The-Valley Handle,** Sterling, 3 1/2 In. 12.00
Bell, **Locomotive,** Solid Brass, Maximum Size 690.00
Bell, **Porcelain,** Victorian Lady, 5 1/2 In. 65.00
Bell, **Post Cradle,** Brass, 12 In. 225.00
Bell, **Santa Claus,** China 5.00
Bell, **School,** Brass, Large 55.00
Bell, **School,** Brass, 6 1/2 In. 25.00
Bell, **School,** Brass, 7 In. 29.00
Bell, **School,** Hand, Brass, Turned Handle, 8 X 4 In.Diameter 38.00
Bell, **School,** Hand, Brass, 3 1/2 In.Diameter X 6 In.High 30.00
Bell, **School,** Hand, Brass, 8 1/2 In. 40.00
Bell, **School,** Maple Handle, 7 1/4 X 4 In.Diameter 35.00
Bell, **School,** Metal, Pine Handle, 9 3/4 In. 42.50
Bell, **School,** Metal, Wooden Rod, Wooden Pulley For Rope, 4 In. 40.00
Bell, **School,** Teacher's, Brass, 7 1/2 In. 35.00
Bell, **School,** Wood Handle, Brass Cone Finial, 7 1/4 In. 48.00
Bell, **School,** Wooden, Round, Bell In Center, 5 In. 6.50
Bell, **Schoolhouse,** Iron 100.00
Bell, **Servant,** Acanthus, Brass 15.00
Bell, **Servant,** Wall, Swivel For Remote Control, Victorian 22.00
Bell, **Service,** Parrot Handle 24.00
Bell, **Shop,** Coiled Spring, Brass 30.00

Bell, Sleigh, Brass, Keyed To Buckled Harness Straps.Graduated	165.00
Bell, Sleigh, 24 Graduated Brass Bells, Keyed To Buckled Strap	165.00
Bell, Sleigh, 24 Graduated Brass Bells, No.2 Through No.11, Leather Strap	175.00
Bell, Sleigh, 27, Brass	75.00
Bell, Steam Locomotive, Cast Iron Bracket, Brass, 19 X 12 In.Diameter	550.00
Bell, Store, Country, Hanging Over Door, Spring Mounted	35.00
Bell, Table, Rung By Spinning 1 Or 2 Knobs, Nickel Over Brass	65.00
Bell, Town Crier, Rosewood Handle, Brass, 10 In.	62.00
Bell, Troika, Brass, High Arched Iron Strap, Set	75.00
Bell, Trolley, Dated 1884, Iron	35.00
Bell, Trolley, Starr Bros. Bell Co.	90.00
Bell, Trolley, 1900, Brass	55.00
Bell, Victorian Lady, Open Mouth, Metal Clapper, C.1895, Brass	30.00
Bell, Woman, Full-Skirted, Brass, 4 In.	18.00
Bell, Woman, Victorian, Brass	22.00

Belle Ware was made in 1903 by Carl V. Helmschmied. In 1904 he started a corporation known as the Helmschmied Manufacturing Company. His factory closed in 1908 and he worked on his own until his death in 1934.

Belle Ware, Box, Covered, Pink, Blue & White, Blossom On Top, 7 X 3 In.	235.00
Belle Ware, Box, Hand-Painted, Brass Collar, C.1903, Signed, 4 1/4 X 2 In.	205.00
Belle Ware, Box, Hinged, Pink Body, Roses On Lid, Signed, 7 In.Diameter	295.00
Belle Ware, Box, Hinged, Pink, Roses, 6 In.Square	168.00
Belle Ware, Box, Jewel, Pebbled, Pink Rose & Buds, Signed, 3 1/2 In.	300.00
Belle Ware, Salt, Sanded, Decorated, Signed, 4 In.	75.00
Belle Ware, Shaker, Red Berries, Original Top, Marked, Pair	150.00

Belleek china is made in Ireland, other European countries, and the United States. The glaze is creamy yellow and appears wet. The first Belleek was made in 1857.

Belleek, see also Ceramic Art Co., Haviland, Lenox, Matt Morgan, Ott & Brewer

Belleek, Barrel, Biscuit, Green Mark, 7 In.	45.00
Belleek, Basket, Hand Holding, Bracelet On Wrist & Bow On Basket, 1870 Mark	185.00
Belleek, Basket, Oval, 8 In.Long	195.00
Belleek, Basket, 3 Strand Shamrock, 5 1/2 In.Diameter	185.00
Belleek, Basket, 3 Strand, 1st Period, 8 1/2 X 7 In.	590.00
Belleek, Biscuit Jar, Green Mark	50.00
Belleek, Bottle, Perfume, Willets, 3 1/2 In.	45.00
Belleek, Bowl & Creamer, 3rd Black Mark	100.00
Belleek, Bowl, Shell, Oval, 3rd Black Mark, 5 In.	55.00
Belleek, Bowl, Willets, Green Ground, Stylized Leaves, 8 3/4 In.Diameter	84.00
Belleek, Bowl, Willets, Green Iridescent, Gold Handles, 2 1/2 X 4 1/2 In.	35.00
Belleek, Bowl, Willets, Stylized Leaves, Signed, 3 1/4 X 8 3/4 In.Diameter	84.00
Belleek, Bowl, 6 Point, Black Mark, 5 X 3 1/2 In.	55.00
Belleek, Box, Trinket, Covered, 1st Black Mark, 6 X 2 In.	205.00
Belleek, Cake Basket, 4 Strand, 10 1/2 In.	270.00
Belleek, Centerpiece, The Prince Of Wales, White, 1st Black Mark, 13 In.	1800.00
Belleek, Cider Set, Grape & Vines, Silver Overlay, Brown, 7 Piece, 6 In.	475.00
Belleek, Coffee Set, Limpet, 3rd Mark, Irish, 11 Piece	550.00
Belleek, Coffee Set, Willets, Pedestaled, Ivory With Gold Scrolls, 11 In.	150.00
Belleek, Coffeepot, Coral Handled, Ivory Glaze, 3rd Black Mark, 9 1/2 In.	250.00
Belleek, Compote, Pedestaled, Twig Handled, Gold Trim, 3 1/2 X 6 In.	95.00
Belleek, Compote, Willets, Gold & Blue, Iridescent Interior, 10 1/2 In.	175.00
Belleek, Cooler, Wine, 2nd Black Mark, 9 In.	690.00
Belleek, Creamer & Sugar, Shamrock, Irish	45.00
Belleek, Creamer & Sugar, Yellow Ivy, Irish	80.00
Belleek, Creamer, Double Shell, Pink Trim, 2nd Black Mark	55.00
Belleek, Creamer, Grasses, Lavender Trim, Gilt Edge, 1st Black Mark	120.00
Belleek, Creamer, Irish Pot, Black Mark	37.00
Belleek, Creamer, Irish Pot, Celtic Design, 2nd Black Mark	45.00
Belleek, Creamer, Ivy, 1st Black Mark	95.00
Belleek, Creamer, Leaf, Green Mark	15.00
Belleek, Creamer, Lily, Pink Handle, Yellow Luster Inside, 3rd Blue Mark	48.00
Belleek, Creamer, Lotus, Black Mark	40.00
Belleek, Creamer, Neptune, White, 1st Black Mark	35.00
Belleek, Creamer, Pink Handle & Rim, Irish	45.00
Belleek, Creamer, Pink Handle, Luster Inside, 3rd Black Mark, 7 1/4 In.Diam.	35.00

Belleek, Creamer, Shamrock & Basket Weave, Black Mark, 4 1/2 In.	35.00
Belleek, Creamer, Shamrock, Irish	45.00
Belleek, Creamer, Shell, Green Trim, Irish	50.00
Belleek, Creamer, Willets, Gold Trim, Enamel Flowers	25.00
Belleek, Creamer, Yellow Luster Ribbons, Green Mark	16.00
Belleek, Cup & Saucer, Armorial, Gold & Black Trim, 1st Mark	85.00
Belleek, Cup & Saucer, Black Mark	49.00
Belleek, Cup & Saucer, Bouillon, Willets, Hand-Painted, Blossom Handles	50.00
Belleek, Cup & Saucer, Demitasse, Green Trim, 2nd Mark, 2 1/4 In.	85.00
Belleek, Cup & Saucer, Demitasse, Nautilus Shell Shaped, Palette Mark	39.00
Belleek, Cup & Saucer, Demitasse, Pink Inside, White Outside, Ribbed	45.00
Belleek, Cup & Saucer, Demitasse, Willets, 2 Handles, Purple Palette Mark	65.00
Belleek, Cup & Saucer, Grasses Pattern, Purple Luster On White	100.00
Belleek, Cup & Saucer, Hawthorne, Brown Handle & Trim, 1st Black Mark	25.00
Belleek, Cup & Saucer, Hexagon, Pink Trim, 2nd Black Mark, Unglazed	50.00
Belleek, Cup & Saucer, Institute, Farmer's Size, 1st Black Mark	110.00
Belleek, Cup & Saucer, Neptune, Blue & Gold Trim, 2nd Black Mark	90.00
Belleek, Cup & Saucer, Ott & Brewer, Tridacna Pattern	55.00
Belleek, Cup & Saucer, Pink Trim, Gilt Border, Black Mark	115.00
Belleek, Cup & Saucer, Shamrock & Basket Weave, Black Mark	38.00
Belleek, Cup & Saucer, Shamrock, 2nd Black Mark	45.00
Belleek, Cup & Saucer, Shell Pattern, Green Mark	25.00
Belleek, Cup & Saucer, Tridacna, Irish, 2nd Black Mark	49.00
Belleek, Cup & Saucer, Tridacna, Pink Trim, 2nd Black Mark	46.50
Belleek, Cup & Saucer, Tridacna, 1st Black Mark	30.00 To 85.00
Belleek, Cup & Saucer, Willets, Floral Chain, Gold, Cup On Raised Base	75.00
Belleek, Cup & Saucer, Willets, Oversized, Pedestal, Gold Handle & Stem	95.00
Belleek, Cup, Limpet, Yellow Luster Handle, 3rd Black Mark	30.00
Belleek, Cup, Tea, Cone, 2nd Black Mark	25.00
Belleek, Cup, Tea, 3rd Black Mark	25.00
Belleek, Dish, Bread, Limpet, 3rd Black Mark	58.00
Belleek, Dish, Heart Shaped, Shell	18.50
Belleek, Dish, Leaf, Sycamore, 3rd Black Mark	26.50
Belleek, Dish, Nut, Heart Shape, Shell Pattern, 3rd Green Mark, 6 In.	42.00
Belleek, Dish, Willets, Pleated, Scalloped Gold Rim, 6 1/4 In.	65.00
Belleek, Eggcup, Coral Feet, 2nd Black Mark	57.50
Belleek, Ewer, Roses & Leaves, 3rd Black Mark, 6 In.	75.00
Belleek, Ewer, Willets, Handle, Berries & Blossoms, Black Mark, 10 1/8 In.	92.00
Belleek, Figurine, Leprechaun, 3rd Black Mark	135.00
Belleek, Figurine, Pig, Irish, Green Mark, 4 5/8 In.	21.00
Belleek, Figurine, Pig, Sitting, Green Mark, 3 1/2 In.	28.50
Belleek, Figurine, Swan, Black Mark, 5 1/2 In.	80.00
Belleek, Figurine, Tay Fox	15.00
Belleek, Frame, Shadow Box, C.1880, 16 In.	1400.00
Belleek, Honey Pot, Grasses Pattern, Ist Black Mark, 6 1/2 In.	270.00
Belleek, Honey Pot, Green Mark, Shamrock	38.00
Belleek, Jardiniere, Flower & Leaf Design, 2nd Black Mark, 10 1/2 X 6 In.	680.00
Belleek, Jug, Cream, Green Mark	25.00
Belleek, Jug, Green Trim, Ornate, Marked, 9 1/2 In.	390.00
Belleek, Jug, Milk, Grasses Pattern, 3rd Black Mark, 6 In.	225.00
Belleek, Marmalade, Barrel, 3rd Black Mark	125.00
Belleek, Mug, Dragon Handle, Willets, 6 In.	110.00
Belleek, Mug, Earthenware, Transfer Hunt Scene, 4 1/4 In.	150.00
Belleek, Mug, Hand-Painted Grapes, Handle & Bottom In Gilt, Signed, 5 In.	95.00
Belleek, Mug, Hand-Painted Monk, Signed, 5 1/2 In.	115.00
Belleek, Mug, Russet To Yellow, Hand-Painted Corn, Signed, 5 1/2 In.	85.00
Belleek, Mug, Tankard, Full Figure Devil, Motto, 7 In.	135.00
Belleek, Mug, Willets, Child Sleeping Near Beerkeg, Brown, Artist Signed	115.00
Belleek, Mug, Willets, Gilded Pattern, Green Ground, 5 1/2 In.	95.00
Belleek, Mug, Willets, Hand-Painted Grapes & Leaves, Gilt Handle, 5 1/4 In.	50.00
Belleek, Mug, Willets, Hand-Painted Grapes, Purple, 4 1/2 In.	45.00
Belleek, Mug, Willets, Red Berries & Branches On Iridescent Body, 7 1/4 In.	75.00
Belleek, Paperweight, Frog, Brown & White, 5 1/2 X 3 1/4 X 2 1/4 In.	850.00
Belleek, Pitcher, Cider, Hand-Painted Apples, Palette Mark	75.00
Belleek, Pitcher, Cider, Willets, Green, Gold Ground, 1905-10 Mark, 6 1/2 In.	285.00
Belleek, Pitcher, Cream, Fish Scale, 3 1/2 In.	22.50
Belleek, Pitcher, Druid Face, 3rd Black Mark, 5 In.	125.00

Belleek, Pitcher, Embossed Grass Design, Hound, Harp & Tower, 3 1/2 In.	26.00
Belleek, Pitcher, Milk, Basket Weave, Shamrock, 2nd Black Mark, 6 1/2 In.	65.00
Belleek, Pitcher, Tankard, Multicolor Grapes, Vines & Leaves, Signed, 15 In.	250.00
Belleek, Pitcher, Water, Child's, Oval Star With Gold	32.00
Belleek, Pitcher, White & Gold, Artist Dated, 1911	60.00
Belleek, Pitcher, Willets, Painted Grapes, Signed, Dated 1910, 15 1/2 In.	275.00
Belleek, Plate, Black & White, Ulster Pattern, 1st Mark, 10 1/2 In.	35.00
Belleek, Plate, Cake, Black Mark, 10 1/2 In.	95.00
Belleek, Plate, Dragon Seeking The Pearl Of Wisdom, Brown, 15 In.	990.00
Belleek, Plate, Limpet, Green Edge, 9 In.	45.00
Belleek, Plate, Scallop Shell, Pink & Gold Trim, 1st Black Mark, 8 3/4 In.	65.00
Belleek, Plate, Shamrock, Black Mark, 7 In.	32.00
Belleek, Plate, Shamrock, 3rd Black Mark, 7 1/2 In.	35.00
Belleek, Plate, Tridacna, Gold Edging, 1st Black Mark, 7 1/4 In.	35.00
Belleek, Plate, Tridacna, 1st Black Mark, 6 In.	38.00
Belleek, Plate, Woven, 10 In.Diameter	100.00
Belleek, Rose Bowl, Willets, Shell & Seaweed, Enameled, Pink	175.00
Belleek, Rose Bowl, Willets, Shell & Seaweed, Enameled, Yellow	175.00
Belleek, Salt Dip, Gold Trim, Serpent Mark	11.00
Belleek, Salt, Black Mark	25.00
Belleek, Salt, Master, Shell Plateau, 1st Mark	85.00
Belleek, Salt, Shamrock, 1st Black Mark	25.00
Belleek, Saucer, Neptune, 2nd Black Mark	18.00
Belleek, Shell, Clam, Intricate Design, Marked, 5 In.	525.00
Belleek, Shell, Conch, Coral, Pink Trim, Marked, 4 1/2 In.	400.00
Belleek, Shell, Orange Coral Branches, C.1860, Black Mark, 8 X 7 X 3 3/4 In.	275.00
Belleek, Sherbet, Gold Paste, Floral, Gold Handles & Rim, 3 1/2 In.	65.00
Belleek, Stack Set, Sugar & Creamer, Cleary Pattern, 2nd Green Mark	57.00
Belleek, Stein, Willet, Grapes, 7 In.	52.00
Belleek, Stein, Willets, Dragon's Body Handle, Signed, 6 In.	50.00
Belleek, Sugar & Creamer, Artichoke, Green Mark	30.00
Belleek, Sugar & Creamer, Blackberry Design, Green Mark, 3 In.	50.00
Belleek, Sugar & Creamer, Bow Tie & Swirl, Green Mark	45.00
Belleek, Sugar & Creamer, Cleary, 2nd Green Mark, Open Sugar	35.00
Belleek, Sugar & Creamer, Corset Shape, C.1900, Black Mark	75.00
Belleek, Sugar & Creamer, Gilded Limpet, 3rd Black Mark, 3 In.	100.00
Belleek, Sugar & Creamer, Lily, Pink Trim, 3rd Black Mark	45.00
Belleek, Sugar & Creamer, Open, Shamrocks, Twig Handles, Castle Mark	44.00
Belleek, Sugar & Creamer, Pearlized Bow & Tassel, Black Mark	95.00
Belleek, Sugar & Creamer, Ribbed Bases, Gold Borders, Green Palette Mark	165.00
Belleek, Sugar & Creamer, Ribbon, Black Hound, Harp & Tower Mark, C.1857	125.00
Belleek, Sugar & Creamer, Saucer Shape, Gold Handled, Green Palette Mark	135.00
Belleek, Sugar & Creamer, Toy Shell	35.00
Belleek, Sugar & Creamer, Willets, Lattice & Scroll, Silver Twig Handles	185.00
Belleek, Sugar, Covered, Willets, Hand-Painted, Gilded, 4 1/2 X 4 1/2 In.	58.00
Belleek, Sugar, Creamer, Tray, Basket-Weave, Black Mark, 10 1/2 X 5 1/4 In.	110.00
Belleek, Sugar, Ivy, 3rd Black Mark	49.00
Belleek, Sugar, Yellow Luster Ribbons, Green Mark	10.00
Belleek, Swan, Green Mark, 4 1/2 In.	25.00
Belleek, Swan, 1st Black Mark	100.00
Belleek, Swan, 2nd Black Mark, 4 In.	175.00
Belleek, Tankard, Cinnamon Colored, Reserves Of Jonquils, 15 In.	275.00
Belleek, Tankard, Grapes & Leaves, Initialed, Dated Mch.'98, 15 In.	100.00
Belleek, Tankard, Peacocks, Pastel Colors, Signed J. Lubbin, 1916, 7 1/2 In.	150.00
Belleek, Tankard, Willets, Hand-Painted, Signed	225.00
Belleek, Tea Set, Grasses Pattern, Marked, 3 Piece	350.00
Belleek, Tea Set, Pink Trim, Hexagon Pattern, 2nd Black Mark, 5 1/2 In.	395.00
Belleek, Tea Set, Roses, Gold Trim, Pink, Turquoise, Pedestaled, Marked	265.00
Belleek, Teakettle, Grass, Black Mark	310.00
Belleek, Teapot, Basket Weave & Shamrock, 3rd Black Mark	200.00
Belleek, Teapot, Cone, Irish, 2nd Black Mark	163.50
Belleek, Teapot, Creamer & Sugar, Shamrock & Basketweave, 2nd Black Mark	175.00
Belleek, Teapot, Echinus Pattern, 2nd Black Mark	325.00
Belleek, Teapot, Grasses Pattern, 1st Black Mark, 7 In.Long	290.00
Belleek, Teapot, Green Trim, Tridacna, 2nd Mark, 9 1/2 In. 225.00 To	320.00
Belleek, Teapot, Green, Hexagon Pattern, 2nd Black Mark	195.00
Belleek, Teapot, Limpet, 1st Green Mark	125.00

Belleek, Teapot, Morgan, Wide Gold Center Band, Gold Handle & Spout 75.00
Belleek, Teapot, Neptune, Ivory & Pink, 1st Black Mark 225.00
Belleek, Teapot, Shamrock, Basket Weave, White, 1st Black Mark, 8 In. 225.00
Belleek, Teapot, Shamrocks, Green Mark 68.00
Belleek, Teapot, Shell, Green Mark, 6 Cup 50.00
Belleek, Teapot, Tridacna, Green Trim, 2nd Black Mark, 5 In. .... 165.00 To 175.00
Belleek, Teapot, Tridacna, Green Trim, 2nd Black Mark, 9 1/2 In. 220.00
Belleek, Tray, Echinus, 1st Black Mark, 15 1/2 X 12 1/2 In. 260.00
Belleek, Tray, Hexagonal, Edged 235.00
Belleek, Tray, Neptune Cabaret Set, 2nd Black Mark, Green Trim, 17 In. 550.00
Belleek, Tray, Tridacna, Pink Edge, 2nd Black Mark, 17 X 14 In. 280.00
Belleek, Tumbler, Fan, 2nd Black Mark, 2 1/2 In. 45.00
Belleek, Tumbler, White, 1st Black Mark, 3 1/4 In. 45.00
Belleek, Vase, Applied Roses, Palette Mark, 5 1/2 In. 95.00
Belleek, Vase, Corn, Green Leaves, First Black Mark, 6 In. 295.00
Belleek, Vase, Corn, Pink Leaves, First Black Mark, 6 In. 225.00
Belleek, Vase, Cornucopia, 2nd Black Mark, 9 1/2 In. 200.00
Belleek, Vase, Cranes, Shaded Green Forest & Winding Stream, 15 1/2 In. 150.00
Belleek, Vase, Ewer, Roses, Leaves, 3rd Black Mark, 6 In. 75.00
Belleek, Vase, Fish & Butterfly, Red, Blue, Yellow, & Tan, Marked, 12 1/2 In. 990.00
Belleek, Vase, Harp, 2nd Black Mark, 6 1/2 In. 225.00
Belleek, Vase, Lenox, Handles, Peonies, Palette Mark, 18 3/4 In. 275.00
Belleek, Vase, Lily, Signed, American, 14 1/2 In. 290.00
Belleek, Vase, Nile, Applied Flowers, 2nd Black Mark, 13 In. 225.00
Belleek, Vase, Nile, 1st Black Mark, 9 1/2 In. 210.00
Belleek, Vase, Owl, 3rd Mark, 8 In., Pair 110.00
Belleek, Vase, Raised Colored Flowers, Irish, 3 In. 40.00
Belleek, Vase, Shell On A Flying Fish, 1st Black Mark, 4 3/4 In. 290.00
Belleek, Vase, Six-Sided, 2nd Green Mark, 5 X 6 1/4 In. 32.00
Belleek, Vase, Swirled Body, Applied Roses, 3rd Black Mark, 3 1/2 In. 95.00
Belleek, Vase, Thistles, Leaves, 3rd Black Mark, Lease No.512 .... 108.00
Belleek, Vase, Tree Trunk, Irish, 6 In. 40.00
Belleek, Vase, Two-Handled, Dated 1904, 5 In. 60.00
Belleek, Vase, White Ground, Palette Mark, 11 1/2 In. 225.00
Belleek, Vase, Willets, Art Deco, 9 In. 75.00
Belleek, Vase, Willets, Birds & Plants, Brown & Tan Base, 15 In. 235.00
Belleek, Vase, Willets, Blown Pink & Yellow Roses, Shaded, 10 In. 95.00
Belleek, Vase, Willets, Gold Scalloped Rim, Green Ground, 15 1/2 In. 148.00
Belleek, Vase, Willets, Hand-Painted, Green & Cream Ground, Signed, 15 In. 210.00
Belleek, Vase, Willets, Mountain Scene, Lake, Signed C.M.Kingbury, 16 In. 115.00
Belleek, Vase, Willets, Pink Roses, Signed, 10 In. 125.00
Belleek, Vase, Willets, Pomegranates, Coral, Green, White Ground, 11 In. 60.00
Belleek, Vase, Willets, Water Lily Bud On Side, White & Gold, 3 In. 95.00
Belleek, Vase, Willets, White Roses On Green Ground, 11 In. 65.00
Belleek, Vase, Willets, 6-Sided, Signed Rean, 12 In. 160.00
Belleek, Wall Pocket, Blue Bamboo Design, Flowers 28.00

Bennington ware was the product of two factories working in Bennington, Vermont. Both firms were out of business by 1896. The wares include brown and yellow mottled pottery, Parian, scroddled ware, stoneware, graniteware, yellowware, and Staffordshire-like vases.

Bennington, see also Rockingham

Bennington Type, Cuspidor, Mottled Yellow & Brown 35.00
Bennington Type, Doorknob, Mottled, Pair .... 27.50 To 45.00
Bennington Type, Planter, Bark Exterior, Glazed Interior, 4 1/2 X 5 In. 30.00
Bennington Type, Spittoon, Brown & Green, 5 X 7 In.Diameter 24.00
Bennington Type, Teapot, Rachael At The Well, 9 In. .... 25.00 To 70.00
Bennington, Basket, Dipping, 11 In. 75.00
Bennington, Bowl & Pitcher, Child's 100.00
Bennington, Box, Oval, Sleeping Baby In Reflief On Lid, 4 1/2 X 3 1/2 In. 52.00
Bennington, Bust, Taft, 11 In. 95.00
Bennington, Cracker Jar, Peacock At Fountain 20.00
Bennington, Creamer, Cow 275.00
Bennington, Creamer, Heart Rim, Signed 345.00
Bennington, Crock, Birds, Leaves, F.D.Norton, 5 Gallon 125.00
Bennington, Crock, Blue Butterfly, 4 Gallon 125.00
Bennington, Crock, Signed E. & L.P.Norton, 6 Gallon 350.00

Bennington, Cuspidor, Diamond Pattern, Ornate Shape	125.00
Bennington, Cuspidor, 7 In.	85.00
Bennington, Dish, Covered, With Under Plate, Wheat	95.00
Bennington, Frame, Oval, Brown & White, Flint, 8 1/2 X 9 1/2 In.	200.00
Bennington, Inkwell, Dog	385.00
Bennington, Jug, Bird-On-Branch, N.Norton & Co., 1 Gallon	115.00
Bennington, Jug, Blue Leaves, Julius Norton, Vermont, 2 Gallon	150.00
Bennington, Mug, Parrot In Relief, Brown, 5 In.	60.00
Bennington, Pitcher, Brown Shades To Light Brown Tulip, 6 In.	45.00
Bennington, Pitcher, Cupid & Psyche, Cream & Brown Glaze, 3 Quart, 9 1/4 In.	120.00
Bennington, Pitcher, Fat Boy, 8 In.	200.00
Bennington, Pitcher, Hunting Scene, 7 1/2 In.	125.00
Bennington, Pitcher, Unglazed, Glazed Inside, 10 In.	220.00
Bennington, Pitcher, Water, Chartered Oak, White, Signed	110.00
Bennington, Pitcher, Water, Flower Spray Rim, Dark Brown, Flint Glaze, 4 Qt.	125.00
Bennington, Plate, Pie, Mottled Glaze, 11 In.	85.00
Bennington, Plate, Pie, 9 1/2 In.	65.00
Bennington, Platter, Oval, Cupid & Psyche, 13 1/4 X 10 1/4 X 1 5/8 In.	100.00
Bennington, Spittoon, Flint Enameled, Signed, 1849	140.00
Bennington, Spittoon, Petal Design	65.00
Bennington, Toby	275.00
Bennington, Vase, Cottage Type, Woman, Scrollwork, 1850-58, 7 1/2 In., Pair	450.00
Bennington, Vase, Parian, Handles, Grapes, Vines & Tendrils, 17 1/2 In.	125.00
Beswick, Ashtray, Quail	7.00
Beswick, Figurine, Champion Horse & Jockey, 8 1/4 In.	85.00
Beswick, Figurine, Chihuahua On Red Pillow, 2 1/2 In.	10.50
Beswick, Figurine, Eagle, Wings Spread, Large	25.00
Beswick, Figurine, Haitian Woman On Donkey	35.00
Beswick, Figurine, Hunter, 9 1/4 In.	150.00
Beswick, Figurine, King Charles Spaniel, 7 1/2 X 5 1/4 In.	25.00
Beswick, Figurine, Palomino, 6 3/4 In.	25.00
Beswick, Figurine, Pony, 6 1/2 In.	65.00
Beswick, Figurine, Royal Canadian Mounted Police, 9 1/4 In.	150.00
Betty Boop, Pendant, Charm	8.50
Bicycle, High Wheel, First Place Road Race, C.1895	350.00
Bicycle, Tandem, Wooden Rims, Wooden Skirt Guard, C.1890	300.00
Bicycle, Velocipede, Victorian	200.00
Bicycle, Women's, 3 Wheel, Wicker Seat, Foot Rod Pedal, 57 In.	900.00

Bing and Grondahl is a famous Danish factory making fine porcelains from 1853 to the present. Their Christmas plates are especially well known.

Bing & Grondahl, Dish, Leaf Shape, Handle, Seagull Design, 5 1/2 X 6 3/4 In.	22.50
Bing & Grondahl, Figurine, Brown & White Springer Spaniel, No. 2095, 8 In.	65.00
Bing & Grondahl, Figurine, Cat, Sitting, Gray & White, 5 In.	60.00
Bing & Grondahl, Figurine, Lamb, Gray, 3 X 4 In.	37.50
Bing & Grondahl, Figurine, Madonna, No.2332, White, 9 In.	38.00
Bing & Grondahl, Figurine, Puppy, Brown & White, 6 1/2 X 4 In.	75.00
Bing & Grondahl, Figurine, Robin, Mouth Open, 2 1/2 In.	33.00
Bing & Grondahl, Figurine, Tall Boy Dancng With Girl, No.1845, 8 1/4 In.	85.00
Bing & Grondahl, Figurine, Youthful Boldness, No. 2162, 7 In.	105.00
Bing & Grondahl, Mug, The Old Inn, 5 In.	35.00
Bing & Grondahl, Plate, Christmas, 1895	3000.00
Bing & Grondahl, Plate, Christmas, 1910	60.00
Bing & Grondahl, Plate, Christmas, 1972, Greenland	20.00
Bing & Grondahl, Plate, Christmas, 1973, Country Christmas	20.00
Bing & Grondahl, Vase, Lily-Of-The-Valley, 7 In.	65.00
Binoculars, Brass, Whale Bone, 19th Century	48.00
Birdcage, Brass, Round	47.50
Birdcage, Dome-Shaped, Tin, Blue, Gold, Victorian	35.00
Birdcage, Round, Brass, Stand, Hendryx, 67 In.	125.00
Birdcage, Wood, Porcelain Water Holder	18.00
Birdcage, Wooden, 10 1/2 In.Square X 12 1/2 In.High	33.00

Bisque is an unglazed baked porcelain. Finished bisque has a slightly sandy texture with a dull finish. Some of it may be decorated with various colors. Bisque gained favor during the late Victorian era when thousands of bisque figurines were made.

Bisque, see also named porcelain factories

Bisque, Basket, Peach, Green Twig Handle, German	18.00
Bisque, Cake Set, Circus Animals, Original Box, Japan	25.00
Bisque, Figurine, Andy Gump, Comic, Nodder	55.00
Bisque, Figurine, Bathing Beauty, Germany, 4 In.	60.00
Bisque, Figurine, Black Babies On Potty, German	57.50
Bisque, Figurine, Black Boy On Watermelon, Eating, 4 1/2 In.	27.00
Bisque, Figurine, Black Child & White Child Sitting On Potty, 3 In.	85.00
Bisque, Figurine, Bowl, Fish In Net, Tans & Gold, 10 X 11 In.	200.00
Bisque, Figurine, Boy & Girl, Pair, 8 3/4 In.	45.00
Bisque, Figurine, Boy Dressed Like Benjamin Franklin, 4 1/2 In.	35.00
Bisque, Figurine, Boy With Goat, French, Pink & Green Trim, 10 In.	175.00
Bisque, Figurine, Bride & Groom, Hand-Painted, 4 In.	10.00
Bisque, Figurine, Bulldog, German, 4 In.	22.50
Bisque, Figurine, Cherub Under Arbor, Riding Wheelbarrow, Gold Beads, 8 In.	89.00
Bisque, Figurine, Child Sprawled Out & Sleeping In Wheelbarrow	35.00
Bisque, Figurine, Child, Blue Cap, German, 4 1/2 In.	40.00
Bisque, Figurine, Cupid Sitting On Shoe Blowing Horn, German, 6 X 7 1/2 In.	80.00
Bisque, Figurine, Demon, Figure Dancing On Marine Monster, 1800s, 10 In.	90.00
Bisque, Figurine, Dennis The Menace, C.1950	18.00
Bisque, Figurine, Dog Carrying Basket Of Puppies, German, 5 1/2 In.	65.00
Bisque, Figurine, French, Girl With Basket, Gold & Floral Trim, 12 3/4 In.	150.00
Bisque, Figurine, French, Standing Girl Leaning On Stump, 21 In.	365.00
Bisque, Figurine, Geisha Girl, 7 In.	12.00
Bisque, Figurine, German Shepherd, Two Puppies, German, 1 1/4 In.	25.00
Bisque, Figurine, Girl Standing With Chickens, Germany, 11 In.	69.00
Bisque, Figurine, Girl, Match Pocket, Pink, White, Gold, C.1880, 5 In.	22.50
Bisque, Figurine, Greyhound, Front Of Tree Stump, 5 X 5 X 5 In.	125.00
Bisque, Figurine, Kitten With Horn, Germany	25.00
Bisque, Figurine, Lady With Swan, Blue, Purple, White, German, 6 In.	88.00
Bisque, Figurine, Lady, Coat, Hat, Blonde Hair, Blue Eyes, Glasses, Holds Dog	40.00
Bisque, Figurine, Man & Woman In Costume, French, 9 1/2 In.	65.00
Bisque, Figurine, Mark Twain In Chair, 5 In.	65.00
Bisque, Figurine, Monkey Troubador Serenading Moon, Gold Stars, 4 3/4 In.	175.00
Bisque, Figurine, Newsboy, 13 In., Glass Dome, Signed Antonio Benni, 9 In.	45.00
Bisque, Figurine, Old Woman Who Lived In A Shoe, 6 Kids, Woman, Original Box	72.50
Bisque, Figurine, Shoe, Angel Holding Horn, Flowers, German, 6 X 7 1/2 In.	80.00
Bisque, Figurine, Sitting Boy, Blue Suit, Yellow Hat, German, 4 In.	60.00
Bisque, Figurine, Sleeping Cat, 6 3/4 In.	22.00
Bisque, Figurine, Squirrel, Oak Leaves & Acorns, Full Color, Signed, 10 In.	35.00
Bisque, Figurine, The Angelus, German, 10 1/4 X 2 5/8 In.Diameter, Pair	150.00
Bisque, Figurine, Three Children On Sled, Germany	32.00
Bisque, Figurine, Whippet, Sitting, Pedestal Base, 4 1/2 In.	10.00
Bisque, Fishbowl Babies, Germany, Pair	45.00
Bisque, Font, Holy Water, Child Angel, 6 In.	22.00
Bisque, Font, Holy Water, Flying Angel	15.00
Bisque, Group, Boy & Girl, Intaglio Eyes, 11 In.	300.00
Bisque, Hair, Receiver, Fairy & Cherub 2 Sides, Blue, Numbered	59.00
Bisque, Holder, Toothbrush, 3 Pigs	20.00
Bisque, Match Holder, Figural Head, Ruffled Collar, Black	75.00
Bisque, Night Light, Cat Head, Eyes Light When Candle Lit, 4 3/8 In.	165.00
Bisque, Night Light, Gray Cat, Green Glass Eyes, 4 In.	175.00
Bisque, Night Light, Owl Head, Amber Glass Eyes, 3 3/8 X 3 1/4 In.Diameter	125.00
Bisque, Night Light, White Owl, Blue Glass Eyes, 4 1/2 In.	175.00
Bisque, Plaque, Wall, Lovers In Victorian Dress, Oval, Blue, Pink, Green, Pair	135.00
Bisque, Plate, Allover High Relief Surface, Woodland Scene, 7 1/2 In.	65.00
Bisque, Salt & Pepper, Barney Google & Snuffy Smith	9.50
Bisque, Salt, Figural Emperor & Empress, Painted Faces, Pair	70.00
Bisque, Teapot, Gray, Pink Applied Flowers, Oriental	58.00
Bisque, Toothpick Holder, Green, Pink Pig Sitting, 2 1/2 X 3 In.	20.00
Bisque, Vase, Ivory Ground, Footed, 2 Handles, Gold Trim, Austrian, 12 In.	75.00
Bisque, Vase, Kissing Children, 16 5/8 In.	157.00

Black amethyst glass appears black until it is held to the light, then a dark purple can be seen. It was made in many factories from 1860 to the present time.

Black Amethyst, Blotter, Rocker, Figural Elephant	12.00 To 35.00

Black Amethyst, Bonbon, 2 Handled, 8 1/2 X 7 In. 10.00
Black Amethyst, Bowl, Ivy, Hobnail, Footed 10.00
Black Amethyst, Bowl, Raised Poppy Design, 5 X 6 In.Diameter 29.00
Black Amethyst, Bowl, 9 In. 18.00
Black Amethyst, Candleholder, Satin Glass, Classic Design, 8 1/2 In., Pair 26.50
Black Amethyst, Candlestick, Etched, Gold Enameling, Pair 20.00
Black Amethyst, Compote, Open, Sterling Silver Overlay 30.00
Black Amethyst, Cup & Saucer 12.00
Black Amethyst, Dish, Candy, Nude, Stemmed 49.00
Black Amethyst, Dish, Pedestal, Straw Mark, 5 X 9 In.Diameter 20.00
Black Amethyst, Inkwell, 2 Piece .... 18.00 To 65.00
Black Amethyst, Jar, Pomade, Figural Bear 85.00
Black Amethyst, Lamp, Removable Font, Mary Gregory 525.00
Black Amethyst, Pitcher, Water, Dewey Portrait 80.00
Black Amethyst, Plate, Cake, Low Pedestal, 10 3/4 In. 17.50
Black Amethyst, Plate, Pierced Border, 7 In.Square 15.00
Black Amethyst, Platter, 2 Handled, 14 X 10 In. 17.50
Black Amethyst, Rose Bowl, Blown Out Florals, 5 X 6 In. 25.00
Black Amethyst, Sugar & Creamer, Indian 10.00
Black Amethyst, Sugar Shaker, Beading, Gilt 22.00
Black Amethyst, Vase, All-Over Etching, 9 In. 59.00
Black Amethyst, Vase, Bottle Shape, Stopper, Blown Flower Shaped, 9 In. 14.50
Black Amethyst, Vase, Double Handle, 7 In. 37.50
Black Amethyst, Vase, Hand-Painted White Flowers, 9 In., Pair 75.00
Black Amethyst, Vase, Pilgrim Shape, Enameled, Mallards, 8 1/4 In., Pair 900.00
Black Amethyst, Vase, Raised Heart, Dancing Girls, 7 In. .... 20.00 To 85.00
Black Amethyst, Vase, Silver Overlay Design, 6 1/2 In. 20.00
Black Amethyst, Vase, Silver Overlay, , Souvenir, New Orleans, 1917, 6 In. 22.50
Black Amethyst, Vase, Urn Shape, 2 Handle, Snake Dance 12.00
Black, Baby Seated On Potty Crying, Mouth Wide Open, Metal, 7 In. 32.00
Black, Boy, Yellow Hat, Holding Chicken, Bisque, 6 In. 28.00
Black, Doll, Whiskbroom 15.00
Black, Humidor, Bandana Lid 55.00
Black, Mug, Coon & Possum From Pass Christian, Mississippi 25.00
Black, Pin, Skirt, Ring In Ear, White Eyeballs & Teeth, Cast Metal, 2 In. 65.00
Black, Sign, Restroom, Enamel, 2 X 10 In. 11.00
Black, Spoon, Rest, Figural, Man 9.00
Black, Statue, Bisque, Bride 4.50
Black, Statue, Bisque, Groom 4.50
Black, Sugar & Creamer, Figural, Aunt Jemima & Uncle Moses 15.00
Bloor Derby, Dish, Hand-Painted Landscape, 1820-40, 8 1/2 X 11 1/2 X 2 In. 150.00
Bloor Derby, Jug, Cream, 1825, 5 1/2 In. 55.00

*Blown glass was formed by forcing air through a rod into molten glass.
Early glass and some forms of art glass were hand blown. Other types of
glass were molded or pressed. The McKearin numbers refer to the book
"American Glass" by George and Helen McKearin.*

Blown Glass, Compote, Green, New York State, 8 1/2 X 7 In.Diameter 525.00
Blown Glass, Cruet, Blue, European, 8 3/4 In. 50.00
Blown Glass, Cruet, 16 Ribbed, Flint, Molded 30.00
Blown Glass, Inkwell, Green, New York State 185.00
Blown Glass, Oil Lamp Filler, Applied Handle & Spout, 4 In. 190.00
Blown Glass, Pan, Milk, Foldover Rim, Depressed Pouring Spout, Pontil, 17 In. 275.00

Blown Glass, Pitcher, Lily Pad, Aqua,
Handle Crack, 2 Quart

Blown Glass, Pitcher, Lily Pad, New York,
Crack, C.1800-40

Blown Glass, Pitcher, Lily Pad, Aqua, Handle Crack, 2 Quart .... *Illus*	575.00
Blown Glass, Pitcher, Lily Pad, New York, Crack, C.1800-40 .... *Illus*	350.00
Blown Glass, Rolling Pin, Amethyst	50.00
Blown Glass, Sock Darner, Light Blue, Rough Pontil	22.00
Blown Glass, Tumbler, Gold, Pink, Blue, Yellow, Twist Ribbons, 4 1/2 In.	110.00

Blue Amberina, see Bluerina
Blue Glass, see Cobalt Blue
Blue Onion, see Onion

Blue Willow pattern has been made in England since 1780. The pattern
has been copied by factories in many countries, including Germany, Japan, and
the United States. It is still being made. Willow was named for a
pattern that pictures a bridge, birds, willow trees, and a Chinese landscape.

Blue Willow, Bowl, Allerton, 10 In.	25.00
Blue Willow, Bowl, H.A. & Co., L.England, 9 X 7 In.	18.00
Blue Willow, Casserole, Covered, Square	45.00
Blue Willow, Creamer, Allerton	22.50
Blue Willow, Creamer, Etruria, Wedgwood	10.00
Blue Willow, Cup & Saucer, Demitasse, Ridgway	8.00
Blue Willow, Cup & Saucer, Farmers, Enoch Wood's Ware	9.50
Blue Willow, Dish, Butter, Buffalo Pottery	75.00
Blue Willow, Dish, Vegetable, Open, Allerton, Octagonal	25.00
Blue Willow, Dish, Vegetable, Open, Oval, Allerton	22.50
Blue Willow, Gravy Boat, Allerton	22.50
Blue Willow, Gravy Boat, Ridgway, England	45.00
Blue Willow, Pitcher, Bulbous, Semi-Vitreous, Buffalo Pottery, 19 In.	55.00
Blue Willow, Pitcher, Cream, Buffalo, 1905	20.00
Blue Willow, Plate, Fluted Border, Gilded Rim, Crossed Swords Mark, 6 In.	15.00
Blue Willow, Plate, Ridgway, 10 In.	7.00
Blue Willow, Platter, Dudson Wilcox & Till, 8 1/2 X 11 1/2 In.	25.00
Blue Willow, Platter, People On Bridge, 18 1/2 X 14 In.	55.00
Blue Willow, Platter, Ridgway, 9 X 15 In.	18.00
Blue Willow, Platter, Till & Son, 6 X 7 1/2 In.	21.00
Blue Willow, Platter, 12 3/4 X 10 1/2 In.	35.00
Blue Willow, Sugar, Adams, Acorn Finial, Covered	37.50
Blue Willow, Tureen, Covered, Octagonal, Allerton, 11 In.	35.00
Blue Willow, Vegetable, Red, 5 1/4 In.	8.00

Bluerina is a type of art glass which shades from light blue to ruby. It is
often called blue amberina.

Bluerina, Tumbler	85.00
Bluerina, Vase, 7 1/2 In.	35.00
Bluerina, Wine, Decorated, 5 In.	135.00
Boat, Canoe, Old Town, Wood & Canvas, Sail Rig, 18 Foot	650.00
Boch, Vase, Stylized Green Leaves & Purple Floral, Signed, 11 1/2 In.	135.00

Bohemian glass is an ornate, overlay, or flashed glass made during the
Victorian era. It has been reproduced in Bohemia, which is now a part of
Czechoslovakia. Glass made from 1875 to 1900 is preferred by collectors.

Bohemian Glass, Beaker, Overlay, Cranberry To Green, Gilded .... *Illus*	190.00
Bohemian Glass, Beaker, Overlay, Olive Green Cut To Amber .... *Illus*	175.00
Bohemian Glass, Bell, Etched, Clear Handle, Faceted Clapper	29.00

Bohemian Glass, Bell, Ruby, 6 In. 25.00
Bohemian Glass, Bottle, Etched Flowers, Clear Stopper, Ruby, 5 1/4 In. 75.00
Bohemian Glass, Bowl, Finger, Lime Green, Grape & Leaf Pattern, 4 1/2 In. 12.00
Bohemian Glass, Box, Powder, Ruby Glass Top, Flying Bird, Deer, Castle 65.00
Bohemian Glass, Candy, Grapes & Leaves, Ruby & Clear, Footed, Lid, 9 In. 32.00
Bohemian Glass, Compote, Deer, Castle, Lid, Pedestal Base, 9 In. 125.00
Bohemian Glass, Compote, Fruit, Ruby To Clear, Deer & Castle, 8 X 7 In. 38.00
Bohemian Glass, Cordial Set, Bottle, 6 1/2 In., Ground Stopper, 6 Glasses 135.00
Bohemian Glass, Cruet, Deer & Building, Cut With Leaves, Original Stopper 75.00
Bohemian Glass, Decanter, Topaz Over Clear, Hallmarked European Sterling 225.00
Bohemian Glass, Decanter, Vintage Pattern, Etched, 15 1/2 In. 75.00
Bohemian Glass, Goblet & Cover, Ruby Flashed, Flowers, 1800s, 11 In., Pair 450.00
Bohemian Glass, Goblet, Overlay Blue, Stag, Hound, Trees, C.1850, 15 In. 600.00
Bohemian Glass, Mug, Etched Rabbit, Trees, Foliage, Amber, 4 3/4 In. 35.00
Bohemian Glass, Pickle Castor, Ruby Red Insert, Silver Plate Holder, Tongs 75.00

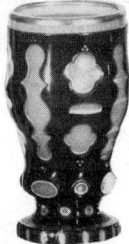

Bohemian Glass, Beaker, Overlay,
Cranberry To Green, Gilded
(See Page 33)

Bohemian Glass, Beaker, Overlay,
Olive Green Cut To Amber
(See Page 33)

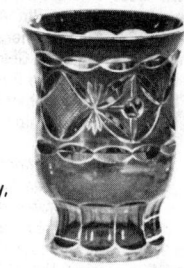

Bohemian Glass, Plate, Dinner, Red, Stag & Castle, 10 3/4 In., Set Of 12 .... 700.00
Bohemian Glass, Tumbler, White Overlay, Clear Glass, Geometric Design, 3 In. 65.00
Bohemian Glass, Vase & Cover, Deer In Woodland, Ruby, 1800s, 24 In. 700.00
Bohemian Glass, Vase & Cover, Enameled, Gilt Green, Knop, C.1800, 17 In. 1000.00
Bohemian Glass, Vase, Birds, Castle, Scrolls, Paperweight Type Base, 9 In. 115.00
Bohemian Glass, Vase, Birds, Gilt Hand Decoration, Red, 10 In., Pair 50.00
Bohemian Glass, Vase, Bulbous, 2 Gold Bow Handles, Ladowitz, 7 1/2 In. 117.50
Bohemian Glass, Vase, Castle & Deer, Ruby Overlay, 19 1/2 In. 115.00
Bohemian Glass, Vase, Ruby Cut To Green, To Clear, 9 1/2 In. 225.00
Bohemian Glass, Vase, Topaz Cut To Clear, Gravic Cut Flowers, 8 1/4 In. 45.00
Bohemian Glass, Water Set, Cobalt Cut To Clear, 7 Piece 165.00
Bohemian Glass, Wine, Blue & Cranberry, Gold Enamel, Set Of 12 .... 390.00
Bohemian Glass, Wine, Ruby, Frosted Cherries 15.00
Bonn, Plate, Cake, Cottage Scene, FM Castle Mark, 11 In. 27.50
   Boston & Sandwich Co., see Sandwich, Fireglow, Lutz

*Bottle collecting has become a major American hobby. There are several
general categories of bottles such as historic flasks, bitters, household,
figural, and others. The McK numbers refer to the book "American
Glass" by George and Helen McKearin and "American Bottles and
Flasks and Their Ancestry" by Helen McKearin and Kenneth
Wilson. For modern bottle prices and more old bottle prices see the book
"Kovels' Complete Bottle Price List" by Ralph and Terry Kovel.*

Bottle, Apothecary, Cobalt, Original Stopper, Syr-Sennae, Reverse On Glass 55.00
Bottle, Apothecary, Cylindrical, Cork & Label, Cobalt Blue, 9 In. 14.50
Bottle, Apothecary, Green, Original Stopper, Strichnine Label, C.1890, 7 In. 45.00
Bottle, Apothecary, Pink Luster, Lid, C.1870, Latin Label, 5 In. 35.00
Bottle, Apothecary, Ribbed, Latin Label, Chloroform, 8 In. 45.00
Bottle, Atomizer, Iridescent, Melon Ribbed, Crystal, White Cased, Pair 35.00

*Avon started in 1886 as the California Perfume Company. It was not
until 1929 that the name Avon was used. In 1939 it became Avon
Products, Inc. Each year Avon sells many figural bottles filled with
cosmetic products. Ceramic, plastic, and glass bottles are made in limited editions.*

Bottle, Avon, Alpine Flask 40.00

Bottle, Avon, Dueling Pistols, Red Lining	40.00
Bottle, Avon, Figurine, Bird Of Paradise, Full	9.00
Bottle, Avon, Whale Organizer, Boxed	25.00
Bottle, Baby, Double Nursing Place Each End, England	35.00
Bottle, Bar, Horn Of Plenty, Original Stopper, 12 In.	235.00
Bottle, Barber, Allover Enameling Of White Daisies, Silver Overlay	95.00
Bottle, Barber, Allover Enameling, White Daisies, Cobalt Blue	85.00
Bottle, Barber, Amber, Hobnail, Ground Pontil, 7 1/2 In.	55.00
Bottle, Barber, Amethyst, Enamel White Beading, 8 In.	48.00
Bottle, Barber, Amethyst, White Enameled, Blown, 8 3/4 In.	55.00
Bottle, Barber, Brokunier, Cranberry, Opalescent	90.00
Bottle, Barber, Bulbous, Clear, Hobnails & Waves, 5 1/2 In.	35.00
Bottle, Barber, Cafe-Au-Lait, Floral Border, Blown, 7 X 2 In.	60.00
Bottle, Barber, Chartreuse, Enamel Beading, Blown, 8 3/4 In.	42.00
Bottle, Barber, Clambroth, Marked T.Noonan, Boston	15.00
Bottle, Barber, Clear Panels, Original Porcelain Top & Cork	24.00
Bottle, Barber, Cobalt, Porcelain Stopper, White Enamel, 8 1/2 In.	55.00
Bottle, Barber, Cranberry Hobnail, Opalescent On Cranberry Coupe Hobs	46.00
Bottle, Barber, Cranberry With Enameled White Flowers	27.00
Bottle, Barber, Cranberry With White Opalescent Striping, Spout	48.00
Bottle, Barber, Cranberry, Opalescent Stripes	38.00
Bottle, Barber, Crystal & Opalescent Stars & Stripes, Polished Pontil	125.00
Bottle, Barber, Enamel Floral Design, Bulbous Top, Green, 7 3/4 In.	95.00
Bottle, Barber, Graphic Cut, Porcelain Stopper	75.00
Bottle, Barber, Hand-Painted, Amethyst, Original Stopper	85.00
Bottle, Barber, Harvard Yard	32.00
Bottle, Barber, N. Wapler, New York, Green	25.00
Bottle, Barber, Opalescent Swirl, Silver Plated Top, 6 1/2 In.	85.00
Bottle, Barber, Opaque White, Rolled Lip, 8 In.	35.00
Bottle, Barber, Pointed Hobnail, Clear To Opaque	24.00
Bottle, Barber, Stopper, Enameled Floral Trim, Blue	65.00
Bottle, Barber, Tulip Shaped, Matching Stopper, Clear	15.00
Bottle, Barber, Vertical Opalescent Stripe, Satin Finish	55.00
Bottle, Barber, White, Enameled, Satin Glass, 6 1/2 In.	40.00
Bottle, Barber, Witch Hazel, Hand-Painted, Hummingbird, Milk Glass	65.00
Bottle, Barber, Yellow, Enameled Flowers, Satin Glass, 8 In.	45.00
Bottle, Bay Rum, Flowers Engraved, Faceted Stopper	50.00
Bottle, Beer, Balboa, Enamel & Glass, 1940s	12.00
Bottle, Beer, Craft, Quart	3.50
Bottle, Beer, E.Wagner, Manchester, N.H., Applied Blob Top, Amber, 8 1/2 In.	4.00
Bottle, Beer, Ginger, Robert Carruthers, 7 1/2 In	21.50
Bottle, Beer, Ginger, Stone, Printed	7.50
Bottle, Beer, Munch, Aqua	9.50
Bottle, Beer, Royal Ruby, Schlitz, 7 Ounce	45.00
Bottle, Beer, Schaefer, Quart	4.00
Bottle, Bitters, Appetine, St.Paul, 2 In.	200.00
Bottle, Bitters, Atwood, Aqua	10.00
Bottle, Bitters, Cross Hatching & Meter Cut, American	75.00
Bottle, Bitters, Diamond Thumbprint, Flint	85.00
Bottle, Bitters, Doyle's Hop, Embossed, Cork, 1872, Amber	18.00
Bottle, Bitters, Dr.J. Hostetter's Stomach Bitters	10.00
Bottle, Bitters, Electric Brand, Label	18.00
Bottle, Bitters, Four Log Cabin, Amber	55.00
Bottle, Bitters, Green Cut To Clear, Pewter Top, 5 1/2 In.	35.00
Bottle, Bitters, Hostetter, Amber	8.00
Bottle, Bitters, Indian Restorative, Dr.George Pierce's, Aqua, 7 In.	27.50
Bottle, Bitters, Old Sachem Bitters & Wigwam Tonic, Gothic Arch, 4 Piece	125.00
Bottle, Bitters, Pepsin Calisaya, R.Russell Medicine Co., Green	75.00
Bottle, Bitters, Phoenix, Hand Blown	40.00
Bottle, Bitters, Rush's, Square, Amber	35.00
Bottle, Blue Enameled, Floral Motif, Stopper, 11 1/2 In., Pair	30.00
Bottle, Calabash, Hunter, Fisherman, Amber, American, 19th Century, Pair	200.00
Bottle, Calabash, Jenny Lind, Embossed Bust & Glass House, C.1850	90.00
Bottle, Calabash, Jenny Lind, Sapphire, Blue, 19th Century, 1 Quart	1700.00
Bottle, Coca-Cola, see Coca-Cola, Bottle	
Bottle, Cologne, All-Over Design, Bulbous Neck, 1800s, France, 6 In.	78.00

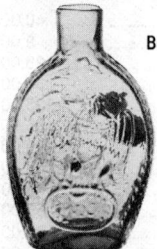

Bottle, Flask, McK G II-011, Aqua, 1/2 Pint

Bottle, Flask, McK G IX-010, Scroll, Yellow, Pint

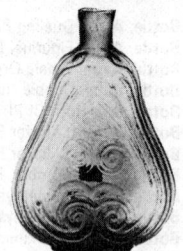

Bottle, Cologne, Baccarat, 5 In.	35.00
Bottle, Cologne, Cranberry Cut To Crystal, 10 In.	125.00
Bottle, Cologne, Green To Clear, Lacy Gold Scrolls, Cut Stopper, 9 3/4 In.	125.00
Bottle, Cologne, Hartford Silver Company, 5 1/2 In.	50.00
Bottle, Cologne, Tulip Top, Pontil Mark, 7 1/2 In.	22.00
Bottle, Decanter, Back-Bar, Old I.W.Harper, Original Stopper	20.00
Bottle, Figural, Cigar Shape, Amber, 5 1/2 In.	37.50
Bottle, Figural, Cigar, Clear	15.00
Bottle, Figural, Ear Of Corn, Clear With Paint, 1910	25.00
Bottle, Figural, Eiffel Tower, Commemorative, Gold Paint & Stopper, 18 In.	38.00
Bottle, Figural, Female Soldier, Cap As Stopper, French, 11 3/4 In.	130.00
Bottle, Figural, Grant's Tomb	265.00
Bottle, Figural, Grape Cluster	10.00
Bottle, Figural, Hessian Soldier	32.00 To 50.00
Bottle, Figural, Horse, Dawes, Porcelain	115.00
Bottle, Figural, Hound, Stopper, Porcelain	6.00
Bottle, Figural, Indian, Arrowhead Spring Water, Amber	35.00
Bottle, Figural, Kangaroo, Bols, Miniature, Full & Mint	18.50
Bottle, Figural, Klondike Nugget, Original Marked Top	55.00
Bottle, Figural, Lady's Shoe, Raised Laces & Buttons, 4 1/4 In.	35.00
Bottle, Figural, Oriental, Bisque	14.50
Bottle, Figural, Owl, Milk Glass, 5 1/2 In.	27.50
Bottle, Figural, Pilgrim's, Amber	175.00
Bottle, Figural, Pretzel	10.00
Bottle, Figural, Rip Van Winkle, Blown, Clear	95.00
Bottle, Figural, Skeleton On Barrel, Bisque, German	75.00
Bottle, Figural, Statue Of Liberty	155.00
Bottle, Figural, Teddy Roosevelt With Dog, Clear, 13 1/2 In.	55.00
Bottle, Figural, Trenton Spirits Limited, John Adams	10.00
Bottle, Figural, Zepplin, Frosted	75.00
Bottle, Flagon, Applied Handle, Brass Neck, Blown, Brown, 9 X 6 In.Diameter	47.50
Bottle, Flask, American Eagle, Pair, 19th Century	175.00
Bottle, Flask, Cobalt Blue, Rounded Shoulders, 6 X 3 1/2 In.Square	75.00
Bottle, Flask, Commemorative, Initialed T.U., Dated 1792, 9 In.	750.00
Bottle, Flask, Cornucopia & Urn, Amber, Pint	110.00
Bottle, Flask, Cut Glass & Sterling Casing, Hinged Top & Mounting	35.00
Bottle, Flask, Double Eagle, Aquamarine, 1/2 Pint	55.00
Bottle, Flask, F.A. & Co., Union & Clasped Hands, Flag On Reverse, 1/2 Pint	65.00
Bottle, Flask, General Taylor Never Surrenders, Pair, 19th Century, 1 Pint	1800.00
Bottle, Flask, Guinness Stout, Label, Green	12.50
Bottle, Flask, Haig, Sterling Overlay, Sterling Stopper	110.00
Bottle, Flask, Health-O-Meter, Bisque, German, C.1900	30.00
Bottle, Flask, Indian With Bow, Reverse, Eagle With Shield, Aqua, Quart	85.00
Bottle, Flask, Jackson Portrait, 19th Century, 1 Pint	600.00
Bottle, Flask, Lady's, Goebel, Early Crown Mark	35.00
Bottle, Flask, Lafayette Portrait, 19th Century, 1 Pint	475.00
Bottle, Flask, Masonic, Eagle, Keene, Amber, Pint	175.00
Bottle, Flask, McK G II-011, Aqua, 1/2 Pint ......Illus	160.00
Bottle, Flask, McK G II-014, American Eagle, Aquamarine, 1/2 Pint	475.00
Bottle, Flask, McK G IX-010, Scroll, Yellow, Pint ......Illus	450.00
Bottle, Flask, Pitkin, 32 Rib Broken Swirl, Green	280.00
Bottle, Flask, Raised Eagle On Front & Back, Pittsburgh, Penna., 7 1/2 In.	55.00
Bottle, Flask, Regiment Pointing One Side, Regiment Number On Other, German	75.00
Bottle, Flask, Scroll, Golden-Yellow, 1 Pint, 19th Century	550.00

Bottle, Flask, Sea-Green, Broken Swirl, Pitkin	280.00
Bottle, Flask, Sheaf Of Wheat, Westford Glass Co., Amber, Pint	90.00
Bottle, Flask, Soldier & Dancer, Bubbled, Pale Green	120.00
Bottle, Flask, Stoddard, Polished Pontil, Amber, 1/2 Pint	25.00
Bottle, Flask, Success To The Railroad, Horse & Cart, Pontil, Pint	250.00
Bottle, Flask, Tooled Lip, Tapering Neck, 1800s, 9 In.	75.00
Bottle, Flask, Union, Clasped Hands, 13 Stars, Aqua, Pint	85.00
Bottle, Flask, Washington Portrait, 1 Pint, 19th Century	200.00
Bottle, Flask, Westford, Connecticut, Wheat, Amber, 1/2 Pint	100.00
Bottle, Flask, Whiskey, Pictorial, 19th Century, 2 Quart	300.00
Bottle, Flask, Wyeth, Cobalt, Eyecup Stopper	15.00
Bottle, Food, Mrs.Butterworth, Amber	4.00
Bottle, Fruit Jar, Atlas E-Z Seal, Pint	15.00
Bottle, Fruit Jar, Bloeser	80.00
Bottle, Fruit Jar, Clark's Peerless, Green	8.00
Bottle, Fruit Jar, Eagle, Quart	70.00
Bottle, Fruit Jar, Flaccus Steer Head, Clear, Pint	75.00
Bottle, Fruit Jar, Flaccus Steer Head, Threaded Glass Lid, 1 Pint	55.00
Bottle, Fruit Jar, Galloway Everlasting Jar, 1879, Stoneware	18.00
Bottle, Fruit Jar, Glass Lid, Metal Screw Lock, Green, Whitall	25.00
Bottle, Fruit Jar, Mason, Patent November 30, 1858, Green	12.00
Bottle, Fruit Jar, Mason's, 1858, Reverse Tudor Rose, Clear	22.00
Bottle, Fruit Jar, Millville Atmospheric, 1 Quart	20.00
Bottle, Fruit Jar, Millville Atmospheric, 2 Quart	30.00
Bottle, Fruit Jar, The Empire, February, 1866	35.00
Bottle, Fruit Jar, The Magic Star	45.00
Bottle, Fruit Jar, The Puritan, Embossed Sailing Ship, Aqua, 1 Quart	225.00
Bottle, Fruit Jar, Victory, Patent February, 1864, 2 Quart	38.00
Bottle, Fruit Jar, Wide Mouth, Aqua, 1 Pint	225.00
Bottle, Gin, Square, Brown To Gold, South America	75.00
Bottle, Ink, Amber Glass, Cone Shape	10.00
Bottle, Ink, Aqua Glass Teakettle, Octagon, C-1252, 1 5/8 In.	125.00
Bottle, Ink, Aqua Umbrella, C.1860, Blown	22.50
Bottle, Ink, Beni Wall 1699, Sealed Spirits, Amber, 6 3/8 In. .... *Illus*	850.00
Bottle, Ink, Carter's, Gray, Pottery, Pint	10.00
Bottle, Ink, Carter's, Large Cathedral, Cobalt	55.00
Bottle, Ink, Clear Glass Cabin, C-679, 2 5/16 In.	225.00
Bottle, Ink, Conical Octagon Paneled, Amber, C-180, 2 1/4 In.	75.00
Bottle, Ink, Rolled Collar, Conical Octagon Paneled, 2 1/2 In.	75.00
Bottle, Ink, Sanford, 2 1/4 Ounce	5.00
Bottle, Ink, Stoneware, 5 In.	9.00
Bottle, Ink, Teakettle Type, Octagon, Red, Gold Flowers, 2 1/16 In.	275.00
Bottle, Ink, 12 Sided, Green, Wide Flat Applied Collar, 3 1/8 In.	95.00
Bottle, Medicine, Blue, Embossed Top, Z Mold, 1912, Cork Stopper	25.00
Bottle, Medicine, Ground Stopper With Drop Grooves, Rack	65.00
Bottle, Medicine, Labeled, Filled, Set Of 6	59.00
Bottle, Medicine, McNess Germicide, Aqua	4.00
Bottle, Medicine, Moxie Nerve Food, Blob Top, BIMAL, 10 1/2 In.	5.00
Bottle, Medicine, Paine's Celery Compound, Embossed, Amber	4.50
Bottle, Medicine, Warner's Safe & Kidney Remedy, Amber	15.00
Bottle, Medicine, William Warner Chemists, Philadelphia	13.00
Bottle, Medicine, 12 Sided, Amber, Spavin Cure	5.00
Bottle, Milk, Amber	3.50
Bottle, Milk, Associated Dairies, Los Angeles, Embossed Child's Face	20.00
Bottle, Milk, Baby's Face	12.00

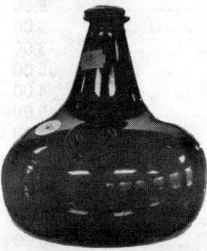

Bottle, Ink, Beni Wall 1699,
Sealed Spirits, Amber, 6 3/8 In.

Bottle, Milk, Country Club Dairy, Set Of 24	6.00
Bottle, Milk, Embossed Seattle	5.00
Bottle, Mineral Water, Pig, Aqua, Embossed Lettering	27.00
Bottle, Nursing, Acme, Oval, 8 Ounce	25.00
Bottle, Nursing, Embossed Mother Cat & Two Kittens, C.1920	4.50
Bottle, Nursing, Papoose Shape	30.00
Bottle, Nursing, Triptite, Double End	19.75
Bottle, Opaline, French, Steeple Stoppers, Applied Jewels, 21 1/2 In., Pair	225.00
Bottle, Perfume, Art Deco, Reclining Nude, Stopper, 6 1/2 In.	30.00
Bottle, Perfume, Cobalt Blue, 3 X 1/2 In.	5.00
Bottle, Perfume, Decanter Shaped, Intaglio, Signed Pitkins & Brooks, 6 In.	45.00
Bottle, Perfume, Diamond Point With Panels	12.00
Bottle, Perfume, Figural Glass Pipe	4.00
Bottle, Perfume, Green, Opaline	45.00
Bottle, Perfume, Hand Holding Bottle, Ribbed Stopper, 9 1/4 In.	18.00
Bottle, Perfume, Intaglio Cut Stopper, Cupids, Green Glass	30.00
Bottle, Perfume, Silver Container, Sterling Capped, Set Of 3	35.00
Bottle, Perfume, Silver Repousse Over Etched Crystal, Figural Stopper	60.00
Bottle, Perfume, Slag, 4 Color, Stopper, 4 1/2 In.	35.00
Bottle, Perfume, With Mirror, 4 In. _Illus_	8.00
Bottle, Perfume, Yellow, Flower Stoppers, Bavarian, Pair	9.00
Bottle, Pickle, Cathedral Arches, Aqua, Large	100.00
Bottle, Poison, Cobalt Blue, Raised Lattice & Knotted Embossing, Signed	45.00
Bottle, Poison, Mold-Blown, Pontil Mark, Set Of 3, 19th Century, 5 3/4 In.	175.00
Bottle, Scent, Sandwich Glass, Pewter Cap, 2 1/2 In.	30.00
Bottle, Scent, Sandwich, Opaque White	30.00
Bottle, Seltzer, Pewter Top, Chantilly, Paris	75.00
Bottle, Smelling Salts, Sterling Cover, Green, 2 1/2 In.	15.00
Bottle, Smelling Salts, Stopper, Green, Marked Preston Of New Hampshire	5.00
Bottle, Snuff, Blue & White, 5 Cockerels, Ivory Spoon, Signed On Base, 1700s	325.00
Bottle, Snuff, Brass & Enamel Peacock, Agate Top, Brass Dabber	47.50
Bottle, Snuff, Carved Amber	75.00
Bottle, Snuff, Carved Cinnabar, Lacquer With Coromandel Panels	100.00
Bottle, Snuff, Carved Fishbone, Oriental Scene, Red	25.00
Bottle, Snuff, Carved Horn, Jade Top	125.00
Bottle, Snuff, Carved Lapis, Ruby Top	250.00
Bottle, Snuff, Carved Malachite, Gold Thread Design	300.00
Bottle, Snuff, Carved Mother-Of-Pearl Fish	90.00
Bottle, Snuff, Carved, Chinese Design, 1 1/2 In.	195.00
Bottle, Snuff, Carved, Oriental Garden Scene, Silver Plated	9.00
Bottle, Snuff, Enameled Aqua, Dragon Center, Front & Back, C.1920	150.00
Bottle, Snuff, Enameled Panels, Silver Spoon, Amethyst Stopper, 1800s	200.00
Bottle, Snuff, Enameled, Jade Stopper, Chinese	95.00
Bottle, Snuff, Figural, Fish, Enameled, Agate Top	35.00
Bottle, Snuff, Figural, Horse, Enameled, Agate Top	35.00
Bottle, Snuff, Figural, Monkey, Rock Crystal, Carved Seated Monkey, 3 1/2 In.	185.00
Bottle, Snuff, Figural, Peacock, Enameled, Agate Top	35.00
Bottle, Snuff, Frosted & Painted Inside, Chinese	135.00
Bottle, Snuff, Frosted Glass, Chinese Figures & Scenes, Painted Inside	120.00
Bottle, Snuff, Hollowed-Out Brown Agate, C.1850	195.00
Bottle, Snuff, Monkey Holding Tiger-Eye Turtle As Stopper, 3 1/2 In.	175.00
Bottle, Snuff, Oriental Quartz, Body Relief Carved, Tinted Marble Stopper	40.00
Bottle, Snuff, Reverse Painting, Two Sides, 2 1/4 In.	90.00
Bottle, Snuff, Seated Maiden Painted Inside, Blue	85.00
Bottle, Snuff, Serpentine Bird	165.00
Bottle, Soda, Orange Crush, July 4, 1920	8.50
Bottle, Soda, Aqua, Embossed, Kirksville, Missouri	3.00
Bottle, Soda, Ginger Beer, Smith & Clody, Pottery, 7 In. _Illus_	3.00
Bottle, Soda, Koszciuszko On Horse, Plonia Bottling Co., Chicago	35.00
Bottle, Soda, Mission Dry Sparkling Soda, Black Glass	4.00
Bottle, Soda, Moxie, Green	5.00
Bottle, Soda, Moxie, Nerve Food, Trademark, Aqua, 10 1/4 In.	4.00
Bottle, Soda, Polonia Bottling Co., Koszciuszko On Horse, 1 Quart	25.00
Bottle, Soda, 1902, Lahainalce Works, Lahaina Maui	16.00
Bottle, Soda, 7 Up, Brown	25.00
Bottle, Spirit, Graphite Pontil, Hand Blown, Black, 10 In.	22.50
Bottle, Stiegel Type, Diamond Rose Pattern, Amethyst, Blown, 1800s, 5 1/2 In.	550.00

Bottle, Stiegel Type, Expanded Diamond Pattern, Amethyst, Blown, 5 1/2 In.	700.00
Bottle, Toilet, Cut Crystal, 6 1/2 In.	25.00
Bottle, Toilet, Green Slag, Ball Stopper	8.00
Bottle, Water, Lead Jointed, Perfection Bottle Co., March 30, 1897	37.50
Bottle, Water, Middleton, Vermont, Amber, 1 Quart	19.50
Bottle, Whiskey, Blake's Rye & Bourbon Whiskey, Barrels Embossed, Marked	4.00
Bottle, Whiskey, Embossed Paul Jones Louisville Kentucky, 1914, Amber, Quart	5.00
Bottle, Whiskey, Golden Wedding, Patent & Raised Markings, 9 1/2 In.	16.00
Bottle, Whiskey, Kummel Bear, Black Amethyst	45.00
Bottle, Whiskey, Old Peerless, Tennessee	45.00
Bottle, Whiskey, Spider Web, 1 Pint	5.50
Bottle, Whiskey, Stopper, Brown Glass, Ornated Silver, 12 1/4 In.	250.00
Bow, Figurine, Putto, Pierced Rococo Scroll Base, C.1770, 6 1/8 In.	450.00

Bottle, Soda, Ginger Beer, Smith & Clody, Pottery, 7 In.

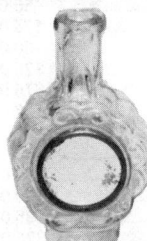

Bottle, Perfume, With Mirror, 4 In.

Boxes of all kinds are collected. They were made of thin strips of inlaid wood, metal, tortoiseshell, embroidery, or other material.

Box, see also Ivory, Box; Porcelain, Box; Shaker, Box; Store Box; Tin, Box; and various porcelain categories

Box, Advertising, Loose Wiles Biscuit, Art Nouveau Scene, Round, Covered	55.00
Box, Agate, Oval, 19th Century, 1 1/2 In.	90.00
Box, Amber Glass, Golden, Round, Hinged, Footed, Bird, Flowers, 4 3/4 In.	275.00
Box, Art Deco, Silver, Green Enamel Striped, Oriental Figure, French	550.00
Box, Battersea, see Battersea, Box	
Box, Bible, Chip Carved Pine, Rectangular, 19th Century, 19 3/4 In.	200.00
Box, Bible, Oak, Tulips, M.F.1772, Iron Lock, Hinges, 22 1/2 X 7 1/4 In.	205.00
Box, Black Lacquer, Gold & Silver Nashiji, Edo Meiji Period, 9 X 7 3/4 In.	950.00
Box, Blanket, Blue, 46 X 19 1/2 X 20 1/2 In.	225.00
Box, Bride's, Abstract Linear Designs, Red, White, Brown, 1800s, 16 3/4 In.	150.00
Box, Bride's, Oval, Painted Free-Hand, 19th Century, 16 1/4 In.	225.00
Box, Bride's, Winged Standing Figure, Scrolls, Tulips, 1800s, Oval, 17 1/2 In.	450.00
Box, Candle, Hanging, Old Red	115.00
Box, Candle, Old Blue, 9 1/2 X 20 X 6 In.	100.00
Box, Candle, Quartered, Oak, Sliding Cover, Hanger	225.00
Box, Candle, Red, Monadnock Region, Doved, 31 X 14 3/4 X 11 3/4 In.	200.00
Box, Chinese, Cinnabar, Round, 3 1/4 In.	60.00
Box, Chinese, Red, Yellow 5 Claw Dragon, Enameled, Covered, 18th Century	100.00
Box, Cigarette Case, Art Deco, Gold & Enamel, French, 3 5/8 In. ....*Illus*	1500.00
Box, Cigarette, Gold & Ruby, Rectangular, C.1920	450.00
Box, Cigarette, Silver, Lion Attacking Antelope, Chain, 3 3/4 X 4 In.	50.00
Box, Cinnabar, Lacquer, Globular, Mark Of Ch'ien Lung, C.1800, 13 1/2 In.	175.00
Box, Cloisonne, Enamel, Globular Form, Medallion Showing Carp Cover, 7 In.	475.00
Box, Compact, Silver & Gold, Enameled, Jewels, Paris, 5 1/8 In. ....*Illus*	1150.00
Box, Coromandel, 3 Scent Bottles, Silver Mounts, C.1874, London, 6 1/4 In.	175.00
Box, Deed, Yellow, Roses, Leaves, Red, Green, Flat Topped, 6 1/2 X 2 5/8 In.	165.00
Box, Desk, Pine & Oak, Slant Lid, Pigeonholes & Drawers, 15 1/2 X 29 1/4 In.	500.00
Box, Document, Curly Maple, Federal, Pierced Heart Crest, 1800s, 10 1/4 In.	450.00
Box, Document, Pine, Dovetailed Sides, Prayer On Inside Lid, C.1860	38.00
Box, Document, Tin, Diary Inside Dated 1866, Decorated, Painted	48.00
Box, Document, Wood-Grained Tin, Brass Bandings	50.00
Box, Dough, Dovetailed Poplar, Removeable Top, 18 3/4 X 36 X 30 In.	125.00
Box, Dough, Pine, Covered, Rectangular, Shaped Base, American, 1800s, 23 In.	250.00
Box, Dovetailed, Red, Cotter Pin Hinges, Ditty Box, 20 X 10 X 10 1/2 In.	95.00
Box, Dovetailed, Walnut, 10 X 5 X 6 In.	28.00
Box, Dresden, Meissen, Blue, Ormolu Mounts, Flower Interior, 15 1/2 In.	950.00
Box, Earthenware, Hotei Figure, Japanese, Covered, 1800s, 6 1/2 In.	175.00

Box, Figural, Hand Bag Shaped, American, Hallmarked	129.00
Box, Figural, Pink Rose, Butterfly Adorns Top, Bavaria	49.00
Box, Glove, Mahogany, Inlaid Mother-Of-Pearl & Onyx, Floral, 11 X 4 X 3 In.	95.00
Box, Hinged, Green & Amethyst Threading, Ormolu Fitting, 4 1/2 X 2 In.	175.00
Box, Inlaid Ivory Circles, Insert Porcupine Quills, 4 X 6 1/2 X 2 In.	22.50
Box, Jade Belt Buckle, Confronting Dragons, Metal, Lidded, Hinged	175.00
Box, Jewel, Cranberry, 3 Cast Brass Feet, Gold White Enamel, 4 1/2 X 4 In.	150.00
Box, Jewel, Gilt Metal, Enameled, Scene Of Children, French, 1800s, 4 3/4 In.	500.00
Box, Jewel, Portrait, Hinged, Tufted Lining, Brass Ormolu, 6 X 4 In.	165.00
Box, Jewel, Raised Holly & Berries, Silver Plated, Scroll Feet, 4 3/4 In.	15.00
Box, Jewel, 5 Drawer, Brass, & Mother-Of-Pearl Inlay, 12 1/4 X 8 X 6 In.	125.00
Box, Jewelry, Metal Corners, Key Hole Lid, Name Plate, Satin Lining, Tray, Oak	35.00
Box, Jewelry, Scottish, Agate, Key Lock In Silver	675.00
Box, Knife, Decorative, Pennsylvania, C.1850	55.00
Box, Knife, Inlaid Mahogany, Federal, Serpentine Case, C.1800, 13 3/4 In.	175.00
Box, Knife, Mahogany, Dovetailed, Birdseye Maple Divider, 5 1/2 X 13 1/2 In.	60.00
Box, Knife, Mahogany, Ebony & Beechwood Inlay, George III, 12 1/4 In.	325.00
Box, Knife, Mahogany, George III, 1700s, 15 X 9 X 11 1/2 In., Pair	675.00
Box, Knife, Pine, Drawer In End, 9 1/4 X 14 3/4 X 6 1/2 In.	112.50
Box, Knife, Scrolled Tapering Sides, Divider, Pierced, Handle, Maple, C.1800	425.00
Box, Korean, Black Lacquer, Mother-Of-Pearl, 14 1/4 X 8 3/4 X 9 1/2 In.	350.00
Box, Lacquer, Gold Ground, Hotei's Sack, Flowers, Emblems, Edo Period, 3 In.	850.00
Box, Lacquered, Mother-Of-Pearl, Millefleurs Design, 3 Drawer, 4 In.	1100.00
Box, Lacquered, Oriental, Copper Iridescent Finish	195.00
Box, Lotus Scroll Roundel, Mottled Gray, Covered, 7 1/4 In.	325.00
Box, Mandarin Medallion, Oblong, Covered	375.00
Box, Miniature, Tole Domed-Top, 3 In.	35.00
Box, Money, Brass, Indian, C.1800, 12 In.	285.00
Box, Money, Tin, Model Of Queen's Doll House, Chubb & Son, London, 3 1/4 In.	75.00
Box, Oval, Old Green Over Original Red, Impressed ZHearsey, 7 1/2 In.	105.00
Box, Pantry, Birchbark, MicMac	90.00
Box, Pantry, Blue-Black Paint, 6 3/4 In.	24.00
Box, Pantry, Blue-Gray, 6 1/8 In.Deep	24.00
Box, Pantry, Blue-Green Paint, 10 3/4 In.	45.00
Box, Pantry, Dark Brown Paint, Gin Written On Side, 6 1/2 In.	35.00
Box, Pantry, Green, 7 1/4 In.Deep	26.00
Box, Pantry, Original Light Brown Paint, 6 1/2 In.	30.00
Box, Pantry, Pegged & Split Lace, Oval	55.00
Box, Persian, Lacquered, Polychrome & Gilt, 3 3/4 X 2 1/4 X 1 1/4 In.	45.00
Box, Picnic, Black Lacquer, Mother-Of-Pearl, Korean, 5 Tiered, 12 In.	200.00
Box, Pin, Round, Flat, Lift-Off Lid, 2 3/4 In.	12.50
Box, Powder, Enameled, Cartouche Shape, Riverscape, Samson, 1870s, 6 1/4 In.	400.00
Box, Powder, Pink, White Medallion On Lid, Florals, Marked Germany	10.50
Box, Powder, Portrait Of Woman, Enameled, French	975.00
Box, Powder, Silver Gilt & Enamel, Continental, Late 1800s, 3 1/2 In.	120.00
Box, Puzzle, Hearts & Pinwheels, Chip-Carved, Pennsylvania, C.1741	395.00
Box, Red & Black Graining, 12 X 8 X 5 1/2 In.	30.00
Box, Salt, Painted, 18th Century, Pair	350.00
Box, Salt, Wooden, Hanging, 11 In., Pair	120.00
Box, Sewing Equipment, Oak, Crowley's Needles, White Porcelain Pulls, 10 In.	130.00
Box, Sewing, Pine, Molded Drawer Front, 4 Spool Holders	135.00
Box, Silver, Diana & Suitor, 4 Females, Cupid, Oval, C.1650, 2 1/4 In.	800.00
Box, Snuff, Bone, Polished & Carved, Oblong, Lift-Off Lid, 1 1/2 X 2 1/2 In.	20.00

Box, Cigarette Case, Art Deco, Gold
& Enamel, French, 3 5/8 In.
(See Page 39)

(See Page 39)

Box, Compact, Silver & Gold, Enameled,
Jewels, Paris, 5 1/8 In.

Bradley & Hubbard, Lamp,
Ribbed Glass, Stamped, 24 In.

(See Page 42)

Box, Snuff, Coal Miner's, Brass, Welch, C.1900	48.00
Box, Snuff, Enameled, Rape Of The Sabine Women, German, C.1760, 3 1/2 In.	1900.00
Box, Snuff, Georgian Silver, Birmingham, 1832, Willmore, 2 3/8 X 1 1/2 In.	265.00
Box, Snuff, Gold & Enamel, Madonna, Raphael, Swiss, C.1805, 3 1/2 In.	5000.00
Box, Snuff, Gold & Red, Hunting Scene, Repousse, German, C.1760, 3 1/4 In.	5000.00
Box, Snuff, Pewter, Oval, Incised J.L.In Fancy Script	65.00
Box, Snuff, Scottish, Mounted On Horns, 7 3/4 In.	35.00
Box, Snuff, Silver, C.1880, Hallmarked, Russian, Niello	345.00
Box, Snuff, Silver, George III, Scottish, R.Keay Of Perth, C.1810, 3 In.	325.00
Box, Spice, Provincial Carved Fruitwood, Louis XVI, 1730s, 17 X 8 1/2 In.	225.00
Box, Tea, Pine, Inscribed A & L, 1796 Within Oval Reserve, 11 X 16 In.	400.00
Box, Strong, Wheels, Chinese, Brass, 12 In.	75.00
Box, Thai, Gilded Phoenix On Cover, Set With Colored Glass, Covered, 8 In.	25.00
Box, Thread, Ivory Rimmed Thread Hole, Lift-Off Lid, Clan Albert, 2 3/4 In.	28.00
Box, Tin, Gloria Swanson, Rectangular, Beaute	22.00
Box, Tinder, Ives Patent, 5 1/2 In.	195.00
Box, Tobacco, Brass & Copper, Keppelman, German, C.1762, 5 3/4 In.	550.00
Box, Tobacco, Brass, Dutch, Dated 1772, 6 1/8 In.	300.00
Box, Toilette, Divided Tray, 2 Drawers, Stand, Hinged, Japanese, 10 1/4 In.	40.00
Box, Tortoise Shell & Mother-Of-Pearl, Crawford, 4 In.	32.00
Box, Tramp Art, House Shaped, Top Lifts Off, 15 X 11 X 8 In.	75.00
Box, Trinket, Enamel On Copper, Bronze Wash, 3 Compartments, Turquoise, Blue	85.00
Box, Trinket, Portrait, Green Porcelain, Beading, 2 X 2 In.	32.00
Box, Viennese, Scenic, Couple In Landscape Cover, Enamel, Silver, 2 1/4 In.	550.00
Box, Wooden, Black Lacquer, Inlaid Abalone Design, 2 1/2 X 5 1/2 In.	20.00
Box, Wooden, Oriental, Lacquered, Chop Sticks, 1949, Pair	28.00
Boy Scout, Altimeter, Cardboard, Metal Weight, 1917	48.00
Boy Scout, Book, Boy Scouts To The Rescue, Maitland	20.00
Boy Scout, Book, Boy Scouts Victory, D.J. Dunston, 1921	8.00
Boy Scout, Book, Hickory Ridge Boy Scouts Under Canvas	20.00
Boy Scout, Bugle, Brass, Marked, Offical & Licensed	20.00
Boy Scout, Calendar, 1918, 11 X 14 In.	55.00
Boy Scout, Calendar, 1944, Norman Rockwell	12.00
Boy Scout, Calendar, 1966, 13 Rockwell Prints, 6 1/4 X 7 3/4 In.	10.00
Boy Scout, Canteen, Metal Fasteners	5.00
Boy Scout, Clip, Money, Cub	6.50
Boy Scout, Flashlight, Emblem	5.00
Boy Scout, Fountain Pen, Cub	12.50
Boy Scout, Game, Progress, 1924	28.00
Boy Scout, Handbook, Linen Cover, 1923	12.00
Boy Scout, Handbook, Patrol Leader, 1944, 444 Pages	15.00
Boy Scout, Handbook, Rockwell Cover, 1941	4.00
Boy Scout, Handbook, Rockwell Cover, 1956	5.00
Boy Scout, Handkerchief, Scout Picture Each Corner	10.50
Boy Scout, Hatchet, Be Prepared	20.00
Boy Scout, Hatchet, Plumb	23.50
Boy Scout, Knife, Imperial, Providence, R.I.	15.00
Boy Scout, Lighter, Cigarette, Made Like Pocket Watch, 1917	35.00
Boy Scout, Mess Kit, Canvas Wrap, Strap, Dated 1915	15.00
Boy Scout, Morse Code, Original Box, 1922	30.00
Boy Scout, Pin, Flag, 1918	12.00
Boy Scout, Pin, War Service, 1919, Metal	14.00
Boy Scout, Pistol, Cap, Floral Handle, 1890	21.00
Boy Scout, Watch	95.00
Bradley & Hubbard, Base, Lamp, Kerosene, Steel, Signed	30.00
Bradley & Hubbard, Base, Lamp, 2-Light, Brass, Signed	40.00
Bradley & Hubbard, Blotter, 2 1/2 X 4 In.	12.00
Bradley & Hubbard, Bookends, Bust Of Whittier, Verse Below, Signed	35.00
Bradley & Hubbard, Bookends, Gilded Bust Of Dickens, Bronzed, Pair	45.00
Bradley & Hubbard, Bookends, Mt.Pleasant, Philadelphia, Bronzed	20.00
Bradley & Hubbard, Bookends, Whittier & Emerson, Bronzed	27.50
Bradley & Hubbard, Bookrack, Brass, Expandable, Signed	31.00
Bradley & Hubbard, Box, Cigarette, Brass	22.00
Bradley & Hubbard, Box, Stamp, Brass, Hinged Cover, 2 Compartments	20.00
Bradley & Hubbard, Candleholder, Brass, Signed, 4 X 5 In.	12.00
Bradley & Hubbard, Candlestick, 10 In., Pair	95.00

Bradley & Hubbard, Chamberstick, Brass, 4 1/4 In. 28.00
Bradley & Hubbard, Desk Set, Bronze, 3 Piece 75.00
Bradley & Hubbard, Desk Set, Inkwell, Insert, Pen Tray, Letter Opener 55.00
Bradley & Hubbard, Desk Set, Inkwell, Pen Tray, Blotter Holder, Brass 68.00
Bradley & Hubbard, Desk Set, Inkwell, Stamp Box, Art Deco, Signed, 4 Piece 150.00
Bradley & Hubbard, Frame, Man Of Mountain At Top, Gilt, 9 X 15 In. 50.00
Bradley & Hubbard, Holder, Letter, Brass 55.00
Bradley & Hubbard, Holder, Letter, Open Work, Nude Figures, 8 In. 38.50
Bradley & Hubbard, Humidor, Glass Insert, Brass 20.00
Bradley & Hubbard, Inkwell, Brass, Pentray, Green Patina, 8 1/2 X 4 X 2 In. 22.00
Bradley & Hubbard, Inkwell, Deer, Signed 125.00
Bradley & Hubbard, Inkwell, Flower On Cover 30.00
Bradley & Hubbard, Inkwell, Stag Head, Long Antlers, Brass 95.00
Bradley & Hubbard, Lamp, Amber Panels, Signed, 16 In. 465.00
Bradley & Hubbard, Lamp, Banquet, Complete, Marked, 31 1/2 In. 600.00
Bradley & Hubbard, Lamp, Banquet, Tripod & Milk Glass Shade, Pot Metal Base 95.00
Bradley & Hubbard, Lamp, Bend Glass Shade, Signed, 16 In. 375.00
Bradley & Hubbard, Lamp, Boudoir, 4 Panel Bent Slag Shade, Signed, 15 In. 300.00
Bradley & Hubbard, Lamp, Brass Base, 6 Paneled Caramel Glass, Signed, 23 In. 425.00
Bradley & Hubbard, Lamp, Brass Font, Flowers On Globe, 31 In. 195.00
Bradley & Hubbard, Lamp, Carmel Glass Shade, Ornate Base, Signed 459.00
Bradley & Hubbard, Lamp, Gone With The Wind, Oil, Iron Base, 30 In. 650.00
Bradley & Hubbard, Lamp, Hanging, Kerosene, Signed 375.00
Bradley & Hubbard, Lamp, Junior Size, Green Cased Shade, Pair 95.00
Bradley & Hubbard, Lamp, Kerosene, Brass, Milk Glass Shade, 18 1/2 In. 140.00
Bradley & Hubbard, Lamp, Kerosene, Table, Scrolled Iron Base, Brass 125.00
Bradley & Hubbard, Lamp, Leaded, Mottled Slag Glass, Signed, 14 In.Diameter 350.00
Bradley & Hubbard, Lamp, Oil, Pull Down, Dated 1895, Signed, 14 In.Diam. 395.00
Bradley & Hubbard, Lamp, Ribbed Glass, Stamped, 24 In. .... *Illus* 400.00
Bradley & Hubbard, Lamp, Scenic, Reverse Painted, Pebbled Shade, 14 In. 450.00
Bradley & Hubbard, Lamp, Smoking, Brass, Signed 200.00
Bradley & Hubbard, Lamp, Square Shaped Shade, Tree Overlay, Signed, 14 In. 325.00
Bradley & Hubbard, Lamp, Table, Brass, 8 Panels, Signed 365.00
Bradley & Hubbard, Lamp, Wall, Hanging, Brass, Ruby Hobnail Globe 125.00
Bradley & Hubbard, Lamp, 8 Paneled, Yellow Slag Shade, Signed, 19 In. 575.00
Bradley & Hubbard, Letter Opener, Bronze, 9 In. 12.00
Bradley & Hubbard, Planter, Hanging, Brass, 5 1/4 X 2 1/2 X 4 In. 18.00
Bradley & Hubbard, Stand, Smoking, Match Holder, Art Nouveau, Brass 85.00
Bradley & Hubbard, Urn, Ewer Form, 15 1/2 In., Pair 55.00

Brass has been used for decorative pieces and useful tablewares since ancient times. It is an alloy of copper, zinc, and other metals.

Brass, see also Bell, Tool, Trivet, etc.

Brass, Ashtray, Art Nouveau, Girl Reclining On Edge Of Shell 17.50
Brass, Ashtray, Baby, Holding Out Skirt To Form Tray, 5 X 5 In. 30.00
Brass, Ashtray, Caterpillar Bulldozers 18.00
Brass, Ashtray, Coronation, Elizabeth II 8.00
Brass, Ashtray, Egyptian, Camels, Pyramids, Red, Green 4.00
Brass, Ashtray, English Breweries, Mansfield, 4 1/2 In., Pair 20.00
Brass, Ashtray, H.C. Spaulding Fire Equipment, C.1890, 4 1/2 X 6 1/4 In. 25.00
Brass, Badge, Cudahy Employee, 1921 .... 3.00
Brass, Basket, Fireplace 35.00
Brass, Bed Warmer, Floral Engraved Lid, Turned Wooden Handle 225.00
Brass, Bed Warmer, Miniature, Wooden Handle, 9 1/2 In. 65.00
Brass, Bed Warmer, Pierced, Iron Handle, Stamped 1ST, 1700s, 40 3/4 In. 450.00
Brass, Bed Warmer, Wooden Handle, 42 X 9 3/4 In. 185.00
Brass, Bleeder, Wiegand & Snowden, Philadelphia, 1 3/4 In. 75.00
Brass, Bob, Plumb, Ovoid Body, Screw Top, William Marples 48.00
Brass, Bookend, Irish Setter 22.00
Brass, Bookrack, Expandable, Copper Over Brass, Art Nouveau 150.00
Brass, Boot, Lady's, Iron Buttons, 4 3/4 In. 40.00
Brass, Box, Cigarette, Cedar Lined, Chinese, 3 3/4 X 3 1/4 X 1 1/2 In. 55.00
Brass, Box, Patch, Flowers, Leaves, Butterfly, 1 1/2 X 2 In. 60.00
Brass, Box, Porcelain Miniature On Top, Oval, Hinged Lid, 3 In. 285.00
Brass, Box, Stamp, Brass Insert, 1 3/4 X 3 In. 40.00
Brass, Bucket, Iron Bale, 18 In. 85.00
Brass, Bucket, Rat Tail Handle, 14 In. 78.00

Brass, Bucket, Spun, Wrought Iron Handle, American, 10 Quart, 12 In.	50.00
Brass, Can, Milk, 20 In.	425.00
Brass, Candelabra, 3 Cup, Pair, 12 1/2 In.	75.00
Brass, Candelabra, 7 Branch, 10 In.	65.00
Brass, Candleholder, Beehive & Diamond, Good Pushers, English, 9 In., Pair	75.00
Brass, Candleholder, Curved Leaf, Swedish, Signed Ystad Metall, 5 In., Pair	40.00
Brass, Candleholder, Enamel & Brass, Extends Like Flame, 8 In., Pair	130.00
Brass, Candleholder, Saucer Base, Match Holder & Striker In Base, 6 In.	40.00
Brass, Candleholder, Swedish, Tulip Leaf, Signed, Pair	50.00
Brass, Candleholder, Wall, 3 Tier, Pair	29.00
Brass, Candleholder, 22 1/2 In.	60.00
Brass, Candleholder, 5 Candles Each Stick, Chinese, 12 In., Pair	95.00
Brass, Candlestick Holder, Queen Anne Type, Octagonal Base, 1700s, 7 1/2 In.	135.00
Brass, Candlestick, Altar, 1903, 16 In.	75.00
Brass, Candlestick, Beehive, 8 1/2 In., Pair	35.00
Brass, Candlestick, C.1820, Pair	95.00
Brass, Candlestick, Continental, Turned Standard, 17th Century, 5 3/4 In.	90.00
Brass, Candlestick, English, Rope Twist, Open Work, 16 In., Pair	175.00
Brass, Candlestick, English, Square Footed Base, 8 1/2 In., Pair	125.00
Brass, Candlestick, English, Stepped Square Base, 1800s, 12 In.	145.00
Brass, Candlestick, Middrip, Push-Up, 8 In., Pair	275.00
Brass, Candlestick, Miniature, 3 1/2 In., Pair	18.00
Brass, Candlestick, Octagonal, Entwining Dragons Column, 9 In., Pair	175.00
Brass, Candlestick, Open Spiral Design, 12 In.	26.00
Brass, Candlestick, Prickett Type, 12 In.	22.50
Brass, Candlestick, Prisms, Twist Design Stem, 11 In., Pair	60.00
Brass, Candlestick, Push-Up, Beehive, Register Number, 12 In., Pair	110.00
Brass, Candlestick, Push-Up, Federal, 19th Century, 9 1/2 In., Pair	160.00
Brass, Candlestick, Push-Up, 9 1/4 In., Pair	88.00
Brass, Candlestick, Queen Anne, Elongated Candlesocket, 1750, 7 1/4 In., Pair	400.00
Brass, Candlestick, Reeded, Fluted, Leaf Tip Rim, Concave Nozzle, 16 In.	100.00
Brass, Candlestick, Robert R.Jarvie, C.1901, Script Name, 12 In.	500.00
Brass, Candlestick, Sharp Turning, Square Base, Push-Rod, C.1825, 8 3/4 In.	39.00
Brass, Candlestick, Square Base & Shaft, Engraved, C.1790, 6 In., Pair	125.00
Brass, Ceiling Light, Frosted Etched Shade, 25 In.	575.00
Brass, Chamberstick, Ring Form Handle, English, C.1800, 6 1/4 In., Pair	130.00
Brass, Chamberstick, Saucer-Base, Ejector Socket, 19th Century, 4 3/4 In.	200.00
Brass, Cherub Head, Wing Sconce, Wax Saucer & Holder On Head, 9 In., Pair	25.00
Brass, Cherub Stick, Victorian, 8 In., Pair	60.00
Brass, Chimney Ornament, Chinamen, C.1800, 4 In., Pair	75.00
Brass, Chocolate Pot, Double Eagle Seal, Russian, Hinged Cover, 13 1/2 In.	159.00
Brass, Coffeepot, Double Eagle Seal, Russian, Hinged Cover, 12 1/2 In.	165.00
Brass, Coffeepot, Hinged Cover, 19th Century, Double Eagle Mark, Russian	149.00
Brass, Coffeepot, Russian Marks, Hinged Cover, 10 X 7 In.	145.00
Brass, Corkscrew, Will & Finck	45.00
Brass, Corn Husker, C.1882	20.00
Brass, Cuspidor, 6 In.	15.00
Brass, Door Knocker, American Eagle, 4 3/4 X 8 3/4 In.	100.00
Brass, Door Knocker, Lady's Head, Leafy Hairdress, 7 1/2 X 5 1/2 In.	32.00
Brass, Door Knocker, Lion, 3 Piece	35.00
Brass, Door Latch, Chippendale Scrolled Plate, C.1780	37.50
Brass, Doorknob, Cut Glass Handles, Set Of 4	75.00
Brass, Doorknob, Embossed, Pair	7.00
Brass, Doorstop, Pirate With Sword & Dagger, 7 In.	50.00
Brass, Doorstop, Swashbuckling Pirate	48.00
Brass, Easel, Floor, Holds 34 In.Painting, Acorn Finules, C.1880, 62 In.	150.00
Brass, Eyeglasses, 18th Century	28.00
Brass, Figurine, Horse Tether With Paw Foot, 15 1/4 In.	40.00
Brass, Figurine, Lizard, 6 3/4 In.	22.00
Brass, Figurine, Prancing Horse, C.1880, Oriental Mark, 10 X 13 In.	185.00
Brass, Figurine, Ram, On Base, Marked China, 5 In.	40.00
Brass, Fork, Child's, Embossed Mother Cat & 3 Kittens	10.00
Brass, Fork, Toasting, Ship Handle, 19th Century, English, 20 1/2 In.	28.00
Brass, Gong, Dinner, Suspended In U-Shaped Brass Arch, Oak Base, 6 In.	45.00
Brass, Handle & Plate, Door Of German Building, Pair	50.00
Brass, Hinge, Door, 6 X 6 In., Set Of 4	18.00
Brass, Hook, Jamb, 18th Century, Pair	78.00

Brass, Horn, Canal Teamster	37.00
Brass, Horn, English Taxi	10.00
Brass, Horseshoe, Man Riding Horse In Center, Signed, 4 1/4 X 4 1/4 In.	15.00
Brass, Horseshoe, Take Simmon's Liver Regulator	30.00
Brass, Humidor, Lined, Embossed, La Palina Senators	20.00
Brass, Humidor, Russian, Coat Of Arms On Side	7.95
Brass, Incense Burner, Part Animal With Eagle Head, 9 X 9 In.	75.00
Brass, Incense, Burner, Animal Handle, China, C.1900, 4 3/4 X 3 1/2 In.	40.00
Brass, Jardiniere, Elephant Head Handles, Oriental, 13 In.	60.00
Brass, Jardiniere, Inset Dragons, Quadripod Grotesque Feet, Chinese, 12 In.	65.00
Brass, Kettle, American, 19th Century, 5 3/4 X 6 1/4 In., Pair	175.00
Brass, Kettle, Candy, Wrought Iron Handles, Copper Rivets, 8 1/2 In.	39.00
Brass, Kettle, Jelly, Wrought Iron Handle, 11 Quart	95.00
Brass, Kettle, Swirled Iron Stand, Brass Burner	40.00
Brass, Lamp, Lucerna, 12 In.	65.00
Brass, Lamp, Shop, Phoebe Design, Inverted Funnel Base, 18th Century	385.00
Brass, Lantern, Skater's, Blown-In Mold Paneled Globe, Brass Arm Loop, 8 In.	85.00
Brass, Letter Holder, Jasperware Medallion, Woman Playing Violin, 6 In.	95.00
Brass, Letter Opener, Floral, Atlas Plaster Supply Co., Shawnee	6.50
Brass, Letter Opener, M.B.Sheffield, Faribault, Minnesota	8.00
Brass, Letter Rack, Hammered Sheet Brass Over Wood, 8 X 3 X 3 1/2 In.	15.00
Brass, Letter, N, 12 X 3/4 In.	10.00
Brass, Letter, O, 12 X 3/4 In.	10.00
Brass, Letter, T, 12 X 3/4 In.	10.00
Brass, Letter, U, 12 X 3/4 In.	10.00
Brass, Letter, Y, 12 X 3/4 In.	10.00
Brass, Lock, Fish Shape	25.00
Brass, Matchbox, Figural, Seated Cat, Chinese, 1 3/4 In.	14.00
Brass, Matchbox, Figural, Standing Deer, Chinese, 1 3/4 In.	14.00
Brass, Mirror, Jenny Lind, Framed, Stand, 21 In.	145.00
Brass, Mold, Hard Candy, For Machine, 12 Fish	40.00
Brass, Mold, Hard Candy, For Machine, 12 Semi-Circles	40.00
Brass, Mold, Hard Candy, For Machine, 24 Fruits	40.00
Brass, Mortar & Pestle, Flared Rim, Side Knobs, 4 In.	24.00
Brass, Mortar & Pestle, Miniature, 2 3/4 In.	49.00
Brass, Mortar & Pestle, Polished, Pine Rack, 4 3/4 X 2 3/4 In.	95.00
Brass, Mortar & Pestle, 3 Engraved Rings Around Body, Miniature, 1 1/4 In.	22.00
Brass, Nutcracker, Crested Bird's Head End	19.00
Brass, Nutcracker, Squirrel	28.00
Brass, Opener, Letter, Deere One Side, Velie Other Side	32.50
Brass, Pail, Iron Bail, American, 5 3/4 X 9 In.	42.00
Brass, Pail, Late 1800s, 16 In.	70.00
Brass, Pan, Gold Miner's, Iron Handle, 12 In.	18.00
Brass, Paper Clip & Pen Holder, Trees, Birds, K & C Mark	50.00
Brass, Paperweight, Lizard, 10 In.	18.00
Brass, Pipe Tamper, Fat Man With Pipe, 1 1/2 In.	45.00
Brass, Pipe Tamper, King Charles, 2 3/4 In.	57.50
Brass, Pipe Tamper, Lady's Leg, 2 1/2 In.	37.50
Brass, Pipe Tamper, Napoleon, 2 In.	57.50
Brass, Pipe Tamper, Scotsman, 2 3/8 In.	57.50
Brass, Pole, Merry-Go-Round	35.00
Brass, Pot, Fern, Russian Mark	65.00
Brass, Pot, Fern, 3 Claw Feet, Hammered, Russian	135.00
Brass, Pot, Fern, 3 Legged, Hand Hammered	65.00
Brass, Pot, Oval, Cabriole Legs, Paw Feet, 2 Side Handles, 6 1/4 X 8 In.	85.00
Brass, Pump, Beer, Bar Top, Brass Cylinder, Wooden Handle	22.00
Brass, Quadruptych, Pointed Arch Panels, Russian, 5 1/2 X 3 1/2 In.	450.00
Brass, Rack, 2 Pipe, Rearing Horse, 4 1/8 In.	7.00
Brass, Roasting Jack, Iron Wheel & Hooks, English	90.00
Brass, Samovar, Porcelain Handles & Knobs, 27 In.	225.00
Brass, Samovar, Russian, Wooden Handles, 20 In.	165.00
Brass, Samovar, Tea Set, Oriental, 9 In., 4 Piece	150.00
Brass, Sconce, Copper Sockets, Mirrored, 13 1/2 In.	90.00
Brass, Sconce, Wall, Molded & Pierced Back, Dutch, 9 3/4 In., Pair	500.00
Brass, Shoe Shine Foot Rests, Pair	50.00
Brass, Skimmer, Handle Marked Richard Lee, Springfield, Vermont, 15 In.	750.00
Brass, Skimmer, Pierced & Engraved, American Eagle, C.1760, 22 In.	600.00

Brass, Snuffer & Tray, Scissors Form Snuffer, Pear Shape Tray	40.00
Brass, Soap & Glass Holder, Dolphin Stem	12.00
Brass, Spittoon, Redskin Chewing Tobacco, Indian Chief Head Both Sides	130.00
Brass, Sprinkler, Church, Wood Handle	20.00
Brass, Stand, Flower, Church, Copper Insert, 60 In., Pair	300.00
Brass, Stand, Umbrella, Russian, Double Eagle Mark, 21 X 8 In.	169.00
Brass, Stencil, Apples, Baldwin's No. 1 & 2, 2 In.	25.00
Brass, Tea Caddy, British Empire Exhibition, 1925, Lipton	25.00
Brass, Teakettle, Alcohol Burner, Brass Stand, 10 1/2 X 4 In.	85.00
Brass, Teakettle, Alcohol Burner, Caster, Crown Mark, Empress N.Y.S.Co.	55.00
Brass, Teakettle, On Stand, Warming Iron, George IV, C.1860, 16 In.	720.00
Brass, Teapot, Queen Anne, Domed Lid, Beaded Border, 19th Century, 10 1/2 In.	150.00
Brass, Torch, Hand, Kerosene, Cylinder	7.00
Brass, Tray, Embossed Design, Morocco, 23 In.Diameter	85.00
Brass, Tray, Gallery, 48 In.Diameter	43.00
Brass, Tray, Handled, Russian, Eagle Mark, 9 X 15 In.	55.00
Brass, Tray, Stamped With State Seal In Cyrillic, Russian, 6 In.	20.00
Brass, Triptych, Gothic, Hand-Painted, Saint Inside, 6 1/2 In.	100.00
Brass, Trivet, C.1820	45.00
Brass, Trivet, Masonic, C.1840	55.00
Brass, Urn, Russian, Double Eagle Mark, 8 X 5 In.	95.00
Brass, Vase, Engraved Dragon All Around, China	8.50
Brass, Vase, Pot Belly, 2 Handles, 9 In.	12.50
Brass, Wall Sconce, Candle Arm, 1900s, 6 X 6 In., Pair	17.50
Brass, Whistle, Mockingbird, Factory Size, 3 1/2 Feet	450.00
Brass, Whistle, Steam, Lonergan, 5 X 3 In.	75.00
Bread Plate, see various Pressed Glass patterns.	
Bretby, Match Holder, Black Boy Head, Signed	20.00

*Brides' baskets of glass were usually one-of-a-kind novelties made in
American and European glass factories. They were especially popular about
1880 when the decorated basket was often given as a wedding gift. Cut glass
baskets were popular after 1890. All brides' baskets lost favor about 1905.*

Bride's Basket, Amber, Silver Overhead Handles, 10 1/2 X 6 1/2 X 10 In.	145.00
Bride's Basket, Art Glass, Cranberry Overlay, Enamel Design, Derby, 10 In.	180.00
Bride's Basket, Blue Cased, Gold Trim, Frame With 3 Brass Feet, 4 1/2 In.	165.00
Bride's Basket, Cased Pink & White, Silver Plated Frame, 10 1/2 In.	135.00
Bride's Basket, Cobalt Blue, Inside Satin, Enameled Flowers, 12 X 4 1/2 In.	250.00
Bride's Basket, Cranberry Insert, Rigaree, 4 Feet, 7 X 7 In.	125.00
Bride's Basket, Cranberry To White, Ruffled & Fluted, 10 In.	125.00
Bride's Basket, Footed Frame, Pink Cased Insert, Signed, 9 In.Diameter	145.00
Bride's Basket, Mt.Washington, Opalescent, Holder, 9 1/2 X 11 1/2 In.	325.00
Bride's Basket, Opal Basket Weave, Green Handle, Pontil Mark, 4 X 5 In.	38.00
Bride's Basket, Opalescent Hobnail, Twisted Handle At Top, 5 X 6 In.	55.00
Bride's Basket, Opalescent, Amber Looped Handles, Flowers, Custard, Pair	400.00
Bride's Basket, Opaline Bowl, Silver Claw Feet	115.00
Bride's Basket, Oval, Green Glass, Gold Flowers, Holder	85.00
Bride's Basket, Pairpoint Frame, Amberina Overlay, 4 X 11 In.	1000.00
Bride's Basket, Pedestal Base, White & Pink, Ruffled Border, 10 In.	120.00
Bride's Basket, Pigeon Blood, Ruffled Silver Frame, Footed, 11 In.	235.00
Bride's Basket, Pink & White, Enameled Leaves, Footed Frame, Meriden, 9 In.	225.00
Bride's Basket, Pink Inside & White Outside, Holder	145.00
Bride's Basket, Pink To Cranberry, Applied Crystal Around Curved Lip	237.50
Bride's Basket, Pink With Orange Enameling, Silver Plate Frame	225.00
Bride's Basket, Rubina Verde, Opalescent Hobnail	375.00
Bride's Basket, Satin Glass, Blue Shading, Enameled Gold	150.00
Bride's Bowl, Cranberry Dish, Silver Plate Cupid Holds Bowl, C.1890, 13 In.	325.00
Bride's Bowl, Opalescent, Hobnails, Crimped, 11 In.Diameter	45.00
Bride's Bowl, Pink Overlay, Silver Plate Horse & Holder, 12 X 11 In.Diam.	395.00
Bride's Bowl, Shaded Rose To Pink, Crimped Edges, 11 1/2 In.Diameter	65.00
Bride's Bowl, 2 In.Border Threaded Cranberry, Opalescent Lining, 11 In.	85.00

*Bristol glass was made in Bristol, England, after the 1700s. The
Bristol glass most often seen today is a Victorian, lightweight opaque glass
that is often blue. Some of the glass was decorated with enamels.*

Bristol, Bottle, Dresser, Original Stopper, Enameled	45.00
Bristol, Bottle, Perfume, Blue, Gold Enameled Flowers & Dots, 3 1/2 In.	75.00

Bristol, Condiment Set, Rectangular Silver Plate Holder, Footed	150.00
Bristol, Decanter, Marked In Gold, C.1790, Pair	300.00
Bristol, Dish, Cheese, Floral Trim, Covered, English	25.00
Bristol, Epergne, Blue, Enamel, 10 X 7 In.	89.00 To 110.00
Bristol, Epergne, White Enameled Flowers, 10 X 7 In.	129.00
Bristol, Jar, Biscuit, Blue, Flowers, Leaves, Silver Plated Rim, Lid, 7 In.	110.00
Bristol, Jar, Biscuit, Turquoise, Enameled, Silver Plated Handle, 6 3/4 In.	135.00
Bristol, Jar, Rose, Cover, Bulbous, Varigated Roses, 6 1/2 In., Pair	95.00
Bristol, Jar, Sweetmeat, Enameled, Brass Top & Handle, 4 3/4 X 3 5/8 In.	55.00
Bristol, Jar, Sweetmeat, Turquoise Blue, Enameled Flowers, 5 1/2 X 3 1/4 In.	75.00
Bristol, Lamp, Ball Shade, Green With Roses, Pair	195.00
Bristol, Lamp, Banquet, Clusters Of Orchids, Fluted Matching Shade, 24 In.	350.00
Bristol, Lamp, Raised Paste Flowers, Leaves, Butterfly, Rose, 2 Section, Shade	175.00
Bristol, Mantel Set, Multicolored Beige, 11 In.	195.00
Bristol, Mug, Enameled Lady With Large Hat, 4 1/2 In.	45.00
Bristol, Mug, Friendship, 4 In.	28.00
Bristol, Plate, Hand-Painted Autumn Leaves, 8 In.	13.00
Bristol, Rose Bowl, Crimped Top, Gold Floral Design	80.00
Bristol, Salt & Pepper, Hand-Decorated	40.00
Bristol, Smoke Set, Footed Wood Base	165.00
Bristol, Sweetmeat, Flowers, Silver Rim, Cover, Handle, Blue, 6 X 3 In.	55.00
Bristol, Vase, Enameled Flowers, Scenic Madallion, 9 In.	40.00
Bristol, Vase, Enameled Heron On Reeds, 11 1/2 In.	95.00
Bristol, Vase, Fireglow, 9 3/4 In.	27.50
Bristol, Vase, Flowers, Fluted, Gold Trim, 9 In.	18.00
Bristol, Vase, Green & Blue, Crimped Rim, 8 1/2 In.	32.50
Bristol, Vase, Hand-Blown, Crimped Ruffled Top, Hand-Painted, 11 In., Pair	100.00
Bristol, Vase, Hand-Painted, Roses & Leaf Design, Cranberry, 17 X 8 In.	45.00
Bristol, Vase, Narrow Neck, Enameled Butterflies, C.1890, 10 1/2 In.	45.00
Bristol, Vase, Pedestal, Hand-Painted, Fluted Lip & Pontil, 11 1/2 In.	85.00
Bristol, Vase, Pink To White, Ruffled Top, 12 In.	26.00
Bristol, Vase, Pink, Enameled Butterflies & Flowers, 14 In., Pair	130.00
Bristol, Vase, Tubular, Gold, Lime Green, 11 In., Pair	86.00
Bristol, Vase, White Lining, Multi-Color Flowers, 5 1/2 In., Pair	35.00
Bristol, Vase, White, Original Enamel, 11 In.	35.00
Bristol, Vase, World's Columbian Exposition, 1893	25.00
Britannia, see Pewter	
Bronze, Ashtray, Art Nouveau, Feathered Fan Forms Bowl	58.00
Bronze, Ashtray, Cat Head	10.00
Bronze, Ashtray, Cowboy On Bucking Horse, 7 1/2 In.	28.00
Bronze, Ashtray, Reclinging Nude, Shawl Over Middle, 3 1/2 X 7 In.	38.00
Bronze, Base, Lamp, Urn Shape, Signed O.B.Bach, 13 1/2 In.	75.00
Bronze, Basket, Vienna, 2-Handled, Wren Perched On Handle, 4 1/2 X 5 1/2 In.	125.00
Bronze, Bell Pusher, Form Of Wild Boar, Vienna	45.00
Bronze, Bell, Archaic Style, Rows Of Knobs, Rosettes, C.1800, 9 In.	125.00
Bronze, Bell, Evolution, 2-Sided Face, 8 In.	60.00
Bronze, Bookends, Baby At Tree Trunk, Frog Below, Signed Moreni	150.00
Bronze, Bookends, Buddha In Classic Seated Position, Dark Patina, 6 3/4 In.	55.00
Bronze, Bookends, Dante & Beatrice, Signed J.B., 5 1/2 X 4 X 5 1/2 In.	140.00
Bronze, Bookends, Embossed Cowboy On Horse Lasooing Cow	40.00
Bronze, Bookends, Lady & Man	45.00
Bronze, Bookends, Male Nudes Wrestling, Signed	150.00 To 200.00
Bronze, Bookends, Man Seated On Bench, Signed K, 6 X 3 1/2 X 4 1/4 In.	75.00
Bronze, Bookends, Nude Girl Sitting On Rock, Armour Bronze Co., Signed	95.00
Bronze, Bookends, Pointer, Standing, Copper Trim	65.00
Bronze, Bookends, Relief Castle Scene, 4 1/2 In.	35.00
Bronze, Bookends, Sailing Ships, Marked N.Y.B.	45.00
Bronze, Bookends, Scottie Dogs, Signed Edith Parsons, Pair	225.00
Bronze, Box, E.Laurent, People In Tavern, Signed, 10 1/2 X 7 X 4 In.	245.00
Bronze, Box, Japanese, Priest On Cover, 19th Century, 5 1/4 In.Diameter	425.00
Bronze, Box, Turtle, Signed, Vienna, 7 In.	310.00
Bronze, Bust, A.Carrier, Head Of Young Woman, Golden Tiara, Signed, 8 1/2 In.	495.00
Bronze, Bust, Boehm, Queen Victoria, Signed, 9 1/2 In.	375.00
Bronze, Bust, C.Kauba, Shakespeare, Marble Base, Signed, 8 1/2 In.	250.00
Bronze, Bust, F.Barbedienne, Lady With Long Curls, 28 In.	2400.00
Bronze, Bust, F.Remington, Savage, 1908, Marble Base, Signed, 13 In.	895.00
Bronze, Bust, Francois, Crying Baby, 7 X 3 3/4 In.	295.00

Bronze, Bust, Georges Clemenceau, Artist Signed, 3 1/2 X 3 1/4 X 1 3/4 In.	350.00
Bronze, Bust, Greil, American Revolutionary Figure, 6 1/2 In.	300.00
Bronze, Bust, Head Of The Buddha, Wood Stand, 1800s, Thai, 8 3/4 In.	175.00
Bronze, Bust, J.A.Houdon, George Washington, Dated 1898, 18 In.	800.00
Bronze, Bust, Jenny Lind, Art Nouveau, A.Falguiere, Paris, 9 1/2 X 6 In.	850.00
Bronze, Bust, Venus, Barbedienne Foundry	1450.00
Bronze, Bust, Young Girl, Hair Piled On Head, Signed, Foundry Mark, 18 In.	600.00
Bronze, Candelabra, Marble Base, Pendants, Pair	97.50
Bronze, Candelabra, 7 Light, Mounted Marble, 1800s, 27 3/4 In., Pair	3500.00
Bronze, Candleholder, Cobra, Wall Hung, 22 In., Pair	100.00
Bronze, Candlestick, Figure, Cherub On Top, 1868, 4 1/2 In.	95.00
Bronze, Chandelier, Dore, From French Cathedral, For 22 Candles, 4 Ft.	425.00
Bronze, Chandelier, 12 Light, Scrolls, Foliage, Tri-Form Cupola, 29 In.	1300.00
Bronze, Compote, France, Embossed, Handled, 5 1/2 X 5 1/2 In.	90.00
Bronze, Corkscrew, Dachshund, Tail Is Corkscrew	18.00
Bronze, Corkscrew, Scottie, Germany	15.00
Bronze, Cutter, Cigar, Form Of Maiden, 2 In.	45.00
Bronze, Door Knocker, Animal Head	100.00
Bronze, Door Knocker, Cornish Pixies, 4 1/4 X 1 1/2 In.	15.00
Bronze, Door Knocker, Cutty Sark, 4 1/2 X 1 1/2 In.	15.00
Bronze, Door Knocker, Figural, Cat & Fiddle, 1 1/4 X 3 In.	15.00
Bronze, Door Knocker, Figural, Grotesque Imp, 1 1/4 X 3 In.	15.00
Bronze, Door Knocker, Lady's Jeweled Hand, Mexican	65.00
Bronze, Door Knocker, Sun Gold Head	80.00
Bronze, Ewer, Brass Plated, Inverted Feather Design, Ornate, 18 1/2 In.	150.00

Bronze Figurines

Bronze, Figurine, A. Jacquemarts, Coyoye, 5 1/4 In.	225.00
Bronze, Figurine, A.De Wever, Mephistopheles, C.1875, Signed, 11 1/2 In.	1375.00
Bronze, Figurine, A.Leonard, Fox Killing Pheasant, Signed, 8 1/2 X 5 In.	450.00
Bronze, Figurine, A.Varnier, 2 German Police Dogs Chained Up, 15 X 11 In.	1650.00
Bronze, Figurine, Armorer, Square Marble Base, C.1800, Waltet, 11 1/4 In.	650.00
Bronze, Figurine, Athlete, Faiger, Marble Base, Signed, 15 1/4 In.	385.00
Bronze, Figurine, Aug.Morell, Lady With Jug, 9 In.	145.00
Bronze, Figurine, Barye, Lion & Captured Gazelle, Signed, 9 1/2 X 4 In.	725.00
Bronze, Figurine, Barye, Lion & Serpent, Signed, 12 X 10 In.	1100.00
Bronze, Figurine, Barye, Lion Holding Gazelle, Marble Base, Signed, 7 In.	725.00
Bronze, Figurine, Barye, Panther Of Tunis, Marble Base, 9 1/2 X 4 1/2 In.	475.00
Bronze, Figurine, Barye, Pug Dog Playing With Rat, Marble Base, 6 X 4 In.	325.00
Bronze, Figurine, Barye, Seated Lion, Signed, 7 1/2 In.	525.00
Bronze, Figurine, Bassin, Standing Dog, Barking, Signed, 6 In.	150.00
Bronze, Figurine, Benjamin Franklin, Verte Base, French, 1800s, 22 1/2 In.	3850.00
Bronze, Figurine, Blicker, Cannon & Ball, Lion & Serpent On Cannon	250.00
Bronze, Figurine, Brian, Nude Holding Hoop, Art Deco, 11 1/2 In.	360.00
Bronze, Figurine, Buddha Sitting On Lotus Throne, C.1700, 11 1/4 In.	450.00
Bronze, Figurine, Buddha Sitting On Throne, Cambodian, 28 In.	400.00
Bronze, Figurine, Buhner, Young Boy, Short Pants, Signed, 7 In.	325.00
Bronze, Figurine, Bulldog Sitting On Rug, Recess In Back, Signed, Austrian	60.00
Bronze, Figurine, C.E.Dalin, The Scout, 1910, 9 In.	1100.00
Bronze, Figurine, C.Masson, Mouse Eating Sugar, Signed, 3 In.	200.00
Bronze, Figurine, C.Valton, Boston Terrier, 6 1/2 In.	200.00
Bronze, Figurine, Cain, Donkey, A.C. On Flank, 5 X 6 In.	650.00
Bronze, Figurine, Carlier, French Soldier Charging, C.1880, 34 In.	2250.00
Bronze, Figurine, Ch.Malfray, Draped Nude, Cire Perdue, 17 1/2 X 4 1/4 In.	850.00
Bronze, Figurine, Child Praying, 5 1/2 X 3 1/2 In.	180.00
Bronze, Figurine, Chinese Gold Of Grain, 8 3/4 In.	205.00
Bronze, Figurine, Cipriana, Nude, Kneeling Position, Aiming Arrow, 18 In.	1800.00
Bronze, Figurine, Cossack, Rifle, Banded Malachite Socket, Russian, 7 In.	450.00
Bronze, Figurine, Delabrierre, Dogs & Deer, Signed, 8 In.	400.00
Bronze, Figurine, Derby Winner, Mounted On Marble Base, Signed, 13 1/4 In.	1650.00
Bronze, Figurine, DeWeaver, Gold Wash Mephistopheles, 11 1/2 In.	1375.00
Bronze, Figurine, Dodge, Otter, U.S.A., 2 X 2 1/4 In.	50.00
Bronze, Figurine, Du Bois, Florentine Singer, Collas Stamp, 24 1/2 In.	2900.00
Bronze, Figurine, Dubucand, Group Of Horses & Two Borzoi Dogs, 9 In.	950.00
Bronze, Figurine, Dubucand, Stag & Doe, 6 1/2 X 5 1/2 In.	375.00
Bronze, Figurine, E.Carlier, Foreign Legion Soldier, 10 1/2 In.	385.00
Bronze, Figurine, E.Fremiet, Knight On Horseback, Gold, Marble Base	400.00

Bronze, Figurine, Flapper, Ivory,
C.1925

Bronze, Figurine, Maiden,
C.1880, 25 1/2 In.

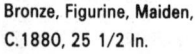

Bronze, Figurine, Tiger & Alligator,
Japanese, C.1880, 32 In.

Bronze, Figurine, E.Fremiet, Seated Setter, Signed, 6 1/4 In, High	275.00
Bronze, Figurine, E.Fremiet, Stretching Dog, Marble Base, 3 1/2 X 7 1/2 In.	750.00
Bronze, Figurine, E.Villanes, Nude Slave Girl, Signed, 10 In.	425.00
Bronze, Figurine, Edouard Sandoz, Moroccan In Traditional Garb, C.1915	250.00
Bronze, Figurine, Elephant Attached By 3 Tigers, 1800s, Ruishin Sano, 42 In.	4000.00
Bronze, Figurine, Elephant, Beset, Japanese, Signed, C.1880	2000.00
Bronze, Figurine, Elephant, Blankets & Water Jars On Back, 6 In., Pair	595.00
Bronze, Figurine, F. Barbedienne, Crocodile, 7 1/2 In.	650.00
Bronze, Figurine, F.Cambria, Buzzard On Pedestal, 6 1/4 In.	500.00
Bronze, Figurine, Flamingo On Back Of Turtle, 16 In.	250.00
Bronze, Figurine, Flapper, Ivory, C.1925	*Illus* 4750.00
Bronze, Figurine, Fratin, Bear, Signed, 3 In.	150.00
Bronze, Figurine, Frog, Holes On Top For Fountain Spray	450.00
Bronze, Figurine, Frog, Japanese, Seated, Signed, 3 1/4 In.	75.00
Bronze, Figurine, Fu Lion, Paw Touching Pierced Ball, Wood Stand, 16 In.	600.00
Bronze, Figurine, G.Salkowski, Goat, Signed	175.00
Bronze, Figurine, Garnier, Woman With Grapes, Naked Infant, 21 1/2 In.	1800.00
Bronze, Figurine, Geschutz, Greyhound, Original Polychrome, 6 X 5 In.	350.00
Bronze, Figurine, Gladys Bros., Great Dane, Signed	150.00
Bronze, Figurine, Greyhound, Sitting, G Emblem Mark, 4 1/2 In.	125.00
Bronze, Figurine, Gus Moreau, Lady With Urn, 31 Ounce, Signed	374.00
Bronze, Figurine, H.Faiken, Boy & Girl, Self Bronze Base, Signed, 4 In., Pair	210.00
Bronze, Figurine, H.Gaudet, Flamenco Dancer, C.1900, 16 1/2 In.	1200.00
Bronze, Figurine, Hazel, Phidias, Pensive Pose, Signed, 1800s, Base, 19 1/4 In.	800.00
Bronze, Figurine, Hercules & Lichas, Nemean Lion, C.1800, 54 1/2 In.	2750.00
Bronze, Figurine, Horse, Teakwood Stand, Chinese	550.00
Bronze, Figurine, I.Bonheur, Hound, 12 1/4 In.	925.00
Bronze, Figurine, Iffland, Barefoot Boy, Marble Base, 6 1/2 In.	400.00
Bronze, Figurine, Industrial Smithie, Stepped Marble Base, 1800s, 11 1/2 In.	650.00
Bronze, Figurine, Ista Stoddart, Stallion, 13 X 13 In.	345.00
Bronze, Figurine, J.Guillot, Cavalier, Standing, Signed, 6 1/2 In.	500.00
Bronze, Figurine, J.M.Lambeaux, Erotica, Marble Base, 5 X 3 In.	600.00
Bronze, Figurine, Jacquemart, Coyote, 5 1/4 In.	275.00
Bronze, Figurine, Jambhala, Seated On Dragon, Mongoose, Nepalese, 7 1/2 In.	400.00
Bronze, Figurine, Jeanne D'Arc-Enfant, Signed, 11 1/2 In.	1450.00
Bronze, Figurine, Jester, Seated On Marble Block, Ivory Face	185.00
Bronze, Figurine, Joseph Boehm, Queen Victoria, 9 1/2 In.Tall	375.00
Bronze, Figurine, Kauba, Armoured Warrior, On Running Horse, Signed	1850.00
Bronze, Figurine, Kauba, Canoe & Indian, Signed, 26 1/2 X 14 1/2 In.	7500.00
Bronze, Figurine, Kauba, Indian, Seated, Headdress, Signed, 5 1/2 In.	575.00
Bronze, Figurine, Kauba, Two Bears Around Tree, Signed, 17 In.	2000.00
Bronze, Figurine, Kuan Yin Seated, Holding Scroll, Wood Stand, 1800s, 7 In.	250.00
Bronze, Figurine, Kuan Yin, Seated In Lalitasana, Hand On Knee, 5 In.	125.00
Bronze, Figurine, Lecourtier, Guard Dog, Beaux Arts, 1878 On Base, 13 1/4 In.	800.00
Bronze, Figurine, Lefeuvre, French Peasant Woman Carrying Boy, 24 1/2 In.	1200.00
Bronze, Figurine, Little Girl, C.1875, 13 1/2 In.	625.00
Bronze, Figurine, Lorenze, Napoleon, Full Figure, Marble Base, 14 In.	360.00

Bronze, Figurine, M.Queste, Nude Woman On Stylized Rock, Signed, 9 1/2 In. 350.00
Bronze, Figurine, Maiden Holding Musical Instrument, Japanese, 30 1/2 In. 1300.00
Bronze, Figurine, Maiden, C.1880, 25 1/2 In. .... *Illus* 750.00
Bronze, Figurine, Medieval Knight In Armor, Marble Pedestal, Signed, 15 In. 1400.00
Bronze, Figurine, Modello, Nude Man, Green Patina, 15 In. 450.00
Bronze, Figurine, Moigniez, Retriever, Signed, 8 X 12 1/2 In. 925.00
Bronze, Figurine, Moigniez, Standing Bull, 3 1/2 X 2 3/4 In. 350.00
Bronze, Figurine, Moigniez, Two Mastiff Dogs Playing, 4 1/2 X 3 1/2 In. 525.00
Bronze, Figurine, Morath, Nude Girl In Art Nouveau Position, Signed, 13 In. 425.00
Bronze, Figurine, Nam Greb, Dancing Girl On Ashtray, Skirt Goes Up, 5 In. 395.00
Bronze, Figurine, Nam Greb, Oasis Scene, 19th Century, 13 X 12 1/2 In. 1650.00
Bronze, Figurine, Nam Greb, Palm Trees, Camel & Master, 12 3/4 X 13 In. 1650.00
Bronze, Figurine, Negro Boy, Head & Shoulders, 13 1/4 In. 60.00
Bronze, Figurine, O'Merth, Harlequin, Ivory Face, Holding Puppet, Signed 500.00
Bronze, Figurine, Young Harlequin, Ivory Face, Puppet Punch, O'Merth 450.00
Bronze, Figurine, Old Man With Dog, Signed, 7 X 5 In. 195.00
Bronze, Figurine, Old Woman With Cat, Signed, 7 X 5 In. 195.00
Bronze, Figurine, P.J.Mene, Arabian Stallion, 12 In. 1650.00
Bronze, Figurine, P.J.Mene, Bovine Cow Nursing Her Calf, Dark Patina, 13 In. 1400.00
Bronze, Figurine, P.J.Mene, Cow Feeding Calf, Signed, 5 In. 425.00
Bronze, Figurine, P.J.Mene, Greyhound, 8 In.Marble Base, Signed, 7 In. 435.00
Bronze, Figurine, P.J.Mene, Horse, D'Jinne, Signed, 16 X 12 In.High 3500.00
Bronze, Figurine, P.J.Mene, Horses, Flundry Mark Susse, 6 In. 500.00
Bronze, Figurine, P.J.Mene, Hunting Dog, Crouching On Point, Signed 425.00
Bronze, Figurine, P.J.Mene, Pointer & Setters, 5 X 2 In. 435.00
Bronze, Figurine, P.J.Mene, Pointer, 7 1/2 X 5 1/2 In. 360.00
Bronze, Figurine, P.J.Mene, Ram, 8 1/4 X 9 In. 650.00
Bronze, Figurine, P.Kovhairemski, Semi-Nude Huntress, 13 In. 750.00
Bronze, Figurine, P.Tereszizuk, Maiden Lying Down, Signed, 8 1/2 In. 365.00
Bronze, Figurine, Paul DuBois, Florentine Singer, C.1865, 24 1/2 In. 2250.00
Bronze, Figurine, Pautrot, Pointer With Hare On Stake, 6 X 6 In. 495.00
Bronze, Figurine, Peter Breuer, Sword Dancer, Marble Pedestal, 16 1/2 In. 1275.00
Bronze, Figurine, Picault, Prima Spoila, Signed, 14 In. 65.00
Bronze, Figurine, R. Bonheur, Grazing Ewe, 8 1/2 X 6 In. 825.00
Bronze, Figurine, Raul, Laughing Mermaid, 1919, Signed, 8 1/2 In. 1250.00
Bronze, Figurine, Roland, Ivory Figure Of Clown, Enameled, 14 1/2 In. 675.00
Bronze, Figurine, Russian Troika, 3 Horses & People, Signed, C.1880 .... 1750.00
Bronze, Figurine, S.Kinsburger, Marie Antoinette As Shepherdess, 17 1/2 In. 650.00
Bronze, Figurine, Silhouette Head Of Lincoln, 3 1/2 In. 59.00
Bronze, Figurine, Spanish Lady With Tambourine, Signed Theo, 13 In. 800.00
Bronze, Figurine, Spirit Of Industry Posed By Anvil, Signed, 12 In. 275.00
Bronze, Figurine, St.Michael Slaying The Dragon, Signed, 11 1/2 In. 875.00
Bronze, Figurine, Stag At Bay, 6 Dogs, Marble Base, 6 1/2 X 4 1/2 In. 250.00
Bronze, Figurine, T.Somme, Old Man With Basket Of Flowers, C.1910, 20 In. 1990.00
Bronze, Figurine, Tiger & Alligator, Japanese, C.1880, 32 In. .... *Illus* 1200.00
Bronze, Figurine, Tiger, Patina, Signed On Bottom In Japanese, 4 1/2 In. 350.00
Bronze, Figurine, Titze, Stag, Reclining, Rocker Blotter, Signed 175.00
Bronze, Figurine, Troudoux, Pheasant, Base Has Trees & Growth, 7 X 7 1/2 In. 475.00
Bronze, Figurine, Van Der Stretton, Gibson Girl, Seated, Signed, 12 1/2 In. 675.00
Bronze, Figurine, Venus De Milo, Lauriage, Signed, 13 1/2 In. 465.00
Bronze, Figurine, Vienna, Alligator Has Black Boy By Seat Of Pants 105.00
Bronze, Figurine, Vienna, Bird, 19th Century, Polychrome, Signed, 3 X 4 In. 185.00
Bronze, Figurine, Vienna, Bulldog Sitting In Lady's Glove, 1 1/4 X 3 In. 95.00
Bronze, Figurine, Vienna, Cat On Chair Reading Times, Signed, 1 3/4 In. 105.00
Bronze, Figurine, Vienna, Cat On Potty, Signed, 1 3/4 In. 115.00
Bronze, Figurine, Vienna, Chick 40.00
Bronze, Figurine, Vienna, Dachsund On Blue Pillow, Signed, 2 In. 90.00
Bronze, Figurine, Vienna, Italian Troubador, 3 In. 85.00
Bronze, Figurine, Vienna, Lady In Riding Habit, Signed, 4 In. 185.00
Bronze, Figurine, Vienna, Love Birds Facing Each Other, 2 3/4 X 1 3/4 In. 75.00
Bronze, Figurine, Vienna, Setter, 2 3/4 In. 45.00
Bronze, Figurine, Vienna, Swallow 32.00
Bronze, Figurine, Vienna, 2 Puppies Peeking Out Of Knapsack, 1 X 1 1/8 In. 95.00
Bronze, Figurine, Waagan, Great Dane, Playing With Ball, 7 X 5 1/4 In. 495.00
Bronze, Figurine, Walking Buddha, Sukhothai Style, Wood Plinth, 28 In. 300.00
Bronze, Figurine, Whippet Dog Looking At Ball, 3 1/2 In. 125.00

Bronze, Figurine, Whippet, Marble Plinth, French, 1800s, 8 3/4 In., Pair 3400.00
Bronze, Figurine, Woman Holding Lantern, Japanese, C.1900, Signed, 32 In. 1800.00

Bronze Group
Bronze, Group, A.Varnier, 2 Police Dogs, Green Marble Base, 11 X 15 In. 1650.00
Bronze, Group, Barye, Two Turkeys, Cock & Hen, 3 1/2 In. 195.00
Bronze, Group, Clodion, Bacchante & A Baby, 34 In. 3200.00
Bronze, Group, E.Fremiet, Gallic Chieftain On Horse, Signed, 14 X 12 In. 950.00
Bronze, Holder, Card, 6 X 3 1/2 X 1 In. 125.00
Bronze, Holder, Letter, Oriental Design 12.00
Bronze, Incense Burner, Fu Lion Surmounted, Tripod Feet, 1800s, 12 In. 125.00
Bronze, Incense Burner, Grillwork Has Hinged Door, 28 In., Pair 190.00
Bronze, Lamp, Art Nouveau, Jewels, 25 In. 850.00
Bronze, Lamp, Floor, 6 Light, German Soldier Blowing Horn, 1800s, 45 In. 1000.00
Bronze, Lamp, Full Figure, Putti, Gold Finish Handle, Floral Sprays, 35 In. 78.00
Bronze, Lamp, Nam Greb, Semi-Nude Slaves, Enamel Work, 14 1/2 X 11 1/2 In. 2450.00
Bronze, Letter Slot, Embossed 12.00
Bronze, Miniature, Russian Troika, Malachite Base, C.1880, Signed 1750.00
Bronze, Mold, Spoon 175.00
Bronze, Mold, Toy, Baby Bear, Kitten With Bonnet, Sun Rubber, Barberton, Ohio 25.00
Bronze, Mold, Toy, Baby Bear, Sun Rubber, Barberton, Ohio 18.00
Bronze, Mold, Toy, Dog, Sun Rubber, Barberton, Ohio 18.00
Bronze, Mold, Toy, Doll, Sun Rubber, Barberton, Ohio 32.50
Bronze, Mold, Toy, Kitten, Sun Rubber, Barberton, Ohio 25.00
Bronze, Mold, Toy, Lamb, Sun Rubber, Barberton, Ohio 35.00
Bronze, Paper Clip, 4 Leaf Clover, Art Nouveau, 2 1/2 X 3 In. 40.00
Bronze, Paperweight, Art Nouveau, Girl With Flowing Hair, Signed, A.Forster 225.00
Bronze, Paperweight, Crouching Lion, 4 1/2 X 1 X 1 3/4 In., Pair 75.00
Bronze, Paperweight, Female Figure Reclining On Flower Stem, Rubin, 11 In. 225.00
Bronze, Plaque, Heads Of 3 Different Dogs, Signed R.Plaght, 3 1/4 X 4 In. 85.00

Bronze, Tray, Pin, Art Nouveau, C.1900

Bronze, Sconce, Wall, Lion's Head, 3 Light 58.00
Bronze, Sconce, Winged Animal, Pair 900.00
Bronze, Seal, Woman Wearing Riding Costume, 4 1/4 In. 125.00
Bronze, Shoe, Mice On Back Is Match Striker, 2 1/2 In. 59.00
Bronze, Spurs, Lady's, Rowels With Chains & Leather Straps, Engraved 85.00
Bronze, Spurs, Man's, Rowels, Leather Straps, Hand Engraved 85.00
Bronze, Stein, Pictures & Scrolls In Danish & English 50.00
Bronze, Sundial, Bird Pointer, Embossed Wings & Hour Glass, 11 In.Diam. 95.00
Bronze, Sundial, Grow Old Along With Me, The Best Is Yet To Be, Roman Nos. 135.00
Bronze, Torchere, Chinese, Applied Bronze Birds & Flowers, 6 1/2 Ft. 825.00
Bronze, Tray, Card, Nouveau Form, Fulats Corp., 7 1/2 X 5 In. 45.00
Bronze, Tray, Pin, Art Nouveau, C.1900 .... *Illus* 850.00
Bronze, Urn, Cloisonne Decoration, Flared Neck, Outset Handles, 24 In. 425.00
Bronze, Urn, Green Enameled Leaves, Japanese, 35 1/2 In. 200.00
Bronze, Urn, Handled, Art Nouveau, Signed F.Levellian, 5 1/2 In. 125.00
Bronze, Vase, Art Nouveau, 2 Handled, C.1900 .... *Illus* 225.00
Bronze, Vase, Ceramic Inlay, Chinese, 18 1/2 In. 600.00
Bronze, Vase, Dancing Man & Woman, Applied, Signed, 19th Century, 10 1/2 In. 425.00
Bronze, Vase, Engraved Floral Sprays, 6 X 2 1/2 In.Diameter 35.00
Bronze, Vase, Gilt, Art Nouveau, Charles Korschann, C.1900 .... *Illus* 500.00
Bronze, Vase, Japanese, Scenic, Children & Animals, 19th Century, 11 In., Pr. 1250.00
Bronze, Vase, Lohan, Dragon, Girl, Covered, Stand, C.1800, 83 In. 4500.00
Bronze, Vase, Ovoid Body, Dragon Handles, Japanese, 1800, 16 1/2 In., Pair 400.00

Bronze, Vase, Silver, Copper, Birds, 10 Inches 95.00
Brownie, Plate, Palmer Cox, Goat Scene, 7 In. 28.00
Brownie, Plate, Palmer Cox, Skipping Rope, Multi-Enamel Colors, 7 In. 42.00
Buck Rogers, Battlecruiser, Tootsietoy 45.00
Buck Rogers, Blast Attack Ship, Red & White, Tootsietoy 95.00
Buck Rogers, Book, City Of Floating Globes 35.00
Buck Rogers, Book, Kelloggs, 1933 .... 25.00
Buck Rogers, Book, Pop Up, 1934 Series, Dangerous Mission 70.00
Buck Rogers, Book, The City Below The Sea 15.00
Buck Rogers, Box, Pencil, Red, With Contents 30.00
Buck Rogers, Game, All Fair, Card, 1934 .... 150.00
Buck Rogers, Game, Rubber Band Cardboard Gun, 1940 .... 15.00
Buck Rogers, Gun, Daisy Ray 40.00
Buck Rogers, Handbook, Solar Scout, 1936 .... 150.00
Buck Rogers, Pistol, Atomic, Daisy 70.00
Buck Rogers, Puzzle, Inlaid, 1952 .... 15.00
Buck Rogers, Ray Gun, 25th Century, C.1930s 45.00
Buck Rogers, Rocket Pistol, Xz-34, 1934 .... 200.00
Buck Rogers, Rocket Police Patrol, Original Box, 1927 .... 250.00
Buck Rogers, Rubber Stampers, Set Of 7 .... 35.00
Buck Rogers, Strato-Kite, Illustrated Envelope, Dated 1946 .... 25.00
Buck Rogers, Toy, Battle Cruisers, Ships, Tootsietoy, 4 Piece 128.00
Buck Rogers, Watch, Pocket, Original 150.00
Buffalo China, Plate, Hotel Astor, Commercial, Straus & Sons, 9 In. 28.00
Buffalo China, Sugar & Creamer, Covered, Dated 1920, Bungalow 20.00

> *Buffalo pottery was made in Buffalo, New York, after 1902. The company was established by the Larkin Company, famous manufacturers of soap. The wares are marked with a picture of a buffalo and the date of manufacture. Deldare ware is the most famous pottery made at the factory. It is a khaki-colored transfer-decorated ware.*

Buffalo Pottery, Bowl, Roosevelt Bears, 6 In. 120.00
Buffalo Pottery, Creamer, Blue Willow, 1911 .... 20.00
Buffalo Pottery, Deldare, Bowl, Breakfast At Three Pigeons, 12 In. 400.00
Buffalo Pottery, Deldare, Bowl, Cereal, Ye Olden Days, 6 1/2 In. 175.00
Buffalo Pottery, Deldare, Bowl, Fruit, Ye Village Tavern, 9 In. 350.00
Buffalo Pottery, Deldare, Bowl, Sugar, Covered, Village Inn Ye Olden Days 185.00
Buffalo Pottery, Deldare, Bowl, Vegetable, Breaking Cover, 9 In. 400.00
Buffalo Pottery, Deldare, Bowl, Vegetable, Ye Village Scene, 9 In. 300.00
Buffalo Pottery, Deldare, Bowl, Ye Village Tavern, 9 1/4 In. 500.00
Buffalo Pottery, Deldare, Candlestick, 9 1/2 In., Pair 450.00

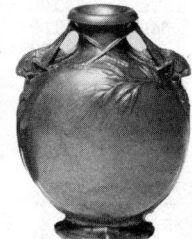

Bronze, Vase, Art Nouveau, 2 Handled, C.1900

Bronze, Vase, Gilt, Art Nouveau, Charles Korschann, C.1900

Buffalo Pottery, Deldare, Charger, An Evening At Ye Lion Inn, 13 1/2 In.	475.00
Buffalo Pottery, Deldare, Creamer, Village Life In The Olden Days, Tardy	145.00
Buffalo Pottery, Deldare, Creamer, Ye Olden Days	240.00
Buffalo Pottery, Deldare, Cup & Saucer, The Hunt	250.00
Buffalo Pottery, Deldare, Cup & Saucer, Ye Olden Days, Artist Signed	235.00
Buffalo Pottery, Deldare, Dish, Relish, The Death	300.00
Buffalo Pottery, Deldare, Dish, Sauce, The Hunt, 5 1/4 X 1 1/4 In.	175.00
Buffalo Pottery, Deldare, Hair Receiver, Ye Village Street	275.00
Buffalo Pottery, Deldare, Mug, Breakfast At The Three Pigeons, 4 1/2 In.	250.00
Buffalo Pottery, Deldare, Mug, The Death, 4 1/2 In.	250.00
Buffalo Pottery, Deldare, Mug, Ye Lion Inn, 4 1/4 In.	225.00
Buffalo Pottery, Deldare, Pitcher, Annual Rent, 1908, 8 In.	375.00
Buffalo Pottery, Deldare, Pitcher, Eight-Sided, Breaking Cover, 7 In.	375.00
Buffalo Pottery, Deldare, Pitcher, Eight-Sided, The Return, 8 In.	400.00
Buffalo Pottery, Deldare, Pitcher, Hunt Supper, 12 1/2 In.	475.00
Buffalo Pottery, Deldare, Pitcher, To Spare An Old Broken Soldier, 7 In.	300.00
Buffalo Pottery, Deldare, Pitcher, Village Scene, Signed, 7 In.	265.00
Buffalo Pottery, Deldare, Plate, Breaking Cover, 10 In.	250.00
Buffalo Pottery, Deldare, Plate, Chop, The Start, 13 5/8 In.	475.00
Buffalo Pottery, Deldare, Plate, Dr.Syntax, Tulip Hall, 8 1/2 In.	350.00
Buffalo Pottery, Deldare, Plate, Lion Inn, 6 1/4 In.	108.00
Buffalo Pottery, Deldare, Plate, Soup, Fallowfield Hunt	225.00
Buffalo Pottery, Deldare, Plate, Star Of Fallowfield Hunt, Old Blue, 9 In.	175.00
Buffalo Pottery, Deldare, Plate, The Death, 8 1/2 In.	165.00
Buffalo Pottery, Deldare, Plate, The Start, 1906, 14 In.	500.00
Buffalo Pottery, Deldare, Plate, The Start, 1908, 9 1/2 In.	185.00
Buffalo Pottery, Deldare, Plate, Town Crier, 8 1/4 In.	160.00
Buffalo Pottery, Deldare, Plate, Ye Lion Inn, 6 1/4 In.	95.00
Buffalo Pottery, Deldare, Plate, Ye Olden Times, 9 1/4 In.	140.00 To 150.00
Buffalo Pottery, Deldare, Plate, Ye Town Crier, 8 1/4 In.	120.00 To 155.00
Buffalo Pottery, Deldare, Plate, Ye Village Street, 7 1/4 In.	115.00
Buffalo Pottery, Deldare, Platter, Round Ye Village Gossips, Signed, 10 In.	169.00
Buffalo Pottery, Deldare, Platter, Ye Olden Times, Artist Signed, 1906, 10 In.	175.00
Buffalo Pottery, Deldare, Platter, Ye Village Gossips, Artist Signed, 1908	175.00
Buffalo Pottery, Deldare, Salt & Pepper, Art Nouveau, Emerald	550.00
Buffalo Pottery, Deldare, Saucer, Olden Days	65.00
Buffalo Pottery, Deldare, Saucer, The Hunt, 6 In.	100.00
Buffalo Pottery, Deldare, Sugar & Creamer, Dr.Syntax, Signed, 1911, 3 In.	625.00
Buffalo Pottery, Deldare, Sugar, Covered, Scenes Of The Village	250.00
Buffalo Pottery, Deldare, Sugar, Ye Olden Days	250.00
Buffalo Pottery, Deldare, Teapot, Village Life In Olden Days, 3 3/4 In.	325.00
Buffalo Pottery, Deldare, Teapot, Ye Olden Days, 3 3/4 In.	300.00
Buffalo Pottery, Deldare, Tray, Card, Ye Lion Inn, C.1908, M.L.Newman	200.00
Buffalo Pottery, Deldare, Tray, Dancing Ye Minuet	450.00
Buffalo Pottery, Deldare, Tray, Pin, Ye Olden Days, 6 1/4 In.	200.00
Buffalo Pottery, Deldare, Tray, Relish, Ye Olden Times, 12 X 6 I	340.00 To 350.00
Buffalo Pottery, Deldare, Tray, Ye Lion Inn, Signed, 9 X 12 In.	399.00
Buffalo Pottery, Dish, Child's, Katzenjammer Kids	55.00
Buffalo Pottery, Dish, Feeding, Campbell Kids, 8 In.	15.00 To 32.00
Buffalo Pottery, Dish, Soup, Willow Ware, Set Of 6	65.00
Buffalo Pottery, Dish, Vegetable, Covered, Blue Willow, 7 1/2 X 9 In.	28.00
Buffalo Pottery, Fish Set, Platter & 5 Plates, Signed	135.00
Buffalo Pottery, Gravy Boat, Blue Willow	12.00
Buffalo Pottery, Jar, Salt	37.50
Buffalo Pottery, Jar, Slop, Cairo Pattern	75.00
Buffalo Pottery, Mug, Purple, With Elk, B.P.O.E.	35.00
Buffalo Pottery, Mug, Vacation	54.00
Buffalo Pottery, Pitcher, Blue Willow, Dated 1911, Trademark	42.75
Buffalo Pottery, Pitcher, Buffalo Hunt	225.00
Buffalo Pottery, Pitcher, Chrysanthemum, Green On White, 7 In.	40.00
Buffalo Pottery, Pitcher, Cinderella, Dated 1906	275.00
Buffalo Pottery, Pitcher, Gaudy Willow, 1907	300.00
Buffalo Pottery, Pitcher, George Washington	265.00 To 345.00
Buffalo Pottery, Pitcher, Geranium, Green-Blue, Dated 1911	165.00
Buffalo Pottery, Pitcher, Geranium, Multicolored	200.00
Buffalo Pottery, Pitcher, Glorianna, Blue	275.00
Buffalo Pottery, Pitcher, Landing Of Roger Williams	295.00 To 325.00

Buffalo Pottery, Pitcher, Pilgrim	500.00
Buffalo Pottery, Pitcher, Robin Hood	275.00
Buffalo Pottery, Pitcher, Roosevelt Bears, 1907	385.00
Buffalo Pottery, Pitcher, Water, Tea Rose Pattern	35.00
Buffalo Pottery, Pitcher, Whirl Of The Town	300.00
Buffalo Pottery, Plate, Deer, Signed, 9 1/4 In.	33.00
Buffalo Pottery, Plate, Dr.Syntax Reading His Tour, White, Blue, 9 1/2 In.	185.00
Buffalo Pottery, Plate, Dusky Grouse, 9 1/4 In.	62.00
Buffalo Pottery, Plate, Fallowfield Hunt Breaking Cover, Olde Ivory, 7 In.	275.00
Buffalo Pottery, Plate, Faneuil Hall, 10 In.	25.00
Buffalo Pottery, Plate, Fish, Green Band Borders, Gold Trim, Signed Beck	38.00
Buffalo Pottery, Plate, George Washington, 11 In.	225.00
Buffalo Pottery, Plate, Independence Hall, Green, 10 In.	14.00
Buffalo Pottery, Plate, Independence Hall, 7 1/2 In.	60.00
Buffalo Pottery, Plate, Jack Dempsey's Picture In Center, 7 1/4 In.Square	65.00
Buffalo Pottery, Plate, Lafayette Square, Buffalo, New York, Green, 7 1/2 In.	150.00
Buffalo Pottery, Plate, Modern Woodmen Of America, 7 1/2 In.	55.00
Buffalo Pottery, Plate, Moose With Doe In Background, 9 In.	25.00
Buffalo Pottery, Plate, Mt.Vernon, Blue & White, 10 In.	30.00
Buffalo Pottery, Plate, Niagara Falls, Green & White, 10 In.	30.00
Buffalo Pottery, Plate, Niagara Falls, 7 1/2 In.	35.00
Buffalo Pottery, Plate, Statue Of Liberty, 7 1/2 In.	75.00
Buffalo Pottery, Plate, The Gunner	50.00
Buffalo Pottery, Plate, White House, 10 In.	25.00
Buffalo Pottery, Sugar, Covered, Blue Willow, 1911	20.00
Buffalo Pottery, Toddy Set, 4 Cups & Bowl, Mocha, Claret Band	185.00
Buffalo Pottery, Tureen, Covered, Roses Around Top	30.00
Buffalo Pottery, Tureen, Soup, Bonrea Pattern	44.00
Buggy, Perambulator, Doll, C.1870	325.00
Buggy, Push-Type, Burton & Whitney, C.1870	2400.00

Burmese glass was developed by Frederick Shirley at the Mt.Washington Glass Works in New Bedford, Massachusetts, in 1885. It is a two-toned glass, shading from peach to yellow. Some have a pattern mold design. A few Burmese pieces were decorated with pictures or applied glass flowers of colored Burmese glass.

Burmese, see also Gunderson

Burmese, Biscuit Jar, Cockle Shell, Flowers Front & Back	225.00
Burmese, Bowl, Mt.Washington, Tri-Cornered, 2 X 5 1/8 In.Diameter	225.00
Burmese, Bowl, Ruffled, Signed Queen's, Thomas Webb, 5 X 2 1/2 In.	625.00
Burmese, Bowl, Tri-Corner, Acid Finish, Flinty Ring, Mt.Washington	275.00
Burmese, Bride's Basket, Daisy Design, Silver Plate Frame, Cherub Figures	1300.00
Burmese, Charger, Leaves With Cluster Of Enamel Flowers, Signed, 11 3/4 In.	525.00
Burmese, Creamer, Minature, Yellow Rim To Pink At Base, 2 1/2 In.	315.00
Burmese, Creamer, Satin Finish, Mt.Washington, 5 1/4 In. *Illus*	140.00
Burmese, Dish, Mt.Washington, Crimped Top, 1 1/2 X 4 1/2 In.Diameter	225.00
Burmese, Dish, Peach To Yellow, Triangular, 5 X 2 1/2 In.	310.00
Burmese, Dish, Sauce, Fluted Sides, Set Of 3	250.00
Burmese, Fairy Lamp, Signed Clark Base, 3 3/4 In. Tall, Pair	185.00
Burmese, Glass, Juice, Satin Finish, 3 In.	125.00
Burmese, Glass, Lemonade, Mt.Washington, Diamond-Quilted, Handled, 4 3/4 In.	375.00
Burmese, Lamp Shade, Ruffled, Glossy, Yellow To Salmon, 4 1/2 X 2 In.	250.00
Burmese, Lamp, Fairy, Ivy Decorated, Clear Marked Clarke Base, 4 3/4 In.	350.00
Burmese, Pitcher, Tankard, Enameled Flowers, 3 3/4 In.	395.00
Burmese, Pitcher, Webb, Acid Finish, Applied Yellow Handle, 5 1/2 In.	395.00
Burmese, Rose Bowl, Graduated Color, Ruffled Top, 3 In.	295.00
Burmese, Rose Bowl, Satin Finish, Triangular & Pinch Pleated Top, 3 In.	450.00
Burmese, Rose Bowl, Triangular, Ruffled Top	450.00
Burmese, Saltshaker, Green & Wine Painted Flowers, Metal Spout, 1 1/2 In.	60.00
Burmese, Shade, Acid Cut Outside, Glossy Inside, Ruffled	85.00
Burmese, Shade, Lamp, Salmon To Yellow, 5 1/2 In.	275.00
Burmese, Shade, Ruffled, 5 In.Diameter	300.00
Burmese, Toothpick, Acid Finish, Mt.Washington, Square Top	225.00
Burmese, Toothpick, Diamond Quilted, Tri-Foil Top, Folded In, Mt.Washington	320.00
Burmese, Toothpick, Glossy, 6-Sided Top	220.00
Burmese, Toothpick, Tri-Corner, Daisy Decoration	350.00
Burmese, Toothpick, Tri-Corner, Enameled Floral Design, Yellow	220.00

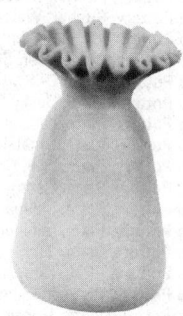

Burmese, Tumbler, Roses,
Poem By Thomas Hood,
Mt.Washington

Burmese, Creamer, Satin Finish,
Mt.Washington, 5 1/4 In.

(See Page 53)

Burmese, Vase, Flaring Ruffled
Rim, Conical Shape, 4 1/4 In.

Burmese, Tumbler, Juice, Satin Finish, 3 In.	125.00
Burmese, Tumbler, Roses, Poem By Thomas Hood, Mt.Washington ....*Illus*	1100.00
Burmese, Vase, Ball Shaped, Ruffled Top, Pink & Yellow, 3 3/8 In.Diameter	225.00
Burmese, Vase, Beaded Enamel Around Lip, Floral Design, Bulbous, 12 In.	625.00
Burmese, Vase, Body Flaring To Crimped Top, Lemon Yellow, 4 In.	235.00
Burmese, Vase, Bulbous, Flares To 7 Petal Top, Acid Finish, 3 1/4 In.	315.00
Burmese, Vase, Corset Shape, Rolled Star Top, 3 1/2 In.	300.00
Burmese, Vase, Enamel Floral Spray, Square Top, Bulbous Base, 2 3/4 In.	175.00
Burmese, Vase, Flaring Ruffled Rim, Conical Shape, 4 1/4 In. ....*Illus*	225.00
Burmese, Vase, Jack-In-The-Pulpit, 1950s, 12 1/2 In.	85.00
Burmese, Vase, Lily Form, 3 Fired, 7 In.	225.00
Burmese, Vase, Lily Form, 3 Fired, 10 1/2 In.	500.00
Burmese, Vase, Lily, Acid Finish, Bled-Out Yellow Edge, 13 In.	1250.00
Burmese, Vase, Lily, Acid Finish, Yellow Bled-Out Edge, Mt.Washington, 13 In.	995.00
Burmese, Vase, Lily, Mt.Washington, Peg Base, Tri-Ruffle Top, 7 3/4 In.	200.00
Burmese, Vase, Rose, Enameled Birds, 8 In.	195.00
Burmese, Vase, Stick Neck, 4-Sided Dimpled Base, Queen's Burmese Label	275.00
Burmese, Vase, Stick, Ivy Around, 7 1/2 In.	340.00
Burmese, Vase, Tri-Cornered Pedestal Trumpet, Mt.Washington, 9 In.	250.00
Burmese, Vase, Tri-Cornered, Acid Finish, Ground Pontil, 6 In.	210.00
Burmese, Vase, Trumpet, Webb, Petal Crimped Top, 4 In.	135.00
Burmese, Vase, Webb, Fluted Top, Satin Finish, 3 1/2 X 2 7/8 In.Diameter	295.00
Burmese, Vase, Webb, Ruffled Top & Pedestal, 4 3/8 X 2 1/2 In.Diameter	225.00
Burmese, Vase, Webb, Ruffled Top, Bulbous Body, Signed, 2 3/4 In.	325.00
Burmese, Vase, Webb, Scalloped Top, Enameled Flowers, Signed, 3 3/4 In.	365.00
Burmese, Webb, see Webb Burmese	
Buster Brown, Bank, Buster & Tige	90.00
Buster Brown, Bill Hook, Picture Of Buster & Tige, 2 1/2 In.Diameter	4.00
Buster Brown, Book, Buster Brown On Uncle Jack's Farm, 1907	20.00
Buster Brown, Book, Latest Frolics, Color, 1907, 11 1/2 X 16 1/2 In.	37.50
Buster Brown, Book, 1910, Brown's Shoe Co., 12 Color Pages, 7 X 5 In.	17.00
Buster Brown, Camera, Box, No.2	20.00
Buster Brown, Cards, Playing, Cartoons, Original Box, 1 3/4 X 2 1/2 In.	27.50
Buster Brown, Clicker, Advertising	4.50 To 10.00
Buster Brown, Dish, Sauce	35.00
Buster Brown, Embroidery Set, Buster & Tige	7.00
Buster Brown, Eyeglasses, Gold Chain, Original Case	20.00
Buster Brown, Figurine, Roly Poly, Celluloid	80.00
Buster Brown, Football	10.00
Buster Brown, Fork & Spoon	35.00
Buster Brown, Game, Necktie Party, 1900	47.00
Buster Brown, Knife, Fork & Spoon, Plate Over Brass, Embossed Handle	35.00
Buster Brown, Knife, Pocket	65.00

Buster Brown, Mannequin, With Tige, Pedestal, Original Clothes, 29 In. 95.00
Buster Brown, Mask, Advertising 6.50
Buster Brown, Mirror, Pocket, Buster & Tige 4.00
Buster Brown, Necktie, Pin On, With Tige, Signed, Outcault 100.00
Buster Brown, Periscope 6.00
Buster Brown, Scarf, Ed McConnell 7.00
Buster Brown, Shoe Tree, Original Package, Pair 7.50
Buster Brown, Spoon 15.00
Buster Brown, Statue, Boy & Girl, Display, 29 In. 135.00
Buster Brown, Tape Measure, Retractable 17.00
Buster Brown, Toy, Tige, Dog Cart, 8 In. 125.00
Buster Brown, Valentine, Postcard, Outcault 12.00
    Butter Mold, see Kitchen, Mold, Butter
    Buttermilk Glass, see Custard Glass

*   Buttons have been known throughout the centuries, and there are millions of*
*   styles. Only a few of the most common types are listed for comparison.*
Button, Art Nouveau, English Silver, Embossed Tulips, 7/8 In., Set Of 5 .... 175.00
Button, Art Nouveau, Head On Each, Birmingham, 1902, 5/16 In., Set Of 6 .... 180.00
Button, Collar, Uncle Sam 6.00
Button, Cut Out Figure King Neptune, English Silver, Hallmarked, Set Of 6 .... 150.00
Button, Gibson Girl, Portrait, Made Into Earrings 22.00
Button, Green Faceted Glass, Jewel Cluster, Set In Brass, 1 3/8 In.Set Of 6 .... 60.00
Button, Indian Head Nickel, 1937, Pair 8.50
Button, Mikado Yum Yum 5.00
Button, Miniature, Glass, Stippled Heart 35.00
Button, N.Y.C. Fire Department, Uniform, Silver Plated 3.00
Button, Paperweight Type, Horse's Head, Under Glass Dome, 1 3/4 In.Diameter 25.00
Button, Porcelain, Multicolored, Gold Edge, Porcelain Shank 12.00
Button, Portrait, Men, Satsuma, 5/8 In. 12.00
Button, Rumplestiltskin 4.00
    Buttonhook, see Silver, Sterling; Buttonhook, Store; Buttonhook
Bybee, Creamer, Blue, Matte Glaze 14.50
    Calcite, see also Steuben
Calcite, Sherbet & Plate, Gold 150.00

*   Calendar plates were very popular in the United States from 1906 to 1929.*
*   Since then plates have been made every year. A calendar, the name of a*
*   store, a picture of flowers, a girl, or a scene was featured on the plate.*
Calendar, Paper, Print, Winchester, 1927 .... 125.00
Calendar, Paper, 1882, Calendar Of The Seasons, Kate Greenaway, 8 Pages 38.00
Calendar, Paper, 1883, Thomas & Co., Cigar Factory, 8 1/2 X 12 In. 12.00
Calendar, Paper, 1891, Willimantic Thread Co., Complete, 4 3/4 X 6 In. 6.50
Calendar, Paper, 1892, Hood's 16.00
Calendar, Paper, 1892, Wood Farm Machinery, 2-Sided, 9 1/2 X 12 1/2 In., Pair 30.00
Calendar, Paper, 1893, Horsford 30.00
Calendar, Paper, 1894, Hood's Sarsaparilla 8.00
Calendar, Paper, 1894, Prang Flower Fancies 25.00
Calendar, Paper, 1896, Garland Stoves, Children Pictured, 10 1/2 X 6 1/4 In. 8.00
Calendar, Paper, 1896, Hood's 38.00
Calendar, Paper, 1896, John Hancock, 13 1/2 X 16 1/2 In. 55.00
Calendar, Paper, 1897, John Hancock, 13 1/2 X 16 1/2 In. 55.00
Calendar, Paper, 1898, Diecut, Victorian Girl With Kitten 15.00
Calendar, Paper, 1898, Three Fold, Couples Pictured, Equitable Insurance 20.00
Calendar, Paper, 1898, Youth's Companion, Chromolithographic, 11 X 24 In. 29.00
Calendar, Paper, 1899, Compliments Carson Lime Co, Riverton, Va. 5.00
Calendar, Paper, 1899, McKinley, Dewey, & Uncle Sam With Eagle 75.00
Calendar, Paper, 1900, Abbey's Effervescent Salt 25.00
Calendar, Paper, 1900, John Hancock, 13 1/2 X 16 1/2 In. 55.00
Calendar, Paper, 1900, Tuck, Golden Memories 8.00
Calendar, Paper, 1900, Youth Companion, 28 X 9 1/4 In. 5.00
Calendar, Paper, 1901, Beautiful Women, 3-Section, 25 X 8 In. 5.00
Calendar, Paper, 1901, Kittens, Lattice Work & Figural, All Date, Month 25.00
Calendar, Paper, 1901, Prudential, Pretty Woman, 10 X 9 In. 15.00
Calendar, Paper, 1902, Fairbank's Fairy Art, Framed, 10 X 14 In. 40.00
Calendar, Paper, 1902, Shelton Commission Co., 2 Pointer Dogs 12.50
Calendar, Paper, 1902, Victorian Lady, Chromolithographic, 10 X 12 3/4 In. 45.00

Calendar, Paper, 1904, Hood's Sarsaparilla, Colonel's Daughter 22.00
Calendar, Paper, 1904, Hood's, Pretty Lady, 4 1/4 X 15 In. 25.00
Calendar, Paper, 1906, Slade's Spices, Child 12.50
Calendar, Paper, 1908, Sweet Bouquet, Violets, 13 X 6 In. 6.00
Calendar, Paper, 1909, A Girl You Ought To Know, Brochure On Artist, Carlyle 10.00
Calendar, Paper, 1909, Krebs Coffee Co., Bloomington, Dog Center 25.00
Calendar, Paper, 1912, Pratt's 30.00
Calendar, Paper, 1913, Buster Brown Shoes, Oak Frame, 21 X 13 In. 37.50
Calendar, Paper, 1914, Springfield Breweries 100.00
Calendar, Paper, 1915, DeLaval, 12 X 24 In. 38.00
Calendar, Paper, 1917, DeLaval 38.00
Calendar, Paper, 1918, Mary Pickford, Pompeian Cream 22.50
Calendar, Paper, 1919, DeLaval Cream Separator, Signed, 12 X 24 In. 85.00
Calendar, Paper, 1921, Ice Cream, Sine's Woman Eating, 18 X 33 1/2 In. 165.00
Calendar, Paper, 1931, DeLaval, Norman Price Illustrator 12.00
Calendar, Paper, 1932, Firestone, Man & Girl Playing Checkers, Complete 25.00
Calendar, Paper, 1932, Nehi 55.00
Calendar, Paper, 1934, Simmons Keen Kutter, Tools & Supplies, Complete 35.00
Calendar, Paper, 1935, Negroes Picking Cotton By Cabin, 12 X 16 In. 2.00
Calendar, Paper, 1936, Franklin D.Roosevelt, Art Deco Border, 22 X 14 In. 3.00
Calendar, Paper, 1936, Franklin D.Roosevelt, Art Deco Border, 45 X 21 In. 5.00
Calendar, Paper, 1936, Franklin D.Roosevelt, Art Deco, 33 1/2 X 15 3/4 In. 4.00
Calendar, Paper, 1937, Dionne Quintuplets 12.00
Calendar, Paper, 1937, Ruppert 18.00
Calendar, Paper, 1938, Dionne Quintuplets 12.00
Calendar, Paper, 1939, Art Deco Nude, A Modern Venus, 23 3/4 X 14 In. 3.00
Calendar, Paper, 1939, Texaco 12.00
Calendar, Paper, 1940, Hello Everybody, Opulent Woman, 17 X 14 In. 2.50
Calendar, Paper, 1940, Toddler Holding Phone 5.00
Calendar, Paper, 1940, Woman, Hello Everybody, 17 X 14 In. 2.50
Calendar, Paper, 1941, Dionne Quintuplets 12.00
Calendar, Paper, 1942, Pepsi-Cola, Complete, 17 X 22 3/4 In. 55.00
Calendar, Paper, 1952, Cowboys, Original Envelope 6.00
Calendar, Paper, 1956, Spokane, Portland, Seattle Railroad 8.00
Calendar, Paper, 1961, Hummel 6.00
Calendar, Plate, 1906, Four Seasons, Scranton, Penn., 9 In. 40.00
Calendar, Plate, 1908, Colored Flags Center, Souvenir La Belle, 8 In. 12.00
Calendar, Plate, 1908, Crossed Flags 8.00
Calendar, Plate, 1908, Santa 35.00
Calendar, Plate, 1908, Thistle Flowers 35.00
Calendar, Plate, 1909, Dog In Center, 9 In. 21.00
Calendar, Plate, 1909, Dog With Advertising 20.00
Calendar, Plate, 1909, Forget-Me-Nots, Blue 15.00
Calendar, Plate, 1909, Girl In Sailor Dress, Flower Border, 9 1/4 In. 28.00
Calendar, Plate, 1909, Hazelton, Pennsylvania 18.00
Calendar, Plate, 1909, Huron, South Dakota 17.50
Calendar, Plate, 1909, Lake & Mountain Scene, Semi-Porcelain 27.50
Calendar, Plate, 1909, Rose Center .... 18.00 To 28.00
Calendar, Plate, 1909, South Dakota 20.00
Calendar, Plate, 1909, Souvenir, Roses 19.00
Calendar, Plate, 1910, Cupids, Hourglass, Bell 21.00
Calendar, Plate, 1910, Flowers 10.00
Calendar, Plate, 1910, Four Seasons, Nantucket, Mass. 28.00
Calendar, Plate, 1910, Girl With Horse 25.00
Calendar, Plate, 1910, Hound Dog 18.00
Calendar, Plate, 1910, J.W.Griever Co., Portrait On Front 29.50
Calendar, Plate, 1910, Jas.Whitcomb Riley Verse, Pond Scene, Boys Swimming 28.00
Calendar, Plate, 1910, Luther, Wyoming, Lilacs In Center 22.00
Calendar, Plate, 1910, New Year, Cupids 17.00
Calendar, Plate, 1910, Old Men With Scythe, New Britain, Conn., 8 1/2 In. 26.00
Calendar, Plate, 1910, Portrait Of Indian, Souvenir, 7 1/2 In. 22.50
Calendar, Plate, 1910, Washington's Home, Side Porch View 26.00
Calendar, Plate, 1911-12, Compliments Of H.B.Walker 22.50
Calendar, Plate, 1911, Ducks, Eaton Ice Co., Quincy Mass. 35.00
Calendar, Plate, 1911, Flowers In Center, 8 In. 14.00
Calendar, Plate, 1911, Girl Gathering Apples 30.00
Calendar, Plate, 1911, Hen & Chicks 27.50

Calendar, Plate, 1911, Hunter With Dog, Quail 20.00
Calendar, Plate, 1911, Orange & Yellow Carnations, 8 In. 20.00
Calendar, Plate, 1911, Setting Sun With Morning Glories 25.00
Calendar, Plate, 1911, Water Scene, Leaves & Roses 30.00
Calendar, Plate, 1912, Airplanes, 8 In. 30.00
Calendar, Plate, 1912, Balloon & Calendar In Center, 8 In. 30.00
Calendar, Plate, 1912, Indian Maid 23.00
Calendar, Plate, 1912, Indian Maiden Husking Corn 34.00
Calendar, Plate, 1912, Kennedy's New Market, N.H. 25.00
Calendar, Plate, 1912, Kitty Hawk, Calendars Around Border, 8 3/4 In. 28.00
Calendar, Plate, 1912, Men In Balloon, Flow Blue Style Border 36.00
Calendar, Plate, 1912, Owl On Calendar Book, 8 In. 22.00
Calendar, Plate, 1912, Planes Flying Over Land & Sea 35.00
Calendar, Plate, 1912, South Dakota 20.00
Calendar, Plate, 1912, Ticonderoga, New York 13.50
Calendar, Plate, 1913, A.M.Phillip's Department Store, Farm Scene 29.50
Calendar, Plate, 1913, Black Swans 16.00
Calendar, Plate, 1913, Early Airplane 30.00
Calendar, Plate, 1914, Child In Tattered Clothing, 8 In. 11.00
Calendar, Plate, 1914, Girl, Horse Jumping Stone Wall 26.00
Calendar, Plate, 1914, The People's Bottling Co., Woman On Horse, 7 1/2 In. 24.00
Calendar, Plate, 1914, Transfer Of Washington At Valley Forge 35.00
Calendar, Plate, 1915, Butterflies Between Months Border, 9 1/4 In. 23.00
Calendar, Plate, 1915, Panama Canal In Center, Flow Blue Edge 20.00
Calendar, Plate, 1916, Eagle & American Flag Center, 7 1/4 In. 21.00
Calendar, Plate, 1916, German Children, Advertising 20.00
Calendar, Plate, 1918, Game Birds In Center & Border, 9 1/4 In. 28.00
Calendar, Plate, 1919, Flag Decoration 27.50
Calendar, Plate, 1919, Flags Of 3 Nations, U.S.Flag Center 25.00
Calendar, Plate, 1919, Point Arena, California 25.00
Calendar, Plate, 1920, Peace 10.00
Calendar, Plate, 1920, Sheldon, Iowa, W.W.I 23.00
Calendar, Plate, 1920, Victory .... 24.00 To 35.00
Calendar, Plate, 1920, World War I, Victory, 8 In. 19.00
Calendar, Plate, 1928, Roses, Back Marked Harker, Arrow Mark 35.00
Calendar, Plate, 1929, Four Scenes, Blue 40.00
Calendar, Plate, 1953, Homer Laughlin 8.50
Calendar, Plate, 1959, Pink Border, Gold Calendar 10.00
Calendar, Plate, 1962, Gold Months Of Year 5.00
Calendar, Plate, 1968, Robert Kennedy, Memorial 8.00
Calendar, Plate, 1972, American Gothic 12.00
Calendar, Plate, 1972, God Bless Our House 9.00
Camark, Frog, Ball Shape, Green & Blue, 5 In.High, 6 1/4 In.Diameter 18.00

*Cambridge art pottery was made in Cambridge, Ohio, from about 1895 until
World War I. The factory made brown glazed decorated wares marked with
a variety of marks including an acorn, the name Cambridge, the name Oakwood,
or the name Terrhea.*

Cambridge Pottery, Vase, Corset Shape, Brown & Green Striations, 7 In. 95.00
Cambridge Pottery, Vase, Nasturtiums Design, Marked, 6 1/2 In.Diam. 245.00

*The Cambridge Glass Company made pressed glass in Cambridge, Ohio.
The words "near-cut" were used after 1906. It was marked with a C in
a triangle about 1916.*

Cambridge, Ashtray, Caprice, Gold, 4 Toed, Set Of 4 .... 24.00
Cambridge, Ashtray, Caprice, Round, 3 .... 35.00
Cambridge, Basket, Decagon, Pink, Etched 996, 11 In. 30.00
Cambridge, Bonbon, Decagon, Apple Green, Signed 16.00
Cambridge, Bonbon, Rosepoint, Handled, Footed, 5 1/4 In. 32.50
Cambridge, Bookend, Eagle, Pair 55.00
Cambridge, Bookend, Lady's Leg, Green, Pair 30.00
Cambridge, Bookend, Scottie Dog, Pair 55.00
Cambridge, Bookend, Solid Crystal, Eagle, Near Cut 175.00
Cambridge, Bottle, Cologne, Buzz Saw, Near Cut 25.00
Cambridge, Bowl & Candleholder, Sterling Overlay Bowl, Signed, 11 3/4 In. 75.00
Cambridge, Bowl, Amberina, Signed, Ebony Base, 9 3/4 In.Diameter 75.00
Cambridge, Bowl, Amberina, 10 In. 85.00

Cambridge, Bowl, Azurite, Footed, Gold Encrusted, 10 In. 35.00
Cambridge, Bowl, Caprice, Crystal, Floral, Footed, 13 In. 28.50
Cambridge, Bowl, Caprice, Handled, Footed, Ice Blue, 12 In. 35.00
Cambridge, Bowl, Caprice, 4-Footed, Oval, 11 In. 20.00
Cambridge, Bowl, Centerpiece, Caprice, Footed, Moonlight Blue, 11 X 7 In. 32.00
Cambridge, Bowl, Centerpiece, Caprice, Ruffled, Footed, Moonlight Blue, 13 In. 38.00
Cambridge, Bowl, Centerpiece, Crown Tuscan, Seashell With Nude, 10 In. 145.00
Cambridge, Bowl, Centerpiece, Honeycomb, Amberina, 10 In. 89.00
Cambridge, Bowl, Crown Tuscan, Flying Nude, Seashell, 12 In. 140.00
Cambridge, Bowl, Crown Tuscan, Seashell Pattern, Footed, 9 In. 65.00
Cambridge, Bowl, Crown Tuscan, Seashell, 3-Toed, Signed, 10 In. 65.00
Cambridge, Bowl, Crown Tuscan, Shell, 8 1/2 In. 50.00
Cambridge, Bowl, Crown Tuscan, Signed, 12 In. 50.00
Cambridge, Bowl, Everglade, 3-Footed, Pearl Mist Finish, 14 In.Diameter 37.50
Cambridge, Bowl, Heliotrope, Gold Band, 3 1/4 X 11 3/4 In.Diameter 65.00
Cambridge, Bowl, Pedestal, Flying Nude, Crown Tuscan 140.00
Cambridge, Bowl, Primrose, 8 In.Diameter 30.00
Cambridge, Bowl, Ruffled Top, Cobalt Blue, Marked, 10 In. 50.00
Cambridge, Bowl, Silver Overlay, Crystal, Signed, 11 In. 22.50
Cambridge, Box, Cigarette, Covered, Caprice 10.00
Cambridge, Box, Cigarette, Covered, Crown Tuscan, Dolphin Feet 60.00
Cambridge, Box, Cigarette, Covered, Hand-Painted Roses, Crown Tuscan 25.00
Cambridge, Butter, Crystal, Rosepoint 85.00
Cambridge, Butter, Inverted Strawberry, Near Cut 65.00
Cambridge, Butter, Rosepoint .... 75.00 To 145.00
Cambridge, Candleholder, Caprice, Moonlight Blue, Prism 15.00
Cambridge, Candleholder, Caprice, 2 1/2 in., Pair 15.00
Cambridge, Candleholder, Chantilly, Scalloped, Pair 16.00
Cambridge, Candleholder, Double, Crown Tuscan 125.00
Cambridge, Candleholder, Double, Decagon, Blue, Pair 38.50
Cambridge, Candleholder, Everglade, Blue, 3-Footed, Signed, 3 In., Pair 55.00
Cambridge, Candleholder, Nude Stem, Crown Tuscan, 9 In. 70.00
Cambridge, Candleholder, 3 Light, Rosepoint 55.00
Cambridge, Candlestick, Azurite, 7 1/2 In., Pair 30.00
Cambridge, Candlestick, Black, No.627, 4 In., Pair 36.00
Cambridge, Candlestick, Brocaded Acorns, Pair 18.00
Cambridge, Candlestick, Calla Lily, Green, Pair 30.00
Cambridge, Candlestick, Caprice, 3 Light, Blue 15.00
Cambridge, Candlestick, Crown Tuscan, Nude, 8 3/4 In., Pair 175.00
Cambridge, Candlestick, Crown Tuscan, Ram's Head, 6 In., Pair 75.00
Cambridge, Candlestick, Dolphin, Pair 95.00
Cambridge, Candlestick, Dolphin, 2 Light, Cambridge, Pair 200.00
Cambridge, Candlestick, Jade, Twisted, 8 1/2 In. 25.00
Cambridge, Candlestick, Light Green, Plate Etch No.704, 10 In., Pair 45.00
Cambridge, Candlestick, No.3900, Crystal, 4 In. 15.00
Cambridge, Candlestick, Nude Lady, Crown Tuscan, Pair 215.00
Cambridge, Candlestick, Pink, No.646, Pair 30.00
Cambridge, Candlestick, Prism, Caprice, 7 In., Pair 21.00
Cambridge, Candlestick, Ram's Light, 2 Lights, 6 Ram's Heads, Pair 125.00
Cambridge, Candlestick, Rosepoint, Gold, 5 1/2 In. 15.00
Cambridge, Candlestick, Rubena, 10 In., Pair 60.00
Cambridge, Candy Container, Flowers, Gold Trim, Crown Tuscan, 3 Pints 45.00
Cambridge, Candy Dish, Pedestaled, Gold Border, Green 32.50
Cambridge, Champagne, Caprice, Long Stem, Moonlight Blue 16.00
Cambridge, Champagne, Diane, Tall Stem, No.3122 .... 5.00
Cambridge, Cheese & Cracker, Covered, Gold Etched, Portia, 12 1/4 In.Diam. 45.00
Cambridge, Cocktail, Figural, Black Figure 72.00
Cambridge, Cocktail, Rose Point, No.101 .... 175.00
Cambridge, Cocktail, Seafood, Icer & Liner, Rosepoint 50.00
Cambridge, Compote, Crown Tuscan, Footed, C In Triangle, 7 In. 65.00
Cambridge, Compote, Crown Tuscan, Shell, Hand-Painted, 8 X 7 1/4 In. 105.00
Cambridge, Compote, Crystal, Nude Stem, 8 In. 60.00
Cambridge, Compote, Inverted Strawberry, Marigold, 9 In. 125.00
Cambridge, Compote, Nude Stem, Shell Top, Crown Tuscan, 5 3/8 In. 75.00
Cambridge, Compote, Nude Stem, Shell, Flowers, Crown Tuscan, 8 X 7 In. 105.00
Cambridge, Compote, Nude, Crystal Stem, Blue Scalloped Top, 8 1/4 In. 90.00
Cambridge, Compote, Open, Pedestal, Shell Shaped, Rose Design, Crown Tuscan 55.00

Cambridge, Compote, Rubena, 7 In. 185.00
Cambridge, Compote, Ruby Bowl In Farber Holder, 6 In. 25.00
Cambridge, Compote, Shell, Footed, Crown Tuscan, 6 X 4 1/4 In. 40.00
Cambridge, Compote, Shell, Footed, Crown Tuscan, 8 In. 30.00
Cambridge, Console Set, Honeycomb Bowl, 10 In., 2 Candlestick, 4 In., Signed 50.00
Cambridge, Cordial Set, Farberware Holder, Amethyst, 7 Piece 35.00
Cambridge, Cornucopia, Caprice, Moonlight Blue, 12 In., Pair 28.00
Cambridge, Cornucopia, Crown Tuscan, 5 In. 13.50
Cambridge, Cornucopia, Set In Bronze, Ram's Head, Flared, Marble Base, Pair 150.00
Cambridge, Cornucopia, Shell Feet, Crown Tuscan, 10 In. 65.00
Cambridge, Cracker Jar, Cover, Wheat Sheaf, Crystal 40.00
Cambridge, Cracker Jar, Near Cut, Feather, No.2651, 2 Handles, Signed 95.00
Cambridge, Creamer, Amber, Signed, 3 1/2 X 3 1/2 In. 12.50
Cambridge, Creamer, Fernland, Cobalt 30.00
Cambridge, Creamer, Gadroon, Royal Blue 15.00
Cambridge, Cruet, Caprice 20.00
Cambridge, Cruet, Duchess, Clear 24.00
Cambridge, Cruet, Ice Blue, Stopper, Pair 35.00
Cambridge, Cruet, Rosepoint 85.00
Cambridge, Cup & Saucer, Amber, Floral Etching 12.50
Cambridge, Cup & Saucer, Rosepoint 35.00
Cambridge, Decanter, Ball Shape, Clear, Stopper, Tumbler, 4 X 2 1/8 In. 25.00
Cambridge, Decanter, Pinch, Amethyst, 6 Matching Tumblers 25.00
Cambridge, Decanter, Pinched, Black Glass 39.95
Cambridge, Dish, Candy, Caprice, Moonlight Blue, Lid, 6 In. 29.00
Cambridge, Dish, Candy, Caprice, Open, Moonlight Blue, 8 3/4 In. 24.00
Cambridge, Dish, Candy, Clear, Gold Decoration On Edge, Etching 35.00
Cambridge, Dish, Candy, Covered, 3 Handles, Crown Tuscan .... 35.00 To 55.00
Cambridge, Dish, Candy, Ram's Head On Lid, Sterling Overlay, Golfers 110.00
Cambridge, Dish, Candy, Three Section, Pink 30.00
Cambridge, Dish, Divided, Acadia, Farber Holder, Chrome Cover, Blue 18.00
Cambridge, Dish, Divided, Gold Encircled, 4 3/4 X 8 In. 18.00
Cambridge, Dish, Gadroon, Handled, Covered, Crystal, 6 In. 17.00
Cambridge, Dish, Mayonnaise, Glass Spoon, Rosepoint 17.50
Cambridge, Dish, Nut, Crown Tuscan 12.00
Cambridge, Dish, Nut, Place Card Holder, Crown Tuscan, Set Of 4 .... 38.00
Cambridge, Dish, Nut, Yellow, Caprice, Footed 5.00
Cambridge, Dish, Pickle, Rosepoint, 9 1/2 In. 27.50
Cambridge, Dish, Relish, Serpentine, Yellow 17.50
Cambridge, Dish, Relish, 2 Compartments, Caprice 10.00
Cambridge, Dish, Relish, 2 Section, Rosepoint 35.00
Cambridge, Dish, Relish, 3 Compartments, Caprice 14.00
Cambridge, Dish, Relish, 3 Section, Crown Tuscan, 3 Handled, Covered 95.00
Cambridge, Dish, Relish, 3 Section, Rosepoint 47.50
Cambridge, Dish, Relish, 5 Section, Calla Lily 65.00
Cambridge, Dish, Sauce, 3-Toed, Orange, Caprice 8.00
Cambridge, Dish, Serving, Portia, 3 Section, 12 1/2 X 8 In. 22.00
Cambridge, Dish, Turtle Cover, Green, Frog Insert, 8 1/2 X 6 In. 29.00
Cambridge, Dish, Underplate, Caprice, Blue 12.00
Cambridge, Dish, 3 Section, Handle, Wildflower, Gold Encrusted 20.00
Cambridge, Dish, 3 Section, 3-Handled, Crown Tuscan, 8 In.Diameter 20.00
Cambridge, Dresser Set, Tussy, Ebony, Signed, 5 Piece 45.00
Cambridge, Figurine, Bashful Charlotte, Amber, 9 In. 65.00
Cambridge, Figurine, Bashful Charlotte, 8 In. 36.00
Cambridge, Figurine, Swan, Apple Green, Signed, 3 1/4 In. 22.00
Cambridge, Figurine, Swan, Apple Green, 4 1/2 In. 38.00
Cambridge, Figurine, Swan, Crystal, Signed, 3 1/4 In. 14.00
Cambridge, Figurine, Swan, Ebony, Marked, 3 In. 50.00
Cambridge, Figurine, Swan, Pink, 9 1/2 In. 80.00
Cambridge, Flower Frog, Bashful Charlotte, 13 In. 85.00
Cambridge, Flower Frog, Bashful Maiden, Green, 8 1/2 In. 85.00
Cambridge, Flower Frog, Draped Nude, 13 In. 89.00
Cambridge, Flower Frog, Flying Sea Gull, Clear, 9 1/2 X 6 In. 38.50
Cambridge, Flower Frog, Heron, Clear, 8 3/4 In. 65.00
Cambridge, Flower Holder, Bashful Charlotte, Crystal, 9 In. 35.00
Cambridge, Flower Holder, Sea Gull, 9 1/2 In. .... 27.00 To 34.00
Cambridge, Glass, Ice Tea, Caprice, Blue, 12 Oz. 17.50

Cambridge, Glass, Ice Tea, Chantilly	16.00
Cambridge, Glass, Ice Tea, Rosepoint	25.00
Cambridge, Glass, Juice, Caprice, Footed, 3 3/4 In.	12.00
Cambridge, Glass, Juice, Rondo, Set Of 12	180.00
Cambridge, Glass, Juice, Rosepoint	27.50
Cambridge, Glass, Mount Vernon, Red, Footed, 10 Oz.	7.90
Cambridge, Goblet, Caprice, Moonlight Blue	13.00
Cambridge, Goblet, Caprice, Short Stem, Moonlight Blue	17.00
Cambridge, Goblet, Diane, No.3122, 9 Ounce	20.00
Cambridge, Goblet, Rosepoint, No.3121	25.00
Cambridge, Goblet, Rosepoint, 10 Oz.	16.00
Cambridge, Ice Bucket, Cleo, Green	35.00
Cambridge, Ice Bucket, Ebony & Farberware	35.00
Cambridge, Ice Bucket, Rosemary, No.851	32.00
Cambridge, Ice Bucket, Rosepoint	125.00
Cambridge, Ice Bucket, Ruby Frosted Ribbon, Bail Handle	30.00
Cambridge, Ice Bucket, Tally Ho, Cobalt	45.00
Cambridge, Ivy Ball, Amber, Keyhole Base, 8 In.	20.00
Cambridge, Ivy Ball, Amethyst Bowl, Crystal Nude Stem, 9 1/2 In.	70.00
Cambridge, Ivy Ball, Amethyst, Clear, Ring Stem	40.00
Cambridge, Ivy Ball, Amethyst, Keyhole Base, 8 In.	30.00
Cambridge, Ivy Ball, Blue, Keyhole Base, 8 In.	35.00
Cambridge, Ivy Ball, Carmen, Footed	40.00
Cambridge, Ivy Ball, Crown Tuscan, Melon Rib, Ring Stem	53.00
Cambridge, Ivy Ball, Crystal, Ring Stem	17.00
Cambridge, Jelly, Feather, 7 1/4 In.	25.00
Cambridge, Jelly, Wild Rose, Cut, 4 1/2 In.	15.00
Cambridge, Jug, Amethyst, Ice Lip, Crystal Handle, 48 Oz.	35.00
Cambridge, Jug, Ball, Amethyst, Ice Lip	32.00 To 34.00
Cambridge, Jug, Ebony, Ice Lip Tilt	34.00
Cambridge, Jug, Elaine, No.3400-14, 80 Ounce	35.00
Cambridge, Jug, Silver Overlay, Black Amethyst	55.00
Cambridge, Juice Set, Vertical Optic Rib, Pitcher, 12 Glasses	42.50
Cambridge, Lemonade Set, Sponge Acid Finish, Pitcher, 6 Mugs, Signed	295.00
Cambridge, Mayonnaise & Ladle, Paneled Edge, Pedestaled, Gold Edge	35.00
Cambridge, Nutcup, Caprice, Shell Shape, Footed, Moonlight Blue	11.00
Cambridge, Pitcher, Cobalt, Ball Shaped, 9 1/2 In.	47.00
Cambridge, Pitcher, Cranberry Opal, Bulbous, Clear Handle, 5 1/4 In.	50.00
Cambridge, Pitcher, Ice Tea, Wildflower	100.00
Cambridge, Pitcher, Rosepoint, Bulbous, No.3800, Ice Lip, 20 Ounce	195.00
Cambridge, Pitcher, Rosepoint, Flared Lip, 76 Ounce	120.00 To 235.00
Cambridge, Pitcher, Water, Tally Ho, Carmine, Clear Handle, 9 In.	70.00
Cambridge, Plate, Apple Blossom, Ebony & Silver, 12 In.	45.00
Cambridge, Plate, Black Amethyst, 8-Sided, 8 In.	8.00
Cambridge, Plate, Caprice, Moonlight Blue, 8 1/2 In.	11.50
Cambridge, Plate, Cascade, 8 In.	7.50
Cambridge, Plate, Decagon, Green, Signed, 8 In., Set Of 4	20.00
Cambridge, Plate, Decagon, Pink, 8 In.	3.00
Cambridge, Plate, Rosepoint, Scalloped Rim, 14 In.	45.00
Cambridge, Plate, Torte, Gold Scalloped Rim, Signed, 14 In.	70.00
Cambridge, Punch Bowl Set, Carmen, Footed, 9 Crystal Cups	500.00
Cambridge, Punch Bowl Set, Tally Ho, Cobalt, 14 Punch Mugs	300.00
Cambridge, Punch Bowl, Marjorie Pattern, 2-Part, Near Cut, Signed	120.00
Cambridge, Punch Bowl, Near Cut, 14 X 6 In.	45.00
Cambridge, Punch Cup, Swan, Clear	47.00
Cambridge, Salt & Pepper, Amethyst, Farber Holders	14.00
Cambridge, Salt & Pepper, Chantilly, Sterling Lids	16.00
Cambridge, Salt & Pepper, Cobalt, Farber Holders, Tilted	9.50
Cambridge, Salt & Pepper, Rosepoint	15.00 To 45.00
Cambridge, Salt & Pepper, Tray, Caprice, Blue	40.00
Cambridge, Salt, Swan, Green, 2 1/2 In.	28.00
Cambridge, Saucer, Amethyst, Marked	6.00
Cambridge, Server, Cobalt Blue, Turned Up Edge, 13 1/2 In.	55.00
Cambridge, Server, Cookie, Decagon, Blue, Keyhole Handle	7.50
Cambridge, Server, Lemon, Handle, Crown Tuscan, Shell, Pink	14.00
Cambridge, Shell, Crown Tuscan, Enameled Rose, Footed, 9 1/2 In.	65.00
Cambridge, Sherbet, Caprice, Blue, Short	15.00

Cambridge, Sherbet, Caprice, Blue, Tall	16.00
Cambridge, Sherbet, Portia, Etched	12.95
Cambridge, Sherbet, Rondo, Set Of 12	180.00
Cambridge, Sherbet, Rosepoint, Low, 7 Oz.	15.00
Cambridge, Spooner, Colonial, Cobalt	30.00
Cambridge, Sugar & Creamer, Amber, Marked	12.00
Cambridge, Sugar & Creamer, Caprice	12.00 To 13.00
Cambridge, Sugar & Creamer, Caprice, Moonlight Blue, Pair	24.00 To 29.00
Cambridge, Sugar & Creamer, Cascade, Green	17.50
Cambridge, Sugar & Creamer, Chantilly, Sterling Bottoms	25.00
Cambridge, Sugar & Creamer, Dahlia	37.50
Cambridge, Sugar & Creamer, Gadroon	12.00
Cambridge, Sugar & Creamer, King Edward Cut, Sterling Base	45.00
Cambridge, Sugar & Creamer, Rosepoint	20.00 To 35.00
Cambridge, Sugar Shaker, Forget-Me-Nots, Blue, Gold Top, Signed, C.1907	24.50
Cambridge, Sugar, Caprice	6.00
Cambridge, Sugar, Near Cut, Open	35.00
Cambridge, Swan, Aqua, 3 1/2 In.	29.50
Cambridge, Swan, Black, Signed, 3 In.	45.00
Cambridge, Swan, Clear, 6 1/2 In.	20.00
Cambridge, Swan, Crown Tuscan, Crystal, 6 1/2 In.	30.00
Cambridge, Swan, Crown Tuscan, Green, Signed, 3 1/2 In.	22.00
Cambridge, Swan, Ebony, Marked, 8 In.	87.50
Cambridge, Swan, Mandarin Gold, Signed, 8 1/2 In.	85.00
Cambridge, Table Set, Child's, Colonial, Sugar, Creamer, Butter, Spooner	75.00
Cambridge, Tile, Silhouettes, The Letter, The Answer, 4 X 4 1/2 In., Pair	35.00
Cambridge, Toothpick, Susann 1907, Gold	21.50
Cambridge, Tray, Card, Flat Shell, Gold Trim, Crown Tuscan, 5 1/2 In.	30.00
Cambridge, Tray, Everglades, 16 In.	35.00
Cambridge, Tray, Sandwich, Center Handle, Etched Sprays, Red, 10 In.Square	55.00
Cambridge, Tray, Sandwich, Rosepoint, 16 In.	36.00
Cambridge, Tray, Wildflower, Gold Encrusted, 16 X 11 In.	30.00
Cambridge, Tumbler, Carmen, 9 Ounce	10.00
Cambridge, Tumbler, Hunt Scene, Cone Shape, Pink Top, Green Feet, 4 In.	14.95
Cambridge, Tumbler, Iced Tea, Carmen Red, Georgian	30.00
Cambridge, Tumbler, Rosepoint, Footed, 10 Ounces, 7 In.	20.00
Cambridge, Tumbler, Rosepoint, Footed, 10 Ounces, 7 In., Set Of 3	20.00
Cambridge, Vase, Ball, Cobalt, 4 In.	28.00
Cambridge, Vase, Basket Weave, Red Top, Blue Base, 10 In., Pair	225.00
Cambridge, Vase, Cathedral, Crystal, 18 In., Pair	90.00
Cambridge, Vase, Chantilly, 8 In.	32.00
Cambridge, Vase, Cornucopia, Crown Tuscan, Shell Foot, 11 In.	55.00
Cambridge, Vase, Cornucopia, Seashell, 7 In., Pair	50.00
Cambridge, Vase, Crown Tuscan, Black Trim, Acid Stamped Signature, 12 In.	145.00
Cambridge, Vase, Crown Tuscan, Cornucopia, Artist Mark, 8 3/4 In.Diameter	25.00
Cambridge, Vase, Crown Tuscan, Cornucopia, Shell Base, 5 In.	35.00
Cambridge, Vase, Crown Tuscan, Cornucopia, Shell Foot, 10 In., Pair	125.00
Cambridge, Vase, Crown Tuscan, Rosepoint, Gold Encrusted, 10 3/4 In.	85.00
Cambridge, Vase, Crown Tuscan, Seashell Pattern On Base, 9 1/2 In., Pair	115.00
Cambridge, Vase, Diane, Amber, Etched, 13 In., Pair	35.00
Cambridge, Vase, Ebony, No.402, 12 In.	18.00
Cambridge, Vase, Fan Shape, Diamond Peg With Panels, 8 1/4 In.	20.00
Cambridge, Vase, Gold Rose Point Pattern, Footed, Crown Tuscan, 11 In.	85.00
Cambridge, Vase, Heliotrope, Sweet Pea, Gold Rim, 7 In.	50.00
Cambridge, Vase, Horn Of Plenty, Crown Tuscan, 5 In.	17.50
Cambridge, Vase, Keyhole Base, Black	75.00
Cambridge, Vase, Keyhole Base, Green	44.00
Cambridge, Vase, Keyhole Base, Pink	37.50
Cambridge, Vase, Peacock, Green, Etched, 12 In.	40.00
Cambridge, Vase, Pillow, Crown Tuscan, 8 1/2 In.	69.00
Cambridge, Vase, Portia, Crystal With Gold Etching, 10 1/2 In.	45.00
Cambridge, Vase, Rose Point, 10 In.	85.00
Cambridge, Vase, Rosepoint, Clear Keyhole Stem, 10 In.	28.00
Cambridge, Vase, Rosepoint, Clear Keyhole Stem, 12 In.	35.00
Cambridge, Vase, Rosepoint, Trefoil, 10 In.	42.00
Cambridge, Vase, Royal Blue, Crystal Foot, 10 In.	65.00
Cambridge, Vase, Trumpet, Clear, 10 In., Pair	110.00

Cambridge, Vase, Trumpet, Crown Tuscan, 10 In. 45.00
Cambridge, Wine, Chantilly 20.00
Cambridge, Wine, Crown Tuscan, Nude 80.00
Cambridge, Wine, Ebony, Nude Stem .... 35.00 To 55.00
Cambridge, Wine, Mandarin, Gold Cascade 15.00
Cambridge, Wine, Rosepoint, 5 Oz. 32.00

Cameo glass was made in layers in much the same manner as a cameo in jewelry.
Part of the top layer of glass was cut away to reveal a different colored
glass beneath. The most famous cameo glass was made during the nineteenth
century.

Cameo, Bottle, Perfume, English, Hallmark, 1905, 5 1/4 In. 775.00
Cameo, Bottle, Perfume, English, Stand-Up, Miniature, Silver Top, 2 In. 350.00
Cameo, Bottle, Scent, Chartreuse, White, Floral, English, 4 1/2 X 3 1/4 In. 1200.00
Cameo, Compote, French, Art Deco, Black Pedestal Foot, 5 1/2 X 8 In. 195.00
Cameo, Console Set, Bowl, 12 X 5 In., Low Candlesticks, Signed 475.00
Cameo, English, Jug, Claret, Blue Ground, Flowers Carved In White 1950.00
Cameo, English, Jug, Silver Handle & Top, Carved, Blue, 8 In. 1795.00
Cameo, English, Rose Bowl, Citron, Carved In White, 3 X 4 1/2 In. 595.00
Cameo, English, Vase, Burnt Orange, Camphor Frosted Handles, 8 1/2 In. 1250.00
Cameo, Flask, Cranberry, Floral, Hallmarked Birmingham, 1890, 4 1/4 In. 1350.00
Cameo, Goblet, French, Stemmed, Frosted Bowl, Acid Cut, Signed, 7 3/4 In. 450.00
Cameo, Jar, Gray, Reddish-Brown Leaves, B.Raspiller, 6 1/2 X 4 In. 240.00
Cameo, Jug, Claret, Blue, Flowers & Leaves, English, Top & Handle Silverplate 1950.00
Cameo, Rose Bowl, Citron Background, White Flowers, English, 4 1/2 X 3 In. 850.00
Cameo, Rose Bowl, English, Citron Ground, 3 X 4 1/2 In.Diameter 850.00
Cameo, Rose Bowl, English, Miniature, Blue & White 375.00
Cameo, Rose Bowl, English, Pedestaled, Flowers & Foliage 1750.00
Cameo, Rose Bowl, English, Red, White Wild Roses, 4 In. 1150.00
Cameo, Shot Glass, One Cutting, Set Of 4 .... 225.00
Cameo, Syrup, Green, Topaz, Enameled, Iris, Leafage, C.1900, 5 In. 225.00
Cameo, Tumbler, French, Translucent, Scenic, Acid Cutting, Signed, 3 3/4 In. 175.00
Cameo, Vase, Baluster Shape, Frosted Background, Signed, 3 1/2 In. 325.00
Cameo, Vase, Burnt Orange, Camphor Frosted Handles, Urn Shaped, 8 1/2 In. 1750.00
Cameo, Vase, Chinese, Green On White, Birds In Flight, 13 In. 840.00
Cameo, Vase, Cranberry, Gold Acorn Design, 3 In. 110.00
Cameo, Vase, Cranberry, Gold Flowers, Overlay, 11 3/4 In. ....*Illus* 150.00

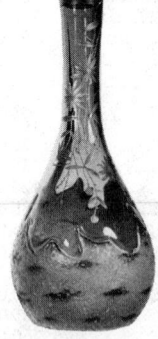

Canton, Jardiniere, Famille Rose,
C.1800, 14 X 12 In.
(See Page 66)

Cameo, Vase, Cranberry, Gold Flowers,
Overlay, 11 3/4 In.

Cameo, Vase, Cranberry, White, Carved Leaves & Berry, 7 In. 1250.00
Cameo, Vase, Cylindrical, Flared Base, Magenta To Translucent, Honesdale 275.00
Cameo, Vase, English, Acorns & Oak Leaves On Green Body, Signed, 4 1/2 In. 650.00
Cameo, Vase, English, Blue Ground, Flowers & Branches, Bird On Front, 8 In. 2500.00
Cameo, Vase, English, Burnt Orange Coloring, Frosted Handles, 8 1/2 In. 1750.00
Cameo, Vase, English, Pink, White, Acanthus Leaves, Flower, 4 In. 2100.00
Cameo, Vase, English, Square Top, Opaque White Flowers, Cranberry Top, 6 In. 1250.00
Cameo, Vase, English, White Flowers & Leaves, Raisin Colored, 3 3/4 In. 945.00
Cameo, Vase, English, White Leaves, Berries, Citron Ground, 9 1/2 In. 1700.00
Cameo, Vase, English, White On Red, 5 1/2 In. 1400.00
Cameo, Vase, Figure Of Classical Lady, The Sybil, Signed, 7 3/4 In. 1250.00
Cameo, Vase, Fishscale, Gold Trim, Marked Rd.39086, 4 3/4 X 4 1/4 In. 446.00

Cameo, Vase, Floral, Red & Gold, French, Signed D'Aurys, 6 1/4 X 4 1/2 In.	325.00
Cameo, Vase, French, Acid Cut Scenic Design, Frosted Ground, Moda, 4 1/2 In.	385.00
Cameo, Vase, French, Acid Cut, Mountain Scent, Signed, R.Chateau, 10 1/2 In.	450.00
Cameo, Vase, French, Art Deco, Geometric Design, Signed, 4 In.	250.00
Cameo, Vase, French, Boats, Scenic, Acid Cut, Signed Gauthier, 10 3/4 In.	350.00
Cameo, Vase, French, Groups Of Mice, Pink, Frosty Green, 5 In.	1450.00
Cameo, Vase, French, Outer Layer Red To Orange, Deep Cut Florals, 13 In.	500.00
Cameo, Vase, French, Sea Life, Signed D'Argental, 14 In.	1950.00
Cameo, Vase, French, Signed LeVerre, 7 In.	165.00
Cameo, Vase, French, White Lining, Purple & Lavender, Signed, 12 1/4 In.	450.00
Cameo, Vase, Frosted Finish, Gilding, Enameled Sunflowers, 13 In.	195.00
Cameo, Vase, German, Trumpet Shape, Acid Cut Back, 14 In.	325.00
Cameo, Vase, Marsh Plants, Yellow & Smoke Pink, Thouvenin	375.00
Cameo, Vase, Palm Trees, Mountains, Lake, Green Cut To Clear	125.00
Cameo, Vase, Poynoud, Stain Finish, 6 1/2 X 10 In.	45.00
Cameo, Vase, Windmill Scene, Cobalt To Clear, 3 1/2 In.	110.00
Campaign, see Political Campaign	
Campbell Kid, Spoon, Soup, Boy	7.50
Campbell Kid, Spoon, Soup, Silver Plated, Full Figure Of Girl	6.00

*Camphor glass is a cloudy white glass that has been blown or pressed. It
was made by many factories in the Midwest during the mid-nineteenth century.*

Camphor Glass, Ashtray, Brass & Iron Cannon On Edge, Jamestown, Va.	12.00
Camphor Glass, Box, Powder, Colonial Lady	25.00
Camphor Glass, Box, Powder, German Shepherd On Lid	12.00
Camphor Glass, Box, Powder, Nudes	12.50
Camphor Glass, Bulldog, Seated, Amber, 1 1/2 In.	5.50
Camphor Glass, Candlestick, Draped Nude, 8 1/2 In.	22.00
Camphor Glass, Compote, Yellow, Footed, 10 1/4 In.	25.00
Camphor Glass, Cruet, Cased Pink, White Looping	65.00
Camphor Glass, Figurine, Boston Bull, Amber, 3 In.	32.00
Camphor Glass, Figurine, Spanish Couple Dancing, Marked, 10 1/2 In.	48.00
Camphor Glass, Jar, Powder, Standing Bulldog Cover, Pink	25.00
Camphor Glass, Lamp, Nursery, Clown Base, Merry-Go-Round Shape	35.00
Camphor Glass, Plate, 3 Kittens	18.00
Camphor Glass, Saltshaker, Leaves & Vines Traced In Yellow, Five Lobed	35.00
Camphor Glass, Server, Sandwich, Center Handle, Hand-Painted, 10 1/4 In.	44.50
Camphor Glass, Shade, Gold Outlined Lavender Flowers, 14 In.	65.00
Camphor Glass, Sugar & Creamer, Quilted, Reeded Frosted Handles	55.00
Camphor Glass, Vase, White, 9 1/2 In.	35.00
Canary Glass, see Vaseline Glass	
Candelabrum, Marble, Ormolu Mounted, Hurricane Form, Bell Form, 17 In., Pair	175.00
Candleholder, see also Brass, Candleholder; Sandwich Glass, Candleholder, Wooden, Candleholder, and various porcelain categories.	
Candleholder, Brass, Tulip Leaf Design, Sweden, 5 X 8 In., Pair	50.00
Candleholder, Cupid & Horserider, Glass	125.00
Candleholder, Rush Light, Side Light, 11 In.	148.00
Candlestick, see also Brass, Candlestick; Pewter, Candlestick; Sandwich Glass, Candlestick; Silver, Sterling, Candlestick; Vaseline Glass, Candlestick and various porcelain categories	
Candlestick, Amethyst & Topaz, Steuben, 12 In., Pair	175.00
Candlestick, Art Deco, Nude, Camphor Glass, 8 In.	49.00
Candlestick, Barley Twists, Oak, 12 In.Brass Pans	20.00
Candlestick, Brass Twisted Stem, 7 3/4 In., Pair	45.00
Candlestick, Brass, Altar Type, 25 In.	70.00
Candlestick, Brass, From Dismantled Church Altar, Spool Design, 37 In.	225.00
Candlestick, Brass, Round Dish Type Base, 7 In., Pair	35.00
Candlestick, Brass, Russian, Platform, 10 In., Pair	145.00
Candlestick, Brass, Spike For Candle, 11 In., Pair	45.00
Candlestick, Brass, Spun Brass Base, Islamic Inscription, 16 1/2 In.	30.00
Candlestick, Brass, 3 Cherubs Entwined, French, C.1780, 7 In.	500.00
Candlestick, Bronze, Oriental, Dragon Shaped, 12 3/4 In., Pair	155.00
Candlestick, Capstan Base, Engraving, 8 1/4 In., Pair	120.00
Candlestick, Ceremonial, Silver, Russian, 13 In., Pair	845.00
Candlestick, Chamber, Brass, Oval, C.1800, 8 In., Pair	425.00
Candlestick, Clear Glass Crucifix, Ripley	95.00
Candlestick, Continental Silver, Figural, 10 In., Pair	400.00

Candlestick, **Continental Silver,** Marked, Lion Rampant, C.1825, 12 In., Pair 1000.00
Candlestick, **Copper & Brass,** Weighted, 10 In., Pair 75.00
Candlestick, **Crucifix,** Milk Glass 25.00
Candlestick, **Dolphin,** Amber Glass, Petal Cup, 6-Sided Base, 9 1/2 In. 45.00
Candlestick, **Dragon Handle,** Saucer Base, Brass, 5 In., Pair 55.00
Candlestick, **Embossed Brass,** Silver Plate, 26 In., Pair 145.00
Candlestick, **Figural,** Sailor, Palmer Cox, Pair 100.00
Candlestick, **Figural,** Wild Boar, Porcelain, Crossed Swords Mark, 9 In. 95.00
Candlestick, **French Empire,** Raised Surface, C.1810, 11 1/2 In., Pair 290.00
Candlestick, **Glass,** Blown & Molded, Applied Handle, 19th Century, 6 1/2 In. 350.00
Candlestick, **Glass,** Fiery Opalescent, Pittsburgh, 9 1/2 In. 500.00
Candlestick, **Glass,** Sandwich, Blue Petal & Loop, Pair 850.00
Candlestick, **Green Glass,** Etched, 12 In., Pair 35.00
Candlestick, **Hog Scraper,** Hook & Lift, Iron, 6 1/2 In. 30.00
Candlestick, **Hog Scraper,** Push-Up, Hook, 5 In. 45.00
Candlestick, **Hog Scraper,** Signed Shaw, 9 In. 130.00
Candlestick, **Hog Scraper,** Wrought Iron, 18th Century, With Push-Up 50.00
Candlestick, **Lady & Soldier,** Applied Flowers, Thuringian, 12 In. 180.00
Candlestick, **Mercury Glass,** Pair 18.00
Candlestick, **Miniature,** Brass, 2 3/4 In., Pair 19.00
Candlestick, **Neoclassical,** Bell Metal, Round Base, C.1790, Pair 350.00
Candlestick, **Neoclassical,** Fluted Columnar Stem, Brass, 9 1/4 In., Pair 495.00
Candlestick, **Notched Corners,** Square Base, Brass, C.1760, 6 7/8 In., Pair 595.00
Candlestick, **Open Work Dragon With Touches Of Gold,** Iron, 7 1/2 In., Pair 28.00
Candlestick, **Petal Base,** Brass, C.1750, 7 3/8 In., Pair 750.00
Candlestick, **Pricket,** Brass, Dutch, Baroque, 11 1/2 In., Pair 400.00
Candlestick, **Push-Up,** Tin, 6 1/2 In. 25.00
Candlestick, **Quadruple,** Baroque Bottom, Victor Silver Co., 10 In. 18.00
Candlestick, **Rib,** Milk Glass, Pair, 7 1/4 In. 45.00
Candlestick, **Roseville Freesia,** Orange, 2-Handle, Pair 15.00
Candlestick, **Rounded Corners,** Notched Square Base, Brass, C.1745, 7 In. 275.00
Candlestick, **Standing Cobra,** Brushed Green, Brass, 7 In., Pair 28.00

Candy containers, especially those made of glass, were popular during the late Victorian era.

Candy Container, **Airplane,** Army Bomber 19.50
Candy Container, **Apple,** Tin, Shenandoah Valley, 3 1/2 In. 20.00
Candy Container, **Auto,** 4-Door, West Bros. 38.00
Candy Container, **Barn Lantern,** Silver Gilt Base 20.00
Candy Container, **Baseball** 12.50
Candy Container, **Basket** 16.00
Candy Container, **Battleship,** Filled, Miniature 20.00
Candy Container, **Beehive Honey,** Footed 10.00
Candy Container, **Billiken** 45.00
Candy Container, **Binoculars,** Ruby Glass, Gold Trim 45.00
Candy Container, **Boston Kettle,** Strap Handle, Brown Paint 12.50
Candy Container, **Camera** 70.00
Candy Container, **Cat Head,** Jack-O-Lantern 12.00
Candy Container, **Charlie Chaplin,** Borgfeldt 50.00
Candy Container, **Chicken** 32.00
Candy Container, **Chicken On Nest** 12.00
Candy Container, **Circus Dog** 3.50
Candy Container, **Clown On Horse** 65.00
Candy Container, **Coach-Type** 24.00
Candy Container, **Colt Pistol,** Black Paint, Never Opened 20.00
Candy Container, **Dog,** 2 1/2 In. 3.50
Candy Container, **Doll Nurser** .... 3.50 To 10.00
Candy Container, **Donkey With Cart** 6.00
Candy Container, **Easter Chick,** Nodding, 2 Part 7.00
Candy Container, **Electric Coupe** 20.00
Candy Container, **Electric Iron** 15.00
Candy Container, **Fire Engine,** Cardboard Bottom 10.00
Candy Container, **Fire Truck With Driver** 22.50
Candy Container, **Flag Box** 5.00
Candy Container, **George Washington,** 3 Corner Hat 6.00
Candy Container, **Girl With 2 Geese** 13.00
Candy Container, **Gun,** Large Clear Revolver No.1 .... 13.00

Candy Container, Gun, 3 3/4 In.	10.00
Candy Container, Gun, 4 In.	10.00
Candy Container, Happi-Fats On Drum	30.00
Candy Container, Hatchet, Pressed Composition	6.00
Candy Container, Hearse	60.00
Candy Container, Hen On Oblong Nest	8.00
Candy Container, Horse Head	12.00
Candy Container, Hound Pup	8.00
Candy Container, Jeep With Driver	17.50
Candy Container, King Tut, Bust, Germany	15.00
Candy Container, Lantern	10.00 To 13.00
Candy Container, Lantern, Metal Top	6.00
Candy Container, Learned Fox	30.00
Candy Container, Locomotive, Man In Window	22.00
Candy Container, Locomotive, Original Closure, Patented 12/20/1892	75.00
Candy Container, Military Hat, Thread Glass, Amber	30.00
Candy Container, Moon Mullins	22.00
Candy Container, Mug	10.00
Candy Container, Pail, Lovell & Covell, Jack Of Hearts, Tin	33.00
Candy Container, Peter Rabbit, Round, Tin	18.00
Candy Container, Pistol, Metal Cap	12.00
Candy Container, Pistol, Round Butt	12.00
Candy Container, Powder Horn	20.00
Candy Container, Rabbit In Egg Shell	45.00
Candy Container, Rabbit With Basket On Arm	55.00
Candy Container, Rabbit, Laid Back Ears	55.00
Candy Container, Rabbit, Papier-Mache	17.50
Candy Container, Rabbit, Standing	18.00
Candy Container, Red Barn Lantern, Tin Base	5.00
Candy Container, Revolver, Mercury Glass, 7 1/2 In.	16.00
Candy Container, Round Butt Revolver, 7 5/8 In.	17.50
Candy Container, Santa Claus Boot	7.00
Candy Container, Santa In Chimney	45.00
Candy Container, Santa's Boot, Merry Xmas Label	15.00
Candy Container, Scottie Dog	12.50
Candy Container, Scottie, Standing, Cardboard Bottom	10.00
Candy Container, Sitting Bulldog, 4 1/4 In.	25.00
Candy Container, Skater's Lamp, Part Aluminum, 4 In.	27.50
Candy Container, Skookum, Tree Trunk	75.00 To 120.00
Candy Container, Spark Plug, Horse, 1923	50.00 To 65.00
Candy Container, Speed Boat	16.50
Candy Container, Spirit Of Good Will, Victory	25.00
Candy Container, Suitcase, Handle & Closure, 3 1/2 X 2 1/4 X 1 1/2 In.	22.00
Candy Container, Suitcase, Milk Glass	50.00
Candy Container, Tank, Driver, Never Opened	10.00
Candy Container, Telephone, Tin Bottom	8.00
Candy Container, Tinsel Xmas Tree	6.00
Candy Container, Toonerville Trolley, Conductor, Wheels	65.00
Candy Container, Trunk, Round Top, Milk Glass	50.00
Candy Container, Tune In, Radio	55.00
Candy Container, Two Man Fire Engine, Jeannette, Pennsylvania, 4 1/2 In.	32.00
Candy Container, Victory Lines Bus	17.50
Candy Container, Whistle	5.00
Cane, Bamboo, Carved Peacock, 35 In.	12.50
Cane, Carved Grotesque Man's Head, Glass Eyes	150.00
Cane, Carved Whalebone Hand Holding Club	75.00
Cane, Carved, Handle Is Head Of Man With Mustache, 19th Century, 26 1/2 In.	350.00
Cane, China Dog Head, 34 In.	6.50
Cane, Glass, Curved Handle, Amberina Center	50.00
Cane, Gold Knob	20.00
Cane, Handle Carved Into Snake	30.00
Cane, Handle, Carved In Figure Of Goblin	75.00
Cane, Handle, Cloisonne	40.00
Cane, Handle, Ivory, Horse's Head, Glass Eyes	175.00
Cane, Handle, Jockey Riding Race Horse, Weighted Celluloid	25.00
Cane, Handle, Tiffany, Signed	38.00
Cane, Horn Handle, Signed Captain John M.Urann, Sullivan, Maine	75.00

Cane, Ivory, Reticulated Sterling Silver Handle	65.00
Cane, Ivory, Wood, Silver Mounted, Shell Cameo, Marked, German, C.1884	250.00
Cane, King Leopold II Of Belgium, Shows His Cities, Industries, People	800.00
Cane, Lad's Battered Button-Up Shoe, Victorian, Silver Plate	75.00
Cane, Polka Dotted Snake	45.00
Cane, Porky Pig Head, Wood, 34 In.	6.50
Cane, Spiraled Blue Threading On White, Shepherd's Crook Handle, 42 In.	48.00
Cane, Sword, Brass Lion's Head Pommel, 24 In.	15.95
Cane, Sword, Hand Carved, Brass Tip & Ferrule, American, 28 In.	125.00
Cane, To Captain Jack Nelson, Silver Handle	34.00
Cane, Umbrella Type, Metal Snake Wrapped Around Below Handle	15.00
Cane, Walking Stick & Yardstick	12.00
Cane, Walking Stick, Dog Head, Hickory	50.00
Cane, Walking Stick, Indian Head	10.00
Cane, Walking Stick, Japanese, Bamboo, Carved Fish	27.50
Cane, Walking, Gold Handle, From A Friend, 1891	35.00
Cane, Whale Tooth Knob, 18K Gold Band, 1862, Mt.Vernon	75.00
Cane, Wood & Painted Porcelain, Japanese Writing, Brass Ring, Ivory Handle	39.50

Canton china is a blue-and-white ware made near Canton, China, from about 1785 to 1895. It is hand-decorated with Chinese scenes.

Canton, Bowl, Reticulated Sides, Oval, 10 X 8 1/2 X 3 1/2 In.	180.00
Canton, Bowl, Rice, C.1840s, 4 1/2 In.	65.00
Canton, Bowl, Round, 10 1/2 In.	250.00
Canton, Bowl, Soup, C.1840, 6 In.	65.00
Canton, Bowl, Sugar, Lid, Strawberry Finial, Celery Handles	165.00
Canton, Charger, Blue Brocade & Center Medallion, 14 In.Diameter	175.00
Canton, Charger, Medallions, Animal Faces, 11 1/2 In.	95.00
Canton, Creamer	98.00
Canton, Cup & Saucer, Twig Handle	65.00
Canton, Cup, Cover, Syllabub	98.00
Canton, Dish, Ducks, Water, Blossoms, 6 In.Diameter	10.00
Canton, Dish, Fish Bone, Pair	45.00
Canton, Dish, Pickle, Leaf Shape, 8 In.	165.00
Canton, Dish, Shrimp	196.00
Canton, Flower Pot, Hexagonal, Footed, 2 1/2 In.	20.00
Canton, Flower Pot, Hexagonal, Footed, 4 In.	35.00
Canton, Gravy Boat	95.00
Canton, Jar, Ball, Recessed Wood Cover, 10 X 9 In.	175.00
Canton, Jar, Tea, Cover	45.00
Canton, Jardiniere, Famille Rose, C.1800, 14 X 12 In. *Illus*	900.00
Canton, Jug, Milk, 6 3/4 In.	375.00
Canton, Planter, Floral, Square Concave Corners, Footed, Orange Peel Glaze	28.00
Canton, Plate, Bread, 8 1/2 In.	45.00
Canton, Plate, C.1840, 8 In.	95.00
Canton, Plate, C.1840, 9 1/2 In.	125.00
Canton, Plate, Hot Water	175.00
Canton, Plate, Soup	25.00
Canton, Plate, 8 1/2 In.	35.00
Canton, Plate, 9 In.	35.00
Canton, Platter, C.1820, 10 In.	65.00
Canton, Platter, Octagonal, C.1800, 12 X 15 In.	265.00
Canton, Platter, Orange Peel Back, 14 X 11 In.	135.00
Canton, Platter, 15 1/2 X 12 1/2 In.	150.00
Canton, Sugar, Covered, Hand-Painted	95.00
Canton, Teapot, Low Lighthouse Form, Twined Handle, 6 In.	400.00

Capo-Di-Monte porcelain was first made in Naples, Italy, from 1743 to 1759. The factory moved near Madrid, Spain, and reopened in 1771 and worked to 1834. Since that time the Doccia factory of Italy acquired the molds and style, even using the N and crown mark, which was made famous by the factory.

Capo-Di-Monte, Ashtray, 8 1/4 In.	12.50
Capo-Di-Monte, Bowl, Gargoyle Face Handles, Signed, 20 X 9 1/2 In.	140.00
Capo-Di-Monte, Box, Erotic Scene Inside Cover, Blue N & Crown, 2 X 3 In.	150.00
Capo-Di-Monte, Box, Hinged, Scalloped, C.1900, 4 In.Diameter	85.00
Capo-Di-Monte, Box, Patch, Cupid On Top, Crown N. 2 X 4 X 3 In.	135.00

Capo-Di-Monte, **Box,** Protruding Children, Claw Feet, Signed, 6 X 4 1/2 In.	112.00
Capo-Di-Monte, **Casket,** Jewel, Standout Children, Splay Legs, Signed	168.00
Capo-Di-Monte, **Centerpiece Set,** 2 Ewers, Bowl, 19 1/4 X 9 3/4 X 7 In.	210.00
Capo-Di-Monte, **Coffer,** Mythological Scenes, Multi-Color, 1800s, 7 X 11 In.	1500.00
Capo-Di-Monte, **Cup & Saucer,** Demitasse, Repousse Flowers, Cherubs	35.00
Capo-Di-Monte, **Ewer,** Footed, Blue Mark, 19 1/4 X 9 3/4 X 7 In., Pair	200.00
Capo-Di-Monte, **Figurine,** Bull Baiting, 3 Dogs Pulling Bull, 6 X 7 In.	495.00
Capo-Di-Monte, **Figurine,** Goose Girl, Signed & Marked, 12 X 14 In.	200.00
Capo-Di-Monte, **Figurine,** Group Of 2 Putti, Rock Base, C.1900, 19 1/4 In.	300.00
Capo-Di-Monte, **Figurine,** Lady In Dress, Blue Crown Over N, 10 In.	150.00
Capo-Di-Monte, **Figurine,** Man Holding Violin, 6 1/2 In.	135.00
Capo-Di-Monte, **Figurine,** Rooster, Pair	85.00
Capo-Di-Monte, **Figurine,** Sir Francis Bacon, Blue Crown	82.00
Capo-Di-Monte, **Figurine,** Woman With Jug, Gold Except Features, 7 1/4 In.	135.00
Capo-Di-Monte, **Figurine,** Woman, Blonde Hair, VIII N, 4 X 10 In.Wide	125.00
Capo-Di-Monte, **Figurine,** Woman, Multi Colored, Signed, 7 In.	95.00
Capo-Di-Monte, **Pitcher,** Standing Lion Handle, Marked, 7 In.	160.00
Capo-Di-Monte, **Plaque,** Mythological Scene, Crown N Mark, Oval, C.1800, 17 In.	350.00
Capo-Di-Monte, **Plate,** Armorial, 18th Century, 9 1/2 In., Pair	360.00
Capo-Di-Monte, **Plate,** Blue, Hand-Painted, Scalloped Edge, 9 1/2 In.	20.00
Capo-Di-Monte, **Stein,** Allegorical Motif, Covered, 12 1/2 In.	180.00
Capo-Di-Monte, **Stein,** Animal Scene, C.19th Century, Crown N Mark, 10 1/2 In.	895.00
Capo-Di-Monte, **Stein,** C.1860, Dolphins, 1 Liter	750.00
Capo-Di-Monte, **Stein,** Puttis & Dolphins, Loose Cover, C.1860, 1 Liter	750.00
Capo-Di-Monte, **Urn,** Covered, Ram's Head Handles, 7 1/2 In.	75.00
Capo-Di-Monte, **Vase,** Classical Figures, Blue Crown N Mark, 9 In., Pair	300.00
Captain Marvel, Puzzle, Jigsaw	3.00
Captain Midnight, Decoder, 1935	20.00
Captain Midnight, Decoder, 1942	12.00
Captain Midnight, Decoder, 1948	28.00
Captain Midnight, Decoder, 1949	35.00 To 37.00
Captain Midnight, Manual, Decoder, 1947, 16 Pages	75.00
Captain Midnight, Medal, Membership, 1940, Skelly Oil	8.00
Captain Midnight, Mug, Red	10.00
Captain Midnight, Neckerchief, Straight Arrow	19.00
Captain Midnight, Secret Squadron Decoder	38.00
Captain Midnight, Weather Wings	12.00
Caramel Slag, see Chocolate Glass	
Card, see also Postcard	
Card, Advertising, Bovine Beef, Hold To Light, Girl Sees Bull	12.00
Card, Animal, Planters Peanuts, 2 Big Game Peanut Blocks, 1934, Set	500.00
Card, Arbuckle Coffee, Advertising, 3 X 5 In., Set Of 50	50.00
Card, Baseball, 1958, Set Of 84	55.00
Card, Christmas & New Year Greetings, Red Fringe, Prang, 4 1/2 X 7 In.	25.00
Card, Christmas, Double, Opens, Fringed, Prang	14.00
Card, Playing Double Deck, Frisco, Boxed In Wrappers	10.00
Card, Playing, Amtrak	3.50
Card, Playing, Betty Boop	25.00
Card, Playing, Chessie Cats, Boxed, Pair	9.00
Card, Playing, Colorado Pictures, 1933	12.50
Card, Playing, Columbian World's Fair, John T.Story Co., Boxed	35.00
Card, Playing, Denver & Rio Grande Railroad	7.00
Card, Playing, Famewill Fire-Alarm	8.00
Card, Playing, Ford Motor 75th Anniversary	6.00
Card, Playing, Franklin 5 Cent Cigars, C.1910	20.00
Card, Playing, Greyhound Bus System	4.00
Card, Playing, Hard-A-Port Cut Plug	225.00
Card, Playing, Nazi	7.00
Card, Playing, Packard Twin Six Automobile, 1922	15.00
Card, Playing, Panama Canal, Inaugural Edition	250.00
Card, Playing, Penn Central, Boxed	12.00
Card, Playing, Santa Fe, Boxed, Set	5.75
Card, Playing, Wheat	35.00
Card, Playing, World Columbian Expo, 1893	39.50
Card, Playing, World's Fair, 1933, Original Box	7.50
Card, Playing, 1904 World's Fair, St.Louis, Original Box	25.00
Card, Valentine, Handmade, Cut-Out Center, Verses, London, Dated 1830	50.00

Card, Valentine, Heart-Shaped, Buster Brown & Tige, Signed Outcault 17.50
Card, Valentine, Lacy Pull-Out, C.1910, Germany 25.00
Card, Valentine, Lacy, C.1880, 4 1/2 X 6 1/2 In. 50.00
Card, Valentine, Lacy, Embossed Envelope, Watermarked 1851, Towgood 150.00
Card, Valentine, Lacy, Embossed Envelope, 2 1/4 X 3 In. 65.00
Card, Valentine, Lacy, 1900 .... 8.50
Card, Valentine, Mansell, 4 1/2 X 7 In. 125.00
Card, Valentine, Meek 15.00
Card, Valentine, Nister 25.00
Card, Valentine, Raphael Tuck 25.00
Card, Valentine, Snow White & 7 Dwarfs, Pull Tab, Dwarfs Move, 1938 .... 15.00
Card, Valentine, Three Part, Victorian, Satin Cord & Tassel 6.00
Card, Valentine, Whitney 15.00
Card, Valentine, Wood, 3 1/2 X 5 1/2 In. 125.00
Card, Valentine, 3-D, Teacher With Students 12.50
   Carder, see Steuben, Aurene

   Carlsbad, Germany, is a mark found on china made by several factories in
   Germany. Most of the pieces available today were made after 1891.
Carlsbad, Bowl, Raised Star, Classic Scene, Signed Kauffmann 125.00
Carlsbad, Bowl, Tapestry, Peacock Iridescent, 4 Handles, 8 X 4 1/2 In. 215.00
Carlsbad, Cup & Saucer, Demitasse, Kaiserin Maria Theresia, Set Of 4 .... 32.00
Carlsbad, Cup & Saucer, Gold Scroll Around Edges, Austria 6.00
Carlsbad, Ewer, Floral, Ecru Ground, Mask Spout, Handle, 7 In. 24.00
Carlsbad, Ewer, Pierced Handle, Flowers, 6 In. 10.00
Carlsbad, Fish Set, Platter, 10 Plates, Pansies, Gold Rim 185.00
Carlsbad, Fish Set, 9 Piece 285.00
Carlsbad, Pitcher, Gold Flowers & Twist Handle, Bulbous, Yellow, 6 In. 80.00
Carlsbad, Pitcher, Helmet Type, Gold Trim, Hand-Painted, 11 In. 65.00
Carlsbad, Pitcher, Helmet, Hand-Painted Scene, 11 In. 60.00
Carlsbad, Plate, Leaf Shaped, Luster Finish, Yellow, 7 1/2 In. 10.00
Carlsbad, Plate, Portrait 10.00
Carlsbad, Plate, Victoria, Maria Antoinette & Louis XVI, Swirl, Gold, Pair 42.50
Carlsbad, Sugar & Creamer, Covered, Thistle Design, 7 1/2 In. 50.00
Carlsbad, Tray, Pink & Gold, Hand-Painted, 10 X 8 In. 26.00
Carlsbad, Vase, Ivory Background, Green Floral, Purple, 9 1/2 X 16 1/2 In. 60.00
Carlsbad, Vase, Ivory Ground, Enameled, Gold Design, Signed, 3 1/2 X 8 In. 65.00
Carlsbad, Vase, 4 Handles, Iridescent, 6 X 3 In. 155.00
Carlton Ware, Biscuit Jar, Petunia Pattern, Silver Plated Rim, Handle, 7 In. 75.00
Carlton Ware, Biscuit Jar, Raised Figures Of Dancing Ladies, 7 In. 95.00
Carlton Ware, Dish, Rouge Royal, 2-Handled, Pedestaled, 6 In. 15.00
Carlton Ware, Jar, Tobacco, Lidded, White Reliefs, Hunting Scene, 6 In., Pair 88.00
Carlton Ware, Muffineer, Silver Plated Dome, Rose 25.00
Carlton Ware, Tea Set, Royal Rouge, 5 Cups & Saucers, Pot, Sugar & Creamer 95.00
Carlton Ware, Tray, Cheese, Pearlized Cover, Slant Top, China, Marked 38.00
Carlton Ware, Vase, Oriental Design, Black Background, 6 In. 58.00
Carnelian, Figurine, Pug, Sitting, Carved, 2 In. 125.00
Carnelian, Paperweight, Curved Beveled Edges, 3 3/8 X 2 1/4 In. 110.00

   Carnival, or taffeta, glass was an inexpensive, pressed, iridescent glass made
   from about 1900 to 1920. Over 200 different patterns are known.
   Carnival glass is currently being reproduced. If the letter N for
   Northwood is included in the description it appears on the piece of glass.
   Carnival Glass, see also Northwood
Carnival Glass, Ashtray, Dutch Boy, Marigold 30.00
Carnival Glass, Ashtray, Florentine No.1, Pink 17.50
Carnival Glass, Ashtray, Polo Pony, Marigold 30.00
Carnival Glass, Banana Boat, Grape & Cable, Marigold .... 120.00 To 150.00
Carnival Glass, Banana Boat, Grape & Cable, Purple .... 175.00 To 195.00
Carnival Glass, Banana Boat, Grape, Marigold 65.00
Carnival Glass, Banana Boat, Kitten, Marigold 75.00
Carnival Glass, Banana Boat, Stippled Petals, Dome Footed, Peach 65.00
Carnival Glass, Banana Boat, Thistle, Marigold 105.00
Carnival Glass, Banana Boat, Waterlily & Cattail, Blue 125.00
Carnival Glass, Basket, Bubble In Bottom, White, Northwood 85.00
Carnival Glass, Basket, Daisy Bouquet, Marigold 20.00
Carnival Glass, Basket, Handle, Three Fruit, Footed, Marigold, 4 X 5 In. 40.00

Carnival Glass, Basket, Lacy Edge, Marigold, 6 3/4 In.	15.00
Carnival Glass, Basket, Northwood, Flared Sides, Marigold	47.00
Carnival Glass, Basket, Open Lattice, Ice Green, Fenton	55.00
Carnival Glass, Berry Bowl, Butterfly & Berry, Marigold	45.00
Carnival Glass, Berry Bowl, Diamond & Lace, Amethyst	25.00
Carnival Glass, Berry Bowl, Fenton's Heavy Grape, Marigold	22.00
Carnival Glass, Berry Bowl, Fruits & Flowers, Marigold, Iridescent	35.00
Carnival Glass, Berry Bowl, Grape & Cable, Amethyst	25.00
Carnival Glass, Berry Bowl, Grape & Cable, Green	30.00
Carnival Glass, Berry Bowl, Grape & Cable, Marigold	20.00
Carnival Glass, Berry Bowl, Imperial Grape, Green, 5 In.	12.00
Carnival Glass, Berry Bowl, Millersburg Blackberry Wreath, Green	25.00
Carnival Glass, Berry Bowl, Millersburg Peacock & Urn, Marigold	39.00
Carnival Glass, Berry Bowl, Orange Tree, Blue, 10 In.	125.00
Carnival Glass, Berry Bowl, Peacock At The Fountain, Marigold	55.00
Carnival Glass, Berry Dish, Butterfly & Berry, Claw & Ball Footed, Ruffled	135.00
Carnival Glass, Berry Dish, Jeweled Heart, Marigold, Opalescent Beading	70.00
Carnival Glass, Berry Set, Acorn, Purple, 7 Piece	325.00
Carnival Glass, Berry Set, Butterfly & Berry, Marigold, 7 Piece	115.00
Carnival Glass, Berry Set, Dahlia Pattern, White 4 Saucers	475.00
Carnival Glass, Bonbon, Butterfly, Green, Northwood	35.00
Carnival Glass, Bonbon, Fruits & Flowers, Marigold	25.00
Carnival Glass, Bonbon, Fruits & Flowers, Smoky Lavender	100.00
Carnival Glass, Bonbon, Fruits & Flowers, Stemmed, Blue	45.00
Carnival Glass, Bonbon, Fruits & Flowers, White, Stemmed, Northwood	75.00
Carnival Glass, Bonbon, Fruits & Flowers, 2 Handles, Pedestal, Blue	65.00
Carnival Glass, Bonbon, Grape & Cable, Marigold	25.00
Carnival Glass, Bonbon, Grape & Cable, Marigold, 2-Handled	32.00
Carnival Glass, Bonbon, Paneled Holly, Marigold, Northwood	18.00
Carnival Glass, Bonbon, Persian Medallion, Blue	32.00
Carnival Glass, Bonbon, Stippled Rays, Marigold, Handled, 7 In.	15.00
Carnival Glass, Bonbon, Vintage, Marigold	9.00
Carnival Glass, Bonbon, Waterlily, Footed, Aqua, 6 In.	30.00
Carnival Glass, Bottle, Cologne, Grape & Cable, Iridescent, Purple	175.00
Carnival Glass, Bottle, Water, Imperial Grape, Green	125.00
Carnival Glass, Bowl, Acanthus, Millersburg, Marigold, 8 In.	30.00
Carnival Glass, Bowl, Acorn Burrs, Purple Amethyst, Marked N, 9 1/2 In.	100.00
Carnival Glass, Bowl, Acorn, Green, 8 In.	35.00
Carnival Glass, Bowl, Amethyst, Grape Leaves, Northwood, 9 In.	43.00
Carnival Glass, Bowl, Australian Kangaroo, Purple, 9 1/2 In.	145.00
Carnival Glass, Bowl, Autumn Acorns, Cobalt, 9 In.	25.00
Carnival Glass, Bowl, Autumn Acorns, Marigold, 8 1/2 In.	27.50
Carnival Glass, Bowl, Banana, Cherry, Red	525.00
Carnival Glass, Bowl, Banana, Grape & Cable, Marigold	150.00
Carnival Glass, Bowl, Banana, Marigold, Kittens	75.00
Carnival Glass, Bowl, Banana, Wreathed Cherry, Purple	110.00
Carnival Glass, Bowl, Bellair Goodwill Tour, Marigold, 6 3/4 In.Deep	50.00
Carnival Glass, Bowl, Berry, Butterfly & Berry, Marigold, 8 1/2 In.	65.00
Carnival Glass, Bowl, Berry, Grape & Cable, Green, Fluted	69.00
Carnival Glass, Bowl, Berry, Iris & Meander, Small, Amethyst	22.00
Carnival Glass, Bowl, Berry, Panther, Blue, Small	35.00
Carnival Glass, Bowl, Blackberries & Leaves, Green, 9 In.	50.00
Carnival Glass, Bowl, Blackberry Wreath, Marigold, Millersburg, 9 In.	49.00
Carnival Glass, Bowl, Blackberry Wreath, Millersburg, Amethyst, 8 In.	35.00
Carnival Glass, Bowl, Blackberry Wreath, Millersburg, Green, 6 In.	19.50
Carnival Glass, Bowl, Butterfly & Berry, Footed, Blue, 9 In.	45.00
Carnival Glass, Bowl, Candy, Leaf & Beads, Green, Northwood, 8 1/2 In.Diam.	36.00
Carnival Glass, Bowl, Captive Rose, Amethyst, Ribbon Candy Edge, 8 1/2 In.	38.50
Carnival Glass, Bowl, Carnival Holly, Candy Ribbon Edge, 8 3/4 In.	45.00
Carnival Glass, Bowl, Cereal, Kittens, Marigold 75.00 To 125.00	
Carnival Glass, Bowl, Cherry Chain, Orange Tree Outside, Marigold, 9 1/2 In.	35.00
Carnival Glass, Bowl, Chrysanthemum & Windmill, Amethyst, 9 In.	45.00
Carnival Glass, Bowl, Chrysanthemum, Marigold, Iridescent, Footed, 11 In.	60.00
Carnival Glass, Bowl, Coin Dot, Amethyst, 8 In.Diameter	28.00
Carnival Glass, Bowl, Coin Spot, Ruffled, Purple, 8 1/2 In.Diameter	18.00
Carnival Glass, Bowl, Comet, Blue, 8 1/2 In.	50.00
Carnival Glass, Bowl, Cosmos Variant, Amethyst, 11 In.	70.00

Carnival Glass, Bowl, Curved Star Outside, Headdress, Marigold, 12 In. 20.00
Carnival Glass, Bowl, Diamond Lace, Ruffled, Amethyst, 9 In. 40.00
Carnival Glass, Bowl, Diamond Ring, Marigold, 9 In. 25.00
Carnival Glass, Bowl, Dragon & Lotus, Fluted, Blue, 9 In. 28.00
Carnival Glass, Bowl, Dragon & Lotus, Low, Crimped, Marigold, 9 In. 20.00
Carnival Glass, Bowl, Dragon & Strawberry, Marigold, Footed, 10 In. 195.00
Carnival Glass, Bowl, Feather, Blue, 6 X 2 In. 60.00
Carnival Glass, Bowl, Fenton's Peacock & Urn, Marigold, Ruffled, 8 1/2 In. 37.50
Carnival Glass, Bowl, Fleur-De-Lis, Marigold, Domed, Footed, 9 In. 55.00
Carnival Glass, Bowl, Flowers & Frames, Purple, Ruffled, 7 1/2 In. 45.00
Carnival Glass, Bowl, Flowers, Green, 5 1/2 In. 28.00
Carnival Glass, Bowl, Fluted, Ice White, 12 In.Diameter 95.00
Carnival Glass, Bowl, Fluted, Kittens, Marigold 45.00
Carnival Glass, Bowl, Fluted, Star Of David & Bow Knots, N., 7 In. 65.00
Carnival Glass, Bowl, Fluted, Thumbprint, Rayed Base, Marigold, 9 In. 35.00
Carnival Glass, Bowl, Fluted, White Ice, 12 In.Diameter 135.00
Carnival Glass, Bowl, Footed, Ruffled, Double Stem, Marigold, 9 In. 27.50
Carnival Glass, Bowl, Footed, Stag & Holly, Marigold, 10 1/2 In. 80.00
Carnival Glass, Bowl, Four Flowers, Ruffled Edge, Purple, 10 1/2 In. 75.00
Carnival Glass, Bowl, Fruit, Peach & Pear, Marigold 60.00
Carnival Glass, Bowl, Fruits, Ruffled Collar, Signed Northwood, 9 In. 45.00
Carnival Glass, Bowl, Good Luck, Fluted, Amethyst, 9 In. 65.00
Carnival Glass, Bowl, Good Luck, Green, Iridescent, N., 8 1/2 In. 135.00
Carnival Glass, Bowl, Good Luck, Marigold, Northwood, 8 3/4 In. 55.00
Carnival Glass, Bowl, Good Luck, Raspberry, 8 1/2 In. 80.00
Carnival Glass, Bowl, Goodwill Tour, Marigold, Bellaire, 7 1/4 In. 40.00
Carnival Glass, Bowl, Grape & Cable, Amethyst, 8 1/2 In. 45.00
Carnival Glass, Bowl, Grape & Cable, Blue Fenton, Iridescent, 7 In. 30.00
Carnival Glass, Bowl, Grape & Cable, Blue, Footed, 8 In. 50.00
Carnival Glass, Bowl, Grape & Cable, Footed, Marigold, 8 In. 30.00
Carnival Glass, Bowl, Grape & Cable, Green, Northwood, 7 3/4 In. 30.00
Carnival Glass, Bowl, Grape & Cable, Green, Northwood, 8 1/2 In. 35.00
Carnival Glass, Bowl, Grape & Cable, Marigold, 8 1/4 In. 30.00
Carnival Glass, Bowl, Grape & Cable, Spatular Foot, Northwood, 9 In. 45.00
Carnival Glass, Bowl, Grape & Leaf, Purple, 3 Feet, 6 X 4 In. 40.00
Carnival Glass, Bowl, Grape Leaves, Clambroth, Ruffled, 9 In., Northwood 45.00
Carnival Glass, Bowl, Grape Leaves, Marigold, Pastel, Northwood, 8 1/2 In. 32.50
Carnival Glass, Bowl, Grape Leaves, Purple, 9 In. 35.00
Carnival Glass, Bowl, Grape Outside, Peacock & Dahlia, Marigold, 7 In. 17.50
Carnival Glass, Bowl, Grape Pattern Reverse, Leaf Chain, Marigold, 7 In. 12.50
Carnival Glass, Bowl, Grape, Ruffled, Green, 6 1/2 In. 40.00
Carnival Glass, Bowl, Hanging Cherries, Millersburg, Amethyst, 7 1/2 In. 37.00
Carnival Glass, Bowl, Headdress, Marigold, 12 In. 30.00
Carnival Glass, Bowl, Heart & Vine, Amethyst, 7 In. 45.00
Carnival Glass, Bowl, Heart & Vine, Blue, Crimped, 7 1/2 In. 45.00
Carnival Glass, Bowl, Heart & Vine, Ribbon Candy Edge, Amethyst, 7 1/2 In. 45.00
Carnival Glass, Bowl, Hearts & Flowers, Electric Blue, 9 In. 79.00
Carnival Glass, Bowl, Hearts & Flowers, White, Ruffled, 8 3/4 In. 75.00
Carnival Glass, Bowl, Heavy Grape, Marigold, 9 In. 35.00
Carnival Glass, Bowl, Holly, Marigold, 9 In. 25.00
Carnival Glass, Bowl, Holly, Red, 9 1/4 In. 325.00
Carnival Glass, Bowl, Holly, Whirl, Millersburg, Green, 6 1/2 In. 39.00
Carnival Glass, Bowl, Holly, Whirl, Millersburg, Purple, 8 In. 37.50
Carnival Glass, Bowl, Holly, 8 Point Star Center, Amethyst, 8 In. 75.00
Carnival Glass, Bowl, Horse's Heads, Green, 7 In. 75.00
Carnival Glass, Bowl, Horse's Heads, Jack-In-The-Pulpit Shape, Marigold 65.00
Carnival Glass, Bowl, Ice Cream, Grape & Cable, Green, 11 In., Northwood 185.00
Carnival Glass, Bowl, Ice Cream, Grape & Cable, Purple, N Mark, 11 In. 169.00
Carnival Glass, Bowl, Ice Cream, Grape & Cable, White, 10 3/4 In. 295.00
Carnival Glass, Bowl, Ice Cream, Peacock & Urn, Ice Blue, 10 In. 295.00
Carnival Glass, Bowl, Ice Cream, Persian Garden, White, 11 1/2 In. 185.00
Carnival Glass, Bowl, Imperial Grape, Marigold, 5 In. 12.00
Carnival Glass, Bowl, Imperial Grape, Marigold, 10 1/2 In. 15.00
Carnival Glass, Bowl, Imperial Grape, Scalloped Edge, Marigold, 10 In. 30.00
Carnival Glass, Bowl, Imperial Open Rose, Green, 9 In. 27.50
Carnival Glass, Bowl, Inverted Strawberry, Marigold, Signed, 6 3/4 In. 19.00
Carnival Glass, Bowl, Isaac Benesch, Purple, 6 In. 145.00

Carnival Glass, Bowl, Lion, Marigold, 7 3/4 In.	65.00
Carnival Glass, Bowl, Little Fishes, Footed, Aqua, 5 In.	75.00
Carnival Glass, Bowl, Little Flowers, Green, 6 In.	17.50 To 27.50
Carnival Glass, Bowl, Little Flowers, Millersburg, Green, 8 1/2 In.	38.00
Carnival Glass, Bowl, Lotus & Grape, Footed, Ruffled, 6 1/2 In.	35.00
Carnival Glass, Bowl, Mayfair, Blue, 12 In.	25.00
Carnival Glass, Bowl, Medallion, Collar Base, Persian, 9 1/2 In.	43.00
Carnival Glass, Bowl, Miss America, Crystal, Curved-In, 8 In.	22.50
Carnival Glass, Bowl, Nesting Swan, Millersburg, Green, 10 In.	210.00
Carnival Glass, Bowl, Octagon, Marigold, 8 1/2 In.	25.00
Carnival Glass, Bowl, Old Windmill, Marigold, 8 In.	25.00
Carnival Glass, Bowl, Open Rose, Marigold, 8 1/2 In.	29.00
Carnival Glass, Bowl, Orange Tree, Blue, 9 In.	35.00
Carnival Glass, Bowl, Oval, Cherries In & Out, Blue, 32 In.Diameter	186.00
Carnival Glass, Bowl, Pansy, Purple, 8 1/2 In.	35.00
Carnival Glass, Bowl, Panther, Marigold, Footed, 5 3/4 In.	28.00
Carnival Glass, Bowl, Peacock & Dahlia, Marigold, 7 In.	30.00
Carnival Glass, Bowl, Peacock & Grape, Amethyst, Footed, 7 1/2 In.	45.00
Carnival Glass, Bowl, Peacock & Grape, Clambroth, 9 In.	38.00
Carnival Glass, Bowl, Peacock & Grape, Footed, Marigold, 8 In.	25.00
Carnival Glass, Bowl, Peacock & Grape, Green, 8 3/4 In.	37.50
Carnival Glass, Bowl, Peacock & Grape, Purple, Collar Base, 9 In.	37.50
Carnival Glass, Bowl, Peacock & Urn, Green, Collar Base, 8 1/2 In.	35.00
Carnival Glass, Bowl, Peacock & Urn, Millersburg, Green, 10 1/4 In.	130.00
Carnival Glass, Bowl, Peacock & Urn, Millersburg, Purple, 10 1/2 In.	155.00
Carnival Glass, Bowl, Peacock & Urn, Northwood, Purple, 5 1/2 In.	55.00
Carnival Glass, Bowl, Peacock & Urn, Scalloped, Blue, Iridescent, 10 In.	145.00
Carnival Glass, Bowl, Peacock & Urn, White, 9 In.	69.00
Carnival Glass, Bowl, Peacock At Fountain, 3-Footed, Marked N, 11 X 5 In.	245.00
Carnival Glass, Bowl, Peacock Eye, Amethyst, 8 In.	40.00
Carnival Glass, Bowl, Peacock On Fence, Blue, 8 1/2 In.Diameter	175.00
Carnival Glass, Bowl, Peacock On Fence, Marigold, 8 3/4 In.	95.00
Carnival Glass, Bowl, Peacock On Fence, Marigold, 9 In.	79.00
Carnival Glass, Bowl, Peacock On Fence, Purple, 9 In., Northwood	90.00
Carnival Glass, Bowl, Peacock Tail, Amethyst, 6 1/2 In.	15.00
Carnival Glass, Bowl, Peacock Tail, Purple, Horlacher Embossed, 6 In.	45.00
Carnival Glass, Bowl, Peacock, Marigold, 8 3/4 X 2 1/2 In.	52.00
Carnival Glass, Bowl, Peacock, Marigold, 9 X 2 In.	99.00
Carnival Glass, Bowl, Persian Garden, Marigold, Ruffled, 9 In.	32.00
Carnival Glass, Bowl, Persian Garden, Ruffled, 10 3/4 In.	135.00
Carnival Glass, Bowl, Persian Garden, White, 6 In.	25.00 To 45.00
Carnival Glass, Bowl, Persian Medallion, Amethyst, 9 In.	37.50
Carnival Glass, Bowl, Persian Medallion, Green, 10 In.	40.00
Carnival Glass, Bowl, Persian Medallion, Marigold, 8 In.	28.00
Carnival Glass, Bowl, Petal & Fan, White, Jeweled Heart Back, 11 In.	75.00
Carnival Glass, Bowl, Pine Cone, Blue, 6 In.	35.00
Carnival Glass, Bowl, Pleating, Ruby, 8 1/4 X 2 1/2 In.	25.00
Carnival Glass, Bowl, Poinsetta, Footed, Scalloped, Marigold, 10 In.	35.00
Carnival Glass, Bowl, Pony Head, Ruffled, Greek Key Rim, Marigold, 7 3/4 In.	75.00
Carnival Glass, Bowl, Poppy Show, White, 8 3/4 In.	240.00
Carnival Glass, Bowl, Punch With Base, Many Fruits, Purple	415.00
Carnival Glass, Bowl, Punch, Grape & Cable, Northwood	385.00
Carnival Glass, Bowl, Punch, Orange Tree, 5 Cups, White	350.00
Carnival Glass, Bowl, Punch, Passion, 6 Cups, Marigold, 10 X 10 1/2 In.	200.00
Carnival Glass, Bowl, Punch, 2 Piece, 9 Matching Cups, Vintage, Marigold	175.00
Carnival Glass, Bowl, Punch, 7 Cups, Base, Crab Claw, 9 1/2 X 12 1/2 In.	195.00
Carnival Glass, Bowl, Raindrops, Purple, 9 In.	45.00
Carnival Glass, Bowl, Rays & Ribbons, Millersburg, Ruffled, Purple, 10 In.	65.00
Carnival Glass, Bowl, Ribbon Tie, Amethyst, Ruffled, 9 1/2 In.	35.00
Carnival Glass, Bowl, Ribbon Tie, Marigold, 9 In.	20.00
Carnival Glass, Bowl, Rose Show, White, 9 In.	195.00
Carnival Glass, Bowl, Roundup, White, Ruffled, 9 1/2 In.	75.00
Carnival Glass, Bowl, Roundup, White, 9 In.	65.00
Carnival Glass, Bowl, Sailboats, Blue, 6 In.	22.50
Carnival Glass, Bowl, Sailboats, Ruffled, Violet, 6 In.	25.00
Carnival Glass, Bowl, Scale Band, Marigold, Ruffled, 7 In.	10.00
Carnival Glass, Bowl, Single Flower, Peach Opalescent, 8 1/2 In.	35.00

Carnival Glass, Bowl, Ski Star, Peach Opalescent, 11 In. 49.00
Carnival Glass, Bowl, Ski Star, Purple, 11 1/4 In. 85.00
Carnival Glass, Bowl, Soup, Iris, Iridescent, Flat 10.50
Carnival Glass, Bowl, Stag & Holly, Cobalt, 8 In. 45.00
Carnival Glass, Bowl, Stag & Holly, Footed, Marigold, 8 1/2 In. 65.00
Carnival Glass, Bowl, Stag & Holly, Footed, Purple, 8 1/2 In. 85.00
Carnival Glass, Bowl, Stag & Holly, Green, Footed, 8 In. .... 38.00 To 79.00
Carnival Glass, Bowl, Stag & Holly, Marigold, Footed, 9 In. 65.00
Carnival Glass, Bowl, Stag & Holly, 3-Footed, Marigold, 11 In. 70.00
Carnival Glass, Bowl, Stag & Holly, 3-Footed, Marigold, 12 In. 85.00
Carnival Glass, Bowl, Star Of David, Purple, 8 1/2 In. 55.00
Carnival Glass, Bowl, Stippled Rays, Amethyst, Marked Northwood, 9 In. 30.00
Carnival Glass, Bowl, Strawberry, Clambroth, Northwood, 8 1/2 In. 49.00
Carnival Glass, Bowl, Strawberry, Marigold, Millersburg, 7 In. 33.00
Carnival Glass, Bowl, Strawberry, Marigold, 9 In. 27.50
Carnival Glass, Bowl, Strawberry, Purple, Stippled, 9 In. 47.00
Carnival Glass, Bowl, Swan Bowl, Marigold, 10 In. 135.00
Carnival Glass, Bowl, Swan, Emerald Green, 10 In. 180.00
Carnival Glass, Bowl, Swirl, Marigold, Northwood, 8 In. 18.00
Carnival Glass, Bowl, Ten Mums, Cobalt, 9 1/2 In. 75.00
Carnival Glass, Bowl, Three Fruits, Aqua, 9 In. 125.00
Carnival Glass, Bowl, Three Fruits, Green, 8 In. 35.00
Carnival Glass, Bowl, Three Fruits, Purple, 8 1/2 In. 45.00
Carnival Glass, Bowl, Trout & Fly, Green Base, Millersburg, 9 In. 225.00
Carnival Glass, Bowl, Two Flowers, Footed, Blue, 7 1/2 In. 25.00
Carnival Glass, Bowl, Victorian, Iridescent, Purple, 11 1/2 In. 125.00
Carnival Glass, Bowl, Vintage, Blue, 9 1/2 In.Diameter 48.00
Carnival Glass, Bowl, Vintage, Purple, 9 In. 31.00
Carnival Glass, Bowl, Waterlily, Aqua Opalescent, Footed, 6 In. 79.00
Carnival Glass, Bowl, Whirling Leaves, Millersburg, Purple, 9 1/2 In. 85.00
Carnival Glass, Bowl, Wildflower, Blue Iridescent, 8 1/4 In. 40.00
Carnival Glass, Bowl, Windflower, Blue, 9 In. 45.00
Carnival Glass, Bowl, Windflower, Peach, Ruffled, Collar Base, 8 1/2 In. 42.00
Carnival Glass, Bowl, Windmill, Amethyst, 8 1/2 In. 30.00
Carnival Glass, Bowl, Windmill, Chrysanthemum, Amethyst, 8 In. 45.00
Carnival Glass, Bowl, Windmill, Red Marigold, 22 In.Diameter 46.50
Carnival Glass, Bowl, Wishbone & Spades, Purple, 5 3/4 In. 40.00
Carnival Glass, Bowl, Wishbone, Footed, Marigold, 8 X 3 In. 42.00
Carnival Glass, Bowl, Wishbone, Footed, Purple, 8 1/2 In. 50.00
Carnival Glass, Bowl, Wishbone, Footed, White, 8 1/2 In. 110.00
Carnival Glass, Bowl, Zig-Zag, Green, Millersburg, 9 1/2 In. 50.00
Carnival Glass, Box, Powder, Grape & Cable, Purple, Signed 32.00
Carnival Glass, Box, Powder, Orange Tree, Marigold 43.50
Carnival Glass, Bride's Basket, Jeweled Heart, Petal, Northwood, 11 1/2 In. 90.00
Carnival Glass, Bride's Basket, Stippled Rays, Square, 10 1/2 In. 65.00
Carnival Glass, Butter, Birds On Cover, Orange-Gold 110.00
Carnival Glass, Butter, Butterfly & Berry, Marigold, Covered 65.00
Carnival Glass, Butter, Creamer & Sugar, Field Thistle, Marigold 195.00
Carnival Glass, Butter, Grape & Cable, Purple, Covered, Northwood 200.00
Carnival Glass, Butter, Grape & Gothic Arches, Marigold, Covered 75.00
Carnival Glass, Butter, Iris, Iridescent 16.00
Carnival Glass, Butter, Moonprint, Marigold 75.00
Carnival Glass, Butter, Princess, Pink .... 52.50 To 60.00
Carnival Glass, Butter, Singing Bird, Northwood, Purple 145.00
Carnival Glass, Candleholder, Block, Green 16.00
Carnival Glass, Candleholder, Brocaded Palm, Pink 27.50
Carnival Glass, Candleholder, Cornucopia, Ice Blue 85.00
Carnival Glass, Candlestick, Grape & Cable, Green 145.00
Carnival Glass, Candlestick, Grape & Cable, Purple 95.00
Carnival Glass, Castor, Pickle, Poppy, Green, Circle Mark 25.00
Carnival Glass, Celery, Peacock, Amythyst Glaze, 8 In. 12.50
Carnival Glass, Celery, Quilted Outside, Marigold, 9 X 5 1/2 In. 25.00
Carnival Glass, Cologne, Grape & Cable, Marigold 59.00
Carnival Glass, Compote, Birds & Cherries, Amethyst 45.00
Carnival Glass, Compote, Blackberry Bramble, Green .... 29.50 To 45.00
Carnival Glass, Compote, Boutonniere, Millersburg, Marigold, Ruffled 38.00
Carnival Glass, Compote, Butterfly & Tulip, Purple, Footed 750.00

Carnival Glass, Compote, Candy, Hearts & Flowers, Stemmed, Cobalt Blue 55.00
Carnival Glass, Compote, Constellation Inside, S-Repeat Outside 26.00
Carnival Glass, Compote, Cover, Grape & Cable, Marked, Purple, 9 1/2 X 6 In. 295.00
Carnival Glass, Compote, Daisy & Plume, Pattern Inside, Purple 39.50
Carnival Glass, Compote, Flannel Flower, Purple 125.00
Carnival Glass, Compote, Grape & Cable, Purple, Northwood, 4 1/2 X 6 1/4 In. 125.00
Carnival Glass, Compote, Hearts & Flowers, Stemmed, Cobalt Blue, Northwood 60.00
Carnival Glass, Compote, Holly, Marigold, Miniature 40.00
Carnival Glass, Compote, Iris, High Standard, Millersburg, Marigold 45.00
Carnival Glass, Compote, Iris, Millersburg, Purple 45.00
Carnival Glass, Compote, Marigold, Grape & Cable, Covered, Iridescent 1500.00
Carnival Glass, Compote, Mikado, Marigold 85.00
Carnival Glass, Compote, Open Dolphin, Pink Amber, Stretch, 6 3/4 In. 65.00
Carnival Glass, Compote, Peacock At Urn, Fern Frond, Marigold, 5 X 5 3/4 In. 110.00
Carnival Glass, Compote, Peacock, Marigold Bowl, Clear Stem 25.00
Carnival Glass, Compote, Prism, Millersburg, 2-Handled, Marigold 80.00
Carnival Glass, Compote, Vintage, Green 35.00
Carnival Glass, Compote, Wreath Of Roses, Stemmed, 2-Handled, Amethyst 45.00
Carnival Glass, Cookie Jar, Grape & Cable, Handled, Purple 375.00
Carnival Glass, Cookie Jar, Grape & Cable, Marigold 145.00
Carnival Glass, Cracker Jar, Grape & Cable, Inverted Feather, Green 115.00
Carnival Glass, Creamer, Acorn Burr, Purple, Northwood 45.00
Carnival Glass, Creamer, Beaded Shell, Marigold 27.50
Carnival Glass, Creamer, Butterfly & Berry, Blue, Claw Footed 79.00
Carnival Glass, Creamer, Butterfly & Berry, Marigold 35.00
Carnival Glass, Creamer, Cathedral, Marigold 27.50
Carnival Glass, Creamer, Cosmos & Cane, White 150.00
Carnival Glass, Creamer, Dahlia, Footed, Purple, Northwood 85.00
Carnival Glass, Creamer, Dahlia, Purple 55.00
Carnival Glass, Creamer, Grape & Cable, Purple, Northwood 125.00
Carnival Glass, Creamer, Grape & Gothic Arches, Marigold 30.00
Carnival Glass, Creamer, Lea, Footed, Marigold 25.00
Carnival Glass, Creamer, Maple Leaf, Marigold 20.00
Carnival Glass, Creamer, Millersburg Cherry, Purple 70.00
Carnival Glass, Creamer, Pansy, Marigold 18.00
Carnival Glass, Creamer, Pineapple, Marigold 35.00
Carnival Glass, Creamer, Pineapple, Purple 35.00
Carnival Glass, Creamer, Shell And Jewel, Marigold 30.00
Carnival Glass, Creamer, Singing Bird, Northwood, Purple 75.00
Carnival Glass, Creamer, Stippled Strawberry, Marigold 13.00
Carnival Glass, Cruet, Buzz-Saw, Original Stopper, Miniature, Green 485.00
Carnival Glass, Cup & Saucer, Kittens, Marigold .... 118.00 To 165.00
Carnival Glass, Cup, Loving, Fenton's Orange Tree, Marigold 115.00
Carnival Glass, Cup, Loving, Orange Tree, Green 100.00
Carnival Glass, Cup, Punch, Acorn Burr, Green 22.00
Carnival Glass, Cup, Punch, Fashion, Marigold 9.00
Carnival Glass, Cup, Punch, Grape & Cable, Marigold 10.00
Carnival Glass, Cup, Punch, Grape & Cable, Marigold, Set Of 6 .... 85.00
Carnival Glass, Cup, Punch, Leaves & Grapes, Bird, Purple, Pair 29.00
Carnival Glass, Cup, Punch, Memphis, Marigold, Marked Northwood 15.00
Carnival Glass, Cup, Punch, Orange Tree, White 28.00
Carnival Glass, Cup, Punch, S-Repeat, Amethyst 20.00
Carnival Glass, Cup, Punch, Star Medallion, Marigold 10.00
Carnival Glass, Cup, Punch, Stippled Grape & Cable, Cobalt Blue, Set Of 6 .... 150.00
Carnival Glass, Cup, Punch, Stippled, Marigold 11.00
Carnival Glass, Cup, Punch, Vintage Grape, Marigold 10.00
Carnival Glass, Cuspidor, Ladies', Marigold 75.00
Carnival Glass, Decanter, Diamond & Sunburst, Purple 125.00
Carnival Glass, Decanter, Grapes, Purple 100.00
Carnival Glass, Decanter, Imperial Grape, Green 59.00
Carnival Glass, Decanter, Imperial Grape, Marigold 40.00
Carnival Glass, Decanter, Octagon, Marigold .... 35.00 To 39.00
Carnival Glass, Decanter, Whiskey, Grape & Cable, Marigold, Stopper 350.00
Carnival Glass, Dish, Acorn, Marigold, 7 1/2 In. 12.00
Carnival Glass, Dish, Basket Weave, Ruffled, Open Lace Edge, Blue, 5 1/2 In. 32.00
Carnival Glass, Dish, Blackberry Pattern, Red, 6 1/2 In. 125.00
Carnival Glass, Dish, Brocaded Acorn, 2-Handled, Ice Blue, 7 In. 12.00

Carnival Glass, Dish, Brooklyn Bridge, 8 1/2 In.	250.00
Carnival Glass, Dish, Candy, Beaded Block, Marigold	8.00
Carnival Glass, Dish, Candy, Blackberry, Peach	20.00
Carnival Glass, Dish, Candy, Drapery, Green, Northwood	45.00
Carnival Glass, Dish, Candy, Fenton Basket, Green	50.00
Carnival Glass, Dish, Candy, Pond Lily, Marigold	28.00
Carnival Glass, Dish, Candy, Ten Mums, Marigold, 9 1/2 In.Diameter	65.00
Carnival Glass, Dish, Candy, Wild Rose, Northwood, 3-Footed, Green	29.50
Carnival Glass, Dish, Candy, Wild Rose, Northwood, 3-Footed, Marigold	25.00
Carnival Glass, Dish, Candy, Wild Rose, Northwood, 3-Footed, Purple	35.00
Carnival Glass, Dish, Cosmos, Green, 6 In.	30.00
Carnival Glass, Dish, Footed, Grapes & Butterfly, Blue, 4 1/2 In.Diam., Pair	39.00
Carnival Glass, Dish, Hat Shaped, Red, 5 3/4 In.	155.00
Carnival Glass, Dish, Ice Cream, Grape & Cable, Purple, Footed	35.00
Carnival Glass, Dish, Ice Cream, Millersburg Peacock & Urn, Purple	40.00
Carnival Glass, Dish, Ice Cream, Peacock & Urn, Ice Blue, Northwood	65.00
Carnival Glass, Dish, Ice Cream, Peacock & Urn, Marigold	30.00
Carnival Glass, Dish, Nut, Vintage, Blue, 6-Footed	25.00 To 33.00
Carnival Glass, Dish, Pickle, Pansy, Amber	42.50
Carnival Glass, Dish, Relish, 2-Handled, Boat Shape, Leaf, Marigold	12.50
Carnival Glass, Dish, Wild Strawberry, Basketweave Back, Northwood, 10 In.	85.00
Carnival Glass, Dresser Tray, Grape & Cable, Purple	185.00
Carnival Glass, Epergne, Lily, Wide Panel, Marigold	175.00
Carnival Glass, Glass, Water, Tiger Lily, Green, Set Of 6	115.00
Carnival Glass, Goblet, Double Dolphin, Ice Blue	85.00
Carnival Glass, Goblet, Flute, Marigold, Set Of 4	39.50
Carnival Glass, Goblet, Imperial Grape, Marigold	25.00 To 33.00
Carnival Glass, Goblet, Orange Tree, Marigold	15.00 To 67.50
Carnival Glass, Goblet, Wildflower, Purple	75.00
Carnival Glass, Gravy Boat, One Handle, Windflower, Marigold	27.50
Carnival Glass, Hat, Peacock Tail, Advertising Delmar Gardens, Green	32.00
Carnival Glass, Hat, Spray, Blackberry, Red	175.00
Carnival Glass, Hatpin Holder, Bat & Stars, Silver Iridescent	35.00
Carnival Glass, Hatpin Holder, Bumble Bee, Cobalt Blue	35.00
Carnival Glass, Hatpin Holder, Butterfly, Cobalt Blue	17.50
Carnival Glass, Hatpin Holder, Grape & Cable, Amethyst	149.00
Carnival Glass, Hatpin Holder, Grape & Cable, Green	137.00 To 150.00
Carnival Glass, Hatpin Holder, Grape & Cable, Marigold	80.00
Carnival Glass, Hatpin Holder, Grape & Cable, Purple	98.00 To 235.00
Carnival Glass, Hatpin Holder, Grape & Cherry, Green	135.00
Carnival Glass, Hatpin Holder, Rooster, Amethyst	30.00
Carnival Glass, Humidor, Grape & Cable, Purple	65.00
Carnival Glass, Jar, Biscuit, Illinois Daisy, Marigold	45.00
Carnival Glass, Jar, Cracker, Inverted Feather, Green, Covered	175.00
Carnival Glass, Jar, Powder, Grape & Cable, Amethyst	45.00
Carnival Glass, Jar, Powder, Grape & Cable, Purple, Stippled	85.00
Carnival Glass, Jar, Powder, My Lady, Covered, Marigold	55.00
Carnival Glass, Jar, Powder, Orange Tree, Amethyst, Lid	69.00
Carnival Glass, Jar, Powder, Orange Tree, Marigold	30.00
Carnival Glass, Jar, Powder, Tree Of Life, Marigold, Covered	20.00
Carnival Glass, Jar, Powder, Vintage, Marigold, Covered	35.00
Carnival Glass, Jar, Tobacco, Grape & Cable, Marigold	385.00
Carnival Glass, Jar, Tobacco, Grape & Cable, Purple	310.00
Carnival Glass, Lamp, Zippered Loop, Marigold	185.00
Carnival Glass, Loving Cup, Orange Tree, Blue	182.50
Carnival Glass, Master Berry, Butterfly & Berry, Marigold	45.00
Carnival Glass, Master Berry, Imperial Grape, Purple	50.00
Carnival Glass, Mug, Banded Vintage, Marigold	13.00
Carnival Glass, Mug, Beaded Shell, Purple	55.00 To 75.00
Carnival Glass, Mug, Bo-Peep, Marigold	135.00
Carnival Glass, Mug, Bowl, Advertising, Isaac Benesch, Purple, 6 In.Diameter	125.00
Carnival Glass, Mug, Dandelion, Purple	150.00
Carnival Glass, Mug, Fisherman, Marigold	175.00
Carnival Glass, Mug, Fisherman's Net, Purple	70.00
Carnival Glass, Mug, Handle, Orange Tree, Marigold	20.00
Carnival Glass, Mug, Little Bo Peep, Marigold	125.00
Carnival Glass, Mug, Orange Tree, Blue	35.00 To 65.00

Carnival Glass, Mug, Orange Tree, Marigold .... 15.00 To 25.00
Carnival Glass, Mug, Robin, Marigold .... 35.00 To 50.00
Carnival Glass, Mug, Singing Birds, Blue 90.00
Carnival Glass, Mug, Singing Birds, Marigold .... 29.00 To 45.00
Carnival Glass, Mug, Singing Birds, Purple .... 45.00 To 47.00
Carnival Glass, Mug, Stork & Rushes, Marigold .... 16.00 To 20.00
Carnival Glass, Nappy, Fruits & Flower, Purple 35.00
Carnival Glass, Nappy, Grape & Cable, Marigold .... 20.00 To 45.00
Carnival Glass, Nappy, Grape & Cable, One-Handled, Green 79.50
Carnival Glass, Nappy, Grape & Cable, Purple 75.00
Carnival Glass, Nappy, Holly Spray, Purple, Handled 45.00
Carnival Glass, Nappy, Leaf Rays, Purple, Handled 25.00
Carnival Glass, Nappy, Leaf Rays, Purple, Lisbon, New Hampshire 45.00
Carnival Glass, Nappy, Leaf Rays, White 35.00
Carnival Glass, Nappy, Marigold 3.50
Carnival Glass, Nappy, Stippled Leaves, Star In Center, Purple 25.00
Carnival Glass, Nappy, Windflower, Marigold 36.00
Carnival Glass, Orange Bowl, Grape Arbor, Footed, Marigold 65.00
Carnival Glass, Pin Tray, Grape & Cable, Marigold 52.00
Carnival Glass, Pitcher, Cream, Peacock At The Fountain, Amethyst, Signed 68.00
Carnival Glass, Pitcher, Fenton Cannonball, Marigold, Enameling 65.00
Carnival Glass, Pitcher, Floral & Grape, Amethyst 150.00
Carnival Glass, Pitcher, Milk, Fans, Marigold 35.00
Carnival Glass, Pitcher, Milk, Flute & Cane, Marigold, 5 3/4 In. 135.00
Carnival Glass, Pitcher, Milk, Poinsettia, Marigold 45.00
Carnival Glass, Pitcher, Milk, Raspberry, Purple 139.00
Carnival Glass, Pitcher, Milk, Star Medallion, Marigold 35.00
Carnival Glass, Pitcher, Milk, Star Medallion, Pastel, Marigold 25.00
Carnival Glass, Pitcher, Milk, Windmill & Mums, Marigold 50.00
Carnival Glass, Pitcher, Milk, Windmill, Medallion, Green 125.00
Carnival Glass, Pitcher, Singing Bird, Marigold, N, 8 1/2 In. 175.00
Carnival Glass, Pitcher, Tree Bark, Marigold, 8 3/4 In. 20.00
Carnival Glass, Pitcher, Water, Blueberry, Blue 400.00
Carnival Glass, Pitcher, Water, Crab Claw, Marigold 150.00
Carnival Glass, Pitcher, Water, Diamond Lace, Purple .... 200.00 To 235.00
Carnival Glass, Pitcher, Water, Engraved Grape, Marigold 150.00
Carnival Glass, Pitcher, Water, Field Flower, Green 115.00
Carnival Glass, Pitcher, Water, Floral & Grape, Amethyst 125.00
Carnival Glass, Pitcher, Water, Frosted Ribbon, Marigold 40.00
Carnival Glass, Pitcher, Water, Grapes & Leaves, Purple 40.00
Carnival Glass, Pitcher, Water, Luster Rose, Green 125.00
Carnival Glass, Pitcher, Water, Magnolia & Drape, Marigold, Bulbous 75.00
Carnival Glass, Pitcher, Water, No.474, Marigold 125.00
Carnival Glass, Pitcher, Water, Octagon, Marigold .... 69.00 To 80.00
Carnival Glass, Pitcher, Water, Peacock At Fountain, White 400.00
Carnival Glass, Pitcher, Water, Raspberry, Purple, Northwood 275.00
Carnival Glass, Pitcher, Water, Scale Band, Marigold 65.00
Carnival Glass, Pitcher, Water, Vineyard, Marigold 105.00
Carnival Glass, Pitcher, Water, Windmill, Marigold 40.00
Carnival Glass, Plate, Cherry Chain, Blue, 6 1/2 In. 45.00
Carnival Glass, Plate, Chop, Heavy Grape, Marigold 95.00
Carnival Glass, Plate, Concord, Purple 450.00
Carnival Glass, Plate, Dragon Lotus, Red Iridescent, Marigold, 8 1/2 In. 37.50
Carnival Glass, Plate, Fenton's Heavy Grape, Purple, 8 In. 52.00
Carnival Glass, Plate, Fishscale & Beads, Marigold, 7 In. 29.00
Carnival Glass, Plate, Floral & Optic, White, Footed, 10 In. 65.00
Carnival Glass, Plate, Good Luck, Purple, 9 In., Northwood 180.00
Carnival Glass, Plate, Grape & Cable, Amethyst, Footed, 9 1/2 In. 70.00
Carnival Glass, Plate, Grape & Cable, Footed, Marigold 65.00
Carnival Glass, Plate, Grape & Cable, Green, Old Rose Distillery, 9 In. 165.00
Carnival Glass, Plate, Grape & Cable, Marigold, 6 In. 30.00
Carnival Glass, Plate, Grape & Cable, Marigold, 9 In. 40.00
Carnival Glass, Plate, Grape & Cable, Northwood, Purple, 6 1/2 In. 75.00
Carnival Glass, Plate, Grape & Cable, Purple, Handgrip, 8 In., Northwood 75.00
Carnival Glass, Plate, Grape & Cable, Wicker Back, Amethyst, 9 In. 127.50
Carnival Glass, Plate, Green Lustre Rose 50.00
Carnival Glass, Plate, Heart & Vine, Blue, 9 In. 150.00

Carnival Glass, Plate, Hearts & Flowers, Marigold, 9 In.	135.00
Carnival Glass, Plate, Holly-Berry, Blue, 9 1/2 In.	85.00
Carnival Glass, Plate, Holly, Blue, 10 In.	95.00
Carnival Glass, Plate, Holly, Marigold, 9 In.	52.50
Carnival Glass, Plate, Imperial Grape, Amber	40.00
Carnival Glass, Plate, Imperial Jewels, Red, 8 1/4 In.	55.00
Carnival Glass, Plate, Leaf Chain, Blue, 7 1/2 In.	46.00
Carnival Glass, Plate, Leaf Chain, Green, 9 In.	69.00
Carnival Glass, Plate, Leaf Chain, White, 9 In.	80.00
Carnival Glass, Plate, Millersburg Peacock & Urn, Amethyst, 6 1/4 In.	175.00
Carnival Glass, Plate, Millersburg Posies & Pods, Peach, 6 1/2 In.	50.00
Carnival Glass, Plate, Open Rose, Marigold, 9 In.	35.00
Carnival Glass, Plate, Orange Tree, White, 9 In.	85.00
Carnival Glass, Plate, Panther, Blue	650.00
Carnival Glass, Plate, Peacock & Grape, Footed, Flat, Green, 9 In.	150.00
Carnival Glass, Plate, Peacock & Urn, Blue, 9 1/2 In.	145.00
Carnival Glass, Plate, Peacock & Urn, Marigold, 9 In.	125.00
Carnival Glass, Plate, Peacock On Fence, Green, 9 In.	95.00 To 165.00
Carnival Glass, Plate, Peacock On Fence, Marigold, 9 In.	125.00
Carnival Glass, Plate, Peacock On Fence, White, 9 In.	115.00
Carnival Glass, Plate, Peacocks At The Gate, 9 In.	185.00
Carnival Glass, Plate, Persian Garden, White, 7 In.	79.00
Carnival Glass, Plate, Persian Medallion, Marigold, 9 1/2 In.	70.00
Carnival Glass, Plate, Pine Cones, Marigold, 6 In.	30.00
Carnival Glass, Plate, Poppy Show, Marigold, 9 1/2 In.	110.00
Carnival Glass, Plate, Poppy Show, White, 9 1/4 In.	265.00
Carnival Glass, Plate, Pretzel, Round-Up, Peach Opalescent, 9 In.	140.00
Carnival Glass, Plate, Ribbon Tie, Ruffled, Blue, 9 1/2 In.	125.00
Carnival Glass, Plate, Rose Show, Blue, 9 1/4 In.	250.00
Carnival Glass, Plate, Scales, Green Ruffled Edge, Northwood, 11 In.	65.00
Carnival Glass, Plate, Scalloped, Rose Show, 1 3/4 In.Deep	250.00
Carnival Glass, Plate, Strawberry, Marigold, 9 In.	60.00
Carnival Glass, Plate, Strawberry, Purple, Northwood, 9 In.	68.00
Carnival Glass, Plate, Thistle & Thorn, Footed, Marigold, 8 In.	25.00
Carnival Glass, Plate, Three Fruits, Amethyst, 9 In.	60.00
Carnival Glass, Plate, Three Fruits, Aqua Opalescent, 9 In.	450.00
Carnival Glass, Plate, Three Fruits, Basket Weave Outside, Marigold, 9 In.	55.00
Carnival Glass, Plate, Three Fruits, Green, 9 In.	38.00
Carnival Glass, Plate, Three Fruits, Marigold, 9 In.	65.00
Carnival Glass, Plate, Three Fruits, Purple, Stippled, Northwood, 9 In.	75.00
Carnival Glass, Plate, Vintage, Green, 7 In.	45.00
Carnival Glass, Plate, Windflower, Marigold, 9 In.	60.00
Carnival Glass, Plate, Wishbone, Blue, 10 In.	45.00
Carnival Glass, Pump, Town, Novelty Tree Bark & Hobnail, Purple	550.00
Carnival Glass, Punch Bowl, Acorn Burr, White	79.00
Carnival Glass, Punch Bowl, Many Fruits, Purple, Ruffled Base	295.00
Carnival Glass, Punch Bowl, Memphis, Ice Green	79.00
Carnival Glass, Punch Cup, Memphis, Marigold	15.00
Carnival Glass, Punch Cup, Memphis, Purple	25.00
Carnival Glass, Punch Set, Fashion, Marigold, Bowl, Base & 5 Cups	175.00
Carnival Glass, Punch Set, Grape & Cable, 6 Cups, 11 In.Bowl Base, Amethyst	500.00
Carnival Glass, Punch Set, Orange Tree, Marigold, 10 Piece	145.00
Carnival Glass, Punch Set, Pillar & Drape, White, 7 Piece	350.00
Carnival Glass, Punch Set, Waffle Back, Marigold, 8 Piece	125.00
Carnival Glass, Rose Bowl, Beaded Cable, Aqua Opalescent, Northwood	130.00
Carnival Glass, Rose Bowl, Beaded Cable, Marigold	35.00
Carnival Glass, Rose Bowl, Daisy & Plume, Deep Purple, Footed	55.00
Carnival Glass, Rose Bowl, Daisy & Plume, Stemmed, Marigold	25.00 To 37.00
Carnival Glass, Rose Bowl, Drapery, Aqua Opalescent, Northwood Circle	130.00
Carnival Glass, Rose Bowl, Drapery, Blue	75.00
Carnival Glass, Rose Bowl, Fenton's Flowers, Blue	45.00
Carnival Glass, Rose Bowl, Finecut & Roses, Green	70.00
Carnival Glass, Rose Bowl, Finecut & Roses, Ice Blue	169.00
Carnival Glass, Rose Bowl, Finecut & Roses, Purple	59.00 To 75.00
Carnival Glass, Rose Bowl, Garland, Green	55.00
Carnival Glass, Rose Bowl, Garland, Marigold	45.00 To 48.00
Carnival Glass, Rose Bowl, Grape & Cable, Hobnail, Marigold	55.00

Carnival Glass, Rose Bowl, Grape Delight, White, 6 Legs 90.00
Carnival Glass, Rose Bowl, Grape, 6-Footed, White 90.00
Carnival Glass, Rose Bowl, Horse's Head, Marigold 72.50
Carnival Glass, Rose Bowl, Imperial, Green, 8 In. 65.00
Carnival Glass, Rose Bowl, Kokomo, Marigold 38.00
Carnival Glass, Rose Bowl, Leaf & Beads, Green, Northwood 23.00
Carnival Glass, Rose Bowl, Leaf & Beads, Purple .... 55.00 To 65.00
Carnival Glass, Rose Bowl, Louisa, Green, Footed 50.00
Carnival Glass, Rose Bowl, Vintage Grape, 6-Footed, Marigold 55.00
Carnival Glass, Rose Bowl, Wreath Of Roses, Marigold 35.00
Carnival Glass, Salt & Pepper, Block, Green, Footed 13.00
Carnival Glass, Sauce, Apple Blossoms, Marigold 18.00
Carnival Glass, Sauce, Butterfly & Berry, Marigold 20.00
Carnival Glass, Sauce, Peacock & Urn, Blue, Northwood, 6 In. 27.50
Carnival Glass, Sauce, Peacock At Fountain, Purple 26.00
Carnival Glass, Sauce, Scroll Embossed & File, Purple, 5 1/2 In. 21.00
Carnival Glass, Shade, Lamp, Hand-Painted Castle, Scene, Marigold 43.50
Carnival Glass, Shade, Lamp, Marigold, Signed, 6 In.Diameter 95.00
Carnival Glass, Shade, Marigold, Set Of 6 .... 120.00
Carnival Glass, Shade, Medallion & Stars, Beaded 15.00
Carnival Glass, Shade, NuArt, Marigold 30.00
Carnival Glass, Shade, Primrose, Marigold, Set Of 3 .... 75.00
Carnival Glass, Shade, Starlite, Green, 4 In. 30.00
Carnival Glass, Shade, White, Drapery, Northwood, Signed 25.00
Carnival Glass, Shaving Mug, Orange Tree, Marigold On Blue 150.00
Carnival Glass, Sherbet, Grape & Cable, Amber, Stemmed, Northwood 45.00
Carnival Glass, Sherbet, Grape & Cable, Amethyst, Stemmed 42.00
Carnival Glass, Sherbet, Grape & Cable, Purple 35.00
Carnival Glass, Spooner, Butterfly & Berry, Marigold 35.00
Carnival Glass, Spooner, Cherry, Marigold, Northwood 52.00
Carnival Glass, Spooner, Circled Scroll, Marigold 45.00
Carnival Glass, Spooner, Grape & Cable, Green .... 79.00 To 95.00
Carnival Glass, Spooner, Grape & Cable, Purple .... 45.00 To 150.00
Carnival Glass, Spooner, Peacock At Fountain, White, Signed .... 97.50 To 110.00
Carnival Glass, Spooner, Singing Bird, Northwood 65.00
Carnival Glass, Sugar & Creamer, Grape & Cable, Purple, Northwood 150.00
Carnival Glass, Sugar & Creamer, Lustre Flute, Green 45.00
Carnival Glass, Sugar & Creamer, Pansy Spray, Violet .... 50.00 To 65.00
Carnival Glass, Sugar & Creamer, Shell & Jewel, Mint Green, 5 In. 65.00
Carnival Glass, Sugar & Creamer, Stippled Rays, Marigold 25.00
Carnival Glass, Sugar & Creamer, Strutting Peacock, Purple 75.00
Carnival Glass, Sugar, Cover, Butterfly & Berry, Marigold 38.00
Carnival Glass, Sugar, Covered, Hanging Cherries, Gold 20.00
Carnival Glass, Sugar, Covered, White, Northwood's Peach 75.00
Carnival Glass, Sugar, Flute, Marigold 36.00
Carnival Glass, Sugar, Grape & Cable, Purple .... 100.00 To 105.00
Carnival Glass, Sugar, Lustre Flute, Amethyst 45.00
Carnival Glass, Sugar, Millersburg Cherry, Marigold, Covered 62.00
Carnival Glass, Sugar, Orange Tree, Blue, Footed 90.00
Carnival Glass, Sugar, Shell & Jewel, Marigold 10.00
Carnival Glass, Sugar, Strutting Peacock, Purple 20.00
Carnival Glass, Sweetmeat, Grape & Cable, Purple, Covered, Northwood 215.00
Carnival Glass, Syrup, Fish Net & Poppy, Marigold, Original Tin Top 135.00
Carnival Glass, Table Set, Grape & Cable, Marigold, 4 Pieces 365.00
Carnival Glass, Table Set, Memphis, Green, Gold Trim 200.00
Carnival Glass, Table Set, Peach, Green & Gold, 4 Piece 335.00
Carnival Glass, Toothpick, Flute, Amethyst 50.00
Carnival Glass, Toothpick, Flute, Marigold .... 38.00 To 39.00
Carnival Glass, Top Hat, Marigold, 1 3/4 In. 10.00
Carnival Glass, Tray, Card, Grape & Cable, Northwood 150.00
Carnival Glass, Tray, Card, Three Fruits, Purple, Northwood, 7 1/2 In. 75.00
Carnival Glass, Tray, Dresser, Grape & Cable, Amethyst 135.00
Carnival Glass, Tray, Dresser, Grape & Cable, Marigold 165.00
Carnival Glass, Tray, Dresser, Grape & Cable, Purple 189.00
Carnival Glass, Tray, Dresser, Pansy, Amber, Oval 85.00
Carnival Glass, Tray, Dresser, Pansy, Marigold, Pastel, 7 In. 45.00
Carnival Glass, Tray, Dresser, Pansy, Marigold, 9 3/4 X 6 3/4 In. 40.00

Carnival Glass, Tray, Peacock At Fountain, Marigold, 9 3/4 X 6 3/4 In. 65.00
Carnival Glass, Tray, Pin, Seacoast, Green .... 130.00 To 135.00
Carnival Glass, Tray, Wine, S-Repeat, Blue 50.00
Carnival Glass, Tumbler, Acorn Burr, Green 65.00
Carnival Glass, Tumbler, Acorn Burr, Marigold .... 29.00 To 35.00
Carnival Glass, Tumbler, Acorn Burr, Purple 45.00
Carnival Glass, Tumbler, Apple Tree, Cobalt Blue 45.00
Carnival Glass, Tumbler, Apple Tree, Marigold .... 18.00 To 18.50
Carnival Glass, Tumbler, Banded Ribs, Marigold 10.00
Carnival Glass, Tumbler, Beaded Shell, Blue 55.00
Carnival Glass, Tumbler, Blueberry, Blue 50.00
Carnival Glass, Tumbler, Bouquet, Marigold .... 25.00 To 30.00
Carnival Glass, Tumbler, Butterfly & Berry, Blue 20.00
Carnival Glass, Tumbler, Butterfly & Berry, Marigold 12.00
Carnival Glass, Tumbler, Butterfly & Fern, Blue 35.00
Carnival Glass, Tumbler, Butterfly & Fern, Green 55.00
Carnival Glass, Tumbler, Butterfly & Fern, Marigold 35.00
Carnival Glass, Tumbler, Butterfly & Plume, Amethyst 40.00
Carnival Glass, Tumbler, Concave Diamond, Pastel Blue .... 39.00 To 45.00
Carnival Glass, Tumbler, Cosmos & Cane, Marigold 36.00
Carnival Glass, Tumbler, Crab Claw, Marigold .... 20.00 To 35.00
Carnival Glass, Tumbler, Daisy & Lattice, Marigold 15.00
Carnival Glass, Tumbler, Dandelion, Amethyst, Northwood 32.50
Carnival Glass, Tumbler, Dandelion, Marigold 38.00
Carnival Glass, Tumbler, Dandelion, Purple, Northwood .... 45.00 To 49.00
Carnival Glass, Tumbler, Diamond & Daisy Cut, Marigold 40.00
Carnival Glass, Tumbler, Diamond Lace, Purple 45.00
Carnival Glass, Tumbler, Diamond, Amethyst 37.50
Carnival Glass, Tumbler, Double Star, Green 35.00
Carnival Glass, Tumbler, Engraved Grape, Marigold 39.00
Carnival Glass, Tumbler, Fashion, Marigold 25.00
Carnival Glass, Tumbler, Fashion, Purple 175.00
Carnival Glass, Tumbler, Field Flowers, Green 52.00
Carnival Glass, Tumbler, Field Thistle, Marigold 90.00
Carnival Glass, Tumbler, File, Marigold 35.00
Carnival Glass, Tumbler, Floral & Grape, Amethyst .... 16.00 To 29.00
Carnival Glass, Tumbler, Floral & Grape, Marigold 15.00
Carnival Glass, Tumbler, Fluffy Peacock, Marigold 45.00
Carnival Glass, Tumbler, Fluffy Peacock, Purple Amethyst 50.00
Carnival Glass, Tumbler, Flute Number 3, Teal Blue 220.00
Carnival Glass, Tumbler, Fruit Luster, Marigold 10.00
Carnival Glass, Tumbler, God & Home, Blue 135.00
Carnival Glass, Tumbler, Gothic Arches, Marigold 14.00
Carnival Glass, Tumbler, Grape & Cable, Green 40.00
Carnival Glass, Tumbler, Grape & Cable, Marigold 22.00
Carnival Glass, Tumbler, Grape & Cable, Northwood .... 28.50 To 37.00
Carnival Glass, Tumbler, Grape & Cable, Purple .... 25.00 To 40.00
Carnival Glass, Tumbler, Grape & Cherry, Marigold 14.00
Carnival Glass, Tumbler, Grape & Gothic Arches, Blue .... 25.00 To 30.00
Carnival Glass, Tumbler, Grape & Gothic Arches, Marigold 24.00
Carnival Glass, Tumbler, Grape & Gothic Arches, Pearl 95.00
Carnival Glass, Tumbler, Grape & Thumbprint, Marigold, Northwood 30.00
Carnival Glass, Tumbler, Grape & Thumbprint, Purple, Signed N 45.00
Carnival Glass, Tumbler, Grape Arbor, Marigold 35.00
Carnival Glass, Tumbler, Grape Arbor, Purple 49.00
Carnival Glass, Tumbler, Grape Arbor, White 85.00
Carnival Glass, Tumbler, Grapevine & Lattice, Light Blue 60.00
Carnival Glass, Tumbler, Grapevine & Lattice, Purple 35.00
Carnival Glass, Tumbler, Greek Key, Marigold, Pastel 85.00
Carnival Glass, Tumbler, Harvest Flowers, Green Base 125.00
Carnival Glass, Tumbler, Hobstar Band, Marigold 35.00
Carnival Glass, Tumbler, Imperial Grape, Marigold .... 15.00 To 16.00
Carnival Glass, Tumbler, Imperial Grape, Purple .... 29.00 To 45.00
Carnival Glass, Tumbler, Inverted Coin Dot, Marigold 35.00
Carnival Glass, Tumbler, Iris, Purple .... 45.00 To 75.00
Carnival Glass, Tumbler, Jewel Heart, Marigold 75.00
Carnival Glass, Tumbler, Lattice & Daisy, Marigold .... 12.50 To 15.00

Carnival Glass, Tumbler, Lustre Rose, Clambroth 35.00
Carnival Glass, Tumbler, Lustre Rose, Green 39.00
Carnival Glass, Tumbler, Lustre Rose, Marigold .... 10.00 To 12.00
Carnival Glass, Tumbler, Lustre Rose, Purple 45.00
Carnival Glass, Tumbler, Maple Leaf Variant, Blue 65.00
Carnival Glass, Tumbler, Maple Leaf, Amethyst 45.00
Carnival Glass, Tumbler, Maple Leaf, Purple 30.00
Carnival Glass, Tumbler, Octagon, Marigold 29.00
Carnival Glass, Tumbler, Octagon, Purple 55.00
Carnival Glass, Tumbler, Orange Tree Orchard, Blue 49.00
Carnival Glass, Tumbler, Orange Tree Variant, Marigold 39.00
Carnival Glass, Tumbler, Orange Tree, Marigold 40.00
Carnival Glass, Tumbler, Oriental Poppy, Marigold 29.00
Carnival Glass, Tumbler, Oriental Poppy, Purple .... 45.00 To 49.00
Carnival Glass, Tumbler, Paneled Dandelion, Marigold 20.00
Carnival Glass, Tumbler, Paneled Dandelion, Purple 29.00
Carnival Glass, Tumbler, Peacock At Fountain, Cobalt Blue 32.00
Carnival Glass, Tumbler, Peacock At Fountain, Marigold 28.00
Carnival Glass, Tumbler, Peacock At Fountain, Purple ..... 27.50 To 30.00
Carnival Glass, Tumbler, Peacock, Footed, Blue 15.00
Carnival Glass, Tumbler, Perfection, Amethyst 325.00
Carnival Glass, Tumbler, Pretty Panels, Ice Blue 29.00
Carnival Glass, Tumbler, Rambler Rose, Marigold 19.00
Carnival Glass, Tumbler, Raspberry, Marigold .... 18.00 To 20.00
Carnival Glass, Tumbler, Rex, Marigold 16.00
Carnival Glass, Tumbler, Robin, Marigold 35.00
Carnival Glass, Tumbler, Scale Band, Marigold 25.00
Carnival Glass, Tumbler, Singing Birds, Green .... 35.00 To 40.00
Carnival Glass, Tumbler, Singing Birds, Marigold .... 25.00 To 27.00
Carnival Glass, Tumbler, Singing Birds, Marigold, Set Of 6 .... 28.00
Carnival Glass, Tumbler, Singing Birds, Purple .... 35.00 To 45.00
Carnival Glass, Tumbler, Springtime, Marigold 40.00
Carnival Glass, Tumbler, Star Medallion 25.00
Carnival Glass, Tumbler, Stork & Rushes, Blue 20.00
Carnival Glass, Tumbler, Stork & Rushes, Marigold ...... 16.00 To 17.00
Carnival Glass, Tumbler, Stork & Rushes, Marigold, Banded 25.00
Carnival Glass, Tumbler, Stork In Bulrushes, Blue 40.00
Carnival Glass, Tumbler, Strawberry Scroll, Marigold 140.00
Carnival Glass, Tumbler, Swirl, Northwood, Marigold 25.00
Carnival Glass, Tumbler, Ten Mums, Blue 25.00
Carnival Glass, Tumbler, Ten Mums, Marigold 28.00
Carnival Glass, Tumbler, Tiger Lily, Marigold .... 15.00 To 25.00
Carnival Glass, Tumbler, Vineyard, Marigold .... 18.00 To 21.00
Carnival Glass, Tumbler, Vineyard, Purple .... 35.00 To 45.00
Carnival Glass, Tumbler, Waterlily & Cattails, Marigold 13.00
Carnival Glass, Tumbler, Wide Panel, Marigold, Handled 24.00
Carnival Glass, Tumbler, Windmill, Marigold 15.00
Carnival Glass, Tumbler, Wreath Cherry, Purple 49.00
Carnival Glass, Vase, Beading On 3 Sides, Tornado, Northwood, 6 X 4 In., Pair 225.00
Carnival Glass, Vase, Bull's-Eye, Beaded, Marigold, 10 In. 15.00
Carnival Glass, Vase, Drapery Variant, Marigold, 8 1/2 In., Northwood 25.00
Carnival Glass, Vase, Footed, Serrated Edge, Stag & Holly, Marigold, 8 In. 55.00
Carnival Glass, Vase, Hat-Shaped, Imperial Jewels, Marigold, 5 In. 40.00
Carnival Glass, Vase, Hat-Shaped, Stork & Rushes, Marigold, 4 3/4 X 3 In. 30.00
Carnival Glass, Vase, Horizontal Ribbing, Green, 7 3/4 In. 45.00
Carnival Glass, Vase, Jack-In-The-Pulpit Top, Purple, 6 1/2 In. 40.00
Carnival Glass, Vase, Lattice, White Lined, 9 In. 75.00
Carnival Glass, Vase, Lined Lattice, Purple, 11 3/4 In. 25.00
Carnival Glass, Vase, Lustre Flute, Purple, Northwood, 4 In. 35.00
Carnival Glass, Vase, Poppy Show, Marigold, 12 1/2 In. 215.00
Carnival Glass, Vase, Ribbed, Cobalt Blue, 9 1/2 In. 12.00
Carnival Glass, Vase, Ribbed, Purple, 7 In. 20.00
Carnival Glass, Vase, Rippled, Marigold, 7 In., Pair 20.00
Carnival Glass, Vase, Ruffled Scalloped Edge, Loop & Column, 9 1/2 In. 85.00
Carnival Glass, Vase, Rustic, Purple, 14 In.High 18.00
Carnival Glass, Vase, Stag & Holly, Footed, Purple, 3 5/8 X 7 5/8 In.Diam. 58.00
Carnival Glass, Vase, Tree Bark, Orange Iridescent, Lady Fingers Top, 16 In. 35.00

Carnival Glass, Vase, Tree Trunk. Signed N, Purple, 13 In.	40.00
Carnival Glass, Vase, Tri-Cornered, Drapery, Blue, 9 In.	65.00
Carnival Glass, Vase, Waffle Pattern, Iridescent, Purple, Marked, 10 1/2 In.	22.00
Carnival Glass, Water Set, Amethyst, 1973 Grape, Pitcher & 6 Goblets	65.00
Carnival Glass, Water Set, Banded Drape, Marigold, 7 Piece	195.00
Carnival Glass, Water Set, Butterfly & Plume, Marigold, 7 Piece	379.00
Carnival Glass, Water Set, Cherries & Blossoms, Blue, 7 Piece	210.00
Carnival Glass, Water Set, Crab Claw, Marigold	325.00
Carnival Glass, Water Set, Diamond Lace, Purple, 6 Piece	395.00
Carnival Glass, Water Set, Diamond Pattern, Marigold, Millersburg, 7 Piece	355.00
Carnival Glass, Water Set, Fashion, Marigold, 7 Pieces	230.00
Carnival Glass, Water Set, Field Flower, Marigold, 7 Piece	185.00
Carnival Glass, Water Set, Grape & Cable, Purple, 7 Piece	360.00 To 395.00
Carnival Glass, Water Set, Grape Arbor, Marigold, 7 Piece	350.00
Carnival Glass, Water Set, Imperial Grape, Marigold, 7 Piece	120.00
Carnival Glass, Water Set, Lattice & Daisy, Marigold, 7 Piece	165.00
Carnival Glass, Water Set, Lustre Rose, Clambroth, 7 Pieces	350.00
Carnival Glass, Water Set, Lustre Rose, Marigold, 7 Piece	105.00
Carnival Glass, Water Set, Mayflower, 4 Tumblers, Marigold	195.00
Carnival Glass, Water Set, Millersburg Diamond, Purple, 5 Piece	395.00
Carnival Glass, Water Set, Northwood's Handpainted, Pitcher, 4 Tumblers	375.00
Carnival Glass, Water Set, Oriental Poppy, Purple, 7 Piece	789.00
Carnival Glass, Water Set, Painted Cherry, Cobalt Blue, 6 Piece	149.00
Carnival Glass, Water Set, Peach, Green With Gold, Northwood, 7 Piece	235.00
Carnival Glass, Water Set, Peacock At The Fountain, Marked N., Blue, 8 Piece	435.00
Carnival Glass, Water Set, Raspberry, Green, 7 Piece	339.00
Carnival Glass, Water Set, Raspberry, Purple, 6 Piece	345.00
Carnival Glass, Water Set, Reverse Drape & Floral, Marigold, 7 Piece	260.00
Carnival Glass, Water Set, Tiger Lily, Grape & Cable, Marigold	130.00
Carnival Glass, Water Set, Tiger Lily, Marigold, 6 Pieces	195.00
Carnival Glass, Water Set, Vineyard, Orange, 7 Piece	110.00
Carnival Glass, Water Set, 6 Tumblers, Azure Blue, Imperial	325.00
Carnival Glass, Whiskey, Palm Beach, Marigold	50.00
Carnival Glass, Wine, Grape & Cable, Green	22.00
Carnival Glass, Wine, Imperial Grape, Marigold	15.00
Carnival Glass, Wine, Octagon, Marigold	19.00
Carnival Glass, Wine, Orange Tree, Blue	45.00 To 50.00
Carnival Glass, Wine, Vintage, Marigold	17.00
Carnival Glass, Wine, Wine & Roses, Marigold, Stemmed	30.00
Carousel, Band Organ, Limonair, Children's	6500.00
Carousel, Camel, French	2750.00
Carousel, Cat, French, Boyol Plaque, 60 In.	2950.00
Carousel, Cat, French, Glass Eyes, Bushy Tail, 60 In.Long	3500.00
Carousel, Chariot, Carving Each Side, Parker, 1/2 Size	150.00
Carousel, Chariot, Carving, Full Size	150.00
Carousel, Dog, Spillman	1600.00
Carousel, Elephant, Old Paint, Looff	4800.00
Carousel, Goat, Small	1200.00
Carousel, Horse, Brass Pole & Stirrup, Cast Iron Coca-Cola Base, 1920s	800.00
Carousel, Horse, Carmel-Borelli	2650.00
Carousel, Horse, Cast Aluminum	500.00
Carousel, Horse, Dentzel Mare, C.1905, Hand-Carved	2750.00
Carousel, Horse, Dentzel Prancer, Original Eyes	2100.00
Carousel, Horse, Herchell Spillman, Wood	500.00
Carousel, Horse, Illions, Inside Row, 43 X 45 In.	1700.00
Carousel, Horse, Illions, Jeweled, Outside Row, 63 X 54 In.	3500.00
Carousel, Horse, Illions, Middle Row, 53 X 48 In.	2500.00
Carousel, Horse, Jewels, Glass Eyes, Brass Pole & Top, Parker	1950.00
Carousel, Horse, Jumper, Tonawanda, 1900, American	995.00
Carousel, Horse, Spillman Jumper, Glass Eyes, Hair Tail, 1915	850.00
Carousel, Horse, Two-Seated, English, C.H.Spooner	1695.00
Carousel, Horse, Wood Body, Metal Head, Legs & Tail, Allan Herchell	300.00
Carousel, Mirror, Lights	35.00
Carousel, Pig, Hand Carved, C.1909, Dentzel	3500.00
Carousel, Pig, Iron Stand	1800.00
Carousel, Tiger, Heyn	3900.00
Carriage, Buckboard, Two Horse, Team Drawn	1000.00

Carriage, Buggy, 4 Passenger, 2 Seats, One Horse 1000.00
Carriage, Cutter, 2 Passenger, Sleigh Bells, Horse Drawn 700.00
Carriage, Jenny Lind Buggy, Black Satin Finish, Lights, Shafts 1650.00
Carriage, Peddler's Wagon, Upholstered, Brakes, Shafts 1650.00
Carriage, Pony, Wicker Sides, Rubber Tires, Sleigh Runners 950.00
Carriage, Sleigh, One Horse, Wicker 415.00
Carriage, Surrey, Pony 985.00
Carriage, Wakefield Tarran Co., Carriage No.0141, Boston, Mass. 375.00
Carriage, 2 Passenger, Side Curtains, Lights, Horse Drawn 1000.00

Cased glass is made with one thin layer of glass over another layer or layers
of colored glass. Many types of art glass were cased. Cased glass is
usually a well-made piece by a reputable factory.
Cased Glass, Epergne, Silver Plate Holder, 10 1/2 In. 125.00
Cased Glass, Sugar Shaker, Cone Pattern, Original Pewter Top, Rose, 5 In. 85.00
Cash Register, Combination Keys On Side, Lift Top, Oak, 1881 .... 275.00
Cash Register, Crank Or Electric, Bronze On Oak Base, 28 X 33 In. 2700.00
Cash Register, Mahogany Case, Inlaid Shells, Scrolls, Fans On Its Face, 1893 .... 1100.00
Cash Register, Metal Ticket Holder, Monitor, Wooden, Patented 1900 .... 200.00
Cash Register, Model 452, Brass 450.00
Cash Register, Monitor, Oak, Decals 500.00
Cash Register, N.C.R., Nickeled Brass 425.00
Cash Register, National, Barber, Brass, Model No.130 .... 325.00
Cash Register, National, Brass, 1905 .... 425.00
Cash Register, National, Brass, 1914, Model 356-G 315.00
Cash Register, National, Bronze, Dated 10-13-17, 10 In. 450.00
Cash Register, National, Floor Model, Oak, Marble Front, 6 Feet .... 1475.00 To 1975.00
Cash Register, National, Floor Model, 5 Drawer, J.E.Hood 1295.00
Cash Register, National, Mahogany, Inlaid Shells, Scrolls, April 4, 1890 ...... 1100.00
Cash Register, National, Model 216, Brass 595.00
Cash Register, National, Model 235-D, Hotel One Side, Cigar On Other 250.00
Cash Register, National, Model 313, Locks 385.00
Cash Register, National, Model 333 .... 400.00
Cash Register, National, Model 349 .... 400.00
Cash Register, National, Model 4121, 1930s 150.00
Cash Register, National, Purchase Sign, Brass 895.00
Cash Register, National, Slotted Top, 2 Glass Sides, 6 In.Square 110.00
Cash Register, Remington, Hotel, Model A-431-S, Marble, Glass & Numbers 230.00
Cash Register, St.Louis, Rings To 4.99 .... 175.00

Castor Set, see also various porcelain and glass categories
Castor Set, Silver Frame & Tongs, Inset Clear Bull's-Eye, 11 1/2 In. 75.00
Castor Set, 3 Bottle, Breakfast, Silver Plate Frame, English 40.00
Castor Set, 3 Bottle, Miniature, Leaf & Lattice Bottles, 6 In. 55.00
Castor Set, 4 Bottle, Cut Crystal, Sheffield Silver, Hallmarked 125.00
Castor Set, 4 Bottle, Cut Glass Bottles, Metal Frame 39.50
Castor Set, 4 Bottle, Glass Frame, 3-Mold Bottles 125.00
Castor Set, 4 Bottle, Glass Holder, Metal Ring Handle 55.00
Castor Set, 4 Bottle, Matched Brilliant Cut, Silver Plate Holder 125.00
Castor Set, 4 Bottle, Miniature, American Shield, Pewter Frame 60.00
Castor Set, 4 Bottle, Paneled, Fine Cut, Matching Glass Holder 150.00
Castor Set, 5 Bottle, Chasing On Skirt, V Shape Bail, Trim, 15 In. 125.00
Castor Set, 5 Bottle, Cut & Polished, Figural Bail 95.00
Castor Set, 5 Bottle, Cut Glass Bottles, Sheffield 125.00
Castor Set, 5 Bottle, Etched, Silver Plate Frame, Meriden 60.00
Castor Set, 5 Bottle, Gothic Pattern, Pewter Frame, Beaded Handle 75.00
Castor Set, 5 Bottle, Massachusetts, 1883, Shelbourne 125.00
Castor Set, 5 Bottle, Pewter Caster, Mustard Spoon 115.00
Castor Set, 5 Bottle, Revolving Stand, Open Handle, Honeycomb Cutting 75.00
Castor Set, 5 Bottle, Revolving, Loop Bail, Gothic Arch, Silver Plate Stand 75.00
Castor Set, 6 Bottle, Crystal, Cut Diamond Pattern, 9 X 6 7/8 X 8 1/4 In. ... 145.00
Castor Set, 6 Bottle, Embossed, Wide Skirt, Trimmed Bail, Revolving 125.00
Castor Set, 6 Bottle, Revolving, Pedestal Base, Cut Bottles, Signed 150.00
Castor Set, 7 Bottle, Ground Glass Bottles, 22 In. 195.00
Castor, Pickle, see also various glass categories
Castor, Pickle, Apple Green Insert, Enameling 200.00
Castor, Pickle, Blue, Starred Button Insert, Silver Frame & Tongs 110.00
Castor, Pickle, Bull's-Eye & Daisy Square Bottles, Server 69.00

Castor, Pickle, Cane Pattern Jar, Tongs, Blue	97.50
Castor, Pickle, Cherubs On Frame, Sapphire Blue Insert, Tongs	150.00
Castor, Pickle, Clear Glass, Silver Lid & Bottom	45.00
Castor, Pickle, Clear Insert, Chicken Finial, Silver Plate	55.00
Castor, Pickle, Clear, Paneled Insert	68.00
Castor, Pickle, Cranberry Insert, Tongs, 4-Footed Frame, 9 3/4 In.	180.00
Castor, Pickle, Cupid & Stag On Frame, Pillar & Diamond Cut	79.50
Castor, Pickle, Cupid & Venus, Plated Lid	32.00
Castor, Pickle, Cut Glass Inserts, Footed, Reed & Barton, Silver Plate	170.00
Castor, Pickle, Diamond Cut, Tongs	69.50
Castor, Pickle, Double Inserts, 4-Footed, Ornate Finials, Silver Plate	125.00
Castor, Pickle, Embossed Scene, Clear Panel Jar, Silver Plate Lid	62.00
Castor, Pickle, Enameled Frame, Blue	265.00
Castor, Pickle, Floral Feet, Flowers & Fish Top, Tongs, Silver Lid	195.00
Castor, Pickle, Footed Frame, Bail, Rippled Jars, Frosted Chick On Lid	135.00
Castor, Pickle, Footed, Full Figure, Bird Finial, Enameled Insert	390.00
Castor, Pickle, Footed, Inverted Thumbprint Insert, Enameled Coralene	400.00
Castor, Pickle, Fork, Cranberry, Paneled Sprig, Enamel Flowers, Insert	200.00
Castor, Pickle, Fork, Silver Plate Lid, Clear Insert, Reed & Barton	71.00
Castor, Pickle, Inverted Thumbprint Insert, Cranberry, Tongs	200.00
Castor, Pickle, Inverted Thumbprint, Cobalt Blue Insert, Enameled Design	185.00
Castor, Pickle, Paneled Sprig, Cranberry, Tongs, Frame	225.00
Castor, Pickle, Peacocks In Garden Around Base, Embossed Lid	65.00
Castor, Pickle, Plume, Engraved, Original Cover & Frame, Ruby Stained	245.00
Castor, Pickle, Pressed Glass, Vertical Plume, Tulips & Leaves, Red Flashed	245.00
Castor, Pickle, Ruby Glass, Mary Gregory, Marked Footed Frame	425.00
Castor, Pickle, Satin Glass, Enameled Flowers, Footed Tufts Frame	400.00
Castor, Pickle, Shape Of Huge Acorn, Cranberry	167.00
Castor, Pickle, Silver Frame, 4 Feet, Tongs, King's Crown Pattern, 11 1/2 In.	135.00
Castor, Pickle, Silver Plate Frame & Tongs, Elk Medallion	110.00
Castor, Pickle, Silver Plate Frame, Lid & Tongs	100.00
Castor, Pickle, Threaded, Engraved Insert In Claw & Ball Footed Holder	85.00
Castor, Pickle, Thumbprint, Enameled Dragonflies, Tongs, Amber	235.00
Castor, Pickle, Tongs, Inverted Thumbprint Art Glass, Enameled Jars	215.00
Castor, Pickle, Tongs, Silver Plate, Hartford Silver Company	60.00
Castor, Pickle, Tongs, Swirl Cut & Diamond	80.00
Castor, Pickle, Wilcox Silver Plate Co., Figures Around Base Of Holder	95.00

Catalogue, see Paper, Catalogue
Caughley, see also Salopian

Caughley, Cup & Saucer, Blue & White, C.1795	85.00
Caughley, Sauce Boat, Taj Mahal, Elephant Parade, Salopian	125.00

*The firm of Cauldon Limited worked in Staffordshire, Great Britain,
and went through many name changes. John Ridgway made porcelain at Cauldon
Place, Hanley until 1855. The firm of John Ridgway Bates and Co.
of Cauldon Place worked from 1856 to 1859. It became the Bates,
Brown-Westhead-Moore and Co. from 1859 to 1862. Brown-Westhead,
Moore and Co. worked from 1862 to 1904. About 1890 this firm started
using the word Cauldon or Cauldon ware as part of the mark. Cauldon
Ltd. worked from 1905 to 1920, Cauldon Potteries from 1920 to 1962.*

Cauldon, see also Indian Tree

Cauldon, Cup & Saucer, White, Gold Decoration	25.00
Cauldon, Eggcup	10.00
Cauldon, Plate, Portrait Of English Bulldog, Signed, 10 1/4 In.	40.00
Cauldon, Plate, Tiffany & Co., 8 In.	18.00

*Celadon is a Chinese porcelain having a velvet-textured green-gray glaze.
Japanese and Korean factories also made a celadon-colored glaze.*

Celadon, Bottle, Perfume, Green On White, Gold Hearts, Cased, 4 In.	30.00
Celadon, Bottle, Perfume, White Cased Glass	30.00
Celadon, Bowl, Covered, Cloverleaf, Green, Raised Sprigs, 4 In.	70.00
Celadon, Bowl, Red & Green, Gold Sprays, 2 5/8 X 6 In.Diameter	40.00
Celadon, Bowl, 3 Feet, Chinese, Early Mid-Ching, 5 1/2 X 4 1/2 In.	250.00
Celadon, Brushpot, Green Jade, Carved, Scenic, Seal Of Ch'ien Lung, 6 1/4 In.	9000.00
Celadon, Charger, Design Under Green Glaze, Enameled Figures, 14 1/2 In.	350.00
Celadon, Cracker Jar, Overall Enameling, Silver Top, Shrine Shaped Handle	165.00
Celadon, Dish, Glazed, Japanese, C.1800, Painted Seal Mark, 15 In.	150.00
Celadon, Dish, Soap, Hanging, White Insert, 5 X 4 X 3 3/4 In.	65.00

Celadon, Figurine, Boy, Dragon Issuing Flaming Pearl, Jade, 1800s, 5 1/2 In.	1300.00
Celadon, Garden Seat, 2 Rows Of Bosses Molded, Chinese, 18 1/4 In., Pair	2000.00
Celadon, Holder, Brush, 4 In.	30.00
Celadon, Holder, Spoon, Raised Enamel Flowers, 5 X 2 In.	27.50
Celadon, Jar, Ball, Covered, 8 In.	159.00
Celadon, Jardiniere, Embossed Underglaze, 4-Sided & Footed, 7 1/2 X 8 In.	275.00
Celadon, Jardiniere, Octagonal, Flower & Bird In Relief, 9 3/4 X 12 1/2 In.	450.00
Celadon, Pitcher, Water, High Bulbous, 9 In.	75.00
Celadon, Planter, Scrolling Dragon In Relief, Footed, 2 X 1 1/4 X 1 1/2 In.	20.00
Celadon, Plate, Birds, Butterflies & Flowers, 7 1/4 In.	40.00
Celadon, Plate, Flower & Fence, Chinese Export, Ming Dynasty, 7 7/8 In.	75.00
Celadon, Plate, Raised Flowers, Intermingled Gold Design, 8 1/2 In.	40.00
Celadon, Pot, Wine, Melon-Form, Sea-Green Glaze, C.1200, 8 1/4 In.	1000.00
Celadon, Teapot, Wrapped Wire Handle, Intermingled Gold Design	70.00
Celadon, Umbrella Stand, Raised Design Of Bird In Flight, 6-Sided, 24 In.	450.00
Celadon, Vase, Enameled, Oriental, 9 1/2 In., Pair	200.00
Celadon, Vase, Green & Blue, Glazed Porcelain, C.1800s, 16 1/2 In.	245.00
Celadon, Vase, Hexagonal, Bird & Flower Design, 9 1/2 In.	135.00
Celadon, Vase, Korean Style, Inlaid, Flowers, 11 1/2 In.	225.00
Celadon, Vase, Plants, Leaves, Dragon & Jui-I Fungus Motif, 1736-95, 9 In.	150.00
Celadon, Vase, Raised Pink Floral, Green, Cylindrical, 6 1/4 In.	75.00
Celadon, Vase, Willow Trees, Grasses, Ovoid Body, Korean, 7 In.	50.00
Celluloid, Album, Photo, Musical, 2 Tunes	45.00
Celluloid, Album, Photograph, Signed	45.00
Celluloid, Bookmark, Kimball Pianos	6.00
Celluloid, Boudoir Set, Clock, Vase, Boxes, Brushes, 12 Piece	69.00
Celluloid, Box, Collar	45.00
Celluloid, Box, Dresser, Footman & 2 Children Jumping Rope	24.00
Celluloid, Box, Glove, Raised Cherub, Brass Latch & Hinges, 11 In.	18.00
Celluloid, Brush & Comb Set, Infant, Art Deco, 1930	12.00
Celluloid, Case, Stamp, Collier Company	6.00
Celluloid, Case, Watch, Scrolled	8.50
Celluloid, Clock & Dresser Set, Bud Vase, 3 Boxes, 9 Piece	75.00
Celluloid, Comb, Hair, Jeweled	12.50
Celluloid, Comb, Lady's, Curved, Painted Flowers, Set Of 12	30.00
Celluloid, Doll, Carnival	10.00
Celluloid, Doll, Dutch Girl, 8 1/2 In.	23.00
Celluloid, Dresser Set, Amber With Ivory Color, 5 Piece	18.00
Celluloid, Dresser Set, Art Deco, 9 Piece	70.00
Celluloid, Dresser Set, Boxed	65.00
Celluloid, Dresser Set, Yellow, 3 Piece	12.00
Celluloid, Fan, Chain, Toronto, Canada	10.00
Celluloid, Figurine, Boy Pulling Rickshaw, Lady & Parasol, 6 1/2 In.	25.00
Celluloid, Figurine, Santa, Pack On Back, 2 1/2 In.	10.00
Celluloid, Frame, Easel Type, 4 1/4 X 5 1/2 In.	5.50
Celluloid, Hair Receiver	3.50
Celluloid, Holder, Cigarette	5.00
Celluloid, Mirror, Hand, Dated 1892	5.00
Celluloid, Opener, Letter, Advertising, Jones-McDuffle China Merchants	7.00
Celluloid, Opener, Letter, Leg Shape Handle, Percy Legge, Worsted Mohair	15.00
Celluloid, Pincushion	1.75
Celluloid, Pulls, Curtain, Victorian Child, Pair	7.00
Celluloid, Rattle, Decorated	14.00
Celluloid, Rattle, Sunbonnet Baby, 1 End, Clown On Other	25.00
Celluloid, Santa Claus	12.00
Celluloid, Shoehorn, Colored Like Ribbon Candy, 15 In.	12.00
Celluloid, Shoehorn, Long Handle	3.00
Celluloid, Stretcher, Glove	7.00
Celluloid, Tag, Luggage, Champion Harvesting Machines	29.00
Celluloid, Tape Measure, General Electric	8.00
Celluloid, Toothpick, Bourier Gin	7.00

 The Ceramic Art Company of Trenton, New Jersey, was established in 1889 by J. Coxon and W. Lenox, and was an early producer of American Belleek porcelain. Some lines are still being manufactured.

Ceramic Art Co., Pitcher, Cider, Belleek, Portrait Indian Chief	135.00
Ceramic Art Co., Pitcher, Cider, Hand-Painted Foliage	65.00

Ceramic Art Co., Pitcher, Cylindrical, Belleek, Palette, 14 In. 95.00

Chalkware is really plaster of Paris decorated with watercolors. The pieces were molded from known Staffordshire and other porcelain models and painted and sold as inexpensive decorations. Most of this type of chalkware was made from about 1820 to 1870.

Chalkware, Bank, Elephant, Standing Tub, 12 In.	9.00
Chalkware, Betty Boop, 15 In.	200.00
Chalkware, Bookends, Cat	15.00 To 17.00
Chalkware, Boy With Basket Of Fruit, Victorian, 10 In.	55.00
Chalkware, Bunny In Chair, 5 In.	5.00
Chalkware, Bust, Esther Hunt, Lotus Bud	29.50
Chalkware, Candlestick, Pair	5.00
Chalkware, Cat, Glass Eyes, Black, 10 In.	26.00
Chalkware, Cat, 4 In.	35.00
Chalkware, Charlie McCarthy, 15 1/2 In.	22.00
Chalkware, Counter Pig, The Taste Is So Good, 13 3/4 In.	190.00
Chalkware, Dog, Collie, 11 1/2 In.	7.50
Chalkware, Dog, Spaniel, From Carnival	8.50
Chalkware, Dog, Victor, 4 1/2 In.	17.50
Chalkware, Donald Duck, Carnival	12.50
Chalkware, Figurine, Majorette	5.00
Chalkware, Flapper	10.00
Chalkware, Girl In Tennis Dress, Racket In Hand, 12 1/2 In.	28.00
Chalkware, Girl, Bobbed Hair, Tam, Trousers, Sweater, 9 In.	7.50
Chalkware, Half Doll, Dressed As Flapper, Marked Circle, 1925	30.00
Chalkware, Kewpie, Carnival, 8 In.	8.00
Chalkware, Kewpie, 7 3/4 In.	14.00
Chalkware, Kitten, Yellow, Streaked Red, 19th Century, 7 1/2 In.	425.00
Chalkware, Lion, On Base, 19 In.	25.00
Chalkware, Lone Ranger, Carnival	12.50
Chalkware, Pinocchio, Carnival	12.50
Chalkware, Rabbit, Seated, Hollow, Ears Extended	295.00
Chalkware, Sailor Boy, 9 In.	7.50
Chalkware, Sailor Girl, Cap, Blouse, Long Pants, 12 1/4 In.	7.50
Chalkware, Santa, Hand-Painted, 10 In.	15.00
Chalkware, Seated Black Boy, 11 In.	50.00
Chalkware, Snow White, 14 In.	20.00
Chalkware, Soldier, World War I	18.00
Chalkware, Whooping Crane, 12 In.	10.50
Chalkware, Young Woman Standing At Wall, Green Base, 14 1/2 In.	45.00
Chantilly, Cache-Pot, Hunting Horn Mark In Red, Kakiemon, C.1735, 5 1/2 In.	3300.00
Chantilly, Dish, Quatrefoil, Red Mark, Kakiemon, C.1735, 9 3/4 In.	700.00
Chantilly, Plate, Horn Mark, Letter E, C.1760, 9 1/2 In.	150.00
Chantilly, Pot, Rouge, Cover, 3 X 2 1/2 In.	115.00
Charlie Chaplin, Book, Cartoon, Up In The Air, 1917, Donohue Co.	45.00
Charlie Chaplin, Clock, Desk, 1917, Portrait Of Charlie	170.00
Charlie McCarthy, Bank, Composition	70.00
Charlie McCarthy, Box, School Kit, Pictures Of Charlie, 1938	18.00
Charlie McCarthy, Doll, Tin	50.00
Charlie McCarthy, Doll, Tuxedo, Composition	65.00
Charlie McCarthy, Game, Question & Answer, 1937, 6 X 8 In.	25.00
Charlie McCarthy, Game, Radio Party, 1938	15.00
Charlie McCarthy, Game, Rummy, 1938	8.00
Charlie McCarthy, Hand Dummy, Dated 1938, Original Box	45.00
Charlie McCarthy, Puzzle, Original Box	12.00
Charlie McCarthy, Spoon, Detective, Silver Plate	12.00

Chelsea grape pattern was made before 1840. A small bunch of grapes in a raised design, colored with purple or blue luster, is on the border of the white plate. Most of the pieces are unmarked. The pattern is sometimes called Aynsley or Grandmother.

Chelsea Grape, Plate, Purple Luster, 9 In.	12.50
Chelsea Grape, Plate, 7 In., Pair	12.00
Chelsea Sprig, Cup & Saucer, Purple Luster	35.00
Chelsea Sprig, Plate, Cake, Purple Luster	55.00
Chelsea Sprig, Tea Set	195.00

Chelsea Keramic Art Works, see Dedham

Chelsea porcelain was made in the Chelsea area of London from about 1745 to 1784. Recent copies of this work have been made from the original molds.

Chelsea-Derby, Candlestick, Bocage, Hunting Scene, Gold Anchor Mark, 12 In.	500.00
Chelsea, Figurine, Dalmatians, Gold Anchor, Pair	90.00
Chelsea, Figurine, Mother & Pup, Gold Band On Base, Gold Anchor Mark, Pair	185.00
Chelsea, Mug, Globular Body, Loop Handle, Gilt Border, C.1780, 3 7/8 In.	350.00
Chelsea, Tea Set, Teapot, Creamer, Sugar, Waste, 6 Plates, Cups & Saucers	650.00
Chelsea, Teapot, Violets & Grapes, C.1844	125.00
Chelsea, Vase, Birds & Flowers, Gold Anchor, 9 In., Pair	2800.00

Chinese export porcelain is all the many kinds of porcelain made in China for export to America and Europe in the eighteenth and nineteenth centuries. Included in the category are Nanking, Canton, Chinese Lowestoft, Armorial, Jesuit, and other types of the ware.

Chinese Export, see also Canton, Celadon, Nanking

Chinese Export, Bowl & Saucer, Montgomerie Quartering Eglinton, Gilt, C.1790	200.00
Chinese Export, Bowl, Aqua Interior, Pastel Flowers Outside, 2 X 8 In.Diam.	40.00
Chinese Export, Bowl, Black Floral & Festoons, 1770-80, 10 1/2 X 4 1/2 In.	525.00
Chinese Export, Bowl, Famille Rose, Floral Scene, C.1750, 9 In., Pair	1000.00
Chinese Export, Bowl, Handle, Garden Scenes, Porcelain, 10 In.Diameter	385.00
Chinese Export, Bowl, Mandarin Palette, Floral, Insects, Pomegranates, Scrolls	100.00
Chinese Export, Bowl, Rice, Blue & White, Canton, 5 1/4 In.Diameter	65.00
Chinese Export, Bowl, Rose Canton, Oriental Landscape, C.1775, 11 1/4 In.	225.00
Chinese Export, Bowl, Shipping, Interior Floral Cluster, C.1775, 10 1/8 In.	700.00
Chinese Export, Bowl, Soup, Blue & White, Canton, C.1840, 6 In.Diameter	65.00
Chinese Export, Charger, Cabbage Leaf, 1830-50, 14 5/8 In.Diameter	175.00
Chinese Export, Charger, Famille Rose, Meadow Scene, Sheep, 1750s, 13 5/8 In.	500.00
Chinese Export, Creamer, Black Floral Design On White, Helmet, 1770-80	185.00
Chinese Export, Cup & Saucer, Demitasse, Blue & White, Cup, 2 1/8 In.	65.00
Chinese Export, Cup, Coat Of Arms & 2 Roses, Blue Flowers Inside, 2 1/2 In.	55.00
Chinese Export, Cup, Rose Design, Set Of 4	60.00
Chinese Export, Dish, Vegetable, Covered, Blue Fitzhugh, 1790-1810, 9 5/8 In.	375.00
Chinese Export, Figurine, Peacock, Enameled, 19th Century, 19 5/8 In.	800.00
Chinese Export, Figurine, Puppy, Seated, Wears Collar With Bell, 18th Century	650.00
Chinese Export, Jar, Ginger, Armorial, Flowers	185.00
Chinese Export, Jar, Ginger, Hand-Painted, Marked, 3 1/2 In.	32.00
Chinese Export, Jug, Milk, Brown Fitzhugh, Helmet Shaped, C.1820, 5 In.	275.00
Chinese Export, Jug, Milk, Green Floral, Helmet Shaped, Splayed Foot, C.1790	145.00
Chinese Export, Lamp, Famille Rose, Birds & Flowers, 15 1/2 In., Pair	1200.00
Chinese Export, Pitcher, Helmet, Brown Floral Design, C.1800	195.00
Chinese Export, Plate, Birds, Flowering Tree, Stream, Fenced Garden, Lacquer	400.00
Chinese Export, Plate, Blue & Imari Red Prunus, Cobalt Blue Border, 9 In.	45.00
Chinese Export, Plate, Crested, C.1770, Set Of 6, 8 7/8 In.	200.00
Chinese Export, Plate, Famille Rose, Central Bouquet, C.1740, 8 7/8 In., Pair	300.00
Chinese Export, Plate, Famille Rose, Ch'ien Lung Period, 9 In.	160.00
Chinese Export, Plate, Famille Rose, K'ang-Hsi Period, 1662-1723, 9 In.	165.00
Chinese Export, Plate, Fitzhugh, Green, 10 In.	125.00
Chinese Export, Plate, Hunter, Sweetheart Seated, Tree, Hounds, Castle, Scrolls	500.00
Chinese Export, Plate, Medallion, Boats, River, Scroll, Bellflowers, Egg & Dart	325.00
Chinese Export, Plate, Orange Fitzhugh, American Eagle, 7 3/4 In., Pair	4100.00
Chinese Export, Plate, Polychrome Floral Enamel, 9 In.	65.00
Chinese Export, Plate, Soup, Famille Rose, Forest Scene, 8 7/8 In., Pair	525.00
Chinese Export, Plate, Soup, Jefferson Crest, C.1790, Set, 9 3/4 In.	400.00
Chinese Export, Plate, Soup, Orange Fitzhugh, American Eagle, 1800s, 10 In.	2300.00
Chinese Export, Plate, Soup, Yellow Fitzhugh, C.1800, 7 7/8 In., Pair	2100.00
Chinese Export, Plate, 1000 Butterflies, 9 1/2 In.	125.00
Chinese Export, Platter & Plate Set, En Suite, Green Fitzhugh, C.1820	575.00
Chinese Export, Platter & Strainer, Mollusks, Crustaceans, Seaweed, Gilding	1200.00
Chinese Export, Platter, Armorial, Continental Coat Of Arms, Floral, Stand	450.00
Chinese Export, Platter, Famille Rose, Scenic, C.1760, 10 5/8 In., Pair	550.00
Chinese Export, Platter, Orange Fitzhugh, American Eagle, 1800s, 12 In.	3400.00
Chinese Export, Punch Bowl, Enameled, C.1775, 15 3/4 In.	2700.00
Chinese Export, Punch Bowl, English Hunting Scenes, C.1780-90, 11 1/2 In.	900.00
Chinese Export, Punch Bowl, Famille Rose, Hunting, C.1780, 15 3/8 In.	2300.00

Chinese Export, Punch Bowl, Famille Rose, Ormolu Mounted, 10 3/4 In., Pair 3000.00
Chinese Export, Punch Bowl, Rose Medallion, C.1775, 15 1/4 In. 1600.00
Chinese Export, Sauceboat, Fitzhugh, Blue & White, 7 1/2 X 2 1/2 In. 145.00
Chinese Export, Saucer, Made For Persia, C.1790-1820, Set Of 3, 11 In. 100.00
Chinese Export, Sugar, Paneled, Gadroon Rim, Leaf Capped Scroll Handles, Lid 375.00
Chinese Export, Table, Game, Gold Lacquer, 3 Dragon Feet, 1840, 30 X 36 In. 1800.00
Chinese Export, Tankard, Oriental Figures, C.1750, 5 1/4 In. 375.00
Chinese Export, Tea Set, Berry Finial On Sugar, C.1780, 3 Piece 1085.00
Chinese Export, Teabowl & Saucer, Brown Fitzhugh, Butterflies, Blossoms 200.00
Chinese Export, Teacup, Hand-Painted Coat-Of-Arms, Scalloped Rim, 2 In. 65.00
Chinese Export, Teapot, Black Floral Design On White, C.1770-80 .... 385.00
Chinese Export, Teapot, Gilt Design, Strap Handle, Strawberry Finial 85.00
Chinese Export, Teapot, Globular Body, C.1740, 4 1/4 In. 375.00
Chinese Export, Teapot, Lobed Bombe Sides, Gadroon Rim, Shells, Scroll Handle 500.00
Chinese Export, Teapot, Mandarin Palette, 5 Figures, Lid, 1780s, 5 3/4 In. 250.00
Chinese Export, Urn, Flowering Tree Design, Signed, 14 1/2 X 22 In.Diameter 155.00
Chinese Export, Vase, Blue On White, Birds In Trees, 1890-1910, 8 In., Pair 75.00
Chinese Export, Vase, Cafe-Au-Lait Ground, Leaf Shape Panels, Floral, Fruits 800.00
Chinese Export, Vase, Famille Rose, Garden Scene, Ovoid, 1780s, 10 5/8 In. 550.00
Chinese Export, Vase, Gourd Shape, Hand-Painted, 19th Century, 4 1/4 In. 40.00
Chinese Export, Vase, Rectangular, Round Base, Flowers, C.1850 .... 135.00
Chinese Export, Wine Cooler, Rose Canton, 2-Handled, C.1765, 6 5/8 In. 1100.00

Chocolate glass, sometimes mistakenly called caramel slag, was made by the Indiana Tumbler and Goblet Company of Greentown, Indiana, from 1900 to 1903.

Chocolate Glass, Berry Bowl, Cactus, 4 In.Diameter 35.00
Chocolate Glass, Berry Set, Cactus, Greentown, 7 Piece 185.00
Chocolate Glass, Berry Set, Leaf Bracket, 7 Piece 225.00
Chocolate Glass, Berry Set, 5 Sauces 450.00
Chocolate Glass, Bowl, Berry, Master, Geneva, Oval, Greentown 75.00
Chocolate Glass, Cat On A Hamper, Tall 195.00
Chocolate Glass, Compote, Footed, 3 1/2 In. 45.00
Chocolate Glass, Compote, Jelly, Cactus 105.00
Chocolate Glass, Compote, Jelly, Knob Stem, Greentown 100.00
Chocolate Glass, Cracker Jar, Lid, Cactus, Greentown 189.00
Chocolate Glass, Creamer, Austrian 75.00
Chocolate Glass, Creamer, Dewey, Greentown 50.00
Chocolate Glass, Creamer, Shuttle Decoration, Greentown 75.00
Chocolate Glass, Cruet, Cactus .... 90.00 To 175.00
Chocolate Glass, Cruet, Leaf Bracket, Original Stopper .... 115.00 To 165.00
Chocolate Glass, Dish, Butter 90.00
Chocolate Glass, Dish, Butter, Cover, Leaf Bracket 105.00
Chocolate Glass, Dish, Butter, Leaf Pattern, Greentown 295.00
Chocolate Glass, Dish, Dolphin 175.00
Chocolate Glass, Dish, Rabbit On Nest 195.00
Chocolate Glass, Dish, Relish 110.00
Chocolate Glass, Dish, Sauce, Cactus 40.00
Chocolate Glass, Figurine, Cat On A Hamper, Greentown, Tall 165.00
Chocolate Glass, Jar, Cactus, 12 X 11 1/2 In. 60.00
Chocolate Glass, Lamp, Table, Dome Inserted Into Openwork Frame, Metal Base 1300.00
Chocolate Glass, Lamp, 7 Panel, Fancy Frame Work & Base 175.00

Chocolate Glass, Pitcher, Cactus Pattern,
Greentown, 6 In.

Chocolate Glass, Mug, Cactus, Greentown, 3 1/2 In. 75.00
Chocolate Glass, Mug, Serenade 65.00
Chocolate Glass, Mug, Shuttle, 3 1/4 In. 48.00
Chocolate Glass, Nappy, Cactus, Triangular 48.00
Chocolate Glass, Nappy, Leaf Bracket 40.00
Chocolate Glass, Pitcher, Cactus Pattern, Greentown, 6 In. .... Illus 80.00
Chocolate Glass, Pitcher, Cactus, Red Agate Feet 150.00
Chocolate Glass, Plate, Serenade, 8 1/2 In. .... 100.00 To 125.00
Chocolate Glass, Salt & Pepper, Leaf Bracket, Greentown 60.00
Chocolate Glass, Saucer, Cactus, 4 In. 35.00
Chocolate Glass, Spooner, Leaf Bracket .... 55.00 To 58.00
Chocolate Glass, Stein, Castle, Pouring Spout .... 75.00 To 85.00
Chocolate Glass, Sugar, Covered, Leaf Bracket, Greentown 65.00
Chocolate Glass, Sugar, Geneva 45.00
Chocolate Glass, Syrup, Cactus, Dewey Lid 85.00
Chocolate Glass, Syrup, Cord Drapery .... 145.00 To 185.00
Chocolate Glass, Syrup, Shuttle, Greentown 74.00
Chocolate Glass, Tumbler, Cactus .... 29.00 To 40.00
Chocolate Glass, Tumbler, Cactus Pattern, Set Of 6 .... 210.00
Chocolate Glass, Tumbler, Holly Amber 375.00
Chocolate Glass, Tumbler, Leaf Bracket 50.00
Chocolate Glass, Tumbler, Sawtooth 40.00
Chocolate Glass, Tumbler, Shuttle .... 48.00 To 55.00
Chocolate Glass, Uneeda Milk Biscuit 80.00
Christmas Plate, see Collector, Plate

Christmas Tree, Light Bulb,
Made In Japan, Set Of 19

Christmas Tree, Candleholder, Amber 9.00
Christmas Tree, Candleholder, Green 9.00
Christmas Tree, Candleholder, Metal Spring, Flower Shape, 1890s 45.00
Christmas Tree, Light Bulb, Andy Gump 23.00
Christmas Tree, Light Bulb, Ball With Stars, Green 4.00
Christmas Tree, Light Bulb, Ball With Stars, Red 4.00
Christmas Tree, Light Bulb, Bird, 1890s 10.00
Christmas Tree, Light Bulb, Birdcage 4.50
Christmas Tree, Light Bulb, Bluebird 4.00
Christmas Tree, Light Bulb, Fat Santa 10.00
Christmas Tree, Light Bulb, Father Christmas 10.00
Christmas Tree, Light Bulb, Frog 20.00
Christmas Tree, Light Bulb, Girl Hand To Mouth 8.00
Christmas Tree, Light Bulb, Grapes, Purple, Set Of 8 .... 15.00
Christmas Tree, Light Bulb, Japanese Lantern, Milk Glass 3.00
Christmas Tree, Light Bulb, Lantern 10.00
Christmas Tree, Light Bulb, Lantern, Blue & White, 1890s 6.00
Christmas Tree, Light Bulb, Lantern, Green, Red & Yellow 10.00
Christmas Tree, Light Bulb, Made In Japan, Set Of 19 .... Illus 55.00
Christmas Tree, Light Bulb, Parrot .... 4.00 To 4.50
Christmas Tree, Light Bulb, Red House, Snow On Roof 12.00
Christmas Tree, Light Bulb, Rose 4.00
Christmas Tree, Light Bulb, Santa Claus, Red Face Each Side, 1890s 16.00
Christmas Tree, Light Bulb, Santa On Both Sides, Milk Glass, 3 In. 20.00
Christmas Tree, Light Bulb, Santa With Pack, Full Length, Milk Glass 8.00
Christmas Tree, Light Bulb, Santa, Head, 2 Faces 8.50
Christmas Tree, Light Bulb, Santa, Milk Glass 15.00

Christmas Tree, Light Bulb, Santa, Standing	8.50
Christmas Tree, Light Bulb, Santa, 8 1/2 In.	22.00
Christmas Tree, Light Bulb, Snowman	3.50 To 8.50
Christmas Tree, Light, Candleholder, Set Of 35	15.00
Christmas Tree, Light, Cobalt	18.00
Christmas Tree, Light, Milk Glass, Blue	15.00
Christmas Tree, Ornament, Angel & Santa Claus, Bisque, Pair	15.00
Christmas Tree, Ornament, Angel Head & Wings, 1890s, 10 X 6 In.	10.00
Christmas Tree, Ornament, Angel Heads On Diamond Shape, 1890s	6.00
Christmas Tree, Ornament, Angel, Composition Face, White Hair, Wings	15.00
Christmas Tree, Ornament, Angel, Spun Glass	17.50
Christmas Tree, Ornament, Angel, Wax	39.00
Christmas Tree, Ornament, Baby, Diecut, Cotton Dress, 1890s, 15 1/2 X 7 In.	15.00
Christmas Tree, Ornament, Ball, Mercury, Cobalt Blue, 2 1/2 In.	20.00
Christmas Tree, Ornament, Ball, Mercury, Gold, Brass Connector, 3 In.	15.00
Christmas Tree, Ornament, Ball, Mercury, Green, Brass Connector, 4 In.	20.00
Christmas Tree, Ornament, Ball, Mercury, Silver, Brass Connector, 3 In.	15.00
Christmas Tree, Ornament, Ball, Mercury, Silver, 2 In.	10.00
Christmas Tree, Ornament, Ball, Opalescent	7.00
Christmas Tree, Ornament, Basket Of Flowers, Dove, 1890s, 7 X 7 In.	8.00
Christmas Tree, Ornament, Bell	4.00
Christmas Tree, Ornament, Bell, Papier-Mache, Set Of 3	8.50
Christmas Tree, Ornament, Bell, Santa Claus	5.00
Christmas Tree, Ornament, Bird, Blue, Wing Hair Tail	15.00
Christmas Tree, Ornament, Boat	20.00
Christmas Tree, Ornament, Camel, 2-Sided, Dresden Paper	28.00
Christmas Tree, Ornament, Clamp On Bird, Mercury Glass	12.50
Christmas Tree, Ornament, Doll Head, Glass, Painted Face, China Eyes	50.00
Christmas Tree, Ornament, Doll's Head, Thin Glass, Painted Face, China Eyes	65.00
Christmas Tree, Ornament, Fish, Blown Glass	18.00
Christmas Tree, Ornament, Flower	15.00
Christmas Tree, Ornament, Heart	4.00
Christmas Tree, Ornament, Horn	8.00
Christmas Tree, Ornament, Icicle, Twisted Blown Glass	4.00
Christmas Tree, Ornament, Kugel, Round, Mercury Glass	25.00
Christmas Tree, Ornament, Lady, Pressed Cotton	20.00
Christmas Tree, Ornament, Parasol, Wire Wrapped, Closes & Opens	28.00
Christmas Tree, Ornament, Pinecone	5.00
Christmas Tree, Ornament, Santa Claus, Blown Glass	12.00
Christmas Tree, Ornament, Santa Claus, Cotton	20.00
Christmas Tree, Ornament, Santa Claus, Hand Blown, Hand-Painted	15.00
Christmas Tree, Ornament, Santa Claus, Head Turns	45.00
Christmas Tree, Ornament, Santa Claus, Paper & Spun Glass	22.50
Christmas Tree, Ornament, Snow White, 7 Dwarfs, 1939 Disney Enterprises	500.00
Christmas Tree, Ornament, Snowman	38.00
Christmas Tree, Ornament, Star, Beaded	9.00
Christmas Tree, Ornament, Strawberry With Leaves, Bisque, Tin Clip	3.00
Christmas Tree, Ornament, Swan, Blown Glass	9.00
Christmas Tree, Ornament, Table Lamp, Old Fashioned	15.00
Christmas Tree, Ornament, Teapot	18.00
Christmas Tree, Ornament, Tinsel Trimmed Paper, Angels, Santas, Children	42.50
Christmas Tree, Ornament, Umbrella	18.00
Christmas Tree, Ornament, Vase, Tinsel Wrapped Glass	17.50
Christmas Tree, Ornament, Violin	14.00
Christmas Tree, Ornament, Wire Balloon With Cupid	18.00
Cigar Cutter, see Store, Cutter, Cigar	
Cigar Store Figure, Darkie, C.1900, Holding Cigars	750.00
Cigar Store Figure, Indian, Princess, Holding Cigars, 19th Century	750.00
Cigar Store Figure, Tout, C.1900, Holding Cigars	750.00

Cinnabar is a vermilion or red lacquer. Some pieces are made with hundreds of thicknesses of the lacquer that is later carved.

Cinnabar, Base, Lamp, Electrified, Vase Height, 13 In.	350.00
Cinnabar, Box, Lacquer, Covered, 5 1/2 In.	160.00
Cinnabar, Figurine, Male, Robed, Stand, 13 In.	80.00
Cinnabar, Holder, Matchbox, Design Both Sides, 2 3/8 X 1 5/8 In.	32.50
Cinnabar, Horse, Ch'ien Lung, Jade, Turquoise Inlay, 10 1/2 X 13 1/2 In., Pair	2500.00

Cinnabar, Jar, Ginger, Red, Carved Characters In Garden, Marked, 6 1/2 In.	105.00
Cinnabar, Vase, Black Lacquer Overlay, Flower Design, 8 In.	100.00
Cinnabar, Vase, Bulbous, Carved, Chinese Design, 7 1/2 X 14 In.Diameter	250.00
Cinnabar, Vase, Dimensional Carving, Brown Ground, 6 1/2 In.	55.00
Cinnabar, Vase, Floral, Squared Mid-Section, Lacquer, 9 1/8 In., Pair	110.00
Cinnabar, Vase, Carving, Oriental Scene, 11 In.	135.00

*Civil War mementos are important collectors' items. Most of the pieces
are military items used from 1861 to 1865.*

Civil War, Album, Documenting 150th Regiment, Photos, Generals, 8 X 10 In.	400.00
Civil War, Arm Badge	4.95
Civil War, Atlas, 821 4-Color Maps, 408 Pages, 13 X 16 In.	59.95
Civil War, Ax, U.S. Military Issue, Belt Size, Wood Handle, 5 In. Head	125.00
Civil War, Backpack, Dated 1864	18.00
Civil War, Bag, Medical, Marked Bottles	89.00
Civil War, Bag, Saddle, Medical With Bottles	75.00
Civil War, Belt, Leather, Cartridge Container, Confederate	40.00
Civil War, Binocular, Confederate	40.00
Civil War, Book, Hymns & Hints, 1862, Calendar Inside	22.50
Civil War, Box, Cartridge Plate, Oval Brass, Raised C.S.A.	10.00
Civil War, Box, Dresser, Hand Made, General Stewart & Horse On Top, Bisque	135.00
Civil War, Box, Snuff, Copper, Double Wall, 5 Line Poem, 2 3/4 X 3 1/2 In.	450.00
Civil War, Buckle, Federal Officer's, Embossed Eagle, Brass	55.00
Civil War, Buckle, With Shoulder Loop, U.S.Regulation, 1874	36.00
Civil War, Bugle, Brass, J.W.York, Grand Rapids	85.00
Civil War, Cannon Ball	50.00
Civil War, Canteen, Bull's-Eye, Gettysburg Battlefield	44.00
Civil War, Canteen, Confederate, 30th Reunion	85.00
Civil War, Canteen, Medical	45.00
Civil War, Canteen, Miniature, Chain & Cord, Original Cork, 3 In.Diameter	16.00
Civil War, Canteen, Round, Canvas Cover, Pewter Spout & Cork Stopper	30.00
Civil War, Canteen, Strap, Pewter	25.00
Civil War, Catalog, Ridabock Co., N.Y., Helmets, Shako Caps, Epaulets, Etc.	35.00
Civil War, Cup, Collapsible, Hard Rubber, Folds Flat, 1 In., Open, 2 1/2 In.	79.50
Civil War, Cutlass, Scabbard, Navy, Brass Hilt	70.00
Civil War, Diary, Captain Cooke	100.00
Civil War, Diary, Tintype Of Soldier To Whom It Belonged	335.00
Civil War, Envelope, Anti General Scott Cartoon	5.00
Civil War, Epaulets, Colonel's, Gold Bullion Boards, Silk Embroidery, Box	425.00
Civil War, Flag, Veteran's, Set Of 12	11.00
Civil War, Flask, Powder With Baffle, 9 1/2 X 6 1/2 X 1 1/2 In.	192.50
Civil War, Flask, Powder, Tin	35.00
Civil War, Holster, Cavalry Gear, Pouch For Horseshoe, Dragoon Pattern	395.00
Civil War, Kit, Field, Canteen, Plate, Utensils, C.1860, 3 3/4 X 8 1/2 In.	225.00
Civil War, Knapsack	60.00
Civil War, Knuckle, Fighting, Found On Battlefield At Lexington	12.00
Civil War, Measure, Cannon Powder, Made From Steer Horn	90.00
Civil War, Medal Of Honor	1200.00
Civil War, Mold, Hat, West Point Cadet, Wooden	65.00
Civil War, Musket Sling	15.00
Civil War, Photograph, Soldier In Full Dress, 4 X 6 In.	10.00
Civil War, Pouch, Dress, Officer's, Gilt Frame, Buckle & Mounts	350.00
Civil War, Pouch, Leather, Infantry, U.S. Plate On Flap, Shoulder Strap	225.00
Civil War, Revolver, Remington, Cap & Ball	215.00
Civil War, Saber, Infantry Officer, Inscribed C.W.	265.00
Civil War, Sword, N.C.O., 1861	60.00
Civil War, Sword, U.S.Cavalry, Dated 1865	145.00
Civil War, Trivet, Fireplace, Hand Forged	32.00
Civil War, Tumbler, Whiskey, Emblem & 13 Star Flag, Flint	85.00
CKAW, see Dedham	

*Clambroth glass, popular in the Victorian era, is a grayish color and is
semiopaque like clambroth*

Clambroth, Bottle, Barber, Witch Hazel, Original Top	57.50
Clambroth, Bottle, Bay Rum, Original Stopper	22.00
Clambroth, Bottle, Cologne, Original Stopper, Bellflower, 9 1/2 In.	175.00
Clambroth, Candleholder, With Pewter, 10 1/2 In.	150.00

Clambroth, Candlestick, Crucifix 35.00
Clambroth, Candlestick, Dolphin, Sandwich 325.00
Clambroth, Candlestick, Opalescent, Teardrop In Stem, 7 1/4 In., Pair 150.00
Clambroth, Candlestick, Petal & Loop, Sandwich Glass, 7 In., Pair 300.00
Clambroth, Dish, Cupped Hands, Blue 25.00
Clambroth, Dresser Set, 2 Bottles, Candleholder, Jar, Yellow, 3 Piece 95.00
Clambroth, Eggcup, Diamond Point, Flint 110.00
Clambroth, Flower Frog, Footed 27.00
Clambroth, Goblet, Cut Bellflower, Flint 225.00
Clambroth, Lamp, Miniature, 6 In. 35.00
Clambroth, Lamp, Whale Oil, Gold, Ribbed Shaft Overlay, Opaque 850.00
Clambroth, Lamp, Whale Oil, Paneled Font, Baluster Base, 8 3/4 In. 225.00
Clambroth, Lamp, White Shade, Round Wick & Pontil, 22 In., Pair 270.00
Clambroth, Mug, Bird Design, Footed 32.50
Clambroth, Pipe, Battle Creek, Michigan, Glass 15.00
Clambroth, Plate, Souvenir, Little Sioux Savings Bank 14.00
Clambroth, Salt, Waffle Base, Flint 40.00
Clambroth, Tumbler, Whiskey 165.00

Clewell ware was made in limited quantities by Charles Walter Clewell of Canton, Ohio, from 1902 to 1955. Pottery was covered with a thin coating of bronze, then treated to make the bronze turn different colors. Pieces covered with copper, brass, or silver were also made. Mr. Clewell's secret formula for blue patina bronze was burned when he died in 1965.

Clewell, Mug, Nailhead Copper 100.00
Clewell, Vase, Green, Rustic, 7 1/2 X 6 X 4 In. 75.00

Clews pottery was made by George Clews & Co.of Brownhill Pottery, Tunstall, England, from 1806 to 1861.

Clews, see also Flow Blue
Clews, Cup & Saucer, American Eagle On Urn, Deep Blue 250.00
Clews, Cup & Saucer, Hunting Dogs, Dark Blue 85.00
Clews, Cup & Saucer, Jessamine, Mulberry 65.00
Clews, Plate, Burning Of Merchants Exchange, N.Y., Black & White, 10 1/4 In. 110.00
Clews, Plate, Dr.Syntax Reading His Tour, C.1820, Marked, 9 In.Diameter 195.00
Clews, Plate, Landing Of Lafayette, Blue, 6 3/4 In. 185.00
Clews, Plate, Landing Of Lafayette, 9 In. 340.00
Clews, Plate, Newburgh, Hudson River, Sepia, 17 1/2 In. 95.00
Clews, Plate, Peace & Plenty, Dark Blue, 9 In. 245.00
Clews, Plate, Soup, Sancho Meets Dapple, Blue, 8 3/4 In. 155.00
Clews, Plate, States, 10 1/2 In. 275.00
Clews, Platter, Hudson River, Black & White, 15 1/2 In. 100.00

The Clifton Pottery was founded by William Long in Clifton, New Jersey, in 1905. He worked there until 1908 making a line called Crystal Patina.

Clifton, Mug, Indian Ware, 4 In. 45.00
Clifton, Mug, Rust & Black Design 42.00
Clifton, Pot, Four-Mile Ruin, Indian Ware, 3 1/2 In. 45.00
Clifton, Teapot, Indian Ware, Art Pottery, With Lid 95.00
Clifton, Tobacco Jar, Indian Ware, With Lid 95.00
Clifton, Vase, Bulbous, Yellow Design On Terra Cotta, Signed 55.00
Clifton, Vase, Crystal Patina, 2 Handles, Signed, 6 3/4 X 8 In. 175.00
Clifton, Vase, Indian Ware, 3 1/2 In. 35.00
Clifton, Vase, Raised Blossoms, Monogramed & Dated, 1906, 9 1/2 In. 115.00
Clock, Advertising, Sta-Brand Shoes 22.00
Clock, Alarm, Bambi, Animated 85.00
Clock, Alarm, Brass, West German 32.50
Clock, Alarm, Mickey Mouse, Hands Are Clock Hands, Marked W.D.P., Germany 35.00
Clock, American, Regulator, Wall, Office, Walnut 225.00
Clock, Anheuser-Busch Emblem, Michelob Light In Center 17.50
Clock, Ansonia, Bonn, Porcelain, Open Escapement 450.00
Clock, Ansonia, Cockatoo, Rose Color, China 325.00
Clock, Ansonia, Crown Crystal Regulator 500.00
Clock, Ansonia, Crystal, Porcelain Dial, Exposed Escapement 275.00
Clock, Ansonia, Figural, Double Statue .... *Illus* 750.00
Clock, Ansonia, Gallery, 14 Day, Oak, Octagonal Shaped, 13 In.Dial 165.00

Clock, Ansonia, Figural, Double Statue

Clock, Ansonia, Gilt Bronze, Strikes Hour & Half Hour	650.00
Clock, Ansonia, Huntress Swing, All Original	1200.00
Clock, Ansonia, Kitchen, Beehive	125.00
Clock, Ansonia, Knight Model, Statue Figure Clock, Visible Escapement	225.00
Clock, Ansonia, La Duchesse, Cast Iron, Mantel, C.1886, Porcelain Dial	75.00
Clock, Ansonia, Long Drop, Walnut, Second Hand, 8 Day, Time & Strike, 32 In.	390.00
Clock, Ansonia, Mantel, Black Enamel, Dated June 18, 1882	225.00
Clock, Ansonia, Mantel, Japanned Finish	250.00
Clock, Ansonia, Mantel, Marble, June 18, 1882, New York	375.00
Clock, Ansonia, Mantel, Time & Strike	110.00
Clock, Ansonia, Miniature, Windsor, Mirror Sides	350.00
Clock, Ansonia, Parisian, Walnut Case, Teardrop Case, 8 Day, Time & Strike	210.00
Clock, Ansonia, Pizarro & Cortez, Hour & Half Hour Strike, 21 In.	995.00
Clock, Ansonia, Regulator, Crystal, Bronze Figure, Mercury Pendulum, 16 In.	625.00
Clock, Ansonia, Regulator, Exposed Escapement, Brass & Beveled Glass Case	195.00
Clock, Ansonia, Regulator, Long Drop, Strike	325.00
Clock, Ansonia, Regulator, Office, Golden Oak, Time & Strike, 3 1/2 Feet	1000.00
Clock, Ansonia, Royal Bonn Porcelain, 8 Day, Time & Strike, Gold Trim	340.00
Clock, Ansonia, School, Time & Calendar, Walnut	325.00
Clock, Ansonia, Shelf, Brass Plated, 13 1/2 In.	275.00
Clock, Ansonia, Statue, Seated Scholar, 8 Day, Time & Strike, 14 X 11 In.	295.00
Clock, Ansonia, Tear Drop, 8 Day, C.1878	450.00
Clock, Ansonia, Wall, Beveled Mirror, C.1920, 2 1/2 Ft.	95.00
Clock, Ansonia, 8 Day, Seated Bronze Statue, Porcelain Dial, Time & Strike	315.00
Clock, Art Nouveau, Green Metal, Cherubs Each Side, Dog Scene	95.00
Clock, Art Nouveau, Runner Holding Clock In Right Hand	75.00
Clock, Babe Ruth	425.00
Clock, Baby Ben, Alarm, Repeat, 1927	15.00
Clock, Baird, Regulator, Advertising	350.00
Clock, Banjo, Dial, Brass Bezel, Acorn Finial, Eglomise Panel, Brass Fillets	1800.00
Clock, Banjo, Floral Glasses, Howard Style	850.00
Clock, Bartholomew Wells, Shelf, Wooden Works, Time, Strike & Alarm, C.1830	275.00
Clock, Bavarian, China, 2 Matching Vases, Country Scenes, 9 In., 3 Piece	125.00
Clock, Big Ben, Alarm, Deluxe	15.00
Clock, Birge & Fuller, Split Column, 8 Day, Time & Strike	375.00
Clock, Birge & Mallory, Weight, Brass Dial	175.00
Clock, Black Forest, Cuckoo, Weight Driven, Hour & Half Hour, 14 X 10 In.	28.00
Clock, Blinking Eye, Shelf, Squire Model, C.1860, 16 In.	525.00
Clock, Boardman & Wells, Wooden Works, 3 Weight, Time, Strike & Alarm	300.00
Clock, Boston Clock Co., Regulator, Cherry Case, Signed Movement, 36 In.	1250.00
Clock, Bracket, Ebonized Case, Brass Dial, 8 Day, Moon Phase Mechanism	250.00
Clock, Brewster Ingraham, Steeple, 8 Day, Etched Glass	225.00
Clock, Brocot, French, Inlaid Case, 8 Day, 21 In.	400.00
Clock, Bronze & Onyx, Set, Clock, 23 X 9 In., 2 Knights In Armor, 22 In., Set	3750.00
Clock, Bulle, Battery Operated, 11 In.	190.00
Clock, Burwell & Carter, Calendar, Weight Driven, No.2	925.00
Clock, Calendar, Double Dial, Seth Thomas	1075.00
Clock, Calendar, School, Large, Walnut	450.00
Clock, Carriage, Alarm, Porcelain Dial, Brevette, 2 In.	50.00
Clock, Carriage, French, Beaded Design, Beveled Glass, 8 Day, Time & Strike	625.00
Clock, Carriage, French, Beveled Glass, Brass, Key, 8 Day	295.00

Clock, Carriage, French, Time & Strike	350.00
Clock, Carriage, French, Wood & Glass Case, 30 Hour	80.00
Clock, Carriage, French, 1/2 Hour Repeater, Bigelow-Kennart & Co.	535.00
Clock, Carriage, French, 8 Day, Brass, Beveled Glass, 3 X 4 1/4 X 2 3/8 In.	200.00
Clock, Carriage, French, 8 Day, Key Set, Brass	175.00
Clock, Carriage, French, 8 Day, Time & Bell Strike, C.1820, Signed, 11 In.	235.00
Clock, Carriage, German, Brass, Leather Case, Bail Handle, 3 In.Square	86.00
Clock, Carriage, Music Box, Nickel On Brass	135.00
Clock, Carriage, 8 Day & Repeat	750.00
Clock, Carved Mahogany, Austrian, Labeled Ant.Oliwa Wien, 1800s, 99 In.	2800.00
Clock, Chauncey Ives, Pillar & Scroll, Shelf, Walnut, Brass Works, Dated 1832	1000.00
Clock, Chelsea Clock Co., Ship's, Key Wind, Time & Seconds, 4 In.Diameter	250.00
Clock, Chelsea Clock Co., 8 Day, Bronze Tambour, Tiffany & Co., 17 In.	300.00
Clock, Chelsea, Desk, Bronze, Ship's Wheel Around Dial, Signed Tiffany	175.00
Clock, Chelsea, Ship, 8 Day	110.00
Clock, Chelsea, Ship, 8 Inch Dial, Raised Numerals, Bronze Case, Signed	375.00
Clock, Chelsea, Weight Driven Regulator, Reverse Painted Door, Marked	725.00
Clock, Chess, Mahogany Frame, Trip Lever, C.1900, Pair	125.00
Clock, Chicago World's Fair, 1933	180.00
Clock, Chicago, Watchman's, Leather Carrying Case, 8 Day	47.50
Clock, Columbus Discovering America, Shape Of Ship, 1891, Cast Iron	65.00
Clock, Columbus, Wooden Works, One Weight, C.1890	150.00
Clock, Crystal Regulator, Porcelain Face, Outside Escapement, Marked	675.00
Clock, Cuckoo, Weight Driven, Floor Model, Walnut, 1800s, 5 Ft., 6 In.	225.00
Clock, Delft, Blue & White China, Windmill & House, Brass Pendulum, German	59.50
Clock, Delft, Porcelain, Scenic, German, 7 3/4 X 4 5/8 In.	175.00
Clock, Desk, 8 Day, Silver & Enamel, Swiss, C.1920, 2 1/2 In.	375.00
Clock, Dresden China, 4 Seasons, Meissen, C.1870-90, 20 X 12 X 6 In.	2800.00
Clock, Dresser, Music Box, Alarm, Le Coulture	175.00
Clock, Dutch Hood, Ship Painted On Face, Carved Figures, 11 Ft. X 19 In.	1450.00
Clock, E.Howard, Banjo, No.4	1800.00
Clock, E.Howard, Banjo, Rosewood Case	1400.00
Clock, E.Howard, Cherry Case, Saxon Lamp Co., Form Of Brass Lamp, 50 In.Long	225.00
Clock, E.Ingraham, Ionic, Wall, 8 Day, Time & Strike, Reverse Painted Door	350.00
Clock, E.N.Welch, Beehive, Shelf, Mahogany Veneer, Brass 8 Day, Time & Strike	725.00
Clock, E.O.Hausburg, Watchman's	48.00
Clock, Early Bird, Animated	160.00
Clock, Eastlake, Kitchen Mantel, Dated 1881, Brass Barometer, Alarm, 24 In.	185.00
Clock, Eli Terry & Sons, Pillar & Scroll, Mahogany, Shelf	1700.00
Clock, English Drop Fusee	175.00
Clock, English, Astronomical Regulator, Mahogany *Illus*	2100.00
Clock, English, Astronomical Regulator, Oak *Illus*	1700.00
Clock, English, Astronomical Regulator, Walnut *Illus*	2700.00
Clock, English, Bracket, Fusee Movement, 8 Day, Time & Strike, Mahogany	450.00
Clock, English, Double Fusee, Bracket, Chimes, C.1900, 13 1/2 X 8 1/2 In.	450.00
Clock, English, Grandfather, C.1800, 2 Weight, 3 Finials, Painted Face	2500.00
Clock, English, Mantel, Inlaid Swag & Shell, Brass Columns, C.1870	1225.00
Clock, Everready Shaving, Advertisement	325.00
Clock, Exterior, Say It With Neon, Octagon Shape, Tin, 3 Feet	235.00
Clock, Figural, Man Stepping On Globe, Metal	75.00
Clock, Fireman's, Brass Bell On Top, Rings On Hour	125.00
Clock, French, A.Mezard, Black Onyx, Brass Urn On Top, C.1860	545.00
Clock, French, Acorn, Thermometer & Barometer	375.00
Clock, French, Black Onyx Case, C.1890	495.00
Clock, French, Bracket, Planchon	800.00
Clock, French, Brass & Glass, Mercury Pendulum	365.00
Clock, French, Brass Trim On Sides & Base, Sunburst Around Face, Strikes	600.00
Clock, French, Brass, Satin Wood Inlay, Ormolu Trim, E.T.Paris, 18 In.	175.00
Clock, French, Bronze Figure Playing Lute	475.00
Clock, French, Bronze, Figural *Illus*	1000.00
Clock, French, Chimes Half Hour & Hour, Pendulum, 2 Candelabra	1400.00
Clock, French, Crystal Regulator, Marble Columns, Lion *Illus*	525.00
Clock, French, Crystal, Porcelain Dial, Mercury Pendulum	250.00
Clock, French, Empire Column, Silvered Brass Dial	225.00
Clock, French, Lemothe, Engraved Black Face, Spelter Soldier On Top, C.1890	495.00
Clock, French, Mantel, Chimes, Strike, Candelabra, 1878	1400.00
Clock, French, Mantel, Marble Base, Anemone Statue, 2 Oil Burning Lamps, 1876	1600.00

Clock, English, Astronomical
Regulator, Mahogany

Clock, English, Astronomical
Regulator, Oak

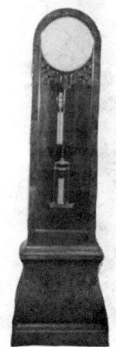

Clock, English, Astronomical
Regulator, Walnut

Clock, French, Bronze, Figural

Clock, French, Crystal Regulator,
Marble Columns, Lion

Clock, French, 2 Piece, Cossack
Figure, Porcelain

Clock, French, Mantel, Marble, Inlaid Case, Porcelain Dial, Escapement	135.00
Clock, French, Mantel, Marble, 8 Day, Time & Strike, 5 In. Bronze Figures	225.00
Clock, French, Mantel, Red Marble, 8 Day Time & Strike, Porcelain Dial	300.00
Clock, French, Mantel, Works Signed, Self Adjusting, Brass, 65 Pounds	1200.00
Clock, French, Marble Case, Porcelain Face, Spelter Statue On Top, C.1890	545.00
Clock, French, Mercury Pendulum, Crystal, Porcelain Dial	250.00
Clock, French, Mercury Pendulum, Crystal, 8 Day, Time & Strike	250.00
Clock, French, Mercury Pendulum, Dated 1889, Marble Case, Matching Urns	895.00
Clock, French, Oval Case, Porcelain Dial, Gold Bands, Mercury Pendulum	395.00
Clock, French, Picture-Frame, Hand-Painted Face, Lacquer Case, 24 X 19 In.	400.00
Clock, French, Porcelain Face, 11 In.	250.00
Clock, French, Regulator, Bowfront Crystal	350.00
Clock, French, Stag Horn, Victorian	75.00
Clock, French, Three Piece Set, Gold Dore, Hand-Painted Porcelain Inserts	750.00
Clock, French, Time & Strike, China	145.00
Clock, French, 2 Piece, Cossack Figure, Porcelain *Illus*	710.00
Clock, George Marsh, Wooden Works & Dial, Reverse Painting	350.00
Clock, German, Cuckoo, 9 In.	25.00
Clock, German, Musical Alarm, Signed, Wenzib	135.00
Clock, German, Nursery Rhyme, Porcelain Face, 8 Characters, 8 Day, 10 X 9 In.	90.00
Clock, German, Regulator, Oak, Beveled Glass	175.00

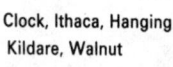
Clock, Gustav Becker, Free
Swinger, Mahogany

Clock, Ithaca, Hanging
Kildare, Walnut

Clock, Hatch, Regulator

Clock, Ithaca, No.3 1/2, Parlor
Model, Walnut

Clock, Lenzkirch, German,
Music Box, Oak,
Polychrome, 96 In.

Clock, Gilbert, Alarm, Oak Case	125.00
Clock, Gilbert, Alarm, Round, Metal, 1929	10.00
Clock, Gilbert, Barbershop, 11 In.Dial, 15 X 31 In.	275.00
Clock, Gilbert, Cottage, Rosewood, 8 Day	90.00
Clock, Gilbert, Grandfather, Paw Feet, Cut Glass Door, Brass Dial, Mahogany	4800.00
Clock, Gilbert, Mantel, Brass & Black Iron, Chimes	185.00
Clock, Gilbert, Mantel, Brass Lions	40.00
Clock, Gilbert, Mantel, Lacquered Wood, Gilt Columns & Feet	80.00
Clock, Gilbert, Old Mr.Boston, Shape Of Bottle, 8 Day, 22 In.	295.00
Clock, Gilbert, Regulator, Golden Oak, No.11	950.00
Clock, Gilbert, Schoolhouse, Octagon, Pendulum	250.00
Clock, Gilbert, Shelf, Rosewood, 8 Day, Alarm	95.00
Clock, Gilbert, Time & Strike, China, Tree Design	200.00
Clock, Gilbert, Wind-Up, Mantel, Wood Case	14.00
Clock, Gilbert, 30 Hour, Time & Strike, Tear Drop Style Case	75.00
Clock, Gilt Bronze & Marble, Empire, 2 Lady Astronomers, 1800s, 16 In.	2250.00
Clock, Gilt Bronze & Sevres Mounted, Surmounted By Urn, C.1800, 17 In.	1100.00
Clock, Glass Dome, 400 Day, Porcelain Face, German	50.00
Clock, Grandfather, Ithaca, 85 1/2 X 18 In.	725.00
Clock, Grandfather, Mahogany, Moon Dial, C.E.Gillett, Manchester, 92 In.	1400.00
Clock, Grandfather, Miniature, Pyrographic, Carved Case, 15 In.	95.00
Clock, Grandfather, Oak, Beveled Glass, Lenz Kirch, Works, 7 Feet High	750.00
Clock, Grandfather, Walnut, Gothic Case, Moon Phase, 8 Day, Brass Weights	2000.00
Clock, Gustav Becker, Bracket	275.00
Clock, Gustav Becker, Free Swinger, Mahogany .... Illus	1000.00
Clock, Gustav Becker, Medaille, No.530440, 42 In.	475.00
Clock, Gustav Neumann, Vienna, 8 Day, Time & Strike	225.00

Clock, Haddon, Figural House, Lady In Rocking Chair, Animated	46.00
Clock, Hatch, Regulator *Illus*	1400.00
Clock, Henry Loomis, Shelf, Wooden Works	350.00
Clock, Herschedes, Mantel, Westminster & Canterbury Chimes, Silver Dial	175.00
Clock, Howard, Banjo, No.1	4200.00
Clock, Howard, Bank Timer	200.00
Clock, Howard, Figure Eight Case, Reverse Painted Throat, 8 Day, Marked	650.00
Clock, Howard, Split Plate Model, Size L, 14K Yellow Gold Filled	600.00
Clock, Hula Girl, Animated	99.00
Clock, I.B.M., Time Clock, Pendulum, Key Wind, C.1895	575.00
Clock, Ingraham, Alarm, Original Stenciled Case, Oak	125.00
Clock, Ingraham, Banjo, 8 Day, Time & Strike, Ship Decoration, 32 In.	250.00
Clock, Ingraham, Bugs Bunny, Alarm	115.00
Clock, Ingraham, Calendar Dial, Barometer, Time & Strike, 8 Day	225.00
Clock, Ingraham, Calendar, Mosaic, Original Dials	975.00
Clock, Ingraham, Calendar, Oak, Gingerbread	185.00
Clock, Ingraham, Calendar, Parlor, Walnut	1050.00
Clock, Ingraham, Calendar, Wall, Rosewood	350.00
Clock, Ingraham, Gingerbread Calendar, Oak, 8 Day, Time & Strike	175.00
Clock, Ingraham, Kitchen, Gothic Design, Alarm, 8 Day, Stenciling, 22 In.	135.00
Clock, Ingraham, Kitchen, Walnut Case, 8 Day, Alarm	175.00
Clock, Ingraham, Kitchenette, Oak, Large	95.00
Clock, Ingraham, Kitchenette, Oak, Small	75.00
Clock, Ingraham, Mantel, Black, Lion Head Sides	57.50
Clock, Ingraham, Mantel, Columned, Black	85.00
Clock, Ingraham, Mantel, Doric Style, Time & Alarm, 16 In.	115.00
Clock, Ingraham, Mantel, Wood Case	75.00
Clock, Ingraham, Regulator, Postal, Oak, Long Drop	485.00
Clock, Ingraham, Regulator, Store, Oak, 8 Day	225.00
Clock, Ingraham, School	185.00
Clock, Ingraham, School House, Wall Case, Hexagon Drop, Face, 11 1/2 In.	200.00
Clock, Ingraham, Shelf, Cherry, Carved	195.00
Clock, Ingraham, Shelf, Doric Style, 8 Day	110.00
Clock, Ingraham, Wall, Golden Oak, 8 Day, Maxim Model, 14 1/2 In.	150.00
Clock, Ingraham, Wall, Navarre, Mahogany, 7 In.Dial	250.00
Clock, Ingraham, Wall, Open Pendulum, Brass Covered	165.00
Clock, Ingraham, Wall, Rosewood, Round Top & Bottom, 8 Day	175.00
Clock, Ingraham, Yellow, Red & Green Painted Decoration	95.00
Clock, International, Time Recorder, 27 In.Wheel In Front	300.00
Clock, Italian, Commemorative, Battle Of Tripoli	160.00
Clock, Italian, Commemorative, John F.Kennedy	150.00
Clock, Ithaca, Calendar, Chronometer Model	1200.00
Clock, Ithaca, Calendar, Farmer's Model, Walnut Case	350.00
Clock, Ithaca, Cottage, 30 Day, Double Dial	750.00
Clock, Ithaca, Hanging Kildare, Walnut *Illus*	1800.00
Clock, Ithaca, No.3 1/2, Parlor Model, Walnut *Illus*	2300.00
Clock, Ithaca, 30 Day, Double Dial Calendar, Shelf	700.00
Clock, Japy Freres, Black Onyx Case	175.00
Clock, Jerome & Co., Ogee, Brass Dial, Tablet Hand-Painted	275.00
Clock, Jerome & Co., Steeple, 20 In.	190.00
Clock, Jerome & Darrow, Weight, Wood Dial	200.00
Clock, Jerome, Ogee, 30 Hour, 32 In.	90.00 To 235.00
Clock, Jerome, Shelf, 8 Day Brass Works & Bezel, Key, 14 1/4 In.	165.00
Clock, Johann, Regulator, Open Swinger, German, 1860	475.00
Clock, Junghans, Mantel, Westminster Chime	195.00
Clock, Junghans, Mantel, Westminster Chime, Oak, 8 Day, C.1890, 18 1/2 In.	440.00
Clock, Junghans, Mantel, 30 Hour, Time & Strike	75.00
Clock, Junghans, Mantel, 8 Day, Time & Strike, C.1890, 16 In.	290.00
Clock, Kitchen, Time & Strike, Alarm, Oak, Gilding On Glass, Pendulum, 22 In.	185.00
Clock, Kitchen, Time & Strike, Alarm, 8 Day.Oak	100.00
Clock, Kitchen, 8 Day, Time & Strike & Alarm, Golden Oak	125.00
Clock, Kroeber, Shelf, Parlor, Ebony & Walnut	275.00
Clock, Lantern, William & Mary, Brass Chapter Ring, 1600s, 19 1/2 In.	2600.00
Clock, Lantern, 4 Legs, Bell At Top	1400.00
Clock, Lenzkirch, German, Music Box, Oak, Polychrome, 96 In. *Illus*	9400.00
Clock, Lenzkirch, Regulator, Single Weight, No.137959	375.00

Clock, Lux, Cuckoo, Miniature, Bobbing Red Bird, Keywind, 6 X 4 In. 24.00
Clock, Lux, Cuckoo, 8 Day, Keywind, Tin Bird, Pendulum, 10 X 6 1/2 In. 38.00
Clock, Lux, Happy Days 150.00
Clock, Lux, Shoeshine Boy 150.00
Clock, Manning-Bowman, Mantel, Electric 26.00
Clock, Mantel, Applied Carving, Embossed Brass Face, Oak Case 125.00
Clock, Mantel, French, Achille Petite, Time & Strike, 18 X 18 In. 450.00
Clock, Mantel, French, Birds & Pastoral Scene, 16 X 9 In. 575.00
Clock, Mantel, French, Cobalt & Gold Trim, Porcelain Insets, 14 X 9 In. 575.00
Clock, Mantel, Gilt Bronze, Figure Of Girl, Child, Scrolled Motifs, 18 In. 175.00
Clock, Mantel, Gilt Bronze, Gray Marble, Louis XVI Style, 1800s, 23 In 2250.00
Clock, Mantel, Gilt Bronze, Pedestal Base, Impressed L.Charpentier, 22 In. 750.00
Clock, Mantel, Meissen, Stand, Underglazed Blue Crossed Swords, 20 1/2 In. 2250.00
Clock, Mantel, Napoleon III, Ormolu, Cherubs, 1800s, Sevres, 16 1/2 In. 1750.00
Clock, Mantel, Ormolu, Louis XVI, No.38, 1700s, 13 1/2 X 11 1/2 In. 2700.00
Clock, Mantel, Spanish American War, Soldier, Sailor 68.00
Clock, Mantel, Tole Case, C.1819 .... 985.00
Clock, Mantel, Will Rogers 110.00
Clock, Miller, Banjo, Lyre, 8 Day, Strike 675.00
Clock, Morbier, French, Crown Wheel Escapement, Porcelain Dial, 2 Weight 450.00
Clock, Mother-Of-Pearl, 8 Day & Strike, Iron 225.00
Clock, New Haven, Banjo, Ship Scene, 32 In. 250.00
Clock, New Haven, Banjo, 25 In. 145.00
Clock, New Haven, Banjo, 40 In. 275.00
Clock, New Haven, Calendar, Drop, Walnut 350.00
Clock, New Haven, Cathedral Shape, Solid Brass, 4 In. 35.00
Clock, New Haven, Cottage, Rosewood, 8 Day 90.00
Clock, New Haven, Double Dial Calendar, Oak, 30 Day, 50 In. 1000.00
Clock, New Haven, Marine Lever, 12 In. Dial 100.00
Clock, New Haven, Miniature, C.1905, Oak, Paper Label, 12 X 3 1/2 In. 250.00
Clock, New Haven, Octagon Drop, Decorated Glass 250.00
Clock, New Haven, Office Regulator, 8 Day, Walnut 200.00
Clock, New Haven, One-Half Column, 30 Hour, Metal Dial 150.00
Clock, New Haven, Parlor, Walnut, C.1890, Lattice Wood Trim, Brass Pendulum 150.00
Clock, New Haven, Regulator, Advertising Gold Lion Tonic 475.00
Clock, New Haven, Regulator, Double Dial, Oak Case, 30 Day, 50 In. 975.00
Clock, New Haven, Regulator, Goulding's Manures, Best For Crops, 32 In. 675.00
Clock, New Haven, Regulator, Outside Escapement 275.00
Clock, New Haven, Regulator, 2 Weight, Walnut 525.00
Clock, New Haven, School, Calendar 265.00
Clock, New Haven, School, Long Drop, Oak 235.00
Clock, New Haven, Scroll, Walnut, Time & Strike 295.00
Clock, New Haven, Shelf, Time, Strike & Alarm, 30 Hour 125.00
Clock, New Haven, Steeple, Rosewood, 19th Century, 19 3/4 X 10 In. 325.00
Clock, New Haven, Tom-Tom, Alarm, Chrome, Octagon 24.00
Clock, New Haven, Two Weight Regulator, Saturn Model 550.00
Clock, New Haven, Walnut & White Victorian Gingerbread 115.00
Clock, New Haven, 12 Day, Time Only, Painted Scene 140.00
Clock, New Haven, 8 Day, Railroad Regulator 325.00
Clock, Novelty, Bobbing Bird, Columbia Time Products 28.00
Clock, Oak & Mahogany, Boxwood Inlay, Shell Motif Inlay, 1780, 20 X 89 In. 2400.00
Clock, Oak, Gingerbread, 8 Day, Time, Strike & Alarm, Time Is Money 115.00
Clock, Orange Crush, Regulator 600.00
Clock, Phinney Walker, Auto, Rim-Wind, Rim Set 35.00
Clock, Phinney Walker, 8 Day, Key Wind 20.00
Clock, Pinocchio, Animated 85.00
Clock, Pluto, Animated 85.00
Clock, Plymouth, Banjo .... 200.00 To 225.00
Clock, Plymouth, Banjo, 8 Day, Time & Strike, Mt.Vernon Glass, 29 In. 195.00
Clock, Pratt & Frost, Shelf, Pristine 350.00
Clock, Red Goose Shoes, Lighted, Electric 95.00
Clock, Regency, English, Fusee Movement, Mahogany, 8 Day, C.1830, 19 In. 425.00
Clock, Regulator, Crystal, Tiffany 425.00
Clock, Regulator, French, Porcelain Face, Bow Glass Door, 10 X 6 1/2 In. 325.00
Clock, Regulator, German, 25 In. 175.00
Clock, Regulator, New Haven, Wall, Time & Calendar 250.00
Clock, Regulator, Provincial Oak, French, Brass Dial, 1700s, 92 In. 1600.00

Clock, Regulator, Top Centerpiece, 4-Corner Finials, Lever Movement	550.00
Clock, Regulator, Wall, 2 Sets Of Chimes, 3 Weight, 58 In.	850.00
Clock, Remke, Office, 3 Feet, Battery Wound Pendulum Driven, C.1900	350.00
Clock, Round Gallery, 8 Day, Hour Strike, 14 In.Diameter	75.00
Clock, Royal Bonn, China, Ansonia Works, Open Escapement, 13 X 12 In.	395.00
Clock, Royal Bonn, China, Ansonia Works, Porcelain Face, 13 X 9 1/2 In.	325.00
Clock, Royal Bonn, China, Floral, Ansonia Works, 9 1/2 X 11 1/2 In.	275.00
Clock, S.J.Bibby, Grandfather, Dated 1875, Rocking Ship, Signed	1500.00
Clock, Sambo, Blinking Eye, 30 Hour, Original Paint	700.00
Clock, School, Welch, Octagon, Original Paper Label	225.00
Clock, School, 8 Day, Hour Strike, 20 In.	75.00
Clock, Seagram 7, Digital Desk, 1954	42.50
Clock, Self Winding Clock Co., Western Union, Wall, C.1930, 15 In.Square	58.00
Clock, Sessions, Banjo, Electric, Mt.Vernon On Glass, 23 In.	35.00
Clock, Sessions, Banjo, Halifax, 8 Day, 2 Tone Strike	145.00
Clock, Sessions, Banjo, 8 Day, Nantucket Model, 22 In.	75.00
Clock, Sessions, Boudoir, Flower & Cane Pattern, 5 1/2 In.	185.00
Clock, Sessions, Cross Wood Bottom, 20 In.	55.00
Clock, Sessions, Goodyear Power Cushion Tire, 5 1/2 In.Diameter	27.50
Clock, Sessions, Kitchen, Golden Oak, 8 Day, Strike	95.00
Clock, Sessions, Mantel, Pendulum, Oak, 1/2 Hour Strike, 14 X 12 In.	58.00
Clock, Sessions, Miniature, Regulator, Pressed Design Oak Case, Red	195.00
Clock, Sessions, School, Octagon	190.00
Clock, Sessions, School, Time Only, Oak Case	169.50
Clock, Sessions, Wall, Mission	90.00
Clock, Sessions, Westminster Wall Regulator, Walnut	175.00
Clock, Sessions, 2 Weight, Office, A Frame, Long Drop	175.00
Clock, Sessions, 8 Day, Time & Strike, Reverse Painting, 20 In.	160.00
Clock, Seth Thomas, Banjo, Brass Eagle	210.00
Clock, Seth Thomas, Banjo, 8 Day, Time & Strike, Mt.Vernon Glasses	250.00
Clock, Seth Thomas, Carriage, Nickel On Brass, Alarm, Second Hand, 5 3/4 In.	105.00
Clock, Seth Thomas, Cottage, Rosewood, 30 Hour, Alarm	100.00
Clock, Seth Thomas, Eclipse Lyre	275.00
Clock, Seth Thomas, Empire Style Case, Cottage, 30 Hour, Plymouth Movement	100.00
Clock, Seth Thomas, Gallery, Copper On Mahogany, 24 In.	550.00
Clock, Seth Thomas, Gallery, Large Seconds Bit, Walnut, Dial, 13 In.	150.00
Clock, Seth Thomas, Gallery, 8 Day, 16 In.Square Quartered Oak Case	135.00
Clock, Seth Thomas, Grandfather, Carved Figwood, 1828, 7 Ft. 10 In.	8000.00
Clock, Seth Thomas, Grandfather, Wooden Works, Masonic & Flowers, 7 Feet	1750.00
Clock, Seth Thomas, Mantel, Hand-Painted Roses On Dial & Door, 14 In.	185.00
Clock, Seth Thomas, Mantel, Key Wind, 8 Day, China	250.00
Clock, Seth Thomas, Mantel, Label Inside, Key & Pendulum, C.1870	105.00
Clock, Seth Thomas, Mantel, Rosewood Veneer, 8 Day, Time & Strike	95.00
Clock, Seth Thomas, Mantel, 8 Day, Bronze, Original Key	1000.00
Clock, Seth Thomas, Mantel, 8 Day, 1/2 Hour Strike, Mahogany, 11 1/4 In.	95.00
Clock, Seth Thomas, Navy Boat	85.00
Clock, Seth Thomas, Neward, Walnut	195.00
Clock, Seth Thomas, Office, Calendar, No.4	975.00
Clock, Seth Thomas, Open Face, Coin Case	125.00
Clock, Seth Thomas, Parlor, Rosewood & Walnut, C.1860, Mirrored Pendulum	250.00
Clock, Seth Thomas, Regulator, Empire No.17, Porcelain Dial	450.00
Clock, Seth Thomas, Regulator, Model No.2, Walnut	600.00
Clock, Seth Thomas, Regulator, No.2	550.00
Clock, Seth Thomas, Regulator, One Weight, Flat Weight, Label	800.00
Clock, Seth Thomas, Schoolhouse, Oak, Round Top, 7 In.Dial	250.00
Clock, Seth Thomas, Second & Alarm Dial, 1890s	25.00
Clock, Seth Thomas, Senora Chimes, Rosewood Case, Pillar Style	235.00
Clock, Seth Thomas, Ship's Bell	265.00
Clock, Seth Thomas, Short Drop, Strike	245.00
Clock, Seth Thomas, Three Weight Regulator, Rosewood Veneer	1100.00
Clock, Seth Thomas, Watchman's, Quarter Hewn Oak, 30 Day, 50 In.	950.00
Clock, Seth Thomas, 2 Weight, Scene On Glass, Walnut Frame, Original Label	325.00
Clock, Seth Thomas, 3 Decker, 8 Day, Time & Strike, Rosewood	435.00
Clock, Seth Thomas, 30 Hour, Keywind, Weight Driven, Wall	325.00
Clock, Seth Thomas, 30 Hour, Time & Strike	175.00
Clock, Shelf, Arched Bonnet, Brass Quarter Columns, 8 Day, D.W.Newbury Port	700.00
Clock, Shelf, Blinking Eye, 30 Hour, Bradley & Hubbard Case, C.1865, 16 In.	450.00

Clock, Shelf, Time, Strike & Alarm, Walnut 97.00
Clock, Shelf, Wood & Brass, Open Pendulum 850.00
Clock, Ship, Chelsea, Bells, Stand 250.00
Clock, Ship, 14 1/2 In.Diameter 550.00
Clock, Smith Of London, Lantern, Miniature, Brass 155.00
Clock, Standard Electric Time Co., Master, Battery Driven, 12 In.Dial 10.00
Clock, Steeple, Reverse Glass Painting, Original Label, C.1850 .... 250.00
Clock, Steeple, 2 Tier, Cherry Wood, Hand-Painted Glass Panels 200.00
Clock, Stennis, Grandmother, Roxbury Case, Westminster Chime 1555.00
Clock, Sunburst, Continental, Silvered Wood, Arabic Numerals, 60 In. 550.00
Clock, T.Lynch, Carriage, Brass Case, Beveled Glass, French, 2 3/4 In. 350.00
Clock, Table, Brass, Calendar, Moon Phases, Lucas Weidman, Cracow, C.1680 .... 0500.00
Clock, Tall Case, Hepplewhite Style, Joshua Bates, C.1816 .... 1600.00
Clock, Tall Case, Mahogany, Art Deco, C.1925 .... *Illus* 850.00
Clock, Tall Case, Mahogany, Brass Inlaid, George 11, John Seddon, 87 In. 2500.00
Clock, Tall Case, Mahogany, Federal, Inlaid, Thompson, Baltimore, 1799, 8 Feet 7000.00
Clock, Tall Case, Mahogany, Inlaid, George 111, 1800s, 99 In. 1700.00
Clock, Tall Case, Pine, Bonnet Hood, Wooden Dial, 1800s, 83 X 17 In. 750.00
Clock, Tall Case, Walnut Case, Hand-Painted Wood Dial, C.1800, 7 Feet ... 800.00
Clock, Tall Case, Wooden Works, Decorated Case & Dial 1200.00
    Clock, Tiffany, see Tiffany, Clock
Clock, Tiffany Dore, Bronze, 25 In. 1200.00
Clock, Tiffany, Carriage, Repeat & Alarm 675.00
Clock, Tiffany, Grandfather, Tubular Chimes, Moon Face, 8 Feet 2875.00
Clock, Time & Strike, 8 Day, Walnut 95.00
Clock, Traveling, Enameled, Silver, Signed Udall & Balldu, C.1900, 1 5/8 In. 350.00
Clock, Victorian, Cobalt Blue, Ladies, Gold Medallion, Austria, 5 1/2 X 4 In. 165.00
Clock, Vienna, One Weight, Oak Case, Art Deco 145.00
Clock, Vienna, Rectangular, 8 Day, Striking Brass Movement 65.00
Clock, Vienna, Regulator, Wall, 8 Day, 3 Weight, Porcelain Dial, Walnut Case 650.00
Clock, Vienna, 8 Day, Strike Brass Movement 65.00
Clock, W.Howard, Regulator, Walnut Case, Reverse Painted Glass, 8 Day, 60 In. 3100.00
Clock, W.N.Welsh, School, 8 Day, Double Wind, Long Drop 225.00
Clock, Wag-On-The-Wall, Time, Strike & Rope Alarm 325.00
Clock, Wall, Carved Case In Form Of Lion & Lioness, Time & Strike, Oak ... 850.00
Clock, Wall, Carved Oak, Copper & Metal Face, Copper Pendulum 290.00
Clock, Wall, Mission, 8 Day, T & S, Brass Numbers, Pendulum 75.00
Clock, Wall, Painted, Beveled Mirror Plate, Arched Top, Swiss, 11 1/4 In. .. 225.00
Clock, Wall, 8 Day, Mission Oak 80.00
Clock, Waltham Clock Company, Mahogany, Silvered & Gilt Face, 92 X 31 In. 3000.00
Clock, Waltham, Grandfather, Moon Dial, Mahogany, Bonnet, 7 Ft.8 In. ... 2450.00
Clock, Waltham, Mantel, Inlaid Case, 8 Day, Time & Strike 100.00
Clock, Waltham, Railroad Regulator, Wall, 5 1/4 Feet 2200.00
Clock, Waltham, Travel Watch, 8 Day 35.00
Clock, Waterbury, Alarm, Daybreak 17.50
Clock, Waterbury, Alarm, Oak Case 125.00
Clock, Waterbury, Carriage, Miniature, 2 1/2 In. 85.00
Clock, Waterbury, Carriage, Nickel & Brass 125.00
Clock, Waterbury, Carriage, Repeater, 1897 .... 450.00
Clock, Waterbury, Carriage, The Magnet, C.1880, 78 Glass Sides, Alarm ... 125.00

Clock, Tall Case, Mahogany, Art Deco,
C.1925

Clock, Waterbury, Cottage, Rosewood, 30 Hour	80.00
Clock, Waterbury, Gallery, Strike & Time, 30 Day	185.00
Clock, Waterbury, Gingerbread, Calendar	175.00
Clock, Waterbury, Ionic-Type, Calendar, Bahia Model	350.00
Clock, Waterbury, Kitchen, Time & Strike, 8 Day, Alarm	125.00
Clock, Waterbury, Kitchen, Walnut Cased, 8 Day	115.00
Clock, Waterbury, Mantel, Glass & Brass, 8 Day, Time & Strike, Beveled Glass	200.00
Clock, Waterbury, Mantel, Time & Strike	100.00
Clock, Waterbury, Mantel, 8 Day, Time & Strike, Oak, 12 X 8 In.	60.00
Clock, Waterbury, Mosaic, Walnut & Maple	325.00
Clock, Waterbury, Mr.Boston	150.00
Clock, Waterbury, On Stem From Base, Temperature Gauge, Lux Clock Co.	145.00
Clock, Waterbury, Parlor, Time & Strike, Walnut Finish	115.00
Clock, Waterbury, Regulator, 30 Day	350.00
Clock, Waterbury, School House Regulator, Marquetry Drop Panel	250.00
Clock, Waterbury, School, Calendar, Oak Case	365.00
Clock, Waterbury, School, Octagon Shape, Long Pendulum	300.00
Clock, Waterbury, Shelf, Key	50.00
Clock, Waterbury, Shelf, Painted Panel	50.00
Clock, Waterbury, Shelf, 8 Day, Time & Strike, Gold Leaf Decal	85.00
Clock, Waterbury, Ship's Bell, Spokes	260.00
Clock, Waterbury, Steeple, 15 In.	115.00
Clock, Waterbury, Steeple, 8 Day	225.00
Clock, Waterbury, Wood Frame, Factory Picture, Alarm, 16 X 22 In.	200.00
Clock, Waterbury, 2 Weight Regulator, Time, Cherry	550.00
Clock, Wedgwood, Tempus Fugit, Blue & White Jasper, C.1860	435.00
Clock, Welch Mfg., Co., Steeple, Strike & Alarm, Brass Works, Key	350.00
Clock, Welch, Parlor, Walnut, C.1870, Patti Type Pendulum	150.00
Clock, Welch, Venetian, 8 Day, Rosewood Case, Round Top, Label	185.00
Clock, Westclox Big Ben, Tin	25.00
Clock, Western Union, Self-Winding, Wood Case, 21 In.Square	295.00
Clock, Woody Woodpecker, Animated, Original Box	190.00

Cloisonne Glass, Vase, Inlaid, Metal
Base & Rim Ring, 3 3/4 In.

*Cloisonne enamel was developed during the nineteenth century. A glass
enamel was applied between small ribbonlike pieces of metal on a metal base.
Most cloisonne is Chinese or Japanese.*

Cloisonne Glass, Vase, Inlaid, Metal Base & Rim Ring, 3 3/4 In.	*Illus*	350.00
Cloisonne, Ashtray, Morning Glories, Turquoise Ground, 4 In.Square		45.00
Cloisonne, Ashtray, Six Color, Carved Jade Insert, 4 1/2 In.Diameter		50.00
Cloisonne, Ashtray, Yellow Florals, Green Interior, Marked China, 3 3/4 In.		36.00
Cloisonne, Base, Candlestick Lamp, Blue Enamel, 14 1/2 In.		135.00
Cloisonne, Base, Lamp, Aztec & Floral Design, White Ground, 9 3/4 In.		200.00
Cloisonne, Boat, Turquoise Blossoms, White Ground, 5 X 1 1/2 In.Deep		28.00
Cloisonne, Bottle, Snuff, Bird & Floral Scenes		175.00
Cloisonne, Bottle, Snuff, Blue Background, Floral Decoration		150.00
Cloisonne, Bottle, Snuff, Double, Yellow Background, Floral Decoration		225.00
Cloisonne, Bottle, Snuff, Green, 5 Claw Dragon, Ivory Spoon, Jade Stopper		400.00
Cloisonne, Bowl, Black Background, Mums & Leaves, Folded Rim, 10 In.Diameter		350.00
Cloisonne, Bowl, Foil, Roses Inside & Out, Silver & Copper Wire, 9 1/2 In.		325.00
Cloisonne, Bowl, Green Interior, White Floral, 2 X 4 In.Diameter		16.50
Cloisonne, Bowl, Medallion Containing Dragon, Leaves, Lotus, 7 1/2 In.		325.00
Cloisonne, Bowl, Turquoise Ground, Flowers, 8 1/2 In.		50.00
Cloisonne, Bowl, White Ground, Wire Scrolls & Outlined Flowers, 1 3/8 In.		20.00
Cloisonne, Bowl, 5 Clawed Dragons, Seal On Base, 3 X 10 In.Diameter		500.00
Cloisonne, Box, Blossoms, Leaves, Brass Foo Dog Finial, Cylindrical, Marked		145.00
Cloisonne, Box, Cigarette, Ashtray, Matchbox Holder, Blue & White		150.00
Cloisonne, Box, Cigarette, Matchholder, Round		80.00

Cloisonne, Box, Clouds, 2 Geese, Blue Interior, Marked, 5 X 2 In. 65.00
Cloisonne, Box, Cover, Goldstone, Phoenix On Lid, Round, 1 1/2 X 2 3/4 In. 210.00
Cloisonne, Box, Covered, Enameled, Hinged, Girls On Cover, 3 In.Long 120.00
Cloisonne, Box, Covered, Mons & Symbols, Gilt Wire Scroll, 3 3/4 X 2 In. 515.00
Cloisonne, Box, Cylindrical, Cover, Water Fowl Design, 3 1/4 X 3 In.Diameter 75.00
Cloisonne, Box, Cylindrical, Dragon, Pearl On Cover, 8 X 5 In. 350.00
Cloisonne, Box, Dome Lid, 3 X 3 1/2 X 2 1/4 In. 75.00
Cloisonne, Box, Double Compartment, Hinged Cover, 6 X 4 X 1 In. 75.00
Cloisonne, Box, Dragon Design, 1 X 3/4 In.Round 30.00
Cloisonne, Box, Dragonfly, Green & Blue, 5 In. 35.00
Cloisonne, Box, Floral, Green, 4 Compartments, China, Footed, 6 X 4 1/2 In. 75.00
Cloisonne, Box, Footed, Multi-Colored Millefiori, 4 3/4 X 3 3/8 X 2 5/8 In. 145.00
Cloisonne, Box, Heart Shaped, Butterflies & Flowers 125.00
Cloisonne, Box, Lidded, Turquoise Trim, Multicolor Flowers, 4 X 5 In.Diam. 59.00
Cloisonne, Box, Millefiori Decoration, Cover, Round, 3 In. 95.00
Cloisonne, Box, Mutton Jade Carved Insert, Flower Design, 5 X 3 X 2 1/2 In. 250.00
Cloisonne, Box, On Silver, Oriental Marking, 3 X 2 X 1 1/2 In. 200.00
Cloisonne, Box, Phoenix Bird On Yellow Background, 4 X 5 1/4 X 2 1/4 In. 175.00
Cloisonne, Box, Powder, Green Geometric Ground, Flowers, 3 3/4 In.Diameter 55.00
Cloisonne, Box, Powder, Green Ground, Blue, Red & White Flowers 10.00
Cloisonne, Box, Red With All Over Floral, Ball Feet, 3 1/2 X 3 Inches 30.00
Cloisonne, Box, Round, Black Dragon, Footed, 2 1/8 X 3 In.Diameter, Pair 210.00
Cloisonne, Box, Round, Floral Sprays, Marked China, 5 In. 45.00
Cloisonne, Box, Stamp, Footed, Hinged Cover, Wire Scrolls, 1 1/2 X 3 1/2 In. 40.00
Cloisonne, Box, Stamp, Teal Blue, Brass Mounts, 4 1/2 X 1 1/2 X 1 1/2 In. 57.50
Cloisonne, Box, Taoist Symbols, Bronze Foo Dog Finial, 5 In.Diameter 85.00
Cloisonne, Buckle, Belt, Butterfly Shape, Fishscale, 3 X 2 In. 75.00
Cloisonne, Candleholder, Dragon With Flaming Pearl 95.00
Cloisonne, Candleholder, Teacup Shape, Flowers & Leaves 85.00
Cloisonne, Candlestick, Mustard Yellow, 6 1/2 In., Pair 200.00
Cloisonne, Case, Baluster Shaped, Blue Ground, 6 1/2 In. 112.50
Cloisonne, Charger, Multi-Colors, Dragon Center, 14 In. 400.00
Cloisonne, Charger, Solid Blue Ground, Diaper Edge, 12 In. 260.00
Cloisonne, Charger, Turquoise Ground, Geese Flying, 12 In.Diameter 525.00
Cloisonne, Chocolate Pot, Miniature, Wisteria, Butterflies, Foliage, Goldstone 395.00
Cloisonne, Cigarette Case, 2 Dragons On Front, Larger Dragon On Back 95.00
Cloisonne, Compote, Covered, Pink, White & Blue Mums, 9 In. 185.00
Cloisonne, Crane, 7 In., Pair 825.00
Cloisonne, Cup, Libation, Ram's Head, 5 1/2 X 3 In., Pair 775.00
Cloisonne, Dish, Brass Band, All Over Scrolls, China, 5 1/8 In.Diameter 30.00
Cloisonne, Dish, Brass Scrolls, Colored Flowers, China, 5 In. 30.00
Cloisonne, Dish, Candy, Covered, Cobalt Blue, Green Diaper, Marked, 2 1/2 In. 100.00
Cloisonne, Ewer, Aqua Butterflies, Flowers, Copper Outlined, 4 3/4 In. 155.00
Cloisonne, Figurine, Mythological Sitting Turtles, Dragons, 3 3/4 X 6 In. 800.00
Cloisonne, Figurine, Sitting Turtles, Removable Back, 3 1/2 X 6 In., Pair 590.00
Cloisonne, Holder, Match Box 25.00
Cloisonne, Incense Burner, Globular Body, Lotus Knob, Ch'ien Lung, 13 In. 1600.00
Cloisonne, Incense Burner, Globular Vase On Elephant, 18 1/2 In., Pair 2600.00
Cloisonne, Incense Burner, Horse, Removable Saddle, Enameled, 11 In., Pair 1800.00
Cloisonne, Inkwell, Purple Flowers, Bulbous, 3 Feet, Cover With Knob, 4 In. 125.00
Cloisonne, Jar, Bronze Finial, Medallions, Black Ground, C.1880, 2 1/2 In. 65.00
Cloisonne, Jar, Covered, Goldstone, Butterflies, Flowers, 4 1/2 In. 285.00
Cloisonne, Jar, Ginger, Bark Ground, Bird & Butterfly On Lid, 7 1/2 X 6 In. 300.00
Cloisonne, Jar, Ginger, Miniature, Goldstone 175.00
Cloisonne, Jar, Ginger, Multicolored Flowers, Turquoise Ground, Pair 275.00
Cloisonne, Jar, Ginger, Treebark Exterior, Snowflakes, 5 1/2 In. 185.00
Cloisonne, Jar, Ginger, Yellow, Flowers, Cloud Cloisons, 5 1/2 In. 145.00
Cloisonne, Jug, Saki, 3 Cups, Dragon Design 35.00
Cloisonne, Matchbox, Yellow Ground, Wire Scrolls, 1 1/2 X 3 1/2 In. 25.00
Cloisonne, Napkin Ring, Black, Green & Red Flowers, 1 1/4 In.Wide 55.00
Cloisonne, Napkin Ring, Floral Pattern, Chinese 15.00
Cloisonne, Napkin Ring, Phoenix Bird, Blooming Flowers 75.00
Cloisonne, Napkin Ring, Pink Flowers, 2 In.Diameter 16.50
Cloisonne, Pipe, Opium, Enameled Branches, Blue Fretwork, Agate Ends 450.00
Cloisonne, Planter, Champleve, 11 1/2 X 12 In. 185.00
Cloisonne, Plate, Birds, Blue Ground, 9 1/2 In. 150.00

Cloisonne, Plate, Footed, Center Medallion, Footed, 9 In.	115.00
Cloisonne, Plate, Hawk Attaching Goose, Pink, Waver Border, 1900s, 12 1/2 In.	275.00
Cloisonne, Plate, Phoenix Medallion, Japanese, 14 In.	155.00
Cloisonne, Plate, Pin, Bird Design, Blue & Pink, 1 3/4 In.Diameter	18.50
Cloisonne, Pot, Wine, Horse, Scrolling Foliate, 9 1/2 In., Pair	1000.00
Cloisonne, Rose Bowl, Melon Ribbed, Enameled Inside, 5 1/2 X 7 In.	375.00
Cloisonne, Rose Jar, Green Background, Japanese, 2 In.	75.00
Cloisonne, Rose Jar, Twisted Wire, Birds & Butterflies, 4 In.	140.00
Cloisonne, Salt & Pepper, Aqua, Pink & Yellow Flowers, 2 In.	20.00
Cloisonne, Salt & Pepper, Brass Filigree, White & Pink Flowers, 2 In.	35.00
Cloisonne, Salt & Pepper, Footed, Imperial Dragon Design, 1 In.	55.00
Cloisonne, Salt & Pepper, Green Ground, Lace Trimmed With Cobalt	125.00
Cloisonne, Salt, Pepper & Sugar, Footed, Fishscale Design	105.00
Cloisonne, Salt, White Background, Blue Interior	22.50
Cloisonne, Salt, White, Blue, Flowers, Leaves, Chinese, 1 7/8 X 1 1/4 In.	22.50
Cloisonne, Screen, 4 Panel, Enameled, Dragons, Each Panel 28 1/2 X 7 In.	1200.00
Cloisonne, Smoke Set, White Scrolls, Lotus, Red, Marked China, 3 Piece Set	60.00
Cloisonne, Stirrups, Floral Decoration, Bronze, 6 In.	180.00
Cloisonne, Teapot, Butterflies & Flower, Dark Green, 4 1/2 X 3 1/2 In.	250.00
Cloisonne, Teapot, Butterflies, Colored Flowers, Goldstone, 2 3/4 In.	155.00
Cloisonne, Teapot, Butterflies, Flowers, Pear Shape, Green, Chinese, 3 7/8 In.	225.00
Cloisonne, Teapot, Floral Decoration, 3 In.	175.00
Cloisonne, Teapot, Miniature, Panels Around Flowers & Butterflies, Handle	115.00
Cloisonne, Teapot, Miniature, Teakwood Stand, Butterflies, Colored Foil	250.00
Cloisonne, Thimble, Chinese, 20th Century	22.00
Cloisonne, Toothpick, Flowers, 2 In.	35.00
Cloisonne, Tray, Brass Rim & Base, Marked China, 7 In.Square	215.00
Cloisonne, Tray, Bright Blue Background, 6 3/4 In.	150.00
Cloisonne, Tray, Thousand Flower, Brass Greek Key Rim, 15 In.Diameter	700.00
Cloisonne, Tub, Jade Trees, Mid 19th Century, 8 1/2 X 4 1/2 In.Diam., Pair	225.00
Cloisonne, Tub, Jade Trees, 19th Century, 3 1/2 X 4 1/2 In.Pair	275.00
Cloisonne, Tumbler, Brass Scrolls, Yellow Dragon, Chinese, 3 3/8 In.	50.00
Cloisonne, Turtle, Back Removes, Scroll, Dragons, Cobalt Blue, 4 X 6 In., Pair	550.00
Cloisonne, Turtle, Lidded, Scrolls, Dragon In Design, 3 1/2 X 6 In., Pair	800.00
Cloisonne, Urn, Bronze, Enamel, F.Barbedienne, C.1880, 14 1/2 In. *Illus*	900.00
Cloisonne, Vase, Apple Blossom On Branch, Gold Trim, 3 In., Pair	95.00
Cloisonne, Vase, Aztec Design, 10 1/2 In.	70.00
Cloisonne, Vase, Baluster Form, Flowers On Ground, 10 In., Pair	675.00
Cloisonne, Vase, Bamboo Trees, 15 In. Tall	125.00
Cloisonne, Vase, Banjo, 19th Century, Japanese, 5 1/2 In.	385.00
Cloisonne, Vase, Bird & Flower, Turquoise, 9 1/2 In.	225.00
Cloisonne, Vase, Birds & Morning Glories, Pink, Lavender Foil, 5 3/4 In.	195.00
Cloisonne, Vase, Black Ground, Fishscale Dragons, 4 In., Pair	45.00
Cloisonne, Vase, Black Ground, Yellow Leaves & Flowers, 5 In.	150.00
Cloisonne, Vase, Black, Brown, White, Dragon, Confronted Ho-O, 1850s, 12 In.	75.00
Cloisonne, Vase, Blue Ground, Goldstone Flecks On Copper, 7 1/2 In.	210.00
Cloisonne, Vase, Blue Ground, Mushroom Blossoms, Marked, 10 1/2 In.	200.00
Cloisonne, Vase, Blue Ground, Red & Blue Irises, 10 In.	145.00
Cloisonne, Vase, Blue Ground, 4 Medallions, 12 In., Pair	400.00
Cloisonne, Vase, Blue, Floral, Stamped China, 4 1/8 In., Pair	75.00
Cloisonne, Vase, Blue, Pink Flowers, Stand, 6 1/2 In., Pair	275.00
Cloisonne, Vase, Blue, 5 Claw Imperial Dragons, 1700s, 6 1/2 In., Pair	200.00

Cloisonne, Urn, Bronze, Enamel, F.Barbedienne,
C.1880, 14 1/2 In.

Coca-Cola, Glass, 1920
(See Page 104)

Cloisonne, Vase, Bulbous, Black Ground, Flowers, 9 1/2 In., Pair 125.00
Cloisonne, Vase, Butterflies, Phoenix Bird, Flowers, Multi-Color, 4 1/2 In. 175.00
Cloisonne, Vase, Chevron Pattern, Roses, Green Ground, 7 In. 230.00
Cloisonne, Vase, Cobalt Blue Ground, Winding Dragon, 3 Claws, 7 1/4 In. 225.00
Cloisonne, Vase, Cobalt Blue, Pheasants In Garden, 17 1/2 X 7 In., Pair 2300.00
Cloisonne, Vase, Colored Enamels, 10 1/2 In. 225.00
Cloisonne, Vase, Dragon Coils Around Vase, 19th Century, 9 1/2 In. 350.00
Cloisonne, Vase, Dragons Fighting, Lotus Flower Neck, 10 1/2 In., Pair 350.00
Cloisonne, Vase, Egrets In Bushes, Olive Ground, 19th Century, 7 3/4 In. 495.00
Cloisonne, Vase, Enamel & Bronze, Japanese Figures, 13 1/2 X 7 1/2 In. 975.00
Cloisonne, Vase, Enameled, Pierced Bronze Base, Continental, 11 1/4 In., Pair 1300.00
Cloisonne, Vase, Fish & Enameled Fish Net, 4 1/2 In. 525.00
Cloisonne, Vase, Fish & Sea Growths On Green Ground, 5 In. 575.00
Cloisonne, Vase, Floral On Blue, Silver Rim, 7 1/2 In. 150.00
Cloisonne, Vase, Floral Scrollwork, Flared Neck, 9 1/2 In., Pair 500.00
Cloisonne, Vase, Flowers, Dragons, Circular Bands Of Black, 7 1/2 In. 195.00
Cloisonne, Vase, Flowers, Gold Stone Flecks, 5 In. 45.00
Cloisonne, Vase, Flying Cranes, Geometric Design, C.1880, Signed, 9 1/2 In. 345.00
Cloisonne, Vase, Foil, Silver Cloisons, Flowers, 10 In. 500.00
Cloisonne, Vase, Gold Ground, Black Lotus Flower, Impressed Mark, 10 1/2 In. 195.00
Cloisonne, Vase, Gold Ground, Multi-Colored Flowers, 20th Century, 13 In. 140.00
Cloisonne, Vase, Goldstone, Arabesque Design, 19th Century, 8 1/2 In. 295.00
Cloisonne, Vase, Green Ground, Transparent Enamel, Silver Foil, 9 3/4 In. 275.00
Cloisonne, Vase, Green, Floral Pattern, Stamped China, 8 1/2 In. 150.00
Cloisonne, Vase, Inverted Pyriform, Millefleurs Design, 9 1/2 In., Pair 425.00
Cloisonne, Vase, Japanese, Banjo Shape, Arabesque, 19th Century, 6 In., Pair 250.00
Cloisonne, Vase, Japanese, Scenic Band And Arabesque Medallions, 7 In. 85.00
Cloisonne, Vase, Kyoto School, Flowers, Black Ground, 19th Century, 9 3/4 In. 585.00
Cloisonne, Vase, Multi-Colored Foil, Inset Blocks, Aqua, Green, 5 3/4 In. 165.00
Cloisonne, Vase, Ovoid Body, Textured Foil, Iris, Pinks, C.1900, 10 In. 250.00
Cloisonne, Vase, Ovoid Form, Purple & White Wisteria, Japanese, 37 In. 500.00
Cloisonne, Vase, Panels Of Phoenix Bird & Dragon, 12 In., Pair 700.00
Cloisonne, Vase, Panels Of Sacred Blossoms, Cobalt Ground, 12 1/2 In., Pair 500.00
Cloisonne, Vase, Pearlized Green & Turquoise Insets, 1850, 8 In. 175.00
Cloisonne, Vase, Pink & White Flowers, Teakwood Stand, 6 In. 85.00
Cloisonne, Vase, Red Chrysanthemums, Japan, 12 In. 225.00
Cloisonne, Vase, Robin Blue Ground, Mountain Scene, 7 1/2 In. 90.00
Cloisonne, Vase, Round, 3 Curved Feet, Covered, 11 1/2 X 7 1/2 In.Diam., Pair 1500.00
Cloisonne, Vase, Russet Ground, Green Interior, 4-Panel, 6 In. 100.00
Cloisonne, Vase, Speckled Dots, Cloison Latticework, C.1880, 6 1/2 X 6 In. 450.00
Cloisonne, Vase, Spill, Footed, Japanese, 8 1/2 In. 290.00
Cloisonne, Vase, Tree Bark Texture, Flowers & Birds, 8 1/2 In., Pair 390.00
Cloisonne, Vase, Tree Bark Texture, Relief Work On Bark, 8 1/2 In., Pair 375.00
Cloisonne, Vase, Trumpet Neck, Fretwork On Turquoise, 10 1/2 In. 175.00
Cloisonne, Vase, Urn Shape, Flowers, Scrolls & Leaf Designs, 4 In. 58.00
Cloisonne, Vase, White Flowers, Green Background, Marked China, 5 In. 45.00
Cloisonne, Vase, Wisteria Tree, Flowers, Bird, Pearl Grey, Japanese, 7 In. 290.00
Cloisonne, Vase, Wisterias, Green Leaves, Red Ground, 19th Century, 8 1/2 In. 295.00
   Clothing, see Textile

*Cluthra glass is a two-layered glass with small air pockets that form white
spots. The Steuben Glass Works of Corning, New York, made it after
1903. Kimball Glass Company of Vineland, New Jersey, made Cluthra
from about 1925.*
   Cluthra, see also Steuben
Cluthra, Bottle, Perfume, Brown & White, Crystal Stopper, 6 In. 450.00
Cluthra, Bowl, Raspberry, Controlled Bubbles, 5 X 7 In. 275.00
Cluthra, Candlestick, Rosaline, Alabaster Wafers, Signed, 12 In., Pair 750.00
Cluthra, Compote, Alabaster Stem & Foot, Rosaline, Signed, 5 X 10 1/4 In. 325.00
Cluthra, Vase, Form Of Elongated Rose Bowl, Orange, Signed, 5 1/2 In. 145.00
Cluthra, Vase, Green & White, 7 1/2 In. 450.00
Cluthra, Vase, Mottling White On Clear, Random Markings In Blue, 8 In. 85.00
Cluthra, Vase, Pink, Signed, 8 1/4 In. 750.00

*Coalbrookdale was made by the Coalport porcelain factory of England
during the Victorian period. The pieces are heavily decorated with floral
encrustations.*

Coalbrookdale, Vase, Flowers, 8 1/2 In. 350.00

Coalport ware has been made by the Coalport Porcelain Works of England from 1795 to the present time.

Coalport, see also Indian Tree

Coalport, Box, Cover, Chicago Exhibition 1893, 1891 Mark, 1 1/2 X 3 1/2 In.	350.00
Coalport, Breakfast Set, Bridal, Sugar, Creamer, Teapot, 2 Cups & Saucers	81.00
Coalport, Cup & Saucer, Anniversary, Gold & White	20.00
Coalport, Cup & Saucer, Blue Flowers On Gold, Gold Handle & Inside Cup, Mark	85.00
Coalport, Cup & Saucer, Demitasse, Gold Filigree, Medallions	15.00
Coalport, Cup & Saucer, Harebell	18.00
Coalport, Demitasse Set, Red & Gold, Flowers, Set Of 6	90.00
Coalport, Plate, Anniversary, Gold & White, 8 In.	25.00
Coalport, Plate, Aurora, 8 In.	5.00
Coalport, Plate, Belfort Pattern, 8 In.	8.00
Coalport, Plate, Cobalt Border, Gold Inside Band, C.1910, 8 5/8 In., Set Of 6	75.00
Coalport, Plate, Dessert, Molded Border, Enamel Flower, 8 5/8 In., Set Of 12	150.00
Coalport, Plate, Floral Centers, Green, Gold, C.1820, 8 3/4 In., Pair	120.00
Coalport, Plate, Floral Medallion Center, 1891-1920 Mark, 9 1/2 In.	39.00
Coalport, Plate, Gold & White Flowers, Outer Third Fluted, Marked, 9 1/4 In.	45.00
Coalport, Urn, Cobalt & Gold, Butterflies	85.00
Coalport, Urn, Covered, Multi-Colors, Marked, 7 1/2 In.	120.00
Coalport, Urn, Miniature, Gilt Handles & Feet, 1891 Mark, Signed, 5 In.	225.00
Coalport, Vase, Blown Out Hexagonal Panels, Gilt Neck, 3 1/4 X 3 1/2 In.	125.00
Coalport, Vase, Floral Encrusted, Scrolled Handles, C.1840, 10 1/2 In., Pair	175.00

Cobalt blue glass was made using oxide of cobalt. The characteristic bright dark blue identifies it for the collector. Most cobalt glass found today was made after the Civil War.

Cobalt Blue, see also Shirley Temple

Cobalt Blue, Ashtray, Souvenir, Cincinnati, Ohio	7.00
Cobalt Blue, Bottle, Hand Blown, Ground Stopper, Square Base, 5 In.	75.00
Cobalt Blue, Bottle, Poodle	25.00
Cobalt Blue, Bowl, Good Luck, 9 In.	125.00
Cobalt Blue, Box, Patch, Hinged, Enameled, 1 X 2 In.	110.00
Cobalt Blue, Dish, Candy, Covered, Arcadia, Divided	12.00
Cobalt Blue, Figurine, Doves, Tulip Vase Back, 3 1/2 In.	85.00
Cobalt Blue, Figurine, Poodles, White, Blue Basket In Mouth, Pair	215.00
Cobalt Blue, Goblet, Diamond Patterned Ball On Standards, 6 3/4 In., Set Of	66.00
Cobalt Blue, Lamp Base, Miniature, Crocodile Tears, Blue	35.00
Cobalt Blue, Mayonnaise Set, Tin Lid	8.00
Cobalt Blue, Nappy, 2-Handled, Serrated Ruffled Rim, Pond Lily Pattern	20.00
Cobalt Blue, Pitcher, Pedestal, Enamel Floral Sprays, Handled, 9 1/2 In.	35.00
Cobalt Blue, Pitcher, Water, Applied Reeded Crystal Handle, Ice Lip	28.00
Cobalt Blue, Pitcher, 7 Glasses, Rib	65.00
Cobalt Blue, Salt, Silver Plated Stand, Footed, Japan	12.50
Cobalt Blue, Sherbet, 4 In., Set Of 6	48.00
Cobalt Blue, Spooner, Teardrop & Thumbprint	49.00
Cobalt Blue, Sugar & Creamer, Handled, Pedestal, 1860s, 5 In.	100.00
Cobalt Blue, Sugar & Creamer, Pedestal Base, Hand Blown, C.1860, 5 In.	100.00
Cobalt Blue, Sugar, Cover, Sawtooth	140.00
Cobalt Blue, Teapot, Gold Design, Pedestal, Blue Maple Leaf	120.00
Cobalt Blue, Tumble-Up, Cut & Etched To Clear, C.1910, 8 In.	37.50
Cobalt Blue, Tureen, Platter, Gold Tracing, Tureen, 16 X 9 In.	1287.00
Cobalt Blue, Vase, Bulbous Base, Urn Shaped, 12 1/4 In.	15.00
Cobalt Blue, Vase, Clear Base, 8 In.	12.00
Cobalt Blue, Vase, Diamond Quilted, Pedestaled, 1920s, 8 1/4 In.	35.00
Cobalt Blue, Vase, Frilly Top, Decorated, 12 1/2 In.	55.00
Cobalt Blue, Vase, Ormolu Mounts, Cupids, Enameled, 9 7/8 In., Pair	225.00
Cobalt Blue, Vase, Pedestaled, Diamond Quilted, C.1920s, 8 1/4 In.	35.00
Cobalt Blue, Vase, 2 Handles, Full Figure Draped Maiden, Bisque, 6 3/4 In.	16.00
Cobalt Blue, Water Set, Leaf Medallion, Blue, 7 Piece	575.00
Cobalt Blue, Wine, 5 In., Set Of 6	60.00

Coca-Cola advertising items have become a special field for collectors.

Coca-Cola, Bag, Over Night	9.00
Coca-Cola, Blotter, 1930s, 3 1/2 X 7 1/2 In.	4.00

Coca-Cola, Bonnet, Baby, Found At Foley Beach, South Carolina, 1930s 7.00
Coca-Cola, Bookmark, 1905, Lillian Nordica 60.00
Coca-Cola, Bottle Opener & Cap Catcher, Sprite Boy, 1950's 10.00
Coca-Cola, Bottle, Amber 35.00
Coca-Cola, Bottle, Anchorage, Alaska, Embossed On Bottom 7.50
Coca-Cola, Bottle, Aqua, Round Base, Square Body, Hexagonal Neck, Oklahoma 27.00
Coca-Cola, Bottle, Brown, 1 Quart 18.50
Coca-Cola, Bottle, Oversize, 1923, 20 In. 125.00
Coca-Cola, Bottle, Perfume, 1930, Shaped Like Coke Bottle 29.00
Coca-Cola, Bottle, 2 1/2 Liter 13.00
Coca-Cola, Bottle, 50th Anniversary, Gold Medallion 45.00
Coca-Cola, Box, Ice, Cooler, 2 Door Top, 1934 .... 185.00
Coca-Cola, Box, Pill, Round, Metal, Thimble On Top, Sprite Boy, 1941 .... 2.75
Coca-Cola, Calendar, 1918, June Caprice, 5 X 9 In. .... 45.00 To 55.00
Coca-Cola, Calendar, 1922 .... 250.00
Coca-Cola, Calendar, 1922, Baseball Background 175.00
Coca-Cola, Calendar, 1925 .... 200.00
Coca-Cola, Calendar, 1942 .... 55.00
Coca-Cola, Calendar, 1947 .... 10.00
Coca-Cola, Calendar, 1951 .... 20.00
Coca-Cola, Calendar, 1957 .... 10.00
Coca-Cola, Candy Container 60.00
Coca-Cola, Card, Nature Study, Original Box, Set Of 96 .... 25.00
Coca-Cola, Card, Nature, Set Of 36 .... 18.00
Coca-Cola, Card, Playing, Never Opened 40.00
Coca-Cola, Card, Playing, 1939, Boxed 27.50
Coca-Cola, Card, Trade, World Of Nature, Set Of 96 .... 35.00
Coca-Cola, Carrier, Vendor's, 1940 .... 35.00
Coca-Cola, Carrier, Yellow, Wood, Rope Handles 10.00
Coca-Cola, Carrier, 1 Dozen Bottles, Wire 20.00
Coca-Cola, Case, Needle, 1924 .... 40.00
Coca-Cola, Case, Needle, 1925 .... 45.00
Coca-Cola, Chest, Stainless Interior 45.00
Coca-Cola, Clock, Gilbert 450.00
Coca-Cola, Clock, Logo, Wooden, Tin Front, Electric, 16 In.Square 175.00
Coca-Cola, Clock, Wall, Electric, Drink Coca-Cola In Bottles, 16 X 16 In. 100.00
Coca-Cola, Coin Changer 150.00
Coca-Cola, Cooler, 2 Door Top, 1934 .... 185.00
Coca-Cola, Cufflinks, 1923 .... 75.00
Coca-Cola, Cutter, Cigar 15.00
Coca-Cola, Dish, Pretzel, 1935 .... 60.00
Coca-Cola, Dispenser, Bottle, Red & White, Model F 83, 1949 .... 100.00
Coca-Cola, Dispenser, Syrup, China 275.00
Coca-Cola, Fan, 1942 .... 14.00
Coca-Cola, Glass, 1920 .... Illus 15.00
Coca-Cola, Ice Pick 18.00
Coca-Cola, Knife, Bottle Opener, One Blade 75.00
Coca-Cola, Lighter, Cigarette, Bottle Shaped 5.00
Coca-Cola, Lighter, Cigarette, Musical, 1940s 75.00
Coca-Cola, Machine, Dispensing, 5 & 10 Cent, Curved Top, 1940s, 5 Feet 285.00
Coca-Cola, Machine, Miniature, Westinghouse, Dispenses Book Matches, 1950s 27.00
Coca-Cola, Marker, Book, 1-Sided, 1899 .... 250.00
Coca-Cola, Marker, Crosswalk, Brass, Safety First, 3 3/4 In.Diameter 35.00
Coca-Cola, Mirror, Pocket, 1904 St.Louis Fair 125.00
Coca-Cola, Mirror, Pocket, 1912 .... 45.00
Coca-Cola, Mirror, Pocket, 1917 .... 45.00 To 120.00
Coca-Cola, Opener, Bottle, Ice Pick, Wood Handle 28.00
Coca-Cola, Opener, Have A Coke, Wire 2.00
Coca-Cola, Opener, Wall, Iron 4.00
Coca-Cola, Paperweight, Chattanooga Bottling Co., 3 1/2 In. 8.50
Coca-Cola, Pencil Kit, 1937 .... 25.00
Coca-Cola, Poster, Girl In White Bathing Suit, Dated, 1938, 50 X 30 In. 35.00
Coca-Cola, Radio, Cooler Shape, 1949 .... 165.00 To 225.00
Coca-Cola, Ruler, 1935 .... 5.00
Coca-Cola, Sharpener, Pencil, Bottle Shape 28.00
Coca-Cola, Sign, Bottle Shaped, Tin, 1923, 36 In. 85.00
Coca-Cola, Sign, Drink Coca Cola, Take Home A Carton, 6 Bottles 25 Cents 55.00

Coca-Cola, Sign, Drink Coca-Cola, Double Sided, Dated 1938, 8 1/2 X 18 In. 55.00
Coca-Cola, Sign, Drink Coca-Cola, Mirror, Walnut Frame 23.00
Coca-Cola, Sign, Fountain Service, Drink Coca-Cola, 1935, 23 X 25 In. 60.00
Coca-Cola, Sign, Old Type Bottle, Big 5 Cent, Tin 35.00
Coca-Cola, Sign, Series Of Fans, 1929 Lithograph, 3 Feet Across, Pair 80.00
Coca-Cola, Sign, 1923 Christmas Bottle, 34 3/4 X 11 1/2 In. 45.00
Coca-Cola, Sign, 1936, Christmas Bottle, Tin 65.00
Coca-Cola, Thermometer, Bottle Shape, Tin, 16 In. 15.00
Coca-Cola, Thermometer, Bottle Shape, 24 In. 45.00
Coca-Cola, Thermometer, Bottle Shape, 29 In. .... 32.00 To 55.00
Coca-Cola, Thermometer, Celsius, Made In Canada, 1950 .... 9.00
Coca-Cola, Thermometer, Cigar Shape, 29 In. 42.00
Coca-Cola, Thermometer, Drink Coca-Cola In Bottles, Steel, 12 In.Diameter 35.00
Coca-Cola, Thermometer, Things Go Better With Coke, 27 In. 45.00
Coca-Cola, Thermometer, 1935, Christmas, 17 In. 32.00
Coca-Cola, Thermometer, 1937, Red Oval, Gold Bottom 48.00
Coca-Cola, Thermometer, 1942, Art Deco, 2 Bottles, 16 X 7 In. 65.00
Coca-Cola, Thermometer, 1950, Convex, 17 In. 17.00
Coca-Cola, Token, Free Drink, 1904 World's Fair, Metal 8.00
Coca-Cola, Tongs, Ice 22.50
Coca-Cola, Tray, Please Pay When Served, Wood, 1940s 48.00
Coca-Cola, Tray, Tip, 1900, Hilda Clark 600.00
Coca-Cola, Tray, Tip, 1904, St.Louis Fair .... 120.00 To 250.00
Coca-Cola, Tray, Tip, 1909, Coca-Cola Girl 85.00
Coca-Cola, Tray, Tip, 1912, Girl With Rose In Hat .... 60.00 To 85.00
Coca-Cola, Tray, Tip, 1914, Betty .... 42.50 To 125.00
Coca-Cola, Tray, Tip, 1917, Elaine .... 20.00 To 100.00
Coca-Cola, Tray, Tip, 1920, Oval, Girl In Yellow Dress, Hat .... 85.00 To 100.00
Coca-Cola, Tray, Tip, 1934, St.Louis 150.00
Coca-Cola, Tray, Wood Six Pack 29.00
Coca-Cola, Tray, 1900, Hilda Clark, 9 3/4 In.Diameter 800.00
Coca-Cola, Tray, 1904, Lillian Russell .... 100.00 To 800.00
Coca-Cola, Tray, 1905, Juanita, Oval 850.00
Coca-Cola, Tray, 1912, Girl With Rose In Her Hat 225.00
Coca-Cola, Tray, 1914, Betty, Oval .... 160.00 To 325.00
Coca-Cola, Tray, 1914, Betty, 13 1/4 X 10 1/2 In. .... 60.00 To 85.00
Coca-Cola, Tray, 1917, Elaine .... 35.00 To 85.00
Coca-Cola, Tray, 1920, Garden Girl, Oval .... 50.00 To 425.00
Coca-Cola, Tray, 1921, Summer Girl .... 140.00 To 165.00
Coca-Cola, Tray, 1923, Flapper Girl .... 65.00 To 70.00
Coca-Cola, Tray, 1924, Smiling Girl 125.00
Coca-Cola, Tray, 1925, Girl At Party In White Fox Fur .... 50.00 To 55.00
Coca-Cola, Tray, 1926, Sports Couple .... 165.00 To 225.00
Coca-Cola, Tray, 1927, Bobbed Hair .... 75.00 To 125.00
Coca-Cola, Tray, 1927, Soda Jerk 85.00
Coca-Cola, Tray, 1929, Bottle 145.00
Coca-Cola, Tray, 1929, Holding Glass .... 90.00 To 110.00
Coca-Cola, Tray, 1930, Bathing Beauty .... 90.00 To 95.00
Coca-Cola, Tray, 1930, Girl With Telephone 115.00
Coca-Cola, Tray, 1932, Yellow Bathing Suit 210.00
Coca-Cola, Tray, 1934, Weissmuller, & O'Sullivan 60.00
Coca-Cola, Tray, 1937, Running Girl 38.00
Coca-Cola, Tray, 1938, Girl In The Afternoon 32.00
Coca-Cola, Tray, 1939, Springboard Girl, Near Mint 57.00
Coca-Cola, Tray, 1941, Girl Ice Skater, Near Mint 40.00
Coca-Cola, Tray, 1942, Two Girls At Car, Near Mint 49.00
Coca-Cola, Tray, 1943, Girl With Wind In Her Hair 35.00
Coca-Cola, Tray, 1950, Girl With Menu, 10 1/2 X 13 1/4 In. .... 13.00 To 20.00
Coca-Cola, Tray, 1968, Lillian Russell 30.00
Coca-Cola, Truck, Miniature, Barclay Bottle Series 10.00
Coca-Cola, Truck, Original Paint, 10 Original Bottles 175.00
Coca-Cola, Wallet, Leather, 1940s 16.00
Coca-Cola, Watch Fob, C.1908 .... 60.00

Coffee grinders, home size, were first made about 1894. They lost favor by
the 1930s.
Coffee Grinder, Arcade 25 .... 35.00

Coffee Grinder, Arcade, Glass & Iron, Wall Model	29.00
Coffee Grinder, Arcade, No. 4, Wall Mount	30.00
Coffee Grinder, Arcade, Wall Hanging, Telephone Model, 1890	150.00
Coffee Grinder, Clamps On Table, Dated 1909, Universal, Iron, 12 In.	35.00
Coffee Grinder, Coles, Electric, Hopper, Drawer, Pouring Spout, 31 X 16 In.	145.00
Coffee Grinder, Covered Wagon Model, Favorite No.17	45.00
Coffee Grinder, Dovetailed Edge, Pyramid Shape, Brass Hopper & Knob, Marked	60.00
Coffee Grinder, Dovetailed, Drawer, Iron Crank, Pine, 6 In.Square	65.00
Coffee Grinder, Elgin, Illinois Company, Eagle Finial, 29 In.	500.00
Coffee Grinder, Elma, Tin	30.00
Coffee Grinder, Enterprise, Counter Top, Original Decals	425.00
Coffee Grinder, Enterprise, Double Wheel, No.4	350.00
Coffee Grinder, Enterprise, Double Wheel, No.9	550.00
Coffee Grinder, Enterprise, Eagle Finial, 1873, 18 In.	225.00
Coffee Grinder, Enterprise, Floor Model, Original Paint	1500.00
Coffee Grinder, Enterprise, No.7, Original Paint	425.00
Coffee Grinder, Enterprise, No.9, Original Paint, 25 In.	395.00
Coffee Grinder, Enterprise, Wall Mount	35.00
Coffee Grinder, Enterprise, 2 Wheel, Dated 1876, Wheel 12 3/4 In.Diameter	295.00
Coffee Grinder, Fairbanks Morse, Floor Model, 2-Wheel	250.00
Coffee Grinder, Glass Jar, Parker, No.441	62.50
Coffee Grinder, Golden Rule	125.00
Coffee Grinder, Iron, Marked Weigall & Hardell	20.00
Coffee Grinder, Lap, Barrel Shaped, Ribbed Metal & Wood	65.00
Coffee Grinder, Miniature, Little Tot, Paper Label	67.00
Coffee Grinder, Miniature, 2 Wheels & Drawer	36.00
Coffee Grinder, PeDe Koffie, Blue Ceramic	75.00
Coffee Grinder, Red, Drawer, Enterprise Mfg., Philadelphia, 16 In.	350.00
Coffee Grinder, Scroll, Iron Top, Dovetailed, 2 Quart	100.00
Coffee Grinder, Star Mill, 2 Wheel	225.00
Coffee Grinder, Table Model, Brass Pull, Porcelain Lined, Iron, Signed	65.00
Coffee Grinder, Tin, The Swift Mill, Drawer, 1875, Lane Bros., 14 In.	175.00
Coffee Grinder, Turkish, Brass, 10 In.	15.00
Coffee Grinder, Vogel, Brass Cup, Delft Celluloid Panels	40.00
Coffee Grinder, Wall Type, Crystal Brand, Glass Top & Bottom	62.50
Coffee Grinder, Wall, Arcade Crystal No.3, Glass	37.50
Coffee Grinder, Wall, Mounted On Original Board, Parker, Tin & Iron	39.00
Coffee Grinder, Wood, Cylinder Shape, Drawer, Original Label, 12 X 7 1/2 In.	115.00
Coffee Grinder, Wooden Dovetailing, Japanning, Model No.2	100.00
Coffee Grinder, Wooden, Iron Handle On Top, 6 In., Square, 5 In.High	48.00
Coffee Grinder, 2 Wheel, National Specialty Co., Brass Hopper, 20 In.	225.00
Coffee Grinder, 26 In.High Wheels, Commercial, Elgin National Coffee Mill	250.00
Coin Spot, Banana Stand, Opalescent, 7 X 5 X 4 1/2 In.	22.50
Coin Spot, Bowl, Ruffled Edges, 6 1/4 In.	18.00
Coin Spot, Bowl, Ruffled Top, Blue Opalescent, 8 In.Diameter	45.00
Coin Spot, Bowl, Ruffled Top, White, 9 1/2 In.	45.00
Coin Spot, Box, Powder, Cranberry	95.00
Coin Spot, Category, Pitcher, Water, Green	85.00
Coin Spot, Cruet, Opalescent	72.00
Coin Spot, Cup, Crackle Glass, Clear, Set Of 3	20.00
Coin Spot, Dish, Pickle	150.00
Coin Spot, Jug, Syrup, Opalescent	110.00
Coin Spot, Lamp, Miniature, Cranberry, Nutmeg Burner, Ball Shade, 9 1/2 In.	90.00
Coin Spot, Pitcher, Blue, 4 In.	50.00
Coin Spot, Pitcher, Ruffled Rim, Opalescent, 6 1/2 In.	37.00
Coin Spot, Pitcher, Water, Blue	95.00
Coin Spot, Pitcher, Water, Bulbous, White, Opalescent, Ruffled	110.00
Coin Spot, Pitcher, Water, Opalescent, Green	110.00
Coin Spot, Pitcher, Water, Square Neck, Opalescent, Blue	95.00
Coin Spot, Pitcher, Water, White	65.00
Coin Spot, Pitcher, Water, White Opalescent, Bulbous	110.00
Coin Spot, Sugar Shaker, Blue, Top Dated 1904	55.00
Coin Spot, Syrup, Applied Handle, Opalescent	47.50
Coin Spot, Syrup, Cranberry	165.00
Coin Spot, Syrup, Opalescent, Blue	115.00
Coin Spot, Syrup, Opalescent, Blue, Tin Top	90.00
Coin Spot, Syrup, Rubena, Opalescent	210.00

Coin Spot, Syrup, White Opalescent, Applied Handle	55.00
Coin Spot, Tumbler, Blue	25.00
Coin Spot, Tumbler, Cranberry	17.50
Coin Spot, Tumbler, Opalescent, Green	20.00
Coin Spot, Vase, Blue Rainbow Stripe, White Lining, Dimpled Sides, 9 In.	650.00
Coin Spot, Vase, Flared, Ruffled Top, White, 8 In.	40.00
Coin Spot, Vase, Ruffled & Crimped Top, Cranberry, 6 1/4 In.	85.00
Coin Spot, Water Set, Cranberry, Opalescent, 7 Pieces	285.00

Collector plates are modern plates produced in limited editions. Some will be found listed under the company. Pictures and more price information can be found in "Kovels' Price Guide for Collector Plates, Figurines, Paperweights, and Other Limited Editions."

Collector, Plate, Anri, Father's Day, 1972	100.00
Collector, Plate, Anri, Father's Day, 1975	60.00
Collector, Plate, Anri, Mother's Day, 1972	85.00
Collector, Plate, Anri, Mother's Day, 1973	70.00
Collector, Plate, Belleek, Christmas, 1971	75.00
Collector, Plate, Belleek, Christmas, 1972	70.00
Collector, Plate, DeGrazia, Festival Of Lights, 1976	95.00
Collector, Plate, Ferrandiz, Christmas, Wooden, 1973	139.00
Collector, Plate, Goebel Hummel, Annual, 1971	995.00
Collector, Plate, Goebel Hummel, Annual, 1972	63.00 To 95.00
Collector, Plate, Goebel Hummel, Annual, 1973	175.00 To 185.00
Collector, Plate, Goebel Hummel, Annual, 1974	89.00 To 95.00
Collector, Plate, Goebel Hummel, Annual, 1975	68.00 To 85.00
Collector, Plate, Goebel Hummel, Annual, 1976	75.00
Collector, Plate, Goebel, Wildlife, 1977	28.00
Collector, Plate, Haviland, Chistmas, 1971	30.00
Collector, Plate, Haviland, Christmas, 1970	165.00
Collector, Plate, Haviland, Christmas, 1973	30.00
Collector, Plate, Haviland, Christmas, 1974	30.00
Collector, Plate, Haviland, Mother's Day, 1974	29.95
Collector, Plate, Haviland, Mother's Day, 1976	38.00
Collector, Plate, Hutschenreuther, Christmas, 1978	250.00
Collector, Plate, Kaiser, Mother's Day, 1971	23.50
Collector, Plate, Lalique, Annual, 1967	275.00
Collector, Plate, Lalique, Annual, 1968	175.00
Collector, Plate, Lalique, Annual, 1969	175.00
Collector, Plate, Lalique, Annual, 1970	65.00
Collector, Plate, Lalique, Annual, 1973	45.00
Collector, Plate, Lenox, Annual, 1973	55.00
Collector, Plate, Lenox, Annual, 1974	29.00
Collector, Plate, Leyendecker, Christmas, 1975	20.00
Collector, Plate, Leyendecker, Mother's Day, 1976	15.00
Collector, Plate, Limoges, Christmas, 1972	6.00
Collector, Plate, Mettlach, Christmas, 1977	139.00 To 175.00
Collector, Plate, Orrefors, Mother's Day, 1971	12.95
Collector, Plate, Orrefors, Mother's Day, 1972	14.95
Collector, Plate, Orrefors, Mother's Day, 1976	32.95
Collector, Plate, Pickard, Christmas, 1976	250.00
Collector, Plate, Pickard, Christmas, 1977	90.00
Collector, Plate, Porsgrund, Christmas, 1969	8.00 To 10.00
Collector, Plate, Porsgrund, Christmas, 1970	9.00
Collector, Plate, Porsgrund, Christmas, 1971	8.00 To 19.95
Collector, Plate, Porsgrund, Christmas, 1975	24.95
Collector, Plate, Porsgrund, Mother's Day, 1971	2.95
Collector, Plate, Porsgrund, Mother's Day, 1974	7.00
Collector, Plate, Rorstrand, Christmas, 1971	11.95
Collector, Plate, Rorstrand, Christmas, 1974	44.00
Collector, Plate, Rorstrand, Mother's Day, 1971	6.95
Collector, Plate, Rorstrand, Mother's Day, 1973	28.75
Collector, Plate, Rosenthal, Christmas, 1975	175.00
Collector, Plate, Royal Bayreuth, Christmas, 1976	30.00
Collector, Plate, Royal Bayreuth, Mother's Day, 1975	75.00
Collector, Plate, Royal Copenhagen, see Royal Copenhagen	
Collector, Plate, Royal Devon, Christmas, 1975	30.00

Collector, Plate, Royal Doulton, Christmas, 1973	22.50
Collector, Plate, Royal Worcester, Annual, 1976	89.50
Collector, Plate, Runci, Mother's Day, 1977	36.00
Collector, Plate, Spode, Christmas, 1971	11.95
Collector, Plate, Svend Jensen, Mother's Day, 1971	25.00
Collector, Plate, Svend Jensen, Mother's Day, 1974	75.95
Collector, Plate, Svend Jensen, Mother's Day, 1976	16.95
Collector, Plate, Wedgwood, Christmas, 1970	14.50
Collector, Plate, Wedgwood, Christmas, 1971	21.50
Collector, Plate, Wedgwood, Christmas, 1977	20.00
Collector, Plate, Wedgwood, Christmas, 1978	38.00
Collector, Plate, Wedgwood, Mother's Day, 1971	10.00
Collector, Plate, Wedgwood, Mother's Day, 1972	10.00

Commemorative items have been made to honor members of royalty and those of great national fame. World's fairs and important historical events are also remembered with commemorative pieces.

Commemorative, see also Coronation, World's Fair

Commemorative, Cup, Visit To Canada, Queen Elizabeth, King George, 1939	10.00
Commemorative, Goblet, Knights Of Pythias, Rochester, N.Y., 1900, Scene, 5 In.	75.00
Commemorative, Mug, 1901 Exposition, Buffalo, Whites	155.00
Commemorative, Mug, 60th Year Of Queen Mary's Reign, 6 1/4 In.High	40.00
Commemorative, Plate, Champlain Memorial, Plattsburg, N.Y., 10 1/2 In.	25.00
Commemorative, Plate, Harvard Buildings, Wedgwood, 10 1/2 In.	15.00
Commemorative, Plate, Longfellow House, Wedgwood, 10 1/2 In.	25.00
Commemorative, Plate, Portland, Maine, Wedgwood, 10 1/2 In.	25.00
Commemorative, Plate, St.James's Palace, Wedgwood	18.00
Commemorative, Plate, Trafalgar Square, Wedgwood	18.00
Commemorative, Plate, World War II, Bundles For Britain, Inc.	25.00
Commemorative, Teapot, Foch, Wilson, Hughes, George V & Queen, Dated 1919	150.00

Coors ware was made by a pottery in Golden, Colorado, owned by the Coors Beverage Company. It was produced from the turn of the century until the pottery was destroyed by fire in the 1930s. It resembles Homer Laughlin lines such as Fiesta. The name Coors is marked on the back.

Coors, Bowl, Console, Tepco, Blue, 3 Figural Buddhas	13.00
Coors, Bowl, Punch, Miniature, Whirligig	13.00
Coors, Cookie Jar, Covered, Signed	11.00
Coors, Honey Pot, Cover, 2-Handled, Rose Finial	15.00
Coors, Honey Pot, Covered, Rosebud, 3 Feet, Blue, 4 1/2 In.Square	22.00
Coors, Jug, Water, Rosebud, Blue, 7 X 7 X 3 In.	22.00
Coors, Mortar & Pestle	10.00
Coors, Mug, Miniature	4.00
Coors, Pitcher, Rosebud, Green	12.00
Coors, Salt & Pepper, Beer Bottle Shape, Pottery	13.50
Coors, Tumbler, Miniature, Flute	4.00
Coors, Vase, Black Cameo	14.00
Coors, Vase, Blue, Double Handled, 9 1/2 In.	16.50
Coors, Vase, Blue, Handles, White Interior, 7 5/8 In.	18.00

W.T.Copeland & Sons, Ltd., ran the Spode Works in Staffordshire, England, from 1847 to the present. Copeland & Garrett was the firm name from 1833 to 1847.

Copeland Spode, see also Flow Blue

Copeland Spode, Cup & Saucer, Primrose	23.00
Copeland Spode, Jug, Ale	80.00
Copeland Spode, Mustard, Cover, Blue & White, Ribbed, 5 In.	30.00
Copeland Spode, Pitcher, Cameo Blue & White, 8 In.	175.00
Copeland Spode, Plate Woodcock, 10 1/4 In.	40.00
Copeland Spode, Plate, Bird, Blue, White, Plover, 10 1/4 In.	45.00
Copeland Spode, Plate, Bird, Blue, White, Wild Ducks, 10 1/4 In.	45.00
Copeland Spode, Plate, Bird, Blue, White, Woodcock, 10 1/4 In.	45.00
Copeland Spode, Plate, Plover, Blue & White, 10 1/4 In.	40.00
Copeland Spode, Plate, Wild Ducks, Blue & White, 10 1/4 In.	40.00
Copeland Spode, Soup, Cobalt Blue & Gold, Pair	25.00
Copeland Spode, Teapot, Cowslip	30.00
Copeland Spode, Toby, Winston Churchill, 8 1/4 In.	60.00

Copeland, see also Spode

Copeland, Creamer & Sugar, Shell Shaped, C.1870	85.00
Copeland, Creamer, Sitting Chinese, Queue Forms Handle, White, Old Mark	70.00
Copeland, Cup & Saucer, Festoon Of Roses, Hand-Painted	45.00
Copeland, Figurine, Woman In Clinging Gown, 10 In.	48.00
Copeland, Jug, Ale, Spode	80.00
Copeland, Jug, Blue & White, 8 In.	80.00
Copeland, Mug, Centennial 1876, G.Washington, Eagle & Flags, Philadelphia	60.00
Copeland, Plate, Luncheon, Hand-Painted Flowers, Gold Net Print, Set Of 1i	150.00
Copeland, Salt, Blue Willow, Demitasse, C.1860	18.50
Copeland, Tea Set, Miniature, Blue & White, 3 Piece	75.00
Copeland, Vase, Shell Shaped, C.1870, 6 1/4 In., Pair	85.00

Copper Luster, see Luster, Copper

Copper, Bedwarmer, Long Turned Hardwood Handle	195.00
Copper, Boiler, Lid	29.50 To 45.00
Copper, Boiler, Wash, Never Used, Original Box	100.00
Copper, Bookends, Spanish Galleon	17.50
Copper, Bowl, Hand Hammered, Signed, K.L.F., 6 In.Diameter	30.00
Copper, Bowl, Imperial Russian, Hand Hammered, Handled, 4 1/4 X 9 1/4 In.	65.00
Copper, Box, Cigar, Upright, Hammered	14.00
Copper, Box, Deed, Hinged & Handled, 11 X 13 X 4 1/4 In.	92.00
Copper, Box, Tobacco, Gilded, 17th Century, 5 1/4 In.	350.00
Copper, Bucket, Tapered Sides, 2 1/2 Gallon	45.00
Copper, Can, Milk, 20 In.	425.00
Copper, Can, Watering	85.00
Copper, Candlesnuffer, Scrolled End, 9 1/4 In.	12.50
Copper, Candlestick, Charles Rohlfs, Oak, R/1905, 19 1/2 In.	1250.00
Copper, Chair, Rocking, Doll's, Wooden Seat	55.00
Copper, Coffee Urn, Brass Spigot, 10 Gallon	50.00
Copper, Coffeepot, Engraved, Gooseneck Spout, Ebony Handle, Victorian, 9 In.	75.00
Copper, Dipper, Kirkland, Glen Falls, N.Y., 3 X 1 1/2 In.	30.00
Copper, Dish, Craftsman Workshop, C.1906, Kan, Stickley Mark, 6 In.Diam.	100.00
Copper, Dispenser, Coffee Bean, Cylinder Shape	700.00
Copper, Ferner, 3 Paw Feet, Russian, 8 X 4 In.	110.00
Copper, Fob, Watch, Taft Emblem	30.00
Copper, Foot Warmer, Oval, 14 X 9 In.	35.00
Copper, Funnel, Beer, Brass Mechanical Thumblift, 9 1/2 In., 1 Quart	49.50
Copper, Funnel, Brass Nozzle, H.Strater, Boston, 5 In.	18.00
Copper, Funnel, Brass Nozzle, H.Strater, Boston, 10 In.	28.00
Copper, Funnel, Finger Release Valve On Handle, 10 X 6 3/4 In.Diameter	22.00
Copper, Funnel, H.Strather & Sons, Boston, Massachusetts, C.1893, 12 In.	38.00
Copper, Funnel, H.Strather & Sons, Boston, Massachusetts, 1893, 7 In.	18.00
Copper, Humidor, Paneled Centerband, Brass Figural Marine, 7 3/4 In.	45.00
Copper, Ice Cube Holder, Porcelain Insert	20.00
Copper, Icebucket, German, C.1907, Cast Brass, 14 X 12 In.Diameter	350.00
Copper, Kettle, Apple-Butter	75.00
Copper, Kettle, Hand-Hammered, Iron Bale & 3 Feet, 14 X 16 In.Diameter	165.00
Copper, Letter Holder, Indian Head, Quill Pens	40.00
Copper, Measure, Dry, Swing Handle, Manufacturers Plaque, Impressed No.4, 1892	60.00
Copper, Measure, Liquid, 1 Quart	20.00
Copper, Measure, 2 Gallon	85.00
Copper, Mold, Food, Basket Form, 4 1/4 X 3 In.	20.00
Copper, Mold, Rabbit	45.00
Copper, Mug, Ale, Tin Lined, 4 1/4 In.	32.00
Copper, Mug, Beer, Barrel Shape, Pair	8.50
Copper, Mug, Beer, 1934 World's Fair	15.00
Copper, Mug, Pot Belly, 2 Rings Around	19.00
Copper, Pan, Dovetail Bottom, Franklin, New Hampshire, 10 In.	95.00
Copper, Pan, Dovetail Bottom, Franklin, New Hampshire, 12 In.	105.00
Copper, Pan, Dovetailed, Handle, 7 In.	115.00
Copper, Pan, Iron Handle & Rivets, Tin Lined, 3 Piece, 9 In., 8 In., 7 In.	165.00
Copper, Pan, Preserving, Loop Handles, 19 1/4 In.	200.00
Copper, Pan, Sauce, Iron Handle, Covered	36.00
Copper, Pitcher, Duckbill Spout, Handmade, 5 In.	18.50
Copper, Pitcher, Luster, 2 Men Fighting, Polychrome Floral Band, 6 3/4 In.	17.50
Copper, Pot, Glue, Copper Insert, Wire Bail, 2 Part	50.00

Copper, Pot, Pineapple Finial, Handles, Chased Floral Design, Rings 110.00
Copper, Sink, Overflow Drain, Copper Pipes, Hand Made, Oval, 19 3/4 X 14 In. 180.00
Copper, Skimmer, Hand-Wrought Iron, Round, Ring End, 12 1/2 In. 75.00
Copper, Smoker, Bee, Wooden Bellows, 9 1/4 X 3 1/2 In.Diameter 85.00
Copper, Steamer, Porcelain Gas Jet, Brass Hardware, 12 1/2 X 18 X 11 In. 180.00
Copper, Still, Teakettle, Copper Coils, 9 1/2 In.Spout, Copper 285.00
Copper, Strainer, Apple Cider Jelly, Punched Drain, Strap, 14 In.Diam. 125.00
Copper, Tea Set, Brass Handled Tray, 13 1/2 In.Diameter, Brass Legs 130.00
Copper, Teakettle, Brass Finial, Dovetailed Bottom, Fixed Handle, 11 In. 100.00
Copper, Teakettle, Brass Footed, Tilting Stand, Alcohol Burner, 13 1/4 In. 150.00
Copper, Teakettle, Good Luck Horseshoe, Dovetailed 115.00
Copper, Teakettle, Gooseneck, Wide Dovetailing Bottom 145.00
Copper, Teakettle, Miniature, , Brass Finial, Copper Rivets, C.1850, 8 X 8 In. 50.00
Copper, Teapot, Aladdin's Lamp 23.00
Copper, Teapot, English, Christopher Dresser, C.1880 .... 375.00
Copper, Teapot, Engraved Scenes, Chinese, C.1800, 13 1/2 In. 165.00
Copper, Thermometer, Candy, Brass Calibrations 28.00
Copper, Tray, G.Stickley, C.1906, Kan, Stickley Mark, 3 1/2 X 10 In.Diam. 100.00
Copper, Tray, Hammered, Russian Eagle Mark, 23 X 14 In. 135.00
Copper, Urn, Cast Brass Handles, C.1900, 18 X 26 In.Diameter 300.00
Copper, Warmer, Bed, Tulip Design, Brass 110.00
Coral, Figurine, Rabbit, 18th Century, Chia-Ch'ing Period, 1/2 In. 55.00

Coralene glass was made by firing many small colored beads on the outside of glassware. It was made in many patterns in the United States and Europe in the 1880s. Reproductions are made today.

Coralene, Bowl, Covered, Floral Insets, Green Coralene Band 75.00
Coralene, Bowl, Pink Satin, Herringbone Design, Signed Webb 300.00
Coralene, Bowl, Ruffled Neck, Cupid Riding A Dolphin Base, 1870s, 11 1/4 In. 275.00
Coralene, Bowl, Scalloped Upstanding Rim, Beaded, Marked, 5 1/4 In.Diam. 195.00
   Coralene, Japanese Pottery, see Japanese Coralene
Coralene, Jar, Bulbous Stopper, Enamel Looped Edging, 6 In. 139.00
Coralene, Jar, Jam, Pink, Mother-Of-Pearl, Satin Glass, 6 In. .... *Illus* 250.00
Coralene, Mustache Cup, Green Fernery, Gold Gilding, Think Of Me 40.00
Coralene, Tumbler, Peachblow Ground .... 85.00 To 125.00
Coralene, Urn, Burial, Art Nouveau, Glass Insert, 16 In. 225.00
Coralene, Vase, Blue Above, Cream Body, 8 In. 335.00
Coralene, Vase, Blue Asters, Bisque Finish, Dated 1909, 9 In. 225.00
Coralene, Vase, Blue Satin Ground, Sea Weed Pattern, 8 In. 250.00
Coralene, Vase, Cabinet, Miniature, Beaded, White Shades Into Rose, 3 3/4 In. 184.00
Coralene, Vase, Coral Beading, White Ground, 5 In. 135.00
Coralene, Vase, Corset Shape 195.00
Coralene, Vase, Cylindrical, Green To Blue, Nippon, 9 In. 260.00
Coralene, Vase, Double Handle, Fluted Top, Signed, 6 In. 185.00
Coralene, Vase, Fan, Black Satin, 7 In. 85.00
Coralene, Vase, Frosted Satin, Flowers, 12 1/2 In. 115.00
Coralene, Vase, Gold Beading, Flowers, 1909, 7 In. 350.00
Coralene, Vase, Gold Flowers, Pinched Top, White & Yellow, 8 X 7 In., Pair 750.00
Coralene, Vase, Green Satin Ground, Stylized Roses, 1909, 7 In. 145.00
Coralene, Vase, Green To Blue, Beaded Flowers, Gold Leaves, 5 In. 150.00
Coralene, Vase, Hand-Painted Wisteria, Shaded Satin Ground, 1909, 8 3/4 In. 150.00
Coralene, Vase, Handled, Coralene Applied Over Roses, Mark 1909, 10 In. 295.00
Coralene, Vase, Matte, Orange To Green Ground, Gold Handles, 9 In. 150.00
Coralene, Vase, Orchids, Yellow, Orange, Green, Blue, Marked, 12 1/2 In. 250.00
Coralene, Vase, Peacock, Opalescent Crystal, Shell Feet, 8 In. 750.00
Coralene, Vase, Pink Decoration, Green, Patented 1909, 5 1/2 In. 85.00
Coralene, Vase, Reticulated Shoulder, Beaded Roses, Bisque Ground, 9 3/4 In. 285.00
Coralene, Vase, Satin Glass, 3 Footed, Webb, Patent, 7 1/2 In. .... *Illus* 350.00
Coralene, Vase, Seaweed Pattern, Satin Glass, 7 1/2 In. 425.00
Coralene, Vase, Squat Flower Shape, Gold On Lip & Base, 1909, 6 In. 225.00
Coralene, Vase, White Lining, Yellow Seaweed Pattern, 5 3/8 In. 395.00
Coralene, Vase, Yellow Satin, Seaweed, 6 In. 185.00
Coralene, Vase, Yellow Shading To White, Coralene Applied Bands 230.00
Cordey, Bust, Lady, Lace Mantilla, Gold Scrolling, 6 1/2 In. 35.00
Cordey, Bust, Lamp, China Lady, 17 In. 125.00
Cordey, Figurine, Marie Antoinette, Louis XVI, 11 1/2 In., Pair 162.00

Coralene, Vase, Satin Glass, 3 Footed,
Webb, Patent, 7 1/2 In.

Coralene, Jar, Jam, Pink, Mother-Of-Pearl,
Satin Glass, 6 In.

Cordey, Figurine, Vineyard Worker, Full Figure, No.905, Signed, 16 In.	350.00
Cordey, Lamp, Base Attached, Lady	150.00
Cornet, Bowl, Roses Inside & Out, Gold Bank, Signed	87.50
Cornet, Plate, Fish, Gold Gorder, Artist Signed, 9 In.	55.00
Cosmos, Butter, Flowers, Pink Band, Pink, Blue, Yellow	145.00 To 185.00
Cosmos, Condiment Set, Scroll, Milk Glass, White	130.00
Cosmos, Creamer	120.00
Cosmos, Lamp, Miniature, Clear	40.00 To 55.00
Cosmos, Lamp, Miniature, Original Burner & Chimney, 8 3/4 In.	75.00 To 135.00
Cosmos, Muffineer, Blue Band, Apple Blossom Pattern	95.00
Cosmos, Pitcher, Water, Pink Band	195.00
Cosmos, Salt & Pepper, Original Tops	75.00
Cosmos, Saltshaker, Cased Pink Glass	25.00
Cosmos, Saltshaker, Pink Band, No Top	37.50
Cosmos, Spooner	85.00
Cosmos, Sugar, Covered	175.00
Cosmos, Syrup	75.00 To 135.00
Cosmos, Tumbler, Pink Band	65.00
Country Store, see Store	

*Cowan pottery was made in Cleveland, Ohio, from 1913 to 1920. Most pieces
of the art pottery were marked with the name of the firm in various ways.*

Cowan, Bowl, Blue Luster, 7 In.Diameter	18.00
Cowan, Bowl, Console, Orange Rim, Green Interior, Seahorse Handle, 16 X 5 In.	32.00
Cowan, Figurine, Art Deco, Signed, White	22.00
Cowen, Console Set, Bowl & 2 Candleholders, Seahorse Design, 17 X 6 In.	65.00

*Crackle glass was originally made by the Venetians, but most of the ware
found today dates from the 1800s. The glass was heated, cooled, and refired so
that many small lines appeared inside the glass. It was made in many
factories in the United States and Europe.*

Crackle Glass, see also Fry

Crackle Glass, Cruet, Green, Handled, Teardrop Glass Stopper	25.00
Crackle Glass, Cup, Cream, Glazed, Cylindrical, Japanese, 1800s, 3 3/4 In.	350.00
Crackle Glass, Decanter, Cranberry Flashed, Victorian, 8 In., Pair	95.00
Crackle Glass, Decanter, Pontiled, Applied Berry Feet	25.00
Crackle Glass, Jar, Apothecary, Lidded, Flowers, Serpent	65.00
Crackle Glass, Pitcher, Applied Green Handle, Clear	25.00
Crackle Glass, Pitcher, Applied Handle, Amber, 5 In.	25.00
Crackle Glass, Pitcher, Yellow Dragon In Relief, Chinese, 1 1/4 In.	30.00
Crackle Glass, Toothpick, Hat, Blue, 2 1/2 X 2 In.	35.00
Crackle Glass, Tumbler, 4 Applied Rosette Prunts, Cranberry, 5 In.	100.00
Crackle Glass, Vase, Cranberry, Round, 5 1/2 In.	16.00
Crackle Glass, Vase, Depressed Sides, Enameled Corners, 5 In.	35.00

*Cranberry glass is an almost transparent yellow red glass. It resembles
the color of cranberry juice.*

Cranberry Glass, see also Northwood, Rubena Verde, etc.

Cranberry Glass, Ball, Witch, Open End, 3 In.Diameter	42.00
Cranberry Glass, Bell, Wedding, Swirl, Clear Handle	265.00
Cranberry Glass, Bell, Wedding, Swirl, Opalescent Rim, Clear Handle	285.00
Cranberry Glass, Berry Bowl, Frosted, Opalescent, Chrysanthemum Base	95.00
Cranberry Glass, Berry Set, Chrysanthemum, Bowl & 6 Sauce Bowls	295.00
Cranberry Glass, Bottle, Barber, Cone Shape, Opalescent	95.00

Cranberry Glass, Bottle, Barber, Pink & Green Flowers, Enameled, 9 In.	30.00
Cranberry Glass, Bottle, Barber, Stars & Stripes, Opalescent	59.00
Cranberry Glass, Bottle, Cologne, Crimped Rim, Stopper, 8 1/2 In.	35.00
Cranberry Glass, Bottle, Cologne, Original Stopper, Gold Floradora	130.00
Cranberry Glass, Bottle, Perfume, Enameled, Gold Trim, 1/4 X 1 1/2 In.Diam.	79.00
Cranberry Glass, Bottle, Perfume, Silver Overlay, Signed Alvin, 5 In.	195.00
Cranberry Glass, Bottle, Wine, Enameled Decoration, Gold Trim, 8 1/2 In.	95.00
Cranberry Glass, Bowl, Applied Mat-Su-Noke Flowers, Marked, 2 5/8 In.	550.00
Cranberry Glass, Bowl, Clear Applied Feet, 6 In.	42.00
Cranberry Glass, Bowl, Finger, Blown, Bell Toned, Polished Pontil	38.00
Cranberry Glass, Bowl, Finger, Inverted Rib, 2 1/2 X 5 1/4 In., Set Of 6	144.00
Cranberry Glass, Bowl, Finger, Inverted Thumbprint	36.00
Cranberry Glass, Bowl, Finger, Overshot, Gold Rim, 5 1/8 In.	95.00
Cranberry Glass, Bowl, Finger, Top Threading, Ruffled Edge	36.00
Cranberry Glass, Bowl, Fruit, Reverse Swirl, Pleated Rim, 8 In.Diameter	175.00
Cranberry Glass, Bowl, Punch, 8 Cups, Reverse Swirl, Tray, 18 In.Diameter	900.00
Cranberry Glass, Bowl, Ribbed, Opalescent, Crimped Rim, 7 1/2 In.Square	87.50
Cranberry Glass, Bowl, Rose, Applied Rigaree Feet	95.00
Cranberry Glass, Bowl, Sugar, Pewter Lid	50.00
Cranberry Glass, Bowl, Swirled, White Frilly Edge, 9 In.	110.00
Cranberry Glass, Box, Blue & White, Gilt Flowers, 1 3/4 In.	36.00
Cranberry Glass, Box, Enamel, Iridized Green & Blue, Hinged Lid, 5 In.	180.00
Cranberry Glass, Box, Hinged, Enameled Mary Gregory Figure On Lid	175.00
Cranberry Glass, Bride's Basket, Crystal Applique, 9 1/2 X 11 In.Diameter	350.00
Cranberry Glass, Carafe, Blown, Ground Pontil, Flute Cut Neck	75.00
Cranberry Glass, Castor, Pickle, Baby Thumbprint, Silver Plate Frame	165.00
Cranberry Glass, Castor, Pickle, Inverted Thumbprint, Tongs	175.00
Cranberry Glass, Castor, Pickle, Original Tongs	295.00
Cranberry Glass, Castor, Pickle, Panelled Sprig, Silver Plate Holder & Lid	225.00
Cranberry Glass, Castor, Pickle, Swirl, Clear	35.00
Cranberry Glass, Celery, Clear Applied Handle, 7 1/4 In.	70.00
Cranberry Glass, Celery, Ribbed Lattice, Opalescent	85.00
Cranberry Glass, Chalice, Double Teardrop Stem, Ring Center, 11 1/2 In.	72.00
Cranberry Glass, Compote, Cut Overlay, Footed	230.00
Cranberry Glass, Creamer, Clear Petal Feet, Flared Top, 4 In.	32.00
Cranberry Glass, Creamer, Square Mouth, Gold Trim, Enameled, 4 1/4 In.	145.00
Cranberry Glass, Creamer, Thumbprint, Applied Reeded Handle, 4 In.	20.00
Cranberry Glass, Creamer, 10 Rows Embossed Circular Ribs, 5 3/4 In.	70.00
Cranberry Glass, Cruet, Bulbous Body, Cut Stopper	52.50
Cranberry Glass, Cruet, Bulge Body, Tricorne Spout, Inverted Thumbprint	60.00
Cranberry Glass, Cruet, Clear Applied Handle, Enameled Sprays, 9 1/2 In.	135.00
Cranberry Glass, Cruet, Diamond Pattern, Blown	65.00
Cranberry Glass, Cruet, Diamond Quilted, Clear Scalloped Base, 7 In.	80.00
Cranberry Glass, Cruet, Fern, Opalescent	225.00
Cranberry Glass, Cruet, Leaf & Umbrella, C.1890, Clear Handle	145.00
Cranberry Glass, Cruet, Quilted, Pair	49.00
Cranberry Glass, Cruet, Steeple Stopper, Blown Crystal Handle, 8 1/2 In.	62.00
Cranberry Glass, Cruet, Vinegar, Applied Handle, Bubble Stopper, 6 3/4 In.	70.00
Cranberry Glass, Cruet, Wine, Gargoyle Heads, Pewter Encased, 11 1/2 In.	185.00
Cranberry Glass, Cup & Saucer, Clear Applied Handle, Enameled Gold	125.00
Cranberry Glass, Cup & Saucer, Demitasse, Leaf Shaped Saucer, Gold Trim	25.00
Cranberry Glass, Cup & Saucer, White Enamel, Gold Scrolls, 3 1/2 In.	95.00
Cranberry Glass, Cup, Clear Applied Handle, 1 1/2 In.	35.00
Cranberry Glass, Decanter Set, Inverted Thumbprint	55.00
Cranberry Glass, Decanter, Bell Shape, Clear Stopper, 12 In.	35.00
Cranberry Glass, Decanter, Blown, Stopper, Pontil, 8 1/2 In.	90.00
Cranberry Glass, Decanter, Bubble Stopper, Sterling Overlay, 12 3/8 In.	450.00
Cranberry Glass, Decanter, Crystal Stopper & Handle, Pontil Mark, 10 In.	160.00
Cranberry Glass, Decanter, Engraved Design, Stopper, 8 1/2 X 5 1/2 In.	295.00
Cranberry Glass, Decanter, Sterling Silver Overlay, Hallmarked, 9 In.	375.00
Cranberry Glass, Decanter, Thumbprint, Clear Applied Handle, Stopper, 10 In.	80.00
Cranberry Glass, Dish, Butter, Covered, Mary Gregory Enameling	39.00
Cranberry Glass, Dish, Candy, Silver Plated Swan Base, Handles	350.00
Cranberry Glass, Dish, Jam, Clear Crimped Border, Silver Frame	95.00
Cranberry Glass, Dish, Jam, Grape & Leaf Silver Frame	95.00
Cranberry Glass, Dish, Sweetmeat, Ormolu Holder, Gold Key, 5 3/8 In.Diam.	85.00
Cranberry Glass, Epergne, Fluted, Three Branches, Clear Rigaree Of Crystal	395.00

Interior, Phyfe room G

Interior, McIntire room

Interior, Georgia dining room J

Interior, DuPont dining room

Interior, Empire parlor

Armchair, Baltimore,
1805–1815

Curly maple tall clock,
John Paul, Pennsylvania,
1815

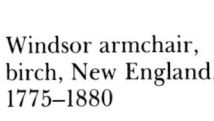

Windsor armchair,
birch, New England,
1775–1880

Mahogany side chair,
Philadelphia, 1760–1770

Painted tulipwood
spoon rack, United
States, 1750–1800

Painted tulipwood miniature chest,
Pennsylvania, 1785

Maple easy chair, New
England, 1720–1740

Drop-leaf table, New England,
1700–1725

Painted tin basket, Maria Osmer,
possibly Pennsylvania, 1860–1880

Ormolu mantel clock,
Dubuc, Paris, 1800–1819

Pine jardiniere, Hallam
Whiting, Connecticut,
1810–1830

Tea box, wood and alloy
of zinc and lead, China,
1850–1900

Box, velvet over wood with paper
trim, England, 1815–1830

Maple rolling pin, mold, probably
Pennsylvania, 1780–1825

Ornamental stand, glass
dome, earthenware
figures, shells, China,
1800–1900

Box with game of dominoes, mahogany and ivory, United States, 1775–1825

Spool stand, wood and ivory, United States, 1825–1860

Splint basket, United States, 1825–1900

Cast-iron andirons, England or United States, 1760–1800

Box, wood, reptile skin, silver, and velvet, England, 1797–1798

Iron toaster, United States,
1750–1800

Pewter mug, Peter Young,
New York, 1772–1800

Teapots, painted tinned iron, probably
Pennsylvania, 1840–1860

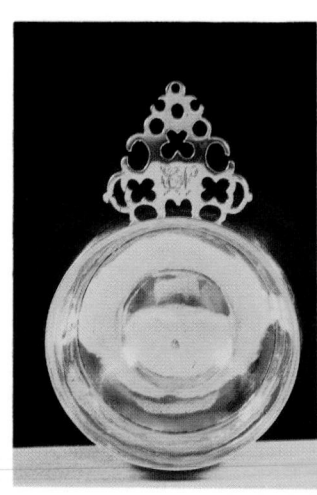

Silver porringer, Samuel
Vernon, Rhode Island,
1715–1725

Fire board, painted trompe
l'oeil design on white pine,
United States, 1830–1850

Painted tulipwood watch holder, United States, 1800–1850

Chinese export porcelain dinner service, China, 1800–1830

Staffordshire platter, "Palestine," William Adams & Sons, England, 1830–1840

Earthenware figure of a lion, John Bell, Pennsylvania, 1840–1865

Earthenware muffin pan or jelly mold, possibly New England, 1800–1875

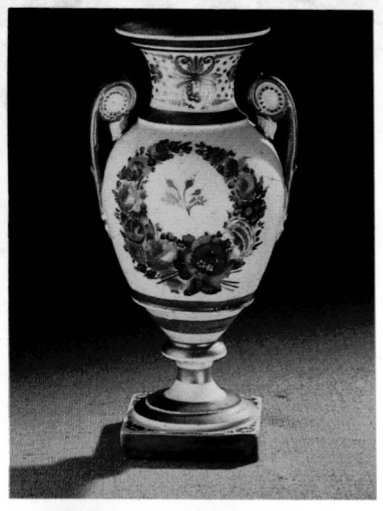

Porcelain vase, William Ellis
Tucker or successor,
Philadelphia, 1825–1838

"Liverpool" pitcher, England,
1830

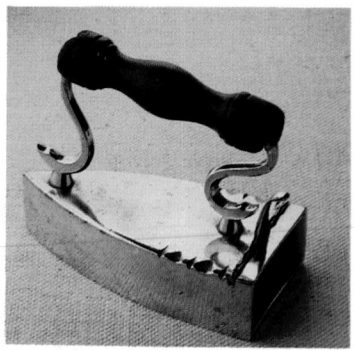

Brass pressing iron, probably
England, 1790–1810

Covered cup, painted maple,
Pennsylvania, 1850–1900

Cranberry Glass, Epergne, Ruffled Base, Applied Spiral Trim, 22 1/4 In.	325.00
Cranberry Glass, Epergne, Ruffled Center Vase, Baskets, 21 X 12 In.Diam.	295.00
Cranberry Glass, Epergne, 2 Piece, Base & Vase, 9 3/8 In.	36.00
Cranberry Glass, Epergne, 3 Lilies, Ruffled, 14 In.	250.00
Cranberry Glass, Epergne, 3 Lilies, 2 Twisted Canes, Rigaree, 20 In.	350.00
Cranberry Glass, Fairy Lamp, Ruffled Base & Candle Cup, 6 3/4 X 8 In.Diam.	395.00
Cranberry Glass, Finger Bowl, Matching Plate	52.00
Cranberry Glass, Finger Bowl, Opalescent, Blown, Pair	60.00
Cranberry Glass, Finger Bowl, Set Of Six	90.00
Cranberry Glass, Glass, Juice, Gold Decoration, 3 1/2 X 2 In.	95.00
Cranberry Glass, Glass, Juice, Set Of 6	60.00 To 75.00
Cranberry Glass, Glass, Liqueur, Clear Stem, Set Of 4	40.00
Cranberry Glass, Goblet, Wine, Inverted Rib, 5 1/2 X 2 1/2 In., Set Of 8	136.00
Cranberry Glass, Jar, Biscuit, Bail & Lid Silver Plate	45.00
Cranberry Glass, Jar, Biscuit, Van Bergh Holder, Enamel Decoration, 7 X 4 In.	245.00
Cranberry Glass, Jar, Jam, Covered, Crystal Leaf Finial, 6 3/8 In.	98.00
Cranberry Glass, Lamp, Banquet, Gold Flower Design, 25 X 7 In., Pair	2150.00
Cranberry Glass, Lamp, Hanging, Brass Font & Holder, Crystal Prisms	750.00
Cranberry Glass, Lamp, Hanging, Inverted Thumbprint, Brass Fittings, 19 In.	275.00
Cranberry Glass, Lamp, Kerosene, Miniature, Applied Handle, 6 X 4 1/2 In.	125.00
Cranberry Glass, Lamp, Miniature, Beaded Ribbed	335.00
Cranberry Glass, Lamp, Miniature, Beaded Swirl, Embossed	325.00
Cranberry Glass, Lamp, Miniature, Inverted Thumbprint	90.00
Cranberry Glass, Lamp, Oil, Milk Glass Base, Brass Fittings, Pair	90.00
Cranberry Glass, Lamp, Ribbed, Opalescent, 45 In.	895.00
Cranberry Glass, Lamp, Table, Millefiori Mushroom Shade, Matching Base	1195.00
Cranberry Glass, Liquor Set, 6 Handled Liquors, Round Tray, Enameled	295.00
Cranberry Glass, Master Salt, Cut, 3 5/8 In.	55.00
Cranberry Glass, Muffineer, Brass Top	58.00
Cranberry Glass, Muffineer, Paneled, Gold Lid	42.50
Cranberry Glass, Mustard Pot, Criss Cross	85.00
Cranberry Glass, Mustard Pot, Reverse Swirl, Opalescent	65.00
Cranberry Glass, Nappy, Hobnail	25.00
Cranberry Glass, Pipe, 18 In.	250.00
Cranberry Glass, Pitcher, Blown, Ruffled Top, Clear Applied Handle, 9 In.	275.00
Cranberry Glass, Pitcher, Bulbous, Footed, 5 1/2 In.	60.00
Cranberry Glass, Pitcher, Clear Applied Handle, Hobnail, 5 In.	75.00
Cranberry Glass, Pitcher, Clear Applied Handle, 5 1/4 In.	48.00
Cranberry Glass, Pitcher, Cream, Blue, Opalescent White, Footed, 5 3/4 In.	125.00
Cranberry Glass, Pitcher, Diamond-Quilted, Reeded Applied Handle, 7 1/8 In.	145.00
Cranberry Glass, Pitcher, Enameled, 3 Glasses, 12 In.	50.00
Cranberry Glass, Pitcher, Inverted Thumbprint, Bulbous, Reed Handle	65.00
Cranberry Glass, Pitcher, Inverted Thumbprint, Crimped Rim, 9 In.	30.00
Cranberry Glass, Pitcher, Inverted Thumbprint, Reeded Handle, 7 1/2 In.	165.00
Cranberry Glass, Pitcher, Melon Shape, Clear Applied Handle, 5 In.	55.00
Cranberry Glass, Pitcher, Quilted, Fluted Top, Clear Applied Handle, 8 In.	130.00
Cranberry Glass, Pitcher, Ribbing, Fluted Rim, Polished Pontil, 7 3/4 In.	85.00
Cranberry Glass, Pitcher, Ruffled Top, Applied Petal Shaped Feet, 6 1/2 In.	62.00
Cranberry Glass, Pitcher, Ruffled Top, Clear Applied Handle, 6 X 9 In.	200.00
Cranberry Glass, Pitcher, Tankard Shape, Clear Applied Handle, 7 5/8 In.	120.00
Cranberry Glass, Pitcher, Tankard Shape, Clear Handle, 5 In.	50.00
Cranberry Glass, Pitcher, Three-Spout, Clear Applied Handle, 5 In.	40.00
Cranberry Glass, Pitcher, Twisted Swirl, Craquelle, Clear Handle, 8 In.	195.00
Cranberry Glass, Pitcher, Water, Coinspot On Swirl, Applied Handle, English	135.00
Cranberry Glass, Pitcher, Water, Crimped Top, Handle, Bulbous, 9 X 22 In.	150.00
Cranberry Glass, Pitcher, Water, Crystal Rope Handle, Bulbous, 7 1/2 In.	165.00
Cranberry Glass, Pitcher, Water, Square Mouth, Clear Rope Handle, 7 7/8 In.	350.00
Cranberry Glass, Pitcher, 3-Spout, Applied Handle, Optic Bottom, 10 In.	45.00
Cranberry Glass, Pitcher, 6 Tumblers, Ruffled Top, Inverted Thumbprint	260.00
Cranberry Glass, Pokal, Ruby Red, Engraved Animals, Footed	130.00
Cranberry Glass, Rose Bowl, Cut, 2 1/4 In.	87.00
Cranberry Glass, Rose Bowl, Enameled Flowers, 2 7/8 X 3 3/8 In.Diameter	125.00
Cranberry Glass, Rose Bowl, Miniature, Crystal Applied Feet, 3 1/2 X 3 In.	105.00
Cranberry Glass, Rose Bowl, Wheeling Drape, Vaseline Rigaree At Top, 4 In.	95.00
Cranberry Glass, Rose Bowl, 8-Crimp Top, Gold Trim, Enameled, 2 1/2 In.Diam.	60.00
Cranberry Glass, Salt & Pepper, Embossed Tops	125.00

Cranberry Glass, Salt & Pepper, Handblown, Swirl Rib, Enameled, Pewter Top 95.00
Cranberry Glass, Salt & Pepper, Inverted Thumbprint, 3 3/4 In. 77.50
Cranberry Glass, Salt & Pepper, Raised Enamel Florals, Holder 95.00
Cranberry Glass, Salt, Crystal Feet, Hallmarked Silver Rim, 2 X 2 In. 78.00
Cranberry Glass, Salt, Enameled Flowers, 2 1/2 In. 32.50
Cranberry Glass, Salt, Gold Plated Leaf Umbrella Holder, 4 Feet 99.00
Cranberry Glass, Salt, Master, Vaseline Applied Ruffled Overlay, Pontil, Mark 50.00
Cranberry Glass, Saltshaker, Barrel Shape, Original Stopper 27.50
Cranberry Glass, Saltshaker, Flower & Butterfly, 3 1/2 X 2 In. 60.00
Cranberry Glass, Saltshaker, Opalescent, Reverse Swirl 28.00
Cranberry Glass, Saltshaker, Opalescent, 4 In., Pair 40.00
Cranberry Glass, Saltshaker, Reverse Swirl, Bulbous, Original Lid, 3 In. 48.00
Cranberry Glass, Saltshaker, Swirl 18.00
Cranberry Glass, Shaker, Sugar, Silver-Plated Mount 39.00
Cranberry Glass, Sugar & Creamer, Camphor, Quilted 55.00
Cranberry Glass, Sugar & Creamer, White Thread Decoration 96.00
Cranberry Glass, Sugar Shaker, Cut Panels, Silver Plated Top, 5 3/4 In. 48.00
Cranberry Glass, Sugar Shaker, Cut Panels, Silver Top, Finial 68.00
Cranberry Glass, Sugar Shaker, Cut Panels, 6 In. 68.00
Cranberry Glass, Sugar Shaker, Fern & Flower 60.00
Cranberry Glass, Sugar Shaker, Paneled 50.00
Cranberry Glass, Sugar Shaker, Ribbed Opal Lattice, Original Top 75.00
Cranberry Glass, Sugar Shaker, Ribbed Opal Lattice, Tall 125.00
Cranberry Glass, Sugar Shaker, Ring Neck, Diamond-Quilted 100.00
Cranberry Glass, Sugar Shaker, Umbrella Leaf 275.00
Cranberry Glass, Sugar Shaker, Venetian Diamond, Ring Neck 95.00
Cranberry Glass, Syrup, Venetian Diamond 145.00
Cranberry Glass, Tankard, Inverted Thumbprint, Polished Pontil, Fuchsia 145.00
Cranberry Glass, Toothpick Holder, Opal Swirl 52.00
Cranberry Glass, Toothpick, Beatty, Opalescent, Ribbed 20.00
Cranberry Glass, Toothpick, Swirl, Chrysanthemum Base 75.00
Cranberry Glass, Tumble-Up, Crackle Ware 125.00
Cranberry Glass, Tumble-Up, Melon Ribbed Inside 210.00
Cranberry Glass, Tumbler, Blue Flowers 16.50
Cranberry Glass, Tumbler, Gold Stripe Top, 4 3/4 In High, 2 3/4 In.Diameter 30.00
Cranberry Glass, Tumbler, Inverted Thumbprint 27.50
Cranberry Glass, Tumbler, Inverted Thumbprint, Enameled 40.00
Cranberry Glass, Tumbler, Opalescent Overlay, 3 5/8 In. 55.00
Cranberry Glass, Tumbler, Opalescent Thumbprint, Set Of 6 .... 160.00
Cranberry Glass, Tumbler, Opalescent, Coin Spot 35.00
Cranberry Glass, Tumbler, Overshot 85.00
Cranberry Glass, Tumbler, Reverse Swirl .... 45.00 To 48.00
Cranberry Glass, Tumbler, Reverse Swirl, Opalescent .... 36.00 To 55.00
Cranberry Glass, Tumbler, Scroll, Opaque, Blue 35.00
Cranberry Glass, Tumbler, Swirl, Opalescent 35.00
Cranberry Glass, Tumbler, Thumbprint, Raised Enamel Flowers, 4 In. 35.00
Cranberry Glass, Tumbler, White Enameled Figure Of Woman, Paneled 55.00
Cranberry Glass, Tumbler, Windows, Opalescent .... 29.00 To 39.00
Cranberry Glass, Urn, Gold, Medallion, Portrait, 16 3/4 In., Pair ....Illus 800.00
Cranberry Glass, Vase, Applied Flower, Clear Leaf & Vine, 8 3/4 In. 50.00
Cranberry Glass, Vase, Applied Rigaree Spiral Trim, 12 1/2 In. 195.00
Cranberry Glass, Vase, Ball Foot, Flowers, 10 In. 20.00
Cranberry Glass, Vase, Bud, Flared Bottom, Glass Overlay, 7 In. 85.00

Cranberry Glass, Urn, Gold, Medallion,
Portrait, 16 3/4 In., Pair

Cranberry Glass, Vase, Bud, Gold Decoration, 6 X 1 1/4 In.	90.00
Cranberry Glass, Vase, Bulbous, Handled, Hand Blown, Diamond Quilted, 15 In.	125.00
Cranberry Glass, Vase, Bulbous, Opalescent, Hobnail, 5 In.	27.00
Cranberry Glass, Vase, Chipped Ice Texture, Enameled, 16 X 4 1/2 In.	225.00
Cranberry Glass, Vase, Clear Applied Crimped Top, 7 In., Pair	102.00
Cranberry Glass, Vase, Clear Applied Top, 4 1/2 In.	78.00
Cranberry Glass, Vase, Cornucopia & Dolphin, Marble, 1900, 9 1/4 In., Pair	325.00
Cranberry Glass, Vase, Crimped Top, Gold Trim, 8 1/2 In.	50.00
Cranberry Glass, Vase, Crystal Rigaree, 10 1/2 In.	75.00
Cranberry Glass, Vase, Cylindrical, Enameled Flowers, 16 In.	195.00
Cranberry Glass, Vase, Daisy & Rail Fence, 11 X 3 In.	155.00
Cranberry Glass, Vase, Diamond Quilted, Applied Crystal Top, 4 X 3 3/4 In.	68.00
Cranberry Glass, Vase, Enameled Band Around Middle, 4 1/8 In., Pair	75.00
Cranberry Glass, Vase, Etched Flowers, 11 1/2 In.	55.00
Cranberry Glass, Vase, Etched Front, White Base, Flat, 12 3/4 X 6 In.	85.00
Cranberry Glass, Vase, Flashed, Etching Of Thistle, 10 1/2 In.	65.00
Cranberry Glass, Vase, Flowers, Leaves, White, Pink, 12 3/4 X 2 7/8 In., Pair	310.00
Cranberry Glass, Vase, Fluted & Ruffled Top, Thumbprint Base, 7 In.	85.00
Cranberry Glass, Vase, Footed, Clear Applied Ruffled Edge, 12 1/2 In.	325.00
Cranberry Glass, Vase, Gold Decoration, Brass Rim & Handles, 4 X 4 In.	120.00
Cranberry Glass, Vase, Gold Decoration, Silver Plated Holder, Marked, 9 In.	190.00
Cranberry Glass, Vase, Gold Enamel Leaves, White & Blue Flowers, 10 1/2 In.	85.00
Cranberry Glass, Vase, Gold Flowers, Enameled, 5 1/2 X 2 1/2 In., Pair	115.00
Cranberry Glass, Vase, Golden Enameled Iris, 12 3/4 In.	65.00
Cranberry Glass, Vase, Jack-In-The-Pulpit, Opaque Loopings, 7 3/4 In.	115.00
Cranberry Glass, Vase, Melon Shaped, 4 In., Pair	80.00
Cranberry Glass, Vase, Miniature, Lily-Of-The-Valley, 3 X 1 1/2 In.	195.00
Cranberry Glass, Vase, New York World's Fair 1940, 3 3/4 In.	10.00
Cranberry Glass, Vase, Opalescent Swirl, Turned Down Top, 10 In.	75.00
Cranberry Glass, Vase, Opalescent Window, Ruffled Top, 6 In.	50.00
Cranberry Glass, Vase, Oval, Molded Shell Design, Applied Handles, 8 In.	95.00
Cranberry Glass, Vase, Reverse Swirl, White Spatter, 6 In.	24.00
Cranberry Glass, Vase, Ribbed Rustic Crimped Top, Applied Feet, 6 In., Pair	102.00
Cranberry Glass, Vase, Ribbed, 2 Clear Applied Handles, 6 1/2 In.	58.00
Cranberry Glass, Vase, Rigaree Spiral Trim, Enameled Flowers, 12 1/4 In.	195.00
Cranberry Glass, Vase, Swirled Bulbous Body, Fluted Top, 4 In.	45.00
Cranberry Glass, Vase, Trumpet Shape, Ruffled Top, 10 In.	85.00
Cranberry Glass, Vase, Trumpet, Umbrella Shape, Brass Base, 6 1/2 In.	95.00
Cranberry Glass, Vase, Tulip Shaped Body, Rubena, 9 1/2 X 5 In.	195.00
Cranberry Glass, Water Set, Bedside, Gold Rim, Hand-Painted, 7 1/2 X 4 In.	110.00
Cranberry Glass, Water Set, Swirl, Bulbous, Alabaster Handle, 6 Tumblers	537.50
Cranberry Glass, Wine, Bowl Covered With Gold Leaves, 4 5/8 In., Set Of 6	335.00
Cranberry Glass, Wine, Hollow Cut Stem, Acid Gold, 6 3/4 In., Pair	145.00

Creamware, or queensware, was developed by Josiah Wedgwood about 1765. It is a cream-colored earthenware that has been copied by many factories.

Creamware, see also Wedgwood

Creamware, Chamber Pot, White Band, 2 X 3 1/2 In.	20.00
Creamware, Plate, Enameled Rose In Red, Yellow & Green, 8 1/8 In.	90.00
Creamware, Plate, Laurel Swags & Feathered Edges, 1775-85, 10 In.	175.00
Creamware, Plate, Underglaze-Blue, Fluted Rim, C.1767, 9 1/8 In.	175.00
Creamware, Spittoon, Green Band	125.00
Creamware, Tea Caddy, Cover, Enameled, English, C.1775, 7 Piece Set	300.00
Creil, Dish, Covered, Montereau, Armorial Anchor & Flag, 9 In.	35.00
Creil, Plate, Gold Rim, Armorial Anchor & Flag, 10 In.	60.00
Creil, Plate, La Caravane, Camel, Arabs, Soldiers, 8 In.	45.00
Creil, Plate, La Vavandiere, Girl Serving Wine To Soldier, 8 In.	45.00
Creil, Plate, Perolla Offre A Son Pere De Tuer Annibal, 8 In.	30.00

Croesus, see Pressed Glass, Croesus

Crown Derby is the nickname given to the works of the Royal Crown Derby Factory which began working in England in 1859. An earlier and more famous English Derby factory existed from 1750 to 1848. The two factories were not related. Most of the porcelain found today with the Derby mark is the work of the later Derby factory.

Crown Derby, see also Royal Crown Derby

Crown Derby, Ewer, Gold & Silver Raised Flowers, 1888, 7 1/2 In.	375.00

Crown Derby, Figurine, Bearded, Hatted Man, Red Jacket, 1877-89, 8 In. 475.00
Crown Derby, Figurine, Dwarf, 7 In., Pair 385.00
Crown Derby, Plate, Scenic, Hand-Painted Medallion With Cat, 9 1/4 In. 125.00
Crown Derby, Vase, Birds & Flowers, Handles Ending With Heads, 6 In. 195.00

Crown Milano glass was made by Frederick Shirley about 1890. It had a plain biscuit color with a satin finish. It was decorated with flowers, and often had large gold scrolls.

Crown Milano, Biscuit Barrel, Jeweled, Scrolls, 4 Sides, 5 3/4 In. 589.00
Crown Milano, Biscuit Barrel, Melon Ribbed, Silver Top, 7 X 7 In.Diameter 575.00
Crown Milano, Biscuit Jar, Gold Design, Silver Plate Rim & Cover, Signed 675.00
Crown Milano, Biscuit Jar, Melon Ribbed, Silver Plated Bail & Cover, Signed 650.00
Crown Milano, Biscuit Jar, Swirl Pattern, Beaded Enamel, Stylized Flower 295.00
Crown Milano, Bowl, Open, Diamond Quilted, Silver Plate Cover, 4 1/4 X 3 In. 350.00
Crown Milano, Bride's Bowl, Holder, Signed, 14 In. ....*Illus* 3000.00
Crown Milano, Cookie Jar, Burmese Coloring, Oak Leaves & Acorns 325.00
Crown Milano, Dish, Sweetmeat, Melon Shape, Embossed Shell Design, Signed 395.00
Crown Milano, Ewer, Opalescent, Raised Floral Design, Paper Label 200.00
Crown Milano, Humidor, Cigars In Gold 595.00
Crown Milano, Jar, Marmalade, Pastel Pansies, C.1890 .... 1000.00
Crown Milano, Jar, Sweetmeat, Albertine Coloring 535.00
Crown Milano, Jar, Sweetmeat, Jeweled, Fantasy Design, Signed, 5 In. 1000.00
Crown Milano, Jar, Sweetmeat, Melon Sectioned, Enameled Flowers, Signed 800.00
Crown Milano, Plate, Wreath & Crown, Pansy Outlined In Gold, 7 1/2 In. 300.00
Crown Milano, Sugar & Creamer, Silver Top & Handle, Melon Shape, Signed 750.00
Crown Milano, Syrup, Gold Fern Design, Gold Top & Handle, Signed 200.00
Crown Milano, Syrup, Melon Shape, Pewter Top, Floral Design 55.00
Crown Milano, Tumbler, White Opalescent Ground, Leaves & Scrolls, 3 3/4 In. 450.00
Crown Milano, Vase, Bud, Flared, Bulbous Body, Gilt Leaf & Vine, 8 1/2 In. 375.00
Crown Milano, Vase, Pansies Outlined In Gold, Lusterless White, 4 1/2 In. 185.00
Crown Milano, Vase, White Opalescent, Squat, Raised Gold Design, Paper Label 825.00
Crown Tuscan, see Cambridge

Cruets of glass or porcelain were made to hold vinegar or oil. They were especially popular during Victorian times.

Cruet Set, Cranberry, Blue & White Opalescent Bottles, Claw Feet & Owl 425.00
Cruet Set, 4 Cut Bottles In Holder, Sheffield 125.00
Cruet, see also other glass sections
Cruet, Amber, Dice & Block, Amber Stopper 55.00
Cruet, Amber, Inverted Thumbprint, Fluted Trefoil Lip, Clear Ribbed Handle 35.00
Cruet, Beveled Star, Clear, Clear Stopper 28.00
Cruet, Blue Finecut, Clear Stopper 65.00
Cruet, Blue Opalescent, Daisy & Fern 75.00
Cruet, Bohemian Glass, Intaglio Cut 25.00
Cruet, Checkerboard, Clear 24.00
Cruet, Chocolate Glass, Hobstar, Imperial 29.00
Cruet, Cranberry Thumbprint, Pair, 6 3/4 In. 42.50
Cruet, Cut Glass, Facet Cut Stopper, Strawberry & Diamond Cut, 6 In. 35.00
Cruet, Cut Glass, Original Stopper, 7 1/2 In. 60.00
Cruet, Deer & Castle, Ruby Glass, Bohemian 5.00
Cruet, Emerald Green, Leaf Medallion 135.00
Cruet, Miniature, Green Swirl, Original Stopper, 3 In. 18.00
Cruet, Moon & Star, Clear 20.00
Cruet, Purple Slag 29.00
Cruet, Squared Bulbous Shape, Blue Applied Handle, Enamel Flower, 7 3/4 In. 88.00
Cruet, Vinegar, Amber Glass, Applied Handle, Round Mouth, 8 In. 50.00
Cruet, Vinegar, Cobalt Blue, Applied Handle, Matching Stopper, 6 1/2 In. 88.00
Cruet, Wild Bouquet, Stopper, White 72.00
CT Germany, Chocolate Set, 6 Cups & Saucers, Flowers & Leaves 80.00
CT Germany, Plate, Classical Figures, Cobalt Blue, Gold, 9 1/4 In. 27.50
CT Germany, Plate, Eagle With Cherries, 8 1/2 In. 30.00

Cup plates are small glass or china plates that held the cup, while a gentleman of the mid-nineteenth century drank his coffee or tea from the saucer. The most famous cup plates were made of glass at the Boston and Sandwich Factory located in Massachusetts.

Crown Milano, Bride's Bowl,
Holder, Signed, 14 In.

Custard Glass, Bottle, Cologne, Grape
& Cable, Blue, Northwood

(See Page 118)

Cup Plate, American Villa, Staffordshire	95.00
Cup Plate, Beaded Hearts	25.00
Cup Plate, Blue Transfer Scene, Staffordshire, Marked	15.00
Cup Plate, Bridge, Sheep, Boatman, Staffordshire	40.00
Cup Plate, Bunker Hill	25.00
Cup Plate, Cadmus Pattern	10.00 To 25.00
Cup Plate, California, Flow Blue	24.00
Cup Plate, Castle Garden, Wood, Blue	85.00
Cup Plate, Eagle, Cut Glass	27.50
Cup Plate, Fort Pitt Eagle, Sandwich	75.00
Cup Plate, Franklin Kite, Staffordshire	60.00
Cup Plate, Hairpin, Opalescent	65.00
Cup Plate, Hearts, Opalescent	95.00
Cup Plate, Hyena, Quadruped, Dark Blue	60.00
Cup Plate, Interlacing Circles Pattern	15.00
Cup Plate, Italian Buildings, Medium Blue, 1822-41	26.00
Cup Plate, Livingston, Blue-Green	450.00
Cup Plate, Log Cabin	450.00
Cup Plate, Paddle Wheeler, Mid-Western	450.00
Cup Plate, Ship, Sandwich Glass, 3 1/2 In.	18.00
Cup Plate, Steamboat With Shields Border, Octagonal	95.00
Cup Plate, Sun Burst, Olive Green	70.00
Cup Plate, The Wedding Day & 3 Weeks After, 3 1/2 In.	12.00
Cup Plate, Twelve Hearts	10.00
Cup Plate, Valentine, Blue	150.00

Currier & Ives made the famous American lithographs marked with their name from 1857 to 1907.

Currier & Ives, Calendar, Winter In The Country	2.00
Currier & Ives, Clipper Ship In A Hurricane	150.00
Currier & Ives, Early Winter, C.1869, 9 5/8 X 17 In.	1300.00
Currier & Ives, Lightning Express, Trains Leaving Junction, C.1863	1600.00
Currier & Ives, New England Home, Crisscross Frame	35.00
Currier & Ives, Pleasures Of The Country, Framed	125.00
Currier & Ives, Roses Of May	45.00
Currier, Burning Of The Henry Clay	100.00
Currier, Lady Of The Lake	40.00
Currier, Little Martha, Butterfly Frame	35.00
Currier, Presidents Of The United States, 1844	85.00
Currier, Prince & Princess Of Wales	40.00

Custard glass is an opaque glass sometimes known as buttermilk glass. It was first made in America after 1886 at the La Belle Glass Works, Bridgeport, Ohio.

Custard Glass, see also Maize

Custard Glass, Argonaut Shell, Bowl, Berry, Master	225.00
Custard Glass, Argonaut Shell, Compote, Jelly	125.00
Custard Glass, Argonaut Shell, Spooner	100.00
Custard Glass, Banana Boat, Louis XV	150.00 To 160.00
Custard Glass, Bell, Souvenir, Hotel Cumberland, New York	135.00
Custard Glass, Berry Bowl, Chrysanthemum Sprig, Blue	395.00
Custard Glass, Berry Bowl, Chrysanthemum Sprig, Gold	185.00
Custard Glass, Berry Bowl, Geneva, Green & Red Decoration, Oval, Medium Size	80.00
Custard Glass, Berry Bowl, Georgia Gem	100.00
Custard Glass, Berry Bowl, Intaglio, Green Decoration	50.00

Custard Glass, Bowl, Orange, Grape
& Cable, Pink, Northwood

Custard Glass, Berry Bowl, Ribbed Drape	40.00
Custard Glass, Berry Set, Cherry & Scales, 7 Piece	375.00
Custard Glass, Berry Set, Chrysanthemum Sprig, Blue, Northwood	1100.00 To 1300.00
Custard Glass, Berry Set, Intaglio Pattern, 6 In.Pedestal Bowl, 4 Cups	375.00
Custard Glass, Berry Set, Memphis, Green With Gold, 7 Piece	200.00
Custard Glass, Berry Set, Ring Band, Rose Decoration, 6 Piece	400.00
Custard Glass, Berry Set, 4 Saucers, Gold Trim, Louis XV	295.00
Custard Glass, Berry Set, 6 Piece, Grape & Cable	350.00
Custard Glass, Bonbon, Grape & Thistle, Green, 2 Handled, Crimped Edges	39.00
Custard Glass, Bonbon, Prayer Rug	23.00 To 32.00
Custard Glass, Bottle, Cologne, Grape & Cable, Blue, Northwood	*Illus* 425.00
Custard Glass, Bowl, Footed, Beaded Circle, 4 1/4 In.	39.00
Custard Glass, Bowl, Footed, Scalloped, Peacock & Urn, 5 1/2 In.	39.00
Custard Glass, Bowl, Fruit, Argonaut Shell, Large	225.00
Custard Glass, Bowl, Fruit, Everglades, Decorated	200.00
Custard Glass, Bowl, Fruit, Georgia Gem, Round, Large	95.00
Custard Glass, Bowl, Fruit, Intaglio	185.00
Custard Glass, Bowl, Fruit, Louis XV, Large	135.00
Custard Glass, Bowl, Gem, Footed, 9 In.	75.00
Custard Glass, Bowl, Inverted Fan & Feather, Gold Trim, 5 1/2 X 10 In.Diam.	270.00
Custard Glass, Bowl, Orange, Grape & Cable, Pink, Northwood	*Illus* 425.00
Custard Glass, Bowl, Sugar, Chrysanthemum, Signed, Northwood	85.00
Custard Glass, Bowl, Sugar, Individual, Diamond Peg, Souvenir	29.50
Custard Glass, Butter, Beaded Circle, Lid	325.00
Custard Glass, Butter, Cherry & Scale	295.00
Custard Glass, Butter, Chrysanthemum Sprig, Gold, Lid, Signed	275.00
Custard Glass, Butter, Geneva, Green & Red Decoration, Lid	145.00
Custard Glass, Butter, Indiana, Lid	55.00
Custard Glass, Butter, Intaglio, Blue, Lid	195.00
Custard Glass, Butter, Intaglio, Green, Lid	235.00
Custard Glass, Butter, Louis XV, Lid	165.00
Custard Glass, Butter, Maple Leaf, Lid, Northwood	195.00 To 250.00
Custard Glass, Butter, Tarentum Victoria, Green, Lid	250.00
Custard Glass, Butter, Vermont, Lid	225.00
Custard Glass, Candle Holders, Penumbra, Pair	50.00
Custard Glass, Celery, Pillow	45.00
Custard Glass, Centerpiece Set, Geneva, Red & Green	415.00
Custard Glass, Compote, Fruit, Intaglio, Large, Blue Trim	225.00
Custard Glass, Compote, Intaglio, Gold, 9 In.	175.00
Custard Glass, Compote, Jelly, Chrysanthemum Sprig	42.00 To 85.00
Custard Glass, Compote, Jelly, Grape N	77.00
Custard Glass, Compote, Jelly, Intaglio, Green Decoration	95.00
Custard Glass, Cracker Jar, Silver Collar, Lid & Bail, Enameling, Green	175.00
Custard Glass, Creamer, Argonaut, Colorful, Signed Northwood	145.00
Custard Glass, Creamer, Bulging Ribs	35.00
Custard Glass, Creamer, Child Size, Diamond Peg	30.00
Custard Glass, Creamer, Chrysanthemum Sprig, Gold	120.00
Custard Glass, Creamer, Chrysanthemum, Signed, Northwood	60.00
Custard Glass, Creamer, Florida	45.00
Custard Glass, Creamer, Louis XV	95.00
Custard Glass, Creamer, Maple Leaf	85.00 To 105.00
Custard Glass, Creamer, Souvenir, Conneaut Lake, Pa., Beading	30.00
Custard Glass, Cruet, Argonaut Shell, Original Stopper	475.00
Custard Glass, Cruet, Chrysanthemum Sprig	250.00 To 400.00
Custard Glass, Cruet, Fluted Scroll, Flower Band, Northwood	75.00
Custard Glass, Cruet, Frosted Stopper, Ring Band, Gold Leaf Decoration	190.00
Custard Glass, Cruet, Louis XV, Stopper, Gold	275.00

Custard Glass, Cruet, Ringband, Frosted Stopper	195.00
Custard Glass, Cruet, Winged Scroll	145.00
Custard Glass, Cup, Tea, Souvenir, Ottawa, Kansas, Red Flower	30.00
Custard Glass, Dish, Bluebirds, No. 458	47.50
Custard Glass, Dish, Bon-Bon, Prayer Rug	50.00
Custard Glass, Dish, Grape & Cable, Scalloped, 8 In.	40.00
Custard Glass, Dish, Master Ice Cream, Peacock & Urn, 9 5/8 In.	195.00
Custard Glass, Dish, Prayer Rug, 2 Handles, 7 1/4 In.Diameter	18.00
Custard Glass, Ewer, Green, Metal Top & Base, 5 In	32.00
Custard Glass, Globe, Light, Glass, Medium	45.00
Custard Glass, Goblet, Beaded Loop, Rose Spray, Dennison, Minnesota, 6 In.	80.00
Custard Glass, Goblet, Beaded Swag	37.50
Custard Glass, Goblet, Grape & Arches	55.00
Custard Glass, Goblet, Rose, Tarrentum, Thumbprint, St.Elmo, Illinois	55.00
Custard Glass, Hat, Blackberry, Pink Shading	28.00
Custard Glass, Hat, Grape Arbor, Signed, Northwood	62.00
Custard Glass, Jelly, Chrysanthemum Sprig	90.00
Custard Glass, Jelly, Geneva, Green & Gold	78.00
Custard Glass, Jelly, Green With Gold	78.00
Custard Glass, Juicer, Sunkist	20.00
Custard Glass, Lamp, Finger, Heart With Thumbprint	110.00
Custard Glass, Lamp, Flat Finger, Heart, Green	135.00
Custard Glass, Mug, Diamond Peg, 2 3/4 In.	40.00
Custard Glass, Mug, Montezuma, Iowa	19.00
Custard Glass, Mug, Serenade	35.00
Custard Glass, Mug, Singing Birds, With Nutmeg	65.00
Custard Glass, Mug, Souvenir, Belgrade Lakes, Maine, Punty & Star	32.00
Custard Glass, Mug, Souvenir, Conneaut Lake, Pa., Diamond Peg	35.00
Custard Glass, Mug, Souvenir, Twin Mountain, New Hampshire, Punty & Star	32.00
Custard Glass, Mug, Thumbprint, Green	20.00
Custard Glass, Mug, Tom & Jerry, Set Of 4	20.00
Custard Glass, Mug, Wide Band Of Stars, Bull's-Eye, 3 1/2 In.	25.00
Custard Glass, Pitcher, Fan, Northwood	210.00
Custard Glass, Pitcher, Milk, King Crown	58.00
Custard Glass, Pitcher, Souvenir, Chariton, Iowa	17.50
Custard Glass, Pitcher, Souvenir, Clara City, Minnesota	25.00
Custard Glass, Pitcher, Thumbprint, Courthouse, Ebensburg, Pa., 4 In.High	33.00
Custard Glass, Pitcher, Water, Cased In Pink, Ribbon Overlay	175.00
Custard Glass, Pitcher, Water, Chrysanthemum Sprig, Gold	350.00
Custard Glass, Pitcher, Water, Georgia Gem	135.00
Custard Glass, Pitcher, Water, Grape Arbor, Pink, Northwood .... Illus	1900.00
Custard Glass, Pitcher, Water, Jackson, 2 Tumblers	225.00
Custard Glass, Pitcher, Water, Louis XV	195.00
Custard Glass, Pitcher, Water, Ring Band	195.00
Custard Glass, Pitcher, Winged Scroll Tankard	150.00
Custard Glass, Plate, Grape & Cable, Signed N, 9 In.	50.00
Custard Glass, Plate, Nutmeg, Grape & Cable	30.00
Custard Glass, Punch Bowl, Grape & Cable, 2 Piece, Blue, 6 Cups .... Illus	1600.00
Custard Glass, Rose Bowl, Fine Cut & Roses, Designed Interior, Footed	65.00
Custard Glass, Rose Bowl, Roses, Footed, 4 1/4 In.	75.00
Custard Glass, Salt & Pepper, Chrysanthemum Sprig, Blue	435.00 To 500.00
Custard Glass, Salt & Pepper, Chrysanthemum Sprig, Gold	175.00
Custard Glass, Salt & Pepper, Corn Pattern	80.00
Custard Glass, Salt & Pepper, Floral Trim, Original Tops, Erie Twist	85.00
Custard Glass, Salt & Pepper, Inverted Fan & Feather, Pink	350.00
Custard Glass, Salt & Pepper, Jefferson Optic	65.00
Custard Glass, Salt & Pepper, Rose, Jefferson Optic	85.00
Custard Glass, Saltshaker, Fluted Scrolls, Blue Flowers & Gold Trim	68.00
Custard Glass, Sauce, Argonaut Shell	50.00
Custard Glass, Sauce, Chrysanthemum Sprig	35.00
Custard Glass, Sauce, Chrysanthemum Sprig, Blue	125.00
Custard Glass, Sauce, Diamond Peg, Gold, Souvenir	20.00
Custard Glass, Sauce, Louis XV, Gold On Feet & Rim, Oval, Northwood, 5 In.	50.00
Custard Glass, Sauce, Tarentum's Victoria	40.00
Custard Glass, Shade, Tulip Shape, Opalescent	70.00
Custard Glass, Shaker, Souvenir, Courthouse, Cresco, Iowa	30.00

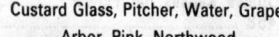

Custard Glass, Pitcher, Water, Grape
Arbor, Pink, Northwood   *(See Page 119)*

Custard Glass, Punch Bowl, Grape & Cable, 2 Piece, Blue, 6 Cups

(See Page 119)

Custard Glass, Shot Glass, Hot Springs, South Dakota	22.50
Custard Glass, Spooner, Argonaut Shell	100.00
Custard Glass, Spooner, Beaded Circle	100.00
Custard Glass, Spooner, Beaded, Swag	60.00
Custard Glass, Spooner, Chrysanthemum Sprig	79.00 To 95.00
Custard Glass, Spooner, Diamond In Peg, Coney Island	65.00
Custard Glass, Spooner, Diamond Peg, Conneaut Lake, Pennsylvania	65.00
Custard Glass, Spooner, Diamond Peg, Rose Decoration, 1916	80.00
Custard Glass, Spooner, Everglades, Gold, Decoration	115.00
Custard Glass, Spooner, Geneva, Green, Red	70.00
Custard Glass, Spooner, Honeycomb, Flower Rim, Blue Trim, Vermont	75.00
Custard Glass, Spooner, Intaglio, Gold, Enamel	85.00
Custard Glass, Spooner, Louis XV	70.00 To 85.00
Custard Glass, Spooner, Maple Leaf, Northwood	95.00
Custard Glass, Spooner, York Herring	37.00
Custard Glass, Sugar Shaker, Melon Shaped, Original Top, 4 In.	50.00
Custard Glass, Sugar Shaker, Paneled Teardrop, Green	110.00
Custard Glass, Sugar, Chrysanthemum Sprig	60.00
Custard Glass, Sugar, Covered, Argonaut, Color & Gold	210.00
Custard Glass, Sugar, Covered, Chrysanthemum Sprig, Gold, Signed	185.00 To 225.00
Custard Glass, Sugar, Covered, Diamond Peg, Coney Island	95.00
Custard Glass, Sugar, Covered, Louis XV	95.00 To 110.00
Custard Glass, Sugar, Covered, Maple Leaf	70.00

Custard Glass, Sugar, Covered, Trip, Triangle Shape 45.00
Custard Glass, Sugar, Grape & Cable, Nutmeg .... 55.00 To 75.00
Custard Glass, Syrup, Ivorina Verde, Gold Trim 150.00
Custard Glass, Syrup, Winged Scroll, Gold Trim 250.00
Custard Glass, Table Set, Argonaut Shell, Signed, Northwood 675.00
Custard Glass, Table Set, Chrysanthemum Sprig, Gold Trim, 4 Piece 575.00
Custard Glass, Table Set, Geneva, Green & Red Design, 4 Piece .... 400.00 To 435.00
Custard Glass, Table Set, Georgia Gem, Green Opaque, 4 Piece 585.00
Custard Glass, Table Set, Intaglio, Green Decoration, 4 Piece 475.00
Custard Glass, Table Set, Louis XV, 4 Piece 475.00
Custard Glass, Table Set, Maple Leaf, Butter, Sugar, Creamer, Spooner, Green 600.00
Custard Glass, Toothpick, Argonaut Shell 325.00
Custard Glass, Toothpick, Bulbous Shape, Ivorina Verde 80.00
Custard Glass, Toothpick, Chrysanthemum Sprig, Signed, Northwood 250.00
Custard Glass, Toothpick, Classical Figures, Scalloped Rim, C.1880 .... 55.00
Custard Glass, Toothpick, Diamond With Peg, Hand Painted Flowers 50.00
Custard Glass, Toothpick, Georgia Gem 40.00
Custard Glass, Toothpick, Harvard 18.00
Custard Glass, Toothpick, Souvenir, Caspian Lake, Vermont 26.00
Custard Glass, Toothpick, Souvenir, Diamond Peg, Coney Island 83.00
Custard Glass, Toothpick, Souvenir, Grand Lake Stream, Maine 24.00
Custard Glass, Toothpick, Souvenir, Houghton, Michigan, Hand-Painted, Beaded 40.00
Custard Glass, Toothpick, Souvenir, Orange, Massachusetts, Fluted Base 22.00
Custard Glass, Toothpick, Souvenir, Pepperell, Massachusetts 24.00
Custard Glass, Toothpick, Souvenir, Thumbprint, Darlington, Wisconsin 85.00
Custard Glass, Tray, Dresser, Winged Scroll 150.00
Custard Glass, Tray, Grape & Cable, Large 385.00
Custard Glass, Tray, Pin, Delaware, Roses, 7 In. 65.00
Custard Glass, Tray, Pin, Ivorina Verde, 3 X 4 In. 95.00
Custard Glass, Tumbler, Argonaut Shell 75.00
Custard Glass, Tumbler, Chrysanthemum Sprig 60.00
Custard Glass, Tumbler, Chrysanthemum Sprig, Blue 150.00
Custard Glass, Tumbler, Diamond Peg, Souvenir .... 45.00 To 50.00
Custard Glass, Tumbler, Geneva 50.00
Custard Glass, Tumbler, Grape Arbor, Pink, Northwood, Set Of 6 .... *Illus* 100.00
Custard Glass, Tumbler, Green, Delaware 65.00
Custard Glass, Tumbler, Intaglio 55.00
Custard Glass, Tumbler, Intaglio, Blue Decoration 50.00
Custard Glass, Tumbler, Intaglio, Green Decoration 50.00
Custard Glass, Tumbler, Inverted Fan & Feather 85.00
Custard Glass, Tumbler, Louis XV .... 40.00 To 95.00
Custard Glass, Tumbler, Ribbed Drape 42.00
Custard Glass, Tumbler, Signed Krystol 55.00
Custard Glass, Tumbler, Souvenir, Bloomer, Wisconson, Thumbprint 40.00
Custard Glass, Tumbler, Souvenir, Garden Of Gods, Colorado 43.00
Custard Glass, Tumbler, Souvenir, Overbrook Kansas, Rose Decoration 75.00
Custard Glass, Tumbler, Souvenir, Starkweather, North Dakota, Red Roses 65.00
Custard Glass, Tumbler, Winged Scroll 50.00
Custard Glass, Vase, Drapery, Nutmeg Stain 50.00
Custard Glass, Vase, Grape Arbor, Ruffled 75.00
Custard Glass, Vase, Thumbprint, Courthouse, Ebensburg, Pa., 6 In.High 33.00
Custard Glass, Water Set, Argonaut Shell .... 800.00 To 900.00
Custard Glass, Water Set, Fan & Feather, Northwood 825.00
Custard Glass, Water Set, Geneva, Green & Red Decoration, 7 Piece 595.00
Custard Glass, Water Set, Georgian Gem, Gold, 6 Piece 475.00
Custard Glass, Water Set, Inverted Fan & Feather .... 800.00 To 850.00
Custard Glass, Wine, Diamond Peg, Rockaway Beach, New York 35.00

*Cut glass has been made since ancient times, but the large majority of the
pieces now for sale date from the brilliant period of glass design, 1880 to
1905. These pieces had elaborate geometric designs with a deep miter cut.*

Cut Glass, Atomizer, Perfume, Allover Harvard 45.00
Cut Glass, Banana Boat, Pinwheels With Circle Of Hobstars, Cane, 11 1/4 In. ... 110.00
Cut Glass, Banana Boat, Strawberry Fan Cutting 95.00
Cut Glass, Barber Pole, Lights Up, Hangs On Wall, 4 Feet 500.00
Cut Glass, Basket, Applied Handle, Cane Border, Rayed Base, 5 1/4 In.Diam. ... 300.00
Cut Glass, Basket, Dorflinger's Marlboro Pattern, Twisted Handle, 5 In. 450.00

Cut Glass, Basket, Floral, Double Bull's-Eye Handle, Rayed Base, 7 X 8 In.	75.00
Cut Glass, Basket, Handled, St.Louis, Honeycomb, Hobstar Bottom, 10 X 10 In.	375.00
Cut Glass, Basket, Harvard & Cosmos, 16 X 12 In.Diameter	295.00
Cut Glass, Basket, Rope Handle, Brilliant Period, 7 X 8 1/2 X 1 1/2 In.	225.00
Cut Glass, Basket, Verticle Step Cuttings, Harvard, 20 X 13 In.Across	825.00
Cut Glass, Basket, White Rose Pattern, Irving, 16 In.	690.00
Cut Glass, Basket, 16-Point Hobstars, Intaglio, Notched Handle, 10 X 8 In.	355.00
Cut Glass, Berry Bowl, Gladys Pattern, Hawkes, 1 1/2 X 5 In.Diam., Set Of 6	160.00
Cut Glass, Berry Bowl, Golf Pattern, 10 In.	70.00
Cut Glass, Biscuit Jar, English, Sheffield Silver Rim, Cover & Handle	75.00
Cut Glass, Boat, Harvard Cut, Star On Bottom, 11 In.	90.00
Cut Glass, Bonbon, Hobstars, Pinwheels, 6 In.	35.00
Cut Glass, Bonbon, Maple Leaf Shape, Magnet Pattern, Bergen, 9 X 7 In.	95.00
Cut Glass, Bonbon, Marquis Pattern, Signed Hoare, 9 In.	150.00
Cut Glass, Bonbon, S-Shape, Hobstars, Diamonds, Buzz Stars, 7 1/4 X 4 In.	45.00
Cut Glass, Bottle, Cologne, Flute Cut, Dated 1876, Faceted Stopper, Pair	50.00
Cut Glass, Bottle, Cologne, Hourglass Shape, Cane Cutting, 9 3/4 In.	140.00
Cut Glass, Bottle, Perfume, Brilliant Cut, Bulbous, 6 In.	30.00
Cut Glass, Bottle, Perfume, Double Pedestal, Flame Finial, Stopper, 5 1/2 In.	25.00
Cut Glass, Bottle, Perfume, Harvard Cut, Sterling Cover, Stopper, 2 1/2 In.	30.00
Cut Glass, Bottle, Perfume, Pyramid Shaped, Jewel Cap, 3 3/4 In.	18.00
Cut Glass, Bottle, Perfume, Starred Base, Hobstar, Fans, Stopper, 6 1/4 In.	70.00
Cut Glass, Bottle, Perfume, Sterling Lid, Ground Stopper, English, 4 In.	50.00
Cut Glass, Bottle, Perfume, Sterling Top, English, 1898, 5 In.	37.00
Cut Glass, Bottle, Scent, Sterling Hinged Top, Cross Cut, 2 1/2 X 1/2 In.	55.00
Cut Glass, Bottle, Whiskey, Plymouth, Meriden, 11 In.	375.00
Cut Glass, Bottle, Worcestershire Sauce, Split Square	145.00
Cut Glass, Bowl, All Hobstars, Signed Clark, 9 In.Diameter	215.00
Cut Glass, Bowl, Alternating Stars & Hobstars, 3/4 In.Rim Teeth, 9 In.Diam.	465.00
Cut Glass, Bowl, American Brilliant Period, Floral Design, 11 1/2 X 7 In.	85.00
Cut Glass, Bowl, Cane Cut, Engraved Flowers, Sinclair, 7 1/4 X 5 In.	110.00
Cut Glass, Bowl, Console, Pedestal, Copper Wheel Cut Flowers, 4 X 11 3/4 In.	95.00
Cut Glass, Bowl, Daisy & Button & Roses, Straus, 9 In.	125.00
Cut Glass, Bowl, Daisy & Button, 8 X 3 1/2 In.	85.00
Cut Glass, Bowl, Drape Pattern, 10 In.Diameter	245.00
Cut Glass, Bowl, Expanding Star Pattern, 8 X 4 In.	135.00
Cut Glass, Bowl, Fan & Hobstar, Crosshatching, 8 In.Diameter	95.00
Cut Glass, Bowl, Fern & Pinwheel, Signed Clark, 8 X 3 3/4 In.	175.00
Cut Glass, Bowl, Fern, Applied Feet, Hobstars, Rayed Base, 4 1/2 In.Diam.	95.00
Cut Glass, Bowl, Fern, Horseshoe Pattern, Harvard Border, 8 In.Diameter	150.00
Cut Glass, Bowl, Finger, Russian Cut, 3 X 5 In.Diam., Set Of 8	700.00
Cut Glass, Bowl, Finger, Strawberry Diamond & Fan	13.50
Cut Glass, Bowl, Flashed Fans, Star, Medallions, 17 In.Diameter	62.00
Cut Glass, Bowl, Fruit, Russian Pattern, Medallions, Hobstar Base, 12 In.	160.00
Cut Glass, Bowl, Fruit, Step Cut Base, Star With Hobstar, 5 1/2 X 8 In.Diam.	195.00
Cut Glass, Bowl, Geometric & Star Motifs, American, Oval, 1900, 12 3/4 In.	300.00
Cut Glass, Bowl, Harvard & Floral Panels, 9 In.	75.00
Cut Glass, Bowl, Hobs In Mitered Vesicas, Diamonds, Beading, 9 In.	105.00
Cut Glass, Bowl, Hobs, Diamonds, Signed Straus, 9 In.	250.00
Cut Glass, Bowl, Hobstar, Strawberry Diamond, 8 In.	70.00
Cut Glass, Bowl, Hobstars, Fans, Scalloped & Notched Rim, 9 1/2 X 4 In.	85.00
Cut Glass, Bowl, Hobstars, Hobstar Base, Pedestal, 8 1/4 X 5 1/2 In.	250.00
Cut Glass, Bowl, Hobstars, Miter Framed Surrounded By Cane, 8 1/2 In.	90.00
Cut Glass, Bowl, Hunt Royal Pattern, Signed, 8 In.Diameter	160.00
Cut Glass, Bowl, Intaglio Fruits, 3 X 10 In.Diameter	250.00
Cut Glass, Bowl, Kalana Pansy, Dorflinger, Flaring Rim, 7 X 3 1/2 In.	115.00
Cut Glass, Bowl, Low, Expanding Star, 9 In.	185.00
Cut Glass, Bowl, Low, Hindoo, Signed Hoare, 8 In.	235.00
Cut Glass, Bowl, Low, Pluto, Signed Hoare, 8 In.	195.00
Cut Glass, Bowl, Low, Royal, Signed Hunt, 7 In.	195.00
Cut Glass, Bowl, Mayonnaise, Underplate, Florence, Signed Bergen	195.00
Cut Glass, Bowl, Orange, Lotus, Signed Egginton, 10 X 7 1/4 In.	450.00
Cut Glass, Bowl, Pedestal, Kismet, 5 In.Tall	155.00
Cut Glass, Bowl, Pinwheel, Fan & Hobstar, 8 In.Deep	85.00
Cut Glass, Bowl, Pluto Pattern, Hoare, 8 In.	195.00
Cut Glass, Bowl, Punch, Allover Cut, Matching Pedestal, 28 In.Diameter	387.00
Cut Glass, Bowl, Punch, American, Allover Cut, Pedestal 30 In.Around	293.00

Cut Glass, Bowl, Punch, Brilliant Period, 8 In. Pedestal, 14 X 12 In.Diam.	6800.00
Cut Glass, Bowl, Punch, Miniature, Crossed Cut Vesicas, 3 3/4 In.Diam.	125.00
Cut Glass, Bowl, Punch, Standard Corinthian, 27 In.Diameter	367.00
Cut Glass, Bowl, Rex Pattern, Intaglio Cut Wild Flowers, Tuthill, 8 In.	195.00
Cut Glass, Bowl, Russian Cut, 10 1/4 In.	225.00
Cut Glass, Bowl, Salad, Venice, 9 In.	115.00
Cut Glass, Bowl, Scalloped Sawtooth Rim, 4 X 8 In.	55.00
Cut Glass, Bowl, Scalloped Tooth Rim, Harvard Pattern, 8 In.Diameter	85.00
Cut Glass, Bowl, Shallow, Russian Cut, 7 In.	260.00
Cut Glass, Bowl, Star Button, Folded Sides, Russian, 10 In.	775.00
Cut Glass, Bowl, Strawberry, Diamond, Hobs, 28 In.Diameter	112.00
Cut Glass, Bowl, Strawberry, Diamond, Hobstars, Signed Hoare, 8 In.	190.00
Cut Glass, Bowl, Tangerine, Shield Cut Rim, 25 In.Diameter	198.00
Cut Glass, Bowl, Triple Square Pattern, Signed, Clark, 8 In.	225.00
Cut Glass, Bowl, Triple Square, Signed Clark, 6 3/4 In.	140.00
Cut Glass, Bowl, Vesicas, Leaves, Hobstars, 8 In.Diameter	63.50
Cut Glass, Bowl, Vesicas, Strawberries, Diamond, 26 In.Diameter	89.00
Cut Glass, Bowl, Webster, Higgins & Seiter, 8 In.	215.00
Cut Glass, Bowl, Whipped Cream, Step Cut Foot, 7 In.	125.00
Cut Glass, Box, Covered, Green Cut To Clear, Signed, 2 1/2 X 4 1/4 In.	495.00
Cut Glass, Box, Covered, Hinged, Cane, Cut Tulip, 5 In.	95.00
Cut Glass, Box, Dresser, Bohemian Cut, Ruby, 6 In.Square	69.00
Cut Glass, Box, Heart Shape, Harvard & Cosmos & Leaf, Footed, Lid, 6 X 6 In.	129.00
Cut Glass, Box, Hinged, Florence Star, 8 X 4 1/2 In.	495.00
Cut Glass, Box, Hinged, Flowers & Leaves, 32 Pint, 6 X 3 In.	175.00
Cut Glass, Box, Hinged, Hobstar On Cover & Base, 8 In.Diameter	550.00
Cut Glass, Box, Hinged, Round, Florence Pattern, 6 In.	235.00
Cut Glass, Box, Hinged, Silsbee Pattern, 6 1/2 In.Diameter	175.00
Cut Glass, Box, Powder, Covered, Harvard Pattern, 5 In.Diameter, Pair	190.00
Cut Glass, Box, Powder, Harvard Pattern, Round	135.00
Cut Glass, Box, Powder, Hinged, All Over Hobstars, 8 In.	550.00
Cut Glass, Box, Powder, Leaf & Flower Intaglio, Libbey, Covered	115.00
Cut Glass, Box, Powder, Strawberry Diamond & Fan, 16 Star Bottom, Round, Pair	98.00
Cut Glass, Brandy Set, Flashed Pinwheels, Cut Stopper, 6 Piece	185.00
Cut Glass, Bucket, Champagne, Flashed Hobstars, 7 X 7 1/2 In.Diameter	350.00
Cut Glass, Bucket, Champagne, Sawtooth Rim, 5 X 4 3/4 In.Diameter	120.00
Cut Glass, Bucket, Ice, Curved Sides, C On Bottom, 7 1/4 X 3 1/2 In.	90.00
Cut Glass, Bucket, Ice, Daisy & Button, Tab Handles, 4 1/2 X 7 In.Diameter	125.00
Cut Glass, Bucket, Ice, Ovoid, Harvard Cut, Tab Handles, 5 1/2 In.	350.00
Cut Glass, Bucket, Ice, Polished Intaglio, Lilies On Pond, 5 1/4 X 10 In.	550.00
Cut Glass, Butter Tub, Adams Pattern, Signed Sinclaire	330.00
Cut Glass, Butter, Covered, Blown Bubbles, Hobs, Prisms, Fans	265.00
Cut Glass, Butter, Covered, Harvard & Floral Pattern	150.00
Cut Glass, Butterpat, Diamonds, Strawberries, Fans, 3 1/4in.Diam., Set Of 6	99.00
Cut Glass, Candelabra, Sunburst Pattern, Silver Top, 3 Candle Holder, 14 In.	325.00
Cut Glass, Candlestick, American Brilliant Cut, 12 In., Pair	150.00
Cut Glass, Candlestick, Blown Hollow Stems, Punties, St.Louis, 13 In., Pair	525.00
Cut Glass, Candlestick, Flute Cut, Teardrop Stem, 4 3/4 In., Pair	250.00
Cut Glass, Candlestick, Flute Pattern, Signed Tuthill, Pair	460.00
Cut Glass, Candlestick, Notched Prism, Silver Plate Top, 8 In., Pair	125.00
Cut Glass, Candlestick, Steuben Cut By Hawkes, Airtwist Stem	70.00
Cut Glass, Candlestick, Teardrop Stem, Bull's-Eye, Rayed Base, 9 In., Pair	175.00
Cut Glass, Candlestick, 32 Point Hobstar Base, Teardrops, 12 In., Pair	595.00
Cut Glass, Canoe, Harvard, 12 In.	135.00
Cut Glass, Canoe, Miniature, Hobstars, Strawberries, Diamonds, 3 1/2 In.	65.00
Cut Glass, Carafe, Step Cutting Up Neck, Pinwheels, Hobstar	65.00
Cut Glass, Carafe, Thumbprint, Notched Prisms, Chain Of Hobstars	45.00
Cut Glass, Carafe, Water, Dorflinger, Middlesex	125.00
Cut Glass, Celery, Blossom Shaped Stars, Leaves, Hoare, 3 X 7 In.	75.00
Cut Glass, Celery, Cluster Of Hobstars, 13 X 5 1/2 In.	125.00
Cut Glass, Celery, Crossed Ovals	95.00
Cut Glass, Celery, Hobs, Cane, Cross Hatching, Signed Tuthill, 12 X 4 3/4 In.	225.00
Cut Glass, Celery, Hobstars, Fans, 11 In.	39.00
Cut Glass, Celery, Vase, Knop Stem, Scalloped Rim, Ashburton, 10 1/2 In.	125.00
Cut Glass, Center Piece, All Over Hobstars, American, 8 1/4 In.Diameter	295.00
Cut Glass, Champagne, Kalana Lily Pattern, Dorflinger, Hollow Stem, 5 In.	45.00
Cut Glass, Champagne, Parisian, Hobstar Foot, 4 5/8 In.	65.00

Cut Glass, Cheese & Cracker Plate, Hobstar Center, One Piece, 10 In.Diam.	525.00
Cut Glass, Compote, Adelaide Pattern, Clear To Pink, 6 1/2 X 6 1/2 In., Pair	135.00
Cut Glass, Compote, Airtwist Stem, Pinwheels, 6 In.	75.00
Cut Glass, Compote, Airtwist Stem, Signed Clark, 5 X 5 In.	245.00
Cut Glass, Compote, Allover Intaglio Cut, 4 1/2 X 7 In., Pair	35.00
Cut Glass, Compote, Base Ground, Initial Shield C, Dorflinger, 9 1/2 X 9 In.	300.00
Cut Glass, Compote, Bedford Pattern, Bergen, 8 In.Diameter	195.00
Cut Glass, Compote, Bishop's Hat, Signed G.Clapperton, 9 X 4 1/2 In.Diam.	125.00
Cut Glass, Compote, Cane Pattern, Pedestal, 9 In.	95.00
Cut Glass, Compote, Cane, Hobstar & Single Star, 9 In.High X 6 In.	100.00
Cut Glass, Compote, Chalice Shape, Hobstar & Fan, Notched Stem, 6 1 /2 In.	140.00
Cut Glass, Compote, Expanding Star, Hobstar Base, 9 In.	235.00
Cut Glass, Compote, Flaring, Creswick, Signed Eggington, 7 3/4 X 9 In.Diam.	575.00
Cut Glass, Compote, Hobstars, Honeycomb Stem, Signed Hoare, 12 X 9 In.	650.00
Cut Glass, Compote, Jelly, Step Cut Pedestal, Harvard Border, 4 1/4 X 5 In.	45.00
Cut Glass, Compote, Panels Of Roses, Crosshatching & Fans, 1920s, 5 In.	50.00
Cut Glass, Compote, Pedestal, Cane Pattern, 9 In.Diameter	95.00
Cut Glass, Compote, Strawberry, Diamond & Fan, 9 1/4 In.Wide, 7 1/2 In.High	175.00
Cut Glass, Compote, Teardrop Notched Stem, Signed Clark, 6 In.	95.00
Cut Glass, Compote, Tooth Cut Rim, Fluted Notch Cut Stem, Teardop, 12 In.	375.00
Cut Glass, Compote, Variation Of Arcadia, Bergen, 2 Part, 9 1/2 X 8 1/4 In.	570.00
Cut Glass, Compote, Vaseline, 6 X 9 1/2 In.Diameter	325.00
Cut Glass, Compote, York, 7 X 7 In.	120.00
Cut Glass, Compote, 24 Point Rayed Base, Tear-Drop In Stem, 8 1/2 X 6 In.	145.00
Cut Glass, Compote, 32 Point Hobstar Base, Notched Teardrop, Fans, 12 In.	890.00
Cut Glass, Cookie Jar, Rayed Lid, Prisms, Signed Libbey, 9 1/2 X 5 1/2 In.	350.00
Cut Glass, Cordial, Frosted Block, Stemmed, 7 In.	30.00
Cut Glass, Creamer & Sugar, Pinwheel Pattern	60.00
Cut Glass, Creamer, Butterflies & Flowers	20.00
Cut Glass, Creamer, Hobstars & Fan	20.00
Cut Glass, Creamer, Pear Shape, Prisms, Leaves, Flowers, 4 1/4 In.	35.00
Cut Glass, Creamer, Scalloped Edge, 6 Rows Opalescent Hobnails, 4 1/2 In.	45.00
Cut Glass, Cruet, Blazed Stars & Hobstars, St.Louis Diamond Handle	90.00
Cut Glass, Cruet, Bulge Body, Pinwheels, Tricornered Spout	52.00
Cut Glass, Cruet, Crosshatching & Star Bursts, Zipper Cut Neck	25.00
Cut Glass, Cruet, Decanter Shape, Intaglio Maple Leaves, 7 In.	95.00
Cut Glass, Cruet, Floral Panels, Chain Of Hobstars, Sinclaire, 8 1/2 In.	110.00
Cut Glass, Cruet, Hobs & Vesica, 6 In., Pair	125.00
Cut Glass, Cruet, Honeycomb Handle, Clear Button, Russian, 4 3/4 In.	210.00
Cut Glass, Cruet, Primrose Pattern, Signed Tuthill	345.00
Cut Glass, Cruet, Renaisssance Pattern, Stopper, 5 1/2 In.	50.00
Cut Glass, Cruet, Ship's, Imperial Pattern, Straus	225.00
Cut Glass, Cup, Punch, Green To Clear	27.50
Cut Glass, Cup, Punch, Hobstar & Fan	125.00
Cut Glass, Cup, Punch, Hobstar Within Diamond Forms, Vertical Cut, Set Of 8	170.00
Cut Glass, Cup, Punch, Hobstars, Fand & Swags, Signed Black	30.00
Cut Glass, Cup, Punch, Hobstars, Single Star, Crosshatching, Signed Tuthill	55.00
Cut Glass, Cup, Punch, Monarch Pattern, J.Hoares	85.00
Cut Glass, Cuspidor, Lady's, Sailor Hat Shape, Libbey, 9 1/4 In.Diameter	495.00
Cut Glass, Decanter, All Over Cane Pattern, Lapidary Stopper, 9 In.	250.00
Cut Glass, Decanter, Alternate Hobstars & Crosses, Faceted Stopper	160.00
Cut Glass, Decanter, Arcadia, Sterling Cut Glass Co., 10 1/2 In.	195.00
Cut Glass, Decanter, Bohemian Cut, 12 In.	69.00
Cut Glass, Decanter, Bowling Pin, Harvard, Horizontal Cut Neck, 13 1/2 In.	395.00
Cut Glass, Decanter, Brandy, Triple Notch Handle, Original Stopper, 7 In.	110.00
Cut Glass, Decanter, Captain's, Star & Button, 9 3/4 In.	90.00
Cut Glass, Decanter, Cut Stopper, Hobstars, Fans, Vesicas, Step Cut Neck	72.00
Cut Glass, Decanter, Dorflinger, Silver Diamond, Teardrop Stopper, 14 In.	450.00
Cut Glass, Decanter, Grecian, Stopper *Illus*	3600.00
Cut Glass, Decanter, Handle, Harvard Pattern, 12 1/2 In.	350.00
Cut Glass, Decanter, Hobstar & Crosses Alternating	145.00
Cut Glass, Decanter, Hobstars, Cross Cut Diamond, Flute Cut Neck, 13 In.	400.00
Cut Glass, Decanter, Panel Cut, 10 X 4 In., Pair	125.00
Cut Glass, Decanter, Pedestaled, Cut Stopper, Raised Hobnail, 14 In.	295.00
Cut Glass, Decanter, Perfume, Sterling Silver Top, C.1905, 3 In.	12.00
Cut Glass, Decanter, Russian Cut, Air Bubble Through Handle, 12 In., Pair	425.00
Cut Glass, Decanter, Sawtooth, 6 1/2 In.	50.00

Cut Glass, Decanter, Silver Diamond Pattern, Teardrop Stopper, 14 In.	450.00
Cut Glass, Decanter, Sterling Top, 4 Shot Glasses, Zipper & Bull's-Eye	325.00
Cut Glass, Decanter, Strawberry Diamond, Stopper, 13 In.	185.00
Cut Glass, Decanter, Whiskey, Strauss Bontemps Pattern, Handled, 9 1/2 In.	325.00
Cut Glass, Decanter, Wine, Emerald Green, Cut To Clear, 15 In.	175.00
Cut Glass, Decanter, Wine, Ruby, Cut To Clear, C.1900, 12 Wines, 8 1/2 In.	650.00
Cut Glass, Decanter, 4 Tumblers, Diamond Cut Stopper, Band Of Cane, 12 In.	175.00
Cut Glass, Decanter, 9 Panels, Double Ring Neck, Lattice, Mushroom Facet Top	72.50
Cut Glass, Dish, Boat-Shaped, Crosshatching, Hobstars, Signed, 8 In.Diameter	95.00
Cut Glass, Dish, Butter, Covered, Hobs, Notched Prism, Blown Blanks	250.00
Cut Glass, Dish, Butter, Covered, Pinwheel & Hobstar	285.00
Cut Glass, Dish, Butter, Dome, Fan, Quartz Crystal	78.50
Cut Glass, Dish, Butter, Hobstars, Diamond Filled Vesicas, Pair	695.00
Cut Glass, Dish, Candy, Club Shaped, Hobstars, Notching, 8 1/4 X 8 1/4 In.	125.00
Cut Glass, Dish, Candy, Flashed Star Center, Curved Miters, 6 In.Diam.	48.00
Cut Glass, Dish, Celery, Drape Pattern, Straus, 12 In.	65.00
Cut Glass, Dish, Celery, Medallions In Loops, 7 In.	70.00
Cut Glass, Dish, Chain Of Hobstars, Signed Sinclair, 9 1/4 X 6 In.	95.00
Cut Glass, Dish, Cheese, Covered, Clusters Of Hobstars	425.00
Cut Glass, Dish, Cheese, Dome & Matching Plate, Chains Of Hobstars	450.00
Cut Glass, Dish, Cheese, Dome, Underplate, Harvard Pattern, 7 X 9 In.Diam.	395.00
Cut Glass, Dish, Cheese, Domed Cover, Hobstar & Diamond Point, 6 In.	100.00
Cut Glass, Dish, Cheese, Domed, Elongated Harvard Pattern, Under Plate, 7 In.	495.00
Cut Glass, Dish, Cheese, Plate 9 In., Dome 6 1/4 In., 7 In.Tall	250.00
Cut Glass, Dish, Cut Leaves & Stems, Signed Hoare, 7 1/2 In.Diameter	65.00
Cut Glass, Dish, Hobstars, Fans, Flare Tall Ends, Oval, 7 X 4 In.	40.00
Cut Glass, Dish, Jewel Pattern, Clarke, Square	45.00
Cut Glass, Dish, Leaf Shaped, Starred Buttons, Russian, 8 In.	150.00
Cut Glass, Dish, Mint, Footed, Border Of Diamond, Notch & Fan, 4 3/4 In.Diam.	35.00
Cut Glass, Dish, Nut, Tazza, Hobstars, Buzz, Paperweight Bottom, 8 1/2 X 8 In.	475.00
Cut Glass, Dish, Olive, Hobstars, Fans, Strawberry Diamond, Argo, 7 3/4 In.	45.00
Cut Glass, Dish, Relish, Harvard, 8 3/4 X 5 In.	95.00
Cut Glass, Dish, Relish, Hobstars, Cane, Signed Hoare, 11 X 4 1/2 In.	125.00
Cut Glass, Dish, Relish, Intaglio Cut, Signed Clark, 7 1/2 X 5 3/4 In.	125.00
Cut Glass, Dish, Relish, Royal Pattern, 11 1/2 X 5 1/2 In.	185.00
Cut Glass, Dish, Round, Signed J.Hoare & Co., 5 In.Diameter	96.00
Cut Glass, Dish, Russian Cut, 7 In.	125.00
Cut Glass, Dish, Serving, Hobstars, Fan, Split Vesicas, 3-Sided	68.00
Cut Glass, Dish, Signed, Hoare, Corning, 6 In.	70.00
Cut Glass, Dish, 4 Section, 12 X 9 In.	165.00
Cut Glass, Dome, Cheese, Flute Cut Knob, Cane Diamond & Fan, 6 1/2 In.Diam.	85.00
Cut Glass, Dome, Lamp, Cross Hatching, Fans, Prisms, Brass Base, 22 In.	1000.00
Cut Glass, Dresser Set, Powder Jar, Hair Receiver, Pin Jar, C.1901, Signed	375.00
Cut Glass, Ferner, Wheel Pattern, Split Vesica, 3 Legs, 3 X 7 1/2 In.Diam.	75.00
Cut Glass, Ferner, 4-Footed, Six-Sided, Cane Pattern	125.00
Cut Glass, Finger Bowl, Vendome Pattern, Signed Eggington	50.00
Cut Glass, Flask, Lady's, Allover Cane, Sterling Top, 9 1/4 In.	195.00
Cut Glass, Frame, Picture, Harvard & Flowers, American, 7 X 5 3/4 In.	140.00
Cut Glass, Frame, Picture, Vintage Pattern, Sterling Border, 10 X 13 In.	250.00
Cut Glass, Fruit Bowl, 1897 Presentation Piece, Silver Rim, 9 1/2 X 5 In.	175.00
Cut Glass, Glass, High Ball, Greek Key, Alhambra Pattern	115.00
Cut Glass, Goblet, Harvard, 16 Point Star In Center, Notched Prism Stem	55.00
Cut Glass, Goblet, Water, Double Teardrop, Hobstar Base, Ribbon Star, 4 Piece	350.00
Cut Glass, Harvard Center & Border, Cut Corn Flowers, 17 X 10 In.	225.00
Cut Glass, Holder, Flower, Cuspidor Shape, Sterling Rim, 10 In.Base	1300.00
Cut Glass, Humidor, Hobstar, Monogrammed Sterling Knob, Dorflinger, 9 In.	695.00
Cut Glass, Humidor, Iris, Intaglio, Sterling Silver Lid	145.00
Cut Glass, Humidor, Middlesex Pattern, Lid, 10 In.	795.00
Cut Glass, Humidor, Renaissance, Dorflinger	175.00
Cut Glass, Humidor, Sterling Lid, Strawberry, Diamonds & Fans, 7 In.	75.00
Cut Glass, Humidor, Sterling Top, Art Nouveau Face, Zippered Bottom	175.00
Cut Glass, Humidor, Zipper Pattern	75.00
Cut Glass, Ice Bucket, Harvard, Hobstar Bottom, Tabs, 3 1/2 In.	95.00
Cut Glass, Inkwell, Harvard Pattern, Sterling Rim, Cover, 1 1/4 X 3/4 In.	60.00
Cut Glass, Inkwell, Notched Panel Cut, Gold, Hinged Lid, 3 1/2 In.	40.00
Cut Glass, Inkwell, Repeated Diagonal Cut, Hinged Lid, 2 In.Square	25.00
Cut Glass, Inkwell, Sunburst Bottom, Silver Plate Ball Shape Lid, 4 In.	65.00

Cut Glass, Inkwell, Swivel Embossed Silver Lid, Rococo, Signed, 8 1/2 In.	60.00
Cut Glass, Jar, Camphor, Harvard Pattern, 4 1/2 In.	50.00
Cut Glass, Jar, Cotton Puff, Up & Down Cuts, Original Top, 2 1/4 X 2 1/2 In.	32.00
Cut Glass, Jar, Pomade, Notched Prism, Gorham Sterling Silver Lid	25.00
Cut Glass, Jar, Powder, Covered, Butterfly	145.00
Cut Glass, Jar, Powder, Notched Prism, Sterling Silver Lid, Gorham	45.00
Cut Glass, Jar, Powder, 32 Point Star Bottom, 5 In.Diameter	129.00
Cut Glass, Jar, Rouge, Cross Cut & Fan, Sterling Silver Cover, 1 1/2 In.	35.00
Cut Glass, Jar, Tobacco, Panel Cut, Rayed Base, Sterling Top, 5 X 4 In.	75.00
Cut Glass, Jar, Tooth Powder, Brass Dispenser, Sterling Cap, 3 1/2 In.	25.00
Cut Glass, Jardiniere, Hobstars & Caning, Meriden Co., 5 1/2 In.	150.00
Cut Glass, Jug, Brandy, 24 Point Star Base, Art Nouveau, Gorham, 8 1/4 In.	80.00
Cut Glass, Jug, Claret, Diamond Cutting, Sheffield Top & Handle, 10 1/2 In.	155.00
Cut Glass, Jug, Whiskey, Brilliant & Heavy Cut, Diamond Cut Stopper	185.00
Cut Glass, Jug, Whiskey, Starred Base, Art Nouveau Sterling Stopper	95.00
Cut Glass, Juice, Buzz Stars, Crosscut Diamonds, Fans, Set Of 4	75.00
Cut Glass, Knife Rest, Cut Knob Ends, 4 1/2 In.	25.00
Cut Glass, Knife Rest, Dumbbell Ends, Zipper Pattern, 6 In.	35.00
Cut Glass, Knife Rest, Dumbbell Shape, Single Star Cut, 3 7/8 In.Long	22.50
Cut Glass, Knife Rest, Notched Center Bar, Star Cut On Ends, 4 1/2 In.	45.00
Cut Glass, Knife Rest, Tear Drop, Signed Hoare, 6 In.	65.00
Cut Glass, Knife Rest, 5 In.	30.00
Cut Glass, Lamp, see Lamp	
Cut Glass, Loving Cup, Hobstars, Fans, Sterling Silver, Gorham, 1880, 7 In.	475.00
Cut Glass, Marmalade Set, 2 Jar, Cut Stand, American Diamond	160.00
Cut Glass, Mayonnaise & Underplate, Hobstars, Fan	110.00
Cut Glass, Mayonnaise Bowl & Underplate, Flowers & Cane	155.00
Cut Glass, Mayonnaise Bowl, Underplate, Scalloped Tooth Rim, 5 3/4 X 7 In.	150.00
Cut Glass, Mayonnaise Set, Cane & Strawberry Diamond, Dorflinger	135.00
Cut Glass, Mayonnaise Set, Florence Pattern, Bergen	150.00
Cut Glass, Mayonnaise Set, Flowers, Cane & Strawberry Diamond, Dorflinger	150.00
Cut Glass, Mayonnaise Set, Hobstar & Fan, Scalloped Edge	125.00
Cut Glass, Mayonnaise Set, Hobstars & Cane, Square Shape	175.00
Cut Glass, Mayonnaise, Dish, Attached Plate, Cut Flowers, Sterling Lid	50.00
Cut Glass, Mayonnaise, Underplate, Cut Floral & Leaf Design	65.00
Cut Glass, Muffineer, Hobstar Center, Stars, Cane, Silver Top	85.00
Cut Glass, Mustard Pot, Diamond Point & Fan	35.00
Cut Glass, Mustard, Jar, Notched Prisms, Lid	42.00
Cut Glass, Mustard, Matching Under Plate, Vertical Notched Prism, Hobstars	65.00
Cut Glass, Napkin Ring, see Napkin Ring	
Cut Glass, Nappy, Applied Double Notch Handle, 7 In.Across	40.00
Cut Glass, Nappy, Brilliant Period, Eggington's Cluster, 7 In.Diameter	135.00
Cut Glass, Nappy, Brilliant Period, Pin Wheel, 6 X 7 1/2 In.	50.00
Cut Glass, Nappy, Buzz Star & Rosette	65.00
Cut Glass, Nappy, Crystal Clear Cutting, Handled, Divided, 8 X 11 In.	145.00
Cut Glass, Nappy, Cut Vesicas, Hobstars, Bull's-Eye Cut Handles, 8 In.	95.00
Cut Glass, Nappy, Heart Shape, Pinwheels & Fan, Handle, 6 X 9 In.	45.00
Cut Glass, Nappy, Lotus Pattern	65.00
Cut Glass, Nappy, Ribbon, Fan, Double Handled, 9 1/2 X 3 In.	60.00
Cut Glass, Nappy, Roses & Buds, 6 In.	40.00
Cut Glass, Nappy, Rosette Pattern	55.00
Cut Glass, Nappy, Sultana Pattern, Heart Shape, Dorflinger	95.00
Cut Glass, Nappy, 2 Handled, 4 Section, Corinthian, 11 In.Long	195.00
Cut Glass, Perfume Vial, Cane, Sterling Cap, Marked	75.00
Cut Glass, Perfume, Lay Down, Harvard Pattern, Sterling Hinged Top, 11 In.	175.00
Cut Glass, Pitcher, American Brilliant, 11 X 6 In.	250.00
Cut Glass, Pitcher, Applied Notched Handle, Starred Base, 6 3/4 In.	125.00
Cut Glass, Pitcher, Bulbous, Hobstars, 3 Pint	135.00
Cut Glass, Pitcher, Champagne, Bull's-Eye & Hobstars, 11 In.	100.00
Cut Glass, Pitcher, Cream, Strawberry-Diamond Cut, Applied Handle, 5 1/4 In.	110.00
Cut Glass, Pitcher, Double Notched Handle, 7 1/2 In.High, 4 3/4 In., Bottom	185.00
Cut Glass, Pitcher, Grape Intaglio Cutting, Double Notched Handle, 13 In.	60.00
Cut Glass, Pitcher, Harvard Cut, Hobstars At Top, Diamond Handle, 9 1/2 In.	175.00
Cut Glass, Pitcher, Harvard Pattern, Straight Sided, 8 In.	185.00
Cut Glass, Pitcher, Harvard, Triple Notched Handle, 9 1/4 In.	195.00
Cut Glass, Pitcher, Hobstars Separated With Bands Of Cane, 10 1/2 In.	285.00
Cut Glass, Pitcher, Lemonade, With Top, American, 9 In.	115.00

Cut Glass, Pitcher, Lotus Pattern, 10 In. 475.00
Cut Glass, Pitcher, Maple Leaf Cut, Hobstar & Cane, Signed, 11 In. 295.00
Cut Glass, Pitcher, Milk, Pinwheel & Hobstars, 4 1/2 In. 75.00
Cut Glass, Pitcher, Notched Prism Pattern, 8 In. 235.00
Cut Glass, Pitcher, Pinwheel, Lead, 9 1/4 In. 95.00
Cut Glass, Pitcher, Rose, Double Bull's-Eye Handle, Caning, 9 1/2 In. 100.00
Cut Glass, Pitcher, Sawtooth Top, Star, Pinwheel & Diamond, 10 1/2 In. 115.00
Cut Glass, Pitcher, Sterling Silver Rim, Applied Ribbed Handle, 9 1/2 In. 165.00
Cut Glass, Pitcher, Vertical Rows Of Hobstars, Signed Clark, 9 In. 175.00
Cut Glass, Pitcher, Water, Creswick Pattern, Hoare 125.00
Cut Glass, Pitcher, Water, Intaglio Flower Pattern, Signed Hawkes, 6 Glasses 275.00
Cut Glass, Pitcher, 2 Pinwheels, Hobstar, Strawberry Diamond, 10 3/4 X 5 In. 197.50
Cut Glass, Pitcher, 6 Tumblers, Intaglio Daisy, Butterfly, Signed, 9 1/2 In. 395.00
Cut Glass, Planter, Clear Buttons, Russian Cut Bottom, 7 X 6 In. 175.00
Cut Glass, Planter, Russian Cut, Cut Even At Bottom, 7 In.Wide 225.00
Cut Glass, Plate, Acid Etched, Kalana Hawthorne, Dorflinger, 7 In. 40.00
Cut Glass, Plate, Carolyn Variation, Signed Hoare, 8 1/4 In. 225.00
Cut Glass, Plate, Cheese & Cracker, 2 Level, 9 In. 115.00
Cut Glass, Plate, Chop, Turned Up Edge, Round 225.00
Cut Glass, Plate, Concentrics & Floral Pattern, Sawtooth Edging, 7 In. 45.00
Cut Glass, Plate, Dessert, Block Cut Center, Fan Edge, 8 In. 60.00
Cut Glass, Plate, Flute Pattern, Flashed Star Base, 6 1/2 In. 35.00
Cut Glass, Plate, Ice Cream, Harvard & Cosmos, 17 X 10 In. 195.00
Cut Glass, Plate, Primrose Pattern, Signed Tuthill, 10 In. 315.00
Cut Glass, Plate, Roland, Signed P. & B., 8 In. 185.00
Cut Glass, Plate, Russian Pattern, Flashed Star Base, 6 1/2 In. 45.00
Cut Glass, Plate, Shell Pattern, 7 In., Set Of 4 .... 280.00
Cut Glass, Plate, Tuthill, Wild Rose Pattern 500.00
Cut Glass, Plate, Wafer Pedestal, Primrose, Signed Tuthill, 6 In. 115.00
Cut Glass, Plate, Willow, Blue Cut To Clear, 8 In. 300.00
Cut Glass, Punch Bowl, Harvard & Floral, 2 Piece, 10 In. 300.00
Cut Glass, Punch Bowl, Harvard, Flowers & Leaves, 12 X 10 In., 2 Piece 225.00
Cut Glass, Punch Bowl, Hobstars & Shooting Stars, 2 Piece, 11 1/2 X 12 In. 550.00
Cut Glass, Punch Bowl, Strawberry, Diamond, Fan, 14 1/2 X 7 1/2 In. 450.00
Cut Glass, Relish, Primrose, Geometric, Signed Tuthill, 7 1/2 X 3 1/2 In. 225.00
Cut Glass, Relish, 2 Sections, Clark, 7 1/2 X 5 3/4 In. 125.00
Cut Glass, Rose Bowl, Allover Cut, Hobnail, 7 X 8 In.Diameter 200.00
Cut Glass, Rose Bowl, Fans, Stars, Panel, Signed Sinclaire, 5 In. 185.00
Cut Glass, Rose Bowl, Hobstars, Hobnail, Fans, Hobstar Base, 6 X 6 In. 375.00
Cut Glass, Rose Bowl, Hobstars, Oval Sunburst, 6 X 7 In.Diameter 195.00
Cut Glass, Rose Bowl, Intaglio Cut, Green To Clear, Signed, 2 1/4 In.Diam. 75.00
Cut Glass, Salad Set, Russian, Pairpoint 475.00
Cut Glass, Salt & Pepper, Ivory Inserts On Tops 40.00
Cut Glass, Salt & Pepper, Ribbed Hobstars, Sterling Tops, 2 1/2 In. 22.50
Cut Glass, Salt Shaker, Sterling Silver Top 3.25
Cut Glass, Salt, Bucket Shape, Basket Weave Cutting, Ruby, 5 1/2 In.Diam. 45.00
Cut Glass, Shade, Lamp, Hobstar, 12 In. 500.00
Cut Glass, Sherry, Cream, Dorflinger, Teardrop In Stem, 4 1/2 In. 55.00
Cut Glass, Shot Glass, Drape Pattern 55.00
Cut Glass, Spooner, Applied Double Notch Handles, Tooth Rim, 4 1/2 In. 135.00
Cut Glass, Spooner, Pinwheel, Strawberry, Diamond & Fan, 4 1/4 In. 75.00
Cut Glass, Spooner, Russian Cut, Scalloped Tooth Rim, 5 X 4 In.Diameter 135.00
Cut Glass, Spooner, Scalloped, Hobstars, Strawberries, Rayed Base, 4 1/2 In. 75.00
Cut Glass, Sugar & Creamer, Arcadia, Sterling Glass Co. 160.00
Cut Glass, Sugar & Creamer, Bedford, Bergen 80.00
Cut Glass, Sugar & Creamer, Buzz Stars, Cross Hatching, Applied Handles 65.00
Cut Glass, Sugar & Creamer, Clover-Leaf Shaped Feet & Handle 235.00
Cut Glass, Sugar & Creamer, Crosscut Diamonds, Flowers & Leaves, Oval 95.00
Cut Glass, Sugar & Creamer, Cut Handles, Teeth, Harvard 95.00
Cut Glass, Sugar & Creamer, Diamond, Fan, Triple Notched Handles, 2 1/8 In. 85.00
Cut Glass, Sugar & Creamer, Geometric, Hobstars, Notched Prisms 50.00
Cut Glass, Sugar & Creamer, Harvard, Hobstar & Cane 185.00
Cut Glass, Sugar & Creamer, Hunt's Royal 275.00
Cut Glass, Sugar & Creamer, Joan, Straus 150.00
Cut Glass, Sugar & Creamer, Magnet Pattern 107.50
Cut Glass, Sugar & Creamer, Pinwheel Pattern, Notched Handles 85.00
Cut Glass, Sugar & Creamer, Royal, Hunt 275.00

Cut Glass, Sugar & Creamer, 3-Footed, Pinwheel Pattern	195.00
Cut Glass, Sugar Shaker, Strawberry Diamond & Fan, Cylinder Shape	68.00
Cut Glass, Sugar Shaker, Strawberry Diamond & Fan, Rayed Base, Lid	48.00
Cut Glass, Sugar Shaker, Strawberry, Diamond & Fan, Cover	35.00
Cut Glass, Syrup, Mums, Hallmarked Sterling Silver Top, 5 1/2 X 4 1/2 In.	50.00
Cut Glass, Syrup, Silver Plate Top, Deep Mitres, 6 1/2 In.	110.00
Cut Glass, Table Set, Mustard, Salt & Vinegar, Stand, Etched, 3 Piece	74.50
Cut Glass, Tankard, Grecian	*Illus* 2900.00
Cut Glass, Tankard, Notched Handle, Star, Fans, Rosetted Base, 9 1/2 In.	95.00
Cut Glass, Tankard, Sterling Top & Lip, Applied Handle, Tiffany, 12 1/2 In.	360.00
Cut Glass, Toothpick, Block, Etched, Pair	20.00
Cut Glass, Toothpick, Diamond Shape & Diamond-Quilted	35.00
Cut Glass, Toothpick, Pedestaled, Hobstars & Fans, 5 In., Pair	275.00
Cut Glass, Torte Stand, Arcadia On Brilliant Blank, 8 X 3 1/2 In.	425.00
Cut Glass, Tray, Bread, Cluster Of Hobstars, 13 X 15 1/2 In.	115.00
Cut Glass, Tray, Cake, Hobstars Four Corners & Center, 12 In.Diameter	425.00
Cut Glass, Tray, Center Handle, Intaglio Cutting, Four Panels, 12 In.	125.00
Cut Glass, Tray, Cosmos, Harvard Band & Center, 17 X 10 1/2 In.	275.00
Cut Glass, Tray, Harvard, Star, Diamond, Cane, 12 In.Diameter	250.00
Cut Glass, Tray, Hobstar Center, Hobstars, Cane & Diamond, 12 In.Diameter	225.00
Cut Glass, Tray, Ice Cream, Bakers Gothic, Clark, 14 1/2 X 8 In.	475.00
Cut Glass, Tray, Ice Cream, Diamond & Stars, Signed Clark, 14 1/2 X 10 In.	395.00
Cut Glass, Tray, Ice Cream, Hobstar Medallions, 78 Teeth, 14 1/4 In.	155.00
Cut Glass, Tray, Ice Cream, Hobstars, Strawberry Diamond, Vesica, 14 X 7 In.	150.00
Cut Glass, Tray, Ice Cream, Intaglio Flowers & Leaves, 13 1/2 X 8 In.	130.00
Cut Glass, Tray, Ice Cream, Miniature, Canton Pattern, 4 1/2 X 2 1/4 In.	60.00
Cut Glass, Tray, Ice Cream, Nelson, Empire Cut Glass Company, 14 X 7 1/2 In.	225.00
Cut Glass, Tray, Ice Cream, Scalloped Tooth Rim, Vesicas, 14 X 7 1/2 In.	165.00
Cut Glass, Tray, Oval, All Over Harvard Pattern, 7 1/4 X 5 1/2 In.	45.00
Cut Glass, Tray, Russian, Starred Buttons, Scalloped Rim, 10 1/4 X 5 In.	225.00
Cut Glass, Tray, Russian, Clear Buttons, 12 In.Diameter	750.00
Cut Glass, Tray, Scalloped, Diamond Point Rim, Signed, 7 X 5 1/2 In.	155.00
Cut Glass, Tray, Sugar Cube, Hobstar & Pyramid, Ear Handles, 2 X 8 3/4 In.	95.00
Cut Glass, Tray, 8 Sided, Step Cutting, Signed Tuthill, 9 1/4 X 6 3/4 In.	275.00
Cut Glass, Tumbler, Cut Rose Pattern, Tuthill	65.00
Cut Glass, Tumbler, Diamond & Prism, Thistle Blossom Shaped	30.00
Cut Glass, Tumbler, English, Signed Webb & Corbett	160.00
Cut Glass, Tumbler, Harvard, Rayed Base, 16 Point, Set Of 4	125.00
Cut Glass, Tumbler, Heart Pattern, Pineapple Cut	38.50
Cut Glass, Tumbler, Hobstar & Fans, Signed Clark, Set Of 8	200.00
Cut Glass, Tumbler, Lotus Pattern, Eggington	24.00
Cut Glass, Tumbler, Pineapple & Fan, English, 4 1/2 X 3 In.Diameter	23.00
Cut Glass, Tumbler, Strawberry Diamond & Star, Clark	35.00
Cut Glass, Urn, Covered, Intaglio Cut Scene, Knopped Mushroom Finial, 17 In.	325.00
Cut Glass, Vase, Black Crystal, Signed Sinclaire, 10 In.	165.00
Cut Glass, Vase, Blown, Yellow Olive, Baluster Body, 1800s, 10 In.	125.00
Cut Glass, Vase, Canadian, Pedestal, Sawtooth Band, 12 In.	96.00
Cut Glass, Vase, Celery, Chalice Type, Pedestal, 10 In.	495.00
Cut Glass, Vase, Cone Shape, Sawtooth Top, Beaded & Ribbed, 10 1/2 In.	95.00
Cut Glass, Vase, Cornucopia, Intaglio Flowers & Ives, 10 3/4 X 5 1/4 In.	500.00
Cut Glass, Vase, Corset Shape, Geometric Pattern, Tuthill, 14 In.	375.00
Cut Glass, Vase, Corset Shape, Harvard, Intaglio Flower, 10 X 4 1/2 In.	45.00
Cut Glass, Vase, Cranberry To Clear, Strawberry Diamonds, Mitres, 12 In.	450.00
Cut Glass, Vase, Cut Velvet, Diamond Quilt, Ruffled Top, Blue, 6 3/4 In.	150.00
Cut Glass, Vase, Diamond Cut Ferns & Flowers, 12 In.	125.00
Cut Glass, Vase, Fanshaped, Hobstar Straw, 7 In.	145.00
Cut Glass, Vase, Floral Band Of Strawberry Diamonds, Cross Hatch, 9 3/4 In.	50.00
Cut Glass, Vase, Footed, Strawberry Diamond Within Diamond, P.Brooks, 8 In.	200.00
Cut Glass, Vase, Geometric & Intaglio, Signed Tuthill, 10 In.	275.00
Cut Glass, Vase, Henry VIII, Signed Clark, 8 In.	80.00
Cut Glass, Vase, Hobstar & Strawberry Diamond, Fan Shaped, 7 In.	145.00
Cut Glass, Vase, Hobstar Base, Bengal Pattern, Signed Sinclaire, 14 In.	525.00
Cut Glass, Vase, Hobstar, Strawberry Diamond, Fan, 16 X 6 3/4 In.	160.00
Cut Glass, Vase, Hobstars, Cross Hatching, Fans, Cane, Portland, 10 1/2 In.	775.00
Cut Glass, Vase, Hobstars, Fine Diamond, Fans, Signed Libbey, 14 In.	300.00
Cut Glass, Vase, Hobstars, Harvard, Fine Diamond, Buzz, 14 In.	475.00

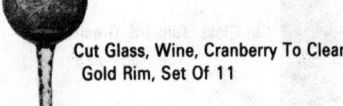

Cut Glass, Wine, Cranberry To Clear,
Gold Rim, Set Of 11

Cut Glass, Wine, Overlay,
Green To Clear, England,
Set Of 12

Cut Glass, Wine, Overlay,
Green To Clear, Twisted Stem,
Set Of 9

Cut Glass, Vase, Hobstars, Hobnail, Cane, Hour Glass Shape, Pedestal, 14 In.	375.00
Cut Glass, Vase, Hourglass Shape, Signed Taylor, 12 In.	245.00
Cut Glass, Vase, Limousine, Hobstars, Notched Prisms, Cane, 9 In.	225.00
Cut Glass, Vase, Middlesex, Pitkins & Brooks, 13 In.	198.00
Cut Glass, Vase, Monarch Pattern, Hobstar Foot, Signed Hoare	595.00
Cut Glass, Vase, Notched Prism, Five Sided Strawberry Diamond Figure, 9 In.	125.00
Cut Glass, Vase, Octagon Base, Horizontal Step Cutting, 4 X 6 1/2 In.Diam.	95.00
Cut Glass, Vase, Pedestal, Buzz, Hobstars, Hobnail & Fans, 10 1/2 In.	420.00
Cut Glass, Vase, Pedestal, Wheel Polished, 14 In.	450.00
Cut Glass, Vase, Pillars, Hobstars & Flute At Top, 12 In.	150.00
Cut Glass, Vase, Pinwheel, Fan, Strawberry Cuttings, 4 1/2 X 3 In.	40.00
Cut Glass, Vase, Pinwheels, Step Cut Center, 12 1/2 In.	135.00
Cut Glass, Vase, Prism Hexagonal Stem, 24 Point Star, Cane, 10 In.	80.00
Cut Glass, Vase, Rayed Footing, Hobstar, Canes, 12 1/4 In.	125.00
Cut Glass, Vase, Rayed Stars At Bottom, Hobstars, Fans, Flute Top, 12 1/4 In.	195.00
Cut Glass, Vase, Silsbee, 10 In.	225.00
Cut Glass, Vase, Starflower By Ideal Cut Glass, 18 In.	195.00
Cut Glass, Vase, Steffin's Daisy Pattern, Mt. Washington, Ball Stem, 14 In.	425.00
Cut Glass, Vase, Tri-Cornered, Hobstars, Vesicas Of Hobnail, 8 1/4 In.	195.00
Cut Glass, Vase, Triple Square, Clark, 10 In.	195.00
Cut Glass, Vase, Trumpet Shape, Graduated Hobstar & Oval Prisms, 15 1/2 In.	800.00
Cut Glass, Vase, Trumpet Shape, Pedestal Base, 14 In.	30.00
Cut Glass, Vase, Trumpet, Cut To Clear, Harvard, 8 1/4 In., Pair	750.00
Cut Glass, Vase, Trumpet, Emerald Cut To Clear, 12 In.	625.00
Cut Glass, Vase, Trumpet, Hobs, Fans & Stars, 16 In.	100.00
Cut Glass, Vase, Trumpet, Hobstars, Fan & Verticle Notch, 14 In.	160.00
Cut Glass, Vase, Wheel Grind, Floral Design, Signed Sinclaire, 5 In.	100.00
Cut Glass, Vase, Zipper Cuts, Bull1s-Eyes, 11 1/2 In.	85.00
Cut Glass, Vase, 3 Pinwheels Separated By Bands Of Hobstars, 12 X 5 In.	425.00
Cut Glass, Water Set, Bulbous, Enameling Of Forget-Me-Nots, 5 Tumblers	155.00
Cut Glass, Water Set, Dauntless Pattern, Bergen, 6 Piece	595.00
Cut Glass, Water Set, Hobstar & Pinwheel, Tankard Pitcher, 7 Piece	225.00
Cut Glass, Water Set, Ribbed, Floral, Signed Fry, 7 In., 6 Piece	375.00
Cut Glass, Water, Set, 4 Glasses, Feather, Fan, Diamond Point, 8 1/2 In.	225.00
Cut Glass, Whiskey, Cistern, Irish, 1860	745.00
Cut Glass, Wine, Clear, Cranberry Cut, Mitre Cut With Thumbprint, 8 In.	55.00
Cut Glass, Wine, Cranberry To Clear, Gold Rim, Set Of 11 .... *Illus*	400.00
Cut Glass, Wine, Crosscut Diamonds & Fans, Hawkes, Set Of 6	275.00
Cut Glass, Wine, Encore Pattern, Amber Cut To Clear, 4 3/4 In.	175.00
Cut Glass, Wine, Overlay, Green To Clear, England, Set Of 12 .... *Illus*	160.00
Cut Glass, Wine, Overlay, Green To Clear, Twisted Stem, Set Of 9 .... *Illus*	500.00
Cut Glass, Wine, Stemmed, Each .... *Illus*	150.00

*Cut velvet is a special type of art glass made with two layers of blown
glass, which shows a raised pattern. It usually had an acid finish or
velvetlike texture. It was made by many glass factories during the late
Victorian years.*

Cut Velvet, Pitcher, Water, Glossy, Tall Tankard, Blue 225.00

Cut Glass, Decanter, Grecian, Stopper
(See Page 124)

Cut Glass, Tankard, Grecian
(See Page 128)

Cut Glass, Wine, Stemmed, Each
(See Page 129)

D'Argental, Goblet, Landscape,
Leaf & Vine Stem & Base

D'Argental was a French cameo glassmaker of the late Victorian period. The D'Argental factory made multilayered, acid-cut cameo glass in France in the late nineteenth century. The glass is decorated with floral or scenic designs.

D'Argental, Atomizer, Perfume, Floral To Amber Satin, Blue, Signed, 7 In		300.00
D'Argental, Goblet, Landscape, Leaf & Vine Stem & Base	*Illus*	525.00
D'Argental, Vase, Cameo, Blue Lining, Landscape Scene, Signed, 13 7/8 In		900.00
D'Argental, Vase, Cameo, Chateau, Scenic, French, Signed, 10 5/8 X 3 1/2 In		495.00
D'Argental, Vase, Cameo, Cut Intaglio, Scenic, Signed, 10 1/2 In		1250.00
D'Argental, Vase, Cameo, Flower Form, Red & Brown, Orange Ground, 14 In		585.00
D'Argental, Vase, Cameo, Ovoid, Frosted Amber Ground, Signed, 10 In		790.00
D'Argental, Vase, Cameo, Slate Black, 6 In		695.00
D'Argental, Vase, Cameo, Storks Nesting On Roof, Signed, 10 In		985.00
D'Argental, Vase, Cameo, Translucent White Satin Ground, Signed, 6 In		395.00
D'Argental, Vase, Gold Frosted Ground, 2 Acid Cuttings, Signed, 5 3/4 In		300.00
D'Argental, Vase, Moonlight Venice, Man In Gondola, French, Signed, 7 In		650.00
D'Argental, Vase, Ovoid Shape, Magenta, Berries, Leaves, Signed, 10 In		790.00
D'Argental, Vase, Red Leaves & Berries, Red & Yellow Body, Signed, 5 In		475.00
D'Argental, Vase, Reddish-Orange Shaded To Yellow, Scenic, Signed, 10 In		650.00
D'Argental, Vase, Scenic, Acid Cuttings, French, Signed, 17 In		1495.00
D'Argental, Vase, Scenic, Frosted Gold Ground, Acid Cut, Signed, 10 5/8 In		495.00
D'Argental, Vase, Translucent Satin Ground, Water Scene, Signed, 6 In		395.00

Daum Nancy is the mark used by Auguste and Antonin Daum on pieces of French cameo glass made after 1875.

Daum Nancy, Apricot, Etched & Enameled, 5 3/4 In., Pair	*Illus*	550.00
Daum Nancy, Bowl, Carved Leaves, Twigs & Bows, 6 X 6 1/2 In.Diameter		425.00
Daum Nancy, Bowl, Centerpiece, Amethyst, Signed, 5 1/2 X 10 1/2 In		250.00
Daum Nancy, Bowl, Cross Of Lorraine, Acid Cut, Signed, 5 1/2 X 5 1/2 In		89.00
Daum Nancy, Bowl, Fruit Design, Yellow Ground, Signed, 2 1/4 X 5 1/4 In		275.00
Daum Nancy, Bowl, Gilt Bronze, Stand, Frosted, Intaglio Cut, Signed, 12 In		390.00
Daum Nancy, Bowl, Green Cut To Mottled Yellow, Signed	*Illus*	275.00
Daum Nancy, Bowl, Mottled Art Glass, Four Crimpings, 4 1/2 X 4 1/2 In		100.00
Daum Nancy, Bowl, Oval, Green On Acid Pink, Tulips, Signed, 4 X 12 1/2 In		425.00
Daum Nancy, Bowl, Oval, Winter Scene, Golden Ground, 6 1/2 In.Diameter		595.00
Daum Nancy, Bowl, Paneled Prism Cut, Crystal, Emerald Green, France, 4 In		135.00
Daum Nancy, Bowl, Peacock Feather Design Circles Bowl, 4 X 7 In		950.00
Daum Nancy, Bowl, Peacock Feather, Marquetry Circles Bowl, 4 X 7 In.Diam		1250.00
Daum Nancy, Bowl, Quatrefoil Shape, Frosted, Signed, 4 1/4 X 2 1/2 In		750.00
Daum Nancy, Chandelier, Brown, Yellow, Orange, Green, Grapes, Leaves, 16 In		1800.00
Daum Nancy, Compote, Footed, Sculptured Lines, Signed, 2 3/4 X 2 In.Diam		110.00
Daum Nancy, Ewer, Cameo, Miniature, Applied Handle, Signed		495.00
Daum Nancy, Inkwell, Covered, Scenic, Signed		1100.00
Daum Nancy, Lamp, Lower Tree Trunk, Clouds Above, Signed, Paper Label, 17 In		2500.00
Daum Nancy, Lamp, Marble, Intaglio Carved, Iron, C.1925	*Illus*	2500.00
Daum Nancy, Lamp, Variegated Berries & Leaves, Fretwork Cover, 6 In		425.00
Daum Nancy, Pitcher, Cameo, Frosted, Gold Trim, Signed, 5 1/8 In		435.00
Daum Nancy, Pitcher, Yellow Orange Splatter, Applied Handles, Signed, 8 In		300.00
Daum Nancy, Plate, Blue Floral, Decoration On Pale Blue, Signed		38.00
Daum Nancy, Plate, Red Flowers, Green Leaves, Sides Turned Up, 6 X 4 1/2 In		295.00
Daum Nancy, Plate, Turned Up Sides, Brown & Yellow Ground, 6 X 4 1/2 In		295.00

Daum Nancy, Rose Bowl, Mottled White Ground, Leaves, Large 575.00
Daum Nancy, Rose Bowl, Purple & Cream, Gold Trim, Signed, 2 3/4 X 3 In. 255.00
Daum Nancy, Salt, Cameo Flowers, Gold Enamel, Oval, Signed 115.00
Daum Nancy, Salt, Green, Gold Decoration, Signed, 1 1/8 In. 205.00
Daum Nancy, Salt, Tub Shape, Rain Scene, Enameled, 1 1/2 X 1 3/4 In.Diam. 295.00
Daum Nancy, Shot Glass, Barrel Shape, Late Spring Scene, 2 X 1 5/8 In.Diam. 265.00
Daum Nancy, Tumbler, Abc, Mistletoe Pattern, Barrel Shape, Frosted 85.00
Daum Nancy, Tumbler, Acid Carved, Chipped Ice Ground, Signed, 4 3/4 In. 145.00
Daum Nancy, Tumbler, Barrel Shape, Gold, Brown Frosted Ground, Signed, 5 In. 295.00
Daum Nancy, Tumbler, Barrel Shape, Mottled Gold, Frosted Ground, 4 5/8 In. 325.00
Daum Nancy, Tumbler, Barrel Shape, Poppies, Frosted Ground, Signed, 2 3/8 In. 325.00
Daum Nancy, Tumbler, Berries & Leaves, Barrel Shape, Signed, 4 3/4 In. 295.00
Daum Nancy, Vase, Acid Cut & Gilded Thistle, Cross Of Lorraine, 8 3/4 In. 475.00
Daum Nancy, Vase, Aqua Hydrangeas, Green Leaves, 23 1/2 In. 1050.00
Daum Nancy, Vase, Art Deco, Raised Spatter Pattern, Signed, 7 X 7 In. 150.00
Daum Nancy, Vase, Autumn Scene, Signed, No.2034, 8 1/2 In. 475.00
Daum Nancy, Vase, Blown Out Berries, Handled, Signed, 7 1/2 In. 300.00
Daum Nancy, Vase, Boats On Water, Green Top, Signed, 5 3/4 In. 550.00
Daum Nancy, Vase, Brown Base, Flowers Rise From Base, Signed, 8 1/2 In. 265.00
Daum Nancy, Vase, Burgundy, Iris, Gold Decoration, Signed, 9 1/2 In. 235.00
Daum Nancy, Vase, Cabachons, Enameling, Rainbow Swirled, 8 In. 1395.00
Daum Nancy, Vase, Cameo & Enamel Fleur-De-Lis, Signed, 6 In. 225.00
Daum Nancy, Vase, Cameo, Autumn Scene, 6 1/2 In. 895.00
Daum Nancy, Vase, Cameo, Browns, Gold, Green Leaves, 11 X 6 In. 375.00
Daum Nancy, Vase, Cameo, Carved & Enameled, Square Form, 5 1/2 In. 250.00
Daum Nancy, Vase, Cameo, Carved Mice, Pink, Green Background, French, 5 In. 1150.00
Daum Nancy, Vase, Cameo, Clear To Pink Background, Signed, 6 3/8 In. 775.00
Daum Nancy, Vase, Cameo, Enameled Free Form, Wild Flowers, 4 3/4 X 3 In. 365.00
Daum Nancy, Vase, Cameo, Enameled Jewels, 2 Bees, Pink Stripes, 8 In. 1395.00
Daum Nancy, Vase, Cameo, Flowers, Leaves, Stems, Purple, Blue, Signed, 17 In. 595.00
Daum Nancy, Vase, Cameo, Gold Ground, Striping, Acid Cut, Signed, 4 7/8 In. 195.00
Daum Nancy, Vase, Cameo, Goose Girl, 4 Geese Front, 3 Back, Signed, 4 In. 450.00
Daum Nancy, Vase, Cameo, Mottled Inside, Frosted Coral Ground, 4 3/4 In. 375.00
Daum Nancy, Vase, Cameo, Pink & Green Cabochons, 10 1/2 In. 975.00
Daum Nancy, Vase, Cameo, Rustic Design, 14 1/2 In. 850.00
Daum Nancy, Vase, Cameo, Scenic, Acid Cutting, Enameled, Signed, 11 1/2 In. 450.00
Daum Nancy, Vase, Cameo, 4 Color Sweet Peas, Mottled, 12 1/2 In. 650.00
Daum Nancy, Vase, Cameo, 4 Color, Sailboat Scene, Signed, 5 3/8 X 5 1/2 In. 325.00
Daum Nancy, Vase, Clear, Acid Cut, Gold & Silver Gilt, 5 In. 650.00
Daum Nancy, Vase, Cut Thistles, Amber Acidized Ground, Signed, 5 In., Pair 525.00
Daum Nancy, Vase, Cylindrical, Scenic, Signed, 6 In. 650.00
Daum Nancy, Vase, Cylindrical, Sunset Landscape Scene, Signed, 11 7/8 In. 750.00
Daum Nancy, Vase, Diamond Shape, Summer Scene, Pink, Signed, 4 1/4 In. 685.00
Daum Nancy, Vase, Egg Shaped, Frosted Background, Signed, 6 1/2 X 4 3/8 In. 425.00
Daum Nancy, Vase, Enamel, Flowers & Buds, 4 1/2 In. 295.00
Daum Nancy, Vase, Enameled Jewels, 2 Bees, Rainbow Swirled Stripes, 8 In. 1395.00
Daum Nancy, Vase, Enameled, Spring Scenic, Signed, 4 3/4 In. 675.00
Daum Nancy, Vase, Flare-Out Opening, Amber Over Bubble, Signed, 6 1/2 In. 110.00
Daum Nancy, Vase, Flowers Outlined In Gold, Signed, 9 3/4 In. 185.00
Daum Nancy, Vase, Flowers, Clear To Pink Mottled Ground, Signed, 4 3/4 In. 495.00
Daum Nancy, Vase, Four Boat Scene, 4 Cuttings, Acid & Wheel, 8 1/2 In. 850.00

Daum Nancy, Bowl, Green Cut
To Mottled Yellow, Signed

Daum Nancy, Lamp, Marble,
Intaglio Carved, Iron, C.1925

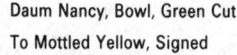
Daum Nancy, Apricot, Etched &
Enameled, 5 3/4 In., Pair

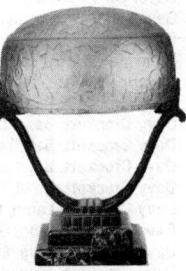

Daum Nancy, Vase, Green, Acid & Wheel Cut, Gold Gilt Trim, Signed, 10 1/2 In.	475.00
Daum Nancy, Vase, Groups Of Mice, Pink & Green Ground, 5 In.	1150.00
Daum Nancy, Vase, Hexagonal Lilacs, Enameled, Signed, 1898, 11 1/4 In.	250.00
Daum Nancy, Vase, Intaglio Etched Cupids, Signed, 5 In.	165.00
Daum Nancy, Vase, Iridescent, Enameled, Gold Trim, Signed, 3 1/4 X 8 3/4 In.	385.00
Daum Nancy, Vase, Lake Scene, Black Enameling, Signed, 4 1/2 X 4 1/2 In.	345.00
Daum Nancy, Vase, Lavender Flowers, Gold Enamel, Signed, 3 In.	180.00
Daum Nancy, Vase, Leaves & Grapes On Yellow Ground, Footed, 12 In.	425.00
Daum Nancy, Vase, Light Rustic Ground, Cameo, 14 1/2 In.	850.00
Daum Nancy, Vase, Mauve Roses, Green Cabochons Scattered, 10 1/2 In.	975.00
Daum Nancy, Vase, Mimosas, Gilded Leaves, Clear Ground, Signed, 5 3/4 In.	285.00
Daum Nancy, Vase, Mottled Blue Frosted Ground, Acid Cutting, Enameled, 6 In.	695.00
Daum Nancy, Vase, Multicolor, Berries Blown Out, Cameo, Signed, 7 1/2 X 6 In.	300.00
Daum Nancy, Vase, Orchid Pattern, 2 Cut Spider Webs, 5 In.	350.00
Daum Nancy, Vase, Orchids, 2 Spider Webs, Rectangular, Signed, 4 3/4 In.	425.00
Daum Nancy, Vase, Pink & Green Jewels, Trumpet Shaped, 10 1/2 In.	850.00
Daum Nancy, Vase, Pink Ground, Defined Pine Trees, 14 In.	1150.00
Daum Nancy, Vase, Purple Flowers & Leaves, 4 1/2 In.	140.00
Daum Nancy, Vase, Red Berries, Green Leaves, Cameo & Enamel, 14 1/2 In.	750.00
Daum Nancy, Vase, Scenic, Acid Cuttings, Signed, 17 1/8 In.	1050.00
Daum Nancy, Vase, Scenic, Mottled Ground, Signed, Wafer Feet, 8 In.	539.00
Daum Nancy, Vase, Scenic, Trees Bent, Blowing Storm, Signed, 4 3/4 In.	1175.00
Daum Nancy, Vase, Spring Scene, Acid Cut, Enameling, Signed, 13 1/2 In.	1100.00
Daum Nancy, Vase, Spring Scene, Frosted Ground, Signed, 13 5/8 In.	1100.00
Daum Nancy, Vase, Square, Yellow Mimosa, Signed, 3 7/8 X 1 3/8 In.Diameter	210.00
Daum Nancy, Vase, Summer Scenic, Frosted Background, Acid Cut, 23 1/8 In.	1000.00
Daum Nancy, Vase, Transparent Blue Ground, Irises & Leaves, Signed, 15 In.	595.00
Daum Nancy, Vase, Tumbler Shape, Pink Flowers, Signed, 3 1/2 In.	325.00
Daum Nancy, Vase, Winter Scene, Bulbous, Signed, 3 1/4 In.	675.00
Daum Nancy, Vase, Winter Scene, Deep Yellow Background, 13 In.	850.00
Daum Nancy, Vase, Yellow Sunflowers, Mustard Background, Bulbous, 10 In.	650.00
Daum Nancy, Vase, 4-Color Flowers, Etched & Wheel Cut, Signed, 11 In.	600.00
Daum, Nancy, Bowl, Footed, Prism Cut, Emerald Green, 2 1/2 X 4 In.	95.00
Daum, Nancy, Box, Camera, Raised Cameo Flowers, Gold Enamel, 6 1/2 In.Diam.	425.00

DAVENPORT
LONGPORT
STAFFORDSHRE

Davenport pottery and porcelain were made at the Davenport Factory in Longport, Staffordshire, England, from 1793 to 1887. Earthenwares, creamwares, porcelains, ironstone wares, and other products were made. Most of the pieces are marked with a form of the word Davenport.

Davenport, Biscuit Jar, Silver Plated Holder, Signed, 8 3/4 In.	165.00
Davenport, Bowl, Covered, 2 Handled, Flowers & Birds, Marked, 5 In.	38.00
Davenport, Charger, Alpine Amusement, Blue, Anchor Mark, 15 1/4 In.	75.00
Davenport, Creamer, Blue, Damask Rose, 9 1/2 In.	45.00
Davenport, Ewer, Gold Griffen Handle, C.1880, 6 X 6 In.	135.00
Davenport, Inkwell, Flower Cluster On Leaf, C.1880	300.00
Davenport, Mug, Child's, Black & White, Feeding The Rabbit, 2 5/8 In.	90.00
Davenport, Mug, Dark Blue Willow, C.1830	40.00
Davenport, Mug, The Little Plunderer, C.1805, Boy Robbing Nest	40.00
Davenport, Pitcher, Blue & Pink, C.1820, Signed, 6 3/4 In.	70.00
Davenport, Plate, Alpine Amusement, Anchor Mark, 15 In.	70.00
Davenport, Plate, Imari Colors, 1793-1806, 10 In., Pair	45.00
Davenport, Plate, Reticulated Edge, Garden Scene, Impressed Anchor, Set Of 6	225.00
Davenport, Platter, Amoy, C.1844, 15 3/4 X 12 In.Diameter	175.00
Davenport, Platter, Cyprus, Mulberry	150.00
Davenport, Platter, Marine Anchor, Cable Rim, Juice Well, Marked, 18 X 14 In.	97.50
Davenport, Vase, Butterfly Handles, Signed, 1870-86, 9 3/4 In.	130.00
Davenport, Vase, Japan Pattern, Pot-Pourri, 1870-86, Crowned Mark, 6 In., Pair	300.00
Davy Crockett, Bank, Pony Express, Canvas, Lock & Key	10.00
Davy Crockett, Base, Lamp, Ceramic, Dated 1955, 8 In.	7.50
Davy Crockett, Belt, Leather	10.00
Davy Crockett, Bowl & Mug, Set	10.00
Davy Crockett, Bowl, Cereal, Red & White	8.00
Davy Crockett, Lamp, Original Shade	40.00
Davy Crockett, Mug, Green & White	8.00
Davy Crockett, Mug, Milk Glass	3.50
Davy Crockett, Mug, Red & White	8.00

De Vez is a name found on special pieces of French cameo glass made by the Cristallerie de Pantin about 1890. Monsieur de Varreux was the art director of the glassworks and he signed pieces "De Vez."

De Vez, Atomizer, Cameo, Butterflies, Brown On Yellow, Signed	330.00
De Vez, Bottle, Perfume, Iridescent Amethyst, Signed, 5 1/2 In.	58.00
De Vez, Bowl, Cameo, Diamond Shape, Scenic, Acid Cutting, Signed, 4 X 4 In.	395.00
De Vez, Light, Night, Scenic, Gold Sky Ground, 7 1/4 In.	950.00
De Vez, Vase, Blue, Signed, 2 3/4 In.	200.00
De Vez, Vase, Cameo, Creamy Translucent Ground, Scenic, Signed, 7 5/8 In.	495.00
De Vez, Vase, Cameo, Frosted Gold Ground, Acid Cut, Signed, 9 7/8 In.	525.00
De Vez, Vase, Cameo, Harbor Scene, 12 1/2 In.	1295.00
De Vez, Vase, Cameo, Opaque Lavender, Cameo Cut Grapes, Signed, 8 1/2 In.	325.00
De Vez, Vase, Cameo, Satin Ground, Scenic, Signed, 9 3/4 In.	575.00
De Vez, Vase, Cameo, Scalloped Top, Frosted Ground, Footed, Signed, 9 5/8 In.	495.00
De Vez, Vase, Cameo, Scenic, Acid Cutting, Signed, 5 1/4 X 2 1/2 In.Diameter	375.00
De Vez, Vase, Cameo, Scenic, Satin Ground, Acid Cut, Signed, 7 3/4 In.	595.00
De Vez, Vase, Cameo, Translucent Ground, Castle On Crag, Signed, 9 1/2 In.	750.00
De Vez, Vase, Cameo, Translucent Satin Ground, Acid Cut, Signed, 9 7/8 In.	595.00
De Vez, Vase, Cameo, Translucent White Ground, Acid Cut, Signed, 6 3/4 In.	295.00
De Vez, Vase, Cameo, White Satin Ground, Pedestal Foot, Signed, 9 5/8 In.	550.00
De Vez, Vase, Cameo, Yellow Translucent Ground, Signed, 10 X 3 3/8 In.Diam.	750.00
De Vez, Vase, Cameo, 3 Acid Cuttings, Scenic, 10 X 3 1/4 In.Diam.	645.00
De Vez, Vase, French Cameo, Harbor Scene, Signed, 12 1/2 In.	1295.00
De Vez, Vase, French, Maritime Scene, Cameo, Signed, 8 In.	520.00
De Vez, Vase, Frosted Yellow Ground, Scenic, Signed, 10 In.	525.00
De Vez, Vase, Frosted, Blue & Pink, Signed, Cameo, 9 In.	575.00
De Vez, Vase, Harbor Scene, 12 1/2 In.	1050.00
De Vez, Vase, Man In Boat, Village Scene, Satin Ground, Signed, 13 7/8 In.	895.00
De Vez, Vase, Mosque & Palm Trees Scenic, Acid Cut, Signed, 10 In.	725.00
De Vez, Vase, Mountain Lake Scene, Gold Frosted Ground, Signed, 9 1/2 In.	645.00
De Vez, Vase, Mountain Scene, Translucent Ground, Blue, Signed, 5 1/4 In.	395.00
De Vez, Vase, Mountains & Trees, Frosted Ground, Acid Cut, Signed, 11 3/4 In.	595.00
De Vez, Vase, Pine Trees & Mountain Scenic, Acid Cut, Signed, 17 1/8 In.	1000.00
De Vez, Vase, Scalloped Top, Translucent Ground, Acid Cut, Signed, 9 5/8 In.	495.00
De Vez, Vase, Scenic, Cabin In Forest, Signed, 7 In.	695.00
De Vez, Vase, Scenic, Multi-Colored, French, Signed, 16 1/4 X 6 1/2 In.	1800.00
De Vez, Vase, Translucent Satin Ground, Castle Scene, Signed, 9 7/8 In.	595.00
De Vez, Vase, Translucent White, Mountain Scene, Signed, 9 5/8 In.	550.00
De Vez, Vase, Water, Flowers, Mountains, Trees, Bushes, Islands, Signed, 5 In.	425.00

Decoys are carved or turned wooden copies of birds. The decoy was placed in the water to lure flying birds to the pond for hunters.

Decoy, Balsa Wood, Papier-Mache Head	9.00
Decoy, Black Duck, Joseph W. Lincoln	350.00
Decoy, Black Duck, Lloyd Johnson	500.00
Decoy, Blue Wing Teal Hen, Wooden, Painted Eyes, 12 1/2 In.	27.50
Decoy, Canada Geese, Johnson, Folding, Wire Frames, 26 X 30 In., Pair	18.00
Decoy, Canada Goose, Hand-Painted, 19 X 9 In.	150.00
Decoy, Canvas Back Canada Goose, Manie Heywood, Curituck Sound, C.1910	135.00
Decoy, Crow, Papier-Mache, Full Body Form	10.00
Decoy, Drake, Blue Wing Teal, Painted Eyes, Capt.Harry Jobes, 13 1/4 In.	27.50
Decoy, Drake, Canvasback, Black, White, Red, Lead Weights, 15 1/2 In.	29.00
Decoy, Drake, Canvasback, New England	30.00
Decoy, Drake, Wooden Head, Cork Body	55.00
Decoy, Duck, Canvas Covers Wooden Frame & Head, Burt Hunt, 1800s, 26 In.	250.00
Decoy, Duck, Cork	20.00
Decoy, Duck, Glass Eyes, George Crossen, Backbay, Virginia	225.00
Decoy, Duck, Hand Carved, 15 In.	15.00
Decoy, Duck, Hand-Carved, Green Spot On Wings	75.00
Decoy, Duck, Mallard, Male & Female, Pair	125.00
Decoy, Duck, Oversize, Ira Hudson	150.00
Decoy, Duck, Plugged Chests, Hollow	35.00
Decoy, Duck, Preening, Black, John B. Belport, C.1930, Glass Eyes	500.00
Decoy, Fish, Carved Tail & Mouth, Tin Fins, Gray, Red	60.00
Decoy, Goose, Miniature, Original Black & White Paint, 2 X 3 1/4 In.	75.00
Decoy, Goose, 42 In.Long	125.00

Decoy, Mallard Duck, Hand-Carved Cedar, Glass Eyes 9.75
Decoy, Mallard, Cedar, Glass Eyes 9.75
Decoy, Mallard, Hand-Carved, Swivel Head, Glass Eyes 160.00
Decoy, Merganser, 20th Century, F.Dobbins 105.00
Decoy, New England Duck, Hand-Carved, Solid Body 27.00
Decoy, Owl, Papier-Mache, Full Body Form, 13 In. 20.00
Decoy, Owl, Papier-Mache, Full Body Form, 16 In. 25.00
Decoy, Owl, Papier-Mache, 13 In. 20.00
Decoy, Owl, Papier-Mache, 16 In. 25.00
Decoy, Pintail Duck, Glass Eyes, Solid Wood, Pair 54.50
Decoy, Plover, White Underside, Black Breast, Folding, Tin, 9 In. 150.00
Decoy, Redhead, Glass Eyes 12.95
Decoy, Ruddy Duck, Saucer Shape, White Jaws, Chubby Body, John Williams 600.00
Decoy, Stretched Canvas On Wooden Frame, Wooden Head, 19th Century, 26 In. ... 250.00
Decoy, Swan, White, Backwards Stretching Neck, Delaware, 1900s, 24 In. 115.00
Decoy, Swift, 24 In.Long 55.00
Decoy, Teal, Green Winged, 20th Century, F.Dobbins 95.00
Decoy, Yellowlegs, Shore Bird, Folding, Spotted Back, Tin, C.1874, 11 1/4 In. 150.00

 The Dedham Pottery Company of Dedham, Massachusetts, started making pottery in 1866. It was reorganized as the Chelsea Pottery Company in 1891, and became the Dedham Pottery Company in 1895. The factory was famous for its crackleware dishes, which picture blue outlines of animals, flowers, and other natural motifs.

Dedham, Bowl, Bunny Rabbits All Around, Crackled, Signed, 5 1/2 X 1 3/4 In. 75.00
Dedham, Bowl, Grape, Shaped Rim, 8 1/2 In. 220.00
Dedham, Bowl, Grape, 3 X 7 In. 145.00
Dedham, Bowl, Rabbit, 8 1/2 In.Diameter 185.00
Dedham, Bowl, Sugar, Rabbit Covered, Handled 75.00
Dedham, Candlestick, Flower Pattern, Marked, Pair 145.00
Dedham, Creamer, Rabbits, Squatty, 3 1/2 X 5 1/2 In. 72.00
Dedham, Dish, Celery, Rabbit Border, Signed, 10 X 6 In. 70.00
Dedham, Dish, Handkerchief Folds In Center, Rabbit Border, 6 In.Square 75.00
Dedham, Egg Cup, Double, Rabbit 120.00
Dedham, Egg Cup, Grape 155.00
Dedham, Jug, Cream, Rabbit On Blue Ground, 3 In. 95.00
Dedham, Mug, Tankard, Rabbit Border, 5 1/4 In. 175.00
Dedham, Pitcher, Night & Morning, 5 In. 320.00
Dedham, Plate, Azalea, 6 In. 50.00
Dedham, Plate, Baby's, Four Rabbits 50.00
Dedham, Plate, Bunny Rabbits All Around, Signed, 8 In.Diameter 75.00
Dedham, Plate, Bunny, 6 In. 38.00
Dedham, Plate, Butterflies, 6 In. 38.00
Dedham, Plate, Duck Border, 8 1/2 In. 82.00
Dedham, Plate, Duck, 6 In. .... 38.00 To 65.00
Dedham, Plate, Duck, 6 1/2 In. 45.00
Dedham, Plate, Duck, 8 1/2 In. 125.00
Dedham, Plate, Duck, 10 In.
Dedham, Plate, Grape 85.00
Dedham, Plate, Iris, 6 In. 38.00
Dedham, Plate, Iris, 8 1/2 In. 95.00
Dedham, Plate, Moth, 10 In. 175.00
Dedham, Plate, Pond Lily, 8 1/2 In. 125.00
Dedham, Plate, Rabbit, One Ear, 8 1/2 In. 70.00
Dedham, Plate, Rabbit, 6 In. .... 36.00 To 41.00
Dedham, Plate, Rabbit, 7 1/2 In. 65.00
Dedham, Plate, Rabbit, 8 1/2 In. 85.00
Dedham, Plate, Rabbit, 8 3/8 In. 85.00
Dedham, Plate, Rabbit, 10 In. 75.00
Dedham, Plate, Snowtree, 6 In. .... 50.00 To 65.00
Dedham, Plate, Swan, 8 1/2 In.Diameter 145.00
Dedham, Plate, Turkey, 8 1/2 In.Diameter 125.00
Dedham, Plate, Water Lily, 6 In. 38.00
Dedham, Plate, Water Lily, 10 In. 68.00
Dedham, Salt & Pepper, Rabbits 125.00
Dedham, Saucer, Butterfly 45.00
Dedham, Sugar, Rabbits & Apples, Lid, 5 In. 175.00

Dedham, Tray, Elephant Border, Round, 7 1/2 In. 195.00
Dedham, Vase, Blue Over Green Volcanic Drip, Rabbit Mark 225.00
Dedham, Vase, Brown Glaze Over Green, Signed, 3 1/2 X 4 1/2 In. 400.00
Dedham, Vase, Flambe Glaze, C.1899-1908, Thrown By H.C.Robertson, 11 1/2 In. 750.00
Dedham, Vase, Pottery, Four-Leaf Clover Overall, Signed, 5 1/2 In., CKAW 445.00
DeFeure, Vase, Charcoal Gray Frosted, Raised Figures, 5 1/2 In. 75.00
DeGue, Centerpiece Bowl, Infused Leaves, Signed, 9 1/2 X 9 1/2 In.Diam. 195.00

Delatte glass is a French cameo glass made by Andre Delatte. It was first made in Nancy, France, in 1921. Lighting fixtures and opaque glassware in imitation of Bohemian opaline were made.

Delatte, Vase, Cameo, Opaque Ground, 2-Handled, Signed, 18 In. 595.00
Delatte, Vase, Cameo, 2 Handles, Pink Ground, Canal Scene, Signed, 6 In. 632.00
Delatte, Vase, Mauve Flowers, Pink Ground, Signed, 10 In. 475.00
Delatte, Vase, Mottled Yellow, Bulbous, Cylinder Neck, Signed, 26 In.Tall 245.00

Delaware, see Pressed Glass, Custard Glass
Deldare, see Buffalo Pottery, Deldare

Delft is a tin-glazed pottery that has been made since the seventeenth century. It is decorated with blue on white or with colored decorations. Most of the pieces sold today were made after 1891, and the name Holland appears with the Delft factory marks.

Delft, Ashtray, Windmill, Silver Top Edge 20.00
Delft, Bottle, Liquor, Dutch House, No.9, Blue & White 7.50
Delft, Canister Set, Salt Box, Wind Mills, House Scene, 12 Piece 135.00
Delft, Coffee Grinder, Wall, Wood, Glass, China 75.00
Delft, Condiment Set, Amstel, Germany, 15 Pieces 235.00
Delft, Cow, Polychrome, Milking Boy, 18th Century 850.00
Delft, Creamer, Cow, Porcelain, Windmills & Sail Boats, 7 X 4 1/2 In. 38.00
Delft, Dish, Oval, Narrow On One End, Crossed Pipes, Germany 24.00
Delft, Figurine, Charger, Blue & White Floral Resembles Peacock Tail 180.00
Delft, Figurine, Dutch Boy, Pocket Vase In Rear, Polychrome, 4 1/4 In. 18.50
Delft, Gravy Boat, Attached Saucer, Duck Handle, Windmill On Side 85.00
Delft, Humidor, Hand-Painted, Amphora, Indians Smoking Pipes, 7 In. 110.00
Delft, Jar, Lid, Peacock & Flowers, Blue & White, C.1890, 13 In. 195.00
Delft, Jar, Paneled Ovoid Body, Foo Dog Finial, Dutch, 21 1/2 In. 850.00
Delft, Pitcher, Blue & White, Fish Lying Down, 10 1/2 In. 135.00
Delft, Pitcher, Embossed Design, Blue Boat Scene, Ornate Handle, 6 In. 15.00
Delft, Plaque, Dutch Couple & Children, Signed, 15 1/2 In.Diameter 65.00
Delft, Plate, Blue & White, Vase Of Flowers, C.1700s, 9 In. 98.00
Delft, Plate, Blue & White, Vase Of Flowers, C.1800, 9 In. 98.00
Delft, Plate, Bristol, Polychrome, C.1730, 12 3/4 In.Diameter 400.00
Delft, Plate, Hanging, Dutch Scene Center, Floral Rim, 8 1/2 In. 23.00
Delft, Plate, London, Polychrome, Pair, C.1750, 7 3/4 In. 425.00
Delft, Plate, Polychrome Griffin In Center, 9 1/2 In. 22.00
Delft, Salt & Pepper, Windmill 7.50
Delft, Stein, Dutchman Seated At Table, Pewter Lid, Dash Handle, 1700s 165.00
Delft, Stein, Hinged Pewter Lid & Base, Church Yard Scene 120.00
Delft, Teabowl & Saucer, Dutch, White, 18th Century, 2 1/2 In. & 4 3/8 In. 375.00
Delft, Tile, Blue Cavalier On White, 18th Century, 5 1/4 In. 15.00
Delft, Tile, Sailboats & Steepled Building, 5 1/8 In.Square, Pair 25.00
Delft, Tray, Windmills & Water Scene, Blue, 12 X 8 In. 120.00
Delft, Wash Bowl & Pitcher, Blue & White, English 125.00

Dentist, see Doctor

Depression glass was an inexpensive glass manufactured in large quantities during the 1920s and early 1930s. It was made in many colors and patterns by dozens of factories in the United States. The name depression glass is a modern one.

Depression Glass, Ashtray, Adam, Green 9.00
Depression Glass, Ashtray, Adam, Pink 9.50
Depression Glass, Ashtray, Florentine No.2, Topaz, 1/2 In. 24.00
Depression Glass, Ashtray, Shamrock, Black 42.00
Depression Glass, Ashtray, Sunflower, Pink 4.00
Depression Glass, Basket, English Hobnail, 4 1/2 In. 15.00
Depression Glass, Berry Bowl, Cherry Blossom, Pink, Iridescent, 4 3/4 In. 4.50

Depression Glass, Berry Bowl, Daisy, Amber, 9 3/8 In.	7.00
Depression Glass, Berry Bowl, Doric, Pink	7.00
Depression Glass, Berry Bowl, Holiday, Pink	3.50
Depression Glass, Berry Bowl, Madrid, Pink	3.00
Depression Glass, Berry Bowl, Normandie	1.25
Depression Glass, Berry Bowl, Parrot, Green, 5 In.	5.00
Depression Glass, Berry Bowl, Sharon, Amber, 8 1/2 In.	2.75
Depression Glass, Berry Bowl, Sharon, Pink, 5 In.	3.00
Depression Glass, Berry Set, Coronation, Ruby, 7 Piece	25.00
Depression Glass, Berry Set, Royal Ruby, 7 Piece	25.00
Depression Glass, Bottle, Vinegar, Cameo, Green	15.00
Depression Glass, Bowl, Apple Blossom, Green, 8 1/2 In.	35.00
Depression Glass, Bowl, Avocado, 8 In.	5.00
Depression Glass, Bowl, Block Optic, Green, 8 In.	7.00
Depression Glass, Bowl, Bubble, Blue, 4 1/2 In.	2.75
Depression Glass, Bowl, Cameo, Green, 8 1/4 In.	9.50
Depression Glass, Bowl, Cameo, 5 1/2 In.	2.00
Depression Glass, Bowl, Cereal, Adam, Green	12.00
Depression Glass, Bowl, Cereal, American Sweetheart, Pink	4.75
Depression Glass, Bowl, Cereal, Cherry Blossom, Pink	12.00
Depression Glass, Bowl, Cereal, Moderntone, Pink	1.00
Depression Glass, Bowl, Cereal, Normandie	2.00
Depression Glass, Bowl, Cereal, Princess, Green	8.00
Depression Glass, Bowl, Cereal, Queen Mary, Pink	1.75
Depression Glass, Bowl, Cereal, Sandwich, Yellow	3.00
Depression Glass, Bowl, Cherry Blossom, Delphite, 9 In.	10.00
Depression Glass, Bowl, Cherry Blossom, Green, Footed, 10 1/2 In.	22.00
Depression Glass, Bowl, Cherry Blossom, Handled, Blue, 9 In.	18.00
Depression Glass, Bowl, Cherry Blossom, Handled, Pink, 9 In.	8.00
Depression Glass, Bowl, Console, Cherry Blossom, Pink, Footed	25.00
Depression Glass, Bowl, Console, Cherry Blossom, 3 Legs, Pink	28.50
Depression Glass, Bowl, Console, Madrid	4.00
Depression Glass, Bowl, Console, Madrid, Pink	10.00
Depression Glass, Bowl, Console, Swirl, Ultramarine	15.00
Depression Glass, Bowl, Coronation, Master Berry, Ruby Red	14.00
Depression Glass, Bowl, Diamond Quilted, Pink, Fluted, 6 1/2 In.	3.00
Depression Glass, Bowl, Diana, Amber, 11 In.	8.00
Depression Glass, Bowl, Diana, 12 In.	10.00
Depression Glass, Bowl, Doric, Pink, 8 1/4 In.	7.00
Depression Glass, Bowl, Floral, Green, Covered, 8 In.	20.00
Depression Glass, Bowl, Florentine No.2, Yellow, Covered, 9 In.	19.00
Depression Glass, Bowl, Fruits, Pink, 10 1/2 In.	17.00
Depression Glass, Bowl, Hobnail & Panel, Pink, 10 1/2 In.	10.00
Depression Glass, Bowl, Hobnail, Blue, Handled, 7 In.	14.00
Depression Glass, Bowl, Iris, Ruffled, Iridescent, 11 In.	6.00
Depression Glass, Bowl, Lace Edge, Pink, 9 1/2 In.	4.00
Depression Glass, Bowl, Manhattan, Lace Edge, Pink, 9 1/2 In.	5.00
Depression Glass, Bowl, Mayfair, Pink, Handled, 10 In.	10.00
Depression Glass, Bowl, Mixing, Hex Optic, Pink, 8 3/4 In.	6.00
Depression Glass, Bowl, Nut, Moderntone, Blue, Ruffled, Handled	6.00
Depression Glass, Bowl, Petalware, Monax, 5 3/4 In.	3.00
Depression Glass, Bowl, Pineapple & Floral, 5/8 In.	2.50
Depression Glass, Bowl, Princess, Green, 9 1/2 In.	12.50
Depression Glass, Bowl, Ribbed, Lace Edge, Pink, 9 1/2 In.	5.00
Depression Glass, Bowl, Royal Lace, Straight Sided, Cobalt, 10 In.	40.00
Depression Glass, Bowl, Salad, Cameo, Green, Square	14.00
Depression Glass, Bowl, Salad, Madrid, Pink, 9 1/2 In.	17.50
Depression Glass, Bowl, Sawtooth, Pink, Footed, 8 In.	15.00
Depression Glass, Bowl, Sharon, Amber, 9 1/2 In.	4.00
Depression Glass, Bowl, Sharon, Green, 10 In.	15.00
Depression Glass, Bowl, Sharon, Pink, 8 In.	5.50
Depression Glass, Bowl, Sharon, Pink, 10 1/2 In.	10.00 To 12.00
Depression Glass, Bowl, Swirl, Ultramarine, Footed, 10 In.	10.00
Depression Glass, Bowl, Vegetable, American Sweetheart, Monax	25.00
Depression Glass, Bowl, Vegetable, Chinex, Ivory, 9 In.	10.00
Depression Glass, Bowl, Vegetable, Royal Lace, Oval, Blue	16.00
Depression Glass, Bowl, Vegetable, Sharon, Green	10.00

Depression Glass, Box, Powder, English Hobnail, Green, Covered	35.00
Depression Glass, Box, Powder, Hobnail, Black, 7 In.	18.00
Depression Glass, Bucket, Ice, Diamond Quilted, Tongs, Green	30.00
Depression Glass, Butter, Adam, Pink	35.00 To 50.00
Depression Glass, Butter, Block Optic, Green, Oblong	12.00
Depression Glass, Butter, Cameo, Green	55.00
Depression Glass, Butter, Cherry Blossom, Green, Covered	55.00
Depression Glass, Butter, Colonial, Covered	25.00
Depression Glass, Butter, Doric, Pink	38.00
Depression Glass, Butter, Floral	35.00
Depression Glass, Butter, Florentine No.1, Yellow	22.00
Depression Glass, Butter, Florentine No.2, Yellow	80.00
Depression Glass, Butter, Georgian	45.00
Depression Glass, Butter, Georgian, Green	45.00
Depression Glass, Butter, Holiday, Pink	20.00
Depression Glass, Butter, Iris	20.00
Depression Glass, Butter, Iris, Iridescent	21.00
Depression Glass, Butter, Lace Edge, Pink	22.50 To 32.50
Depression Glass, Butter, Mayfair, Pink	45.00
Depression Glass, Butter, Patrician, Amber	47.50
Depression Glass, Butter, Patrician, Pink	150.00
Depression Glass, Butter, Royal Lace	15.00
Depression Glass, Butter, Royal Lace, Pink	45.00
Depression Glass, Butter, Sharon, Green	45.00
Depression Glass, Butter, Sharon, Pink	30.00 To 35.00
Depression Glass, Butter, Sierra, Pink	15.00 To 37.50
Depression Glass, Butter, Windsor	16.00
Depression Glass, Butter, Windsor, Pink	25.00
Depression Glass, Cake Stand, Mayfair, Pink, Open	12.00
Depression Glass, Candleholder, Iris, 2 Branch, Pair	10.00
Depression Glass, Candleholder, Windsor, Pink, 6 3/4 In., Pair	28.00
Depression Glass, Candlestick, Adam, Pink	15.00
Depression Glass, Candlestick, Cameo, Green, Pair	32.00
Depression Glass, Candlestick, Dolphin Feet, Pink, 4 In.	15.00
Depression Glass, Candlestick, Floragold, Pair	12.50
Depression Glass, Candlestick, Floral, Gold, Pair	14.00
Depression Glass, Candlestick, Holiday, Pink, Pair	22.50
Depression Glass, Candlestick, Indiana Sandwich, Pair	12.00
Depression Glass, Candlestick, Iris, Pair	10.00
Depression Glass, Candlestick, Madrid, Amber, Pair	9.00
Depression Glass, Candlestick, Swirl, Pair	17.50
Depression Glass, Candlestick, Swirl, Ultramarine, Pair	15.00
Depression Class, Candy Container, Block Optic, Green, Covered	13.50
Depression Glass, Candy Container, Cameo, Green, 6 1/2 In.	75.00
Depression Glass, Candy Container, Cube, Pink, Covered, 6 1/2 In.	13.50
Depression Glass, Candy Container, Doric, Green	20.00
Depression Glass, Candy Container, Doric, Pink, Covered	17.00 To 25.00
Depression Glass, Candy Container, Floral, Green, Covered	20.00
Depression Glass, Candy Container, Floral, Pink, Covered	18.00
Depression Glass, Candy Container, Fortune, Pink, Covered	6.00
Depression Glass, Candy Container, Iris	45.00
Depression Glass, Candy Container, Miss America, Cover	35.00
Depression Glass, Candy Container, Miss America, Pink, Covered, 11 1/2 In.	65.00
Depression Glass, Candy Container, Moonstone, Covered	10.00
Depression Glass, Candy Container, Princess, Green, Covered	12.50
Depression Glass, Candy Container, Princess, Pink, Covered	20.00
Depression Glass, Candy Container, Sharon, Pink, Covered	18.00
Depression Glass, Candy Container, Swirl, Pink	45.00
Depression Glass, Casserole, Bubble, Covered, 7 In.	3.50
Depression Glass, Ceiling Light, English Hobnail, 12 1/2 In.	55.00
Depression Glass, Celery, Miss America, Pink	7.50
Depression Glass, Celery, Miss America, 10 1/2 In.	4.50
Depression Glass, Centerpiece, Grape, Green, Oval	30.00
Depression Glass, Coaster, Cherry Blossom, Green	5.00
Depression Glass, Coaster, Cube, Pink	2.25
Depression Glass, Coaster, Diana, Pink	2.50
Depression Glass, Coaster, Florentine No.2, Green	6.00

Depression Glass, Coaster, Iris 22.50
Depression Glass, Cocktail Shaker, Cobalt, 6 Glasses & Sticks 45.00
Depression Glass, Cocktail Shaker, Moondrops, Red, Chrome Top 32.00
Depression Glass, Coffeepot, Cherry Blossom, Red 30.00
Depression Glass, Compote, Diamond Quilted, Blue, 7 In. 12.00
Depression Glass, Compote, English Hobnail, Ball Stem, Pink, 8 3/4 In. 85.00
Depression Glass, Console Set, Madrid, Amber 20.00
Depression Glass, Console Set, Mayfair, Pink 45.00
Depression Glass, Console, Madrid, Amber, 11 In. 7.50
Depression Glass, Cookie Jar, Cameo, Green 20.00
Depression Glass, Cookie Jar, Lace Edge, Covered 18.50
Depression Glass, Cookie Jar, Madrid, Amber, Covered 22.00
Depression Glass, Cookie Jar, Madrid, Pink, Covered 20.00
Depression Glass, Cookie Jar, Mayfair, Ice Blue 40.00
Depression Glass, Cookie Jar, Mayfair, Pink, Covered 18.00
Depression Glass, Cookie Jar, Princess, Green 17.00
Depression Glass, Cookie Jar, Princess, Pink, Covered 18.00
Depression Glass, Cookie Jar, Royal Lace, Blue 29.00
Depression Glass, Cookie Jar, Royal Lace, Green, Covered 25.00
Depression Glass, Cookie Jar, Royal Lace, Pink, Covered 18.00
Depression Glass, Cookie Jar, Sandwich, Amber 3.95
Depression Glass, Cookie Jar, Sandwich, Green 14.00
Depression Glass, Creamer, American Sweetheart, Monax 4.50
Depression Glass, Creamer, Beaded Block, Green, Footed 7.50
Depression Glass, Creamer, Block Optic, Green 3.00
Depression Glass, Creamer, Bubble, Green 8.00
Depression Glass, Creamer, Cherry Blossom, Child's, Pink 18.50
Depression Glass, Creamer, Cherry Blossom, Delphite 15.00
Depression Glass, Creamer, Criss Cross, Green 6.00
Depression Glass, Creamer, Dogwood, Pink 4.50
Depression Glass, Creamer, Doric, Pink 3.75
Depression Glass, Creamer, Holiday, Pink 2.00
Depression Glass, Creamer, Mayfair, Pink 8.00
Depression Glass, Creamer, Moondrops, Amber 3.50
Depression Glass, Creamer, Moonstone 4.00
Depression Glass, Creamer, Patrician, Green 5.00
Depression Glass, Creamer, Royal Ruby 2.75
Depression Glass, Creamer, Sharon, Pink .... 4.00 To 6.50
Depression Glass, Creamer, Starlight 2.50
Depression Glass, Creamer, Windsor 6.00
Depression Glass, Cup & Saucer, Adam, Pink .... 12.00 To 12.50
Depression Glass, Cup & Saucer, American Sweetheart, Monax ... 7.00 To 8.00
Depression Glass, Cup & Saucer, Block Optic, Green 4.00
Depression Glass, Cup & Saucer, Bubble, Blue .... 1.50 To 4.00
Depression Glass, Cup & Saucer, Cherry Blossom, Pink 10.50
Depression Glass, Cup & Saucer, Florentine No.1, Green .... 3.50 To 5.00
Depression Glass, Cup & Saucer, Florentine No.1, Pink 5.00
Depression Glass, Cup & Saucer, Holiday, Pink 4.00
Depression Glass, Cup & Saucer, Madrid, Blue 10.00
Depression Glass, Cup & Saucer, Mayfair, Blue 25.00
Depression Glass, Cup & Saucer, Moderntone, Amethyst 6.00
Depression Glass, Cup & Saucer, Moon Drops, Amethyst 6.00
Depression Glass, Cup & Saucer, Moonstone, Amethyst 6.00
Depression Glass, Cup & Saucer, Newport, Amethyst 5.25
Depression Glass, Cup & Saucer, Normandie, Amber 5.50
Depression Glass, Cup & Saucer, Patrician, Pink 7.00
Depression Glass, Cup & Saucer, Royal Lace 5.00
Depression Glass, Cup & Saucer, Shamrock, Pink 3.75
Depression Glass, Cup & Saucer, Sharon, Amber 4.00
Depression Glass, Cup & Saucer, Sharon, Pink 6.00
Depression Glass, Cup & Saucer, Sierra, Pink 6.00
Depression Glass, Cup & Saucer, Spiral, Green 2.00
Depression Glass, Cup & Saucer, Vernon, Green 14.00
Depression Glass, Cup, American Sweetheart, Monax 7.00
Depression Glass, Cup, Bowknot, Green 2.00
Depression Glass, Cup, Cameo, Green 6.00
Depression Glass, Cup, Cherry Blossom, Green 9.50

Depression Glass, Cup, Cloverleaf, Black	4.50
Depression Glass, Cup, Cloverleaf, Pink	2.50
Depression Glass, Cup, Madrid, Green	3.50
Depression Glass, Cup, Measuring, Bubble, Blue	2.50
Depression Glass, Cup, Normandie, Iridesdcent	2.00
Depression Glass, Cup, Normandie, Pink	2.50
Depression Glass, Cup, Princess, Pink	4.00
Depression Glass, Cup, Shamrock, Black	4.50
Depression Glass, Cup, Shamrock, Pink	2.50
Depression Glass, Cup, Sharon, Pink	3.00
Depression Glass, Custard, Block Optic, Yellow	24.50
Depression Glass, Decanter, Indiana Sandwich, Stopper	27.50
Depression Glass, Decanter, Mayfair, Pink, Stopper	57.50
Depression Glass, Decanter, Ring, Decorations, Stopper	12.50
Depression Glass, Demitasse Set, Diana, Gold Trim	30.00
Depression Glass, Dinner Set, Miss America, 56 Piece	295.00
Depression Glass, Dish, American Sweetheart, Monax, Oval, 11 In.	29.50
Depression Glass, Dish, Candy, Aunt Polly, 2 Handled, Blue	12.00
Depression Glass, Dish, Candy, Covered, Sharon, Pink	20.00
Depression Glass, Dish, Candy, Cube, Green, Covered	15.00
Depression Glass, Dish, Candy, Floragold, Iridescent, Covered	23.00
Depression Glass, Dish, Candy, Fortune, Covered	6.00
Depression Glass, Dish, Candy, Iris	45.00
Depression Glass, Dish, Candy, Mayfair, Blue, Covered	75.00
Depression Glass, Dish, Candy, Miss America, Covered	17.00
Depression Glass, Dish, Candy, Miss America, Pink, Covered	59.00
Depression Glass, Dish, Candy, Princess, Covered, Pedestal	20.00
Depression Glass, Dish, Candy, Sharon, Amber, Covered	18.00
Depression Glass, Dish, Candy, Sharon, Pink, Covered	20.00
Depression Glass, Dish, Cheese, Sandwich, Metal Cover	15.00
Depression Glass, Dish, Pickle, Beaded Block, Iridescent, 2 Handled	12.00
Depression Glass, Dish, Poinsettia, Green, Divided, Oval, 8 In.	8.00
Depression Glass, Dish, Relish, Adam, Pink	5.50
Depression Glass, Dish, Relish, Beaded Block, Pink, Oval, Handles, 6 1/2 In.	15.00
Depression Glass, Dish, Relish, Cameo, Green	4.00
Depression Glass, Dish, Relish, Hobnail, Opalescent	5.00
Depression Glass, Dish, Relish, Madrid, Amber, 10 1/4 In.	6.00
Depression Glass, Dish, Relish, Mayfair, Pink, 4-Part	6.00
Depression Glass, Dish, Relish, No.612, Green	7.00
Depression Glass, Dish, Relish, 3-Part, Adam, Pink	19.00
Depression Glass, Dish, Relish, 4-Part, Miss America, Pink	7.50
Depression Glass, Dish, Soup, Florentine No.2, Pink	4.00
Depression Glass, Dish, Soup, Madrid, Amber	6.00
Depression Glass, Dish, Sundae, American Sweetheart, Metal Holder	5.00
Depression Glass, Glass, Cherry Blossom, Set Of 5	20.00
Depression Glass, Goblet, Block Optic, Green, 6 In.	6.00
Depression Glass, Goblet, Cape Cod, Ruby, 9 Ounces	14.00
Depression Glass, Goblet, Colonial, Green	9.00
Depression Glass, Goblet, Dellia Robbia, 6 In.	5.00
Depression Glass, Goblet, English Hobnail, Yellow, 6 In.	10.00
Depression Glass, Goblet, Iris, 5 1/2 In.	12.00
Depression Glass, Goblet, Iris, 5 3/4 In.	6.00
Depression Glass, Goblet, Mayfair, Pink, Footed, 5 3/4 In.	22.00
Depression Glass, Goblet, Miss America, Pink	19.00
Depression Glass, Ice Bucket & Tongs, Royal Ruby	25.00
Depression Glass, Ice Bucket, Block Optic, Green, Bail	12.00
Depression Glass, Ice Bucket, Cameo, Frosted White, Gold Trim, 9 X 6 In.	450.00
Depression Glass, Ice Bucket, Sportsman's Series, Cobalt, Dancing Sailor	10.00
Depression Glass, Ice Tub, Cameo, Green	62.00
Depression Glass, Ice Tub, Swirl, Green	6.00
Depression Glass, Jar, Candy, Covered, Sharon, Pink	18.00
Depression Glass, Jar, Cookie, Cameo, Green, Covered	16.50
Depression Glass, Jar, Jam, Spiral, Green, Covered	8.00
Depression Glass, Jar, Mayonnaise, Cameo, Green	14.00
Depression Glass, Jar, Powder, Cube, Pink, 3-Legged, Covered	7.00
Depression Glass, Jello Mold, Madrid, Amber	4.25
Depression Glass, Jug, Iris, Iridescent, 60 Ounces	12.00

Depression Glass, Jug, Madrid, Amber, Square 35.00
Depression Glass, Jug, Mayfair, Pink, 60 Ounce 27.50
Depression Glass, Juice, Florentine No.2, Footed, Yellow, 5 Ounce 8.00
Depression Glass, Lamp, Floral, Green 80.00
Depression Glass, Lamp, Hobnail, Crystal & Green 20.00
Depression Glass, Lamp, Oil, English Hobnail, Pink 60.00
Depression Glass, Lazy Susan, Waterford 2.00
Depression Glass, Mold, Jello, Madrid, Amber 4.00
Depression Glass, Mug, Cherry Blossom, Child's, Green 88.00
Depression Glass, Nappy, Cameo, Green, 8 1/2 In. 13.00
Depression Glass, Nappy, Cherry Blossom, Pink, 8 1/2 In. 11.50
Depression Glass, Nappy, Diamond Quilted, Green, Handled, 5 1/2 In. 3.50
Depression Glass, Nappy, Georgian, Green, 4 1/2 In. 4.00
Depression Glass, Pitcher, Block Optic Green, 8 In. 20.00
Depression Glass, Pitcher, Cherry Blossom, Green, Footed, 8 In. 16.00
Depression Glass, Pitcher, Cherry Blossom, Pink, 6 3/4 In.Base 24.00
Depression Glass, Pitcher, Colonial, 68 Oz. 16.00
Depression Glass, Pitcher, Floral, Pink, 32 Ounces 12.00
Depression Glass, Pitcher, Holiday, Pink, 7 In. 18.00
Depression Glass, Pitcher, Juice, Cherry Blossom, Pink 8.00
Depression Glass, Pitcher, Juice, Mayfair, Pink .... 15.00 To 18.00
Depression Glass, Pitcher, Juice, Sandwich, Green, 6 In. 65.00
Depression Glass, Pitcher, Lemonade, Adam, Pink, Square Base 25.00
Depression Glass, Pitcher, Lemonade, Floral, Cone Shape, Pink, 48 Ounce 110.00
Depression Glass, Pitcher, Madrid, Green, 8 In. 125.00
Depression Glass, Pitcher, Manhattan, 42 Ounce 6.00
Depression Glass, Pitcher, Mayfair, Pink, 8 In. 14.00
Depression Glass, Pitcher, Mayfair, 8 1/2 In. 25.00
Depression Glass, Pitcher, New Century, Cobalt, Ice Lip, 80 Ounce 20.00
Depression Glass, Pitcher, Normandie, Amber, 8 In. 42.50
Depression Glass, Pitcher, Patrician, Pink, 8 In. 90.00
Depression Glass, Pitcher, Poinsettia, Pink, 8 In. 12.00
Depression Glass, Pitcher, Princess, Pink, 8 In. 20.00
Depression Glass, Pitcher, Princess, Yellow, 60 Ounces 70.00
Depression Glass, Pitcher, Royal Lace, Green, 8 1/2 In. 85.00
Depression Glass, Pitcher, Water, Cherry Blossom, Blue Delphite 50.00
Depression Glass, Pitcher, Water, Floragold, Iridescent 12.00
Depression Glass, Pitcher, Water, Floral, Green 15.00
Depression Glass, Pitcher, Water, Florentine No.2, Yellow, 7 1/4 In. 12.50
Depression Glass, Pitcher, Water, Fruits, Green 55.00
Depression Glass, Pitcher, Water, Madrid, Blue 110.00
Depression Glass, Pitcher, Water, New Century, Cobalt 25.00
Depression Glass, Pitcher, Windsor, Pink, 48 Ounce 15.00
Depression Glass, Pitcher, Windsor, 4 1/2 In. 6.00
Depression Glass, Pitcher, Windsor, 52 Ounce 10.00
Depression Glass, Plate, Adam,Green, 8 In. 6.00
Depression Glass, Plate, Adam, Green & Gold, 11 In. 8.00
Depression Glass, Plate, Adam, Pink, 6 In. 2.50
Depression Glass, Plate, Adam, Pink, 7 3/4 In. 6.00
Depression Glass, Plate, American Sweetheart, Monax 8.00
Depression Glass, Plate, American Sweetheart, Pink, 12 In. 6.00
Depression Glass, Plate, American Sweetheart, Pink, 8 In. 3.00
Depression Glass, Plate, Block Optic, Green, 6 In. 1.00
Depression Glass, Plate, Cake, Cameo, Green, 10 1/4 In. 6.00
Depression Glass, Plate, Cake, Cherry Blossom 12.00
Depression Glass, Plate, Cake, Cherry Blossom, Pink 5.00
Depression Glass, Plate, Cake, Dogwood, Green 30.00
Depression Glass, Plate, Cake, Dogwood, Pink, 13 In. 25.00
Depression Glass, Plate, Cake, Mayfair, Pink 11.00
Depression Glass, Plate, Cake, Miss America, Pink 17.50
Depression Glass, Plate, Cake, Sharon .... 5.00 To 8.00
Depression Glass, Plate, Cake, Sharon, Pink 12.00
Depression Glass, Plate, Cameo, Green, 8 In. 3.75
Depression Glass, Plate, Cherry Blossom, Pink, 9 In. ....Illus 7.00
Depression Glass, Plate, Chop, Windsor, Pink, 15 In. ....Illus 10.00
Depression Glass, Plate, Cube, Green, 6 In. ....Illus 1.00

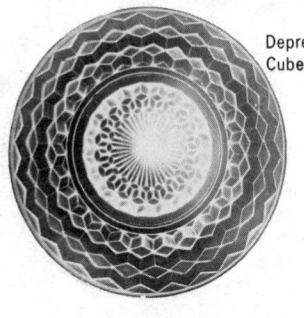

Depression Glass, Plate,
Cube, Green, 6 In.

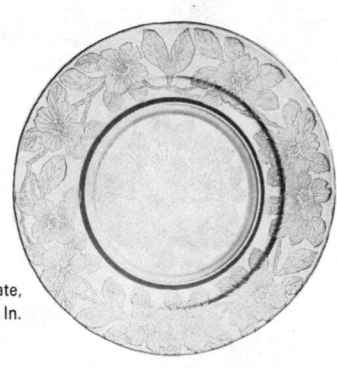

Depression Glass, Plate,
Dogwood, 6 In.
(See Page 143)

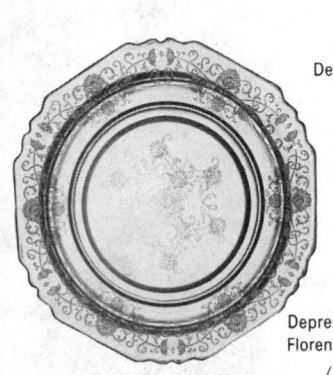

Depression Glass, Plate,
Dinner, Floral, Pink
(See Page 143)

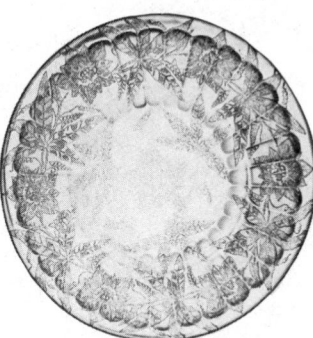

Depression Glass, Plate,
Florentine No.I, Green, 8 1/2 In.
(See Page 143)

Depression Glass, Plate,
Florentine No.2, Yellow, 8 1/2 In.
(See Page 143)

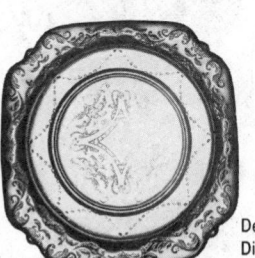

Depression Glass, Plate,
Dinner, Madrid, Amber
(See Page 143)

Depression Glass, Plate,
Dinner, Mayfair, Pink
(See Page 143)

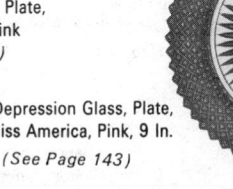

Depression Glass, Plate,
Miss America, Pink, 9 In.
(See Page 143)

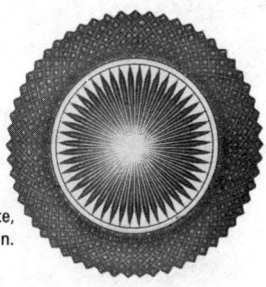

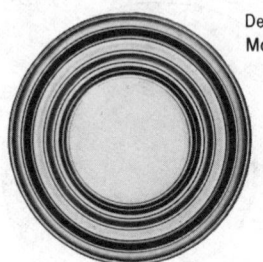

Depression Glass, Plate,
Moderntone, Cobalt, 9 In.

Depression Glass, Plate,
No.612, Yellow, 11 1/4 In.

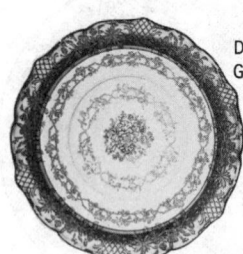

Depression Glass, Plate,
Grill, Normandie, 11 In.

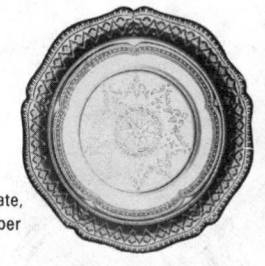

Depression Glass, Plate,
Salad, Patrician, Amber

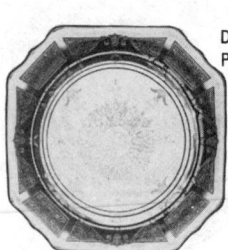

Depression Glass, Plate,
Princess, Yellow, 6 In.

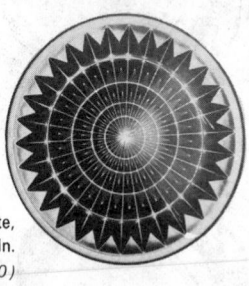

Depression Glass, Plate,
Chop, Windsor, Pink, 15 In.
(See Page 140)

Depression Glass, Plate,
Cherry Blossom, Pink, 9 In.
(See Page 140)

Depression Glass, Plate,
Dinner, Sharon, Amber, 7 1/2 In.

Depression Glass, Plate, Dessert, Adam, Green 4.50
Depression Glass, Plate, Diamond Quilted, Blue, 8 In. 4.50
Depression Glass, Plate, Diamond Quilted, Pink, 8 In., Set Of 9 .... 16.00
Depression Glass, Plate, Diana, Amber, 9 1/2 In. 2.50
Depression Glass, Plate, Diana, 9 In. 1.75
Depression Glass, Plate, Dinner, Adam, Pink 6.00
Depression Glass, Plate, Dinner, Block Optic, Green .... 3.00 To 5.00
Depression Glass, Plate, Dinner, Cameo, Green 5.75
Depression Glass, Plate, Dinner, Cameo, Yellow, Pair 12.00
Depression Glass, Plate, Dinner, Cherry Blossom, Green .... 8.50 To 10.00
Depression Glass, Plate, Dinner, Cherry Blossom, Pink 7.50
Depression Glass, Plate, Dinner, Dogwood, Pink, 9 1/4 In. 7.50
Depression Glass, Plate, Dinner, Floral, Pink .... *Illus* 6.75
Depression Glass, Plate, Dinner, Indiana Sandwich, 10 1/2 In. 6.00
Depression Glass, Plate, Dinner, Madrid, Amber .... *Illus* 15.00
Depression Glass, Plate, Dinner, Madrid, Green 8.00
Depression Glass, Plate, Dinner, Mayfair, Pink .... *Illus* 15.00
Depression Glass, Plate, Dinner, Miss America, Pink, Set Of 3 .... 28.00
Depression Glass, Plate, Dinner, Moderntone, Cobalt 3.00
Depression Glass, Plate, Dinner, Queen Mary, Pink 7.50
Depression Glass, Plate, Dinner, Sharon, Amber 4.50
Depression Glass, Plate, Dinner, Sharon, Amber, 7 1/2 In. .... *Illus* 4.00
Depression Glass, Plate, Dinner, Sierra, Green 3.50
Depression Glass, Plate, Dogwood, 6 In. .... *Illus* 2.00
Depression Glass, Plate, Doric & Pansy, 6 In. 5.00
Depression Glass, Plate, Doric, Pink, 9 In. 3.25
Depression Glass, Plate, Florentine No.1, Green, 8 1/2 In. .... *Illus* 4.00
Depression Glass, Plate, Florentine No.2, Yellow, 8 1/2 In. .... *Illus* 3.50
Depression Glass, Plate, Fruits, Green, 8 In. 3.00
Depression Glass, Plate, Grill, Bubble, Blue 5.00
Depression Glass, Plate, Grill, Cameo, Yellow 3.75
Depression Glass, Plate, Grill, Cherry Blossom, Pink 8.00
Depression Glass, Plate, Grill, Madrid 2.50
Depression Glass, Plate, Grill, Mayfair, Blue 15.00
Depression Glass, Plate, Grill, Mayfair, Pink 10.00
Depression Glass, Plate, Grill, Normandie, 11 In. .... *Illus* 2.00
Depression Glass, Plate, Grill, Princess, Pink 5.00
Depression Glass, Plate, Grill, Royal Lace, Blue 12.00
Depression Glass, Plate, Holiday, Pink, 8 1/2 In. 3.00
Depression Glass, Plate, Homespun, Pink, 6 In. 1.00
Depression Glass, Plate, Lace Edge, Pink, 8 In. 4.00
Depression Glass, Plate, Lace Edge, Pink, 10 In. 4.00
Depression Glass, Plate, Luncheon, Block Optic, Green, 8 In. 1.75
Depression Glass, Plate, Luncheon, Dogwood, Pink, Set Of 3 .... 6.00
Depression Glass, Plate, Luncheon, Madrid, Amber, 9 In. 3.00
Depression Glass, Plate, Luncheon, No.612, Green 3.00
Depression Glass, Plate, Luncheon, Royal Lace, Blue, 8 1/2 In. 6.00
Depression Glass, Plate, Mayfair, Pink, 8 In. 6.00
Depression Glass, Plate, Miss America, Pink, 9 In. .... *Illus* 4.00
Depression Glass, Plate, Miss America, 6 In. 2.25
Depression Glass, Plate, Moderntone, Cobalt, 9 In. .... *Illus* 3.25
Depression Glass, Plate, Mt.Pleasant, Cobalt, Scalloped, 8 In. 8.00
Depression Glass, Plate, No.612, Yellow, 11 1/4 In. .... *Illus* 7.00
Depression Glass, Plate, Pie, Bubble, Blue, 8 1/2 In. 8.50
Depression Glass, Plate, Princess, Yellow, 6 In. .... *Illus* 1.50
Depression Glass, Plate, Rosemary, Amber, 9 1/2 In. 3.00
Depression Glass, Plate, Salad, American Sweetheart, Red 90.00
Depression Glass, Plate, Salad, Iris 22.50
Depression Glass, Plate, Salad, Madrid 3.75
Depression Glass, Plate, Salad, Miss America, Pink, 8 1/2 In. 5.00
Depression Glass, Plate, Salad, Patrician, Amber .... *Illus* 3.50
Depression Glass, Plate, Sandwich, Queen Mary, Pink, 12 In. 5.00
Depression Glass, Plate, Shamrock, Pink, 8 In. 2.50
Depression Glass, Plate, Shamrock, 8 In. 5.00
Depression Glass, Plate, Torte, Adam, Pink, 12 In. 33.50
Depression Glass, Platter, Adam, Pink, 10 In. 4.50

Depression Glass, Platter, Cherry Blossom, Divided, Green, 13 In.	20.00
Depression Glass, Platter, Cherry Blossom, Divided, Green, 16 In.	20.00
Depression Glass, Platter, Cherry Blossom, Divided, Pink, 13 In.	18.00
Depression Glass, Platter, Laurel, Jade Green, 11 1/2 In.	12.50
Depression Glass, Platter, Miss America, Pink, 12 In.	10.00
Depression Glass, Platter, Sharon, Oval, Green, 12 1/2 In.	10.00
Depression Glass, Salt & Pepper, Adam, Pink	24.00
Depression Glass, Salt & Pepper, American Sweetheart, Monax	225.00
Depression Glass, Salt & Pepper, Block Optic, Green	12.00
Depression Glass, Salt & Pepper, Cameo, Green	30.00
Depression Glass, Salt & Pepper, Cube, Green	13.00
Depression Glass, Salt & Pepper, Cube, Pink	14.00
Depression Glass, Salt & Pepper, Della Robbia	20.00
Depression Glass, Salt & Pepper, Floragold, Iridescent, Plastic Tops	25.00
Depression Glass, Salt & Pepper, Floral, Green, Footed, Pair	22.50
Depression Glass, Salt & Pepper, Floral, Pink, Footed, 4 In.	20.00
Depression Glass, Salt & Pepper, Florentine No.2, Yellow	25.00
Depression Glass, Salt & Pepper, Hex Optic, Green	10.00
Depression Glass, Salt & Pepper, Jadite	10.00
Depression Glass, Salt & Pepper, Madrid, Amber, Footed	40.00
Depression Glass, Salt & Pepper, Manhattan	10.00
Depression Glass, Salt & Pepper, Manhattan, Pink	14.00 To 20.00
Depression Glass, Salt & Pepper, Mayfair, Pink	25.00
Depression Glass, Salt & Pepper, Miss America	18.00
Depression Glass, Salt & Pepper, Miss America, Pink	35.00
Depression Glass, Salt & Pepper, Moderntone, Blue	13.50
Depression Glass, Salt & Pepper, Normandie, Amber	25.00
Depression Glass, Salt & Pepper, Patrician, Amber	22.00
Depression Glass, Salt & Pepper, Princess, Pink, 4 1/2 In.	25.00
Depression Glass, Salt & Pepper, Queen Mary	10.00
Depression Glass, Salt & Pepper, Shamrock, Green	15.00 To 18.00
Depression Glass, Salt & Pepper, Sharon, Amber	30.00
Depression Glass, Salt & Pepper, Sharon, Green	45.00
Depression Glass, Salt & Pepper, Sharon, Pink	15.00 To 25.00
Depression Glass, Saltshaker, Adam, Pink	12.50
Depression Glass, Saltshaker, American Sweetheart, Monax	55.00 To 75.00
Depression Glass, Saltshaker, American Sweetheart, Pink	75.00
Depression Glass, Saltshaker, Cameo, Green	15.00
Depression Glass, Saltshaker, Floral, Green, Footed, 4 In.	22.00
Depression Glass, Saltshaker, Miss America	17.50
Depression Glass, Saltshaker, Parrot, Green	45.00
Depression Glass, Saltshaker, Royal Lace, Blue	150.00
Depression Glass, Saltshaker, Sierra, Pink	12.00
Depression Glass, Salver, American Sweetheart, Blue, 12 In.	145.00
Depression Glass, Salver, American Sweetheart, Monax, 12 In.	9.00 To 12.00
Depression Glass, Salver, American Sweetheart, Pink, 12 In.	7.00
Depression Glass, Salver, American Sweetheart, 12 In.	12.00
Depression Glass, Salver, Dogwood, Pink, 12 In.	10.50
Depression Glass, Salver, Petalware, Pink, 11 In.	3.50
Depression Glass, Salver, Vernon, 12 In.	15.00
Depression Glass, Sauce, American Sweetheart, Monax	1.25 To 4.00
Depression Glass, Sauce, Madrid, Amber	1.25
Depression Glass, Sauce, Normandie	1.25
Depression Glass, Saucer, Block Optic, Green	1.00
Depression Glass, Saucer, Diana, Amber	2.00
Depression Glass, Saucer, Dogwood, Pink, Set Of 5	10.00
Depression Glass, Saucer, Madrid, Green	2.50
Depression Glass, Saucer, Mayfair, Blue	7.00
Depression Glass, Saucer, Swirl, Green, 2 3/4 In.	10.00
Depression Glass, Server, Sandwich, Mayfair, Blue	30.00
Depression Glass, Server, Sandwich, 3-Tiered	12.50
Depression Glass, Sherbet, Adam, Pink	8.00
Depression Glass, Sherbet, American Sweetheart, Pink, 4 In.	6.00
Depression Glass, Sherbet, Anniversary, Pink	3.00
Depression Glass, Sherbet, Aunt Polly, Blue, Set Of 4	5.50
Depression Glass, Sherbet, Block Optic, Green, Footed	3.00

Depression Glass, Sherbet, Block Optic, Green, Stemmed	5.00
Depression Glass, Sherbet, Cameo, Green, 4 7/8 In.	22.50
Depression Glass, Sherbet, Cherry Blossom, Pink	6.75
Depression Glass, Sherbet, Colonial, Pink	2.75
Depression Glass, Sherbet, Doric, Blue, Set Of 3	12.00
Depression Glass, Sherbet, Floral & Diamond Band, Green	2.75
Depression Glass, Sherbet, Floral, Pink	3.50
Depression Glass, Sherbet, Georgian, Green	5.00
Depression Glass, Sherbet, Hobnail, Set Of 6	11.00
Depression Glass, Sherbet, Holiday, Pink	1.75
Depression Glass, Sherbet, Holiday, Pink, Footed, Set Of 8	16.00
Depression Glass, Sherbet, Iris, 4 In.	4.50
Depression Glass, Sherbet, Lace Edge, Pink	32.00
Depression Glass, Sherbet, Madrid	1.75
Depression Glass, Sherbet, Madrid, Green	4.50
Depression Glass, Sherbet, Mayfair, Pink, 3 1/4 In., Set Of 9	6.00
Depression Glass, Sherbet, Moderntone, Amethyst	4.25
Depression Glass, Sherbet, Moonstone, Opalescent, Hobnails	3.00
Depression Glass, Sherbet, Mt.Pleasant, Cobalt	9.00
Depression Glass, Sherbet, Newport, Amethyst	3.50 To 4.00
Depression Glass, Sherbet, Normandie	2.00
Depression Glass, Sherbet, Normandie, Pink	5.00
Depression Glass, Sherbet, Patrician, Amber	13.50
Depression Glass, Sherbet, Patrician, Green	6.00
Depression Glass, Sherbet, Pineapple & Floral	6.00
Depression Glass, Sherbet, Pink Holiday, Footed, Set Of 8	16.00
Depression Glass, Sherbet, Princess, Green	6.00
Depression Glass, Sherbet, Ring, Green	2.00
Depression Glass, Sherbet, Shamrock	4.00
Depression Glass, Sherbet, Sharon, Amber	4.00
Depression Glass, Sherbet, Sharon, Pink	5.00
Depression Glass, Sherbet, Tea Room, Pink	9.00
Depression Glass, Shot Glass, Hobnail, Set Of 6	15.00
Depression Glass, Soup Dish, Cherry Blossom, Green, Flat	20.00
Depression Glass, Soup Dish, Cherry Blosssom, Green	18.00
Depression Glass, Soup Dish, Chinex, Ivory	5.00
Depression Glass, Soup Dish, Cream, Daisy	2.00
Depression Glass, Soup Dish, Cream, Diana, Pink	6.00
Depression Glass, Soup Dish, Cream, Petalware, Monax	4.00
Depression Glass, Soup Dish, Florentine No.2, Pink	4.00
Depression Glass, Soup Dish, Iris, Iridescent, Flat	14.50
Depression Glass, Soup Dish, Madrid, Amber	6.00
Depression Glass, Soup, Cream, American Sweetheart, Pink	8.00 To 9.50
Depression Glass, Soup, Cream, Florentine No.2, Green	4.50
Depression Glass, Soup, Cream, Newport, Handled, Cobalt	7.00
Depression Glass, Soup, Cream, Pineapple & Floral, Amber	12.00
Depression Glass, Soup, Cream, Rosemary, Amber	4.50
Depression Glass, Soup, Cream, Royal Lace, Blue	7.75
Depression Glass, Soup, Cream, Royal Lace, Pink	5.00
Depression Glass, Soup, Cream, Sharon, Pink	9.00
Depression Glass, Sugar & Creamer, Beaded Block, Opalescent Green	35.00
Depression Glass, Sugar & Creamer, Block Optic, Green	5.00
Depression Glass, Sugar & Creamer, Block Optic, Pink	5.50
Depression Glass, Sugar & Creamer, Bubble, Blue	2.50
Depression Glass, Sugar & Creamer, Cameo, Green, 3 In.	8.00
Depression Glass, Sugar & Creamer, Cape Cod, Footed	6.00
Depression Glass, Sugar & Creamer, Cherry Blossom, Covered, Pink	14.00

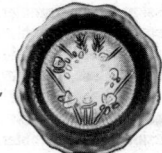

Depression Glass, Sherbet,
Iris, Iridescent

Depression Glass, Sugar & Creamer, Cherry Blossom, Delphite	32.50
Depression Glass, Sugar & Creamer, Cherry Blossom, Green	20.00
Depression Glass, Sugar & Creamer, Colonial, Green	15.00
Depression Glass, Sugar & Creamer, Dogwood, Pink	4.75
Depression Glass, Sugar & Creamer, Doric, Pink	14.00
Depression Glass, Sugar & Creamer, Florentine No.2, Yellow	16.00
Depression Glass, Sugar & Creamer, Holiday, Pink	15.00
Depression Glass, Sugar & Creamer, Iris, Covered	12.00
Depression Glass, Sugar & Creamer, Lace Edge	15.00
Depression Glass, Sugar & Creamer, Lotus, Gold Overlay	25.00
Depression Glass, Sugar & Creamer, Miss America	12.50
Depression Glass, Sugar & Creamer, Moderntone, Amethyst	3.50
Depression Glass, Sugar & Creamer, Moderntone, Blue	8.00
Depression Glass, Sugar & Creamer, Moondrops, Amber, 3 1/4 In.	12.00
Depression Glass, Sugar & Creamer, Normandie, Amber	10.00
Depression Glass, Sugar & Creamer, Parrot, Green, Covered	30.00
Depression Glass, Sugar & Creamer, Princess, Yellow	12.00
Depression Glass, Sugar & Creamer, Round Robin	3.25
Depression Glass, Sugar & Creamer, Royal Lace, Blue	30.00
Depression Glass, Sugar & Creamer, Royal Ruby, Footed, Covered	11.00
Depression Glass, Sugar & Creamer, Shamrock, Black	7.00
Depression Glass, Sugar & Creamer, Sharon, Pink	10.00 To 14.00
Depression Glass, Sugar & Creamer, Tea Room, Green, 4 In.	15.00
Depression Glass, Sugar & Creamer, Windsor Diamond, Pink	4.50
Depression Glass, Sugar & Creamer, Windsor, Pink, Covered	12.50
Depression Glass, Sugar, American Sweetheart, Covered, Green	150.00
Depression Glass, Sugar, American Sweetheart, Monax	4.00
Depression Glass, Sugar, Avocado, Green	10.00
Depression Glass, Sugar, Block Optic, Green	3.00
Depression Glass, Sugar, Cameo, Green	3.50
Depression Glass, Sugar, Cameo, Yellow	6.50
Depression Glass, Sugar, Cherry Blossom, Delphite	12.00 To 12.50
Depression Glass, Sugar, Cherry Blossom, Pink	6.00
Depression Glass, Sugar, Cherry Blossom, Pink, Open	5.00
Depression Glass, Sugar, Cloverleaf, Yellow	4.00
Depression Glass, Sugar, Colonial, Green	4.00
Depression Glass, Sugar, Cube, Green, Covered	4.50
Depression Glass, Sugar, Floragold, Iridescent, Covered	5.00
Depression Glass, Sugar, Mayfair, Blue, Open	24.00
Depression Glass, Sugar, Mayfair, Pink	12.00
Depression Glass, Sugar, Moondrops, Red, Open, 4 In.	8.00
Depression Glass, Sugar, Shamrock, Yellow	4.00
Depression Glass, Sugar, Sharon, Amber, Open	5.00
Depression Glass, Sugar, Sharon, Green, Open	6.00
Depression Glass, Sugar, Waterford, Pink, Open	2.25
Depression Glass, Sugar, Windsor Diamond, Pink, Covered	4.50
Depression Glass, Syrup, Cameo, Rope Top, Green, 5 3/4 In.	105.00
Depression Glass, Teapot, Swirl, Green, Lid, 2 In.	17.50
Depression Glass, Tray, Bread, Bubble, Blue, 2 Loaf	3.50
Depression Glass, Tray, Cake, Dogwood, Pink	75.00
Depression Glass, Tray, Cherry Blossom, Pink, Handled, 10 1/2 In.	7.00
Depression Glass, Tray, Doric, Green, Handles	6.50
Depression Glass, Tray, Torte, Floragold, Iridescent, 13 In.	7.75
Depression Glass, Tumbler, Adam, Green, Footed, 5 1/2 In.	17.00
Depression Glass, Tumbler, Adam, Green, 4 1/2 In.	9.50
Depression Glass, Tumbler, Adam, Pink, 4 1/2 In.	9.50
Depression Glass, Tumbler, American Sweetheart, Pink, 9 Oz., Set Of 7	18.50
Depression Glass, Tumbler, Block Optic, Green, 3 In.	4.00
Depression Glass, Tumbler, Block Optic, Pink	3.75
Depression Glass, Tumbler, Block Optic, Yellow, Footed, 9 Ounces	8.00
Depression Glass, Tumbler, Bottoms Up, Jadite	24.00
Depression Glass, Tumbler, Bubble, 7 In.	5.50
Depression Glass, Tumbler, Cameo, Footed, 3 Ounce	23.00
Depression Glass, Tumbler, Cameo, Green, Footed, 3 Ounces	32.50
Depression Glass, Tumbler, Cameo, Yellow, Footed, 5 In.	7.00
Depression Glass, Tumbler, Cherry Blossom, Delphite, Pedestal	15.00
Depression Glass, Tumbler, Cherry Blossom, Pink, Footed	11.00

Depression Glass, Tumbler, Cherry Blossom, Pink, 9 Ounce	9.00
Depression Glass, Tumbler, Colonial, Green, Footed, 3 Ounce	15.00
Depression Glass, Tumbler, Colonial, Pink	5.00
Depression Glass, Tumbler, Doric	15.00
Depression Glass, Tumbler, Doric & Pansy, Ultramarine	20.00
Depression Glass, Tumbler, Doric, Pink, 4 In.	15.00
Depression Glass, Tumbler, Fire King, 7 In.	5.50
Depression Glass, Tumbler, Florentine No.1	18.00
Depression Glass, Tumbler, Florentine No.1, Green, Footed, 4 3/4 In.	9.00
Depression Glass, Tumbler, Florentine No.2	15.00
Depression Glass, Tumbler, Hobnail, Red Trim, 12 Ounces	4.00
Depression Glass, Tumbler, Holiday, Iridescent, Footed, 4 In.	2.00
Depression Glass, Tumbler, Homespun, Pink, Footed, 4 In.	4.00
Depression Glass, Tumbler, Iris, Footed, 7 In.	8.50
Depression Glass, Tumbler, Lace Edge, Footed, Pair	16.50
Depression Glass, Tumbler, Lace Edge, Pink	6.00
Depression Glass, Tumbler, Lace Edge, Pink, Footed	16.00
Depression Glass, Tumbler, Mayfair, Blue, Footed	15.00
Depression Glass, Tumbler, Mayfair, Pink, Footed	18.00
Depression Glass, Tumbler, Mayfair, Pink, 5 1/2 In., Set Of 4	12.00
Depression Glass, Tumbler, Moderntone, Blue	6.00
Depression Glass, Tumbler, New Century, Pink, 4 In.	4.50
Depression Glass, Tumbler, Patrician, Amber, Footed, 8 Ounces	22.00
Depression Glass, Tumbler, Princess, Yellow, Footed, 5 1/2 In.	12.00
Depression Glass, Tumbler, Royal Lace	54.00
Depression Glass, Tumbler, Royal Lace, Blue	125.00
Depression Glass, Tumbler, Royal Lace, Green, 4 In.	12.00
Depression Glass, Tumbler, Royal Lace, Pink, 4 1/8 In.	8.00
Depression Glass, Tumbler, Royal Ruby, 10 Oz., Set Of 6	24.00
Depression Glass, Tumbler, Royal Ruby, 13 Oz., Set Of 6	36.00
Depression Glass, Tumbler, Shamrock	80.00
Depression Glass, Tumbler, Shamrock, Black	34.00
Depression Glass, Tumbler, Shamrock, Green, Footed, 5 3/4 In.	14.00
Depression Glass, Tumbler, Sharon	44.00
Depression Glass, Tumbler, Sharon, Amber, 9 Oz.	10.00
Depression Glass, Tumbler, Sharon, Pink, Footed, 6 1/2 In.	17.00
Depression Glass, Tumbler, Sharon, Pink, 4 In.	15.50
Depression Glass, Tumbler, Sunflower, Green, Footed, 4 3/4 In.	10.00
Depression Glass, Tumbler, Swirl, Pink, Footed, 9 Ounce	7.00
Depression Glass, Tumbler, Swirl, Ultramarine, Footed, 9 Ounce	10.00
Depression Glass, Tumbler, Windsor, Pink, 5 In.	6.00
Depression Glass, Vase, Anniversary, 6 1/2 In.	3.00
Depression Glass, Vase, Cameo, Green, 5 3/4 In.	75.00
Depression Glass, Vase, Hobnail, Pink, Flared, 7 In.	45.00
Depression Glass, Vase, Iris, 9 In.	8.00
Depression Glass, Vase, Lace Edge, Frog, Ribbed, Pink, 4 In.	8.00
Depression Glass, Vase, Swirl, Green, 8 X 6 In.	15.00
Depression Glass, Vase, Swirl, Ultramarine, 8 1/2 In.	12.00
Depression Glass, Vegetable, Adam, Pink, Covered	16.00 To 20.00
Depression Glass, Vegetable, American Sweetheart, Pink, Oval	10.00
Depression Glass, Vegetable, Floral, Green, Oval	7.00
Depression Glass, Vegetable, Madrid, Amber, Oval	5.50 To 6.00
Depression Glass, Vegetable, Normandie, Iridescent, Oval	6.00
Depression Glass, Vegetable, Parrot, Green, Oval	12.50
Depression Glass, Water Set, Madrid, Amber	50.00
Depression Glass, Water Set, Mayfair, Pink	135.00
Depression Glass, Water Set, New Century, Amethyst, Ice Lip, 7 Piece	75.00
Depression Glass, Water Set, Optic Diamond, Green	32.00
Depression Glass, Water Set, Sharon, Pink	88.00
Depression Glass, Whiskey, Hobnail, 1 1/2 Ounces	2.00
Depression Glass, Wine, Cameo, Green	29.50
Depression Glass, Wine, Hobnail, Footed	3.50
Depression Glass, Wine, Iris, Iridescent	12.50
Depression Glass, Wine, Iris, 4 1/2 In.	7.00
Depression Glass, Wine, Iris, 5 3/4 In.	8.00
Depression Glass, Wine, Miss America, Pink	20.00
Depression Glass, Wine, Royal Ruby, Footed	7.50

Derby porcelain was made in Derby, England, from 1756 to the present. The factory changed names and marks several times. Chelsea Derby (1770-1784), Crown Derby (1784-1811), and the modern Royal Crown Derby are some of the most famous periods of the factory.

Derby, see also Chelsea, Crown Derby, Royal Crown Derby

Derby, Bowl, Pedestal, Cherubs, Flowers, Silver Plate	45.00
Derby, Bowl, Vegetable, Oval, C.1780	125.00
Derby, Figurine, Dr.Syntax Landing At Calais, Numbered, 1800s, 4 3/4 In.	250.00
Derby, Figurine, Dr.Syntax, Standing In Tree, Cow, 1800s, 6 In.	275.00
Derbyshire, Urn, Spar, Ormolu Mounted, Napoleon III, 1850s, 16 In., Pair	2000.00
DeVilbiss, Atomizer, Black, Signed, 4 In.	50.00
DeVilbiss, Atomizer, Blue Opalescent, 6 In.	23.00
DeVilbiss, Atomizer, Gold & Amber, 4 In.	25.00
DeVilbiss, Atomizer, Gold Crackle	20.00
DeVilbiss, Atomizer, Opaque Orchid, Paper Label, 4 1/4 In.	19.00
DeVilbiss, Atomizer, Perfume, Black Amethyst, Gold Band, Pair	85.00
DeVilbiss, Atomizer, Silver & Gold Craquelle, Paper Label	30.00
DeVilbiss, Atomizer, White Opalescent	20.00
DeVilbiss, Atomizer, White Opalescent Swirl	15.00
DeVilbiss, Bottle, Perfume, Paper Label, Gold Crackle	14.00
Dick Tracy, Badge, Pictured, 1 1/2 In.	12.00
Dick Tracy, Badge, Republic Serial	22.50
Dick Tracy, Badge, Secret Patrol, 2nd Year	15.00 To 20.00
Dick Tracy, Book, Big Little Book, Dick Tracy On The High Seas	12.00
Dick Tracy, Book, Coloring, 1946	15.00
Dick Tracy, Button, Detective, Red, White & Blue, 1 1/2 In.	2.00
Dick Tracy, Button, Picture, Red, White & Blue	2.50
Dick Tracy, Camera	13.50 To 15.00
Dick Tracy, Flashing Light & Siren Car	35.00
Dick Tracy, Game, Cardboard Figures, Boxed, 1962	11.00
Dick Tracy, Gun, Cap, Cast Iron	8.00
Dick Tracy, Police Station	125.00
Dick Tracy, Puzzle, Comic Strip, 1943, Jaymar	15.00
Dick Tracy, Radio, Wrist, Star Wars	8.75
Dick Tracy, Secret Code Maker	7.50
Dick Tracy, Wristwatch, Boxed	125.00
Dick Tracy, Wristwatch, Round	85.00
Dickens Ware, see Weller, Royal Doulton	
Dionne Quintuplets, Bowl, Figural, Signed	12.50
Dionne Quintuplets, Calendar, 1935	9.00
Dionne Quintuplets, Calendar, 1940	19.00
Dionne Quintuplets, Dish, Feeding, Signed	11.50
Dionne Quintuplets, Doll, Human Hair, Old Blue Pajamas, 14 In.	145.00
Dionne Quintuplets, Doll, Toddlers, Sleep Eyes, Name Pins, 11 1/2 In., Set	750.00
Dionne Quintuplets, Fan, Hand, Cardboard	7.50
Dionne Quintuplets, Picture, Framed, 1935, 9 X 15 In.	12.50
Dionne Quintuplets, Postcard, 1930	8.50
Dionne Quintuplets, Spoon, Annette	15.00
Dionne Quintuplets, Spoon, Emilie	15.00
Disneyana, Album, Record, Three Little Pigs, 1949	12.50
Disneyana, Bag, Marble, Mickey Mouse	12.00
Disneyana, Blocks, Mickey Mouse, Original Box	50.00
Disneyana, Book, Coloring, Mickey Mouse, Crayons, Original Box	17.50
Disneyana, Book, Coloring, Snow White & The Seven Dwarfs, 1938	25.00
Disneyana, Book, Donald Duck, Big Little Book	4.00
Disneyana, Book, Donald Duck, Linen, 1935	85.00
Disneyana, Book, Hard Cover, Mickey Mouse, Mickey Sees U.S.A., 1944	15.00
Disneyana, Book, School Days In Disneyville, C.D.Emerson, 1939	12.00
Disneyana, Book, Song, 24 Pages, 1938	16.00
Disneyana, Bottle, Hot Water, Donald Duck	7.00
Disneyana, Bottle, Mickey Mouse, Stopper	12.50
Disneyana, Bottle, Stopper, Pluto	12.50
Disneyana, Bowl, Donald Duck, Magic Eyes, Plastic	2.50
Disneyana, Bubble Blower, Donald Duck, Plastic	12.00
Disneyana, Button, Mickey Mouse Globetrotter Member	2.75
Disneyana, Cards, Playing, Dopey	30.00
Disneyana, Cards, Playing, Miniature, Snow White	25.00

Disneyana, **Clock,** Alarm, Mickey Mouse, 1946, Decorated Box 300.00
Disneyana, **Clock,** Alarm, Wind-Up, Animated, Big Bad Wolf, C.1934, Ingersoll 400.00
Disneyana, **Clock,** Big Bad Wolf & 3 Little Pigs, Wolf's Head Bobs 160.00
Disneyana, **Clock,** Big Bad Wolf, Animated, Ingersoll 350.00
Disneyana, **Cookie Jar,** Donald Duck 18.00
Disneyana, **Cookie Jar,** Dumbo, Walt Disney 22.00
Disneyana, **Cookie Jar,** Snow White & 7 Dwarfs 20.00
Disneyana, **Creamer,** Dumbo 13.00
Disneyana, **Dipsy Car,** Mickey Mouse, Marx 125.00
Disneyana, **Doc,** 3 In. 12.00
Disneyana, **Doll,** Mickey Mouse, Rubber, 1946 .... 7.50
Disneyana, **Doll,** Minnie Mouse, 1940s, 13 In. 65.00
Disneyana, **Doll,** Mouseketeer, Rubber, Jointed, 12 In. 15.00
Disneyana, **Doll,** Snow White, Composition, 19 In. 55.00
Disneyana, **Dominoes,** Mickey Mouse, Original Box 45.00
Disneyana, **Drum,** Mickey Mouse, Early Forties 65.00
Disneyana, **Figurine,** Doc, Bisque, 2 1/2 In. 14.00
Disneyana, **Figurine,** Donald Duck, Chalkware, 13 In. 19.50
Disneyana, **Figurine,** Donald Duck, Riding Scooter, Bisque, 6 1/2 In. 30.00
Disneyana, **Figurine,** Donald With Arm Around Mickey, Minnie, Bisque 95.00
Disneyana, **Figurine,** Dopey, Bisque, 4 In. 16.00
Disneyana, **Figurine,** Felix The Cat, Cast Iron, 2 1/2 In. 42.00
Disneyana, **Figurine,** Grumpy, Bisque, 4 In. 16.00
Disneyana, **Figurine,** Mickey Mouse, Green Pants, Long Nose, Bisque, 2 3/4 In. 23.00
Disneyana, **Figurine,** Mickey Mouse, Moveable Arms, Bisque, 6 In. 55.00
Disneyana, **Figurine,** Mickey Mouse, Moveable Tail, Straw Filled, 9 1/2 In. 55.00
Disneyana, **Figurine,** Mickey Wiping Pluto's Nose, Bisque 95.00
Disneyana, **Figurine,** Minnie Mouse, Bisque 25.00
Disneyana, **Figurine,** Snow White, Bisque, 4 In. 12.00
Disneyana, **Fishing Pole,** Mickey Mouse, On Original Card, 1950s 7.00
Disneyana, **Flashlight,** Mickey, Minnie & Pluto Lithograph On Casing, 1935 .... 225.00
Disneyana, **Fork,** Snow White 15.00
Disneyana, **Game,** Card, Donald Duck 6.50
Disneyana, **Game,** Mickey Mouse, Magic Adder 8.00
Disneyana, **Gun,** Mickey Mouse, Bubble Buster, Original Box, 1936 .... 65.00 To 100.00
Disneyana, **Holder,** Pencil, Wall, Donald Duck, Copeland's Bread 23.00
Disneyana, **Knife,** Pocket, Davy Crockett, 3 In. 12.50
Disneyana, **Lamp,** Figural, Snow White 8.50
Disneyana, **Lantern,** Slide, Cinderella, Wooden Frame, Set Of 8 .... 125.00
Disneyana, **Lunch Box,** Thermos 12.50
Disneyana, **Lunch Pail,** Disney Characters 20.00
Disneyana, **Marionette,** Minnie Mouse 14.00
Disneyana, **Marionette,** Olive Oyl 14.00
Disneyana, **Marionette,** Pinocchio, Composition Head, Hands & Feet, 13 1/2 In. 30.00
Disneyana, **Mug,** Bugs Bunny, Plastic 3.50
Disneyana, **Mug,** Humpty Dumpty, Pink 25.00
Disneyana, **Mug,** Little Pigs, Disney Productions 30.00
Disneyana, **Night Light,** Snow White, Box 20.00
Disneyana, **Pail,** Sand, Donald Duck 30.00
Disneyana, **Pen,** Fountain, Mickey, Inkograph, 1935 .... 12.00
Disneyana, **Pencil Sharpener,** Donald Duck 8.00
Disneyana, **Pencil Sharpener,** Pluto 5.00
Disneyana, **Pinocchio,** Fully Jointed, Wooden 10.00
Disneyana, **Plate,** Minnie Mouse, Playing Coronet, Chased By Cats, 6 In. 50.00
Disneyana, **Pocket Watch,** Mickey Mouse, Mice On Second Hand, Fob 325.00
Disneyana, **Popcorn Popper,** Mickey Mouse 65.00
Disneyana, **Puzzle,** Mickey Mouse, C.1940 .... 7.00
Disneyana, **Radio,** Mickey Mouse Sing-A-Long 40.00
Disneyana, **Ring,** Donald Duck, Head Turns, Mouth Opens 15.00
Disneyana, **Rocker,** Wood, Panel Shows Mickey Floating, 35 X 17 In. 65.00
Disneyana, **Rug,** Snow White & Seven Dwarfs, 38 X 21 In. 12.00
Disneyana, **Salt & Pepper,** Donald Duck, Hand-Painted, C.1940 .... 8.00
Disneyana, **Salt & Pepper,** Dumbo, Disney Productions, 3 1/2 In. 15.00
Disneyana, **Scarf,** Snow White & The Seven Dwarfs, 24 X 24 In. 15.00
Disneyana, **Song Sheet,** Snow White & Seven Dwarfs, 1937 .... 15.00
Disneyana, **Spoon,** Mickey Mouse 12.00
Disneyana, **Tea Set,** Mickey Mouse, China 38.00

Disneyana, Teapot, Donald Duck	4.50 To 10.00
Disneyana, Teapot, Sugar & Creamer, Bambi	25.00
Disneyana, Toothbrush Holder, Donald Duck, Bisque	95.00
Disneyana, Toothbrush Holder, Mickey Mouse	95.00
Disneyana, Toothbrush Holder, Mickey Mouse & Minnie, Bisque	75.00
Disneyana, Toothbrush Holder, Mickey Mouse, Minnie & Pluto, Bisque	30.00
Disneyana, Toothbrush Holder, Three Little Pigs, Bisque	45.00 To 55.00
Disneyana, Toothpick, Pinocchio, Bisque	11.00
Disneyana, Toy, Dipsy Car, Mickey Mouse, Marx	125.00
Disneyana, Toy, Disneyland Ferriswheel, Tin, Windup, Chein	180.00
Disneyana, Toy, Donald Duck, Pulling Cart, Fischer-Price	22.50
Disneyana, Toy, Duet, Donald Duck & Goofy, Windup	125.00
Disneyana, Toy, Mickey Mouse, Mechanical Golf Game	125.00
Disneyana, Toy, Talkie-Jector, Mickey Mouse, 1929	150.00
Disneyana, Toy, Xylophone, Donald Duck-Mickey Mouse, Tin, Lithographed	20.00
Disneyana, Tray, 1939, Donald Duck, Tin	25.00
Disneyana, Tub Toy, Donald Duck, Sun Rubber, 12 In.	10.00
Disneyana, Uniform Patch, Donald Duck, 1942	12.00
Disneyana, Watch Fob, Mickey Mouse, Half Dollar Size	85.00
Disneyana, Watch, Pocket, Ingersoll, Mickey Mouse, 1935	160.00
Disneyana, Watch, Pocket, Mickey Mouse, With Fob, Ingersoll, 1930s	225.00
Disneyana, Wrist Watch, Bugs Bunny	25.00
Disneyana, Wrist Watch, Cinderella	15.00 To 45.00
Disneyana, Wrist Watch, Donald Duck, Ingersoll, Round	60.00
Disneyana, Wrist Watch, Mickey Mouse, Ingersoll, Oblong	75.00 To 125.00
Disneyana, Wrist Watch, Mickey Mouse, Ingersoll, 1922, Original Box	170.00
Disneyana, Wrist Watch, Mickey Mouse, Original Band & Box	135.00
Disneyana, Wrist Watch, Mickey Mouse, Sweep Second Hand, Dated 1937	210.00
Disneyana, Wrist Watch, Mickey Mouse, 1946, Round, Long Tailed Mickey	220.00
Disneyana, Wrist Watch, Mickey Mouse, 3-Mice Second Hand, 1936	175.00
Disneyana, Wrist Watch, Porky Pig, Ingraham, 1949	50.00
Disneyana, Wrist Watch, Snow White	38.00
Disneyana, Wrist Watch, Snow White, Ceramic Figure, 1960	30.00
Disneyana, Wrist Watch, Zorro	35.00
Doctor, see Medical	

Doll entries are listed by marks printed or incised on doll, if possible.
If there are no marks, the doll is listed by name of subject or country.

Doll, A.B.G. 1352, Baby, Flirty Eyed, 19 1/2 In.	275.00
Doll, A.B.G., Baby, Chubby, Breather, 24 In.	315.00
Doll, A.M., see also Doll, Armand Marseille	
Doll, A.M., Boy, Kid Body, Ball Joint Arms, Navy Blue Knickers, 16 In.	125.00
Doll, A.M., Floradora, Bisque Head & Arms, Kid Body, Paperweight Eyes, 15 In.	165.00
Doll, A.M., Floradora, Dressed As Scarlett O'Hara, Jointed Body, 20 In.	200.00
Doll, A.M., Floradora, Kid Body, Bisque Hands, Human Wig, 27 In.	185.00
Doll, A.M., Girl, Bisque Head, Black Eyes, Kid Body, 10 In.	100.00
Doll, A.M., Mohair Wig, Pierced Ears, Ball Jointed Body, 30 In.	285.00
Doll, A.M., Scarlett O'Hara, Green Eyes, Cry Box, Ball Jointed Body, 20 In.	180.00
Doll, A.M., Sleep Eyes, Long Blond Hair, Ball Joint Body, 18 In.	125.00
Doll, A.M., Toddler, Composition Body, Brown Sleep Eyes, 7 1/2 In.	145.00
Doll, A.M., 210, Kid Body, Flowered Dress, Germany, 19 In.	145.00
Doll, A.M., 3200, Jester, Marotte, Plays Music, 6 In.	450.00
Doll, A.M., 323, Googly, Composition Body, 7 1/2 In.	550.00
Doll, A.M., 351, Rock-A-Bye-Baby, Black, 7 1/2 In.	185.00
Doll, A.M., 351, Rock-A-Bye, Black, Solid Dome, 17 In.	295.00
Doll, A.M., 351, Rock-A-Bye, Black, Solid Dome, 18 1/2 In.	300.00 To 400.00
Doll, A.M., 351, Rock-A-Bye, Black, Solid Dome, 19 1/2 In.	325.00
Doll, A.M., 351, Rock-A-Bye, Brown Eyed, Solid Dome, 22 3/4 In.	345.00
Doll, A.M., 370, Bisque Head, Composition Hands, Leather Body, 21 1/2 In.	180.00
Doll, A.M., 370, Boy, Kid Body, Composition Limbs, Dressed, 16 In.	135.00
Doll, A.M., 370, Curl Wig, Bisque Head, Celluloid Forearms, Marked, 27 In.	150.00
Doll, A.M., 370, Lashed Sleep Eyes, Kid Torso, Bisque Hands, Dressed, 19 In.	95.00
Doll, A.M., 370, Leather Body, Bisque Hands	125.00
Doll, A.M., 370, White Leather Body, Bisque Head, 19 In.	300.00
Doll, A.M., 390, Bisque, Ball Jointed Body, Velvet Dress & Hat, 26 In.	225.00
Doll, A.M., 390, Blue Sleep Eyes, Fully Jointed, 24 In.	175.00
Doll, A.M., 390, Mohair Wig, Old Clothes, 25 In.	170.00

Doll, A.M., 590, Composition, Moveable Eyes, Jointed Legs, 8 1/2 In. 150.00
Doll, A.M., 971, Character, Composition Baby Body, 11 In. 225.00
Doll, A.M., 975, Character Baby, 10 In.Head Circumference 170.00
Doll, A.M., 980, Boy, Toddler, Straight Legged, 19 In. 275.00
Doll, A.M., 985 M, Baby, Bent Limb Body, 12 In. 175.00
Doll, A.M., 990, Baby, Character, Blue Eyes, 22 In. 275.00
Doll, Acme, Baby Grumpy 28.00
Doll, Acrobat, Male, Bisque Head, Original Clothes, Schoenhut 175.00
    Doll, Alexander, see Doll, Madame Alexander
Doll, Alma, Kid Body, A.M.Germany, 19 In. 175.00
Doll, Alma, Kid Body, Bisque Head, Open Mouth, 18 In. 125.00
    Doll, Armand Marseille, see Doll, A.M.
Doll, American Indian, Bisque, Composition Body, Berman, 9 In. 165.00
Doll, Bahr & Proschild, Baby, Bent Limb, 25 In. 350.00
Doll, Bahr & Proschild, Toddler, Jointed, 20 In. 325.00
Doll, Barbie, Ponytail, Red Lips & Nails 35.00
Doll, Baseball Player, 1930s, 8 In. 9.00
Doll, Bebe Jumeau, Bisque, Paperweight Eyes, Original Box & Clothes, 22 In. 1500.00
Doll, Belton Type, Kid Body, Bisque Arms, Completely Original, 13 In. 595.00
Doll, Belton, Brown Eyes, Closed Mouth, Human Hair Wig, 15 In. 475.00
Doll, Belton, Closed Mouth, Bisque, Paperweight Eyes, French, 22 1/2 In. 1100.00
Doll, Belton, Concave Head, Blue Eyes, Wood, Composition Jointed Body, 14 In. 450.00
Doll, Bestor, Original Clothes, Ball Jointed Body, 1919, Signed 100.00
Doll, Betsy McCall, 36 In. 45.00
Doll, Betty Boop, Jointed, Wooden 55.00
Doll, Bill Price, No.585, Baby, 15 In. 275.00
Doll, Bisque Bald Head, Composition Body, Sleep Eyes, White Rompers 150.00
Doll, Bisque, Character Baby, Jointed, Boy, German, 7 In. 85.00
Doll, Bisque, Glass Eyes, Cloth Body & Legs, Kid Arms & Hands, 21 1/2 In. 295.00
Doll, Bisque, Glass Eyes, Pierced Ears, Kid Body, Legs & Arms, 15 1/2 In. 375.00
Doll, Bisque, Indian Boy & Girl, Colorful, Japan, Original Box, 3 3/4 In. 15.00
Doll, Bisque, Miniature, Bathing Beauty, German, 2 1/2 In. 60.00
Doll, Bisque, One Piece Body, Swivel Head, Molded & Painted Socks & Shoes 85.00
Doll, Black Baby Twins, In Wicker-Like Baskets, Diapered, Bisque, 2 1/2 In. 20.00
Doll, Black Baby, Bisque, Afro Wig, Googly Eyes, 18 In. 85.00
Doll, Black Girl, Papier-Mache, 12 In., Pair 385.00
Doll, Black, Walnut Head, Small, Rag 35.00
Doll, Boy, Amish, Composition, 10 In. 30.00
Doll, Boy, Cloth & Papier Mache, Original Clothes 45.00
Doll, Boy, Sailor, Composition Head & Hands, World War I, 30 In. 150.00
Doll, Boy, Soldier, Composition Head & Hands, World War I, 30 In. 150.00
Doll, Bozo The Clown, Cloth 18.00
Doll, Brass Head, Tin Shoulders, Sawdust Filled, Kid Body, 13 In. 60.00
Doll, Bru, Toddler, Nursing, Human Hair, Dressed In Rompers, 16 In. 1800.00
Doll, Buggy, Wicker, Wooden Handle 30.00
Doll, Bye-Lo Baby, Bisque Head, Cloth Body, Dressed, 14 In. 750.00
Doll, Bye-Lo Baby, Bisque, Marked, 12 In. 500.00
Doll, Bye-Lo Baby, Blue Sleep Eyes, Cloth Body, Made In Germany, 13 In. 425.00
Doll, Bye-Lo Baby, Celluloid Hands, 12 In. 350.00
Doll, Bye-Lo Baby, Sleep Eyes, Bisque Head & Body, Fully Marked, 12 In. 325.00
Doll, Bye-Lo Body, Stamped, Celluloid Head, 7 1/2 In. 55.00
Doll, Bye-Lo, Baby, Bisque Head, 10 1/2 In.Head Circumference 350.00
Doll, Bye-Lo, Baby, Jointed Arms, Legs, Bisque Head, Circle Signed, 6 In. 415.00
Doll, Bye-Lo, Baby, Sleep Eyes, Wig, Bisque, 6 In. 500.00
Doll, Bye-Lo, Blue Eyes, Original Dress & Blue Label Pin, 10 In. 395.00
Doll, Bye-Lo, Brown Eyes, Signed Head & Body, 13 In. 350.00
Doll, Bye-Lo, Painted Eyes, Bisque, 4 1/2 In. 285.00
Doll, Bye-Lo, Pillow Baby, Brown Sleep Eyes 195.00
Doll, Bye-Lo, Sleep Blue Eyes, Original Body, 10 In. 285.00
    Doll, C.M.Bergmann, see also Doll, S.&H., Doll, Simon & Halbig
Doll, C.M.Bergmann, Ball Jointed Body, Sleep Eyes, Original Clothes, 16 In. 125.00
Doll, C.M.Bergmann, Composition Body, Pink Dress, 27 In. 275.00
Doll, C.M.Bergmann, Open Mouth, Ball Jointed, Pierced Ears, 32 In. 475.00
Doll, C.M.Bergmann, Tin Head, 15 In. 95.00
Doll, Campbell Kid, Horsman, Composition, All Original, 12 In. 145.00
Doll, Campbell Kid, Rubber, 10 In. 15.00
Doll, Celluloid, Jointed, Elaborate Hairdo & Costume, 1920s 15.00

Doll, Chad Valley Dutch Boy & Girl, Blue Glass Eyes	65.00
Doll, Charlie Chaplin, Vinyl, Bamboo Cane, Milton Bradley, 19 In.	23.50
Doll, Charlie Weaver, Bartender	25.00
Doll, Chase, Boy, Rubber Head, Stockinette Body, Sailor Suit, 16 In.	195.00
Doll, Chase, Boy, Stockinette, 24 1/2 In.	275.00
Doll, Chatty Baby, Black	85.00
Doll, China, Black Hair, China Arms & Legs, Undressed, 6 In.	25.00
Doll, China, Black Molded Curls, All Original, 12 In.	55.00
Doll, Chinese Royal, Wood, Composition, Sawdust Body, 20 In. *Illus*	85.00
Doll, Clootles, Composition Head, Rubber Body, 14 In.	55.00
Doll, Cloth, Emma Adams, Columbian, Ink Stamp, 19 In.	1200.00
Doll, Clown, Cymbalist, Bellow Mechanism, Wood Legs, Feet, Gold Outfit, 18 In.	125.00
Doll, Clown, Jointed, Composition Face, Red, White & Black, 9 In.	37.50
Doll, Coleman, Walker, 29 In.	100.00
Doll, Cow, Elsie Borden	15.00
Doll, Cuno & Otto Dressel, Baby, Dressed, 26 1/2 In.	385.00
Doll, D'r 101, Marie, Brown Eyes, 17 In.	2000.00
Doll, D'r 122, Character Baby, 14 In.	305.00
Doll, D'r 126, Baby, Flirty Eyed, 21 In.	345.00

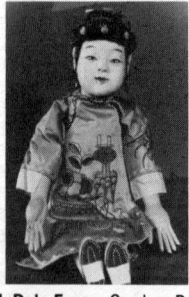

Doll, Chinese Royal, Wood, Composition,
Sawdust Body, 20 In.

Doll, Dale Evans, Cowboy Dress	35.00
Doll, Deanna Durbin, Composition, Original Clothes, Human Hair, 18 In.	200.00
Doll, Dimples, Composition, Straight Legged, 19 In.	48.00
Doll, Dolly Sister, 5 Black Celluloid Dolls, Arms Jointed, Boxed	35.00
Doll, Donald Duck, Lars Of Italy, 1940s	150.00
Doll, Dream Baby, Original, 7 In.Head Circumference	165.00
Doll, Dream Baby, 9 In. Circumference	325.00
Doll, Dressel, Girl, Ball-Jointed, Bisque, 1912, Original Clothes	225.00
Doll, Dwarf, Happy, Walt Disney, 12 In.	60.00
Doll, Eden Bebe, Closed Mouth, Straight Wrists, Blue Eyes, 18 In.	875.00
Doll, Edith Lonely, Large Gold Hoop Earrings, 15 In.	85.00
Doll, Effanbee, Anne Shirley, 1939	95.00
Doll, Effanbee, Baby	35.00
Doll, Effanbee, Betty Boop	150.00
Doll, Effanbee, Bubbles, Composition Body, Dressed, 23 In.	50.00
Doll, Effanbee, Candy Kid, Composition, Swivel Head, Sleep Eyes	37.50
Doll, Effanbee, Candy Kid, Original Red Dress, 12 In.	65.00
Doll, Effanbee, Charlie McCarthy, 30 In.	135.00
Doll, Effanbee, Fluffy, Molded Hair, 8 1/2 In.	20.00
Doll, Effanbee, Honey Walker, Original Bridal Outfit, Human Hair, 18 In.	45.00
Doll, Effanbee, Little Lady, Composition, 20 In.	85.00
Doll, Effanbee, Little Lady, Cotton Floss Wig, Original Dress, 18 In.	75.00
Doll, Effanbee, Lovums, Blonde Curly Wig, Composition, 16 In.	45.00
Doll, Effanbee, Patsy Ann, Tag On Wrist, 19 In.	120.00
Doll, Effanbee, Patsy Jr., Molded Hair, Painted Eyes, Composition, 11 1/2 In.	110.00
Doll, Effanbee, Patsy Lou, Brown Mohair Wig, All Original	250.00
Doll, Effanbee, Patsy Ruth, 27 In.	350.00
Doll, Effanbee, Patsy, Compostion, Dressed, Sleep Eyes, Molded Hair, 13 In.	59.50
Doll, Effanbee, Rosemary, Long Curl Wig, Tin Eyes, Tagged Clothes, 24 In.	135.00
Doll, Effanbee, Rosey Posey	29.95
Doll, Effanbee, Sugar Plum	31.95
Doll, Effanbee, Suzanne, Pigtails, Composition, 14 In.	60.00
Doll, Effanbee, Sweet Sue, American Character	20.00

Doll, Effanbee, Sweetie Pie, 16 In.	65.00
Doll, Einco, Baby, Bald Dome, Mold Band Across Head, 13 1/2 In.	225.00
Doll, Einco, Girl, Jointed Body, 23 In.	325.00
Doll, Ella Cinders, Label On Dress, 20 In.	500.00
Doll, Emma Clear, Grape Lady, Satin Dress, Undies & Earrings, 1947, 18 In.	350.00
Doll, English, Poured Wax, Blue Glass Eyes, Original Clothes, 16 1/2 In.	395.00
Doll, F S. & Co., Toddler, No.1295	250.00
Doll, F.G., Closed Mouth, French, 17 In.	1275.00
Doll, F.G.Gesland, Blue Eyes, Closed Mouth, Extra Large, 31 In.	2750.00
Doll, Felix, Dressed In G.I. Clothes, Composition, 13 1/2 In.	65.00
Doll, First Ladies, 1976, Mint In Box, Set	325.00
Doll, Floradora, Composition Body, Jointed, Bisque Head, Dressed, 20 In.	125.00
Doll, Floradora, Papier-Mache Body, All Original, 16 1/2 In.	145.00
Doll, Fredrich, Sound Of Music, Mint In Box	100.00
Doll, French, All Bisque, Girl, Glass Eyes, Original Clothes, 3 1/2 In.	150.00
Doll, French, China Fashion, Original Kid Body & Wig & Cork Plate, C.1860	2500.00
Doll, French, Oriental Couple, Bisque, 4 In., Pair	300.00
Doll, French, Peasant, Stockinette, 22 In., Pair	500.00
Doll, Frozen Charlie, China, Pink Tinted Face, Gray Eyes, Light Hair, 15 In.	465.00
Doll, Frozen Charlie, 15 1/2 In.	285.00
Doll, Frozen Charlie, 16 In.	245.00
Doll, Frozen Charlotte, Bisque, Moveable Arms, Stand Alone, 6 1/2 In., Pair	60.00
Doll, Frozen Charlotte, In Tub, 2 1/2 In.	65.00
Doll, Frozen Charlotte, Moveable Arms, Molded Hair, Marked Germany	75.00
Doll, Frozen Charlotte, Sitting In Chair, 1 1/2 In.	20.00
Doll, Fulper, Baby, Blue Eyes, Open Mouth, Old Baby Dress, Human Hair, 18 In.	325.00
Doll, Gans & Seyfarth, Ball Joint Body, Sleep Eyes, Old Clothes, 23 In.	135.00
Doll, Geisha, Carrying Theater Mask, Silk Robes, Japanese, Glass Case, 17 In.	80.00
Doll, General Douglas MacArthur, Original Clothes, 19 In.	75.00
Doll, Georgene Averill, Baby, Bald Head, Brown Eyes, Bisque, 18 In.	515.00
Doll, Georgene Averill, Baby, Bald Head, Painted Hair, 12 In.	725.00
Doll, Georgene Averill, Bonnie Babe, Christening Gown, Bisque, 10 In.	450.00
Doll, German, American Indian, Bisque Face, Rest Composition, 9 3/4 In.	160.00
Doll, German, Flapper, Bisque Head, 13 In.	450.00
Doll, German, Frozen Bonnet, On Swing, Marked, 3 In.	75.00
Doll, German, 326B, Character Baby, Solid Dome Head, Brown Eyes, 14 In.	400.00
Doll, Giggles, Rose O'Neill, Composition, Hair In Bun, 12 In.	100.00
Doll, Girl, Molded Hair, Ribbon, Signed, Nippon.7 In.	65.00
Doll, Googly, Papier-Mache, Original, 11 1/2 In.	250.00
Doll, Greiner, Sailor Boy, Bisque Head, Papier-Mache Body, Marked, 8 In.	350.00
Doll, Gutta-Percha, Clown, Steiff, 16 In.	75.00
Doll, H.W.38W, Baby, 15 In.	275.00
Doll, Handwerck BJ, Girl, Old Clothes, Hat, Bisque Head	350.00
Doll, Handwerck 99-DEP, 33 In.	625.00
Doll, Handwerck, Baby, Bisque Head, Slant Eyes, Cries, 15 In.	235.00
Doll, Handwerck, Girl, Ball Jointed, Pierced Ears, Dressed, 23 In.	300.00
Doll, Handwerck, Girl, Blonde Mohair Wig, Blue Sleep Eyes, 22 In.	275.00
Doll, Handwerck, Toddler, Bent Limb, Germany	295.00
Doll, Happifat, Girl, Jointed Arms, Molded Clothes, Bisque, German, 4 1/2 In.	200.00
Doll, Happy Hooligan, Original Paint, Schoenhut	250.00
Doll, Henlen W.Janson, Gladdie, Open Mouth, Stuffed Body, Germany, 20 In.	600.00
Doll, Herm Steiner, Baby, All Original, 6 In.	120.00
Doll, Heubach Koppelsdorf, Baby, Sleep Eyes, Christening Dress, 9 In.	110.00
Doll, Heubach Koppelsdorf 275, Bisque Head, Leather Forehands, 14 In.	135.00
Doll, Heubach Koppelsdorf 275, Kid Body, Original Wig & Clothes, 22 In.	165.00
Doll, Heubach Koppelsdorf 300-7, Bent Limb Body, 21 In.	315.00
Doll, Heubach Koppelsdorf 342, Toddler, Straight Leg, 21 In.	275.00
Doll, Heubach Koppelsdorf 342, Toddler, Straight Legged, 18 1/2 In.	245.00
Doll, Heubach Koppelsdorf 350, Baby, Blue Sleep Eyes, 5 1/2 In.Cir.	130.00
Doll, Heubach Koppelsdorf 399, Black Baby, Bisque Head, 12 In.	395.00
Doll, Heubach Koppelsdorf, Babies, Automation, On Music Box, Crank, C.1900	1900.00
Doll, Heubach Koppelsdorf, Baby Stuart, Leather Body, Christening Dress	550.00
Doll, Heubach Koppelsdorf, Baby, Bent Limb, Intaglio Eyes, Marked, 9 In.	185.00
Doll, Heubach Koppelsdorf, Baby, Molded Blond Hair, Ribbon, 8 In.	395.00
Doll, Heubach Koppelsdorf, Boy, Open/Closed Mouth, Intaglio Eyes, 9 1/2 In.	325.00
Doll, Heubach Koppelsdorf, Character Girl, Dressed In Purple Velvet, 16 In.	285.00

Doll, Heubach Kopplesdorf, Girl, Pleated Dress, Slippers, Bisque, 11 1/2 In.	95.00
Doll, Heubach Kopplesdorf, Girl, Sleep Eyes, Blonde, Jointed Torso, 18 In.	475.00
Doll, Heubach Kopplesdorf, Googly, Sleep Blue Eyes, 5 Piece Body 6 1/2 In.	275.00
Doll, Heubach Kopplesdorf, Pouty Baby, Intaglio Eyes, Baby Dress, 6 1/4 In.	250.00
Doll, Heubach Kopplesdorf, Sleep Eyes, Wig, Molded Shoes, Bisque Head, 10 In.	115.00
Doll, Heubach Kopplesdorf, Toddler, Flirty Eye, Bisque, 25 In.	375.00
Doll, Heubach Kopplesdorf, Toddler, Flirty Eye, 22 In.	385.00
Doll, Heubach Koppelsdorf, Toddler, Straight Leg, 9 In.	155.00
Doll, Heubach Kopplesdorf, Toddler, 4 Teeth, Dress & Pinafore, 18 In.	1150.00
Doll, Holz-Masse, Lori, Bisque, Intaglio Eyes, 16 In.	825.00
Doll, Howdy Doody, Composition, Cloth, 13 In.	25.00
Doll, Hula Dancing, Key Wind, Composition, 16 In.	95.00
Doll, Hummel, Girl Sweeper, Vinyl, 8 In.	45.00
Doll, Ideal, Daddy's Little Girl, 35 In.	35.00
Doll, Ideal, Flossie Flirt, Dressed, 18 In.	35.00
Doll, Ideal, Kissy, Blonde Hair, Blue Sleep Eyes, Socket Head, 1962, 16 In.	30.00
Doll, Ideal, Nancy, Original Velvet Jacket, Skirt, Straw Hat, 18 In.	85.00
Doll, Ideal, Patty, Original, 36 In.	55.00
Doll, Ideal, Snoozie, Baby, 1949, Vinyl	75.00
Doll, Ideal, Toni, Brunette, Permanent Set Hair, 14 In.	65.00
Doll, Ideal, Trilby, 3 Faces	30.00
Doll, Ideal, Winsome Winnie, 1929, Rubber Arms, Composition Legs, 22 In.	35.00
Doll, Indian, see also Indian, Doll	
Doll, Indian, Maid & Man, Bisque Head, Jointed Shoulders & Hips, 6 In., Pair	200.00
Doll, Indian, Original Cloth Body, Bisque, 14 In.	125.00
Doll, J.D.K., see also Doll, Kestner	
Doll, J.D.K.211, Baby, Sleep Eyes, Brown, 16 In.	335.00
Doll, J.D.K.257, Baby, 15 In.	335.00
Doll, Jumeau, Blue Eyes, Open Mouth, Signed Body, 1907, 35 In.	1495.00
Doll, Jumeau, Closed Mouth, Marked Head, Original Silk Clothing, 20 In.	750.00
Doll, Jumeau, Cloth Body, Turned Bald Dome Head, Paperweight Eyes	500.00
Doll, Jumeau, Cork Pate & Wig, Papier-Mache, Wood, 19 In. .... Illus	1850.00
Doll, Jumeau, Girl, Blue Paperweight Eyes, 26 In.	475.00
Doll, Jumeau, Laughing Baby, Brown Sleep Eyes, Human Hair Wig, 16 In.	1200.00
Doll, Jumeau, Open Mouth, Human Hair, Blue Eyes, Original Clothes, 23 1/2 In.	750.00
Doll, Jumeau, Sleep Blue Eyes, Unis France, Label On Wrist, 21 In.	250.00
Doll, K & H, Girl, Cloth & Compostiion Body, Sleep Eyes, Cries, 18 In.	165.00
Doll, K * R 100, Baby, 19 In.	800.00
Doll, K * R 100, Bisque Head, Composition, Jointed Body, Marked, 15 1/2 In.	1475.00
Doll, K * R 114, Pouty Boy	500.00
Doll, K * R 126, Baby, Flirty Blue Eyes, Original Body, 30 In.	795.00
Doll, K * R 126, Toddler, Flirt, Ball Jointed, 22 1/4 In.	375.00
Doll, K * R 126, Toddler, 11 In.	215.00
Doll, K * R 127, Boy Toddler, Molded Hair, Sleep Eyes, 15 In.	695.00
Doll, K * R 403, Open & Close Eyes, Human Hair, Ball Jointed Body, 23 In.	475.00
Doll, K * R 728/10, Celluloid Head, Flirty Eyes, 21 In.	195.00
Doll, Kaiser, Baby, Deep Molding, 11 In. Head, Dressed	465.00
Doll, Kaiser, Baby, Papier-Mache, 15 In.	110.00
Doll, Kathe Kruse, Girl, Celluloid, 13 In.	100.00
Doll, Kathe Kruse, Girl, Original Clothes, 20 1/2 In.	135.00
Doll, Kelly, Blue Organdy Party Dress, 22 In.	75.00
Doll, Kestner, see also Doll, J.D.K.	
Doll, Kestner Z226, Baby, Wobble Tongue, Open Mouth, Bent Limb, 15 In.	300.00
Doll, Kestner 129, Open Mouth, Brown Eyes, Blonde Mohair Wig, 12 1/2 In.	275.00
Doll, Kestner 150, Toddler, 11 In.	275.00
Doll, Kestner 151, Baby, Brown Molded Tongue, 2 Upper Teeth, 23 In.	455.00
Doll, Kestner 152, Character Baby, 6 3/4 In.	130.00
Doll, Kestner 154, Bisque Arms, Kid Body, 17 In.	150.00
Doll, Kestner 164, Girl, Original Dress & Shoes, 27 In.	395.00
Doll, Kestner 164, Sleep Blue Eyes, Ball Jointed, 20 In.	245.00
Doll, Kestner 478, Brown Eyes, Large, 36 In.	750.00
Doll, Kestner 1123, Turned Head, Stationary Blue Eyes, 30 In.	385.00
Doll, Kestner, Baby, Blue Eyes, Closed Mouth, Cloth Body, Marked, 18 1/2 In.	650.00
Doll, Kestner, Baby, Long Dress, Sleep Eyes, Undies, Marked Gb., 16 In.	320.00
Doll, Kestner, Ball Jointed, Stationary Eyes, Long Human Hair, 12 In.	135.00
Doll, Kestner, Bisque Head, Jointed Composition Limbs, Open Mouth, 29 In.	375.00

Doll, Kwanjo, Maid Of Honor, Swivel Head, Glass Eyes, 8 In.

Doll, Jumeau, Cork Pate & Wig, Papier-Mache, Wood, 19 In.

Doll, **Kestner**, Bisque Shoulder Head, Kid Body, Original Clothes, 14 In.	150.00
Doll, **Kestner**, Blonde Wig, Sleep Eyes, Open Mouth, Bisque, 6 In.	130.00
Doll, **Kestner**, Boy, Velvet Suit, 18 In.	260.00
Doll, **Kestner**, Closed Mouth, Blue Painted Eyes, Molded Hair, Bisque, 6 In.	225.00
Doll, **Kestner**, Lady, Bisque Head, Kid Body, Paperweight Eyes, 21 In.	295.00
Doll, **Kestner**, Leather Body, Bisque Head, Human Hair, 33 In.	600.00
Doll, **Kestner**, Sleep Eyes, Fur Eyebrows, Ball Jointed, 29 In.	325.00
Doll, **Kestner**, Sleep Eyes, Human Hair, Crown Mark, 9 1/2 In.	260.00
Doll, **Kewpie, see Kewpie, Doll**	
Doll, **Konig & Wernicke 99/16**, Baby, Bent Limb, 24 In.	350.00
Doll, **Kwanjo**, Maid Of Honor, Swivel Head, Glass Eyes, 8 In. *Illus*	55.00
Doll, **Limoges**, Bru Body, Kid & Wood, Paperweight Eyes, Ed Tasson, 30 In.	3900.00
Doll, **Little Women**, Walkers, Jointed Knee, Set Of 5	225.00
Doll, **Lizzy**, Kid Body, 21 In.	275.00
Doll, **Lori**, Baby, Marked D.V., Stamp, 11 In.	600.00
Doll, **Lovums**, Composition, Laughing, Cloth Body	125.00
Doll, **M.M.**, Lady, Ears Exposed, Bun In Back, 14 In.	350.00
Doll, **Madame Alexander**, Agatha, Dressed In Blue, 21 In.	165.00
Doll, **Madame Alexander**, Alice In Wonderland, Mint In Box, 8 In.	125.00
Doll, **Madame Alexander**, Baby Butch, Composition Head, Dressed, 11 In.	95.00
Doll, **Madame Alexander**, Baby McGuffey, 23 In.	125.00
Doll, **Madame Alexander**, Barbara Jane, Vinyl, Cloth Body, 34 In.	80.00
Doll, **Madame Alexander**, Billy & Wendy, Scarlet Caps, 8 In., Pair	175.00
Doll, **Madame Alexander**, Bridesmaid, All Original, 20 In.	65.00
Doll, **Madame Alexander**, Bubble, Blue Sleep Eyes, Lacy Dress, 18 In.	45.00
Doll, **Madame Alexander**, Butch, Sleep Eyes, Molded Hair, Rompers, 12 In.	48.00
Doll, **Madame Alexander**, Chatterbox, 24 In.	60.00
Doll, **Madame Alexander**, Cherie, Ball Jointed, Open Mouth, Bisque, 25 In.	650.00
Doll, **Madame Alexander**, Cissette, Red Dress & Underwear, 9 In.	50.00
Doll, **Madame Alexander**, Deanna Durbin, Knitted Outfit	245.00
Doll, **Madame Alexander**, Dionne Babies, Sun Suits, Name Pins, 7 In., Set Of 5	550.00
Doll, **Madame Alexander**, Dionne Baby, Sleep Eyes, Molded Hair, Marked, 12 In.	60.00
Doll, **Madame Alexander**, Dionne Quintuplets, In Bag, Never Dressed, 7 1/4 In.	75.00
Doll, **Madame Alexander**, Dolly Dryper, 11 In.	20.00
Doll, **Madame Alexander**, Fanny Brice, 1939, 12 In.	75.00
Doll, **Madame Alexander**, Flora McFlimsey, Freckle Faced, Red Head, 15 In.	165.00
Doll, **Madame Alexander**, Flora McFlimsey, 12 In.	125.00
Doll, **Madame Alexander**, Girl, Dress, Gloves, Vinyl Face, Ball Jointed, 17 In.	125.00
Doll, **Madame Alexander**, Jackie Kennedy, Inaugural Ball Gown, Tag, 21 In.	375.00
Doll, **Madame Alexander**, Jane Withers, 13 In.	450.00
Doll, **Madame Alexander**, Janie, 36 In.	150.00
Doll, **Madame Alexander**, Joanie, 35 In.	135.00
Doll, **Madame Alexander**, Kathy, 21 In.	20.00
Doll, **Madame Alexander**, Kelly, Blue Party Dress, 23 In.	95.00
Doll, **Madame Alexander**, Little Genius, Painted Blue Eyes, 16 In.	52.50
Doll, **Madame Alexander**, Margot, Plastic Walker, 14 In.	85.00
Doll, **Madame Alexander**, Marme, Original Clothes, 13 In.	60.00
Doll, **Madame Alexander**, McGuffey Ana, 1968, 14 In.	100.00
Doll, **Madame Alexander**, Mime, 31 In.	150.00
Doll, **Madame Alexander**, Orphan Annie, 14 In.	85.00
Doll, **Madame Alexander**, Patsy Mae, All Original, 30 In.	185.00

Doll, **Madame Alexander**, Poor Cinderella, 12 In.	14.00
Doll, **Madame Alexander**, Portrette Scarlett, 10 In.	125.00
Doll, **Madame Alexander**, Princess Elizabeth, Crown, Ball Gown, 23 In.	175.00
Doll, **Madame Alexander**, Princess Elizabeth, Peach Dress, Crown, 15 In.	160.00
Doll, **Madame Alexander**, Renoir Girl, 1969, 14 In.	65.00
Doll, **Madame Alexander**, Scarlett O'Hara, Original Paper Tag, 11 In.	165.00
Doll, **Madame Alexander**, Shari Lewis, Rose Taffeta Dress, 14 In.	225.00
Doll, **Madame Alexander**, Sir Winston & Lady Churchill, 18 In., Pair	450.00
Doll, **Madame Alexander**, Smarty, Dressed In Artist Smock, 12 In.	25.00
Doll, **Madame Alexander**, Sonja Henie, Tagged Clothes, 15 In.	125.00
Doll, **Madame Alexander**, Vinyl, Brown Hair, Blue Sleep Eyes, 18 In.	38.00
Doll, **Madame Alexander**, Wendy Ann, Swivel Waist, Riding Habit, 13 In.	145.00
Doll, **Mammy**, Stuffed Figure, Late 19th Century, 27 1/2 In.	500.00
Doll, **Man From U.N.C.L.E.**, Boxed	17.50
Doll, **Mary Hoyers**, Composition, 18 In.	85.00
Doll, **Mary Poppins**, Horsman, Jointed, Original Box, 12 In.	16.50 To 35.00
Doll, **Max & Moritz**, Original Pants & Shirts, Schoenhut	550.00
Doll, **Mechanical**, Clockwork, On Tricycle	650.00
Doll, **Minerva**, Brown Eye, Tin Head, Straw Body, 11 In.	180.00
Doll, **Minerva**, Girl, Tin Head, Straw Body, 11 In.	70.00
Doll, **Morimura**, Ball Jointed Body, Fixed Blue Eyes, Rose Dress, 22 In.	180.00
Doll, **Mortimer Snerd**, Walking	90.00
Doll, **Mutt**, Metal Ball Jointed, Felt Clothes, Switzerland, 8 In.	125.00
Doll, **Negro**, Rag, Original Clothes, Mother, 23 In., Son, 18 In., Pair	350.00
Doll, **Nippon**, Bisque Baby, Solid Dome Head, Oriental Eyes	225.00
Doll, **Olive Oyl**, King Features	25.00
Doll, **P.M. 914**, Baby, Molded Tongue, 15 1/2 In.	235.00
Doll, **Paper, see Paper, Doll**	
Doll, **Papier-Mache & Wax**, Glass Eyes, Leather Boots, Blonde Hair, 26 In.	155.00
Doll, **Papier-Mache**, Boy's Day Figure, 8 In. *Illus*	30.00
Doll, **Papier-Mache**, Clown, Squeeze Stomach, Plays Cymbals	100.00
Doll, **Papier-Mache**, Excelsior Filled, Paperweight Eyes, Mohair Wig, 33 In.	185.00
Doll, **Papier-Mache**, Mechanical, Push Tummy, Mouth Opens, Dated 1885, 12 In.	185.00
Doll, **Papier-Mache**, Samurai Warrior, Swivel Head, 12 In. *Illus*	55.00
Doll, **Papier-Mache**, Warrior, Swivel Head, Gofun Finish, 7 In. *Illus*	25.00
Doll, **Patsy Pocketbook**, Composition Head, Straw & Cloth Body	18.00
Doll, **Pincushion, see Pincushion Doll**	
Doll, **Popeye & Olive Oyl**, Rubber, 8 In., Pair	30.00
Doll, **Popeye**, Fully Wood Jointed, Original Sea Bag, 12 In.	250.00
Doll, **Popeye**, Wood, Jointed, Carries Original Sea Bag, 10 In.	250.00
Doll, **Princess Elizabeth**, Blonde Braids, Brown Eyes, Composition, 15 In.	75.00
Doll, **Princess Elizabeth**, Ermine Cape, 19 In.	85.00
Doll, **Queen Elizabeth**, Original Clothes, 14 In.	75.00
Doll, **Queen Louise**, Blue Eyes, Blonde Wig, Bisque & Composition, 34 In.	375.00
Doll, **Queen Louise**, Sleep Blue Eyes, Fully Jointed, 24 In.	275.00
Doll, **Queen Louise**, Sleep Brown Eyes, 25 In.	275.00
Doll, **R & B**, Bride, Nancy Lee, Original, Wrist Tag	65.00
Doll, **R & B**, Debuteen, Composition, Cloth Body, All Original, 18 In.	75.00
Doll, **R & B**, Jack & Jill, In Suitcase, Carrying Red Wooden Bucket, 8 In.	150.00
Doll, **R & B**, Sonja Henie, Composition, 21 In.	45.00
Doll, **Re-Wax Over Composition**, Straw Filled Body, 28 In.	150.00
Doll, **Revalo**, Ball Jointed Body, Fixed Eyes, White Clothes, 14 In.	160.00
Doll, **S & H, see also Doll, C.M.Bergmann, Doll, Simon & Halbig**	
Doll, **S & H 210**, Baby, Character Face, 22 In.	325.00
Doll, **S & H 1079**, Chunky, Brown Eyes, 36 In.	575.00
Doll, **S & H 1906**, Girl, Jointed Body, 31 In.	385.00
Doll, **S.F.B.J.**, Bisque Head, Molded Teeth, Real Hair, Marked, 13 In.	425.00
Doll, **S.F.B.J.**, Bisque Head, Open & Close Eyes, Pierced Ears, Marked, 14 In.	425.00
Doll, **S.F.B.J.**, Girl, Molded Teeth, Pierced Ears, Glass Eyes, Marked, 36 In.	1050.00
Doll, **S.F.B.J.247**, French Toddler, Rare Number And Size, 28 In.	2500.00
Doll, **S.F.B.J. 251**, Toddler, Brown Eyes, Bisque, 28 In.	1350.00
Doll, **S.F.B.J.301**, Paris, Blue Eyes, Open Mouth, 26 In.	950.00
Doll, **Samurai Warrior**, Carved In Wrinkles, Gray Hair, 8 In. *Illus*	65.00
Doll, **Santa Claus**, Rag, Printed Cloth, C.1900	75.00
Doll, **Sax Over Pouty Mouth**, Bulgy Blue Eyes, 18 In.	165.00
Doll, **Schoenau & Hoffmeister**, Bisque, Sleep Eyes, Blonde Human Hair, 25 In.	285.00

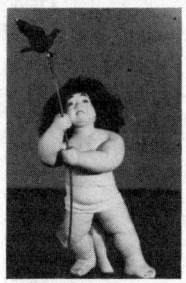

Doll, Papier-Mache, Boy's Day
Figure, 8 In.

Doll, Papier-Mache, Samurai
Warrior, Swivel Head, 12 In.

Doll, Papier-Mache, Warrior,
Swivel Head, Gofun Finish, 7 In.

Doll, Samurai Warrior, Carved
In Wrinkles, Gray Hair, 8 In.

Doll, Schoenhut, Girl, Good Paint,
2 Minor Flaws, 16 In.
(See Page 158)

Doll, Simon & Halbig, Black Child,
12 In.
(See Page 158)

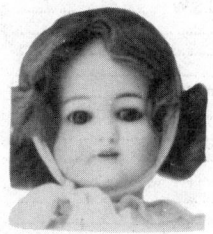

Doll, Simon & Halbig & C.M.Bergmann,
Dolly Face, German, 24 In.
(See Page 158)

Doll, Simon & Halbig, 1199, Burmese,
Golden Bisque, 17 1/2 In.
(See Page 158)

Doll, Schoenhut, Barney Google & Spark Plug 475.00
Doll, Schoenhut, Boy & Girl, 19 In., Pair 875.00
Doll, Schoenhut, Boy, Pouty, 15 In. 375.00
Doll, Schoenhut, Clown, Rolly-Dolly 150.00
Doll, Schoenhut, Girl, Good Paint, 2 Minor Flaws, 16 In. ....*Illus* 480.00
Doll, Schoenhut, Girl, Sleep Blue Eyes, 22 In. 495.00
Doll, Schoenhut, Happy Hooligan 315.00
Doll, Schoenhut, Hobo .... 85.00 To 140.00
Doll, Schoenhut, Maggie & Jiggs, Rolling Pin & Cabbage Pail 885.00
Doll, Schoenhut, Policeman 195.00
Doll, Schoenhut, Pouty, Brown Eyes, 21 In. 495.00
Doll, Schoenhut, Ringmaster, Two Part Face, Original Clothes 175.00
Doll, Schoenhut, Walker, Blue Painted Eyes, Mohair Wig, Dressed, 17 In. 345.00
Doll, Scotty Boy, Composition, Original Clothes, 12 1/2 In. 65.00
    Doll, Shirley Temple, see Shirley Temple
    Doll, Simon & Halbig, see also Doll, C.M.Bergmann; Doll, S.&H.
Doll, Simon & Halbig & C.M.Bergmann, Dolly Face, German, 24 In. ....*Illus* 550.00
Doll, Simon & Halbig, Black Child, 12 In. ....*Illus* 850.00
Doll, Simon & Halbig, Open Mouth, Pierced Ears, Jointed, 13 1/2 In. 450.00
Doll, Simon & Halbig, Walking, Head Turns As It Walks 175.00
Doll, Simon & Halbig, 1039, Flirty Eyed, Open Mouth, Bisque Head, 22 In. 695.00
Doll, Simon & Halbig, 1078, Bavarian Dress 250.00
Doll, Simon & Halbig, 1079, Oriental Appearance, Bisque, 21 In. 475.00
Doll, Simon & Halbig, 1079, Sleep Blue Eyes, 26 In. 285.00
Doll, Simon & Halbig, 1199, Burmese, Golden Bisque, 17 1/2 In. ....*Illus* 2650.00
Doll, Simon & Halbig, 1249, Santa, Sleep Blue Eyes, 21 In. 375.00
Doll, Simon & Halbig, 1279, Character Doll, 15 In. 595.00
Doll, Sleeping Beauty, Box, 21 In. 325.00
Doll, Snow Baby, Shoulder Head Doll, Cloth Body, 7 1/2 In. 225.00
Doll, Snow White, Composition, 15 In. 90.00
Doll, Soldier, World War 1, Walking, 6 1/2 In. 14.00
Doll, Sonja Henie, Skating Outfit, Skates, Marked, 15 In. 125.00
Doll, Splash Me, Red Wig, Original Label, Dated 1919 .... 20.00
Doll, Squaw With Papoose, Skookum, 7 1/2 In. 40.00
Doll, Stationary Eyes, Real Hair, Cloth Stuffed Body, Poured Wax, 17 In. 250.00
Doll, Steiff, Mickey Mouse, Green Pants, Tag In Ear, Disney Stamp, 6 1/2 In. .. 325.00
Doll, Steiner, French, Wire Eyes, 2 Rows Teeth, 18 In. 1300.00
Doll, Steiner, Le Parisien A3, Closed Mouth, Marked Body, 10 In. 1000.00
Doll, Superior P.M., Original Clothes, 36 In. 310.00
Doll, Teddy Bear, Jointed, Mohair, Small 12.50
Doll, Terri Lee, Scottish Outfit 95.00
Doll, Tete Jumeau, Brown Eyes, Closed Mouth, Applied Ears, 32 In. 2750.00
Doll, Tiny Tears, Rubber Body, Hand-Painted Head 22.00
Doll, Tiny Terri Lee, Original Dress, 10 In. 45.00
Doll, Toddler, Composition, 12 In. 20.00
Doll, Tommy Tucker, Bisque Swivel Head, Blue Glass Eyes, Marked B.S.W. 650.00
Doll, Vargas, Grandpa & Grandma, Original Clothes & Chairs, Pair 200.00
Doll, Vogue, Miss Ginny, Original Clothes, 12 In. 35.00
Doll, Wanda The Magical Walking Doll, Hand-Painted, 18 In. 45.00
Doll, Wanda The Unaided Walking Doll, Sleep Eyes, Sides Pull Apart, 19 In. 70.00
Doll, Wax Over Pouty Mouth, Bulgy Blue Eyes, 18 In. 165.00
Doll, Wee Whimsies, Black Sambo 25.00
Doll, Wee Whimsies, Red Riding Hood 25.00
Doll, Whiskbroom, Flapper, German 25.00
Doll, Winker Boy, 1913, All Original 35.00
Doll, Wooden, Stack, Early 1900s, Pair 30.00
    Donald Duck, see Disneyana
    Doorstop, see Iron, Doorstop
Dorchester, Jug, Stopper, Blue Flowers, 5 In. 45.00
Dorchester, Plate, Blueberry Design, 8 In. 55.00
Dorchester, Sugar & Creamer, Scrolling On White Ground, Signed 32.50
Dorchester, Syrup, Pottery, Pinecone, Marked I.M.E.H.H., 6 In. 75.00
Dorchester, Vase, Pottery, Yellow, 8 In. 85.00

Doulton pottery and porcelain were made by Doulton & Co. of Burslem,
England, after 1882. The name Royal Doulton appeared on their wares after 1902.

Doulton, see also Royal Doulton

Doulton, **Biscuit Jar,** Burslem, Iris Outlined In Gold, Marked	225.00
Doulton, **Bowl,** Punch, Burslem, Hand-Painted, Signed, 6 X 14 In.Diameter	200.00
Doulton, **Clock,** Cased, Floral, Blue, Pink, Beige, 14 In.	175.00
Doulton, **Cookie Jar,** Burslem, Blue & White With Gilt	92.00
Doulton, **Cracker Jar,** Tapestry Birds & Flowers, 1872 Mark, Signed	160.00
Doulton, **Cup,** Loving, Burslem, 3 Handled, Lettering Spells Advice To Drinkers	150.00
Doulton, **Dish,** Burslem, Flowers, Signed C.Hart, 8 X 8 In.	71.00
Doulton, **Dish,** Vegetable, Covered, Burslem, 12 X 8 In.	30.00
Doulton, **Ewer,** Burslem, Cobalt Iris, Gold Trim, 8 1/2 In.	110.00
Doulton, **Ewer,** Burslem, Gold Outlines Flowers, Fish Handle, Signed, 16 In.	235.00
Doulton, **Figurine,** Mouse Group In Boat, Holding Bowls, Frog At Wheel, Signed	1600.00
Doulton, **Jar,** Covered, Fluted, Gold Scallops, Signed, Burslem, 4 1/2 X 6 In.	150.00
Doulton, **Jardiniere,** Slatters, Green Ground, Flowers, 8 1/4 X 9 1/2 In.	216.00
Doulton, **Jug,** Brown Glaze, Green Leaves, Purple Grapes, Lambeth, 6 1/4 In.	135.00
Doulton, **Jug,** Brown, Beige, Blue, Flowers, C.1880-91, Signed & Numbered, 9 In.	165.00
Doulton, **Jug,** Bulbous, Lambeth, Brown, Blue, Flowers, Pewter Top, C.1891, 8 In.	125.00
Doulton, **Jug,** Incised Goat, Leaf Wreath, Hannah Barlow, C.1872, 9 1/2 In.	420.00
Doulton, **Jug,** Lambeth, Classical Dieties, Logo, Marked, 5 In.	125.00
Doulton, **Jug,** Sea Shanty, Pictures & Songs Printed	97.50
Doulton, **Jug,** Whiskey, Raised Ship Design, Tan & Brown, Lambeth	30.00
Doulton, **Lamp,** Oil, Stoneware, Geometric Design, Oil Reservoir, C.1885, 9 In.	280.00
Doulton, **Mustard Pot,** Stoneware, Raised Design Of Gods, Silver Lid, 4 In.	45.00
Doulton, **Paperweight,** Cheshire Cat, Grinning, M.V.Marshall, 3 X 4 In.	150.00
Doulton, **Pitcher,** Ball Tilt, 80 Oz.	105.00
Doulton, **Pitcher,** Blue With Rust, Yellow Flowers, C.1900, 9 In.	70.00
Doulton, **Pitcher,** Bulbous, Impressed Leaves, Lambeth, 6 3/4 In.	95.00
Doulton, **Pitcher,** Burslem, Adelaide Pattern, 6 In.	60.00
Doulton, **Pitcher,** Burslem, Corset Shaped, Ye Old Crown & Sceptre, 8 3/4 In.	95.00
Doulton, **Pitcher,** Burslem, Floral Decoration, 8 In.Tall	95.00
Doulton, **Pitcher,** Burslem, Gold Handle & Mouth Interior, Signed, 8 In.	125.00
Doulton, **Pitcher,** Gold Handle, Brown Collar, Poppy Design, 1885 Mark, 12 In.	60.00
Doulton, **Pitcher,** Lambeth, Incised Brown Ground, Pearl Beading, C.1880, 6 In.	175.00
Doulton, **Pitcher,** Lambeth, Incised Design, Dated 1885, Signed, 6 3/4 In.	108.00
Doulton, **Pitcher,** Leatherware, C.1891, 11 3/4 X 21 In.	235.00
Doulton, **Pitcher,** Old Seadogs, 6 In.	60.00
Doulton, **Pitcher,** Pewter Lid, Flowers On Buff Lace Ground	75.00
Doulton, **Pitcher,** Pewter Lid, Orange & White Flowers, Signed, 8 1/4 In.	75.00
Doulton, **Pitcher,** Raised Decoration, Braided Handle, Impressed Mark	32.00
Doulton, **Pitcher,** Stoneware, Drinking Verse, 7 In.	85.00
Doulton, **Pitcher,** Syrup, Lambeth, 3 1/2 In.	77.50
Doulton, **Pitcher,** Tan Lace Ground, Pewter Lid, 8 1/4 In.	75.00
Doulton, **Pitcher,** Water, Watteau	125.00
Doulton, **Plate,** Burslem, Gaudy Orange & Blue, Mark, 10 In.	55.00
Doulton, **Plate,** Madras, 10 1/2 In.	30.00
Doulton, **Plate,** Melrose, Flow Blue, 9 In.	34.00
Doulton, **Punch Bowl,** Hand-Painted, Large Peonies, Signed, 6 1/2 X 14 In.	185.00
Doulton, **Sugar & Cream Jug,** Bayeux Tapestry, Marked, 2 1/4 X 2 1/4 In.	55.00
Doulton, **Tankard,** Three Musketeers, 6 In.	46.00
Doulton, **Tea Set,** Burslem, Pot, Sugar & Creamer, 2 Cups & Saucers	205.00
Doulton, **Teapot,** Burslem, Bulbous, Jacobean Flow Blue Pattern	145.00
Doulton, **Teapot,** Monk & Ladies, So Farther & Fare Worse, Beige & Blue	85.00
Doulton, **Tobacco Jar & Match Holder,** Signed & Dated 1885, 6 3/4 In.	285.00
Doulton, **Tumbler,** Leatherware, Sterling Rim, C.1891, 4 3/4 X 10 In.	75.00
Doulton, **Vase,** Bowling Pin Shaped, Enameling, Signed, 11 In., Pair	275.00
Doulton, **Vase,** Burslem, Gilt Handles, Beige Ground, Hand-Painted, 11 3/4 In.	121.00
Doulton, **Vase,** Burslem, Gilt Handles, Beige Ground, 5 3/4 In., Pair	84.00
Doulton, **Vase,** Burslem, Hand-Painted, Gold Trim, Signed, 18 1/2 In.	235.00
Doulton, **Vase,** Carrara Ware, Geometric Design, Hand-Painted, 7 1/2 In.	185.00
Doulton, **Vase,** Carrara, Pale Rose, Geometric Banding, Enameled, C.1889, Pair	185.00
Doulton, **Vase,** Cylindrical, Lambeth, 1871, Raised Foliate Border, 12 In.	325.00
Doulton, **Vase,** Earthenware, Handled, Signed, 6 1/2 In.	150.00
Doulton, **Vase,** Glossy Ground For Leaves & Branches, Marked, 10 1/8 In.	95.00
Doulton, **Vase,** Gold, Blue, 3 Handled & Footed, C.1891, Signed, 7 X 8 In.	175.00
Doulton, **Vase,** Lambeth, Scenic, Dated 1887, Blue Lining, 14 1/2 In., Pair	895.00
Doulton, **Vase,** Lambeth, 1884, Artist Signed, 9 In.	165.00

Doulton, Vase, No.1349, Lambeth Faience, 11 1/4 In. 98.00
Doulton, Vase, Persian Ware, Turquoise, Blue Band, Marked 210.00
Doulton, Vase, Purple Flowers, Impressed Mark & Word Ivory, 10 7/8 In. 145.00
Doulton, Vase, Spill, Mottled Blue, 11 In. 145.00
Doulton, Vase, Tapestry, Beige, Blue, Green, Gold, Flowers, C.1900, 10 In., Pair 250.00
    Dr.Syntax, see Adams, Staffordshire

*Dresden china is any china made in the town of Dresden, Germany. The
most famous factory in Dresden is the Meissen factory.*
Dresden, see also Meissen
Dresden, Basket, Floral, Vines As Handles, Lattice Allover, 1 1/2 X 4 In. 40.00
Dresden, Bell, Blue Background, Male & Female Subjects 225.00
Dresden, Bell, Dinner, Swags Of Purple Flowers, Gold Gilding, 4 1/2 In. 50.00
Dresden, Bowl, Scalloped, Hand-Painted, Lion Head Handles, 18 X 12 In. 250.00
Dresden, Bowl, 1700s Huntsman Scene, Oval, Footed, Snake Handles, 18 3/4 In. 400.00
Dresden, Box, Pierced Sides & Lid, Blue Flowers, Marked, 2 1/2 X 2 1/2 In. 68.00
Dresden, Butter Tub, Cover, Marked, 3 X 5 1/2 In. 45.00
Dresden, Cache Pot, White, Pink, 2 Kittens, Flowers, 7 X 8 1/2 In. 125.00
Dresden, Candlestick, Applied Flowers, Marked, 10 1/2 In., Pair 375.00
Dresden, Chocolate Set, Dresden Flowers, Signed 450.00
Dresden, Clock, White & Pink Flowers, Blue Mark 205.00
Dresden, Compote, Footed, Hand Decorated, 19th Century, 5 X 7 In.Diam. 50.00
Dresden, Compote, Footed, Pierced Rim, Marked, 5 X 6 1 /2 In. 75.00
Dresden, Cup & Saucer, Bouillon, Openwork, Hand-Painted Flowers, Set Of 4 .... 50.00
Dresden, Cup & Saucer, Demitasse, Canterbury Bells, Gold Trim, Marked 47.50
Dresden, Dish, Asparagus, Flowers & Gold Design 350.00
Dresden, Dish, Leaf Shape, Handled, Gold Rim, Eagle Mark, 11 X 8 1/2 In. 59.00
Dresden, Figurine, Angel, Sleeping On Red Cushion, 3 1/4 X 6 In. 85.00
Dresden, Figurine, Ballerina, No.13580, Blue Mark 75.00
Dresden, Figurine, Ballerina, No.2002, 3 1/2 In. 65.00
Dresden, Figurine, Boy Playing Flute, 2 Lambs & Goat At Side, 4 1/2 In. 210.00
Dresden, Figurine, Cherub, Playing Accordion, Gilt & Marble Base, 11 In. 195.00
Dresden, Figurine, Chinese Dog, Seated, Porcelain, 12 In. 300.00
Dresden, Figurine, Doe, Grazing, R Mark, 3 3/4 In. 79.00
Dresden, Figurine, Girl With Dog, Underglaze-Blue Crowned Mark, 9 1/2 In. 200.00
Dresden, Figurine, Lady At Her Toilet, Lace Clothing, Reds, 16 X 14 In. 850.00
Dresden, Figurine, Lady In Chair, Gent Standing, No.1050E 75.00
Dresden, Figurine, Macaws Perched On Tree Stump, Greenish Yellow, 7 In.Pair 260.00
Dresden, Figurine, Male & Female Dancers, Gold Mark 125.00
Dresden, Figurine, Napoleon, Riding Horse, 11 X 10 In. 385.00
Dresden, Figurine, Orchestra, White, Blue, Black, Red, Marked, 20 X 9 In. 950.00
Dresden, Figurine, Oriental Lady, Nodding Head, Gilded Clothing, 6 1/2 In. 290.00
Dresden, Figurine, Pug & Puppy, Mother Pug With Raised Paw, Nursing, 10 In. 290.00
Dresden, Figurine, Pug, Sitting, Collar Of Yellow Bells, 7 In., Pair 245.00
Dresden, Figurine, Skiers, White Glaze With Gold Trim, Art Deco, C.1925, Pair 350.00
Dresden, Figurine, Swimming Swans With Head Erect, 11 1/2 X 9 1/2 In. 450.00
Dresden, Figurine, Trumpet Swan, Swimming, Head Erect, 11 1/2 X 9 1/2 In. 225.00
Dresden, Figurine, Woman, Long Gown, Wolfhound, Made Into Lamp, 10 In. 300.00
Dresden, Figurine, Women Holding Flowers, Wolfhound, 10 X 10 In. 225.00
Dresden, Holder, Place Card, Crossed Sword, Set Of 12 .... 75.00
Dresden, Inkwell & Underplate, Blue Forget-Me-Nots, Signed, Germany 125.00
Dresden, Lamp, Boudoir, Painted Children, Silk Shade, Germany 250.00
Dresden, Letter Holder, Signed 65.00
Dresden, Mirror, Beveled, Flowers & Cherubs On Frame, 9 1/2 In. 300.00
Dresden, Pitcher, Pompadour Pink, Gilding, 10 In. 185.00
Dresden, Plaque, Bacchanal, H.G.Poetz, Signed, Framed, C.1800, 14 3/4 X 12 In. 3250.00
Dresden, Plaque, Young Maiden, Rectangular, Framed, C.1800, 12 1/2 X 8 In. 2250.00
Dresden, Plate, Bread & Butter, Floral Design, 5 7/8 In., Set Of 7 .... 140.00
Dresden, Plate, Cake, Scrolled Gold Border, 13 In. 65.00
Dresden, Plate, Pink, Signed With Klemm's 1869 Mark, 9 In. 65.00
Dresden, Plate, Reticulated, C.1885, 9 1/2 In.Square 125.00
Dresden, Plate, Scalloped, Open Work Border, Marked, 8 1/4 In.Diam., Pair 75.00
Dresden, Plate, Square Reticulated, C.1885, 9 1/2 In. 125.00
Dresden, Tea Set, Teapot, Creamer, Sugar, 4 Cups & Saucer, Plates, Marked 250.00

Duncan & Miller glass was made at the George A. Duncan and Sons Company in Washington, Pennsylvania. The company was started in 1894, with James E. Duncan, president, and Edwin C. Miller, secretary.

Duncan & Miller, **Ashtray,** Duck, Pair	12.00
Duncan & Miller, **Basket,** Canterbury, 9 X 10 1/4 In.	85.00
Duncan & Miller, **Basket,** Clear, Handled, 9 1/2 In.	22.00
Duncan & Miller, **Basket,** Cosmos Cut, 7 1/2 In.	25.00
Duncan & Miller, **Basket,** Handle, Scalloped Edge, Intaglio Cut, 12 1/4 In.	55.00
Duncan & Miller, **Berry Bowl,** Sylvan, Berries & Cream Divider, 11 1/2 In.	24.00
Duncan & Miller, **Bowl & Ladle,** Mayonnaise, Diamond	18.00
Duncan & Miller, **Bowl,** Canterbury, Fluted Sides, Wavy & Scalloped Top, Feet	35.00
Duncan & Miller, **Bowl,** Flared, Pink Opalescent, 10 In.	40.00
Duncan & Miller, **Bowl,** Fruit, Pink Opalescent, Shell Shape, 12 1/2 In.Diam.	65.00
Duncan & Miller, **Bowl,** Irregular Edge, Opalescent, 8 In.	30.00
Duncan & Miller, **Bowl,** Murano, Pink Opalescent, 10 In.	40.00
Duncan & Miller, **Bowl,** Murano, 11 1/4 In.Diameter	45.00
Duncan & Miller, **Bowl,** Salad, Sanibel, Yellow, Deep, 11 In.	60.00
Duncan & Miller, **Bowl,** Salad, Sapphire Blue, Shallow, 12 X 13 In.	35.00
Duncan & Miller, **Bowl,** Swan, Clear, 12 1/2 In.	20.00
Duncan & Miller, **Bowl,** Swan, Ruby Body, Clear Neck & Head, 7 1/2 X 5 1/4 In.	35.00
Duncan & Miller, **Bowl,** Swan, Ruby, 10 1/2 In.	40.00
Duncan & Miller, **Box,** Cigarette, Covered, Canterbury	18.00
Duncan & Miller, **Candelabra,** 5 Light, 50 Prisms, Sandwich, 16 X 13 In.	225.00
Duncan & Miller, **Candleholder,** American Way, Pair	10.00
Duncan & Miller, **Champagne,** Green	6.00
Duncan & Miller, **Champagne,** Stemmed, Dover, Ruby	10.00
Duncan & Miller, **Compote,** Canterbury, Vaseline, 5 1/2 In.	45.00
Duncan & Miller, **Compote,** Footed, Tepee, 7 X 8 In.	25.00
Duncan & Miller, **Cornucopia,** Blue Opalescent, Swirl Shape	75.00
Duncan & Miller, **Cornucopia,** Chartreuse	65.00
Duncan & Miller, **Cornucopia,** Clear, 14 In.	24.50
Duncan & Miller, **Cornucopia,** Lying Down, Pink Opalescent, 12 In.	100.00
Duncan & Miller, **Cornucopia,** 3 Feather, Floral Etching, Crystal	27.00
Duncan & Miller, **Cruet,** Crystal, Teardrop, Pair	25.00
Duncan & Miller, **Dish,** Divided, Sanibel, Pink Opalescent	22.00
Duncan & Miller, **Dish,** Divided, Teardrop Crystal	5.00
Duncan & Miller, **Dish,** Mayonnaise, Underplate, Canterbury	16.50
Duncan & Miller, **Dish,** Nut, 2 Compartment, Handled, 6 In.Diamter	6.00
Duncan & Miller, **Dish,** Pink Opalescent, Sylvan, 6 In.	12.00
Duncan & Miller, **Dish,** Relish, Canterbury Crystal	12.50
Duncan & Miller, **Dish,** Relish, 2 Compartment, Canterbury, 6 In.Diameter	30.00
Duncan & Miller, **Dish,** Relish, 2 Section, Sanibel, Blue	15.00
Duncan & Miller, **Dish,** Relish, 2 Section, Sanibel, Pink, 8 1/2 In.	15.00
Duncan & Miller, **Dish,** Sandwich, Handled, Puritan, Green	15.00
Duncan & Miller, **Glass,** Tom Collins, Etched Seahorse	12.50
Duncan & Miller, **Goblet,** Canterbury, Ball Stem	6.50
Duncan & Miller, **Goblet,** Canterbury, Short Stem	10.00
Duncan & Miller, **Goblet,** Caribbean, Blue, 8 Oz., Pair	18.00
Duncan & Miller, **Goblet,** Egg-In-Sand	24.50
Duncan & Milller, **Goblet,** First Love, 5 3/4 In.	12.00
Duncan & Miller, **Goblet,** Hobnail, Pink Opalescent	32.00
Duncan & Miller, **Goblet,** Paneled Long Jewels	19.50
Duncan & Miller, **Goblet,** Scroll With Flowers	24.50
Duncan & Miller, **Goblet,** Teardrop	16.50
Duncan & Miller, **Ivy Ball,** Hobnail, Green	30.00
Duncan & Miller, **Mayonnaise Set,** Teardrop, 3 Piece	12.50
Duncan & Miller, **Nappy,** Handled, Mardi Gras	15.00
Duncan & Miller, **Paperweight,** Duck	65.00
Duncan & Miller, **Pitcher,** Ice Lip, 60 Oz.	50.00
Duncan & Miller, **Plate,** Green, 6 In.	2.00
Duncan & Miller, **Plate,** Salad, Blue Opalescent, Sanibel	22.00
Duncan & Miller, **Plate,** Salad, Sanibel, Yellow, 8 In.	35.00
Duncan & Miller, **Rose Bowl,** Dawn	30.00
Duncan & Miller, **Shade,** No.42, 7 1/2 In.	22.50
Duncan & Miller, **Sherbet & Liner,** Canterbury, Chartreuse, 3 5/8 In.	20.00
Duncan & Miller, **Sugar & Creamer,** Canterbury	16.50

Duncan & Miller, Sugar, Canterbury, 3 1/4 In.	11.50
Duncan & Miller, Swan, Applied Clear Neck, Amber, 5 1/4 X 5 1/4 In.	15.50
Duncan & Miller, Swan, Avocado, 10 1/2 In.	40.00
Duncan & Miller, Swan, Black, Solid, 5 In.	25.00
Duncan & Miller, Swan, Blue Opalescent, 8 In.	45.00
Duncan & Miller, Swan, Clear Neck, Green, 5 1/4 X 5 1/4 In.	15.50
Duncan & Miller, Swan, Clear, 7 In.	9.00 To 21.00
Duncan & Miller, Swan, Clear, 7 1/2 In.	12.50
Duncan & Miller, Swan, Clear, 12 In.	20.00 To 21.00
Duncan & Miller, Swan, Crystal Neck, Dark Green Body, 10 1/2 In.	40.00
Duncan & Miller, Swan, Crystal Neck, Ruby Body, 7 In.	45.00
Duncan & Miller, Swan, Emerald Green, 12 In.	55.00
Duncan & Miller, Swan, Opalescent, Pink, 12 In. Wing Spread	135.00
Duncan & Miller, Swan, Red, Clear Neck, 11 1/2 X 9 1/2 In.	58.00
Duncan & Miller, Swan, Ruby, Clear Neck, 7 In.	38.00
Duncan & Miller, Swan, Ruby, 4 In.	65.00
Duncan & Miller, Swan, Ruby, 10 1/2 In.	60.00
Duncan & Miller, Swan, Ruby, 12 In.	95.00
Duncan & Miller, Swan, Smoke, 10 1/2 In.	60.00
Duncan & Miller, Swan, Sylvan, 7 In.	12.00
Duncan & Miller, Swan, Topaz, 7 In.	22.50
Duncan & Miller, Table Set, Butter, Spooner, Sugar & Creamer, Green, Gold	350.00
Duncan & Miller, Toothpick, Tepee	20.00
Duncan & Miller, Tray, Muffin, Sanibel, Blue, 13 In.	28.00
Duncan & Miller, Tray, Sanibel, Opalescent, Handled, Yellow, 13 X 9 1/4 In.	60.00
Duncan & Miller, Tray, 3 Section, Opalescent Blue, Sanibel, 14 In.	28.00
Duncan & Miller, Tumbler, Hobnail, Pink Opalescent	14.00
Duncan & Miller, Vase, Chartreuse, 8 1/2 In.	35.00
Duncan & Miller, Vase, Opalescent, Blue, 5 In.	15.00
Duncan & Miller, Vase, Tepee, 10 In.	20.00
Duncan & Miller, Vase, Trumpet, No.42, 8 In.	12.00

Durand glass was made by Victor Durand from 1879 to 1935 at several factories. Most of the iridescent Durand glass was made by Victor Durand, Jr., from 1912 to 1924 at the Durand Art Glass Works in Vineland, New Jersey.

Durand, Bowl, Acid Cutback, Floral, Signed, C.1925-32, 6 3/4 In. *Illus*	1000.00
Durand, Bowl, Footed, Spanish Yellow, Green Scalloped Rim, 5 1/4 X 2 1/2 In.	55.00
Durand, Bowl, Iridescent, Gold, 5 X 11 3/4 In.	450.00
Durand, Bowl, Spanish Yellow, Scalloped Rim, Footed, 2 1/2 X 5 1/4 In.Diam.	55.00
Durand, Candlestick, Orange Iridescent, Signed, 10 In.	175.00
Durand, Candy Dish, Blue Crackle Finish, Shallow, 7 3/4 In.	90.00
Durand, Compote, Blue & Gold, Signed, 4 In.Diameter	250.00
Durand, Compote, Underplate, 2 Layer Gold Iridescent Inside, Calcite	185.00
Durand, Lamp, Gold Aurene Interior, Egyptian Crackle, 17 In., Pair	800.00
Durand, Lamp, Gold Threading, Jade Butterfly Finial, Marked, 28 1/2 In.	450.00
Durand, Lamp, Iridescent Crackle Glass & Bronze, Bracket Feet, 10 1/2 In.	525.00
Durand, Lamp, Table, Threading, Colored Leaves, Metal & Marble Base, 27 In.	425.00
Durand, Night Light, Opalescent Shade In Silver Plated Base	275.00
Durand, Plate, Flashed Ruby, Opal Pulled Feather, Charles Link, 8 In.	395.00
Durand, Rose Bowl, Gold Luster Spider Webbing, Footed, 4 3/4 X 4 1/2 In.	675.00
Durand, Rose Bowl, Green Leaves, Cream Lining, Signed In Silver, 5 5/8 In.	725.00
Durand, Shade Set, Gold & Green Leaves, Gold Threading, Scalloped Base, 3	75.00
Durand, Shade, Crackle Glass, Gold, Green, C.1925-32, 3 1/4 In. *Illus*	150.00
Durand, Shade, Gold Spider Webbing, Gold Iridescent Ground, Pair	185.00
Durand, Shade, King Tut, Green On Orange, No.297, 6 1/2 In.	250.00
Durand, Vase, Beehive, Iridescent Peacock Blue, Signed & Numbered, 6 In.	750.00
Durand, Vase, Blue & Rainbow Iridescent, Signed, 10 In.	750.00
Durand, Vase, Blue Iridescent, Ovoid, Inscribed 1710-10, 1905-25, 10 1/4 In.	350.00
Durand, Vase, Blue Iridescent, Ruffled Rim, Signed, 9 In.High	375.00
Durand, Vase, Blue Iridescent, Signed, 12 1/2 X 25 In.Diameter	650.00
Durand, Vase, Blue Iridescent, Signed, 7 1/2 In.	335.00 To 350.00
Durand, Vase, Blue Iridescent, White, Hearts, Vines, 1905-25, 7 1/8 In.	350.00
Durand, Vase, Car, Tear Drop Form, Gold Threading, 8 In.	295.00
Durand, Vase, Embedded Threading On Opalescent, 8 In.	165.00
Durand, Vase, Gold & Pink Iridescent, Signed, No.1982-16, 16 1/2 In.	450.00

Durand, Bowl, Acid Cutback,
Floral, Signed, C.1925-32, 6 3/4 In.

Durand, Shade, Crackle Glass,
Gold, Green, C.1925-32, 3 1/4 In.

Durand, Vase, Gold Iridescent,
Threaded, Unsigned, 6 3/4 In.

Durand, Vase, Gold Calcite, Signed, 7 1/4 X 6 1/4 In.	750.00
Durand, Vase, Gold Iridescent, Threaded, Unsigned, 6 3/4 In. ....*Illus*	225.00
Durand, Vase, Iridescent Blue, Classic Shape, Signed, 6 3/4 In.	295.00
Durand, Vase, Iridescent Gold, Gold Threading, Signed, No.1710-4, 4 1/2 In.	385.00
Durand, Vase, Iridescent Gold, King Tut Pattern, Signed, 9 In.	900.00
Durand, Vase, Iridescent Gold, Signed & Numbered, Bulbous, 4 1/2 In.	340.00
Durand, Vase, King Tut, Gold & Green Design, Gold Inside, 8 In.	675.00
Durand, Vase, King Tut, Gold & White, Signed, 6 3/4 In.	465.00
Durand, Vase, King Tut, Green & Gold Iridescent, Pink & Blue, Signed, 7 In.	875.00
Durand, Vase, King Tut, Pontil Finished With V, Iridescent, 6 1/2 In.	325.00
Durand, Vase, Orange, Green Leaf & Vine, Signed, 8 X 8 In.	850.00
Durand, Vase, Sapphire Blue, Silver Feathering, Pewter Frame, 10 1/2 In.	625.00
Durand, Vase, Silver-Blue Iridescent, Signed, 4 X 6 In.	285.00
Durand, Vase, White Body, Hearts All Over, 1/2 Blue, 1/2 Gold, Signed, 8 In.	575.00
Elvis Presley, Bracelet, Charm, All Shook Up	12.00
Elvis Presley, Bracelet, 1956	10.00
Elvis Presley, Button, Flasher, Black & White	12.00
Elvis Presley, Card, Lobby, Movie, 11 X 18 In.	12.00
Elvis Presley, Card, Trade, 450	15.00
Elvis Presley, Cover, Pillow, Figural, Pair	21.00
Elvis Presley, Doll, Bisque Head & Hands, White Jump Suit, 24 In.	50.00
Elvis Presley, Necklace, 1956	10.00
Elvis Presley, Paperweight, 1971, Marble, 4 1/2 X 3 In.	18.00
Elvis Presley, Pencil, Set Of 12 Colors, Picture, Packaged In Cellophane	35.00
Elvis Presley, Picture, Movie Still, 8 X 10 In.	7.50 To 10.00
Elvis Presley, Postcard	5.00
Elvis Presley, Poster, Girls, Girls, Girls, 1960, 14 X 36 In.	65.00
Elvis Presley, Record, Sun, Baby Let's Play House, I'm Left, You're Right	250.00
Elvis Presley, Record, 45 Rpm, Sun	95.00
Elvis Presley, Scarf, Signed Las Vegas Hilton, Elvis Presley	35.00
Elvis Presley, Spoon, Demitasse, Gold Plated, 1960, With Picture	9.00
Elvis Presley, Tape Measure, Heart Shape	1.50
Elvis Presley, Tape Measure, Love Me Tender	10.00
Enamel Ware, see Graniteware	
Enamel, Austrian, Vase, Foliate Gold Scrolls, Castle Scene, Green, 16 1/2 In.	89.00
Enamel, Chinese, Box, Hinged Cover, C.1860, 3 1/2 X 3 X 1 1/2 In.	15.00
Enamel, Chinese, Box, Hinged, Enamel On Copper, 7 X 4 In.	85.00
Enamel, Chinese, Tray, Scene Of Crane In Pond	25.00
Enamel, English, Box, The Gift Of A Friend	125.00
Enamel, French, Box, Blue Lilacs, Lily Of The Valley, Brass Feet, Lid	76.00

Enamel, French, Cross, Mounted On Cream Colored Marble, 4 X 6 1/2 In.	175.00
Enamel, French, Dresser Box, Portrait On Lid	875.00
Enamel, French, Frame, Rococo, 9 1/2 X 5 In.	100.00
Enamel, Russian, see also Faberge	
Enamel, Russian, Bowl, Salt, Silver Gilt, 3 Ball Feet, I.Saltikov	300.00
Enamel, Russian, Case, Cigarette, Blue In Border Of Blue Beads, Maker GK	725.00
Enamel, Russian, Case, Cigarette, Gold Washed Interior, 3 1/2 X 21/2 In.	950.00
Enamel, Russian, Cup & Saucer, Floral Motifs, Scrolling, 4 Color, Maker A.N.	550.00
Enamel, Russian, Cup, Coronation	175.00
Enamel, Russian, Decanter, Rigarees & Steeple Stopper, Ruby Glass, Pair	125.00
Enamel, Russian, Handle, Umbrella Or Cane, Signed & Marked	950.00
Enamel, Russian, Kovsch, Maria Semenova, 5 1/2 In.	5650.00
Enamel, Russian, Pad, Writing, Maker TO, 3 In.	375.00
Enamel, Russian, Salt, Footed, Maker G.I.C.	250.00
Enamel, Russian, Salt, Master, Champleve, Maker AL	275.00
Enamel, Russian, Scoop, Seven Colors, Marked 84	1100.00
Enamel, Russian, Snuffbox, Niello, Hallmarked	315.00
Enamel, Russian, Spoon, Coffee, Moscow, 1885	125.00
Enamel, Russian, Spoon, Jelly, Marked A.K.	245.00
Enamel, Russian, Spoon, Serving, Gilded, Scene On Bowl, Maker AE, 7 In.	345.00
Enamel, Russian, Strainer, Tea, Multicolor & Floral Design	355.00
Enamel, Viennese, Box, Jewelry, Plaques All Around, 8 In.	2150.00
Enamel, Viennese, Ewer, Bronze Mount	550.00

End-of-day glass is now an out-of-fashion name for spattered glass. The glass was made of many bits and pieces of colored glass. Traditionally, the glass was made by workmen from the odds and ends left from the glass used during the day. Actually it was a deliberately manufactured product popular about 1880 to 1900, and some of it is still being made.

End-Of-Day, Basket, Clear Thorn Applied Handle, White Lining, 5 5/8 In.	125.00
End-Of-Day, Basket, Twisted Thorn Handle, 9 X 6 In.	115.00
End-Of-Day, Bowl, Black Inside, Colorful Outside, Cased, 7 X 3 In.	79.00
End-Of-Day, Bowl, Finger	22.50
End-Of-Day, Bowl, Flared, Collar Base, 11 In.Diameter	55.00
End-Of-Day, Bowl, Squatty, 6 In.Diameter	69.00
End-Of-Day, Cruet, Jug Shaped, Pink, Blue & Red	75.00
End-Of-Day, Cruet, Tortoiseshell Colors	95.00
End-Of-Day, Cruet, Yellow & Pink, Clear Trim	165.00
End-Of-Day, Dish, Butter, Covered, Ball Finial, Yellow Lining, 4 X 5 3/4 In.	70.00
End-Of-Day, Ewer, Applied Rib Handle	45.00
End-Of-Day, Lamp, Art Nouveau, Gold Plated, 6 1/2 In. Ball Shade, 1924	165.00
End-Of-Day, Pitcher, Pedestal, White Lining, Cylindrical Shape, 4 1/2 In.	45.00
End-Of-Day, Pitcher, White Lining, Bulbous, Clear Applied Handle, 6 In.	65.00
End-Of-Day, Shoe Boot, Applied Leaf	75.00
End-Of-Day, Sign, Marble, White, Green, Pink Center, 1 3/4 In.Diameter	135.00
End-Of-Day, Tumbler, Pink & Gold	25.00
End-Of-Day, Vase, Applied Rigaree Handles, 6 In.	22.00 To 25.00
End-Of-Day, Vase, Blue, White & Ruby Flecks, 5 In.	125.00
End-Of-Day, Vase, Bulbous, Quilted & Swirled, Fluted Top, 10 1/2 In., Pair	250.00
End-Of-Day, Vase, Burgundy Base, Applied White Opalescent Looping, 10 In.	38.50
End-Of-Day, Vase, Cased, Applied Feet, 8 In.	45.00
End-Of-Day, Vase, Clear Applied Handle, Amphora Shape, 6 3/4 In., Pair	150.00
End-Of-Day, Vase, Cranberry Lining, Millefiori Insets, 6 1/2 In.	85.00
End-Of-Day, Vase, Fluted Top, Pinched Base, Pontil, 8 1/2 In., Pair	95.00
End-Of-Day, Vase, Fluted, Bulbous, Pedestaled, Maroon, Yellow Green, Gold, 7 In.	50.00
End-Of-Day, Vase, Jack-In-The-Pulpit, White, Pink, Lavender, 8 In.	60.00
End-Of-Day, Vase, Jack-In-The-Pulpit, 7 1/2 In.	32.00
End-Of-Day, Vase, Metallic Flecks Inside, Cased, 12 In.	25.00
End-Of-Day, Vase, Purple & Multicolor, Pairpoint, 6 In.	38.00
ES Germany, Ashtray, 4 Card Suit, Pearlized, Gold Trim, Set Of 4	25.00
ES Germany, Basket, Fruit, Red Nosegays, Double Handled, 10 In.	75.00
ES Germany, Bowl, Summer Season, Portrait, Gold Iridescent, 11 1/2 In.	175.00
ES Germany, Bowl, 2 Handled, Hand-Painted, 7 1/2 X 6 1/2 In.Square	65.00
ES Germany, Candleholder, Hand-Painted Gold Flowers, Porcelain	15.00
ES Germany, Creamer, Birch Trees, Water, Boat	15.00
ES Germany, Dish, Butterfly Shaped, Flowers In Base Of Wings, 5 X 8 In., Mark	35.00

ES Germany, Dish, Windmill Scene, Handled, 7 In.	28.00
ES Germany, Hatpin Holder, Roses, Gold Trim	27.50
ES Germany, Plate, Cake, Roses, Prov Saxe, Handled	33.00
ES Germany, Plate, Irregular Edge, Gold Trim, Floral Center, 10 1/2 In.	80.00
ES Germany, Plate, Lady Pictorial, Green & Gold, 12 In.	85.00
ES Germany, Plate, Portrait, Indian, Left Hand Bear	40.00
ES Germany, Plate, Portrait, Marked, 11 1/2 In.	195.00
ES Germany, Vase, Birch Trees, Water, Boat Man, Handles, 8 In.	50.00
ES Germany, Vase, Classical Semi-Nudes Portrait, Burgundy, 4 Mark, 9 In.	225.00
ES Germany, Vase, Fox Hunt Scene, 8 In.	70.00
ES Germany, Vase, Mottled Colors On Silver, Marked, 8 In.	20.00
ES Germany, Vase, Portrait, Woman Holding Bird, 10 1/2 In.	125.00
ES Germany, Vase, Portrait, 2 Handled, Marked, 7 In.	195.00
ES Germany, Vase, Yellow Roses, Gold Garland Trim, Red Handles, 9 In.	40.00
ES Prussia, Celery, Orange Poppies	50.00
ES Prussia, Hatpin, Pink Roses	34.00
ES Prussia, Plate, Cream Flowers, Gold Trim, Signed, 8 1/2 In.	25.00
ES Prussia, Rose Bowl, Gold Trim, 12 In.	48.00
ES Prussia, Tray, Pin, Ivory Ground, Violets	35.00
ES Prussia, Vase, Figure Of Woman, Birds, Iridescent, Gold, 7 In.	65.00
Eskimo, Carving, Walrus Head, Soapstone	18.00
Eskimo, Kayak, Seal Skin, Skin Stretched Over Carved Frame, 8 In.	45.00
Eskimo, Knife, Antler Handle & Whalebone Blade	35.00
Etling, Vase, Frosted & Clear, Birds In Flight, Art Deco, Signed, 7 In.	95.00
Etling, Vase, Full Figure Nude Both Sides, Opalescent, Signed, 12 In.	450.00
Etruscan Majolica, see Majolica	

КФ Faberge was a firm of jewelers and goldsmiths founded in St. Petersburg, Russia, in 1842, by Gustav Faberge. Peter Carl Faberge, his son, was jeweler to the Russian Imperial Court from about 1870 to 1914.

Faberge, Cup, Vodka, Enamel, Signed, Dated 1885, 2 1/2 In.	575.00
Faberge, Figurine, Donkey, Blue-Gray Chalcedony, Standing, 3 1/2 X 3 1/4 In.	495.00
Faberge, Spoon, Serving, Silver	625.00
Faience, Bowl, Hand-Painted Fish, 9 In.Diameter	22.00
Faience, Charger, Yellow Dove Center, 18th Century, 12 In.	295.00
Faience, Inkwell, Flower Design	48.50
Faience, Jar, Drug, Blue & White, Savona, 18th Century, 8 3/8 In.	750.00
Faience, Jardinere, 2 Handle, Slip Painting, 4 3/4 X 9 X 20 In.	275.00
Faience, Jug, Pewter-Mounted, 18th Century, Austrian, 10 In.	575.00
Faience, Pitcher, Basket-Weave Pattern, Turquoise Leaves, Signed	35.00
Faience, Plaque, Yellow, Cobalt, Green, Cherubs, Pastoral Scene	150.00
Faience, Plate, Roses, Hand-Painted, Marked	35.00
Faience, Vase, Applied Coral & Yellow Roses, White Ground, Marked, 4 In.	125.00
Faience, Vase, Frosted Icicles Draped At Top, Signed, 14 1/2 X 4 1/2 In.	140.00
Faience, Vase, Rhododendron On Yellow & Gold, C.1882	185.00

Fairings are small souvenir china boxes sold at country fairs during the nineteenth century.

Fairing, Figurine, A Pastoral Visit By The Rev.Jones	97.50
Fairing, Going To Market	65.00
Fairing, Match Holder, Fresh Chestnuts Sir	85.00
Famille Rose, see Chinese Export	
Fan, see also Store, Fan	
Fan, Bamboo Spokes, Black Silk Covered, Cut Work	6.00
Fan, Bamboo, Refresh Yourself, , Made In China	20.00
Fan, Beaded Satin, Ormolu Bases, C.1800, English, 16 In.	150.00
Fan, Black Silk, Sequins, Carved Spokes, Hand-Painted, Box, 8 1/2 X 16 In.	65.00
Fan, Black Teak & Satin	12.00
Fan, Black, Silver Sticks, Black Silk With Silver Sequins, 12 In.	15.00
Fan, Brussels Lace, Mother-Of-Pearl Fingers, Original Box	70.00
Fan, Building Of International Exhibition, Philadelphia, 1876	55.00
Fan, Carved, Painted White, Pink Daisies, 23 In.	35.00
Fan, Child's, Folding, Depicts Children At Play, Victorian	16.00
Fan, Cloth, Hand-Painted Silver Flowers, Wooden Sticks, Opens To 13 1/2 In.	15.00
Fan, Colonial Couple, Painted, Black Carved Sticks, 21 In.	45.00

Fan, Dancing Girl On Border, Celluloid	10.00
Fan, Embroidered, Ivory Frame, Green, 1902	35.00
Fan, Folding, Advertising, Walter Baker Co., Baker Lady	29.50
Fan, Folding, Bissell's Carpet Sweeper	4.00
Fan, Goodyear, 1940s, Paper	6.00
Fan, Green Silk, Hand-Painted Flowers, Gold Wooden Sticks, Opens To 24 In.	25.00
Fan, Ivory Beige Lace, Painted Birds, 26 In.	25.00
Fan, Ivory Spokes, Flowers On Silk, 12 3/4 In.	65.00
Fan, Ivory, Gold Sequins, Lace Ruffle, 8 In.	25.00
Fan, Ivory, Spokes, Carved, White Silk, 4 Leaf Sequins, Lace Top	20.00
Fan, Mother-Of-Pearl Endsticks, Battenburg Lace, 8 1/2 X 17 In.	60.00
Fan, Mother-Of-Pearl, Gold & Silver Inlay, 2 Diamonds, C.1860, Boxed, Key	275.00
Fan, Moxie, 1925	10.00
Fan, Order Of Worship On Back, 1897	15.00
Fan, Painted, Ivory, Chinese Scenes, C.1850, 8 In.	250.00
Fan, Paper, Black, 14 X 35 In.	11.00
Fan, Paper, Colonial Scene, Opens To 20 In.	25.00
Fan, Peacock Feather, Ivory Handle, Green Silk Tassel	55.00
Fan, Peacock Feathered, Hand-Painted, Openwork Sticks, Opens To 18 In.	25.00
Fan, Pierce Work Wood, Hand-Painted	15.00
Fan, Pink Silk & Mother-Of-Pearl, Occupied Japan	55.00
Fan, Putnam Dyes	8.00
Fan, Red Satin, Hand-Painted Flowers, Wooden Sticks, Opens To 23 In.	25.00
Fan, Red Silk, 14 In.	30.00
Fan, Satin, Hand-Painted, Marabou Feathers, Carved Sticks, 23 In.Spread	95.00
Fan, Silk Roses, Hand-Painted, 9 In.	15.00
Fan, Silk, Dragons, Original Lacquer Box, Oriental, 15 In.	27.50
Fan, Silk, Ivory Spokes, 13 X 23 In.	15.00
Fan, Silk, Ivory Stays, Black Lacquered Case, 1800s, 16 In.	130.00
Fan, Silk, Scenic, 17 In.	40.00
Fan, Silk, Souvenir Of Missouri	5.00
Fan, Souvenir, Shelburne Grill	10.00
Fan, Tortoise Shell Sticks, Black Ostrich Feathers, 17 1/2 In.Spread	45.00
Fan, White Silk, Ivory Sticks, Opens To 18 In.	25.00
Fan, White Sticks, Paper, Painted Flowers, 15 In.	15.00

Fenton Art Glass Company, founded in Martins Ferry, Ohio, by Frank L.Fenton, is now located in Williamstown, West Virginia. It is noted for early carnival glass produced between 1907 and 1920. Many other types of glass were also made.

Fenton, Bonbon, Topaz, Lid	32.00
Fenton, Bowl, Holly, Ruffled, Blue, 8 In.	40.00
Fenton, Compote, Jefferson, Blue	125.00
Fenton, Cracker Jar, Imperial, Marigold	45.00
Fenton, Dish, Candy, Basket Weave, Iridescent	27.00
Fenton, Epergne, Blue Opalescent, 4 Piece	85.00
Fenton, Fruit Bowl, Celeste Blue, 7 1/2 In.	18.00
Fenton, Goblet, Lincoln Inn	12.00
Fenton, Jar, Candy, Stretch Glass, Velvarose, 1 Lb.	34.00
Fenton, Jardiniere, Dancing Lady, Hook Earred, Amber	75.00
Fenton, Lamp, Swing Hearts, Blue	175.00
Fenton, Lemonade Set, Vertical Stripes, Cobalt Handles, 6 Tumblers	325.00
Fenton, Plate, Celeste Blue, Collar Foot, 11 3/4 In.	22.50
Fenton, Plate, Custard, Bird & Flower, 9 1/4 In.	26.50
Fenton, Vase, Cased, Melon Ribbed, White Outside, Pink Inside, 8 In.	38.00
Fenton, Vase, Sheffield, Ruby With Amber Rim, 6 In.	22.00
Fenton, Water Set, Imperial, Blue	125.00

Fiesta dinnerware was introduced in 1936 by the Homer Laughlin China Co., redesigned in 1969, and withdrawn in 1973. The simple design was characterized by a band of concentric circles, beginning at the rim. Cups had full-circle handles until 1969, when partial-circle handles were made. Harlequin and Riviera were related wares.

Fiesta Ware, Ashtray, Medium Green	17.00
Fiesta Ware, Bowl, Fiesta Red, 9 1/2 In.	15.00
Fiesta Ware, Bowl, Medium Green, 4 3/4 In.	3.50

Fiesta Ware, Bowl, Medium Green, 5 1/2 In.	4.00
Fiesta Ware, Bowl, Medium Green, 8 1/2 In.	6.00
Fiesta Ware, Bowl, Soup, Yellow, 8 In.	6.00
Fiesta Ware, Bowl, Turquoise Blue, 5 1/2 In.	4.00
Fiesta Ware, Bowl, Yellow, 8 1/2 In.	6.00
Fiesta Ware, Canister, Ball Shape, Yellow	57.50
Fiesta Ware, Carafe, Green	35.00
Fiesta Ware, Casserole, Yellow, Covered, 8 1/2 In.	25.00
Fiesta Ware, Fork, Green	20.00
Fiesta Ware, Jug, Blue, 2 Pint	20.00
Fiesta Ware, Jug, Medium Green, 2 Pint	10.00
Fiesta Ware, Marmalade, Yellow	45.00
Fiesta Ware, Mixing Bowl, Green, Large	27.50
Fiesta Ware, Mug, Green	18.00
Fiesta Ware, Pitcher, Juice, Gray	32.50
Fiesta Ware, Plate, Medium Green, 6 In.	1.00
Fiesta Ware, Plate, Turquoise Blue, 12 In.	8.00
Fiesta Ware, Plate, Turquoise Blue, 15 In.	9.00
Fiesta Ware, Plate, Turquoise Blue, 6 In.	1.00
Fiesta Ware, Plate, Yellow, 6 In.	1.00
Fiesta Ware, Platter, Medium Green, Oval, 12 In.	6.75
Fiesta Ware, Relish, Fiesta Red	25.00
Fiesta Ware, Relish, Fiesta Red, Divided	40.00
Fiesta Ware, Saucer, Blue	.75
Fiesta Ware, Saucer, Medium Green	.75
Fiesta Ware, Saucer, Old Ivory	.75
Fiesta Ware, Saucer, Turquoise Blue	.75
Fiesta Ware, Seucer, Yellow	.75
Fiesta Ware, Teapot, Yellow	24.00
Fiesta Ware, Vase, Bud, Green	15.00

Findlay, or onyx, glass was made using three layers of glass. It was manufactured by the Dalzell Gilmore Leighton Company about 1889 in Findlay, Ohio. The silver, ruby, or black pattern was molded into the glass. The glass came in several colors, but was usually white or ruby.

Findlay Onyx, Bowl, Sugar, White Glass, Fluted Neck, Daisy Embossed Body	100.00
Findlay Onyx, Celery, White With Silver	220.00 To 350.00
Findlay Onyx, Spooner, 4 1/4 In.	395.00
Findlay Onyx, Sugar Shaker, Ivory	475.00
Findlay Onyx, Sugar Shaker, Platinum Trim, Original Top	650.00
Findlay Onyx, Tumbler	225.00
Fire, Andiron, Art Moderne, Joseph Urban, C.1935, Pair *Illus*	1200.00
Fire, Andiron, Black Youth, Iron, American, C.1800, 12 In., Pair	400.00
Fire, Andiron, Brass & Knife-Blade, New England, 1770-90, 24 1/2 In.	475.00
Fire, Andiron, Brass, R.Wittingham, New York, Signed, 1800s, 17 1/4 In., Pair	1500.00
Fire, Andiron, Bronze, Baroque, Flame Finials, Bracket Feet, 24 In., Pair	200.00
Fire, Andiron, Bronze, Rampant Lion, C.1800, 35 In., Pair	1200.00

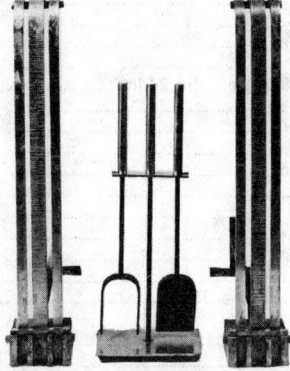

Fire, Andiron, Art Moderne,
Joseph Urban, C.1935, Pair

Fire, Andiron, Couchant Animal Feet, North Italy, 1600s, 46 1/2 In., Pair 5500.00
Fire, Andiron, Gilt Bronze, Fluted Column, Ionic Capital, 35 In., Pair 550.00
Fire, Andiron, Hessian Soldier, Marching, Iron, C.1800, 20 In., Pair 425.00
Fire, Andiron, New England, John Molineux, Boston, 18th Century, Pair 225.00
Fire, Andiron, Trivet & Tongs, Brass, Federal, Pair, C.1810, 18 In. 275.00
Fire, Andiron, Urn & Flame Finial, Fluted Columns, Claw Feet, 27 1/2 In. 175.00
Fire, Andiron, Wrought Iron, Loop Finial, 18th Century, 20 In. 150.00
Fire, Andirons, Bell Form Finial, Octagonal Standard, Arch Supports, Pair 200.00
Fire, Andirons, Brass Cannon Ball Finials, Pair 85.00
Fire, Andirons, Brass Figureheads, Baroque, Pair 450.00
Fire, Andirons, Brass, Boston, 17 X 18 1/2 In., Pair 325.00
Fire, Andirons, Brass, Screen, Dated 1919 .... 90.00
Fire, Andirons, Brass, Sheraton, Fluted, Pair 95.00
Fire, Andirons, Copper, Inlay Pair 350.00
Fire, Andirons, Figural, Black Man, Half Round, 19th Century, 18 1/2 In., Pair 1000.00
Fire, Andirons, Gooseneck, Arch Brass & Iron Trivet, Brass Jamb Hook, 5 Piece 400.00
Fire, Andirons, Iron, Gooseneck Ball Finial, 18th Century, 12 1/4 In. 195.00
Fire, Andirons, Iron, Gooseneck, 19 In.Log Rest, C.1850, 19 In.Tall 45.00
Fire, Bellows, Embossed Brass Ship On Wood, Leather Strap 15.00
Fire, Bellows, Wooden, Original Leather, C.1850 .... 36.00
Fire, Box, Alarm, Iron, Bronze Front, 2 3/4 X 4 1/4 In. 17.00
Fire, Box, Alarm, Telegraph, Iron 90.00
Fire, Bucket, Attentive David Dudley 1820, Clasped Hands, Red Ground 450.00
Fire, Bucket, H.B.Norton No. I., Leather 285.00
Fire, Bucket, Leather, Marked Engine No.17, Wooden Bottom, Handle 150.00
Fire, Bucket, Leather, Painted Black, Dated 1735, 10 In. 225.00
Fire, Bucket, Leather, Painted, Pair, C.1800, 12 1/4 In. 1100.00
Fire, Bucket, Waterproof Canvas, Folding Metal Frame, Bail Handle, Wood Grip 35.00
Fire, Chenets, Brass, Louis XV Style, Figural Form, C-Scrolls, 14 In., Pair 250.00
Fire, Crane, Brace, Wrought Iron, 31 In. 45.00
Fire, Crane, Forged, 29 In. 45.00
Fire, Extinguisher, Auto, Eagle 35.00
Fire, Extinguisher, Brass & Copper, Guardene 22.50
Fire, Extinguisher, Junior Firefighters, Fyr-Fyter, Iron Bracket, 18 In. 22.50
Fire, Extinguisher, La France, N.Y.C., R.R. 15.00
Fire, Extinguisher, Phoenix Dry Powder, 22 In. 10.00
Fire, Extinguisher, Pyrene, Brass 15.00
Fire, Extinguisher, Solid Copper, Polished & Lacquered 26.50
Fire, Extinguisher, Swan 20.00
Fire, Fender, Brass, Shelf Top, 47 1/2 X 12 X 6 In. 45.00
Fire, Fender, Bronze Mounted, Steel, 5 Feet, Tongs, Shovel, Poker 300.00
Fire, Fender, Ormolu, Napoleon III, Mid 19th Century, 9 3/4 X 72 In. 650.00
Fire, Fender, Pierced Brass, Lion's Paw Feet, 46 In. 225.00
Fire, Fender, Steel & Brass Trim, 33 X 9 In. 175.00
Fire, Fender, Wire, Federal, Brass Top, D-Shaped, C.1800, 49 1/2 In. 300.00
Fire, Fireback, Arched Crest, 3 Tulips, Iron, Dated 1794, 22 1/2 X 14 1/2 In. 400.00
Fire, Fireback, 2 Piece, Gothic Church Form, Whitehead & Law, 34 1/2 In. 1600.00
Fire, Fireplace Cover, Tin, Copper Wash, Art Nouveau 125.00
Fire, Fireplace Cover, Victorian, Art Nouveau, Tin, Copper Wash 100.00
Fire, Fork, Gargoyle, Brass, 18 In. 20.00
Fire, Heater, Gas, Economy Stove Company 795.00
Fire, Helmet, Captain P.F.D., Brass Eagle, Leather Liner 150.00
Fire, Horn, Funnel Shaped End, Brass Tweeter, Wooden Mouthpiece, Tin, 21 In. 35.00
Fire, Hose Wagon, 2 Wheel, 2 Men To Pull 300.00
Fire, Nozzle, Adaptor, Copper With Brass Couplings, 25 1/2 In. 65.00
Fire, Nozzle, Brass, Chrome Plated, 17 X 3 3/4 In.Diameter 60.00
Fire, Nozzle, Brass, Elkhart, Open & Close Handle, 8 1/2 In. 28.00
Fire, Nozzle, Brass, Elkhart, Spray Type, 5 1/2 In. 22.00
Fire, Nozzle, Eureka Co., 1800-90s, Brass, 12 1/2 In. 46.00
Fire, Nozzle, Fogger, Hand Hold Valve, Brass, Chrome Plated 45.00
Fire, Pull Cart, 2-Man Fire Hose, 4 Foot Wheels 625.00
Fire, Screen, Iron Base, Adjustable, Victorian, 61 In.Tall 195.00
Fire, Screen, Rosewood & Needlepoint, Victorian, Swiveling Frame, 38 In. 205.00
Fire, Stove, see Stove
Fire, Toaster, Hand Wrought, Rotating, Original 149.00
Fire, Tong, Hand-Wrought Iron, 14 In. 20.00

Fire, Tong, Hand-Wrought Iron, 18 In.	20.00
Fire, Tongs, Ember, Hand Wrought	16.00
Fire, Tongs, Faceted Ball, Pair	12.00
Fire, Trivet, Legs, Open-Work, Iron, 5 X 11 In.	30.00
Fire, Trivet, 10 In.Handle, 7 In.Ring, Three 5 In.Legs	90.00
Fire, Trumpet, Fireman's	450.00

Fireglow glass resembles English Bristol glass, But a reddish-brown color can be seen when the piece is held to the light. It is a form of art glass made by the Boston and Sandwich Glass Co.of Massachusetts, and other companies.

Fireglow, Vase, Autumn Leaves, Mt.Washington, 8 X 6 In.	95.00
Fireglow, Vase, Bud, Tan, Enameled Green Leaf & Orange Twig, 4 1/2 In.	45.00
Fireglow, Vase, Mauve Flowers, Blue, Green & Brown Leaves, 8 X 6 In.	95.00
Fireplace Tools, see Fire, Tongs, etc.	

Fischer porcelain was made in Herend, Hungary. The factory was founded in 1839, and has continued working into the twentieth century. The wares are sometimes referred to as Herend porcelain.

Fischer, Egg, Opens To Form Box, Gilt Trim, 4 1/2 X 3 In.Diameter	125.00
Fischer, Figurine, Sitting Cat, White Porcelain, Green Eyes, 4 1/2 In.	40.00
Fish Set, Platter, 6 Plates, 8 1/2 In., Gold Rim, Cobalt, France	275.00
Fish Set, Underwater Scene, 24 1/2 In.Platter, 8 Plates, Gravy Boat, Marked	400.00
Flag, see Textile, Flag	
Flash Gordon, Book, Witch Queen Of Mongo, Big, Little Book	20.00
Flash Gordon, Compass, Original Card	45.00
Flash Gordon, Compass, Wrist Band, Plastic & Vinyl, 1950s	20.00
Flash Gordon, Pistol	40.00 To 45.00
Flash Gordon, Pistol, Water	40.00 To 45.00
Flash Gordon, Puzzle, Inlaid, 1951, King Feature	56.00
Flash Gordon, Radio Pistol	40.00
Flash Gordon, Space Outfit, Watch, Belt, Glasses, On Card	26.00

Flow blue, or flo blue, was made in England about 1830 to 1900. The plates were printed with designs using a cobalt blue coloring. The color flowed from the design to the white plate so the finished plate had a smeared blue design. The plates were usually made of ironstone china.

Flow Blue, Berry Bowl, Athens, 5 In.	18.00
Flow Blue, Berry Bowl, Fairy Villas, 6 In.	20.00
Flow Blue, Biscuit Jar, Cover, Romance, Staffordshire	45.00
Flow Blue, Bone Dish, Gironde, W.H.Grindley	15.00
Flow Blue, Bowl, Cereal, Fairy Villas, 6 3/4 In.	24.00
Flow Blue, Bowl, Cereal, Lancaster, 7 X 2 In.	16.00
Flow Blue, Bowl, Conway, New Wharf Pottery, 9 In.	25.00
Flow Blue, Bowl, Conway, 9 In.	35.00
Flow Blue, Bowl, Covered, Oval, Devon, Burslem, England, 11 In.	65.00
Flow Blue, Bowl, Fairy Villas, 8 1/2 In.	40.00
Flow Blue, Bowl, Floral, Pagoda, 10 X 2 1/4 In.	42.00
Flow Blue, Bowl, Jenny Lind, 8 In.	65.00
Flow Blue, Bowl, Keswick, 9 X 12 X 1 3/4 In.	39.00
Flow Blue, Bowl, Kyber, Ribbed, 8 In.	80.00
Flow Blue, Bowl, Lotus, 11 X 8 1/2 In.	40.00
Flow Blue, Bowl, Lugano, Ridgway, 9 1/2 In.	22.50
Flow Blue, Bowl, Oval, Touraine, Alcock & Stanley, 8 1/2 In.	60.00
Flow Blue, Bowl, Regent, 9 In.	34.00
Flow Blue, Bowl, Vegetable, Belmont	25.00
Flow Blue, Bowl, Vegetable, Blue Rose	25.00
Flow Blue, Bowl, Vegetable, Covered, Iris	40.00
Flow Blue, Bowl, Vegetable, Covered, Ladas, Ridgway	50.00
Flow Blue, Bowl, Vegetable, Covered, Lakewood	80.00
Flow Blue, Bowl, Vegetable, Covered, Le Pavot	45.00
Flow Blue, Bowl, Vegetable, Covered, Oval, Lorraine	75.00
Flow Blue, Bowl, Vegetable, Covered, Pansy	65.00
Flow Blue, Bowl, Vegetable, Covered, Regent, 12 In.	47.50
Flow Blue, Bowl, Vegetable, Covered, Seville, 11 X 8 1/2 In.	75.00
Flow Blue, Bowl, Vegetable, Covered, Stanley, 9 X 6 1/2 In.	65.00
Flow Blue, Bowl, Vegetable, Covered, Vermont, 12 In.	65.00

Flow Blue, Bowl, Vegetable, Marie, 8 In. 25.00
Flow Blue, Bowl, Vegetable, Oblong, Melbourne 125.00
Flow Blue, Bowl, Vegetable, Oval, Covered, Florida, Grindley 75.00
Flow Blue, Bowl, Vegetable, Oval, Covered, Grenada, Alcock 75.00
Flow Blue, Bowl, Vegetable, Oval, Covered, Louise, New Wharf Pottery 75.00
Flow Blue, Bowl, Vegetable, Oval, Fleur-De-Lis, Meakin, 6 X 8 In. 30.00
Flow Blue, Bowl, Vegetable, Oval, Gironde, Grindley, 9 X 6 1/2 In. 35.00
Flow Blue, Bowl, Vegetable, Oval, Keswick, Wood, 9 X 11 In. 28.00
Flow Blue, Bowl, Vegetable, Oval, Pekin 38.00
Flow Blue, Bowl, Vegetable, Oval, Pelew, 9 In. 65.00
Flow Blue, Bowl, Vegetable, Oval, Regent, 9 In. 40.00
Flow Blue, Bowl, Vegetable, Pedestal, Covered, Tonquin, Heath 245.00
Flow Blue, Bowl, Vegetable, Round, Ayr, Corn, 8 1/2 In. 35.00
Flow Blue, Bowl, Vegetable, Round, Louis, New Wharf Pottery 32.00
Flow Blue, Bowl, Vegetable, Round, Osborne, Grindley, 9 In. 40.00
Flow Blue, Bowl, Vegetable, Round, Trilby, Wood 34.00
Flow Blue, Bowl, Vegetable, Round, Watteau, New Wharf Pottery 32.00
Flow Blue, Bowl, Vegetable, Scinde, 8 X 11 In. 135.00
Flow Blue, Bowl, Vegetable, Togo, 8 1/4 In. 24.00
Flow Blue, Bowl, Vegetable, Touraine, 9 1/4 In. 45.00
Flow Blue, Bowl, Vegetable, Touraine, 10 In. 45.00
Flow Blue, Bowl, Waste, Kyber 48.00
Flow Blue, Bowl, Waste, Touraine, Stanley 55.00
Flow Blue, Bowl, Watteau, 9 In. 40.00
Flow Blue, Butter Pat, Alhambra, Set Of 6 .... 35.00
Flow Blue, Butter Pat, Argyle 7.50
Flow Blue, Butter Pat, Argyle, Set Of 9 .... 90.00
Flow Blue, Butter Pat, Fairy Villas 15.00
Flow Blue, Butter Pat, Gironde, W.H.Grindley 10.00
Flow Blue, Butter Pat, Ideal, C.1891 .... 10.00
Flow Blue, Butter Pat, La Francaise, Set Of 4 .... 20.00
Flow Blue, Butter Pat, Marlborough, Grindley 12.00
Flow Blue, Butter Pat, Nonpareil, Set Of 3 .... 40.00
Flow Blue, Butter Pat, Touraine, Alcock & Stanley 15.00
Flow Blue, Butter, Covered, Elsie 125.00
Flow Blue, Butter, Covered, Grenada, Alcock 40.00
Flow Blue, Butter, Covered, Iris 65.00
Flow Blue, Butter, Covered, Regent, 8 In. 65.00
Flow Blue, Butter, Covered, Scinde, 7 3/4 X 3 In. 95.00
Flow Blue, Butter, Covered, Touraine, Stanley 100.00
Flow Blue, Butter, Covered, Willow 55.00
Flow Blue, Butter, Drainer, Temple 165.00
Flow Blue, Cake Stand, Cashmere, 5 X 9 In. 200.00
Flow Blue, Charger, La Belle, 13 In. 85.00
Flow Blue, Chocolate Pot, La Belle 75.00
Flow Blue, Creamer, Argyle 48.50
Flow Blue, Creamer, Cashmere 140.00
Flow Blue, Creamer, Chapeau, Hughes 135.00
Flow Blue, Creamer, Copper Luster, Red Decoration, Dahlia 50.00
Flow Blue, Creamer, Davenport, Wood & Sons, 3 1/4 In. 45.00
Flow Blue, Creamer, Eclipse, Johnson Brothers 45.00
Flow Blue, Creamer, Gironde, Grindley 25.00
Flow Blue, Creamer, Iris, A.Wilkinson, 4 In. 45.00
Flow Blue, Creamer, Ladas, Ridgway 25.00
Flow Blue, Creamer, Lobelia, Phillips 95.00
Flow Blue, Creamer, Louise, New Wharf Pottery 50.00
Flow Blue, Creamer, Pedestal, Geneva, New Wharf Pottery, 5 1/2 In. 50.00
Flow Blue, Creamer, Red, Green & Gold Overglaze, Japanese, C.1875 .... 55.00
Flow Blue, Creamer, Touraine, Stanley .... 65.00 To 75.00
Flow Blue, Creamer, Waldorf 65.00
Flow Blue, Cup & Saucer, Abbey 20.00
Flow Blue, Cup & Saucer, Argyle, Grindley .... 32.50 To 40.00
Flow Blue, Cup & Saucer, Ayr, Corn 5.00
Flow Blue, Cup & Saucer, Chocolate, Warwick Pansy, Set Of 5 .... 150.00
Flow Blue, Cup & Saucer, Coffee, Garland, Corn 25.00
Flow Blue, Cup & Saucer, Conway, New Wharf Pottery 40.00

Flow Blue, Cup & Saucer, Demitasse, Osborne, Ridgway	35.00
Flow Blue, Cup & Saucer, Demitasse, Watteau, Register Mark	25.00
Flow Blue, Cup & Saucer, Gironde, Grindley	25.00
Flow Blue, Cup & Saucer, Handleless, Athens	55.00
Flow Blue, Cup & Saucer, Handleless, Chusan	60.00
Flow Blue, Cup & Saucer, Handleless, Indian Jar	65.00
Flow Blue, Cup & Saucer, Handleless, Manilla, Podmore, Walker	62.00
Flow Blue, Cup & Saucer, Handleless, Pelew, Challinor	96.00
Flow Blue, Cup & Saucer, Handleless, Temple	58.00
Flow Blue, Cup & Saucer, Handleless, Temple, P.W. & Co., C.1850	86.50
Flow Blue, Cup & Saucer, Holland, Johnson	32.50
Flow Blue, Cup & Saucer, Iris	45.00
Flow Blue, Cup & Saucer, Nonpareil	38.00
Flow Blue, Cup & Saucer, Oriental, Ridgway, Set Of 8	300.00
Flow Blue, Cup & Saucer, Oriental, Ridgway, Set Of 6	300.00
Flow Blue, Cup & Saucer, Regout's Flower	35.00
Flow Blue, Cup & Saucer, Touraine	32.00 To 45.00
Flow Blue, Cup & Saucer, Touraine, Alcock	19.50
Flow Blue, Cup & Saucer, Waldorf	20.00 To 45.00
Flow Blue, Cup Plate, Amoy	35.00
Flow Blue, Cup Plate, California	25.00
Flow Blue, Cup Plate, Chusan	28.00
Flow Blue, Cup Plate, Gothic, Furnival	35.00
Flow Blue, Cup Plate, Indian Stone, Walley	38.00
Flow Blue, Cup Plate, Lobelia	28.00
Flow Blue, Cup Plate, Nankin	30.00 To 36.00
Flow Blue, Cup Plate, Rhone, Mayer	28.00 To 32.00
Flow Blue, Cup Plate, Scinde	45.00
Flow Blue, Cup Plate, Tivoli, Furnival	28.00 To 35.00
Flow Blue, Cup Plate, Troy, Meigh	38.00
Flow Blue, Cup, Custard, Handled, Covered, Buccleuch, C.1845, 3 3/4 In.	50.00
Flow Blue, Cup, Handleless, Amoy	40.00
Flow Blue, Dish, Cheese, Blue Rose	95.00
Flow Blue, Dish, Cheese, Covered, Verona	125.00
Flow Blue, Dish, Honey, Tivoli, T.Furnival, C.1845, 4 In.	38.00
Flow Blue, Ewer, Gold Neck & Handle, Pedestal Base, Peony, 8 1/2 X 6 In.	77.00
Flow Blue, Gravy Boat & Underplate, Grenada, Alcock	15.00
Flow Blue, Gravy Boat & Underplate, Kenworth, Johnson Bros.	65.00
Flow Blue, Gravy Boat & Underplate, Madras, Grindley	75.00
Flow Blue, Gravy Boat & Underplate, Melbourne, W.H.Grindley	75.00
Flow Blue, Gravy Boat & Underplate, Regent, 8 In.	55.00
Flow Blue, Gravy Boat & Underplate, Tokio, Johnson Bros.	52.00
Flow Blue, Gravy Boat & Underplate, Touraine	40.00
Flow Blue, Gravy Boat & Underplate, Versailles	65.00
Flow Blue, Gravy Boat & Underplate, Versailles, Furnival	65.00
Flow Blue, Gravy Boat, Albany	26.00
Flow Blue, Gravy Boat, Argyle, Grindley	42.00
Flow Blue, Gravy Boat, Clarissa	50.00
Flow Blue, Gravy Boat, Denton	30.00
Flow Blue, Gravy Boat, Denton, Grindley	30.00
Flow Blue, Gravy Boat, Duchess	30.00
Flow Blue, Gravy Boat, Iris	30.00
Flow Blue, Gravy Boat, Kyber	65.00
Flow Blue, Gravy Boat, Olympia	50.00
Flow Blue, Gravy Boat, Olympia, Grindley	40.00
Flow Blue, Gravy Boat, Ovando, A.Meakin	40.00
Flow Blue, Gravy Boat, Pedestal, Scinde, Alcock	138.00
Flow Blue, Gravy Boat, Royston, Johnson Bros.	35.00
Flow Blue, Gravy Boat, Seville	50.00
Flow Blue, Gravy Boat, Touraine, Stanley	65.00
Flow Blue, Gravy, Duchess, Grindley	30.00
Flow Blue, Holder, Toothbrush, Lily	38.00
Flow Blue, Jug, Hogburg, German, 2 Quart	125.00
Flow Blue, Mug, Pekin, T.Dimmock, C.1845, 3 1/4 X 3 1/2 In.	98.00
Flow Blue, Pitcher & Washbowl Set, Royal, F.Winkle	125.00
Flow Blue, Pitcher, Clarence, Grindley, 5 In.	45.00
Flow Blue, Pitcher, Cream, Bulbous Base, Baroque Handle, Regent, 6 In.	55.00

Flow Blue, Pitcher, Cream, Hong Kong, Charles Meigh, 5 In.	125.00
Flow Blue, Pitcher, Cream, Regent, Bulbous Base, Baroque Handle, 6 In.	55.00
Flow Blue, Pitcher, Milk, Chapoo, Wedgwood, 1 1/2 Quart	150.00
Flow Blue, Pitcher, Milk, Chapoo, 5 1/2 In.	135.00 To 165.00
Flow Blue, Pitcher, Milk, Nonpareil, 1 Quart	95.00
Flow Blue, Pitcher, Milk, Oriental, Ridgeway, 2 1/4 Quart	135.00
Flow Blue, Pitcher, Milk, Portman, Grindley, 5 1/2 In.	65.00
Flow Blue, Pitcher, Milk, Staffordshire, England, 7 In.	75.00
Flow Blue, Pitcher, Milk, Touraine, Stanley, 6 In.	135.00
Flow Blue, Pitcher, Portman, W.H.Grindley, 6 In.	55.00
Flow Blue, Pitcher, Serpent Handle, Willow, 14 In.	200.00
Flow Blue, Pitcher, Tulip, 7 1/2 In.	95.00
Flow Blue, Pitcher, Warwick, 8 In.	125.00
Flow Blue, Pitcher, Water, Linda, J.Maddock & Sons	85.00
Flow Blue, Plate, Alaska, 10 In.	45.00
Flow Blue, Plate, Amoy, Davenport, 7 1/4 In.	32.00
Flow Blue, Plate, Amoy, Davenport, 9 1/4 In.	40.00
Flow Blue, Plate, Amoy, 7 1/2 In.	26.00
Flow Blue, Plate, Amoy, 8 In.	25.00
Flow Blue, Plate, Amoy, 10 1/2 In.	60.00
Flow Blue, Plate, Amoy, 7 1/4 In.	35.00
Flow Blue, Plate, Arcadia, A.Wilkinson, 10 In.	30.00
Flow Blue, Plate, Argyle, Grindley, 10 In.	35.00
Flow Blue, Plate, Ashburton, Grindley, Artist Initialed, 10 In.	25.00
Flow Blue, Plate, Ashburton, 8 1/2 In.	18.00
Flow Blue, Plate, Athens, 10 1/2 In.	50.00
Flow Blue, Plate, Blue Rose, Grindley, 8 In.	18.00
Flow Blue, Plate, Blue Rose, W.H.Grindley, 8 In., Set Of 10	250.00
Flow Blue, Plate, Brunswick, New Wharf Pottery, 9 In.	18.50
Flow Blue, Plate, Burton, Grindley, Artist Initialed, 10 In.	25.00
Flow Blue, Plate, Cake, Chaing, C.1870, 10 In.	65.00
Flow Blue, Plate, Cake, Nonpariel	23.00
Flow Blue, Plate, Cecil, Till & Sons, 10 In.	35.00
Flow Blue, Plate, Celtic, 8 1/2 In.	15.00
Flow Blue, Plate, Chop, La Belle, 12 In.	85.00
Flow Blue, Plate, Conway, New Wharf Pottery, 9 In.	20.00
Flow Blue, Plate, Chen-Si, John Meir, C.1835, 7 1/2 In.	38.50
Flow Blue, Plate, Conway, New Wharf Pottery, 10 In.	30.00
Flow Blue, Plate, Cup, Rimmed, Fairy Villas II, Adams, 9 In., Set Of 5	100.00
Flow Blue, Plate, Del Monte, Johnson Bros., 9 In.	18.00
Flow Blue, Plate, Del Monte, 10 In.	22.50
Flow Blue, Plate, Denton, W.W.Grindley	13.00
Flow Blue, Plate, Duchess, 10 In.	21.00
Flow Blue, Plate, Dudley, Ford & Sons, 10 In.	15.00
Flow Blue, Plate, Dundee, 9 In.	22.00
Flow Blue, Plate, Fairy Villas, 7 In.	20.00
Flow Blue, Plate, Fairy Villas, 9 In.	25.00
Flow Blue, Plate, Fairy Villas, 10 In.	45.00
Flow Blue, Plate, Florida, Grindley, 9 In.	20.00
Flow Blue, Plate, Florida, Grindley, 10 In.	22.50 To 25.00
Flow Blue, Plate, Gironde, Grindley, 8 1/2 In.	17.00
Flow Blue, Plate, Gironde, Grindley, 9 In.	12.00 To 15.00
Flow Blue, Plate, Gironde, Grindley, 10 In.	15.00
Flow Blue, Plate, Gironde, Grindley, 8 In.	10.00
Flow Blue, Plate, Gothic, Furnival, 10 1/2 In.	32.00
Flow Blue, Plate, Gothic, 10 1/2 In.	50.00
Flow Blue, Plate, Grace, Grindley, 6 1/2 In.	15.00
Flow Blue, Plate, Hindostan, Maddock, 9 1/2 In., Pair	96.00
Flow Blue, Plate, Hofburg, Grindley, 10 In.	16.00
Flow Blue, Plate, Holland, Johnson, 9 In.	20.00
Flow Blue, Plate, Holland, 10 In.	23.00
Flow Blue, Plate, Hong Kong, C.1845, 10 1/4 In.	55.00
Flow Blue, Plate, Hong Kong, Charles Meigh, 8 1/4 In.Set Of 6	250.00
Flow Blue, Plate, Hong Kong, Charles Meigh, 9 1/4 In., Set Of 4	200.00
Flow Blue, Plate, Hong Kong, 9 In.	45.00
Flow Blue, Plate, Hong Kong, Meigh, 10 In.	55.00

Flow Blue, Plate, Hong Kong, 10 1/2 In.	45.00
Flow Blue, Plate, Iris, Royal Staffordshire Burslem, Round, 8 In.	7.00
Flow Blue, Plate, Jeddo, Brown, Westhead & Moore, 8 In.	15.00
Flow Blue, Plate, Kenworth, Johnson Bros., 7 In.	15.00
Flow Blue, Plate, Kenworth, Johnson Bros., 8 In.	17.00
Flow Blue, Plate, Kenworth, Johnson Bros., 9 In.	22.00
Flow Blue, Plate, Kyber, 6 In.	20.00
Flow Blue, Plate, Kyber, 8 In.	25.00
Flow Blue, Plate, Kyber, 9 In.	35.00
Flow Blue, Plate, Kyber, 10 In.	45.00
Flow Blue, Plate, Ladas, Ridgway, 8 In.	18.00
Flow Blue, Plate, Ladas, Ridgway, 9 In.	20.00
Flow Blue, Plate, Ladas, Ridgway, 10 In.	20.00
Flow Blue, Plate, Lancaster, 9 In.	19.00
Flow Blue, Plate, Le Pavot, Grindley, 10 In.	25.00
Flow Blue, Plate, Lobelia, C.1845, 9 1/2 In.	27.00
Flow Blue, Plate, Lucania, 9 In.	18.00
Flow Blue, Plate, Luncheon, Denton, W.W.Grindley	11.00
Flow Blue, Plate, Mandarin, C.1850, 8 In.	32.00
Flow Blue, Plate, Manhattan, Alcock, 7 3/4 In.	17.00
Flow Blue, Plate, Manilla, 9 1/2 In.	40.00 To 45.00
Flow Blue, Plate, Manilla, 10 1/4 In.	60.00
Flow Blue, Plate, Manilla, Podmore Walker & Company, 7 1/2 In.	32.00
Flow Blue, Plate, Marechal Niel, Grindley, 8 In.	17.00
Flow Blue, Plate, Melbourne, 7 In.	15.00
Flow Blue, Plate, Melbourne, 8 3/4 In.	20.00
Flow Blue, Plate, Melbourne, 10 In.	28.00
Flow Blue, Plate, Melrose, Doulton, 9 In.	26.00
Flow Blue, Plate, Melrose, Doulton, 10 In.	22.00
Flow Blue, Plate, Nonpareil, 7 3/4 In.	18.00
Flow Blue, Plate, Nonpareil, 9 3/4 In.	28.50
Flow Blue, Plate, Nonpariel, 10 1/4 In.	40.00
Flow Blue, Plate, Normandy, 10 In.	32.00
Flow Blue, Plate, Oregon, 9 1/2 In.	42.00
Flow Blue, Plate, Oriental, England, Beehive Mark, 8 3/4 In.	30.00
Flow Blue, Plate, Oriental, Ridgway, 8 1/4 In., Set Of 4	128.00
Flow Blue, Plate, Ormonde, Meakin, 9 In.	35.00
Flow Blue, Plate, Ormonde, 8 1/2 In.	32.00
Flow Blue, Plate, Osborne, Ridgway, 5 3/4 In.	12.00
Flow Blue, Plate, Osborne, Ridgway, 9 3/4 In.	25.00
Flow Blue, Plate, Persian, 7 In.	25.00
Flow Blue, Plate, Persian, 10 In.	25.00
Flow Blue, Plate, Pekin, Doulton, 10 1/2 In.	15.00
Flow Blue, Plate, Pekin, Doulton, 6 1/2 In.	8.00
Flow Blue, Plate, Pie, Conway, New Wharf Pottery, 6 In.	20.00
Flow Blue, Plate, Pie, Dundee, Ridgway	12.00
Flow Blue, Plate, Pie, Grace, 6 In.	20.00
Flow Blue, Plate, Pie, Normandy, 6 1/4 In.	15.00
Flow Blue, Plate, Pie, Osborne, Ridgway, 5 3/4 In.	12.00
Flow Blue, Plate, Progress, Grindley, 9 In.	18.00
Flow Blue, Plate, Progress, Grindley, 10 In.	20.00
Flow Blue, Plate, Raleigh, 9 In.	18.00
Flow Blue, Plate, Ruins, Copeland, Late Spode, Dated 9-15-1848	47.50
Flow Blue, Plate, Scalloped Edge, Portman, Grindley, 6 3/4 In., Set Of 4	55.00
Flow Blue, Plate, Scinde, Alcock, 10 1/2 In.	70.00
Flow Blue, Plate, Scinde, Alcock, 9 1/2 In., Set Of 6	360.00
Flow Blue, Plate, Scinde, 8 In.	24.00
Flow Blue, Plate, Scinde, 8 1/4 In.	40.00
Flow Blue, Plate, Scinde, 9 1/4 In.	50.00
Flow Blue, Plate, Scrolls, Flowers, C.1850-60, 10 In.	31.00
Flow Blue, Plate, Seville, Wood, 9 In., Set Of 4	75.00
Flow Blue, Plate, Shanghai, J.Furnival, 8 1/2 In.	42.00
Flow Blue, Plate, Shanghai, 10 1/4 In.	50.00
Flow Blue, Plate, Shapoo, 9 1/2 In.	50.00
Flow Blue, Plate, Shell, 10 In.	50.00
Flow Blue, Plate, Shusan, 10 In.	50.00

Flow Blue, Plate, Soup, Fairy Villas, 9 1/2 In. 25.00
Flow Blue, Plate, Syrian, Stanley, 7 1/2 In. 13.50
Flow Blue, Plate, Tea, Melrose, Doulton, C.1899, 7 1/4 In. 19.00
Flow Blue, Plate, Temple, Podmore Walker Company, 7 1/4 In. 37.00
Flow Blue, Plate, Temple, Podmore Walker Company, 7 1/4 In., Set Of 6 .... 250.00
Flow Blue, Plate, Temple, Podmore Walker Company, 9 1/2 In., Pair 75.00
Flow Blue, Plate, Temple, 10 In. 32.50
Flow Blue, Plate, Temple, 8 In. 35.00
Flow Blue, Plate, Temple, 9 3/4 In. 50.00
Flow Blue, Plate, Touraine 13.00
Flow Blue, Plate, Touraine, Alcock & Stanley, 6 1/2 In. 18.00
Flow Blue, Plate, Touraine, Alcock & Stanley, 8 1/4 In. 22.00
Flow Blue, Plate, Touraine, Alcock & Stanley, 9 In. 25.00
Flow Blue, Plate, Touraine, Alcock & Stanley, 10 In. 45.00
Flow Blue, Plate, Touraine, Alcock, 6 1/2 In. 18.00
Flow Blue, Plate, Touraine, Alcock, 8 3/4 In. 22.00
Flow Blue, Plate, Touraine, Alcock, 9 In. 22.00
Flow Blue, Plate, Touraine, Stanley, 10 In. 35.00
Flow Blue, Plate, Touraine, 9 In., Set Of 6 .... 150.00
Flow Blue, Plate, Trieste, Johnson Bros., 9 In., Set Of 4 .... 35.00
Flow Blue, Plate, Trilby, Compliments, Fuller Co., Mansfield, Mass., 10 In. 38.50
Flow Blue, Plate, Turkey, Doulton, C.1900, 10 In. 45.00
Flow Blue, Plate, Verona, 9 In. 25.00
Flow Blue, Plate, Vinranka, Sweden 22.00
Flow Blue, Plate, Waldorf 17.50
Flow Blue, Plate, Waldorf, Medallion Border, New Wharf Pottery, 10 In. 35.00
Flow Blue, Plate, Waldorf, New Wharf Pottery, England, 8 3/4 In. 20.00
Flow Blue, Plate, Waldorf, New Wharf Pottery, 8 In. 25.00
Flow Blue, Plate, Waldorf, 9 In. 10.00
Flow Blue, Plate, Watteau, Doulton, 8 1/2 In. 22.00
Flow Blue, Platter, Alexandria, C.1850, 17 X 13 In. 89.00
Flow Blue, Platter, Argyle, C.1891, 17 X 12 In. 95.00
Flow Blue, Platter, Argyle, 9 X 13 In. 45.00
Flow Blue, Platter, Astoria, New Wharf Pottery, 9 X 12 In. 40.00
Flow Blue, Platter, Beauties Of China, 14 In. 110.00
Flow Blue, Platter, Chapoo, 10 3/4 X 8 In. 95.00
Flow Blue, Platter, Chusan, W.Ridgway, C.1850, 16 3/4 X 13 In. 155.00
Flow Blue, Platter, Chusan, 16 In. 170.00
Flow Blue, Platter, Coburg, Edwards, 10 X 7 1/2 In. 170.00
Flow Blue, Platter, Coburg, Edwards, 15 X 12 In. 165.00
Flow Blue, Platter, Coburg, Edwards, 17 1/2 X 13 1/2 In. 140.00
Flow Blue, Platter, Coburg, 14 In. 95.00
Flow Blue, Platter, Conway, New Wharf Pottery, 10 1/2 X 8 In. 60.00
Flow Blue, Platter, Cut Corners, Scinde, 15 1/2 X 12 In. 190.00
Flow Blue, Platter, Del Monte, Johnson Bros. 30.00
Flow Blue, Platter, Etruscan, W.Ridgway, C.1850, 17 1/2 X 14 In. 180.00
Flow Blue, Platter, Florida, Grindley, 12 In. 30.00
Flow Blue, Platter, Florida, Grindley, 14 In. .... 45.00 To 55.00
Flow Blue, Platter, Gironde, Grindley, 12 In. 27.00
Flow Blue, Platter, Gironde, Grindley, 9 X 13 In. 35.00
Flow Blue, Platter, Holland, 11 X 14 1/2 In. 46.00
Flow Blue, Platter, Kyber, 12 In. 80.00
Flow Blue, Platter, Lorne, 14 X 10 1/2 In. 38.50
Flow Blue, Platter, Lozenge Shape, Waldorf, 10 1/2 X 8 In. 65.00
Flow Blue, Platter, Manila, 15 1/2 X 12 In. 150.00
Flow Blue, Platter, Manilla, R.Ridgway, C.1850, 22 X 17 1/2 In. 225.00
Flow Blue, Platter, Manilla, 15 1/2 X 12 In. 150.00
Flow Blue, Platter, Manilla, 16 In. 160.00
Flow Blue, Platter, Marechal Niel, 12 1/2 X 9 In. 25.00
Flow Blue, Platter, Morning Glory, 19 X 14 1/2 In. 85.00
Flow Blue, Platter, Nonpareil, Burgess & Leigh, 15 X 12 1/2 In. 110.00
Flow Blue, Platter, Nonpareil, Burgess & Leigh, 17 1/4 X 14 1/2 In. 185.00
Flow Blue, Platter, Normandy, 10 1/4 In. 35.00
Flow Blue, Platter, Octagonal, Rhone, 17 1/2 In. 140.00
Flow Blue, Platter, Octagonal, Kyber, 10 X 7 1/2 In. 65.00
Flow Blue, Platter, Oriental, Ridgway, 15 X 12 1/2 In. 100.00

Flow Blue, Platter, Ormonde, Meakin, 16 X 11 In.	85.00
Flow Blue, Platter, Oval, Agra, W.Ridgway, C.1850, 18 X 14 In.	95.00
Flow Blue, Platter, Oval, Ceylon, Furnival, 18 In.	150.00
Flow Blue, Platter, Oval, Kenworth, Johnson Bros., 12 3/4 X 9 3/4 In.	45.00
Flow Blue, Platter, Oval, Kenworth, Johnson Bros., 14 1/2 X 10 1/4 In.	65.00
Flow Blue, Platter, Oval, Keswick, 9 1/4 X 12 In.	35.00
Flow Blue, Platter, Oval, Le Pavot, Grindley, 15 X 10 1/2 In.	48.00
Flow Blue, Platter, Oval, Touraine, Stanley, 12 X 8 In.	35.00
Flow Blue, Platter, Oval, Verona, Meakin, 12 X 8 In.	16.00
Flow Blue, Platter, Peach, Johnson Bros., 12 1/2 X 9 1/2 In.	24.00 To 35.00
Flow Blue, Platter, Pheasant, Scalloped Rim, Signed, 14 1/2 In.	48.00
Flow Blue, Platter, Scinde, Alcock, 10 1/2 X 13 1/4 In.	125.00
Flow Blue, Platter, Scinde, 16 In.	110.00
Flow Blue, Platter, Segapore, W.Ridgway, C.1850, 18 X 13 1/2 In.	155.00
Flow Blue, Platter, Sobraon, C.1850, 16 X 12 In.	175.00
Flow Blue, Platter, Temple, 14 In.	120.00
Flow Blue, Platter, Tonquin, 12 1/2 X 9 1/2 In.	75.00
Flow Blue, Platter, Touraine, Alcock & Stanley, 12 1/2 In.	65.00
Flow Blue, Platter, Touraine, Stanley, 12 1/2 In.	55.00
Flow Blue, Platter, Touraine, 15 X 10 In.	40.00
Flow Blue, Platter, Vinranka, Sweden, 7 1/2 X 9 In.	22.00
Flow Blue, Platter, Waverly, 16 1/2 X 12 1/2 In.	57.00
Flow Blue, Platter, Well & Tree, Chinese, W.Ridgway, C.1850, 19 X 15 In.	350.00
Flow Blue, Platter, Well & Tree, Chinese, 19 X 15 In.	375.00
Flow Blue, Relish, Formosa	75.00
Flow Blue, Relish, Long Shell, Formosa, Mayer, 9 In.	110.00
Flow Blue, Relish, Manilla	85.00
Flow Blue, Relish, Scinde	55.00
Flow Blue, Relish, Shell-Shaped, Pagoda	65.00
Flow Blue, Relish, Shell, Shanghai, J.Furnival, 7 1/2 In.	95.00
Flow Blue, Sauce, Ashburton	15.00
Flow Blue, Sauce, Fairy Villas, 5 In.	15.00
Flow Blue, Sauce, Florida, Grindley, 5 In.	8.00
Flow Blue, Sauce, Gironde, Grindley	7.50
Flow Blue, Sauce, Lancaster	3.00
Flow Blue, Sauce, Malta, 6 In.	8.00
Flow Blue, Sauce, Raleigh	15.00
Flow Blue, Sauce, Raleigh, Burgess & Leigh	14.00
Flow Blue, Sauce, Richmond, Johnson Bros., C.1891	12.00
Flow Blue, Sauce, Scinde	38.00
Flow Blue, Sauce, Touraine, H.Alcock	15.00
Flow Blue, Sauce, Waldorf	8.00
Flow Blue, Server, Cake, Nonpareil	68.00
Flow Blue, Soup, Dish, Bentick	20.00
Flow Blue, Soup, Dish, Delft, 9 1/2 In.	18.00
Flow Blue, Soup, Dish, Fairy Villas	25.00
Flow Blue, Soup, Dish, Fairy Villas, Adams	40.00
Flow Blue, Soup, Dish, Fairy Villas, 9 1/2 In.	25.00
Flow Blue, Soup, Dish, Flange, Olympia	25.00
Flow Blue, Soup, Dish, Hong Kong	50.00
Flow Blue, Soup, Dish, Kyber, 9 In.	30.00
Flow Blue, Soup, Dish, Marechal Niel, Grindley, 9 In.	25.00
Flow Blue, Soup, Dish, Neil, Manilla, Rim, 10 In.	46.00
Flow Blue, Soup, Dish, Olympia, Grindley	20.00
Flow Blue, Soup, Dish, Progress, Grindley	15.00
Flow Blue, Soup, Dish, Scinde, Alcock, 10 1/2 In.	75.00
Flow Blue, Soup, Dish, Seville	18.00
Flow Blue, Soup, Dish, Touraine	25.00
Flow Blue, Soup, Dish, Touraine, Alcock & Stanley, 9 In.	30.00
Flow Blue, Soup, Dish, Virginia	20.00
Flow Blue, Soup, Osborne, Ridgways	20.00
Flow Blue, Soup, Virginia, Maddock	20.00
Flow Blue, Sugar & Creamer, Covered, Argyle	125.00
Flow Blue, Sugar & Creamer, Manhattan	115.00
Flow Blue, Sugar & Creamer, Marechal Niel	150.00
Flow Blue, Sugar Bowl, Covered, Touraine, Large	85.00

Flow Blue, Sugar, Covered, Baltic 45.00
Flow Blue, Sugar, Covered, Coburg, Edwards, 5 3/4 In. 125.00
Flow Blue, Sugar, Covered, Gironde, Grindley 35.00
Flow Blue, Sugar, Covered, Gothic 95.00
Flow Blue, Sugar, Covered, Manilla, Podmore, Walker 145.00
Flow Blue, Sugar, Covered, Oregon, Mayer 145.00
Flow Blue, Sugar, Covered, Tonquin 165.00
Flow Blue, Sugar, Eglantine 65.00
Flow Blue, Sugar, Florida, Grindley 65.00
Flow Blue, Sugar, Holland, Johnson 65.00
Flow Blue, Sugar, Olympia, Grindley 35.00
Flow Blue, Sugar, Scinde, Alcock 95.00
Flow Blue, Sugar, Touraine, Alcock & Stanley 95.00
Flow Blue, Syrup, Candia, Melon Ribbed, Pewter Top, Cauldon 95.00
Flow Blue, Teapot, Amoy 225.00
Flow Blue, Teapot, Atalanta 135.00
Flow Blue, Teapot, Chapoo 295.00
Flow Blue, Teapot, Creamer & Covered Sugar Bowl, Gothic 350.00
Flow Blue, Teapot, Indian 195.00
Flow Blue, Teapot, Lahore 260.00
Flow Blue, Teapot, Manilla 250.00
Flow Blue, Teapot, Persian Moss 160.00
Flow Blue, Teapot, Touraine, Alcock 185.00
Flow Blue, Toothbrush, Oregon 26.00
Flow Blue, Tray, Bread, Oval, Conway, 10 1/2 X 8 In. 45.00
Flow Blue, Tureen & Tray, Vermont 350.00
Flow Blue, Tureen, Open, Scinde, 13 In. 75.00
Flow Blue, Tureen, Soup, Rectangle, Oriental, Ridgway, 2 1/2 Quarts 165.00
Flow Blue, Tureen, Vegetable, Covered, Touraine, 12 X 7 1/2 In. 65.00
Flow Blue, Vase, Spill, Cattle Groups, W.Adams & Sons, 6 1/2 X 3 In. 35.00
Flow Blue, Vegetable, Covered, Ashburton 75.00
Flow Blue, Vegetable, Covered, Bolingbroke 75.00
Flow Blue, Vegetable, Covered, Chiswick 75.00
Flow Blue, Vegetable, Covered, English Views 55.00
Flow Blue, Vegetable, Covered, Keele, Grindley, C.1891 .... 75.00
Flow Blue, Vegetable, Covered, Marguerite, Grindley 26.00
Flow Blue, Vegetable, Covered, Oval, Grenada, Alcock 55.00
Flow Blue, Vegetable, Persian Moss 25.00
Flow Blue, Washbowl & Pitcher, Adams, Pitcher, 13 In., Bowl, 16 1/2 In. 495.00
Flow Blue, Washbowl & Pitcher, Regal, Bowl, 16 In., Pitcher, 13 In. 425.00

*Foo dogs are mythical Chinese figures, part dog and part lion. They were
made of pottery, porcelain, carved stone, and wood.*

Foo Dog, Chinese, 10 In., Pair 450.00
Foo Dog, Porcelain, Brown Base, Gold & Green, 1920s, 14 1/2 In. 110.00
Foo Dog, Porcelain, Drip Glaze, Gray, Black & Green, 7 In. 45.00
Foo Dog, Temple Dogs, Male & Female, Tans, Greens & Yellows, 17 In. 535.00

FOSTORIA *Fostoria glass was made in Fostoria, Ohio, from 1887 to 1891. The factory
was moved to Moundsville, West Virginia, and most of the glass seen in
shops today is a twentieth-century product.*

 Fostoria, see also Milk Glass

Fostoria, Bookends, Rearing Horses 35.00
Fostoria, Bowl, Console, American Pattern, 10 In.Diameter 20.00
Fostoria, Bowl, Console, Pink, Ruffled, Rolled Edge 16.00
Fostoria, Bowl, Fruit, Pressed Leaf, Signed, Ruby 85.00
Fostoria, Bowl, Punch, Glass Ladle, Early American, 13 In. 43.00
Fostoria, Bowl, Versailles, Green, 5 In. 5.00
Fostoria, Cake Stand, Square, American Lady 35.00
Fostoria, Candleholder, Matching Console Bowl, Versaille, Green, 5 In. 50.00
Fostoria, Candleholder, American, 2 Light, Pair 35.00
Fostoria, Candleholder, Etched Roses, Crystal, 12 In. 50.00
Fostoria, Candleholder, June, Yellow, 2 In., Pair 22.00
Fostoria, Candleholder, Navaire, Clear, Etched 15.00
Fostoria, Candleholder, Purple Iridescent, Label, 3 1/2 In. 32.00
Fostoria, Candlestick, June, Blue, Pair 25.00

Fostoria, Candlestick, Squatty, Versailles, Topaz	15.00
Fostoria, Centerpiece, Dish & 2 Candleholder Dishes, Pink, Star Fish Shape	90.00
Fostoria, Champagne, Tall Stem, Mulberry	10.00
Fostoria, Cocktail, June	12.00
Fostoria, Compote, Baroque, Blue, 5 In.	12.00
Fostoria, Compote, Grape Brocade, Green, 7 In.	25.00
Fostoria, Compote, Orange Top, Iridescent Stem, 9 In.	25.00
Fostoria, Compote, Royal, Green, 6 In.	25.00
Fostoria, Creamer, Fairfax, Green, 3 3/4 In.	5.50
Fostoria, Cup & Saucer, Versailles, Pink	14.00
Fostoria, Cup, Baroque, Yellow	4.00
Fostoria, Dish, Relish, Divided, Versailles, Amber, 8 3/4 In.	14.00
Fostoria, Figurine, Colt, Lying Down, 2 1/4 X 2 3/4 In., Pair	42.00
Fostoria, Figurine, Colt, Standing, 3 7/8 X 2 1/2 In., Pair	42.00
Fostoria, Figurine, Deer, Standing, 4 1/2 X 2 In., Pair	42.00
Fostoria, Figurine, Mermaid, 10 In.	65.00
Fostoria, Figurine, Pelican, 4 X 4 1/2 In., Pair	65.00
Fostoria, Figurine, Penguin	40.00
Fostoria, Figurine, Rabbit, Green, Small	10.00
Fostoria, Figurine, Squirrel, Blue	15.00
Fostoria, Figurine, Squirrel, Rectangular Base	40.00
Fostoria, Goblet, Leaf & Dart	18.00
Fostoria, Goblet, Mikado Fan	18.00
Fostoria, Goblet, Mulberry	12.00
Fostoria, Goblet, Pan Dewdrop	16.00
Fostoria, Goblet, Vernon, Green	14.00
Fostoria, Ice Bucket, Chintz, No.2496	25.00
Fostoria, Ice Bucket, Versailles, Topaz	25.00
Fostoria, Jug, Syrup, Victoria, Frosted & Clear	65.00
Fostoria, Plate, Cake, Trogan, Yellow, 12 1/4 In.	12.00
Fostoria, Plate, Sweetmeat, Baroque, Blue	10.00
Fostoria, Plate, Versailles, Pink, 9 1/2 In.	10.00
Fostoria, Plate, Versailles, 10 1/2 In.	10.00
Fostoria, Relish, American Pattern, & Compartment, 10 In.	10.00
Fostoria, Rose Bowl, American Pattern	14.00
Fostoria, Shade, Gold & Green, Opalescent Zipper, Gold Lining, Ruffled Edge	125.00
Fostoria, Shade, Gold Crisscrossing, Gold Lining, Ruffled Bottom	70.00
Fostoria, Sherbet, Baroque, Crystal	3.50
Fostoria, Sherbet, June, Clear	12.00
Fostoria, Sherbet, Pink, Etched, Green Base, Set Of 6	25.00
Fostoria, Soup, Cream, Versailles	10.00
Fostoria, Sugar & Creamer, American, Pink, Individual	12.00
Fostoria, Sugar & Creamer, June	22.00
Fostoria, Sugar & Creamer, Shirley	14.00
Fostoria, Sugar, Fairfax, Amber, 3 1/8 In.	5.50
Fostoria, Toothpick, Rosby, No.1704	20.00
Fostoria, Tumbler, Stemmed, Versailles, 9 Ounce, Set Of 6	90.00
Fostoria, Tumbler, Vernon Orchid, 5 1/2 In., Set Of 3	15.00
Fostoria, Vase, American, Crystal, Square Footed, 6 1/2 In.	20.00
Fostoria, Vase, Baroque, Blue, 8 In.	12.00

Foval, see Fry Foval
Frame, see Furniture, Frame

Francisware is an amber hobnail glassware made by Hobbs Brockunier and Company, Wheeling, West Virginia, in the 1880s.

Francisware, Bowl, Master Berry, Unfrosted, 7 In.Square	50.00
Francisware, Dish, Butter, Swirl, Frost With Amber	70.00
Francisware, Lemonade Set, Pitcher, Cloverleaf Tray, Waste Bowl, 2 Tumblers	375.00
Francisware, Match Holder, Frosted, Amber Top	58.75
Francisware, Pitcher, Frosted, 8 1/2 In.	125.00
Francisware, Pitcher, Water, Swirl	195.00
Francisware, Sauce, 4 In.Square	16.00
Francisware, Spooner, Swirl	65.00
Francisware, Sugar, Covered, Frosted Swirl	50.00
Francisware, Tumbler, Frosted, Stained Amber Rim	38.00
Francisware, Water Set, Child's Pitcher, 4 Tumblers	325.00

Francisware, Water Set, 5 Tumblers, Honeycomb, 8 Piece 225.00
Francisware, Water Set, 7 Piece 375.00

*Frankoma Pottery was originally known as The Frank Potteries when
John F. Frank opened shop in 1933. The factory is now working in
Sapulpa, Oklahoma.*
Frankoma, Boot, Red, 4 1/4 In. 12.00
Frankoma, Bowl & Candlesticks, Green & Brown, Set 18.00
Frankoma, Candlestick, Double, Brown & White 7.50
Frankoma, Casserole, Covered, Wagon Wheel 12.00
Frankoma, Console Set, 3 Piece, Green & Brown 18.00
Frankoma, Cookie Jar, Blue, Large 14.00
Frankoma, Creamer, Marked, Red Ware, Wagon Wheel 8.50
Frankoma, Pitcher, Art Deco 12.00
Frankoma, Plate, Cherokee Alphabet, 2 Indian Heads, Set Of 3 .... 25.00
Frankoma, Plate, Dealer's Sign, Brown 25.00
Frankoma, Plate, Signers Of Declaration Of Independence, 1973 .... 10.00
Frankoma, Vase, Brown & Green, 8 In. 8.50
Frankoma, Vase, Pillow, Silver Overlay 75.00
Frankoma, Vase, Sea Shell, Black, Pair 17.50
Frankoma, Vase, 2-Handled, Rose, 11 In. 22.50
Fruit Jar, see Bottle, Fruit Jar

*Fry glass was made by the famous H.C.Fry Glass Company of
Rochester, Pennsylvania. It includes cut glass, but the famous Fry glass
today is the foval, or pearl, art glass. This is an opal ware decorated with
colored trim. It was made from 1922 to 1933.*
Fry, see also Cut Glass
Fry Foval, Beverage Set, Covered Pitcher, 4 Handled Mugs, Applied Handle 245.00
Fry Foval, Bowl, Swirl Stripes, 5 X 6 In. 49.00
Fry Foval, Candlestick, Blue Threading & Trim, 12 In. 125.00
Fry Foval, Candlestick, Blue Threading, 10 1/2 In., Pair 150.00
Fry Foval, Candlestick, Looped Festoons, Pearl Base, 12 In., Pair 275.00
Fry Foval, Candlestick, Twisted Stem, Blue Trim, 12 In., Pair 250.00
Fry Foval, Candlestick, White Opalescent, 2 Green Rings, 10 In., Pair 250.00
Fry Foval, Casserole, Trivet, Lid 30.00
Fry Foval, Compote, Blue Trim, 11 1/2 In.Diameter 125.00
Fry Foval, Compote, Delft Blue Stem & Rim, 5 X 9 3/4 In. 155.00
Fry Foval, Compote, Jade Stem, Sterling On Rim & Foot, 5 X 9 In.Diameter 225.00
Fry Foval, Compote, Silver Overlay & Green Stem, 7 In. 175.00
Fry Foval, Creamer, Blue Opaline 45.00
Fry Foval, Cup & Saucer, Applied Pearl Glass Handles 95.00
Fry Foval, Cup & Saucer, Delft Handle 38.00
Fry Foval, Glass, Iced Tea, Green Handles 50.00
Fry Foval, Lemonade Set, Covered Pitcher, 6 Glasses, Applied Cobalt Handles 275.00
Fry Foval, Mug, Opalescent Green, Striped, Applied Cobalt Handles, 4 3/4 In. 40.00
Fry Foval, Pitcher, Bee-Hive Shape, Applied Handle, Signed, 7 In. 155.00
Fry Foval, Pitcher, Cream, Opalescent, Gold Handle, 3 1/4 In. 55.00
Fry Foval, Pitcher, Lemonade, Green Handles, Four Tumblers 300.00
Fry Foval, Pitcher, Lemonade, Vaseline Opalescent Stripes, Cobalt Handle 135.00
Fry Foval, Pitcher, Pearl Glass, Blue Finial & Handle, Covered, 12 In. 249.00
Fry Foval, Plate, Cake, Green Ball Feet, Green Handles, 10 In. 185.00
Fry Foval, Sugar & Creamer, Cobalt Handles 150.00
Fry Foval, Tea Set, White Opalescent Pot, 6 Cups, Green Handles & Saucers 585.00
Fry Foval, Teapot, Attached Silver, Tea Infuser, Glass 130.00
Fry Foval, Teapot, 6 Cups & Saucers, Opaline, Jade Handle & Spout 350.00
Fry Foval, Toothpick Holder, Scalloped Rim, 2 Blue Handles 67.25
Fry Foval, Tumble-Up, Opalescent Stripe, Green 75.00
Fry Foval, Tumbler, Cone, Blue 50.00
Fry Foval, Tumbler, Frosted Yellow Crackle, Amber Base, Set Of 6 .... 60.00
Fry Foval, Tumbler, Lemonade, Blue Handle, Green Opalescent 27.50
Fry Foval, Vase, Blue Loops & Blue Top Band, 9 1/2 In. 225.00
Fry Foval, Vase, Clear Crackle, 3 Applied Black Leaves, 12 In. 70.00
Fry Foval, Vase, Opalescent, Green Drag Loop & Rim, Cylinder Shaped, 8 In. 145.00
Fry Foval, Vase, Pink, Cobalt Handles, 7 1/2 In. 150.00
Fry Foval, Vase, Sweet Pea, Delft Blue Expanded Base, Rolled Rim, 5 In. 185.00

Fry, Bowl, Turned Down Rim, Half Moons & Miter, Signed, 10 In.Diameter	175.00
Fry, Casserole, Covered, Metal Frame	20.00
Fry, Compote, Hobstars, Diamond, Fan, Honeycomb, Signed, 12 In.	350.00
Fry, Cookie Jar, Glass Tops, Flashed Stars, Fans, Prisms, Signed, 7 In., Pair	1000.00
Fry, Cup, Custard, Opalescent Ovenware, Dated 1927, Signed, Set Of 6	35.00
Fry, Dish, Divided, Ovenware, 7 X 10 1/2 In.	12.50
Fry, Jar, Cigar, Freedom, Signed	475.00
Fry, Juicer, Orange, Fluted, Glass	10.00
Fry, Nappy, Venice, Signed, 6 In.	45.00
Fry, Reamer, Opalescent, 6 1/2 In.	15.00
Fry, Vase, Intaglio Flowers, Harvard Band, Corset Shape, Signed, 10 In.	135.00
Fry, Water Set, Intaglio Floral Design, 4 Tumblers, Signed, 10 In.	235.00

Fulper is the mark used by the American Pottery Company of Flemington, New Jersey. The art pottery was made from 1910 to 1929. The firm had been making bottles, jugs, and housewares from 1805. Doll heads were made about 1928. The firm became Stangl Pottery in 1929.

Fulper, see also Doll

Fulper, Basket, Pink Outside, Moss Inside, Signed, 6 1/2 In.	75.00
Fulper, Bookend, Figural, Egyptian Lion Mask, Green Glaze	50.00
Fulper, Bowl, Blue Flambe & Dark Blue, 10 1/2 In.	32.00
Fulper, Bowl, Blue Matte Incised Exterior, Crystalline Interior, 10 1/2 In.	40.00
Fulper, Bowl, Centerpiece, Silver Crystals Among Green Satin Glaze, 11 In.	45.00
Fulper, Bowl, Curled-In Top, Blue Flambe, White Matte, Signed, 5 X 12 In.	90.00
Fulper, Bowl, Eggshell Rose Outside, Iridescent Glaze, 6 X 1 3/4 In.	30.00
Fulper, Bowl, Green Crystalline Glaze, Stamped, C.1914, 2 3/4 X 10 1/2 In.	150.00
Fulper, Bowl, Scalloped Edge, Yellow & Green, Raised Mark, 11 In.	45.00
Fulper, Bowl, 10 Sided, Flambe Glaze, Black Mark, 1915, 8 3/4 X 2 1/2 In.	96.00
Fulper, Bowl, 2 Handles, Crystalline Finish, Marked, 12 X 6 1/2 X 3 1/4 In.	75.00
Fulper, Box, Powder, Art Deco Lady	55.00
Fulper, Candlestick, Blue Glossy & Matte Glaze, 4 X 5 1/2 In.Diameter, Pair	58.00
Fulper, Candlestick, Handled, Purple & Blue, Paper Label, Pair	55.00
Fulper, Candlestick, Molded Fruit & Leaves, Pair	12.00
Fulper, Flower Frog, Seated Nude, Turtles Around, Marked, 6 1/4 In.	32.00

Fulper, Jar, Flaring Rim, Handled, C.1910-30, Pair

Fulper, Jar, Flaring Rim, Handled, C.1910-30, Pair ....*Illus*	350.00
Fulper, Lamp, Base & Shade Signed, 15 Pieces Leaded Glass In Shade, 18 In.	2700.00
Fulper, Lamp, Perfume, Ballerina, Signed	85.00 To 145.00
Fulper, Pitcher, Coil Design, Signed, 4 Cup	49.00
Fulper, Vase, Beehive, Handles, Blue Crystals, 9 In.	70.00
Fulper, Vase, Black Drip Over Green, 3 3/4 In.	40.00
Fulper, Vase, Blue Crystalline Glaze, Applied Handles, C.1914, 10 1/2 In.	400.00
Fulper, Vase, Bud, Footed, Metallic Brown, 9 In.	35.00
Fulper, Vase, Bud, Mottled Beige Streaking, Footed, 9 In.	36.00
Fulper, Vase, Bud, Mustard, Brown Drippings, Signed, 8 In.	22.00
Fulper, Vase, Crystalline, 3 Handles, Blue, 6 3/4 In.	40.00
Fulper, Vase, Drip-Blue Glaze, Handled, 5 In.	14.00
Fulper, Vase, Fan Shaped, Art Deco Design, Signed, 3 1/2 X 6 X 2 3/4 In.	55.00
Fulper, Vase, Fan, Footed, Side Handled, Crystalline, 8 X 6 1/2 In.	75.00
Fulper, Vase, Green Matte Glaze, Impressed Mark, 11 1/2 In.	40.00
Fulper, Vase, Green, Mauve & Lavender, 2 Handled, 8 In.	44.00
Fulper, Vase, Handled, Horizontal Ribs, Rose Glaze, 6 In.	28.00
Fulper, Vase, Mythological Dragon Climbing Down Neck, 8 In.	250.00
Fulper, Vase, Snowdrops, Rust & Cream Flambe, 8 In.	38.00
Fulper, Vase, Urn Type, Mottled Green, Paper Label, 12 X 8 In.	45.00
Fulper, Vase, 2 Handled, Coiled Body, Gunmetal Splotches, Signed, 9 In.	115.00

Furniture, Armchair, Charles II Style

Furniture, Armchair, Chinese, Lacquered, Landscape, Scrollwork

Furniture, Armchair, Oak, Carolean Style, Pair

Furniture, Armchair, High Back, Carolean Style, Pair

Furniture, Armchair, Papier-Mache & Lacquer, Victorian, Pair

Furniture, Armchair, Walnut, George II, English, Arms Later

Furniture, Armchair, Walnut, George III, Adjustable, 1800s

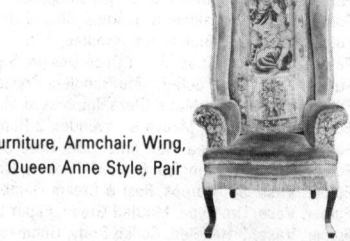

Furniture, Armchair, Wing, Queen Anne Style, Pair

Fulper, Vase, 4 Sided, Red Matte Glaze, 8 1/2 In. 24.00
Furniture, Armchair, Bannister Back, 18th Century 1500.00
Furniture, Armchair, Black & Green Painted Wood, Continental, Pair 1500.00
Furniture, Armchair, Bow Back Windsor, Carved Knuckle Arms 975.00
Furniture, Armchair, Bow Back, Windsor, Simple Carved Knuckle Arms 975.00
Furniture, Armchair, Bow Back, 7 Turned Spindles, Molded Seat, Ring Turn Legs 450.00
Furniture, Armchair, Brace Back, Windsor, C.1795, Black & Brown Striping 1100.00
Furniture, Armchair, Carved Oak, Rush Ladder Back, 12 In. 125.00
Furniture, Armchair, Charles II Style .... Illus   420.00
Furniture, Armchair, Child's, Windsor, Painted, New England, C.1790 .... 1300.00
Furniture, Armchair, Chinese, Huang Huali, Caned Seat, 1600-1700, Pair 6500.00
Furniture, Armchair, Chinese, Lacquered, Landscape, Scrollwork .... Illus   650.00
Furniture, Armchair, Chinese, Painted Back Panel, Fretwork, 1800s, Pair 2000.00
Furniture, Armchair, Chippendale, Blue-Green, Quebec 2750.00
Furniture, Armchair, Chippendale, Carved Mahogany, Philadelphia, 1760-80 .... 1600.00
Furniture, Armchair, Corner, Carved Oak, Continental, Oak Leaf Splats, 1700s 600.00
Furniture, Armchair, Curved Crestrail, 7 Turned Spindles, Incised Seat 100.00
Furniture, Armchair, Federal, C.1800, Scrolled Splat, Central Flowerhead 200.00
Furniture, Armchair, Gentleman's, Laminated Rosewood, Victorian, Carved Legs 1000.00
Furniture, Armchair, Gustav Stickley, Oak 165.00
Furniture, Armchair, Hand Carved Fruitwood Frame, 1900s 590.00
Furniture, Armchair, High Back, Carolean Style, Pair .... Illus   800.00
Furniture, Armchair, Mahogany, Federal, Robert Carter, C.1790, Pair 2700.00
Furniture, Armchair, Mahogany, George II, Drop-In Seat, 1700s 600.00
Furniture, Armchair, Mahogany, Georgian, Cabriole Legs, Claw & Ball Feet 450.00
Furniture, Armchair, Mahogany, Lyre Form, Turned Spindles In Arms, 1900s 175.00
Furniture, Armchair, Oak & Ash, Ladder-Back, Rush Seat, Baluster Legs 650.00
Furniture, Armchair, Oak, Carolean Style, Pair .... Illus   500.00
Furniture, Armchair, Open, Library, Mahogany, Late 1850s 775.00
Furniture, Armchair, Papier-Mache & Lacquer, Victorian, Pair .... Illus   2000.00
Furniture, Armchair, Queen Anne, Ladder Back, Turned Posts, Ring Turned Legs 400.00
Furniture, Armchair, Rosewood, Carved & Laminated, New York, C.1840-50 .... 2000.00
Furniture, Armchair, Rosewood, Manner Of Charles Baudovune, New York, 1800s 7000.00
Furniture, Armchair, Sheraton, Cane Seat, Black Paint 170.00
Furniture, Armchair, Shield Back, Flowerheads, Square Tapered Legs, Silk Seat 4500.00
Furniture, Armchair, Stickley Bros., Grand Rapids 95.00
Furniture, Armchair, Theater, Brass 250.00
Furniture, Armchair, Walnut, George II, English, Arms Later .... Illus   1200.00
Furniture, Armchair, Walnut, George III, Adjustable, 1800s .... Illus   400.00
Furniture, Armchair, Walnut, Rococo, Victorian, C.1850, 22 X 26 X 38 In. 400.00
Furniture, Armchair, Walnut, Victorian, Fruit Crest, C.1860 .... 120.00
Furniture, Armchair, Windsor, Painted, Fan-Back, New England, C.1700 .... 1000.00
Furniture, Armchair, Windsor, Turned & Painted, Connecticut, C.1790 .... 2100.00
Furniture, Armchair, Wing, Queen Anne Style, Pair .... Illus   850.00
Furniture, Armchair, Wing, Walnut, Queen Anne, Arched Cresting, Pad Feet 2750.00
Furniture, Armoire, Bamboo & Maplewood, Louis Philippe, 1830s, 92 X 41 In. 800.00
Furniture, Armoire, Bamboo, Cane & Lacquer, Mirrored Door, Drawer, 72 In. 800.00
Furniture, Armoire, Carved, 2 Mirrored Doors, 104 X 60 In. 750.00
Furniture, Armoire, Golden Oak, 72 In. 750.00
Furniture, Armoire, Oval, Beveled Mirrors, English 195.00
Furniture, Armoire, Provincial Carved Oak, Louis XV, C.1750, 88 X 63 In. 2200.00
Furniture, Armoire, Red, Gold, Lacquer, Rectangular, C.1800s, 72 X 39 1/2 In. 2500.00
Furniture, Armoire, Walnut, 85 X 59 X 21 In. 500.00
Furniture, Back Bar & Bar, Oak, Victorian, 5 Mirrors, 14 X 18 Feet 3500.00
Furniture, Back Bar & Columns, Large Mirror, 20 Ft.Long 900.00
Furniture, Back Bar & Columns, 4 Leaded Windows, Marble Top, 12 Ft.Long 5500.00
Furniture, Back Bar & Front, Mirrors, Columns On Each Side, Oak, 18 Ft.Long 900.00
Furniture, Back Bar, Art Deco, 9 Feet 500.00
Furniture, Back Bar, Barber, 3 Stations, Hat & Coat Rack, Koch Chairs 5000.00
Furniture, Back Bar, Barber's, Mirrors, 1880s 800.00
Furniture, Back Bar, Brass Hinges, Doors, Mahogany, 12 Ft.Long 600.00
Furniture, Back Bar, Mirror Top, Oak, Shelves, 8 X 6 Feet 1000.00
Furniture, Back Bar, Oak Turnings & Carvings, 2 Mirrors, 12 Feet 750.00
Furniture, Back Bar, 8 Section, Leaded Glass Door, 40 Drawers, 10 Feet 5000.00
Furniture, Banquette, Provincial Carved Oak, Louis XV, 56 In. 875.00
Furniture, Basket, Plant, Oak Pedestal, Wood Bottom, 8 1/2 X 7 In.Diameter 27.50

Furniture, Basket, Toiletries, Baby's, White Wicker, 1914 .... 15.00
Furniture, Bed Steps, English Mahogany & Pine, Sheraton 145.00
Furniture, Bed, Baby, Brass 225.00
Furniture, Bed, Canopy, Cherry Finish, C.1815, 84 X 4 1/4 In. 950.00
Furniture, Bed, Carved Walnut, 1/2 Testor 1850.00
Furniture, Bed, Child's, Mahogany, Oak, 4 Post, Tester, 1800s, 67 X 64 In. 450.00
Furniture, Bed, Chinese, Figural Panels, Canopy, Lacquered Frame, 88 X 88 In. 3400.00
Furniture, Bed, Day, Chinese, Rectangular, Fretwork, Silk Cushions, 31 In. 1700.00
Furniture, Bed, Day, Mahogany, Queen Anne Style, Cabriole Legs, 68 In. 350.00
Furniture, Bed, Double, Solid Brass 1000.00
Furniture, Bed, Eastlake Style, Oak, High Headboard 800.00
Furniture, Bed, Four-Post, Elizabethan Style, Canopy Frame .... Illus 3800.00
Furniture, Bed, Four-Post, Hepplewhite, C.1790, Curtains & Spread 1000.00
Furniture, Bed, Four-Post, Mahogany, Tapering Square Posts, C.1850 .... 100.00
Furniture, Bed, Four Post, Pineapple Finials, Acanthus Carved Posts 450.00
Furniture, Bed, Four-Post, Rope, Cherry 500.00
Furniture, Bed, Full Size, Brass 325.00
Furniture, Bed, Hand-Carved, Crotch Walnut, Gold Leaf Trim, Double 2000.00
Furniture, Bed, Hired Man's, Red Paint, 66 Inside Rails, 39 In. 175.00
Furniture, Bed, Iron, Brass Finials & Roundels, Black, 1800s, 54 In. 200.00
Furniture, Bed, Mahogany, American, Empire, 1800s, 43 X 60 In. 125.00
Furniture, Bed, Mahogany, Four-Post, Victorian, Rope & Leaf Motifs, 1800, 94 In. 3000.00
Furniture, Bed, Mahogany, Neoclassical Style, Inlaid, Single, Pair 400.00
Furniture, Bed, Mahogany, Rope Twist Finials, Tear Drops, C.1850 .... 1250.00
Furniture, Bed, Maple, Acorn Posts, 3/4 Size 525.00
Furniture, Bed, Nickle-Plated Brass, French, C.1800, Double 800.00
Furniture, Bed, Poster, Sheraton, Canopy Frame, Maple & Pine, C.1810 .... 1375.00
Furniture, Bed, Poster, Tiger Maple, Cherry Head & Foot Board, C.1815, 6 Ft. 2750.00
Furniture, Bed, Rope, Cherry 400.00
Furniture, Bed, Rope, Cream Paint, C.1820 .... 265.00
Furniture, Bed, Rope, Hired Man's, Curly Maple, C.1820, 41 3/4 X 82 In. 850.00
Furniture, Bed, Shaker Type, Low Poster, Painted 285.00
Furniture, Bed, Spool Turned, Single, 19th Century 100.00
Furniture, Bed, Tester, Sheraton, Spiral Reeded Posts 1100.00
Furniture, Bed, Trundle, Maple 150.00
Furniture, Bed, Walnut, C Scrolls & Grapes, Victorian, C.1860, Double, 70 In. 725.00
Furniture, Bedroom Set, Art Deco, Bed, Dresser, Chairs, 1920s 899.00
Furniture, Bedroom Set, Bed, Marble Step-Down Dresser, Walnut Finish 1595.00
Furniture, Bedroom Set, Bed, Mirrored Bureau, Half Commode, Marble Top 1400.00
Furniture, Bedroom Set, Burl Trim, Marble Tops, Carved, 9 Feet, 4 Piece 5000.00
Furniture, Bedroom Set, Eastlake, Walnut 850.00
Furniture, Bedroom Set, Headboard, Marble Top Dresser & Washstand, Oak 3500.00
Furniture, Bedroom Set, Victorian, Renaissance, Bed & Dresser .... Illus 2250.00
Furniture, Bedroom Set, Victorian, Renaissance, Bed & Dresser .... Illus 5250.00
Furniture, Bedroom Set, Walnut, New Orleans, 1870s, 3 Piece .... Illus 1500.00
Furniture, Bedroom Set, 8 Ft., Headboard, Marble Top Dresser, Beveled Mirror 3500.00
Furniture, Bedroom Suite, Art Moderne, Altman, N.Y., 7 Piece .... Illus 1700.00
Furniture, Bench, Bucket 165.00
Furniture, Bench, Cobbler's, Pine, American, 50 In. 130.00
Furniture, Bench, Lawn, Cast Iron, C.1860 .... 150.00
Furniture, Bench, Painted & Decorated, Pine, Pennsylvania, 1800s, 6 Ft. 800.00
Furniture, Bench, Park, Wooden, Green 4.00
Furniture, Bench, Pine, Red Paint, 15 1/2 X 44 X 21 In. 40.00
Furniture, Bench, Pine, Whittled Oak Legs, 49 1/2 X 13 X 25 In. 45.00
Furniture, Bench, Settle, Spindle Back, Turned Legs, Shaped Arms, 84 In. 235.00
Furniture, Bench, Shoe-Shine, Amish, 5 Feet 75.00
Furniture, Bench, Two-Seater, Folding, Hardwood, Contoured Back & Seat 25.00
Furniture, Bench, Upholstered Top, Chrome Supports, Stretchers, 19 In. 700.00
Furniture, Bench, Water 150.00
Furniture, Bench, Water, Pine, C.1850 .... 425.00
Furniture, Bergeres A La Reine, Gilt Wood, C.1850, Pair 1900.00
Furniture, Bin, Pine, 2 Section Interior, 16 X 35 X 21 1/4 In. 105.00
Furniture, Bookcase, Burl Walnut, Aluminum, Art Deco, C.1930 .... Illus 2300.00
Furniture, Bookcase, Federal, Mahogany, C.1815, 51 1/4 X 32 In. 600.00
Furniture, Bookcase, Leaded Glass Doors, 3 Stack, Mahogany 365.00
Furniture, Bookcase, Mahogany, George II, 4 Drawer, 1750s, 103 X 43 In. 1800.00

Furniture, Bed, Four-Post, Elizabethan
Style, Canopy Frame

Furniture, Bedroom Set, Victorian,
Renaissance, Bed & Dresser

Furniture, Bedroom Set, Victorian,
Renaissance, Bed & Dresser

Furniture, Bedroom Set, Walnut,
New Orleans, 1870s, 3 Piece

Furniture, Bedroom Suite,
Art Moderne, Altman, N.Y., 7 Piece

Furniture, Bookcase, Burl Walnut,
Aluminum, Art Deco, C.1930

Furniture, Cabinet, China, Walnut,
Glass Sides & Door, Missouri
(See Page 184)

Furniture, Bookcase, Mahogany, 2 Glass Doors, 97 1/2 X 56 In. 1000.00
Furniture, Bookcase, Oak, Rococo Columns Flanking Shelves, 59 1/2 X 16 In. 150.00
Furniture, Bookcase, Open, Oak, L. & J.G.Stickley, C.1910, 55 1/2 X 49 In. 950.00
Furniture, Bookcase, Victorian, Walnut, 5 Shelf, 6 Ft. 2 In. X 13 3/4 In. 295.00
Furniture, Bookcase, 2 Door, L. & J.G.Stickley, C.1908, 55 1/2 X 49 X 12 In. 1200.00
Furniture, Bookcase, 3 Door, L. & J.G.Stickley, C.1908, 55 1/2 X 69 1/2 In. 1750.00
Furniture, Bookcase, 3 Stack, Leaded Glass Doors, Mahogany 365.00
Furniture, Box, Blanket, 30 3/4 X 24 In. 35.00
Furniture, Box, Dowry, Hand Tooled Leather Trim, Pennsylvania, 14 X 8 In. 115.00
Furniture, Box, Storage, Green, Blue, Salem, Massachusetts, 24 X 18 X 9 In. 85.00
Furniture, Breakfront, Fruitwood, Marquetry, 99 X 66 5/8 In. 2700.00
Furniture, Buffet, Beveled Mirror, Gargons, Claw Feet, C.1876 .... 1500.00
Furniture, Buffet, China, Dragons Carved On Doors 500.00
Furniture, Buffet, China, Old Man Of The North, Golden Oak 950.00
Furniture, Buffet, Fruitwood, Marquetry, French, C.1900, 77 1/2 X 51 In. 2000.00
Furniture, Bureau, Cylinder, Mahogany, Ormolu Mounted, 1800s, 82 X 58 In. 4500.00
Furniture, Bureau, Hepplewhite Style, Matching Mirror 750.00
Furniture, Bureau, Mahogany, George III, 3 Drawer, C.1780 .... 1900.00
Furniture, Bureau, Sheraton, Mahogany, 4-Drawer, Bowed Top, French Feet 375.00
Furniture, Cabinet, Black Lacquer, Inlaid Mother-Of-Pearl, Cinnabar, 86 In. 3000.00
Furniture, Cabinet, Brass Mounted, 3 Doors, 4 Drawers, Korean, 66 X 43 In. 800.00
Furniture, Cabinet, China, Corner, Oak, Curved Glass Door, 26 X 46 In. 750.00
Furniture, Cabinet, China, Oak, Cloverleaf Glass Shelves, Mirror Back, C.1880 .... 850.00
Furniture, Cabinet, China, Oak, Curved Glass 550.00
Furniture, Cabinet, China, Walnut, Glass Sides & Door, Missouri .... Illus 2000.00
Furniture, Cabinet, Collector's, Austrian, Baroque Style, Milco, 29 X 33 In. 1400.00
Furniture, Cabinet, Corner, Medicine, Oak 40.00
Furniture, Cabinet, Corner, 12 Pane, Two Part, Cherry 700.00
Furniture, Cabinet, Curio, Mahogany & Glass, Mirrored Back, 21 X 11 X 56 In. 150.00
Furniture, Cabinet, Curio, Shelves, Victorian, Free Standing, 9 X 15 In. 15.00
Furniture, Cabinet, Curio, Shelves, Victorian, Wall Hanging, 14 X 28 In. 25.00
Furniture, Cabinet, Cylinder Records 225.00
Furniture, Cabinet, Disc Records, Pop Out 175.00
Furniture, Cabinet, Display, Black Lacquer, Revolving Drawers, Signed 4250.00
Furniture, Cabinet, Display, 3 Bracket Shelves, 38 X 18 X 37 In. 250.00
Furniture, Cabinet, Ebonized, Brass Inlaid, Napoleon III, 1800s, 44 In. 650.00
Furniture, Cabinet, Hoosier, Miniature, Pine, Doors Open, 17 X 15 1/2 X 7 In. 150.00
Furniture, Cabinet, Hoosier, Oak, Frosted Glass Doors, Sugar Jar, Flour Bin 285.00
Furniture, Cabinet, Letter, Inlaid Rosewood, Silver, Ivory, 13 3/4 X 10 In. 280.00
Furniture, Cabinet, Linen, Barber Shop Chair, Shoe Shine Chair, Oak, 3 Piece 1500.00
Furniture, Cabinet, Mahogany, Ormolu Mounted, Continental, 1850s, 78 In. 1400.00
Furniture, Cabinet, Music, Bleached Mahogany, Porcelain Mounted, 46 X 23 In. 300.00
Furniture, Cabinet, Oak, Carved Figures On Doors & Sides, Paw Feet 2000.00
Furniture, Cabinet, Ormolu Mounted, French, 54 1/2 X 26 X 14 In. 950.00
Furniture, Cabinet, Padouk Wood, Hanging Medal, George II, 1700s, 49 In. 1500.00
Furniture, Cabinet, Phonograph, Oak, Floor Model, Without Phonograph, 4 Feet 165.00
Furniture, Cabinet, Record, Cylinder, Oak, Holds 216 Records 385.00
Furniture, Cabinet, Side, Giltwood, Neoclassical Style, C.1876, 44 X 49 In. 1000.00
Furniture, Cabinet, Side, Philippine Padouk, Inlaid, 1800s, 43 X 64 In. 900.00
Furniture, Cabinet, Side, Rococo Burl Walnut, Marble Top, Victorian, 42 In. 1300.00
Furniture, Cabinet, Spice, Many Tiny Drawers, Yellow, Hanging 275.00
Furniture, Cabinet, Spice, Oak & Pine, Wall Hanging, 8 Drawer 85.00
Furniture, Cabinet, Spice, 9 Drawer, Old Brown Paint 135.00
Furniture, Cabinet, Vitrine, Mahogany, Louis XV Style, 65 In. .... Illus 500.00
Furniture, Cabinet, Walnut, Ormolu Mounted, Marble Top, 1800s, 37 In., Pair 1000.00
Furniture, Cabinet, 10 Drawer, Graduated Depth, Oak, 32 X 32 In. 250.00
Furniture, Cabinet, 2 Cockerels, Ivory Knobs, Japanese, 1800s, 8 1/2 X 7 In. 225.00
Furniture, Candlestand, Adjustable, C.1800, 25 1/2 In.High, 17 1/2 In. Diam. 600.00
Furniture, Candlestand, Chippendale, Carved Mahogany, Dish Top, 29 1/4 In. 3400.00
Furniture, Candlestand, Chippendale, Carved Walnut, Dish Top, 1770s, 27 In. 2800.00
Furniture, Candlestand, Chippendale, Tilt Top, Birdcage Support, Claw Feet 5250.00
Furniture, Candlestand, Chippendale, Walnut, 27 1/2 In.High, 18 In.Diam. 800.00
Furniture, Candlestand, Dish Top, Ring Turned & Arched Snake Feet, Mahogany 600.00
Furniture, Candlestand, Federal, C.1780, 29 In.High, 29 1/4 In.Wide 650.00
Furniture, Candlestand, Mahogany, Federal, Tilt-Top, C.1810, 27 1/2 X 24 In. 450.00
Furniture, Candlestand, Maple, Federal, Circular, 1700s, 15 In. 350.00

Furniture, Candlestand, Maple, Hepplewhite, Tilt-Top, C.1790 .... 650.00
Furniture, Candlestand, Maple, Queen Anne, Painted, 1750-80, 25 X 17 1/4 In. 400.00
Furniture, Candlestand, Tiger Maple, Snake Foot, Shaped Top, C.1760 .... 600.00
Furniture, Candlestand, Tilt-Top Birdcage, Salem 750.00
Furniture, Candlestand, Tilt-Top, Mahogany, Federal, C.1800, 30 X 19 1/2 In. 325.00
Furniture, Candlestand, William & Mary, C.1710, 26 1/4 In.High, 15 In.Diam. 275.00
Furniture, Candlestand, 2 Light, William & Mary, 18th Century, 34 1/2 In. 550.00
Furniture, Casket, Monkey, Carved Walnut, French, 18th Century 900.00
Furniture, Cedar Chest, 1920s, Child's 27.50
Furniture, Chair & Stool, Hepplewhite, Serpentine Seat, Mahogany 325.00
Furniture, Chair, Arrowback, Original Chrome Yellow Paint, Set Of 5 .... 750.00
Furniture, Chair, Arrowback, Set Of 6 .... 550.00
Furniture, Chair, Balloon-Back, Zoar, Original Graining, Set Of 6 .... 950.00
Furniture, Chair, Bamboo, Carved Maple, C.1880 .... 85.00
Furniture, Chair, Barber, Brass Trim, Oak, C.1870-80 .... 645.00
Furniture, Chair, Barber, Emil Paidar 100.00
Furniture, Chair, Barber, Lion Head On Sides, Wood 375.00
Furniture, Chair, Barber, Porcelain 295.00
Furniture, Chair, Barber's, Brass Trim, Oak, C.1870-80 .... 645.00
Furniture, Chair, Billiard Watcher 150.00
Furniture, Chair, Bird's-Eye & Tiger Maple, Cane Seated, Hitchcock, Set Of 5 .... 650.00
Furniture, Chair, Buffalo Horn, Hooves On Legs 1750.00
Furniture, Chair, Cane Seat, Original Paint & Stencil, Sheraton, C.1825 .... 500.00
Furniture, Chair, Carved Back & Turned Rungs, Cane Bottom, Walnut 75.00
Furniture, Chair, Child's, Ladderback, Kentucky, 13 In. 85.00
Furniture, Chair, Child's, Morris, Oak, Green Velvet 98.00
Furniture, Chair, Child's, Plank Seat 30.00
Furniture, Chair, Child's, Rush Seat, Oak, Black With Yellow Trim 225.00
Furniture, Chair, Child's, Windsor, Stickback 90.00
Furniture, Chair, Chippendale, Hairy Ball & Claw Feet, Carved, Dolphin Arms 900.00
Furniture, Chair, Corner, Maple & Ash, Triangular Rush Seat, Shaped Cresting 250.00
Furniture, Chair, Corner, Queen Anne, Horseshoe Backrest, Baluster Splats 2400.00
Furniture, Chair, Corner, Sheraton, Fruitwood With Inlay, 19th Century, Pair 480.00
Furniture, Chair, Corset Back, Lady's & Man's, Finger Carved, Walnut 750.00
Furniture, Chair, Crest, Old Black, C.1720 .... 675.00
Furniture, Chair, Dining Room, Chippendale, Straight Leg, Set Of 14 .... 4000.00
Furniture, Chair, Dining, Gustav Stickley, Set Of 6 .... 750.00
Furniture, Chair, Dining, Spindle Oak, Pressed 150.00
Furniture, Chair, Duncan Phyfe School, Signed ID 975.00
Furniture, Chair, Folding, Leg-O-Matic, Bridgeport, Connecticut 22.50
Furniture, Chair, Gambler's, Converts To Table, Oak 250.00
Furniture, Chair, Gentleman's, Rosewood, Victorian, Pair ....*Illus* 2250.00
Furniture, Chair, Gothic Benton, Carved Gargoyles, Walnut, C.1820, Pair 650.00
Furniture, Chair, Hepplewhite, 6 Side, 2 Arm, Shield Back, Plume 950.00
Furniture, Chair, Hickory, Bent Wood, Caned Seat 97.50
Furniture, Chair, Hitchcock Type, Stencil & Rush Seat, Set Of 4 .... 175.00
Furniture, Chair, Ice Cream Parlor, Bentwood, Set Of 4 .... 110.00
Furniture, Chair, Ice Cream Parlor, Set Of 6 .... 300.00
Furniture, Chair, Ice Cream, Table, Child's 489.00
Furniture, Chair, Ice Cream, Table, Glass Top, 4 .... 400.00

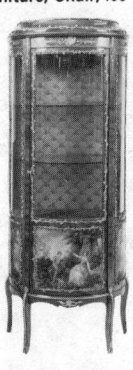

Furniture, Cabinet, Vitrine, Mahogany,
Louis XV Style, 65 In.

Furniture, Chair, Gentleman's,
Rosewood, Victorian, Pair
(See Page 185)

Furniture, Chair, Oak,
James II Style, Set Of 4

Furniture, Chair, Oak, Savonarola

Furniture, Chair, Side, Federal, Rush Seat,
New England, Set Of 6

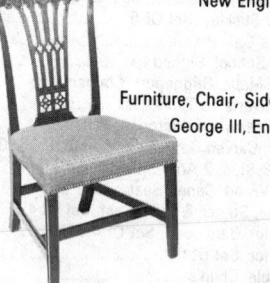

Furniture, Chair, Side, Mahogany,
George III, English, 1700s

Furniture, Chair, Side, Beechwood, Louis XVI,
French, Pair

Furniture, Chair, Side,
Classical Revival, Pair

Furniture, Chair, Side, Rosewood,
Belter Style, New York, Pair
(See Page 188)

Furniture, Chaise, Corner, Rosewood,
Belter Style, New York
(See Page 188)

Furniture, **Chair**, J.Swint, Cabinetmaker, Green, Set Of 3	995.00
Furniture, **Chair**, Ladderback, Maple, New England, C.1780	850.00
Furniture, **Chair**, Laminated Rosewood, Carved, Belter Type	850.00
Furniture, **Chair**, Laminated Rosewood, Victorian, C & S Curves, Set Of 4	5500.00
Furniture, **Chair**, Library, Mahogany, Leather, Roycroft, 26 In.	350.00 To 1300.00
Furniture, **Chair**, Mahogany, Chippendale, Ribbon Split Back, C.1840, Set Of 4	2100.00
Furniture, **Chair**, Maple, Banister Back, Portsmouth, New Hampshire, 1700s	350.00
Furniture, **Chair**, Maple, Ladderback, 19th Century, Set Of 4	1200.00
Furniture, **Chair**, Oak, James II Style, Set Of 4 *Illus*	1700.00
Furniture, **Chair**, Oak, Savonarola *Illus*	600.00
Furniture, **Chair**, Office, Pressed Back Oak	425.00
Furniture, **Chair**, Portrait Of Gentleman On Top Rail, Baltimore, Set Of 4	2500.00
Furniture, **Chair**, Potty, Bentwood, Oak	30.00
Furniture, **Chair**, Potty, Lift-Top, Oak	20.00
Furniture, **Chair**, Potty, New England, C.1880, Graniteware Bowl, 17 In.	45.00
Furniture, **Chair**, Potty, Pressed Back, High Back	125.00
Furniture, **Chair**, Pressed Back, Cane Bottom, Set Of 6	90.00
Furniture, **Chair**, Pressed Back, Caned, Set Of 7	560.00
Furniture, **Chair**, Pressed Back, Oak, Pair	49.00
Furniture, **Chair**, Pressed Back, Solid Bottom, Oak, Set Of 6	65.00
Furniture, **Chair**, Queen Anne, Duck Feet, Carved Splat	1000.00
Furniture, **Chair**, Reclining, L. & J.G.Stickley, C.1910, Leather, 42 1/2 In.	750.00
Furniture, **Chair**, Reclining, Roycroft, C.1914, Leather, 46 X 37 1/2 In.	1300.00
Furniture, **Chair**, Rocker, Mission Oak, Marked Stickley Bros.	165.00
Furniture, **Chair**, Rocker, Walnut, Inlaid Wood, Caned Seat	60.00
Furniture, **Chair**, Rocker, Wicker, Brown Painted Finish	45.00
Furniture, **Chair**, Rococo Revival, Cherubs, Griffins, Serpents, Pair	925.00
Furniture, **Chair**, Rope Wicker, High Back, No Arms	200.00
Furniture, **Chair**, Sheraton Style, Cut-Out Panels, Gold Leaves, Set Of 6	2400.00
Furniture, **Chair**, Sheraton, Flowers, Cream Background, C.1810-30	165.00
Furniture, **Chair**, Sheraton, Seven-Spindle, Windsor, Bamboo Turnings, Set Of 6	1575.00
Furniture, **Chair**, Side, Beechwood, Louis XVI, French, Pair *Illus*	1500.00
Furniture, **Chair**, Side, Carved Walnut, Queen Anne, Philadelphia Area, 1750s	2500.00
Furniture, **Chair**, Side, Child's, Crest Rail, Rush Seat, Taper Legs	125.00
Furniture, **Chair**, Side, Chippendale, Carved Mahogany, Thomas Tufft, 1770s	1600.00
Furniture, **Chair**, Side, Chippendale, Carved Walnut, Philadelphia	1300.00 To 2300.00
Furniture, **Chair**, Side, Chippendale, Carved Walnut, 1760-80, Pair	4000.00
Furniture, **Chair**, Side, Chippendale, Mahogany, Carved Knees, 19th Century, Pr.	600.00
Furniture, **Chair**, Side, Classical Revival, Pair *Illus*	250.00
Furniture, **Chair**, Side, Dutch, Marquetry, Drop-In Seat, Saber Legs, 1800s	300.00
Furniture, **Chair**, Side, Federal, C.1810, Set Of 4	750.00
Furniture, **Chair**, Side, Federal, Rush Seat, New England, Set Of 6 *Illus*	6000.00
Furniture, **Chair**, Side, Flared Stiles, Leafage, Balloon Seat, Claw Feet, Pair	3800.00
Furniture, **Chair**, Side, Heart & Crown Type, Reeded Banisters	450.00
Furniture, **Chair**, Side, Hepplewhite, English, Shield Back, 3 Heads Of Wheat	165.00
Furniture, **Chair**, Side, Laminated Rosewood, New York, Carved Legs, C.1800	800.00
Furniture, **Chair**, Side, Mahogany, Brass Inlaid, Empire, Saber Legs, Pair	300.00
Furniture, **Chair**, Side, Mahogany, George III, Domed Crest Rail, 1850s	125.00
Furniture, **Chair**, Side, Mahogany, George III, English, 1700s *Illus*	425.00
Furniture, **Chair**, Side, Mahogany, Late Empire, Carved Back, 1840-60, Pair	240.00
Furniture, **Chair**, Side, Mahogany, Philadelphia Chippendale	2700.00
Furniture, **Chair**, Side, Maple, Queen Anne, Leather Covered, C.1730	3500.00
Furniture, **Chair**, Side, Prince-Of-Wales, Carved Crest Banister Back	950.00
Furniture, **Chair**, Side, Queen Anne, C.1750-70	400.00
Furniture, **Chair**, Side, Queen Anne, Cupid's Bow Crestrail, Scroll Ears	3000.00

Furniture, Chair, Side, Queen Anne, Turned Legs, Front Stretcher	500.00
Furniture, Chair, Side, Rosewood, Belter Style, New York, Pair .... *Illus*	3250.00
Furniture, Chair, Side, Sausage Turning Base, Turned Posts, Fluted Ears	460.00
Furniture, Chair, Side, Walnut, C.1850, 18 X 21 1/2 X 35 In., Pair	500.00
Furniture, Chair, Side, Walnut, Directoire, Italian, Dolphin Splats, Pair	500.00
Furniture, Chair, Side, Walnut, Queen Anne, Balloon Seat, New England, 1750s	3000.00
Furniture, Chair, Side, Walnut, Queen Anne, Shell Carved, Pad Feet, C.1750	4250.00
Furniture, Chair, Side, Walnut, Renaissance, Burl Walnut Panel, Pair	160.00
Furniture, Chair, Side, Walnut, Victorian, Renaissance	75.00
Furniture, Chair, Side, Windsor, Brace Back, New England, C.1780-1800	2000.00
Furniture, Chair, Six 1/2 Spindle, Plank	390.00
Furniture, Chair, T-Back, Oak, Set Of 4	100.00
Furniture, Chair, Teacher's Writing, Dovetailed Drawer, Kidney Shaped Arm	1000.00
Furniture, Chair, Tubback, Olivewood, Egyptian, Mother-Of-Pearl Inlaid, Pair	5000.00
Furniture, Chair, Wicker, Large	65.00
Furniture, Chair, Windsor, Bow Back, Brace Back, C.1790-1810, 18 In.	575.00
Furniture, Chair, Windsor, Double Step-Down, Front Stretcher	300.00
Furniture, Chair, Windsor, Knuckle Arm, Bow Back, Black Paint	1250.00
Furniture, Chair, Windsor, Rabbit Ear, Signed, F.Raymond, Black	45.00
Furniture, Chair, Wing Back, American, Connecticut, C.1800	1250.00
Furniture, Chair, Yachting, Victorian	228.00
Furniture, Chaise Lounge, Gilt Wood, Alligator Form Legs, Regency, 1800s	3250.00
Furniture, Chaise, Corner, Rosewood, Belter Style, New York .... *Illus*	3250.00
Furniture, Chest-On-Chest, Chippendale, Bonnet Top, Walnut, Pennsylvania	9500.00
Furniture, Chest-On-Chest, Chippendale, Carved Walnut, Flat Top, 68 In.	3250.00
Furniture, Chest-On-Chest, Chippendale, Japanned Pine, 1760-80, 69 3/4 In.	1000.00
Furniture, Chest-On-Chest, Mahogany, George III, 1750s, 79 X 39 In.	1600.00
Furniture, Chest-On-Chest, Mahogany, Sawtooth Inlay, 18th Century	2250.00
Furniture, Chest-On-Frame, Carved Walnut, Queen Anne, Pennsylvania, 1760s	3500.00
Furniture, Chest, Apothecary, 27 Drawers, 3 Bottom Drawers, 45 X 13 X 46 In.	450.00
Furniture, Chest, Austrian, Walnut, Empire, 3 Drawer, Block Feet, 34 In.	500.00
Furniture, Chest, Bachelor, Bow Front, American, C.1780	2000.00
Furniture, Chest, Bird's-Eye Maple, Carved Drawer Fronts	435.00
Furniture, Chest, Blanket, Chippendale, Painted Poplar, C.1797, 27 X 50 In.	1300.00
Furniture, Chest, Blanket, Federal, New England, 1800-30, 33 X 37 3/4 In.	500.00
Furniture, Chest, Blanket, Lift-Top, C.1820-35, 41 3/4 X 40 1/2 In.	800.00
Furniture, Chest, Blanket, Lift-Top, Green, 2 Drawer, 18th Century	375.00
Furniture, Chest, Blanket, New England, 1800-30, 33 X 37 3/4 In.	500.00
Furniture, Chest, Blanket, Pine, Dovetailed, Tulips, 50 X 21 X 24 In.	2000.00
Furniture, Chest, Blanket, Pine, 2 Drawer, C.1780, 45 X 35 In.	485.00
Furniture, Chest, Blanket, Poplar, Turned Feet, 43 X 18 1/2 X 23 1/2 In.	110.00
Furniture, Chest, Blanket, Removeable Till, I.Morton, 37 3/4 X 21 X 23 In.	675.00
Furniture, Chest, Blanket, Walnut, 18 X 12 In.	300.00
Furniture, Chest, Blanket, 2 Drawer, Bun Feet, Fluted Waist, C.1730	2700.00
Furniture, Chest, Blanket, 3 Drawer, 37 1/2 X 38 X 15 In.	265.00
Furniture, Chest, Blanket, 6-Board, Bootjack, Yellow	395.00
Furniture, Chest, Bow Front Variant, Maine	450.00
Furniture, Chest, Bow Front, French Feet, C.1800, 41 X 22 X 37 In.	2250.00
Furniture, Chest, Bow Front, Hepplewhite, C.1820, 43 X 21 1/2 X 41 1/2 In.	650.00
Furniture, Chest, Bow Front, Sheraton, Original Brass, C.1800, Mahogany	650.00
Furniture, Chest, Bow Front, 4 Drawer, Portsmouth, N.H.	1350.00
Furniture, Chest, Cedar, Colonnaded Front, Long Drawer, Curved Legs, 25 In.	130.00
Furniture, Chest, Charles II, 3 Drawers, 30 X 20 1/2 X 32 In.	350.00
Furniture, Chest, Cherry, Birch, New England, 4 Drawer, Molded Edge, C.1780	695.00
Furniture, Chest, Cherry, Graduated Drawers, Scrolled Back	235.00
Furniture, Chest, Cherry, Ogee Foot, Rosewood Graining, 18th Century	1750.00
Furniture, Chest, Cherry, 11 Drawer, Dovetailed	365.00
Furniture, Chest, Child's, Curly Maple, 1780-1820, 13 1/2 X 15 In.	375.00
Furniture, Chest, Chippendale, Carved Birch, 4 Drawer, C.1780, 32 1/2 In.	1000.00
Furniture, Chest, Chippendale, Carved Cherrywood, 4 Drawer, 37 1/4 In.	3500.00
Furniture, Chest, Chippendale, Carved Walnut, 4 Drawer, 34 3/4 X 38 1/4 In.	2100.00
Furniture, Chest, Chippendale, Cherry, 5 Drawer, Bracket Base, Thumbnail Top	1600.00
Furniture, Chest, Chippendale, Country, Tiger Maple	475.00
Furniture, Chest, Chippendale, Mahogany, Oxbow, Wallace Nutting	1800.00
Furniture, Chest, Chippendale, Mahogany, 4 Drawer, New England, 36 X 40 In.	1050.00
Furniture, Chest, Chippendale, Walnut, Bracket Feet, 3 X 2 X 4 Feet	3250.00

Furniture, Chest, Chippendale, 3 Drawer, Mahogany, Pennsylvania, 65 In.	2750.00
Furniture, Chest, Continental, Carved Oak, Paneled Sides, 27 X 55 In.	500.00
Furniture, Chest, Curly Maple & Mahogany, 5 Drawer, 1800s, 13 X 11 In.	225.00
Furniture, Chest, Curly Maple, Federal, Bow Front, 4 Drawer, 38 1/4 X 43 In.	1100.00
Furniture, Chest, Dower, Pennsylvania Dutch, Decorated, Signed	825.00
Furniture, Chest, Dower, Studding, Dome Top, Iron Lock, 24 X 12 X 9 3/4 In.	110.00
Furniture, Chest, Empire, Cherry, Bird's-Eye Maple, 43 1/2 X 20 1/4 X 51 In.	325.00
Furniture, Chest, Federal, Pine, Painted, Grained, Bow Front, 38 3/4 In.	2300.00
Furniture, Chest, Hepplewhite, Cherry, Banding, Apron Base	995.00
Furniture, Chest, Hepplewhite, Cherry, 4 Drawer, Tiger Maple, Brasses	950.00
Furniture, Chest, Hepplewhite, 4 Drawer, Inlay, Bow Front	1350.00
Furniture, Chest, Hepplewhite, 4 Drawer, Inlay, Pennsylvania, C.1790	950.00
Furniture, Chest, Hungarian, Hand-Carved, 1700s	1650.00
Furniture, Chest, Inlaid Rim, Crossband Drawers, Valanced Skirt, Bracket Feet	2500.00
Furniture, Chest, Korean, Brass Mounted, Bracket Feet, 4 Doors, 1800s, 55 In.	700.00
Furniture, Chest, Korean, Brass Mounted, 4 Hinged Doors, 1800s, 25 1/4 In.	350.00
Furniture, Chest, Mahogany Inlays & Case, Boston, C.1800-10, 40 In.	1475.00
Furniture, Chest, Mahogany, Pennsylvania, Fluted, C.1810	1250.00
Furniture, Chest, Mahogany, Pine, 3 Drawer, 2 On Top, 38 X 42 X 29 In.	125.00
Furniture, Chest, Mahogany, 4 Drawer, Boston, C.1800-10, 40 In.	1475.00
Furniture, Chest, Mahogany, 4 Drawer, 46 X 43 X 20 In.	200.00
Furniture, Chest, Mahogany, 4 Drawers, 2 Drawers On Top, 50 X 48 X 22 In.	200.00
Furniture, Chest, Medicine, 6 Rows Of Drawers, Lock & Key, 44 X 38 In.	500.00
Furniture, Chest, Miniature, Inlaid Mahogany, C.1820, 19 1/2 X 19 1/2 In.	475.00
Furniture, Chest, Mule, Pine, Dovetailed Drawer, 41 1/4 X 21 X 39 3/4 In.	1200.00
Furniture, Chest, Oak, 1600s, Frisian, North German, 52 X 24 X 32 In.	5000.00
Furniture, Chest, Pilgrim, Carved Oak, Lift Top, C.1600, 28 X 53 1/4 In.	2400.00
Furniture, Chest, Pine, Empire, New England, 1800s, 49 1/4 In. *Illus*	1900.00
Furniture, Chest, Pine, Lift Top, New England, 1800s, 23 1/4 In. *Illus*	5500.00
Furniture, Chest, Pine, Lift Top, New England, 1800s, 25 In. *Illus*	3750.00
Furniture, Chest, Pine, Red, C.1775, 44 3/4 X 16 3/4 In.	1350.00
Furniture, Chest, Poplar, 4 Drawer, Cherry Finish, 43 1/2 X 40 1/2 X 21 In.	175.00
Furniture, Chest, Queene Anne, Walnut, 5 Drawer, New England, 36 1/4 In.	700.00
Furniture, Chest, Red Lacquer, 3 Drawer, Hand-Painted, 6 1/2 X 5 1/4 In.	27.50
Furniture, Chest, Sewing, Victorian, Walnut, Lift-Top, 20 1/2 X 19 X 31 In.	85.00
Furniture, Chest, Sheraton, Cherry, 42 1/2 X 20 1/2 X 45 1/2 In.	410.00
Furniture, Chest, Spice, Graduated Drawers, Stepback, Original Finish	210.00
Furniture, Chest, Spice, 6 Drawer	55.00
Furniture, Chest, Swell Front, Walnut, Mahogany Veneer, 41 In.	125.00

Furniture, Chest, Pine, Empire,
New England, 1800s, 49 1/4 In.

Furniture, Chest, Pine, Lift Top, New England,
1800s, 23 1/4 In.

Furniture, Chest, Pine, Lift Top, New England,
1800s, 25 In.

Furniture, Chest, Tea, Rosewood, George IV, Rectangular Top, 1800s, 12 In.	100.00
Furniture, Chest, Tiger Maple Front, Cherry Case, 4 Drawer, 48 X 38 X 19 In.	300.00
Furniture, Chest, Tiger Maple, Cherry & Walnut, 7 Drawer, Glass Pulls	300.00
Furniture, Chest, Victorian, Mahogany, 4 Drawer, American, 1800s, 54 In.	1050.00
Furniture, Chest, Victorian, Walnut, Burr, Inlaid, Ebonized & Gilt, 97 In.	1100.00
Furniture, Chest, Walnut & Cherry, 5 Drawer, 2 Bird's-Eye Maple Drawers	275.00
Furniture, Chest, Walnut, Basque, Carved, 16th Century	1500.00
Furniture, Chest, Walnut, Carved, Handkerchief Drawers	165.00
Furniture, Chest, Walnut, Hanky Drawer, 4 Drawers, Wood Pulls, 38 X 53 In.	245.00
Furniture, Chest, Wedding, Chinese, 24 X 11 X 11 1/2 In.	55.00
Furniture, Chest, Yew Wood, F.A.Rawlence Design, 34 1/2 X 50 1/2 In.	3500.00
Furniture, Chest, 4 Drawer, New England, Curly Maple, C.1820	1650.00
Furniture, Church Pew, Mahogany, 3 Feet Long	110.00
Furniture, Clothes Rack, Cast Iron Base, Large Ring To Hold Clothes	250.00
Furniture, Coffer, Ebony, Inlaid Tortoiseshell & Mother-Of-Pearl, 1800s	475.00
Furniture, Commode, Eastlake, Walnut, Inset Marble Top, Drawer & Door	300.00
Furniture, Commode, Fruitwood, Ormolu Mounted, Louis XV, 1800s, 37 X 54 In.	6750.00
Furniture, Commode, Marble Top, Walnut	265.00
Furniture, Commode, Pine, 1 Door, 1 Drawer	75.00
Furniture, Commode, Tulip & King Wood, Louis XV, M.Bary, 1700s	6500.00
Furniture, Commode, Tulip & King Wood, Louis XV, Transitional, 45 X 40 In.	2000.00
Furniture, Commode, Walnut, Victorian, Marble Top, Wooden Pulls, 30 1/2 In.	100.00
Furniture, Console, Carved Giltwood, Eagle Form, George II, Marble Top	1400.00
Furniture, Console, Giltwood, Continental, Marble Top, 35 1/2 In., Pair	4000.00
Furniture, Console, Painted Wood, Marble Top, Parcel Gilt, Italy, 36 In., Pair	2100.00
Furniture, Couch, Fainting, Lady's, Red Velvet, Victorian	695.00
Furniture, Couch, Mission Oak, Pullman, Black Velvet, 6 Feet Long	200.00
Furniture, Cradle-Crib, Latches, Dated 1875, Oak	750.00
Furniture, Cradle, Cherry, Shaped Rockers & Ends, 17 X 40 X 20 In.	205.00
Furniture, Cradle, Hooded, Handwrought Nails, Dated 1774	350.00
Furniture, Cradle, Old Blue, Dovetailed	100.00 To 175.00
Furniture, Cradle, Red & Black Tole Decoration, Tin	165.00
Furniture, Cradle, Walnut, American, 1800s, 4 1/2 In.	400.00
Furniture, Crib, Cannonball Top, Slide Sides, Brass	650.00
Furniture, Crib, Golliwog Finials, 4 Posts, Iron, English	2200.00
Furniture, Cupboard Top, Red, 38 X 42 X 16 In.	110.00
Furniture, Cupboard, Bedside, Elm, Burr, Inlaid, Victorian, 1800, 29 1/2 In.	600.00
Furniture, Cupboard, Bedside, Mahogany, Tambour Door, English, C.1790	690.00
Furniture, Cupboard, Cherry, 2 Piece, Pie Shelf, 2 Drawer, 3 Glass Panes	650.00
Furniture, Cupboard, Cherry, 2 Piece, 6 Pane Doors, 64 1/4 X 22 X 91 3/4 In.	4700.00
Furniture, Cupboard, Corner, Cherry, 2 Piece, 2 8-Light Doors, 1820, 88 In.	2950.00
Furniture, Cupboard, Corner, Chippendale, Carved & Painted Pine, 83 1/4 In.	1600.00
Furniture, Cupboard, Corner, Double Door, 16 Pane, Pine, 2 Drawer	950.00
Furniture, Cupboard, Corner, Kentucky Cherry, 7 Ft., 1 In. X 4 Ft., X 35 In.	1175.00
Furniture, Cupboard, Corner, Kentucky Cherry, 85 X 28 X 35 In.	1175.00
Furniture, Cupboard, Corner, Pine, Barrelback, 80 3/4 X 35 1/2 In.	300.00
Furniture, Cupboard, Corner, Pine, 1 Piece, Panel Doors, 46 X 24 1/2 X 83 In.	1700.00
Furniture, Cupboard, Corner, Upper & Lower Interiors Shelved, 4 Doors, 2 Part	600.00
Furniture, Cupboard, Corner, Walnut, 4 Panes Of Glass	900.00
Furniture, Cupboard, Corner, 4 Panel Doors, 75 In.	470.00
Furniture, Cupboard, Court, Oak, Pilgrim, Carved, Painted, 1600s, 48 1/2 In.	2500.00
Furniture, Cupboard, Curly Maple, 2-Drawer, Ogee Feet, C.1810, 86 X 53 In.	4500.00
Furniture, Cupboard, Double Door, New England, Pine, 40 X 16 1/2 X 78 In.	420.00
Furniture, Cupboard, Glass Door, Inlaid Corner, Ohio	1600.00
Furniture, Cupboard, Hanging Corner, Pine & Poplar, 2 Shelves, 27 In.	185.00
Furniture, Cupboard, Hanging, Dovetailed, Original Green Paint, 24 X 24 In.	105.00
Furniture, Cupboard, Honey, Stepback, 4 Single Doors, Cornice, Bootjack	380.00
Furniture, Cupboard, Jam, 2 Drawers & Doors, High Back, Shelf, Victorian	180.00
Furniture, Cupboard, Jelly, Cherry, Apron, 2-Drawer	375.00
Furniture, Cupboard, Jelly, One Door, Cutout End, Ohio, 43 X 33 1/2 In.	210.00
Furniture, Cupboard, Jelly, Reddish Brown, Paint-Grained, 19th Century	410.00
Furniture, Cupboard, Kitchen, Japanese Dutch, Complete	300.00
Furniture, Cupboard, Kitchen, 2 Piece, Pine, 12 Glass Panes	1250.00
Furniture, Cupboard, Mahogany, Cross Band, Hanging, George III, 35 X 24 In.	200.00
Furniture, Cupboard, Mahogany, Sycamore Inlaid, Hanging, Corner, 1850s, 36 In.	250.00
Furniture, Cupboard, Oak & Walnut, Ivory Inlaid, Continental, 39 X 22 In.	200.00

Furniture, Cupboard, Oak, Dutch Baroque, Bun Feet, 1650s, 78 X 63 In. 1500.00
Furniture, Cupboard, Oak, Knight In Relief, 1832, 41 1/4 X 19 1/2 In., Pair 200.00
Furniture, Cupboard, Pie, Country Sheraton, 12 Tulip Tins, Red Paint 450.00
Furniture, Cupboard, Pie, Maine 115.00
Furniture, Cupboard, Pie, Pierced Tin, Pine, Dutch 395.00
Furniture, Cupboard, Pie, Tulips & Baskets Of Flowers, Blind Doors Below 395.00
Furniture, Cupboard, Pie, Walnut Case, Gallery, 6 Star Tins, 2 Drawers 295.00
Furniture, Cupboard, Pine, C.1800, 67 X 48 X 19 In. 480.00
Furniture, Cupboard, Pine, Dovetailed Case, 18 1/4 X 11 1/4 X 23 3/4 In. 310.00
Furniture, Cupboard, Pine, Dovetailed Top, 75 X 40 X 12 1/2 In. 995.00
Furniture, Cupboard, Pine, Pewter, Pennsylvania, C.1785, 80 X 29 1/2 X 17 In. 895.00
Furniture, Cupboard, Pine, Red, 76 1/2 X 44 X 17 In. ....Illus 475.00
Furniture, Cupboard, Pine, 1 Piece, Barrelback, 11 Pane Doors, 53 X 93 In. 660.00
Furniture, Cupboard, Pine, 2 Drawer, Bracket Base, 41 X 27 X 15 In. 495.00
Furniture, Cupboard, Pine, 4-Panel Door, Shaker Style 560.00
Furniture, Cupboard, Primitive, C.1750-80, 6 Feet, 2 In. X 43 1/2 In. 850.00
Furniture, Cupboard, Red, 2 Drawers & Doors, Gallery Sides & Back 255.00
Furniture, Cupboard, Red, 2 Single Doors 225.00
Furniture, Cupboard, Shaker, Walnut, Mount Union, Ohio, 50 X 42 1/2 In. 575.00
Furniture, Cupboard, Sheraton, 2 Piece, Walnut, Arched Glazed Doors 750.00
Furniture, Cupboard, Southern Ohio, Walnut, 2 Door, 39 X 78 In. 645.00
Furniture, Cupboard, Three Shelf, Original Paint, Shaker 750.00
Furniture, Cupboard, Wall, Cherry, 2 Piece, Curly Maple, 57 X 21 X 85 3/4 In. 1025.00
Furniture, Cupboard, Wall, 2 Breadboard Doors, One Above Other 215.00
Furniture, Cupboard, 2 Door, Mustard Color Inside, Pine, C.1860, 79 X 31 In. 285.00
Furniture, Cupboard, 5 Shelves, Natural Finish, Butternut 290.00
Furniture, Daybed, Chippendale, Canted Back, Scroll Ears, Pierced Splat, Seat 1600.00
Furniture, Desk & Dressing Table, Mahogany, Adams, English, 39 X 21 X 34 In. 1550.00
Furniture, Desk, Adirondack, Open Pigeon Holes, Rustic Chair, Pair 500.00
Furniture, Desk, Auto Stencillor, Scale, Paint, 6 Drawer, 13 X 22 In. 175.00
Furniture, Desk, Bird's-Eye Maple Interior, 4 Drawer, 60 1/2 X 39 1/2 In. 995.00
Furniture, Desk, Butler's, Cherry & Walnut, C.1820 .... 1675.00
Furniture, Desk, Butler's, Mahogany, Federal, New York, C.1800, 42 In. 1000.00
Furniture, Desk, Captain's, Walnut 795.00
Furniture, Desk, Carved & Inlaid Mahogany, Federal, Cylinder Front, 42 In. 4250.00
Furniture, Desk, Cherry, Slant Top, Free Columns, Tiger Interior, C.1815 .... 1650.00
Furniture, Desk, Chippendale, Carved Mahogany, Block Front, 45 1/4 In. 5250.00
Furniture, Desk, Chippendale, Walnut, Block Front, 42 3/4 X 39 1/4 In. 2000.00
Furniture, Desk, Counting House, Pine, Rev.S.Ripley, 3 Shelves, 52 1/2 In. 900.00
Furniture, Desk, Country Store, Oak 350.00
Furniture, Desk, Curved Display Doors, Inlay, Hand-Painting 1400.00
Furniture, Desk, Double Secretary, Oak, Victorian, Original Finish 1200.00
Furniture, Desk, Fall Front, Federal, Inlay & Serpentine, 3 Drawer 500.00
Furniture, Desk, Fall Front, Pine 200.00
Furniture, Desk, Hepplewhite, Cherry, Slant Front, Pennsylvania, C.1790 .... 1750.00
Furniture, Desk, Hepplewhite, Slant Front, C.1790-1800, England 3800.00
Furniture, Desk, Lady's, Curved Doors, Satin Wood Inlay 1100.00
Furniture, Desk, Lady's, Fall Front Opening, Drawers Inside, 1 Out Drawer 550.00
Furniture, Desk, Lady's, Fall Front, Mahogany, 3 Drawer, Carved Panels 600.00
Furniture, Desk, Lady's, Federal, C.1800, 34 1/4 X 29 In. 900.00
Furniture, Desk, Lady's, Hepplewhite, English, 24 3/4 X 14 1/2 X 44 In. 500.00
Furniture, Desk, Lap, Angle Surface, Felt Lined, Brass Trim, 8 X 12 X 4 In. 35.00
Furniture, Desk, Lap, Lacquer, Mother-Of-Pearl Inlay 100.00
Furniture, Desk, Lap, Mother-Of-Pearl Inlay, Footed 185.00
Furniture, Desk, Lap, Rosewood, Lock, Key, Pen Holder, 8 1/2 X 11 3/4 X 5 In. 95.00
Furniture, Desk, Lap, Rosewood, Original Inkwell 50.00
Furniture, Desk, Lap, Silver Inlay, Rosewood 375.00
Furniture, Desk, Larkin, Mirror, Oak 135.00
Furniture, Desk, Oak, Kidney Shaped, Victorian 900.00
Furniture, Desk, Partner's, Crotch Walnut, C.1830, 60 1/4 X 35 1/2 In. 4250.00
Furniture, Desk, Plantation, Pine 275.00
Furniture, Desk, Polychrome, Hepplewhite, Decorated 950.00
Furniture, Desk, Roll Top, C.1869, Walnut, 54 X 54 In. 2000.00
Furniture, Desk, Roll Top, C.1910, Mahogany, 64 X 42 X 32 In. 1000.00
Furniture, Desk, Roll Top, Child's, Swivel Chair, Oak, 39 X 33 X 19 1/2 In. 275.00
Furniture, Desk, Roll Top, Flame Grain, Beveled Inside & Out, Carved Pulls 2500.00

Furniture, Desk, Roll Top, Oak, Beveled Panels Inside & Out, American 2500.00
Furniture, Desk, Roll Top, Oak, 47 X 32 In. 450.00
Furniture, Desk, Roll Top, Quarter Sawed Oak, 201 Compartments, Dated 1911 .... 3500.00
Furniture, Desk, Roll Top, Raised Panels, S-Curve, Oak, 50 In. 1150.00
Furniture, Desk, Roll Top, S Roll, Oak .... 825.00 To 1100.00
Furniture, Desk, Roll Top, S Roll, Oak, 45 In. 325.00
Furniture, Desk, Roll Top, S Roll, Swivel Chair, Oak, 48 In. 650.00
Furniture, Desk, Roll Top, S Roll, Victorian, Key, 48 In.High 1000.00
Furniture, Desk, Roll Top, S Roll, 31 Drawers, 50 Cubby Holes, 66 X 53 In. 3500.00
Furniture, Desk, Roll Top, S-Curve, Oak, 19 Drawers, Lock & Key, 48 In. 1050.00
Furniture, Desk, Roll Top, Walnut 475.00
Furniture, Desk, Schoolmaster's, C.1820-50 .... 375.00
Furniture, Desk, Schoolmaster's, Double Iron Inkwells, Drawers, C.1896, Oak 350.00
Furniture, Desk, Schoolmaster's, Oak & Fir 210.00
Furniture, Desk, Schoolmaster's, Pine, Cast-Iron Legs 495.00
Furniture, Desk, Schoolmaster's, Pine, Slant Top, 33 1/2 X 22 X 37 In. 220.00
Furniture, Desk, Schoolmaster's, Stretcher Base, Maple & Pine, New England 215.00
Furniture, Desk, Slant Front, Cherry, Free Columns, Tiger Interior, C.1815 .... 875.00
Furniture, Desk, Slant Front, Chippendale, Mahogany, 38 X 43 X 32 In. 1550.00
Furniture, Desk, Slant Front, Hepplewhite, Walnut, Inlaid, Interior, C.1795 .... 1000.00
Furniture, Desk, Slant Front, Sheraton, Cherry, Tiger Maple Interior, C.1800 .... 1250.00
Furniture, Desk, Slant Front, Walnut Hepplewhite, Cross Banded Lid, C.1795 .... 1650.00
Furniture, Desk, Slant Front, 4 Drawer, Scalloped Apron 2150.00
Furniture, Desk, Slant Top, Ball & Claw Feet, Chippendale, Birch & Mahogany 3200.00
Furniture, Desk, Slant Top, Cherry, Graduated Drawers, Hepplewhite 1800.00
Furniture, Desk, Slant Top, Chippendale, Walnut, Ogee Feet 3250.00
Furniture, Desk, Slant Top, Hepplewhite, Walnut With Poplar, American, 42 In. 2450.00
Furniture, Desk, Sorting, Post Office, Oak & Walnut, Pigeon Holes 100.00
Furniture, Desk, Tambour, Sheraton, Cherry & Mahogany, Inlaid, Massachusetts 1800.00
Furniture, Desk, Walnut & Mahogany, Wooten, C.1874, Indianapolis, 65 X 46 In. 3900.00
Furniture, Desk, Walnut, Slant Front, Pennsylvania, 27 1/4 X 23 In. 1000.00
Furniture, Desk, Wooten, Oak, S-Curve, Roll Top, Multi-Drawer, Brass Tag 2300.00
Furniture, Dining Room Set, Refectory, Oak 350.00
Furniture, Dining Set, Jacobean, Cupboard, Buffet, 8 Side & 2 Arm Chairs, Oak 5500.00
Furniture, Door, Grained, 18th Century 80.00
Furniture, Door, Oak, Beveled Oval Glass, Brass Hardware, 32 X 80 In. 550.00
Furniture, Door, Oak, Glass, Double .... Illus 3300.00
Furniture, Dresser & Chest, Beveled Glass, Louis XV, Bird's-Eye Maple 1800.00
Furniture, Dresser & Washstand, Marble Top, Brass Pulls, Beveled Mirrors 750.00
Furniture, Dresser Set, Flowers On Blue, Pink, White, 4 Piece 115.00
Furniture, Dresser Set, Roses, Blue & Pink, Artist Signed K.A., 4 Piece 125.00
Furniture, Dresser, Beveled Mirror, Claw Feet, Oak 150.00
Furniture, Dresser, Beveled Mirror, Maple 235.00
Furniture, Dresser, Burl Walnut, Marble Top 350.00
Furniture, Dresser, Carved Oak, Later Rack, English, 66 X 43 In. 550.00
Furniture, Dresser, Cottage, Mirror 115.00
Furniture, Dresser, Marble Top, Mirror, Burl Walnut 550.00
Furniture, Dresser, Marble Top, Walnut, Mirror, 6 Drawer, Brass Pulls 200.00
Furniture, Dresser, Marble Top, Walnut, 4 Drawer, Beveled Mirror, Wood Pulls 475.00
Furniture, Dresser, Oak, William & Mary, 3 Paneled Doors, 39 1/2 X 78 In. 450.00
Furniture, Dresser, Princess, Bird's-Eye Maple, Beveled Mirror, Larkin 95.00
Furniture, Dresser, Swing-Mirror, 4 Drawer, 13 1/2 X 22 1/2 X 38 1/2 In. 125.00
Furniture, Dresser, Walnut, Victorian, Marble Top, Mirror, Brass Pulls, 88 In. 350.00
Furniture, Dresser, 5 Drawer, Pine, 42 X 36 X 19 In. 250.00
Furniture, Dry Sink, Walnut, Dovetailed Top & Drawers 850.00
Furniture, Dry Sink, 3 Drawer, High Back, Amish, Chestnut, Poplar, 29 In.Wide 465.00
Furniture, Dumbwaiter, Mahogany, Beaded Revolving Top, 12 In.Diameter 100.00
Furniture, Dumbwaiter, Mahogany, Three-Tier, George III, 1700s, 43 In. 550.00
Furniture, Etagere, Carved, Rosewood, 105 X 69 X 21 1/2 In. 6500.00
Furniture, Etagere, Walnut .... Illus 450.00
Furniture, Etagere, Walnut .... Illus 1000.00
Furniture, Fireplace Screen, Victorian, Iron Base, Adjustable, 61 In. 195.00
Furniture, Footstool, Cast Iron, Victorian, Needlepoint Covering, 13 In. 100.00
Furniture, Footstool, Cut Velvet Top, Button Feet, 6 X 6 In. 35.00
Furniture, Footstool, Lady's, Victorian, Cast Iron Legs 25.00
Furniture, Footstool, Spool Legs, Tapestry Upholstery, Walnut, 10 X 14 In. 18.00

Furniture, Cupboard, Pine, Red,
76 1/2 X 44 X 17 In.

Furniture, Door, Oak, Glass, Double
(See Page 191)

Furniture, Etagere, Walnut   Furniture, Etagere, Walnut

Furniture, Footstool, Velvet Covered, Metal Legs, Salesman Sample, 2 1/4 In.	28.00
Furniture, Fountain, Soda, Marble Stand, 8 Glass Shades, Ball Top, 44 In.	1500.00
Furniture, Frame, Black Walnut, Gold Liner, 2 In.Depth, 11 X 13 In.	60.00
Furniture, Frame, Easel-Back, Florentine Mosaic, Oval Opening, 7 X 8 In.	68.00
Furniture, Frame, Gilt Liner, Black Walnut, Oval, 11 X 13 In.	27.00
Furniture, Frame, Hand-Carved Wreath Of Flowers, Oval, 6 3/4 X 4 1/2 In.	68.00
Furniture, Frame, Heart Shaped, Redwood Burl, Double, Dated 1916	195.00
Furniture, Frame, Mosaic, Oval For Picture, 2 1/4 X 3 1/2 In.	42.00
Furniture, Frame, Oak, 17 1/2 X 13 1/2 In.	75.00
Furniture, Frame, Oval, Gold Liner, Black Walnut, C.1860, 11 X 13 In.	60.00
Furniture, Frame, Oval, Walnut, Grooved With Gold Liner, 8 X 10 In.	30.00
Furniture, Frame, Pine, Blue Smoked Paint, 10 X 12 In.	37.50
Furniture, Frame, Red Velvet, 10 X 7 1/2 In.	17.00
Furniture, Frame, Shadow Box, Mourning Wreath, Hair	45.00
Furniture, Frame, Silvered Metal, Rococo, Topped By Crown, 8 X 8 In.Diam.	55.00
Furniture, Frame, Standing, Brass, Oval, 4 3/4 X 3 3/4 In.	20.00
Furniture, Frame, Walnut, Original Gold Leaf Liner, Victorian, 8 X 10 In.	27.50
Furniture, Hall Tree, Beveled Mirror, Oak, Small	175.00
Furniture, Hall Tree, Carved, Oak	550.00
Furniture, Hall Tree, Miniature, Brass, 15 In.	65.00
Furniture, Hall Tree, Miniature, Brass, 15 In., Pair	65.00
Furniture, Hall Tree, Walnut, Victorian *Illus*	675.00
Furniture, Hamper, Corner, Lift Top, Loops, Wicker, C.1880, 14 X 20 In.	45.00
Furniture, Hat Rack, Expanding, Walnut, Porcelain Tips	35.00
Furniture, Headboard, Parcel Gilt, Painted, Classical, 1800s, 67 X 74 In.	750.00
Furniture, High Chair-Stroller, Pressed Back, Cast Iron Wheels, Walnut	225.00
Furniture, High Chair, Pressed Back	75.00
Furniture, High Chair, Wicker & Wood	185.00
Furniture, Highboy, Carved Maple, Queen Anne, 2 Part, Flat Top, 61 1/2 In.	2100.00
Furniture, Highboy, Cherrywood, Queen Anne, Flat Top, 1760-90, 66 1/4 In.	9500.00
Furniture, Highboy, Chippendale, Curly Maple, Flat-Top, 17 X 73 X 3 In.	3500.00
Furniture, Highboy, Queen Anne, Bonnet Top	1200.00
Furniture, Highboy, Queen Anne, Curly Maple Front	650.00
Furniture, Highboy, Queen Anne, Maple, Birch & Pine, 2 Piece	2250.00
Furniture, Highboy, William & Mary, Maple	2200.00
Furniture, Highchair-Stroller, Cast Iron Wheels, Oak	147.50
Furniture, Hutch Base, Pennsylvania, 2 Doors, Pine, C.1830, 37 X 50 In.	245.00
Furniture, Icebox, Mansion, 4 Drawer, Oak, Solid Brass Trim, 50 X 36 1/2 In.	400.00
Furniture, Icebox, McCray, 4 Door, Brass Hardware, Oak, 4 1/2 X 6 Feet	750.00
Furniture, Icebox, Oak, Triple Glass Doors, 4 Doors, 68 X 54 X 32 In.	750.00

Furniture, Kas, Canadian, Pine, Inlaid Diamonds, 53 1/2 X 54 1/9 In. 1300.00
Furniture, Kas, Marriage, Faux Bois, Swiss, Muller, Widtmer, 1819, 70 X 76 In. 6600.00
Furniture, Lamp, Stand, S.Rohlfs, 1903, Oak, Copper, 2 Shelf, 17 1/2 X 18 In. 1100.00
Furniture, Linen Press, Cherrywood, Queen Anne, Connecticut, 1700s, 74 In. 3200.00
Furniture, Linen Press, Federal Inlaid Mahogany, C.1800, 89 X 47 1/2 In. 1600.00
Furniture, Linen Press, Kentucky Walnut, C.1840, 7 Ft., 2 In. X 56 X 21 In. 2100.00
Furniture, Linen Press, Pull Out Shelves, Mahogany, Ebony Inlay 1200.00
Furniture, Living Room Set, Lion's Head On Back, Cherry, 4 Piece 800.00
Furniture, Love Seat & Two Matching Chairs, Walnut, Victorian 750.00
Furniture, Love Seat & 2 Chairs, Green Velvet, Cameo Heads & Cupid Dolls 995.00
Furniture, Love Seat & 2 Side Chairs, Victorian Medallion, Original Covers 700.00
Furniture, Love Seat, Cabriole Legs, Serpentine Back, 58 In. 400.00
Furniture, Love Seat, Cameo Back, Carved Cupids, Black Walnut, C.1850-60 .... 550.00
Furniture, Love Seat, Cast Iron, Squirrels On Ferns 325.00
Furniture, Love Seat, Shellback, 3 Chairs, Original Finish & Upholstery 1650.00
Furniture, Love Seat, Turkish Style, C.1840, Pair 675.00
Furniture, Love Seat, Victorian, Walnut, Carved Back, Cabriole Legs 500.00
Furniture, Love Seat, Walnut, Finger Carved Frame, Cabriole Legs, 58 In. 400.00
Furniture, Love Seat, White Wicker, High-Back, Victorian Veranda, C.1890 .... 375.00
Furniture, Lowboy, Mahogany, Queen Anne Duck Feet, 38 X 21 3/4 X 30 1/2 In. 400.00
Furniture, Lowboy, Mahogany, Queen Anne, Cabriole Legs, 29 X 42 In. 650.00
Furniture, Lowboy, Queen Anne, Mahogany, 29 X 42 In. 550.00
Furniture, Lowboy, Queen Anne, Walnut, American, C.1740-60, 29 X 29 3/4 In. 0000.00
Furniture, Lowboy, William & Mary, Queen Anne Cabriole Legs, C.1700 .... 5000.00
Furniture, Magazine Rack, Hanging, Carved Walnut, Victorian, 17 X 28 In. 55.00
Furniture, Mail Cupboard, Cubicles, Conn, 31 X 15 3/4 X 10 3/4 In. 630.00
Furniture, Mantel, Federal, Carved Pine, C.1800, 55 3/4 X 6 Feet, 6 1/2 In. 950.00
Furniture, Mantel, Pillars, Beveled, Oval Mirror 350.00
Furniture, Mantel, Pine, 47 X 44 In. 110.00
Furniture, Mirror, Art Deco, Oval Plaster Frame, Shelf, 1930, 16 X 13 1/2 In. 25.00
Furniture, Mirror, Carved Gilt Wood, Louis XV, C.1750, 74 X 44 In. 2700.00
Furniture, Mirror, Chippendale, Carved, C.1770-1800, 18 1/2 X 11 1/4 In. 200.00
Furniture, Mirror, Chippendale, Gold Bird At Top, 21 In. 280.00
Furniture, Mirror, Chippendale, Inlaid & Parcel Gilded Walnut, 54 In. 1800.00
Furniture, Mirror, Chippendale, Pennsylvania, C.1770, 21 X 13 In. 275.00
Furniture, Mirror, Convex, Gold Leafed, Stylized Eagle On Top, 6 In. 17.50
Furniture, Mirror, Courting, Queen Anne, Reverse Painting Slip Inset, 18 In. 1600.00
Furniture, Mirror, Courting, Traveling Case, C.1790, 16 1/4 X 11 1/4 In. 600.00
Furniture, Mirror, Dressing Table, Mahogany, Parcel Gilt, George I, 2 1/2 In. 150.00
Furniture, Mirror, Empire, Divided, Corner Gesso, 9 X 13 1/2 In. 45.00
Furniture, Mirror, Empire, Gold Leaf, Scenic Reverse Glass Top, 15 X 30 In. 85.00
Furniture, Mirror, Federal, 2 Part Split, Gold Leaf, 25 X 37 In. 250.00
Furniture, Mirror, Florentine, Gesso & Gold Leaf Frame, 13 X 27 In. 45.00
Furniture, Mirror, Framed, 2 Drawer, 19th Century, 20 X 17 3/4 In. 125.00
Furniture, Mirror, Gesso Medallions, Reverse Painting, 26 X 52 1/2 In. 135.00
Furniture, Mirror, Hall, Victorian Renaissance, Hand Carving, 8 X 6 Ft. 650.00
Furniture, Mirror, Mahogany On Pine, Beveled, 18 1/2 X 24 1/2 In. 25.00
Furniture, Mirror, Mahogany, Scroll, 16 1/2 X 28 1/2 In. 2500.00
Furniture, Mirror, Neoclassical, Venetian, 61 X 38 In. 2100.00
Furniture, Mirror, Oval, 17 X 21 In. 30.00
Furniture, Mirror, Overmantel, Eglomise Panels, Gilt Leaves, Landscape Center 550.00
Furniture, Mirror, Overmantel, Empire Carved & Gilded, 3 Part, C.1830, 25 In. 100.00
Furniture, Mirror, Pier, Columns, Beveled Mirror, 8 Feet Tall 125.00
Furniture, Mirror, Pier, Gilt Wood, Neoclassical, Italian, 1700s, 90 X 35 In. 1900.00
Furniture, Mirror, Pier, Set Of 4 .... 200.00
Furniture, Mirror, Pier, Victorian, Walnut, Eastlake Carving, Free Standing 175.00
Furniture, Mirror, Pier, Walnut, Marble Shelf, 7 Feet 225.00
Furniture, Mirror, Pierced Crest, 40 In. 175.00
Furniture, Mirror, Plateau, Beveled, Footed, Ornate Metal, 12 In.Diameter 125.00
Furniture, Mirror, Plateau, Silver Mounting 30.00
Furniture, Mirror, Queen Anne, Parcel Gilded, C.1740, 34 1/2 X 14 In. 400.00
Furniture, Mirror, Rococo, French, Silver & Velvet Frame, 19 X 17 In. 180.00
Furniture, Mirror, Rococo, Gilt Gesso Over Wood, C.1840, 79 X 42 In. 1350.00
Furniture, Mirror, Shaving, Mahogany, English, Ogee Feet, 17 X 7 1/2 X 24 In. 265.00
Furniture, Mirror, Sheraton, Eglomise Tablet, C.1839, 10 1/2 X 13 In. 125.00
Furniture, Mirror, Tri-Fold, Victorian, Each Beveled Panel, 10 X 10 In. 189.00

Furniture, Mirror, Vanity, Triple, Traveling, Brass Frame, 14 X 20 In.	30.00
Furniture, Mirror, Venetian, Blue Frame, Rectangular, C.1800, 65 X 36 In.	2700.00
Furniture, Mirror, Victorian Renaissance Revival, Hand Carving, 8 X 6 Feet	650.00
Furniture, Mirror, Wall, Convex, Federal, C.1820, 40 1/2 X 23 1/2 In.	600.00
Furniture, Mirror, Wall, Federal, New England, C.1790, 20 1/8 X 12 In.	200.00
Furniture, Mirror, Wall, Inlaid & Parcel-Gilded Walnut, C.1740, 55 In.	1600.00
Furniture, Mirror, Wall, Pierced Crest, 40 In.	175.00
Furniture, Mirror, Wall, Queen Anne, C.1750, Beveled Mirror, 24 1/2 In.	450.00
Furniture, Mirror, Wall, Rococo Frame, Leaf Motif, Lattice Crest, 32 In.	50.00
Furniture, Panel, Oak, Renaissance, Relief Bust, C.1550, 3 1/2 In., Pair	800.00
Furniture, Parlor Set, Eastlake, Settee, Armchair, 2 Side Chairs	800.00
Furniture, Parlor Set, Medallion Back, Walnut & Burl, 5 Piece	2200.00
Furniture, Parlor Set, Rocker, Straight Chair, Love Seat	600.00
Furniture, Parlor Set, Sofa, Rocker, Chair, C.1900	495.00
Furniture, Parlor Set, 6 Ft., Settee, Recliner, Chair, Mission Oak, Stickley	3200.00
Furniture, Parlor Table, Flame Mahogany, J.W.Bancroft, C.1840	475.00
Furniture, Pedestal, Plant, Mahogany, 36 In.	65.00
Furniture, Pedestal, Walnut, 36 X 13 1/4 In.	120.00
Furniture, Pie Safe, Pine, 2 Pierced Tin Doors, 1 Board Side	345.00
Furniture, Pie Safe, Walnut Case With Gallery, 6 Star Tins, 2 Drawers	295.00
Furniture, Pool Table, Brunswick Monarch, Golden Oak, Solid Slate	1200.00
Furniture, Pool Table, Brunswick, Oak Base, Mother-Of-Pearl Inlaid	2650.00
Furniture, Pool Table, Brunswick, 1920s, 6 Legs, Leather Pockets, 1920-24	5000.00
Furniture, Porch Set, Wicker, Loveseat, Rocker, Table	350.00
Furniture, Press, Cherry, Glass Door, Kentucky Jackson	1700.00
Furniture, Rack, Clothes, Art Deco, 5 Bronze Hooks	275.00
Furniture, Rack, Hat, Beveled Edge Mirror, Brass Hangers, 17 1/2 In.Square	75.00
Furniture, Rack, Hat, Expanding, Walnut, Porcelain Tips	35.00
Furniture, Rack, Hat, Folding, White Porcelain Tips, Opens To 36 X 31 In.	85.00
Furniture, Rack, Magazine, God Bless Our Home, 30 1/2 X 17 1/2 In.	90.00
Furniture, Rack, Magazine, Green & White Knobs, Wall, Victorian	60.00
Furniture, Rack, Magazine, Hanging, Folding Oak, Turned Spool	165.00
Furniture, Rack, Magazine, Wall Type, White Knobs, Victorian	60.00
Furniture, Rack, Magazine, Wall, Victorian, God Bless Our Home	60.00
Furniture, Rack, Plate, Red & Brown Grain, 42 X 28 In.	265.00
Furniture, Rack, Towel, Golden Oak, 23 In.	15.00
Furniture, Rack, Towel, 8 Wooden Lift-Up Arms	11.00
Furniture, Rocker, Arrow Back, Rush Seat, Connecticut, 1800s ....*Illus*	1100.00
Furniture, Rocker, Child's, Bentwood, Cane Seat, Austria	175.00
Furniture, Rocker, Child's, Hardwood, Red Velvet Seat	85.00
Furniture, Rocker, Child's, Oak Split Seat, C.1830	195.00
Furniture, Rocker, Child's, Victorian, 26 1/2 X 11 In.	85.00
Furniture, Rocker, Child's, Wicker	135.00
Furniture, Rocker, Child's, Windsor, Saddle Seat, 7 Spindles, C.1800	200.00
Furniture, Rocker, Double Step-Down, Comb Back, Windsor	475.00
Furniture, Rocker, Hand Turned Oak Spool, Posts To Floor, Oak	750.00
Furniture, Rocker, Ladder Back, C.1820	185.00
Furniture, Rocker, Lady's, Burl Walnut, Victorian	350.00
Furniture, Rocker, Lady's, L.J.& G.Stickley	110.00
Furniture, Rocker, Lady's, Oak, Signed Gustave Stickley	145.00
Furniture, Rocker, Lincoln, Cane Seat & Back	325.00

Furniture, Rocker, Arrow Back, Rush Seat,
Connecticut, 1800s

Furniture, Hall Tree, Walnut, Victorian
(See Page 193)

Furniture, Secretary, Front,
Walnut, Barrel, 108 In.

Furniture, Settee, Armchair, & Sidechair,
Eastlake, C.1880

Furniture, Settee, Knole, Charles I Style

Furniture, Rocker, Oak, Spring Carpet	65.00
Furniture, Rocker, Painted, Federal, American, C.1820	225.00
Furniture, Rocker, Pressed Back, Oak	195.00
Furniture, Rocker, Shaker	185.00
Furniture, Rocker, Slat-Back, Splint Seat, C.1830	85.00
Furniture, Rocker, Tiger Maple, Pennsylvania Dutch, C.1840	1250.00
Furniture, Rocker, Windsor, Horseshoe Back Rest, C.1810, New England	250.00
Furniture, Rocker, Windsor, 7-Spindle	235.00
Furniture, Rug, Caucasian Type, 2 X 4 Feet	150.00
Furniture, Salon Set, Louis XV, Couch & 6 Chairs, Rosewood Frame, C.1836	6000.00
Furniture, Screen, English, Tooled, 4 Fold	1200.00
Furniture, Screen, Fire, Mahogany, Victorian, 1800s, 47 X 25 1/2 In.	275.00
Furniture, Screen, Hardstone & Ivory Inlaid, Floral, 4 Panel, 24 X 18 In.	70.00
Furniture, Screen, Oriental, Lacquer With Ivory Inlay, 2 Panel, 30 X 28 In.	225.00
Furniture, Screen, Teakwood Stand, 3 Type Of Jade, C.1910, 18 X 11 In.	750.00
Furniture, Screen, 2 Fold, Ivory, Pearl, Figures, Signed, Chinese, 66 X 69 In.	400.00
Furniture, Screen, 2 Fold, Walnut, Floral Needlepoint, 7 1/2 X 14 1/2 In.	22.50
Furniture, Screen, 3 Fold, Chinese, Red Silk & Satin Panel, 96 X 25 In.	250.00
Furniture, Screen, 3 Fold, Glass, Bronze, Pine Needle Pattern, 7 In.High	175.00
Furniture, Screen, 4 Fold, Gold, Japanese, C.1800, 69 X 102 In., Pair	950.00
Furniture, Screen, 4 Fold, Mother-Of-Pearl, Softstone Mounted, 72 X 64 In.	1000.00
Furniture, Screen, 4 Fold, Painted Canvas, Continental, 1800s, 84 X 116 In.	1300.00
Furniture, Screen, 6 Fold, Chinese, Lacquer, Chinoiserie, 84 1/2 In.	3000.00
Furniture, Screen, 6 Fold, Cloisonne Inlaid, Still Life Scenes, 89 X 96 In.	2250.00
Furniture, Screen, 6 Fold, Japanese, Peonies, Irises, Orchids, 54 In.High, Pair	1800.00
Furniture, Screen, 6 Fold, Landscape, Soga Shohaku, 1700s, 60 X 111 In	1050.00
Furniture, Screen, 6 Fold, Mother-Of-Pearl, Softstone Mounted, 72 In.High	2000.00
Furniture, Screen, 8 Fold, Black Lacquer, Courtyard Scene, 7 Feet High	2000.00
Furniture, Screen, 12 Fold, Chinese, Coromandel, Pavilion Scene, 46 In. High	3000.00
Furniture, Seat, Elephant Supporting Seat, Southeast Asia, 20 3/4 In., Pair	350.00
Furniture, Seat, Hall, Bamboo, Cane & Lacquer, Mirror, 1900s, 79 X 42 X 14 In.	600.00
Furniture, Seat, Window, Satinwood, Half Round Armrests, C.1850, 23 In.	275.00
Furniture, Secretary-Bookcase, Chippendale, Curly Maple, Bonnet Top	7000.00
Furniture, Secretary, Base, Drop Front, Walnut, 21 X 46 1/2 In.	175.00
Furniture, Secretary, Beveled Mirror, Oak	625.00

Furniture, Secretary, Cherry & Bird's-Eye Maple, Empire, 2 Piece 1250.00
Furniture, Secretary, Cherry Wood, Honey Colored, 1800s, 62 1/2 X 37 1/4 In. 895.00
Furniture, Secretary, Eastlake Carving, Walnut, C.1870, Glass Door Top 1075.00
Furniture, Secretary, Front, Walnut, Barrel, 108 In. .... *Illus* 3300.00
Furniture, Secretary, Hanging, Kentucky Cherry, 5 Feet Tall 850.00
Furniture, Secretary, Hepplewhite, Cathedral Doors, Mahogany, 1784, Signed 5500.00
Furniture, Secretary, Mahogany, Flame Mahogany, American Empire, C.1835 .... 1250.00
Furniture, Secretary, Mahogany, Hepplewhite, Inlay Woods, C.1830, 72 1/2 In. 1800.00
Furniture, Secretary, Rolltop, Cylinder, Walnut, 8 Feet High 950.00
Furniture, Secretary, Tiger Maple, Northern Vermont, 38 X 8i In. 7200.00
Furniture, Secretary, Triple, Golden Oak, 6 Double Rollers, 1874, 64 X 80 In. 2150.00
Furniture, Secretary, Walnut & Burl Veneer, Pierced Fret, 1 Drawer, 30 In. 1250.00
Furniture, Settee, Armchair, & Sidechair, Eastlake, C.1880 .... *Illus* 850.00
Furniture, Settee, Armchair, 2 Side Chairs, Eastlake 800.00
Furniture, Settee, Jacobean Style, Walnut, 3 Section Back, Carved 375.00
Furniture, Settee, Knole, Charles I Style .... *Illus* 300.00
Furniture, Settee, Mahogany, Empire, S-Scroll Fronts, C.1820, 93 1/2 In. 500.00
Furniture, Settee, Mahogany, Ormolu Mounted, Empire, Hoof Feet, 1800s, 41 In. 2100.00
Furniture, Settee, Mission Oak 335.00
Furniture, Settee, Oak, Gothic Style .... *Illus* 1500.00
Furniture, Settee, Rosewood, Rococo, Victorian, Brass Casters, 64 X 41 In. 900.00
Furniture, Settee, Satinwood, Double Shield Back, Painted, 41 In. 550.00
Furniture, Settee, Victorian, Walnut 430.00
Furniture, Settee, Walnut, Burr, Victorian, Upholstered, Strapback, 80 In. 1300.00
Furniture, Settee, Walnut, Rococo, Victorian, C.1850, 80 X 35 X 40 In. 675.00
Furniture, Settee, Walnut, Rococo, Victorian, 3 Part Open Back, 1850s, 64 In. 800.00
Furniture, Settee, Windsor, Bamboo Turnings, 8 Legs 750.00
Furniture, Settee, Windsor, Bamboo, Turned, C.1800, 5 Feet, 8 3/4 In.Long 1300.00
Furniture, Settee, 2 Matching Arm Chairs, Louis XV, C.1885, Silk Brocade 3000.00
Furniture, Settle, Oak, Leather Cushion, G.Stickley, C.1910, 28 X 32 In.Deep 950.00
Furniture, Settle, Pine, English, High Backed, Armrests, C.1700, 71 In. 450.00
Furniture, Shelf, Clock, Chestnut & Walnut Trim, Drawer In Top, 33 X 20 In. 115.00
Furniture, Shelf, Corner Wall, Rococo Styling, Gold Finish, 12 X 30 In. 15.00
Furniture, Shelf, Hanging, Pine, Stained, 6 Shelves, Pair Of Drawers, 48 In. 120.00
Furniture, Shelf, Poplar, Yellow, 29 3/4 X 11 3/4 X 4/ In. 110.00
Furniture, Shelf, Spice, Pine, 8 Drawer, Old Green Paint 195.00
Furniture, Side Table, D-Top, Gilt Stencil Of Neo Classical Devices, Fruits 850.00
Furniture, Sideboard, Carved Crest, Wolf Head, Walnut, 6 1/2 X 7 1/2 Feet 2500.00
Furniture, Sideboard, Cherry & Mahogany, Veneer On Cherry, 65 X 22 X 40 In. 300.00
Furniture, Sideboard, China Cabinet Top, Oak 725.00
Furniture, Sideboard, China Hutch Top, Hand-Carving, Oak 725.00
Furniture, Sideboard, Claw Feet, Carving, Oak 975.00
Furniture, Sideboard, Gargoyle Heads, Ornate Carving, Oak 695.00
Furniture, Sideboard, Hepplewhite, Inlaid Mahogany, 35 X 28 In. .... *Illus* 2000.00
Furniture, Sideboard, Inlaid Mahogany, Federal, Serpentine Front, 72 In. 2100.00
Furniture, Sideboard, Leaded Glass Door, Carved Figures, 66 X 72 X 15 In. 3000.00
Furniture, Sideboard, Mahogany, Classical, 6 Drawer, 1800s, 44 1/2 X 80 In. 1300.00
Furniture, Sideboard, Mahogany, Empire, 72 3/4 X 28 1/4 X 48 1/2 In. 425.00
Furniture, Sideboard, Mahogany, Georgian, C.1820, 37 X 66 3/4 X 24 3/4 In. 3400.00
Furniture, Sideboard, Mahogany, Hepplewhite, Veneered, 1790, 41 X 72 X 24 In. 1200.00
Furniture, Sideboard, Mahogany, Hepplewhite, 1900s, 60 X 24 1/4 X 39 In. 275.00
Furniture, Sideboard, Mahogany, Satinwood Inlaid, George III, 37 X 72 In. 1800.00
Furniture, Sideboard, Mahogany, Sheraton, England, C.1780, 72 X 36 1/2 In. 7000.00
Furniture, Sideboard, Mahogany, 4 Door, Brass Bails, Pulls & Gallery, 95 In. 925.00
Furniture, Sideboard, Miniature, Walnut, Brass Fittings, 12 X 20 1/2 In. 350.00
Furniture, Sideboard, Mission Oak, Leaded Glass Doors 300.00
Furniture, Sideboard, Oak, Gustav Stickley, C.1910, 47 3/4 X 55 15/16 In. 2000.00
Furniture, Sideboard, Pine, 7 Dovetailed Drawers, 51 X 19 X 71 In. 500.00
Furniture, Sideboard, Renaissance, Walnut 2900.00
Furniture, Sideboard, Rosewood, Mirrored Back, 2 Drawer, 5 Feet X 67 In.High 595.00
Furniture, Sideboard, Serpentine Case, 3 Frieze Drawers, Bowed Doors, Bottle 1100.00
Furniture, Sideboard, Sheraton, Bowfront, C.1780, 36 X 73 In. 4900.00
Furniture, Sideboard, Walnut & Burl Veneer, D-Shaped Case, Mirror Top 2000.00
Furniture, Sink, Dry, Pine, Pegged, C.1800, 33 1/2 X 42 1/2 X 14 1/4 In. 370.00
Furniture, Sleigh Bed, 4 Sleighed Ends, Full Size 1775.00
Furniture, Sofa, American Sheraton, Reeded Legs, Birch Inlays, 6 Ft.Long 2500.00

Furniture, Settee, Oak, Gothic Style
(See Page 197)

Furniture, Table, Card, Mahogany, Federal,
1810, 29 1/4 X 35 In.
(See Page 201)

Furniture, Sideboard, Hepplewhite, Inlaid Mahogany, 35 X 28 In.
(See Page 197)

Furniture, Table, Card, Mahogany,
Federal, 1810, 29 1/4 X 35 In.
(See Page 201)

Furniture, Table, Console,
Tiger & Bird's-Eye Maple, 29 In.
(See Page 201)

Furniture, Table, Game, Lacquer
& Gilt, Oriental Scenes, 25 In.
(See Page 202)

Furniture, Table, Oak, Mission,
G.Stickley, 30 1/4 X 54 X 32 In.
(See Page 202)

Furniture, Sofa, Empire, Carved Mahogany, Acanthus Carved Claw Feet, C.1830	350.00
Furniture, Sofa, Empire, Walnut Frame, Red Velvet Upholstery	450.00
Furniture, Sofa, Gold Leaf, Velvet, Victorian	500.00
Furniture, Sofa, Laminated Rosewood, New York, C & S Curves	4500.00
Furniture, Sofa, Mahogany & Bird's-Eye Maple, Federal, Massachusetts, 79 In.	3400.00
Furniture, Sofa, Mahogany, American Empire, Old Patina, C.1835	1250.00
Furniture, Sofa, Mahogany, Crest Carving, Horsehair Cover, C.1840	1200.00
Furniture, Sofa, Mahogany, Federal, School Of Duncan Phyfe, 1810s, 87 1/2 In.	6500.00
Furniture, Sofa, Oriental, Carved Fret Panels In Back & Arms, 76 In.	325.00
Furniture, Sofa, Wicker, Original Beige Paint, Rolled Paper "wicker"	500.00
Furniture, Sofa, 5 Matching Rockers, Wicker, Backs Curve To Form Arms	500.00
Furniture, Staircase, Spiral, Oak, Mahogany Rail, French, 13 Ft., 7 In.	2000.00
Furniture, Stand, Birdcage Basket Below, Cherry	445.00
Furniture, Stand, Cherry, 2 Dovetailed Drawers, 17 X 22 X 28 3/4 In.	95.00
Furniture, Stand, Cherrywood, Federal, 1 Drawer, New England, 1800s, 26 In.	275.00
Furniture, Stand, Curly Maple, Tilt-Top	425.00
Furniture, Stand, Dressing, Mahogany & Walnut, English, C.1800	210.00
Furniture, Stand, Federal, Pine & Curly Maple, C.1810, 28 3/4 X 20 3/4 In.	450.00
Furniture, Stand, Fern, Maple, 28 In.	39.50 To 49.50
Furniture, Stand, Hanging What-Not, Walnut, 4 Shelved, 34 In.	12.50
Furniture, Stand, Magazine, Wicker, Handle	22.00
Furniture, Stand, Oblong Top, Single Drawer, Square Tapered Legs, Red, Pine	100.00
Furniture, Stand, Oval Topped, Victorian	65.00
Furniture, Stand, Round Top, 3 Legs, Leaf Design In Gold & White, 26 1/4 In.	50.00
Furniture, Stand, Shaving, Mahogany, Baltimore Hepplewhite, C.1790, 19 In.	850.00
Furniture, Stand, Shaving, Oval Mirror, Oak	200.00
Furniture, Stand, Smoking, Handwrought, Bucks Co., Pennsylvania	125.00
Furniture, Stand, Teakwood, Blossoms & Birds, Marble Insert, 28 In.	250.00
Furniture, Stand, Teakwood, Inset Marble Top, C.1800, 12 X 24 1/2 In.	200.00
Furniture, Stand, Teakwood, Oriental, Marble Insert, Round, Carved Apron	275.00
Furniture, Stand, Teakwood, Pierced Floral, Drum Shaped, Marble Top, 21 In.	350.00
Furniture, Stand, Tip-Top, Walnut & Mahogany	675.00
Furniture, Stand, Turned Curly Maple, Federal, Pennsylvania, 32 1/4 In.	1000.00
Furniture, Stand, Umbrella, Oak, Copper Tray, G.Stickley, C.1908, 33 1/2 In.	200.00
Furniture, Stand, Urn, Chippendale & Cherrywood, C.1780, 22 1/4 X 12 1/2 In.	175.00
Furniture, Stand, Wig, Mercury Glass, French, Concrete Base, 17 1/2 In.	40.00
Furniture, Stand, 1-Drawer, Tiger Maple, Cherry Inlay, Bird's-Eye Maple	375.00
Furniture, Stand, 17 In.Platter Inset, As End Table	440.00
Furniture, Stand, 2-Drawer, Dish Top, Shaker	550.00
Furniture, Stool, Cloverleaf Shape, Legs Are Horns	18.00
Furniture, Stool, Curule, Louis XVI Style, Corrugation Fluting, 28 1/2 In.	150.00
Furniture, Stool, Gilt Wood, Continental, 18 In., Pair	700.00
Furniture, Stool, Ice Cream Parlor, Cast Iron, 1920s, Set Of 5	65.00
Furniture, Stool, Ice Cream, Porcelain, Set Of 5	485.00
Furniture, Stool, Mahogany, George II, Oval, 1700s, 22 In.	3200.00
Furniture, Stool, Milking, Cast Iron Base, 12 In.	15.00
Furniture, Stool, Organ, Glass Ball & Claw Feet	49.50
Furniture, Stool, Organ, Lift Seat, Burl Walnut Panels, Turned Spindles	69.50
Furniture, Stool, Organ, Lift Seat, Walnut, Needlepoint Seat	59.50
Furniture, Stool, Organ, Turned Legs & Arms, Upholstered Saddle Seat	49.50
Furniture, Stool, Organ, 3 Legs, Red Cover & Fringe, Iron	55.00
Furniture, Stool, Piano, Iron Claw, Glass Ball Inserts	35.00
Furniture, Stool, Piano, Mahogany, Federal, Ring Turned Legs, 19 1/4 In.	350.00
Furniture, Stool, Piano, Rosewood, Regency, 3 Scrolled Legs, 1800s, 21 1/2 In.	125.00
Furniture, Stool, Piano, Walnut, Pattern Back, Swivel, Glass Ball & Claw Feet	155.00
Furniture, Stool, Piano, 3 Legged, Glass Ball Claw Feet, Oak	100.00
Furniture, Stool, Tiger Maple	65.00
Furniture, Stool, Walnut, George II, On Leg Stamped S.G.W.	1000.00
Furniture, Stool, Wood, Cut-Out Base, Mortised, 8 X 15 In.	35.00
Furniture, Stool, 1 Drawer, Pine	165.00
Furniture, Table & 6 Spindle Chairs, Golden Oak, Carvings & Brass, 1885	1750.00
Furniture, Table Cabinet, Ebony, Ivory Mounted, Italian, 19 1/2 X 23 In.	1000.00
Furniture, Table En Chiffoniere, Parquetry, Ormolu Mounted, 29 X 16 In.	1300.00
Furniture, Table, Altar, Chinese, Pierced Fretwork, Carved Legs, 16 X 31 In.	525.00
Furniture, Table, Altar, Mother-Of-Pearl Inlaid, 1700s, 33 3/4 In.	4500.00
Furniture, Table, Baker's Dough, Fruitwood, French, 1700s, 64 X 28 X 28 In.	2250.00

Furniture, Table, Banquet, Mahogany, C.1900, Cabriole Legs, 5 Leaves 725.00
Furniture, Table, Birch, Hepplewhite, Pembroke, 15 3/4 X 36 X 8 1/2 In. 225.00
Furniture, Table, Breakfast, Drop-Leaf, Federal, C.1810, 29 X 48 3/4 In. 1400.00
Furniture, Table, Butler's Tray, English, Separate Sheraton Base 650.00
Furniture, Table, Butterfly, C.1895, Pair 300.00
Furniture, Table, Card, Chippendale, Swing Leg, Bird's-Eye Drawer 400.00
Furniture, Table, Card, Demi-Lune, Adams, 39 3/4 X 19 3/4 X 30 1/4 In. 375.00
Furniture, Table, Card, Gate Supports, Federal, C.1800, 29 X 37 In. 850.00
Furniture, Table, Card, Mahogany, Federal, C.1800, 29 1/2 X 36 In. 325.00
Furniture, Table, Card, Mahogany, Federal, 1810, 29 1/4 X 35 In. .... Illus 550.00
Furniture, Table, Card, Mahogany, Hepplewhite, Line Inlay, New York, C.1790 .... 575.00
Furniture, Table, Card, Mahogany, Sheraton, 29 3/4 X 36 In. .... Illus 2600.00
Furniture, Table, Card, Swivel Top, D-Shape, Crossband, Frieze, Leaves, Paw Feet 600.00
Furniture, Table, Carved Flowers, Vines, Teakwood, C.1870, 18 In.Square 269.00
Furniture, Table, Carved Walnut, Victorian, Quadrupedal Pedestal, 31 In. 800.00
Furniture, Table, Center, Gilt Wood, Acanthus Leaf Feet, 26 1/2 X 29 In. 50.00
Furniture, Table, Center, Mahogany, Carved Shell Knees, Claw Feet, 34 In. 125.00
Furniture, Table, Center, Painted & Grained, Empire, C.1825, 41 1/4 In.Diam. 650.00
Furniture, Table, Cherry, Pembroke, American, C.1810, 28 1/4 X 34 3/4 In. 175.00
Furniture, Table, Cherry, Sheraton, Inlaid Maple Ovals On Drawer Fronts 1600.00
Furniture, Table, Cherry, 1-Drawer, Rope Turned Legs, C.1820 .... 295.00
Furniture, Table, Chippendale, Drop Leaf, San Domingo Mahogany, C.1770 .... 1600.00
Furniture, Table, Claw Foot, Round, 48 In. 150.00
Furniture, Table, Console, Demi-Lune, Adams, 42 1/2 X 20 3/4 X 33 In. 1000.00
Furniture, Table, Console, French, Leaves & Flowers, 1800s, 28 X 49 X 30 In. 370.00
Furniture, Table, Console, French, Marble Top, 1800s, 25 X 99 3/4 X 38 In. 750.00
Furniture, Table, Console, Marble Top, 8 Tapering & Fluted Legs, 1800s 0000.00
Furniture, Table, Console, Neoclassical, Parcel Gilt, Rome, 1800s, 33 X 69 In. 700.00
Furniture, Table, Console, Regency Coramandel Wood, C.1810, Nolan & Sons 2600.00
Furniture, Table, Console, Tiger & Bird's-Eye Maple, 29 In. .... Illus 275.00

Furniture, Table, Dining, Satinwood,
Art Deco, Leytens Freres, 1900s

Furniture, Table, Corner, Rosewood & Mahogany, Brass Inlaid, English, 29 In. 325.00
Furniture, Table, Curly Maple, Drop Leaf, 6 Leg, 18 1/2 X 44 1/4 X 20 In. 385.00
Furniture, Table, Dark Wood, Marble Top, Porcelain Casters, 1850, 29 X 31 In. 265.00
Furniture, Table, Dining, Carved Base, Detailed Runner, C.1860, 78 X 32 In. 3000.00
Furniture, Table, Dining, Chippendale, Carved Mahogany, Drop-Leaf, 53 1/2 In. 4250.00
Furniture, Table, Dining, Claw Foot, 5 Leaves, Oak, 48 In.Diameter 750.00
Furniture, Table, Dining, Drop Leaf, Beaded Apron, Ring & Spiral Taper Legs 400.00
Furniture, Table, Dining, Drop Leaf, Scalloped Apron, Cabriole Legs, Pad Feet 2000.00
Furniture, Table, Dining, Mahogany, Ormolu Mounted, Continental, 26 1/2 In. 2500.00
Furniture, Table, Dining, Oak, 4 Leaves, Carved Legs, C.1890, 54 In.Diameter 2500.00
Furniture, Table, Dining, Satinwood, Art Deco, Leytens Freres, 1900s .... Illus 1600.00
Furniture, Table, Dining, Sheraton, Mahogany, Reeded Leg 375.00
Furniture, Table, Dining, Wicker, Oak Top, 45 In., Round 395.00
Furniture, Table, Dining, Wicker, Round 125.00
Furniture, Table, Dining, 3 Pedestal, George III, 1770s, 29 X 130 In. 6500.00
Furniture, Table, Dining, 3-Part, Mahogany, 2 D-Ends, 29 X 11 Feet 2 In. 2750.00
Furniture, Table, Draw Leaf, Oak, Late 17th Century, 90 In. 1500.00
Furniture, Table, Draw Leaf, Walnut, Late 17th Century, 32 X 88 In. 1000.00
Furniture, Table, Dressing, Beveled Mirror, Maple 225.00
Furniture, Table, Dressing, Mahogany, Classical, Lyre Base, C.1810, 57 1/2 In. 2500.00
Furniture, Table, Dressing, Queen Anne, Curly Maple Front, Matching Stool 275.00
Furniture, Table, Dressing, 2-Drawer, Sheraton 365.00
Furniture, Table, Drop Leaf, Child's, Round Drop, Top Swivels, 12 In. 150.00
Furniture, Table, Drop Leaf, Empire, Walnut, 2 Drawer, 36 X 46 In. 180.00
Furniture, Table, Drop Leaf, Golden Oak, Drawer & Under Shelf, C.1890 .... 350.00

Furniture, Table, Drop Leaf, Mahogany, Child's, 28 1/2 X 19 X 22 In. 33.00
Furniture, Table, Drop Leaf, Mahogany, George III, 1 Drawer, 28 X 28 In. 200.00
Furniture, Table, Drop Leaf, Mahogany, Shell Inlay, 1800s, Miniature, 7 In. 225.00
Furniture, Table, Drop Leaf, Mahogany, 1 Drawer, 28 3/4 X 34 1/4 In. 400.00
Furniture, Table, Drop Leaf, Miniature, 19th Century, 19 X 21 5/8 In. 200.00
Furniture, Table, Drop Leaf, Original Red, C.1820, Opens To 40 X 42 In. 165.00
Furniture, Table, Drop Leaf, Sheraton, Cut Corner, 1 Drawer, 1 Board, 24 In. 290.00
Furniture, Table, Drop Leaf, Trestle Feet, Gate Supports, Oak, 27 In. 350.00
Furniture, Table, Drop Leaf, Walnut Queen Anne, C.1750, 42 X 27 In. 2250.00
Furniture, Table, End, Wicker, 27 3/4 X 22 3/4 X 12 In. 75.00
Furniture, Table, Farm, Poplar, Long & Short Drawer, Turned Legs, C.1840 .... 585.00
Furniture, Table, Game, Burl Walnut, George I, Money Wells, 1700s, 29 X 33 In. 2500.00
Furniture, Table, Game, Lacquer & Gilt, Oriental Scenes, 25 In. ....Illus 850.00
Furniture, Table, Game, Mahogany, Half Round, Queen Anne, Pad Feet 350.00
Furniture, Table, Game, New England, C.1800 .... 425.00
Furniture, Table, Game, Triple Top, D-Shaped, George II, 1700s, 29 X 32 In. 1300.00
Furniture, Table, Game, Triple-Top, Walnut, English, C.1725, 30 1/2 In. 6900.00
Furniture, Table, Gilt Bamboo, Vitrine, Red Lacquer, Glass Top, 1800s, 31 In. 2400.00
Furniture, Table, Gilt Wood, Specimen & Tesserae Marble Top, 1800s, 28 In. 950.00
Furniture, Table, Harvest, 19th Century, 10 Feet 1200.00
Furniture, Table, Hepplewhite, Console, Swing Leg, Flat Top, C.1770 .... 175.00
Furniture, Table, Hutch, Pine, New York State, Red Paint 1350.00
Furniture, Table, Hutch, Top, 48 X 34 1/2 In. 595.00
Furniture, Table, Hutch, Yellow Base, Connecticut, 4 Feet Diameter, C.1810 .... 3900.00
Furniture, Table, Lamp, Chinese Teakwood, Carved Dogs For Legs, 1800s 950.00
Furniture, Table, Lamp, Louis XVI Style, Ormolu Mounted, 1800s, 52 X 24 In. 250.00
Furniture, Table, Lamp, Pedestal, Octagon, Walnut, 32 In. 185.00
Furniture, Table, Lamp, Porcelain Casters, Oak, 26 In.Square 245.00
Furniture, Table, Lamp, Walnut, Victorian, Marble Top, Finger Carved Supports 200.00
Furniture, Table, Library, Carved & Inlaid Mahogany, Federal, 27 1/4 In. 1800.00
Furniture, Table, Library, Eastlake Carved Drawer & Apron, C.1870, Felt Top 200.00
Furniture, Table, Library, L. & J.G.Stickley, C.1910, 29 X 59 1/2 In. 850.00
Furniture, Table, Library, Mahogany, Federal, Drop-Leaf, C.1810, 28 1/2 In. 2100.00
Furniture, Table, Library, Rosewood, Veneered, Victorian, 2 Drawer 225.00
Furniture, Table, Library, Spool Legs, China Casters, 60 X 35 X 32 In.High 800.00
Furniture, Table, Library, Walnut, 1 Drawer, Carved & Shaped Sides 1150.00
Furniture, Table, Library, 2 In.Top, Spool Legs, 2-Drawer, 60 X 35 X 32 In. 800.00
Furniture, Table, Mahogany, Victorian, Ornate Legs, Circular, 32 X 29 In. 210.00
Furniture, Table, Mahogany, 2 Drawer, 1 Shelf, 28 X 46 X 30 In. 70.00
Furniture, Table, Malachite, Ormolu Mounted, Continental, 1800s, 24 X 24 In. 2000.00
Furniture, Table, Marble, Jaune De Verone, Italian, C.1800, 31 X 42 In. 2600.00
Furniture, Table, Marble, Oval, Walnut, Gold Incised Carving, 18 X 32 In. 450.00
Furniture, Table, Oak, Bulbous Legs, Block Feet, Round, 1900s, 30 X 36 In. 400.00
Furniture, Table, Oak, Claw Foot, 55 In.Diameter 1395.00
Furniture, Table, Oak, Claw Pedestal, Leaves, 4 Gargoyles, 60 In.Diameter 900.00
Furniture, Table, Oak, Gustav Stickley, Signed, 38 In.Diameter 845.00
Furniture, Table, Oak, L. & J.G.Stickley, C.1910, 29 1/4 X 24 In.Diameter 300.00
Furniture, Table, Oak, Mission, G.Stickley, 30 1/4 X 54 X 32 In. ....Illus 700.00
Furniture, Table, Oak, Removable Plank Top, Bun Feet, 1650s, 34 X 60 In. 1300.00
Furniture, Table, Oak, Stickley Bros., Metal Tag, 24 X 29 3/4 In.Diameter 200.00
Furniture, Table, Oak, 48 In.Diameter 225.00
Furniture, Table, Oriental Pedestal, Carved, Turned Leg, Lacquered, 30 In. 165.00
Furniture, Table, Pembroke, Chippendale, Carved Walnut, Philadelphia, 1770s 1000.00
Furniture, Table, Pembroke, Mahogany, Chippendale, 20 X 31 X 28 1/2 In. 500.00
Furniture, Table, Pembroke, 1 Drawer, Drop Leaves, 28 X 16 X 24 In. 60.00
Furniture, Table, Pier, Marble Top, Recessed Arch, Brass Columns, Ebony Feet 700.00
Furniture, Table, Poker, Ornate Pedestal 425.00
Furniture, Table, Porcelain & Sevres, Ormolu Mounted, 1800s, 24 1/2 In. 6000.00
Furniture, Table, Provincial Oak, Louis XV, Cabriole Legs, 26 1/2 In. 950.00
Furniture, Table, Pub, Marble Top, Cast Iron 265.00
Furniture, Table, Pub, Wood Top, Cast Iron 220.00
Furniture, Table, Queen Anne, Drop Leaf, Valanced Apron, Cabriole Legs, Padded 3000.00
Furniture, Table, Rectangular, White Marble Top, Walnut, Victorian 175.00
Furniture, Table, Red On Top & Base, Scrubbed Top, 5 1/2 In. 300.00
Furniture, Table, Refectory, Oak, Pedestal, Baroque, 1600s, 31 X 192 1/2 In. 1200.00
Furniture, Table, Rosewood, Inlaid Mother-Of-Pearl, Scenic, 60 In. 3250.00

Furniture, Table, Satinwood, Mahogany, 3 Pedestal, George III, 29 X 130 In.	8750.00
Furniture, Table, Satinwood, Pembroke, Inlaid, George III, 1700s, 27 In.	2600.00
Furniture, Table, Sewing, Black, Gold Lacquer, Chinese, C.1840, 29 1/2 In.	925.00
Furniture, Table, Sewing, Drop Leaf, C.1800-10, American	895.00
Furniture, Table, Sewing, Mahogany & Maple Wood, Massachusetts, 1800s, 31 In.	850.00
Furniture, Table, Sewing, Mahogany, American, C.1800, 27 In.High	1650.00
Furniture, Table, Sewing, Mother-Of-Pearl Inlaid, Black, Chinese, 30 X 15 In.	300.00
Furniture, Table, Sewing, Sheraton, 3 Center Drawers, 2 Side Compartments	50.00
Furniture, Table, Sheraton, Dovetailed Drawer, Pine, 36 X 18 X 35 1/4 In.	300.00
Furniture, Table, Sheraton, 3-Part, Centennial, Walnut Leaves	3500.00
Furniture, Table, Side, Fruitwood, 2 Tier, Marquetry, French, 1900s, 31 1/2 In.	300.00
Furniture, Table, Side, Mahogany, George II, Brass Paw Feet, 33 X 60 In.	1200.00
Furniture, Table, Side, Mahogany, George III, 1 Drawer, Square Legs, 28 In.	200.00
Furniture, Table, Side, Oak, 1 Shelf, 25 In.	25.00
Furniture, Table, Side, Rosewood, Inlaid Mother-Of-Pearl, 2 Drawer, 37 In.	1700.00
Furniture, Table, Side, Sheraton, Banded Inlay & Reeded Legs	150.00
Furniture, Table, Side, Walnut, Victorian, Oval Top, Carved, Base, 27 X 29 In.	125.00
Furniture, Table, Sofa, Mahogany, Federal, Brass Paw Casters, 29 X 66 In.	1300.00
Furniture, Table, Sofa, Rosewood & Mahogany, Regency, 2 Drawer, 28 X 60 In.	2700.00
Furniture, Table, Steamboat, Cherry, C.1840, 4 Leaves, 48 X 96 In.	1500.00
Furniture, Table, Tap, Cherry Hepplewhite	145.00
Furniture, Table, Tavern, Cherrywood, Oval Top, New England, 1750s, 28 In.	750.00
Furniture, Table, Tavern, English, Tripod Base, Shelf, 26 1/2 X 28 1/4 In.	140.00
Furniture, Table, Tavern, Maple & Pine, Turned Legs, 1800s, 26 In.	600.00
Furniture, Table, Tavern, Oblong Top, Plain Skirt, Square Tapered Legs, Pine	300.00
Furniture, Table, Tavern, Tapered & Splayed Legs, Red Finish, 24 X 27 In.	350.00
Furniture, Table, Tavern, 18th Century, Grain Paint	2700.00
Furniture, Table, Tavern, 18th Century, 26 1/4 X 46 3/4 In.	950.00
Furniture, Table, Tea, Chippendale, Carved Mahogany, Piecrust Edge, 37 In.	4000.00
Furniture, Table, Tea, Mahogany, English Tilt Top, 29 3/4 X 27 1/2 In.	475.00
Furniture, Table, Tea, Queen Anne, Walnut, 18th Century, 28 1/2 X 34 5/8 In.	500.00
Furniture, Table, Tea, Tilt Top, Snake Feet	375.00
Furniture, Table, Tea, Tray Top, Drawer, Cyma Curved Apron, Cabriole Legs	3600.00
Furniture, Table, Teak, Marble Top, Chinese, 38 In.Diameter	575.00
Furniture, Table, Teakwood, Florals In Mother-Of-Pearl, 1800s, 38 X 28 In.	550.00
Furniture, Table, Teakwood, Flowers & Leaves In Relief, Carved	75.00
Furniture, Table, Tiger Maple, Drop Leaf, Cherry Apron & Legs	550.00
Furniture, Table, Tilt Top, Bird Cage Candlestand, Salem	750.00
Furniture, Table, Tilt Top, Tiger Maple, Birdcage, Serpentine Feet, 32 In.	385.00
Furniture, Table, Tilt Top, With Bird Cage	850.00
Furniture, Table, Tip & Turn, Carved Tripod, Irish, C.1760-70, 28 In.	2000.00
Furniture, Table, Trestle, C.Rohlfs, C.1907, Oak, 29 X 78 X 42 In.	6500.00
Furniture, Table, Trestle, Pine & Walnut, Spanish Baroque, 31 X 63 In.	500.00
Furniture, Table, Turtle Top, Walnut, Carved Apron, Cabriole Legs, C.1860	425.00
Furniture, Table, Walnut, Harvest, Primitive, 6 X 2 1/2 In.	750.00
Furniture, Table, Walnut, Marquetry, Mother-Of-Pearl, Pewter, Bone, 29 1/2 In.	1300.00
Furniture, Table, Walnut, Pegged, H-Bulbous Stretcher, Bucks Co., Redfield	165.00
Furniture, Table, Walnut, Victorian, Carved Base, Oval Top, 20 1/2 X 26 In.	110.00
Furniture, Table, Work, Canted, Outset-Rounded Corners, Drawer, Section Inside	2100.00
Furniture, Table, Work, Carved & Inlaid Mahogany, Federal, 30 X 26 3/4 In.	1500.00
Furniture, Table, Work, Cream Paint, C.1830	195.00
Furniture, Table, Work, Curly Maple, Federal, 30 In.High, 15 3/8 In.Wide	325.00
Furniture, Table, Work, Federal, C.1800-10, 30 1/2 In X 20 1/2 In.	1400.00
Furniture, Table, Work, Federal, Mahogany, C.1815, 28 1/4 X 22 In.	750.00
Furniture, Table, Work, Mahogany, American, C.1815, 22 X 15 X 30 In.High	835.00
Furniture, Table, Work, Mahogany, Hepplewhite, American, 28 X 13 3/4 X 28 In.	200.00
Furniture, Table, Work, Taper Leg, Single-Board, Scrub-Top	425.00
Furniture, Table, Work, Tiger Maple, 1-Drawer	595.00
Furniture, Table, Writing, Bank, Sloped Either Side, 3 Drawers, Mahogany	500.00
Furniture, Table, Writing, Black, Gold, Lacquer, Fretwork, 32 X 51 In.	2700.00
Furniture, Table, Writing, Hepplewhite, Mahogany Veneer, 4 Drawers	250.00
Furniture, Table, Writing, Library, Mahogany, English, C.1850-60, 30 X 53 In.	700.00
Furniture, Table, Writing, Mahogany, Federal, Slope Front, 31 3/4 X 27 In.	1000.00
Furniture, Table, Writing, Mahogany, George III, 3 Drawer, 30 1/4 X 57 In.	3800.00
Furniture, Table, Writing, Mahogany, Parcel Gilt, Ormolu, 1800s, 29 In.	3750.00
Furniture, Table, Writing, Mahogany, Regency, Kneehole, 9 Drawer, 30 X 39 In.	650.00

Furniture, Throne, Bishop's, Oak, Gothic Style, 1800s

Furniture, Table, Writing, Mahogany, 3 Dovetailed Drawers, 51 X 22 X 30 In.	310.00
Furniture, Table, Writing, Poplar & Pine, 2-Drawer, Shelf	260.00
Furniture, Table, 4 Legged, Oak, Signed Gustav Stickley, 38 In.Diameter	845.00
Furniture, Tabourette, Oak, Tile Top, Stickley, C.1909, 22 1/2 X 17 X 17 In.	850.00
Furniture, Telephone Stand, Caned Sides & Matching Chair, Walnut	425.00
Furniture, Throne, Bishop's, Oak, Gothic Style, 1800s ....Illus	1700.00
Furniture, Throne, Ecclesiastical, Storage In Bottom, 8 Feet High	1200.00
Furniture, Tobacco Stand, Copper Lined, Magazine Rack, Walnut, C.1920	65.00
Furniture, Tray, Bed, Kidney Shaped, Wicker & Wood, Folding, 26 In.	23.00
Furniture, Tray, Butler's, Mahogany, Dovetailed, Folding Stand, 34 1/2 In.	125.00
Furniture, Tray, Butler's, Mahogany, George III, C.1780, 29 1/2 In.	550.00
Furniture, Tray, Wicker, Glass Over Print, Dated 1915, 12 In.Diameter	20.00
Furniture, Umbrella Stand, Lion's Head Handles, Cylinder, China	85.00
Furniture, Umbrella Stand, Saucer Base, Iron, Double Arm	45.00
Furniture, Vanity & Dresser, Bird's-Eye Maple	500.00
Furniture, Vitrine, Table, Ormolu Mounted, Continental, 1800s, 18 1/2 In.	1800.00
Furniture, Wardrobe, Curly Maple, 2 Section Doors, 14 3/4 X 38 3/4 In.	950.00
Furniture, Warmer, Foot, Carpet Covered, Drawer For Briquettes	14.00
Furniture, Warmer, Foot, Heart Pierced, Spooled Posts, Pegged Maple Frame	83.00
Furniture, Wash Stand & Dresser, Marble Top, Walnut, 1890 Period	600.00
Furniture, Washstand, Towel Bar, Clawfoot, Maple	210.00
Furniture, Weapon Case, Revolving, Oak, 3 Ft.Square X 6 Ft.	2200.00
Furniture, What-Not, Papier Mache & Lacquer, Victorian, Mirror, 1800s, 52 In.	700.00
Furniture, Window Seat, Mahogany, Rectangular Seat, C.1815, 5 Feet 6 In.	1300.00

G-ARGY-
ROUSSEAU

Gabriel Argy-Rousseau, born in 1885, was a French glass artist who produced a variety of objects in Art Deco style. His mark, G. Argy-Rousseau, was usually impressed.

G.Argy-Rousseau, Bowl, Frosted Ground, Pate-De-Verre, Signed, 3 1/2 In.	250.00

Galle

Galle glass was made by the Galle Factory founded in 1874 by Emile Galle of France. The firm made cameo glass, furniture, and other Art Nouveau items, including some pottery. After Galle's death in 1904, the firm continued in production until 1935.

Galle, Atomizer, Amethyst Pedestal Base, Brass Top, Original Label	250.00
Galle, Atomizer, Brown Flowers & Leaves, Frosted Ground, Signed	240.00
Galle, Atomizer, Original Rubber Fittings, Green Ground, Signed, 8 3/4 In.	775.00
Galle, Atomizer, Red On Honey, 7 In.	250.00
Galle, Bottle, Perfume, Original Stopper, Signed, 4 X 4 In.	350.00
Galle, Bottle, Perfume, Pink Ground, Crystal Ball Stopper, Signed, 5 In.	475.00
Galle, Bottle, Perfume, Purple Flowers, Stopper, 7 1/2 In. .... 950.00 To	1250.00
Galle, Bottle, Pilgrim, Orange, Signed, 5 1/2 In.	590.00
Galle, Bowl, Cameo With Fern Design, 5 1/2 In.Diameter	325.00
Galle, Bowl, Cameo, Wide Mouthed, Cut With Scrolling, Signed, 4 3/4 In.Diam.	190.00
Galle, Bowl, Finger, Underplate, Violet, Signed, 2 1/2 X 4 3/4 In.	875.00
Galle, Bowl, Purple Over Gray, Signed, 4 3/4 In.	290.00
Galle, Bowl, Trefoil Mottled Gray & Yellow, Blossoms, Signed, 4 3/4 In.	650.00
Galle, Bowl, Trefoil Yellow, Overlay, Signed, 4 3/4 In.	650.00
Galle, Bowl, 2 Acid Cuttings, Cameo Of Fern, Foliage, Signed, 5 In.	400.00

Galle, Bowl, 4 Points On Rim, Cameo, Signed, 7 3/4 X 4 In.	300.00
Galle, Box, Cameo, Autumn Colors, Round, Covered, 4 In.	650.00
Galle, Box, Covered, Bleeding Hearts On Frosted Blue Ground, 5 In.Diameter	575.00
Galle, Box, Covered, Yellow Ground, Leaves & Berries, 6 In.Square	425.00
Galle, Box, Frosted Background, Signed, 4 X 3 1/2 In.	495.00
Galle, Box, Octagon, Ebony Inlaid Ivory, Inlaid Quill, 8 1/2 In.	115.00
Galle, Box, Powder, Flowers, Leaves, Gray Ground, Signed, 3 1/2 X 2 1/4 In.	275.00
Galle, Cordial, Boy Blowing Bubbles, Crystal & Enamel, Signed, 5 In.	275.00
Galle, Cruet, Green Swirl, Overlay, Stopper, Signed, 13 In.	475.00
Galle, Decanter Set, 5 Glasses, Enameled, Tiered Stopper, Signed, 9 1/2 In.	950.00
Galle, Jardiniere, Acid Etched Ground, Enameled, Gold Trim, Signed, 6 In.	750.00
Galle, Jardiniere, Hallmarked Collar, Paperweight Leaves, 5 X 8 1/2 In.Wide	1950.00
Galle, Lamp Base, Red Morning Glories, 3 Acid Cuttings, 12 In.	550.00
Galle, Night Light, White Ground, 4 Acid & Wheel Cuttings, Signed, 9 1/4 In.	1500.00
Galle, Pottery, Bowl, Bulb, Delft Type Scene, 3 1/2 X 6 1/2 In.	260.00
Galle, Pottery, Bowl, Nautilus Shell, Signed	450.00
Galle, Pottery, Figurine, Cat, Yellow, Blue Hearts, Glass Eyes	75.00
Galle, Pottery, Plate, Oriental Peasant Design, Signed, 10 In.	275.00
Galle, Rose Bowl, Cameo, Floral, Leaves Sprout From Soil, Iridescent, Signed	750.00
Galle, Rose Bowl, Orange On Clear, Signed, 2 1/4 X 3 In.Diameter	375.00
Galle, Rose Bowl, Purple, Flowers & Leaves, Signed, 2 3/4 X 3 In.	325.00
Galle, Rose Bowl, Violet On Pale Pink, Signed, 2 1/4 X 3 In.Diameter	375.00
Galle, Salt, Pedestal, Rippled Green Ground, Flower Enameling	135.00
Galle, Tray, Marquetry, Inlaid Wood, Hunter, Wife, Child On Horse, 16 X 25 In.	650.00
Galle, Tray, Oblong, Double Handled, Footed, 17 X 10 In.	350.00
Galle, Tumbler, Enameled, Dragon & Flowers, Opalescent Amber, 2 1/2 In.	800.00
Galle, Tumbler, Scenic, Forest, Lake Skyline, Pink Ground, Signed, 3 1/2 In.	425.00
Galle, Urn, Covered, 3-Footed, Birds, Signed, 28 X 8 1/2 In.Diameter	1500.00
Galle, Urn, Monumental, Cherry & Leaf Cameo, Mottled Inside, Signed, 14 In.	2600.00
Galle, Vase & Jar, Covered, White Beading, Vase, 5 3/4 In., Jar, 5 In., Set	675.00
Galle, Vase, Acid Cuttings, Lavender Flowers, Signed, 5 In.	425.00
Galle, Vase, Acid Cuttings, Wine Flowers, Green Stems, Signed, 13 In.	675.00
Galle, Vase, Amber Cut Back, Water Lillies, Signed, 4 In. ....Illus	325.00
Galle, Vase, Amber Cut Leaves & Blossoms, White Ground, 13 3/4 In.	625.00
Galle, Vase, Applied Sterling Silver Repousse, Iris Pattern, 17 In.	600.00
Galle, Vase, Apricot Flowers & Leaves, Miniature	275.00
Galle, Vase, Arum Lily Shaped, Hammered Ground, Signed, 5 1/4 X 5 1/2 In.	1250.00
Galle, Vase, Baluster Shape, 3 Cameo Layers, Melon Pink Frosted, Signed	675.00
Galle, Vase, Banjo Shaped, Brown Grapes, Vine Cut To Deep Yellow, 11 In.	495.00
Galle, Vase, Blossoms & Leaves Deep Grape, Signed In Cameo, 5 X 3 1/4 In.	450.00
Galle, Vase, Blue & Green, Lake, Mountain & Trees, Signed, 7 In. ....Illus	700.00
Galle, Vase, Blue Ground, Scattered Purple Phlox, 14 1/2 In.	975.00
Galle, Vase, Boat Shape, Red Berries, Leaves, Orange, Red, White, Signed, 5 In.	545.00
Galle, Vase, Boat Shaped, Enameled Beach Scene, 9 X 3 1/2 X 4 In.	95.00
Galle, Vase, Bright Orange, White Frosted Background, 6 1/2 In.	285.00
Galle, Vase, Brown & Orange, Seaweed Design, Signed, 3 In.	295.00
Galle, Vase, Brown Leaves, Blue Fuchsia, Gourd Shaped, Signed, 5 1/2 In.	375.00
Galle, Vase, Brown, Man Fishing, Trees, Water, Fence, 9 1/2 In.	1350.00
Galle, Vase, Bud, Cameo, Wheel-Polished, Lavender & Purple, Signed, 6 1/2 In.	425.00
Galle, Vase, Bud, Fire Polished, Signed, 5 1/2 In.	325.00
Galle, Vase, Bud, Flowers, Leaves, Purple, Yellow, Beige, Cameo, Signed, 2 In.	275.00
Galle, Vase, Bud, Orange, Signed, 4 1/8 In.	425.00
Galle, Vase, Bulbous, Lime, Peach, Frosted White Ground, 3 1/4 In.	275.00
Galle, Vase, Cameo Cut, Poppies, Footed, Signed, 8 In.	475.00
Galle, Vase, Cameo, Amethyst On Frosted Ground, 8 1/2 In.	300.00
Galle, Vase, Cameo, Baluster Form, Everted Mouth, Orange Ground, Signed, 5 In.	390.00
Galle, Vase, Cameo, Baluster Form, Orange Background, Signed, 5 In.	390.00
Galle, Vase, Cameo, Berry & Leaf, Signed, French, 8 1/2 In. ....Illus	450.00
Galle, Vase, Cameo, Carved Flowers On Frosted Ground, Signed, 4 7/8 In.	345.00
Galle, Vase, Cameo, Columbine, Frosted Ground, Acid Cut, 5 1/2 X 1 7/8 In.	245.00
Galle, Vase, Cameo, Enameled, Floral, 2 Handled, C.1885 ....Illus 2100.00	2100.00
Galle, Vase, Cameo, Flower & Leaf Design, C.1895 ....Illus 1100.00	1100.00
Galle, Vase, Cameo, Frosted Blue To Gold, Acid Cut, Signed, 6 3/4 In.	395.00
Galle, Vase, Cameo, Frosted Peach Ground, 2 1/4 X 2 7/8 In.Diameter	245.00
Galle, Vase, Cameo, Magenta On Pink Frosted, Signed, 4 3/4 In.	390.00
Galle, Vase, Cameo, Purple & Blue, Opaque White Background, Signed, 14 In.	585.00

Galle, Vase, Blue & Green,
Lake, Mountain & Trees.
Signed, 7 In.
(See Page 205)

Galle, Vase, Iris On White Ground,
Signed, 7 1/2 In.

Galle, Vase, Amber
Cut Back, Water Lillie
Signed, 4 In.
(See Page 205)

Galle, Vase, Green & White,
Berried Branches, Signed, 5 In.

Galle, Vase, Lime Green,
Aubergine Leaves & Pods,
Signed, 5 In.

Galle, Vase, Cameo, Enameled,
Floral, 2 Handled, C.1885

Galle, Vase, Cameo, Flower
& Leaf Design, C.1895

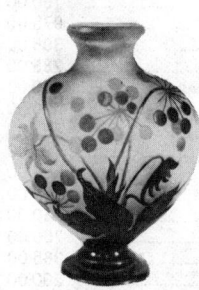

Galle, Vase, Cameo, Berry & Leaf,
Signed, French, 8 1/2 In.
(See Page 205)

Galle, Vase, Cameo, Russet To Salmon, 5 In.	250.00
Galle, Vase, Cameo, Stick, Frosted Gray, Signed, 5 In.	450.00
Galle, Vase, Cameo, Thistles Carved Each Side, Opaque Ground, Signed, 8 In.	895.00
Galle, Vase, Cameo, Wheel Polished Wild Flowers, Signed, 4 7/8 In.	675.00
Galle, Vase, Cameo, Yellow Background, Signed, 7 1/4 In.	650.00
Galle, Vase, Cameo, 2 Acid Cuttings, Wheel Cutting, Tri-Color, Signed, 5 In.	450.00
Galle, Vase, Cameo, 3-Ribbed Melon Shape, Long Neck, Peach Ground, 10 1/2 In.	450.00
Galle, Vase, Cherries & Leaves On Frosted Ground, 4 In.	300.00
Galle, Vase, Columbine Floral, Frosted Yellow, Signed, 5 1/7 X 1 7/8 In.	245.00
Galle, Vase, Cone Shape, Matching Covered Dish, Beading, 5 1/2 In., Set	650.00
Galle, Vase, Cream Frost & Velvet Brown Leaves, 16 In.	90.00
Galle, Vase, Cream, Green & Pink, Acorns & Oak Leaves, 16 1/2 In.	700.00
Galle, Vase, Cross Of Lorraine, Enameled, Footed, C.1878, Signed, 6 In.	475.00
Galle, Vase, Crystal & Enamel, Multi-Colored, 3 1/2 In.	285.00
Galle, Vase, Enameled, Oriental Signature, 9 3/4 In.	1100.00
Galle, Vase, Enameled, Tiger Lilies, Hexagonal, Signed, 3 1/2 X 4 1/2 In.	875.00
Galle, Vase, Flask Shape, Blown-Out Pilgrim, Flowers, 8 1/2 X 5 In.	3400.00
Galle, Vase, Floral Stalks, Celadon Colored Ground, Pinched Neck, 9 1/4 In.	850.00
Galle, Vase, Floral, Purple, Green To White, Signed, 5 1/2 In.	415.00
Galle, Vase, Flowers On Cream, Acid Finish Background, Signed, 8 1/4 In.	650.00
Galle, Vase, Folded Leaf Shape, Castle In Country, People, Blues, 11 In.	425.00
Galle, Vase, Footed, Chinese Junkets, Blue & Purple, Signed, 4 1/2 X 9 In.	1900.00
Galle, Vase, Footed, Frosted Colors, Pedestal Foot, Signed In Cameo, 4 In.	325.00
Galle, Vase, Four Color, Purple Base, Signed, 7 3/4 In.	1100.00
Galle, Vase, French Cameo, Poppy Blossoms, 8 In.	450.00
Galle, Vase, French Cameo, Round Shape, Pointed Lip Top, 13 In.	2200.00
Galle, Vase, Frost Ground, Lavender Foliage, Signed, 3 3/4 In.	140.00
Galle, Vase, Frosted Ground, Flowers In Two Layers, Signed, 5 1/2 In.	375.00
Galle, Vase, Frosted White Ground, Blue Flowers, Signed, 15 1/2 In.	490.00
Galle, Vase, Frosted White, Green & Pink Poppies, 13 3/4 In.	450.00
Galle, Vase, Frosted, Olive Green To Pink, 13 3/4 In.	500.00
Galle, Vase, Fuchsia, Wheel Polished, Orange Ground, Signed, 10 1/2 In.	975.00
Galle, Vase, Golden Ground, Red & Burgundy Roses, 11 In.	975.00
Galle, Vase, Golden Ground, Roses, Wheel Polished, 11 In.	975.00
Galle, Vase, Golden Hued, Carved, Signed, 6 1/4 In.	250.00
Galle, Vase, Grasshopper & Floral, Bronze Mountings, Signed, 10 In.	475.00
Galle, Vase, Green & White, Berried Branches, Signed, 5 In. *Illus*	425.00
Galle, Vase, Hanging Fuchsia On Frosted Background, Deep Cut, 9 In.	850.00
Galle, Vase, Honeycomb Shape, Honey Colored, C.1890s, Signed, 5 1/2 In.	1850.00
Galle, Vase, Inverted Gourd Shape, Blue & Purple Flowers, Signed, 7 3/4 In.	1700.00
Galle, Vase, Iris On White Ground, Signed, 7 1/2 In. *Illus*	700.00
Galle, Vase, Iris, Purple, Yellow Frosted Ground, Signed, 6 1/2 In.	350.00
Galle, Vase, Lake Scene With Trees, Baluster Shaped, Wine, Green, Pink, 10 In.	675.00
Galle, Vase, Lavender & Purple On Frosted Ground, Crocus, Signed, 3 1/4 In.	285.00
Galle, Vase, Lavender & White Floral, Frosted Background, Signed, 5 1/2 In.	375.00
Galle, Vase, Leaves & Flowers, Butterfly On Neck, Signed, 4 X 2 In.	250.00
Galle, Vase, Lime Green, Aubergine Leaves & Pods, Signed, 5 In. *Illus*	400.00

Galle, Vase, Miniature, Cameo, Single Cut Lavender Leaves, Flowers On Opaque	240.00
Galle, Vase, Miniature, Flowers, Purple, Frosted, Rose Bowl Shape, 2 In.	150.00
Galle, Vase, Mountains, Trees, Lake, Wheelcut, 3 Color, Signed, 6 1/2 In.	975.00
Galle, Vase, Narrow At Mouth, Wider Base, Brown Leaves & Berries, 3 1/4 In.	395.00
Galle, Vase, Orange Flowers On White, Signed, 3 7/8 In.	285.00
Galle, Vase, Oriental Style, Brown Floral, Orange Body, Signed, 6 In.	450.00
Galle, Vase, Pansies, Leaves, Green, Pink, Frosted, Signed, 12 In.	525.00
Galle, Vase, Pedestal, Wheel Polished, Gold Iridescent, Signed, 8 In.	895.00
Galle, Vase, Pedestal, Wheel Polished, Yellow Ground, Signed, 4 7/3 In.	495.00
Galle, Vase, Pink Frosted Ground, Lilac, 8 In.	550.00
Galle, Vase, Polished Brown Leaves, Yellow Ground, 4 1/2 In.	300.00
Galle, Vase, Portrait Of Bride & Groom, Crystal & Enamel, Signed, 5 In.	250.00
Galle, Vase, Portrait Of Lady & Puppy, Crystal & Enamel, Signed, 5 In.	250.00
Galle, Vase, Pulled In At Top & Ruffled, Frosted Body, 4 3/4 In.	385.00
Galle, Vase, Purple Flowers, Frosted Base, 4 In.	200.00
Galle, Vase, Purple, Frosted Yellow, Leaves, Buds, Iris, Signed, 6 1/4 In.	350.00
Galle, Vase, Satin Rose, Purple & Charcoal Floral, Beige Background, 5 In.	275.00
Galle, Vase, Scene Of Trees In Forest, Purple & Gold, 4 1/2 In.	650.00
Galle, Vase, Scenic, Brown To Yellow, Gray Ground, 15 1/2 In.	1000.00
Galle, Vase, Scenic, Cameo, Lake & Trees, Green, Brown, Rose & White, 7 In.	525.00
Galle, Vase, Scenic, Layers Of Cutting, Polished In Foreground, 16 In.	1950.00
Galle, Vase, Scenic, Wheel Polished, Pink Ground, Signed, 8 In.	965.00
Galle, Vase, Sea Green Background, Green Leaves, Blue Flowers, 6 1/2 X 5 In.	2750.00
Galle, Vase, Slender Stick, Ruffled Base & Top, Signed, 9 1/4 In.	375.00
Galle, Vase, Squatty Base, Narrowing To Stick Top, 4 3/4 In.	495.00
Galle, Vase, Star Cameo, Lime, Peach, Frosted White, Bulbous, 3 1/4 In.	275.00
Galle, Vase, Stick, Cameo, Magenta Flowers & Leaves, Frosted Gray, 5 In.	450.00
Galle, Vase, Stick, Floral, Lavender Tones, Signed, 8 1/2 In.	295.00
Galle, Vase, Stick, Leaves & Vines, Green, 3 Cuttings, 17 1/2 In.	1250.00
Galle, Vase, Stick, 3 Large Cuttings, Leaves & Flowers, 23 1/2 In.	1500.00
Galle, Vase, Tri-Colored, Teal Ground, Brown Base, 8 1/4 In.	600.00
Galle, Vase, Tri-Colored, Yellow Ground, Red & Cranberry, Signed, 8 1/2 In.	900.00
Galle, Vase, Violets & Leaves On Peach, Signed With Star, 2 1/2 In.	350.00
Galle, Vase, Wild Flowers, Clear & Yellow Ground, Signed, 4 1/4 In.	585.00
Galle, Vase, Wisteria Vine, Gold, Magenta & Brown, 19 In	1850.00
Galle, Vase, Woodland Scene, Impressed Signature, 9 1/2 In.	595.00
Galle, Vase, Yellow, Orange, Maroon, Cameo, Signed Star, 2 3/4 In.	200.00
Galle, Vase, Yellow, Weaving Blossoms & Leafage, Signed In Cameo, 5 1/2 In.	525.00
Galle, Vase, 3 Colors, Berries & Leaves, Yellow & Frosted Ground, 2 1/2 In.	275.00
Galle, Vase, 4 Color Overlay, Elm Tree & Seeds, Signed, 24 In.	1700.00
Galle, Vase, 4 Colored Floral, Pink, Blue, White, Cameo Signed, 16 In.	750.00

Game plates are any type of plate decorated with pictures of birds, animals, or fish. The game plates usually came in sets consisting of twelve dishes and a serving platter. These game plates were most popular during the 1880s.

Game Plate, Bird Landing Over Water & Marshes, Limoges, Signed, 9 In.Diam.	45.00
Game Plate, Bird Landing Over Water & Marshes, Signed, Limoges, 9 In.Diam.	45.00
Game Plate, Bird, Rococo Scalloped Border, Hand-Painted, Limoges, 12 3/8 In.	175.00
Game Plate, Bird, Standing, Rococo Scalloped Border, 10 1/4 In.	110.00
Game Plate, Birds Near Water, Baroque Gold Border, Limoges, Signed, 13 In.	375.00
Game Plate, Duck, Limoges, 9 1/2 In.	60.00
Game Plate, Gold Rim, Pheasants In Woods, White, Nippon, 8 1/2 In.	55.00
Game Plate, Goose, Green Head, Scalloped Gold Rim, Limoges, Signed, 9 1/2 In.	50.00
Game Plate, Goose, Green Head, Scalloped Gold Rim, Signed, Limoges, 9 1/2 In.	50.00
Game Plate, Mountain Partridge, Limoges, 9 1/2 In.	60.00
Game Plate, Three Boars In Snow, McNicol, 11 1/2 In.	35.00
Game Plate, Thrush, Foliage, Gold Baroque Border, Blue Beehive Mark, Limoges	275.00
Game Plate, Wild Turkey, Limoges, 9 1/2 In.	60.00
Game Plate, Winged Birds, Water, Baroque Border, Signed, Crown Mark, 10 In.	150.00
Game Set, Platter, 12 X 18 In., Two 9 In.Plates, 6 Lemon Plates, Haviland	1500.00
Game, Aces High, Tin, Plunger Type	35.00
Game, All, Kennedy Family, Boxed, 1962	12.00
Game, Alley Oop	10.00
Game, Anagram, McLaughlin, 1901	12.00
Game, Andy Gump His Game, Parker Bros.	19.00
Game, Authors, Box, 1910	9.00

Game, Barney Google, Spark Plug, Boxed	68.00
Game, Baseball For Dad & Son	15.00
Game, Baseball, Board Opens To Ball Diamond, Metal Figures, 1886	125.00
Game, Baseball, Carl Hubbell, Metal	9.00
Game, Baseball, Pinball Type, Metal, C.1910, 14 X 10 X 3 In.	35.00
Game, Batman, Card	4.00
Game, Big Business, Transogram Co., 1937, 5 X 6 In.	7.50
Game, Bingo, Whitman, 1940	3.00
Game, Brownie, Jump-Up, Tin, 1920s, Boxed	35.00
Game, Card, Game Of Flowers, 1899	15.00
Game, Cat & Witch, Whitman, 1930s, 8 X 10 In.	10.00
Game, Cavalry, 60 Soldiers With Stands, Bradley, 1890s, 22 X 9 X 1 1/2 In.	75.00
Game, Check & Double Check, Milton Bradley, Original Box, 1930	15.00
Game, Checker & Chess, Inlaid Wood, Anri	22.50
Game, Checkerboard, Hires	150.00
Game, Checkerboard, Mother-Of-Pearl, Crystal Pearl Mfg., Co., 7 X 7 In.	65.00
Game, Chess Set, Bone, Velvet Lined Box, Inlaid Ivory & Ebony, 32 Piece Set	275.00
Game, Chess Set, Hand Carved Ivory, Oriental, C.1880	745.00
Game, Chess Set, Ivory, Cantonese, 19th Century ....Illus	814.00
Game, Chess Set, Ivory, John Company Style, C.1780 ....Illus	6820.00
Game, Chess Set, Ivory, Painted, South Indian, 19th Century ....Illus	3520.00
Game, Chess Set, Johnson, Kennedy, Eisenhower, Unused	25.00
Game, Chinese Checkers, 1940	5.00
Game, Corn And Beans, E.G.Selchow & Co., Dated 1875	22.00
Game, Cribbage Board, Walrus Tusk, Nipper Design, Scrimshaw	120.00
Game, Crisscross Spelling Slips, McLoughlin Bros.	20.00
Game, Dart Board, Sambo, Tin	35.00
Game, Davy Crockett Rescue Race, Walt Disney	4.50
Game, Dice Wheel, Schowalter, 30 In.	225.00
Game, Dog Race, Transogram Co., 1937, 11 X 14 In.	17.50
Game, Dominoes, Ebony & Bone, 55 Piece	45.00
Game, Dominoes, Hand Made, Ivory, 26 In Box	45.00
Game, Dominoes, Ivory & Ebony, Mahogany Box	25.00
Game, Dominoes, Through Double 12s, Embossed Lion On Backs, U.S.A.	15.00
Game, Dominos, Embossed Dragons, Wood	8.00
Game, Eddie Cantor's Tell It To The Judge	14.00
Game, Fibber McGee, 1936	12.50
Game, Fish Pond, McLoughlin, Lithograph	22.00
Game, Fourteen Game Combination Board, Milton Bradley, Early 20s	20.00
Game, Funny Faces, Construct Funny Characters, Ideal, 1912	35.00
Game, Gambling Wheel, Carnival, Numbered Both Sides, Wood	100.00
Game, Game Of Jack Straws, Parker Bros.	7.50
Game, Gee Whiz, Racing, Wolverine	35.00
Game, Geography Up To Date, Parker Bros.	15.00
Game, Happy Hooligan, 1925	40.00
Game, Hi Ho Silver, The Lone Ranger Card Game, 1938, Parker Bros.	9.50
Game, History Up To Date, Parker Bros.	15.00
Game, Horse Race, Lowe	3.00
Game, Horse Race, Parlor, 8 Horses, French, 14 In.Base	525.00
Game, Horse Race, Tin, Spinner Game, Chein, 8 In.Diameter	20.00
Game, Jack & Jill, Milton Bradley, 1920	20.00
Game, Judge, Eddie Cantor, Boxed	10.00
Game, Little Black Sambo, Cadaco, 1945	8.00
Game, Lotto, Antique Train On Top Of Box, English	8.00
Game, Lotto, J.W.Spear & Sons, London, Wood Numbers, Original Box	15.00
Game, Lotto, 1940	5.00
Game, Mah Jong, Ivory & Bamboo Tiles, Brass Bound Wood Box	58.00
Game, Mah Jong, Teakwood Box, Dragon Handle, Ivory Pulls, 7 1/4 X 8 In.	450.00
Game, Mah Jong, Wooden Tiles, 3 Pullout Drawers, Parker Bros.	30.00
Game, Midway Monster Gun Rifle	125.00
Game, Modern Authors, Bradley	5.00
Game, Motoring, Passengers In Electric Car, C.1903, 20 X 12 X 1 1/2 In.	45.00
Game, My Mother Sends Me To The Grocery Store, Parker	20.00
Game, New Merchant Marine, 5 Ships, Spinner, McLaughlin Bros., 1920	25.00
Game, Numbers Game, All Fair Game Co., 1936, 11 X 14 In.	15.00
Game, Numerica, Parker Bros., 1894	8.00

Game, Chess Set, Ivory, Cantonese, 19th Century

(See Page 209)

Game, Chess Set, Ivory, John Company Style, C.1780

(See Page 209)

Game, Chess Set, Ivory, Painted, South Indian, 19th Century

(See Page 209)

Game, Old Gypsy Fortune, Whitman, 1936, 5 X 7 In.	10.00
Game, Old Maid, Milton Bradley	5.00
Game, Old Woman & The Pig, McLoughlin, 1891	75.00
Game, Our Country Puzzle, U.S.A., Obverse, Laboratory Puzzle, 11 X 18 In.	99.00
Game, Parcheesi, Royal Game Of India, 1890	25.00
Game, Parlor Horse Race, Mason Co., 16 In.At Base	450.00
Game, Pinball, Jet Age, Metal & Glass, Boxed	12.00
Game, Pinball, Rufus, Rastus, Eruption, King Hobo Cole	35.00
Game, Pit, 1903	15.00
Game, Pokena, Original Box	14.00
Game, Pollyanna	8.00
Game, Poosh-M-Up, Junior Pinball	8.00
Game, Popeye The Jiggler	75.00
Game, Puzzle, Avenue Of Flags, Chicago World's Fair	12.00
Game, Puzzle, Hood's Bride, Obverse, Wedding In Catland, 10 X 14 In.	99.00
Game, Puzzle, Jigsaw, Advertising Aprons & Coat Rentals	8.50
Game, Puzzle, Jigsaw, Rankin Flying School	8.50
Game, Puzzle, Locomotive, Wooden Box, Milton Bradley	35.00
Game, Puzzle, Norman Rockwell, Saturday Evening Post	4.00
Game, Puzzle, Palmer Cox Brownies, Block Set, 12 X 10 In.	95.00
Game, Puzzle, Sky Ride, Chicago World's Fair	12.00
Game, Puzzle, Superman, Original Box, 1940	22.00
Game, Puzzle, Victor, Artists In Front Of Phonograph, 9 X 8 In.	75.00
Game, Quiz Kids, 1940, Boxed	12.50
Game, Radio, Milton Bradley	10.00
Game, Rainy Day Puzzle, Obverse, Balloon Puzzle, Hood's, 10 1/2 X 15 In.	99.00
Game, Ring My Nose, Clown With Peg Nose To Catch Rings, C.1925, Bradley	17.50
Game, Ring Toss, J.Pressman	4.50
Game, Ring Toss, Wooden Rabbit, 2 Rings, 1921, Fisher	15.00
Game, Rotation Rummy, 1944	2.00
Game, Roulette Table, Bird's-Eye Maple, Rosewood Wheel, Clawfoot Base	8500.00
Game, Roulette Table, Claw Feet Inlaid Wheel, C.1890, 5 X 3 X 8 Feet	2750.00
Game, Roulette Wheel, Square, Case, 60 Numbers, C.1830, 18 1/2 In.	395.00
Game, Sambo Target, All Metal Products Co., Gun & 3 Darts	25.00
Game, Scouting, Milton Bradley	25.00
Game, Sew Hat, Campbell Kids	25.00
Game, Shooting Gallery, Uncle Remus, 13 X 20 In.	20.00
Game, Streamline Ching Cong Oriental Checkers, Gabriel Sons & Co.	25.00
Game, Table Tennis, Original Box, 1930, Milton Bradley	20.00
Game, The New Pretty Village, Church Set, 1897, McLaughlin Bros.	50.00
Game, The Three Guardsmen, Milton Bradley	25.00
Game, Three Musketeers, Milton Bradley	7.50
Game, Tiddley Winks, Cobalt Blue Glass, J.Pressman	3.50
Game, Tiddly Winks, Dated 1890	8.00
Game, Tootie Kazootie Puppet Show, 3 Puppets	10.00
Game, Toss-O, 1930	12.00
Game, Touring, Card Game	4.50
Game, Traffic, All Fair Game Co., 1936, 10 X 14 In.	15.00
Game, Traveling, Ebony, Various Games, English, 19th Century, 7 X 12 3/4 In.	300.00
Game, Treasure Island, 1922	10.00
Game, U.S. Vs. Spain, Hoods	18.00
Game, Uncle Wiggily, 4 Metal Figures, Complete	10.50
Game, Wheel Of Fortune, Carnival, Hand-Painted, Stops, 30 In.Diameter	175.00
Game, Window, 2 Mice, Traps, Kitchen Scene	15.00
Game, Words & Sentences, Wooden Box, Milton Bradley	20.00
Game, Zorro, Disney's, 1966	8.00
Game, Zorro, Walt Disney Productions, Original Box, 1950s	14.00

*Gaudy Dutch pottery was made in England for America from about 1810 to
1820. It is a white earthenware with Imari style decorations of red, blue,
green, yellow, and black. Only sixteen patterns of Gaudy Dutch were made —
Butterfly, Carnation, Dahlia, Double Rose, Dove, Grape, Leaf,
Oyster, Primrose, Single Rose, Strawflower, Sunflower, Urn,
War Bonnet, Zinnia, and No Name. Other similar wares are called
Soft Paste, Gaudy Ironstone, or Gaudy Welsh.*

Gaudy Dutch, Bowl, Shallow, Dove Pattern	250.00

Gaudy Dutch, Saucer, Grape Pattern, 5 1/2 In. 265.00
Gaudy Dutch, Saucer, Oyster Pattern, 5 1/2 In. 265.00
Gaudy Ironstone, Cracker Jar, Brass Bail, Copper Luster Border Butterfly 75.00
Gaudy Ironstone, Cracker Jar, Davenport 95.00
Gaudy Ironstone, Pitcher, Cobalt & Red, Animal Handle, 6 In. 95.00
Gaudy Ironstone, Pitcher, Oriental Scent, Reptile Handle, C.1829, 4 1/2 In. 65.00
Gaudy Ironstone, Pitcher, Peking Pattern, Ford & Sons, Ltd., 6 1/2 In. 52.00
Gaudy Ironstone, Platter, Ivory Ground, Flowers, Round, Signed, 15 In. 120.00

*Gaudy Welsh is an Imari decorated earthenware with red, blue, green, and
gold decorations. It was made after 1820.*

Gaudy Welsh, Biscuit Jar, Silver Plated Top, Rope Handle, 7 1/2 In. 75.00
Gaudy Welsh, Bowl & Creamer, Oyster 45.00
Gaudy Welsh, Bowl, Sugar, Basket Pattern 80.00
Gaudy Welsh, Creamer, Grape Decoration, 4 In. 40.00
Gaudy Welsh, Creamer, Oyster Pattern, 4 X 3 In. .... 35.00 To 40.00
Gaudy Welsh, Cup & Saucer, Floral Pattern 40.00
Gaudy Welsh, Cup & Saucer, Tulip 35.00
Gaudy Welsh, Cup & Saucer, Wagon Wheel 38.00
Gaudy Welsh, Jar, Tobacco, Covered 39.00
Gaudy Welsh, Mug, Florals & House 50.00
Gaudy Welsh, Mug, Grape Pattern, Straight Side 65.00
Gaudy Welsh, Mug, Oyster, Applied Handles, 3 In. 36.00
Gaudy Welsh, Mug, Wagon Wheel, 2 3/4 In. 55.00
Gaudy Welsh, Pitcher, Milk, Cobalt Blue Glazing On White, 4 1/2 In. 45.00
Gaudy Welsh, Pitcher, Oyster Pattern, 4 In. 50.00
Gaudy Welsh, Pitcher, Oyster Pattern, 4 1/2 In. .... 52.00 To 65.00
Gaudy Welsh, Plate, Oyster Pattern, Pink Luster Rim, 8 1/2 In. 30.00
Gaudy Welsh, Plate, Oyster Pattern, Pink Luster Rim, 9 In. 40.00
Gaudy Welsh, Plate, Tulip, 6 In. 30.00
Gaudy Welsh, Plate, Wagon Wheel, 5 1/2 In. 35.00
Gaudy Welsh, Pot, Chamber, Oriental Scenes, 2 X 3 In.Diameter 30.00
Gaudy Welsh, Sugar, Cover, Corey Hill 52.00
Gaudy Welsh, Tea Set, Child's, Oyster, Service For 6, Waste Bowl, Cake Plate 550.00
Gaudy Welsh, Tea Set, 6 Cups & Saucers, 2 Trays, Tulip Pattern, 24 Piece 595.00
Gaudy Welsh, Vase, Tulip Pattern, 4 In. 38.50
Gaudy Welsh, Washbowl & Pitcher, C.1830 .... 185.00
Gene Autry, Badge, Official Club 12.00
Gene Autry, Book, Famous Cowboy Songs, 68 Pages 25.00
Gene Autry, Book, Paint, 1944 .... 10.00
Gene Autry, Boots, Snow, Red & White Rubber, Size 9 .... 15.00
Gene Autry, Gun, Cap, White Handle, Spring Trigger 55.00
Gene Autry, Gun, Horse Head On Handle, Pair 26.00
Gene Autry, Music, Sheet, 1927 .... 15.00
Gene Autry, Pencil, Figural, Battery Operated 6.00
Gene Autry, Pencil, Figural, Mechanical 5.00
Gene Autry, Pistol, Cap 35.00
Gene Autry, Poster, Movie, Back In The Saddle 6.00
Gene Autry, Statue, Handmade By Hollywood Ceramics, 8 In. 27.50
Gene Autry, Watch, Sixty Shots A Minute, Animated, Original Box 175.00

*Black and blue decorated Gibson Girl plates were made in the early 1900s.
Twenty-four different 10 1/2-inch plates were made by the Royal Doulton
Pottery at Lambeth, England. Another set of twelve 9-inch plates
featuring pictures of the Gibson girl by the artist Charles Dana
Gibson had all blue decoration.*

Gibson Girl, Plate, A Quiet Dinner With Dr.Bottles, 10 1/2 In. .... 60.00 To 65.00
Gibson Girl, Plate, Comments Of People About Retirement, 10 1/2 In. 65.00
Gibson Girl, Plate, Drifting, Fellow & Girl, Signed, 6 1/4 In. 14.00
Gibson Girl, Plate, Fancy Dress Ball As Juliet, 10 1/2 In. .... 60.00 To 65.00
Gibson Girl, Plate, Fishing, Royal Doulton, 10 1/2 In. .... 45.00 To 60.00
Gibson Girl, Plate, Hat & Fan In Hand, Bavaria Green Crown Mark, 8 1/2 In. 50.00
Gibson Girl, Plate, Hostile Criticism, 10 1/2 In. .... 60.00 To 65.00
Gibson Girl, Plate, Message From The Outside World ....
Gibson Girl, Plate, Message From The Outside World, 10 1/2 In. .... 50.00 To 60.00
Gibson Girl, Plate, Miss Babbles, Calls & Reads, 10 1/2 In. .... 60.00 To 65.00

Gibson Girl, Plate, Mr.Waddles Arrives Late & Finds Her Card Filled	65.00
Gibson Girl, Plate, Mr.Waddles Finds Card Filled, 10 1/2 In.	60.00 To 65.00
Gibson Girl, Plate, Mrs.Diggs & Safety Of Child, 10 1/2 In.	54.00 To 60.00
Gibson Girl, Plate, Portrait, Blue Border, Royal Doulton, Signed, 9 1/4 In.	25.00
Gibson Girl, Plate, Portrait, C.1900, Warwick, 10 In.	16.00
Gibson Girl, Plate, Portrait, Faces Right, 1899, 9 1/2 In.	55.00 To 65.00
Gibson Girl, Plate, She Contemplates The Cloister, Marked, 10 1/2 In.	65.00
Gibson Girl, Plate, She Decides To Die, Dr.Bottles, 10 1/2 In.	45.00 To 68.00
Gibson Girl, Plate, She Longs For Seclusion In Milder Climate, 10 1/2 In.	60.00
Gibson Girl, Plate, She Looks For Relief, Old Ones, 10 1/2 In.	60.00 To 72.50
Gibson Girl, Plate, Skating, 10 1/2 In.	60.00
Gibson Girl, Plate, Winning New Friends, 10 1/2 In.	60.00
Gibson Girl, Portfolio, Artist Proof, 1909, Signed, 17 X 12 In., Set Of 8	125.00
Gibson Girl, Print, Ivory & Black, Portfolio Of 23, 10 X 14 In.	200.00

GILLINDER   *Gillinder pressed glass was first made by William T. Gillinder of Philadelphia in 1863. Many pressed glass items were made for the Centennial.*

Gillinder, Figurine, Ruth The Gleaner	100.00
Gillinder, Figurine, Shakespeare	125.00
Gillinder, Shoe, 1876 Centennial, Bow On Front, 5 1/2 In.	22.00
Gillinder, Sugar Shaker, Melon, Blue Flowers	85.00
Girandole, Candlesticks & Solar Lamp, Pair, C.1850, 17 To 22 1/2 In.	175.00
Girandole, Marble Base, Prisms, Lady & Child, Set Of 3	210.00
Girl Scout, Camera, 1930s	7.50
Girl Scout, Handbook, 1954	2.50
Girl Scout, Lunch Pail	7.00
Girl Scout, Stamp, Rubber, Brownie	4.00
Glasses, Ben Franklin, Sliding, Adjustable Sides, Case, C.1870	25.00
Glasses, Lorgnette, Gold On Sterling	125.00
Glasses, Lorgnette, Hidden, Tortoise Shell, 8 In.	29.50
Glasses, Lorgnette, Loop For Hanging, 18K Gold, 5 In.	55.00
Glasses, Lorgnette, Rope Chain, Sterling Silver	42.50
Glasses, Lorgnette, Snap Closure, Embossed, 10K Gold	32.00
Glasses, Lorgnette, Tortoise Shell, 11 In.	34.00
Glasses, Lorgnette, With Hair Pin	15.00
Glasses, Opera, Mother-Of-Pear & Gilt	25.00
Glasses, Reading, Wire, Tinted Glass, Leather Case, Lens 1 In.Wide	25.00
Gold, American, Lighter, Cigar, Table, Tiffany & Co., C.1920, 2 In.	1650.00
Goldscheider, Figurine, Prince Of Wales, Artist Signed, 6 1/2 In.	40.00
Goldscheider, Figurine, Wedding Bells, Artist Signed, 6 1/2 In.	40.00
Golf Club, see Toy, Golf Club	
Gonder, Basket, Pink	12.00
Gonder, Ewer, Handled, Pink Interior, Mottled Blue, 6 In.	15.00
Gonder, Figurine, Chinaman	10.00

Goofus glass was made from about 1900 to 1920 by many American factories. It was originally painted gold, red, green, bronze, pink, purple, and other bright colors.

Goofus Glass, Basket	55.00
Goofus Glass, Bowl, Fluted, Ruffled, Red Roses, 8 1/2 In.	12.00
Goofus Glass, Bowl, Gold With Red Flowers, Green, Marked N, 7 In.Diameter	20.00
Goofus Glass, Bowl, 9 In.Diameter	15.00
Goofus Glass, Box, Powder, Rose	12.00
Goofus Glass, Decanter	20.00
Goofus Glass, Dish, Monk, Clear	12.00
Goofus Glass, Dish, Ruffled, 7 In.Diameter	12.00
Goofus Glass, Jar, Powder, Roses, Hand-Painted	21.50
Goofus Glass, Lamp, Miniature, Burner & Chimney	45.00
Goofus Glass, Lamp, Table, Birds, Grapes	22.00
Goofus Glass, Plate, Apples, 8 1/2 In.	10.00
Goofus Glass, Plate, Roses, 10 In.	10.00
Goofus Glass, Vase, Dancing Lady, 12 1/2 In.	40.00
Goofus Glass, Vase, Hand-Painted Flowers, 14 In.	10.00
Goofus Glass, Vase, Lovebirds, 10 1/2 In.	25.00
Goofus Glass, Vase, Mums, 15 In.	25.00

Goofus Glass, Vase, Statue Of Liberty, 12 1/2 In.	55.00
Goofus, Bowl, Ruffled, Red Flowers, 11 In.	25.00
Goofus, Bowl, Wild Roses, 9 In.	15.00

Goss china has been made since 1858. English potter William Henry Goss first made it at the Falcon Pottery in Stoke-on-Trent. In 1934 the factory name was changed to Goss China Company when it was taken over by Cauldon Potteries. Goss china resembles Irish Belleek in both body and glaze. The company also made popular souvenir china.

W.H.COSS

Goss, Bell, Cow, Swiss, Maldon Crest, Clapper, Porcelain	35.00
Goss, Bowl, Fountain, St.Ives, Cornwall, Crest On Inside .... *Illus*	37.20
Goss, Bust, Sir Walter, Parian	50.00
Goss, Can, Milk, Guernsey, Lid, 5 1/2 In. .... *Illus*	26.97
Goss, Candle Snuffer, Falcon Mark	17.50
Goss, Cottage, Prince Llewelyn's House, Beddgelert, Wales .... *Illus*	126.48
Goss, Cottage, St.Nicholas Chapel, St.Ives, 2 In. .... *Illus*	334.80
Goss, Cup & Saucer, Demitasse, Blue Enamel, Sussex Crest	32.00
Goss, Cup & Saucer, Demitasse, City & Cathedral Of Peterbororough Crests	32.00
Goss, Jug, Falcon Mark, 3 1/2 In.	20.00
Goss, Model Of Eddystone Lighthouse, Exeter Crest, Hawk Mark	18.00
Goss, Pitcher, Grasmere Crest, Hawk Mark, 3 In.	12.00
Goss, Pitcher, Thistle, Small	25.00
Goss, Rose Bowl, Four Belgian Armorials, 5 In.	20.00

327
SCHOONHOVEN
HOLLAND
COREL
E

Pottery has been made in Gouda, Holland since the 17th century. Two firms, The Zennith pottery, established in the 18th century, and the Zuid-Hollandsche pottery made the brightly colored art nouveau wares marked Gouda from 1880 to about 1940.

PLAZUID
GOUDA
HOLLAND
A.M.P.SMIT.

Gouda, Ashtray, Black Background, Round	35.00
Gouda, Ashtray, Floral On Green Glaze, Areo Royal Zuid, 5 In.	25.00
Gouda, Ashtray, Plazuid, 4 1/2 In.Diameter	28.00
Gouda, Basket, Turquoise, Orange & Brown, 8 1/2 X 5 1/4 In.Diameter	95.00
Gouda, Bottle, Windmill Form, Pastel Coloring, 4 1/2 In.	65.00
Gouda, Bowl, Flower, Symmetric Design, Serma, 3 X 5 In.	38.50
Gouda, Bowl, Gray Ground, Yellow, Green & Red Flowers, 14 1/2 In.Diameter	98.00
Gouda, Bowl, Leaves & Flowers, Mustard Banding, 6 X 2 1/2 In.	38.00
Gouda, Bowl, 2 Handled, Flowers & Leaves, Holland, 8 In.Diameter	38.00
Gouda, Box, Powder, Covered, Black, Gold & White, Signed, 4 1/2 In.Diameter	150.00
Gouda, Candlestick, Floral, Rust, Turquoise, Jonka House Mark, 6 In., Pair	95.00
Gouda, Candlestick, Green, Red, Blue & Yellow, Marked Ngra, 12 In.	35.00
Gouda, Candlestick, Handle, Black Trim, Marked, Bowl, 6 In.	45.00
Gouda, Compote, Flowers, Gray, Areo Royal & Housemark, Signed	45.00
Gouda, Compote, House Mark, 7 In.	87.00

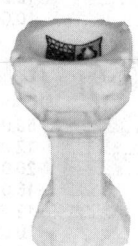

Goss, Bowl, Fountain, St.Ives,
Cornwall, Crest On Inside

Goss, Cottage, St.Nicholas Chapel,
St.Ives, 2 In.

Goss, Can, Milk, Guernsey,
Lid, 5 1/2 In.

Goss, Cottage, Prince Llewelyn's
House, Beddgelert, Wales

Gouda, Dish, Candy, Covered, Cream, Brown & Green	45.00
Gouda, Ewer, Matte Finish, Pedestal Base, Signed, 8 1/2 In.	85.00
Gouda, Humidor, Indian Smoking, Ship, Blue Cartouche, Brass Lid	125.00
Gouda, Jar, Covered, Black, Green & Rose, 4 1/2 In.	20.00
Gouda, Jar, Tobacco, 163 Corel Schoonhoven, C.1900	95.00
Gouda, Jug, Dutch Mother & Child, Windmill, Impressed Marks, 5 3/4 In.	38.00
Gouda, Nappy, Flared Edge & Handle, Yellow Tulip, Signed, 7 In.	45.00
Gouda, Pitcher, Colorful Flowers, Light Background, House Mark, 6 In.	50.00
Gouda, Pitcher, Metallic Luster, Iridescent Tones, House Marked, 7 1/2 In.	165.00
Gouda, Pitcher, Multicolored On Black, House Mark, 5 In.	45.00
Gouda, Pitcher, Souvenir, Regina, 2 1/2 In.	20.00
Gouda, Pitcher, Tulip Pattern, 5 In.	35.00
Gouda, Plate, Openwork Border, Flowers, 8 In.	35.00
Gouda, Plate, Windmill & Cottage Scene, 8 3/4 In.	40.00
Gouda, Shoe, Dark Colors, House Mark, 4 In.	22.00
Gouda, Shoe, Dutch, Scene Across Top Of House, Marked, 5 1/2 In.	35.00
Gouda, Shoe, Whimsey, Ivy, Marked, 4 1/2 In.	25.00
Gouda, Vase, Beige Flowers, House Mark, Anjea, 8 In., Pair	125.00
Gouda, Vase, Bulbous, MN 55a, 10 1/4 In.	85.00
Gouda, Vase, Cabinet, Gold Flowers On Black, 3 1/2 In.	30.00
Gouda, Vase, Carma Pattern, Glazed, 10 In.	95.00
Gouda, Vase, Double, Olive Ground, Gold Trim, Iridescent, Marked, 8 In.	150.00
Gouda, Vase, Ecru Ground, Pansies, House Mark, 9 In.	80.00
Gouda, Vase, Floral, Bulbous, Long Neck, Signed Chrisonta, Holland, 6 1/2 In.	110.00
Gouda, Vase, I-Handled, Low Pedestal, Art Nouveau Forms, House Mark, 10 In.	95.00
Gouda, Vase, Regina Mark, 3 In.	77.00
Gouda, Vase, Regina Pattern, Graduated Ringed Body, Crown Mark, 10 In.	75.00
Gouda, Vase, Signed B.Nicole, 6 In.	27.00
Gouda, Vase, Simson, House Mark, 8 In., Pair	95.00
Gouda, Vase, Stylized Pattern, Signed, 7 In.	70.00
Gouda, Vase, 2-Handled, Regina Rosario, Multi-Floral, 7 In.	75.00

Graniteware is an enameled tinware that has been used in the kitchen from the late nineteenth century to the present. Earlier graniteware was green or turquoise blue, with white spatters. The later ware was gray with white spatters. Reproductions are being made in all colors.

Graniteware, Bed Pan, Blue Trim	15.00
Graniteware, Boiler, Coffee, Gray	29.50
Graniteware, Boiler, Coffee, Nesco Royal Granite, 2 Gallon	40.00
Graniteware, Can, Cream, 1 Quart	28.00
Graniteware, Chamber Pot	30.00
Graniteware, Coffee Boiler, Green & White Swirl, Large	40.00
Graniteware, Coffeepot, Blue & White Enamel, Large	28.00
Graniteware, Coffeepot, Blue Spout & Lid Handle, 9 3/4 In.	12.00
Graniteware, Coffeepot, Granite Lid, Gray	18.50
Graniteware, Coffeepot, Gray, 11 Quart	25.00
Graniteware, Coffeepot, Lid, 7 In.	20.00
Graniteware, Coffeepot, Long Spout, Gray Gasket, 9 In.	18.00
Graniteware, Coffeepot, Pewter Trim, Spout, Collar, Copper Base Rim	115.00
Graniteware, Coffeepot, Tin Lid, Domed, Blue & White, 6 Quart, 12 1/2 In.	23.00
Graniteware, Colander, Gray, 10 1/2 In.	7.00
Graniteware, Cup & Saucer, Blue Swirl	18.00
Graniteware, Cuspidor	7.00
Graniteware, Dish, Blue & White, Spongeware Design, 8 X 2 In.	12.50
Graniteware, Dish, Soup, White, Black Rim	2.00
Graniteware, Dishpan, Gray	8.00
Graniteware, Double Boiler	22.50
Graniteware, Funnel	12.00
Graniteware, Gravy Boat, White With Blue Trim	12.50
Graniteware, Jar, Slop, Lid, Bulbous Shape, Turquoise & White, Wood Grip	55.00
Graniteware, Kettle, Large Dipper	7.00
Graniteware, Kettle, Tin Top, Bail Handle, 17 X 9 In.	27.50
Graniteware, Ladle, Pierced	3.50
Graniteware, Lunch Box	32.50
Graniteware, Measure, 2 1/2 In.	32.00
Graniteware, Mold, Fluted, Gray & Splotched, 10 1/2 X 2 1/4 In.	18.00

Graniteware, Mold, Tube, Octagon, 8 In.	16.00
Graniteware, Pail, Berry, Knob	15.00
Graniteware, Pail, Cream, Gray, Tin Lid	25.00
Graniteware, Pail, Dinner, Complete	28.00
Graniteware, Pan, Cake, Angel Food, Gray	8.50
Graniteware, Pan, Frying	12.00
Graniteware, Pan, Green & Cream, 2 Handles	12.00
Graniteware, Pan, Muffin, 6 Cup, Tin	14.00
Graniteware, Pan, Roasting, Signed Nesco, Early 1900s	14.00
Graniteware, Pan, Vegetable, 9 1/2 In.	4.50
Graniteware, Pan, 9 In.	12.50
Graniteware, Pitcher, Water, 8 In.	35.00
Graniteware, Pitcher, Wide Lip, 1 Gallon	14.00
Graniteware, Plate, Pie, Blue & White	3.00
Graniteware, Potty, Side Handle	18.00
Graniteware, Rack, Kitchen, 4 White Utensils	100.00
Graniteware, Roaster, Covered, Round, 11 In.	8.50
Graniteware, Scoop, Grain, Large	32.50 To 45.00
Graniteware, Skimmer & Dipper, Long Handle	7.00
Graniteware, Spittoon, Removable Top, Black Rim, 5 1/4 X 11 1/2 In.Diam.	16.00
Graniteware, Sugar, Lid, Blue Trim On White	15.00
Graniteware, Teakettle, Blue	14.00
Graniteware, Teakettle, Cobalt & White, Iron Range Co., St.Louis	65.00
Graniteware, Teakettle, Iron Range Co., St.Louis, Cobalt & White	65.00
Graniteware, Teakettle, Tan, Stainless Top	15.00
Graniteware, Teapot, Gooseneck, Tin Lid, 7 In.	25.00
Graniteware, Tub, Baby's, Oval, White, 1914	18.00
Graniteware, Tumbler, Blue & White	10.00
Graniteware, Wash Basin	3.00
Graniteware, Wash Pan & Soap Dish, 7 In.	9.50
Graniteware, Washboard	47.00

Greentown glass was made by the Indiana Tumbler and Goblet Company of Greentown, Indiana, from 1894 to 1903. In 1899, the factory name was changed to National Glass Company. A variety of pressed, milk, and chocolate glass was made.

Greentown, see also Chocolate Glass, Custard Glass, Holly Amber, Milk Glass, Pressed Glass

Greentown, Bowl, Footed, Cactus, Scalloped Rim & Base, 3 1/4 X 7 1/4 In.	80.00
Greentown, Bowl, Oval, 4 1/2 X 7 1/4 In.	18.00
Greentown, Bowl, Sugar, Covered, 6-Sided, Handled	45.00
Greentown, Butter, Creamer, Spooner & Open Sugar, Teardrop & Tassel	110.00
Greentown, Compote, Teardrop & Tassel, 8 1/4 In.Diameter	34.00
Greentown, Creamer, Frosted Green Wild Rose & Bow Knot	55.00
Greentown, Creamer, Vaseline, 4 1/2 In.	55.00
Greentown, Cruet, Dewey, Original Stopper, Green	700.00
Greentown, Decanter, Straight-Sided, Stopper, Leaf Bracket, 5 In.	16.00
Greentown, Dish, Butter, Covered, Chocolate Glass	75.00
Greentown, Dish, Cord Drapery, Clear, 7 In.	15.00
Greentown, Dish, Hen Cover, Blue	95.00
Greentown, Dish, Hen Cover, Green	115.00
Greentown, Dish, Mitted Hand	20.00 To 30.00
Greentown, Dish, Rabbit On Nest, Blue	125.00
Greentown, Dish, Relish, Dewey Serpentine, Clear	18.00
Greentown, Master Berry, Leaf Bracket, Clear	35.00
Greentown, Match Holder, Nile Green	110.00
Greentown, Mug, Blue Opaque, Elves	39.00
Greentown, Mug, Blue Opaque, Troubadour	39.00
Greentown, Mug, Dewey, Clear	20.00
Greentown, Mug, Serenade, Blue, Opaque	32.00
Greentown, Mug, Serenade, Green	33.00 To 75.00
Greentown, Mug, Serenade, Opaque, Blue	48.00
Greentown, Mug, Troubador, Blue	35.00
Greentown, Pitcher & Five Glasses, Teardrop & Tassel	400.00
Greentown, Pitcher, Cord Drapery, Clear	40.00
Greentown, Pitcher, Teardrop & Tassel, Honoring Admiral Simpson Lindsay	65.00

Greentown, Pitcher, Water, Cord Drapery, Clear 45.00
Greentown, Pitcher, Water, Deer Alert 90.00
Greentown, Plate, Frosted Serenade, 6 In. 30.00
Greentown, Smoke Set, Frosted Gold & Colors, Wild Rose & Bowknot 95.00
Greentown, Spooner, Austrian, Clear 30.00
Greentown, Stein, Indoor Drinking Scene, Pouring Spout, Green 125.00
Greentown, Stein, Serenade, Custard 60.00
Greentown, Sugar & Creamer, Austrian, Clear, 4 1/2 In. 38.00
Greentown, Sugar, Cord Drapery, Covered 28.50
Greentown, Sugar, Covered, Dewey, Green, Small 35.00
Greentown, Syrup, Herringbone Buttress, Clear 75.00
Greentown, Toothpick, Clear Holly 65.00
Greentown, Tray, Dewey, Serpentine, Amber 45.00
Greentown, Tray, Dewey, Serpentine, Clear, Small 20.00
Greentown, Tumbler, Austrian 15.00
Greentown, Tumbler, Chocolate Glass, Cactus Pattern 37.50
Greentown, Tumbler, Connecticut Skillet 27.50
Greentown, Tumbler, Lemonade, No.11 .... 6.50
Greentown, Tumbler, Paneled Holly 50.00
Greentown, Vase, Herringbone Buttress, Clear, 6 In. 14.00
Greentown, Water Set, Brazen Shield, Blue, 5 Pieces 250.00
Greentown, Water Set, Rose With Bowknot, Frosted, 7 Piece 125.00

Grueby Faience Company of Boston, Massachusetts, was incorporated in 1897 by William H. Grueby. Garden statuary, art pottery, and architectural tiles were made until 1920.

Grueby, Bowl, Matte Blue Glaze, 6 1/2 X 5 In. 350.00
Grueby, Scarab, Bluegreen Matte Glaze, 2 3/4 In. 150.00
Grueby, Tile, Green, 4 In.Square 12.00
Grueby, Tile, 2 X 6 In. 24.00
Grueby, Vase, Blue, 4 1/2 In. 275.00
Grueby, Vase, Dark Green Matte Glaze, 3 X 3 3/4 In. 150.00
Grueby, Vase, Double Gourd, Mottled Green, 6 3/4 X 6 In. 195.00
Grueby, Vase, Flaring Rim, Bulbous, C.1893-1903 .... *Illus* 350.00
Grueby, Vase, Green Matte Glaze, 3 X 3 3/4 In. 145.00
Grueby, Vase, High Green, 6 1/2 In. 150.00
Grueby, Vase, Leafage, C.1893-1903, Pair .... *Illus* 2600.00
   Gum Ball Machine, see Store, Machine
   Gun, see Weapon, Gun

Gunderson glass was made at the Gunderson Pairpoint Works of New Bedford, Massachusetts, from 1952 to 1957. Gunderson Peachblow is especially famous.

Gunderson, Ashtray, Rose Bowl Shape, Air Traps, 2 1/2 X 3 1/2 In.Diameter 45.00
Gunderson, Peachblow, Compote, White To Raspberry, Threading, 6 In. 225.00
Gunderson, Tumbler, Peachblow, Raspberry Shading To Pink At Base, 3 1/2 In. 140.00
Gunderson, Vase, Flared, Bulbous, Burmese, 11 X 5 1/2 In. 80.00
Gunderson, Vase, Lily, 3 Petal Top, Acid Finish, Burmese, 10 1/2 In. 325.00
   Gutta-Percha, see also Photography, Daguerreotype Case
Gutta-Percha, Box, Collar, Wheat Design, 4 1/2 X 4 1/2 In. 25.00
Gutta-Percha, Frame, Floral Embossing, Dated 1868, 7 3/4 X 6 In. 50.00
Gutta-Percha, Match Safe, Arm & Hammer 25.00
Gutta-Percha, Match Safe, Sea Horses, Fish Dragon, Sterling Silver 65.00
Gutta-Percha, Mirror, Folding, Oval, Greek Key Outline, 4 1/4 X 7 In. 110.00
Gutta-Percha, Mirror, Hand, Raised Leaf Design 13.00

The Haeger Brick and Tile Company of Dundee, Illinois, was founded in 1871 by David Haeger. His son Edmund H. Haeger decided to produce an art pottery in 1914. The name of the firm was changed to The Haeger Potteries, Inc. The firm is still in operation.

Haeger, Centerpiece, Green, Black, Sculptured Leaf, Green Fruit Cluster 23.00
Haeger, Figural Planter, Higlaze Ivory Girl, 10 X 12 1/2 X 6 1/2 In. 32.00

Hall China Company started in East Liverpool, Ohio in 1903. The firm made all types of wares, including Autumn Leaf pattern dishes. It is still working.

Grueby, Vase, Leafage, C.1893-1903, Pair
(See Page 217)

Grueby, Vase, Flaring Rim, Bulbous,
C.1893-1903
(See Page 217)

Hall, see also Autumn Leaf

Hall, Bowl, Mixing, Set Of 3	28.00
Hall, Coffeepot, Poppy, Golden Key, Red	20.00
Hall, Dish, Covered, Art Deco, Chrome Cradle, Geometric Design	30.00
Hall, Lamp, Cranberry Shade, All Original	260.00
Hall, Pitcher, Tilt, Poppy, Orange	14.00
Hall, Teapot, Creamer, Jug, Chinese Red	35.00
Hall, Teapot, Turned Spout, Green	10.00
Hammersley, English Bone China, Victorian Violets, 48 Pieces	200.00

Hampshire pottery was made in Keene, New Hampshire, between 1871 and 1923. Hampshire developed a popular line of colored glazed works as early as 1883, which included a Royal Worcester-type pink, olive green, blue, and mahogany.

Hampshire, Bowl & Pitcher Set, Rose & Fishscale	140.00
Hampshire, Chamberstick, Hooded, C.1900, Matte Green Glaze, Marked, 7 In.	75.00
Hampshire, Creamer, Green Glaze, Marked	30.00
Hampshire, Crock, Butter, Eagle Shield, Grapes & Little Men, 6 X 9 1/2 In.	125.00
Hampshire, Dish, Transfer Scene, Soldier's Monument, Star Shaped, 5 1/2 In.	25.75
Hampshire, Ewer, Sweetpeas, 7 1/2 In.	55.00
Hampshire, Jar, Powder, Covered, Hand Molded, C.1890	40.00
Hampshire, Jug, Green, Pouring Spout, Handled, 4 In.	45.00
Hampshire, Lamp, Base, Blue & Green, Marbleized Glaze, Signed, 12 1/2 In.	300.00
Hampshire, Mug, Landing Of The Pilgrims, 4 1/8 In.	65.00
Hampshire, Mug, Leaves & Berries, Marked, Keene, New Hampshire	35.00
Hampshire, Mug, Matte Green, Line Design Top & Bottom, Signed, 7 In.	30.00
Hampshire, Mug, Red Boats On Gold & Green, Marked JST & Co., 5 1/2 In.	70.00
Hampshire, Mug, Root Beer, Men Drinking Around Barrel	35.00
Hampshire, Strainer, Tea, Signed	40.00
Hampshire, Tankard, Green, 4-Band Panels & Stylized Leaf, Handle, 9 In.	65.00
Hampshire, Teapot, Bird Design, Signed	45.00
Hampshire, Teapot, Deco Sweeping Handle, Butterfly Finial	45.00
Hampshire, Urn, Thistle, Green Matte Finish, 5 1/2 X 6 In.	45.00
Hampshire, Vase, Cylinder, Blue, 7 In.	26.00
Hampshire, Vase, Mottled Blue, Cylinder, 7 In.	24.00

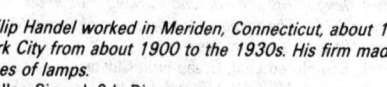

Philip Handel worked in Meriden, Connecticut, about 1885 and in New York City from about 1900 to the 1930s. His firm made art glass and other types of lamps.

Handel, Bowl, Brass Collar, Signed, 6 In.Diameter	79.00
Handel, Bowl, Cased, Copper Rim, Signed, 5 1/2 X 2 1/2 In.	79.00
Handel, Bowl, Fruit, Poppies, Gold Trim, Signed, 1909, 2 X 12 In.	85.00
Handel, Chandelier, Painted, Leafage, Birds, Patinated Metal .... *Illus*	1700.00
Handel, Humidor, Bulldog, Signed, 5 In.	195.00

Handel, Humidor, Frosted Pebble Exterior, Green, Signed	195.00
Handel, Humidor, Hand-Painted, Brass Trim, Signed, 7 1/2 X 6 In.Diameter	275.00
Handel, Humidor, Mare & Dog Front Panel, Square, Pipe On Top, Signed, 7 In.	335.00
Handel, Humidor, Owl On Branch, Squat Shape	250.00
Handel, Humidor, Portrait Of Bulldog, Handle, 5 In.	225.00
Handel, Jar, Tobacco, Bird Dog Portrait, Brass Trim, Brown Shades, Signed	295.00
Handel, Jar, Tobacco, Miniature, Cover	95.00
Handel, Jar, Tobacco, Treasure Island, Teroma Finish, Stopper, Signed, 9 In.	375.00
Handel, Lamp, All Over Floral, Blue & Pink, Signed, 14 In.Diameter	1100.00

Handel, Vase, Trees & Sunset,
Signed & Numbered, 8 In.

Handel, Chandelier, Painted, Leafage,
Birds, Patinated Metal

Handel, Lamp, Apple Blossom, Tree Trunk Base, 30 In.	2900.00
Handel, Lamp, Art Deco, Table, Tripod Base, Signed, 18 In.	1775.00
Handel, Lamp, Black-Eyed Susan, Leaded, Signed, 20 In.	87.50
Handel, Lamp, Boudoir, Border Flowers, Signed, 9 In.	425.00
Handel, Lamp, Boudoir, Reverse Pointing, Acorn Pull, Signed, 14 1/2 In.	475.00
Handel, Lamp, Bridge, Green Shade, Brass, Signed	410.00
Handel, Lamp, Bronze Finish, 3 Socket, Pull Chain, Signed, 22 In.	165.00
Handel, Lamp, Chipped Ice Shade, Owl Base, Indian Encampment, 18 In.	835.00
Handel, Lamp, Chipped Ice Shade, Signed & Numbered, 18 In.	1575.00
Handel, Lamp, Chipped Ice Shade, Tree Design, Base Signed, 14 In.	450.00
Handel, Lamp, Confetti Glass, Artichokes & Leaves, Signed, 16 In.	850.00
Handel, Lamp, Double Row Floral Leaded Lamp, Tree Trunk Base, Signed, 20 In.	2685.00
Handel, Lamp, Egyptian Leaded Shade, 3 Lions At Base, Signed, 20 In.	1485.00
Handel, Lamp, Floral Border, Signed, 18 In.	1485.00
Handel, Lamp, Flying Butterfly, Floral Border, Cream, Signed, 18 In.	1250.00
Handel, Lamp, Geometric Pattern, Acorn Pull Chain, 16 In.	1675.00
Handel, Lamp, Gold & Green Flowers, Signed, 14 In.Diameter	1100.00
Handel, Lamp, Indian Encampment, Indian In Canoe, Signed, 16 In.	1450.00
Handel, Lamp, Lavender & Blue, Signed Base & Shade, 17 In.	4700.00
Handel, Lamp, Leaded Shade, Tree Trunk Base, Signed, 8 In.	425.00
Handel, Lamp, Leaded, Multi-Colored, Signed, 22 In.	1850.00
Handel, Lamp, Painted, Trees, Bronze Base & Finial *Illus*	700.00
Handel, Lamp, Reverse Painted, Same On Shade, Signed Rim & Base, 22 In.	900.00
Handel, Lamp, Sunset Palm Trees Overlay, Signed, 20 In.	2150.00
Handel, Lamp, Surface Painted Pine Tree Shade, Signed, 25 In.	1400.00
Handel, Lamp, Three Panel Shade, Signed On Base	300.00
Handel, Lamp, Wall, Pond Lily, Green & White, 1890, Signed	85.00
Handel, Lamp, Wooded Scene, Sunset In Colors, No.6628, Signed, 18 In.	1800.00
Handel, Shade, Brass Filigree Over 6 Bent Panels, 5 In.	285.00
Handel, Shade, Geometric, Brass & Metal Base, Label On Bottom	450.00
Handel, Shade, Hanging, Forest Scene, Original Tassel, 8 1/2 X 12 1/2 In.	850.00
Handel, Shade, Mushroom Cap Shape, Opaque, Signed, 24 In.Opening	150.00
Handel, Vase, Beaded Brass Collar, Hand-Painted Roses, 12 In.	195.00
Handel, Vase, Grecian Motif, 9 In.	59.00
Handel, Vase, Trees & Sunset, Signed & Numbered, 8 In. *Illus*	480.00

*Harlequin dinnerware was produced by the Homer Laughlin Company
from 1938 to 1964, and sold without trademark by the F. W. Woolworth
Co. It had a concentric ring design like Fiesta, but the rings were*

separated from the rim by a plain margin and cup handles were angular in shape

Harlequin Ware, Bowl, Salad, Mauve	3.50
Harlequin Ware, Casserole, Rose, Covered	13.00
Harlequin Ware, Casserole, Yellow, Covered	16.00
Harlequin Ware, Creamer, Mauve	3.50
Harlequin Ware, Cup & Saucer, Turquoise	2.00
Harlequin Ware, Cup, Dark Green	1.25
Harlequin Ware, Cup, Nut, Rose	3.00
Harlequin Ware, Dish, Nut, Blue	5.00
Harlequin Ware, Duck, Maroon	30.00
Harlequin Ware, Plate, Chartreuse, 6 In.	1.00
Harlequin Ware, Rose Bowl, Blue, 7 In.	3.00
Harlequin Ware, Soup, Cream, Turquoise	3.50
Harlequin Ware, Sugar, Yellow, Covered	3.00
Hatpin Holder, see also Porcelain and various porcelain categories	
Hatpin Holder, Dog Winking, 5 In.	14.00
Hatpin Holder, Gold & Green Borders, Nippon, R.C. Mark	20.00
Hatpin Holder, Gold, Flowers	25.00
Hatpin Holder, Hand-Painted, Signed, Bavarian	22.50
Hatpin Holder, Multi-Colored Roses, German	32.50
Hatpin Holder, Nippon, Red Roses, Beaded	32.50
Hatpin Holder, Pink Violets, Austria	40.00
Hatpin Holder, Saucer, Oriental	69.00
Hatpin Holder, Wall Hanging, Neo Classic Design, French Bisque, Cameo Lady	250.00
Hatpin, Filigree, Signet Top, Gold	10.00

HAVILAND & CO. *Haviland china has been made in Limoges, France, since 1842. The factory was started by the Haviland Brothers of New York City. Other factories worked in the town of Limoges making a similar chinaware.*

Haviland, Berry Set, Pedestal Type Bowl, 6 Saucers, Signed	250.00
Haviland, Bone Dish, Baltimore Rose, Gold Trim	10.00
Haviland, Bone Dish, Hand-Painted Flowers, Birds, Butterflies, Set Of 6	45.50
Haviland, Bowl, Acorns Inside & Out, Pedestaled, Short, Brown & Beige Tones	40.00
Haviland, Bowl, Centerpiece, Roses Inside & Out, Gold Border, 12 In.	145.00
Haviland, Bowl, Covered, Hand-Painted Grapes, Signed, 9 1/2 In.Diameter	350.00
Haviland, Bowl, Cyma Edge, Gold Trim, Marked, 10 1/2 In.	50.00
Haviland, Bowl, Floral Border In & Outside, Gold Trim, 9 In.	30.00
Haviland, Bowl, Vegetable, White, Gold Trim	20.00
Haviland, Butter Pat, Chrysanthemum	6.00
Haviland, Butter Pat, No.59	8.00
Haviland, Butter, Cover, Strainer, Chrysanthemum	35.00
Haviland, Butter, Covered, No.18, Insert	50.00
Haviland, Butter, Garlands Of Roses, Lid	33.00
Haviland, Butter, Lid, Liner, Pink Flowers	55.00
Haviland, Chocolate Set, Floral, Gold Edges, Pink, Field Mark, 13 Piece	275.00
Haviland, Coffeepot, Red Roses, Green Leaves, Ivory Background	85.00
Haviland, Creamer & Sugar, No.5 Star	65.00
Haviland, Creamer, Floral Decoration, Limoges, 5 1/2 In.	15.00
Haviland, Creamer, Garlands Of Roses, Small	20.00

Handel, Lamp, Painted, Trees, Bronze Base & Finial

(See Page 219)

Haviland, Creamer, Gramercy 20.00
Haviland, Cup & Saucer Set, Demitasse, Set Of 4 .... 49.00
Haviland, Cup & Saucer, Chocolate, Flowers 12.00
Haviland, Cup & Saucer, Chocolate, White 15.00
Haviland, Cup & Saucer, Cream, White With Gold, Gold Handle, Pedestal Foot 20.95
Haviland, Cup & Saucer, Demitasse, Brushed Gold, Set Of 6 .... 105.00
Haviland, Cup & Saucer, Garland, English Ivy & Flower, Gold Trim, Pair 95.00
Haviland, Cup & Saucer, My Garden 18.50
Haviland, Cup & Saucer, No.5 Star 25.00
Haviland, Cup & Saucer, No.19 .... 26.00
Haviland, Cup & Saucer, No.152 .... 12.00
Haviland, Cup & Saucer, Pink Spray 22.50
Haviland, Cup & Saucer, Roses, Gold Outlined, Scalloped Saucer, Pink, Limoges 11.50
Haviland, Cup, Georgia 20.00
Haviland, Cup, Touraine 20.00
Haviland, Dish, Leaf Shape, Baltimore Rose, 8 X 9 In. 30.00
Haviland, Dish, Pancake Cover, Scalloped Gold Trimmed Edge, Handle, Marked 58.00
Haviland, Dish, Vegetable, Covered, Chrysanthemum 18.00
Haviland, Dish, Vegetable, Covered, No.59, Oval 40.00
Haviland, Dish, Vegetable, Gramercy 22.50
Haviland, Dish, Vegetable, My Garden 25.00
Haviland, Dish, Vegetable, No.59 .... 25.00
Haviland, Dish, Vegetable, Peonies 25.00
Haviland, Dish, Vegetable, Verlaine 22.00
Haviland, Ewer, Satin Quilted, Green, 19 In., Pair 275.00
Haviland, Fish Set, 21 1/2 In.Platter, 10 Plates, Signed 395.00
Haviland, Gravy Boat, Apple Blossom 35.00
Haviland, Gravy Boat, Attached Plate, Chrysanthemum 12.00
Haviland, Gravy Boat, Gramercy 35.00
Haviland, Gravy Boat, Orange Blossom 35.00
Haviland, Gravy Boat, Pink Spray 35.00
Haviland, Ice Cream Set, Pink Flowers, Gray Green Ives, 14 Piece 100.00
Haviland, Mug, Shaving, Pink, White, Gold, Signed C.F.H., Gold Name 40.00
Haviland, Mustache Cup & Saucer, Deer & Rabbit Scene, Hand-Painted 30.00
Haviland, Pitcher, Quilted, Leaves, Currants, Gold Handle & Rim, Signed, 8 In. 130.00
Haviland, Plate, Baltimore Rose, 9 1/2 In. 30.00
Haviland, Plate, Bread & Butter, My Garden 7.50
Haviland, Plate, Bread & Butter, Orange Blossom 9.00
Haviland, Plate, Bread & Butter, Springtime 9.00
Haviland, Plate, Chrysanthemum, 7 In. 7.00
Haviland, Plate, Floral, Gold, Silver, Artist Signed Bardos 37.50
Haviland, Plate, Gainsborough, 10 In. 12.50
Haviland, Plate, Gramercy, 10 In. 12.50
Haviland, Plate, Gramercy, 6 In. 9.00
Haviland, Plate, Hand-Painted Scene, Gold Trim, Marked, 7 1/2 X 9 1/4 In. 40.00
Haviland, Plate, Hand-Painted, Aura Argenta Linear, Signed, 9 In. 37.50
Haviland, Plate, Lake Scene, Hills, Flowers, Leaves, Gold Rim, Signed, 8 1/2 In. 30.00
Haviland, Plate, My Garden, 10 In. 12.50
Haviland, Plate, My Garden, 7 In. 8.50
Haviland, Plate, No.19, 10 In. 15.00
Haviland, Plate, No.19, 7 1/2 In. 13.00
Haviland, Plate, No.30-B, 10 In. 12.50
Haviland, Plate, No.30-B, 6 In. 7.00
Haviland, Plate, No.59, 6 In. 7.50
Haviland, Plate, Orange Blossom, 7 In. 10.00
Haviland, Plate, Oyster, Center Well, Signed, 9 In.Diameter 25.00
Haviland, Plate, Oyster, Floral, 6 Sections, Signed, 9 In. 34.00
Haviland, Plate, Oyster, Ivory Ground, Hand-Painted, Gold Rim 15.00
Haviland, Plate, Pink Roses, Gold Trim, Artist Signed, 9 In. 30.00
Haviland, Plate, Pink Spray, 10 In. 12.50
Haviland, Plate, Pink Spray, 6 In. 9.00
Haviland, Plate, Pink Spray, 7 In. 10.00
Haviland, Plate, Red Rose Design, Signed, 9 1/4 In. 55.00
Haviland, Plate, Roses, Blue Ground, Artist Signed, 9 In. 32.00
Haviland, Plate, Roses, Gold Trim, 6 In. 8.00
Haviland, Plate, Roses, Gold Trim, 7 In. 10.00

Haviland, Plate, Roses, Gold Trim, 8 1/2 In.	12.50
Haviland, Plate, White, 6 In.	6.50
Haviland, Platter, Bacon, No.30-B	25.00
Haviland, Platter, Fish, Roses & Leaves Full Length, Signed, 23 1/2 In.	225.00
Haviland, Platter, Gold Trim, 16 X 12 In.	25.00
Haviland, Platter, Gramercy, 12 X 14 In.	25.00
Haviland, Platter, Hand-Painted, Scalloped, 13 1/2 X 9 1/2 In.	45.00
Haviland, Platter, No.333, 14 In.	35.00
Haviland, Platter, Orange Blossom, 14 In.	25.00
Haviland, Platter, Peonies, 11 In.	27.50
Haviland, Platter, Ranson, 11 1/2 In.	34.00
Haviland, Platter, Ranson, 13 3/4 In.	34.00
Haviland, Platter, Springtime, 14 In.	25.00
Haviland, Platter, Troy, Round, 12 1/2 In.	25.00
Haviland, Ramekin & Matching Plate, Wide Lip, Marked, C.F.Haviland	10.00
Haviland, Ramekin, No.22	8.00
Haviland, Ramekin, Porcelain, Green Floral Pattern, Green Mark, Set Of 5	60.00
Haviland, Relish, No.30-B	18.50
Haviland, Relish, No.59, Leaf Shaped	30.00
Haviland, Sauce Boat, Underplate, Leaf Shape, Red & Green Mark, 8 In.Diam.	35.00
Haviland, Sauce, Baltimore Rose	12.00
Haviland, Sauce, Gladiola	4.50
Haviland, Sauce, Gramercy	5.50
Haviland, Sauce, No.5 Star	5.00
Haviland, Sauce, Springtime	5.50
Haviland, Soup, Cream, Saucer, Gladiola	20.00
Haviland, Soup, Dish, Gramercy	11.50
Haviland, Soup, Dish, Hand-Painted Scene, 19th Century, 9 1/2 In., Set Of 7	125.00
Haviland, Soup, Dish, My Garden	9.00
Haviland, Soup, Dish, White	7.50
Haviland, Spittoon, Pink Peonies & Leaves, Open Area Handles	35.00
Haviland, Sugar & Creamer, Diamond Shaped, Butterflies, Flowers, C.1800	75.00
Haviland, Sugar & Creamer, No.5 Star	65.00
Haviland, Sugar & Creamer, The Miramar, Curved Mark	48.00
Haviland, Tea Set, Impressed Mark, C.1879, Wedding Ring Pattern, 3 Piece	90.00
Haviland, Tray, Baltimore Rose, 10 1/2 X 8 1/2 In.	42.50
Haviland, Tray, Pink Flowers, Beige Ground, Signed, 11 In.Diameter	75.00
Haviland, Tureen, Painted Flowers, Spattered Gold Gilding, 11 X 5 In., Pair	125.00

T.G.Hawkes & Company of Corning, New York, was founded in 1880. The firm cut glass made at other firms until 1962. Many pieces are marked with the trademark, a trefoil ring enclosing a fleur-de-lis and two hawks.

Hawkes, see also Cut Glass	
Hawkes, Bottle, Bitters, Signed	47.00
Hawkes, Bottle, Cordial, Queens Pattern, Signed, 7 1/2 In.	215.00
Hawkes, Bottle, Dressing, Engraved Design, Signed & Numbered	48.00
Hawkes, Bottle, Oil, Engraved Flowers, Signed	38.00
Hawkes, Bottle, Perfume, Venetian, Original Faceted Stopper, 5 1/2 In.	180.00
Hawkes, Bottle, Prohibition, Sterling Hinged Cap, Signed, 11 1/2 In.	325.00
Hawkes, Bottle, Vinegar, Hand Hammered Sterling Stopper, Signed, 1916, 8 In.	75.00
Hawkes, Bowl, Dessert, Intaglio Stars, Lines, Amber Stained Comets, 4 In.	30.00
Hawkes, Bowl, Intaglio Cut, Footed, Turned Down Rims, Signed, 8 In.	125.00
Hawkes, Bowl, Iris, Three Applied Feet, Clover Shape, Signed, 6 X 8 In.Diam.	525.00
Hawkes, Bowl, Miniature, Gladys, 1 3/4 X 3 3/8 In.	65.00
Hawkes, Bowl, Polished Acorns & Oak Leaves, Signed Gravic, 8 X 3 1/2 In.	285.00
Hawkes, Bowl, Roll Over Rim, 8 1/4 In., 2 Vases, Pedestal, 8 1/4 In., Signed	350.00
Hawkes, Bowl, Scalloped, All Over Cut, 3 X 8 1/2 In.Diameter	112.00
Hawkes, Bowl, Star Of David, Etched Flowers, Signed, 8 X 4 In.	145.00
Hawkes, Bowl, Strawberry Pattern, Signed, 8 1/2 In.Diameter	295.00
Hawkes, Bowl, Venetian Pattern, 8 In.	295.00
Hawkes, Bucket, Ice, Handled, Gladys, Signed, 5 1/2 X 9 3/4 In.	415.00
Hawkes, Bucket, Ice, 2 Handled, Brazilian Pattern, 6 1/4 X 10 1/2 In.Diam.	550.00
Hawkes, Candlestick-Vase, Intaglio Flowers & Leaves, Signed, 6 In., Pair	230.00
Hawkes, Candlestick, Bull's-Eye, Crosshatch, Strip, Signed, 6 X 5 In., Pair	450.00
Hawkes, Candlestick, Tear Drop, Scalloped Base, Old Mark, 9 In., Pair	250.00
Hawkes, Carafe, Notched Prism Neck, Mitered Fans, Marked, 7 1/4 In.	750.00

Hawkes, Carafe, Water, Navarre Pattern, Signed	200.00
Hawkes, Celery, Hobstars, Fine Cut, Fans, Signed	65.00
Hawkes, Chalice, Etched, Sterling Silver Foot, Signed, 6 In.	65.00
Hawkes, Champagne, Cut Flowers & Strawberry Diamonds, 4 In.	12.00
Hawkes, Champagne, Honeycomb & Rosettes, Signed	24.00
Hawkes, Compote, Footed, Signed, 5 1/2 X 4 3/4 In.	42.50
Hawkes, Compote, Gravic, Rose Pattern, Signed, 9 In.	495.00
Hawkes, Compote, Green Stem & Foot, Clear Bowl, Signed, 4 X 9 In.	95.00
Hawkes, Compote, Leaf & Ribbon, Green Base & Stem, 4 X 8 In.	85.00
Hawkes, Compote, Open, Green Base & Stem, Clear Bowl, Signed, 4 X 8 In.Diam.	85.00
Hawkes, Compote, Panel Pattern, Signed, 6 1/4 X 9 1/4 In.	325.00
Hawkes, Compote, Rolled Rim, Signed, 9 In.Diameter, Pair	375.00
Hawkes, Compote, Teardrop Fluted Stem, 10 In.	135.00
Hawkes, Cruet, Brilliant Cut	50.00
Hawkes, Cruet, Copper Wheel Cut, Applied Handle, Marked, 4 1/2 In.	35.00
Hawkes, Cruet, Hobstars, Crosscut, Diamond & Fans, Signed	85.00
Hawkes, Cruet, Mushroom Stopper, Copper Wheel Cut, Signed, 4 1/2 In.	35.00
Hawkes, Cruet, Oil & Vinegar, Original Stopper, Signed & Dated	40.00
Hawkes, Cup & Saucer, Copper Wheel Engraved, Wreaths, Signed	140.00
Hawkes, Decanter, Beading, Fans, Notched Prisms, Signed, 11 1/2 In.	275.00
Hawkes, Decanter, Brazilian Pattern, 12 In.	210.00
Hawkes, Decanter, Bull's-Eye, Original Stopper, Signed, 13 In.	97.00
Hawkes, Decanter, Cross Cut Diamonds & Fans, Signed On Rim, 8 In.	135.00
Hawkes, Decanter, Golf Course Scene, 19th Hole, Lick, Marked, 1 Quart	75.00
Hawkes, Dish, Bishop Hat, Signed, 10 In.Wide	1050.00
Hawkes, Dish, Bonbon, Kohinoor Pattern, 6 In.	115.00
Hawkes, Dish, Brunswick, Signed, 10 1/4 X 3 1/4 In.	395.00
Hawkes, Dish, Candy, Covered, Sterling Finial, 10 In.	95.00
Hawkes, Dish, Leaf Shape, Scalloped Sawtooth Edge, 6 3/4 X 7 In.	95.00
Hawkes, Glass, Juice, Signed, Set Of 6	65.00
Hawkes, Goblet, Antique Green, Etched, Signed, 6 In.	60.00
Hawkes, Goblet, Copper Wheel Cut Floral & Garlands, Signed, 5 1/2 In.	60.00
Hawkes, Goblet, Cut Ovals Around Bowl, Signed	12.00
Hawkes, Goblet, Plain With Silver Rims, 6 1/2 In.	12.00
Hawkes, Goblet, Wheat & Star Cut, Stars Repeated On Base, Signed	50.00
Hawkes, Goblets, Wine, Cross Hatched Diamonds, 6 In., Set Of 5	55.00
Hawkes, Humidor, Barrel Shaped, Notched Prism, Sterling Top, Signed, 7 In.	225.00
Hawkes, Inkwell, Millicent Pattern, Signed, 2 1/2 X 3 1/2 In.Diameter	125.00
Hawkes, Jam Pot, Apple Shape, Apple Stem Handle, Sterling Silver Lid, Paneled	35.00
Hawkes, Jar, Jam, Sterling Cover & Bail, Signed	69.00
Hawkes, Mustard, Lid, Gladys, Signed	80.00
Hawkes, Napkin Ring, Wreath Engraving, Signed, Pair	135.00
Hawkes, Nappy, Aberdeen Pattern, Handle, 6 X 7 1/2 In.	75.00
Hawkes, Nappy, Scalloped Sawtooth Top, Cross Hatching, Marked, 5 In.	50.00
Hawkes, Nappy, Six Gravic Florals, Line Bands, Signed	40.00
Hawkes, Pitcher, Cider, Signed, 7 1/2 In.	165.00
Hawkes, Pitcher, Duck In Marsh Pattern, Signed, 8 1/2 In.	195.00
Hawkes, Pitcher, Gladys Pattern, Reeded Handle, Sterling Top, 9 3/4 In.	235.00
Hawkes, Pitcher, Milk, Cut Handle, 24 Point Base, 8 1/2 In.	125.00
Hawkes, Plate, Cake, Hobstar Outer Edge, Medallion Center, Signed	210.00
Hawkes, Plate, Centauri, Signed, 7 In.	75.00
Hawkes, Plate, Gladys, 6 3/4 In.	25.00
Hawkes, Plate, Star Cut, Signed, 8 In., Set Of 4	75.00
Hawkes, Plate, Star Pattern, Crystal, Signed, 8 1/2 In., Set Of 12	195.00
Hawkes, Rose Bowl, Navarre, Signed, 6 In.	425.00
Hawkes, Rose Bowl, Queen's, Signed, 6 In.	750.00
Hawkes, Salt, Intaglio, Cut Glass, Set Of 4	58.00
Hawkes, Salt, Pepper & Horse Radish, Sterling Tops, Signed	75.00
Hawkes, Sherbet, Signed, Set Of 6	275.00
Hawkes, Sugar & Creamer, Greek Key & Flute, Signed	115.00
Hawkes, Sugar & Creamer, Pedestal, Frosted Panels, Signed	165.00
Hawkes, Sugar & Creamer, Verre De Soie, Engraved, Signed	225.00
Hawkes, Tray, Floral Etched, Signed, 12 1/4 X 10 In.	35.00
Hawkes, Tray, Punty & Hobstar, Signed, 3 1/4 X 7 3/8 In.	80.00
Hawkes, Tray, Two Layer, Rock Crystal, Sterling Handle, Signed, 9 X 6 1/2 In.	110.00
Hawkes, Tumbler, Ice Tea, Ribbon Pattern, Flaring At Top, 5 1/4 In., Pair	70.00

Hawkes, Tumbler, Strawberry Diamond & Fan, Signed, Set Of 7	125.00
Hawkes, Tumbler, Tea, Ribbon Pattern, Flared Top, Signed, 5 1/4 In.	55.00
Hawkes, Vase, Brunswick, 16 Point Hobstar Base, Signed	95.00
Hawkes, Vase, Corset Shaped, Brunswick Pattern, Signed, 8 In.	325.00
Hawkes, Vase, Enameled, Silver Overlay Rim, Signed, 9 1/2 In.	109.00
Hawkes, Vase, Fan Shape, Green Etched Leaves, 7 1/2 In.	50.00
Hawkes, Vase, Intaglio Iris, Signed On Glass & Sterling Base, 10 In.	550.00
Hawkes, Vase, Loving Cup Shape, Copper Wheel Engraved, Signed, 3 1/8 In.	65.00
Hawkes, Vase, Navarre Pattern, Signed, 17 In.	900.00
Hawkes, Vase, Notched Edge, Signed, 12 In.	175.00
Hawkes, Vase, Panel Pattern, Signed, 12 In.	180.00
Hawkes, Vase, Paperweight Base, Trumpet, Hobstar On Bottom, 14 In., Pair	475.00
Hawkes, Vase, Rock Crystal, Flowers & Ives, Signed, 10 In.	140.00
Hawkes, Vase, Shaded Blue To Clear, Signed, 11 1/4 In.	95.00
Hawkes, Vase, Sterling Base, Optic Cut, Trumpet Shape, Signed, 6 1/2 In.	150.00
Hawkes, Vase, Trumpet, Cut Fluted Body, Greek Key Cutting, Signed, 12 In.	135.00
Hawkes, Vase, Trumpet, 2 Intaglio Roses, Signed, 10 In.	50.00
Hawkes, Vase, Verre De Soie, Copper Wheel Engraved, Signed, 6 3/4 In.	135.00
Hawkes, Vase, Vertical Bands Of Cross Hatch, Sterling Base, Signed, 11 In.	325.00
Hawkes, Water Set, Squat Pitcher, 6 Tumblers, Scalloped, Marked, 6 1/4 In.	300.00
Hawkes, Wine, Green, Cut To Clear, Tall, Signed, Pair	360.00
Hawkes, Wine, Red, Copper Wheel Engraving, Signed, 4 1/4 In.	55.00
Hearse, Virginia City, Montana, Horse-Drawn	6500.00

H   *Heisey glass was made from 1895 to 1958 in Newark, Ohio, by A.H. Heisey and Co., Inc.*

Heisey, see also Custard Glass

Heisey, Ashtray, Duck, 4 1/4 In.	100.00
Heisey, Ashtray, MacArthur Hat	22.00
Heisey, Ashtray, Ridgeleigh, Spade	10.00
Heisey, Basket, Cut Floral Design, Flaring Rim, 15 In.	95.00
Heisey, Basket, Double Rib & Panel, Flamingo, 8 1/2 In.	65.00
Heisey, Basket, Notched Handle, Star Bottom, Dated, 8/17/15, 9 3/4 In.	85.00
Heisey, Basket, Panel Design, Flared, Signed, Crystal, 11 X 8 1/4 In.	35.00
Heisey, Bell, Colonial, Signed	75.00
Heisey, Berry Bowl, Beaded Swag	40.00
Heisey, Berry Set, Colonial, 7 Piece	40.00
Heisey, Berry Set, Queen Anne, 7 Piece	75.00
Heisey, Berry Set, Sunburst & Fan, 7 Piece	110.00
Heisey, Bonbon, Queen Anne, Sahara, Footed, Handled, 6 In.	25.00
Heisey, Bookend, Frosted, Horse Head	95.00
Heisey, Bookend, Rearing Horse, Pair	165.00
Heisey, Bottle, Bitters, Colonial	18.50
Heisey, Bottle, Carafe, Sunburst	35.00
Heisey, Bottle, Cologne, Cracked Ice Effect, Flat Stopper, Marked, 6 1/4 In.	65.00
Heisey, Bottle, Perfume, Sterling, Enameled Stopper	45.00
Heisey, Bottle, Water, Beaded Panel & Sunburst	38.50
Heisey, Bowl, Beaded Panel & Sunburst, Gold Panels, 8 In.	35.00
Heisey, Bowl, Colonial, Signed, 9 In.Diameter	15.00
Heisey, Bowl, Console, Lariat, Wavy Edges, 12 In.	27.00
Heisey, Bowl, Console, Wampum, 12 In., Pair Of Candlesticks	46.00
Heisey, Bowl, Enameled Red & Blue Roses, Star Base, Signed, 10 1/2 In.	50.00
Heisey, Bowl, Floral, Crystolite, 13 1/2 In.	35.00
Heisey, Bowl, Flower, Crystolite, Oval, 13 In.Diameter	30.00
Heisey, Bowl, Orchid, 12 1/2 In.	38.50
Heisey, Bowl, Pinwheel & Fan, Marked, 8 In.	60.00
Heisey, Bowl, Plantation, 3 Compartment, 11 In.	30.00
Heisey, Bowl, Punch, Colonial, Signed, 15 In.Diameter	125.00
Heisey, Bowl, Punch, Colonial, 12 Cups.Signed, 14 In.	195.00
Heisey, Bowl, Punch, Ridgeleigh, 12 Cups, Signed	125.00
Heisey, Bowl, Punch, Wedding Band, Base, 4 Cups	195.00
Heisey, Bowl, Puritan, Footed, 8 X 8 1/2 In.	30.00
Heisey, Bowl, Salad, Orchid, 12 In.	35.00
Heisey, Bowl, Swirl Design, 4 Feet, Green, 3 X 12 In.	30.00
Heisey, Bowl, Swirl, Clear, Oval, 4 Feet, Marked, 12 X 10 In.	25.00
Heisey, Bowl, Underplate, Old Colony, Etched, 5 1/2 In.	27.50

Heisey, Bowl, Yeoman, Rimmed, 8 In.	15.00
Heisey, Box, Cigarette, Ridgeleigh	22.00
Heisey, Box, Puff, Crystolite, Cover, 4 3/4 In.	40.00
Heisey, Bust, Owens, Dated, Libbey Glass	87.50
Heisey, Butter, Beaded Swag, Etched, Covered	79.50
Heisey, Butter, Covered, Banded Flute	85.00
Heisey, Butter, Covered, Beaded Swag	75.00
Heisey, Butter, Covered, Colonial, Signed	47.50
Heisey, Butter, Covered, Peerless, Embossed Underside Of Lid, Clear	85.00
Heisey, Butter, Covered, Pineapple & Fan, Green With Gold	90.00
Heisey, Butter, Covered, Revere, Cut Cover, 5 1/2 In.	45.00
Heisey, Butter, Locket On Chain, Clear, Covered	79.00
Heisey, Butter, Puritan	50.00
Heisey, Butter, Winged Scroll, Green With Gold	135.00
Heisey, Candelabra, Prism Block, 3 Light, Signed, Pair	250.00
Heisey, Candle Block, Crystolite, 4 In.	40.00
Heisey, Candleholder, Cornucopia, Single Light, Pair	35.00
Heisey, Candleholder, Cornucopia, Three Light, Pair	49.00
Heisey, Candleholder, Crystolite, 3 Light, Crystal, Pair	20.00
Heisey, Candleholder, Horn Of Plenty, Double	15.00
Heisey, Candleholder, Lariat, Triple, Pair	55.00
Heisey, Candleholder, Orchid, Pair	38.00
Heisey, Candleholder, Parallel Quarters, Pair	44.00
Heisey, Candlestick, Old Sandwich, Cobalt, Pair	350.00
Heisey, Candletstick, No.113, Pink, Signed, 3 1/2 In., Pair	18.00
Heisey, Candy Container, Recessed Panel, Signed, 1/4 Pound	35.00
Heisey, Candy Jar, Footed, Amethyst, No.1405, 10 In., Signed	35.00
Heisey, Celery, Crystolite, 12 X 3 1/2 In.	16.00
Heisey, Celery, Greek Key	29.00
Heisey, Champagne, Danish Princess, Cut	9.00
Heisey, Champagne, Pied Piper, Etched	19.00
Heisey, Champagne, Rib & Panel	12.00
Heisey, Claret, Oxford, Stem, Etched Fisherman, Signed	35.00
Heisey, Coaster, Ridgeleigh, 3 1/2 In.Diameter, Set Of 8	28.00
Heisey, Cocktail Shaker, Intaglio Cut, Strainer	65.00
Heisey, Cocktail Shaker, Orchid, Etched	125.00
Heisey, Cocktail Shaker, Rooster Head	85.00
Heisey, Cocktail, Crystolite, 3 1/2 Oz	8.00
Heisey, Cocktail, Fancy Loop, Footed	40.00
Heisey, Cocktail, Orchid, Etched	10.00
Heisey, Cocktail, Pied Piper, Stem, 4 Ounce	16.00
Heisey, Cocktail, Wabash, Stem, 4 Ounce	16.00
Heisey, Compote, Colonial, Pedestal, Signed, 6 1/4 X 8 1/2 In.	25.00
Heisey, Compote, Etched & Cut, Signed, 6 X 5 In.	32.00
Heisey, Compote, Jelly, Twist, 2 Handled, 6 In.	13.50
Heisey, Compote, Moonglo, Covered, Low Footed, 6 In.	65.00
Heisey, Compote, Plantation, 12 In.Diameter	47.50
Heisey, Compote, Plantation, 5 In.	22.00
Heisey, Compote, Queen Anne, Pink, Marked, 6 X 6 In.	22.50
Heisey, Compote, Tulip, 5 1/4 X 4 3/4 In.Diameter	27.50
Heisey, Console Set, Grape & Vine, Bowl, Candleholder, Cut, 3 Piece	200.00
Heisey, Cordial, Old Williamsburg, 4 In.	9.50
Heisey, Cornucopia, 7 In.	30.00
Heisey, Cornucopia, 9 In., Signed	38.00
Heisey, Creamer & Sugar, Lariat, Signed	15.00
Heisey, Creamer, Beaded Swag, Opalescent, Painted Flowers	50.00
Heisey, Creamer, Fandango, Individual	28.50
Heisey, Creamer, Prince Of Wales, Gold Trim	35.00
Heisey, Cruet, Banded Flute, 7 In.	32.50
Heisey, Cruet, Colonial, Original Stopper, Signed	30.00
Heisey, Cruet, Crystolite, 3 1/2 In.	45.00
Heisey, Cruet, Fandango	60.00
Heisey, Cruet, Flat Panel, Original Sticker	48.50
Heisey, Cruet, No.451, Cross Lined Flute, Stopper	36.50
Heisey, Cruet, Plantation	25.00
Heisey, Cruet, Ridgeleigh	18.00

Heisey, Cruet, Sawtooth Band	45.00
Heisey, Cup & Saucer, Crystolite, Signed	11.50
Heisey, Cup & Saucer, Empress, Round	30.00
Heisey, Cup & Saucer, Empress, Square	30.00
Heisey, Cup & Saucer, Oceanic, Green	12.00
Heisey, Cup & Saucer, Octagon, Pink	10.00
Heisey, Cup & Saucer, Optic Tooth, Marked, Set Of 6	90.00
Heisey, Cup & Saucer, Orchid, Etched	15.00
Heisey, Cup & Saucer, Queen Anne	11.00 To 22.00
Heisey, Cup & Saucer, Rose, Etched	45.00
Heisey, Cup & Saucer, Twist, Signed	15.00
Heisey, Cup, Custard, Old Williamsburg, 5 Oz., Set Of 6	30.00
Heisey, Cup, Punch, Colonial, Set Of 8	40.00
Heisey, Cup, Punch, Greek Key	10.00 To 23.00
Heisey, Cup, Punch, Plantation	10.00 To 12.00
Heisey, Cup, Punch, Puritan	7.00
Heisey, Cup, Punch, Victoria, Cut	5.00 To 6.00
Heisey, Decanter, Peerless, Handled, Original Stopper	17.50
Heisey, Dish, Candy, Crystolite, Brass Cover, Cherry Wood Apple Finial	30.00
Heisey, Dish, Candy, Crystolite, Gorham Sterling Cover, Signed	45.00
Heisey, Dish, Nut, Flamingo, Queen Anne Dolphin, Footed, Set Of 6	55.00
Heisey, Dish, Nut, Individual, Moonglo	12.50
Heisey, Dish, Plantation, Divided, Oval, 8 In.	25.00
Heisey, Dish, Relish, Colonial, 5 Section, Marked, 9 1/2 X 13 In.	40.00
Heisey, Dish, Relish, Crystolite, 3 Compartment, 8 In.	35.00
Heisey, Dish, Relish, Greek Key, Oval, 9 In., Pair	21.00
Heisey, Dish, Relish, Oceanic, Green, Signed, 13 X 14 1/4 In.	28.00
Heisey, Dish, Relish, Oceanic, Pink, Signed, 12 X 4 In.	12.50
Heisey, Dish, Relish, Prism Pattern, 8 X 3 1/2 In.	6.50
Heisey, Dish, Relish, Ridgeleigh, 5 Compartment, Signed	28.00
Heisey, Dish, Soap, Flat Panel, Covered	20.00
Heisey, Dish, Soup, Pied Piper, 8 In.	13.50
Heisey, Dish, Sterling Silver Cover, Man With Basket & Duck Knob, 5 In.	65.00
Heisey, Dish, Sundae, Colonial, Clear, Signed, 5 1/2 In.	14.00
Heisey, Dish, Sundae, Williamsburg, Marked	22.00
Heisey, Figurine, Bull, Signed, 4 In.	1000.00
Heisey, Figurine, Bunny, Head Up, 2 3/8 In.	90.00
Heisey, Figurine, Cygnet, 2 1/8 In.	90.00
Heisey, Figurine, Giraffe, Head Back, 11 In.	150.00
Heisey, Figurine, Giraffe, Head Turned, 11 In.	150.00
Heisey, Figurine, Goose, Wings Down, 2 3/4 In.	75.00
Heisey, Figurine, Goose, Wings Half Way, 4 1/2 In.	90.00
Heisey, Figurine, Goose, Wings Up, 6 1/2 In.	100.00
Heisey, Figurine, Mallard, Wings Half Way, 5 In.	125.00
Heisey, Figurine, Plug Horse	65.00 To 75.00
Heisey, Figurine, Plug Horse, 4 In.	65.00 To 75.00
Heisey, Figurine, Pony, Standing, 5 In.	75.00
Heisey, Figurine, Rearing Pony, 3 3/4 In.	125.00
Heisey, Figurine, Scottie, 3 1/2 In.	25.00 To 85.00
Heisey, Figurine, Sparrow, 2 1/4 In.	70.00
Heisey, Figurine, Swan, 7 In.	85.00
Heisey, Flower Frog, Duck Insert, C.1920	97.50
Heisey, Glass, Juice, Etched Fisherman, Signed, 6 1/2 Oz.	35.00
Heisey, Glass, Juice, Pied Piper, 5 Ounce	10.00
Heisey, Glass, Shot, Hartman	22.00
Heisey, Glass, Wine, Rib & Panel, Signed, 3 Oz.	11.00
Heisey, Goblet, Banded Flute	22.00
Heisey, Goblet, Danish Princess, Cut	16.00
Heisey, Goblet, Greek Key, Clear, Signed	45.00
Heisey, Goblet, Minuet, No.5010	25.00
Heisey, Goblet, Moonglo, Signed, 10 Oz.	35.00
Heisey, Goblet, New Era	15.00
Heisey, Goblet, Optic Tooth, 8 In.	20.00
Heisey, Goblet, Orchid, Etched, 7 In.	16.00
Heisey, Goblet, Pied Piper, Marked, Set Of 6	135.00
Heisey, Goblet, Rib & Panel, Signed, 8 Oz.	10.00

Heisey, Goblet, Rose	27.00
Heisey, Goblet, Victorian, Ball Stem, Set Of 6	58.00
Heisey, Goblet, Wabash, 10 Ounce	15.00
Heisey, Hair Receiver, Cut Glass, Cherub, Silver Plated Cover	65.00
Heisey, Ice Bucket, Crystolite, Tab Handled, Marked	15.00
Heisey, Jar, Candy, Olive, Covered, 12 In.	38.00
Heisey, Jar, Candy, Waverly, Footed, Etched	150.00
Heisey, Jar, Jam, Crystolite, Covered	40.00
Heisey, Jar, Jam, Diamond Point, Pair	10.00
Heisey, Jar, Jam, Greek Key, Handles	28.00
Heisey, Jar, Jam, Rib & Panel, 2 Handled	19.00
Heisey, Jar, Jelly, Lariat, Covered	24.00
Heisey, Jug, Colonial, Signed, 6 1/2 In.	35.00
Heisey, Jug, Crystolite, 1/2 Gal.	45.00
Heisey, Mayonnaise Set, Crystolite, Marked	10.00
Heisey, Mug, Pineapple & Fan, Handled, 7 Oz.	32.50
Heisey, Mug, Punty Band, Red, 3 1/4 In.	25.00
Heisey, Mustard Pot, Colonial, Signed	25.00
Heisey, Mustard Pot, Crystolite, Covered, Miniature	50.00
Heisey, Mustard Pot, Ridgeleigh	5.00
Heisey, Mustard Pot, Victorian	22.50
Heisey, Nappy, Intercepted Flute, 4 1/4 In.	35.00
Heisey, Nappy, Narrow Flute, 4 1/2 In.	8.50
Heisey, Nappy, Pinwheel & Fan, Signed, 5 In., Set Of 6	65.00
Heisey, Nappy, Prison Stripe, 4 1/2 In.	14.00
Heisey, Pitcher, Colonial, No.353, 1/2 Gallon	42.00
Heisey, Pitcher, Ice, Old Sandwich, 1/2 Gallon	27.50
Heisey, Pitcher, Molasses, Williamsburg, Etched Flowers, 8 Oz.	12.00
Heisey, Pitcher, Moonglo, Marked, 6 In.	55.00
Heisey, Pitcher, Narrow Flute, Marked, 4 1/2 In.	30.00
Heisey, Pitcher, Plain Panel Recess, Dated 1910, 1/2 Gallon	47.50
Heisey, Pitcher, Tankard, Banded Flute, Crystal, Signed, 8 1/2 In.	45.00
Heisey, Pitcher, Tankard, Greek Key	105.00
Heisey, Pitcher, Water, Banded Flute	50.00
Heisey, Pitcher, Water, Rib & Panel, 6 Goblets, Set	140.00
Heisey, Plate, Cake, Orchid, Etched, Handled, Open, 12 In.	27.00
Heisey, Plate, Coarse Rib, Moonglo, 7 1/2 In.	7.50
Heisey, Plate, Coaster, Panel Rim, Star Bottom, Signed, Set Of 8	30.00
Heisey, Plate, Crinoline, Etched, 7 1/2 In.	12.50
Heisey, Plate, Dinner, Empress, 9 In.	20.00
Heisey, Plate, Dinner, Queen Anne, Sahara, Square, 10 1/2 In.	42.50
Heisey, Plate, Empress, Sahara, 6 In.Square	18.00
Heisey, Plate, Empress, 7 In.	8.00
Heisey, Plate, Empress, 8 In.	100.00
Heisey, Plate, Greek Key, 4 1/2 In.	10.00
Heisey, Plate, Ipswich, Crystal, Signed, 7 In.	8.50
Heisey, Plate, Luncheon, Empress, 8 In.Square	20.00
Heisey, Plate, Luncheon, Pied Piper, 8 In.	10.00
Heisey, Plate, Octagon, Moonglo, 8 In.	8.25
Heisey, Plate, Optic Tooth, 8 In., Set Of 6	30.00
Heisey, Plate, Orchid, Dolphin Center Handle, 14 In.	75.00
Heisey, Plate, Orchid, Etched, 6 In.	10.00
Heisey, Plate, Orchid, Etched, 8 In.	15.00
Heisey, Plate, Panel, 3 1/2 In.	4.00
Heisey, Plate, Queen Anne, Pink, Signed, 10 1/2 In.	25.00
Heisey, Plate, Queen Anne, 7 In.Square	15.00
Heisey, Plate, Salad, Empress, 7 In.Square	15.00
Heisey, Plate, Salad, Pied Piper, 7 In.	7.00
Heisey, Plate, Salad, Queen Anne, Clear, 7 In.	7.00
Heisey, Plate, Snack, Crystolite, 2 Handles, 7 In.	25.00
Heisey, Plate, Supper, Empress, 9 In.	20.00
Heisey, Plate, Torte, Whirlpool, 18 In.	18.00
Heisey, Plate, Twist, 8 In.	6.00
Heisey, Punch Bowl, Greek Key, Pedestal, 12 Cups, Signed, 15 In.	375.00
Heisey, Punch Set, Colonial, 17 Pieces	300.00
Heisey, Punch Set, Greek Key, 13 Pieces	400.00

Heisey, Punch Set, Old Williamsburg, Bowl & 12 Cups, Marked	115.00
Heisey, Punch Set, Prison Stripe, Bowl, Base & 8 Cups	550.00
Heisey, Punch Set, Whirlpool, Signed, 14 Piece	150.00
Heisey, Salt & Pepper, Moonglo, Original Tops, Marked	55.00
Heisey, Salt & Pepper, No.24, Signed	20.00
Heisey, Salt & Pepper, Old Williamsburg, Marked	20.00
Heisey, Salt & Pepper, Plantation, Marked	25.00
Heisey, Salt, Colonial, Mother-Of-Pearl Shaker Top	18.50
Heisey, Salt, Fancy Loop, Clear	15.00
Heisey, Salt, Greek Key, Footed	9.00
Heisey, Sherbet, Colonial Pattern, Ruffled Edge	6.00
Heisey, Sherbet, Crinoline, No.5010, Etched, Low Footed	12.50
Heisey, Sherbet, Frontenac, Set Of 3	12.00
Heisey, Sherbet, Greek Key, Signed, Set Of 7	40.00
Heisey, Sherbet, Ipswich	13.00
Heisey, Sherbet, Jamestown, Stem, Barsolina Cut	14.00
Heisey, Sherbet, Moonglo	15.00
Heisey, Sherbet, Old Williamsburg, Marked	40.00
Heisey, Sherbet, Orchid, Etched	17.50
Heisey, Sherbet, Pied Piper, 6 Ounce	10.00
Heisey, Sherbet, Tyrolean, Stemmed, Set Of 6	72.00
Heisey, Sherbet, Wabash, Stem, 6 Ounce	10.00
Heisey, Sherbet, Wedding Band, Footed, Set Of 6	62.00
Heisey, Spooner, Greek Key	50.00
Heisey, Spooner, Peerless	23.00 To 27.50
Heisey, Spooner, Pineapple & Fan, Green & Gold	50.00
Heisey, Spooner, Prison Stripe	32.50
Heisey, Spooner, Sawtooth Band, Cut, Gold Trim	25.00
Heisey, Sugar & Creamer, Chrysanthemum, Silver Overlay	22.00
Heisey, Sugar & Creamer, Cornucopia, Individual	30.00
Heisey, Sugar & Creamer, Crystolite, Signed	15.00 To 35.00
Heisey, Sugar & Creamer, Cut Block	23.00
Heisey, Sugar & Creamer, Moonglo, Green	35.00
Heisey, Sugar & Creamer, New Era	20.00
Heisey, Sugar & Creamer, Octagon	22.50
Heisey, Sugar & Creamer, Octagon, Sahara, Marked	42.50
Heisey, Sugar & Creamer, Orchid, Etched	25.00 To 36.00
Heisey, Sugar & Creamer, Orchid, Pedestal, Crystal	40.00
Heisey, Sugar & Creamer, Plantation, Cut	28.00
Heisey, Sugar & Creamer, Pointed Oval	45.00
Heisey, Sugar & Creamer, Queen Anne, Footed, Dolphin	27.50
Heisey, Sugar & Creamer, Queen Anne, Individual	20.00
Heisey, Sugar & Creamer, Ridgleigh, Amethyst, Miniature	10.00
Heisey, Sugar & Creamer, Square, Triple Mitre Cross Sections	75.00
Heisey, Sugar & Creamer, Victorian, Signed	25.00
Heisey, Sugar & Creamer, Winged Scroll, Open	135.00
Heisey, Sugar Shaker, Optic Tooth, Zircon, Footed	22.00
Heisey, Sugar Shaker, Plantation	47.50
Heisey, Sugar, Greek Key, Round	18.00
Heisey, Syrup, Peerless	28.00
Heisey, Table Set, Child's, Sawtooth Band, 4 Piece	135.00
Heisey, Table Set, Winged Scroll, Custard, 4 Piece	500.00
Heisey, Tankard, Old Williamsburg, 1/2 Gallon	35.00
Heisey, Tankard, Wabash Stem, 3 Pint	85.00
Heisey, Toothpick, Beaded Swag, Opalescent	35.00
Heisey, Toothpick, Beaded Tray, Dresser, Colonial, Oval, Rayed Bottom	38.00
Heisey, Toothpick, Cherub	40.00
Heisey, Tray, Crystolite, Oval, 13 In.	30.00
Heisey, Tray, Spice, Colonial, 5 Section, Signed, 13 1/2 X 9 1/2 In.	45.00
Heisey, Trivet, Crystolite, 3 Footed, 6 1/4 In.	23.50
Heisey, Tub, Ice, Greek Key, 5 1/2 In.Diameter	50.00
Heisey, Tumbler, Beaded Swag, Opalescent, Colored Daisy	25.00
Heisey, Tumbler, Colonial, 2 Oz.	15.00
Heisey, Tumbler, Cross Lined Flute	22.00
Heisey, Tumbler, Hartman, 6 In.	22.00
Heisey, Tumbler, Moonglo, Cut	10.00

eisey, Tumbler, Old Sandwich, Footed	16.00
eisey, Tumbler, Pineapple & Fan, Gold, Set Of 6	300.00
eisey, Tumbler, Ridgeleigh, 6 In.	22.00
eisey, Tumbler, St.Louis Exposition Souvenir, Ruby, Marked, 3 3/4 In.	30.00
eisey, Tumbler, Thumbprint, Cobalt, Signed	65.00
eisey, Tumbler, Victorian, 10 Ounce	9.00
eisey, Vase, Bud, Pineapple & Fan, Green & Gold	28.00
eisey, Vase, Candle, Ipswich, Prisms & Inserts, Pair	80.00
eisey, Vase, Colonial, Signed, 20 In.	85.00
eisey, Vase, Cornucopia, Cobalt Blue, Signed, 8 In.	35.00
eisey, Vase, Cornucopia, Warwick, Cobalt Blue, Signed, 7 1/2 In., Pair	286.00
eisey, Vase, Cornucopia, 9 In.	85.00
eisey, Vase, Crinoline, No.353, 10 In.	45.00
eisey, Vase, Crinoline, No.353, 15 In.	65.00
eisey, Vase, Figural Seahorse Handles, Fish On Sides, Frosted, 7 X 6 3/4 In.	55.00
eisey, Vase, Greek Key, 6 1/2 In.	200.00
eisey, Vase, Pineapple & Fan, 10 In.	16.50 To 22.00
eisey, Vase, Ribbed, Crystal, 9 In.	24.00
eisey, Vase, Rooster, 6 1/2 In.	60.00 To 85.00
eisey, Vegetable, Orchid, 3 Part, Etched, 11 In.	30.00
eisey, Water Set, Beaded Swag, Pitcher, 6 Tumblers, Gold Trim	175.00
eisey, Wine, Greek Key, Signed	19.50
eisey, Wine, Orchid, Etched	12.00
eisey, Wine, Orchid, Set Of 6	35.00
eisey, Wine, Paneled Cane, Gold	10.50
eisey, Wine, Yorktown, Set Of 6	59.00
Herend, see Fischer	
Heubach, Dish, Jasper, Full Headdress Indian, Fan Mark, 6 X 5 In.	65.00
Heubach, Figurine, Baby Sitting In Snow	85.00
Heubach, Figurine, Boy Sitting On Chair, 7 In.	45.00
Heubach, Figurine, Boy With Broom, Bisque, 13 1/2 In.	95.00
Heubach, Figurine, Boy, Red Mark, 14 In.	185.00
Heubach, Figurine, Crawling Baby, Bisque, 5 X 3 1/2 In.	125.00
Heubach, Figurine, Dancing Girl, Holding Sides Of Dress, 7 In.	45.00
Heubach, Figurine, Girl In Nightgown, Hands Clasped, Bisque, Marked, 10 In.	110.00
Heubach, Figurine, Girl With Baskets Of Apples, Bisque, Marked, 12 1/2 In.	165.00
Heubach, Figurine, Girl With Watering Can, Impressed Mark, 13 In.	175.00
Heubach, Figurine, Itchy Puppy, White With Gray Patches, 5 X 6 In.	62.50
Heubach, Figurine, Peasant Girl Playing Tambourine, Signed, 14 In.	160.00
Heubach, Figurine, Sailor Boy, Lavender & Green Outfit, Marked, 9 3/8 In.	110.00
Heubach, Figurine, Seated Boy, Bisque, 7 In.	125.00
Heubach, Pincushion Doll, With Pincushion, 11 In.	150.00
Heubach, Plate, Girl Holding Hen, Impressed Mark, 10 In.	48.50
Heubach, Toothpick, Boy Straddling Chair	60.00
Heubach, Vase, Lotus Type Porcelain, Figural, Signed, 5 In.	145.00
Heubach, Vase, Pate-Sur-Pate, Art Nouveau Woman, Lavender, 3 1/2 In.	35.00

(H I G)   *Higbee glass was made by the J.B. Higbee Company of Bridgeville, Pennsylvania, about 1900.*

Higbee, see also Pressed Glass

Higbee, Cakestand, Rayed Scalloped Bottom, Bee Mark, 9 1/4 In.Diameter	25.00
Higbee, Candlestick, Square Base, Pair, Marked, 6 3/4 In.	27.50
Higbee, Creamer, Flute	7.00
Higbee, Dish, Butter, Crystal	5.00
Higbee, Vase, Rayed Scalloped Base, Bee Mark, 15 1/2 In.	25.00
Higbee, Water Set, Child's, Oval Star, 5 Piece	65.00
Historic Blue, see Adams, Clews, Ridgway, Staffordshire	

Hobnail glass is a pattern of glass with bumps in an allover pattern.

Hobnail, Butter, Ruffled Lid, Clear	25.00
Hobnail, Celery, Blown In Mold, Ground & Polished Pontil	22.50
Hobnail, Celery, Flat, Fan Top	23.75
Hobnail, Decanter, Matching Stopper, Quart	45.00
Hobnail, Goblet, Amber	27.50
Hobnail, Goblet, Blue	30.00
Hobnail, Mug, Vaseline	18.00

Honesdale, Vase, Acid Cut, Green,
Gold, Frosted, Signed, 6 3/4 in.

Holly Amber, Tumbler, Leafage

Hobnail, Pitcher, Water, Amber, 6 Tumblers	170.0
Hobnail, Salt, Blue, Lid	14.0
Hobnail, Sugar Shaker, Green	45.0
Hobnail, Toothpick, Amber	19.0
Hobnail, Toothpick, Blue	18.0
Hobnail, Tray, Water, Amber	30.0
Hobnail, Vase, Crimped Top, 7 1/2 In.	16.0

*Holly amber, or golden agate, glass was made by the Indiana Tumbler and
Goblet Company from January 1, 1903, to June 13, 1903. It is a pressed
glass pattern featuring holly leaves in the amber shaded glass.*

Holly Amber, Bowl, 1 3/4 X 7 1/2 In.	500.0
Holly Amber, Compote, Jelly, Open	500.0
Holly Amber, Cruet	1500.0
Holly Amber, Dish, Butter	450.0
Holly Amber, Sugar, Open, 3 3/4 In.	300.0
Holly Amber, Syrup	850.0
Holly Amber, Toothpick, Annealing Lines	250.0
Holly Amber, Tumbler, Leafage *Illus*	400.0
Holly Amber, Tumbler, 4 X 3 In.Diameter	450.0
Honesdale, Vase, Acid Cut, Green, Gold, Frosted, Signed, 6 3/4 In. *Illus*	175.0
Honesdale, Vase, Etched, Footed, Narrow Neck, Center 8 In.Diameter	200.0
Hopalong Cassidy, Bank, White Plastic Head	24.0
Hopalong Cassidy, Banner, Felt	8.0
Hopalong Cassidy, Binoculars	25.0
Hopalong Cassidy, Book, Sticker	12.0
Hopalong Cassidy, Bottle, Figural, 1950	20.0
Hopalong Cassidy, Bowl, Cereal, Signed, China	20.0
Hopalong Cassidy, Camera, Box & Literature, 1941	70.0
Hopalong Cassidy, Case, Pencil, Folder & Supplies	15.0
Hopalong Cassidy, Clock, Alarm	85.0
Hopalong Cassidy, Cup, Coffee, Picture Of Hopalong Cassidy	12.0
Hopalong Cassidy, Drum	25.0
Hopalong Cassidy, Film, 16mm., Bar 20 Rides Again, Boxed	7.5
Hopalong Cassidy, Game, Canasta, Revolving Saddle Tray, Score Pad, 1950	22.0
Hopalong Cassidy, Game, Dominoes, Boxed	14.0
Hopalong Cassidy, Game, Ring Toss	7.2
Hopalong Cassidy, Glass, Milk Glass	7.00 To 12.0
Hopalong Cassidy, Gun, 6 Shooter, 1950	15.0
Hopalong Cassidy, Jar, Cookie, Bar 20 Cookie Corral, 6 1/2 X 8 In.	18.5
Hopalong Cassidy, Knife, Child's, Figure & Name Both Sides, Stainless	12.5
Hopalong Cassidy, Knife, Pocket	15.00 To 30.0
Hopalong Cassidy, Knife, With Horse	15.0
Hopalong Cassidy, Lamp, Bar 20 Ranch, Revolving Color Cylinder Insert, 1949	75.0
Hopalong Cassidy, Mug, Blue	6.0
Hopalong Cassidy, Mug, Milk Glass	2.25 To 6.0
Hopalong Cassidy, Mug, Red	7.0
Hopalong Cassidy, Nightlight, Figural, Aladdin Alacite Holster, Switch	55.0
Hopalong Cassidy, Paper, Writing Kit	20.0
Hopalong Cassidy, Pennant, Cole Bros., Circus	6.0
Hopalong Cassidy, Plate, Dinner	12.00 To 15.0

Hopalong Cassidy, Puzzle, Box Of 4	15.00
Hopalong Cassidy, Puzzle, Jigsaw	4.00
Hopalong Cassidy, Radio, Black & Silver	125.00
Hopalong Cassidy, Radio, Table	35.00
Hopalong Cassidy, Ring	10.00 To 20.00
Hopalong Cassidy, Shirt, Cowboy, White Trim, Hoppy Buttons, Size 14	15.00
Hopalong Cassidy, Spurs	23.00
Hopalong Cassidy, Star Badge	8.50
Hopalong Cassidy, Thermos	34.50
Hopalong Cassidy, Tie Bar, Boxed	15.00
Hopalong Cassidy, Wrist Watch	45.00 To 75.00
Horn, Candlestick, Ivory & Gold, C.1889	175.00
Horn, Corkscrew, Sterling	65.00
Howdy Doody, Bag, Shoulder, Canvas	18.00
Howdy Doody, Beanie	15.00
Howdy Doody, Camera, Sun Ray, Original Card	8.50
Howdy Doody, Doll, String Activates His Eyes & Mouth, 14 In.	40.00
Howdy Doody, Dummy, Ventriloquist, Hard Head, Stuffed Body, 20 In.	28.00
Howdy Doody, Earmuffs	10.00
Howdy Doody, Game, Chart, 1949, Boxed	12.00
Howdy Doody, Glass, Blue Plastic	10.00
Howdy Doody, Handkerchief, 1950s, Signed Bob Smith	12.00
Howdy Doody, Marionette	28.00
Howdy Doody, Mask	10.00
Howdy Doody, Mug, Princess On Other Side	13.00
Howdy Doody, Puppet, Hand	8.00
Howdy Doody, Teaspoon	8.00

Hull pottery is made in Crooksville, Ohio. The factory started in 1903 as the Acme Pottery Company. Art pottery was first made in 1917.

Hull, Bank, Pig, No.196	6.50
Hull, Basket, Bow Knot, B25, 6 1/2 In.	30.00
Hull, Basket, Bow Knot, Pink To Blue, 10 1/2 In.	48.00
Hull, Basket, Ebb Tide, Maroon, Fish On Handle, 7 X 8 In.	25.00
Hull, Basket, Twig Handle, 5 1/2 In.	17.50
Hull, Basket, Zinnia, 602, 6 1/2 In.	25.00
Hull, Bowl, Console, Bow Knot, Footed, 8-16, 13 1/2 In.	30.00
Hull, Bowl, Speckle, Pink, 2 X 2 X 6 In.	3.00
Hull, Centerpiece, Magnolia, Footed, 13 In.	20.00
Hull, Console Set, Wildflower, 3 Piece, No.W-21, 12 In.	40.00
Hull, Console Set, Woodland, 3 Piece, No.W-29	45.00
Hull, Cookie Jar, Figural, Little Red Riding Hood, No.135889	35.00
Hull, Cookie Jar, Little Red Riding Hood, No.967	20.00
Hull, Cornucopia, Magnolia, 19 X 8 1/2 In.	12.00
Hull, Cornucopia, Wild Flower, No.W-10, 8 1/2 In.	25.00
Hull, Cornucopia, Woodland, Green To Pink, 11 In.	15.00
Hull, Creamer, Magnolia	9.50
Hull, Creamer, Magnolia, No.24, 3 3/4 In.	9.50
Hull, Ewer, Tulip, No.109-33, 12 In.	50.00
Hull, Lavabo, Blue & Pink Butterflies, Wall Hanger	20.00
Hull, Pitcher, Magnolia, 5 In.	12.00
Hull, Pitcher, Matte Ivory, 13 5/8 In.	29.00
Hull, Pitcher, Pink Glazed, Yellow Flowers, Green Leaves, 6 X 6 In.	11.50
Hull, Planter, Hanging, 5 3/4 In.	18.00
Hull, Planter, Pink & Green Oval, Bird In Flight On Rim, 7 X 8 In.	14.00
Hull, Planter, 2 Swans, White, 8 X 10 In.	18.00
Hull, Platter, Double Duck, Green, 9 1/2 In.	16.00
Hull, Pot & Lid, Miniature, Parchment & Pine	29.00
Hull, Tea Set, Bow Knot, 3 Piece	20.00
Hull, Vase, Bow Knot, Pink To Green, Bulbous, 5 In.	18.00
Hull, Vase, Bow Knot, Yellow Flower, No.6-13, 10 1/2 In.	20.00
Hull, Vase, Bud, Double, Woodland, No.W-15, 8 1/2 In.	20.00
Hull, Vase, Cornucopia, No.B-5, 7 1/2 In.	18.00
Hull, Vase, Cornucopia, Parchment & Pine, No.S6R, 11 3/4 In.	30.00
Hull, Vase, Ebb Tide, Shrimp Color, 2 Fish & Large Shell, 9 X 10 In.	24.00
Hull, Vase, Magnolia, No.2, 8 1/2 In.	20.00

Hull, Vase, Narcissus, No.406, 8 1/2 In. 20.00
Hull, Vase, Orchid, No.301, 8 In. 20.00
Hull, Vase, Parchment & Pine, Footed, No.S-4, 10 1/2 In. 27.00
Hull, Vase, Pinecone, No.65, 6 1/2 In. 18.00
Hull, Vase, Poppy, No.607, 4 3/4 In. 15.00
Hull, Vase, Serenade, Yellow, 9 In. 14.00
Hull, Vase, Wild Flower, 10 X 8 1/2 In. 22.00
Hull, Vase, Woodland, No.W-16, 8 1/2 In. 20.00
Hull, Wall Pocket, Ebb Tide 15.00

> Hummel figurines, based on the drawings of Berta Hummel, are made by the
> W.Goebel Porzellanfabrik of Oeslau, Germany. They were first made in
> 1934. The mark has changed slightly through the years. The "crown" mark
> dates 1935 to 1949; "U. S. Zone, Germany" dates 1946 to 1948; "West
> Germany" dates after 1949; "incised bee" dates 1950 to 1955; "full bee" dates
> 1950 to 1959; "stylized bee" dates 1960 to 1972; "three line mark" dates
> after 1968.

Hummel, Ashtray, Singing Lesson, No.34 .... 120.00
Hummel, Bookend, Apple Boy & Girl, No.252/A & B, Stylized Bee, 4 1/2 In., Pr. 100.00
Hummel, Candleholder, Angel Duet, No.193, Full Bee, 5 In. 91.75
Hummel, Candleholder, Angel Joyous News, 111/39/1, Bee & Germany, 2 3/4 In. 55.00
Hummel, Figurine, Accordion Boy, No.185, Full Bee, Black, Germany, 5 1/4 In. 120.00
Hummel, Figurine, Accordion Boy, No.185, Stylized Bee, 5 1/4 In. 73.00
Hummel, Figurine, Adoration, No.23, Stylized Bee, Western Germany, 9 In. 250.00
Hummel, Figurine, Adoration, No.28/11, Full Bee, Black, Germany, 7 1/2 In. 295.00
Hummel, Figurine, Angel Cloud, No.206, Font, Full Bee, 4 3/4 In. .... 350.00 To 475.00
Hummel, Figurine, Angel Serenade, No.83, Crown Mark, 5 In. 600.00
Hummel, Figurine, Angel Serenade, No.83, Full Bee, Black, Germany, 5 In. 450.00
Hummel, Figurine, Apple Tree Boy, No.142/1, Crown Mark, Germany, 6 1/2 In. 325.00
Hummel, Figurine, Apple Tree Boy, No.142, Full Bee, Black, Germany 225.00
Hummel, Figurine, Apple Tree Boy, No.142, Stylized Bee, 6 In. 150.00
Hummel, Figurine, Apple Tree Boy, 142/3/0, Full Bee & Germany, 4 In. 95.00
Hummel, Figurine, Apple Tree Girl, Crown Mark, U.S.Zone, Germany, 6 In. 325.00
Hummel, Figurine, Apple Tree Girl, No.141/1, Full Bee, 6 1/2 In. 175.00
Hummel, Figurine, Apple Tree Girl, No.141/3/0, Full Bee, 4 1/2 In. 140.00
Hummel, Figurine, Apple Tree Girl, No.141, Stylized Bee, 6 In. 69.50
Hummel, Figurine, Auf Wiedersehen, No.153, Full Bee, Incised Crown, 7 In. 450.00
Hummel, Figurine, Auf Wiedersehen, No.153, Stylized Bee, 7 In. 124.50
Hummel, Figurine, Auf Wiedersehen, Stylized Bee, 5 1/4 In. 110.00
Hummel, Figurine, Baker, Stylized Bee, No.128, 5 In. 80.00
Hummel, Figurine, Band Leader, No.129, Full Bee, Split Base, 5 1/4 In. 120.00
Hummel, Figurine, Band Leader, No.129, Stylized Bee, 5 1/4 In. 82.00
Hummel, Figurine, Barnyard Hero, No.195, Stylized Bee, Western Germany, 4 In. 65.00
Hummel, Figurine, Battle Prayer, No.20, Full Bee, 4 1/4 In. .... 150.00 To 150.00
Hummel, Figurine, Be Patient, No.197, 3 Line Mark, 4 1/4 In. 107.50
Hummel, Figurine, Begging His Share, Hollow Cake. West Germany 350.00
Hummel, Figurine, Begging His Share, No.9, Stylized Bee, No Hole, 5 1/2 in. 75.00
Hummel, Figurine, Bird Duet, No.169, Full Bee, Split Base, 5 In. 110.00
Hummel, Figurine, Bird Duet, No.169, Stylized Bee, Black, Western Germany 65.00
Hummel, Figurine, Birthday Serenade, No.218, 3 Line Mark, 4 1/4 In. 68.00
Hummel, Figurine, Book Worm, No.8, Full Bee, Black, Germany, 4 In. 175.00
Hummel, Figurine, Book Worm, No.8, Stylized Bee, 4 In. 82.00
Hummel, Figurine, Boots, No.143/0, Crown, 5 1/4 In. 190.00
Hummel, Figurine, Boots, No.143/1, Stylized Bee, Western Germany, 6 3/4 In. 250.00
Hummel, Figurine, Boots, No.143, Crown Mark, 6 3/4 In. 600.00
Hummel, Figurine, Boots, No.143, Full Bee, Black, Germany, 5 1/4 In. 135.00
Hummel, Figurine, Boy With Toothache, No.217, Full Bee, Germany, 5 1/2 In. 1600.00
Hummel, Figurine, Brother, No.95, Stylized Bee, 5 1/2 In. 81.75
Hummel, Figurine, Builder, No.305, Full Bee, 5 1/2 In. 85.00
Hummel, Figurine, Candlelight, No.192, Stylized Bee, 6 3/4 In. 117.50
Hummel, Figurine, Celestial Musician, No.188, Full Bee, 7 In. 124.00
Hummel, Figurine, Chick Girl, No.57, Crown Mark, 3 1/2 In. 250.00
Hummel, Figurine, Chick Girl, No.57, Full Bee, 3 1/2 In. 40.00
Hummel, Figurine, Chimney Sweep, No.12/1, Full Bee, 5 1/2 In. 105.00
Hummel, Figurine, Chimney Sweep, No.12/1, Stylized Bee, 5 1/2 In. 68.00

ummel, Figurine, Chimney Sweep, No.12/2/0, Full Bee, Hollow Base, 4 In. 90.00
ummel, Figurine, Chimney Sweep, No.12, Full Bee, Germany 6 1/4 In. 175.00
ummel, Figurine, Congratulations, No.17/0, Stylized Bee, No Socks, 6 In. 175.00
ummel, Figurine, Congratulations, No.17, No Socks, Full Bee, Germany, 6 In. 250.00
ummel, Figurine, Congratulations, No.17, 3 Line Mark, 5 3/4 In. 55.00
ummel, Figurine, Coquettes, No.179, Full Bee, 5 1/4 In. 165.00
ummel, Figurine, Coquettes, No.179, Stylized Bee, 5 1/4 In. 105.00
ummel, Figurine, Culprits, No.56/a, Full Bee, Hollow Base, 6 1/4 In. 150.00
ummel, Figurine, Doctor, No.127, Full Bee, 4 3/4 In. .... 120.00 To 160.00
ummel, Figurine, Doctor, No.127, Stylized Bee, Black, W.Germany, 4 3/4 In. 75.00
ummel, Figurine, Doll Mother, No.67, Full Bee, 4 3/4 In. .... 135.00 To 192.00
ummel, Figurine, Eventide, No.99, Stylized Bee, 4 3/4 In. 140.00
ummel, Figurine, Farewell, No.65, Full Bee, 5 In. .... 225.00 To 350.00
ummel, Figurine, Farm Boy, No.66, Full Bee, Black, Germany, 5 1/4 In. 175.00
ummel, Figurine, Farm Boy, No.66, Stylized Bee, 5 1/4 In. 79.00
ummel, Figurine, Favorite Pet, No.361, Stylized Bee, 4 1/4 In. 85.00
ummel, Figurine, Feathered Friends, No.344, Full Bee, 4 3/4 In. 75.00
ummel, Figurine, Feeding Time, No.199, Full Bee, Germany, 5 3/4 In. 200.00
ummel, Figurine, Festival Harmony, No.172, Stylized Bee, 10 3/4 In. 325.00
ummel, Figurine, Festival Of Harmony, Flute, No.173, Stylized Bee, Germany 300.00
ummel, Figurine, Flower Madonna, No.10, Color, Stylized Bee, 11 1/2 In. 200.00
ummel, Figurine, Flower Madonna, White, No.10, Full Bee, Germany, 8 1/4 In. 175.00
ummel, Figurine, For Father, No.87, Full Bee & Germany Mark, 5 1/2 In. 135.00
ummel, Figurine, For Father, No.87, Incised Bee, Black, W.Germany, 5 1/2 In. 110.00
ummel, Figurine, For Father, No.87, Stylized Bee, West Germany, 5 1/2 In. 75.00
ummel, Figurine, Friends, No.136/v, Full Bee, Black, Germany, 10 3/4 In. 800.00
ummel, Figurine, Girl With Nosegay, No.115, Full Bee, 3 3/4 In. 110.00
ummel, Figurine, Globe Trotter, No.79, Full Bee, Black, Germany, 5 In. 250.00
ummel, Figurine, Going To Grandma's, No.52, Full Bee, Germany, 4 3/4 In. 280.00
ummel, Figurine, Going To Grandma's, No.52, Stylized Bee, 4 3/4 In. 111.00
ummel, Figurine, Going To Grandma's, No.52, Stylized Bee, 6 In. 395.00
ummel, Figurine, Good Friends, No.182, Full Bee, 4 In. .... 125.00 To 200.00
ummel, Figurine, Good Friends, No.182, Hollow Mold, Full Bee, 4 In. ....
ummel, Figurine, Good Shepherd, No.42, Full Bee, 6 1/4 In. .... 175.00 To 200.00
ummel, Figurine, Goose Girl, No.47, Crown Mark, 7 1/2 In. 400.00
ummel, Figurine, Goose Girl, No.47, Full Bee, Black, Germany, 7 1/2 In. 150.00
ummel, Figurine, Goose Girl, No.47, Stylized Bee, 7 1/2 In. 327.00
ummel, Figurine, Happiness, No.86, Crown Mark, 4 3/4 In. 180.00
ummel, Figurine, Happy New Year, No.163, Stylized Bee, W.Germany, 7 1/4 In. 1350.00
ummel, Figurine, Happy Pastime, No.69, Full Bee, Black, Germany, 3 1/4 In. 260.00
ummel, Figurine, Happy Traveller, No.109, Full Bee, Black, Germany, 5 In. 100.00
ummel, Figurine, Happy Traveller, No.109, Stylized Bee, Germany, 5 1/4 In. 59.00
ummel, Figurine, Happy Traveller, No.109, Stylized Bee, 8 In. 74.50
ummel, Figurine, Hear Yel, No.15, Full Bee, Black, Germany, 5 3/4 In. 250.00
ummel, Figurine, Heavenly Angel, No.21, Stylized Bee, 8 3/4 In. .... 145.00 To 545.50
ummel, Figurine, Heavenly Lullaby, No.262, 3 Line Mark, 3 1/2 X 5 In. 100.00
ummel, Figurine, Heavenly Protection, No.88, Crown Mark, 9 1/2 In. 800.00
ummel, Figurine, Heavenly Protection, Stylized Bee, 9 1/4 In. 325.00
ummel, Figurine, Hello, No.124, Green Pants, Pink Vest, Full Bee, 6 1/2 In. 250.00
ummel, Figurine, Hello, Stylized Bee, Green Pants, 6 In. 165.00
ummel, Figurine, Holy Child, No.70, Stylized Bee, 6 3/4 In. 83.00
ummel, Figurine, Home From Market, No.198, Full Bee, Germany, 6 In. 225.00
ummel, Figurine, Home From Market, No.198, 3 Line Mark, 4 3/4 In. 65.00
ummel, Figurine, Infant Of Krumbad, No.78, Stylized Bee, 10 In. 130.00
ummel, Figurine, Infant Of Krumbad, No.78, 3 Line Mark, 7 3/4 In. 75.00
ummel, Figurine, Joyful, No.53, Full Bee, Black, Germany, 4 1/2 In. 200.00
ummel, Figurine, Just Resting, No.112/3/0, Stylized Bee, 3 3/4 In. 75.00
ummel, Figurine, Just Resting, No.112, Full Bee, Basket, 5 In. .... 165.00 To 200.00
ummel, Figurine, Just Resting, No.112, 3 Line Mark, 3 3/4 In. 75.00
ummel, Figurine, Kiss Me, No.311, Full Bee, 6 In. 85.00
ummel, Figurine, Kiss Me, No.311, 3 Line Mark, 6 In. 98.25
ummel, Figurine, Knitting Lesson, No.256, 3 Line Mark, 7 1/2 In. 175.00
ummel, Figurine, Latest News, No.184, Crown Mark, 5 1/4 In. 225.00
ummel, Figurine, Latest News, No.184, Full Bee, Black, Germany, 5 1/4 In. 210.00
ummel, Figurine, Let's Sing, No.110, Full Bee, Black Germany, 3 7/8 In. 180.00
ummel, Figurine, Let's Sing, No.110, 3 Line Mark, 3 1/4 In. 90.00

Hummel, Figurine, Little Cellist, No.89, Stylized Bee, 8 In. 250.0
Hummel, Figurine, Little Drummer, No.240, 3 Line Mark, 4 1/4 In. 58.0
Hummel, Figurine, Little Fiddler, No.4, Crown Mark, 4 3/4 In. 210.0
Hummel, Figurine, Little Fiddler, No.4, Full Bee, Black, Germany, 4 3/4 In. 130.0
Hummel, Figurine, Little Fiddler, No.4, Stylized Bee, 4 3/4 In. 90.2
Hummel, Figurine, Little Gabriel, No.32, Stylized Bee, 5 In. 70.0
Hummel, Figurine, Little Gardener, No.74, Full Bee, Black, Germany, 4 1/4 In. 125.0
Hummel, Figurine, Little Goat Herder, No.200, Full Bee Mark, 5 1/2 In. 295.0
Hummel, Figurine, Little Helper, No.73, Full Bee, Hollow Base, 4 1/4 In. 80.0
Hummel, Figurine, Little Helper, No.73, Stylized Bee, 4 1/4 In. 70.0
Hummel, Figurine, Little Hiker, No.16, Stylized Bee, 5 1/2 In. .... 60.00 To 92.5
Hummel, Figurine, Little Pharmacist, No.322, Stylized Bee, 6 In. 110.0
Hummel, Figurine, Little Pharmacist, No.322, 3 Line Mark, 6 In. 48.0
Hummel, Figurine, Little Shopper, No.96, Stylized Bee, 4 3/4 In. 53.0
Hummel, Figurine, Little Sweeper, No.171, Full Bee, 4 1/2 In. 68.0
Hummel, Figurine, Little Thrifty, No.118, Full Bee, 5 1/2 In. 280.0
Hummel, Figurine, Little Tooter, , 214H, 3 Line Mark, 3 3/4 In. 45.0
Hummel, Figurine, Little Tooter, No.214/h, Full Bee, 3 3/4 In. .... 90.00 To 100.0
Hummel, Figurine, Lost Sheep, No.68, Full Bee, Germany, Donut Base, 6 1/2 In. .... 140.00 To 175.0
Hummel, Figurine, Madonna Praying, No.46, Full Bee, 10 1/4 In. 90.0
Hummel, Figurine, Mail Coach, No.226, 3 Line Mark, 4 1/4 X 6 1/4 In. 350.0
Hummel, Figurine, Mail Pouch, No.226, Full Bee, Black, Germany, 6 1/4 In. 650.0
Hummel, Figurine, Max & Moritz, No.123, Full Bee, Black, Germany, 5 1/4 In. 170.0
Hummel, Figurine, Meditation, No.13, Full Bee, Black, Germany, 6 In. 350.0
Hummel, Figurine, Meditation, No.13, Stylized Bee, 5 1/4 In. 75.0
Hummel, Figurine, Meditation, No.13, 3 Line Mark, 4 1/4 In. 48.0
Hummel, Figurine, Merry Wanderer, No.11, Full Bee, Black, Germany, 5 1/2 In. 125.0
Hummel, Figurine, Mother's Darling, No.175, Full Bee, Germany, 5 1/2 In. 265.0
Hummel, Figurine, Mother's Helper, No.133, Full Bee, 5 In. 130.0
Hummel, Figurine, Not For You, No.317, 3 Line Mark, 6 In. 98.2
Hummel, Figurine, O Hear Ye, No.15, Stylized Bee, 7 1/2 In. 100.0
Hummel, Figurine, Out Of Danger, No.56/b, Eyes Open, Full Bee, 6 3/4 In. 245.0
Hummel, Figurine, Out Of Danger, No.56/b, Stylized Bee, Girl, 7 In. 110.0
Hummel, Figurine, Photographer, No.178, Full Bee, Black, Germany, 4 3/4 In. 135.0
Hummel, Figurine, Playmates, No.58/0, Full Bee, Black, Germany, 4 In. 65.0
Hummel, Figurine, Playmates, No.58, Double Crown Mark, 4 In. 450.0
Hummel, Figurine, Playmates, No.58, Stylized Bee, 4 1/2 In. 134.0
Hummel, Figurine, Postman, No.119, Full Bee & Germany Mark, 5 1/4 In. 135.0
Hummel, Figurine, Puppy Love, No.1, Full Bee, Black, Germany, 5 In. 150.0
Hummel, Figurine, Puppy Love, No.1, Stylized Bee, 5 In. 76.0
Hummel, Figurine, Retreat To Safety, No.201, Full Bee, 4 In. 138.0
Hummel, Figurine, Retreat To Safety, No.201, Full Bee, 5 1/2 In. 213.0
Hummel, Figurine, Ring Around The Rosie, No.348, 3 Line Mark, 6 3/4 In. 1400.0
Hummel, Figurine, School Boy, No.82, Full Bee, 7 1/2 In. 135.0
Hummel, Figurine, School Boy, No.82, Stylized Bee, Black, Germany, 5 In. 58.0
Hummel, Figurine, School Girl, No.81, Full Bee, Gray Socks, 5 1/4 In. 110.0
Hummel, Figurine, School Girls, No.177, Stylized Bee, 7 1/2 In. 800.0
Hummel, Figurine, Sensitive Hunter, Incised Full Bee, 4 3/4 In. 90.0
Hummel, Figurine, Sensitive Hunter, No.6, Incised Full Bee, 4 3/4 In. 90.0
Hummel, Figurine, Serenade, No.85, Full Bee, Black, Germany, 4 3/4 In. 100.0
Hummel, Figurine, Serenade, No.85, Stylized Bee, 4 3/4 In. 250.0
Hummel, Figurine, She Loves Me, No.174, Full Bee, Open Eyes, 4 1/4 In. 210.0
Hummel, Figurine, She Loves Me, No.174, Stylized Bee, 4 1/4 In. .... 85.00 To 135.0
Hummel, Figurine, Shepherd Boy, No.64, Full Bee, Black, Germany, 5 1/2 In. 175.0
Hummel, Figurine, Shepherd Boy, No.64, Stylized Bee, 5 1/2 In. 106.7
Hummel, Figurine, Signs Of Spring, No.203, Crown, 5 In. 220.0
Hummel, Figurine, Signs Of Spring, No.203, Full Bee, 2 Shoes, 5 In. 500.0
Hummel, Figurine, Signs Of Spring, No.203, 3 Line Mark, 4 In. 60.0
Hummel, Figurine, Singing Lesson, No.63, Full Bee, 2 3/4 In. 110.0
Hummel, Figurine, Singing Lessons, No.63, Crown Mark, 2 3/4 In. 250.0
Hummel, Figurine, Sister, No.98, Stylized Bee, 5 3/4 In. 81.7
Hummel, Figurine, Skier, No.59, Full Bee, Black, Germany, Wood Poles 200.0
Hummel, Figurine, Smart Little Sister, No.346, 4 3/4 In. 95.0
Hummel, Figurine, Soloist, No.135, Full Bee, Black, Germany, 4 3/4 In. 100.0
Hummel, Figurine, Soloist, No.135, Stylized Bee, West Germany, 4 3/4 In. 55.0
Hummel, Figurine, Spring Cheer, No.72, Stylized Bee, 5 In. .... 53.00 To 95.0

Hummel, Figurine, Star Gazer, No.132, Incised Full Bee, 4 3/4 In. 130.00
Hummel, Figurine, Star Gazer, No.132, Stylized Bee, Black, Germany, 4 3/4 In. 85.00
Hummel, Figurine, Stormy Weather, No.71, Double Crown Mark, 6 1/4 In. 750.00
Hummel, Figurine, Stormy Weather, No.71, Full Bee, 6 1/4 In. 325.00
Hummel, Figurine, Stormy Weather, No.71, Stylized Bee, 6 1/4 In. .... 275.00 To 350.00
Hummel, Figurine, Street Singer, No.131, Full Bee, Black, Germany, 5 In. 100.00
Hummel, Figurine, Street Singer, No.131, Stylized Bee, 5 In. 66.00
Hummel, Figurine, Strolling Along, No.5, Full Bee, Eyes To Side, 4 3/4 In. 160.00
Hummel, Figurine, Strolling Along, No.5, Stylized Bee, Germany, 4 3/4 In. 65.00
Hummel, Figurine, Surprise, No.94, Crown, 5 1/2 In. 260.00
Hummel, Figurine, Surprise, No.94, Full Bee, Black, 4 1/4 In. 90.00
Hummel, Figurine, Sweet Music, No.186, Full Bee, 5 1/4 In. .... 85.00 To 115.00
Hummel, Figurine, Telling Her Secret, No.196, Full Bee, 6 3/4 In .... 475.00 To 500.00
Hummel, Figurine, To Market, No.49, Full Bee, Germany, 5 1/2 In. .... 110.00 To 240.00
Hummel, Figurine, To Market, No.49, Stylized Bee, 5 1/2 In. .... 105.00 To 148.00
Hummel, Figurine, Trumpet Boy, No.97, Crown Mark, 4 3/4 In. 165.00
Hummel, Figurine, Trumpet Boy, No.97, Stylized Bee, 4 3/4 In. 69.75
Hummel, Figurine, Umbrella Boy, No.152/a, Stylized Bee, 8 In. 700.00
Hummel, Figurine, Umbrella Girl, No.152/b, Full Bee, 8 In. 425.00
Hummel, Figurine, Village Boy, No.51/0, Full Bee, 6 In. .... 150.00 To 175.00
Hummel, Figurine, Village Boy, No.51, Stylized Bee, 6 In. 100.00
Hummel, Figurine, Volunteers, No.50, Stylized Bee, 5 1/2 In. 105.00
Hummel, Figurine, Waiter, No.154, Full Bee Mark, Germany, 6 In. 125.00
Hummel, Figurine, Wayside Devotion, No.28, Full Bee, Germany, 8 1/2 In. 310.00
Hummel, Figurine, Wayside Devotion, No.28, Stylized Bee, 8 1/2 In. 320.00
Hummel, Figurine, Wayside Harmony, No.111, Full Bee, Germany, 3 3/4 In. 102.00
Hummel, Figurine, Wayside Harmony, No.111, 3 Line Mark, 3 3/4 In. 91.75
Hummel, Figurine, We Congratulate, No.220, Stylized Bee, 4 In. 92.50
Hummel, Figurine, We Congratulate, No.220, Three Line, 4 In. 57.00
Hummel, Figurine, Weary Wanderer, No.204, Stylized Bee, Black, Germany, 6 In. 85.00
Hummel, Figurine, Weary Wanderer, No.204, Three Line, 6 In. 59.00
Hummel, Figurine, Worship, No.84/0, Full Bee, 5 In. 165.00
Hummel, Figurine, Worship, No.84/0, Stylized Bee, 5 In. 75.00
Hummel, Figurine, Worship, No.84, Crown Mark, 5 In. 275.00
Hummel, Lamp, Apple Tree Girl, No.229, Crown Mark 200.00
Hummel, Plate, Annual, Globetrotter, 1973, No.266, 7 1/2 In. 280.00
Hummel, Plate, Annual, Hear Ye, Hear Ye, 1972, No.265, 3 Line Mark, 7 1/2 In. 165.00
Hummel, Plate, Annual, Heavenly Angel, 1971, No.264, 7 1/2 In. 1200.00
Hummel, Vase, Seagull Flying, Full Bee In V, 3 In. 28.00
Hummel, Vase, Wall, C.1958, No.360B, Pair 800.00

Hutschenreuther Porcelain Company of Selb, Germany, was established in 1814 and is still working.

Hutschenreuther, Cup & Saucer, Ivory, White & Gold 7.00
Hutschenreuther, Cup & Saucer, The Ferndale 12.50
Hutschenreuther, Dresser Set, Powder Box, Hair Receiver, Pin Tray, Green 65.00
Hutschenreuther, Dish, Poppy, Gold Borders, Selb Bavarian, 5 3/4 In., Pair 80.00
Icebox, see Kitchen, Icebox
Hutschenreuther, Figurine, Beagle, Standing, 4 X 5 1/2 In. 65.00
Hutschenreuther, Figurine, Bremen Musicians, Porcelain, 7 1/2 In. 140.00
Hutschenreuther, Figurine, Bull Dog, Sitting, Tan & Brown, 4 In. 50.00
Hutschenreuther, Figurine, Butterfly, Wings Over Foliage, 2 X 2 1/2 In. 55.00
Hutschenreuther, Figurine, Cat, Persian, Sitting, Artist Signed, 4 1/2 In. 100.00
Hutschenreuther, Figurine, Cat, Sitting, 7 X 7 In., Pair 260.00
Hutschenreuther, Figurine, Chihuahua, Standing, 4 X 4 In. 63.00
Hutschenreuther, Figurine, Colt, Rearing On Hind Legs, 6 In. 650.00
Hutschenreuther, Figurine, Couple Dancing, Art Deco, Pastel, 11 In. 175.00
Hutschenreuther, Figurine, Dachshund, Standing, Long Hair, 5 X 9 1/2 In. 125.00
Hutschenreuther, Figurine, Dachshund, Standing, Smooth Hair, 5 X 9 In. 100.00
Hutschenreuther, Figurine, Dancing Couple, Marked U.S. Zone, 11 In. 175.00
Hutschenreuther, Figurine, Dolphin, Jumping From Rolling Waves, Signed, 5 In. 65.00
Hutschenreuther, Figurine, Donkey, Lying, Gray, 3 1/4 X 4 In. 50.00
Hutschenreuther, Figurine, Donkey, Standing, Gray, 5 X 6 1/2 In. 60.00
Hutschenreuther, Figurine, Fawn, Lying, Spotted, 4 X 4 3/4 In. 90.00
Hutschenreuther, Figurine, Figure Skater, All White Porcelain 65.00
Hutschenreuther, Figurine, Gazelle, Signed Granget 85.00

Hutschenreuther, Figurine, Hummingbird Over Nest With Egg, 3 X 2 1/2 In.	78.00
Hutschenreuther, Figurine, Hummingbird, High Glaze Finish, 4 1/2 In.	68.00
Hutschenreuther, Figurine, Hummingbird, Matt Finish, 2 3/4 In.	65.00
Hutschenreuther, Figurine, Jumping Russian Wolfhounds, Signed	400.00
Hutschenreuther, Figurine, Lizard On Rock, 2 X 3 1/2 In.	52.00
Hutschenreuther, Figurine, Mermaid Holding Fish, Signed, 6 In.	75.00
Hutschenreuther, Figurine, Monkey Sitting In A Flowering Tree, 5 In.	100.00
Hutschenreuther, Figurine, Musicians Of Bremen, 7 5/8 In.	75.00
Hutschenreuther, Figurine, Owl On Perch, 6 1/2 In.	78.00
Hutschenreuther, Figurine, Parakeet Roosting On Stump, 5 In.	70.00
Hutschenreuther, Figurine, Persian Cat, Sitting, Bisque, Signed, 5 In.	125.00
Hutschenreuther, Figurine, Rabbit, Sitting, Brown, 5 1/2 X 4 1/2 In.	50.00
Hutschenreuther, Figurine, Rearing White Stallion, 4 1/4 X 4 In.	39.00
Hutschenreuther, Figurine, Salamander, On Rock Ledge, Signed, 2 X 4 In.	40.00
Hutschenreuther, Figurine, Scottie	45.00
Hutschenreuther, Figurine, Seahorse, Signed, 5 1/4 In.	85.00
Hutschenreuther, Figurine, Siamese Cat, Sitting, Signed Granget, 6 1/2 In.	70.00
Hutschenreuther, Figurine, Spotted Fawn, Standing, 5 1/2 X 5 In.	137.00
Hutschenreuther, Figurine, Standing Brown Pekinese, 3 1/2 X 4 1/2 In.	60.00
Hutschenreuther, Figurine, Standing Fawn Colored Foal, 5 1/2 X 4 3/4 In.	54.00
Hutschenreuther, Figurine, Swimming Fish, Signed Granget, 3 1/2 X 4 In.	65.00
Hutschenreuther, Figurine, Tammy Cat, Artist Signed, 7 In.	95.00
Hutschenreuther, Figurine, Tammy Cat, Signed, 3 1/2 X 6 In.	90.00
Hutschenreuther, Figurine, Tan Colt Lying, Head Over Back, 3 X 5 1/2 In.	73.00
Hutschenreuther, Figurine, Tommy Cat, Sitting, Tiger Eye, 6 1/4 X 4 1/4 In.	105.00
Hutschenreuther, Figurine, Two Running Deer, Marked	80.00
Hutschenreuther, Figurine, Two Standing Foxes, 7 X 11 In.	215.00
Hutschenreuther, Figurine, White Bear Sitting, Paws Extended, Signed, 7 In.	85.00
Hutschenreuther, Figurine, Yellow Warbler, Holding Worm In Mouth, 5 3/4 In.	150.00
Hutschenreuther, Group, Two Cherubs Kissing, 3 X 5 X 4 In.	45.00
Hutschenreuther, Plate, Gold Border, Scene, Goddess With Child, 10 In.	45.00
Hutschenreuther, Plate, Ivory & Pink Border, 8 In.	12.50
Hutschenreuther, Platter, The Ferndale, 12 In.	20.00
Hutschenreuther, Platter, The Ferndale, 15 In.	25.00
Hutschenreuther, Tureen, Ivory White & Gold	39.00
Hutschenreuther, Vase, Art Deco, Hand-Painted, 11 In.	65.00
Icon, Bronze, 5 X 4 In.	167.00
Icon, Tin, Mary With Crown Of Roses & Dove, 4 1/4 X 6 1/2 In.	72.50

*Imari patterns are named for the Japanese ware decorated with orange and
blue stylized flowers. The design on the Japanese ware became so
characteristic that the name Imari has come to mean any pattern of this type.
It was copied by the European factories of the eighteenth and early
nineteenth centuries.*

Imari, Bowl, Asymmetric Design, 19th Century, Porcelain, 9 3/4 In.	85.00
Imari, Bowl, Cobalt, Panels, Scalloped Rim, 2 X 4 In.Diameter	10.00
Imari, Bowl, Enameled Inside & Out, Oriental Figures, 10 In.	200.00
Imari, Bowl, Fish, Figure Panels, Butterflies, Underglaze Blue, 1800, 23 In.	1600.00
Imari, Bowl, Flower Panels, Scalloped Rim, Gold Trim, 2 1/4 X 5 In.Diameter	24.00
Imari, Bowl, Fluted, Floral Decoration, 10 X 5 In.	75.00
Imari, Bowl, Medallions Of Dragons G Birds, Cobalt, Red, Gold, 6 In.	60.00
Imari, Bowl, Panel Scenes Inside & Out, Blue & White, 3 1/2 X 8 In.Diameter	70.00
Imari, Bowl, Panel Scenes Of Winged Creatures, Ribbed, 3 X 7 1/4 In.Diam.	60.00
Imari, Bowl, Paneled, Flying Cranes, Flowers On Back Flange, 3 X 8 In.	90.00
Imari, Bowl, Red & Blue Panels, Scalloped Top, 10 In.	55.00
Imari, Bowl, Red, Blue, Gilt Scrolls, 1800s, Pseudo-Reign Mark, 10 In., Pair	400.00
Imari, Bowl, Red, Gold, Blue Design Outer Rim, 6 In.	45.00
Imari, Bowl, Ribbed Sides, Blue Design, 4 X 8 1/2 In.	50.00
Imari, Bowl, Scalloped Edge, C.1800, 8 3/4 In.	142.00
Imari, Bowl, Scalloped Edge, 5 In.	28.00
Imari, Bowl, Scalloped, Over-All Coloring, 8 1/2 In.	65.00
Imari, Bowl, Victorian, Scalloped Edge, Japanese, 8 1/4 In.	37.00
Imari, Bowl, 3 Panels, Heron In Flight, Scalloped Rim, Edo Period, 11 3/8 In.	160.00
Imari, Charger, Blue & Rust, 11 In.	125.00
Imari, Charger, Blue & White, C.1800, 18 In.	395.00
Imari, Charger, Panels, Serpents, Butterfly, Birds, Gold, C.1830, 23 3/4 In.	550.00

Imari, **Charger**, Rust, Green, White Ground, 1800s, 14 1/2 In. 240.00
Imari, **Charger**, Teak Stand, Signed, 16 Pounds, 24 In.Diameter 5200.00
Imari, **Dish**, Blue & White, Birds, Fruit, Flowers, Arita, 1600s, 15 1/4 In. 875.00
Imari, **Dish**, Blue & White, Spotted Carp, Water Weeds, Arita, 1800s, 18 1/2 In. 325.00
Imari, **Dish**, Characteristic Palette, Cranes, Figures, 1870s, 18 In., Pair 1000.00
Imari, **Dish**, Medallion, Crane Vignettes, Seal Mark, 1800s, 18 In., Pair 1000.00
Imari, **Jar**, Covered, Lion Dog Finial, C.1850, 8 1/2 In. 114.00
Imari, **Jar**, Temple, Flying Cranes, Foo Dog Finial, Lid, Blue, Rust, White, Gold 125.00
Imari, **Jardiniere**, Flowering Plum Trees, Lobed Body, C.1800, 13 In. 1200.00
Imari, **Plate**, Crane, C.1850, 14 1/2 In. 222.00
Imari, **Plate**, Fans, Gold, 8 In. 30.00
Imari, **Plate**, Floral, Red, Blue, 10 In. 55.00
Imari, **Plate**, Flower Basket Center, Birds In Panels, 8 1/4 In. 38.00
Imari, **Plate**, Fluted Edge, Herringbone, Blue & Green Enamel, 8 1/2 In. 45.00
Imari, **Plate**, Iron-Red Border, Blue Center, 8 1/2 In. 30.00
Imari, **Plate**, Palette, Figure On Elephant, Attendants, 1800s, 18 1/2 In. 550.00
Imari, **Plate**, Red & Blue Floral, 10 In. 45.00
Imari, **Plate**, Ruffled Edge, 9 1/2 In. 85.00
Imari, **Plate**, Scalloped & Ribbed, Geometric Design, 8 1/2 In. 35.00
Imari, **Plate**, Under-Water Scene, Red Character Signature, 7 In. 67.50
Imari, **Plate**, 6 Panel, Oriental, 9 1/2 In. 45.00
Imari, **Platter**, Flowers, Ships, Grotesque Animal, 19th Century, 9 X 11 In. 135.00
Imari, **Pot**, Brush 40.00
Imari, **Punch Bowl**, Lakeside Panels, Peony Bands, Rounded, 1800s, 19 1/4 In. 1000.00
Imari, **Teapot**, Reserve Panels Of Phoenix, Peacocks & Prunus, Domed Lid 68.00
Imari, **Vase**, Bird On Reverse Side, Geometric Pattern Each Side, 7 In. 175.00
Imari, **Vase**, 4 Panels, Gold Foo Dogs, Ovoid, Narrow Neck, 10 In. 185.00

IMPE
RIAL   *Imperial Glass Corporation was founded in Bellaire, Ohio, in 1902.*
       Stretch glass and art glass are two of the many kinds of glass made.

Imperial, **Bowl**, Grape, Helios, 11 1/2 In. 100.00
Imperial, **Candlestick**, Blue Iridescent Top & Base, Label, 10 3/4 In., Pair 365.00
Imperial, **Compote**, Footed, Gold & Blue Leaf, Paper Label, 5 1/2 X 4 1/2 In. 275.00
Imperial, **Dish**, Covered, Purple Slag Owl, Glass Eyes, 6 1/2 In. 65.00
Imperial, **Figurine**, Swan, Rubigold, 8 In. 40.00

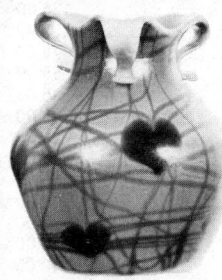

Imperial, Vase, Iridescent Gold Bronze,
O.Eckstead, 6 1/2 In.

Imperial, **Glass**, Shot, Calvert Pure Rye Whiskey 10.00
Imperial, **Pitcher**, Colonial, Signature & Cross, 9 In. 10.00
Imperial, **Pitcher**, Grape, Helios, 9 In. 200.00
Imperial, **Vase**, Free Hand, Blue, White, Marble Swirl, Luster Throat, 9 1/2 In. 135.00
Imperial, **Vase**, Iridescent Gold Bronze, O.Eckstead, 6 1/2 In. .... *Illus* 200.00
Imperial, **Vase**, Jewel, Greek Shape, Signed, 5 In. 125.00
Imperial, **Vase**, Jewel, Iridescent Amethyst, Signed, Cross Mark, 5 1/2 In. 75.00
Imperial, **Vase**, Mother-Of-Pearl, Orange Throat, White, 9 1/2 In. 70.00
Imperial, **Vase**, Orange & Black Mirror Finish, Pedestal, 10 1/2 In.High 110.00
Imperial, **Vase**, Orange Luster, Cobalt Blue Rim & Feet, 11 In. 225.00

    Indian Tree is a china pattern that was popular during the last half of
    the nineteenth century. It was copied from earlier patterns of English
    China that were very similar. The pattern includes the crooked branch of a
    tree and a partial landscape with exotic flowers and leaves. It is colored
    green, blue, pink, and orange.
Indian Tree, **Cup & Saucer**, Bouillon, Coalport 15.00

Indian Tree, Plate, Coalport, 10 In.	30.00
Indian Tree, Plate, Set Of 6, 7 3/4 In.	38.00
Indian Tree, Vase, Doric Shape, Coalport, 12 In.	20.00

Indian art from North America has attracted the collector for many years.
Each tribe has its own distinctive designs and techniques. Baskets, jewelry,
and leatherwork are of greatest collector interest.

Indian, Apache, Burden Basket, Tassels, 3 1/2 X 3 In.	25.00
Indian, Armband, Arapaho, Pair	38.00
Indian, Awl, Eskimo, Ivory, 4 1/2 In.	55.00
Indian, Bag, Corn Husk, Six Pine Trees, 12 X 14 In.	175.00
Indian, Bag, Nez Perce, Beaded, Geometric Design, 10 X 12 In.	125.00
Indian, Bag, Nez Perce, Buckskin, Beaded, Fringe	50.00
Indian, Bag, Pipe, Beaded, Woodland, C.1840, Buckskin, Floral Design, 27 In.	375.00
Indian, Bag, Pipe, Sioux, Beaded Both Sides	400.00
Indian, Bag, Seed, Sewn With Raw Hide, Made From Cow's Udder	75.00
Indian, Bag, Tepee, Sioux, Quilled, Beaded, Buffalo Hide, 21 X 15 In.	375.00
Indian, Basket Tray, Pima, Black Swirl Design, 11 In.Diameter	135.00
Indian, Basket, Algonquin, Potato Stamp Design, 2 Handles, 16 X 16 X 6 In.	110.00
Indian, Basket, Apache, Burden, C.1906, 11 1/2 X 14 In.Diameter	250.00
Indian, Basket, Apache, Winnowing, Fine Weave, C.1906, 5 1/2 X 22 In.Diam.	700.00
Indian, Basket, Birchbark, Lid, Geometric Design, 14 In.	200.00
Indian, Basket, Birchbark, Nesting, Largest, 5 X 5 In., Set Of 5	285.00
Indian, Basket, Coil Plate, 10 In.	30.00
Indian, Basket, Cone Shaped, Birchbark, 10 In.	40.00
Indian, Basket, Corn, 20 In.Diameter	150.00
Indian, Basket, Covered, Geometric, 3 3/4 In.	40.00
Indian, Basket, Covered, Popago, 4 1/2 X 4 1/2 In.	17.50
Indian, Basket, Fretwork Design, 15 In.Diameter	300.00
Indian, Basket, Globular Pine, Needlebirch Bark, 4 1/2 X 2 1/2 In.	10.00
Indian, Basket, Hopi, Coil Weave, Yucca Reim, 1920, 4 X 5 In.	110.00
Indian, Basket, Hopi, 2nd Mesa Coil	185.00
Indian, Basket, Hupa-Karok H., 8 X 4 In.Diameter	175.00
Indian, Basket, Kootenai, Porcupine Quill On Birch Bark, Geometric Design	350.00
Indian, Basket, Micmac, Round, Blue Polychrome, 8 X 12 In.Diameter	45.00
Indian, Basket, Modoc, Twine Weave, Sedge Fiber, Post-1900, 5 X 9 In.	135.00
Indian, Basket, Papago, Feather Weave, Covered, Round, 4 X 6 In.Diameter	28.00
Indian, Basket, Papago, Feather Weave, Round, 4 X 5 1/2 In.Diameter	25.00
Indian, Basket, Papago, Footed, Geometric Designs, 6 X 6 In.Diameter	55.00
Indian, Basket, Papago, Fret Work, Devil's Claw, C.1940, 5 X 11 In.	45.00
Indian, Basket, Pima H., Early Blue Trade Beads On Rim, 5 X 4 In.Diameter	125.00
Indian, Basket, Pima H., 6 X 5 In.Diameter	75.00
Indian, Basket, Pima, Geometric Design, Footed, 8 In.	30.00
Indian, Basket, Polychrome Twine, Cover, Octagon Shape	55.00
Indian, Basket, Tlingit, Openwork, 4 X 5 In.	50.00
Indian, Basket, Waso, Hide Around Top, 7 Human Figures, 6 X 6 In.	425.00
Indian, Basket, Yucca, Geometric Design, Dyed Blue, 15 Coil, 5 1/4 In.Diam.	85.00
Indian, Beaded Bag, Sioux, Sinew, C.1880	110.00
Indian, Belt, Beaded, 36 In.Long	105.00
Indian, Belt, Navajo, Silver Conchos, Leather, Late 1800s	1500.00
Indian, Belt, 9 Sterling Silver Conchos & Silver Buckle, 28 In.	195.00
Indian, Blanket, Horse, Chichimeca, Handwoven, 30 X 60 In.	27.50
Indian, Blanket, Lightning Design, Beige Ground	600.00
Indian, Blanket, Navajo, Red Ground, Diamond Shape Design, 52 X 82 In.	400.00
Indian, Blanket, Saddle, Double, Red, Gray, Geometrics, 43 X 29 In.	100.00
Indian, Blanket, Saddle, Navajo	150.00
Indian, Blanket, Saddle, Navajo, 29 1/2 X 31 1/2 In.	125.00
Indian, Blanket, Saddle, Single, Red Black, Gray Geometrics, 28 X 30 In.	50.00
Indian, Blanket, Saddle, Single, Red, Black, White & Yellow, 29 X 30 In.	50.00
Indian, Blanket, Spirit Lines, Orange, Brown & Beige, 3 1/2 Feet X 6 Feet	1500.00
Indian, Bonnet, Chief, War, Feathers On Full Leather Cap, Beaded, Medallions	250.00
Indian, Boots, Buckskin, Beaded Toe & Top	55.00
Indian, Bow & Arrow, Plains	95.00
Indian, Bow, Plains, Painted, 44 In.	25.00
Indian, Bow, Wooden, With Papers, Maine	55.00
Indian, Bowl, Food, Northwest, Human Head Shape	165.00

Indian, Bowl, Hop, Red Clay, Expanded Rim, 3 1/2 In.	38.00
Indian, Bowl, Hope, Dark Geometric Design, Polished Red Clay, 10 In.	45.00
Indian, Bowl, Mesa, Geometric Design, Polished Red Clay, 8 In.	45.00
Indian, Box, Quill, 2 X 2 In.Diameter	23.00
Indian, Bracelet, Pawnee, Turquoise, 45 Stones, Sterling Silver	150.00
Indian, Breech Clout, Apache, C.1875-90, Deerskin, 26 X 16 In.	450.00
Indian, Cradle Board, Nez Perce, On Buckskin, Beaded, 27 In.	275.00
Indian, Crow, Beaded Bag, Moose Hide, 7 1/2 X 17 In.	50.00
Indian, Dance Wand, Crow, Horn With Carved Wood Handle, C.1890	150.00
Indian, Doll, Buckskin Clothing	10.00
Indian, Doll, Crow, Man & Woman, Beaded On Buckskin, C.1900, Pair	250.00
Indian, Doll, Leather & Cloth, Beaded, 10 3/4 In.	22.50
Indian, Doll, Leather, Hand Made, 9 In.	35.00
Indian, Doll, Maid & Man, Bisque Head, Jointed Shoulders & Hips, 6 In., Pair	200.00
Indian, Doll, Maiden, Original, Bisque, 7 1/2 In.	65.00
Indian, Doll, Original Cloth Body, Bisque, 14 In.	125.00
Indian, Doll, Skookum, Chief, Beads & Feathers, 23 In.	225.00
Indian, Dress, Squaw, Blue & Silver, Size 14, 1950s	15.00
Indian, Drum, Red Painted Design, Both Sides, 13 In.Across	200.00
Indian, Fork & Spoon, Handmade, Silver, Decorated	40.00
Indian, Gauntlets, Sioux, Beaded, Crossed Flags, C.1910	150.00
Indian, Hoe, Sioux, Buffalo Shoulder Bones, 1800s	45.00
Indian, Jar, Apache, Grain, C.1906, 9 X 8 In.Diameter	250.00
Indian, Jar, Apache, Oval, Figures Of People & Animals, C.1906, 9 1/2 In.	300.00
Indian, Leg Bands, Geometric Design, Braided Yarn Ties & Tassels	45.00
Indian, Leggings, Crow, Beaded, Trade Cloth	175.00
Indian, Loom, Bead, Wooden	10.00
Indian, Masher, Grain, Sitting Bird, Stoneware	125.00
Indian, Mat, Bolivian, Hand Woven, Wool, 35 X 34 In.	100.00
Indian, Mat, Bolivian, Hand Woven, Wool, 39 X 35 In.	100.00
Indian, Moccasins, Apache, Raw Hide	75.00
Indian, Moccasins, Cheyenne, C.1900	125.00
Indian, Moccasins, Deer Skin, Blue Beadwork	75.00
Indian, Moccasins, Deer Skin, Red Beads, White Bead Design	75.00
Indian, Moccasins, Leather, Beaded, 4 In., Pair	12.00
Indian, Moccasins, Mohawk, Child's, Beaded, 6 In.	60.00
Indian, Moccasins, Plains Indian, Child's, Fully Beaded	125.00
Indian, Moccasins, Sioux, Beaded, Man's, Sinew Sewn	85.00
Indian, Moccasins, Squaw, Fully Beaded	110.00
Indian, Neck Piece, Beaded, Sinew Sewed, 4 X 29 In.	110.00
Indian, Necklace, Bear Claw, Cobalt & Crystal Beads, Framed	150.00
Indian, Necklace, Medicine, Sioux, Beaded Fetish, C.1880	250.00
Indian, Necklace, Nez Perce, Seed Bud, Tassel, 28 In.	18.00
Indian, Necklace, Zuni, Inlaid Turquoise, Mother-Of-Pearl, Coral, 8 In.	225.00
Indian, Necklace, 7 Wolverine Claws, Red & Blue Trade Beads	85.00
Indian, Necklace, 8 Bear Claws, White Glass & Clay Trade Beads	85.00
Indian, Pillow, Navajo, Eagle On Both Sides, 1920s, 18 In.Square	115.00
Indian, Pin Cushion, Beadwork, C.1900	12.00
Indian, Pin, Zuni, Intarsia & Silver, Apache Crown Dancer	100.00
Indian, Pipe, Catlnite, Cherry Stem, 12 In.	75.00
Indian, Pipe, Catlnite, Chief's Head Carved Bow, Etched Stem, 15 In.	200.00
Indian, Pipe, Peace, Tomahawk, Brass Over Iron	350.00
Indian, Pipe, Tomahawk, Hand Forged, Bowl Integral With Ax, Wooden, 7 1/2 In.	225.00
Indian, Pipe, Tomahawk, Relief Ring Turning, C.1840-60, 8 In.	395.00
Indian, Pitcher, Huichole, Grecian Type, Long Handle, Signed, 12 In.	35.00
Indian, Plate, Reed, Wheat Design, 7 In.Diameter	10.00
Indian, Pot, Acoma, Signed Flute Man, 1 1/2 In.	35.00
Indian, Pot, Lid, Huichole, Black & Brown, Signed, 19 X 9 In.Diameter	65.00
Indian, Pot, San Juan, 1908, 8 X 13 In.Diameter	775.00
Indian, Pot, Seed, Brown-Red Clay, Lucy Year, Signed, 3 In.Diameter	68.00
Indian, Pots, Black, Signed Maria & Julian, 4 In.	500.00
Indian, Pouch, Beaded, Iroquois	35.00
Indian, Pouch, Medicine, Draw String	165.00
Indian, Purse, Sioux, Beaded, Crossed Flags, Dated 1915, 3 X 5 In.	75.00
Indian, Quilt, Appliqued Butterflies, White Ground, Twin Size, Pair	125.00
Indian, Quirt, Cheyenne, Beaded, C.1880, 16 In.	250.00

Indian, Rug, Black & White Stripes & Geometrics, 30 X 60 In.	60.00
Indian, Rug, Ceremonial, Tapestry Weave, Red, Yellow, Red, 72 X 42 In.	350.00
Indian, Rug, Navajo, Geometric Design, 65 X 43 In.	200.00
Indian, Rug, Navajo, Gray, Green & Yellow, Hand Woven, Wool, 56 1/2 X 37 In.	200.00
Indian, Rug, Navajo, Gray, Red & Black, 7 Feet, 2 In. X 4 Feet, 2 In.	700.00
Indian, Rug, Navajo, Multi-Colored, 4 Ft., 3 In. X 2 Ft., 7 In.	114.00
Indian, Rug, Navajo, Rug, 46 X 67 In.	125.00
Indian, Rug, Navajo, Tan, Black & White, Hand Woven, Wool, 62 X 42 In.	300.00
Indian, Rug, Navajo, Vari-Colored, 51 X 31 In.	116.00
Indian, Rug, Navajo, Wool, 1947, 63 X 33 In.	500.00
Indian, Rug, Shimayo, Wool, White Fringe, 4 1/2 X 6 3/4 Feet	95.00
Indian, Rug, Yei Rainbow Gold, Wool, 35 X 62 In.	62.00
Indian, Scraper, Hide, Sioux, Elk Horn, 1890s	85.00
Indian, Shoehorn, Eskimo, Whaler's, Ivory, Dated 1760	50.00
Indian, Spike, Tomahawk, Tapered Spiked Top, C.1780, 12 In.	225.00
Indian, Spoon, Sioux, Horn	25.00
Indian, Tomahawk, Leather Thongs, 9 In.	55.00
Indian, Tool, Bone, 6 1/2 X 1 In.	45.00
Indian, Trade Beads, Glass, Cobalt, 40 In.	100.00
Indian, Tray, Basket, 12 In.Diameter	55.00
Indian, Vase, Corn, Clue, 5 X 6 In.Diameter	600.00
Indian, Vase, Huichole, Black, Signed, 22 1/2 In.	65.00
Indian, Vase, Huichole, Grecian Shape, 2 Handles, Signed, 18 In.	45.00
Indian, Vase, Sioux, Pottery, 10 1/4 X 10 1/2 Diameter	35.00
Indian, Vase, 2 Handled, Matte Black Design, Signed P.S.Clar, 6 In.	85.00
Indian, Vest, Crow, Fully Beaded Front, Partial Back, Floral Design	650.00
Indian, Vest, Santee Sioux, Quilled, Lady's, Buckskin, Cloth Back, C.1880	575.00
Indian, Wall Pocket, Chippewa	25.00
Indian, War Club, Iroquois, Wood, Ball-Headed, 18th Century, 21 In.	250.00
Inkstand, Domed Inkwell, Original Liner, Brass, 10 1/4 X 3 In.	125.00
Inkstand, Glass Snail Inkwells, Revolve, Calendar, Brass Pen Rail, 9 X 6 In.	150.00
Inkstand, Marble, 2 Hinged Wells, Bronze Dog Between, 3 1/4 X 3 1/2 In.	70.00
Inkstand, Pen & Double, Crystalline Blue, Covered, 4 3/4 In.	225.00
Inkstand, Rosewood, Victorian, Wells Of Crystal, 2 Hinged, 11 X 6 1/2 In.	79.00
Inkstand, 5 In.Round Stepped Brass Base, Pewter Lid	40.00
Inkwell, see also Brass, Inkwell;Pewter, Inkwell; and various porcelain categories	
Inkwell, Art Deco, Pyramid Shape, Silver Inlay, Bronze, 5 X 5 X 3 In.	48.00
Inkwell, Art Nouveau, Painted Iron, Geschutz	35.00
Inkwell, Art Nouveau, Pyramid Shape, Bronze	25.00
Inkwell, Attached Underplate, Swirled Bottle & Cap, Brass Hinge, 4 In.	30.00
Inkwell, Blown, 3 Mold, Round, Amber, Stoddard Glass	150.00
Inkwell, Blue Hinged Top, Colored Glass, 2 1/4 In.Square	65.00
Inkwell, Bronze Well, Geometric Silver Inlay On Lid, 5 In.	55.00
Inkwell, Bust Of Lady, Sweeping Hat, Art Nouveau	65.00
Inkwell, Caldron On Log Fire, Black Iron, Marble Base	30.00
Inkwell, Carved Marble, Glass Ink Pot, Lid, 3 1/2 X 3 In.Diameter	17.50
Inkwell, Character, Kettle Shape, French Pottery, C.1850	235.00
Inkwell, Clear Base Design, Sterling Top, 3 1/2 X 2 1/2 In.	65.00
Inkwell, Copper & Sterling, Glass Insert	85.00
Inkwell, Counting House, Gilt, Original Label, Silliman	85.00
Inkwell, Covered, Hinge, Pewter, C.1845, Signed Whitcomb	70.00
Inkwell, Crystal & Sterling, Hinged Top, Cut Glass Base, 3 1/2 In.Square	190.00
Inkwell, Crystal, Cut Edges, Pressed Glass Top, 1 1/2 In.Square	15.00
Inkwell, Crystal, Sterling Hinged Cover, 4 1/2 X 4 1/2 In.	175.00
Inkwell, Cut Clear Crystal, Double Well, Hinged, 3 1/2 X 1 3/4 X 3 In.	85.00
Inkwell, Cut Glass, Blue, 1 3/4 In.	145.00
Inkwell, Deep Inset Top, Insert At Center, 4 Quill Holes, Pewter, 1 3/4 In.	65.00
Inkwell, Double Glass Inserts, Hinged Lid, Letter Holder, 3 Pen Rack, 1879	75.00
Inkwell, Double, Snail Shape, Tilting Wells, Iron Base	34.00
Inkwell, Elk, Large Antler, Acorn Base, Bronze, 5 1/2 X 6 In.	95.00
Inkwell, Fashioned Out Of World War II Shell, Brass	35.00
Inkwell, Figural, Camel, Glass Insert, Hinged Saddle	60.00
Inkwell, Figural, Camel, Metal Base, Saddle Opens To Show Well, 9 X 6 In.	145.00
Inkwell, Figural, Camel, Original Paint, White Metal, 5 1/2 X 10 X 3 In.	25.00
Inkwell, Figural, Dog, Carved, Glass Eyes, Wood	50.00

Inkwell, Figural, Horse Pulling Plow, Log Cover On Porcelain Wells, 14 In.	205.00
Inkwell, Figural, Indian Head, Headdress Lifts Up To Get Ink, 4 1/2 In.	65.00
Inkwell, Figural, Lion, Well In Jaws	27.50
Inkwell, Figural, Ma & Pa Carter, Germany	60.00
Inkwell, Figural, Mephistopheles Head, Ears Are Penholders, 2 1/2 X 3 In.	45.00
Inkwell, Figural, Monkey, Arms Hold Pen, Tray, Bronze, Geschutz, 5 X 6 1/2 In.	235.00
Inkwell, Figural, Moose Head, Clear Swirl, Wells In Front, 4 In.	38.00
Inkwell, Figural, Negro, Bronze	38.00
Inkwell, Figural, Owl Head, Iron, 10 1/2 In.	65.00
Inkwell, Figural, Owl, Pen Holder At Side, Porcelain, 4 1/2 In.	75.00
Inkwell, Figural, Seated Satyr, Cap Lifts, Bronze, English	45.00
Inkwell, Figural, 2 Poodles, Tree Trunk Is Inkwell, Staffordshire, 5 X 5 In.	50.00
Inkwell, Glass Insert, Metal Holder, Mech & Company	42.00
Inkwell, Glass, Three-Mold, Pair, 19th Century, 1 1/2 In. To 2 In.	150.00
Inkwell, Gondola Shape, Double Wells Inside Cabin	40.00
Inkwell, Hat-Shaped, Hand-Carved, Bottle Insert	25.00
Inkwell, Helmet Shape, Opens, Tin, 3 1/4 In.	35.00
Inkwell, Hinged Sterling Cover, Cut Crystal, 4 1/2 X 4 1/2 In.	175.00
Inkwell, Hinged Top, Blue, Cut Glass, 1 3/4 X 2 1/4 In.	85.00
Inkwell, Hinged Top, Hallmarked, Silver, 2 3/4 In.	25.00
Inkwell, Hinged, Porcelain Ink Pot, Wooden, 3 X 2 1/2 In.	40.00
Inkwell, Indented All Around, Cut Glass, Amber, 2 X 2 1/2 In.	85.00
Inkwell, Knight's Armor, Visor Lifts For Ink	35.00
Inkwell, Marble, Grain, Beige, Oval, Hinged Well, Spot For Pens	75.00
Inkwell, Metal Embossed Cover, Ice Blue Pyramid	20.00
Inkwell, Non-Spillable, Ridged Side, 2 X 2 In.Diameter	10.00
Inkwell, Panel With Man In Roadster, 3 Piece	125.00
Inkwell, Paperweight, Silver Collar & Dome, Turtle Mark, 3 1/2 X 3 In.Diam.	135.00
Inkwell, Pine Needle, Dore, Large	290.00
Inkwell, Plymouth Rock, Paperweight, 1876	35.00
Inkwell, Porcelain Insert, Hinged Lid, Open-Work, Cast Iron	32.00
Inkwell, Pressed & Cut Cane Pattern, Lid, Faceted Edge, 2 3/4 In.Square	75.00
Inkwell, Puppy Dining From Old Flat Nurser, China	85.00
Inkwell, Pyramid Shape, Geometric Silver Inlay Lid, Bronze, 5 X 5 X 3 In.	60.00
Inkwell, Quill Pen, 1 In.Square At Bottom To 3/4 In.Square Top, American	75.00
Inkwell, Rhinoceros Foot	50.00
Inkwell, Round, Art Nouveau, Form Of Waves, Reclining Mermaid Atop Cover	350.00
Inkwell, School Desk, Bakelite Top, Set Of 10	4.50
Inkwell, Scottie Dog, Head Opens To Reveal Well, Clear Glass	50.00
Inkwell, Scrolled Brass Holder, Cover, Souvenir Sheehan Co., Druggists	40.00
Inkwell, Set Goes Into A Meriden Silver Tray, Hinged Dover, 6 X 3 In.	65.00
Inkwell, Single, 6 Petal Base, Footed, Hinged Lid, Milk Glass Liner	24.00
Inkwell, Spike Helmet, Glass, White Metal Top	35.00
Inkwell, Square Cut Crystal, Hinged Cover, 2 1/2 In.	65.00
Inkwell, Square, Beveled Corners, C.1790, Soapstone, 2 1/4 X 1 1/2 In.	45.00
Inkwell, Sterling Tray, Crystal Cut Well, Sterling Top	30.00
Inkwell, Teakettle, Clear, Flint Glass, Brass Covered Spout	200.00
Inkwell, Tiffany, see Tiffany, Inkwell	
Inkwell, Traveler's, Blown Glass Well, Civil War Era, Lignum Vitae	18.50
Inkwell, Traveling, Barrel, Treen	135.00
Inkwell, Traveling, Brass	18.00
Inkwell, Tray For Pens, Square Marble Inkwell, Hinged Lid, Brass, 6 X 10 In.	85.00
Inkwell, Wooden, Round, Glass Insert, 3 Quill, Signed Silliman	60.00
Inkwell, Young Girl By Log, Bisque, Brass Hinged Top, Porcelain Liner	195.00

Insulators of glass or pottery have been made for use on telegraph or telephone poles since 1844.

Insulator, Armstrong, Amber	5.00
Insulator, Bennington Type	.75
Insulator, C.N.R., Purple	26.00 To 32.00
Insulator, Canadian Pacific Railroad, Dining Car, Stanley	15.00
Insulator, Canadian Pacific Railroad, Milk Glass, Stamped	1.50
Insulator, Canadian Pacific Railroad, Purple	12.00
Insulator, CD 728, Threadless	65.00
Insulator, Ceramic, Impressed Mushroom Mark, 6 X 3 In.	6.00
Insulator, Hemingray-O, Blue, Set Of 3	5.00

Insulator, Hemingray, Aqua, Patent 1893	10.00
Insulator, Hemingray, Blue, Set Of 3	5.00
Insulator, Hemingray, No.16-56	2.00
Insulator, Maydwell 20, Milk Glass	9.00
Insulator, Maydwell 42, Purple	7.00
Insulator, Pyrex CD 234, Carnival Glass	12.00
Insulator, Pyrex, Carnival Glass	12.00 To 15.00
Insulator, Pyrex, Carnival Glass, Rainbow Colored, 10 In.	15.00
Insulator, Western Union Co., Continental Rubber Works, Pair	7.50
Insulator, Westinghouse, Columbia Type, Granite, Threadless	50.00
Insulator, Whitehall, Tatum, Carnival Glass	10.00
Iron, see also Kitchen, Tool, Store	
Iron, American Eagle, Wings Spread, Perched On Rockwork Base, C.1915, 14 In.	250.00
Iron, Ashtray, Kaiser Beer, Figural Coal Miner Drinking Beer, 5 In.	48.00
Iron, Bank, Boy Scout	60.00
Iron, Basin, Flared Rim, Signed Langdon, 11 X 3 In.Deep	100.00
Iron, Basin, 8 3/4 In.	30.00
Iron, Boiler, Rotary, 22 1/2 In.	55.00
Iron, Book Press, C.1865, Victorian, 11 1/2 X 17 X 15 In.	75.00
Iron, Bookends, Dutch Girl, Yoke On Shoulder, 2 Pails, Pair	8.50
Iron, Bookends, Egyptian Sphinx	6.50
Iron, Bookends, Liberty Bell	10.00
Iron, Bookends, Lincoln Log Cabin, Bronze Finish	18.00
Iron, Bookends, Lost Indian, Pair	29.00
Iron, Bookends, Mayflower Ship, Pair	8.00 To 15.00
Iron, Boot Scraper, Dachshund, Black, Open Mouth, Red Tongue, 18 X 5 In.	65.00
Iron, Boot Scraper, Dachshund, 5 3/4 X 15 In.	22.00
Iron, Boot Scraper, Queen Anne Style, Mortised	195.00
Iron, Boot Scraper, Ram Horn Shape	35.00
Iron, Bootjack & Scraper, Steer Head, Horns Form Scraper, 10 In.	50.00
Iron, Bootjack, Dirty Nellie	12.50
Iron, Bootjack, Double Ended	25.00
Iron, Bootjack, Elk	25.00
Iron, Bootjack, Hand-Wrought	25.00
Iron, Bootjack, Naughty Nellie, Old Fashioned Bathing Suit	25.00 To 31.00
Iron, Bracket, Shelf, Open Scroll Design, 5 1/2 X 8 In.	12.00
Iron, Bracket, Supporting Scrolls, Hanging Ring, 24 X 40 1/2 In.	45.00
Iron, Broiler, Rotating, Good Handle	160.00
Iron, Bucket, 9 X 11 In.Diameter	25.00
Iron, Bust, Deity, Ming Dynasty, 21 3/4 In.	110.00
Iron, Bust, Knute Rockne	25.00
Iron, Candleholder, Miner's, Sticking Tommy	48.00
Iron, Candleholder, Wall, 3 Light, Hand-Forged, C.1890	150.00
Iron, Chameleon, Curled Tail, Sherwin-Williams Co., 8 1/2 In.	28.00
Iron, Claw Feet, 3 In.Glass Ball Inserts, For Parlor Table, Set Of 4	50.00
Iron, Coffee Grinder, see Coffee Grinder	
Iron, Crane, Fireplace, 17 1/2 In.	25.00
Iron, Cuspidor, Turtle, Step On Head, Shell Opens, 14 1/2 In.	95.00
Iron, Cutter, Paper, Sensible, Small, Paper Roll	22.00
Iron, Cutter, Triumph Tobacco	22.50
Iron, Diamond Kerosene Iron, Pump In Handle	12.50
Iron, Dispenser, Cigarette, Elephant	28.00
Iron, Dog, Whippet, Painted White, Facing Forward, 1800s, 38 In., Pair	1600.00
Iron, Door Knocker, Woman's Hand Holding Ball	28.00

Iron doorstops have been made in all types of designs. The vast majority of the doorstops sold today are cast iron and were made from about 1890 to 1930. Most of them are shaped like people, animals, flowers, or ships.

Iron, Doorstop, Airdale	38.00
Iron, Doorstop, Basket Of Flowers, Original Paint, 9 1/2 In.	20.00
Iron, Doorstop, Basket Of Flowers, Small	10.00
Iron, Doorstop, Black Cat, Green Eyes, Original Paint, 8 1/4 In.	36.00
Iron, Doorstop, Black Minstrel Man	35.00
Iron, Doorstop, Boot, Foot Sized	22.50
Iron, Doorstop, Boston Terrier, Standing, 8 In.	40.00
Iron, Doorstop, Bouquet Of Flowers	10.00

Iron, Doorstop, Boxer Dog	25.00
Iron, Doorstop, Bulldog, Black & White, 11 In.	40.00 To 50.00
Iron, Doorstop, Bulldog, 9 X 10 In.	30.00
Iron, Doorstop, Clown	75.00
Iron, Doorstop, Coach, Driver, Bugler & Horses	35.00
Iron, Doorstop, Cottage	25.00
Iron, Doorstop, Dog	35.00
Iron, Doorstop, Duck, 25 Lbs.	40.00
Iron, Doorstop, Elephant	35.00 To 48.00
Iron, Doorstop, English Coach, Team Of Horses, 2 Men, 12 1/4 X 7 1/4 In.	37.50
Iron, Doorstop, German Shepherd, Original Paint, 9 X 9 In.	30.00
Iron, Doorstop, Grazing Saddled Horse	18.50
Iron, Doorstop, Horsehead, Brass Whip	38.00
Iron, Doorstop, Lighthouse, Rock Base, Open Windows, 13 1/2 In.	60.00
Iron, Doorstop, Mail Coach	30.00
Iron, Doorstop, Mammy Doll	40.00
Iron, Doorstop, Mayflower Ship	20.00
Iron, Doorstop, Negro Mammy	8.50
Iron, Doorstop, Parrot, 8 In.	25.00
Iron, Doorstop, Ram, Black, Cast Iron, 6 1/2 X 9 1/2 In.	60.00
Iron, Doorstop, Rearing Lion, 15 In.	40.00
Iron, Doorstop, Rearing Lion, 18 In.	15.00
Iron, Doorstop, Rin Tin Tin, Embossed World Radio	35.00
Iron, Doorstop, Sailing Ship	25.00
Iron, Doorstop, Scottie, Standing, 10 X 8 1/4 In.	35.00
Iron, Doorstop, Seated Scottie, Marked Wilton, 7 3/4 In.	22.00
Iron, Doorstop, Shape Of Man Sitting	19.00
Iron, Doorstop, Ship, Full Sail, 11 In.	24.00
Iron, Doorstop, Sitting Cat, Yellow Eyes	32.00
Iron, Doorstop, Spanish Galleon, , 10 1/2 X 11 In.	32.50
Iron, Doorstop, Squirrel, With Nut, 6 In.	35.00
Iron, Doorstop, St.Bernard	25.00
Iron, Doorstop, Stagecoach	32.00
Iron, Doorstop, Sunbonnet Girl	35.00
Iron, Doorstop, Waitress	17.50
Iron, Doorstop, Windmill	25.00
Iron, Dryer, Corn, Hanging, Set Of 3	37.50
Iron, Dutch Oven, Matching Cover, Deep Flange, 19th Century, 11 In.	250.00
Iron, Eagle, Half-Round, Facing Left, 30 In.High X 64 In.Long	2800.00
Iron, Fence, Double Gate & Posts, 195 Feet	1500.00
Iron, Fence, Gate, 250 Feet	3000.00
Iron, Figurine, El Capitan, Marching Soldier	68.00
Iron, Figurine, Royal Mounted Police Horseback	15.00
Iron, Fork, Hearth, Heart Terminus, 3 Tine, 19th Century, 11 1/2 In.	75.00
Iron, Fork, Toasting, Brass Elephant Handle	10.00
Iron, Griddle, Hearth, Top 10 X 13 1/2 In.	35.00
Iron, Hair Curler	12.00
Iron, Hanger, Horse Whip	14.00
Iron, Harness, Hames With Brass Knobs, Pair	14.50
Iron, Hitching Post, Black Stable Boy Form, Ragged Clothes, 19th Century	1700.00
Iron, Hitching Post, Horse	18.00
Iron, Holder, String, Beehive Shape, Dated 1855	30.00
Iron, Holder, String, Shape Of Ball Of Twine, 2 Piece	55.00
Iron, Hook, Hog	5.00
Iron, Hook, Meat, Hand-Forged, Hanging Ring, 10 X 1/ In.Diameter	30.00
Iron, Hook, Meat, Three Prong	30.00
Iron, Horse's Head, Form Of Hitching Posts Fitted With Ring, 14 In., Pair	225.00
Iron, Ice Pick, Punxy Beer	12.00
Iron, Incense Burner, Rooster	125.00
Iron, Jardiniere, Scrolled Iron Work, 1800s, 3 X 5 Feet, Pair	225.00
Iron, Juicer, Lemon	12.00
Iron, Kettle, Contoured, Barstow Stove Co., 11 1/2 X 8 1/2 In.	37.50
Iron, Kettle, Flanged Top, C.1860, 100 Gallon	225.00
Iron, Kettle, Goose Neck Spout, Bail Handle, Flat Bottom	48.00
Iron, Key, Folding, Large	6.50
Iron, Key, Large Jail, Ranch, 5 To 7 In.Long	3.50

Iron, Knocker, Door, Shape Of Basket Of Flowers 10.00
Iron, Ladle, Double Lipped, Long Handle, 3 3/4 X 19 In. 16.00
Iron, Lamp, Betty, Wick Pick, American, 18th Century 145.00
Iron, Lighter, Cigarette, Dog, Hinged Head, 2 1/2 In. 20.00
Iron, Mailbox, Name & Dated 1889 .... 65.00
  Iron, Match Holder, see also Match Holder
Iron, Match Safe, Bulldog On Lid, Striker Inside, 3 1/3 X 2 In. 22.00
Iron, Mold, Chocolate, Santa 65.00
Iron, Mold, Cornucopia, Oval, 4 1/4 X 5 3/4 In. 140.00
Iron, Nutcracker, Dog, 11 In. 35.00
Iron, Nutcracker, Dog, 14 In. 25.00
Iron, Nutcracker, Mounted On Wood 9.00
Iron, Nutcracker, Perfection 16.00
Iron, Nutcracker, Sergeant 18.00
Iron, Nutcracker, Shape Of Dog, Tail Is Handle, Mouth Cracks Nut, 4 1/4 In. ... 20.00
Iron, Opener, Bottle, Pink Elephant 20.00
Iron, Pan, Hanging Hook, American, 18th Century, 2 7/8 X 2 3/4 In. 110.00
Iron, Pan, Muffin, 11 Holes 18.00
Iron, Paperweight, Merode Knit Underwear, Wakefield, Mass. 17.50
Iron, Plaque, Teddy Roosevelt, Bronzed, Signed, 1920 .... 65.00
Iron, Plate, Raised Border, Raised Painted Indian 90.00
Iron, Porringer, Kenrick 55.00
Iron, Porringer, Leaf Handle, Baldwin, 5 1/2 In. 70.00
Iron, Porringer, Marked W.T., 6 1/2 In.Diameter 70.00
Iron, Pot, Bean, On Legs 12.00
Iron, Press, Meat, Screw 27.00
Iron, Pulley, Well 6.50
Iron, Pump, Cistern, Brass Sleeve 14.75
Iron, Rack, Corn Drying 12.00
Iron, Ratchet, Hanging Betty Lamp, 12 In. 90.00
Iron, Riveter, Harness, Iron, Dated 1900 .... 10.00
Iron, Roaster, Chestnut, Pierced Lid, Brass Agitator, 18th Century 195.00
Iron, Rosette, 3 Piece 18.00
Iron, Safe, Floor, Skeleton Key 65.00
Iron, Shaver, Ice, New Bregleton, Penna. 15.00
Iron, Shoes, High Button, 5 1/4 In., Pair 25.00
Iron, Shovel, Fireplace, Hand-Wrought 50.00
Iron, Skillet, Fireplace, 3 Foot Handle 90.00
Iron, Skillet, Fireplace, 4 Foot Handle 125.00
Iron, Snuffer, Candle .... 10.00 To 22.00
Iron, Snuffer, Candle, Footed, Heart Shape In Handle 35.00
Iron, Speculum, Mouth, Veterinarians 5.00
Iron, Spindle, Bill 6.00
Iron, Spit, For Fireplace Oven, Pair 50.00
Iron, Spittoon, One Footed, Corset Shape, Porcelain Lined, Weighted Bottom ... 20.00
Iron, Spur, Fighting Cock, Kirby, Pair 75.00
Iron, Spur, Silver Engraved Mounting, Single 45.00
Iron, Spur, Silver Inlay, Western, Pair 45.00
Iron, Spur, Spanish, 1800s, Large Rowels 10.00
Iron, Spur, 2 In.Rowel, Etched Design, Pair 9.00
Iron, Stair Case, From Theater, Circular, 13 Feet 1500.00
Iron, Stand, Copper Wash Basin, Handmade, 41 In. 260.00
Iron, Stove Figurine, George Washington, Academic Gown, Painted, 47 In. ... 1000.00
Iron, Strap Hinges, Burnished & Cleaned, Pair 55.00
Iron, Strongbox, Wells Fargo, Original Stenciled Name Stamped In Carcass ... 325.00
Iron, Swift, Standing, Table Model, 15 In. 85.00
Iron, Teakettle, Gooseneck, Flat Bottom, 3 1/2 X 6 1/2 In. 69.50
Iron, Teakettle, Hanging, Wrought Handle, 18th Century 85.00
Iron, Teazel, Butter Stamp, 18th Century, 4 3/4 In. 150.00
Iron, Tie Backs, Basket Of Flowers, 3 1/2 X 3 In., 6 1/2 In.Shaft, Set Of 3 ... 37.50
Iron, Toaster, Fireplace, Long Handled 115.00
Iron, Toaster, Hearth, 4 Footed, Swivel Handle, C.1780, 13 1/2 X 27 In. 170.00
Iron, Tongs, Blacksmith's 5.00
Iron, Tongs, Ember, 29 In. 35.00
Iron, Tongs, For Hot Coals, Hand-Forged, Pipe Tongs, 11 In. 95.00
Iron, Tongs, Ice, Ice Plant, Lift 300 Pound Block 15.00

Iron, Tsuba, Figures In Garden, Gold & Silver,
1700s, 3 1/4 In.

Iron, Tongs, Ice, Small	6.50
Iron, Trammel, Fireplace	45.00
Iron, Trap, Wolf, Hand-Forged, 18th Century, 20 In.	95.00
Iron, Trimmer, Wick, Scissor Type, C.1810, Signed J.Rodgers & Co., C.1810	20.00
Iron, Trivet, Entwined Hearts, Lovebirds	15.00
Iron, Trivet, Kettle, 14 In.	95.00
Iron, Tsuba, Figures In Garden, Gold & Silver, 1700s, 3 1/4 In. ....Illus	400.00
Iron, Wall Pocket, Double, Bracket	24.00

*Ironstone china was first made in 1813. It gained its greatest popularity
during the mid-nineteenth century. The heavy, durable, off-white pottery was
made in white or was colored with any of hundreds of patterns. Much flow
blue pottery was made of ironstone. Some of the pieces had raised
decorations.*

**Ironstone, see also Chelsea Grape, Gaudy Ironstone, Moss Rose,
Staffordshire, Wedgwood**

Ironstone, Bowl & Pitcher, Octagon Shape, Oriental Scenes, Mason's	250.00
Ironstone, Bowl, Footed Base, C.1815-20, Mason, 3 1/2 X 9 In.Diameter	150.00
Ironstone, Bowl, Paneled, 9 1/2 In.Square	32.50
Ironstone, Bowl, Ribbed	12.00
Ironstone, Bowl, Sugar, Ribbon Finial, J.G. Meakin	22.00
Ironstone, Bowl, Vegetable, Covered, Signed, 12 1/2 X 8 1/2 In.	85.00
Ironstone, Bowl, Vegetable, Vista, 9 1/2 In.	15.00
Ironstone, Chamber Pot, Lid, Sawtooth Design, White	25.00
Ironstone, Coffeepot, Twig Handle, Embossed, 19th Century, 9 In.	45.00
Ironstone, Coffeepot, White, Bridgwood & Sons, 1885	95.00
Ironstone, Creamer, Wheat, 6 1/2 In.	28.00
Ironstone, Cup & Saucer & Plate, Handleless, Columbia, Plate 8 1/2 In.	35.00
Ironstone, Cup & Saucer, Handleless, Child's, Pair	28.00
Ironstone, Cup & Saucer, Handleless, Johnson Brothers	15.00
Ironstone, Cup & Saucer, Handleless, White, England	15.00
Ironstone, Dish, Soap, Insert & Cover, Powell & Bishop	37.50
Ironstone, Jar, Lidded, C.1845, Mason's, 15 In.	230.00
Ironstone, Jug, Mason's, Oriental Family, Reptile Handle, 1830, 4 1/2 In.	65.00
Ironstone, Jug, Oriental Design, Medallions, C.1829, Mason's	75.00
Ironstone, Mold, Pudding, Melon & Flower, 9 X 6 In.	20.00
Ironstone, Mug, Shaving, Scuttle Shape, White	16.00
Ironstone, Mug, Triple X Root Beer	15.00
Ironstone, Pitcher & Bowl, Octagonal, C.1840, Mason's, Bowl, 8 1/2 In.	175.00
Ironstone, Pitcher & Bowl, Polychrome Colors, C.1845, Mason's	295.00
Ironstone, Pitcher, Cream, Ribbon Finial	10.00
Ironstone, Pitcher, Mason's, Oriental Figures, C.1850, 5 1/4 In.	88.00
Ironstone, Pitcher, Milk, Gray Glaze, Blue Medallions Of Cows, 8 In.	45.00
Ironstone, Pitcher, Milk, Wheat, 8 In.	85.00
Ironstone, Pitcher, Syrup, Pewter Top, Dated 1872	62.50
Ironstone, Pitcher, U.S.Pottery Co., 12 In.	28.00
Ironstone, Pitcher, Wash, Acanthus Scrolls, Johnson	50.00
Ironstone, Plate, Alleghany, Blue & White, 9 1/4 In.	35.00
Ironstone, Plate, Athens, 9 In.	20.00
Ironstone, Plate, Bread, View Of Historical Niagara Falls, Johnson Bros.	39.00
Ironstone, Plate, Chinese Garden Scene, Black Border, 8 In.	20.00
Ironstone, Plate, Feather Edge, Blue	8.00
Ironstone, Plate, Handles, Black Chinese Pattern, Flowers, Square	27.50
Ironstone, Plate, Mason's, Flowers & Bird, 10 1/2 In.	25.00

Ironstone, Plate, Mason's, Oriental Symbols, 10 1/2 In.	25.00
Ironstone, Platter & Covered Vegetable, Rope Twisted Handles, Set	38.50
Ironstone, Platter, Blue & White Flowers, Mason's, 17 X 21 In.	135.00
Ironstone, Platter, E.Challinor, Rose, 14 X 18 In.	110.00
Ironstone, Platter, Embossed Floral & Leaf Border, Marked, 18 1/4 X 14 In.	52.00
Ironstone, Platter, Handled, Alcock, 13 In.	12.00
Ironstone, Platter, Mulberry, Neva, 12 X 15 1/2 In.	95.00
Ironstone, Platter, Palestine Pattern, C.1842, Scotland, 12 3/4 X 10 In.	27.50
Ironstone, Platter, Prague Porcelain, 10 X 13 In.	20.00
Ironstone, Platter, Vista, 13 3/4 In.	30.00
Ironstone, Platter, Wheat Border, White, 17 In.	15.00
Ironstone, Saucer, Ford Motor Co.	6.50
Ironstone, Soup, Dish, White, Rimmed, Corn Pattern, Wedgwood, C.1863, 10 In.	25.00
Ironstone, Sugar & Creamer, Fruit Basket, Mason's	25.00
Ironstone, Sugar, Senate, Handled, Covered, 6 In.	20.00
Ironstone, Syrup, Pewter Top, White	45.00
Ironstone, Tea Leaf, Bowl, Commode, Wedgwood	65.00
Ironstone, Tea Leaf, Bowl, Vegetable, Royal Ironstone Grindley	45.00
Ironstone, Tea Leaf, Coffeepot, Wedgwood	50.00
Ironstone, Tea Leaf, Cup	65.00
Ironstone, Tea Leaf, Cup & Saucer, Handleless, Gold Trim	42.50
Ironstone, Tea Leaf, Dish, Butter, Insert, Square, Signed	65.00
Ironstone, Tea Leaf, Pitcher, Luster, Mayer Pottery, C.1885, 5 1/2 In.	49.00
Ironstone, Tea Leaf, Plate, Bread, Luster, 9 1/2 In.	25.00
Ironstone, Tea Leaf, Plate, Wedgwood, 9 1/2 In.	15.00
Ironstone, Tea Leaf, Plate, 9 In.	15.00
Ironstone, Tea Leaf, Platter, Acanthus Leaves, 16 1/4 X 12 1/4 In.	35.00
Ironstone, Tea Leaf, Platter, Burslem, 15 In.	60.00
Ironstone, Tea Leaf, Platter, Luster, Scalloped, 10 1/4 X 14 1/4 In.	25.00
Ironstone, Tea Leaf, Platter, Luster, 12 In.	17.50
Ironstone, Tea Leaf, Platter, Meakin, 8 X 11 In.	25.00
Ironstone, Tea Leaf, Platter, Mellor, Taylor, 10 X 13 In.	30.00
Ironstone, Tea Leaf, Platter, Ribbed Border, Wedgwood & Co., 8 1/2 X 12 In.	35.00
Ironstone, Tea Leaf, Shaving Mug	
Ironstone, Tea Leaf, Teapot, Burslem	60.00
Ironstone, Tea Leaf, Teapot, Child's, 5 In.	24.00
Ironstone, Tea Leaf, Wash Bowl & Pitcher	285.00
Ironstone, Tea Pot, Burgess, Goddard, Lion, Dragon, White	30.00
Ironstone, Teapot, Blue Trim, Twig Handle, Moss Rose	38.00
Ironstone, Teapot, Bulbous, Grape Pattern, White, Marked, 10 In.	45.00
Ironstone, Teapot, Feather Pattern, C.1800	35.00
Ironstone, Teapot, Marked Powell & Bishop, England, White, 8 1/2 In.	48.00
Ironstone, Tureen, Attached Underplate, Finial Nut On Lid, White	15.00
Ironstone, Tureen, Covered, Meakin, 10 1/2 In.	24.00
Ironstone, Tureen, Covered, Meakin, 13 In.	32.50
Ironstone, Tureen, Soup, Oval, 1880 Mark, T. & R.Boote, 14 1/2 X 11 In.	89.00
Ironstone, Urn, Flow Blue & White Enamel Flowers, Gold Trim, Large, Pair	325.00
Ivorex, Plaque, Glasgow Cathedral, Signed, A.Osborne, 1906	30.00
Ivory, Ball, Billiard, 1/2 Pound	20.00
Ivory, Basket, Painted, Royal Bayreuth, Black Mark	185.00
Ivory, Beads, African, Graduated, 77 Beads, 44 In.	300.00
Ivory, Box, Chinese Game Of Loo, Figure On Top & Inside Cover, French	275.00
Ivory, Box, Covered, Cylindrical, 4 Carved Scenes, 4 X 3 1/2 In.	150.00
Ivory, Box, Miniature Portrait, Tortoise Lined	168.00
Ivory, Brushpot, Cover, Footed, Tigers & Elephants In Relief, 19th Century	775.00
Ivory, Bust, African, Hand-Carved	75.00
Ivory, Case, Carved, 4 X 2 In.	195.00
Ivory, Case, Lady's, Victorian, Silver & Crystal Trim, 1860, 24 In.Wide	100.00
Ivory, Comb, Butterflies & Flowers, French	65.00
Ivory, Comb, Hand-Carved Rosebuds, 19th Century, China, Box, 8 In.	30.00
Ivory, Container, Perfume Bottle, Girl & Flowers	37.50
Ivory, Corkscrew, Sterling Marked Cap, 8 1/2 In.	125.00
Ivory, Dagger, In Sheath, Carved, Scrimshaw, 9 In.	150.00
Ivory, Doctor's Doll, On Base, Signed	200.00
Ivory, Doctor's Lady, Reclining Nude Lady, Pedestal	125.00
Ivory, Eagle Head, 5 Inches	275.00

Ivory, Elephant Tusk, Carved Into Alligator, 16 In.	130.00
Ivory, Fetish, Duck & Bird, Eskimo, 7/8 To 1 1/4 In., Set Of 4	125.00
Ivory, Figurine, Bird, Tail & Wings Tinted Blue, C.1900, 2 1/2 In., Pair	100.00
Ivory, Figurine, Buddha, Wooden Base, 20th Century, 4 In.	95.00
Ivory, Figurine, Child Holding Enameled Box, Signed Preiss, 6 In.	950.00
Ivory, Figurine, Chinese Lohan, 18th Century, 8 In.	375.00
Ivory, Figurine, Court Jester, Carved Wood Plinth, Dancing, C.1800, 8 1/4 In.	700.00
Ivory, Figurine, Crane, 6 In.	85.00
Ivory, Figurine, Diety Of Thousand Hands, 8 1/2 In.	150.00
Ivory, Figurine, Doctor's Lady, 7 In.	175.00
Ivory, Figurine, Elephant God, Wooden Base, 4 1/2 In.	50.00
Ivory, Figurine, Elephant God, Wooden Base, 5 1/8 In.	135.00
Ivory, Figurine, Elephant, Hand-Carved, 2 In.	30.00
Ivory, Figurine, Empress & Emperor On Throne, 6 1/2 X 3 1/2 In., Pair	1000.00
Ivory, Figurine, Fisherman, Chinese Mark, 3 1/2 In.	75.00
Ivory, Figurine, Goddess Of A Thousand Hands, Koon Yum, Carved, 8 1/2 In.	195.00
Ivory, Figurine, Hoeti, Seated, Hand-Carved, 3 In.	30.00
Ivory, Figurine, Kwan Yin Holding Flower Basket, Bird At Feet, 32 In.	2000.00
Ivory, Figurine, Lion, 2 Dog's Heads Carved On Side, 1 1/2 X 5 3/4 In.	225.00
Ivory, Figurine, Man In Medieval Costume, Austrian, 3 In.	285.00
Ivory, Figurine, Man On Bench Smoking Pipe, Lunch At His Side, 4 1/2 In.	225.00
Ivory, Figurine, Monk With Staff, Hair & Beard White, Amber, 4 1/4 In.	75.00
Ivory, Figurine, Native Man & Woman, African, Wooden Stand, 9 In., Pair	175.00
Ivory, Figurine, Nude Woman, Art Deco, French, Wood Base, 14 In.	650.00
Ivory, Figurine, Oriental Diety, Koom Lum, God Of Thousand Hands, 8 1/2 In.	225.00
Ivory, Figurine, Oriental Lady & Fan, Hand-Carved, 4 In.	30.00
Ivory, Figurine, Owl, Raised Feathers, C.1900, 2 In.	48.00
Ivory, Figurine, Rabbi, Standing, Body In Different Position, 4 In., Set Of 6	525.00
Ivory, Figurine, Saint George & Dragon, Wooden Base, 1900s, 5 1/4 In.	135.00
Ivory, Figurine, Standing Woodsman With Foot On Axe, Signed, 8 1/4 In.	475.00
Ivory, Figurine, Warrior, Sword & Arrows By Side, Chinese, Stand, 18 1/2 In.	1600.00
Ivory, Figurine, Warrior, 2 Galloping Horses, Wood Stand, 16 1/2 In.	1500.00
Ivory, Figurine, Whale, Carved, From Sperm Whale Teeth, Coral Base, 5 In., Pair	200.00
Ivory, Figurine, Woman, Half Clothed, Ivory Stand, 14 In.	475.00
Ivory, Figurine, 4 Immortals, Seated On Base, Wood Stand, 15 In., Pair	3000.00
Ivory, Grouping, Japanese, Man & Child, Man Holds Toy Elephant, Signed, 8 In.	335.00
Ivory, Hair Receiver, Carved, Victorian, 3 3/4 X 3 3/4 In.	225.00
Ivory, Handle, Cane, Silver Mounted, Horse's Head, Glass Eyes, 4 3/4 In.	800.00
Ivory, Holder, Cigarette, Dragon Head, 6 7/8 Inches	37.50
Ivory, Holder, Cigarette, Hand-Carved, 3 1/2 In.	25.00
Ivory, Irish Setter, 1 1/2 In.	12.50
Ivory, Medallion, Buddha, 2 3/8 In., Pair	115.00
Ivory, Napkin Ring, Carved Figures & Garden Scene Around Edge	25.00
Ivory, Necklace, Carved Elephants, Large Elephant Pendant	195.00
Ivory Netsuke, see Netsuke	
Ivory, Okimono, Man & Girl On Toy Horse, Mother-Of-Pearl, Ichiro Inada	800.00
Ivory, Pagoda, Japanese, 19th Century, 15 X 10 In.	1400.00
Ivory, Painting, Child, Gold Liner Frame	175.00
Ivory, Patience Ball, 5 3/4 In.	85.00
Ivory, Plaque, Art Nouveau, Carved Female Nude Covered By Waves, 6 In.	900.00
Ivory, Plaque, Depicting Couple In Landscape, Oval, 1700s, 2 1/2 In.	300.00
Ivory, Puzzle Ball, Stand, 7 Layers, Dragons, 5 1/4 In.	60.00
Ivory, Rattle, Hand-Painted, 2 1/2 In.	19.00
Ivory, Seal, Woman's Face & Hair, 4 3/4 In.	125.00
Ivory, Shoehorn, Woman, Child, Figural Handle	24.00
Ivory, Skull, Miniature	60.00
Ivory, Spoon, Salt, Hand Carved, C.1850, 2 1/2 In.	12.50
Ivory, Spoon, Salt, Scoop Type	6.50
Ivory, Stand, Carved Elephants, Lady's, Snacks, Dogs & Birds, 38 In.	540.00
Ivory, Stickpin, Carved Flower, Gold Nugget Center	9.00
Ivory, Tabernacle, Cameo Photos Of King George V & Queen Mary	275.00
Ivory, Tankard, Silver Base & Lid, Figural Finial, German, 1900, 13 1/4 In.	3750.00
Ivory, Tankard, Silver Domed Lid, German, Ivory Finial, C.1800, 17 In.	4000.00
Ivory, Tray, Inlay Mother-Of-Pearl	12.00
Ivory, Triptych, Marie Antoinette, Skirt Opens To 3 Scenes, 5 1/4 In.	800.00
Ivory, Tusk, Elephant, 65 Pounds, 6 Feet	4900.00

Ivory, Tusk, Spiraling Snake, Lions, Birds, Snails, African, 21 In., Pair	175.00
Ivory, Tusk, Walrus, 29 Inches	345.00
Ivory, Wagon, 3 Figures & Brahma Bulls, India, Carved, C.1850, Miniature	450.00
Ivory, Watch Fob, Carved Horse's Head, 14K Gold, Bridle	39.50
Ivory, Whale, Figurine, Polar Bear, Standing On All Fours, 1 1/2 In.	22.00
Jack Armstrong, Flashlight	12.00 To 15.00
Jack Armstrong, Gun, In Box	25.00
Jack Armstrong, Hikeometer	10.00
Jack Armstrong, Pedometer, Silver	16.00
Jack Armstrong, Propeller Gun, Original Mailer	65.00
Jack Armstrong, Telescope	20.00

Jack-In-The-Pulpit vases were named for their odd trumpetlike shape that resembles the wild plant called-jack-in-the-pulpit. The design originated in the late Victorian years.

Jack-In-The-Pulpit, Bowl, Opaline, Crimped, 3 Talon Feet	95.00
Jack-In-The-Pulpit, Bowl, Opaline, Talon Feet, 8 X 4 In.	99.00
Jack-In-The-Pulpit, Bowl, 3 Talon Feet, Opaline, 8 In.Diameter	135.00
Jack-In-The-Pulpit, Rose Bowl, Yellow, White, 5 In.	55.00
Jack-In-The-Pulpit, Vase, Amberina Swirl, Amber Applied Rim, 11 X 5 In.	195.00
Jack-In-The-Pulpit, Vase, Amberina, Applied Amber Foot & Edging, 12 3/4 In.	175.00
Jack-In-The-Pulpit, Vase, Applied Feet, Flower Shaped Top, 7 1/4 In.	85.00
Jack-In-The-Pulpit, Vase, Blown, White Opalescent, 4 In.	35.00
Jack-In-The-Pulpit, Vase, Blue, Opalescent, 12 In.	48.00
Jack-In-The-Pulpit, Vase, Cased Dark Green & White, 9 X 5 In.	59.00
Jack-In-The-Pulpit, Vase, Coil Stem, Footed, Opalescent Green, 9 1/4 In.	65.00
Jack-In-The-Pulpit, Vase, Cranberry, 7 In.	58.00
Jack-In-The-Pulpit, Vase, Flower Shaped Top, Rose Overlay, 7 1/4 In.	85.00
Jack-In-The-Pulpit, Vase, Green Hobnail Interior, White, 6 1/2 In.	55.00
Jack-In-The-Pulpit, Vase, Green Overlay, White Outside, 7 7/8 In.	60.00
Jack-In-The-Pulpit, Vase, Green Transparent To Blue Opalescent, 12 1/2 In.	60.00
Jack-In-The-Pulpit, Vase, Green, White Casing, 7 X 13 In.Base	50.00
Jack-In-The-Pulpit, Vase, Multicolor Rainbow Stripes, Footed, 9 1/2 In.Tall	175.00
Jack-In-The-Pulpit, Vase, Opalescent Frill, Slim, Green, 6 3/4 In.	35.00
Jack-In-The-Pulpit, Vase, Pink & White Overlay, 6 1/4 In.	48.00
Jack-In-The-Pulpit, Vase, Pink Inside, White Outside, 9 In.	45.00
Jack-In-The-Pulpit, Vase, Quilted Blue Ruffle, Enamel Accents, 5 In.	85.00
Jack-In-The-Pulpit, Vase, Ribbed, Swirled Stem, Enameled Roses, 10 3/4 In.	68.00
Jack-In-The-Pulpit, Vase, Ruffled Edge, Vaseline Pedestal Feet, 7 7/8 In.	65.00
Jack-In-The-Pulpit, Vase, Spatters Of Pink Enamel, Crimped Rim, 7 In.	55.00
Jack-In-The-Pulpit, Vase, Thin Rib, Satin Iridescent, Aqua, 10 1/2 In.	120.00
Jack-In-The-Pulpit, Vase, White Opalescent, Red & Black Shaded Lip, 7 In.	60.00

Jackfield ware was originally a black glazed pottery made in Jackfield, England, from 1750 to 1775. A yellow glazed ware has also been called Jackfield ware. Most of the pieces referred to as Jackfield are black pieces made during the Victorian era.

Jackfield, Dish, Candy, Decorated	75.00
Jackfield, Figurine, Spaniel, Pair	150.00
Jackfield, Pitcher, Turquoise Buds & Gold Leaves, Pewter Lid, 6 X 3 1/2 In.	45.00
Jackfield, Sugar, Creamer & Teapot, Eagle Head Handles, C.1840	98.00
Jackfield, Teapot, Oval, Green Ivy, Gilt Against Black	39.75
Jacob Petit, Inkwell, France, C.1796-1868	175.00
Jacob Petit, Vase & Stand, J.P. In Underglaze Blue, 16 In.	400.00
Jacob Petit, Vase, Cornucopia, Scrolls, Flowers, 1830, 11 In., Pair	475.00
Jade, Basket, Applied Clear Handle, Polished Pontil, Purple, 7 1/2 In.	125.00
Jade, Bottle, Snuff, Incised With Stylized Bat, Stopper Carved In Bird Form	70.00
Jade, Bowl & Cover, White, Ribbed Sides, Matching Stand, 1800s, 6 In.	3700.00
Jade, Bowl, Green, Circular, Flaring Rim, Bears Steuben Stamp, 8 1/2 In.	150.00
Jade, Bowl, White, Metal & Enamel Stand, Lipped Rim, Ch'ien Lung, 6 5/8 In.	2100.00
Jade, Box, Covered, White, Carved, 3 1/2 X 5 In.Diameter	450.00
Jade, Bracelet, Carved, Entwined Rope, Pale Green Stone, 1800s, 3 In.	950.00
Jade, Dice, Numbers In Gold, Pair	145.00
Jade, Dish, Flower Shape, 12 Petal Lobes, Coiled Stem, Green, 7 1/2 In.	450.00
Jade, Fan-Tail Goldfish, Plum, Teakwood Stand, 2 1/2 X 2 3/4 In.	190.00
Jade, Figurine, Bird Among Lotus Leaves, Fei T'sui, 3 1/4 In.	300.00

Jade, Figurine, Boy Riding On A Buffalo, Greenish White, 2 In. 225.00
Jade, Figurine, Fantail Goldfish, Outstretched Fins, Plum, 1 1/2 X 2 1/2 In. 160.00
Jade, Figurine, Foo Dog, Serpentine Carved & Sculptured, 6 1/2 X 9 1/2 In. 1200.00
Jade, Figurine, Lohan, Staff & A Prunus, Chinese, 5 In. 100.00
Jade, Figurine, Maiden, Holding Lotus Blossom, Wood Stand, 8 1/2 In. 150.00
Jade, Figurine, Water Buffalo, Standing, Rose, 3 X 5 1/2 In. 400.00
Jade, Foo Dog, With Ball, Ming Dynasty, 1 1/4 X 1 3/4 In. 100.00
Jade, Goldfish, Apple Green, Teakwood Stand, 3 1/2 X 3 In. 175.00
Jade, Grapes, Bunch, Green 45.00
Jade, Inkstand, Lid Pierced With Birds, 2 Inkwells & Liners, 7 1/2 In. 1300.00
Jade, Match Holder, Brass Trim, Signed, Green & White 295.00
Jade, Pendent, Carved Mutton Fat, Peapods, Leaves, Tendrils, 1700s, 2 1/4 In. 450.00
Jade, Puff Box, Covered, Alabaster Finial, Footed Base, Yellow, 6 In. 125.00
Jade, Urn, White, Covered, Cornelian Bead Knob, 5 X 6 X 2 In.Diameter 950.00
Jade, Vase, Fan, Glass Pedestal, Dolphin Handles 28.00
Jade, Vase, Foo Dog Sculptured Top, Loops & Rings On Cover, Green, 5 3/4 In. 750.00
Jade, Vase, Geometric Motifs, Elephant Head Handles, Stand, Cover, 8 3/4 In. 400.00
Jade, Vase, Landscape, Dragon Finial, Elephant Head Handles, Cover, 5 In. 350.00
Jade, Vase, Lid Has Crab Face, Hinged, 2 Handled, 5 1/2 X 3 3/4 In., Pair 550.00
Jade, Vase, 4 Animal Mask Neck, Figurines, Ring Handles, Cover, 9 In. 600.00
Japanese, Cloisonne, Vase, On Pottery, Pair, 9 1/4 In. 220.00

> *Japanese Coralene is a pottery decorated with small raised beads and dots.*
> *It was first made in the nineteenth century. Later wares made to imitate*
> *coraline had dots of enamel.*

Japanese, Coralene, Vase, Beehive, Portrait, 10 In. 135.00
Japanese, Coralene, Vase, Cylindrical, Green To Blue, 9 In. 260.00
Japanese, Coralene, Vase, Floral, U.S.Pat.Feb.9, 1909, 9 In. 275.00

> *Jasperware is a fine-grained pottery developed by Josiah Wedgwood in*
> *1755. The jasper was made in many colors including the most famous, a light*
> *blue. It is still being made.*

Jasperware, see also Various Art Potteries, Wedgwood
Jasperware, Chocolate Pot, Dark Blue, Covered, 8 1/2 In. 150.00
Jasperware, Hair Receiver, Green, Heart Shaped 65.00
Jasperware, Jug, Claret, Silver Plate Handle, Dark Blue Lid, 11 In. 190.00
Jasperware, Medallion, Cameo, Porcelain, American 75.00
Jasperware, Pitcher, Pewter Top, Three Cherubs, 1850s, 7 In. 185.00
Jasperware, Plate, Two Cupids, Lady With Harp, Pink & White, 6 In.Diameter 35.00
Jasperware, Sugar, Metal Cover, Attached Tongs, Adam, 5 X 4 In. 95.00
Jasperware, Tankard, Silver Rim, Hallmarked, Wedgwood, Silversmith 235.00
Jasperware, Teapot, Queen Elizabeth Coronation, C.1953 .... 165.00
Jasperware, Vase, Classic Woman Entwined In Florals, 7 X 3 1/2 In. 32.00
Jasperware, Vase, Grey & White, 5 In., Pair 165.00
Jasperware, Vase, Raised Profile Of Diana, Bark Finish, 4 1/2 X 3 In.Diam. 47.50
Jewel Tea, see Autumn Leaf
Jewelry, Beads, Agate, Orange & White Graduated, 28 In. 35.00
Jewelry, Beads, Amethyst Quartz, Graduated, 19 In. 42.50
Jewelry, Beads, Amethyst, Vermeil Clasp, 24 In. 175.00
Jewelry, Beads, Art Deco, Vaseline, 16 In. 19.50
Jewelry, Beads, Baltic Amber, Cloudy & Clear Yellows, 20 1/2 In. 150.00
Jewelry, Beads, Black Amethyst, Beaded Teardrop, 16 In. 15.00
Jewelry, Beads, Black Jet, Faceted Carnival Beads, Tassels, 34 In. 48.50
Jewelry, Beads, Carnelian, Oval, Separated By Crystal Discs, 32 In. 75.00
Jewelry, Beads, Cherry Amber, Graduated Beads, 14 In. 75.00
Jewelry, Beads, Cherry Amber, Graduated, 12 In. 50.00
Jewelry, Beads, Coral, Interspersed 14K Gold Beads, 27 In. 37.00
Jewelry, Beads, Coral, 5-Strand, Chinese Silver Clasp, Separators 325.00
Jewelry, Beads, Crystal, Amber & Clear, Graduated, 24 In. 20.00
Jewelry, Beads, Faceted, Engraved Link Chain, Czechoslovakian, 16 1/2 In. 47.50
Jewelry, Beads, Gold Over Sterling Clasp, Jade, 20 In. 56.00
Jewelry, Beads, Graduated, Amber, 32 In. 75.00
Jewelry, Beads, Jet, Whitby, England, 11 In. 45.00
Jewelry, Beads, Peking Glass, Interspersed With 14K Gold Beads, 18 In. 59.00
Jewelry, Beads, Peking Glass, 51 In. 125.00
Jewelry, Beads, Reverse-Painted Peking Glass, Unstrung, 1 5/8 X 2 In.Diam. 125.00

Jewelry, Beads, Rosary, Wooden, Copper Stations 14.00
Jewelry, Beads, Rough Cut Garnets, 46 In.Long 125.00
Jewelry, Bracelet, Art Nouveau, Moonstones, 3 Sapphires, 14K Gold 400.00
Jewelry, Bracelet, Bangle, Gold & Enamel, Greek Key Pattern, C.1865 .... 650.00
Jewelry, Bracelet, Charm, 1 In.Wide, 14K Gold 110.00
Jewelry, Bracelet, Gold & Woven Hair, Pair, Mid-19th Century 175.00
Jewelry, Bracelet, Gold Links Are Head & Tail Of Snake, Pearl Eyes 295.00
Jewelry, Bracelet, Gold Mesh, 18K Pink Gold 255.00
Jewelry, Bracelet, Gold, Diamonds, Cobalt Blue Enamel, French, C.1860 .... 5000.00
Jewelry, Bracelet, Hair, Wide 90.00
Jewelry, Bracelet, Marcasite Links, Flexible, Carnelian Center, 7 In.Long 75.00
Jewelry, Bracelet, Mesh Slide, Victorian, Pearls 45.00
Jewelry, Bracelet, Nephrite, Relief Kylins, Mottled Brown & White 75.00
Jewelry, Bracelet, Siberian Amethyst, Engraved Snake Outline, Ruby Eyes 165.00
Jewelry, Bracelet, Spider Web Blue Diamond Turquoise Stone, Signed F.M. 295.00
Jewelry, Bracelet, Tiger-Eye, Cameo, Gold Filled Mesh, Victorian 52.00
Jewelry, Bracelet, Twin Yellow Gold Bars, Held By 14K Gold Bar 450.00
Jewelry, Brooch & Earring Set, Pinchback, Fringed, C.1830 .... 159.00
Jewelry, Brooch & Earrings, Pietra Dura, Black Stone, White Flowers, Set 195.00
Jewelry, Brooch, Art Nouveau, Enamel Flowers 45.00
Jewelry, Brooch, Art Nouveau, Portrait, Sterling Silver, 2 1/2 X 2 In. 75.00
Jewelry, Brooch, Brass Framed Courtier & Lady, Limoges 28.00
Jewelry, Brooch, Cameo, Filigree Frame, 14K Gold 80.00
Jewelry, Brooch, Cameo, Gold Border Of C-Scrolls, Female Profile, Oval, 1850s 150.00
Jewelry, Brooch, Cameo, Set In Gold, Victorian, 2 1/2 X 1 1/2 In. 115.00
Jewelry, Brooch, Cameo, Shell, Set In Solid Gold, 14K 135.00
Jewelry, Brooch, Cameo, Tri-Color, Wedgwood 35.00
Jewelry, Brooch, Cameo, White, Face Of Josiah Wedgwood, Jasperware, 4 1/2 In. 20.00
Jewelry, Brooch, Cameo, Yellow Gold Mount 45.00
Jewelry, Brooch, Carnelian, Surrounded By Marcasites, Sterling 38.00
Jewelry, Brooch, Carved Ivory Rose, Pierced Border 30.00
Jewelry, Brooch, Garnet, Moon Type With Arrow Across 30.00
Jewelry, Brooch, Gold & Enamel, Alpine Lake Scene, Swiss, C.1840, 1 1/4 In. 500.00
Jewelry, Brooch, Gold Mounting, Blue Jasper, Wedgwood 75.00
Jewelry, Brooch, Gold, Citrine & Enameled, Swiss, C.1840, 3 1/2 In. 900.00
Jewelry, Brooch, Gold, Enamel & Diamond, Scrolled Ribbon, C.1880, 2 In. 1500.00
Jewelry, Brooch, Jade, Enameled Flowers, Sterling Frame, 1 1/4 X 1 1/2 In. 200.00
Jewelry, Brooch, Oriental Scene, Ivory, Filigree 125.00
Jewelry, Brooch, Portrait, Porcelain, Countess Potocka, Signed, 2 X 1 1/2 In. 110.00
Jewelry, Brooch, Silver Mounting, Blue Jasper, Wedgwood 75.00
Jewelry, Brooch, Tintype, Mustached Man 10.00
Jewelry, Brooch, Wing Spread Peacock, Enameled Body, Feather Ends, 2 In. 65.00
Jewelry, Buckle, B.P.O.E., Sterling With 14K Gold Inlay 20.00
Jewelry, Buckle, Belt, Lady's, Cut Steel 3.00
Jewelry, Buckle, French Paste, Dress, Silver, Oval, 2 1/4 In. 28.00
Jewelry, Buckle, Mother-Of-Pearl, Brass Fittings 10.00
Jewelry, Buckle, Shoe, Cut Steel On Velvet, Pair 7.50
Jewelry, Case, Cigarette, Chrome, Simulated Tortoise Shell 6.50
Jewelry, Chain, Albert, Each Link Hallmarked, 14K Gold 260.00
Jewelry, Chain, Attached Coin & Picture Holder, 18K Gold 265.00
Jewelry, Chain, Braided Hair 37.50
Jewelry, Chain, Custom Linked, 14K Gold, 15 1/2 In. 72.00
Jewelry, Chain, Religious Medal, Cuban, 18K Gold, 25 In. 360.00
Jewelry, Chain, Rope, Art Nouveau, Openwork Pendant, 14K Gold 72.00
Jewelry, Chain, Rope, Brown Enamelled Pear Pendant, 14K Gold 21.00
Jewelry, Chain, Rope, Florentined, Twisted, 14K Gold, 17 1/2 In. 56.00
Jewelry, Chain, Watch, Gold Filled, Bar & Clasp, 11 In. 18.50
Jewelry, Chain, Watch, Handmade, Large Links, English, 9K Gold, 14 1/2 In. 250.00
Jewelry, Chain, Watch, Lady's, Diamond In Slide 36.00
Jewelry, Chain, Watch, Large Link, 14K Solid Gold, 13 1/2 In. 165.00
Jewelry, Chain, Watch, Made Of Hair, Gold Filled Fittings 40.00
Jewelry, Chain, Watch, 1 3/4 In. Match Safe Attached, Hallmarked18 In. 75.00
Jewelry, Chain, Watch, 14K Yellow & White Gold Links, 15 In. 120.00
Jewelry, Charm, Brass Banjo, Mother-Of-Pearl, 1 5/8 In. 7.50
Jewelry, Charm, Prancing Horse, Miniature, 14K Gold 19.00
Jewelry, Charm, Tambourine, Miniature, 14K Gold 15.00

Jewelry, Chatelaine, 3 Filigree Drops, Mirror, Pencil Holder & Pad 88.00
Jewelry, Clip, Clam Shell, Diamond & Rubies, 14K Gold, 1 1/2 In. 500.00
Jewelry, Clip, Fruit & Leaf Design, Oval, Sterling, Georg Jensen, 1 3/4 In. 60.00
Jewelry, Collar Button, Eyes Red Stones, 1900 .... 12.00
Jewelry, Cuff Links, Bride Of The Waves, Unger Brothers 100.00
Jewelry, Cuff Links, Emerald & Shirt Button With Emerald, 14K Gold 85.00
Jewelry, Cuff Links, Enamel, Blue 4 Leaf Clover, Enamel 24.00
Jewelry, Cuff Links, Hieroglyphs Gold Band, Carnelian Scarab Rotating 275.00
Jewelry, Cuff Links, Oval Link Joins, D.S.In Italics, American Gold, Pair 400.00
Jewelry, Earrings, Art Nouveau Woman, Sterling 13.00
Jewelry, Earrings, Emerald, Set In 14K Gold Stud, 1 Carat 175.00
Jewelry, Earrings, Enamelled, English Crystal, Reverse Painting, 18K Gold 150.00
Jewelry, Earrings, Etruscan Style, Dangling Cluster Of Pearl, 14K Gold 49.00
Jewelry, Earrings, Flower Design, Georg Jensen, Denmark 45.00
Jewelry, Earrings, Garnet, Czechoslovakian, Screw Type 26.00
Jewelry, Earrings, Gold Loops, Mounted With 2 Diamonds, C.1880 .... 425.00
Jewelry, Earrings, Gold, Turquoise, Diamond & Pearl, 1 7/8 In. .... *Illus* 2100.00
Jewelry, Earrings, Moonstone Centers, Sterling, Georg Jensen 150.00
Jewelry, Earrings, Rose Diamonds, Emeralds, Sapphires, Georgian 220.00
Jewelry, Earrings, Tassel, 28K Gold 64.00
Jewelry, Earrings, Wedgwood, Jasper, Screw-Type 85.00
Jewelry, Flip Ring, Cameo On One Side, 1939 On Other, 14K Gold 95.00
Jewelry, Fob Chain, Pink Gold Heart With 3 Pearls, 14K Gold 69.00
Jewelry, Garnet Set, Lavalier & Screw Back Earrings, 1800s, Seed Pearls 475.00
Jewelry, Hatpin, Gold, Enameled Flowers & Leaves 225.00
     Jewelry, Indian, see Indian
Jewelry, Ivory Rose, 14K Gold Chain 25.00
Jewelry, Locket, Blue Sapphire One Side, Monogram, E.J.B., Other Side, Fold 55.00
Jewelry, Locket, Coral In Gold Front, Matching Bale, 18K Gold 160.00
Jewelry, Locket, Gold, Enamel, Diamond, C.1890 .... *Illus* 850.00
Jewelry, Lorgnette, Art Nouveau, Scrolled & Embossed, 14K Gold, 7 1/2 In. 400.00
Jewelry, Lorgnette, Scrolled & Engraved, French Sterling 90.00
Jewelry, Necklace, Amber, Cherry, 12 In. 50.00
Jewelry, Necklace, Choker, Coral & Copper Luster, 3 Strand 35.00
Jewelry, Necklace, Gold & Turquoise, Austrian, C.1850, Matching Brooch 700.00
Jewelry, Necklace, Gold Ropework, Pearls & Diamonds Mounts, C.1880 .... 800.00
Jewelry, Necklace, Gold Ropework, 7 Carnelian Intaglios, C.1865 .... 3200.00
Jewelry, Necklace, Italian Cameo, Separates To Make 2 Bracelets 245.00
Jewelry, Necklace, Ivory, Carved Elephants, Lace Balls 65.00
Jewelry, Necklace, Silver, Turquoise, Coral, Agate, Mandarin, 30 In. 40.00
Jewelry, Necklace, Squash Blossom, Blue Turquoise, Navajo 400.00
Jewelry, Pearls, Oriental, Tiffany Mounted 45.00
Jewelry, Pendant & Chain, Art Nouveau Woman, Sterling 13.00
Jewelry, Pendant & Chain, Parrot On Perch, Sterling 16.00
Jewelry, Pendant & Chain, Woman With Wand, Art Nouveau, Sterling 15.00
Jewelry, Pendant Locket, Gold, Enamel, Oriental Style, Falize, French, 1865 ..... 2300.00
Jewelry, Pendant, Aquamarine, Pear-Shaped Bezel Drop, Victorian, 2 Carats 165.00
Jewelry, Pendant, Art Nouveau Silver, French, Enamel, 1900s .... *Illus* 275.00
Jewelry, Pendant, Cameo, Amber, Surrounded By Seed Pearls 75.00
Jewelry, Pendant, Diamond Heart, Chain, 16 Diamonds, 14K White Gold 165.00
Jewelry, Pendant, Foo Dog, Jade 90.00
Jewelry, Pendant, Gold & Turquoise, Art Nouveau, C.1910 .... *Illus* 375.00
Jewelry, Pendant, Gold Horseshoe, 12 Pearls & 1 Diamond, Victorian 55.00
Jewelry, Pendant, Gold, Enamel, Amethyst & Pearl Pendant .... *Illus* 2800.00
Jewelry, Pendant, Ivory, Carved Rose, 2 In.Diameter 28.00
Jewelry, Pendant, Jade, Carved, Handmade Silver Chain, 20 In. 125.00
Jewelry, Pendant, Jet, 3 1/4 In. 25.00
Jewelry, Pendant, Pear Shaped Garnet, Gold Frame, 14K Gold 26.00
Jewelry, Pendant, Shell Carved Cameo, Solid Gold Frame, Heavy Rope Chain ... 185.00
Jewelry, Pin & Earrings, Chinese Mutton Fat Jade, Carved, Enameling, C.1880 ... 600.00
Jewelry, Pin & Earrings, Coral, Victorian 150.00
Jewelry, Pin, Art Nouveau, Floral Form, Gold, 1 In. 85.00
Jewelry, Pin, Art Nouveau, 14K Flower, 9 Pearls, 8 Diamonds 100.00
Jewelry, Pin, Bar, Filigree, 3 Diamonds, 14K Gold & Platinum 55.00
Jewelry, Pin, Bar, Filigree, 3 Diamonds, 18K Gold 160.00
Jewelry, Pin, Bar, Oval Golden Topaz, English, 9K Gold 42.00

Jewelry, Earrings, Gold, Turquoise,
Diamond & Pearl, 1 7/8 In.
(See Page 251)

Jewelry, Locket, Gold, Enamel,
Diamond, C.1890
(See Page 251)

Jewelry, Pendant, Gold,
Enamel, Amethyst & Pearl Pendant
(See Page 251)

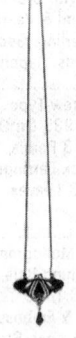

Jewelry, Pendant. Art Nouveau
Silver, French, Enamel, 1900s
(See Page 251)

Jewelry, Pendant, Gold
Turquoise, Art Nouveau, C.19
(See Page 251)

Jewelry, Pin, Bar, Victorian, 5 Blue Moonstones, 14K Gold	45.00
Jewelry, Pin, Bar, 2 Rows Garnets, Gold On Silver	155.00
Jewelry, Pin, Bird Design, Open Work, Sterling, Georg Jensen, 1 1/2 In.	90.00
Jewelry, Pin, Bow Knot, 14K Gold, 1940s, 1 3/4 In.	125.00
Jewelry, Pin, Cameo, Carnelian, Florentined, 14K Gold	60.00
Jewelry, Pin, Carved Carnelian, Oval Carved, Pierced Floral Spray	35.00
Jewelry, Pin, Carved Jade, Gold Mount	45.00
Jewelry, Pin, Cinnabar, Marked China, Oblong	15.00
Jewelry, Pin, Circle, 4 Diamonds & 4 Sapphires, White Gold	350.00
Jewelry, Pin, Double Horseshoe, Turquoises Set In Sterling Silver	25.00
Jewelry, Pin, Fish Design, 2 Porpoises, Sterling, Georg Jensen, 1 1/2 In.	150.00
Jewelry, Pin, Floral Design, Oval, Sterling, Georg Jensen, 2 In.	45.00
Jewelry, Pin, Hair, Damascene, 4 1/2 In.	33.00
Jewelry, Pin, Horseshoe, Bohemian Garnets, 11 Rose Cut Garnets	59.00
Jewelry, Pin, Ivory & Mosaic, 1 1/4 In.Diameter	17.50
Jewelry, Pin, Ladies Of The Maccabees, 6 Female Pictures	15.00
Jewelry, Pin, Lady's, Art Nouveau, Sterling	65.00
Jewelry, Pin, LaFollette & Wheeler Picture, Bronze	9.50
Jewelry, Pin, Mosaic, St.Peter's Basilica & Square In Rome, Onyx & Silver	265.00
Jewelry, Pin, Scimitar, Separates From Scabbard, Chain Connected, Sterling	110.00
Jewelry, Pin, Wishbone Shape, Ruby In Center, 14K Gold, 1 1/8 In.	29.00
Jewelry, Pin, 2 Twisted-Work Bars, Crescent Woven, 15K Gold, Hallmarked	35.00
Jewelry, Ring, Art Deco, Ox-Blood Coral, 15K Gold Bezel	49.00
Jewelry, Ring, Art Nouveau, Cabochon Triangular Garnet, 14K Gold	175.00
Jewelry, Ring, Bumble Bee, Atop Branch, Sterling	9.00
Jewelry, Ring, Cameo, 2 Faces, Victorian, Yellow Gold	80.00
Jewelry, Ring, Center Diamond, Sapphire Baguettes, Victorian, 18K Gold	75.00
Jewelry, Ring, Cluster, Diamond & Enamel, Victorian, 14K Gold	350.00
Jewelry, Ring, Coral & Rose Diamond, Early French, Yellow Gold	150.00

Jewelry, Ring, Gold, Enamel,
Diamond & Pink Topaz, 1800s, 7/8 In.

Jewelry, Ring, Czechoslovakian Amber, Raised Setting, Sterling, Hallmarked	95.00
Jewelry, Ring, Diamond Shape Setting, Art Deco, 18K Platinum	350.00
Jewelry, Ring, Erotic, Menage-A-Trois Scene, 14K Gold	170.00
Jewelry, Ring, Florentined Rose, Center Pearl, 14K Gold	65.00
Jewelry, Ring, Garnet, Victorian Setting, 12 Stones, 14K Yellow Gold	450.00
Jewelry, Ring, Gold Accents, Center Mine Cut Diamond, Victorian, 14K Gold	59.00
Jewelry, Ring, Gold Filigree, Emerald Set, 18K Gold	42.00
Jewelry, Ring, Gold, Enamel, Diamond & Pink Topaz, 1800s, 7/8 In. _____ *Illus*	1200.00
Jewelry, Ring, Hair, Cross On Top, Pearls In Center, 14K Gold, Set Of 3	85.00
Jewelry, Ring, Lady's, White On Black Cameo, Victorian, 10K Gold	50.00
Jewelry, Ring, Love With Diamond, 14K Gold	13.00
Jewelry, Ring, Man's, Persian Turquoise, Victorian, Hallmarked	70.00
Jewelry, Ring, Onyx & Angel Skin Coral Cameo, Yellow Gold	105.00
Jewelry, Ring, Pierced & Engraved Mounting 3 Garnets, Victorian, 14K Gold	75.00
Jewelry, Ring, Pouting Face Of Bulldog, Sterling	13.00
Jewelry, Ring, Princess, 19 Diamonds, 14K Gold	525.00
Jewelry, Ring, Rectangle Of Imperial Jade, Filigree Setting, Engraved	175.00
Jewelry, Ring, Remington Arms Co., 25 Years Loyal Service, 10K Gold	75.00
Jewelry, Ring, Rose Cut Garnet, Yellow Gold Deco Mount	40.00
Jewelry, Ring, Snake Coiled In 5 Bands, Oval Turquoise In Head, 14K Gold	89.00
Jewelry, Ring, Snake, Ruby Eyes, 14K Gold	49.00
Jewelry, Ring, Squirrel Eating Nut, Sterling	13.00
Jewelry, Ring, Tiffany Set, 15 Pt.Mine Cut Diamond, Victorian, 14K Gold	69.00
Jewelry, Ring, Wedding, Hair In Center, 14K Gold	75.00
Jewelry, Ring, White Gold Filigree Mount, Large Bloodstone	48.00
Jewelry, Ring, 3 Blue Moonstones, Victorian, 14K Gold	65.00
Jewelry, Ring, 3 Peridots, 4 Rose Diamonds, 14K Yellow Gold	55.00
Jewelry, Ring, 4 Emeralds Set In Ornate Ball, 18K Yellow Gold, 7 1/2 In.	200.00
Jewelry, Ring, 7 Rose Diamonds, Victorian, 14K Yellow Gold	185.00
Jewelry, Slide, Opal, Engraved, 14K Gold	28.00
Jewelry, Slide, Openwork, Center Emerald, 14K Gold	29.00
Jewelry, Stickpin, Bicycle	8.00
Jewelry, Stickpin, Bird Holding Garnet, 14K Gold	38.00
Jewelry, Stickpin, Butterfly Set With 7 Opals, 14K Gold	36.00
Jewelry, Stickpin, Cabochon Milano Citrine, White Enamel, 14K Gold	35.00
Jewelry, Stickpin, Cameo, Pink Coral, Woman's Head, 4 Pearls, Solid Gold	28.00
Jewelry, Stickpin, Carved Amethyst Flower, Diamond Center, 14K Gold	55.00
Jewelry, Stickpin, Cluster Of 7 Garnets, 14K Gold	36.00
Jewelry, Stickpin, Crescent With Bird, Diamond & Seed Pearls, 14K Gold	45.00
Jewelry, Stickpin, Figural Soldier With Helmet	25.00
Jewelry, Stickpin, Frame Around Moonstone, 14K Yellow Gold	45.00
Jewelry, Stickpin, Gold Butterfly, Emerald In Center, 14K Gold	28.00
Jewelry, Stickpin, Gold Horseshoe, 14K Gold	24.00
Jewelry, Stickpin, Gold Turtle, Garnet Eyes, 1/2 X 3/4 In.	58.00
Jewelry, Stickpin, Goldplate Wishbone, Genuine Opal	12.00
Jewelry, Stickpin, Horseshoe & 4 Leaf Clover, 14K Pink Gold	32.00
Jewelry, Stickpin, Jeweled Floral Spray, Sapphire & Ruby On Each Side	65.00
Jewelry, Stickpin, John Deere	14.00
Jewelry, Stickpin, Leaf With Green Scarab, 14K Gold	35.00
Jewelry, Stickpin, Libby	6.00
Jewelry, Stickpin, Marquise Cut Amethyst, 14K Gold	30.00
Jewelry, Stickpin, Mexican Opal	35.00
Jewelry, Stickpin, Moline Plow	7.50
Jewelry, Stickpin, Mosaic Of Dog With Ball, 14K Gold, 3/4 In.Oval	125.00
Jewelry, Stickpin, Opal	15.00
Jewelry, Stickpin, Opal With Blue Fire, 1/2 X 3/4 In.	35.00
Jewelry, Stickpin, Pearl Set In Openwork, 10K Gold, 3/8 In.Diameter	32.00
Jewelry, Stickpin, Pink Enamel Flower With Pearl, 10K Gold	26.00
Jewelry, Stickpin, Pinwheel, Small Diamond, 14K Gold	34.00

Jewelry, Stickpin, Rumely Plow, Advertisement	9.00
Jewelry, Stickpin, Swan, 14K Gold	24.00
Jewelry, Stickpin, Swastika, Green, Enamel	8.00
Jewelry, Stickpin, Teddy Bear	8.00
Jewelry, Stickpin, Tiger Eye, Tiny Pearl, 14K Gold	30.00
Jewelry, Stickpin, Winchester Shotgun Shell	25.00
Jewelry, Stickpin, Woman's Head On Blue, Bisque	45.00
Jewelry, Stickpin, 8 Seed Pearls In Square, Diamond In Center, 14K Gold	100.00
Jewelry, Stud, C.1739, , Muller, Sterling, 7/8 In.Square	225.00
Jewelry, Stud, Collar, Lady's, Enameled With Turquoise Stones	14.00
Jewelry, Tie Bar, Fox Head In Center, Ruby Eyes, Gold, 1 7/8 In.	150.00
Jewelry, Tie Pin, Indian, Motorcycle, Indian's Head	22.50
Jewelry, Tie Pin, Saw, Power Saw Blade, Hand Saw, Silver, Atkins	20.00
Jewelry, Toothpick, Retractable, Gold	60.00
Jewelry, Watch, see Watch	

John Rogers statues were made from 1859 to 1892. The originals were bronze, but the thousands of copies made by the Rogers Factory were of painted plaster. Eighty different figures were made.

John Rogers, Chess, Gray-Brown, 21 1/4 In.	700.00
John Rogers, Group, Picket Guard, 2nd Version, 14 1/2 In.	300.00
Judaica, Candelabrum, Hanukkah Menorah, Porcelain, 5 X 8 1/4 X 4 1/2 In.	225.00
Judaica, Candelabrum, Lions, Star Of David, Oil Burning, 9 X 8 1/2 In.	425.00
Judaica, Cup, Kiddush, Russian, Silver, 1909, 2 1/2 In.	55.00
Judaica, Figurine, Studying Of Talmud, Ivory, Billiard Ball Size	165.00
Judaica, Lamp, Whale Oil, Rabbi's, 2 Spouts, Saucer Base, Brass, 11 1/2 In.	60.00
Judaica, Menorah, Star Of David, Lions, Sterling, Oil Burning, 8 X 9 In.	400.00
Judaica, Menorah, 7-Branch, Brass, 17 In.	75.00
Judaica, Spice Holder, Castle, 4 Turrets, Sterling, 7 In.	250.00
Judaica, Spice Holder, Pyramid Form With Flags, Sterling, 7 In.	150.00
Judaica, Spice Holder, Round Turret, 7 In.	170.00
Judaica, Spice Holder, 4 Small, 1 Large Tower, Doors, Silver, 7 In.	260.00
Judaica, Spice Holder, 6 Sided Turret, Flying Flags, Hinged Door, 8 1/2 In.	250.00
Judaica, Triptych, Carved Ivory, Feasts Of Tabernacle, Blessing Children	175.00

Jugtown pottery refers to pottery made in North Carolina as far back as the 1750s. In 1915 Juliana and Jacques Busbee set up a training and sales organization for what they named Jugtown Pottery. In 1921 they built a shop at Jugtown, North Carolina, and hired Ben Owen as a potter in 1923. The Busbees moved the Village Store where the pottery was sold and promoted to 37 East Sixtieth Street in New York City. Juliana Busbee sold the New York store in 1926 and moved into a log cabin near the Jugtown Pottery. The pottery ended production in 1958.

Jugtown, Inkwell, Mottled Blue, 3 In.	22.00
Jugtown, Pitcher, Pinch Spout, Brown & Green, Signed, 8 In.	75.00
Jugtown, Vase, White Glaze, Marked, 6 In.	17.00
Jummel, Box, Candy, Joyful, No.111/53, Full Bee, 6 In.	165.00

Kate Greenaway, who was a famous illustrator of children's books, drew pictures of children in high-waisted Empire dresses. She lived from about 1846 to 1901. Her designs appear on china, glass, and other pieces.

Kate Greenaway, Bell & Teething Ring, Ivory	45.00
Kate Greenaway, Book, Alphabet, 2 1/2 X 2 3/4 In.	45.00
Kate Greenaway, Book, Pictures & Rhymes, Color, Under The Window	50.00
Kate Greenaway, Cup & Saucer, Brown, Girls	65.00
Kate Greenaway, Doll, Soap	6.00
Kate Greenaway, Fan, Children Skipping Rope, Shuttle Cock, Blind Man's Bluff	55.00
Kate Greenaway, Figurine, Boy, Basket, Royal Worcester, 9 3/8 X 4 3/8 In.	495.00
Kate Greenaway, Figurine, Girl & Boy, Porcelain, 7 X 5 In., Pair	119.00
Kate Greenaway, Figurine, Grandma & Grandpa, Pair, Germany	89.00
Kate Greenaway, Figurine, 2 Standing Girls, Long Dresses, Hats, Bisque, 6 In.	85.00
Kate Greenaway, Inkwell, Two Figures On Reticulated Base, Bronze	180.00
Kate Greenaway, Match Holder, Slippers, Boy & Girl, Pair	139.00
Kate Greenaway, Napkin Ring, Figural, Boy & Dog Under Ring, Mother	190.00
Kate Greenaway, Napkin Ring, Figural, Infant	200.00
Kate Greenaway, Napkin Ring, Girl Standing In Front Of Ring	115.00

Kate Greenaway, Plate, Boy & Girl Playing Ball, Bramble, Wedgwood, 14 In. 65.00
Kate Greenaway, Plate, Bread, Seesaw, Frosted 75.00
Kate Greenaway, Plate, Cake, Hand-Painted, C.1884, Doulton, 8 3/4 In.Diameter 95.00
Kate Greenaway, Salt & Pepper, Boy & Girl In Period Clothing, Pair 85.00
Kate Greenaway, Salt & Pepper, Girl In Bonnet, Boy In Top Hat, 3 1/8 In.Pr. 50.00
Kate Greenaway, Salt, Figural, Hand Painted 28.00
Kate Greenaway, Saltshaker, Boy In Double Breasted Coat, 4 1/2 In. 33.00
Kate Greenaway, Saltshaker, Girl, Crossed Arms, Wicker Carrier, 3 1/4 In. 27.00
Kate Greenaway, Shaker, Salt, Girl 22.50

*Kauffmann refers to the type work done by Angelica Kauffmann, a painter
and decorative artist for Adam Brothers in England between 1766 and 1781.
She designed small-scale pictorial subjects in the neoclassic manner. Most
porcelains signed Kauffmann were made in the nineteenth century.*

Kauffmann, Bowl, Gold, Green, Scenic, Austria, Beehive, 5 1/4 In., Pair 55.00
Kauffmann, Bowl, Portrait, Sleeping Maiden & Cupid, Signed, 13 In.Diameter 38.00
Kauffmann, Cup & Saucer, Allegorical Scene, Crown & No.302 Mark, Pair 23.00
Kauffmann, Cup & Saucer, Scenic, Signed, Marked Crown, Set 23.00
Kauffmann, Cup & Saucer, 4 Ladies In Garden, Signed 35.00
Kauffmann, Jar, 4-Panel, Maidens & Cupid, Each Signed, Gold Tracery, Marked 45.00
Kauffmann, Plate, Greek Scene, 7 In. 20.00
Kauffmann, Plate, Hanging, Blue Border, Gold Design, Beehive Mark, 10 In. 85.00
Kauffmann, Plate, Maidens & Cupids, Green Border, Gold Trim, 8 5/8 In. 15.00
Kauffmann, Plate, Portrait, Cobalt Blue Border, Signed, 8 1/2 In. 45.00
Kauffmann, Plate, Scalloped Gold Edge, Lover's Scene, Signed, Beehive, 8 In. 89.00
Kauffmann, Vase, Bud, Handles, 7 1/2 In. 25.00
Kauffmann, Vase, Bulbous, Footed, Signed, 4 1/2 In. 25.00
Kauffmann, Vase, Carlsbad, 3 Women With Cherub, Bulbous, 10 1/2 In. 75.00
Kauffmann, Vase, Portrait Of 2 Maidens & Man, Signed, 16 In. 68.00
Kayserzinn; see Pewter

KELVA *Kelva glassware was made by the C.F. Monroe Company of Meriden,
Connecticut, about 1904. It is a pale pastel painted glass decorated with
flowers, designs, or scenes.*

Kelva, Box, Cigar, Lettering In Gold, Moisture Fixture In Lid, Signed 425.00
Kelva, Box, Jewel, Roses On Green Leaves, Signed, 7 In.Diameter 350.00
Kelva, Box, Jewel, White Daisies, Peach Ground, Signed, 7 In.Diameter 535.00
Kelva, Box, Open, Green & Pink Flowers, 6 In.Diameter 125.00
Kelva, Box, Ring, Hand-Painted, Silk Lined, Blue, 4 In. 175.00
Kelva, Box, 8 Sided, Flowers, Metal Around Rim, Signed, 4 1/2 In. 100.00
Kelva, Humidor, Mottled Green, Azaleas, Signed 375.00
Kelva, Vase, Apricot Color, Ormolu Footed Base & Collar, Marked, 17 In. 450.00
Kelva, Vase, Bronze Feet & Handles, Pink Ground, 10 1/2 In. 275.00
Kelva, Vase, Mottled Apricot, Silver Rim, Signed, 8 In. 175.00
Kelva, Vase, Ormolu Handles & Base, Apricot, 9 In. 180.00
Kelva, Vase, Spongeware Blue, Pink, Ormolu Base, 8 1/2 In. 225.00

*Kemple glass was made by John Kemple of East Palestine, Ohio, and
Kenova, West Virginia, from 1945 to 1970. The glass was made from old
molds. Many designs and colors were made. Kemple pieces are usually
marked with a K on the bottom.*

Kemple, Box, Dresser 12.00
Kemple, Compote, Small 12.00
Kemple, Match Holder, Indian 12.00
Keramic Club, Vase, Bisque Exterior, Green Interior, Signed, 1891, 7 In. 395.00

*Kew blas is the name used by the Union Glass Company of Somerville,
Massachusetts. The name refers to an iridescent golden glass made from the
1890s to 1924.*

Kew Blas, Candlestick, Iridescent Gold, Twisted Stem, Signed, 10 In., Pair 550.00
Kew Blas, Candlestick, Swirled Stem, Signed, Pair, 8 In. 425.00
Kew Blas, Glass, Wine, Bowl Widens Then Narrows, Signed, 5 In. 125.00
Kew Blas, Rose Bowl, Orange Speckled Body, Green Pulls, Signed, 3 1/2 In. 510.00
Kew Blas, Vase, Bowl Shape, Orange Iridescent, King Tut, Signed, 4 1/4 In. 675.00
Kew Blas, Vase, Gold Lily, Pink, Triangular Top, Signed & Labeled, 10 In. 375.00
Kew Blas, Vase, Gold Lily, Triangular Top, Forms Lip, Signed, 10 In. 375.00

Kewpies were first pictured in the 'Ladies' Home Journal' by Rose O'Neill. The pixielike figures became an immediate success, and Kewpie dolls started appearing in 1911. Kewpie pictures and other items soon followed.

Kewpie, Bank, Figural Kewpie, Marked, Glass	55.00
Kewpie, Bank, Tin Lid, Glass	65.00
Kewpie, Book, Love Of Edway, Rose O'Neill	16.00
Kewpie, Bowl, Cereal, 6 Action Kewpies, Marked, 6 In.	85.00
Kewpie, Bowl, Mug, Plate, Divided, Kewpies In Action, Set	110.00
Kewpie, Bowl, 8 Kewpies, Signed, Royal Rudolstadt, Relief Star	138.00
Kewpie, Cameo, Rubber, 10 In.	25.00
Kewpie, Candy Container, Bank Form, Kewpie Next To Barrel	85.00
Kewpie, Card, Christmas, Signed	12.00
Kewpie, Creamer, Jasperware, Blue, Signed O'Neill	125.00
Kewpie, Creamer, Kewpies Front & Back, Signed Royal Rudalstadt, 4 3/4 In.	75.00
Kewpie, Creamer, Rose O'Neill, 4 Kewpies On Front & 3 On Back, 2 1/2 In.	195.00
Kewpie, Cup & Saucer, Boat Scene, Signed Rudolstadt	65.00
Kewpie, Cup & Saucer, Rose O'Neill, Child's	50.00
Kewpie, Cup & Saucer, Royal Rudolstadt, Rose O'Neill	125.00
Kewpie, Dish, Feeding	30.00
Kewpie, Dish, Feeding, Royal Rudolstadt	225.00
Kewpie, Doll, Bisque, Bride & Groom, Pair	5.50
Kewpie, Doll, Bisque, Free Standing, Blue Wings, 4 1/2 In.	2.00
Kewpie, Doll, Bisque, Free Standing, Jointed Arms, Blue Wings, 5 In.	3.00
Kewpie, Doll, Bisque, On Chain, 2 1/2 In.	200.00
Kewpie, Doll, Bisque, Signed Rose O'Neill, 5 1/2 In.	45.00
Kewpie, Doll, Bisque, Signed, 5 In.	125.00
Kewpie, Doll, Bisque, 11 In.	485.00
Kewpie, Doll, Black Cloth Body, 14 In.	80.00
Kewpie, Doll, Blue Wings, Bisque, Signed O'Neill, 2 1/4 In.	48.00
Kewpie, Doll, Blue Wings, Eyes Right, Moveable Arms, Signed O'Neill, 8 In.	140.00
Kewpie, Doll, Blunder 600 On Slab, Signed, 3 1/4 In.	350.00
Kewpie, Doll, Bride & Groom, Attached, Original Clothes, 2 In.	85.00
Kewpie, Doll, Bride, Moveable Arms, Dressed, Rose O'Neill Label, 8 In.	385.00
Kewpie, Doll, Celluloid, Green Wings, 1936, 3 In.	8.00
Kewpie, Doll, Composition Body, Bisque, Nippon, 7 3/4 In.	75.00
Kewpie, Doll, Composition, Jointed, Dressed In Original Sun Suit	45.00
Kewpie, Doll, Dish, Candy, No.2862	100.00
Kewpie, Doll, Flannel Square, R.O'Neill	25.00
Kewpie, Doll, Holding Cover Over Front, Blue Wings, Bisque, Numbered, 5 In.	62.00
Kewpie, Doll, Hugger-Lovers, Bisque, 3 5/8 In.	110.00
Kewpie, Doll, Huggers, 2 1/4 In.	250.00
Kewpie, Doll, Huggers, 3 1/4 In.	95.00
Kewpie, Doll, Jointed Legs & Arms, Dressed, Composition	65.00
Kewpie, Doll, Lying On Stomach, Signed, 3 1/2 In.	350.00
Kewpie, Doll, Moveable Arms, All Bisque, Signed, O'Neill, 7 In.	150.00
Kewpie, Doll, Sitting On Name Tag, Playing Mandolin, 2 In.	175.00
Kewpie, Doll, Sitting, Holding Rose, 1 1/2 In.	175.00
Kewpie, Doll, Sitting, Holding Rose, 2 In.	350.00
Kewpie, Doll, Sitting, Signed, Rose O'Neill, 5 1/2 In.	145.00
Kewpie, Doll, Standing, Arms Up, 2 In.	75.00
Kewpie, Doll, Standing, Signed Fulper, Made In U.S.A., 9 In.	1200.00
Kewpie, Doll, The Thinker, Signed Rose O'Neill, 6 In.	195.00
Kewpie, Doll, The Thinker, Signed Rose O'Neill, 6 1/4 In.	195.00
Kewpie, Doll, Winged, Standing, Moveable Arms, Bisque, Signed, 4 3/4 In.	85.00
Kewpie, Doll, With Italian Soldier Cap, Signed, 2 1/4 In.	500.00
Kewpie, Doodle Dog, Bisque, Signed, 5 In.	2000.00
Kewpie, Figurine, Seated On Chair, Bronze, 3 1/4 In.	150.00
Kewpie, Flannel, Clipping The Top Knott, Rose O'Neill	18.50
Kewpie, Flannel, Playing Soldier, Rose O'Neill	18.50
Kewpie, Flannel, Wag Riding A Fish, Rose O'Neill	18.50
Kewpie, Hair Receiver, Signed Rose O'Neill	75.00
Kewpie, Hatpin Holder, Blue Jasperware, Signed Rose O'Neill	185.00
Kewpie, Hatpin Holder, Green Jasper, 3 Pink Kewpies, Signed Rose O'Neill	200.00
Kewpie, Jar, Powder, Signed Rose O'Neill	75.00
Kewpie, Lamp, Thinker, Fringe Shade, Chalkware	37.50

Kewpie, Napkin	4.00
Kewpie, Pitcher, Cream, Luster, Signed Rose O'Neill, 2 3/4 In.	75.00
Kewpie, Pitcher, Jasper, 4 Action Kewpies, Signed Rose O'Neill, 4 1/4 In.	225.00
Kewpie, Planter, Blue	4.00
Kewpie, Planter, Blue, White & Pink	65.00
Kewpie, Plate, Feeding, Rose O'Neill, Milk Glass, 8 In.	75.00
Kewpie, Plate, Playing Instruments, Marked Royal Rudolstadt, Prussia	75.00
Kewpie, Plate, 6 Kewpies Hand-Painted, White Ground, Royal Rudolstadt, 7 In.	25.00
Kewpie, Postcard, Atop Haystack	18.00
Kewpie, Postcard, 2 In Wicker Basket	28.00
Kewpie, Poster, Handler's Ice Cream, Signed R. O'Neill, 18 X 7 3/8 In.	75.00
Kewpie, Salt & Pepper, Pink, China, Japan, 2 In.	25.00
Kewpie, Salt & Pepper, Sterling, Japan, 2 1/4 In.	175.00
Kewpie, Stickpin, Sterling Silver, 2 1/8 In.	10.50
Kewpie, Stickpin, Sterling, 1 In.	10.50
Kewpie, Tally Card, Rose O'Neill	15.00
Kewpie, Thimble	5.00
Kewpie, Toothpick Holder, Clear	65.00
Kewpie, Tray, Ice Cream, Kewpie With Tray, Signed, 11 1/2 X 17 1/2 In.	155.00
Kewpie, Tray, Velvet Ice Cream, Tin, 12 X 13 1/2 In.Square	90.00
Kewpie, Tray, 12 Kewpies Picking Blackberries, Signed, Rose O'Neill, C.1920	225.00
Kewpie, Vase, Blue & White, 2 Handled, 4 Kewpies, Signed R. O'Neill	95.00
King's Rose, see Soft Paste	
Kitchen, see also Iron, Store, Tool, Wooden	
Kitchen, Apple, Peeler, see Kitchen, Peeler, Apple	
Kitchen, Barrel, Salt, Wooden Rings, 27 In.	32.50
Kitchen, Basket, Egg, 8 X 6 In.	20.00
Kitchen, Beater, Egg, Pushup & Down Ratchet, 4 Blades, Tin	22.50
Kitchen, Board, Bread, Word Bread Carved, 12 In.Diameter	35.00
Kitchen, Board, Dough, Hand-Hewn, Wooden, 21 X 12 1/2 In.	45.00
Kitchen, Board, Kraut Cutting, Cherry, Heart Cutout In Arched Top	95.00
Kitchen, Board, Pie, Paddle Shaped, Round, One Piece Walnut, 14 X 19 In.	38.00
Kitchen, Board, Pie, Round, 12 Sided	35.00
Kitchen, Board, Slaw, Hard Wood, 9 X 21 In.	28.00
Kitchen, Bowl, Butter, Wood, Apples & Tree Limbs Carved Inside & Out, 10 In.	59.00
Kitchen, Bowl, Chopping, Handled, Oblong, Hand Hewn Wood, 5 X 1k X 25 In.	150.00
Kitchen, Bowl, Dough, Handmade, C.1850, Spoon, 17 X 12 In.	52.50
Kitchen, Bowl, Dough, Maple & Burl, One Piece Turned Wood, 22 In.Diameter	295.00
Kitchen, Box, Donut, Original Yellow Paint, Penna., Origin, 10 In.Diam.	290.00
Kitchen, Box, Knife, Center Grip Handle, Handmade, 9 1/2 X 2 1/2 In.	30.00
Kitchen, Box, Pantry, Figs, Lapped With Nails, Wood Pegs, Oval, 3 X 4 1/2 In.	24.00
Kitchen, Box, Salt, Hanging, Dovetailed Pine	55.00
Kitchen, Box, Salt, Hanging, Hinged Wood Cover, German	49.00
Kitchen, Box, Salt, Hanging, Wooden Lid, Pottery, Germany	40.00
Kitchen, Box, Salt, Slant Front, C.1830, 5 1/2 X 5 1/2 X 7 1/4 In.	75.00
Kitchen, Box, Spice, Round, Japanned, Gold Trim, Set Of 6	25.00
Kitchen, Bread Board, Grooved Rim, 9 1/2 In.Diameter	16.00
Kitchen, Breadmaker, Tabletop, Universal, Tin	16.00
Kitchen, Broiler, American, C.1790	75.00
Kitchen, Broiler, Rotating, European, C.1820	210.00
Kitchen, Broom, Hand Hewn, Birch Splint, 18th Century, 16 In.	75.00
Kitchen, Bucket, Apple Butter, Handle, Lid, Wooden	45.00
Kitchen, Bucket, Mincemeat, Cover	32.00
Kitchen, Bucket, Salt, Lid	30.00
Kitchen, Bucket, Wooden, Covered, Metal Banding, Bail Handle	28.00
Kitchen, Butter, Mold, see Kitchen, Mold, Butter	
Kitchen, Canister Set, Assorted Spices, 6 Piece	18.50
Kitchen, Canister Set, Cobalt Blue, Windmills, German Lettering, 6 Piece	75.00
Kitchen, Carrier, Pie, Wood Handle, Amish, 5 Pie Capacity	80.00
Kitchen, Cherry, Pitter, see Kitchen, Pitter, Cherry	
Kitchen, Chest, Flour, 2 Section, Sliding Breadboard, Rolling Pin, Pine	150.00
Kitchen, Chest, Spice, 11 Drawers, Molded Fronts, 15 X 14 X 9 1/2 In.	195.00
Kitchen, Chipper, Potato, All In One Tool, Cored, Peeled, C.1893	12.50
Kitchen, Chopper, Food, Crescent Shaped, Tiger Maple Crossbar Handle, Iron	20.00
Kitchen, Chopper, Food, Iron, Wood Handle	12.50
Kitchen, Chopper, Food, Keen Kutter	8.00

Kitchen, Chopper, Food, Wrought Iron, Moon Blade, 6 1/2 In.	9.00
Kitchen, Chopper, Meat, Enterprise, Patent, April 13, 1886	20.00
Kitchen, Chopper, Right Angle Handled, Hand Forged Iron	30.00
Kitchen, Churn, Butter, Barrel Type, The Favorite	89.00
Kitchen, Churn, Butter, Barrel, Hawthorn	125.00
Kitchen, Churn, Butter, Glass, Daisy	22.50
Kitchen, Churn, Butter, Red Wing	79.00
Kitchen, Churn, Cedar, Tall	185.00
Kitchen, Churn, Crank, Tin, 2 Gallon	35.00
Kitchen, Churn, Daisy, Red Ovate Gear Box, 1 Gallon	30.00
Kitchen, Churn, Daisy, 1/2 Gallon	25.00
Kitchen, Churn, Dasher, Tin, Wooden Dasher, 5 1/4 In.Diameter	85.00
Kitchen, Churn, Dazey, Square, Tin, Cast Iron Flywheel	35.00
Kitchen, Churn, Oak Stave, Dasher, 44 X 11 In.Diameter	160.00
Kitchen, Churn, Red Enamel, Gear Box, Daisy, 1 Gallon	32.50
Kitchen, Churn, Round, Wooden Paddles, Tin	32.00
Kitchen, Churn, Treadle Dog, 2 Sections, Treadle, Arm Connector	360.00
Kitchen, Churn, Wood, Brass Bands, 18 In.	95.00
Kitchen, Churn, Wood, 10 Gallon	140.00
Kitchen, Cleaver, Meat, Incised Fish Scales, Initialed M.K., Brass	175.00
Kitchen, Cleaver, Single Blade, U-Shaped Clamp, 7 1/2 X 8 X 2 In.	35.00
Kitchen, Coffee Container, Attached Dispenser, China, Hall	20.00
Kitchen, Coffee Grinder, see Coffee Grinder	
Kitchen, Colander, Copper, Long Handles	15.00
Kitchen, Colander, Green Outside, White Inside	20.00
Kitchen, Corker, Bottle, Plunger, Brass Fittings, Maple, 11 In.	28.00
Kitchen, Corkscrew, Figural, Scottie, Bronze, German	15.00
Kitchen, Crimper, Maple	22.50
Kitchen, Crimper, Pie, Pewter Wheel, Wooden	45.00
Kitchen, Crimper, Pie, Whalebone	125.00
Kitchen, Crimper, Pie, Wood	17.00
Kitchen, Crimper, Pie, Wooden Wheel, C.1890, 5 In.	15.00
Kitchen, Crock, Butter, Blue & White Apricots, Lid & Bail, 3 Pound	85.00
Kitchen, Crock, Butter, Butterflies, Blue & White, 2 Pound	40.00
Kitchen, Crock, Canning, 1892, Weir, Quart	15.00
Kitchen, Crock, Churn, Brown, 2 Gallon	25.00
Kitchen, Curd Breaker, Crank Handle, Slant Sides, Wooden	150.00
Kitchen, Cutter, Biscuit, Cast Iron	6.50
Kitchen, Cutter, Cookie, Double Fluting Top & Bottom, 2 3/4 In. Diameter	10.00
Kitchen, Cutter, Cookie, Fluted, Handle, Tin, 4 In.Diameter	5.00
Kitchen, Cutter, Cookie, Goose, Arched Neck & Head, Tin, C.1820, 5 X 6 In.	40.00
Kitchen, Cutter, Cookie, Handle, Sitting Cat, Tin	10.00
Kitchen, Cutter, Cookie, Heart, 2 X 1 1/2 In.	4.00
Kitchen, Cutter, Cookie, Horse, Handled, Tin.3 1/2 X 6 In.	25.00
Kitchen, Cutter, Cookie, Horse, Tin, 2 X 3 1/2 In.	35.00
Kitchen, Cutter, Cookie, Lion, Seal, Chick & Pig	22.50
Kitchen, Cutter, Cookie, Tulip, Tin	15.00
Kitchen, Cutter, Donut, Rumford, C.1890	6.00
Kitchen, Cutter, Egg, Chicken-Shape, German	15.00
Kitchen, Cutter, Kraut, Cabbage Holder, 35 In.	60.00
Kitchen, Drainboard, Grooved, Porcelain Lip, Golden Oak, 20 X 25 In.	20.00
Kitchen, Drainer, Cheese, Slant Sides, Slat Bottom	120.00
Kitchen, Egg Beater, Triangular Paddles, Tin	17.00
Kitchen, Egg Cooker, Green, Hankscraft, Original Instructions	25.00
Kitchen, Food Chopper, Wooden Handle, Landers & Frary, 7 X 7 In.	10.00
Kitchen, Fork, Bone Handled, 2 Tined, C.1840, 6 3/4 In.	5.00
Kitchen, Fork, Bone Handled, 2 Tined, Set Of 3, C.1840, 8 1/4 In.	15.00
Kitchen, Fork, Forged Iron, American, C.1780	55.00
Kitchen, Fork, Pewter Inlay, Bone-Handled, Set Of 5	8.00
Kitchen, Fork, Toasting, Brass, Extends	15.00
Kitchen, Fork, Toasting, 2 Tine, Hand-Forged Iron, Ring Handle	30.00
Kitchen, Fork, Wrought Iron, Twisted Handle	47.50
Kitchen, Funnel, Fill Coffee Bean Bag, 1840, Brass, 6 X 7 In.	36.00
Kitchen, Funnel, Maple, Rounded Rim, 6-Sided Spout, 7 1/4 In.	86.00
Kitchen, Grater, Hand Punched, Cylinder Shape, Tin, 6 1/2 In.	38.00
Kitchen, Grater, Hand-Pierced, Original Wood, Tin	30.00

Kitchen, Grater, Hand-Pierced, Tin, Handle, 21 In.	45.00
Kitchen, Grater, Hand-Pierced, Tin, Long Handled Pine Board	35.00
Kitchen, Grater, Hand, Mouli Products	9.00
Kitchen, Grater, IDEAL, Tin, 7 X 1i In.	18.00
Kitchen, Grater, Nutmeg, Pierced, Edgar, Tin	28.00
Kitchen, Grater, Nutmeg, Silver Over Copper, 2 1/2 X 1 X 3/4 In.	8.50
Kitchen, Griddle, Air Slots On Side, Cast Iron, 1893	25.00
Kitchen, Griddle, Round, Cast Iron	2.50
Kitchen, Griddle, 3 Footed, Cast Iron	79.00
Kitchen, Grinder, Food, Keen Kutter, Model Kk11	12.00
Kitchen, Grinder, Food, Regal, Cast Iron	12.00
Kitchen, Grinder, Nutmeg, Crank Handle	4.25
Kitchen, Grinder, Peanut Butter	18.50
Kitchen, Grinder, Sausage, Keen Kutter	10.00
Kitchen, Grinder, Sausage, Keystone	10.00
Kitchen, Holder, String, Hinged, Shape Of Ball Of Twine, Iron, 1860	65.00
Kitchen, Hook, Pot, Iron	12.00
Kitchen, Hook, Three-Prong, Cast Iron	14.00
Kitchen, Ice Cream Maker, Instant Freezer Co., Fitchburg, Massachusetts	78.00
Kitchen, Icebox, Brass Hardware, Oak, McCray, 4 Doors, 4 1/2 X 6 Feet	750.00
Kitchen, Icebox, Carvings, Buffalo Oak, Small	265.00
Kitchen, Icebox, New Iceberg, Oak	350.00
Kitchen, Icebox, Oak, Porcelain Lined	300.00
Kitchen, Icebox, Oak, 7 Feet Square	695.00
Kitchen, Icebox, 7 Feet Square	695.00
Kitchen, Iron, Brass, Chinese	45.00
Kitchen, Iron, Flounce, One Piece, Pointed, 3 1/2 X 5 In.	20.00
Kitchen, Iron, Fluting, Base Dated 1866, Geneva	38.00
Kitchen, Iron, Fluting, Crank Type, Brass Rollers, 1879	38.50
Kitchen, Iron, Fluting, Hand, Geneva, Illinois	28.00
Kitchen, Iron, Fluting, The Best, S.W.Whitfield, 2 Piece	30.00
Kitchen, Iron, Fluting, 1880	20.00
Kitchen, Iron, Gas	20.00
Kitchen, Iron, Goffering, Signed E. & T.Clark	120.00
Kitchen, Iron, Hand, 1 Piece, Signed Ober, Chagrin Falls, S.C.	12.00
Kitchen, Iron, Silk, Chinese, Enamel Handle	18.00
Kitchen, Iron, Waffle, Cast Iron, Stand	15.00
Kitchen, Iron, Waffle, Diamond Point Pattern, Stand	19.50
Kitchen, Iron, Waffle, Fleur-De-Lis Pattern, Stand	19.50
Kitchen, Iron, Waffle, Griswold, Base	12.50
Kitchen, Iron, Waffle, Hand Wrought Iron	45.00
Kitchen, Iron, Waffle, Heart & Star, Dated 1920, Cast Iron	85.00
Kitchen, Iron, Waffle, Spring Handles, Ideal 8	15.00
Kitchen, Iron, Waffle, Stove Top, Flip Lid, Circular Diamond Pattern	16.00
Kitchen, Juicer, Enterprise Extractor	15.00
Kitchen, Juicer, Lemon, Iron	18.00
Kitchen, Juicer, Parsnip, Looks Like Inside Of Shark's Mouth	6.50
Kitchen, Kettle, Bail Handle, Brass, 10 In.Diameter	75.00
Kitchen, Kettle, Candy, Brass, Rat Tail Handle, 14 In.Diameter, 9 In.Deep	45.00
Kitchen, Kettle, Candy, Forged Handles, Copper, C.1840, 7 1/2 X 17 In.Diam.	295.00
Kitchen, Kettle, Candy, 2 Iron Handles, Copper, 26 In.Diameter	225.00
Kitchen, Kettle, Stew, Dovetailed, Brass Braised, Iron Ring Bail, Copper	65.00
Kitchen, Kettle, 3 Legged, Cast Iron, 6 X 12 In.Diameter	35.00
Kitchen, Knife & Fork, Carving, Ivory Handled, 1878	12.50
Kitchen, Knife, Butcher, Winchester, Oak Handle, 7 1/2 In.Blade	39.00
Kitchen, Knife, Chef, Winchester, Ebony Handle, 12 In.Blade	75.00
Kitchen, Knife, Chopping, Wooden Handle, Crescent Blade	4.00
Kitchen, Knife, Fruit, Agate Handles, Set Of 4, 18th Century, 8 1/2 In.	100.00
Kitchen, Ladle, Hand Forged, Iron	110.00
Kitchen, Lifter, Pie, Dated 1875, Cast Iron	27.50
Kitchen, Lifter, Pie, Wire, Wooden Handle, C.1870	18.50
Kitchen, Masher, Potato, Round, 11 In. X 2 3/4 In.Diameter	5.00
Kitchen, Masher, Potato, Wood	5.00 To 6.50
Kitchen, Masher, Turned Handle, Mushroom Top, Wooden	10.00
Kitchen, Match Safe , see Match Safe	
Kitchen, Measure, Lard, Celluloid	6.00

Kitchen, Measure, Wood, 1 Quart To 1/2 Bushel, Signed, Henniker, N.H., Set 75.00
    Kitchen, Mold, Ice Cream, see Pewter, Mold, Ice Cream
    Kitchen, Mold, see also Pewter, Mold, Tin, Mold
Kitchen, Mold, Baking, Fish Design, Handled, Iron, California 39.50
Kitchen, Mold, Boar's Head, 2 X 3 In. 5.00
Kitchen, Mold, Brown Bread, Tin, 10 In. 19.00
Kitchen, Mold, Butter, Acorn Pattern, Pat Size 30.00
Kitchen, Mold, Butter, Cow Pattern, Wooden Plunger, Glass, 3 1/2 X 4 1/2 In. 65.00
Kitchen, Mold, Butter, Deep Acorns & Leaves, 4 1/2 In. 60.00
Kitchen, Mold, Butter, Dovetailed, Wooden 12.00
Kitchen, Mold, Butter, Eagle, One Piece, 18th Century 195.00
Kitchen, Mold, Butter, Eagle, Star, Carved, 4 In.Diameter 175.00
Kitchen, Mold, Butter, Fern Leaf Pattern, 3 Rings, 3 1/2 In. 38.50
Kitchen, Mold, Butter, Floral, 4 In.Diameter 15.00
Kitchen, Mold, Butter, Hand-Cut, Flower Design, 4 In.Diameter 49.00
Kitchen, Mold, Butter, Leaf, 4 In. 36.00
Kitchen, Mold, Butter, Pineapple 45.00
Kitchen, Mold, Butter, Pineapple & Rings, 4 3/4 In. 50.00
Kitchen, Mold, Butter, Pineapple Design, Dated 1866, 5 In. 40.00
Kitchen, Mold, Butter, Pineapple Design, 1866, Wood 60.00
Kitchen, Mold, Butter, Pineapple, 4 1/2 In. 40.00
Kitchen, Mold, Butter, Plunger Type, Sheaf Of Wheat, Half Circle Of Leaves 35.00
Kitchen, Mold, Butter, Plunger Type, Wooden, Double Acorn, 4 1/2 In.Diameter 40.00
Kitchen, Mold, Butter, Round Plunger, Carved Flowers & Leaves 35.00
Kitchen, Mold, Butter, Shield, Flowers, Round 35.00
Kitchen, Mold, Butter, Strawberry With Leaves, 3 1/4 In.Diameter 45.00
Kitchen, Mold, Butter, Three Leaf Fern, 3 3/4 In. 32.00
Kitchen, Mold, Butter, Three Leaf Fern, 5 In.Diameter 45.00
Kitchen, Mold, Butter, Wheat Design, Round, 1 Pound 30.00
Kitchen, Mold, Butter, Wheat Imprint, 3 X 3/4 In.Diameter, Handle 4 1/4 In. 48.50
Kitchen, Mold, Butter, Wood Rectangle, 2 Piece, 1 Handle 15.00
Kitchen, Mold, Butter, 3 Leaf Design, 3 1/2 In.Diameter 36.00
Kitchen, Mold, Cake, Heart-Shaped, Tin, Hand-Made, 8 X 8 X 2 1/2 In. 22.00
Kitchen, Mold, Cake, Lamb, Cast Iron 75.00
Kitchen, Mold, Cake, Pineapple Shape, Tin 2.25
Kitchen, Mold, Candy, Santa Claus, 8 In. 55.00
Kitchen, Mold, Chocolate, Baker's, Lady's Top & Bottom, 19 X 10 X 2 In. 55.00
Kitchen, Mold, Chocolate, Easter Egg 14.00
Kitchen, Mold, Chocolate, Egg, Man In The Moon, 1915, 3 In. 4.00
Kitchen, Mold, Chocolate, Liberty Bell, 4 X 5 In. 25.00
Kitchen, Mold, Chocolate, Rabbit, Locking Piece, 9 In. 28.00
Kitchen, Mold, Chocolate, 36 Crescent Candies, Signed, Berlin, 8 X 10 1/2 In. 16.00
Kitchen, Mold, Cookie, Carved Figures, J.V.Watkins, New York, 11 X 11 In. 550.00
Kitchen, Mold, Cookie, Dog & Ship, Hand-Carved 68.00
Kitchen, Mold, Cookie, Double Cornucopia, Iron, 3 1/2 X 5 1/2 In. 50.00
Kitchen, Mold, Cookie, Oval, Acorn, 2 Oak Leaves, Iron, 4 X 6 In. 66.00
Kitchen, Mold, Cookie, 3 Birds, One Girl & 3 Others, 7 Piece 29.00
Kitchen, Mold, Copper Base, Tin, 8 X 6 1/2 In. 35.00
Kitchen, Mold, Copper, Round, Squirrel, 8 1/2 X 4 1/2 In. 45.00
Kitchen, Mold, Creamware, 19th Century, 9 X 7 1/2 In. 15.00
Kitchen, Mold, Curved, Foliated, Fluted, Tin, 2 X 3 In. 4.00
Kitchen, Mold, Fish, American, Tin, Signed, 5 X 11 In. 44.00
Kitchen, Mold, Fish, Dreamer, Straight, Tin, 5 X 13 In. 35.00
Kitchen, Mold, Fish, Tin, 11 In. 15.00
Kitchen, Mold, Food, Pineapple, Tin, 7 X 4 In. 15.00
Kitchen, Mold, Food, Rooster Shape, 2 Part, 2 1/4 X 5 1/2 X 7 In. 40.00
Kitchen, Mold, Food, Sheaf Of Wheat, Tin, 7 X 4 In. 15.00
Kitchen, Mold, Gingerbread, Shape Of American Indian, Copper, 6 In. 31.50
Kitchen, Mold, Loaf Pan, Dated 1860, 3 Triangular Shape 15.00
Kitchen, Mold, Maple Sugar, Fluted, Tin, Set Of 5 .... 12.50
Kitchen, Mold, Maple Sugar, Vermont, Tin, 8 1/2 X 15 In.32 Sections 35.00
Kitchen, Mold, Maple, 4 Sizes, Pegged Wooden Mallet, Pewter Lined 100.00
Kitchen, Mold, Plum Pudding, Bail Handle, 1 Quart 15.00
Kitchen, Mold, Pudding, Ear Of Corn Impressed In Bottom 20.00
Kitchen, Mold, Pudding, Grapes, Tin 20.00
Kitchen, Mold, Push Out With Star 27.00

Kitchen, Mold, Rabbit, Hinged	40.00
Kitchen, Mold, Rice Cake, Hand-Carved Designs, Korean, 12 In.	20.00
Kitchen, Mold, Rice, Wooden, Hand-Carved Designs, 12 In.	9.00
Kitchen, Mold, Snow White & The Seven Dwarfs, Double, 11 1/2 X 4 1/2 In.	58.00
Kitchen, Mold, Tin Lined, Mixed Fruit Design	20.00
Kitchen, Mortar & Pestle, Maple, C.1850, 4 1/2 X 7 1/2 In.	46.50
Kitchen, Mortar & Pestle, 18th Century, Mortar, 17 3/4 In., Pestle, 9 1/4 In.	375.00
Kitchen, Oven, Raosting, Spit, Tin	230.00
Kitchen, Paddle, Butter, Curved, Wood	6.50
Kitchen, Pan, Bread Baking, Corrugated, Round, 2 Piece	20.00
Kitchen, Pan, Bread, 5 Loaves In One Unit, 19 X 10 X 3 In.	7.50
Kitchen, Pan, Bundt, American, Copper, 6 1/2 In.	75.00
Kitchen, Pan, Bundt, Cast Iron, 5 X 10 In.Diameter	60.00
Kitchen, Pan, Fireplace, Swivel Ring, Cast Iron Spout & Handle	55.00
Kitchen, Pan, Frying, Handwrought Iron, Rattail Handle, Scroll Hook End	85.00
Kitchen, Pan, Frying, Long Handled	135.00
Kitchen, Pan, Hearts, Diamonds, Clubs Spades, 2 X 9 In.	22.50
Kitchen, Pan, Muffin, Cast Iron, 11 Muffin Size	14.00
Kitchen, Pan, Muffin, 12 Section, Half-Rounds, Iron	12.00
Kitchen, Pan, Pork Pie, Hat Shape, Tin	65.00
Kitchen, Pastry Wheel & Jigger, Double Wheel & Crimped End, Brass & Iron	60.00
Kitchen, Peel, Oven, Hand Wrought Iron, Ram's Horn Handle, 43 In.	65.00
Kitchen, Peel, Oven, Handle, Wrought Iron, 35 In.	45.00
Kitchen, Peeler, Apple, Baystate, 2 Table Clamps	38.00
Kitchen, Peeler, Apple, Clampon, Cast Iron, 3 Gears	48.00
Kitchen, Peeler, Apple, Dated January, 1882	32.00
Kitchen, Peeler, Apple, Dated March 1869	27.50
Kitchen, Peeler, Apple, Dated 1856	27.50
Kitchen, Peeler, Apple, F.W.Munson's, Iron Clamp, 1862	38.00
Kitchen, Peeler, Apple, H.Keyes, Patent 1856, Cast Iron	30.00
Kitchen, Peeler, Apple, Iron, Reading, Pennsylvania, 1868	40.00
Kitchen, Peeler, Apple, Little Star, 1885	30.00
Kitchen, Peeler, Apple, Original Blue-Green Paint, Belt Driven, Wooden	150.00
Kitchen, Peeler, Apple, Turn Table, Cast Iron, 1856	22.50
Kitchen, Peeler, Apple, White Mountain, Goodell Co., Antrim, N.H.	30.00
Kitchen, Peeler, Apple, Wooden, 11 1/2 In.Base, 5 1/2 In.	160.00
Kitchen, Pie Safe, Hanging, Pierced Tin, 4 Sided, Pennsylvania	275.00
Kitchen, Piebird, China, Black Crow	12.50
Kitchen, Pitcher, Clown Reamer Top	20.00
Kitchen, Pitter, Cherry, Brighton, Pennsylvania	27.50
Kitchen, Pitter, Cherry, Cast Iron, 1903	10.00
Kitchen, Pitter, Cherry, Clamps To Table, Pits 2 At A Time, 1880	45.00
Kitchen, Pitter, Cherry, Dated 1867	45.00
Kitchen, Pitter, Cherry, 4 Legs, Patent 1866, Iron	17.50
Kitchen, Pot, 3 Footed, Cast Iron, 5 In.Diameter	30.00
Kitchen, Press, Cheese, Plunger, 2 Iron Bands, 13 In.Diameter	35.00
Kitchen, Press, Fruit, Footed, Iron, 4 Quarts	18.50
Kitchen, Range, Gas, Kalamazoo	100.00
Kitchen, Range, Green Enamel	150.00
Kitchen, Reamer, Clown, Peach, 6 In.	34.00
Kitchen, Reamer, Detachable Cone, Silver Plate	85.00
Kitchen, Reamer, Duck, 1 Piece	32.00
Kitchen, Reamer, Iron, 9 1/4 In.	12.00
Kitchen, Reamer, Lemon, Goebel, 2 Piece	37.00
Kitchen, Reamer, Lemon, Maple, Lignum Vitae Head	65.00
Kitchen, Reamer, Orange For Baby, Ceramic	35.00
Kitchen, Reamer, Orange Shape, Bavaria	22.50
Kitchen, Reamer, Pear, 3 Piece	33.00
Kitchen, Reamer, Sunkist, Opalescent	20.00
Kitchen, Reamer, Sunkist, Yellow	27.00
Kitchen, Refrigerator, G.E., Monitor Top	75.00
Kitchen, Riser, Bread, Cover, Tin	30.00
Kitchen, Roller, Cookie, Corrugated Head, Single Handle, Maple, 6 1/2 In.	21.50
Kitchen, Roller, Strudel, Tapered, Tiger Maple	58.00
Kitchen, Rolling Pin, Blown, C.1890, 14 In.	45.00
Kitchen, Rolling Pin, Creamware, Wooden Handles, 14 In.	85.00

Kitchen, Rolling Pin, Glass, Blue, 14 In.	32.00
Kitchen, Rolling Pin, Glass, Metal Screw	15.00
Kitchen, Rolling Pin, Glass, Screw Cap End	12.50
Kitchen, Rolling Pin, Hand-Blown Amber Glass, 16 In.	32.00
Kitchen, Rolling Pin, Impressed Imperial, Dated, Milk Glass	40.00
Kitchen, Rolling Pin, Maple, 27 In.	14.50
Kitchen, Rolling Pin, Milk Glass, Wood Handles, 19 In.	20.00
Kitchen, Rolling Pin, Milk Glass, Wooden Handle, Dated June 26, 1921	45.00
Kitchen, Rolling Pin, One Piece Tiger Maple, 18th Century	20.00
Kitchen, Rolling Pin, Solid Oak	12.00
Kitchen, Rolling Pin, Tiger Maple, One Piece	110.00
Kitchen, Rolling Pin, Tin Screw Cap, Glass	6.00
Kitchen, Rolling Pin, White Ironstone China, Wooden Handles	45.00
Kitchen, Rolling Pin, Wooden Springerle	35.00
Kitchen, Sadiron, Wooden Handle	6.50
Kitchen, Scale, Egg, Cast Iron, Zenith	10.00
Kitchen, Scoop, Draw-Shaved, Hooked Handle, Wooden, 15 1/2 In.	25.00
Kitchen, Scoop, Flour, Brass, 9 In.	22.00
Kitchen, Scoop, Flour, Tin	10.00
Kitchen, Scoop, Ice Cream, Cone Shape, Iron & Tin, Dated 1905	20.00
Kitchen, Scoop, Molasses, Wood, Hand Made	10.00
Kitchen, Scoop, Spice, Tin	8.00
Kitchen, Scraper, Dough, Hand-Wrought Iron	16.00
Kitchen, Seeder, Cherry, Table Clamp	10.00
Kitchen, Seeder, Raisin, Dated 1897	13.00
Kitchen, Seeder, Raisin, Wood Handle, Wire Slicer, Signed, The Everett	30.00
Kitchen, Sheller, Bean, Fastens To Table, Cast Iron	35.00
Kitchen, Sheller, Corn, Patent 1870	35.00
Kitchen, Shovel, Placing Bread In Fire, Handforged, Iron, 37 In.	125.00
Kitchen, Sink, Dry, Maple, Lift Top, 2 Drawer, Pegged Construction	195.00
Kitchen, Skillet, No.4, Griswold Co., Erie, Pennsylvania	12.00
Kitchen, Skimmer, Brass Bowl, Wrought Iron Handle, Ring, 18 1/2 In.	95.00
Kitchen, Skimmer, Copper, Iron Handle, 19 In.	45.00
Kitchen, Skimmer, Cream, Hand-Style, Tin	5.50
Kitchen, Slicer, Cabbage, 1876, Clinton, Ithaca, N.Y.	125.00
Kitchen, Slicer, French Bean, Cast Iron	20.00
Kitchen, Slicer, Onion, Little Shaver, J.M.Mast Fg., Co., U.S.A., Wood	22.00
Kitchen, Spatula, Hand-Forged Iron Hook Handle, York Co., Penna., 12 In.	135.00
Kitchen, Spatula, Iron	5.00
Kitchen, Spice Cabinet, 8 Drawer	65.00
Kitchen, Spice Set, Grand Union Tea Co., Tin	38.00
Kitchen, Spinning Wheel, see Tool, Spinning Wheel	
Kitchen, Stamp, Butter, Carved U.S. Eagle & Shield	185.00
Kitchen, Stove, see Stove	
Kitchen, Strainer, Pudding, Loop Feet, Oval, 2 Piece	39.00
Kitchen, Strainer, Tin, Pierced, Tin Lapped Seams, 11 In.	35.00
Kitchen, Tea Cozy, Stockinette Face	15.00
Kitchen, Teakettle, Coil Handle, Iron	11.50
Kitchen, Teakettle, Copper Handle, Brass Finial, American Copper, 10 1/2 In.	140.00
Kitchen, Teakettle, Copper, Curved Spout, Rochester, 9 In.Diameter	35.00
Kitchen, Teakettle, Copper, Majestic, Dated 1898, 9 In.Diameter	30.00
Kitchen, Teakettle, D.Bentley & Sons, Copper	250.00
Kitchen, Teakettle, Gooseneck Spout, Rat-Tailed Bail, Cast Iron	79.50
Kitchen, Teakettle, Gooseneck, Footed, Ball Shaped, Iron	185.00
Kitchen, Teakettle, Gooseneck, 4 Feet, Wooden Handle, Brass	75.00
Kitchen, Teakettle, Solid Copper, Polished & Lacquered	24.50
Kitchen, Tenderizer, Wood Handle, Stoneware, Dated 1877	40.00
Kitchen, Thermometer, Candy, Brass, Tin Backing, 6 1/2 In.	20.00
Kitchen, Timer, Figural, Dutch Girl Holding Timer, Porcelain, 3 In.	25.00
Kitchen, Toaster, Bread, Arched Feet, American, Iron, 18th Century	140.00
Kitchen, Toaster, Hearth, 4 Bars, Wrought Iron, 18th Century, 16 In.Long	175.00
Kitchen, Toaster, Pyramid, Tin	5.00
Kitchen, Toaster, Rotating, 4 Feet, 18th Century, Iron	260.00
Kitchen, Toaster, Simple Details, Wrought Iron, 18 In.	145.00
Kitchen, Toaster, Stove-Top, 4 Sides, Tin & Metal	6.00
Kitchen, Toaster, Swing Handle, Wrought Iron, C.1840	70.00

Kitchen, Toaster, Wrought Iron, Hinged Handle, Horseshoe-Shaped, 38 In. 275.00
Kitchen, Tong, Egg, Tin, Spring Valley Butter Co., Kansas City, Missouri 5.00
Kitchen, Trammel, Hole Adjustments, Adjusts From 22 To 31 In. 36.00
Kitchen, Trammel, Saw-Tooth, Adjusts 36 To 54 In. 60.00
Kitchen, Tray, Cutlery, Handled, Chestnut 22.00
Kitchen, Tray, Dough, Ovoid, Maple, 12 X 19 In. 30.00
Kitchen, Tray, Sorting Sieve, Adjusts From Square To Diamond Shape 49.00
Kitchen, Trough, Dough, Pine, 7 Foot 250.00
Kitchen, Tub, Ice Cream Freezer, Cedar, 8 In. 23.00
Kitchen, Utensil Rack, Wrought Iron, Scrolled & Twisted Members, 19 1/2 In. 205.00
Kitchen, Wafer, Iron Handle, Musical Instruments, 27 In. 85.00
Kitchen, Washboard, Bentwood, 19 In. 28.00
Kitchen, Washboard, Metal 12.00
Kitchen, Washer, Fairy, Salesman's Sample .... *Illus* 575.00
Kitchen, Whipper, Egg, Squeeze Handle To Operate, Wire 20.00
Knife, A.K. & B., In Kit, 8 Attachments 55.00
Knife, Adolphus Busch, See Him In Peep Hole, 3 Blade 90.00
Knife, American Automatic Gun Buyers, 2 Blade 8.00
Knife, Artillery, Spanish, Curved Blade, Pistol Grip, 12 In. 32.50
Knife, Barlow, One Blade, Bone Handle, Keen Kutter On Blade, 5 In. 75.00
Knife, Bolo, U.S.Model 1917, Iron Guard, Walnut Grips, 10 1/4 In. 37.50
Knife, Bowie, Brass, Guard, Clip Blade, Death To Yankees, Civil War, Wood Grip 195.00
Knife, Bowie, California, German Silver Grip 275.00
Knife, Bowie, Etched Panel, Scroll Design, C.1860, 13 1/4 In. 325.00
Knife, Bowie, German Silver Cross Guard, Stag Grips, 5 3/4 In. 145.00
Knife, Bowie, Murray & Gray Co., Marked V.R., 1863 .... 350.00
Knife, Bowie, Sheath, Civil War, Silver Handle, Fluted Shell Design, 7 In. 150.00
Knife, Bowie, Sheffield, Holster, Bone Handle, 8 3/4 In. 90.00
Knife, Bowie, Sheffield, Leather Scabbard, Bone Handle 90.00
Knife, Bowie, Sheffield, Scabbard, Manhattan Cutler 85.00
Knife, Bowie, Sheffield, Silver Handle 110.00
Knife, Bowie, Sheffield, Stag Handle, Sheath 120.00
Knife, Bowie, Wostenholm & Sons, Marked, Stag Handle, 12 1/2 In. 195.00
Knife, British Navy, War Of 1812, Ivory Hilt & Pommel, Brass Sheath, 9 In. 225.00
Knife, Bulldog Case, Stag Handle, U.S.A. 100.00
Knife, Camillus Grand Daddy Barlow 40.00
Knife, Camillus, Wildlife, Deer On Handle 50.00
Knife, Central Fire Truck Corp., 2 Blade, 3 5/8 In. 12.50
Knife, Clasp, Pearl Handle, 4 Blade, Tools, Opened, 10 1/2 In. 225.00
Knife, Clasp, Spanish, In-Curved Blade, Wood Grips, 18th Century, 12 1/2 In. 74.50
Knife, Dutch Naval, C.1820, Brass Hilt, Ivory Grips, Sheath, 11 In. 295.00
Knife, Electrician's, Pal Blade Co., Stag Like Handle, 3 In. .... 20.00 To 37.50
Knife, Electrician's, Pal Blade Company, 3 1/2 In. 20.00
Knife, Embossed Reindeer Pulling Man On Sled, 2 Blade, 3 1/4 In. 15.00
Knife, Fish, Winchester, One Blade 18.50
Knife, Four Blade, Corkscrew, Water Scene, Leather Case, 3 3/4 In. 25.00
Knife, German Savings Bank, 2 Blade, Sterling 25.00
Knife, Gold Fill, Loop For Chain, 2 Blades, Meriden Knife Co. 35.00
Knife, Golden Rule Cutlery, Girlie Knife, 2 Blade, 3 1/4 In. 25.00
Knife, Hand-Carved Bone Handle, George Westenholm XL 24.00
Knife, Howard Co., Two Blade, Pearl Handle, Germany, 2 7/8 In. 15.00
Knife, Hunting, Aluminum Handle, Brown Leather Discs, Mexico, 8 In. 6.50
Knife, Hunting, Cattaragus, Leather Entwined Handle, 10 1/2 In. 21.50
Knife, Hunting, German, Brass Hilt, Engraved Blades, 17 In. 94.50
Knife, Hunting, Ka-Bar, Leather Handle, 4 In.Blade 10.50
Knife, Hunting, Remington, Double Edge, Pair 30.00
Knife, Hunting, Remington, RH32, Sheath, 4 1/2 In.Blade 45.00
Knife, Hunting, Remington, RH4, Stag Handle, 4 In.Blade 35.00
Knife, Imperial, Souvenir, Statue Of Liberty, Empire State Bldg., 1 Blade 17.50
Knife, Jack, Case Brothers Cutlery Co., 4 Blade 95.00
Knife, Jack, Remington, No.R-1072, Whetted Back Blades 18.50
Knife, Jack, Remington, Silver, Franklin Fire Insurance Co., 1829-1929 .... 98.00
Knife, Jack, Schrade Waldon, Senator's Presentation, 14K Gold 125.00
Knife, Jack, Shape Of Woman's Leg, High Heel Shoe, Utica Club, 3 1/8 In. 50.00
Knife, Key Chain, Chevrolet, Kansas City, 2 3/8 In. 10.00
Knife, Knuckle, Wooden Handle, Sheath, U.S., 1917 .... 50.00

Knife, Metropolitan Life Insurance Co., Building On One Side	30.00
Knife, Mother-Of-Pearl Handle, 2 Blades, Challange Cutlery Co., Conn.	28.00
Knife, Mother-Of-Pearl Handle, 2 Blades, Soling, Germany	15.00
Knife, Mother-Of-Pearl, Escanaba, Michigan	4.00
Knife, One Blade, Shape Of Baseball Bat & Ball, Striped Handle, 7/8 In.	20.00
Knife, Pabst Blue Ribbon	7.50
Knife, Pen, Mother-Of-Pearl, Marked I-Xl, Wostenholm, Sheffield, England	13.50
Knife, Pen, Shoe, 2 In.	20.00
Knife, Plug Bayonet, Eliptical Iron Cross Guard, C.1860, 9 In.	195.00
Knife, Pocket, A.Busch, Silver Handle, Jan. 1, 1900	200.00
Knife, Pocket, Buster Brown	37.50
Knife, Pocket, Camillus, Razor Type Blade	15.00
Knife, Pocket, Chicago World's Fair, 1933	15.00
Knife, Pocket, Cigar Cutting, Silver Handled	8.50
Knife, Pocket, Double Bladed, Engraved Design, Sterling Silver, 2 3/4 In.	18.00
Knife, Pocket, Embossed Lady's Head, Ornate Blade, Silver, 2 Blade	25.00
Knife, Pocket, Geo.Meuhlebach Brewing Co., 80th Anniversary, 3 In.	27.50
Knife, Pocket, Golden Wedding, Pull To Snap Open	15.00
Knife, Pocket, Imperial, 3 Blades, Green Pearlized Case	7.50
Knife, Pocket, Irish Military	9.95
Knife, Pocket, Keen Kutter, Emblem On Blade & Stag Handle	12.50
Knife, Pocket, Kentucky Rifle	45.00
Knife, Pocket, Kungshal Cruise, Swedish American Line	25.00
Knife, Pocket, Kutmaster, 2 Blade, Purina Checkerboard Handle	12.50
Knife, Pocket, Made By I-Xl, 18K White Gold	100.00
Knife, Pocket, Mother-Of-Pearl, 2 Blades, 1 In.	10.00
Knife, Pocket, Niagara Falls, Richland	3.00
Knife, Pocket, Pacific Imports Company, Japan, Brass, 2 1/2 In.	5.00
Knife, Pocket, Purina, 2 Blade	10.00
Knife, Pocket, Remington Circle, Bone	26.00
Knife, Pocket, Remington, Blue Fleck Handle, 3 In.	40.00
Knife, Pocket, Remington, Bone Handle	18.00
Knife, Pocket, Remington, No.R7925, 2 Blade	25.00
Knife, Pocket, Remington, No.1623, 2 Blade	75.00
Knife, Pocket, Remington, Purina	25.00
Knife, Pocket, Remington, R 485	19.00
Knife, Pocket, Remington, R.B.44	75.00
Knife, Pocket, Remington, Ring, Brown Bone Handle, Boy Scout	28.00
Knife, Pocket, Remington, R2083	25.00
Knife, Pocket, Remington, R2203	80.00
Knife, Pocket, Remington, R6949, Visible Logo, Metal Handle	37.50
Knife, Pocket, Remington, 2 Blade	18.00
Knife, Pocket, Remington, 2 Blade, Blue Handle	15.00
Knife, Pocket, Remington, 2 Blade, Stag Grips, Signed In Circle	26.50
Knife, Pocket, Robeson, Pearl	15.00
Knife, Pocket, St.Louis Exposition, 1940, Building Each Side	18.00
Knife, Pocket, Winchester, Model 2902	40.00
Knife, Pocket, Winchester, No.4321, Pearl Handle	75.00
Knife, Pocket, Winchester, 2 Blade	35.00
Knife, Pocket, Winchester, 2 Blade, Bone Handle, Embossed Blade, 4 In.	55.00
Knife, Pocket, Winchester, 2 Blade, 3 1/8 In.	40.00
Knife, Pocket, Winchester, 3 Blade	30.00
Knife, Pocket, 2 Blade, Cattaraugus Stag Bone	35.00
Knife, Pocket, 2 Blade, Shine-All, Hillyard Chemical, 2 3/8 In.	12.50
Knife, Pruning, Remington	26.00
Knife, Sailor, Schrade Walden	7.50
Knife, Shape Of Pipe Wrench, 2 Blade, Japan	20.00
Knife, Sharpener, Bagley Old Colony Tobacco	20.00
Knife, Sheath, British Naval Officer's, C.1799, Ivory Grips, 15 In.	550.00
Knife, Sheath, Mermaid Design, C.1810, British Naval, Brass Hilt, 12 In.	795.00
Knife, Sheath, U.S. Army Hospital, 1912	100.00
Knife, Sheffield, 2 Blades, Scissors, Pearl Handle, 3 1/2 In.	25.00
Knife, Shoe, Folding, Small	17.50
Knife, Shoe, Roger Johnson Rand Shoe Co., Ivory Colored	65.00
Knife, Six-Dot, Concave, Plain Blade	40.00
Knife, Souvenir, Seahorse, Florida, 2 Blade	8.50

Knife, Stone, Sharpening, Winchester	12.00
Knife, Tie Tack, Brass & Pearl Handle, 1 In.	12.50
Knife, Two Blade, Corkscrew, Wood Grain Handle, Germany, 3 3/8 In.	15.00
Knife, Utica Club Beer, High Button Boot Shape, 2 Blade	45.00
Knife, Wadsworth & Son, Stag Handle, 3 Blade	10.00
Knife, 5-Dot, Kentucky, Green Handle, One Blade	20.00
Knife, 7-Dot, Dr.Knife Case, One Blade	20.00

Knowles, Taylor & Knowles, see KTK, Lotus Ware

Koch, Cup, Chocolate, Grapes, Signed	14.00
Koch, Plate, Fruit, Apples & Grapes, 8 1/2 In., Pair	45.00
Koch, Plate, Fruit, Apples, 7 1/2 In.	18.00
Koch, Plate, Fruit, Apples, 8 5/8 In.	29.00
Koch, Plate, Fruit, Louise Bavaria, Signed, 8 5/8 In.	27.00
Koch, Plate, Fruit, 2 Color Grapes & Leaves, 8 5/8 In.	27.00
Koch, Plate, Grapes, Shaded Ground, Signed, 8 1/2 In.	28.00
Koch, Plate, Grapes, Signed, 7 1/2 In.	18.00
Korean Ware, Humidor, Figures Of 3 Men, Medallion Signature, 7 1/4 In.	250.00
Korean Ware, Lamp, Children Playing Hide And Seek, 13 In.	128.00
Korean Ware, Matchstrike, Red Pottery, Drip Glaze, Marked	120.00
Korean Ware, Mug, Handles, Applied Figure	65.00
Korean Ware, Mug, Red & Gray, Applied Boy & Dog	110.00
Korean Ware, Mug, Water Lilies In Porcelain, Seal Signed, 5 In.	45.00
Korean Ware, Plate, Incised Design, 6 In.	55.00
Korean Ware, Teapot, Crab Holding Man By Ear, Signed	250.00
Korean Ware, Teapot, Drip Glaze, Porcelain Seal, Covered	220.00
Korean Ware, Teapot, Incised Floral Design, C.1910, Seal On Bottom	65.00
Korean Ware, Vase, Man On Rocks, Drip Glaze, Signed, 8 1/2 In.	150.00
Korean Ware, Vase, Tree Trunk Shape, Poo Ware, 6 1/2 X 6 1/2 In.	90.00
Korean Ware, Vase, 3-Hole, Crouching Man, Seal	85.00

K.P.M

KPM is part of one of the marks used about 1723 by the Meissen Factory Konigliche Porzellan Manufaktur. Other firms using the letters include the Royal Manufactory of Berlin, Germany, that worked from 1832 to 1847. A factory in Scheibe, Germany, used the mark in 1928. The mark was also used in Waldenburg, Germany, and other German cities during the twentieth century.

KPM, Bowl, Molded Flowers Inside, Scepter K.P.M., Green, 8 1/2 In.Diameter	30.00
KPM, Bowl, Molded Flowers, Pink Inside Walls, Green Mark, 1 1/2 X 8 In.Diam.	30.00
KPM, Bowl, Pink Inside Walls, 19th Century, Green Scepter Mark, 8 In.Diam.	35.00
KPM, Chocolate Pot, Paneled, Flowers, Gold Handle & Trim, White, 9 In.	27.50
KPM, Creamer, Silesia, Onion Pattern, 4 In.	18.00
KPM, Cup & Bowl, Scepter Mark, 1760-1800, Set Of 6	200.00
KPM, Cup & Saucer, Chinoiserie Design, C.1840, Blue Scepter Mark	35.00
KPM, Cup & Saucer, Gilded, Red, Yellow, 1834 Mark, 5 X 5 1/2 In.	290.00
KPM, Frame & Picture, Girl Showing Mother Flowers, 8 1/4 X 5 1/2 In.	600.00
KPM, Mug, Barber, Red Splotched, Bust Of Lady, Signed	50.00
KPM, Plaque, Berlin, C.Melt, Signed, Impressed, 1800s, 15 1/4 In.	3000.00
KPM, Plaque, Berlin, I.Sturm, Impressed, Signed, C.1882, 18 1/4 In.	2000.00
KPM, Plaque, Berlin, Van Der Werff, Impressed, C.1800, 7 1/2 In.	9500.00

Kitchen, Washer, Fairy, Salesman's Sample
(See Page 263)

KPM, Plaque, Fisher Boy,
Maidens, Scepter Mark, 13 In.
(See Page 266)

KPM, Plaque, Child, Berlin, Impressed Scepter, 1880, 9 1/4 In.	5250.00
KPM, Plaque, Fisher Boy, Maidens, Scepter Mark, 13 In. ....*Illus*	4250.00
KPM, Plaque, Gypsy Boy, Framed	825.00
KPM, Plaque, Signed Wagner, Oval Frame, 7 In.	650.00
KPM, Plaque, Young Boy In Forest, Signed Fr.Till, Dresden, C.1880, 6 1/8 In.	475.00
KPM, Plate, Cake, Blue Background, Pink Roses, Gold Handled, 10 In.	58.00
KPM, Plate, Cherries & Apples, Scepter Mark, 6 3/4 In.	10.00
KPM, Plate, Dessert, Hand-Painted Flowers, 8 1/4 In., Set Of 6	300.00
KPM, Plate, Gold & Black Design, Open Handles, 10 In.	11.00
KPM, Plate, Kaiser Wilhelm Family Service, Orange, White, Gilding, 9 1/2 In.	350.00
KPM, Platter, White & Gold Band, 13 In.	10.00
KPM, Ramekin Set, Blue & Green Floral, Underliners, C.1900, Marked, 6 Piece	70.00
KPM, Salt, Pepper, Mustard & Spoon	45.00
KPM, Shaving Mug, Scuttle	28.00
KPM, Tureen, Soup, Cover, Roses & Gold Trim, White Porcelain	35.00
KPM, Vase, Forest Scene, White Satin Finish, Germany, Flat, Oval, 9 1/2 In.	175.00
KPM, Vase, Goat Head Handles, Scenic Panels, 19th Century, 6 3/4 In., Pair	585.00
KPM, Vase, Hanging, Brown Mask With Orb & Cross, 9 In.	150.00

K.T.&K.
CHINA *KTK are the initials of the Knowles, Taylor and Knowles Company of East Liverpool, Ohio, founded by Isaac W. Knowles in 1853. They made Lotus Ware.*

KTK Lotus Ware, see Lotus Ware

KTK, Plate, White, Brown Transfer, 8 In.	20.00
Ku Klux Klan, Book, Women's Ritual Book, 40 Pages	18.50
Ku Klux Klan, Booklet, 1921	12.00
Ku Klux Klan, Robe	50.00

Kutani ware is a Japanese porcelain made after the mid-seventeenth century. Most of the pieces found today are nineteenth century.

Kutani, Bowl, Red Stoneware, 8 1/2 In.	95.00
Kutani, Bowl, Red, 3 X 9 In.Diameter	125.00
Kutani, Bowl, Terra Cotta, Signed, 8 1/2 X 2 1/2 In.	119.00
Kutani, Chocolate Set, Butterflies, Ivory, Blue, Green, Rust, C.1900	225.00
Kutani, Cup & Saucer, Satsuma Style Decoration, Eggshell Porcelain, Signed	35.00
Kutani, Cup, Saki, Gold Band, Orange Kutani Mark, Flying Phoenix	15.00
Kutani, Ginger Jar, Cover, Gold Tracery, Oriental Signature, 7 1/2 In.	89.00
Kutani, Plate, Bird Design, 9 1/2 In.	60.00
Kutani, Plate, Set Of 6, 7 In.	35.00
Kutani, Saki Set, Whistling Bottle, 5 Cups, Geisha Head In Bottom	50.00
Kutani, Salt, Master, Translucent Panels	22.50
Kutani, Sugar & Creamer, Covered, Birds & Flowers, Red Handles & Rims	65.00
Kutani, Tea Service, Gold Scene, Geisha Girl Head In Cup Bottoms, 6 Settings	135.00
Kutani, Tea Set, Courtesans, Cobalt Blue, C.1890, 3 Piece	165.00
Kutani, Tea Set, 6 Cups & Saucers, Scenic In Platinum	250.00
Kutani, Teapot, Birds & Flowers, C.1880, 8 In.	70.00
Kutani, Teapot, Bulbous, 5 Panels, Garden Scene, 5 X 8 In.	85.00
Kutani, Teaset, Beaded, Raised Brown, Dragon Head Spout, 12 Piece	95.00
Kutani, Urn, Covered, Decorated With Figures, Signed, 3 X 3 In., Pair	150.00
Kutani, Vase, Kaga Province, 19th Century, 12 X 6 In.	295.00
Kutani, Vase, Orange Tree, 19th Century, 12 In. X 8 In.Diameter	85.00
Kutani, Vase, Scenic, People In Garden, Finial Of Temple Dog.11 1/2 In.	250.00
Kutani, Vase, Women In Garden Scene, 5 In., Pair	70.00
Lacquer, Bowl, Nut, 6 Small Bowls & Spoon, Karovan	25.00
Lacquer, Box, Chinese Scene On Top, Black & Gold, 7 X 5 X 2 In.	22.00
Lacquer, Box, Russian, Troika Scene, Signed Vishniff, 1 1/2 X 2 In.Diam.	95.00
Lacquer, Desk Set, Gold & Red Dragons, Made In Foochow, China, 11 Piece	190.00
Lacquer, Vase, Black, Over Cinnabar, Floral Trellis, Sticker, 8 In., Pair	95.00

R.LALIQUE

LALIQUE *Lalique glass was made by Rene Lalique in Paris, France, between the 1890s and his death in 1945. The glass was molded, pressed, and engraved in Art Nouveau and Art Deco styles. Pieces were marked with the signature, "R. Lalique." Lalique glass is still being made. Pieces made after 1945 bear the mark "Lalique."*

Lalique, Ashtray, Cable Rim, Masted Sailing Ship, Signed, 7 In.Diameter	60.00
Lalique, Ashtray, Etched Frosted Nude, Signed, 4 X 4 In.	75.00

alique, **Ashtray,** Frosted Chain Motif, 6 1/4 In.	25.00
alique, **Ashtray,** German Shepard Finial	30.00
alique, **Ashtray,** Jamaique	40.00
alique, **Ashtray,** Large Fish, Bubbles, Marked	39.00
alique, **Ashtray,** Round, Frosted, Pheasant, 4 X 4 In.	25.00
alique, **Atomizer,** Frosted, Gold Wash, Plunger Style, Marked, 5 1/4 In.	475.00
alique, **Atomizer,** 4 Vertical Panels Of Art Nouveau Ladies, Gold Top	225.00
alique, **Bell,** Crystal, Bird Top, 5 1/2 In.	75.00
alique, **Bonbon,** Covered, Fish On Top, Opalescence, Signed, 10 1/2 In.	1450.00
alique, **Bonbon,** Hanging Leaves From Raised Center Cluster, Signed, 6 In.	450.00
alique, **Bookends,** Crystal Birds, Signed, 6 X 3 X 3 1/2 In.	225.00
alique, **Bottle,** Brown Stain, Epines, Dome Formed, Stopper	235.00
alique, **Bottle,** Cologne, 8 Tiny Faces Blowing Frost Down Sides, 4 In.Diam.	155.00
alique, **Bottle,** Molded With Thorn Branches, Stopper, Dome Form, 4 1/2 In.	225.00
alique, **Bottle,** Nudes Around, Heads Around Stopper, 11 In.	150.00
alique, **Bottle,** Perfume, Amber Wash, Floral, Matching Stopper, Signed, 4 In.	225.00
alique, **Bottle,** Perfume, Art Deco, Tiers, Turquoise Stopper, 5 1/2 In.	125.00
alique, **Bottle,** Perfume, Art Deco, Tiers, Vertical Ribbing, 5 X 2 In.	195.00
alique, **Bottle,** Perfume, Ball Shape, Frosted, Trefoil Stopper, Signed, 5 In.	58.00
alique, **Bottle,** Perfume, Bird On Top, Marked	35.00
alique, **Bottle,** Perfume, Blue, Stopper, Molded Mark, Flat, Circular, 3 1/4 In.	115.00
alique, **Bottle,** Perfume, Border Of Roses In Center, Signed, Pair, 5 3/4 In.	150.00
alique, **Bottle,** Perfume, Camille, Satin Glass, Geometric Shape, 2 1/2 In.	210.00
alique, **Bottle,** Perfume, Canarina Molded Into Stopper, Boxed	260.00
alique, **Bottle,** Perfume, Coral Color Decoration, In Box, Signed, 4 X 2 In.	150.00
alique, **Bottle,** Perfume, Embossed Tulips, Tulip Stopper, Orange Wash	175.00
alique, **Bottle,** Perfume, Enamel Tipped Hobnails, Signed, 5 1/2 In.	135.00
alique, **Bottle,** Perfume, Falcon Enfants, Cherubs Holding Flowers, 3 1/2 In.	250.00
alique, **Bottle,** Perfume, Flying Swallows, Carre Hirondelles, Signed	225.00
alique, **Bottle,** Perfume, Frosted Double Flower	38.00
alique, **Bottle,** Perfume, Frosted, 3 Arch Stopper, Signed, France, 6 1/4 In.	295.00
alique, **Bottle,** Perfume, Orange & Black Enameled, Fringed Atomizer	70.00
alique, **Bottle,** Perfume, Side-By-Side Flowers	60.00
alique, **Bowl,** Cherries, Raised On Back, Clear, Signed, 3 X 8 1/2 In.	340.00

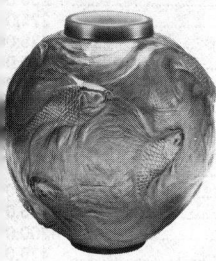

Lalique, Bowl, Formose, Molded Glass, C.1925

alique, **Bowl,** Clam Shell, Opalescent, Signed & Numbered, 8 In.	200.00
alique, **Bowl,** Clear & Blue, Raised Fruits & Berries, Signed, 8 1/2 X 3 In.	225.00
alique, **Bowl,** Coupe Chicoree, 9 In.	195.00
alique, **Bowl,** Crouching Nude Women Around Center, Signed, 8 1/2 X 10 In.	1450.00
alique, **Bowl,** Crystal, Frosted, Inverted Flowers, Black Enamel, 10 In.	380.00
alique, **Bowl,** Dessert, Blue Stain, Frieze Of Leaping Fish, 4 1/2 In.Diam.	45.00
alique, **Bowl,** Fern Pattern, Frosted, 5 In.	75.00
alique, **Bowl,** Finger, Clear, Signed In Block Letters, 2 1/2 In., Pair	135.00
alique, **Bowl,** Fishscale, Frosted Amber, Signed, 9 In.	425.00
alique, **Bowl,** Formose, Molded Glass, C.1925 .... *Illus*	1100.00
alique, **Bowl,** Frosted & Cut, Chaffinches, 4 X 9 1/4 In. Wide	145.00
alique, **Bowl,** Frosted Cherries & Leaf Design, Signed, 3 In.	225.00
alique, **Bowl,** Frosted Snake Chain Design, Clear Bull's-Eyes, 4 In.Diam.	35.00
alique, **Bowl,** Frosted, Leaves, Cherries, Signed, 9 1/2 In.	90.00
alique, **Bowl,** Incurved Body, Stylized Leaves, Blue Stain, 8 1/2 In.Diameter	225.00
alique, **Bowl,** Molded In Intaglio, Berries In Relief, 10 In.Diam.	295.00
alique, **Bowl,** Opalescent, Fish Encircling, Signed In Block Letters, 8 In.	165.00
alique, **Bowl,** Opalescent, Nude, Molded Mark, 3 X 8 In.Diameter	275.00
alique, **Bowl,** Opalescent, Starfish Design, Signed, 9 1/4 In. Diameter	265.00

Lalique, Bowl, Opalescent, Starfish, Signed R. Lalique, 3 Inches	265.00
Lalique, Bowl, Opalescent Starfish, Signed, 3 X 9 1/2 In.Diameter	265.00 To 450.00
Lalique, Bowl, Opalescent, Overlapping Scallop Shells, 9 1/2 In.	275.00
Lalique, Bowl, Opalescent, Petal Form, Molded Petals, Medallion, 10 In. Diam	275.00
Lalique, Bowl, Opalescent, Petal Molded Into Shell-Like Medallion, 10 In.	250.00
Lalique, Bowl, Opalescent, Shell, Signed, 9 1/2 In.Diameter	225.00
Lalique, Bowl, Opalescent, 6 Molded Female Nudes, Signed, 3 X 8 In.Diameter	250.00
Lalique, Bowl, Raised Cherries In Relief, Signed, 3 X 9 1/2 In.	250.00 To 300.00
Lalique, Bowl, Rows Or Circles, Scallops, 10 In.	265.00
Lalique, Bowl, Sprays Of Berry-Laden Branches, 10 In.	195.00
Lalique, Bowl, Star Fish, Opalescent, Signed, 3 X 9 1/2 In.	325.00 To 450.00
Lalique, Bowl, Stylized Petals On Underside, Green Stain, 12 1/2 In.Diam.	235.00
Lalique, Bowl, Underplate, Blue Opalescent, Signed, 8 In.	350.00
Lalique, Bowl, Wheat Design, Signed & Numbered, 9 1/4 In.Diameter	175.00
Lalique, Bowl, 12 Swirling Fish, Bubbles On Base, Signed, 4 In. X 9 In.Diam.	235.00
Lalique, Bowl, 3 Molded Gazelles, Flared Base, Signed, 1 3/4 X 11 3/4 In.	385.00
Lalique, Box, Cigarette, Covered, Clear, Molded Ginko Leaf On Cover, Signed	115.00
Lalique, Box, Cigarette, Covered, Rectangular, Stylized Swallow	165.00
Lalique, Box, Cigarette, Floral & Leaf, Amber, Ribbed Herringbone, 4 X 3 In.	250.00
Lalique, Box, Crystal Blocks Each Side, Floral Sides, Round, Lid, Signed, 6 In.	160.00
Lalique, Box, Frosted, Nudes Encircled, Covered, No.492, 4 In.	175.00
Lalique, Box, Frosted, 8 Panels, Coquilles, Covered, Signed, 2 3/4 X 1 1/2 In.	350.00
Lalique, Box, Opalescent, Dinard, Oval, Covered, Signed, 4 1/2 In.	495.00
Lalique, Box, Peacock With Black Stain, Script Signed, 5 In.Diameter	135.00
Lalique, Box, Powder, Brown Wash, Flower Design, Marguerites, 4 In.Diameter	150.00
Lalique, Box, Powder, D'Orsay, Floral, Red, Signed, 4 In. *Illus*	275.00
Lalique, Box, Powder, Flowers In Relief On Cover, Frosted, 3 1/2 In.	145.00
Lalique, Box, Powder, Frosted Cupids & Flowers, Oval Shape, 5 1/4 In.	145.00
Lalique, Box, Powder, Frosted Flowers On Cover, D'Orsay, 4 In.Diameter	160.00
Lalique, Box, Powder, Frosted Nudes, Heavy Circular, 4 In.	125.00 To 200.00
Lalique, Box, Powder, Frosted, 3 Nudes Dancing, Signed, 3 3/4 X 1 1/2 In.	150.00
Lalique, Box, Powder, Marguerites	175.00 To 185.00
Lalique, Box, Powder, Opalescence, Puff Flowers, 5 1/2 In.Diameter	185.00
Lalique, Box, Powder, Powder Puff Design, Houppes, Signed, 5 1/2 In.	295.00
Lalique, Box, Powder, 3 Female Nudes On Cover, Signed, 4 In.Diameter	235.00
Lalique, Box, Powder, 3 Nudes Dancing On Lid, 1 1/2 X 3 1/2 In.	225.00
Lalique, Box, Powder, 4 Dragonflies, Frosted, Brown Wash, Signed, 3 1/2 In.	225.00
Lalique, Box, Thistle Pattern, Flared Sides, Signed, 5 X 10 In.	285.00
Lalique, Burner, Perfume, Frosted Nude, 4 Panels, Countersunk, 6 X 5 In.	135.00
Lalique, Car Mascot, Archers, Signed, C.1925, 5 1/4 In. *Illus*	2600.00
Lalique, Chandelier, Frosted, Blown-Out Globe, 4 Bronze Rings, Signed, 19 In.	950.00
Lalique, Chandelier, Frosted, Leaf Design, Hanging, Signed, France, 19 In.	950.00
Lalique, Christmas Plate Set, 1965-1973	1800.00
Lalique, Clock, Frosted, Leaf Design, Signed, France, No.725, 6 1/2 In.	375.00
Lalique, Clock, Two Pair Love Birds, Blue Stain, 4 1/2 In.Square	475.00
Lalique, Clock, 2 Figurines, Signed, C.1936, 14 3/4 In.	5200.00
Lalique, Compote, Blown-Out Bulbous Pattern, Pedestal, Signed, 11 3/4 In.	425.00
Lalique, Compote, Pedestaled, Frosted Amber, 7 X 8 In.Diameter	145.00
Lalique, Cordial, Females In Classical Dress, Signed, 4 3/4 In.Set Of 6	500.00
Lalique, Cufflinks, Nude & Grapes, Signed, 1 1/4 In.	120.00
Lalique, Decanter, Raised Nudes, Signed R.Lalique, 11 Inches	295.00
Lalique, Dish, Candy, 2 Acid Etched Semi-Nude Dancers, 4 1/2 In.Diam.	250.00
Lalique, Dish, Opalescent, 3 Flowerheads, Form The Feet, 9 In.Diameter	185.00
Lalique, Dish, Pin, Frosted, 2 1/2 X 5 1/4 In.	40.00
Lalique, Dish, Rectangular, Beaded Rim, Signed, 9 X 3 1/4 X 1 1/2 In.	135.00
Lalique, Dish, Swirl, Milk Blue Coloring, Signed, 10 1/2 In.	325.00
Lalique, Dish, 3 Flowerheads, Centers Forming Feet, 9 In.	185.00
Lalique, Figurine, Bear, Frosted Lavender, Signed, 3 1/2 X 2 In.	100.00
Lalique, Figurine, Bird On Pedestal, Signed, 3 1/2 In.	185.00
Lalique, Figurine, Bird, Crystal, Head Up, Satin Finish, Signed, 5 X 3 In.	55.00
Lalique, Figurine, Bird, Head Down, Satin Finish, Signed, 5 X 3 In.	55.00
Lalique, Figurine, Blue & Amber Opalescent, No.831, 5 1/2 In.	950.00
Lalique, Figurine, Eagle, Head, Clear & Frosted, Signed, 4 1/4 X 5 1/2 In.	300.00
Lalique, Figurine, Fish, Green, 2 X 2 In., Pair	60.00
Lalique, Figurine, Frosted Bird, 3 1/2 In.	18.00
Lalique, Figurine, Frosted, Nude Couple Embracing, Black Stand, 10 1/2 In.	275.00

Lalique, Box, Powder, D'Orsay,
Floral, Red, Signed, 4 In.

Lalique, Vase, Cluny, Bronze Mounts,
Blown, C.1925

Lalique, Figurine, Guinea Hens, Male, 7 In., Female, 5 1/2 In., Signed	350.00
Lalique, Figurine, Madonna & Child, 12 In.	225.00
Lalique, Figurine, Man & Woman In 1700s Formal Dress, 5 3/4 In., Pair	125.00
Lalique, Flacon, Frosted, Enameled, Decorated, Stopper, Signed, 4 1/2 X 4 In.	295.00
Lalique, Holder, Business Card, Art Nouveau, Nude Woman, Blue, 6 X 2 1/2 In.	50.00
Lalique, Holder, Place Card, Domed, Frosted, Signed, 1 3/4 X 1 In., Set Of 4	50.00
Lalique, Jar, Powder, Beaded, Blown Out Nude Children, Cover	195.00
Lalique, Lamp Shade, 4 Scalloped Shells, Shallow Hemispherical Form, 12 In.	495.00
Lalique, Medallion, Molded With Flowerheads, Frosted, 1 3/4 In.Diameter	295.00
Lalique, Ornament, Hood, Naked Archer, 1930s, Marked	650.00
Lalique, Ornament, Hood, Peacock	395.00
Lalique, Ornament, Hood, Rooster, 8 In.	275.00 To 430.00
Lalique, Paperweight, Art Nouveau Nude Female, Arms In Back Of Head	235.00
Lalique, Paperweight, Frosted, Nude Female, Signed, 2 3/4 X 1 1/2 In.	195.00
Lalique, Pendant, Fioret, Crystal	295.00
Lalique, Perfume, Frosted Flowers All Over, Signed, 7 1/2 In.	75.00
Lalique, Perfume, Plunger Type, 5 Draped Nudes, Chain Guard Over Opening	85.00
Lalique, Perfume, 8 Sided, Draped Nudes, Chrome Top Atomizer, Signed, 4 In.	55.00
Lalique, Plaque, Menu, Frosted Grapes, 3 1/2 X 5 7/8 In.	165.00
Lalique, Plate, Blue Between Swirls, Signed, 10 1/2 In.Diameter	295.00
Lalique, Plate, Crescent Shape, Crystal, Engraved Pineapples, Signed, 7 In.	50.00
Lalique, Plate, Dessert, Crystal, Molded Block Letter Sign, 7 In.	30.00
Lalique, Plate, Incurved Rim, Fish Spiraling Toward Center, 12 In.	245.00
Lalique, Plate, Leaf, 6 1/2 In.	20.00
Lalique, Plate, Sculptured Leaves, Black, Signed, 10 In.	85.00
Lalique, Pot, Jam, Clear, Paneled, Etched Flowers, Sterling Top	28.00
Lalique, Rose Bowl, Pink, Stylized Tulip Bulb Design, 9 1/2 In.	525.00
Lalique, Shade, Lamp, Hanging, Hemispherical Body, Panels, 14 In.Diameter	595.00
Lalique, Shaker, Martini, 3 Pieces, 9 In., 8 Matching Glasses, Script Signed	500.00
Lalique, Spittoon, Lady's, Fontainebleau, Etched	150.00
Lalique, Tray, Pin, Opalescent Bird In Center, 4 In.	55.00
Lalique, Tumbler, Black Enamel Flower Center, Signed, 3 In.	80.00
Lalique, Urn, Lion Head Two Sides, 3 3/4 X 3 1/2 In.Diameter	100.00
Lalique, Vase, Blue Stain Feathers, Signed, 8 1/4 In.	575.00
Lalique, Vase, Bordieres Epines, Brown Toning, Signed, 7 3/4 X 4 In.	250.00
Lalique, Vase, Bud, Raised Nudes, Signed R. Lalique, 5 Inches	150.00
Lalique, Vase, Camellias, Frosted, Signed In Block Letters, 8 In.	295.00
Lalique, Vase, Cerises, Clear, Frosted, Cherries, 8 In.	900.00
Lalique, Vase, Ceylon, 8 Love Birds, 9 1/2 In.	675.00
Lalique, Vase, Cluny, Bronze Mounts, Blown, C.1925	*Illus* 5500.00
Lalique, Vase, Coqs Et Plumes, Frosted, 6 In.	325.00
Lalique, Vase, Cupids & Birds, Frosted, 6 In.	95.00
Lalique, Vase, Cylindrical Shape, Roosters, Shafts Of Grass, 6 In.	285.00
Lalique, Vase, Dandelion Leaf, Frosted, 8 1/4 X 8 In.	335.00
Lalique, Vase, Escargot, Frosted, Signed, No.931, 8 1/2 X 8 In.	275.00
Lalique, Vase, Flared, Satyrs Crouching Among Foliage, Script France, 7 In.	850.00
Lalique, Vase, Flower Bud Base, Eucalyptus, Signed, 6 1/2 In.	285.00
Lalique, Vase, Formose, Opalescent, Fish In High Relief, 6 1/2 In.	975.00
Lalique, Vase, Graines, Beaded Design, Pink To Blue, 7 1/2 In.	725.00
Lalique, Vase, Gray, Thistle, Signed In Script, France, 8 3/8 In.	550.00
Lalique, Vase, Herd Of Deer Feeding From Tree, Frosted, Signed, 6 1/2 In.	550.00
Lalique, Vase, Honfleur, Blue Stain, Scrolling Vines, 5 1/2 In.	335.00
Lalique, Vase, Lievres, Frieze Of Rabbits Mold, Opalescent, 6 X 5 1/2 In.	350.00
Lalique, Vase, Molded Cherries, Leaves, 7 1/4 In.	55.00
Lalique, Vase, Molded Lovebirds, Frosted, Signed, C.1930, 10 In.	750.00

Lalique, Vase, Nude Panels, Blue Satin, Clear Vase, 7 1/2 In.	1350.00
Lalique, Vase, Nude Sirens, Frosted, Blue Wash, Signed, 5 X 3 1/2 In.	550.00
Lalique, Vase, Opaline Camelias & Vines, Camelia, Flaring Neck, 6 1/2 In.	425.00
Lalique, Vase, Orange Wash, Blown-Out Thistles, Signed, 8 1/2 In.	500.00
Lalique, Vase, Ovoid, Molded Fern On Side, Smoky Cast, 7 X 6 In.Diameter	275.00
Lalique, Vase, Palissy, Frosted, Spherical Body With Snails, 6 1/2 In.	350.00
Lalique, Vase, Parakeet, Corn Stalk, Frosted, Signed, 10 1/4 X 9 In.	900.00
Lalique, Vase, Parakeets, Frosted, Engraved Lalique, France, C.1910, 9 1/2 In.	510.00
Lalique, Vase, Rampillon, Topaz, 5 In.	425.00
Lalique, Vase, Rooster, Bottom Border, Tall Blades Of Grass, 6 In.	265.00
Lalique, Vase, Sophora, Frosted Satin Ground, 10 1/2 X 10 In.Diameter	895.00
Lalique, Vase, Squirrels, Gray, Signed In Block Letters, 7 1/2 In.	435.00
Lalique, Vase, Swimming Fish In Relief, Seahorse Handle, Signed, 7 In.	250.00
Lalique, Vase, Thistle, Bulbous, Smoky Dark Crystal, 8 1/2 In.	675.00
Lalique, Vase, Thistles, Frosted, Signed, 9 1/2 In.	285.00
Lalique, Wine, Crystal, Amber Toning, Signed, France, 3 1/4 In., Pair	75.00
Lalique, Wine, Geometric Frosted Pattern At Base, Signed, 4 1/2 In.	45.00
Lalique, Wine, Stem Forms Rooster, Signed, 6 In.	40.00
Lamartine, Vase, Summer Scene, Mottled Ground, Signed, 8 1/2 In.	785.00
Lamp, see also Bradley & Hubbard, Lamp; Burmese, Lamp	
Handel, Lamp; Pairpoint, Lamp; Tiffany, Lamp	
Lamp, Aladdin, Alacite, Lincoln Drape	67.50
Lamp, Aladdin, Alacite, Lincoln Drape, Scalloped Base	150.00
Lamp, Aladdin, B-100, Venetian, Model A	65.00
Lamp, Aladdin, B-108, Cathedral, Green, 10 In.	60.00
Lamp, Aladdin, B-166, Rose, Moonstone	85.00
Lamp, Aladdin, B-40, Washington Drape, Green	65.00
Lamp, Aladdin, B-52, Washington Drape, Amber	75.00
Lamp, Aladdin, B-55, Washington Drape, Amber	60.00
Lamp, Aladdin, B-60, Lincoln Drape, Alacite	65.00 To 90.00
Lamp, Aladdin, B-77, Lincoln Drape, Red, Tall	300.00
Lamp, Aladdin, B-80, Beehive, Clear	35.00
Lamp, Aladdin, B-82, Beehive, Amber	85.00
Lamp, Aladdin, B-83, Ruby Crystal	175.00
Lamp, Aladdin, Beehive, Amber, B-82	85.00
Lamp, Aladdin, Beehive, Clear, B-80	35.00
Lamp, Aladdin, Bracket, Model 6	52.50
Lamp, Aladdin, Copper Over Brass, 9 X 7 In.	85.00
Lamp, Aladdin, Figural Pineapple Shape, Alacite, Electric	15.00
Lamp, Aladdin, Hanging, Brass Font, White Satin Glass Shade	195.00
Lamp, Aladdin, Hanging, Moonstone Font, Satin Glass Shade, 24 1/2 In.	225.00
Lamp, Aladdin, Hanging, No.6, Shade	140.00
Lamp, Aladdin, Hanging, Satin Shade, No.8 Generator	300.00
Lamp, Aladdin, Lincoln Drape, Alacite	67.50
Lamp, Aladdin, Lincoln Drape, Alacite, Scalloped Base	150.00
Lamp, Aladdin, Nickel, No.9	30.00
Lamp, Aladdin, No.12, Brass	85.00
Lamp, Aladdin, No.1231, Vase	75.00
Lamp, Aladdin, No.1241 Vase	80.00
Lamp, Aladdin, No.1245, Vase	75.00
Lamp, Aladdin, No.1248, Vase	80.00
Lamp, Aladdin, Orientale, B-130	50.00
Lamp, Aladdin, Pedestal, Model 12, Nickel	37.50
Lamp, Aladdin, Rose Design, Alacite, Electric, 26 In.	30.00 To 33.00
Lamp, Aladdin, Shade, No.301	80.00
Lamp, Aladdin, Shade, No.501	75.00
Lamp, Aladdin, Shade, No.6205	200.00
Lamp, Altar, Catholic Church, Cobalt & Red Glass, Brass Frame, 30 3/4 In.	250.00
Lamp, American Shield & Stars, Crimped Handle	80.00
Lamp, Argand, Marble Base, Fluted Stem, Brass Font, Cut Prisms, 23 3/8 In.	210.00
Lamp, Art Deco, Nude Lady Standing On Brass Base, 32 In.	165.00
Lamp, Art Deco, Shade Has 4 Sailboats, Signed	200.00
Lamp, Art Nouveau, Nude Figural, Bronze	55.00
Lamp, Art Nouveau, 2 Nudes Supporting Pagoda House, Bird Finial	163.50
Lamp, Astral, Original Burner, Label W.Carleton, Boston	225.00
Lamp, Banquet, Brass Base, Gold Fleur-De-Lis On Cased Globe, 1889, 29 In.	350.00

Lamp, Banquet, Brass, Cranberry Inverted Thumbprint Shade, Wired	350.00
Lamp, Banquet, Enameled, Blue Background Over Brass, Cranberry Shade, 36 In.	475.00
Lamp, Banquet, Fern Like Branches On Shade, 30 In.	375.00
Lamp, Banquet, Font Dated 1890, Pairpoint Puffed Out Satin Globe, 26 In.	295.00
Lamp, Banquet, Kerosene, Brass Cherub Stem, Amber Fount & Ball Shade	250.00
Lamp, Banquet, Miller New Vestal, Floral, Cream Shade, Onyx, Brass, 30 In.High	225.00
Lamp, Banquet, Miniature, 3 Tier, Red Satin Glass, 18 1/2 In.	495.00
Lamp, Banquet, Miniature, 3 Tier, Yellow Cased Glass, 20 In.	295.00
Lamp, Banquet, Olive Green Globe, Brass Plated Base, Victorian, 33 In.	210.00
Lamp, Banquet, Satin Ball Shade, Step-Up Base, Pink Gold & Silver, 31 In.	550.00
Lamp, Banquet, Slip In Font, Thistles In Globe, Signed, 1895, 29 1/2 In.	295.00
Lamp, Banquet, Winged Cherub Base, Dated 1897, Roses On Globe	250.00
Lamp, Base, Brass Font & Burner, Kerosene, Handled, 4 Scrolled Feet	195.00
Lamp, Base, Bronze, Rayed, 5 Ball Feet, Signed & Numbered, Torchere, 9 In.	130.00
Lamp, Base, Ram's Head, Bronze, 18 In.	125.00
Lamp, Base, Rayed Base, 5 Ball Feet, Desk, Signed & Numbered, 12 In.	130.00
Lamp, Base, Steuben, Acid Cut Back, Yellow Jade Floral, 20 In.	375.00
Lamp, Basket Of Fruit, Handled, Crystal Facet Beads, Art Nouveau	155.00
Lamp, Basket, Glass Flowers, Crystal Beads, Brass Trim, Victorian, 10 In.	125.00
Lamp, Betty, Screw Top, Iron Spout & Wick, Copper, 7 1/2 X 3 1/2 In.	75.00
Lamp, Betty, Sculptured Head At End Of Handle, 17th Century, Brass	120.00
Lamp, Betty, Tin	30.00
Lamp, Bicycle, Old Sol, Carbide	18.00
Lamp, Bicycle, Solar, Gadger Brass Co., Kenosha, Wisc., 7 In.	40.00
Lamp, Bicycle, Wick, Red Glass Windows	45.00
Lamp, Blown & Cut, Double Tube Burner, Applied Handle, 4 In.	165.00
Lamp, Blown Cone Font, Pressed Base, Tin & Cork Drop Burner, 10 In.	90.00
Lamp, Blue Cut To White To Clear, Marble Base, Brass Stem, 1900s, 12 1/2 In.	55.00
Lamp, Boudoir, Etched Prisms & Globe, Bronzed Man Holding Sword, 26 In.	150.00
Lamp, Boudoir, German China, Colonial Figures Base, 5 In.	10.95
Lamp, Boudoir, Jefferson, Cylinder Shape, Covered, Art Glass, Pair	695.33
Lamp, Bracket, Brass Collar, Blown Chimney	30.00
Lamp, Bracket, Clarks, Quilted Background, Signed	75.00
Lamp, Bracket, Swing Arm, Glass, Victorian	25.00
Lamp, Bracket, Wall, Iron Gilt, 1880s	42.00
Lamp, Bracket, With Reflector, Tin	35.00
Lamp, Bradley & Hubbard, see Bradley & Hubbard, Lamp	
Lamp, Brass Mounted, Onyx, Victorian, Tripod Stand, Wolf Heads, 62 1/2 In.	700.00
Lamp, Brass Oil Guard, Mercury Reflector, 1870, 12 In.	90.00
Lamp, Brass, Bell-Shaped, Fluid Lamp, American	18.00
Lamp, Bronze Holders, 3 Lily Shades, Gold Aurene, Green, Buffalo, 12 In.	390.00
Lamp, Bronze, Oriental Jar Base, Birds, Blossoms, Wooden Base, 21 1/2 In.	115.00
Lamp, Camphene, 3-Printie Pattern, Appled Handle, 3 1/2 In.	165.00
Lamp, Candelabra, Marble Base, 20 Cut Pendants, Bronze, 15 In., Pair	97.00
Lamp, Candle, Diamond Quilted, Bulbous Font, Green, 16 X 8 In.Diameter	150.00
Lamp, Candlestick, Art Nouveau, Lavender Blown Prisms, Pair	50.00
Lamp, Canting, Double Lard Oil Wick Supports, Filler Cap	165.00
Lamp, Cap, Carbide, Z.A.R. Mfg., Co., New York, 1913	100.00
Lamp, Carbide, Universal Lamp Co., Springfield, Illinois	32.00
Lamp, Carlisle, Cobalt Blue, 8 In.	135.00
Lamp, Carriage, Beveled Side Glass, Oval Front, French, Brass, 17 1/2 In.Pair	150.00
Lamp, Carriage, Dutch, Silverplate, 22 In.	355.00
Lamp, Chandelier, Brass & Copper, 5 Mottled Shades Signed Muller Freres	250.00
Lamp, Chandelier, Brass & Glass, 12 Light, 5 Tiers, Glass Drops Hung, 48 In.	850.00
Lamp, Chandelier, Brass, Bronze, Red Glass, 6 Light, Victorian, 1800s, 39 In.	1900.00
Lamp, Chandelier, Brass, Electric & Gas, 80 Prisms, 4 Bulb	1700.00
Lamp, Chandelier, Brass, Slag Glass Inserts, 4 Branch, C.1912, 26 X 17 In.	250.00
Lamp, Chandelier, Bronze & China, 8 Light, Electrified, Signed K.P.M.	1500.00
Lamp, Chandelier, Bronze, 5 Glass Shades, Signed Mueller	460.00
Lamp, Chandelier, Cast Iron, Glass Oil Fonts, 2 Branch, Frosted Shades	159.50
Lamp, Chandelier, Crystal Lusters, 4 Branch, Victorian, 34 X 30 In.	170.00
Lamp, Chandelier, Crystal, 5 Branch, Hanging Festoons & Lusters, 27 In.	75.00
Lamp, Chandelier, Cut & Blown Glass, 12 Light, Continental, 42 X 30 In.	275.00
Lamp, Chandelier, Cut Glass, Regency, 52 X 23 In.	750.00
Lamp, Chandelier, Gas Light, Etched Greek Key Shade, Brass, 25 X 21 In.	189.00
Lamp, Chandelier, Mottled Glass, 4 Light, Wrought Iron, 1900s, 15 1/2 In.	350.00

Lamp, Chandelier, Multicolored Leaded Glass, Bronze, C.1890s, 36 In. 8500.00
Lamp, Chandelier, Ormolu, Russian, 8 Light, Pineapple Finial, 1800s, 47 In. 3500.00
Lamp, Chandelier, Pressed & Cut Glass, S-Scroll Arms, 1800s, 40 X 36 In. 1700.00
Lamp, Chandelier, Red Glass, Gilt-Metal, Russian, C.1800, 50 X 32 In. 3200.00
Lamp, Chandelier, Victorian, Mother-Of-Pearl Inlaid, Lacquer, 38 X 35 In. 250.00
Lamp, Charles Rohlfs, Oil, Copper & Shell Shade, C.1900, 18 In. 850.00
Lamp, Chocolate Glass Shade, Matching Base, 2 Lights In Shade, 1 In Base 495.00
Lamp, Clambroth, Baroque Base, Bull's-Eye Font, Burner & Chimney, 19 In. 125.00
Lamp, Clambroth, Base, Acanthus 750.00
Lamp, Cobalt, Nutmeg 68.00
Lamp, Coolidge Drape, Flint 70.00
Lamp, Copper, Mica Inserts, C.1915, 14 X 8 In.Diameter 450.00
Lamp, Copper, Mica Inserts, C.1915, 20 X 13 In.Diameter 600.00
    Lamp, Cosmos, see Cosmos, Lamp
Lamp, Crackle Glass & Bronze, Durand, Egyptian, Bronze Base, 10 1/2 In. 475.00
Lamp, Cranberry, Glass Lusters, Hurricane Shade, 1900s, 24 3/4 In., Pair 700.00
Lamp, Cranberry, Opalescent Hobnails, Ribbon Candy Pleated Top 100.00
Lamp, Crusie, Wrought Iron, Iron Hanger, Wick Pick, 6 In. 70.00
Lamp, Cut Glass, Ball Shape, Hobstar Cutting, 12 In. 450.00
Lamp, Cut Glass, Banquet, Round Dome, 23 1/2 In. 1450.00
Lamp, Cut Glass, Boudoir, Mushroom Shaped Dome, Cane, Prisms, 14 X 6 1/4 In. 425.00
Lamp, Cut Glass, Boudoir, 13 In. 150.00
Lamp, Cut Glass, Cut Flowers, 30 Prisms, 6 In.Strawberry Shade, 13 In. 210.00
Lamp, Cut Glass, Dome Shaped, Hobstar, Hobnail & Cross Hatch, Prisms, 23 In. 1750.00
Lamp, Cut Glass, Fairy, Diamond Point, Amber, Clarke 45.00
Lamp, Cut Glass, Harvard Cut, Matching Top & Bottom, Prisms, 21 In. 1750.00
Lamp, Cut Glass, Harvard, Pierced Rim, Glass Beaded Fringe, 13 1/2 In. 475.00
Lamp, Cut Glass, Mushroom Shade, Harvard Pattern, 39 Prisms, 19 1/2 In. 935.00
Lamp, Cut Glass, Mushroom Shade, Hobstar Center, 22 Prisms, 16 1/2 In. 575.00
Lamp, Cut Glass, Shade Has 12 Point Hobstar Center, 12 Panels, 16 X 10 In. 900.00
Lamp, Daisy & Button, Blue, 11 1/2 In. 225.00
Lamp, Daum Nancy, Grapes & Leaves, Lighted Base, Acid Cutting, 16 In. 3500.00
Lamp, Desk, Emeralite, Shade 100.00
Lamp, Desk, Nautilus Shell, Bronzed Lily Pad Base 75.00
Lamp, Dietz, Kerosene, U.S.A., Dubrown & Hearne 25.00
Lamp, Dome, Brooks Mfg.Co., C.1951, Wood & Leaded Glass, 28 X 20 In. 300.00
Lamp, Double Overlay, Blue, White & Clear, Burner, 11 1/2 In. 575.00
Lamp, Driving, Red Bull's-Eye In Back, Dietz Union, Brass Front, 11 In. 50.00
    Lamp, Fairy, Burmese, see Burmese , Lamp, Fairy
Lamp, Fairy, Clarke Cricklite, 3 Piece, Signed 48.00
Lamp, Fairy, Clear Base, Diamond-Quilted, Acid Finish 135.00
Lamp, Fairy, Cranberry Glass, Mary Gregory Type, 6 In. 45.00
Lamp, Fairy, Decorated Base, Royal Doulton, Webb Burmese Globe 565.00
Lamp, Fairy, Hand-Painted, Tower Of Notre Dame, 18K Gold Gild, C.1810 .... 138.00
Lamp, Fairy, Lithophane, One Piece Dome, Victorian Couple, 9 In. 200.00
Lamp, Fairy, Nailsea, Citron 135.00
Lamp, Fairy, Peach To Yellow, Signed Clarke & Webb, 6 1/2 In., 3 Piece 700.00
Lamp, Fairy, Pedestal, Pink Satin Edged, Frosted Glass 675.00
Lamp, Fairy, Pressed Crystal Glass, Marked Clarke 18.00
Lamp, Fairy, Two Faced, Man & Monkey, Pink Hat, 5 In. 295.00

Lamp, Figural, Moroccan, C.1900,
Cold-Painted, Marked, 12 1/4 In.

Lalique, Car Mascot, Archers,
Signed, C.1925, 5 1/4 In.
(See Page 268)

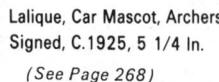

Lamp, Fairy, Verre Moire, Blue, Cut Glass Pedestal Base, Clarke, 14 3/4 In.	275.00
Lamp, Farm House Scene, Jefferson, Signed, 22 In.	800.00
Lamp, Fat, Tin	125.00
Lamp, Figural, Moroccan, C.1900, Cold-Painted, Marked, 12 1/4 In. .... Illus	600.00
Lamp, Finger, Amethyst, Applied Handle, Star & Scroll Embossing	175.00
Lamp, Finger, Applied Blue Handle, Opalescent Coin Spot, Dated	125.00
Lamp, Finger, Arched Loop, Emerald Green	85.00
Lamp, Finger, Cobalt Blue, Paneled, Pedestal Base, 9 In.	150.00
Lamp, Finger, Eyebrow, Pedestal Base	50.00
Lamp, Finger, Flat, Clear, 1870, Oil Guard	48.00
Lamp, Finger, Kerosene, Blue Opalescent, Stripe Clear Chimney	135.00
Lamp, Finger, Oil, Coolidge Drape	50.00
Lamp, Finger, Paneled Sides & Beading, 1870	28.00
Lamp, Finger, Pedestal, Brass Insert, Cobalt, 6 In.	95.00
Lamp, Finger, Peloton Glass, White, Multi-Colored Threadings	460.00
Lamp, Finger, Riveted Handle, 4 1/2 In.Top Of Burner, 4 In.Base	40.00
Lamp, Finger, Sperm Oil, Double Bull's-Eye Pattern, 3 In.	125.00
Lamp, Floor, Brass & Tole, Leaves & Flowers, Art Nouveau, Lights	450.00
Lamp, Floor, Oriental, Carved Owls, Wooden Base, Black Lacquer, 66 1/2 In.	135.00
Lamp, Floor, Wicker	80.00
Lamp, Fluid, Blown Lead Glass, Bell-Shaped Font, 12 In., Pair	70.00
Lamp, Frosted Florette, Green, Electrified Through Font	175.00
Lamp, Girl, Leaves, Marble Base, France, Signed Rosseau, 24 In.	125.00
Lamp, Glass, Clear Font & Base, Blue Stem, New England Glass Co., 10 1/4 In.	1650.00
Lamp, Glass, Clear, Sandwich, Tulip Font, Column Base, 12 In.	165.00
Lamp, Glass, Coolidge Drape Hand, 9 1/2 In.	45.00
Lamp, Glass, Double Bull's-Eye, Globe	125.00
Lamp, Glass, Flowers, Leaves, Smith Brothers, Mt.Washington, White, Pair	250.00
Lamp, Glass, Frosted Drape, Oil, Original, 17 In.	65.00
Lamp, Glass, Hall, Federal Brass & Blown, Brass Collar, 19th Century, 16 In.	325.00
Lamp, Glass, King's Crown	75.00
Lamp, Glass, Ribbed Acorn, Copper Stem, Marble Base	150.00
Lamp, Glass, White Loopings, Pear Shaped Font, New England	800.00
Lamp, Globe, Blue & Red Cranberry, Hall	95.00
Lamp, Globe, Red Cranberry, 9 X 7 1/2 In.Diameter, Pair	95.00
Lamp, Globe, Satellite, Lighted, Clock & Pictures, 24 In.	350.00
Lamp, Gone With The Wind, Acanthus, Pink & White	380.00
Lamp, Gone With The Wind, Base, Red Satin Glass	225.00
Lamp, Gone With The Wind, Beaded Drape, Satin, Original, Electric	550.00
Lamp, Gone With The Wind, Blown Out Roses, Red Satin Glass	595.00
Lamp, Gone With The Wind, Blown White Faces, 24 1/2 In.	450.00
Lamp, Gone With The Wind, Brass Base, Pear-Shape Bottom, Bull's-Eyes, 25 In.	265.00
Lamp, Gone With The Wind, Cranberry Glass, 11 In.	225.00
Lamp, Gone With The Wind, Diamond Pattern, Red Satin, Electrified, 27 In.	400.00
Lamp, Gone With The Wind, Farm Scene, Signed B. & H.	375.00
Lamp, Gone With The Wind, Fuchsia Tea Roses, 26 1/2 In.	495.00
Lamp, Gone With The Wind, Green Satin	175.00
Lamp, Gone With The Wind, Hand-Painted Fleur-De-Lis, 20 In.	295.00
Lamp, Gone With The Wind, Kerosene, Bedroom Size, Milk Glass	175.00
Lamp, Gone With The Wind, Lion Face, Desert Scene, Embossed Brass Font	550.00
Lamp, Gone With The Wind, Oil, The New Rochester, Original, 25 In.	460.00
Lamp, Gone With The Wind, Pink, Blue, Trees, Birs, Signed E.J.Duplex & Co.	350.00
Lamp, Gone With The Wind, Pink, White Lilies, Original, 23 In.	425.00
Lamp, Gone With The Wind, Puffed Out Fishnet & Scroll, Kerosene, C.1890	395.00
Lamp, Gone With The Wind, Red Background, Enameled Chrysanthemums, 20 In.	295.00
Lamp, Gone With The Wind, Red Satin Glass, Dated 1895, Original	795.00
Lamp, Gone With The Wind, Red Satin Glass, 26 In.	525.00
Lamp, Gone With The Wind, Red Satin, Melon Rib, 9 1/2 In.	250.00
Lamp, Gone With The Wind, Red Satin, 10 In.Diameter, 10 In.High	225.00
Lamp, Gone With The Wind, Red, Satin Glass, Blown Out Fruit, 26 In.	650.00
Lamp, Gone With The Wind, Rose & Ruffle Design, Green Satin Glass, 17 In.	435.00
Lamp, Gone With The Wind, Satin Glass, Dated 1895, Large	600.00
Lamp, Gone With The Wind, Satin Glass, Yellow Moire, 10 In.	165.00
Lamp, Gone With The Wind, Wave Crest, Peachblow Color, 10 In.Shade, 17 In.	395.00
Lamp, Gone With The Wind, White Satin Glass, Raised Grape & Leaf Design	275.00
Lamp, Gone With The Wind, Wild Rose, Umbrella Shade & Base, 13 In.	255.00

Lamp, Gone With The Wind, Yellow To Fuchsia Background, Enameled Flowers	495.00
Lamp, Grease, 4 Spout, Wrought Iron, Hanger, 8 1/2 In.	30.00
Lamp, Greek Key, Miniature, Acorn Burner	50.00
Lamp, Hall, Hanging, Etched Glass Shade, Brass Frame, Chain	120.00
Lamp, Hall, Hanging, Swirl Cranberry, Pull Down Canopy, Kerosene	275.00
Lamp, Hall, Kerosene, Brass Fittings, Pink Opalescent Swirl	175.00
Lamp, Hall, Red Satin Ball, Hanging, 10 In.	225.00
Lamp, Hall, Shade Frosted To Clear For Candle, Victorian	70.00
Lamp, Hand, Amber, Ten Panel	65.00
Lamp, Hand, Bull's-Eye, Flat	85.00
Lamp, Hand, Log Cabin, Milk Glass	250.00
Lamp, Hand, Lomax	55.00
Lamp, Hand, Peacock Feather	55.00
Lamp, Hand, Tin, 6 1/4 In.	75.00
Lamp, Hand, Zipper	125.00
Lamp, Handel, see Handel, Lamp	
Lamp, Hanging Dome, 534 Leaded Pieces, Leaves Around Bottom, 24 In.Diam.	975.00
Lamp, Hanging, Candle Burning, Pull Down Canopy, Brass, 17 In.	195.00
Lamp, Hanging, Ceiling, Double Bracket, Victorian, Kerosene, Cast Iron, 14 In.	285.00
Lamp, Hanging, Chain & Smoke Bell, Flared Shade, Tin	125.00
Lamp, Hanging, Chandelier, Brass Chain, White Dome, C.1910	200.00
Lamp, Hanging, Country Store, White Shade, Embossed Font	169.50
Lamp, Hanging, Flowered Ball Shade, Brass Font Holder, Rachet Ceiling Piece	225.00
Lamp, Hanging, Hand-Painted, Brass Frame, Original, 14 In.	350.00
Lamp, Hanging, Hobnail Shade, Cranberry Glass, Brass, Prisms, 14 In.	600.00
Lamp, Hanging, Jeweled, Pull Down Canopy, Candle Burning, Cast Bronze	395.00
Lamp, Hanging, Kitchen, White Shade, Pattern Glass Font, Cast Iron	225.00
Lamp, Hanging, Miniature, Filigreed, All-Over Jewels, Ceiling Canopy	275.00
Lamp, Hanging, Pink Satin, Aurora Borealis Prisms, Shade 13 1/2 In.	850.00
Lamp, Hanging, Prism, Brass Font, Pink Flowers On Shade, 14 In.	265.00
Lamp, Hanging, Prism, Brass Frame, 14 In.Flowered Shade, Pattern Glass Font	295.00
Lamp, Hanging, Prism, Brass Frame, 14 In.Flowered Shade, Patterned Font	297.50
Lamp, Hanging, Pull Down, Opalescent, Candle Burning, Brass Fittings	149.00
Lamp, Hanging, Ruby Glass Font, Prisms, Brass Frame, Electrified	250.00
Lamp, Hanging, White Shade, Brass Frame, Pattern Font	149.50
Lamp, Hanging, White Shade, Brass Frame, Pull-Down Ceiling Piece	169.50
Lamp, Hooded, Hanging, Kerosene, Tin, Original Green Paint	65.00
Lamp, Hurricane, Cambridge, Rosepoint, No.1617, Pair	250.00
Lamp, Hurricane, Candle, Intaglio Cut Shade, 8 Prisms, Swirl, 15 1/2 In.	45.00
Lamp, Iron, Figure, End-Of-Day Globe, 21 In.	95.00
Lamp, Jefferson, Reverse & Surface Painted Scene, Signed, 23 In.	850.00
Lamp, Jefferson, Scenic, Signed, 18 In.Diameter	850.00
Lamp, Jefferson, 4 In.Band Of Roses At Bottom, 6-Sided	975.00
Lamp, Karl Kipp, Copper, Slag Glass Panels, C.1915, 20 1/2 In.	700.00
Lamp, Kerosene, Bracket, Glass Font, Tin Reflector	39.00
Lamp, Kerosene, Brass Column, Black Metal Base, Clear Font	55.00
Lamp, Kerosene, Camphor Glass, Hand Stem	75.00
Lamp, Kerosene, Clambroth Fluted, Brass Joins Top & Base, 10 1/2 In.	60.00
Lamp, Kerosene, Clear Font, Vaseline Base, Belmont	120.00
Lamp, Kerosene, Country Scene, House & Fence, Bristol, 18 1/2 In.	210.00
Lamp, Kerosene, Cylindrical, Hall Light, Inverted Thumbprint	275.00
Lamp, Kerosene, Glass Jug Swings On Chain, Wood Holder, 1914, 27 In.	35.00
Lamp, Kerosene, Green, Cable & Fish Scale, 19 1/2 In.	150.00
Lamp, Kerosene, Hand-Painted Flowers, Milk Glass	36.00
Lamp, Kerosene, Mirror-Backed, Blue Glass Reservoir	35.00
Lamp, Kerosene, Relief Scrolls, Beaded Base, Milk Glass, 14 1/2 In.	89.00
Lamp, Kerosene, Table, Peacock Feather, 10 In.	55.00
Lamp, Kerosene, Turkeman, Copper Bottom, Pottery Wick Holder, C.1828	275.00
Lamp, Kissing Lovebirds, C.1920, Art Deco, 10 1/2 In.	75.00
Lamp, Lantern, Police, Dietz, Sliding Tin Screen, Cone Top, Bronze Paint	30.00
Lamp, Lard Oil, Saucer Base, Tin, Removable Cup Burner, 7 In.	90.00
Lamp, Leaded Glass, Hanging, Victorian, 14 1/2 In.Square	250.00
Lamp, Library, Brass Frame, Prisms, Ceiling Canopy, Signed, 14 In.Shade	395.00
Lamp, Library, Kerosene, Hand-Painted Shade, C.1890	395.00
Lamp, Library, Pull-Down, Prisms, Dated 1893, Maroon Ground, Signed, 14 In.	395.00
Lamp, Library, Pull Down, 14 In.Shade & Font, Flowers, Butterflies, Signed	395.00

Lamp, Lincoln Drape, Alacite, Pair	195.00
Lamp, Lincoln Drape, Miniature, Clear, Swirl Chimney, 6 1/2 In.	35.00
Lamp, Long Loop, Green, 9 In.	95.00
Lamp, Loom Light, 19 In.	65.00
Lamp, Meeting House, Wall Bracket, Brass, Penacook, N.H., 15 In., Pair	175.00
Lamp, Metal, Figural, Female, Muse De Bois, Plants Form Sockets, 1900s, 39 In.	200.00
Lamp, Milk Glass, Flat Bowl, Rounded Foot & Stem, 9 In.	60.00
Lamp, Milk Glass, Oil, Blue, Ribbed, Turnip Shape	130.00
Lamp, Milk Glass, Oriental Figures & Writing, Blue, 7 1/2 In.	45.00
Lamp, Milk Glass, Spider Web, Original Chimney	95.00
Lamp, Milk Glass, Versailles, 8 In.	105.00
Lamp, Miner's, Carbide, Polished Brass	10.00
Lamp, Miner's, Brass, Miniature	33.00
Lamp, Miner's, Brass, Wales	55.00
Lamp, Miner's, Monongahela, Penna., Hook & Spout, Signed	20.00
Lamp, Miner's, Sunshine, Dunlap, Pittsburgh	15.00
Lamp, Miniature, Amber Glass Base, Shade In Moon & Star, Brass Burner	135.00
Lamp, Miniature, Amber Satin Glass, Beaded Swirl Base	200.00
Lamp, Miniature, Banquet, Brass Base, Satin Cranberry Etched Globe, 9 In.	195.00
Lamp, Miniature, Base, Cosmos, Glass Chimney	30.00
Lamp, Miniature, Beaded Drape, White Satin Ball Shade	135.00
Lamp, Miniature, Beaded Swirl, Cranberry	275.00
Lamp, Miniature, Bracket, Nickel, Brass, Signed, 6 In., Milk Glass Shade, 1890	159.00
Lamp, Miniature, Brass, Little Jewel	65.00
Lamp, Miniature, Bristol Glass, Country Scenes On Base & Shade	245.00
Lamp, Miniature, Camphor Glass, Chimney, Signed	18.00
Lamp, Miniature, Greek Key	55.00
Lamp, Miniature, Hall, Brass Chains, Cranberry Swirl, 20 In.	150.00
Lamp, Miniature, Inverted Thumbprint, Amber Shade & Chimney	295.00
Lamp, Miniature, Inverted Thumbprint, Cranberry Glass, Acorn Burner, 9 In.	175.00
Lamp, Miniature, Lincoln Drape, Shade	52.50
Lamp, Miniature, Little Buttercup, Cobalt, Applied Handle	68.00
Lamp, Miniature, Little Duchess, Milk Glass	57.50
Lamp, Miniature, Little Jewel, Embossed, Complete With Shade	135.00
Lamp, Miniature, Milk Glass, Green Base & Matching Ball Shade	225.00
Lamp, Miniature, Nellie Bly, Blue Shade	165.00
Lamp, Miniature, Nellie Bly, Orange	135.00
Lamp, Miniature, Nutmeg	18.00
Lamp, Miniature, Octagonal Shade & Base, Milk Glass	125.00
Lamp, Miniature, Oil, Blue Satin Beaded Drape	245.00
Lamp, Miniature, Oriental Figures, Milk Glass, Blue, 7 In.	45.00
Lamp, Miniature, Pearl Glass, Embossed Design, Signed Chimney	195.00
Lamp, Miniature, Porcelain, Spectacle Dragon, Ivory Coloring, Signed	300.00
Lamp, Miniature, Quilted Phlox	375.00
Lamp, Miniature, Red Satin Glass, Petal-Type Shade	265.00
Lamp, Miniature, Rochester Jr., Dated 1886	135.00
Lamp, Miniature, Rubena Crystal, Diamond-Quilted, Gold Enamel	225.00
Lamp, Miniature, Ruffled, Bull's-Eye	35.00
Lamp, Miniature, Satin Glass, Tulip Shade	100.00
Lamp, Miniature, Smith, Pedestal Base, Clear	45.00
Lamp, Miniature, Tiny Juno, Embossed, Complete With Shade	135.00
Lamp, Miniature, Triple Extract Jockey Club, Marked, 1898, 2 1/2 In.	65.00
Lamp, Miniature, Wall Hung, Embossed, Brass Reflector, Milk Glass, Blue	165.00
Lamp, Miniature, White Milk Glass	165.00
Lamp, Miniature, 6 Glass Jewels Around 6 1/8 In. Shade, Marked, 12 3/4 In.	195.00
Lamp, Moe Bridges, Reverse Painted, Signed, 12 X 7 In.Diameter	250.00
Lamp, New England Glass Co., Clear Font, Sapphire Blue Stem, 10 1/4 In.	1500.00
Lamp, New England Glass Company, Opaque White	320.00
Lamp, Newelpost, Nouveau Lady, 3 Lights, Bronze Finish	125.00
Lamp, Night Light, Head Of Negro Boy, Blue Paperweight Eyes, 3 1/4 In.	115.00
Lamp, Night, Milk Glass Shade, Comet	38.00
Lamp, Nippon, Cascading Flowers, 10 1/2 In.	85.00
Lamp, Northwood, Base, Frosted Cranberry, Vaseline, Leaf Mold	150.00
Lamp, Nutmeg, Miniature, Brass Ting & Handle, Green, Clear Chimney	75.00
Lamp, Oil, Aquarius, Amber, 9 In.	120.00
Lamp, Oil, Atterbury, Burst Bubbles On Rim, Dated 1872	35.00

Lamp, Oil, Beaded Heart Pattern, Green, C.1850	150.00
Lamp, Oil, Blue Opalescent, Enameled Flowers, 23 In.	95.00
Lamp, Oil, Blue Opalescent, Square Font, Clear Stem, Fluted Shade, 17 1/2 In.	175.00
Lamp, Oil, Brass Stem, Coin Spot, 17 In.	110.00
Lamp, Oil, Bull's-Eye & Peanut Pattern, Clear Glass, 3 Pint	80.00
Lamp, Oil, Bull's-Eye, Green, 8 1/2 In.	115.00
Lamp, Oil, Chimney, Birds & Insects, Frosted, Cranberry Flashings, 9 1/2 In.	40.00
Lamp, Oil, Erin Fan, Green, 9 In.	125.00
Lamp, Oil, Erin Fan, Handled, 10 In.	115.00
Lamp, Oil, Etched Glass & Brass, Empire, Stepped Marble Base, 1850s, 22 In.	250.00
Lamp, Oil, Finger, Greek Key, Dated 1870	40.00
Lamp, Oil, Finger, Lomax, Dated 1870	33.00
Lamp, Oil, Finger, Prince Edward, C.1870	45.00
Lamp, Oil, Grecian, Bronze, Tiffany Studios, 20 In.	450.00
Lamp, Oil, Heart, Green, 9 In.	95.00
Lamp, Oil, Horn Of Plenty, Whale	165.00
Lamp, Oil, Miniature, Clear, Blown Out Base & Shade, Acid Etched Leaf, Pair	200.00
Lamp, Oil, Miniature, Cupid Carrying Fire Buckets, Brass, 3 3/4 In.	28.00
Lamp, Oil, Peacock, Clear, 7 In.	38.00
Lamp, Oil, Peanut, Handled, Green, 7 In.	115.00
Lamp, Oil, Pink Satin Glass, Melon Panels & Beading, 26 1/2 In.	395.00
Lamp, Oil, Pink, Gold On White, Lacey Base	42.00
Lamp, Oil, Pressed Glass, Iron Base, Brass Burner & Chimney	35.00
Lamp, Oil, Pressed Glass, Whale, Pair	250.00
Lamp, Oil, Ratchet Spout, Tin, 3 1/2 In.	35.00
Lamp, Oil, Rayo, Dated On Burner, November, 1894	65.00
Lamp, Oil, Thumbprint & Fan Base, Amber, 7 In.	95.00
Lamp, Oil, Turkey Foot, Blue, 8 1/2 In.	155.00
Lamp, Oil, Vasa Murrhina	500.00
Lamp, Oil, Vaseline Font, Dated 1876, 14 In.	75.00
Lamp, Organ, Floor Style, Wrought Iron, Adjustable, 48 In.	125.00
Lamp, Owl, Miniature, Original Chimney	925.00
Lamp, Pairpoint, see Pairpoint, Lamp	
Lamp, Panel, Art Nouveau, Mushroom Caramel Slag Shade, Matched Base, 21 In.	325.00
Lamp, Panel, 6 Panels, Caramel Slag, Gold Base	200.00
Lamp, Paperweight, 3 Sections, Red Flowers, Pewter Finial, 30 In.	250.00
Lamp, Parrot, Blue, Orange Head, Black Base, Pottery, 13 1/2 In.	250.00
Lamp, Pedestal, Fishscale, 2 Finger, Green	110.00
Lamp, Peg-Lamp, Lard Oil, Ribbed Font	80.00
Lamp, Peg, Blown Glass, Wooden Base, 7 X 4 1/4 In.	60.00
Lamp, Peg, Swirl Base, Maroon To Pink, Sterling Silver, 15 1/2 In.	350.00
Lamp, Peg, 10 Ribbed, Clear Paneling, Insert Rod For Candle Cup, C.1850	99.00
Lamp, Petticoat, Candle Socket, Drip Pan, Bell Shaped Base, Blown, 6 1/4 In.	165.00
Lamp, Pewter, Double Wick Burner, Scroll Handle, American, 4 X 4 1/4 In.	150.00
Lamp, Piano, Acorn Shade, Figure Of Woman, 55 In.	175.00
Lamp, Pool Table Light, 6 Bulb, Hangs 4 Feet From Ceiling, Brass Link Chain	2500.00
Lamp, Porcelain, Chinese, Reverse Floral, Ju-I Heads, 17 1/4 In., Pair	1700.00
Lamp, Porcelain, Coach, Horses, Cinderella	30.00
Lamp, Pottery Grease, Dark Brown Shiny Glaze, 4 1/2 In.	350.00
Lamp, Pressed Glass, Greek Key, Kerosene, Square	55.00
Lamp, Pressed Glass, Hand, 6 In.	45.00
Lamp, Pressed Glass, Janice, 8 1/2 In.	45.00
Lamp, Pressed Glass, Paneled Sawtooth, 7 1/2 In.	45.00
Lamp, Pressed Glass, Peacock Feather, Kerosene, Base	42.00
Lamp, Pressed Glass, Swirled Rosettes, 8 1/2 In.	35.00
Lamp, Pressed Glass, Torpedo, Finger	60.00
Lamp, Pressed Glass, Turkey Foot, Finger	48.00
Lamp, Pressed Glass, Waffle Cube, 7 1/2 In.	55.00
Lamp, Pressed Glass, Zipper, Kerosene	160.00
Lamp, Projector, Paraffin, 27 X 13 In.Diameter	125.00
Lamp, Pull-Down, Hand-Painted Shade, , W. & S. Little Giant, Shade 14 In.	495.00
Lamp, Pull-Down, Milk Glass Font & Shade, Hand-Painted, Brass Frame	295.00
Lamp, Rayo, Original Shade, Blown Out Diamond Quilted, 1882, Amber, 21 In.	135.00
Lamp, Reverse Painted Shade, Art Deco Base, 16 In.	110.00
Lamp, Reverse Painted, Diamond Medallions, Gilt Metal Base, 24 In.	375.00
Lamp, Reverse Painted, Satin Glass Base, 12 In.	195.00

Lamp, Reverse Painted, 4 Panels, Scene Each Side, 12 X 5 In.Diameter	95.00
Lamp, Reverse Painting On Shade, Bronze Base, Greek Key Design, 25 In.	210.00
Lamp, Revolving, Budweiser Clydesdale	1000.00
Lamp, Sandwich Glass, Brass Stem, Marble Base, Original Burner & Chimney	45.00
Lamp, Sandwich Glass, Oil, Cobalt Blue, White Swirl, Opalescent Base	2500.00
Lamp, Sandwich Glass, Red Flashed Font, Brass Stem, Marble Base	90.00
Lamp, Sandwich Glass, Sterling Base, Overlay, White & Clear	700.00
Lamp, Sandwich Glass, Tulip Font, Column Base, 12 In.	165.00
Lamp, Sandwich Glass, Whale Oil, Bull's-Eye Font, Clambroth Base, 11 In.	125.00
Lamp, Sandwich Glass, Whale Oil, Light-Bulb Font, Pressed Base	85.00
Lamp, Sandwich Glass, Whale Oil, Star & Punty, Pair	225.00
Lamp, Sandwich Glass, Whale Oil, Tube Burner, Acanthus Leaf, Pear Shape Bowl	95.00
Lamp, Satin Glass, see Satin Glass, Lamp	
Lamp, Satin Glass, Small Blownout Roses, Brass Mountings, Red, 26 In.	825.00
Lamp, Sconce, Brass, English Victorian, Wired, Pair	300.00
Lamp, Sconce, Queen Anne, 3 Arm, Brass, Pair	600.00
Lamp, Sconce, Wall, Bronze, Cut Glass, 9 Light, Classical Figures, 39 In., Pair	1000.00
Lamp, Shade, Amberina, Ball, Enameled Flowers, 21 In.Outside, 2 1/2 In.Bottom	75.00
Lamp, Shade, Inverted Thumbprint, Amber, Ruffled Edge, 8 1/2 X 5 In.	35.00
Lamp, Shade, Leaded Glass, Bent Glass Corners, 14 Petals, 22 In.Diameter	1000.00
Lamp, Shade, Leaded Glass, 375 Panels, Acorn Pulls & Finial, 17 In.Diameter	495.00
Lamp, Silver Plated, Corinthian Column, Flowers, 1900s, 27 1/2 In.	350.00
Lamp, Single Spout, Made From Pet Milk Can, 5 In.	12.50
Lamp, Six Panel, Caramel Base & Shade, 20 In.	175.00
Lamp, Slag, Blue, 6 Panel, Umbrella Shade, Egyptian Design, 1920s, 25 In.	350.00
Lamp, Slag, Green, Oak Frame & Base, 12 In.Diameter	75.00
Lamp, Smith Brothers, Bronze & China, Heron & Reeds	350.00
Lamp, Store, Brass Font, Slipdown Shade, 1890-95, 32 In.	175.00
Lamp, Store, Brass, Signed Miller, Waffle Shade, Bell Dated 1895, 15 In.	175.00
Lamp, Store, Hanging, Tin Shade, Juno Lamp Co., Electrified, Polished	175.00
Lamp, Street, St.Louis, Missouri, Cast Base, Glass Globe, Oak Posts, 10 Feet	69.95
Lamp, Student, American, Green Glass Font, Perfection 1881, Green Overlay	475.00
Lamp, Student, Brass, 2 Swirled Green Glass Shades, C.1800, 29 In.	525.00
Lamp, Student, Dated May 23, 1876, Manhattan Brass Co.	295.00
Lamp, Student, Manhattan Brass Co., 1879, Electrified, Green Swirl Shade	225.00
Lamp, Student, Oil, White Shade, 1878	225.00
Lamp, Student, Rochester, Dated 1894, Green Cased Shade, 10 In.	495.00
Lamp, Student, Signed Schneider, 1870, 7 In.Shade	350.00
Lamp, Student, Single Arm, Pink Cased Glass Shade, Brass	275.00
Lamp, Sweetheart, Miniature, Green	150.00
Lamp, Table, Agate Stem & Prisms, Brass	385.00
Lamp, Table, Alabaster, 1920	27.50
Lamp, Table, Brass Stem, Marble Base, 12 In.Burner, Marked	700.00
Lamp, Table, Bronze, Caramel Slag Glass Shade, 24 In.	150.00
Lamp, Table, Bronze, In Shape Of Gondola, 17 1/2 In.	55.00
Lamp, Table, Burnished Brass, 1890, Ribbed Spatter Shade, 21 1/2 In.	195.00
Lamp, Table, Cherub & Lamb Stem, Frosted Font	34.50
Lamp, Table, Chocolate Glass, Cast Base, Art Nouveau	200.00
Lamp, Table, Cut & Pressed Dome, Dated 1905, 30 Prisms, Sharon Pattern	195.00
Lamp, Table, Famille Rose, Figure Of Kuan Yin, C.1800, 21 1/2 In., Pair	700.00
Lamp, Table, King Tut Pattern, Durand	395.00
Lamp, Table, Leaded, Brown Swags & Red Center, Carved Brass Base	650.00
Lamp, Table, Opaline Glass, Blue, Napoleon III, C.1875, 21 In., Pair	500.00
Lamp, Table, Oriental Brass Base, 25 In.	60.00
Lamp, Table, Painted Scenic, Mottled Opalescent Art Glass, Landscape	475.00
Lamp, Table, Pink, Yellow, Green, Petticoat Shade, Brass Base, Miller, 17 In.	325.00
Lamp, Table, Silvered-Metal, Floral Scrolls In Relief, 1900s, 38 1/2 In.	100.00
Lamp, Table, Tenaud, Red Slag, Bent Glass Shade, 23 In.	500.00
Lamp, Tiffany, see Tiffany, Lamp	
Lamp, Time, Miniature, Milk Glass, Beehive Shade	110.00
Lamp, Tin, Camphene	75.00
Lamp, Twin Horsehead, Pincushion Paperweight, 10 X 4 X 7 In.	75.00
Lamp, Two Branch, Pendant Lanterns, C.1915, Copper, Amber Slag, 22 In.	1250.00
Lamp, Vapo-Cresolene, Original Box	38.00
Lamp, Wedding, Chinese, White Porcelain, 1920s, 11 X 21 In.	165.00
Lamp, Weller, Aurelian, Oil, Artist Signed, 10 In,	495.00

Lamp, Weller, Louwelsa, Large Jonquil, 12 In.	65.00
Lamp, Weller, Urn Shape, Sicard, Original Paper Shade, 9 In.	425.00
Lamp, Whale Oil, American Pewter, Marked Morey & Ober	225.00
Lamp, Whale Oil, Argand Style, C.1800, 17 In., Pair	995.00
Lamp, Whale Oil, Base Weighted, Tin	85.00
Lamp, Whale Oil, Basket Of Flowers, Lion Heads, Blown Font, Clear	325.00
Lamp, Whale Oil, Blown & Pressed, Threaded Pewter Collar, 4 1/2 In.	185.00
Lamp, Whale Oil, Blown Font & Stem, 13 In.	125.00
Lamp, Whale Oil, Blown, Tin Drop Burner, Stamped Patent, 1800s, 3 1/2 In.	185.00
Lamp, Whale Oil, Blue Acanthus Leaf Font, Brass Stem, Marble Base, 9 In., Pr.	525.00
Lamp, Whale Oil, Brass Burner, Saucer & Cone, 4 X 2 1/2 In.	30.00
Lamp, Whale Oil, Brass, 6 1/4 In.	48.00
Lamp, Whale Oil, Brass, 8 In.	70.00
Lamp, Whale Oil, Bull's-Eye, Fleur-De-Lis & Heart Pattern, Pair	295.00
Lamp, Whale Oil, Clambroth Base, Gold Trim, Overlay Font, Ribbed Shaft	850.00
Lamp, Whale Oil, Colonial, Pedestal	95.00
Lamp, Whale Oil, Conical, Hexagonal Paneled Font, Pewter Collar	40.00
Lamp, Whale Oil, Cut Overlay, Ribbed Shaft, White Cut To Opaque Green	850.00
Lamp, Whale Oil, Dolphin, Hexagonal Font & Base, Amber	78.00
Lamp, Whale Oil, Finger, Waffle & Thumbprint, Flint, 3 In.	95.00
Lamp, Whale Oil, Gilt Brass Columns, Marble Base, Sawtooth Pattern, 13 In.	285.00
Lamp, Whale Oil, Glass, Clambroth, Paneled Font, Baluster Base, 8 3/4 In.	225.00
Lamp, Whale Oil, Hand, Pressed Glass, Moon & Star	65.00
Lamp, Whale Oil, Horn Of Plenty, Original Top, 11 In.	220.00
Lamp, Whale Oil, Miniature, Pewter Collar, Blown-In-Mold, 2 3/4 In.	45.00
Lamp, Whale Oil, Onion Font, Blown Ball & Knops, 8 1/4 In.	110.00
Lamp, Whale Oil, Pewter, Double Spout, Cylindrical Font, Sauce Base, 7 In.	160.00
Lamp, Whale Oil, Police, Bull's-Eye, Japan, 2 Spout, C.1840, 7 In.	65.00
Lamp, Whale Oil, Ribbed Font, 6 Sided Base, Green Glass, Pair	115.00
Lamp, Whale Oil, Star & Punty, 6 Panel Bowl, Pewter Collar, 10 1/2 In.	110.00
Lamp, Whale Oil, Twin Spouts, Blown In Mold, C.1830, 8 1/2 In., Pair	450.00
Lamp, Whale Oil, Urn Style, Weighted Base, 7 1/2 In.	125.00
Lamp, Whale Oil, Waffle Font, 6 Sided Dolphin Base, 11 1/2 In., Pair	425.00
Lamp, Whale Oil, Wine Glass, Knob Stem, Circular Feet, Freeblown, 3 1/4 In.	165.00
Lamp, Wrought Iron, Domical Shade Etched Muller Fres, Luneville, 22 In.	550.00
Lantern, Arched Top, Pierced Smoke Chamber, Rectangular, Tin, 19th Century	145.00
Lantern, Barn, Copper Bottom, G.T.Ham Mfg., Co.	40.00
Lantern, Bicycle, Jim Dandy, Plated Brass	35.00
Lantern, Boat, Luck-E-Lite, Kerosene, Red Globe	27.50
Lantern, Buckeye, Inside & Outside Globe	150.00
Lantern, Buggy, Hand, Metal Back	12.50
Lantern, Candle, Tin, Glass, 10 In.	30.00
Lantern, Candle, Tin, 12 In.	125.00
Lantern, Candle, 4 Glass Sided, Pierced Tin Cone, Boston, Mass., Signed	140.00
Lantern, Carbide, Just-Rite, Brass	25.00
Lantern, Coleman, Polished & Lacquered	19.50
Lantern, Dietz, Fire King, Brass	110.00
Lantern, Half-Round, Tin, Pierced Door	155.00
Lantern, Hatch, Removable Font, Brass, 15 1/2 In.X 10 In.	70.00
Lantern, Horn, 3 Horn Lights, Candle Socket, Chamberstick, Punched Top	325.00
Lantern, Railroad, see, Railroad, Lantern	
Lantern, Skater's, Brass, 7 In.	49.00
Lantern, Skater's, Jewel, Green Globe	45.00
Lantern, Toleware, Yellow, Chinoiserie Scene, C.1810, French, 15 1/4 X 8 In.	275.00
Lantern, Wagon, Bail Handle, Clear Bull's-Eye Reflector, Dietz, Tin	45.00
Lantern, Whale Oil, Bull's-Eye Lens, Tin, 8 In.	36.00
Lantern, Whale Oil, Glass Font, Bail Ring	125.00
Lantern, Whale Oil, Pierced Top & Base, Tin, Bail Handle, 16 1/2 In.	75.00
Lapis Lazuli, Figurine, Hoeti, Seated, Carved, 2 1/2 X 2 1/4 In.	285.00

Le Verre Francais cameo glass was made in France between 1920 and 1933 by the C. Schneider Factory. It is mottled and usually decorated with floral designs, and bears the incised signature *Le Verre Francais.*

Le Verre Francais, Bowl, Punch, Cobalt & Orange Flowers, Signed, 10 3/4 In.	650.00
Le Verre Francais, Bowl, 7 In.Diameter, 4 In.Tall	220.00

Le Verre Francais, Lamp, Tortoiseshell Shades, Flowers, Signed .... *Illus*	900.00
Le Verre Francais, Planter, Stylized Cameo, Art Deco, Signed, 6 1/2 X 4 In.	250.00
Le Verre Francais, Planter, Stylized Cameo, Signed, 4 1/2 X 6 1/2 In.	195.00
Le Verre Francais, Vase, Abstract Cut, Signed With Candy Cane, 13 3/4 In.	150.00
Le Verre Francais, Vase, Cameo Cut, Bulbous, Maroon Shades, Signed, 9 In.	260.00
Le Verre Francais, Vase, Cameo, Floral, Acid Cut, Maroon, Pink, Signed, 5 In.	165.00
Le Verre Francais, Vase, Cameo, Orange, 7 1/2 X 10 In.	275.00
Le Verre Francais, Vase, Cobalt, Yellow & Orange, Art Deco, 17 In.	325.00
Le Verre Francais, Vase, Footed, Deep Cut, , 6 X 4 In.	359.00
Le Verre Francais, Vase, Wisteria & Tortoise, Bulbous, Signed, 10 X 8 In.	450.00
Leather, Box, Snuff, Hand-Painted Polychrome Lid, Figural Shoe, 3 In.	145.00
Leather, Case, Attache, Alligator, Matched Hides	400.00
Leather, Case, Cigarette, Fatima Cigarettes, 1914, Boston Auto Show	18.50
Leather, Collar, Horse, Steel Hames, Brass Knobs	27.50
Leather, Deed, Sheepskin, Switzerland County, Indiana, Signed J.Monroe	95.00
Leather, Desk Pad & Pen Wiper, Roycroft Shop, C.1917, 17 X 12 In.	100.00
Leather, Flask, Bullet, Thong For Suspension, Handmade, 3 1/8 X 4 3/4 In.	48.00
Leather, Footstool, Goat's Feet	60.00
Leather, Glove, Falconer's, Mesh Chain Mail	24.00
Leather, Hat, Miner's, Bull's-Eye Lens, Tin Lamp, Fluted Cone Top, Lard Oil	135.00
Leather, Polisher, Lignum Vitae, Flat Bottom, One Piece, Handled	22.00
Leather, Purse, Shoulder Strap, 2 Compartments, Alligator	150.00

LEEDS POTTERY. *Leeds pottery was made at Leeds, Yorkshire, England, from 1774 to 1878. Most Leeds ware was not marked. Early Leeds pieces had distinctive twisted handles with a greenish glaze on part of the creamy ware. Later ware often had blue borders on the creamy pottery.*

Leeds, Bowl, Blue, White, Criss-Cross & Scallop Banded, Pinwheel Base, 3 In.	38.00
Leeds, Bowl, Creamware, Matching Tray, Oval, 18th Century	225.00
Leeds, Bowl, Variegated Pearlware, C.1805, 8 5/8 In.Diam.	150.00
Leeds, Cup & Tea Bowl, Child's, Handleless, Rust & Green Border	48.00
Leeds, Plate, Blue Feather Edge, Embossed Sign, Soft Paste, 10 1/4 In.	45.00
Leeds, Plate, Eagle Design, Feather Border, 8 In.	285.00
Leeds, Plate, Mother & Child, To My Mother, Feather-Edged, Green, Creamware	125.00
Leeds, Plate, Soup, Green Feather Edge, Embossed Flowers & Leaves, 10 In.	60.00
Leeds, Platter, Creamware, Feathered Edge, 16 X 12 In.	125.00
Leeds, Pot, Blue, Dome Top, 11 1/4 In.	500.00
Leeds, Sugar, Covered, Child's, Finial Lid	45.00

LEGVAS *Legras glass was made by August J. F. Legras in Saint-Denis, France, between 1864 and 1914. Cameo, acid cut, and enameled glass were made.*

Legras, Bowl, Butterscotch Ground, Caramel Cased Inside, 3 1/2 X 6 1/4 In.	300.00
Legras, Bowl, Pulled Corners, Butterscoth, Caramel Cased, 4 3/4 X 3 1/4 In.	300.00
Legras, Lamp, Art Glass, Mushroom Shade, Enameled Shell Design, 16 1/2 In.	900.00
Legras, Rose Bowl, Raised Enamel Florals, Mottled Yellow Ground, 5 X 4 In.	90.00
Legras, Rose Bowl, Spherical, Cameo Cut, Magenta Leaf & Berry, Signed	120.00
Legras, Vase, Acid Cut, Decorated With Gold, 8 In.	400.00
Legras, Vase, Acid Cut, Drapes & Swags, Signed, 6 1/2 In.	350.00
Legras, Vase, Acid Cut, Hand-Painted Enamel, Signed, 13 3/4 X 7 In.Diam.	650.00
Legras, Vase, Acid Etched, Covered In Maroon Enameled Leaves, Signed, 11 In.	465.00
Legras, Vase, Art Deco, Acid Cut, Stylized Leaves, Signed, 6 1/2 In.	200.00
Legras, Vase, Berries On Branch, Frosted Body, Maroon Shades, Signed, 12 In.	135.00
Legras, Vase, Blood Red Cut To Bright Red, Signed, 16 In.	375.00
Legras, Vase, Cameo & Enamel, Pink With Lavender, Signed, 10 1/2 In.	215.00
Legras, Vase, Cameo & Enamel, Underwater Plants, Bulbous, Signed, 7 1/4 In.	475.00
Legras, Vase, Cameo, Cranberry, Frosted Crystal, 7 3/4 X 3 3/4 X 3 1/2 In.	250.00
Legras, Vase, Cameo, Gold Ground, Mountain Scene, 8 1/2 X 2 1/2 In.Square	300.00
Legras, Vase, Cameo, Lavender Wisteria & Brown Luster, 13 In.	590.00
Legras, Vase, Cameo, Mountain & Lake Scene, Green, Lavender, 4 X 4 1/2 In.	495.00
Legras, Vase, Cameo, Purple Leaves, Frosted Wine Background, 11 In.	445.00
Legras, Vase, Cameo, Shepherd Scene, 13 In.	250.00
Legras, Vase, Cameo, 2 Shades Of Green On Orange, Mint & White, 11 1/4 In.	700.00
Legras, Vase, Carved, Scenic, Square, Signed, 8 In.	165.00
Legras, Vase, Cylinder Shaped, Polychrome Flowers, Enamel Signature, 3 In.	215.00
Legras, Vase, Cylindrical, Polychrome Flowers, Enamel, Signed, 3 X 2 1/2 In.	215.00

Legras, Vase, Diamond Shaped, Open, Scenic, Signed, 8 In.	475.00
Legras, Vase, Enameled Blue Flowers, Mottled Glass, Signed, 16 In., Pair	1650.00
Legras, Vase, Lavender Mountains, Green Lake & Bushes, Scenic, 4 X 4 1/2 In.	495.00
Legras, Vase, Multi-Colored Ground, Enameled, Signed, 2 3/4 X 2 1/2 In.	150.00
Legras, Vase, Orange & Green, Trees, Lake House, Enameled, 9 1/2 In.	150.00
Legras, Vase, Scenic, Shades Of Green, 4 Casings, 7 1/4 X 4 In.	465.00
Legras, Vase, Scenic, Tangerine Ground, Layers Of Cutting, 4 In.	395.00
Legras, Vase, Shades Of Green, Trees, Water, 7 1/4 In.	410.00
Legras, Vase, Stick, Maroon Autumn Leaves, Acid Cut, 6 In.	150.00
Legras, Vase, Stick, Maroon Leaves Entwining Frosted Ground, Signed, 6 In.	345.00

Lenox china was made in Trenton, New Jersey, after 1906. The firm also makes a porcelain similar to Belleek.

Lenox, see also Ceramic Art Co.

Lenox, Ashtray, Shell Shaped, Green Mark	7.00
Lenox, Bottle, Perfume, Ivory, 2 Yellow Trim Lines, Green Wreath Mark	50.00
Lenox, Bowl, Belleek, Pedestal, Swag Of Garlands, Palette Mark, 5 X 3 1/8 In.	72.50
Lenox, Bowl, Camels & Elephants, Orange Trim, Palette Mark, 9 In.Diam.	75.00
Lenox, Bowl, Flanged Gilt Rims, Nested Pair, 9 1/4 & 8 3/4 In.	110.00
Lenox, Bowl, Footed, Belleek, Palette Mark, 3 X 4 In.Diameter	35.00
Lenox, Bowl, Fruit, Sterling Overlay, Floral & Leaf Design, 8 1/2 In.	65.00
Lenox, Bowl, Gilt Edge, Oval, 1 3/4 X 7 In.	45.00
Lenox, Bowl, Nautilus, Coin Gold Drip Edge, Green Wreath, 6 X 4 In.	25.00
Lenox, Bowl, Oval, Ivory, Enameled Peacocks, Signed Hicks, Belleek, 10 1/2 In.	150.00
Lenox, Bowl, Shell Shape, Scrolled Handle, Pink, Gold Rim, Green Wreath, 8 In.	22.00
Lenox, Box, Gold Leaf Finial, Gray, Green Wreath Mark	42.00
Lenox, Box, Hattie Carnegie, Figural Finial	67.50
Lenox, Box, Ming, Knob On Lid, 6 X 2 1/2 In.	45.00
Lenox, Candleholder, Form Of Curved Horns, 7 In., Pair	45.00
Lenox, Candlestick, Delft Design Top, Gold Rim, Marked, 11 In., Pair	67.50
Lenox, Candlestick, Dutch Scenes, Green Wreath Mark, 8 In., Pair	155.00
Lenox, Cider Set, Austria Fruit & Leaves, Signed, Belleek, 7 Piece	365.00
Lenox, Coffee Set, Pot, 10 1/2 In., Sugar & Creamer, Silver Overlay	135.00
Lenox, Compote, Belleek, 2-Handled, Swag Of Garlands, Palette Mark, 5 X 9 In.	98.00
Lenox, Compote, Green Wreath Mark, 4 1/4 X 5 3/4 In.	45.00
Lenox, Compote, Oval, Extended Handles, Green Wreath, 7 In.Diameter	29.00
Lenox, Compote, Oval, Handles, Wreath Mark, 7 X 4 1/2 In.	31.00
Lenox, Cornucopia, Green Mark, 4 1/2 In.	25.00
Lenox, Cup & Saucer, Belleek, Ivory, Silver Overlay On Rims, Set Of 4	120.00
Lenox, Cup & Saucer, Demitasse, Belleek, Hilt Handle, Hand-Painted Flowers	35.00
Lenox, Cup & Saucer, Demitasse, Green & Ivory Lined	15.00
Lenox, Cup & Saucer, Demitasse, Hand-Painted, Gold Trim & Handle	30.00
Lenox, Cup & Saucer, Demitasse, Ming Pattern	25.00
Lenox, Cup & Saucer, Demitasse, Nydia	9.00
Lenox, Cup & Saucer, Demitasse, Sterling Footed Holder	25.00
Lenox, Cup & Saucer, Demitasse, Sterling Saucers & Holders, Set Of 8	225.00
Lenox, Cup & Saucer, Ivory, Silver Overlay, Belleek, Palette Mark, Set Of 4	120.00
Lenox, Cup & Saucer, Mount Vernon Pattern	95.00
Lenox, Cup & Saucer, Red Rose, Coin-Gold Leaves, Green Wreath	22.00
Lenox, Cup & Saucer, Victorian Pattern, Made For Tiffany & Co., 1911, Pair	95.00
Lenox, Cup, Bouillon, Sterling Holder, Green Mark	20.00
Lenox, Cup, Bouillon, Underplate, Handled, Ming Pattern	35.00
Lenox, Cup, Pedestal, 2 Cherubs, Clouds, Green Wreath Mark, 3 3/4 In.	75.00
Lenox, Decanter, Jade Green, Silver Overlay	165.00
Lenox, Dinner Set, Gold Medallion Center, 8 Place Setting	300.00
Lenox, Dish, Candy, Crimped, Gold Trim	18.00
Lenox, Dish, Candy, Silver Plate Footed Holder, Green Mark, 6 In.Diameter	60.00
Lenox, Dish, Leaf Shape, Pink, White Handle, 3 1/2 X 6 X 2 In.	25.00
Lenox, Dish, Leaf Shape, White, Handled, 3 1/2 X 6 X 2 In.	25.00
Lenox, Dish, Leaf, Gold Border, White Handle, Belleek, Green Mark, 9 X 5 In.	35.00
Lenox, Dish, Mayonnaise, Blossom Shape, Silver Overlay, 6 1/4 X 3 1/2 In.	55.00
Lenox, Dish, Pin, Souvenir, Knights Templar, 1903, Red Wreath Mark, 6 In.	28.00
Lenox, Dish, Relish, Divided, Imperial, Oval, 11 In.	30.00
Lenox, Ewer, Pink Cream Base & Handle, 10 1/2 X 15 In.	50.00
Lenox, Figural, Swan, Belleek, Palette Mark	8.00
Lenox, Figurine, Bird, Crossed Wings, Green Wreath Mark, 3 1/2 In.	30.00

Lenox, Figurine, Bird, On Base, Long Tail, Green Wreath Mark, 7 In.	45.00
Lenox, Figurine, Bird, Pink, Green Mark, 6 1/2 In.	40.00
Lenox, Figurine, Bird, White Glazed, Green Mark, 3 X 2 In.	30.00
Lenox, Figurine, Parian Nude, Bathing Beauty Reclining, Green Mark, 6 In.	125.00
Lenox, Flower Holder, Bird On Tree Stump, Gold Trim, Bird, 2 In.	42.00
Lenox, Game Plate, Silver Edge, Center Decal By Singer, 10 1/2 In.	24.00
Lenox, Hand, White, Art Deco, Green Mark	21.00
Lenox, Jar, Covered, Belleek, Gold With Orange, 4 1/2 X 2 3/4 In.	45.00
Lenox, Jar, Jam, Belleek, Underplate, Grapes, Lemons, Gold Handles & Trim	68.00
Lenox, Jar, Jam, Plate, Gold Band, Green Wreath	40.00
Lenox, Jar, Jam, Sterling Overlay	45.00
Lenox, Lamp, Boudoir, Pink Body, Swan Handles, Ivory Pedestal, 19 In.	40.00
Lenox, Mayonnaise Set, Sterling Overlay, Blossom Shape, Green Mark, 6 In.	65.00
Lenox, Mug, Belleek, Bulbous, Ears Of Corn, Palette Mark, 5 In.	55.00
Lenox, Mug, Belleek, Hand-Painted Grapes, 5 In., Pair	35.00
Lenox, Mug, Belleek, Monk Scene, Palette Mark	95.00
Lenox, Mug, Belleek, Monk, Stag Horn Shaped Handle	28.00
Lenox, Mug, Belleek, Pinecone Design, Brown	55.00
Lenox, Mug, Child's, Uncle Wiggily, Goosey Gander	20.00
Lenox, Pitcher, Belleek, 6 Jeweled Butterflies, Palette Mark, 7 1/4 In.	150.00
Lenox, Pitcher, Impressed Dimples, Footed, Green Mark, 3 X 5 X 7 1/2 In.	115.00
Lenox, Pitcher, Mask Spout, Scroll Handle, Green Wreath Mark, 3 X 5 X 7 In.	95.00
Lenox, Pitcher, Pink Bulbous Swirl Bottom, Handle, 5 X 15 In.	22.50
Lenox, Pitcher, Scroll Handle, Shell Lip, Blue Gray, White, Green Mark, 5 In.	48.00
Lenox, Pitcher, Silver Overlay, Hand-Painted, 9 In.	120.00
Lenox, Pitcher, Tankard, Belleek, Blackberries & Leaves, Palette Mark, 15 In.	250.00
Lenox, Plate, Brook Trout, Signed, 9 In.	115.00
Lenox, Plate, Maiden, B.Geyer, Signed, Impressed Mark, C.1900, 10 1/4 In.	900.00
Lenox, Plate, Ming, 8 1/2 In.	15.00
Lenox, Plate, Scenes Of Old N.Y., Coin-Gold Borders, Signed, 10 1/2 In.Diam.	28.00
Lenox, Plate, The Autumn, Black Mark, 12 1/2 In.	35.00
Lenox, Plate, The Croton Reservior 1850, 10 In.	47.50
Lenox, Plate, Weak Fish, Signed, 9 In.	115.00
Lenox, Ramekin & Underplate, Gold Embossed Borders, C.1912, Pair	55.00
Lenox, Ramekin, 2 Gold Bands, Pierced Holders, Sterling Silver, Set Of 4	95.00
Lenox, Relish, Belleek, 8 Ruffled Petals, Green Wreath Mark	20.00
Lenox, Salt & Pepper, Gold Band, Green Mark	18.00
Lenox, Salt & Pepper, R.C.A. Victor Dog	12.00
Lenox, Salt Dip, Floral, M Wreath	7.50
Lenox, Salt, Belleek, Hand-Painted, Gold Rims, Set Of 6	58.00
Lenox, Salt, Floral, Open, Belleek, Biedelman, 1914	12.00
Lenox, Salt, Open, Belleek, Pink Luster, Gold Trim, Palette Mark, Set Of 4	28.00
Lenox, Shade, Ivory, Embossed Grape & Leaf, C.1930, Green Mark, 11 3/4 In.	95.00
Lenox, Shade, Lamp, 8 X 12 1/4 In.Diameter	15.00
Lenox, Stein, Monk At Barrel, Copper Thumbrest & Lid, Marked, 6 1/2 In.	250.00
Lenox, Sugar & Creamer, Covered, Brown, Silver Overlay	95.00
Lenox, Sugar & Creamer, Footed, The Colonial, Blue & Gold	58.00
Lenox, Sugar & Creamer, Ivory, Sterling Silver Floral Overlay	75.00 To 95.00
Lenox, Sugar Shaker, Belleek, 6 Sided, 6 3/4 In.	35.00
Lenox, Swan, Gold Trim, Salmon, 5 In.	45.00
Lenox, Swan, Green Wreath Mark, 2 1/4 In., Pair	20.00
Lenox, Swan, Green Wreath, 4 1/2 X 3 1/8 In.	27.50
Lenox, Swan, Pink, Green Mark, 4 1/2 X 3 In.	35.00
Lenox, Swan, Salmon Colored, Gold Rim, 4 1/4 In.	40.00
Lenox, Swan, White, Green Mark, 4 In.	11.00
Lenox, Tankard, Monk Seated Before Barrel Holding Open Stein, Green Wreath	145.00
Lenox, Tea Caddy, Cover, Oriental Shape, Silver Overlay, 5 1/2 In.	175.00
Lenox, Tea Set, Belleek, Teapot, Sugar & Creamer, Coin Gold Handles, & Trim	120.00
Lenox, Tea Set, Sterling Overlay, 4 Demitasse Cups, Saucers, Green Wreath	350.00
Lenox, Teapot, Ming, 6 1/2 X 10 1/2 In.	60.00
Lenox, Teapot, Sterling Silver Overlay, Pastel Blue	65.00
Lenox, Toby Mug, William Penn, White, Green Wreath Mark	90.00
Lenox, Tray, Pin, Signed, Green Wreath Mark, 7 In.	45.00
Lenox, Tumbler, Belleek, Gold Leaf, Enameled, Green Palette Mark, 5 1/2 In.	135.00
Lenox, Vase, Art Nouveau, Palette Mark, 6 X 4 1/2 In., Base	70.00
Lenox, Vase, Belleek, Hand-Painted, Art Nouveau, Signed, Palette Mark, 8 In.	68.00

Lenox, Vase, Belleek, Ovoid, Pink, White Pedestal, Swan Handles, 10 1/4 In.	35.00
Lenox, Vase, Belleek, Purple, 6 1/2 In.	35.00
Lenox, Vase, Birds, 15 In.	165.00
Lenox, Vase, Black, Gold Trim, Art Deco Shape, 8 In.	30.00
Lenox, Vase, Bud, Metallic Raspberry Luster, Palette Mark, Belleek, 5 In.	27.00
Lenox, Vase, Bud, Pink Rose, Gold Leaves, Belleek, Green Mark, 7 1/2 In.	20.00
Lenox, Vase, Bud, 4 Finger, Green Wreath Mark, 8 1/2 In.	45.00
Lenox, Vase, Cream, Green Body, Flared Top, 2-Handled, 5 1/2 X 6 In., Pair	80.00
Lenox, Vase, Ivory, Pink Base & Handles, 6 In.	30.00
Lenox, Vase, Lavender & White Orchids, Green Wreath Mark, 10 In.	140.00
Lenox, Vase, Low Foot, Bulbous, Fluted Neck, Green Wreath, 8 In.	35.00
Lenox, Vase, Meadowbrook Pattern, Green Wreath, 10 In.	32.00
Lenox, Vase, Pink Bird, 6 In.	25.00
Lenox, Vase, Pink Fluted, Gold Edge, Cream Base & Inside, 9 X 15 In.	55.00
Lenox, Vase, Pink Swan Handles, Cream Base, 8 3/4 In., Pair	100.00
Lenox, Vase, Purple Iris, Pink Background, Signed, Belleek, 10 1/2 In.	150.00
Lenox, Vase, Round In Lower Half, Fluted Neck, 7 In.	25.00
Lenox, Vase, Round Lower Half With Tall Narrow Neck, Green Mark, 9 In.	25.00
Lenox, Vegetable, 2 Handles In Ming Design, 10 X 3 1/2 In.	40.00
Letter Opener, Advertising, Lone Star Masonary Cement	5.50
Letter Opener, Art Nouveau, Scissors, Red Leather Scabbard, German	25.00
Letter Opener, Black Boy Holding Alligator Head, Pencil Inside, Celluloid	23.00
Letter Opener, Bone Scrimshaw, Eskimo	10.00
Letter Opener, Brass Ruler, Allen Bookbinders	8.00
Letter Opener, Bronze, Nude, Gorham Co., Artist Initial, 9 1/4 In.	12.00
Letter Opener, Carved Camel, 3 Small Ones, Ivory, 7 In.	14.00
Letter Opener, Carved Wood, Peking Glass Trim	12.00
Letter Opener, Carved Wooden Bulldog, Glass Eyes, Brass Collar, 9 1/2 In.	35.00
Letter Opener, Clown Head, Scrolling On Blade, Brass, England, 8 1/2 In.	18.50
Letter Opener, Copper, Horse Head One End	21.00
Letter Opener, Dupont Explosives	24.00
Letter Opener, Enameled, Turquoise Center, Israel, 9 In.	10.00
Letter Opener, Etched Bear On Handle, Jade, 6 1/2 In.	18.00
Letter Opener, Figural, Coes Wrench	8.00
Letter Opener, Figural, Dog	8.00
Letter Opener, Figural, Old Sleepy Eye, Copper	25.00
Letter Opener, Figural, Turkey Claw, Metal	12.50
Letter Opener, Figural, Yellow Boy, Uneeda Biscuits, 1906, 8 1/2 In.	55.00
Letter Opener, Filigree Handle, French Silver, 8 In.	22.00
Letter Opener, Hand-Carved Scabbard, 13 Elephants, Ivory	30.00
Letter Opener, Home Life Insurance Co., Nickel Plate	4.00
Letter Opener, Indian Head, Great Sun Council, 1915, Bronze, 8 1/4 In.	60.00
Letter Opener, Ivory, French	5.00
Letter Opener, Ivory, Scrimshaw Ship, 1861	45.00
Letter Opener, Jensen, Denmark, Sterling Silver	110.00
Letter Opener, Kennedy Space Center, Leather Case	5.00
Letter Opener, Kirk, Marked, Sterling	35.00
Letter Opener, Knife Shape, Bronze, Fleer's Double Bubble Gum, 7 3/4 In.	15.00
Letter Opener, Knife, Brass, Clarence O'Brien On Handle	12.00
Letter Opener, Lebanon, Silver Handle	6.00
Letter Opener, Metropolitan Life Insurance, Brass, 7 In.	5.00
Letter Opener, Mother-Of-Pearl, Sterling Handle	10.00
Letter Opener, Mozart In Raised Letters, Bust On Top, Bronze, 7 3/4 In.	65.00
Letter Opener, O'Brien & Berman Trademark, Attorneys, Washington, Brass	5.00
Letter Opener, Owl, Brass	10.00
Letter Opener, Salt Lake City, Copper	5.00
Letter Opener, Scrimshaw Handle, Polar Bear Chasing Seal, Ivory, 6 In.	28.00
Letter Opener, Souvenir, Salt Lake Route, Wood	3.50
Letter Opener, Spanish Galleon, Copper, Handmade, 9 In.	35.00
Letter Opener, Sterling Handle, String Cutter	12.50
Letter Opener, Tortoise Shell, 6 1/4 In.	7.50
Letter Opener, University Of Illinois, Charter Seal	9.00
Letter Opener, Whale Bone, Carved In Shape Of Sperm Whale, Baleen Eyes	28.00
Letter Opener, Wood, Bamboo Inlaid, Philippines	5.00
Letter Opener, Yale & Towne Mfg., Embossed Lock & Padlock, 7 1/2 In.	37.50
Libbey, Basket, Intaglio Design, Horeshoe Handles, Signed, 11 1/2 In.	325.00

Libbey, Basket, Panel Cut Sides, Prism Cut Handle, Signed, 4 1/2 X 5 In.	68.00
Libbey, Bell, World's Fair Of 1893, Columbian Exposition	125.00
Libbey, Bowl, Boat Shape, Oval, Thistle & Straw Flower, 12 X 4 1/2 In.	265.00
Libbey, Bowl, Celery, American Brilliant, Signed	159.00
Libbey, Bowl, Diana Pattern, Signed, 3 X 9 In.	275.00
Libbey, Bowl, Elsmere Pattern, Signed, 9 X 4 In.	250.00
Libbey, Bowl, Punch, Tulip Shape, 2 Piece, 11 In.	685.00
Libbey, Bowl, Ribbon Star With Hobstars Fan, 8 X 4 In.	175.00
Libbey, Bowl, Sugar, Platform Base, Frosted Intaglio Cutting, Signed	98.50
Libbey, Bowl, Twining Roping, Buzzwheels & Snowflakes, 2 X 8 1/2 In.	125.00
Libbey, Box, Brilliant Cut, Florence Pattern, Cover, 5 X 4 3/8 In.	250.00
Libbey, Brandy Snifter, Squirrel Silhouette, Crystal Stem	85.00
Libbey, Candleholder, Intaglio Cut.Stylized Floral Design, Signed	65.00
Libbey, Candlestick, Air Twist Stem, Signed, 8 In., Pair	325.00
Libbey, Candlestick, Black Cut To Clear, Signed, 12 In., Pair	330.00
Libbey, Candlestick, Copper Wheel Cut, Stem Enlarges Toward Top, 10 In.	115.00
Libbey, Candlestick, Panels & Bull's-Eye, Rayed Base, Signed, 8 1/4 In.	175.00
Libbey, Candlestick, Trapped Air Stem, Intaglio Design, Signed, 10 In., Pair	285.00
Libbey, Candlestick, Wheel Cut Flowers & Scrolls, Signed, 3 5/8 In.	35.00
Libbey, Carafe, 32 Point Star Base, Panel Notched Neck, Signed, 8 1/2 In.	130.00
Libbey, Celery, Neola Pattern, Signed, 11 1/2 X 4 1/2 In.	160.00
Libbey, Celery, Wisteria, Signed, 11 1/4 In.	250.00
Libbey, Center Piece, Empress Pattern, 10 In.	550.00
Libbey, Champagne, Hollow Stem, Cut Glass, Signed, Pair	115.00
Libbey, Champagne, Rabbit Silhouette, Signed	52.00
Libbey, Champagne, Squirrel Silhouette, Opalescent Stem	85.00
Libbey, Champagne, States, Signed	35.00
Libbey, Claret, Bear Silhouette, Black Stem, Signed	200.00
Libbey, Claret, Bear Silhouette, Opalescent Stem, Signed	85.00
Libbey, Cocktail, American Eagle Silhouette, Crystal Stem	10.00
Libbey, Cocktail, Crow Silhouette, Crystal Stem	20.00
Libbey, Cocktail, Kangaroo Silhouette, Frosted Stem	85.00
Libbey, Compote, Engraved Flowers & Leaves, Signed, 7 In.	125.00
Libbey, Compote, Intaglio Cut Base & Bowl, Baluster Stem, Signed, 8 In.	140.00
Libbey, Compote, Intaglio, Diamond Twisted Base, Signed, 5 3/4 X 7 1/4 In.	200.00
Libbey, Compote, Intaglio, Flowers, Leaves, Signed, 5 1/4 In.	95.00
Libbey, Compote, Intaglio, Twisted Stem, Bowl & Base, 5 1/2 X 7 1/4 In.	150.00
Libbey, Compote, Ribbon Star, Hobstar Base, Notched Stem, 9 X 5 3/4 In.	195.00
Libbey, Compote, Ribbon Star, 8 In.	175.00
Libbey, Container, Pansy, Quilted-Diamond, Brass Frog Top, 5 1/2 In.	225.00
Libbey, Cordial, Greyhound Silhouette, Opalescent Stem, Signed	125.00
Libbey, Creamer, 2 In.Square Base, Knickerbocker, Crystal, 4 1/4 In.	20.00
Libbey, Cruet, All Over Cut, Signed	120.00
Libbey, Cruet, Cross Hatching, Single Star Neck, Stopper, Signed, 7 1/2 In.	250.00
Libbey, Cup, Punch, Princess, Set Of 6	110.00
Libbey, Dish, Butter, Corinthian, Dome, 6 In., Plate, 8 In.	250.00
Libbey, Dish, Heart-Shaped, Signed, 10 In.Diameter	275.00
Libbey, Goblet, Cat Silhouette, Opalescent Stem, Signed	85.00
Libbey, Goblet, Liberty Bell, American Eagle Stem	20.00
Libbey, Goblet, Teardrop Stems, Hobstars, Strawberries, Fans, Signed, Set Of 6	600.00
Libbey, Goblet, Water, Floral & Leaf Cut, Signed	25.00
Libbey, Parfait, Cut Glass, Signed, 7 3/4 In.	55.00
Libbey, Pilsner, Malmaison Pattern, C.1933, Set Of 4	75.00
Libbey, Pitcher, Cider, Sultana, Signed	325.00
Libbey, Pitcher, Double Lozenge, Signed, 2 Quart	250.00
Libbey, Pitcher, Reverse Amberina, Parallelogram Shape, Applied Handle	350.00
Libbey, Plate, Cake, Hobstar & Intaglio, Signed, 10 1/4 In.	250.00
Libbey, Plate, Corinthian, Signed, 12 In.	430.00
Libbey, Plate, Ice Cream, Daisy & Stem Pattern, Sword, Signed, 8 3/4 In.Diam.	225.00
Libbey, Plate, Neola, 7 In.	125.00
Libbey, Rose Bowl, Florence Pattern, 5 X 6 1/2 In.	250.00
Libbey, Rose Bowl, Intaglio Cut Flowers & Leaves, Signed, 4 1/2 X 5 In.	145.00
Libbey, Sherbet, Rabbit Silhouette, Opalescent Stem, Signed	85.00
Libbey, Sherry, Monkey Silhouette, Opalescent Stem, Signed	85.00
Libbey, Sign, Advertising, 2 Piece	275.00
Libbey, Tray, Thistles, Flowers & Leaves, Hobnail Center, 12 In.Diam.	325.00
Libbey, Tumbler, Cut Glass, Signed	85.00

Libbey, Tumbler, Saber, Signed, Set Of 13	235.00
Libbey, Tumbler, Star & Feather Pattern, Sword Signature, Set Of 4	160.00
Libbey, Vase, Amberina, Fuchsia Shading To Blue, C.1921, Signed	475.00
Libbey, Vase, Bud, Fuchsia, Ribbed, Bulbous, Amberina, 5 1/4 In.	215.00
Libbey, Vase, Flared Top, Scalloped Base, Saber Mark, Signed, 14 In.	275.00
Libbey, Vase, Intaglio Flowers & Ives, Ball Stem, Teardrop, Signed, 9 1/2 In.	295.00
Libbey, Vase, Panel Of Inverted Thumbprint & Cable, Cylindrical, 12 In.	385.00
Libbey, Vase, Pedestal, Engraved, Signed, 12 In.	165.00
Libbey, Vase, Pedestal, Ruffled Top, Hobstars, Bull's-Eye, Rayed Foot, 12 In.	225.00
Libbey, Vase, Rabbit Silhouette, Opalescent Stem, Signed, 10 1/2 In.	162.00
Libbey, Vase, Russian Vesicas, Pedestal, 18 In.	1075.00
Libbey, Vase, Tear Drop In Stem, Signed, 7 In.	125.00
Libbey, Vase, Trumpet, Bull's-Eye, Prism, Chain Of Hobstars, Signed, 16 In.	395.00
Libbey, Vase, Tulip Shaped, Graduated Stem, Star-Cut Foot, Signed, 13 1/2 In.	250.00
Libbey, Wine, Kangaroo Stem, Signed, 6 In.	95.00

Lighting Devices, see Candleholder, Candlestick, Lamp, etc.

Lightning rod balls are collected for their variety of shape and color.
These glass balls were at the center of the rod that was attached to the
roof of a house or barn to avoid lightning damage.

Lightning Rod, Ball, Red Etched Tail, Kretzer	40.00
Lightning Rod, Ball, Ruby Glass	35.00
Lightning Rod, Ball, Wrought Iron	50.00
Lightning Rod, Copper	42.50

  Limoges porcelain has been made in Limoges, France, since the
mid-nineteenth century. Fine porcelains were made by many factories, including
Haviland, Ahrenfeldt, Guerin, Pouyat, Elite, and others.

Limoges, see also Haviland

Limoges, Ashtray, Pearlized, 2 Brownies, Gilt Trim	30.00
Limoges, Atomizer, Flowers, Gold, Porcelain	17.00
Limoges, Barrel, Cracker, Hand-Painted, Pinecones	40.00
Limoges, Basket, Flowers Inside, White Outside, Rope Handle, 7 1/2 X 5 In.	30.00
Limoges, Basket, Gold Outlined Flowers, 1891-97, 7 X 4 1/2 In.	29.00
Limoges, Basket, Hand Painted Roses, Gold, Stouffer, 4 1/2 In.	35.00
Limoges, Basket, Pearlized Interior, Roses, Signed, 5 1/2 In.	45.00
Limoges, Basket, Violets, Lavender, Ground, Gold Bow Handle, 4 1/2 In.	42.00
Limoges, Basket, 14K Gold Leaf, Arched Handle, Signed, 6 X 8 In.	65.00
Limoges, Bell, Hand-Painted, Artist Signed, 3 In.	25.00
Limoges, Bell, Table, Holly & Berries	17.00
Limoges, Berry Set, Covered Master Bowl, All Pieces Signed, Tray 12 In.	265.00
Limoges, Berry Set, Pink Roses On Green Ground, 7 Piece	45.00
Limoges, Blotter, Ink, White, Flowers	26.00
Limoges, Bonbon, Hand-Painted Butterflies, Gold Handle, Signed	35.00
Limoges, Bookends, Birds With Outspread Wings, Heavy Figural Glass, Pair	35.00
Limoges, Boot, Lady's, 4 In.	15.00
Limoges, Bowl, Covered, Art Deco, 5 In.	22.00
Limoges, Bowl, Covered, Flowers, 10 In.Diameter	29.00
Limoges, Bowl, Covered, Oval, 3 Handles, 9 1/2 In	34.00
Limoges, Bowl, Cream, Gold Trim, Cupid Design In Center, Large	85.00
Limoges, Bowl, Footed, Peaches On Tree, Gold Rim, Signed, 9 1/2 In.	125.00
Limoges, Bowl, Gold Overlay, Green & Purple Grapes, June 6, 1895, 15 1/4 In.	425.00
Limoges, Bowl, Irregular Shaped, Gold Trim, 6 In., Set Of 12	68.00
Limoges, Bowl, Punch, Allover Gold & Grapes, 14 1/2 In.Diameter	188.00
Limoges, Bowl, Punch, Fluted Top, Gold Rim, Hand-Painted, 13 X 6 In.	350.00
Limoges, Bowl, Punch, Full-Blown Roses Inside & Out, Signed, 14 1/2 In.Diam.	395.00
Limoges, Bowl, Punch, Rococo Gold & Trim, 5 Portraits, Marked, 14 X 9 1/2 In.	495.00
Limoges, Bowl, Soup, Bouquets Of Hand-Painted Florals, Signed, 9 In.	20.00
Limoges, Bowl, Underplate, Hand-Painted, Scalloped Gold Rococo Rims, 9 In.	65.00
Limoges, Bowl, 3-Footed, Hand-Painted Berries, Signed, 9 In.	45.00
Limoges, Bowl, 3-Legged, Blackberries, Flowers, Signed, 9 1/2 In.Diameter	42.50
Limoges, Box, Collar Button, Forget-Me-Not- Flowers, Signed, 1 X 2 1/2 In.	18.00
Limoges, Box, Covered, Lid, Roses & Gold Trim, 3 1/4 X 6 5/8 In.	70.00
Limoges, Box, Floral, Hand Painted, Round, Covered, French, 3 1/2 X 6 In.	55.00
Limoges, Box, Footed, Flowers On Lid, 4 In.Square	17.50

Limoges, Box, Pin, Portrait Of Marie Louise	35.00
Limoges, Box, Powder, Floral, Gold Edged Leaves, Lavender, Pink, Artist Signed	50.00
Limoges, Box, Sardine, Shell Shaped Underplate, Sea Shell & Weed Design	95.00
Limoges, Box, Sides Form Shirt Collar With Bow Tie, Stud Finial, 2 1/2 In.	35.00
Limoges, Box, Trinket, Gold & Floral Design	18.00
Limoges, Butter Pat, Cherub	14.00
Limoges, Butter Tub, Underplate, 2 Gold Leaf Handles, 1 On Lid, Marked	35.00
Limoges, Butter, Insert, Pink Wild Roses, Gold	38.50
Limoges, Butter, Tub, Attached Underplate, Gold Leaf Handles, Marked	35.00
Limoges, Buttermilk Set, Grapes On Green, Gold Ground, Hand-Painted, 7 Piece	425.00
Limoges, Cachepot, Flaring Top & Bottom, 5 1/2 X 5 1/2 In.	38.00
Limoges, Candlestick, Blackberries, Pink & White, Artist Signed, 9 In., Pair	38.00
Limoges, Candlestick, Daisies, Artist Signed, 7 In., Pair	35.00
Limoges, Candlestick, White, Gold Trim, 8 In.	20.00
Limoges, Celery, Hand-Painted Jonquils, Signed	45.00
Limoges, Chalice, Portrait, In Oval, Artist Signed, 10 In.	295.00
Limoges, Charger, Gold Handles, Signed B.Hall, 16 In.	125.00
Limoges, Charger, Indian Chief Eagle Track, Hand-Painted, Signed, 12 In.	285.00
Limoges, Charger, 2 Gold Handles, Signed, 16 In.Diameter	89.00
Limoges, Chocolate Pot, Blue Flowers, Gold Trim, GDA Mark, 9 1/2 In.	32.00
Limoges, Chocolate Pot, Embossed Gold Design, C.1842-98, 8 1/2 In.	75.00
Limoges, Chocolate Pot, Flowers, Green & Red Mark	40.00
Limoges, Chocolate Pot, Gold & Rose Garlands, 8 1/2 In.	85.00
Limoges, Chocolate Pot, Pink Roses, Gold Trim, Marked, 3 In.	24.00
Limoges, Chocolate Pot, Poppy Decoration, Pale Green Background, Signed	75.00
Limoges, Chocolate Pot, Roses, Pink, Marked, Elite, 3 In.	25.00
Limoges, Chocolate Pot, Scalloped Base, Marked, Haviland	75.00
Limoges, Chocolate Pot, Spider Web Design, Signed, 9 X 1i In.	100.00
Limoges, Chocolate Pot, Sprays Of Flowers, Gold Trim, Marked	125.00
Limoges, Chocolate Pot, Triumph, Pastel Orchid	20.00
Limoges, Chocolate Set, Hand-Painted, Cake Set, Nut Dish, Signed, 23 Pieces	350.00
Limoges, Chocolate Set, Yellow Ground, Gold Handles, 5 Cups & Saucers	110.00
Limoges, Cider Set, Pitcher, 5 1/2 In., 5 Mugs, Apples, Leaves, Marked	165.00
Limoges, Cider Set, Pitcher, 6 In., Bulbous, 4 Mugs, 3 3/4 In., Gold Beaded	275.00
Limoges, Coffee Set, Lille Pattern, Gold Trim, 6 Cups & Saucers	125.00
Limoges, Cracker & Cheese, Raised Gold Band, Gold Banded, Leaves, Floral Rim	42.00
Limoges, Cracker Jar, Poppies & Wildflowers, Blue Ground	100.00
Limoges, Cracker Jar, White Ground, Pink Roses	75.00
Limoges, Creamer, Hand-Painted, Gilded Borders & Handle, 4 X 5 X 2 1/2 In.	30.00
Limoges, Cup & Saucer, Bouillon, Flowers	14.00
Limoges, Cup & Saucer, Demitasse, Blue Forget-Me-Nots, Yellow & Gold	25.00
Limoges, Cup & Saucer, Demitasse, Pink Garland, Gold Border, Set Of 6	84.00
Limoges, Cup & Saucer, Demitasse, Scalloped Gold Edge, Set Of 6	85.00
Limoges, Cup & Saucer, Pink & Blue Flowers	15.00
Limoges, Dish, Boat Shaped, Signed, 5 X 8 X 1 1/2 In.	18.00
Limoges, Dish, Bone, Green, Pink & Yellow, Fluted, Hand-Painted, Set Of 6	30.00
Limoges, Dish, Butter, Covered, Insert, Green Scrolls	30.00
Limoges, Dish, Cake, Gold Handled, Hand-Painted, Signed, Xmas, 1905, 11 In.	49.00
Limoges, Dish, Candy, Double Slotted Handles, Gold Trim, Signed, 8 In.	30.00
Limoges, Dish, Nut, Rose Lei, 14K Gold Leaf, Signed, Set Of 6	50.00
Limoges, Dish, Pancake, Cover, Yellow Rose Clusters, 10 In.	45.00
Limoges, Dish, Relish, Inserts, Silver Frame	84.00
Limoges, Dish, Serving, Covered, Basketweave Handles, Signed	45.00
Limoges, Dish, Vegetable, Covered, Handles, The Athena, Gold Trim, Oval, 12 In.	25.00
Limoges, Double Dish, Florals, Berries & Details, 13 X 10 In.	47.50
Limoges, Dresser Set, Blue, Gold Trim, 2 Bowls, Tray, 7 1/2 X 11 In., 3 Piece	95.00
Limoges, Egg, Miniature, Gold Pastoral, Opens In Half	10.00
Limoges, Eggcup, Blown Out Faces	15.00
Limoges, Ewer, Burnished Gold Inside, Matte Finish, 13 In.	196.00
Limoges, Ewer, Burnished Gold Inside, Pouring Lip, Gold Tracery, 13 In.	135.00
Limoges, Ewer, Green, White Lavender, Floral, Leaves, Gold Handle, 10 In.	60.00
Limoges, Ewer, Hand-Painted, Floral, Marked, ITA SHIELDS, 12 In., Pair	150.00
Limoges, Ewer, Roses & Gold Tracery, 13 In.	95.00
Limoges, Ewer, Roses, Greenery, Gold Handle, Signed & Dated 1907, 9 In.	65.00
Limoges, Fernery, Pink & Red Roses, 4 Gold Rococo Legs, Turquoise Center	135.00
Limoges, Fish Set, Gold Rim, Baby Design In Middle, 10 Piece	445.00

Limoges, Fish Set, Hand-Painted, 9 In.Plates, Platter, 24 In., 11 Piece	395.00
Limoges, Fish Set, Platter, 5 Plates, Different Fishes, Artist Signed	300.00
Limoges, Fish Set, Platter, 8 1/2 In.Plates, 5 Signed Rene	250.00
Limoges, Fish Set, Scalloped Edges, Platter, 20 X 8 1/2 In.7 Piece	200.00
Limoges, Game Plate, Coronet, Signed Max, 9 3/4 In.	50.00
Limoges, Game Plate, Cows In Pasture, Signed, 12 1/2 In.	175.00
Limoges, Game Plate, Each A Different Bird, C.1889, Signed, Set Of 12	800.00
Limoges, Game Plate, Hanging Game, Gold Rococo Border, Signed, 13 In.	150.00
Limoges, Game Plate, Hanging Grouse, Signed, 13 In.	125.00
Limoges, Game Plate, Pheasants & Quail, Scalloped, 13 In.Diameter, Pair	250.00
Limoges, Game Plate, Quail & Partridge, Shaded Ground, Signed Max, 10 In.	70.00
Limoges, Game Plate, Wild Boars, Artist Signed, 10 In.	75.00
Limoges, Game Plate, Wild Boars, Signed	55.00
Limoges, Game Set, Platter, Bowl, Ten Plates, Artist Signed	650.00
Limoges, Game Set, Platter, 18 7/8 X 13 5/8 In., 10 Plates, Gold Rim, Signed	575.00
Limoges, Gravy Boat, Attached Tray, Scalloped, Floral Clusters Inside	25.00
Limoges, Gravy Boat, Floral Clusters Inside & Out, Scalloped	25.00
Limoges, Gravy Boat, Hand-Painted, Fish & Floral, Gold Edge	18.00
Limoges, Hair Receiver & Powder Jar, White, Gold Trim, Pair	30.00
Limoges, Hatpin Holder, Forget-Me-Nots, 5 In.	25.00
Limoges, Hatpin Holder, Goldenrod Decoration, Saucer Base	16.00
Limoges, Inkwell, Boat Shaped Cover, Floral Design, Well, 4 X 6 1/2 In.	135.00
Limoges, Inkwell, Double, Green With Gold	75.00
Limoges, Inkwell, Double, Hand-Painted, Tray & Stand, Signed, 1894	85.00
Limoges, Jar, Cookie, Pink Roses, Blue Forget-Me-Nots, Gold Handle & Trim	75.00
Limoges, Jar, Cracker, Gold & Floral Design, 8 In.	90.00
Limoges, Jar, Powder, Dan Cupid, Florals On Side, Marked Elite, Limoges, France	15.00
Limoges, Jar, Powder, Holly, Signed	22.00
Limoges, Jardiniere, Clawfoot Stand, Hand-Painted, Signed, 14 X 15 In.	250.00
Limoges, Jardiniere, Multicolored Roses On White, 8 X 10 In.Diameter	135.00
Limoges, Jardiniere, Pansies, Gold, D. & C. Mark	65.00
Limoges, Jardiniere, Roses, Gold Trim, Signed, 7 1/2 X 10 1/2 In.	145.00
Limoges, Lemonade Set, Red & Purple Grapes, 7 Piece, Pitcher 5 3/4 In.	165.00
Limoges, Matchbox Holder, Signed, 3 1/2 In.	35.00
Limoges, Mug, Gold Rim, Pastel Ground, Marked, 3 1/2 In.	28.00
Limoges, Mug, Indian Scene	55.00
Limoges, Mug, Monk, Green, Pair	65.00
Limoges, Mug, Painted Indian	14.50
Limoges, Mug, Pastel Blue Ground, Dogwood Flowers, 6 In.	55.00
Limoges, Mug, Rooster, Hand-Painted	63.00
Limoges, Mug, Yellow, Gold Rim, 3 1/2 In.	28.50
Limoges, Mug, 2 Fighting Cocks, Dragon Handle, Signed, 5 3/4 In.	45.00
Limoges, Mustache Cup & Saucer, Hand-Painted, Gold Garlands, Signed	75.00
Limoges, Mustache Cup, Cobalt Blue	25.00
Limoges, Nappy, Finger Loop Handle On Top, 14K Gold Trim, Signed	29.50
Limoges, Oyster Plate, Flowers, Brushed Gold Rim, Green Mark, 7 3/4 In.	25.00
Limoges, Painting On Enamel, Deux Enfants, Framed, 7 X 9 1/2 In.	300.00
Limoges, Pitcher, Bird, Butterfly, Wild Rose, 5 In.	24.50
Limoges, Pitcher, Bulbous Base, Hand-Painted, C.1890, 9 1/2 In.	95.00
Limoges, Pitcher, Cider, Dragonflies, Studded Handle, Brown, Tan, Gold	50.00
Limoges, Pitcher, Cider, Green, Cherries & Leaves, T. & V.	85.00
Limoges, Pitcher, Cider, Hand-Painted Berries, Signed	45.00
Limoges, Pitcher, Cider, Purple At Base, Leaves & Blackberries, Gold Handle	48.00
Limoges, Pitcher, Cider, Purple, Red, Green Grapes & Leaves, 5 1/2 X 25 In.	115.00
Limoges, Pitcher, Cider, Signed A.M.Chapman, 1904, 6 In.	105.00
Limoges, Pitcher, Cream, Bulbous, Hand-Painted, Open Work At Handle, Signed	25.00
Limoges, Pitcher, Grape Design, Signed, 12 1/4 X 4 In.Diameter	145.00
Limoges, Pitcher, Green & White, Art Deco Decoration, 8 In.	40.00
Limoges, Pitcher, Hand-Painted, Turquoise & Pink, Scrolled Handle, 12 In.	135.00
Limoges, Pitcher, Lemonade, Hand-Painted, Beaded, Gold Handle, 6 1/2 In.	85.00
Limoges, Pitcher, Lemonade, Hand-Painted, Gold Edge, 8 X 6 1/4 In.Diameter	55.00
Limoges, Pitcher, Water, Bulbous, Red Flowers, Gold Ground, Signed	125.00
Limoges, Planter, Footed, Hand-Painted Waterlilies, Signed & Dated 1911	75.00
Limoges, Plaque, Flowers In Basket, Gold Rococo Border, Signed, 10 1/4 In.	65.00
Limoges, Plaque, Game, Drawing Room Scene, Signed, 15 1/2 In.	300.00
Limoges, Plaque, Game, 2 Hanging Birds, Signed Dubois, 13 1/4 In.	150.00

Limoges, Plaque, Gold Rococo Border, Artist Dubois, 13 In.Diameter	275.00
Limoges, Plaque, Portrait, Nude Maiden, Child, Blue Sky, 11 1/2 In.	95.00
Limoges, Plaque, Portraits Of Brittany Maids, 13 1/4 In., Pair	395.00
Limoges, Plaque, Victorian Couple, Swans, Gold, Artist Signed, 10 In.	235.00
Limoges, Plaque, Victorian Girl, Fur Coat, Fur Muff, Puppy Peeks Out, Gold Rim	135.00
Limoges, Plaque, 2 Cardinals, Signed A.R.Shortland, 1850-1950, 12 X 16 In.	800.00
Limoges, Plate, Applied Gold Leaf, Pansy Center, 12 In.	35.00
Limoges, Plate, Asparagus, Irregular Rim, Rococo Gold, 10 In.Diam., Set Of 6	195.00
Limoges, Plate, Cake, Reticulated Handles, Marked Elite, 10 1/2 X 9 In.	28.00
Limoges, Plate, Cake, White With Roses, Gold Trim, 9 3/4 In.	10.00
Limoges, Plate, Charger, Deco Design, Gold Trim, 14 In.	28.00
Limoges, Plate, Chop, Art Deco, Stylized Flowers, Gold Edge, 12 1/4 In.	38.00
Limoges, Plate, Chop, Gold Rim, Hand-Painted, Signed, 13 In.	165.00
Limoges, Plate, Chop, Roses, Scalloped Edge, Pastel, 14 In.	120.00
Limoges, Plate, Chop, 3 Poppies, 3 Buds, Vines, Gold Rim, Coronet, Signed, 13 In.	62.50
Limoges, Plate, Cookie, Leaf Shaped, White, 9 X 9 1/4 In., Pair	12.50
Limoges, Plate, Coronet, Monk, 9 1/2 In.	25.00
Limoges, Plate, Cupids Playing, Pastel Background, Marked, Pair, 6 1/2 In.	40.00
Limoges, Plate, Fish, Pink & Gold Scalloped Shell Edge, Set Of 8	150.00
Limoges, Plate, Fish, Scalloped Edge, 9 In., Set Of 6	85.00
Limoges, Plate, Fishermen In Boat, Signed Duval, 10 In.	38.00
Limoges, Plate, Flambeau, Pink Carnations, Artist Signed, 8 1/2 In.	25.00
Limoges, Plate, Floral, Branches, Thorns, Scalloped, Gold Rim, Art Nouveau, Pair	50.00
Limoges, Plate, France, Flying Bird, Tinted Background, 12 1/2 In.Signed Max	42.50
Limoges, Plate, Game, Bird, Artist Signed, Marked L.Straus Sons, 10 In.	125.00
Limoges, Plate, Game, Coronet, Quail, Gold Edges, Signed Dileron, 9 In., Pair	90.00
Limoges, Plate, Game, Flying Bird, Rococo Edge, Artist Signed, 9 In.	39.50
Limoges, Plate, Gilded Border, Horses At Pond, 19th Century, 11 In.	165.00
Limoges, Plate, Gold Beaded Flowers, Hand-Painted Birds, Signed	125.00
Limoges, Plate, Gold Edge, Green Ground, Hand-Painted Dog Portrait, 9 In.	75.00
Limoges, Plate, Gold Fruit & Leaves, Hand-Painted, Signed, 8 1/2 In.	12.00
Limoges, Plate, Gold Handle, Daisy Design, Signed, 8 1/2 In.Diameter	30.00
Limoges, Plate, Gold Irregular Border, Poppies, Signed, 11 In.	65.00
Limoges, Plate, Green Border, Gold Edge, 10 In., Set Of 12	180.00
Limoges, Plate, Green With Roses, Signed, 8 3/4 In.	15.00
Limoges, Plate, Hand-Painted Dogwoods & Bumble Bees, Signed, 12 In.	75.00
Limoges, Plate, Hand-Painted, Butterfly On Rose, Gold Edge, 9 1/2 In.	20.00
Limoges, Plate, Hand-Painted, Scalloped Edge, Gold Trim, 8 1/2 In.	18.00
Limoges, Plate, Hanging, Hand-Painted, Signed Piusoye, 11 In.	45.00
Limoges, Plate, Holly, Irregular Gold Border, Marked, 8 In.	30.00
Limoges, Plate, Holly, Red Berries, Gold Border, 8 In.	30.00
Limoges, Plate, Hunting Dog, 9 1/2 In., Set Of 8	250.00
Limoges, Plate, Mandolin Player With Girl, 9 In.	35.00
Limoges, Plate, Pink Carnations, Flambeau, Artist Signed, 8 1/2 In.	25.00
Limoges, Plate, Pink Garland Design, Gold Border, 6 1/4 In.Set Of 6	45.00
Limoges, Plate, Pink Roses, Blue Forget-Me-Nots, Pierced Handles, 11 In.	35.00
Limoges, Plate, Pointer Entering Into Misty Area, 9 1/2 In.	55.00
Limoges, Plate, Presentation Piece, 1882, Indian Girl On Brick Wall, 13 In.	290.00
Limoges, Plate, Quail, Gold Rim, Signed, 10 1/2 In.	125.00
Limoges, Plate, Scene Of Castle, Sunset, Hand-Painted, 11 In.	78.00
Limoges, Plate, Service, Cobalt Blue Trim, T. & V. Bell Mark, Set Of 12	450.00
Limoges, Plate, White & Yellow Roses, Tan Ground, 10 In.	40.00
Limoges, Plate, Wild Goose, Gold Scalloped Rim, Signed, 9 1/2 In.Diameter	50.00
Limoges, Plate, Wild Goose, Signed, 9 In., Pair	75.00
Limoges, Platter, Grape & Leaf, Irregular Gold Border, Marked, 13 X 16 In.	100.00
Limoges, Platter, Haviland, 12 1/2 In.Diameter	25.00
Limoges, Platter, Poppies, 14 X 9 1/2 In.	22.50
Limoges, Platter, Scalloped Edge, Gold Trim, Roses, 13 X 7 In.	28.00
Limoges, Platter, Wild Goose, Signed, 16 X 11 In.	149.00
Limoges, Portrait, Plate, Baby Sitting On Cushion, Marked, 9 in.	75.00
Limoges, Portrait Plate, Bust Of Girl, Long Hair, Floral Border, 9 1/2 In.	38.00
Limoges, Portrait Plate, Cavalier On Barrel Playing Guitar, Signed, 10 /n.	165.00
Limoges, Portrait Plate, Full Figure, Gold Border, Signed, 12 1/2 In.	85.00
Limoges, Portrait Plate, Monk	40.00
Limoges, Pot, Chocolate, Gold Trim Handle, Spout, Edges Of Pot, Cover, Roses	85.00
Limoges, Powder Jar & Hair Receiver, Artist Signed, Old Mark	50.00

Limoges, Ramekin & Underplate, Green Leaves & Gold Bank, Marked, 24 Piece 100.00
Limoges, Ramekin, Handled, Sterling Holder, Marked, 1 1/4 X 1 1/2 In., Pair 39.00
Limoges, Ramekin, Long Handles, Sterling Holders, 1 1/2 In.Diam., Set Of 4 .... 78.00
Limoges, Ramekin, Sterling Holder, Underplate, Pink 24.00
Limoges, Ramekin, Underplate, Scalloped Rims, Gold Trim, Set Of 6 .... 45.00
Limoges, Ring Tree, Hand-Painted 9.00
Limoges, Salt, White Doves, Marked, 3 In., Pair 15.00
Limoges, Sardine Set, Covered Dish & Tray, White, Pastel Seashell 65.00
Limoges, Server, Cheese, Lid, Hand Painted, MWC, 13 X 7 X 7 In. 135.00
Limoges, Server, Cheese, Roses, 1i X 8 In. 135.00
Limoges, Shaving Mug, Hand-Painted Chestnuts 35.00
Limoges, Shaving Mug, White, Gold Writing 22.50
Limoges, Shoe, Lady's, Flowers, Gold Trim, 1 In. 5.00
Limoges, Shoe, White, Gold Flower, Signed, 3 1/2 In. 30.00
Limoges, Slipper, Lady's, Flowers, Gold Trim, 1 In. 5.00
Limoges, Sugar & Creamer, Coin-Gold Handle, Signed 38.00
Limoges, Sugar & Creamer, Cream Ground, Gold Trim, 1910 .... 25.00
Limoges, Sugar & Creamer, Etched Grape, Footed 40.00
Limoges, Sugar & Creamer, Gold Luster, Branch Handle 50.00
Limoges, Sugar & Creamer, Pink Blue Luster, Marked PL, Artist Signed 16.00
Limoges, Tankard Set, Syrquist, Gold Scroll Handles, Raspberries, Blossoms 425.00
Limoges, Tankard, Floral, Bird Of Paradise, Gold Handle Neck & Base, 10 In. 95.00
Limoges, Tankard, Hand-Painted, Grapes & Leaves, 7 1/2 In. 30.00
Limoges, Tankard, Sgraffito, Monk Pouring Wine Into Mug, Signed, 13 1/2 In. 275.00
Limoges, Tankard, White Glaze, Signed, 13 3/4 In. 40.00
Limoges, Tea Caddy, Hand-Painted, Morning Glory Flowers, 3 X 4 In. 22.00
Limoges, Tea Set, Gold Encrusted Teapot, Creamer, Sugar, Signed Jesse Dean 100.00
Limoges, Tea Set, Solid Gold Decoration, C.1865, 3 Piece 100.00
Limoges, Tea Set, Square Pedestal, Gold Trim, Hand-Painted Thistle, 3 Piece 100.00
Limoges, Tea Set, Wild Roses, Gold Trim, Footed, 3 Piece 105.00
Limoges, Teapot, Dragons, Flowers, Gold Spout & Handle, M.Redon, 7 In. 70.00
Limoges, Tile, Hand-Painted Roses, 11 X 8 1/4 In. 65.00
Limoges, Tray & Candleholder, Lavender, Tray 12 In., Holders, 10 1/2 In. 95.00
Limoges, Tray, Dresser, Hand-Painted, Footed, Signed, 7 X 9 1/2 X 1 1/2 In. 89.50
Limoges, Tray, Dresser, Hand-Painted, 14K Gold Leaf, Signed, 4 1/4 X 15 In. 79.50
Limoges, Tray, Dresser, Lovers In Garden, Gold Scrolling, 9 1/2 X 7 In. 95.00
Limoges, Tray, Dresser, Scalloped Gold Border, Center Handle, 11 X 6 1/2 In. 65.00
Limoges, Tray, Dresser, White With Roses, Gold Trim, 11 In. 16.00
Limoges, Tray, Irregular Scallops, Purple Flowers, Signed, 9 In.Long 28.00
Limoges, Tray, Multi-Colored Grapes, Leaves, Artist Signed, 18 In.Diameter 245.00
Limoges, Tray, Pin, Forget-Me-Nots & Gold 10.00
Limoges, Tray, Pinecone, 10 X 4 In. 24.00
Limoges, Tray, Scene Of Wine Cellar, Cavalier Drinking, 2 Handles, 10 In. 145.00
Limoges, Tray, Serving, 2-Handled, Etched Gold, Signed, 14 X 6 1/2 In. 55.00
Limoges, Tray, Spoon, Hand-Painted Roses, Gold Trim, 3 3/4 X 7 1/4 In. 45.00
Limoges, Tray, 3 Section, Gold Handle, Violet, Green Leaves, Signed 65.00
Limoges, Tray, 6 Lobed, Raised Flower Handle, 10 1/2 In. 40.00
Limoges, Tureen, Soup, Covered, Six Soup Plates, Floral Border 60.00
Limoges, Vase, Birds Roosting In Trees, Gray Ground, 11 In., Pair 55.00
Limoges, Vase, Bulbous, Roses, Gold On Rim, 9 X 8 In. 159.00
Limoges, Vase, Cherries, C.1895, Signed Burghoff, 12 In. 135.00
Limoges, Vase, Daisy & Leaves, Green Background, Gold Trim, 8 In. 22.00
Limoges, Vase, Grape Clusters, Artist Signed, 10 In. 135.00
Limoges, Vase, Hand-Painted Band, Art Nouveau Design, Gold Ground, Signed 150.00
Limoges, Vase, Hand-Painted Birds, Dated 1910, Signed, 10 1/2 In. 95.00
Limoges, Vase, Hand-Painted Cherries, Signed Burghoff, 10 In. 122.00
Limoges, Vase, Man & Woman In Garden, Dragon Head Handles, 16 In. 165.00
Limoges, Vase, Pink, Violets, Gilt Edge Top & Bottom, Signed, 6 In., Pair 65.00
Limoges, Vase, Rose Garland On Pale Green, Marked A.Lanternier, 4 In. 20.00
Limoges, Vase, Roses, Signed, T. & V., 11 In. 107.00
Limoges, Vase, Silver Body, Enameled, Red, Salmon, C.1925, Signed 1500.00
Limoges, Vase, Squatty, J.P.L., France, 7 In. 45.00
Limoges, Vegetable, Blue & Pink Flowers, J.P.L.France, 12 X 7 X 5 In. 55.00
Limoges, Washbowl & Pitcher Set, Blue Garlands & Pink Bouquets 325.00
Limoges, Wine, Set, Tankard & 5 Mugs, Red, Blue & Green Grape Clusters 350.00
Lindbergh, Bookends, The Aviator, Bronze 28.00

Lindbergh, Booklet, Speech, 1941	2.25
Lindbergh, Box, Photo Under Glass, Metal, 7 1/2 X 3 3/4 X 2 3/4 In.	45.00
Lindbergh, Hat	16.00
Lindbergh, Pennant, On Stick, Welcome Lindbergh, Red	15.00
Lindbergh, Pillowcase, Eagle, Plane & Lindy, Pair	25.00
Lindbergh, Record, Phonograph, 1926	18.00
Lindbergh, Tapestry, New York & Paris Scenes, France, 55 X 20 In.	85.00
Lindbergh, Watch, New York To Paris, Plane Model	55.00

Lithophanes are porcelain pictures made by casting clay in layers of various thicknesses. When a piece is held to the light, a picture of light and shadow is seen through it. Most lithophanes date from the 1825 to 1875 period. A few are still being made.

Lithophane, Candlestand, Pandora's Box, 5 3/4 X 4 1/4 In.	225.00
Lithophane, Children, 1 1/4 X 1 3/4 In.	27.50
Lithophane, Composer Puccini, Mounted In Leaded Frame, 7 1/2 X 8 In.	110.00
Lithophane, Lamp, American Views, Brass Base, Glass Font, Shade, 16 In.	575.00
Lithophane, Mug, Coronation, Edward VII, Irlan District Council, 2 1/2 In.	75.00
Lithophane, Portrait, Full Face Man, Leaded Glass Frame, 7 7/8 X 7 1/2 In.	165.00
Lithophane, Screen, Girls At Play, Candle At Back, 7 1/4 X 5 3/4 In.	225.00
Lithophane, Screen, Meissen, Crossed Swords Mark, 8 3/4 X 7 1/2 In.	255.00
Lithophane, Shade, Lamp, Clamp To Bulb, Metal Framed Panels, Pair	200.00
Lithophane, Shade, 5 Sided, Different Scene Each Panel, 15 1/2 X 6 1/2 In.	550.00
Lithophane, Stein, Monk, 7 X 6 In.	250.00
Lithophane, Tea Warmer, 4 Scenic Panels, Burner, 6 In.	140.00
Lithophane, Tray, Admiral Dewey, Porcelain, Admiral's Cap Shape, 3 In.Diam.	125.00
Lithophane, Warmer, Tea, Rural Scene	145.00
Lithophane, Warmer, Toddy, White, Shade, Round	150.00
Lithyalin, Beaker, Bohemian Glass, Mustard Brown, Gilded Bands .... *Illus*	100.00

Liverpool, England, has been the site of several pottery and porcelain factories from 1716 to 1785. Some earthenware was made with transfer decorations. Sadler and Green made print-decorated wares from 1756. Many of the pieces were made for the American market and featured patriotic emblems such as eagles, flags, and other special-interest motifs.

Liverpool, Jug, St.Patrick, Reverse Flower Girl & Verse, 10 In.	275.00
Lobmeyr, Cordial, Enameled, Full Figure Person, Signed, 4 3/4 In.	115.00
Locke Art, Bowl, Footed, Engraved & Etched, Signed, 3 1/2 X 4 1/2 In.Diam.	175.00
Locke Art, Bowl, Intaglio Cut, Engraved Poppies, Footed, Signed, 4 1/2 In.	165.00
Locke Art, Cracker Jar, Blown Out, Raspberries, Signed	125.00
Locke Art, Goblet, Etched Flowers	70.00
Locke Art, Goblet, Harvard Pattern, Notched Stem & Starred Foot	45.00
Locke Art, Goblet, Poppy, Signed, 6 In.	95.00
Locke Art, Goblet, Water, Etched Grape, Signed, Set Of 8	480.00
Locke Art, Sherbet, Poppy Pattern, Signed	70.00
Locke Art, Wine, Wild Rose Design, Signed, Pair	125.00

Loetz glass was made in Austria in the late nineteenth century. Many pieces are signed Loetz, Loetz-Austria, or Austria, and a pair of crossed arrows in a circle. Some unsigned pieces are confused with Tiffany glass.

Loetz, Atomizer, Burnt Orange, Cameo, Signed, 6 In.	170.00
Loetz, Basket, Iridescent, Satin Inside, Deep Rose Rim, 18 1/2 X 12 In.	150.00
Loetz, Basket, Iridescent, 8 1/2 X 8 In.Diameter	260.00
Loetz, Biscuit Jar, Iridescent, Blown-Out Sides, Bail Handle, 6 1/2 In.	175.00

Le Verre Francais, Lamp, Tortoiseshell Shades,
Flowers, Signed
(See Page 279)

Lithyalin, Beaker, Bohemian Glass,
Mustard Brown, Gilded Bands

Loetz, Bowl, Custard Cut, Flat Base, Ruffled Top, 7 1/2 In.Diameter	295.00
Loetz, Bowl, Dimpled Sides, Iridescent, Scalloped Top, Signed, 6 X 7 In.Diam.	450.00
Loetz, Bowl, Finger, Cranberry Threaded Glass, Opalescent Top, 2 X 5 In.	55.00
Loetz, Bowl, Free-Form, Shallow, Undulating Rim, Striated Texture, 12 In.	165.00
Loetz, Bowl, Purple Iridescent, Fluted Inverted Rim, 2 3/4 X 8 In.	165.00
Loetz, Bowl, Ruffled Top, Web Design, Iridescent Finish, 5 1/2 In.Diameter	100.00
Loetz, Bowl, 4 Snake Handles, Blue Iridescent, Signed, 6 In.Diameter	350.00
Loetz, Box, Yellow Ground, Blue Florals, Lidded, Signed, 5 1/4 X 3 1/2 In.	424.00
Loetz, Compote, Blue Iridescent, Multi-Colored, 8 1/2 X 4 In.	250.00
Loetz, Compote, Iridescent, Rolled Rim, Brass Base, 9 X 9 1/2 In.Diameter	250.00
Loetz, Cruet, Blue Iridescent, Polished Pontil, Signed & Numbered	185.00
Loetz, Floral, Lid, Yellow, Blue, Signed, 5 1/4 In.	422.00
Loetz, Hatpin Holder, Iridescent Blue & Green, 9 X 1 1/4 In.	38.00
Loetz, Inkwell, Hinged Cover, Inner Well, Amber Ground, Signed, 3 1/4 In.	285.00
Loetz, Inkwell, Square, Frosted Loopings, Brass Collar & Lid, Signed	200.00
Loetz, Paperweight, Blue Aurene, Feather Design, Signed, 2 1/2 X 3 1/4 In.	215.00
Loetz, Pitcher, Green Iridescent, Silver Lid & Handle, Signed, 8 In.	165.00
Loetz, Pitcher, Vertical Ribbed Raised Lines, Green Ground, Signed, 6 In.	195.00
Loetz, Rose Bowl, Art Deco, Raised Design, Iridescent, Brass Top	75.00
Loetz, Rose Bowl, Blown-Out Rose, Pulled Threads, Signed, 4 1/2 In.	249.00
Loetz, Rose Bowl, Gold Iridescent, Signed, 4 X 6 1/2 In.Diameter	125.00
Loetz, Rose, Bowl, Blown Body, Iridescent Purple Threads, Signed, 4 3/4 In.	235.00
Loetz, Saltshaker, Mottled Blue Iridescent, Sterling Top, Signed, 3 1/2 In.	210.00
Loetz, Vase, Amber Iridescent, Oil Spot Glaze, Flaring Neck, 1900s, 6 1/8 In.	100.00
Loetz, Vase, Amber Iridescent, Ovoid & Inverted Baluster Form, 10 In., Pair	200.00
Loetz, Vase, Applied Leaves, Flared Bottom, Green, 5 1/2 In.	127.50
Loetz, Vase, Art Nouveau, Swirled, Bronze Ormolu, Green Iridescence, 12 In.	175.00
Loetz, Vase, Blue Feather Decoration On Iridescent Glass, Pontil, 4 In.	65.00
Loetz, Vase, Blue Inside, Bronze Rim, 13 In.	145.00
Loetz, Vase, Brass Frog Top Cover, Pink & Green, 6 In.	80.00
Loetz, Vase, Bulbous, Green Iridescence, Signed, 4 1/2 X 7 In.	160.00
Loetz, Vase, Bulbous, Oil Spots, Signed, 9 1/4 In.	175.00
Loetz, Vase, Bulbous, Pinched, 7 In.	115.00
Loetz, Vase, Bulbous, Purple, Green & Blue, Iridescent, Signed, 7 3/4 In.	250.00
Loetz, Vase, Bulbous, Signed, 9 1/4 In.	250.00
Loetz, Vase, Cameo, Orange & Brown, Opaque Background, Signed, 13 In.	985.00
Loetz, Vase, Clear Iridescent, Applied Teardrops, Ruffled Top, 6 1/2 In.	75.00
Loetz, Vase, Cuspidor Shape.Ruffled Rim, Blown Out Design, 5 X 6 1/2 In.	155.00
Loetz, Vase, Fluted Rim, Orange Iridescent, Signed, 5 1/2 In.	150.00
Loetz, Vase, Gold Iridescent, Lap Top, Signed, 11 In.	375.00
Loetz, Vase, Gourd Shape, Inverted Quilt Pattern, Incised Loetz, 11 1/2 In.	700.00
Loetz, Vase, Green & Blue Iridescent, Austria, Signed, 7 In.	145.00
Loetz, Vase, Green Iridescent, Applied Gold Handles, Trails & Rim, 5 1/2 In.	95.00
Loetz, Vase, Green Iridescent, Signed, 9 In.High	135.00
Loetz, Vase, Green Mottling, Red Crabs Up Sides, Signed, 9 1/2 In.	1200.00
Loetz, Vase, Green, Gold Splashes, Twisted Curl Top, Signed, 10 1/2 X 6 In.	220.00
Loetz, Vase, Iridescent Gold, Marked, 3 In.	95.00
Loetz, Vase, Iridescent Green, Tree Bark, 11 In.	65.00
Loetz, Vase, Iridescent Green, 3 Applied Lily Pads On Neck, 10 In.	300.00
Loetz, Vase, Iridescent Purple & Green, 5 1/4 In.	85.00
Loetz, Vase, Iridescent, Gold & Purple, Ruffled Top, Signed, 6 1/8 In.	115.00
Loetz, Vase, King Tut Type, 4 Corner Freeform Shape, 4 3/4 In.	175.00
Loetz, Vase, King Tut, Blue, Gold Splashes, Pinched Body, 4 3/4 In.	175.00
Loetz, Vase, Lava Design, Red Color, Signed, 7 X 4 1/2 In.Diameter	350.00
Loetz, Vase, Line Design, Blue Iridescence, Signed, 5 1/2 In.	75.00
Loetz, Vase, Mother-Of-Pearl, White Swag Design, 5 In.	135.00
Loetz, Vase, Pearlized Green Spatter, Blown Mold Design, 4 In.	78.00
Loetz, Vase, Pinched & Twisted, Pink, Brown & Cream, 12 1/2 In.	90.00
Loetz, Vase, Pinched Shoulders, Green Interior, Amber Oil Spots, 11 In.	155.00
Loetz, Vase, Random Threading, Mulberry, 5 X 4 In.	95.00
Loetz, Vase, Red Color, Signed, 7 X 4 1/2 In.	30.00
Loetz, Vase, Sea Form Design, Iridescent, 6 In.	78.00
Loetz, Vase, Silver-Green Iridescence, Petal Top, Signed, 13 In.	295.00
Loetz, Vase, Silver, Blue Damascene Pattern, Red Glass Inside, 8 1/2 In.	350.00
Loetz, Vase, Triangle Opening, Gold Iridescence, Bronze Holder, 8 In.	85.00
Loetz, Vase, Trumpet Shape, Iridescent, 10 In.	145.00

Loetz, Vase, 2 Shades Of Red On Orange Body, Cameo Carved, Signed, 7 1/2 In.	650.00
Loetz, Vase, 3 Handled, Bulbous Base, Green, 4 In.	165.00
Lone Ranger, Badge, Deputy, C.1950s, On Card	7.50
Lone Ranger, Badge, Merita Bread, Star	6.00
Lone Ranger, Badge, Safety Club	10.00
Lone Ranger, Board Game, 1966, Boxed	4.50
Lone Ranger, Flashlight	9.00
Lone Ranger, Game, Target Board, 1938	8.00 To 24.00
Lone Ranger, Handcuffs	11.00
Lone Ranger, Hat, Cowboy, 1966	7.50
Lone Ranger, Holder, Toothbrush, On Horse, 1938	12.00 To 28.00
Lone Ranger, Holster, Boxed	10.00
Lone Ranger, Knife, Pocket, On Card	22.00 To 35.00
Lone Ranger, Knife, Pocket, Picture & Slogans, 3-D Bullet	18.50
Lone Ranger, Knife, Pocket, With Silver Bullet	10.00
Lone Ranger, Paperweight, Snow Globe	12.00 To 30.00
Lone Ranger, Pedometer, Silver	20.00
Lone Ranger, Pencil Box, Set	8.00
Lone Ranger, Pinback, Hi-Ho Silver, 1938, Picture On Horse	8.50
Lone Ranger, Pistol, Click, Tin, Boxed	35.00
Lone Ranger, Poster, 1940s	12.00
Lone Ranger, Radio	66.50
Lone Ranger, Ring, Atom Bomb	30.00
Lone Ranger, Ring, Flashlight, Original Battery	35.00
Lone Ranger, Ring, Six-Shooter	30.00
Lone Ranger, Ring, Weather	40.00
Lone Ranger, Shirt, Original Bag	12.00
Lone Ranger, Sparking Pistol	42.00
Lone Ranger, Viewer, 3 Films, Acme	18.00
Lone Ranger, Wrist Watch	55.00
Lone Ranger, Wristwatch, 1939, Original Box	250.00
Longwy, Jardiniere, Allover Enameled Flowers, 7 In.	80.00

Lonhuda Pottery Company of Steubenville, Ohio, was organized in 1892 by William Long, W. H. Hunter, and Alfred Day. Brown underglaze slip decorated pottery was made. The firm closed in 1896.

Lonhuda, Bowl, Yellow & Orange Flowers, Marked L.F., Denver, 6 1/4 In.	175.00
Lonhuda, Ewer, Zanesville Mark, 9 1/2 In.	375.00
Lonhuda, Vase, Flowers, 3 Feet, 3 Handles, Denver, 3 3/4 X 3 3/4 In.	275.00
Lonhuda, Vase, Green, Denver, Denaura, 5 1/2 In.	450.00
Lonhuda, Vase, High Floral, Bulbous, Narrow Flaring Neck, 6 3/4 In.	185.00
Lonhuda, Vase, Signed Elizabeth Ayers, 8 1/2 In.	345.00
Lonhuda, Vase, Slip Relief, Brown Background, Signed, 4 1/2 X 5 1/2 In.	175.00

Lotus ware was made by the Knowles, Taylor & Knowles Company of East Liverpool, Ohio, from 1890 to 1900.

Lotus Ware, Bowl, Gold Beaded & Ruffled Edge, Medallions, Signed K.T.K.	375.00
Lotus Ware, Bowl, Sugar, Green & Gold On Cream, Marked K.T.K., 3 1/2 In.	250.00
Lotus Ware, Creamer, Fishnet & Pink Flowers, Signed	175.00
Lotus Ware, Pitcher, K.T.K., Molded Leaf Design, Bamboo Handle, 4 1/2 In.	85.00
Lotus Ware, Rose Bowl, Green Fishscale Band, Floral, Gold Foilage, Marked	450.00
Lotus Ware, Tea Set, Raised Blossoms, Gold Trim, 3 Piece	350.00
Lotus Ware, Teapot, Green & Gold On Cream, Marked K.T.K.	150.00
Lotus Ware, Vase, Floral, Aqua Puffed Handles, Gold Beading, Artist Signed	485.00
Lotus Ware, Vase, Gold Beading, Puffed Handle, Signed, 4 1/4 X 5 1/2 In.	450.00
Lotus Ware, Vase, K.T.K., White Ball Feet, Net Pattern, Signed, 8 X 5 In.	200.00

J.&J.G.LOW *Low art tiles were made by the J. and J.G. Low Art Tile Works of Chelsea, Massachusetts, from 1877 to 1902. A variety of art and other tiles were made.*

Low, Tile, Floral, Green, 3 In.	15.00

The Lowestoft factory in Suffolk, England, worked from 1757 to 1802. They made many commemorative gift pieces and small dated, inscribed pieces of soft-paste porcelain.
Lowestoft, see also Chinese Export

Lowestoft, Bowl, Sugar, Soft-Paste, Swan Finial On Cover, C.1762, English 90.00
   Loy-Nel-Art, see McCoy
Ludwigsburg, Charger, Basketwork, Marked, C.1770, Pair, 14 1/4 In. 1600.00
Ludwigsburg, Dish, Marked, C.1770, Pair, 9 1/8 In. 950.00
Ludwigsburg, Dish, Oval, Marked, C.1770, Pair, 8 3/8 In. 475.00

     Luneville, a French faience factory, was established in 1731 by Jacques
     Chambrette. It is best known for its fine biscuit figures and groups and
     for large faience dogs and lions. The early pieces were unmarked. The
     Terre de Lorraine of T.D.L.impression was used after 1766.
Luneville, Vase, White Lilies, Gold Outlined, Blue To Green, Marked, 8 X 4 In. 68.00

     Lusterware was meant to resemble copper, silver, or gold. It has been used
     since the sixteenth century. Most of the luster found today was made during
     the nineteenth century.
  Luster, Sunderland, see Sunderland
Luster, Blue, Cup, Loving, Miniature, 3-Handled, Orange Interior, 2 X 2 In. 165.00
Luster, Bowl, Mother-Of-Pearl Interior, Octagonal, 4 1/2 In. 235.00
Luster, Canary, Jug, Success To The United States, 5 X 5 In. 695.00
Luster, Canary, Pitcher, Embossed Figures, Polychrome, C.1810, 8 In., Pair 295.00
Luster, Copper, Bowl, Band Of Flowers, 2 7/8 In. 15.00
Luster, Copper, Bowl, Centerpiece, 14 X 8 In. 100.00
Luster, Copper, Bowl, Embossed Deer, Made In England, 8 X 3 1/4 In. 47.00
Luster, Copper, Bowl, Round Footed, Scenes Around Side & Top, 4 5/8 In.Diam. 65.00
Luster, Copper, Bowl, Sugar, House Decoration, Pink Luster Trim 125.00
Luster, Copper, Cream Jug, Decorated Band, Blue, 4 1/4 In. 46.00
Luster, Copper, Creamer, Pink Flowers, Hanley, England, 3 In. 25.00
Luster, Copper, Creamer, 4 5/8 In. 40.00
Luster, Copper, Cup & Saucer, Beige Band 52.00
Luster, Copper, Jug, Hand-Painted, English 45.00
Luster, Copper, Jug, Milk, 2 Ivory Bands Decorated With Pink Luster, 7 In. 110.00
Luster, Copper, Mug, Brush Mark Decoration, Yellow Band, 3 In. 32.00
Luster, Copper, Mug, Decorated Band, 3 In. 50.00
Luster, Copper, Mug, Handles, Tan Band, Copper Design, 3 1/4 X 3 1/4 In. 40.00
Luster, Copper, Mug, Mustard Band, Flaring Shape, English, C.1830, 2 3/4 In. 30.00
Luster, Copper, Mug, Orange With Raised Flowers, Large 20.00
Luster, Copper, Mug, Yellow Band, Pink Inside Rim, 2 1/2 In. 20.00
Luster, Copper, Pitcher, Blue Band, Gold Scrolls, 3 1/2 In. 25.00
Luster, Copper, Pitcher, Blue Dancing Figures 55.00
Luster, Copper, Pitcher, Children Dancing, 6 1/2 In. 75.00
Luster, Copper, Pitcher, Colored Flowers At Top, 5 In. 45.00
Luster, Copper, Pitcher, Cream, Blue Band, 3 In. 35.00
Luster, Copper, Pitcher, Cream, Bulbous, 5 In. 40.00
Luster, Copper, Pitcher, Dancers, Embossed Blue, 7 In. 59.00
Luster, Copper, Pitcher, Diamond Pattern, Leaves & Flowers, 5 In. 35.00
Luster, Copper, Pitcher, Diamond Pattern, Leaves & Flowers, 6 In. 45.00
Luster, Copper, Pitcher, Duck Head, Serpent Handle, 7 1/4 In. 75.00
Luster, Copper, Pitcher, Embossed Deer & Band, 6 1/2 In. 52.00
Luster, Copper, Pitcher, Face On Spout, Applied Flowers, 4 1/2 In. 65.00
Luster, Copper, Pitcher, Floral Bands, 7 In. 85.00
Luster, Copper, Pitcher, Hand-Painted, Diamond Mold Base, 6 1/4 In. 75.00
Luster, Copper, Pitcher, Milk, Children Dancing, Blue Scroll, 6 3/4 In. High 67.50
Luster, Copper, Pitcher, Sand Bands, 3 In. 35.00
Luster, Copper, Pitcher, Tan Band, Gold Luster Flowers, 5 1/2 In. 55.00
Luster, Copper, Pitcher, 2 Tan Luster Bands, Decorated, 6 In. 65.00
  Luster, Copper, Tea Leaf, see Ironstone, Tea Leaf
Luster, Copper, Teapot, Bird Handle 69.00
Luster, Copper, Tumbler, Bar, Blue Band, Copper Leaves, 3 1/4 X 2 3/4 In. 35.00
  Luster, Fairyland, see Wedgwood, Fairyland Luster
Luster, Gold, Bowl, 8 In.Diameter 50.00
Luster, Green, Bowl, Candy, Applied Cherubs, Steeple Mark 135.00
Luster, Match Striker On Stand, Pink & White Boots, German, 4 In. 35.00
Luster, Matchholder, Pair Shoes, Striker On Back, German, 2 1/2 In. 20.00
Luster, Pink, Bowl, 5 3/4 In.Diameter 45.00
Luster, Pink, Candleholder, Snuffer, 6 1/2 In.Wide 32.00
Luster, Pink, Coffeepot, Child's, Gold Trim, 6 In. 12.00

Luster, Pink, Cup & Saucer, Applied Flowers, German 24.00
Luster, Pink, Cup & Saucer, Faith & Hope In Black Transfer, Charity Saucer 40.00
Luster, Pink, Cup & Saucer, Flowers 20.00
Luster, Pink, Cup & Saucer, Handleless, School House Pattern 40.00
Luster, Pink, Cup & Saucer, Pink & Green Flowers 15.00
Luster, Pink, Cup & Saucer, Raised Flowers, Victorian 11.50
Luster, Pink, Cup & Saucer, Temperance Star, Be Thou Faithful Unto Death 85.00
Luster, Pink, Jug, Coronet, Classical Figures On Blue, 5 In. 60.00
Luster, Pink, Pitcher, House Design, Copper Trim, 5 1/4 In. 145.00
Luster, Pink, Pitcher, Yellow Flowers, Marked, 5 X 17 1/4 In.Diameter 55.00
Luster, Pink, Plate, House, Wide Luster Border, Scalloped Edge, 8 1/2 In. 320.00
Luster, Pink, Pot, Chamber, Miniature, Sunderland, Compass On Front 125.00
Luster, Pink, Shoe 23.00
Luster, Pink, Spooner, Gold Flowers & Bird Design, Ruffled Top 28.00
Luster, Pink, Sugar, Open 45.00
Luster, Pink, Tea Set, 12 Cups & Saucers, Creamer, Sugar, Teapot, 2 Plates 350.00
Luster, Pink, Teapot, Portrait 40.00
Luster, Pink, Tray, Chain Design Border, 19th Century, 7 1/2 X 6 In. 22.50
Luster, Pink, Tumbler, Birthplace Of Daniel Webster, Marked Germany 14.50
Luster, Pink, Tumbler, Hand-Painted Clipper Ship 22.00
Luster, Pink, Vase, Souvenir, Terre Haute, Indiana 15.00
Luster, Purple, Pitcher, Yellow Flowers, Gray Pottery, England, 17 1/2 In. 65.00
Luster, Purple, Pitcher, 5 1/2 X 7 In. 75.00
Luster, Silver, Creamer, Queen Anne, Flaring Lip, English, C.1810 .... 65.00
Luster, Silver, Goblet, Copper Luster Lined, 5 In. 30.00
Luster, Silver, Jug, Foliage & Fruit On Vine, 6 In. 145.00
Luster, Silver, Mug, Lavender Lined, 5 1/4 In. 45.00
Luster, Silver, Pitcher, Hexagon Shape, 5 1/2 X 4 1/2 In. 75.00
Luster, Silver, Pitcher, Ribbed Pattern, 5 X 3 3/4 In. 65.00
Luster, Silver, Sugar & Creamer, Schwarzenhammer Crest 70.00
Luster, Silver, Teapot, C.1850s, Hinged Pewter Lid, 5 Cup 70.00
Luster, Silver, Vase, Bud, Cobalt Glass, Pair 35.00
Luster, Silver, Vase, Porcelain Lined, Bulbous Shape, 10 In. 40.00
Luster, Yellow & Green, Demitasse Set, Pot, Creamer, Sugar, 4 Cups & Saucers 460.00

*Lustre Art Glass Company was founded in Long Island, New York, in
1920 by Conrad Vahlsling and Paul Frank. The company made lampshades
and globes that are almost indistinguishable from those made by Quezal.*

Lustre Art, Shade, Gold Webbing Over Green & Gold Leaves, Opal Glass, Lined 110.00
Lustre Art, Shade, Green Feather, Gas, Signed, Set Of 4 .... 440.00
Lustre Art, Shade, Opal Feather With Green Edge On Gold, Notched Rim 95.00

*Lustres are mantel decorations, or pedestal vases, with many hanging glass
prisms. The name really refers to the prisms, and it is proper to refer to a
single glass prism as a lustre. Either spelling, luster or lustre,
is correct.*

Lustres, Vase, Overlay Glass, Victorian, Prisms, Bohemian, 11 1/2 In., Pair 375.00

*Lutz glass was made in the 1870s by Nicholas Lutz at the Boston and
Sandwich Company. He made a delicate and intricate threaded glass of
several colors. Other similar wares are referred to as Lutz.*

Lutz, Bowl & Dish, Finger, Threaded, Pink To Opalescent At Rim, Pontil 160.00
Lutz, Bowl, Crimped & Scalloped Rim, Gold & White Latticinio, 5 In., Diameter 57.50
Lutz, Bowl, Finger, Underplate, Pink To Opalescent, Ruffled Edge, Threaded 160.00
Lutz, Plate, Alternating Stripes Of Filigree, Gold Twists, 7 In. 57.50
Lutz, Plate, Filigree Canes, Multicolor, 6 1/2 In. 50.00
Lutz, Toothpick, Gold Sprinkled, Hand Blown Fluted Top, 1/2 X 2 In. 90.00

*Petrus Regout established the De Sphinx pottery in Maastricht,
Holland, in 1836. The firm was noted for its transfer-printed earthenware.
Many factories in Maastricht are still making ceramics.*

Maastricht, Bowl, Hong Pattern, 4 1/2 X 8 In. 22.00
Maastricht, Plate, Blue Stick Spatter Border, Gaudy Cobalt, 8 In. 17.00
Maastricht, Plate, Leaf Design On Border, Crystal, 4 1/4 In., Set Of 12 .... 85.00
MacIntyre, Biscuit Jar, Blue & Cream, Impressed Mark, 1852-62 .... 60.00
MacIntyre, Coffeepot, Dated 1899, Green Design, Tan Ground, 7 In. 265.00

Maize glass, sold by the W.L. Libbey & Son Company of Toledo, Ohio,
was made by Joseph Locke in 1889. It is pressed glass formed like an ear
of corn. Most pieces were made for household use.

Maize, Biscuit Jar, Cased, Ear Of Corn Finial, Pink	140.00
Maize, Bowl, Fruit, Blue Husks, Ivory, 9 In.	195.00
Maize, Celery, Libbey, Gold Iridescent, 6 1/4 In.	115.00
Maize, Pitcher, Water, Applied Handle, 8 1/2 In.	200.00
Maize, Pitcher, Water, Blue Opalescent	170.00
Maize, Salt, Libbey	45.00
Maize, Sugar Shaker	165.00 To 225.00
Maize, Toothpick, Green-Yellow Leaves	235.00
Maize, Tumbler, Yellow Leaves Outlined In Gold, Libbey	75.00
Maize, Vase, Celery, Green Leaves, 6 1/2 In.	55.00
Maize, Vase, Celery, Stained Glass, 6 1/2 In.	135.00
Maize, Vase, Celery, 6 1/2 X 4 In.Diameter	120.00

Majolica is any pottery glazed with a tin enamel. Most of the majolica
found today is decorated with leaves, shells, branches, and other natural shapes
and in natural colors. It was a popular nineteenth-century product.

Majolica, see also Wedgwood

Majolica, Ashtray, Cigar Stand, Striker, Black Boy Carries Watermelon	90.00
Majolica, Basket, Basket Weave With Leaves, Twisted Rope Handle, 10 X 6 In.	42.00
Majolica, Basket, Floral, Green, Pink, Blue	18.00
Majolica, Bowl, Cherub On Tiger In Center, Garland Border, 10 In.	45.00
Majolica, Bowl, Etruscan, Shell & Seaweed, 8 In.	36.00 To 75.00
Majolica, Bowl, Footed, Cream Ground, Pink Interior, 9 1/4 X 5 1/2 In.	55.00
Majolica, Bowl, Sugar, Birds & Flowers	12.50
Majolica, Bowl, Sugar, Etruscan, Cauliflower Handled	75.00
Majolica, Butter Pat, Begonia Leaf	22.00
Majolica, Butter Pat, Geranium Leaf	20.00
Majolica, Cake Plate, Pedestal, Leaf Pattern, Green	16.00
Majolica, Candleholder, Shape Of Sailor	45.00
Majolica, Candlestick, Boy & Girl Beside Stem, Pedestal Base, Pair	65.00
Majolica, Checker Set, Complete, 19th Century, 8 1/4 X 8 1/4 In.	147.00
Majolica, Compote, Top Resting On Cherub, 7 In.	82.00
Majolica, Creamer, Shell & Seaweed, Signed, 4 In.	85.00
Majolica, Cup, Shells & Seaweed, Pink, Green, Cream	38.00
Majolica, Cuspidor, Green, Yellow & Brown	38.00
Majolica, Dish, Begonia Leaf, 7 1/2 In.	12.00
Majolica, Dish, Butter, Bird & Fan	65.00
Majolica, Dish, Oval, Reclining Women, Molded Rim, C.1860, 15 In.	850.00
Majolica, Eggcup, Basket Caddy, Footed, Twig Handle, Set Of 4	85.00
Majolica, Ewer, Crossed Bands Front, Relief Flowers, England, 9 In.	80.00
Majolica, Figurine, Cherub Seated Next To Basket, Pink, C.1880	325.00
Majolica, Figurine, Playing Bagpipes, Mustache, Blue Hat, Cape, C.1890, 8 In.	90.00
Majolica, Humidor, Arab, Turban, Black Mustache, 5 In.	60.00
Majolica, Humidor, Bear, Blue Jacket, Holding Pipe, 6 In.	55.00
Majolica, Humidor, Egyptian Queen, Green Head, Turban, 6 In.	60.00
Majolica, Humidor, Elephant, Gray & Pink Jacket, Pipe In Mouth, 7 In.	65.00
Majolica, Humidor, Frog, Green & Pink Jacket, Pipe In Mouth, 6 1/2 In.	65.00
Majolica, Humidor, Monk, Skull Cap, Curly Gray Hair, 5 In.	60.00
Majolica, Humidor, Pig, Yellow, Green Apron, Pipe In Mouth, 6 1/2 In.	65.00
Majolica, Inkwell, Atop Footed Pen Tray, 8 X 3 In.	95.00
Majolica, Jar, Covered, Beige Glaze, Cows & Flowers, 4 1/2 X 5 In.Diameter	70.00
Majolica, Jar, Tobacco, Lion's Head With Hat	60.00
Majolica, Jar, Tobacco, Monk's Head	60.00
Majolica, Jar, Tobacco, Pig, Apron, Broom, Pipe	27.00
Majolica, Jar, Tobacco, Tiger's Head With Hat	27.00
Majolica, Jug, Duck, Pouring Spout Through Beak, 12 In.	35.00
Majolica, Jug, Parrot, Pouring Spout Through Beak, 12 In.	35.00
Majolica, Jug, Syrup, Stippled Cream, Daisies, Leaves, Metal Top, Dated 1872	63.00
Majolica, Match Holder, Black Boy On Bridge, Eating Corn, 7 In.	95.00
Majolica, Match Holder, Comic Dog Figure	33.50
Majolica, Match Holder, Dog Holds Matches, Striker, Oriental Figures	40.00
Majolica, Pitcher, Asters & Lily Pad Leaves, 9 1/4 In.	45.00
Majolica, Pitcher, Basket Weave, Daisy, Cream Background, 6 In.	28.00

Majolica, Pitcher, Blue Bow, Brown Handle, 5 In. 18.00
Majolica, Pitcher, Brown Tree Bark Pattern, Pink Interior, 8 1/2 In. 55.00
Majolica, Pitcher, Cream, Yellow & Brown Flowers, 5 In. 12.00
Majolica, Pitcher, Dragonfly Relief, 8 1/4 In. 60.00
Majolica, Pitcher, Etruscan, 5 In. 60.00
Majolica, Pitcher, Figural Owl, Lavender Interior, 10 In. 85.00
Majolica, Pitcher, Figural, Monkey Sitting, 7 In. 65.00
Majolica, Pitcher, Grape Leaf All Over, Brown Vine Handle, Marked, 7 In. 38.00
Majolica, Pitcher, Green, Yellow, Brown, Pink Lining, Bird, 6 3/4 In. 22.00
Majolica, Pitcher, Impressed Multicolor Flowers, Bird Head Handle, 10 In. 35.00
Majolica, Pitcher, Pineapple Shape, Green & White, 5 In. 125.00
Majolica, Pitcher, Pink Intaglio, Goats, 7 1/2 In. 24.00
Majolica, Pitcher, Raised Corn Design, Yellow & Green, 4 1/4 In. 15.00
Majolica, Pitcher, Roses, Leaves, Vines, Brown Tree Bark, Green, Pink, 9 In. 67.50
Majolica, Pitcher, Syrup, Etruscan, Sunflower Design, Pewter Top, 8 1/2 In. 125.00
Majolica, Pitcher, Syrup, Pink Lining, Aqua Outside, Single Stem Flower 40.00
Majolica, Pitcher, Toby, Blue Inside, 5 In. 92.00
Majolica, Pitcher, Violet Asters, Lily Pod Leaves, Green, Brown, 9 1/4 In. 45.00
Majolica, Pitcher, Water, Apple Blossom Decoration, Lavender Lining 27.50
Majolica, Pitcher, Wedding Of Edward To Princess Alexandria, 1870 .... 275.00
Majolica, Pitcher, 4 Vertical Fish, Lined In Pink, Applied Handle, 9 In. 35.00
Majolica, Plate Set, Different Fruits, France, Set Of 5 .... 40.00
Majolica, Plate, Apples & Raspberries, Marked Etruscan, 9 1/4 In. 48.00
Majolica, Plate, Basket Weave Border, Grecian Figures In Center, 8 In. 12.50
Majolica, Plate, Cauliflower Pattern, Impressed, 8 In. 45.00
Majolica, Plate, Cauliflower, Etruscan, 9 In. 35.00
Majolica, Plate, Dog, Sausage On Plate, Wavy Edge, 11 In. 45.00
Majolica, Plate, Fish, Round Fish, Plate Is Puffed Up, 9 In. 24.00
Majolica, Plate, Flowered Border, Raised Dog In Center, Etruscan Mark, 9 In. 32.00
Majolica, Plate, Greek Key Border, HBC & Co., Choisy Le Roi, 9 In. 15.00
Majolica, Plate, Green Basket Weave, Raised Pink Flowers, Set Of 3, 8 In. 25.00
Majolica, Plate, Leaf Border, Lattice Edge, C.1872, Pair 150.00
Majolica, Plate, Leaf, 12 In. 12.00
Majolica, Plate, Man On Keg Drinking Beer, Brown Edge, Pink, 11 In. 18.00
Majolica, Plate, Oyster, Registry Mark, Dated 1846, Minton 50.00
Majolica, Plate, Turquoise Basket Weave, Large Orange In Center, 9 In. 27.00
Majolica, Smoker, Square Base, Place For Pipe, Tobacco & Matches, 8 In. 62.00
Majolica, Spittoon, Flared Top, Raised Birds, Large 85.00
Majolica, Stein, Pewter Top, Signed M 40.00
Majolica, Sugar, Covered, Bamboo, Etruscan 75.00
Majolica, Sugar, Lid, Cauliflower 45.00
Majolica, Teapot, Acorn Shape, Squirrel Handle, 7 In. 15.00
Majolica, Teapot, Cabbage Ware, Dark Green, 5 X 7 In.Diameter 37.50
Majolica, Teapot, Cauliflower, Lid 85.00
Majolica, Teapot, Shell & Tassel, Etruscan, 6 X 5 In.Diameter 140.00
Majolica, Teapot, Shells & Seaweed, Pink, Green, Cream 162.00
Majolica, Tobacco Jar, Indian Chief, 5 1/2 In. 62.00
Majolica, Toby Jug, Parrot, Twig Handle & Base, Marked, 13 1/2 In. 125.00
Majolica, Tray, Oval, Green & Gray Dragon Flies, 12 In. 25.00
Majolica, Tureen, Covered, Footed, Melon Ribbed, Pear Finial, 4 Quart 56.00
Majolica, Vase, Figure Of Nubian Boy, 12 In. 75.00
Majolica, Vase, Fish, Tail Is Handle, Open Mouth Is Vase, 9 In. 40.00
Majolica, Vase, Flower Form, Nubian Lad, 12 In. 69.00
Majolica, Vase, Mayer, England, C.1840 .... 22.00
Majolica, Vase, Monkey, 11 In. 50.00
Majolica, Vase, Orange With Blue, 1860s, 10 1/2 In., Pair 310.00
Majolica, Vase, Zigzag Bands Of Contrasting Colors, Schramberger, 11 In. 50.00
Majolica, Vase, 2-Handled, Fish Mouth, Green, 10 1/2 In. 35.00
Majolica, Wall Bracket, Cupid, Brown & White Glaze, Wedgwood, 9 X 4 In. 750.00
Malachite, Ball, Banded, 2 1/2 In.Diameter 475.00
Malachite, Ball, Billiard, Banded, 2 1/4 In. 395.00
Malachite, Figurine, Kuan Yin Holding Flowers, 2 Attendants, 7 1/2 In. 1000.00
Malachite, Jar, Powder, Birds, Flowers, Cherub, Covered 40.00
Malachite, Vase & Cover, Dragons Contesting Flaming Pearls, 10 In. 800.00
Malachite, Vase, Footed, Jade Green, Embossed, 10 X 4 In. 75.00
Malachite, Vase, 3 Classic Nudes, Jade Green, 8 1/2 In. 75.00

Marble Carving, Boy & Girl,
Sculpture Group, Unsigned

Marble Carving, Grecian Women
With Children, 21 1/2 In.

Marble Carving, Bust, Woman
With Roses In Her Hair, 22 In.

Marble Carving, Statue,
Venus Di Milo, Copy, 35 In.

Mantel, see Furniture, Mantel

Marbles of glass were made during the nineteenth century. Venetian swirl,
clear glass, sulfides, and marbles with frosted white animal figures embedded in
the glass were popular. Handmade clay marbles were made in many places, but
most of them came from the pottery factories of Ohio and Pennsylvania.
Occasionally, real stone marbles of onyx, carnelian, or jasper can be found.

Marble Carving, Ashtray, Lion's Head On Side, Rubylike Stones In Mouth	23.50
Marble Carving, Boy & Girl, Sculpture Group, Unsigned ....*Illus*	375.00
Marble Carving, Bust, Child In Bonnet, Galli Rizzard, 21 In.	535.00
Marble Carving, Bust, Classical Female Figure, 22 In.	575.00
Marble Carving, Bust, Classical Male Figure, White, Prof.O.Puertze, 11 In.	70.00
Marble Carving, Bust, Classical Male Figure, 21 In.	350.00
Marble Carving, Bust, Sophocles, White, Circular Marble Plinth, 25 3/4 In.	450.00
Marble Carving, Bust, Victorian Woman With Cap, Signed F.Cornacchia, 1913	290.00
Marble Carving, Bust, White Head, Curly Hair & Beard, 28 In.	2400.00
Marble Carving, Bust, Woman With Roses In Her Hair, 22 In. ....*Illus*	325.00
Marble Carving, Bust, Woman, Alabaster, 20 In.	350.00
Marble Carving, Figure, Young Girl Sewing, Seated On Plinth, 1900s, 28 In.	1600.00
Marble Carving, Grecian Women With Children, 21 1/2 In. ....*Illus*	450.00
Marble Carving, Statue, Classical Maiden, Legs Crossed, C.1900, 44 In.	2250.00
Marble Carving, Statue, Juan Yin, Holding Ambrosia Vase, Lotus Base, 45 In.	700.00
Marble Carving, Statue, Venus Accompanied By Dolphin, Italian, 1800s, 61 In.	2750.00
Marble Carving, Statue, Venus Di Milo, Copy, 35 In. ....*Illus*	500.00
Marble Carving, Urn Stand, White, Square Top, Plastform Base, 39 In., Pair	1500.00
Marble, Bennington, Blue, Approximately 60 3/4 In.Diameter	50.00
Marble, Bennington, Blue, 1 1/4 In.Diameter	10.00
Marble, Bennington, 1 1/8 In.	14.50
Marble, Bennington, 5 In.Diameter	25.00
Marble, Chinese, Decorated, Unglazed, 1 1/8 In.	17.00
Marble, Comic, Annie	25.00
Marble, Comic, Annie & Sandy, Pair	45.00
Marble, Comic, Betty Boop	27.00
Marble, Comic, Bimbo	30.00
Marble, Comic, Emma	35.00
Marble, Comic, Herbie	30.00
Marble, Comic, Koko	30.00
Marble, Comic, Sandy	25.00 To 30.00

Marble, Comic, Smitty	25.00
Marble, Goldstone	20.00
Marble, Latticinio, White Core, Red, Yellow, Green & Blue Ribbons, 1 3/4 In.	42.50
Marble, Latticinio, Yellow Core, Red & White Ribbons, 1 7/8 In.	45.00
Marble, Onionskin Swirl, Red, White & Blue, 1 5/8 In.	40.00
Marble, Planters Peanut	7.50
Marble, Sulfide, Bear, Standing, 1 1/2 In.	40.00
Marble, Sulfide, Begging Cat, Bluish Tint, 1 3/4 In.	90.00
Marble, Sulfide, Bird, Green Swirl	70.00
Marble, Sulfide, Bird, 2 In.	95.00
Marble, Sulfide, Boy On Stump, 5/8 In.	65.00
Marble, Sulfide, Cat, Seated, 1 1/4 In.	35.00
Marble, Sulfide, Chicken, 7/8 In.	45.00
Marble, Sulfide, Crow, Clear, 5 In.Diameter	60.00
Marble, Sulfide, Dog, Seated, White, 1 1/2 In.	65.00
Marble, Sulfide, Dog, Seated, 9/16 In.	35.00
Marble, Sulfide, Dog, Standing, 7 1/4 In.	55.00
Marble, Sulfide, Dog, 1 1/2 In.	40.00
Marble, Sulfide, Dog, 6 In.	74.00
Marble, Sulfide, Dog, 6 1/2 In.	68.00
Marble, Sulfide, Fish, 1 3/8 In.	45.00
Marble, Sulfide, Frog	85.00
Marble, Sulfide, Hen	45.00
Marble, Sulfide, Horse, 2 In.	115.00
Marble, Sulfide, Kangaroo	125.00
Marble, Sulfide, Lamb	15.00
Marble, Sulfide, Lamb, 2 In.	45.00
Marble, Sulfide, Monkey, 1 3/19 In.	50.00
Marble, Sulfide, Monkey, 2 In.	110.00
Marble, Sulfide, Rabbit, Running, 2 In.	45.00
Marble, Sulfide, Rabbit, 1 3/4 In.	35.00
Marble, Sulfide, Reclining Lion, 1 1/4 In.	25.00
Marble, Sulfide, Seated Cat, 1 1/4 In.	35.00
Marble, Sulfide, Sheep & Lamb Nursing, 13/16 In.	55.00
Marble, Sulfide, Spaniel, Seated, 1 1/2 In.	65.00
Marble, Sulfide, Squirrel, 5 In.	62.00
Marble, Sulfide, Wild Turkey, 1 7/8 In.	85.00
Marble, Swirl, Black & White, 1 1/2 In.	40.00
Marble, Swirl, Blue & White, White Center Core, 7/8 In.	12.00
Marble, Swirl, Blue & White, White Core, 1/2 In.	10.00
Marble, Swirl, Candy Stripe, 1/2 In.	12.50
Marble, Swirl, Candy Stripe, 2 In.	47.50 To 52.50
Marble, Swirl, Latticinio, 1 5/8 In.	29.00
Marble, Swirl, Latticinio, 9 X 1/2 In.	19.00
Marble, Swirl, Multicolor, Silver Flecking, 1 3/4 In.	65.00
Marble, Swirl, Multicolored From Center Out, 1 3/4 In.Diameter	35.00
Marble, Swirl, Multicolored Latticino Center, 1 1/4 In.Diameter	24.00
Marble, Swirl, Multicolored Ribbon Center, White Outer Swirl, 4 1/2 In.	45.00
Marble, Swirl, Multicolored Ribbon, Glass, 3/4 In.	8.50
Marble, Swirl, Multicolored, White Core, Swirl On Outer Side, 5/8 In.	14.00
Marble, Swirl, Multicolored, 1 3/4 In.	25.00
Marble, Swirl, Red, White & Blue, Yellow Center Core, Blown, 1 7/8 In.	48.00
Marble, Swirl, Split Core, 2 In.	85.00
Marble, Swirl, 1 1/8 In.	24.00
Marble, Swirl, 1 1/4 In.	24.00 To 35.00
Marble, Swirl, 1 1/2 In.	20.00 To 22.50

The Marblehead Pottery was founded in 1905 as a rehabilitative program for the patients of a Marblehead, Mass., sanitarium by Dr. J. Hall. Two years later it was separated from the sanitarium, and it continued operations until 1936. Many of the pieces were decorated with marine motifs.

Marblehead, Bowl, 2 Color Leaf Garland, Artist Signed, 5 In.	285.00
Marblehead, Candlestick, Purple Glaze, Original Label, Pair	80.00
Marblehead, Candlestick, Scroll Handles, Green, Pair	42.50
Marblehead, Pitcher, Cream, Blue, 3 1/2 In.	45.00

Marblehead, Pitcher, Cream, Tan, 4 1/2 In.	55.00
Marblehead, Rose Bowl, 8 In.	25.00
Marblehead, Tea Set, Matte Blue Glaze, Signed, Teapot, Sugar, Creamer	150.00
Marblehead, Tile, Blue & White Sailing Ship, 5 In.	10.00
Marblehead, Vase, Blue, 3 3/4 In.	30.00 To 42.00
Marblehead, Vase, Bulbous, Green, 3 1/2 In.	26.00
Marblehead, Vase, Butterflies, Flowers, Blue Ground, 4 1/4 X 4 In.	350.00
Marblehead, Vase, Cylinder, 10 1/2 In.	50.00
Marblehead, Vase, Fan Shape, Blue, 5 3/4 In.	30.00
Marblehead, Vase, Matte Finish, Blue, 8 1/2 In.	32.00
Marblehead, Vase, Stick, 5 3/4 In.	52.50
Marblehead, Vase, Stylized Flowers At Top, Gray Ground, Signed, 5 1/4 In.	330.00
Marblehead, Vase, 7 Sided, Medallions, Signed, 3 1/2 X 4 1/4 In.	340.00
Marblehead, Wallpocket, Brown, 5 In.	25.00

Marine, see Nautical

Mary Gregory glass is identified by a characteristic white figure painted on dark glass. It was made from 1870 to 1910. The name refers to any glass decorated with a white silhouette figure and not just the Sandwich glass originally painted by Miss Mary Gregory.

Mary Gregory, Ale, Footed, Amber, 7 In.	58.00
Mary Gregory, Basket, Dutch Boy, Green	135.00
Mary Gregory, Biscuit Jar, Lid, White Figure Of Child	145.00
Mary Gregory, Bottle, Barber, Boy & Girl, Amethyst, Pair	250.00
Mary Gregory, Bottle, Emerald Green, Young Girl Picking Flowers, 9 In.	135.00
Mary Gregory, Bottle, Perfume, Boy, Clear, 6 In.	115.00
Mary Gregory, Bottle, Perfume, Tinted Features, White, 5 3/4 X 3 In.	135.00
Mary Gregory, Bottle, Wine, Baby Thumbprint, Boy Figure	65.00
Mary Gregory, Bottle, Wine, White Enamel On Clear, 12 In.	35.00
Mary Gregory, Bowl, Sugar, Clear Glass	20.00
Mary Gregory, Box, Brass Rigaree, Girl, Enamel, Periwinkle, 5 3/8 X 5 7/8 In.	325.00
Mary Gregory, Box, Jewel, Amber, 2 1/2 In.Diameter	80.00
Mary Gregory, Box, Patch, Cranberry	175.00
Mary Gregory, Box, Powder, Beading, Brass Collar, Hinged, 3 3/4 X 3 1/2 In.	90.00
Mary Gregory, Carafe, Water, Tumbler, Boy With Kite, Girl On Tumbler, Blue	225.00
Mary Gregory, Carafe, Water, Tumbler, Girl On Both, Green, 9 1/4 In.	175.00
Mary Gregory, Castor Set, Amber	85.00
Mary Gregory, Cruet, All White Girl, Clear	125.00
Mary Gregory, Cruet, Applied Handle, Green, 10 1/2 In.	250.00
Mary Gregory, Cruet, Blown Stopper, White Figures, Boy & Girl, 10 In.	175.00
Mary Gregory, Cruet, Boy With Cane, In Woods, Original Stopper, Green	175.00
Mary Gregory, Cruet, Green	29.00 To 150.00
Mary Gregory, Cruet, Green, Young Boy Lying On Grass, Stopper, 4 1/2 In.	165.00
Mary Gregory, Cruet, Inverted Thumbprint, Emerald, 8 1/2 In.	145.00
Mary Gregory, Cruet, Squared, Bulbous, Cranberry, 3 Petal Top, White, 8 In.	195.00
Mary Gregory, Cruet, Tinted Features, Girl At Fence, White Enamel, 7 3/4 In.	225.00
Mary Gregory, Cup, Punch, White Boy, Souvenir De Nice, Amber	50.00
Mary Gregory, Decanter, Cranberry, Child Decoration, Mushroom Stopper, 7 In.	52.00
Mary Gregory, Decanter, Girl, Tinted Face, White Enamel, Blue, 10 1/2 In.	95.00
Mary Gregory, Decanter, Inverted Thumbprint, White Figures, 8 3/4 In., Pair	350.00
Mary Gregory, Decanter, Wine, 2 Wines, Tray, 9 In.Diameter	350.00
Mary Gregory, Decanter, 3 Petal Top, Girl & Foliage, White Enamel, 9 1/4 In.	165.00
Mary Gregory, Ewer, Applied Handle, White Figures, 10 In., Pair	350.00
Mary Gregory, Figurine, Girl With Basket Of Flowers, Francois, 4 1/8 In.	80.00
Mary Gregory, Glass, Ale, Boy On One, Girl On Other, Footed, 6 3/4 In., Pair	80.00
Mary Gregory, Glass, Cordial, Blue With Boy In White, Enamel, 2 1/2 In.	55.00
Mary Gregory, Glass, Juice, Expanded Base, Enamel, Girl	54.00
Mary Gregory, Goblet, Boy & Girl, Amber, Pair	175.00
Mary Gregory, Goblet, Boy On One, Girl On Other, Amber, Pair	165.00
Mary Gregory, Jar, Cover, 3 Legs, White Boy, Green, 9 1/2 In.	67.00
Mary Gregory, Jar, Pomade, Cranberry, 3 In.	150.00
Mary Gregory, Jar, Powder, Covered, Clear, 3 1/2 X 5 In.Diameter	90.00
Mary Gregory, Match Safe, White Enameled, Clear, 3 1/4 X 2 In.	55.00
Mary Gregory, Mug, Cranberry, 3 In.	66.00
Mary Gregory, Mug, Cupid In White, 3 1/2 In.	58.00
Mary Gregory, Mug, Handled, Honey Amber, Boy	114.00

Mary Gregory, **Mug,** Inverted Thumbprint, Honey Amber, Boy 60.00
Mary Gregory, **Paperweight,** Black Glass, White Figure Of Boy, Square, 2 In. 185.00
Mary Gregory, **Pitcher,** Applied Handles, Olive, 4 X 2 In., Pair 130.00
Mary Gregory, **Pitcher,** Crystal, Girl Picking Flowers, Applied Handle, 11 In. 120.00
Mary Gregory, **Pitcher,** Dark Green, Blown, All White Girl, 6 In. 125.00
Mary Gregory, **Pitcher,** Emerald Green, Girl With Sprig In Hand, 5 3/4 In. 140.00
Mary Gregory, **Pitcher,** Hand Blown, Frosted, White Dress, 9 3/4 In. 95.00
Mary Gregory, **Pitcher,** Milk, White Girl, Cranberry, Clear Handle, 7 In. 150.00
Mary Gregory, **Pitcher,** Miniature, 3 In. 45.00
Mary Gregory, **Pitcher,** Water, Ruffled Top, Boy & Birds, White, 8 3/4 In. 325.00
Mary Gregory, **Pitcher,** White Figure Girl, Clear, 9 1/2 In. 105.00
Mary Gregory, **Spooner,** Girl Feeding Birds, White, Black Amethyst 95.00
Mary Gregory, **Sugar & Creamer,** Green 165.00
Mary Gregory, **Tankard,** Girl By Tree, Hat In Hand, Blue, 11 In. 295.00
Mary Gregory, **Tankard,** Girl, Hat & Staff In Hands, White Tree, Blue, 12 In. 255.00
Mary Gregory, **Tea Warmer,** Metal Frame, Lavender, White Figures, 9 1/2 In. 125.00
Mary Gregory, **Toothpick,** Boy With Pack, Blue 32.00
Mary Gregory, **Toothpick,** Indian Chief 45.00
Mary Gregory, **Tray,** Pin, Cranberry, 4 1/2 In. 72.00
Mary Gregory, **Tumbler,** Clear, Girl Holding Flowers, White Enamel, 3 3/4 In. 35.00
Mary Gregory, **Tumbler,** Girl With Twig In Hand 55.00
Mary Gregory, **Tumbler,** Inverted Rib, Green, White Figured Boy, 4 In. 45.00
Mary Gregory, **Tumbler,** Little Girl, Lime Green Garment Trim, Cranberry 48.50
Mary Gregory, **Tumbler,** Paneled, Blue 70.00
Mary Gregory, **Tumbler,** Tinted Face Lady, Pair 28.00
Mary Gregory, **Tumbler,** White Enamel, Boy & Girl 35.00
Mary Gregory, **Tumbler,** White Figures, Boy & Girl, Green, 5 1/4 In., Pair 67.50
Mary Gregory, **Vase,** All White, One Boy, Other Girl, 5 1/2 In., Pair 185.00
Mary Gregory, **Vase,** Applied Crystal Trim, Boy, Girl, Facing, 9 7/8 In.Pair 250.00
Mary Gregory, **Vase,** Applied Prunts On Sides, Clear, 8 In. 95.00
Mary Gregory, **Vase,** Black Amethyst, Girl Feeding Bird, 4 1/2 X 3 In. 85.00
Mary Gregory, **Vase,** Blown Glass, Green, 15 In. 90.00
Mary Gregory, **Vase,** Boy On One & Girl On Other, Amber, 11 1/4 In., Pair 425.00
Mary Gregory, **Vase,** Boy Sitting On Mound, Green, White Enamel, 8 7/8 In. 110.00
Mary Gregory, **Vase,** Boy With Hat, All White Enamel, Cranberry, 8 1/4 In. 145.00
Mary Gregory, **Vase,** Boy, Girl, White Figures, Cranberry Ground, 7 1/2 In., Pr. 50.00
Mary Gregory, **Vase,** Boy, White Enamel, Cranberry, 7 In. 115.00
Mary Gregory, **Vase,** Boy, White Enamel, Inverted Thumbprint, 7 3/4 In. 135.00
Mary Gregory, **Vase,** Cranberry, 5 In. 85.00
Mary Gregory, **Vase,** Cerulean, Blue, 11 In. 179.00
Mary Gregory, **Vase,** Chartreuse, Green, Young Girl, 4 X 2 1/4 In. 69.00
Mary Gregory, **Vase,** Clear To Green, 11 In. 165.00
Mary Gregory, **Vase,** Clear, White Figures, Rigaree Sides, 11 X 4 In. 145.00
Mary Gregory, **Vase,** Cranberry, Little Boy 110.00
Mary Gregory, **Vase,** Crimped Edge, White Boy, Shield & Arrow, 6 In. 45.00
Mary Gregory, **Vase,** Double Figure, All White Enamel, 13 5/8 In. 325.00
Mary Gregory, **Vase,** Emerald Green, White Boy Blowing Horn, 7 1/4 In. 75.00
Mary Gregory, **Vase,** Facing Pair, Young Boy, Girl, White Enamel, 4 1/8 In., Pr. 210.00
Mary Gregory, **Vase,** Front Enameling, Girl, Ruffled Edging In Gold, 8 In. 110.00
Mary Gregory, **Vase,** Girl Picking Apples From Tree, Scalloped, Blue, 12 In. 165.00
Mary Gregory, **Vase,** Girl With Apron, All White Satin Enamel, Green, 9 In. 175.00
Mary Gregory, **Vase,** Gold Reeded Handles, Facing Pair, 13 3/8 In., Pair 795.00
Mary Gregory, **Vase,** Gourd Shape, Cranberry, 11 In. 29.00
Mary Gregory, **Vase,** One Girl, One Boy, Facing, Amber, 6 1/4 In., Pair 110.00
Mary Gregory, **Vase,** Ruby Boy, Blowing Bubbles, 9 In. 115.00
Mary Gregory, **Vase,** Ruffled Top, Facing Pair, White Enamel, 6 3/8 In., Pair 185.00
Mary Gregory, **Vase,** Sapphire Blue, Blown, 8 In. 45.00
Mary Gregory, **Vase,** Sapphire Blue, White Enamel, 5 7/8 X 4 7/8 In.Diameter ... 195.00
Mary Gregory, **Vase,** Stick, Boy & Girl Facing, White Figures, 7 In., Pair 250.00
Mary Gregory, **Vase,** Stick, Optic Panel, Cranberry, 7 In., Pair 325.00
Mary Gregory, **Vase,** Stick, Optic Panels, Girl Holding Leaves, Cranberry, 7 In. ... 125.00
Mary Gregory, **Vase,** Trumpet Shape, Clear Base, 10 1/2 In. 149.00
Mary Gregory, **Vase,** White Enamel, Facing Pair, Cranberry, 8 7/8 In., Pair 365.00
Mary Gregory, **Vase,** White Enameled Girl, 5 1/2 In. 95.00
Mary Gregory, **Vase,** White Girl, Cobalt, 10 In. 150.00
Mary Gregory, **Water Set,** Bulbous, Clear White Figures, 7 Glasses, 8 1/2 In. 340.00

Mary Gregory, Water Set, White Enameling, 6 In.Tumbler, Pitcher, 11 In.	295.00
Mary Gregory, Wine Set, Boy On Bottle, Sail Boat On Glass, Cranberry	675.00

Masonic Shrine glassware was made from 1893 to 1917. It is occasionally called Syrian Temple Shrine glassware. Most pieces are dated.

Masonic, Ashtray & Match Holder, Mother-Of-Pearl Shell	11.00
Masonic, Book, Degrees Of Free Masonry, Dated 1867, 300 Pages, Leather Bound	10.00
Masonic, Bookends, Bronzed Cast Iron	25.00
Masonic, Button, G.Washington Wearing Masonic Apron, C.1896	8.50
Masonic, Candlestick, Shrine, Egyptian Figures, Brass, 10 1/2 In.	27.00
Masonic, Chalice, Syria Shrine, 1908	50.00
Masonic, Champagne, Louisville, Ky., 1909, Gold Swords, Iridescent	65.00
Masonic, Champagne, New Orleans, 1904, Neptune Head, Alligator Sides	48.00
Masonic, Champagne, New Orleans, 1910, Alligators On Side, Old Man	75.00
Masonic, Champagne, Pittsburgh, New Orleans, 1910, Figural Alligators	65.00
Masonic, Champagne, Pittsburgh, Pennsylvania, Clear Carnival	145.00
Masonic, Champagne, Syria Shrine, New Orleans, 1910	70.00
Masonic, Compact, Chain, Place For Change & Bills, Shrine	15.00
Masonic, Compact, Eastern Star, Bronze	10.00
Masonic, Cup, Fish Handle, Atlantic City, July 13, 1904, Pittsburgh	50.00
Masonic, Dish, Footed, Dated 1890, Pittsburgh, Pennsylvania	35.00
Masonic, Flashlight, Keychain, Shriner Emblem, Engraved	17.00
Masonic, Flask, Round, Shriner Scene, 1912	20.00
Masonic, Fob, Compliments Of C.G.Braxmar Co.	10.00
Masonic, Goblet, Rochester, N.Y., July 1900	45.00
Masonic, Goblet, Syria, Los Angeles, 1907, Pittsburgh	60.00
Masonic, Handkerchief, Knights Templar, Boston, 1895	9.00
Masonic, License Attachment, Mirza, Pittsburgh, Kansas, 5 X 5 1/2 In.	12.50
Masonic, Match Holder, Table, Ironstone	8.00
Masonic, Match Safe, Cambridge, Mass., Commandery, 1906, Silver Plate	18.50
Masonic, Mirror, Celluloid Case & Handle, Murat Temple, Indianapolis	65.00
Masonic, Mug, Atlantic City, 1904, Bathing Beauty, Sword Handle	45.00
Masonic, Mug, Chirhicapuia Apache, Osiris Temple, Wheeling, W.Va., 1904	65.00
Masonic, Mug, Commemorative, Nantucket Beach, 1895, Gold Symbols, Legend	75.00
Masonic, Mug, Knights Templar, Syracuse, 1909	22.00
Masonic, Mug, Osiris Temple, Wheeling, W.Va., 1909, Warwick, 4 1/2 In.	55.00
Masonic, Mug, Shrine, Saratoga, 1903	65.00
Masonic, Mug, Shriner's, July, 1904, Atlantic City, Fish Handle	45.00
Masonic, Mug, Syria On Handle, Indian On Front	75.00
Masonic, Mug, 3 Handled, Central City Commandery, June, 1909, Cobalt Blue	22.50
Masonic, Nappy, Greentown Glass, Star On Bottom	105.00
Masonic, Paperweight, Emblem Inside	25.00
Masonic, Paperweight, Metal, 4 In.	20.00
Masonic, Pin, Lapel, Shriner, 26 Small Pearls	65.00
Masonic, Plate, Antiquarian Society, Maryland, General Shryock, 1910	25.00
Masonic, Plate, Chicago, 1961, Spode	9.00
Masonic, Plate, Desert Scene, Camel Rider, Symbos On Edge, Tin, 10 In.	47.50
Masonic, Plate, Detroit, 1967, Spode	9.00
Masonic, Plate, Los Angeles, 1906, Syria Shrine, 6 In.	25.00
Masonic, Plate, Pittsburgh Commandery, Dated 1898	30.00
Masonic, Plate, Pittsburgh Commandery, Dated 1906	25.00
Masonic, Plate, Pittsburgh, Syria Shrine, May, 1906, 6 In.	36.00
Masonic, Plate, Pittsburgh, 1967, Spode	9.00
Masonic, Plate, Zembo Temple, Harrisburg, 9 1/2 In.	45.00
Masonic, Ring, Diamond, Yellow Gold	90.00
Masonic, Ring, Emblem On Onyx, 10K Gold	32.00
Masonic, Ring, Initialed J.E.E., Patent 1884	25.00
Masonic, Ring, 32nd Degree, 10K Gold, Minecut Diamond	21.00
Masonic, Shaving Mug, Mason Charles Preston, Washington Post	8.00
Masonic, Shaving Mug, Scottish Rite	25.00
Masonic, Stick Pin, Chip Diamond, Shrine	15.00
Masonic, Sword & Scabbard, Dress, Knight Of Columbus	45.00
Masonic, Sword & Scabbard, Grand Master's, C.1858	300.00
Masonic, Sword & Scabbard, Knights Of Pythias, C.1870s	48.00
Masonic, Sword, Knights Templar, Marked Charles A. Upham	55.00
Masonic, Sword, Pittsburgh, 1909, Pair	75.00

Masonic, Tankard, 60th Anniversary, Newark, 1853-1913, 12 1/2 In.	80.00
Masonic, Tray, Pin, Morocco Temple, 1911, Brass	15.00
Masonic, Trowel, Miniature, 1811-1936, Delaware, Ohio, 4 1/4in.	9.50
Masonic, Trowel, Sterling, 3 Handled, C.1919, 4 In.	35.00
Masonic, Tumbler, Flashed Ruby, 1893 World's Fair	29.00
Masonic, Tumbler, Souvenir, Louisville, Ky., 1901	20.00
Masonic, Watch Fob, Rochester, N.Y., Emblem In Circle	14.00
Masonic, Watch Fob, 1916	12.00
Masonic, Wine, Pittsburgh, St.Paul, 1908, Gold Sheaths Of Wheat	65.00

J.Massier fils   *Massier pottery is iridescent French art pottery made by Clement Massier in Golfe-Juane, France, in the late nineteenth and early twentieth centuries. It is characterized by a metallic luster glaze.*

Massier, Candlestick, Handle In Mottled Green, Tan & Brown, 13 In.	150.00
Massier, Jardiniere & Pedestal, Chocolate Ground, Art Nouveau	500.00
Massier, Vase, Figures Of Man & Woman, 7 X 6 1/2 In.	375.00
Massier, Vase, Surface Gilt Luster, Dragonflies, C.1900 ....*Illus*	450.00
Match Holder, see also Iron, Match Holder; Staffordshire,	
Match Holder; Store, Match Holder	
Match Holder, Aladdin, Copper	15.00
Match Holder, Ashtray, Fatima Turkish Cigarettes, China, Marked Nippon	50.00
Match Holder, Ashtray, Red Raven Bottle	70.00
Match Holder, Bonnet Baby Hugging Frog, Bisque	15.00
Match Holder, Book, Ivory Celluloid, Seagram Whiskey	7.00
Match Holder, Book, Sterling	27.50
Match Holder, Boot, Iron	30.00
Match Holder, Booty, Blue	35.00
Match Holder, Boy On Barrel, Striker, Bisque	28.00
Match Holder, Brass, German, Gott Mit Uns	10.00

Massier, Vase, Surface Gilt Luster,
Dragonflies, C.1900

Match Holder, Brown, Poppies & Gold, Signed, Haviland	40.00
Match Holder, Ceresota Flour	22.00
Match Holder, Chattanooga Plows, Whitehead & Hoag	65.00
Match Holder, China & Brass, Dog On Top	8.00
Match Holder, Commemorative, Jumbo, The Circus Elephant, Glass, 7 In.	7.00
Match Holder, Consolidated Ice Co., China	42.00
Match Holder, Dated 1864, Cast Iron, 5 1/2 X 3 1/2 In.	20.00
Match Holder, Dated 1899, U.S., Over Crossed Rifles, Cast Iron, 9 X 5 In.	55.00
Match Holder, De Laval	45.00
Match Holder, De Laval, Lithograph, Tin	65.00
Match Holder, Double, Wall, Enameled Boy & Girl	35.00
Match Holder, Dutch Girl, Striker, Copper Luster & Color, Bisque	42.00
Match Holder, Elephant, Head, Glass, Wall	25.00
Match Holder, Elmer Fudd	8.00
Match Holder, English Bobby, Body Opens To Hold Matches	85.00
Match Holder, English Bobby, Body Opens To Hold Matches, Metal, 4 1/2 In.	85.00
Match Holder, Fireplace, Iron	30.00
Match Holder, Flute Playing Figure, Bisque, 6 In.	42.50
Match Holder, Foliated Horseshoe Background, U Shape, Striker, 5 In.	8.00
Match Holder, Frog, Striker, Pointer Stoves, Iron, 4 In.	42.50
Match Holder, Geometric Pattern, Ironstone, Syracuse China	8.00
Match Holder, Girl Holding Doll, Striker, Germany, Glazed	25.00
Match Holder, Gott Mit Uns	15.00

Match Holder, Hanging, Bisque, Lady's Head, Open Topped Hat 20.00
Match Holder, Hanging, Boot Shape, Amethyst Glass 22.00
Match Holder, Hanging, Slippers, Metal 15.00
Match Holder, High Button Shoe, Iron, 5 In. 30.00
Match Holder, Indian Head 12.00
Match Holder, Indian On Front, Nippon 30.00
Match Holder, Kneeling Colonial Man, On Stand With Striker 14.00
Match Holder, Mantel, Asphaltum Striking Surface, 5 1/2 X 2 3/4 In. 30.00
Match Holder, Metal, Lid On One, Pair 10.00
Match Holder, Monk With Crossed Legs, Bronzed Metal, Striker 40.00
Match Holder, Monk, Brown, Striker On Bottom, Milk Glass 12.50
Match Holder, Monkey Head, Open Mouth, Victorian, China 67.50
Match Holder, O.V.B.Hardware, Metal 12.00
Match Holder, Old Judge Whiskey, J.C. Stevens, Kansas City, Missouri, Tin 27.50
Match Holder, Pedestal, Figural Lid, Dog, Iron 25.00
Match Holder, Picnic Basket, Straw Covered, Mouse On Top, Silver Plate 50.00
Match Holder, Pig, Striker On Belly, Hinged Head, Brass 38.00
Match Holder, Pumpkin, Ceramic 55.00
Match Holder, Safe Home Matches, Tin 18.00
Match Holder, Shoes Form Holders, Brass 15.00
Match Holder, Skull On Book, Bisque 15.00
Match Holder, Spiked Helmet Design, Brass 8.00
Match Holder, Sterling, Pedestal Urn, 2 3/4 In. 28.00
Match Holder, Striker, Art Nouveau, Head Of Roman, Hanging 37.50
Match Holder, Table, Cherubs, Impressed M.Loewenstein, N.Y., Brass 22.00
Match Holder, Tin, Wall, Holder For Burnt Matches 12.00
Match Holder, Triple Swan, Milk Glass 30.00
Match Holder, Trousers, Goodman The Clothier 90.00
Match Holder, Turkey, Amber Glass 10.00
Match Holder, Universal Stoves, Tin 38.00
Match Holder, Urn, Wall, Cast Iron 12.00
Match Holder, Verdun Emblem, Copper, Smoke Y-B's & B-Y's 12.50
Match Holder, Wall Plaque, Bisque, Boy & Girl 45.00
Match Holder, Wall, Juicy Fruit, Mr.Wriggley, Tin 20.00
Match Holder, World's Fair, Red Flash 35.00
    Match Safe, see also Silver, Sterling, Match Safe
Match Safe, Abraham Lincoln, Silver Plate, 1902, 2 5/8 X 1 1/2 In. 65.00
Match Safe, Alaga Syrup, Montgomery 18.00
Match Safe, Albany, New York Capitol 9.00
Match Safe, Anheuser Busch, Embossed Trace-Mark, Brass 62.00
Match Safe, Anheuser Busch, Stamped Trade-Mark, St.Louis, Train On Back 48.00
Match Safe, Art Nouveau, Sterling Silver 30.00
Match Safe, Art Nouveau, Woman With Flowing Hair 24.00
Match Safe, B.P.O.E., Elk's Head On Front, Sterling 50.00
Match Safe, Beetle Form, Wings Lift, Interior Compartments, Cast Iron, 4 In. 28.00
Match Safe, Bitters Bottle, Celluloid Picture 45.00
Match Safe, Blatz Beer 48.00
Match Safe, Boy & Girl On Fence 59.00
Match Safe, Cigar Makers Union, 1905, Celluloid Cover 27.00
Match Safe, Civil War, Eagle On Shield, Sterling 8.00
Match Safe, Cleopatra 34.00
Match Safe, Columbian Fair, Showing Columbus With Dates, Silver Plate 45.00
Match Safe, Coronation Of King Edward, 1902, Silver Plate, 2 X 1 1/2 In. 35.00
Match Safe, Cremola Wheat Food, Waldorf Oats 16.50
Match Safe, De Cazanove Champagne 15.00
Match Safe, Diamond Match Co., Tin 9.50
Match Safe, Dr.Shoop's Lax-Ets, Tin 30.00
Match Safe, Economy Clothing, Scranton, Pa. 28.00
Match Safe, Elephant, Ivory Tusks, Hang Loop, Brass, 1 1/2 X 2 1/8 In. 95.00
Match Safe, Embossed German Writing, Tin 12.00
Match Safe, Embossed Horseshoe, Lady On Horse, Striker Inside, 3 1/2 In. 25.00
Match Safe, English Bobby, Not Pocket 85.00
Match Safe, Fire Place, Crane & Kettle, 2 Pocket, Brass 36.00
Match Safe, Fireman's Picture 10.00
Match Safe, Floral Engraved, Sterling Silver 25.00
Match Safe, Flowers, Sterling 32.00

Match Safe, For The Good Husband, Shoe Shape	27.00
Match Safe, Four Dogs	47.50
Match Safe, Frogs Under Toadstool	8.00
Match Safe, German Silver	18.00
Match Safe, Gillette, Nickel Plate	7.00
Match Safe, Girl & Boy Under Umbrella, Both Sides	23.00
Match Safe, Girl On Cliff	74.00
Match Safe, Golfer Carrying Bag Of Clubs, Silver Plate, 1 7/8 X 1 1/2 In.	50.00
Match Safe, Grapes, Sterling	32.00
Match Safe, Great Northern	29.00
Match Safe, Hanging, American Steel Farm Fence, Tin, 3 X 5 In.	20.00
Match Safe, Hanging, Crimped, Scalloped Top	30.00
Match Safe, Hanging, Lady's High Shoe, Nickel Plated Brass, 5 In.	45.00
Match Safe, Hanging, Self-Closing, Dated 1864, New Haven, 2 1/2 X 4 In.	28.00
Match Safe, Heilman Brewing Co., Pictured Gentleman	20.00
Match Safe, Hinged Lid, Embossed Fruit, Marked, Sterling Silver	32.00
Match Safe, Horseshoe, Horse's Head, Aluminum	10.50
Match Safe, Hunter With Dogs	70.00
Match Safe, Ideal Heaters, Boston	15.00
Match Safe, Indian & Dog	30.00
Match Safe, International Tailoring, Indian, Woman & Lion	25.00
Match Safe, Jenny Lind, Clear, Dated	46.00
Match Safe, Kate Greenaway, Copper	45.00
Match Safe, Leather Book, Brown, Carved White Jade	38.00
Match Safe, Man Fishing	58.00
Match Safe, Marble's, Screw Type	8.00
Match Safe, Nude Lady & Pig, Plated Silver & Celluloid, 2 3/4 X 1 1/2 In.	48.00
Match Safe, Odd Fellows Lodge, Designs All Over	20.00
Match Safe, One End For Matches, Head Pops Out Thumbing Nose Other End	1200.00
Match Safe, Oriental Dragon In Relief, Both Sides, Brass	40.00
Match Safe, Pan American Exposition, Nude	45.00
Match Safe, Pig, Brass	35.00
Match Safe, Porcelain, Beehive	18.00
Match Safe, Rainbow, Packing Peerless Rubber Co.	25.00
Match Safe, Raised Oriental Figures, Compass, 2 1/2 X 1 3/8 In.	65.00
Match Safe, Rococo Design, Sterling Silver	40.00
Match Safe, Scalloped Top, Self-Closing, Cast Iron	30.00
Match Safe, Schlitz, World Globe One Side, Cigar Cutter	35.00
Match Safe, Sealy Cigars, Confectionery, Wickford, R.I.	15.00
Match Safe, Seated Pig, Head Opens At Neck, Silver Plated Brass, 2 In.	75.00
Match Safe, Shape Of Deer Leg, Leather Covered	35.00
Match Safe, Shape Of Oyster Shell, Marked	32.00
Match Safe, Shape Of Sideboard, Hinged Cover, Footed, Brass, 4 X 4 3/8 In.	26.00
Match Safe, Silver, German, Masonic Emblem	14.50
Match Safe, St.Louis Fair, 1904, Cascades & Transportation Building	19.00
Match Safe, Stevens' Whiskey, 1905, Tin, Man & Child, 4 X 6 In.	27.00
Match Safe, Tansill's Punch Cigar, Chicago, Brass	28.00
Match Safe, The Best Dueber Watch Case, Brass	27.50
Match Safe, Two Compartment, Urn Form, Saucer Base, 1871	22.00
Match Safe, U.S. Injector Steam	20.00
Match Safe, U.S. Mail, One Side, Letters On Other, Mailbag Shape	22.00
Match Safe, Union Made Cigars	12.00

Matt Morgan, Vase, Brown & Green,
Bird, Leafage, C.1880
(See Page 304)

Match Safe, Wall Type, Self-Closing, 1864	15.00
Match Safe, Warren's Stone Surface Ready Roofing	20.00
Match Safe, Whole Pig On Cover	78.00

MATT MORGAN
—CIN. O—
ART POTTERY Cº Matt Morgan opened an art pottery company in Cincinnati, Ohio, in 1883.
It lasted in business for only a year, closing because of money problems.

Matt Morgan, Vase, Blue Glaze & Gold Design In Panels, 11 3/4 In., Pair	250.00
Matt Morgan, Vase, Brown & Green, Bird, Leafage, C.1880 .... Illus	650.00
Matt Morgan, Vase, 2 Handled, Blue Glaze, Raised Hispano Moresque, 4 1/2 In.	285.00

McCoy

McCoy pottery is made in Roseville, Ohio. The J. W. McCoy
Pottery was founded in 1899. It became the Brush McCoy Pottery
Company in 1911. The name changed to the Brush Pottery in 1925. The
Nelson McCoy Sanitary and Stoneware Company was founded in
Roseville, Ohio, in 1910. This firm made art pottery after 1926. In 1933
it became the Nelson McCoy Pottery. Pieces marked McCoy were
made by the Nelson McCoy Company.

McCoy, Basket, Green, Applied Berries	10.00
McCoy, Basket, Handled, 10 In.	10.00
McCoy, Basket, Oval, Brown, Acorn, 5 X 7 1/2 In.	18.00
McCoy, Bowl, Fruit, Stemmed, Pink, 10 In.	6.00
McCoy, Bowl, Ice, Manhattan, Crystal, Metal Handle & Tongs	8.50
McCoy, Bowl, Loy Nel Art, 2 Handled, Signed, 8 X 3 In.	115.00
McCoy, Candleholder, Double, Candlewick, Crystal, Pair	15.00
McCoy, Clock, Flapper, Blue Onyx, 4 1/2 In.	80.00
McCoy, Cookie Jar, Antique Stove	12.00
McCoy, Cookie Jar, Apple	12.00
McCoy, Cookie Jar, Basket, Lid	12.00
McCoy, Cookie Jar, Bear On Clock	10.00
McCoy, Cookie Jar, Bear, Cookies In Vest	15.00
McCoy, Cookie Jar, Blue Windmill	11.00
McCoy, Cookie Jar, Bunch Of Bananas	22.00
McCoy, Cookie Jar, Bushel Basket Of Fruit	38.00
McCoy, Cookie Jar, Chef Head	25.00
McCoy, Cookie Jar, Clown Bust	15.00
McCoy, Cookie Jar, Clown In Barrel	22.00
McCoy, Cookie Jar, Coffee Grinder	7.00 To 12.00
McCoy, Cookie Jar, Cookie Cabin	18.00
McCoy, Cookie Jar, Cookie House	25.00
McCoy, Cookie Jar, Cookstove, Black	6.00 To 12.00
McCoy, Cookie Jar, Country Stove	12.00
McCoy, Cookie Jar, Covered Wagon	10.00 To 28.00
McCoy, Cookie Jar, Dog On Basket Weave	9.00
McCoy, Cookie Jar, Duck On Basket Weave	12.50 To 18.00
McCoy, Cookie Jar, Duck With Picnic Basket	29.00
McCoy, Cookie Jar, Dutch Boy	8.00 To 12.00
McCoy, Cookie Jar, Elephant	10.00
McCoy, Cookie Jar, Engine	28.00
McCoy, Cookie Jar, English Cottage	25.00
McCoy, Cookie Jar, Figural Cabin	18.00
McCoy, Cookie Jar, Floral	7.00
McCoy, Cookie Jar, Grandfather Clock	18.00
McCoy, Cookie Jar, Happy Face, 3 Mugs	20.00
McCoy, Cookie Jar, Hillbilly Bear	12.00 To 30.00
McCoy, Cookie Jar, Hobby Horse	25.00 To 28.00
McCoy, Cookie Jar, Honey Bear	20.00 To 25.00
McCoy, Cookie Jar, Indian	85.00
McCoy, Cookie Jar, Indian Tepee	40.00
McCoy, Cookie Jar, Kangaroo, Baby In Pouch	18.00
McCoy, Cookie Jar, Kitten On Basket Weave	18.00
McCoy, Cookie Jar, Kittens On Ball Of Yarn	15.00
McCoy, Cookie Jar, Little Clown	25.00
McCoy, Cookie Jar, Lollipop	15.00 To 18.00
McCoy, Cookie Jar, Mammy, Cookies, Cauliflowers	25.00
McCoy, Cookie Jar, Mr. & Mrs. Owl	25.00
McCoy, Cookie Jar, Oaken Bucket	10.00

McCoy, Cookie Jar, Pineapple	20.00
McCoy, Cookie Jar, Turkey	18.00 To 50.00
McCoy, Cookie Jar, White Cylinder	12.00
McCoy, Cookie Jar, Wishing Well	8.00 To 18.50
McCoy, Cookie Jar, World Globe	40.00
McCoy, Creamer, Green & Brown High Glaze	10.00
McCoy, Creamer, Ivy, Glaze	8.00
McCoy, Fower Pot & Saucer, Brown, 3 1/2 In.	5.00
McCoy, Gondola, Green	8.50
McCoy, Jardiniere, Diamond-Quilted, Bow Handles, 9 X 12 In.Diameter	15.00
McCoy, Jardiniere, Turquoise Glaze, Diamond Quilted, Leaves, 8 1/2 In.	9.00
McCoy, Lamp, Boot, Shade	35.00
McCoy, Mug, Railroad Engine, 1897	35.00
McCoy, Pitcher & Washbowl, Windmills	25.00
McCoy, Pitcher, Buttermilk, Iris, 8 1/2 In.	55.00
McCoy, Pitcher, Fish Handle	25.00
McCoy, Pitcher, Matte Gray, 1950s	7.00
McCoy, Planter, Alligator	7.00
McCoy, Planter, Bird Bath, With Bird	10.00
McCoy, Planter, Chinese Man With Wheelbarrow	10.00
McCoy, Planter, Dog With Cart, Signed, 9 X 4 In.	12.00
McCoy, Planter, Duck, 1951	7.50
McCoy, Planter, Frog, 1950	10.00
McCoy, Planter, Gondola, Green	8.00
McCoy, Planter, Old Mill	12.00
McCoy, Planter, Spinning Wheel, Brown Glaze, 6 1/2 In.	10.00
McCoy, Planter, Swan, 1946	12.00
McCoy, Planter, Turtle, Green Glaze	15.00
McCoy, Planter, Wishing Well, 1950	12.50
McCoy, Pot, Bean, Handle, Brown, 1956	18.00
McCoy, Pot, Flower, Quilted, Turquoise	5.00
McCoy, Punchbowl, Brown Glaze, Tiger Lily, Incised Olympia & McCoy	300.00
McCoy, Punchbowl, Royal Ruby, 12 Cups	45.00
McCoy, Shoe, Dutch, Blue, Pink Flower	8.00
McCoy, Sprinkler, Turtle, Green Glaze	12.00
McCoy, Sugar & Creamer, Ivy	15.00
McCoy, Tankard Set, Brown Glazed, 1910, Set Of 7	95.00
McCoy, Tankard, Pottery, Loy-Nel Art, 15 3/4 In.High	250.00
McCoy, Tankard, 2 Handle, Loy-Nel Art Olympia, 15 3/4 In.	180.00
McCoy, Tea Set, Ivy, 3 Piece	22.00
McCoy, Tea Set, Pinecone, 3 Piece	24.00 To 38.00
McCoy, Teakettle, Copper Luster	13.00
McCoy, Vase, Amber Base, Old Wishing Well, Signed, 6 1/2 X 7 In.	12.00
McCoy, Vase, Arcature, Red Bird	11.00
McCoy, Vase, Birds & Berries, Signed, Turquoise, Signed, 8 In.	15.00
McCoy, Vase, Blue, 9 In.	12.00
McCoy, Vase, Brown, Blooming Jonquils, Loy-Nel Art, 9 In.	95.00
McCoy, Vase, Bunch Of Grapes	12.00
McCoy, Vase, Calla Lily	5.00
McCoy, Vase, Capricorn, 9 In., Pair	8.00
McCoy, Vase, Cat Shaped, Gray, 14 In.	25.00
McCoy, Vase, Cylindrical, Embossed Floral Design, 8 In.	18.50
McCoy, Vase, Handled, Leaf Spray, Turquoise, Signed, 9 In.	12.00
McCoy, Vase, Hyacinth	16.00
McCoy, Vase, Lavender Chrysanthemums, Marked & Paper Label	14.00
McCoy, Vase, Republican	10.00
McCoy, Vase, Rib Swirl, Signed, 6 1/2 X 4 1/4 In.	9.50
McCoy, Vase, Sunbonnet Lady, 8 In.	8.00
McCoy, Vase, Swan, Blue, 9 In.	12.00
McCoy, Vase, Triple Lily	14.00
McCoy, Vase, Two Handles, Aqua, 8 In.	7.00
McCoy, Vase, Uncle Sam	13.00
McCoy, Vase, Wall Pocket, Yellow Birdbath, Blue Bird, 7 3/4 In.	8.00
McCoy, Vase, Wild Rose, 14 1/4 In.	18.00
McCoy, Wall Pocket, Blossom Time	18.00
McCoy, Wall Pocket, Cuckoo Clock	22.00

McCoy, Wall Pocket, Green Mail Box	18.00
McCoy, Wall Pocket, Pink Lily, 6 In., Pair	6.00

PRESCUT *The McKee name has been associated with various glass enterprises in the U.S. since 1836, including J. & F. McKee (1850), Bryce, McKee & Co. (1850-1854), McKee and Brothers (1865), and National Glass Co. (1899). In 1903 the McKee Glass Company was formed in Jeanette, Pennsylvania; it became McKee Division of the Thatcher Glass Co. in 1951, and was bought out by the Jeanette Corporation in 1961. Pressed glass, kitchenware, and tableware were produced.*

McKee, Berry Set, Pres Cut, Signed, 5 Piece	25.00
McKee, Bottoms-Up, Holder, Green	45.00
McKee, Bowl, Centerpiece, Footed, Amber, 12 X 5 1/2 In.	35.00
McKee, Bowl, Pregue, Custard, 11 In.	28.50
McKee, Champagne, Ruby, 4 Oz.	25.00
McKee, Clock, Mantel, Tambour, Art Glass, Black	500.00
McKee, Compote, Covered, Tidy Pattern, Barberry Finial	75.00
McKee, Compote, Dolphin, Clear & Opalescent	55.00
McKee, Cooler, Water, Green, 18 In.	125.00
McKee, Creamer, Four Petals, Pre-Civil War	125.00
McKee, Creamer, Ray	16.00
McKee, Cup, Pouring, Opaque, Signed	7.00
McKee, Dish, Candy, Red Top, Crystal Bottom, 7 In.Diameter	20.00
McKee, Dish, Dove On Basket Weave Nest, Vaseline, 4 1/2 In.	125.00
McKee, Glass, Art Nouveau Period, Bottoms Up, Green	30.00
McKee, Glass, Nudes On Sides, 8 1/2 In.	25.00
McKee, Goblet, Custard, Signed McK, 4 1/2 In., 5 Piece Set	45.00
McKee, Goblet, Red Rock Crystal	18.00
McKee, Juicer, Opaque, Green	5.00
McKee, Juicer, Rainbow	9.00
McKee, Mug, Tom & Jerry, Ivory, Set Of 6	32.00
McKee, Plate, Scroll & Waffle, Milk Glass, Signed	39.00
McKee, Salt & Pepper, Black Amethyst, 5 In.	22.50
McKee, Sherbet, American Rock Crystal	10.00
McKee, Shot Glass, Jolly Golfer	30.00
McKee, Vase, Nude, Green Custard, 9 In.	35.00
Mechanical Bank, see Bank, Mechanical	
Medical, Bag, Leather, 4 Section, 48 Vials, Civil War, Dr.C.W.Martin	150.00
Medical, Bag, 72 Marked & Filled Bottles, Civil War Era	89.00
Medical, Bleeder, Folding, Brass	45.00
Medical, Bleeder, German, Small Box	65.00
Medical, Box, Doctor Shocking Device, Oak	42.00
Medical, Box, First Aid, Wood, Compartmented, Signed Red Cross Co., 1906	28.00
Medical, Cabinet, Dental, 14 Drawer, Milk Glass Pulls, 58 X 40 X 14 In.	595.00
Medical, Cabinet, Optometrist, Lens, Oak, 5 Drawer, 14 X 15 1/2 X 20 1/2 In.	165.00
Medical, Cabinet, Wall, Pratt's Veterinary, Tin Front, Oak	375.00
Medical, Canister, Dentist's, Twin Clamps, C.1880, Burnished Brass, 4 X 6 In.	75.00
Medical, Case, Display, Glass, Optometrist	275.00
Medical, Case, Syringe, Davidson, 1878	4.00
Medical, Chair, Dentist, Adjustable Head & Backrest, Iron	100.00
Medical, Cup, Eye, John Bull, Green, Dated 1917	28.50
Medical, Dental Set, Georgian Steel & Ivory, 18th Century	650.00
Medical, Desk, Dentist's, Roll Top, Bin, Cupboard, 13 Drawers, Oak	600.00
Medical, Dictionary, Dunglison's, Leather Bound, 1874	10.00
Medical, Drill, Dentist, Complete	75.00
Medical, Ear Horn, Flexible Tube, 38 In.	50.00
Medical, Ear Horn, Flexible Tube, 42 In.	45.00
Medical, Eyecup, Cobalt	10.00
Medical, Eyecup, John Bull, Clear	6.00
Medical, Eyecup, John Bull, Clear, Blue, Green, Set Of 3	48.00
Medical, Eyecup, John Bull, Clear, Ribbed	4.00
Medical, Eyecup, John Bull, Green, Dated 1917	28.50
Medical, Eyecup, John Bull, Green, Pedestal	8.00
Medical, Eyecup, Made In England, White, Clear & Green, Set Of 3	30.00

Medical, Eyecup, Milk Glass	6.00
Medical, Feeder, Infant, Porcelain, White, Blue & Gold, Late 18th Century	18.00
Medical, Feeder, Invalid, Blue & White, Bamboo Design	20.00
Medical, Feeder, Shape Of Lady's Shoe, Glass, Clear	7.50
Medical, Field Instrument Set, Walnut Case, Civil War, 3 1/2 X 9 In.	185.00
Medical, Fixtures, Pharmacy, 68 Ft.Wall Cabinet, 7 Glass Cases, Mirror, Fan	4500.00
Medical, Glass, Dose, Impressed Dr.Gram's Grandmother's Medicine	5.00
Medical, Glass, Dose, Impressed Dr.Harter's, Small	5.00
Medical, Hearing Aid, Flexible Conversation Tube, Black Silk Cover	20.00
Medical, Invalid Set, Homestead Ware, England, 10 Piece	37.50
Medical, Lamp, Dr.Siegel's Patent, Strap Handle, Beehive Shape, Tin & Brass	150.00
Medical, Lens, Optometrist's, Brass, Set Of 26	9.00
Medical, Measurer, Owl, Glass	27.50
Medical, Microscope, Wooden Box, English, Brass, 6 In.	65.00
Medical, Mixer, Chemical, 4 Brass Pedestals, Oak Case, 26 X 23 In.	125.00
Medical, Mortar & Pestle, Glass, 5 1/4 In.Diameter	35.00
Medical, Outfit, Sick Call, Oak Box & Contents, C.1897	75.00
Medical, Pump, Breast, Davol, Glass, Box	5.00
Medical, Pump, Stomach, Brass & Ivory, Fitted Wooden Case, C.1875	600.00
Medical, Ruler, Self Optical Test, For Ordering Lenses Through Catalog	18.00
Medical, Table, Examining, Oak	250.00
Medical, Tool, Bleeding, Case, 5 In.Diameter	5.50
Medical, Tools, Veterinarian, 8 Tools For Worming Horses, Case	23.00
Medical, Tooth Puller, Whalebone Handle, Signed Biddle	60.00
Medical, Toothbrush, Removable Brushes, Child's, Sterling Silver Handle	16.00
Medical, Witch Doctor, Fortune Telling Device, Carved Ivory	200.00

Meerschaum pipes and other carved pieces of meerschaum date from the nineteenth century to the present time.

Meerschaum, Cigar Holder, Amber, Case	18.00
Meerschaum, Cigar Holder, Carved Horse & Dog, Box	65.00
Meerschaum, Cigar Holder, Case, 4 In.	25.00
Meerschaum, Cigar Holder, Man On Horse	175.00
Meerschaum, Cigarette Holder, Carved Animal's Head One End, Boxed, 4 In.	25.00
Meerschaum, Cigarette Holder, Carved Horse On Middle, Original Case	35.00
Meerschaum, Cigarette Holder, Man Lying On Back	95.00
Meerschaum, Holder, Cigarette, Carved Animal's Head One End, Boxed, 4 In.	25.00
Meerschaum, Holder, Cigarette, Carved Horse On Middle, Original Case	35.00
Meerschaum, Holder, Cigarette, Man Lying On Back	95.00
Meerschaum, Pipe, Carved Knight, Shield, Armor, Brass Lid, 9 X 4 1/2 In.	75.00
Meerschaum, Pipe, Curved Sterling, Fitted Case, Hallmark, Birmingham, 1909	40.00
Meerschaum, Pipe, Dark Amber Stem, 3 1/2 In.	45.00
Meerschaum, Pipe, Elk Standing, Doe Reclining, Amber Stem, 5 In.	115.00
Meerschaum, Pipe, Gold Plated Rim	25.00
Meerschaum, Pipe, Hand-Carved Ivory Stallions, Amber Stem, 5 In.	250.00
Meerschaum, Pipe, Horse & Fox Running In The Wind, Amber Stem	125.00
Meerschaum, Pipe, Looks Like 3 Crab Claws, Amber Stem, Case	50.00
Meerschaum, Pipe, Moose & Doe, Antlered, Tree Back Of Moose, Amber Stem	125.00
Meerschaum, Pipe, Original Suede Case, 1913, 4 In.	45.00
Meerschaum, Pipe, Running Deer, Amber Stem, Leather Case, 2 3/4 In.	115.00
Meerschaum, Pipe, Running Horses	40.00
Meerschaum, Pipe, Scholar's Head, Tassled Cap, Mustache & Beard, 7 In.	48.00
Meerschaum, Pipe, 2 Dogs Carved On Bowl, Case, 4 In.	65.00

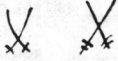

Meissen is a town in Germany where porcelain has been made since 1710. Any china made in that town can be called Meissen, although the famous Meissen Factory made the finest porcelains of the area.

Meissen, see also Dresden, Onion

Meissen, Bowk, Oval, Cobalt, White & Gold, 1700s, Signed	125.00
Meissen, Bowl, Centerpiece, Cobalt & Floral, Crossed Swords	145.00
Meissen, Bowl, Floral Bouquet In Bottom, Crossed Swords, 8 1/2 In.	48.00
Meissen, Bowl, Fruit, Cobalt Blue, White Leaf, Crossed Swords, 10 X 12 In.	200.00
Meissen, Bowl, Gilt Handles, Crossed Swords Mark, 14 1/4 X 9 In.	347.50
Meissen, Bowl, Low, Oval, Cobalt, White & Gold, 1700s, Signed	125.00

Meissen, Bowl, Raised Leaves, Gold Trim, Crossed Swords, 12 X 8 In. 48.00
Meissen, Box, Covered, Fuchsia With Gold, 18th Century, 2 3/4 In.Diameter 150.00
Meissen, Box, Covered, Oval, Attached Stand, Numbered, C.1745, Pair, 9 1/2 In. 900.00
Meissen, Candelabra, 5 Light, Incised G 128-9, C.1800, 18 In., Pair 1200.00
Meissen, Charger, Floral, Vines, Relief, Gold Crossed Swords, C.1860, 11 In. 195.00
Meissen, Chocolate Pot, Blue & Gold On White, Crossed Swords Mark, 10 In. 225.00
Meissen, Chocolate Pot, Covered, Mask Spout, Crossed Swords 185.00
Meissen, Chocolate Pot, Mauve Background, Scenic, Signed 150.00
Meissen, Compote, Reticulated, Crossed Swords, 9 X 8 1/2 In. 175.00
Meissen, Cup & Saucer, Castle Scene, Crossed Swords 65.00
Meissen, Cup & Saucer, Heavy Gold Covers, 3 Sprays Of Flowers, C.1820 .... 175.00
Meissen, Cup & Saucer, Multi-Colored Flowers, Square Handle, Crossed Swords 135.00
Meissen, Cup & Saucer, Portrait 75.00
Meissen, Cup & Saucer, Raised Design, Pink, Crossed Swords 190.00
Meissen, Cup & Saucer, Scalloped Top, Crossed Swords Mark 75.00
Meissen, Demitasse Set, 6 Cups & Saucers, Sugar & Creamer, Crossed Swords 280.00
Meissen, Dish, Floral Center, Medallions, Crossed Swords Mark, Pair 300.00
Meissen, Dish, Leaf-Shaped, Crossed Swords, C.1750, 8 1/2 In. 400.00
Meissen, Dish, Leaf, Handles, Applied Flowers, Gold Rim, 7 1/2 In. 135.00
Meissen, Ewer, Allegorical, Galleons, Dolphins, Neptune, C.1800, 18 In. 750.00
Meissen, Feeder, Invalid, Onion 22.00
Meissen, Figurine, Amor In Chains, Rose Garlands, Crossed Swords, 7 1/2 In. 700.00
Meissen, Figurine, Barefooted Boy, Minor Chips, 4 1/2 In. 325.00
Meissen, Figurine, Boar, Standing, Porcelain, Crossed Swords Mark, 2 X 3 In. 195.00
Meissen, Figurine, Boston Terrier, White With Brown & Black, 6 In. 495.00
Meissen, Figurine, Boy & Girl, Blue & White, 4 3/4 In., Pair 325.00
Meissen, Figurine, Boy Catching Fish, Crossed Swords Mark, 4 1/2 In. 475.00
Meissen, Figurine, Boy Feeding Geese, Crossed Swords Mark, 5 In. 550.00
Meissen, Figurine, Boy In Loin Cloth, Crossed Swords Mark, 5 1/4 In. 295.00
Meissen, Figurine, Boy Playing Flute, Crossed Swords Mark, 5 1/2 In. 550.00
Meissen, Figurine, Cardinal, Rocky Base, Crossed Swords, 1900s, 8 1/4 In. 225.00
Meissen, Figurine, Celebration Group, Incised D 96 & D 93, 1800s, 19 In. 3000.00
Meissen, Figurine, Country Swain With Flute, Crossed Swords Mark, 5 1/2 In. 325.00
Meissen, Figurine, Crinoline Lady, Underglaze, Crossed Swords Mark, 8 In. 350.00
Meissen, Figurine, Cupid, Crossed Swords, Incised R 123 & R 122, 7 In. 750.00
Meissen, Figurine, Family Group, 6 1/2 In. 900.00
Meissen, Figurine, Feeding Gaggle Of Geese, Crossed Swords Mark, 5 In. 585.00
Meissen, Figurine, Flutist In Costume, Crossed Swords Mark, 5 3/4 In. 325.00
Meissen, Figurine, Girl Carrying Basket Of Fruit, Incised, 7 1/2 In. 125.00
Meissen, Figurine, Goat, Atop Saucer, Crossed Sword Mark, 5 1/2 X 5 1/2 In. 285.00
Meissen, Figurine, Goddess, Chains, Rose Garlands, Crossed Swords, 7 1/2 In. 700.00
Meissen, Figurine, Group Emblematic Of Autumn, 7 1/2 In. 600.00
Meissen, Figurine, Group Of Proposal, Base Cracked, 12 In. 950.00
Meissen, Figurine, Group Of 4 Children Playing, 5 3/4 In. 650.00
Meissen, Figurine, Hessian Grenadier, 18th Century 395.00
Meissen, Figurine, Huntsman, Crossed Swords, 1800s, 11 1/4 In., Pair 800.00
Meissen, Figurine, Huntsman, 1800s, Minor Chips, 5 In. 500.00
Meissen, Figurine, Lady Holding Box, Minor Chips, 4 1/2 In. 450.00
Meissen, Figurine, Lady Listening To Bird, 5 1/2 In. 700.00
Meissen, Figurine, Lady Looking Into Mirror, 5 1/2 In. 525.00
Meissen, Figurine, Lady Playing Spinet, 4 3/4 In. 625.00
Meissen, Figurine, Lady Sniffing Flower, Minor Chips, 5 1/2 In. 525.00
Meissen, Figurine, Lady With Sheep 175.00
Meissen, Figurine, Man In 18th Century Costume, Flute, Swords Mark, 5 1/2 In. 295.00
Meissen, Figurine, Monkey Playing Horn, C.1895, 5 1/2 In. 95.00
Meissen, Figurine, Nodding Mandarin, Crossed Swords, 1800s, 5 3/4 In., Pair 1500.00
Meissen, Figurine, Peasant Girl, Barefoot, Apron, Flowers In Hand, Mark, 6 In. 295.00
Meissen, Figurine, Peasant Woman Holding Box, Animal, 5 1/2 In. 325.00
Meissen, Figurine, Peasant Woman, 1880, Crossed Swords, 6 1/2 In. 450.00
Meissen, Figurine, Pug Dog, Sitting, Green Collar, Crossed Swords, 6 1/2 In. 300.00
Meissen, Figurine, Pug With Head Over Back Wearing Blue Collar, Gold Bells 225.00
Meissen, Figurine, Pug, Seated, Green Collar, Crossed Swords Mark, 6 In. 30.00
Meissen, Figurine, Rabbit, White, Crossed Swords, 7 In. 220.00
Meissen, Figurine, Shepherd With Woman, Crossed Swords Mark, 10 X 10 In. 700.00
Meissen, Figurine, Soldier Musician, Crossed Swords Mark, 5 1/4 In. 295.00
Meissen, Figurine, Underglazed Blue Crossed Swords & Dot, 16 In., Pair 1700.00

Meissen, Figurine, Vintager, Minor Chips, 4 3/4 In.	275.00
Meissen, Figurine, Violinist, Minor Repair, 4 1/2 In.	200.00
Meissen, Figurine, White Turkey, 18th Century, 2 1/8 In.	120.00
Meissen, Figurine, Winter, Boy & Girl On Sleigh, Crossed Swords Mark	395.00
Meissen, Figurine, Winter, 5 1/4 In.	150.00
Meissen, Figurine, Woman Beggar, Seated, Plays Instrument, Child Begs, 8 In.	395.00
Meissen, Figurine, Young Boy, Minor Chips, 4 3/4 In.	275.00
Meissen, Fruit Cooler, Zoology Scenes, Covered, 4 Reserves, Marked, 7 5/8 In.	1100.00
Meissen, Fruit Stand, Onion Pattern, 3-Tiered, Blue & White, 22 In., Pair	1000.00
Meissen, Group, Amphitrite, Incised D 81, C.1800, 9 In.	800.00
Meissen, Group, Love Restrained, Incised F-82, 1800s, 12 3/4 In.	1900.00
Meissen, Group, Putti Fisherboys, Incised D 84, 1800s, 5 3/4 In.	1200.00
Meissen, Group, The Proposal, Incised F 63, C.1800, 9 1/2 In.	1300.00
Meissen, Holder, Pen, Floral, Crossed Swords, 9 X 2 1/2 In.	55.00
Meissen, Jar, Powder, Gold Edge, Signed, Crossed Swords, 2 1/4 X 5 In.Diam.	36.00
Meissen, Jug, Cream, Scenic Panels, Crossed Swords Mark, 3 1/4 X 2 3/8 In.	95.00
Meissen, Knife Rest, Brass Jack Stands, Onion	35.00
Meissen, Lamp, Banquet, Hand-Painted Globe, French Scenes	750.00
Meissen, Luncheon Set, Bowl, 12 Cups, Saucers, Plates, C.1820, Crossed Swords	1200.00
Meissen, Napkin Ring, Held Between Pair Of Saddle Bags, Crossed Swords	175.00
Meissen, Pitcher, Angel Near Top, Scroll Work, Gold Lined, Signed, 9 1/2 In.	175.00
Meissen, Plate, Blue, Bisque Foot Rim, Blue Crossed Swords, C.1850, 9 3/4 In.	38.00
Meissen, Plate, Cake, Fruit, Butterflies, Crossed Swords Mark, 11 3/4 In.	250.00
Meissen, Plate, Cake, Multi-Colored, 6 7/8 In., Set Of 8	240.00
Meissen, Plate, Cake, Rose In Center, Blue Crossed Swords, 6 In.Diameter	15.00
Meissen, Plate, Cream Soup, Floral Pattern, 8 1/4 In., Set Of 8	160.00
Meissen, Plate, Dessert, Raised Scroll & Shell Border, 8 1/2 In., Set Of 6	240.00
Meissen, Plate, Floral, White, Crossed Swords, 8 1/4 In.	95.00
Meissen, Plate, Flowers, Black Background, Crossed Swords, Set Of 6	250.00
Meissen, Plate, Gilded On White, Crossed Swords, 10 In.	175.00
Meissen, Plate, Green & Gold, Crossed Swords, 12 1/2 In.	230.00
Meissen, Plate, Openwork Rim, Gold Trim, Man & Woman In Center, 11 In.	375.00
Meissen, Plate, Star Edges, Gold Encrusted, 11 In.	135.00
Meissen, Plate, Troubadour & Lady, Cobalt Field, 19th Century, 10 In.	275.00
Meissen, Plate, Two People In Center, Cobalt Blue, 8 In.	175.00
Meissen, Platter, Floral Design, Gold Trim, Crossed Swords Mark, 12 In.	78.00
Meissen, Platter, Pink Flowers, 18 1/2 X 13 1/4 In.	95.00
Meissen, Salt, Master, Oval, Floral, Gold Accents, 4 1/2 X 3 1/2 X 1 1/2 In.	125.00
Meissen, Salt, Master, Oval, Gold Accents, Mid 18th Century, Crossed Sword	140.00
Meissen, Sauce, Chinese Design, 4 3/4 In.Diameter	35.00
Meissen, Sauce, Green Ivy, Crossed Swords, 6 In.	25.00
Meissen, Slipper, Scene Of Dresden, Crossed Swords, 2 X 2 1/4 X 6 1/2 In.	195.00
Meissen, Snuff Box, Figural, Bulldog, Bonbonniere, 18th Century	950.00
Meissen, Sugar, Covered, Floral Design, Finial, Crossed Swords Mark	75.00
Meissen, Teapot, Cobalt, White Oval Medallions, Crossed Swords Mark	215.00
Meissen, Teapot, Gold Mask Spout, Gold Molding, Crossed Swords Mark	185.00
Meissen, Trivet, White & Gold Encrustation, Pair	135.00
Meissen, Vase, Gilt Borders, Cylindrical, Crossed Swords Mark, 5 1/4 In.	95.00
Meissen, Vase, Orange Dragon On White, Blue Crossed Swords, 5 In.	95.00
Meissen, Vase, Snake Handle, Raised Figures, Crossed Swords, 1850, 11 In., Pr.	520.00
Meissen, Vase, White, Pedestal Base, Gold Trim, 2 Handles, Marked, Pair, 11 In.	350.00

*Mercury, or silvered, glass was first made in the 1850s. It lost favor for a
while but became popular again about 1910. It looks like a piece of silver.*

Mercury Glass, Ball, Witches, Open Pontil, 12 1/2 In.Diameter	15.00
Mercury Glass, Ball, Witches, Open Pontil, 13 In.Diameter	20.00
Mercury Glass, Candlestick, Frosted, Nude, Silver Overlay, 12 In., Pair	35.00
Mercury Glass, Dish, Candy, Gold Inside, Grapes & Leaves Outside	45.00
Mercury Glass, Goblet, Footed, Gold Interior, Birds & Flowers, 5 1/2 In.	45.00
Mercury Glass, Rose Bowl, 4 1/2 In.	22.50
Mercury Glass, Salt, Master, Pedestal Base, Varnish & Co., London, 3 X 3 In.	105.00
Mercury Glass, Salt, Pedestal, Pair	25.00
Mercury Glass, Tieback, Pewter Post, Pair	19.50 To 50.00
Mercury Glass, Vase, Gold & Blue Enamel, 8 1/2 In.	40.00
Mercury Glass, Vase, Gold Liner, Leaf Decoration, 10 In.	22.00
Mercury Glass, Vase, Hand-Painted Bouquet, 10 1/2 In.	38.00

Mercury Glass, Vase, Hand-Painted Flowers, 12 In.	35.00
Mercury Glass, Vase, Hand-Painted Flowers, 6 1/2 X 2 1/2 In.Diameter	18.00
Mercury Glass, Vase, Pumpkin Shaped, 5 1/2 In.	24.00
Mercury Glass, Vase, White Flowers, 10 1/2 In., Pair	40.00
Mercury, Vase, Floral Design, 10 In., Pair	24.00
Merrimac, Vase, Corset Shape, Matte Drip Over Red Clay, Signed, 4 X 4 In.	125.00

Mettlach, Germany, is a city where the Villeroy and Boch factories worked. Steins from the firm are known as Mettlach steins. They date from about 1842. PUG means painted under glaze.

Mettlach, Ale Set, Pewter Lidded, 4 Mugs, No.1028, Applied Coloring	400.00
Mettlach, Beaker, No.1023 & No.1093, PUG Handled	100.00
Mettlach, Beaker, No.2327/1023, 1/4 Liter, Man With Feathered Hat	48.00
Mettlach, Beaker, No.2327/1024, 1/4 Liter, Minstrel Playing Flute, PUG	48.00
Mettlach, Beaker, No.2327/1190, 1/4 Liter, PUG	48.00
Mettlach, Beaker, No.2327/1191, 1/4 Liter, PUG	48.00
Mettlach, Beaker, No.2327, 1/4 Liter, Seattle, Washington	95.00
Mettlach, Beaker, No.2368, 1/4 Liter, Elk's Club	49.00
Mettlach, Beaker, State Of Indiana	45.00
Mettlach, Bowl, No.1248, Silver Plated Rim, Floral Design, Marked, 4 1/4 In.	50.00
Mettlach, Bowl, No.2087, Punch, Underplate	150.00
Mettlach, Bowl, Sugar, Cover, Acorn Finial	18.00
Mettlach, Cracker Jar, Floral Design	185.00
Mettlach, Jardiniere, No.2167, Bacchanalian Scenes, 6 X 6 In.Diameter	350.00
Mettlach, Jardiniere, Pastoral Scene, Hand Painted, Blue On White, 7 1/4 In.	95.00
Mettlach, Jug, Pouring, Barrel Shape, Brown, Copper Handle & Rim, Signed	225.00
Mettlach, Mug, Atlantic Garden, 1908	45.00
Mettlach, Mug, No.1909, 4/10 Liter, Black Transfer	45.00
Mettlach, Mug, No.1909, 5 In.	45.00
Mettlach, Mug, No.2077/98, Mercury Mark, Villeroy & Boch, 1/2 Liter	45.00
Mettlach, Mug, No.2189, 1/4 Liter, Villeroy & Boch, Tan	15.00
Mettlach, Mug, No.3533, 3/10 Liter, Children In Relief	65.00
Mettlach, Mug, South Bend Brewing Co., Picture Of Brewery	85.00
Mettlach, Pitcher & Bowl, Odillo Pattern, Silver Over Ivory, Mercury Mark	175.00
Mettlach, Pitcher, 1 Liter, Pewter Base, Collar & Thumblift, 9 1/4 In.	89.50
Mettlach, Planter, No.2787, Art Deco, 5 X 14 In.	110.00
Mettlach, Plaque, No.1011, St.Goar, Castle Scene, 12 In.	120.00
Mettlach, Plaque, No.1384, Etched, Knight With Banner, 14 1/2 In.	700.00
Mettlach, Plaque, No.1385, Etched, Knight With Spear, 14 1/2 In.	700.00
Mettlach, Plaque, No.2195, Etched, Castle On Lake, C.1907, 17 1/4 In.	600.00
Mettlach, Plaque, No.2621, Cavalier Pouring Wine, 7 In.	250.00
Mettlach, Plaque, No.2625, Troubador Playing Mandolin, Etched, 7 In.	395.00
Mettlach, Plaque, No.2648, Etched, Knight And Girl, 9 1/2 In.	295.00
Mettlach, Plaque, No.3131, Farm Scene, 11 3/4 In.	150.00
Mettlach, Plaque, No.3164, Etched, River Sirens And Castle, 11 3/4 In.	150.00
Mettlach, Plaque, No.7026, Scene From Lohengrin, Signed, 16 X 9 In.	1800.00
Mettlach, Plaque, No.7069, Woman In Flowing Gown, Cameo, Oval	220.00
Mettlach, Plaque, No.7341 & 7045, Lovers In Woods, C.1902, 16 X 9 In., Pair	1800.00
Mettlach, Punch Bowl, No.418, Floral Decoration, Relief, 2 Quart	400.00
Mettlach, Stein, No.100C, 1/4 Liter, Coat Of Arms, Gray, Marked	135.00 To 140.00
Mettlach, Stein, No.1005, 1 Liter, 3 Panels, Figures, Relief	350.00
Mettlach, Stein, No.1028, Maiden & Man With Scythe, Relief	225.00
Mettlach, Stein, No.1028, 1/2 Liter, Tree Trunk, Relief	75.00
Mettlach, Stein, No.1028, 1/2 Liter, Woodsman & Maiden, Winking Man Lid	210.00
Mettlach, Stein, No.1053, 1 Liter, 3 Dwarfs, Etched	650.00
Mettlach, Stein, No.1069, Signed Worth	550.00
Mettlach, Stein, No.1105, 1/2 Liter, Geometric Floral, Inlaid Lid	165.00
Mettlach, Stein, No.1146, 1/2 Liter, Drinking Scene, Signed Warth, 1891	425.00
Mettlach, Stein, No.1164, 1/2 Liter, 5 Drinking Figures, Etched	395.00
Mettlach, Stein, No.1174, 1/2 Liter, Raised Stylized Flowers, Mosaic	500.00
Mettlach, Stein, No.1286, Villeroy & Boch, Geschutzt, 5 1/2 In.	310.00
Mettlach, Stein, No.1403, 1/2 Liter, 7 People Bowling, Etched	460.00
Mettlach, Stein, No.1467, 1/2 Liter, 4 Seasons, Relief	175.00
Mettlach, Stein, No.1477, 1/2 Liter, Dwarfs Carrying Grapes, Etched	375.00
Mettlach, Stein, No.1526, 1/2 Liter, Princeton Coat Of Arms	75.00
Mettlach, Stein, No.1526, 4/10 Liter, Harvard U., 1893-1913	65.00 To 110.00

Mettlach, Stein, No.1577, 5 Liter, Dinner Scene, Etched 2000.00
Mettlach, Stein, No.1643, 1/2 Liter, Student Drinking, Holding Dog, Tapestry 325.00
Mettlach, Stein, No.1645, 1 Liter, Man With Beer & Mandolin, Tapestry 450.00
Mettlach, Stein, No.1654, 1/2 Liter, Geometric Floral, Mosaic 300.00
Mettlach, Stein, No.1655, 1/2 Liter, Dancing Scene, Etched .... 400.00 To 460.00
Mettlach, Stein, No.1656, 1/2 Liter, Man & Woman, Etched 200.00
Mettlach, Stein, No.1675, 1/2 Liter, Heidelberg, Etched 400.00
Mettlach, Stein, No.171, 1/4 Liter, 5 Figures, Blue & White, Relief 145.00
Mettlach, Stein, No.1797, 1/2 Liter, 4 Panels, Musicians 400.00
Mettlach, Stein, No.1856, 1 Liter, German Eagle, Postman, Etched 650.00
Mettlach, Stein, No.1901, Bowler, PUG 255.00
Mettlach, Stein, No.1909, 1/4 Liter, Alice Hotel, British Columbia 65.00
Mettlach, Stein, No.1909, 3/10 Liter, Bartholomay's, Rochester 110.00
Mettlach, Stein, No.1947, 1/2 Liter, Man With Cat 450.00
Mettlach, Stein, No.1968, 1/2 Liter, Lovers In Floral Background, Etched 450.00
Mettlach, Stein, No.1972, 1/4 Liter, 4 Seasons, Etched .... 285.00 To 365.00
Mettlach, Stein, No.1997, 1/2 Liter, Medallion, Portrait, Etched .... 325.00 To 475.00
Mettlach, Stein, No.2002, 1 Liter, Houses, City Scene, Etched 600.00
Mettlach, Stein, No.2002, 1/2 Liter, Houses, City Scene, Etched 350.00
Mettlach, Stein, No.2024, 1/2 Liter, City Of Berlin, Glazed .... 375.00 To 600.00
Mettlach, Stein, No.2025, 3/10 Liter, Playing Cherubs, Etched 250.00
Mettlach, Stein, No.2027, 1 Liter, King Of The Hops, C.1897 .... 475.00
Mettlach, Stein, No.2035, 1/2 Liter, Satyrs & Drinkers, Etched 475.00
Mettlach, Stein, No.2036, 1/2 Liter, Mettlach Owl, Cameo 750.00
Mettlach, Stein, No.2039, 1/2 Liter, Playing Cards, Etched .... 595.00 To 750.00
Mettlach, Stein, No.2057, 1/2 Liter, Dancing Figures, Etched 250.00
Mettlach, Stein, No.2057, 3/10 Liter, Dancing Figures, Etched 275.00
Mettlach, Stein, No.2065, 3 Liter, Girl, Cavalier, Birdcage, Etched 1250.00
Mettlach, Stein, No.2076, 3 Liter, German Eagle, Owls, Relief 395.00
Mettlach, Stein, No.2077, 3/10 Liter, Red, Cream, Pedestal Base 110.00
Mettlach, Stein, No.2086, 1/2 Liter, Figures Dancing, Relief .... 225.00 To 260.00
Mettlach, Stein, No.2089, 1/2 Liter, Angel, Cherubs, Etched .... 450.00 To 525.00
Mettlach, Stein, No.2090, 1/2 Liter, Husband, Wife .... 325.00 To 500.00
Mettlach, Stein, No.2092, 1/2 Liter, Whiskered Man, Clock, Etched .... 425.00 To 525.00
Mettlach, Stein, No.2094, 1/2 Liter, Lady, Bass Fiddle, Etched .... 450.00 To 675.00
Mettlach, Stein, No.2097, 1/2 Liter, Music, Etched .... 400.00 To 550.00
Mettlach, Stein, No.2100, 3/10 Liter, Roman Soldier, Etched 300.00
Mettlach, Stein, No.2131, 1 Liter, Three Panels, People, Relief 450.00
Mettlach, Stein, No.2184, 3/10 Liter, Elves, Relief 385.00
Mettlach, Stein, No.2204/II, 1/2 Liter, Black German Eagle, Glazed 575.00
Mettlach, Stein, No.2217, 4/10 Liter, Minnesota Brew Co., B.P.O.E., 1897 .... 60.00
Mettlach, Stein, No.2231, 1/2 Liter, Polychrome Knights & Cavaliers, Etched 190.00
Mettlach, Stein, No.2271/1107, Men In Forest, PUG 225.00
Mettlach, Stein, No.2278, 1/2 Liter, Figures Of Athletes, Relief 400.00
Mettlach, Stein, No.2285, 1/2 Liter, Lovers, Etched 400.00
Mettlach, Stein, No.2382, 1 Liter, Thirsty Rider, Etched 1100.00
Mettlach, Stein, No.2382, 1/2 Liter, Thirsty Rider, Etched 595.00
Mettlach, Stein, No.2388, 1/2 Liter, Pretzel, Glazed 450.00
Mettlach, Stein, No.2391, 1/2 Liter, Romeo And Juliet, Etched 900.00
Mettlach, Stein, No.2394, 1/2 Liter, Siegfried, Etched 600.00
Mettlach, Stein, No.2402, 1/2 Liter, Wedding Party, Etched 675.00
Mettlach, Stein, No.2428, 4 Liter, Knights In Tavern, Etched 1250.00
Mettlach, Stein, No.2440, 1/2 Liter, Ten Girls, Relief 575.00
Mettlach, Stein, No.2479, 1/2 Liter, Three Panel 600.00
Mettlach, Stein, No.2530, 1 Liter, Boar Hunting, Cameo 1300.00
Mettlach, Stein, No.2580, 1/2 Liter, Scene Of Castle, Etched 700.00
Mettlach, Stein, No.2607, 2 Liter, Three Paired Couples, Cameo 950.00
Mettlach, Stein, No.2632, 1/2 Liter, Inlaid Lid, Bowling Scene .... 415.00 To 425.00
Mettlach, Stein, No.2693, 1/2 Liter, Troubador And Knight, Etched 550.00
Mettlach, Stein, No.2757, Man And Girl Dancing, Cameo 600.00
Mettlach, Stein, No.2778, 1/4 Liter, Scene Inside Castle, Etched 350.00
Mettlach, Stein, No.2784, 3 Liter, Man Playing Mandolin, PUG 550.00
Mettlach, Stein, No.2802, 1/2 Liter, Panels, Etched 75.00
Mettlach, Stein, No.2828, 1/2 Liter, Black Forest, Glazed 1350.00
Mettlach, Stein, No.2833-B, 1/2 Liter, Evening In Forest, Etched 400.00
Mettlach, Stein, No.2833-C, 3/10 Liter, Lorelei, Etched 325.00

Mettlach, Stein, No.2833-E, 3/10 Liter, Couple Under Tree, Etched 475.00
Mettlach, Stein, No.2845, 1/2 Liter, Alpine Scene, 1902, Glazed 450.00
Mettlach, Stein, No.2871, 1 Liter, Cornell University, Etched 1400.00
Mettlach, Stein, No.2892, 1/2 Liter, Green & White Artichokes, Etched 250.00
Mettlach, Stein, No.2893, 3 Liter, German Eagle & 12 State Shields, PUG 325.00
Mettlach, Stein, No.2900, 1/2 Liter, Argentina, Etched 325.00
Mettlach, Stein, No.2936, 1/2 Liter, Elk's Club, Etched 375.00
Mettlach, Stein, No.2957, 1/2 Liter, Bowling Alley, Etched .... 400.00 To 425.00
Mettlach, Stein, No.2958, 3 Liter, Bowling Scene, Etched 900.00
Mettlach, Stein, No.3070, 1/2 Liter, Monkey & Man 250.00
Mettlach, Stein, No.3095, Drink Hires Root Beer .... 90.00 To 99.00
Mettlach, Stein, No.3168, 1/2 Liter, Fox Hunter, Etched 450.00
Mettlach, Stein, No.3172, Man With Umbrella, Etched 395.00
Mettlach, Stein, No.485, 1 Liter, Ten People Dancing, Drinking, Relief 450.00
Mettlach, Stein, No.5005, 1/2 Liter, Blue Delft 350.00
Mettlach, Stein, No.6, 3 Liter, Justice, Noah, Relief 450.00
Mettlach, Stein, No.675, 1/2 Liter, Keg, Acorn Finial, Glazed .... 180.00 To 225.00
Mettlach, Trivet, Footed, Poppy Design, 7 In.Square 32.00
Mettlach, Trivet, Poppy Decoration, Footed, 7 In. 32.00
Mettlach, Tumbler, No.2327, Winged Mercury Stamp 60.00
Mettlach, Tumbler, No.8085, Purple Grapes, Villeroy & Boch, Set Of 5 .... 125.00
Mettlach, Vase, Art Deco, Green, White & Red, 10 In. 75.00
Mettlach, Vase, Etched & Enameled, Floral Design, Castle Mark, 12 3/4 In. 385.00
Mettlach, Vase, No.1046, Applied Cherubs, V. & B., 10 In. 95.00
Mettlach, Vase, No.1591, Etched & Enameled Children, Castle Mark, 12 3/4 In. 385.00
Mettlach, Vase, No.1591, Etched & Enameled, Castle Mark, 14 In. 425.00
Mettlach, Vase, No.2242, Etched, 14 In. 150.00
Mettlach, Vase, No.2414, Handled, Gray Background, Dated 1909, 13 1/2 In., Pr. 750.00
Mettlach, Vase, No.2733, Blue & Black, 16 X 10 In. 189.00
Mettlach, Vase, No.3014, Magenta & Green, Mercury Mark 139.00
   Mickey Mouse, see Disneyana, Mickey Mouse

Milk glass was named for its milky white color. It was first made in
England during the 1700s. The height of its popularity in the United
States was from 1870 to 1880. It is now correct to refer to some colored
glass as blue milk glass, black milk glass, etc. The letter B before the
numbers xx refers to the book "Milk Glass" by E. Belknap.
   Milk Glass, see also Cambridge, Cosmos
Milk Glass, Ashtray, Dobbs Hat, Black 12.00
Milk Glass, Basket, Blackberry Pattern, 6 1/2 X 4 1/4 X 3 3/4 In. 37.50
Milk Glass, Basket, Clear Applied Handle 20.00
Milk Glass, Basket, Flat Reeded Handle, Opalescent, 12 1/2 X 7 1/2 In. 55.00
Milk Glass, Basket, Hen On Handle 40.00
Milk Glass, Basket, Hobnail, Pink Interior, Amber Thorn Handle, 6 In. 135.00
Milk Glass, Basket, Ruffled, Gold Flecks Inside, Applied Twisted Handle 265.00
Milk Glass, Berry Bowl, American Sweetheart, Pink, 3 1/4 In., Set Of 6 .... 100.00
Milk Glass, Berry Set, Bowl, 9 In., 6 4 1/2 In.Bowls, Leaf Design 40.00
Milk Glass, Berry Set, Pattee Cross, U.S. Glass, Green, 7 Piece 75.00
Milk Glass, Block, Flower, Blue 14.75
Milk Glass, Bootie, Daisy & Button, Open 22.00
Milk Glass, Bottle, Base, Statue Of Liberty 190.00
Milk Glass, Bottle, Dresser, Actress 55.00
Milk Glass, Bottle, Dresser, Chrysanthemum, Globe Stopper, 9 1/2 In., Pair 90.00
Milk Glass, Bottle, Dresser, Rose & Poppy, Blown Out Head, 11 In. 65.00
Milk Glass, Bottle, Dresser, Stopper, Jenny Lind 30.00
Milk Glass, Bottle, Ink, House, Window, Door, Mansard Roof, 4 3/4 X 2 In. 375.00
Milk Glass, Bottle, Souvenir, Hemisphere 11.00
Milk Glass, Bottle, Statue Of Liberty 125.00
Milk Glass, Bowl, Acanthus Leaf, Blue, 4 In. 45.00
Milk Glass, Bowl, Atterbury, Pedestaled, Hand-Painted Center, 11 In. 38.00
Milk Glass, Bowl, Basketweave Edge, Opalescent, 9 In. 22.00
Milk Glass, Bowl, Florette, 10 In. 95.00
Milk Glass, Bowl, Honeycomb, Flint, 8 In 35.00
Milk Glass, Bowl, Lattice Edge, Bell-Toned, Applied Blossom, 8 In. 32.00
Milk Glass, Bowl, Raised Floral, White, 9 1/4 X 5 3/4 In. 58.50
Milk Glass, Bowl, Scroll & Eye, Blue, 6 1/2 In. 29.50

Milk Glass, Bowl, Sugar, Waffle Pattern, Blue 29.75
Milk Glass, Bowl, Tree Of Life With Daisy, Portland, 8 In. 45.00
Milk Glass, Box, Card, Footed, Scrolls & Heart 12.50
Milk Glass, Box, Covered, Raised Flowers & Scrolls, 6 1/2 X 3 In. 29.50
Milk Glass, Box, Covered, 3 Kittens On Lid, 3 In. 18.00
Milk Glass, Box, Dresser, Covered, Butterfly Shape 4.00
Milk Glass, Box, Powder, Cat On Drum 55.00
Milk Glass, Box, Trinket, 3 Kittens On Top, 3 1/2 In.Square 28.00
Milk Glass, Butter, Blue Knob & Rim, Beaded Swag, Signed 150.00
Milk Glass, Butter, Coreopsis 115.00
Milk Glass, Butter, Covered, Miniature 18.50
Milk Glass, Butter, Duchess, Green & Gold 68.00
Milk Glass, Butter, Heisey Beaded Swag, Cornflower Trim 95.00
Milk Glass, Butter, Hobnail, Scalloped Edge Underplate, Crown Finial, 7 In. 35.00
Milk Glass, Butter, Wild Rose, Covered, Child Size 70.00
Milk Glass, Cake Stand, Hand-Painted Flowers 30.00
Milk Glass, Candleholder, Angle, Pair 30.00
Milk Glass, Candleholder, Scrolled Feet & Top, 4 X 4 1/2 In. 22.50
Milk Glass, Candlestick, Blue, 8 In., Pair 85.00
Milk Glass, Candlestick, Blue, 8 1/2 In., Pair 59.00
Milk Glass, Candlestick, Reeded Columns, 9 In., Pair 69.00
Milk Glass, Candlestick, Reeded, Blue, 7 In., Pair 69.00
Milk Glass, Canoe, Souvenir, Berton, South Dakota 12.50
Milk Glass, Cat Cover, Oblong, Signed W. 75.00
Milk Glass, Celery, Ivy In Snow 25.00
Milk Glass, Celery, Sawtooth 29.00
Milk Glass, Compote, Basket Weave, Lid, Dated June 30, 1874, 11 In. 125.00
Milk Glass, Compote, Basket Weave, Pedestal, Lattice Edge 46.00
Milk Glass, Compote, Hexagon Shape, 8 X 7 1/2 In. 35.00
Milk Glass, Compote, Partially Draped Nude Stem, Flowers, Lid 37.50
Milk Glass, Condiment Set, White, For-Get-Me-Not 65.00
Milk Glass, Condiment Set, 3 Bottle, Fan Shaped Base, Butterflies 42.00
Milk Glass, Cowboy Hat, Blue, 6 In.Diameter 28.00
Milk Glass, Creamer, Cloud Band 20.00
Milk Glass, Creamer, Covered, Basket Weave, Blue, 6 X 4 In. 69.00
Milk Glass, Creamer, Covered, Chain Handle, Blue 30.00
Milk Glass, Creamer, Diamond Shape, Scroll 52.00
Milk Glass, Creamer, Flattened Diamond & Sunburst 10.00
Milk Glass, Creamer, Florette, Pink Satin 90.00
Milk Glass, Creamer, Sawtooth .... 15.00 To 20.00
Milk Glass, Creamer, Tappan 25.00
Milk Glass, Cruet, Diamond Design, Skirted, Original Stopper 65.00
Milk Glass, Cruet, Grape & Leaf 95.00
Milk Glass, Cruet, Sprig, Decorated 75.00
Milk Glass, Cup, Fleur-De-Lis & Drape 16.50
Milk Glass, Cup, Punch, Nursery Rhymes 18.00
Milk Glass, Cup, Punch, Wild Rose 17.00
Milk Glass, Decanter, Perfume, Hand-Painted, 10 In. 22.00
Milk Glass, Decanter, Scroll Variant, Bulbous Stopper 17.50
Milk Glass, Dish, Battleship Maine Cover 30.00
Milk Glass, Dish, Boat Shape, Swan Handles, Marked, Chartreuse, 5 1/2 In. 55.00
Milk Glass, Dish, Camel Cover, English, 6 In. 60.00
Milk Glass, Dish, Cat Cover, Glass Eyes, 8 In. 40.00
Milk Glass, Dish, Cat Cover, Split Rib Base, 5 1/2 X 4 1/4 In. 40.00
Milk Glass, Dish, Cat, Cover, Glass Eyes, Dated 1889 .... 100.00
Milk Glass, Dish, Chick & Eggs, Cover, Dated 1889, Lacy Base 100.00
Milk Glass, Dish, Chicken, Cover, White Head, Blue .... 35.00 To 39.00
Milk Glass, Dish, Conestoga Wagon 75.00
Milk Glass, Dish, Dewey Cover, Oval, Inscribed Dewey, 6 3/4 In. ....*Illus* 32.00
Milk Glass, Dish, Dog Cover, Lying On Mat, 3 5/8 X 4 5/8 X 4 1/4 In. 88.00
Milk Glass, Dish, Dog Cover, Ribbed Base 30.00
Milk Glass, Dish, Dog On Oblong Floral Embossed Base 115.00
Milk Glass, Dish, Dove Cover, 1889, Green Eye 115.00
Milk Glass, Dish, Duck Cover, Atterbury, Amethyst Head 75.00
Milk Glass, Dish, Duck Cover, Wavy Base, Opalescent 72.00
Milk Glass, Dish, Duck Cover, 5 3/8 In. 25.00

Milk Glass, Dish, Dewey Cover, Oval,
Inscribed Dewey, 6 3/4 In.
(See Page 313)

Milk Glass, Dish, Entwined Fish Cover, Atterbury, 1889	132.00 To 165.00
Milk Glass, Dish, Figural, Shell	5.00
Milk Glass, Dish, Fish Cover, Impressed Patent, 1887, 9 In.	45.00
Milk Glass, Dish, Fox Cover, Dated 1889	110.00
Milk Glass, Dish, Fox Cover, Lacy Edge Base, Atterbury	89.00
Milk Glass, Dish, Fox Cover, Lattice Base	75.00
Milk Glass, Dish, Hand & Dove Cover, Blue Stone Eyes, Dated 1889	100.00
Milk Glass, Dish, Hen & Eggs Cover	65.00
Milk Glass, Dish, Hen Cover	55.00
Milk Glass, Dish, Hen Cover, Amber	165.00
Milk Glass, Dish, Hen Cover, American	75.00
Milk Glass, Dish, Hen Cover, Basket Weave Base, Vallerystahl, 5 X 4 In.	45.00
Milk Glass, Dish, Hen Cover, Basket Weave, Vallerystahl, 3 1/4 X 2 1/2 In.	35.00
Milk Glass, Dish, Hen Cover, Blue Head, White, 5 1/2 In.	37.50 To 40.00
Milk Glass, Dish, Hen Cover, Blue Head, 5 In.	35.00
Milk Glass, Dish, Hen Cover, Blue, 6 In.	40.00
Milk Glass, Dish, Hen Cover, Marble, Blue, Fenton Base, 8 1/2 In.	20.00
Milk Glass, Dish, Hen Cover, Miniature	7.50
Milk Glass, Dish, Hen Cover, Red Comb, White, 7 In.	18.00
Milk Glass, Dish, Hen Cover, White Head, Blue, 7 In.	45.00
Milk Glass, Dish, Hen On Chick Cover, 6 1/4 In.	145.00 To 185.00
Milk Glass, Dish, Hen On Nest Cover, Blue	40.00 To 50.00
Milk Glass, Dish, Hen On Nest Cover, Brown Basket, Glass Eyes	135.00
Milk Glass, Dish, Hen On Nest Cover, Glass Eyes	135.00
Milk Glass, Dish, Lamb Cover, Picket Base	40.00
Milk Glass, Dish, Lion Cover, Dated 1889	125.00
Milk Glass, Dish, Lion Cover, Picket Base	45.00
Milk Glass, Dish, Lion Cover, Split Rib Case	40.00
Milk Glass, Dish, Moses In The Bullrushes Cover	165.00
Milk Glass, Dish, Mule-Earred Rabbit Cover	22.50 To 40.00
Milk Glass, Dish, Pear Cover	45.00
Milk Glass, Dish, Pintail Duck Cover, 5 1/2 In.	35.00
Milk Glass, Dish, Quail Cover	18.00 To 35.00
Milk Glass, Dish, Rabbit Cover, Atterbury, 9 1/2 In.	145.00
Milk Glass, Dish, Relish, Fish, Blue Eyes	65.00
Milk Glass, Dish, Robed Santa Cover	90.00
Milk Glass, Dish, Rooster Cover, Red Eyes	35.00
Milk Glass, Dish, Rooster Cover, Ribbed Base, Red & Black, 5 1/2 X 4 1/4 In.	35.00
Milk Glass, Dish, Scottie Dog Cover	30.00
Milk Glass, Dish, Snail On Strawberry Cover	60.00
Milk Glass, Dish, Swan Cover, Basket Weave Base, 10 In.	45.00
Milk Glass, Dish, Uncle Sam Cover	40.00 To 50.00
Milk Glass, Easter Egg, Large	10.00
Milk Glass, Egg Cup, Blue, 4 1/2 In.	22.00
Milk Glass, Egg Plate, With Loving Easter Thoughts, Floral, 6 In.	22.50
Milk Glass, Egg, Blown, Pontiled	6.00
Milk Glass, Egg, Chick Coming Out Of Egg	27.50
Milk Glass, Egg, Easter, Decorated, Large	28.00
Milk Glass, Egg, Embossed Easter Greetings, 6 1/2 X 4 In.	20.00
Milk Glass, Egg, Horseshoe, Embossed, 6 X 4 In.Diameter	20.00
Milk Glass, Epergne, Lily Shaped Candlesticks, 17 In., Set	145.00
Milk Glass, Epergne, Single Lily In Pedestal Base, 11 In.	65.00
Milk Glass, Holder, Spoon, Scenic, Flared Scalloped Top, Bulbous	65.00
Milk Glass, Inkwell, Boat Shape, Dated	88.00
Milk Glass, Inkwell, Snail	55.00

Milk Glass, Jar, Actress, White Opalescent, Lid	30.00
Milk Glass, Jar, Candy, Covered, Cloverleaf, Green	35.00
Milk Glass, Jar, Eagle	85.00
Milk Glass, Jar, Mustard, Bull's Head, Ladle	135.00
Milk Glass, Jar, Owl, Lid Insert	99.00
Milk Glass, Jar, Spice Rack, Griffith	15.00
Milk Glass, Jar, Sterilizer, Barber Shop, Copper Lid	12.00
Milk Glass, Label, Westmoreland Spec.Co.Prepared Must.	15.00
Milk Glass, Lamp, see Lamp, Milk Glass	
Milk Glass, Lighter, Electric, Green & Pumpkin Stripe, Footed, Round	20.00
Milk Glass, Match Holder, Shape Of Book, Floral Cover, 2 Section Striker	25.00
Milk Glass, Match Holder, Triple Swan	28.00
Milk Glass, Match Holder, Words In Gold, For Burnt Matches	17.00
Milk Glass, Muffineer, Blue Floral Decoration, 5 3/4 In.	24.00
Milk Glass, Mug, Child's, Peacock, Stork On Reverse, 2 5/8 X 2 1/2 In.	40.00
Milk Glass, Mug, Elves, Greentown	16.00
Milk Glass, Mug, Liberty Bell	138.00
Milk Glass, Mug, Lidded, Knights & Serenade, Greentown	35.00
Milk Glass, Mug, Pedestal Base, Swan Forms Handle & On Base	35.00
Milk Glass, Mustard Dish, Cow, Ladle	145.00
Milk Glass, Paperweight, Kellogg's Corn Flakes, Baby In Wicker Basket	65.00
Milk Glass, Pepper Shaker, Cosmos, Pink, Yellow, Blue, Flowers, Original Top	60.00
Milk Glass, Pitcher, Cream, Blue	35.00
Milk Glass, Pitcher, Cream, Roses & Gold Trim, Versailles, 5 In.	29.50
Milk Glass, Pitcher, Cream, Swan In Cattails, Handle Is Swan's Neck	20.00
Milk Glass, Pitcher, Silverplated Spout & Dragon Handle, Victorian, 9 In.	70.00
Milk Glass, Pitcher, Syrup, Hand-Painted, Hinged Tin Lid, White	27.50
Milk Glass, Pitcher, Syrup, Red Morning Glories	45.00
Milk Glass, Pitcher, Water, Applied Handle, Scroll Design, 9 1/2 In.	45.00
Milk Glass, Pitcher, Water, Curtain Pattern, Gold Trim Lip & Handle	100.00
Milk Glass, Pitcher, Water, Curtain, 6 Tumblers	195.00
Milk Glass, Pitcher, Water, Scroll, 9 In.	40.00
Milk Glass, Pitcher, Water, Waffle Pattern, Chartreuse, 7 1/2 In.	85.00
Milk Glass, Planter, Hanging, Embossed Grapes & Leaves, Chain, 2 1/2 X 3 In.	15.00
Milk Glass, Planter, Open Edge, Cupid & Venus, 7 1/2 In.	18.00
Milk Glass, Plate, Balking Mule	40.00
Milk Glass, Plate, Battleship Maine	25.00
Milk Glass, Plate, Bread, Basket Weave, Give Us This Day, Dated 1874	56.00
Milk Glass, Plate, Bust Of Dewey, Openwork Border, 7 In. .... *Illus*	12.00
Milk Glass, Plate, Cake, Fenton, 6 1/2 In.High, 10 In.Square	30.00
Milk Glass, Plate, Easter Rabbits	42.00
Milk Glass, Plate, Flag, Eagles & Fleur-De-Lis Border, 1903	20.00
Milk Glass, Plate, Frank Bros., Store, Chicago, 7 In.	15.00
Milk Glass, Plate, Indian Head, 7 1/2 In.	30.00
Milk Glass, Plate, Molded Cherries, Blue, 8 1/2 In.	30.00
Milk Glass, Plate, Persian Garden, White, 7 In.	69.00
Milk Glass, Plate, Rabbit, Whole Body	37.50
Milk Glass, Plate, Scroll & Waffle, Signed McKee	29.00
Milk Glass, Plate, Scroll With Eye, Hand-Painted, 10 In.	45.00
Milk Glass, Plate, Serenade, 6 In.	45.00
Milk Glass, Plate, Souvenir, Frank Bros., Store, Chicago, 7 In.	20.00
Milk Glass, Plate, Souvenir, State Capital, Des Moines, Iowa, Open Border	25.00
Milk Glass, Plate, Toddy, Oak Leaves, Reticulated Border, 5 1/2 In.	28.00

Milk Glass, Plate, Bust Of Dewey,
Openwork Border, 7 In.

Milk Glass, Plate, 20 Hearts All Around	35.50
Milk Glass, Platter, Diamond Grill	28.50
Milk Glass, Platter, Dog Swimming After Duck, 13 1/2 In.	85.00 To 150.00
Milk Glass, Punch Set, Nursery Rhymes, Bowl, 6 Cups, 7 Piece	185.00
Milk Glass, Punchbowl Set, Pedestal Base, 12 Cups, Daisy & Button	36.00
Milk Glass, Rolling Pin, Metal Handles	40.00
Milk Glass, Rolling Pin, Wood Handles	35.00
Milk Glass, Salt & Pepper, Acorn, Blue	25.00
Milk Glass, Salt & Pepper, Colored Animals Bottom Border	17.00
Milk Glass, Salt & Pepper, Creased Bale, Blue	35.00
Milk Glass, Salt & Pepper, Embossed Gold Rabbits, Hen & Chicks	42.00
Milk Glass, Salt & Pepper, London's Trafalger Square, St.Paul's	10.00
Milk Glass, Salt & Pepper, Quilted Phlox	28.00
Milk Glass, Salt & Pepper, Rabbits, Egg Shaped	50.00
Milk Glass, Salt & Pepper, Refrigerators, 3 In.	15.00 To 25.00
Milk Glass, Salt & Pepper, Sunset Pattern, I Blue, I White, Original Tops	19.75
Milk Glass, Salt & Pepper, Sunset, Pink	48.00
Milk Glass, Salt Shaker, Pink, Embossed Flowers	17.50
Milk Glass, Salt, Master, Cabbage Rose	22.00
Milk Glass, Salt, Scroll & Net, Blue	19.00
Milk Glass, Saltshaker, Apple Blossom, Pair	50.00
Milk Glass, Saltshaker, Beehive	18.00 To 36.00
Milk Glass, Saltshaker, Corn Husk	16.00
Milk Glass, Saltshaker, Heart	22.00
Milk Glass, Saltshaker, Panel Sprig	28.00
Milk Glass, Shade, Petticoat Style, Flat	4.50
Milk Glass, Shell, Oval, Footed, 8 1/2 In.	25.00
Milk Glass, Shoe, Man's, Laced Up, Head Of Cat In Shoe	58.00
Milk Glass, Smoke Bell, Flint, Ruffled Edge, C.1880, 7 1/2 In.Diameter	20.00
Milk Glass, Spooner, Blackberry	10.00
Milk Glass, Spooner, Cattail & Waterlily	65.00
Milk Glass, Spooner, Grape, 1870	13.00
Milk Glass, Spooner, Horse Heads On Each Side, Handles	12.50
Milk Glass, Spooner, Iris	25.00
Milk Glass, Spooner, Sawtooth	9.00 To 13.00
Milk Glass, Spooner, Versailles	13.00
Milk Glass, Spooner, Wild Rose	55.00
Milk Glass, Stein, Lid, Elves	35.00
Milk Glass, Stein, Lid, 4 Knights	35.00
Milk Glass, Stein, Monk	40.00
Milk Glass, Sugar & Creamer, Covered, Coreopsis, Red Satin	275.00
Milk Glass, Sugar & Creamer, Covered, Crown	25.00
Milk Glass, Sugar & Creamer, Covered, Hand-Painted, Footed, 8 In.	48.50
Milk Glass, Sugar & Creamer, Paneled Wheat	65.00
Milk Glass, Sugar & Creamer, Portieux, Miniature, Pig Finial	175.00
Milk Glass, Sugar Shaker, Blown Out Grapes	35.00
Milk Glass, Sugar Shaker, Florette	125.00
Milk Glass, Sugar Shaker, Inverted Flowers	29.00
Milk Glass, Sugar Shaker, Lustered Colors, Grape & Leaf, Northwood	55.00
Milk Glass, Sugar Shaker, Netted Oak	45.00
Milk Glass, Sugar Shaker, Pinecone, Green	75.00
Milk Glass, Sugar, Covered, Square, Blackberry Pattern, Berry Finial	50.00
Milk Glass, Sugar, Creamer & Spooner, Gothic Arch, Grape, Northwood	95.00
Milk Glass, Syrup, Alba, Decorated	25.00
Milk Glass, Syrup, Catherine Ann	45.00
Milk Glass, Syrup, Enameling, Honeycomb Veining, Bulbous Base	70.00
Milk Glass, Syrup, French Primrose	55.00
Milk Glass, Syrup, Gold Decoration, Grape & Vine	40.00
Milk Glass, Syrup, Grape Design	38.50
Milk Glass, Syrup, Hinged Tin Top, Hand-Painted Flowers	27.50
Milk Glass, Syrup, Hobnail	75.00
Milk Glass, Syrup, Honeycomb, Raised Net Design	70.00
Milk Glass, Syrup, Netted Ribbons	50.00
Milk Glass, Syrup, Tin Cover, Alba	35.00
Milk Glass, Toothpick, Blue, Fan Shaped, Basketweave With Rope Trim, C.1880	35.00
Milk Glass, Toothpick, Hat With Parrot	35.00

Milk Glass, Toothpick, Horseshoe & Clover	33.00
Milk Glass, Toothpick, Pansy, 3 Handled	35.00
Milk Glass, Toothpick, Scroll, Acanthus, Purple Slag	85.00
Milk Glass, Toothpick, Swimming Fish, Shell On Back, 5 X 2 1/2 In.	35.00
Milk Glass, Tray, Beaded Edge, 8 1/4 In.Square	15.00
Milk Glass, Tray, Bread, Basket Weave, C.1874	42.00
Milk Glass, Tray, Buffalo Heads Each End, Beading, M On Base, 9 X 5 In.	18.50
Milk Glass, Tray, Fish, Open, Dated June 4, 1872, Atterbury, 10 In.	75.00
Milk Glass, Tray, Triangle, Pointed Hobs, 7 1/4 In.	15.00
Milk Glass, Tumbler, Bumper To The Flag, Union Forever	85.00
Milk Glass, Tumbler, Curtain Pattern	30.00
Milk Glass, Tumbler, Gold Ribs, Beaded Rib	14.00
Milk Glass, Tumbler, Grape & Cable, Red & Gold	19.00
Milk Glass, Tumbler, Grape & Leaf	29.00
Milk Glass, Tumbler, Guttate	23.00
Milk Glass, Tumbler, Hand-Painted, Raised Molded Leaves	35.00
Milk Glass, Tumbler, Louisiana Purchase	15.00
Milk Glass, Tumbler, Nestor	39.00
Milk Glass, Tumbler, Netted Oak	29.00
Milk Glass, Tumbler, Scroll, Blue, Set Of 6	175.00
Milk Glass, Tumbler, Single Rose	40.00
Milk Glass, Tumbler, St.Louis World's Fair	13.00
Milk Glass, Vase, Bud, Paneled, Scalloped Top, 15 1/4 In.	20.00
Milk Glass, Vase, Crimped & Fluted, Swirl Pattern, Lavender Lining, Blue	125.00
Milk Glass, Vase, Daisy Pattern, Black, 7 In.	18.00
Milk Glass, Vase, Jack-In-The-Pulpit, Cerulean Blue, Bulbous, 9 1/2 In.Tall	40.00
Milk Glass, Water Set, Torquay, 4 Tumblers	85.00
Millefiore, Vase, Double Gourd Shape, Paperweight Pastry Canes, 5 1/2 In.	100.00

*Millefiori means many flowers. It is a type of glasswork popular in
paperweights. Many small flowerlike pieces of glass are grouped together to
form a design.*

Millefiori, see also Paperweight

Millefiori, Bowl, 2 Handled, White, Pastry Canes Multicolored, 6 In.	85.00
Millefiori, Cup & Saucer	50.00
Millefiori, Lamp Base, Blue & Green, Dated 1910, Miniature	200.00
Millefiori, Lamp, Dome Shade, Electric, C.1908, 15 In.	495.00
Millefiori, Paperweight Inkwell	120.00
Millefiori, Paperweight, Blue, Red, Yellow, White Cane Flowers, 2 In.	35.00
Millefiori, Paperweight, Concentric Rows, 1800s, 1 1/8 X 1 1/2 In.	125.00
Millefiori, Paperweight, Egg-Shaped	300.00

Millefiori, Pitcher, Colorful Canes,
Stripled Handle, 7 1/2 In.

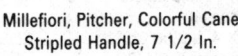

Millefiori, Paperweight, Flowers	12.50
Millefiori, Paperweight, Shape Of Coffee Pot	15.00
Millefiori, Pitcher, Colorful Canes, Stripled Handle, 7 1/2 In. ......*Illus*	125.00
Millefiori, Slipper, High Heel, 5 1/2 In.	135.00
Millefiori, Slipper, Persian Shape	10.00
Millefiori, Vase, 150 Canes, Red, Yellow, Green, Triple Loop Handles, 7 In.	147.00
Millersburg, Bowl, Ice Cream, Peacock, Amethyst	195.00
Millersburg, Bowl, Nesting Swan, Amethyst, 9 1/2 In.Diameter	195.00
Millersburg, Goblet, Buttermilk, Iris, Green	60.00
Millersburg, Goblet, Buttermilk, Iris, Marigold	85.00

Minton china has been made in the Staffordshire region of England from 1793 to the present. Many marks have been used; the one shown dates from c. 1873 to 1911.

Minton, Biscuit Jar, Silver Plate Bale & Lid, Flow Blue Type	32.50
Minton, Bowl, Decorated With Fruits, Inside Pattern, 11 In.Diameter	100.00
Minton, Bowl, Delft Blue & White, 10 1/2 In.	45.00
Minton, Bowl, Gravy, Underplate, C.1870s	35.00
Minton, Bowl, Luster Ware, Multicolored Rooster, Signed, 8 In.Diam.	120.00
Minton, Charger, Cats On Rooftop, 1888-1914 Mark, 14 In.	95.00
Minton, Chocolate Pot, Miniature, 7 X 5 In.	49.00
Minton, Compote, Blue Border, Center Sprays, Signed, 2 3/4 X 8 1/2 In.Diam.	42.00
Minton, Cup & Saucer, Deep Dish, English Soft Paste, C.1828, Marked	40.00
Minton, Dinner Service, Ancestral, Service For 8, 49 Pieces	325.00
Minton, Eggcup, Pink Flowers, Marked	17.50
Minton, Figurine, Clorinda, Parian, Arrow & 3 Dots, John Bell, 1848.14 In.	275.00
Minton, Gravy Boat, Oval, Handles, Lid, Chinese Blossom, C.1863	50.00
Minton, Oyster Plate, Shells On Turquoise Ground, Dated 1872, Signed, 9 In.	50.00
Minton, Pitcher, Raised Cherubs, Lined, Branch Handle, 1894 Mark, 15 1/2 In.	325.00
Minton, Plate, Canada Goose, Gold Border, Artist Signed, 8 In.	42.50
Minton, Plate, Castle Scene, Floral Border, 1836-41, Marked, 10 1/4 In., Pair	75.00
Minton, Plate, Dinner, Blue Border, Gold Edging, 10 1/4 In., Set Of 12	130.00
Minton, Plate, Enameled Floral Center, Gold Edge, 8 In.	20.00
Minton, Plate, Fish, Underwater Scene, Lacy Gold Borders, Signed, 9 In.	25.00
Minton, Plate, Hand-Painted, Alexandria, C.1868, Signed, 9 1/2 In.Diameter	225.00
Minton, Plate, Lattice, Children Center, Signed Boullemeier, 9 1/4 In., Pair	550.00
Minton, Plate, Portrait Center, Gold Rim, Green Crowned Globe, 8 1/2 In.	150.00
Minton, Platter, Butterfly Pattern, November 3, 1868, Marked, 19 1/2 X 15 In.	85.00
Minton, Platter, Dutch Boy & Girl, C.1875, 13 In.	30.00
Minton, Platter, Fish Serving, Majolica, Impressed Minton, 1876, 23 1/2 In.	200.00
Minton, Tile, Anthony & Cleopatra	30.00
Minton, Tile, Girl Picking Flowers, 6 In.	15.00
Minton, Tile, King Lear	30.00
Minton, Tile, Much Ado About Nothing	30.00
Minton, Tile, Romeo & Juliet	30.00
Minton, Toby Jug, Winston Churchill, Man Of The Year, 4 X 4 1/2 In.	30.00
Minton, Tray, Relish, Collection Of Fruit In Center, 6 3/4 In.	75.00
Minton, Urn, Hand-Painted Orchids, Birds, Signed Musfitt, C.1883, 20 In., Pr.	2000.00
Minton, Vase, Bottle, Gold Encrusted Flowers, C.1878, 9 3/4 In.	175.00
Minton, Vase, Brown Ground, Enameled Circles, Green Interior, C.1860, 10 In.	75.00
Minton, Vase, 2 Panel, Bird At Side, Multicolored Rooster, 8 In.	135.00
Minton, Wash Set, Green & White	185.00

Mirror, see Furniture, Mirror

Mocha ware is an English-made product that was sold in America during the early 1800s. It is a heavy pottery with pale coffee and cream coloring. Designs of blue, brown, green, orange, or black or white were added to the pottery.

Mocha, Bowl, Blue, Seaweed, 10 In.	65.00
Mocha, Bowl, Yellow Band, Green Seaweed, 12 1/2 In.Diameter	35.00
Mocha, Bowl, Yellowware, 12 In.Diameter X 5 3/4 In.High, Pair	125.00
Mocha, Chamber Pot, Seaweed	135.00
Mocha, Jug, Cat's Eye, 6 X 4 1/2 In.	145.00
Mocha, Jug, Seashell Design, 6 X 4 1/2 In.	145.00
Mocha, Mug, Earthworm, Brown, Cream & Blue, C.1810, 3 5/8 In.	245.00
Mocha, Mug, Ribs Flanking Gray Band With Circlets, Cylindrical, 19th Century	100.00
Mocha, Mug, Seaweed Decoration, 5 In.	75.00
Mocha, Mug, Transparent Green Glaze Top, Creamware, 4 5/8 In.	255.00
Mocha, Mug, Tree Pattern, Blue Band, 5 X 3 3/4 In.Diameter	65.00
Mocha, Mug, 3 Feather Type Design, Gray-Green Band, 5 X 3 1/2 In.	175.00
Mocha, Pitcher, Banded Yellowware, 7 X 4 3/4 In.	125.00
Mocha, Pot, Pepper, Cat's Eye Pattern, Dome Top, C.1800, 5 In.	235.00

Mold, Candle, see Kitchen, Mold, Candle; Tin, Mold, Candle
Mold, Bullet, see Weapon, Mold, Bullet
Mold, Ice Cream, see Pewter, Mold, Ice Cream

Monart, Vase, Scotch Cluthra, Pink, Goldstone At Top, Signed, 6 In.	95.00
Monmouth, Jar, Beater, Blue Band, Store Advertising	30.00

Monmouth, Urn, Indian Design, Stoneware, 14 1/2 X 24 In.Diameter 150.00
Monmouth, Vase, Blue, Art Deco, 14 In. 225.00
Monroe, Box, Powder, Hobstar & Fluting, Silver Fitted, Marked, 5 3/4 In.Diam. 300.00
  Mont Joye, see Mt.Joye

Moorcroft Pottery was founded in Burslem, England, in 1914 by William Moorcroft. The earlier wares are similar to those made today, but color and marking will help indicate the age.

Moorcroft, Ashtray, Green, Floral Center, Script Signature 23.00
Moorcroft, Base, Lamp, Orchids, Green Initials, Paper Label, 13 In. 155.00
Moorcroft, Basket, Handle, Pomegranate, Signed, Dated 1914 .... 150.00
Moorcroft, Boot, Footed, Wisteria, Signed, 6 X 8 In.Diameter 110.00
Moorcroft, Bowl, Flambe, Marked, 9 1/4 X 4 In. 135.00
Moorcroft, Bowl, Floral, 5 In. 55.00
Moorcroft, Bowl, Footed, Signed, Royal Mark, 2 X 4 1/4 In. 38.00
Moorcroft, Bowl, Leaf & Berry Design, Flambe Glaze, Signed, 4 X 9 1/2 In. 110.00
Moorcroft, Bowl, Miniature, Embossed Flowers, 4 3/4 X 1 1/2 In. 75.00
Moorcroft, Bowl, Pomegranate, Pedestal Base, 4 X 9 3/4 In.Diameter 98.00
Moorcroft, Bowl, Raised Pansies On Blue, Green Inside, Marked, 4 X 1 1/2 In. 40.00
Moorcroft, Bowl, Raised Pansies, Blue, Green, Marked, 4 In. 35.00
Moorcroft, Bowl, Red & Yellow Hibiscus, Off White, 10 In. 60.00
Moorcroft, Bowl, Script Signed, C.1945, 3 X 9 1/2 In.Diameter 75.00
Moorcroft, Bowl, 2 Handled, Spanish, Green Mark, 7 In. 265.00
Moorcroft, Box, Lidded, Dahlias In Pastels, Signed, 6 In.Diameter 130.00
Moorcroft, Butter Pat, Pansy On Cobalt, Mark, 3 In. 7.50
Moorcroft, Candlestick, Floral, Yellow, Green, Signed, Pair, 3 1/2 Inches 45.00
Moorcroft, Candlestick, Florian Ware, MacIntyre Mark, Pair, 9 3/4 In. 550.00
Moorcroft, Cooler, Wine, Pappy Design, Macintyre Mark, 6 3/4 In. 400.00
Moorcroft, Inkwell, Pomegranates, Blue, Burslem, Marked 65.00
Moorcroft, Jar, Ginger, Pomegranate, Hand-Painted, C.1914, Signed, 6 X 5 In. 350.00
Moorcroft, Jug, Cobalt Blue, Pink & White Flowers, 4 1/2 In. 60.00
Moorcroft, Lamp, Blue & Green Flowers, Signed, 27 In., Pair 350.00
Moorcroft, Lamp, Script Signature, Paper Label 95.00
Moorcroft, Match Striker, Pomegranate & Grapes, Marked, 1914, 2 1/2 In. 50.00
Moorcroft, Plate, Heart Shape, Floral, Blue, 5 In. 18.00
Moorcroft, Pomegranate, Green Signature, 4 1/2 In. 85.00
Moorcroft, Rose Bowl, Miniature, Poppies, 3 1/4 X 3 1/2 In. 75.00
Moorcroft, Salt, England, 3 In. 16.00
Moorcroft, Vase & Candlesticks, Salmon Flowers, Signed, Vase, 8 1/4 In. 105.00
Moorcroft, Vase & Candlesticks, Vase, 8 1/4 In., Candlesticks, 3 1/2 In. 115.00
Moorcroft, Vase, Blue & White, 3 1/2 In. 65.00
Moorcroft, Vase, Blue Background, Signed, 9 In. 70.00
Moorcroft, Vase, Blue, Green Grapes, 3 1/2 In. 65.00
Moorcroft, Vase, Bulbous, Tapered Neck, Rouge, Flower Design, Signed, 12 In. 75.00
Moorcroft, Vase, Burslem Cornflower, Marked, C.1914, 6 1/2 X 3 1/2 In. 450.00
Moorcroft, Vase, Cobalt Blue, Pomegranates & Grapes, 7 1/2 In. 70.00
Moorcroft, Vase, Cornflower Pattern, Mottled Green, C.1916, 13 X 8 In. 1300.00
Moorcroft, Vase, Flambe, Bulbous Bottom, Long Neck, 9 1/2 X 17 1/2 In. 180.00
Moorcroft, Vase, Flambe, Scenic, Landscape, C.1921, Marked, 10 1/2 X 5 1/2 In. 510.00
Moorcroft, Vase, Fruit, Leaves & Pomegranates, Royal Blue, Marked, 4 In. 115.00
Moorcroft, Vase, Lemons, Plums, Cobalt Glaze, Sterling Rim, 5 In. 80.00
Moorcroft, Vase, Miniature, Pansies, 3 1/2 X 2 3/4 In., Pair 95.00
Moorcroft, Vase, Pansies On Blue Ground, 7 In. 95.00
Moorcroft, Vase, Pansies On White Ground, MacIntyre Mark, 5 3/4 In. 155.00
Moorcroft, Vase, Pink & Purple Flowers, Signed, Blue Script, 5 In. 55.00
Moorcroft, Vase, Pomegranate & Pansy, 7 1/4 In. 70.00
Moorcroft, Vase, Pomegranate Trimmed Inside, Green, Script Signed, 4 1/2 In. 90.00
Moorcroft, Vase, Pomegranate, Bulbous, 7 In. 88.00
Moorcroft, Vase, Pomegranate, Green, Signature, 4 1/2 In. 85.00
Moorcroft, Vase, Pomegranate, Green, Signed, 8 In. 98.00
Moorcroft, Vase, Purple, Pink, Original Paper Label, Signed In Script, 6 In. 45.00
Moorcroft, Vase, Raised Pansies, 2 In. 34.00
Moorcroft, Vase, Stick, Florian, Green, Dated 1898, Signed, 10 In. 240.00
Moorcroft, Vase, Wisteria On Cobalt, 7 In. 70.00
Moorcroft, Vase, Yellow Flower, Cream Ground, Paper Label, 5 1/4 In. 36.50
Moorcroft, Vase, 2-Handled, Poppies On Inside, C.1897, Signed, 5 X 3 1/4 In. 425.00

Moore, Vase, Beige & Tan Marbleized, Signed, 7 In.	152.00
Moore, Vase, Blue Dragons On Beige, Signed, 5 3/4 In.	152.00

Moriage is used to identify Japanese pottery to which a raised overglaze decoration has been added. This relief ornamentation may be elaborate. The term applies to the style or technique.

Moriage, Candlestick, Green Putti, Leaves & Medallions, 11 In.	195.00
Moriage, Cup & Saucer, Bouillon, Enameling, Scarlet Rose Design	45.00
Moriage, Cup & Saucer, Drago On Gray Ground, 1 1/2 In.	9.50
Moriage, Ewer, Green Ground, Orchids, 8 In.	210.00
Moriage, Ewer, Green Slip, Medallions, 7 In.	125.00
Moriage, Ewer, Jewels & Beads, Magenta Flowers, Petal Medallions, 6 In.	125.00
Moriage, Humidor, Floral Panels, Red Accents, Green, 6 1/2 In.	108.00
Moriage, Muffineer, Deep Red Roses, 4 X 3. 1/2 In.	45.00
Moriage, Pitcher, Lip & Body Beaded & Jeweled, Medallions	200.00
Moriage, Plate, Flowers & Gold, 9 1/2 In.	78.00
Moriage, Plate, Long Tail Bird, 7 1/4 In.	48.00
Moriage, Plate, Scalloped, Green Slip, 3 Medallions, 10 1/2 In.	95.00
Moriage, Platter, Turned Edges, Butterflies, 9 In.	62.00
Moriage, Saki Set, Jeweled Dragon, Swirled Ground, Lithophane In Cups	45.00
Moriage, Tea Set, Dragon Ware, 4 Cups & Saucers, 6-7 1/2 In.Plate, 17 Piece	150.00
Moriage, Tea Set, Sugar & Creamer, Covered Teapot, Slip Decoration	225.00
Moriage, Tea Set, 6 Cups & Saucers, Gold Mark, 15 Piece	80.00
Moriage, Teapot, Miniature, Dragon Ware	10.00
Moriage, Teapot, Sugar & Creamer, Medallions In Burgundy, White Trim	150.00
Moriage, Vase, Bolted, Green, Red Flowers, 15 In.	100.00
Moriage, Vase, Camel, 7 In.	60.00
Moriage, Vase, Flowers & Leaves, 8 X 16 In.Diameter, Pair	150.00
Moriage, Vase, Gold Encrusted, Jeweling In Gold, Sawtooth Top, 15 In.	200.00
Moriage, Vase, Gray Ground, Dragon On Front, Enamel Eyes, M In Wreath, 13 In.	175.00
Moriage, Vase, Handled, Swan On Water, Green Ground, 7 In.	240.00
Moriage, Vase, Heart Shaped, Wisteria, 10 In.	165.00
Moriage, Vase, Moon, Green Dotted Ground, Loop Handles, 7 1/2 In.	125.00
Moriage, Vase, Owls, Mottled Green Ground, C.1930, 12 In.	95.00
Moriage, Vase, Swan On Water, Green Ground, 7 In.	260.00
Moriage, Vase, Winter Scene Top Half, Oriental Handles, Gold Beading, 6 In.	70.00

Mosaic Tile Company of Zanesville, Ohio, was started by Karl Langenbeck and Herman Mueller in 1894. Many types of plain and ornamental tiles were made until 1959. The company closed in 1967.

Mosaic Tile Co., Ashtray	28.00
Mosaic Tile Co., Tile, General Pershing, Original Box	50.00
Mosaic Tile Co., Tile, Lincoln, White On Blue	25.00
Mosaic Tile Co., Woodrow Wilson Profile	40.00

Moser glass was made by Ludwig Moser and Sohne, a Bohemian glasshouse founded in 1857. Art Nouveau type glassware and iridescent glassware were made. The firm is still working.

Moser, Atomizer, Clear To Green At Top, All Over Gold, 4 1/2 In.	50.00
Moser, Atomizer, Paneled, Cranberry, Signed	25.00
Moser, Bell, Colors & Clear	24.50
Moser, Bell, Milk Glass Overlay, Enamel Decoration	150.00
Moser, Bottle, Acorn Decorated, Amberina, Enameled Signature, 8 1/2 In.	850.00
Moser, Bottle, Blue, Decorated, Fluted Top, Stopper, Signed, 7 1/2 In.	85.00
Moser, Bottle, Perfume, Blue Cut To Clear, Jewelled Top, Signed, 7 In.	425.00
Moser, Bottle, Perfume, Clear To Yellow, Intaglio Cut, 4 In.	30.00
Moser, Bottle, Perfume, Gold Band Of Nymphs, Green, Signed	100.00
Moser, Bottle, Perfume, Intaglio Cut Stopper, Diamond Shaped Body, 5 In.	195.00
Moser, Bottle, Scent, Amethyst, Signed, 4 In.	65.00
Moser, Bottle, Scent, Brass Cover, Stopper, Cranberry, Signed, 3 3/4 In.Long	95.00
Moser, Bowl, Acorn Decorated, Yellow To Blue, Signed, No.D.180, 2 1/2 In.	1100.00
Moser, Bowl, Alexandrite, Coin Gold, White Enamel, Signed, 4 1/2 In.Diameter	150.00
Moser, Bowl, Amethyst To Clear, Gilt, Enameled Flowers, 8 1/2 X 3 1/2 In.	125.00
Moser, Bowl, Black Amethyst, Gold Band, 4 1/2 X 10 1/2 In.	65.00
Moser, Bowl, Clear, Intaglio Cut, Signed, 12 X 7 In.	75.00
Moser, Bowl, Enameled, Peach, Green Scalloped Rim, 13 In.	345.00

Moser, Bowl, Finger, Matched Underplate, Square Top, Pedestal, Signed 250.00
Moser, Bowl, Finger, Underplate, Pedestal, Enameled Design, Karlsbad 450.00
Moser, Bowl, Gold Crown Inside Center, 8 In. 495.00
Moser, Bowl, Gold Trim, 5 1/2 X 9 In.Diameter 75.00
Moser, Bowl, Mayonnaise, Underplate & Ladle, Gold Engraved Band, Marked 75.00
Moser, Bowl, Underplate, Thumbprint Design, Bowl, 2 X 4 1/2 In.Diameter 35.00
Moser, Box, Enamel On Clear Glass, 4 Ormolu Feet, Karlsbad, 5 1/4 X 7 In. 299.00
Moser, Box, Gold Decoration, Blue, 2 1/2 X 3 1/4 In. 260.00
Moser, Box, Gold Decoration, Blue, 4 X 3 In. 295.00
Moser, Box, Hinged, Enameled Flowers On Lid, Signed, 3 X 4 In. 110.00
Moser, Box, Jewel, Beaded Enameling & Medallions, 4 Feet, 5 X 5 1/2 In.Diam. 225.00
Moser, Box, Jewel, Hinged, Enamel, Blue Satin Frosted, Signed, 4 1/4 X 5 In. 70.00
Moser, Box, Patch, Hinged, Enameling & Gold, Signed 195.00
Moser, Chalice, Applied Enamel, Gold Trim, Green, Signed, 14 In. 250.00
Moser, Compote, Covered, Footed, Cased Glass, Label, 8 X 6 In. 159.00
Moser, Compote, Cranberry, Cut Overlay, Moser Label, 9 X 6 In. 155.00
Moser, Compote, Scallop Rim, Gold Trim, 8 X 6 In.Diameter 395.00
Moser, Cruet, Acorn Design, Blue To Clear, Enameled, Signed, 6 1/2 In. 975.00
Moser, Cruet, Green To Clear, Gold Band, Enameled Scroll, Signed, 10 1/2 In. 150.00
Moser, Cruet, Oil & Vinegar, Enameled, Amber, Swan Stopper, Signed 375.00
Moser, Cup & Saucer, Demitasse, Raised Gold Work, Signed 125.00
Moser, Decanter, Amethyst To Clear, Cased Stopper, Enameled Flowers, 8 In. 250.00
Moser, Decanter, Cut & Gravic, Signed, 14 In., Pair 185.00
Moser, Decanter, Cut To Cranberry, Decorated, Overlay, 15 X 7 In. 210.00
Moser, Decanter, Matching Stopper, Handle, Enamel Over Cranberry, 14 In. 750.00
Moser, Decanter, Seven Wines, Swirl Stem, Ruby With Gold, Signed 250.00
Moser, Decanter, Stopper, Gold Handle, Enamel Over Cranberry, 14 In. 950.00
Moser, Dish, Enameled Flowers & Birds, Ruby, Signed, 5 X 6 In. 115.00
Moser, Dresser Set, Cut Emerald Green Lip, Signed, 3 Piece 200.00
Moser, Dresser Set, 2 Perfumes, Box, Brass Frame, White Enameling, Signed 310.00
Moser, Dresser Set, 3 Perfume Bottles, Hinged Box, Gold Enamel, Signed 335.00
Moser, Ewer, Applied Handle, All Over Gold, Signed 4206 D.8 Moser, 4 5/8 In. 495.00
Moser, Glass, Juice, Applied Acorns, Signed, Gold Mark, 3 7/8 In., Set Of 4 .... 700.00
Moser, Glass, Juice, Cranberry, Enamel Decoration, 3 1/2 X 2 In. 95.00
Moser, Glass, Wine, Clear Stem, Gold Knobs, Gold Trim, Pair 95.00
Moser, Glass, Wine, Gold Swag & Lion's Head, Set Of Six 200.00
Moser, Goblet, Gold Lions, Scroll & Swag 50.00
Moser, Goblet, Gold Swag, Lion's Head, Set Of 6 .... 200.00
Moser, Goblet, Intaglio Cut Roses, Gold Rim, Wafer Foot, Signed, 9 In. 226.00
Moser, Goblet, Wine, Cranberry, Gold Leaves, Gold Rim, 6 1/2 In. 65.00
Moser, Goblet, Wine, Gold Leaves, Clear Top, Gold Rim, Signed, 6 1/2 In. 85.00
Moser, Lamp, Greek Warrior Scene, Wood Base, Patina 325.00
Moser, Liquor Set, Round Tray, Decanter, 2 Glasses, Enameled, Signed 595.00
Moser, Match Holder, Alexandrite, Square Top, Bulbous, Honeycomb, 3 In. 550.00
Moser, Mug, Alexandrite, Bird In Flight, Marsh Plants, Signed, 4 1/2 In. 110.00
Moser, Mug, Etched Scenic Design, Alexandrite, Signed 90.00
Moser, Perfume, Finger, Gold & Enamel Decoration, Amber, 3 X 1 1/4 In. 140.00
Moser, Perfume, Gold Decoration, Cranberry, 4 1/2 X 2 1/4 In. 230.00
Moser, Pitcher, Water, Gold Acid Cut, Trefoil Mouth, Cobalt Blue, 8 1/2 In. 225.00
Moser, Plate, Overlay Cut, Ice Blue, Footed, Label, 9 1/2 In. 159.00
Moser, Plate, Porcelain, Blue, Green & Gold, C.1914, 10 1/2 In., Pair 125.00
Moser, Rose Bowl, Gold Decoration, Cranberry, 5 1/2 X 5 1/2 In. 310.00
Moser, Rose Bowl, Gold Warrior Band, Amber, 4 X 4 1/2 In. 225.00
Moser, Salt & Pepper, 1 Amber, 1 Blue, Applied Fish, Worms, Flowers 225.00
Moser, Tumbler, Applied Acorns, Cranberry Glass, Enameled, 4 In. 225.00
Moser, Tumbler, Cranberry, Enamel Floral, Gold Edge, 4 In. 60.00
Moser, Tumbler, Cut In Strawberry Diamond, Bull's-Eye, Flutes, Gilt Band 50.00
Moser, Tumbler, Enameled, Applied Luster Acorns, Signed, 3 7/8 In. 595.00
Moser, Tumbler, Enameled, Green 15.00
Moser, Tumbler, Etched, Deer In The Woods, Carlsbad, 3 1/2 In. 12.50
Moser, Tumbler, Grape Leaf Enameling, Applied Grapes, Signed, 4 In. 65.00
Moser, Tumbler, Stag & Doe, Trees & Foliage, Signed, 6 1/4 In. 110.00
Moser, Vase, Acid Etched, Enameled, Classical Figures, C.1900, 14 1/2 In. 250.00
Moser, Vase, Alexandrite, Flaring Top, 7 X 4 In.Diameter 185.00
Moser, Vase, Alexandrite, Silver Sleeve, Signed, 12 1/2 In. 385.00
Moser, Vase, Amber, Gold Etched Warrior Band, 8 1/2 In. 65.00

Moser, Vase, Amethyst, Intaglio Cut, Applied Carved Flower, 6 1/4 In.	425.00
Moser, Vase, Bird & Acorn, Pink Opalescent, Amber Feet & Trim, Signed, 8 In.	1195.00
Moser, Vase, Bud, Marquetry, Intaglio Flowers, Clear Ground, 5 In.	350.00
Moser, Vase, Clear To Green Gold Decoration, Signed, 16 In., Pair	275.00
Moser, Vase, Clear To Green, Floral Intaglio Cut, 10 In.	75.00
Moser, Vase, Coin Gold Flowers, Enameling, Signed, Karlsbad, 9 In.	235.00
Moser, Vase, Crackle Glass, 2 Handled, Enameled Fish, 7 In.	200.00
Moser, Vase, Cranberry, Enameled, Applied Grapes, 18 In.	600.00
Moser, Vase, Crystal Paneled, Cut Satin Intaglio, Signed, 6 In.	110.00
Moser, Vase, Cut Paperweight, Gold, Clear To Purple, 9 X 3 In.	140.00
Moser, Vase, Dancing Nudes, Green Jade, Signed, 10 In.	190.00
Moser, Vase, Emerald Green To Clear, Pilsner Shaped, Signed, 12 1/2 In.	135.00
Moser, Vase, Enamel Decoration, Applied Blue Lizard, Amber, 6 1/2 X 2 In.	295.00
Moser, Vase, Enameled & Applied Grapes, Cranberry, 18 In.	450.00
Moser, Vase, Enameled Flowers, Amethyest, Gold Base, Signed, 14 In.	265.00
Moser, Vase, Enameled Insects, Applied Acorns, Bulbous Neck, 4 1/2 In.	225.00
Moser, Vase, Enameled, Gold Trim, Amethyst Background, 12 In.	135.00
Moser, Vase, Enameling, Applied Grapes, Pedestaled, Cranberry, 18 In.	375.00
Moser, Vase, Gold Grecian Figures, Cobalt Blue, Czechoslovakia, 10 1/2 In.	60.00
Moser, Vase, Gold Stem, 13 Gold Bees Overall, Paper Label, 18 In.	450.00
Moser, Vase, Golden Amber Ground, Scenic, Cameo, Signed, 11 1/2 In.	685.00
Moser, Vase, Green Shamrocks, Gold On Front, Signed Karlsbad, 5 3/4 In.	60.00
Moser, Vase, Green, Silver Deposit, 8 In.	85.00
Moser, Vase, Hunting Figures, Cobalt Blue, Gold Ground, Signed, 9 1/2 In.	98.00
Moser, Vase, Intaglio Carved, Base Inscribed Moser Karlsbad, 1900s, 21 In.	275.00
Moser, Vase, Intaglio In 3 Colors, Clear Ground, Signed, 12 In., Pair	1850.00
Moser, Vase, Karlsbad, Amber Acid Cutting, Scenic, 24K Gold Band, Signed	3000.00
Moser, Vase, Lemon Colored Crackle, Handled, Enamel Fish, 7 In.	165.00
Moser, Vase, Lilies, Cranberry Glass, Signed, 10 In., Pair	380.00
Moser, Vase, Overlay Glass, Amber Foot, Gold Trim, 4 5/8 X 1 3/4 In. Diameter	175.00
Moser, Vase, Panels Of Enameled Flowers, Gilt Collar, Signed, 16 In.	225.00
Moser, Vase, Paperweight, Crystal Bottom, Gold Enameling, Signed, 5 1/2 In.	85.00
Moser, Vase, Peachy Pink, Opalescent, Signed, 4 1/8 In., Pair	175.00
Moser, Vase, Smoke, Enamel Decoration, Applied Teardrops, 7 X 6 In.	275.00
Moser, Vase, Yellow, Intaglio Cut, Signed, 2 3/4 X 3 In.	50.00
Moser, Whiskey Taster, Amethyst, Enameled Grape Clusters & Leaves, Gold	25.00
Moser, Wine Set, Six 3 1/4 In. Tumblers, Decanter, Signed, 14 In.	125.00
Moser, Wine, Enameled Cherub Faces, Gold Overlay, 5 In.	110.00
Moser, Wine, Gold Swag & Lion's Head, Set Of 6	185.00

Moss rose china was made by many firms from 1808 to 1900. It refers to any china decorated with the moss rose flower.

Moss Rose, Coffee Pot, Haviland, 8 In.	60.00
Moss Rose, Creamer, Gold Edge	25.00
Moss Rose, Pitcher, Milk, Ironstone, Crazed, 7 In.	27.50
Moss Rose, Tea Pot, Gold Edge	45.00

Mother-of-pearl glass, or pearl satin glass, was first made in the 1850s in England and in Massachusetts. It was a special type of mold-blown satin glass with air bubbles in the glass, giving it a pearlized color.

Mother-of-Pearl, Satin Glass, see also Satin Glass, Smith
Brothers, Tiffany Glass, etc.
Mother-of -Pearl, see also Pearl

Mother-Of-Pearl, Bowl, Finger, Quilted, Ruffled Top, 3 In.	50.00
Mother-Of-Pearl, Bowl, Ruffled Tricorn, 2 1/2 X 7 In.	225.00
Mother-Of-Pearl, Bride's Basket, Ruffled, Frame	495.00
Mother-Of-Pearl, Pitcher, Melon Ribbed, Diamond-Quilted, Blue, 5 In.	75.00
Mother-Of-Pearl, Pitcher, Raindrop, 7 In.	165.00
Mother-Of-Pearl, Pitcher, Water, Diamond-Quilted, C.1885, 8 In.	350.00
Mother-Of-Pearl, Plate, Herringbone Pattern, Blue, Applied Feet, 4 3/4 In.	80.00
Mother-Of-Pearl, Rose Bowl, American Beauty Rose, White Lining, 2 3/4 In.	325.00
Mother-Of-Pearl, Rose Bowl, Butterscotch Raindrop, Crimped Rim	145.00
Mother-Of-Pearl, Rose Bowl, Crimped Top, Diamond-Quilted, Webb, 2 3/8 In.	295.00
Mother-Of-Pearl, Rose Bowl, Crimped Top, White Interior Casing, 3 1/2 In.	150.00
Mother-Of-Pearl, Rose Bowl, Diamond-Quilted, Applied Burmese Berries	100.00
Mother-Of-Pearl, Rose Bowl, Diamond-Quilted, 6 Crimp Top, 2 1/2 In.	300.00

Mother-Of-Pearl, Rose Bowl, Egg Shape, Herringbone, White Lining, 3 1/2 In. 195.00
Mother-Of-Pearl, Rose Bowl, Miniature, Crimped Top, 2 X 2 5/8 In. 275.00
Mother-Of-Pearl, Rose Bowl, Ten Crimp Top, White Lining, 2 3/4 X 3 3/4 In. 325.00
Mother-Of-Pearl, Salt & Pepper, Silver Tops, Satin Glass, 3 1/2 In. 275.00
Mother-Of-Pearl, Saltshaker, Christmas, Marked Brass Top With Agitator 165.00
Mother-Of-Pearl, Screen, 4 Panel, Flower-Filled Vases, Birds, 26 X 27 In. 125.00
Mother-Of-Pearl, Sugar, Creamer & Spooner, Diamond-Quilted, Pink, Set 895.00
Mother-Of-Pearl, Tankard, Diamond-Quilted, Pink, Enameled Flowers, 9 1/2 In. 750.00
Mother-Of-Pearl, Tumbler, Diamond-Quilted, Yellow 145.00
Mother-Of-Pearl, Vase, Applied Camphor Footed Base, Satin Glass, 6 In. 115.00
Mother-Of-Pearl, Vase, Apricot Herringbone, Flattened Oval Shape, 7 In. 225.00
Mother-Of-Pearl, Vase, Bud, Herringbone, Blue, 6 In. 95.00
Mother-Of-Pearl, Vase, Bulbous Body, Diamond-Quilted, Satin Glass, 7 1/4 In. 110.00
Mother-Of-Pearl, Vase, Bulbous, Pink Quilted, Goose Neck, 9 In. 135.00
Mother-Of-Pearl, Vase, Butterscotch, Rain Drop, Satin Glass, 6 1/2 In. 125.00
Mother-Of-Pearl, Vase, Celery, Silver Holder, Diamond-Quilted, 8 1/4 In. 495.00
Mother-Of-Pearl, Vase, Diamond-Quilted, Frosted Amber, 2 Sided, 7 3/4 In. 265.00
Mother-Of-Pearl, Vase, Diamond-Quilted, Ruffled Top, Satin Glass, 6 5/8 In. 145.00
Mother-Of-Pearl, Vase, Herringbone, Ruffled Top, Blue, 3 1/2 In.Diameter 265.00
Mother-Of-Pearl, Vase, Herringbone, Ruffled Top, Satin Glass, 9 1/2 In. 150.00
Mother-Of-Pearl, Vase, Herringbone, Ruffled Top, 6 3/4 In. 345.00
Mother-Of-Pearl, Vase, Herringbone, Satin Glass, White Lining, 6 In. 175.00
Mother-Of-Pearl, Vase, Peach, Diamond-Quilted, White Lining, 7 In. 125.00
Mother-Of-Pearl, Vase, Raindrop Pattern, White, Bulbous Base, 11 In. 210.00
Mother-Of-Pearl, Vase, Ruffled Top, Satin Glass, White Lining, 5 7/8 In. 175.00
Mother-Of-Pearl, Vase, Ruffled, Diamond Quilted, Rose Satin, 9 5/8 In. 195.00
Mother-Of-Pearl, Vase, Satin Glass Handle, Diamond-Quilted, Dimpled, 7 In. 450.00
Mother-Of-Pearl, Vase, White Lining, Diamond-Quilted, Pearl Satin, 6 5/8 In. 145.00
Mother-Of-Pearl, Vase, 4 Petal Top, White Lining, Diamond-Quilted, 7 In. 225.00
Moustache Cup, see Mustache Cup

Mont Joye is an enameled cameo glass made in the late nineteenth and the twentieth centuries by Saint-Hilaire Touvoir de Varraux and Co. of Pantin, France. This same company produced De Vez glass.

Mt.Joye, Bowl, Enameled Poppies, Gold Leaves, Signed, 10 In.Diameter 239.00
Mt.Joye, Bowl, Green Mica Glass Ground, Gold Enamel, Signed, 4 In. 145.00
Mt.Joye, Vase, Cameo, Floral, French, Signed, 9 3/4 X 4 3/8 In. 295.00
Mt.Joye, Vase, Cameo, Frost Acid Cut, Green Ground, Gold Flowers, 5 In. 170.00
Mt.Joye, Vase, Cameo, Twist, Enameled, Poppy, Gilt, Signed, 5 X 2 In. 450.00
Mt.Joye, Vase, Clear Crystal, Enameled Flowers, Leaves, Signed, 10 In. 185.00
Mt.Joye, Vase, Irises, Gold Acid Border, Purple, Yellow, White, Signed, 7 In. 175.00
Mt.Joye, Vase, Orchid Flowers, Gold Leaves, Pink, 9 1/2 In. 210.00
Mt.Joye, Vase, Raised Chrysanthemum, Green Tinted, Gilt, Etched, 13 1/2 In. 225.00
Mt.Joye, Vase, Vertical Sided, Frosted, Gold Enamel, Gold Mark, 6 In. 250.00

Mt.Washington Glass was made at the Mt.Washington Glass Co. located in New Bedford, Massachusetts. Many types of art glass were made there from 1850 to the 1890s.

Mt.Washington, see also Burmese, Crown Milano

Mt.Washington, Barrel, Biscuit, Uranium Glass Decorated, Enamel Dots, 7 In. 850.00
Mt.Washington, Basket, Looped Handle, Turquoise Interior, 10 1/2 In. 165.00
Mt.Washington, Biscuit Jar, Blue Dot Florals, Pink & White, Pair 145.00
Mt.Washington, Biscuit Jar, Squatty, Ribbed, Silver Fittings, 7 In.Diameter 210.00
Mt.Washington, Bottle, Perfume, Morning Glory Bouquet, 4 1/2 In. 75.00
Mt.Washington, Bowl, Burmese, 3 1/4 In. 250.00
Mt.Washington, Bowl, Tricornered, Burmese, 6 In. 225.00
Mt.Washington, Box, Dresser, Hand-Painted, Blue 15.00
Mt.Washington, Box, Patch, Satin Finish, 2 In. 75.00
Mt.Washington, Box, Powder, American Hobnail, Canary Tint, C.1848, Lid 135.00
Mt.Washington, Castor, Pickle, Bird Finial, Quadrangle Plate Holder 425.00
Mt.Washington, Cracker Jar, Enameled Flowers, Satin Glass, 5 1/2 In.Diam. 98.00
Mt.Washington, Cracker Jar, Enameling Outlined In Gold, Pairpoint Silver 325.00
Mt.Washington, Cracker Jar, Melon Ribbed, Panels Of Pansies 255.00
Mt.Washington, Cracker Jar, Opalescent Glass, Silver Plate Rim, Bail, Cover 110.00
Mt.Washington, Cracker Jar, Pansy Design, Silver Plated Cover, Rim 210.00
Mt.Washington, Cracker Jar, Ribbed, Orchids, Silver Plated Top 285.00

Mt.Washington, Cracker Jar, Silver Plate Top, Enameled Flowers	160.00
Mt.Washington, Cracker Jar, Uranium, Enameled, Gold Trim, Marked, 6 3/4 In.	950.00
Mt.Washington, Creamer, Burmese, Hollow Handle, Acid Finish	350.00
Mt.Washington, Cruet, Acid Cut	600.00
Mt.Washington, Cruet, Burmese, Glossy	700.00
Mt.Washington, Egg, Flat End, Pair	82.50
Mt.Washington, Holder, Egg, Original Tops	37.50
Mt.Washington, Jar, Cracker, Satin Glass, Burmese Coloring, Signed In Cover	225.00
Mt.Washington, Jar, Pickle, Verona, Diamond Quilt, Gold Spider Mums, Frosted	190.00
Mt.Washington, Jug, Syrup, Lusterless White, Pewter Lid, Dated	90.00
Mt.Washington, Lamp, Burmese, Top & Bottom Light Up, Signed, 15 1/2 In.	2100.00
Mt.Washington, Muffineer, Egg	86.00
Mt.Washington, Muffineer, Pewter Top, Peach Ground, 4 1/2 X 3 1/4 In.	154.00
Mt.Washington, Mustard, Spoon, Silver Flip-Top, Yellow To White, 3 In.	75.00
Mt.Washington, Plate, Burmese, Forget-Me-Nots In Center, Sticker, 11 1/2 In.	575.00
Mt.Washington, Plate, Hand-Painted Flowers, 7 In.	10.00
Mt.Washington, Plate, Hand-Painted Rose, Lusterless White, 10 In.	20.00
Mt.Washington, Plate, Hand-Painted, Cat Face, 4 3/4 In.	35.00
Mt.Washington, Rose Bowl, Enameled Daisy Spray, Blue	135.00
Mt.Washington, Rose Bowl, Purple & Yellow Pansies, 7 X 6 1/4 In.Diameter	108.00
Mt.Washington, Rose Jar, Mushroom Form, Hand-Painted, 3 1/2 X 6 1/2 In.	950.00
Mt.Washington, Salt & Pepper, Burmese, Silver Holder, Acid Finish, 4 In.	350.00
Mt.Washington, Salt & Pepper, Crown Milano	70.00
Mt.Washington, Salt & Pepper, Egg Shaped, Yellow & Blue Flowers, Pair	70.00
Mt.Washington, Salt & Pepper, Figural, Floral, Opaque White, Original Tops	98.00
Mt.Washington, Salt & Pepper, Floral, Pewter Tops, Satin, Pair	87.00
Mt.Washington, Salt & Pepper, Laydown Egg, Forget-Me-Not Design	95.00
Mt.Washington, Salt & Pepper, Melon Shape, Silver Plate Holder	295.00
Mt.Washington, Salt & Pepper, Tomato, Original Tops, Enameled	75.00
Mt.Washington, Salt & Pepper, 6 Section, Squat, Pewter Tops	135.00
Mt.Washington, Salt Shaker, Egg Shaped, 2 1/2 In., Pair	125.00
Mt.Washington, Salt, Egg, Single	50.00
Mt.Washington, Salt, Lusterless, Pewter Top, Enameled Flowers, White, Pair	65.00
Mt.Washington, Salt, Master, Melon Rib, Buff Ground, Richmond, Indiana	60.00
Mt.Washington, Saltshaker, Burmese, Hand-Painted Flowers, Barrel Shape	295.00
Mt.Washington, Saltshaker, Egg In Blossom, Original Top, Pansies, Pink Base	36.00
Mt.Washington, Saltshaker, Egg Shaped, Pastel Ground, Original Top	30.00
Mt.Washington, Saltshaker, Egg, Blue, Pink Flower	40.00
Mt.Washington, Saltshaker, Egg, Flat End, Pewter Top, Original Flowers	35.00
Mt.Washington, Saltshaker, Egg, Queen's Ware Enameling, Paper Label	225.00
Mt.Washington, Saltshaker, Egg, White, Morning Glory	35.00
Mt.Washington, Saltshaker, Fig Shape, Hand-Painted, Original Tops	75.00
Mt.Washington, Saltshaker, Fig, Cranberry, Dotted Decoration	100.00
Mt.Washington, Saltshaker, Fig, Glossy, Yellow Flower	75.00
Mt.Washington, Saltshaker, Fig, Red Cranberry, Florals	145.00
Mt.Washington, Saltshaker, Palmer Cox Brownies On Sides, Original Top	71.50
Mt.Washington, Saltshaker, Pink Wild Roses, Ball Shaped, Pair	75.00
Mt.Washington, Saltshaker, Squat, Hand-Painted, Melon	40.00
Mt.Washington, Saltshaker, Tomato, Blue, Cobalt & Pink Enameling	48.00
Mt.Washington, Saltshaker, Tomato, Blue, Leaf & Berry	35.00
Mt.Washington, Saltshaker, Tomato, Original Top, Purple	48.00
Mt.Washington, Saltshaker, Tomato, Original Top, Yellow With Enameling	48.00
Mt.Washington, Saltshaker, Yellow & White Flower, Barrel Satin, Ribbed	70.00
Mt.Washington, Sauce, Burmese, Acid Finish	115.00
Mt.Washington, Shade, Melon Ribbed, 2 Owls On Branches, 4 1/2 In.	95.00
Mt.Washington, Sugar & Creamer, Blown Out Flowers, Silver Handles & Rims	100.00
Mt.Washington, Sugar Shaker, Cranberry, Enameled Decoration, Original Top	595.00
Mt.Washington, Sugar Shaker, Egg Shaped, Satin Glass, 4 1/2 In.	135.00
Mt.Washington, Sugar Shaker, Egg, Pink To White, Dotted Flower Design	125.00
Mt.Washington, Sugar Shaker, Egg, White, Blue & White Dotted Flowers	120.00
Mt.Washington, Sugar Shaker, Erie Twist, Original Top	165.00
Mt.Washington, Sugar Shaker, Fig, Clear Frosted Blue, Flowers	275.00
Mt.Washington, Sugar Shaker, Floral Enamel, Burmese Color	165.00
Mt.Washington, Sugar Shaker, Melon Ribbed, Embossed Basket On Top, 4 In.	235.00
Mt.Washington, Sugar Shaker, Melon Shape, Hand-Painted, 1 1/2 X 2 1/4 In.	60.00
Mt.Washington, Sugar Shaker, Ribbed, Blue Flower, World's Fair 1893	150.00

Mt.Washington, Sugar Shaker, Ribbed, Enameled Blossoms, Original Top	295.00
Mt.Washington, Sugar Shaker, Tomato, Blue & White Dotted Flowers	195.00
Mt.Washington, Sugar Shaker, Tomato, Blue & White, Pink Flower	185.00
Mt.Washington, Sugar Shaker, Tomato, Enameled In Blue & Orange, Silver Top	200.00
Mt.Washington, Sugar Shaker, Transparent Coloring	450.00
Mt.Washington, Sugar Shaker, White, Pink Flower, Ribbed, 5 1/2 In.	140.00
Mt.Washington, Sugar, Bail & Lid, Burmese	225.00
Mt.Washington, Sugar, Blue, White, Enameled Daisies, Egg Shape, Signed	125.00
Mt.Washington, Sugar, Burmese, Pansies, Pewter Top, Egg Shape, 4 1/2 In.	175.00
Mt.Washington, Toothpick, Burmese, Bulbous Bottom, Square Top	235.00
Mt.Washington, Toothpick, Enameled Floral, Crimped Top, Swirled Rib, 2 In.	85.00
Mt.Washington, Toothpick, Fig Mold, Hand-Painted, Lobed Top, Opaque Glass	150.00
Mt.Washington, Toothpick, Hat Shape, White Satin, Polished Pontil	145.00
Mt.Washington, Toothpick, Pink & Yellow, 4 Sided, Burmese, 2 In.	336.00
Mt.Washington, Toothpick, Rose Berries, Green Leaves, Acid Finish	275.00
Mt.Washington, Toothpick, White Satin Hat, Polished Pontil	145.00
Mt.Washington, Tumbler, Inverted Thumbprint, Amberina	125.00
Mt.Washington, Vase, Blue Diamond-Quilted Satin, Melon Ribbed Base, 7 In.	145.00
Mt.Washington, Vase, Burmese, Kate Greenaway Girls On Fence, 7 In.	3800.00
Mt.Washington, Vase, Burmese, Pinch-Pleated Top, 17 In., Pair	895.00
Mt.Washington, Vase, Colored Birds, 7 In.	162.00
Mt.Washington, Vase, Cut Velvet, Turquoise, White Lining, 3 In.Diameter	160.00
Mt.Washington, Vase, Cylinder Top, Dimpled Bottom, Beading At Top, 10 In.	200.00
Mt.Washington, Vase, Double, Cut Velvet, Ribbed, Blue, 3 X 2 3/8 In.Diam.	145.00
Mt.Washington, Vase, Fish Among Seaweed, Crackle, 2 Handled, 7 In.	135.00
Mt.Washington, Vase, Melon Ribbed, Roses Outlined In Gold, 4 3/4 In.	110.00
Mt.Washington, Vase, Mum, Signed Napoli, 17 In.	400.00
Mt.Washington, Vase, Pink Rain Drop Satin, Melon Ribbed, 7 In.	145.00
Mt.Washington, Vase, Stick, Acid Finish, Burmese, 10 In.	395.00
Mt.Washington, Vase, Trumpet, Ruffled & Crimped Top, 8 In.	350.00
Muffineer, Flint, Cut, Plated Top	55.00
Muffineer, Garlands Of Daisies, Roses, Sterling Silver, Gorham	70.00
Muffineer, Spanish Lace, Cranberry, 5 In.	65.00

Mulberry Ware, see Staffordshire

Muller Freres, French for Muller Brothers, made cameo and other art glass from the early 1900s to the late 1930s. Their factory was first located in Luneville and later moved to Croismaire, France.

Muller Freres, Cameo, Vase, Purple Iris, Light Ground, Signed, 7 In.	295.00
Muller Freres, Cameo, Vase, Triple Gourd Shape, Teal Ground, 10 1/2 In.	425.00
Muller Freres, Lamp, Hanging Shades, Art Deco Wrought Iron, Signed, 15 In.	450.00
Muller Freres, Lamp, Luneville, Orange Mottled, Signed Base & Shade, 12 In.	600.00
Muller Freres, Lamp, Table, Double, Hanging Shades, Cut Leaf & Berry, Signed	900.00
Muller Freres, Light, Night, Luneville, Butterflies Holding Shade, 5 1/2 In.	150.00
Muller Freres, Vase, Art Deco, Acid Cut, Smoke Color, 11 1/2 X 12 In.Diam.	350.00
Muller Freres, Vase, Bud, Cameo, Irises Cut Down To Foot, Polished, 7 In.	450.00
Muller Freres, Vase, Bulbous Shape, Mourning Scene, 7 1/4 In.	395.00
Muller Freres, Vase, Cameo, Frosted, Blue Birds In Flight, Signed, 10 X 8 In.	175.00
Muller Freres, Vase, Cameo, Red Butterflies, Luneville, Signed, 14 1/2 In.	950.00
Muller Freres, Vase, Cameo, Triple Gourd Shape, Blue, Purple, French, 11 In.	475.00
Muller Freres, Vase, Cameo, Triple-Gourd Shape, Passion Flowers, 10 1/2 In.	650.00
Muller Freres, Vase, Cameo, 8 Parrots, Each Different, Acid Cut, 7 1/2 In.	750.00
Muller Freres, Vase, Marbleized Satin Glass, Blues, Greens, Pink, 11 X 6 In.	110.00
Muller Freres, Vase, Scenic Cut Cameo, 8 1/2 In.	169.00
Muller Freres, Vase, 3 Acid Cuttings, Flowers, Frosted, Signed, 7 1/4 In.	1100.00
Muller, Freres, Vase, Cameo, Luneville, Native Stalking Elephant, 5 3/4 In.	325.00
Muller, Freres, Vase, Iris On Light Ground, Polished, 7 In.	325.00
Music, Accordion, Italian, Mother-Of-Pearl Keys, Carrying Case	300.00
Music, Accordion, Italian, 90 Treble, 5 Stops, 120 Bass With 1 Stop	250.00
Music, Autoharp, Zimmerman, C.1894	55.00
Music, Autoharp, Zimmerman, Original Cardboard Box, Tuning Key, 1894	49.00
Music, Autoharp, Zimmerman, 2 Sheets Of Music	70.00
Music, Automaton, Striking Bells, Rabbit .... *Illus*	850.00
Music, Autopiano, Coinola, Type O, Tinky-Tink	2800.00
Music, Banjo Mandolin, Gibson, Original Case, C.1915	155.00
Music, Banjo Mandolin, Leather Case, Ivory Keys, Mother-Of-Pearl Frets	95.00

Music, Banjo, Folk, 6 String, Oval .... 60.00 To 75.00
Music, Banjo, Maggie & Jiggs, Adult 47.50
Music, Banjo, Tenor, Golden Dragon, 1932 Epiphone 2000.00
Music, Banjo, Weymann, Tenor, Wooden Top 100.00
Music, Box, Adler, Upright, 22 M Discs 2500.00
Music, Box, Bell & Drum Cylinder, Rosewood Case, 10 Tune, 26 X 12 X 10 In. 2250.00
Music, Box, Bird In Cage Swings, Jewelry 150.00
Music, Box, Bremond, Hidden Drum & Bell Box, 10 1/2 In. 925.00
Music, Box, Bremond, Hidden Drum & Bell Box, 11 In. 325.00

Music, Automaton, Striking Bells, Rabbit

(See Page 325)

Music, Box, Carousel, Miniature Of Adult Ride, C.1890, 39 X 27 X 20 In. 7500.00
Music, Box, Carousel, Wooden, 33 Animals, Panels, Mirrors, Crank, 12 X 14 In. 6000.00
Music, Box, Case, Flat Front, 15 1/2 In.Disc Changer, Oak 695.00
Music, Box, Chalet, Cylinder, Time & Strike Clock, 8 Tune, 24 X 1i X 18 In. 1500.00
Music, Box, Cylinder 6500.00
Music, Box, Cylinder Piccolo Zither Movement, 37 In. 3200.00
Music, Box, Cylinder, Maple Panels, Rosewood Borders, Swiss, 1800s, 31 1/2 In. 2000.00
Music, Box, Cylinder, 12 Tune, Gutta-Percha Scene, 7 1/2 X 28 1/2 In. 3750.00
Music, Box, Cylinder, 3 Comb, Inlay Top, Matching Table, 37 In.Long 4500.00
Music, Box, Disk Type, 19 Disks, 20th Century, 9 1/2 X 6 X 5 1/2 In. 300.00
Music, Box, Empress, Concert Grand, Double Comb, Mahogany Case, 23 Discs 4750.00
Music, Box, Forte, Tune Sheet, 17 In.Cylinder 1200.00
Music, Box, George Baker Co., 10 Tune, Orchestra Music, Drum & Bell 2000.00
Music, Box, Graphophone, Busy Bee, 5 Cylinder Records 325.00
Music, Box, Graphophone, Columbia, Type B2 .... 525.00
Music, Box, Heart Shape, I Love You Truly, Jewelry, Victorian, 3 In. 125.00
Music, Box, Imperial Symphonium, Key, 15-15 In.Discs.20 X 23 X 10 In. 1950.00
Music, Box, Inlaid Brass Medallion, Single Comb, 8 Tunes, 19 X 8 X 6 1/2 In. 650.00
Music, Box, Jewelry, Bird In Cage Swings 150.00
Music, Box, Jewelry, Heart Shape, I Love You Truly, Victorian, 3 In. 125.00
Music, Box, Jewelry, Victorian, 4 Tune Opera, Hand Carved, 5 X 5 In. 125.00
Music, Box, Lecoultre, Brecht, Rosewood, 6 Tunes, 3 Striker Bells, C.1850 .... 2500.00
Music, Box, Mandolin, I Opera & Waltz Cylinder, 43 X 16 X 11 In. 950.00
Music, Box, Mermod Freres, Marche Cylinder Box, 31 X 13 X 10 In. 1950.00
Music, Box, Mermod Freres, 11 In.Cylinder, Inlaid Case, 8 Tunes .... 875.00 To 975.00
Music, Box, Mira, Fifteen 15 1/2 In.Discs 2250.00
Music, Box, Olympia, Double Comb, Mahogany Case, 12 Tune Discs, 15 1/2 In. 2250.00
Music, Box, Olympia, Mahogany Finish, 77 Teeth Comb, 1898, 15 1/2 In.Disc 1500.00
Music, Box, Paillard, Zither Attachment, 4 Changeable Cylinders, 40 In. 2500.00
Music, Box, Polyphon, Coin Operated, Extra Disc, Walnut, 19 1/2 Feet 3000.00
Music, Box, Polyphon, Serpentine Case, Style 41R, 8 1/4 In. 500.00
Music, Box, Polyphon, Transfer Design On Lid, 16 Discs, C.1897 .... 350.00
Music, Box, Polyphon, 12 Discs, German, C.1850, 5 3/4 X 10 X 8 3/4 In. 850.00
Music, Box, Regina Sublima, No.1236, Motor & Coin Chute 4000.00
Music, Box, Regina, Automatic Changer, Mahogany, 12 Discs, 27 In. 9950.00
Music, Box, Regina, Coin Operated, Double Comb, Golden Oak Case, 15 1/2 In. 1995.00
Music, Box, Regina, Coin-Operated, Oak, 15 1/2 In. 1950.00
Music, Box, Regina, Double Comb, Mahogany Case, 15 Discs, 12 1/4 In. 1200.00
Music, Box, Regina, Double Comb, Mahogany Case, 8 Discs, 11 In. 1050.00
Music, Box, Regina, Double Comb, Short Bedplate, Oak, 25 Discs, 15 In. 2250.00
Music, Box, Regina, One Comb, Style 11a, Golden Oak Case, 12 Discs, 15 1/2 In. 1450.00
Music, Box, Regina, Parlor Model, Automatic Changer, 12 Discs, 15 1/2 In.Disc 8495.00
Music, Box, Regina, Serpentine, Bedplate & Sliding Shelf, 20 3/4 In. 4250.00
Music, Box, Regina, Short Bed Plate, Banjo Attachment, 20 3/4 In. 3500.00

Music, Box, Regina, Table Model, Golden Oak, 8 1/2 In.	995.00
Music, Box, Regina, Table Model, Serpentine Case, Cupola Lid, 20 3/4 In.	4000.00
Music, Box, Regina, 20 Single Comb, Oak Case, 8 Discs, 11 In.	1000.00
Music, Box, Regina, 3 Dancing Girls, 15 1/2 In.Disc, Coin Operated, 30 In.	2800.00
Music, Box, Reginaphone, Style 240, Carved Lion's Heads	3900.00
Music, Box, Singing Bird, Snuff, Mechanical, C.Bruguier, 1788-1862, Signed	6500.00
Music, Box, Singing Bird, Tortoise Shell Case, C.1800s	1250.00
Music, Box, Stella, 25 Steel Discs	1000.00
Music, Box, Swiss, Brass Cylinder, 8 Tunes, Inlaid Mahogany Case, Tune Card	375.00
Music, Box, Swiss, Cylinder, Bells, Insects, Drum, Inlaid Lid, 9 X 12 X 23 In.	2495.00
Music, Box, Swiss, Darling I Am Growing Old, Walnut, 4 X 8 In.	195.00
Music, Box, Swiss, Inlaid, Double Lid, 8 Tunes, 18 In.	1250.00
Music, Box, Swiss, Napoleon, 12 Tunes, 28 X 15 In.	1250.00
Music, Box, Swiss, Orchestrion, 48 Airs, Tune Card, 6 Cylinders	5900.00
Music, Box, Swiss, 10 Tune Cylinder, Rosewood Case, Indicator & Tune Card	1200.00
Music, Box, Swiss, 3 Bells, 6 In.Cylinder, 8 Tunes	1500.00
Music, Box, Symphonion, Double Comb, Cherry, 18 In.Discs, 11 X 21 X 27 In.	2200.00
Music, Box, Symphonion, Double Comb, 7 Discs, 10 1/2 In.	750.00
Music, Box, Table Model, Serpentine Case, Raised Cupola Lid, 20 3/4 In.	4000.00
Music, Box, Zither Tremolo Cylinder, Flower Inlay, 6 Tunes, 18 X 9 X 6 In.	900.00
Music, Box, 3 Dancing Girls, Coin Slot, 15 1/2 In.Disc, 3/ X 42 X 13 In.	2800.00
Music, Box, 4 Tune Opera, Hand-Carved, Jewelry, Victorian, 5 X 5 In.	125.00
Music, Box, 8 Tune, Inlaid Case, 3 Bells, 13 3/4 X 9 1/2 X 8 1/4 In.	725.00
Music, Bugle, Military, Copper & Brass, 19th Century	75.00
Music, Bugle, U.S. Regulation, Brass, C.1920	38.50
Music, Calliope, Tangley, 43 Note, Spencer Blower, Manual & Automatic	8800.00
Music, Clarinet, Ebony, Marked Buffet, Silver Keys, Paris, Original Box	225.00
Music, Clarinet, Geib, Case	80.00
Music, Clarinet, Othello, Ebony, Silver Trim On Case	35.00
Music, Coronet, Brass, Original Velvet Lined Case	50.00
Music, Disc, Regina, Ave Maria, 27 In.	100.00
Music, Disc, Regina, Monastery Bells, 27 In.	60.00
Music, Disc, Regina, William Tell Overture, 27 In.	50.00
Music, Graphophone, Columbia, Type Q, Small Horn	185.00
Music, Graphophone, Columbia, 2 Minute, Oak Case, Daisy Horn	350.00
Music, Graphophone, Cylinder, Penny Operated, Oak, 1897, Decals	2600.00
Music, Guitar, Fender, 8 String, Country Western, Steel, Pedals, Case	195.00
Music, Harmonica, Borrah Minnevitch, Harmonica Rascals, Boxed, 1934	15.00
Music, Harmonica, Butterfly, Occupied Japan	12.50
Music, Harmonica, Hohner, Little Lady	6.00
Music, Harmonica, Hohner, Marine Band Tremolo, 7 X 2 In.	10.00 To 25.00
Music, Harmonica, Hohner, Plays Both Sides, 7 In.	15.00
Music, Harmonica, Hohner, The Auto	37.00
Music, Harmonica, Hohner, 64 Chronomica, Germany	40.00
Music, Harmonica, Mutt & Jeff, 1923	25.00
Music, Harmonica, Panama, Pacific Exposition, 1915, Original Box	20.00
Music, Horn, Berliner, Zinc	175.00
Music, Horn, Morning Glory For Old Phonograph, Tin	50.00
Music, Hurdy Gurdy, Cocchi-Bacigalupe & Graffigna, 23 Note, Inlaid Front	5250.00
Music, Hurdy Gurdy, Crown, Oak, Cylinders	600.00
Music, Hurdy Gurdy, 32 Note, Extra 49 Note Keyboard, Una-Fon-Deagan	1000.00
Music, Jukebox, A.J.I., Model A	425.00
Music, Jukebox, Ami, Model C, C.1949	500.00
Music, Jukebox, Bing Crosby Junior, 78 R.P.M., Counter Top	250.00 To 295.00
Music, Jukebox, Edison Eclipse, Coin Operated, Single Cylinder, 1905	2000.00
Music, Jukebox, Link Piano Co., Autovox, 10 Turntables	5000.00
Music, Jukebox, Mills, Empress	700.00
Music, Jukebox, Mills, Ferris Wheel, 12 Selections, C.1930	450.00 To 1750.00
Music, Jukebox, Mutoscope, 5 Reel Selectomatic, Wood Cabinet	1850.00
Music, Jukebox, Rock-Ola, Model 1422, 78 R.P.M., 1946	1395.00
Music, Jukebox, Rock-Ola, Model 1428	350.00 To 795.00
Music, Jukebox, Seeburg Barrel 148, Blonde	375.00
Music, Jukebox, Seeburg G, Model B	225.00 To 250.00
Music, Jukebox, Seeburg, Bear Gun	500.00
Music, Jukebox, Seeburg, Coon Hunt	250.00
Music, Jukebox, Seeburg, Model B	225.00 3250.00

Music, Jukebox, Seeburg, Model 147S, Matching Wall Speakers, C.1947		1000.00
Music, Jukebox, Seeburg, Model 148M		900.00
Music, Jukebox, Seeburg, Model 8800		850.00
Music, Jukebox, Seeburg, Mystic Pen		750.00
Music, Jukebox, Seeburg, R-100, 45 Selections, 1955		475.00
Music, Jukebox, Wurlitzer, Model 50		1850.00
Music, Jukebox, Wurlitzer, Model 61		900.00
Music, Jukebox, Wurlitzer, Model 71, Counter Top		1250.00
Music, Jukebox, Wurlitzer, Model 412, C.1936	250.00 To	1000.00
Music, Jukebox, Wurlitzer, Model 616	300.00 To	350.00
Music, Jukebox, Wurlitzer, Model 780E		3000.00
Music, Jukebox, Wurlitzer, Model 800	800.00 To	1550.00
Music, Jukebox, Wurlitzer, Model 1015, Original Plastic	2000.00 To	2600.00
Music, Jukebox, Wurlitzer, Model 1250		295.00
Music, Jukebox, Wurlitzer, Model 1400		350.00
Music, Jukebox, Wurlitzer, Model 503, Wood Cabinet		850.00
Music, Jukebox, Wurlitzer, Model 700	750.00 To	1175.00
Music, Jukebox, Wurlitzer, Model 750	900.00 To	1500.00
Music, Jukebox, Wurlitzer, Model 780, Wood Cabinet, Wheel In Center		1850.00
Music, Mandolin, Ditson Empire, Ivory Keys, Mother-Of-Pearl Inlaid, C.1915		85.00
Music, Mandolin, Washburn		120.00
Music, Medlodeon, Stilwell & Genung, Ivory Keys & Buttons, C.1850		2500.00
Music, Melodeon, C. & S.Sawyer & Co., Rosewood, C.1850		1500.00
Music, Melodeon, Jewett & Goodman, Rosewood		550.00
Music, Melodeon, Mason & Hamlin		450.00
Music, Melodeon, R.G.Green, Rosewood, Chicago		1500.00
Music, Melodeon, Rosewood, R.G. Green, Chicago		1500.00
Music, Melodeon, Whitney Slayton, 6 Octaves, 4 Stops, Rosewood		1000.00
Music, Mouth Organ, Horner, Chrome Finish, Bird's-Eye Wood, Germany		14.00
Music, Mouth Organ, Sweet Potato, Signed, Austria, 5 1/2 In.		16.00
Music, Nickelodeon, Capital, Violin Pipes		5995.00
Music, Nickelodeon, Cremona, Coin Operated, Bench		3500.00
Music, Nickelodeon, Cremona, Mandolin Attachment, Oak, 3-10 Tune Rolls		2950.00
Music, Nickelodeon, Cremona, Style A, Art Glass, 7 Rolls	5000.00 To	5500.00
Music, Nickelodeon, Cupid, Coinola, Mandolin & Xylophone, 36 X 21 X 54 In.		5500.00
Music, Nickelodeon, Electrova, 12 Rolls		3900.00
Music, Nickelodeon, Mills Troubador, Ferris Wheel Type		2000.00
Music, Nickelodeon, Mira, 20 Discs, 9 1/4 In.		795.00
Music, Nickelodeon, National Electric Changer	2500.00 To	5000.00
Music, Nickelodeon, Seeburg L, Cabinet Style		5500.00
Music, Nickelodeon, Seeburg, Kt Orchestrion		9800.00
Music, Nickelodeon, Seeburg, Style A		4500.00
Music, Nickelodeon, Western Electric, Cabinet Style		4850.00
Music, Nickelodeon, Western Electric, Derby		7600.00
Music, Orchestrion, Coin Operated, Beveled Glass Ovals, 10 Tunes		4800.00
Music, Orchestrion, Losche, Jazzband		7900.00
Music, Orchestrion, 48 Airs, Tune Card, 6 Cylinder, Organ, Drum, Bells, Swiss		590.00
Music, Organ, Ami Rivenc, Bell Box, 6 Tune		1500.00
Music, Organ, Ariston, Hand Crank, 25 Discs		495.00
Music, Organ, Band, Limonair Freres, Child's Carousel, Ornate Facade		6500.00
Music, Organ, Band, North Tonawanda, Brass		9500.00
Music, Organ, Band, Wurlitzer, Degan Unafon, 1911, Tandem Mounted		5500.00
Music, Organ, Bruder, 59 Keyless Duplex Roll Operated		8500.00
Music, Organ, Chautauqua Roller	375.00 To	650.00
Music, Organ, Chicago Organ Co., Pump, Cottage, Round Stool		5000.00
Music, Organ, Concert Roller, Oak, 15 X 18 X 12 In.	245.00 To	795.00
Music, Organ, Concert Roller, 6 Cobs		450.00
Music, Organ, Crown, Reed, Carved		5000.00
Music, Organ, Estey, Church, Electric, Double Keyboard, Wooden Works		2500.00
Music, Organ, Estey, Pump Bellows, Carved Spool Trim, Mahogany, 6 1/2 Ft.Tall		375.00
Music, Organ, Gem Roller, Labeled Sears Roebuck-Chicago		500.00
Music, Organ, Gem Roller, Patented 1887, 8 Extra Musical Cobs		285.00
Music, Organ, Gem Roller, 10 Cobs	425.00 To	495.00
Music, Organ, Gem Roller, 5 Cobs		300.00
Music, Organ, Gem Roller, 6 Cobs	375.00 To	1300.00
Music, Organ, Gem Roller, 8 Cobs, C.1887		350.00

Music, Organ, Grand, Roller, 6 Cobs 1300.00
Music, Organ, Hamilton, Pump, Walnut, Ornate 600.00
Music, Organ, Kimball, Walnut, 5 Ft.8 In. X 48 1/2 In. 350.00
Music, Organ, Mason & Hamlin, Chapel, 19 Stops, Quartered Oak, 72 X 70 In. 2000.00
Music, Organ, Mason & Hamlin, No.2, American Reed Organ, Cabinet 1200.00
Music, Organ, Mechanical Orguinette Company, C.1877, Walnut 325.00
Music, Organ, Miller, Oil Lamp Holders, Spindle Shelves, Dated 1892 .... 210.00
Music, Organ, Paper Roller, Mechanical Orguinette Company, 1877 .... 325.00
Music, Organ, Pipe, Aeolian Duo Art, 100 Rolls, Harp, 2 Manual Console 4750.00
Music, Organ, Pipe, Aeolian, Hand-Carved Oak, Matching Bench 5000.00
Music, Organ, Pipe, Kimball, 11, Drums, Bells, Marimbas 2500.00
Music, Organ, Preacher's, Folds Into Compact Carrying Case, Oak 125.00
Music, Organ, Pump, Beckwith, Walnut, 6 Octaves, 17 Stops, 4 Reeds 2000.00
Music, Organ, Pump, Estey, Bellows, Carved Trim, Mahogany, 6 1/2 Ft.Tall 375.00
Music, Organ, Pump, Estey, Candle Stands, Beveled Mirrors, Oak, 1900s 1000.00
Music, Organ, Pump, Kimball .... 500.00 To 1000.00
Music, Organ, Pump, Kimball, 1889 .... 500.00 To 1000.00
Music, Organ, Pump, Mason & Hamlin Co., Walnut, Fretwork, 1800s, 41 X 51 In. 275.00
Music, Organ, Pump, William & Son, 52 Key 500.00
Music, Organ, Reed, Estey, Carved, Solid Walnut, Two Manual 2000.00
Music, Organ, Reed, Seybold 800.00
Music, Organ, Reed, Sterling Piano Company, Derby, Connecticut, C.1900 .... 350.00
Music, Organ, Street, Carl Frei, 132 Pipes, Coliola Rolls, On Cart 8500.00
Music, Organ, Tournaphone Music Co., Hand, 5 Rolls 650.00
Music, Organ, Treadle, Waters, No.32068, Ivory Keys, Cherry Wood 1200.00
Music, Organ, W.W.Kimball, Pump, Walnut, Hand-Carving, Dated 1887, Stool 1875.00
Music, Organ, Waters, Parlor, Built 1870 .... 1350.00
Music, Organette, Celestina, Paper Roll 425.00
Music, Organette, Melodia 300.00

*The Phonograph, invented by Thomas Edison in the 1880s, has been made by
many firms.*

Music, Phonograph, Amberola, Model 30, Matching Cylinder Cabinet 400.00
Music, Phonograph, Amberola, Model 75, 12 Edison, 4 Minute Cylinders 300.00
Music, Phonograph, Columbia Q, Cylinder, Oak Case .... 175.00 To 250.00
Music, Phonograph, Columbia, Serpentine Case, Mahogany, Matching Wood Horn 1000.00
Music, Phonograph, Columbia, 2 Minute Cylinders, Brass Bell Horn, 1897 .... 375.00
Music, Phonograph, Edison Amberola, Matching Cylinder Cabinet 500.00
Music, Phonograph, Edison Amberola, Model 75, 4 Minute Cylinders 300.00
Music, Phonograph, Edison, Concert, Model A 1500.00
Music, Phonograph, Edison, Cylinder, Model 75, 3 Drawers 400.00
Music, Phonograph, Edison, Cylinder, Morning Glory Horn, Stand .... 375.00 To 450.00
Music, Phonograph, Edison, Cylinder, Type D.C. 150.00
Music, Phonograph, Edison, Fireside, Two 4 Minute Records, Horn .... 300.00 To 375.00
Music, Phonograph, Edison, Home, Morning Glory Horn 450.00
Music, Phonograph, Edison, Model Triumph, Model O Reproducer, Bammer 650.00
Music, Phonograph, Edison, Standard Home, Horn .... 275.00 To 400.00
Music, Phonograph, Edison, Standard, C Reproducer, Red Horn .... 325.00 To 335.00
Music, Phonograph, Edison, Standard, Reproducer, 14 In.Brass Bell Horn 250.00
Music, Phonograph, Edison, Standard, Suitcase Type, 14 In.Horn 350.00
Music, Phonograph, Edison, Standard, 20 In.Brass Bell Horn, 29 In.Long 265.00
Music, Phonograph, Edison, Triumph, 4 Minute Record, Morning Glory Horn 495.00
Music, Phonograph, Grafanola Deluxe, Lion Head Case 1750.00
Music, Phonograph, Keen-O-Phone, Mahogany Horn In Lid, 1913 .... 995.00
Music, Phonograph, Phonola, Portable 45.00
Music, Phonograph, Polly Oscillator, Portable, Folding Cardboard Horn 110.00
Music, Phonograph, Victor I, Horn 425.00
Music, Phonograph, Victor M, Horn .... 450.00 To 600.00
Music, Phonograph, Victor 222 .... 450.00
Music, Phonograph, Victor, Model Z, Pewter Horn 550.00
Music, Phonograph, Victor, Orthaphonic, Windup, 1921 .... 35.00 To 45.00
Music, Phonograph, Victrola, Edison, Standard, Hombe & Amberola, No.30 .... 225.00
Music, Phonograph, Victrola, Portable, No.2, 1906 .... 75.00 To 110.00
Music, Phonograph, 78S, Portable, Built In Horn, 15 X 15 X 9 In. 125.00
Music, Pianino, Seeburg, 5 Cent, 10 Tune Roll, Oak, 21 X 48 X 62 In. 5000.00
Music, Piano, Ampico, Chickering, Parlor Grand, Ivory Keys, Dated 1832 .... 2500.00

Music, Piano, Ampico, Fischer, 1930, 5 Feet, 4 In. 8800.00
Music, Piano, Ampico, Grand, Haines Bros., Reproducing, Upright 1650.00
Music, Piano, Ampico, Grand, Lacquered, Matching Bench, 5 Feet, 4 In. 6750.00
Music, Piano, Ampico, Marshall & Wendel, Upright 1750.00
Music, Piano, Ampico, Reproducing, Keyboard & Paper Rolls, Cherry 1200.00
Music, Piano, Baby Grand, Oriental Style, Red, Bench, London, D.Forty, 41 In. 5000.00
Music, Piano, Baldwin, No.79744, Baby Grand, Ebonized 2100.00
Music, Piano, Barrel Cart, Plays 6 Christmas Songs, Triangle & Drum 950.00
Music, Piano, Barrel, Coin Operated, 10 Play, England, 1890-1900 .... 1000.00
Music, Piano, Barrel, French, Automatic, 10 Tunes, 1890-1910 .... 3500.00
Music, Piano, Barrel, 8 Tunes 900.00
Music, Piano, Chickering Ampico, Model A, Upright 1500.00
Music, Piano, Coin Operated, Plays 9 Percussion Instruments 2500.00
Music, Piano, Coin Operated, Reproduction, 10 Instruments 2300.00
Music, Piano, Conway, Reproducing, Upright, 88 Note 550.00
Music, Piano, Cunningham-Welte, Reproducing, Upright, Mahogany, Bench 3750.00
Music, Piano, Drum, Coin Operated, Plays 10 Songs, C.1880 .... 3500.00 To 5600.00
Music, Piano, Dubois & Warriner, Petite Grand, Rosewood, Inlaid 2000.00
Music, Piano, F.G.Otto & Sons, Disc Operated, 12 Original Discs 3500.00
Music, Piano, Fischer, C.1920, 6 Feet, 2 In. 4000.00
Music, Piano, Grand, Henry Miller, C.1881, Stool 2000.00
Music, Piano, Grand, Knabe, Rosewood, Moorish Design, Square, C.1850 .... 950.00
Music, Piano, Grand, Knabe, Square, Scroll Legs 900.00
Music, Piano, Grand, Knabe, 1923, 5 Feet, 8 In. 3800.00
Music, Piano, Grand, Mahogany, Steinway, C.1891 .... 7500.00
Music, Piano, Grand, Marshall & Wendell, Square, Carved Legs 1000.00
Music, Piano, Grand, Mason & Hamlin, Ampico, 5 Feet, 8 In. 9800.00
Music, Piano, Grand, New England Piano Co., Carved, Mahogany, Square 1800.00
Music, Piano, Grand, Rosewood, Fruit Carved Legs, Steinway & Sons, C.1871 .... 3200.00
Music, Piano, Grand, Square, No.16935, Rosewood, Built 1875, Swivel Stool 8000.00
Music, Piano, Grand, W.P.Haines, New York, Rosewood, Carved 3250.00
Music, Piano, Grand, Weber Duo Art, Art Case, Inlaid, Music Desk, 5 Ft. 6 In. 5500.00
Music, Piano, Grand, Welte Mignon Reproducer, Art Case, Matching Bench 0500.00
Music, Piano, Grand, 1917 Weber, Player 2000.00
Music, Piano, Grande, E.G.Harrington & Company, Upright, 1875 .... 700.00
Music, Piano, Grobesteen & Fuller, 1871, Rosewood, Square Grand 2800.00
Music, Piano, Haines Bros., Reproducer Player, Ampico Marquie, Walnut 4500.00
Music, Piano, Haines Brothers, Ampico Reproducing Grand, Bench, 75 Rolls 5500.00
Music, Piano, Hohler & Campbell, 61 Note, Upright, Chinese Art Case, Bench 2495.00
Music, Piano, Hupfeld Concerto, Mechanical, Coin Operated 2500.00
Music, Piano, Hupfeld, Concerto, Coin Operated, Operates On Book Music 2500.00
Music, Piano, Kimball & Welte, Reproducer Grand, Rolls .... 2500.00 To 3500.00
Music, Piano, Kranich & Bach, Welte-Mignon Mechanism, 5 Feet, 4 In. 3700.00
Music, Piano, Manx, Baillie Scott Design, C.1869, 46 X 56 X 26 1/2 In. 7500.00
Music, Piano, Marshall & Wendell, Grand Ampico, 5 Feet 5000.00
Music, Piano, Mason & Hamlin, Concert Grand, Fruitwood, 6 Feet, 2 In. 4950.00
Music, Piano, Mason & Hamlin, Grand, Reproducer Ampico A, 300 Rolls 7500.00
Music, Piano, Mathushek, Square, Grand, Rosewood 1800.00
Music, Piano, Meister, Upright, Matching Bench, 1904, Oak 650.00
Music, Piano, Player, Baldwin 850.00
Music, Piano, Player, Chien, 4 Rolls 150.00
Music, Piano, Player, Grenell Pianola, Bench, Oak, 1924 .... 1895.00
Music, Piano, Player, Hupfeld Phonola 1500.00
Music, Piano, Player, Little Empress, 10 Style C Rolls 3500.00
Music, Piano, Player, Stark, Burled Walnut, Bench, Simplex Action 2250.00
Music, Piano, Player, Weaver, E.P.Johnson Co., Ottawa, Illinois 600.00
Music, Piano, Schomacker Welte, Upright 525.00
Music, Piano, Seeburg, A Roll, Xylophone, Art Glass 5900.00
Music, Piano, Seeburg, 5 Cent, 10 Tune Roll, Oak, 21 X 49 X 62 In. 5000.00
Music, Piano, Seeburg, 51 Note, Non-Mechanical, Matching Bench 1495.00
Music, Piano, Steinway & Sons, Square, Grand, Bench, 80 1/2 X 40 X 38 In. 1000.00
Music, Piano, Steinway Duo-Art, Cabinet, Bench, Player, 5 Feet, 8 In. 6600.00
Music, Piano, Steinway Grand, Square, 1884, 39 1/2 X 79 1/2 X 36 In. 1500.00
Music, Piano, Steinway 1857, Rosewood Cabinet, Square 3500.00
Music, Piano, Steinway, Upright, Electric, No.168762 .... 8000.00
Music, Piano, Steinway, Vertigrand, 1908, Bird's-Eye Maple Case, 1908 .... 6995.00

Music, Piano, Stroud, Duo Art, Upright, 1928	2195.00
Music, Piano, Thomas Tomkison, George III, Soho, Mahogany, 1810, 33 X 67 In.	1000.00
Music, Piano, Upright, J.H.Lee, Storage Bench, Rosewood Case, English	1195.00
Music, Piano, Weber Duo Art, Reproducing, Art Case, 5 Feet, 6 In.	5500.00 To 7000.00
Music, Piano, Weber, Carved Legs, C.1875, Black Walnut, Square	1250.00
Music, Piano, Weber, Carved Legs, Walnut, Square, C.1878	1800.00
Music, Piano, Wurlitzer, No.1015	1200.00
Music, Piano, Wurlitzer, Red, Gold, Chinese Taste, Figures, 1930, 41 X 40 In.	750.00
Music, Pianola, Weber Duo Art, Mahogany, Motor In Separate Case, 72 In.	8500.00
Music, Polyphon, Disc Storage Cabinet Below, Double Combination, 19 3/4 In.	8500.00
Music, Polyphon, Double Combination, 23 Discs, 24 3/4 In.	3000.00
Music, Polyphon, Excelsior Model, Walnut, 10 Discs, 15 1/2 In.	1850.00
Music, Pump Organ, Beckwith, Walnut, 6 Octaves, 17 Stops, 4 Reeds	2000.00
Music, Radio & Phonograph, United Unidyne, 4 Tube Radio With Crank	200.00
Music, Radio, Scott, Turntable, 1932	285.00
Music, Radio, Shape Of Official League Baseball	155.00
Music, Radio, WEKZ, Microphone Shaped, 14 In.	50.00
Music, Record Player, Ami, Model B, 40 Selections, 45 R.P.M., 1947	850.00
Music, Record Player, Rockola, Model 1428, 20 Selections, 45 R.P.M., 1948	1250.00
Music, Record Player, Wurlitzer, Model 2500, 100 Selections, 45 R.P.M., 1961	350.00
Music, Record Player, Wurlitzer, Model 600, 24 Selections, 1938	850.00
Music, Record, Santa's Child, 1948, 8 In.	8.00
Music, Record, Sweet September, Al Jolson, Columbia	5.00
Music, Reginaphone, Columbia, Lion Heads, Table Model, 15 1/2 In.	3850.00
Music, Reginaphone, Phonograph Conversion, Serpentine Front, 15 1/2 In.Disc	2000.00
Music, Sheet, Amelia Earhart's Last Flight, 1939	15.00
Music, Sheet, Barney Google & Spark Plug	7.00 To 10.50
Music, Sheet, Blue Hawaii, Elvis Presley	10.00
Music, Sheet, Bromo Seltzer, C.1890	9.95
Music, Sheet, Chant Of The Jungle, 1929, Joan Crawford Cover	5.00
Music, Sheet, Charles Magnus, Lithographed	20.00
Music, Sheet, Curly Top's Birthday	20.00
Music, Sheet, Down In Old Nantucket, 1913	15.00
Music, Sheet, G.I.Blues, Elvis Presley	10.00
Music, Sheet, Going My Way, Bing Crosby	5.00
Music, Sheet, Henry's Made A Lady Out Of Lizzi	5.00
Music, Sheet, I May Be Gone For A Long Long Time, 1917	4.00
Music, Sheet, I Want To Go Home, World War I	15.00
Music, Sheet, I Want You, I Need You, I Love You, Elvis Presley	10.00
Music, Sheet, If I Had My Way, Bing Crosby, 1939	10.00
Music, Sheet, If I Had My Way, Picture Of Bing Crosby, 1939	10.00
Music, Sheet, Little Nemo	40.00
Music, Sheet, Love Me, Elvis Presley, 1954	10.00
Music, Sheet, Maggie, Jiggs & Rosie, 1914	12.00
Music, Sheet, Moxie Song	10.50
Music, Sheet, My Daddy's Coming Home, W.W.I	15.00
Music, Sheet, Over There, Rockwell Cover, 1917	15.00
Music, Sheet, Over There, Rockwell, 1917	15.00
Music, Sheet, Remembering, Duncan Sisters, 1923	8.00
Music, Sheet, Smiles, 1917	3.00
Music, Sheet, That Wonderful Something, Joan Crawford Cover, 1929	5.00
Music, Sheet, That Wonderful Something, Joan Crawford, 1929	5.00
Music, Sheet, True Love, Bing Crosby, 1956	5.00
Music, Sheet, True Love, 1956, Bing Crosby Cover	5.00
Music, Stand, For Guitar Or Cello, Wood	20.00
Music, Stand, Wood, For Table Model Jukebox	45.00
Music, Symphonion, Disc, Upright, C.1895, Germany, 6 Ft. X 23 X 14 In.	1950.00
Music, Talking Machine, Model A, Case, Reproducer & Horn, Ten 10 In. Records	325.00
Music, Tambourine, Greenwich Village Follies, New York's Latin Quarter	19.50
Music, Trombone, Busher, 1914	800.00
Music, Trombone, Paramont Deluxe, Brass, Made In Elkart, Ind.	75.00
Music, Trumpet, Fireman's, Brass, Braided Tassel Cord	175.00
Music, Trumpet, Mother-Of-Pearl On Keys, Brass	45.00
Music, Ukulele, Wood	25.00
Music, Violano-Virtuosos, 35 Vintage Rolls, Original Box	9000.00
Music, Violano, Mills, Quartered Oak Case	7500.00 To 8500.00

Music, Violin, Bow, Case, Marked Stradivarius, Germany, 22 In. 35.00
Music, Zither, Oscar Schmidt, Eagle Decal, Tuning Key 95.00
Music, Zither, Pearl & Silver Inlay, Case, Tuner, Hartmann Bros. 285.00
    Musket, see Weapon, Musket

Mustache cups were popular from 1850 to 1900. A ledge of china or silver
held the hair out of the liquid in the cup.
Mustache Cup & Saucer, Blown Out Ribs, Crossed Sword Mark 42.50
Mustache Cup & Saucer, Blown, Ribbed, Gold Edging, White, Marked 42.50
Mustache Cup & Saucer, Floral, 3 Crown Mark 30.00
Mustache Cup & Saucer, Hand-Painted, Star Mark, Scalloped Edge 65.00
Mustache Cup & Saucer, Holly Sprigs, Germany 30.00
Mustache Cup & Saucer, Pink Luster, Gold & Wine Leaves 25.00
Mustache Cup & Saucer, Raised Cupids & Garland, Capo-Di-Monte 125.00
Mustache Cup & Saucer, Silver Plate 40.00
Mustache Cup, Edward VII Coronation, 1902 .... 115.00
Mustache Cup, For A Gift, Feather Design, Red & Gold 45.00
Mustache Cup, Gold Band .... 15.00 To 16.00
Mustache Cup, Hand-Painted Roses, Bavaria 38.00
Mustache Cup, Handle, Footed, Tree Limb Design 38.00
Mustache Cup, Horses, China, Victorian 8.50
Mustache Cup, Kettle Shaped, Footed 60.00
Mustache Cup, Leaf Design, Remember Me, In Gold, Germany 30.00
Mustache Cup, Left-Handed, Embossed & Painted Flowers 55.00
Mustache Cup, Locomotive With Wood-Burning Tender 90.00
Mustache Cup, Matching Saucer, Pictures Owl 37.00
Mustache Cup, Multi-Colored Flowers, Gold Relief, Germany 38.00
Mustache Cup, Octagon, Maple Leaves 25.00
Mustache Cup, Pastel Flowers, Raised Poppies, Left-Handed 60.00
Mustache Cup, Pink Flower, Green Fernery, Gold Coralene, Think Of Me 34.00
Mustache Cup, Racing Scene 25.00
Mustache Cup, Repousse Around, Derby Silver Co. 42.00
Mustache Cup, Roses, Maroon Background, German 28.00
Mustache Cup, Saucer, Beading Pansies, Green Edging On Plate & Cup 32.50
Mustache Cup, Saucer, Cream To Green, Nippon, Wreath Mark 45.00
Mustache Cup, Saucer, Figural Angel Handle .... 48.00 To 55.00
Mustache Cup, Saucer, Orange Banding, Amethyst Striations, Marked 1849 .... 34.50
Mustache Cup, Saucer, Sunderland Luster, Flying Cloud Transfer 75.00
Mustache Cup, White, Affections Offering, China 15.00
Mustache Cup, 3 Footed, Flowers 50.00

MZ Austria is a mark used by Moritz Zdekauer from about 1900. The
firm worked in the town of Alt-Rohlau, Austria.
MZ Austria, Berry Set, Orange Bead Border, Ivory, Gold Artist Signature 115.00
MZ Austria, Bowl, Dessert, Saucer, Scalloped Edge, Roses, Gold Trim, Set Of 4 .... 40.00
MZ Austria, Chocolate Pot, 2 Cups & Saucers, Floral Border, Handpainted 65.00
MZ Austria, Cup & Saucer, Dessert, Greek Key Design, Set Of 6 .... 55.00
MZ Austria, Milk & Mush Set, Hand-Painted Roses, 3 Piece 75.00
MZ Austria, Mush Set, Hand-Painted Roses, 3 Piece 75.00
MZ Austria, Plate, Bird, Goose In Blue Flying, White Moon, 8 3/4 In., Pair 30.00
MZ Austria, Plate, Cake, Pink Roses, Gold Trim, 10 In. 10.00
MZ Austria, Plate, White Narcissi, Green, 9 1/2 In.Diameter 13.75
MZ Austria, Plate, White, Pink Flowers, Gold, 6 In. 35.00
MZ Austria, Ramekin & Underplate, Pink Roses, White Ground, Set Of 6 .... 70.00
MZ Austria, Sugar & Creamer, Artist Signed & Dated, 1915 .... 30.00
MZ Austria, Sugar & Creamer, 6-Sided, Encrusted Gold, Signed 35.00
MZ Austria, Tea Set & Tray, Hand-Painted, Imari Pattern 150.00

Nailsea glass was made in the Bristol District in England from 1788 to
1873. Many pieces were made with loopings of colored glass as decorations.
Nailsea, Bottle, Perfume, Laydown 25.00
Nailsea, Bottle, Perfume, Mica Stripping, Blown Glass Stopper 45.00
Nailsea, Bottle, Perfume, Sterling Silver Flower, Embossed Cover, 6 3/4 In. 265.00
Nailsea, Cruet, Blue, 9 In. 85.00
Nailsea, Fairy Lamp, Satinized Cranberry, Signed Clark Base, 4 3/4 In.Tall 190.00
Nailsea, Flask, Pewter Top, 7 3/4 In. 88.00

Nailsea, Flask, Reclining, White On Cranberry	95.00
Nailsea, Flask, White, Blue & Pink Loops, Pontil	165.00
Nailsea, Flask, White, Blue Loops, 7 1/2 In.	185.00
Nailsea, Globe, Applied Cranberry Threading, Pair	139.00
Nailsea, Globe, Cranberry Threading, White On Clear, Opening, 4 In.Diameter	159.00
Nailsea, Lamp, Fairy Lite, Amber Ground, White Loopings, Clarke, 5 In.	110.00
Nailsea, Pipe, Victorian, Red & White, 14 In.	162.00
Nailsea, Rolling Pin, Cranberry Swirl, 3 In.Diameter, 17 In.Long	230.00
Nailsea, Rose Bowl, White Loopings, Blue Cased Interior	125.00
Nailsea, Tumbler, Blue Threaded Base	50.00
Nailsea, Vase, Clear Handle, 10 1/2 In., Pair	135.00

NAKARA *Nakara is a trade name for a white glassware made around 1900 that was decorated in pastel colors. It was made by the C. F. Monroe Company of Meriden, Connecticut.*

Nakara, Ashtray, Floral & White Dot, Ormolu Rim, Bar Holder	185.00
Nakara, Biscuit Barrel	169.00
Nakara, Box, Cover, Pink, Signed, 4 1/2 In.	225.00
Nakara, Box, Covered, Blown-Out Orange Poppy, Green, Signed	350.00
Nakara, Box, Hinged, Blue, Pink Scrolling & Beading, Matched Lining	235.00
Nakara, Box, Hinged, Cherry Branch & Blossoms, Enameled	200.00
Nakara, Box, Hinged, Enameled Flowers, Beige, 5 1/2 In.Diameter	295.00
Nakara, Box, Hinged, Oval, Blue Ground, Rust Flowers, Signed, 5 3/4 X 4 In.	350.00
Nakara, Box, Jewel, Kate Greenaway Children, Signed C.F.M.Co., 6 In.	435.00
Nakara, Box, Jewel, Kate Greenaway's Children Having A Tea Party, Signed	435.00
Nakara, Box, Jewel, Ormolu Feet, Enameled Flowers, 6-Sided Oval, Signed, 5 In.	275.00
Nakara, Box, Jewel, Pink, Shades To Soft Yellow At Back, C.F.M.Company, 5 In.	225.00
Nakara, Box, Jewelry, Opaque, White On Cream, Signed, 2 In.Square	100.00
Nakara, Box, Lidded, Apricot, 2 Cherubs On Top, Beading, Marked	226.00
Nakara, Box, Powder, Orange, Yellow, Signed	125.00
Nakara, Casket, Covered, Hinged, Beaded Rim, Children In Center, 12 In.	394.00
Nakara, Casket, Jewel, Enameled Flowers, Ormolu Base, Signed, 15 In.Diameter	495.00
Nakara, Dish, Pin, Ormolu Rim & Handles, Beading, Signed	175.00
Nakara, Fernery, Brown, Orange Flowers, Brass Rim	160.00
Nakara, Fernery, Copper Insert, Enameled, Beaded Center, 4 1/2 X 8 In.Diam.	345.00
Nakara, Flower Arranger, Six Scallops, Enameled Orchids, Signed, 7 In.	235.00
Nakara, Hair Receiver, Enameled, Dotted Scrolls, Signed, 4 In.Diameter	165.00
Nakara, Humidor, Green Ground, Pink Flowers, Molding, Signed	365.00

Nanking china is a blue-and-white porcelain made in China for export during the eighteenth century.

Nanking, Plate, 10 In.	45.00
Nanking, Platter, Oval, Reticulated Border, 9 6/8 X 8 3/8 In.	95.00

Napkin rings were popular from 1869 to about 1900.

Napkin Ring, Bee & Flower, Set Of 6	40.00
Napkin Ring, Blue & White, Cloisonne	20.00
Napkin Ring, Bone China, Floral	4.00
Napkin Ring, Cut Glass, Diamond, Can, Fan, American	85.00
Napkin Ring, Cut Glass, Greek Key Pattern	50.00
Napkin Ring, Cut Glass, Harvard, 5/8 X 2 In.Diameter, Set Of 6	225.00
Napkin Ring, Cut Glass, Starburst, Beveled Rims	28.00
Napkin Ring, Cut Out, Flower Medallions, Sterling, 3/4 In.Wide	25.00
Napkin Ring, Embossed, Couples Dancing, Sterling Silver, Edwin	52.00
Napkin Ring, Figural, Baby Bird On Nest, Opens Mouth For Feeding	140.00
Napkin Ring, Figural, Barrel With Branch & Leaf Each Side, Silver Plate	38.00
Napkin Ring, Figural, Barrel With Staves, Leaf, Branches	45.00
Napkin Ring, Figural, Baseball Player With Bat In Hand	165.00
Napkin Ring, Figural, Bird On Ring, Pepper & Open Salt Each Side	225.00
Napkin Ring, Figural, Bird On Top, Oblong Base	53.50
Napkin Ring, Figural, Bird With Extra Long Tail, Reed & Barton	82.00
Napkin Ring, Figural, Bird, Leaf & Stem In Mouth, Silver Plate	75.00 To 120.00
Napkin Ring, Figural, Boy Bust Holding Ring Over Head	52.50
Napkin Ring, Figural, Boy Pulling Sled, Meridan	110.00
Napkin Ring, Figural, Bulldog & Ornate Ring On Pedestal, Signed Webb	115.00
Napkin Ring, Figural, Cat Aside Napkin Ring, 1 1/2 In.	55.00

Napkin Ring, Figural, Cat With Yellow Glass Eyes, Sitting Next To Ring 95.00
Napkin Ring, Figural, Cat, Glass Eyes, Silver Plated 175.00
Napkin Ring, Figural, Chair With Ring On Seat 74.00
Napkin Ring, Figural, Cherub Holds Vase Against Ring 150.00
Napkin Ring, Figural, Cherub On Stool Reading Book 85.00
Napkin Ring, Figural, Cherub, Bird Beside Ring 96.00
Napkin Ring, Figural, Cherubs, Winged, Holds Up Napkin Ring, 3 In. 150.00
Napkin Ring, Figural, Chick With Ring, 1 1/2 In. 20.00
Napkin Ring, Figural, Chick, Scrolled Legs On Ring Base, Silver Plate 59.00
Napkin Ring, Figural, Dachshund, Ring On Back 65.00
Napkin Ring, Figural, Deer, Meriden 115.00
Napkin Ring, Figural, Dog & Cat, Iron, 1 3/4 In., Pair 28.00
Napkin Ring, Figural, Dog With Wishbone In Mouth On Top Of Napkin Ring 70.00
Napkin Ring, Figural, Dog, Pail & Handle In Mouth Sets On Side Of Barrel 200.00
Napkin Ring, Figural, Double Cupid, Roger & Smith & Co., Meriden 85.00
Napkin Ring, Figural, Doves Either Side, Silver Plate 50.00
Napkin Ring, Figural, Eagles On Both Sides, Silver Plated 38.50
Napkin Ring, Figural, Fancy Leaf, Bird, Rogers Mark 85.00
Napkin Ring, Figural, Fans, Butterfly, Rogers 38.00
Napkin Ring, Figural, Floral Within Horseshoe, Silver Plate, Signed 83.00
Napkin Ring, Figural, Girl Feeding Dog, Standing On Hind Legs, Silver Plate 125.00
Napkin Ring, Figural, Girl Standing Behind Ring, Sterling Silver, 3 3/4 In. 150.00
Napkin Ring, Figural, Goat Pulling Cart, Moveable Wheels 185.00
Napkin Ring, Figural, Goodluck Horseshoe, Silver Plate 6.50
Napkin Ring, Figural, Horse Pulling Ring, Moving Wheels, Meriden 220.00
Napkin Ring, Figural, Horse Pulling Tong On Wheels 85.00
Napkin Ring, Figural, Horseshoe Leans On Ring 45.00
Napkin Ring, Figural, Kangaroo & Emu, Signed EPNS, SS Australia, 5 In. 70.00
Napkin Ring, Figural, Kewpie 4.00
Napkin Ring, Figural, Leaf Base, Pond Lily, Meriden Silver Co. 47.00
Napkin Ring, Figural, Lion On Rectangular Base, Ring On Back, Silver 55.00
Napkin Ring, Figural, Lion, Silver 48.00
Napkin Ring, Figural, Miner Holds Pick & Rock, Hand On Triangle Ring, Signed 185.00
Napkin Ring, Figural, Morning Glory & Leaf, Meriden 27.50
Napkin Ring, Figural, Owl & 2 Small Owls At Side, Leaves & Vines, Silver 200.00
Napkin Ring, Figural, Owl Perched On Book, Silver Plate, 2 In. 25.00
Napkin Ring, Figural, Pear & Leaves 70.00
Napkin Ring, Figural, Ring Form Of Vest, Silver Plate 20.00
Napkin Ring, Figural, Ring Nestles In Horseshoe, Silver Plate 80.00
Napkin Ring, Figural, Ring On Base, Bird On Top, Wm.Roger, Numbered 68.00
Napkin Ring, Figural, Ring Resting On Leaf, Detailed Bird On Stem 68.00
Napkin Ring, Figural, Scottie, Silver 48.00
Napkin Ring, Figural, Seated Kate Greenaway Girl 65.00
Napkin Ring, Figural, Sitting Cat, Silver Plated 45.00
Napkin Ring, Figural, Soldier Each Side Of Ring, Bracket Base 52.50
Napkin Ring, Figural, Spanish Comb Against Ring 65.00
Napkin Ring, Figural, Tai Bird On Ring, Reed & Barton 83.00
Napkin Ring, Figural, Triangular, With Wishbones 24.00
Napkin Ring, Figural, Two Turtles On Fern Fronds, Silver Plate 85.00
Napkin Ring, Figural, Two Turtles, Ring On Backs, Sterling Silver 100.00
Napkin Ring, Figural, Vertical Upright Held By 4 Posts, Silver Plate 95.00
Napkin Ring, Figural, Warrior Each Side, Ball Feet, Reed & Barton 110.00
Napkin Ring, Figural, Water Lily Pad, Bud On Curled Stem Forms Handle 60.00
Napkin Ring, Figural, Wingless Cherub, Hand Out, Reed & Barton, 3 3/4 In. 150.00
Napkin Ring, Figural, Wishbone, Merry Wishes 26.00
Napkin Ring, Figural, Woman On Each Side 30.00
Napkin Ring, Fitted Removeable Wood Base, Sterling Silver 45.00
Napkin Ring, Fox, Dated, M.G.Atterbury 175.00
Napkin Ring, Glass, Diamond Peg, Ruby Flashed 65.00
Napkin Ring, Ivory, Chain Of Elephants, Set Of 4 .... 45.00
Napkin Ring, Ivory, Curved 20.00
Napkin Ring, Ivory, Oriental Scene, Pair 30.00
Napkin Ring, Openwork Centers, Sterling Silver, Georg Jensen, Set Of 6 .... 225.00
Napkin Ring, Oriental Ladies, Enameled Trees, Red & Gold, Nippon 45.00
Napkin Ring, Porcelain, Gold Beading & Roses 14.00
Napkin Ring, Psyche & Cupid, Medallions, Sterling Silver, Unger Bros. 75.00

Napkin Ring, Sailboats & Camels, Oriental, Silver, Set Of 5 .... 30.00
Napkin Ring, Salt & Pepper Set, All On One Stand, Glass 40.00
Napkin Ring, Sterling Silver, Christine, 1 1/2 In. 15.00
Napkin Ring, Sterling Silver, Victorian, Ida 35.00
Napkin Ring, Styled Like Watch, Attached Band, Opens To Insert Napkin, Pair 45.00
Napkin Ring, Unger Brothers, Sterling Silver 35.00
Napkin Ring, 1937 Coronation 17.00

Nash glass was made in Corona, New York, by Arthur Nash and his sons
after 1919. He worked at the Webb Factory in England and for the
Tiffany Glassworks in the United States.

Nash, Candlestick, Embossed, Gold, Rounded Shape, Wafer Base, 4 1/2 In., Pair 225.00
Nash, Compote, Chintz, Signed 615.00
Nash, Cordial Set, Handled Decanter & 6 Handled Cordials, Lily Pads 295.00
Nash, Goblet, Balled Footed, Blue & Green Stripe, Signed, 7 In. 150.00
Nash, Goblet, Blue Chintz, Signed, 5 In. 50.00
Nash, Salt, Bronze & Purple Iridescent, 1 In.Wide Rim, Signed, 4 In.Diameter 175.00
Nash, Sherbet, Footed, Chintz Glass, Brown & Gold Stripe, 2 3/4 X 4 1/4 In. 150.00
Nash, Stemware, Chintz, Blue & Green Pulls, Signed, 4 In. 55.00
Nash, Stemware, Chintz, Blue & Green Pulls, Signed, 5 1/4 In. 65.00
Nash, Vase, Bud, Gold Iridescent, Wafer Foot, 7 7/8 In. 350.00
Nash, Vase, Bud, Wafer Foot, Signed, 7 3/4 In. 350.00
Nash, Vase, Floriform, Amber Iridescent, Inscribed Nash 544, 1928-31, 4 In. 275.00
Nash, Vase, Gold & Lavender Highlights, Pedestal Foot, Signed, 12 In. 250.00
Nash, Vase, Green & Red Vertical Striping, Chintz, 14 1/2 In. ....*Illus* 300.00

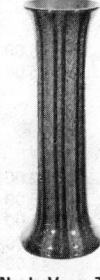

Nash, Vase, Green & Red Vertical Striping,
Chintz, 14 1/2 In.

Nash, Vase, Trumpet, Blue Chintz Glass, Signed, 16 In. 225.00
Nautical, see also Scrimshaw
Nautical, Anchor, C.1820, Gilt Finish, Carved Of One Piece Of Wood, Pair 250.00
Nautical, Anchor, Lake Erie Boat, 36 X 56 In. 150.00
Nautical, Bell, Brackets, Original Clapper, Bronze, 6 X 8 In.Diameter 35.00
Nautical, Bell, Seth Thomas, Brass Case, 6 In.Dial 265.00
Nautical, Boat, Model, The Frigate, U.S.S.Constitution, 1797, Eldredge 2000.00
Nautical, Bucket, Tar, Nelson, Trafalgar Era, C.1800, 12 X 9 In.Diameter 195.00
Nautical, Card, Clipper Ship, Coleman's California Line, 4 X 6 1/2 In. 195.00
Nautical, Chest, Iron Bands, Handles, Pine, Hannibal, Missouri 100.00
Nautical, Chest, Sea Captain's, Leather, Brass Latch & Key, 1867, 8 X 15 In. 175.00
Nautical, Chest, Swiss Immigrant's, 1880s, Wood & Iron Hinges 40.00
Nautical, Chest, Wooden, C.1860, Carved Eagle & Border, 11 X 15 X 9 In. 550.00
Nautical, Chimes, Dinner 100.00
Nautical, Clock, Seth Thomas, 2 Springs, 8 Day Lever, Thomaston, Connecticut 135.00
Nautical, Clock, U.S.Navy, 1941 .... 50.00
Nautical, Compass, Draftsman's Beam, Box, C.1880-1900 .... 15.00
Nautical, Compass, Leather Covered Box, Brass Hinge & Hook, Round 20.00
Nautical, Compass, Pocket, Dated 1862, Signed, 1 1/2 In. 25.00
Nautical, Crochet Hook, Hand-Carved Ivory, Dice Design 15.00
Nautical, Eagle, Pilot House, Hand-Carved, 19th Century, Gold Paint, 28 In. 1650.00
Nautical, Epaulet, Naval Officer, Tin Case 50.00
Nautical, Flag, 13 Star Standard, Union Steamer Mendota, 1862 .... 350.00
Nautical, Gauge, Pressure, Brass, Iron Back, 6 In. 20.00
Nautical, Globe, Celestial, 19th Century, 12 In.Diameter, 18 1/2 In. 550.00
Nautical, Harpoon, Whaling, Single Barb 75.00
Nautical, Horn, Fog, Brass, Navy 60.00

Nautical, Horn, Fog, Hand Pumped, Protruding Horn 200.00
Nautical, Horn, Signal, Foot Or Hand Operated, C.1860, 9 X 16 In.Diameter 125.00
Nautical, Kayak, 2 Hole, Nome, Alaska, 1904 Golden Gate Hotel, 35 Feet 250.00
Nautical, Lance, Whale Killing, C.1840, Leaf-Shaped Blade, 52 In. 250.00
Nautical, Lantern, Beveled Glass, Brass Hinges, Kerosene Burner, 18 1/2 In. 95.00
Nautical, Lantern, Lovell, Arlington, N.J., Ribbed Glass Globe, Brass 150.00
Nautical, Lantern, Signal, Perko, 8 1/2 In. 29.00
Nautical, Lantern, 2 Handles, For Wave Rocking, Red Globe, 12 In. 125.00
Nautical, Light, Bulkhead, Brass In Brass Cage, 8 X 3 In. 35.00
Nautical, Light, Search, G.E., Brass, 28 In. 90.00
Nautical, Light, Trouble, Brass, Mahogany Handle 60.00
Nautical, Model, Ship, The Brig Boxer, 1831, 19 1/4 X 26 In. 1000.00
Nautical, Model, Ship, The Endeavour, Fully Equipped For Battle, 25 1/2 In. 1200.00
Nautical, Nameboard, Sailing Vessel, Carved, 4 In.Letters, 10 Feet 375.00
Nautical, Plate, U.S.S. Maine, Open Work, Opaque 17.50
Nautical, Propeller, Brass, 20 In.Diameter, Pair 275.00
Nautical, Propeller, Bronze, 24 In. 90.00
Nautical, Propeller, Evinrude Motor, 1920s, Brass 47.50
Nautical, Sign, Brass Plate, Kelvin, Bottomley & Baird Ltd., 12 X 36 In. 395.00
Nautical, Sign, Hinson & Stowman, Wooden Letters, 63 X 12 1/2 In. 275.00
Nautical, Telegraph, Brass, C.1943, 45 In. 650.00
Nautical, Telescope, Braid Covered Handle, Brass, Open To 40 In. 75.00
Nautical, Telescope, Brass, C.1850, Lens Cover, Opens To 23 In. 115.00
Nautical, Telescope, Brass, Cutts, London, Opens 41 In. 125.00
Nautical, Telescope, High Powered, Brass, Adjustable Tripod, 1860-70 .... 2000.00
Nautical, Wheel, Submarine, Bronze 300.00
    Needlework, see Textile, Sampler
    Negro, see Black
Nautical, Whistle, Bos'n, Silk Braided Lanyard, Sterling Silver, 5 1/2 In. 125.00
Nautical, Whistle, Distress, Lake Winnebego, Oshkosh Ferry, Brass, 15 In. 325.00

    *Netsuke are small ivory, wood, metal, or porcelain pieces used as the button on
    the end of a cord holding a Japanese money pouch. The earliest date from
    the sixteenth century.*
Netsuke, Chick In Egg, 1 1/2 In. 42.00
Netsuke, Ivory, Boy Brushing Man's Hair, Japanese, 1 3/4 In. 115.00
Netsuke, Ivory, Boy Holding Onto Fish In Tub, 1 1/4 In. 275.00
Netsuke, Ivory, Cat With Kitten, Signed 45.00
Netsuke, Ivory, Changing Faces, Signed 49.00
Netsuke, Ivory, Chick In Egg, Signed 39.00
Netsuke, Ivory, Dancer, Kabuk I, Revolving Face 39.00
Netsuke, Ivory, Dragon, Hand-Carved 65.00
Netsuke, Ivory, Face, Revolving, From Anger To Happy, 2 In. 45.00
Netsuke, Ivory, Hotei Seated With Child In Front, Holding Fan, 1 1/4 In. 300.00
Netsuke, Ivory, Insect, Hand-Carved 65.00
Netsuke, Ivory, Kabuki Dancer, Revolving Face 35.00
Netsuke, Ivory, Large Cat, Small Kitten, Artist Signed 45.00
Netsuke, Ivory, Mask, Pendant 65.00
Netsuke, Ivory, Mask, Signed 49.00
Netsuke, Ivory, Monster Head With Moveable Jaws, Signed 250.00
Netsuke, Ivory, Noh Masks, Signed 33.00
Netsuke, Ivory, Peapods Forming The Himotashi 200.00
Netsuke, Ivory, Samurai, Signed Isshi, 1 1/4 In. 125.00
Netsuke, Ivory, Tiger Confronted By Snake In Front Of Rock, Munemitsu 400.00
Netsuke, Ivory, Wild Boar, Kneeling, 2 In. 50.00
Netsuke, Wood, Gamma Sennin With Frog Companion Resting On Shoulders 125.00
    New Martinsville, see also Peachblow
New Martinsville, Bottle, Perfume, Long Dauber, Amethyst, Marked, Pair 22.50
New Martinsville, Bowl, Janice, 3-Toed, 10 1/2 In. 18.00
New Martinsville, Bowl, Silver Deposit, 3 Toed, Janice 25.00
New Martinsville, Bowl, Sunglow, Custard Coloring & Iridescence, Small 65.00
New Martinsville, Cocktail, Moondrops, Ruby 8.00
New Martinsville, Creamer, Individual, Ruby 8.00
New Martinsville, Dish, Candy, Viking Bird, Covered, Blue 25.00
New Martinsville, Dish, Relish, Swan, Clear, Cobalt Head & Neck, 9 1/2 In. 22.00
New Martinsville, Figurine, Baby Bear 40.00

Salt box, painted white
pine, Pennsylvania, 1797

Wooden tankard,
probably
Connecticut,
1750–1830

Quilt, cotton and silk,
probably Baltimore, 1854

Wool winder, maple and
birch, Shaker community of
Canterbury, New
Hampshire, 1800–1900

Grecian couch, cherry and ash, New York, c. 1820–1835

Covered sewing box, Shaker, United States, 1900–1930

Sideboard, wood, glass, and marble, attributed to Antoine G. Quervelle, Philadelphia, c. 1825–1835

Pier table, Philadelphia, c. 1825–1840

Canterbury, rosewood, pine, tulip, brass,
and ivory, New York or Pennsylvania,
1825–1840

Center table, wood, marble, and
mother of pearl, New York,
1830–1845

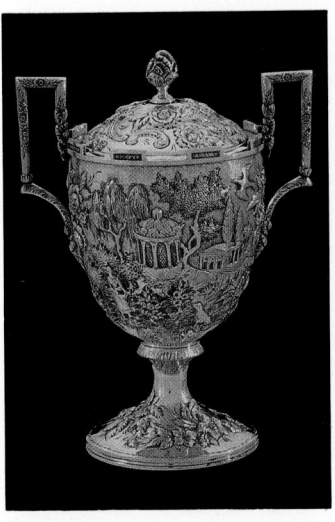

Silver sugar bowl, Samuel
Kirk, Baltimore, 1828

Andirons, brass and iron, Richard
Wittingham, Sr., New York, c. 1795–1810

Bellows, John Eckstein & R. B. Richardson, Philadelphia, c. 1819–1822

Agateware teapot, Staffordshire, England, 1750–1770

Silver tray, Samuel Coleman, New Jersey, c. 1790–1820

Cotton handkerchief, Cocheco Manufacturing Co., United States, 1892

Blue glass candlestick,
United States, 1845–1865

Wool carpet, corner
knot, selvage warp,
Axminster or
Exeter factories,
Axminster,
England, 1765

Pitcher, glass, New York, 1830–1850

Candelabrum, glass and
ormolu, probably
England, c. 1800

Hooked rug, wool and linen,
northeastern United States or Canada,
1830–1870

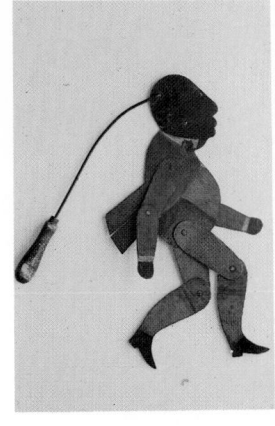

Toy, jointed figure of
a Negro man, United
States, 1860–1930

Maple rocking armchair,
Shaker, United States,
1820–1870

Watch and watch case,
T. Selrat, London,
1760–1790

Card table, mahogany
veneer, white pine, tulip,
and cherry, Philadelphia,
1820–1830

Looking glass, wood,
gesso, gilt, and glass,
probably New York,
1790–1810

Earthenware wine cups,
Staffordshire, England, 1800–1805

Pincushions, steel and
brass, Russia, 1800–1820

Brass snuffer stand,
England, 1720–1770

Carved and painted white pine
eagles, attributed to Wilhelm
Schimmel, Pennsylvania, 1865–1890

"Gaudy Dutch" tea service,
King's Rose, Staffordshire,
England, 1810–1850

Interior, Lebanon bedroom

New Martinsville, Figurine, Bear, Glass, 3 In. 38.00
New Martinsville, Figurine, Bear, Glass, 4 1/2 In. 38.00
New Martinsville, Figurine, Bunny, Sitting Upright, Ears Up, 7 In. 22.50
New Martinsville, Figurine, Elephant 50.00
New Martinsville, Figurine, Fighting Duck, Sitting 32.50
New Martinsville, Figurine, Frosted Seal 68.00
New Martinsville, Figurine, Hobo 85.00
New Martinsville, Figurine, Hunter 95.00
New Martinsville, Figurine, Mama Bear, 4 1/2 In. 30.00
New Martinsville, Figurine, Prancing Horses, Clear, 7 1/2 X 6 1/4 In., Pair 38.00
New Martinsville, Figurine, Prancing Horses, Red, Amber Base, 8 X 6 In., Pair 48.00
New Martinsville, Figurine, Rabbit 65.00
New Martinsville, Figurine, Rooster, 8 1/2 X 8 1/2 In. 68.00
New Martinsville, Figurine, Seal, Ball On Nose, 4 1/2 In..Pair 45.00
New Martinsville, Figurine, Seal, Crystal 65.00
New Martinsville, Figurine, Seal, Small 45.00
New Martinsville, Figurine, Sitting Panther, Clear 65.00
New Martinsville, Figurine, Standing Pony, 12 In. 95.00
New Martinsville, Figurine, Swan, Clear, 9 In. 27.00
New Martinsville, Figurine, Swan, Crystal Neck, Emerald 35.00
New Martinsville, Figurine, Swan, Elongated, Ruby, 7 1/2 In. 24.50
New Martinsville, Figurine, Swan, Green, Clear Neck, 6 In. 24.00
New Martinsville, Figurine, Viking Fish, C.1960, Pair 45.00
New Martinsville, Figurine, Wolfhound 65.00
New Martinsville, Pitcher, Water, Carnation, 2 Tumblers 230.00
New Martinsville, Plate, Cake, 11 In. 16.00
New Martinsville, Platter, Moondrops, Ruby, Oval, 12 In. 16.50
New Martinsville, Water Set, Heart In Sand, Clear, 6 Tumblers, Pitcher 95.00

*Newcomb Pottery was founded by Ellsworth and William Woodward at
Sophie Newcomb College, New Orleans, Louisiana, in 1896. The work
continued through the 1940s. Pieces of this art pottery are marked with the
letter N inside the letter C.*

Newcomb, Bowl, Blue & Green, 2 1/2 In. 135.00
Newcomb, Bowl, Daffodils, Leaves Over Blue Band, Green Ground, 4 X 7 1/2 In. 375.00
Newcomb, Bowl, Floral, NC Mark, 7 3/4 X 2 1/4 In. 300.00
Newcomb, Bowl, Floral, Signed AFS, 5 1/2 X 2 1/4 In. 225.00
Newcomb, Bowl, Floral, Signed AFS, 8 1/4 X 3 3/4 In. 325.00
Newcomb, Bowl, Flower Frog, Pink Over Blue, Irvine, 4 X 1 5/8 In. 100.00
Newcomb, Bowl, Flowers, Irvine, Paper Sticker, 5 3/8 X 2 1/4 In. 275.00
Newcomb, Bowl, Narcissus, Irvine, 9 3/8 X 3 In. 375.00
Newcomb, Bowl, Narcissus, Pink, Lavender Ground, 2 3/4 X 5 In.Diameter 250.00
Newcomb, Candlestick, Dogwood, Irvine, 9 3/4 In., Pair 1000.00
Newcomb, Creamer, Sea Gull Scene, Blue, 3 1/2 In. 35.00
Newcomb, Match Holder, Daisies On Blue Matte, Signed 225.00
Newcomb, Match Holder, Daisies On Pink, Semi-Gloss, Signed, 2 In. 325.00
Newcomb, Mug, 2-Tone Green, 4 1/2 In. 200.00
Newcomb, Pitcher, Open Cut Handle, Blue, Paper Sticker, 1 3/4 X 3 In. 42.00
Newcomb, Tile, Oak Tree & Moss, Signed, 6 X 10 In. 250.00
Newcomb, Vase, Blue & Green Tones, Bulbous, Marked, 4 In. 95.00
Newcomb, Vase, Blue Floral Design, Irvine, 6 1/2 X 3 1/2 In. 350.00
Newcomb, Vase, Blue Flowers & Leaves Around Shoulder, 5 1/2 X 4 1/4 In. 250.00
Newcomb, Vase, Blue Glaze, Incised Design, Signed 800.00
Newcomb, Vase, Blue, Beige Band Around Rim.7 1/4 X 4 1/2 In. 250.00
Newcomb, Vase, Bulbous Bottom, 4 Rings At Throat, 6 1/2 In. 375.00
Newcomb, Vase, Floral, Bailey, 5 1/4 X 4 In. 325.00
Newcomb, Vase, Floral, 8 X 3 1/4 In. 325.00
Newcomb, Vase, Flowers, Irvine, 5 1/4 In. 350.00
Newcomb, Vase, Glaze Drip, Blue To Gray, Marked 185.00
Newcomb, Vase, Irvine, Art Nouveau Swirls, 3 1/2 X 3 In. 100.00
Newcomb, Vase, Narcissus, Blue, Irvine, 8 3/8 X 3 1/4 In. 475.00
Newcomb, Vase, Oleander Blossoms, Signed, Paper Label, 5 In. 335.00
Newcomb, Vase, Pink Cherries On Blue, Irvine, 3 1/2 X 3 In. 375.00
Newcomb, Vase, Pink Narcissus, JH, AFS, 7 1/2 X 4 1/2 In. 400.00
Newcomb, Vase, Scenic, Moon & Trees At Lakeside, 12 X 5 In. 650.00
Newcomb, Vase, Scenic, Purple Trees, Red Sunset, Irvine, 3 5/8 X 3 5/8 In. 375.00

Newcomb, Vase, Semi-Gloss, Blue, Band Of Pink Flowers, Signed, 6 X 6 1/2 In. 185.00
Newcomb, Vase, Squatty, J.N.Joor, 4 X 1 5/8 X 1 1/2 In. 125.00
Newcomb, Vase, Squatty, Yellow, Signed, 1 5/8 X 4 In.Diameter 125.00
Newcomb, Vase, Transitional Higlaze, Blue Floral, Irvine, 4 1/2 X 2 1/8 In. 325.00
Newcomb, Vase, 3 Handled, Ribbed, Irvine, 4 3/4 X 4 3/4 In. 300.00

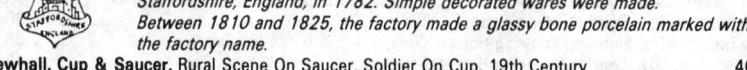

Newhall Porcelain Manufactory was started at Newhall, Shelton,
Staffordshire, England, in 1782. Simple decorated wares were made.
Between 1810 and 1825, the factory made a glassy bone porcelain marked with
the factory name.

Newhall, Cup & Saucer, Rural Scene On Saucer, Soldier On Cup, 19th Century 40.00
Niello, Match Safe, Russian 60.00

Niloak Pottery (Kaolin spelled backwards) was made at the Hyten
Brothers Pottery in Benton, Arkansas, between 1909 and 1946.
Although the factory did make cast and molded wares, collectors are
most interested in the marbleized art pottery line.

Niloak, Bowl, Swirl, Red, Cream, Blue, Green, 5 X 2 5/8 In. 25.00
Niloak, Canoe, Rose, 10 In. 12.00
Niloak, Cornucopia, Pink Monochrome, 4 In. 10.00
Niloak, Ewer, Embossed Eagle & Stars, Mauve, 10 In. 15.00
Niloak, Ewer, Purple, 6 3/4 In., Pair 35.00
Niloak, Figurine, Elephant, Circus, Signed 8.50
Niloak, Figurine, Southern Belle, Ruffled Hoopskirt, Paper Label, 9 1/2 In. 32.00
Niloak, Pitcher, Embossed Pink Flowers, Marked, 7 In. 20.00
Niloak, Planter, Polar Bear, Matte Glaze 25.00
Niloak, Planter, Squirrel 12.00
Niloak, Planter, Swan 10.00
Niloak, Vase, Bud, Swirl, Cream Ground, 8 X 3 1/2 In. 37.00
Niloak, Vase, Bud, Swirl, 6 1/2 In. 25.00
Niloak, Vase, Cornucopia, Brown & Green, 3 In. 18.00
Niloak, Vase, Cylindrical, 9 1/2 X 3 In.Diameter 22.50
Niloak, Vase, Ivory, Blue & Brown Swirls, Signed, 4 3/4 In. 26.00
Niloak, Vase, Swirl, Red, Tan, Blue & Cream, 5 1/4 X 3 1/2 In. .... 27.50 To 30.00
Niloak, Vase, Swirled Colors, Matte Finish, 13 1/2 In. 38.00
Niloak, Vase, White With Red & Blue, 5 In. 40.00

Nippon-marked porcelain was made in Japan from 1891 to 1921. "Nippon" is
the Japanese word for "Japan."

Nippon, Ashtray, Blown-Out, Tan Ground, Box Of Matches Raised In Center 195.00
Nippon, Ashtray, Enamel Beading, Hand-Painted Rooster Inside, Signed 50.00
Nippon, Ashtray, Matched Box Curved Holder, Fatima Cigarettes 45.00
Nippon, Ashtray, Pinecones 32.00
Nippon, Ashtray, Scenic, Green Wreath Mark 55.00
Nippon, Ashtray, Trees, House 19.00
Nippon, Ashtray, 4 Feet, Landscape Scene, Enamel Dots, 5 1/2 In.Square 65.00
Nippon, Asparagus Set, Dish With Well, Sauce Boat, Five 7 1/2 In.Plates 115.00
Nippon, Basket, Bisque, Blown-Out Plums, Basket Weave, 6 In. 65.00
Nippon, Basket, Hand-Painted Windmill Scene, Gold Handle, 8 1/4 X 6 In. 65.00
Nippon, Basket, Hand-Painted Windmill Scene, Gold Trim, Leaf Mark, 6 X 8 In. 65.00
Nippon, Basket, Multicolor Butterflies, 10 X 7 1/2 In. 125.00
Nippon, Berry Bowl, Blown-Out Child's Face, 5 1/4 In. 22.00
Nippon, Biscuit Jar, Bulbous, Footed, 4 Puffed Panels, Oriental Mark 40.00
Nippon, Biscuit Jar, Hand-Painted, Violets, Gold Trim, Marked 175.00
Nippon, Biscuit Jar, Poppies, Gold Eagles, Green Wreath Mark 125.00
Nippon, Biscuit Jar, Portrait, Cobalt, Footed 225.00
Nippon, Bonbon, Cradled In Pierced Copper Pedestal Stand 115.00
Nippon, Bonbon, Footed, Gold Handles, Matte Finish, M Mark, 7 In. 28.00
Nippon, Bottle, Barber, Junks In Pink, Signed 20.00
Nippon, Bottle, Perfume, Gold Trim, Beading, Royal Crown, 5 1/2 In., Pair 125.00
Nippon, Bottle, Perfume, Porcelain, Gold Trim, Magenta M Mark, 5 In., Pair 90.00
Nippon, Bowl & Saucer, 3 Gold Feet, M In Wreath, Bowl, 5 1/8 In.Diameter 16.00
Nippon, Bowl, Azalea Border, Gold Edge, Oval, 6 In. 9.00
Nippon, Bowl, Bisque, 4 Blown-Out Acorns, Enameled, Jewels 65.00
Nippon, Bowl, Blown-Out Acorns, Footed, 7 In. 35.00
Nippon, Bowl, Blown-Out Flower, 7 1/2 In. 45.00

Nippon, Bowl, Blown-Out Nuts, Yellow & Brown Double Handle, Green Wreath 110.00
Nippon, Bowl, Blown-Out Peanut Shell, 7 X 6 In. 48.00
Nippon, Bowl, Butter, Enameled, Gold Beads, Porcelain Insert, Signed 86.00
Nippon, Bowl, Candy, Hand-Painted Acorns, Tan Ground, Enameled, Green Wreath 40.00
Nippon, Bowl, Cereal, Child's Face & Body, 5 In.Diameter 40.00
Nippon, Bowl, Clover Shape, 3 Handles, Scenic, Green Wreath, 7 In. 45.00
Nippon, Bowl, Cream Background, Gold Beading, 10 In. 75.00
Nippon, Bowl, Fluted, Brown Leaf Design, Leaves & Flower In Relief, 7 In. 85.00
Nippon, Bowl, Fluted, Pierced Handles, Roses, Maple Leaf Mark, 9 1/2 In. 45.00
Nippon, Bowl, Folded Style, Gold Lace Border, Maple Leaf Mark, 7 1/4 In. 65.00
Nippon, Bowl, Footed, Blown Out Flowers, 3 1/2 X 5 1/2 In.Diameter 20.00
Nippon, Bowl, Footed, Pearlized, Hand-Painted, Maple Leaf Mark, 9 1/4 In. 119.00
Nippon, Bowl, Footed, Scalloped Edge, Melon Ribbed, Signed, 4 X 7 1/4 In. 90.00
Nippon, Bowl, Footed, Scalloped, Gold Trim, Blue Maple Leaf, 7 In.Diameter 45.00
Nippon, Bowl, Four Section, Open Handles, Green Wreath Mark, 10 X 2 In. 25.00
Nippon, Bowl, Gold & Enameling, 6 Panel, Meadow Scene, Green Mark, 10 In. 110.00
Nippon, Bowl, Green Glaze, Footed, Beaded Edge, Maple Leaf, 9 1/4 In. 119.00
Nippon, Bowl, Hand-Painted Flowers Inside, Gold Border, Green Wreath, 9 In. 55.00
Nippon, Bowl, Hand-Painted, Ear Handles, M Mark, 8 In. 30.00
Nippon, Bowl, Hand-Painted, Gold Border, Beading, 19th Century, 7 3/4 In. 48.00
Nippon, Bowl, Hand-Painted, Gold Trim, Green Wreath, 6 1/2 In. 28.00
Nippon, Bowl, Japanese Scenes, Royal Kaga Mark, 4 X 8 In. 100.00
Nippon, Bowl, Pansies Trimmed In Black & Gold, Open Handles, 10 1/4 In. 22.00
Nippon, Bowl, Pedestal, Brown Leak Design, 3 Walnuts In Relief, 8 In. 85.00
Nippon, Bowl, Persian Design, 10 In. 45.00
Nippon, Bowl, Petal Shape, Gilt Handle, Green M Mark, 6 X 9 1/2 In. 28.00
Nippon, Bowl, Pheasants, Gold Handles, Green Wreath Mark, 10 In. 55.00
Nippon, Bowl, Relief Chestnuts, Hand-Painted Leaves, Wreath Mark, 7 In. 38.00
Nippon, Bowl, Roses & Green Leaves, 8 1/4 In. 35.00
Nippon, Bowl, Roses Outlined In Black, Gold Border, Marked, 2 X 8 In.Diam. 60.00
Nippon, Bowl, Shaped As Porringer, Moriage, 6 In. 240.00
Nippon, Bowl, Stand, Matte Landscape Interior, Green Wreath Mark, 10 X 7 In. 225.00
Nippon, Bowl, Strawberry, Scalloped Rim, Signed, Torii Mark, 7 1/2 In. 79.00
Nippon, Bowl, Sugar, Pedestal, Gold Beading, Cobalt Blue Ground, 5 1/4 In. 140.00
Nippon, Bowl, 2 Handled, Orange Flowers, Green M, 4 3/4 In. 15.00
Nippon, Bowl, 2 Handled, Rural Scene, Hand-Painted, Green Wreath, 6 3/4 In. 35.00
Nippon, Bowl, 2 Rope Handles, Blown Out Nuts, Bisque Finish, 7 In. 85.00
Nippon, Bowl, 3 Ball Feet, 5 Sided, Water Scene, 7 In. 75.00
Nippon, Bowl, 3 Blown-Out Peanuts, 7 In., Diameter 62.00
Nippon, Bowl, 4 Gold Wreath Border, Beading, Maple Leaf Mark, 10 1/2 In. 98.00
Nippon, Box, Collar Button 15.00
Nippon, Box, Covered, Footed, Scenic, Beaded Edges, 4 X 2 1/4 In. 25.00
Nippon, Box, Covered, Gold Beaded Trim, Green M In Wreath, 4 X 3 1/2 In. 25.00
Nippon, Box, Covered, Gold Beading, Round, Green Wreath, 5 1/2 X 3 In. 53.00
Nippon, Box, Covered, Hand-Painted Boat Scene, Green Wreath, 3 1/2 X 4 In. 55.00
Nippon, Box, Covered, White, Gold Border, Royal Crown Mark, 6 In.Diameter 40.00
Nippon, Box, Dresser, Geese, Heavy Gold Beading 150.00
Nippon, Box, Jewel, Beads & Gold, Maple Leaf Mark, 5 1/2 X 3 1/2 In. 59.00
Nippon, Box, Oriental Carving, Wood, Round, 3 1/4 In. 20.00
Nippon, Box, Powder, Matching Hair Receiver, Footed, Gold Trim, Signed 35.00
Nippon, Box, Powder, Round, 5 In.Diameter 26.00
Nippon, Box, Trinket, Burnished Gold Design, M In Wreath Mark 30.00
Nippon, Burner, Incense, Foo Dog Finial, Marked, 4 1/2 In. 12.00
Nippon, Burner, Incense, Pierced Lid, 3 Footed, Embossed, 3 1/4 X 3 1/2 In. 30.00
Nippon, Butter Pat, Blue & Brown, Handle, 3 3/4 In., Set Of 3 .... 6.50
Nippon, Butter Pat, Double, Open Handled, Green Mark, 2 1/2 In.Diam.Set Of 6 .... 14.00
Nippon, Cake Set, Blue Band, Forget-Me-Nots, Crown Mark, 7 Piece 48.00
Nippon, Cake Set, White Slip Dragon, 7 Piece 95.00
Nippon, Cake Set, Yellow Ground, Blue Birds, 10 In. 55.00
Nippon, Cake Set, 11 In.Cake Plate, 6 6 1/2 In.Plates, Green Wreath Mark 68.00
Nippon, Candleholder, Pastel Iris Outlined In Gold, M In Wreath 30.00
Nippon, Candleholder, Scene Outlined In Gold, Marked, 6 In., Pair 65.00
Nippon, Candlestick, Black & Gold Scene On White, Green M Mark, 6 1/2 In. 45.00
Nippon, Candlestick, Black, Gold & White, Scenic, 6 1/2 In. 80.00
Nippon, Candlestick, Portrait, Square Base, Jeweling, Blonde Lady, 9 In. 115.00
Nippon, Candy Dish, Floral, Gold Trim & Beading, Handled 12.50

Nippon, Celery & Salt, Gold Encrusted, Pink Flowers, Red & Green Mark 77.50
Nippon, Celery Set, Pink Flowers & Gold, 5 Pieces 22.00
Nippon, Celery Set, Women On Shore, 6 Salts, Royal Karga, 13 X 6 X 1 1/2 In. 125.00
Nippon, Celery, Open Handled, Roses, 12 1/2 X 5 1/2 In. 22.00
Nippon, Celery, Open Handles, Gold Trim, Blue Rising Sun Mark 35.00
Nippon, Celery, Palm Trees, Sailboat, Rolled Ends, Slotted 40.00
Nippon, Chocolate Pot, Cobalt, Gold Trim, Puffed Lid, Corolene Beading 145.00
Nippon, Chocolate Pot, Floral Design, 13 In. 88.00
Nippon, Chocolate Pot, Gold Outlined Lilacs, Royal Kinran Mark, 10 X 8 In. 85.00
Nippon, Chocolate Pot, Japanese Ladies In Garden, Flowers, Marked, 9 1/2 In. 60.00
Nippon, Chocolate Pot, Roses & Beading, 10 In. 95.00
Nippon, Chocolate Pot, Scenic Panels On White, 7 In. 65.00
Nippon, Chocolate Pot, White & Pink Flowers, Raised Gold, Green Leaves 50.00
Nippon, Chocolate Pot, Wisteria Clusters, Green Wreath Mark 95.00
Nippon, Chocolate Set, Gold & White, 4 Cups & Saucers 45.00
Nippon, Chocolate Set, Gold Flowers, Pot & 6 Cups & Saucers, Signed 85.00
Nippon, Chocolate Set, Gold Trim, 4 Cups & Saucers 95.00
Nippon, Chocolate Set, Hand-Painted, Rising Sun Mark, 11 Piece 65.00
Nippon, Chocolate Set, Pink & Red Flowers, Cobalt Trim, White, 9 Piece 68.00
Nippon, Chocolate Set, Rising Sun, Pink, Blue, Gold Trim, 4 Cups & Saucers 69.00
Nippon, Chocolate Set, Sailboats At Sunrise, Green M In Wreath, 13 Piece 225.00
Nippon, Chocolate Set, Scenic, Water, Sail Boat, Pot, 6 Cups & Saucers 135.00
Nippon, Chocolate Set, White & Gold, 9 Piece 125.00
Nippon, Chocolate Set, Yellow, Raised Gold Rim, Swans, Lilies 145.00
Nippon, Chocolate Set, 4 Cups & Saucers, Violets, Rising Sun Mark 165.00
Nippon, Chocolate Set, 5 Cups & Saucers, Hand-Painted, Beaded, R.C. Mark 250.00
Nippon, Coaster, Flying Bluebird, Flowers, Crown Mark, 3 3/4 In.Diameter 6.00
Nippon, Coaster, Large Owl In Flight, Set Of 5 .... 65.00
Nippon, Coaster, Sail Boats, Lavender Ground, Green Wreath Mark, Set Of 4 .... 55.00
Nippon, Coffee Set, Moriaga, Signed, 10 Piece 95.00
Nippon, Compote, Footed & Handled, Signed, 6 In.Diameter 25.00
Nippon, Compote, Footed, Green & Gold, Undulating Sides, Jewels, 7 1/2 In. 70.00
Nippon, Compote, 2 Handles, Wild Flowers, 9 In.Diameter 18.00
Nippon, Condiment Set, Mustard, Toothpick, Salt & Pepper, Tray, Marked 45.00
Nippon, Condiment Set, Ring Handle, Hand-Painted, Green Wreath M, 2 5/8 In. 18.00
Nippon, Condiment Set, Scene, Brown Beaded Borders, M In Wreath, 4 Pieces 58.00
Nippon, Condiment Set, Tray, Mustard, Pair Of Shakers, Red, Green, Gold 75.00
Nippon, Condiment Set, Violets, Rising Sun Mark, 3 Piece 27.50
Nippon, Container, Condensed Milk, White Ground, Blue Forget-Me-Nots, Signed 50.00
Nippon, Cookie Jar & Matching Underplate, Vignettes On Blue & Gold 235.00
Nippon, Cookie Jar, Cobalt, Gold Scrolls, Scenes, Red, 7 1/2 In. 57.00
Nippon, Cookie Jar, Covered, Hand-Painted, Green Wreath 110.00
Nippon, Cookie Jar, Gold Loop Finial, Scenic, Hand-Painted, Green Wreath 110.00
Nippon, Cookie Jar, Pearlized Luster Ground, Roses, Signed, 8 1/2 In. 135.00
Nippon, Cookie Jar, Under Plate, 9 X 8 In. 225.00
Nippon, Cracker Jar, Autumn Scenic 45.00
Nippon, Cracker Jar, Bulbous, Melon Shape, Scenic, Gold Trim, 8 1/2 In. 275.00
Nippon, Cracker Jar, Clusters Outlined & Beaded In Gold, Blue Maple Leaf 150.00
Nippon, Cracker Jar, Covered, Melon Shape, Moriaga Dragon, Green Wreath Mark 145.00
Nippon, Cracker Jar, Encrusted With Gold, 2 Handled, Maple Leaf Mark 125.00
Nippon, Cracker Jar, Footed, Gold Beading, Fuchsia To Pink, Geometric Design 135.00
Nippon, Cracker Jar, Hand-Painted Flowers, Gold Trim, 9 1/2 In.Diameter 135.00
Nippon, Cracker Jar, Melon Ribbed, Cobalt Blue, Gold Trim 185.00
Nippon, Cracker Jar, Melon Shape, Covered, Footed, Scattered Flowers, Marked 95.00
Nippon, Creamer & Sugar, Covered, White, Pastel Flowers, Raised Gilding 45.00
Nippon, Creamer, Child's Blown-Out Face, 3 In. .... 40.00 To 145.00
Nippon, Creamer, Gaudy Design, Red Border 26.00
Nippon, Creamer, Rural Scene Of Lake, Cottages 6.00
Nippon, Cruet, Indian In Headdress, Enamel Beading, Signed 285.00
Nippon, Cruet, Salt & Pepper, Trees Landscape, Brown Beading 16.00
Nippon, Cup & Saucer, Blue Bird, Pink Floral Motif 8.50
Nippon, Cup & Saucer, Bouillon, Gold & Black Landscape On White, Set Of 4 .... 85.00
Nippon, Cup & Saucer, Bouillon, Pink Floral, Garlands, Gold 15.00
Nippon, Cup & Saucer, Chocolate, Cobalt Blue, Gold Flowers 45.00
Nippon, Cup & Saucer, Chocolate, Gold Bands, Beading, M In Wreath 8.00
Nippon, Cup & Saucer, Demitasse, Pink Florals, Gold Trim, M In Wreath Mark 9.00

Nippon, Cup & Saucer, European Castle, White Ground, Decal Designs	20.00
Nippon, Cup & Saucer, Flowers, Blue Maple Leaf Mark, Set Of 6	32.00
Nippon, Cup & Saucer, Hand-Painted, Beaded Gold Banding, Green M Mark	12.00
Nippon, Cup & Saucer, Hand-Painted, Gold Beading, 3 Curved Feet, Wreath Mark	35.00
Nippon, Cup & Saucer, Lavender, Brown, Windmills, Geometric Border	15.00
Nippon, Cup & Saucer, Wild Roses, Gold, Maple Leaf	15.00
Nippon, Cup, Handleless, Royal Sometuke, Pair	15.00
Nippon, Cup, Loving, Pink Azaleas & Gold, Pair	25.00
Nippon, Demitasse Set, Slim Pot, Gold Beaded Embroidery, 4 Cups & Saucers	165.00
Nippon, Desk Set, Inkwell, Pen Tray, Blotter, 2 Corners, Gold Trim, R.C. Mark	250.00
Nippon, Dish, Beaded Edge, Cobalt Bird, Green Wreath Mark, 6 1/2 In.	55.00
Nippon, Dish, Butter, Covered, Floral Border, Green Wreath Mark, 7 3/4 In.	45.00
Nippon, Dish, Butter, Covered, Geometric Design, Red Crown Mark	40.00
Nippon, Dish, Butter, White Ground, Pink Flowers, Signed	70.00
Nippon, Dish, Candy, Butterflies & Flowers, R.C. Mark, 6 1/2 In.	10.50
Nippon, Dish, Candy, Cover, Gold & Pastels, Hand-Painted, Signed, 6 1/2 In.	29.00
Nippon, Dish, Candy, Open Handle, Gold Beading, Cobalt Blue, 7 1/2 X 7 In.	59.00
Nippon, Dish, Candy, Oviform, Eared, Six Colors, Jewels, 8 In.	22.00
Nippon, Dish, Canoe Shape, Indian In Canoe, 11 In.	65.00
Nippon, Dish, Cheese, Slant Cover, 8 X 4 In.	35.00
Nippon, Dish, Cheese, Wedge Cover, Bands Of Roses	30.00
Nippon, Dish, Cucumber, Matching Underplate, Gold Trim	28.00
Nippon, Dish, Diamond Shape, Violets, Green Design, 12 1/2 X 8 1/2 In.	25.00
Nippon, Dish, Divided, Center Handle, Magenta M, 7 In.	15.00
Nippon, Dish, Domed Lid, Gold On Loop Handle, Rising Sun Mark, 9 In.	40.00
Nippon, Dish, Footed, Autumn Tones, Green Wreath Mark, 6 In.Diameter	25.00
Nippon, Dish, Hand-Painted, Lake Scene, Beaded Banding, Green M Mark, 7 In.	30.00
Nippon, Dish, Hot Food, Hand-Painted, Gold Diapered Borders, 9 In.Diam.	35.00
Nippon, Dish, Kidney Shaped, Flowers Inside, 7 X 4 In.	8.00
Nippon, Dish, Mayonnaise, Hand-Painted Blue Birds Flying	10.00
Nippon, Dish, Mayonnaise, Ladle, 3 Feet, Hand-Painted	48.00
Nippon, Dish, Nut, Blown-Out Nut, Hand-Painted, M In Wreath Mark, 6 1/2 In.	125.00
Nippon, Dish, Pierced Handles, Boat Scene, Marked M, Green Wreath, 5 In.	20.00
Nippon, Dish, Powder, Snow Scene On Top, White	55.00
Nippon, Dish, Relish, Flowers, Gold Beading, 7 1/2 In.	12.00
Nippon, Dish, Relish, Oval, 2 Handles, Water Scene, Hand-Painted, 7 1/2 In.	10.50
Nippon, Dish, Relish, Poppies, Sun Mark, 6 1/4 In.	12.00
Nippon, Dish, Sailboat & Lake Scene, Matte, Handled, 6 In.	22.00
Nippon, Dish, Scalloped, Gold Beading, Maple Leaf Mark, 13 X 7 In.	88.00
Nippon, Dresser Set, Applied Dragon, Enamel Trim, Green Wreath Mark, 3 Piece	145.00
Nippon, Dresser Set, Pink Roses, Blue & White Border, Green Wreath Mark	50.00
Nippon, Dresser Set, Red Flowers, Gold Beading, Marked, 5 Piece	85.00
Nippon, Dresser Set, Scenic, 3 Piece	32.50
Nippon, Egg Warmer, Flowers, Gold Trim, Warmer Cap, 4 Holders, Rising Sun Mark	85.00
Nippon, Eggcup, Gold Rims, Rising Sun, Set Of 6	30.00
Nippon, Ewer, Art Deco, Cranes, 9 In.	68.00
Nippon, Ewer, Gold Beaded Band Top & Bottom, Hold Handles, 11 In., Pair	250.00
Nippon, Ewer, Gold Beading & Overlay, Bulbous, Cobalt Handle, 14 In.	165.00
Nippon, Ewer, Gold Roses, Scenic Background, 12 1/2 X 7 3/4 In.	145.00
Nippon, Ewer, Landscape, Signed, Blue M, 9 1/4 In.	135.00
Nippon, Ewer, Moriage Handle & Veining, Green Ground, 8 In.	205.00
Nippon, Ewer, Portrait, Floral Medallions, 3 Feet, Maple Leaf Mark, 9 In.	250.00
Nippon, Ewer, Portrait, 2 Women, Gold Beading, Maple Leaf Mark, 7 1/2 In.Base	220.00
Nippon, Ewer, Red & Pink Roses, Gold Trim, Marked, 6 1/4 In.	48.00
Nippon, Ewer, Roses, Cobalt Blue & Gold Trim, 9 1/2 In.	65.00
Nippon, Fernery, Beaded Legs, Etched, M In Green Wreath, 7 1/4 X 4 3/4 In.	139.00
Nippon, Fernery, Floral Medallions, Octagonal, 8 In.	32.00
Nippon, Fernery, Footed, Gold Trim, Enamel Jewels, 6 X 8 In.Diameter	95.00
Nippon, Fernery, Hexagon, Lake Scene, Oriental Handles, Blue Leaf, 7 In.	45.00
Nippon, Fernery, 3 Corner, Egyptian Design, 6 In.Sides	55.00
Nippon, Fernery, 4 Beaded Legs, Green M In Wreath, 7 1/2 X 4 3/4 In.	139.00
Nippon, Figurine, Black Rhinoceros, 2 1/2 In.	35.00
Nippon, Figurine, Dog With Bone, Bisque, Marked, 4 In.	35.00
Nippon, Figurine, Girl, Molded Hair In Bun, Skirted, Blue Dress, 3 1/4 In.	12.00
Nippon, Flask, Talcum, Pink Roses, Solid Gold Top	58.00
Nippon, Game Set, 6 8 1/2 In.Plates, 8 Birds, Green Wreath Mark, 17 X 11 In.	575.00

Nippon, Hair Receiver & Powder Jar, Beading Overlay, Maple Leaf Mark .... 100.0￠

Nippon, Hair Receiver, Cover, Hand-Painted, Gold & Beads, Maple Leaf .... 43.0￠

Nippon, Hair Receiver, Gold Beaded Trim, Pink & Blue Floral, Signed .... 28.0￠

Nippon, Hatpin Holder, Gold Beads & Jewels, Maple Leaf Mark .... 40.0￠

Nippon, Hatpin Holder, Hourglass Shape, 5 In. 37.0

Nippon, Hatpin Holder, Ivory & Blue Flowers .... 18.0￠

Nippon, Hatpin Holder, Scenic, Beading, Bisque .... 35.0￠

Nippon, Holder, Sugar Cube, Gold Beading, Hand-Painted, 6 3/4 X 1 3/4 In. .... 55.0￠

Nippon, Humidor, Bisque Finish, Design Of Pipe, Cigar & Matched .... 138.0￠

Nippon, Humidor, Bisque, Jeweled .... 65.0￠

Nippon, Humidor, Black Bottom & Lid, Branch & Owl On Upper Half, 5 1/2 In. .... 65.0￠

Nippon, Humidor, Blown-Out Dog Heads, Beige & Brown, 6 1/2 In. .... 600.0￠

Nippon, Humidor, Blown-Out Indian Heads, In Full Headdress .... 90.0￠

Nippon, Humidor, Blown-Out, Bulbous, Pirate Smoking Pipe On Lid, Green M .... 175.0￠

Nippon, Humidor, Circular, Beaded Cover, Enameling, Green Wreath Mark, 6 In. .... 185.0￠

Nippon, Humidor, Collie, Blown Out, Green Wreath Mark .... 400.0￠

Nippon, Humidor, Gold & Magenta Enamel, Beaded, Green Maple Leaf, 6 In. .... 185.0￠

Nippon, Humidor, Hexagon, Bisque Finish, Camels & Pyramids .... 65.0￠

Nippon, Humidor, Horse-Pulled Carriage, Driver & Lady Rider .... 395.0￠

Nippon, Humidor, Hunt Scene, Red Coated Riders, Marked .... 175.0￠

Nippon, Humidor, Indian Design, With Deer, Blue Wreath Mark, 6 In. .... 110.0￠

Nippon, Humidor, Man Playing Guitar, Green .... 395.0￠

Nippon, Humidor, Pirate Smoking Pipe, Blown-Out, Green Mark .... 175.0￠

Nippon, Humidor, Playing Card Design, Leaf Mark .... 135.0￠

Nippon, Humidor, Roses, Pink, Red, Lid .... 47.5￠

Nippon, Humidor, Scenic, Moriaga Rim & Knob, Orange, Blue, Signed, 5 In. .... 75.0￠

Nippon, Humidor, Stag & Doe, Ball Shape, Footed, Green M, 5 1/4 In. .... 195.0￠

Nippon, Humidor, Yellow & Tan Ground, Yellow Roses, Signed, 9 In. .... 225.0￠

Nippon, Humidor, 4-Sided, Horses' Heads, Bisque, Green M In Wreath, 6 In. .... 250.0￠

Nippon, Humidor, 6 Sided, Pictured Pipe, Cigar & Cigarette, Signed, 4 1/2 In. .... 135.0￠

Nippon, Incense Burner, Foo Lion Handle, Incised Mark .... 32.0￠

Nippon, Incense Burner, Terra Cotta Decoration .... 40.0￠

Nippon, Inkwell, Desert Isle Scene, Yellow, Brown, Green Wreath Mark .... 35.0￠

Nippon, Inkwell, Flowers Outlined In Gold, Superior Mark .... 55.0￠

Nippon, Jar, Ginger, Blue & White, Prunus Blossoms, 5 In. .... 65.0￠

Nippon, Jar, Ginger, Covered, Overall Beading, Leaf Mark, 4 3/4 In. .... 65.0￠

Nippon, Jar, Jam, Covered, Gold Band, M In Wreath .... 21.0￠

Nippon, Jar, Jam, Handled, Underplate, Gold Rims & Beading, Gold Finial .... 39.0￠

Nippon, Jar, Powder, Beaded, Raised Gold, Maple Leaf Mark .... 42.0￠

Nippon, Jar, Sachet, Roses, Green, Gold, Label On Bottom, 5 1/2 X 14 In. .... 85.0￠

Nippon, Jug, Bisque Scenes, Enameled, 4-Sided Stoppered, Multicolored .... 275.0￠

Nippon, Jug, Stopper, Bulldog, Champion Bromley Crib .... 255.0￠

Nippon, Jug, Syrup & Underplate, Purple M Mark .... 35.0￠

Nippon, Jug, Whiskey, Raised Gold Oriental Scenes, Black Panels, Green Mark .... 285.0￠

Nippon, Jug, Wine, Eagle Design Cork Stopper .... 135.0￠

Nippon, Lemonade Set, Pitcher & 6 Mugs, Enamel Flowers .... 83.0￠

Nippon, Lemonade Set, Pitcher & 7 Mugs, Gold Beading .... 225.0￠

Nippon, Lemonade Set, 5 Mugs, Bisque Finish, Farm Scene, Mark 37 .... 75.0￠

Nippon, Luncheon Set, Ormonde, Bassett, Green Wreath And M.30 Piece .... 120.0￠

Nippon, Match Holder & Ashtray, Duck Shaped, Green, Signed .... 10.0￠

Nippon, Match Holder, Pink Roses, Butterfly .... 20.0￠

Nippon, Match Holder, Scenic, Jeweled In Top Corners, Green Wreath .... 25.0￠

Nippon, Match Holder, Striker On Bottom, Gold & Blue, Marked .... 28.5￠

Nippon, Mayonnaise & Underplate, Pink Floral, Gold Scallop & Swag .... 17.5￠

Nippon, Mayonnaise Set, Footed, 3 Piece, Red M Mark .... 30.0￠

Nippon, Mayonnaise Set, Scenic, Geishas, Royal Koga, 3 Piece .... 38.0￠

Nippon, Mayonnaise Set, 3 Ball Feet, Raised Gold Floral, Green Wreath Mark .... 35.0￠

Nippon, Mug, Blown-Out Googly-Eyed Boy .... 45.00 To 115.0￠

Nippon, Mug, Dragons, Beaded Handle, Oak Leaf Mark, 5 1/2 In. .... 150.0￠

Nippon, Mug, Shaving, White, Black Band Around Top .... 60.0￠

Nippon, Mush Set, Creamer & Bowl, Scenic, Blue Leaf .... 28.0￠

Nippon, Mustache Cup & Saucer, Cobalt Blue, Panels Of Flowers, Marked .... 75.0￠

Nippon, Mustache Cup & Saucer, Gold, Peach, Light Green, Maple Leaf Mark .... 135.0￠

Nippon, Mustache Cup & Saucer, Red & Orange Roses, Gold Beading, Marked .... 135.0￠

Nippon, Mustard & Underplate, Roses & Webbing, Blue Mapleleaf Mark .... 25.0￠

Nippon, Mustard Pot, Attached Underplate, Cobalt Border, Beading .... 22.0￠

Nippon, Mustard Pot, Attached Underplate, Egyptian Scene, Cobalt Trim	23.00
Nippon, Mustard Pot, Spoon, Violets, Gold Trim, Blue Rising Sun Mark	32.50
Nippon, Mustard Pot, Spoon, White Ground, Gold Trim, Murisama Mark	22.50
Nippon, Mustard Pot, Underplate, Gold Rigaree, Green Wreath Mark, 8 In.	40.00
Nippon, Napkin Ring, Gold Outline, Jeweled Berries, Flower Mark	45.00
Nippon, Napkin Ring, Scenic, Flowers, Gold, Green Wreath Mark	65.00
Nippon, Napkin Ring, Triangular, Flowers, Gold Trim	35.00
Nippon, Nappy, Covered, Scalloped Rim, Gold Tracery, Hand-Painted, Signed	29.00
Nippon, Nappy, House, Trees, Lake, Bisque Finish, 6 3/4 In.	26.00
Nippon, Nappy, Leaf Shape, Raised Enamel Trim, Blue Mark, 5 1/2 X 7 1/4 In.	37.50
Nippon, Nut Set, Footed, Gold Trim, Green Mark With Wreath, 7 Piece	75.00
Nippon, Nut Set, Hand-Painted, 7 1/4 In.Bowl & 6 Dishes	125.00
Nippon, Nut Set, Six 3-Footed Cups & Serving Bowl, Hand-Painted	55.00
Nippon, Pitcher, Child's Blown-Out Face, 3 In.	35.00 To 45.00
Nippon, Pitcher, Cider, Six Handled Mugs, Yellow & White Flowers	150.00
Nippon, Pitcher, Cider, 2 Mugs, Cream To Green, Wreath Mark	52.00
Nippon, Pitcher, Gold, Beading, Hand-Painted Scene, Nagoya, 16 In.	145.00
Nippon, Pitcher, Hand-Painted Roses, Gold Rim, Base & Handle, 10 In.	160.00
Nippon, Pitcher, Lemonade, 2 Tumblers, Cream Ground, Violets	60.00
Nippon, Pitcher, Milk, Beaded, Gold Trim, 4 1/2 In.	12.00
Nippon, Pitcher, Milk, Covered, Boat Scene, Beaded Rim, Maple Leaf, 7 1/4 In.	149.00
Nippon, Pitcher, Milk, Covered, Boat Scene, Maple Leaf Mark, 7 1/4 In.	145.00
Nippon, Pitcher, Rising Sun, Blown Googly Faced Girl, Red, Marked, 3 In.	65.00
Nippon, Pitcher, Water, Hand-Painted Violets	35.00
Nippon, Planter, Jeweled, Footed, Pastels, M In Wreath, 6 1/2 X 4 1/2 In.	115.00
Nippon, Planter, Triangular Shape, Raised Enamel Design, 3 1/2 In.	95.00
Nippon, Plaque, Antlered Moose, Raised Enamel Tree, M In Wreath, 8 3/4 In.	95.00
Nippon, Plaque, Blown-Out Moose, Green Mark, Signed, 10 1/2 In.	375.00
Nippon, Plaque, Fall Scene, Bisque Finish, Pierced For Hanging, 9 In.	40.00
Nippon, Plaque, Five Horses Blown, Green Mark, Signed, 10 1/2 In.	550.00
Nippon, Plaque, Lions On Rocky Mountain, Blown, Green Mark, Signed, 11 In.	425.00
Nippon, Plaque, Oriental Scene, Blue Wreath Mark, 9 1/2 In.	95.00
Nippon, Plaque, Spotted Deer, Dogs, Foliage, Laurel Mark, 10 5/8 In., Pair	750.00
Nippon, Plaque, Spring Scene, Bisque Finish, Pierced For Hanging, 9 In.	40.00
Nippon, Plate, Azalea, 7 1/2 In.	7.00
Nippon, Plate, Blue Windmill, Boats, Water Scene, 8 3/4 In.Diameter	22.00
Nippon, Plate, Boats & Cargo On Shore, Matte, Beaded, 9 In.	65.00
Nippon, Plate, Cake, Autumn Scene, Set Of 6	45.00
Nippon, Plate, Cake, Gold Border, Banding, Handled	20.00
Nippon, Plate, Cake, Kutani Style Scene, Gold Trim, M In Wreath, 10 1/4 In.	36.00
Nippon, Plate, Cake, Open Handled, Gold Banded, Gold Beading	35.00
Nippon, Plate, Cake, Pierced Handles, Roses, Maple Leaf Mark	32.00
Nippon, Plate, Celery, Hand-Painted, 13 In.	25.00
Nippon, Plate, Desert Scene Border, Enameled Inner Circle, Green Mark, 9 In.	37.50
Nippon, Plate, Flying Phoenix, 8 In.	25.00
Nippon, Plate, Game, Raised Gold Floral Rim, 7 1/2 In., Pair	85.00
Nippon, Plate, Geisha, Cobalt Scalloped Border, 7 1/2 In.	55.00
Nippon, Plate, Gold & Enamel Border, Flying Geese, 8 In.	85.00
Nippon, Plate, Gold Beading, Green M, 7 1/2 In.	9.00
Nippon, Plate, Gold, Handpainted, Open Handle, 11 In.	150.00
Nippon, Plate, Hand-Painted Boat Scene, Green Wreath, 19 In.Diameter	65.00
Nippon, Plate, Hand-Painted, Gold Border, Green Wreath, 8 3/4 In.	45.00
Nippon, Plate, Hand-Painted, Gold Edge, Snowberries, 6 1/4 In.	25.00
Nippon, Plate, Imari Coloring, Marked, 8 1/4 In.	17.50
Nippon, Plate, Indian Tree, 6 In., Set Of 5	15.00 To 25.00
Nippon, Plate, Lake & Cottage Scene, Green M Wreath, 10 In.	30.00
Nippon, Plate, Multicolor Matte Scene, Green Wreath Mark, 12 In.	250.00
Nippon, Plate, Nile Scene, Gold Border, Green M Mark, 10 In.	55.00
Nippon, Plate, Palm Tree & Lake Scene, Matte Finish, 8 In.	25.00
Nippon, Plate, Pheasants, Green Wreath Mark, 9 1/2 In.	47.50
Nippon, Plate, Purple Orchids, Gold Scroll Around Plate, 10 In.	35.00
Nippon, Plate, Scenic, Raised Stork Handles, Green M, 9 In.	32.00
Nippon, Plate, Slip Rim, Jewel Each Curve, Royal Crown Mark, 10 In.	55.00
Nippon, Plate, Swans, Lake, Windmill, Gold Trim, Green M, 7 1/2 In.	30.00
Nippon, Plate, White, Pink Border, Black Ground, Marked, 7 In.	5.00
Nippon, Plate, Windmill, Water Scene, Green Maple Leaf, 6 In., Set Of 6	55.00

Nippon, Platter, Butterflies, Black Ground, Red Mark, 13 X 10 1/2 In.	50.00
Nippon, Platter, Kiva, Green Wreath Mark, 16 X 12 In.	20.00
Nippon, Platter, Red Flowers On Black Ground, Signed, 13 X 10 1/2 In.	100.00
Nippon, Pot, Demitasse, Lighthouse Shape, Encrusted Gold, Blue Leaf	22.00
Nippon, Pot, Demitasse, Raised Gold On White, Blue Mark	35.00
Nippon, Pot, Demitasse, 4 Cups & Saucers, Embroidery & Webbing, 9 3/4 In.	165.00
Nippon, Punch Set, Bowl, Handled, 6 Handled Cups, 12 In.Tray, Gold Trim	195.00
Nippon, Punch Set, Encrusted Gold Trim, Claw Feet, 5 Pedestal Cups, Signed	625.00
Nippon, Rack, Letter, Art Nouveau, Gold Handle, Signed, 6 1/4 X 3 1/2 X 5 In.	135.00
Nippon, Rack, Toast, Double Size, White Ground, Signed	85.00
Nippon, Relish, Pink Floral, Beading, Green Trim, Leaf Mark, 7 1/2 X 4 3/4 In.	12.50
Nippon, Ring Tree, Outstretched Gold Hand, Boats In Background	45.00
Nippon, Salt & Pepper, Green & Grey Moriye, Floral, Flowers & Leaves, Pair	50.00
Nippon, Salt & Pepper, Sailboats, Green M	14.00
Nippon, Salt, Blown-Out Nut Shell Shape	16.00
Nippon, Salt, Footed, Boat Scene	9.50
Nippon, Sauceboat & Underliner, Pink Flowers, Gold Beading, Green Mark	35.00
Nippon, Server, Pancake, Covered, Royal Kaga Design	85.00
Nippon, Server, Sardine, Lid & Underplate, Geometric Design, Signed	72.00
Nippon, Serving Set, Bowl, Underplate & Ladle, Signed	35.00
Nippon, Shaving Mug, Hand-Painted Purple Pansies	80.00
Nippon, Shaving Mug, Porcelain, Floral Border, Rising Sun Mark, 3 1/4 In.	45.00
Nippon, Shaving Mug, Scenic, Enameled & Jeweled Handle, Green Wreath & M	95.00
Nippon, Stein, Beaded Rim & Handle, Green Wreath Mark	40.00
Nippon, Stickpin Holder, Saucer Bottom, Purple Violets, White Beading	42.00
Nippon, Strainer, Tea, Flying Turkey	20.00
Nippon, Strainer, Tea, Green & Gold	25.00
Nippon, Strainer, Tea, Holder, Cobalt Blue, Gold Trim, Blue Maple Leaf	55.00
Nippon, Strainer, Tea, Red & Pink Roses, Gold Beading, Marked	48.00
Nippon, Strainer, Tea, Roses On Green Background, Red, Yellow, Maple Leaf Mark	60.00
Nippon, Strainer, Tea, Violets, Gold Beading	45.00
Nippon, Sugar & Creamer, Blue & Pink Flowers	65.00
Nippon, Sugar & Creamer, Bluebirds, Roses, Gold Border, Crown Mark	22.00
Nippon, Sugar & Creamer, Bulbous, Gold Trim & Beading, Signed, Royal Crown	50.00
Nippon, Sugar & Creamer, Bulbous, 3 Gold Feet, Gold Oriental Mark	45.00
Nippon, Sugar & Creamer, Cobalt Blue Border, Pink Flowers	40.00
Nippon, Sugar & Creamer, Cover, Raised Gold Design, Beading, Jewels, Marked	65.00
Nippon, Sugar & Creamer, Covered, Gold-On-Gold Vintage Grape & Leaf	110.00
Nippon, Sugar & Creamer, Footed, Gold Trim, White Inside	40.00
Nippon, Sugar & Creamer, Footed, Pink & Yellow Roses, Gold Trim, Signed	55.00
Nippon, Sugar & Creamer, Geometric Border, Gold Outlining, Imperial Mark	48.00
Nippon, Sugar & Creamer, Gold Beaded Border, Green Wreath Mark	50.00
Nippon, Sugar & Creamer, Gold Footed, Gold Tracery & Beading, Blue Leaf	45.00
Nippon, Sugar & Creamer, Gold Handles & Trim, Hand-Painted, M In Wreath	40.00
Nippon, Sugar & Creamer, Gold Lower, Red Upper, White Gold Trim & Handles	45.00
Nippon, Sugar & Creamer, Gold On Handles, Top Rim, Finials, M In Wreath	28.00
Nippon, Sugar & Creamer, Hand-Painted Roses, Gold Trim	27.00
Nippon, Sugar & Creamer, Hand-Painted, Scenic, Cobalt Band, M In Wreath	45.00
Nippon, Sugar & Creamer, Jeweled Bird, Pink Flowers, Marked	27.00
Nippon, Sugar & Creamer, Lavender, Brown, Windmills, Geometric Border	25.00
Nippon, Sugar & Creamer, Lid, Flying Turkey	27.50
Nippon, Sugar & Creamer, Lid, Scenic, Green Wreath	25.00
Nippon, Sugar & Creamer, Pedestal, Gold Overlay, Maple Leaf	120.00
Nippon, Sugar & Creamer, Roses On Gold Stems, Blue Rising Sun	20.00
Nippon, Sugar & Creamer, Royal Sometuke, 8 Cups & Saucers	50.00
Nippon, Sugar & Creamer, Satin Finish, Beading.Blue Jewels	28.00
Nippon, Sugar & Creamer, Scenic, Gold Trim, Green Wreath & M	38.00
Nippon, Sugar & Creamer, 6-Sided, Roses Framed In Gold Jewels, Finial, 5 In.	50.00
Nippon, Sugar Shaker, Apple Blossoms, Gold Trim, Round, Marked	42.00
Nippon, Sugar Shaker, Barrel Shape, Bands Of White Jewels, 4 1/2 In.	85.00
Nippon, Sugar Shaker, Cobalt & Gold Trim, Holes Outlined In Beading	70.00
Nippon, Sugar Shaker, Gold & Pink Flowers, Green Mark	40.00
Nippon, Sugar Shaker, Porcelain Handle, Gold Trim	17.00
Nippon, Sugar Shaker, 6-Sided, Poppies, Gold Trim	48.00
Nippon, Syrup, Gold Beading, Raised Gold, Maple Leaf Mark	39.00
Nippon, Syrup, Gold Handle & Beading, Gold Tracings, R.C.Mark	39.00

Nippon, Syrup, Pastel Scene, 1/2 Gallon, Green Mark, 9 1/2 In.	100.00
Nippon, Syrup, Underplate, Loop Handle & Spout, Moriaga Trim	45.00
Nippon, Tankard & Mugs, Floral Moriage Beaded Work, Set Of 4, Signed	295.00
Nippon, Tankard, Flowers In Center, 12 In.	50.00
Nippon, Tankard, Marked Royal Nippon, 6 Sided, 12 In.	145.00
Nippon, Tankard, Red To Green Ground, Gold Overlay, Royal Nishiki, 12 In.	150.00
Nippon, Tea Caddy, Blue, Yellow & Gold, Green M Mark	120.00
Nippon, Tea Set, Blue, Red & Yellow Flowers, 6 Cups & Saucers, 15 Piece	95.00
Nippon, Tea Set, Melon Ribbed, Floral, Gold Trim, Leaf Mark	175.00
Nippon, Tea Set, Roses Outlined In Gold, Pot, 6 In.	110.00
Nippon, Tea Set, Roses, Cobalt, Gold, Multi-Colored, 13 Piece	120.00
Nippon, Tea Set, Scenic Panels, Beading, 6 Cups & Saucers, Blue Mark	150.00
Nippon, Tea Set, White Flowers, Gold Outline, Apricot, Imperial Mark, 13 Piece	125.00
Nippon, Tea Set, Yellow Flowers & Stem, Signed, 3 Piece	69.00
Nippon, Tea Set, 4 Cups & Saucers, Scenes In Raised Gold Ovals, Wreath Mark	250.00
Nippon, Tea Set, 5 Cups & Saucers, 3 Cake Plates, Platter, M In Green Wreath	155.00
Nippon, Teapot, Bulbous, Rural Scene, Cottages, 4 1/2 In.	18.00
Nippon, Teapot, Footed, White, Gold Trim, Green M Wreath	55.00
Nippon, Teapot, Houses, Volcano, Gold Trim, Nagoya Mark	57.00
Nippon, Teapot, Oriental Scenes, Geishas, Pink, Green, Gold Trim, 8 1/2 In.	65.00
Nippon, Teapot, Pink Roses, Rising Sun Mark	22.00
Nippon, Teapot, Sugar & Creamer, Dragon, Black Matte, Flower Mark	175.00
Nippon, Teapot, Sugar & Creamer, Footed, Gold & Silver Flowers, Fluted	125.00
Nippon, Teapot, Sugar & Creamer, Ladies In Garden, Marked	85.00
Nippon, Teapot, Sugar & Creamer, Ladies In Garden, White Ground, Marked	65.00
Nippon, Teapot, 17 Medallions, Turquoise, Gold & Green, 5 X 6 In.	70.00
Nippon, Tile, 8 Sided, Black & Gold Geometric Design, Green Wreath Mark	14.00
Nippon, Toothpick, Figural, Grotesque Bird, Made In Japan	45.00
Nippon, Toothpick, Hand-Painted Floral Border	6.00
Nippon, Toothpick, Lake Scene, 2 Handled	18.00
Nippon, Toothpick, Water Scene, Green M	18.00
Nippon, Toothpick, 2 Gold Handles, Pinecones	25.00
Nippon, Toothpick, 3 Feet, Handles, Black With Flowers	25.00
Nippon, Tray & Cup, Pink, Gold Leaves, Rising Sun Mark	12.00
Nippon, Tray, Border Print Of Pink Roses, 11 X 7 1/2 In.	25.00
Nippon, Tray, Bread, Scalloped Edge, Fruits, Beading & Gold Trim, 13 1/2 In.	85.00
Nippon, Tray, Celery, Cranes Outlined In Gold, Green Crown Mark, 12 In.	35.00
Nippon, Tray, Celery, Gold Border, Jewels, Blue Mark, 12 X 5 1/2 In.	30.00
Nippon, Tray, Double Tiered, Beaded Border, Rising Sun Mark, 8 3/4 In.Diam.	38.00
Nippon, Tray, Dresser, Gold Trim, White, 7 X 12 In.	30.00
Nippon, Tray, Farm Scene, Bisque, Green Wreath Mark, 8 3/4 X 4 In.	48.00
Nippon, Tray, Floral Sprays Outlined In Gold, Impressed Mark, 9 X 6 In.	38.00
Nippon, Tray, Floral Sprays, Gold Trim, Impressed Oriental Mark, 9 X 6 In.	38.00
Nippon, Tray, Flowers, Multi-Colored, Cobalt, 15 In.	185.00
Nippon, Tray, Gold Handles, Signed, Green Wreath, 10 In.	32.00
Nippon, Tray, Gold Outlined Flowers & Leaves Border, Handled, 10 In.	25.00
Nippon, Tray, Mountain Scene, Gold Scroll, Green Beads Outlined In Gold, Mark	59.00
Nippon, Tray, Pin, Butterfly Shape, Gold Beading, Green Wreath	18.50
Nippon, Tray, Trinket, Jeweled & Scenic, Green Wreath Mark, 6 1/2 X 3 In.	25.00
Nippon, Tray, Violets, Rising Sun Mark, 9 X 6 In.	16.00
Nippon, Tumbler, With Coaster, Bisque Finish, Playing Cards, Green Wreath	75.00
Nippon, Urn, Covered, Scenic, Gold Trim, 14 In.	295.00
Nippon, Urn, Twin Ring Handles, Hand-Painted, Green M In Wreath, 9 1/2 In.	130.00
Nippon, Vase, All Over Roses & Gold, 12 In.	195.00
Nippon, Vase, Arab On Camel In Oasis, 6 Ball Feet, 2 Handled, 6 In.	70.00
Nippon, Vase, Art Nouveau, 9 In.	129.00
Nippon, Vase, Beach Scene, Shoulder & Foot Raised Designs *Illus*	125.00
Nippon, Vase, Beaded Dragon, 6 1/2 In., Pair	100.00
Nippon, Vase, Beaded Handles & Base, Geometric Throat, Green M Mark, 11 In.	70.00
Nippon, Vase, Black Ground, Bands Of Gold & Green, Green Wreath Mark, 8 In.	55.00
Nippon, Vase, Black Handles, Pearlized Beige, 5 3/4 In.	15.00
Nippon, Vase, Black Silhouette Cowboy On Horse, 8 Inches	40.00
Nippon, Vase, Blue Panels On White, Gold Urn Handles, Hand-Painted, 10 In.	80.00
Nippon, Vase, Blue, Pink, Flowers, 2 Birds, Gold Handle & Trim, 9 1/2 In.	70.00
Nippon, Vase, Brown & Gold, Swan Scene, Handled, 12 In., Pair	125.00
Nippon, Vase, Brown Ground, Scenic Jewels, Gold, Superior Mark, 6 In.	75.00

Nippon, Vase, Bulbous Shape, Scenic Medallions, Ram's Head Handles, 10 In. 250.00
Nippon, Vase, Bulbous, Raised Leaves, Acorns, Green Wreath Mark, 6 In. 85.00
Nippon, Vase, Burnished Gold, Matte, Gold Outlines, M In Wreath, 10 In. 145.00
Nippon, Vase, Claw Footed, Elephant Head Handles, M In Wreath, 8 1/2 In. 135.00
Nippon, Vase, Corset Shaped, Gold Collar, Tapestry, 8 1/2 In. 325.00
Nippon, Vase, Country Scene, Geometric Beaded Gold, Green M Wreath, 8 In. 48.00
Nippon, Vase, Desert Scene, Arabic Pattern, M In Green Wreath, 9 1/2 In. 98.00
Nippon, Vase, Double Handle, Egyptian Design, 7 1/2 In. 85.00
Nippon, Vase, Double Handled, Scenic, Gold Scrolling & Beading, 14 In. 135.00
Nippon, Vase, Egyptian Desert Scene, Green Mark, 9 1/2 In. .... Illus 250.00
Nippon, Vase, Egyptian Shape, Beaded Jewels, Handles, Signed, 11 1/2 In. 89.00
Nippon, Vase, Flared, Geometric Design, Beading, Green Wreath Mark, 5 In. 40.00
Nippon, Vase, Floral, Gold, Enamel Beading, Green M In Wreath, 11 3/8 In. 80.00
Nippon, Vase, Floral, 2 Handled, Gold, Purple, Pink, Signed, 7 In. 75.00
Nippon, Vase, Flower Form, Raised Gold Beading, Roses, Gold, Pink, Red, 6 In. 90.00
Nippon, Vase, Flower Panel, Cobalt, Gold Trim, 4 Handles, 12 1/4 In. 130.00
Nippon, Vase, Fluted Top, 2 Handles, Hand-Painted, Green Wreath, 6 In. 35.00
Nippon, Vase, Footed, Beaded Rim, Gold Ring Handles, Maple Leaf, 8 1/4 In. 98.00
Nippon, Vase, Footed, Gold Beading, Gold Trim, Leaf Mark, 14 1/2 In. 165.00
Nippon, Vase, Gold Design & Silhouette Scene Of Cottage, 5 1/2 In. 40.00
Nippon, Vase, Gold Rippled Handles, Gold Beaded, Florals, M In Wreath, 10 In. 175.00
Nippon, Vase, Gold Square Handles, Beaded Neck, 1 Jewel, M In Wreath, 11 In. 185.00
Nippon, Vase, Gold Trim, 2 Gold Curled Handles, Maple Leaf Mark, 7 1/2 In. 65.00
Nippon, Vase, Grapes, Leaves, Gold Design, Tapestry, 5 1/2 In. 325.00
Nippon, Vase, Gray Background, Raised Flowers Around Sunset, 6 1/2 In. 35.00
Nippon, Vase, Gray Top & Bottom, Scene In Center, No.34, 9 1/2 In. 80.00
Nippon, Vase, Green & Gold Scenic, Grecian Arms, Signed, 6 X 12 In. 135.00
Nippon, Vase, Green, White & Purple Flowers, 4 Lobed Base, 8 1/2 In. 60.00
Nippon, Vase, Greenery Outlined In Gold, Handled, 6 1/2 In. 85.00
Nippon, Vase, Hand-Painted Parrots & Medallions, 13 In., Pair 350.00
Nippon, Vase, Hand-Painted Pink Flowers, Green Leaves, Green Wreath, 9 In. 55.00
Nippon, Vase, Hand-Painted, Cowboys & Sunset, 13 3/4 In. .... Illus 325.00
Nippon, Vase, Hand-Painted, Desert Ruins, 8 3/4 In. .... Illus 200.00
Nippon, Vase, Hand-Painted, Enamel, Scenes, C.1880, Signed, 10 In., Pair 259.00
Nippon, Vase, Hand-Painted, Flamboyant, Boat Scene, Green Wreath, 8 1/2 In. 75.00
Nippon, Vase, Hand-Painted, Indian In Canoe, 8 3/4 In. .... Illus 250.00
Nippon, Vase, Hand-Painted, Pink Flowers, 8 1/2 In., Pair .... Illus 275.00
Nippon, Vase, Hanging, Hand-Painted, Applied Dragon, Black Mark, 6 In. 30.00
Nippon, Vase, Irises, Dark Green, 7 1/2 In. 45.00
Nippon, Vase, Jeweled Neck, Cartouche Sides, Ivory Ground, 7 In., Pair 195.00
Nippon, Vase, Lake Scene, Hand-Painted, Green Wreath Mark, 10 In. 65.00
Nippon, Vase, Lavender & Pink Ground, Gold Handles At Base, 9 1/2 In., Pair 180.00
Nippon, Vase, Lavender & Yellow Floral, Gold Outline, Gold, Marked, 8 In. 120.00
Nippon, Vase, Melon Ribbed, Cobalt Blue Top, Signed, Blue Oak Leaf, 8 1/2 In. 60.00
Nippon, Vase, Melon Ribbed, Matte, Poppies, M In Wreath, 8 1/4 In. 100.00
Nippon, Vase, Moriaga Design Of 12 Birds In Flight, 8 In. 195.00
Nippon, Vase, Moriaga, Dragon, Feet, Green Wreath Mark, 4 3/4 In. 60.00
Nippon, Vase, Multicolored Flowers, Gold Trim, Green M In Wreath, 11 In. 75.00
Nippon, Vase, Orange Peel Finish, Raised Sea Serpent, 9 1/2 In. 24.00
Nippon, Vase, Orange Semi-Gloss, Black Rim & Streaks, 7 1/2 In. 21.50
Nippon, Vase, Oval, Bulbous, Hand-Painted Flowers, Moriaga, 3 1/2 X 7 In. 125.00
Nippon, Vase, Ovoid Shape, Beading, Signed, Maple Leaf, 6 1/2 In. 64.00
Nippon, Vase, Pink Floral Outlined In Gold, Leaves, Blue Leaf, Signed, 8 In. 100.00
Nippon, Vase, Pink Flowers, Moriaga Trim, 7 3/4 In. 40.00
Nippon, Vase, Portrait, Hand-Painted, Gold Trim & Beading, 2 Handled, 9 In. 350.00
Nippon, Vase, Raised Gold Landscape, Gold Handles, Green M Mark, 7 1/2 In. 155.00
Nippon, Vase, Raised Gold, Green Wreath Mark, 13 In. 285.00
Nippon, Vase, Raised Leaves & Enamel Flowers, 2 Handled, Signed, 10 3/4 In. 75.00
Nippon, Vase, Ring Handled, Hand-Painted, Blue & White, 8 1/2 In. 185.00
Nippon, Vase, Rose Design, Yellow, Orange, 10 In. 75.00
Nippon, Vase, Roses, Leaves, Gold Beading & Handles, Pink, Green, , 8 1/2 In. 48.50
Nippon, Vase, Satin Finish, Roses & Leaves Cover Ground, M Wreath, 8 In. 115.00
Nippon, Vase, Scenic Design, 2-Handled, Green Wreath Mark, 6 In. 29.00
Nippon, Vase, Scenic, Pink & White Blossoms, Hand-Painted, Marked, 13 In. 100.00
Nippon, Vase, Scenic, Ribbon Handles, Green M, 10 In. 100.00

Nippon, Vase, Beach Scene,
Shoulder & Foot Raised Designs
(See Page 345)

Nippon, Vase, Egyptian
Desert Scene, Green
Mark, 9 1/2 In.

Nippon, Vase, Hand-Painted,
Cowboys & Sunset, 13 3/4 In.

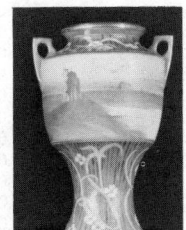

Nippon, Vase, Hand-Painted,
Desert Ruins, 8 3/4 In.

Nippon, Vase, Hand-Painted,
Indian In Canoe, 8 3/4 In.

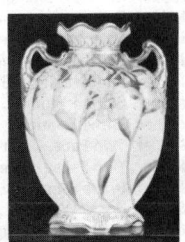

Nippon, Vase, Hand-Painted,
Pink Flowers, 8 1/2 In., Pair

Nippon, Vase, Scenic, Turquoise & Gold Around Base, Maple Leaf, 10 1/2 In. 85.00
Nippon, Vase, Scenic, White, Green, Pillow Shaped, Blue Wreath, 6 1/2 In. 165.00
Nippon, Vase, Scenic, Yellow & Green, Gold Trim, Green M In Wreath, 6 1/2 In. 30.00
Nippon, Vase, Scroll Work On Body, Victorian Lady, Green M Mark, 12 1/2 In. 75.00
Nippon, Vase, Shepherdess & Sheep, Handles, Hand Painted, 9 1/2 In.Tall 100.00
Nippon, Vase, Square, Mosaic, 4 Handles, 6 In. 129.00
Nippon, Vase, Squat, Gold Frames, 6 Floral Panels, 6 In. 95.00
Nippon, Vase, Tree Scene, Jeweled, 10 1/2 In. 75.00
Nippon, Vase, Urn Shape, Gold & Beads, Gold Handles, Marked, 11 1/4 In. 95.00
Nippon, Vase, Urn Shaped, 2-Handled, Green Ground, Signed, 6 1/2 In. 45.00
Nippon, Vase, Violets On Blue Ground, Gold Beaded, 9 In. 120.00
Nippon, Vase, Water Scene, Blue Background, 12 In. 100.00
Nippon, Vase, White & Yellow Florals, Grey Background, Gold Edge, 12 In. 85.00
Nippon, Vase, White Set In Stones Form Floral Decoration, M Wreath, 9 In. 150.00
Nippon, Vase, White, Pastel Flowers, Gilt Edging, Floral Spray, 11 1/2 In. 90.00
Nippon, Vase, White, Roses, Beaded Band, Hand-Painted, Handled, 8 X 7 In. 75.00
Nippon, Vase, Yellow & Gilt, Hand-Painted, Green Mark, 6 1/2 In. 45.00
Nippon, Vase, Yellow Background, Two Blue Birds, 12 In. 275.00
Nippon, Warmer, Pancake, Red & Gold, Leaf Mark 55.00
Nippon, Witch's Pot, Handled, Footed, Bisque, Woods Scene, Signed, 3 1/4 In. 55.00

*Nodders or nodding figures, or pagods, are porcelain figures with heads and
hands that are attached to wires. Any slight movement causes the parts to
move up and down. They were made in many countries during the eighteenth and
nineteenth centuries.*

Nodder, Avery, Comic Strip, Bisque, German, 3 1/2 In.	62.50
Nodder, Bearded Man, Germany	24.00
Nodder, Bell, Oriental Lady Holding Baskets, Head Is Nodder, Skirt Is Bell	55.00
Nodder, Bisque, Negro Woman Dressed In Oriental Costume, German, 3 3/4 In.	115.00
Nodder, Black Man With Derby, Cigar, Ashtray, Tin & Brass	42.00
Nodder, Boy & Girl, Bisque, German, Pair	32.00
Nodder, Boy, Molded & Painted Hair & Features, Hat & Clothes, Germany	25.00
Nodder, Cat, Papier-Mache, Black, 6 In.	30.00
Nodder, Chinese Man, Sitting, Holding Fan Behind Head, 7 X 3 In.	335.00
Nodder, Dancing Couple, Wind-Up, Celluloid, Japanese	58.00
Nodder, Elephant, Celluloid	6.00
Nodder, Emmy, Bisque, 4 In.	35.00
Nodder, Genie, 2 1/2 In.	20.00
Nodder, Girl Dressed As Grandmother, Holding Basket Of Fruit, German, 7 In.	140.00
Nodder, Girl Holding Dog, Dressed As Clown, German, 7 1/4 In.	125.00
Nodder, Girl, Molded & Painted Hair, Dressed, Jointed, Germany, 2 1/2 In.	30.00
Nodder, Halloween, 3 Jack-O-Lanterns, 1920s	78.00
Nodder, Hawaiian Girl	5.00
Nodder, Irish Couple, Pair	75.00
Nodder, Man In Barrel, I Never Feel Dry, Striped Robe, Bisque, Germany	125.00
Nodder, Man Seated In Dentist Chair, Head & Tongue Nod, 6 In.	175.00
Nodder, Man, Oriental, Arm Raised, Holding Fan, Matte, 7 X 7 In.	330.00
Nodder, Mickey Mantle, Miniature, Boxed	10.00
Nodder, Monk, Standing, Holding Key & Three Bottles Of Wine, 7 1/4 In.	160.00
Nodder, Monkey, Sitting, Holding A Pipe, German, 5 1/2 In.	110.00
Nodder, Monkey, Sitting, Wearing Jacket, 5 In.	115.00
Nodder, Oriental Woman Playing Piano, Head & Hands Move, German, 9 X 7 In.	300.00
Nodder, Oriental Woman With Fan Behind Head, Porcelain, German, 6 1/2 In.	155.00
Nodder, Salt & Pepper, Man & Woman In China Scenic Holder, Ireland	30.00
Nodder, Santa, Bisque, Germany, Marked	35.00
Nodder, Seated Woman, Oriental, Head & Hand Move, Porcelain, 7 1/2 In.	335.00
Nodder, Three Beatles	30.00
Nodder, Two-Face, Oriental, Black Face, Sitting, Bisque, 4 1/2 In.	195.00
Nodder, Two-Faced, Other Face Frowning, German, 2 1/2 In.	125.00
Nodder, Uncle Bim, Bisque, 4 In.	35.00
Nodder, Uncle Walt, Bisque, 3 In.	50.00
Nodder, Uncle Walt, Bisque, 4 In.	35.00

Noritake-marked porcelain was made in Japan after 1904 by Nippon Toki Kaisha.

Noritake, Ashtray, Art Deco Clown Astride	25.00
Noritake, Basket, Oblong, Yellow & Orange Mums, Coin Gold Handle, 8 In.	28.00
Noritake, Berry Set, Azalea, 6 Sauces, Lilies Extend Into Bowls	75.00
Noritake, Berry Set, Raised Gold, Hand-Painted Flowers, Green Mark	45.00
Noritake, Bowl, Azalea, Round, 10 In.	20.00
Noritake, Bowl, Blown-Out Acorns, Footed, 7 In.	35.00
Noritake, Bowl, Console, Azalea	30.00
Noritake, Bowl, Covered, Blue Birds & Gold Trim	12.00
Noritake, Bowl, Cream Soup, Flying Phoenix	30.00
Noritake, Bowl, Iridescent & Silver Overlay, Domed, Enamel Flowers, 9 In.	35.00
Noritake, Bowl, Luster Exterior, Ram's Head Handles, Green M Mark, 11 In.	32.00
Noritake, Bowl, Molded Walnuts, Open Handled, 7 In.	20.00
Noritake, Bowl, Nut, Molded Nuts, Twig Handles, 6 In.	35.00
Noritake, Bowl, Punch, Gold Claw Feet Base, Inside Scene, Spoke Mark	295.00
Noritake, Bowl, Vegetable, Azalea, Oval, 10 1/2 In.	18.00
Noritake, Bowl, Vegetable, Hand-Painted, 2 Handles, 8 1/2 In.	25.00
Noritake, Butter Tub, Azalea, Liner	22.00
Noritake, Castor, 5 Bottle, Ribbed Swirling, Revolving Stand, 15 1/2 In.	75.00
Noritake, Celery, Azalea, 9 3/4 In.	125.00
Noritake, Chocolate Pot, Green & Ivory	25.00
Noritake, Chocolate Set, 5 Cups & Saucers, Lake Scene, Gilt On Blue Border	135.00
Noritake, Coffeepot, Demitasse, Tree In Meadow	200.00
Noritake, Coffeepot, Tree In The Meadow	165.00
Noritake, Compote, Azalea	45.00
Noritake, Compote, Handled, Hand-Painted Scene, Gold Rim	40.00
Noritake, Condiment Set, Lake Scene, Hand-Painted, Green M Mark	25.00

Noritake, Condiment Set, Tree In Meadow	18.00
Noritake, Console Set, Azalea, 3 Piece	55.00
Noritake, Cracker Jar, 2-Handled, Lake Scene	25.00
Noritake, Creamer, Arlene	4.00
Noritake, Creamer, Gramatan	5.00
Noritake, Cruet, Stopper, Azalea	138.00
Noritake, Cup & Saucer, Arlene	7.00
Noritake, Cup & Saucer, Azalea	7.50 To 12.00
Noritake, Cup & Saucer, Bouillon, Azalea	12.00
Noritake, Cup & Saucer, Hand-Painted, White Ground, M In Wreath	14.00
Noritake, Cup, Nut, 3 Feet, Set Of 4	25.00
Noritake, Dish, Butter, Azalea, Drainer	45.00
Noritake, Dish, Candy, Hand-Painted Flowers, 7 In.	55.50
Noritake, Dish, Cheese, Covered, Azalea	55.00
Noritake, Dish, Cheese, Malay Pattern, Signed, Nippon	25.00
Noritake, Dish, Cheese, Slant Lid, Purple, Blue Feature Stripes	18.50
Noritake, Dish, Condiment, Beige, Painted Apples, 1 Piece	12.50
Noritake, Dish, Nut, Open Handle, Red Wreath Mark, 6 1/4 In.Diameter	8.00
Noritake, Dish, Relish, Two Section, Tree In Meadow	16.00
Noritake, Dish, Relish, 4 Compartment, Azalea	60.00
Noritake, Dish, Sauce, Azalea	5.50
Noritake, Dish, Serving, Covered, Azalea	35.00
Noritake, Dish, Serving, Oval, Azalea, 10 1/2 In.	20.00
Noritake, Dish, Serving, Round, Azalea, 10 In.	20.00
Noritake, Dish, Shell, Azalea	170.00
Noritake, Dish, Shell, Tree In Meadow	78.00
Noritake, Dish, Vegetable, Arlene	9.00
Noritake, Dish, Vegetable, Covered, Canton	12.50
Noritake, Dish, Vegetable, Flying Turkey, Blue & White, C.1915, 10 In.Diam.	30.00
Noritake, Eggcup, Azalea	20.00
Noritake, Fish, Relish, Azalea, Oval	10.00
Noritake, Humidor, Blown-Out, Fox, Bark Handle, Green Mark, 6 1/4 In.	325.00
Noritake, Jar, Honey, Blue Luster, Wreath Mark	35.00
Noritake, Jar, Jam, Underplate, White Ground, Encrusted Gold, M In Wreath	35.00
Noritake, Jug, Milk, Azalea, 5 5/8 In.	88.00
Noritake, Mayonnaise Set, Azalea, Ruffled Edge, 3 Piece	150.00
Noritake, Mayonnaise Set, Flowers, Silver Leaves, Red Wreath Mark, 3 Piece	25.00
Noritake, Mayonnaise Set, Petal Underplate, Rosebud Finial, Pink	18.00
Noritake, Muffineer, Hand-Painted, Pagoda Scene	24.00
Noritake, Mustard Pot, Azalea	18.00
Noritake, Napkin Ring, Azalea	15.00
Noritake, Nappy, Hand-Painted, 6 In.	9.00
Noritake, Nut Set, Hand-Painted, Peanut Shape Bowl, 6 Serving Bowls, 1920	125.00
Noritake, Pitcher, Milk, Crusted Gold, Gold Beading, Nippon Mark, 3 In.	65.00
Noritake, Plate, Azalea, Pierced, 9 1/2 In.	20.00
Noritake, Plate, Azalea, 10 In.	8.50
Noritake, Plate, Bread & Butter, Azalea	3.50
Noritake, Plate, Cake, Azalea	15.00 To 20.00
Noritake, Plate, Colburn, 10 In.	4.00
Noritake, Plate, Dinner, Arlene	5.00
Noritake, Plate, Dinner, Azalea	8.00 To 9.50
Noritake, Plate, Dinner, Flying Phoenix	14.00
Noritake, Plate, Figure Of Mitsui Line Freighter At Sea, Marked, 10 5/8 In.	75.00
Noritake, Plate, Lemon, Azalea	15.00
Noritake, Plate, Lunch, Azalea	9.50
Noritake, Plate, Salad, Arlene	3.00
Noritake, Plate, Salad, Azalea	4.00
Noritake, Plate, Soup, Azalea	9.00 To 10.00
Noritake, Plate, 2 Handled, Hand-Painted, 6 1/2 In.	12.00
Noritake, Platter, Ashleigh, 14 In.	10.00
Noritake, Platter, Azaela, 16 In.	175.00
Noritake, Platter, Azalea, 12 In.	23.00
Noritake, Platter, Azalea, 14 In.	27.00
Noritake, Platter, Azalea, 16 In.	175.00
Noritake, Platter, Detailed Fully Bodied Red Lobster, 13 In.Diameter	75.00
Noritake, Pot, Demitasse, Tree In The Meadow	100.00

Noritake, Salt & Pepper, Azalea, Bulbous	15.00
Noritake, Salt & Pepper, Azalea, 2 3/4 In.	12.00
Noritake, Salt & Pepper, Azalea, 3 1/2 In.	6.00
Noritake, Sauce, Arlene	3.00
Noritake, Saucer, Azalea, 5 1/4 In.	5.50
Noritake, Serving Set, 1 Large Bowl & 6 Small Serving Bowls, Walnut, 1920	100.00
Noritake, Soup, Dish, Arlene	4.00
Noritake, Spoon Holder, Azalea	40.00
Noritake, Spooner, Azalea	30.00 To 45.00
Noritake, Spooner, Lay Down, Handled, Hand-Painted Farm Scene, 8 In.	18.50
Noritake, Sugar & Creamer, Ashleigh	12.50
Noritake, Sugar & Creamer, Azalea	18.00 To 21.00
Noritake, Sugar & Creamer, Azalea, Gold Finial	75.00 To 90.00
Noritake, Sugar & Creamer, Cover, Tree At The Lake Mark	25.00
Noritake, Sugar & Creamer, Cream, Turquoise, Floral, Red Wreath Mark, 7 In.	30.00
Noritake, Sugar & Creamer, Gold Handles & Rims, Green Wreath Mark	12.00
Noritake, Sugar & Creamer, Hand-Painted Scene, Green Wreath Mark	19.50
Noritake, Sugar & Creamer, Pearlized Ground, Black Trim, M In Wreath	18.50
Noritake, Sugar & Creamer, Turquoise & White, Gold Bird In Tree	8.00
Noritake, Sugar & Creamer, Yellow Band, Rose In Panel, Green Wreath Mark	18.00
Noritake, Sugar Shaker & Creamer, Azalea	68.00 To 79.00
Noritake, Sugar Shaker & Creamer, Gold Trim, Green M In Wreath, 6 3/4 In.	35.00
Noritake, Sugar Shaker, Azalea, Footed, 6 1/2 In.	38.00
Noritake, Sugar Shaker, Fruit Baskets, Garlands, Gold Dome, 6 1/2 In.	17.00
Noritake, Sugar, Arlene	3.00
Noritake, Sugar, Open, Linden	4.00
Noritake, Syrup & Underplate, Azalea	55.00 To 69.00
Noritake, Tea Strainer, Flowers, Orchid Edging	25.00
Noritake, Teapot, Arlene	12.00
Noritake, Teapot, Azalea	25.00
Noritake, Tile, Tea, Scenic	9.00 To 16.00
Noritake, Toothpick, 6 Sided	75.00
Noritake, Tray, Snack, Azalea, Pallet Shape, 7 1/2 X 8 In., Pair	28.00
Noritake, Tub, Butter, Drainer, Azalea	22.50 To 27.50
Noritake, Urn, Blue Mottled, Covered, Spoke Mark, Gold, 13 1/2 In., Pair	395.00
Noritake, Vase, Azalea, Footed, Fan Shape	50.00
Noritake, Vase, Blue Luster Bands, Hand-Painted, Green Mark, 6 In.	20.00
Noritake, Vase, Cobalt Border, Lake Scene, Gold Handles, 7 In., Pair	60.00
Noritake, Vase, Fan, Azalea	60.00 To 115.00
Noritake, Vase, 2-Handled, Water Scene, Gold Trim, 10 1/2 In.	35.00

The North Dakota School of Mines was established in 1892 at the
University of North Dakota.

North Dakota School Of Mines, Pitcher, Prairie Flower, Signed	140.00
North Dakota School Of Mines, Tile, Impressed Flowers, Signed, 6 In.Diam.	55.00
North Dakota School Of Mines, Vase, 3 In.	9.00

Northwood Glass Company worked in Martins Ferry, Ohio, in the 1800s
to c.1923. They marked some pieces with the underlined letter N. Many
pieces of carnival glass were made by this company.

Northwood, see also Carnival Glass; Custard Glass; Goofus Glass;
Pressed Glass

Northwood, Banana Boat, Grape & Cable, Gold, 12 In.	85.00
Northwood, Basket, Leaf & Flower, Handled	95.00
Northwood, Berry Set, Bowl & 6 Bowls, Cherry Design, Crystal, 9 X 3 1/2 In.	130.00
Northwood, Berry Set, Pecan, Green With Gold Trim, 6 Piece	150.00
Northwood, Bowl, Beads, Opalescent, Green	25.00
Northwood, Bowl, Block, Green, 8 1/2 In.	25.00
Northwood, Bowl, Canary Yellow Cactus, Opalescent, 8 X 4 X 6 In.	25.00
Northwood, Bowl, Green, 8 In.	20.00
Northwood, Bowl, Ice Cream, Grape & Cable, White	195.00
Northwood, Bowl, Jolly Bear, White Opalescent, 8 In.	95.00
Northwood, Bowl, Reverse 44, Gold, 8 X 5 In.High	25.00
Northwood, Butter, Covered, Cable With Thumbprint, Cherry, Signed	67.50
Northwood, Butter, Near Cut, Gold With Ruby Dot	105.00
Northwood, Butter, Singing Birds, Amber	150.00

Northwood, Celery, Chrysanthemum Sprig, Gold, Signed	350.00
Northwood, Celery, Clear, Thumbprint & Cable	85.00
Northwood, Compote, Blue Opalescent, Dolphin	50.00
Northwood, Cookie Jar, Cherry Thumbprint, Signed N	110.00
Northwood, Creamer, Leaf Umbrella, Lemon Cased	75.00
Northwood, Creamer, Memphis, Emerald Green & Gold	45.00
Northwood, Creamer, Near Cut, Gold With Ruby Dot	45.00
Northwood, Creamer, Peach, Memphis, Emerald Green & Gold	45.00
Northwood, Creamer, Purple & Gold, Leaf Bracket	45.00
Northwood, Dish, Berry, Small, Set Of 6	90.00
Northwood, Dish, Butter, Covered, Regal, Green Opalescent	100.00
Northwood, Dish, Sauce, Cherry Pattern	9.00
Northwood, Dish, Sweet Meat, Covered, Strawberry & Cable	50.00
Northwood, Fruit Set, Footed, Wildflower Pattern, Amber, Bowl, 7 In.	22.50
Northwood, Goblet, Strawberry & Cable	30.00
Northwood, Jar, Candy, Stretch Topaz, No. 636, 1 Lb.	40.00
Northwood, Pitcher & 4 Glasses, Opalescent, Cobalt Blue, Signed, 8 X 5 In.	360.00
Northwood, Pitcher & 6 Tumblers, Drapery, Blue Opalescent, Signed	450.00
Northwood, Pitcher, Raspberries, Purple, Signed, 7 1/4 In.	175.00
Northwood, Pitcher, Water, Fan, 4 Tumblers	385.00
Northwood, Pitcher, Water, Leaf Umbrella, Cranberry	295.00
Northwood, Rose Bowl, Basket Weave, Strawberry, Ice Green, 9 In.	65.00
Northwood, Rose Bowl, Daisy & Plume, Opalescent, Green	30.00
Northwood, Rose Bowl, Daisy & Plume, Opalescent, White	20.00
Northwood, Rose Bowl, Fine Cut & Roses, 3 Footed, Purple	55.00
Northwood, Shade, Orange Carnival Glass, Signed, 6 In. X 5 1/2 In.Diam.	50.00
Northwood, Spooner, Grape & Cable	25.00
Northwood, Spooner, Memphis, Emerald Green & Gold	35.00
Northwood, Spooner, Near Cut, Gold With Ruby Dot	35.00
Northwood, Spooner, Peach, Memphis, Emerald Green & Gold	35.00
Northwood, Sugar & Creamer, Cover, Peach Pattern	100.00
Northwood, Sugar & Creamer, Covered, Peacock At The Fountain, Marigold	95.00
Northwood, Sugar & Creamer, Flute, Red Tint, Gold Trim	40.00
Northwood, Sugar, Near Cut, Covered, Gold With Ruby Dot	55.00
Northwood, Sugar, Peach, Memphis, Emerald Green & Gold	65.00
Northwood, Tumbler, Cherry Lattice, Gold & Flashing, Signed	15.00
Northwood, Water Set, Cara Nome, Frosted With Enameled Pansies, 7 Piece	250.00
Northwood, Water Set, Drape, Blue Opalescent, Pitcher & 4 Glasses, Signed	320.00
Northwood, Water Set, Leaf Mold, Pink & White, Cased Overlay, 7 Piece	785.00
Northwood, Water Set, Oriental Poppy, Emerald Green & Gold, 7 Piece	275.00

Nymphenburg, a German porcelain factory, was established at Neudeck-ob-der-Au in 1753 and moved to Nymphenburg in 1761. The company is still in existence. Modern marks include a shield superseded by a star or crown, and a crowned CT with a checkered shield.

Nymphenburg, Figurine, Birds Nibbling Grapes, Signed, 7 3/4 In., Pair	395.00
Nymphenburg, Figurine, Polar Bear, Impressed Mark, 8 1/2 In.	395.00
Nymphenburg, Toothpick, Shape Of Tree Trunk, Marked, 3 In.	45.00
Nymphenburg, Toothpick, Tree Trunk Shape, Owl In Relief, 3 In.	47.00
Obert, Plate, Fruit, Peaches On Green, Signed	25.00
Obert, Plate, Red & Yellow Apples, 8 1/2 In.	20.00

Occupied Japan is the mark used on pieces of pottery and porcelain made during the American occupation of Japan after World War II. Collectors are now buying these pieces. The items were made for export to the United States.

Occupied Japan, Ashtray, Negro Baby	10.00
Occupied Japan, Bowl, Blue Willow, 6 In.	8.00
Occupied Japan, Car, Windup, Studebaker	12.00
Occupied Japan, Compote, Copper, Silver Plate, Floral Design, 4 X 5 1/2 In.	26.00
Occupied Japan, Condiment Set, Melon Ribbed, Gold Trim, Set Of 6	30.00
Occupied Japan, Cup & Saucer, Demitasse, Florals, Gold, Octagonal	5.00
Occupied Japan, Cup & Saucer, Pedestaled, Cream Ground, Gold Trim, Signed	12.50
Occupied Japan, Cup & Saucer, Strawberries & Vines, Set	10.00
Occupied Japan, Doll, Hula Dancer, Celluloid, Tin, 18 In.	20.00
Occupied Japan, Figurine, Bride & Groom, Bisque, 3 In.	14.00

Occupied Japan, Figurine, Court Gentleman With Mandolin, Moriyama Bisque	25.00
Occupied Japan, Figurine, French Court, Lady & Gentleman, 7 1/2 In., Pair	50.00
Occupied Japan, Figurine, Girl & Boy Playing With Dogs, 8 In.	20.00
Occupied Japan, Figurine, Lady & Man, Fancy Attire, 10 In., Pair	35.00
Occupied Japan, Figurine, Lady, Bisque, 7 1/2 In.	9.50
Occupied Japan, Figurine, Oriental Lady, 5 In.	5.50
Occupied Japan, Figurine, Paulo, Bisque, 8 In.	20.00
Occupied Japan, Figurine, Scottie, Mechanical, Original Box, 4 n.	10.00
Occupied Japan, Figurine, Shepherdess, Basket Over Arm, Bisque, 12 In.	32.00
Occupied Japan, Figurine, Shepherdess, Muted Colors, Bisque, 8 In.	25.00
Occupied Japan, Fishing Boy, Shelf Sitter, Bisque	8.50
Occupied Japan, Lamp, Boy Against Tree, Bisque, 12 In.	13.00
Occupied Japan, Lamp, Colonial Woman & Man	27.00
Occupied Japan, Lighter, Cigar, Original Box, Figural Horse	20.00
Occupied Japan, Match Holder, Wall, Boy & Girl With Baskets, Bisque	30.00
Occupied Japan, Mug, Old Man, Donkey Handle	30.00
Occupied Japan, Pitcher, Applied China Roses, 3 1/2 In.	8.00
Occupied Japan, Planter, Goose, 4 In.	7.00
Occupied Japan, Plaque, Gent & Lady In Garden, 6 1/4 X 5 1/4., Pair	42.00
Occupied Japan, Plate, Bisque, Hand-Painted, Lakeside Scene, Signed, 9 In.	40.00
Occupied Japan, Pot, Demi, Dragons, Gold Trim & Handle, 7 3/4 In.	29.00
Occupied Japan, Pot, Demitasse, Gray & Red Moriage, Gold Handle	27.00
Occupied Japan, Scale & Basket, Baby, China, 6 1/2 In.	16.50
Occupied Japan, Scissors, Fisherman's Net, Surgical Steel, 4 In.	5.00
Occupied Japan, Shelf, Curio, Lacquer, Black & Gold On Wood, 19 In.	28.00
Occupied Japan, Sugar & Creamer, Lid, Aladdin Lamp, Hollandia, Gold Edged	29.00
Occupied Japan, Sugar & Creamer, Swan Handles & Finials	25.00
Occupied Japan, Teapot, Dragons, Gold Trim, 7 1/4 In.	24.00
Occupied Japan, Toothpick, Souvenir Of Long Beach, Mississippi	15.00
Occupied Japan, Toy, Ukelele, Tin & Wood	10.00
Occupied Japan, Vase, Mum, Gold Leaves, Apple Blossom Reverse, 12 X 9 In.	65.00

G. E. OHR, BILOXI. *Ohr pottery was made by George E.Ohr in Biloxi, Mississippi, between 1883 and 1918. The pieces were made of very thin clay and were twisted, folded and dented into odd, graceful shapes.*

Ohr, Bowl, Brown Drips, Impressed Mark, 3 X 4 1/2 In.Diameter	225.00
Ohr, Bowl, Figural, Caterpillar On Rim, Script Signature, 3 1/2 X 5 1/2 In.	325.00
Ohr, Bowl, Folded Lip, Green & Brown Glaze, 2 X 4 1/2 In.Diameter	120.00
Ohr, Bowl, Striated Reds, Crumbled, 4 X 5 In.	185.00
Ohr, Bowl, Yellow & Green Glaze, 2 1/2 X 4 In.	110.00
Ohr, Card Holder, Shell Motif, Mustard Yellow	112.00
Ohr, Mug, Green Glaze, Puzzle	85.00
Ohr, Mug, Speckled Green Glaze, Impressed Motto, 5 3/4 In. *Illus*	190.00
Ohr, Pitcher, Handled, Green, 4 X 5 In.	250.00
Ohr, Plaque & Pen Holder, Donkey Head, Signed, 6 X 4 In.	175.00
Ohr, Pot, Crimped, Twisted Form, Metallic Glaze, Signed, 4 1/2 In.	295.00
Ohr, Pot, Glossy Brown Glaze, Signed, Biloxi, Miss., 3 In.	165.00
Ohr, Pot, Metallic, Gun Metal Glaze, Signed, 3 In.	140.00
Ohr, Teapot, Pink Raku Glaze, Applied Snake, 5 1/4 In. *Illus*	400.00
Ohr, Vase, Brown Glaze, Pleated & Pinched Body, Marked, 3 1/4 X 5 1/4 In.	275.00
Ohr, Vase, Bulbous Top, Wide Base, Incised Mark, 3 5/8 X 4 3/8 In.	240.00
Ohr, Vase, Bulbous, Flared Rim, Runny Black Luster, Marked, 2 3/4 X 3 1/4 In.	85.00

Ohr, Mug, Speckled Green Glaze,
Impressed Motto, 5 3/4 In.

Ohr, Teapot, Pink Raku Glaze,
Applied Snake, 5 1/4 In.

Ohr, Vase, Dark Lead Glaze,
Double Neck, 5 3/4 In.

Ohr, Vase, Dark Green, Dark Mauve, 6 1/4 In.	285.00
Ohr, Vase, Dark Lead Glaze, Double Neck, 5 3/4 In. .... *Illus*	170.00
Ohr, Vase, Folded Neck, Lead Glaze, 4 3/4 X 4 In.Diameter	150.00
Ohr, Vase, Green & Tan Mottling, Snake, 6 1/2 In.	335.00
Ohr, Vase, Green, Brown Ground, Bulbous Top, Incised Mark, 3 5/8 X 4 3/8 In.	240.00
Ohr, Vase, Green, Orange, 2-Handled, Red Clay, 3 1/4 X 3 1/4 In.	225.00
Ohr, Vase, Mottled Black & Red, Die Stamped Geo.E.Ohr, Biloxi, 3 X 3 In.	225.00
Ohr, Vase, Orange & Green, 2 Handles, Stamped G.E. Ohr, 3 1/4 X 3 1/4 In.	225.00
Ohr, Vase, Pinched Rim, Dimples, Incised Mark, 3 1/4 X 3 1/2 In.Diameter	275.00
Ohr, Vase, 2 Snakes, Medium Brown Glaze, 5 In.	325.00

Old ivory china was made in Silesia, Germany, at the end of the nineteenth century. It is often marked with a crown and the word Silesia. The pattern numbers appear on the base of each piece.

Old Ivory, Berry Set, No.16, 7 Piece	145.00 To 155.00
Old Ivory, Bowl, No.16, 2 1/2 X 9 3/4 In.	55.00
Old Ivory, Bowl, Pierced Handles, Square, 8 1/2 X 9 3/4 In.	30.00
Old Ivory, Bowl, 5 3/4 In.	20.00
Old Ivory, Bowl, 6 1/2 In.	18.50 To 24.00
Old Ivory, Bowl, 9 1/2 In.	60.00
Old Ivory, Butter Pat, No.11	35.00
Old Ivory, Cake Set, Handled Plate, Six 4 In.Plates	140.00
Old Ivory, Cake Set, Plate, 10 1/4 In., 4 Serving Plates, 6 1/2 In.Diam.	65.00
Old Ivory, Cake Set, 7 Piece	145.00 To 175.00
Old Ivory, Celery, Silesia	25.00
Old Ivory, Celery, 5 3/4 X 11 3/4 In.	46.00
Old Ivory, Celery, 9 In.	20.00
Old Ivory, Chocolate Pot	195.00
Old Ivory, Chocolate Pot, Pink Thistle Pattern	68.00
Old Ivory, Chocolate Set, Thistle Pattern, Pot & 3 Cups & Saucers	95.00
Old Ivory, Cracker Jar	195.00
Old Ivory, Creamer, No.84	42.00
Old Ivory, Cup & Saucer	32.50 To 35.00
Old Ivory, Cup & Saucer, Bracelet Pattern, Set Of 6	150.00
Old Ivory, Cup & Saucer, Gold Daisies Around Edge	40.00
Old Ivory, Cup & Saucer, No.84, Chocolate, Silesia	35.00
Old Ivory, Cup & Saucer, Pink & Lilac Flowers	15.00
Old Ivory, Dish, Relish, 6 1/2 X 4 1/2 In.	30.00
Old Ivory, Hair Receiver, Royal Bayreuth, 3 1/2 In.	25.00
Old Ivory, Mustard Pot	75.00 To 88.50
Old Ivory, Nappy, Handled	40.00
Old Ivory, Nappy, No.26, Handled	55.00
Old Ivory, Pitcher, Milk, 5 In.	26.00
Old Ivory, Plate, Cake, No.84	65.00
Old Ivory, Plate, Cake, Variegated Brown Roses, 10 1/4 In.	45.00
Old Ivory, Plate, Clairon, 7 1/2 In.	24.00
Old Ivory, Plate, Eglantine	28.00
Old Ivory, Plate, Luncheon, No.75, Crown Mark	28.00
Old Ivory, Plate, No.12, 6 In.	15.00
Old Ivory, Plate, No.82, 13 In.	45.00
Old Ivory, Plate, 6 In.	15.00
Old Ivory, Plate, 6 1/4 In.	22.00 To 24.00
Old Ivory, Plate, 6 3/4 In.	24.00
Old Ivory, Plate, 8 1/2 In.	14.00
Old Ivory, Platter, No.16, 11 In.	50.00

Old Ivory, Platter, Oval, 8 X 11 1/2 In. 48.00
Old Ivory, Salt & Pepper .... 60.00 To 65.00
Old Ivory, Sauce 13.50
Old Ivory, Sauce Boat, Underplate, La Touraine 39.00
Old Ivory, Sauce, Underplate 55.00
Old Ivory, Sauce, 5 1/2 In. 16.50
Old Ivory, Sauce, 5 3/4 In., Set Of 6 .... 70.00
Old Ivory, Sugar & Creamer, No.16 .... 85.00
Old Ivory, Sugar & Creamer, No.69 .... 145.00
Old Ivory, Sugar Shaker, No.78, Pink Roses, Green Leaves 155.00
Old Ivory, Teapot, 7 1/2 In. 145.00

Onion, originally named "bulb pattern," is a white ware decorated with cobalt blue. Although it is commonly associated with Meissen, other companies made the pattern in the latter part of the nineteenth century.

Onion, Bowl, Cereal, Crossed Swords, Meissen .... 23.00 To 45.00
Onion, Bowl, Vegetable, Covered, Crossed Swords, Meissen, 10 In. 225.00
Onion, Canister, Round, Lid, Meissen 34.00
Onion, Compote, Lattice Open Work, Star Mark, Meissen, 5 3/4 X 9 In. 110.00
Onion, Compote, Meissen, Crossed Swords, 8 1/4 X 9 In. 185.00
Onion, Cup & Saucer, Demitasse, Crossed Swords, Meissen 35.00
Onion, Plate, Crossed Swords, Meissen, 10 In. 45.00
Onion, Plate, Crossed Swords, Meissen, 6 In. 15.00
Onion, Plate, Crossed Swords, Meissen, 6 1/2 In. 15.00
Onion, Platter, Meissen, Hot Water Jacket 118.00
Onion, Platter, Oval, Mercury Mark, 13 3/4 X 9 1/2 In. 42.00
Onion, Rack, Spice, Blue, 10 Jars, 2 Drawers, 13 1/2 In. 18.00
Onion, Salt & Pepper, Meissen 38.50
Onion, Sauce, Crossed Swords, Meissen, 5 1/2 In. 20.00
Onion, Strainer, Tea, Wooden Handle, Meissen 35.00
Onion, Tureen, Lid, Underplate, Crossed Swords, 7 X 5 1/4 X 2 3/4 In. 165.00
Onion, Tureen, Meissen, Covered, Crossed Swords 150.00

Opalescent glass is translucent glass that has the bluish-white tones of the opal gemstone. It is often found in pressed glassware made in Victorian times. Some dealers use the terms opaline and opalescent for any of the bluish-white translucent wares.

Opalescent, Banana Boat, Everglades 150.00
Opalescent, Berry Bowl, Diamond Point, Cobalt Blue 85.00
Opalescent, Berry Bowl, Fluted Scrolls, Vaseline, 8 1/2 In.Diameter 65.00
Opalescent, Berry Bowl, Intaglio, Blue 22.00
Opalescent, Berry Bowl, Intaglio, White 68.00
Opalescent, Berry Bowl, Shell And Wreath, Blue 18.50
Opalescent, Berry Bowl, Tokyo, Blue, 4 Sauces 175.00
Opalescent, Berry Bowl, Water Lily & Cattails, Amethyst, 11 In. 60.00
Opalescent, Berry Set, Alaska, Vaseline, 7 Piece 325.00
Opalescent, Berry Set, Fluted Scrolls, Vaseline, Enameled Flowers, 6 Sauces ... 235.00
Opalescent, Berry Set, Hobnail, Vaseline, 7 Piece 150.00
Opalescent, Berry Set, Jewelled Heart, Ruffled, 7 Piece 75.00
Opalescent, Berry Set, Regal, White, 7 Piece .... 150.00 To 165.00
Opalescent, Berry Set, Shell & Wreath, Blue, 7 Piece 295.00
Opalescent, Bottle, Perfume, Opal Swirl, 4 1/2 In. 40.00
Opalescent, Bowl, Basketweave, Vaseline, 4 1/2 In.Diameter 40.00
Opalescent, Bowl, Beaded Drape, Footed, Ruffled, 8 In. 30.00
Opalescent, Bowl, Daisy & Plume, Green 35.00
Opalescent, Bowl, Daisy & Plume, Marigold 35.00
Opalescent, Bowl, Diamond Point, Marked N, 8 In.Diameter 40.00
Opalescent, Bowl, Greek Key & Ribs, White, Marked N 38.00
Opalescent, Bowl, Leaf & Beads, Dome, Footed, Gold Paint On Design 26.50
Opalescent, Bowl, Northwood's Block, Footed, 9 In. 24.00
Opalescent, Bowl, Northwood's Drape, Blue, 8 1/2 X 4 In. 57.50
Opalescent, Bowl, Pearl Flowers, Scalloped Rim, Blue, 6 1/2 X 4 1/2 In. 35.00
Opalescent, Bowl, Pearl Flowers, White .... 28.00 To 30.00
Opalescent, Bowl, Ruffles & Rings, Blue, 8 1/2 In. 28.00
Opalescent, Bowl, Ruffles & Rings, Footed, 8 In. 25.00
Opalescent, Bowl, Ruffles & Rings, 3 Feet, Blue, 9 In. .... 35.00 To 45.00

Opalescent, Bowl, Vintage, 9 In.	22.00
Opalescent, Bowl, Water Lily With Cattails, Amethyst, Fluted, 10 In.	45.00
Opalescent, Box, Puff, Fluted Scrolls, Blue	45.00
Opalescent, Box, Puff, Fluted Scrolls, White, Covered	35.00
Opalescent, Butter, Beatty's Swirl Opal, Blue	175.00
Opalescent, Butter, Covered, Alaska, Blue	68.00
Opalescent, Butter, Covered, Everglades, Blue	245.00
Opalescent, Butter, Covered, Feathers, Green	95.00
Opalescent, Butter, Covered, Regal, Blue	255.00
Opalescent, Butter, Covered, Shell & Wreath, Vaseline	175.00
Opalescent, Butter, Covered, Vaseline	68.00
Opalescent, Butter, Fluted Scrolls, White	85.00
Opalescent, Butter, Hobnail, Vaseline	135.00
Opalescent, Butter, Intaglio, White	125.00
Opalescent, Butter, Reverse Swirl, White	65.00
Opalescent, Butter, Shell & Wreath	175.00
Opalescent, Butter, Swag With Brackets, Green	95.00 To 150.00
Opalescent, Butter, Swag With Brackets, Vaseline	135.00
Opalescent, Butter, Tokyo, Green	165.00
Opalescent, Butter, Tokyo, White	75.00
Opalescent, Butter, Wreath & Shell, Canary, Covered	155.00
Opalescent, Cake Stand, Tokyo, Blue	59.00
Opalescent, Celery, Beatty's Ribbed Opal, Blue	50.00
Opalescent, Celery, Beatty's Swirl Opal	69.00
Opalescent, Celery, Lattice Medallions, Cranberry	75.00
Opalescent, Celery, Northwood's Block, Blue	40.00
Opalescent, Chalice, Leaves, Green	35.00
Opalescent, Chalice, Pump & Trough, Northwood	100.00
Opalescent, Compote, Beaded Fleur-De-Lis, Green, 4 1/2 X 8 In.	42.50
Opalescent, Compote, Blue, Argonaut Shell, 5 X 5 1/2 X 3 1/4 In.	39.00
Opalescent, Compote, Dolphin Handles, Pedestal, Blue, 7 In.	39.00
Opalescent, Compote, Jelly, Argonaut Shell	125.00
Opalescent, Compote, Jelly, Blue, Scroll With Acanthus	45.00
Opalescent, Compote, Jelly, Blue, Tokyo	45.00
Opalescent, Compote, Jelly, Intaglio	20.00 To 38.50
Opalescent, Compote, Jelly, Intaglio, Blue	44.00
Opalescent, Compote, Jelly, Intaglio, Vaseline	25.00 To 38.50
Opalescent, Compote, Jelly, Iris With Meander	45.00
Opalescent, Compote, Jelly, Maple Leaf, Green	35.00
Opalescent, Compote, Jelly, Scroll With Acanthus, Green	25.00
Opalescent, Compote, Jelly, Swag With Brackets, Green	25.00
Opalescent, Compote, Jelly, Tokyo, Green	25.00
Opalescent, Creamer & Spooner, Alaska, Vaseline	160.00
Opalescent, Creamer, Alaska, Blue	89.00
Opalescent, Creamer, Alaska, Northwood	65.00
Opalescent, Creamer, Alaska, Vaseline	50.00 To 95.00
Opalescent, Creamer, Alaska, White	35.00
Opalescent, Creamer, Argonaut Shell, Blue	80.00
Opalescent, Creamer, Argonaut Shell, Custard	95.00
Opalescent, Creamer, Beatty's Ribbed Opal, Blue	45.00
Opalescent, Creamer, Beatty's Ribbed Opal, White, 2 In.	25.00
Opalescent, Creamer, Cross Bar, Blue	22.50
Opalescent, Creamer, Drapery, Blue	50.00
Opalescent, Creamer, Drapery, White, Gold Trim	30.00
Opalescent, Creamer, Fluted Scroll, Blue	40.00
Opalescent, Creamer, Fluted Scroll, Vaseline	60.00
Opalescent, Creamer, Gold Trim, Argonaut Shell	105.00
Opalescent, Creamer, Hobnail, Blue	38.00
Opalescent, Creamer, Hobnail, Northwood, White	25.00
Opalescent, Creamer, Intaglio, Blue	45.00
Opalescent, Creamer, Intaglio, White	20.00 To 45.00
Opalescent, Creamer, Iris With Meander, Clear	25.00
Opalescent, Creamer, Jewel & Flower, Blue	110.00
Opalescent, Creamer, Jeweled Heart, Blue	40.00
Opalescent, Creamer, Miniature, Beatty's Ribbed Opal	14.00
Opalescent, Creamer, Regal, Gold Trim, Green	65.00

Opalescent, Creamer, Swag With Brackets, Blue 75.00
Opalescent, Creamer, Swag With Brackets, Vaseline 85.00
Opalescent, Creamer, Tokyo, Blue 50.00
Opalescent, Cruet, Alaska, Emerald Green 165.00
Opalescent, Cruet, Alaska, Vaseline 225.00
Opalescent, Cruet, Blue, Fern Sprays 105.00
Opalescent, Cruet, Blue, Scroll With Acanthus 100.00
Opalescent, Cruet, Daisy & Plume, Blue 75.00
Opalescent, Cruet, Daisy & Plume, Yellow 55.00
Opalescent, Cruet, Fluted Scroll, Blue 120.00
Opalescent, Cruet, Hobnail, White 98.00
Opalescent, Cruet, Hobnail, White, Miniature, Pair 25.00
Opalescent, Cruet, Intaglio, Blue 115.00
Opalescent, Cruet, Intaglio, White, Original Stopper 55.00
Opalescent, Cruet, Jewel & Flower, Clear 45.00
Opalescent, Cruet, Windows, Swirled Blue 125.00
Opalescent, Cup, Blue, Ribbed Spiral 42.50
Opalescent, Cup, Ribbed Basket 38.50
Opalescent, Cup, Ribbed Stripe 37.50
Opalescent, Cup, Shell, Pink & White 25.00
Opalescent, Dish, Berry, Hobnail, Cranberry, 5 In.Diameter 48.00
Opalescent, Dish, Berry, Hobnail, Vaseline, 5 In.Diameter 48.00
Opalescent, Dish, Candy, Blue, Hobnail, Covered, 7 1/2 In. 22.00
Opalescent, Dish, Coral, Blue, 8 In. 22.00
Opalescent, Dish, Covered, Fluted Scrolls, Blue 48.00
Opalescent, Dish, Intaglio, Ruffled, Small, Vaseline 20.00
Opalescent, Epergne, 3 Trumpet, White, Hobnail In Square 100.00
Opalescent, Finger Bowl, Stars & Stripes, White 15.00
Opalescent, Gas Shade, Candy Ribbon Rim, Hobnail, 8 In.Diameter 50.00
Opalescent, Goblet, Hobnail, White 27.00
Opalescent, Goblet, Plumes 18.50
Opalescent, Jar, Powder, Covered, Fluted Scrolls, Blue 42.00
Opalescent, Jar, Puff, Fluted Scrolls, Vaseline 55.00
Opalescent, Jar, Puff, Fluted Scrolls, White 30.00
Opalescent, Jar, Puff, Lidded, Fluted Scroll, Blue 45.00
Opalescent, Master Berry Bowl, Fluted Scrolls, Vaseline 55.00
Opalescent, Master Berry Bowl, Iris With Meander, Blue 125.00
Opalescent, Master Berry Bowl, Jewel & Flower, Gold & Red Design 105.00
Opalescent, Master Berry Bowl, Paneled Holly, Clear, Red & Gold Trim 45.00
Opalescent, Master Berry Bowl, Regal, Blue 85.00
Opalescent, Master Berry Bowl, Shell & Wreath, Vaseline 125.00
Opalescent, Master Berry Bowl, Shell & Wreath, 3 Sauces, White 90.00
Opalescent, Master Berry Bowl, Tokyo, Green .... 35.00 To 38.00
Opalescent, Muffineer, Hobnail 50.00
Opalescent, Nappy, Sea Spray, Blue, Finger Ring, 5 1/2 In. 35.00
Opalescent, Pitcher, Blue, Buttons & Braids 165.00
Opalescent, Pitcher, Buttons And Braid, Clear 80.00
Opalescent, Pitcher, Drapery, Applied Handle, Blue 45.00
Opalescent, Pitcher, Hobnail, Clear Threaded Handle, 4 In. 32.50
Opalescent, Pitcher, Hobnail, Squat Base, Reeded Handle, Ground Pontil, 8 In. 185.00
Opalescent, Pitcher, Water, Alaska, Blue 335.00
Opalescent, Pitcher, Water, Beads & Braids, Ruffled, Blue 97.50
Opalescent, Pitcher, Water, Beatty Swirl, Blue 115.00
Opalescent, Pitcher, Water, Buttons & Braid 50.00
Opalescent, Pitcher, Water, Fluted Scrolls, Blue 225.00
Opalescent, Pitcher, Water, Hobnail, Square Top, Vaseline 175.00
Opalescent, Pitcher, Water, Honeycomb, White With Clear Handle, 9 3/4 In. 100.00
Opalescent, Pitcher, Water, Reverse Swirl, Clear, 2 Tumblers 155.00
Opalescent, Pitcher, Water, Ribbed Basket, Clear 125.00
Opalescent, Pitcher, Water, Swag With Brackets, Vaseline 185.00
Opalescent, Pitcher, Water, Swirl, Cranberry, Bulbous, Fluted Top 145.00
Opalescent, Pitcher, Water, Tokyo, Green 135.00
Opalescent, Pitcher, Water, Tokyo, White 95.00
Opalescent, Pitcher, Water, Windows, Blue Applied Handle 175.00
Opalescent, Plate, Iris With Meander, Green, 7 In. .... 25.00 To 30.00
Opalescent, Plate, White, Iris With Meander, 8 In. 20.00

Opalescent, Rose Bowl, Beaded Drape, Blue 28.00
Opalescent, Rose Bowl, Beaded Drape, Footed, Cranberry Border 34.00
Opalescent, Rose Bowl, Beaded Drape, White 25.00
Opalescent, Rose Bowl, Fan & Feather, Inverted, Blue 75.00
Opalescent, Rose Bowl, Footed, Piasa Bird, Blue 35.00
Opalescent, Rose Bowl, Inverted Fan & Feather, Blue .... 47.00 To 78.00
Opalescent, Rose Bowl, Opal Swirl, Blue 35.00
Opalescent, Rose Bowl, Plumes, Footed, Vaseline 59.00
Opalescent, Rose Bowl, Spool, Blue, 4 In. 45.00
Opalescent, Salt & Pepper, Fluted Scrolls, Enameling, Vaseline 95.00
Opalescent, Salt, Blue, Jackson 55.00
Opalescent, Saltshaker, Beatty Waffle, Blue, Pair 45.00
Opalescent, Saltshaker, Beatty's Ribbed Opal, Blue, Original Top 45.00
Opalescent, Saltshaker, Hobnail, Blue 16.00
Opalescent, Saltshaker, Opalescent Swirl, Blue 22.00
Opalescent, Saltshaker, Ribbon Stripe, Blue 30.00
Opalescent, Sauce, Alaska 22.00
Opalescent, Sauce, Alaska, Blue 62.00
Opalescent, Sauce, Berry, Jeweled Heart, Ruffled, Green 18.00
Opalescent, Sauce, Drapery, White, Signed Northwood 12.50
Opalescent, Sauce, Fan, Blue, Signed D 25.00
Opalescent, Sauce, Footed, Intaglio, Blue 20.00
Opalescent, Sauce, Green, Regal 28.00
Opalescent, Sauce, Intaglio, Bouquet 32.50
Opalescent, Sauce, Jewel & Flower, White With Gold Flashing 35.00
Opalescent, Sauce, Jeweled Heart, Ruffled, White 12.00
Opalescent, Sauce, Palm Beach, Vaseline 45.00
Opalescent, Sauce, Scroll With Acanthus, White 16.00
Opalescent, Sauce, Shell & Wreath, Blue 38.00
Opalescent, Shade, Gas, Hobnail, Ruffled, 4 X 5 1/4 X 8 1/2 In. 65.00
Opalescent, Shade, Gas, Swirl, Ruffled, 4 X 8 3/4 X 4 1/2 In. 60.00
Opalescent, Spooner & Creamer, Alaska, White 35.00
Opalescent, Spooner, Alaska, Blue .... 50.00 To 69.00
Opalescent, Spooner, Alaska, Vaseline .... 38.00 To 55.00
Opalescent, Spooner, Alaska, White 35.00
Opalescent, Spooner, Argonaut Shell, Custard 95.00
Opalescent, Spooner, Beatty's Swirled Opal 24.00
Opalescent, Spooner, Drapery, Blue .... 55.00 To 60.00
Opalescent, Spooner, Drapery, White 22.00
Opalescent, Spooner, Flora, Blue 100.00
Opalescent, Spooner, Flora, Clear 45.00
Opalescent, Spooner, Fluted Scrolls, Blue .... 48.00 To 65.00
Opalescent, Spooner, Fluted Scrolls, Pinched, Vaseline 75.00
Opalescent, Spooner, Fluted Scrolls, Vaseline .... 32.50 To 60.00
Opalescent, Spooner, Fluted Scrolls, White 47.00
Opalescent, Spooner, Idyll, Blue 80.00
Opalescent, Spooner, Intaglio, Blue .... 40.00 To 75.00
Opalescent, Spooner, Intaglio, White .... 30.00 To 42.00
Opalescent, Spooner, Iris With Meander, Clear 30.00
Opalescent, Spooner, Jackson, Blue 40.00
Opalescent, Spooner, Jewel & Flower, Vaseline 95.00
Opalescent, Spooner, Northwood Hobnail, Blue, Thumbprint 45.00
Opalescent, Spooner, Palm Beach, Vaseline 75.00
Opalescent, Spooner, Regal, Blue 78.00
Opalescent, Spooner, Shell & Wreath, Blue 85.00
Opalescent, Spooner, Shell & Wreath, Enameling, Vaseline 85.00
Opalescent, Spooner, Swag With Brackets, Blue 75.00
Opalescent, Spooner, Swag With Brackets, Vaseline 65.00
Opalescent, Spooner, Tokyo, Green 65.00
Opalescent, Spooner, Water Lily & Cattails, Blue .... 35.00 To 55.00
Opalescent, Spooner, Water Lily & Cattails, Green 55.00
Opalescent, Spooner, Wreath & Shell, Enameled 125.00
Opalescent, Sugar & Creamer, Alaska, Clear 70.00
Opalescent, Sugar & Creamer, Hobnail, Blue, 2 3/4 In. 45.00
Opalescent, Sugar & Creamer, Hobnail, Small 10.00
Opalescent, Sugar & Creamer, Lid, Argonaut Shell, Script Signed, Blue 225.00

Opalescent, Sugar Bowl, Fluted Scroll, Clear 15.00
Opalescent, Sugar Shaker, Fern 80.00
Opalescent, Sugar Shaker, Opalescent Swirl, Blue 75.00
Opalescent, Sugar, Covered, Alaska, Enameling 125.00
Opalescent, Sugar, Covered, Beatty's Swirled Opal, Blue 95.00
Opalescent, Sugar, Covered, Drapery 30.00
Opalescent, Sugar, Covered, Fluted Scrolls, White 25.00
Opalescent, Sugar, Covered, Hobnail, Vaseline 95.00
Opalescent, Sugar, Covered, Iris With Meander 80.00
Opalescent, Sugar, Covered, Jewel & Flower, Vaseline 145.00
Opalescent, Sugar, Covered, Northwood's Block, White 42.50
Opalescent, Sugar, Covered, Swag With Brackets, Green 80.00
Opalescent, Sugar, Covered, Swirl Windows, Blue 110.00
Opalescent, Sugar, Covered, White, Beatty Ribbed Opal 42.50
Opalescent, Sugar, Drapery, White 45.00
Opalescent, Sugar, Intaglio, Blue 150.00
Opalescent, Sugar, Palm Beach, Vaseline 30.00
Opalescent, Sugar, Regal, Blue .... 120.00 To 135.00
Opalescent, Sugar, Regal, Gold Trim, Green 85.00
Opalescent, Sugar, Regal, White 55.00
Opalescent, Sugar, Swag With Brackets, Blue 40.00
Opalescent, Sugar, Swag With Brackets, Green 75.00
Opalescent, Sugar, Swag With Brackets, Vaseline 95.00
Opalescent, Syrup, Coin Spot, Blue, Original Top 127.50
Opalescent, Syrup, Coin Spot, Original Lid, Blue 95.00
Opalescent, Syrup, Coin Spot, Ring Neck, Blue 130.00
Opalescent, Syrup, Daisy & Plume, Tin Lid, Blue 110.00
Opalescent, Syrup, Sea Spray, Original Top, Blue 265.00
Opalescent, Table Set, Circled Scroll, White 275.00
Opalescent, Table Set, Fluted Scrolls, Blue 575.00
Opalescent, Table Set, Fluted Scrolls, Vaseline .... 375.00 To 425.00
Opalescent, Table Set, Opal Swag With Brackets, Green 375.00
Opalescent, Table Set, Pitcher, Sugar, Creamer, Butter, Spooner, Sauce, 7 Piece 125.00
Opalescent, Table Set, Tokyo, White 250.00
Opalescent, Toothpick, Beatty's Ribbed Opal 42.50
Opalescent, Toothpick, Diamond Point, Green 65.00
Opalescent, Toothpick, Diamond Stem, Cobalt 95.00
Opalescent, Toothpick, Iris With Meander, Blue 95.00
Opalescent, Tray, Beatty's Ribbed Opal, Ribs Rayed To Center, 8 1/2 X 5 In. 40.00
Opalescent, Tray, Celery, Alaska, Blue 90.00
Opalescent, Tray, Water, Beatty's Swirl, Blue 65.00
Opalescent, Trough, Northwood Block, Blue 45.00
Opalescent, Tumble-Up, Drape, Vaseline, 7 In. 150.00
Opalescent, Tumble-Up, Loop, 7 1/4 In. 85.00
Opalescent, Tumbler, Alaska, Blue 48.00
Opalescent, Tumbler, Beaded Drape, Green 48.00
Opalescent, Tumbler, Beatty's Swirled Opal, White 20.00
Opalescent, Tumbler, Blue, Water Lily & Cattails 38.50
Opalescent, Tumbler, Buttons & Braid, Blue 25.00
Opalescent, Tumbler, Christmas Snowflake, Blue 60.00
Opalescent, Tumbler, Coin Spot, Blue 35.00
Opalescent, Tumbler, Daisy & Plume, Yellow 18.00
Opalescent, Tumbler, Drapery, White, Set Of 6 .... 110.00
Opalescent, Tumbler, Everglades, Vaseline 100.00
Opalescent, Tumbler, Hobnail, Blue 35.00
Opalescent, Tumbler, Hobnail, Cranberry, 4 3/4 In. 25.00
Opalescent, Tumbler, Hobnail, Vaseline 19.00
Opalescent, Tumbler, Hobnail, 10 Row Hobs, Cranberry 65.00
Opalescent, Tumbler, Idyll, Blue 40.00
Opalescent, Tumbler, Idyll, Gold Trim, Green 23.00
Opalescent, Tumbler, Inverted Fan & Feather, Blue 58.00
Opalescent, Tumbler, Iris With Meander, Vaseline 55.00
Opalescent, Tumbler, Jefferson Drape, Green 16.00
Opalescent, Tumbler, Jeweled Heart, Clear 39.00
Opalescent, Tumbler, Paneled Holly, White .... 35.00 To 45.00
Opalescent, Tumbler, Poinsettia, Blue 30.00

Opalescent, Tumbler, Ribbed Stripe, White	20.00
Opalescent, Tumbler, S-Repeat, Blue	45.00
Opalescent, Tumbler, Shell & Wreath, Vaseline	35.00 To 50.00
Opalescent, Tumbler, Stars & Stripes, Blue	18.00
Opalescent, Tumbler, Swag With Brackets, Vaseline	50.00
Opalescent, Tumbler, Turrons And Braids	20.00
Opalescent, Tumbler, Water Lily & Cattails, Blue	27.50 To 35.00
Opalescent, Vase, Applied Leaves & Flowers, 8 1/2 In.	135.00
Opalescent, Vase, Blue, Vertical Ribbed, Scalloped Rim, 13 In.	27.00
Opalescent, Vase, Celery, Northwood's Block, Green	18.00
Opalescent, Vase, Celery, Seaweed, Blue	70.00
Opalescent, Vase, Coin Spot, Cranberry, Ruffled Top, 6 1/2 X 6 1/2 In.	65.00
Opalescent, Vase, Corn Vase, Vaseline, 8 In.	95.00
Opalescent, Vase, Corn, Blue	85.00 To 100.00
Opalescent, Vase, Corn, White	39.00
Opalescent, Vase, Diamond Point, Blue, Marked N, 9 3/4 In.	26.00
Opalescent, Vase, Drapery, Green, 11 1/2 In.	28.00
Opalescent, Vase, Fan, Flared Ruffled Top, 6 In.	15.00
Opalescent, Vase, Fluted Scrolls, 6 In.	25.00
Opalescent, Vase, Hobnail, Cranberry, Bulbous Bottom, 6 In.	40.00
Opalescent, Vase, Hobnail, Flared Ruffled Top, Blue, 7 X 2 In.	20.00
Opalescent, Vase, Hobnail, Ruffled Edge, Pink To White, 8 In.	45.00
Opalescent, Vase, Jefferson Wheel, Green To White, 6 1/2 In.	25.00
Opalescent, Vase, Rib & Diamond Point, White, 10 1/2 In.	20.00
Opalescent, Vase, Tree Trunk, Blue, 11 1/2 In.	20.00
Opalescent, Vase, Wheel & Block, Jefferson Glass Company, 4 1/4 In.	24.00
Opalescent, Water Set, Arabian Nights, Blue	450.00
Opalescent, Water Set, Beatty's Ribbed Opal, Blue, 6 Piece	395.00
Opalescent, Water Set, Coin Spot, Blue, Bulbous, 5 Piece	180.00
Opalescent, Water Set, Daisy & Fern, Cranberry, 6 Pieces	300.00
Opalescent, Water Set, Drape, Cobalt Handle, 10 Glasses, Vaseline	400.00

Opaline glass, or opal glass, was made in white, apple green, and other colors. The glass had a matte surface and a lack of transparency. It was often gilded or painted. It was a popular mid-nineteenth-century European glassware.

Opaline, Box, Blown, Pink, Hinged	115.00
Opaline, Dish, Candy, Hand-Painted Scene, Brass Finial & Dome, 6 1/2 In.	32.50
Opaline, Pitcher, Green, Applied Handle, Gold Band & Trim, 4 X 2 1/4 In.	50.00
Opaline, Vase, Blue Ball Feet, Pulled Feather, 6 X 6 In.	169.00
Opera Glasses, Brass, Fold Flat In Original Leather Case, French, C.1900	105.00
Opera Glasses, French, Hounds Chasing Stag Scene	20.00
Opera Glasses, Jumelle Ducheffel	15.00
Opera Glasses, Mother-Of-Pearl Sides, Leather Case	35.00
Opera Glasses, Mother-Of-Pearl, Brass, Chevalier, Paris, C.1900	13.00
Opera Glasses, Mother-Of-Pearl, Leather Case, Signed C In Star	25.00
Opera Glasses, Paris, Mother-Of-Pearl & Brass	20.00
Opera Glasses, Red & Silver Brocade, Steel Frame, Snap-Up Case	35.00
Organ, see Music, Organ	
Orphan Annie, Bandana	34.00
Orphan Annie, Book, Comic, 1930s	2.50
Orphan Annie, Book, Secret Society, 8 Pages	23.50
Orphan Annie, Bowl & Plate	6.50
Orphan Annie, Bowl, Breakfast Of Champions	20.00
Orphan Annie, Bracelet	34.00
Orphan Annie, Clicker, Safety Guard	15.00
Orphan Annie, Decoder, 1935	20.00
Orphan Annie, Decoder, 1936	12.00
Orphan Annie, Decoder, 1937	16.00 To 20.00
Orphan Annie, Doll, 7 In.	5.00
Orphan Annie, Game, Radio Treasure Hunt, 1938, Ovaltine Premium	45.00
Orphan Annie, Game, Travel, Box & Board	10.75
Orphan Annie, Mug, Annie & Sandy, Signed Harold Gray	50.00
Orphan Annie, Mug, Beetleware	12.00 To 16.00
Orphan Annie, Mug, China	25.00
Orphan Annie, Neckerchief, Straight Arrow	15.00

Orphan Annie, Pin, Sandy	2.25
Orphan Annie, Pin, Secret Society	8.00
Orphan Annie, Purse, Leather	25.00
Orphan Annie, Ring	12.00
Orphan Annie, Shaker, Ovaltine, Covered, Annie & Sandy, Beetleware	25.00
Orphan Annie, Stove, Figural	18.00
Orphan Annie, Toy, Windup	95.00

Orrefors Glassworks, located in the Swedish Province of Smaaland, was established in 1916.

Orrefors, Bottle, Perfume, Script, Signed	30.00
Orrefors, Bowl, Crystal, Crimped Base, 8 In.	40.00
Orrefors, Decanter, Intaglio Carved, S.Gate, 1284 R.A3, C.1825, 10 1/2 In.	850.00
Orrefors, Vase, Crystal, Satyr Playing Flute, Nymph Lady Dancing, 11 1/2 In.	175.00
Orrefors, Vase, Etched Fish, Signed & Dated 1916, 9 1/2 In.	975.00
Orrefors, Vase, Mother Of Mercy Figure, Signed A.Kunft 1950, 13 1/2 X 8 In.	1000.00
Orrefors, Vase, Naked Maidens Celebrating, Marked, Signed, C.1930, 9 In.	550.00
Orrefors, Vase, Paperweight, Fish Design, Painted Inside, Signed, 5 1/2 In.	350.00
Orrefors, Vase, Prismatic Smoke Gray Decoration, Signed, 7 In.	125.00

Ott & Brewer Company operated the Etruria Pottery at Trenton, New Jersey, from 1863 to 1893. It was under the direction of William Bromley, Sr., from the Belleek factory at Belleek, Ireland, from 1883.

Ott & Brewer, Plate, Gold Paste Thistle Design, Crown & Sword, 6 1/2 In.	85.00
Ott & Brewer, Platter, Blue Rim, Fishscale Pattern, 15 1/4 In.	25.00
Ott & Brewer, Shell, Gold Fluted, 2 Shell Feet, Floral, Stems, Leaves, Handle	145.00

OWENS UTOPIAN

Owens Pottery was made in Zanesville, Ohio, from 1891 to 1928. The first art pottery was made after 1896. Utopian Ware, Cyrano, Navarre, Feroza, and Henri Deux were made. Pieces were usually marked with a form of the name Owens. About 1907 the firm began to make tile and gave up the art pottery wares.

Owens, Base, Lamp, Utopian, Cherries, 13 In.	165.00
Owens, Basket, Hanging, Green	70.00
Owens, Bottle, Utopia, 1885	120.00
Owens, Jardiniere, Dragons, Streaked Background, Utopian, 15 In.Diameter	695.00
Owens, Jug, Alpine, Left-Handed, Signed, 6 1/2 In.	95.00
Owens, Jug, Handle, Utopian, Corn On Side, 7 1/2 In.	100.00
Owens, Letter Holder, Utopian, Frank Ferrell, 5 1/2 In.	195.00
Owens, Mug, Utopian, Cherries & Leaves, 5 In.	75.00
Owens, Mug, Utopian, Grape & Leaf, Brown, Yellow Ground, 5 X 5 1/2 In.	65.00
Owens, Mug, Utopian, Handle, Signed Tot Steele	75.00
Owens, Pitcher, Tankard, Utopian, Cherries, Signed, 12 In.	245.00
Owens, Tankard & 4 Mugs, Cherries, Signed	500.00
Owens, Tankard, Utopian, Pansies, 12 1/4 In.	170.00
Owens, Vase, Brown Glaze, Raised Pansy, Marked, 12 In.	95.00
Owens, Vase, Bud, Utopian , Twisted Shape, Orange Flowers, 4 1/2 In.	85.00
Owens, Vase, Cattails, Utopian, 10 1/2 In.	135.00
Owens, Vase, Cyrano, Footed, Crescent Shape, 5 1/2 In.	140.00
Owens, Vase, Jug, Utopian, Ear Of Corn, Signed, 5 X 20 In.Diameter	275.00
Owens, Vase, Leaves, Brown, Orange, Green, Marked, Signed CA, 7 1/2 In.	115.00
Owens, Vase, Matte Green, 2 Handled, Signed, 8 1/4 In.	70.00
Owens, Vase, Rose Decoration, MC-7-Owens Utopian-127, 7 X 3 3/8 In.	100.00
Owens, Vase, Utopian, Buttercup, Foliage, Artist Signed, 5 1/2 In.	90.00
Owens, Vase, Utopian, Cattails, 10 1/2 In.	135.00
Owens, Vase, Utopian, Floral, Artist Signed, 10 X 5 In.	150.00
Owens, Vase, Utopian, Matte, 13 In.	135.00
Owens, Vase, Utopian, Sanches Apache, Brown & Yellow, Signed, 11 In.	2000.00
Owens, Vase, Woman's Profile, Flowing Hair Forms Handles	285.00
Owens, Vase, 2 Handles, Matte Green, Owensart, 8 In.High	85.00
Oyster Plate, Clam Shape, Embossed Fish & Seaweed, 1881, 8 1/2 In.	55.00
Oyster Plate, Covered, Wild Rose Pattern, C.1915, Buffalo Pottery	30.00
Oyster Plate, Divided Bed, Middle Sauce Cup	32.00
Oyster Plate, Elite, Pink Flowers, Gold Edge, Limoges, 8 1/2 In., Set Of 10	185.00
Oyster Plate, Gold Trim, Limoges	7.50

Oyster Plate, Open Handles, Embossed Design, , Set Of 4	45.00
Oyster Plate, Shell & Seaweed, Majolica	60.00
Oyster Plate, White Background, Clam Shape, 10 1/2 In.	68.00
Oyster Plate, 5 Wells, Shells & Seaweed Decoration, Limoges, 8 1/4 In.	21.00
Oyster Plate, 6 Insets, Pink, Yellow, White, 8 1/4 In.Diameter	130.00
Paden City, Figurine, Squirrel On Log	55.00
Paden City, Lamp, Handy, Apple Green, Sapphire Blue, Turquoise	68.00
Painting, Oil On Paper, Von Hindenberg, C.1900, 6 In.Oval	250.00
Painting, On Celluloid, Spanish Lady, Reds, Framed, Signed	90.00
Painting, On Ivory, Bust Of Woman, C.1890, 3 1/4 X 2 3/4 In.	45.00
Painting, On Ivory, Court Lady, Framed, C.1800, Signed, 4 3/4 X 5 1/2 In.	135.00
Painting, On Ivory, Court Lady, Ivory Frame, Signed Vigee Le Brun	750.00
Painting, On Ivory, Girl Sitting, Curls, Gold Leaf Frame, American, 4 X 5 In.	450.00
Painting, On Ivory, Josephine, Bronze Frame, Artist Signed, 4 X 5 In.	325.00
Painting, On Ivory, Josephine, Signed, Black Wooden Frame, 2 3/4 X 3 1/2 In.	125.00
Painting, On Ivory, Lady, Bronze & Tortoise Shell Frame, 2 1/2 X 3 1/4 In.	150.00
Painting, On Ivory, Man Wooing Woman, 2 In.Diameter	130.00
Painting, On Ivory, Marquises De Montessar, Framed, Signed, 5 1/2 X 4 In.	225.00
Painting, On Ivory, Miniature, Moses, Case, 3 In.Oval	100.00
Painting, On Ivory, Missy, Eyelet Gown, Carved Wood Frame, 3 1/2 X 4 1/2 In.	250.00
Painting, On Ivory, Napoleon, Signed, Black Wood Frame, 2 3/4 X 3 1/2 In.	125.00
Painting, On Ivory, Persian, Hunt Scene, 4 X 6 In.	21.00
Painting, On Ivory, Pink Roses, Signed Sinclair, Oval, 3 1/2 X 3 1/2 In.	325.00
Painting, On Ivory, Portrait Of Court Lady, Sterling Filigree Mounting	50.00
Painting, On Ivory, Portrait, Flirty, Signed, Sinclair, Framed, 5 X 6 In.	325.00
Painting, On Ivory, Portrait, Josephine, Signed French, 3 1/4 X 4 In.	175.00
Painting, On Ivory, Portrait, Lady, Signed Kidia, Framed, 5 X 5 In.	250.00
Painting, On Ivory, Portrait, Mosaic, Jeweled Frame, 2 1/2 X 3 In.	125.00
Painting, On Ivory, Portrait, Pearl, Signed Plimer, Oval, 5 X 6 In.	250.00
Painting, On Ivory, Portrait, Plumes, Signed Lebrun, 4 1/2 X 5 1/2 In.	250.00
Painting, On Ivory, Portrait, Ringlets, Brass Narrow Frame, 4 1/2 X 5 In.	65.00
Painting, On Ivory, Portrait, Russian, Signed Borty, 4 1/2 X 4 1/2 In.	175.00
Painting, On Ivory, Shadow Box Frame, C.1860, 4 X 6 In.	225.00
Painting, On Ivory, Victorian Lady, Signed, 2 1/2 X 3 In.	165.00
Painting, On Ivory, Young Lady, Bronze Frame, Signed, 5 1/2 X 4 1/2 In.	225.00
Painting, On Porcelain, Baker's Chocolate Lady, Brass Frame, 3 X 2 1/4 In.	85.00
Painting, On Porcelain, Bare Chested Lady, 2 1/4 X 2 1/2 In.	125.00
Painting, On Porcelain, Child With Woman, 5 3/4 X 8 3/4 In.	750.00
Painting, On Porcelain, Courting Scene, 18th Century, 2 X 3 1/4 In.	35.00
Painting, On Porcelain, French Court Lady, Oval, 4 X 3 In.	85.00
Painting, On Porcelain, Girl Holding Jug, 7 3/4 X 4 In.	750.00
Painting, On Porcelain, Lady Holding Jug, Metal Frame, 2 1/4 X 2 1/2 In.	125.00
Painting, On Porcelain, Lady, Gold Frame, 2 1/4 X 3 1/2 In.	150.00
Painting, On Porcelain, Lady, Roses, Leaves, Framed, Limoges, 13 X 16 In.	650.00
Painting, On Porcelain, Lady, 2 1/4 In.Square	48.00
Painting, On Porcelain, Madame Vegee Leburn, Signed Shoery, 2 In.Round	125.00
Painting, On Porcelain, Man & Woman, Bronze Frame, C.1860, 7 X 9 In.	1250.00
Painting, On Porcelain, Nude Coming Out Of Water, 7 1/4 X 5 1/2 In.	750.00
Painting, On Porcelain, Robed Woman, Wooden Frame, French, 4 3/4 In.Diameter	225.00
Painting, On Porcelain, Virgin Mary, Signed Dininger, 16 X 13 1/8 In.	750.00
Painting, On Porcelain, Women Looking Into Water, Framed, 5 1/4 X 7 3/8 In.	450.00
Painting, On Porcelain, Young Beauty, Signed Geyer, 3 3/4 X 2 1/2 In.	150.00
Painting, On Porcelain, Young Girl, C.1880, Framed, 6 3/4 X 5 1/2 In.	65.00
Painting, On Rice Paper, Chinaman, Isinglass Cover, 3 1/4 X 4 1/2 In.	18.00
Painting, On Velvet, White Roses, Unframed, 9 1/2 X 19 1/2 In.	75.00
Painting, Reverse On Glass, Christmas Eve, Framed, 33 X 19 In.	125.00
Painting, Reverse On Glass, Lady In Ribboned Hat, Chinese, 8 1/2 In.	1300.00
Painting, Reverse On Glass, The Weary Hunter, Chinese, 13 1/2 In.	1500.00
Painting, Watercolor On Velvet, 19th Century, 14 X 15 1/2 In.	650.00
Painting, Watercolor, Fruit Filled Bowl, 19th Century, 20 X 27 In.	600.00
Painting, Watercolor, Marriage Record & Portrait, , 1833, 11 1/2 X 9 1/4 In.	5000.00
Painting, Wax On Velvet, Uni Aequis Virturte, 1779, Framed, 6 1/4 X 5 In.	395.00

Pairpoint Corporation was a silver and glass firm founded in New Bedford, Massachusetts, in 1880.

Pairpoint, Base, Bubble-Ball Connector In Stem, 11 1/2 In.	150.00

Pairpoint, **Base,** Lamp, Brass, Marked, 16 In. 85.00
Pairpoint, **Basket,** Pierced Work, Twisted Handle, Plated, 6 In. 45.00
Pairpoint, **Bottle,** Perfume, Blue Tulip, Clear Leaf Top, Applied Separately 175.00
Pairpoint, **Bottle,** Perfume, Stopper, Paperweight, Melon Ribbed, 7 In., Pair 190.00
Pairpoint, **Bowl,** Controlled Bubble, Ruby, 12 In. 78.00
Pairpoint, **Bowl,** Enameled Glass, Silver Base, Signed, 5 1/4 X 7 1/2 In.Diam. 95.00
Pairpoint, **Bowl,** Finger, Under Plate, Deep Cobalt, Original Label 32.00
Pairpoint, **Bowl,** Merry Widow, Cut Glass, 14 In. .... 85.00 To 125.00
Pairpoint, **Bowl,** Squirrel In Relief, Gold Wash Inside, 3 X 11 In. 155.00
Pairpoint, **Box,** Covered, Heart Shaped, Gold Leaves, Signed, 2 1/2 X 6 In. 300.00
Pairpoint, **Box,** Enameled Opalescent Glass Top, Silver Hinged, 2 1/4 X 6 In. 215.00
Pairpoint, **Box,** Handkerchief, Lid, Silver Rim, Crosscutting, 6 1/2 In.Square 475.00
Pairpoint, **Box,** Lid, Silver Bindings & Clasp, Label, 6 X 6 1/2 X 3 In. 235.00
Pairpoint, **Box,** Round, Hinged, Cut Glass, 6 X 6 1/2 X 3 In. 235.00
Pairpoint, **Box,** Silver Body, Opalescent Cover, Signed, 6 In.Diameter 225.00
Pairpoint, **Box,** 4 Petal Shape, Covered, Raised Scroll Work, Signed, 7 X 6 In. 310.00
Pairpoint, **Candleabra,** 5 Cup, Quadruple Plate, Marked, 11 1/2 In. 165.00
Pairpoint, **Candleholder,** Blown, Blue, 14 In., Pair 110.00
Pairpoint, **Candlestick,** Art Nouveau Pond Lily, Verde Patina, Signed, 10 In. 42.00
Pairpoint, **Candlestick,** Art Nouveau, Chased Flowers, Silver, 8 In. 20.00
Pairpoint, **Candlestick,** Blown, Hollow Stem, Pair, 14 In. 105.00
Pairpoint, **Candlestick,** Controlled Bubble In Stem, 11 1/2 In., Pair 125.00
Pairpoint, **Candlestick,** Teardrop, Colonial Pattern, 11 In., Pair 395.00
Pairpoint, **Castor Set,** 4 Bottles, Cut & Etched 60.00
Pairpoint, **Chalice,** Etched Foliage On Bowl & Foot, Blue Ribbon, 7 In. 115.00
Pairpoint, **Chest,** Liquor, Captain's, Decanter & Glasses 725.00
Pairpoint, **Compote,** Amethyst, , 7 1/4 In., Pair 115.00
Pairpoint, **Compote,** Ball In Stem, Ruby Glass, Early 1900s, 6 In. 125.00
Pairpoint, **Compote,** Clear Bubbled Knob, Amber, Cut Leaves, 12 In., Pair 275.00
Pairpoint, **Compote,** Controlled Bubble, Ball In Stem, Ruby Glass, 6 X 6 In. 125.00
Pairpoint, **Compote,** Footed, Amber Rim & Knot In Stem, Intaglio, 7 X 8 In. 75.00
Pairpoint, **Compote,** Red, Clear Bubble Paperweight Base, 12 X 5 1/2 In. 65.00
Pairpoint, **Console Set,** Bowl, 14 In., Candlesticks, 12 In.Apple Green 350.00
Pairpoint, **Console Set,** Bubble Ball Connector Candlesticks, Bowl, 14 In. 295.00
Pairpoint, **Cordial,** Richmond, Polished Pontil, Base Cut, Pair 65.00
Pairpoint, **Cracker Jar,** Purple Flowers, Green Ground, Signed 295.00
Pairpoint, **Dish,** Candy, Footed Silver Holder, Handle, Signed, 4 1/2 In.Oval 32.00
Pairpoint, **Dish,** Sweet Meat, Melon Ribbed, Cover Stamped MW, Signed 350.00
Pairpoint, **Figurine,** Swan, Swimming, Peachblow, 7 1/4 X 6 1/2 In. 45.00
Pairpoint, **Flower Holder,** Flower Stylized, Brass Stand, Green Vase, 5 In. 45.00
Pairpoint, **Glass,** Wine, Set Of 7 .... 45.00
Pairpoint, **Globe,** Gas, Acid Etched 45.00
Pairpoint, **Goblet,** Cobalt Blue, Hobstar Pedestal Base, 6 In.Set Of 6 .... 75.00
Pairpoint, **Goblet,** Engraved, Silver Plated Base, Boy On Dolphin, Signed 135.00
Pairpoint, **Goblet,** Hobnail Standard, Clear Crystal Stem, 6 3/4 In., Set Of 6 .... 60.00
Pairpoint, **Goblet,** Hobstar Pedestal Base, Cobalt Blue, Set Of 6 .... 75.00
Pairpoint, **Goblet,** Ruby, Clear Stem, 6 In., Set Of 4 .... 75.00
Pairpoint, **Holder,** Cigarette, Bubble Stem 45.00
Pairpoint, **Holder,** Pen, Oriental Figure, Silver Plate 45.00
Pairpoint, **Holder,** Pickle, Double, Cranberry Jars, 12 3/4 In. 795.00
Pairpoint, **Inkwell,** Hinged Lid, Sterling, Bubbles, Large 85.00
Pairpoint, **Jar,** Candy, Pedestal, Cobalt Finial & Stem, 10 1/2 In. 95.00
Pairpoint, **Knife Rest,** Figural, Squirrel Each End 75.00
Pairpoint, **Ladle,** Teardrop, Cane, Hobstars 325.00
Pairpoint, **Lamp,** Astral, Cut Glass, St.Aubin No.82, Shade No.83 .... 800.00
Pairpoint, **Lamp,** Boudoir, Closed Top Shade, Reverse Painted Flowers, Signed 875.00
Pairpoint, **Lamp,** Boudoir, 8 In.Blown-Out Shade, Brass Columnar Base, Marked 800.00
Pairpoint, **Lamp,** Cornucopia, Marina Blue, Bubbly Ball Base, 6 In. 45.00
Pairpoint, **Lamp,** Daisy Pattern, 14 X 6 1/2 In. 295.00
Pairpoint, **Lamp,** Desk, 2 Arm Candlelight, Cut Glass Amber Shade, 18 In. 275.00
Pairpoint, **Lamp,** Desk, 6 In.Raised Diamond, Domed Top, Signed, 7 X 7 In. 400.00
Pairpoint, **Lamp,** Flowers, Signed, Shade, 16 In.Diameter 1250.00
Pairpoint, **Lamp,** Gold Coralene Beads On Shade, Fleur-De-Lis Pattern, 22 In. 950.00
Pairpoint, **Lamp,** Gold Coralene Shade, Fleur-Di-Lis Pattern, 22 In. 950.00
Pairpoint, **Lamp,** Green & Yellow Shade, 21 In. 1500.00
Pairpoint, **Lamp,** Hummingbird & Roses, Gold Satin Ground, Signed, 14 In. 2000.00

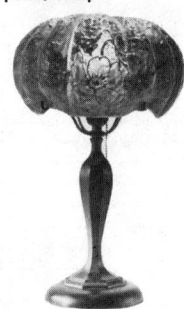  

Pairpoint, Lamp, Painted,
Floral, Patinated Metal

Pairpoint, Lamp, Painted,
Lake Scene, Patinated Metal

Pairpoint, Lamp, Reverse Painted,
Scenic, Stamped, 22 3/4 In.

Pairpoint, Lamp, Painted Mountain Scene	1400.00
Pairpoint, Lamp, Painted, Floral, Patinated Metal *Illus*	1200.00
Pairpoint, Lamp, Painted, Lake Scene, Patinated Metal *Illus*	1100.00
Pairpoint, Lamp, Puffy Grape, Grape Base, Signed, 14 In.Diameter	2750.00
Pairpoint, Lamp, Puffy Yellow Rose Bouquet, Filigree Base, 10 In.	2500.00
Pairpoint, Lamp, Reverse Painted, Scenic, Stamped, 22 3/4 In. *Illus*	1000.00
Pairpoint, Lamp, Roses On Shade, 15 In.Diameter, Signed, 24 In.	4500.00
Pairpoint, Lamp, Scenic Reverse Painted Shade, Signed, 15 In.	525.00
Pairpoint, Lamp, Table, Painted Glass, Silvered Metal, Lake Scene, 17 1/2 In.	900.00
Pairpoint, Lamp, Viscaria, Silverplate Bottom, 13 In. Base	65.00
Pairpoint, Matchsafe, Embossed Dog With Pheasant, Signed, Numbered	40.00
Pairpoint, Napkin Ring, Base Is Frog On Leaf, Fly On Top, Glass Eyes	225.00
Pairpoint, Napkin Ring, Figural Rabbits, One Standing, One Sitting	240.00
Pairpoint, Napkin Ring, Figural, Cockatoo Sits On Ball, Round Base	65.00
Pairpoint, Napkin Ring, Figural, Turtle, Ring On Back	225.00
Pairpoint, Napkin Ring, Figural, Wheelbarrow	100.00
Pairpoint, Orange Holder, Silver Plated, No.6303	37.00
Pairpoint, Paperweight, Life Size Bird, Bubbles	28.00
Pairpoint, Paperweight, Millefiori, 3 In.	60.00
Pairpoint, Paperweight, Pear, End-Of-Day	15.00
Pairpoint, Paperweight, Yellow Rose, Magnum	80.00
Pairpoint, Pickle Castor, Double, Etched Jars, Tongs	165.00
Pairpoint, Pitcher, Cobalt Blue, Clear Base & Handle, 8 1/2 X 4 1/2 In.	50.00
Pairpoint, Plate, Butterfly & Daisy, 10 In.Diameter	175.00
Pairpoint, Plate, Fish & Bug Motif, Hammered Quadruple, 6 In.	20.00
Pairpoint, Salt, Master, Nautilus, 3 1/2 In.	48.50
Pairpoint, Saltshaker, Egg, Violet Flower, 2-Piece Top	25.00
Pairpoint, Shade, Metal Encased, Signed, Pair, 9 1/2 In.	250.00
Pairpoint, Sherbet, Hobnail Standard, Blue Crystal Stem, 4 In.Set Of 6	48.00
Pairpoint, Tea Set, Floral Repousse, Teapot, Sugar Creamer, Waste	175.00
Pairpoint, Tray, Bread, Silsbee Pattern, 12 3/4 X 6 In.	135.00
Pairpoint, Urn, Ruby, Footed, Crystal Ball Stem, 13 1/2 In.	58.00
Pairpoint, Vase, Bubble Ball Connector In Stem, 11 1/2 In.	150.00
Pairpoint, Vase, Bubble, Blown, Scalloped, Pink Threading, 7 X 6 In.	65.00
Pairpoint, Vase, Bud, Amberina, 7 In.	60.00
Pairpoint, Vase, Bud, Sheffield Silver Standard, Hallmarked, 8 5/8 In.	150.00
Pairpoint, Vase, Cornucopia, Red, Paperweight Base	125.00
Pairpoint, Vase, Deep Purple, Bubble Ball, 12 In.	99.00
Pairpoint, Vase, Enameled Flowers, Tavern Glass, 5 In.	35.00
Pairpoint, Vase, Honey Amber, Blackberry Engraving, Flip Shape, 8 In.	45.00
Pairpoint, Vase, Silver Base, Enameled Bowl, Poppies, 5 1/2 In.	125.00
Pairpoint, Vase, Urn With Flame, 8 In.	215.00
Pairpoint, Wine, Hobnail Standard & Footing, Crystal Stem, 5 In.Set Of 6	60.00
Pantin, Vase, Gladiolas, Humming Bird, Dragon Flies, Signed	310.00
Paper, Album, Victorian, Brass Trim, Secret Storage, Green Velvet	40.00
Paper, Almanac Diary, Kate Greenaway, 1897	55.00
Paper, Almanac, N.Y. Telephone Company, 1955	7.50
Paper, Almanac, N.Y.Telephone Company, 1952	7.50
Paper, Almanac, Shaker, 1886, 32 Pages	5.00

Paper, Bill Of Sale, J.A. & C.W.Underwood, Dated 1866	60.00
Paper, Book, American Printer, T.Mackellar, 1872, 7th Edition	40.00
Paper, Book, Big Little Book, Buck Jones, 1935	7.00
Paper, Book, Big Little Book, Buffalo Bill, 1936	4.00
Paper, Book, Big Little Book, Bugs Bunny	3.50
Paper, Book, Big Little Book, Charlie Chan Solves New Mystery	10.00
Paper, Book, Big Little Book, Lone Ranger, 1938	10.00
Paper, Book, Big Little Book, Popeye & The Jeep	12.00
Paper, Book, Big Little Book, Saalfield No. 1085, Movie Scenes	22.50
Paper, Book, Big Little Book, Terry & The Pirates	12.00
Paper, Book, Campbells Kids, At Home	8.50
Paper, Book, Campbells Kids, Have A Party	8.50
Paper, Book, Chemistry Of Light & Photography, Bogel, 1875	40.00
Paper, Book, Christmas Book For Little People, 1886	10.00
Paper, Book, Christmas Fairy Book, C.1900, 10 Color Illustrations	21.00
Paper, Book, Don Quixote, Clothbound, Gustave Dore, Illustrator, 198 Pages	25.00
Paper, Book, Frank Merriwell At Yale, 1936	15.00
Paper, Book, Hole Book, Peter Newell, 1908	30.00
Paper, Book, Horace Greeley, Autograph, Pen Signature, 1863, 5 1/2 X 8 In.	85.00
Paper, Book, Kindergarten Book Of Folk Songs, Schirmer, 1922	6.50
Paper, Book, Land Of Oz, 1939	22.00
Paper, Book, Lone Ranger, Feature Book No.21	45.00
Paper, Book, Lottie & Dottie, Sunbonnet Girls On Cover, C.1880	15.00
Paper, Book, Maggie & Jiggs, McManus, Autographed, Unpublished	150.00
Paper, Book, Mandrake The Magician, 1935	15.00
Paper, Book, McGuffey's Reader	6.00
Paper, Book, Mutt & Jeff, Hard Cover, 1919	38.00
Paper, Book, Nipper The Little Bull Pup, English, 1943	3.00
Paper, Book, Overall Boys, A First Reader, Grover & Corbett	65.00
Paper, Book, P.T.Barnum's Circus, Hard Cover, 1888, 12 1/2 X 10 1/2 In.	125.00
Paper, Book, Pinocchio, 1927	5.00
Paper, Book, Return Of Tarzan, Edgar Rice Burroughs, 1915	7.00
Paper, Book, Slant Book, Peter Newell, 1910	23.00
Paper, Book, Song Of The Cardinal, Gene Stratton Porter, 1915, Illustrated	10.00
Paper, Book, Tale Of Squirrel Nutkin, 1903, B. Potter	18.00
Paper, Booklet, Fold-Out, Barnum & Bailey, 1892	35.00
Paper, Booklet, He's From Missouri, Story Of Harry S. Truman	5.00
Paper, Booklet, Jello, Maxfield Parrish, 1924	10.00
Paper, Calendar, see Calendar, Paper	
Paper, Calligraphy, Loose Cardboard Cover, Spiral Bound, 10 7/8 X 17 In.	45.00
Paper, Catalog, General Motors Fire Trucks, 1924, 24 Pages	150.00
Paper, Catalog, M.Abbott Frazar Company, Taxidermists .... *Illus*	7.00
Paper, Catalog, Macy's Fall & Winter, 1911, 449 Pages, 7 1/4 X 9 1/2 In.	25.00
Paper, Catalog, Men's Fashion Prints, Fabric Samples, C.1911 .... *Illus*	17.50
Paper, Catalog, Montgomery Ward Fall & Winter, 1927	25.00
Paper, Catalog, Mt.Washington Glass Co., 800 Illustrations	7.50
Paper, Catalog, Steven's Gun, 1900s	30.00
Paper, Catalog, Toys, Edward K.Tryon Co., 1940	35.00
Paper, Catalog, Wiss Scissors	11.00
Paper, Chart, McGuffey's, Reading, Hanging, Illustrated, 1880, 25 X 32 In.	195.00

Paper, Catalog, M.Abbott
Frazar Company, Taxidermists

Paper, Catalog, Men's Fashion Prints, Fabric
Samples, C.1911

Paper, Deed, Hand Written, 1796	12.00
Paper, Doll, Captain Marvel, Packaged, C.1944	12.00
Paper, Doll, Linda Darnell, Uncut	20.00
Paper, Doll, Molly Mansing, 8 Outfits	8.00
Paper, Doll, Oo La-La, For Car Window, Pull String & Skirt Lifts	3.00
Paper, Doll, Rhonda Fleming, Uncut	20.00
Paper, Doll, Uncut, From Book Called Scissors Play	25.00
Paper, Magazine, First 6 Issues Of Life	50.00
Paper, Magazine, Look, 1930-1950s, Each	.75
Paper, Magazine, Police Gazette, 1930s, Movie Star Cover	5.00
Paper, Map, Connecticut, 1799, 9 1/4 X 7 1/4 In.	36.00
Paper, Map, Geological Survey, 1898-1902, New England, N.Y., N.J., Set Of 85	50.00
Paper, Map, Latin America, Lithographs, 1850-80, Set Of 8	50.00
Paper, Map, Lloyd's, Military Map Of Southern States	20.00
Paper, Map, New York State, 1842, 39 X 35 In.	30.00
Paper, Map, Panama Canal, 1906	29.00
Paper, Mask, Halloween, Cisco Kid	4.00
Paper, Menu, Airport Diner, Roosevelt Field, 1930s	20.00
Paper, Money Order, Wells Fargo, Receipts, Framed, Set Of 8	25.00
Paper, Noisemaker, Halloween, 1921	6.50
Paper, Shakespeare, 9 Volumes, Published Berlin 1867, German	75.00
Paper, Trunk, Chinese, Maidens On Landscape Terrace, 1800s, 31 X 15 In., Pair	550.00
Paperweight, Abe Lincoln, Impressed Head, Frosted	45.00
Paperweight, Allegheny Transfer Co., Horse Drawn Moving Wagon	35.00
Paperweight, Anvil, To Forge Our Friendship, Brass, 1922	12.50
Paperweight, Arkansas Portland Cement Co., Cement Shaped Barrel	16.50
Paperweight, Bakewell, Thumbprint Pattern, Finial, C.1840, 3 3/8 In.Diam.	250.00
Paperweight, Banford, Purple & Striped Primrose, Signed, 2 1/4 In.	110.00
Paperweight, Bank Note, Brass, 6 In.Long	12.00
Paperweight, Bell Telephone, New York, Blue	50.00
Paperweight, Ben Franklin Walking To Boston, 5 1/2 X 3 3/4 In.	55.00
Paperweight, Bird Inside, Glass, Round	8.25
Paperweight, Bronze, Capital Fuel Company, Cleveland, Ohio	3.50
Paperweight, Brown's Tested Seeds, Early Wooden Seed Cabinet	32.00
Paperweight, Bulldog, Iron, Advertising	35.00
Paperweight, Chalmers Motor Company, Detroit, Michigan, Factory, 2 Cars, Brass	42.50
Paperweight, Chinese, 4 Concentric Circles & Center Canes, 2 1/2 In.	30.00
Paperweight, Clown, Rookwood, C.1923	82.00
Paperweight, Columbian Exposition, Libbey	20.00
Paperweight, Columbian Exposition, 1893	6.50
Paperweight, Columbian World's Fair, Fish & Fisheries Building, 1893	35.00
Paperweight, Columbian, World's Fair, Iridescent, Glass, 1893, 4 X 2 3/4 In.	18.00
Paperweight, Crouched Lion, American Insurance Of Kentucky	20.00
Paperweight, Derby Hat, Cast Iron, 3 1/2 In.	15.00
Paperweight, Dice With Thermometer	10.00
Paperweight, E.Brandt, Symbol Of Speed, Iron, Signed, 4 1/2 X 1 3/4 X 8 In.	150.00
Paperweight, Elephant, Rookwood, C.1923	82.00
Paperweight, Embossed Lincoln Head, Jasperware, 1911	18.00
Paperweight, Embossed, Kansas City Southern Lines, Octagon Shape, 5 7/8 In.	25.00
Paperweight, Fellerman, No.5, 1974	28.00
Paperweight, Figural, Fish, Spatter Design Inside, Crystal	36.00
Paperweight, Figural, Stove, Reeves Mfg., Company, Dover, Ohio	25.00
Paperweight, Fish Riding Waves, Benton County Guide, Warsaw, Missouri, 2 In.	12.50
Paperweight, Frosted Lion, Centennial Exhibition, Gillinder & Sons, 1876	125.00
Paperweight, Gillinder & Son, Lion	250.00
Paperweight, Glass With Brass Top & Picture, Marked HA	5.00
Paperweight, Grandfather, Mountain Scene, Glass	5.00
Paperweight, Hippopotamus, Amercite, Hand-Painted Flowers, 5 In.	10.00
Paperweight, Japanese Pansy	120.00
Paperweight, Joe St.Clair, Pink Flower	85.00
Paperweight, Kaziun, Yellow Lily, Signed, No.1	225.00
Paperweight, Kewpie, Iron	47.50
Paperweight, Lady's Hand, Brass, 3 1/2 In.	16.50
Paperweight, Leaning Tower Of Pisa, Metal	4.00
Paperweight, Lily, Signed Robert Haman	85.00
Paperweight, Lincoln Park, Chicago, Ill., Place For Pencil	8.50

Paperweight, Lion, Engineered Castings, Inc., Brass	12.50
Paperweight, Little Jayhawk, Kansas University	9.50
Paperweight, Marble, National Cash Register, Gold Register, Pen Holder	27.50
Paperweight, Marble, Pen Holder, John Deere Track Crawler	25.00
Paperweight, Memorial Hall 1776-1876, Frosted & Clear, Oval	150.00 To 325.00
Paperweight, Mirror & Rouge, Kremola Makes The Skin Beautiful	27.50
Paperweight, Mirrored Bottom, Iridescent, Horseshoe Falls	7.00
Paperweight, Monkey On Book, Rookwood, C.1923	82.00
Paperweight, Nailsea, Flower In A Pot	1100.00
Paperweight, New England, Pear	300.00
Paperweight, New York Telephone Co., Blue, Straw Mark	57.50
Paperweight, Pairpoint, see Pairpoint, Paperweight	
Paperweight, Pepsin Gum, 1916	35.00
Paperweight, Photo & Caption Of William McKinley, Flat, Rectangular	15.00
Paperweight, Pinchbeck, Moses In The Bulrushes	650.00
Paperweight, Pink Snake On Jasper Ground	150.00
Paperweight, Plymouth Rock, Inscription At Bottom, Large	33.00
Paperweight, Plymouth Rock, Inscription At Bottom, Small	25.00
Paperweight, Regina State College, Marble, 1882	13.00
Paperweight, Round, Multi-Floral, Dated 1878, Signed, 3 In.	100.00
Paperweight, Sandwich Fruit Weight	650.00
Paperweight, Sandwich Poinsettia, Blue On Jasper Ground	600.00
Paperweight, Sandwich, Double Clematis	600.00
Paperweight, Seven Pointed Star, Magnifying	12.50
Paperweight, Skull, Bronze Over Plaster	10.00
Paperweight, Snow, Saluting Wave	35.00
Paperweight, Squirrel, Danville Stove Co., Pa., Cast Iron, 1898	20.00
Paperweight, St. Louis Fair, 1904	12.00
Paperweight, St.Louis Art Directors Club, 1960, Bronze	22.50
Paperweight, St.Louis, Close Millefiori, 8 Pentagons Around Dog	1400.00
Paperweight, Temple Of Music, Pan American Exposition, Rectangle, Glass	20.00
Paperweight, Tiger, Iron	12.50
Paperweight, Trumpeting Elephant, Cast Brass, 3 In.	9.00
Paperweight, Turtle, Celluloid Back, Bullups, Richmond	10.00
Paperweight, Turtle, Moving Parts, Glass	110.00
Paperweight, World War I, Haig, Pershing & Foch	10.00
Paperweight, World's Fair, 1893, Ferris Wheel Scene	12.00

Papier-mache is a decorative form made from paper mixed with glue, chalk, and other ingredients, then molded and baked. It becomes very hard and can be decorated. Boxes, trays, and furniture were made of papier-mache. Some of the early-nineteenth-century pieces were decorated with mother-of-pearl.

Papier-Mache, Box, Collar, Black With Gold Stars	6.00
Papier-Mache, Box, Covered, Russian, Iris & Leaf Design, 5 In.Diameter	55.00
Papier-Mache, Box, Glove, Painted On Top	12.50
Papier-Mache, Box, Lid, Tree In The Meadow	30.00
Papier-Mache, Box, Mother-Of-Pearl, Floral, Square, C.1850, 11 X 4 In.	125.00
Papier-Mache, Box, Snuff, Hinged, Silver Inlay On Top	12.50
Papier-Mache, Box, Snuff, Lid, Black Lacquered, Pewter Inlay, 1 X 2 In.	20.00
Papier-Mache, Box, Snuff, Water Color Under Glass, C.1830, Round, 2 3/4 In.	45.00
Papier-Mache, Box, Stamp, Double, Black	36.00
Papier-Mache, Cat, Glass Eyes	8.00
Papier-Mache, Cat, Jack-In-The-Box	40.00
Papier-Mache, Christmas Bell, 4 In.	6.00
Papier-Mache, Clown, Wood Limbs, Fur Hair, Bellows, 9 1/2 In.	135.00
Papier-Mache, Creche, Holy Figures, Wise Men, Manger, Cradle, 1900s, 26 Piece	125.00
Papier-Mache, Desk, Lap, Inlaid Mother-Of-Pearl, Gold Designs, English	115.00
Papier-Mache, Easter Egg, Marked Germany	20.00
Papier-Mache, Figures, Manger Scene, 10 Piece, Germany	25.00
Papier-Mache, Figurine, Man In Coat, Large Head, 1920s, 17 In.	75.00
Papier-Mache, Figurine, Shepherd	20.00
Papier-Mache, Rabbit With Basket, 6 1/2 In.	8.00
Papier-Mache, Rabbit, With Basket, 11 In.	20.00
Papier-Mache, Rabbit, With Basket, 5 1/2 In.	5.00
Papier-Mache, Santa Claus, 4 In.	8.00
Papier-Mache, Santa, 10 In.	15.00

Papier-Mache, Soldiers, With Trench, Marked Duro, Austria 165.00
Papier-Mache, Tea Caddy, 3 Medallion Seal, Russian, 2 3/4 X 3 5/8 In. 125.00
Papier-Mache, Tray, Mother-Of-Pearl Inlaid, Painted, Victorian, 1800s, 30 In. 50.00
Papier-Mache, Wig & Mannequin, High Fetched, 19th Century, 15 In. 130.00
　　Parasol, see Umbrella

Parian is a fine-grained, hard-paste porcelain named for the marble it resembles. It was first made in England in 1846 and gained in favor in the United States about 1860. Figures, tea sets, vases, and other items were made of Parian at many English and American factories.

Parian, Box, Covered, Greyhound On Tasseled Cushion Lid, 5 X 4 1/2 In. 125.00
Parian, Bust, Child, 8 In. 38.00
Parian, Bust, Clytie, Goddess Metamorphasing Into Sunflowers, 1870, 7 In. 100.00
Parian, Bust, Goddess Diana, C.1870, 9 1/2 In. 55.00
Parian, Bust, Lincoln, C.1870, 9 In. 90.00
Parian, Bust, Pope Leo XIII, 5 In. .... 16.00 To 32.50
Parian, Bust, Schiller, 2 In. 19.00
Parian, Bust, Thomas Sampson, Hero Of Spanish American War, 5 In. 30.00
Parian, Bust, William Penn, 8 X 6 In. 89.00
Parian, Clock, Elephant Standing On It, 7 1/4 In. 75.00
Parian, Cup & Saucer, Lily Pad Pattern 75.00
Parian, Dish, Blue Embossed Grapes, Leaves & Stems, 9 3/4 X 6 5/8 In. 50.00
Parian, Figurine, Boy With Horn, No.7772, 8 In. 35.00
Parian, Figurine, Child, Rocky Base, C.1880, 7 1/4 In., Pair 100.00
Parian, Figurine, Children At Play, White, 6 X 7 3/4 In. 175.00
Parian, Figurine, Draped Maiden With Bird, 13 In. 95.00
Parian, Figurine, Draped Maiden, Holding Bird, 13 1/4 In. 95.00
Parian, Figurine, Fishnet Lady, Man Holding Basket Of Fish, 7 1/2 In., Pair 135.00
Parian, Figurine, Man Holding Door, Lady With Lamb, Hand-Painted, 9 In., Pair 250.00
Parian, Figurine, President Garfield, 12 In. 160.00
Parian, Figurine, St.Joseph, 15 In. 65.00
Parian, Jug, Woman's Head & Flowers, Open Work Handle, C.1855, 9 1/2 In. 150.00
Parian, Pitcher, White & Blue Design, 8 1/2 In. 135.00
Parian, Plate, Scalloped Rim, Raised Vine Border, 6 5/8 In. 25.00
Parian, Tray, Bread, Give Us This Day, Wheat Sheaf, 11 3/4 X 6 1/2 In. 55.00
Parian, Vase, Cornucopia Type, 2 Seated Dogs, Jewel Work, 6 1/2 In. 40.00
Parian, Vase, Grapes & Tendrils, C.1858, Bennington, 7 In. 57.50
Parian, Vase, Grapes, 8 In. 55.00

Paris, or Old Paris, is porcelain ware that is known to have been made in Paris in the eighteenth or early nineteenth century but has no identifying manufacturer's mark.

Paris, Bottle, Cologne, Cobalt Flowers, Gold Scrollwork 25.00
Paris, Bowl, Pink Ground, Gilt Bronze Mounted, 4 Pierced Feet, 1880s, 17 In. 500.00
Paris, Cup & Saucer, Gilded, Velvet Pink, C.1810 .... 175.00
Paris, Cup & Saucer, 12 Panels, Gold Band Inside Cup 65.00
Paris, Dessert Set, Cup & Saucer, Dessert Plate, C.1840, 2 Of Each 60.00
Paris, Matchbox & Cover, View Of Baltimore, 19th Century, 3 7/8 In. 450.00
Paris, Pot De Creme Set, Tray & Set Of 6 .... 135.00
Paris, Tea Set, Bulbous Teapot, Hand-Painted, 4 Cups, Saucers, Plates 100.00
Paris, Teacup & Saucer, View Of Philadelphia, 1820-40, Initialed 275.00
Paris, Vase, Biscuit, Glazed Blue, Lovers, Scrolled Handles, 1860, 16 In., Pair 90.00
Paris, Vase, Bronze Dore Mountings, Signed Louchet, 14 1/2 In. 950.00
Paris, Vase, Campana Form, Mask Terminal Handle, Scenes, C.1840, 13 In., Pair 1000.00
Paris, Vase, Double Lipped Neck, Foliate Handles, C.1800, 22 3/4 In., Pair 350.00
Paris, Vase, Floral, Gold Trim, 13 1/2 In. 155.00
Paris, Vase, Gilt Ground, Vasiform Body, Swan Head Handle, 1800s, 11 In., Pair 250.00
Paris, Vase, Panel Of Children, Flowers, Dragon Handles, Pink, 18 3/4 In. 130.00
Paris, Vase, Scenes Of Lovers, Pale Blue Ground, 1880, 16 In., Pair 200.00
Paris, Vase, Urn-Form, Gilt Mask Handles, C.1815, 12 1/2 In. 550.00
Paris, Vase, Vincennes Blue, Vignettes, 19th Century, 20 X 10 In., Pair 875.00

Pate de verre is an ancient technique in which glass is made by blending and refining powdered glass of different colors into molds. The process was revived by French glassmakers, especially Galle, around the end of the nineteenth century.

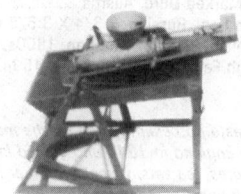

Patent Model, Can Filler, Funnel
Tilt Top, Wood Frame, 12 In.

Patent Model, Egg Box, Woo
3 Drawer, A.Lucas, C.1976, 9

Pate-Sur-Pate, Vase, Angel,
Minton, Signed L.Solon, 8 3/4 In.

Patent Model, Washing Machine,
Thomas Austin, C.1880, 8 1/2 In.

Patent Model, Folding Chair,
Wood, Metal Frame, 11 1/2 In.

Pate De Verre, see also A. Walter

Pate De Verre, Ashtray, Yellow & Orange, Green Lizard, Signed, 4 1/2 X 3 In.	850.00
Pate De Verre, Bowl, Green, Purple, Leaves, Floral, G.Argy Rousseau, 2 In.	350.00
Pate De Verre, Bowl, Head Of Bacchus Protruding, 6 In.Diameter	2250.00
Pate De Verre, Bowl, Miniature, Amber Body, Signed, 3 1/2 In.Diameter	385.00
Pate De Verre, Figurine, Frog On Top Of Turtle, Signed	1400.00
Pate De Verre, Figurine, Mythological Nude, Flesh To Gold, 5 1/2 In.Long	1950.00
Pate De Verre, Figurine, Mythological Nude, Flesh Tone, Signed, 5 1/2 In.	1950.00
Pate De Verre, Figurine, Pan Blowing Pipes, Green Base, Signed, 3 1/2 In.	500.00
Pate De Verre, Figurine, Pan Blowing Pipes, Yellow Base, Signed, 3 1/2 In.	550.00
Pate De Verre, Plaque, Yellow, Raised Dancer, La Danse, Daum, 10 X 6 In.	550.00
Pate De Verre, Seal, Yellow, Walter, Nancy, H.Mercier, C.1910, 6 3/8 In., Pair	1100.00
Pate De Verre, Tray, Carved Out Flower, Signed	595.00
Pate De Verre, Vase, Lemon Tinged With Green, Signed, 6 1/2 In., Pair	2800.00
Pate De Verre, Vase, Lime, Green, Purple, G.Argy Rousseau, 6 1/2 In., Pair	3500.00
Pate De Verre, Vase, Ovoid Body, Orange, Greens, Rousseau, C.1920, 7 1/8 In.	1300.00

*Pate-sur-pate means paste on paste. The design was made by painting layers
of slip on the ceramic piece until a relief decoration was formed. The
method was developed at the Sevres factory in France about 1850. It
became even more famous at the English Minton factory about 1870.*

Pate-Sur-Pate, Atomizer, Nude On Cloudbank, Blue & White, 2 7/8 X 2 1/2 In.	70.00
Pate-Sur-Pate, Box, Circular, Cover, Signed, Limoges, 2 X 3 1/2 In.	145.00
Pate-Sur-Pate, Box, Covered, Warrior In Chariot, Limoges, 8 1/2 In.Diameter	275.00
Pate-Sur-Pate, Cup & Saucer, Cobalt, Gold-Lined Cup, Cherub, Blue Beehive	90.00
Pate-Sur-Pate, Milk & Mush Set, Aqua Luster, Raised Figures, Porcelain	250.00
Pate-Sur-Pate, Milk & Mush Set, Classical White Figures, Aqua Ground	250.00
Pate-Sur-Pate, Mirror, Hand, Maiden With Cupid, Silver Frame & Handle, 9 In.	180.00
Pate-Sur-Pate, Pitcher, Cupid Design, W.R. & Son Cobridge, 6 1/4 In.	65.00
Pate-Sur-Pate, Plate, Classical Figures, Gold, Blue, White, Marked, 9 In., Pair	40.00
Pate-Sur-Pate, Vase, Angel, Minton, Signed L.Solon, 8 3/4 In.	*Illus* 1200.00
Pate-Sur-Pate, Vase, Meissen, Sky Blue, Marked, 18 In.	*Illus* 1800.00

Patent Model, Can Filler, Funnel Tilt Top, Wood Frame, 12 In. ....*Illus*   80.00
Patent Model, Egg Box, Wood, 3 Drawer, A.Lucas, C.1976, 9 In.   ....*Illus*   80.00
Patent Model, Folding Chair, Wood, Metal Frame, 11 1/2 In. ....*Illus*   45.00
Patent Model, Washing Machine, Thomas Austin, C.1880, 8 1/2 In. ....*Illus*   50.00

Paul Revere pottery was made at several locations in and around Boston
between 1906 and 1942. The pottery was operated as a settlement-house type
of program for teen-aged girls. Many pieces were signed S.E.G. for
Saturday Evening Girls. The firm concentrated on children's dishes
and tiles. Decorations were outlined in black and filled in with color.

Paul Revere, Butter, Hen & Chick, S.E.G., C.1918, Signed E.P., 8 In. 225.00
Paul Revere, Creamer, Yellow Chick, Off White, Signed, 3 1/4 In. 68.00
Paul Revere, Plate, Mustard Color, Impressed Mark, 7 1/2 In. 25.00
Paul Revere, Vase, Blue Drip Over Dark Blue & Green, Marked, 9 In. 45.00

Peachblow glass originated about 1883 at Hobbs, Brockunier and Company
of Wheeling, West Virginia. It is a glass that shades from yellow to
peach. It was lined in white. New England peachblow is a one-layer
glass shading from red to white. Mt. Washington peachblow shades from pink
to blue. Reproductions of peachblow have been made, but they are of poor
quality and can be detected.

Peachblow, Webb, see Webb, Peachblow
Peachblow, Bottle, Perfume, Butterfly, Coin Gold, London, 4 3/4 In. 547.00
Peachblow, Bowl, Acid Finish, Gold Blossoms, Butterflies, Webb, 2 1/2 In. 275.00
Peachblow, Bowl, Finger, Matching Underplate, Pie Crust Edging 475.00
Peachblow, Bowl, Footed, Pink To White, Gunderson, 10 X 4 In. 185.00
Peachblow, Bowl, Tri-Cornered, Blue Inside, New England, 2 1/2 X 5 1/2 In. 325.00
Peachblow, Box, Powder, Covered, Cherry To Pink, 5 In.Diameter 100.00
Peachblow, Box, Powder, 14 Panel, Covered 100.00
Peachblow, Creamer, Applied Reeded Handle, Raspberry To White, Gunderson 165.00

Pate-Sur-Pate, Vase, Meissen,
Sky Blue, Marked, 18 In.

Peachblow, Cruet, Wheeling, Hobbs,
Brockunier & Co., C.1890

Peachblow, Creamer, Drape Pattern 1250.00
Peachblow, Cruet, Amber Handle & Stopper, Wheeling, West Virginia 950.00
Peachblow, Cruet, Wheeling, Hobbs, Brockunier & Co., C.1890 ....*Illus* 1050.00
Peachblow, Cruet, Wheeling, Teardrop 900.00
Peachblow, Cup, Punch, Wheeling 300.00
Peachblow, Darner, Ball Shape, Hollow Handle, 5 1/2 In. 135.00
Peachblow, Darner, New England, Pear Shape, Pink To White, 5 In. 225.00
Peachblow, Darner, New England, Round Bottom, Long Handle, 5 3/4 In. 145.00
Peachblow, Darning Egg, Bulbous, Salmon Pink, White At Handle, 5 In. 110.00
Peachblow, Dish, Butter, Cover, Metal Finial, Enamel Floral Design, 5 In. 195.00
Peachblow, Egg, Darning, Salmon Pink, White At Handle, , 4 1/4 X 5 1/2 In. 300.00
Peachblow, Ewer, Applied Amber Handle, 7 In., Pair 235.00
Peachblow, Figurine, Swimming Swan, Trumpet Shaped, Bryden, Pairpoint, 7 In. 60.00
Peachblow, Gunderson, see Gunderson, Peachblow
Peachblow, Lamp, Fairy, Silver Plated Stand, Base Marked Clarke, 8 1/4 In. 550.00
Peachblow, Lamp, Hanging, Diamond Pattern, Brass Frame, 9 1/2 X 19 In.Diam. 475.00
Peachblow, Lamp, Miniature, Overlay 385.00
Peachblow, Muffineer, Multi-Colored, 5 1/4 In. 450.00
Peachblow, Pear, Acid Cut, New England 395.00
Peachblow, Rose Bowl, Crimped Top, Homogenous Roses, New England, 3 3/8 In. 325.00
Peachblow, Rose Bowl, New England, 3 X 3 In. 285.00

Peachblow, Rose Bowl, Wheeling, Small Neck, 4 In.	450.00
Peachblow, Rose Bowl, 7 Crimp Top, Satin Finish, 2 1/2 X 2 7/8 In.	235.00
Peachblow, Sock Darner, New England, Pear Shape, Stem, Pink To White, 5 In.	225.00
Peachblow, Sugar, Mt.Washington, Wishbone Feet, Open, 4 1/4 In. .... Illus	1000.00
Peachblow, Syrup, Pink, Acorn Pattern, Original Lid	125.00
Peachblow, Syrup, Reverse Swirl, Clear Opalescent, Tin Lid	75.00
Peachblow, Toothpick, New England, Glossy, Square Top	375.00
Peachblow, Toothpick, Raspberry & White, Square Top, New England	325.00
Peachblow, Tumbler, Acid Finish, Raspberry Top, Pink Base, 3 1/2 In.	110.00
Peachblow, Tumbler, Gunderson, Raspberry & Pink, 3 1/2 In.	135.00
Peachblow, Tumbler, Raspberry To Yellow, Case Lined, Wheeling	395.00
Peachblow, Tumbler, Raspberry, Pink & White At Base, Acid Finish, 3 1/2 In.	135.00
Peachblow, Tumbler, Water, Wheeling	175.00
Peachblow, Tumbler, Wheeling, White Lining, Red Shading, 3 3/4 In.	365.00
Peachblow, Tumbler, White To Raspberry, New England, Glossy	395.00
Peachblow, Tumbler, Wild Rose Design	300.00
Peachblow, Vase, Bud, Red To White, 7 In.	125.00
Peachblow, Vase, Fluted Top, Raspberry Color, New England	550.00
Peachblow, Vase, Lily, New England, 6 1/2 In.	295.00
Peachblow, Vase, Lily, Shading From Raspberry To White, 10 1/4 In.	450.00
Peachblow, Vase, Matte Finish, Griffin Base	1250.00
Peachblow, Vase, Red To Fuchsia, White Lining, Wheeling, 6 1/8 In.	850.00
Peachblow, Vase, Stick, Mahogany Shading To Yellow, Wheeling, 8 1/2 In.	900.00
Peachblow, Vase, Swirl Pattern, Applied Frosted Binding, Acid Finish, 7 In.	325.00
Peachblow, Vase, Wheeling, Matte Finish, Griffin Base	1250.00
Peachblow, Vase, Wheeling, Morgan	1750.00
Peachblow, Vase, White Lining, Satin Finish, Dimpled, Slender Neck, 9 In.	225.00
Peachblow, Vase, Wild Rose, Tapered Cylinder, 13 1/2 In.	450.00
Peachblow, Vase, Yellow Shading To Rose, Wheeling	800.00
Pearl, Opera Glasses, see Opera Glasses	

Peking glass is a Chinese cameo glass of the eighteenth and nineteenth centuries.

Peking Glass, Bottle, Snuff, Overlay, Stopper, Pair	90.00
Peking Glass, Bottle, Snuff, Reverse Painting Around Bottle	65.00
Peking Glass, Bottle, Snuff, Reverse Painting, Scenic	85.00
Peking Glass, Bottle, Snuff, Ruby, Hermit & Deer In Woods, Ivory Spoon, 1700s	275.00
Peking Glass, Bowl, Cameo, Signed, 6 In., Pair	285.00
Peking Glass, Bowl, Imperial Yellow, Everted Rim, Wood Stand, 1800s, 9 In.	750.00
Peking Glass, Bowl, Red Veining On Base, Carved Stand, 7 3/8 In.	400.00
Peking Glass, Bowl, Topaz, Teakwood Base, 3 X 6 1/2 In.	395.00
Peking Glass, Bowl, 9 1/4 In., Pair Of Ribbed Finger Bowls, Undertray	50.00
Peking Glass, Box, Lid, Carved Lotus Blossoms, White, 2 X 3 5/8 In.	185.00
Peking Glass, Jar & Cover, Yellow, Ovoid Form, Phoenix, 1800s, 7 In., Pair	750.00
Peking Glass, Vase, Amethyst On White, 9 In., Pair	795.00
Peking Glass, Vase, Cameo Cut, Green To Chinese White, 9 In., Pair	250.00
Peking Glass, Vase, Cameo, Red Birds, White Clouds, 9 3/4 In., Pair	575.00
Peking Glass, Vase, Cameo, Red Flowers, Teakwood Base, 9 3/4 In. .... Illus	175.00
Peking Glass, Vase, Crimson & White, 3 In.	122.00
Peking Glass, Vase, Red Flowers & Bee, 6 In., Pair	395.00
Peking Glass, Vase, Red Swans, Foliage, Cameo Cutting, 10 In.	800.00

Peking Glass, Vase, Cameo, Red Flowers,
Teakwood Base, 9 3/4 In.

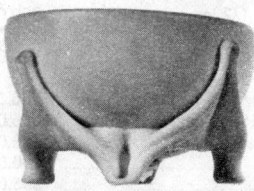

Peachblow, Sugar, Mt.Washington,
Wishbone Feet, Open, 4 1/4 In.

Peking Glass, Vase, 3 Reverse Painted Medallions, Red Cameo, 8 In. 550.00

Peloton glass is European glass with small threads of colored glass rolled onto the surface of clear or colored glass. It is sometimes called spaghetti, or shredded coconut glass

Peloton, Biscuit Jar, Blue Body, 5 3/4 X 7 In. 990.00
Peloton, Condiment Set, 2 Shakers, Mustard Pot & Tray 165.00
Peloton, Rose Bowl, Applied Feet, Ribbed Ground, Coconut Strings, 3 7/8 In. 295.00
Peloton, Tumbler, Blue Threads On White Satin, 3 1/2 In. 70.00
Peloton, Vase, Bulbous, Black, Red & White Coconut Threading, 8 In. 285.00
Peloton, Vase, Bulbous, Folded Over Tricorne Shaped Top, 4 X 4 3/4 In. 325.00
Peloton, Vase, Colored Threads Sealed In Clear, 4 1/2 In. 360.00
Peloton, Vase, Tricorne Top, Opaque, Ribbed Ground, 3 7/8 X 4 3/4 In., Diam. 325.00
Peloton, Vase, White On Clear, 1 In.Stem Opening, 5 In.Globe 25.00
Pen Sharpener, Quill, Bone Handled, Sheffield, 5 In. 12.50
Pen Sharpener, Quill, Ebony Handle, 6 1/4 In. 10.00
Pen, Drafting, Bone Handle 6.00
Pen, Esterbrook, Black Glass Pen Holder & Pen 6.50
Pen, Folding, Gold, Clasp Case, Looks Like Rolling Pin 25.00
Pen, Fountain, Miniature, Peter Pan 12.00
Pen, Fountain, Parker, Gold Bands & Tip, 1892 .... 12.50
Pen, Fountain, Silver Overlay 25.00
Pen, Fountain, Wearever 12.50
Pen, Lady's, Gold Band & Pen Point, Satin Lined Case, Clasps, 6 1/2 In. 35.00
Pen, Lady's, Pearl Handled, Gold Band 18.00
Pen, Moore's, 1898, Embossed, Gold Cap, Gold Tip & Nib, 1/2 X 4 3/4 In. 35.00
Pen, Mother-Of-Pearl, Gold Plate, Case 15.00
Pen, Mother-Of-Pearl, Gold Tip, Presentation Case 8.00
Pen, Parker, Duofold, Orange, Pencil 100.00
Pen, Parker, Duofold, Pen & Pencil Set, Coral 150.00
Pen, Parker, Duofold, Red, Split Rings On Cap 80.00
Pen, Parker, Duofold, Red, 1928 .... 50.00
Pen, Sheaffer, Cartridge 25.00
Pen, Sheaffer, Cartridge, 15K Gold 20.00
Pen, Sheaffer, Pencil, In Case 10.00
Pen, Vest, Gold Point, Loop For Chain, C.1920 .... 10.00
Pen, Waterman's Ideal, Dip Pen, Sterling Overlay 40.00
Pen, Waterman's Repousse, Gold 82.00
Pen, Wooden, Onyx Holder, Wahl, Trimmed In Gold 24.50
Pencil Box, Art Deco, Wooden, 10 In. 12.00
Pencil Box, Papier-Mache & Pewter Inlay 10.00
Pencil Holder, Brocade & Velvet Covered, Victorian 25.00
Pencil Holder, Dragon On Both Sides, Hanging Chain, Sterling, 3 1/4 In. 20.00
Pencil, Eversharp, Lady's, Gold Filled 5.00
Pencil, Head Of Girl, Pull Ring, Opens On Bottom, Metal, 1 1/2 In. 45.00
Pencil, Mechanical, Bat Shape, Souvenir 1939 World Series 28.00
Pencil, Mechanical, Eagle Co., Picture Of Popeye, 12 X 3/4 In.Diameter 18.00
Pencil, Mechanical, Missouri Pacific Lines, Picture Of Engine 4.00
Pencil, Mechanical, Mr.Peanut 3.75
Pencil, Mechanical, Mr.Peanut, Floats In Oil 12.00
Pencil, Mechanical, Nude, Everlast, Logansport, Indiana 27.50
Pencil, Mechanical, Souvenir, End Has Oil Can, Globe Oil Co. 12.50
Pencil, Mechanical, 18K Gold, Marked Tiffany & Co., 5 In. 125.00
Pencil, Parker, Duofold, Coral 65.00
Pencil, Parker, Duofold, Green Onyx 25.00
Pencil, Sterling, 1899 .... 15.00
Pennsbury, Sugar, Covered, Rooster 9.50

ZP
ZANE WARE
MADE IN U.S.A

Peters and Reed Pottery Company of Zanesville, Ohio, was founded by John D. Peters and Adam Reed in 1897. Chromal, Landsun, Montene, Pereco, and Persian are some of the art lines that were made until the company closed in 1920.

Peters & Reed, see also Zane
Peters & Reed, Jug, Brown Glazed, Sprig On Head 70.00
Peters & Reed, Jug, Higlaze, Gold Lion's Head & Grapevine, 4 X 4 1/2 In. 45.00
Peters & Reed, Pitcher, Snail Design, Cavalier Heads, 7 X 6 In. 75.00

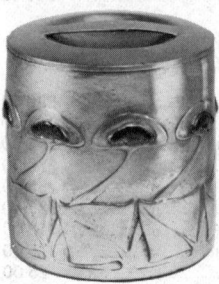

Pewter, Box, Biscuit, Enamel,
Tudric, Liberty & Co., 1900s

Pewter, Clock, Enamel, Tudric,
Liberty & Co., London, 1900s

Peters & Reed, Vase, 3 Legged, Floral Sprig Above Each Leg, 4 X 5 In.Diam.	55.00
Peters & Reed, Wall Pocket, Sign, Aztec, Ferrell	50.00
Petrous Regout, see Maastricht	
Pewabic, Ashtray, Art Deco, Green & Pink Luster, 4 In.	35.00
Pewabic, Vase, Iridescent, Turquoise & Silver Drip, Marked, 2 1/2 In.	48.50
Pewabic, Vase, Yellow Glaze, Bulbous Bottom, Marked, 12 X 7 1/2 In.	275.00

Pewter is a metal alloy of tin and lead. Some of the pewter made after about 1840 has a slightly different composition and is called Britannia metal.

Pewter, Ashtray, Sesquicentennial	10.00
Pewter, Basin, American, 5 1/2 In.Diameter X 2 In.Deep	50.00
Pewter, Basin, Eagle Mark Of Gershom Jones, 7 3/4 X 1 3/4 In.	380.00
Pewter, Beaker, Flared Sides, C.1820, 2 1/2 X 3 In.	58.00
Pewter, Beaker, Flaring Lip, Oliver Trask, Beverly, 1830s, 5 1/4 In., Set Of 6	3750.00
Pewter, Box, Biscuit, Enamel, Tudric, Liberty & Co., 1900s .... *Illus*	475.00
Pewter, Box, Tobacco, Molded Foot, 19th Century, 7 In.	800.00
Pewter, Can, Oil, Brass Threaded Screw, 3 1/2 In.	9.00
Pewter, Candleholder, Liberty Tudric, Hammered, Pair	40.00
Pewter, Candlestick, England, C.1830, 4 1/8 In.Pair	210.00
Pewter, Candlestick, 1 In Center, 2 Crossed Arms Hold 5 Candles	125.00
Pewter, Charger, English, 13 1/2 In.	195.00
Pewter, Clock, Enamel, Tudric, Liberty & Co., London, 1900s .... *Illus*	550.00
Pewter, Coffee Set, Kayserzinn, Art Nouveau, Signed	800.00
Pewter, Coffee Set, Miniature, Melon Ribbed, 4 Cups, Saucers, Spoon, 3 1/2 In.	95.00
Pewter, Coffeepot, Dunham, C.1830, 10 1/2 In.	395.00
Pewter, Coffeepot, Kayserzinn, Hugo Leven Design, 7 1/2 In.	350.00
Pewter, Coffeepot, Lighthouse Shape, H.B.Ward, 11 In.	425.00
Pewter, Coffeepot, Sheldon & Feltman, 12 1/2 In.	235.00
Pewter, Coffeepot, Sugar & Creamer, 16 In.Tray, Wallace	125.00
Pewter, Coffeepot, Wallingford, Connecticut, 1830, Charles Yale, 10 1/2 In.	470.00
Pewter, Communion Set, James Dixon & Sons, 3 Piece	325.00
Pewter, Compote, American, 6-Panel, Fluted Top, Flagg & Homan, 5 7/8 In.Diam.	60.00
Pewter, Cruet, Encased Orange, Pedestal Foot, French	100.00
Pewter, Cup, Loving, Kayserzinn, 4 3/4 In.	75.00
Pewter, Cup, Wedding, Kayserzinn, Peacocks & Moths, 3 Handled, 8 In., Pair	250.00
Pewter, Dish, Figural, Cupid Holding Up Bowl, 7 In.	30.00
Pewter, English, Salt, 3 Lion Head & Paw Feet, Glass Insert, 2 1/4 In.	22.50
Pewter, Ewer, Kayserzinn, No.4220, 8 In.	125.00
Pewter, Flagon, Ball Shape, Hebrew Inscription, Shaped Thumbrest, 10 1/2 In.	125.00
Pewter, Flagon, Bud Terminal, Domed Lid, Double S-Scroll Handle, 11 3/8 In.	1100.00
Pewter, Flagon, H.Sachs In Shield On Lid, 1709 Nuremburg Mark, 8 In.	1200.00
Pewter, Flagon, Roswell Gleason, C.1840, Marked, 10 In.	450.00
Pewter, Flagon, W.Calder, Providence, R.I., C.1835, 11 3/4 In. .... *Illus*	700.00
Pewter, Inkwell, Hinged Cover, Glass Insert, 2 3/4 X 2 In.	48.00
Pewter, Inkwell, Hinged Cover, 5 Holes, 4 3/4 In.	70.00
Pewter, Inkwell, Kayserzinn, Figural Pear Attached To Tray	175.00
Pewter, Inkwell, 18th Century, English, 8 1/4 X 5 1/2 In.	200.00
Pewter, Inkwell, 6 Quill Pen Holdes, American, 4 X 2 1/4 In.	75.00

Pewter, Flagon, W.Calder,
Providence, R.I., C.1835, 11 3/4 In.

Pewter, Teapot, C.1820, George Richardson,
Marked, 7 1/2 In.
(See Page 375)

Pewter, Lamp, Whale Oil,
Roswell Gleason, C.1830, 7 1/2 In.

Pewter, Shaving Mug, G.Richardson,
C.1820, Marked, 4 1/2 In.
(See Page 375)

Pewter, Pitcher, Rufus Dunham,
Westbrook, Maine, C.1840, Quart
(See Page 374)

Pewter, Jug, Water, C.1830, Porter, Westbrook, Maine, 6 1/2 In.	265.00
Pewter, Knife Rest, Kayserzinn, Figural Panther, 4 3/4 In.	45.00
Pewter, Knife Rest, Kayserzinn, Figural, Greyhound	45.00
Pewter, Knife Rest, Rabbit	18.00
Pewter, Ladle, Wooden Handle, 15 In.	35.00
Pewter, Lamp, Bell Shape, Applied Ring Handle, 3 1/2 In.	185.00
Pewter, Lamp, Camphene, Brass Spouts, Cap On Chain, C.1830-60, 9 1/2 In.	185.00
Pewter, Lamp, Kayserzinn, Aladdin, Art Nouveau, 10 In.	150.00
Pewter, Lamp, Whale Oil, Roswell Gleason, C.1830, 7 1/2 In. .... *Illus*	325.00
Pewter, Lavabo, Ogee Shape, Hallmarked, 24 In., 3 Piece	105.00
Pewter, Measure, Signed James Yates, 3 1/2 In.	85.00
Pewter, Measure, 6 Graduated Bulbous, 1 Quart Down To 1/4 Gill, Set	300.00
Pewter, Mold, Choclate, Easter Egg With Rabbits, 6 X 8 In.	65.00
Pewter, Mold, Chocolate, Rabbits	35.00
Pewter, Mold, Chocolate, Row Of Rabbits	22.50
Pewter, Mold, Horseshoe Design	45.00
Pewter, Mold, Ice Cream Oriental Man	65.00
Pewter, Mold, Ice Cream, Artichoke	19.00
Pewter, Mold, Ice Cream, Banana, Small	12.00
Pewter, Mold, Ice Cream, Beaver, E. & Co.	40.00
Pewter, Mold, Ice Cream, Bell, 3 1/2 X 3 3/4 In.	28.50
Pewter, Mold, Ice Cream, Bowl, 1 X 3 In.Diameter	5.00
Pewter, Mold, Ice Cream, Boy On Bicycle	60.00
Pewter, Mold, Ice Cream, Bunch Of Grapes	20.00
Pewter, Mold, Ice Cream, Chicken	25.00
Pewter, Mold, Ice Cream, Cradle	22.00
Pewter, Mold, Ice Cream, Ear Of Corn	12.00
Pewter, Mold, Ice Cream, Elephant	22.00

Pewter, Mold, Ice Cream, English Gentleman, 5 In.	58.00
Pewter, Mold, Ice Cream, Father Christmas, 4 1/2 In.	50.00
Pewter, Mold, Ice Cream, Flag	25.00
Pewter, Mold, Ice Cream, Flower	18.00
Pewter, Mold, Ice Cream, Four Cherries	20.00
Pewter, Mold, Ice Cream, Four Leaf Clover	18.00
Pewter, Mold, Ice Cream, George Washington	30.00
Pewter, Mold, Ice Cream, Grandfather Clock	16.00
Pewter, Mold, Ice Cream, Harp, 1800s	28.00
Pewter, Mold, Ice Cream, Indian	25.00
Pewter, Mold, Ice Cream, Kewpie, Marked, 6 1/2 In.	65.00
Pewter, Mold, Ice Cream, Lemon	12.00
Pewter, Mold, Ice Cream, Man On Bike	25.00
Pewter, Mold, Ice Cream, Masonic Emblem	18.00 To 20.00
Pewter, Mold, Ice Cream, Masonic Emblem, S.E. & Co.	21.50
Pewter, Mold, Ice Cream, Morning Glory	20.00
Pewter, Mold, Ice Cream, Pair Of Doves On Nest	48.00
Pewter, Mold, Ice Cream, Pear	12.00
Pewter, Mold, Ice Cream, Pumpkin	9.50
Pewter, Mold, Ice Cream, Road Roller	55.00
Pewter, Mold, Ice Cream, Rose	20.00
Pewter, Mold, Ice Cream, Santa	25.00
Pewter, Mold, Ice Cream, Tulip	20.00
Pewter, Mold, Ice Cream, Tulip Form	18.00
Pewter, Mold, Ice Cream, Turkey, 2 Hinged Sections, 3 X 5 In.	60.00
Pewter, Mold, Ice Cream, W.C.Fields	25.00
Pewter, Mug, American, Handled, Signed Manning Bowman, C.1830, 1 Pint	115.00
Pewter, Mug, Cylindrical Body, Bud Terminal, Early 17th Century, 5 7/8 In.	500.00
Pewter, Mug, Double C Handle, American, Hall & Cotton, 4 3/8 In.	500.00
Pewter, Mug, English, Baluster Shaped, C.1825, 1 Pint	150.00
Pewter, Mug, Glass Bottom, Engraved Dragons, Chinese	22.50
Pewter, Mug, Handled, American, Signed Morey & Ober, Boston, 1/2 Pint	350.00
Pewter, Napkin Ring, see Napkin Ring	
Pewter, Nappy, Kayserzinn, Dragon Fly Forms Handle, 9 3/4 X 6 1/2 In.	95.00
Pewter, Pitcher, C.1850, Flagg & Homan	150.00
Pewter, Pitcher, Insert Of Jewel, Tudric, Liberty & Co.	150.00
Pewter, Pitcher, Marked R.Dunham, 6 1/2 In.	600.00
Pewter, Pitcher, Rufus Dunham, Westbrook, Maine, C.1840, Quart ....*Illus*	375.00
Pewter, Pitcher, Water, Kayserzinn, Mephistopheles, 13 1/2 In.	175.00
Pewter, Planter, Kayserzinn, Footed, Art Nouveau Design, 17 X 9 X 5 1/4 In.	185.00
Pewter, Plate, Concave Rim, Molded Edge, Thomas Badger, Boston, 13 1/2 In.	375.00
Pewter, Plate, Edgar Curtis, London, C.1780	125.00
Pewter, Plate, Gershom Jones, 8 3/8 In.	325.00
Pewter, Plate, Hot Water, English	135.00
Pewter, Plate, Kayserzinn, Clover Leaf, No.4098, Raised Flowers & Insects	85.00
Pewter, Plate, Kayserzinn, Palette Shape, Thistle Flower Design, 9 1/2 In.	55.00
Pewter, Plate, Love, 7 3/4 In.	285.00
Pewter, Plate, Marked London, 8 1/2 In.	60.00
Pewter, Plate, Raised Thistle Pattern, German, 8 In.Diameter	55.00
Pewter, Plate, Service, C.1810, Set Of 6	575.00
Pewter, Plate, Solid Center, Filigree Rim, Mark New Amsterdam, 10 In.	28.00
Pewter, Platter, Kayserzinn, Floral Border, 20 1/2 In.	88.00
Pewter, Platter, Kayserzinn, Floral Design, 17 X 12 X 3 In.	175.00
Pewter, Platter, Kayserzinn, 21 1/2 X 10 1/2 In.	125.00
Pewter, Porringer, American, Pierced Handle, Pairpoint, 4 3/4 In.Diameter	60.00
Pewter, Porringer, Crown Handle, Marked, 1700s, 8 In. ....*Illus*	400.00
Pewter, Porringer, Flowered Handle, Out Flaring Lip, Rounded Sides, 5 1/4 In.	60.00
Pewter, Porringer, Geometric Handle, 18th Century, 7 1/4 In. ....*Illus*	400.00
Pewter, Porringer, Handle, 4 1/2 In.Diameter	95.00
Pewter, Porringer, L.B.Smith, Boston	16.00
Pewter, Porringer, Ornate Handle, 3 In.Diameter	40.00
Pewter, Porringer, Pierced & Scroll Handle, C.1790, 7 1/2 In. ....*Illus*	1500.00
Pewter, Porringer, Pierced & Scroll Handle, 1700s, 6 3/8 In. ....*Illus*	425.00
Pewter, Porringer, Pierced Heart Handle, Marked, 1700, 4 3/4 In. ....*Illus*	225.00
Pewter, Pot, Mustard, Cobalt Liner	55.00
Pewter, Server, Pancake, Kayserzinn, Fish & Seashell Design	195.00

Pewter, Shaving Mug, G.Richardson, C.1820, Marked, 4 1/2 In. .... *Illus*	500.00
Pewter, Spoon, Luther Boardman	18.00
Pewter, Spoon, Wedding, Dutch	18.00
Pewter, Spoon, Wreath & Fleur-De-Lis, Broyon Ernest	30.00
Pewter, Stein, Kayserzinn, Art Deco, Double Acorn Thumblift	95.00
Pewter, Stein, Kayserzinn, Art Nouveau, 3 Liter, Duck Billed Lid	325.00
Pewter, Strainer, Tea, Attached Drip Cup	10.00
Pewter, Sugar & Creamer, American, Domed Foot, Revere 498, 3 1/4 In.Diameter	32.50
Pewter, Sugar Shaker, American, Thomas Danforth III	295.00
Pewter, Syringe, Wooden Plunger, 12 3/4 In.	37.50
Pewter, Syrup, Continental, C.1840, 7 In.	37.50
Pewter, Tankard, Kayserzinn, Art Nouveau, Floral Relief, 15 In.	195.00
Pewter, Tea Set, Child's, Teapot.Sugar, Creamer, 4 Cups & Saucers, Tongs	135.00
Pewter, Tea Set, Teapot, Creamer, Sugar & Spooner, Flower Mark	195.00
Pewter, Tea Strainer, Germany	10.00
Pewter, Teapot, Acorn Final, 8 In.	120.00
Pewter, Teapot, A.Griswold, 1830, Meriden, Connecticut, 7 In.	325.00
Pewter, Teapot, Acorn Finial, Signed T.D. & S.Boardman, 9 In.	200.00
Pewter, Teapot, American, C.1840, Samuel Simpson, 8 1/2 In.	450.00
Pewter, Teapot, Boardman & Hart, N.Y., 8 In.	375.00
Pewter, Teapot, C.1820, George Richardson, Marked, 7 1/2 In. .... *Illus*	1500.00
Pewter, Teapot, Chinese, Cup Stand, Jade Handle, Carnelian Inlay	125.00
Pewter, Teapot, Dixon & Sons, 11 1/2 In.	125.00
Pewter, Teapot, G.Richardson, Sr., Boston, 9 In.	345.00
Pewter, Teapot, Hallmarked, C.1780, English	60.00
Pewter, Teapot, Middletown, 1825, Josiah Danforth, 6 1/2 In.	310.00
Pewter, Teapot, Pedestal, Fluted Sides, Wooden Handle, Dixon & Son, 10 In. ...	125.00
Pewter, Teapot, 17 In.Around Middle, Marked, T.D. & S.B., 9 3/4 In.	195.00
Pewter, Tray, Bread, American, Scalloped Panels, Revere 319, 12 7/8 X 7 In. ..	38.50
Pewter, Tray, Copper Wash, House & Trees, Oriental, 10 1/2 X 3 1/4 In.	22.50
Pewter, Tray, Crumb, Kayserzinn, Signed, 7 X 10 In.	65.00
Pewter, Tray, English, Lion & Crown On Lid, James Yates, 1800s, 22 In.	350.00
Pewter, Tray, Kayserzinn, Art Nouveau Design, 10 1/2 X 5 3/4 In.	65.00
Pewter, Tray, Kayserzinn, Oval, No.4624, Raised Design, 21 X 12 In.	95.00
Pewter, Tray, Kayserzinn, Oval, Signed, 21 1/2 X 10 1/2 In.	125.00
Pewter, Tray, Marked Federal Solid Pewter, 7 1/2 X 13 In.	24.50
Pewter, Tray, Oval, 8 3/4 In.	13.00
Pewter, Tray, Porcelain Inserts, Jade Handles, C.1815	650.00
Pewter, Tray, 4-Leaf Clover Shape, Garden Scene, 11 1/2 X 9 1/2 In.	115.00
Pewter, Tureen, Kunstzinn, Art Nouveau, Lobster Finial	95.00
Pewter, Urn, Coffee, American, Signed Manning, Bowman & Co., C.1869	550.00
Pewter, Vase, Art Nouveau, Liberty Tudric, Hand Hammered, 11 In.	95.00
Pewter, Vase, Brass Floral Overlay, Chinese, 18 X 7 In.Diameter	65.00
Pewter, Vase, Kayserzinn, Hammered, German Coin Trim, Trumpet Shape, 11 In. ..	95.00
Pewter, Vase, Morning Glory, Early American Co., 10 1/2 X 8 In.	35.00
Pewter, Vase, Purple Iridescent, Glass, Riceszinn, No.642, 7 1/4 In.	200.00
Pewter, Whistle, Dog's Head	75.00

*Phoenix Bird, or flying Phoenix, is the name given to a blue and
white chinaware made between 1900 and World War II. A variant
is known as the Flying Turkey.*

Phoenix Bird, Cup & Saucer	15.00
Phoenix Bird, Eggcup	5.00
Phoenix Bird, Plate	10.00

*Phoenix Glass Company was founded in 1880 in Pennsylvania. The firm
made commercial products such as lampshades, bottles, glassware. Collectors
today are interested in the sculptured glassware made by the company from the
1930s until the mid-1950s.*

Phoenix, Base, Lamp, Sculptured Cameo, Acidized Background, 14 In.	55.00
Phoenix, Bowl, Console, Diving Nude, Oval, Original Sticker	125.00
Phoenix, Bowl, Goldfish Outside, Waterlilies Inside, 16 1/4 In.	150.00
Phoenix, Box, Lid, Round, Hummingbirds & Roses, 6 3/4 X 3 1/2 In.	57.00
Phoenix, Bust Of Lady, Cream Color Iridescence, 10 In.	65.00
Phoenix, Candlestick, Green, 7 In., Pair	135.00
Phoenix, Dish, Covered, Cameo Decoration, 8 X 2 X 4 In.	75.00

Phoenix, Dish, Powder, Sculptured Birds & Roses, Purple	65.00
Phoenix, Lamp, Brass Base, White, Pink Berries, Green Leaves	265.00
Phoenix, Lamp, Raised Flowers, Brass Base & Mounts, 25 In.	95.00
Phoenix, Lamp, Table, Sculptured White, Brown Dogwood	185.00
Phoenix, Plate, Clear & Frosted, Frolicking Nudes	38.00
Phoenix, Plate, Dancing Nudes, Frosted Green, 18 In.	98.50
Phoenix, Plate, Dancing Nudes, Satin Frosted, 6 3/4 In.	38.00
Phoenix, Plate, Dancing Nudes, 8 1/2 In.	25.00
Phoenix, Rose Bowl, Open, Footed, 10 X 5 In.	52.00
Phoenix, Tumbler, Footed, Purple, 5 1/4 In.	9.00
Phoenix, Vase, Aqua Lovebirds On Tan, 10 In.	90.00
Phoenix, Vase, Art Deco, Pearly Cream Iridescence, Lady Covers All, 10 In.	65.00
Phoenix, Vase, Bell, White, Pink Flowers, Leaves, 7 X 8 1/2 In.	125.00
Phoenix, Vase, Birds & Cherries, Blue, Frosted, 7 In.	55.00
Phoenix, Vase, Branches & Berries In Cameo, Green, 9 1/2 In.	65.00
Phoenix, Vase, Camphor & White Sculptured Pinecone Pattern	30.00
Phoenix, Vase, Coral Blossoms, Beige Foliage, 10 1/2 In.	137.00
Phoenix, Vase, Cosmos, White On Gray, Oval Cross Section, 7 1/2 X 7 1/2 In.	50.00
Phoenix, Vase, Cream & White, Feather Leaves, 7 1/2 In.	27.50
Phoenix, Vase, Custard Ground, Bittersweet, 9 1/2 In.	60.00
Phoenix, Vase, Dahlia, Clear Frosted Flowers, Bulbous, 9 1/4 X 9 1/2 In.	120.00
Phoenix, Vase, Dancing Nudes, 12 In.	125.00
Phoenix, Vase, Dogwood Center, White Ground, 11 X 7 In.	90.00
Phoenix, Vase, Dogwood, Rose, Beige, Aqua On White Center, 10 In.	85.00
Phoenix, Vase, Dogwood, 12 In.	30.00
Phoenix, Vase, Dogwood, 17 In.Tall	90.00
Phoenix, Vase, Dragon Fly & Rushes On White, 6 In.	32.00
Phoenix, Vase, Ewer Shaped Handle, Natural Irridescent, 6 1/2 In.	240.00
Phoenix, Vase, Fairy, Arcs & Flowers, Pale Green, 7 1/2 In.	50.00

Pewter Porringer *(l. to r.):* Crown Handle; Geometric Handle; Pierced & Scroll Handle, 7 1/2 In.; Pierced & Scroll Handle, 6 3/8 In.; Pierced Heart Handle. *(See Page 374)*

Phoenix, Vase, Fan Shaped, Grasshopper, Green, 8 1/2 In.	35.00
Phoenix, Vase, Fern, Sculptured, 7 In.	47.50
Phoenix, Vase, Flowers On Pink Ground, 4 1/2 In.	37.50
Phoenix, Vase, Flying Geese, Beige & White, 9 1/2 X 11 1/2 In.	125.00
Phoenix, Vase, Flying Gulls, Aqua Birds, Custard Ground, 10 3/4 X 10 In.	110.00
Phoenix, Vase, Freesia, Frosted Clear On Blue, 8 1/4 In.	48.00
Phoenix, Vase, Frosted Birds & Flowers, 5 1/2 In.	18.00
Phoenix, Vase, Frosty White, Grasshoppers, 7 1/2 X 8 In.	60.00
Phoenix, Vase, Goldfish, White, Rectangular, 9 In.	72.00 To 75.00
Phoenix, Vase, Ivory Ground, Lavender Flowers, 7 In.	39.00
Phoenix, Vase, Little Owls, Sculptured, 6 In.	57.50
Phoenix, Vase, Lovebirds, Chartreuse, 6 3/8 X 5 1/2 X 3 1/2 In.	38.00
Phoenix, Vase, Lovebirds, Iridescent, 6 3/8 X 5 1/2 X 3 1/2 In.	35.00
Phoenix, Vase, Madonna, 10 In.	95.00
Phoenix, Vase, Nudes, Triangular, Sculptured, 8 1/2 In.	45.00
Phoenix, Vase, Pan & Dancing Nudes, 12 In.	225.00
Phoenix, Vase, Pan And Dancing Nudes, Raised Detail, 12 In.	225.00
Phoenix, Vase, Persimmon, White Geese, Flower Form, Oval, 12 X 10 In.	250.00
Phoenix, Vase, Pink & Green Fern, Phoenix Glass Label, 8 In.	75.00
Phoenix, Vase, Pink, White Flowers, Label, 7 3/4 In.	60.00
Phoenix, Vase, Praying Mantis, 7 1/4 X 8 In.	80.00
Phoenix, Vase, Purple & Clear Lovebirds On Branch, Rectangular, 6 1/4 In.	72.50

Phoenix, Vase, Purple Blackberries, 18 In.	250.00
Phoenix, Vase, Raised Figure Of God Pan, Nudes, Green Ground, 11 1/2 X 9 In.	150.00
Phoenix, Vase, Rectangular, Iridescent, Lovebirds, 6 3/8 X 5 1/2 In.	40.00
Phoenix, Vase, Salmon & White Carnations, 7 1/2 X 6 1/2 In.	65.00
Phoenix, Vase, Sculptured Fan Tailed Fish, Green, 9 In.	105.00
Phoenix, Vase, Sculptured Flowers, Pink Background	75.00
Phoenix, Vase, Sculptured Leaves, Persimmon Ground, Paper Label, 11 In., Pair	225.00
Phoenix, Vase, Smoke Colored Glass, Frosted Finish, Art Deco, 6 1/4 In.	40.00
Phoenix, Vase, White Ground, Yellow Birds, Pink Flowers, Pair	490.00
Phoenix, Vase, White Nude Dancers, Blue Ground, 11 X 9 In.	195.00
Phoenix, Vase, White, Blue Sculptured Flowers, 7 In.	55.00
Phoenix, Vase, White, Goldfish, 9 In.	75.00
Phoenix, Vase, White, Grasshoppers, 7 1/4 X 9 In.	55.00
Phoenix, Vase, White, Lovebirds, 6 1/4 X 5 1/2 X 3 1/2 In.	35.00
Phoenix, Vase, 12 White Seagulls, Blue & Aqua, 10 3/4 X 9 3/4 In.	490.00
Phonograph, see Music, Phonograph	
Photography, Album, Celluloid Roses & Leaves On Cover, Blue	22.00
Photography, Album, Celluloid, 11 X 8 1/2 In.	45.00
Photography, Album, Ivory Celluloid, Blue Velvet Spine, 7 X 16 In.	75.00
Photography, Album, Oval Tintypes, Brass Clasp, 3 1/2 In.	16.00
Photography, Ambrotype, Bilateral Cover, Embossed Lady, Leather Case	15.00
Photography, Ambrotype, Black Mammy Holding White Child In Lap	100.00
Photography, Ambrotype, Civil War Soldier, Tinted, Brass Clasp	85.00
Photography, Ambrotype, Corporal In Richmond Guard, Pre-Civil War	105.00
Photography, Ambrotype, Girl In Gingham, Rocking Chair, Gilt, 2 X 2 1/2 In.	7.50
Photography, Ambrotype, Lincoln	1100.00
Photography, Ambrotype, Resting Dog, One-Sixth	35.00
Photography, Ambrotype, Woman In Bloomers, Case	40.00
Photography, Ambrotype, Young Soldier, Gilt Frame, Cover, 2 X 2 1/2 In.	37.50
Photography, Brooch, Swiveling Case, Daguerreotype, 1 1/4 X 1 1/2 In.	75.00
Photography, Camera, Ansco, Folding, Case	12.00
Photography, Camera, Ansco, Folding, Wood, C.1915	75.00
Photography, Camera, Anthony & Scovill 1894, Ansco, No. 4	28.00
Photography, Camera, B. & J.Fexoette	10.00
Photography, Camera, Brownie Hawkeye Flash, Duaflex Flash	12.00
Photography, Camera, Brownie, Ball Bearing	85.00
Photography, Camera, Brownie, Box, No.2-A	18.00
Photography, Camera, Brownie, Hawkeye, Flash Model, Attachment, Leather Case	12.50
Photography, Camera, Brownie, No.3 Box	25.00
Photography, Camera, Cartridge Tremo, No.2	7.50
Photography, Camera, Conley Kewpie, No.3a	12.50
Photography, Camera, Coronet Midget, England, 1 X 2 1/2 In.	20.00
Photography, Camera, Eastman Kodak, Crown Tripod, 1903	35.00
Photography, Camera, Folding, Horizontal Format, 2A Pocket Brownie	20.00
Photography, Camera, Girl Scout	10.00
Photography, Camera, Jiffy Kodak 6-16	16.00
Photography, Camera, Keystone, Hand Crank, 35 Mm, 1927	80.00
Photography, Camera, Keystone, 8mm, Model K-8	25.00
Photography, Camera, Kodak Dedauist, 3 Lens Filter, Case	85.00
Photography, Camera, Kodak Special, Rangefinder 3a	38.00
Photography, Camera, Kodak 1a, Pocket	10.00
Photography, Camera, Kodak 35, Rapid F 3.5	30.00
Photography, Camera, Kodak, Folding, Autographic 4-A	22.00
Photography, Camera, Kodak, Folding, Vigilant Jr.	27.50
Photography, Camera, Kodak, Hawkeye, No. 2a Cartridge, Original Box	7.50
Photography, Camera, Kodak, Red Bellows	24.00
Photography, Camera, Kombi, Original Box	80.00
Photography, Camera, Leica, No.144849, Ernst Leitz, D.R.P.	225.00
Photography, Camera, Miniature, Univex	15.00
Photography, Camera, Pocket Kodak, No.I-A	10.00
Photography, Camera, Poco B Rochester	55.00
Photography, Camera, Portrait, Agfa-Ansco, Attachments, C.1900	450.00
Photography, Camera, Seneca Uno, Bubble Level, Postcard Size Photos	15.00
Photography, Camera, Seroco, Folding, Tripod Plate Holders	60.00
Photography, Camera, Tripod, Graflex Automatic, Folmer, Schwing	87.50
Photography, Camera, Universal Univex, Af2, Art Deco, Miniature	12.00

Photography, Camera, Univex, 1930s	7.50
Photography, Carte De Visite, Civil War Celebrities & Washington	15.00
Photography, Carte De Visite, Civil War Generals, Admirals	35.00
Photography, Carte De Visite, General Grant Center, Dry Goods Store, Boston	15.00
Photography, Case, Gutta-Percha, Girl With Basket, 6 1/4 X 3 3/4 In.	85.00
Photography, Daguerreotype Case, Embossed Hearts, Gilt Frame, 2 X 3 In.	17.50
Photography, Daguerreotype Case, Gutta-Percha, Civil War Soldier	42.50
Photography, Daguerreotype Case, Gutta-Percha, Cupid & Wounded Stag	85.00
Photography, Daguerreotype Case, Gutta-Percha, Faithful Hound, 6 X 4 In.	85.00
Photography, Daguerreotype Case, Gutta-Percha, Mother, Son, Signed, 3 3/4 In.	55.00
Photography, Daguerreotype Case, Gutta-Percha, Ornate Cross	48.00
Photography, Daguerreotype Case, Gutta-Percha, Sir Henry Havelock	125.00
Photography, Daguerreotype Case, Gutta-Percha, 3 Children Playing	55.00
Photography, Daguerreotype Case, Men, Women & Children, 3 1/2 X 3 In.	275.00
Photography, Daguerreotype Case, The Scroll, Constitution & The Laws, Man	48.00
Photography, Daguerreotype Case, Woman Dressed In Victorian Clothing	75.00
Photography, Daguerreotype Case, Woman Holding Girl & Cat, 3 X 4 3/4 In.	165.00
Photography, Daguerreotype, Bearded Man	35.00
Photography, Daguerreotype, Boy All Togged Out, 3 X 2 1/4 In.	24.50
Photography, Daguerreotype, Civil War Soldier, Case, 5 X 3 1/2 In.	44.00
Photography, Daguerreotype, Couple Holding Booksixth Plate	45.00
Photography, Daguerreotype, Couple, Leather Case, 2 1/4 X 3 1/4 In.	30.00
Photography, Daguerreotype, Couple, Oval Mat, Early Plastic Frame, 5 1/2 In.	85.00
Photography, Daguerreotype, Elderly Lady, Leather Case, 2 1/4 X 3 1/2 In.	45.00
Photography, Daguerreotype, French Navy Officer, Black Frame	250.00
Photography, Daguerreotype, Gentleman, Checkered Vest, 6th Plate, Anson	40.00
Photography, Daguerreotype, Gentleman, Half Plate, Cased	45.00
Photography, Daguerreotype, Girl In Chair Holding Doll, Dated 1853	450.00
Photography, Daguerreotype, Lady In White Hood, Hard Case, 3 1/2 X 3 In.	34.00
Photography, Daguerreotype, LaFayette, Greeted By Man & Ladies, 5 X 4 In.	63.00
Photography, Daguerreotype, Man With Beard, Hard Case	32.00
Photography, Daguerreotype, Musician Playing Accordion, 6th Plate	75.00
Photography, Daguerreotype, Naval Officer, Signed, 1/6 Plate	135.00
Photography, Daguerreotype, Naval Officer, 1/9 Plate	90.00
Photography, Daguerreotype, Naval Officer, 1840s, 1/6 Plate	125.00
Photography, Daguerreotype, Older Woman, Velvet Insert, Eagle, Evans, Phila.	22.00
Photography, Daguerreotype, Quaker Man & Lady, C.1850, 3 1/4 X 4 In., Pair	89.00
Photography, Daguerreotype, Seated Girl, Leather Case, 2 3/4 X 3 1/4 In.	25.00
Photography, Daguerreotype, Store, Men, Horses & Wagon, 1/4 Plate	335.00
Photography, Daguerreotype, Two Brothers, 3 X 3 1/4 In.	27.50
Photography, Daguerreotype, Union Soldier	125.00
Photography, Daguerreotype, Woman & Child	12.00
Photography, Daguerreotype, Woman In Victorian Dress, Papier-Mache Case	75.00
Photography, Magic Lantern, Brass Trim, Slides In Color, 9 X 9 1/2 In.	95.00
Photography, Magic Lantern, Children, Comic, Brass & Tin, 1893, German	150.00
Photography, Magic Lantern, Kerosene, Glass Slides	170.00
Photography, Magic Lantern, Oil Burner, 1890, Slides, 11 1/2 X 12 In.	85.00
Photography, Magic Lantern, Open Model, Brass Lamp, 20 Slides, 4 X 7 X 9 In.	65.00
Photography, Magic Lantern, Wood Cabinet, 30 Slides	69.00
Photography, Magnesium Views, Mammoth Cave, 7 Slides	60.00
Photography, Negative, Glass, Family With Children, Set Of 18	30.00
Photography, Photograph, Chief Black Thunder, Chief Tall Man Dan, Pair	6.00
Photography, Print, Abe Lincoln, Pine Frame & Glass, 19 X 13 1/2 In.	20.00
Photography, Projector, Magic Image, Bulbs	25.00
Photography, Projector, Mirroscope Postcard, Red & Gold, Electric	50.00
Photography, Projector, Movie, 16 M.J., Victor, Sound-On-Film Animatophone	75.00
Photography, Projector, Slide, Carbide	95.00
Photography, Stereo, see Stereo	
Photography, Tintype, Baby Boy In Woman's Lap, Gilt Foil, 2 X 2 1/2 In.	4.50
Photography, Tintype, Boy & Girl, Civil War Dress, 7 3/4 X 5 1/2 In.	15.00
Photography, Tintype, Boy On Submarine At Sea, Comic, 6th Plate	5.00
Photography, Tintype, Child Holding China Doll, 9th Plate	5.00
Photography, Tintype, Children Holding Sandpails & Shovels, 6th Plate	5.00
Photography, Tintype, Civil War Soldier Groups	65.00
Photography, Tintype, Civil War Soldier, Sergeant, Gold Frame	40.00
Photography, Tintype, Civil War, Soldier Holding Rifle, With Wife, Cased	38.00

Photography, Tintype, Clapboard House, Picket Fence, 2 3/4 X 3 1/2 In. 27.50
Photography, Tintype, Fireman With Hat 25.00
Photography, Tintype, Freak, 40 Pound Man, 3 1/4 X 4 1/4 In. 30.00
Photography, Tintype, Girl Holding Fruit Jar, 6th Plate 4.00
Photography, Tintype, Hound Dog With Master, 6th Plate 5.00
Photography, Tintype, Infantryman, Civil War, 2 3/4 X 3 1/2 In. 42.50
Photography, Tintype, Infantryman, Full Length, Holding Rifle, 2 X 3 1/4 In. 20.00
Photography, Tintype, Ladies At Tea, 6th Plate 6.00
Photography, Tintype, Man Reading Newspaper, Smoking Cigar, 6th Plate 6.00
Photography, Tintype, Soldier, Leather Case 32.50
Photography, Tintype, Spaniel, Caged Outdoors, 6th Plate 10.00
Photography, Tintype, Standing Union Officer, Gilt Frame, Box, 2 1/2 X 3 In. 64.50
Photography, Tintype, Two Men Drinking, Bottle To Lips, 6th Plate 6.00
Photography, Tintype, U.S. Infantryman, Upper Body, Hatless, 2 X 2 1/2 In. 29.50
Photography, Tintype, Waitresses, 1 Seated, 1 Pouring Tea 10.00
Photography, Tintype, Young Girl, 1840, 8 1/2 X 6 1/2 In. 15.00
Photography, Tintype, 2 Cavalrymen, Civil War, 2 X 3 3/4 In. 54.50
Photography, Tintype, 2 Men On Bicycles 12.00
Photography, Tintype, 3/4 View Infantryman, Tinted, 2 1/2 X 3 1/4 In. 34.50
Photography, Tintype, 8 Ladies Blowing Horns, Flags, 6th Plate 7.00
Photography, Viewer, Stereoscope 25.00
Photography, Viewer, Sterographoscope, Burled Walnut, Z-Fold, C.1865 .... 360.00
Photography, Viewer, True-Vue, Rock Island, Illinois, 1937, 7 Films 25.00
Piano, see Music, Piano

> About 1880 the well-decorated home had a shawl draped over the piano. The
> bisque piano baby was designed to help hold the shawl in place. They range
> in size from about 6 to 18 inches. Most of the figures were made in
> Germany.

Piano Baby, Bisque, 2 1/2 X 1 3/4 In. 25.00
Piano Baby, Blue Eyes & Ties, German, 5 3/4 In. 80.00
Piano Baby, Boy Holding Cat, Bisque, French 45.00
Piano Baby, Heubach, Reclining, 7 In. 100.00
Piano Baby, Holding Pocket Watch To Ear, Bisque, German, 6 1/2 In. 165.00
Piano Baby, Intaglio Eyes, Molded Brown Hair, Bulldog Under Arm, White Gown 70.00
Piano Baby, Seated Boy & Girl, Pink Bonnet, Yellow Hat, Marked, 12 In. 295.00
Piano Baby, Seated, G.Heubach Mark, 8 1/4 In. 190.00
Piano Baby, Sitting, Blue Dress, 7 1/2 X 8 In. 40.00
Piano Baby, Sitting, Hand-Painted, Girl, Head Cocked, Signed, 5 1/2 In. 75.00
Piano Baby, Sitting, Touching Toes, Signed, Heubach 145.00
Piano Baby, Stone Bisque, Kate Greenaway 35.00
Piano Baby, Twins On Basket, Bisque 175.00
Piano, Fischer Ampico, Story & Clark, Standard Grand 2500.00

> Pickard china was started in 1898 by Wilder Pickard. Hand-painted china
> was a featured product. The firm is still working in Antioch, Illinois.

Pickard, Berry Set, Fruit Border, Signed H.Tolley 195.00
Pickard, Bowl & Underplate, Fruit & Flowers, Signed, 5 In. 70.00
Pickard, Bowl, Baskets Of Pink Flowers, Gold Band, 4 1/2 X 8 1/2 In. 45.00
Pickard, Bowl, Blackberries, Flowers, 1898 Mark, Signed, 7 1/4 In. 72.00
Pickard, Bowl, Blue Band, Apricot, Gold Border, Pedestal Base, 9 1/2 In.Diam. 245.00
Pickard, Bowl, Florence James, Gold Trim & Handles, 1912, 9 1/2 In. 65.00
Pickard, Bowl, Footed, Hickory Nuts, Gold Leaf Mark, 8 In. 125.00
Pickard, Bowl, Fruit, Faces, Double Handle, Pedestaled, Signed C.Rosel, 13 In. 360.00
Pickard, Bowl, Gold Etched Inside, Plain Gold Outside, 6 X 13 1/2 In. 75.00
Pickard, Bowl, Gold Rim, Green Band, Easter Lilies, Signed, 10 In. 225.00
Pickard, Bowl, Hand-Painted Violets, Maple Leaf Mark, 7 3/4 In.Diameter 22.00
Pickard, Bowl, Handled, Oval, Overall Gold Flowers, 6 1/2 In. 10.00
Pickard, Bowl, Landscape Scene, Gold Sides To Rim, 1912, Signed, 9 In. 95.00
Pickard, Bowl, Octagonal, Gold Etched Inside & Out, 7 1/2 In. 135.00
Pickard, Bowl, Oval, Gold Trim, Gold & Ivory Bands, Signed, 3 1/2 In. 265.00
Pickard, Bowl, Pedestal Base, Strawberry Design, 1895 Mark, Signed, 7 1/2 In. 85.00
Pickard, Bowl, Poppies, Gold & Green On Ivory, Marked, 10 3/4 In.Diameter 195.00
Pickard, Bowl, Poppies, Handled, Deep, 5 3/4 In. 45.00
Pickard, Bowl, Poppies, Shallow, Signed, 6 1/2 In. 40.00
Pickard, Bowl, Punch, Figural Handles, Pedestal Base, Signed, 14 1/2 In.Diam. 335.00

Pickard, Bowl, Punch, Fruit Border, Signed, 6 1/2 X 14 1/2 In.Diameter	295.00
Pickard, Bowl, Red To Yellow, Scalloped, Rean, 1894-1904, 9 3/8 X 4 1/2 In.	265.00
Pickard, Bowl, Scalloped, Yellow Interior, Leroy, 1898-1904, 10 1/4 In.Diam.	165.00
Pickard, Bowl, Sugar, Dutch Girl, 1912, Signed	12.00
Pickard, Bowl, Underplate, Art Nouveau Shape, Flower Design	65.00
Pickard, Bowl, Water Lily Swirl Inside & Out, Artist Signed Blazek, 1895	265.00
Pickard, Bowl, 1895 Mark, Signed C.Hohn, 5 3/4 In.Diameter	35.00
Pickard, Bowl, 3 Silhouetted Nudes On Sides, Art Deco, Artist James, 9 In.	130.00
Pickard, Box, Trinket, Covered, 1905, Signed, 3 1/4 In.	90.00
Pickard, Butter Tub, Underplate, Signed	65.00
Pickard, Candlestick, Floral, On Gold, Blue, Green, 1905-1910	95.00
Pickard, Candlestick, Gold, Pink & Green Decoration On White, Mark, 1912, Pair	75.00
Pickard, Candlestick, Signed, 6 1/2 In., Pair	155.00
Pickard, Charger, Italian Garden, Marble Columns, 1912-19, Gasper, 12 1/4 In.	295.00
Pickard, Chocolate Pot, Gold Handle, Finial, 1895-98, Signed, 11 1/2 In.	195.00
Pickard, Coffee Pot, Rosenthal Blank, 1 Quart, 8 1/2 In.	85.00
Pickard, Coffee Set, Aura Argenta Linear, 1905-1910, Signed Vobor, 3 Piece	365.00
Pickard, Coffee Set, Venetian Renaissance, 1912, Cameos Each Side, Set	350.00
Pickard, Compote, Encrusted Linear, 1912, Signed, 8 1/2 In.Diameter	135.00
Pickard, Compote, Gold Trim Handles & Base, Vokray, 1912-11, 11 1/2 In.Diam.	185.00
Pickard, Compote, Violets, Gold Edge, Maple Leaf Mark, Signed Marker, 7 In.	40.00
Pickard, Creamer, Gold, Hand-Painted Acorns, Signed	18.00
Pickard, Creamer, Hand-Painted, Dutch Design, Signed	50.00
Pickard, Cup & Saucer, Enameled, Beading, Artist Signed	85.00
Pickard, Cup & Saucer, Flowers, Gold Border, 1910 Mark, Signed	55.00
Pickard, Cup & Saucer, Gold Grapes & Leaves, Circle Mark	20.00
Pickard, Cup & Saucer, Gold, Lilies, Pedestal, Artist Signed, 1910-12 Mark	45.00
Pickard, Cup, Punch, Antique Chinese Enamel, Signed, Maple Leaf Mark, 3 In.	50.00
Pickard, Decanter, Scotch Plaid, Lion Crest, Gold Stopper, Signed, 8 1/2 In.	165.00
Pickard, Dessert Set, Dutch Maiden, 11 In.Handled Plate, Six 8 In.Plates	195.00
Pickard, Dish, Candy, Blossom Shape, Gold Inside, 1930-38 Mark, 4 X 5 In.	35.00
Pickard, Dish, Grapevine Winds To Become Border, Marked, 4 X 7 In.	55.00
Pickard, Dish, Mayonnaise, Undertray, Gold Trim, 1898 Mark, Signed	75.00
Pickard, Dish, Oval, Pierced Handles, Gold Outside, 1922-25, 5 X 8 1/2 In.	35.00
Pickard, Dish, Pale Green, Roses, Leaves, Buds, Signed, 7 1/4 In.Diameter	65.00
Pickard, Dish, Relish, Easter Lily, 1910 Mark, Signed, Pierced Handles, 7 In.	48.00
Pickard, Dish, Relish, Handles, Oak Leaves, Gold Trim, 1905-10 Mark, 5 1/2 In.	30.00
Pickard, Dish, Relish, Open Handled, Gold Leaf Mark, 13 In.	60.00
Pickard, Dish, Relish, Pierced Handles, Maple Leaf Mark, 8 In.	22.00
Pickard, Dish, Scalloped Rim, 1905-10, Signed, 7 1/4 In.	65.00
Pickard, Hair Receiver, Stylized Lotus, 1912 Leaf Mark	28.00
Pickard, Hair Receiver, Sweet Peas, Gold Trim, Artist Signed	55.00
Pickard, Jar, Covered, Double Handles, Hand-Painted, Signed, 5 X 3 1/2 In.	110.00
Pickard, Jar, Covered, Forget-Me-Nots, Gold Trim, Signed	35.00
Pickard, Jar, Jam, Cherries On White, 3 Gold Feet, Artist Signed, Thomas	32.50
Pickard, Jug, Whiskey, Stalks Of Corn Decoration, Brown Mark, Signed	155.00
Pickard, Jug, Whiskey, Stopper, Decorated With Stalks Of Corn, Brown Mark	185.00
Pickard, Lamp, Black, Gold Encrusting, Hand-Painted Peacock, Signed, 14 In.	200.00
Pickard, Mug, Gold Trim, Painted, Marked & Artist Signed, 3 3/4 In.	65.00
Pickard, Nappy, Handled, Gold Trim, Fruit, Marked, 8 In.	65.00
Pickard, Nappy, 2 Handled, Floral Inside & Out, 6 1/2 In.	35.00
Pickard, Pitcher, Black, Gold & Purple, Signed Hess, 12 In.	185.00
Pickard, Pitcher, Cider, Etched Gold Flowers, 1930-38 Mark, 6 X 6 1/2 In.	85.00
Pickard, Pitcher, Cider, Impressionistic Forest, Signed Challinor, 6 1/4 In.	300.00
Pickard, Pitcher, Cider, Poppies, Signed, Fuchs	205.00
Pickard, Pitcher, Cider, 1905, Signed Aura	240.00
Pickard, Pitcher, Gold Tracing & Border, 5 In.	105.00
Pickard, Pitcher, Grape Bunches, Purple, Black, Gold, White, Signed Hess, 12 In.	300.00
Pickard, Pitcher, Irises On Gold, Blue Panels At Top, 1905-10, 3 1/4 In.	45.00
Pickard, Pitcher, Lemonade, Green Matte, Gold Top Band, 5 1/2 X 8 1/2 In.	150.00
Pickard, Pitcher, Lemonade, Octagon Shape, Signed	140.00
Pickard, Pitcher, Milk, Gold Trim, Artist Signed, Hand-Painted, 6 In.	65.00
Pickard, Pitcher, Nasturtiums, Dorique, June '84, Signed, 3 1/4 In.	85.00
Pickard, Pitcher, Puffed Panels, Gold Top & Handle, Blaha, 1898-1904, 10 In.	250.00
Pickard, Pitcher, Red Carnations, Cream & Gold Base, Signed, 9 In.	275.00
Pickard, Pitcher, 6 Sided, Artist Signed, Maple Leaf Mark, 8 1/2 X 8 1/2 In.	175.00

Pickard, Plate, Art Deco, Signed, 8 1/2 In.Diameter 35.00
Pickard, Plate, Bentlich, Berries & Foliage, Gold Band, 1905, 8 1/2 In.Diam. 75.00
Pickard, Plate, Cake, Double Open Handled, Signed, 11 In. 125.00
Pickard, Plate, Cake, Open Handle, Artist Signed, 13 1/2 In. 255.00
Pickard, Plate, Cake, Open Handled, Stylized Flowers, Signed, 1910-12, 11 In. 110.00
Pickard, Plate, Cake, Pink & Blue Florals , Gold Designs, C.1912, 10 1/2 In. 30.00
Pickard, Plate, Cake, Pink & Blue Flowers, Gold Design, 1902, 10 1/2 In. 30.00
Pickard, Plate, Cake, Violets, Gold Trim, Signed, 1905-10 Mark, 8 5/8 In. 60.00
Pickard, Plate, Chop, Gold Border On White, 12 In.Diameter 36.00
Pickard, Plate, Chop, Pin & Green, Gold Designs, 1912, 12 1/4 In. 50.00
Pickard, Plate, Clover Design With Bee, Gold Edge, Signed, 9 In. 75.00
Pickard, Plate, Cornyn, Hand-Painted Flowers, 1910, 9 In. 75.00
Pickard, Plate, Easter Lilies, 1 1/2 In.Gold Border, Circle Mark, 8 3/4 In. 70.00
Pickard, Plate, Flower, Pansy, Lilac, Haviland, Signed, 8 5/8 In. 40.00
Pickard, Plate, Flowers, Gold Border, 1910 Mark, Signed, 8 1/2 In. 55.00
Pickard, Plate, Forest & Lake, Signed, 8 1/2 In. 175.00
Pickard, Plate, Fruit, Marked & Artist Signed, 8 1/2 In. 45.00
Pickard, Plate, Garden Scene, Vellum, Signed, 7 In. 110.00
Pickard, Plate, Gold & Black Tracery, Pastel Ground, 8 3/4 In. 75.00
Pickard, Plate, Gold Encrusted Flowers, Luster Design, Marked, 9 In. 45.00
Pickard, Plate, Gold Scalloped Rim, 1905, Hand-Painted, 8 5/8 In. 50.00
Pickard, Plate, Gold Trim, Pink Flowers, Bladed Propeller Design, 9 In. 75.00
Pickard, Plate, Gold Wheat & Florals, Artist Signed, C.1905, 8 1/2 In. 50.00
Pickard, Plate, Green & White Flowers, Gold Rim, 6 1/4 In. 35.00
Pickard, Plate, Green, Pink & Wheat Leaves, 8 In. 45.00
Pickard, Plate, Hand-Painted Columbine, Gold Rim, 1898, Signed, 8 1/4 In. 65.00
Pickard, Plate, Hand-Painted, Violets, Signed, 9 In. 98.00
Pickard, Plate, Iridescent Red Flowers, 7 3/4 In. 70.00
Pickard, Plate, Irregular Border Of Gold, Circle Mark, 8 1/2 In. 60.00
Pickard, Plate, Italian Garden Scene, Handled, Artist Signed, 11 In. 225.00
Pickard, Plate, Lilies, Iridescent Leaves, Beaded Rim, Marked, 7 1/2 In. 45.00
Pickard, Plate, Lind, Cherries, Flowers, Enamel, 1905, 8 3/4 In. 75.00
Pickard, Plate, Mountain & Lake, Signed, 8 1/2 In. 175.00
Pickard, Plate, Nut Design, 1905, Artist Signed, 8 3/4 In. 85.00
Pickard, Plate, Open Handle, Gold Border, Easter Lilies, Signed, 10 1/2 In. 125.00
Pickard, Plate, Open Handles, Gold Rimmed, Scenic, Signed, 10 1/2 In. 65.00
Pickard, Plate, Opened Handle, Scenic, Marked, Signed, 13 1/2 In. 245.00
Pickard, Plate, Orange Flowers, Gold Trim, Signed E.Chalinor, 8 In. 40.00
Pickard, Plate, Pink Dogwood, Gold Scalloped Border, 1898 Mark, 8 In. 60.00
Pickard, Plate, Scenic Path Of Palm Trees, Signed, 8 1/2 In. 165.00
Pickard, Plate, Scenic, Bisque Finish, 1912-19, Signed Challinor, 8 1/2 In. 150.00
Pickard, Plate, Scenic, Gold Band, Satin Finish, 9 In. 150.00
Pickard, Plate, Stylized Blue Flowers, Gold Band, 8 1/2 In. 50.00
Pickard, Plate, Vokral, Different Nuts, Gold Rim, 1905, 8 3/4 In.Diameter 85.00
Pickard, Plate, Wisteria Decoration, Shaded, James, C.1905, 8 1/2 In. 55.00
Pickard, Platter, 2 Handles, Forest Scene, Vellum, Signed, 12 In. 250.00
Pickard, Platter, 2 Handles, Scenic, Vellum, Signed, 12 In. 215.00
Pickard, Punchbowl, 10 Pedestal Cups, Vintage Grape, Signed 695.00
Pickard, Salt & Pepper, Flowers, White Ground, Gold Band At Top 22.50
Pickard, Salt & Pepper, Gold Etched, 3 1/2 In. 50.00
Pickard, Salt & Pepper, Monochromatic Green Leaf, Gold Tops, 4 1/2 In. 45.00
Pickard, Salt & Pepper, Multi-Floral, 2 1/8 In. 75.00
Pickard, Salt & Pepper, Pedestal Feet, Engraved Gold On Body, Signed 20.00
Pickard, Salt & Pepper, Stylized Flowers, Circle In Leaf Mark 24.00
Pickard, Stein, Gold & Green, Gold Border & Handle, Lind, 7 In. 175.00
Pickard, Stein, Gold Trim, Red Poinsettias, 1898-1904, Signed, 7 In. 195.00
Pickard, Sugar & Creamer 75.00
Pickard, Sugar & Creamer, Beading On Top In Gold, Signed 50.00
Pickard, Sugar & Creamer, Covered, Flowers & Gold Design 29.95
Pickard, Sugar & Creamer, Floral Decoration, C.1910 .... 75.00
Pickard, Sugar & Creamer, Gold & Green 75.00
Pickard, Sugar & Creamer, Lind, Foliage Outlined In Gold, 1905 .... 85.00
Pickard, Sugar & Creamer, Metallic Grape, 1905-1910, Signed F.H. 130.00
Pickard, Sugar & Creamer, Poppies, Green Leaves, Gold, Pedestaled, Signed 165.00
Pickard, Sugar & Creamer, Rose Tones Of Calla Lilies, Circle Mark, 3 In. 110.00
Pickard, Sugar & Creamer, Stylized Cornflowers, Gold Handles 75.00

Pickard, Sugar & Creamer, Violets, Gold, 2nd Mark, Signed	68.00
Pickard, Tankard, Boughs Of Apples, Signed, 12 In.	245.00
Pickard, Tankard, Green Matte, Gold Overlay, 1905, Signed, 10 In.	250.00
Pickard, Tea Set, Pot, Sugar & Creamer, Dutch Girl, Signed	170.00
Pickard, Tea Set, Solid Gold Raised Flowers All Over, Signed	55.00
Pickard, Tea Set, Stylized Corn & Flowers, Dragon Head Spout, 1898, Signed	285.00
Pickard, Tea Set, Teapot, 4 Cups & Saucers, Playing Cards Design	22.50
Pickard, Tray, Gold, 2 Pierced Handles, 1922-25 Mark, 5 X 8 1/2 In.	35.00
Pickard, Vase, Allover Gold, Square, Mark, 5 3/4 In.	10.00
Pickard, Vase, Aura Argenta Linear Pattern, Artist Signed Hess, 1905-1910	190.00
Pickard, Vase, Bulbous, Forest Scene, Handles & Rim In Gold, 8 In.	340.00
Pickard, Vase, Bulbous, 1898-1904, Water Scene, Signed, 6 In.	190.00
Pickard, Vase, Corset Shape, Lilies In Art Nouveau Style, Signed, 9 1/2 In.	135.00
Pickard, Vase, Deserted Garden Scene, Signed, 1912-19, 8 1/4 In.	235.00
Pickard, Vase, Deserted Garden, Scenic, Hand-Painted, 1912, 8 In.	125.00
Pickard, Vase, Etched Gold Flowers, Gold Handles, Marked, 10 1/2 In.	75.00
Pickard, Vase, Flower Medallion, Gold Etched Body, Gold Leaf Mark, 8 In.	125.00
Pickard, Vase, Footed, Bisque, Tropical Scene, Artist Marker, 5 1/2 In.	195.00
Pickard, Vase, Forest, Lake & Mountains, Signed, 8 In.	175.00
Pickard, Vase, Garden Wall, Pink Flowers, 1912 Mark, E.Challinor, 7 In.	125.00
Pickard, Vase, Gold Flowers, Black Outline, Signed, 7 In.	65.00
Pickard, Vase, Gold Rimmed, Autumn Scene, Signed, 7 In.	175.00
Pickard, Vase, Green & Gold Tulips, Scalloped, Artist Signed O.Goess, 7 In.	110.00
Pickard, Vase, Hand-Painted, Striping, Circle Mark, Signed, 5 1/2 In.	65.00
Pickard, Vase, Lind, Green, Hand-Painted, C.1905, 6 X 13 In.Diameter	100.00
Pickard, Vase, Moonlit Impressionist, 2 Handled, Signed Challinor, 9 In.	300.00
Pickard, Vase, Purple & Gold Grape Clusters, Black Satin, 9 In.	160.00
Pickard, Vase, Purple Iris, Gold Swirls, Cream Ground, 1898-1904, 7 In.	145.00
Pickard, Vase, Roses, Gold Trim, 1898-1904, Signed A.Burton, 11 1/2 In.	465.00
Pickard, Vase, Scenic, Scene Of Trees & Vines, Signed, 1912, 9 1/2 In.	195.00
Pickard, Vase, Seagulls, Red, Green, Artist Signed, 6 In.	310.00
Pickard, Vase, Trees, Mountains, R.S.Tillowitz Mark, Signed Marker, 7 3/4 In.	145.00
Picture, see also Painting, Print	
Picture Frame, see Furniture, Frame	
Picture, Calligraphy, W.S.Fabens, May Morning Poem, Salem, Mass., 1835	65.00
Picture, Woven Hair, Flowers, Shadow Box Frame, 1860s, 22 1/2 X 23 In.	85.00
Pigeon Blood, see Cranberry Glass, Ruby Glass	
Pilkington, Console Set, Candleholders, Dish, Covered, 5 1/2 In.Diameter	45.00
Pilkington, Dish, Geometric Design, Signed, Dated 1923, 11 In.Diameter	250.00
Pilkington, Vase, Royal Lancastrian, Crystaline Glaze, 5 3/4 In.	175.00
Pincushion Dall, Arms Away From Body, Legs, German	55.00
Pincushion Doll, Arms & Hands Away From Body, Germany, 2 3/4 In.	35.00
Pincushion Doll, Arms Away From Body, German	65.00
Pincushion Doll, Arms On Hips.Porcelain, 5 In.	25.00
Pincushion Doll, Art Deco, Needle Holder Attached	60.00
Pincushion Doll, Bathing Beauty, Pink Bisque Bathing Sue, Cap, Germany	25.00
Pincushion Doll, Bisque Head, Brown Sleep Eyes, Open Mouth, 4 Teeth	75.00
Pincushion Doll, Black Hair, Orange Hat, Fan In Hand, Germany, 4 In.	18.50
Pincushion Doll, Blonde Hair, Blue Ribbon, Germany, 3 In.	20.00
Pincushion Doll, Blonde Hair, Green Sash, China	16.00
Pincushion Doll, Blonde Hair, Lace & Satin Ribbon Skirt, Germany	23.00
Pincushion Doll, Blonde Hair, 1 Arm On Waist, Germany, 1 3/8 In.	30.00
Pincushion Doll, Blonde, White Bonnet, Flowers In Hand, Germany, 2 1/2 In.	22.00
Pincushion Doll, Blue Comb In Black Hair, Germany, 3 In.	20.00
Pincushion Doll, Blue Ribbon Around Hair, Yellow Bows, Germany, 4 In.	27.50
Pincushion Doll, Bonnet Girl, Both Hands On Collar	25.00
Pincushion Doll, Child, Wearing Dutch Cap, German	28.00
Pincushion Doll, China, German, 4 In.	75.00
Pincushion Doll, China, Germany, 3 In.	38.00
Pincushion Doll, China, 4 1/2 In., Pair	15.00
Pincushion Doll, Clown Head, 1 1/2 In.	35.00
Pincushion Doll, Dancer, Germany, 3 In.	25.00
Pincushion Doll, Dressed, Holds Fan	35.00
Pincushion Doll, Dutch Dress, Holding Ball Of Yarn, Signed, 3 In.	95.00
Pincushion Doll, Dutch Girl, Bisque, Jointed Arms, 2 1/2 In.	85.00
Pincushion Doll, Fan Against Shoulder, Germany, 2 1/2 In.	20.00

Pincushion Doll, Flapper Girl With Fan, Germany, 3 1/2 In.	25.00
Pincushion Doll, Flapper Girl With Hat & Fan	35.00
Pincushion Doll, Flapper Girl, Black Hair, Bow	25.00
Pincushion Doll, Flapper Girl, Blonde Hair	20.00
Pincushion Doll, Flapper, Extended Hand Holds Fan, Germany, 5 1/2 In.	125.00
Pincushion Doll, Flapper, Nude, Germany, 4 1/4 In.	115.00
Pincushion Doll, Flowers In Hair, Satin Dress, Germany, 3 1/2 In.	27.50
Pincushion Doll, German, One Arm Raised Behind Head, 3 1/2 In.	20.00
Pincushion Doll, Girl Holding A Dog, Marked, Germany	18.00
Pincushion Doll, Girl With Flowers In Hair, Germany, 3 1/2 In.	25.00
Pincushion Doll, Girl With Roses, Germany, 3 In.	30.00
Pincushion Doll, Gray Hair, Blue Ribbon Band, Yellow Bows, Germany, 4 In.	16.50
Pincushion Doll, Gray Hair, Blue Ribbon, Dress, Germany, 3 1/2 In.	17.50
Pincushion Doll, Gray Hair, Tricorn Hat, Flowers In Hand, Cushion Attached	25.00
Pincushion Doll, Half, Crocheted Base Cover, Matching Bonnet, Bisque	14.00
Pincushion Doll, Hands On Waist, Large, Germany	45.00
Pincushion Doll, Heubach, Large	165.00
Pincushion Doll, Lady, Arms Out Holding Book, Victorian, 8 1/2 In.	225.00
Pincushion Doll, Lady, Blonde With Blue Ribbon, German, 3 In.	22.50
Pincushion Doll, Lady, Victorian, Bisque, Arms Out, 5 1/2 In.	225.00
Pincushion Doll, Lamp, Wire Hoop Skirt	27.50 To 30.00
Pincushion Doll, Legs, Pink Satin Skirt, 7 In.	57.50
Pincushion Doll, Marie Antoinette, Yellow Bonnet, Germany	27.50
Pincushion Doll, Miniature, Girl With Sunflower For Hat, German, 2 3/4 In.	20.00
Pincushion Doll, Molded Hair, Legs Peep From Skirt, 8 In.	65.00
Pincushion Doll, Molded Painted Hair, Germany, 2 1/2 In.	30.00
Pincushion Doll, Moveable Arms, Open Mouth, Bisque, 1 3/4 In.	95.00
Pincushion Doll, Moveable Arms, Original Romper & Bonnet, Japan, 3 5/8 In.	24.00
Pincushion Doll, Oriental Girl, Arms Open, Holding Fan, Japan, 3 1/2 In.	12.00
Pincushion Doll, Pierrette, Arms Away, Hands Pressed Together	40.00
Pincushion Doll, Pink Dress, Blue Ribbon, German	42.50
Pincushion Doll, Pink Skirt, Composition, 4 In.	8.00
Pincushion Doll, Porcelain, Both Hands Out, 3 1/4 In.	55.00
Pincushion Doll, Porcelain, Both Hands To Chest, 2 3/8 In.	28.00
Pincushion Doll, Rose Velvet & Lace, Marked, Alice, 8 In.	50.00
Pincushion Doll, Silk Wig, No.5694, Bisque, German, 2 3/4 In.	125.00
Pincushion Doll, Spanish Dancer, German	12.00
Pincushion Doll, Spanish Lady Holding Pink Hat, Pink Shawl, China	19.00
Pincushion Doll, Spanish Lady, Arms Open, German, 2 1/2 In.	26.00
Pink Slag, see Slag, Pink	
Pinocchio, see Disneyana	
Pipe, Bird, Effigy, Stone	350.00
Pipe, Box, Dovetailed Drawer, Wooden	65.00
Pipe, Briar & Ivory, Curved, Bowl Cover, Deer On Bowl	50.00
Pipe, Calabash, Meerschaum Bowl, Sherlock Holmes Type	34.00
Pipe, Carved Burl, Battle Names, Civil War	200.00
Pipe, Carved Head Of Dog, Glass Eyes, Leather Case	58.00
Pipe, Clay Bowl, Happy Hooligan	9.00
Pipe, Clay Ram's Head Bowl, Cherry Wood Stem, 11 In.	35.00
Pipe, Clay, Jacob, Paris	50.00
Pipe, Clay, Short Stem, Footed, 5 In.	9.00
Pipe, Enamel On Copper, Oriental	40.00
Pipe, German, Porcelain, Long Stem	40.00
Pipe, Hand-Carved, Curved Handled, Head Of Man With Beard As Bowl	40.00
Pipe, Holder, English Bulldog Reclining, Brass, 5 X 1 5/8 In.	25.00
Pipe, Holder, Figural, Lady	9.50
Pipe, Holder, Footed, Spoon Shape, Advertising, 4 In.	22.00
Pipe, Hooka, Waterpipe, Brass Trim, India	14.00
Pipe, King George V, English	45.00
Pipe, Lady's, Art Deco, Red Bowl, Black Stem, Rhinestones, 5 In.	13.00
Pipe, Meerschaum, see Meerschaum, Pipe	
Pipe, Meerschaum, Bird On Nest On Bowl, Amber Stem, Velvet Box, 5 In.	58.00
Pipe, Meerschaum, Bushy Tailed Fox Near Tree Trunk, Original Case	75.00
Pipe, Meerschaum, Hand Carved, Animal Design, Original Felt Lined Case	35.00
Pipe, Opium, Ivory & Cloisonne Table Pipe, 2 Traveling Pipes	80.00
Pipe, Opium, Teak & Ivory	135.00

Pipe, Paktong, Gold Inlay, 17th Century, Bowl 3/8 In.Diam.6 In.Long 150.00
Pipe, Rest, Japanese, Kiriwood, Nut Ojimi 200.00
Pipe, Rest, Will Rogers On Rearing Horse, Metal 12.00
Pipe, Stuffer, Indian Head, Brass 1.75
Pipe, Tamper, Mr.Pickwick, Brass 15.00

Pirkenhammer is a porcelain manufactory started in 1802 by Friedrich Holke and J. G. List.

Pirkenhammer, Plaque, Young Girl, Odaliske Nach J.Richter, 15 In. 800.00
Pirkenhammer, Plate, 6 Rose Center, 6 Iris Center, 9 In., Set Of 12 .... 150.00

Pisgah pottery pieces that are marked Pisgah Forest Pottery were made in North Carolina from 1926 until the present. Vases, teapots, jugs, candlesticks, and many other items were made.

Pisgah Forest, Bowl, Glazed, Wine Color, 5 In. 25.00
Pisgah Forest, Bowl, Purple, 4 In. 10.00
Pisgah Forest, Jardiniere, 3 X 4 In. 10.00
Pisgah Forest, Jug, 1946, Signed Stephan 80.00
Pisgah Forest, Pitcher, Turquoise & Pink, Signed Stephan 30.00
Pisgah Forest, Sugar & Creamer 25.00
Pisgah Forest, Sugar & Creamer, Blue, Pink Interior, 2 1/2 In., Pair 20.00
Pisgah Forest, Sugar & Creamer, Covered, Pink Interior, Signed 50.00
Pisgah Forest, Sugar, Crystalline, Covered 65.00
Pisgah Forest, Teapot, Lid, Green Outside, Pink Inside, Dated 1935 .... 47.00
Pisgah Forest, Vase, Turquoise Transparent Glaze, 1940, 5 In. 45.00
Pisgah Forest, Vase, Turquoise, 1937, 4 1/2 In. 65.00
Pisgah Forest, Vase, Turquoise, 8 In. 40.00
Pistol, See Weapon, Pistol ....
Plate, see under special types such as ABC, Calendar, Christmas

Plated amberina was patented June 15, 1886 by Edward D. Libbey and made by the New England Glass Works. It is similar to amberina, but is characterized by a cream-colored or chartreuse lining (never white) and small ridges or ribs on the outside.

Plated Amberina, Pitcher, Syrup 4800.00
Plated Silver, see Silver Plate

Plique a jour is an enameling process. The enamel was laid between thin raised metal lines and heated. The finished piece has transparent enamel held between the thin metal wires.

Plique A Jour, Spoon, Flowers, Gold Gilt, 2 In.Bowl, 6 In. 350.00
Plumbing, Bath Tub, White Enamel, Ball & Claw Feet 100.00
Plumbing, Water Heater, Ruud, C.1890 .... 400.00
Political Campaign, Book Matches, Inauguration, Eisenhower & Nixon, 1953 ...... 3.50
Political Campaign, Book, Facts About The Candidate, 1904, T.Roosevelt 25.00
Political Campaign, Book, President William McKinley, Hardbound 7.00
Political Campaign, Book, Republican Song Book, Abe Lincoln, C.1860 .... 45.00
Political Campaign, Bottle, Perfume, Goldwater 5.00
Political Campaign, Box, Ballot, Non-Tamper Slot, 11 X 16 X 8 1/2 In. 65.00
Political Campaign, Box, Cigar, Cleveland, Thurman 100.00
Political Campaign, Box, Cigar, James Blaine 35.00
Political Campaign, Brochure, Republican, 28 Page, 1891, 4 X 8 In. 6.00
Political Campaign, Bust, Lyndon Johnson, Composition, 5 In. 7.50
Political Campaign, Button, Al Smith, Corning, 7/8 In. 29.50
Political Campaign, Button, Al Smith, Picture 8.00
Political Campaign, Button, Americanism Roosevelt, Flag In Center, 7/8 In. 10.00
Political Campaign, Button, Boat Shaped, Kennedy 60, Brass, 1 3/4 In. 30.00
Political Campaign, Button, Brass, Profile Roosevelt & Garner 15.00
Political Campaign, Button, Bryan, Portrait 45.00
Political Campaign, Button, Bull Moose, Embossed P.T.A.P. 15.00
Political Campaign, Button, Collar, McKinley 23.00
Political Campaign, Button, Coolidge, Dawes 10.00
Political Campaign, Button, Dewey & Warren, 1948, 7/8 In. 2.50
Political Campaign, Button, Elephant, Embossed G.O.P. 15.00
Political Campaign, Button, Elephant, Embossed Hoover 15.00
Political Campaign, Button, F.D.R., A Gallant Leader 10.00

Political Campaign, Button, F.D.Roosevelt, Picture, New Deal In Penna.	8.00
Political Campaign, Button, F.D.Roosevelt, Picture, 3 1/2 In.	18.50
Political Campaign, Button, Flasher Picture, Ike, 1953, With Ribbon	8.50
Political Campaign, Button, For Governor Charles Hughes, Picture, 7/8 In.	6.50
Political Campaign, Button, For President, Warren G.Harding, 5/8 In.	6.50
Political Campaign, Button, Franklin Roosevelt, Picture, 1 1/4 In., V Sign	4.50
Political Campaign, Button, Franklin Roosevelt, 1944, V Sign, 1 1/4 In.	4.50
Political Campaign, Button, Goldwater Picture, Lithograph	8.50
Political Campaign, Button, Henry Wallace For President, Picture, 1 1/4 In.	9.50
Political Campaign, Button, Hoover, Enamel On Brass	8.00
Political Campaign, Button, Hoover, Gray Enamel Elephant, GOP	28.00
Political Campaign, Button, Hughes, Fairbanks	24.00
Political Campaign, Button, Humphrey-Muskey	2.00
Political Campaign, Button, I Like Ike, White & Blue, 1952-56, 3/4 In.	2.50
Political Campaign, Button, I Want Roosevelt Again	5.00
Political Campaign, Button, John Kennedy, Jugate	10.00
Political Campaign, Button, John W.Davis, 1924	85.00
Political Campaign, Button, LaFollette, Wheeler, Bronze, Jugate, 1 In.	9.95
Political Campaign, Button, Landon, Knox, 1 In.	19.50
Political Campaign, Button, Lowden For Governor, Picture, 7/8 In.	7.00
Political Campaign, Button, Mayor's Committee, Jimmy Walker, 1926, Metal	14.00
Political Campaign, Button, McClellan, Bronze	28.00
Political Campaign, Button, McKinley Picture In Brass Frame, 1 1/2 In.	49.50
Political Campaign, Button, Mechanical, Uncle Sam Hanging Hitler	20.00
Political Campaign, Button, Member Kennedy For President Club	19.95
Political Campaign, Button, Nelson Rockefeller, Oval, 6 X 8 In.	18.00
Political Campaign, Button, Picture, Dante League For Roosevelt	29.50
Political Campaign, Button, Picture, Franklin Roosevelt, 7/8 In.	3.00
Political Campaign, Button, Picture, McCloskey	69.50
Political Campaign, Button, Picture, Teddy Roosevelt, 1912, 1 3/4 In.	60.00
Political Campaign, Button, Re-Elect Governor Smith, 7/8 In.	8.00
Political Campaign, Button, Rockefeller, Always Looking Ahead	19.50
Political Campaign, Button, Roosevelt, Picture, Friends Of F.Roosevelt	15.00
Political Campaign, Button, Roosevelt, 1912, Moose	10.00
Political Campaign, Button, Shield Of Beardless Abe Lincoln, Flag, 7/8 In.	6.50
Political Campaign, Button, Smith, Robinson	20.00
Political Campaign, Button, Socialist Party, C.1920, 3/4 In.	10.00
Political Campaign, Button, T.Roosevelt, Equality, 1904, 1 1/4 In.Diameter	1300.00
Political Campaign, Button, Taft, Picture, 7/8 In.	8.50
Political Campaign, Button, Teaneck For McGovern	10.00
Political Campaign, Button, Teddy Roosevelt & Fairbanks, 1904, 5/8 In.	12.50
Political Campaign, Button, Teddy Roosevelt, Jugate, 7/8 In.	15.00
Political Campaign, Button, Truman, The Won't Do Congress, Won't Do	39.50
Political Campaign, Button, We Don't Want Eleanor Either	3.50
Political Campaign, Button, Wendell Willkie	5.00
Political Campaign, Button, William Randolph Hearst For Governor, Picture	9.00
Political Campaign, Button, Willian Howard Taft, 1 In.	10.00
Political Campaign, Button, Willkie, Enamel Picture	5.95
Political Campaign, Button, Willkie, Set Of 6	24.00
Political Campaign, Button, Wilson, 7/16 In.	32.00
Political Campaign, Cane Head, McKinley, Metal	28.00
Political Campaign, Cane, Figural Head Of Taft, Silver Plate	35.00
Political Campaign, Cane, McKinley	75.00
Political Campaign, Cane, McKinley, Whistle Top, Tin	65.00
Political Campaign, Card, Change-Over, Roosevelt Or Parker, Pull Tab	75.00
Political Campaign, Card, Cleveland & Harrison, On Bikes	15.00
Political Campaign, Card, Inaugural Ball Dance, 1901	10.50
Political Campaign, Card, White House, With Best Wishes, Lady Bird Johnson	25.00
Political Campaign, Cigar, Humphrey, 10 In.	10.95
Political Campaign, Cigar, McGovern, 10 In.	10.95
Political Campaign, Cigar, Nixon, 10 In.	12.95
Political Campaign, Clock, Alarm, Lester Maddox, Wake Up America	13.00
Political Campaign, Cufflinks, 3/4 In.Letters, Spell Ike	26.00
Political Campaign, Doll, Richard Nixon	15.00
Political Campaign, Elephant, Hoover, Curtis, Enamel	15.00
Political Campaign, Envelope, Picture Of William McKinley	7.50

Political Campaign, Figurine, Elephant, G.O.P. On Side, Dirksen Other, 2 In.	10.00
Political Campaign, Flag, Again With Roosevelt, Picture, 1 X 1 3/4 In.	4.95
Political Campaign, Flag, Teddy Roosevelt, Caricatures, 1912, 19 X 19 In.	65.00
Political Campaign, Fob, Key, Cox, Roosevelt	30.00
Political Campaign, Glass, William McKinley, Our Next President	25.00
Political Campaign, Goblet, Grant, Wilson, Bust Of Both, 1872	225.00
Political Campaign, Handkerchief, Bryan & Sewall, 1897, Eagle At Bottom	95.00
Political Campaign, Hat, Cleveland, Thurman	50.00
Political Campaign, Hat, Nixon & Lodge	5.00
Political Campaign, Hat, Straw, Roosevelt	20.00
Political Campaign, Hat, 1972, Nixon Now	35.00
Political Campaign, Holder, Pencil, Desk, Eisenhower	8.50
Political Campaign, Jugate, Cleveland, Hendricks, Oval Pictures	60.00
Political Campaign, Jugate, Dewey-Warren, 3 1/2 In.	15.00
Political Campaign, Jugate, John Kennedy	4.50
Political Campaign, Jugate, McKinley, Roosevelt	15.00
Political Campaign, Jugate, Robert Kennedy	4.50
Political Campaign, Jugate, Roosevelt, Garner, Bronze	9.50
Political Campaign, Jugate, Seymour, Clair, Brass Shell	350.00
Political Campaign, Jugate, Theodore Roosevelt, Fairbanks	12.00
Political Campaign, Jugate, Wm.Bryan & Kern, Post Card	25.00
Political Campaign, Key Chain, Nixon, 1968	8.50
Political Campaign, Key Fob, Cox, Roosevelt	30.00
Political Campaign, Key, Gold Colored, 1909, Taft Inauguration	45.00
Political Campaign, Knife, McGovern, Eagleton	6.00
Political Campaign, Knife, Pocket, Wilson & Marshall, White House Reverse	200.00
Political Campaign, Lapel Stud, Hoover, Metal Rim, 13/16 In.	25.00
Political Campaign, License Plate, Hoover For President	30.00
Political Campaign, Medal, Tammany, Democratic Convention, 1908, 1 1/4 In.	35.00
Political Campaign, Mirror, Anti-Nixon, 1973	5.00
Political Campaign, Mirror, Jerry Ford	5.00
Political Campaign, Mirror, Wallace	8.00
Political Campaign, Mug, Bobby For President	9.00
Political Campaign, Mug, Miniature Liberty Bell, Hayes & Wheeler	75.00
Political Campaign, Mug, Toby, Napoleon, McKinley, Marked	300.00
Political Campaign, Parasol, Lady's, I Like Ike, Maple Handle, Sateen Fringe	45.00
Political Campaign, Pass, Floor, Democratic National Convention, Humphrey	5.00
Political Campaign, Pen, Woodrow Wilson, Colored	29.00
Political Campaign, Pencil, Mechanical, Win With Stevenson & Sparkman	7.50
Political Campaign, Pennant, F.D.Roosevelt, Picture, Our President, 28 In.	25.00
Political Campaign, Pennant, Goldwater	8.00
Political Campaign, Pennant, Johnson	8.00
Political Campaign, Pin Ribbon, Roosevelt, Donkey, Large	20.00
Political Campaign, Pin, Al Smith, Brass & White Enamel	20.00
Political Campaign, Plate, Nixon	10.00
Political Campaign, Plate, Taft, Sherman, Jugate, 1908	110.00
Political Campaign, Plate, Theodore Roosevelt, Birth & Death Date, 9 In.	50.00
Political Campaign, Poster, F.D.R. And Garner, 24 In.Wide	15.00
Political Campaign, Poster, Johnson, Humphrey For The U.S.A., 20 X 29 In.	10.00
Political Campaign, Poster, Kennedy For President, A Time For Greatness	10.00
Political Campaign, Poster, McGovern, 1972, 21 X 28 In.	2.25
Political Campaign, Poster, Nixon, Color Portrait, 22 X 15 In.	8.00
Political Campaign, Poster, Taft & Sherman, 1908, 27 1/2 X 21 In.	14.00
Political Campaign, Poster, This Is A Hoover Home, Picture, 11 X 11 In.	22.00
Political Campaign, Poster, Wm.E.Miller, Vp/usa, 1964, Signed, 16 X 13 In.	25.00
Political Campaign, Program, Democratic National Convention, 1948	15.00
Political Campaign, Puzzle, Spiro Agnew, 1970, Boxed	3.50
Political Campaign, Ribbon, Inaugural, President Johnson	2.50
Political Campaign, Ribbon, Lapel, Abe Lincoln, Hannibal Hamlin, 1860	280.00
Political Campaign, Ribbon, Silk, Republican State Rally, 1888	10.00
Political Campaign, Ribbon, Woman's Christian Temperance Union, C.1900	15.00
Political Campaign, Shot Glass, McKinley, Bryan, 1883	70.00
Political Campaign, Sign, Women's Suffrage Assoc., November 2nd, Tin	18.00
Political Campaign, Silhouette, Teddy Roosevelt, Framed	15.00
Political Campaign, Soap Baby, McKinley	28.00
Political Campaign, Stickpin, Grover Cleveland	8.50

Political Campaign, Stickpin, Teddy Roosevelt	20.00
Political Campaign, Stud, Lapel, Cox	12.50
Political Campaign, Stud, McKinley, Hobart, Jugate	15.00
Political Campaign, Stud, Teddy Roosevelt Picture, Cloth Rim	14.00
Political Campaign, Stud, The Money We Want, McKinley	15.00
Political Campaign, Teapot, Musical, Hail To The Chief	28.00
Political Campaign, Thimble, Coolidge & Dawes	8.00
Political Campaign, Thimble, Nixon, Plastic	2.50
Political Campaign, Ticket, For President Abraham Lincoln Of Illinois	10.00
Political Campaign, Ticket, Vice President Andrew Jackson Of Tennessee	10.00
Political Campaign, Tie Clip, Seal Of President, Signed, Richard Nixon	17.50
Political Campaign, Tie Pin, Democrat	12.50
Political Campaign, Torch, Kerosene, Wooden Handle, Tin	18.00
Political Campaign, Torch, Parade, Kerosene Burner, Trunnion Mounting, Tin	30.00
Political Campaign, Toy, 2 Elephants On Ramp, I Like Ike, Original Box	55.00
Political Campaign, Tray, Admiral Dewey, Picture With Flag & Eagle Border	45.00
Political Campaign, Tray, Card, Republican National Convention, 1900	20.00
Political Campaign, Tray, Keep Roosevelt In The White House, Tin	38.00
Political Campaign, Tray, Remember The Maine, Battleship With Flag Border	35.00
Political Campaign, Tray, T.Roosevelt, Rough Riders, 1903, 16 X 14 In.	100.00
Political Campaign, Tray, Taft, Sherman, G.O.P.	40.00
Political Campaign, Umbrella, Pictures Of McKinley & Hobart, Wood Parts	175.00
Political Campaign, Umbrella, 4 Pictures Of McKinley & Hobart, All Wood	175.00
Political Campaign, Watch Fob, Bryan, Kern, Jugate	25.00
Political Campaign, Watch Fob, Carter, Picture	12.50
Political Campaign, Watch Fob, Cox, Roosevelt, Jugate	95.00
Political Campaign, Watch Fob, Harding, Coolidge, Jugate	95.00
Political Campaign, Watch Fob, Harry S.Truman, Embossed Picture	47.50
Political Campaign, Watch Fob, Republican National Convention, 1952	15.00
Political Campaign, Watch Fob, Roosevelt, Century Of Progress 1933, Picture	57.50
Political Campaign, Watch Fob, Taft, Sherman, Jugate	25.00
Political Campaign, Watch Fob, To The White House, William H.Taft, 1908	28.50
Political Campaign, Watch Fob, W.Wilson, Pen Is Mightier Than The Sword	8.50
Political Campaign, Watch Fob, William Jennings Bryan's Picture, Fiber	27.50
Political Campaign, Watch Fob, Willkie, Porcelain Front	40.00
Political Campaign, Watch Fob, Wilson Picture	17.00

Pomona glass is clear with a soft amber border decorated with pale blue or rose-colored flowers and leaves. The colors are very, very pale. The background of the glass is covered with a network of fine lines. It was made from 1885 to 1888 by the New England Glass Company.

Pomona, Bowl, Crimped Sides, Amber Stained Upper Third, 4 X 2 In.	78.00
Pomona, Bowl, Finger, Blue Straw Flower, Ruffled Edge	95.00
Pomona, Bowl, Finger, Ruffled Top, 2nd Grind	85.00
Pomona, Bowl, Finger, Ruffled, First Grind	35.00
Pomona, Bowl, Gold Fluted Rim, First Ground, 5 X 2 In.	135.00
Pomona, Bowl, Ruffled Top, lst Grind, 2 1/4 X 5 1/4 In.Diameter	125.00
Pomona, Cup, Punch, Amber Band & Handle, First Grind	85.00
Pomona, Cup, Punch, Cornflower, Amber Stain, First Grind	200.00
Pomona, Pitcher, Applied Feet & Handle, Crimped Top, First Grind, 7 1/2 In.	400.00
Pomona, Pitcher, Applied Handle, Inverted Thumbprint, Enameled	195.00
Pomona, Pitcher, Blue Cornflowers, 1st Grind, 7 1/2 In.	375.00
Pomona, Pitcher, Water, Floral, Applied Handle	110.00
Pomona, Toothpick, Ruffled Amber Top, Matching Handle	95.00
Pomona, Toothpick, Swirl Neck, 1st Grind, 2 1/2 In.	165.00
Pomona, Tumbler, Amber, Diamond Quilted, 2nd Grind Lower 2/3, 4 1/2 In.	85.00
Pomona, Tumbler, Blue Cornflower, 2nd Grind, 4 X 2 1/2 In.	100.00
Pomona, Tumbler, Cornflower, Second Grind, 3 3/4 In.	150.00
Pomona, Tumbler, Diamond Quilted, Second Grind, Amber Above, 4 1/2 In.	85.00
Pomona, Tumbler, Diamond Quilted, Second Grind, 4 1/2 In.	115.00
Pomona, Tumbler, Scalloped Amber Rim	70.00
Pomona, Tumbler, Second Grind, Enameled Apple Blossom	45.00
Pomona, Vase, Bulbous Bottom, Crimped Top, 2nd Grind, 5 1/2 X 5 In.Diam.	140.00
Pomona, Vase, Leaf Design, 1st Grind, 6 1/2 In.	290.00
Pontypool, see Tole	
Poo Ware, see Banko	

Popeye, Bank, Coin 12.00
Popeye, Book, Animated, 1945 .... 16.00
Popeye, Book, Punch-Out, Uncut, 1936 .... 85.00
Popeye, Box, Pencil, C.1950, Cloth 7.50
Popeye, Box, Pencil, Graphics On Both Sides 68.00
Popeye, Box, School Supply 15.00
Popeye, Button, Pinback, C.1940, 1 1/4 In. 15.00
Popeye, Doll, Wood Jointed, 4 1/2 In. .... 50.00 To 60.00
Popeye, Game, The Juggler .... 65.00 To 75.00
Popeye, Game, Toss 15.00
Popeye, Kazoo 3.50
Popeye, Paint Set, 1949 .... 25.00
Popeye, Pin, Enameled, Popeye's Dog 22.00
Popeye, Toy, Carrying Parrot Cage, Windup, Tin 135.00
Popeye, Toy, In Spinach Can, Popup 12.00
Popeye, Toy, Popeye In A Barrel, Chein 145.00
Popeye, Toy, Tin, Popeye Pushing Wheelbarrow 85.00
Popeye, Tumbler, Pair 6.50
Popeye, Wagon, Paddle, Corgi 35.00
    Porcelain, see also Copeland, Nippon, R.S.Prussia, etc.
Porcelain Drawer Pull, Black Lettering, Red Trim, 2 X 3 1/4 X 1 1/4 In. 1.25
Porcelain Tray, Paris, Hand-Painted, Marked, 8 5/8 In. 85.00
Porcelain, Basket, Handled, Hand-Painted, C.1890, Signed, Oval, 4 X 6 3/4 In. 45.00
Porcelain, Bottle, Scent, Flowers With Gold, German, 6 1/2 In. 55.00
Porcelain, Bottle, Scent, French, Blue Floral With Gold, 7 In. 65.00
Porcelain, Bowl, Apple Blossoms On Green Background, 9 1/2 X 3 1/2 In. 225.00
Porcelain, Bowl, Chinese, Blue & Gray, 3 1/4 X 1 1/4 In. 25.00
Porcelain, Bowl, Chinese, Porcelain On Metal, C.1885, 9 1/2 In. 175.00
Porcelain, Bowl, Chinese, White Paste Body, Ming Dynasty, 4 1/4 In. 130.00
Porcelain, Bowl, Dragons & Scrolls, Blue & White, Marked, Chinese, 7 In. 350.00
Porcelain, Bowl, Fish, Famille Rose, Colorfully Painted, 1800s, 20 1/2 In. 3200.00
Porcelain, Bowl, Ho-O & Dragons, Seal Mark In Underglaze Blue, 11 3/4 In. 180.00
Porcelain, Box, Food, Chinese, 4-Tier, 19th Century, 8 1/2 X 8 In. 365.00
Porcelain, Box, Patch, Insect Shaped, Fisher-Meig, 2 1/2 X 4 1/2 In. 100.00
Porcelain, Bust, Maiden, Colored-Biscuit, French, A.Carrier, C.1900, 15 In. 350.00
Porcelain, Bust, Maiden, Hautin & Boulenger, Choisy-Le-Roy, 1800s, 30 1/4 In. 650.00
Porcelain, Bust, Richard Wagner, Signed, Scheibe Mark, 8 In. 85.00
Porcelain, Can, Watering, Flowers, Butterflies, Encrusted Gold, Pierced Spout 22.00
Porcelain, Candle Snuffer, Boy's Head In Southwester Hat 45.00
Porcelain, Candle Snugger, Figural, Woman In Black Hat Holding Basket 45.00
Porcelain, Candlestick, Violets, Gold Numbers, Pair 10.00
Porcelain, Case, Wall, Hanging, Scrolled Rococo Border, 10 X 7 X 3 In. 123.00
Porcelain, Centerpiece, Schierholze, German, C.1890, 10 In. 395.00
Porcelain, Coffee Pot, Napoleon Portrait, Nast A Paris Marked Base, 11 In. 80.00
Porcelain, Coffee Pot, Pewter, Long Legged Heron In March, 10 1/2 In. 125.00
Porcelain, Compote, 6 Cherubs Hold Bowl, Signed, Crown & Arch, 12 X 8 In. 550.00
Porcelain, Creamer, Cow, Germany 18.00
Porcelain, Cup & Saucer, Apple Blossoms & Butterfly, White 7.50
Porcelain, Cup & Saucer, Purple Transfer Of Lady & Man At Church 15.00
Porcelain, Desk Set, Hand-Painted, Handled Box, Tray, 3 X 4 In. 32.50
Porcelain, Dish, Butter, Kusnetzov, Dulevo Mark, Russian 125.00
Porcelain, Dish, Cheese, Matching Plate, S.D. & F., 9 In. 385.00
Porcelain, Dish, Seagull, Square, 9 X 8 1/2 X 2 1/2 In. 32.00
Porcelain, Ewer, Stag, Brown Background, Elkhorn Handle, Germany, 5 In. 25.00
Porcelain, Figurine, Ballerina, Lace Costume, Blue Crown Mark, 3 1/2 In. 50.00
Porcelain, Figurine, Bird, Parakeet, On Tree Trunk, Signed, 5 In. 35.00
Porcelain, Figurine, Birds Copulating, Rooster & Chicken, German, 4 X 6 In. 150.00
Porcelain, Figurine, Boy Playing Mandolin, Mark, Red P Over R & Germany 75.00
Porcelain, Figurine, Cherub Standing On Cornucopia, Gebruder & Oloff 450.00
Porcelain, Figurine, Cow, Calf Lying On Stomach, Head Over Cow's Back, 7 In. 50.00
Porcelain, Figurine, Dalmatian, Turned Head, Ludwigsburg, 5 In., Pair 125.00
Porcelain, Figurine, Dancing Girl, Signed, German 125.00
Porcelain, Figurine, Dog, Spaniel, Signed, HR Germany, 3 1/2 In. 20.00
Porcelain, Figurine, E.Barlach, Child Drinking From Vessel, 2 1/2 In. 425.00
Porcelain, Figurine, Flower Frog, Nude, White, Marked Germany, 4 1/4 In. 22.00
Porcelain, Figurine, Japanese, Buddha, Gilt Body, Coraline Robe, 14 In. 15.00

Porcelain, Figurine, Kneeling Nude, No.5729, Artist Signed, Herend, 9 1/4 In. 145.00
Porcelain, Figurine, Lady, Coach Drawn By 4 Horses, C.1800, Saxe, 24 In. 700.00
Porcelain, Figurine, Mother Bird Over Nest, Feeding Young, German, 9 In. 215.00
Porcelain, Figurine, Oriental Woman, Seated, Holding Fan, 2 3/4 In. 30.00
Porcelain, Figurine, Pillow Boy Crouching, Glazed, C.1900 .... 300.00
Porcelain, Figurine, Polo Player With Horse Rearing By Post, 15 1/2 In. 1100.00
Porcelain, Figurine, Temple Dog, Green, Gold, Gray, Chinese, 22 X 25 In. 600.00
Porcelain, Figurine, Woman In 1800 Costume, French, Paul Duboy, 23 1/2 In. 425.00
Porcelain, Fruit Stand, Pierced, Potschappel, Monogram Mark, 1900s, 7 In. 100.00
Porcelain, Holder, Watch, Russian, Figural, 7 X 5 1/2 In. 250.00
Porcelain, Jar, Ginger, Chien Lung, 18th Century, 10 In., Pair 975.00
Porcelain, Jar, Ginger, Prunus, Covered, Dark Blue & White, Large 270.00
Porcelain, Jar, Temple, Kutani-Kyoto Province, 19th Century, Japanese 250.00
Porcelain, Jar, Tobacco, Googly-Eyed Policeman, Marked Germany 165.00
Porcelain, Jar, White Glazed, Ovoid Body, Narcissus Decorated, 13 3/4 In. 100.00
Porcelain, Jardiniere, Enameled Figures, Flowers, C.1900, Oshima, 17 1/2 In. 800.00
Porcelain, Jardiniere, Rose Vignette, German, Rococco, 9 X 9 In. 195.00
Porcelain, Knob, Door, 11 White, 2 Black, Set 40.00
Porcelain, Lemon Reamer, White, 3 1/2 In. 8.75
Porcelain, Mug, Child's Three Children On Fence, German 25.00
Porcelain, Napkin Ring, see Napkin Ring
Porcelain, Pitcher, Full Figure Of Betty Prig, Wearing Cape, Dress, 3 In. 45.00
Porcelain, Plaque, Bats, Geisha Girl, Shou Lau, Spotted Deer, Chop Mark, Signed 750.00
Porcelain, Plaque, Continental, Austrian, Schner, Signed, 1800s, 18 1/2 In. 1500.00
Porcelain, Plaque, English, Circular, C.1860, Signed W.Mitchell, 14 1/4 In. 400.00
Porcelain, Plaque, Herta, Shield Mark In Blue, Circular, Vienna, 1800s 2000.00
Porcelain, Plaque, Still-Life, Continental, 1800s, 9 1/4 In., Pair 475.00
Porcelain, Plaque, Young Girl, Oval, Framed, 7 In. 495.00
Porcelain, Plaque, Young Maiden, German, Impressed Numerals, 1800, 5 X 7 In. 650.00
Porcelain, Plaque, 2 Young Girls, E.M.Bevridge, Signed, C.1800, 10 1/2 In. 600.00
Porcelain, Plate, Flying Horse, Ming, Chinese, 16th Century 200.00
Porcelain, Plate, Kakiemon, Underglaze Blue Mark, Japanese, 1700s, 8 1/4 In. 160.00
Porcelain, Plate, Marsh Birds, Anchor Mark, 9 3/4 In., Pair 210.00
Porcelain, Plate, Portrait, Cavalier & Lady Seated, Signed, 9 3/4 In. 85.00
Porcelain, Plate, Portrait, Enameled Dog, 8 3/4 In. 125.00
Porcelain, Plate, Portrait, Estalla, Gold Details, Signed, C.1850, 9 1/2 In. 550.00
Porcelain, Plate, Portrait, Feuer, Gold Border, Signed, C.1850, 9 1/2 In. 450.00
Porcelain, Plate, Portrait, French Enamel, Signed & Framed 335.00
Porcelain, Plate, Portrait, Lady In Park, Marked H & C Selb, 9 3/4 In. 40.00
Porcelain, Plate, Portrait, Lady Sitting On Bench, Signed, C.1850, 9 1/2 In. 450.00
Porcelain, Plate, Portrait, Lady, Gold Border, Marked Silesia, 9 1/2 In. 50.00
Porcelain, Plate, Portrait, Malerei & Rossler, Signed, C.1850, 9 1/2 In. 450.00
Porcelain, Plate, Portrait, Ruth, Gold, Red Border, Signed, C.1850, 9 1/2 In. 550.00
Porcelain, Plate, Portrait, Tludienkopt, C.1850, Signed, 10 In. 450.00
Porcelain, Plate, Stoke On Trent, Hand-Painted, Two Maidens, 13 In.Diameter 70.00
Porcelain, Platter, Fruit, Flowers, Ivory Background, French, 11 X 7 1/2 In. 125.00
Porcelain, Salt Dip, Neptune, Coral Handle, Shell Feet 20.00
Porcelain, Saltshaker, Red Tomato 20.00
Porcelain, Shoe, Rose Decoration, Scalloped Edge, 5 X 4 1/4 X 6 1/4 In. 60.00
Porcelain, Shoe, Turned Up Toe, Pipe Across Instep, Victorian, 7 In. 24.00
Porcelain, Spittoon, Lady's, German 68.50
Porcelain, Statuette, Lady Holding Basket, Famille Rose, Chinese, 21 1/2 In. 575.00
Porcelain, Sugar & Creamer, 2-Headed Black Eagle, Imperial Russia, Pair 250.00
Porcelain, Tea Service, 3 Piece, Scalloped Edges, Gold Rims, 6 Cup, Austria 45.00
Porcelain, Teapot, Oriental, Polychrome Enameled Figures, 4 1/2 In. 50.00
Porcelain, Teapot, Oriental, 5 Color Glaze, Mark On Base, 4 3/4 In. 85.00
Porcelain, Tumbler, Souvenir, St.Louis World's Fair, Austria, 4 1/4 In. 39.00
Porcelain, Urn, Floral, Austrian, Covered, Dated 1893, 16 3/4 In. .... *Illus* 900.00
Porcelain, Vase & Cover, Lovers, Helena Wolfsohn, Bud Knop, 1800s, 13 3/4 In. 325.00
Porcelain, Vase, Austrian, 4 Arms, C.1900 .... *Illus* 175.00
Porcelain, Vase, Butterflies, Peony, Glazed, Cylindrical, 34 In. 172.00
Porcelain, Vase, Cabinet, Grecian Lady Making Up Her Face, Handmaiden, 5 In. 60.00
Porcelain, Vase, Chinese, 4 Women In Different Poses, 10 1/2 X 3 In. 125.00
Porcelain, Vase, Ducks, Wildflower, Famille Rose, C.1800s, 2 1/2 In., Pair 700.00
Porcelain, Vase, Floral Panels, Dark Blue , Gold, C.1850, 12 3/4 In., Pair 485.00
Porcelain, Vase, Pink, Colorful Flowers, Ruffled Top, Victorian, 5 1/2 In. 190.00

Porcelain, Vase, Reticulated, Gold Iguana Handles, 11 X 8 In.	175.00
Porcelain, Vase, 2 Handles, Cobalt Blue & Gold, 7 1/2 In.	39.00
Porcelain, Whistle, Clown Shape, Brown Luster, 4 In.	45.00

Postcards were first legally permitted in Austria on October 1, 1869.
The United States passed postal regulations allowing the card in 1873.
Most of the picture postcards collected today date from 1910.

Postcard, Airplane, U.S.Mail Service, Celluloid, 1912, Gold	22.50
Postcard, Airplane, U.S.Mail Service, Celluloid, 1912, Silver	22.50
Postcard, Album, Greeting Cards, Set Of 230	55.00
Postcard, Album, Holiday & View Cards, Set Of 75	23.00
Postcard, Album, 70 Cards, 1900-10	35.00
Postcard, Album, 100 California Cards	12.00
Postcard, Album, 200 Cards, 50 Views Of Early Florida	75.00
Postcard, Alcatraz Island, 1908	3.00
Postcard, American Troops Arrive In Europe	3.00
Postcard, Arizona, Wooden	12.00
Postcard, Boats, Ferry, Set Of 16	9.75
Postcard, Buster Brown & Tige, Pair	11.00
Postcard, Campbell Kids, 1910	12.00
Postcard, Chicago World's Fair	1.00
Postcard, Cracker Jack, Bear	14.00
Postcard, Depots & Trains, Set Of 307	237.00
Postcard, Earthquake, San Bernardino, 1925	4.00
Postcard, Easter Sunrise Service Mt.Ribidoux, California	3.00
Postcard, European Royalty, Set Of 11	50.00
Postcard, Ferris Wheel, World's Fair Chicago, 1893	5.00
Postcard, Five Owls, Dated 1911	8.00

Porcelain, Urn, Floral, Austrian,
Covered, Dated 1893, 16 3/4 In.
(See Page 389)

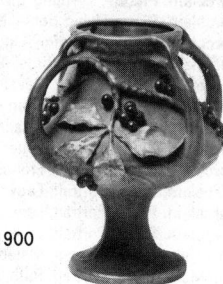

Porcelain, Vase, Austrian, 4 Arms, C.1900
(See Page 389)

Postcard, Folding Brochure, Buffalo Bill Show, 1911	20.00
Postcard, French, Embroidered Silk	6.00
Postcard, Gassaway, Mon Dieu	5.00
Postcard, Germany, Sample Folder, 1911, 2 Piece	10.00
Postcard, Good Old Days	50.00
Postcard, Graf Zeppelin In Hangar	10.00
Postcard, Graf Zeppelin In Sky	8.00
Postcard, Grant's Tomb, Hold To Light	12.00
Postcard, Greeting, 1892 Columbian Exposition, Hold To Light, 5 X 6 In.	50.00
Postcard, Hands Across The Sea, R.M.S. Mauretania	35.00
Postcard, Harvard & Yale Football Game	10.00
Postcard, Harvard University, 1909	2.00
Postcard, Hitler, Postmarked Late 30s	6.75
Postcard, Holes Around Edge For Ribbon, Leather	2.00
Postcard, Indian Canoeing	50.00
Postcard, Indian, Monument	50.00
Postcard, Leather, 1902	3.00
Postcard, Lindbergh In Foyer Of Boston Theater	10.00
Postcard, Louisiana Purchase Expo	2.00
Postcard, Mexican Bullfights, Album	22.00
Postcard, Mount Vesuvius Erupting, 1906, 4 Scenes	8.00

Postcard, Napoleon & Napoleon Museum, Color, Set Of 10 .... 5.00
Postcard, New England States, 83 In Set 40.00
Postcard, New York City, Set Of 35 .... 12.50
Postcard, Now I Lay Me Down To Sleep 7.50
Postcard, Old New York State, Set Of 700 .... 80.00
Postcard, Panama Pacific Exposition, 1915 .... 5.00
Postcard, Pope Paul VI, Commemorating 1965 Visit To New York 2.50
Postcard, Roosevelt, Lehman & Jack Dempsey, Three Champions, 1936 .... 8.50
Postcard, Sailing Ship, 85 Piece 100.00
Postcard, Savin Rock, Connecticut, C.1920 .... 5.00
Postcard, Ship, Hold To Light 22.00
Postcard, Ships, Lakes & Rivers, 1930s, Set Of 101 .... 114.00
Postcard, Soldiers, Colored, C.1885, Set Of 9 .... 50.00
Postcard, Teddy Bears, Leather 7.50
Postcard, Thanksgiving, Set Of 100 .... 15.00
Postcard, U.S. Ships, Views On Board, Set Of 34 .... 47.00
Postcard, Valentine, German, Set Of 10 .... 15.00
Postcard, Valentine, Lovers Kissing & Dan Cupid, C.1930 .... 1.00
Postcard, Washington, D.C., Hold To Light 15.00
Postcard, Zeppelin Schwaben, 1913 .... 10.00
Postcard, 1938 Hurricane, Connecticut 2.50
Postcard, 1939 World's Fair, Set Of 20 .... 3.00
Postcard, 5 Kewpies & 3 Birds On Tree Limb, Christmas 22.50
    Potlid, see also Pratt
Potlid, Persuasion 55.00
Potlid, The Prince Consort, Albert Seated At Desk 85.00
    Pottery, see also Buffalo Pottery, Staffordshire, Wedgwood, etc.
Pottery, Biscuit Jar, English, Scene Of Old World Garden, Square, 6 1/8 In. 68.00
Pottery, Biscuit Jar, English, Silver Plated Top & Handle, 6 1/2 In. 75.00
Pottery, Cookie Jar, Cream Tapestry Ground, Crown Albion, 6 1/2 X 5 1/4 In. 110.00
Pottery, Crock, Bird, New York Stoneware Company, 1 1/2 Gallon 140.00
Pottery, Frog, Flower, Blue, 4 1/2 X 2 3/4 In. 8.00
Pottery, Harvest Ring, Brown Glaze, Southern, 19th Century, 10 1/4 In. 275.00
Pottery, Jar, Snuff, Weymans, Covered With Cigar Bands 12.00
Pottery, Mug, Woman Herding 3 Cows, Lockhart & Sons Mark, Scottish, 4 In. 38.00
Pottery, Orange, Ceramic, Irphila Art Pottery, Czechoslovakia 40.00
Pottery, Pitcher, Batter, Chocolate Brown Glaze, 1/2 Gallon 35.00
Pottery, Salt & Pepper, Tobies, Prestopans, Scotland, 1830-40, Pair 95.00
Pottery, Tobacco Jar, Matching Lid, William Dracott, December, 19, 1854, 6 In. 100.00
Pottery, Vase, Maroon & Olive Green Matte, Signed Grumbach, 14 In. 75.00
Pottery, Vase, The Descent To Hell, Earthenware, Seal Mark, 1850s, 24 In. 800.00
Pottery, Whippet, Solomon Bell, Early 19th Century, 6 3/4 In. 3250.00
    Powder Flask, see Weapon, Powder Flask
    Powder Horn, see Weapon, Powder Horn

PRATT FENTON   *Pratt ware means two different things. It was an early Staffordshire pottery, cream colored with colored decorations, made by Felix Pratt during the late eighteenth century. There was also Pratt ware made with transfer designs during the mid-nineteenth century in Fenton, England.*

Pratt, Bottle, Snuff, C.1775-1805 .... 20.00
Pratt, Frog Mug, One Handled, 4 1/4 In. 100.00
Pratt, Frog Mug, 2 Handled, 5 1/4 In. 110.00
Pratt, Jar, Ointment, Hunting Scene, Blue, 4 1/4 In. 42.00
Pratt, Jar, Snuff, Blue, Transfer Scene, Wild Boar Hunt, 4 In. 22.50
Pratt, Jug, Toby, C.1790 .... 575.00
Pratt, Plaque, Figure Seated On Mound, Blue Leafage, C.1800, 11 1/8 In. 350.00
Pratt, Plate, Animals In Water & Women Washing, 9 In. 50.00
Pratt, Plate, Haddon Hall, Castle, Cottage, Cows, Gold Border Of Maidens, 9 In. 60.00
Pratt, Plate, Portrait, Blue & Gold, 8 1/2 In. 52.00
Pratt, Plate, Sebastopol, Harbor Scene, 8 1/2 In. 60.00
Pratt, Plate, The Village Wedding, 7 1/2 In. 55.00
Pratt, Platter, Indian, 19 X 15 In. 145.00
Pratt, Potlid, Best Card 75.00
Pratt, Potlid, Charing Cross 85.00
Pratt, Potlid, Cries Of London, Primroses 30.00
Pratt, Potlid, Embarking For The East 100.00

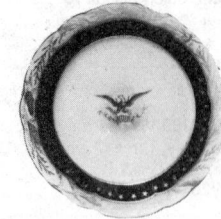

Presidential China *(l. to r.)*: Bowl, Soup; Plate, Harrison; Plate, Lincoln.

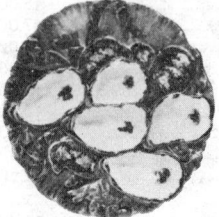
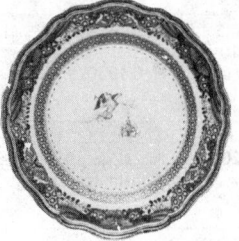

Presidential China, Plate, Oyster, Hayes, Haviland, Set Of 3

Presidential China, Plate, Washington's Order, Cincinnati

Pressed Glass, Admiral Dewey, Plate, Clear, 5 1/2 In.

Pratt, Potlid, Fishbarrow, Raised Rim, Lace Border	75.00
Pratt, Potlid, Good Dog	65.00
Pratt, Potlid, I See You My Boy	56.00
Pratt, Potlid, Queen Victoria	84.00
Pratt, Potlid, Queen Victoria, England's Pride, Framed	100.00
Pratt, Potlid, Red Bull Inn, Large	90.00
Pratt, Potlid, Second Appeal, Blue Border	85.00
Pratt, Potlid, Shakespeare's Birth Place, Interior & Exterior	50.00
Pratt, Potlid, Tam O'Shanter & Souter Johnny	125.00
Pratt, Potlid, Westminster Abbey, London	150.00
Pratt, Potlid, Who'll Buy My Lavender	55.00
Pratt, Potlid, Wolf And Lamb	70.00
Pratt, Vase, Shakespeare, 4 In.	25.00
Presidential China, Bowl, Soup, Hayes, Limoges, C.1880, 9 In. ....*Illus*	500.00
Presidential China, Plate, Harrison, Limoges, 8 1/2 In. ....*Illus*	800.00
Presidential China, Plate, Lincoln, Haviland, C.1873, 8 1/4 In. ....*Illus*	350.00
Presidential China, Plate, Oyster, Hayes, Haviland, Set Of 3 ....*Illus*	175.00
Presidential China, Plate, Washington's Order, Cincinnati ....*Illus*	800.00

Pressed glass was first made in the United States in the 1820s after the invention of pressed-glass machines. Hundreds of patterns of pressed glass were made in complete table settings. Although the Boston and Sandwich Works was the most famous of the pressed glass factories, there were about sixteen other factories making pressed glass from 1830 to 1850, and still more from 1850 to 1900, when pressed glass reached its greatest popularity. It is now being widely reproduced.

Pressed Glass, A Good Girl, Mug, Amber, 3 1/2 In.	22.50
Acanthus, see Ribbed Palm	
Pressed Glass, Acanthus Scroll, Butter	25.00
Acme, see Butterfly & Spray	
Pressed Glass, Acorn Band, Spooner	24.00
Acorn Medallion, see Beaded Acorn Medallion	
Pressed Glass, Acorn, Goblet	25.00 To 26.50
Pressed Glass, Actress, Bread Plate, Pinafore, 7 X 11 1/4 In.	44.50 To 70.00
Pressed Glass, Actress, Celery	95.00
Pressed Glass, Actress, Celery, Pinafore	95.00 To 135.00
Pressed Glass, Actress, Compote, Covered	95.00

Pressed Glass, Actress, Compote, Covered, 8 1/4 In.	60.00
Pressed Glass, Actress, Compote, 10 In.	75.00
Pressed Glass, Actress, Creamer	45.00 To 60.00
Pressed Glass, Actress, Dish, Cheese, Covered	110.00
Pressed Glass, Actress, Dish, Cheese, Frosted	225.00
Pressed Glass, Actress, Dish, Cheese, Two Dromios	150.00
Pressed Glass, Actress, Goblet	58.00 To 125.00
Pressed Glass, Actress, Jar, Jam, Covered	75.00
Pressed Glass, Actress, Pitcher, Water	175.00
Pressed Glass, Actress, Plate, Pinafore	50.00
Pressed Glass, Actress, Sauce, Clear & Frosted, Flat, 4 In.	15.00
Pressed Glass, Actress, Sauce, Clear & Frosted, Footed, 4 In.	15.00 To 19.00
Pressed Glass, Actress, Sauce, Clear, Footed, 4 1/2 In.	20.00
Pressed Glass, Actress, Sauce, Footed	12.00
Pressed Glass, Admiral Dewey, Plate, Clear, 5 1/2 In.	12.00
Pressed Glass, Adonis, Celery	18.00
Pressed Glass, Adonis, Spooner	10.50
Pressed Glass, Akron Block, Sauce, Square	5.00
Pressed Glass, Alabama, Creamer, Large	29.00
Pressed Glass, Alabama, Pitcher, Water	65.00
Pressed Glass, Alabama, Relish, Oval	18.00
Pressed Glass, Alabama, Toothpick	22.00
Pressed Glass, Alaska, Bowl, Master Berry, Opalescent	120.00
Pressed Glass, Alaska, Creamer, Blue	95.00
Pressed Glass, Alaska, Creamer, Green	45.00
Pressed Glass, Alaska, Creamer, Opalescent	95.00
Pressed Glass, Alaska, Creamer, Opalescent, Vaseline	95.00
Pressed Glass, Alaska, Creamer, Spooner, Sugar, Covered, Green	110.00
Pressed Glass, Alaska, Spooner, Enameled Florals, Green	55.00
Pressed Glass, Alaska, Spooner, Green	37.50
Pressed Glass, Alaska, Sugar	55.00
Pressed Glass, Alaska, Sugar, Covered, Ship Finial	40.00
Pressed Glass, Alaska, Tray, Jewel	65.00
Pressed Glass, Alligator Scales With Spearpoint, Goblet, Etched	16.00
Pressed Glass, Alligator Scales, Goblet	15.00
Pressed Glass, Almond Thumbprint, Celery, Pedestal	29.00
Pressed Glass, Almond Thumbprint, Champagne	16.00
Pressed Glass, Almond Thumbprint, Compote, Scalloped Rim, Low Foot, 9 In.	32.50
Pressed Glass, Almond Thumbprint, Glass, Ale, Flint	21.00
Pressed Glass, Almond Thumbprint, Goblet	10.00 To 22.00
Pressed Glass, Almond Thumbprint, Sugar, Flint	25.00
Pressed Glass, Almond Thumbprint, Tumbler, Flint	28.00
Pressed Glass, Almond Thumbprint, Wine, Gold	14.50
Pressed Glass, Amazon, Creamer, Miniature	7.00
Pressed Glass, Amazon, Dish, Covered, Oval, Lion Handles	40.00
Pressed Glass, Amazon, Nappy, 3-Cornered, Lion Handle	20.00
Amberette, see Klondike	
Pressed Glass, Ambidextrous, Spooner	28.50
Pressed Glass, Angora, Goblet	12.50
Pressed Glass, Anvil, Toothpick	17.50
Pressed Glass, Apollo, Celery, Etched	27.50 To 28.50
Pressed Glass, Apollo, Celery, Pedestal, Frosted Top	35.00
Pressed Glass, Apollo, Goblet, Etched	20.00
Pressed Glass, Apollo, Goblet, Frosted	20.00
Pressed Glass, Arch & Forget-Me-Not, Creamer	18.00
Pressed Glass, Arch, Tumbler, Bar, Amethyst	65.00
Pressed Glass, Arched Fans, Creamer	40.00
Pressed Glass, Arched Fleur-De-Lis, Banana Boat, 11 X 5 1/2 In.	25.00
Pressed Glass, Arched Fleur-De-Lis, Banana Stand	25.00
Pressed Glass, Arched Fleur-De-Lis, Bowl, Flared Edge, 9 In. Square	25.00
Pressed Glass, Arched Grape, Goblet	15.00 To 24.50
Pressed Glass, Arched Grape, Spooner	35.00
Pressed Glass, Arched Leaf, Spooner, Flint	75.00
Pressed Glass, Arched Leaf, 12 Plates & 2 Cake Plates, C.1850	150.00
Pressed Glass, Arched Ovals, Creamer	22.50
Pressed Glass, Arched Ovals, Toothpick, Clear With Pink Blush	18.00

Pressed Glass, Arched Grape, Goblet

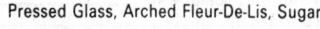

Pressed Glass, Arched Fleur-De-Lis, Sugar

Pressed Glass, Arched Ovals, Tumbler, Ruby & Clear	20.00
Argonaut Shell, see Nautilus	
Pressed Glass, Argosy, Goblet, Flint	15.00
Argus, see also Cut Argus	
Pressed Glass, Argus, Cordial	30.00
Pressed Glass, Argus, Eggcup	25.00
Pressed Glass, Argus, Eggcup, Flint	19.50 To 23.00
Pressed Glass, Argus, Goblet, Bulb Stem	25.00
Pressed Glass, Argus, Goblet, Flint	32.50 To 50.00
Pressed Glass, Argus, Goblet, Flint, Set Of 8	300.00
Pressed Glass, Argus, Mug, Applied Handle	45.00
Pressed Glass, Argus, Spill, Flint	35.00
Pressed Glass, Argus, Tumbler, Bar, Flint	37.00
Pressed Glass, Argus, Tumbler, Flint	45.00
Pressed Glass, Argus, Tumbler, Footed, Flint, 5 1/4 In.	28.00
Pressed Glass, Argus, Tumbler, Reverse, Flint	60.00
Pressed Glass, Argus, Water Set, Etched, 4 Glasses, Pitcher, 10 1/2 In.	115.00
Pressed Glass, Argus, Whiskey	25.00
Pressed Glass, Argus, Wine	35.00
Pressed Glass, Arrowhead In Oval, Cake Stand, 6 1/2 In.Diameter	23.00
Art Novo, see Dogwood	
Pressed Glass, Art, Bowl, Crystal, 3 3/4 X 8 1/4 In.Diameter	30.00
Pressed Glass, Art, Celery	18.00 To 30.00
Pressed Glass, Art, Creamer	30.00
Pressed Glass, Art, Sugar, Covered	28.00 To 30.00
Pressed Glass, Artichoke, Butter, Covered, Frosted	85.00
Pressed Glass, Artichoke, Compote, Frosted, Clear, Covered	95.00
Pressed Glass, Artichoke, Creamer, Frosted	75.00
Pressed Glass, Artichoke, Pitcher, Water, Frosted, Clear	85.00
Pressed Glass, Artichoke, Plate, Frosted, 6 In.	37.00
Pressed Glass, Artichoke, Sauce, Flat	18.00
Pressed Glass, Artichoke, Spooner, Frosted, Clear	20.00
Pressed Glass, Artichoke, Spooner, Handled, Frosted	30.00
Pressed Glass, Artichoke, Sugar, Covered, Frosted	50.00
Pressed Glass, Ashburton With Sawtooth, Whiskey, Applied Handle, 4 In.	73.00
Pressed Glass, Ashburton, Celery, Plain Rim, Flint	75.00
Pressed Glass, Ashburton, Celery, Scalloped Rim, Flint	100.00
Pressed Glass, Ashburton, Cordial, Flint	25.00
Pressed Glass, Ashburton, Creamer, Flint	175.00
Pressed Glass, Ashburton, Eggcup	20.00 To 27.00
Pressed Glass, Ashburton, Eggcup, Flint	12.50 To 23.00
Pressed Glass, Ashburton, Goblet	35.00
Pressed Glass, Ashburton, Goblet, Flint	19.50 To 34.00
Pressed Glass, Ashburton, Tumbler	50.00
Pressed Glass, Ashburton, Tumbler, Bar, Flint	37.00
Pressed Glass, Ashburton, Tumbler, Flint	50.00
Pressed Glass, Ashburton, Tumbler, Historical Scenes In Ovals, Flint	350.00
Pressed Glass, Ashburton, Wine, Clear, Flint, 4 1/2 In.	40.00
Pressed Glass, Ashburton, Wine, Creased, Flint	35.00
Pressed Glass, Ashburton, Wine, Flint	22.00 To 28.00

Pressed Glass, Ashburton, Champagne, Presentation Piece

Pressed Glass, Ashburton, Bottle, Amethyst, Tumbler Mold

Pressed Glass, Ashman, Celery	35.00
Pressed Glass, Ashman, Compote, Covered	43.00
Pressed Glass, Ashman, Creamer	47.50
Pressed Glass, Ashman, Goblet, Etched	35.00
Pressed Glass, Ashman, Spooner	25.00
Pressed Glass, Asonis, Pitcher, Water	32.50
Pressed Glass, Astro, Bowl, Ruffle, Clear, Opalescent	28.00
Pressed Glass, Atlanta, Compote, Open, Scalloped Top, Lion Heads, 8 In.	45.00
Pressed Glass, Atlanta, Goblet	13.50
Pressed Glass, Atlas, Celery, Flat	20.00
Pressed Glass, Atlas, Dish, Butter, Covered, Etched	20.00
Pressed Glass, Atlas, Goblet	25.00
Pressed Glass, Atlas, Goblet, Etched	24.00
Pressed Glass, Atlas, Spooner	17.50 To 18.50
Pressed Glass, Atlas, Tankard, Copper Wheel Engraving, Birds & Flowers	145.00
Pressed Glass, Atlas, Tumbler	20.00
Pressed Glass, Aurora, Pitcher, Water, Applied Handle	45.00
Pressed Glass, Aurora, Tray, Water, 11 In.	15.00
Pressed Glass, Aurora, Wine	15.50
Pressed Glass, Aurora, Wine, Etched Tulip	18.00
Pressed Glass, Austrian, Creamer, Amber	20.00
Pressed Glass, Austrian, Spooner, Clear With Gold	40.00
Pressed Glass, Austrian, Vase, 8 1/2 In.	27.00
Pressed Glass, Aztec, Wine	10.00
Pressed Glass, Baby Face, Knife Rest	55.00
Pressed Glass, Baby Lion, Celery, Cable Base	35.00
Baby Thumbprint, see Dakota	
Pressed Glass, Bakewell Block, Goblet, Flint	85.00
Balder, see also Pennsylvania	
Pressed Glass, Balder, Celery, Flat	12.00
Pressed Glass, Balder, Cup, Punch	15.00
Pressed Glass, Balder, Goblet	16.00
Pressed Glass, Balder, Sugar, Covered	20.00
Pressed Glass, Balder, Toothpick	65.00
Pressed Glass, Balder, Whiskey	8.00
Pressed Glass, Balder, Wine	12.00
Balky Mule, see Currier & Ives	
Pressed Glass, Ball & Swirl Band, Cake Stand	20.00
Pressed Glass, Ball & Swirl, Compote, Open, Etched, 8 1/4 X 7 In.	25.00
Pressed Glass, Ball & Swirl, Creamer	22.50
Pressed Glass, Ball & Swirl, Goblet	28.50
Pressed Glass, Ball & Swirl, Pitcher, Tankard, Etched	25.00
Pressed Glass, Ball & Swirl, Sauce, Footed	8.50
Pressed Glass, Ball & Swirl, Spooner	16.00
Pressed Glass, Ball & Swirl, Spooner, Etched	29.00
Pressed Glass, Ball & Swirl, Tankard, Pitcher, Water	47.50

Pressed Glass, Ball & Swirl, Wine	7.50
Pressed Glass, Balloon, Goblet, Footed, Amber, 5 In.	16.50
Pressed Glass, Baltimore Pear, Butter, Covered	35.00
Pressed Glass, Baltimore Pear, Compote, Open, 6 In.	45.00
Pressed Glass, Baltimore Pear, Jar, Jam, Lid	30.00
Pressed Glass, Band, Goblet, Etched	12.00

Banded Beaded Grape Medallion, see Beaded Grape Medallion, Banded

Pressed Glass, Banded Buckle, Sauce, Flint	20.00
Pressed Glass, Banded Buckle, Spooner	16.00 To 28.50
Pressed Glass, Banded Buckle, Sugar	15.00
Pressed Glass, Banded Buckle, Tumbler	32.50
Pressed Glass, Banded Buckle, Wine	24.50 To 26.00

Banded Portland when flashed with pink is sometimes called Maiden Blush

Pressed Glass, Banded Portland, Bottle, Cologne, Original Stopper, 10 In.	55.00
Pressed Glass, Banded Portland, Butter Pat	12.00
Pressed Glass, Banded Portland, Celery	27.00
Pressed Glass, Banded Portland, Claret, 5 In.	35.00
Pressed Glass, Banded Portland, Compote, Petal Cover	90.00
Pressed Glass, Banded Portland, Dish, Pickle, 8 1/2 X 4 In.	30.00
Pressed Glass, Banded Portland, Dish, Relish	30.00 To 31.50
Pressed Glass, Banded Portland, Goblet	28.00
Pressed Glass, Banded Portland, Goblet, Frosted	24.00
Pressed Glass, Banded Portland, Goblet, Gold	29.00
Pressed Glass, Banded Portland, Jar, Pomade, Covered	25.00
Pressed Glass, Banded Portland, Syrup, Covered	50.00
Pressed Glass, Banded Portland, Syrup, Dated 1872	58.00
Pressed Glass, Banded Portland, Tankard	80.00
Pressed Glass, Banded Portland, Toothpick	15.00
Pressed Glass, Banded Portland, Toothpick, Gold	16.50
Pressed Glass, Banded Portland, Tumbler	35.00
Pressed Glass, Banded Portland, Vase, 8 In.	22.50
Pressed Glass, Banded Portland, Wine	34.00

Banded Raindrop, see Candlewick

Pressed Glass, Banded Star, Creamer, Footed	30.00
Pressed Glass, Banded Star, Dish, Covered, Footed	20.00
Pressed Glass, Banded Star, Pitcher, Water	45.00

Other "Banded" patterns, see under name of basic pattern; e.g.: Banded Honeycomb, see Honeycomb, Banded

Pressed Glass, Bar & Block, Tankard, Milk	36.50

Bar & Diamond, see Kokomo

Pressed Glass, Bar & Flute, Creamer, Ruby Stained	55.00
Pressed Glass, Bar & Swirl, Bread Plate	15.00
Pressed Glass, Bar Waffle, Goblet	10.00
Pressed Glass, Barberry, Celery	21.50 To 24.50
Pressed Glass, Barberry, Eggcup	22.50
Pressed Glass, Barberry, Goblet	16.50 To 19.00
Pressed Glass, Barberry, Pitcher, Water	55.00 To 58.50
Pressed Glass, Barberry, Pitcher, Water, Applied Handle	65.00
Pressed Glass, Barberry, Plate, 6 In.	18.00 To 22.00
Pressed Glass, Barberry, Salt, Master, Oval Berries, Footed	25.00
Pressed Glass, Barberry, Sauce, Footed	8.00
Pressed Glass, Barberry, Sauce, Footed, 4 In.	10.00
Pressed Glass, Barberry, Spooner	18.50
Pressed Glass, Barberry, Sugar, Covered	38.00

Barley & Oats, see Wheat & Barley
Barley & Wheat, see Wheat & Barley

Pressed Glass, Barley, Bread Plate	20.00 To 41.00
Pressed Glass, Barley, Cake Stand	25.00
Pressed Glass, Barley, Celery, Pedestal	30.00
Pressed Glass, Barley, Compote, Covered, 8 1/2 In.	45.00
Pressed Glass, Barley, Creamer	22.00
Pressed Glass, Barley, Goblet	15.00 To 26.00
Pressed Glass, Barley, Jar, Jam, Covered	25.00
Pressed Glass, Barley, Pitcher, Water	26.00 To 45.00

Pressed Glass, Barley, Sauce, Flat	8.50
Pressed Glass, Barley, Spooner	16.00
Pressed Glass, Barley, Wine	12.00 To 18.00
Pressed Glass, Barred Forget-Me-Not, Goblet	19.00
Pressed Glass, Barred Forget-Me-Not, Plate, Bread	25.00
Pressed Glass, Barred Forget-Me-Not, Wine	19.00
Barred Ovals, see Banded Portland	
Pressed Glass, Barred Star, Pitcher, Water	25.00
Pressed Glass, Barrel Argus, Goblet, Flint	30.00
Pressed Glass, Barrel Ashburton, Goblet, Flint	30.00
Pressed Glass, Barrel Excelsior, Celery	55.00
Pressed Glass, Barrel Excelsior, Goblet, Flint	35.00
Pressed Glass, Barrel Huber, Goblet, Flint	15.00
Barreled Block, see Red Block	
Bartlett Pear, see Pear	
Pressed Glass, Basket Weave, Basket, Handled, Blue	24.50
Pressed Glass, Basket Weave, Goblet	12.50
Pressed Glass, Basket Weave, Pitcher, Milk, Blue, 7 In.	35.00
Pressed Glass, Basket Weave, Pitcher, Rose	18.00
Pressed Glass, Basket Weave, Pitcher, Water	15.00
Pressed Glass, Bead & Scroll, Salt	10.00
Pressed Glass, Beaded Acorn Medallion, Goblet	25.00
Pressed Glass, Beaded Acorn With Leaf Band, Spooner, Flint	45.00
Pressed Glass, Beaded Arch Panels, Creamer	13.00
Pressed Glass, Beaded Band, Compote, Covered, 11 In.	30.00
Pressed Glass, Beaded Band, Goblet	16.00 To 22.00
Pressed Glass, Beaded Band, Pitcher	40.00
Pressed Glass, Beaded Band, Sauce, Footed	10.00
Pressed Glass, Beaded Band, Sugar, Covered	28.50
Beaded Bull's-Eye & Drape, see also Alabama	
Pressed Glass, Beaded Circle, Compote, Jelly, Green	45.00
Pressed Glass, Beaded Circle, Jelly, Green, Decorated	40.00
Pressed Glass, Beaded Dart Band, Castor, Pickle, Silver Plate Frame	75.00
Pressed Glass, Beaded Dart Band, Goblet	18.00
Pressed Glass, Beaded Dewdrop, Cake Stand, 10 In.	32.00
Pressed Glass, Beaded Dewdrop, Celery	30.00
Pressed Glass, Beaded Dewdrop, Dish, Square, 4 1/4 X 1 1/2 In.	6.50
Pressed Glass, Beaded Dewdrop, Master Salt	21.00
Pressed Glass, Beaded Dewdrop, Pitcher, Water	52.00
Pressed Glass, Beaded Dewdrop, Plate, 7 In.Square	22.50
Pressed Glass, Beaded Dewdrop, Sauce, Flat	6.50
Pressed Glass, Beaded Dewdrop, Spooner	16.00
Pressed Glass, Beaded Dewdrop, Sugar Shaker	45.00
Pressed Glass, Beaded Dewdrop, Toothpick, 3 Legged	25.00
Pressed Glass, Beaded Dewdrop, Tray, Pickle, 5 X 10 In.	22.00
Pressed Glass, Beaded Dewdrop, Wine	45.00
Pressed Glass, Beaded Ellipse, Creamer	20.00
Pressed Glass, Beaded Ellipse, Pitcher, Water	23.00
Pressed Glass, Beaded Fine Cut, Pitcher, Water	31.50
Pressed Glass, Beaded Finecut, Pitcher, Water	31.50
Pressed Glass, Beaded Finecut, Sugar & Creamer	30.00
Pressed Glass, Beaded Frog's Eye, Goblet	17.00
Pressed Glass, Beaded Grape Medallion, Eggcup	22.50 To 25.00
Pressed Glass, Beaded Grape Medallion, Eggcup, Banded	17.00
Pressed Glass, Beaded Grape Medallion, Goblet	16.50 To 28.50
Pressed Glass, Beaded Grape Medallion, Spooner	18.00 To 22.00
Pressed Glass, Beaded Grape, Butter, Emerald, Covered	62.00
Pressed Glass, Beaded Grape, Celery	18.00
Pressed Glass, Beaded Grape, Cruet	25.00
Pressed Glass, Beaded Grape, Dish, Square, Green, 8 1/4 In.	30.00
Pressed Glass, Beaded Grape, Pitcher, Water, Green	85.00
Pressed Glass, Beaded Grape, Table Set, Green, Gold, 4 Piece	335.00
Pressed Glass, Beaded Grape, Toothpick, Green	50.00
Pressed Glass, Beaded Grape, Tumbler, Green	13.50
Pressed Glass, Beaded Grape, Water Set, Green, Round Pitcher, 7 Piece	225.00
Pressed Glass, Beaded Grape, Water Set, Green, 7 Piece	195.00

Pressed Glass, Beaded Grape, Wine	14.00
Pressed Glass, Beaded Heart, Cruet, Original Stopper	45.00
Pressed Glass, Beaded Loop, Berry Set, 5 Piece	40.00
Pressed Glass, Beaded Loop, Cake Stand, Oregon, 8 3/4 In.	22.75
Pressed Glass, Beaded Loop, Cake Stand, 9 1/4 In.	24.50
Pressed Glass, Beaded Loop, Dish, Pickle, 7 1/4 In.	9.00
Pressed Glass, Beaded Loop, Dish, Relish, Flat Oval, Clear, 4 1/2 X 9 In.	10.00
Pressed Glass, Beaded Loop, Goblet	32.00
Beaded Medallion, see Beaded Mirror	
Pressed Glass, Beaded Mirror, Goblet	18.00
Pressed Glass, Beaded Mirror, Salt	15.00
Pressed Glass, Beaded Mirror, Spooner	16.00
Pressed Glass, Beaded Mirror, Spooner, Boston & Sandwich Co., 5 1/2 In.	25.00
Pressed Glass, Beaded Mirror, Spooner, Flint	20.00
Pressed Glass, Beaded Mirror, Sugar, Open	20.00
Pressed Glass, Beaded Oval & Scroll, Berry Set, 9 Piece	100.00
Pressed Glass, Beaded Oval & Scroll, Creamer	16.50
Pressed Glass, Beaded Oval & Scroll, Goblet	7.50
Pressed Glass, Beaded Panel, Compote, Open	35.00
Pressed Glass, Beaded Panel, Tumbler, Water	14.50
Pressed Glass, Beaded Swag, Tumbler, Ruby	45.00
Pressed Glass, Beaded Swirl & Disc, Bowl, 8 1/2 In.	20.00
Pressed Glass, Beaded Swirl & Disc, Creamer	8.00
Pressed Glass, Beaded Swirl & Disc, Pitcher, Water	18.00
Pressed Glass, Beaded Swirl & Disc, Spooner, 6 In.	24.00
Pressed Glass, Beaded Swirl & Dot, Creamer, Clear	28.00
Pressed Glass, Beaded Swirl, Berry Bowl, Green	27.50
Pressed Glass, Beaded Swirl, Butter, Covered, Green With Gold	70.00
Pressed Glass, Beaded Swirl, Tumbler, Ruby Stained	24.00
Pressed Glass, Beaded Swirl, Water Set, Green With Gold, 7 Piece	225.00
Pressed Glass, Beaded Tulip, Butter, Covered	42.00 To 42.50
Pressed Glass, Beaded Tulip, Compote, Scalloped, 8 1/4 Diameter	35.00
Pressed Glass, Beaded Tulip, Creamer	25.00
Pressed Glass, Beaded Tulip, Goblet, Pair	30.00
Pressed Glass, Beaded Tulip, Pitcher, Milk	45.00
Pressed Glass, Beaded Tulip, Pitcher, Water	42.50 To 43.00
Bearded Man, see Viking	
Pressed Glass, Beatrice, Goblet	8.00
Pressed Glass, Beatty Rib, Celery, Opalescent	32.50
Pressed Glass, Beatty Rib, Creamer, Clear To Opalescent, 3 In.	25.00
Pressed Glass, Beatty Rib, Pitcher, Water	29.50
Pressed Glass, Beatty Rib, Toothpick	25.00
Pressed Glass, Beautiful Lady, Cake Stand, 6 In. Diameter	25.00
Pressed Glass, Beehive, Bread Plate	65.00
Pressed Glass, Beehive, Goblet	20.00
Pressed Glass, Beehive, Plate, Sandwich, Octagonal, Flint, 9 1/4 In. Diameter	165.00
Pressed Glass, Beehive, Salt, Marigold, Lid	18.00
Pressed Glass, Beetle Band, Creamer	35.00
Pressed Glass, Bella Donna, Sugar, Covered, Green & Gold	25.00
Pressed Glass, Bellflower, Castor Set	165.00
Pressed Glass, Bellflower, Celery, Flint	125.00
Pressed Glass, Bellflower, Celery, Scalloped Rim, Ribs To Top, Flint	140.00
Pressed Glass, Bellflower, Compote	45.00
Pressed Glass, Bellflower, Compote, Covered, 6 In.	20.00
Pressed Glass, Bellflower, Compote, Inverted Bowl Base, 8 X 5 In.	40.00
Pressed Glass, Bellflower, Compote, Scalloped Edge, Coarse Rib, 8 X 5 In.	40.00
Pressed Glass, Bellflower, Compote, Single Vine, Coarse Rib, Scalloped, Footed	52.00
Pressed Glass, Bellflower, Compote, 8 1/2 In.	24.00
Pressed Glass, Bellflower, Cordial, Knob Stem	55.00
Pressed Glass, Bellflower, Double Vine, Bread Plate	10.00
Pressed Glass, Bellflower, Eggcup	15.00 To 25.00
Pressed Glass, Bellflower, Eggcup, Flint	22.00 To 30.00
Pressed Glass, Bellflower, Goblet	25.00 To 45.00
Pressed Glass, Bellflower, Goblet, Cut, Flint	250.00
Pressed Glass, Bellflower, Goblet, Flint	30.00
Pressed Glass, Bellflower, Goblet, Knob Stem, Flint	40.00

Pressed Glass, Bellflower, Honey	10.00
Pressed Glass, Bellflower, Honey, Scalloped Rim, Flint	12.50
Pressed Glass, Bellflower, Mug, Child's	25.00
Pressed Glass, Bellflower, Pitcher, Buttermilk	45.00
Pressed Glass, Bellflower, Pitcher, Syrup, 10 Panel, Tin Lid	350.00
Pressed Glass, Bellflower, Pitcher, Water, Applied Handle	185.00
Pressed Glass, Bellflower, Pitcher, Water, Flint	200.00
Pressed Glass, Bellflower, Plate, 6 In.	60.00
Pressed Glass, Bellflower, Salt	22.00
Pressed Glass, Bellflower, Sauce	7.00
Pressed Glass, Bellflower, Spooner, Flint	24.50 To 25.00
Pressed Glass, Bellflower, Sugar	20.00 To 23.00
Pressed Glass, Bellflower, Sugar, Double Vine, Single Vine Cover, Flint	70.00
Pressed Glass, Bellflower, Tumbler	55.00 To 65.00
Pressed Glass, Bellflower, Tumbler, Coarse Rib, Flint	75.00
Pressed Glass, Bellflower, Tumbler, Cut Double Vine, Flint	145.00
Pressed Glass, Bellflower, Tumbler, Flint	75.00
Pressed Glass, Bellflower, Wine, Single Vine, Flint, Rayed Base	65.00
Pressed Glass, Belltone, Goblet, Flint	32.00
Pressed Glass, Belmont, Dish, Butter, Amber	88.00
Pressed Glass, Belted Icicle, Goblet	21.00
Belted Worcester, see Worcester, Belted	
Bent Buckle, see New Hampshire	
Berkeley, see Blocked Arches	
Pressed Glass, Berry Cluster, Creamer	13.00 To 16.00
Pressed Glass, Bethlehem Star, Cruet, Clear, Opalescent	21.00
Pressed Glass, Beveled Diamond & Star, Dish, Cheese	37.50
Pressed Glass, Beveled Diamond & Star, Wine	11.00
Pressed Glass, Beveled Star, Bowl, 9 In.	27.50
Pressed Glass, Beveled Star, Creamer, Green	45.00
Pressed Glass, Beveled Star, Jelly, Green	34.00
Pressed Glass, Beveled Star, Spooner, Green	32.50
Pressed Glass, Bible, Bread Plate	35.00
Pressed Glass, Bible, Toothpick	22.00
Big Block, see Henrietta	
Pressed Glass, Bigler, Decanter, Flint, Quart	30.00
Pressed Glass, Bigler, Goblet	25.00
Pressed Glass, Bigler, Goblet, Flint	30.00
Pressed Glass, Birch Leaf, Glass, Buttermilk, Flint	30.00
Pressed Glass, Birch Leaf, Goblet	11.50 To 15.00
Pressed Glass, Bird & Harp, Mug	30.00
Pressed Glass, Bird & Strawberry, Bowl, Oval, Footed	48.00
Pressed Glass, Bird & Strawberry, Bowl, Paint, 9 1/2 In.	40.00
Pressed Glass, Bird & Strawberry, Bowl, Scalloped Top, 10 In.	37.50 To 45.00
Pressed Glass, Bird & Strawberry, Butter, Covered	65.00
Pressed Glass, Bird & Strawberry, Cake Stand	29.00 To 45.00
Pressed Glass, Bird & Strawberry, Candy Container, Heart Shaped	45.00
Pressed Glass, Bird & Strawberry, Celery	32.00 To 65.00
Pressed Glass, Bird & Strawberry, Compote, Covered, 5 1/2 In.	50.00
Pressed Glass, Bird & Strawberry, Compote, Covered, 6 1/2 In.	60.00
Pressed Glass, Bird & Strawberry, Compote, Scalloped Rim, 4 1/2 In.	23.00
Pressed Glass, Bird & Strawberry, Dish, Relish, Heart Shape	20.00
Pressed Glass, Bird & Strawberry, Pitcher, Water	110.00
Pressed Glass, Bird & Strawberry, Plate, 12 In.	65.00
Pressed Glass, Bird & Strawberry, Sauce, Footed	15.00
Pressed Glass, Bird & Strawberry, Sauce, Footed, Paint	17.00
Pressed Glass, Bird & Strawberry, Sauce, 3 Legged	22.50
Pressed Glass, Bird & Strawberry, Sugar, Covered	58.00
Pressed Glass, Bird & Strawberry, Tumbler	28.00 To 34.00
Pressed Glass, Bird & Strawberry, Tumbler, Clear	30.00
Pressed Glass, Bird & Strawberry, Tumbler, Paint	30.00
Pressed Glass, Bird & Strawberry, Water Set	350.00
Pressed Glass, Bird & Strawberry, Wine	28.00 To 32.00
Pressed Glass, Bird & Strawberry, Wine, Clear	42.00
Pressed Glass, Bird Basket, Toothpick, Amber	28.00
Pressed Glass, Bird, Etched, Goblet	30.00

Pressed Glass, Bird, Mug, Amber 28.00
Pressed Glass, Birds & Roses, Goblet, Etched 30.00
Pressed Glass, Birds & Wheat, Mug, Amber 35.00
Pressed Glass, Birds At Fountain, Compote, Pedestal, Covered, 8 In. 75.00
Pressed Glass, Birds At Fountain, Goblet .... 30.00 To 35.00
Pressed Glass, Birds In Swamp, Goblet 30.00
Pressed Glass, Bissing, Goblet 8.00
Pressed Glass, Blackberry Band, Goblet .... 19.50 To 30.00
Pressed Glass, Blackberry Band, Spooner 19.50
Pressed Glass, Blackberry Variant, Goblet 20.00
Pressed Glass, Blackberry, Goblet .... 16.00 To 35.00
Pressed Glass, Blackberry, Spooner, Clear 15.00
Pressed Glass, Bleeding Heart, Cake Stand, 10 In. 85.00
Pressed Glass, Bleeding Heart, Cake Stand, 9 1/2 In. .... 48.00 To 50.00
Pressed Glass, Bleeding Heart, Compote, Covered, 8 1/4 In. 65.00
Pressed Glass, Bleeding Heart, Goblet .... 28.00 To 30.00
Pressed Glass, Bleeding Heart, Goblet, Knob Stem .... 22.00 To 35.00
Pressed Glass, Bleeding Heart, Pitcher, Water, Applied Handle 126.00
Pressed Glass, Bleeding Heart, Plate, Cake, 9 In. 35.00
Pressed Glass, Bleeding Heart, Spooner .... 18.50 To 25.00
Pressed Glass, Bleeding Heart, Sugar, Covered, Heart Finial 29.50
Pressed Glass, Bleeding Heart, Tumbler, Footed 25.00
Pressed Glass, Block & Bar, Pitcher, Water, Flint 100.00
Pressed Glass, Block & Double Bar, Tumbler, Ruby Stained 28.00
Pressed Glass, Block & Fan, Butter, Covered 37.50
Pressed Glass, Block & Fan, Celery .... 12.50 To 22.00

Pressed Glass, Bleeding Heart, Goblet

Pressed Glass, Block & Fan, Cracker Jar, Covered 37.50
Pressed Glass, Block & Fan, Cruet .... 22.50 To 30.00
Pressed Glass, Block & Fan, Goblet .... 42.50 To 45.00
Pressed Glass, Block & Fan, Salt 12.00
Pressed Glass, Block & Fan, Sugar Shaker 30.00
Pressed Glass, Block & Fan, Sugar, Covered 30.00
Pressed Glass, Block & Fan, Wine 35.00
   Block & Finecut, see Finecut & Block
Pressed Glass, Block & Lattice, Pitcher, Water, 5 Tumblers, Amber 350.00
Pressed Glass, Block & Lattice, Sauce, Ruby Stained 22.50
Pressed Glass, Block & Pleat, Celery 25.50
Pressed Glass, Block & Plume, Spooner 20.00
Pressed Glass, Block & Spearpoint, Berry Bowl 14.00
   Block & Star, see Valencia Waffle
Pressed Glass, Block & Star Spearpoint, Goblet, Ruby & Clear 25.00
Pressed Glass, Block & Star, Tankard 39.75
Pressed Glass, Block Band, Wine, St.Mary's, Pa., Ruby 22.00
Pressed Glass, Block Optic, Bottle, Night, Green 15.00
   Block with Stars, see Hanover
Pressed Glass, Block, Creamer, Red, 3 In. 35.00
Pressed Glass, Block, Pitcher, Clear, Applied Handle 55.00
Pressed Glass, Block, Spooner, Ruby & Clear, 2 Handled 30.00
Pressed Glass, Block, Sugar, Open, Flint, 3 X 4 1/4 In. 7.00
Pressed Glass, Block, Tumbler 24.00
Pressed Glass, Block, Tumbler, Red 20.00
   Blockade, see Diamond Block with Fans

Pressed Glass, Broken Column, Goblet

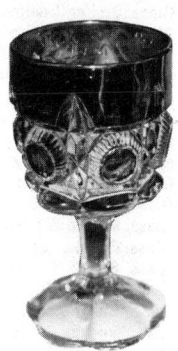

Pressed Glass, Buckle, Goblet

Pressed Glass, Bull's Eye & Daisy, Goblet

Pressed Glass, Bull's Eye & Diamond Point, Goblet, 7 In.

Pressed Glass, Blocked Arches, Cookie Jar, Lid, 8 1/2 In.	38.00
Blockhouse, see Hanover	
Bluebird, see Bird & Strawberry	
Pressed Glass, Boot, Toothpick, Wall Match, Blue	32.00
Pressed Glass, Bow Tie, Cake Stand, 9 In.	45.00
Pressed Glass, Bow Tie, Compote, Open	45.00
Pressed Glass, Bow Tie, Dish, 9 X 5 1/2 In.	32.00
Pressed Glass, Bow Tie, Spooner	18.00
Pressed Glass, Boxed Star, Pitcher, Water	22.50
Pressed Glass, Boy With Pack, Toothpick, Amber	42.00
Bradford Blackberry, see Bradford Grape	
Pressed Glass, Bradford Grape, Goblet, Flint	35.00
Pressed Glass, Bradford Grape, Tumbler, Flint	95.00
Pressed Glass, Braided Belt, Creamer	25.00
Pressed Glass, Branched Tree, Pitcher, Water	55.00
Pressed Glass, Brazen Shield, Tumbler, Blue	40.00
Pressed Glass, Brazilian, Jar, Cracker	35.00
Pressed Glass, Brazilian, Toothpick	18.50
Pressed Glass, Brazilian, Tumbler, Green	15.00
Pressed Glass, Bread Is The Staff Of Life, Bread Plate	32.50
Pressed Glass, Bridle Rosettes, Wine	22.00
Pressed Glass, Brilliant, Goblet, Flint	30.00
Pressed Glass, Brilliant, Spooner, Footed	32.50
Pressed Glass, Brilliant, Tumbler, Flint, 3 1/2 In.	40.00
Pressed Glass, Britannic, Banana Stand	52.00
Pressed Glass, Britannic, Compote	30.00
Pressed Glass, Britannic, Spooner	15.00
Pressed Glass, Britannic, Toothpick	14.00
Pressed Glass, Broken Arch, Cup, Punch	30.00
Pressed Glass, Broken Column, Castor, Pickle, Ruby Glass	175.00
Pressed Glass, Broken Column, Celery	12.50 To 23.00
Pressed Glass, Broken Column, Compote, Covered, Square	45.00
Pressed Glass, Broken Column, Compote, Covered, 5 3/4 X 10 1/2 In.	42.00
Pressed Glass, Broken Column, Dish, Gold Flashed, 5 1/2 X 4 In.	24.50
Pressed Glass, Broken Column, Goblet	35.00
Pressed Glass, Broken Column, Jar, Cracker	52.50
Pressed Glass, Broken Column, Mug, Gold Rim, Blue	45.00
Pressed Glass, Broken Column, Pitcher, Syrup, Dated, January 29, 1884	49.50
Pressed Glass, Broken Column, Spooner	16.50 To 27.00

Pressed Glass, Broken Column, Table Set, Sugar, Creamer, Spooner, Cruet 125.00
Pressed Glass, Broken Column, Tumbler 22.50
Pressed Glass, Brooklyn, Goblet, Flint 45.00
Pressed Glass, Broughton, Berry Set, Child's 65.00
Pressed Glass, Broughton, Creamer, 4 3/4 In. 12.50
Pressed Glass, Broughton, Pitcher, Water, Gold Top, Child's 18.00
Pressed Glass, Broughton, Water Set, Pitcher & 5 Glasses, Child's 58.00
    Bryce, see Ribbon Candy
Pressed Glass, Bubble Lattice, Syrup, Blue 135.00
Pressed Glass, Buckle & Star, Celery .... 18.00 To 22.00
Pressed Glass, Buckle & Star, Creamer 16.50
Pressed Glass, Buckle, Eggcup, Flint 22.00
Pressed Glass, Buckle, Goblet 30.00
Pressed Glass, Buckle, Goblet, Flint .... 23.00 To 32.00
Pressed Glass, Buckle, Sugar, Covered, Flint 35.00
Pressed Glass, Buckle, Sugar, Open, Flint 22.50
Pressed Glass, Buckle, Tumbler 27.50
Pressed Glass, Budded Ivy, Creamer 30.00
Pressed Glass, Budded Ivy, Goblet 25.00
Pressed Glass, Budded Ivy, Spooner .... 20.00 To 22.00
Pressed Glass, Bull's-Eye & Arch, Decanter, Neck-Ring, Flint, Quart 50.00
Pressed Glass, Bull's-Eye & Broken Column, Goblet, Flint 35.00
Pressed Glass, Bull's-Eye & Daisy, Creamer, Cranberry Eyes 30.00
Pressed Glass, Bull's-Eye & Daisy, Goblet 22.00
Pressed Glass, Bull's-Eye & Daisy, Goblet, Cranberry Eyes 23.00
Pressed Glass, Bull's-Eye & Daisy, Goblet, Green Eyes, Gold Trim .... 19.00 To 20.00
Pressed Glass, Bull's-Eye & Daisy, Pitcher, 5 Tumblers, Gold Eyes 185.00
Pressed Glass, Bull's-Eye & Daisy, Sauce, Gold Eyes 7.00
Pressed Glass, Bull's-Eye & Daisy, Spooner, Green Eyes, Gold Trim 15.00
Pressed Glass, Bull's-Eye & Daisy, Tumbler, Green 12.00
Pressed Glass, Bull's-Eye & Diamond Panels, Goblet .... 10.00 To 15.00
Pressed Glass, Bull's-Eye & Diamond Point, Celery, Flint 125.00
Pressed Glass, Bull's-Eye & Diamond Point, Compote, Covered, Frosted 85.00
Pressed Glass, Bull's-Eye & Diamond Point, Dish, Sauce, Flint, 4 1/2 In. 16.00
Pressed Glass, Bull's-Eye & Diamond Point, Goblet, Flint .... 60.00 To 100.00
Pressed Glass, Bull's-Eye & Diamond Point, Tumbler, Water, Flint 125.00
Pressed Glass, Bull's-Eye & Drape, Sugar, Open, Flint 32.00
    Bull's-Eye & Fan, see Daisies in Oval Panels
Pressed Glass, Bull's-Eye & Oval Panels, Creamer, Purple Eyes 17.00
Pressed Glass, Bull's-Eye & Oval Panels, Tumbler, Purple Eyes 14.00
Pressed Glass, Bull's-Eye & Prism, Goblet, Knob Stem, Flint 90.00
Pressed Glass, Bull's-Eye & Spearhead, Decanter 18.00
Pressed Glass, Bull's-Eye & Wishbone, Goblet, Flint 150.00
    Bull's-Eye Band, see Reverse Torpedo
Pressed Glass, Bull's-Eye With Fleur-De-Lis, Celery, Flint 150.00
Pressed Glass, Bull's-Eye With Fleur-De-Lis, Goblet, Flint .... 65.00 To 75.00
Pressed Glass, Bull's-Eye With Fleur-De-Lis, Pitcher, Water, Flint 250.00
Pressed Glass, Bull's-Eye, Bottle, Perfume, Stopper, 7 In. 32.00
Pressed Glass, Bull's-Eye, Butter, Covered, Findlay 37.50
Pressed Glass, Bull's-Eye, Decanter, Bar Lip, Flint, Quart 110.00
Pressed Glass, Bull's-Eye, Decanter, Bar Lip, Quart 110.00
Pressed Glass, Bull's-Eye, Decanter, Stopper, Flint, Pint 42.50

Pressed Glass, Cable With Rings,
Bowl, Footed

Pressed Glass, Cabbage Rose, Mug

Pressed Glass, Bull's-Eye, Dish, Relish, Clear, Gold Wash, 2 X 4 In.Diam.	10.00
Pressed Glass, Bull's-Eye, Eggcup, Flint	38.50
Pressed Glass, Bull's-Eye, Goblet	65.00
Pressed Glass, Bull's-Eye, Goblet, Amethyst Eyes, Gold Trim	22.00
Pressed Glass, Bull's-Eye, Goblet, Flint	50.00 To 65.00
Pressed Glass, Bull's-Eye, Spooner	10.00
Pressed Glass, Bull's-Eye, Spooner, Flint	30.00
Pressed Glass, Bull's-Eye, Tumbler, Flint	110.00
Bull's-Eye Variant, see Texas Bull's-Eye	
Pressed Glass, Bullet Emblem, Butter, Covered	240.00
Pressed Glass, Bullet Emblem, Spooner	95.00
Pressed Glass, Bullet Emblem, Sugar Open	95.00
Pressed Glass, Bunker Hill, Bread Plate	45.00
Pressed Glass, Butterfly & Spray, Mug, Amber	28.00
Pressed Glass, Butterfly, Mug	20.00
Pressed Glass, Butterfly, Salt, Marigold, Lid	24.00
Pressed Glass, Button Arches, Creamer, Frosted Band, Ruby Stained	45.00
Pressed Glass, Button Arches, Creamer, Ruby Stained, Kentucky Fair, 1933	35.00
Pressed Glass, Button Arches, Glass, Souvenir, 1903	20.00
Pressed Glass, Button Arches, Mug, Applied Handle, Ruby	32.50
Pressed Glass, Button Arches, Pitcher, Tankard, Gold Leaf Band, 11 In.	42.50
Pressed Glass, Button Arches, Pitcher, Tankard, Ruby, 12 In.	75.00
Pressed Glass, Button Arches, Spooner, Frosted Band, Ruby Stained	35.00
Pressed Glass, Button Arches, Sugar, Frosted Band, Ruby Stained	58.00
Pressed Glass, Button Arches, Toothpick, Clear With Gold	12.00
Pressed Glass, Button Arches, Water Set, Frosted Band, Ruby Stain, 7 Piece	225.00
Pressed Glass, Button Arches, Wine, Ruby	25.00
Pressed Glass, Button Band, Celery, Etched	27.00
Pressed Glass, Button Band, Compote, Covered, 7 In.	45.00
Pressed Glass, Button Panel, Salt & Pepper, Original Top, Pair	37.50
Pressed Glass, Buttons & Bows, Goblet	24.00
Pressed Glass, Cabbage Leaf, Pitcher, Water, Frosted	80.00
Pressed Glass, Cabbage Rose, Bowl, Amber, Hexagonal Pedestal, 11 X 7 1/2 In.	65.00
Pressed Glass, Cabbage Rose, Butter, Pink	25.00
Pressed Glass, Cabbage Rose, Champagne	22.00
Pressed Glass, Cabbage Rose, Compote, Covered, 7 In.	62.00
Pressed Glass, Cabbage Rose, Goblet	34.50
Pressed Glass, Cabbage Rose, Spooner	30.00
Pressed Glass, Cable With Ring, Sauce	7.00
Pressed Glass, Cable With Ring, Sugar, Covered, Flint	75.00 To 90.00
Pressed Glass, Cable, Butter, Covered	74.00
Pressed Glass, Cable, Celery, Flint	95.00
Pressed Glass, Cable, Compote, Flint, 8 1/4 In.	45.00
Pressed Glass, Cable, Compote, Open, Flint, Low Standard, 7 In.	25.00
Pressed Glass, Cable, Decanter, Cable Stopper, Flint, 1 Quart	65.00
Pressed Glass, Cable, Decanter, Cable Stopper, Quart	225.00
Pressed Glass, Cable, Eggcup, Flint	35.00
Pressed Glass, Cable, Goblet	52.00 To 55.00
Pressed Glass, Cable, Goblet, Flint	50.00 To 55.00
Pressed Glass, Cable, Lamp, Whale Oil, Flint, 7 1/2 In.	100.00
Pressed Glass, Cable, Salt, Master, Footed, Flint	30.00
Pressed Glass, Cable, Sauce, Flat, Flint, 3 1/2 In.	9.00
Pressed Glass, Cable, Spooner	28.00
Pressed Glass, Cable, Spooner, Flint	29.50
Pressed Glass, Cable, Sugar & Creamer, Flint	140.00
California, see Beaded Grape	
Pressed Glass, California Beaded Grape, Pitcher, Water, Green, Gold	95.00
Canadian Drape, see Garfield Drape	
Pressed Glass, Canadian Leaf, Pitcher, Water	24.00
Pressed Glass, Canadian, Bread Plate	28.00
Pressed Glass, Canadian, Compote, Covered, 10 In.	65.00
Pressed Glass, Canadian, Compote, Open, 6 X 7 In.	38.00
Pressed Glass, Canadian, Compote, Open, 6 1/4 In.	25.00
Pressed Glass, Canadian, Creamer	35.00
Pressed Glass, Canadian, Goblet	26.00 To 30.00
Pressed Glass, Canadian, Honey	10.50

Pressed Glass, Cable, Spooner

Pressed Glass, Canadian, Compote, Covered

Pressed Glass, Cathedral, Compote

Pressed Glass, Ceres, Bowl, Covered

Pressed Glass, Chain & Shield, Pitcher

Pressed Glass, Chicken, Jar, Mustard, Frosted, Covered

Pressed Glass, Canadian, Plate, Scene In Extended Handles, 7 In.	32.5
Pressed Glass, Canadian, Plate, 8 In.	23.0
Pressed Glass, Canadian, Sauce, Footed	12.0
Pressed Glass, Canadian, Sugar, Open	20.0
Pressed Glass, Canadian, Wine	22.50 To 35.0
Pressed Glass, Candian, Goblet	22.50 To 30.0
Pressed Glass, Candlewick, Cup & Saucer	20.0
Candy Ribbon, see Ribbon Candy	
Pressed Glass, Cane & Star Medallion, Goblet	15.0
Pressed Glass, Cane, Dish, Cheese, Underplate, 8 1/2 In.	425.0
Pressed Glass, Cane, Goblet	17.0
Pressed Glass, Cane, Goblet, Amber	25.00 To 28.0
Pressed Glass, Cane, Goblet, Green	35.0
Pressed Glass, Cane, Pitcher, Water	29.5
Pressed Glass, Cane, Pitcher, Water, Blue	50.0
Pressed Glass, Cane, Plate, Toddy, Amber	13.0

Pressed Glass, **Cane**, Plate, Toddy, Amber, Pair	15.00
Pressed Glass, **Cane**, Plate, Toddy, Green	16.00
Pressed Glass, **Cannonball**, Butter, Covered, Etched Tulips	28.00
Pressed Glass, **Cannonball**, Pitcher, Water, Etched Tulips	35.00
Pressed Glass, **Cape Cod**, Compote, Covered, 7 In.	68.00
Pressed Glass, **Cape Cod**, Goblet	29.50
Pressed Glass, **Cape Cod**, Mug, 2 In.	28.50
Pressed Glass, **Cape Cod**, Pitcher, Water	55.00
Pressed Glass, **Capitol Building**, Goblet	20.00 To 25.00
Pressed Glass, **Cardinal Bird**, Butter, Covered	50.00
Pressed Glass, **Cardinal Bird**, Creamer	27.50 To 37.50
Pressed Glass, **Cardinal Bird**, Goblet	23.00 To 32.50
Pressed Glass, **Cardinal Bird**, Sauce, Flat, 4 In.	12.00
Pressed Glass, **Cardinal Bird**, Sauce, Footed, 4 In.	14.00
Pressed Glass, **Cardinal Bird**, Sauce, Footed, 4 1/2 In.	15.00
Pressed Glass, **Cardinal Bird**, Spooner	22.50 To 28.00
Pressed Glass, **Cardinal Bird**, Sugar, Covered	40.00
Pressed Glass, **Cardinal**, Creamer	35.00
Pressed Glass, **Cardinal**, Goblet	22.00 To 32.00
Pressed Glass, **Carolina**, Pitcher, Water, 8 1/2 In.	9.00
Pressed Glass, **Cat's-Eye**, Goblet	16.00
Pressed Glass, **Cathedral**, Berry Bowl, Blue	30.00
Pressed Glass, **Cathedral**, Butter, Covered	60.00
Pressed Glass, **Cathedral**, Creamer	24.00
Pressed Glass, **Cathedral**, Sauce, Footed	9.50
Pressed Glass, **Cathedral**, Spooner	21.00 To 23.00
Pressed Glass, **Cathedral**, Sugar, Covered	29.50
Centennial, see also Liberty Bell, Washington Centennial	
Pressed Glass, **Centennial Stippled Star**, Goblet	35.00
Pressed Glass, **Centennial**, Sauce, Footed, Frosted Eagle, C.1876	25.00
Pressed Glass, **Centennial**, Shoe, Frosted, Gillinder	30.00
Pressed Glass, **Ceres**, Creamer	27.50
Pressed Glass, **Chain & Shield**, Bread Plate	32.00
Pressed Glass, **Chain & Shield**, Bread Plate, 12 X 8 1/2 In.	30.00
Pressed Glass, **Chain & Shield**, Creamer	10.50
Pressed Glass, **Chain & Shield**, Goblet	25.00
Pressed Glass, **Chain & Shield**, Pitcher, Water	23.00 To 40.00
Pressed Glass, **Chain Thumbprints**, Pitcher, Water	17.00
Chain with Diamonds, see Washington Centennial	
Pressed Glass, **Chain With Star**, Goblet	17.50
Pressed Glass, **Chain With Star**, Plate, 7 1/2 In.	15.00
Pressed Glass, **Chain**, Butter, Covered	32.00
Pressed Glass, **Chain**, Goblet	12.50 To 18.00
Pressed Glass, **Chain**, Relish, Stippled	12.50
Pressed Glass, **Chain**, Spooner	12.00
Pressed Glass, **Chain**, Wine	28.00
Pressed Glass, **Challinor Forget-Me-Not**, Cruet, Pink, Opaque	50.00
Pressed Glass, **Challinor Forget-Me-Not**, Sugar Shaker, Blue	85.00
Pressed Glass, **Champion**, Toothpick	18.00
Pressed Glass, **Champion**, Toothpick, Clear	12.00
Chandelier, see also Crown Jewels	
Pressed Glass, **Chandelier**, Cake Stand, 10 In.	45.00
Pressed Glass, **Chandelier**, Creamer	30.00
Pressed Glass, **Chandelier**, Goblet	45.00
Pressed Glass, **Chandelier**, Tankard	96.50
Pressed Glass, **Checkerboard**, Pitcher, Milk, Clear	20.00
Pressed Glass, **Checkerboard**, Tumbler	7.50 To 9.00
Pressed Glass, **Cherry & Cable**, Pitcher, Water	100.00
Pressed Glass, **Cherry & Fig**, Pitcher, Milk	25.00 To 48.00
Pressed Glass, **Cherry Lattice**, Pitcher, Water, Gold	110.00
Pressed Glass, **Cherry With Thumbprint**, Spooner, Double Handles, 5 1/2 In.	32.50
Pressed Glass, **Cherry**, Goblet	22.50
Pressed Glass, **Chickens Coming Out Of Shell**, Cup, Stem Is Leg Of Chicken	22.00
Pressed Glass, **Chilson**, Goblet, Flint	125.00 To 145.00
Pressed Glass, **Choked Ashburton**, Goblet, Flint	30.00
Pressed Glass, **Christmas Snowflake**, Pitcher, Lemonade, Applied Handle	150.00

Pressed Glass, Chrysanthemum Leaf, Celery 17.00
Pressed Glass, Chrysanthemum Leaf, Cruet 35.00
Pressed Glass, Chrysanthemum Leaf, Pitcher, Water 30.00
Pressed Glass, Chrysanthemum Leaf, Toothpick 35.00
Pressed Glass, Chrysanthemum Sprig, Tumbler 55.00
Pressed Glass, Chrysanthemum, Cruet, Clear, Satin Finish 150.00
Pressed Glass, Circled Scroll, Spooner, Blue, Opalescent 88.00
Pressed Glass, Classic Medallion, Spooner 16.00
Pressed Glass, Classic Warrior, Bread Plate 100.00
Pressed Glass, Classic, Butter, Covered 190.00
Pressed Glass, Classic, Butter, Covered, Open Feet, 7 1/2 In. 265.00
Pressed Glass, Classic, Celery 125.00
Pressed Glass, Classic, Celery, Collared Base 175.00
Pressed Glass, Classic, Celery, Collared Base, Clear 150.00
Pressed Glass, Classic, Celery, Open Log Feet 195.00
Pressed Glass, Classic, Compote, Open, 8 In. 120.00
Pressed Glass, Classic, Creamer 95.00
Pressed Glass, Classic, Creamer, Log Feet .... 145.00 To 195.00
Pressed Glass, Classic, Goblet .... 165.00 To 185.00
Pressed Glass, Classic, Goblet, Log Feet 185.00
Pressed Glass, Classic, Pitcher, Water 275.00
Pressed Glass, Classic, Pitcher, Water, Collared Base 275.00
Pressed Glass, Classic, Pitcher, Water, Log Feet 275.00
Pressed Glass, Classic, Pitcher, Water, Log Feet, Frosted Panels 245.00
Pressed Glass, Classic, Pitcher, Water, Open Foot, 10 In. 245.00
Pressed Glass, Classic, Plate, Campaign, 1884, 10 1/2 In. 950.00
Pressed Glass, Classic, Plate, Hendricks 225.00
Pressed Glass, Classic, Spooner .... 72.00 To 95.00
Pressed Glass, Classic, Spooner, Log Feet 110.00
Pressed Glass, Classic, Spooner, Open Feet 95.00
Pressed Glass, Classic, Sugar, Covered 170.00
Pressed Glass, Classic, Sugar, Log Feet 95.00
Pressed Glass, Classic, Sugar, Open 80.00
Pressed Glass, Classic, Sugar, Open, Log Feet 65.00
Pressed Glass, Clear Block, Berry Set, 7 Piece 40.00
Pressed Glass, Clear Block, Goblet 12.50
Pressed Glass, Clear Block, Sugar, Covered 24.50
Pressed Glass, Clear Panels With Cord Band, Goblet 11.50
Pressed Glass, Clear Ribbon, Compote, Covered, Etched, 8 In. 45.00
Pressed Glass, Cleat, Decanter, Flint 35.00
Pressed Glass, Cleat, Pitcher, Water, Flint 150.00
Pressed Glass, Clematis, Goblet, Buttermilk 18.00
Pressed Glass, Cleopatra, Bread Plate 50.00
Pressed Glass, Cleopatra, Platter, Bread 50.00
Pressed Glass, Cleveland-Hendricks, Tray 250.00
Pressed Glass, Clio, Pitcher, Water, 8 1/2 In. 25.00
Pressed Glass, Coachman's Cape, Wine 18.00
Pressed Glass, Coarse Diamond Point, Goblet 8.00
Pressed Glass, Coat Of Mail, Sugar Shaker 9.50
Coin Spot, see Coin Spot Category
Pressed Glass, Colonial, Celery, Hexagonal, Flint 40.00
Pressed Glass, Colonial, Goblet, Knob Stem, Flint 30.00
Pressed Glass, Colonial, Pitcher, 6 Tumblers, Silver Overlay 187.00
Pressed Glass, Colorado, Banana Boat, Blue, 9 In. 45.00
Pressed Glass, Colorado, Berry Set, Green, 5 Piece 85.00
Pressed Glass, Colorado, Berry Set, Ruffled Top, Green & Gold, 5 Piece 85.00
Pressed Glass, Colorado, Bowl, , Green, 10 In. 55.00
Pressed Glass, Colorado, Bowl, Fluted, Green & Gold, 10 In. 35.00
Pressed Glass, Colorado, Bowl, Green, 6 1/2 In. 38.50
Pressed Glass, Colorado, Butter, Green 125.00
Pressed Glass, Colorado, Butter, Green, Gold 120.00
Pressed Glass, Colorado, Creamer, Blue & Gold 85.00
Pressed Glass, Colorado, Creamer, Green .... 22.50 To 40.00
Pressed Glass, Colorado, Creamer, Green, Gold 60.00
Pressed Glass, Colorado, Dish, Crimped Edge, Gold Trim, 5 In., Set Of 4 .... 125.00
Pressed Glass, Colorado, Dish, Footed, Cobalt, Gold Trim, 5 In. 23.00

Pressed Glass, Circle & Ellipse, Vase, Canary, 7 1/4 In.

Pressed Glass, Classic, Compote, Covered

Pressed Glass, Clear Diagonal Band, Creamer

Pressed Glass, Colorado, Dish, Green & Gold, 5 1/4 In.	22.50
Pressed Glass, Colorado, Mug, Clambroth, Handled	16.00
Pressed Glass, Colorado, Nappy, Cobalt With Gold, 4 In.	22.00
Pressed Glass, Colorado, Pitcher, Milk, Blue	65.00
Pressed Glass, Colorado, Sauce, Blue	35.00
Pressed Glass, Colorado, Sauce, Footed, Blue	18.00 To 22.00
Pressed Glass, Colorado, Sugar & Creamer, Green	60.00
Pressed Glass, Colorado, Sugar, Covered, Green, Gold	95.00
Pressed Glass, Colorado, Sugar, Creamer, Covered Butter, Clear	95.00
Pressed Glass, Colorado, Sugar, Open	25.00
Pressed Glass, Colorado, Sugar, Open, Green	30.00 To 35.00
Pressed Glass, Colorado, Toothpick	17.00
Pressed Glass, Colorado, Toothpick, Green	35.00 To 42.00
Pressed Glass, Colorado, Tray, Card, Blue	25.00
Pressed Glass, Colorado, Tumbler, Green	15.00
Pressed Glass, Colorado, Tumbler, Souvenir, York, Pa., Green	22.50
Pressed Glass, Colorado, Vase, Green, 12 In.	55.00
Pressed Glass, Colorado, Vase, Green, 12 1/2 In.	95.00
Pressed Glass, Colorado, Vase, Trumpet, Green, 12 In.	45.00
Pressed Glass, Colorado, Vase, Violet, Blue	40.00
Pressed Glass, Columbia, Banana Stand, Etched	47.00
Pressed Glass, Columbia, Toothpick	15.00
Pressed Glass, Columbian Coin, Butter, Covered, Frosted	135.00
Pressed Glass, Columbian Coin, Butter, Covered, Gold Medallion	135.00
Pressed Glass, Columbian Coin, Celery, Frosted	145.00
Pressed Glass, Columbian Coin, Celery, Gold Medallion	145.00
Pressed Glass, Columbian Coin, Claret, 4 3/4 In.	95.00
Pressed Glass, Columbian Coin, Compote, Open, Clear, 8 In.	100.00
Pressed Glass, Columbian Coin, Creamer, Frosted	95.00
Pressed Glass, Columbian Coin, Creamer, Gold Coins	85.00 To 95.00
Pressed Glass, Columbian Coin, Mug, Beer, Frosted Coins	130.00
Pressed Glass, Columbian Coin, Mug, Gold Coins	45.00
Pressed Glass, Columbian Coin, Salt & Pepper	110.00
Pressed Glass, Columbian Coin, Spooner, Clear, 4 1/2 In.	52.00
Pressed Glass, Columbian Coin, Spooner, Frosted	85.00
Pressed Glass, Columbian Coin, Spooner, Gold Medallion	85.00

Pressed Glass, Columbian Coin, Sugar, Covered, Frosted 125.00
Pressed Glass, Columbian Coin, Sugar, Covered, Gold Medallion 125.00
Pressed Glass, Columbian Coin, Wine, Frosted .... 67.50 To 95.00
Pressed Glass, Columbian Exposition, Goblet .... 14.50 To 20.00
Pressed Glass, Columbian Exposition, Mug 15.00
Pressed Glass, Columbian Exposition, Tumbler 16.00
Pressed Glass, Columbus, Mug 80.00
Pressed Glass, Column Block, Pitcher, Water 50.00
Pressed Glass, Columned Thumbprints, Sugar & Creamer, Covered 30.00
Pressed Glass, Comet, Goblet, Flint .... 45.00 To 75.00
Pressed Glass, Comet, Pitcher, Water, Flint 375.00
Pressed Glass, Comet, Tumbler, Flint 110.00
    Compact, see Snail
Pressed Glass, Cone, Sugar Shaker, Pink 75.00
Pressed Glass, Cone, Syrup, Pink Satin, Squatty 125.00
Pressed Glass, Cone, Tumbler, Blue Satin 35.00
Pressed Glass, Cone, Water Set, Pink Cased, 7 Piece 385.00
Pressed Glass, Constitution, Bread Plate 75.00
Pressed Glass, Continental, Compote, Birds, Opaque Interior, 6 1/2 X 10 In. 75.00
Pressed Glass, Cord & Tassel, Compote, Covered, 10 In. 75.00
Pressed Glass, Cord & Tassel, Goblet .... 15.00 To 27.50
Pressed Glass, Cord & Tassel, Spooner 11.50
Pressed Glass, Cord Drapery, Bowl, Fluted, Green, 5 3/4 In.Diameter 80.00
Pressed Glass, Cord Drapery, Creamer 16.50
Pressed Glass, Cord Drapery, Pitcher, Water 45.00
Pressed Glass, Cord Drapery, Sauce .... 7.75 To 8.00
Pressed Glass, Cord Drapery, Spooner 16.50
Pressed Glass, Cordova, Compote, 8 In. 40.00
Pressed Glass, Cordova, Salt 9.50
Pressed Glass, Coreopsis, Berry Dish, Milk Glass 15.00
Pressed Glass, Corn, Tumbler, Blue, Opalescent Swirl 18.00
Pressed Glass, Corn, Vase, Blue, Opalescent 95.00
Pressed Glass, Corn, Vase, White 55.00
Pressed Glass, Corner Medallion, Sugar, Creamer & Spooner 50.00
Pressed Glass, Cornucopia, Pitcher, Water .... 65.00 To 67.50
Pressed Glass, Cornucopia, Wine 14.50
    Pressed Glass, Cosmos, see Cosmos
Pressed Glass, Cosmos, Creamer 120.00
Pressed Glass, Cosmos, Pitcher, Water 185.00
Pressed Glass, Cosmos, Spooner 85.00
Pressed Glass, Cosmos, Sugar, Covered 175.00
Pressed Glass, Cottage, Butter, Covered .... 20.00 To 28.00
Pressed Glass, Cottage, Cake Stand, Electric Blue 68.00
Pressed Glass, Cottage, Compote, Jelly 16.50
Pressed Glass, Cottage, Cup & Saucer 18.00
Pressed Glass, Cottage, Goblet .... 15.00 To 22.00
Pressed Glass, Cottage, Plate, 6 In. 10.00
Pressed Glass, Cottage, Plate, 7 In. .... 10.00 To 12.00
Pressed Glass, Cottage, Spooner 17.00
    Crane, see Stork
    Crisscross, see Rexford
Pressed Glass, Croesus, Berry Bowl, Amethyst, Footed, 6 3/4 In. 165.00
Pressed Glass, Croesus, Berry Bowl, Green 100.00
Pressed Glass, Croesus, Berry Set, Green 225.00
Pressed Glass, Croesus, Bowl, Sugar, Covered 175.00
Pressed Glass, Croesus, Butter 80.00
Pressed Glass, Croesus, Butter, Amethyst 125.00
Pressed Glass, Croesus, Butter, Covered, Creamer & Spooner, Gold Trim 350.00
Pressed Glass, Croesus, Butter, Purple, Covered .... 185.00 To 225.00
Pressed Glass, Croesus, Celery, Amethyst 135.00
Pressed Glass, Croesus, Compote, Jelly, Purple 230.00
Pressed Glass, Croesus, Compote, Open, 7 In. 70.00
Pressed Glass, Croesus, Condiment Set, Amethyst, Salt & Pepper, Tray & Cruet 425.00
Pressed Glass, Croesus, Condiment Set, Saltshakers, Cruet, Stopper & Tray 255.00
Pressed Glass, Croesus, Creamer, Amethyst 159.00
Pressed Glass, Croesus, Creamer, Gold Trim, Green 30.00

Pressed Glass, **Croesus**, Creamer, Green With Gold	75.00
Pressed Glass, **Croesus**, Creamer, Green, Gold On Legs	85.00
Pressed Glass, **Croesus**, Creamer, Individual, Purple	90.00
Pressed Glass, **Croesus**, Creamer, Purple	200.00
Pressed Glass, **Croesus**, Cruet, Purple	250.00
Pressed Glass, **Croesus**, Dish, Sauce, Footed, Set Of 4	75.00
Pressed Glass, **Croesus**, Lamp, Gone With The Wind, Pink Roses, Purple, 18 In.	350.00
Pressed Glass, **Croesus**, Pitcher, Milk, Gold Legs, Handle, Rim, 5 1/2 In.	72.00
Pressed Glass, **Croesus**, Salt & Pepper, Green	90.00
Pressed Glass, **Croesus**, Salt & Pepper, Purple	150.00
Pressed Glass, **Croesus**, Sauce, Green	28.00
Pressed Glass, **Croesus**, Spooner, Amethyst	53.00
Pressed Glass, **Croesus**, Spooner, Green	90.00
Pressed Glass, **Croesus**, Spooner, Green & Gold, Footed	60.00
Pressed Glass, **Croesus**, Spooner, Purple	100.00 To 115.00
Pressed Glass, **Croesus**, Sugar & Creamer, Cover, Gold Trim, Amethyst	145.00
Pressed Glass, **Croesus**, Sugar, Covered, Green	100.00
Pressed Glass, **Croesus**, Sugar, Covered, Green, Gold Trim	117.00
Pressed Glass, **Croesus**, Sugar, Purple, Covered	180.00 To 200.00
Pressed Glass, **Croesus**, Table Set, Purple	610.00
Pressed Glass, **Croesus**, Toothpick, Amethyst	92.50
Pressed Glass, **Croesus**, Toothpick, Green	55.00
Pressed Glass, **Croesus**, Toothpick, Purple	90.00
Pressed Glass, **Croesus**, Tray, Green	85.00
Pressed Glass, **Croesus**, Tumbler, Amethyst, Gold	65.00
Pressed Glass, **Croesus**, Water Set, Green	450.00
Pressed Glass, **Croesus**, Water Set, Green With Gold, 7 Piece	325.00
Pressed Glass, **Croesus**, Water Set, Purple	475.00
Crossbar & Finecut, see Ashman	
Pressed Glass, **Crossed Block**, Sugar & Creamer	30.00
Pressed Glass, **Crossed Cords & Prisms**, Butter, Amber, Covered	34.00
Pressed Glass, **Crowfoot**, Butter	35.00
Pressed Glass, **Crowfoot**, Creamer	22.50
Pressed Glass, **Crowfoot**, Goblet	13.00 To 26.00
Pressed Glass, **Crowfoot**, Spooner	12.00 To 18.00
Pressed Glass, **Crowfoot**, Tumbler, Clear Opalescent	65.00
Pressed Glass, **Crystal Wedding**, Goblet, Ruby Stain	42.00
Pressed Glass, **Crystal Wedding**, Sugar, Ruby	22.00
Pressed Glass, **Crystal**, Celery, Flint	35.00
Pressed Glass, **Crystal**, Eggcup, Flint	12.00
Pressed Glass, **Crystal**, Goblet	5.00
Cube & Diamond, see Milton	
Cube & Fan, see Pineapple & Fan	
Pressed Glass, **Cube**, Goblet	8.50
Cupid & Psyche, see Psyche & Cupid	
Pressed Glass, **Cupid & Venus**, Bread Plate, Round Handle	22.00
Pressed Glass, **Cupid & Venus**, Bread Plate, 10 1/2 In.	25.00 To 35.00
Pressed Glass, **Cupid & Venus**, Bread Plate, 11 X 8 1/2 In.	35.00
Pressed Glass, **Cupid & Venus**, Celery	30.00 To 38.00
Pressed Glass, **Cupid & Venus**, Compote, Footed, 6 1/2 In.Diameter	35.00
Pressed Glass, **Cupid & Venus**, Creamer	35.00 To 46.00
Pressed Glass, **Cupid & Venus**, Goblet	37.00 To 50.00
Pressed Glass, **Cupid & Venus**, Jar, Marmalade, Covered	35.00
Pressed Glass, **Cupid & Venus**, Mug, 2 1/2 In.	28.00
Pressed Glass, **Cupid & Venus**, Pitcher, Milk	35.00 To 80.00
Pressed Glass, **Cupid & Venus**, Pitcher, Water	36.00 To 75.00
Pressed Glass, **Cupid & Venus**, Plate, Handles, 10 1/2 In.	39.00
Pressed Glass, **Cupid & Venus**, Plate, 10 1/2 In.	30.00
Pressed Glass, **Cupid & Venus**, Sauce, Footed, 3 3/4 In.	8.00
Pressed Glass, **Cupid & Venus**, Sauce, Footed, 4 1/2 In.	10.00
Pressed Glass, **Cupid & Venus**, Spooner	25.00 To 40.00
Pressed Glass, **Cupid's Hunt**, Compote, 3 X 8 In.Diameter	30.00
Pressed Glass, **Currant**, Goblet	23.00
Pressed Glass, **Currant**, Pitcher, Water	50.00
Pressed Glass, **Currant**, Spooner	18.00
Pressed Glass, **Currant**, Wine	18.00

Pressed Glass, Currant, Goblet, 5 In.	14.00
Pressed Glass, Currier & Ives, Bread Plate, Train	75.00
Pressed Glass, Currier & Ives, Goblet	14.50 To 24.00
Pressed Glass, Currier & Ives, Relish	9.50
Pressed Glass, Currier & Ives, Salt & Pepper, Original Tops, Amber	35.00
Pressed Glass, Currier & Ives, Syrup	18.00
Pressed Glass, Currier & Ives, Tray, Balking Mule, Blue, 11 In.	65.00 To 85.00
Pressed Glass, Currier & Ives, Tray, Wine, Balky Mule	33.00
Pressed Glass, Currier & Ives, Tumbler, Amber	30.00
Pressed Glass, Currier & Ives, Wine	16.00 To 17.00
Pressed Glass, Curtain Tieback, Goblet	10.00 To 15.00
Pressed Glass, Curtain Tieback, Sauce, Footed, 5 In.	8.00
Pressed Glass, Curtain, Celery	10.00
Pressed Glass, Cut Honeycomb, Goblet	25.00
Pressed Glass, Cut Log, Cake Stand, 9 In.	40.00 To 42.00
Pressed Glass, Cut Log, Cake Stand, 10 In.	49.00 To 50.00
Pressed Glass, Cut Log, Cake Stand, 8 In.	25.00 To 27.50
Pressed Glass, Cut Log, Compote, Covered, 7 In.	60.00
Pressed Glass, Cut Log, Compote, Open, 8 X 6 1/4 In.	45.00
Pressed Glass, Cut Log, Compote, Scalloped Rim, 8 In.	45.00
Pressed Glass, Cut Log, Compote, 8 X 6 1/4 In.	50.00
Pressed Glass, Cut Log, Creamer	12.00 To 28.00
Pressed Glass, Cut Log, Honey, Cover, Square, 7 In.	45.00
Pressed Glass, Cut Log, Mug, 3 1/4 In.	13.50 To 14.50
Pressed Glass, Cut Log, Nappy, Handled	15.00
Pressed Glass, Cut Log, Nappy, 5 In.	14.50
Pressed Glass, Cut Log, Olive Dish, Handled	22.50
Pressed Glass, Cut Log, Pitcher, Water	30.00
Pressed Glass, Cut Log, Pitcher, Water, Tankard, Applied Handle	45.00 To 50.00
Pressed Glass, Cut Log, Relish, 8 X 5 In.	19.00
Pressed Glass, Cut Log, Spooner	21.00 To 24.50
Pressed Glass, Cut Log, Wine	16.00 To 22.50
Pressed Glass, Cyclone, Celery	21.00
Pressed Glass, Dahlia, Bread Plate, Blue, Round	50.00
Pressed Glass, Dahlia, Bread Plate, Oval	40.00
Pressed Glass, Dahlia, Bread Plate, Round	24.00
Pressed Glass, Dahlia, Goblet, Etched	15.00 To 25.00
Pressed Glass, Dahlia, Goblet, Flint	35.00
Pressed Glass, Dahlia, Mug, Child's, Yellow	35.00
Pressed Glass, Dahlia, Pitcher, Water	45.00
Pressed Glass, Dahlia, Pitcher, Water, Amber	65.00
Pressed Glass, Dahlia, Plate, Handled, 9 In.	21.00
Pressed Glass, Dahlia, Sauce, Footed	10.00
Pressed Glass, Dahlia, Wine	25.00 To 35.00
Pressed Glass, Daisies In Diamonds, Butter, Covered	42.00
Pressed Glass, Daisies In Oval Panels, Creamer, Blue	40.00
Pressed Glass, Daisies In Oval Panels, Creamer, Blue With Gold	35.00
Pressed Glass, Daisies In Oval Panels, Goblet	14.00
Pressed Glass, Daisies In Oval Panels, Toothpick	17.50
Pressed Glass, Daisies In Oval Panels, Water Set, Green With Gold, 7 Piece	175.00
Pressed Glass, Daisy & Block, Wine	16.00
Daisy & Button, see also Paneled Daisy & Button	
Pressed Glass, Daisy & Button With Crossbar, Butter, Vaseline, Covered	65.00
Pressed Glass, Daisy & Button With Crossbar, Celery	40.00
Pressed Glass, Daisy & Button With Crossbar, Celery, Vaseline	40.00
Pressed Glass, Daisy & Button With Crossbar, Creamer	37.50
Pressed Glass, Daisy & Button With Crossbar, Creamer & Spooner, Amber	50.00
Pressed Glass, Daisy & Button With Crossbar, Creamer, Vaseline	37.50
Pressed Glass, Daisy & Button With Crossbar, Cruet	35.00
Pressed Glass, Daisy & Button With Crossbar, Goblet	45.00
Pressed Glass, Daisy & Button With Crossbar, Goblet, Blue	35.00
Pressed Glass, Daisy & Button With Crossbar, Pitcher, Water, Vaseline	57.50
Pressed Glass, Daisy & Button With Crossbar, Spooner	40.00
Pressed Glass, Daisy & Button With Crossbar, Spooner, Amber	35.00
Pressed Glass, Daisy & Button With Crossbar, Tumbler, Amber	25.00 To 30.00
Pressed Glass, Daisy & Button With Narcissus, Butter	32.50

Pressed Glass, Clover, Creamer, 3 1/2 In.

Pressed Glass, Colonial, Sugar, Opalescent, Covered

Pressed Glass, Columbian Coin, Salt & Pepper

Pressed Glass, Croesus,
Berry Set, Green

Pressed Glass, Croesus,
Water Set, Green

Pressed Glass,
Croesus, Salt & Pepper,
Green

Pressed Glass, Croesus,
Water Set, Purple

Pressed Glass, Croesus, Table Set, Purple

Pressed Glass, Croesus,
Compote, Jelly, Purple

Pressed Glass, Compote, Bellflower

Pressed Glass, Cupid & Psyche, Creamer

Pressed Glass, Cupid & Venus, Plate, Bread

Pressed Glass, Curtain, Spooner

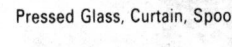

Pressed Glass, Daisies In Oval Panels, Goblet

Pressed Glass, Daisy & Button With Narcissus, Decanter	30.00
Pressed Glass, Daisy & Button With Narcissus, Tray, 10 1/2 In. Diameter	45.00
Daisy & Button with Oval Panels, see Hartley	
Pressed Glass, Daisy & Button With Pointed Panel, Wine	13.00
Pressed Glass, Daisy & Button With Thumbprint, Goblet, Amber Panels	75.00
Pressed Glass, Daisy & Button With V Ornament, Celery, Flat	16.00
Pressed Glass, Daisy & Button With V Ornament, Creamer	17.00
Pressed Glass, Daisy & Button With V Ornament, Pitcher, Water	62.50
Pressed Glass, Daisy & Button With V Ornament, Pitcher, Water, 8 In.	20.00
Pressed Glass, Daisy & Button With V Ornament, Toothpick, Amber	25.00
Pressed Glass, Daisy & Button With V Ornament, Toothpick, Blue	20.00
Pressed Glass, Daisy & Button, Ashtray, Kettle Shape	10.00
Pressed Glass, Daisy & Button, Bell, On Bowl Base, Blue	65.00
Pressed Glass, Daisy & Button, Bowl, Berry, Scalloped Top, 10 In.	30.00
Pressed Glass, Daisy & Button, Bowl, 6 Panel, Etched, Pink, 7 X 9 1/2 In.	25.00
Pressed Glass, Daisy & Button, Bread Plate	20.00
Pressed Glass, Daisy & Button, Cake Stand, Amber Thumbprint, Panel, 10 In.	110.00
Pressed Glass, Daisy & Button, Cake Stand, 9 1/4 In.	12.50
Pressed Glass, Daisy & Button, Canoe, Ruby Flashed	65.00
Pressed Glass, Daisy & Button, Canoe, 10 In.	20.00
Pressed Glass, Daisy & Button, Castor, Pickle, Tongs, Blue	225.00
Pressed Glass, Daisy & Button, Celery, Blue, Tri-Cornered	35.00
Pressed Glass, Daisy & Button, Celery, Panels, Flashed Red, 7 1/2 In.	35.00
Pressed Glass, Daisy & Button, Celery, Scalloped Top, 6 1/2 In.	20.00
Pressed Glass, Daisy & Button, Compote, Covered, Pedestal, Square, Medium	95.00
Pressed Glass, Daisy & Button, Compote, Open, Ruffled, 9 In.	68.00 To 75.00
Pressed Glass, Daisy & Button, Compote, Open, 8 In. High X 7 1/2 In.	70.00
Pressed Glass, Daisy & Button, Dish, Shape Of Whisk Broom, Amber	35.00
Pressed Glass, Daisy & Button, Dish, Whiskbroom, Amber	28.00
Pressed Glass, Daisy & Button, Goblet, Recessed Ovals	12.00
Pressed Glass, Daisy & Button, Holder, Napkin, Canary	75.00
Pressed Glass, Daisy & Button, Pitcher, Water	20.00

Pressed Glass, Daisy & Button, Pitcher, Water, Scalloped Top, 8 3/4 In.	30.00
Pressed Glass, Daisy & Button, Plate, Blue, 7 In.	25.00
Pressed Glass, Daisy & Button, Plate, Red Daisies, 7 1/2 In.Square	20.00
Pressed Glass, Daisy & Button, Plate, Vaseline, 7 In.Square	20.00
Pressed Glass, Daisy & Button, Plate, Yellow Daisies, 7 1/2 In.Square	20.00
Pressed Glass, Daisy & Button, Salt & Pepper, One Blue, One Yellow, 4 In.	45.00
Pressed Glass, Daisy & Button, Saltshaker, Original Top, Square Ornament	24.00
Pressed Glass, Daisy & Button, Saltshaker, Pewter Top, Flint	35.00
Pressed Glass, Daisy & Button, Sauce, Amberette, 4 In.	15.00
Pressed Glass, Daisy & Button, Shoe, Vaseline Buttons, 1886	110.00
Pressed Glass, Daisy & Button, Spooner	22.00
Pressed Glass, Daisy & Button, Spooner, Clear	15.00
Pressed Glass, Daisy & Button, Sugar, Covered	40.00
Pressed Glass, Daisy & Button, Sugar, Covered, Large	40.00
Pressed Glass, Daisy & Button, Sugar, Open, Amber Panels	24.50
Pressed Glass, Daisy & Button, Toothpick	5.00
Pressed Glass, Daisy & Button, Toothpick, Potty	28.00
Pressed Glass, Daisy & Button, Toothpick, Red Dots, Scalloped, 2 1/2 In.	30.00
Pressed Glass, Daisy & Button, Toothpick, Stippled Sides, Footed	35.00
Pressed Glass, Daisy & Button, Tray, Clear, 11 X 28 In.	18.00
Pressed Glass, Daisy & Button, Tumbler	25.00 To 27.00
Pressed Glass, Daisy & Button, Tumbler, Blue	20.00
Pressed Glass, Daisy & Button, Whiskey, Vaseline	20.00
Pressed Glass, Daisy & Fern, Creamer, Gold Trim	14.00
Pressed Glass, Daisy & Fern, Pitcher, Opalescent Cranberry, Reeded Handle	100.00
Pressed Glass, Daisy & Fern, Sugar, Cranberry Opalescent	65.00
Pressed Glass, Daisy & Star, Water Set, 7 Piece	125.00
Pressed Glass, Daisy Band, Goblet, Etched	8.00
Pressed Glass, Daisy Button With Crossbar, Compote	25.00
Pressed Glass, Daisy Panel, Tankard, Milk	38.50
Pressed Glass, Daisy, Celery, Paneled	25.00
Pressed Glass, Daisy, Goblet, Amber Stripe, Clear	6.00
Pressed Glass, Daisy, Goblet, Amber Stripe, Etched	22.50
Pressed Glass, Dakota, Butter	25.00 To 38.50
Pressed Glass, Dakota, Butter, Clear, Opalescent, Covered	38.00
Pressed Glass, Dakota, Butter, Covered	33.00
Pressed Glass, Dakota, Butter, Covered, Etched	38.00 To 57.00
Pressed Glass, Dakota, Butter, Covered, Pie Crust Edge, Etched	60.00
Pressed Glass, Dakota, Cake Basket, Metal Handle	55.00
Pressed Glass, Dakota, Cake Stand, 10 In.	45.00
Pressed Glass, Dakota, Celery	19.50 To 20.00
Pressed Glass, Dakota, Celery Holder, Etched	24.00
Pressed Glass, Dakota, Celery, Etched Bird & Flowers	24.00 To 45.00
Pressed Glass, Dakota, Celery, Etched, Footed	27.00
Pressed Glass, Dakota, Celery, Hotel Style	34.00
Pressed Glass, Dakota, Compote, Open, 7 In.	20.00
Pressed Glass, Dakota, Compote, 7 In.	24.50
Pressed Glass, Dakota, Creamer, Pedestal	35.00
Pressed Glass, Dakota, Creamer, Pedestal, Etched	22.00
Pressed Glass, Dakota, Goblet	17.50 To 18.50
Pressed Glass, Dakota, Goblet, Etched	18.00 To 35.00
Pressed Glass, Dakota, Mug, Souvenir, Ruby Stained, 3 1/2 In.	25.00
Pressed Glass, Dakota, Pitcher, Milk	48.00
Pressed Glass, Dakota, Pitcher, Water, Leaf & Berry	65.00
Pressed Glass, Dakota, Pitcher, Water, Tankard, Clear, Opalescent	46.00

Pressed Glass, Deer & Dog, Goblet

Pressed Glass, Delaware, Pitcher, Rose Color, 9 1/2 In.

Pressed Glass, Dakota, Sherbet, Cobalt 20.00
Pressed Glass, Dakota, Spooner .... 25.00 To 28.00
Pressed Glass, Dakota, Sugar & Creamer 23.00
Pressed Glass, Dakota, Sugar Shaker, Decorated 45.00
Pressed Glass, Dakota, Sugar, Covered 32.50
Pressed Glass, Dakota, Sugar, Covered, Etched 45.00
Pressed Glass, Dakota, Tankard, Etched 85.00
Pressed Glass, Dakota, Tray, Water, 13 In 135.00
Pressed Glass, Dakota, Tumbler, Red Stain 35.00
Pressed Glass, Dakota, Vase, Celery 18.00
Pressed Glass, Dakota, Wine .... 13.00 To 22.00
Pressed Glass, Dakota, Wine, Red Stain .... 38.00 To 52.50
Pressed Glass, Dalton, Spooner, Gold 15.00
Pressed Glass, Dancing Goat, Ale Glass 37.00
Pressed Glass, Dart, Sugar, Covered 28.00
Pressed Glass, Darwin, Toothpick 30.00
Pressed Glass, Deer & Dog, Celery, Etched 52.50
Pressed Glass, Deer & Dog, Celery, Gillinder 120.00
Pressed Glass, Deer & Dog, Compote, Frosted Dog Finial, 8 X 6 1/2 In. 85.00
Pressed Glass, Deer & Dog, Goblet 49.50
Pressed Glass, Deer & Dog, Goblet, Etched .... 40.00 To 75.00
Pressed Glass, Deer & Dog, Sauce, Etched 8.00
Pressed Glass, Deer & Dog, Spooner, Gillinder 65.00
Pressed Glass, Deer & Dog, Sugar, Covered, Frosted Dog Finial 125.00
Pressed Glass, Deer & Pine Tree, Bread Plate .... 32.00 To 47.00
Pressed Glass, Deer & Pine Tree, Bread Plate, Amber 55.00
Pressed Glass, Deer & Pine Tree, Bread Plate, Blue 32.00
Pressed Glass, Deer & Pine Tree, Butter 45.00
Pressed Glass, Deer & Pine Tree, Cake Stand, 12 In.Diameter, 7 In.High 55.00
Pressed Glass, Deer & Pine Tree, Celery, 7 1/2 In. 35.00
Pressed Glass, Deer & Pine Tree, Compote, Covered, 7 X 9 X 12 In. 65.00
Pressed Glass, Deer & Pine Tree, Compote, Open, 6 X 8 X 6 1/2 In. 45.00
Pressed Glass, Deer & Pine Tree, Creamer 38.00
Pressed Glass, Deer & Pine Tree, Dish, Vegetable, Rectangular, 9 X 5 In. 45.00
Pressed Glass, Deer & Pine Tree, Goblet .... 35.00 To 37.50
Pressed Glass, Deer & Pine Tree, Mug, Green, Gold Accents, 2 1/2 In. 25.00
Pressed Glass, Deer & Pine Tree, Mug, Handled, Green 35.00
Pressed Glass, Deer & Pine Tree, Mug, Yellow, 2 1/2 In. 25.00
Pressed Glass, Deer & Pine Tree, Pitcher, Milk 67.50
Pressed Glass, Deer & Pine Tree, Pitcher, Water, 8 1/2 In. 60.00
Pressed Glass, Deer & Pine Tree, Sauce, Footed 16.00
Pressed Glass, Deer & Pine Tree, Tray, Green 55.00
Pressed Glass, Deer & Pine Tree, Tray, Yellow, 8 X 13 In. 50.00
Pressed Glass, Deer & Pine Tree, Tray, 8 X 13 In. 40.00
Pressed Glass, Deer & Pine Tree, Tray, 9 X 15 In. 65.00
Pressed Glass, Deer, Dog, And Hunter, Celery, Etched 52.50
Pressed Glass, Deer, Dog, Celery, Gillinder 120.00
Pressed Glass, Deer, Dog, Spooner, Gillinder 65.00
Pressed Glass, Delaware, Banana Boat, Green & Gold .... 35.00 To 57.50
Pressed Glass, Delaware, Banana Bowl, Rose, Gold 52.00
Pressed Glass, Delaware, Berry Bowl, Boat Shape, Green & Gold 45.00
Pressed Glass, Delaware, Bowl, Cranberry, Gold Trim, Round 125.00
Pressed Glass, Delaware, Bowl, Fruit, Boat Shape, Green, Gold 44.00
Pressed Glass, Delaware, Bowl, Fruit, Gold, Oval, 12 In. 45.00
Pressed Glass, Delaware, Bowl, Gold, Green Exterior, 9 In. 30.00
Pressed Glass, Delaware, Bowl, Green & Gold, Round, 8 In. 36.50
Pressed Glass, Delaware, Bowl, Green, Gold Rim, Octagonal Shape, 9 In. 37.50
Pressed Glass, Delaware, Box, Puff, Green With Gold, Jeweled Glass Lid 175.00
Pressed Glass, Delaware, Bride's Basket, Miniature, Rose, Oval 75.00
Pressed Glass, Delaware, Butter, Green & Gold .... 49.50 To 135.00
Pressed Glass, Delaware, Butter, Rose & Gold 135.00
Pressed Glass, Delaware, Celery, Ruby 95.00
Pressed Glass, Delaware, Creamer, Gold Flowers, Rose Tint Rim .... 28.00 To 35.00
Pressed Glass, Delaware, Cup, Green & Gold 12.50
Pressed Glass, Delaware, Pitcher, Green 70.00
Pressed Glass, Delaware, Pitcher, Rose, Gold 90.00

Pressed Glass, Delaware, Sauce, Boat Shaped, Rose With Gold 20.00
Pressed Glass, Delaware, Sauce, Round, 4 In. 21.50
Pressed Glass, Delaware, Sugar, Covered, Rose With Gold .... 55.00 To 85.00
Pressed Glass, Delaware, Tankard, Pitcher, Green 80.00
Pressed Glass, Delaware, Tumbler 30.00
Pressed Glass, Delaware, Tumbler, Green, Gold .... 22.00 To 39.00
Pressed Glass, Delaware, Vase, Green With Gold, 9 1/2 In. 80.00
Pressed Glass, Delaware, Water Set, Green, Gold, 6 Tumblers .... 250.00 To 275.00
Pressed Glass, Dewberry, Tumbler, Gilt 7.50
Pressed Glass, Dewdrop Bands, Goblet .... 8.00 To 18.00
Pressed Glass, Dewdrop In Points, Goblet 22.00
Pressed Glass, Dewdrop With Sheaf Of Wheat, Bread Plate 27.00
Pressed Glass, Dewdrop With Small Stars, Goblet .... 13.00 To 14.00
Pressed Glass, Dewdrop With Star, Butter, Covered 35.00
Pressed Glass, Dewdrop With Star, Compote, Covered 55.00
Pressed Glass, Dewdrop With Star, Sauce, Footed 10.00
Pressed Glass, Dewdrop, Goblet 17.00
Pressed Glass, Dewdrop, Mug, Applied Handle 15.00
    Dewey, see also Admiral Dewey
Pressed Glass, Dewey, Cruet, Original Stopper, Amber 100.00
Pressed Glass, Dewey, Jar, Puff, Clear, Covered 24.00
Pressed Glass, Dewey, Pitcher, Water .... 29.50 To 68.75
Pressed Glass, Dewey, Plate, 101 Border, 6 In. 15.00
Pressed Glass, Dewey, Relish, Amber, Serpentine Shape 32.50
Pressed Glass, Dewey, Salt & Pepper, Amber 40.00
Pressed Glass, Diagonal Band & Fan, Celery 18.00
Pressed Glass, Diagonal Band & Fan, Champagne 17.50
Pressed Glass, Diagonal Band & Fan, Goblet 18.00
Pressed Glass, Diagonal Band & Fan, Plate, 6 In. 11.00
Pressed Glass, Diagonal Band & Fan, Sugar 5.00
Pressed Glass, Diagonal Band & Flower, Mug 12.50
Pressed Glass, Diagonal Band, Bread Plate 18.00
Pressed Glass, Diagonal Band, Compote, Clear, 7 In. 16.00
Pressed Glass, Diagonal Band, Creamer, Clear 26.50
Pressed Glass, Diagonal Band, Goblet .... 13.00 To 22.00
Pressed Glass, Diagonal Band, Pitcher, Clear, 6 In. 20.00
Pressed Glass, Diagonal Band, Pitcher, Water 23.00
Pressed Glass, Diagonal Band, Wine 26.00
Pressed Glass, Diagonal Block Band, Goblet 12.50
    Diamond, see Umbilicated Sawtooth
    Diamond & Bull's-Eye Band, see Reverse Torpedo
Pressed Glass, Diagonal Block Band, Plate, 8 In., Pair 32.00
Pressed Glass, Diamond & Fan, Goblet 20.00
Pressed Glass, Diamond & Oval Thumbprint, Vase, Green Opalescent 35.00
    Diamond & Sunburst, see also Flattened Diamond & Sunburst
Pressed Glass, Diamond & Sunburst, Goblet 15.00
Pressed Glass, Diamond Band, Goblet 10.00
Pressed Glass, Diamond Beaded Band, Goblet 9.50
Pressed Glass, Diamond Block With Fans, Goblet 18.00
Pressed Glass, Diamond Block With Fans, Pitcher, Water, Footed 27.50
Pressed Glass, Diamond Cut With Leaf, Goblet 12.50
    Diamond Horseshoe, see Aurora
Pressed Glass, Diamond Medallion, Cake Stand, 9 1/2 In. 15.00
Pressed Glass, Diamond Medallion, Celery 16.50
Pressed Glass, Diamond Medallion, Goblet .... 15.00 To 18.00
Pressed Glass, Diamond Medallion, Nappy 13.50
Pressed Glass, Diamond Medallion, Pitcher, Water 22.00
Pressed Glass, Diamond Medallion, Sugar, Covered 18.00
Pressed Glass, Diamond Panels, Glass, Child's, Blue 165.00
Pressed Glass, Diamond Point & Fan, Rose Bowl, Clear, 4 1/2 In. 32.00
Pressed Glass, Diamond Point & Loop, Pitcher, Water, Amber 68.00
    Diamond Point Discs, see Eyewinker
Pressed Glass, Diamond Point Discs, Creamer 17.00
    Diamond Point with Panels, see Hinoto
Pressed Glass, Diamond Point, Celery, Flint .... 49.50 To 60.00
Pressed Glass, Diamond Point, Celery, Knob Stem, Flint, 8 5/8 In. 60.00

Pressed Glass, Diamond Point, Claret .... 59.50 To 87.50
Pressed Glass, Diamond Point, Claret, Flint 87.50
Pressed Glass, Diamond Point, Creamer 150.00
Pressed Glass, Diamond Point, Creamer, Applied Handle 110.00
Pressed Glass, Diamond Point, Decanter With Stopper, Quart 89.50
Pressed Glass, Diamond Point, Goblet .... 10.00 To 40.00
Pressed Glass, Diamond Point, Goblet, Flint .... 39.00 To 45.00
Pressed Glass, Diamond Point, Goblet, Knob Stem, Flint 24.00
Pressed Glass, Diamond Point, Pitcher, Water, Flint 150.00
Pressed Glass, Diamond Point, Salt, Master, Blue Opaque, Flint 48.00
Pressed Glass, Diamond Point, Spillholder 30.00
Pressed Glass, Diamond Point, Tumbler, Flint 55.00
Pressed Glass, Diamond Prisms, Wine 13.50
Pressed Glass, Diamond Quilted, Bowl, Amber, 8 1/4 In. 18.00
Pressed Glass, Diamond Quilted, Celery, Amber 35.00
Pressed Glass, Diamond Quilted, Goblet, Amethyst .... 40.00 To 50.00
Pressed Glass, Diamond Quilted, Spooner, Amber 27.50
Pressed Glass, Diamond Spearhead, Toothpick, Green, Opalescent 45.00
Pressed Glass, Diamond Spearhead, Toothpick, Vaseline, Opalescent 32.00
Pressed Glass, Diamond Splendor, Goblet 12.50
Pressed Glass, Diamond Sunburst Variant, Pitcher, Milk 28.00
Pressed Glass, Diamond Sunburst Variant, Pitcher, Syrup, Hinged Tin Top 25.00
Pressed Glass, Diamond Sunburst Variant, Tumbler, Clear & Ruby 22.00
Pressed Glass, Diamond Sunburst, Tumbler, Ruby Stained 19.50
   Diamond Swag, see Fandango
Pressed Glass, Diamond Thumbprint, Bowl, Queen Victoria Jubilee 43.50
Pressed Glass, Diamond Thumbprint, Carafe, Open, Flint 115.00
Pressed Glass, Diamond Thumbprint, Celery, Flint .... 150.00 To 200.00
Pressed Glass, Diamond Thumbprint, Compote, 11 1/4 X 9 In. 85.00
Pressed Glass, Diamond Thumbprint, Goblet 375.00
Pressed Glass, Diamond Thumbprint, Goblet, Flint .... 350.00 To 375.00
Pressed Glass, Diamond Thumbprint, Pitcher, Water, Flint .... 275.00 To 375.00
Pressed Glass, Diamond Thumbprint, Tumbler, Flint .... 85.00 To 95.00
Pressed Glass, Diamond Thumbprint, Whiskey, Flint 100.00
Pressed Glass, Diamond With Double Fan, Spooner, 6 In. 22.00
Pressed Glass, Diamond With Double Fans, Creamer 13.50
Pressed Glass, Diamond With Double Fans, Lamp, Hand, Loop Handled 32.50
Pressed Glass, Diamond With Double Fans, Spooner 13.50
Pressed Glass, Diamond, Compote, Open, 7 3/4 In.Diameter 35.00
Pressed Glass, Dickinson, Goblet 24.00
Pressed Glass, Diedre, Goblet 8.00
Pressed Glass, Divided Block With Sunburst Variant 13.50
Pressed Glass, Divided Hearts, Eggcup, Flint 35.00
Pressed Glass, Dog With Rabbit In Mouth, Etched, Goblet 80.00
Pressed Glass, Dogwood, Berry Bowl, Amethyst 55.00
Pressed Glass, Dogwood, Berry Bowl, Amethyst Stain, Gold Trim 55.00
Pressed Glass, Dogwood, Creamer, Ruby Stained 34.50
Pressed Glass, Dolly Madison, Spooner, Blue, Opalescent 75.00
Pressed Glass, Dolphin & Herons, Compote, White 37.50
Pressed Glass, Dolphin, Box, Cigarette, Footed 22.50
Pressed Glass, Dolphin, Creamer 30.00
Pressed Glass, Dolphin, Creamer, Frosted 100.00
Pressed Glass, Dolphin, Creamer, Stemmed .... 45.00 To 47.50
   Doric, see Feather
Pressed Glass, Double Beaded Band, Wine 18.00
Pressed Glass, Double Beetle Band, Creamer 21.00
Pressed Glass, Double Beetle Band, Spooner, Amber 25.00
Pressed Glass, Double Block, Tumbler, Ruby 24.00
Pressed Glass, Double Crossroads, Saltshaker, Amber 20.00
Pressed Glass, Double Dahlia & Lens, Sugar & Creamer, Green, Gold Flowers 85.00
Pressed Glass, Double Dahlia & Lens, Wine Set, Cranberry, 7 Piece 185.00
   Double Daisy, see Rosette Band
Pressed Glass, Double Disced Prism Variant, Goblet, Flint 30.00
Pressed Glass, Double Disced Prism, Goblet, Flint 40.00
   Double Loop, see Double Loop & Dart
Pressed Glass, Double Loop & Dart, Goblet, Clear, Set Of 6 .... 65.00

Pressed Glass, Diamond Cut With Leaf, Plate

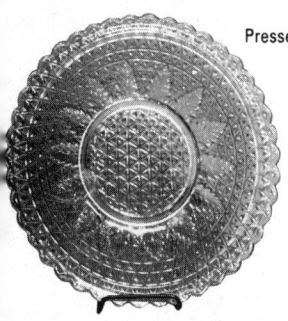

Pressed Glass, Diamond Point, Claret

Pressed Glass, Diamond Thumbprint, Decanter

Pressed Glass, Dolphin, Pitcher, Frosted

Pressed Glass, Egg In Sand, Goblet

Pressed Glass, Egyptian, Goblet

Pressed Glass, Fern Burst, Goblet

Pressed Glass, Excelsior, Bottle, Bitters

Pressed Glass, Double Ribbon, Creamer	22.00
Pressed Glass, Double Rosette, Compote, Jelly	15.00
Pressed Glass, Double Snail, Rose Bowl	21.50 To 28.00
Double Vine, see Bellflower, Double Vine	
Pressed Glass, Double Wedding Ring, Goblet, Flint	45.00
Pressed Glass, Double Wedding Ring, Goblet, Knob Stem, Flint	48.00
Pressed Glass, Double Wedding Ring, Syrup, Flint, Applied Handle	48.00
Pressed Glass, Double Wedding Ring, Tumbler, Flint	65.00
Pressed Glass, Double Wedding Ring, Wine, Flint	35.00
Pressed Glass, Douglas, Toothpick	20.00
Pressed Glass, Dragon, Sugar, Pedestal	115.00
Pressed Glass, Draped Fan, Pitcher	30.00
Pressed Glass, Draped Red Block, Goblet, Ruby	45.00
Pressed Glass, Drapery Band With Stars, Goblet	13.00
Pressed Glass, Drapery, Creamer	15.00 To 22.00

Pressed Glass, Drapery, Eggcup	19.00
Pressed Glass, Drapery, Goblet	15.50 To 24.00
Pressed Glass, Drapery, Pitcher, Water, Blue Opalescent	225.00
Pressed Glass, Drum, Butter, Sugar, Covered, Creamer, Spooner	160.00
Pressed Glass, Drum, Mug, Gold	25.00
Pressed Glass, Drum, Mug, Gold Eagle, Gold Handle	50.00
Pressed Glass, Drum, Sugar, Covered, Miniature	35.00
Pressed Glass, Duchess Loop, Cordial	15.00
Pressed Glass, Duchess Loop, Wine, Flint	10.00
Pressed Glass, Duchess, Relish, Green	35.00
Pressed Glass, Duncan Block, Tumbler, Ruby Stained	24.00
Pressed Glass, Duncan Tepee, Goblet	20.00
Pressed Glass, Dunlop Strawberry, Goblet	18.00
Pressed Glass, Duquesne, Goblet	10.00 To 15.00
Pressed Glass, E.Pluribus Unum, Mug	60.00
Pressed Glass, Eagle, Celery, Frosted	35.00
Pressed Glass, Ear Of Corn, Pitcher, Pink Lining, 5 1/2 In.	35.00
Earl, see Spirea Band	
Pressed Glass, Eastern Star, Goblet	10.00 To 16.00
Pressed Glass, Effulgent Star, Mug, Blue	35.00
Pressed Glass, Egg In Sand, Bread Plate	20.00
Pressed Glass, Egg In Sand, Bread Plate, Double Handles, 12 3/4 In.	15.00
Pressed Glass, Egg In Sand, Goblet	25.00
Pressed Glass, Egg In Sand, Pitcher, Milk	22.50 To 45.00
Pressed Glass, Egg In Sand, Pitcher, Water	35.50
Pressed Glass, Egg In Sand, Spooner	17.00
Pressed Glass, Egyptian, Bread Plate, Cleopatra	30.00 To 49.00
Pressed Glass, Egyptian, Compote, Footed, Sphinx On Base	50.00
Pressed Glass, Egyptian, Compote, Sphinx On Base, Covered	145.00
Pressed Glass, Egyptian, Creamer	27.50 To 36.00
Pressed Glass, Egyptian, Dish, Pickle	17.00
Pressed Glass, Egyptian, Goblet	32.00 To 35.00
Pressed Glass, Egyptian, Pitcher, Water	85.00 To 145.00
Pressed Glass, Egyptian, Plate, Handles	40.00
Pressed Glass, Egyptian, Sauce, Footed, 4 1/2 In.	13.50 To 15.00
Pressed Glass, Egyptian, Spooner	23.50
Pressed Glass, Elaine, Platter, Frosted, One-O-One Border	52.50
Pressed Glass, Elephant, Etched, Goblet	100.00
Pressed Glass, Elk Medallion, Goblet	32.00
Pressed Glass, Ellipse, Spooner, Scalloped Top	15.00
Pressed Glass, Empress, Pitcher, Water, Green	215.00
Pressed Glass, Empress, Spooner, Gold Trim, Green	85.00
Pressed Glass, Empress, Sugar, Covered, Green	125.00
English Hobnail Cross, see Klondike	
Pressed Glass, Esther, Butter, Covered, Green	152.00
Pressed Glass, Esther, Creamer, Green	98.00
Pressed Glass, Esther, Creamer, Green & Gold	48.00
Pressed Glass, Esther, Sugar, Covered	35.00
Pressed Glass, Esther, Sugar, Covered, Green	110.00
Pressed Glass, Esther, Table Set, Covered Sugar, Spooner & Creamer, Green	250.00
Pressed Glass, Esther, Wine	22.00 To 30.00
Etched Band, see Dakota	
Etched Dakota, see Dakota	
Etched Fern, see Ashman	
Etched patterns, see under main pattern, e.g.: Etched Dakota, see	
Dakota	
Pressed Glass, Etruscan, Sugar, Footed	12.00
Pressed Glass, Euclid, Cruet, Rough Pontil	25.00
Pressed Glass, Eugenie, Eggcup, Flint	40.00
Pressed Glass, Eugenie, Goblet, Flint	45.00
Pressed Glass, Eureka, Goblet, Flint	15.00
Pressed Glass, Everglades, Compote, Jelly, Green Opalescent	60.00
Pressed Glass, Excelsior With Maltese Cross, Tumbler, Flint	55.00
Pressed Glass, Excelsior, Bottle, Perfume, Faceted Stopper	35.00
Pressed Glass, Excelsior, Candlestick, Flint	125.00
Pressed Glass, Excelsior, Eggcup, Flint	22.50

Pressed Glass, Excelsior, Goblet	31.50
Pressed Glass, Excelsior, Goblet, Flint	35.00
Pressed Glass, Excelsior, Jar, Pickle, Covered	125.00
Pressed Glass, Excelsior, Pitcher, Water, Flint	150.00
Pressed Glass, Excelsior, Tumbler, Bar	35.00
Pressed Glass, Excelsior, Tumbler, Flint	55.00
Pressed Glass, Excelsior, Tumbler, Footed, Flint	35.00
Pressed Glass, Excelsior, Wine	30.00
Pressed Glass, Eye & Scale, Decanter, Sandwich, 1 Quart	27.00
Pressed Glass, Eyewinker, Butter, Covered	42.00 To 65.00
Pressed Glass, Eyewinker, Cake Stand, 8 1/4 In.	42.00 To 50.00
Pressed Glass, Eyewinker, Cracker Jar	45.00
Pressed Glass, Eyewinker, Creamer	17.00
Pressed Glass, Eyewinker, Salt & Pepper	40.00
Pressed Glass, Eyewinker, Syrup	35.00
Fagot, see Vera	
Pressed Glass, Faith, Hope & Charity, Bread Plate, Round, Handled	65.00
Pressed Glass, Falcon Strawberry, Goblet	16.00 To 22.50
Pressed Glass, Famous, Salt & Pepper	12.00
Pressed Glass, Fan & Star, Carafe, Water, Pewter Rim, Dated 1897	20.00
Pressed Glass, Fan With Crossbars, Wine	20.00
Pressed Glass, Fan With Diamond, Creamer	15.00

Pressed Glass, Fine Rib With Cut Ovals, Cordial

Pressed Glass, Fruit Panels, Goblet

Pressed Glass, Frosted Stork, Goblet

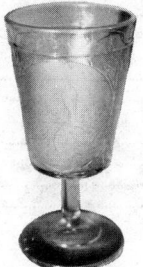

Pressed Glass, Fan With Diamond, Goblet	7.50 To 15.00
Pressed Glass, Fan With Diamond, Wine	19.50
Pressed Glass, Fan With Flute, Goblet, Amber Stained	35.00
Pressed Glass, Fan With Loops, Goblet	16.00
Pressed Glass, Fancy Cut, Glass, Child's	135.00
Pressed Glass, Fancy Loop, Creamer	25.00
Pressed Glass, Fancy Loop, Salt	12.00
Pressed Glass, Fancy Loop, Wine, Clear With Gold	25.00
Pressed Glass, Fandango, Salt	12.00
Pressed Glass, Feather Duster, Creamer	12.00 To 15.00
Pressed Glass, Feather Duster, Creamer, Footed	16.00
Pressed Glass, Feather Duster, Creamer, Green	26.00
Pressed Glass, Feather Duster, Spooner	15.00
Pressed Glass, Feather Duster, Spooner, Green	26.00
Pressed Glass, Feather Duster, Tumbler, Green	30.00
Pressed Glass, Feather, Banana Boat, Low Standard	75.00
Pressed Glass, Feather, Berry Bowl	14.00
Pressed Glass, Feather, Bowl, Pedestal, Covered, 7 1/2 In.	40.00
Pressed Glass, Feather, Butter, Covered	33.00 To 45.00
Pressed Glass, Feather, Butter, Covered, Green	145.00

Pressed Glass, Feather, Cake Stand, 8 X 4 1/4 In. .... 24.50 To 25.00
Pressed Glass, Feather, Cake Stand, 8 1/2 In. 33.00
Pressed Glass, Feather, Cake Stand, 8 3/4 In. 20.00
Pressed Glass, Feather, Cake Stand, 9 1/2 In. 37.50
Pressed Glass, Feather, Celery .... 22.00 To 32.50
Pressed Glass, Feather, Celery, Green 65.00
Pressed Glass, Feather, Compote, Jelly, 4 1/2 In. .... 16.50 To 17.50
Pressed Glass, Feather, Cordial 65.00
Pressed Glass, Feather, Creamer 15.00
Pressed Glass, Feather, Cruet .... 22.00 To 25.00
Pressed Glass, Feather, Cruet, Faceted Stopper 37.50
Pressed Glass, Feather, Dish, Ice Cream, 4 In.Square 10.00
Pressed Glass, Feather, Goblet 45.00
Pressed Glass, Feather, Goblet, Amber 55.00
Pressed Glass, Feather, Honey, 3 1/2 In. 22.50
Pressed Glass, Feather, Jar, Marmalade 90.00
Pressed Glass, Feather, Pitcher, Milk 42.50
Pressed Glass, Feather, Pitcher, Water .... 23.00 To 45.00
Pressed Glass, Feather, Pitcher, Water, Green 175.00
Pressed Glass, Feather, Plate, 10 In. 35.00
Pressed Glass, Feather, Punch Set, Bowl & 8 Cups, Near Cut, Signed 100.00
Pressed Glass, Feather, Relish .... 12.00 To 15.00
Pressed Glass, Feather, Relish, Green, 4 1/2 X 8 3/4 In. 45.00
Pressed Glass, Feather, Spooner .... 15.00 To 17.00
Pressed Glass, Feather, Spooner, Green 55.00
Pressed Glass, Feather, Sugar, Covered .... 22.50 To 30.00
Pressed Glass, Feather, Sugar, Open 16.00
Pressed Glass, Feather, Toothpick 37.00
Pressed Glass, Feather, Tumbler, Green 65.00
Pressed Glass, Feather, Wine 35.00
Pressed Glass, Feather, Wine, Indian Swirl 24.00
Pressed Glass, Feather, Wine, Scalloped Top 35.00
Pressed Glass, Feeding Swan, Celery, Etched 25.00
Pressed Glass, Feeding Swan, Pitcher, Water, Etched 45.00
Pressed Glass, Fern Burst, Goblet 9.00
Pressed Glass, Fern Burst, Goblet, Set Of 6 .... 72.00
Pressed Glass, Fern Burst, Sugar, Covered 18.00
Pressed Glass, Fern, Eggcup, Inverted, Flint 25.00
Pressed Glass, Fernland, Butter, Covered 10.00
Pressed Glass, Fernland, Creamer 15.00
Pressed Glass, Fernland, Creamer, Green 22.00
Pressed Glass, Ferris Wheel, Butter 35.00
    Festoon and Grape, see Grape and Festoon
Pressed Glass, Festoon, Berry Bowl 16.00
Pressed Glass, Festoon, Berry Bowl, 9 1/4 In. 25.00
Pressed Glass, Festoon, Bowl, 9 In. .... 15.00 To 16.50
Pressed Glass, Festoon, Butter, Covered 25.00
Pressed Glass, Festoon, Cake Stand, 9 In. 19.50
Pressed Glass, Festoon, Cake Stand, 9 1/4 X 6 In. 25.00
Pressed Glass, Festoon, Dish, 8 1/4 X 5 In. 14.50
Pressed Glass, Festoon, Pitcher, Water 45.00
Pressed Glass, Festoon, Spooner 19.50
Pressed Glass, Festoon, Tray, Water .... 21.50 To 25.00
Pressed Glass, Festoon, Tumbler 10.00
Pressed Glass, Festoon, Water Set, Tray, Pitcher, 4 Tumblers 145.00
Pressed Glass, Fickle Block, Goblet .... 11.00 To 15.00
Pressed Glass, Fickle Block, Lamp, 8 1/2 In. 45.00
Pressed Glass, Fickle Block, Wine 20.00
Pressed Glass, Fickle, Pitcher, Water 19.00
Pressed Glass, File, Pitcher, Water 40.00
Pressed Glass, File, Sugar, Covered 30.00
Pressed Glass, Fine Prism, Eggcup, Flint 27.50
Pressed Glass, Fine Prism, Goblet, Flint 20.00
Pressed Glass, Fine Rib With Cut Ovals, Goblet, Flint 195.00
Pressed Glass, Fine Rib With Cut Ovals, Tumbler, Flint 145.00
Pressed Glass, Fine Rib, Celery, Flint .... 50.00 To 65.00

Pressed Glass, Grape & Festoon, Cup

Pressed Glass, Garfield Drape, Pitcher, Water

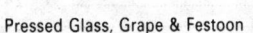

Pressed Glass, Grape & Festoon
With Shield, Goblet

Pressed Glass, Harp, Spill

Pressed Glass, Hairpin, Goblet, Rayed Base

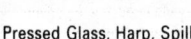

Pressed Glass, Hamilton, Compote

Pressed Glass, Fine Rib, Compote, Flint	45.00
Pressed Glass, Fine Rib, Goblet, Flint	45.00
Pressed Glass, Fine Rib, Pitcher, Water, Flint	275.00
Pressed Glass, Fine Rib, Salt, Flint	11.00
Pressed Glass, Fine Rib, Salt, Master, Flint	23.00
Pressed Glass, Fine Rib, Spooner	55.00
Pressed Glass, Fine Rib, Spooner, Flint	45.00 To 55.00
Pressed Glass, Fine Rib, Tumbler, Flint	35.00
Pressed Glass, Finecut & Block, Butter, Sugar & Creamer, Clear, 1880s	295.00
Pressed Glass, Finecut & Block, Compote	30.00
Pressed Glass, Finecut & Block, Cordial, Clear, 3 1/4 In.	15.00
Pressed Glass, Finecut & Block, Eggcup	19.50
Pressed Glass, Finecut & Block, Relish, Amber, Corset Shape, 8 1/2 In.	17.50
Pressed Glass, Finecut & Block, Spooner, Yellow Blocks	60.00
Pressed Glass, Finecut & Block, Sugar, Covered	35.00
Pressed Glass, Finecut & Feather, Wine	24.50
Pressed Glass, Finecut & Panel, Bowl, Footed, Blue	27.50
Pressed Glass, Finecut & Panel, Goblet	14.00 To 25.00
Pressed Glass, Finecut & Panel, Tray, Handled, 13 In.	23.00
Finecut Medallion, see Austrian	

Pressed Glass, Finecut, Creamer	15.00
Pressed Glass, Finecut, Plate, 10 1/2 In.	46.00
Pressed Glass, Finecut, Toothpick, Blue, Hat	35.00
Pressed Glass, Finecut, Wine	18.00
Pressed Glass, Finecut, Wine Set, Stopper, Green	135.00
Pressed Glass, Fishscale, Berry Bowl, 8 In.	16.00 To 18.00
Pressed Glass, Fishscale, Berry Bowl, 8 1/2 In.	18.50
Pressed Glass, Fishscale, Butter	28.00 To 40.00
Pressed Glass, Fishscale, Celery	22.50 To 28.50
Pressed Glass, Fishscale, Compote, Jelly	14.00 To 18.00
Pressed Glass, Fishscale, Creamer	15.00
Pressed Glass, Fishscale, Goblet	24.50 To 32.50
Pressed Glass, Fishscale, Pitcher, Milk	25.00 To 29.50
Pressed Glass, Fishscale, Pitcher, Water	30.00
Pressed Glass, Fishscale, Plate, Square, 8 In.	25.00
Pressed Glass, Fishscale, Plate, Square, 9 In.	24.50
Pressed Glass, Fishscale, Sauce	5.00
Pressed Glass, Fishscale, Spooner	25.00
Pressed Glass, Flamingo Habitat, Dish, Cheese, Covered	60.00 To 75.00
Pressed Glass, Flamingo Habitat, Goblet	15.00
Pressed Glass, Flamingo Habitat, Sugar	23.50
Flat Diamond & Panel, see Lattice & Oval Panels	
Pressed Glass, Flat Diamond, Celery	35.00
Pressed Glass, Flat Diamond, Goblet	10.00
Pressed Glass, Flat Panel, Berry Bowl, Ruby Stained	20.00
Pressed Glass, Flat Panel, Dish, Oval, Ruby Stained, 9 X 6 In.	20.00
Pressed Glass, Flat Prism Banded, Goblet	6.50
Pressed Glass, Flattened Diamond & Sawtooth, Table Set, Child's	75.00
Pressed Glass, Flattened Diamond & Sunburst, Cup, Punch	6.00
Pressed Glass, Flattened Sawtooth, Spooner, Spill, Flint	28.50
Pressed Glass, Fleur-De-Lis & Drape, Sugar	18.50
Pressed Glass, Fleur-De-Lis & Tassel, Pitcher, Milk	25.00
Pressed Glass, Fleur-De-Lis & Tassel, Pitcher, Milk, Green	45.00 To 65.00
Pressed Glass, Fleur-De-Lis & Tassel, Pitcher, Water, Emerald	38.00
Pressed Glass, Fleur-De-Lis & Tassel, Plate, Green, 8 In.	21.00
Pressed Glass, Fleur-De-Lis, Butter, Covered	38.00
Pressed Glass, Fleur-De-Lis, Butter, Covered, Arched	26.00
Pressed Glass, Fleur-De-Lis, Pitcher, Water, Emerald Green	45.00
Pressed Glass, Fleur-De-Lis, Wine	18.00
Pressed Glass, Flora, Sauce, Vaseline Opalescent, Set Of 6	160.00
Pressed Glass, Flora, Tumbler, Green	22.00
Florida, see Herringbone	
Pressed Glass, Florida Palm, Banana Stand	27.50
Pressed Glass, Florida Palm, Goblet	18.00
Pressed Glass, Flower & Pleat, Sugar Shaker, Original Top	75.00
Pressed Glass, Flower & Quill, Sugar, Covered	28.00
Pressed Glass, Flower Band, Celery	29.50
Pressed Glass, Flower Band, Compote, Oval, Covered, Frosted	125.00
Pressed Glass, Flower Band, Saltshaker, Celluloid Top, 1904, Pink Cased, Pr.	45.00
Flower Flange, see Dewey	
Pressed Glass, Flower Medallion, Creamer	12.00
Pressed Glass, Flower Medallion, Goblet, Flint	35.00
Pressed Glass, Flower Medallion, Tumbler, Set Of 8	100.00
Pressed Glass, Flower Pot, Bread Plate	35.00
Pressed Glass, Flower Pot, Creamer	20.00 To 24.50
Pressed Glass, Flower Pot, Spooner	19.50
Pressed Glass, Flower With Cane, Goblet	18.00
Pressed Glass, Flower With Cane, Water Set, 5 Tumblers	125.00
Pressed Glass, Flower With Cane, Wine, Gold	14.50
Pressed Glass, Flowered Scroll, Pitcher, Water, Amber	125.00
Pressed Glass, Flowered Scroll, Plate, Amber, 8 1/4 In.	35.00
Pressed Glass, Flute, Claret, Flint	27.00
Pressed Glass, Flute, Eggcup, Double	15.00
Pressed Glass, Flute, Eggcup, Flint	16.00
Pressed Glass, Flute, Goblet	30.00
Pressed Glass, Flute, Goblet, Flint	18.00

Pressed Glass, Flute, Pitcher, Covered, Footed, Pewter Top, 6 1/2 In. 25.00
Pressed Glass, Flute, Toothpick, Orange 50.00
Pressed Glass, Flute, Tumbler, 8 Sides, Flint 18.00
Pressed Glass, Flute, Whiskey, Footed, Flint 25.00
Pressed Glass, Fluted Scrolls, Creamer, Blue 45.00
Pressed Glass, Fluted Scrolls, Jar, Puff, Clear, Opalescent 32.00
Pressed Glass, Fluted Scrolls, Spooner, Opalescent, Vaseline 45.00
Pressed Glass, Flying Birds, Goblet 45.00
Flying Robin, see Hummingbird
Pressed Glass, Flying Stork, Compote, Covered, 8 In. 65.00
Pressed Glass, Flying Stork, Goblet .... 39.00 To 45.00
Pressed Glass, Flying Stork, Spooner 26.00
Forget-Me-Not in Snow, see Stippled Forget-Me-Not
Pressed Glass, Forget-Me-Not, Barred, Goblet 20.00
Pressed Glass, Forget-Me-Not, Relish, Paneled, Oblong 8.00
Pressed Glass, Forget-Me-Not, Saltshaker, Blue, Original Top 30.00
Pressed Glass, Forget-Me-Not, Sugar, Melon Ribbed, Green Opaque 85.00
Pressed Glass, Forget-Me-Not, Syrup 55.00
Pressed Glass, Forget-Me-Not, Wine, Stippled 32.50
Pressed Glass, Four Petal, Creamer, Flint 65.00
Pressed Glass, Four Petal, Sugar & Creamer, Covered, Applied Handle, Flint 160.00
Pressed Glass, Four Petal, Sugar, Lid 57.00
Pressed Glass, Fox & Crow, Pitcher, Water, Purpling 90.00
Pressed Glass, Frazier, Tumbler, Cranberry Flashed, Enamel Decoration 20.00
Pressed Glass, Frog With Water Lily, Toothpick 42.00
Frosted patterns, see also under name of main pattern
Pressed Glass, Frosted Band, Cake Stand 38.00
Pressed Glass, Frosted Cabbage Leaf, Compote, Rabbit Head Cover, 8 1/2 In. 75.00
Pressed Glass, Frosted Circle, Berry Bowl 28.00
Pressed Glass, Frosted Circle, Compote 35.00
Pressed Glass, Frosted Circle, Compote, Clear, 6 1/2 In. 19.00
Pressed Glass, Frosted Circle, Goblet, Etched 22.00
Pressed Glass, Frosted Circle, Sugar, Covered 39.50
Frosted Crane, see Frosted Stork
Pressed Glass, Frosted Eagle, Creamer 30.00
Pressed Glass, Frosted Eagle, Creamer, Etched 35.00
Pressed Glass, Frosted Eagle, Spooner, Etched 25.00
Pressed Glass, Frosted Eagle, Sugar, Covered, Etched 85.00
Frosted Flower Band, see Flower Band, Frosted
Pressed Glass, Frosted Fruits, Compote, Lovebirds Finial, C.1870 .... 225.00
Pressed Glass, Frosted Fruits, Pitcher, Water 45.00
Pressed Glass, Frosted Fruits, Tumbler, Water 35.00
Pressed Glass, Frosted Goat's Head, Spooner 58.00
Pressed Glass, Frosted Hobnail, Pitcher, Water 85.00
Pressed Glass, Frosted Leaf, Eggcup, Flint 95.00
Pressed Glass, Frosted Leaf, Goblet, Flint .... 60.00 To 75.00
Pressed Glass, Frosted Leaf, Spooner, Flint 69.50
Pressed Glass, Frosted Lion, Bread Plate, Closed Handles 50.00
Pressed Glass, Frosted Lion, Bread Plate, Frosted Center, Round 55.00
Pressed Glass, Frosted Lion, Bread Plate, Oval, Lions On Handles 75.00
Pressed Glass, Frosted Lion, Butter, Frosted Lion's Head, Covered 85.00
Pressed Glass, Frosted Lion, Celery .... 55.00 To 68.50
Pressed Glass, Frosted Lion, Celery, Frosted Base, 8 X 4 In. 42.50
Pressed Glass, Frosted Lion, Compote, Covered, Frosted Lion Finial, 8 In. 90.00
Pressed Glass, Frosted Lion, Compote, Covered, High Standard, 8 In. 85.00
Pressed Glass, Frosted Lion, Compote, Covered, 8 In. 85.00
Pressed Glass, Frosted Lion, Creamer .... 32.50 To 67.50
Pressed Glass, Frosted Lion, Dish, Relish, Frosted Lion Handles 45.00
Pressed Glass, Frosted Lion, Goblet 45.00
Pressed Glass, Frosted Lion, Jar, Marmalade .... 50.00 To 75.00
Pressed Glass, Frosted Lion, Marmalade, Covered, Lion Head Finial 110.00
Pressed Glass, Frosted Lion, Pitcher, Frosted Base, 6 1/2 In. 50.00
Pressed Glass, Frosted Lion, Spooner .... 22.50 To 57.50
Pressed Glass, Frosted Lion, Sugar, Open 82.50
Pressed Glass, Frosted Petal, Goblet 12.50
Pressed Glass, Frosted Ribbon With Double Bar, Goblet 15.00

Pressed Glass, Frosted Ribbon, Compote, Covered, 8 X 11 In.	55.00
Pressed Glass, Frosted Ribbon, Compote, 12 In.	45.00
Pressed Glass, Frosted Ribbon, Goblet	32.50
Pressed Glass, Frosted Ribbon, Pitcher, Water	87.50
Pressed Glass, Frosted Ribbon, Sugar	65.00
Pressed Glass, Frosted Stork, Bread Plate, Oval, 12 In.	35.00
Pressed Glass, Frosted Stork, Bread Plate, 12 In.	55.00
Pressed Glass, Frosted Stork, Spooner	26.00
Pressed Glass, Frosted Stork, Tray, Water	75.00
Frosted Waffle, see Hidalgo	
Pressed Glass, Frosted Wildrose & Bowknot, Pitcher, Water	42.00
Pressed Glass, Fuchsia, Compote, Scalloped Rim, Etched, 7 In.	32.00
Pressed Glass, Fuchsia, Goblet	22.50
Pressed Glass, G.A.R., Bread Plate	75.00
Pressed Glass, Gaelic, Cruet	15.00
Pressed Glass, Gaelic, Sugar, Covered	22.00
Pressed Glass, Gaelic, Toothpick, Clear With Gold	12.00
Pressed Glass, Galloway, Berry Bowl, 10 1/4 In.	29.50
Pressed Glass, Galloway, Bowl, Fruit	22.50
Pressed Glass, Galloway, Carafe, Water	23.50
Pressed Glass, Galloway, Celery	20.00
Pressed Glass, Galloway, Creamer	20.00 To 24.00
Pressed Glass, Galloway, Cruet	15.00
Pressed Glass, Galloway, Cup	25.00
Pressed Glass, Galloway, Salt & Pepper, Celluloid Insets	20.00
Pressed Glass, Galloway, Salt, Pewter Lid	9.00
Pressed Glass, Galloway, Sauce	7.00
Pressed Glass, Galloway, Sherbet, Footed	12.00
Pressed Glass, Galloway, Spooner	15.00
Pressed Glass, Galloway, Sugar	24.00
Pressed Glass, Galloway, Sugar, Covered	30.00
Pressed Glass, Galloway, Syrup, Original Top	32.00
Pressed Glass, Galloway, Toothpick, Gold At Top	35.00
Pressed Glass, Galloway, Wine	6.50 To 32.50
Pressed Glass, Garden Fruits, Butter, Covered	40.00
Pressed Glass, Garden Fruits, Creamer	30.00
Pressed Glass, Garden Fruits, Goblet	24.00
Pressed Glass, Garden Fruits, Pitcher, Water	48.00
Pressed Glass, Garden Fruits, Sugar, Covered	35.00
Garden of Eden, see Lotus & Serpent	
Pressed Glass, Garfield Drape, Butter, Covered	60.00
Pressed Glass, Garfield Drape, Celery	37.00 To 39.75
Pressed Glass, Garfield Drape, Creamer	18.00 To 35.00
Pressed Glass, Garfield Drape, Goblet	28.00 To 29.00
Pressed Glass, Garfield Drape, Pitcher, Milk	57.50
Pressed Glass, Garfield Drape, Pitcher, Water	50.00 To 70.00
Pressed Glass, Garfield Drape, Sauce, Flat, 4 In.	8.00
Pressed Glass, Garfield Drape, Spooner	20.00 To 38.00
Pressed Glass, Garfield Drape, Sugar, Covered	40.00
Pressed Glass, Garfield, Bread Plate, 11 1/4 In.	30.00
Pressed Glass, Garfield, Tumbler	16.00
Pressed Glass, General Ulysses Grant, Bread Plate	42.00
Pressed Glass, Georgia Gem, Toothpick, Green, Custard	45.00
Pressed Glass, Georgia, Berry Bowl	4.00
Pressed Glass, Giant Bull's-Eye, Goblet, Flint	45.00 To 75.00
Pressed Glass, Giant Prism With Thumbprint Band, Celery, Flint	50.00 To 100.00
Pressed Glass, Giant Prism With Thumbprint Band, Goblet, Flint	75.00
Pressed Glass, Giant Prism With Thumbprint Band, Spooner	24.50
Pressed Glass, Giant Prism, Goblet, Flint	75.00
Pressed Glass, Girl At Play, Plate, Frosted, Egg & Dart Border, 9 In.	32.00
Pressed Glass, Gloved Hands, Pitcher, Water	32.50
Pressed Glass, Golden Rule, Bread Plate	50.00
Pressed Glass, Gonterman Swirl, Creamer, Opalescent & Amber	110.00
Pressed Glass, Gonterman Swirl, Pitcher, Water, Opalescent & Amber	245.00
Pressed Glass, Gonterman Swirl, Sugar, Covered, Amber & Frosted	110.00 To 130.00
Pressed Glass, Gonterman Swirl, Toothpick, Amber, Opalescent	85.00

Pressed Glass, Gonterman Swirl, Tumbler, Opalescent, Amber Band	48.00
Pressed Glass, Gonterman, Berry Bowl, Swirl, Opalescent, Blue Band, 10 In.	135.00
Good Luck, see Horseshoe	
Pressed Glass, Gooseberry, Creamer	26.00
Pressed Glass, Gooseberry, Goblet	20.00
Pressed Glass, Gothic Arch, Celery, Flint	60.00
Pressed Glass, Gothic Arch, Tumbler, Sapphire, Flint, 3 1/4 In.	70.00
Pressed Glass, Gothic, Celery, Flint	100.00
Pressed Glass, Gothic, Celery, Gauffered Rim, Flint	150.00
Pressed Glass, Gothic, Creamer	55.00
Pressed Glass, Gothic, Eggcup, Flint	45.00
Pressed Glass, Gothic, Goblet, Flint	50.00 To 65.00
Pressed Glass, Gothic, Spooner, Flint	50.00
Pressed Glass, Gothic, Sugar, Covered, Flint	87.50
Grand, see Diamond Medallion	
Grand Army of the Republic, see G.A.R.	
Pressed Glass, Grant, Plate, Square	25.50
Grape, see also Beaded Grape, Beaded Grape Medallion, Magnet &	
Grape, Magnet & Grape with Frosted Leaf, Paneled Grape, Paneled	
Grape Band	
Pressed Glass, Grape & Cable, Tumbler Set, 5 Piece	175.00
Pressed Glass, Grape & Festoon With Shield, Goblet	30.00 To 35.00
Pressed Glass, Grape & Festoon With Stippled Leaf, Goblet	15.00
Pressed Glass, Grape & Festoon, Goblet	15.00 To 22.00
Pressed Glass, Grape & Festoon, Pitcher, Water, Applied Handle	60.00
Pressed Glass, Grape & Festoon, Spooner	16.00
Pressed Glass, Grape & Festoon, Spooner, Veined Leaf	22.50
Pressed Glass, Grape & Festoon, Sugar & Creamer, Applied Handle	50.00
Pressed Glass, Grape & Leaf, Bowl, Cover, Panels, 8 In.Deep	38.00
Pressed Glass, Grape & Leaf, Syrup, Opaque Blue, Applied Handle	90.00
Pressed Glass, Grape & Leaf, Syrup, Opaque Green	92.00
Pressed Glass, Grape Band, Goblet	15.00 To 18.50
Pressed Glass, Grape Band, Spooner, Footed	25.00
Pressed Glass, Grape Vine, Spooner	18.00
Pressed Glass, Grape Vintage, Bread Plate	22.50
Pressed Glass, Grape Vintage, Platter, It's A Pleasure	22.50
Pressed Glass, Grape Vintage, Tray, Bread, It's A Pleasure	22.50
Pressed Glass, Grape With Gothic Arches, Creamer, Green	35.00
Pressed Glass, Grape With Scroll Medallion, Creamer	20.00 To 25.00
Pressed Glass, Grape, Celery, Heavy Panel	27.50
Pressed Glass, Grape, Mug, Blue	25.00
Pressed Glass, Grapevine With Ovals, Butter, Covered, Clear, Miniature	55.00
Pressed Glass, Grapevine With Ovals, Creamer, Miniature	30.00
Pressed Glass, Grapevine With Ovals, Sugar, Covered, Miniature	65.00
Pressed Glass, Grasshopper With Insect, Spooner	24.00
Pressed Glass, Grasshopper With Insect, Spooner, Amber	65.00
Pressed Glass, Grasshopper, Bowl, 3 Feet, 8 1/2 In.Diameter	15.00
Pressed Glass, Grasshopper, Creamer	25.00
Pressed Glass, Grasshopper, Spooner	28.00 To 30.00
Pressed Glass, Grasshopper, Spooner, Insect	37.50
Pressed Glass, Greek Key, Spooner, Clear	16.00
Pressed Glass, Greek Key, Tumbler, Ruby Stained	32.50
Pressed Glass, Greentown, Tumbler, No.11	12.00
Pressed Glass, Grogan, Pitcher, Water	22.00
Pressed Glass, Guttate, Sugar Shaker, Pink	105.00
Pressed Glass, Hairpin With Rayed Base, Goblet, Flint	35.00
Pressed Glass, Hairpin With Thumbprint, Eggcup, Double, Flint	20.00
Pressed Glass, Hairpin With Thumbprint, Goblet	55.00
Pressed Glass, Hairpin With Thumbprint, Goblet, Flint	35.00
Pressed Glass, Hairpin, Champagne, Flint	18.50
Pressed Glass, Hairpin, Eggcup, Flint	12.00 To 24.50
Pressed Glass, Hairpin, Spooner, Flint	20.00
Pressed Glass, Halley's Comet, Goblet	30.00
Pressed Glass, Halley's Comet, Pitcher, Water, Etched	15.00
Pressed Glass, Halley's Comet, Tankard, Etched	48.00
Pressed Glass, Halley's Comet, Tumbler	16.00

Pressed Glass, Hamilton, Butter, Covered, Flint	75.00
Pressed Glass, Hamilton, Compote, Scalloped Rim, 5 X 8 In.	85.00
Pressed Glass, Hamilton, Eggcup, Flint	20.00 To 28.50
Pressed Glass, Hamilton, Goblet, Flint	27.50
Pressed Glass, Hamilton, Pitcher, Water, Flint	125.00
Pressed Glass, Hamilton, Platter, Railroad Train	45.00
Pressed Glass, Hamilton, Spooner	38.00
Pressed Glass, Hamilton, Spooner, Flint	25.00
Pressed Glass, Hamilton, Sugar	25.00
Pressed Glass, Hamilton, Tumbler	55.00
Pressed Glass, Hamilton, Tumbler, Flint	65.00
Hand, see Pennsylvania Hand	
Pressed Glass, Hand & Bar, Sugar	51.00
Pressed Glass, Hand With Fan, Toothpick	18.00
Pressed Glass, Hanover, Compote	30.00
Pressed Glass, Harp, Butter, Covered, Flint	135.00
Pressed Glass, Hartley, Goblet	15.00
Pressed Glass, Hartley, Vase, Celery	14.50 To 22.00
Pressed Glass, Hawaiian Lei, Cake Stand, 6 1/4 In. Diameter	23.00
Pressed Glass, Hawaiian Lei, Compote, Jelly	10.00
Pressed Glass, Hawaiian Lei, Salt & Pepper	18.50
Pressed Glass, Hawaiian Pineapple, Goblet, Flint	85.00
Pressed Glass, Hawaiian Pineapple, Tumbler, Flint	85.00
Pressed Glass, Heart & Thumbprint, Berry Bowl, 9 In.	32.50
Pressed Glass, Heart & Thumbprint, Berry Set, 7 Piece	75.00
Pressed Glass, Heart & Thumbprint, Bucket, Ice	31.50 To 65.00
Pressed Glass, Heart & Thumbprint, Cruet	41.00
Pressed Glass, Heart & Thumbprint, Plate, 12 In.	35.00
Pressed Glass, Heart & Thumbprint, Punch Cup	13.50
Pressed Glass, Heart & Thumbprint, Rose Bowl	24.00 To 30.00
Pressed Glass, Heart & Thumbprint, Salt	10.00
Pressed Glass, Heart & Thumbprint, Sugar, Handled	14.50
Pressed Glass, Heart & Thumbprint, Vase, 6 In.	18.00
Pressed Glass, Heart & Thumbprint, Wine	35.00
Pressed Glass, Heart Band, Tumbler, Ruby Stained	20.00
Pressed Glass, Heart Stem, Creamer	25.00
Pressed Glass, Heart With Thumbprint, Bottle, Bitters	68.00
Pressed Glass, Heart With Thumbprint, Cruet	43.00
Pressed Glass, Heart With Thumbprint, Sugar & Creamer, Individual	35.00
Pressed Glass, Heart With Thumbprint, Sugar, Handled, Individual	14.50
Pressed Glass, Heart With Thumbprint, Syrup, Small	38.00
Pressed Glass, Heart, Creamer, Stem	40.00
Pressed Glass, Heart, Cup Plate, Flint	45.00
Pressed Glass, Heart, Goblet	20.00
Pressed Glass, Heart, Honey, Flint	10.00
Pressed Glass, Heart, Sauce, Flint	15.00
Hearts of Loch Laven, see Shuttle	
Pressed Glass, Heavy Drape, Pitcher, Water	37.00
Pressed Glass, Heavy Finecut, Butter, Covered, Amber	50.00
Pressed Glass, Heavy Gothic, Spooner, Ruby Stain	37.50
Heavy Paneled Finecut, see Paneled Diamond Cross	
Pressed Glass, Heavy Thumbprint, Goblet	5.00
Pressed Glass, Henrietta, Celery, Ruby Stained	75.00
Pressed Glass, Henrietta, Creamer, 3 1/4 In.	10.00
Pressed Glass, Henrietta, Sugar, Covered	22.00
Pressed Glass, Hercules Pillar, Syrup	38.00
Pressed Glass, Heron, Celery	29.00
Pressed Glass, Heron, Creamer	28.50
Pressed Glass, Heron, Sugar, Covered	45.00
Pressed Glass, Herringbone Band, Goblet	22.00
Pressed Glass, Herringbone Band, Spooner	14.50
Pressed Glass, Herringbone, Berry Bowl, Emerald Green	35.00
Pressed Glass, Herringbone, Berry Set, 7 Piece	85.00
Pressed Glass, Herringbone, Creamer	20.00
Pressed Glass, Herringbone, Dish, Relish, Green	9.50
Pressed Glass, Herringbone, Dish, Sauce, Emerald Green	8.00

Pressed Glass, Herringbone, Goblet .... 9.00 To 11.50
Pressed Glass, Herringbone, Mustard 15.00
Pressed Glass, Herringbone, Pitcher, Buttermilk 23.50
Pressed Glass, Herringbone, Pitcher, Water, Emerald Green, 8 1/2 In. 40.00
Pressed Glass, Herringbone, Sauce, Flat, Emerald Green 5.00
Pressed Glass, Herringbone, Sauce, Ribbed 8.00
Pressed Glass, Herringbone, Spooner 24.50
Pressed Glass, Herringbone, Tumbler, Green 17.50
Pressed Glass, Hexagon Block, Creamer, Variant, Flint 30.00
Pressed Glass, Hexagon Block, Syrup, Etched, Amber 160.00
Pressed Glass, Hey Diddle Diddle, Plate, 6 In. 22.50
Pressed Glass, Hickman, Goblet .... 20.00 To 22.00
Pressed Glass, Hickman, Goblet, Green 45.00
Pressed Glass, Hickman, Relish, Green 12.00
Pressed Glass, Hickman, Salt 11.00
Pressed Glass, Hidalgo, Celery, Etched .... 15.00 To 18.00
Pressed Glass, Hidalgo, Creamer, Frosted 30.00
Pressed Glass, Hidalgo, Goblet, Frosted .... 12.50 To 18.00
Pressed Glass, Hidalgo, Pitcher, Milk, Frosted 35.00
Pressed Glass, Hinoto, Celery, Flint 50.00
Pressed Glass, Hinoto, Champagne, Flint 20.00
Pressed Glass, Hinoto, Creamer 68.00
Pressed Glass, Hinoto, Creamer, Flint 85.00
Pressed Glass, Hinoto, Goblet, Flint 40.00
Pressed Glass, Hinoto, Sugar, Covered, Flint 70.00
Pressed Glass, Hinoto, Tumbler, Footed .... 25.00 To 28.00
Hobnail & Bars, see Barred Hobnail
Pressed Glass, Hobnail & Paneled Thumbprint, Creamer, Vaseline 75.00
Pressed Glass, Hobnail With Line Band, Pitcher, Water 19.00
Pressed Glass, Hobnail With Thumbprint, Salt 12.00
Pressed Glass, Hobnail With Thumbprint, Salt, Amber 17.00
Pressed Glass, Hobstar & Flower, Cruet 25.00
Holbrook, see Pineapple & Fan
Pressed Glass, Holland, Sugar, Covered 16.50
Pressed Glass, Holly Leaves, Goblet .... 16.00 To 19.00
Pressed Glass, Holly With Cord & Tassel, Spooner 45.00
Pressed Glass, Homestead, Celery, Handled 12.00
Honeycomb, see also Loop & Honeycomb, Vernon Honeycomb
Pressed Glass, Honeycomb & Clover, Berry Bowl, Master 50.00
Pressed Glass, Honeycomb With Diamond, Goblet, Flint 25.00
Pressed Glass, Honeycomb, Butter, Green 35.00
Pressed Glass, Honeycomb, Goblet .... 5.00 To 15.00
Pressed Glass, Honeycomb, Goblet, Buttermilk, Flint 25.00
Pressed Glass, Honeycomb, Goblet, Engraved Floral Band, Flint 24.00
Pressed Glass, Honeycomb, Goblet, Flint .... 18.00 To 22.00
Pressed Glass, Honeycomb, Goblet, Frosted, Etched Grape, Flint 60.00
Pressed Glass, Honeycomb, Jar, Pomade, Metal Cover 35.00
Pressed Glass, Honeycomb, Mug 20.00
Pressed Glass, Honeycomb, Spooner .... 13.00 To 13.50
Pressed Glass, Honeycomb, Tumbler, Footed 7.00
Pressed Glass, Honeycomb, Whiskey, Applied Handle, Flint 35.00
Pressed Glass, Honeycomb, Whiskey, Handled 20.00
Pressed Glass, Hooks & Eyes, Goblet 13.00
Pressed Glass, Hops Band, Cake Stand 20.00
Pressed Glass, Hops Band, Goblet 12.00
Pressed Glass, Horn Of Plenty, Celery, Flint 125.00
Pressed Glass, Horn Of Plenty, Champagne, Flint 125.00
Pressed Glass, Horn Of Plenty, Creamer 148.00
Pressed Glass, Horn Of Plenty, Creamer, Flint 132.00
Pressed Glass, Horn Of Plenty, Decanter, Flange Neck, Flint, Quart 115.00
Pressed Glass, Horn Of Plenty, Eggcup 35.00
Pressed Glass, Horn Of Plenty, Eggcup, Flint .... 32.50 To 35.00
Pressed Glass, Horn Of Plenty, Glass, Shot, Flint, 3 In. 75.00
Pressed Glass, Horn Of Plenty, Goblet, Flint .... 38.50 To 80.00
Pressed Glass, Horn Of Plenty, Plate, Flint, 6 In. .... 47.50 To 85.00
Pressed Glass, Horn Of Plenty, Relish, Flint 31.50

Pressed Glass, Hobnail,
Tumbler, 4 1/2 In.High

Pressed Glass, Hobnail, Pitcher, 8 1/2 In.High

Pressed Glass, Holly Band, Celery

Pressed Glass, Holly, Compote, Covered

Pressed Glass, Horn Of Plenty, Sauce, Flint, 4 In.	14.00
Pressed Glass, Horn Of Plenty, Spill, Flint	25.00
Pressed Glass, Horn Of Plenty, Spooner	35.00
Pressed Glass, Horn Of Plenty, Sugar, Covered, Flint	90.00 To 135.00
Pressed Glass, Horn Of Plenty, Sugar, Flint	50.00 To 52.00
Pressed Glass, Horn Of Plenty, Sugar, Open, Flint	52.00
Pressed Glass, Horn Of Plenty, Tumbler, Flint	75.00
Pressed Glass, Horn Of Plenty, Whiskey, Flint, 3 In.	75.00
Pressed Glass, Horseheads Medallion, Celery	25.00
Pressed Glass, Horseheads Medallion, Spooner	17.00
Pressed Glass, Horsemint, Candy Container, Handled	18.00
Pressed Glass, Horsemint, Pitcher, Water, Gold	25.00
Pressed Glass, Horseshoe, Bowl, 6 In.	8.50
Pressed Glass, Horseshoe, Bread Plate, Give Us This Day	39.50
Pressed Glass, Horseshoe, Bread Plate, 13 1/2 In.	25.00
Pressed Glass, Horseshoe, Cake Stand, 10 In.	35.00 To 70.00
Pressed Glass, Horseshoe, Celery	45.00
Pressed Glass, Horseshoe, Compote, Covered, 8 In.	47.50
Pressed Glass, Horseshoe, Creamer	20.00 To 35.00
Pressed Glass, Horseshoe, Creamer, Good Luck	22.00
Pressed Glass, Horseshoe, Dish, Relish	13.00 To 14.00
Pressed Glass, Horseshoe, Goblet	22.50 To 24.00
Pressed Glass, Horseshoe, Goblet, Knob Stem	25.00 To 35.00
Pressed Glass, Horseshoe, Pitcher	50.00
Pressed Glass, Horseshoe, Plate, Bread, Single Horseshoe Handles, 9 X 13 In.	20.00
Pressed Glass, Horseshoe, Plate, 10 In.	28.50
Pressed Glass, Horseshoe, Plate, 7 In.	35.00
Pressed Glass, Horseshoe, Sauce, Footed	12.00
Pressed Glass, Horseshoe, Spooner	17.50 To 21.00
Pressed Glass, Horseshoe, Sugar, Open, Good Luck	15.00
Pressed Glass, Hotel Argus, Goblet	18.00
Pressed Glass, Hotel Thumbprint, Goblet	5.00
Pressed Glass, Huber, Claret, Flint, Straight	16.00
Pressed Glass, Huber, Decanter, Quart, Flint	25.00

Pressed Glass, Huber, Whiskey, Curled Applied Handle, Flint	45.00
Pressed Glass, Huber, Whiskey, Handled, Flint	47.50
Huckle, see Feather Duster	
Pressed Glass, Hummingbird, Butter, Covered	39.00
Pressed Glass, Hummingbird, Creamer	25.00 To 30.00
Pressed Glass, Hummingbird, Creamer, Amber	35.00
Pressed Glass, Hummingbird, Goblet	39.00
Pressed Glass, Hummingbird, Tumbler	26.00
Pressed Glass, Hundred Eye, Goblet	18.50
Pressed Glass, Icicle, Pitcher, Water	28.00
Ida, see Sheraton	
Pressed Glass, Idyll, Butter, Apple Green, Lid	90.00
Pressed Glass, Idyll, Sugar, Covered, Green & Gold	40.00
Pressed Glass, Illinois Basket, Spooner	45.00
Pressed Glass, Illinois, Creamer	16.50 To 17.50
Pressed Glass, Illinois, Plate, Square, 7 In.	16.50 To 17.00
Pressed Glass, Illinois, Spooner	18.00
Pressed Glass, Illinois, Toothpick	16.00
Pressed Glass, In Remembrance, Plate, 3 Presidents, 12 In.	65.00
Pressed Glass, Independence Hall, Bank, Tin Enclosure	195.00
Indian Tree, see Sprig	
Indiana Swirl, see Feather	
Pressed Glass, Intaglio, Creamer, Blue	90.00
Pressed Glass, Interlocked Hearts, Butter	20.00
Pressed Glass, Inverted Fan & Feather, Dish, Candy, Flared, Canary	18.00
Pressed Glass, Inverted Fan & Feather, Tumbler, Blue Opalescent, Gold	55.00
Pressed Glass, Inverted Fan & Feather, Tumbler, Green	45.00
Pressed Glass, Inverted Fan & Feather, Tumbler, Green, Gold	34.00
Pressed Glass, Inverted Fan & Feather, Water Set, Pitcher & 4 Tumblers	395.00
Pressed Glass, Inverted Fern, Creamer, Flint	60.00
Pressed Glass, Inverted Fern, Eggcup	25.00
Pressed Glass, Inverted Fern, Goblet	25.00 To 27.00
Pressed Glass, Inverted Fern, Goblet, Flint	27.00
Pressed Glass, Inverted Fern, Goblet, Rayed Base	40.00
Pressed Glass, Inverted Fern, Tumbler, Flint	110.00
Pressed Glass, Inverted Heart, Honey, Set Of 6	20.00
Pressed Glass, Inverted Heart, Sauce	8.00
Pressed Glass, Inverted Prism, Goblet, Etched	16.00
Pressed Glass, Inverted Strawberry, Bowl, Punch, Child's	45.00
Pressed Glass, Inverted Strawberry, Tumbler, Ruby Stained	65.00
Pressed Glass, Inverted Thistle, Cake Stand, 6 3/4 X 10 3/4 In.	35.00
Pressed Glass, Inverted Thumbprint, Celery, Amber	17.00
Pressed Glass, Inverted Thumbprint, Cruet, Smoky, Clear Trim	80.00
Pressed Glass, Inverted Thumbprint, Cruet, Square, Blue	75.00
Pressed Glass, Inverted Thumbprint, Syrup, Dated Top, July 15, 1884, Amber	95.00
Pressed Glass, Inverted Thumbprint, Tumbler, Amber	20.00
Pressed Glass, Inverted Thumbprint, Tumbler, Blue	22.50
Pressed Glass, Inverted Thumbprint, Wine	22.00
Pressed Glass, Ionia, Goblet	8.00 To 15.00
Pressed Glass, Iowa, Compote, Jelly	15.00
Pressed Glass, Iowa, Goblet	18.50
Pressed Glass, Iowa, Salt	11.00
Pressed Glass, Iris & Herringbone, Wine, Clear	18.00
Pressed Glass, Iris With Meander, Plate, Clear, Opalescent, 7 In.	12.00
Pressed Glass, Iris With Meander, Toothpick, Green	43.00
Pressed Glass, Iris, Pitcher, Footed, Crystal, 9 1/2 In.	12.00
Pressed Glass, Ivy In Snow, Butter	27.00
Pressed Glass, Ivy In Snow, Cake Stand, 7 In.	12.00
Pressed Glass, Ivy In Snow, Cake Stand, 8 In.	17.00
Pressed Glass, Ivy In Snow, Goblet	19.00
Pressed Glass, Ivy In Snow, Goblet, Buttermilk, Stippled	28.00
Pressed Glass, Ivy In Snow, Pitcher, Water	40.00
Pressed Glass, Ivy In Snow, Spooner	12.50
Pressed Glass, Ivy, Toothpick	70.00
Pressed Glass, Jackson, Creamer	55.00
Pressed Glass, Jacob's Coat, Pitcher, Water	17.00

Pressed Glass, Jacob's Ladder, Celery	21.00
Pressed Glass, Jacob's Ladder, Creamer	29.00 To 30.00
Pressed Glass, Jacob's Ladder, Dish, Pickle, Maltese Cross Handles, Amber	55.00
Pressed Glass, Jacob's Ladder, Goblet	45.00 To 55.00
Pressed Glass, Jacob's Ladder, Pitcher, Water	145.00 To 150.00
Pressed Glass, Jacob's Ladder, Pitcher, Water, Applied Handle	150.00
Pressed Glass, Jacob's Ladder, Plate, 6 In.	25.00
Pressed Glass, Jacob's Ladder, Spooner	24.00 To 35.00
Pressed Glass, Jacob's Ladder, Sugar & Creamer	60.00
Pressed Glass, Jacob's Ladder, Sugar & Creamer, Open	57.00 To 60.00
Pressed Glass, Jacob's Ladder, Sugar, Covered	40.00
Pressed Glass, Jacob's Ladder, Syrup, Metal Top, Thumb Rest, 7 1/2 In.	70.00
Pressed Glass, Jacob's Ladder, Wine	29.00 To 35.00
Jasper, see Late Buckle	
Pressed Glass, Jefferson Davis, Bread Plate	50.00
Pressed Glass, Jefferson's Drape, Tumbler, White Opalescent	45.00
Pressed Glass, Jenny Lind, Bread Plate	30.00
Pressed Glass, Jenny Lind, Compote, Frosted Bust Stem & Flower, 8 X 9 In.	95.00
Pressed Glass, Jersey Swirl, Compote, High Standard, 8 In.	28.50
Pressed Glass, Jersey Swirl, Salt Dip, Blue	12.00
Pressed Glass, Jersey Swirl, Toothpick	14.00
Pressed Glass, Jerusalem Star, Compote, Jelly, 4 1/2 X 5 1/2 In.	12.50
Pressed Glass, Jewel & Dewdrop, Bowl, 8 1/4 X 3 In.	20.00

Pressed Glass, Iconoclast, Goblet

Pressed Glass, Jeweled Heart, Pitcher

Pressed Glass, Jewel & Dewdrop, Bread Plate, Daily Bread, Clear	35.00
Pressed Glass, Jewel & Dewdrop, Butter, Covered, Flange	48.00
Pressed Glass, Jewel & Dewdrop, Cake Stand, High Pedestal, 8 In.Diameter	35.00
Pressed Glass, Jewel & Dewdrop, Cake Stand, Low Pedestal, 8 In.Diameter	35.00
Pressed Glass, Jewel & Dewdrop, Compote, Open, 6 In.Diameter	35.00
Pressed Glass, Jewel & Dewdrop, Dish, Pickle, 3 X 7 In.	22.00
Pressed Glass, Jewel & Dewdrop, Mug	12.00
Pressed Glass, Jewel & Dewdrop, Mug, Whiskey	10.00
Pressed Glass, Jewel & Dewdrop, Pitcher, Water	25.00 To 39.00
Pressed Glass, Jewel & Dewdrop, Sauce, 4 1/2 X 1 1/2 In.	6.50
Pressed Glass, Jewel & Dewdrop, Syrup, Original Tin Lid	68.00
Pressed Glass, Jewel & Fan, Bowl, Oval, 7 In.	9.00
Pressed Glass, Jewel & Flower, Sauce, White With Gold Flashing	35.00
Jewel Band, see Scalloped Tape	
Pressed Glass, Jeweled Drapery, Goblet	14.00
Pressed Glass, Jeweled Heart, Cruet, Blue, Gold Trim	165.00
Pressed Glass, Jeweled Heart, Dish, Berry, Blue Opal, Not Scalloped	23.00
Pressed Glass, Jeweled Heart, Saltshaker, Blue, Pair	50.00
Pressed Glass, Jeweled Moon & Star, Pitcher, Water	65.00
Pressed Glass, Jeweled Moon & Star, Spooner	45.00
Job's Tears, see Art	
Jubilee, see Hickman	
Pressed Glass, Jumbo, Candy Container, Green, 3 1/4 In.	65.00
Pressed Glass, Jumbo, Compote, Frosted, Covered, Finial, 7 1/2 X 12 In.	245.00

Pressed Glass, Jumbo, Spoon Rack 295.00
Pressed Glass, Jumbo, Spooner 60.00
Pressed Glass, Just Out, Toothpick 65.00
Pressed Glass, Just Out, Toothpick, Frosted 62.00
Pressed Glass, Kalbach, Goblet 8.00
Pressed Glass, Kaleidoscope, Creamer 28.00
Kamoni, see Balder
Pressed Glass, Kansas, Bowl, 8 1/4 X 3 In. 20.00
Kansas, see Jewel & Dewdrop
Pressed Glass, Kayak, Spooner 9.50
Pressed Glass, Kennedy Loop, Goblet, Flint 15.00
Pressed Glass, Kentucky, Cake Stand, 8 3/4 In. 35.00
Pressed Glass, Kentucky, Celery 18.00
Pressed Glass, Kentucky, Cruet 25.00
Pressed Glass, Kentucky, Plate, 8 In. 12.00
Pressed Glass, Kentucky, Tumbler, Green 21.00
Pressed Glass, Kentucky, Wine 20.00
Pressed Glass, Keystone Centennial, Goblet 75.00
Pressed Glass, King's Crown, Banana Boat 125.00
Pressed Glass, King's Crown, Berry Set, Master & 6 Sauces, 4 1/4 In. 165.00
Pressed Glass, King's Crown, Bowl, Punch, Footed 225.00
Pressed Glass, King's Crown, Celery .... 58.75 To 65.00
Pressed Glass, King's Crown, Compote, Covered, 6 In. 45.00
Pressed Glass, King's Crown, Compote, Open, 8 1/2 In. 38.00
Pressed Glass, King's Crown, Creamer, Crystal, 3 In. 12.50
Pressed Glass, King's Crown, Creamer, Green Eyes, Gold Trim 22.00
Pressed Glass, King's Crown, Creamer, Yellow Stained, Miniature, 3 In, High 30.00
Pressed Glass, King's Crown, Creamer, Yellow, Squat Shape, 3 In. 30.00
Pressed Glass, King's Crown, Pitcher, Water, Bulbous, Applied Handle 135.00
Pressed Glass, King's Crown, Pitcher, Water, 6 Stemmed 3-Mold Goblets 95.00
Pressed Glass, King's Crown, Salt, Individual .... 35.00 To 45.00
Pressed Glass, King's Crown, Salt, Individual, Rectangular 35.00
Pressed Glass, King's Crown, Saltshaker 30.00
Pressed Glass, King's Crown, Sauce, Boat Shaped, Yellow Stained 25.00
Pressed Glass, King's Crown, Spooner .... 25.00 To 55.00
Pressed Glass, King's Crown, Spooner, Etched 18.00
Pressed Glass, King's Crown, Spooner, 4 3/8 In. 26.00
Pressed Glass, King's Crown, Toothpick, Etched 42.50
Pressed Glass, King's Crown, Tumbler .... 25.00 To 34.50
Pressed Glass, King's Crown, Wine, Footed 6.00
Pressed Glass, King's Curtain, Goblet 14.00
Pressed Glass, King's 500, Tumbler, Cobalt Blue, Gold 24.00
Pressed Glass, Klondike, Bowl, Flared, 11 In. 45.00
Pressed Glass, Klondike, Bowl, Round, 8 In. 45.00
Pressed Glass, Klondike, Butter 85.00
Pressed Glass, Klondike, Celery, Ruby Panels 95.00
Pressed Glass, Klondike, Creamer, Applied Handle 25.00
Pressed Glass, Klondike, Cruet, Yellow Bars 675.00
Pressed Glass, Klondike, Cup, Punch 125.00
Pressed Glass, Klondike, Salt & Pepper .... 125.00 To 195.00
Pressed Glass, Klondike, Salt & Pepper, Frosted & Amber .... 168.00 To 185.00
Pressed Glass, Klondike, Saltshaker, Clear 15.00
Pressed Glass, Klondike, Saltshaker, Clear, Pair 25.00
Pressed Glass, Klondike, Saltshakers, Pair 195.00
Pressed Glass, Klondike, Spooner 50.00
Pressed Glass, Klondike, Sugar Shaker, Pair 195.00
Pressed Glass, Klondike, Sugar, Frosted, Amber Cross With Scalloped Top 195.00
Pressed Glass, Klondike, Table Set, Covered Sugar & Creamer, Butter, Spooner 850.00
Pressed Glass, Klondike, Tray, Cruet 235.00
Pressed Glass, Klondike, Vase, Stemmed, 8 1/4 In. 200.00
Pressed Glass, Klondike, Vase, Trumpet Shape, Frosted, Amber, 8 In. 175.00
Pressed Glass, Knights Of Labor, Bread Plate 95.00
Pressed Glass, Knights Of Labor, Mug 25.00
Pressed Glass, Knights Of Pythias, Goblet, Green 16.00
Pressed Glass, Knives & Forks, Goblet, Flint 12.00
Pressed Glass, Knobby Bull's-Eye, Goblet 18.00

Pressed Glass, Jumbo, Jar, Marmalade

Pressed Glass, Knobby Bull's-Eye, Tumbler, Amethyst Eyes, Gold Trim	12.00
Pressed Glass, Knobby Bull's-Eye, Wine	15.00
Pressed Glass, Kokomo, Compote, Covered, 8 In.	25.00
Pressed Glass, Kokomo, Goblet	15.00 To 19.00
Pressed Glass, Kokomo, Sugar, Covered	25.00
Pressed Glass, Krom, Goblet, Flint	40.00 To 45.00
Lace, see Drapery	
Pressed Glass, Lacy Daisy, Berry Set, 4 In. Diameter, 6 Piece	60.00
Pressed Glass, Lacy Dewdrop, Butter, Covered, C.1880	30.00
Pressed Glass, Lacy Medallion, Mug, Green, Gold, 2 3/4 In.	25.00
Pressed Glass, Lacy Medallion, Toothpick, Green, Trace Of Gold	20.00
Pressed Glass, Lacy Medallion, Tumbler, Green	18.00
Pressed Glass, Ladders, Toothpick	22.00
Pressed Glass, Lamb, Creamer, Child's	48.00
Pressed Glass, Lamp, see Lamp, Pressed Glass	
Pressed Glass, Late Block, Tumbler, Ruby Stained	29.50
Pressed Glass, Late Buckle, Butter, Covered	32.00
Pressed Glass, Late Buckle, Wine	22.00
Pressed Glass, Lattice & Oval Panels, Glass, Ale	55.00
Pressed Glass, Lattice & Oval Panels, Goblet, Flint	75.00
Pressed Glass, Lattice & Oval Panels, Pitcher, Water, Flint	275.00
Pressed Glass, Lattice & Oval Panels, Tumbler, Flint	100.00
Pressed Glass, Lattice & Oval Panels, Wine, Flint	50.00
Pressed Glass, Lattice, Goblet	14.00 To 20.00
Pressed Glass, Lattice, Toothpick, White Opalescent, Ribbed	35.00
Pressed Glass, Leaf & Dart, Butter, Covered	50.00
Pressed Glass, Leaf & Dart, Celery	40.00 To 45.00
Pressed Glass, Leaf & Dart, Celery, Pedestal	25.00
Pressed Glass, Leaf & Dart, Creamer, Applied Handle	35.00
Pressed Glass, Leaf & Dart, Dish, Relish, Oval	15.00
Pressed Glass, Leaf & Dart, Goblet	18.00 To 25.00
Pressed Glass, Leaf & Dart, Goblet, Flint	24.00
Pressed Glass, Leaf & Dart, Master Salt	22.00
Pressed Glass, Leaf & Dart, Pitcher, Water, Applied Handle	85.00
Pressed Glass, Leaf & Dart, Spooner	25.00
Pressed Glass, Leaf & Dart, Sugar, Covered	40.00
Pressed Glass, Leaf & Dart, Tumbler, Footed	25.00
Pressed Glass, Leaf & Dart, Wine	18.00 To 28.00
Pressed Glass, Leaf & Flower, Butter, Amber & Clear	90.00
Pressed Glass, Leaf & Flower, Butter, Covered, Clear & Frosted	35.00
Pressed Glass, Leaf & Flower, Celery, Fluted Top, Amber	52.00
Pressed Glass, Leaf & Flower, Creamer, Amber	62.00
Pressed Glass, Leaf & Flower, Creamer, Amber & Clear	50.00
Pressed Glass, Leaf & Flower, Sugar, Covered, Amber & Clear	65.00
Pressed Glass, Leaf & Flower, Syrup, Amber & Clear	65.00
Pressed Glass, Leaf & Flower, Tankard, Amber & Clear	105.00
Pressed Glass, Leaf & Star, Pitcher, Water, Gold Rim	43.50
Pressed Glass, Leaf Bracket, Butter, Covered, Chocolate	75.00
Pressed Glass, Leaf Medallion, Sauce, Green, Gold	14.00

ressed Glass, **Leaf Mold,** Shaker, Sugar, Cranberry, Spatter	155.00
ressed Glass, **Leaf Umbrella,** Sugar Shaker, Blue	37.00
ressed Glass, **Leaf,** Eggcup, Flint	24.50
ressed Glass, **Leaf,** Eggcup, Frosted, Flint	95.00
ressed Glass, **Leaf,** Sugar, Open	15.00
ressed Glass, **Leaflets,** Creamer	15.00
ressed Glass, **Lee,** Goblet, Flint	125.00
ressed Glass, **Lee,** Tumbler, Flint	95.00
ressed Glass, **Leg Banded Star,** Creamer	21.00
Lens & Star, see Star & Oval	
Leverne, see Star in Honeycomb	
ressed Glass, **Liberty Bell,** Berry Bowl	45.00
ressed Glass, **Liberty Bell,** Butter, Covered	48.00 To 150.00
ressed Glass, **Liberty Bell,** Creamer, Applied Reeded Handle	95.00 To 135.00
ressed Glass, **Liberty Bell,** Creamer, Plain Handle	85.00
ressed Glass, **Liberty Bell,** Dish, Relish, Oval	33.00 To 45.00
ressed Glass, **Liberty Bell,** Goblet	30.00 To 35.00
ressed Glass, **Liberty Bell,** Goblet, Knob Stemmed	37.50
ressed Glass, **Liberty Bell,** Mug, Snake Handle	325.00
ressed Glass, **Liberty Bell,** Plate, 10 In.	75.00
ressed Glass, **Liberty Bell,** Sauce, Footed	22.00
ressed Glass, **Liberty Bell,** Sauce, Scalloped Edge, 1776-1876	18.00
ressed Glass, **Liberty Bell,** Spooner	75.00 To 95.00
ressed Glass, **Liberty Bell,** Sugar, Covered	50.00 To 120.00
ressed Glass, **Lighting,** Celery	22.00
ressed Glass, **Lily Of The Valley,** Celery	27.50 To 40.00
ressed Glass, **Lily Of The Valley,** Dish, Relish	12.00 To 12.50
ressed Glass, **Lily Of The Valley,** Dish, Relish, Egg Shape	7.50
ressed Glass, **Lily Of The Valley,** Eggcup	45.00
ressed Glass, **Lily Of The Valley,** Goblet	32.50
ressed Glass, **Lily Of The Valley,** Goblet, Etched	12.50 To 15.00
ressed Glass, **Lily Of The Valley,** Goblet, Knob Stem, Etched	20.00
ressed Glass, **Lily Of The Valley,** Spooner	22.00
ressed Glass, **Lily Of The Valley,** Tumbler, Etched	18.00
ressed Glass, **Lincoln Drape With Tassel,** Goblet, Flint	95.00 To 105.00
ressed Glass, **Lincoln Drape,** Eggcup, Flint	49.50
ressed Glass, **Lincoln Drape,** Goblet, Flint	55.00 To 65.00
ressed Glass, **Lincoln Drape,** Syrup	65.00
ressed Glass, **Lined Ribs,** Wine	15.00
Lion, see also Frosted Lion	
ressed Glass, **Lion & Baboon,** Spooner	60.00
ressed Glass, **Lion In The Jungle,** Goblet	85.00
ressed Glass, **Lion,** Butter, Covered	75.00
ressed Glass, **Lion,** Butter, Frosted	135.00
ressed Glass, **Lion,** Butter, Frosted Lion Head Finial	75.00
ressed Glass, **Lion,** Cake Plate, Clear, Frosted	35.00
ressed Glass, **Lion,** Celery, Frosted	60.00
ressed Glass, **Lion,** Compote, Covered, Lion Finial, Frosted, 5 1/2 X 9 In.	100.00
ressed Glass, **Lion,** Compote, Lion Head Finial, 7 1/2 In.	125.00
ressed Glass, **Lion,** Creamer, Baboon	67.50

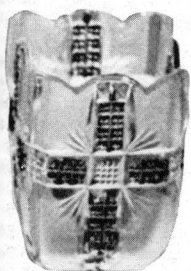

Pressed Glass, Klondike, Toothpick

Pressed Glass, Liberty Bell, Plate

Pressed Glass, Lion, Goblet, Frosted .... 25.00 To 50.0
Pressed Glass, Lion, Goblet, Square 49.0
Pressed Glass, Lion, Jar, Jam, Covered, Frosted 100.0
Pressed Glass, Lion, Marmalade, Covered, Lion Finial, Frosted 135.0
Pressed Glass, Lion, Pitcher, Water, Cable Base 55.0
Pressed Glass, Lion, Pitcher, Water, Cable Base, Small 55.0
Pressed Glass, Lion, Spooner .... 20.00 To 31.5
Pressed Glass, Lion, Spooner, Frosted .... 30.00 To 67.5
Pressed Glass, Lion, Spooner, Reclining 31.5
Pressed Glass, Lion, Sugar & Creamer, Frosted 125.0
Pressed Glass, Lion, Sugar, Covered .... 75.00 To 90.0
    Lion's Leg, see Alaska
    Lippman, see Flat Diamond
Pressed Glass, Little Bo-Peep, Plate, Dancing Bears, 6 1/2 In. 40.0
Pressed Glass, Locket On Chain, Compote, Open, 8 1/2 In. 80.0
Pressed Glass, Log & Star, Cruet 35.0
Pressed Glass, Log & Star, Salt & Pepper 35.0
Pressed Glass, Log & Star, Tray 35.0
Pressed Glass, Log Cabin, Butter, Covered 195.0
Pressed Glass, Log Cabin, Pitcher, Water, Clear 185.0
Pressed Glass, Log Cabin, Spooner 85.0
Pressed Glass, Lone Elk, Sweetmeat, Covered 47.5
Pressed Glass, Long Buttress, Toothpick 16.0
    Loop, see also Seneca Loop, Yuma Loop
Pressed Glass, Loop & Argus, Goblet 10.0
Pressed Glass, Loop & Crystal, Whiskey, Flint 42.5
Pressed Glass, Loop & Dart With Diamond Ornament, Goblet 20.0
Pressed Glass, Loop & Dart With Diamond Ornament, Sugar, Covered 18.5
Pressed Glass, Loop & Dart With Round Ornament, Spooner 32.0
Pressed Glass, Loop & Dart, Compote, 8 In. 65.0
Pressed Glass, Loop & Dart, Creamer, Round Applied Handle 55.0
Pressed Glass, Loop & Dart, Eggcup 21.5
Pressed Glass, Loop & Dart, Eggcup, Flint 18.0
Pressed Glass, Loop & Dart, Goblet .... 15.00 To 22.5
Pressed Glass, Loop & Dart, Spooner 15.0
Pressed Glass, Loop & Dart, Tumbler, Footed 17.0
Pressed Glass, Loop & Ovals, Goblet, Flint 17.0
Pressed Glass, Loop & Pillar, Spooner, 5 3/4 In. 20.0
Pressed Glass, Loop With Dewdrop, Celery .... 15.00 To 28.0
Pressed Glass, Loop With Dewdrop, Creamer 22.5
Pressed Glass, Loop With Dewdrop, Goblet 7.0
Pressed Glass, Loop With Dewdrop, Goblet, 6 Oz. 18.5
Pressed Glass, Loop With Fisheye, Goblet .... 17.00 To 30.0
Pressed Glass, Loop With Honeycomb Band, Goblet, Flint 24.0
Pressed Glass, Loop With Moose Eye, Sugar, Covered, Flint 49.5
Pressed Glass, Loop With Moose Eye, Tumbler, Flint 45.0
Pressed Glass, Loop With Prism, Goblet 17.5
    Loop with Stippled Panels, see Texas
Pressed Glass, Loop, Candlestick, Bluish-Purple, Hexagonal, 7 In. 250.0
Pressed Glass, Loop, Celery 28.0
Pressed Glass, Loop, Compote, Baluster Stem, Flint, 10 In. X 7 In. High 75.0
Pressed Glass, Loop, Eggcup 21.0
Pressed Glass, Loop, Eggcup, Flint 12.0
Pressed Glass, Loop, Glass, Flip, C.1830 .... 48.0
Pressed Glass, Loop, Goblet, Flint 24.0
Pressed Glass, Loop, Pitcher, Water, Applied Handle, Flint 69.0
Pressed Glass, Loop, Spooner, Flint 24.0
Pressed Glass, Loop, Vase, Plain Rim, 11 In. 125.0
Pressed Glass, Loop, Wine, Flint 29.5
Pressed Glass, Looped Hairpin, Compote, Flint 60.0
Pressed Glass, Looped Hairpin, Sugar & Creamer, Cut & Etched 60.0
Pressed Glass, Loops & Fans, Bread Plate 20.0
Pressed Glass, Loops & Fans, Celery 17.5
Pressed Glass, Loops & Fans, Pitcher, Milk 18.5
Pressed Glass, Lotus & Serpent, Bread Plate, 9 X 12 In. .... 28.00 To 30.0
Pressed Glass, Lotus & Serpent, Compote, Covered, 7 In. 45.0

Pressed Glass, Lincoln Drape, Compote, 8 In.

Pressed Glass, Lily Of The Valley, Etched, Goblet

Pressed Glass, Loop With Fisheye, Goblet

Pressed Glass, Lion, Compote, Frosted Stem

Pressed Glass, Lotus & Serpent, Creamer	45.00
Pressed Glass, Lotus & Serpent, Goblet	40.00 To 55.00
Pressed Glass, Lotus & Serpent, Mug	35.00
Pressed Glass, Lotus & Serpent, Plate, Handled, 6 1/2 In.	15.00
Pressed Glass, Lotus & Serpent, Sauce, Handled	10.00
Pressed Glass, Lotus, Bread Plate	38.00
Pressed Glass, Lotus, Goblet	35.00
Pressed Glass, Louis XV, Banana Boat, Green, Gold	65.00
Pressed Glass, Louis XV, Creamer	70.00
Pressed Glass, Louis XV, Spooner	50.00
Pressed Glass, Louisiana Purchase Exposition, Tumbler	18.00 To 22.00
Pressed Glass, Louisiana, Mug, Blue	14.50
Pressed Glass, Lozenges, Wine	16.00
Pressed Glass, Magnet & Grape With Frosted Leaf, Goblet, American Shield	145.00
Pressed Glass, Magnet & Grape With Frosted Leaf, Goblet, Flint	35.00 To 65.00
Pressed Glass, Magnet & Grape With Frosted Leaf, Salt, Footed, Flint	65.00
Pressed Glass, Magnet & Grape With Frosted Leaf, Tumbler, Flint	100.00
Pressed Glass, Magnet & Grape, Eggcup	19.00
Pressed Glass, Magnet & Grape, Eggcup, Flint	60.00
Pressed Glass, Magnet & Grape, Wine, Clear	25.00
Maiden Blush, see Banded Portland	
Pressed Glass, Maine, Bowl, 6 X 8 In.	16.00
Pressed Glass, Maine, Spooner	20.00
Pressed Glass, Maine, Syrup, Tole Lid	42.00
Pressed Glass, Maine, Wine	25.00
Pressed Glass, Majestic, Berry Bowl	12.00
Pressed Glass, Majestic, Butter, Covered	30.00
Pressed Glass, Majestic, Goblet, Flint	45.00
Pressed Glass, Majestic, Goblet, Ruby Stained	45.00

Pressed Glass, **Majestic,** Tumbler, Ruby Stained 28.00
Pressed Glass, **Maltese Cross Excelsior,** Goblet 52.00
Pressed Glass, **Maltese Cross,** Cruet, Green Flashed 15.00
Pressed Glass, **Manhattan,** Bowl, Amber, 4 1/2 In. 7.00
Pressed Glass, **Manhattan,** Bowl, 8 In. 18.00
Pressed Glass, **Manhattan,** Cracker Jar, 9 In. 30.00
Pressed Glass, **Manhattan,** Goblet 12.00
Pressed Glass, **Manhattan,** Pitcher, Water, Clear, Ruby Stain .... 55.00 To 65.00
Pressed Glass, **Manhattan,** Toothpick 17.50
Pressed Glass, **Manting,** Goblet, Flint 22.50
Pressed Glass, **Maple Leaf Band,** Goblet 18.00
Pressed Glass, **Maple Leaf Variant,** Relish 11.00
Pressed Glass, **Maple Leaf,** Bread Plate, Frosted 15.00
Pressed Glass, **Maple Leaf,** Goblet 35.00
Pressed Glass, **Maple Leaf,** Plate, Amber, 10 1/2 In. 24.00
Pressed Glass, **Maple Leaf,** Spooner, Custard 100.00
Pressed Glass, **Marquisette,** Celery 24.00
Pressed Glass, **Marquisette,** Goblet .... 16.50 To 26.00
Pressed Glass, **Marquisette,** Spooner .... 15.00 To 18.50
Pressed Glass, **Marsh Pink,** Sauce 5.00
Pressed Glass, **Martha's Tears,** Wine 15.00
Pressed Glass, **Maryland,** Compote, Jelly 15.00
Pressed Glass, **Maryland,** Goblet 22.00
Pressed Glass, **Maryland,** Pitcher, Water 17.00
Pressed Glass, **Mascotte,** Butter 41.00
Pressed Glass, **Mascotte,** Celery, Etched 25.00
Pressed Glass, **Mascotte,** Compote, Covered, 8 In. 75.00
Pressed Glass, **Mascotte,** Creamer .... 14.50 To 15.00
Pressed Glass, **Mascotte,** Salt Dip, Amber 11.00
Pressed Glass, **Mascotte,** Spooner 19.50
Pressed Glass, **Mascotte,** Wine 12.00
Pressed Glass, **Masonic,** Berry Bowl 15.00
Pressed Glass, **Massachusetts,** Mug 13.00
Pressed Glass, **Massachusetts,** Plate, Scalloped Edge, 8 1/4 In.Round 18.50
Pressed Glass, **Massachusetts,** Rum Jug .... 75.00 To 95.00
Pressed Glass, **Massachusetts,** Shot Glass 10.50
Pressed Glass, **Massachusetts,** Toothpick, Green 20.00
Pressed Glass, **Massachusetts,** Wine 16.00
Pressed Glass, **Master Argus,** Goblet, Flint .... 25.00 To 32.50
Pressed Glass, **Master Argus,** Tumbler 40.00
Pressed Glass, **Maypole,** Sugar Shaker 14.50
Pressed Glass, **McCormick,** Bread Plate 70.00
Pressed Glass, **McKinley,** Bread Plate 42.00
Pressed Glass, **McKinley,** Plate, Protection & Plenty, Frosted, 7 1/4 In. 25.00
Pressed Glass, **Medallion Sprig,** Tumbler, Blue 35.00
Pressed Glass, **Medallion Sunburst,** Pitcher, Water 15.00
Pressed Glass, **Medallion,** Butter, Blue 75.00
Pressed Glass, **Medallion,** Cake Stand, Green, 9 1/4 In. 50.00

Pressed Glass, Maine, Syrup

Pressed Glass, Magnet & Grape With Stippled Leaf, Goblet

Pressed Glass, Medallion, Creamer	70.00
Pressed Glass, Medallion, Goblet	28.00
Pressed Glass, Medallion, Spooner, Amethyst	65.00
Pressed Glass, Melon, Sugar, Blue, Covered	68.50
Pressed Glass, Melon, Sugar, Covered, Dated April 23, 1878, Blue	65.00
Pressed Glass, Melrose, Creamer, Etched	18.00
Pressed Glass, Melrose, Wine, Greentown	16.50
Pressed Glass, Memphis, Berry Set, 7 Piece	275.00
Pressed Glass, Memphis, Bowl, Master Berry, 4 Small Bowls, Green	85.00
Pressed Glass, Memphis, Spooner, Green, Gold Trim	33.00
Pressed Glass, Memphis, Water Set, Green With Gold, 7 Piece	145.00 To 195.00
Pressed Glass, Menagerie, Creamer, Owl	35.00
Pressed Glass, Meteored Diagonal, Celery	15.00
Pressed Glass, Michigan, Creamer, Decorated	15.00
Pressed Glass, Michigan, Goblet, Gold	26.00
Pressed Glass, Michigan, Goblet, Maiden's Blush	40.00
Pressed Glass, Michigan, Mug	16.00
Pressed Glass, Michigan, Pitcher, Water, Maiden's Blush, Gold Trim	95.00
Pressed Glass, Michigan, Spooner, Maiden's Blush & Gold	27.50
Pressed Glass, Mikado Fan, Goblet	20.00
Pressed Glass, Millard, Bowl, Ruby, 9 In.	45.00
Pressed Glass, Millard, Tumbler, Yellow Stained	20.00
Pressed Glass, Milton, Cruet, Original Stopper	25.00
Pressed Glass, Milton, Goblet	9.00 To 14.00
Pressed Glass, Minerva, Bowl, Waste, 6 In.	45.00
Pressed Glass, Minerva, Bread Plate, Handles, 9 X 13 In.	45.00 To 60.00
Pressed Glass, Minerva, Butter	52.00 To 65.00
Pressed Glass, Minerva, Cake Stand, 8 In.	48.00
Pressed Glass, Minerva, Compote, Covered, 7 X 10 3/4 In.	80.00
Pressed Glass, Minerva, Creamer	35.00 To 45.00
Pressed Glass, Minerva, Dish, Relish, Love's Request	18.00
Pressed Glass, Minerva, Goblet	85.00
Pressed Glass, Minerva, Pitcher, 5 1/2 In.	26.00
Pressed Glass, Minerva, Sauce, Footed, 4 In.	10.50 To 12.50
Pressed Glass, Minerva, Spooner	22.50 To 27.00
Pressed Glass, Minerva, Sugar, Covered	55.00
Pressed Glass, Minerva, Table Set, Creamer, Butter, Spooner	175.00
Pressed Glass, Minnesota, Carafe	22.00
Pressed Glass, Minnesota, Goblet	20.00
Pressed Glass, Minnesota, Spooner	15.00
Pressed Glass, Minnesota, Toothpick	14.00 To 17.50
Pressed Glass, Minnesota, Tumbler	40.00
Pressed Glass, Minnesota, Wine	16.00
Pressed Glass, Mirror & Fan, Decanter, Green, Gold, Stopper	30.00
Pressed Glass, Mirror, Goblet, Flint	20.00
Pressed Glass, Mirror, Wine, Flint	29.00
Pressed Glass, Missouri, Butter, Covered, Green	48.00
Pressed Glass, Missouri, Sauce, Green	14.50
Pressed Glass, Mitered Bars, Celery	22.00
Mitered Diamond Point, see Mitered Bars	
Pressed Glass, Mitered Prisms, Goblet	15.00
Pressed Glass, Monkey & Stump, Toothpick, Blue	32.00
Pressed Glass, Monkey, Spooner	45.00 To 75.00
Pressed Glass, Moon & Star, Bowl, 7 In.	23.00
Pressed Glass, Moon & Star, Cake Stand, 10 In.	65.00
Pressed Glass, Moon & Star, Celery	30.00
Pressed Glass, Moon & Star, Compote, Covered, Flint, 7 X 9 In.	40.00
Pressed Glass, Moon & Star, Creamer	35.00
Pressed Glass, Moon & Star, Goblet	25.00 To 27.50
Pressed Glass, Moon & Star, Sugar, Covered, & Creamer, Ruby Stained, Pair	125.00
Pressed Glass, Moon & Star, Sugar, Open, Footed, Flint	85.00
Moon & Stork, see Ostrich Looking at the Moon	
Pressed Glass, Moose Eye In Sand, Goblet	15.00
Pressed Glass, Morning Glory, Honey	45.00
Pressed Glass, Morning Glory, Sauce	64.00
Pressed Glass, Morning Glory, Syrup	35.00

Pressed Glass, My Lady's Workbox, Goblet	14.50
Pressed Glass, Nailhead, Butter, Covered	15.00 To 35.00
Pressed Glass, Nailhead, Cake Stand, 9 In.	16.00 To 27.00
Pressed Glass, Nailhead, Creamer	15.00 To 25.00
Pressed Glass, Nailhead, Goblet	15.00
Pressed Glass, Nailhead, Plate, 9 In.	12.00
Pressed Glass, Nailhead, Sugar, Covered	20.00 To 30.00
Pressed Glass, Nailhead, Wine	14.00 To 25.00
Pressed Glass, Napoleon, Berry Bowl	12.00
Pressed Glass, Nautilus, Banana Dish, Blue, Signed	45.00
Pressed Glass, Nautilus, Creamer, Custard	125.00
Pressed Glass, Near Garland, Tray, Double Handles, 14 1/4 In.	40.00
Pressed Glass, Nearcut Inverted Strawberry, Basket	32.00
Pressed Glass, Nestlings, Celery	35.00
Pressed Glass, Nestor, Creamer, Green, Enameled	39.50
Pressed Glass, Nestor, Spooner, Apple Green, Enameled	18.00
Pressed Glass, Netted Oak, Sugar, Pink, Green Leaves	65.00
Pressed Glass, Nevada, Celery	22.00
Pressed Glass, New England Pineapple, Compote, 4 3/4 X 8 In.	85.00
Pressed Glass, New England Pineapple, Eggcup	32.00
Pressed Glass, New England Pineapple, Eggcup, Flint	28.50
Pressed Glass, New England Pineapple, Goblet, Flint	32.00 To 50.00
Pressed Glass, New England Pineapple, Honey, Flint	14.50
Pressed Glass, New England Pineapple, Salt, Master, Footed	30.00
Pressed Glass, New England Pineapple, Sauce	13.00
Pressed Glass, New England Pineapple, Sauce, Flint	15.00
Pressed Glass, New England Pineapple, Spooner, Flint	32.00
Pressed Glass, New England Pineapple, Tumbler, Flint	85.00
Pressed Glass, New Hampshire, Cruet	20.00
Pressed Glass, New Hampshire, Dish, Relish	9.00
Pressed Glass, New Hampshire, Goblet, Maiden's Blush	35.00
Pressed Glass, New Hampshire, Punch Cup	3.50
Pressed Glass, New Hampshire, Syrup	24.00
Pressed Glass, New Hampshire, Table Set, Clear With Gold, 4 Piece	115.00
Pressed Glass, New Hampshire, Toothpick	17.50
Pressed Glass, New Hampshire, Toothpick, Gold Trim	19.00
Pressed Glass, New Jersey, Berry Bowl, Gold Rim	24.00
Pressed Glass, New Jersey, Butter	35.00
Pressed Glass, New Jersey, Celery, Flat	9.50
Pressed Glass, New Jersey, Dish, Boat Shaped, 7 X 4 1/2 In.	14.50
Pressed Glass, New Jersey, Goblet	25.00
Pressed Glass, New Jersey, Spooner	17.00
Pressed Glass, New Jersey, Sugar, Covered	22.50 To 36.50
Pressed Glass, New Jersey, Tumbler	23.00
Pressed Glass, New Jersey, Water Set	120.00
Pressed Glass, New York Honeycomb, Goblet	16.00
Pressed Glass, New York Honeycomb, Tumbler, Flint	22.00
Pressed Glass, Notched Ovals, Sugar, Gold Flashed, Covered	24.00
Pressed Glass, Nova Scotia Diamond, Dish, Pickle, Canoe Shaped, 7 3/4 In.	35.00
Pressed Glass, Nursery Rhymes, Butter, Covered, Miniature	50.00 To 58.00
Pressed Glass, Nursery Rhymes, Creamer, Child's	48.00
Pressed Glass, Nursery Rhymes, Cup, Punch	15.00
Pressed Glass, Nursery Rhymes, Sugar, Cover, Child's	40.00
Pressed Glass, Nursery Rhymes, Tumbler, Child's	10.00 To 22.00
Pressed Glass, O'Hara Diamond, Spooner, Ruby Stained	37.50
Pressed Glass, O'Hara Diamond, Syrup, Clear, Original Lid	28.00
Pressed Glass, O'Hara Star, Sugar Shaker	32.00
Pressed Glass, Oak Leaf Band, Goblet	16.00
Pressed Glass, Oak Leaf, Dish, Relish, Oblong	7.00
Pressed Glass, Oak Leaf, Spooner	21.50
Pressed Glass, Oaken Bucket, Pitcher, Amethyst, 8 In.	75.00
Pressed Glass, Oaken Bucket, Pitcher, Water	36.00 To 50.00
Pressed Glass, Oaken Bucket, Pitcher, Water, Amber	55.00
Pressed Glass, Oaken Bucket, Pitcher, Water, Amethyst	65.00
Pressed Glass, Oaken Bucket, Spooner, Yellow	25.00
Pressed Glass, Odd Fellows, Goblet	26.00

Pressed Glass, Moon & Star, Bowl, Covered, Footed

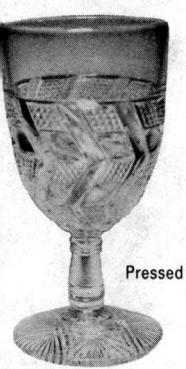

Pressed Glass, Mitered Diamond, Goblet

Pressed Glass, Old Statehouse, Platter, Philadelphia	57.50
Pressed Glass, Old Statehouse, Tray, Large	67.50
One Hundred One, see One-O-One	
Pressed Glass, One-O-One, Bread Plate, Garfield	46.00
Pressed Glass, One-O-One, Butter, Covered, Frosted	55.00
Pressed Glass, One-O-One, Compote, Large	30.00
Pressed Glass, One-O-One, Creamer	15.00 To 18.50
Pressed Glass, One-O-One, Goblet	24.50 To 30.00
Pressed Glass, One-O-One, Spooner	18.50
One-Thousand Eye, see Thousand Eye	
Pressed Glass, Open Plaid, Goblet	12.00
Pressed Glass, Open Rose, Eggcup	18.50
Pressed Glass, Open Rose, Goblet	17.50 To 30.00
Pressed Glass, Open Rose, Sauce, 3 In.	6.00
Pressed Glass, Open Rose, Spooner	18.00 To 22.00
Pressed Glass, Opposing Pyramid, Compote, Covered, 9 X 6 In.	36.00
Pressed Glass, Optic, Sugar Shaker, Original Lid, Red Hobs, Stained	75.00
Oregon, see also Beaded Loop, Skilton	
Pressed Glass, Oregon, Bowl, Ruby, 8 In.	30.00
Pressed Glass, Oregon, Dish, Pickle, 9 1/4 In.	12.00
Pressed Glass, Oriental Poppy, Tumbler, Green, Gold, Northwood	35.00
Pressed Glass, Oriental, Spooner	10.00
Orion, see Cathedral	
Pressed Glass, Ostrich Looking At The Moon, Goblet	65.00
Pressed Glass, Our Daily Bread, Bread Plate	25.00
Pressed Glass, Oval Barberry, Butter, Covered	38.00
Pressed Glass, Oval Barberry, Eggcup	16.50
Pressed Glass, Oval Barberry, Spooner	19.00
Pressed Glass, Oval Basket, Toothpick, Amber	24.00
Oval Loop, see Question Mark	
Pressed Glass, Oval Panels, Goblet	10.00
Pressed Glass, Oval Panels, Goblet, Amber	29.50
Pressed Glass, Oval Panels, Goblet, Blue	25.00
Pressed Glass, Oval Panels, Goblet, Vaseline	26.00
Pressed Glass, Oval Star, Tumbler	5.00
Pressed Glass, Oval Star, Tumbler, Children's Miniature	9.00
Pressed Glass, Oval Star, Water Set, Miniature, 7 Piece	85.00
Pressed Glass, Overshot, Pitcher, Water	87.50
Pressed Glass, Overshot, Pitcher, Water, Reeded, Applied Handle	65.00
Pressed Glass, Overshot, Salt Dip	15.00
Owl, see Bull's-Eye & Diamond Point	
Owl & Fan, see Parrot & Fan	
Pressed Glass, Owl & Possum, Goblet	50.00 To 80.00
Pressed Glass, Owl & Pussycat, Dish, Cheese	295.00 To 325.00
Pressed Glass, Owl In Horseshoe, Goblet	48.00
Pressed Glass, Owl, Compote, Covered, Frosted	85.00
Pressed Glass, Paddle Wheel, Cruet, Stopper	30.00
Pressed Glass, Paisley, Cruet	45.00

Pressed Glass, New England Flute, Goblet

Pressed Glass, New England Pineapple, Pitcher

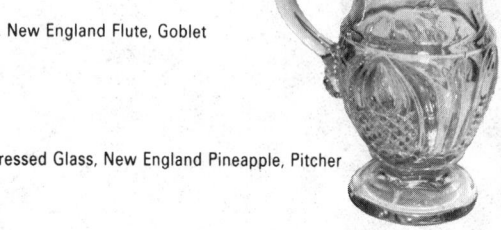

Pressed Glass, Paisley, Dish, Pickle, Red Flared Circles & Gold	32.0
Pressed Glass, Paisley, Table Set, 4 Piece	265.0
Pressed Glass, Paling, Goblet	6.0
Pressed Glass, Palm Beach, 4 Piece Table Set, Red, Green & Gold	395.0
Pressed Glass, Palm Stub, Goblet	10.0
Pressed Glass, Palm Stub, Goblet, Clear, Opalescent	11.0
Pressed Glass, Palmette, Bread Plate	30.0
Pressed Glass, Palmette, Celery	27.5
Pressed Glass, Palmette, Goblet	24.0
Pressed Glass, Palmette, Salt	10.00 To 22.0
Pressed Glass, Pampas Flower, Creamer	15.0
Pressed Glass, Panama, Berry Bowl	10.0
Pressed Glass, Panama, Cruet	18.0
Pressed Glass, Panel & Fine Cut, Wine	60.0
Pressed Glass, Panel & Star, Sugar Shaker	9.9
Pressed Glass, Panel & Star, Wine	8.0
Pressed Glass, Panel, Pitcher, Water, Yellow	45.0
Pressed Glass, Panel, Sauce	14.0
Pressed Glass, Panel, Tumbler, 9 Sides, Flint	21.0
Pressed Glass, Paneled Acorn Band, Goblet	19.0
Pressed Glass, Paneled Beads, Compote, Covered, 11 In.	95.0
Pressed Glass, Paneled Cane, Goblet	16.00 To 25.0
Pressed Glass, Paneled Cane, Wine, Blue	24.00
Pressed Glass, Paneled Cherry, Goblet	18.00 To 28.0
Pressed Glass, Paneled Daisy & Button, Creamer	67.5
Pressed Glass, Paneled Daisy & Button, Spooner, Amber	65.50
Pressed Glass, Paneled Daisy, Cake Stand, 9 In.	20.0
Pressed Glass, Paneled Daisy, Cake Stand, 9 1/2 In.	29.50
Pressed Glass, Paneled Daisy, Celery	25.0
Pressed Glass, Paneled Daisy, Goblet	17.0
Pressed Glass, Paneled Daisy, Mug	30.0
Pressed Glass, Paneled Daisy, Pitcher	40.0
Pressed Glass, Paneled Daisy, Plate, 9 In.	22.50
Pressed Glass, Paneled Daisy, Tankard	49.5
Pressed Glass, Paneled Dewdrop, Bread Plate	32.00
Pressed Glass, Paneled Dewdrop, Goblet, Pattern Base	22.50
Pressed Glass, Paneled Dewdrop, Sugar, Covered	28.0
Pressed Glass, Paneled Diamond Band, Goblet	10.00
Pressed Glass, Paneled Diamond Block, Spooner	15.00
Pressed Glass, Paneled Diamond Cross, Butter	45.00
Pressed Glass, Paneled Diamond Cross, Goblet	12.50
Pressed Glass, Paneled Diamond Point, Goblet	10.00
Pressed Glass, Paneled Diamonds, Goblet	9.00
Paneled Dogwood, see Dogwood	
Pressed Glass, Paneled English Hobnail, Goblet	12.50
Paneled Fan Top, see Shepherd's Plaid	
Pressed Glass, Paneled Forget-Me-Not, Bread Plate	22.0
Pressed Glass, Paneled Forget-Me-Not, Cake Stand, 9 1/2 In.	22.50
Pressed Glass, Paneled Forget-Me-Not, Creamer	24.50
Pressed Glass, Paneled Forget-Me-Not, Dish, Pickle	12.00

Pressed Glass, Paneled Forget-Me-Not, Dish, Relish	12.50
Pressed Glass, Paneled Forget-Me-Not, Goblet	22.00 To 28.50
Pressed Glass, Paneled Forget-Me-Not, Pitcher, Milk, Vaseline	135.00
Pressed Glass, Paneled Forget-Me-Not, Pitcher, Water	26.50
Pressed Glass, Paneled Forget-Me-Not, Sauce	9.50
Pressed Glass, Paneled Forget-Me-Not, Wine	32.50 To 48.00
Pressed Glass, Paneled Grape Band, Spooner	19.50
Pressed Glass, Paneled Grape, Compote, Low Standard, 6 1/2 In.	22.50
Pressed Glass, Paneled Grape, Goblet	12.50 To 17.00
Pressed Glass, Paneled Grape, Goblet, Flint	25.00
Pressed Glass, Paneled Grape, Sauce	5.00
Pressed Glass, Paneled Grape, Spooner	19.50
Pressed Glass, Paneled Heather, Creamer	20.00
Pressed Glass, Paneled Heather, Goblet, Gold Band	12.00
Pressed Glass, Paneled Heather, Wine	13.00
Pressed Glass, Paneled Herringbone, Goblet	9.00
Pressed Glass, Paneled Herringbone, Mustard, Matching Lid, Attached Saucer	22.50
Pressed Glass, Paneled Holly, Mug	20.00
Pressed Glass, Paneled Iris, Wine	10.00
Pressed Glass, Paneled Ivy, Goblet	20.00
Pressed Glass, Paneled Jewels, Goblet	13.50 To 18.00
Pressed Glass, Paneled Jewels, Goblet, Amber	38.00
Pressed Glass, Paneled Long Jewels, Goblet	14.50
Pressed Glass, Paneled Ovals, Goblet, Flint	37.50 To 40.00
Pressed Glass, Paneled Palm, Pitcher, Water	23.00
Pressed Glass, Paneled S, Goblet	26.00
Pressed Glass, Paneled Scroll, Salt, Marigold	14.00
Paneled Star & Button, see Sedan	
Paneled Stippled Bowl, see Stippled Band	
Pressed Glass, Paneled Sunflower, Goblet	15.00
Pressed Glass, Paneled Sunflower, Toothpick	22.00
Pressed Glass, Paneled Thistle, Basket, Twisted Handle	85.00
Pressed Glass, Paneled Thistle, Butter, Bee Mark	45.00
Pressed Glass, Paneled Thistle, Compote, 8 In.	32.00
Pressed Glass, Paneled Thistle, Dish, Relish, Bee With HIG	26.00
Pressed Glass, Paneled Thistle, Goblet	30.00
Pressed Glass, Paneled Thistle, Plate, 8 In.	20.00
Pressed Glass, Paneled Thistle, Wine	26.50
Pressed Glass, Paneled Thumbprint, Goblet	7.50
Pressed Glass, Paneled Wild Daisy, Goblet	10.00
Pressed Glass, Paneled Zipper, Dish, Relish	15.00
Pressed Glass, Paneled 44, Goblet, Some Silver	16.00
Pressed Glass, Panels With Cord Band, Bread Plate	18.00
Pressed Glass, Parrot & Fan, Goblet	18.00 To 25.00
Pressed Glass, Parrot, Punch Cup, Gold Eyes, Blue	15.00
Pressed Glass, Parrot, Salt & Pepper, Green	130.00
Pattee Cross, see Broughton	
Pressed Glass, Pavonia, Berry Set, Bowl & 8 Sauces, Square Shape	45.00
Pressed Glass, Pavonia, Pitcher, Etched	30.00
Pressed Glass, Pavonia, Pitcher, Water, Etched	48.00
Pressed Glass, Pavonia, Tankard	46.50
Pressed Glass, Pavonia, Tankard, Pitcher, Water	55.00
Pressed Glass, Pavonia, Toothpick	12.50
Pressed Glass, Pavonia, Tumbler, Flat, Ruby Stained, 4 1/4 In.	22.50
Pressed Glass, Pavonia, Tumbler, Ruby Stained	22.50
Pressed Glass, Pavonia, Water Set, Etched, Red, 7 Piece	295.00
Pressed Glass, Pavonia, Wine	15.00 To 17.50
Pressed Glass, Peace & Plenty, Creamer, Footed	35.00
Pressed Glass, Peacock & Heron, Mug, Blue	40.00
Pressed Glass, Peacock Feather, Berry Set, 7 Piece	75.00
Pressed Glass, Peacock Feather, Butter, Covered	35.00
Pressed Glass, Peacock Feather, Creamer	25.00
Pressed Glass, Peacock Feather, Pitcher, Water, Clear, Opalescent	35.00
Pressed Glass, Peacock Feather, Spooner	27.50
Pressed Glass, Peacock Feather, Sugar, Covered	40.00
Peacock's Eye, see Peacock Feather	

Pressed Glass, Oval & Crossbar, Tumbler, Whiskey

Pressed Glass, Orange Peel, Goblet

Pressed Glass, Oval Miter, Salt, Footed

Pressed Glass, Pear, Butter, Covered	32.00
Pressed Glass, Pear, Spooner, Footed, Scallop Top	17.50
Pressed Glass, Pearl, Cruet, 6 In.	55.00
Pressed Glass, Peerless, Bread Plate	18.00
Pressed Glass, Peerless, Creamer, Applied Handle	25.00
Pressed Glass, Peerless, Goblet	14.00
Pressed Glass, Peerless, Spooner	17.50
Pressed Glass, Peerless, Water Set, Original Tray, Green, 8 Piece	165.00
Pressed Glass, Pendleton, Goblet	35.00
Pressed Glass, Pendleton, Goblet, Flint	30.00
Pennsylvania Hand, see also Pennsylvania	
Pressed Glass, Pennsylvania Hand, Celery	20.00 To 24.50
Pressed Glass, Pennsylvania Hand, Creamer	42.50
Pennsylvania, see also Balder, Pennsylvania Hand	
Pressed Glass, Pennsylvania, Butter, Covered	44.00 To 45.00
Pressed Glass, Pennsylvania, Creamer	27.00
Pressed Glass, Pennsylvania, Goblet	17.50
Pressed Glass, Pennsylvania, Spooner	22.00
Pressed Glass, Pennsylvania, Spooner, Amber	15.00
Pressed Glass, Pennsylvania, Sugar, Covered	32.50 To 35.00
Pressed Glass, Pennsylvania, Table Set, Miniature, 4 Piece	120.00
Pressed Glass, Pennsylvania, Toothpick	17.50
Pressed Glass, Pennsylvania, Toothpick, Clear With Gold	15.00
Pressed Glass, Pennsylvania, Tumbler	16.50
Pressed Glass, Pennsylvania, Wine	15.00 To 16.50
Pressed Glass, Pennsylvania, Wine, Emerald	25.00
Pressed Glass, Pequot, Sauce, Footed	6.00
Pressed Glass, Petal & Loop, Candlestick, Blue Socket, Clambroth Base	240.00
Pressed Glass, Petal & Loop, Compote, Stemmed Foot, 7 1/4 X 5 1/4 In.	70.00
Pressed Glass, Petal, Salt, Master, Footed, Flint	12.00
Pressed Glass, Petticoat Fluting, Berry Set, Vaseline, 5 Piece	95.00
Pressed Glass, Pheasant, Sugar, Covered, Frosted	85.00
Pressed Glass, Philadelphia Centennial, Goblet	35.00
Pressed Glass, Phoenix, Plate, 8 1/2 In., Pair	19.00
Pressed Glass, Phoenix, Sugar & Creamer	18.00
Pressed Glass, Picket Fence, Spooner	27.50
Pressed Glass, Picket, Compote, Open, 8 In.	23.50
Pressed Glass, Picket, Compote, 8 In.	24.00
Pressed Glass, Picket, Creamer	22.50
Pressed Glass, Picket, Toothpick, Purple Slag	48.00
Pressed Glass, Pigs In Corn, Goblet	115.00 To 180.00
Pillar & Bull's-Eye, see Thistle	
Pressed Glass, Pillar, Claret, Flint	22.50
Pressed Glass, Pillow & Sunburst, Sugar, Covered	12.50
Pressed Glass, Pillow Encircled, Tumbler, Red Flashed	28.00
Pinafore, see Actress	
Pressed Glass, Pineapple & Fan, Biscuit Jar	22.00
Pressed Glass, Pineapple & Fan, Goblet	15.00

ressed Glass, Pineapple & Fan, Rose Bowl	14.00
ressed Glass, Pineapple & Fan, Vase, 7 1/2 In.	8.50
ressed Glass, Pineapple, Goblet, Flint	42.00
ressed Glass, Pineapple, Wine, Flint	95.00
ressed Glass, Pinwheel & Cannon Ball, Goblet	10.00
ressed Glass, Pinwheel, Goblet	10.00
ressed Glass, Pioneer's Victoria, Spooner, Ruby Stained Top & Blocks	35.00
ressed Glass, Pioneer's Victoria, Tumbler, Red Stain	28.00
ressed Glass, Pioneer's Victoria, Tumbler, Ruby Stain	25.00
ressed Glass, Pittsburgh Daisy, Goblet, Flared	15.00
ressed Glass, Pittsburgh Pillar, Pitcher, Milk, 8 Ribs, Applied Handle	290.00
ressed Glass, Pittsburgh, Celery, Pillar-Mold Blown, 9 1/2 In.	60.00
ressed Glass, Pittsburgh, Celery, Strawberry & Fan	225.00
ressed Glass, Pittsburgh, Compote, Folded Rim, Flint, 7 X 7 In.	100.00
ressed Glass, Pittsburgh, Creamer, Applied Base & Handle, 8 Rib, Flint	125.00
ressed Glass, Pittsburgh, Goblet	9.00
ressed Glass, Pittsburgh, Pitcher, Milk, Applied Handle, 8 Ribs	290.00
ressed Glass, Pittsburgh, Pitcher, Water, 8 Ribs, Pillar Mold, Flint	200.00
ressed Glass, Plaid, Plate, 6 In.	25.00
Plain Smocking, see Smocking	
ressed Glass, Plain Sunburst, Goblet	12.50
ressed Glass, Pleasant To Labor, Bread Plate	40.00
ressed Glass, Pleat & Block, Goblet	9.00
ressed Glass, Pleat & Panel, Bowl, 9 X 5 1/2 In.	18.50
ressed Glass, Pleat & Panel, Bread Plate	35.00
ressed Glass, Pleat & Panel, Butter Pat	20.00
ressed Glass, Pleat & Panel, Cake Stand, Footed, 8 In.	40.00
ressed Glass, Pleat & Panel, Celery	19.50 To 40.00
ressed Glass, Pleat & Panel, Creamer	26.00 To 42.50
ressed Glass, Pleat & Panel, Dish, Relish, Oval	25.00
ressed Glass, Pleat & Panel, Goblet	12.00 To 16.00
ressed Glass, Pleat & Panel, Pitcher, Milk	50.00
ressed Glass, Pleat & Panel, Pitcher, Water	39.50
ressed Glass, Pleat & Panel, Plate, 6 In.	13.00 To 14.00
ressed Glass, Pleat & Panel, Plate, 7 In.	15.00 To 22.00
ressed Glass, Pleat & Panel, Sauce, Footed	12.00
ressed Glass, Pleat & Panel, Spooner	22.50 To 25.00
ressed Glass, Pleat & Panel, Sugar, Covered	40.00
ressed Glass, Plume, Berry Bowl, Scalloped, 8 In.	18.00
ressed Glass, Plume, Bowl, Flint, 6 In.	22.00
ressed Glass, Plume, Bowl, Waste	35.00 To 45.00
ressed Glass, Plume, Cake Stand, 9 In.	30.00
ressed Glass, Plume, Celery	16.00
ressed Glass, Plume, Compote, Open, Ruffled Edge, 7 1/2 X 6 In.	25.00
ressed Glass, Plume, Goblet	20.00 To 32.00
ressed Glass, Plume, Goblet, Frosted	23.50
ressed Glass, Plume, Sauce, 4 In.	8.50
ressed Glass, Plume, Spooner	18.00 To 26.00
ressed Glass, Plutec, Berry Set, 7 Piece	60.00
ressed Glass, Pogo Stick, Cake Stand, 10 In.	15.00
ressed Glass, Pogo Stick, Cruet, Clear	13.00
ressed Glass, Pogo Stick, Jelly, Stemmed	12.50
ressed Glass, Poinsettia, Tumbler, Green	30.00
ressed Glass, Poinsettia, Tumbler, Green Opalescent	22.00
ressed Glass, Pointed Hobnail, Wine, Amber	16.00
ressed Glass, Pointed Jewel, Goblet	7.50
ressed Glass, Pointed Jewel, Pitcher, Water	30.00
Pointed Paneled Daisy & Button, see Queen	
Pointed Thumbprint, see Almond Thumbprint	
ressed Glass, Polar Bear, Bowl, Waste	52.00
ressed Glass, Polar Bear, Goblet	70.00 To 95.00
ressed Glass, Polar Bear, Goblet, Frosted	89.00 To 145.00
ressed Glass, Pomona, Cruet, Blue Cornflower, Faceted Stopper	300.00
ressed Glass, Popcorn, Creamer	38.00
ressed Glass, Popcorn, Wine	22.00
ressed Glass, Portland Tree Of Life, Compote, 10 In.	95.00

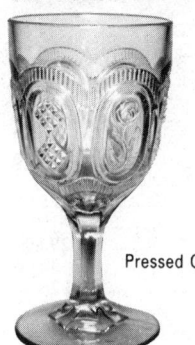

Pressed Glass, Paneled Diamond Cross

Pressed Glass, Paneled Diamond & Flowers, Goblet

Pressed Glass, Portland Tree Of Life, Tumbler, Footed, Gold Rim	48.00
Portland with Diamond Point Band, see Galloway, Virginia	
Pressed Glass, Portland, Celery	28.00
Pressed Glass, Portland, Creamer	18.50
Pressed Glass, Portland, Pitcher, 7 1/2 In.	45.00
Pressed Glass, Portland, Sauce, Leaf Shaped	8.50
Pressed Glass, Portland, Syrup	10.50
Pressed Glass, Portland, Toothpick	12.00 To 14.00
Pressed Glass, Portland, Wine	10.00
Pressed Glass, Post, Celery	32.00
Pressed Glass, Post, Compote, Covered, 7 1/2 In.	85.00
Potted Plant, see Flower Pot	
Pressed Glass, Powder & Shot, Butter, Covered, Flint	75.00
Pressed Glass, Powder & Shot, Creamer	72.00
Pressed Glass, Powder & Shot, Goblet, Flint	38.00 To 48.50
Pressed Glass, Powder & Shot, Goblet, Frosted	40.00
Pressed Glass, Powder & Shot, Spooner, Flint	22.00 To 35.00
Prayer Rug, see Horseshoe	
Pressed Glass, President Grant, Plate, Patriot & Soldier, 9 1/2 In.Square	30.00
Pressed Glass, Pressed Block, Bowl, Flint, 8 1/2 In.	30.00
Pressed Glass, Pressed Diamond, Tumbler, Amber	24.00
Pressed Glass, Pressed Leaf, Eggcup, Set Of 4	60.00
Pressed Glass, Pressed Leaf, Goblet	10.00 To 18.00
Pressed Glass, Pressed Leaf, Pitcher, Water, 8 Goblets, Applied Handle	145.00
Pressed Glass, Pressed Leaf, Spooner	20.50
Pressed Glass, Pressed Leaf, Wine, Flint	31.50
Pressed Glass, Primrose, Pitcher, Water	30.00
Pressed Glass, Primrose, Sugar, Covered	27.50
Princess Feather, see also Lacy Medallion	
Pressed Glass, Princess Feather, Butter	37.00
Pressed Glass, Princess Feather, Compote, Covered, Low, 8 1/2 In.Diameter	44.50
Pressed Glass, Princess Feather, Goblet	15.00 To 25.00
Pressed Glass, Princess Feather, Spooner	15.00 To 26.50
Pressed Glass, Princess Feather, Spooner, Milk White	35.00
Pressed Glass, Princess Feather, Sugar, Covered, Milk White	130.00
Pressed Glass, Printed Hobnail, Pitcher, Water	23.00
Pressed Glass, Priscilla, Bowl, Flat, 10 In.	16.00
Pressed Glass, Priscilla, Creamer, Small	30.00
Pressed Glass, Priscilla, Rose Bowl	22.00
Pressed Glass, Priscilla, Wine	25.00
Pressed Glass, Prism & Clear Panels, Goblet	7.00
Pressed Glass, Prism & Diamond Band, Pitcher, Water	45.00
Pressed Glass, Prism & Diamond Band, Wine	8.00
Pressed Glass, Prism & Flattened Sawtooth, Goblet, Flint	45.00
Pressed Glass, Prism & Flattened Sawtooth, Spill, Flint	40.00
Pressed Glass, Prism & Lobular Loops, Goblet, Flint	30.00
Pressed Glass, Prism & Sawtooth, Goblet, Flint	18.00
Pressed Glass, Prism & Sawtooth, Spill, Opaque Blue	375.00
Pressed Glass, Prism Arc, Goblet	16.00

Pressed Glass, **Prism Bar,** Goblet	10.00
Pressed Glass, **Prism With Diamond Points,** Goblet, Knob Stem, Flint	35.00
Pressed Glass, **Prism With Thumbprint Band,** Celery, Flint	125.00
Pressed Glass, **Prism With Thumbprint Band,** Glass, Ale	40.00
Pressed Glass, **Prism,** Bowl, Clear, Flared, Flint, 4 1/2 X 11 In.	28.00
Pressed Glass, **Prism,** Compote, Flint, 7 1/2 In.	25.00
Pressed Glass, **Prism,** Decanter, Bar Lip, Pewter Stopper, C.1858, Flint, Quart	125.00
Pressed Glass, **Prism,** Goblet, Banded Top	6.00
Pressed Glass, **Prism,** Sugar, Flint, C.1868	32.00
Pressed Glass, **Prismatic,** Creamer	14.00
Pressed Glass, **Prize,** Celery, Ruby Stained	70.00
Pressed Glass, **Prize,** Wine, Green	20.00
Pressed Glass, **Psyche & Cupid,** Celery	24.00
Pressed Glass, **Psyche & Cupid,** Creamer	28.00
Pressed Glass, **Psyche & Cupid,** Goblet	30.00 To 32.50
Pressed Glass, **Psyche & Cupid,** Pitcher, Water	49.00
Pressed Glass, **Pulaski Cube,** Goblet	6.50
Pressed Glass, **Quartered Block,** Bowl, Punch, 2 Piece	75.00
Pressed Glass, **Quartered Block,** Pitcher, Tankard	25.00
Pressed Glass, **Quartered Block,** Salt	5.00
Queen Anne, see Viking	
Pressed Glass, **Queen,** Creamer	39.50
Pressed Glass, **Queen,** Creamer, Gold Trim	35.00
Pressed Glass, **Queen,** Goblet	15.00 To 16.00
Pressed Glass, **Queen,** Goblet, Blue	27.50
Pressed Glass, **Queen,** Sugar, Covered	45.00
Queen's Necklace, see also Crown Jewels	
Pressed Glass, **Queen's Necklace,** Bottle, Cologne, Flower Form Stopper	35.00
Pressed Glass, **Queen's Necklace,** Bottle, Perfume	19.50
Pressed Glass, **Queen's Necklace,** Tumbler	28.50
Pressed Glass, **Queen's,** Necklace, Vase, 10 In.	55.00
Pressed Glass, **Question Mark,** Butter	27.50
Pressed Glass, **Question Mark,** Cordial	12.00
Pressed Glass, **Quilted Phlox,** Sugar Shaker, Amethyst	65.00
Pressed Glass, **Quilted Phlox,** Sugar Shaker, Opaque Green	85.00
Pressed Glass, **Quixote,** Rose Bowl, Green With Some Gold	20.00
Pressed Glass, **Rabbit Tracks,** Goblet	18.00
Pressed Glass, **Racing Deer,** Pitcher, Water	95.00
Pressed Glass, **Rail Fence Band,** Goblet	20.00
Pressed Glass, **Rain & Dewdrop,** Wine	18.00
Pressed Glass, **Raindrop,** Creamer, Amber	28.00
Pressed Glass, **Raindrop,** Pitcher, Water, Opalescent	65.00
Pressed Glass, **Raspberry & Grape,** Creamer	38.00
Pressed Glass, **Ray,** Celery, Flint	45.00
Pressed Glass, **Ray,** Creamer	16.00
Pressed Glass, **Rayed Flower,** Wine, Ruby, Gold	18.00
Recessed Ovals with Block Band, see Recessed Ovals	
Pressed Glass, **Recessed Ovals,** Goblet	12.00 To 18.00
Pressed Glass, **Red Block,** Goblet	30.00 To 38.00

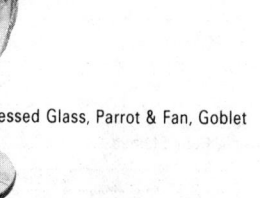

Pressed Glass, Parrot & Fan, Goblet

Pressed Glass, Pennsylvania, Goblet

Pressed Glass, Red Block, Goblet, Ruby 34.50
Pressed Glass, Red Block, Sauce, Ruby Stained 20.00
Pressed Glass, Red Block, Spooner .... 29.50 To 35.00
Pressed Glass, Red Block, Sugar, Ruby, Covered 40.00
Pressed Glass, Red Block, Tumbler 21.00
Pressed Glass, Red Block, Tumbler, Ruby Stained 29.50
Pressed Glass, Red Block, Wine .... 23.00 To 32.00
Pressed Glass, Red Block, Wine, Double Row .... 44.50 To 45.00
   Regal, see Paneled Forget-Me-Not
Pressed Glass, Regal Block, Wine 18.00
Pressed Glass, Reticulated Cord, Creamer 22.00
Pressed Glass, Reverse Colonial, Dish, Sweetmeat, Covered, Flint 30.00
Pressed Glass, Reverse Swirl, Syrup, White 60.00
Pressed Glass, Reverse Torpedo, Banana Boat 95.00
Pressed Glass, Reverse Torpedo, Banana Stand 125.00
Pressed Glass, Reverse Torpedo, Bowl, Fruit, Footed 35.00
Pressed Glass, Reverse Torpedo, Compote, Flint, 8 In. 75.00
Pressed Glass, Reverse Torpedo, Sauce .... 16.00 To 20.00
Pressed Glass, Reverse Torpedo, Spooner 20.00
Pressed Glass, Reverse Torpedo, Tumbler, Water, 5 1/4 In. 15.00
Pressed Glass, Reverse 44, Lemonade Set, Goblets, Gold & Amethyst, 5 Piece 125.00
Pressed Glass, Reverse 44, Water Set, Gold & Pink, 7 Piece 295.00
Pressed Glass, Reverse 44, Water Set, Tumblers, Gold & Amethyst, 6 Piece 125.00
Pressed Glass, Rexford, Celery 16.50
Pressed Glass, Rexford, Goblet 10.00
Pressed Glass, Rexford, Toothpick 15.50
Pressed Glass, Rexford, Water Set 120.00
Pressed Glass, Ribbed Acorn, Honey 10.00
Pressed Glass, Ribbed Clover, Tumbler, Bellflower Variant, Flint 75.00
Pressed Glass, Ribbed Forget-Me-Not, Sugar & Creamer 30.00
Pressed Glass, Ribbed Grape, Goblet 30.00
Pressed Glass, Ribbed Grape, Goblet, Flint .... 30.00 To 47.50
Pressed Glass, Ribbed Grape, Plate, Flint, 6 In. 30.00
Pressed Glass, Ribbed Grape, Spooner, Flint 32.50
Pressed Glass, Ribbed Grape, Sugar, Covered, Flint 85.00
Pressed Glass, Ribbed Ivy, Butter, Covered, Flint .... 72.00 To 95.00
Pressed Glass, Ribbed Ivy, Decanter, 1/2 Pint, Tulip Stopper 225.00
Pressed Glass, Ribbed Ivy, Dish, Sweetmeat, High Standard, Flint 115.00
Pressed Glass, Ribbed Ivy, Eggcup, Flint .... 25.00 To 28.00
Pressed Glass, Ribbed Ivy, Glass, Whiskey, Flint .... 52.50 To 58.00
Pressed Glass, Ribbed Ivy, Goblet, Flint .... 30.00 To 32.00
Pressed Glass, Ribbed Ivy, Salt, Master 27.00
Pressed Glass, Ribbed Ivy, Spooner 25.00
Pressed Glass, Ribbed Ivy, Tumbler, Flint 85.00
Pressed Glass, Ribbed Lattice, Tankard, White, Opalescent 85.00
   Ribbed Leaf, see Bellflower
Pressed Glass, Ribbed Loop, Goblet, Flint 40.00
   Ribbed Opal, see Beatty Rib
Pressed Glass, Ribbed Palm, Celery, Flint 65.00
Pressed Glass, Ribbed Palm, Eggcup 20.00
Pressed Glass, Ribbed Palm, Eggcup, Flint 26.50
Pressed Glass, Ribbed Palm, Goblet .... 22.00 To 50.00
Pressed Glass, Ribbed Palm, Goblet, Flint .... 22.50 To 30.00
Pressed Glass, Ribbed Palm, Goblet, Frosted 30.00
Pressed Glass, Ribbed Palm, Pitcher, Water, Flint 125.00
Pressed Glass, Ribbed Palm, Plate, Flint, 6 In. 48.50
Pressed Glass, Ribbed Palm, Spooner 35.00
Pressed Glass, Ribbed Palm, Sugar, Flint 35.00
Pressed Glass, Ribbed Palm, Sugar, Open, Flint 35.00
Pressed Glass, Ribbed Palm, Tumbler, Flint 85.00
   Ribbed Pineapple, see Prism & Flattened Sawtooth
Pressed Glass, Ribbed Thumbprint, Toothpick, Souvenir, Ruby Stained 20.00
Pressed Glass, Ribbon Candy, Creamer 15.00
Pressed Glass, Ribbon Candy, Spooner, 5 In. 20.00
Pressed Glass, Ribbon Candy, Sugar & Creamer, Square Base ..... 30.00 To 35.00
Pressed Glass, Ribbon Candy, Sugar, Covered 24.00

Pressed Glass, Ribbon, Creamer	40.00
Pressed Glass, Ribbon, Bowl, Waste	50.00
Pressed Glass, Ribbon, Butter	50.00
Pressed Glass, Ribbon, Compote, Covered, 6 In.	30.00
Pressed Glass, Ribbon, Compote, Covered, 7 1/2 In.	45.00
Pressed Glass, Ribbon, Compote, Open, Classic Figure, 6 In.	135.00
Pressed Glass, Ribbon, Compote, 8 1/2 X 4 In.	30.00
Pressed Glass, Ribbon, Creamer	25.00
Pressed Glass, Ribbon, Goblet	10.00 To 34.00
Pressed Glass, Ribbon, Goblet, Scalloped Foot	26.00
Pressed Glass, Ribbon, Sauce, Footed	10.00
Pressed Glass, Ribbon, Spooner	15.00 To 25.00
Pressed Glass, Ribbon, Sugar	50.00
Pressed Glass, Ribbon, Sugar, Covered	40.00
Pressed Glass, Ribbon, Water Tray	80.00
Ripple Band, see Ripple	
Pressed Glass, Ripple, Eggcup	18.00
Pressed Glass, Ripple, Goblet	7.50
Pressed Glass, Rising Sun, Cruet, Pink Sun	50.00
Pressed Glass, Rising Sun, Pitcher, Water	28.50
Pressed Glass, Rising Sun, Toothpick, Gold Suns	18.00
Pressed Glass, Rising Sun, Tumbler, Clear, Green	12.00
Pressed Glass, Riverside's Victoria, Celery, Ruby Stained	89.00
Pressed Glass, Roanoke, Butter, Covered	25.00
Rochelle, see Princess Feather	
Pressed Glass, Roman Key, Celery, Frosted, Flint	65.00
Pressed Glass, Roman Key, Celery, Frosted, Flint, Pair	115.00
Pressed Glass, Roman Key, Compote, Cut Panel Stem, Frosted, 6 1/4 In.	55.00
Pressed Glass, Roman Key, Compote, Flint, Frosted, C.1880, 6 X 5 1/2 In.	45.00
Pressed Glass, Roman Key, Creamer, Clear, Flint	37.00
Pressed Glass, Roman Key, Eggcup, Frosted, Flint	52.50
Pressed Glass, Roman Key, Goblet, Clear	22.00
Pressed Glass, Roman Key, Goblet, Frosted, Flint	27.00 To 40.00
Pressed Glass, Roman Key, Salt, Master, Frosted	25.00
Pressed Glass, Roman Key, Sugar, Covered, Frosted, Flint	45.00
Pressed Glass, Roman Key, Wine, Frosted, Flint	33.00
Pressed Glass, Roman Rosette, Bread Plate	36.00
Pressed Glass, Roman Rosette, Cake Stand, 10 In.	40.00 To 49.00
Pressed Glass, Roman Rosette, Creamer	16.00 To 25.00
Pressed Glass, Roman Rosette, Dish, Pickle	20.00
Pressed Glass, Roman Rosette, Mug, Child's	22.00
Pressed Glass, Roman Rosette, Mug, Child's, Blue	30.00
Pressed Glass, Roman Rosette, Salt & Pepper	25.00
Pressed Glass, Roman Rosette, Spooner	8.00
Pressed Glass, Roman Rosette, Sugar, Covered	17.00 To 30.00
Pressed Glass, Romeo, Goblet	16.00 To 16.50

Pressed Glass, Paneled Nightshade, Goblet

Pressed Glass, Paneled Wheat, Compote, Covered, 7 1/2 In.

Pressed Glass, Pleat & Panel, Bowl

Pressed Glass, Pleat Band, Compote, Covered

Pressed Glass, Viking, Compote, Covered

Pressed Glass, Punty, Syrup, Opalescent

Pressed Glass, Roman Rosette, Sugar & Crea

Pressed Glass, Rose In Snow, Goblet

Pressed Glass, Roosevelt Teddy Bears, Pitcher	375.00
Rope Bands, see Clear Panels with Cord Band	
Pressed Glass, Rope With Thumbprint, Butter, Covered, Blue	70.00
Pressed Glass, Rope With Thumbprint, Syrup, Amber	50.00 To 70.00
Pressed Glass, Rope With Thumbprint, Syrup, Blue	70.00
Pressed Glass, Rose In Snow, Cake Stand, 9 In.	65.00
Pressed Glass, Rose In Snow, Creamer, Square	25.00
Pressed Glass, Rose In Snow, Dish, Pickle	18.50
Pressed Glass, Rose In Snow, Goblet	25.00 To 35.00
Pressed Glass, Rose In Snow, Goblet, Flint	30.00
Pressed Glass, Rose In Snow, Plate, Handle, 10 In.	22.00
Pressed Glass, Rose In Snow, Plate, 5 In.	14.00
Pressed Glass, Rose In Snow, Plate, 7 In.	15.00
Pressed Glass, Rose In Snow, Plate, 8 In.	37.00

Pressed Glass, Rose In Snow, Sauce, 4 In.	7.00
Pressed Glass, Rose Leaves, Goblet	15.00
Pressed Glass, Rose Point Band, Creamer	12.00
Pressed Glass, Rose Point Band, Tumbler, Clear, Gold Top	12.00
Pressed Glass, Rose Sprig, Cake Stand, Blue, Square, 9 In.	58.00
Pressed Glass, Rose Sprig, Creamer, Vaseline	45.00
Pressed Glass, Rose Sprig, Goblet	22.50 To 30.00
Pressed Glass, Rose Sprig, Pitcher, Water	45.00
Pressed Glass, Rose Sprig, Wine	27.00
Pressed Glass, Rosette Band, Sugar, Covered	20.00
Rosette Medallion, see Feather Duster	
Pressed Glass, Rosette With Palms, Banana Stand	32.00
Pressed Glass, Rosette With Palms, Sugar	27.50
Pressed Glass, Rosette With Pinwheels, Spooner	13.00
Pressed Glass, Rosette, Celery	27.00
Pressed Glass, Rosette, Compote, Jelly	13.00 To 18.50
Pressed Glass, Rosette, Creamer	15.00
Pressed Glass, Rosette, Goblet	26.00
Pressed Glass, Rosette, Pitcher, Milk	25.00
Pressed Glass, Rosette, Pitcher, Water	25.00 To 44.00
Pressed Glass, Royal Block, Tankard	35.50
Pressed Glass, Royal Crystal, Berry Bowl, Round	20.00
Pressed Glass, Royal Crystal, Berry, 2 X 4 1/2 In.	16.00
Pressed Glass, Royal Crystal, Bottle, Perfume, 5 1/2 X 2 1/2 In.	25.00
Pressed Glass, Royal Crystal, Bottle, Water	26.00
Pressed Glass, Royal Crystal, Bowl, Square, 1 1/2 X 3 3/4 In.	7.00
Pressed Glass, Royal Crystal, Bowl, Square, 2 1/2 X 5 1/2 In.	10.00
Pressed Glass, Royal Crystal, Bowl, Square, 3 1/4 X 7 X 7 In.	55.00
Pressed Glass, Royal Crystal, Bowl, 1 3/4 X 3 3/4 X 3 3/4 In.	16.00
Pressed Glass, Royal Crystal, Cake Stand, 6 1/2 X 10 1/2 In.	26.00
Pressed Glass, Royal Crystal, Celery, 6 1/2 X 4 In.	27.00
Pressed Glass, Royal Crystal, Compote, Flared Edge, 6 1/2 X 8 1/2 In.	35.00
Pressed Glass, Royal Crystal, Compote, 7 X 7 1/2 In.	35.00
Pressed Glass, Royal Crystal, Creamer	18.00
Pressed Glass, Royal Crystal, Creamer, Ellipse Bordered	40.00
Pressed Glass, Royal Crystal, Cruet & Stopper, Pair	45.00
Pressed Glass, Royal Crystal, Cruet, Clear	19.50 To 28.00
Pressed Glass, Royal Crystal, Dish, Olive, Handled, 1 1/2 X 4 1/2 In.	12.00
Pressed Glass, Royal Crystal, Goblet	38.00
Pressed Glass, Royal Crystal, Jar, Cracker, Covered, 9 1/4 X 6 In.	38.00
Pressed Glass, Royal Crystal, Jug	31.00
Pressed Glass, Royal Crystal, Pitcher, Water	32.00 To 110.00
Pressed Glass, Royal Crystal, Rose Bowl, 6 X 5 3/4 In.	25.00
Pressed Glass, Royal Crystal, Salt & Pepper, Tops	30.00
Pressed Glass, Royal Crystal, Spooner	11.00 To 28.00
Pressed Glass, Royal Crystal, Sugar	28.00
Pressed Glass, Royal Crystal, Sugar, Covered	48.00
Pressed Glass, Royal Crystal, Sugar, Ruby & Clear, Open	25.00
Pressed Glass, Royal Crystal, Syrup	30.00 To 41.50
Pressed Glass, Royal Crystal, Table Set, Ruby Stained	275.00
Pressed Glass, Royal Crystal, Tankard, Lemonade	32.00
Pressed Glass, Royal Crystal, Toothpick	13.00
Pressed Glass, Royal Crystal, Tray, Pin, 11 X 8 X 4 X 8 In.	13.00
Pressed Glass, Royal Crystal, Tumbler	15.00
Pressed Glass, Royal Crystal, Wine	30.00
Pressed Glass, Royal Ivy, Berry Bowl, Clear To Pink, Frosted	28.00
Pressed Glass, Royal Ivy, Berry Bowl, Master, Clear To Pink, Frosted	65.00
Pressed Glass, Royal Ivy, Bowl, Clear To Pink, 9 In.	68.00
Pressed Glass, Royal Ivy, Castor, Pickle, Silver Plate Holder & Lid, Clear	245.00
Pressed Glass, Royal Ivy, Creamer, Frosted & Clear, 4 1/4 In.	50.00
Pressed Glass, Royal Ivy, Cruet, Frosted Crackle	225.00 To 335.00
Pressed Glass, Royal Ivy, Pitcher, Water, Clear To Pink, Frosted	250.00
Pressed Glass, Royal Ivy, Pitcher, Water, Pink	250.00
Pressed Glass, Royal Ivy, Pitcher, Water, Pink To Clear	195.00
Pressed Glass, Royal Ivy, Rose Bowl, Clear To Pink	65.00
Pressed Glass, Royal Ivy, Rose Bowl, Cranberry To Clear	150.00

Pressed Glass, Royal, Butter, Covered

Pressed Glass, Rose Sprig, Goblet

Pressed Glass, Sawtooth, Jar, Pomade

Pressed Glass, Royal Ivy, Saltshaker, Crackle, Northwood	52.00
Pressed Glass, Royal Ivy, Saltshaker, Pink	35.00
Pressed Glass, Royal Ivy, Spooner, Clear To Pink	90.00
Pressed Glass, Royal Ivy, Sugar Shaker, Cased Spatter, Northwood	165.00
Pressed Glass, Royal Ivy, Sugar Shaker, Clear To Pink	115.00
Pressed Glass, Royal Ivy, Sugar, Covered, Clear To Pink	85.00
Pressed Glass, Royal Ivy, Toothpick, Clear To Pink, Frosted	55.00
Pressed Glass, Royal Ivy, Tumbler, Clear To Pink	30.00 To 52.00
Pressed Glass, Royal Lace, Shaker, Green, Set	55.00
Pressed Glass, Royal Lady, Celery	23.00
Pressed Glass, Royal Oak, Butter, Covered, Clear To Pink	165.00
Pressed Glass, Royal Oak, Butter, Covered, Cranberry To Clear, Frosted	120.00
Pressed Glass, Royal Oak, Butter, Cranberry Lid, Acorn Finial	215.00
Pressed Glass, Royal Oak, Rose Bowl, Crackle, Cranberry & Amber, 5 In.	120.00
Pressed Glass, Royal Oak, Saltshaker, Clear To Pink, Pair	70.00
Pressed Glass, Royal Oak, Saltshaker, Pink	35.00
Pressed Glass, Royal Oak, Spooner, Clear To Pink, Frosted	95.00
Pressed Glass, Royal Oak, Sugar	65.00
Pressed Glass, Royal Oak, Sugar, Clear To Pink, Frosted	150.00
Ruby Rosette, see Pillow Encircled	
Ruby Thumbprint, see King's Crown	
Pressed Glass, S Repeat, Butter, Green With Gold	125.00
Pressed Glass, S Repeat, Condiment Set, Green, 5 Piece	165.00
Pressed Glass, S Repeat, Cup, Punch, Amethyst	15.00
Pressed Glass, S Repeat, Saltshaker, Blue	22.50
Pressed Glass, S Repeat, Tray, Condiment, Amethyst	15.00
Pressed Glass, Saint Bernard, Butter, Footed Base	100.00
Pressed Glass, Sandwich Gothic Arch, Celery, Printie Panel Loop, Flint	110.00
Pressed Glass, Sandwich Gothic Arch, Sugar	300.00
Pressed Glass, Sandwich Ivy Leaf, Sugar, Black Amethyst	145.00
Sandwich Loop, see Hairpin	
Pressed Glass, Sandwich Star, Compote, Flint, 7 1/2 In. X 5 1/2 In. High	55.00
Pressed Glass, Sandwich Star, Spill	30.00
Pressed Glass, Sandwich Star, Spill, Flint	38.00
Pressed Glass, Sandwich Star, Spooner, Spill, Flint	65.00
Pressed Glass, Sandwich Tulip, Celery, Flint	30.00 To 45.00
Pressed Glass, Sandwich, Celery, 4-Printie-Block, Scalloped Rim, 10 In.	95.00
Pressed Glass, Sawtooth & Pineapple, Spooner, 6 In.	30.00

Pressed Glass, Sawtooth Mitered, Butter, Covered, Child's	45.00
Pressed Glass, Sawtooth Mitered, Creamer, Child's	30.00
Pressed Glass, Sawtooth Mitered, Spooner, Child's	30.00
Sawtooth with Panels, see Hinoto	
Pressed Glass, Sawtooth, Bottle, Bitters, Stopper	58.00
Pressed Glass, Sawtooth, Butter, Covered, Child's	40.00 To 45.00
Pressed Glass, Sawtooth, Celery, Flint	50.00
Pressed Glass, Sawtooth, Champagne, Flint	60.00
Pressed Glass, Sawtooth, Compote, 7 1/2 In.	35.00
Pressed Glass, Sawtooth, Creamer, Applied Handle	75.00
Pressed Glass, Sawtooth, Creamer, Applied Handle, Flint	75.00
Pressed Glass, Sawtooth, Creamer, Footed	25.00
Pressed Glass, Sawtooth, Creamer, Molded Handle	25.00
Pressed Glass, Sawtooth, Creamer, Ovoid, Applied Handle, Flint	85.00
Pressed Glass, Sawtooth, Eggcup, Flint	35.00
Pressed Glass, Sawtooth, Eggcup, Umbilicated, Flint	22.50
Pressed Glass, Sawtooth, Goblet, Knob Stem	32.00
Pressed Glass, Sawtooth, Pitcher, Milk, Applied Handle	65.00
Pressed Glass, Sawtooth, Pitcher, Water, Applied Handle	82.00
Pressed Glass, Sawtooth, Pitcher, Water, Applied Handle, Flint	85.00
Pressed Glass, Sawtooth, Pitcher, Water, Flint	75.00
Pressed Glass, Sawtooth, Salt, Master, Fiery Opalescent	145.00
Pressed Glass, Sawtooth, Spooner	22.50 To 40.00
Pressed Glass, Sawtooth, Spooner, Child's	30.00
Pressed Glass, Sawtooth, Spooner, Flint	22.00 To 29.50
Pressed Glass, Sawtooth, Spooner, Gold On Base & Rim, Flint	110.00
Pressed Glass, Sawtooth, Spooner, Pair	40.00
Pressed Glass, Sawtooth, Sugar, Covered	55.00
Pressed Glass, Sawtooth, Tumbler, Flint	55.00
Pressed Glass, Sawtooth, Wine, Knob Stem, Flint	60.00
Pressed Glass, Saxon, Celery, Pedestal	35.00
Pressed Glass, Scalloped Daisy & Fan, Goblet, Green	28.00
Pressed Glass, Scalloped Daisy & Fan, Tumbler, Green	18.00
Pressed Glass, Scalloped Lines, Spooner	16.00
Pressed Glass, Scalloped Swirl, Toothpick	22.00
Pressed Glass, Scalloped Tape, Bread Plate	25.00
Pressed Glass, Scalloped Tape, Goblet	16.00
Pressed Glass, Scalloped Tape, Relish	9.50 To 11.00
Pressed Glass, Scalloped Tape, Wine	32.00
Pressed Glass, Scarab, Goblet, Flint	85.00 To 110.00
Pressed Glass, Scroll Medallion, Creamer, Grape	22.50
Pressed Glass, Scroll Medallion, Sugar, Covered, Grape Cluster, C.1870	35.00
Pressed Glass, Scroll With Acanthus, Compote, Jelly	28.00
Pressed Glass, Scroll With Acanthus, Compote, Jelly, Green, Opalescent	35.00
Pressed Glass, Scroll With Acanthus, Creamer, Gold & Enamel Design, Green	55.00
Pressed Glass, Scroll With Acanthus, Jelly, Green	48.00
Pressed Glass, Scroll With Flowers, Goblet	15.00
Pressed Glass, Scroll, Eggcup	14.00
Pressed Glass, Scroll, Goblet	10.00 To 14.00
Pressed Glass, Scroll, Spooner	13.00
Pressed Glass, Sedan, Creamer	22.00
Pressed Glass, Seneca Loop, Celery, Flint	18.00
Pressed Glass, Seneca Loop, Goblet	20.00
Pressed Glass, Seneca Loop, Goblet, Flint	40.00
Pressed Glass, Serpent, Pitcher, Water	120.00
Sheaf & Diamond, see Fickle Block	
Pressed Glass, Sheaf Of Wheat, Bread Plate, Give Us This Day	35.00
Pressed Glass, Shell & Jewel, Pitcher, Water	22.00 To 38.00
Pressed Glass, Shell & Jewel, Sauce, Set Of 4	40.00
Pressed Glass, Shell & Jewel, Tumbler	12.00 To 22.00
Pressed Glass, Shell & Jewel, Tumbler, Green	31.50
Pressed Glass, Shell & Jewel, Tumbler, Water, Green	31.50
Pressed Glass, Shell & Jewel, Water Set, Blue, 5 Piece	195.00
Pressed Glass, Shell & Jewel, Water Set, Green, Pitcher & 4 Tumblers	110.00
Pressed Glass, Shell & Jewel, Water Set, Pitcher & 8 Tumblers	80.00
Pressed Glass, Shell & Seaweed, Toothpick, Opaque Blue	45.00

Pressed Glass, Shell & Tassel, Bowl, Oblong	35.00
Pressed Glass, Shell & Tassel, Bowl, Oval, Amber, Tufts Plated Stand	150.00
Pressed Glass, Shell & Tassel, Bowl, Oval, 10 In.	33.00 To 37.00
Pressed Glass, Shell & Tassel, Bowl, Oval, 10 X 4 1/2 In.	70.00
Pressed Glass, Shell & Tassel, Bowl, Oval, 12 In.	55.00
Pressed Glass, Shell & Tassel, Bowl, Oval, 12 1/4 In.	75.00
Pressed Glass, Shell & Tassel, Bowl, Sugar, Covered, Square	65.00
Pressed Glass, Shell & Tassel, Bowl, 11 1/2 X 5 In.	28.00
Pressed Glass, Shell & Tassel, Cake Stand, 12 In.	65.00
Pressed Glass, Shell & Tassel, Compote, Jelly, 4 1/2 In.	47.50
Pressed Glass, Shell & Tassel, Compote, Open, Square, 8 X 8 1/2 In.	35.00
Pressed Glass, Shell & Tassel, Compote, Open, 10 X 8 1/4 In.	45.00
Pressed Glass, Shell & Tassel, Compote, Open, 4 1/2 In.	28.00 To 37.50
Pressed Glass, Shell & Tassel, Compote, Open, 6 1/2 In.	35.00 To 38.50
Pressed Glass, Shell & Tassel, Compote, Open, 7 3/4 In.	42.00
Pressed Glass, Shell & Tassel, Compote, Open, 8 3/4 In.	36.00
Pressed Glass, Shell & Tassel, Compote, 9 X 9 1/2 In.	85.00
Pressed Glass, Shell & Tassel, Creamer	55.00
Pressed Glass, Shell & Tassel, Creamer, Round	42.50
Pressed Glass, Shell & Tassel, Creamer, Square	45.00 To 49.50
Pressed Glass, Shell & Tassel, Dish, Pickle, 5 X 8 In.	21.00
Pressed Glass, Shell & Tassel, Jar, Jam, Covered, Shell Finial	29.00
Pressed Glass, Shell & Tassel, Pitcher, Water, Red	40.50
Pressed Glass, Shell & Tassel, Plate, 12 X 8 In.Deep	38.50
Pressed Glass, Shell & Tassel, Plate, 14 X 8 1/2 In.Deep	95.00
Pressed Glass, Shell & Tassel, Platter, Handled, 14 X 8 In.	49.50
Pressed Glass, Shell & Tassel, Platter, 11 X 7 In.	40.00
Pressed Glass, Shell & Tassel, Salt & Pepper, Original Top	250.00
Pressed Glass, Shell & Tassel, Sauce	6.00 To 12.00
Pressed Glass, Shell & Tassel, Sauce, Footed, 3 3/4 In.Square	7.50 To 15.00
Pressed Glass, Shell & Tassel, Sauce, Square	7.00
Pressed Glass, Shell & Tassel, Spooner	35.00
Pressed Glass, Shell & Tassel, Spooner, Round	25.00
Pressed Glass, Shell & Tassel, Sugar & Creamer, 5 In.	47.50
Pressed Glass, Shell & Tassel, Sugar, Covered	65.00 To 75.00
Pressed Glass, Shell & Tassel, Sugar, Covered, Square	55.00 To 65.00
Pressed Glass, Shell & Tassel, Sugar, Footed, Cover, Dog Finial	125.00
Pressed Glass, Shell & Tassel, Sugar, Open	19.00
Pressed Glass, Shell & Tassel, Tray, Oval, 13 In.	45.00 To 75.00
Pressed Glass, Shell & Tassel, Tray, 8 X 12 In.	28.00
Pressed Glass, Shepherd's Plaid, Creamer	12.00
Pressed Glass, Sheraton, Compote	17.50
Pressed Glass, Sheraton, Dish, Pickle, Octagonal, Amber, 8 3/4 X 4 1/4 In.	12.00
Pressed Glass, Sheraton, Dish, Relish, Amber	17.00
Pressed Glass, Sheraton, Dish, Relish, Open Handles, Oblong	10.00
Pressed Glass, Sheraton, Pitcher, Cream, Amber	30.00
Pressed Glass, Sheraton, Spooner, Blue	40.00
Pressed Glass, Sheraton, Sugar	23.00
Pressed Glass, Sheraton, Sugar & Creamer, Amber	45.00
Pressed Glass, Shield & Anchor, Goblet	45.00
Pressed Glass, Shield, Sugar, Open	40.00
Pressed Glass, Shields, Goblet	18.00

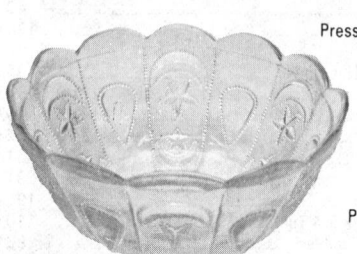

Pressed Glass, Shrine, Bowl

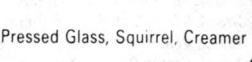

Pressed Glass, Squirrel, Creamer

Pressed Glass, Star & Dewdrop, Butter, Covered

Pressed Glass, Short Loops, Goblet, Flint 22.00
Pressed Glass, Short Swirl, Goblet 6.00
   Short Teasel, see Teasel
Pressed Glass, Shoshone, Banana Stand 30.00
Pressed Glass, Shoshone, Bowl, Six Sided, 6 In. 10.00
Pressed Glass, Shoshone, Bowl, Square, 6 1/2 In. 12.00
Pressed Glass, Shoshone, Cake Stand, 9 In. 20.00
Pressed Glass, Shoshone, Compote, Emerald Green, 8 1/4 X 5 In. 22.50
Pressed Glass, Shoshone, Compote, 8 In. 18.00
Pressed Glass, Shoshone, Creamer & Sugar, Ruby Stained 47.50
Pressed Glass, Shoshone, Creamer, Ruby Stained 55.00
Pressed Glass, Shoshone, Cruet, Green .... 38.00 To 70.00
Pressed Glass, Shoshone, Cruet, Original Stopper, Green .... 100.00 To 135.00
Pressed Glass, Shoshone, Relish, Pear Shaped 8.00
Pressed Glass, Shoshone, Spooner, Ruby Stained 45.00
Pressed Glass, Shoshone, Sugar, Open 20.00
Pressed Glass, Shovel, Pitcher, Syrup, Glass Top 18.50
Pressed Glass, Shrine, Butter, Covered 32.00
Pressed Glass, Shrine, Goblet 32.00
Pressed Glass, Shrine, Pitcher, Lemonade 75.00
Pressed Glass, Shrine, Pitcher, Water .... 35.00 To 48.50
Pressed Glass, Shrine, Tumbler .... 18.50 To 22.00
Pressed Glass, Shrine, Tumbler, Lemonade 30.00
Pressed Glass, Shuttle, Celery 25.00
Pressed Glass, Shuttle, Cup, Punch 7.50
Pressed Glass, Shuttle, Wine .... 12.50 To 13.50
Pressed Glass, Six Flute, Wine, Flared, Hexagonal Stem, Flint 20.00
Pressed Glass, Six Panel, Spooner, Fine Cut Amber Panels 40.00
Pressed Glass, Six Row Kalbach, Goblet 16.00
Pressed Glass, Skilton, Celery 20.00
Pressed Glass, Skilton, Spooner, Ruby Flash 28.00
Pressed Glass, Smocking, Butter, Covered, Flint 52.50
Pressed Glass, Smocking, Creamer, Applied Handle 62.00
Pressed Glass, Smocking, Creamer, Flint 80.00
Pressed Glass, Smocking, Goblet, Flint .... 27.00 To 45.00
Pressed Glass, Smocking, Sugar & Creamer, Covered, Applied Handle, Flint 160.00
Pressed Glass, Smocking, Sugar, Covered, Flint 80.00
Pressed Glass, Smooth Diamond, Creamer 15.00
Pressed Glass, Smooth Diamond, Sugar, Covered 25.00
Pressed Glass, Snail, Banana Stand 75.00
Pressed Glass, Snail, Bowl, 8 In. 30.00
Pressed Glass, Snail, Celery .... 27.50 To 28.00
Pressed Glass, Snail, Celery, Etched 65.00
Pressed Glass, Snail, Cup 11.00
Pressed Glass, Snail, Cup, Punch 38.00
Pressed Glass, Snail, Dish, Relish, Oval, 7 In. 23.00
Pressed Glass, Snail, Goblet .... 45.00 To 55.00
Pressed Glass, Snail, Pitcher, Etched, 9 In. 75.00
Pressed Glass, Snail, Rose Bowl, 7 1/2 In. .... 38.00 To 39.00
Pressed Glass, Snail, Salt & Pepper 37.00
Pressed Glass, Snail, Sauce, 4 In. 16.00
Pressed Glass, Snail, Sauce, 4 3/4 In. 17.00

Pressed Glass, Snail, Spooner 26.00
Pressed Glass, Snail, Spooner, Etched 20.00
Pressed Glass, Snail, Syrup, Original Lid 58.00
Pressed Glass, Snail, Tumbler .... 38.00 To 45.00
Pressed Glass, Snail, Tumbler, Etched 30.00
Pressed Glass, Snake Drape, Goblet .... 14.50 To 25.00
Pressed Glass, Snow Band, Goblet 10.00
Pressed Glass, Snowdrop, Bowl, Waste 23.00
Pressed Glass, Snowdrop, Tray, Ice Cream 30.00
Pressed Glass, Snowflake, Butter, Clear, Opalescent, Covered 22.00
    Spanish American, see Admiral Dewey
    Spanish Coin, see Columbian Coin
Pressed Glass, Spear Point & Daisy Band, Wine 8.00
Pressed Glass, Spear Point Band, Celery, Scalloped Top 17.00
Pressed Glass, Spear Point, Sugar, Covered, Gold 12.00
Pressed Glass, Spearheads, Sugar, Covered 35.00
Pressed Glass, Spiral With Maltese Cross, Creamer 15.00
Pressed Glass, Spirea Band, Bowl, Oval, Blue 28.00
Pressed Glass, Spirea Band, Goblet, Amber 30.00
Pressed Glass, Spirea Band, Goblet, Blue 10.00
Pressed Glass, Spirea Band, Goblet, Blue, Etched Name & 1886 .... 30.00
Pressed Glass, Spirea Band, Spooner, Blue 45.00
Pressed Glass, Spirea, Bread Plate 20.00
Pressed Glass, Spirea, Bread Plate, Amber 32.00
Pressed Glass, Spirea, Bread Plate, Blue 35.00
Pressed Glass, Sprig, Berry Set, 8 Piece 85.00
Pressed Glass, Sprig, Bowl, Footed 20.00
Pressed Glass, Sprig, Bowl, Footed, 8 In.Diameter 18.00
Pressed Glass, Sprig, Cake Stand, 8 In. 28.00
Pressed Glass, Sprig, Celery 27.00
Pressed Glass, Sprig, Compote, Covered, High Standard, 7 In.Diameter 49.50
Pressed Glass, Sprig, Compote, Open, High Standard, 10 In.Diameter 37.50
Pressed Glass, Sprig, Compote, 7 In. 25.00
Pressed Glass, Sprig, Compote, 8 In. 30.00
Pressed Glass, Sprig, Creamer 25.00
Pressed Glass, Sprig, Cup & Saucer 22.50
Pressed Glass, Sprig, Dish, Pickle, 2 Handled 15.00
Pressed Glass, Sprig, Dish, Relish 14.50
Pressed Glass, Sprig, Goblet .... 23.00 To 27.50
Pressed Glass, Sprig, Pitcher, Water 47.50
Pressed Glass, Sprig, Salt, Master, Flat, Oval 40.00
Pressed Glass, Sprig, Sauce, Flat, 4 In. .... 7.00 To 8.00
Pressed Glass, Sprig, Sauce, Footed .... 9.00 To 10.00
Pressed Glass, Sprig, Sauce, Footed, 4 In. 8.00
Pressed Glass, Sprig, Spooner .... 15.00 To 25.00
Pressed Glass, Sprig, Spooner, Blue Custard Chrysanthemum 225.00
Pressed Glass, Sprig, Sugar 10.00
Pressed Glass, Sprig, Sugar, Covered .... 35.00 To 39.50
Pressed Glass, Sprig, Vegetable, Oval, 8 In. 18.00
Pressed Glass, Sprig, Vegetable, Oval, 9 In. 20.00
Pressed Glass, Squirrel In Bower, Pitcher, Water, Frosted Fruits 125.00
Pressed Glass, Squirrel With Nut, Pitcher, Water 98.50
Pressed Glass, Squirrel, Goblet .... 250.00 To 275.00
Pressed Glass, Squirrel, Pitcher, Water .... 85.00 To 95.00
Pressed Glass, Squirrel, Sauce 15.00
Pressed Glass, Star & Bead, Table Set, 4 Piece 155.00
Pressed Glass, Star & File, Bowl, 6 1/2 In. 12.00
Pressed Glass, Star & File, Cake Stand, 8 In. 17.50
Pressed Glass, Star & File, Cup, Punch 7.00
Pressed Glass, Star & File, Sherbet 7.00
Pressed Glass, Star & Honeycomb, Pitcher, Water 41.00
Pressed Glass, Star & Ivy, Cup & Saucer 21.00
Pressed Glass, Star & Oval, Butter, Covered, Frosted & Clear 35.00
Pressed Glass, Star & Oval, Celery, Frosted 15.00
Pressed Glass, Star & Palm, Goblet 14.00
Pressed Glass, Star & Pillar, Pitcher, Water, Bars 45.00

Pressed Glass, Tandem Diamonds
And Thumbprint, Goblet

Pressed Glass, Strawberry,
Creamer, 5 1/2 In.

Star & Punty, see Moon & Star
Pressed Glass, **Star & Rib**, Table Set, Blue, 4 Piece 265.00
Pressed Glass, **Star Arches**, Punch Cup 7.00
Star Band, see also Bosworth
Pressed Glass, **Star Medallion**, Lacy Sandwich, Sauce, Flint 70.00
Pressed Glass, **Star Of Bethlehem**, Pitcher, Water 35.00
Pressed Glass, **Star Of David**, Goblet .... 10.00 To 16.50
Pressed Glass, **Star Rosetted**, Bread Plate, A Good Mother 42.50
Pressed Glass, **Star Rosetted**, Goblet .... 17.50 To 18.00
Pressed Glass, **Star Whorl**, Goblet 14.00
Pressed Glass, **Stars & Bars**, Cruet, Amber 30.00
Pressed Glass, **Stars & Bars**, Cruet, Original Stopper 23.00
Pressed Glass, **Stars & Bars**, Cruet, Original Stopper, Blue 75.00
Pressed Glass, **Stars & Stripes**, Wine .... 5.00 To 15.00
Pressed Glass, **States**, Goblet 26.00
Pressed Glass, **States**, Punch Set, Bowl & 4 Cups 60.00
Pressed Glass, **States**, Saltshaker, Clear, Pair 24.00
Pressed Glass, **Statue Of Liberty**, Jar, 12 1/2 In. 75.00
Pressed Glass, **Statue Of Liberty**, Toothpick, Figural, Amber 95.00
Stayman, see Tidy
Pressed Glass, **Stedman**, Tumbler, Flint 35.00
Pressed Glass, **Stippled Band**, Goblet 9.50
Pressed Glass, **Stippled Chain**, Goblet .... 14.00 To 18.00
Pressed Glass, **Stippled Chain**, Relish 12.50
Pressed Glass, **Stippled Chain**, Sugar, Covered 22.00
Pressed Glass, **Stippled Cherry**, Bread Plate 29.50
Stippled Dahlia, see Dahlia
Pressed Glass, **Stippled Double Loop**, Goblet 15.00
Pressed Glass, **Stippled Fleur-De-Lis**, Goblet, Blue 35.00
Pressed Glass, **Stippled Fleur-De-Lis**, Sauce, Blue, 4 1/2 In. 12.00
Pressed Glass, **Stippled Flower Band**, Goblet 15.00
Pressed Glass, **Stippled Forget-Me-Not**, Celery 38.00
Pressed Glass, **Stippled Forget-Me-Not**, Cup & Saucer 21.50
Pressed Glass, **Stippled Forget-Me-Not**, Pitcher, Water 35.00
Pressed Glass, **Stippled Forget-Me-Not**, Plate, Baby Center 32.00
Pressed Glass, **Stippled Forget-Me-Not**, Plate, Kitten, 9 In. 27.00
Pressed Glass, **Stippled Forget-Me-Not**, Wine 36.50
Pressed Glass, **Stippled Fuchsia**, Goblet 18.50
Pressed Glass, **Stippled Grape & Festoon**, Celery .... 27.00 To 35.00
Pressed Glass, **Stippled Grape & Festoon**, Compote, Covered, 8 In. 45.00
Pressed Glass, **Stippled Grape & Festoon**, Goblet .... 22.50 To 24.00
Pressed Glass, **Stippled Grape & Festoon**, Goblet, Clear Leaf 18.50
Pressed Glass, **Stippled Grape & Festoon**, Spooner .... 11.00 To 30.00
Pressed Glass, **Stippled Grape & Festoon**, Spooner, Clear Leaf 24.50
Pressed Glass, **Stippled Ivy**, Goblet 20.00
Pressed Glass, **Stippled Ivy**, Sugar, Covered 35.00
Pressed Glass, **Stippled Leaf & Flower**, Pitcher, Water 40.00
Pressed Glass, **Stippled Leaf**, Goblet 15.00
Pressed Glass, **Stippled Maiden Hair Fern**, Goblet .... 10.00 To 20.00

Pressed Glass, Stippled Medallion, Goblet 16.00
   Stippled Paneled Flower, see Maine
   Stippled Scroll, see Scroll
   Stippled Star Variant, see Stippled Sandburr
Pressed Glass, Stippled Star, Spooner .... 15.00 To 45.00
   Stork Looking at the Moon, see Ostrich Looking at the Moon
Pressed Glass, Stork, Creamer, Frosted .... 65.00 To 75.00
Pressed Glass, Stork, Pickle Castor, Frosted 100.00
Pressed Glass, Stork, Spooner, Frosted 65.00
Pressed Glass, Stork, Water Tray, Frosted 75.00
Pressed Glass, Straight Ball & Swirl, Wine 7.50
Pressed Glass, Strawberry & Greek Key, Goblet 24.50
Pressed Glass, Strawberry, Compote, Jelly 14.50
Pressed Glass, Strawberry, Goblet 27.00
Pressed Glass, Strawberry, Spooner .... 19.00 To 25.00
Pressed Glass, Stylized Flower, Pitcher, Water 21.00
Pressed Glass, Success To The Railroad, Flask, Horse-Pulled Cart, Pink 275.00
Pressed Glass, Sugar Pear, Goblet 19.50
Pressed Glass, Sunbeam, Plate, Square, Gold Edge, 7 1/4 In. 12.00
Pressed Glass, Sunbeam, Salt & Pepper 25.00
Pressed Glass, Sunbeam, Toothpick 14.00

Pressed Glass, Three Face, Bowl, Covered, Footed

Pressed Glass, Thistle, Goblet

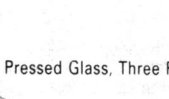

Pressed Glass, Three Printie, Vase, 10 In.

Pressed Glass, Sunbeam, Vase, Green, 6 In. 15.00
Pressed Glass, Sunburst & Bar, Tumbler, Amber 22.00
Pressed Glass, Sunburst, Butter .... 34.50 To 35.00
Pressed Glass, Sunburst, Pitcher, Water, 10 In. 32.50
Pressed Glass, Sunk Daisy, Cake Stand, 10 In. 28.50
Pressed Glass, Sunk Honeycomb, Creamer, Ruby Stained, Tankard Shaped 20.00
Pressed Glass, Sunk Honeycomb, Mug, Ruby Stained 15.00
Pressed Glass, Sunk Honeycomb, Tumbler, Ruby Stained 24.50
Pressed Glass, Sunken Primrose, Creamer, Panel, Flower, Clear, Ruby Stained 45.00
Pressed Glass, Sunken Primrose, Water Set, Gold & Ruby Flashed, 7 Piece 325.00
   Sunrise, see Rising Sun
Pressed Glass, Swag With Brackets, Creamer 138.00
Pressed Glass, Swag With Brackets, Creamer, Blue 45.00
Pressed Glass, Swag With Brackets, Spooner 45.00
Pressed Glass, Swag With Brackets, Spooner, Blue 59.00
Pressed Glass, Swag With Brackets, Spooner, Green 59.00
Pressed Glass, Swag With Brackets, Sugar, Blue Opalescent, Covered 110.00
Pressed Glass, Swag With Brackets, Sugar, Covered, Blue With Gold 80.00
Pressed Glass, Swag With Brackets, Water Set, Blue Opalescent, 7 Piece 425.00
Pressed Glass, Swan With Tree, Creamer 30.00
Pressed Glass, Swan, Mug, Clambroth 30.00
Pressed Glass, Swan, Mustard, Blue 25.00
Pressed Glass, Swan, Pitcher, Water 75.00

Pressed Glass, Swan, Sauce, Footed	13.00
Pressed Glass, Swans & Heron, Tray, Water, 9 X 13 In.	37.00
Pressed Glass, Sweetheart, Glass, Child's	135.00
Pressed Glass, Sweetheart, Spooner	30.00
Pressed Glass, Swirl & Ball, Pitcher, Water	25.00
Pressed Glass, Swirl & Cable, Butter	27.50
Pressed Glass, Swirl & Diamond, Tankard, Etched	59.75
Pressed Glass, Swirl, Pitcher, Water	30.00
Pressed Glass, Swirl, Pitcher, Water, Jefferson Shape	115.00
Pressed Glass, Swirl, Syrup, Opalescent Dots, Tin Top, Blue	85.00
Pressed Glass, Tackle Block, Goblet, Flint	20.00 To 25.00
Pressed Glass, Tacoma, Sauce, Ruby Stained, 4 In.	15.00
Pressed Glass, Talisman Ashburton, Goblet, Flint	35.00
Pressed Glass, Tall Prism, Goblet	6.50
Pressed Glass, Tandem Bicycle, Goblet	18.00 To 25.00
Tape Measure, see Shields	
Pressed Glass, Tape Motto, Tray, Scalloped	25.00
Pressed Glass, Tappan, Butter, Sugar, Covered, Creamer, Sapphire Blue	65.00
Pressed Glass, Teardrop & Tassel, Berry Set, 7 Piece, Blue, Greentown	185.00
Pressed Glass, Teardrop & Tassel, Butter	47.50
Pressed Glass, Teardrop & Tassel, Creamer	32.00
Pressed Glass, Teardrop & Tassel, Pitcher, Water	65.00
Pressed Glass, Teardrop & Tassel, Pitcher, Water, 8 1/2 In.	55.00
Pressed Glass, Teardrop & Tassel, Sugar & Creamer, Covered, Green	110.00
Pressed Glass, Teardrop & Tassel, Tumbler, Blue	25.00
Teardrop & Thumbprint, see Teardrop	
Pressed Glass, Teardrop Bands, Pitcher, Water	17.00
Pressed Glass, Teardrop, Goblet	10.00 To 22.00
Pressed Glass, Teardrop, Wine	10.00
Pressed Glass, Teasel, Goblet	12.00 To 14.00
Pressed Glass, Teasel, Plate, Clear, 9 1/4 In.	14.00
Pressed Glass, Teddy Roosevelt, Bread Plate, Dancing Bear Border, Frosted	125.00
Pressed Glass, Tennessee, Celery	28.00 To 35.00
Pressed Glass, Tennessee, Goblet	8.00
Pressed Glass, Tennessee, Pitcher, Milk	28.00
Pressed Glass, Tennessee, Relish	12.50
Pressed Glass, Tepee, Cruet	35.00
Pressed Glass, Terrace, Bread Plate, Engraved	20.00
Pressed Glass, Terrace, Goblet, Flint	10.00
Pressed Glass, Texas Bull's-Eye, Goblet	15.00
Pressed Glass, Texas Bull's-Eye, Goblet, Ladies	13.50
Pressed Glass, Texas Bull's-Eye, Wine	13.00
Pressed Glass, Texas, Creamer, Gold Trim	10.00
Pressed Glass, Texas, Sauce, Flat	8.50
Pressed Glass, Texas, Toothpick, Clear With Gold	20.00
Pressed Glass, Texas, Vase, 10 In.	18.00
Pressed Glass, Thistle Shield, Goblet	18.50
Pressed Glass, Thistle, Dish, Relish, Oblong	18.00
Pressed Glass, Thistle, Goblet, Flint	50.00
Pressed Glass, Thistle, Pitcher, Water, Flint	125.00
Pressed Glass, Thistle, Wine, Flint	45.00
Pressed Glass, Thompson, Toothpick, Ruby Stained, No.77	16.50
Pressed Glass, Thousand Eye, Butter, Covered, Amber, 3 Knob	32.50
Pressed Glass, Thousand Eye, Celery, Opalescent	75.00 To 100.00
Pressed Glass, Thousand Eye, Celery, Vaseline Knob, Stemmed	45.00
Pressed Glass, Thousand Eye, Compote, Blue, Square, 8 X 5 1/2 In.	45.00
Pressed Glass, Thousand Eye, Creamer	25.00
Pressed Glass, Thousand Eye, Cruet, Knob Stopper, 6 In.	35.00
Pressed Glass, Thousand Eye, Cruet, Yellow	85.00
Pressed Glass, Thousand Eye, Goblet	18.00
Pressed Glass, Thousand Eye, Goblet, Amber	20.00
Pressed Glass, Thousand Eye, Goblet, Knob Stem, Amber	36.50
Pressed Glass, Thousand Eye, Mug, Amber	25.00
Pressed Glass, Thousand Eye, Pitcher, Water	95.00
Pressed Glass, Thousand Eye, Plate, Green, 8 In.Square	28.00
Pressed Glass, Thousand Eye, Saltshaker, Vaseline, Pair	45.00

Pressed Glass, Thousand Eye, Spooner 22.50
Pressed Glass, Thousand Eye, Spooner, Amber 35.00
Pressed Glass, Thousand Eye, Spooner, 3 Knobs On Stem, Blue, 5 1/2 In. 38.00
Pressed Glass, Thousand Eye, Syrup, Green 65.00
Pressed Glass, Thousand Eye, Toothpick 30.00
Pressed Glass, Thousand Eye, Toothpick, Hat 30.00
Pressed Glass, Thousand Eye, Toothpick, Vaseline 35.00
Pressed Glass, Thousand Eye, Tray, Oval, 14 In. 95.00
Pressed Glass, Thousand Eye, Tumbler 25.00
Pressed Glass, Thousand Eye, Tumbler, Amber 32.00
Pressed Glass, Thousand Eye, Wine, Amber 18.50
Pressed Glass, Threaded, Goblet 26.00
Pressed Glass, Three Deer, Goblet, Iowa City 125.00
Pressed Glass, Three Face, Butter 155.00
Pressed Glass, Three Face, Cake Stand, 7 In. 95.00
Pressed Glass, Three Face, Cake Stand, 9 1/2 In. 85.00
Pressed Glass, Three Face, Compote, Covered, 8 1/2 X 13 In. 145.00
Pressed Glass, Three Face, Compote, Covered, 9 In. 95.00
Pressed Glass, Three Face, Compote, 10 In. 100.00
Pressed Glass, Three Face, Compote, 7 In. 35.00
Pressed Glass, Three Face, Goblet 55.00
Pressed Glass, Three Face, Goblet, Etched 75.00
Pressed Glass, Three Face, Pitcher, Water 75.00
Pressed Glass, Three Face, Saltshaker, Pair 75.00
Pressed Glass, Three Face, Spooner, Etched 75.00
Pressed Glass, Three Face, Spooner, Frosted 20.00
Pressed Glass, Three Fruits, Goblet 27.00
Pressed Glass, Three Fruits, Grape Cluster, Pear, Blackberry, Creamer 37.50
  Three Graces, see also Three Face
Pressed Glass, Three Panel, Berry Bowl, Amber 22.00
Pressed Glass, Three Panel, Berry Bowl, Blue 25.00
Pressed Glass, Three Panel, Bowl, Footed, Amber, 7 In. .... 30.00 To 32.00
Pressed Glass, Three Panel, Bowl, Footed, Blue, 7 In. 32.00
Pressed Glass, Three Panel, Celery, Folded Top, Amber .... 60.00 To 65.00
Pressed Glass, Three Panel, Creamer, Blue 48.00
Pressed Glass, Three Panel, Spill 25.00
Pressed Glass, Three Panel, Sugar, Covered 30.00
Pressed Glass, Three Presidents, Bread Plate, Frosted 55.00
Pressed Glass, Three Presidents, Bread Plate, In Remembrance 50.00
  Three Sisters, see Three Face
Pressed Glass, Three-In-One, Toothpick 12.00
Pressed Glass, Thumbprint Windows, Goblet 22.00
Pressed Glass, Thumbprint, Bottle, Bitters 95.00
Pressed Glass, Thumbprint, Celery 125.00
Pressed Glass, Thumbprint, Celery, Flint .... 85.00 To 100.00
Pressed Glass, Thumbprint, Celery, Pattern In Base, Flint 125.00
Pressed Glass, Thumbprint, Compote, High Standard, Ruby Stained, 5 In. 75.00
Pressed Glass, Thumbprint, Compote, Pedestal, Covered, Flint, 5 In. 85.00
Pressed Glass, Thumbprint, Compote, Pedestal, Flint, 8 1/2 In. 155.00
Pressed Glass, Thumbprint, Compote, Scallop Rim, Flared, Flint, 8 1/4 In. 85.00
Pressed Glass, Thumbprint, Creamer & Sugar, Ruby Stained 59.50
Pressed Glass, Thumbprint, Cup & Saucer, Ruby 48.00
Pressed Glass, Thumbprint, Goblet 30.00
Pressed Glass, Thumbprint, Goblet, Baluster Base, Flint 65.00
Pressed Glass, Thumbprint, Goblet, Barrel & Baluster Stem 65.00
Pressed Glass, Thumbprint, Goblet, Ruby 20.00
Pressed Glass, Thumbprint, Goblet, Ruby Stained, Souvenir Of Boston, Mass. 25.00
Pressed Glass, Thumbprint, Honey 18.50
Pressed Glass, Thumbprint, Honey, Flint 18.50
Pressed Glass, Thumbprint, Pitcher, Water, Flint 175.00
Pressed Glass, Thumbprint, Salt & Pepper, Ruby Stained 40.00
Pressed Glass, Thumbprint, Salt, Master, Footed .... 29.00 To 29.50
Pressed Glass, Thumbprint, Saltshaker, Etched Fern & Berry, Ruby Stained 30.00
Pressed Glass, Thumbprint, Spooner, Ruby Stained 45.00
Pressed Glass, Thumbprint, Toothpick, Ruby Stained 22.50
Pressed Glass, Thumbprint, Toothpick, Ruby, Etched 42.50

Pressed Glass, Thumbprint, Tumble-Up, Flint	385.00
Pressed Glass, Thumbprint, Tumbler, Flint	50.00
Pressed Glass, Thumbprint, Tumbler, Ruby Stained	29.50
Pressed Glass, Thumbprint, Whiskey, Footed, Flint	35.00
Pressed Glass, Thumbprint, Wine, Baluster Stem, Flint	60.00
Pressed Glass, Thumbprint, Wine, Barrel & Baluster Stem, Flint	60.00
Pressed Glass, Thumbprint, Wine, Ruby	30.00
Pressed Glass, Tidy, Goblet	11.00 To 15.00
Pressed Glass, Tidy, Pitcher, Water, Applied Handle	40.00
Pressed Glass, Tiger, Goblet, Etched, C.1870	70.00
Pressed Glass, Tiny Finecut, Wine	15.00
Pressed Glass, Tiny Lion, Celery	20.00
Tobin, see Leaf & Star	
Pressed Glass, Toltec, Celery, Footed	18.00
Pressed Glass, Tong, High Standard, Flint, 7 1/2 In. X 12 In. High	55.00
Pressed Glass, Tong, Sugar, Covered, Flint	55.00
Pressed Glass, Torpedo, Bowl, 7 In.	28.00
Pressed Glass, Torpedo, Bowl, 8 In.	28.00
Pressed Glass, Torpedo, Bowl, 9 1/2 In.	30.00
Pressed Glass, Torpedo, Castor, Pickle, Complete	70.00
Pressed Glass, Torpedo, Celery	28.00
Pressed Glass, Torpedo, Compote, Open, 7 X 8 1/2 In.	45.00
Pressed Glass, Torpedo, Compote, Open, 8 In.	29.50
Pressed Glass, Torpedo, Compote, Open, 9 In.	45.00
Pressed Glass, Torpedo, Compote, 7 1/4 In.	52.00
Pressed Glass, Torpedo, Creamer	37.00
Pressed Glass, Torpedo, Creamer, Footed, Applied Handle, 6 In.	32.00
Pressed Glass, Torpedo, Cruet	39.00
Pressed Glass, Torpedo, Cup & Saucer	37.00
Pressed Glass, Torpedo, Goblet	34.50 To 45.00
Pressed Glass, Torpedo, Goblet, Etched	52.00
Pressed Glass, Torpedo, Pitcher, Milk, 9 In.	46.00 To 56.00
Pressed Glass, Torpedo, Sauce, Flat, 4 1/4 In.	16.00
Pressed Glass, Torpedo, Sauce, Footed, 4 1/4 In.	16.00
Pressed Glass, Torpedo, Syrup	49.00
Pressed Glass, Torpedo, Tumbler	37.00
Pressed Glass, Torquay, Creamer, White	38.00
Pressed Glass, Transcontinental Railroad, Bread Plate	75.00
Pressed Glass, Transcontinental Railroad, Platter, 9 X 12 In.	45.00
Pressed Glass, Transverse Ribs, Goblet	20.00
Pressed Glass, Tree Of Life, Bowl, Finger, Blue, Melon Shaped	38.50
Pressed Glass, Tree Of Life, Butter, Pittsburgh	60.00
Pressed Glass, Tree Of Life, Compote, Hand Holds Stem, 10 X 10 In.	110.00
Pressed Glass, Tree Of Life, Compote, Hand Stem, 5 3/4 In.	35.00
Pressed Glass, Tree Of Life, Compote, P.G.Company, 7 1/4 X 9 3/4 In.	110.00
Pressed Glass, Tree Of Life, Compote, Pittsburgh, 9 In.	50.00
Pressed Glass, Tree Of Life, Creamer, Ball & Hand	50.00
Pressed Glass, Tree Of Life, Creamer, Pittsburgh	50.00
Pressed Glass, Tree Of Life, Creamer, Silver Plated Holder	34.00
Pressed Glass, Tree Of Life, Cruet, Opaque Green	80.00
Pressed Glass, Tree Of Life, Dish, Sauce	6.00
Pressed Glass, Tree Of Life, Goblet, Flint	30.00
Pressed Glass, Tree Of Life, Nappy, Leaf Handled	10.00
Pressed Glass, Tree Of Life, Nappy, Leaf Shape	6.50 To 9.00
Pressed Glass, Tree Of Life, Tray, Ice Cream, Signed	48.00
Pressed Glass, Tree Of Life, Tumbler	25.00
Pressed Glass, Tree Of Life, Tumbler, Footed, Signed P.G.C.Patent	60.00
Pressed Glass, Trellis, Goblet	12.50
Pressed Glass, Triangular Prism, Compote, 5 1/2 X 8 1/2 In.	28.50
Pressed Glass, Triangular Prism, Goblet	7.50
Pressed Glass, Triple Band Moiton, Goblet	7.00
Pressed Glass, Triple Triangle, Creamer & Sugar, Open, Ruby Stained	65.00
Pressed Glass, Triple Triangle, Goblet	38.00
Pressed Glass, Triple Triangle, Goblet, Ruby	38.00
Pressed Glass, Triple Triangle, Tumbler, Ruby Stained	34.50
Pressed Glass, Triple Triangle, Wine, Ruby Stained	38.00 To 39.50

Pressed Glass, Tropical Villa, Celery	45.00
Pressed Glass, Tropical Villa, Creamer	55.00
Pressed Glass, Tropical Villa, Goblet	50.00
Pressed Glass, Tropical Villa, Goblet, Etched	45.00
Pressed Glass, Tropical Villa, Sugar, Covered	75.00
Pressed Glass, Truncated Cube, Spooner	45.00
Pressed Glass, Truncated Cube, Toothpick	12.00 To 12.50
Pressed Glass, Tulip & Honeycomb, Bowl, Punch	20.00
Pressed Glass, Tulip & Honeycomb, Punch Bowl, 4 1/2 X 4 1/2 In	16.00 To 50.00
Pressed Glass, Tulip & Honeycomb, Punch Set, Miniature, 7 Piece	75.00
Pressed Glass, Tulip & Honeycomb, Spooner, Child's, 2 Handled	13.50
Pressed Glass, Tulip Band, Compote, Open, Flint, 4 3/4 X 6 1/2 In.	45.00
Pressed Glass, Tulip With Sawtooth, Bowl, Footed	40.00
Pressed Glass, Tulip With Sawtooth, Mug	65.00
Pressed Glass, Tulip With Sawtooth, Pitcher, Water, Flint	175.00
Pressed Glass, Tulip With Sawtooth, Spooner	35.00
Pressed Glass, Tulip With Sawtooth, Tumbler, Flint	75.00
Pressed Glass, Tulip With Sawtooth, Tumbler, Water, Flint	45.00
Pressed Glass, Tulip With Small Flower, Goblet	14.50
Pressed Glass, Tulip, Pitcher, Water, Flint	125.00
Pressed Glass, Tulip, Tumbler, Flint	35.00

Pressed Glass, U.S.Coin, Plate, Bread

Pressed Glass, Twelve Panel, Glass, Whiskey	80.00
Pressed Glass, Twin Snowshoes, Creamer	15.00
Pressed Glass, Twin Snowshoes, Goblet, Gold Flash	18.00
Pressed Glass, Twin Teardrops, Butter	25.00
Pressed Glass, Twin Teardrops, Cake Stand, 9 In.	22.50
Pressed Glass, Twinkle Phlox, Butter	25.00
Pressed Glass, Two Band, Butter	27.50
Pressed Glass, Two Band, Compote, Covered, 7 In.	35.00
Pressed Glass, Two Band, Creamer	18.50
Pressed Glass, Two Band, Spooner	16.00
Pressed Glass, Two Band, Sugar, Covered	30.00
Pressed Glass, Two Panel, Bowl, Waste, Blue	30.00
Pressed Glass, Two Panel, Butter, Oval, Footed, 7 In.	30.00
Pressed Glass, Two Panel, Celery, Clear	16.00
Pressed Glass, Two Panel, Dish, Relish, Amber, 9 X 4 1/2 In.	20.00
Pressed Glass, Two Panel, Goblet, Amber	27.50
Pressed Glass, Two Panel, Goblet, Blue	25.00 To 32.50
Pressed Glass, Two Panel, Pitcher, Cream, Oval, Amber	36.50
Pressed Glass, Two Panel, Pitcher, Water, Green	50.00
Pressed Glass, Two Panel, Pitcher, Water, Waste Bowl & Tray, Amber	135.00
Pressed Glass, U.S.Coin, Bowl, Waste, Flared	250.00
Pressed Glass, U.S.Coin, Bread Plate	265.00
Pressed Glass, U.S.Coin, Bread Plate, Frosted	195.00
Pressed Glass, U.S.Coin, Celery, Quarters	215.00 To 285.00
Pressed Glass, U.S.Coin, Compote, Cover, 7 In.	375.00
Pressed Glass, U.S.Coin, Cruet, Original Stopper	650.00
Pressed Glass, U.S.Coin, Pitcher, Syrup	475.00
Pressed Glass, U.S.Coin, Pitcher, Syrup, Patent Dated	475.00
Pressed Glass, U.S.Coin, Sauce	95.00
Pressed Glass, U.S.Coin, Spooner	165.00
Pressed Glass, U.S.Coin, Sugar, Covered, Half Dollar On Base	475.00

Pressed Glass, U.S.Coin, Toothpick	115.00
Pressed Glass, U.S.Rib, Creamer, Green	38.00
Pressed Glass, U.S.Rib, Pitcher, Water, Green, Gold Trim	85.00
Pressed Glass, U.S.Rib, Sugar & Creamer, Green, Gold	65.00
Pressed Glass, U-Bend, Creamer	15.00
Pressed Glass, Umbilicated Sawtooth, Spill, Flint	18.00
Pressed Glass, Valencia Waffle, Celery, Amber	40.00
Pressed Glass, Valencia Waffle, Goblet	24.00
Pressed Glass, Valencia Waffle, Goblet, Amber	35.00
Pressed Glass, Valencia Waffle, Goblet, Blue	45.00
Pressed Glass, Valencia Waffle, Salt, Green	21.00
Pressed Glass, Valencia Waffle, Spooner, Green	39.50
Pressed Glass, Vermont, Butter, Green	35.00
Pressed Glass, Vermont, Creamer	20.00
Pressed Glass, Vermont, Creamer, Amber	30.00
Pressed Glass, Vermont, Goblet, Green	48.00
Pressed Glass, Vermont, Goblet, Green With Gold	50.00
Pressed Glass, Vermont, Salt & Pepper, Green, Original Tops	35.00
Pressed Glass, Vermont, Sauce, Green	12.00
Pressed Glass, Vernon Honeycomb, Celery, Blue	85.00
Pressed Glass, Vernon Honeycomb, Celery, 10 In.	65.00
Pressed Glass, Vernon Honeycomb, Compote, Flint, 7 1/2 X 11 1/2 In. High	55.00
Pressed Glass, Vernon Honeycomb, Decanter, Quart, Flint	25.00
Pressed Glass, Victoria, Pitcher, Water, Cut Log, 13 In.	40.00
Pressed Glass, Victoria, Pitcher, Water, Green With Gold	140.00
Pressed Glass, Viking, Bread Plate	48.00
Pressed Glass, Viking, Butter	38.00 To 58.00
Pressed Glass, Viking, Celery	26.00 To 42.50
Pressed Glass, Viking, Compote, Cover, 3 Feet, Silver On Finial Helmet Tip	45.00
Pressed Glass, Viking, Compote, Covered, 7 In.	62.50
Pressed Glass, Viking, Compote, Covered, 9 In.	45.00 To 90.00
Pressed Glass, Viking, Compote, Covered, 9 1/2 In.	85.00
Pressed Glass, Viking, Compote, Low, Covered, 8 In. Diameter	60.00
Pressed Glass, Viking, Compote, Low, Oval, Covered, 8 In. Long, 5 1/2 In. Wide	50.00
Pressed Glass, Viking, Creamer	22.50 To 40.00
Pressed Glass, Viking, Dish, Pickle, Oval, Footed	38.00
Pressed Glass, Viking, Dish, Relish	35.00
Pressed Glass, Viking, Jar, Spice	65.00
Pressed Glass, Viking, Master Salt	15.00 To 25.00
Pressed Glass, Viking, Pickle Jar, Cover	85.00
Pressed Glass, Viking, Pitcher, Water	45.00 To 78.00
Pressed Glass, Viking, Pitcher, Water, Frosted Face Under Spout & Base	110.00
Pressed Glass, Viking, Sauce, Footed, 4 In.	8.50 To 12.00
Pressed Glass, Viking, Sauce, Frosted Base, 4 1/2 In.	12.50
Pressed Glass, Viking, Spooner	23.00 To 30.00

Pressed Glass, Waffle &
Thumbprint, Flip Glass

Pressed Glass, Washington Centennial, Relish Dish

Pressed Glass, Viking, Sugar, Covered .... 28.00 To 48.00
Pressed Glass, Viking, Sugar, Open 25.00
Pressed Glass, Viking, Syrup 65.00
Pressed Glass, Vintage, Plate, Blue, 8 In. 30.00
  Virginia, see also Galloway
Pressed Glass, Virginia Dare, Bread Plate 50.00
Pressed Glass, Virginia Dare, Bread Plate, Cupid's Hunt Border 85.00
Pressed Glass, Virginia, Dish, Pickle, Rose Flashed, 8 1/2 In. 25.00
Pressed Glass, Virginia, Jug, Matching Stopper 29.50
Pressed Glass, Virginia, Pitcher, Water, Enameled Flowers 37.50
Pressed Glass, Waffle & Star Band, Toothpick 17.50
Pressed Glass, Waffle & Thumbprint, Celery, Flint .... 60.00 To 85.00
Pressed Glass, Waffle & Thumbprint, Claret, Flint .... 75.00 To 110.00
Pressed Glass, Waffle & Thumbprint, Decanter, Bar Lip, Quart 125.00
Pressed Glass, Waffle & Thumbprint, Goblet, Flint 55.00
Pressed Glass, Waffle & Thumbprint, Pitcher, Water, Flint 375.00
Pressed Glass, Waffle & Thumbprint, Spill 45.00
Pressed Glass, Waffle & Thumbprint, Tumbler, Flint 75.00
Pressed Glass, Waffle Cube, Lamp, 7 1/2 In. 55.00
Pressed Glass, Waffle, Celery, Canary, Sandwich 675.00
Pressed Glass, Waffle, Celery, Flared, Scalloped Top, Flint .... 50.00 To 85.00
Pressed Glass, Waffle, Champagne, Flint 135.00
Pressed Glass, Waffle, Decanter, Sunburst Stopper, Flint, Quart, Pair 250.00
Pressed Glass, Waffle, Eggcup, Flint 17.00
Pressed Glass, Waffle, Goblet, Fan Top 15.00
Pressed Glass, Waffle, Goblet, Flint, 3 Mold 50.00
Pressed Glass, Waffle, Plate, Flint, 6 In. 12.50
Pressed Glass, Waffle, Sugar, Canary, Covered, Sandwich 1100.00
Pressed Glass, Waffle, Wine, Flint 75.00
Pressed Glass, Wahoo, Goblet 14.00
  Washboard, see Adonis
Pressed Glass, Washington & Lafayette, Mug, Clear 30.00
Pressed Glass, Washington Centennial, Cake Stand, 8 1/4 In. .... 35.00 To 42.00
Pressed Glass, Washington Centennial, Cake Stand, 9 1/2 In. .... 50.00 To 68.50
Pressed Glass, Washington Centennial, Celery 52.50
Pressed Glass, Washington Centennial, Champagne 62.50
Pressed Glass, Washington Centennial, Compote, Open, 8 1/4 In. 35.00
Pressed Glass, Washington Centennial, Dish, Relish, Bear Handles, Dated 45.00
Pressed Glass, Washington Centennial, Eggcup 52.50
Pressed Glass, Washington Centennial, Goblet .... 35.00 To 37.50
Pressed Glass, Washington Centennial, Pitcher, Water 85.00
Pressed Glass, Washington, Celery, Flint 60.00
Pressed Glass, Washington, Eggcup, Flint 35.00
  Water Lily, see Rose Point Band
Pressed Glass, Wedding Bells, Pitcher, Water 42.50
Pressed Glass, Wedding Bells, Toothpick 17.50
Pressed Glass, Wedding Bells, Wine .... 14.00 To 17.00
Pressed Glass, Wedding Ring, Goblet 38.50
Pressed Glass, Wedding Ring, Goblet, Flint 36.50
Pressed Glass, Wedding Ring, Wine, Flint 40.00
Pressed Glass, Westmoreland, Goblet 18.00
Pressed Glass, Westmoreland, Spooner .... 11.50 To 13.50
Pressed Glass, Westward Ho, Bread Plate 25.00
Pressed Glass, Westward Ho, Butter .... 75.00 To 95.00
Pressed Glass, Westward Ho, Celery 85.00
Pressed Glass, Westward Ho, Compote, Covered, High Standard, 12 X 6 In. 125.00
Pressed Glass, Westward Ho, Compote, Low Standard, Covered, 8 In. 105.00
Pressed Glass, Westward Ho, Compote, Open, 8 X 8 In. 95.00
Pressed Glass, Westward Ho, Compote, Oval, 8 1/2 X 5 1/2 In. 180.00
Pressed Glass, Westward Ho, Compote, 8 In. 170.00
Pressed Glass, Westward Ho, Goblet .... 45.00 To 75.00
Pressed Glass, Westward Ho, Jar, Marmalade, Covered 175.00
Pressed Glass, Westward Ho, Pitcher, Water 175.00
Pressed Glass, Westward Ho, Sugar, Open 30.00
Pressed Glass, Wheat & Barley, Bread Plate 20.00
Pressed Glass, Wheat & Barley, Butter 35.00

Pressed Glass, Wheat & Barley, Compote, Jelly	32.50
Pressed Glass, Wheat & Barley, Compote, Jelly, Amber	21.50
Pressed Glass, Wheat & Barley, Compote, Jelly, Blue	18.00
Pressed Glass, Wheat & Barley, Creamer	16.50 To 18.00
Pressed Glass, Wheat & Barley, Goblet, Blue	24.00
Pressed Glass, Wheat & Barley, Mug, Amber	22.50
Pressed Glass, Wheat & Barley, Plate, Blue, 7 In.	28.00
Pressed Glass, Wheat & Barley, Spooner	18.00
Pressed Glass, Wheat & Barley, Sugar	50.00
Pressed Glass, Wheat & Barley, Sugar, Covered	24.50
Pressed Glass, Wheat & Barley, Tumbler, Amber	15.00
Pressed Glass, Wheat Sheaf, Goblet	22.50
Pressed Glass, Wheat Sheaf, Pitcher, Water	24.00
Pressed Glass, Wheat, Creamer	30.00
Pressed Glass, Whirligig, Butter	20.00
Pressed Glass, Whirligig, Cup, Punch	8.00
Pressed Glass, Whirligig, Punch Bowl, Pink, 4 1/2 X 4 1/4 In.	40.00
Pressed Glass, Whirligig, Spooner	12.00
Pressed Glass, Wild Bouquet, Jelly, Blue	55.00
Pressed Glass, Wild Bouquet, Spooner, Opalescent	37.50
Pressed Glass, Wild Rose With Bowknot, Cruet, Clear Stopper	85.00
Pressed Glass, Wild Rose, Pitcher, Water, Green, Gold Trim	85.00
Pressed Glass, Wildflower, Compote, Tall, Green	45.00
Pressed Glass, Wildflower, Creamer	15.50
Pressed Glass, Wildflower, Dish, Pickle, Amber, Rectangular, 8 In.	15.00
Pressed Glass, Wildflower, Goblet	5.00 To 17.50
Pressed Glass, Wildflower, Goblet, Amber	20.00
Pressed Glass, Wildflower, Spooner	17.50
Pressed Glass, Wildflower, Spooner, Clear	22.50
Pressed Glass, Wildflower, Sugar, Open	22.50
Pressed Glass, Wildflower, Table Set, Amber, 4 Piece	125.00
Pressed Glass, Wildflower, Tumbler, Amber	25.00
Pressed Glass, Wildflower, Vaseline, Square, 6 1/2 In.	25.00
Pressed Glass, Willow Oak, Cake Stand, Amber	45.00

Pressed Glass, Westward Ho,
Compote, Covered, 7 3/4 In.

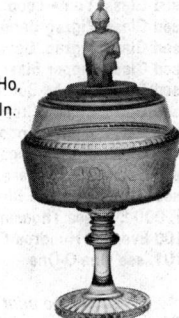

Pressed Glass, Wedding Ring, Syrup, Flint

Pressed Glass, Willow Oak, Compote, Covered, 6 1/2 In.	35.00 To 44.00
Pressed Glass, Willow Oak, Creamer	22.00 To 28.00
Pressed Glass, Willow Oak, Cup, Blue	35.00
Pressed Glass, Willow Oak, Goblet, Amber	45.00
Pressed Glass, Willow Oak, Goblet, Blue	55.00
Pressed Glass, Willow Oak, Pitcher, Milk	45.00

Pressed Glass, Willow Oak, Pitcher, Water	45.00
Pressed Glass, Willow Oak, Plate, 9 In.	32.50
Pressed Glass, Willow Oak, Tumbler	26.00
Pressed Glass, Windflower, Bowl, Apple Green, Square, 6 1/2 In.	25.00
Pressed Glass, Windflower, Creamer	27.50
Pressed Glass, Windflower, Goblet	22.00
Pressed Glass, Windflower, Spooner	17.50 To 24.00
Pressed Glass, Windsor Anvil, Toothpick, Amber	25.00
Pressed Glass, Winged Scrolls, Pitcher, Water, Gold	225.00
Pressed Glass, Winsome, Sugar, Gold, Covered	27.00
Wisconsin, see Beaded Dewdrop	
Pressed Glass, Wooden Pail, Creamer, Blue	12.50
Pressed Glass, Worcester, Belted, Goblet, Flint	25.00
Pressed Glass, Worcester, Belted, Tumbler, Water, Footed	25.00
Pressed Glass, Wreath & Shell, Butter, Opalescent, Canary	155.00
Pressed Glass, Wreath & Shell, Creamer, Opalescent, Canary	95.00
Pressed Glass, Wreath & Shell, Spooner, Blue	50.00
Pressed Glass, Wreath & Shell, Spooner, Enameled	125.00
Pressed Glass, Wreath & Shell, Spooner, Opalescent, Canary	85.00
Pressed Glass, Wreath & Shell, Spooner, Opalescent, Canary, Enameling	125.00
Pressed Glass, Wreath & Shell, Spooner, Vaseline Opalescent, Enameling	72.00
Pressed Glass, Wreath & Shell, Sugar, Opalescent, Canary, Covered	145.00
Pressed Glass, Wyoming, Pitcher, Water	32.50 To 40.00
Pressed Glass, Wyoming, Tumbler, Gold Rim	27.50
Pressed Glass, X-Ray, Spooner, Green	35.00
Pressed Glass, X-Ray, Spooner, Green With Gold	45.00
Pressed Glass, X-Ray, Sugar, Green	45.00
Pressed Glass, X-Ray, Toothpick, Green	35.00
Yale, see Crowfoot	
Pressed Glass, Yoked Loop, Goblet, Flint	25.00
Pressed Glass, Yoked Loop, Sugar, Covered, Flint	70.00
Pressed Glass, Yoked Loop, Sugar, Flint	30.00
Pressed Glass, Yoked Loop, Tumbler, Flint	25.00
Pressed Glass, York Herringbone, Compote, Scalloped Rim, 8 In.Diameter	35.00
Pressed Glass, Young Queen Victoria, Bread Plate	35.00
Pressed Glass, Yuma Loop, Goblet	22.00
Pressed Glass, Yuma Loop, Spooner	16.00 To 16.50
Pressed Glass, Zigzag Band, Creamer	19.00
Pressed Glass, Zigzag, Goblet, Buttermilk	28.00
Pressed Glass, Zipper Slash, Goblet, Etched	14.00
Pressed Glass, Zipper, Butter	35.00
Pressed Glass, Zipper, Creamer	22.00 To 35.00
Pressed Glass, Zipper, Spooner	15.00
Pressed Glass, Zipper, Sugar Shaker	17.50
Pressed Glass, Zipper, Vase, 7 In.	14.00
Pressed Glass, Zippered Block, Goblet	7.00
1, 000-Eye, see Thousand Eye	
100-Eye, see Hundred Eye	
101, see One-O-One	

The size of the print is given, not the overall size with frame.
Print, see also Store, Sign

Print, Audubon, Black & Yellow Warbler, 17 1/8 X 22 1/2 In.	275.00
Print, Audubon, Elephant Folio, Amsterdam Edition, Female Turkey	500.00
Print, Audubon, Elephant Folio, Amsterdam Edition, Male Turkey	1000.00
Print, Audubon, Rose Breasted Grosbeak, 17 1/8 X 22 1/2 In.	275.00
Print, Classical Theme, I.Audran, Signed, French, C.1770, 15 1/2 X 28 In.	35.00
Print, Columbia's Noblest Sons, Kummel & Forster, 1865, 19 X 24 In.	65.00
Print, Country Woman, Water Color, English, Gold Matte & Frame, 16 X 20 In.	37.50
Print, Cox's Famous Brownies, Palmer Cox, 22 1/4 X 17 In., Set Of 3	325.00
Print, Currier, see Currier	
Print, Currier & Ives, see Currier & Ives	
Print, English Sporting, Colored Lithograph, 24 X 31 In.	60.00
Print, Ferrier, Red Riding Hood & Wolf, Framed, C.1912, 10 X 15 In.	14.00
Print, Figures & Heads, George Cruickshank, Pen & Ink, Set Of 2	275.00
Print, Gordon Grant, Lithograph, Two Schooners, Framed, Signed	250.00

Print, **Gould,** Purple Heron, Matted & Gold Frame, 2 X 2 1/2 Feet	250.00
Print, **Grant Wood,** Lithograph, February, Signed, Framed	750.00
Print, **Gray Squirrel,** Signed, Japanese	35.00
Print, **Hand Colored Engraving,** R.Havell, 1832 Mark, 39 3/4 X 26 3/4 In.	1600.00
Print, **Icart,** Baby Doll, 1924	550.00
Print, **Icart,** Coy, Rare Circle	575.00
Print, **Icart,** Etching, 1928, Secrets, Framed	235.00
Print, **Icart,** Finlande, 1940	395.00
Print, **Icart,** Follies, 1935	1295.00
Print, **Icart,** French Doll	465.00
Print, **Icart,** Kittens, 1925	395.00
Print, **Icart,** Laughing, 1930	525.00
Print, **Icart,** Laziness, 1925	575.00
Print, **Icart,** Pastel, Original, 18 X 24 In.	950.00
Print, **Icart,** Pink Alcove	325.00
Print, **Icart,** Recital, Black & White	325.00
Print, **Icart,** The Ritz	1100.00
Print, **Icart,** The Tea	500.00
Print, **Icart,** Waiting, 1927	325.00
Print, **Icart,** White Underwear, 1925	550.00
Print, **Lillian Russell,** Richmond Straight Cut Cigarettes, 8 X 11 In.	22.00
Print, **Lithograph,** Execution Of 38 Sioux Indians, 1862, 14 X 19 In.	350.00
Print, **Lithograph,** George Washington, Walnut Frame, 19 X 28 In.	75.00
Print, **Lithograph,** Hand Colored Aquatints, Published 1840, 13 X 17 In.	650.00
Print, **Lithograph,** Ocean Express, C.Parsons, 1856, 16 1/8 X 24 1/2 In.	250.00
Print, **Lithograph,** Seascape, A.Mayer, 17 X 26 1/2 In.	400.00
Print, **Lithograph,** 3 Reclining Figures, Signed, Henry Moore	925.00
Print, **Mezzotint,** Sir Philip Bowes Vere Broke, 1813, Gilt Frame, 35 X 22 In.	750.00

Print, Mucha, De L'Aiglon, C.1900, 28 1/4 X 76 5/8 In.

Print, Mucha, 3 Seasons Of The Year,
C.1896, 24 X 14 3/4 In.

Print, Mucha, Cours De Composition
D'Art Decoratif

Print, **Mucha,** Cours De Composition D'Art Decoratif	*Illus*	375.00
Print, **Mucha,** De L'Aiglon, C.1900, 28 1/4 X 76 5/8 In.	*Illus*	900.00
Print, **Mucha,** 3 Seasons Of The Year, C.1896, 24 X 14 3/4 In.	*Illus*	950.00
Print, **Nutting,** Fireside Fancies, Lady At Fire, Framed, 15 1/2 X 15 1/2 In.		60.00
Print, **Nutting,** Honeymoon Drive, Color, 15 Inches		30.00
Print, **Nutting,** Interior, Frame, Lady Descending Staircase, Signed		31.00
Print, **Nutting,** The Swimming Pool, Framed, Signed, 15 1/2 X 15 1/2 In.		28.00
Print, **Parrish,** Daybreak, Framed 15 X 12 Inches		40.00
Print, **Parrish,** Daybreak, 18 X 24 In.		75.00
Print, **Parrish,** Dorothy In Birdland, 1904, 10 X 14 In.		18.50
Print, **Parrish,** Dreaming, Original Frame, Signed, 12 X 2/ In.		55.00
Print, **Prang,** Chromolithograph, Original Prang Frame		125.00
Print, **Rockwell,** Window Washer, Signed & Numbered		1000.00
Print, **Russell,** Scotch, Indian Chief, McIntosh, Gold Frame		200.00

Print, 4 Men On Handcar, Signed, 16 X 24 1/2 In.	12.50
Purple Slag, see Slag, Purple	
Purse, Alligator, With Baby Alligator, 9 In.	18.00
Purse, Art Deco, Silver Chain, 1920s	40.00
Purse, Belt, Mad Money	4.50
Purse, Carnival Glass Beads, Wide Loop Handle, Blue, 7 1/2 X 9 In.	75.00
Purse, Change, Leather, 3 Compartment, Carved Ivory Horse & Rider, 2 X 3 In.	20.00
Purse, Change, Man's, Miniature, Leather, 2 1/2 X 2 1/2 In.	35.00
Purse, Chatelaine, Blue Stone Set In Clasp	20.00
Purse, Child's, Victorian, Chain Handle, Pearl Outside, Red Inside	6.00
Purse, Clutch, Handmade, Satin & Petit Point, French	25.00
Purse, Clutch, Paisley, Jeweled Clasp	300.00
Purse, Crochet, Heavy Silver Frame, Holland Scenery	25.00
Purse, Crochet, Shell Pattern, Satin Lined, Ivory Heading, 6 X 8 In.	37.50
Purse, Envelope, Alligator, Art Deco Clasp, 12 1/2 X 8 1/2 In.	45.00
Purse, Evening, Art Deco, Black Enameling, Whiting Davis Co., 3 X 6 In.	30.00
Purse, Evening, Gold Mesh, Rhinestone Clasp, Whiting & Davis	20.00
Purse, Evening, Marcasite Flowered Frame, Glass Ornament, C.1920	55.00
Purse, Evening, Mesh, Hanging Chain At Bottom	12.50
Purse, Evening, Reticulated Handle, Chain Mesh Body, Sterling, 6 5/8 In.	75.00
Purse, Evening, 14K Gold Filled Mesh	27.50
Purse, Feather, Black	10.00
Purse, Fish Scale, Expandable Top	15.00
Purse, Fold Over Metal Top, Embossed Horse Racing Scene, Leather	22.50
Purse, Frame, Sterling, Italian	28.00
Purse, Gold Mesh, Jeweled Clasp, Chain, Whiting & Davis	22.00
Purse, Green Stones, Butterfly & Flower Work, Chain, Art Nouveau	55.00
Purse, Hand Crocheted, Draw String Closure, Beaded, 7 1/2 In.	25.00
Purse, Kid, Child's, Brass, Bead Chain	10.00
Purse, Leather, Metal Top, Art Nouveau	15.00
Purse, Mesh, Chatelaine, 18K Gold Frame & Chain, 2 X 3 In.	350.00
Purse, Mesh, Linked Chain, Silver Composition	15.00
Purse, Mesh, Silver, 2 In., On 49 In. Chain	20.00
Purse, Mesh, Whiting & Davis	20.00 To 27.50
Purse, Money Pouch, 18th Century, Japanese, Tapestry, Silver, Chain, Netsuke	1900.00
Purse, Petite point, Marcasite Catch	20.00
Purse, Pocket, White House Shoes For Men & Women, Leather, 1904	17.50
Purse, Round, Black, Full Figure Art Nouveau Lady	20.00
Purse, Silver Mesh, Sapphire In Closing Bar, Whiting & Davis	45.00
Purse, Suede, Cigar Holder & Ivory Cigarette Holder	22.50
Purse, Taffeta, Black, Embroidered Oriental Ladies, 4 1/2 X 4 1/2 In.	12.00
Quartz, Figurine, Buddha, Seated, Robes, Knotted Hair, Rose, Wood Stand, 6 In.	200.00
Quartz, Figurine, Rabbit, Sitting, Brown Tipped Ears & Paws, 1 3/4 X 2 In.	90.00

Quezal

Quezal glass was made from 1901 to 1920 by Martin Bach, Sr. He made iridescent glass of the same type as Tiffany.

Quezal, Base, Lamp, Bronze Base & Top Border, Signed, 24 In.	685.00
Quezal, Bowl, Diamond-Quilted, Gold Iridescent, Signed, 6 X 2 3/4 In.	195.00
Quezal, Bowl, Iridescent Blue, Signed, 4 X 6 In.	450.00
Quezal, Candlestick, Dark-Blue Iridescence, Pair, 8 In.	575.00
Quezal, Candlestick, Iridescent Blue, Multi-Color, Signed, 10 In.	275.00
Quezal, Compote, Gold Iridescence, Signed, 5 In.	275.00
Quezal, Glass, Dimpled, Rainbow Iridescence, Signed, 3 In.	135.00
Quezal, Globe, Green Feather, Gold Outline, Signed, 7 1/2 In.Diameter	175.00
Quezal, Lamp, Floor, Gold & White Shade, Signed, 10 In.Diameter	950.00
Quezal, Lamp, Iridescent Gold, The Twilight, Shade & Base, No.240, Signed	1500.00
Quezal, Lamp, Table, Aurene Stick Shape, Signed, 17 In.	575.00
Quezal, Mug, Gold With Green Iridescence, Signed, 3 1/2 In.	975.00
Quezal, Salt, Blue & Gold Iridescent, Fluted, Signed	150.00
Quezal, Salt, Marigold, Fluted, Signed	95.00
Quezal, Salt, Rainbow Iridescence, Signed	120.00
Quezal, Salt, Ribbed, Gold Iridescence, Signed	120.00
Quezal, Shade, Art Glass	110.00
Quezal, Shade, Calcite, Gold Interior, Pair	125.00 To 150.00
Quezal, Shade, Fold Feather, Green Edge, Gold Lining, Signed, Pair	175.00
Quezal, Shade, Gas, Gold Feather On White, Calcite, Signed	125.00

Quezal, Vase, Iridescent Blue, Gold Aurene,
Signed, 12 3/4 In.

Quezal, Shade, Gold Feather On Opal Gold Lining, Signed	90.00
Quezal, Shade, Gold Hearts, Gold Threading, Signed	95.00
Quezal, Shade, Gold Hooked Feather, Gold Lining, Signed, No.255, 6 1/4 In.	125.00
Quezal, Shade, Gold Iridescent, Set Of 6, Signed, 5 3/8 In.	495.00
Quezal, Shade, Gold Iridescent, Trumpet Shaped, Dimples, Signed	100.00
Quezal, Shade, Gold King Tut & Zipper On Calcite, Gold Lining, Signed, Pair	175.00
Quezal, Shade, Gold Lines, Stripes Of Dark & Light Opalescent, Signed, 6 In.	95.00
Quezal, Shade, Green & Gold Feathers, Chartreuse, Gold Lining, 6 1/2 In.	120.00
Quezal, Shade, Green Feather On White Gold Interior, 1 1/2 In.	300.00
Quezal, Shade, Hanging, Pulled Feather Design, Signed, 8 In.	525.00
Quezal, Shade, Leaves, Signed, 6 In.	150.00
Quezal, Shade, Mother-Of-Pearl, Signed, 4 In.	225.00
Quezal, Shade, Opalescent Feather, Gold Ribbed, Signed, 4 In., Pair	200.00
Quezal, Shade, Open Feather, Green Edge, Gold Ribbed, 4 In., Pair	200.00
Quezal, Shade, Pulled Feather, Blue, Set Of 5	650.00
Quezal, Shade, Snakeskin	100.00
Quezal, Shade, White & Gold Pulled Feather, Gold Interior	90.00
Quezal, Shade, White Calcite, Aurene Interior, Signed, 5 In.	80.00
Quezal, Shade, White Calcite, Gold Leaf, Signed	85.00
Quezal, Vase, Bud, Gold, Iridescent, Original Holder, Signed, 8 In.	145.00
Quezal, Vase, Bud, Silver Container, Flanged Top, Signed, 20 3/4 In.	475.00
Quezal, Vase, Chalice Shape, Foot & Stem, White Inside, 6 In.	550.00
Quezal, Vase, Gold & Orange, Oriental Shape, Signed, 12 In.	450.00
Quezal, Vase, Gold & White, Signed, 5 1/2 In.	475.00
Quezal, Vase, Gold Hearts & Vines, Opalescent Body, Signed, 6 In.	465.00
Quezal, Vase, Green & Gold Feathers Over Opalescence, Signed, 6 In.	875.00
Quezal, Vase, Green Pulled Feathers, Wafer Foot, Gold Ground, Signed, 8 In.	1150.00
Quezal, Vase, Green Pulled Feathers, Wafer Foot, Signed, 8 In.	950.00
Quezal, Vase, Green, Gold, Opal, Flower-Like Top, Feathers, 6 In.	875.00
Quezal, Vase, Iridescent Amber, Signed, 6 In.	290.00
Quezal, Vase, Iridescent Blue, Gold Aurene, Signed, 12 3/4 In. _Illus_	750.00
Quezal, Vase, Leaf, Vine, Gold Threading, Alabaster, Signed, 6 1/2 In.	350.00
Quezal, Vase, Light Blue Iridescent, Gold Rim, Signed, Footed, 8 1/4 In.	385.00
Quezal, Vase, Lustrous Gold, White Inside, Signed, 6 In.	550.00
Quezal, Vase, Silver Overlay, Iridescent Pink, Blue & Green, 15 In.	2950.00
Quezal, Vase, Silver Overlay, Iridescent Shading, Green To Blue, 5 1/2 In.	1050.00
Quezal, Vase, Silver Overlay, Iridescent, Signed, 15 In.	2250.00
Quezal, Vase, Silver Overlay, Iridescent, Signed, 8 1/2 In.	695.00
Quezal, Vase, Silver Overlay, Silver Morning Glories, Signed, 4 1/2 In.	600.00
Quezal, Vase, Trumpet, Green & Gold Iridescent, Signed, No.Y257, 9 1/2 In.	500.00
Quilt, see Textile, Quilt	

Quimper pottery was made in Finistere, France, after 1900. Most of the
pieces found today were made during the twentieth century. A Quimper factory
has worked in France since the eighteenth century.

Quimper Dutch Shoes, Peasant Design, 2 3/4 In., Pair	15.00
Quimper, Ashtray, 2 X 7 In.Diameter	45.00
Quimper, Bowl, Salad, Signed Henriot, 9 1/2 In.	24.00
Quimper, Box, Man On Cover, Signed Henriot, Covered	45.00
Quimper, Candlestick, Green Horse, 9 In., Pair	260.00
Quimper, Creamer, Peasant Woman, Red, Blue Accents, 3 1/2 In.	42.50
Quimper, Creamer, Woman & Flowers, 3 1/4 In.	20.00

Quimper, Cruet, Double, Wooden Stoppers, 7 In.	32.00
Quimper, Dish, Basket Type, Signed HB France, 8 X 6 In.	20.00
Quimper, Dish, Serving, 3-Section, Handle On Top, 11 1/2 In.	75.00
Quimper, Dish, Suits Of Cards, Set Of 4	45.00
Quimper, Dutch Shoes, Peasant Design, 2 1/2 In., Pair	15.00
Quimper, Eggcup, Attached Base, 4 In.	20.00
Quimper, Eggcup, Spiky Edge, Signed	28.00
Quimper, Figurine, Male & Female Dancers, Signed, 9 1/2 In.	185.00
Quimper, Figurine, Peasant Man, 3 1/2 In.	60.00
Quimper, Figurine, Seated Child, Full Skirt, 5 1/2 In.	68.00
Quimper, Inkwell, Clover Shape, Signed	95.00
Quimper, Jar, Jam, Attached Underplate, Fan Shaped Finial, Signed	28.00
Quimper, Jug, Cider, 6 In.	65.00
Quimper, Mug, Peasant, 4 In.	40.00
Quimper, Pitcher, Green & Brown Design, 7 1/2 In.	25.00
Quimper, Pitcher, Peasant Woman & Flowers, 6 In.	45.00
Quimper, Pitcher, Round Spout, Bail Handle, 6 1/2 In.	35.00
Quimper, Pitcher, Tri-Corner, Tab Handle, Mustard, Flowers, 4 In.	110.00
Quimper, Pitcher, 6 In.	38.00
Quimper, Planter, Swan, 6 3/4 X 8 In., Pair	150.00
Quimper, Plate, Breton Man In Center, Square, Signed, 7 X 7 In.	19.50
Quimper, Plate, Chanticleer, 6 In.	15.00
Quimper, Plate, Peasant Husband & Wife, Signed, 8 In., Pair	150.00
Quimper, Plate, Rooster In Center, 10 In.	32.00
Quimper, Platter, Divided, Round, 11 In.	55.00
Quimper, Platter, 2-Handled, 12 1/2 X 8 1/4 In.	55.00
Quimper, Shoes, Attached	27.00
Quimper, Sugar & Creamer, Signed Henriot	23.00
Quimper, Tray, Pen, Footed, Signed, 9 X 2 1/2 In.	95.00
Quimper, Tumbler, Signed, 3 1/2 In.	75.00
Quimper, Vase, Five Finger, Peach, 5 1/2 In.	55.00
Quimper, Vase, Wall, Yellow, 9 In.	87.00

RADFORD JASPER	*Radford pottery was made by Alfred Radford in Broadway, Virginia, Tiffin and Zanesville, Ohio, and Clarksburg, West Virginia, from 1891 until 1912. Jasperware, Ruko, Thera, Radera, and Velvety Art Ware were made.*	
Radford, Jardiniere, Flowers, Ruko, 11 In.		120.00
Radio, Algonquin Receiver, 5 Tube		90.00
Radio, Arvin, Table Model		85.00
Radio, Atwater-Kent, Deluxe		75.00
Radio, Atwater-Kent, M 44, Matching Speaker, Metal		77.00
Radio, Atwater-Kent, Metal		33.50
Radio, Atwater-Kent, Speaker, Earphones		180.00
Radio, Battery, Tourist, 5 Tubes, Portable		65.00
Radio, Battery, 5 Tube, Kansas City, Missouri		70.00
Radio, Car, Packard		45.00
Radio, Car, United American Bosch Corp., Model 150a		35.00
Radio, Coca-Cola Cooler Shape, Red Case, 1949		350.00
Radio, Crosley, Battery, Model 601, Instructions		55.00
Radio, Crosley, Model H 51, 2 Tube, 1914		20.00
Radio, Crosley, Showbox, 1920s, Matching Speaker		125.00
Radio, Crosley, Two Floating Tubes, C.1915		99.00
Radio, Crystal Set, Instructions		135.00
Radio, Crystal Set, Monarch, Frost, Ear Phones		60.00
Radio, Emerson, Mickey Mouse		450.00
Radio, Five Tube, Marwol Radio Corp		68.00
Radio, Fried Eisman, 6 Tube, Battery		40.00
Radio, General Electric, Cathedral		40.00
Radio, Horn, Magnavox, Gooseneck		50.00
Radio, Hotel, 25 Cents An Hour		40.00
Radio, International, Brass Dial, Wood Case		7.00
Radio, Kolster, 6 Tube Battery		45.00
Radio, Motorola, Portable, Model 5p31a, Ac-Dc, Battery, 1950s		15.00
Radio, R.C.A., Model 100-A, Speaker		20.00
Radio, Stewart-Warner, Table Model, Model 51t56		50.00

Radio, Transitone, Philco, Walnut Case, 7 X 6 X 12 1/2 In.	28.00
Radio, Westinghouse, 1941, Table	15.00
Radio, Zenith, Big Dial	75.00
Radio, Zenith, Wood Cabinet, Model 65152, 23 1/2 X 40 In.	150.00
Railroad, , Platter, N.Y.C., 11 1/2 X 7 1/2 In.	115.00
Railroad, Ash Stand, Lounge Car, Hold 6 Glasses, 26 X 17 In.Diameter	52.00
Railroad, Ashtray, Clinchfield	10.00
Railroad, Ashtray, Marked Turquoise Room, Super Chief	8.00
Railroad, Ashtray, Northern Pacific	4.00
Railroad, Ashtray, Rectangular, Full Name, C. & O.	32.00
Railroad, Ashtray, Rock Island	15.00
Railroad, Ashtray, Youngstown & Northern R.R., Anniversary, 1909-59	5.00
Railroad, Badge, Cap, Baggage Master's, N.Y. & N.H. R.R.	6.50
Railroad, Badge, Centennial Committee, Lackawanna R.R., 1851-1951	16.00
Railroad, Badge, Conductor's, Porcelain, Leather Strap, B. & M.R.R.	35.00
Railroad, Badge, Freight Conductor, Nickel	4.00
Railroad, Bandana, Brotherhood, Blue & White, Train In Center	20.00
Railroad, Bandana, Railroad Track Center, Brotherhood, 24 In.Square	20.00
Railroad, Bell, Locomotive, Brass, 22 In.	675.00
Railroad, Bell, Locomotive, Yoke & Cradle, 17 In.Diameter	625.00
Railroad, Bell, Marked Frisco, Brass, 28 X 16 1/2 In.Diameter	825.00
Railroad, Book Of Rules, P.R.R., 1956	2.50
Railroad, Book, Conductor's, Unused, Marbleized Cover, 1904	18.00
Railroad, Bowl, Salad, Pullman, Indian Tree, 7 1/2 In.Diameter	48.00
Railroad, Box, Conductor's, Cast Iron	85.00
Railroad, Box, First Aid, New York Central System, Tin, 2 X 5 X 8 In.	25.00
Railroad, Box, Patrol Station, To Punch Time Clock, 4 X 2 In.	30.00
Railroad, Box, Ticket, Roll Up Cover, Oak	45.00
Railroad, Box, Tool, N.Y., N.Y. & H.R.R.	45.00
Railroad, Bucket, Fire, Canvas, Folding Metal Frame, Boston & Maine	35.00
Railroad, Bucket, Fire, Collapsible, Canvas, N.Y.Central R.R.	35.00
Railroad, Bucket, Fire, Embossed, Wabash R.Y.	20.00
Railroad, Bucket, Ice, N.Y.C.R.R., Silver Plated	55.00
Railroad, Button, Conductor's Coat, Southern	2.00
Railroad, Button, Embossed Train Engine, Brass	5.00
Railroad, Button, Lapel, Enameled On Brass, Boston & Maine R.R., 5/8 In.	10.00
Railroad, Button, Relief Woodburner Locomotive, C.1870, 5/8 In.	5.00
Railroad, Button, Steam Locomotive, Worcester Salt, 1896, 1 1/4 In.	9.50
Railroad, Button, Uniform, Brass, Woodburner Locomotive, C.1870, 5/8 In.	5.00
Railroad, Cabinet, Ticket, Wooden, 16 In.	65.00
Railroad, Calendar, 1950, Union Pacific Railroad	12.50
Railroad, Calendar, 1961, Union Pacific Railroad	12.50
Railroad, Can, Oil, Brass Tipped Spout, C. & O., 3 Gallon	35.00
Railroad, Can, Oil, Long Spout, Marked P.R.R.	12.50
Railroad, Can, Oil, Lubricator, Rock Island Lines, Side Handle, 8 In.	24.00
Railroad, Can, Oil, Steam Engine, Pint	20.00
Railroad, Can, Water, Embossed, N. & W. N.Y.	15.00
Railroad, Can, Water, Embossed, Wabash N.Y.	15.00
Railroad, Cap, Conductor, Burlington Route	55.00
Railroad, Cap, Station Agent, N.Y.Central, C.1920	65.00
Railroad, Car Mover, Iron, Made By Appleton Car Mover Company	30.00
Railroad, Card, Playing, Double Deck, Chessie On Box, Peake On Cards	18.00
Railroad, Card, Playing, Railroad Scenes, P.R.R.	35.00
Railroad, Cards, Playing, Santa Fe, Boxed Set	5.25
Railroad, Cards, Playing, Train Scenes, Southern Pacific	20.00
Railroad, Clip Board, Meal Check, N. & W., International Silver	80.00
Railroad, Coffeepot, Broadway Service, Pennsylvania, 14 Ounce	34.95
Railroad, Coffeepot, Triangle Logo, R.R. & P., 8 Oz.	62.00
Railroad, Creamer, Covered, Broadway Service, Pennsylvania, 8 Ounce	32.50
Railroad, Creamer, Covered, Fluted, Santa Fe, 8 Ounce	34.95
Railroad, Cuff Links, New York, New Haven & Hartford	19.50
Railroad, Cup & Saucer, Atlantic Coast Line	8.50
Railroad, Cup & Saucer, B. & O.R.R., Shenango China	12.00
Railroad, Cup & Saucer, Demitasse, B. & O., Blue	45.00
Railroad, Cup & Saucer, U.P., Streamliner	22.00
Railroad, Cup & Saucer, 1830-38 Cars, B. & O. Shenango	30.00

Railroad, Cup, Bouillon, A.C.L., Carolina, Marked & Dated 1947	24.00
Railroad, Cup, Bouillon, Lid, M.I.L.W., Traveller	24.00
Railroad, Cup, Bouillon, N.Y.C., R.R., Syracuse China	11.75
Railroad, Cup, Bouillon, Union Pacific, Backstamped Harriman	6.00
Railroad, Cup, Bouillon, W.P., Feather River	16.00
Railroad, Cup, Loving, Sterling Silver, Chicago & Alton R.R., 1911, 6 1/2 In.	85.00
Railroad, Diary, Dated 1864, Between Chattanooga & Atlanta	40.00
Railroad, Dipper, Water, A.T. & S.F., Tin	16.00
Railroad, Dish, Celery, C.P.R., Crest	24.00
Railroad, Dish, Celery, Marked & Dated 1912, A.T.S.G.	55.00
Railroad, Dish, Celery, N.Y.C., Limoges	55.00
Railroad, Dish, Ice Cream, Footed, D.R.G., Prospector	24.00
Railroad, Dish, Soup, N.Y.C. DeWitt Clinton	27.50
Railroad, Eggcup, Double, N.Y.C., Mercury	18.00
Railroad, Eggcup, Footed, M.I.L.W., Peacock	7.00
Railroad, Eggcup, Southern Pacific, Poppy	15.00
Railroad, Extinguisher, Fire, B. & O.R.R., American LaFrance, Brass	40.00
Railroad, Fire Bucket, Canvas, Collapsible, Metal Folding Frame, N.Y.Central	39.00
Railroad, Glass, Double Shot, B. & O., Sleeping Car Department, 4 Oz.	36.00
Railroad, Glass, Wine, Stemmed, New York Central	14.00
Railroad, Globe, Cumberland Valley, Clear, 3 1/4 In.	26.00
Railroad, Globe, N. & W., 5 3/8 In.	50.00
Railroad, Globe, Reading Company, Red, 4 1/4 In.	24.00
Railroad, Goggles, Blue-Green Lens, Gauze String, C.1890, Tin Oval Box	40.00
Railroad, Hammer, Spike, Boston & Maine Railroad	18.50
Railroad, Headlight, Kerosene, C.1870, 27 X 30 In.	550.00
Railroad, Headrest, Buzzsaw & Eagles Logo, M.O.P.A.C.	8.00
Railroad, Holder, Candle, Caboose, Brass	45.00
Railroad, Holder, Menu, Applied Keystone Crest, Pennsylvania	27.50
Railroad, Ice Bucket, Dining Car, Wagner	55.00
Railroad, Ice Bucket, N.Y.C.	55.00
Railroad, Inkwell, Glass, P.R.R.	10.00
Railroad, Key & Receiver, Telegraph, Mounted On Oak Board	17.50
Railroad, Key, Cabin, P.R.R., Brass	4.00
Railroad, Key, Maine Central, Brass, 3 1/2 In.	12.00
Railroad, Ladder, Carpeted Rungs, Car & Bedroom Designation, 48 In.	60.00
Railroad, Lamp, Aladdin, Wall Bracket, Brass	45.00
Railroad, Lamp, Caboose, Bracket, Kerosene, Adam's Westlake	25.00
Railroad, Lamp, Caboose, Wall, Chimney, Aladdin Mark, N.W. Railway Co.	40.00
Railroad, Lamp, Cast Globe, C. & N.W.	40.00
Railroad, Lamp, Marker, Reservoir & Burner, Bull's-Eye Lens, 15 In., Pair	250.00
Railroad, Lamp, Oxweld, Union Carbide	30.00
Railroad, Lamp, Parlor Car, Brass, Large	150.00
Railroad, Lamp, Parlor Car, Candle Burning, Wall Bracketed, Brass, 12 In.	75.00
Railroad, Lamp, Reliable, N. & W.R.R., Red, 5 3/8 In.	30.00
Railroad, Lamp, Semiphore, M.C.R.R., Gray, Boston	45.00
Railroad, Lamp, Wall, Candle Burning, Mail Car, Spring Action, Iron	55.00
Railroad, Lamp, Whale Oil, Cone Shaped, Goose Neck Spout, Lapped Tin	79.00
Railroad, Lamp, Yard, Hooded, Dietz Acme	85.00
Railroad, Lamp, 4 Lens, 5 1/2 In.Bull's Eye Lens, Pair, 15 In.	250.00
Railroad, Lantern Frame & Globe, Brakesman's, Penn., Lines	40.00
Railroad, Lantern, Armspear, L. & N.Red Globe, Marked, Raised Letters	50.00
Railroad, Lantern, Armspear, N. & W., Clear 5 3/8 In., Globe, Raised Letters	50.00
Railroad, Lantern, Bell Bottom, Marked & Dated, New York Central Railroad	60.00
Railroad, Lantern, Brakeman's, Armspear, 1925, P.R.R.	22.50
Railroad, Lantern, Brakeman's, Frame Marked P. & R. Ry.	45.00
Railroad, Lantern, Brakeman's, Marked Pennsylvania Lines, Globe 5 1/4 In.	42.00
Railroad, Lantern, Brakeman's, Marked P.R.R., Red Globe, Hanlon	27.50
Railroad, Lantern, Brakeman's, Red Globe & Frame, P.R.R.	50.00
Railroad, Lantern, C.P.R., Adlake Red Globe	45.00
Railroad, Lantern, Caboose, Adlake, 2 Lens, 8 1/2 In.	75.00
Railroad, Lantern, Caboose, Bail Handle, Reservoir, Bull's-Eye Lens, Tin	69.50
Railroad, Lantern, Canadian National R.R., Wire Guard	24.50
Railroad, Lantern, Conductor's, Nickel Plated, N.Y.C.R.R., Etched On Globe	150.00
Railroad, Lantern, Corrugated Cobalt Globe, N.Y.C.S., Green	35.00
Railroad, Lantern, Erie, Etched Clear Globe	25.00

Railroad, Lantern, Guard, Boston & Maine Railroad, Marked	29.50
Railroad, Lantern, Inspectors, Dietz, Magnifying Lens	89.50
Railroad, Lantern, L.P.M., Piper, Montreal, 4 Rounded Glasses	65.00
Railroad, Lantern, N.P.R. Canada R.R., Blue Glass	35.00
Railroad, Lantern, N.Y. Central Emblem, Clear Globe	25.00
Railroad, Lantern, N.Y.C., Bellbottom, Marked	35.00
Railroad, Lantern, N.Y.Central, Marked Globe & Frame	30.00
Railroad, Lantern, New York Central, Clear Globe	26.00
Railroad, Lantern, Pennsylvania, Red Globe	30.00
Railroad, Lantern, Red Globe, B. & M. R.R., Dietz	32.50
Railroad, Lantern, Red Globe, Great Northern	35.00
Railroad, Lantern, Red Globe, Missouri Pacific	30.00
Railroad, Lantern, Red Globe, New York Central, 5 In.	32.50
Railroad, Lantern, Red Globe, Rock Island R.R.	37.00
Railroad, Lantern, Short Globe, Marked S.P.C.	35.00
Railroad, Lantern, Switchyard, P.R.R., Internal Mirrors, 27 X 14 X 5 In.	150.00
Railroad, Lantern, To Test Color Vision, Electric, A.T. & S.F.	125.00
Railroad, Lantern, Train Marker, 4 Bull's-Eye Lenses, 1914, Pair	135.00
Railroad, Lantern, Vesta, Boston & Albany	30.00
Railroad, Lantern, Vesta, New York Central	25.00
Railroad, Lantern, Wakefield, 1943, England, 12 In.	35.00
Railroad, Lantern, Wire Guard, Rd Glass, Marked Boston & Maine	42.50
Railroad, Lantern, Yard Switch Signal, Erie R.R.	85.00
Railroad, Lantern, 4-Way Switch, B.N.R.Y.	79.50
Railroad, Lap Board, Card Playing, N.Y., N.H. & H., R.R., 29 X 17 In.	25.00
Railroad, Light, Oil, Handled Pot, Spout With Wick, 6 In.	17.50
Railroad, Lock, Switch, Steel, N.Y.C.R.R.	35.00
Railroad, Lock, Tennessee, Steel	10.00
Railroad, Locomotive, Steam, 70 Horse Power, 2 Foot Gauge, 10 X 17 Feet	2000.00
Railroad, Magnet, Cincinnati Railroad Car Company	10.00
Railroad, Map, South New England, Complete Routes, N.Y., N.H. & Hartford	45.00
Railroad, Marker Light, Caboose, Canadian, Bull's-Eye Lens, 5 3/8 In.Cir.	35.00
Railroad, Marker Light, Caboose, Square Top, Adlake, Kerosene, Red, Green Lens	85.00
Railroad, Mustard Pot, Contoured Thumb Grip, Reed & Barton, D.R.G.	85.00
Railroad, Nappy, D.R.G., Prospector, 5 1/2 In.Diameter	22.00
Railroad, Nutcracker, Santa Fe	10.00
Railroad, Oiler, Engine, Large Spout, Copper, 24 In.	45.00
Railroad, Oiler, Engine, Long Snouted, L.V.R.R.	20.00
Railroad, Oiler, R. & M.R.R., Reservoir Base, 5 In.Spout, 7 1/2 In.Handle	21.50
Railroad, Oiler, Reservoir Base, Attached Chain, B. & M.R.R., Eagle	21.50
Railroad, Oiler, Spout, Georgia R.R.	22.00
Railroad, Padlock, A.T. & S.F., Marked	10.00
Railroad, Padlock, Key, Union Pacific Roadway & Bridge, Brass	42.50
Railroad, Paperweight, Passenger Depot, Laconia, N.H., 2 1/2 X 4 In.	15.00
Railroad, Pencil, Eversharp, Rock Island R.R., Rocket & Engine Pictured	8.50
Railroad, Pennant, Baltimore & Ohio R.R., 1827-1927 Centenary, 29 In.	48.00
Railroad, Pillowcase, Stamped Chesapeake & Ohio, Blue & Yellow	28.00
Railroad, Pitcher, Baltimore & Ohio Railway	25.00
Railroad, Pitcher, Hinged Top, P.R.R., Logo On Front	31.00
Railroad, Pitcher, Milk, B. & O., Capitol, 64 Oz.	175.00
Railroad, Pitcher, Syrup, Hinged Lid, International Silver, The Pullman Co.	25.00
Railroad, Plaque, Carbuilder's, Brass, 1 X 3/4 X 18 In.	39.00
Railroad, Plate, Advertising, Woodsville, N.H.	5.00
Railroad, Plate, Bread & Butter, Thomas Viaduct, 6 5/8 In.	26.00
Railroad, Plate, Bread & Butter, Union Pacific Overland Shield, 7 In.	30.00
Railroad, Plate, Cake, Oval, S.P., Sunset, Sept., 1923, 12 In.Diameter	185.00
Railroad, Plate, Commemorative, Baltimore & Ohio.1927, Train Scenes, 9 In.	35.00
Railroad, Plate, Compartment, S.O.U., 10 In.Diameter	55.00
Railroad, Plate, Dinner, C.P.R., Brown Maple Leaf, 9 In.Diameter	24.00
Railroad, Plate, Dinner, P.R.R., Purple Laurel, Bottom Marked, 8 In.Diameter	34.00
Railroad, Plate, Dinner, U.P., Harriman, Blue, Overland Logo, 9 In.	70.00
Railroad, Plate, Dinner, W.A.B., Banner, 9 In.Diameter	55.00
Railroad, Plate, Keystone, Red Logo, 8 3/4 In.	29.00
Railroad, Plate, Luncheon, S.O.U., Peach Blossom, 7 1/2 In.Diameter	44.00
Railroad, Plate, Luncheon, S.P., Harriman, Blue, Logo Topside, 7 In.	44.00
Railroad, Plate, Mohawk, Pacific, Syracuse China	150.00

Railroad, Plate, Oval, B. & O.R.R., Ioga Mark, 6 X 8 In.	35.00
Railroad, Plate, Potomac Valley, Cars 1830-1937, Diesel, 8 1/4 In.	25.00
Railroad, Plate, Pullman, Calumet, 7 1/2 In.	30.00
Railroad, Plate, Soup, Canadian National System, Royal Doulton, 9 In.	15.00
Railroad, Plate, Soup, R.M. & O., Rose, 9 In.Diameter	34.00
Railroad, Platter, A.T.S.F., Griffin, 10 1/2 X 7 1/2 In.	42.00
Railroad, Platter, Mountain & Flowers, Great Northern Railway, 9 In.	23.00
Railroad, Platter, Oval, N.Y.C. DeWitt Clinton, 11 3/4 In.	36.50
Railroad, Platter, Pullman, Indian Tree, September, 1946, 10 1/2 X 7 1/2 In.	54.00
Railroad, Platter, Turkey, A.T.S.F., Bleeding, Blue, 11 1/2 X 16 1/2 In.	225.00
Railroad, Platter, Union Pacific, Backstamped Harriman, 9 In.	7.50
Railroad, Poster, Excursion From Concord To Boston, 1889, 26 X 34 1/2 In.	49.50
Railroad, Ramekin, N.Y.C., Mercury, 4 1/2 In.Diameter	26.00
Railroad, Sauce, Erie, Susquehanna, Rectangular, 5 X 4 1/2 In.	45.00
Railroad, Sauce, P.R.R., Broadway, Bottom Marked, 4 3/4 In.Diameter	28.00
Railroad, Sauce, Union Pacific, Backstamped Harriman	6.00
Railroad, Saucer, Southern R.R., China	7.50
Railroad, Shovel, Coal, St. J. & C.I. Ry., Cast Iron	9.00
Railroad, Sign, Crossing X, Porcelain, 2-Sided, Glass Reflectors	145.00
Railroad, Sign, Crossing, Reflective Surface, C.1920, 36 In.Diameter	42.50
Railroad, Sign, New York Central On Frame & Blue Globe	40.00
Railroad, Sign, Signal, Yellow, 2 Seven-Inch Black Dots	12.50
Railroad, Sign, Southern Railway System, 1911, Tin, 25 3/4 X 37 3/4 In.	185.00
Railroad, Sign, Station, Missouri, Kansas, Texas Lines, Porcelain	150.00
Railroad, Sounder & Key, Telegraph, Morse, On Wood Panel	42.00
Railroad, Spittoon, Pullman Silver Palace Car Co., Weighted, Brass, 11 In.	115.00
Railroad, Spoon, Serving, Silver Plate, New Haven R.R.	12.50
Railroad, Step, Conductor's, Wooden	15.00
Railroad, Stove, Caboose, M.K. & T. Railroad	135.00
Railroad, Strainer, Tea, Silver Bail, Marked, Gorham, N.H., 2 In.Diameter	48.00
Railroad, Sugar & Creamer, International Silver, The Pullman Co.	30.00
Railroad, Sugar, Cover, International Silver, The Pullman Co.	15.00
Railroad, Sugar, Lid, Burlington R.R., 14 Oz., Silver	36.50
Railroad, Sugar, Lid, Burlington Route, 6 Ounce	37.50
Railroad, Sugar, N.Y.C.Western, Silver Cover	30.00
Railroad, Sugar, P.R.R., Dining Car	30.00
Railroad, Sugar, P.R.R., Marked Keystone	8.00
Railroad, Switchlock, Brass, N & W.	20.00
Railroad, Tablecloth, Erie Lackawanna R.R., Large	13.00
Railroad, Teapot, Illinois Central Railroad, Hinged Lid, Siver	35.00
Railroad, Teapot, Lid, B. & O., Shenango	38.00
Railroad, Teapot, Torch Shape	27.00
Railroad, Telegraph Key, Marked Western Electric	22.50
Railroad, Telegraph Key, Side Swing Action	28.00
Railroad, Telephone & Morse Code Ringer, Scissor Type, Earphones	350.00
Railroad, Ticket Punch, Trolley Car, Boston, Massachusetts	3.00
Railroad, Ticket, 10-Day Excursion To Columbian Exposition, 1893	7.50
Railroad, Timetable, Baltimore & Washington, Dated 1904	3.00
Railroad, Timetable, National R.R. Of Mexico, 1903	20.00
Railroad, Tongs, Ice, Southern Pacific	26.50
Railroad, Tray, Bread, N.Y., N.H. & Hartford R.R., Silver Plate, 12 In.	32.00
Railroad, Tray, Bread, Oval, Burlington Route, 11 In.	29.95
Railroad, Tray, Change, Fluted, Santa Fe, 6 In.	17.50
Railroad, Tray, Crumb, Devil's Head Style, D. & H., Reed & Barton	105.00
Railroad, Tray, Juice, Seaboard Air Line, Silver, 5 In.	12.00
Railroad, Tray, Tip, Intercolonial Railway Of Canada	55.00
Railroad, Tumbler, Logo Etched On Side, L.F., 8 Oz.	36.00
Railroad, Tureen, Lid & Underliner, Santa Fe, 20 Ounce	54.95
Railroad, Valve, Foot, Dead Man's, Cast Iron	40.00
Railroad, Vase, Bud, Trumpet Shape, Keystone Logo, P.R.R., 1926, 6 In.	105.00
Railroad, Whistle, Back-Up, Caboose, Brass, Air Brake Control Handle	35.00
Railroad, Whistle, Caboose, Brass, Steam Operated	65.00
Railroad, Whistle, Caboose, Brass, 1 1/4 X 2 1/4 In.	50.00
Railroad, Whistle, Caboose, Brass, 6 In.Long X 1 3/4 In.Diameter	45.00
Railroad, Whistle, Steam Engine, Brass, 12 In.	175.00
Railroad, Whistle, Steam, Brass, 9 3/4 In.	75.00

Railroad, Wrench, Embossed, L. & N. R.R.	20.00
Rainbow, see Mother-of-Pearl, Satin Glass	
Razor, Antone Berg, Eskulstuna, Sweden, 1881	8.50
Razor, Bee Climbing Acorns & Tree, Celluloid	18.00
Razor, Celluloid Case	10.00
Razor, Corn, Pearl Handled, German	15.00
Razor, Durham-Duplex, Original Box	9.50
Razor, Gillette, Swel-Do, Blade Case, Black, Original Lined Box	9.00
Razor, Hackett Diamond	4.50
Razor, Holder, Blade, Grog, Listerine Shaving Cream	6.00
Razor, J.A.Helberg, Eskulstuna	6.50
Razor, Red Injun, No.101, Rope Carved Ivory Handle	9.50
Razor, Reynolds, Sheffield, Tortoise Shell Handle	9.75
Razor, Rolls, Leather Case	39.50
Razor, Safety, Christy, Original Box & Blades	4.00
Razor, Safety, Ender, Case & Instructions	8.00
Razor, Safety, Everready, Tin Case	7.00
Razor, Safety, Gem, Dated 1912	5.00
Razor, Safety, Keen Kutter, Original Box & Blades	10.00
Razor, Safety, Winchester	39.50
Razor, Sharpener, Celluloid Handled Shaving Brush	4.50
Razor, Sharpener, Kriss-Kross	15.00
Razor, Sheffield, Wade & Butcher	5.75
Razor, Souvenir, National Hardware Job Assoc., 4 1/2 In.	20.00
Razor, Stoltz Barber Supplies, San Francisco, Celluloid Case & Handle	10.00
Razor, Straight Edge, Civil War, Engraved Eagle On Blade	27.00
Razor, Straight, Boker	5.00
Razor, Straight, Bone Handle, No.K10	20.00
Razor, Straight, Carved Black Handle	6.00
Razor, Straight, Civil War Era, Etched 3 In.Blade, Figures In Uniform	47.50
Razor, Straight, Eagle On Blade	25.00
Razor, Straight, German Blade, Limerick Leather Case	12.50
Razor, Straight, Ivory Handle, Embossed Scene On Side, Germany, 6 In.	25.00
Razor, Straight, King, Celluloid Handle	6.50
Razor, Straight, Patriotic, Civil War, 3 In.Blade, Horn Handle	64.50
Razor, Straight, Peacock Handle	15.00
Razor, Straight, Sheffield, Bone Handle	5.00
Razor, Straight, Wade & Butcher Sheffield, Cardboard Case	10.00
Razor, Straight, Winchester, Box	49.50
Razor, Straight, Wizard Safety Razor, Patented 1924	8.50
Razor, Straight, World's Columbian Exposition, C.1892, Black, Germany	35.00
Razor, Strop & Case, Late 1860s, Benjamin	12.50
Razor, Strop, Double Duck Leather	15.00
Razor, Strop, Kriss-Kross Safety Blade, Original Box	6.00
Razor, Strop, Valet Auto, Dated 1912, In Case	10.00
Razor, Taft, Sherman	40.00
Razor, Traveling, Eveready Safety, Velvet Box, 6 Radio Steel Blades	45.00
Razor, Winchester, Straight Edge Blade	30.00

The Red Wing Pottery of Red Wing, Minnesota, was a firm started in 1878. It was not until the 1920s that art pottery was made. It closed in 1967. Rumrill pottery was made for George Rumrill by the Red Wing Pottery Company and other firms. It was sold in the 1930s.

Red Wing, Ashtray, 75th Anniversary	15.00
Red Wing, Bowl, Centerpiece, Pair Candlesticks, 7 In.Square	10.00
Red Wing, Bowl, Console, Frog In Form Of Doe, 15 In.	65.00
Red Wing, Bowl, Indian Design, Blue & White, 7 In.	40.00
Red Wing, Bowl, Mixing, Brown's Market, New London, 1 1/2 Quart	40.00
Red Wing, Bowl, Union Stoneware Brushware, Oval Mark, 3 X 9 1/2 In.Diam.	26.00
Red Wing, Candleholder, Figural Grapes, Ivory, Pair	15.00
Red Wing, Candleholder, Pink Bow, Pair	6.00
Red Wing, Candlestick, Form Of Cherubs, Pair	20.00
Red Wing, Chocolate Pot, 9 1/4 In.	6.00
Red Wing, Console & Flower Frog, Figural Deer, Matte Ivory	25.00
Red Wing, Cookie Jar, Davy Crockett	20.00
Red Wing, Cookie Jar, Dutch Girl, Creams, Brown	20.00

Red Wing, Cookie Jar, Figural Baker Man, Blue, 9 X 12 In. 45.00
Red Wing, Cookie Jar, Monk, Blue 25.00
Red Wing, Cookie Jar, Saffron 20.00
Red Wing, Cooler, Water, 3 Gallon 85.00
Red Wing, Crock, Blue Banded, 4 X 7 1/2 In. 38.00
Red Wing, Crock, Bull's-Eye Mark 45.00
Red Wing, Crock, Minnesota Stoneware Mark On Bottom, 2 Gallon 18.00
Red Wing, Dish, 75th Anniversary Red Wing 28.00
Red Wing, Honeypot, Linden Apiary, 6 3/4 X 8 3/4 In.Diameter 40.00
Red Wing, Jar, Fruit, Zinc Lid, Mason Stoneware 30.00
Red Wing, Jar, Fruit, 1/2 Gallon 65.00
Red Wing, Jar, Lard, Bail, 5 Pound 55.00
Red Wing, Jardiniere, Elephant Head Handles, 6 1/2 In. 20.00
Red Wing, Juicer, Pedestal 125.00
Red Wing, Pitcher, Blue Gray, Lily 150.00
Red Wing, Planter, Hat Shape, Ribbed Brim, Blue Mottled, Mauve 6.00
Red Wing, Planter, Speckled Goose 12.00
Red Wing, Pot, Bean, Brown & Cream, Marked 50.00
Red Wing, Sugar & Creamer, Orange, Small 16.00
Red Wing, Swan, Blue 8.50
Red Wing, Teapot, Bobwhite 38.00
Red Wing, Teapot, Yellow Figural Chicken 25.00
Red Wing, Vase, Brown, Textured, 7 In. 12.00
Red Wing, Vase, Cattails, Marked, 7 In. 30.00
Red Wing, Vase, Cylinder, Applied Cupid, Signed 15.00
Red Wing, Vase, Earlike Handles, Blue Mottled, 10 In. 15.00
Red Wing, Vase, Free-Form, Half-Cylinder, Gray, 7 X 5 3/4 X 2 1/2 In., Pair 26.00
Red Wing, Vase, Handled, White, 7 3/4 In. 8.00
Red Wing, Vase, Ivory With Green Interior, No.1203, 10 In. 12.00
Red Wing, Vase, Mottled, Blue, 10 In. 18.00
Red Wing, Vase, Multicolor, 10 In. 45.00
Red Wing, Vase, Pink Lined, Leaf Base, Paper Sticker, 10 1/2 In. X 4 In. 12.50
Red Wing, Vase, Stoneware, Tan, Cattails, Marked, 8 In. 30.00
Red Wing, Vase, Union Stoneware Company, Green, 11 In. 15.00

Redware is a hard red stoneware that originated in the late 1600s and
continues to be made. The term is also used to describe any common clay
pottery that is reddish in color.

Redware, Bird Whistle Whimsey, Cream Slip, Brown Glaze, Birds, 10 In. 800.00
Redware, Bird Whistle, Cream & Dark Brown Slip 800.00
Redware, Bowl, Cream Slip, Green Glaze, 19th Century, 14 1/2 In. 225.00
Redware, Bowl, Manganese Splotching, 6 1/4 In.Diameter 95.00
Redware, Bowl, Orange Glaze With Brown Streaks, 1700s, 13 X 4 X 9 1/2 In. 250.00
Redware, Bowl, Wash, 15 In.Diameter 85.00
Redware, Butter Churn, Baluster-Form, Wood Dasher, 19th Century, 18 1/2 In. 300.00
Redware, Candlestick, Classical Figures, C.1830-59, Signed, 7 3/4 In., Pair 150.00
Redware, Colander, Mug Shaped, Interior Glaze, 19th Century, 4 1/2 X 7 In. 165.00
Redware, Crock, Glazed Exterior, Wide Mouth, 7 1/2 X 5 1/2 In. 45.00
Redware, Crock, Rust & Tan, Signed Wilcock, 21 In. 650.00
Redware, Crock, Tin Cover, Terraced Shoulder, 1/2 Gallon, 7 1/4 In. 150.00
Redware, Crock, Wide Mouthed, Glazed Exterior, 1 Gallon 45.00
Redware, Dish, Deep, Abstract Linear Design, 19th Century, 17 1/8 In. 250.00
Redware, Dish, German Calligraphy, 1783, 13 In.Diameter 850.00
Redware, Dish, Soap, Slanted Side, 7 1/2 X 3 1/4 X 2 1/4 In. 58.00
Redware, Figural Group, Eberly Potters, 1894, 15 1/4 X 15 1/8 In. 2500.00
Redware, Flowerpot & Saucer, Cylindrical, 19th Century, 8 1/2 In. 300.00
Redware, Flowerpot, Attached Saucer, 3 3/4 In. 110.00
Redware, Inkwell, Leather Traveling Case 65.00
Redware, Jar, Covered, Glazed, Massachusetts, 19th Century, 10 1/2 In. 250.00
Redware, Jar, Covered, Tooled Ring, Iridescent Brown, 19th Century, 10 In. 325.00
Redware, Jar, Green To Clear, 3 Incised Bands, Applied Handles, 6 In. 135.00
Redware, Jar, Incised Beaded Circles, 6 3/4 In. 26.00
Redware, Jar, Ovoid, Clear Glaze, 6 In. 35.00
Redware, Jardiniere, Glazed Inside & Out, 3 Gallon 75.00
Redware, Jardiniere, Medallions With Birds & Flowers, 8 In. 65.00
Redware, Jug, Bulbous Body, Incised Reeding, Early 19th Century, 8 1/2 In. 850.00

Redware, Jug, Dark Brown Glaze, 8 1/2 In.	50.00
Redware, Jug, Handles, Black Mottling, Brown Glaze, 1 Gallon, 9 In.	175.00
Redware, Jug, Olive Green Glaze, Orange Spots, Ovoid, 1800s, 10 1/2 In.	300.00
Redware, Jug, Ovoid, C.1810, Brown Glazed Interior, Applied Handle, 8 1/2 In.	150.00
Redware, Lamb, S.Bell & Son, Late 19th Century, 12 In.	1750.00
Redware, Lighting Stand, Greenish Glaze With Brown Sponging, 4 3/4 In.	135.00
Redware, Match Safe, Brown Glaze, 4 X 3 In.	25.00
Redware, Mold, Candle, Wood Frame, 12 Tubes, 19 X 15 In.	950.00
Redware, Mold, Head, Turk, 8 1/2 In.	55.00
Redware, Pan, Milk, Yellowish Red Glaze, 16 In.	55.00
Redware, Pitcher, Baluster-Form Body, S.Bell & Son, 19th Century, 11 In.	425.00
Redware, Pitcher, Celadon-Glazed, John Bell, 19th Century, 7 1/2 In.	950.00
Redware, Pitcher, Presentation, Dated 1881, 11 1/2 In.	500.00
Redware, Plaque, Greek Classical Figs In Relief, Jobenhaven, 8 1/2 In.	22.00
Redware, Plate, Bird & Tulip, Bucks Co., Signed I.S., C.1775, 12 1/2 In.	115.00
Redware, Plate, Easel Back, Flowers, 9 In.	49.00
Redware, Plate, Slip-Decorated, Dated 1822, 9 3/4 In.	1750.00
Redware, Plate, Slip-Decorated, Lafayette, Orange-Brown, 9 1/8 X 11 1/4 In.	700.00
Redware, Plate, 3 Line Yellow Slip, Coggled Edge, 9 In.	220.00
Redware, Pot, Flower, Pie Crust Edge, 9 X 8 In.Diameter	75.00
Redware, Trivet, Molded Design, John Bell, 19th Century, 8 1/2 In.Diameter	475.00
Redware, Vase, Dragon Design, 12 In.	75.00
Redware, Wall Pocket, Cylindrical, Bell Family, 19th Century, 8 1/2 In.	275.00
Redwing, Pitcher, Ivory Background, Brown Embossed Flowers & Leaves, 7 In.	8.00
Redwing, Vase, White Open Rose, 6 In.	12.00

Regout, see Maastricht

Reverse Painting, see Painting, Reverse on Glass

Richard was the mark used on acid-etched cameo glass vases, bowls, night lights and lamps in Lorraine, France, during the 1920s.

Richard, Vase, Brown On Frosted Body, Signed, 7 3/4 In.	325.00
Richard, Vase, Cameo, Baluster Shape, Frosted Background, 3 1/2 In.	325.00
Richard, Vase, Cameo, Brown Thistles Cut To Green, 6 In.	185.00
Richard, Vase, Cameo, Chateau, Scenic, French, Signed, 10 1/2 X 3 1/2 In.	450.00
Richard, Vase, Cameo, Translucent Ground, Scenic, Signed, 10 1/2 In.	450.00
Richard, Vase, Cameo, Yellow, Orange, Brown, Birds In Flight, 5 Inches	415.00
Richard, Vase, Cameo, 2 Cuts, Brown On Yellow Ground, Signed, 5 1/4 In.	295.00
Richard, Vase, Crown Cut To Orange, Scenic, Signed, 15 1/2 In.	1250.00
Richard, Vase, Deep Orange & Brown, Castle, 17 In.	750.00
Richard, Vase, Red & Blue, Wheel & Acid Cut, Free Form Square, 9 1/4 In.	375.00
Richard, Vase, Scenic, Scalloped Top, Pedestal Foot, Signed, 15 1/4 In.	895.00
Richard, Vase, Yellow, Orange & Blue, Castle, 14 In.	750.00
Richard, Wine, Floral, Frosted Yellow Ground, Acid Cut, Signed, 4 5/8 In.	195.00

Ridgway pottery has been made in the Staffordshire District in England since 1808 by a series of companies with the name Ridgway. The transfer-design dinner sets are the most widely known product. They are still being made.

Ridgway, Cake Stand, Persia, Orange Transfer, C.1830	15.00
Ridgway, Dish, Vegetable, Covered, Green & White, Grecian Pattern, 11 In.	48.50
Ridgway, Jug, Slop, Covered, Views Of Holland, C.1893, Delft, 14 In.	165.00
Ridgway, Mug, Black Transfer, Dog Subject, 4 1/8 In.	30.00
Ridgway, Mug, Coaching Days & Coaching Ways, Fresh Teams, 3 7/8 In.	30.00
Ridgway, Mug, Coaching Days & Coaching Ways, Fresh Teams, 4 7/8 In.	37.50
Ridgway, Mug, Coaching Days & Coaching Ways, Walking Up The Hill, 4 7/8 In.	37.50
Ridgway, Mug, Coaching Days & Coaching Ways, 1/2 Pint	30.00
Ridgway, Mug, Silver Luster Rim & Handle, Mr.Pickwick Scene, 3 1/4 In.	30.00
Ridgway, Pitcher, Green, Exotic Birds, Anchor Mark, C.1830, 6 In.	70.00
Ridgway, Pitcher, Tam O'Shanter, 1835, Salt Glaze, 6 In.	65.00
Ridgway, Plate, Child's, Old Curiosity Shop Scenes, Blue, 4 1/2 In., Set Of 4	32.00
Ridgway, Plate, Coaching Days & Coaching Ways, 10 1/2 In.	55.00
Ridgway, Plate, Coaching Days & Coaching Ways, 9 In., Set Of 6	120.00
Ridgway, Plate, Octagon, Church, Boston, Dark Blue, 9 3/4 In.	175.00
Ridgway, Plate, Oriental Blue & White, 9 1/2 In.	22.00
Ridgway, Plate, Pie, Dundee, 6 In.	12.00
Ridgway, Plate, Soup, Octagon, Church, Boston, Blue, 10 In.	185.00

Ridgway, Platter, Coaching Day & Coaching Ways, Trinity College, 8 X 10 In.	90.00
Ridgway, Tea Set, Child's, Maidenhair Fern, Figural Floral Knobs, 5 Piece	125.00
Rifle, American Fowling, C.1780-1800, Shell, Fan Carving, 47 In.	250.00
Rifle, B.B., Red Ryder	13.00
Rifle, Bag & Horn, Kentucky, Rawhide Bag, Strap, 1847, General Taylor	90.00
Rifle, Blunderbuss, Muzzle Loader, Signed & Proof Marked	215.00
Rifle, Carcano, Model 1891, Standard Grade	55.00
Rifle, Confederate, Barrel, 69 Caliber	480.00
Rifle, Curly Maple, Full Stock, 11 Silver Inlays, Marked G.G.Julcher	775.00
Rifle, Curly Maple, Half Stock, 4 Silver Inlays, J.Haberstro, Buffalo, N.Y.	775.00
Rifle, Flask, Copper, Design Both Sides, Laced Rope, 8 1/2 In.	54.50
Rifle, Flintlock, Curly Maple, C.1830, 41 In.Barrel	275.00
Rifle, Flintlock, Full Stock, Kentucky, Brass Patchbox, 53 In.	1250.00
Rifle, German Tschinke, C.1650, Wheelock Mechanism, 17th Century, Inlay	2500.00
Rifle, Harper's Ferry, 1848, Ramrod, 56 In.	285.00
Rifle, Jenning's, Repeating, Magazine Loaded, Ring Trigger, C.1851, 26 In.	2500.00
Rifle, Kentucky Full Stock Tiger Maple, Brass Patch Box	495.00
Rifle, Kentucky Half Stock, Octagon Barrel, German Silver, Trim, 37 In.	375.00
Rifle, Kentucky Half Stock, Percussion, Marked J.Henry, 36 Caliber, 40 In.	695.00
Rifle, Kentucky, Over-Under Double Barrel, 40 Caliber, Silver Inlay, 34 In.	950.00
Rifle, Kentucky, Silver Inlay, C.1810-20, Curly Maple Stock, 41 In.	1950.00
Rifle, Marlin, Lever Action, Top Ejection, Octagon Barrel, 28 In.	295.00
Rifle, Matching Pistol, Flintlock, De Charlesville, 1877, D.D.A. & Seal	3000.00
Rifle, Mauser, Siamese, Model 1887	37.50
Rifle, Maynard, Target, Hooded Front Sight, Pistol Grip Stock, 32 In.	1850.00
Rifle, Mississippi, 54 Caliber, Robbins & Lawrence, 1848, 24 In.	135.00
Rifle, Mule-Ear, Double Barrel, Over-Under, C.1840, 20 Gauge, Brass Trim	275.00
Rifle, Murata, Japanese, Bolt Action, C.1883, 13 In.	115.00
Rifle, New England Underhammer, Percussion, Buggy, 52 Caliber, 28 In.	195.00
Rifle, Percussion, Double Set Trigger, Hunting Pouch & Horn	195.00
Rifle, Percussion, Iron Mounted Half Stock, 54 Caliber	110.00
Rifle, R.S.Mortimer, Double-Barrel, 10-Gauge, Brass Powder Flask	600.00
Rifle, Remington Rolling Block, Military, C.1870, Inspection Mark, 36 In.	135.00
Rifle, Remington-Zouave, Percussion, 58 Caliber, Brass Patch Box	750.00
Rifle, Remington, Rolling Block Action, 24 In.	84.50
Rifle, Springfield, Attached Sling	150.00
Rifle, Springfield, Krag, Dated 1894, Wooden Stock & Barrel Cover, Sling	295.00
Rifle, Springfield, Trapdoor, Model 1873, 4, 000 Made	550.00
Rifle, Springfield, 1873, 45-70 Caliber	185.00
Rifle, Squirrel, Kentucky Half Stock, Curly Maple, Patch Box, 35 Caliber	400.00
Rifle, Stevens' Tip-Up, Interchangeable Barrel, Gilt Finish, 24 In.	795.00
Rifle, Target, Single Shot, German, Decorated, Large Cheekrest, , 32 In.	595.00
Rifle, Trapdoor, No.5971	250.00
Rifle, Trapdoor, Springfield, Original Blue	350.00
Rifle, Winchester 1873, Full Magazine, Mortised Dust Cover, 24 In.	275.00
Rifle, Winchester, Model 73, Original Blue	425.00
Rifle, Winchester, Tang Peep Sight, Long Range	110.00
Rifle, Winchester, 1866, No.131186	1400.00
Rifle, Winchester, 1873, No.194779b, 44 Caliber	400.00
Rifle, Winchester, 1873, No.218128b, 32 Caliber	460.00
Rifle, Winchester, 1873, No.287843b, 32 Caliber	480.00
Rifle, Winchester, 1873, No.321085b, 22 In.	780.00
Rifle, Winchester, 1873, No.363693b, 38 Caliber	400.00
Rifle, Winchester, 1873, No.369524b	800.00
Rifle, Winchester, 1873, No.484063b, 32 W.C.F.	380.00
Rifle, Winchester, 1873, No.629128b	280.00
Rifle, Winchester, 1886, Mp.31737, 40-65 Caliber	700.00
Rifle, Winchester, 1886, No.109869, 45-90 Caliber	860.00
Rifle, Winchester, 1906, 22 Caliber, Repeater	100.00
Rifle, Winchester, 66 Carbine, Brass Frame	850.00

Riviera Ware was made by the Homer Laughlin Co. from 1938 to 1950.
Plates were square and cup handles were squared.

Riviera Ware, Casserole, Covered, Green	15.00
Robj, Bottle, Figural, Art Deco, 9 1/2 To 10 1/2 In., Set Of 8 ....*Illus*	900.00
Robj, Jar, Powder, Covered, All-Over Beading Pattern, Signed, 3 1/2 In.Diam.	45.00

Robj, Bottle, Figural, Art Deco, 9 1/2 To 10 1/2 In., Set Of 8

Roblin, Vase, Pinecones & Branches, Signed, 5 1/2 X 3 1/2 In. 500.00

> *Rockingham in the United States is a brown glazed pottery with a tortoiseshell-like glaze. It was made from 1840 to 1900 by many American potteries. The mottled brown Rockingham wares were first made in England at the Rockingham factory. Other wares were also made by the English firm.*

Rockingham, Bank, Uncle Sam, 4 1/4 In. 155.00
Rockingham, Basket, Blue, Apricot, Flowers, Leaves, C.1830, 7 1/2 X 6 1/4 In. 175.00
Rockingham, Basket, Raised Flowers, Castle, Stone Bridge, C.1840, 11 1/2 In. 550.00
Rockingham, Bowl, Mixing, 11 1/4 X 5 1/2 In. 65.00
Rockingham, Cuspidor, Lady's, Octagonal Shaped, Raised Leaf & Scroll, 8 In. 50.00
Rockingham, Cuspidor, Lady's, Raised Leaf & Scroll, 8 1/4 In.Diameter 55.00
Rockingham, Dish, Oval, 7 X 9 In. 65.00
Rockingham, Dish, Oval, 8 3/4 X 10 3/4 X 2 1/2 In. 80.00
Rockingham, Dish, Salmon-Ground Oval, C.1830, 12 1/4 In. 225.00
Rockingham, Dish, Soap, One Piece Tub Shape, Dappled Brown Glaze 58.50
Rockingham, Dog, Sitting, 10 In.High X 8 In.Long 95.00
Rockingham, Doorstop, Dog, Free Standing Front Legs, 10 3/4 In. 130.00
Rockingham, Figurine, Poodle, Clipped, C.1815, 3 1/2 In., Pair ....*Illus* 160.00
Rockingham, Figurine, Poodle, Parrot, C.1820, 4 1/2 In., Pair 280.00
Rockingham, Figurine, Poodle, Puppy, C.1810-20, 4 1/4 In., Pair 300.00
Rockingham, Loving Cup, Lion Battling Serpent, Interior Has 2 Frogs 200.00
Rockingham, Mug, Shaving, 4 X 3 3/4 In. 18.00
Rockingham, Pitcher, Anchor, Marked S.P.Co., 9 1/2 In. 75.00
Rockingham, Pitcher, Batter, Yellow & Brown, Enameled, 8 1/2 X 5 In.Diam. 35.00
Rockingham, Pitcher, Toby 38.00
Rockingham, Plate, Pie, Mottled Glaze, 9 1/2 In. 62.00
Rockingham, Platter, Octagonal, 10 X 12 3/4 In. 145.00
Rockingham, Toby Jug, Bennington, Franklin Type, Grape Handle 400.00
Rockingham, Toby, Snuff Taker, Brown Glazed, 19th Century, 9 In. 50.00
   Rogers, see John Rogers

> *Rookwood pottery was made in Cincinnati, Ohio, from 1880 to 1960. All of this art pottery is marked, most with the famous flame mark. The R is reversed and placed back to back with the letter P. Flames surround the letters.*

Rookwood Bookend, Cream, Owls On Book, 6 In., Pair 75.00
Rookwood, Ashtray, Fox, 1940 .... 35.00
Rookwood, Ashtray, Green Eagle, XLIV, 5 1/4 In. 37.50
Rookwood, Ashtray, Matte Green, Ohio Knife Co., 1848-1948 .... 30.00
Rookwood, Bookend, Beagle, Green, No.2998, 1946, Pair 58.00
Rookwood, Bookend, Cornucopia, Pink, 1921 .... 65.00
Rookwood, Bookend, Dutch Boy & Girl Leaning On Wall, 1928, Sallie Toohey 158.00
Rookwood, Bookend, Elephant, Green Matte Glaze, 1935, 5 In., Pair 125.00
Rookwood, Bookend, Owls, Greenish White, 6 In., Pair 70.00

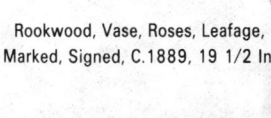

Rookwood, Vase, Roses, Leafage,
Marked, Signed, C.1889, 19 1/2 In.

(See Page 477)

Rockingham, Figurine, Poodle, Clipped, C.1815,
3 1/2 In., Pair

Rookwood, Bowl, Adeliza Sehon, 1889, Standard, 2 In.Tall	145.00
Rookwood, Bowl, Flower, Art Nouveau Figural, Ambroso, Ivory, Signed, L.Abel	185.00
Rookwood, Bowl, Flower, Floral, Stems, Speckling, Inturned Rim, Green, Brown	45.00
Rookwood, Bowl, Flowers In Relief, Squatty, Henschel Signed, C.1912, 10 In.	155.00
Rookwood, Bowl, Matte Glaze, Dated 1916, No.2131, 3 X 5 In.	42.50
Rookwood, Bowl, Running Deer, Glazed, Green, 6 In.	55.00
Rookwood, Bowl, Vellum, 1917, Margaret McDonald, 2 1/2 In.Tall	125.00
Rookwood, Bowl, White Roses, Peach Background, 1891, 12 In.	285.00
Rookwood, Box, Cigar, Western & Southern Railroad, 1934	35.00
Rookwood, Cache Pot, Beige Glaze, Tubular Shape, 1927, 4 1/2 In.	52.00
Rookwood, Cache Pot, Petals, Section At Bottom, Vertical Lines, 1927	52.00
Rookwood, Candleholder, Stylized Flower Buds, 1923, 4 X 2 In., Pair	65.00
Rookwood, Candlestick, Matte Blue, Raised Floral Relief, C.1921, 4 1/2 In.	40.00
Rookwood, Candlestick, Pink Matte, 1922 Paneled Design, Footed, 7 In., Pair	60.00
Rookwood, Candlestick, Pink, Side Handles, XXVII 2981, 2 3/4 X 4 In., Pair	40.00
Rookwood, Candlestick, Yellow Jonquil Leaves & Blossoms, C.1891, 5 1/2 In.	195.00
Rookwood, Candlestick, 2 Handles, Turquoise, Signed, C.1922	37.50
Rookwood, Chamberstick, Inverted Mushroom Form, Matte Green, 1906, 4 1/2 In.	58.00
Rookwood, Chocolate Pot, 1885, Tan	195.00
Rookwood, Creamer, Butterfly Handle, 1898	215.00
Rookwood, Cup, Loving, Ears Of Corn & Wheat Sheaves, 2 Handles, Brown, Signed	395.00
Rookwood, Ewer, Heart Shaped Mouth, Handle, Signed Sally Toohey, 12 In.	395.00
Rookwood, Ewer, Sprays, Lacy Florals, Gold Splashes, Semi Bisque, 1887, 12 In.	625.00
Rookwood, Ewer, Trefoil Lip, Melon Ribbed Body, Handle, C.1893, Signed H.R.S.	475.00
Rookwood, Ewer, Yellow Flower Decoration, C.1894, Artist C.S., 6 In.	225.00
Rookwood, Figurine, Baby Burro, Green, Louise Abel, 1932, 2 1/2 X 5 X 6 In.	110.00
Rookwood, Figurine, Collie, XXVII, Ivory Color, 6 1/2 In.	85.00
Rookwood, Figurine, Deer, Brown, Lying Down, Head Erect, 1934, 4 1/4 In.	85.00
Rookwood, Figurine, Nude Woman Seated, 1928, 4 1/4 In.	115.00
Rookwood, Flower Frog, Satyr With Turtle, Mustard, C.1921	95.00
Rookwood, Flower Frog, Turquoise, High Glaze, Water Lily	27.00
Rookwood, Hatpin Holder, Iris, White, Wine, Signed, Marked, 1912	225.00
Rookwood, Head, Young Woman In White, Matte Glaze, 8 X 8 In.	125.00
Rookwood, Humidor, 2 Handled, Holly & Berries, Brown Glaze, 1891	340.00
Rookwood, Inkwell, Thistle Blossoms, Matte Green, Signed Sallie Coyne, 5 In.	185.00
Rookwood, Jar, Powder, XXIII, 5 1/2 In.	45.00
Rookwood, Jar, Rose, Iris, Matte, A.Daly, No.142D, C.1885, 4 1/2 In.	235.00
Rookwood, Jardiniere, Blue, No.2355, 1921, 5 3/4 X 7 In.	55.00
Rookwood, Mug, Handled, Hand-Painted, Dogwood Sprig, Marked, Signed, 3 3/4 In.	260.00
Rookwood, Paperweight, Blue Nude Figure, C.1943	50.00
Rookwood, Paperweight, 3 Mast Sailing Ship, Waves, Blue Glaze, 4 X 3 1/2 In.	75.00
Rookwood, Pitcher, Cherries Decal, Gold Trim, Signed, 9 1/2 In.	30.00
Rookwood, Pitcher, Glazed, Dandelion Blooms & Leaves, Signed, C.1892, 6 In.	540.00
Rookwood, Pitcher, Milk, Brushed Gold, Dated 1882	665.00
Rookwood, Pitcher, Shaded Mustard Ground, Incised Flowers, 1885, Signed	190.00
Rookwood, Plaque, Mountain Scene, 1914, E.Diers, 9 X 14 1/2 In.	2250.00
Rookwood, Plaque, Scenic, 1913, 4 X 8 In.	550.00
Rookwood, Plaque, Twin Birches, Original Frame, 1921, 5 1/2 X 9 In.	950.00
Rookwood, Plate, Anna Valentien, 1886, Standard Glaze	195.00
Rookwood, Platter, Cabbage Leaf, XL1V, Signed	55.00

Rookwood, Rose Bowl, Rooks In Flight, 1935, 4 1/2 In. 46.00
Rookwood, Teapot & Creamer, Plum & Blue, No.54 Design, Matte Incised 95.00
Rookwood, Tile, Monk Kneeling Before Cross, Mule In Background, Marked 95.00
Rookwood, Tile, Tea, Polychrome Flowers, White Border, Signed, 1946, 5 1/4 In. 75.00
Rookwood, Vase, Abstract Decoration, Blue, William Hentschel, 1913, 8 In. 115.00
Rookwood, Vase, Beige, Band Of Raised Daisies, C.1948, 5 1/2 In. 30.00
Rookwood, Vase, Black-Eyed-Susans, 4 1/2 In. 185.00
Rookwood, Vase, Blackberries, Leaves, Vine, Bulbous, Signed Irene Bishop, 6 In. 310.00
Rookwood, Vase, Blue Panel, 5 Rooks, Trees, 1926, 5 In. 65.00
Rookwood, Vase, Brown Glaze, Scroll Border, 1929, 4 1/4 In. 40.00
Rookwood, Vase, Bud, Constance Baker, Iris Glaze, 5 In.Tall 145.00
Rookwood, Vase, Bud, Matte Green, 1922, 7 In. 26.00
Rookwood, Vase, Bulbous Base, Slender Neck, 1897, Signed, 6 1/2 In. 195.00
Rookwood, Vase, Bulbous, Metallic Black Streaks, 1932, 7 In. 90.00
Rookwood, Vase, Bulbous, Squat, Matte Finish, Greek Key, 4 1/2 In. 75.00
Rookwood, Vase, Butterfly Relief, Blue, XIV 6457, 4 3/4 In. 24.00
Rookwood, Vase, Charles McLaughlin, Blue Vellum, 1914, 4 1/2 In.Tall 125.00
Rookwood, Vase, Coral Interior, Maize, Matte Wax Glaze, Signed, 7 In. 285.00
Rookwood, Vase, Crimson To Blue, 1913, Signed, 8 In. 115.00
Rookwood, Vase, Dated 1926, No.2913, 7 X 5 In. 62.50
Rookwood, Vase, Deus Est Caritas, October 7, 1934, XXX1V, 5 X 4 1/2 In. 135.00
Rookwood, Vase, Elizabeth Barrett, Matte, 1924, 6 1/2 In.Tall 58.00
Rookwood, Vase, Fred Rothenbusch, Iris Glaze, 1905, 7 1/2 In.Tall 175.00
Rookwood, Vase, Gray With Pink Mottling, Matte, 1920s, 5 1/2 In. 35.00
Rookwood, Vase, Greek Key Pattern, Dated 1900, No.1088, 4 1/2 X 6 In. 65.00
Rookwood, Vase, Green Iridescent, XV 219, Porcelain, 4 1/2 X 3 5/8 In. 250.00
Rookwood, Vase, Holly Leaves & Berries, Fluted, Signed, 7 In. 315.00
Rookwood, Vase, Irises, Leaves, Blue, No.827, C.1927, E.T.Hurley, 11 In. 325.00
Rookwood, Vase, Jen Jensen, 1943, 6 3/4 In. 175.00
Rookwood, Vase, Lily-Of-The-Valley, 1902, Artist Signed, 7 In. 165.00
Rookwood, Vase, Matte Finish, Art Deco Design, 1926, 6 1/2 In. 65.00
Rookwood, Vase, Matte, Beaded Leaves & Berries, 827, 1927, Hentschel, 11 In. 185.00
Rookwood, Vase, Matte, 1921, 7 In. 23.00
Rookwood, Vase, Molded Flowers, 1929, 6 In. 17.50
Rookwood, Vase, Orange Leaves, C.1900, No.566d, Signed I.B., 6 1/2 In. 50.00
Rookwood, Vase, Pale Yellow, 1922, 7 In. 30.00
Rookwood, Vase, Pillow, Fish In Low Relief, 1928, 6 1/2 X 8 X 5 In. 95.00
Rookwood, Vase, Rooks Around Top, 1914, 7 1/2 In. 85.00
Rookwood, Vase, Rose, Floral, C.1923, Artist K.Jones, 8 In. 225.00
Rookwood, Vase, Roses, Leafage, Marked, Signed, C.1889, 19 1/2 In. .... Illus 1900.00
Rookwood, Vase, Rust Chrysanthemums On Bisque, Valentien, 16Z, 1885, 11 In. 765.00
Rookwood, Vase, Sara Sax, Iris Glaze, 1923, 6 In.Tall 58.00
Rookwood, Vase, Semi-Porcelain, Mexican Design, 1947, 6 In. 55.00
Rookwood, Vase, Stylized Poppies, Signed Howard Altman, 7 In. 295.00
Rookwood, Vase, Tan Ground, Blue Interior, XX1X, 5 3/8 X 6 3/8 In. 95.00
Rookwood, Vase, Vellum, Iris Blossoms, 1905, 8 In. 198.00
Rookwood, Vase, Vine & Flower, Matte Yellow, 5 In. 45.00
Rookwood, Vase, Wheat, Iris Glaze, 7 1/4 X 3 1/4 In. 250.00
Rookwood, Vase, 3 Fish, Vellum, 1907, Signed, Boxed, 4 In. 235.00
Rookwood, Vase, 3 Yellow & Blue Butterflies On Purple, C.S.Todd, 1913, 6 In. 110.00
Rookwood, Wall Pocket, Blue, 1914, Paper Label, 9 1/2 In. 65.00
Rookwood, Wall Pocket, 3 Lobed Leaves Cover Surface, 1920, 2 X 6 X 7 In. 58.00

*Rosaline glass is a rose-colored jade glass that was made by the Steuben
Glass Works in Corning, New York.*

Rosaline, Creamer, Alabaster Handle, 4 1/8 In. 100.00
Rosaline, Plate, Alabaster Intaglio Cut Wreath, Signed, 6 1/4 In., Pair 200.00

*Rose bowls were popular during the 1880s. Rose petals were kept in the open
bowl to add fragrance to a room. The glass bowls were made with crimped tops,
which kept the petals inside. Many types of Victorian art glass were made
into rose bowls.*

Rose Bowl, Basalt Cameo, English, 5 In. 125.00
Rose Bowl, Blue Opalescent, Seaweed 45.00
Rose Bowl, Blue, White Lining, Satin Glass, 3 1/2 X 4 In.Diameter 45.00
Rose Bowl, Cased Glass, Red Lining, Crimped Top, 6 In. 55.00

Rose Bowl, Egg Shaped, Diamond-Quilted, Deep Relief Over White, 4 In.	190.00
Rose Bowl, Enamel Decoration, Yellow Satin, Shell & Seaweed	215.00
Rose Bowl, Fluted Top, Enameled, Pink Satin	95.00
Rose Bowl, Fox Hunt Scene	69.00
Rose Bowl, Glass, Cased, Applique Flowers & Leaves, 2 7/8 X 4 In.Diameter	85.00
Rose Bowl, Glass, Strawberry Diamond & Fan, 8 X 6 In.	140.00
Rose Bowl, Gold Maple Leaves & Acorns, Smith Brothers, Lion Mark	145.00
Rose Bowl, Hand-Painted Pansies, Amethyst	40.00
Rose Bowl, Iridescent, Held By 2 Seals, Black Milk Glass Pedestal	47.50
Rose Bowl, Melon Ribbed, Mercury, Amethyst	85.00
Rose Bowl, Opalescent, Lavender Blue, Double Looped Top, 3 In.	27.00
Rose Bowl, Rose To Pink, 8 Crimp, 3 3/4 X 4 1/2 In.Diameter	60.00
Rose Bowl, Shell & Seaweed, Satin Glass, 3 1/4 In.	125.00
Rose Bowl, Star Cut Base, Hobstar Pattern, English Milk Glass	21.00
Rose Bowl, White Bristol Glass, Black Spots Rough Pontil	25.00
Rose Bowl, White Satin Glass, Hand-Painted, Mt.Washington, 8 X 8 In.	95.00
Rose Canton, Coffeepot	450.00
Rose Canton, Dish, Covered, Interior, Exterior Design, C.1820, 7 1/2 X 9 In.	250.00
Rose Canton, Eggcup, Set Of 2	50.00
Rose Canton, Mug, Shaving, Handled	100.00
Rose Canton, Plate, Birds & Butterflies, 9 1/2 In.	58.00
Rose Canton, Plate, Made In China, 6 In., Set Of 4	75.00
Rose Canton, Plate, Wicker Holder, Oriental Mark, 7 1/4 In.	30.00
Rose Canton, Plate, 5 3/4 In.	50.00
Rose Canton, Plate, 6 In., Set Of 8	70.00
Rose Canton, Platter, Reticulated, 11 In.	175.00

Rose Medallion china was made in China during the nineteenth and twentieth centuries. It is a distinctive design picturing people, flowers, birds, and butterflies. They are colored in greens, pinks, and other colors.

Rose Medallion, Bowl, Decorated Inside & Out, Scalloped Edge, 10 In.Deep	395.00
Rose Medallion, Bowl, Flared Rim, C.1850, 1 1/2 X 3 1/4 In.Diameter	32.50
Rose Medallion, Bowl, Fruit, Oblong, 6 3/4 X 8 3/4 X 1 3/4 In.	150.00
Rose Medallion, Bowl, Lidded, 5 1/2 In.	198.00
Rose Medallion, Bowl, Lotus Shape, Chinese Markings	175.00
Rose Medallion, Bowl, People, 9 In.Diameter	250.00
Rose Medallion, Bowl, Punch, Birds, 14 1/2 In.	850.00
Rose Medallion, Bowl, Rice, & Spoon	35.00
Rose Medallion, Bowl, Shallow, 8 1/2 In.	55.00
Rose Medallion, Bowl, Waste, 2-Handled, 3 3/4 In.	85.00
Rose Medallion, Bowl, 19th Century, 11 X 4 1/2 In.	345.00
Rose Medallion, Bowl, 4 Panels Outside, Flowers Inside, Signed, 7 In.	110.00
Rose Medallion, Bowl, 4 X 9 1/2 In.Diameter	165.00
Rose Medallion, Bowl, 8 In.Diameter	195.00
Rose Medallion, Brush-Box, Gold In Hair, 7 1/2 X 3 3/4 X 3 1/4 In.	950.00
Rose Medallion, Charger, Butterflies, 13 In.Diameter	275.00
Rose Medallion, Charger, 12 In.	95.00
Rose Medallion, Creamer, C.1850, 4 In.	85.00
Rose Medallion, Cup & Saucer	25.00 To 50.00
Rose Medallion, Cup & Saucer, Bouillon, Lid, 2-Handled	65.00
Rose Medallion, Cup & Saucer, Demitasse	20.00
Rose Medallion, Cup & Saucer, Demitasse, Made In China	30.00 To 60.00
Rose Medallion, Cup & Saucer, Hexagonal Sides, Marked China	45.00
Rose Medallion, Cup & Saucer, Set Of 6	270.00
Rose Medallion, Cup & Saucer, Wishbone Handle, Cup, 4 1/2 In.Diameter	135.00
Rose Medallion, Cup & Saucer, 6 Sided Saucer	85.00
Rose Medallion, Dish, Vegetable, Covered, Porcelain, 8 1/2 X 10 1/2 X 2 In.	150.00
Rose Medallion, Dish, Vegetable, Covered, 8 1/2 X 10 1/2 X 2 In.	135.00
Rose Medallion, Ladle, 4 3/4 In.	12.50
Rose Medallion, Lamp, Oil, Font Container, Brass Footing, 11 X 5 X 4 3/4 In.	395.00
Rose Medallion, Match Holder, English Bobby, Body Opens To Hold Matches	85.00
Rose Medallion, Mug, C.1810, 5 X 4 1/4 In.Diameter	215.00
Rose Medallion, Mustache Cup	195.00
Rose Medallion, Picnic Set, Fitted Wicker Basket, 2 Cups & Teapot	235.00
Rose Medallion, Pitcher, 19th Century, 4 In.	175.00
Rose Medallion, Plate, Butterflies, 10 1/4 In.Diameter	45.00

Rose Medallion, Plate, Dinner, Made In China	42.50
Rose Medallion, Plate, Enameled, 7 1/4 In.	25.00
Rose Medallion, Plate, Enameled, 9 1/2 In.	75.00
Rose Medallion, Plate, Face On Panels, 9 1/2 In.	95.00
Rose Medallion, Plate, Family, Roses, Birds & Butterflies, 10 In.	50.00
Rose Medallion, Plate, Gold Trim Edge, 10 In.	25.00
Rose Medallion, Plate, Hand-Painted, 6 1/2 In., Set Of 6	130.00
Rose Medallion, Plate, Hexagonal, 8 1/2 In.	90.00
Rose Medallion, Plate, Reticulated, 6 1/4 In.	35.00
Rose Medallion, Plate, Roses, Birds, Butterflies, Family, 10 In.	65.00
Rose Medallion, Plate, Scalloped Edge, 6 1/2 In.	47.50
Rose Medallion, Plate, 19 1/2 In.	50.00
Rose Medallion, Plate, 8 1/2 In.	55.00 To 60.00
Rose Medallion, Platter, Enameled, 14 X 10 In.	225.00
Rose Medallion, Platter, Muted Coloring, Oval, 14 1/2 X 11 1/2 In.	200.00
Rose Medallion, Platter, Oval, Red, Marked China, 17 3/4 In.	495.00
Rose Medallion, Platter, People Pictured, Oval, 13 In.	275.00
Rose Medallion, Punch Bowl, 19th Century, 11 X 4 1/4 In.	380.00
Rose Medallion, Seat, Garden, Hexagonal, Flowers, Birds, 18 1/2 In., Pair	3600.00
Rose Medallion, Spoon, Rice	15.00
Rose Medallion, Sugar & Creamer	125.00 To 275.00
Rose Medallion, Teapot & Cup, Wicker Basket, C.1890	170.00
Rose Medallion, Teapot, Genre Scenes, Gold In Woman's Hair	90.00
Rose Medallion, Teapot, Gooseneck Spout, Wire Handles	100.00
Rose Medallion, Teapot, Reed Double Handles, Cylindrical, 5 1/2 In.	115.00
Rose Medallion, Teapot, Satin Ribbon Handle	125.00
Rose Medallion, Teapot, Straight Sided	80.00
Rose Medallion, Teapot, Wire Handle, Interior Scene, 19th Century, 5 X 4 In.	115.00
Rose Medallion, Teapot, Wrapped Handles, Double Wires, 5 1/2 In.	98.50
Rose Medallion, Teapot, Wrapped Wire Handles, 4 Scenes, 5 X 4 In.	115.00
Rose Medallion, Tray, Dresser, 9 3/4 X 7 In.	250.00
Rose Medallion, Tray, Tea, Hold In Hair, Unfired Back	300.00
Rose Medallion, Tureen, Covered, Butterflies, Decorated Inside, 9 X 10 In.	375.00
Rose Medallion, Tureen, Covered, Butterflies, 2 Handled, 6 1/2 X 11 In.Diam.	475.00
Rose Medallion, Tureen, Covered, Hexagonal, C.1900, 8 1/2 X 6 1/2 In.	200.00
Rose Medallion, Umbrella Stand, Gold In Hair, 26 X 9 In.Diameter	2700.00
Rose Medallion, Vase, Flared At Top & Base, Center Bulbous, 15 X 11 X 9 In.	675.00
Rose Medallion, Vase, Raised People & Flowers, 7 1/2 In.	45.00
Rose Medallion, Vase, Spill	98.00
Rose Medallion, Vase, Temple, Lid, C.1850, 13 In., Pair	550.00

Rose O'Neill, see Kewpie

*Rose Tapestry porcelain was made by the Royal Bayreuth Factory of
Germany during the late nineteenth century. The surface of the ware feels
like cloth.*

Rose Tapestry, Ashtray, Pink Flowers, Royal Bayreuth	135.00
Rose Tapestry, Basket, Handled, Royal Bayreuth, Blue Mark, 4 1/4 X 2 1/4 In.	335.00
Rose Tapestry, Basket, Inside Design, Royal Bayreuth, 8 X 3 In.	265.00
Rose Tapestry, Basket, Miniature, Royal Bayreuth	140.00
Rose Tapestry, Basket, Pierced Base, Oblong, Royal Bayreuth, 5 1/2 In.	235.00
Rose Tapestry, Basket, Pierced Base, Royal Bayreuth, Blue Mark, 5 In., 5 In.	375.00
Rose Tapestry, Basket, Pink & Yellow Roses, 3 7/8 X 4 1/4 In.	165.00
Rose Tapestry, Basket, 5 X 5 In.	300.00
Rose Tapestry, Bowl, Apricot & White, Black Mark	210.00
Rose Tapestry, Bowl, Royal Bayreuth, 10 3/4 X 3 1/2 In.	625.00
Rose Tapestry, Box, Dresser, Covered, 3 Gold Feet, Pink & Yellow, Signed	165.00
Rose Tapestry, Box, Powder, Footed, Gibson Girl, Royal Bayreuth	325.00
Rose Tapestry, Box, Powder, 3 Gold Feet, Blue Mark, Royal Bayreuth, 2 1/2 In.	172.50
Rose Tapestry, Box, Powder, 3 Gold Feet, White & Pink Roses, Royal Bayreuth	175.00
Rose Tapestry, Box, Powder, 3 Gold Legs, Blue Mark, 4 1/8 In.Diameter	225.00
Rose Tapestry, Cake Plate, Royal Bayreuth, 7 1/2 In.Diameter	110.00
Rose Tapestry, Candleholder, Man On Horse, Blue Mark, 2 1/2 In.Diameter	65.00
Rose Tapestry, Candlestick, Roses, Handled, Saucer Type, Royal Bayreuth	215.00
Rose Tapestry, Creamer, Corset Shape, Pink, Blue Mark, Royal Bayreuth	130.00
Rose Tapestry, Creamer, Pinch Mouth, Blue Mark, 2 1/2 X 3 1/2 In.	135.00
Rose Tapestry, Creamer, Pinched Spout, Castle & Mountain Scene, 5 In.	395.00

Rose Tapestry, **Creamer,** Straight Shape, Small, Blue Mark	125.00
Rose Tapestry, **Creamer,** Three Color Roses, Black Mark	200.00
Rose Tapestry, **Dish,** Candy, Gold Handle, Black Mark, 8 In.	275.00
Rose Tapestry, **Dish,** Heart Shape	150.00
Rose Tapestry, **Dish,** Leaf, Royal Bayreuth	123.00
Rose Tapestry, **Dish,** Lidded, Royal Bayreuth	155.00
Rose Tapestry, **Dish,** Portrait, Clover Shaped, Ring Handle, Blue Mark	160.00
Rose Tapestry, **Dish,** Relish, Open Handles, Blue, Signed, 8 X 4 1/2 In.	185.00
Rose Tapestry, **Dish,** Relish, Royal Bayreuth, Blue Mark, 8 X 4 In.	125.00
Rose Tapestry, **Dish,** Relish, Ruffled Edge, Royal Bayreuth, Blue Mark, 8 In.	185.00
Rose Tapestry, **Dresser Set,** Tray, Hatpin Holder & Powder, Pink Roses	650.00
Rose Tapestry, **Ewer,** Blown Roses, Gold Jewels, Leaf Mark	375.00
Rose Tapestry, **Hair Receiver,** Mountain Goat, Blue, Gold Legs, Marked	165.00
Rose Tapestry, **Hair Receiver,** Pink & Yellow Roses, Signed, Royal Bayreuth	147.50
Rose Tapestry, **Hair Receiver,** Royal Bayreuth	110.00 To 195.00
Rose Tapestry, **Hair Receiver,** Royal Bayreuth, Golden Legs, 2 Parts, Signed	174.00
Rose Tapestry, **Hatpin Holder**	175.00
Rose Tapestry, **Hatpin Holder,** Lady & Horse, Blue Mark, 4 1/2 In.	295.00
Rose Tapestry, **Hatpin Holder,** Pink Flowers, Royal Bayreuth	225.00
Rose Tapestry, **Hatpin Holder,** Royal Bayreuth	225.00 To 235.00
Rose Tapestry, **Hatpin Holder,** 3 Color Roses, Perforated Gold Scroll, Signed	199.00
Rose Tapestry, **Match Holder,** Tavern Scene, Hanging, Royal Bayreuth	195.00
Rose Tapestry, **Pin Box,** Royal Bayreuth, 4 1/2 In.	185.00
Rose Tapestry, **Pitcher,** Cavaliers, Royal Bayreuth, Signed, 3 3/4 In.	135.00
Rose Tapestry, **Pitcher,** Corset Shape, Royal Bayreuth, 3 1/2 In.	150.00
Rose Tapestry, **Pitcher,** Milk, Corset Shape, Blue Mark, 4 3/4 In.	185.00
Rose Tapestry, **Pitcher,** Pinched Spout, Mountain Goats, Black Mark, 4 In.	185.00
Rose Tapestry, **Pitcher,** Pinched Spout, Royal Bayreuth, Blue Mark, 4 In.	200.00
Rose Tapestry, **Pitcher,** Pinched Spout, 5 Mountain Goats, Blue Mark, 5 In.	335.00
Rose Tapestry, **Pitcher,** Royal Bayreuth, Corinthian, Black, 5 1/2 In.	39.50
Rose Tapestry, **Pitcher,** Royal Bayreuth, Roses, Pinched Spout, Blue Mark, 4 In.	165.00
Rose Tapestry, **Pitcher,** Royal Bayreuth, 4 In.	125.00
Rose Tapestry, **Pitcher,** 3 Color, Royal Bayreuth, 4 3/4 In.	185.00
Rose Tapestry, **Planter,** Insert, Roses, Signed, Black Mark	250.00
Rose Tapestry, **Planter,** Miniature, Forest & Castle Scene	195.00
Rose Tapestry, **Plate,** Blue Mark, 7 1/2 In.	165.00
Rose Tapestry, **Plate,** Cake, Hand-Painted, Royal Bayreuth, Blue Mark, 10 In.	300.00
Rose Tapestry, **Plate,** Molded Border, Royal Bayreuth, 6 In.	135.00
Rose Tapestry, **Plate,** Royal Bayreuth, 6 In.	130.00
Rose Tapestry, **Plate,** Royal Bayreuth, 9 1/2 In.	290.00
Rose Tapestry, **Plate,** Three Colors, Blue Mark, Royal Bayreuth, 7 In.	190.00
Rose Tapestry, **Plate,** Three Colors, Blue Mark, 7 1/2 In.	165.00
Rose Tapestry, **Relish,** Royal Bayreuth, Small Open Ends, 8 X 4 1/4 In.	98.50
Rose Tapestry, **Sugar & Creamer,** Cover, Royal Bayreuth, Blue Mark	300.00
Rose Tapestry, **Sugar,** Covered, Gold Handles, Royal Bayreuth	394.00
Rose Tapestry, **Sugar,** Covered, Lady On Pony, 2 Handles	445.00
Rose Tapestry, **Toothpick,** Coal Hod	115.00
Rose Tapestry, **Tray,** Pin, Blue, Signed, 11 X 7 1/2 In.	250.00
Rose Tapestry, **Tray,** Pink Roses, Blue Mark, Royal Bayreuth, 11 X 7 3/4 In.	225.00
Rose Tapestry, **Tumbler,** Castle Scene, Royal Bayreuth	120.00 To 235.00
Rose Tapestry, **Vase,** Blue Mark, 5 In.	195.00
Rose Tapestry, **Vase,** Purple Grapes, Corset Shaped	195.00
Rose Tapestry, **Vase,** Roses, Blue Mark, 4 In.	150.00
Rose Tapestry, **Vase,** Royal Bayreuth, Scenic, German, 5 3/4 In.	95.00
Rose Tapestry, **Vase,** Royal Bayreuth, 10 In.	195.00
Rose Tapestry, **Vase,** Royal Bayreuth, 2 Handled, Liner, Signed, 3 In.	68.00
Rose Tapestry, **Vase,** Ruffled Top, Original Liner, Royal Bayreuth, 2 3/4 In.	95.00
Rose Tapestry, **Vase,** Scenic, Marked G.H., Germany, 7 In.	150.00
Rose Tapestry, **Vase,** Scenic, Tall Obelisk, Gold Handles, Signed, 13 1/2 In.	195.00
Rose Tapestry, **Vase,** Three Color, Royal Bayreuth, Green Mark, 5 In.	195.00
Rose Tapestry, **Vase,** Three Color, 4 1/2 In.	195.00
Rose Tapestry, **Wall Pocket,** Royal Bayreuth, Roses, Gold Trim, Blue Mark, 9 In.	350.00

MARKE

Rosenthal porcelain was established in Selb, Bavaria, in 1880. The German factory still continues to make fine-quality tableware and figurines.

Rosenthal, Basket, Nut, Gold Flowers, White Ground, Small	8.00
Rosenthal, Basket, Nut, White, Gold Flowers	8.00

Rosenthal, Berry Set, Cameo, Ivory Ground, Beaded Portrait Center, 5 Piece	100.00
Rosenthal, Bowl, Hand-Painted, Poppy Decoration, Gold Borders, 6 In.	155.00
Rosenthal, Bowl, Soup, 3 Reverse Mauve & White Panels, 8 In., Set Of 6	75.00
Rosenthal, Chocolate Pot, Creamer & Covered Sugar, Gold Finials, Crown Mark	125.00
Rosenthal, Chocolate Set, Tray, Pot & 6 Cups, Signed, 8 Piece	225.00
Rosenthal, Coffee Set, White Background, Hand Painted Flowers, Set Of 3	125.00
Rosenthal, Coffeepot, Pompadour, Covered, Ivory, Gold Trim	95.00
Rosenthal, Cup & Saucer, White, Wide Gold Bands	12.00
Rosenthal, Dish, Soup, Phoenix, 8 In.	12.00
Rosenthal, Figurine, Butterfly, Pedestal Base, Hand-Painted, 2 1/2 In.	35.00
Rosenthal, Figurine, Calf Licking Rear Foot, 8 1/2 X 6 In.	42.00
Rosenthal, Figurine, Colt, Rectangular Base, 7 X 7 In.	85.00
Rosenthal, Figurine, Dachshund Puppy, C.1940s, Karner, 6 X 6 In.	85.00
Rosenthal, Figurine, Egyptian Snake Charmer, Art Deco, 1925, 7 3/4 In.	395.00
Rosenthal, Figurine, Egyptian Lady Kneeling With Outstretched Arms, Signed	155.00
Rosenthal, Figurine, Exotic Bird, 5 In.	25.00
Rosenthal, Figurine, Half-Nude, Seated, Raised Arms, Signed, 7 In.	215.00
Rosenthal, Figurine, Horse, Mohammed	95.00
Rosenthal, Figurine, Horse, Rearing, Small	36.00
Rosenthal, Figurine, Nude Woman Seated On Wall, Padded With Robe	150.00
Rosenthal, Figurine, Parian Nude, No.1771, Artist Signed, 3 X 6 X 8 In.	85.00
Rosenthal, Figurine, Pouter Pigeons, Male & Female, Signed, 6 X 7 In., Pair	150.00
Rosenthal, Figurine, Seals Nuzzling, No.1377, Signed, 3 1/2 X 4 X 3 In.	55.00
Rosenthal, Figurine, Terrier, Sitting, Signed, 6 1/2 In.	75.00
Rosenthal, Fish Set, 12 Plates, 2 Tureens & Platter, Gold Borders, 16 Piece	500.00
Rosenthal, Jar, Jam, Covered, Underplate, Gold & Holly Berry, 6 In.	65.00
Rosenthal, Jar, Jam, Hand-Painted Blackberries, Signed Pemmock	75.00
Rosenthal, Pitcher, Pink Flowers, Signed, 5 1/2 In.	35.00
Rosenthal, Plaque, Alpine Retreat On Lake, Watzman Von H.Fink, 7 X 9 In.	145.00
Rosenthal, Plaque, Lake Scene, Mountain Range, Artist Signed, 8 X 9 1/4 In.	210.00
Rosenthal, Plate, Bread & Butter, Dresden, 6 In., Set Of 12	120.00
Rosenthal, Plate, Gold & Orchid Flower Edge, 7 In.	50.00
Rosenthal, Plate, Railroad, New Hampshire, 5 In.	8.00
Rosenthal, Sugar, Pink, Opaque, Tin Cover, Soft & Puffy	75.00
Rosenthal, Teapot, Sugar & Creamer, Cream Color, Floral	75.00
Rosenthal, Tray, Celery, Gold Border, Curved Sides, Signed, 11 X 6 X 2 In.	20.00
Rosenthal, Tray, Dresser, Embossed Garland, Open Handle, Marked, 12 X 8 In.	35.00
Rosenthal, Tumbler, Intaglio Cut, Panel Cut Stem, Signed, 6 1/2 In., Pair	40.00
Rosenthal, Tureen, Covered, 2-Handled, Flowers, 8 X 5 In.	79.00
Rosenthal, Vase, Art Nouveau, Gray, Pink, Blue, Artist Signed, 9 In.	125.00
Rosenthal, Vase, Pompadour, Cobalt With Gold	60.00
Rosenthal, Vase, Wall, Kinstasteibung, Selb, 4 1/2 In.	18.00
Rosenthal, Vase, Wisteria Vines, Artist Signed, R.K., 7 In.	45.00

Roseville
U.S.A.

*Roseville Pottery Co. was organized in Roseville, Ohio, in 1890.
Another plant was opened in Zanesville, Ohio, in 1898. Many types of
pottery were made. The firm closed in 1954.*

Roseville, Ashtray, Peony, No.27, 6 In.	28.00
Roseville, Ashtray, Snowberry, Blue, Marked	17.00
Roseville, Baby Dish, Duck With Hat	35.00
Roseville, Baby Dish, Hickory Dickory Dock	35.00
Roseville, Baby Dish, Rabbit	35.00
Roseville, Basket, Apple Blossom, Pink, 10 In.	36.00
Roseville, Basket, Apple Blossom, Pink, 310-10	45.00
Roseville, Basket, Footed, No.385, 13 X 9 1/2 In.	70.00
Roseville, Basket, Freesia, Blue, 7 In.	25.00
Roseville, Basket, Freezia, Burnt Orange, 7 X 8 1/2 In.	28.00
Roseville, Basket, Gardenia, Gray, 10 3/8 In.	46.00
Roseville, Basket, Hanging, Freesia, 10 In.	38.50
Roseville, Basket, Hanging, Snowberry, Blue, 6 In.	35.00
Roseville, Basket, Hanging, Zephyr Lily, Blue, 6 In.	35.00
Roseville, Basket, Imperial I, 10 In.	45.00
Roseville, Basket, Iris, Pink, 8 In.	25.00
Roseville, Basket, Magnolia, Footed, Blue, No.384, 10 1/4 X 7 1/2 In.	38.00
Roseville, Basket, Magnolia, Green, Footed, 13 X 9 1/2 In.	65.00

Roseville, Basket, Ming Tree, White, No.508, 8 In.	25.00
Roseville, Basket, Pinecone, Attached Flower Holder, 9 X 9 In.	35.00
Roseville, Basket, Pinecone, Green, 10 In.	34.00
Roseville, Basket, Pinecone, Rust, Branch Handle, 14 In.	185.00
Roseville, Basket, Silhouette, White, 8 In.	38.00
Roseville, Basket, Snowberry, Blue, 1bk-12	55.00
Roseville, Basket, Snowberry, Blue, 7 In.	20.00
Roseville, Basket, Thornapple, Blue, 12 In.	45.00
Roseville, Basket, Wincraft, Tan & Brown	27.50
Roseville, Basket, Wincraft, 209-12	45.00
Roseville, Bookend, Apple Blossom, Blue, Pair	40.00
Roseville, Bookend, Burmese Men, Green, Pair	175.00
Roseville, Bookend, Magnolia, Pair	35.00
Roseville, Bowl & Candlesticks, Water Lily, Pink, Green, Matching Set	25.00
Roseville, Bowl, Bleeding Heart, Green, No.651, 4 In.	20.00
Roseville, Bowl, Bushberry, Matching Frog, Blue, 10 In.	41.00
Roseville, Bowl, Carnelian I, 8 1/2 In.	18.00
Roseville, Bowl, Carnelian II, Marbleized, Blue, 9 1/2 In.	25.00
Roseville, Bowl, Cherry Blossom, Brown, Handles, 4 1/2 In.	50.00
Roseville, Bowl, Clematis, Handled, Green, 8 In.	20.00
Roseville, Bowl, Donatello, RV Mark, 7 In.	55.00
Roseville, Bowl, Donatello, 8 1/2 X 3 In.	37.50
Roseville, Bowl, Imperial II, Hand Thrown, Yellow Drip, 4 X 6 1/2 In.	45.00
Roseville, Bowl, Ixia, Handles, 9 In.	27.50
Roseville, Bowl, Mock Orange, Pink, 6 In.	12.50 To 17.50
Roseville, Bowl, Morning Glory, Bulbous, 2 Small Handles, 4 X 7 In.	38.00
Roseville, Bowl, Pinecone, No.263, Green, 14 In.	55.00
Roseville, Bowl, Pinecone, 2 Handled, 5 In.Diameter	25.00
Roseville, Bowl, Poppy, Handled, Green, Matching Frog, 8 In.	32.50
Roseville, Bowl, Poppy, Matching Frog, Handled, Green, 8 In.	32.50
Roseville, Bowl, Silhouette, White, 4 In.	12.50
Roseville, Bowl, Waterlily, Brown, 5 In.	25.00
Roseville, Bowl, Windsor, Blue, Console, 16 In.	70.00
Roseville, Bowl, Wisteria, 4 In.	35.00
Roseville, Cache Pot & Underplate, Magnolia, Green, 5 In.	20.00
Roseville, Candleholder, Bushberry, Green, 1147-Cs, 2 In., Pair	10.00
Roseville, Candleholder, Clematis, Brown, Pair	30.00
Roseville, Candleholder, Fuchsia, Frog, 5 In.	80.00
Roseville, Candleholder, Pink, Snowberry, No.1-Cs-2, 4 1/2 In., Pair	22.50
Roseville, Candleholder, Snowberry, Pink, No.2-Cs-2, 4 1/2 In., Pair	22.50
Roseville, Candleholder, Zephyr Lily, Blue, 2 In., Pair	17.50
Roseville, Candlestick, Columbine, Blue, 2 1/2 In., Pair	22.00
Roseville, Candlestick, Creamware, Storybook Type, Handle, 7 In.	65.00
Roseville, Candlestick, Foxglove, Blue	9.00
Roseville, Candlestick, Magnolia, Brown, 4 1/2 In., Pair	22.00
Roseville, Candlestick, Panel, Brown, 2 In.	12.00
Roseville, Candlestick, Panel, 2 In., Pair	28.00
Roseville, Candlestick, Snowberry, 4 3/4 In., Pair	18.00
Roseville, Celery, Foxglove, Green	22.00
Roseville, Center Piece, Ming, 2 Handles, 4 3/4 X 14 In.	38.00
Roseville, Cookie Jar, Freesia, Brown, 8 In.	40.00
Roseville, Cookie Jar, Magnolia, Pink, 8 In.	90.00
Roseville, Cookie Jar, Water Lily, 8 In.	65.00
Roseville, Cookie Jar, Waterlily	65.00
Roseville, Cornucopia, Apple Blossom, Rose	25.00
Roseville, Cornucopia, Clematis, Green, 6 In.	15.00
Roseville, Creamer, Freesia, Blue	13.00
Roseville, Cuspidor, Rozane	65.00
Roseville, Dish, Baby, Bunnies	25.00
Roseville, Dish, Child's, Santa Claus	75.00
Roseville, Dish, Donatello, Pedestal, 5 X 6 1/2 In.	50.00
Roseville, Dish, Peony, 2 Handles, Pink, 3 X 7 In.	18.00
Roseville, Dish, Pinecone, Oblong, 12 In.	30.00
Roseville, Dish, Rosecraft Vintage, 2 1/4 X 7 1/2 In.	22.00
Roseville, Dish, Windsor, 2 Handle, Marked, Sticker, 2 1/2 X 16 In.	55.00
Roseville, Ewer, Bleeding Heart, Pink, 15 In.	85.00

Roseville, Ewer, Bleeding Heart, Pink, 18 In.	115.00
Roseville, Ewer, Foxglove, Green, 6 1/2 In.	36.00
Roseville, Ewer, Freesia, Green, Purple, 15 In.	55.00
Roseville, Ewer, Freesia, Rust, 6 In.	25.00
Roseville, Ewer, Magnolia, 10 1/2 In.	60.00
Roseville, Ewer, Snowberry, 10 1/2 In.	45.00
Roseville, Flower Frog, Clematis, Green Mark, U.S.A.	14.00
Roseville, Inkwell, Egyptian, Rozane, Green, 5 X 3 1/8 In.	140.00
Roseville, Jardiniere, Apple Blossom, Pink, Pedestal, 31 In.	275.00
Roseville, Jardiniere, Baneda, Rose, 24 In.	450.00
Roseville, Jardiniere, Carnelian, Spongeware, 6 1/4 X 7 In.	50.00
Roseville, Jardiniere, Cherry Blossom, Pink Fence, 8 In.	95.00
Roseville, Jardiniere, Clematis, White, Blue, Pedestal, Marked, 25 X 9 In.	165.00
Roseville, Jardiniere, Corinthian, 8 X 11 In.	100.00
Roseville, Jardiniere, Cosmos, Blue, 4 In.	16.00
Roseville, Jardiniere, Dahlrose, 2 Handles, 12 In.	65.00
Roseville, Jardiniere, Donatello, Bulbous, 28 In.	425.00
Roseville, Jardiniere, Donatello, 10 In.	75.00
Roseville, Jardiniere, Donatello, 6 X 7 1/4 In.	36.00
Roseville, Jardiniere, Foxglove, Pink, No.659, 6 In.	22.00
Roseville, Jardiniere, Freesia, Blue, 8 In.	78.00
Roseville, Jardiniere, Freesia, Green, 24 In.	190.00
Roseville, Jardiniere, Futura, 7 X 10 In.	45.00
Roseville, Jardiniere, Peony, Green, No.661, Pedestal, 10 In.	225.00
Roseville, Jardiniere, Pinecone, Pedestal, 15 In.	185.00
Roseville, Jardiniere, Velmoss II, 6 In.	45.00
Roseville, Jardiniere, Velmoss II, 6 In.Diameter	28.00
Roseville, Jardiniere, White Rose, Brown, No.88, 7 In.	35.00
Roseville, Jug, Tuscany, 10 In.	32.50
Roseville, Lamp, Orian, Electric, 20 1/2 In.	75.00
Roseville, Lamp, Pinecone, Green, Twig Handle, 10 In.	60.00
Roseville, Mug, Dutch	40.00
Roseville, Mug, Dutch, 5 In.	40.00
Roseville, Mug, Elk	40.00
Roseville, Mug, Rozane, Cherries Decoration	110.00
Roseville, Paperweight, Rozane, Pansy Decoration, Signed, Pillsbury	155.00
Roseville, Pinecone Vase, Wincraft, Blue, 6 In.	12.50
Roseville, Pitcher, Boy, Embossed	95.00
Roseville, Pitcher, Child's, Yellow Chicks	19.50
Roseville, Pitcher, Colonial, Blue Sponging, Scallops	55.00
Roseville, Pitcher, Cream, Child's, 3 Faded Bunnies	15.00
Roseville, Pitcher, Peony, Ice Lip, Green, No.1326, 7 1/2 In.	50.00
Roseville, Pitcher, Peony, Water	50.00 To 55.00
Roseville, Pitcher, Tankard, Dutch, 11 1/2 In.	75.00
Roseville, Pitcher, Water, Boy With Horn	50.00
Roseville, Pitcher, Water, Fuchsia	50.00
Roseville, Planter, Apple Blossom, Pink, 8 In.	16.00 To 26.00
Roseville, Planter, Bushberry, Burnt Orange, 12 X 3 In.	20.00
Roseville, Planter, Hanging, Water Lily, Blue, Chain, 8 X 5 1/2 In.	35.00
Roseville, Planter, Tourmaline, Aqua Drizzles, 5 X 13 In.	30.00
Roseville, Planter, Wincraft, Tulip In Open Center, 10 1/2 X 6 In.	25.00
Roseville, Plate & Creamer, Child's, Ducks, Rv Mark	45.00
Roseville, Plate, Child's, Chicks	34.00
Roseville, Pot, Flower, Hanging, Azurine, Chains	45.00
Roseville, Shell, Conch, Blue, No.453, 6 In.	38.00
Roseville, Shell, Conch, Brown, No.454, 8 In.	52.00
Roseville, Shell, Conch, Magnolia, Green	30.00
Roseville, Shell, Conch, Water Lily, Blue, 438-8	38.00
Roseville, Shell, Conch, Water Lily, Brown, 438, 8 In.	45.00
Roseville, Shell, Scalloped, 6 1/2 In.	27.50
Roseville, Sugar & Creamer, Apple Blossom, Blue	32.00
Roseville, Sugar, Magnolia, 3 In.	10.00
Roseville, Tankard, Elk	100.00
Roseville, Tankard, Wild Flower, C.1915	75.00
Roseville, Tea Set, Magnolia, Blue	75.00
Roseville, Tea Set, White Rose, Pink	85.00 8

Roseville, Tea Set, Zephyr Lily, Blue	75.00
Roseville, Teapot & Creamer, Clematis, Rust	65.00
Roseville, Teapot & Creamer, Snowberry, Rose	65.00
Roseville, Teapot, Magnolia, Green	50.00
Roseville, Teapot, Peony, Gold	45.00
Roseville, Tray, Peony, Rose, Handled, 10 3/4 In.	40.00
Roseville, Tray, Zephyr Lily, 14 In.	38.00
Roseville, Urn, Topeo, 6 In.	40.00
Roseville, Urn, Turquoise, Handled, 10 X 25 In.	85.00
Roseville, Vase, Apple Blossom, Handles, Blue, 8 In.	30.00
Roseville, Vase, Aztec, 11 In.	185.00
Roseville, Vase, Baneda, 6 In.	18.00
Roseville, Vase, Baneda, 7 1/4 In.	35.00
Roseville, Vase, Blackberry, 2 Handled, 5 In.	25.00 To 45.00
Roseville, Vase, Bleeding Heart, Handles, Blue, 8 In.	20.00
Roseville, Vase, Bleeding Heart, Pink, Notched Rim, 6 1/4 In.	18.00
Roseville, Vase, Bleeding Heart, Pink, 5 1/2 In.	14.00
Roseville, Vase, Bud, Bushberry, Handled, 7 In.	13.00
Roseville, Vase, Bud, Carnelian, Blue On Blue, 7 In.	20.00
Roseville, Vase, Bud, Dogwood, 8 3/4 In.	18.00
Roseville, Vase, Bud, Handled, Bushberry, 7 In.	13.00
Roseville, Vase, Bud, Magnolia, 7 1/2 In.	25.00
Roseville, Vase, Bushberry, Pedestal, 6 1/4 In.	18.00
Roseville, Vase, Bushberry, 2 Handled, Blue, 15 In.	65.00
Roseville, Vase, Carnelian I, 8 In.	25.00
Roseville, Vase, Carnelian 1, Side Handles, 13 In.	50.00
Roseville, Vase, Carnelian 1, 6 In.	18.00
Roseville, Vase, Carnelian, 11, Pink Mottle, 9 X 6 In.	48.00
Roseville, Vase, Cherry Blossom, Brown, 12 1/2 In.	100.00
Roseville, Vase, Clematis, Blue, 7 In., Pair	30.00
Roseville, Vase, Clematis, Handles, Green, 6 In.	12.50
Roseville, Vase, Cremona, Six Sided, Pink, 4 In.	18.00
Roseville, Vase, Dahlrose, 10 In.	15.00
Roseville, Vase, Dahlrose, 6 X 3 In.	16.00
Roseville, Vase, Donatello, Cherubs, 9 3/4 X 4 In.Diameter	50.00
Roseville, Vase, Double, Donatello, Connecting Panel, 8 X 4 In.	30.00
Roseville, Vase, Earlam, 2 Handled, Crown, Green, 7 X 8 1/2 In.	42.00
Roseville, Vase, Earlam, 7 In.	46.00
Roseville, Vase, Foxglove, Pink, Handles, 8 In.	25.00
Roseville, Vase, Freesia, Blue, Handles, 9 In.	20.00
Roseville, Vase, Freesia, Brown, Handles, 9 In.	20.00
Roseville, Vase, Freesia, Green, Shoulder Handled, 15 1/2 In.	55.00
Roseville, Vase, Freesia, Handled, Green, No.128-15, 10 1/2 In.	60.00
Roseville, Vase, Freesia, No.123, Green, Signed, 9 In.	48.00
Roseville, Vase, Fuschia, 2 Handled, Blue, 8 1/4 In.	34.00
Roseville, Vase, Futura, 5 1/2 X 5 1/2 In.	38.00
Roseville, Vase, Iris, Pink, 4 In.	17.00
Roseville, Vase, Ixia, Fan, Green, 10 In.	37.50
Roseville, Vase, Ixia, Rust, 6 In.	20.00
Roseville, Vase, Jonquil, 8 1/2 In.	45.00
Roseville, Vase, Laurel, Green, 6 In., Pair	45.00
Roseville, Vase, Lotus, Maroon & Beige, 10 In.	75.00
Roseville, Vase, Luffa, Handled, 8 In.	23.00
Roseville, Vase, Luffa, Original Seal, 7 1/2 In.	32.00
Roseville, Vase, Magnolia, Brown, Green, Handled, 8 X 10 In.	41.00
Roseville, Vase, Magnolia, Brown, 6 In.	16.00
Roseville, Vase, Magnolia, Green, 5 In.	12.00
Roseville, Vase, Magnolia, No.95, 10 In.	32.50
Roseville, Vase, Monticello, Green, 4 In.	30.00
Roseville, Vase, Mostique, Glazed, 7 3/4 X 3 3/4 In.	45.00
Roseville, Vase, Mostique, Gray, 6 X 3 1/4 In.	22.00
Roseville, Vase, Mostique, 6 In.	16.00
Roseville, Vase, Orion, Yellow, Aqua, Handled, Original Label, 13 In.	25.00
Roseville, Vase, Peony, Footed, 2 Handles, 6 1/4 In.	14.00
Roseville, Vase, Peony, Gold, 18 In.	165.00
Roseville, Vase, Peony, Green, Footed, Side Handled, 15 1/4 In.	70.00

Roseville, Vase, Peony, No.65, Gold, 9 In.	18.00
Roseville, Vase, Peony, No.66, 10 In.	28.00
Roseville, Vase, Pinecone, Brown, 6 In.	19.00
Roseville, Vase, Pinecone, Green, Footed, Gold Sticker, 10 X 5 In.	29.00
Roseville, Vase, Pinecone, Green, Footed, Handled, No.709-10, 10 3/8 In.	40.00
Roseville, Vase, Pinecone, Green, 10 1/2 In.	55.00
Roseville, Vase, Pinecone, No.711-10, Green, 10 1/4 In.	55.00
Roseville, Vase, Pinecone, No.745, Footed, 7 In.	36.00
Roseville, Vase, Pink, Thornapple, 4 X 6 In.	16.00
Roseville, Vase, Rosecraft, Yellow, Red Mark, 6 In.	28.00
Roseville, Vase, Rozane, Clover Decoration, 5 1/2 In.	87.50
Roseville, Vase, Russco, Green, Cream, 2 Handled, 8 1/4 In.	39.00
Roseville, Vase, Snowberry, 2 Handled, Pedestal Base, Pink, 7 1/4 In.	15.00
Roseville, Vase, Tourist, 9 In.	375.00
Roseville, Vase, Tourmaline, 5 1/4 In.	45.00
Roseville, Vase, Tourmaline, 7 In.	47.50
Roseville, Vase, Volpato, Black Sticker, 6 1/2 In.	85.00
Roseville, Vase, Water Lily, 6 In.	18.00
Roseville, Vase, White Rose, Blue, 6 In.	10.00
Roseville, Vase, Wincraft, No.289, Green, 18 In.	55.00
Roseville, Vase, Wincraft, Tulip, Blue, 8 In.	12.50
Roseville, Vase, Zephyr Lily, Blue, 15 In.	55.00
Roseville, Wall Pocket, Apple Blossom, Pink	20.00
Roseville, Wall Pocket, Clematis	32.00
Roseville, Wall Pocket, Clematis, Brown	25.00
Roseville, Wall Pocket, Clematis, Green	20.00
Roseville, Wall Pocket, Clematis, No.1295, Blue, 8 In.	20.00
Roseville, Wall Pocket, Clematis, Orange	20.00
Roseville, Wall Pocket, Corinthian, 12 In.	35.00
Roseville, Wall Pocket, Corinthian, 12 3/8 In.	40.00
Roseville, Wall Pocket, Corinthian, 9 1/2 In.	25.00
Roseville, Wall Pocket, Cosmos, Double, Green	25.00
Roseville, Wall Pocket, Dogwood 11, Single	25.00
Roseville, Wall Pocket, Dogwood, 11, Double	30.00
Roseville, Wall Pocket, Donatello, 9 1/2 In.	30.00
Roseville, Wall Pocket, Florentine, Brown, 9 1/2 In.	25.00
Roseville, Wall Pocket, Florentine, 12 1/2 In.	40.00
Roseville, Wall Pocket, Freesia, Blue	20.00
Roseville, Wall Pocket, Gardenia, Gray	30.00
Roseville, Wall Pocket, Mayfair, Brown	20.00
Roseville, Wall Pocket, Mostique, 12 In.	30.00
Roseville, Wall Pocket, Panel, Red	25.00
Roseville, Wall Pocket, Peony, Orange	20.00
Roseville, Wall Pocket, Peony, Pink	20.00
Roseville, Wall Pocket, Rosecraft Vintage	45.00
Roseville, Wall Pocket, Rozane Line, 8 In.	35.00
Roseville, Wall Pocket, Rozane, 1917	40.00
Roseville, Wall Pocket, Silhouette, White, 8 In.	28.00
Roseville, Wall Pocket, Snowberry, Blue	20.00
Roseville, Wall Pocket, Snowberry, Pink	15.00 To 28.00
Roseville, Wall Pocket, Snowberry, Rose	25.00
Roseville, Wall Pocket, White Rose, Pink	20.00
Roseville, Wall Pocket, Wincraft	20.00
Roseville, Wall Pocket, Zephyr Lily, Blue	10.00
Roseville, Wall Pocket, Zephyr Lily, Green	20.00
Rosewood, Tea Caddy, Inlaid, Regency, 1800s, Hinged, 7 X 12 In.	250.00
Rouen, Inkstand, Rust & Yellow, Dated 1780, French, 8 X 2 X 6 1/2 In.	75.00

 *Rowland and Marsellus Company is a mark which appears on historical Staffordshire dating from the late nineteenth and early twentieth centuries. Rowland and Marsellus is believed to be the British Anchor Pottery Co. of Longton, England. Many American views were made.*

Rowland & Marsellus, Plate, New Bedford, Massachusetts, Rolled Edge, Blue	25.00
Rowland & Marsellus, Plate, Topeka, Kansas, Rolled Edge, Blue	25.00
Rowland & Marsellus, Plate, William Shakespeare, 10 In.	58.00
Roy Rogers, Album, R.C.A., 78 R.P.M.	12.50

Roy Rogers, Badge, Deputy .... 4.50 To 20.00
Roy Rogers, Bank, Boot, Metal 39.00
Roy Rogers, Belt, Leather 10.00
Roy Rogers, Camera .... 12.00 To 15.00
Roy Rogers, Camera, Box, Flash Attachment 25.00
Roy Rogers, Clicker, Tin 10.00
Roy Rogers, Clock, Alarm, Boxed 65.00
Roy Rogers, Guitar, 29 In. 15.00
Roy Rogers, Hat, Quick Shooter .... 15.00 To 28.00
Roy Rogers, Knife 15.00
Roy Rogers, Lamp, Trigger, Figural 27.95
Roy Rogers, Lantern, Metal Lithograph 4.00
Roy Rogers, Lantern, Tin 10.00
Roy Rogers, Lucky Piece 5.50
Roy Rogers, Lunch Box .... 10.00 To 12.50
Roy Rogers, Lunch Pail, Double R Bar Ranch 6.00
Roy Rogers, Mug, Plastic .... 6.00 To 10.00
Roy Rogers, Pen, Ink 5.00
Roy Rogers, Pistol, Cap 12.00
Roy Rogers, Puzzle 4.00
Roy Rogers, Shirt, Knit, White & Red Trim, Size 8 .... 10.00
Roy Rogers, Truck & Horse Trailer, Tin, Marx, C.1940 .... 18.00
Roy Rogers, Wristwatch, Original Band 40.00
Royal Austria, Bowl, Rose Dubarry, Gold Background, Red Roses 35.00
Royal Austria, Bowl, Serving, Hand-Painted, Autumn Leaves, Signed 37.50
Royal Austria, Bowl, Soup, Hand-Painted Seashells, Artist Initials 35.00
Royal Austria, Candleholder, Hand-Painted, Gold Top, Marked, 4 1/2 In. 25.00
Royal Austria, Cup, Sherbet, Hand-Painted, Set Of 6 .... 108.00
Royal Austria, Plate, Hand-Painted, Pink Morning Glories, 8 3/4 In. 12.50
Royal Austria, Plate, Morning Glories, Hand-Painted, 8 1/2 In. 12.50
Royal Austria, Salt & Pepper, Roses 12.00
Royal Austria, Salt, Hand-Painted, Heart Shape, Set Of 4 .... 18.00
Royal Austria, Tankard, Currants & Flowers, Gold Rim & Handle, 13 1/2 In. 127.00
Royal Austria, Tray, Green To Blue Background, Yellow Roses, Signed, Oblong 42.00

*The Royal Bayreuth factory was founded in Tettau, Bavaria, in 1794.
It has continued to modern times. The marks have changed through the years.
A stylized crest, the name "Royal Bayreuth" and the word "Bavaria"
appear in slightly different form from 1870 to about 1919. Later dishes
include the words "U. S. Zone, " the year of the issue, or do not have
the word "Bavaria."*

Royal Bayreuth, see also Rose Tapestry, Sand Babies, Snow
Babies, Sunbonnet Babies

Royal Bayreuth, Ashtray, Art Deco, Gold & Black, Red Mark, 4 1/4 X 4 3/8 In. 12.50
Royal Bayreuth, Ashtray, Cards, Marked 22.50
Royal Bayreuth, Ashtray, Clown, 7 In.Diameter 120.00
Royal Bayreuth, Ashtray, Corinthian Ware, Black Ground, Acanthus Border 23.00
Royal Bayreuth, Ashtray, Devil Head, Red, Blue Mark 45.00
Royal Bayreuth, Ashtray, Elk, Blue Mark 95.00
Royal Bayreuth, Ashtray, Goose Girl 30.00
Royal Bayreuth, Ashtray, Heart Shaped, Courting Scene, Signed, 5 In. 57.00
Royal Bayreuth, Ashtray, Hillside Scene, 4 Sheep, Triangular, Marked 60.00
Royal Bayreuth, Ashtray, Jack & The Beanstalk, Diamond Shape, Blue Mark 69.00
Royal Bayreuth, Ashtray, Little Boy Blue, Heart Shape, Signed, Blue Mark 69.00
Royal Bayreuth, Ashtray, Moose, Black Mark, 6 X 4 In. 75.00
Royal Bayreuth, Ashtray, Mountain Goats 66.00
Royal Bayreuth, Basket, Donkey, 5 1/2 In. 225.00
Royal Bayreuth, Basket, Scalloped Top, Handle Striped In Gilt, 4 1/4 In. 300.00
Royal Bayreuth, Bell, Wooden Clapper, Fox Hunt Scene, Blue Mark 135.00
Royal Bayreuth, Berry Set, Large Bowl, 6 Small Bowls 165.00
Royal Bayreuth, Bowl, Floral Decoration, Signed, Large 130.00
Royal Bayreuth, Bowl, Jack & Jill Picture & Verse, Black Mark, 6 In. 85.00
Royal Bayreuth, Bowl, Lobster, Blue Mark, 8 In. 95.00
Royal Bayreuth, Bowl, Pearlized Finish, Roses, 11 In. 125.00
Royal Bayreuth, Bowl, Raised Tomatoes, Leaves & White Flowers, 9 1/2 In. 45.00
Royal Bayreuth, Bowl, Red Poppy, Marked, 9 In. 85.00
Royal Bayreuth, Bowl, Salad, Lobster On Lettuce Leaf, 9 1/2 In. 150.00

Royal Bayreuth, Bowl, Salad, Tomato, Green Leaf Pedestal Base, 8 X 4 In.	75.00
Royal Bayreuth, Bowl, Shaded Green, Bunches Of Grapes, 11 In.	85.00
Royal Bayreuth, Box,Powder, Footed, Green & White, Gold Trim	48.00
Royal Bayreuth, Box, Circular, Dome Covered, 4 Gilt Legs, 4 1/4 In.	175.00
Royal Bayreuth, Box, Couple Seated On Rock, Green Mark, 3 X 1 1/2 In.Diam.	85.00
Royal Bayreuth, Box, Covered, Hand-Painted, Blue Mark, 5 1/2 X 3 3/4 In.	70.00
Royal Bayreuth, Box, Covered, Jack & Jill, Blue Mark, 2 1/2 X 2 1/2 In.	75.00
Royal Bayreuth, Box, Covered, Little Bo-Peep, 1 1/2 X 2 3/4 In.	125.00
Royal Bayreuth, Box, Covered, Musicians, Black Mark, 3 In.Diameter	68.00
Royal Bayreuth, Box, Dome Lidded, Three Gold Feet, Blue Mark, 3 1/4 X 4 In.	85.00
Royal Bayreuth, Box, Hunt Scene On Lid, Blue Mark, 5 In.	30.00
Royal Bayreuth, Box, Pin, Castle Scene, Blue Mark	55.00
Royal Bayreuth, Box, Pin, Cover, Pastoral Scene, Signed, Blue Mark, 2 X 4 In.	95.00
Royal Bayreuth, Box, Powder, Hand-Painted Yellow Rose	45.00
Royal Bayreuth, Box, Trinket, Pastoral Scene	32.00
Royal Bayreuth, Box, Trinket, Shield Shape, Blue Mark, 2 X 2 1/2 In.	60.00
Royal Bayreuth, Candleholder, Corinthian, Handle	65.00
Royal Bayreuth, Candlestick, Basset	195.00
Royal Bayreuth, Candlestick, Bent Handle, Cock Fight Scene, Blue Mark	75.00
Royal Bayreuth, Candlestick, Cavalier, Blue Mark	60.00
Royal Bayreuth, Candlestick, Chamber, 2-Handled, Blue Mark, 5 1/2 In.	85.00
Royal Bayreuth, Candlestick, Elk	50.00
Royal Bayreuth, Candlestick, Floral Design, Gold Trim, Blue Mark, 4 In., Pair	50.00
Royal Bayreuth, Candlestick, Fox Hunt, Pair	100.00
Royal Bayreuth, Candlestick, Handled, Black, 5 3/4 In.	54.50
Royal Bayreuth, Candlestick, Jack Horner	110.00
Royal Bayreuth, Candlestick, Little Boy Blue, Shield Back	185.00
Royal Bayreuth, Candlestick, Penguins Walking, Black	25.00
Royal Bayreuth, Celery, Lobster, 12 1/2 In.	75.00
Royal Bayreuth, Celery, Stippled Grape & Festoon, C.1870	45.00
Royal Bayreuth, Chamberstick, Figural Rose, Blue Mark	225.00
Royal Bayreuth, Chamberstick, Handle, Trees, Cows, Blue Mark	125.00
Royal Bayreuth, Chamberstick, Murex Shell	150.00
Royal Bayreuth, Chamberstick, Poppy, Red, Blue Mark	110.00
Royal Bayreuth, Chocolate Pot, Boy With Donkeys, Blue Mark	135.00
Royal Bayreuth, Chocolate Set, Pink Flowers, Gold, White, Blue Mark, 15 Piece	225.00
Royal Bayreuth, Clock, Silver Tapestry, Pink Bouquet, Marked	350.00
Royal Bayreuth, Compote, Pastoral Scene, Signed, Blue Mark, 5 7/8 In.	100.00
Royal Bayreuth, Compote, Pink Roses, Scalloped Border, 2 3/8 X 3 1/2 In.	35.00
Royal Bayreuth, Cracker Jar, Lobster Figural	195.00
Royal Bayreuth, Cracker Jar, Tomato	185.00
Royal Bayreuth, Creamer & Sugar, Overlay Of Gold	75.00
Royal Bayreuth, Creamer, Alligator, Blue Mark	145.00
Royal Bayreuth, Creamer, Apple, Blue Mark	35.00 To 65.00
Royal Bayreuth, Creamer, Art Nouveau, Blue Mark, 4 In.	90.00
Royal Bayreuth, Creamer, Bass, Blue Mark	95.00
Royal Bayreuth, Creamer, Beetle, Blue Mark, Signed	185.00
Royal Bayreuth, Creamer, Bird Of Paradise, Blue Mark	160.00
Royal Bayreuth, Creamer, Black Bear, Blue Mark, 4 1/2 In.	90.00
Royal Bayreuth, Creamer, Black Cat, Red Trim, Black Eyes, Blue Mark	90.00
Royal Bayreuth, Creamer, Black Crow, Blue Mark	95.00
Royal Bayreuth, Creamer, Black Owl, Red Eyes	130.00
Royal Bayreuth, Creamer, Black Water Buffalo	85.00 To 90.00
Royal Bayreuth, Creamer, Blue Mark, 4 1/2 In.	50.00
Royal Bayreuth, Creamer, Blue Top, Dutch Women, Blue Mark	75.00
Royal Bayreuth, Creamer, Bo-Peep, Blue Mark	85.00
Royal Bayreuth, Creamer, Card & Devil, Blue Mark	90.00
Royal Bayreuth, Creamer, Cat, Black	85.00
Royal Bayreuth, Creamer, Cat, Gray, Blue Mark	120.00
Royal Bayreuth, Creamer, Chicken	95.00
Royal Bayreuth, Creamer, Chrysanthemum, Blue Mark	100.00
Royal Bayreuth, Creamer, Clown, Red, Blue Mark	110.00
Royal Bayreuth, Creamer, Clown, Tilted Head, Hat Is Spout	120.00
Royal Bayreuth, Creamer, Coachman, Signed	130.00
Royal Bayreuth, Creamer, Conch Shell, Blue Mark, 4 1/2 In.	55.00
Royal Bayreuth, Creamer, Conch, Iridescent	45.00

Royal Bayreuth, Creamer, Corinthian, Salmon Lining, Black Mark, 4 1/2 In.	48.00
Royal Bayreuth, Creamer, Covered, Lobster On Leaf, Marked, 5 In.	70.00
Royal Bayreuth, Creamer, Cows In Pasture, Blue Mark, Signed, 4 In.	60.00
Royal Bayreuth, Creamer, Cows, Yellow & Brown Ground	55.00
Royal Bayreuth, Creamer, Crow, Black Mark	75.00
Royal Bayreuth, Creamer, Dachshund, Liver Colorations	75.00
Royal Bayreuth, Creamer, Dachshund, Liver & Gray, Signed	125.00
Royal Bayreuth, Creamer, Devil & Cards, Black Mark	58.00 To 70.00
Royal Bayreuth, Creamer, Devil & Cards, Blue Mark	85.00 To 125.00
Royal Bayreuth, Creamer, Duck	95.00
Royal Bayreuth, Creamer, Duck, Signed, Blue Mark	85.00 To 100.00
Royal Bayreuth, Creamer, Dutch Scene	52.50
Royal Bayreuth, Creamer, Eagle, Blue Mark	110.00 To 135.00
Royal Bayreuth, Creamer, Elk	30.00 To 85.00
Royal Bayreuth, Creamer, Elk, Blue Mark, C.1910, 5 In.	55.00
Royal Bayreuth, Creamer, Elk, Blue Mark, 4 1/2 In.	40.00
Royal Bayreuth, Creamer, Farm Scene, Chicken & Rooster, Blue Mark	65.00
Royal Bayreuth, Creamer, Farm Scene, Mountain Goats, Yellow, Green, 3 In.	45.00
Royal Bayreuth, Creamer, Fish	80.00 To 115.00
Royal Bayreuth, Creamer, French Poodle, Signed	160.00
Royal Bayreuth, Creamer, Frog	55.00
Royal Bayreuth, Creamer, Girl & Dog, Black Mark, 3 In.	85.00
Royal Bayreuth, Creamer, Grapes, Mother-Of-Pearl	145.00
Royal Bayreuth, Creamer, Green & Brown Background, Sheep, 4 In.	48.00
Royal Bayreuth, Creamer, Green Oak Leaf Pattern	90.00
Royal Bayreuth, Creamer, Hand-Painted Peasant & Turkeys, 2 5/8 In.	54.00
Royal Bayreuth, Creamer, Horses & Peasant, Signed	145.00
Royal Bayreuth, Creamer, Hunting Scene, 4 In.	60.00
Royal Bayreuth, Creamer, Jack Horner	55.00
Royal Bayreuth, Creamer, Little Boy Blue	85.00
Royal Bayreuth, Creamer, Lobster & Claw Handle, Green, 4 In.	35.00
Royal Bayreuth, Creamer, Man Of The Mountain	97.50
Royal Bayreuth, Creamer, Monkey, Green, Blue Mark	70.00
Royal Bayreuth, Creamer, Mountain Goat	120.00
Royal Bayreuth, Creamer, Mountain Goat, Blue Mark	60.00 To 135.00
Royal Bayreuth, Creamer, Musicians' Scene, 4 X 4 In.	75.00
Royal Bayreuth, Creamer, Old Man Of Mountain, Tettau Mark	55.00
Royal Bayreuth, Creamer, Old Man Of The Mountain	43.00
Royal Bayreuth, Creamer, Orange Frog, Blue Mark	90.00
Royal Bayreuth, Creamer, Orange, Green Leaf & Stem Trim	97.00
Royal Bayreuth, Creamer, Owl, Blue Mark	129.00
Royal Bayreuth, Creamer, Oyster & Pearl Glass	42.50
Royal Bayreuth, Creamer, Pansy, Purple, Blue Mark	95.00
Royal Bayreuth, Creamer, Parakeet, Blue Mark	135.00
Royal Bayreuth, Creamer, Pastoral Scenes, Flared Base, Signed	90.00
Royal Bayreuth, Creamer, Poodle	105.00 To 125.00
Royal Bayreuth, Creamer, Poppy, Signed	50.00
Royal Bayreuth, Creamer, Red Devil, Card	65.00
Royal Bayreuth, Creamer, Red Frog, Blue Mark	60.00
Royal Bayreuth, Creamer, Red Poppy, Blue Mark	85.00
Royal Bayreuth, Creamer, Robin, Blue Mark	100.00 To 142.00
Royal Bayreuth, Creamer, Rooster	115.00
Royal Bayreuth, Creamer, Scene Of Cows, Boats, Flower Border	42.00
Royal Bayreuth, Creamer, Scenic, Cattle, Puckered Spout, 3 In.	89.00
Royal Bayreuth, Creamer, Seagulls, Ship & Woman In Field, 3 3/4 In.	70.00
Royal Bayreuth, Creamer, Seal	175.00
Royal Bayreuth, Creamer, Sheep On Hillside, 4 In.	65.00
Royal Bayreuth, Creamer, Snake, Blue Mark	210.00
Royal Bayreuth, Creamer, St.Bernard	50.00 To 120.00
Royal Bayreuth, Creamer, Strawberry, Marked	68.00
Royal Bayreuth, Creamer, Swans On Pond, Blue Mark, Signed, 4 In.	60.00
Royal Bayreuth, Creamer, Toby	120.00
Royal Bayreuth, Creamer, Tomato, Lettuce Leaf Underplate, Marked	40.00
Royal Bayreuth, Creamer, Tri-Cornered Hat Lid	65.00
Royal Bayreuth, Creamer, Water Buffalo, Black, Red Horns, 3 1/2 In.	110.00
Royal Bayreuth, Creamer, Water Buffalo, Gray & White	95.00

Royal Bayreuth, **Creamer,** 3 Cows In Pasture, Pinched Spout, 3 1/2 In. 65.00
Royal Bayreuth, **Cup & Saucer,** Arab With 2 Horses, Blue Mark 69.00
Royal Bayreuth, **Cup & Saucer,** Blue, Shells & Roses, Green Mark 65.00
Royal Bayreuth, **Cup & Saucer,** Bouillon, Figural, Red Poppy, Blue Mark 55.00
Royal Bayreuth, **Cup & Saucer,** Brittany Women, 3 In.Saucer, 4 3/4 In.Cup, Mark 70.00
Royal Bayreuth, **Cup & Saucer,** Demitasse, Peacock, Yellow Ground, Gold Trim 40.00
Royal Bayreuth, **Cup & Saucer,** Demitasse, Red Rose 225.00
Royal Bayreuth, **Cup & Saucer,** Pedestal Bases, Gold Designs, Set Of 4 .... 220.00
Royal Bayreuth, **Cup & Saucer,** Pink & White 175.00
Royal Bayreuth, **Cup,** Loving, Corinthian Pattern, 3-Handled, Blue Mark 69.00
Royal Bayreuth, **Dinner Service,** Belmont Pattern, Green Mark, 60 Piece 150.00
Royal Bayreuth, **Dish,** Cheese, Cover, Gold Handle, Blue Mark, 2 1/2 X 3 In. 85.00
Royal Bayreuth, **Dish,** Feeding, Jack & The Beanstalk, Blue Mark 120.00
Royal Bayreuth, **Dish,** Feeding, Ring-Around-Rosie, 7 1/2 In. 85.00
Royal Bayreuth, **Dish,** Fishing Scene, Handled, 6 X 3 1/2 In. 75.00
Royal Bayreuth, **Dish,** Leaf, Ear Handle, 6 1/2 In. 35.00
Royal Bayreuth, **Dish,** Mayonnaise, Lobster, Lid 45.00
Royal Bayreuth, **Dish,** Open Handle, Goose Girl With Geese, Signed, 8 X 4 In. 65.00
Royal Bayreuth, **Dish,** Pin, Flowers, 4 3/4 X 4 In. 12.00
Royal Bayreuth, **Dish,** Relish, Handled, Blue Mark, 8 In. 275.00
Royal Bayreuth, **Dish,** Relish, Poinsettia 120.00
Royal Bayreuth, **Dish,** Relish, Tomato 35.00
Royal Bayreuth, **Dish,** Soap, Fishing Scene 65.00
Royal Bayreuth, **Dish,** 2 Girls Sliding On Snow, 4 In.Square 50.00
Royal Bayreuth, **Dish,** 3-Footed, Little Miss Muffet, Blue Mark, 2 X 5 In. 85.00
Royal Bayreuth, **Fernery,** Rose Decoration, Green Mark, 6 3/4 X 9 In. 250.00
Royal Bayreuth, **Figurine,** Duck 85.00
Royal Bayreuth, **Figurine,** Parakeet 40.00
Royal Bayreuth, **Figurine,** St.Bernard 50.00
Royal Bayreuth, **Flower Pot,** Three Color Roses, Blue Mark 165.00
Royal Bayreuth, **Frame,** Picture, Original Glass & Backing, 8 X 6 In. 175.00
Royal Bayreuth, **Grape Set,** Bowl, 9 1/2 In.Diam., 4 Bowls, 5 1/2 In., Signed 175.00
Royal Bayreuth, **Hair Receiver,** Rooster Fight Scene 60.00
Royal Bayreuth, **Hair Receiver,** Roses 95.00
Royal Bayreuth, **Hatpin Holder,** Attached Saucer, Hunt Scene, Blue Mark 85.00
Royal Bayreuth, **Hatpin Holder,** Cavalier Musicians, Signed, Blue Mark 155.00
Royal Bayreuth, **Hatpin Holder,** Ivory 150.00
Royal Bayreuth, **Hatpin Holder,** Miss Muffet, Picture & Verse, Black Mark 78.00
Royal Bayreuth, **Hatpin Holder,** Penguins, Raised Decoration 75.00
Royal Bayreuth, **Hatpin Holder,** Poppy, Mother-Of-Pearl 165.00
Royal Bayreuth, **Hatpin Holder,** Portrait, Lady By Horse, Square, Signed 147.00
Royal Bayreuth, **Hatpin Holder,** Scene Of Farmer & 2 Horses 69.00
Royal Bayreuth, **Hatpin Holder,** 3 Color Roses, Footed, Tapestry, Black Mark 219.00
Royal Bayreuth, **Holder,** String, Figural Rooster, Blue Mark 175.00
Royal Bayreuth, **Humidor,** Corinthian, Wall Of Troy, Blue Mark 125.00
Royal Bayreuth, **Humidor,** Elk, Black Mark 250.00
Royal Bayreuth, **Humidor,** Half Gold & Painted Roses, Gold Cubed Knobs, Marked 225.00
Royal Bayreuth, **Inkwell,** Devil 35.00
Royal Bayreuth, **Jar,** Covered, Jester, Signed Noke 95.00
Royal Bayreuth, **Jar,** Jam, Covered, Spoon, Underplate, Pearlized Silver 95.00
Royal Bayreuth, **Jar,** Jam, Tomato 49.00
Royal Bayreuth, **Jardiniere,** Water, Trees & Cattle, Blue Mark 225.00
Royal Bayreuth, **Lamp,** Red Devil, Electric, 8 1/2 In. 75.00
Royal Bayreuth, **Match Holder,** Clown, Hanging 160.00
Royal Bayreuth, **Match Holder,** Devil & Cards, Black Mark .... 85.00 To 165.00
Royal Bayreuth, **Match Holder,** Man On Horse, Brown & White .... 85.00 To 115.00
Royal Bayreuth, **Match Holder,** Man, Horses, Thatched Roof, Farm, Blue Mark 110.00
Royal Bayreuth, **Match Holder,** Wall, Farm Scene 85.00
Royal Bayreuth, **Match Holder,** Wall, Picture Of Jester, Signed 65.00
Royal Bayreuth, **Mayonnaise Set,** Orange, Green Handle 115.00
Royal Bayreuth, **Mug,** Beer, Elk, Signed, Black Mark 185.00
Royal Bayreuth, **Mug,** Beer, Hunter Scene, Dog & Geese, Blue Mark 85.00
Royal Bayreuth, **Mug,** Beer, Musicians Playing Table, Signed 125.00
Royal Bayreuth, **Mug,** Beer, Souvenir, Devil & Cards, U.S.Zone, Bermuda 65.00
Royal Bayreuth, **Mug,** Card & Devil 95.00
Royal Bayreuth, **Mug,** Three Handles, Storks, Black Mark 55.00

Royal Bayreuth, Mustache Cup, Elk, Black Mark 175.00
Royal Bayreuth, Mustard Pot, Lobster 75.00
Royal Bayreuth, Mustard, Covered, Tomato, Blue Mark .... 30.00 To 40.00
Royal Bayreuth, Mustard, Lid, Red Rose, Twig Handle & Spoon, Blue Mark 90.00
Royal Bayreuth, Mustard, Lobster With Leaf .... 55.00 To 70.00
Royal Bayreuth, Mustard, Rose, Pink & White 155.00
Royal Bayreuth, Nappy, Children Sliding Downhill, Handle 50.00
Royal Bayreuth, Nappy, Handled, Lettuce Leaf, Blue Mark 25.00
Royal Bayreuth, Pincushion, Elk 90.00
Royal Bayreuth, Pitcher, Antlered Deer 42.00
Royal Bayreuth, Pitcher, Cock Fighting Turkey, Signed, Black Mark, 7 In. 125.00
Royal Bayreuth, Pitcher, Conch Shell, Pearlized, Blue Mark, 4 1/4 X 7 In. 50.00
Royal Bayreuth, Pitcher, Cows, Blue Ground, Yellow, 7 1/2 In. .... 75.00 To 110.00
Royal Bayreuth, Pitcher, Cream, Brittany Girl 50.00
Royal Bayreuth, Pitcher, Cream, Corinthian, Green Interior, Blue Mark, 4 In. 85.00
Royal Bayreuth, Pitcher, Cream, Doe & Buck In Snow, Trees, Pink Coral, Marked 80.00
Royal Bayreuth, Pitcher, Cream, Sheep & Cottage, Pinched Out, Blue Mark 65.00
Royal Bayreuth, Pitcher, Cream, White, Rose Buds, Pansies, 2 3/4 In. 15.00
Royal Bayreuth, Pitcher, Crow 85.00
Royal Bayreuth, Pitcher, Elk, Blue Mark 40.00
Royal Bayreuth, Pitcher, Fish, 4 In. 120.00
Royal Bayreuth, Pitcher, Forest, Deer, Lake, Castle, Pinched Spout, 3 1/4 In. 175.00
Royal Bayreuth, Pitcher, Fox Hunting Scene, 5 In. 65.00
Royal Bayreuth, Pitcher, Gibson Girl With Mare, Gold Rim, 3 1/2 In. 195.00
Royal Bayreuth, Pitcher, Girl With Baskets, Blue Mark, 4 In. 75.00
Royal Bayreuth, Pitcher, Hunting Scene, Blue Mark, 2 3/4 In. 45.00
Royal Bayreuth, Pitcher, Hunting Scene, Blue Mark, 3 3/4 In. 48.00
Royal Bayreuth, Pitcher, Hunting Scene, Blue Mark, 8 In. 50.00
Royal Bayreuth, Pitcher, Huntsman & Dog, Blue Mark, 4 In. 95.00
Royal Bayreuth, Pitcher, Jack And The Beanstalk, Large 100.00
Royal Bayreuth, Pitcher, Jester Motif, Blue Mark, Signed Noke, 6 3/4 In. 150.00
Royal Bayreuth, Pitcher, Lemonade, Ring-Neck Pheasant, Blue Mark 135.00
Royal Bayreuth, Pitcher, Lobster, Blue Mark, 7 In. 110.00
Royal Bayreuth, Pitcher, Milk, Alligator 150.00
Royal Bayreuth, Pitcher, Milk, Art Nouveau Lady, Blue Mark 225.00
Royal Bayreuth, Pitcher, Milk, Bass, Blue Mark 145.00
Royal Bayreuth, Pitcher, Milk, Clown, Yellow 175.00
Royal Bayreuth, Pitcher, Milk, Coachman 165.00
Royal Bayreuth, Pitcher, Milk, Dachshund, Blue Mark 140.00
Royal Bayreuth, Pitcher, Milk, Eagle, 4 In. 132.50
Royal Bayreuth, Pitcher, Milk, Elk, Blue Mark 135.00
Royal Bayreuth, Pitcher, Milk, Fish 145.00
Royal Bayreuth, Pitcher, Milk, Hunting Scene, Blue Mark 55.00
Royal Bayreuth, Pitcher, Milk, Lamplighter .... 165.00 To 185.00
Royal Bayreuth, Pitcher, Milk, Lobster, Marked 185.00
Royal Bayreuth, Pitcher, Milk, Moose, Blue Mark, 5 1/4 In. 85.00
Royal Bayreuth, Pitcher, Milk, Orange 100.00
Royal Bayreuth, Pitcher, Milk, Pastoral Scene, Signed, Blue Mark, 7 1/2 In. 155.00
Royal Bayreuth, Pitcher, Milk, Pear, Green Leaf Trim 100.00
Royal Bayreuth, Pitcher, Milk, Seal, Blue Mark 150.00
Royal Bayreuth, Pitcher, Milk, St.Bernard 85.00
Royal Bayreuth, Pitcher, Milk, Tomato, Signed 75.00
Royal Bayreuth, Pitcher, Moose, Black Mark, 7 In. 95.00
Royal Bayreuth, Pitcher, Pearl Shell, 4 In. 76.00
Royal Bayreuth, Pitcher, Pinch Spout, Cherries & Leaves, Blue Mark, 7 In. 185.00
Royal Bayreuth, Pitcher, Pinched, Cows, Brook, Mountains, 8 1/2 In. 275.00
Royal Bayreuth, Pitcher, Polar Bear Scene, Black Mark, 5 In. 95.00
Royal Bayreuth, Pitcher, Tomato, 4 In. 30.00
Royal Bayreuth, Pitcher, Water, Alligator, Mother-Of-Pearl, Blue Mark 350.00
Royal Bayreuth, Pitcher, Water, Apple, Blue Mark 150.00
Royal Bayreuth, Pitcher, Water, Clown, Black Mark 350.00
Royal Bayreuth, Pitcher, Water, Elk 195.00
Royal Bayreuth, Pitcher, Water, Lobster, Blue Mark .... 185.00 To 195.00
Royal Bayreuth, Pitcher, Water, Pastoral Scene, Signed, Blue Mark, 7 In. 200.00
Royal Bayreuth, Pitcher, Water, Tomato .... 140.00 To 150.00
Royal Bayreuth, Pitcher, 2 Handled, 2 Musicians Playing On Bench, 3 3/4 In. 75.00

Royal Bayreuth, Planter, Farm Scene	45.00
Royal Bayreuth, Planter, Pastoral Scene, 3 In.	38.00
Royal Bayreuth, Plate, Arab Scene With Horses, 9 In.	68.00
Royal Bayreuth, Plate, Beach Babies, Playing Giddyap, 6 1/4 In.	56.00
Royal Bayreuth, Plate, Boat Scene, Blue Mark, 6 1/2 In.	38.00
Royal Bayreuth, Plate, Cake, Cows Grazing, Blue Mark, 6 In.	20.00
Royal Bayreuth, Plate, Cake, Handled, Little Boy Blue	155.00
Royal Bayreuth, Plate, Children Playing On Ice, Signed, 6 In.	98.00
Royal Bayreuth, Plate, Chop, Pink Roses & Gold Trim, Blue Mark, 12 In.	115.00
Royal Bayreuth, Plate, Chop, Pink Roses, Gold Band, 12 1/2 In.	115.00
Royal Bayreuth, Plate, Country Scene, Blue, Signed, 10 1/2 In.	70.00
Royal Bayreuth, Plate, Flowers, Gold Trim, 10 In.	9.00
Royal Bayreuth, Plate, Girl With Dog, 4 1/4 In.	15.00
Royal Bayreuth, Plate, Girl With Dog, 8 1/2 In.	80.00
Royal Bayreuth, Plate, Green Leaves, Yellow Flowers, Twig Handle, 7 In.	16.00
Royal Bayreuth, Plate, Jack And The Beanstalk, Blue Mark, 6 1/2 In.	85.00
Royal Bayreuth, Plate, Little Bo-Peep, Picture & Verse, 6 1/2 In.	85.00
Royal Bayreuth, Plate, Lobster Tail Handle, Black Mark, 6 1/2 In.	25.00
Royal Bayreuth, Plate, Pastoral Scene, Cows, Black Mark, 6 In.	25.00
Royal Bayreuth, Plate, Pastoral Scene, Goats, Black Mark, 6 In.	25.00
Royal Bayreuth, Plate, Pastoral Scene, Sheep, Black Mark, 6 In.	25.00
Royal Bayreuth, Plate, Poppy, Blue Mark, 8 1/4 In.	45.00
Royal Bayreuth, Plate, Portrait, Cavalier In Center, Signed, 9 1/4 In.	185.00
Royal Bayreuth, Plate, Portrait, Gold & Floral Rim, Blue Mark, 6 In., Pair	45.00
Royal Bayreuth, Plate, Purple Pansy, Blue Mark, 7 1/2 In.	85.00
Royal Bayreuth, Plate, Rose Color Pansy, Blue Mark, 8 1/2 In.	110.00
Royal Bayreuth, Plate, Sand Babies, Blue Mark, 6 In.	56.00
Royal Bayreuth, Plate, Scalloped Gilt Rim, Octagonal, 9 1/4 In.	300.00
Royal Bayreuth, Plate, Scenic, Lady With Geese, Blue Mark, 8 In.	35.00
Royal Bayreuth, Plate, Snow Scene, Blue Mark, Signed, 6 In.	55.00
Royal Bayreuth, Plate, Sunbonnet Babies Washing, 6 In.	38.00
Royal Bayreuth, Plate, Woman On Shore, 10 1/2 In.	68.00
Royal Bayreuth, Pot & Ladle, Sauce, Figural Lobster, 4 1/4 X 4 1/4 In.	50.00
Royal Bayreuth, Relish, Poinsettia	125.00
Royal Bayreuth, Ring Tree, Attached Saucer, Enameled, 2 1/4 In.	45.00
Royal Bayreuth, Rose Bowl, Little Bo Peep	50.00
Royal Bayreuth, Rose Bowl, Sunbonnet Babies Sweeping, Blue Mark	120.00
Royal Bayreuth, Rose Bowl, Yellow, Medium Size, Blue Mark	175.00
Royal Bayreuth, Salt & Pepper, Conch Shell, Green, Signed	35.00
Royal Bayreuth, Salt & Pepper, Elk, Blue Mark	120.00
Royal Bayreuth, Salt & Pepper, Grape, Blue Mark, Signed	85.00 To 150.00
Royal Bayreuth, Salt & Pepper, Tomato	30.00
Royal Bayreuth, Salt Dip, Poppy, Red	28.00
Royal Bayreuth, Saltshaker, Radish	25.00
Royal Bayreuth, Shoe, Man's	115.00
Royal Bayreuth, Smoke Set, Black, Corinthian, Blue Mark	185.00
Royal Bayreuth, Stein, Handled, Hunter With Dog, Geese, Blue Mark	100.00
Royal Bayreuth, Stickpin Holder, Green Frog In Pin Tray, Maroon, Marked	127.00
Royal Bayreuth, String Holder, Rooster, Signed	180.00
Royal Bayreuth, Sugar & Creamer, Conch Shell, Blue Mark	95.00
Royal Bayreuth, Sugar & Creamer, Corinthian	125.00
Royal Bayreuth, Sugar & Creamer, Cows In Pasture, Blue Mark	50.00
Royal Bayreuth, Sugar & Creamer, Dover, Brittany Girl, Blue Mark	115.00
Royal Bayreuth, Sugar & Creamer, Gold Lattice Work, 4 X 3 1/2 In.	45.00
Royal Bayreuth, Sugar & Creamer, Hunt Scene, Black Mark	80.00
Royal Bayreuth, Sugar & Creamer, Lemon, Black Mark, Pair	230.00
Royal Bayreuth, Sugar & Creamer, Lobster, Blue Mark	80.00 To 125.00
Royal Bayreuth, Sugar & Creamer, Murex	95.00
Royal Bayreuth, Sugar & Creamer, Musicians	135.00
Royal Bayreuth, Sugar & Creamer, Purple Grapes, Blue Mark	175.00
Royal Bayreuth, Sugar & Creamer, Red Poppy, Blue Mark	125.00
Royal Bayreuth, Sugar & Creamer, Tomato, Black Mark	75.00
Royal Bayreuth, Sugar & Creamer, Tomato, Blue Mark	75.00
Royal Bayreuth, Sugar & Creamer, Tray, Dated 1794, Black Mark	125.00
Royal Bayreuth, Sugar, Covered, Conch Shell, Green, Signed	25.00
Royal Bayreuth, Sugar, Covered, Tomato, Blue Mark, 3 In.	10.00 To 20.00

Royal Bayreuth, Sugar, Covered, Tomato, Blue Mark, 4 In.	35.00
Royal Bayreuth, Tea Set, Tomato, 3 Piece	80.00 To 135.00
Royal Bayreuth, Teapot, Apple, Signed	75.00
Royal Bayreuth, Teapot, Orange	85.00
Royal Bayreuth, Teapot, Polar Bear Design	125.00
Royal Bayreuth, Teapot, Tomato, Blue Mark	78.50
Royal Bayreuth, Teapot, Tomato, Blue Mark, 4 1/4 X 7 1/2 In.	58.00 To 70.00
Royal Bayreuth, Teaset, Teapot, Sugar, Creamer, Set Of 3	950.00
Royal Bayreuth, Toothpick, Amber, Pedestal, 3 7/8 In.	65.00
Royal Bayreuth, Toothpick, Elk, Blue Mark	85.00 To 145.00
Royal Bayreuth, Toothpick, Floral, Lavender, 3 Handle	90.00
Royal Bayreuth, Toothpick, Musicians, 4 Corner	65.00
Royal Bayreuth, Toothpick, 3 Handles, Horse With Rider, Blue Mark	120.00
Royal Bayreuth, Tray, Dresser, Devil & Cards, Black Mark	250.00
Royal Bayreuth, Tray, Dresser, Green & Gilt Border, Signed, 8 X 11 In.	60.00
Royal Bayreuth, Tray, G.Washington Portrait Center, Marked, 4 1/4 In.	39.00
Royal Bayreuth, Tray, Little Miss Muffet, 4 In.Square	92.50
Royal Bayreuth, Tray, Pin, Covered, Fox Hunt	55.00
Royal Bayreuth, Tray, Pin, Heart Shaped, Pink Roses, Black Mark	25.00
Royal Bayreuth, Tray, Pin, Hunter, Dog, Woman In Cart, Blue Mark	35.00
Royal Bayreuth, Urn, Cover, Diapered Borders, Gold Trim, Blue Mark, 5 In.	45.00
Royal Bayreuth, Vase, Blue, 2 Polar Bears In Snow, Moon, 8 1/2 In.	350.00
Royal Bayreuth, Vase, Brittany Girl, 4 In.	65.00
Royal Bayreuth, Vase, Bulbous, Fisherman In Boat, Black Mark, 8 In.	145.00
Royal Bayreuth, Vase, Corinthian, Orange, 5 1/2 In., Pair	155.00
Royal Bayreuth, Vase, Country Scene, Blue Mark, 6 1/2 In.	85.00
Royal Bayreuth, Vase, Cows In Pasture, 4 3/4 In., Pair	45.00
Royal Bayreuth, Vase, End Of Day, Pink, Yellow, Cranberry, 5 1/2 In.	17.50
Royal Bayreuth, Vase, Farm Scene, Blue Mark, 8 3/4 In.	95.00
Royal Bayreuth, Vase, Girls & Sheep, 14 In., Pair	75.00
Royal Bayreuth, Vase, Handled, Silver Rim, Sheep, Green Mark, 3 1/4 In.	55.00
Royal Bayreuth, Vase, Hunt Scene, Sterling Top, Green Mark, 3 1/2 In.	60.00
Royal Bayreuth, Vase, Little Boy Blue, Picture, Verse, Black Mark, 3 1/2 In.	95.00
Royal Bayreuth, Vase, Moon Scene, Polar Bear, 8 1/2 In.	375.00
Royal Bayreuth, Vase, Mountain Goats, 2 Handles, Blue Mark, 3 1/2 In.	40.00
Royal Bayreuth, Vase, Picture Of Semi-Nude Lady With Wings, 3 1/2 In.High	45.00
Royal Bayreuth, Vase, Pink Roses, Blue Mark, 3 1/2 In.	25.00
Royal Bayreuth, Vase, Portrait, Gold Handles, Blue Mark, 4 1/2 Inches	45.00
Royal Bayreuth, Vase, Scenic, 7 In.	185.00
Royal Bayreuth, Vase, Sheep In Mountain, Blue Mark, 5 1/2 In.	45.00
Royal Bayreuth, Vase, Silver Rim, Hallmark, Sheep & Trees, Handled, 3 3/4 In.	50.00
Royal Bayreuth, Vase, Turkey Decoration, 4 In.	15.00
Royal Bayreuth, Vase, Twin Handled, Pastoral Scene, Blue Mark, 5 1/2 In.	155.00
Royal Berlin, see KPM	
Royal Bonn, Vase, Lady Head Portrait, Gold Trim, Mottled, Marked, 7 In.	165.00
Royal Bonn, Vase, Old Dutch, Rich Deep Colors, 10 X 7 In.	118.00
Royal Bonn, Vase, Olive Background, 11 X 11 In.	125.00
Royal Bonn, Vase, Painted Rose, Signed, 21 In.Tall	115.00
Royal Bonn, Vase, Pastel Flowers, Raised Goldon Ivory Ground, 15 In.	115.00
Royal Bonn, Vase, Pedestal Base, Bulbous Center, Scenic Tapestry, 8 3/4 In.	125.00
Royal Bonn, Vase, Pedestal, Flowers On Green, Gold Trim, 10 1/4 In.	65.00
Royal Bonn, Vase, Pink Flowers, Gold Trim, Dated, 9 1/4 In.	75.00
Royal Bonn, Vase, Portrait Lady, Green Border, Gold Trim, Marked, 7 3/4 In.	175.00
Royal Bonn, Vase, Portrait, Red Haired Woman, Signed, 10 In.	200.00
Royal Bonn, Vase, Red, Yellow & Pink Roses, Bulbous, 8 In.	42.50
Royal Bonn, Vase, Roses, Yellow, Signed, 10 X 6 1/2 In.	95.00

 Royal Copenhagen porcelain and pottery have been made in Denmark since 1772. They are still being made. One of their most famous wares is the Christmas Plate Series.

Royal Copenhagen, Coffeepot, Immortelle	65.00
Royal Copenhagen, Cup & Saucer, Confetti, Gold Interior	10.00
Royal Copenhagen, Dish, Lady's Deco Head, Stoneware, 3 In.	48.00
Royal Copenhagen, Dish, Powder, Lidded, Crackle Glaze, 3 Wave Mark, 4 In.	30.00
Royal Copenhagen, Figurine, Boy With Horn, 4 1/2 In.	50.00
Royal Copenhagen, Figurine, Boy, Blue & White, 4 3/4 In.	45.00

Royal Copenhagen, Figurine, Cat, Gray, White Face, 4 1/2 X 5 X 3 In.	90.00
Royal Copenhagen, Figurine, Colt, Large	245.00
Royal Copenhagen, Figurine, Crow, Large	225.00
Royal Copenhagen, Figurine, Doves, 5 1/2 In.	65.00
Royal Copenhagen, Figurine, Elephant Standing With Trunk Up, 4 1/2 In.	52.00
Royal Copenhagen, Figurine, Elephant Vocalizing, No.2998, 4 1/2 In.	52.00
Royal Copenhagen, Figurine, Fish, No. 2553, 2 1/4 X 3 1/4 In.	55.00
Royal Copenhagen, Figurine, Goose Girl, 7 In.	95.00
Royal Copenhagen, Figurine, Goose Girl, 9 In.	145.00
Royal Copenhagen, Figurine, Love Birds, No.402, 5 In.	65.00
Royal Copenhagen, Figurine, Resting Deer, Signed, O.P., No.756, 5 1/2 In.	45.00
Royal Copenhagen, Figurine, Rooster, No.1127, Red Comb	45.00
Royal Copenhagen, Figurine, The Sandman, No.1129, 7 In.	85.00
Royal Copenhagen, Figurine, Young Man Carrying Umbrella, 7 In.	85.00
Royal Copenhagen, Lamp, Boudoir, White & Pink Rose	65.00
Royal Copenhagen, Plate, Blue, White, Commemorative, Krog, 1915, 7 In.	135.00
Royal Copenhagen, Plate, Christmas, 1915, Original Paper Label	77.00
Royal Copenhagen, Plate, Christmas, 1962	100.00
Royal Copenhagen, Plate, Christmas, 1963	35.00
Royal Copenhagen, Plate, Christmas, 1965	35.00
Royal Copenhagen, Plate, Soup, Deep, Immortelle, Blue Flower, 9 In.Diameter	22.00
Royal Copenhagen, Platter, Blue & White, 12 In.	45.00
Royal Copenhagen, Sauce Boat, Matching Tray	39.50
Royal Copenhagen, Tray, Change, Advertising Carlsberg Beer	40.00
Royal Copenhagen, Tray, Pin, Portrait	25.00
Royal Copenhagen, Tray, Sandwich, Immortelle, Kidney Shape, 9 1/2 X 7 In.	35.00
Royal Copenhagen, Vase, Art Nouveau Pattern, Rosewood Base, 12 In., Pair	95.00
Royal Copenhagen, Vase, Hand-Painted Mallard, Ocean, Fog, 5 1/2 In.	27.50
Royal Copenhagen, Vase, Sailboat Scene, 6 1/2 In.	75.00

Royal Crown Derby Company, Ltd., was established in England in 1876.

Royal Crown Derby, see also Crown Derby, Derby

Royal Crown Derby, Center Piece, Oval, Lattice Work, Hand-Painted	160.00
Royal Crown Derby, Inkwell, Imari Pattern, Covered	175.00
Royal Crown Derby, Vase, Hand Decorated, Gold Trim, Red Mark, 6 In.	100.00
Royal Crown Derby, Vase, Imari Pattern, Bulbous Shape, 1915 Mark, 5 3/4 In.	110.00

Royal Doulton was the name used on pottery made after 1902. The Doulton Factory was founded in 1815. Their wares are still being made.

Royal Doulton, Ash Bowl, Old Charley, A Mark	55.00
Royal Doulton, Ash Bowl, Paddy, A Mark	55.00
Royal Doulton, Ashtray, Dick Turpin	55.00
Royal Doulton, Ashtray, Dickensware, Center Match Box Holder, Fagin	85.00
Royal Doulton, Ashtray, Paddy, A Mark	55.00
Royal Doulton, Beaker, John Hassell, Boy By A Fishing Hole	85.00
Royal Doulton, Bottle, Dan Sandeman, 4 1/2 In.	125.00
Royal Doulton, Bottle, Flask, Empire Maidens, Crown & Sceptre, 9 In.	95.00
Royal Doulton, Bottle, Perfume, Sung Ware, Noke & F.Allans, 5 1/4 In., Pair	310.00
Royal Doulton, Bottle, Zorro, A Mark, 10 1/2 In.	25.00 To 45.00
Royal Doulton, Bowl, Bill Sykes, Shallow, 5 1/4 In.	25.00
Royal Doulton, Bowl, Blue, Red Flowers, A Mark, 12 In.	60.00
Royal Doulton, Bowl, Chang Ware, Marked, Signed, Noke, 9 1/2 X 3 1/4 In.	585.00
Royal Doulton, Bowl, Chang Ware, Mutton Fat, Purple, Noke, 3 1/4 X 9 1/2 In.	585.00
Royal Doulton, Bowl, Child's, Bunnykins, 5 3/4 In.	15.00
Royal Doulton, Bowl, Dickensware, Alfred Jingle In Street, 5 In.Square	35.00
Royal Doulton, Bowl, Dickensware, Artful Dodger, Signed, 1 3/4 X 6 In.Diam.	48.00
Royal Doulton, Bowl, Dickensware, Bill Sykes, Signed, 6 In.	37.00
Royal Doulton, Bowl, Dickensware, Fagin In Courtyard, Signed, 5 1/4 In.	85.00
Royal Doulton, Bowl, Dickensware, Mr.Pickwick, Signed Noke, 9 X 9 In.	135.00
Royal Doulton, Bowl, Dickensware, Sam Weller, 3 1/2 X 6 1/4 In.Diameter	45.00
Royal Doulton, Bowl, Dr.Johnson At The Temple Bar, Registry Mark, 9 1/4 In.	60.00
Royal Doulton, Bowl, Farmer Plowing Field, C.1902, Marked, 9 1/4 X 2 3/8 In.	157.50
Royal Doulton, Bowl, Medallions, Tan, England, Blue, 4 1/4 X 2 1/2 In.	27.50
Royal Doulton, Bowl, Old English Coaching Scene, Signed, 8 1/2 In.Square	75.00
Royal Doulton, Bowl, Sairey Gamp, 8 X 11 In.	75.00
Royal Doulton, Bowl, Street Scene, Figure Of Nightwatchman, 4 X 10 In.Diam.	65.00
Royal Doulton, Bowl, Woman At Pump, Flowers, 7 In. Diameter	48.00

Royal Doulton, Candlestick, Dickensware, Square Shape, 6 1/2 In., Pair	225.00
Royal Doulton, Candlestick, Gypsys Round A Campfire, 6 1/4 In.	48.00
Royal Doulton, Candlestick, Pilgrim Scenes, Set In Bowl	95.00
Royal Doulton, Candlestick, The Poacher, 4 In.	90.00
Royal Doulton, Candlestick, Welsh Ladies	18.00
Royal Doulton, Canister, Egyptian Motif, Green, Covered, 6 1/2 X 4 In.	100.00
Royal Doulton, Casserole, Covered, The Kirkwood	22.50
Royal Doulton, Chamberpot, Dickens Watchmen On Patrol, 6 X 10 In.	70.00
Royal Doulton, Chamberstick, Woodland Scene	65.00

*Character jugs are modeled of the head and shoulders of the subject. They
were made in four sizes: large - 5 1/4 to 7 inches, small - 3 1/4 to 4 inches,
miniature - 2 1/4 to 2 1/2 inches, and tiny - 1 1/4 inches. Toby mugs depict
a full seated figure. The HN mark has been used by the factory since 1913.*

Royal Doulton, Character Jug, 'Ard Of 'Earing, 3 1/2 In.	350.00
Royal Doulton, Character Jug, 'Ard Of 'Earing, 6 In.	425.00
Royal Doulton, Character Jug, 'Ard Of 'Earing, 7 In.	590.00
Royal Doulton, Character Jug, 'Arriet	105.00
Royal Doulton, Character Jug, 'Arriet, A Mark, 3 1/4 In.	55.00
Royal Doulton, Character Jug, 'Arriet, 3 1/2 In.	47.00
Royal Doulton, Character Jug, 'Arriet, 6 1/2 In.	105.00 To 110.00
Royal Doulton, Character Jug, 'Arry, A Mark, 2 1/2 In.	55.00 To 60.00
Royal Doulton, Character Jug, 'Arry, A Mark, 2 1/4 In.	55.00
Royal Doulton, Character Jug, 'Arry, A Mark, 3 1/4 In.	60.00
Royal Doulton, Character Jug, 'Arry, 1 1/4 In.	100.00
Royal Doulton, Character Jug, 'Arry, 2 1/4 In.	45.00
Royal Doulton, Character Jug, 'Arry, 5 1/4 In.	110.00
Royal Doulton, Character Jug, 'Arry, 6 In.	110.00
Royal Doulton, Character Jug, Auld Mac, A Mark	58.00
Royal Doulton, Character Jug, Auld Mac, A Mark, 1 1/4 In.	30.00 To 65.00
Royal Doulton, Character Jug, Auld Mac, A Mark, 2 1/4 In.	38.00
Royal Doulton, Character Jug, Auld Mac, A Mark, 3 1/4 In.	45.00 To 47.50
Royal Doulton, Character Jug, Auld Mac, 1 1/4 In.	115.00 To 170.00
Royal Doulton, Character Jug, Bacchus, 6 In.	23.00
Royal Doulton, Character Jug, Beefeater, A Mark, 3 1/2 In.	40.00
Royal Doulton, Character Jug, Beefeater, GR Raised On Handle, 6 1/4 In.	65.00
Royal Doulton, Character Jug, Beefeater, Green, 6 1/2 In.	75.00
Royal Doulton, Character Jug, Beefeater, Shorter, England, 7 In.	25.00
Royal Doulton, Character Jug, Beefeater, 2 1/2 In.	15.00
Royal Doulton, Character Jug, Beefeater, 6 1/4 In.	70.00
Royal Doulton, Character Jug, Beswick Pecksniff, 1 1/4 In.	18.00
Royal Doulton, Character Jug, Cap'n Cuttle, Seated, A Mark, 4 1/2 In.	145.00
Royal Doulton, Character Jug, Captain Cuttle, 3 1/2 In.	57.00
Royal Doulton, Character Jug, Captain Hook, 3 1/2 In.	145.00 To 190.00
Royal Doulton, Character Jug, Captain Hook, 6 1/2 In.	175.00 To 240.00
Royal Doulton, Character Jug, Cardinal, A Mark, 1 1/4 In.	45.00
Royal Doulton, Character Jug, Cardinal, A Mark, 6 In.	80.00 To 95.00
Royal Doulton, Character Jug, Cardinal, 1 1/4 In.	180.00
Royal Doulton, Character Jug, Cardinal, 2 1/4 In.	38.00 To 45.00
Royal Doulton, Character Jug, Cardinal, 6 1/2 In.	80.00 To 90.00
Royal Doulton, Character Jug, Cavalier, A Mark	50.00
Royal Doulton, Character Jug, Cavalier, A Mark, Large	72.00
Royal Doulton, Character Jug, Cavalier, A Mark, 6 1/2 In.	72.00 To 95.00
Royal Doulton, Character Jug, Cavalier, 3 1/2 In.	50.00
Royal Doulton, Character Jug, Cavalier, 6 1/2 In.	65.00 To 75.00
Royal Doulton, Character Jug, Cavalier, 6 1/4 In.	95.00
Royal Doulton, Character Jug, Charley, 1 1/4 In.	65.00
Royal Doulton, Character Jug, Clown, White Haired, 1950-55, 6 In.	475.00 To 750.00
Royal Doulton, Character Jug, Clown, 6 In.	775.00 To 800.00
Royal Doulton, Character Jug, Dick Turpin, A Mark, Miniature	40.00
Royal Doulton, Character Jug, Dick Turpin, A Mark, 2 1/2 In.	40.00
Royal Doulton, Character Jug, Dick Turpin, 2 1/2 In.	45.00
Royal Doulton, Character Jug, Dick Turpin, 3 1/2 In.	37.00 To 45.00
Royal Doulton, Character Jug, Dick Turpin, 6 1/2 In.	75.00
Royal Doulton, Character Jug, Dick Whittington, 6 In.	240.00 To 375.00

Royal Doulton, Character Jug, Drake, 3 1/2 In. 50.00
Royal Doulton, Character Jug, Drake, 6 1/2 In. 75.00
Royal Doulton, Character Jug, Falstaff, 6 In. 100.00
Royal Doulton, Character Jug, Farmer John, A Mark, 6 In. .... 150.00 To 180.00
Royal Doulton, Character Jug, Farmer John, 2 1/2 In. 50.00
Royal Doulton, Character Jug, Farmer John, 3 1/2 In. .... 55.00 To 70.00
Royal Doulton, Character Jug, Farmer John, 6 1/2 In. .... 70.00 To 125.00
Royal Doulton, Character Jug, Fat Boy, A Mark, 1 1/4 In. .... 55.00 To 80.00
Royal Doulton, Character Jug, Fat Boy, A Mark, 2 1/4 In. 55.00
Royal Doulton, Character Jug, Fat Boy, A Mark, 7 In. 115.00
Royal Doulton, Character Jug, Fat Boy, 1 1/4 In. .... 75.00 To 95.00
Royal Doulton, Character Jug, Fat Boy, 2 1/4 In. 48.00
Royal Doulton, Character Jug, Fat Boy, 3 1/2 In. 40.00
Royal Doulton, Character Jug, Fortune Teller, 2 1/4 In. 220.00
Royal Doulton, Character Jug, Fortune Teller, 3 1/2 In. .... 180.00 To 225.00
Royal Doulton, Character Jug, Fortune Teller, 6 1/2 In. .... 225.00 To 235.00
Royal Doulton, Character Jug, Friar Tuck, 6 1/2 In. 250.00
Royal Doulton, Character Jug, Full Seated, Toby XX .... 200.00 To 325.00
Royal Doulton, Character Jug, Gladiator, 2 1/4 In. 200.00
Royal Doulton, Character Jug, Gladiator, 3 1/2 In. .... 195.00 To 300.00
Royal Doulton, Character Jug, Gladiator, 6 In. .... 225.00 To 365.00
Royal Doulton, Character Jug, Gladiator, 6 1/2 In. .... 225.00 To 365.00
Royal Doulton, Character Jug, Gondolier, 2 1/4 In. .... 30.00 To 295.00
Royal Doulton, Character Jug, Gondolier, 3 1/2 In. .... 230.00 To 300.00
Royal Doulton, Character Jug, Gondolier, 6 1/2 In. .... 245.00 To 265.00
Royal Doulton, Character Jug, Granny, 6 1/4 In. 65.00
Royal Doulton, Character Jug, Gulliver, Marked, 6 In. .... 290.00 To 350.00
Royal Doulton, Character Jug, Gulliver, 2 1/4 In. .... 290.00 To 295.00
Royal Doulton, Character Jug, Gulliver, 3 1/4 In. 350.00
Royal Doulton, Character Jug, Gulliver, 6 1/2 In. .... 285.00 To 350.00
Royal Doulton, Character Jug, Henry Morgan, 2 1/2 In. 15.50
Royal Doulton, Character Jug, Henry Morgan, 4 In. 24.00
Royal Doulton, Character Jug, Jarge, 3 1/2 In. .... 115.00 To 135.00
Royal Doulton, Character Jug, Jarge, 6 1/2 In. .... 185.00 To 210.00
Royal Doulton, Character Jug, Jester, A Mark 60.00
Royal Doulton, Character Jug, Jester, 3 1/2 In. 63.00
Royal Doulton, Character Jug, John Barleycorn, 2 1/4 In. 40.00
Royal Doulton, Character Jug, John Barleycorn, 3 1/2 In. 37.00
Royal Doulton, Character Jug, John Peel, A Mark 90.00
Royal Doulton, Character Jug, John Peel, A Mark, 2 1/4 In. 40.00
Royal Doulton, Character Jug, John Peel, A Mark, 3 1/4 In. 47.25
Royal Doulton, Character Jug, John Peel, A Mark, 6 In. .... 80.00 To 85.00
Royal Doulton, Character Jug, John Peel, 1 1/4 In. 120.00
Royal Doulton, Character Jug, John Peel, 2 1/4 In. 50.00
Royal Doulton, Character Jug, John Peel, 3 1/2 In. 37.00
Royal Doulton, Character Jug, John Peel, 7 In. 75.00
Royal Doulton, Character Jug, Johnny Appleseed, 6 In. .... 160.00 To 180.00
Royal Doulton, Character Jug, Lord Nelson, 6 In. .... 175.00 To 315.00
Royal Doulton, Character Jug, Mephistopheles, A Mark, 6 In. 800.00
Royal Doulton, Character Jug, Mephistopheles, 3 1/2 In. 375.00
Royal Doulton, Character Jug, Mephistopheles, 6 In. .... 675.00 To 950.00
Royal Doulton, Character Jug, Mephistopheles, 7 In. 950.00
Royal Doulton, Character Jug, Mikado, 2 1/4 In. .... 175.00 To 200.00
Royal Doulton, Character Jug, Mikado, 3 1/2 In. .... 160.00 To 180.00
Royal Doulton, Character Jug, Mikado, 6 1/2 In. .... 190.00 To 220.00
Royal Doulton, Character Jug, Mr. Pickwick, Bust, 1 1/4 In. 45.00
Royal Doulton, Character Jug, Mr.Micawber, A Mark .... 45.00 To 65.00
Royal Doulton, Character Jug, Mr.Micawber, A Mark, 1 1/4 In. 80.00
Royal Doulton, Character Jug, Mr.Micawber, A Mark, 3 1/4 In. 60.00
Royal Doulton, Character Jug, Mr.Micawber, A Mark, 7 In. 140.00
Royal Doulton, Character Jug, Mr.Micawber, Miniature 95.00
Royal Doulton, Character Jug, Mr.Micawber, White, A Mark, 2 1/4 In. 125.00
Royal Doulton, Character Jug, Mr.Micawber, 1 1/4 In. .... 31.00 To 125.00
Royal Doulton, Character Jug, Mr.Micawber, 2 1/2 In. .... 30.00 To 95.00
Royal Doulton, Character Jug, Mr.Micawber, 2 1/4 In. .... 37.00 To 45.00
Royal Doulton, Character Jug, Mr.Micawber, 3 1/2 In. .... 37.00 To 60.00

Royal Doulton, Character Jug, Mr.Pickwick, 1 1/4 In. .... 45.00 To 55.00
Royal Doulton, Character Jug, Mr.Pickwick, 2 1/2 In. 30.00
Royal Doulton, Character Jug, Mr.Pickwick, 5 3/4 In. 95.00
Royal Doulton, Character Jug, Mr.Pickwick, 6 In. 85.00
Royal Doulton, Character Jug, Mr.Pickwick, 6 1/2 In. .... 85.00 To 170.00
Royal Doulton, Character Jug, Old Charley, A Mark 55.00
Royal Doulton, Character Jug, Old Charley, A Mark, 1 1/4 In. 30.00
Royal Doulton, Character Jug, Old Charley, A Mark, 2 1/4 In. .... 25.00 To 40.00
Royal Doulton, Character Jug, Old Charley, A Mark, 3 1/2 In. 32.00
Royal Doulton, Character Jug, Old Charley, Seated, 3 1/2 In. 115.00
Royal Doulton, Character Jug, Old Charley, Seated, 6 In. 150.00
Royal Doulton, Character Jug, Old Charley, 1 1/4 In. .... 70.00 To 90.00
Royal Doulton, Character Jug, Old Charley, 3 1/2 In. .... 28.00 To 30.00
Royal Doulton, Character Jug, Old King Cole, 3 1/2 In. .... 70.00 To 160.00
Royal Doulton, Character Jug, Old King Cole, 6 In. 150.00
Royal Doulton, Character Jug, Old Mack, 1 1/4 In. 85.00
Royal Doulton, Character Jug, Paddy, A Mark, 1 1/4 In. 50.00
Royal Doulton, Character Jug, Paddy, A Mark, 3 1/2 In. 45.00
Royal Doulton, Character Jug, Paddy, White, A Mark, 2 1/4 In. 150.00
Royal Doulton, Character Jug, Paddy, 1 1/4 In. .... 72.00 To 85.00
Royal Doulton, Character Jug, Paddy, 3 1/2 In. 37.00
Royal Doulton, Character Jug, Parson Brown, A Mark 45.00
Royal Doulton, Character Jug, Parson Brown, 3 1/2 In. .... 35.00 To 125.00
Royal Doulton, Character Jug, Parson Brown, 6 In. .... 80.00 To 125.00
Royal Doulton, Character Jug, Pearly Boy, Crown, 2 1/4 In. 400.00
Royal Doulton, Character Jug, Punch & Judy Man, 2 1/4 In. .... 295.00 To 300.00
Royal Doulton, Character Jug, Punch & Judy Man, 3 1/2 In. .... 275.00 To 295.00
Royal Doulton, Character Jug, Punch & Judy Man, 3 1/4 In. 295.00
Royal Doulton, Character Jug, Punch & Judy Man, 6 1/2 In. .... 325.00 To 425.00
Royal Doulton, Character Jug, Regency Beau, 2 1/4 In. 300.00
Royal Doulton, Character Jug, Regency Beau, 3 1/2 In. 290.00
Royal Doulton, Character Jug, Regency Beau, 6 1/2 In. .... 365.00 To 400.00
Royal Doulton, Character Jug, Regency Beau, 7 In. 400.00
Royal Doulton, Character Jug, Robin Hood, 2 1/4 In. 50.00
Royal Doulton, Character Jug, Robin Hood, 3 1/2 In. 40.00
Royal Doulton, Character Jug, Robin Hood, 6 In. .... 65.00 To 100.00
Royal Doulton, Character Jug, Sairey Gamp, A Mark .... 32.00 To 55.00
Royal Doulton, Character Jug, Sairey Gamp, A Mark, Seated, 7 In. 140.00
Royal Doulton, Character Jug, Sairey Gamp, A Mark, 2 1/4 In. 25.00
Royal Doulton, Character Jug, Sairey Gamp, A Mark, 3 1/2 In. 22.50
Royal Doulton, Character Jug, Sairey Gamp, A Mark, 3 1/4 In. .... 25.00 To 40.00
Royal Doulton, Character Jug, Sairey Gamp, 1 1/4 In. .... 65.00 To 80.00
Royal Doulton, Character Jug, Sairey Gamp, 2 1/4 In. .... 18.00 To 40.00
Royal Doulton, Character Jug, Sairey Gamp, 3 1/2 In. 35.00
Royal Doulton, Character Jug, Sairey Gamp, 6 1/4 In. 60.00
Royal Doulton, Character Jug, Sam Johnson, 3 1/2 In. .... 145.00 To 160.00
Royal Doulton, Character Jug, Sam Johnson, 6 1/2 In. $ 150.00 To 200.00
Royal Doulton, Character Jug, Sam Weller, A Mark, 6 In. .... 85.00 To 100.00
Royal Doulton, Character Jug, Sam Weller, 1 1/4 In. .... 69.00 To 80.00
Royal Doulton, Character Jug, Sam Weller, 2 1/2 In. .... 65.00 To 120.00
Royal Doulton, Character Jug, Sam Weller, 6 1/2 In. 85.00
Royal Doulton, Character Jug, Scaramouche, Miniature 240.00
Royal Doulton, Character Jug, Scaramouche, 2 1/4 In. .... 240.00 To 295.00
Royal Doulton, Character Jug, Scaramouche, 3 1/2 In. .... 215.00 To 275.00
Royal Doulton, Character Jug, Scaramouche, 6 1/2 In. .... 285.00 To 300.00
Royal Doulton, Character Jug, Simon The Cellarer, 6 1/2 In. .... 75.00 To 95.00
Royal Doulton, Character Jug, Simple Simon, 6 In. .... 350.00 To 425.00
Royal Doulton, Character Jug, St.George, 4 In. 35.00
Royal Doulton, Character Jug, St.George, 6 In. 70.00
Royal Doulton, Character Jug, The Huntsman, 7 In. 22.00
Royal Doulton, Character Jug, Toby Philpots, A Mark 38.00
Royal Doulton, Character Jug, Tony Weller, A Mark, Miniature 40.00
Royal Doulton, Character Jug, Tony Weller, A Mark, 2 1/2 In. 40.00
Royal Doulton, Character Jug, Tony Weller, A Mark, 3 1/2 In. 42.00
Royal Doulton, Character Jug, Tony Weller, A Mark, 6 In. 85.00
Royal Doulton, Character Jug, Tony Weller, 2 1/2 In. 45.00

Royal Doulton, **Character Jug,** Tony Weller, 3 1/2 In.	37.00 To 45.00
Royal Doulton, **Character Jug,** Touchstone, 6 In.	140.00 To 165.00
Royal Doulton, **Character Jug,** Town Crier, 3 1/2 In.	60.00
Royal Doulton, **Character Jug,** Town Crier, 6 In.	95.00
Royal Doulton, **Character Jug,** Ugly Duchess, 3 1/2 In.	145.00
Royal Doulton, **Character Jug,** Ugly Duchess, 7 In.	125.00 To 200.00
Royal Doulton, **Character Jug,** Uncle Tom Cobleigh, 6 In.	200.00 To 285.00
Royal Doulton, **Character Jug,** Vicar Of Bray, A Mark, 6 In.	150.00 To 165.00
Royal Doulton, **Character Jug,** Vicar Of Bray, 6 In.	135.00 To 175.00
Royal Doulton, **Character Jug,** Viking, 2 1/4 In.	100.00
Royal Doulton, **Character Jug,** Viking, 3 1/2 In.	37.00 To 50.00
Royal Doulton, **Character Jug,** Viking, 6 In.	65.00
Royal Doulton, **Character Jug,** Winston Churchill, Full Figure, 9 In.	65.00
Royal Doulton, **Charger,** Hamlet, 13 1/2 In.	120.00
Royal Doulton, **Charger,** Long John Silver, 15 1/2 In.	120.00
Royal Doulton, **Cigarette & Match Holder,** Side Strike, 3 5/8 X 4 3/8 In.	135.00
Royal Doulton, **Cigarette Lighter,** Bacchus	75.00
Royal Doulton, **Cookie Jar,** Acorn Finial, Square Shape, Warwick, 6 3/4 In.	110.00
Royal Doulton, **Cup & Saucer,** Demitasse, Gold Bands, Green Wreath, Set Of 6	195.00
Royal Doulton, **Cup & Saucer,** Dickensware, Artful Dodger, Bill Sykes	65.00
Royal Doulton, **Cup & Saucer,** Dickensware, Mr.Pickwick, Cup, 2 3/4 In.	55.00
Royal Doulton, **Cup & Saucer,** Indian Tree	12.00
Royal Doulton, **Cup & Saucer,** Old Leeds Spray	10.00
Royal Doulton, **Cup,** Miniature, Bill Sykes, Signed	46.00
Royal Doulton, **Cup,** Saucer & Dessert Plate, Belvedere, 3 Piece Set, 12 Sets	185.00
Royal Doulton, **Dish,** Baby, Bunnykins	35.00
Royal Doulton, **Dish,** Cheese, Underplate, Birds	55.00
Royal Doulton, **Dish,** Child's, Bunnies Bathing	18.00
Royal Doulton, **Dish,** Child's, Three Blind Mice, 8 1/4 In.Diameter	45.00
Royal Doulton, **Dish,** Dickensware, Sairey Gamp, 4 In.Square	15.00 To 18.00
Royal Doulton, **Dish,** Feeding, Boy On Beach	40.00
Royal Doulton, **Dish,** Mr.Pickwick, Octagonal, 8 3/4 X 8 3/4 In.	60.00
Royal Doulton, **Dish,** Nut, Canadian National Steamship, 2 1/4 In.Square	12.50
Royal Doulton, **Dish,** Relish, Dickensware, Little Nell, Hexagon, 5 In.	50.00
Royal Doulton, **Dish,** The Fat Boy, 7 1/4 X 8 3/8 In.	75.00
Royal Doulton, **Eggcup,** Madras	10.00
Royal Doulton, **Ewer,** Relief Head Of Gladstone, Coat Of Arms, C.1890, 8 In.	350.00
Royal Doulton, **Figurine,** A La Mode, HN 2544	145.00
Royal Doulton, **Figurine,** A Victorian Lady, No.728	200.00
Royal Doulton, **Figurine,** Abdullah, 6 1/4 In.	450.00
Royal Doulton, **Figurine,** Adrienne, HN 2152, Purple, 7 5/8 In.	115.00 To 125.00
Royal Doulton, **Figurine,** Airdale, HN 1023	40.00
Royal Doulton, **Figurine,** Anabella, HN 1871	325.00 To 450.00
Royal Doulton, **Figurine,** Angela, HN 1204	475.00
Royal Doulton, **Figurine,** Annette, HN 1471	275.00
Royal Doulton, **Figurine,** Annette, HN 1472	250.00
Royal Doulton, **Figurine,** Annette, HN 1550	250.00
Royal Doulton, **Figurine,** Apple Maid, HN 2160	295.00 To 350.00
Royal Doulton, **Figurine,** At Ease, HN 2473	105.00
Royal Doulton, **Figurine,** Autumn Breeze	80.00
Royal Doulton, **Figurine,** Autumn Breezes, HN 1911, 7 1/2 In.	65.00 To 125.00
Royal Doulton, **Figurine,** Autumn Breezes, HN 1913	89.00 To 125.00
Royal Doulton, **Figurine,** Autumn Breezes, HN 1934	65.00 To 85.00
Royal Doulton, **Figurine,** Babie, HN 1679	28.00
Royal Doulton, **Figurine,** Baby Bunting, HN 2108	165.00
Royal Doulton, **Figurine,** Bachelor, HN 2319	120.00 To 150.00
Royal Doulton, **Figurine,** Ballad Seller, HN 2266, 7 3/4 In.	180.00 To 215.00
Royal Doulton, **Figurine,** Ballerina, HN 2116	150.00 To 205.00
Royal Doulton, **Figurine,** Balloon Man, HN 1954, 7 1/2 In.	54.00
Royal Doulton, **Figurine,** Balloon Seller With Child, HN 583	325.00 To 500.00
Royal Doulton, **Figurine,** Barn Owls, Larger Protecting Smaller, C.1940, 5 In.	390.00
Royal Doulton, **Figurine,** Beggar	350.00
Royal Doulton, **Figurine,** Belle O' The Ball, HN 1997	105.00
Royal Doulton, **Figurine,** Bess, HN 2002	175.00 To 225.00
Royal Doulton, **Figurine,** Biddy, Green, HN 1445	130.00
Royal Doulton, **Figurine,** Biddy, HN 1513, 5 1/2 In.	225.00

Royal Doulton, Figurine, Bunny, HN 2214, 5 In.

Royal Doulton, Figurine, Choir Boy, HN 2141, 4 7/8 In.

Royal Doulton, Figurine, Daffy Down Dilly, HN 1712, 8 1/4 In.

Royal Doulton, Figurine, Diana, HN 1986, 5 1/2 In.

Royal Doulton, Figurine, Black Cocker, HN 1021	62.00
Royal Doulton, Figurine, Blithe Morning, HN 2021	120.00 To 135.00
Royal Doulton, Figurine, Blithe Morning, HN 2065	135.00
Royal Doulton, Figurine, Bluebeard, HN 2105	100.00 To 150.00
Royal Doulton, Figurine, Bo-Peep, HN 1811, 5 In.	55.00
Royal Doulton, Figurine, Bonnie Lassie, HN 1626	195.00 To 245.00
Royal Doulton, Figurine, Boxer, HN 2643	39.50
Royal Doulton, Figurine, Bride, HN 2166	90.00 To 125.00
Royal Doulton, Figurine, Bridesmaid, HN 2148	160.00
Royal Doulton, Figurine, Bridesmaid, HN 2196	55.00
Royal Doulton, Figurine, Bridget, HN 2070	200.00
Royal Doulton, Figurine, Broken Lance, HN 2041	265.00
Royal Doulton, Figurine, Broken Lance, HN 2041	255.00 To 265.00
Royal Doulton, Figurine, Bunny, HN 2214, 5 In.	Illus 40.00
Royal Doulton, Figurine, Buttercup, HN 2309	65.00
Royal Doulton, Figurine, Camellia, HN 1111	200.00 To 220.00
Royal Doulton, Figurine, Carmen, HN 2545	145.00
Royal Doulton, Figurine, Carolyn, HN 2112	250.00
Royal Doulton, Figurine, Carpet Seller, HN 1464, 9 1/4 In.	190.00
Royal Doulton, Figurine, Cat, HN 999, 5 In.	49.00
Royal Doulton, Figurine, Celeste, HN 2237	135.00 To 160.00
Royal Doulton, Figurine, Celia, HN 1727	550.00
Royal Doulton, Figurine, Cellist, HN 2226, 8 1/4 In.	220.00 To 450.00
Royal Doulton, Figurine, Chestnut Mare, HN 2522	375.00
Royal Doulton, Figurine, Child On A Crab, HN 32	475.00
Royal Doulton, Figurine, Child, HN 603B	300.00
Royal Doulton, Figurine, Chloe, HN 1765	190.00
Royal Doulton, Figurine, Choir Boy, HN 2141, 4 7/8 In.	Illus 60.00
Royal Doulton, Figurine, Christmas Time, HN 2110	300.00
Royal Doulton, Figurine, Cissie, HN 1809	40.00 To 41.00
Royal Doulton, Figurine, Claribel, HN 1951, Dated 1942	175.00
Royal Doulton, Figurine, Cobbler, HN 1706	175.00 To 200.00
Royal Doulton, Figurine, Columbine, HN 2185	155.00 To 169.00
Royal Doulton, Figurine, Columbine, HN 2185, 7 1/4 In.	300.00
Royal Doulton, Figurine, Cookie, HN 2218	75.00
Royal Doulton, Figurine, Corgi, HN 2558	95.00
Royal Doulton, Figurine, Craftsman, HN 2284	400.00
Royal Doulton, Figurine, Curly Knob, HN 1627, C.1943	200.00

Royal Doulton, Figurine, Curly Locks, HN 2049 .... 140.00 To 250.00
Royal Doulton, Figurine, Daffy Down Dilly, HN 1712, 8 1/4 In. .... *Illus* 110.00
Royal Doulton, Figurine, Dainty Mae, HN 1656 .... 200.00
Royal Doulton, Figurine, Daisy, HN1961 .... 210.00
Royal Doulton, Figurine, Daphne, HN 2268 .... 105.00
Royal Doulton, Figurine, Darby, HN 2024 .... 145.00
Royal Doulton, Figurine, Darling, HN 1319, 7 1/2 In. 80.00
Royal Doulton, Figurine, Dawn, HN 1858 .... 250.00 To 395.00
Royal Doulton, Figurine, Dawn, HN 1858, Dated 1941, 10 In. 500.00
Royal Doulton, Figurine, Debbie, HN 2385 .... 41.50
Royal Doulton, Figurine, Debutante, HN 2210 .... 250.00
Royal Doulton, Figurine, Delight, HN 1772 .... 110.00 To 195.00
Royal Doulton, Figurine, Delphine, HN 2136 .... 250.00
Royal Doulton, Figurine, Diana, Blue, HN 1716 .... 90.00 To 155.00
Royal Doulton, Figurine, Diana, HN 1986, 5 1/2 In. .... *Illus* 55.00
Royal Doulton, Figurine, Dimity, HN 2169 .... 310.00
Royal Doulton, Figurine, Dinky Do, HN 1678 .... 32.00
Royal Doulton, Figurine, Dog, Spaniel, Reclining, HN 1104, 4 X 2 In. 35.00
Royal Doulton, Figurine, Dorcas, HN 1491 .... 160.00
Royal Doulton, Figurine, Dorcas, HN 1558 .... 195.00 To 205.00
Royal Doulton, Figurine, Dragon, Flambe, 7 1/2 X 10 1/2 In. 295.00
Royal Doulton, Figurine, Easter Day, HN 1976, 7 1/4 In. 295.00
Royal Doulton, Figurine, Easter Day, HN 2039, 7 1/4 In. 255.00
Royal Doulton, Figurine, Elegance, HN 2264, 1960, 7 1/2 In. 100.00
Royal Doulton, Figurine, Elephant, Flambe Mark, 8 1/2 In. 48.00
Royal Doulton, Figurine, Elephant, HN 2644, 6 1/2 In. .... 85.00 To 95.00
Royal Doulton, Figurine, Eliza, HN 2543 .... 145.00
Royal Doulton, Figurine, Ermine Coat, HN 1981 .... 150.00 To 225.00
Royal Doulton, Figurine, Esmerelda, HN 2168 .... 310.00
Royal Doulton, Figurine, Estelle, HN 1802 .... 445.00
Royal Doulton, Figurine, Falstaff, HN 2054 .... 95.00
Royal Doulton, Figurine, Fat Boy, HN 1893, 7 In. 200.00
Royal Doulton, Figurine, First Steps, HN 2242, 6 3/4 In. 380.00
Royal Doulton, Figurine, Fleur, HN 2368 .... 70.00
Royal Doulton, Figurine, Flower Seller's Children, HN 1342, 7 In. 168.75
Royal Doulton, Figurine, Forty Winks, HN 1974 .... 135.00 To 160.00
Royal Doulton, Figurine, Fox, HN 130, Shades Of Brown, 4 1/2 In. 160.00
Royal Doulton, Figurine, French Poodle, HN 2631, 6 1/2 X 6 In. 55.00
Royal Doulton, Figurine, Friar Tuck, HN 2143 .... 250.00 To 295.00
Royal Doulton, Figurine, Gay Morning, HN 2135, 7 In. .... 140.00 To 225.00
Royal Doulton, Figurine, Genevieve, HN 1962 .... 120.00 To 135.00
Royal Doulton, Figurine, Geraldine, HN 2348 .... 63.00 To 85.00
Royal Doulton, Figurine, Giselle, HN 2139 .... 235.00
Royal Doulton, Figurine, Giselle, The Forest Glade, HN 2140, 7 1/4 In. 325.00
Royal Doulton, Figurine, Gladiator, Small 235.00
Royal Doulton, Figurine, Golden Days, HN 2274 .... 85.00
Royal Doulton, Figurine, Good King Wenceslas, HN 2118 .... 125.00 To 150.00
Royal Doulton, Figurine, Good Morning, HN 2671, 8 In. .... 65.00 To 95.00
Royal Doulton, Figurine, Gossips, HN 2025 .... 275.00 To 310.00
Royal Doulton, Figurine, Granny's Heritage, HN 2031 .... 350.00
Royal Doulton, Figurine, Granny's Shawl, HN 1647 .... 325.00
Royal Doulton, Figurine, Greta, HN 1485, 5 1/2 In. .... 150.00 To 260.00
Royal Doulton, Figurine, Gude Grey Mare, HN 2532 .... 250.00 To 285.00
Royal Doulton, Figurine, Gude Grey Mare, HN 2569, Dated 1945 .... 225.00
Royal Doulton, Figurine, Guinea Hen, Flambe, 3 1/2 X 5 3/4 n. 220.00
Royal Doulton, Figurine, Guy Fawkes, HN 98, 10 1/2 In. 525.00
Royal Doulton, Figurine, Gwynneth, HN 1980 .... 300.00
Royal Doulton, Figurine, Gypsy Dance, HN 2230 .... 200.00 To 235.00
Royal Doulton, Figurine, Harlequin, HN 2186 .... 169.00 To 225.00
Royal Doulton, Figurine, Harmony, HN 2824 .... 75.00
Royal Doulton, Figurine, He Loves Me, HN 2046 .... 110.00
Royal Doulton, Figurine, Her Ladyship, HN 1977, 7 In. .... 235.00 To 325.00
Royal Doulton, Figurine, Hinged Parasol, HN 1579 .... 335.00
Royal Doulton, Figurine, Honey, HN 1909 .... 260.00
Royal Doulton, Figurine, Hornpipe, HN 2161 .... 375.00
Royal Doulton, Figurine, Invitation, HN 2170, 5 1/2 In. .... 70.00 To 95.00

Royal Doulton, Figurine, Irene, HN 1621, 6 3/4 In. .... 225.00 To 275.00
Royal Doulton, Figurine, Jack, HN 2060 .... 70.00
Royal Doulton, Figurine, Janice, HN 2165 .... 245.00
Royal Doulton, Figurine, Jean, HN 2032 .... 150.00 To 235.00
Royal Doulton, Figurine, Jennifer, HN 1484 .... 350.00
Royal Doulton, Figurine, Jersey Milkmaid, HN 2057, 6 1/4 In. .... 150.00 To 180.00
Royal Doulton, Figurine, Jolly Sailor, HN 2172 .... 375.00
Royal Doulton, Figurine, Judge, HN 2443 .... 40.00 To 95.00
Royal Doulton, Figurine, Judith, HN 2089 .... 210.00
Royal Doulton, Figurine, Julia, HN 2705 .... 65.00
Royal Doulton, Figurine, Karen, HN 1994 .... 350.00
Royal Doulton, Figurine, Kate, HN 2789 .... 64.00
Royal Doulton, Figurine, Katrina, HN 2327 .... 185.00 To 345.00
Royal Doulton, Figurine, King Charles, HN 404 .... 600.00
Royal Doulton, Figurine, Lady Betty, HN 1967 .... 245.00
Royal Doulton, Figurine, Lady Charmian, HN 1949, 7 1/4 In. .... *Illus* 135.00
Royal Doulton, Figurine, Lady Clare, HN 1465 .... 525.00
Royal Doulton, Figurine, Lady Musicians, Set Of 12 .... 7000.00
Royal Doulton, Figurine, Laird, HN 2361, 8 In. 63.75
Royal Doulton, Figurine, Lambing Time, HN 1890 .... 54.00 To 145.00
Royal Doulton, Figurine, Leading Lady, Blue & Yellow, HN 2269 .... 85.00
Royal Doulton, Figurine, Leisure Hour, HN 2055 .... 300900 To 375.00
Royal Doulton, Figurine, Lily, HN 1798, 5 1/4 In. .... 75.00 To 150.00
Royal Doulton, Figurine, Lisa, HN 2310, 7 In. 85.00
Royal Doulton, Figurine, Little Boy Blue, HN 2062 .... 65.00 To 125.00
Royal Doulton, Figurine, Little Bridesmaid, HN 1433, 5 In. .... 100.00 To 215.00

Royal Doulton, Figurine, Lady Charmian, HN 1949, 7 1/4 In.

Royal Doulton, Figurine, Little Miss Muffet, HN 1936, Red .... 100.00 To 160.00
Royal Doulton, Figurine, Long John Silver, HN 2204 .... 325.00 To 350.00
Royal Doulton, Figurine, Love Letter, HN 2149 .... 200.00
Royal Doulton, Figurine, Lydia, HN 1907, Green 185.00
Royal Doulton, Figurine, Madonna, HN 10 .... 1000.00
Royal Doulton, Figurine, Margaret, HN 1989 .... 210.00 To 250.00
Royal Doulton, Figurine, Margery, HN 1413, 10 1/4 In. 425.00
Royal Doulton, Figurine, Marguerite, HN 1928 .... 225.00
Royal Doulton, Figurine, Marie, HN 1370 .... 32.00 To 75.00
Royal Doulton, Figurine, Market Day, HN 1991 .... 185.00
Royal Doulton, Figurine, Mary, Mary, HN 2044 .... 125.00 To 135.00
Royal Doulton, Figurine, Masquerade, HN 2251 .... 250.00
Royal Doulton, Figurine, Masquerade, HN 2259 .... 200.00
Royal Doulton, Figurine, Maureen, HN 1770, 7 1/2 In. .... 165.00 To 195.00
Royal Doulton, Figurine, Maytime, HN 2113 .... 225.00
Royal Doulton, Figurine, Mendicant, HN 1365 .... 150.00 To 170.00
Royal Doulton, Figurine, Midinette, HN 2090, 7 1/4 In. 235.00
Royal Doulton, Figurine, Minuet, HN 2066 .... 135.00
Royal Doulton, Figurine, Miss Demure, HN 1402 .... 125.00
Royal Doulton, Figurine, Monica, HN 1467, 4 In. 50.00
Royal Doulton, Figurine, Moor, HN 2082 .... 375.00
Royal Doulton, Figurine, Mr.Pickwick, HN 2099 .... 200.00
Royal Doulton, Figurine, My Pet, HN 2238, 4 In. .... *Illus* 55.00
Royal Doulton, Figurine, Nell Gwynn, HN 1887, 6 1/2 In. 280.00
Royal Doulton, Figurine, Newsboy, HN 2244 .... 225.00
Royal Doulton, Figurine, Noelle, NN 2179 .... 250.00

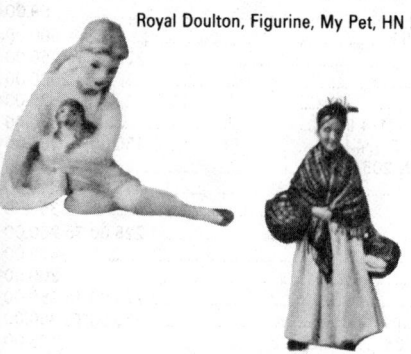

Royal Doulton, Figurine, My Pet, HN 2238, 4 In.

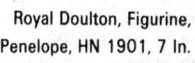

Royal Doulton, Figurine, Penelope, HN 1901, 7 In.

Royal Doulton, Figurine, Orange Lady, HN 1759, 8 In.

Royal Doulton, Figurine, Old Balloon Seller, HN 1315	65.00 To 90.00
Royal Doulton, Figurine, Old Balloon Seller, HN 1315, Dated 1942	80.00
Royal Doulton, Figurine, Old Balloon Seller, HN1315, C.1948, 7 In.	94.00
Royal Doulton, Figurine, Old King, HN 2134	168.75
Royal Doulton, Figurine, Old Meg, HN 2494, 8 In.	100.00
Royal Doulton, Figurine, Olga, HN 2463, 8 1/4 In.	97.00 To 140.00
Royal Doulton, Figurine, Olivia, HN 1995	285.00
Royal Doulton, Figurine, Orange Lady, HN 1759, 8 In.	*Illus* 125.00
Royal Doulton, Figurine, Organ Grinder, HN 2173	450.00
Royal Doulton, Figurine, Paisley Shawl, HN 1392, C.1930, 8 1/2 In.	195.00
Royal Doulton, Figurine, Paisley Shawl, HN 1914	100.00
Royal Doulton, Figurine, Paisley Shawl, HN 1987, 9 In.	240.00
Royal Doulton, Figurine, Paisley Shawl, HN 1988, 9 In.	85.00 To 175.00
Royal Doulton, Figurine, Pantalettes, HN 1362	175.00 To 250.00
Royal Doulton, Figurine, Parisian, HN 2445, 8 In.	100.00
Royal Doulton, Figurine, Patchwork Quilt, HN 1984	285.00 To 325.00
Royal Doulton, Figurine, Patricia, Green, HN 1462	375.00
Royal Doulton, Figurine, Patricia, HN 1414	350.00
Royal Doulton, Figurine, Pearly Boy, HN 1482, A Mark, 5 1/2 In.	125.00
Royal Doulton, Figurine, Pearly Boy, HN 2035, 5 1/2 In.	135.00 To 145.00
Royal Doulton, Figurine, Pearly Girl, HN 2036	160.00
Royal Doulton, Figurine, Peggy, HN 1941, Dated 1942	90.00
Royal Doulton, Figurine, Penelope, HN 1901, 7 In.	*Illus* 150.00
Royal Doulton, Figurine, Penny, HN 2338	25.00
Royal Doulton, Figurine, Phyllis, HN 1420	325.00
Royal Doulton, Figurine, Pillow Fight, HN 2270	150.00
Royal Doulton, Figurine, Polka, HN 2156	175.00 To 225.00
Royal Doulton, Figurine, Polly Peachum, HN 549	295.00 To 310.00
Royal Doulton, Figurine, Polly Peachum, HN 550	325.00
Royal Doulton, Figurine, Poodle, HN 2631	39.50
Royal Doulton, Figurine, Poodle, White, HN 1631	55.00
Royal Doulton, Figurine, Pride Of The Shires, HN 2564	325.00
Royal Doulton, Figurine, Priscilla, HN 1501	295.00
Royal Doulton, Figurine, Regency Beau, HN 1972	385.00
Royal Doulton, Figurine, Riber Boy, HN 2128	75.00 To 110.00
Royal Doulton, Figurine, Rosalind, HN 2393	105.00 To 180.00
Royal Doulton, Figurine, Rose, HN 1368, 4 1/2 In.	75.00
Royal Doulton, Figurine, Rose, HN 1416	60.00
Royal Doulton, Figurine, Sabbath Morn, HN 1982, 7 1/4 In.	185.00
Royal Doulton, Figurine, Sairey Gamp, HN 558	235.00
Royal Doulton, Figurine, Scotch Terrier, HN 1016	24.00
Royal Doulton, Figurine, Sea Harvest, HN 2257, 7 1/8 In.	75.00
Royal Doulton, Figurine, She Loves Me Not, HN 2045, 5 1/2 In.	100.00 To 125.00

Royal Doulton, Figurine, Shepherd, HN 1975, 8 3/4 In. .... 110.00 To 145.00
Royal Doulton, Figurine, Shore Leave, HN 2254 .... 59.00
Royal Doulton, Figurine, Sir Walter Raleigh, HN 1751 .... 600.00
Royal Doulton, Figurine, Skater, HN 2117 .... 225.00 To 250.00
Royal Doulton, Figurine, Smuts 2000.00
Royal Doulton, Figurine, Spaniel, HN 1020 .... 35.00
Royal Doulton, Figurine, Spring Flowers, HN 1807, 7 1/4 In. 250.00
Royal Doulton, Figurine, Spring Morning, HN 1922, 7 1/4 In. .... 150.00 To 185.00
Royal Doulton, Figurine, St.George With Dragon, HN 2051 .... 180.00
Royal Doulton, Figurine, Suitor, HN 2132 .... 315.00 To 350.00
Royal Doulton, Figurine, Summer, HN 2086 .... 350.00
Royal Doulton, Figurine, Sunday Morning, HN 2184 .... 225.00 To 260.00
Royal Doulton, Figurine, Sunshine Girl, HN 1344 .... 475.00
Royal Doulton, Figurine, Susan, HN 2056 .... 200.00
Royal Doulton, Figurine, Suzette, HN 1487 .... 225.00 To 250.00
Royal Doulton, Figurine, Suzette, HN 2026, 7 1/2 In. .... 235.00 To 250.00
Royal Doulton, Figurine, Sweet And Twenty, HN 1298 .... 125.00
Royal Doulton, Figurine, Sweet And Twenty, Small, HN 1589 .... 175.00
Royal Doulton, Figurine, Sweet Anne, HN 1330, 7 In. 220.00
Royal Doulton, Figurine, Sweet Anne, HN 1331 .... 150.00
Royal Doulton, Figurine, Sweet Anne, HN 1453, 7 In. 225.00
Royal Doulton, Figurine, Sweet Dreams, HN 2380 .... 50.00
Royal Doulton, Figurine, Sweet Lavender, HN 1373 .... 400.00
Royal Doulton, Figurine, Sweet Maid, HN 1505 .... 350.00
Royal Doulton, Figurine, Tailor, '56-'59, HN 2174 .... 375.00
Royal Doulton, Figurine, Tall Story, HN 2248 .... 105.00
Royal Doulton, Figurine, Teenager, HN 2203 .... 250.00
Royal Doulton, Figurine, Terrier, HN 1100 .... 20.00
Royal Doulton, Figurine, Terrier, HN 1101 .... 60.00
Royal Doulton, Figurine, The Prince Of Wales, HN 1217 .... 600.00
Royal Doulton, Figurine, Tootles, HN 1680, 4 3/4 In. 55.00
Royal Doulton, Figurine, Top O' Hill, Green, HN 1833 .... 250.00
Royal Doulton, Figurine, Top O' Hill, HN 1849 .... 125.00
Royal Doulton, Figurine, Town Crier, HN 2119, 8 1/2 In. 150.00
Royal Doulton, Figurine, Toymaker, HN 2250 .... 220.00
Royal Doulton, Figurine, Twilight, HN 2256 .... 85.00
Royal Doulton, Figurine, Uriah Heep, HN 1892, Black 300.00
Royal Doulton, Figurine, Vera, HN 1729 .... 450.00
Royal Doulton, Figurine, Veronica, HN 1517 .... 225.00
Royal Doulton, Figurine, Victorian Lady, HN 728 .... 175.00 To 220.00
Royal Doulton, Figurine, Viking, HN 2375 .... 125.00
Royal Doulton, Figurine, Viking, HN 2375 .... 105.00 To 125.00
Royal Doulton, Figurine, Vivenne, HN 2073 .... 185.00
Royal Doulton, Figurine, Votes For Women, HN 2816 .... 112.00 To 140.00
Royal Doulton, Figurine, Wardrobe Mistress, HN 2145 .... 350.00
Royal Doulton, Figurine, Wee Willie Winkie, HN 2050, 5 1/4 In. 195.00
Royal Doulton, Figurine, Welsh Corgi, HN 2559 .... 24.00
Royal Doulton, Figurine, Welsh Corgi, K 16 .... 16.00
Royal Doulton, Figurine, Willy Won't He, HN 1561 .... 295.00
Royal Doulton, Figurine, Willy Won't He, HN 1584, Red, C.1934 .... 225.00 To 325.00
Royal Doulton, Figurine, Winter, HN 2088 .... 350.00
Royal Doulton, Figurine, Wood Nymph, HN 2192 .... 250.00
Royal Doulton, Figurine, Yardley's Mother & Children 375.00
Royal Doulton, Game Dish, Pie, Caneswear, Signed, C.1790 .... 465.00
Royal Doulton, Humidor, Barrel Shaped, Blue Band, Beige Scroll, Signed, 5 In. 30.00
Royal Doulton, Humidor, Dickens Scene, Openings For Pipes On Rim, Signed 135.00
Royal Doulton, Humidor, Scenic, Brown, Yellow, Clamp On Cover 70.00
Royal Doulton, Hunt Jug, Dogs, Huntmaster, Horse, 6 In. 150.00
Royal Doulton, Jar, Tobacco, Mr. Pickwick Proposes A Toast, Signed 275.00
Royal Doulton, Jar, Tobacco, Old Charlie 495.00
Royal Doulton, Jardiniere, Dickensware, Footed, Fruit & Vines, 9 X 12 In. 300.00
Royal Doulton, Jardiniere, Gilt Lace Background, Signed, 7 1/4 In., Pair 250.00
Royal Doulton, Jardiniere, Tapestry, Gold, Green Trim, Slater, 11 X 10 In. 245.00
Royal Doulton, Jug, Dewar's, Egyptian Type Frieze Design 110.00
Royal Doulton, Jug, Dewar's, Thistle Shape, 1905 .... 135.00

Royal Doulton, Jug, Dickens, 1936, Signed Noke & Fenton, 10 X 7 In. 795.00
Royal Doulton, Jug, Dickensware, Micawber, 8 1/2 In. 95.00
Royal Doulton, Jug, Dickensware, Pickwick, Oval, 2 In. 45.00
Royal Doulton, Jug, Dickensware, Sam Weller, Marked, 2 5/8 X 1 5/8 In. 65.00
Royal Doulton, Jug, Dickensware, Square, Sykes, 7 1/2 In. 75.00
Royal Doulton, Jug, Dickensware, Sykes, 3 In. 48.00
Royal Doulton, Jug, Friar Tuck 200.00
Royal Doulton, Jug, Guy Fawkes Limited, 1934 .... 550.00
Royal Doulton, Jug, Hunting Scene, 8 1/4 In. 60.00
Royal Doulton, Jug, Jackdaw Of Rheims, Green Edging, Signed, 6 1/4 In. 85.00
Royal Doulton, Jug, Kingsware, Sir Francis Drake & Friends, Brown, 9 1/2 In. 145.00
Royal Doulton, Jug, Long John Silver, Treasure Island 265.00
Royal Doulton, Jug, Musical, Auld Mac 350.00
Royal Doulton, Jug, Old King Cole 125.00
Royal Doulton, Jug, Shakespeare Limited, 1933 .... 900.00 To 1200.00
Royal Doulton, Jug, Sir Andrew Aguecheek, 7 In. 55.00
Royal Doulton, Jug, Stoneware, Raised Figures, 7 1/4 X 5 1/2 In.Diameter 85.00
Royal Doulton, Jug, Welsh Ladies, 6 X 2 In.Diameter 45.00
Royal Doulton, Jug, Whiskey, Handled, Stopper, Dark Green, Brown 150.00
Royal Doulton, Luncheon Set, Coaching Days, C.1910, Set Of 42 .... 650.00
Royal Doulton, Matchholder, Dickensware, Sam Weller & Mr.Micawber 250.00
Royal Doulton, Mug, Bunnykins, Railroad Station Scene 10.00
Royal Doulton, Mug, Commemorative, Surrey Yeomanry Rifle Club, 5 1/4 In. 75.00
Royal Doulton, Mug, Dickensware, Fish Handle 195.00
Royal Doulton, Mug, Elizabeth At Old Moreton, 5 3/4 In. 42.00
Royal Doulton, Mug, Fox Hunt, Tan & Brown, 4 1/2 In. 65.00
Royal Doulton, Mug, Sailing Ships Scene, 6 1/2 In. 45.00
Royal Doulton, Mug, Villagers At Picnic, 5 5/8 In. 66.00
Royal Doulton, Mustard, White Raised Dogs, Brown & Tan 20.00
Royal Doulton, Pitcher & Bowl Set, Aubrey Pattern, Art Nouveau 355.00
Royal Doulton, Pitcher, Alan-A-Dale, 4 1/2 In. 29.00
Royal Doulton, Pitcher, Autumn Pattern, Horse On Each Side, 6 1/2 In. 75.00
Royal Doulton, Pitcher, Better So Than Worse, Noke, 8 In. 135.00
Royal Doulton, Pitcher, Bunnykins, To The Camp, Signed, 4 1/4 In. 30.00
Royal Doulton, Pitcher, Cavalier & His Lady, Doulton Mark, 4 In. 45.00
Royal Doulton, Pitcher, Come & Welcome, Pass By & No Offense, Noke 85.00
Royal Doulton, Pitcher, Corset Shape, Sir Thomas Belch, Saying, Crazing, 8 In. 75.00
Royal Doulton, Pitcher, Dickensware, Fagin, Green Handle, 2 5/8 In. 60.00
Royal Doulton, Pitcher, Dickensware, Mr.Micawber, Signed, 5 In. 75.00
Royal Doulton, Pitcher, Dickensware, Mr.Pickwick, Black Mark, 6 3/4 In. 79.00
Royal Doulton, Pitcher, Don Quixote, 5 1/2 In. 54.00
Royal Doulton, Pitcher, Edward VII & Alexandria Commemorative, Tan 125.00
Royal Doulton, Pitcher, Eglinton Tournament, 5 1/2 In. 64.00
Royal Doulton, Pitcher, Falstaff, 9 In. 60.00
Royal Doulton, Pitcher, Figure Of Dutch Man & Children, Marked, 2 1/2 In. 55.00
Royal Doulton, Pitcher, Fishing, 7 In. 42.50
Royal Doulton, Pitcher, Floral, 6 3/4 In. 47.50
Royal Doulton, Pitcher, Footed, The Galleon, Burslem Mark, 7 In. 67.50
Royal Doulton, Pitcher, Hand-Painted, Fish, Boat, Seaweed Handle, 8 1/4 In. 55.00
Royal Doulton, Pitcher, Helmet Shaped, Medallion Of Centurian Bust, 7 In. 58.00
Royal Doulton, Pitcher, Indian Tree, Pink, 5 In. 20.00
Royal Doulton, Pitcher, Lord & Lady, Castles, Falcon, Signed, 4 1/2 In. 45.00
Royal Doulton, Pitcher, Miniature, Santa Claus & Reindeer 55.00
Royal Doulton, Pitcher, Morrisian, 6 3/4 In. .... 92.00 To 125.00
Royal Doulton, Pitcher, Old Charley 45.00
Royal Doulton, Pitcher, Old Curiosity Shop, 7 In.Square .... 80.00 To 195.00
Royal Doulton, Pitcher, Old Peggotty, Square, Black Mark, 5 1/8 X 2 1/2 In. 65.00
Royal Doulton, Pitcher, Oliver Asks For More, Square 150.00
Royal Doulton, Pitcher, Oliver Twist With Fagin, Artful Dodger Scenes 25.00
Royal Doulton, Pitcher, Pickwick Papers, Square .... 90.00 To 195.00
Royal Doulton, Pitcher, Poor Jo 50.00
Royal Doulton, Pitcher, Scene, Deaf, 5 1/4 X 3 1/2 In. 35.00
Royal Doulton, Pitcher, Serpent Handled, 1807, 5 1/2 In. 37.50
Royal Doulton, Pitcher, Shakespeare Quotation Each Side, 7 1/2 In. 35.00
Royal Doulton, Pitcher, Sir John Falstaff, No.8328, Incised Mark, 8 1/4 In. 65.00

Royal Doulton, Pitcher, Titanian, Dogs Decoration, Cecil Aldin	85.00
Royal Doulton, Pitcher, Visit Of Elizabeth To Old Moreton Hall, 1589, 5 In.	75.00
Royal Doulton, Pitcher, Watchman What Of The Night, 8 1/4 In.	94.00
Royal Doulton, Pitcher, Watchman What Of The Night, 9 1/4 In.	95.00
Royal Doulton, Pitcher, Water, Coaching Scene	95.00
Royal Doulton, Pitcher, Water, Prince Frederick, Pinch Spout	40.00
Royal Doulton, Pitcher, Welsh Lady, Dog On Front, Marked Noke, 2 1/2 In.	55.00
Royal Doulton, Pitcher, White Hart Inn, White, A Mark, Square	175.00
Royal Doulton, Plaque, Boy Kneeling, Oval, Blue & White, 11 X 8 In.	150.00
Royal Doulton, Plate, Artful Dodger, Signed, 10 In.	42.50
Royal Doulton, Plate, Babes In Woods, 9 In.	110.00 To 195.00
Royal Doulton, Plate, Battle Of Trafalgar, 10 In.	25.00
Royal Doulton, Plate, Bill Sykes, Noke, 6 1/2 In.	40.00
Royal Doulton, Plate, Bill Sykes, 10 In.	35.00
Royal Doulton, Plate, Black Scottie Center, Early Mark, 10 1/2 In.	65.00
Royal Doulton, Plate, Blue Ground, Design Of Parrots & Florals, 10 1/4 In.	20.00
Royal Doulton, Plate, Bookworm, 10 1/2 In.	45.00
Royal Doulton, Plate, Britons All, Hearts, Clover Rim, C.1902, 9 1/2 In.	25.00
Royal Doulton, Plate, Canterbury Pilgrims, Becket's Martyrdom, 10 1/2 In.	45.00
Royal Doulton, Plate, Cavalier, Smiling Visage, 10 1/2 In.	30.00
Royal Doulton, Plate, Child's, Alice In Wonderland, 1921, 8 In.	28.50
Royal Doulton, Plate, Coaching Ways & Coaching Days, 9 In.	35.00
Royal Doulton, Plate, Coaching, 3 Horses, 5 People, C.1921-22, 10 1/2 In.	65.00
Royal Doulton, Plate, Coachman, 10 1/2 In.	30.00
Royal Doulton, Plate, Couching & Hunting Scene, 8 In., Set Of 10	150.00
Royal Doulton, Plate, Dick Swiveller, Signed, 10 In.	55.00
Royal Doulton, Plate, Dickensware, Admiral, 10 In.	46.00
Royal Doulton, Plate, Dickensware, Alfred Jingle, 10 In.	60.00
Royal Doulton, Plate, Dickensware, Artful Dodger	30.00
Royal Doulton, Plate, Dickensware, Fat Boy, 10 1/4 In.	60.00
Royal Doulton, Plate, Dickensware, Judge	46.00
Royal Doulton, Plate, Dickensware, Mr.Squeers, Yellow, Brown, 8 In.	60.00
Royal Doulton, Plate, Dickensware, Parson, 10 In.	46.00
Royal Doulton, Plate, Dickensware, Pickwick	60.00
Royal Doulton, Plate, Dickensware, Poor Jo, 9 1/2 In.	55.00
Royal Doulton, Plate, Dickensware, S.Weller	60.00
Royal Doulton, Plate, Dickensware, Squire	46.00
Royal Doulton, Plate, Dickensware, Swiveller	60.00
Royal Doulton, Plate, Dickensware, Sydney Carton, 9 1/2 In.	75.00
Royal Doulton, Plate, Dr.Johnson At The Cheshire Cheese, 10 1/4 In.	45.00
Royal Doulton, Plate, Dr.Squeers, 8 In.	50.00
Royal Doulton, Plate, Dutchman With Oar, Green Border	28.00
Royal Doulton, Plate, Falconer	37.00
Royal Doulton, Plate, Falstaff, Shakespeare Series, 10 1/2 In.	25.00
Royal Doulton, Plate, Figure Of Falstaff, 9 1/2 In.	65.00
Royal Doulton, Plate, Fox Hunt, Hand-Painted, Dated 1902, 9 1/2 In., 6 Piece	200.00
Royal Doulton, Plate, Fox Hunting, 10 1/2 In.	32.00
Royal Doulton, Plate, Gaffers, Noke, 10 1/2 In.	55.00
Royal Doulton, Plate, Harlequin	75.00
Royal Doulton, Plate, Hunting Dog In Woods, Blue Mark, 10 1/4 In.	60.00
Royal Doulton, Plate, Izaak Walton, Fisherman, 10 1/2 In.	35.00
Royal Doulton, Plate, Izaak Walton, 9 In.	35.00
Royal Doulton, Plate, Jackdaw Of Rheims, 10 1/2 In.	65.00
Royal Doulton, Plate, Johnny Appleseed	170.00
Royal Doulton, Plate, Katherine, 6 In.Square	35.00
Royal Doulton, Plate, Leather Bottle, Old English Inns Series, 10 1/2 In.	25.00
Royal Doulton, Plate, Little Man With Gun	28.00
Royal Doulton, Plate, Little Nell, 10 In.	42.50
Royal Doulton, Plate, Martha Washington, 10 1/2 In.	35.00
Royal Doulton, Plate, Micawber, Dated 1938	45.00
Royal Doulton, Plate, Norfolk Pattern, 1910 Mark, 10 1/4 In.	30.00
Royal Doulton, Plate, Old English Coaching Scene, 7 In.	25.00
Royal Doulton, Plate, Old English Coaching Scenes, 10 1/2 In.	45.00
Royal Doulton, Plate, Pipe Smoker, 10 In.	35.00
Royal Doulton, Plate, Queen Elizabeth At Moreton	30.00
Royal Doulton, Plate, Romeo & Juliet, Blue & White, 10 1/2 In.	32.00

Royal Doulton, Plate, Romeo In Courtyard, 10 In. 40.00
Royal Doulton, Plate, Romeo, 6 In.Square 35.00
Royal Doulton, Plate, Rosalind's, Portrait Of Girl, 9 3/4 In. 38.00
Royal Doulton, Plate, Rustic England, 10 In. 35.00
Royal Doulton, Plate, Sam Weller, Signed, 10 In. 50.00
Royal Doulton, Plate, San Francisco 55.00
Royal Doulton, Plate, Shakespeare 48.00
Royal Doulton, Plate, Soup, Mr.Squeers, Dated 1914, Signed 37.50
Royal Doulton, Plate, Spring Harmony 50.00
Royal Doulton, Plate, The Battle Of Hastings, 1066, 9 1/4 In.Diameter 30.00
Royal Doulton, Plate, The Doctor, 10 1/2 In. 32.00
Royal Doulton, Plate, The Kirkwood, 12 1/2 In.Diameter 17.50
Royal Doulton, Plate, Titanian, 10 1/4 In. 54.00
Royal Doulton, Plate, To Market To Buy A Fat Pig, 7 In. 37.50
Royal Doulton, Plate, Venetian Scene, 10 In. 65.00
Royal Doulton, Plate, Welsh Ladies, 9 In. 45.00
Royal Doulton, Plate, Windmills, 1910 Mark, 10 1/4 In. 30.00
Royal Doulton, Plate, Winston Churchill, Dated 1940 .... 75.00
Royal Doulton, Plate, 3 Children & Dog Sitting At Base Of Tree, 13 1/2 In. 200.00
Royal Doulton, Plate, 4 Children Playing Blindman's Bluff, 15 1/4 In. 225.00
Royal Doulton, Platter, Historic, Henry V111 At Hampton Court, 11 1/2 In. 69.00
Royal Doulton, Platter, Pansy Florals, Hound & Hare, Field, Flowers, Marked 110.00
Royal Doulton, Platter, The Kirkwood, 15 1/2 In. 22.50
Royal Doulton, Portrait Plate, Flower Blue, Welsh Lady, Fruit Border, 11 In. 65.00
Royal Doulton, Pot, Chocolate, Trotty Veck Character, Dickensware, 6 1/2 In. 95.00
Royal Doulton, Shoe, On Skate, Red 25.00
Royal Doulton, Sugar & Creamer, Coaching Days 22.50
Royal Doulton, Sugar & Creamer, Gold Melon Ribbed Sides, Blue & White 45.00
Royal Doulton, Sugar Shaker, Reverse Swirl, Cranberry 85.00
Royal Doulton, Sugar, Open, Dickensware, Fat Boy, 3 1/4 X 6 1/2 In. 85.00
Royal Doulton, Syrup, Pewter Top, Applied Egyptian Figures, 1891, 6 1/2 In. 85.00
Royal Doulton, Tankard, Oliver Twist, 6 In. 175.00
Royal Doulton, Tea Caddy, Kingsware, Old Woman Drinking Tea, 5 In. 125.00
Royal Doulton, Tea Set, Pot, 6 Cups & Saucers, Venice Gondola Scene 150.00
Royal Doulton, Teapot & Creamer, Velluma Ware, Scenic 225.00
Royal Doulton, Teapot, Glamis Thistle, Signed 67.50
Royal Doulton, Teapot, The Gallant Fishers 55.00
Royal Doulton, Tile, Izaak Walton Ware, 2 Fishermen, Signed, 5 3/4 In. 46.00
Royal Doulton, Tile, Tea, Exotic Birds & Foliage 25.00
Royal Doulton, Toby Mug, Captain Cuttle 190.00
Royal Doulton, Toby Mug, Churchill, White, 9 In. 1250.00
Royal Doulton, Toby Mug, Churchill, 5 1/4 In. 20.00
Royal Doulton, Toby Mug, Churchill, 9 In. 27.50
Royal Doulton, Toby Mug, Falstaff, 5 1/4 In. 20.00
Royal Doulton, Toby Mug, Falstaff, 8 1/2 In. 27.50
Royal Doulton, Toby Mug, Fat Boy 185.00
Royal Doulton, Toby Mug, Full Figure George Washington, Higgins, 1896, N.Y. 150.00
Royal Doulton, Toby Mug, Honest Measure, 4 1/2 In. 20.00
Royal Doulton, Toby Mug, Jolly Toby, 6 1/4 2n. 20.00
Royal Doulton, Toby Mug, Mr.Micawber, Seated, 4 1/2 In. .... 135.00 To 145.00
Royal Doulton, Toby Mug, Old Charley, 5 In. 160.00
Royal Doulton, Toby Mug, Old Charley, 8 1/2 In. .... 85.00 To 200.00
Royal Doulton, Toby Mug, Old Town Crier, Signed, 10 In. 65.00
Royal Doulton, Toby Mug, Sairey Gamp 160.00
Royal Doulton, Toby Mug, Sam Weller 170.00
Royal Doulton, Toby Mug, Singer, Full Figure, 6 1/2 In. 45.00
Royal Doulton, Toby Mug, Sleeper, Full Figure, 6 In. 45.00
Royal Doulton, Toby Mug, The Squire, 6 In. 220.00
Royal Doulton, Toothpick, Sairey Gamp 50.00
Royal Doulton, Toothpick, Three-Handled, Dutch Scene 35.00
Royal Doulton, Tray, Cardinal Wolsey, 11 X 5 In. 50.00
Royal Doulton, Tray, Dickensware, Mr.Pickwick, Brown Mark, Noke, 4 1/8 In. 55.00
Royal Doulton, Tray, Dickensware, Poor Jo, 3 1/2 X 4 In. 30.00
Royal Doulton, Tray, Dickensware, Sairey Gamp, 5 X 10 1/2 In. 75.00
Royal Doulton, Tray, Sandwich, Sairey Gamp, Old Mark, 11 3/4 X 7 3/4 In. 59.00
Royal Doulton, Tray, Venice Canal, 17 In. 42.00

Royal Doulton, Vase, Babes In The Woods, 2 Gold Handles, Flow Blue, 7 In.	95.00
Royal Doulton, Vase, Babes In Woods, Flow Blue, Marked, 11 In.	225.00
Royal Doulton, Vase, Babes In Woods, Gold Trim, 7 1/8 X 3 3/8 In.Diameter	175.00
Royal Doulton, Vase, Babes In Woods, Lady With Basket, 11 X 4 1/2 In.Diam.	225.00
Royal Doulton, Vase, Babes In Woods, Sitting By Tree, 8 1/2 In.	295.00
Royal Doulton, Vase, Babes In Woods, Snow Scene, 16 1/2 In.	695.00
Royal Doulton, Vase, Babes In Woods, 2 Handled, 5 In.	159.00
Royal Doulton, Vase, Barrel Shape, Gilt Tracery, Hand-Painted, 6 1/2 In.	80.00
Royal Doulton, Vase, Beige Tapestry, Enameled Flowers, Gold Trim, 9 In., Pair	150.00
Royal Doulton, Vase, Bulbous, Babes In The Woods, Woman With Guitar, 9 In.	275.00
Royal Doulton, Vase, Bulbous, Flared Top, Persian, 13 In.	86.00
Royal Doulton, Vase, Coach Scene, Church Steeple & Woods, 6 1/2 In.	115.00
Royal Doulton, Vase, Coaching Days, Hallmarked Silver Collar, 6 In.	90.00
Royal Doulton, Vase, Country Scene, Gold, Brown, 2 Handled	40.00
Royal Doulton, Vase, Dickensware, Artful Dodger, Black Mark, 5 3/8 In.	60.00
Royal Doulton, Vase, Dickensware, Golfers, Impressed Mark, 7 1/2 In., Pair	550.00
Royal Doulton, Vase, Dickensware, Handled, Barkis, Black Mark, 4 3/8 In.	65.00
Royal Doulton, Vase, Dickensware, Mr.Micawber, Handles, Signed, 2 1/8 In.	55.00
Royal Doulton, Vase, Dickensware, Mr.Pickwick, Double Handle, 6 1/2 In.	85.00
Royal Doulton, Vase, Dickensware, Mr.Squeers, Brown Mark, Signed, 3 X 2 In.	55.00
Royal Doulton, Vase, Dickensware, Sairey Gamp, 5 In.	70.00
Royal Doulton, Vase, Dickensware, Sykes, 3 In.Diameter	48.00
Royal Doulton, Vase, Dickensware, Tony Weller, Green Handles, 5 3/8 In.	68.00
Royal Doulton, Vase, Dickensware, Trumpet Tapley, 7 In.	75.00
Royal Doulton, Vase, Embossed Ware, Sairey Gamp & Mr. Micawber, 7 In.	155.00
Royal Doulton, Vase, Flambe, Noke, Cottage, Daisy Scene, Red, 5 7/8 In.	165.00
Royal Doulton, Vase, Flambe, Red, Purple, Yellow & White, Signed, 7 In.	190.00
Royal Doulton, Vase, Flambe, Sung Style Of Design, Mottled Effect, 9 In.	140.00
Royal Doulton, Vase, Flambe, Veined Sung, Narrow Neck, 4 3/4 In.	30.00
Royal Doulton, Vase, Flambe, Veined Sung, 8 1/2 In.	55.00
Royal Doulton, Vase, Flambe, Woodcut Design, Bulbous Bottom, 4 1/4 In.	55.00
Royal Doulton, Vase, Floral & Leaf, Blue Top, Gray Base, 8 In.	105.00
Royal Doulton, Vase, Flowers, Burslem, 7 In.	90.00
Royal Doulton, Vase, Flowers, Vines, Green, Signed Emily White, 8 1/2 In.	85.00
Royal Doulton, Vase, Foliage Ware, 8 1/2 In.	65.00
Royal Doulton, Vase, Foliage, England, 11 1/4 In.	98.00
Royal Doulton, Vase, Fuchsia, Gray Ground, Green Top, Marked, 7 1/4 In.	110.00
Royal Doulton, Vase, Handles At Base, Hand-Painted Orchids, 8 In.	97.00
Royal Doulton, Vase, Hannah Barlow, 5 Horses, 8 3/4 In.	295.00
Royal Doulton, Vase, Incised Horses & Cows, Beading, Signed, 17 In.	425.00
Royal Doulton, Vase, Iridescent, Mottled Blue Ground, Titanian, 8 X 4 In.	100.00
Royal Doulton, Vase, Iris, Handles, Blue & Gilt, 8 In.Base	97.00
Royal Doulton, Vase, Lambeth Carrara, Signed, 11 In.	125.00
Royal Doulton, Vase, Lambeth, Signed, Tapestry With Cobalt, 12 In.	165.00
Royal Doulton, Vase, Lambeth, Tapestry, Henry Simion, 12 In.	195.00
Royal Doulton, Vase, Monk, Blue On Tan, Signed, 10 In.	55.00
Royal Doulton, Vase, Mountain Scene, Signed, 6 In.	85.00
Royal Doulton, Vase, Portrait, Edward VII & Alexandra, C.1902, 9 1/2 In.	25.00
Royal Doulton, Vase, Pressed Leaf, Leaves In Copper, Marked, 9 3/4 In.	95.00
Royal Doulton, Vase, Roses, Blue, Artist Signed, 13 In.	110.00
Royal Doulton, Vase, Scenic, Porcelain, Marked, 1 3/4 X 1 1/2 In.Diameter	45.00
Royal Doulton, Vase, Scenic, 6 Incised Sheep, Marked, H. Barlow, 3 3/4 In.	295.00
Royal Doulton, Vase, Silicon, Blue Flowers, White Mid Section, 3 1/2 In.	75.00
Royal Doulton, Vase, Small Girl Holding Basket, 6-Sided, 4 X 10 In.	175.00
Royal Doulton, Vase, Squatty, 2 Handles, Dutch Figures, 4 3/4 X 5 1/2 In.	53.00
Royal Doulton, Vase, Squatty, 2 Handles, Dutch Figures, 4 3/4 X 7 3/4 In.	60.00
Royal Doulton, Vase, Titanian, Peacock Design, 8 In.	85.00
Royal Doulton, Vase, Trailing Leaves & Vines, Green, Brown, E.White, 9 In.	75.00
Royal Doulton, Vase, Trumpet, 3 Mice Musicians, Signed, 5 1/2 In.	275.00
Royal Doulton, Vase, Veined Sung, No.1618, Signed Flambe, 9 1/4 In.	72.00
Royal Doulton, Vase, Welsh Ladies, 3 1/2 In.	39.00
Royal Doulton, Vase, Welsh Woman, Signed Noke, 9 In.	68.00
Royal Doulton, Vase, Wood & House Scene, Flambe, 9 1/2 In.	140.00
Royal Doulton, Vase, Woodcut, Flambe, 7 In.	145.00
Royal Doulton, Vase, 2 Long-Haired White Goats, England, Kolsoll, 6 In.	95.00
Royal Doulton, Vase, 3 Children & Dog Sitting, 4 In.	100.00

Royal Doulton, Vase, 3 Children Lost In The Woods, Tapered Shape, 10 In. 150.00
Royal Doulton, Warmer, Bed, Lambeth Stoneware 85.00

Royal Dux is a porcelain made by Duxer Porzellanmanufaktur, a factory established in 1860 in Dux, Bohemia (now Czechoslovakia). Reproductions are being made.

Royal Dux, Bust, Actress Series, 6 1/2 In., Pair 175.00
Royal Dux, Bust, Lady, Hair Clustered, Pink Triangle Mark On Base 450.00
Royal Dux, Bust, Lady, Pink, Green & Beige, Marked, 17 In. 850.00
Royal Dux, Centerpiece, Apple & Leaves Decoration, Pink Triangle Mark 145.00
Royal Dux, Chess Set, Figurine Of Genghis Khan & Entourage, Set 480.00
Royal Dux, Figurine, Art Nouveau, Woman On Edge Of Bowl, 7 X 9 In. 145.00
Royal Dux, Figurine, Bird Dogs, Pink Triangle Mark, 8 X 10 1/2 In. 75.00
Royal Dux, Figurine, Buck, Head Over Back Antlers, Signed, 9 1/2 X 8 In. 95.00
Royal Dux, Figurine, Deer, Seated, Head Back, Antlers, Signed, 9 1/2 X 8 In. 95.00
Royal Dux, Figurine, Elephant, Gold On Gray-Tan, 5 X 7 In. 32.00
Royal Dux, Figurine, Elephant, Trunk Back Over Head, Signed, 6 X 6 1/2 In. 60.00
Royal Dux, Figurine, Fishermen Hauling In Net, Large 150.00
Royal Dux, Figurine, Flapper, 14 In. 160.00
Royal Dux, Figurine, Girl On Shell, Art Nouveau 225.00
Royal Dux, Figurine, Girl Pouring Water, Triangle Mark, 10 In. 185.00
Royal Dux, Figurine, Girl Sitting On Sea Shell, 8 In. 225.00
Royal Dux, Figurine, Hunter Group, Triangle Mark, 20 X 16 X 8 In. 575.00
Royal Dux, Figurine, Hunting Dog, Pheasant In Mouth, 7 In. 225.00
Royal Dux, Figurine, Isadora Duncan, 24 In. 390.00
Royal Dux, Figurine, Lady On Seashell, Coral Triangle Mark, 9 In. 175.00
Royal Dux, Figurine, Lady With Fruit Figure, Triangle Mark, 11 1/8 In. 135.00
Royal Dux, Figurine, Seated Dog With Large Bow Tie 100.00
Royal Dux, Figurine, Sower & Reaper, Matte, Gold Accents, 14 In., Pair 550.00
Royal Dux, Figurine, Victorian Man, Woman, Pink Triangle Mark, 9 & 8 In., Pair 275.00
Royal Dux, Figurine, Woman In Fur Lined Cape, Warming Hands, Signed, 23 In. 475.00
Royal Dux, Vase, Cream Base, Rose & Gold Painting, 9 1/2 In. 65.00
Royal Dux, Vase, Green, Scenic, Art Nouveau, Marked, C.1900, 10 7/8 In. 125.00
Royal Dux, Vase, Raised Apple Design, Handled, Triangle Mark, 15 In., Pair 360.00
Royal Dux, Vase, Roses Applied On Front With Leaves, Marked, 10 In. 78.00
Royal Dux, Vase, Satin Gray Background, Pink Triangle Mark, 10 1/4 In. 195.00

Royal Flemish glass was made during the late 1880s in New Bedford, Massachusetts, by the Mt. Washington Glass Works. It is a colored satin glass decorated in dark colors with gold designs.

Royal Flemish, Cookie Jar, Covered, Gold Enamel Lines, C.1890, 7 In. 1950.00
Royal Flemish, Vase, Roman Coin Design, Triangular 1850.00
Royal Ivy, see Pressed Glass, Royal Ivy.
Royal Lancastrian, Vase, Dated 1927, Gold Leaves, 10 1/2 In. 395.00
Royal Lancastrian, Vase, Red, Brown & Silver, Signed, 3 1/2 In. 245.00
Royal Lancastrian, Vase, Tulips, Silver Background, Dated 1924, Signed, 5 In. 170.00
Royal Lancastrian, Vase, 2 Handle, Silver Birds, Signed, 8 X 8 1/2 In. 425.00
Royal Oak, see Pressed Glass, Royal Oak

Royal Rudolstadt, a German faience factory, was established in Thuringia, Germany, in 1721. Hard paste porcelain was made by E.Bohne after 1854. Late nineteenth- and early twentieth-century pieces are most commonly found today. The later mark is a shield with the letters RW inside superseded by a crown and the words Royal Rudolstadt.

Royal Rudolstadt, see also Kewpie
Royal Rudolstadt, Bonbon, Ivory, Floral, Gilt Trim, Handled 28.00
Royal Rudolstadt, Bonbon, Leaf Shaped, Grapes, Leaves, Gold Trim 35.00
Royal Rudolstadt, Bonbon, Shell Shaped, Purple Flowers, Beige, 8 1/2 In. 52.50
Royal Rudolstadt, Bowl, Gold Trim, Fruit On Bottom, Signed, 10 In. 98.00
Royal Rudolstadt, Bowl, Gold Trim, Hand-Painted, Pink Inside, Signed, 10 In, ... 98.00
Royal Rudolstadt, Bowl, Upturned Shell Shape, Gold Trim, Marked, 10 1/2 In. 95.00
Royal Rudolstadt, Candlestick, Elephant Head Base, Trunk Shank, 11 In. 58.00
Royal Rudolstadt, Celery, Lilies, Green, White, Prussia, 13 X 5 1/2 In. 40.00
Royal Rudolstadt, Chocolate Pot, Pink & Yellow Flowers, Marked, 10 In. 85.00
Royal Rudolstadt, Chocolate Set, Signed, 15 Piece 225.00
Royal Rudolstadt, Cracker Jar, Corset Shape, Six Paneled, 8 In. 85.00

Royal Rudolstadt, Dish, Candy, Cloverleaf Shape, Hand-Painted	20.00
Royal Rudolstadt, Dish, Celery, Lilies On Green Ground, 13 X 5 1/2 In.	40.00
Royal Rudolstadt, Dish, Pickle, Pink Roses & Gold Trim, 7 In.	25.00
Royal Rudolstadt, Jar, Sweetmeat, Swirl Rib Body, Handle, 6 X 7 1/2 In.	130.00
Royal Rudolstadt, Pickle Dish, Pink Roses, Gold Border, Artist Signed, Small	37.50
Royal Rudolstadt, Plate, Open Handles, Peanuts & Vines, 10 In.	27.50
Royal Rudolstadt, Plate, Pastel, Flowers, Gold Trim, 8 1/2 In.	15.00
Royal Rudolstadt, Plate, Pink Band, Yellow & White Roses, 6 In.	11.00
Royal Rudolstadt, Plate, Portrait, Open Handles, Gold Trim, 11 In.	45.00
Royal Rudolstadt, Plate, Sheep In Meadow, Gold Edge, 8 1/2 In.	25.00
Royal Rudolstadt, Plate, White & Peach Roses, 8 In.	23.00
Royal Rudolstadt, Server, Tidbit, Hand-Painted, Gold Design, Art Deco	30.00
Royal Rudolstadt, Sugar & Creamer, Oblong Shape, Gold Handle, Signed	50.00
Royal Rudolstadt, Sugar & Creamer, Pink Roses, Beige Ground	62.00
Royal Rudolstadt, Teapot, Raised Swirl Design	30.00
Royal Rudolstadt, Tray, 4 Chocolate Cups, Hand-Painted, Marked, 10 In.	100.00
Royal Rudolstadt, Vase, Gold Filigree Handles, Ivory Ground, 10 In., Pair	135.00
Royal Rudolstadt, Vase, Gourd Shape, Handles, Encrusted Gold, 5 1/4 In.	32.00
Royal Rudolstadt, Vase, Raised Slip Flowers, Coralene Finish, 7 1/2 In.	50.00
Royal Rudolstadt, Vase, Raised Slip Leaves, Gilded Leaves, 7 In.	80.00
Royal Rudolstadt, Vase, Shaded Ivory To Rosy Beige, Gilt Trim, 11 1/2 In.	60.00
Royal Rudolstadt, Vase, 2 Handled, Red Roses, Gold Design, 4 1/2 In.	16.00
Royal Saxe, Bowl, Portrait, Lady, Holly In Hair, Handles, 11 1/2 In.Diameter	95.00
Royal Saxe, Vase, Ewer Shape, Portrait Medallion, Gold Handle, Signed, 8 In.	95.00
Royal Saxe, Vase, Portrait, Pedestal, Gold Handles, 9 In.	50.00

Royal Vienna was established in Vienna by Claude Innocentius du Paquier in 1719. The factory closed in 1865. Since then, various German and Austrian factories have reproduced Royal Vienna wares, complete with the original beehive mark.

Royal Vienna, see also Beehive

Royal Vienna, Basket, Hanging, Futura, Leaf Design	75.00
Royal Vienna, Basket, Hanging, Twig Handles, Apple Blossoms, 5 1/2 In.Diam.	45.00
Royal Vienna, Basket, Twig Handles, Blue Bushberry, 8 In.	35.00
Royal Vienna, Biscuit Jar, Portrait Scene, Silver Trim	160.00
Royal Vienna, Bowl, 4 Maidens, Scalloped Edge, Beading, Beehive, 12 X 2 In.	125.00
Royal Vienna, Cake Set, Beehive Mark, C.1910, 25 Piece	400.00
Royal Vienna, Candlestick, Black, Pair	45.00
Royal Vienna, Candlestick, Blackberry, 4 X 5 In.	45.00
Royal Vienna, Cup & Saucer, Cobalt Blue & Brown, Bacchanal Scene	35.00
Royal Vienna, Cup & Saucer, Demitasse, Maiden & Cupid, Beehive Mark	30.00
Royal Vienna, Cup & Saucer, Floral, Red, Cobalt, Square, Blue Beehive	40.00
Royal Vienna, Cup, Saucer & Spoon, White & Cobalt, Beehive Mark	75.00
Royal Vienna, Figurine, Bust Of Boy, Feathers On Black Hat, 5 In.	225.00
Royal Vienna, Figurine, Cleopatra, Holding Snake, Beehive Mark, 8 1/2 In.	90.00
Royal Vienna, Jardiniere, Normandy, 8 1/2 X 6 5/8 In.Base	140.00
Royal Vienna, Jardiniere, Rosecraft Vintage, 8 In.	50.00
Royal Vienna, Plaque, Mandolin Player, Wagner, 19 3/4 In. *Illus*	1600.00
Royal Vienna, Plaque, Ulysses, Achilles, C.1800, 15 In. *Illus*	800.00
Royal Vienna, Plate, Bird Medallions, Crown Mark & Beehive, 10 In.	155.00
Royal Vienna, Plate, C.Herr, Signed, Octagonal, Shield Mark, C.1800, 13 1/2 In.	1200.00
Royal Vienna, Plate, Dutch Woman & Children In Potato Field, 10 In.	40.00
Royal Vienna, Plate, Girl Picks From Tree, Beehive Mark, 7 1/4 In., Pair	160.00
Royal Vienna, Plate, Gold Arabesque Design, Blue Shield Mark, 8 7/8 In.	395.00
Royal Vienna, Plate, Gold Tracery, 3 Dutch Women & Baby, Beehive, 10 In.	80.00
Royal Vienna, Plate, Maiden, Young Man, Beehive, Signed Kauffmann, 9 1/2 In.	185.00
Royal Vienna, Plate, Melon Boys, Shooting Dice, Blue Beehive Mark, 9 1/2 In.	295.00
Royal Vienna, Plate, Mother & Children On Shore Looking At Sea, Green	85.00
Royal Vienna, Plate, Portrait, Artist Signed, 9 3/4 In.	375.00
Royal Vienna, Plate, Portrait, Artist Wagner, 8 In.	425.00
Royal Vienna, Plate, Portrait, Fruhlings Lied, Lady, Cupid, C.1870, 9 1/2 In.	325.00
Royal Vienna, Plate, Portrait, Lady With A Torch, Wagner, C.1850, 9 1/2 In.	375.00
Royal Vienna, Plate, Portrait, Malerei V Rossler, Ahne, C.1850, 9 1/2 In.	350.00
Royal Vienna, Plate, Portrait, 1800s, Signed Kaulbach, 14 1/2 In., Pair	500.00
Royal Vienna, Plate, Scenic, Beehive, 13 In.	47.00
Royal Vienna, Plate, Underglaze Blue Beehive Mark, Signed Painting, 9 In.	500.00

Royal Vienna, Plaque, Mandolin
Player, Wagner, 19 3/4 In.

Royal Vienna, Plaque, Ulysses, Achilles, C.1800, 15 In.

Royal Vienna, Plate, Wall, Tristan & Isolde, Shield, C.1900, 18 In.	1300.00
Royal Vienna, Plate, 2 Monks With Steins, A Jolly Table, Signed, 9 1/2 In.	265.00
Royal Vienna, Portrait Plate, En Traum, Cobalt Border, Signed, 8 In.	175.00
Royal Vienna, Stein, Gold Mount, Crown Lift, Beehive Mark, 1/2 Liter	1200.00
Royal Vienna, Sugar & Creamer, Portraits, Gold Beading, Blue, Signed	950.00
Royal Vienna, Table Set, Hand-Painted, Signed Angelica Kauffmann, 7 Piece	900.00
Royal Vienna, Tea Set, Portraits, Signed Richter, 3 Piece	850.00
Royal Vienna, Tray, Dresser, Bust Portrait, Gold Flowers, Beehive	47.50
Royal Vienna, Tray, Dresser, Portrait, Signed Kauffmann, Beehive, 11 X 7 In.	97.50
Royal Vienna, Urn, Classical Scene, Beehive Mark, Signed, 16 1/2 In., Pair	500.00
Royal Vienna, Urn, Cobalt Blue, Signed Painting, Covered, 13 In.	550.00
Royal Vienna, Urn, Covered, Open Gold Handles, Beehive Mark, 16 1/2 In., Pair	600.00
Royal Vienna, Urn, Covered, Portrait, Josephine, Crown Finial, Signed, 10 In.	550.00
Royal Vienna, Urn, Grecian Figures, Beehive Mark, C.1880, 7 1/2 In., Pair	390.00
Royal Vienna, Urn, Portrait Of Josephine, Signed Wagner, 10 In.	550.00
Royal Vienna, Urn, The Wedding, Artist Signed A.Weh, C.1870, 12 1/2 In.	525.00
Royal Vienna, Vase, Florentine, Handle, Ivory, 5 X 8 1/2 In.	50.00
Royal Vienna, Vase, Gold Overlay Flowers, Beehive, C.1850, 9 1/2 In.	365.00
Royal Vienna, Vase, Gold Trim, Iridescent Blue, Ladies, Beehive Mark, 5 In.	225.00
Royal Vienna, Vase, Hand-Painted, Figures Around Entire Vase, 33 In.	1885.00
Royal Vienna, Vase, Handled, Portrait Of Lady With Dog, Crown Mark, 10 In.	350.00
Royal Vienna, Vase, Iridescent, Pinched Neck, Medallion Front & Back, 12 In.	250.00
Royal Vienna, Vase, Ivory Ground, Gold Design & Rim, Signed, 7 3/4 In., Pair	475.00
Royal Vienna, Vase, Maiden, Painted Shield & Numeral, C.1910, 9 1/2 In.	550.00
Royal Vienna, Vase, Ming Tree, 8 In.	45.00
Royal Vienna, Vase, Portrait Marie Antoinette, Gold Handles, 6 3/4 In.	250.00
Royal Vienna, Vase, Portrait, Signed Wagner, 5 1/2 In.	450.00
Royal Vienna, Vase, 2 Women Sitting On Log, Gold & Cobalt, Signed, 5 3/4 In.	165.00
Royal Vienna, Vase, 3 Maids Flowing Gowns, Gilt, Jewels, Pink, Handles, 10 In.	239.00

*Royal Worcester porcelain was made in the later period of Worcester
pottery, which was originally established in 1751. The Royal Worcester
trade name has been used by Worcester Royal Porcelain Company, Ltd.,
since 1862.*

Royal Worcester, Bottle, Vinegar & Oil, Basketweave Design, Green Mark	95.00
Royal Worcester, Bowl, Open Work Top, Embossed, Marked, 9 1/4 In.Diameter	375.00
Royal Worcester, Bowl, Sailing Ship, 2 Cherubs On Swan, 12 X 9 In.	300.00
Royal Worcester, Box, Trinket, Covered, Raised Leaves, Gold Trim, 2 X 4 In.	85.00
Royal Worcester, Cachepot, Hand-Painted Birds, 2 Handles, 2 In.	75.00
Royal Worcester, Candleholder, Cream, 3 Molded Owls, Gold Trim, Signed	150.00
Royal Worcester, Candlesnuffer, Cook, Dress, White Apron, Purple Mark	115.00
Royal Worcester, Candlesnuffer, Girl In Hat, Feather & Ribbon, C.1870-89	105.00
Royal Worcester, Candlesnuffer, Glazed Parian, Greenaway Boy, Purple Mark	85.00
Royal Worcester, Candlesnuffer, Monk & Nun, Black Mark	23.50
Royal Worcester, Candlesnuffer, Mrs.Caudle, Black Mark	27.50
Royal Worcester, Candlesnuffer, Old Granny Snow	100.00
Royal Worcester, Candlesnuffer, Plumed Hat, G. & Co.	120.00
Royal Worcester, Candlestick, Art Nouveau, Dated 1892, 6 1/4 In	335.00 To 350.00
Royal Worcester, Chocolate Pot, Enameled Flowers, Purple Mark	95.00
Royal Worcester, Creamer, White, C.1897, 3 1/4 In.	50.00
Royal Worcester, Cup & Saucer, Cornflowers, Twig Handle, Oversized	12.50

Royal Worcester, Cup & Saucer, Demitasse, Nut On Leaf, 1903, Cup 2 In.	95.00
Royal Worcester, Cup & Saucer, Florizel, Bouillon, Set Of 8	35.00
Royal Worcester, Cup & Saucer, Twig Handle, C.1887	15.00
Royal Worcester, Dinner Service, Watteau, 73 Pieces	400.00
Royal Worcester, Dish, Scalloped Shell, Dolphin Feet, 1886, 4 X 5 1/4 In.	275.00
Royal Worcester, Dish, Shape Of 2 Leaves, Gilt Turtle, Oblong, 1909, 1 X 5 In.	145.00
Royal Worcester, Dish, 3 Shaped Panels, Hand-Painted, Gilt, C.1765, 7 In.	1200.00
Royal Worcester, Dresser Set, 5 Piece	195.00
Royal Worcester, Ewer, Bamboo Handle, Hand-Painted, Purple Mark, 7 In.	95.00
Royal Worcester, Ewer, Bamboo Shoot Handle, 1887, 10 1/2 In.	285.00
Royal Worcester, Ewer, Cherry Blossoms, 1887 Mark, 6 1/2 In. *Illus*	150.00
Royal Worcester, Ewer, Double Walled Reticulated Neck, 1888, 10 1/4 In.	585.00
Royal Worcester, Ewer, Dragon Handled, Raised Gilt, Dated 1888, 7 1/4 In.	295.00
Royal Worcester, Ewer, Flowers & Leaves, Gold Handle, Purple Mark, 5 1/4 In.	95.00
Royal Worcester, Ewer, Flowers Outlined In Gold, C.1880, 8 1/2 In.	165.00
Royal Worcester, Ewer, Gold Top & Handle, Gilted, Green Mark, 12 In.	325.00
Royal Worcester, Ewer, Lid, Gold Flowers & Trim, Purple Mark, 9 1/2 In.	155.00
Royal Worcester, Ewer, Raised Two Tone Gold Design, Dated 1886, 7 In.	185.00
Royal Worcester, Ewer, Reticulated Top, Green Mark, C.1880, 17 1/2 In.	350.00
Royal Worcester, Ewer, Reticulated, Butterflies & Flowers, 18 In.	300.00
Royal Worcester, Ewer, Reticulated, 1890 Mark, Pedestal Base, 11 3/4 In.	585.00
Royal Worcester, Ewer, Satin Finish, Dated 1898, 8 3/4 In.	195.00
Royal Worcester, Figurine, Babes In The Wood, 3381, Double	150.00
Royal Worcester, Figurine, Burmah, F.Doughty, 5 In.	60.00 To 65.00
Royal Worcester, Figurine, Corgi	115.00
Royal Worcester, Figurine, Dutch Girl	70.00
Royal Worcester, Figurine, Eastern Water Carrier, Woman, 11 1/2 X 4 3/4 In.	695.00
Royal Worcester, Figurine, Elephant With Howdah, 1874, Gold Trim, 8 X 9 In.	550.00
Royal Worcester, Figurine, First Dance, Aubergine Dress, Pink Scarf	125.00
Royal Worcester, Figurine, Friday's Child, No. 3261, 6 1/2 In.	55.00 To 82.00
Royal Worcester, Figurine, Girl By Tree Stump, Signed Hadley, 9 In.	325.00
Royal Worcester, Figurine, Girl With Lamb, No.3012, Signed, 9 1/2 In.	149.00
Royal Worcester, Figurine, Girl, Shot Enamel, 1874, 6 1/2 In.	345.00
Royal Worcester, Figurine, Goosie, Goosie, Gander, No. 3304	125.00
Royal Worcester, Figurine, Grandmother's Dress, F.Doughty, 6 1/2 In.	70.00
Royal Worcester, Figurine, Grecian Lady Water Carrier, Marked, 9 1/4 In.	300.00
Royal Worcester, Figurine, Grecian Woman, Bottle On Head, Signed, 19 1/2 In.	425.00
Royal Worcester, Figurine, Group Of Three Spaniels	135.00
Royal Worcester, Figurine, Hound Dog, Seated, D.Lindner, 7 1/2 In.	145.00
Royal Worcester, Figurine, Hummingbird, Dorothy Doughty, 9 1/4 In., Pair	850.00
Royal Worcester, Figurine, Indian Brave & Squaw With Papoose, Gertner, Pair	450.00
Royal Worcester, Figurine, June	75.00
Royal Worcester, Figurine, L'Allegro, Woman In Classical Dress, 1893, 16 In.	495.00
Royal Worcester, Figurine, Lady, Cairo Water Carrier, No. 1250, 9 1/2 In.	495.00
Royal Worcester, Figurine, May, No.3455, Girl Kneeling, 5 1/4 In.	60.00
Royal Worcester, Figurine, Mischief	40.00
Royal Worcester, Figurine, Monk, Black Mark, 5 In.	100.00
Royal Worcester, Figurine, Nun, 4 In.	100.00
Royal Worcester, Figurine, Oriental Woman With Fan, Purple Mark, 7 In.	175.00
Royal Worcester, Figurine, Parakeet Boy, Blue	54.00

Royal Worcester, Pitchers *(l.)* 5 1/4 In.; *(top)* 8 In.; *(r)* 7 In.; *(front)* Ewer, 6 1/2 In.

Royal Worcester, Figurine, Parian, C.1885, 16 In., Pair

Royal Worcester, **Figurine,** Parian, C.1885, 16 In., Pair .... *Illus*	1600.00
Royal Worcester, **Figurine,** Polly Put The Kettle On, No.3303, 6 In.	45.00
Royal Worcester, **Figurine,** Rabbit Running Along Fence, No.1302, 1892, 12 In.	475.00
Royal Worcester, **Figurine,** Robin, No.3197, 2 1/2 In.	45.00
Royal Worcester, **Figurine,** Sabbath Girl .... 65.00 To	82.50
Royal Worcester, **Figurine,** Saturday Boy .... 75.00 To	95.00
Royal Worcester, **Figurine,** Sea Breeze	65.00
Royal Worcester, **Figurine,** Sunday's Child, Boy, Black Mark	75.00
Royal Worcester, **Figurine,** Sunshine	200.00
Royal Worcester, **Figurine,** Thursday Boy .... 65.00 To	82.50
Royal Worcester, **Figurine,** Thursday Girl	82.50
Royal Worcester, **Figurine,** Wednesday Boy .... 65.00 To	82.50
Royal Worcester, **Figurine,** Woodland Dance, No.3076	150.00
Royal Worcester, **Figurine,** Yellow-Headed Blackbird, Signed, 10 1/4 In., Pair	1800.00
Royal Worcester, **Jar,** Cookie, Blue & White, Willow Pattern, 5 1/2 In.	60.00
Royal Worcester, **Jar,** Cookie, Floral, Gold Decoration, Underplate, C.1889	250.00
Royal Worcester, **Jar,** Tobacco, Sabrina Ware, Dated 1906	125.00
Royal Worcester, **Jug,** Flat Back, Hand-Painted, 1887, Purple Mark, 5 1/4 In.	78.00
Royal Worcester, **Jug,** Flat Back, Hand-Painted, 1889, Purple Mark	95.00
Royal Worcester, **Jug,** Floral, Matte Finish, England, C.1896, 4 1/2 In.	65.00
Royal Worcester, **Mug,** Monday's Child	35.00
Royal Worcester, **Mustard Pot,** Miniature, Green, Gold Trim	23.00
Royal Worcester, **October Boy,** Boy Playing With 2 Squirrels, 7 1/2 In.	150.00
Royal Worcester, **Pepper Shaker,** Speckled Plover Egg	18.00
Royal Worcester, **Pitcher,** Beige Satin, Basket Weave, Purple Mark, 6 In.	225.00
Royal Worcester, **Pitcher,** Birds Of Paradise, Dated 1894, 6 1/2 In.	130.00
Royal Worcester, **Pitcher,** Blue Design, 1862-91, 2 1/2 In.	15.00
Royal Worcester, **Pitcher,** Bulbous, Flat Back, Decorated, 4w Mark, 6 1/2 In.	90.00
Royal Worcester, **Pitcher,** Bulbous, Gold Handle, Purple Mark, 8 3/4 In.	325.00
Royal Worcester, **Pitcher,** Cream Background, 1892-91, 2 1/2 In.	15.00
Royal Worcester, **Pitcher,** Divided Top & Spout, Ivory Ground, 1891, 4 1/2 In.	145.00
Royal Worcester, **Pitcher,** Flat Back, Gold Handle, Red Mark, Signed, 5 1/2 In.	90.00
Royal Worcester, **Pitcher,** Floral, Gilt, 1887 Mark, 8 In. .... *Illus*	175.00
Royal Worcester, **Pitcher,** Floral, Gilt, 1889 Mark, 7 In. .... *Illus*	125.00
Royal Worcester, **Pitcher,** Floral, Gilt, 1890 Mark, 5 1/4 In. .... *Illus*	100.00
Royal Worcester, **Pitcher,** Flowers, Gold Trim, Beige Background, 5 In.	85.00
Royal Worcester, **Pitcher,** Gilt Handle, Hand-Painted, 1890, 6 1/4 In.	115.00
Royal Worcester, **Pitcher,** Gold Trim & Handle, C.1892, 3 3/8 In.Base	116.00
Royal Worcester, **Pitcher,** Orchids, Gold On Handle, Signed, 5 In.	78.00
Royal Worcester, **Pitcher,** Recticulations, Beading, Purple Mark, 11 3/4 In.	295.00
Royal Worcester, **Pitcher,** Salamander, Basket Weave, Purple Mark, 6 In.	225.00
Royal Worcester, **Pitcher,** Satin Finish, Marked 1909, Gold Handle, 5 1/8 In.	95.00
Royal Worcester, **Pitcher,** Satin Ground, Gold Flowers, 1899, 8 3/4 In.	195.00
Royal Worcester, **Pitcher,** Scalloped & Scroll Pattern, Marked, 9 1/2 In.	375.00
Royal Worcester, **Pitcher,** Trefoil Shape, Oriental Design, Green Mark, 5 In.	95.00
Royal Worcester, **Pitcher,** Wrap Around Dragon In Gold Over Beige	295.00
Royal Worcester, **Plate,** Bamboo Stem, Open Handles, C.1886, 4 3/4 X 8 1/2 In.	185.00
Royal Worcester, **Plate,** Blue Underglaze, Rococo, 3 Panels, Marked, 8 In.	2200.00
Royal Worcester, **Plate,** Blue, Chinese Pagoda Decoration, C.1878, Set Of 6	45.00
Royal Worcester, **Plate,** Chantilly, Enameled, 9 In., Set Of 6	95.00

Royal Worcester, Plate, Floral Sprays, Gold Scalloped Border, Purple Mark	225.00
Royal Worcester, Plate, Floral, Matte Finish, England, C.1896, 3 In	50.00
Royal Worcester, Plate, Flowers & Pinecones, 8 In.	68.00
Royal Worcester, Plate, Gold Scale Rim, C.1889, 8 1/2 In.Diameter	22.00
Royal Worcester, Plate, Goldfish, Aqua Swirls, Hand-Painted, 10 In.	45.00
Royal Worcester, Plate, Irregular Edge, Leaf Motif, Gold Edged, 8 1/2 In.	52.00
Royal Worcester, Plate, Irregular Shape, Rococo Gold Design, 8 1/2 In.	47.00
Royal Worcester, Plate, Mums & Flying Bird, White Ground, C.1888, 10 In.	18.00
Royal Worcester, Plate, Oyster, Basket Weave, 7 Sections, Shaded Luster, 1888	60.00
Royal Worcester, Plate, Pattern C3100, 1926, H.Davis, 10 1/2 In., Set Of 12	1500.00
Royal Worcester, Plate, Raised Enamel Roses, C.1897, 8 1/4 In.Square	37.50
Royal Worcester, Plate, Supper, Royal Lilly, One Dozen	110.00
Royal Worcester, Platter, Creamware, Dated 1873, Marked, 14 X 10 In.	117.00
Royal Worcester, Rose Jar, Gold Outlining, Matching Lid, 1906, 4 3/8 In.	175.00
Royal Worcester, Salt, Master, Mermaid, White, 4 1/2 In.	32.50
Royal Worcester, Shell, Upturned On Leaf Base, 1897, Marked, 4 In.	28.00
Royal Worcester, Soup, Dish, Rosemary, 8 In.	8.00
Royal Worcester, Sugar & Creamer, Bone China, Green Mark	75.00
Royal Worcester, Sugar & Creamer, Cream Ground, Red, Orange & White Flowers	95.00
Royal Worcester, Sugar & Creamer, Wildflower Pattern, Open Sugar, Pair	225.00
Royal Worcester, Sugar & Creamer, 3-Colored Flowers, Gold Edging	95.00
Royal Worcester, Sugar Shaker, Satin Finish, Flowers, C.1885, 5 X 3 1/8 In.	125.00
Royal Worcester, Tea Set, Cream, Lily Pads, 1881 Mark, 3 Piece .... Illus	425.00
Royal Worcester, Teapot, Bamboo Handle, Purple Mark, 6 1/2 In.	185.00
Royal Worcester, Teapot, Celadon Green, Gold Filagree, Ribbed Design, 5 In.	140.00
Royal Worcester, Teapot, Double Wall, Reticulated, C.1885	400.00
Royal Worcester, Teapot, Floral On Cream Ground, Pre 1900, 6 1/2 In.	80.00
Royal Worcester, Teapot, Globular, Cover, Floral Sprig Finial, C.1770, 6 In.	400.00
Royal Worcester, Teapot, Gold On Handle, Flowers, Purple Mark, 6 3/4 In.	195.00
Royal Worcester, Teapot, Ivory Finish, Dated 1890, Purple Mark, 5 In.	400.00
Royal Worcester, Toby, Cook, Dress, Apron, Purple Mark, 1 3/4 In.	65.00
Royal Worcester, Toby, Woman In Orange Dress, No.2841, Purple Mark	65.00
Royal Worcester, Tray, Shell Shape, Gold & Red Frog, Dated 1883, 5 X 3 In.	295.00
Royal Worcester, Tumbler, Sabrina, Flowers, Blue Ground, Signed	100.00
Royal Worcester, Tureen, Covered, Rose Band, Green Mark, 6 1/2 In.	145.00
Royal Worcester, Tureen, Symmetric Floral, Trunk Handles, Gold Finial, Lid	95.00
Royal Worcester, Tureen, Underplate, C.1887, 6 X 7 In.	90.00
Royal Worcester, Urn, Reticulated Cathedral Cover, 1888, Signed, 9 1/4 In.	375.00
Royal Worcester, Vase, Bamboo Handle, Hand-Painted, Purple Mark, 7 In.	125.00
Royal Worcester, Vase, Banjo, Right & Left, Oriental Style, 1890, 9 In., Pair	575.00
Royal Worcester, Vase, Basketweave, Tan To Beige, C.1897, 3 1/4 In.	95.00
Royal Worcester, Vase, Beige Ground, Flowers, 2 Handles, C.1902, 4 1/4 In.	76.50
Royal Worcester, Vase, Beige, Gold Design & Trim, C.1902, 4 1/2 In.	50.00

Royal Worcester, Tea Set, Cream, Lily Pads,
1881 Mark, 3 Piece

Royal Worcester, Vase, Bronzed, Corrugated Body, Signed, C.1860, 6 1/2 In.	295.00
Royal Worcester, Vase, Bulbous Bottom & Trumpet Top, 9 1/2 In.	250.00
Royal Worcester, Vase, Fan Shape, 7 Openings, 1875, 6 X 11 In.	360.00
Royal Worcester, Vase, Floral, Frieze, Hexagon Neck, 1908, Artist Signed, 7 In.	350.00
Royal Worcester, Vase, Floral, Gold Tracery, Bamboo Neck, C.1890, 9 1/2 In.	175.00
Royal Worcester, Vase, Full Gold Dragon & Leaves, C.1875, 14 1/2 In.	1750.00
Royal Worcester, Vase, Geese In Flight, Raised Gold, 1884, 9 In.Matched Pr.	585.00
Royal Worcester, Vase, Gold Butterflies & Trim, Cream, 9 1/2 In.	265.00
Royal Worcester, Vase, Gold Decoration & Handles, Ram's Head, 6 7/8 In.	145.00
Royal Worcester, Vase, Gold Outlining, Green Mark, 10 In.	150.00
Royal Worcester, Vase, Gourd Shape, Handled, C.1888, 18 In.	400.00
Royal Worcester, Vase, Hand Holding, C.1865, Jewel Inserts, Marked, 6 In.	175.00

Royal Worcester, Vase, Handled, Fall Leaves, Dated 1886, 9 3/4 In.	385.00
Royal Worcester, Vase, Handled, Gold Outlined Flowers, Marked, 6 1/4 In., Pr.	265.00
Royal Worcester, Vase, Handled, Satin Finish, Gold Trim, C.1908, Marked, 6 In.	175.00
Royal Worcester, Vase, Honeycomb Base, Openwork, C.1894, Signed, 7 3/4 In.	295.00
Royal Worcester, Vase, Mazarine Blue Ground, Floral, C.1904, Signed, 6 In.	95.00
Royal Worcester, Vase, Nautilus Shape, Purple Mark, 8 1/4 In.	125.00
Royal Worcester, Vase, Nautilus Shell Shape, Shells On Base, 6 In.	62.00
Royal Worcester, Vase, Porcelain Flowers, 1911, Pair, 10 1/4 In.	395.00
Royal Worcester, Vase, Printed Crown Circle & Date Code For 1883, 11 In.	150.00
Royal Worcester, Vase, Satin Finish, Handled, Gold Trim, 1903, 6 1/4 In.Pair	265.00
Royal Worcester, Vase, Swan, Gold Trim, Purple Mark, Basket Weave, 9 3/4 In.	595.00
Royal Worcester, Vase, Swan, Satin Finish, Gold Trim, Purple Mark, 7 1/4 In.	575.00
Royal Worcester, Vase, Swirled Panel Body, Green Mark, C.1900, 11 In.	195.00
Royal Worcester, Vase, Urn Shape, Flowers Outlined In Gold, Signed, 7 In.	119.00
Royal Worcester, Vase, Water Lilies & Dragon Handle, Gold Trim, 9 In., Pair	435.00
Royal Worcester, Vase, White, Gilded, Colored Flowers, Signed, 12 In.	800.00
Royal Worcester, Violet Globe, Handled, Gold Rim, 4 1/2 X 3 In.Diameter	100.00
Royal Worcester, Wall Pocket, Teardrop Bowl, C.1889, 9 1/2 In., Pair	175.00
Royal Worcester, Whistle, Hound's Head, Purple Mark	75.00

Roycroft products were made by the Roycrofter community of East Aurora, New York, in the late nineteenth and early twentieth centuries. The community was founded by Elbert Hubbard. The products included furniture, metalware, leatherwork, and jewelry.

Roycroft, Ashtray, Copper, C.1924, R In Orb, 2 1/4 X 5 1/4 In.Diameter	75.00
Roycroft, Ashtray, Triangle, Silver Plated On Copper, 5 1/4 In.	20.00
Roycroft, Beanpot, 4 In.	42.00
Roycroft, Bookends, Copper, C.1915, R In Orb, 3 X 5 3/8 In.	75.00
Roycroft, Bookends, Embossed Borders, Floral Design, Copper, 4 1/2 X 5 In.	30.00
Roycroft, Bookends, Hammered Copper, Embossed Design	18.95 To 30.00
Roycroft, Bowl, Bread Crumb Pan, Double Sconce	95.00
Roycroft, Bowl, Copper, C.1924, 2 3/4 X 6 In.Diameter	100.00
Roycroft, Bowl, Wrought Copper, C.1915, R In Orb, 3 X 6 In.Diameter	100.00
Roycroft, Box, Copper & Mahogany, C.1914, R In Orb, 9 1/2 X 23 X 12 In.	350.00
Roycroft, Candleholder, Hammered Copper, 9 In., Pair	60.00
Roycroft, Candlestick, Copper, C.1910, R In Orb, 8 X 3 1/4 In.Diameter	100.00
Roycroft, Candlestick, Hand-Wrought, 12 1/2 In., Pair	90.00
Roycroft, Crumber Set, Hammered Brass, Signed	18.95
Roycroft, Desk Set, Copper, 4 Piece	55.00
Roycroft, Dish, Shell Shaped, Copper, Signed, 3 1/2 X 5 3/4 X 1 In.	25.00
Roycroft, Holder, Pen & Pencil, 5 Cylinder Holders, 4 1/2 X 2 3/4 In.	15.00
Roycroft, Humidor, Copper, Acid Finish, C.1924, R In Orb, 5 X 8 In.	150.00
Roycroft, Inkwell, Copper	35.00
Roycroft, Jar, Pottery, Tan Glaze, 4 1/4 In.	12.00
Roycroft, Jug, Brown Drip Glaze, 5 In.	10.00 To 35.00
Roycroft, Lamp, Copper, Mica, C.1914, R In Orb, 14 X 10 In.Diameter	500.00
Roycroft, Lamp, Desk, Mushroom Shade, Silver Over Copper, 6 In.Diameter	65.00
Roycroft, Letter Opener, Copper, C.1912, R In Orb, 7 1/2 X 1 1/4 In.	75.00
Roycroft, Tray, Copper, K.Kipp Design, C.1917, R In Orb, 10 X 22 In.Diameter	150.00
Roycroft, Tray, Oval, Art Nouveau Design, Marked, 22 X 9 1/2 In.	58.00
Roycroft, Tray, Pen, Hammered Copper	6.00
Roycroft, Vase, Camphor Glass, Hammered Copper, Silver Washed Holder	35.00
Roycroft, Vase, Hat Shape, Handles, Enamel Design, Marked, 5 X 8 In.	38.00
Rozane, see Roseville	
RRP Co., Urn, Handles, Turquoise	17.50

RS Germany porcelain was made at the factory of Rheinhold Schlegelmilch after 1869 in Tillowitz, Germany. It was sold both decorated and undecorated.

RS Germany, Ashtray, Pine Cone, Yellow Interior, 3 3/4 X 1 1/2 In.	27.00
RS Germany, Basket, Double Handle, Tillowitz	65.00
RS Germany, Basket, Etched Floral, Gold, 5 In.	32.00
RS Germany, Basket, Hand-Painted Yellow Poppies, Marked, 7 1/2 X 5 1/2 In.	50.00
RS Germany, Basket, Handled, Artist Signed, Marked, 6 1/2 In.	23.00
RS Germany, Basket, Oval, Melon Boys, Green Mark	250.00
RS Germany, Berry Set, 4 Matching Bowls, Picture Of Bowl Full Of Water	225.00

RS Germany, Berry Set, 4 Saucers, Blown Out Ribs, Ivory Ground, Gold Trim	150.00
RS Germany, Berry Set, 8 Sauce Dishes, Gold Trim, Enameled, Red Mark	110.00
RS Germany, Bonbon, 2 Handled, Blue, Fold Edge	7.50
RS Germany, Bottle, Perfume, Stopper, Roses On Peach Luster, Blue Mark	27.50
RS Germany, Bowl, Castle Scene, Satin Finish, Blown Ribbon Rim, 10 1/2 In.	395.00
RS Germany, Bowl, Cottage Scene, Gold Luster Edge, 10 In. Diameter	125.00
RS Germany, Bowl, Cream, Green & Purple Flowers, 5 In., Set Of 6	30.00
RS Germany, Bowl, Daisies, Peach Ground, Marked, 9 1/4 In.	38.00
RS Germany, Bowl, Free-Form Top, Gold Tracery, Signed, 9 In.	42.00
RS Germany, Bowl, Molded Cabbage Leaf, Hydrangeas Inside, 9 1/2 In.	125.00
RS Germany, Bowl, Petal Shaped, Gold Etched, Star & Wreath, 8 In.	70.00
RS Germany, Bowl, Pink Roses, Green & Ivory Ground, 9 In.	20.00
RS Germany, Bowl, Poppies, Green Ground, Marked, 9 1/4 In. Diameter	35.00
RS Germany, Bowl, Rose Clusters, Green Luster Ground, Marked, 9 1/4 In. Diam.	38.00
RS Germany, Bowl, Roses, Pastel Coloring, 10 1/2 In.	35.00
RS Germany, Bowl, Satin, Green & Gold Trim, 10 In.	65.00
RS Germany, Bowl, Scalloped, Hand-Painted Roses, 5 1/4 In. Diam., Set Of 6	25.00
RS Germany, Bowl, Scenic, Victorian Woman & Children, Signed, 9 1/2 In. Diam.	95.00
RS Germany, Bowl, Scenic, 4-Story House, Marked, 4 1/2 X 4 1/2 In.	75.00
RS Germany, Bowl, Snowballs, 9 In.	35.00
RS Germany, Box, Double Poppy Cover & Sides, 5 3/4 In.	35.00
RS Germany, Cake Plate, Rose Border, Satin Finish, Open Handles, 10 In.	30.00
RS Germany, Cake Set, Double Handled, 6 6 1/2 In. Plates	85.00
RS Germany, Cake Set, Flowers, Leaves, Gold Scroll, White, Green, Brown, 7 Piece	100.00
RS Germany, Cake Set, Roses, Shadow Leaves, White & Blue, 7 Piece	70.00
RS Germany, Candleholder, Yellow Roses, Pair, 4 3/4 In.	35.00
RS Germany, Celery, Double Pierced Handles, 12 3/4 X 5 1/4 In.	45.00
RS Germany, Celery, Easter Lilies & Shadow Flowers, 12 1/4 In.	30.00
RS Germany, Celery, Lilies, Marked, 4 X 8 In.	22.00
RS Germany, Celery, Pink & Yellow Roses & Shadow Flowers, 12 1/2 In.	30.00
RS Germany, Chocolate Pot. Pearlized Roses, Signed, 10 1/2 In.	50.00
RS Germany, Chocolate Pot, 2 Cups & Saucers, Poppy Design, Green Mark	132.50
RS Germany, Chocolate Pot, 3 Cups & Saucers, Ribbed Pot, Black Mark	150.00
RS Germany, Chocolate Set, Orchids, 4 Cups & Saucers	235.00
RS Germany, Chocolate Set, 3 Cups & Saucers, Luster, Gold Rims, Blue Mark	175.00
RS Germany, Chocolate Set, 4 Cups & Saucers, Orchids	185.00
RS Germany, Clematis, Lacy Gold Rim, Marked, 8 1/2 In.	24.00
RS Germany, Compote, Border Of Leaves, Gold Outlined, 3 1/4 X 5 1/2 In.	40.00
RS Germany, Cracker Jar, Satin With Orchids, Signed	65.00
RS Germany, Cracker Jar, White Jonquils	85.00
RS Germany, Creamer, Green & Pink Rose	25.00
RS Germany, Creamer, Yellow Poppies, Marked, 3 In.	10.00
RS Germany, Cruet, Stopper, White, Blue Mark, 4 1/2 In.	45.00
RS Germany, Cup & Saucer, Chocolate, Gold Trim	25.00
RS Germany, Cup & Saucer, Roses On Green Ground, Blue Mark	21.00
RS Germany, Cup, Chocolate, Satin Finish, Tulip	30.00
RS Germany, Cup, Punch, Ruby Flashed, Lillie, 1909	15.00
RS Germany, Dish, Cheese & Cracker, Tiered, Roses	75.00
RS Germany, Dish, Cheese & Cracker, Yellow Roses, Melon Tones, 9 In.	35.00
RS Germany, Dish, Gold Bird & Edge, Blue Luster, Heart Shaped, 6 1/2 In.	18.00
RS Germany, Dish, Relish, Blue Background, Peonies, 8 1/2 In.	18.00
RS Germany, Dish, Relish, Double Pierced Handles, Blue Mark, 8 X 3 3/4 In.	34.00
RS Germany, Dish, Relish, Green Luster, Floral, Handled, Green Mark	20.00
RS Germany, Dish, Relish, Open Handles, Poppies, Luster, 10 1/2 In.	28.00
RS Germany, Dish, Relish, Peach & White Poppies, 12 1/4 In.	55.00
RS Germany, Dish, Ruffled, Magnolias, 8 In.	20.00
RS Germany, Dish, Serving, Orange Luster, Carved Indian Head Top, 5 X 8 In.	35.00
RS Germany, Dresser Set, Tray, Hair Receiver, Pin Tray, 11 X 8 1/4 In.	80.00
RS Germany, Ewer, Rembrandt Night Watch, Green Mark	46.00
RS Germany, Ferner, Bisque Liner, Pink & White Roses, 5 X 9 In., Marked	120.00
RS Germany, Ferner, Roses On Green & Cream Ground, 4 X 8 In.	65.00
RS Germany, Hair Receiver & Powder Box, Covered, Yellow Lilies	65.00
RS Germany, Hair Receiver, Green With Roses, Green Mark	17.50
RS Germany, Hair Receiver, Medallions Of Pink & Yellow, Marked	22.00
RS Germany, Hair Receiver, Yellow Background With Forget-Me-Nots	15.00
RS Germany, Hatpin Holder, Calla Lily	30.00

RS Germany, **Hatpin Holder**, Green Poppy Design, R.S. Prussia Mold 38.00
RS Germany, **Hatpin Holder**, Opalescent Glaze, 4 1/2 In. 45.00
RS Germany, **Hatpin Holder**, Orange Poppy .... 26.00 To 34.00
RS Germany, **Hatpin Holder**, Pussy Willow On Both Sides 47.00
RS Germany, **Hatpin Holder**, Roses, Cork Bottom, Marked Germany 42.50
RS Germany, **Hatpin Holder**, White With Gold Luster, Flowers 28.00
RS Germany, **Hatpin Holder**, White, Gold Decoration, Green & B.I.Germany Mark 20.00
RS Germany, **Hatpin Holder**, Yellow Flowers, Gold Trim, Green Mark 28.00
RS Germany, **Holder**, Toothbrush, White Glaze 35.00
RS Germany, **Inkwell**, Cover, 6-Sided, Enameled, Gold Trim, 6 X 2 1/4 In. 40.00
RS Germany, **Jar**, Jam, Underplate, Gold Filagree 32.50
RS Germany, **Juicer**, Fruit Decoration, Green Mark 90.00
RS Germany, **Mustard Pot**, Footed, Purple Pansies On White 25.00
RS Germany, **Mustard Pot**, Iris Accented With Gold, Blue & Pink Ground 35.00
RS Germany, **Mustard Pot**, Ladle, 8 Sided, Gold Trim & Outline, Marked 28.00
RS Germany, **Mustard Pot**, Tulips On White Ground, Blue Mark 23.00
RS Germany, **Mustard Pot**, White Flowers On Green Ground 22.00
RS Germany, **Nut Set**, Compote Shaped, Master & 6 Green & White Saucers 56.00
RS Germany, **Nut Set**, Satin Magnolias, 7 Piece 110.00
RS Germany, **Pitcher**, Cider, 6 Sides, Gold Leaves, Pink Roses 125.00
RS Germany, **Pitcher**, Lemonade, Matching Lemon & Mint Plate, Green Mark 118.00
RS Germany, **Pitcher**, Lemonade, Pink Roses On Green Ground, Green Mark 105.00
RS Germany, **Pitcher**, Syrup, Calla Lily, 3 1/2 In. 30.00
RS Germany, **Planter**, Scalloped, Green Luster, Applied Gold, Liner, 6 3/4 In. 59.00
RS Germany, **Plate Set**, Orange Poppies, 6 In., Set Of 8 .... 37.00
RS Germany, **Plate**, Apricot Flowers, Scalloped Rim, Gold Beading, 6 1/2 In. 9.00
RS Germany, **Plate**, Black & Ivory, White Roses, Green Mark, 9 In. 25.00
RS Germany, **Plate**, Cake, Dogwood Pattern, Iridescent Edge, 11 3/4 In. 69.00
RS Germany, **Plate**, Cake, Pierced Handles, Rose Ground, Shadow Forms, 10 In. 40.00
RS Germany, **Plate**, Cake, Pink Roses, Marked, 10 In. 35.00
RS Germany, **Plate**, Cake, Pink, Yellow, White Roses, 10 In. 30.00
RS Germany, **Plate**, Cake, Tab Handles, Textured Gold Roses, Orange Ground 48.00
RS Germany, **Plate**, Cake, White Lilies, Open Handled, Scalloped Rim, 9 3/4 In. 22.50
RS Germany, **Plate**, Crimped Edge, Blue Mark, 6 In. 10.00
RS Germany, **Plate**, Dogwood, Raised Gold, Rococo Ruffled, 11 3/4 In. 85.00
RS Germany, **Plate**, Gold Rim, Ecru Ground, Roses, Leaves, Signed, 11 3/4 In. 53.00
RS Germany, **Plate**, Hand-Painted, Gold Rims & Handle, 6 1/2 In., Pair 18.00
RS Germany, **Plate**, Handled, Roses On Yellow & Brown, 10 In. 40.00
RS Germany, **Plate**, Open Handled, Anemone Center, Redchurch Mark, 10 1/2 In. 225.00
RS Germany, **Plate**, Pastel Roses, Tiered, 9 1/2 In. 55.00
RS Germany, **Plate**, Peonies, 8 1/2 In. 18.00
RS Germany, **Plate**, Scalloped, Hand-Painted Flowers, 11 1/4 In. 85.00
RS Germany, **Plate**, Scenic, Stag, Mountains, Marked, 10 In. 145.00
RS Germany, **Plate**, White Flowers On Green Ground, Gold Trim, 8 1/2 In. 20.00
RS Germany, **Plate**, 4 Medallions, Cupids, Pierced Handles, Steeple Mark, 9 In. 65.00
RS Germany, **Relish**, Calla Lily, Open Handles 21.00
RS Germany, **Relish**, Yellow Daffodil Decoration, Gold Rim, 9 1/2 X 4 1/2 In. 34.00
RS Germany, **Rose Bowl**, Pansies, Lavender, 3 1/2 X 3 1/2 In. 25.00
RS Germany, **Rose Bowl**, Silver Luster, Cabbage Leaf Design, Signed 125.00
RS Germany, **Salt**, Gondola Shape, Gold Edge, Marked R.S.Tillowitz, Set Of 6 .... 38.50
RS Germany, **Sauce**, Lake & Windmill Scene, Gold Gorder, Green Mark 37.50
RS Germany, **Sauce**, Pearlized Calla Lily, Pair 15.00
RS Germany, **Sauce**, Roses Allover, Set Of 12 .... 145.00
RS Germany, **Server**, Green Floral, Center Handle, Gold Rim 22.00
RS Germany, **Shaving Mug**, Green Poppy Transfer 35.00
RS Germany, **Shaving Mug**, Orange Poppy, Green Mark 70.00
RS Germany, **Shaving Mug**, Soap Drain, Yellow Roses, Green Mark 55.00
RS Germany, **Sugar & Creamer**, Covered, Fuchsias 29.00
RS Germany, **Sugar & Creamer**, Green Ground, Dogwood Flowers 40.00
RS Germany, **Sugar & Creamer**, Roses, Gold Trim, Red Mark 30.00
RS Germany, **Sugar & Creamer**, Tan & White Luster 10.00
RS Germany, **Sugar & Creamer**, Wild Rose, Hand-Painted, Signed 30.00
RS Germany, **Sugar**, Cottage Scene, Covered 65.00
RS Germany, **Sugar**, Roses, 9 1/2 In. 19.00
RS Germany, **Syrup**, Underplate, Pink Roses, Marked, 3 In. 20.00
RS Germany, **Syrup**, Violets, Marked, 3 In. 23.00

RS Germany, Tea Set, Cottage Scene, Cup & Saucer, Plate, 10 In., 3 Piece	475.00
RS Germany, Tea Set, Pearlized, Silver Trim, Blue Mark, 3 Piece	75.00
RS Germany, Teapot, Creamer & Sugar, Covered, Gold Border & Finials	130.00
RS Germany, Tile, Tea, Blue, Yellow Roses, Marked, 6 1/2 In.	22.00
RS Germany, Toothbrush Holder, Wall Type, Floral	35.00
RS Germany, Toothpick, Hand-Painted, Floral With Gold	20.00
RS Germany, Toothpick, White Ground, Double Handled	40.00
RS Germany, Tray, Bread, Lilies In Pool	35.00
RS Germany, Tray, Cheese & Cracker, Tulips On Blue Ground, 8 1/2 In.Diam.	55.00
RS Germany, Tray, Dresser, Oval, Gold Trim, 9 X 4 1/2 In.	19.00
RS Germany, Tray, Mill Scene, 8 In.	75.00
RS Germany, Tray, Pierced Handles, Wild Rose, Signed, 7 1/2 X 4 In.	24.00
RS Germany, Tray, Pin, Green Ground, Pink Flowers On Lid	20.00
RS Germany, Tray, Pin, Oval, Pierced Handles, 6 X 3 In.	12.00
RS Germany, Vase, Bud, Iris On White Ground, Blue Mark, 4 1/2 In.	36.00
RS Germany, Vase, Bulbous, Gold Leaves, Purple Violets, 5 In.	40.00
RS Germany, Vase, Double Handled, Pink Rose, 5 1/2 In.	35.00
RS Germany, Vase, Flowers, Gold Trim, 3 1/4 In.	12.50
RS Germany, Vase, Green Lilies, Handles, 5 1/2 In.	35.00
RS Germany, Vase, Green Poppies, Handles, 5 1/2 In.	35.00
RS Germany, Vase, Melon Boy, Sterling Rim, 6 In.	85.00
RS Germany, Vase, Pastel Background, Pink Roses, Signed, 6 1/4 In.	35.00
RS Germany, Vase, Roses On Brown Ground, Luster Finish, 5 In., Pair	45.00
RS Poland, Candlestick Holder, Green Ground, Rose Decoration	89.00
RS Poland, Compote, Green To Brown, Rhododendrons, Red Mark, 6 In.	85.00
RS Poland, Dresser Set, Tray, 11 1/2 X 7 In., Hatpin Holder, Hair Receiver	90.00
RS Poland, Hatpin Holder, Bouquet Of Roses, Olive Background, Red Mark	95.00
RS Poland, Hatpin Holder, Saucer Type Bottom, Handles, Hand-Painted	195.00
RS Poland, Vase, Game Bird, Double Handled, 6 1/2 In.	118.00
☆**RS Poland, Vase,** 4 Scenic Oval Panels, Blue Satin Finish, 8 In.	375.00

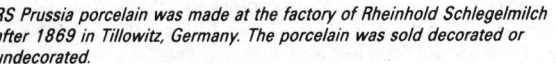

RS Prussia porcelain was made at the factory of Rheinhold Schlegelmilch after 1869 in Tillowitz, Germany. The porcelain was sold decorated or undecorated.

RS Prussia, Basket, Lilac Decoration, Tri-Handle, 5 X 5 In.	108.00
RS Prussia, Berry Set, Blown-Out Flower, Blossoms, 6 Piece, 9 1/2 In.	212.00
RS Prussia, Berry Set, Flowers, Gold Rimmed, Blown Out Panels, 7 Piece	325.00
RS Prussia, Berry Set, Gold Drape, Jewels On Rim, Pink, Red Mark, 7 Piece	385.00
RS Prussia, Berry Set, Rose Design, 9 1/2 In., 7 Piece	115.00
RS Prussia, Berry Set, Six 5 In. Bowls, Pearlized Poppies, Master, 10 In.	225.00
RS Prussia, Berry Set, Water Lily, Red Mark, 7 Piece	695.00
RS Prussia, Berry Set, 4 Sauces, White Ground, Opalescent, 10 3/4 X 3 In.	265.00
RS Prussia, Biscuit Jar, Ivory & Green, White Tulip	185.00
RS Prussia, Bowl & Cake Plate, Cottage Scene, Red Mark, Bowl, 10 In.Diam.	835.00
RS Prussia, Bowl & Cake Plate, Green, Mill Scenery Mark, 10 In.	675.00
RS Prussia, Bowl Set, Group Of Flowers Reflected In Pool Of Water, Set Of 4	175.00
RS Prussia, Bowl, Berry, Medallions, Mill Scenes Around Border, Red Mark	250.00
RS Prussia, Bowl, Berry, 4 Dishes, Opalescent Tint, Scalloped, 10 3/4 X 3 In.	265.00
RS Prussia, Bowl, Blown-Out Feather Design, Red Mark, 10 In.Diameter	195.00
RS Prussia, Bowl, Blown-Out Floral Border, Red Mark, 10, 1/2 In.	130.00
RS Prussia, Bowl, Blown-Out Iris, Gold Rim, Cover, Blue Mark, 10 1/4 In.	150.00
RS Prussia, Bowl, Blown-Out Orchids, Iridescent Edges, Red Mark, 10 1/2 In.	225.00
RS Prussia, Bowl, Blown-Out Orchids, Red Mark, 11 In.	235.00
RS Prussia, Bowl, Blown-Out Panels, Pearlized, Beaded Edge, 10 1/4 In.	150.00
RS Prussia, Bowl, Blown-Out Rays At Bottom, Scalloped Edge, Red Mark, 11 In.	175.00
RS Prussia, Bowl, Blown-Out Violets, 10 1/2 In.	200.00
RS Prussia, Bowl, Boat Scene, Pearlized Finish, Red Mark, 10 In.	478.00
RS Prussia, Bowl, Canterbury Bells, Blown-Out, Gold Border, Roses, 9 In.	125.00
RS Prussia, Bowl, Castle, Red Mark, 11 In.	250.00
RS Prussia, Bowl, Champagne Glass In Center, Red Mark, 10 In.	308.00
RS Prussia, Bowl, Double Edge, Scalloped, 10 1/2 In.Diameter	110.00
RS Prussia, Bowl, Double Scalloped Edge, Flowers, 10 1/2 In.	115.00
RS Prussia, Bowl, Floral Bottom & Sides, Red Mark, 10 5/8 In.Diameter	95.00
RS Prussia, Bowl, Floral Decoration, Red Mark, 10 3/4 In.	155.00
RS Prussia, Bowl, Floral, Pink Roses, Red Mark, 10 In.	125.00
RS Prussia, Bowl, Flowers In Center, Gold Trim & Design, Signed, 10 In.	200.00

RS Prussia, Bowl, Footed, Green & Yellow Luster, Red Mark, 8 In. 95.00
RS Prussia, Bowl, Footed, Water Lilies On Lake, Red Mark, 6 In. 35.00
RS Prussia, Bowl, Footed, 6 Arrows Pointed To Bottom, Red Mark, 6 1/2 In. 75.00
RS Prussia, Bowl, Glazed, Roses, Green & Fuchsia Panels, Red Mark, 11 In. 125.00
RS Prussia, Bowl, Gold Trim, Red Mark, 11 In. 145.00
RS Prussia, Bowl, Gravy, Underplate, Satinized, Red Mark 125.00
RS Prussia, Bowl, Green & White Flowers, Satin Finish, 10 In. 150.00
RS Prussia, Bowl, Green Ground, Blown-Out Sections, Red Mark, 10 1/2 In. 225.00
RS Prussia, Bowl, Green With Roses, Red & Green Mark, 9 In. 68.00
RS Prussia, Bowl, Green, Ivory, Gold, Bell Shape Flowers, Green Wreath, 10 In. 125.00
RS Prussia, Bowl, Hand-Painted Swans & Pine Trees, 11 In. 150.00
RS Prussia, Bowl, Medallion Mold, Peacock, 10 1/2 In. 675.00
RS Prussia, Bowl, Melon Boy Dice Player, Spear, 10 In. 1100.00
RS Prussia, Bowl, Melon Boy, Crapshooter Scene, Red Mark, 10 1/2 In. 1000.00
RS Prussia, Bowl, Molded Flowers Along Edge, Marked, 10 In. 120.00
RS Prussia, Bowl, Octagonal Border, Satin Finish, Red Mark, 11 In.Diameter 150.00
RS Prussia, Bowl, Old Man In The Mountain, 10 In. 900.00
RS Prussia, Bowl, Oval, Open Handles, Roses, 12 X 6 In. 115.00
RS Prussia, Bowl, Ovals, 12 Gold Petal Figures, Signed, Red Mark, 10 3/8 In. 115.00
RS Prussia, Bowl, Pearlized Flowers, Accents Of Gold, Red Mark, 10 In. 200.00
RS Prussia, Bowl, Pearlized, Red Mark, 10 1/2 In. 115.00
RS Prussia, Bowl, Pearlized, 9 In. 130.00
RS Prussia, Bowl, Pink & White Roses, Red Mark, 11 In. 125.00
RS Prussia, Bowl, Pink & White Roses, Satin Finish, Red Mark, 10 1/2 In. 150.00
RS Prussia, Bowl, Pink Roses, Blue Water, Open Handles, Oval, Red Mark, 13 In. 195.00
RS Prussia, Bowl, Portraits Of Napoleon's Court, Red Mark, 5 1/2 In.Diam. 225.00
RS Prussia, Bowl, Puffed Out Flowers, Red Mark, 10 7/8 In.Diameter 135.00
RS Prussia, Bowl, Quiet Cove Or Man In Mountain, Icicle Sides, 10 1/2 In. 875.00
RS Prussia, Bowl, Raised Border, Roses In Center, Scalloped Edge, 10 In. 120.00
RS Prussia, Bowl, Red & Pink Roses, Floral Sprigs, Red Mark, 10 In. 185.00
RS Prussia, Bowl, Red Star, 10 In.Diameter 85.00
RS Prussia, Bowl, Rose, Iris Blow Outs, Satin, 10 1/2 In. 105.00
RS Prussia, Bowl, Roses On Green Ground, Gold Border, Red Mark, 6 In. 60.00
RS Prussia, Bowl, Roses, Pansies, Pink, White, Red Mark, 11 In. 175.00
RS Prussia, Bowl, Ruffled Edge, Gold Line On Edge, 11 1/2 In.Diameter 195.00
RS Prussia, Bowl, Satinized, Lilies-Of-The-Valley, Red Mark, 11 In.Diameter 135.00
RS Prussia, Bowl, Scalloped Edge, Pink, 10 3/4 In.Diameter 165.00
RS Prussia, Bowl, Scalloped Top, Beading & Gold, Red Mark, 10 1/2 In. 95.00
RS Prussia, Bowl, Scalloped, Gold Trim, Red Mark, 5 1/4 In. 55.00
RS Prussia, Bowl, Shell Shape, Hand-Painted Bust Queen Louise, 10 In. 250.00
RS Prussia, Bowl, Tulips, Red Mark, 10 1/2 In. 160.00
RS Prussia, Bowl, Violets, Vines & Ivy, Red Mark, 11 In. 125.00
RS Prussia, Bowl, Water Lilies At Top, 3 Swans, Red Mark, 10 3/4 In. 425.00
RS Prussia, Bowl, White, Gold Rim, Flowers, Red Mark, 10 In.Diameter 195.00
RS Prussia, Bowl, Winter Portrait, Signed, 9 In. 725.00
RS Prussia, Bowl, Yellow & Pink, Blown-Out Flowers On Edge, 8 1/2 In. 48.00
RS Prussia, Bowl, 2 In.Black Trim, Red Mark, 10 In. 100.00
RS Prussia, Bowl, 3-Footed, Beaded Gold Border, Red Mark, 6 In.Diameter 500.00
RS Prussia, Bowl, 5 Fuchsia Heart Panels, Red Mark, 10 1/2 In. 135.00
RS Prussia, Box, Covered, Green Ground, Signed, Red Mark, 5 In.Diameter 85.00
RS Prussia, Box, Jewel, Beaded Edge, Marked, 10 1/2 X 6 1/2 X 5 1/2 In. 98.00
RS Prussia, Cake Set, Pierced Handles, Red Mark, 6 Plates, 6 1/2 In. 225.00
RS Prussia, Celery, Bird Of Paradise, Blue Mark 1250.00
RS Prussia, Celery, Blown-Out Flowers On Border & Form Handle, 12 X 6 In. 90.00
RS Prussia, Celery, Fluted Rim, Red Mark, 12 In. 65.00
RS Prussia, Celery, Tray, Pearlized Roses, Pierced Handles, Red Mark, 12 In. 85.00
RS Prussia, Child's Set, Scenic, Flower Border, 17 Piece .... Illus 3100.00

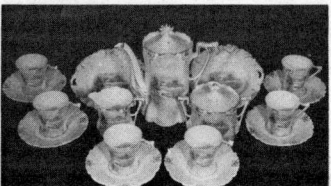

RS Prussia, Child's Set,
Scenic, Flower Border,
17 Piece

RS Prussia, Dresser Set, 5 Piece, Unmarked
(See Page 521)

RS Prussia, Chocolate Cup, Cabbage Roses, Ruffled Top, Footed, Red Mark	55.00
RS Prussia, Chocolate Pot, Flared Top, Green On White, Red Mark	140.00
RS Prussia, Chocolate Pot, Footed, Red Mark, 10 In.	265.00
RS Prussia, Chocolate Pot, Lavender & Gold	235.00
RS Prussia, Chocolate Pot, Paneled, Acorn Finial, 11 In.	135.00
RS Prussia, Chocolate Pot, Pink & Yellow Roses, Signed, 9 1/2 In.	150.00
RS Prussia, Chocolate Pot, Pink Roses, Blown-Out Irises, Flower Finial	225.00
RS Prussia, Chocolate Pot, Roses, Raised Iris Rim, White, Green	45.00
RS Prussia, Chocolate Pot, Swan Decoration, Red Mark	357.50
RS Prussia, Chocolate Pot, Teapot, Sugar & Creamer, Red Mark	590.00
RS Prussia, Chocolate Pot, 2 Cups & Saucers, Red Star Mark, 9 1/4 In.	376.00
RS Prussia, Chocolate Set, Bulbous, Luster, Gold Trim, 6 Cups & Saucers	425.00
RS Prussia, Chocolate Set, Leaf Handles, 6 Cups, Red Mark	350.00
RS Prussia, Chocolate Set, Pearlized Pot, 4 Cups & Saucers, Red Mark	565.00
RS Prussia, Chocolate Set, Pot & 5 Cups & Saucers, Orange Blossom, Red Mark	625.00
RS Prussia, Chocolate Set, Raised Gold, Rib Swirl, Pot, 4 Cups & Saucers	145.00
RS Prussia, Chocolate Set, 6 Cups & Saucers, Carnation, Signed, Luster	595.00
RS Prussia, Chocolate Set, 6 Cups & Saucers, Orange Blossom, Red Mark	660.00
RS Prussia, Chocolate Set, 6 Cups, Gold Rim, Swirled, Raised Stems, Red Mark	600.00
RS Prussia, Cocoa Pot, Green Satin, Roses, Shadow Leaves	285.00
RS Prussia, Coffeepot, Gooseneck Spout, Cream Ground, Leaf Formed Feet	85.00
RS Prussia, Compote, Flowers, Red Mark, 4 1/2 X 6 1/2 In.Diameter	100.00
RS Prussia, Compote, Red Flowers, Gold Beads, Scalloped Rim, 5 X 7 In.	165.00
RS Prussia, Condiment Set, Jam Pot, Spoon, Salt & Pepper Shaker, Toothpick	28.00
RS Prussia, Cookie Jar, Handles, Crease Embossments, Scallops, Red Mark	185.00
RS Prussia, Cracker Jar, Cover, Satinized, Roses, Red Mark	150.00
RS Prussia, Cracker Jar, Covered, Floral, Red Mark	295.00
RS Prussia, Cracker Jar, Handled, Covered, Scalloped Feet, Flowers, Red Mark	150.00
RS Prussia, Cracker Jar, Handled, Pink Roses, Blue Ground, Gold Trim	34.00
RS Prussia, Cracker Jar, Handled, Scalloped Feet, Pink & White, Red Mark	175.00
RS Prussia, Cracker Jar, Large Roses, Gold Design	155.00
RS Prussia, Cracker Jar, Pink Design, Gold Trim, Red Mark	200.00
RS Prussia, Cracker Jar, Satin Finish, Red Mark, 7 X 7 In.Diameter	225.00
RS Prussia, Creamer, Barnyard Scene, Red Mark	225.00
RS Prussia, Creamer, Blown-Out Roses, Indented Rim, Red Mark	50.00
RS Prussia, Creamer, Castle Scene, Footed, Red Mark	375.00
RS Prussia, Creamer, Cottage Scene	75.00
RS Prussia, Creamer, Footed, Dogwood Flowers, Pearl Luster, Red Mark	55.00
RS Prussia, Creamer, Overlapping Petal Formation, Gold Trim	38.00
RS Prussia, Creamer, Scalloped Edge, Pastel Flowers, 4 In.	45.00
RS Prussia, Creamer, Scalloped Edging, 4 In.	45.00
RS Prussia, Creamer, Scene Of 3 Swans, Pine Trees	42.00
RS Prussia, Cup & Saucer, Cabbage Roses, Gold Trim, Footed, Red Mark	60.00
RS Prussia, Cup & Saucer, Demitasse, Blown-Out Carnations, Red Mark	45.00
RS Prussia, Cup & Saucer, Demitasse, Green, White, Pink Roses	45.00
RS Prussia, Cup & Saucer, Demitasse, Roses On Cream Ground, Jewels, Red Mark	45.00
RS Prussia, Cup & Saucer, Floral, Mother-Of-Pearl, Footed, Demitasse, Red Mark	60.00
RS Prussia, Cup & Saucer, Green Vine Ribbed Body, Pink Poppies, Red Mark	35.00
RS Prussia, Cup & Saucer, Ostrich	2000.00
RS Prussia, Cup & Saucer, Pearlized Violet Design	55.00
RS Prussia, Cup & Saucer, Pedestal Footed, Square, Red Mark	50.00
RS Prussia, Cup & Saucer, Pink Jewels, Pink Roses, Red Mark, Pair	125.00
RS Prussia, Cup & Saucer, Roses & White Jewels, Red Mark	40.00
RS Prussia, Cup, Castle Scene	40.00
RS Prussia, Cup, Chocolate, Swirl Shape, Pearl Luster, Gold Trim, Red Mark	25.00
RS Prussia, Cup, Mill Scene	40.00
RS Prussia, Cup, Underplate, Footed, White Dogwood, 6 1/4 In.	55.00
RS Prussia, Cup, White Flowers & Gold Rim On Green	25.00
RS Prussia, Dish, Berry, Fruit In Center, Molded Rims, Gold Trim, Red Mark	40.00
RS Prussia, Dish, Divided, Figural Red Lobster On Center, 10 In.	285.00
RS Prussia, Dish, Footed, Shape Of Open Flower, Red Mark, 6 In.	49.00
RS Prussia, Dish, Leaf-Shape, Gold Dot Outline, Beading, Red Mark	285.00
RS Prussia, Dish, Open Handles, Blue Ground, Center Rose, 3 3/4 X 8 In.Diam.	65.00
RS Prussia, Dish, Pickle, Open Handle, Blown Out Edge, 12 1/2 X 5 1/2 In.	85.00
RS Prussia, Dish, Relish, Handled, Swans & Building, Red Mark, 10 In.	295.00
RS Prussia, Dish, Relish, Open Handled, Flowers, Red Mark, 9 1/2 In.	59.00

RS Prussia, Dish, Relish, Pierced Ends, Pearlized Finish, Red Mark, 9 In. 65.00
RS Prussia, Dish, Relish, Scalloped, Green Corners, Marked, 6 1/4 X 9 3/4 In. 52.00
RS Prussia, Dish, Relish, Swan Shape, Scenic, 8 In. 185.00
RS Prussia, Dresser Set, 5 Piece, Unmarked .... Illus 350.00
RS Prussia, Gravy Boat & Underplate, Satinized, Gold Trim, Red Mark 110.00
RS Prussia, Hair Receiver, Lilies-Of-The-Valley, Ivory Satin, Red Mark 78.00
RS Prussia, Hair Receiver, Old Man In The Mountain, 4 1/2 In.Square 125.00
RS Prussia, Hair Receiver, Olive Green, White & Gold, Red Mark 65.00
RS Prussia, Hatpin Holder & Hairpin Box, Attached, Red Mark 245.00
RS Prussia, Hatpin Holder, Attached Pin Box, Red Mark 135.00
RS Prussia, Hatpin Holder, Bell Shape Flowers, 3 Legs, Red Mark 47.50
RS Prussia, Hatpin Holder, Floral, Jeweled, 3 Legs, Red Mark 65.00
RS, Prussia, Hatpin Holder, Footed, Roses & Daisies, Red Mark 125.00
RS Prussia, Hatpin Holder, Mill & Water Wheel, Girl, 3 Legs, Red Mark 225.00
RS Prussia, Hatpin Holder, Pink Banded Daisies, Gold Rim, 4 1/2 In. 123.00
RS Prussia, Hatpin Holder, Roses, Bulbous, Red Mark, 3 1/4 In. 85.00
RS Prussia, Hatpin Holder, Water Lilies, 4 1/2 In. 150.00
RS Prussia, Holder, Hat Pin, Pink Roses, Red Mark 195.00
RS Prussia, Jar, Cracker, Cabbage Shape, Pin Roses, Curled Handles, Red Mark 195.00
RS Prussia, Jar, Cracker, Double Handle, Red Mark 175.00
RS Prussia, Jar, Cracker, Flowers, Gold Beads, Scalloped Top & Base, 8 In. 225.00
RS Prussia, Jar, Jam, Rose Garland On Green Luster Ground 65.00
RS Prussia, Jar, Mustard, Snow Scene 98.00
RS Prussia, Jar, Powder, White Flowers On Green, Red Mark 85.00
RS Prussia, Jug, Red & Green, Marked, 8 1/2 In. 190.00
RS Prussia, Luncheon Set, 8 1/2 In.Plate, Cup & Saucer, Red Mark 90.00
RS Prussia, Muffineer, Handled, Ruffled Base, Hydrangea Design 145.00
RS Prussia, Muffineer, Pedestal, Satin Finish, Scalloped Foot & Top, Red Mark 195.00
RS Prussia, Mug, Drinking, Footed, Floral On White Ground, Red Mark, Set Of 4 .... 110.00
RS Prussia, Mustache Cup & Saucer, Blue Garlands Of Roses, Red Mark 145.00
RS Prussia, Mustard Pot, Green & White 32.50
RS Prussia, Mustard Pot, Handled, Roses, Red Mark 75.00
RS Prussia, Mustard Pot, Ladle, Footed & Jeweled, Red Mark 125.00
RS Prussia, Mustard Pot, Lid & Spoon, Red Star 37.00
RS Prussia, Mustard Pot, Satin Finish, Footed, Jeweled, Red Mark 145.00
RS Prussia, Mustard, Pale Pink Roses In Panels, Luster Trim 55.00
RS Prussia, Mustard, Roses, Pearlized On 6 Feet, Leaf Finial, Red Mark 125.00
RS Prussia, Mustard, White With Gold Trim, Garlands & Bows 30.00
RS Prussia, Perfume Bottle, With Stopper, Floral, Bulbous, Red Mark 35.00
RS Prussia, Pitcher, Blown-Out Carnation, Gold Trim, Red Mark 450.00
RS Prussia, Pitcher, Bulbous, Melon Ribbed, Blown-Out Leaf Rim, 10 In. 125.00
RS Prussia, Pitcher, Cream, Melon Boy, Red Mark 220.00
RS Prussia, Pitcher, Herringbone Quilting, Green Mark, 12 1/2 In. 295.00
RS Prussia, Pitcher, Lemonade, Green Jeweling, Red Mark, 10 In. 350.00
RS Prussia, Pitcher, Snow Scene, Pie Crust Border, Red Mark, 4 In. 135.00
RS Prussia, Planter, Footed, Gold Fluted Edge, Red Mark, 9 In.Diameter 225.00
RS Prussia, Planter, Footed, Pink Poppies, Gold Fluted Edge, Red Mark 295.00
RS Prussia, Planter, Footed, Poppies, Gold Fluted Edge, Red Mark, 9 In.Diam. 250.00
RS Prussia, Plate, Blue Grapes, White Leaves, Red Wreath Mark, 9 In. 35.00
RS Prussia, Plate, Cake, Beaded Rim, Handled, Green Mark 50.00
RS Prussia, Plate, Cake, Cobalt Blue, White, Gold 55.00
RS Prussia, Plate, Cake, Dice Players, Jeweled .... Illus 1500.00
RS Prussia, Plate, Cake, Handled, Poppy, Blue Ground, Raised Edge, 11 In. 130.00
RS Prussia, Plate, Cake, Handled, Rococo Border, Red Mark 100.00
RS Prussia, Plate, Cake, Handled, 10 In. 79.00
RS Prussia, Plate, Cake, Open Handles, Flowers, Red Mark, 11 1/2 In. 68.00
RS Prussia, Plate, Cake, Open Handles, Lily-Of-The-Valley, Red Mark 115.00
RS Prussia, Plate, Cake, Pearlized, Open Handles, Fluted, Red Mark, 11 1/2 In. 175.00
RS Prussia, Plate, Cake, Pierced Handles, Roses Reflecting On Water, 11 In. 85.00
RS Prussia, Plate, Cake, Snowballs, Roses, Red Mark, 11 In. 145.00
RS Prussia, Plate, Cake, Waterlilies Reflection, Red Mark, 10 In. 175.00
RS Prussia, Plate, Cookie, Handled, Scalloped, Gold & Pink On White, Red Mark 30.00
RS Prussia, Plate, Country Church, Fishing Junk, Red Mark, 6 In. 200.00
RS Prussia, Plate, Country Church, Path, Lake, Signed, Red Mark, 6 In. 225.00
RS Prussia, Plate, Cupids, Easel & Portrait, Satin 1250.00
RS Prussia, Plate, Flowers & Gold, Red Star, 8 1/2 In. 35.00

RS Prussia, Plate,
Cake, Dice Players,
Jeweled

(See Page 521)

RS Prussia, Sugar & Creamer, Portrait, Lebrun & Potocka
RS Prussia, Tankard, Portrait, Madame Recamier, 13 In.

RS Prussia, Plate, Flowers Reflecting In Water, Red Mark, 8 3/4 In.	85.00
RS Prussia, Plate, Flowers, Peonies, Pierced Handle, Green Wreath Mark	125.00
RS Prussia, Plate, Fruits, Cable Edge, White Ground, Red Mark, 8 1/2 In.	105.00
RS Prussia, Plate, Gold Border, Swirls In Relief, Purple Mark, 7 1/2 In.	35.00
RS Prussia, Plate, Jasmine, Red Mark, 8 1/2 In.	65.00
RS Prussia, Plate, Jasmine, White Lilac, Red Mark, 8 In.	65.00
RS Prussia, Plate, Jeweled Border, Gold Trim, Center Rose, 9 1/2 In.	95.00
RS Prussia, Plate, Lilac, Red Mark, 8 1/2 In.	65.00
RS Prussia, Plate, Mill Scene, 10 In.Diameter	363.00
RS Prussia, Plate, Open Handle, Blown Maple Leaves, Red Mark, 10 1/2 In.	90.00
RS Prussia, Plate, Open Handle, Blown-Out Iris, Red Mark, 9 1/2 In.	130.00
RS Prussia, Plate, Open Handle, Centered With Fruit, 11 In.	175.00
RS Prussia, Plate, Open Handle, 4 Swans, Icicle Edge, Red Mark, 11 In.	475.00
RS Prussia, Plate, Open Handles, Roses, Cream Ground, 10 In.	80.00
RS Prussia, Plate, Pearlized, Embossed Sections, Red Mark, 11 In.	200.00
RS Prussia, Plate, Pierced Handles, Blown Out Flowers, 11 In.	165.00
RS Prussia, Plate, Pink Roses, Scalloped Border, Gold Edge Trim, 8 1/2 In.	48.00
RS Prussia, Plate, Portrait, Lady, Marked, 10 In.	285.00
RS Prussia, Plate, Portrait, Madame Recamier, 9 3/4 In.	950.00
RS Prussia, Plate, Raised Plumes, Gold Edge, Red Mark, 9 3/4 In.	135.00
RS Prussia, Plate, Red Mark, 10 3/4 In.	75.00
RS Prussia, Plate, Red Mark, 8 In.	65.00
RS Prussia, Plate, Scalloped Edge, Cluster Of Flowers, Red Mark, 8 1/2 In.	65.00
RS Prussia, Plate, Scalloped, Gold Embossed, Red Mark, 9 7/8 In.	105.00
RS Prussia, Plate, Scalloped, Red Mark, 8 1/2 In.	65.00
RS Prussia, Plate, Snow Ball, Red Mark, 8 1/2 In.	65.00
RS Prussia, Plate, Snowballs, Poppies, Red Mark, 10 1/2 In.	130.00
RS Prussia, Plate, Spring Seasons, Keyhole, 9 In.	1150.00
RS Prussia, Plate, Sunflower Mold, Brown & Red	95.00
RS Prussia, Plate, Violet Design, Red Mark, 9 In.	65.00
RS Prussia, Plate, Violet, Red Mark, 8 1/2 In.	65.00
RS Prussia, Plate, Violets & Jasmine, Red Mark, 8 1/2 In.	65.00
RS Prussia, Plate, White, Red Mark, 8 1/2 In.	65.00
RS Prussia, Portrait Plate, Apple Girl, Satin Finish, 9 In.	700.00
RS Prussia, Portrait Plate, Marked, 10 In.	285.00
RS Prussia, Receiver, Hair, Roses, Petaled Lid, Blue, Red Mark	115.00
RS Prussia, Relish, Floral Decoration, Gold, Red Mark, 9 1/2 X 4 1/2 In.	60.00
RS Prussia, Relish, Fluted, Beading, Gold Trim, Roses, Red Mark	90.00
RS Prussia, Relish, Swan, Scenic, 8 In.	185.00
RS Prussia, Relish, White Roses On Creamy Beige, Gold Trim, Signed	75.00
RS Prussia, Salt & Pepper, Melon Boy, Brown & Yellow	150.00
RS Prussia, Sauce, Satin Finish, Blown-Out Iris Edge, Red Mark, 5 1/2 In.	185.00
RS Prussia, Shaving Mug & Shield Mirror	300.00
RS Prussia, Shaving Mug, Handle, Hand Decorated	48.00
RS Prussia, Shaving Mug, Red Mark	140.00
RS Prussia, Spooner, Raised Star, Hand-Painted	65.00
RS Prussia, Sugar & Creamer, Blue Bird Medallions, Red Mark	295.00

RS Prussia, Sugar & Creamer, Bluebird	350.00
RS Prussia, Sugar & Creamer, Castle & Mill Scene, Green & Black	300.00
RS Prussia, Sugar & Creamer, Covered, 4 Feet, Leaf Finial On Sugar, Red Mark	250.00
RS Prussia, Sugar & Creamer, Flower, Eggshell Ground, Signed, Red Mark	165.00
RS Prussia, Sugar & Creamer, Footed, Blown-Out Bottom, Red Mark	210.00
RS Prussia, Sugar & Creamer, Fruit Design, Red Mark	145.00
RS Prussia, Sugar & Creamer, Fruit Pattern, Red Mark	62.00
RS Prussia, Sugar & Creamer, Pebble Tops With Gold, Portrait On Each	500.00
RS Prussia, Sugar & Creamer, Pedestal Footed, Blue Birds	295.00
RS Prussia, Sugar & Creamer, Pink Roses, Gold Trim, Red Mark	175.00
RS Prussia, Sugar & Creamer, Pink Roses, Green Wreath	55.00
RS Prussia, Sugar & Creamer, Portrait, Lebrun & Potocka .... *Illus*	400.00
RS Prussia, Sugar & Creamer, Satin Finish, Gold Tracery, Red Mark	185.00
RS Prussia, Sugar & Creamer, Scalloped Rim, Flowers, Footed	120.00
RS Prussia, Sugar Shaker, Violets, Red Mark	78.00
RS Prussia, Sugar, Blossoms, 6 In.Across Handles	33.00
RS Prussia, Sugar, Cover, Roses, Beige Background, Red Mark	120.00
RS Prussia, Sugar, Covered, White Flowers, Green Luster	37.00
RS Prussia, Sugar, Mill Scene	300.00
RS Prussia, Sugar, Swan, Icicle Mold	65.00
RS Prussia, Syrup & Underplate, Brown To Ivory, Red Mark	75.00
RS Prussia, Syrup, Underplate, Red Mark	80.00
RS Prussia, Tankard, Flowers, Red Mark, 10 3/4 In.	495.00
RS Prussia, Tankard, Flowers, Red Mark, 13 In.	595.00
RS Prussia, Tankard, Hand-Painted Flowers, Red Mark	325.00
RS Prussia, Tankard, Magnolias, Red Mark, 14 In.	550.00
RS Prussia, Tankard, Medallions Around Top, Red Mark, Signed	300.00
RS Prussia, Tankard, Portrait, Madame Recamier, 13 In. .... *Illus*	3000.00
RS Prussia, Tankard, Shadow Flowers, 12 1/2 In.	300.00
RS Prussia, Tea Set, Blown-Out, Jewels, Red Mark, 3 Piece	350.00
RS Prussia, Tea Set, Hand-Painted Roses, Red Mark	335.00
RS Prussia, Tea Set, Roses, Pink, White, Ivory, Red Mark, 9 Piece	400.00
RS Prussia, Tea Set, Salmon Roses, Red Mark	315.00
RS Prussia, Teapot, Applied Color, Red Mark, 6 In.	200.00
RS Prussia, Teapot, Individual, Underliner Plate, Red Mark	42.50
RS Prussia, Teapot, Jeweled, Red Mark	135.00
RS Prussia, Teapot, Satin, Hand-Painted Swans, Red Mark	395.00
RS Prussia, Toothpick, Floral Sprays, Scalloped Base & Top, Gold Jewels	90.00
RS Prussia, Tray, Beaded Edge, Blown Flowers, Red Mark, 7 1/2 X 11 1/2 In.	100.00
RS Prussia, Tray, Bread, Green Luster, White Dogwood, Red Mark	85.00
RS Prussia, Tray, Bread, Open Handle, Floral Decoration	125.00
RS Prussia, Tray, Bun, Blue, Plume Edges, Red Mark	135.00
RS Prussia, Tray, Bun, Flowers, 13 In.	42.00
RS Prussia, Tray, Bun, Melon Boy, 13 3/4 X 6 1/2 In.	800.00
RS Prussia, Tray, Celery, Pheasant & Pine Trees, Luster, 12 In.	350.00
RS Prussia, Tray, Dresser, Blown-Out Edges, Beading, Red Mark, 8 X 12 In.	210.00
RS Prussia, Tray, Dresser, Open Handle, Flowers, Marked, 11 1/2 In.	95.00
RS Prussia, Tray, Dresser, Oval, Gold Stippling At Edge, Red Mark	90.00
RS Prussia, Tray, Dresser, Satin Finish, Wild Rose Design	95.00
RS Prussia, Tray, Four Blue Bird Medallions, Red Mark, 12 X 6 In.	375.00
RS Prussia, Tray, Handled, Magnolias, Satin Finish, Red Mark, 12 1/4 In.	75.00
RS Prussia, Tray, Handled, Satinized, Puffed Out Areas, Red Mark, 12 X 6 In.	150.00
RS Prussia, Tray, Handled, Swans, Trees, Grass, Red Mark, 12 1/2 X 6 In.	275.00
RS Prussia, Tray, Jewel Floral Rim, White Pink Rose, Marked, 9 1/2 X 5 In.	125.00
RS Prussia, Tray, Lebrun Girl Portrait, Gold Scroll Decoration, 10 1/2 In.	150.00
RS Prussia, Tray, Mill Scene, Tapestry Finish, Handles, Red Mark, 12 X 6 In.	595.00
RS Prussia, Tray, Old Man In The Mountain, Scenic Medallions .... *Illus*	1375.00
RS Prussia, Tray, Open Handled, Lilies, Red Mark, 13 1/2 X 6 1/2 In.	85.00
RS Prussia, Tray, Open Handled, Puffed Out Cabbage, Red Mark, 12 X 6 In.	165.00
RS Prussia, Tray, Open Handled, Ruffled, Beaded Edging, Red Mark, 11 X 7 In.	150.00
RS Prussia, Tray, Open Handled, Satinized, Red Mark, 10 1/4 X 6 In.	50.00
RS Prussia, Tray, Open Handled, Swans, Blue Water, Red Mark, 12 X 6 In.	250.00
RS Prussia, Tray, Perfume, Oval, Gold Edge, Pink Tulips, 11 3/4 X 8 1/2 In.	18.50
RS Prussia, Tray, Pink Flowers, Blue & Green Border, 11 X 6 1/2 In.	175.00
RS Prussia, Tray, Slotted Handles, White Flowers, Signed, Red Mark, 11 In.	110.00
RS Prussia, Tray, 2 Handled, Mill Scene, Gold Trim, Red Mark, 12 1/2 X 6 In.	400.00

RS Prussia, Tureen, Covered, Handles, Hand-Painted, Marked, 5 1/2 X 9 In. 135.00
RS Prussia, Tureen, Pink, Red, Roses, Cut-Out Handles, Covered, Marked, 9 In. 135.00
RS Prussia, Turkey Bowl, Wild Turkey, Trees, Scalloped Edge, 10 1/2 In. 225.00
RS Prussia, Vase, Bulbous, Cottage Scene, Red Mark, 5 In. 425.00
RS Prussia, Vase, Cobalt, Gold Blown Body, Red Mark, 11 In. 345.00
RS Prussia, Vase, Cottage Scene, Red Mark, 4 In. 385.00
RS Prussia, Vase, Handled, Floral Design, Marked, 6 In. 75.00
RS Prussia, Vase, Hanging Basket Of Roses, Red Mark, 11 In. 225.00
RS Prussia, Vase, Perforated Flanges, Gold Handles, Red Mark, 9 1/4 In. 275.00
RS Prussia, Vase, Pink Flowers, Green & Gold Decoration, 9 In. 195.00
RS Prussia, Vase, Raised Enameled Flowers, Round, Steeple Mark 140.00
RS Prussia, Vase, Roses, Leaves, Gold Leaves On Vase, Red Mark, 6 1/2 In. 165.00
RS Prussia, Vase, Sheepherder, Handled, Red Mark, 8 1/2 In. 500.00
RS Prussia, Vegetable, Boat Shaped, Water Lilies, Poppies, Handles, Red Mark 185.00
RS Suhl, Bowl, Mill & Sheepherder Scene, 10 In.Diameter 700.00
RS Suhl, Box, Powder, Bust Portrait, No.8 .... 65.00
RS Teplitz, Dish, Candy, Handled, Pink Flowers On Green Ground 14.00

R.S.Tillowitz porcelain factory was started at Tillowitz near Silesia in 1869 by Rheinhold Schlegelmilch. Table services and ornamental pieces were made.

RS Tillowitz, Bowl, Centerpiece, Silesia, Green Ground, Calla Lilies 97.50
RS Tillowitz, Bowl, Silesia, Roses, Yellow Center, Gold Trim, 9 1/4 In. 32.50
RS Tillowitz, Cruet, Gold Overlay, Mark 21, Artist Signed, Pair 45.00
RS Tillowitz, Dish, Relish, 2 Handled, Bisque, Silesia Mark, 4 X 8 In. 20.00
RS Tillowitz, Pitcher, Condensed Milk, Underplate, Brown Luster Ground 32.50
RS Tillowitz, Plate, Cake, Roses, Slotted Handles, Gold Trim 60.00
RS Tillowitz, Sugar & Creamer, Red Eye, White Pheasant 185.00
RS Tillowitz, Sugar, Blossom & Gold Trim 28.00
RS Tillowitz, Sugar, Covered, 2-Handled, Russet With Gold 23.00
RS Tillowitz, Teapot, Parrot Design, Small 25.00
RS Tillowitz, Tile, Tea 28.00
RS Tillowitz, Vase, Florals, Spittoon Shape 22.00

Rubena Verde is a Victorian glassware that was shaded from red to green. It was first made by Hobbs, Brockunier and Company of Wheeling, West Virginia, about 1890.

Rubena Verde, Bowl, Pedestal, Fluted Rim, 3 1/2 X 5 I/2 In. 75.00
Rubena Verde, Creamer, , 4 1/2 In. 95.00
Rubena Verde, Cruet, Hobnail, Teadrop Stopper, Polished Pontil 165.00
Rubena Verde, Cruet, Vinegar, Petticoat Shape, Original Stopper, 6 1/4 In. 250.00
Rubena Verde, Dish, Crackle Glass, Metal Base, 6 1/4 X 9 3/4 In. 125.00
Rubena Verde, Pitcher, Cream, Inverted Thumbprint, Square Mouth, 4 In. 175.00
Rubena Verde, Toothpick 120.00
Rubena Verde, Tumbler, Enameled 75.00
Rubena Verde, Tumbler, Enameled Flowers & Leaves 65.00
Rubena Verde, Tumbler, Inverted Thumbprint, Cranberry, 3 7/8 In. 50.00

RS Prussia, Tray, Old Man In The
Mountain, Scenic Medallions
(See Page 523)

Rubena Verde, Vase, Bulbous, Melon Ribbed, Enameled Flowers, 6 1/2 In. 250.00
Rubena Verde, Vase, Jack-In-The-Pulpit, Enameled Flowers, 6 In. 65.00
Rubena Verde, Vase, Pinched Sides, C.1890, 12 1/2 In. 95.00
Rubena Verde, Vase, Ribbed Ground, Enameled Florals, Gold, 12 1/4 In., Pair 475.00
Rubena Verde, Vase, Ruffle Top, Hi-Enamel Decoration, Artist Initial 165.00

*Rubena is a glassware that shades from red to clear. It was first made by
George Duncan and Sons of Pittsburgh, Pennsylvania, about 1885.*
Rubena, see also Pressed Glass, Royal Ivy Pressed Glass, Royal Oak
Rubena, Base, Lamp, Miniature, French 140.00
Rubena, Bottle, Cologne, French Bottle, Acid Cut, Gold Trim, 7 1/4 In. 68.00
Rubena, Bottle, Perfume, 9 In. 65.00
Rubena, Carafe 45.00
Rubena, Carafe, Water, Etched Floral Design 45.00
Rubena, Castor, Pickle, Bull's-Eye & Scrolled, Enameled, Bulbous 245.00
Rubena, Castor, Pickle, Bulls-Eye & Scrolled, Enameled, Gold & Silver 245.00
Rubena, Castor, Pickle, Enameled, Inverted Thumbprint Insert, Tufts Silver 265.00
Rubena, Cracker Jar, Inverted Thumbprint, Coralene Decoration, 8 1/2 In. 145.00
Rubena, Cruet, Inverted Thumbprint 90.00
Rubena, Goblets, Frosted, Diamond, Quilted 60.00
Rubena, Jar, Cracker, Silver Plate Lid & Bail 100.00
Rubena, Mug, Clear Applied Handle, 3 1/4 In. 65.00
Rubena, Mustard Pot & Pepper Sauce Shaker, Paneled, Set, 3 In. 58.00
Rubena, Pitcher, Crimped Top, 4 In. 38.00
Rubena, Pitcher, Daisy, Handle 150.00
Rubena, Pitcher, Diamond-Quilted, Applied Clear Handle, 7 1/2 In. 110.00
Rubena, Pitcher, Pedestal Base, Applied Handle, Pleated Top, 4 In. 46.00
Rubena, Pitcher, Tankard, Overshot, Sandwich, 9 In. 125.00
Rubena, Pitcher, Water, Clear, Bulbous 110.00
Rubena, Pitcher, Water, Cranberry Shading, Notch-Cut Top, Handle, 8 1/2 In. 160.00
Rubena, Pitcher, Water, Round Mouth, Reeded Handle, 7 7/8 X 4 3/4 In.Diam. 135.00
Rubena, Rose Bowl, Applied Green Feet, Enamel Design, 6 1/4 In. 185.00
Rubena, Rose Bowl, Sandwich Glass, 5 X 5 1/2 In. 90.00
Rubena, Salt, Swirl Ribbon, Blue Opalescent 25.00
Rubena, Saltshaker, Opalescent Spots, Original Top 35.00
Rubena, Spooner, Frosted Circle 22.00
Rubena, Sugar Shaker, Cut Panels, Brass Screw-On Top, 5 1/2 In. 48.00
Rubena, Sugar Shaker, Melon Ribbed, 8 In. 85.00
Rubena, Sugar, Royal Oak, Frosted 150.00
Rubena, Syrup, Opalescent, Coinspot, Original Lid 125.00
Rubena, Toothpick, Inverted Thumbprint, Decorated 85.00
Rubena, Tumbler, Remember The Maine, Eagle Holding 2 Flags, Etched 15.00
Rubena, Vase, Bud, Bulbous Base, Narrow Neck, 5 1/2 In. 45.00
Rubena, Vase, Drape, Green Rickery, 10 X 3 In. 195.00
Rubena, Vase, Frosted Hobnail Ruffled, 9 1/2 In. 175.00
Rubena, Vase, Rigaree, Spiraled To Top, Verde, Smith & Williams 230.00
Rubena, Vase, Trumpet Shaped, Ruffled Rim, Enameled Flowers & Leaves, 14 In. 95.00
Rubena, Water Set, Five Tumblers, Pitcher, 9 3/4 In. 285.00

*Ruby glass is a dark red color. It was a Victorian and twentieth-century
ware. The name means many different types of red glass.*
Ruby Glass, see also Cranberry Glass, Pressed Glass, Souvenir
Ruby Glass, Ashtray, Duck, Small 75.00
Ruby Glass, Bell, Merry Christmas, Gold Rim, Clear Handle, W.M.Saunders 450.00
Ruby Glass, Berry Bowl, Fancy Diamonds 35.00
Ruby Glass, Berry Set, Pillow Encircled, 7 Piece 125.00
Ruby Glass, Berry Set, Roanoke, 7 Piece 95.00
Ruby Glass, Bowl, Fruit, Hexagon Block, 10 In. 55.00
Ruby Glass, Butter, Box In Box 95.00
Ruby Glass, Butter, Bull's-Eye, U.S.Glass Co. 65.00
Ruby Glass, Butter, Covered, Beaded Swag 95.00
Ruby Glass, Butter, Covered, Beveled Star & Diamond 65.00
Ruby Glass, Butter, Covered, Co-Op Block 85.00
Ruby Glass, Butter, Covered, Minton 60.00
Ruby Glass, Butter, Covered, O'Hara Diamond 75.00

Ruby Glass, Butter, Covered, Prize	95.00
Ruby Glass, Butter, Covered, Red Block	80.00
Ruby Glass, Butter, Covered, Riverside Victoria	95.00
Ruby Glass, Butter, Covered, Shoshone	95.00
Ruby Glass, Butter, Covered, Triple Triangle	60.00
Ruby Glass, Butter, Zipper Block	100.00
Ruby Glass, Celery, Block & Star, Etched	45.00
Ruby Glass, Celery, Thumbprint, Tall	40.00
Ruby Glass, Compote, Covered, Petaled Medallion, High Standard	95.00
Ruby Glass, Compote, Hexagon Block, 8 In.	75.00
Ruby Glass, Compote, Jelly, Prize	38.00
Ruby Glass, Compote, O'Hara Diamond, 7 X 7 1/2 In.Diameter	125.00
Ruby Glass, Creamer & Covered Butter, Jewel & Flower, Clear	125.00
Ruby Glass, Creamer, Block & Star, Etched	40.00
Ruby Glass, Creamer, Late Washington, 3 1/4 In.	14.00
Ruby Glass, Creamer, O'Hara Diamond, Etched	55.00
Ruby Glass, Creamer, Pleating	35.00
Ruby Glass, Creamer, Plume	75.00
Ruby Glass, Creamer, Ruby Thumbprint	55.00
Ruby Glass, Creamer, Wedding, Crystal	75.00
Ruby Glass, Cruet, Beaded Swirl, Ruby, Clear Stopper	65.00
Ruby Glass, Cruet, Block & Lattice	130.00
Ruby Glass, Cruet, Grandma From Edie, Revere Beach, 1908, Mointon	55.00
Ruby Glass, Cruet, Sunk Honeycomb, Original Stopper	48.50
Ruby Glass, Cruet, Thumbprint	150.00
Ruby Glass, Cup, Punch, Beaded Swag	22.50
Ruby Glass, Decanter, Horseshoe, Original Stopper & Lip	65.00
Ruby Glass, Decanter, Wine, Frosted Grapes, Pontil, Bohemian, 13 3/4 In.	35.00
Ruby Glass, Decanter, Wine, Sunk Honeycomb, Etched	110.00
Ruby Glass, Goblet, Dakota, Etched	42.00 To 50.00
Ruby Glass, Goblet, Double Beaded Band, Augusta, Me.	22.00
Ruby Glass, Goblet, Duncan Block, Etched	40.00
Ruby Glass, Goblet, Oregon	37.50
Ruby Glass, Goblet, Red Block	32.00 To 35.00
Ruby Glass, Goblet, Roanoke	35.00
Ruby Glass, Goblet, Ruby Thumbprint	38.00
Ruby Glass, Goblet, Thumbprint, Etched	65.00
Ruby Glass, Goblet, Triple Triangle	38.00
Ruby Glass, Goblet, Truncated Cube	22.00 To 28.00
Ruby Glass, Goblet, Yorked Loop	25.00
Ruby Glass, Hat, Blown, Turned Over Sides, Flint, 4 In.	85.00
Ruby Glass, Liquor Set, Decanter & 6 Shot Glasses, Wheat Pattern	50.00
Ruby Glass, Mug, Button Arches, Souvenir, Plymouth, Mass., 3 In.	15.00
Ruby Glass, Mug, Etched, D.E.House, August 24th, 1904	200.00
Ruby Glass, Mug, Souvenir, Sioux Falls, 1918	15.00
Ruby Glass, Mug, Souvenir, The Dells, 1906	22.50
Ruby Glass, Mug, Souvenir, Woodland Beach Park	15.00
Ruby Glass, Mug, Thumbprint, Handled, Honeycomb	16.00
Ruby Glass, Pitcher, Button Arches, Eva, 1901, 4 1/2 In.	35.00
Ruby Glass, Pitcher, Milk, Button Arches, Applied Handle	55.00
Ruby Glass, Pitcher, Tankard, Button & Arches, Frosted Band	90.00
Ruby Glass, Pitcher, Water, Block & Lattice	60.00
Ruby Glass, Pitcher, Water, Flower & Pleat	85.00
Ruby Glass, Pitcher, Water, Footed, Sheaf & Block	60.00
Ruby Glass, Pitcher, Water, Lorraine	95.00
Ruby Glass, Pitcher, Water, Pillow Encircled	95.00
Ruby Glass, Pitcher, Water, Plume	150.00
Ruby Glass, Pitcher, Water, Sheaf & Block	48.00
Ruby Glass, Pitcher, Water, Sunken Honeycomb	95.00
Ruby Glass, Rose Bowl, Majestic	48.00
Ruby Glass, Salt & Pepper, Georgian Pattern, Metal Tops, 4 1/2 In.	110.00
Ruby Glass, Salt & Pepper, Souvenir, Askoo, Minnesota	19.50
Ruby Glass, Salt & Pepper, Zipper Borders	45.00
Ruby Glass, Salt, Flower Shape, Silver Plate Handle, 3 X 2 3/4 In.Diameter	50.00
Ruby Glass, Salt, Original Top, Diamond With Peg, Ed Williams, 1910	17.50
Ruby Glass, Spooner & Creamer, Vincent Valentine	200.00

Ruby Glass, Spooner, Block & Lattice	45.00
Ruby Glass, Spooner, Gold Rose	40.00
Ruby Glass, Spooner, O'Hara Diamond	15.00
Ruby Glass, Spooner, Plume	68.00
Ruby Glass, Spooner, Ruby Thumbprint	30.00
Ruby Glass, Spooner, Ruby Thumbprint, Etched	45.00
Ruby Glass, Spooner, Scalloped Swirl	32.00
Ruby Glass, Spooner, Thumbprint, Etched	65.00
Ruby Glass, Spooner, Truncated Cube	25.00
Ruby Glass, Spooner, Wedding, Crystal	65.00
Ruby Glass, Spooner, Whitton	50.00
Ruby Glass, Sugar & Creamer, Pearl	70.00
Ruby Glass, Sugar & Creamer, Souvenir, Green Bay	35.00
Ruby Glass, Sugar, Covered, Scroll With Cane Band	75.00
Ruby Glass, Sugar, Covered, Thumbprint	95.00
Ruby Glass, Sugar, Open, O'Hara Diamond	23.00
Ruby Glass, Sugar, Scroll With Cane Band, Clear	75.00
Ruby Glass, Sugar, Wedding, Crystal	85.00
Ruby Glass, Syrup, Zipper Borders, Original Lid	150.00
Ruby Glass, Table Set, Box In Box, 4 Piece, Etched	425.00
Ruby Glass, Table Set, Frosted Band, Button Arch, 4 Piece	250.00
Ruby Glass, Table Set, Loop & Block, 4 Piece	265.00
Ruby Glass, Table Set, Red Block, 4 Piece	235.00
Ruby Glass, Table Set, Royal Crystal, 4 Piece	265.00
Ruby Glass, Table Set, Tarentum's Tiny Thumbprint Pattern	350.00
Ruby Glass, Table Set, Triple Triangle, 4 Piece	195.00 To 250.00
Ruby Glass, Toothpick, Souvenir, Niagara Falls, C.1907	15.00
Ruby Glass, Toothpick, Souvenir, Royal Coops	15.00
Ruby Glass, Toothpick, Thumbprint, Etched	35.00
Ruby Glass, Tumble-Up, Cut To Clear	38.00
Ruby Glass, Tumbler, Block & Double Bar	25.00
Ruby Glass, Tumbler, Block & Lattice	28.00
Ruby Glass, Tumbler, Co-Op Block	20.00
Ruby Glass, Tumbler, Dogwood, Gold Flowers, Set Of 3	100.00
Ruby Glass, Tumbler, O'Hara Diamond, Etched	30.00
Ruby Glass, Tumbler, Scroll With Cane Band	27.50
Ruby Glass, Tumbler, Torpedo	28.00
Ruby Glass, Vase, Bulbous Base, Frosted Bird In Round Medallion, 9 1/2 In.	38.50
Ruby Glass, Vase, Floral Enameled Decoration, Crystal Lusters, 14 In., Pair	250.00
Ruby Glass, Vase, Globe, Blown, 10 1/4 X 10 1/4 In.	125.00
Ruby Glass, Water Set, Button Arches, Frost & Gold Band, 7 Piece	250.00
Ruby Glass, Water Set, Button Arches, Sister, Atlantic City, 1904, 6 Tumblers	95.00
Ruby Glass, Water Set, Co-Op Block, 7 Piece	235.00
Ruby Glass, Water Set, Pavonia, Etched, 5 Piece	235.00
Ruby Glass, Water Set, Red Block, 7 Piece	265.00
Ruby Glass, Water Set, Thumbprint, 5 Piece	285.00
Ruby Glass, Water Set, Triple Triangle, 7 Piece	255.00
Ruby Glass, Wine, Box-In-Box	30.00
Ruby Glass, Wine, Red Block	28.00
Ruby Glass, Wine, Star Motifs, Fruiting Vine, 1900s, 8 1/4 In., Set Of 12	400.00
Ruby Glass, Wine, Thumbprint	35.00
Ruby Glass, Wine, Truncated Cube	30.00
Rudolstadt, Bowl, Hand-Painted, Ribbon Handles, R.W.Mark, 7 1/2 X 5 1/2 In.	75.00
Rudolstadt, Bowl, Violets, Raised Gold, Buff Ground, Oval, RW Mark, 11 In.	50.00
Rudolstadt, Cake Set, Open Handle Plate & 6 Tea Plates, Thuringia	55.00
Rudolstadt, Cup & Saucer, Demitasse, Chinoiserie, Signed	45.00
Rudolstadt, Dish, Feeding, Happifats	45.00
Rudolstadt, Jar, Powder & Underplate, Covered	450.00
Rudolstadt, Pitcher, Floral, Gold Handle & Trim, Lobate Melon Shaped, 9 In.	65.00
Rudolstadt, Teapot, Gold Scroll Handle, Woman's Face On Spout, Signed, 9 In.	48.00
Rudolstadt, Vase, Canteen Shape, 4 Gold Feet & Handles, 7 1/4 X 6 In.	48.00
Rudolstadt, Vase, Purple Violets, Cream Background, Marked, 8 1/2 In.	90.00
Rudolstadt, Vase, 2 Gold Handles, Scalloped Edge, Gold Trim, 10 In.	60.00
Rudolstadt, Vase, 2 Handled, Scalloped Top, Gold Trim, 10 In.	75.00
Rudolstadt, Vase, 4 Paw Feet, Buff Ground, Sculptured Handles, C.1875, 6 In.	35.00

Rug, see Textile, Rug

RumRill

Rumrill Pottery was designed by George Rumrill of Little Rock, Arkansas. From 1930 to 1933, it was produced by the Red Wing Pottery of Red Wing, Minnesota. In 1938 production was transferred to the Shawnee Pottery, Zanesville, Ohio.

Rumrill, Basket, Blue	15.00
Rumrill, Ewer, Blue, 11 In.	18.00
Rumrill, Vase, Mottled Blue, Handled, 8 In.	9.00
Ruskin, Vase, Bulbous, Purple Iridescence, Converted To Lamp Base	30.00
Ruskin, Vase, Iridescent Blue, Green, 1923, 10 3/4 In.	42.00
Russel Wright, Dinner Service, American, C.1937, 13 Piece ....*Illus*	150.00

SABINO FRANCE

Sabino glass was made in the 1920s and 1930s in Paris, France. Founded by Marius-Ernest Sabino, the firm was noted for Art Deco lamps, vases, nudes, figures and animals in clear, colored and opalescent glass. Production stopped during World War II, but resumed in the 1960s with manufacture of nudes and small opalescent glass animals. The new pieces are a slightly different color and can be recognized.

Sabino France

Sabino, Bookend, Rabbit	22.00
Sabino, Bookend, Ram, Pair	150.00
Sabino, Bookend, Scottie Dog	50.00
Sabino, Bookend, Squirrel	27.00
Sabino, Bottle, Perfume, Opalescent, 6 Nudes In High Relief, Signed, 6 In.	48.00
Sabino, Bottle, Perfume, 6 Standing Nudes In Relief, Signed, 6 In.	48.00
Sabino, Dish, Snail Shell Shape, 3 X 2 1/2 X 1 1/2 In.	35.00
Sabino, Figurine, Butterfly, Miniature, Signed	25.00
Sabino, Figurine, Elephant, Signed, 2 1/4 In.	19.00
Sabino, Figurine, Elephant, Trunk Up, Signed	35.00
Sabino, Figurine, Mocking Bird, Opalescent, Signed	48.00
Sabino, Figurine, Nude Woman Kneeling, Holding 3 Pigeons, 6 1/4 In.	225.00
Sabino, Figurine, Nude, Female, Opalescent, Signed, 6 In.	80.00 To 90.00
Sabino, Figurine, Pekingese Dog, Opalescent, 2 1/2 X 4 In.	45.00
Sabino, Figurine, Pheasant, Opalescent, Tails Raised, 3 3/4 X 2 1/4 In., Pair	50.00
Sabino, Figurine, Rabbit, Signed, 1 1/4 X 2 In.	18.00
Sabino, Figurine, Scottie, 3 1/4 X 4 In.	50.00
Sabino, Knife Rest, Cut Glass, Signed	16.00
Sabino, Plate, 1970	93.00
Sabino, Tray, Oyster-Shell, Orange-Red Highlights, Molded Mark, 4 X 7 In.	50.00
Sabino, Tumbler, Female Nude In Opalescent Glass, Signed, 6 In.	80.00
Sabino, Vase, Frosted & Clear, Art Nouveau, Signed, 10 1/4 In.	375.00

Russel Wright, Dinner Service, American, C.1937, 13 Piece

Sabino, Vase, Praying Mantis, Cone Shape, Signed, 8 In.	190.00
Salt & Pepper, see Pressed Glass, Porcelain, etc.	

Salt glaze is a hard, shiny glaze that was developed for pottery during the eighteenth century. It is still being made.

Salt Glaze, Crock, Blue & White, 4 In.	18.00
Salt Glaze, Crock, Butter, Blue Flowers	12.00
Salt Glaze, Flask, Cathedral Shape, Marked Green, Lambeth, C.1835	115.00
Salt Glaze, Match Holder, Beehive Shape, 2 3/4 In.	15.00
Salt Glaze, Mug, Beer, Man & Tavern Scene	18.00
Salt Glaze, Pitcher, Bas Relief, Fox Hunt, Empressed 18, 5 1/8 In.	45.00
Salt Glaze, Pitcher, Blue Floral Pattern, 6 5/8 In.	18.00
Salt Glaze, Pitcher, Brown Ground, White Raised Cartouche, Marked, 6 1/2 In.	150.00
Salt Glaze, Pitcher, Figures Around Body, Banded Vine Handle, Marked, 10 In.	70.00
Salt Glaze, Pitcher, Flowers & Draped Figures, Shell Base, Signed, 8 1/2 In.	155.00
Salt Glaze, Pitcher, Lily Pad Design, Dated 1857, English, 10 In.	55.00
Salt Glaze, Pitcher, Pear Shape, Raised Floral, Jet Black Reverse, 6 1/2 In.	38.00
Salt Glaze, Pitcher, Pewter Lid, English, 9 1/2 In.	110.00

Samson, Figurine, 12 Piece Canine Orchestra, Conductor, 5 In.

Salt Glaze, Pitcher, Tan, C.1845, Signed, 8 1/2 In.	150.00
Salt Glaze, Pitcher, Tan, W.Ridgway, 1835, 7 1/2 In.	150.00
Salt Glaze, Pitcher, The Gleaners, English Mark, Dated 1858, 10 1/2 In.	100.00
Salt Glaze, Pitcher, Wheat Pattern, Applied Handle, 8 In.	75.00
Salt Glaze, Plate, Rococo Molded, Pierced Panels, C.1750	145.00 To 245.00
Salt Glaze, Plate, Scalloped & Gadrooned Edge, 10 1/4 In.	60.00
Salt Glaze, Syrup, Bennett's, May 12, 1855	37.50
Salt Glaze, Syrup, Fruit	125.00
Salt Glaze, Syrup, Grapes	85.00
Sampler, see Textile, Sampler	

Samson and Company, a French firm specializing in the reproduction of collectible wares of many countries and periods, was founded in Paris in the early nineteenth century. Chelsea, Meissen, Famille Verte, and Oriental Lowestoft are some of the wares that have been reproduced by the company. The company uses a variety of marks to distinguish its reproductions. It is still in operation.

Samson, Box, Grape, Faux Crossed Swords In Underglaze Blue, 4 1/2 In., Pair	100.00
Samson, Box, Miniature, Enameled, Hinged, Signed	125.00
Samson, Figurine, Conversation Group, Crossed Swords, 1800s, 5 In.	400.00
Samson, Figurine, Group Of Conspiring Lovers, 1910, Marked, 7 3/4 In.	175.00
Samson, Figurine, 12 Piece Canine Orchestra, Conductor, 5 In. ....*Illus*	620.00
Samson, Plate, Armorial, Rose & Purple Festooned Border, 9 In.	85.00
Sand Babies, Dish, Child's, Blue Mark, Royal Bayreuth	95.00
Sand Babies, Mug, Royal Bayreuth	75.00
Sand Babies, Pitcher, 2 1/2 X 4 In.	75.00
Sand Babies, Tray & Box, Pin, Royal Bayreuth, Running, Black Mark, 5 In.	109.00
Sand Babies, Vase, Double Handles, Sterling Rim, Royal Bayreuth, 3 1/4 In.	85.00

Sandwich glass is any one of the myriad types of glass made by the Boston and Sandwich Glass Works in Sandwich, Massachusetts, between 1825 and 1888. It is often very difficult to be sure whether a piece was really made at the Sandwich factory because so many types were made there and similar pieces were made at other glass factories. The McK numbers refer to the book "American Glass" by George P. and Helen McKearin.

Sandwich Glass, see also Pressed Glass, etc.

Sandwich Glass, **Basket,** Diamond Quilted, Queen Victoria Head Handle, 8 In.	195.00
Sandwich Glass, **Bottle,** Colgne, Cobalt Blue Cut To Clear, 6 7/8 In.	265.00
Sandwich Glass, **Bottle,** Cologne, Amber, Flint	80.00
Sandwich Glass, **Bottle,** Scent, Pewter Lid, Amethyst	75.00
Sandwich Glass, **Bottle,** Scent, Pewter Lid, Blue	75.00
Sandwich Glass, **Bottle,** Scent, Pewter Lid, Emerald Green	75.00
Sandwich Glass, **Bottle,** Scent, 8 Sided, Corseted, Emerald Green, 4 1/2 In.	175.00
Sandwich Glass, **Bottle,** Smelling, Clear, Blown & Molded, Pewter Cap	39.00
Sandwich Glass, **Bowl,** Expanded Honeycomb, Scalloped Rim, Flint, 7 1/2 In.	30.00
Sandwich Glass, **Bowl,** Fruit, Footed, Loop, Blue, Flint, 3 X 10 In.Diameter	195.00
Sandwich Glass, **Bowl,** Industry, Agriculture, Commerce & Industry	225.00
Sandwich Glass, **Bowl,** Lacy, Oak Leaf, 7 1/4 In.	95.00
Sandwich Glass, **Bowl,** Peacock Eye, Beads Between Concave Eyes & Rim, 6 In.	35.00
Sandwich Glass, **Bowl,** Princess Feather, 7 1/2 In.	38.00
Sandwich Glass, **Bowl,** Scalloped, Sandwich Industry	195.00
Sandwich Glass, **Box,** Hinged, Applied Flowers, Footed, 5 1/2 X 4 1/2 In.Diam.	270.00
Sandwich Glass, **Butter,** Peachblow, Floral In Gold & Enamel, Covered, 5 In.	195.00
Sandwich Glass, **Candlestick,** Canary Petal & Loop, Round Base, 7 In., Pair	275.00
Sandwich Glass, **Candlestick,** Clambroth Petal & Loop, Pair	330.00
Sandwich Glass, **Candlestick,** Clambroth, Column, One Has Socket Check, Pair	275.00
Sandwich Glass, **Candlestick,** Clambroth, Petal & Loop, Pair	330.00
Sandwich Glass, **Candlestick,** Dolphin, Pair	1500.00
Sandwich Glass, **Candlestick,** Electric Blue Petal & Loop, Pair	850.00
Sandwich Glass, **Candlestick,** Milk-White, Petal & Loop, Pair	450.00
Sandwich Glass, **Candlestick,** Opaque White Base, Hexagonal	300.00
Sandwich Glass, **Candlestick,** Petal & Loop, Canary	325.00
Sandwich Glass, **Candlestick,** Petal & Loop, Flint, 7 In., Pair	300.00
Sandwich Glass, **Candlestick,** Petal Top, Vaseline, Octagon Base, Pair	150.00
Sandwich Glass, **Candlestick,** 6-Sided Base & Shaft, Opaque Holder	300.00
Sandwich Glass, **Compote,** Funnel Shape, Scalloped Rim, 9 3/4 In., Diameter	58.00
Sandwich Glass, **Compote,** Petal & Loop, Base Design, Belltone, C.1850, 11 In.	245.00
Sandwich Glass, **Creamer,** Ivy, Pedestal Foot, Flint	55.00
Sandwich Glass, **Crossed Peacock Eye,** Bowl, Rayed Center, Flint, 7 3/8 In.	65.00
Sandwich Glass, **Cruet,** Melon Shape, Amber, Pink, Amber Stopper	65.00
Sandwich Glass, **Cup Plate, see Cup Plate**	
Sandwich Glass, **Cup,** Punch, Amber	25.00
Sandwich Glass, **Cup,** Punch, Footed, Vaseline	35.00
Sandwich Glass, **Decanter,** Bull's-Eye Sunburst, Rigaree Rings, Blown, 1 Quart	265.00
Sandwich Glass, **Decanter,** Ground Neck, Square, 1 Quart	37.50
Sandwich Glass, **Decanter,** Sunburst, Blown, 3 Mold Quart	245.00
Sandwich Glass, **Decanter,** 32 Point Star Bottom, Threaded & Leaf On Handle	150.00
Sandwich Glass, **Dish,** Double Horn Of Plenty, 8 X 5 1/2 In.	150.00
Sandwich Glass, **Dish,** Honey, Peacock Eye, 4 1/2 In.	16.00
Sandwich Glass, **Dish,** Lacy Beehive, Octagonal, Flint, 9 1/4 In.	110.00
Sandwich Glass, **Drawer Pull,** Octagonal, Canary Yellow, Set Of 6	140.00
Sandwich Glass, **Drawer Pull,** Opalescent, 2 In., Set Of 6	85.00
Sandwich Glass, **Drawer Pull,** Sunburst Faces, Canary Yellow, Set Of 6	140.00
Sandwich Glass, **Eggcup,** Loop Pattern, Opalescent	65.00
Sandwich Glass, **Ewer,** Clear Thorny Applied Handle, Swirled Rib, 11 7/8 In.	225.00
Sandwich Glass, **Goblet,** Morning Glory	75.00 To 135.00
Sandwich Glass, **Holder,** Spill, Sandwich Star, Flint	35.00
Sandwich Glass, **Honey Dip,** Ribbed Acorn, Pair	15.00
Sandwich Glass, **Inkwell,** Hinged Mushroom Lid, Pyramid Shape, 4 In.	110.00
Sandwich Glass, **Jar,** Pomade, Black Amethyst, Bear, V-Shaped Neck Chips	75.00
Sandwich Glass, **Lamp, see Lamp**	
Sandwich Glass, **Mustard,** Peacock-Eye, Lacy Handle, Flint	40.00
Sandwich Glass, **Pitcher,** Lemonade, Ice Lip, Green, 1/2 Gallon	45.00
Sandwich Glass, **Pitcher,** Overshot, Applied Clear Handle, 6 3/4 In.	135.00
Sandwich Glass, **Pitcher,** Sahara, 18 Ounces, 5 In.	75.00
Sandwich Glass, **Pitcher,** Stippled Design Of Arch & Chain	185.00
Sandwich Glass, **Pitcher,** Water, Old Blue, Twisted Rope Handle	140.00
Sandwich Glass, **Plate,** Dinner, Lacy Octagonal Beehive, Stars, Grapes	140.00
Sandwich Glass, **Plate,** Gold Threaded, Cranberry Center, 6 1/4 In.	36.00
Sandwich Glass, **Plate,** Lacy, Peacock Eye & Thistle, 8 In.	125.00
Sandwich Glass, **Plate,** Oak Leaf, Scalloped, 8 In.	55.00

Sandwich Glass, Plate, Peacock Eye & Thistle, 8 In. 125.00
Sandwich Glass, Plate, Rayed With Chain Border, Flint, 6 In. 32.00
Sandwich Glass, Plate, Shell, 6 In. 45.00
Sandwich Glass, Plate, Star Pattern, C.1860-80, 11 In. 25.00
Sandwich Glass, Plate, Tea, Flint, 6 In. 50.00
Sandwich Glass, Plate, Toddy, Peacock Eye, Clear, 4 1/4 In.Diameter 45.00
Sandwich Glass, Pull, Draw, Opalescent, Set Of 4 .... 45.00
Sandwich Glass, Salt & Pepper, Pine Cone, Pink & Blue 110.00
Sandwich Glass, Salt, Circle Design 6.00
Sandwich Glass, Salt, Master, Tulip, Footed, Flint 28.50
Sandwich Glass, Salt, Opalescent Yellow, Green, Fluted 50.00
Sandwich Glass, Salt, Original Dated Tops With Agitators, Christmas 70.00
Sandwich Glass, Salt, Petal Shape, Round 18.00
Sandwich Glass, Sauce, Beaded Scale With Daisy Center, Flint, 3 1/2 In. 50.00
Sandwich Glass, Sauce, Lacy Peacock-Eye, Flint 20.00
Sandwich Glass, Sauce, Lacy, Crossed Swords, Flint 18.00
Sandwich Glass, Sauce, Lacy, Opalescent Plume, Acorn Base, 4 In. 110.00
Sandwich Glass, Sauce, Plume, Clear, 4 3/8 In., Set Of 4 .... 65.00
Sandwich Glass, Shade, For Ceiling Fixture, Birds & Foliage, 10 1/2 In. 60.00
Sandwich Glass, Slipper, Daisy & Button, Amber, 8 1/2 X 2 In. 110.00
Sandwich Glass, Sugar & Creamer, Loaf, Ivy, Flint 85.00
Sandwich Glass, Sugar, Acanthus Leaf, Blue & Ruby, Covered 2800.00
Sandwich Glass, Sugar, Footed, Ivy, Amber 135.00
Sandwich Glass, Sugar, Gothic Arch, Opaque Blue 300.00
Sandwich Glass, Sugar, Open, Wheat & Barley 17.50
Sandwich Glass, Sweet Meat, Honeycomb, Covered, Flint 75.00
Sandwich Glass, Taster, Whiskey, Opalescent 230.00
Sandwich Glass, Tieback, Cobalt 35.00
Sandwich Glass, Tieback, Floral, Canary, 3 In., Pair 65.00
Sandwich Glass, Tieback, Opalescent, Original Stems, 4 1/4 In. 28.00
Sandwich Glass, Tieback, Pewter Fittings, 4 1/2 In.Round, Pair 50.00
Sandwich Glass, Tieback, Pewter Pin, Opalescent, 3 In.Diameter, Set Of 4 .... 100.00
Sandwich Glass, Tieback, White Opalescent, 3 In., Pair 10.00
Sandwich Glass, Tieback, 2 Color, Pewter Stem & Cap, Canary Fan Edge, 4 Pr. 260.00
Sandwich Glass, Tray, Hearts & Stars Border, 7 X 4 1/2 In. 65.00
Sandwich Glass, Tray, Scrolled Leaf, 6 1/2 X 5 In. 65.00
Sandwich Glass, Tray, Tidbit, 2 Tier, Crystal, Hocking 15.00
Sandwich Glass, Tumbler, Lacy, French, C.1840, 4 1/4 X 3 5/8 In. 195.00
Sandwich Glass, Tumbler, Lemonade, Amber 40.00
Sandwich Glass, Tumbler, Lemonade, Clear With Cranberry 45.00
Sandwich Glass, Tumbler, Lemonade, Threaded, Crackle Top 50.00
Sandwich Glass, Tumbler, Miniature, Punty Pattern, Green 65.00
Sandwich Glass, Tumbler, Overshot, Gilt Trim, Footed 45.00
Sandwich Glass, Vase, Bull's-Eye, Fleur-De-Lis, Knob Stem, Footed, 9 3/4 In. 425.00
Sandwich Glass, Vase, Celery, 4 Printie Block, Clear, 10 In. 95.00
Sandwich Glass, Vase, Enamel Flowers, Birds & Butterfly, 9 1/2 In., Pair 135.00
Sandwich Glass, Vase, Loop, Amethyst, Pair 1150.00
Sandwich Glass, Vase, White, Blue Leaves As Handles, 5 3/4 In., Pair 265.00

Satin Glass, Bowl, White, Blue, Pink, Melon Ribbed, 4 1/4 In.
(See Page 532)

Satin Glass, Ewer, Gold Leaf & Flowers, Silver Lid, 8 In.
(See Page 532)

Sandwich Glass, Whiskey Taster, Peacock Blue	85.00
Sandwich Glass, Whiskey, Canary	55.00
Sandwich Glass, Window Pane, Blue, Concentric Circle Design, 5 3/4 In.	24.00
Sandwich Glass, Wine, Diagonal Sawtooth Band, Flint	18.00
Sandwich, Vase, Trevaise, Iridescent Ivory, Gold Leaf, 12 In.	500.00

Sarreguemines pottery was first made in Lorraine, France, about 1770. *Most of the pieces found today date from the late nineteenth century.*

Sarreguemines, see also Kate Greenaway

Sarreguemines, Bowl, Pedestal Base, Handles, 1858 Mark, 5 X 12 In.Diameter	65.00
Sarreguemines, Plate, Cupids, Green Trim, 8 1/2 In.	18.00
Sarreguemines, Plate, French Nursery Rhymes, Fluted, 7 1/2 In., Set Of 12	80.00
Sarreguemines, Plate, Hand-Colored Scene, 19th Century, Signed	25.00
Sarreguemines, Plate, Napoleonic, French Captions, 7 1/4 In., Set Of 8	115.00
Sarreguemines, Plate, Opera, Scene From Lohengrin, Portrait Of Wagner, 9 In.	22.50
Sarreguemines, Plate, Serving, Floral Bouquets, Signed, Set Of 12, 9 3/4 In.	95.00
Sarreguemines, Plate, Strawberries, Leaves, Impressed Mark, 7 1/2 In.	22.00
Sarreguemines, Plate, White, Narrow Blue Band, Basket-Weave Border, 7 In.	14.00
Sarreguemines, Vase, Blue & White On Light Brown, 5 In.	45.00
Sarreguemines, Vase, 3-Handled, Incised Leaves, Zigzag Design, Marked, 5 In.	45.00

Satin glass is a late-nineteenth-century art glass. It has a dull finish that is caused by a hydrofluoric acid vapor treatment. Satin glass was made in many colors and sometimes had applied decorations.

Satin Glass, Atomizer, Pedestal, Blue Body, Vaseline Base	28.00
Satin Glass, Atomizer, Pink, Melon, Ribbed	95.00
Satin Glass, Basket, Blue, Camphor Handle, Ruffled Edge, 6 1/2 In.	65.00
Satin Glass, Bell, Camphor Handle	35.00
Satin Glass, Biscuit Jar, Metal Lid, Sections Blown-Out, Pink	275.00
Satin Glass, Bowl, Blue Overlay, Enameled Foliage, 11 1/2 In.Diameter	195.00
Satin Glass, Bowl, Footed, Diamond Pattern, 8 In.	50.00
Satin Glass, Bowl, Rose Lining, Diamond-Quilted, Frosted Prunt, 5 3/4 In.	595.00
Satin Glass, Bowl, Round Ridges, Pink & White, 3 1/2 X 8 In.Diameter	95.00
Satin Glass, Bowl, White, Blue, Pink, Melon Ribbed, 4 1/4 In. *Illus*	750.00
Satin Glass, Bride's Basket, Blue & White Spatter	195.00
Satin Glass, Bride's Bowl, Pink Overlay, Silver Plate Basket, 12 In.	275.00
Satin Glass, Butter, Pink Cone, Acid Finish	185.00
Satin Glass, Candlestick, Figural, Madonna, Pair	25.00
Satin Glass, Chamberstick, Embossed Design, Gilt	15.00
Satin Glass, Compote, Pebbled Bottom, Crimped, Crass Base, Marked, 9 1/2 In.	125.00
Satin Glass, Compote, Twisted Stand, Sky Blue, Acid Finish, 7 X 7 1/2 In.	42.50
Satin Glass, Cookie Jar, Silver Top, Lid & Handle	265.00
Satin Glass, Cracker Jar, Drape & Vertical Beading, Red	170.00
Satin Glass, Cracker Jar, Enameled Flowers, Meridian, Conn., 6 In.High	60.00
Satin Glass, Cracker Jar, Puffy Pink Quilted, White Lining, Silver Lid	125.00
Satin Glass, Cracker Jar, Silver Rim, Bail & Lid, 11 1/2 In.	105.00
Satin Glass, Cruet, Yellow Quilted	65.00
Satin Glass, Dish, Cheese, Covered, Ruffled Pink To Yellow	55.00
Satin Glass, Dish, White Cased Blue, Plated Stand, 9 1/2 In.	84.00
Satin Glass, Epergne, Cased, 1 Trumpet & 3 Jack-In-The-Pulpit, 9 In.	165.00
Satin Glass, Epergne, Fluted Bowl & Lily, Victorian, 16 1/2 In.	245.00
Satin Glass, Epergne, Lily, Footed Brass Holder, Ribbed Bowl, 10 1/2 In.	250.00
Satin Glass, Ewer, Blue Diamond-Quilted, Mother-Of-Pearl, Handle, 13 In.	395.00
Satin Glass, Ewer, Frosted Applied Handles, White Lining, 9 1/2 In., Pair	175.00
Satin Glass, Ewer, Gold Leaf & Flowers, Silver Lid, 8 In. *Illus*	400.00
Satin Glass, Ewer, Melon Ribbed, Enameled Flowers, Frosted Handle, 9 In.	145.00
Satin Glass, Ewer, Ribbed Apricot, Ribbon Candy Top, Frosted Handle, 10 In.	96.00
Satin Glass, Ewer, White Lining, Ruffled Top, Frosted Applied Handle, 8 In.	95.00
Satin Glass, Hatpin Holder, Cranberry, Ostrich Egg Decorated	175.00
Satin Glass, Inkwell, Cherubs Holding Flowers, Signed, 3 1/2 In.	190.00
Satin Glass, Jar, Cracker, Red, Draped Panels & Beading, Silver Plate Collar	165.00
Satin Glass, Jar, Jam, Quilted, Pink	45.00
Satin Glass, Jug, Syrup, White, Heart Arches	165.00
Satin Glass, Lamp, Blown-Out Leaves & Flowers, Matching Shade, Pink, 14 In.	795.00
Satin Glass, Lamp, Embossed Scrolled Design, Enameled Sprays, Red	125.00
Satin Glass, Lamp, Fairy, Lighthouse, Blue, 6 In.	150.00

Satin Glass, Lamp, Fairy, Matching Cup Base, Rose Swirl, 4 5/8 In.	295.00
Satin Glass, Lamp, Fairy, Mother-Of-Pearl, Rose, Diamond Quilted, 4 1/2 In.	195.00
Satin Glass, Lamp, Oil, Lincoln Drape, Blue, 10 In.	110.00
Satin Glass, Lamp, Reverse Painted, Landscape Scene, 7 1/2 In.	100.00
Satin Glass, Lemonade Set, Red Swirl, White To Pink, Pitcher, 6 Tumblers	800.00
Satin Glass, Mustard Pot, Mother-Of-Pearl, Rose Red Ribbon, 4 X 2 In.	135.00
Satin Glass, Pitcher, Cased With Shades Of Pink At Top, 8 1/2 In.	250.00
Satin Glass, Pitcher, Diamond-Quilt, Pink, Camphor Handle, 10 In.	350.00
Satin Glass, Pitcher, Pink, Frosted Applied Handle, 8 1/2 In.	200.00
Satin Glass, Pitcher, Rose Pink Overlay, Diamond Quilted, 3 1/4 X 3 In.	245.00
Satin Glass, Pitcher, Shaded Pink To Rose, 5 X 7 1/2 In.	169.00
Satin Glass, Pitcher, Water, Crimped Rim, Applied White Handle	42.00
Satin Glass, Pitcher, Water, Florette, Frosted Handle, Bulbous, Rose, 7 In.	175.00
Satin Glass, Plate, Pansies, White Satin, Hand-Painted, Enameled, 11 1/2 In.	20.00
Satin Glass, Rose Bowl, Applied Flowers, Blue, White Lining, 4 1/4 In.	125.00
Satin Glass, Rose Bowl, Apricot, Frosted Applied Feet, 4 1/2 X 4 1/4 In.	135.00
Satin Glass, Rose Bowl, Blue Ribbed, White Lining, 4 In.	65.00
Satin Glass, Rose Bowl, Blue, Orange Flowers	85.00
Satin Glass, Rose Bowl, Cherubs, Pink	85.00
Satin Glass, Rose Bowl, Crimped Edge, Cut Lining, Blue To Light Blue	65.00
Satin Glass, Rose Bowl, Crimped Top, Pink, 3 1/2 In.	25.00
Satin Glass, Rose Bowl, Diamond-Quilted, Cut Velvet, 3 1/4 X 3 5/8 In.Diam.	185.00
Satin Glass, Rose Bowl, Diamond-Quilted, Rainbow Striped, 3 1/2 In.	100.00
Satin Glass, Rose Bowl, Diamond-Quilted, 5 3/4 In.Diameter	295.00
Satin Glass, Rose Bowl, Dimpled Sides, Enameled Flowers, 5 3/8 X 5 1/8 In.	150.00
Satin Glass, Rose Bowl, Egg Shaped, Blue Overlay, 5 7/8 X 3 3/4 In.	135.00
Satin Glass, Rose Bowl, Embossed Flowers & Leaves, Pink Overlay, 3 1/4 In.	110.00
Satin Glass, Rose Bowl, Gold & White Enameled Daisies & Bees, Blue, 7 In.	97.50
Satin Glass, Rose Bowl, Shaded, Crimped Rim, Blown, Blue, 4 In.	45.00
Satin Glass, Rose Bowl, Shell & Seaweed, Blue, 5 1/2 In.	129.00
Satin Glass, Rose Bowl, Shell & Seaweed, Pink, Enameled, 5 X 5 1/4 In.Diam.	195.00
Satin Glass, Rose Bowl, Shell & Seaweed, Yellow, 6 In.Diameter	248.00
Satin Glass, Rose Bowl, Six-Crimp Top, Blue Ground, 2 1/2 In.Diameter	60.00
Satin Glass, Rose Bowl, White Lining, Blue, 8 Crimp Top, 3 1/4 X 3 7/8 In.	110.00
Satin Glass, Rose Bowl, White Lining, C.1880, Blue, 4 1/2 X 5 In.Diameter	75.00
Satin Glass, Rose Bowl, Yellow Diamond Quilted, Mother-Of-Pearl, 4 5/8 In.	195.00
Satin Glass, Rose Bowl, Yellow To White, White Lining, 4 In.	75.00
Satin Glass, Rose Bowl, 4 Applied Frosted Feet, Enameled, 4 5/8 X 4 5/8 In.	135.00
Satin Glass, Rose Bowl, 5 1/2 X 5 1/4 In.	89.00
Satin Glass, Salt & Pepper, Ships Wheel & Honey Pot, Brownie	50.00
Satin Glass, Saltshaker, Apricot-To-White, Raindrop, 3 1/2 In.	100.00
Satin Glass, Saltshaker, Floral, Melon Ribbed, 1 1/4 In.	65.00
Satin Glass, Saltshaker, Leaf Mold, Blue	40.00
Satin Glass, Saltshaker, Pink, Guttate	45.00
Satin Glass, Saltshaker, Quilted, Pink, Pewter Lid	45.00
Satin Glass, Shade, Art Glass, Red, Cone Shaped, Blown-Out Pattern, 9 In.	135.00
Satin Glass, Shade, Orange Tulips, Green Leaves, 2 1/8 In.Opening, Set Of 5	84.50
Satin Glass, Sugar & Creamer, Floral, Melon Ribbed, White	125.00
Satin Glass, Sugar & Creamer, Silver Plate Lid & Frame, Red	165.00
Satin Glass, Sugar, Bead & Drape, Red	150.00
Satin Glass, Sugar, Cone, Lemon	125.00
Satin Glass, Sugar, Florettes, Pink	39.00
Satin Glass, Table Set, Ruffled Top, 4 Piece	225.00
Satin Glass, Toothpick, Blue, Florette	45.00
Satin Glass, Tumbler, Cased, Enameled Flowers, Gold Beaded Stems & Buds	125.00
Satin Glass, Tumbler, Cased, White, Pink Lining	47.50
Satin Glass, Tumbler, Mother-Of-Pearl, Yellow	85.00
Satin Glass, Tumbler, Pink Swirl	50.00
Satin Glass, Tumbler, Yellow, Mother-Of-Pearl, Diamond-Quilted	85.00
Satin Glass, Vase, Blue Overlay, Melon Sectioned, Ruffled Top, 12 In.	225.00
Satin Glass, Vase, Blue Overlay, White Liner, Enameled Flowers, 11 In.	95.00
Satin Glass, Vase, Blue, Applied Frosted Edging, Raindrop Pattern, 6 In.	125.00
Satin Glass, Vase, Camphor Thorn Handles, Blue, 6 1/2 In., Pair	300.00
Satin Glass, Vase, Cased Glass, Fluted Top, Aqua, 5 1/2 In.	40.00
Satin Glass, Vase, Cased, Blue To White, Coralene Beading, 4 In.	40.00
Satin Glass, Vase, Cased, Green To White, Enamel Flowers, 10 In.	35.00

Satin Glass, Vase, Cased, Mother-Of-Pearl Teardrop, Pinched Neck, 9 1/2 In.	90.00
Satin Glass, Vase, Cased, Pink & White Lining, Applied Handles, 8 In., Pair	240.00
Satin Glass, Vase, Celery, Diamond-Quilted, Silver Plated Holder, 8 1/4 In.	495.00
Satin Glass, Vase, Cerulean Blue, Rust Floral, Enameled Leaves, 8 In.	45.00
Satin Glass, Vase, Cranberry, Hand-Painted, Floral, 10 In., Pair	80.00
Satin Glass, Vase, Cream, Diamond Quilted Overlay, Bulbous, 16 In.	67.50
Satin Glass, Vase, Crimped Ruffled Top, Applied Frosted Edging, 6 In.	140.00
Satin Glass, Vase, Crimped Top, White, 6 1/2 In.	45.00
Satin Glass, Vase, Diamond-Quilted, Blue, 6 In.	85.00
Satin Glass, Vase, Diamond-Quilted, White Lining, Blue, 5 1/4 X 6 1/4 In.	130.00
Satin Glass, Vase, Ducks, Iris, Flared, 15 X 7 In., Pair	335.00
Satin Glass, Vase, Enameled Birds, Crimped Edge, Frosted Handles, 8 In.Tall	195.00
Satin Glass, Vase, Enameled Flowers, Yellow Scrolls, 7 5/8 In., Pair	165.00
Satin Glass, Vase, Footed, Enameled Flowers, Blue, 10 In., Pair	136.00
Satin Glass, Vase, Footed, White Lining, Facing Pair, Blue, 9 1/8 In., Pair	195.00
Satin Glass, Vase, Footed, White Lining, Scalloped Points Top, 9 7/8 In.	100.00
Satin Glass, Vase, Frosted Feet, Shaded Peach, Melon Sectioned, 9 In., Pair	195.00
Satin Glass, Vase, Gourd Shape, Handled, Gold Leaves On Front, 10 In.	65.00
Satin Glass, Vase, Jack-In-The-Pulpit, Pink & White, Striped, 9 1/2 In.	175.00
Satin Glass, Vase, Jack-In-The-Pulpit, White, Camphor Petal Feet, 6 1/2 In.	120.00
Satin Glass, Vase, Melon Ribbed, Raindrop, Blue, 8 X 3 In.	195.00
Satin Glass, Vase, Mother-Of-Pearl, Camphor Edge, Amberina Moire, 7 In.	325.00
Satin Glass, Vase, Mother-Of-Pearl, Pink, Diamond-Quilted, 6 3/8 X 4 1/4 In.	295.00
Satin Glass, Vase, Muted Tangerine To Blue, Fluted, 8 In.	110.00
Satin Glass, Vase, Pale Green, Hand Painted, Owl Perched On Tree, 7 In.	80.00
Satin Glass, Vase, Pink At Ruffled Top, Footed, Pink Overlay, 8 1/4 In.	65.00
Satin Glass, Vase, Pink Melon Section, Rope Handle, White Lining, 9 1/2 In.	95.00
Satin Glass, Vase, Pink Overlay, White Lining, 9 3/4 In., Pair	175.00
Satin Glass, Vase, Pink To White, 9 In.	185.00
Satin Glass, Vase, Pink, Diamond-Quilted, Mother-Of-Pearl, 7 1/4 X 4 1/2 In.	135.00
Satin Glass, Vase, Pink, Diamond-Quilted, Mother-Of-Pearl, 9 1/4 In., Pair	950.00
Satin Glass, Vase, Pink, Double Crimped Rim, Cased In White, 9 1/2 In.	55.00
Satin Glass, Vase, Raindrop, Pinched Sides, Pink, White Interior, 8 In.	240.00
Satin Glass, Vase, Raindrop, Ruffled & Crimped Rim, Blue, 10 X 6 In.	275.00
Satin Glass, Vase, Ruffled Top, White Lining, Beaded Coralene, 8 1/4 In.	495.00
Satin Glass, Vase, Shaded Pink With Herringbone Texture, 6 1/2 In.	149.00
Satin Glass, Vase, Stick, Bulbous, Gold Enameling, Hand Blown, 8 1/4 In.	115.00
Satin Glass, Vase, Trumpet, White To Raspberry, Enamel Design, 14 In.	90.00
Satin Glass, Vase, White Lining, Facing Pair, Blue, 9 1/8 In., Pair	195.00
Satin Glass, Vase, White To Apricot, Enamel Decoration, 7 In.	44.00
Satin Glass, Vase, Yellow, Green, Enameled Flowers, 10 In., Pair	120.00
Satin Glass, Water Set, Florette, Pink, 7 Piece	300.00
Satin Glass, Water Set, Quilted Phlox, Pink, 7 Piece	350.00
Satin Glass, Webb, see Webb	

Satsuma is a Japanese pottery with a distinctive creamy beige crackled glaze. Most of the pieces were decorated with blue, red, green, orange, or gold. Almost all the Satsuma found today was made after 1860. Japanese faces are often a part of the decorative scheme.

Satsuma, Berry Set, Bowl & 4 Sauces, Diapered Border, 10 In.	135.00
Satsuma, Bottle, Butterfly Handles & Knob On Lid, Ribbed Sides, 7 X 5 In.	65.00
Satsuma, Bottle, Point, Painted Genre Scenes, Signed, 1868-1912, 3 1/4 In.	52.50
Satsuma, Bowl, Design Inside & Out, 1800s, Gold Mark, 2 1/8 X 4 3/4 In.	575.00
Satsuma, Bowl, Earthenware, Landscape, Figures, Enameled, C.1900, 8 1/4 In.	125.00
Satsuma, Bowl, Garden Scene, Petal Edge, Brocade Border, Signed, 5 In.	90.00
Satsuma, Bowl, Pedestal, 3 Booted, Enameling, Pagoda Scenes, 18 1/2 In.	145.00
Satsuma, Bowl, Scalloped Edge, Millefleurs Design, 2 Seal Marks, 12 In.	500.00
Satsuma, Bowl, 19th Century, 4 3/4 In. .... *Illus*	1100.00
Satsuma, Box & Cover, Gilt Mark, 19th Century, 6 1/4 In. .... *Illus*	400.00
Satsuma, Box, Cover, Bulbous Ribbing, Diapered Band, Enameling, 4 1/4 X 5 In.	48.00
Satsuma, Box, Cover, Demon Face Handles, Marked, 2 3/4 X 3 3/4 In.	395.00
Satsuma, Box, Swirl, Ribbing, Flowers, Pink To Tan, Blue, White, Lid, 5 In.	180.00
Satsuma, Button, 3 Geisha Girls & Butterflies, 1 In.Diameter	45.00
Satsuma, Cookie Jar, Shishi Handles & Finial, C.1920	85.00
Satsuma, Cup & Saucer & 6 Plates, C.1850, Kin Ko Zan	250.00
Satsuma, Cup & Saucer, Gold, Scenic, Dragon Handle, Marked, 1868-1912, Pair	50.00

Satsuma, Cup & Saucer, Six 7 In.Plates, C.1850, Kin Ko Zan	250.00
Satsuma, Cup & Saucer, 6-Sided, Scalloped Rim, Flowers, Butterflies	22.00
Satsuma, Dish, Nut, Flowers, Signed	15.00
Satsuma, Dish, Pumpkin, Covered, Marked	95.00
Satsuma, Handle, Parasol, Multi-Hued Butterfly, 1 1/2 In.Diameter	30.00
Satsuma, Holder, Thousand Faces, Oriental Signature, 2 In.	125.00
Satsuma, Humidor, Abstract Design, Coralene & Enamel, Wood Finial, 7 1/2 In.	75.00
Satsuma, Incense Burner, Oriental Figures, Foo Lion Finial & Handle, 9 In.	35.00
Satsuma, Jar, Brocade Patterning, Ring Handle, Covered, 6 1/2 In.	45.00
Satsuma, Jar, Covered, Shishi Finial, C.1910, 8 In.	110.00
Satsuma, Jar, Faience, Geishas, Foo Dog Handles & Finials, Covered, 33 In.	180.00
Satsuma, Koro & Cover, Nikko, 19th Century *Illus*	375.00
Satsuma, Koro, Floral, Crackle, Metal Cover, Base Signed, 1868-1912	85.00
Satsuma, Lunch Set, 4 Cups & Saucers, Six 7 In.Plates, C.1850, Kinkozan	250.00
Satsuma, Plate, Birds, Red & Gold, Signed, Cross In Circle, 10 In.	65.00
Satsuma, Plate, Geisha Girls, Pagoda, 7 1/2 In.	22.00
Satsuma, Salt, 3 Men In Bowl, Gold, 1 1/4 In.Square	65.00
Satsuma, Sugar & Creamer, Brown Ground, Enameled, Marked, Japan	82.00
Satsuma, Sugar & Creamer, Gold Beading & Faces, Dragon Finial & Spout	65.00
Satsuma, Tea Caddy, Lift Off Top, Enameled, Signed, 3 3/4 X 4 1/2 In.	78.00
Satsuma, Tea Caddy, Morning Glories, Mums, Foliage, Square, Round Lid, Marked	80.00
Satsuma, Tea Set, Cobalt, Gold Trim, Bamboo Design, 6 Cups & Saucers	325.00
Satsuma, Tea Set, Crackled Buff Ground, Padded Velvet Box, 15 Pieces	375.00
Satsuma, Tea Set, Showa Period, 21 Piece	200.00
Satsuma, Tea Set, Teapot, 10 In., 12 Cups & Saucers, Thousand Faces	1500.00
Satsuma, Tea Set, Wisteria Pattern, 6 Cups & Saucers, 15 Pieces	300.00
Satsuma, Tea Set, 4 Cups & Saucers, Crackled, Hand-Painted, Signed, 11 Piece	225.00
Satsuma, Teapot & Cover, Hododa, 19th Century, 8 In. *Illus*	400.00
Satsuma, Teapot, Black Ground, Gold Tracery Of Garden Scene, 4 X 7 In.	90.00
Satsuma, Teapot, Black Ground, Scene Of Garden, Gold Gilding, 4 1/2 X 7 In.	85.00
Satsuma, Teapot, Blue Eyed Dragon Handle & Spout, Raised Gold, Marked, 6 In.	395.00
Satsuma, Teapot, Gold, Scenic, Dragon Spout & Handle, Marked, 1868-1912	75.00
Satsuma, Teaset, Covered Pot, Sugar, Creamer, 6 Cups & Saucers	175.00
Satsuma, Tray, Brush Mark Green & Black Corner Design, Square, 7 3/4 In.	7.50
Satsuma, Vase, Azaleas, C.1890, Drilled For Lamp Base, 15 In.	175.00
Satsuma, Vase, Banjo Shape, Pedestal, Geisha Portrait, 11 1/4 In.	70.00
Satsuma, Vase Bilateral Handles, Oriental Figures, C.1850, 3 3/4 In.	25.00
Satsuma, Vase, Blue Birds, 15 1/2 X 8 In.	110.00
Satsuma, Vase, Blue, Gold Outline Boat Scene, 13 In., Pair	140.00
Satsuma, Vase, Blue, Pink, Apricot, Floral, Butterfly Handle, 18 1/2 In., Pair	395.00
Satsuma, Vase, Body Set On Back Of Spotted Shi-Shi, Enameled, 6 In.	250.00
Satsuma, Vase, Brown & Cream, Lord & Lady, Enamel & Gold, 9 In.	120.00
Satsuma, Vase, Continual Scene, Geishas, Enamel Design, C.1920s, 9 3/4 In.	60.00
Satsuma, Vase, Cream Ground, Red, Beads, Scholar, 8 In.	32.50
Satsuma, Vase, Cylinder, Cranes & Floral, Signed, 7 1/2 In.	40.00
Satsuma, Vase, Dancers On A Straw Mat Base, 10 In., Pair	250.00
Satsuma, Vase, Dragon In Relief, 5 Heads Of Immortals, 10 In.	95.00
Satsuma, Vase, Emperor & Empress In Gold Jeweled Robes, Black, 6 In.	65.00
Satsuma, Vase, Enamel & Gold Work Raised, Satsuma Cross Mark, 3 3/4 In.	295.00
Satsuma, Vase, Facing, Lord & Lady, Enamel & Gold, Satsuma Crest, 12 In., Pair	295.00
Satsuma, Vase, Falcon Hunt Scene, 19th Century, Signed, 15 1/2 X 10 In.	1200.00
Satsuma, Vase, Figural View, Bulbous Shape, 2 Character Seal Marks, 18 In.	1050.00
Satsuma, Vase, Figural, Enamel, C.1915, 12 In.	100.00
Satsuma, Vase, Flare Top, Bulbous Middle, 35 In., Figural Scenes, 25 In.	550.00
Satsuma, Vase, Floral & Trailed Enamel Work, 10 1/2 In.	70.00
Satsuma, Vase, Floral Design, C.1910, 10 1/2 In.	225.00
Satsuma, Vase, Gold Ground, 4 Panels Depicting Japanese Life, 5 3/4 In.	200.00
Satsuma, Vase, Green Ground, Gold Phoenix, C.1910, 12 1/2 In.	165.00
Satsuma, Vase, Hand-Painted, Bust Of Woman, 10 In.	45.00
Satsuma, Vase, Heads Of 2 Immortals, Raised & Beaded Enamel, 12 1/2 In.	125.00
Satsuma, Vase, Hexagon, 2 Panels, 1910 Mark, Dark Blue, 6 1/2 In.	70.00
Satsuma, Vase, Jeweled, Mandarin Figures, 12 X 6 1/2 In.	145.00
Satsuma, Vase, Jeweled, Moriaga, 12 X 6 1/2 In.	129.00
Satsuma, Vase, Kirin Handles, Pink & Blue, C.1900, 16 1/2 In.	130.00
Satsuma, Vase, Lord & Lady, Raised Enamel, 9 In.	120.00
Satsuma, Vase, Male Figures, Rust, Brown, Gold, Crazing, 6 1/2 In., Pair	65.00

Satsuma, Bowl, 19th Century, 4 3/4 In.
(See Page 534)

Satsuma, Box & Cover, Gilt Mark,
19th Century, 6 1/4 In.
(See Page 534)

Satsuma, Teapot & Cover,
Hododa, 19th Century, 8 In.
(See Page 535)

Satsuma, Koro & Cover, Nikko, 19th Century
(See Page 535)

Satsuma, Vase, Polychrome Enamels,
Relief Decoration, 24 In.

Satsuma, Vase, 19th Century, Marked, 7 1/4 In.

Satsuma, Vase, Man & Woman Seated, Enameling, Satsuma Crest, 12 In., Pair 325.00
Satsuma, Vase, Man On Each Side, Handled, 13 In. 75.00
Satsuma, Vase, Miniature, Raised Gold & Enamel, Gold Mark, 3 5/8 In. 295.00
Satsuma, Vase, Orange Ground & Flowers, C.1885, 13 1/2 In. 110.00
Satsuma, Vase, Ovoid Body, Figure Panels, Figural Knob, 57 In., Pair 0000.00
Satsuma, Vase, Pearl Shaped, Lakeside Scene, Wood Stand, 16 1/4 In., Pair 700.00
Satsuma, Vase, Phoenix Handles, Enameling, C.1905 .... 225.00
Satsuma, Vase, Pink & Blue, C.1900, 16 In. 65.00
Satsuma, Vase, Polychrome Enamels, Relief Decoration, 24 In. .... *Illus* 7500.00
Satsuma, Vase, Raised Gold & Enamel, Egrets, Red & Black Mark, 4 3/4 In. 325.00
Satsuma, Vase, Rust Beige, Gray, 2 Paneled, Elephant Handles, 7 1/2 In. 90.00
Satsuma, Vase, Scholars & Students, Gold Designing, 12 1/4 In. 185.00
Satsuma, Vase, Six-Sided, Thousand Faces, Signed In Japanese, 4 X 4 In. 550.00
Satsuma, Vase, Trumpet Shape, 6 Panels, Black & Gold Mark, 7 1/4 In. 675.00
Satsuma, Vase, Two Panels, Cobalt, Enameled Flowers, Marked, 12 In. 525.00
Satsuma, Vase, 19th Century, Marked, 7 1/4 In. .... *Illus* 850.00
Scale, Analytical, In Glass Case, Brass Weights 450.00
Scale, Apothecary, Hanging, Wooden Pans, 3 In.Diameter 75.00
Scale, Art Nouveau, Brass Trays, Woman At Center Platform, Iron, 18 In. 110.00
Scale, Balance, Brass, Mahogany Box, 10 X 4 1/2 X 2 In. 67.50
Scale, Balance, Fairbank's, Brass, 1896 .... 79.00
Scale, Balance, Marble Base, 2 Brass Pans 39.00
Scale, Beam, Handing, 2 Tin Pans, Old Red Paint, C.1830, 8 1/2 In.Diameter 120.00
Scale, Calculating Beam, Pelouze, Cast Iron Base, 10 In.Nickel Scoop, 2 Lbs 40.00
Scale, Candy, Spring Balance, Brass Tray, Shield, 13 X 14 1/4 In. 100.00
Scale, Candy, Toledo, White Porcelain, 1924 .... 40.00
Scale, Candy, Tradesman's, Dayton, Brass Pan, Dated 1906, 7 1/2 X 10 1/2 In. 115.00
Scale, Catalog, Fairbanks, 1854, Illustrated, Woodblock Cuts, 54 Pages 35.00
Scale, Chatillion, New York, Weighs To 75 Lbs., 13 1/2 In. 17.50
Scale, Christian Becker, Walnut Case, 18 In. 195.00
Scale, Columbia, Wooden 150.00
Scale, Computing, Dayton, Yellow Brass 20.00
Scale, Counter, Double Round Tray, Brass Scoop, Cast Iron, 19 X 5 X 9 In. 85.00
Scale, Counter, Pennies & Nickels By Weight, C.1920 .... 50.00
Scale, Dairy, Hanson, Model 60 .... 15.00
Scale, Dayton, Fan Type 20.00
Scale, Diamond, Mahogany Case, Dutch, 1800s, 7 X 2 In. 135.00
Scale, Druggist, Beveled Glass, Ornate Mechanism, 20 X 10 X 8 In. 180.00
Scale, Egg, One Weight For Ounce 45.00
Scale, Egg, Zenith, Earlville, N.Y., Iron, Original Paint 10.00
Scale, Fortune, 1 Cent, 200 Readings, Watling 145.00
Scale, Glass Lid, Marble Base, Oak Case, 2 Brass Pans, 13 X 7 1/2 In. 125.00
Scale, Gold & Money, French, Set Of Cup Weights, 1760-8-, 7 X 2 In. 250.00
Scale, Gold, Brass Pans, Fitted Wood Case, Printed Values, Colonial Days 22.00
Scale, Gold, Hand-Held, Original Box 20.00
Scale, Guinea, 1/2 Sovereign Flap, English, 18th Century, 5 1/4 X 1 In. 200.00
Scale, Hanging, Brass Face, Dated 1867 .... 17.50
Scale, Hanging, Brass Face, 3 Chains, Round 11 In.Pan, 20 Pound 65.00
Scale, Hanging, Marked In Kilos & Pounds, C.Forschner, N.Y., 18 In. 25.00
Scale, Hanging, 2 Pans, 5 Weights, Chamois Lined, Brass, 5 1/2 X 2 1/2 In. 55.00
Scale, Hide, Brass & Iron, Calibrated In Kilos, 2 Hooks, Colonial 20.00
Scale, Ice, Hanson, Model 893, 300 Pounds 25.00
Scale, Kitchen, Upright, Pewter Washed Tray, Marked Alexanderwerk 69.50
Scale, Letter, Brass, Hardwood Base, Weights Included 25.00
Scale, Miniature, Red, Iron, Tin Scoop, 4 1/2 In. 27.50
Scale, Pharmaceutical, Brass Pans, Marble & Cherry Base, All Weights, C.1870 .... 395.00
Scale, Platform, Brass Sliding Weight & Rod, Red, 19 In. 55.00
Scale, Pocket, Brass Weighing Pans, 1 1/2 In., Box, 2 X 5 In. 40.00
Scale, Postage, Brass, Wood Base, Five Original Weights, 6 X 12 In. 100.00
Scale, Postage, Brass, Wooden Base, Five Weights, 6 X 12 In. 145.00
Scale, Postage, 5 Cent Letter, Black Tole 14.75
Scale, Postal, Brass, Oak Base, 4 Weights, 7 X 4 X 3 1/2 In. 25.00
Scale, Postal, Fairbanks, Brass, Iron Base 34.00
Scale, Postal, Hanging, Nickel Finish, Small 4.50
Scale, Postal, Hanson, First Class Mail, 3 Cents, 1953, 9 1/2 In. 25.00
Scale, Postal, Nested Weights, English, Brass 175.00

Scale, Postal, U.S., Dated 1939, Brass Balance Beam, 0 To 10 Ounce 45.00
Scale, Rag Picker, Brass Face 8.00
Scale, Scoop, Brass Plated, 10 X 7 In. 14.00
Scale, Shopkeeper's, Brass Pans, Wood Frame 300.00
Scale, Silver, Balance, Colorado, Brass Pans, Iron Center Balance 95.00
Scale, Spring, Brass, 100 Pound Weight, Iron Hooks, Brass Front, 19 In. 25.00
Scale, Spring, Excelsior, Brass 12.00
Scale, Spring, Hanging, Cylinder, Brass Faced, Large 12.00
Scale, Stillyard, Whitmore-52, Weighing Fowl 18.50
Scale, Store, Cylinder Head Quilt Finish, Iron, Weights Up To 75 Lbs. 125.00
Scale, Store, Hanging, Porcelain Tray, Brass Trim, 13 5/8 X 16 In.Diameter ... 85.00
Scale, Table, Wrigley's Spearmint Gum, Brass Face & Scoop, 20 X 24 In. 65.00
Scale, Tradesmen's, Double Brass Fulcrum, Brass Tray, 10 X 18 X 5 In. 145.00
Scale, Vending Operator's, Weigh Pennies, Dial Shows Amount 50.00
Scale, W.A.Stimpson Scales, Marble Top 250.00
Scale, Watling, Fortune Telling, Penny 125.00
Scale, Weighing Buffalo Hides, Germany, 3 X 3 1/2 In. 30.00
Scale, Weight, A.B.T. Corp., 1 Cent, Free If You Guess Your Weight 500.00
Scale, Weight, Peerless, 1 Cent, Brass Platform, Dated 1914, Cast Iron 595.00
Scale, Weight, Watling, 1 Cent, Oak Case, Brass Platform & Trim, 62 In. 1225.00

Schneider
Schneider Glassworks was founded in 1903 at Epinay-sur-Seine, France, by Charles and Ernest Schneider. Art glass was made between 1903 and 1930. The company still produces clear crystal glass.

Schneider, Base, Lamp, Purple Cluthra, 8 1/2 X 5 In.Diameter 110.00
Schneider, Bowl, Cone Shape, Blown In Wrought Iron Holder, 8 In. 225.00
Schneider, Bowl, Pedestal Foot, Mottled Pink & White, Signed, 4 X 3/4 In. ... 40.00
Schneider, Charger, Mottled Yellow, Orange & Amethyst, 16 In.Diameter 195.00
Schneider, Compote, Mottled Yellow, Amethyst Stem & Base, Signed, 6 In. ... 165.00
Schneider, Compote, Orange To Blue, Amethyst Stem, Iron Base, Signed, 14 In. ... 750.00
Schneider, Dish, Bell Form, Circular Foot, Sloping Body, C.1925, 5 In. 140.00
Schneider, Ewer, Fawn Base, Applied Amethyst Handle, Signed, 6 3/8 In. 150.00
Schneider, Finger Bowl & Plate, Tango Orange To Mottled Camphor 145.00
Schneider, Vase, Bulb Shape, Blue & Rose Mottling, Signed, 7 In. 135.00
Schneider, Vase, Flared, Blue & Yellow, 9 In. 90.00
Schneider, Vase, Flower Shaped, Signed, 7 In. 255.00
Schneider, Vase, Footed, Art Deco, Frosted Fingers, Smoked Clear Glass, 6 In. ... 85.00
Schneider, Vase, Pink, Yellow, Orange & White, 17 In. 335.00

Scrimshaw is bone or ivory or whales' teeth carved by sailors and others for entertainment during the sailing-ship days. Some scrimshaw was carved as early as 1800.

Scrimshaw, see also Nautical
Scrimshaw, Antler, Caribou, 17 Inches 150.00
Scrimshaw, Bone, Knife & Sheath, 7 1/2 Inches 95.00
Scrimshaw, Caribou, Eskimo Knife Handle, Scene On Bone Blade 85.00
Scrimshaw, Crochet Hook, Flag, Brass, Pair 7.50
Scrimshaw, Crochet Hook, Hand-Carved Ivory, Dice Design 15.00
Scrimshaw, Figurine, Dancing Joe, Black Man, Articulated, 15 In. 1000.00
Scrimshaw, Jagging Wheel With Fork, Abalone Inlay 475.00
Scrimshaw, Jigger, Pastry Wheel, Handle, C.1840, 5 1/4 In. 55.00
Scrimshaw, Napkin Ring, Ivory 40.00
Scrimshaw, Necklace, Eskimo Pulling Seal, Signed 30.00
Scrimshaw, Opener, Letter, Ivory Pen Holder 22.50
Scrimshaw, Powder Horn, Engraved J.B., 1756, Ft.Crown Point, N.Y., 11 1/2 In. ... 265.00
Scrimshaw, Walrus Tusk, Ladies & Dancer, Reverse, American Eagle, 23 In. ... 650.00
Scrimshaw, Whale Tooth, George Washington & Ship, 4 In. 250.00
Scrimshaw, Whale Tooth, Gibson Girl, 3 1/2 In. 73.00
Scrimshaw, Whale Tooth, Whaling Scene, Signed M.Patrick, 5 In. 250.00
Scrimshaw, Whale Tooth, 3 Shakespearean Characters, 6 1/2 In. 200.00
Scrimshaw, Whale's Tooth, Abe Lincoln On Front, Civil War Scene On Back ... 125.00
Scrimshaw, Whale's Tooth, American Eagle, Young Girl, Black & Red, 8 In. ... 1400.00
Scrimshaw, Whale's Tooth, Carved Buddha, 1 1/2 In. 18.00
Scrimshaw, Whale's Tooth, Carving Of General Lee, Dixie Insignia On Back ... 450.00
Scrimshaw, Whale's Tooth, Eskimo Attacking Walrus With Harpoon, 3 1/2 In. ... 55.00
Scrimshaw, Whale's Tooth, General Lee & Dixie, 5 In. 450.00

Sevres, Cup, Bleu Celeste, Ormolu Mounts,
Cover, 7 1/2 In., Pair

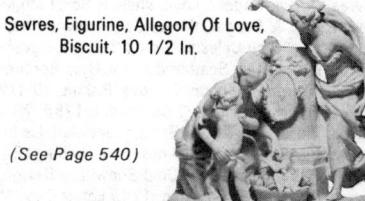

Sevres, Figurine, Allegory Of Love,
Biscuit, 10 1/2 In.

(See Page 540)

Sevres, Urn, Bleu-De-Roi, Ormolu,
Mungeir, C.1800, 24 1/2 In.

(See Page 540)

Sevres, Urn, Bleu Celeste, Ormolu, Jeweled,
10 1/4 In., Pair

Scrimshaw, Whale's Tooth, Lincoln Assassination, Large	2750.00
Scrimshaw, Whale's Tooth, Men Pursuing Whales, Woman Reading, 6 1/2 In.	2200.00
Scrimshaw, Whale's Tooth, Patterson Park, Baltimore, Maryland, 8 1/4 In.	1400.00
Scrimshaw, Whale's Tooth, Portrait Of General Lee, Dixie Symbol On Reverse	450.00
Scrimshaw, Whale's Tooth, Ship, Cannon Eagle, Star & Weather Vane, 5 In.	170.00
Scrimshaw, Whale's Tooth, Sperm Whale, Whaling Ships, 8 In.	900.00
Scrimshaw, Whale's Tooth, Whaling Ship, Full Sail, Signed, 4 In.	85.00

Scuttle Mug, see Shaving Mug, Scuttle
SEG, see Paul Revere Pottery

Sevres porcelain has been made in Sevres, France, since 1769. Many copies of the famous ware have been made. The name originally referred to the works of the Royal Factory. The name now includes any of the wares made in the town of Sevres, France.

Sevres, Basket, Gold & White, Oval, 1814-24, 14 In.	800.00
Sevres, Bowl, Birds Sitting In Foliage Inside, Bronze, Gilt, 1926, Signed	1050.00
Sevres, Box, Hinged, C.1771, Signed, 5 In.	265.00
Sevres, Box, Jewel, Blue & White, Ormolu Mounted, 10 1/2 X 4 1/2 In.	750.00
Sevres, Box, Pheasants On Lid, Gold Trim, Signed, 7 1/4 X 3 1/2 X 2 1/2 In.	310.00
Sevres, Bust, Marie Antoinette, Pedestal In Celeste Blue, Gold Trim	450.00
Sevres, Bust, Marie Antoinette, Pedestal, Blue, Gold Accents, 17 In.	450.00
Sevres, Candelabra, 3 Light, China Base, Gold Beading, 22K Gold, 13 5/8 In.	225.00
Sevres, Casket, Bleu-De-Roi Ground, Gilt Metal Mounted, 1800s, 8 1/4 In.	750.00
Sevres, Centerpiece Set, Blue, Medallions, Covered Bowl, 2 Wines	350.00
Sevres, Centerpiece, Art Nouveau, Silver Rim, Yellow Glaze, Signed, 7 X 3 In.	195.00
Sevres, Centerpiece, Napoleon III, Ormolu Mounted, 1800s, 11 X 21 In.	1600.00
Sevres, Compote, Covered, Ormolu, Pompadour Pink, 13 In.	375.00
Sevres, Compote, Hand-Painted Gold Rim, French Scene, 8 3/4 X 8 3/4 In.	147.50
Sevres, Cup & Saucer, Czarina Elizabeth Of Russia Portrait, C.1840	150.00
Sevres, Cup & Saucer, Gilt & Biscuit, 1800s, Underglaze-Red Mark	90.00

Sevres, Cup & Saucer, Gilt Border, Scalloped Shell, Marked, 1760	300.00
Sevres, Cup & Saucer, Louis Phillipe, Royal Monogram, Blue & White	290.00
Sevres, Cup & Saucer, White, Gold Crowned N On Each, Dated, 12 Oz.	175.00
Sevres, Cup, Bleu Celeste, Ormolu Mounts, Cover, 7 1/2 In., Pair *Illus*	1600.00
Sevres, Dish, Shell, Scattered Floral, Gold Border, Marked, 1769, 8 3/4 In.	300.00
Sevres, Figurine, Allegory Of Love, Biscuit, 10 1/2 In. *Illus*	2750.00
Sevres, Figurine, Bisque, 2 Childred, C.1755, 7 In.	1900.00
Sevres, Plate, Bleu-De-Roi Ground, Jeweled, L's In Blue Enamel, 9 1/2 In.	550.00
Sevres, Plate, Chateau Tuileries, Blue Border, 1844 Mark, 9 1/2 In., Set Of 8	850.00
Sevres, Plate, Cobalt Rim, Gold Snowflake Design, 9 In.	35.00
Sevres, Plate, Cobalt, Scenic, 1765 Letter Date, Morin, 8 1/2 In.	225.00
Sevres, Plate, Dinner, Date Letters, 18th Century, Set Of 14, 9 1/2 In.	9500.00
Sevres, Plate, Gilded Pierced Border, Marked & Dated, 4 1/2 In.	115.00
Sevres, Plate, Palace Of St.Cloud & Chateau Chantilly, 9 In., Pair	250.00
Sevres, Plate, Portrait, Duchesse De Bourgogne, Signed, 9 1/4 In.	275.00
Sevres, Plate, Portrait, Gold Borders, Each Different, 9 1/4 In., Set Of 6	1800.00
Sevres, Plate, Portrait, Gold Crustings, Hand-Painted, Signed, 9 1/2 In.	135.00
Sevres, Plate, Portrait, Marie Leczinska, Signed, 9 1/4 In.	140.00
Sevres, Plate, Portrait, Royal Family, 1846, 9 1/2 In., Set Of 4	600.00
Sevres, Plate, Portrait, Shepherd, Maiden, Floral, Scrolls, Enamel, Gold, 10 In.	155.00
Sevres, Plate, Sprays Of Flowers, Woman & Man, Gold Rim, Signed, 9 In.	167.50
Sevres, Tureen, Sauce, Attached Stand, Date Letter, 1768, 9 1/2 In.	950.00
Sevres, Urn, Bleu Celeste, Ormolu, Jeweled, 10 1/4 In., Pair *Illus*	850.00
Sevres, Urn, Bleu-De-Roi, Ormolu, Mungeir, C.1800, 24 1/2 In. *Illus*	2000.00
Sevres, Urn, Chrubs & Flowers, Gilt Scrollwork, Ormolu Mounted, 13 In., Pair	950.00
Sevres, Urn, Cover, Gold & Cobalt Blue On Neck, Bronze Ormolu, Signed, Pair	750.00
Sevres, Urn, Covered, Courting Scene, Hand-Painted, Ormolu Mounts, Signed	1500.00
Sevres, Urn, Pink, Ormolu Mounted, Covered, 7 3/4 In.	190.00
Sevres, Urn, White Biscuit, Louis XVI, C.1800, 16 1/2 In., Pair	750.00
Sevres, Urn, 1700 Figures, Landscape, Foliate Ormolu, 1800s, 28 1/2 In., Pair	4200.00
Sevres, Vase & Cover, Azure Blue Ground, Ovoid Body, 1800, 23 3/4 In., Pair	1300.00
Sevres, Vase & Cover, Blue Celeste-Ground, Jeweled Borders, 17 3/4 In., Pair	1600.00
Sevres, Vase & Cover, Gilt Bronze Mounted, Ovoid Body, Collot, 1880, 35 In.	2500.00
Sevres, Vase & Cover, Green Ground, Ovoid Body, Signed, 1800, 26 In.	1000.00
Sevres, Vase & Cover, Jeweled, Painted Interlaced L's, 1800, 10 In., Pair	600.00
Sevres, Vase, Floral Panels, Ovoid Body, C.1850, 24 1/2 In., Pair	375.00
Sevres, Vase, Galante Scene, Gilt Cartouche, 1800s, 29 In., Pair	700.00
Sevres, Vase, Gilt-Bronze Mounted, Ovoid Body, Miguel, Signed, 23 In., Pair	1600.00
Sevres, Vase, Green & Brown On Light Green, 11 In.	225.00
Sevres, Vase, Gros Blue, Ormolu Mounted, Napoleon III, C.1850, 27 In.	950.00
Sevres, Vase, Incised Date Code For 1833, Printed Sevres Mark, 13 1/2 In.	400.00
Sevres, Vase, Ormolu Mounted, Couple, Flowers, Leafage, Marked, 31 In., Pair	800.00
Sevres, Vase, Potpourri, Flowers, Birds, Scrolled Feet, 1800s, 5 1/4 In., Pair	300.00

Sewer tile figures were made by workers in the sewer tile factories in the Ohio area during the late nineteenth and early twentieth centuries.

Sewer Tile, Ashtray, Husky Dog	14.00
Sewer Tile, Boot	10.00
Sewer Tile, Cross-Eyed Indian, Ohio, 10 1/2 In.	175.00
Sewer Tile, Deer & Doe, Wall Hanging	10.00
Sewer Tile, Frog, On Rectangular Base, Hand Moulded, 3 1/2 X 4 1/4 In.	17.50
Sewer Tile, Lion, Laying Down	85.00
Sewer Tile, Lion, On Oval Base, Hand Tooled, Initialed R.L.W., 12 1/2 In.	40.00
Sewer Tile, Shoe	5.00
Sewer Tile, Skull, Initialed E.J.E., 5 1/2 In.	90.00
Sewer Tile, Spaniel Dog, Ohio, 11 In.	185.00
Sewing, Basket Pincushion, Grass, Natural With Pink, 1 1/2 X 1 3/4 In.Diam.	8.50
Sewing, Basket, Attached Needle Holder & Scissors Case, 2 Thimbles, German	28.00
Sewing, Basket, Brocade Lining, Wicker, 7 1/2 In.Diameter	15.00
Sewing, Basket, French, Directoire Period, Brass Feet, Satin Lined, Drawers	150.00
Sewing, Basket, Sweet Grass, Covered, 6 In.Diameter	10.00
Sewing, Basket, Thimble	5.00
Sewing, Basket, Wicker, Round	10.00
Sewing, Bird, Clamp On, Cushion, Brass	48.00
Sewing, Bird, Dated 1853, Pincushion Top	85.00
Sewing, Bird, Double Cushion, Metal, 4 1/2 In.	95.00

Sewing, Bird, Floral Design On Bracket, Velvet Cushions, Dated 1853	85.00
Sewing, Bird, For Braiding Rugs, Shape Of Duck, Iron	90.00
Sewing, Bird, Heart Screw Clamp, Iron	89.00
Sewing, Bird, Pincushion At Feet, Serves As Nest, Table Clamp, C.1850s	95.00
Sewing, Bird, Silver Plated, 2 Pincushions, Dated 1853	70.00
Sewing, Book, Butterick Dressmaker, 1921	4.00
Sewing, Book, Needle, Dirigible Shape	6.00
Sewing, Box, Clark's Cotton Spool	18.00
Sewing, Box, Dovetailed, White Knobs, 2 Lids, Handle	50.00
Sewing, Box, Inlaid Sprays Of Shamrock, Cherry, 6 1/2 X 10 1/2 X 4 In.	130.00
Sewing, Box, Needle, Souvenir, Crystal Palace, Thimble, Pincushion, Lined	85.00
Sewing, Box, Sewing, Spool Drawer, Coffee Grinder Shape, 9 Spindles	35.00
Sewing, Box, Thread, Advertising Playing Cards	12.50
Sewing, Box, Tiered, Single Drawer, Lift Top, 8 Spindles, 5 1/2 X 7 In.	32.50
Sewing, Box, Walnut, Original Satin Lining, Key, 7 3/4 X 10 3/4 X 5 1/2 In.	115.00
Sewing, Box, Wooden, Dovetailed, Cane Trim, Red Lining, 8 X 12 In.	12.00
Sewing, Cabinet, Braid, Three 3 In.Drawers, Oak, 24 X 17 X 12 In.	100.00
Sewing, Cabinet, Mock Bookcase Front & Mirror, Oak	195.00
Sewing, Cabinet, Needle, Crawley's	85.00
Sewing, Case, Needle, Carved Ivory	24.00
Sewing, Case, Needle, Chinese Silver, 2 In.	105.00
Sewing, Case, Needle, Ivory, Book Form	35.00
Sewing, Case, Needle, Push-Up Type, Picture Of Woman	15.00
Sewing, Case, Needle, Revolving Counter Type, Boye, 1929, Shuttles & Bobbins	55.00
Sewing, Case, Needle, Ribbon Rolls Out To Hold Needles, C.1880	15.00
Sewing, Case, Scissors, Fitted For 2 Pair, Marked Drummond, 7 In.Long	32.00
Sewing, Case, Thimble, Shape & Size Of Hen Egg, Brass Chain	50.00
Sewing, Case, Thread & Thimble, 1 1/2 In.	6.50
Sewing, Clamp, Quilting, Hand-Wrought Iron, Set Of 4	28.00
Sewing, Darner & Needle Holder, Handle Unscrews For Needles, Birch	8.00
Sewing, Darner, Blown Glass, Pink	20.00
Sewing, Darner, Double Ended, Wood	4.50
Sewing, Darner, Ebony & Sterling	25.00
Sewing, Darner, Glove, Sterling Shank, Painted Wood Ends	28.00
Sewing, Dressing Set, Traveling, Mother-Of-Pearl Handle, Box, 11 Piece	75.00
Sewing, Egg, Darning, Blown Cased Glass, Marbleized, 3 X 4 1/4 In.	95.00
Sewing, Egg, Darning, Mauchline, Opens For Needle Case	25.00
Sewing, Egg, Darning, Sterling Handle	22.00
Sewing, Egg, Darning, Whalebone, Wood Handle	55.00
Sewing, Egg, Darning, Wooden, Handle	6.00
Sewing, Egg, The Columbian Egg, Needle Case Inside	55.00
Sewing, Goose, Tailor's, Large	18.00
Sewing, Guard, Knitting Needle, Sterling, 1 1/4 In.	8.00
Sewing, Holder, Needle, Tankard, Wood, Revolving Top	15.00
Sewing, Holder, Spool, Circular Base, Pincushion Top, C.1880, Maple	30.00
Sewing, Holder, Spool, 6 Spindles, Tri-Footed, Thimble Finial, 4 In.	15.00
Sewing, Holder, Thimble, Glass Shoe, Gold & Enamel	26.00
Sewing, Holder, Thimble, Mother-Of-Pearl	38.50
Sewing, Holder, Thimble, Straw	2.50
Sewing, Holder, Yarn, Four Branches, Maple	95.00
Sewing, Kit, Leather, Sterling Fittings	60.00
Sewing, Lacemaker, Set, Bone Handles, 6 Piece	40.00
Sewing, Loom, Weaver's Delight, Davenport, Iowa, Accessories, 4 Feet	250.00
Sewing, Machine, Hand, Needles & Table Clamp, Smith & Egge, 1901	85.00
Sewing, Machine, New Home Sewing Machine, 6 Drawers, C.1879	130.00
Sewing, Machine, Table Model, Wilcox & Gibbs 1883	80.00
Sewing, Machine, Wilcox & Gibbs, Patent, July 15, 1857	65.00
Sewing, Needle Case, Hire's Condensed Milk, 1899	22.00
Sewing, Needle, Boyd, Flat Tin, Dated 1912	2.75
Sewing, Needle, Emery, Velvet Cat	9.00
Sewing, Needle, Knitting, Eureka, Cylinder Shape, Tin Picture, C.1900	40.00
Sewing, Needles & Threader, Dollard Coal Company	3.00
Sewing, Pin Cushion & Tape Measure	10.00
Sewing Pincushion, see also Pincushion Doll	
Sewing, Pincushion & Thimble Holder, World Globe, Base Is Tape Measure	22.50
Sewing, Pincushion, Beaded, Velvet, Victorian, 7 1/2 In.	28.00

Sewing, Pincushion, Bird, Brass, Cushion By The Neck	95.00
Sewing, Pincushion, Clamp On, Tiger Maple	20.00
Sewing, Pincushion, Figural, Apple, Silk, Victorian, C.1880	36.50
Sewing, Pincushion, Hitler, Hotzi Notzi, Dated 1941	38.00
Sewing, Pincushion, Indian Woman	5.00
Sewing, Pincushion, Luster, Japan, 2 1/2 In.	7.00
Sewing, Pincushion, Metal, Occupied Japan	3.50
Sewing, Pincushion, Mockland	22.00
Sewing, Pincushion, Pillow, Beaded, 5 X 7 1/2 In.	35.00
Sewing, Pincushion, Rabbit, White Metal	14.00
Sewing, Pincushion, Red Velvet, Beaded, Victorian, 7 1/2 X 6 In.	35.00
Sewing, Pincushion, Revolving, Piano Stool Shape	10.00
Sewing, Pincushion, Shoe, Papier-Mache	15.00
Sewing, Pincushion, Strawberries, Green Velvet	12.00
Sewing, Scissors & Emery, Silk Case, Painted, Chinese	9.00
Sewing, Scissors, Buttonhole	5.50 To 7.50
Sewing, Scissors, Figural Stork, Gilted Body Feathers, Germany, 4 1/2 In.	12.50
Sewing, Scissors, Folding, Marked Belmont, Germany	4.00
Sewing, Scissors, Keen Kutter, 6 In.	3.00
Sewing, Scissors, Stork, Head Of Man As Mark Of Maker, Steel, 3 1/2 In.	15.00
Sewing, Shuttle, Tatting, Needle & Thread Case, Tape Measure, Lydia Pinkham	48.00
Sewing, Tape Measure & Sewing Kit, G.E.Vacuum Cleaner	8.00
Sewing, Tape Measure, Basket Of Flowers, Celluloid	25.00
Sewing, Tape Measure, Carved Ivory	16.00
Sewing, Tape Measure, Clock	17.50
Sewing, Tape Measure, Cowboy On Horse, Kansas City, Missouri	8.50
Sewing, Tape Measure, Dog, German, 4 1/2 In.	27.50
Sewing, Tape Measure, Fab	12.50
Sewing, Tape Measure, Felt, Flapper Face Painted On Cloth	15.00
Sewing, Tape Measure, Figural Ship	25.00
Sewing, Tape Measure, Figural, Pig, Dated August 25/96	45.00
Sewing, Tape Measure, Firestone	7.00
Sewing, Tape Measure, Fishing Reel, Wooden, Ivory & Brass Handle	55.00
Sewing, Tape Measure, Goodyear	7.00
Sewing, Tape Measure, Green Piggy, Celluloid, 3 In.Diameter	12.50
Sewing, Tape Measure, Hoover Sweeper	17.50
Sewing, Tape Measure, Hose Supporter, Celluloid	15.00
Sewing, Tape Measure, Iona Savings Bank, Tilton, N.H., Celluloid, C.1880	22.50
Sewing, Tape Measure, Ivory, Stanhope	35.00
Sewing, Tape Measure, Leather Covered, Brass Bound, Dated 1908	5.00
Sewing, Tape Measure, Miniature, Alarm Clock, Big Ben	40.00
Sewing, Tape Measure, Owl	29.00
Sewing, Tape Measure, Pig, Sterling, 2 X 1 In.	92.00
Sewing, Tape Measure, Pig, Tail Winds The Tape	44.00
Sewing, Tape Measure, Puppy On Pincushion	22.00
Sewing, Tape Measure, R.C.A.	5.00
Sewing, Tape Measure, Scene Of Niagara Falls, Celluloid	14.00
Sewing, Tape Measure, Standing Figure Of Hunter Atop, 1 3/4 X 1 In.Diam.	22.00
Sewing, Tape Measure, Statue Of Liberty Pictured	7.50
Sewing, Tape Measure, Tiffany	32.00
Sewing, Tape Measure, Victorian, Sterling, 1 1/8 In.	45.00
Sewing, Tatting Shuttle	5.00
Sewing, Thimble Case, Size & Shape Of Hen Egg, Brass Chain, Chased Design	85.00
Sewing, Thimble, Boat, Lighthouse, Sterling	20.00
Sewing, Thimble, Carnelian Inset Top, Coin Silver	32.00
Sewing, Thimble, Chased Border, Building Scene, Dated November I, 1910, Gold	95.00
Sewing, Thimble, Coca-Cola	3.00
Sewing, Thimble, Embossed Scrolls, Crown Is Sterling, Other Is 14K Gold	35.00
Sewing, Thimble, Engraved Band, Sterling Silver, Size 11	19.00
Sewing, Thimble, Floral Engraved, 10K Gold	45.00
Sewing, Thimble, Flower Decoration, Royal Worcester	12.00
Sewing, Thimble, Gold, Hand-Carved Case Shape Of Walnut	85.00
Sewing, Thimble, Gold, 3 Cartouche Around, Diamond Design Border, Size 7	63.50
Sewing, Thimble, Hoover, Home Happiness	7.50
Sewing, Thimble, Leroy Sanatorium	7.50
Sewing, Thimble, Narrow Scroll Band, 10K Gold	55.00

Sewing, Thimble, Nugrape	7.50
Sewing, Thimble, One Scallop Top, Other Flowered Border, Pair	45.00
Sewing, Thimble, Open-Ended, Sterling	11.00
Sewing, Thimble, Pepsi-Cola	3.00
Sewing, Thimble, Raised Cherubs, November 21, 1885, Sterling	32.00
Sewing, Thimble, Razor & Wire Needle Threader	22.50
Sewing, Thimble, Red Goose Shoes	7.50
Sewing, Thimble, Snowflake Design, Sterling Silver	30.00
Sewing, Thimble, Sterling Silver, Ornate Border	14.00
Sewing, Thimble, Westinghouse	7.50
Sewing, Thimble, Wide Ornate Band, Sterling Silver	28.00
Sewing, Thread Holder, Round, Lift Off Lid, Clarks, 3 1/3 In.Diameter	29.00
Sewing, Threader, Ribbon, Beaded Edges	22.00
Sewing, Threader, Ribbon, Sterling	23.00
Sewing, Winder, Skeins Into Balls, Umbrella Fold, Table Clamping, 29 In.	125.00
Shaker, Basket, Covered, Lined, 5 1/2 In.Square	55.00
Shaker, Basket, Sewing, Canterbury Shakers, Sweetgrass, C.1890, 4 1/2 X 2 In.	125.00
Shaker, Basket, Sewing, Straw, 2 Button Clasps, Silk Lining, 12 1/2 X 2 In.	95.00
Shaker, Box, Black Graining, Top Initialed B.F.M., Oval, 4 In.	39.00
Shaker, Box, Candle, Slide Cover, Enfield, Connecticut	200.00
Shaker, Box, Candle, Slide Lid, Brown, Dovetailed, Massachusetts	95.00
Shaker, Box, Cheese, Interwoven Laps, Darkened Wood	95.00
Shaker, Box, Document, Flat-Top, Yellow, New Lebanon, 12 X 17 X 4 1/2 In.	400.00
Shaker, Box, Poplar, Sabbathday Lake, Signed	45.00
Shaker, Box, Sewing, Sabbathday Lake, Maine, Pincushion, Signed, Square, 6 In.	160.00
Shaker, Can, Oil Filler, Tin	39.00
Shaker, Carrier, Cherry, Handle, 2 Slide Lids, G.Wilcox.16 X 3 3/4 In.	345.00
Shaker, Cheese Form, Sabbathday Lake	45.00
Shaker, Comb, Wooden, Round, Early	40.00
Shaker, Drainer, Wooden	125.00
Shaker, Furniture, see Furniture	
Shaker, Hetchel, Dovetailed Cover, Paper Attests Aurelia Mace, 19 In.	270.00
Shaker, Mold, Box, Solid Wood, Bentwood Boxes, Oval, 8 In.	65.00
Shaker, Pie Crimper, Bone, Wood	20.00
Shaker, Pin, Clothes, Tin Band	5.00
Shaker, Rack, Shoe, Four Cross Members	110.00
Shaker, Sewing Kit, Completley Fitted, Leather, 6 1/2 In.Square	70.00
Shaker, Sewing Kit, Leather Ends & Cover, Fitted, 4 X 1 1/2 In.	65.00
Shaker, Shawl, Dark Gray & Black	65.00
Shaker, Sifter, Horse Hair	100.00
Shaker, Sorter, Bean, Adjustable, Slatted Bottom, Wooden	75.00

Shaving mugs were popular from 1860 to 1900. Many types were made, including occupational mugs featuring pictures of the man's job. There were scuttle mugs, silver-plated mugs, glass-lined mugs, and others.

Shaving Mug, Applied Grapes & Leaves	27.50
Shaving Mug, B.P.O.E. Elk	75.00
Shaving Mug, B.P.O.E., Marked Goy's Lunch	67.50
Shaving Mug, Blue & Green Background, Trailing Flowers	21.00
Shaving Mug, Brush Holder, Silver Over Brass	65.00
Shaving Mug, Brush, Lady's, Celluloid Covered Box	38.00
Shaving Mug, Copper Luster	25.00
Shaving Mug, Drain, Flowers	18.00
Shaving Mug, Elk, Brown & Tan	25.00
Shaving Mug, Embossed Elk, Bisque	30.00
Shaving Mug, Embossed Face Of Bearded Man, Milk Glass, 1894	95.00
Shaving Mug, Floral, Drain Tray	15.00
Shaving Mug, Fraternal, Eagle, American Flag, Name	40.00
Shaving Mug, Gold Bands, Name	25.00
Shaving Mug, Gold Rim, H.B.Hinman	16.50
Shaving Mug, Golden Knight Shaving Soap	22.00
Shaving Mug, Hand-Painted Roses	13.50
Shaving Mug, Holder, Wall Mounted, Brass	25.00
Shaving Mug, Insert, Dated 1907, Pairpoint Quadruple Plate	35.00
Shaving Mug, Lake & Mountain Scene, Marked, Frank Gardiner	27.50
Shaving Mug, Leaves & Flowers, Silver Plate	40.00

Shaving Mug, Lettered A Present, German	22.50
Shaving Mug, Lithophane, Rollicking Tavern Scene	110.00
Shaving Mug, Masonic, Symbol 32nd Degree, Name In Gold	95.00
Shaving Mug, Matching Brush, Sterling, Gorham	55.00
Shaving Mug, Number 15 In Gold, Royal China	15.00
Shaving Mug, Occupational, B.F. & S.R.Ry., Electric Car	75.00
Shaving Mug, Occupational, Baker, Cone Oven, Loaves Of Bread	125.00
Shaving Mug, Occupational, Bartender, Carl Christman In Gold, Signed Koken	165.00
Shaving Mug, Occupational, Bird Dog, Shotgun, Rod, Creel, Fish	125.00
Shaving Mug, Occupational, Blacksmith Shoeing Horse, Forge & Anvil	140.00
Shaving Mug, Occupational, Boot Black & Shoe, R.R.Chandler	75.00
Shaving Mug, Occupational, Brick Layer, Limoges	110.00
Shaving Mug, Occupational, Bricklayer, Trial & Hammer	95.00
Shaving Mug, Occupational, Caboose, Red	65.00
Shaving Mug, Occupational, Dentist, Pulling Teeth	135.00 To 175.00
Shaving Mug, Occupational, Drapes, Name	65.00
Shaving Mug, Occupational, Dray With Driver & Horses	75.00
Shaving Mug, Occupational, Farmer Plowing, 2 Horses, Gold Band	95.00
Shaving Mug, Occupational, Farmer, Man With Basket Of Potatoes, Wagon	100.00
Shaving Mug, Occupational, Fisherman, Walking Toward Boat, Austria	65.00
Shaving Mug, Occupational, Fraternal, W.D.Dietz, A.O.K. Of M.C.	80.00
Shaving Mug, Occupational, Horsedrawn Funeral Carriage, Limoges	125.00
Shaving Mug, Occupational, Horses Pulling 4 Wheeled Buggy	110.00
Shaving Mug, Occupational, Jockey, Horse's Head In Horseshoe, Name In Gold	95.00
Shaving Mug, Occupational, Livery Stable	140.00
Shaving Mug, Occupational, Man On Scaffolding, Painting, Gold Band	100.00
Shaving Mug, Occupational, Musician, Silver Overlay	75.00
Shaving Mug, Occupational, Painless Dentist, False Teeth Picture	100.00
Shaving Mug, Occupational, Railroad Wood Burning Engine, Name, Gold	110.00
Shaving Mug, Occupational, Sportsman, Dog, Bird, Fish, Creel, Pole, Gun	95.00
Shaving Mug, Occupational, Stationery Engineer	115.00
Shaving Mug, Occupational, Surveyor, Marked C.F.H.	105.00
Shaving Mug, Occupational, Theatrical Drape, Name & Gold	65.00
Shaving Mug, Occupational, Track Foreman, Name In Gold	90.00
Shaving Mug, Occupational, Trainman On Caboose, Limoges	70.00
Shaving Mug, Occupational, Trolleycar	140.00
Shaving Mug, Palmer Cox Brownies, China	55.00
Shaving Mug, Peach Luster Bands, Excelsior, 1870	35.00
Shaving Mug, Picture Of Train, France	22.50
Shaving Mug, Pink Luster, Beading	22.50
Shaving Mug, Scuttle, Blue & Fuchsia Flowers	26.00
Shaving Mug, Scuttle, Gold Trim, Pink Luster	30.00
Shaving Mug, Scuttle, Lavender & Yellow Flowers	34.50
Shaving Mug, Scuttle, Pink Roses, Gilt Trim, Germany	20.00
Shaving Mug, Scuttle, Roses	22.00
Shaving Mug, Scuttle, Signed Union Shaving Mug, 1870	25.00
Shaving Mug, Scuttle, Strap Handle, Seamed Brush Spout, C.1850	35.00
Shaving Mug, Scuttle, Yellow & White, Gold Flowers	25.00
Shaving Mug, Seaforth	15.00
Shaving Mug, Shepherdess, Lambs, Purple Luster, Germany	30.00
Shaving Mug, Shield On Front, Silver Plate	12.00
Shaving Mug, Tole, Tin	50.00
Shaving Mug, University Of Tennessee, Gold Lettering	18.50
Shaving Mug, Violets, Name, Limoges	14.00
Shaving Mug, White & Gold, Limoges	35.00
Shaving Mug, White Background, Pink Rose & Buds, Gold Banded, 3 1/2 In.	20.00
Shaving Mug, White, Gold Bands & Trim, Name In Gold	25.00

Shawnee   Shawnee pottery was made in Zanesville, Ohio, from 1935 until 1961.
USA   Shawnee also produced pottery for George Rumrill during the late 1930s.

Shawnee, Bowl, Corn	21.00
Shawnee, Butter, Corn	25.00
Shawnee, Butter, Oblong	12.50
Shawnee, Casserole, Corn	28.00
Shawnee, Casserole, Covered, Corn, Large, Original Sticker	18.50
Shawnee, Casserole, Covered, 11 In.	38.50

Shawnee, Cookie Jar, Mrs. Pig With Bank Top	20.00
Shawnee, Cookie Jar, Mrs.Winnie	30.00
Shawnee, Cookie Jar, Puss'n Boots	20.00 To 32.00
Shawnee, Cookie Jar, Reclining Clown, Seal With Ball On Tummy, Signed	25.00
Shawnee, Cookie Jar, Smiley The Pig	18.00
Shawnee, Creamer, Elephant	7.00 To 9.50
Shawnee, Creamer, Pig	7.50
Shawnee, Creamer, Puss 'n Boots	9.00
Shawnee, Dish, Puss-In-Boots	30.00
Shawnee, Holder, Flower Pot, Clown	7.50
Shawnee, Mug, Corn	5.00
Shawnee, Pitcher, Blue Boy	15.00
Shawnee, Pitcher, Bo Peep, 8 In.	19.00
Shawnee, Pitcher, Bo-Peep, 7 1/2 In.	12.50
Shawnee, Pitcher, Chanticleer Rooster	15.00
Shawnee, Pitcher, Figural, Sailor Boy	15.00
Shawnee, Pitcher, Little Bo Peep, 7 1/2 In.	14.00
Shawnee, Pitcher, Milk, Smiley Pig	9.00
Shawnee, Pitcher, Sailor Boy	10.00
Shawnee, Planter, Dutch Boy & Girl	5.00
Shawnee, Planter, Oriental Girl	5.00
Shawnee, Planter, Pup With Doghouse	8.00
Shawnee, Planter, Wishing Well, Dutch Girl & Boy	7.50
Shawnee, Salt & Pepper, Corn, 5 1/2 In.	12.00
Shawnee, Salt & Pepper, Lamb	2.50
Shawnee, Salt & Pepper, Pigs	2.50
Shawnee, Saltshaker, Owl	8.00
Shawnee, Saltshaker, Puss 'n Boots	9.00
Shawnee, Teapot, Corn	18.50 To 22.50
Shawnee, Teapot, Granny Ann	17.00
Shawnee, Teapot, Granny Annie, Flowers & Colors	30.00
Shawnee, Teapot, Tom Tom The Piper's Son	22.00

Shirley Temple, Doll, Original Clothes With Tag, Marked, 22 In.

(See Page 546)

Shawnee, Vase, Figural, Rooster, Tan	5.00
Shawnee, Vase, Wall, Jack Horner	6.00
Shearwater, Vase, Purple, 9 1/4 In.High	85.00
Sheffield, see Silver, Sheffield	
Ship, see Nautical	

Shirley Temple dishes, blue glassware, and any other souvenir-type objects with her name and picture are now collected.

Shirley Temple, Bank, Staten Island Bank, 1930s, Metal	60.00
Shirley Temple, Book, Five Books About Me, 1935	50.00
Shirley Temple, Book, Rebecca Of Sunnybrook Farm	14.00
Shirley Temple, Book, Stories That Never Grow Old	8.00
Shirley Temple, Book, Treasury, Hard Cover	10.00
Shirley Temple, Buggy, Wicker	325.00 To 475.00
Shirley Temple, Cards, Playing	6.00
Shirley Temple, Carriage, Wooden With Medallions	425.00
Shirley Temple, Cereal Set, Mug, Creamer, Bowl	85.00
Shirley Temple, Charm, Sterling Silver	14.50
Shirley Temple, Creamer	15.00 To 25.00
Shirley Temple, Doll, Blond Wig, Blue Eyes, Fully Jointed, Bisque, 16 In.	65.00

Shirley Temple, Doll, Blue Dress, 24 In.	80.00
Shirley Temple, Doll, Cheer Leader Costume, Marked, 18 In.	180.00
Shirley Temple, Doll, Composition, Marked Head & Body, 20 In.	225.00
Shirley Temple, Doll, Composition, 13 Inches	145.00
Shirley Temple, Doll, Hard Plastic, Original Purse & Jewelry, 17 In.	78.00
Shirley Temple, Doll, Original Clothes With Tag, Marked, 22 In. .... Illus	375.00
Shirley Temple, Doll, Original Red & White Dotted Dress, Fur Coat, 18 In.	275.00
Shirley Temple, Embroidery Kit, Boxed, 1959	20.00
Shirley Temple, Mirror, Fox Film Corp	28.00
Shirley Temple, Mirror, Picture, Pink, Brown, Imprint, Round, 2 1/4 In.	4.00
Shirley Temple, Mirror, Pocket, America's Sweetheart, 2 1/4 In.Diameter	4.50
Shirley Temple, Mug	27.00 To 35.00
Shirley Temple, Paper Dolls, Set	13.50
Shirley Temple, Paperweight, Love Shirley, Mirror On Reverse	6.00
Shirley Temple, Pitcher, Blue, Portrait	19.00 To 22.00
Shirley Temple, Purse, Picture Play Money, 7 X 6 In.	35.00
Shirley Temple, Salt, Figural, 3 In.	15.00
Shirley Temple, Stand, Wooden Cut Out, Life Sized, Used In Theatre Lobby	225.00
Shirley Temple, Store Display, Stand-Ups & Shirley Temple Cereal Box, 1938	135.00
Shirley Temple, Teapot, Pink, Plastic, 2 Cups	62.00
Shirley Temple, Viewer, Picture Film Boxes	6.50
Shotgun, see Weapon, Shotgun	
Silesia, Chocolate Pot, White Ground, Pink & Lavender Flowers	45.00
Silesia, Creamer, Wild Roses, Blue, 6 In.	10.00
Silesia, Jar, Gold & Blue Squares.Handles, Marked, 3 1/2 X 4 1/2 In.	28.00
Silesia, Plate, Beaded Edge, Artist Signed, 9 In., Pair	50.00
Silesia, Plate, Cake, Scalloped Edge, Gold Beaded Trim, 9 1/2 In.	45.00
Silesia, Sugar & Creamer, Hand-Painted, 1915, Signed	30.00
Silesia, Vase, Hand-Painted Showing A Woman	25.00
Silhouette, see Picture, Silhouette	

*Silver deposit glass was made during the late nineteenth and early twentieth
centuries. Solid sterling silver was applied to the glass by a chemical
method so that a cutout design of silver metal appeared against a clear or
colored glass. It is sometimes called silver overlay.*

Silver Deposit, Bottle, Cologne, Art Nouveau, Steuben	150.00
Silver Deposit, Bottle, With Hazel, Clambroth	25.00
Silver Deposit, Cruet, Original Stopper, 6 1/2 In.	30.00
Silver Deposit, Decanter, Swirl, Floral	22.00
Silver Deposit, Mug, Green Glass, Floral Vine, 5 In. Tall	125.00
Silver Deposit, Pitcher, Large Lip & Shoulder, 5 X 7 X 8 In.	45.00
Silver Deposit, Vase, Art Nouveau, Footed Base, Signed Tiffany, 12 1/4 In.	350.00
Silver Plate, see also Silver, Sheffield	
Silver Plate, Basket, Flower, Forbes Silver Co., Quadruple, 16 1/2 In.	100.00
Silver Plate, Basket, Footed, Handle, Raised Figures, J.W.Tufts, 11 1/2 In.	135.00
Silver Plate, Basket, Fruit, Repousse Center, Pairpoint, 11 1/2 X 9 1/2 In.	75.00
Silver Plate, Basket, Stationary Handle, Ribbing, Forbes, 12 1/2 X 7 In.	22.00
Silver Plate, Bowl, Fruit, Footed, Art Nouveau Trim, Webster Co., C.1886, 9 In.	85.00
Silver Plate, Bowl, Nut, Cabbage Leaf Forms Bowl, Pairpoint, 10 1/2 X 7 In.	85.00
Silver Plate, Box, Ball Feet, Rabbit & Word Pins On Top	25.00
Silver Plate, Brush, Bust Of Lady, Art Nouveau	10.00
Silver Plate, Butter, Cow Standing On Top	55.00
Silver Plate, Butter, Figural, Cow, Deer In Circle, Hartford	75.00
Silver Plate, Butter, Roll Top, Glass Insert, Paw Feet, Rogers	25.00
Silver Plate, Butter, Round, Insert, Pairpoint	25.00
Silver Plate, Candelabra, 5 Arm, Converts To Single, 19 X 14 In., Pair	300.00
Silver Plate, Candlestick, Swing Back, 3 Socket, Pair, 7 1/2 X 10 1/2 In.	85.00
Silver Plate, Castor, see Castor	
Silver Plate, Chamberstick, Floral Handle, Swirl, Bead, Open Scallop, 3 In.	22.00
Silver Plate, Coffeepot, Fluted Legs, Claw Feet, English, C.1860, 14 1/2 In.	675.00
Silver Plate, Coffin Plate, Woodman Of The World	5.00
Silver Plate, Compote, Art Nouveau, Clover & Leaf, Derby, 13 In.	48.00
Silver Plate, Cooler, Water, Double Walled, Greek Key, 12 In.	125.00
Silver Plate, Cooler, Water, Double Walled, Victorian, 13 In.	165.00
Silver Plate, Cooler, Water, Porcelain Lined, Meriden Company, Victorian	150.00
Silver Plate, Cooler, Water, Porcelain Lined, Meriden, 11 In.	145.00

Silver Plate, Crumb Tray, Grape, Adelphi Silver Company 29.00
Silver Plate, Cup, Egg, On Stand, Set Of 4 .... 55.00
Silver Plate, Dish, Candy, Figural Finial, Meriden, 13 1/2 In. 135.00
Silver Plate, Dresser Set, Art Deco, Alvin, Set Of 5 .... 75.00
Silver Plate, Egg, Decapitator, Figural Rooster, Germany 22.00
Silver Plate, Epergne, Ruffled Top, Green Iridescent, Hallmarked Stand 50.00
Silver Plate, Figurine, Dancing Lady, Art Nouveau 25.00
Silver Plate, Figurine, Elephant, Niagara Falls On Back, Occupied Japan 10.00
Silver Plate, Flask, Cap, Hammered Design 20.00
Silver Plate, Humidor, Figural Horse & Man On Top, Large 215.00
Silver Plate, Humidor, 2 Compartments, Scrolled Sides, Meriden, 11 In. 215.00
Silver Plate, Kettle, Burner, Bone Handle, Marked Foehr 800 Stuttgart 425.00
Silver Plate, Kettle, Triplet Base, Swivel, J.A.Stimpson Company, 18 1/2 In. 275.00
Silver Plate, Knife Rest, Figural, Cat & Dog On Fence 49.00
Silver Plate, Knife Rest, Wolf Hounds 16.50
Silver Plate, Ladle, Gravy, Adoration, 1847 Rogers 5.00
Silver Plate, Ladle, Punch, Cut Glass Handle, Marked J.D.Bergen Co. 210.00
Silver Plate, Ladle, Soup, Royal, 1887, Gorham 35.00
Silver Plate, Mirror, Plateau, Feet & Scroll Sides, 10 In. 35.00
Silver Plate, Mug, Child's, Little Boy Blue, Cows 30.00
Silver Plate, Mug, King Edward VIII Coronation 17.50
Silver Plate, Mustache Cup, see Mustache Cup
Silver Plate, Napkin Ring, see Napkin Ring
Silver Plate, Pail, Wine, Swag Handles, English, C.1860, 11 1/2 In., Pair 660.00
Silver Plate, Pan, Dust, Grape, Adelphi Silver Company 35.00
Silver Plate, Pitcher, Syrup, Egyptian Head On Handle & Finial, 8 In. 55.00
Silver Plate, Pitcher, Syrup, Footed, Lid, Victorian, 5 3/4 In. 45.00
Silver Plate, Pitcher, Water, Double Wall, Lid, Spout, Derby Silver, 12 In. 125.00
Silver Plate, Receiver, Card, Cherub, Meriden & Co., 4 1/4 In. 225.00
Silver Plate, Ring Box, Figural, Tote Bag, 4 X 5 In. 147.00
Silver Plate, Salt, 2 Cellars Set In Viking Shop 15.00
Silver Plate, Shears, Grape, E.P. Hallmark, English 42.00
Silver Plate, Spoon, Demitasse, Gold Wash Bowl, Henninger, Set Of 12 .... 95.00
Silver Plate, Spoon, Napkin Ring, Eggcup, Boxed 25.00
Silver Plate, Spoon, Souvenir, see Souvenir, Spoon, Silver Plate
Silver Plate, Spooner, Bird Finial, Scroll Handles, 12 Hooks, Rogers 97.00
Silver Plate, Spoonholder, Ovoid Body, 12 Spoon Hooks, Side Handles, Rogers 110.00
Silver Plate, Sugar & Creamer, Equitable Life Of Iowa, Logo On Side 35.00
Silver Plate, Tea Service, Teapot, Sugar, Butter, Creamer, 1887 .... 495.00
Silver Plate, Tea Set, Teapot, Sugar & Creamer, Spooner, Wilcox 65.00
Silver Plate, Tongs, Pickle, Sweden 12.00
Silver Plate, Toothpick, see Toothpick
Silver Plate, Tray, Bread, Buck Silver Co., 12 3/4 X 6 1/4 In. 16.00
Silver Plate, Tray, Double Crystal Inkwells, Pen Holder 95.00
Silver Plate, Tray, Inkwell, Crystal Inkwells, Wilcox, 5 1/4 In.Square 85.00
Silver Plate, Tureen, Handled, Melon Ribbed, Berry Finial, 7 1/2 In.Diameter 115.00
Silver Plate, Tureen, Soup, Notched Cover, Meriden, 8 X 10 1/2 In.Diameter 60.00
Silver Plate, Tureen, Soup, Round, Lion Head, Ring Handles, English, C.1870 .... 450.00
Silver Plate, Urn, Coffee, Middletown Plate Co., 1879, 16 Cup 175.00
Silver Plate, Vase, Celery, Figural Rabbits, Reticulated, 10 In. 28.00
Silver Plate, Water Set, Ice, Tilting, Dated 1889 .... 295.00
Silver Plate, Wax Jack, Sheffield, 18th Century, 5 1/4 X 4 3/8 X 4 1/4 In. 145.00
Silver, American, see also Tiffany Silver, Silver, Sterling
Silver, American, Basket, Cake, Tiffany & Co., C.1900, 15 1/2 In. 550.00
Silver, American, Basket, Sweetmeat, Oval, Swing Handle, C.1865, 6 In. 130.00
Silver, American, Bowl, Kalo Shops, 1914-18, 8 3/4 Oz., 7 In.Diameter 95.00
Silver, American, Bowl, Monteith, Repousse, Flowers, Fruit, Notched Rim, 11 In. 1000.00
Silver, American, Bowl, Sugar, Stebbins & Co., C.1840, 8 3/4 In. 650.00
Silver, American, Box, Cigarette, The Gorham Co., Providence, R.I., 1920 .... 80.00
Silver, American, Brilliant Cut, Coffin End, D.Smith, Philadelphia, Pair 75.00
Silver, American, Butter, Cover & Stand, Scroll Handles, 1858, 7 In. 225.00
Silver, American, Castor, Diaper Panels, Scrolls, Baluster Finial, Foot, C.1770 .... 5000.00
Silver, American, Centerpiece, Ball, Black & Co., New York, C.1860, 13 In. 475.00
Silver, American, Centerpiece, Oval, Handled, Gorham Co., 1894, 10 3/4 In. 750.00
Silver, American, Centerpiece, Reed & Barton, Taunton, Mass., 1900, 17 1/2 In. 2400.00
Silver, American, Coffin End, A.S. Script Mark 35.00

Silver, American, Compact, Art Deco, Elgin, 5 1/2 In.Diameter 30.00
Silver, American, Creamer & Basket, Sweetmeat, 19th Century, 6 X 7 1/4 In. 500.00
Silver, American, Creamer, John Letelier, Philadelphia, C.1790 .... 425.00
Silver, American, Creamer, Leaf Capped Scroll Handle, Gadroon Rim, Baluster 190.00
Silver, American, Creamer, Marked J.D., C.1785, 6 3/8 In. 375.00
Silver, American, Creamer, Reeded Handle, E.Moulton, C.1800, 5 3/8 In. 200.00
Silver, American, Creamer, Samuel Casey, Coin, 3 3/4 In. 1650.00
Silver, American, Cup, Art Nouveau, 3 Handled, Gorham, 1900s .... *Illus* 1700.00
Silver, American, Dessert & Tea, J.Conning, Mobile, Set Of 12 .... 750.00
Silver, American, Dish, Entree, Gadroon Rim, Reversible Lid, Handle Removes 200.00
Silver, American, Dish, Grape, C.1900, 12 X 13 In. 300.00
Silver, American, Dish, Serving, Stone Associates, Massachusetts, 10 In. 200.00
Silver, American, Flask, Engraved, Screw Top, George Unite, 1854-5 .... 235.00
Silver, American, Flatware, Fiddle, Shell Terminals, C.1840, 30 Piece 350.00
Silver, American, Fork, Olive, S.Wilmont, 6 7/8 In., Set Of 10 .... 485.00
Silver, American, Fork, Seth E. Brown, Coin, Set Of 6 .... 350.00
Silver, American, Goblet, Engraved Design, C.1890, Coin 150.00
Silver, American, Initialed A.L.W., C.1850, Repousse Body, 7 3/4 In. 275.00
Silver, American, Knife, Butter, Master, S.H.Johnson, C.1840 .... 35.00
Silver, American, Knife, Caviar, Mother-Of-Pearl Blade, C.1900, Set Of 12 .... 190.00
Silver, American, Knife, Fruit, Wheat, Coin 18.00
Silver, American, Knife, J.Moulton 1V, Massachusetts, C.1850, Set Of 11 .... 240.00
Silver, American, Knife, Pocket, Albert Coles, Coin 35.00
Silver, American, Ladle, Coffin End, Saunders Pitman, Rhode Island, 1800s 110.00
Silver, American, Ladle, Cream, Asa Blanchard, Kentucky 110.00
Silver, American, Ladle, Mustard, Marked Wm.Thomson 85.00
Silver, American, Ladle, Newell Matson, New York, Ohio, Wisconsin, C.1850 .... 40.00
Silver, American, Ladle, Soup, Coffin End, Marcus Merriman, 12 In. 285.00
Silver, American, Ladle, Upturned Fiddle, J.B. Wheeling, Coin, 13 1/2 In. 400.00
Silver, American, Mayonnaise Ladle, Fiddle Thread, James Conning, Coin 55.00
Silver, American, Mug, Chased Cartouche, Dated 1859, Coin 225.00
Silver, American, Mug, Chinoiserie, Pair, C.1850, 3/34 X 5 1/4 In. 500.00
Silver, American, Mug, Pear & Bacall, 19th Century, Coin 150.00
Silver, American, Mug, Scroll Handle, Burried Leafage, Scrolls, Inscribed, Pair 150.00
Silver, American, Mug, Tapered Cylindrical, Reeded Bands, C.1850, 4 3/4 In. 300.00
Silver, American, Pap Boat, John Arnell, 1775 .... 225.00
Silver, American, Pastry Server & Sugar Sifter, Coin, Gorham, Set 95.00
Silver, American, Pitcher, Cream, Eoff & Shepherd, New York, C.1840, 6 3/4 In. 250.00
Silver, American, Pitcher, Cream, Helmet, C.1790-1800 .... 400.00
Silver, American, Pitcher, Cream, J.Owens, C.1810, Coin 495.00
Silver, American, Pitcher, Water, Gilt, Tapered Shape, C.1900, 10 3/4 In. 230.00
Silver, American, Pitcher, Water, Philadelphia, R. & W.Wilson, 14 1/2 In. 600.00
Silver, American, Pitcher, Water, Repousse Bulbous Body, C.1859, 15 In. 525.00
Silver, American, Pitcher, Water, Tiffany & Co., C.1875, 37 Ounces, 8 3/4 In. 850.00
Silver, American, Plate, Dinner, Watson & Attleboro Co., C.1910, Set Of 12 .... 1000.00
Silver, American, Plate, T.C. Shop, Chicago, 1910-23, 5 1/2 Oz., 6 5/8 In. 35.00
Silver, American, Salt, Master, Footed, Bigelow Bros. & Kennard, Coin 45.00
Silver, American, Salver, Beaded, Panel & Scroll Feet, Shell, C.1850, 8 1/2 In. 325.00
Silver, American, Salver, Gorham, Providence, Rhode Island, C.1901, 12 7/8 In. 260.00
Silver, American, Salver, Oval, G.Boyce, C.1849, 17 1/4 In. 800.00

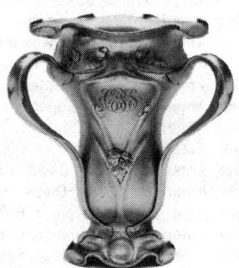

Silver, American, Cup, Art Nouveau, 3 Handled, Gorham, 1900s

Silver, American, Salver, S.Kirk & Son Co., C.1900, 14 1/4 In.Diameter 400.00
Silver, American, Sauce Boat, F.Marquand, C.1820, 15 Ounces, 7 1/4 In. 800.00
Silver, American, Scoop, Cracker, Josephine, Gorham, Coin 85.00
Silver, American, Server, Pastry, Farrington & Hunnewell, Boston, C.1850 .... 75.00
Silver, American, Snuff Box, Shell-Shaped, Marked Ps In Oval Cartouche 500.00
Silver, American, Spoon, Dessert, E.Pelletreau, 1726-1810, 8 In. 350.00
Silver, American, Spoon, Egg, Fiddle-Thread, J.A. Hommedieu, 5 1/2 In. 75.00
Silver, American, Spoon, Salt, William Moulton IV, Fiddle 45.00
Silver, American, Spoon, Serving, Davis & Brown, Boston, Mass.1810-12 .... 35.00
Silver, American, Spoon, Serving, J.Moulton, 1835 To 1850, Coin 29.00
Silver, American, Spoon, Serving, Shell Shaped, Mulford & Wendell, C.1850 .... 55.00
Silver, American, Strainer, Bell Shaped Handles, Boston, 1750-60, 10 1/4 In. 200.00
Silver, American, Sugar & Creamer, Pear Shape, Birds, Butterflies, Flowers 550.00
Silver, American, Sugar & Creamer, Ruby Liners, Victorian 55.00
Silver, American, Sugar Urn, Covered, William Faris, Annapolis, C.1800 .... 1200.00
Silver, American, Tablespoon, C.Warner, Coin 75.00
Silver, American, Tablespoon, E. & D.Kinsey, Ohio, C.1840, Set Of 6 .... 210.00
Silver, American, Tablespoon, Fiddle Thread, Large, S.Kirk 55.00
Silver, American, Tablespoon, Fiddle, S.Baker, Coin, Set Of 6 .... 80.00
Silver, American, Tablespoon, Geissler & Delang, Fiddle, C.1850, Coin 23.00
Silver, American, Tablespoon, Goodwin & Dodd, C.1812, Coin 35.00
Silver, American, Tablespoon, H.C.Robinson, C.1830 .... 50.00
Silver, American, Tablespoon, Hanoverian, A.Hays & M.Myers, Set Of 3, C.1770 ...... 475.00
Silver, American, Tablespoon, Harding & Co., Boston, C.1830, Coin 16.00
Silver, American, Tablespoon, J.Shoemake, Philadelphia, C.1810 .... 30.00
Silver, American, Tablespoon, James Mix, Jr., Albany, Coin 25.00
Silver, American, Tablespoon, S.Dodge, Coin 50.00
Silver, American, Tablespoon, Upturned Fiddle, J.Bishop Wheeling, Coin 60.00
Silver, American, Tablespoon, Wm.Dugin, Concord, N.H., Coin, Pair 40.00
Silver, American, Tablespoon, Wood & Hughes, New York, Coin 15.00
Silver, American, Tea & Coffee Set, Kalo Shop, 1700s, 6 Piece .... Illus 950.00
Silver, American, Tea & Coffee Set, Repousse, Gorham, 5 Piece .... Illus 500.00
Silver, American, Tea Kettle On Stand, Lincoln & Foss, Boston, C.1850, 16 In. 550.00
Silver, American, Tea Set, C.1810, Marked Jenkins, Coin.3 Piece 1950.00
Silver, American, Tea Set, Charter & Bros., New York, C.1855, 3 Piece 95.00
Silver, American, Tea Set, James W. Tufts, Boston, 4 Piece 195.00
Silver, American, Tea Set, Lobed, Oblong, Shells & Flowers Band, Scroll Handle 1200.00
Silver, American, Teapot, William G.Forbes, New York, C.1780-90 .... 1250.00
Silver, American, Teaspoon, Basket Of Flowers, H.Pearce, C.1825 .... 50.00
Silver, American, Teaspoon, Bright-Cut, Oval End, John McMullin 45.00
Silver, American, Teaspoon, Bright-Cut, Oval End, Thos.Clark, C.1780, Set Of 4 .... 220.00
Silver, American, Teaspoon, Brokhouse, Salem, Coffin 40.00
Silver, American, Teaspoon, C.A. Hoyt, New York, C.1830, Set Of 6 .... 90.00

Silver, American, Tea & Coffee Set, Kalo Shop, 1700s, 6 Piece

Silver, American, Tea & Coffee Set, Repousse, Gorham, 5 Piece *(See Page 549)*

Silver, American, Teaspoon, C.C.Beard, C.1810	35.00
Silver, American, Teaspoon, Clark Lindsey, C.1850, Coin	50.00
Silver, American, Teaspoon, Coffin End, Petit, M.P.Matthew	35.00
Silver, American, Teaspoon, Coffin-End, David Greenleaf, Jr.	40.00
Silver, American, Teaspoon, D.Van Woophs, Pair	300.00
Silver, American, Teaspoon, E.Mead, C.1850, Set Of 12	125.00
Silver, American, Teaspoon, Fiddle Thread, Stebbins & Co., C.1840, Set Of 6	150.00
Silver, American, Teaspoon, Fiddle Tip, Pointed Bowl, W.Kendrick, Coin, Pair	30.00
Silver, American, Teaspoon, Fiddle, John Adam, Alexandria , Va.	5.00
Silver, American, Teaspoon, Fiddle, P.P.Hayes	22.00
Silver, American, Teaspoon, Fiddle, Richard Matthews, Set Of 9	400.00
Silver, American, Teaspoon, Fiddle, S.Baker, Coin, Set Of 6	80.00
Silver, American, Teaspoon, Flared & Pointed Handle, Zachariah Brigden	85.00
Silver, American, Teaspoon, G.Hulton, C.1805, Set Of 6	175.00
Silver, American, Teaspoon, H.C.Robinson, C.1830	30.00
Silver, American, Teaspoon, H.Lewis, C.1811, Set Of 6	175.00
Silver, American, Teaspoon, Hood & Tobey, C.1849, Coin	15.00
Silver, American, Teaspoon, J.I.Lemon, C.1860	25.00
Silver, American, Teaspoon, J.Jackson, Baltimore, Coin	16.00
Silver, American, Teaspoon, J.Sargent, C.1824	30.00
Silver, American, Teaspoon, J.Tanguy, Philadelphia, C.1810, Set Of 6	175.00
Silver, American, Teaspoon, Joseph Foster, C.1790	40.00
Silver, American, Teaspoon, Josiah Flagg, C.1770	45.00
Silver, American, Teaspoon, Low's Ball & Co., Coin, Set Of 6	48.00
Silver, American, Teaspoon, Pointed-End, J.Moulton II	57.00
Silver, American, Teaspoon, R.Clayton, C.1830, Set Of 6	100.00
Silver, American, Teaspoon, S.Baker & Son, C.1822, Set Of 6	200.00
Silver, American, Teaspoon, Shepherd & Boyd, , Coin, C.1810, Set Of 9	275.00
Silver, American, Teaspoon, Signed, W.J.Bogert, Coin	12.00
Silver, American, Teaspoon, Taylor & Hunsdale, C.1825, Set Of 6	150.00
Silver, American, Teaspoon, W.M.Root, Coin	15.00
Silver, American, Teaspoon, W.Wise, Coin	12.00
Silver, American, Teaspoon, Wm.Durgin, Concord, N.H., Coin	12.50
Silver, American, Tongs, Applied Shell, Engraved Fiddle, Coin	95.00
Silver, American, Tongs, Basket Of Flowers, Coin, 7 In.	95.00
Silver, American, Tongs, Shell Pattern, C.A.Burnett	160.00
Silver, American, Tongs, Sugar, Asa Blanchard, Kentucky	160.00
Silver, American, Tongs, Sugar, Eagle-Claw, Coin	15.00
Silver, American, Tongs, Sugar, Fiddle, Oval Nopper, S.C.Brown, 6 1/2 In.	45.00
Silver, American, Tongs, Sugar, Marked Burnett & Ryder	95.00
Silver, American, Tongs, Sugar, Marked Ezekiel Burr	95.00
Silver, American, Tongs, Sugar, Marked Pitman	95.00
Silver, American, Tongs, Sugar, Marked W.Roe	125.00
Silver, American, Tongs, Sugar, McFee & Feeder, C.1795	125.00
Silver, American, Tray, Footed, Bigelow Brothers & Kennard, C.1850, 24 In.	1400.00
Silver, American, Tray, Gorham, Oval, Footed, Coin	400.00
Silver, American, Trumpet, Fireman's, Repousse, Foliage, Eagles Heads, Rings	550.00
Silver, American, Vase, Art Nouveau, George Shiebler & Co. *Illus*	400.00
Silver, American, Vase, Flower, Tiffany & Co., New York, C.1900, 17 In.	225.00
Silver, American, Vinaigrette, Nathaniel Mills, C.1834	220.00
Silver, Austrian, Drinking Horn, Enameled, H.Bohm, Vienna, 1850s, 17 3/4 In.	3100.00

Silver, American, Vase,
Art Nouveau, George
Shiebler & Co.

Silver, Chinese, Tsuba, Carved Dragon,
Seppo Hidetomo, 3 1/8 In.

Silver, Chinese, Tsuba, Cloisonne,
Hirata Style, 1800s, 3 7/8 In.

Silver, Continental, Coach With Horses, 1900s, 10 1/8 In.

Silver, Danish, Bowl, Georg Jensen,
Copenhagen, C.1930

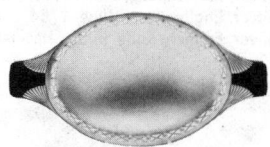

Silver, Danish, Dish, Art Deco,
2 Handled, Georg Jensen, 1900s

(See Page 554)

Silver, English, Teapot, Thomas Holland,
London, C.1805

Silver, Austrian, Mirror, Table, Dressing, Vienna, C.1840, 20 1/4 In.	1000.00
Silver, Chinese, Case, Card, Curved, Applied Dragon, Signed, 1 7/8 X 3 1/8 In.	85.00
Silver, Chinese, Koro, Flower Finial, Bird Handles, Cover, 1800s, 4 1/2 In.	1800.00
Silver, Chinese, Tsuba, Carved Dragon, Seppo Hidetomo, 3 1/8 In. .... Illus	210.00
Silver, Chinese, Tsuba, Cloisonne, Hirata Style, 1800s, 3 7/8 In. .... Illus	1000.00
Silver, Continental, Coach With Horses, 1900s, 10 1/8 In. .... Illus	500.00
Silver, Danish, Bowl, Georg Jensen, Copenhagen, C.1930 .... Illus	750.00
Silver, Danish, Dish, Art Deco, 2 Handled, Georg Jensen, 1900s .... Illus	600.00
Silver, Danish, Fork & Spoon, Jensen	225.00
Silver, Danish, Letter Opener, Acorn, Jensen	95.00
Silver, Danish, Letter Opener, Acorn, Signed, Jensen, Denmark, 7 1/2 In.	65.00
Silver, Danish, Scoop, Sugar, Jensen	45.00
Silver, Danish, Server, Cake, Jensen	125.00
Silver, Danish, Spirit Cup, Hammered Surface, G.Jensen, 2 Ounce, 2 In.	22.00
Silver, Dutch, Bowl, Brandy, 2 Handled, Casparus Janszonius, Haarlem, 6 In.	900.00
Silver, Dutch, Box, Biscuit, Anton Paap, Amsterdam, C.1804, 6 1/4 In., Pair	3400.00
Silver, Dutch, Teapot, Bullet Shape, Eise Andeles II, C.1759, 4 1/2 In.	3300.00
Silver, Dutch, Tray, Rectangular Section, Molded Rim, C.1942, 16 5/8 In.	350.00
Silver, English, Basket, Cake, 1773, William Plummer, 13 X 10 1/2 In.	3000.00
Silver, English, Basket, Shell, Edwardian, G.Fox, London, C.1909, 10 In., Pair	3500.00
Silver, English, Basket, 4 Footed Handled Openwork, C.1797-1805, 8 1/2 In.	150.00
Silver, English, Bowl, Arts & Crafts, Liberty & Co., C.1909, Pair .... Illus	350.00

Silver, English, Bowl, Fruit, George III, Pitts & Preedy, London, 1799, Pair	2800.00
Silver, English, Box, Ovate, Wedgwood Insert On Top, Hallmarked, 3 X 4 In.	95.00
Silver, English, Candlestick, Arts & Crafts, Jones, Ltd., Pair *Illus*	325.00
Silver, English, Candlestick, George II, Gurney & Co., C.1743, 7 In., Pair	1900.00
Silver, English, Candlestick, 1771, Ebenezer Coker, 11 In., Set Of 4	1000.00
Silver, English, Case, Card, Scrollwork, 4 X 2 3/4 In.	145.00
Silver, English, Castor, Pepper, Pyriform Shape, 1781, Hester Bateman, 6 In.	875.00
Silver, English, Castor, Signed, 1751-79, 4 3/4 X 5 1/8 In., Pair	450.00
Silver, English, Coaster, Double, Wood Base, 1794, R.Hennell, 5 In.Diam., Each	1850.00
Silver, English, Coaster, Ovolo Rim, 1809, R.Emes & E.Barnard, 6 In.Diam.	375.00
Silver, English, Coaster, Wine, Cymric, Liberty & Co., C.1905 *Illus*	500.00
Silver, English, Coffee & Tea Set, Melon Design, 1873, J.C.Edington, 4 Piece	4500.00
Silver, English, Coffeepot, Bird's Neck Spout, 1765, Henry Corry, 27 Oz.	3600.00
Silver, English, Coffeepot, George II, Fosey, London, 1736, 8 In.	2500.00
Silver, English, Coffeepot, George III, Smith & Sharp, London, 11 3/4 In.	2700.00
Silver, English, Coffeepot, Lighthouse Shape, 1730, J.Swift, 26 Oz., 8 3/4 In.	7500.00
Silver, English, Creamer, George II, Samuel Meriton, London, C.1753, 4 In.	225.00
Silver, English, Dish, Entree, Hallmarked, 1808, R.Cooke, 11 X 8 X 5 In., Pair	4750.00
Silver, English, Epergne, George II, J.Robins, London, C.1794, 16 3/4 In.	4500.00
Silver, English, Ewer, Victorian, E.H., London, C.1884, 11 In., Pair	1400.00
Silver, English, Ewer, Victorian, Hunt & Roskell, London, C.1869, 12 1/2 In.	1100.00
Silver, English, Fork, Fiddle Pattern, 1824, William Sumner, Set Of 12	775.00
Silver, English, Fork, Fiddle, Thread & Shell, 1841, W. & E. Eaton, Set Of 6	385.00
Silver, English, Fork, Old English, 1835-06-07, W.Eley & W.Fearn, Set Of 6	425.00
Silver, English, Fork, Toasting, Wooden Handle, 1823, W.Eley & W.Fearn, 16 In.	395.00
Silver, English, Fruit Stand, Victorian, Robert Garrard, London, 1853, Pair	2600.00
Silver, English, Funnel, Wine, 1804, Charles Chesterman 11, 5 1/4 In.Long	375.00
Silver, English, Goblet, Ovoid, 1788, John Wall, 6 3/4 X 3 3/4 In., Set Of 4	1750.00
Silver, English, Jug, Claret, Victorian, Etched Glass, J.Hunt, London, Pair	1200.00
Silver, English, Jug, Cream, Greek Key Design, 1802, John Emes, 1/2 Pint	475.00
Silver, English, Jug, Wine, 1784, John Scofield, 27 Oz., 12 1/4 In.	2500.00
Silver, English, Knife, Butter, Hallmarked	5.00

(See Page 551)

Silver, English, Bowl, Arts & Crafts,
Liberty & Co., C.1909, Pair

Silver, English, Candlestick,
Arts & Crafts, Jones, Ltd., Pair

Silver, English, Coaster, Wine, Cymric,
Liberty & Co., C.1905

Silver, English, Spoon, Coronation, Enamel, Cymric, C.1901

Silver, English, Knife, Dessert, Queen's, 1831, A.Hadfield, 9 In., Set Of 6	265.00
Silver, English, Knife, Fish, Maltese Cross	8.00
Silver, English, Label, Feather Edge, Claret, C.1770, R.Binley	115.00
Silver, English, Label, Port, London, C.1812	60.00
Silver, English, Label, Sherry & Port, 1807, Elizabeth Morley, 1 1/4 In., Pair	215.00
Silver, English, Label, Sherry, London, C.1812	60.00
Silver, English, Label, Threaded Edge, 1814, R.Phipps, E.Robinson, J.Phipps	90.00
Silver, English, Label, Vine-Leaf, Sherry, 1829, Taylor & Perry	95.00
Silver, English, Ladle, Cream, Old English, 1812, Samuel Hennell, 4 1/4 In.	48.00
Silver, English, Ladle, Gravy, Old English, 1811, W.Eley, Fearn & Chawner, Pair	175.00
Silver, English, Ladle, Gravy, Queen's Pattern, 1836, Jacob Wintle	100.00
Silver, English, Ladle, Irish Bright-Cut, 1767, Dublin, John Locker	495.00
Silver, English, Ladle, Mustard, Old English, 1863, George Adams, 4 1/4 In.	48.00
Silver, English, Ladle, Oval Bowl, Fiddle Thread, 1802, William Ellerby	295.00
Silver, English, Ladle, Punch, Fiddle, 1817, Glasgow, F.Newlands, 14 1/2 In.	315.00
Silver, English, Ladle, Sauce, Twisted Handle, Glasgow, 1848, D.C.R., 7 1/2 In.	125.00
Silver, English, Ladle, Sauce, 1789, 6 In.	120.00
Silver, English, Ladle, Soup, Robert Cruickshank, 1786 London, 13 In.	265.00
Silver, English, Ladle, Tea, Kidney Shaped, 1804, Cocks & Bettridge, 2 1/4 In.	220.00
Silver, English, Loving Cup, S Shaped Handles, 10 In.	200.00
Silver, English, Match Safe, Figural Boar	150.00
Silver, English, Mug, Bands Of Reeding, 1772, William Peaston, Pint	850.00
Silver, English, Mug, Child's, Pedestal Base, 1859, E. & J. Barnard, 3 In.	225.00
Silver, English, Mug, Thomas Whipham, London, 1742, 13 Ounces, 5 In.	775.00
Silver, English, Mug, William Cox, London, 1775, 6 1/3 Ounces, 4 In.	425.00
Silver, English, Mustard Pot, Drum Shape, 1842, J.C.Edington, 2 3/4 In.Diam.	345.00
Silver, English, Mustard Pot, Hinged Cover, Peter & Ann Bateman, London	285.00
Silver, English, Page Turner, Children On Handle, Tortoise Blade, 16 In.	165.00
Silver, English, Pan, Sauce, Wooden Handle, 1817, Emes & Barnard, 7 1/2 Oz.	850.00
Silver, English, Pap Boat, John Arnell, C.1775	225.00
Silver, English, Rack, Toast, Sheffield, 1835, H.Wilkinson, 6 1/2 In.Long	425.00
Silver, English, Salt, Pedestal, 1822, William Eaton, 3 1/4 In., Set Of 4	975.00
Silver, English, Salver, George III, Crouch & Hannam, C.1791, 19 1/2 In.	2500.00
Silver, English, Salver, Panel Feet, 1781, D.Smith & R.Sharp, 10 In.Diam.	1750.00
Silver, English, Salver, 4 Molded Feet, W.& H.Co., Ltd., London, 1912, 12 In.	425.00
Silver, English, Sauce, Applied Gadrooning, 1762, W.Robertson, 9 In.Long, Pr.	4200.00
Silver, English, Scoop, Marrow, Cropped Rat-Tail, 1742, M.Daintry, 8 1/4 In.	250.00
Silver, English, Scoop, Marrow, Deep Bowl, 1818, T. & G. Hayter, 9 1/2 In.	155.00
Silver, English, Scoop, Marrow, Slender Scoop, 1809, P. & W.Bateman, 9 In.	190.00
Silver, English, Server, Fish, Cock's Head, 1809, Thomas Streetin	155.00
Silver, English, Server, Fish, King's Hourglass, 1807, W.Eley & W.Fearn	225.00
Silver, English, Server, Fish, King's Pattern, 1841, William Eaton	195.00
Silver, English, Serving Set, Fish, Dublin, 1836, Peter Weeks, 12 3/4 In.	400.00
Silver, English, Shears, Fruit, 1838, Charles Reilly & George Storer, 7 In.	450.00
Silver, English, Shell, Butter, Crests, 1787, J.Wakelin & W.Taylor, Pair	750.00
Silver, English, Shovel, Cheese, King's Husk, 1852, H. & H.Lias, 8 3/4 In.	295.00
Silver, English, Shovel, Cheese, Pusher, Ivory Handle, 1876, Sheffield, 10 In.	245.00
Silver, English, Skewer, Flat Shoulder, 1822, Robert Rutland, 8 1/2 In.	175.00
Silver, English, Skewer, Oval, Flat Ring, 1805, F.P. & J.G., 12 1/2 In.	185.00
Silver, English, Skewer, Shell Top, 1802, W.Eley & W.Fearn, 13 In.	375.00
Silver, English, Skewer, 1792, Peter & Ann Bateman, 13 In.	225.00
Silver, English, Spoon, Caddy, Pear Bowl, Solomon Hougham, 1817	58.00
Silver, English, Spoon, Coronation, Enamel, Cymric, C.1901 ....*Illus*	575.00
Silver, English, Spoon, Egg, Fiddle Thread, 1854, Elizabeth Eaton, 4 3/4 In.	30.00
Silver, English, Spoon, Fiddle, Double Eagle, 1820, Francis Higgins, Set Of 9	265.00
Silver, English, Spoon, Fruit, Fluted Bowl, 1833, William Chawner, 9 3/4 In.	145.00
Silver, English, Spoon, Gravy, Georgian Irish, Dublin, 1812, R.Sawyer, 13 In.	395.00
Silver, English, Spoon, Gravy, Peter, Ann & William Bateman, 1802, 12 In.	112.00
Silver, English, Spoon, Heraldic Antelope, 1807, E. & W. Fearn, Set Of 6	195.00
Silver, English, Spoon, King's Pattern, 1835, William Eaton	195.00
Silver, English, Spoon, Mote, Boarbed Ends, 1750, 4 1/4 In.	125.00
Silver, English, Spoon, Mote, Vine Engraving, 1765, J.Innocent, 5 1/2 In.	125.00
Silver, English, Spoon, Mustard, William Eaton, 1830, Set Of 4	50.00
Silver, English, Spoon, Old English Bead, 1863, S.Hayne, D.Cater, 5 3/4in., Six	135.00
Silver, English, Spoon, Old English Bright-Cut, 1873, George Adams	135.00
Silver, English, Spoon, Rattail, George II, Richard Hussey, London, 1758	80.00

Silver, English, Spoon, Salt, King's Pattern, 1865, G.Adams, 4 1/2 In., Pair	50.00
Silver, English, Spoon, Salt, Lias Brothers, 1829, Set Of 3	33.00
Silver, English, Spoon, Scottish Pointed, 1802, Edinburgh, A.Henderson	140.00
Silver, English, Spoon, Serving, Rattail, Pair	120.00
Silver, English, Spoon, Sifter, Fiddle Pattern, 1846, S.Hayne & D.Cater, 6 In.	85.00
Silver, English, Spoon, Sifter, Fiddle Pattern, 1861, H. & H.Lias, 6 1/4 In.	85.00
Silver, English, Spoon, Sifter, Ladle Shape, 1859, Jacob Wintle, 6 1/2 In.	125.00
Silver, English, Spoon, Snuff, Old English, 1800, W.Eley & W.Fearn, 3 1/2 In.	65.00
Silver, English, Spoon, Strainer, Bright-Cut, Irish, 1798, J.Brady, 12 3/4 In.	325.00
Silver, English, Spoon, Stuffing, London, 1826, William Elliott	95.00
Silver, English, Spoon, Sugar, King's Pattern, 1873, George Adams, 5 3/4 In.	85.00
Silver, English, Spoon, Tea Caddy, Hand Shape, 1805, Josiah Snatt, 2 1/2 In.	450.00
Silver, English, Spoon, Tea Ladle, Fiddle Thread, 1816, W.Pugh, 3 1/2 In.	110.00
Silver, English, Spoon, Tea Ladle, Fluted Bowl, 1811, Joseph Taylor, 2 3/4 In.	155.00
Silver, English, Spoon, Tea Ladle, 1809, R.Crossley & G.Smith, 3 3/4 In.	115.00
Silver, English, Tablespoon, Feather Edge, Hester Bateman, London, 1773	100.00
Silver, English, Tablespoon, Hanoverian Picture, Henry Bayley, London, C.1760	55.00
Silver, English, Tablespoon, Provincial Brightcut, Joseph Hicks, Exeter 1800	48.00
Silver, English, Tablespoon, William Welch, Exeter 1832, Set Of 3	74.00
Silver, English, Tankard, Charles II, D.S., London, C.1863, 6 1/8 In.	2000.00
Silver, English, Tea Caddy, George III, Pineapple Finial, Reeded, Shields	1200.00
Silver, English, Tea Caddy, Knight Finial, 7 1/4 In.	150.00
Silver, English, Teapot Stand, Cartouche Center, 1790, E.Jones, 7 X 5 1/4 In.	425.00
Silver, English, Teapot, George III, Hester Bateman, London, 1787, 5 3/4 In.	650.00
Silver, English, Teapot, George III, P.& W.Bateman, London, 1800s, 6 1/8 In.	700.00
Silver, English, Teapot, Ribbed & Footed, Acorn Finial	125.00
Silver, English, Teapot, Thomas Holland, London, C.1805 .... Illus	400.00
Silver, English, Teaspoon, Joseph Wilmore, 1816	33.00
Silver, English, Teaspoon, William Bateman, 1827	57.00
Silver, English, Toast Warmer, 8 1/2 X 9 In.	125.00
Silver, English, Tongs, Asparagus, Fiddle, Thread & Shell, 1831, Eaton, 10 In.	375.00
Silver, English, Tongs, Asparagus, King's Hourglass, 1833, Esterbrook, 10 In.	335.00
Silver, English, Tongs, Brite-Cut, Wallis & Hayne, London, 1811-12	45.00
Silver, English, Tongs, Scissor-Type, Scroll Design, 1750, J.Jennings, 5 In.	195.00
Silver, English, Tongs, Scissor-Type, 1735, Gawen Nash, 4 3/4 In.	225.00
Silver, English, Tongs, Scissor-Type, 1765, W. & J.Deane, 5 In.	195.00
Silver, English, Tongs, Sugar, English Bright-Cut, C.1780, Hester Bateman	135.00
Silver, English, Tongs, Sugar, King's Pattern, C.1845, John Walton	55.00
Silver, English, Tongs, Sugar, Old English Bead, 1807, Thomas Wallis	55.00
Silver, English, Tongs, Sugar, Shell Bowls, 1822, Edinburgh, W.W.	55.00
Silver, English, Tongs, Sugar, Stephen Adams, 1791	35.00
Silver, English, Tray, Filagree Handle, Marked Rand, 8 1/2 In.Diameter	24.00
Silver, English, Tray, Rococo Border, Animals, 4 Helmeted Heads, 25 1/2 In.	3100.00
Silver, English, Tray, Snuffer, Gadroon Border, 1803, John Emes, 10 X 4 In.	450.00
Silver, English, Tray, Venison, Warmer, Covered, Sheffield, 19 1/2 X 25 In.	700.00
Silver, English, Tumbler, Elizabeth Beteux, 1731	500.00
Silver, English, Tumbler, Thomas Parr, 1720	500.00
Silver, English, Urn, George III, Wright, London, 1780, 2 Handled, 14 1/2 In.	600.00
Silver, English, Vase, Goblet Shape, Hallmarked, London, 1904, 9 1/2 X 5 In.	195.00
Silver, English, Waiter, George IV, W.Edwards, London, C.1835, 6 3/8 In.	275.00
Silver, English, Whistle, Regimental, Victorian, B & P, Birmingham, C.1891	170.00
Silver, English, Wine Cooler, Victorian, John Hunt, London, C.1844, 10 1/2 In.	4750.00
Silver, French, Bowl, Louis XIV, 2 Handled, C.G., Morlaix, C.1680, 6 1/4 In.	5500.00
Silver, French, Box, Tobacco, 3 People On Hinged Lid, 1768-74	600.00
Silver, French, Centerpiece, Empire, Boat Shaped, J.Odiot, Paris, 14 1/2 In.	3900.00
Silver, French, Dish, Serving, Berried Foliage Border, Paris, 1900, 16 In.	225.00
Silver, French, Ewer, Louis XVI, Marked, J.Outrebon, Paris, C.1788, 11 In.	6000.00
Silver, French, Wine Taster, Snake Handle, Paris, 1798-1809, 3 1/4 In.	150.00
Silver, German, Box, Sugar, Bombe Sides, S.Bergkstadt, Dresden, C.1750, 4 In.	1900.00
Silver, German, Cup, Gilt, Arabesques, Stemmed, Dome Base, C.1580, 5 1/2 In.	2700.00
Silver, German, Spoon, Salt, Rose In Handle, Set Of 3	28.00
Silver, German, Tea Caddy, Porcelain Bowls In Drip Bottom, Stand, 8 1/2 In.	20.00
Silver, German, Tea Set, Art Deco, Teapot, Sugar & Creamer, Initialed	375.00
Silver, Holland, Apostle, Triple Silver Plate	72.00
Silver, Holland, Grater, Nutmeg, Flop Open Lid, Scenes, Hallmarked	275.00
Silver, Irish, Chocolate Pot, George I, Hamilton, Dublin, 1715, 10 3/4 In.	4200.00

Silver, Irish, Coffee Pot, George II, J.Pittar, Dublin, C.1750, 10 In. 2200.00
Silver, Italian, Lamp, Oil, Diana, Hound, V.Belli II, Rome, 1840s, 14 In. 1300.00
Silver, Itialian, Altar Stick, Continental, C.1800, 29 In., Pair 350.00
Silver, Plate, Bottle, Witch Hazel, Clambroth 25.00
Silver, Portuguese, Coffee & Tea Pot, Sugar & Creamer, Libson, C.1840 .... 1300.00
Silver, Portuguese, Ewer & Basin, Baluster Form, Scrolls & Flowers, 13 In. 2100.00
    Silver, Russian, see also Faberge
Silver, Russian, Belt, Enameled, 32 Oval Sections, C.K., Moscow, 29 In. 1000.00
Silver, Russian, Box, Circular, Cloisonne, Gilt & Enamel, C.1895 .... Illus   900.00
Silver, Russian, Box, Pill, Heart Shaped, Gold Washed, Hallmarked 200.00
Silver, Russian, Box, Snuff, Scene Front & Back, Moscow, 1777-1816, Niello 550.00
Silver, Russian, Brandy Warmer, Covered, St.Petersburg, 1850-56, 7 In. 350.00
Silver, Russian, Candlestick, Signed, Hallmarked, 13 1/4 In. 1200.00
Silver, Russian, Case, Cigarette, Art Nouveau, Nude Holding Caduceus, Marked 575.00
Silver, Russian, Case, Cigarette, Niello Stripes 120.00
Silver, Russian, Chair, Miniature, Seat Lift For Salt, Hallmarked 1876, 3 In. 255.00
Silver, Russian, Changer, 3 Coin 65.00
Silver, Russian, Cigarette Case, Engraved Buildings, Flowers & Birds, C.1888 .... 200.00
Silver, Russian, Cigarette Case, Niello, Fully Hallmarked 315.00
Silver, Russian, Flatware Set, Fiddle & Thread, Make MAA, 48 Piece 1125.00
Silver, Russian, Salt, Floral Engraved, 1 In.Tall, 1 1/4 In.Diameter 110.00
Silver, Russian, Spoon, Dessert, Gilded, Twisted Handles, Case, Set Of 6 .... 125.00
Silver, Russian, Spoon, Etched, Hallmarked 45.00
Silver, Russian, Spoon, Serving, Niello, By Faberge 625.00
Silver, Scottish, Tea Caddy, William IV, T.A.F., Edinburgh, C.1835, 7 In. 1500.00
    Silver, Sheffield, see also Silver Plate
Silver, Sheffield, Argyle, Ball Finial, Detachable Lid, C.1790, 4 1/2 In. 375.00
Silver, Sheffield, Basket, Cake, George III, Roberts & Co., C.1808, 13 In. 600.00
Silver, Sheffield, Candlestick, Chamber, Matthew Boulton Co., C.1810, 4 In. 220.00
Silver, Sheffield, Decanter Trolley, Ivory Wheels & Handle, C.1830 .... 325.00
Silver, Sheffield, Inkstand, Boat Shaped, 4 Blue Glass Liners, C.1790, 11 In. 625.00
Silver, Sheffield, Meat Dish Cover, Scroll Border, Ring Handle, 1840, 19 In. 70.00
Silver, Sheffield, Tray, Beaded Border, 4 Panel Feet, Oval, 18 1/8 In. 325.00
Silver, Sheffield, Wine Cooler, Baron's Coronet, C.1790, 7 3/8 In., Pair 1100.00
Silver, Sheffield, Wine Cooler, Crest Engraved, Boulton Co., 11 In., Pair 1200.00

    Sterling silver is made with 925 parts of silver out of 1,000 parts of metal.
    The word sterling is a quality guarantee used in the United States after
    about 1860.
    Silver, Sterling, see also Silver, American; Silver, English;
    etc.
Silver, Sterling, Ashtray, 3.6 Oz., Shreve, Crump & Low Co., Set Of 4 .... 50.00
Silver, Sterling, Basket, Miniature, Marked Cartier, 2 X 2 3/8 X 3 In. 29.00
Silver, Sterling, Basket, Openwork, 4 Feet, Ruffled Cobalt Insert, 6 In. 85.00
Silver, Sterling, Beaker, Marked W.M. 650.00
Silver, Sterling, Bell, Cactus, Georg Jensen, 3 1/4 In. 45.00
Silver, Sterling, Bell, Victorian Flowers, 3 3/4 In. 18.00
Silver, Sterling, Bib Holder, Mary & Lamb 22.00
Silver, Sterling, Bonbon, Openwork, 4 Floral Embossed Feet, Tiffany, 3 In. 85.00
Silver, Sterling, Bonbon, 4 Ounce, 4 3/4 In.Diameter 25.00
Silver, Sterling, Bookmark, Jensen 28.00
Silver, Sterling, Bowl & Plate, Child's, William B. Kerr 135.00
Silver, Sterling, Bowl, Cut Glass Liner, Gorham, 11 In. 225.00
Silver, Sterling, Bowl, Footed, Repousse, C.1880, Kirk, 9 In. 1500.00
Silver, Sterling, Bowl, Fruit, Pierced Work, C.D.Peacock, 10 1/4 In.Diameter 300.00
Silver, Sterling, Bowl, Raised Floral Rim, 2 In.Deep, 10 1/4 In.Diameter 85.00
Silver, Sterling, Bowl, Revere Type, A.Stone, 1920-36, 7 Ounce, 5 1/4 In.Diam. 45.00
Silver, Sterling, Box, Cigarette, Cedar Lined, Towle, 4 X 3 1/4 X 1 1/2 In. 47.00
Silver, Sterling, Box, Cigarette, 2 Applied Fish, Gorham, 6 X 4 X 2 In. 200.00
Silver, Sterling, Box, Heart Shaped, Hinged, Scroll Work, English 32.00
Silver, Sterling, Box, Jewel, Heart Shape, Howard & Co., No.134, 2 X 5 In. 135.00
Silver, Sterling, Box, Powder, Art Nouveau, Unger Bros. 85.00
Silver, Sterling, Box, Repousse Figural Scene, French, 3 X 2 1/4 In. 195.00
Silver, Sterling, Box, Repousse Work, Flowers, Fernery, Gorham, 3 X 4 1/2 In. 165.00
Silver, Sterling, Broom, Whisk, Loves Dream, Unger Bros. 75.00
Silver, Sterling, Brush, Clothes, Ovoid Shape, Unger Brothers 25.00

Silver, Sterling, Brush, Clothes, Tortoise Trim, Pair 30.00
Silver, Sterling, Brush, Comb, Mirror, Buffer, Initial T 95.00
Silver, Sterling, Brush, Hair, Art Deco 20.00
Silver, Sterling, Brush, Hair, Love's Dream, Unger Brothers, 9 In. 125.00
Silver, Sterling, Brush, Hair, Man's, Love's Voyage, Unger Bros. 50.00
Silver, Sterling, Brush, Hair, Men's Military, Pair 25.00
Silver, Sterling, Brush, Shaving, Repousse 42.00
Silver, Sterling, Buckle, Woman With Flowing Hair, Unger Bros., 6 1/4 In. 400.00
Silver, Sterling, Buttonhook, Flower Vase Shape 18.50
Silver, Sterling, Buttonhook, Gadrooned Rim 17.00
Silver, Sterling, Buttonhook, Hanging Ring At Top 7.50
Silver, Sterling, Buttonhook, Knopped Shank, Vase Shape 17.00
Silver, Sterling, Buttonhook, Knurled, Chased Silver, Extra Long 19.00
Silver, Sterling, Buttonhook, Ornate Handles 22.00
Silver, Sterling, Buttonhook, Oval, Chase Silver 18.00
Silver, Sterling, Buttonhook, Projected Beading 14.75
Silver, Sterling, Buttonhook, Puffed Out Silver, Knurled Shank 21.00
Silver, Sterling, Buttonhook, Raised Design, 6 3/4 In. 14.00
Silver, Sterling, Buttonhook, Repousse, Kirk, 1846-61, 6 3/4 In. 30.00
Silver, Sterling, Buttonhook, Ringed Shank, Allover Design 17.50
Silver, Sterling, Buttonhook, Six Large Open Flowers 18.50
Silver, Sterling, Buttonhook, Vase Shape, Blown-Out Next To Shaft 21.00
Silver, Sterling, Carving Set, Mythologique, 2 Piece 135.00
Silver, Sterling, Carving Set, Ornate Handles, C.1878, 14 In.2 Piece 38.50
Silver, Sterling, Case, Book Match, 14K Gold Stripes, 2 1/2 X 1 3/4 In. 55.00
Silver, Sterling, Case, Card, Calling, Monogrammed, Repousse 45.00
Silver, Sterling, Case, Card, Floral, Leaves & Scroll, Link Chain Handle 65.00
Silver, Sterling, Case, Card, Hinged, October 13, 1858 .... 95.00
Silver, Sterling, Case, Cigar, Hinged, Embossed, C.1892 .... 115.00
Silver, Sterling, Case, Cigarette, Fox Chase, Unger Bros. 200.00
Silver, Sterling, Case, Cigarette, Jewel Catch, 1908 .... 27.50
Silver, Sterling, Case, Cigarette, Oriental Scene 25.00
Silver, Sterling, Case, Comb, Scroll Work, Drinking Scene, 5 In. 12.00
Silver, Sterling, Case, Stamp, Large, Unger Brothers 45.00
Silver, Sterling, Castor, Twist Finial, I.M. & I.D., London, 1767, 4 3/4 In. 175.00
Silver, Sterling, Challis, Ceremonial, Amethyst Jewels, 8 1/2 In. 115.00
Silver, Sterling, Chamberstick, Repousse, By D. & H. 275.00
Silver, Sterling, Cigarette Case, European, Enameled Horse's Head Lid, Mark 55.00
Silver, Sterling, Cigarette Case, Raised Flower, Georg Jensen, Denmark 150.00
Silver, Sterling, Coaster, Wine, Embossed Grapes, Wood Insert, E.G.Webster 95.00
Silver, Sterling, Coffee Service, Gorham, Adams Pattern, 4 Piece 950.00
Silver, Sterling, Collar, Dog, Padlock, Applied Prince On Front, 3/4 In. 325.00
Silver, Sterling, Comb Case, Drinking Scene, Scroll, Hall Marked, 5 In. 12.00
Silver, Sterling, Comb, Mustache, Cartier 25.00
Silver, Sterling, Compact, Green Enamel 28.00
Silver, Sterling, Compote, Georg Jensen, 3 1/2 X 5 1/2 X 5 1/4 In. 250.00
Silver, Sterling, Corkscrew, Whale's Tooth, Design 65.00
Silver, Sterling, Creamer, C.1810, Hallmarked, English, 4 1/4 X 3 X 2 5/8 In. 195.00
Silver, Sterling, Creamer, Cow, Embossed Insect On Lid, 4 1/2 X 7 In. 345.00
Silver, Sterling, Creamer, David Tyler, Boston, C.1785, 7 1/4 X 5 In.Diam. 950.00
Silver, Sterling, Creamer, Long Horn Cow, Insect On Lid, 4 X 6 1/2 In. 350.00
Silver, Sterling, Cup, Julep, First Kentucky Winner, 1883, 3 3/4 In. 475.00
Silver, Sterling, Curler, Mustache 30.00
Silver, Sterling, Desk Set, Art Nouveau, 7 Piece 800.00
Silver, Sterling, Dish, Candy, Intaglio Fruit, English, 1889, 8 X 4 3/4 In. 125.00
Silver, Sterling, Dish, Nut, Daffodils Down Handle, Pierced Stars 20.00
Silver, Sterling, Dish, Nut, Flowers, Art Nouveau, 3 1/2 In.Diameter 45.00
Silver, Sterling, Dish, Nut, Leaf On Threaded Border, Set Of 6, 3 X 2 1/4 In. 42.00
Silver, Sterling, Dish, Nut, Strasbourg, Set Of 4 .... 85.00
Silver, Sterling, Dish, Pierce Work, 3 Jade Stones, Art Deco, 4 1/2 X 6 In. 240.00
Silver, Sterling, Dresser Set, Love's Dream, Unger Bros., 6 Pieces 350.00
Silver, Sterling, Epergne, 3 Dragons Form Base, Conical Stem, 13 In. 185.00
Silver, Sterling, Figurine, Bulldog Standing, 2 X 4 In. 145.00
Silver, Sterling, Figurine, Lioness, Walking, 2 1/4 X 3 1/2 In. 120.00
Silver, Sterling, Figurine, Pheasant With Vermeil On Body & Tail, 3 X 9 In. 185.00
Silver, Sterling, Figurine, Prancing Stallion, 5 X 5 1/2 In. 300.00

Silver, Sterling, Figurine, Pug Dog, Standing, 2 1/4 X 2 1/4 In.	75.00
Silver, Sterling, Figurine, Whippet, Paws Outstretched, 1 X 2 1/2 In.	77.00
Silver, Sterling, Flask, Grape & Leaf Decoration, Alvin	150.00
Silver, Sterling, Food Pusher, Cat, Kerr	25.00
Silver, Sterling, Food Pusher, Etruscan, Gorham	18.00
Silver, Sterling, Fork, Cocktail, Persian, Whiting, 5 3/4 In., Set Of 6	65.00
Silver, Sterling, Fork, Cold Meat, 7 1/4 In.	23.00
Silver, Sterling, Fork, Ice Cream, Nile, Wallace, Set Of 12	125.00
Silver, Sterling, Fork, Lettuce, Mazarin, Dominick & Haff	35.00
Silver, Sterling, Fork, Lobster, Blackinton, Beed & Barton, 6 In.	15.00
Silver, Sterling, Fork, Sardine, Marguerite, Gorham	24.00
Silver, Sterling, Fork, Serving, Arts & Crafts, Shreve & Co., Wide	80.00
Silver, Sterling, Frame, Engraved Flowers & Ivy, 9 1/2 X 11 1/2 In.	350.00
Silver, Sterling, Funnel, Gold Wash Interior, 2 In.Diameter, 1 1/2 In.Deep	25.00
Silver, Sterling, Gravy Boat, Grape Repousse, Baltimore, A.G.Schultz	250.00
Silver, Sterling, Hairbrush, Mermaid, Unger Brothers, 4 1/2 X 2 1/2 In.	125.00
Silver, Sterling, Hatpin, 3 Dimensional Duck In Flight, Unger Bros., 2 In.	150.00
Silver, Sterling, Infuser, Tea, Hinged Lid, Pierced, 5 1/2 In.	42.00
Silver, Sterling, Jar, Puff, Repousse, Covered	125.00
Silver, Sterling, Knife Set, Fruit, Handle, Reed & Barton, 6 In., Set Of 6	85.00
Silver, Sterling, Knife, Pie & Cake, Mt.Vernon.Lunt, 9 3/4 In.	30.00
Silver, Sterling, Knight, Standing, Embossed Armour, Vermeil, Ivory Face, 6 In.	230.00
Silver, Sterling, Label, Brandy, With Chain, Birmingham	58.00
Silver, Sterling, Ladle, Cut Glass Handle, Teardrop Hobstars, 15 In.	255.00
Silver, Sterling, Ladle, Mustard, Cottage, Gorham	22.00
Silver, Sterling, Ladle, Sauce, Daffodils Down Handle, Gold Wash	20.00
Silver, Sterling, Ladle, Sauce, Frontenac, International	45.00
Silver, Sterling, Letter Opener, Mother Of Pearl Blade	27.50
Silver, Sterling, Liquor, Raised Band, Redlich & Co., Hallmarked, 3 In.	50.00
Silver, Sterling, Locket, Heart Shaped, Cupid Kissing Woman, Unger Bros.	200.00
Silver, Sterling, Lorgnette, Gold Gilt Wash, Art Nouveau, Unger Bros.	425.00
Silver, Sterling, Lorngette, Sterling Rope Chain	40.00
Silver, Sterling, Loving Cup, Gorham, 7 1/2 In.	95.00
Silver, Sterling, Match Safe, Art Nouveau, Unger Bros.	120.00
Silver, Sterling, Match Safe, Lily Upon Leaf Design, Frog Peeking Out	125.00
Silver, Sterling, Measure, Whiskey, Dumbbell Shape, Marked	15.00
Silver, Sterling, Mirror & Brush Set, Floral Pattern, Unger Bros., 2 Piece	275.00
Silver, Sterling, Mirror, Dresser, Embossed Flowers	45.00
Silver, Sterling, Mirror, Hand, Art Deco	30.00
Silver, Sterling, Mirror, Hand, Love's Dream, Unger Brothers, 9 1/2 In.	165.00
Silver, Sterling, Mirror, Queen Anne, English, Original Glass	225.00
Silver, Sterling, Mug, John Shcofield, London, 1777, 11 1/2 Ounce, 5 In.	700.00
Silver, Sterling, Napkin Ring, see Napkin Ring	
Silver, Sterling, Pencil, Lead	12.00
Silver, Sterling, Pencil, Telescopic, Amethyst Top	35.00
Silver, Sterling, Pepper, Light House Shape, Set Of 6, 1 1/2 In.	28.00
Silver, Sterling, Pin, Art Nouveau, Cupid Kissing Lady, 1 3/4 In.	75.00
Silver, Sterling, Pin, Cupid Playing Violin, Art Nouveau, 2 In.	115.00
Silver, Sterling, Pin, Figure Of Cupid, 2 In.	45.00
Silver, Sterling, Pitcher, Water, Chased Grapes & Vines, Howard & Co., N.Y.	750.00
Silver, Sterling, Pitcher, Water, Dolphin Head Handle, 36 Ounce, 12 In.	185.00
Silver, Sterling, Pitcher, Water, Pedestal Base, Mexican, 36 Ounce, 11 3/4 In.	185.00
Silver, Sterling, Pitcher, Water, Pedestal Footing, 2 3/4 X 2 3/4 In.	14.00
Silver, Sterling, Rattle, Baby, Celluloid Ring	28.00
Silver, Sterling, Rattle, Bell, Pearl Ring	9.50
Silver, Sterling, Rattle, Dog Body, Tail Is Handle, Whistle, 2 Bells	35.00
Silver, Sterling, Rattle, Dumbbell Shape	12.00
Silver, Sterling, Rattle, Golliwog Figural, Hallmarked	125.00
Silver, Sterling, Rattle, Large Fat Rabbit, Attached Ring	42.00
Silver, Sterling, Rattle, Whistle, Head Of Jester In Shape Of Foot	225.00
Silver, Sterling, Rose Bowl, Repousse, Kirk, C.1880, Footed, C.1880, 5 In.Diam.	425.00
Silver, Sterling, Salad Set, Parcel-Gilt & Ivory, Gorham	275.00
Silver, Sterling, Salt & Pepper, Gorham, 1 1/4 X 3/4 In., Pair	15.00
Silver, Sterling, Salt & Pepper, 3 In.	12.00
Silver, Sterling, Salt & Pepper, 4 1/2 In.	15.00
Silver, Sterling, Salt, Hoof Feet, D.H., London, 1776, 2 1/2 In. Diam., Pair	170.00

Silver, Sterling, Salt, Master, Mussel Shell Shaped, Gorham, 1860, 5 X 1 In. 75.00
Silver, Sterling, Salt, Ritter & Sullivan 45.00
Silver, Sterling, Salt, Vermeil Top, Miniature, Tiffany & Co.2 1/2 In. 40.00
Silver, Sterling, Salver, Ball & Claw Footed, S.Kirk & Son, 8 In. 175.00
Silver, Sterling, Salver, Oval, C.1860, Gorham, 11 X 15 X 3/4 In. 425.00
Silver, Sterling, Scissors, , Manicure, 3 3/4 In. 20.00
Silver, Sterling, Scoop, Cheese, Mille Fleurs, International 35.00
Silver, Sterling, Server, Ice Cream, Lily, 1870 Gorham, Boxed 125.00
Silver, Sterling, Server, Pie, Shell Handle, Bigelow & Kennard 38.00
Silver, Sterling, Shaker, Cocktail, Shreve, Crump & Low, Boston, 6 In. 58.00
Silver, Sterling, Shaving Brush, Repouse Decoration, Marked 42.00
Silver, Sterling, Shears & Blades, Grape, 6 In. 55.00
Silver, Sterling, Shears, Grape, Foxes Eyeing Grapes, Gorham 110.00
Silver, Sterling, Shoehorn, Black, Starr & Frost, 7 1/2 In. 45.00
Silver, Sterling, Shoehorn, Handled, 9 In. 18.00
Silver, Sterling, Sifter, Sugar, Lily, 1880 Gorham, Boxed 50.00
Silver, Sterling, Spoon, Art Nouveau, Cattails, Woman & Fish 24.50
Silver, Sterling, Spoon, Baby, Turquoise, Navajo 12.00
Silver, Sterling, Spoon, Berry, Arts & Crafts, Shreve & Co., 9 1/4 In. 80.00
Silver, Sterling, Spoon, Berry, Curved Handle, Berry On End, George Jensen 21.00
Silver, Sterling, Spoon, Bonbon, Open Work In Bowl 12.50
Silver, Sterling, Spoon, Cream Soup, Queen Anne, Dominick & Haff 12.00
Silver, Sterling, Spoon, Demitasse, Biegelow & Kennard, Boston, Set Of 12 .... 125.00
Silver, Sterling, Spoon, Demitasse, Each Has Semiprecious Stone, Set Of 6 .... 135.00
Silver, Sterling, Spoon, Dessert, Knowles & Ladd Warren 15.00
Silver, Sterling, Spoon, Dessert, Monroe, St.Louis 30.00
Silver, Sterling, Spoon, Dessert, Scroll & Floral, Hamilton & Dresinger 10.00
Silver, Sterling, Spoon, Dessert, Sheaf-Of-Wheat, John Naile 50.00
Silver, Sterling, Spoon, Dessert, William Cassidy, C.1850, Set Of 6 .... 180.00
Silver, Sterling, Spoon, Egg, Rococo, Dominick & Haff 9.00
Silver, Sterling, Spoon, Flower Stem, Demi-Tasse, Gold Washed Bowls, Set Of 8 .... 75.00
Silver, Sterling, Spoon, Ice Tea, Cartier, Set Of 12 .... 150.00
Silver, Sterling, Spoon, Lidded, Floral Repousse Work Of Roses, 6 In. 40.00
Silver, Sterling, Spoon, Plique A Jour, Shiebler, Set 125.00
Silver, Sterling, Spoon, Serving, Shell-Shaped, Jenkins & Jenkins 110.00
   Silver, Sterling, Spoon, Souvenir, see Souvenir, Spoon, Sterling
   Silver
Silver, Sterling, Spoon, St.George & Dragon, Moscow, 1824, Marked, 8 1/4 In. 67.50
Silver, Sterling, Spoon, Sugar, Mme. Royale 15.00
Silver, Sterling, Spoon, Tea Maker, Lidded & Hinged, 6 1/4 In. 45.00
Silver, Sterling, Stamp, Sealing Wax, Form Of Heart 22.00
Silver, Sterling, Standing Elephant, Ivory Tusks, 4 1/2 X 6 1/2 In. 385.00
Silver, Sterling, Stirrup, Lady's, 1 1/2, 18th Century, 1 1/2 Lb.Silver 595.00
Silver, Sterling, Strainer, Tea, Single Handle, Pierced & Ribbed Bowl 27.00
Silver, Sterling, Strainer, Tea, Sterling Rimmed Glass Drip Bowl 22.00
Silver, Sterling, Sugar Scoop, Dated 1897, Fessenden Alice, Reed & Barton 19.00
Silver, Sterling, Tablespoon, Basket-Of-Flowers, Chauncey Johnson 95.00
Silver, Sterling, Tablespoon, Bright-Cut, William Moulton 95.00
Silver, Sterling, Tablespoon, Brilliant Cut, A.Moulton 75.00
Silver, Sterling, Tablespoon, Brilliant Cut, W. Grigg, Albany 80.00
Silver, Sterling, Tablespoon, Coffin-End, Ward & Bartholemew, Hartford, Pair 150.00
Silver, Sterling, Tablespoon, T.Bruff, Maryland, C.1790 .... 85.00
Silver, Sterling, Tablespoon, W.G. Forges, New York, C.1810, Set Of 5 .... 175.00
Silver, Sterling, Tea & Coffee Service, Kalo, 5 Piece 1950.00
Silver, Sterling, Tea & Coffee Set, Georgian Rose, Reed & Barton, 4 Piece 1500.00
Silver, Sterling, Tea & Coffee Set, Hand Chased, Floral Decoration, Prisner 775.00
Silver, Sterling, Tea & Coffee Set, L.Andrews & Co., 5 Piece .... Illus 1900.00
Silver, Sterling, Tea & Coffee Set, Royal Danish, 5 Piece Set 675.00
Silver, Sterling, Tea & Coffee Set, 5 Piece Set, Weight, 18 1/2 Pounds Avoir 1950.00
Silver, Sterling, Tea Caddy, Cylinder, Embossed Scenes, Continental, 3 In. 125.00
Silver, Sterling, Tea Caddy, Hexagon Shape, Whiting, 4 1/2 In. 65.00
Silver, Sterling, Tea Infuser, Commonwealth 40.00
Silver, Sterling, Tea Set, Georg Jensen, 3 Piece 1200.00
Silver, Sterling, Tea Set, John Adamson, Chester, 1784, 3 Piece 1250.00
Silver, Sterling, Tea Set, Tray, 25 X 18 In., 1867 Meriden Co., 5 Piece 795.00
Silver, Sterling, Tea Strainer, Plymouth 40.00

Silver, Sterling, Tea Strainer, 27th N.Y. Division Insignia 8.00
Silver, Sterling, Teapot, Gooseneck Spout, Ivory Heat Stops, 9 In. 135.00
Silver, Sterling, Teapot, 4 Paw Feet, C.1810, Peter Targee, N.Y. 1500.00
Silver, Sterling, Teaspoon, Bowie Knife Shape, Dated 1818, Texas Star 125.00
Silver, Sterling, Teaspoon, Bright Cut, Knowles & Ladd 10.00
Silver, Sterling, Teaspoon, Chippendale, Watson 6.00
Silver, Sterling, Teaspoon, Lid, Floral Reposse Of Roses, Pierced, 6 1/4 In. 45.00
Silver, Sterling, Teaspoon, Oval End, Joseph Richardson 50.00
Silver, Sterling, Teaspoon, Pineapple Pattern, Georg Jensen 18.50
Silver, Sterling, Teaspoon, Queen Anne, Dominick & Haff 4.00
Silver, Sterling, Teaspoon, Versailles, Gorham, Set Of 12 .... 210.00
Silver, Sterling, Teaspoon, Warren, Knowles & Ladd 8.00
    Silver, Sterling, Thimble, see Sewing Tool, Thimble, Sterling
Silver, Sterling, Thimble Case 22.00
Silver, Sterling, Tie Bar, Shell & Fish Design, Georg Jensen 60.00
Silver, Sterling, Toilet Set, Man's, Tiffany, Set Of 8 .... 350.00
Silver, Sterling, Tongs, Sugar, Bailey & Kitchen 55.00
Silver, Sterling, Tongs, Sugar, Marked F.M. 95.00
Silver, Sterling, Tongs, Sugar, Mythologique, Gorham 28.00
Silver, Sterling, Toothpick, Flaring Rim, Durgin, Victorian, 2 1/2 In. 28.00
Silver, Sterling, Tray, Bread, Embossed Flowers & Wheat, Whiting, 11 Oz. 80.00
Silver, Sterling, Tray, Footed, Scalloped Edge, England, 10 In. 250.00
Silver, Sterling, Tray, Pin, Cupid & Satyr Faces, Kerr 40.00
Silver, Sterling, Tray, Pin, Heart Shape, Love's Dream, Unger Brothers 35.00
Silver, Sterling, Tray, Pipe, Nude Blowing Bubbles, Unger Bros., Signed 85.00
Silver, Sterling, Vegetable, Covered, Unger Brothers, 11 X 8 In. 400.00
Silver, Sterling, Vinaigrette, 18th Century, Dutch, 3/4 X 1 5/8 X 1 3/8 In. 65.00
Silver, Sterling, Wager Cup, Woman Holds Bowl Over Head, Floral, 4 1/2 In. 125.00
Silver, Sterling, Wine Taster, Grande Baroque 20.00
Silver, Swedish, Tongs, P.Norlin, Malmo, 1796, Pricked Letters, 6 In. 65.00
Silver, Swiss, Box, Singing Bird, Enamel, Alpine Lake Scene, C.1850, 3 3/4 In. 4500.00
Silver, Turkish, Scribe's Case, Foliage Borders, 1800s, 12 3/4 In. 375.00

Sinclaire cut glass was made by H.P.Sinclaire and Company of Corning, New York, between 1905 and 1929. Pieces were made of crystal as well as amber, blue, green, or ruby. Only a small percentage of Sinclaire glass is marked.

Sinclaire, Ashtray, Engraved, 4 X 3 X 3/4 In., Set Of 3 .... 30.00
Sinclaire, Bowl, Hand Blown, Scalloped Edge, Green, 9 X 2 1/2 In. 20.00
Sinclaire, Bowl, Turn Down Rim, Green, Signed, 11 1/2 In. 50.00
Sinclaire, Candleholder, Engraved Body, Domed Base, Ruby & Gold, 4 In., Pair 125.00
Sinclaire, Candlestick, Amber, Signed, Pair 65.00
Sinclaire, Candlestick, Swirled Body, Amber, Signed, 10 In., Pair 200.00
Sinclaire, Cologne, Farrar II, Sterling Silver Top, 1067 .... 98.00
Sinclaire, Compote, Grape & Vine, Air Twist Stem, Green, 10 In. 450.00
Sinclaire, Cordial, Cut & Engraved Flowers, Long Stem, Set Of 10 .... 325.00
Sinclaire, Decanter, Pedestal, Flute Cut, Sterling Top, Signed 195.00
Sinclaire, Dish, Amber, Low Stemmed, Footed, Signed 35.00
Sinclaire, Plate, Dessert, Hand Blown, Green, 8 1/2 In., Set Of 10 .... 100.00
Sinclaire, Sugar & Creamer, Queen Louise, Signed 225.00
Sinclaire, Tray, Mint, Flowers, Signed, 8 X 2 1/2 In. 40.00
Sinclaire, Vase, Acid Etched Design, Signed, 20 In.Tall 90.00

Silver, Russian, Box, Circular, Cloisonne, Gilt & Enamel, C.1895
(See Page 555)

Sinclaire, Vase, Intaglio, Iris, Sterling Rim & Base, Leaves, 11 In.	265.00
Sinclaire, Vase, Lightly Cut, Signed, 8 1/4 In.	39.00
Sinclaire, Vase, Roses Pattern, 10 3/4 X 8 1/2 In.	195.00
Sinclaire, Vase, Trumpet, 3 Hobs, Floral Etch Rim, Cut No.1023, Signed, 14 In.	140.00
Sinclaire, Vase, Wheel Grind Floral Design, Cut Neck, Signed, 5 In.	100.00
Sinclaire, Water Set, Stratford, Pitcher & 4 Glasses, Signed	520.00
Sitzendorf, Figurine, Cupid Playing Drums, 4 1/4 X 4 In.	75.00
Sitzendorf, Figurine, Young Man, Reddish & Gold Coat, Holding Rosebud, 6 In.	115.00
Skull, Walrus, Lower Jaw, Tusks & Teeth	350.00
Sky King, Ring, Teleblinker	55.00
Sky King, Spy Detecto Writer	35.00

Slag glass is streaked with several colors. There were many types made from about 1880. Pink slag was an American Victorian product of unknown origin. Purple and blue slag were made in American and English factories. Red slag is a very late Victorian product. Other colors are known, but are of less importance to the collector. The numbers B-xx refer to the book "Milk Glass" by E. Belknap.

Slag, Blue, Candleholder, Flower Pattern, Pair	35.00
Slag, Blue, Match Holder	30.00
Slag, Blue, Plate, Open Panel Border, 8 3/4 In.	25.00
Slag, Blue, Vase, Embossed, 7 1/2 X 5 In.	110.00
Slag, Caramel, see Chocolate Glass	
Slag, Green, Bowl, Spaced Rib	35.00
Slag, Green, Box, Covered Rooster	40.00
Slag, Green, Creamer, Owl	15.00
Slag, Green, Jar, Perfume, Renaud Paris, Original Label	23.50
Slag, Green, Pitcher, Wide Mouth, Openwork Edge, 4 1/4 X 4 1/2 In.	55.00
Slag, Green, Pot, Honey	16.00
Slag, Green, Swan, 4 In.	14.00
Slag, Green, Table Set, Creamer, Spooner, Sugar, Butter, Atterbury	225.00
Slag, Lamp, Hanging, Metal Frame, 9 Panels, Different Colors, 14 1/4 In.	150.00
Slag, Pink, Berry Bowl, Inverted Fan & Feather	125.00
Slag, Pink, Butter Dish, Inverted Fan & Feather *Illus*	500.00
Slag, Pink, Creamer, Inverted Fan & Feather *Illus*	275.00
Slag, Pink, Dish, Four Footed, Scalloped Top, 2 1/2 X 4 In.Diameter	575.00
Slag, Pink, Sauce, 3 Legs, Fan & Feather	250.00
Slag, Pink, Spooner, Inverted Fan & Feather *Illus*	175.00
Slag, Pink, Tumbler, Inverted Fan & Feather *Illus*	275.00
Slag, Purple, Boot, With Spur	50.00
Slag, Purple, Bowl, Dart Bar, 8 In.Diameter	38.00
Slag, Purple, Butter, Chicken Head Top	145.00
Slag, Purple, Cake Stand, Dart Bar, 11 In.Diameter	75.00
Slag, Purple, Cake Stand, Ringed Foot, 9 In.Diameter	55.00
Slag, Purple, Celery, Fluted	55.00
Slag, Purple, Celery, Jewel Pattern	100.00
Slag, Purple, Compote, English, Signed	90.00
Slag, Purple, Compote, Stemmed, Scroll With Acanthus	50.00
Slag, Purple, Compote, Tall Standard, Dart Bar, 8 In.Diameter	70.00
Slag, Purple, Compote, 5 In.	95.00
Slag, Purple, Creamer, Flower & Panel	67.00
Slag, Purple, Creamer, Sunflower	45.00
Slag, Purple, Cruet, Pair	55.00
Slag, Purple, Dish, Candy, 2 Handled, Signed	67.50
Slag, Purple, Glass, Whiskey, Just A Thimble Full, C.1880, Marked, 2 Ounce	85.00
Slag, Purple, Holder, Match, Ring Handles, English Mark	49.00
Slag, Purple, Match Holder, Bushel Basket, 2 Handled, Marbleizing	45.00
Slag, Purple, Match Holder, Square, Footed, 3 3/4 In.	32.50
Slag, Purple, Match Holder, Square, 4 Feet, 3 3/4 In.	42.50
Slag, Purple, Pitcher, Pleat & Bead Pattern, 7 3/4 In.	117.00
Slag, Purple, Plate, Open Edge, 10 1/4 In.	95.00
Slag, Purple, Platter, 13 X 9 1/2 In.	59.50
Slag, Purple, Shoe, Upper Vaseline	115.00
Slag, Purple, Spooner, Scroll With Acanthus	42.00
Slag, Purple, Tumbler, English Mark, 4 1/2 In.	21.00
Slag, Purple, Vase, Celery, Fluted Pattern, Scalloped Top, 8 1/4 In.	88.00

Argand lamp, brass, jasper, and glass, Miller, England, 1825–1875

Tortoiseshell comb, attributed to Alfred Willard, probably Boston, 1820–1840

Mahogany bottle case and bottles, England, 1800–1825

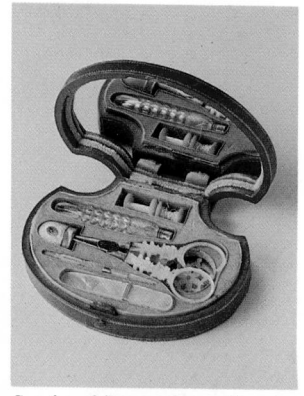

Sewing kit, mother of pearl, probably Europe, 1820–1850

Pincushion, wool and cotton, United States, 1776

Pocketbooks, wool, silk, canvas, and linen, probably United States, 1700–1800

Dresser, American pewter, probably Pennsylvania, 1750–1825

Hutch cupboard, painted white pine, Pennsylvania, 1750–1800

Rug, wool and cotton, probably New England, 1800–1830

Painted tulipwood chest, dome top, tinned sheet iron Pennsylvania, 1814

ainted white pine
ooster, attributed to
Vilhelm Schimmel,
Pennsylvania, 1865–1890

Painted white pine
whirligig, United States,
1825–1900

Argand lamp, brass, glass,
nd copper, probably
England, 1800–1830

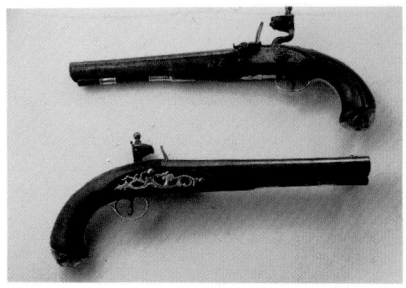

Pistols, Frederick Zorger,
Pennsylvania, 1765–1780

Hooked rug, cotton, wool, and
burlap, Maritime Provinces or
New England, 1870–1925

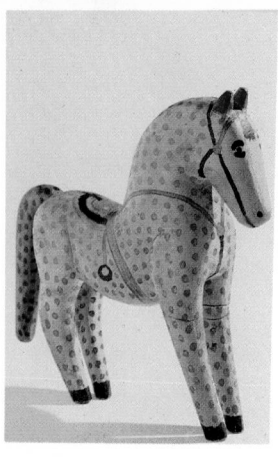

Wooden horse,
painted tulipwood,
Pennsylvania, c. 1840

Springerle mold,
probably applewood,
probably Pennsylvania,
1750–1850

Scrimshaw jagging wheel or pastry
wheel, whalebone, United States,
1825–1900

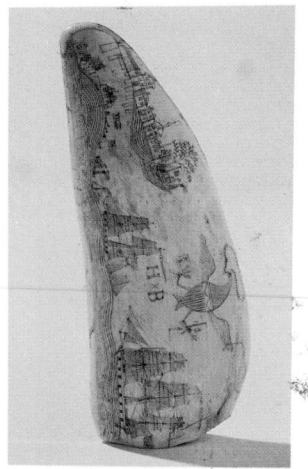

Scrimshaw, whale tooth,
United States,
1825–1860

Lamp, glass and brass,
probably New England,
1840–1860

Chinese porcelain platter, 11½ inches, 1842

Glass candlesticks, New England Glass Co., Massachusetts, c. 1860–1880

Wooden statue of Justice, attributed to Simeon Skillin, Jr., Boston, c. 1790–1806

White pine figure of an Indian, possibly Massachusetts, 1830–1880

Tape loom, painted white pine, Pennsylvania, 1795

The Van Pelt highboy,
mahogany, tulip, white
cedar, oak, and yellow pine,
Pennsylvania, 1765–1780

Fishing reel, iron, bone, and
wood, Europe or United States,
1770–1830

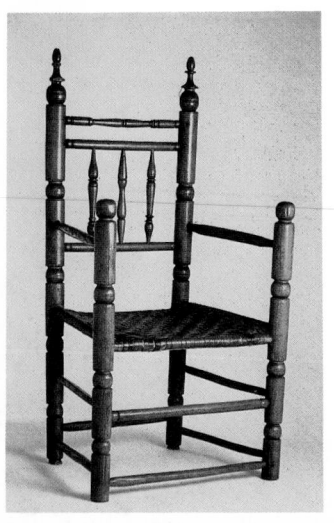

Blanket chest, pine, ash,
oak, and maple, New
England, 1710–1725

Armchair, oak, ash, and
hickory, New England,
1660–1700

Kettle, copper and brass,
Robert Reed,
Pennsylvania, 1780–1795

Coverlet, wool and
cotton, woven by I. Myer,
Ohio, 1836

Weathervane, pine and metal,
New York, 1800–1840

Brass candlesticks, probably
England, c. 1660

Basket, wood, United States,
1800–1850

Leather fireman's hat, Philadelphia,
1820–1830

Toy humming top, satinwood, United
States, 1800–1860

Mahogany knife
boxes, England or
United States,
1790–1800

Slag, Pink, Tumbler, Inverted Fan & Feather
(See Page 560)

Silver, Sterling, Tea & Coffee Set, L.Andrews & Co., 5 Piece   *(See Page 558)*

Slag; Pink *(l. to r.)*: Creamer; Butter Dish; Dish, Four Footed.   *(See Page 560)*

Slag, Purple, Vase, Grapes, 3 Reticulated Twigs, 6 In. 42.50
Slag, Purple, Vase, 11 1/2 In. 20.00
Slag, Red, Bowl, Melon Rib Sides, Scalloped Edge, Oval, 10 1/4 X 12 1/2 In. 175.00
Slag, Red, Vase, Peacock & Floral 80.00

Sleepy Eye pottery was made to be given away with the flour products of the Sleepy Eye Milling Co., Sleepy Eye, Minnesota, from about 1893 to 1952. It is a heavy stoneware with blue decorations, usually the famous profile of an Indian.

Sleepy Eye, Bookend, Tan, 7 1/2 In. 145.00
Sleepy Eye, Bowl, Butter 395.00
Sleepy Eye, Bowl, Salt, Blue & Gray 395.00
Sleepy Eye, Creamer 150.00
Sleepy Eye, Crock, Butter 300.00
Sleepy Eye, Crock, Salt 250.00
Sleepy Eye, Mug, Blue & White 60.00
Sleepy Eye, Pitcher, Blue & White, 8 In. 125.00
Sleepy Eye, Pitcher, Marked Monmouth, 9 In. 125.00
Sleepy Eye, Postcard 65.00
Sleepy Eye, Spoon .... 95.00 To 125.00
Sleepy Eye, Stein, Cobalt Blue, Marked 850.00
Sleepy Eye, Stein, Gray, Blue, Indian Profile Handle 375.00
Sleepy Eye, Vase, Blue & Gray, Signed, 9 In. 285.00
Sleepy Eye, Vase, Blue, Gray, Cylinder, 8 1/2 In. 135.00
Sleepy Eye, Vase, Flemish Blue & Gray, Dragonfly, Signed, 8 1/2 In. 175.00
Sleepy Eye, Vase, Indian On Front, Blue & Gray Stoneware, 9 In. 200.00

Slip is a thin mixture of clay and water, about the consistency of sour cream, that is applied to the pottery for decoration.

Slipware, Dish, Divided, C.1800, 14 In. 110.00
Slipware, Plate, Red, Orange Cast, Coggle Edge, 18th Century, 9 3/4 In. 110.00
Slipware, Plate, Redware Glaze, Virginia, Coggle Edge, 18th Century, 11 In. 125.00
Slipware, Plate, Set Of 3, 19th Century, 6 3/4 To 10 1/4 In. 325.00
Slipware, Plate, Three Rows Yellow Squiggles, 9 In. 275.00

Slot Machine, see Store, Machine

Smith Bros. Co.

Smith Brothers glass was made after 1878. The owners had worked for the Mt.Washington Glass Company in New Bedford, Massachusetts, for seven years before going into their own shop. Some of the designs were similar.

Smith Brothers, Biscuit Jar, Ribbon Design, 4 Sides & 4 Rounded Panels 725.00
Smith Brothers, Bookends, Rearing Horse 27.50
Smith Brothers, Bottle, Cologne, Multi-Color Maple Leaves, Signed, 5 1/4 In. 325.00
Smith Brothers, Bottle, Perfume, Blue Scrolls, Multi-Color Leaves, 5 In. 170.00
Smith Brothers, Bowl, Melon Ribbed, Enameled Flowers, 10 1/4 In. 275.00
Smith Brothers, Box, Covered, Melon Ribbed, Gold Base & Lid, 3 X 4 In.Diam. 290.00
Smith Brothers, Box, Covered, Melon Ribbed, Shasta Daisy, 6 X 3 1/2 In. 235.00
Smith Brothers, Box, Powder, Daisy On Ivory Background Lid, 3 In. 225.00
Smith Brothers, Chandelier, Blue Teardrop Prisms, Top & Base Light, 3 Ft. 650.00
Smith Brothers, Cracker Jar, Flower Petal Finial, Signed, 8 In. 300.00
Smith Brothers, Cracker Jar, Jeweled, Signed 275.00
Smith Brothers, Cracker Jar, Melon, Lion Mark 45.00
Smith Brothers, Lamp, Bronze And China Cylinder 350.00
Smith Brothers, Muffineer, Original Lid, Ribbed, Cream, Signed 185.00
Smith Brothers, Plate, Lily, Outline In Gold, Blue Edge & Gold, 7 In. 140.00
Smith Brothers, Plate, Santa Maria, Odd Shape, Signed, 7 3/4 In. 200.00
Smith Brothers, Rose Bowl, Hand-Painted, Beaded Rim 150.00
Smith Brothers, Rose Bowl, Red Rampant Lion, Creamy White To Lavender, 4 In. 175.00
Smith Brothers, Salt Shaker, Original Top, Enameled, Fig Shape 85.00
Smith Brothers, Shade, Lamp, White Glass, Beige Ground, 5 In., Pair 250.00
Smith Brothers, Sugar Shaker, Cabin Scene, Pewter Lid 115.00
Smith Brothers, Vase, Cylindrical, Heron In Water Scene, 6 X 2 1/8 In. 75.00
Smith Brothers, Vase, Decorated In Gold, Signed, 4 X 2 X 3 1/2 In. Diameter 290.00
Smith Brothers, Vase, Hand-Painted, Heron, Pink Bands, 6 In. 60.00
Smith Brothers, Vase, Rampant Lion, Hand-Decorated, Signed, 5 3/4 In. 150.00
Smith Brothers, Vase, Scenic, Cranes, Pair, 7 In. 55.00

Snow Babies, Arms Out, German, 2 X 2 1/4 In.	35.00
Snow Babies, Baby Being Pulled On Sled By Two Dogs	25.00
Snow Babies, Baby On Deer, 1 1/2 In.	50.00 To 75.00
Snow Babies, Baby On Skis, Pair	40.00
Snow Babies, Baby On Sled	65.00
Snow Babies, Baby On Stomach	45.00
Snow Babies, Baby Pulling Sled	45.00
Snow Babies, Baby Seated, Germany	45.00 To 60.00
Snow Babies, Baby Seated, 2 1/4 In.	45.00
Snow Babies, Baby Sitting On Red Sled, German	37.50
Snow Babies, Baby Sliding Down Roof	75.00
Snow Babies, Baby, Arms Outstretched, Germany, 2 In.	49.00
Snow Babies, Baby, Rosy Cheeks, Lying, Germany	30.00
Snow Babies, Baby, Rosy Cheeks, Sitting, Germany	30.00
Snow Babies, Baby, Rosy Cheeks, Standing, Germany	30.00
Snow Babies, Bear On Yellow Sled, German	25.00 To 45.00
Snow Babies, Bear, Germany	45.00
Snow Babies, Boy, Lying On Sled, German, 2 In.	45.00
Snow Babies, Boy, Sliding With Sled On Snow, Gold Handles, 3 X 3 1/2 In.	50.00
Snow Babies, Boy, Waving	25.00
Snow Babies, Children Dancing, Bisque, 2 1/2 In.	55.00
Snow Babies, Dish, Relish, Royal Bayreuth	115.00
Snow Babies, Girl On Skis	75.00
Snow Babies, Pincushion	35.00
Snow Babies, Seated Baby, Japan, 1 In.	10.00
Snow Babies, Standing Snowman, German	45.00
Snow Babies, Twins, 1 1/2 In.	35.00
Snow Babies, Vase, Royal Bayreuth, Blue Mark, 3 X 3 In.	65.00
Snuff Bottle, see Bottle, Snuff	
Snuffbox, Black Lacquer, Shoe Shape, Hinged Lid & Cuban Heel, 3 1/4 In.	32.00
Snuffbox, Brass Mounted & Hinged, Cherubs, Sevres Mark, 2 1/4 X 2 In.	38.00
Snuffbox, Carved Horn, Oval, Lift-Off Lid, 1 1/2 X 2 1/2 X 1 In.	30.00
Snuffbox, Oil Painting Of Harbor Scene	75.00
Snuffbox, Shoe, Small Man	22.50
Snuffbox, Tortoise Shell, Hanged Lid, 1 1/2 X 2 1/2 X 1/2 In.	30.00
Snuffbox, Tortoise Shell, Silver Rim, 800 Mark, 1 1/2 X 1 1/4 In.	110.00

Soapstone is a mineral that was used for foot warmers or griddles because of its heat-retaining properties. Soapstone was carved in many countries in the nineteenth and twentieth centuries.

Soapstone, Ashtray, Leaf-Shape	30.00
Soapstone, Bookends, Carved Flower Pot & Foliage, Brown & Beige, Pair	175.00
Soapstone, Bookends, Carved With Protruding Flowers & Birds	135.00
Soapstone, Box, Covered, Chinese, Lavender & White, 4 1/2 X 3 1/4 In.	20.00
Soapstone, Chinese Seal, Bodhidarma With Image Of Kwan Yin In His Heart	90.00
Soapstone, Figurine, Brown, 3 Monkeys, 3 3/4 X 3 1/4 In.	45.00
Soapstone, Figurine, Buddhist Priest, Seal Base	58.00
Soapstone, Figurine, Carved Dragon, Cranes, Flowers, Vases, 7 3/4 X 6 In.	95.00
Soapstone, Figurine, Condor, Red Jasper, Gold Feet, 6 1/4 In.	675.00
Soapstone, Figurine, Mandarin, Flowing Robe, Sword At Waist, Green, 10 In.	75.00
Soapstone, Figurine, Quan Yin, Carved, 6 1/2 In.	17.50
Soapstone, Figurine, Seal, Carved With A Fu Lion, 3 In., Pair	125.00
Soapstone, Figurine, Walrus, Ivory Tusks, 3 In.	26.00
Soapstone, Footwarmer, Tin Case, Bail Handle, 4 1/4 X 8 In.	37.50
Soapstone, Griddle, Iron Banding, Iron Loops, C.1840	30.00
Soapstone, Holder, Cigarette & Match, 3 1/2 In.	20.00
Soapstone, Mask, Central American Indian, Carved, 11 In.	65.00
Soapstone, Muff Warmer & Black Seal Muff, 5 3/4 1 1/2 In.	45.00
Soapstone, Owl, Dark Green, 2 1/2 Inches Tall, 2 Inches Wide	20.00
Soapstone, Seal, Foo Dog, Chinese, 2 1/8 In.	38.00
Soapstone, Seal, Foo Dog, Chinese, 3 In.	50.00
Soapstone, Tray, Pin	17.50
Soapstone, Vase, Fish & Undersea Foliage, China, 5 In., Pair	50.00
Soapstone, Vase, Meandering Vine, 7 In.	35.00
Soapstone, Vase, Souvenir, St.Louis World's Fair, 1904	95.00
Soapstone, Walrus, Light Green, 6 Inches Long, 3 1/4 Inches Tall	40.00

Soapstone, Warmer, Tin Holder, C.1850, 5 1/2 X 9 X 1 1/2 In. 22.50
Soft Paste, Basket, Imari Red, Bow Porcelain Co., English, 9 In., Pair 160.00
Soft Paste, Bowl, Footed, Floral Design, Marked Pompeii, 3 1/2 X 13 In.Diam. 47.50
Soft Paste, Bowl, Sugar, Castle Landscape, Flower Finial, C.1800 .... 27.00
Soft Paste, Cup & Saucer, Handleless, Chintz Pattern, C.1810 .... 28.00
Soft Paste, Cup & Saucer, Oriental Scene, C.1820, Cup, 2 1/8 In., Set Of 9 .... 225.00
Soft Paste, Cup & Saucer, Purple Luster, Polychrome Enameling 18.00
Soft Paste, Cup, Wash Vase, Handleless 30.00
Soft Paste, Pitcher, Blue Transfer, Silver Resist Rim 90.00
Soft Paste, Plate, Hannibal Crossing Alps, 10 In. 35.00
Soft Paste, Plate, King's Rose, Red, Pink, Green, Yellow, 8 1/8 In. 125.00
Souvenir, Ashtray, Ford, 1939 World's Fair, Picture Of Car 22.00
Souvenir, Creamer, Municipal Building, Des Moines 8.00
Souvenir, Cup, Fort Pitt Block House, Bavarian 8.00
Souvenir, Goblet, Grand Army Of The Republic Reunion, Milwaukee, 1887 .... 35.00
Souvenir, Goblet, U.S.S.Kentucky, Cherry 20.00
Souvenir, Hatchet, George Washington, Inaugural, April 30, 1789 .... 28.00
Souvenir, Hatchet, 1893 World's Fair, Blue 28.00
Souvenir, Mug, Lake Gogebic, Michigan, Custard Glass 47.00
Souvenir, Pillow, Chicago 6.00
Souvenir, Pillow, Minnesota 6.00
Souvenir, Pillow, Nebraska 6.00
Souvenir, Pitcher, Detroit, Cleveland Steamship Lines, 6 1/4 In. 18.00
Souvenir, Plate, Pioneer White Wings Flour Co., 90th Anniversary 85.00
Souvenir, Plate, Yellowstone Park, Adams Crown Mark, Blue & White, 10 In. 23.00
Souvenir, Platter, Pioneer White Wings Flour Co., 90th Anniversary, 12 In. 62.00
Souvenir, Salt & Pepper, Lucky Strike Club, Las Vegas 3.50
Souvenir, Spoon, Silver Plate, A Century Of Progress, 1933, Embossed Bowl 12.50
Souvenir, Spoon, Silver Plate, Flagship Olympia, Battle Of Manila, 1898 .... 12.00
Souvenir, Spoon, Silver Plate, Norma Talmadge, Signature & Face On Handle 15.00
Souvenir, Spoon, Silver Plate, Oklahoma, State Seal, 1907 .... 10.00

Spangle Glass, Vase, Multicolor, Melon Ribbed, Swirl, 3 1/2 In.

Souvenir, Spoon, Silver Plate, Pola Negri, Signature & Face On Handle 15.00
Souvenir, Spoon, Silver Plate, Yogi Bear 6.00
Souvenir, Spoon, Sterling Silver, Alaska, Totem Pole 10.00
Souvenir, Spoon, Sterling Silver, All American Indian, Mackinac Island 35.00
Souvenir, Spoon, Sterling Silver, April 12.00
Souvenir, Spoon, Sterling Silver, Ashland, Wisconsin High School 12.50
Souvenir, Spoon, Sterling Silver, B.P.O.E., Figural Elk Head & Clock, 1906 .... 15.00
Souvenir, Spoon, Sterling Silver, Bexley Hall, Ruby Eyes On Tip 15.00
Souvenir, Spoon, Sterling Silver, Buffalo, New York, Figural Buffalo On End 15.00
Souvenir, Spoon, Sterling Silver, California State, Gold Wash Bowl 15.00
Souvenir, Spoon, Sterling Silver, City High School, Junction City, Kansas 15.00
Souvenir, Spoon, Sterling Silver, Columbia River Salmon 15.00
Souvenir, Spoon, Sterling Silver, Denver, Colorado, Indian, Cowboy, Horse 15.00
Souvenir, Spoon, Sterling Silver, El Garce Hotel, Needles, California 15.00
Souvenir, Spoon, Sterling Silver, Elk Point, South Dakota, 7 1/2 In. 6.00
Souvenir, Spoon, Sterling Silver, Elks 55.00
Souvenir, Spoon, Sterling Silver, Figural Mining Pan, Denver 15.00
Souvenir, Spoon, Sterling Silver, Frog Under Umbrella, Oregon Webfoot, 1898 .... 15.00
Souvenir, Spoon, Sterling Silver, Garden Of Gods, Colorado Gateway 12.00
Souvenir, Spoon, Sterling Silver, Gloucester, Fisherman On Handle, Demitasse 10.50
Souvenir, Spoon, Sterling Silver, Kansas, Steer On Handle 12.00
Souvenir, Spoon, Sterling Silver, Kentucky, Men Shaking Hands & Horse 10.00
Souvenir, Spoon, Sterling Silver, Massachusetts Seal 12.00

Souvenir, Spoon, Sterling Silver, May	12.00
Souvenir, Spoon, Sterling Silver, North American Indian	90.00
Souvenir, Spoon, Sterling Silver, Oklahoma	18.00
Souvenir, Spoon, Sterling Silver, Park Springs, Eldorado, Montana	15.00
Souvenir, Spoon, Sterling Silver, Pasadena	15.00
Souvenir, Spoon, Sterling Silver, Portland, Oregon, Demitasse	15.00
Souvenir, Spoon, Sterling Silver, Santa Barbara Mission	12.00
Souvenir, Spoon, Sterling Silver, Skyline, Vancouver, Openwork Handle	22.00
Souvenir, Tumbler, Green, Niagara Falls	15.00

Spangle glass is multicolored glass made from odds and ends of colored glass rods. It includes metallic flakes of mica covered with gold, silver, nickel, or copper. Spangle glass is usually cased with a thin layer of clear glass over the multicolored layer.

Spangle Glass, see also Vasa Murrhina

Spangle Glass, Basket, Amber Cased, Twig Handle, 6 In.	150.00
Spangle Glass, Basket, Mica Under Surface, White Lining, 7 X 5 3/4 In.Diam.	87.75
Spangle Glass, Basket, Thorn Handle, White Interior, Cased, 3 X 5 1/2 In.	125.00
Spangle Glass, Paperweight, Mushroom, Gold Mica Flakes, Color Streaks	125.00
Spangle Glass, Pitcher, Bulbous, Cranberry, Silver Mica, 8 3/4 In.	135.00
Spangle Glass, Vase, Multicolor, Melon Ribbed, Swirl, 3 1/2 In. *Illus*	40.00
Spangle Glass, Vase, Pink, Cobalt, Charteuse, Mica Flakes, Rigaree, English	35.00
Spangle Glass, Vase, Silver Mica Flakes, Applied Rusching, 10 In.	95.00
Spanish American War, Eagle, From Dress Helmet, U.S.	10.00
Spanish American War, Pin, Shape Of Rifle With Eagle	8.00
Spanish American War, Pouch, Cartridge, Belt, Flap Cover, Brass Rosettes	250.00

Spanish lace is a Victorian glass pattern that seems to have white lace on a colored background. Blue, yellow, cranberry, and clear glass was made with this distinctive white pattern. It was made in the United States and England after about 1885.

Spanish Lace, Bottle, Barber, Opalescent, Yellow	75.00
Spanish Lace, Bowl, Sugar, Cranberry, Opalescent, Twig Knob, 6 In.	95.00
Spanish Lace, Lamp, Cranberry, Electric	100.00
Spanish Lace, Lamp, Miniature, Silver Filigree, Blue	225.00
Spanish Lace, Pitcher, Water, Ruffled Opalescent Top, Blue, 9 1/4 In.	125.00
Spanish Lace, Pitcher, Water, White Opalescent	70.00
Spanish Lace, Rose Bowl	30.00
Spanish Lace, Saltshaker, Opalescent	28.00
Spanish Lace, Spooner, Opalescent, Vaseline	50.00 To 75.00
Spanish Lace, Sugar Shaker, Blue	120.00
Spanish Lace, Tankard, Applied Handle, Green, 11 1/2 In.	250.00
Spanish Lace, Toothpick	18.00
Spanish Lace, Vase, Fluted Rim, Blue, 6 In.	40.00
Spanish Lace, Vase, Opalescent, Blue, Flared & Ruffled Top, 1800s, 6 In.	50.00
Spanish Lace, Vase, Ruffled Lip, Opalescent Vaseline Color, 6 1/2 In.	55.00
Spanish Lace, Vase, Yellow To Clear, Bulbous Bottom, 6 In.	45.00
Spanish Lace, Water Set, Ruffled Top Pitcher, Cranberry, 6 Tumblers	130.00

Spatter glass is a multicolored glass made from many small pieces of different colored glass.

Spatter glass, see also End-of-Day Glass

Spatter Glass, Basket, Diamond Shape Opening, Twisted Thorn Handle	225.00
Spatter Glass, Basket, Opalescent Over Clear, Twisted Handle, 6 X 5 1/2 In.	35.00
Spatter Glass, Basket, Wishbone Handle, 7 1/2 In.High	60.00
Spatter Glass, Bowl, Red & Green Flowers, Spattered Border, 11 In.	48.00
Spatter Glass, Cruet, Bulbous, Clear Applied Handle, Cut Stopper, 7 In.	100.00
Spatter Glass, Fairy Lamp, Clear Petal Base, Green Overshot, 5 1/4 In.	195.00
Spatter Glass, Mug, Lady's, Geometric Band, White Porcelain, 3 3/4 In.	25.00
Spatter Glass, Pitcher, Blown, Daisy, Green Leaves, White, Victorian, 9 In.	110.00
Spatter Glass, Pitcher, Blue On Gray, 9 In.	125.00
Spatter Glass, Pitcher, Bulbous, Pink & White, Clear Handle, 8 In.	90.00
Spatter Glass, Pitcher, Water, Cranberry & White, Applied Handle, 8 In.	105.00
Spatter Glass, Rose Bowl, White, Black Spatter, 4 In.	26.00
Spatter Glass, Saltshaker, Leaf Mold, Rose & White, Original Top	52.00
Spatter Glass, Sugar Shaker, Green Opalescent, Feather Pattern	65.00

Spatter Glass, Sugar Shaker, Pink & White	50.00
Spatter Glass, Syrup, Ring Necked	120.00 To 135.00
Spatter Glass, Vase, Cased, Green & Pink, Applied Clear Base, 8 In.	45.00
Spatter Glass, Vase, Flared Top, 9 In.	47.00
Spatter Glass, Vase, Melon Ribbed, Ruffled Rim, Bulbous, 5 1/2 In., Pair	45.00
Spatter Glass, Vase, Multi-Color, 3 Layer, 2 Slip Rings, 5 1/2 In.	97.50
Spatter Glass, Vase, Urn Shape, Satin Finish, 5 X 5 In.	22.00
Spatter Glass, Vase, White On Amber, 4 1/2 In.	35.00

Spatterware is a creamware or soft-paste dinnerware decorated with spatter designs. The earliest pieces were made during the late eighteenth century, but most of the wares found today were made from 1800 to 1850. The spatterware dishes were made in the Staffordshire district of England for sale on the American market.

Spatterware, see also Spongeware

Spatterware, Bowl & Saucer, Tea, Queen's Rose Pattern	26.00
Spatterware, Bowl, Buff, Brown & Green, 9 1/2 In.	95.00
Spatterware, Bowl, Green & Brown On Tan, 2 1/2 X 6 In.Diameter	17.50
Spatterware, Bowl, Hand-Painted, Blue Stick Starflowers, Nesting, 8 To 4 In.	125.00
Spatterware, Bowl, Mixing, Blue, White & Red Sponge, 9 X 5 In.	48.00
Spatterware, Bowl, Paneled Sides, 6 In.Diameter	15.00
Spatterware, Bowl, Paneled Sides, 7 1/4 In.Diameter	17.50
Spatterware, Bowl, Stick Spatter, Black Diamonds, Red Striping, 7 1/4 In.	20.00
Spatterware, Bowl, Sugar, Red & Blue Rainbow	95.00
Spatterware, Bowl, Vertical Paneled Sides, 3 X 7 1/4 In.Diameter	20.00
Spatterware, Cup & Saucer, Handleless, Flower In Bottom Of Cup	165.00
Spatterware, Cup & Saucer, Handleless, Red Flower	135.00
Spatterware, Cup & Saucer, Overall Spatter Flower & Leaf Design, 4 In.	85.00
Spatterware, Cup Plate, Blue & Yellow	45.00
Spatterware, Dish, Cheese, Green & Multicolored, 11 X 8 1/2 In.	65.00
Spatterware, Mug, White, Blue Band, Brown Stick Design, 4 In.	85.00
Spatterware, Pitcher, Enameled Daisy, Victorian Blown Glass, 9 In.	110.00
Spatterware, Pitcher, Soft Paste, Roses & Leaves, 3 3/4 In.	115.00
Spatterware, Plate, Blue Border Eagle	125.00
Spatterware, Plate, Cut Sponge Border, 10 In.	85.00
Spatterware, Plate, Morning Glory	210.00
Spatterware, Plate, Peacock, Red, Green, Blue, Marked, 9 1/4 In., Set Of 6	600.00
Spatterware, Plate, Peafowl, Carmine Spatter, Impressed Adams, 9 1/2 In.	185.00
Spatterware, Plate, Rabbit & Frog Border, Polychrome Center, 9 1/2 In.	125.00
Spatterware, Plate, Rabbit, Open Border, 3 Rabbits In Center	75.00
Spatterware, Plate, Red & Yellow Tulip & Green Leaves, 6 1/2 In.	75.00
Spatterware, Plate, Red, Blue & Green, Malkin & Co., 8 3/4 In.	37.50
Spatterware, Plate, Red, Blue, Green Peafowl, Davenport, 1848, 8 1/4 In.	150.00
Spatterware, Platter, Landscape Center, Red, Green & Blue, 14 1/2 X 10 In.	375.00
Spatterware, Soup, Cut Sponge, Flowing Blue, 8 1/2 In.	85.00
Spatterware, Sugar, Blue & White, Crazed Inside, 5 In.	55.00
Spatterware, Sugar, Covered, Blue	110.00

Spinning Wheel, see Tool, Spinning Wheel

Spode pottery, porcelain, and bone china were made by the Stoke-on-Trent Factory of England founded by Josiah Spode about 1770. The firm became Copeland and Garrett from 1833 to 1847, then W.T.Copeland or W.T.Copeland and Sons until the present time. The word Spode appears on many pieces made by the Copeland Factory. Most collectors include all the wares under the more familiar name of Spode.

Spode, see also Copeland

Spode, Basket, Sweetmeat, C.1840, 9 X 5 1/2 In.	40.00
Spode, Coffeepot, Billingsley Rose	45.00
Spode, Creamer, Blue Background, White Raised Figures	23.00
Spode, Cup & Saucer, Demitasse, Cobalt, Japanese Birds, Enameling, 1778	70.00
Spode, Dinner Service, Loralie, Service For 8, 48 Pieces	250.00
Spode, Jar, Lidded, Animal Finial, Oriental Decoration, Signed, 10 1/2in.	118.00
Spode, Jug, Ale, Grapevine On Neck, Cameo Cut Men, Good Old Ale, 7 1/2 In.	100.00
Spode, Jug, Hand-Painted Flowers, White Ground, C.1820, 2 In.	150.00
Spode, Mug, Coffee, Temple, C.1810, 2 1/2 In.	70.00
Spode, Plate, Bird Center, Black Border, Embossed Flowers, 8 In.	45.00

Spode, Plate, Blue Willow, Turner's Engraving, C.1820, 10 In. 45.00
Spode, Plate, Hand-Painted Peacock, 7 1/2 In., Set Of 6 .... 75.00
Spode, Plate, Hot Water, Blue, C.1820, Spode Tower California, 10 In. 85.00
Spode, Plate, The Kill, 11 In. 12.00
Spode, Plate, 1805-15, Marked Spode Newstone 40.00
Spode, Platter & Mazarine, Coral, Cobalt, Blue & Gold, C.1820 .... 525.00
Spode, Platter, Oval, Castile 34.50
Spode, Sugar & Creamer, Gainsborough 25.00
Spode, Vase, Floral Motifs, Imari Style, Stand, 1820, 14 In., Pair 1400.00
Spode, Vegetable, Flowers & Birds, Black Transfer, 7 3/4 X 11 1/4 In. 35.00

*Spongeware is very similar to spatterware in appearance. The designs were
applied to the ware by daubing the color. Many dealers do not differentiate
between the two wares and use the names interchangeably.*

Spongeware, Bowl, Blue & Brown, 9 1/2 In. 48.00
Spongeware, Bowl, Blue & Rust, 10 1/4 & 9 1/4 In.Diameter, Set Of 2 .... 38.00
Spongeware, Bowl, Blue, Brown On White, 6 In. 45.00
Spongeware, Bowl, Embossed Arch, Blue, 6 1/2 X 12 1/4 In.Diameter 85.00
Spongeware, Bowl, Green On Yellow, 6 1/4 X 2 1/2 In. 25.00
Spongeware, Bowl, Mixing, Blue & Rust Daubing, 5 1/4 X 3 1/2 In.Deep 25.00
Spongeware, Bowl, Mixing, Blue & Rust Daubing, 7 1/4 X 4 1/2 In.Deep 40.00
Spongeware, Bowl, Mixing, Blue & Rust Daubing, 8 1/4 X 5 In.Deep 45.00
Spongeware, Bowl, Mixing, Blue Lines Around Middle, White, 7 1/2 In. 60.00
Spongeware, Bowl, Mixing, Red & Blue Spatter, 1 1/2 Quart 28.00
Spongeware, Bowl, Mixing, Red & Blue Spatter, 2 1/2 Quart 38.00
Spongeware, Bowl, Molded Rib Exterior, Brown On Tan, 5 1/2 X 9 3/4 In.Diam. 35.00
Spongeware, Bowl, Molded Rib Exterior, 5 1/2 X 9 3/4 In. 25.00
Spongeware, Bowl, Tan With Blue Splotching 65.00
Spongeware, Casserole, Brown 32.00
Spongeware, Chamber Pot, Blue & White, Blue Band 45.00
Spongeware, Cooler, Water, Blue Banded, Lid & Bail 125.00
Spongeware, Cooler, Water, Blue With Cream, 12 1/2 In. X 8 In.Diameter 225.00
Spongeware, Cooler, Water, Covered, Brass Spigot, Blue & White, 5 Gallon 185.00
Spongeware, Cooler, Water, Sponge Lid, Brass Spigot, 5 Gallon 175.00
Spongeware, Creamer 10.00
Spongeware, Cup Plate, Blue, Cream, Underside Has Asterisk Impression 30.00
Spongeware, Cup, Custard, Brown & Cream 11.50
Spongeware, Cup, Custard, Pair 58.00
Spongeware, Cup, Custard, Yellow-Brown, Set Of 3 .... 15.00
Spongeware, Cuspidor, Blue & White, Blue Banding, 8 In. 68.00
Spongeware, Cuspidor, Blue & White, Open, 5 1/4 X 7 1/4 In. 95.00
Spongeware, Dish, Butter, Basket Weave, Lid 100.00
Spongeware, Dish, Soap, Blue & Green 70.00
Spongeware, Dish, Soap, Blue, Burford Bros. 55.00
Spongeware, Dish, Souffle, Blue & White, 7 In. 45.00
Spongeware, Figurine, Whimsey, Blue & White, Monkey, 4 In. 110.00
Spongeware, Flask, Lady's, Cream & Brown, Original Stopper, 4 In. 50.00
Spongeware, Foot Warmer, Logan Pottery, Blue & White 55.00
Spongeware, Jug, Blue, Cream Background, 1 Gallon 95.00
Spongeware, Jug, Brown, Tan, Green On Cream, Rotund Shape, 5 X 3 3/4 In. 110.00
Spongeware, Pitcher, Black, Cream, 6 1/2 In. 65.00
Spongeware, Pitcher, Blue & White, 7 In. .... 60.00 To 155.00
Spongeware, Pitcher, Blue & White, 8 In. 40.00
Spongeware, Pitcher, Blue, 8 3/4 In. 87.50
Spongeware, Pitcher, Brown & Buff, Peacock Under Palm Tree 72.00
Spongeware, Pitcher, Cow, Blue 90.00
Spongeware, Pitcher, Cream, Green & Brown, Advertising, 4 1/2 In. 24.00
Spongeware, Pitcher, Gray, Rust, Cream, 6 1/2 In. 75.00
Spongeware, Pitcher, Milk, Blue & White, 6 1/2 In. 65.00
Spongeware, Pitcher, Milk, 9 In. 135.00
Spongeware, Pitcher, Raised Floral Sprays, 9 In. 197.00
Spongeware, Pitcher, Raised Floral, Yellow, Brown, Gold, 12 X 4 X 6 In. 65.00
Spongeware, Pitcher, Rust On Yellow, Raised Flowers, 9 1/4 In. 35.00
Spongeware, Pitcher, Tankard Shape, Blue & White, 9 In. 75.00
Spongeware, Pitcher, Wash, Blue & White, Pointed Scrolls At Base 65.00
Spongeware, Pitcher, Wash, Bowknot, Blue & White 65.00

Spongeware, Pitcher, White Interior, Black Handle, 8 1/2 In.	17.50
Spongeware, Pitcher, Yellow, Rust & Green, Embossed Flowers, 9 1/2 In.	110.00
Spongeware, Plate, Bow & Sash, Blue & Green, 9 In.	78.00
Spongeware, Plate, Brown & White, Tight Sponge Design, 5 1/4 In.	72.00
Spongeware, Platter, Blue & White, Scalloped Sides, Oval, 10 X 13 1/2 In.	75.00
Spongeware, Platter, Blue Stoneware, Blue, Oval, 12 X 8 In.	145.00
Spongeware, Saucer, Stick, Brown & White, 3 3/4 In.	16.00
Spongeware, Spittoon, Blue & White, Ladies, 4 1/2 In.	55.00
Spongeware, Spittoon, Green On White	95.00
Spongeware, Vase, Applied Handles, Blue & Cream, 8 In.	75.00

Spool Cabinet, see Store, Cabinet

Staffordshire is a district in England where pottery and porcelain have been made since the 1900s. Thousands of types of pottery and porcelain have been made in the hundreds of factories that worked in the area. Some of the most famous factories have been listed separately. See Royal Doulton, Royal Worcester, Spode, Wedgwood, and others.

Staffordshire, see also Flow Blue, Ridgway

Staffordshire, Bank, Old English House, 2 Chimneys, 4 1/2 X 4 1/4 In.	50.00
Staffordshire, Barrel, Rum, Rectangular, 1850s, Brass Faucet, 14 In.	250.00
Staffordshire, Bowl, American Eagle On Urn, 6 1/2 In.	150.00
Staffordshire, Bowl, Girl Milking, Blue, 5 In.	55.00
Staffordshire, Bowl, Serving, Fairy Villas, W.Adams & Co., 10 In.	50.00
Staffordshire, Bowl, Sugar, Open, Mulberry Ware, Corean	58.00
Staffordshire, Bowl, Vegetable, Covered, Mulberry Ware, 12 X 10 1/2 In.	135.00
Staffordshire, Bowl, Vegetable, Mulberry Ware, 7 X 9 In.	40.00
Staffordshire, Bowl, Vegetable, Open, Mulberry Ware, Jeddo, 10 In.	45.00
Staffordshire, Bowl, Verbena, Flow Blue, 10 In.Diameter	41.00
Staffordshire, Bowl, Waste, Christmas Eve, Dark Blue, Clews' Wilkie Series	225.00
Staffordshire, Bowl, Waste, Mulberry Ware, Corean, 4 X 6 1/2 In.	55.00
Staffordshire, Bowl, Yellow Glazed Earthenware, C.1820, 6 3/8 In.	300.00
Staffordshire, Bowl, 12 Sided, Foliage, Flow Blue, 9 In.	15.00
Staffordshire, Box, Dog On Cushion Before Mirror	40.00
Staffordshire, Box, Footed, Oval, 4 Cameos On Lid, 3 1/2 X 2 1/2 In.	35.00
Staffordshire, Box, Fox With Hen On Lid, 5 3/4 In.Square	50.00
Staffordshire, Box, Gold Frame, Crown & Scepter On Lid, 4 X 3 1/8 In.	60.00
Staffordshire, Box, Lid Is Roof, Children Under Umbrella, 4 1/2 In.	65.00
Staffordshire, Box, Powder, Boy With Parakeet, 8 1/2 In.	25.00
Staffordshire, Box, Powder, Lady Holding Dog, 8 1/2 In.	85.00
Staffordshire, Box, Powder, Sitting Spaniel, 7 1/2 In.	35.00
Staffordshire, Box, Ring, Bisque Bird On Lid, White Glaze, 4 1/2 X 3 1/4 In.	47.50
Staffordshire, Box, Snuff, Enameled, Scene Of Lovers, C.1765, 3 1/8 In.	125.00
Staffordshire, Box, Trinket, Boy With Hoop, Base Is Fireplace, 3 X 4 In.	48.00
Staffordshire, Box, Trinket, Fireplace Shape, Boy Rolling Hoop, 3 X 2 In.	48.00
Staffordshire, Box, Trinket, Fox With Pheasant On Lid, Bisque, 3 X 3 1/4 In.	37.50
Staffordshire, Box, Trinket, Girl On Lid, Feeding Puppy, 5 1/2 In.	85.00
Staffordshire, Box, Trinket, On Pillars	18.00
Staffordshire, Box, Trinket, Oval, Cameos On Lid, Wild Rose Scene	35.00
Staffordshire, Box, Trinket, Pocket Watch & Fob On Cover	47.00
Staffordshire, Box, Trinket, Watch & Ring On Cover, 2 In.	35.00
Staffordshire, Box, Trinket, Watch With Ring & Seal On Sides, 2 3/4 X 2 In.	39.00
Staffordshire, Bust, George Washington, 8 In.	225.00
Staffordshire, Chamberpot, Marbleized	35.00
Staffordshire, Charlotte Mourning At The Tomb Of Werther, C.1800, 9 In.	125.00
Staffordshire, Clock Figures, C.1830-40, 5 1/2 In.	75.00
Staffordshire, Coffeepot, Franklin's Tomb, Wood, 12 In. ....Illus	850.00
Staffordshire, Coffeepot, Mulberry Ware, 8-Sided, Scenic, C.Meich, C.1840	160.00
Staffordshire, Coffeepot, Vincennes, Mulberry Ware, 11 1/2 In.	165.00
Staffordshire, Compote, Oriental Design, Fan Mark, 3 X 9 1/2 In.Diam., Pair	20.00
Staffordshire, Cottage, One Smoke Stack, 5 In.	45.00
Staffordshire, Cottage, 2 Smoke Stacks, 5 1/2 In.	45.00
Staffordshire, Creamer, Corean, Mulberry Ware	105.00
Staffordshire, Creamer, Cow, Cover, Transfer, C.1890	60.00
Staffordshire, Creamer, Pelew, Mulberry Ware, C.1850, 5 In.	75.00
Staffordshire, Creamer, Skenectady On Mohawk River, Purple, 4 1/2 In.	195.00
Staffordshire, Creamer, Washington, Mulberry Ware	65.00

Staffordshire, Coffeepot, Franklin's Tomb, Wood, 12 In.

Staffordshire, Cup & Saucer, Bird & Bug, Ladybug On Inside, Cobalt & Gold	30.00
Staffordshire, Cup & Saucer, Child's, C.1820, Saucer, 4 1/4 In.	50.00
Staffordshire, Cup & Saucer, Chowder, Red Willow, JM & S England Mark	25.00
Staffordshire, Cup & Saucer, Cottage Scene, Dark Blue	85.00
Staffordshire, Cup & Saucer, Dark Blue Transfer Of 2 Dogs, Stevenson	85.00
Staffordshire, Cup & Saucer, Draped Urn & Floral, Dark Blue	80.00
Staffordshire, Cup & Saucer, Goats & Floral, Dark Blue, Stubbs	95.00
Staffordshire, Cup & Saucer, Groups Of Peasants With Birdcage, Adams	80.00
Staffordshire, Cup & Saucer, Handleless, C.1840, Marked, 11 Piece	27.50
Staffordshire, Cup & Saucer, Handleless, Corean, Mulberry Ware, Set Of 5	275.00
Staffordshire, Cup & Saucer, Handleless, Cyprus, Davenport, Mulberry	40.00
Staffordshire, Cup & Saucer, Handleless, Vincennes, Mulberry Ware, C.1857	38.00
Staffordshire, Cup & Saucer, Linnet, Birds, Flowers, Beaded Design, C.1835-40	42.00
Staffordshire, Cup & Saucer, Mycena, Brown Transfer	15.00
Staffordshire, Cup & Saucer, Tea, Alhambra, Sepia, Pair	20.00
Staffordshire, Cup Plate, Battery, Blue, Wood	145.00
Staffordshire, Cup Plate, Belzoni, Enoch Wood, Red Transfer	30.00
Staffordshire, Cup Plate, Broadlands, Hampshire, Hall, Dark Blue, 4 In.	75.00
Staffordshire, Cup Plate, Cadmus, Blue	65.00
Staffordshire, Cup Plate, Corean, Mulberry, C.1850	25.00
Staffordshire, Cup Plate, Fruit Basket, C.1845, Brown Transfer, 4 1/2 In.	20.00
Staffordshire, Cup Plate, Genoa, Davenport, 12-Sided	16.00
Staffordshire, Cup Plate, Giraffe	34.00
Staffordshire, Cup Plate, Red Transfer Of Girl, Wood	35.00
Staffordshire, Cup, Child's, Forget-Me-Not	18.00
Staffordshire, Cup, Franklin Flying Kite One Side, Independence Hall Other	28.00
Staffordshire, Cup, Handleless, Missouri, Mulberry Ware	20.00
Staffordshire, Cup, Handleless, William Cowper's Birthplace, Hartfordshire	35.00
Staffordshire, Cup, Stirrup, Fox Head, 6 In.	55.00
Staffordshire, Dinner Set, Blue, Butterflies & Florals, Miniature, 50 Pieces	800.00
Staffordshire, Dish, Cheese, Covered, 1901	35.00
Staffordshire, Dish, Hen On Nest Cover	95.00
Staffordshire, Dish, Hen On Nest, Yellow, 3 1/2 In.	35.00
Staffordshire, Dish, Hen On Nest, 6 1/2 In.	135.00
Staffordshire, Dish, Soup, Don Quixote And Sancho Panza, Larsen, 9 In.	160.00
Staffordshire, Dish, Vegetable, Corean, Mulberry Ware, , 7 X 9 In.	75.00
Staffordshire, Dish, Vegetable, Corean, Mulberry Ware, 6 X 8 In.	65.00
Staffordshire, Dish, Vegetable, Cyprus, Covered, Mulberry, 9 In.	125.00
Staffordshire, Dish, Vegetable, Skenectady On The Mohawk River, U.S.	150.00
Staffordshire, Dish, Vegetable, Transfer Design, J.Dimmick & Co.	15.00
Staffordshire, Dish, Vegetable, Vincennes, Covered, Mulberry, 10 In.	135.00
Staffordshire, Dish, Washington Vase, Open, Mulberry, 11 In.	75.00
Staffordshire, Eggcup, Double Ended, Floral Design	8.50
Staffordshire, Figure, Samuel & Eli, C.1850, 11 In.	240.00
Staffordshire, Figurine, Bird On Log, 3 In.	57.50
Staffordshire, Figurine, Bird Perched On Tree Trunk, Signed, 7 1/2 In.	65.00
Staffordshire, Figurine, Boy & Girl On Tree Stump, Basket Of Eggs	55.00
Staffordshire, Figurine, Burns & Mary In Arbor, 12 In.	65.00
Staffordshire, Figurine, Cat, Black, White, Gold Ribbon, 7 In., Pair	65.00
Staffordshire, Figurine, Cat, Brown & White, Glass Eyes, Pair	500.00
Staffordshire, Figurine, Cat, Gray, Glass Eyes, Gold Ribbon, 12 In.	185.00
Staffordshire, Figurine, Cat, Lemon Yellow, 8 In., Pair	57.50
Staffordshire, Figurine, Cat, Sitting, Glass Eyes, No.523391, 11 1/2 In.	185.00

Staffordshire, Dog: *(top)* Poodle, Pink, Pair; *(center)* Poodle & Puppy, 4 1/2 In., Pair and Poodle, Clipped, Pair; *(bottom)* Poodle & Puppy, 3 3/4 In., Pair

Staffordshire, Figurine, Dalmatian, Oval Base, Gold Necklace & Chain, 7 In.		37.50
Staffordshire, Figurine, Dalmatian, Sitting On Haunches, 4 In., Pair		35.00
Staffordshire, Figurine, Dog, Copper Luster, 10 In., Pair		350.00
Staffordshire, Figurine, Dog, Glass Eyes, Pair		200.00
Staffordshire, Figurine, Dog, Paperweight Eyes, Pair, 10 1/2 In.		90.00
Staffordshire, Figurine, Dog, Poodle & Puppy, C.1815, 4 1/2 In., Pair	*Illus*	300.00
Staffordshire, Figurine, Dog, Poodle & Puppy, C.1835, 3 3/4 In., Pair	*Illus*	210.00
Staffordshire, Figurine, Dog, Poodle, Clipped, 3 1/4 In., Pair		320.00
Staffordshire, Figurine, Dog, Poodle, Clipped, 5 3/5 In., Pair	*Illus*	60.00
Staffordshire, Figurine, Dog, Poodle, Pink, 5 1/2 In., Pair	*Illus*	180.00
Staffordshire, Figurine, Dog, Yellow Eyes, Gold Chain & Locket, 12 In., Pr.		295.00
Staffordshire, Figurine, Girl & Cat, 6 In.		35.00
Staffordshire, Figurine, Lady On Horse, Dogs, Thermometer, 6 In.		115.00
Staffordshire, Figurine, Lady, Pink, Crimson Tinting, Mama Impressed, 11 In.		160.00
Staffordshire, Figurine, Lion, Brown Glaze, 9 1/2 X 11 1/2 In.		65.00
Staffordshire, Figurine, Little Red Riding Hood		22.00
Staffordshire, Figurine, Man Talking To Lady, 19th Century, 4 1/2 In.		35.00
Staffordshire, Figurine, Mislabeled Washington, Ben Franklin, C.1820		2000.00
Staffordshire, Figurine, Opening At Base For Watch, 11 In.		65.00
Staffordshire, Figurine, Poodle, Gold Luster Collar, Facing, 5 In., Pair		35.00
Staffordshire, Figurine, Prince Charlie, Astride White Horse, 11 1/2 In.		47.50
Staffordshire, Figurine, Prodigal's Return, 14 1/2 In.		190.00
Staffordshire, Figurine, Reclining Lions, 7 In., Pair		45.00

Staffordshire, Figurine, Seated Dog, 11 1/2 In., Pair	160.00
Staffordshire, Figurine, Sheep, Trunk Flower Holder, C.1810, Pair	250.00
Staffordshire, Figurine, Spaniel, Golden Brown & Tan, 12 In., Pair	395.00
Staffordshire, Figurine, Spaniel, Pebbled, Gold Collar & Lock, 4 3/4 In., Pr.	50.00
Staffordshire, Figurine, Spaniels, Tan & White, Gold Trim, Glass Eyes, 13 In.	155.00
Staffordshire, Figurine, The Shepherdess, Flat Back, 13 In.	75.00
Staffordshire, Figurine, Two Men, Plumed Hats, Cow Over Clock Face	48.50
Staffordshire, Figurine, Uncle Tom & Little Eva, 9 In.	195.00
Staffordshire, Figurine, Whippet, Tan & White, 4 In.	15.00
Staffordshire, Figurine, Woman, Green Dress, Carrying Flowers, 12 1/2 In.	25.00
Staffordshire, Figurine, Wooly Dogs, Cobalt Base, Mother & 2 Pups, 5 1/4 In.	135.00
Staffordshire, Gravy Boat, Burslem, Gilded	15.00
Staffordshire, Holder, Spill, Boy & Girl, Bird & Flowers	40.00
Staffordshire, Holder, Spill, Cow & Calf, Cauliflower Protrusions, Pair	225.00
Staffordshire, Holder, Toothbrush, Beatrice Pattern, C.1875, Brown Transfer	18.00
Staffordshire, Holder, Watch, Castle, 2 Cherubs, Towers, Vines, 10 X 8 In.	115.00
Staffordshire, Holder, Watch, Open Orchid, Tiny Flowers Around Base	65.00
Staffordshire, Holder, Watch, 3 Graces, 11 1/2 X 7 1/2 In.	155.00
Staffordshire, Humidor, Covered, Blue Boar, Tavern Scene, 8 1/2 X 6 1/2 In.	60.00
Staffordshire, Inkstand, Flower Inserts, C.1820, 6 3/4 X 2 3/4 X 2 3/4 In.	70.00
Staffordshire, Inkstand, Reclining Hound On Cobalt Base, Signed With Blue V	110.00
Staffordshire, Inkwell, C.1820, 7 X 2 3/4 In.	120.00
Staffordshire, Inkwell, Two Sanded Poodles, Vase Back	175.00
Staffordshire, Jar, Tobacco, Boot, Black Boy, 11 In. *Illus*	600.00
Staffordshire, Jug, Blue Floral Transfer	55.00
Staffordshire, Jug, Canary Yellow, C.1815, Pair, 5 7/8 In.	300.00
Staffordshire, Jug, Coronation, Blue, Large	220.00
Staffordshire, Jug, Elizabeth Evans, 1831, 3 In.	130.00
Staffordshire, Jug, Yellow Glazed Earthenware, Single Rose, 1820s, 6 7/8 In.	1100.00
Staffordshire, Knob, Mirror, Set Of 6, 18th Century, 1 5/8 To 1 3/4 In.	125.00
Staffordshire, Ladle, Peace, Blue, 1838-41, Child & Lion, 6 In.	38.00
Staffordshire, Mug, Alphabet, Polychrome Decoration	65.00
Staffordshire, Mug, Billy Buttons Journey To Brentford, 2 5/8 In.	125.00
Staffordshire, Mug, Child's, A Present For My Dear Girl, 2 3/4 In.	125.00
Staffordshire, Mug, Child's, ABC, Inscription, Brown On Yellow, 2 3/4 In.	125.00
Staffordshire, Mug, Child's, Blue & White, Mill With Water Wheel; 2 1/2 In.	50.00
Staffordshire, Mug, Child's, Children Playing Game	25.00
Staffordshire, Mug, Child's, Lost Time Is Never Found	95.00
Staffordshire, Mug, Child's, Mother & Children Church Bound, 2 1/4 In.	125.00
Staffordshire, Mug, Child's, Pink & White, 2 1/2 In.	125.00
Staffordshire, Mug, Child's, The Diligent Spinner Has A Large Shift	95.00
Staffordshire, Mug, Child's, 2 Gentlemen In Park, Brown Transfer, 2 1/2 In.	125.00
Staffordshire, Mug, Cries Of London, Set Of 6	50.00
Staffordshire, Mug, Frog	79.00 To 85.00
Staffordshire, Mug, Frog Inside, 5 1/2 In.	35.00
Staffordshire, Mug, Luster, Abraham Lincoln's Head	42.50
Staffordshire, Mug, Toby, Man Standing With Snuff	150.00
Staffordshire, Ornament, Castle, Clock On Turret, Dated 1849, 6 X 6 1/2 In.	75.00
Staffordshire, Pastille Burner, Rockingham, C.1815, 7 In. *Illus*	500.00
Staffordshire, Penholder, Man With Stove Pipe Hat, Basket Holds Quill	10.00
Staffordshire, Pepper Pot, Toby, Fill Hole In Pants, C.1840, 5 1/2 In.	55.00
Staffordshire, Pitcher, Blue & White, 1870, 9 In.	45.00
Staffordshire, Pitcher, Canova, Signed T.Mayer, Green, 5 In.	32.00
Staffordshire, Pitcher, Corean, Mulberry, 13 In.	105.00
Staffordshire, Pitcher, Cream, Boat Shape, Scenic View, 5 X 5 In.	22.50
Staffordshire, Pitcher, Mulberry Ware, Corean, 13 In.	105.00
Staffordshire, Pitcher, Toby, Blue, Polychrome Enameling, 9 1/2 In.	175.00
Staffordshire, Pitcher, Water, Harvest Scene, Farm Tools Border, 1820, Purple	100.00
Staffordshire, Plate, Acorn Border, Park Theatre, New York, 10 In.	225.00
Staffordshire, Plate, Alphabet, Helping Little Brother	45.00
Staffordshire, Plate, American Marine, 9 1/4 In.	35.00
Staffordshire, Plate, American Villa, Dark Blue, 7 1/2 In.	95.00
Staffordshire, Plate, Arms Of New York, Signed, 10 In.Diameter	495.00
Staffordshire, Plate, Arms Of The State Of New York, Marked, 9 7/8 In.	495.00
Staffordshire, Plate, Ashbury Park, N.J., Gray & Blue, 8 1/4 In.	12.50
Staffordshire, Plate, Athens, Mulberry, 10 In.	28.00

Staffordshire, Jar, Tobacco,
Boot, Black Boy, 11 In.

Staffordshire, Pastille Burner,
Rockingham, C.1815, 7 In.

(See Page 571)

(See Page 571)

Staffordshire, Plate, Aurora, Beech Hancock, C.1845, 7 In.	9.50
Staffordshire, Plate, Aurora, D.F.Morley, Mulberry, C.1870, 10 1/4 In.	28.00
Staffordshire, Plate, Baker's Falls, Hudson River, Black, 8 3/4 In.	85.00
Staffordshire, Plate, Battery, New York, Blue, 7 3/4 In.	68.00
Staffordshire, Plate, Blue, Villa, C.1835, 10 1/2 In.	30.00
Staffordshire, Plate, Blue, Winter View Of Pittsfield, Clews, 10 1/2 In.	300.00
Staffordshire, Plate, Boston State House, 10 In.	125.00
Staffordshire, Plate, Buenos Aires, 10 In.	95.00
Staffordshire, Plate, Cadmus Cup, Wood, Trefoil Border	125.00
Staffordshire, Plate, Catskill Mt.House, Adams, Carmine, 10 1/2 In.	72.00
Staffordshire, Plate, City Hall, N.Y., 10 In.	170.00
Staffordshire, Plate, City Of Albany, State Of New York, Dark Blue, 10 In.	295.00
Staffordshire, Plate, Colorado Springs, Blue, 10 In.	28.00
Staffordshire, Plate, Corean, Mulberry, 7 In.	24.00
Staffordshire, Plate, Corean, Mulberry, 7 3/4 In.	24.00
Staffordshire, Plate, Corean, Mulberry, 8 1/2 In.	28.00
Staffordshire, Plate, Corean, Mulberry, 8 3/4 In.	27.00
Staffordshire, Plate, Corean, Mulberry, 9 3/4 In.	40.00
Staffordshire, Plate, Cup, Corean, Mulberry	30.00
Staffordshire, Plate, Dam & Waterworks, Philadelphia, 10 In.	245.00
Staffordshire, Plate, Davenport, 1805-20, Gold Overglaze, 9 1/2 In.	42.00
Staffordshire, Plate, Don Quixote And Sancho Panza, 6 1/4 In.	150.00
Staffordshire, Plate, Eagles, Floral Relief On Rim, C.1800, Marked, 7 In.	75.00
Staffordshire, Plate, Eashing Park, Surrey, 7 In.	25.00
Staffordshire, Plate, Faces Of Montmorenci, Blue, 9 In.	250.00
Staffordshire, Plate, Fairmont At Philadelphia, Blue, 10 In.	145.00
Staffordshire, Plate, Faulkbourn Hall, Dark Blue Transfer, 10 1/4 In.	70.00
Staffordshire, Plate, Fishing Scene, Impressed Clews, 8 7/8 In.	70.00
Staffordshire, Plate, Fishkill, Hudson River, Blue, 10 In.	60.00
Staffordshire, Plate, Flora, C.1840, Thomas Walker, 8 1/2 In.	17.50
Staffordshire, Plate, Franklin Kite, Blue Transfer, 2 In.	75.00
Staffordshire, Plate, Gentlemen's Cabin, Black Transfer, C.1840, 9 In.	30.00
Staffordshire, Plate, Ghaut Of Cutwa, Hall's Oriental Series, 8 X 2 In.	50.00
Staffordshire, Plate, Green, Underglaze, Hybla, Brougham & Mayer, 9 1/2 In.	28.00
Staffordshire, Plate, Hospital, Boston, Blue, 9 In.	225.00
Staffordshire, Plate, Italian Buildings, Blue, 10 In.	22.00
Staffordshire, Plate, John & Priscilla, Floral Border	42.00
Staffordshire, Plate, Landing Of Fathers, Wood, Medium Blue, 8 1/2 In.	90.00
Staffordshire, Plate, Landing Of Lafayette, Blue, 8 In.	225.00
Staffordshire, Plate, Landing Of LaFayette, 6 3/4 In.	185.00
Staffordshire, Plate, Landing Of The Pilgrims, Blue, 1820-40, 10 In.	110.00
Staffordshire, Plate, Landing Of The Pilgrims, Medium Blue, Wood, 8 1/2 In.	110.00
Staffordshire, Plate, Llanarth Court, Monmouthshire, Wood, Dark Blue, 10 In.	55.00
Staffordshire, Plate, Marine Hospital, Louisville, Ky., Dark Blue, 8 3/8 In.	250.00
Staffordshire, Plate, Mohawk Trail, Indian Center, 7 In.	15.00
Staffordshire, Plate, Moulin Sur La Marne A Charenton, 1820-40, 9 1/4 In.	120.00
Staffordshire, Plate, Niagara Falls, Floral Border	42.00
Staffordshire, Plate, Nonpareil, 10 1/2 In.	20.00
Staffordshire, Plate, Oriental Scenery, Blue, 10 In.	85.00
Staffordshire, Plate, Oriental, Ridgway, Green, 9 1/4 In.	27.00
Staffordshire, Plate, Palestine, Adams, Black Transfer, C.1830, 8 In.	29.00
Staffordshire, Plate, Palestine, Adams, 9 1/2 In.	28.00

Staffordshire, Plate, Palestine, Black Transfer, 7 1/4 In. 24.00
Staffordshire, Plate, Palestine, Pink, 8 1/2 In., Pair 66.00
Staffordshire, Plate, Park Theatre, New York, Stevenson, 10 In. 220.00
Staffordshire, Plate, Pass In Catskill Mts., Wood, Dark Blue, 7 1/2 In. 250.00
Staffordshire, Plate, Patrick Henry Delivering His Speech, Brown Transfer 85.00
Staffordshire, Plate, Penn's Treaty, Brown, 7 In. 65.00
Staffordshire, Plate, Peru, Mulberry, 9 3/4 In. 20.00
Staffordshire, Plate, Pink Rim, Black Center, J.Ridgway, C.1835, 9 In. 22.00
Staffordshire, Plate, Playing At Draughts, 7 3/4 In. 115.00
Staffordshire, Plate, Ponte Rotto, Italian Historical, 10 In. 40.00
Staffordshire, Plate, President's House, Washington, Pink, 10 1/4 In. 100.00
Staffordshire, Plate, Quebec, Blue, 9 In. 250.00
Staffordshire, Plate, Raised Eagles, Verse In Center, C.1800, 7 1/4 In. 75.00
Staffordshire, Plate, Sancho And The Priest And The Barber, 7 1/2 In. 150.00
Staffordshire, Plate, Saratoga Scenes, Sailboat Center, 10 In. 30.00
Staffordshire, Plate, Scenic View, Incised Ivory, Mulberry, 10 In. 38.00
Staffordshire, Plate, Scrolls, Leaves, Flowers, Flow Blue, 10 In. 28.00
Staffordshire, Plate, States, Clews, 10 1/2 In. 265.00
Staffordshire, Plate, Temperance Motto, Octagonal 30.00
Staffordshire, Plate, Texian Campaign, Blue, 9 1/2 In. 88.00
Staffordshire, Plate, Texian Campaign, 8 1/4 In. 75.00
Staffordshire, Plate, The Temple, C.1850, Mulberry, 10 In. 32.00
Staffordshire, Plate, Toddy, Boreham House, Essex, Stevenson, 5 3/4 In. 45.00
Staffordshire, Plate, Tyrolean, C.1830-54, 10 1/2 In. 17.00
Staffordshire, Plate, Upper Ferry Bridge, Eagle Border, Stubbs, 8 3/4 In. 185.00
Staffordshire, Plate, View Of Liverpool, American Flag, Blue, 10 In. 250.00
Staffordshire, Plate, Vincennes, 7 1/4 In. 32.00
Staffordshire, Plate, Washington Vase, Mulberry, 8 3/4 In. 25.00
Staffordshire, Plate, Wilkie Series, Christmas Eve, Clews, 6 3/4 In. 175.00
Staffordshire, Plate, Wilkie Series, Christmas Eve, Clews, 9 In., Pair 400.00
Staffordshire, Plate, Wilkie Series, Valentine, Clews, 10 In. 275.00
Staffordshire, Plate, Winter View, Pittsfield, Mass., Blue, Clews, 10 1/2 In. 285.00
Staffordshire, Plate, 1776 Independence Hall, Brown Transfer 85.00
Staffordshire, Platter, Black Transfer, C.1830, 12 1/2 X 14 3/4 In. 150.00
Staffordshire, Platter, Blue Feather Edge, 10 1/4 X 13 In. 12.50
Staffordshire, Platter, Blue, Kenmont Castle, Stevenson, 16 1/2 In. 250.00
Staffordshire, Platter, Canova, Black, Gray, White, Mayer, 15 In. 95.00
Staffordshire, Platter, Clews, Windsor Castle, Crown Mark, 17 1/4 X 13 In. 395.00
Staffordshire, Platter, Corean, Mulberry, 12 X 16 In. 65.00
Staffordshire, Platter, Corean, Mulberry, 13 1/2 X 10 1/2 In. 110.00
Staffordshire, Platter, Corean, Mulberry, 14 In. 75.00
Staffordshire, Platter, Corean, Mulberry, 16 In. 95.00
Staffordshire, Platter, Corean, Mulberry, 16 X 12 1/4 In. 130.00
Staffordshire, Platter, Fruit & Flower Border, Boughton House, 13 In. 225.00
Staffordshire, Platter, Italian Building, C.1830, 12 1/2 X 14 3/4 In. 150.00
Staffordshire, Platter, Jeddo, Mulberry, 15 1/2 In. 55.00
Staffordshire, Platter, Limehouse Dock, Enoch Wood, 14 3/4 In. 335.00
Staffordshire, Platter, London Views, St.George Chapel, Regent St., Wood 130.00
Staffordshire, Platter, Mulberry, Woodlands, 11 3/4 X 9 1/2 In. 45.00
Staffordshire, Platter, Oval, Scenic, Pink, 12 In. 25.00
Staffordshire, Platter, St.Charles Church, R.Hall, 19 In. .... *Illus* 300.00
Staffordshire, Platter, The Villagers, Blue, 16 3/4 X 13 In. 110.00
Staffordshire, Platter, Tyrolean, Ridgway, Green Scenic, 1820-40, 14 3/4 In. 75.00
Staffordshire, Platter, Views Of Church & School, R.Hall, 19 X 14 1/2 In. 245.00
Staffordshire, Platter, Villa, Pink, Marked JR 45.00
Staffordshire, Platter, Vincennes, Mulberry, 17 1/2 X 13 1/2 In. 75.00

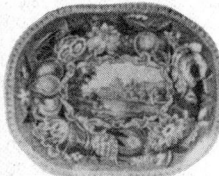

Staffordshire, Platter, St.Charles Church, R.Hall, 19 In.

Staffordshire, **Platter,** Windsor Castle, C.1810-32, 20 1/2 X 30 In.	525.00
Staffordshire, **Punch Pot,** Cover, Elijah Mayer, 1790-1804, 6 3/4 In.	375.00
Staffordshire, **Relish,** Cyprus Shell, Mulberry Ware	40.00
Staffordshire, **Salt Shaker,** Toby, Brown Suited, 1800s, 5 In.	38.00
Staffordshire, **Saucer,** Corean, Mulberry	40.00
Staffordshire, **Soup,** Dish, Meeting Of Sancho And Dapple, 8 3/4 In.	165.00
Staffordshire, **Soup,** Dish, Oriental, Mulberry Ware, 9 In.	20.00
Staffordshire, **Soup,** Dish, Sancho Meets Dapple, 8 3/4 In.	155.00
Staffordshire, **Soup,** Dish, Sancho Panza At The Boar Hunt, 9 3/4 In.	165.00
Staffordshire, **Soup,** Dish, Table Rock, Niagara, Blue	275.00
Staffordshire, **States Plate,** Clews, 10 In.	250.00
Staffordshire, **Sugar & Creamer & Plate,** Sepia Transfer, C.1840, 5 1/4 In.	24.00
Staffordshire, **Sugar & Creamer,** Jenny Lind, Pink & White	45.00
Staffordshire, **Sugar & Milk Pitcher,** Blue Transfer, Palestine, C.1875, 8 In.	95.00
Staffordshire, **Sugar Bowl,** Transfer Portrait, Impressed Mark, C.1862	35.00
Staffordshire, **Sugar,** Covered, Blue & White, Pippin Pattern	19.50
Staffordshire, **Sugar,** Covered, White Ribbed, C.1830	45.00
Staffordshire, **Tea Set,** Child's, Clyde, 1860-72, 17 Piece	275.00
Staffordshire, **Tea Set,** Child's, Davenport, 19 Piece	100.00
Staffordshire, **Tea Set,** Child's, Italy, Edge Malkin 1873, 17 Piece	250.00
Staffordshire, **Teapot,** Blue & Red Swag, Rim Footed, Lid, C.1800	175.00
Staffordshire, **Teapot,** Corean, Walker, Mulberry	175.00
Staffordshire, **Teapot,** Franklin's Tomb, Phillips, Spout Chip .... *Illus*	400.00
Staffordshire, **Toby Mug,** Admiral Nelson, Tree Forms Handle, C.1830, 11 In.	475.00
Staffordshire, **Toby Mug,** Beefeater, 9 5/8 In.	32.00
Staffordshire, **Toby Mug,** King Neptune, 7 1/4 In.	42.00

Staffordshire, Teapot, Franklin's Tomb, Phillips, Spout Chip

Staffordshire, **Toby Mug,** Punch & Judy, Seated, Removable Hat, 12 In., Pair	295.00
Staffordshire, **Toby,** John Hull, Full Figure, 5 In.	25.00
Staffordshire, **Toby,** Pepper Pot, Man's Breeches Hold Mug, 5 1/2 In.	55.00
Staffordshire, **Toby,** Snuff Holder, Gray Hair, 19th Century, 9 1/2 In.	195.00
Staffordshire, **Tureen,** Castle Scene, Medium Blue, Covered, Handled	400.00
Staffordshire, **Tureen,** Covered, Platter, Lake Pattern, 14 X 8 In.	137.50
Staffordshire, **Tureen,** Fort Ticonderoga, Jackson, Covered, Mulberry	145.00
Staffordshire, **Tureen,** Gravy, Gypsy, 8 Sided, 5 1/2 In.	115.00
Staffordshire, **Tureen,** Gravy, Holly & Berry Border, Scenery, 7 1/2 X 6 In.	65.00
Staffordshire, **Tureen,** Gravy, Thorn Pattern, C.1872	25.00
Staffordshire, **Tureen,** Sauce, Corean, Mulberry	95.00
Staffordshire, **Tureen,** Sauce, Lid, Ladle, Tray, Dyber, Meir, Mulberry	125.00
Staffordshire, **Tureen,** Soup, Chinese Birds, Brown, White, Davenport, 10 In.	245.00
Staffordshire, **Tureen,** Soup, Covered, Aladdin, Tray, 12 1/2 In.	235.00
Staffordshire, **Tureen,** Soup, Thorn Pattern, C.1872	65.00
Staffordshire, **Vase,** Cobalt Blue, Floral Decoration, 3 In., Pair	53.00
Staffordshire, **Vase,** Mother Goose, C.1910	75.00
Staffordshire, **Vase,** Spill, Cow & Calf	95.00
Staffordshire, **Vase,** Spill, Yellow Glazed Earthenware, Marked, 4 7/8 In.	250.00
Staffordshire, **Vase,** Washington, Mulberry, 13 In.	100.00
Staffordshire, **Vegetable,** Brown Leaf, Fern Transfer, J.Dimmick	13.50
Staffordshire, **Vegetable,** Covered, Handles, Flower Finial, Marked, 7 X 10 In.	85.00
Staffordshire, **Vegetable,** Pink, Acropolis, Open, 10 1/4 X 8 1/4 In.	58.00
Staffordshire, **Wash Set,** Bowl, Pitcher, Toothbrush Vase, Cobalt	250.00
Stained Glass, see Windowpane	

 Stangl pottery was organized in 1929, succeeding the Fulper Pottery Company. Stangl porcelain birds are popular collectibles.

Stangl, Bird, Bird Of Paradise, No.3408, 5 1/2 In.	45.00 To 85.00
Stangl, Bird, Blue Headed Vireo, No.3448, Blue Stamp, Signed, 4 1/4 In.	32.00

Stangl, Bird, Bluebird, No.3276, 5 In.	45.00
Stangl, Bird, Bluebirds, No.3276D, 8 1/2 In.	38.00
Stangl, Bird, Broadtail Hummingbird, No.3626, Yellow & Blue, 6 In.	37.50
Stangl, Bird, Cardinal, Gray	15.00
Stangl, Bird, Cerulean Warbler, No.3456, Marked, 4 1/4 In.	28.00
Stangl, Bird, Chestnut-Sided Warbler, No.3812, 4 In.	50.00
Stangl, Bird, Cockatoo, No.3405, 6 In.	22.00 To 30.00
Stangl, Bird, Cockatoo, No.3580, 9 In.	75.00 To 85.00
Stangl, Bird, Cockatoo, No.3584, Signed Jacob, 12 In.	135.00
Stangl, Bird, Cockatoos, No.3405D, 9 1/2 In.	50.00 To 100.00
Stangl, Bird, Group Of Goldfinches, No.3635, 4 X 11 1/2 In.	120.00
Stangl, Bird, Hen, Yellow, No.3446, 7 In.	37.50
Stangl, Bird, Hummingbirds, No.3599D, 8 X 10 1/2 In.	75.00 To 160.00
Stangl, Bird, Kentucky Warbler, No.3598, 3 In.	25.00
Stangl, Bird, Lovebird, No.3400, Gold, Green Ground, Rose Breast, 4 In.	30.00
Stangl, Bird, Oriole, No.3402, 3 1/4 In.	18.00 To 30.00
Stangl, Bird, Orioles, No.3402D, 5 1/2 In.	55.00
Stangl, Bird, Painted Bunting, No.3452, 5 In.	50.00
Stangl, Bird, Parakeets, No.3582D, 7 In.	55.00
Stangl, Bird, Parula Warbler, No.3583, 4 3/4 In.	24.00
Stangl, Bird, Prothonatary Warbler, No.3447, 5 In.	35.00 To 45.00
Stangl, Bird, Red-Faced Warbler, No.3594, 3 In.	35.00
Stangl, Bird, Redstarts, No.3490D, 9 In.	75.00
Stangl, Bird, Rieffers Hummingbird, No.3628, 4 1/2 In.	85.00
Stangl, Bird, Rivoli Hummingbird, No.3627, 6 In.	90.00
Stangl, Bird, Rooster, No.3445, Yellow, 9 In.	37.50
Stangl, Bird, Rufous Hummingbird, No.3585, 3 In.	35.00
Stangl, Bird, Titmouse, No.3592, 2 1/2 In.	18.00
Stangl, Bird, Wilson Warbler, No.3597, 3 1/2 In.	18.00 To 25.00
Stangl, Bird, Wren, No.3401, 3 1/2 In.	18.00 To 25.00
Stangl, Pitcher, Tilt, Green, 7 1/2 In.	7.00
Stangl, Planter, Figural, Bust Of Woman, Art Deco, 7 X 7 In.	20.00
Stangl, Vase, Cornucopia, Terra Rose, 10 1/2 X 13 In.	25.00

Star Holly is a milk glass type of glass made by the Imperial Glass Company of Bellaire, Ohio, in 1957. The pieces were made to look like Wedgwood jasperware. White holly leaves appear against colored borders of blue, green, or rust. It is marked on the bottom of every piece.

Star Holly, Plate, Green, 10 In.	55.00

Steins have been used for over 500 years. They have been made of ivory, porcelain, stoneware, faience, silver, pewter, wood, or glass in sizes up to nine gallons. Although some were made by Meissen, Capo-Di-Monte, and other famous factories, most were made in Germany. The words Geschutz or Musterschutz on a stein are the German for patented or registered design, not company names.

Stein, Apostle, Stoneware, Glazed Figures, C.1909	175.00
Stein, Art Nouveau, Etched, Inlay Lid, 2 Liter	165.00
Stein, Artillery Shell, Marked J.Reinemann, Munich	350.00
Stein, Barrel Shape, Die Kehl Kost Veel	75.00
Stein, Bowling Pin Shape, Musterschutz, Signed	350.00
Stein, Character, Skull, Bisque, Pewter Thumbpiece, 4 3/8 In.	265.00
Stein, Commemorative, George Washingon, Musical	27.50
Stein, Double Face, Skull & Bones, Incised Anchor, 4 3/4 In.	385.00
Stein, German Officer's, Bismarck, Baltimore, 1/2 Liter	145.00
Stein, German, Bull's-Eye Cut Glass, Pewter Top, Dated 1883, 1/2 Liter	85.00
Stein, German, Clear Ribbed Glass, Pewter Lid, Enameled Top, 1802	120.00
Stein, German, Deutsches Trunfest 1908, Frankfurt, 1/2 Liter	110.00
Stein, German, Fox Handle, Hunter Lid, 2 Liter, 17 1/2 In.	100.00
Stein, German, No.1038, 1/2 Liter, Man & Woman, Dragons	75.00
Stein, German, Pewter Domed Lid & Thumb Rest, 5 Liter, Signed, 21 In.	180.00
Stein, German, Pewter Top, Dated 1913, German Writing	125.00
Stein, German, 1/2 Liter, Schlitz, 537 S.Main.L.A., Cal.	60.00
Stein, Geschutzt, No.802, 1/2 Liter, Musical Instruments	90.00
Stein, Geschutzt, No.9734, 1/2 Liter, 3 Men Pulling Beer Cask	105.00
Stein, Glass, Man On Lid, Student Prince, Springfield, Massachusetts	45.00

Stein, Hunting Club Coat Of Arms, Gray, Salt Glaze, Pewter Lid	60.00
Stein, Lion's Head, Blue, Pewter Lid	20.00
Stein, Lithophane Bottom, Blue Onion, Pewter, 6 1/2 In.	195.00
Stein, Lithophane, Buildings, Porcelain	70.00
Stein, Lithophane, Town Scene, Porcelain	70.00
Stein, Lithophane, 1/2 Liter, Munich Maid	145.00
Stein, Merkel Boch & Wick, 1/2 Liter	85.00
Stein, Merkel, Boch & Wick, 2 Liter, Hand-Painted	150.00
Stein, Mettlach, see Mettlach, Stein	
Stein, Monk Scene, 1/2 Liter, Columbian Art Pottery	45.00
Stein, Monk, Cobalt Blue & Gray Stoneware, 6 7/8 In.	165.00
Stein, Monk, Lithophane Bottom, 7 In.	250.00
Stein, Monkeys & Skull, No.1257, 5 Liter	400.00
Stein, Monks, Lenox	250.00
Stein, Munich Child, 1/2 Liter, Buff Ground, Holding Book	95.00
Stein, Munich Maid, J.Reinemann Munchen, 1/2 Liter	170.00
Stein, Munich Maid, 1/4 Liter, Hand-Painted	45.00
Stein, Musterschutz, Bicycle, Lithophane	325.00
Stein, Musterschutz, Bismark	600.00
Stein, Musterschutz, Cat With Hangover	550.00
Stein, Musterschutz, Drunken Monkey	450.00
Stein, Musterschutz, Happy & Unhappy Radish, Pair	800.00
Stein, Musterschutz, Happy Radish, 1/2 Liter	450.00
Stein, Musterschutz, L.A.W. Bicycle, 1/2 Liter	450.00
Stein, Musterschutz, Law	450.00
Stein, Musterschutz, No.459, Van Holte	850.00
Stein, Musterschutz, Pewter Lid, Scenic Cameo, 1/2 Liter	105.00
Stein, Musterschutz, Sad Radish, Pewter Mounted Lid, 6 3/4 In.	300.00
Stein, Musterschutz, Sad Radish, 1/2 Liter	450.00
Stein, Musterschutz, Seated Ram	650.00
Stein, Musterschutz, Singing Pig, 1/2 Liter	450.00
Stein, Musterschutz, Smoking Pig, 1/2 Liter	450.00
Stein, Musterschutz, Village Dancers Cameo, 1/2 Liter	125.00
Stein, Nun, Lithophane Bottom, 7 In.	250.00
Stein, Pabst Brewing Co., 5 Gnomes Holding Beer Mugs, Theumler Mfg.	95.00
Stein, Paneled Blown Glass, Brass Cover & Thumblift, Figural Elf, 1 Liter	65.00
Stein, Pewter Cover, German Folk On Front, Bark Handle, Signed, 11 In.	95.00
Stein, Pewter Lid, Engraved In German, Troubadour Blowing Horn, 10 1/2 In.	45.00
Stein, Porcelain, Goose Man Of Nuremberg, I Liter	550.00
Stein, Porcelain, Hand-Painted Lid, Eagle Thumblift, Dated 1871	125.00
Stein, Pottery, Dwarfs Drinking, 1/2 Liter	100.00
Stein, Pottery, Dwarfs On Lid, 1/2 Liter	75.00
Stein, Puzzle Jug, Faience, French, Late 1800's	225.00
Stein, Regimental, Dated 1911, Germany	135.00
Stein, Regimental, World War I, Removable Lid, Jewel Under Lid, Lithophane	475.00
Stein, Regimental, 23rd, Bavarian Infantry, Decorated For A Drummer	225.00
Stein, Regimental, 28th Saxon Artillery	225.00
Stein, Salt Glaze, Music Box, 1/2 Liter	85.00
Stein, Skull, 1/2 Liter	325.00
Stein, Stone Mason, Pewter Top, Lithophane	135.00
Stein, Stoneware, Hand-Painted, 1 Liter	85.00
Stein, Stoneware, 1/2 Liter, Pewter Pagoda Lid, Marked T.W.	200.00
Stein, Tankard, Deutsches Turnfest, Open Winged German Falcon, Crest, 1863	35.00
Stein, Wood, Hand Carved, Bulldog Chained To Doghouse, 10 1/2 In.	185.00
Stein, 1/2 Liter, Skeleton Head On Book	400.00
Stein, 3-Panel, Peasant Scenes, C.1890, Pewter Top & Thumblift, 1 1/2 Liter	80.00
Stein, 4 Playing Cards In Relief, Gold Trim, Marked & Numbered	190.00

Stereo cards that were made for stereopticon viewers became popular after 1840. Two almost identical pictures were mounted on a stiff cardboard backing so that, when viewed through a stereoscope, a three-dimensional picture could be seen.

Stereo, Card, Agriculture, Set Of 15	8.00
Stereo, Card, Animals & Birds, Set Of 12	8.00
Stereo, Card, Black, Set Of 6	5.00
Stereo, Card, British Isles, Set Of 16	8.00

Stereo, Card, Children With Dolls & Toys, Set Of 8	12.00
Stereo, Card, Comic & Sentimental, Set Of 10	6.00
Stereo, Card, Industry, Set Of 15	9.00
Stereo, Card, Ingersal Colored Travel Views, Set Of 500	49.50
Stereo, Card, Italy, Set Of 11	6.00
Stereo, Card, Jerusalem, Palestine & The Holy Land, Set Of 100	39.50
Stereo, Card, Keystone Imperial, Anatomy Of Head & Neck, 136 Views	90.00
Stereo, Card, McKinley Cortege	1.50
Stereo, Card, McKinley's Blue Room	1.50
Stereo, Card, Mexico, Set Of 10	9.00
Stereo, Card, New England Mountains, Set Of 12	7.00
Stereo, Card, Niagara Falls, Set Of 7	5.00
Stereo, Card, Niagara, Set Of 20	10.00
Stereo, Card, Palestine, Set Of 15	7.00
Stereo, Card, President Grant & Family, 1872	15.00
Stereo, Card, Spanish, American War, Set Of 10	8.00
Stereo, Card, St.Louis Fair, Color, 1904, Set Of 20	40.00
Stereo, Card, Switzerland, Set Of 12	7.00
Stereo, Card, W.W.I, Set Of 23	11.00
Stereo, Card, Watkins Glen, Set Of 12	7.00
Stereo, Card, World War I, Set Of 8	8.00
Stereo, General Sherman	35.00
Stereo, Lincoln	85.00
Stereo, Queen Victoria	35.00
Stereo, Slide, 1876 Centennial Exhibition, Philadelphia, Set Of 35	200.00
Stereo, Wild Bill Hickok	42.00

Stereoscopes, or stereopticons, were used for viewing the stereo cards. The hand viewer was invented by Oliver Wendell Holmes, although more complicated table models were used before his was placed in production in 1859.

Stereoscope, Fairchild F-71, Magnifying, Instructions & Case	65.00
Stereoscope, Keystone, Eye Comfort, View Cards, Instructions	50.00
Stereoscope, Viewer, Becker's, In Cabinet, C.1859	240.00
Stereoscope, Viewer, Table, Standing, With Graphoscope	95.00
Stereoscope, Viewmaster, 92 View Cards	75.00

Sterling Silver, see Silver, Sterling

Steuben glass was made at the Steuben Glass Works of Corning, New York. The factory, founded by Frederick Carder and T.C.Hawkes, Sr., was purchased by the Corning Glass Company. They continued to make glass called Steuben. Many types of art glass were made at Steuben. The firm is still producing glass of exceptional quality.

Steuben, see also Aurene

Steuben, Ashtray, Aurene, 3 Cornered, Signed	285.00
Steuben, Atomizer, Aurene, 9 1/2 In.	195.00
Steuben, Ball, Crystal, Wave Base Of Sterling Silver, Signed, 5 1/2 In.	800.00
Steuben, Base, Bud, Verre De Soie, Swirl Design, 4 1/4 In.	325.00
Steuben, Base, Lamp, Smoked Crystal Over Brown Jade, No.3-6094, 12 In.	275.00
Steuben, Basket, Calcite, Lined With Gold Aurene, Fluted Rim	450.00
Steuben, Basket, Intaglio Sunflowers, St.Louis Diamond Handle, 15 1/2 In.	245.00
Steuben, Basket, Verre De Soie, Handle, 11 X 8 1/2 In.Diameter	250.00
Steuben, Bonbon, Green Swirled Crystal, 4 Sided, Green, Signed, 2 3/4 In.	35.00
Steuben, Bonbon, Yellow Ribbed & Flared Bowl, 2 1/2 X 5 In.Diameter	45.00
Steuben, Bookends, Gazelle, Signed	200.00
Steuben, Boot, Drinking, Clear, 15 In.	275.00
Steuben, Bottle, Cologne, Black Reeds, Stopper, Crystal, Fleur-De-Lis, Signed	125.00
Steuben, Bottle, Cologne, Blue Aurene, Signed, 7 3/4 In., Pair	575.00
Steuben, Bottle, Cologne, Blue Swirled Crystal, Signed, 5 In.	85.00
Steuben, Bottle, Cologne, Green Swirled Crystal, Signed, 5 In.	85.00
Steuben, Bottle, Cologne, Lavender Swirled Crystal, Signed	85.00
Steuben, Bottle, Perfume, Alabaster Flame Stopper & Pedestal, 7 3/4 In.	195.00
Steuben, Bottle, Perfume, Bird Stopper, Pair	32.00
Steuben, Bottle, Perfume, Original Stopper, 7 3/4 In.	95.00
Steuben, Bottle, Perfume, Rosaline, Alabaster Foot, Stopper, Signed, 8 In.	195.00
Steuben, Bottle, Perfume, Rosaline, Alabaster Stopper, Signed, 7 In.	225.00

Steuben, Bottle, Perfume, Rosaline, 4 3/4 In. 250.00
Steuben, Bottle, Perfume, Rose Lavender, Blue Stopper, 5 In. 145.00
Steuben, Bowl, Acid But Back, Art Deco, Stylized Flowers, 7 X 7 In. 825.00
Steuben, Bowl, Acid Cut, Geometric Floral & Leaves, Signed, 7 X 8 In. 1800.00
Steuben, Bowl, Amber, Aurene & Calcite, Ruffled Rim, Ovoid, 1902-32, 5 1/2 In. 175.00
Steuben, Bowl, Amethyst, Flint, Pontil, Crimped Rim, Signed, 11 3/4 X 4 In. 400.00
Steuben, Bowl, Aurene, Blue Iridescence, Urn Shape, Signed, 5 1/2 X 10 In. 595.00
Steuben, Bowl, Aurene, Calcite, 10 In. 175.00
Steuben, Bowl, Aurene, Triangular Shape, Green Feathering, Signed, Small 650.00
Steuben, Bowl, Aurene, Urn Shape, Iridescent, Blue, Signed, 5 1/2 X 10 In. 595.00
Steuben, Bowl, Blue Aurene, Footed, Signed, 2 1/2 X 10 In.Diameter 625.00
Steuben, Bowl, Calcite, Gold Aurene Lining, 7 In.Diameter 145.00
Steuben, Bowl, Calcite, Gold Interior, 10 In. 195.00
Steuben, Bowl, Calcite, Gold Lining, 10 X 2 3/4 In. 185.00
Steuben, Bowl, Calcite, Iridescent Gold Lining, 10 X 2 3/4 In. 185.00
Steuben, Bowl, Calcite, Iridescent, Pinched Rim, 6 In. 395.00
Steuben, Bowl, Calcite, Orange, Bronze, Gold Lining, 10 X 2 3/4 In. 175.00
Steuben, Bowl, Calcite, Pinched Rim, Iridescence, 6 In.Diameter 358.00
Steuben, Bowl, Calcite, Turned Down Stretched Rim, Aurene, 14 In. 295.00
Steuben, Bowl, Candy, Calcite, Silver Plate Holder 110.00
Steuben, Bowl, Celeste Blue, Turned Down Rim, 11 X 3 1/4 In. 95.00
Steuben, Bowl, Centerpiece, Rosaline, 12 X 5 In. 275.00
Steuben, Bowl, Centerpiece, Silenium Red, Bronze Holder, 20 In. 165.00
Steuben, Bowl, Centerpiece, Topaz, Celeste Blue Rim, Signed, 10 1/4 In. 65.00
Steuben, Bowl, Centerpiece, Yellow-Green, Signed, 5 X 12 1/4 In.Diameter 60.00
Steuben, Bowl, Double Ball Stem, Flute Paneled, Signed, 7 In.Diameter 45.00
Steuben, Bowl, Electric Blue, Spider Web-Like Threads, Signed, 4 1/2 In. 85.00
Steuben, Bowl, Etched Grapes, Signed, 7 1/2 In.Diameter 48.50
Steuben, Bowl, Finger, Thistle Pattern, Clear, Signed 35.00
Steuben, Bowl, Finger, Underplate Set, Pale Green, Set Of 3 .... 25.00
Steuben, Bowl, Finger, Underplate, Ribs Form Scalloped Edge, Lead, Set Of 10 ..... 225.00
Steuben, Bowl, Finger, Underplate, Selenium Red, Crystal 25.00
Steuben, Bowl, Gold Aurene & Calcite, Flared 195.00
Steuben, Bowl, Gold Aurene Interior, Stretch Finish, 10 3/4 X 2 1/4 In. 145.00
Steuben, Bowl, Gold Calcite, Cased Glass, 12 1/2 In.Diameter 200.00
Steuben, Bowl, Green To Clear, Grotesque, Signed, 6 X 12 X 7 In. 195.00
Steuben, Bowl, Ivorene, Based, 5 In. 55.00
Steuben, Bowl, Ivorene, Flared, 2 1/4 X 5 1/2 In.Diameter 55.00
Steuben, Bowl, Light Blue Jade, Signed, 6 In.Diameter 525.00
Steuben, Bowl, Molded, Hand Finished, Jet Black, Signed, No.6890, 12 In. 145.00
Steuben, Bowl, Polished Pontil, Flaring Mouth, Cobalt, 3 X 12 In.Diameter 120.00
Steuben, Bowl, Red Reeding, No.6640, 12 In.Diameter 40.00
Steuben, Bowl, Rolled Rim, Selenium Red, 2 1/2 X 13 In. 65.00
Steuben, Bowl, Rosaline, Alabaster Foot, Signed, 3 X 8 In.Diameter 115.00
Steuben, Bowl, Round, Calcite, Gold Lining, 2 In.Deep 50.00
Steuben, Bowl, Verre De Soie, Etched Florals, Wide Amber Rim, 10 In. 155.00
Steuben, Bowl, Verre De Soie, 12 In.Diameter .... 58.00 To 60.00
Steuben, Bucket, Ice, 2 Blue Rings Applied At Top, Amber, Marked, 6 1/2 In. 135.00
Steuben, Cake Stand, Pedestal, Blue, 10 In.Diameter 85.00
Steuben, Candelabra, 2 Light, Art Deco, Signed, 10 In. 150.00
Steuben, Candleholder & Center Compote, Selenium Red, Fruit On All Pieces 485.00
Steuben, Candleholder, Domed Base, Threaded, Controlled Bubbles, 3 In.Pair 95.00
Steuben, Candleholder, Melon Half Shape, Signed, 4 1/8 In.Diameter, Pair 295.00
Steuben, Candleholder, Rock Crystal, Amethyst, 14 In., Pair 175.00
Steuben, Candleholder, Signed, 2 1/4 X 5 1/4 In.Diameter 60.00
Steuben, Candlestick, Amethyst & Topaz, 12 1/4 In., Pair 450.00
Steuben, Candlestick, Aurene, Blue, Signed, 12 In., Pair 1450.00
Steuben, Candlestick, Blue & Topaz, Marked, 10 In., Pair 185.00
Steuben, Candlestick, Bristol Yellow, Signed, 4 In. 50.00
Steuben, Candlestick, Diagonal Swirl, Prunted Middle, Signed, 3 3/4 In. 45.00
Steuben, Candlestick, Green Swirled Crystal, Signed, 4 1/2 In., Pair 125.00
Steuben, Candlestick, Prunted Middle, Green Swirl, Signed, 3 3/4 In. 45.00
Steuben, Candlestick, Quilted Foot, Pink Reeding, Signed, 6 In., Pair 200.00
Steuben, Candlestick, Twisted Stem, Green, Polished Pontil, 10 In., Pair 165.00
Steuben, Candlestick, Verre De Soie, Twisted Stem, 10 In.Tall 100.00
Steuben, Centerpiece, Amethyst, Turned Down Rim, No.3579, 13 1/2 In. 60.00

Steuben, Centerpiece, Clear To Cerise, No.7091, Signed, 11 X 7 In. 195.00
Steuben, Centerpiece, Grotesque, Clear To Cerise, Signed, 7 X 11 In. 200.00
Steuben, Centerpiece, Grotesque, No.7091, Signed, 12 X 9 1/4 X 6 1/2 In. 75.00
Steuben, Centerpiece, Ivory Pedestal, Pillars, 7 1/2 X 6 1/2 X 6 In. 225.00
Steuben, Champagne, Clear Stems, Folded Rim Base, 4 1/2 In. 13.50
Steuben, Champagne, Gold, Blue & Red 225.00
Steuben, Chandelier, Brass, 5 Signed Ivorene Shades 450.00
Steuben, Compote, Alabaster Base, Jade Green, 4 X 12 In.Diameter 145.00
Steuben, Compote, Alabaster, Jade, 8 X 3 X 2 In. 75.00
Steuben, Compote, Amber Crystal, Turquoise Stripes, 2 3/4 X 6 In. 145.00
Steuben, Compote, Aurene, Signed, 6 X 8 In.Diameter 550.00
Steuben, Compote, Aurene, Swelled Stem & Flat Foot, Etched Aurene 2642 .... 225.00
Steuben, Compote, Black Edging, Pedestal Base, 7 3/4 X 8 1/4 In.Diameter 90.00
Steuben, Compote, Black Reeding, Signed, 2 3/4 X 6 In.Diameter 60.00
Steuben, Compote, Black Reeding, 3 3/4 In. 55.00
Steuben, Compote, Blue Aurene, Signed, 10 In. 425.00
Steuben, Compote, Braided Stem, Green, 6 In. 85.00
Steuben, Compote, Bubbly, Ruffled Reeded Rim, Teardrop Stem, Signed, 5 In. 75.00
Steuben, Compote, Calcite, Blue, Iridescent, White Stem, 6 In. 550.00
Steuben, Compote, Gold & Calcite, Turned Down Rim, 3 X 5 1/2 In. 175.00
Steuben, Compote, Gold & Calcite, Turned Over Rim, No.5090, 5 1/2 In. 135.00
Steuben, Compote, Gold Aurene, Blue On Foot, Signed, 7 X 8 In. 595.00
Steuben, Compote, Green, Braided Stem, 6 In. 85.00
Steuben, Compote, Low, Calcite, Blue, 4 1/2 X 6 1/2 In.Diameter 500.00
Steuben, Compote, Oriental Jade, Opalescent Braided Stem & Base, 7 X 7 In. 650.00
Steuben, Compote, Ribbed Topaz, Green Stem, Signed, 8 In. 75.00
Steuben, Compote, Rosaline, Alabaster Stem & Base, 6 X 3 In. 255.00
Steuben, Compote, Ruffled Threaded Top, Controlled Bubbles, 5 1/2 X 8 In. 95.00
Steuben, Compote, Topaz, 3 X 6 In.Diameter 45.00
Steuben, Compote, Vintage Pattern, Teardrop Stem, 6 1/4 X 6 1/2 In. 85.00
Steuben, Compote, White Jade, Black Edging At Pip, Ovington Label, 7 3/4 In. 125.00
Steuben, Console Set, Candlesticks & Bowl, Amber, Signed 250.00
Steuben, Cordial, Gold Aurene, Twist Stem, Signed 150.00
Steuben, Cordial, Topaz, Blue Rim & Applied Prunts, Signed, 5 3/4 In., Pair 90.00
Steuben, Cruet Set, Joined, Sterling Overlay, Black Stopper & Handle, Signed 89.00
Steuben, Cruet, Oil & Vinegar, Sterling Top, Signed Hawkes 150.00
Steuben, Cup & Saucer, Blue Jade, Alabaster Handle, Set 145.00
Steuben, Cup & Saucer, Demitasse, Verre De Soie 85.00
Steuben, Cup & Saucer, Green Jade, Alabaster Ring Handle, Set 85.00
Steuben, Cup & Saucer, Rosaline With Alabaster Handle 110.00
Steuben, Cup, Loving, 4 Handles, Flares From Base To Top, Signed, 5 In. 750.00
Steuben, Cup, Punch, Handled, Amber & Blue, Set Of 5 .... 120.00
Steuben, Darner, Aurene, Blue 110.00
Steuben, Dish, Butter, Blue Knob, Signed 75.00
Steuben, Dish, Candy, Aurene, Signed, 6 In. .... 155.00 To 175.00
Steuben, Dish, Candy, Rosaline To Alabaster, 3 X 6 In. 200.00
Steuben, Dish, Candy, Royal Blue Jade, Signed, 6 1/2 X 8 1/4 In. 1250.00
Steuben, Dish, Caviar, Gold Iridescence, Signed, 3 X 6 In.Diameter 395.00
Steuben, Dish, Circular, Calcite, Amber Iridescent Interior, 5 3/4 In. 95.00
Steuben, Dish, Salt, Ruffled, Green, Signed 26.50
Steuben, Egg With Ovoid Bubble, On Aluminum Ring, Signed, 4 In. 285.00
Steuben, Figurine, Arctic Fisherman, Silver Mounted, Ice Block, 6 1/4 In. 1300.00
Steuben, Figurine, Cat, Clear, Green Eyes, Signed, 6 In. 130.00
Steuben, Figurine, Ice Hunter, Silver Mounted, Ice Arch, Fitted Case, 6 In. 1600.00
Steuben, Figurine, Mermaid Standing On Sea Shell, Marked, 10 1/2 In. 95.00
Steuben, Figurine, Owl, Signed, Clear 195.00
Steuben, Figurine, Snail, Crystal, 3 1/4 In. 68.00
Steuben, Figurines, Pheasants, Cut Glass, Pair 1800.00
Steuben, Fixture, Light, Hanging, Calcite, Medallions, Brass Hardware 140.00
Steuben, Glass, Black Reeding, Clear, Signed, 2 1/2 In. 22.00
Steuben, Glass, Cordial, Selenium Red, 4 1/2 In. 30.00
Steuben, Glass, Whiskey, Pomona Green Reeding, 2 1/2 Ounce 35.00
Steuben, Goblet, Alabaster Pedestal, Rosaline 150.00
Steuben, Goblet, Braided Alabaster Stem, Green Top, 8 In. 85.00
Steuben, Goblet, Bristol Yellow, Purple Swirled Stem, Signed, 5 1/4 In. 75.00
Steuben, Goblet, Bubbles, Green Reeding, Clear, 9 In. 65.00

Steuben, Goblet, Cintra Braided Stem, Opalescent Top	110.00
Steuben, Goblet, Clear Bubbly, Pomona, Green Reeding, Signed, 9 In.Tall	65.00
Steuben, Goblet, Emerald Green, Swirl Bowl, Clear Stem, Signed	45.00
Steuben, Goblet, Fleur-De-Lis Intaglio Cut, Square Base, 6 In.	255.00
Steuben, Goblet, Gray Bowl, Amethyst Stem, Set Of 7	100.00
Steuben, Goblet, Iridescence, Aurene, Signed, 6 3/8 In.	225.00
Steuben, Goblet, Opalescent Stem & Foot, Oriental Poppy, 8 1/4 In.	225.00
Steuben, Goblet, Pedestal, Selenium Red, Double Ball Stem, Signed, 6 3/4 In.	50.00
Steuben, Goblet, Pomona, Green Reeding, Signed, 9 In.	65.00
Steuben, Goblet, Purple Swirled Stem, Signed, 8 1/2 In.	75.00
Steuben, Goblet, Red Cut To Clear, 10 In.	195.00
Steuben, Goblet, Reeded Bowl, Optic Twist Stem, Signed, 5 1/2 In., Pair	95.00
Steuben, Goblet, Rosaline, Alabaster Base	250.00
Steuben, Goblet, Selenium Red, Wafer Stem, Ribbed Body	43.00
Steuben, Goblet, Twisted Alabaster Stem & Base, Copper Wheel Cut, Jade	195.00
Steuben, Goblet, Water, Green Jade & Alabaster, Braided Stem, 8 In.	125.00
Steuben, Goblet, Water, Lavender Center Braided Stem, Opalescent Top	135.00
Steuben, Goblet, Wine, Selenium Red, 6 In., Set Of 6	210.00
Steuben, Hour Glass, In Double Void, Red Satin Lined Box, Signed, 4 1/4 In.	725.00
Steuben, Ice Bucket, Rosa, Pink Amber, 2 French Blue Rings, Marked, 6 1/2 In.	135.00
Steuben, Jar, Covered, Selenium Red, Paperweight Finial	650.00
Steuben, Lamp, Aurene, Threads Running Through, Iridescence, Blue, 28 In.	750.00
Steuben, Lamp, Boudoir, Acid Cut Into 12 Panels, Acorn Finial, Signed, 16 In.	450.00
Steuben, Lamp, Hanging, Stylized Flowers, Oxidized Copper Accents, 18 In.	245.00
Steuben, Lamp, Luminor, Carved Nudes Pouring Water From Jug, Signed, 10 In.	1750.00
Steuben, Lamp, Oriental Poppy, Bronze Mounting, Goat Heads & Hooves	895.00
Steuben, Lamp, Plum Jade, Double Acid Cut-Back & Gourd, 13 In.	2000.00
Steuben, Luminor, Carved Nudes, Art Deco Base, Signed, 10 In.Square	1450.00
Steuben, Mayonnaise Set, Wheel Etched, Selenium Red, Signed	650.00
Steuben, Paperweight, Crystal Horse's Head, Signed, 5 In.	185.00
Steuben, Perfume, Gold Aurene, Teardrop Stopper, Signed, 5 In.	175.00
Steuben, Perfume, Verre De Soie, Blue Flame Stopper, 4 1/2 In.	150.00
Steuben, Pitcher, Applied Black Handle, Green, Signed, 9 1/4 In.	450.00
Steuben, Pitcher, Bristol, Yellow, Black Threading, 10 1/2 In.	150.00
Steuben, Pitcher, Green Jade, Black Handle, Signed, 9 1/4 In.	400.00
Steuben, Pitcher, Jade & Alabaster, Handled, Signed, 9 1/2 In.	245.00
Steuben, Plate, Crystal, Pink Reeding, Signed, 8 1/2 In.	75.00
Steuben, Plate, Green Jade, 8 1/2 In.	20.00 To 35.00
Steuben, Plate, Rosaline, 6 1/2 In.	85.00
Steuben, Plate, Selenium Red, 8 1/2 In.	47.50
Steuben, Plate, Swirl Pattern, Amber, 8 1/2 In., Set Of 4	110.00
Steuben, Rose Bowl, Plum Jade, Signed, 2 1/2 X 6 In.	575.00
Steuben, Salt Dip, Footed, Pedestaled, Silver Foot, Verre De Soie Engraved	150.00
Steuben, Salt, Aurene, Flattened Rose Bowl Shape, Blue, Signed, 3 In.	275.00
Steuben, Salt, Aurene, Ruffled Turned Out Edge, Signed, 3 1/2 In.	295.00
Steuben, Salt, Blue Calcite, Ruffled, Blue Iridescence	165.00
Steuben, Salt, Master, Aurene, Ruffled Edge, 3 1/2 In.Diameter	425.00
Steuben, Salt, Rosa	95.00
Steuben, Shade, Aurene, Gold, Ribbed, Signed, 5 3/4 In.	70.00
Steuben, Shade, Calcite, Gold Aurene Interior, 4 1/2 In.	65.00
Steuben, Shade, Calcite, Signed Sconce, 4 X 4 In.	350.00
Steuben, Shade, Crystal Feather, Diamond-Quilted, Gold	175.00
Steuben, Shade, Flared Melon Shape, Gold Aurene On Calcite, Signed, Pair	180.00
Steuben, Shade, Fleur-De-Lis, Drawn Feather, Amber, White, 5 3/4 In., Pair	500.00
Steuben, Shade, Gold Aurene, Signed, 4 1/4 In.	85.00
Steuben, Shade, Gold Aurene, White Feathering, Fixture, Signed, Set Of 4	435.00
Steuben, Shade, Gold Iridescent, Calcite Lining, 4 In.	80.00
Steuben, Shade, Green Drape On Calcite, Pair	210.00
Steuben, Shade, Hanging, Calcite, Cut Medallions	95.00
Steuben, Shade, Hooked Feather, White Ground, Signed, 6 In., Pair	370.00
Steuben, Shade, Lime Green Feather, Gold On Opal, Gold Lining, Signed	100.00
Steuben, Shade, Pearlized Exterior, Luster Inside, 5 1/4 In. Pair	160.00
Steuben, Shade, Rubbed Umbrella Shape, Calcite Interior, Signed, 17 In.Diam.	110.00
Steuben, Shade, Square, Gold With Calcite Lining, 4 3/4 In.	125.00
Steuben, Shade, Tulip Shape, Gold & Colored Highlights, 5 1/4 In., Set Of 5	425.00
Steuben, Sherbet & Under Plate, Aurene, Calcite	225.00

Steuben, Sherbet, Alabaster Foot, 5 In. 50.00
Steuben, Sherbet, Alabaster Pedestal, Rosaline 125.00
Steuben, Sherbet, Braided Alabaster Stem, Green Top, 3 In. 50.00
Steuben, Sherbet, Calcite, Gold Lining 100.00
Steuben, Sherbet, Green Jade & Alabaster, 3 X 5 In. 50.00
Steuben, Sherbet, Green Opalescent, Cintra Collar, Signed, 4 1/2 In. 85.00
Steuben, Sherbet, Oriental Jade, Opalescent Foot 145.00
Steuben, Sherbet, Paneled, Cerise Reeding Around Bowl, Footed, 4 X 4 In. 35.00
Steuben, Toothpick, Jade Green, Signed 75.00
Steuben, Tumble-Up, Blue Aurene, Signed Aurene No.3064 .... 695.00
Steuben, Tumbler, Oriental Jade 135.00
Steuben, Tumbler, Pomona Green Reeding On Clear Glass, Signed, 4 1/2 In. 45.00
Steuben, Urn, Cluthra, Royal Blue, Classical Shape, Signed In Script, 9 In. 675.00
Steuben, Urn, Footed, Green, Ribbed Body, 5 In. 65.00
Steuben, Urn, Royal Blue, Classical Shape, Cluthra, Signed, 9 In. 850.00
Steuben, Urn, Stylized Tulips Engraved, Signed, 10 In. 250.00
Steuben, Vase, Acid Cut Back, Carp, Turtle, Fish, , Black & Gray, Signed, 10 In. 1950.00
Steuben, Vase, Acid Cutback, Fleur-De-Lis, Jade Green, Signed, 4 In. 850.00
Steuben, Vase, Amber Top, Engraved Floral Wreaths, Signed, 8 1/2 In. 80.00
Steuben, Vase, Amber, Aurene Iridescent, Steuben Aurene 2689, 1902-32, 8 In. 250.00
Steuben, Vase, Amber, Blue Rim, 8 In. 90.00
Steuben, Vase, Amethyst, Stylized Tulips & Urns Engraved, Signed, 10 In. 250.00
Steuben, Vase, Aurene, Calcite, 7 In. 250.00
Steuben, Vase, Aurene, Classic Shape, Blue, 5 1/4 X 4 1/4 In. 350.00
Steuben, Vase, Aurene, Classical Shape, Blue, 11 1/2 In. 375.00
Steuben, Vase, Aurene, Flared, Ruffled, Hour-Glass Shape, Signed, 6 1/2 In. 350.00
Steuben, Vase, Aurene, Gold, Ribbed, Iridescent, Signed, 5 In. 295.00
Steuben, Vase, Aurene, Inscribed Bottom, Fluted, 8 X 4 In.Diameter 700.00
Steuben, Vase, Aurene, Pedestal, Calcite, Paper Label, 7 In. 235.00
Steuben, Vase, Aurene, 3-Prong Tree Trunk, Blue, Signed, 6 1/4 In. 650.00
Steuben, Vase, Blue Aurene, Bulbous, Signed, 4 X 8 In. 475.00
Steuben, Vase, Blue Aurene, Shade Shape, 5 In. 275.00
Steuben, Vase, Blue Aurene, Stick, Signed, 6 In. 275.00
Steuben, Vase, Blue Calcite, Flared, Pedestal, 6 In. 325.00
Steuben, Vase, Bristol Yellow, Fan Shape, Ball & Wheel Stem, 8 1/2 In. 75.00
Steuben, Vase, Bristol Yellow, Spiral Ribbed, Ovoid Body, 1902-30, 8 1/4 In. 100.00
Steuben, Vase, Bubbly Ribbed, Green Reeding, 6 3/4 In. 55.00
Steuben, Vase, Bud, Aurene, Blue, Signed & Numbered, 7 In. 300.00
Steuben, Vase, Bud, Aurene, Wafer Base, Signed Aurene, 12 In. 195.00
Steuben, Vase, Bud, Rosaline Jade, F.D.L. Mark, 9 In. 245.00
Steuben, Vase, Calcite & Aurene, Trumpet, 6 In. 185.00
Steuben, Vase, Cigarette, Bulbous, Amber, Signed Aurene, 2 1/2 X 2 1/2 In. 150.00
Steuben, Vase, Classic Shape, Alabaster Foot, Blue Jade, Signed, 5 In. 400.00
Steuben, Vase, Cluthra, Amethyst, Signed, 8 1/2 In. 475.00
Steuben, Vase, Cornucopia Shape, Ivorene, Signed, 6 In. 250.00
Steuben, Vase, Crystal, Green, Inverted Ribs, Signed, 8 In. 50.00
Steuben, Vase, Diagonal Swirl, Amber, No.6030, Signed, 10 In. 70.00
Steuben, Vase, Diagonal Swirl, Green & Bristol Yellow, 6-Sided, 8 1/4 In. 120.00
Steuben, Vase, Emerald Green, 3 Prong, Rustic, Signed, 6 In.Tall 115.00
Steuben, Vase, Fan Shape, Footed, Blue & Amber, Signed, 7 X 6 In. 169.00
Steuben, Vase, Fan, Emerald Base, Amber Fan, Signed, 9 X 7 In. 185.00
Steuben, Vase, Fan, Green Top Amber Stem & Foot, Marked, 8 1/4 In. 75.00
Steuben, Vase, Fan, Rose Amber, Cobalt Blue, Fan Top, 9 X 8 1/2 In. 150.00

Steuben, Vase, Gold Decoration, Aurene, 10 In.
(See Page 582)

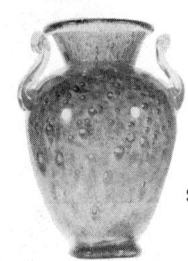

Steuben, Vase, Pink, Cluthra, Alabaster Handles, 10 In.

Steuben, Vase, Finger, Blue Aurene, Signed, 9 1/2 X 7 1/4 In. 425.00
Steuben, Vase, Flared Top, Blue & Orange Threading, Signed, 9 In. 100.00
Steuben, Vase, Flared Top, Ivory, No.7311, 6 In. 265.00
Steuben, Vase, Flared, Amber & Celeste Blue, Fluted Sides, 8 In. 95.00
Steuben, Vase, Gold Aurene Leaf & Vine Decoration, Calcite, 6 1/2 In. 295.00
Steuben, Vase, Gold Aurene, Flared Body, Pinched Waist, Signed, 6 1/4 In. 350.00
Steuben, Vase, Gold Aurene, Signed, 10 1/2 In. 150.00
Steuben, Vase, Gold Decoration, Aurene, 10 In. ....*Illus* 475.00
Steuben, Vase, Gold Iridescent, Fleur-De-Lis, Marked, 9 1/4 In. 185.00
Steuben, Vase, Gold Ruby Footed, Chalice Shape, Signed, 8 1/4 X 5 In.Diam. 95.00
Steuben, Vase, Green Base, 6 Sided Upper, Bristol Yellow, 8 1/4 In. 120.00
Steuben, Vase, Green Diagonal Swirl, No.6441, Signed, 10 In. 75.00
Steuben, Vase, Green Jade Over Alabaster, Bird Design, 9 In. 950.00
Steuben, Vase, Green Jade, Alabaster Cut, Matzu Pattern, 7 1/4 X 7 1/4 In. 575.00
Steuben, Vase, Green Jade, Birds & Floral, A.C.B., Oriental Shape, 10 In. 950.00
Steuben, Vase, Green Jade, M Handles, No.8508, 10 In. 350.00
Steuben, Vase, Green Jade, No.6207, Alabaster Lion's Head Medallions, 8 In. 175.00
Steuben, Vase, Green Reeding, No.6031, 7 In. 55.00
Steuben, Vase, Green Ribbed Crystal, Signed, 6 1/4 In. 60.00
Steuben, Vase, Green, Stylized Design, Acid Cutback, Signed, 7 1/2 X 8 In. 850.00
Steuben, Vase, Green, Wheel Engraved, Ovoid Vessel, 1902-32, 8 3/4 In. 175.00
Steuben, Vase, Grotesque Shape, Pink To Clear, Signed, 9 In. 125.00
Steuben, Vase, Ice Bucket, Diamond Thumbprint, Black Reeding, 7 In. 95.00
Steuben, Vase, Ivorene, Pedestal, Rainbow Iridescence, Signed, 8 1/4 In. 475.00
Steuben, Vase, Ivory, Black Jade Foot, Signed, 6 1/2 In. 285.00
Steuben, Vase, Ivory, No.8508, Black M Handles, 10 In. 350.00
Steuben, Vase, Jade & Alabaster Stem & Foot, Signed, 6 In. 150.00
Steuben, Vase, Jade Swirled, Signed, 10 In. 325.00
Steuben, Vase, Lavender, Signed Cluthra, 8 1/2 In. 485.00
Steuben, Vase, Light Blue Jade, Alabaster Pedestal, Signed, 5 1/4 In. 400.00
Steuben, Vase, Lily, Amber Crystal, Turquoise Stripes, No.1686, 6 In. 165.00
Steuben, Vase, Lily, Calcite, Wafer Base, Gold Iridescence Inside, 8 In. 350.00
Steuben, Vase, Oriental Poppy, Ribbing, 7 In. 825.00
Steuben, Vase, Ovoid, Stylized Flowers, Signature In Acid, 7 1/2 In. 875.00
Steuben, Vase, Pedestal, Alabaster, Rosaline Tazza, 2 1/2 X 9 3/4 In.Diam. 225.00
Steuben, Vase, Pink To Clear, Grotesque, Signed, 9 In. 75.00
Steuben, Vase, Pink, Cluthra, Alabaster Handles, 10 In. ....*Illus* 775.00
Steuben, Vase, Red Reeding, Bubble Glass, Round, 7 X 6 In.Diameter 95.00
Steuben, Vase, Ribbed Amber Crystal, Signed, 10 In. 75.00
Steuben, Vase, Ribbed Body, Lavender Crystal, Signed, 6 1/4 In. 60.00
Steuben, Vase, Ribbed Crystal, Wisteria Color, Signed, 6 In. 135.00
Steuben, Vase, Ribbed, Amethyst, Signed, 6 In. 125.00
Steuben, Vase, Ribbed, Flared, Ivory, 5 1/2 In. 135.00
Steuben, Vase, Rose Du Barry, Black Foot, 8 In. 220.00
Steuben, Vase, Ruffled Top, Ivory, 6 In. 100.00
Steuben, Vase, Sea Green, Ground Pontil, 8 1/4 In. 75.00
Steuben, Vase, Stick, Aurene, Blue Iridescence, Signed, 8 1/4 In. 295.00
Steuben, Vase, Topaz Crystal Pedestal, Flare Top, Signed, 12 1/4 In. 75.00
Steuben, Vase, Topaz Diagonal Swirl Shape, Signed, 10 In. 70.00
Steuben, Vase, Topaz, Signed, 10 1/2 X 8 In.Diameter 75.00
Steuben, Vase, Tree-Trunk, 3 Prong, Topaz Crystal, Signed, 6 In. 125.00
Steuben, Vase, Trumpet Shape, Jade With Alabaster Foot, Signed, 7 1/2 In. 125.00
Steuben, Vase, Trumpet, Footed, Ribbed, Bristol Yellow, Signed, 8 1/4 In. 75.00
Steuben, Vase, Tulip Shape, Optic Rib Pattern, Iridescent Gold, Signed, 7 In. 575.00

Steuben, Vase, Verre De Soie, Green, Signed, 5 In. 135.00
Steuben, Vase, Verre De Soie, Quilted, Pink Threading, 8 In. 295.00
Steuben, Vase, White Base, Blue, Jade, Flint, 10 In. 145.00
Steuben, Vase, White Cluthra, Signed, 6 1/2 X 5 1/2 In.Diameter 550.00
Steuben, Vase, Window Sill, Acid Cutback, Calla Lily Design, Signed, 9 In. 475.00
Steuben, Wine, Aurene, Gold Swirl, Signed, 4 X 3 In.Diameter, Pair 230.00
Steuben, Wine, Braided Opalescent Stem, Oriental Jade 185.00
Steuben, Wine, Clear Bowl, Twisted Rosa Stem, 6 In. 85.00
Steuben, Wine, Flat Alabaster Base, 4 1/2 In. 95.00
Steuben, Wine, Gold Aurene, Twisted Stem, Marked, 5 In., Pair 130.00
Steuben, Wine, Jade Green, Alabaster Stem, 6 1/4 In. 60.00
Steuben, Wine, Oriental Jade .... 175.00 To 235.00
Steuben, Wine, Rosaline, No.7284, 7 In. 75.00

*Stevengraphs are woven pictures made like ribbons. They were manufactured
by Thomas Stevens of Coventry, England, and became popular in 1862.*

Stevengraph, Angelus, Framed, 10 1/2 X 12 In. 125.00
Stevengraph, Are You Ready 185.00
Stevengraph, Bookmark, A Birthday Gift, 9 X 2 In. 40.00
Stevengraph, Bookmark, A Merry Xmas To You 65.00
Stevengraph, Bookmark, A Wish, 6 X 1 1/2 In. 35.00
Stevengraph, Bookmark, Compliments Of The Season 35.00
Stevengraph, Bookmark, G.Washington Centennial, First In Peace, 10 X 2 In. 135.00
Stevengraph, Bookmark, General George Washington, First In Peace 65.00
Stevengraph, Bookmark, George Washington, Father Of Our Country 62.00
Stevengraph, Bookmark, Good Wishes, Hope Thee Of Soul, 9 X 2 In. 45.00
Stevengraph, Bookmark, Joy Greet The Day, 6 1/2 X 1 1/2 In. 40.00
Stevengraph, Bookmark, Many Happy Returns Of The Day, 11 X 2 In. 65.00
Stevengraph, Bookmark, May The Bestower Of Bliss, 9 1/2 X 2 In. 65.00
Stevengraph, Bookmark, Our Saviour, 7 1/2 X 1 1/2 In. 40.00
Stevengraph, Bookmark, The Old Arm Chair, With Music Score, 10 1/2 X 2 In. 85.00
Stevengraph, Bookmark, Thy Will Be Done 65.00
Stevengraph, Bookmark, To My Dear Brother, 6 1/2 X 1 1/2 In. 35.00
Stevengraph, Bookmark, To My Friend, 7 1/2 X 1 1/2 In. 45.00
Stevengraph, Bookmark, To One I Love, Bright Be Thy Life, 9 1/2 X 2 In. 65.00
Stevengraph, Bookmark, Unchanging Love, 6 1/2 X 2 In. 45.00
Stevengraph, Columbian Expostion, Mounted & Framed, 7 1/2 X 10 1/2 In. 165.00
Stevengraph, Columbus Leaving Spain, Mounted & Framed, 7 1/2 X 10 1/2 In 165.00
Stevengraph, Crossbow, Man And Boy, Framed, 11 1/2 X 15 In. 275.00
Stevengraph, Death 150.00
Stevengraph, Declaration Of Independence, Framed, 7 1/2 X 10 1/2 In. 165.00
Stevengraph, Don't Tell Anyone, Signed, 8 X 12 1/2 In. 45.00
Stevengraph, Elizabeth II, Crowned 2nd June, 1953, Picture Of Queen 35.00
Stevengraph, Finish 123.00
Stevengraph, Finish, Framed 225.00
Stevengraph, First Point 150.00
Stevengraph, Full Cry 150.00
Stevengraph, Full Cry, Framed .... 145.00 To 250.00
Stevengraph, General U.S.Grant, Dated 1865, Signed 125.00
Stevengraph, Robert Burns, Framed 200.00
Stevengraph, U.S.Grant, Richmond, 1865, Framed 110.00
Stevengraph, Wellington & Blucher Meeting After Battle Of Waterloo 155.00

S ✦ W *Stevens & Williams of Stourbridge, England, made many types of glass,
including layered, etched, cameo, and art glass, between the 1830s and
the 1930s. Some pieces are signed S and W.*

Stevens & Williams, Basket, Applied Flowers & Leaves, Handle, Feet, 7 In. 200.00
Stevens & Williams, Bell, Marriage, Opalescent Trim, Clapper, 1850, 12 In. 195.00
Stevens & Williams, Bottle, Cologne, Crystal Intaglio, 8 3/4 In. 195.00
Stevens & Williams, Bowl, Applied Strap Handles, 11 1/2 X 9 1/4 In. 175.00
Stevens & Williams, Bowl, Matsu-No-Ke Decoration, Cranberry, 6 1/8 In.Diam. 575.00
Stevens & Williams, Bowl, Rock Crystal, Chinoiserie, Engraved, 8 1/2 In. 400.00
Stevens & Williams, Bucket, Ice, Amber Glass Form Legs & Handles, Custard 285.00
Stevens & Williams, Compote, Intaglio Cut, Willow Pattern, 5 1/4 In. 450.00
Stevens & Williams, Cracker Jar, White Exterior, Applied Leaves 385.00
Stevens & Williams, Creamer, Applied Strawberry & Vine Form Handle, 5 In. 135.00

Stevens & Williams, Cruet, Amber, Blue Pincered Decorations, Signed, 8 In.	145.00
Stevens & Williams, Dish, Footed, Threaded Glass Edge, Fluted, 8 1/2 In.	125.00
Stevens & Williams, Epergne, 1 Lily, 3 Canes, Hanging Basket, 1890, Cranberry	650.00
Stevens & Williams, Fingerbowl & Underplate, Moire Pattern, Signed	220.00
Stevens & Williams, Garniture Set, 1 Large Vase & 2 Small Vases, Signed	275.00
Stevens & Williams, Jar, Cracker, Candy Stripe	200.00
Stevens & Williams, Jar, Sweetmeat, Vaseline Cover, Cut Design, 5 1/2 In.	165.00
Stevens & Williams, Jug, Claret, Silver Plated Mount, Signed, 11 In.	3495.00
Stevens & Williams, Pitcher, Water, Opalescent, Diamond Quilted, 8 In.	125.00
Stevens & Williams, Rose Bowl, Box Pleated Top, Frosted Green, 4 5/8 In.	195.00
Stevens & Williams, Rose Bowl, Egg Shape, Swirl Mother-Of-Pearl, 6 1/4 In.	650.00
Stevens & Williams, Rose Bowl, Fluted Top, Applied Cherries, 3 3/4 In.	165.00
Stevens & Williams, Rose Bowl, Satin Lining, Box Pleats, 3 1/4 X 4 1/4 In.	195.00
Stevens & Williams, Rose Bowl, 3 1/2 X 5 In.Diameter	145.00
Stevens & Williams, Vase, Applied Cherries, Gold Highlights, Signed, 13 In.	825.00
Stevens & Williams, Vase, Blue Opalescent, Appliqued Fruit, 6 1/8 In.	595.00
Stevens & Williams, Vase, Blues, Applied Glass Cherrries & Leaves, 13 In.	625.00
Stevens & Williams, Vase, Cranberry, Intaglio Cut, Royal Brieley, Signed	345.00
Stevens & Williams, Vase, Crystal, 6 Elongated Green Eyes, 12 In.	125.00
Stevens & Williams, Vase, Double Gourd Shape, Cased Over Pink, 5 1/2 In.	65.00
Stevens & Williams, Vase, Intaglio, Pink Cut To White, 5 1/2 In.	650.00
Stevens & Williams, Vase, Jewel Pattern, Amber, Fluted Top, 5 X 5 In.	145.00
Stevens & Williams, Vase, Opalescent Overlay, Flowers & Leaves, 9 In.	300.00
Stevens & Williams, Vase, Protruding Applied Flowers, Handles, 14 3/8 In.	295.00
Stevens & Williams, Vase, Pull Up, White Lining, 3 X 3 3/4 In.Diameter	445.00
Stevens & Williams, Vase, Reversed Amberina, Enameled, 9 1/4 In.	995.00
Stevens & Williams, Vase, Swirl, Satin, Aqua & Blue Lining, 18 1/2 In.	1050.00
Stevens & Williams, Vase, White, Frosted Blue, No.674-4 1/2, Cameo, 8 In.	1150.00
Stevens & Williams, Vase, 2 Color Cameo Glass, 1800s, 12 1/2 In.	2600.00
Stiegel Type, Bottle, Etched, Hand Blown	95.00
Stiegel Type, Bottle, Toilet, Blown, 3 Mold, Blue	160.00
Stiegel Type, Bowl, Sugar, Footed, 12 Rib Mold, Cobalt Blue, 6 3/4 In.	1025.00
Stiegel Type, Cordial, Blown & Cut	10.00
Stiegel Type, Creamer, 16-Diamond, Cobalt Blue, Flint	325.00
Stiegel Type, Decanter, Ring Neck, Pint, Flint	35.00
Stiegel Type, Flip Glass, Flint	150.00
Stiegel Type, Inkwell, Amber	140.00
Stiegel Type, Salt, Footed, 11-Diamond, Blue	225.00
Stiegel Type, Salt, Pedestal Footed, Sapphire Blue, 20 Rib Mold, 3 1/4 In.	155.00
Stiegel Type, Salt, 12 Rib, Swirled To Left	110.00
Stiegel Type, Top Hat, Trapped Air Bubbles, Polished Pontil	55.00

Stoneware is a coarse glazed and fired potter's ware that is used to make crocks, jugs, etc.

Stoneware, Bottle, Birresborn Mineral Wasser, Winter Scene, 11 1/2 In.	50.00
Stoneware, Bottle, Ginger Beer, World War I	9.00
Stoneware, Bottle, Ink, Brown Glaze, Short Neck, 4 1/4 X 2 1/4 In.Diameter	12.00
Stoneware, Bottle, Ink, Tan & Cream Glaze, Round, 2 In.	15.00
Stoneware, Bottle, Ink, Tan, C.1860, 2 1/2 In.	12.00
Stoneware, Bottle, Ink, 6 1/2 In.	11.00
Stoneware, Bottle, Pig, Albany Slip, Incised Eyes & Mouth, 7 3/4 In.	155.00
Stoneware, Bottle, 12-Sided, Dr.Conck's Sarsaparilla Beer, 10 In.	68.00
Stoneware, Bowl & Pitcher Set, Rose & Fishscale, Blue & Gray	150.00
Stoneware, Bowl, Blue & White Chain, 6 1/2 In.	20.00
Stoneware, Bowl, Blue & White, Apricot, Original Bail & Handle, 10 In.	75.00
Stoneware, Bowl, Blue & White, Pyramid, 7 X 3 1/2 In.	45.00
Stoneware, Bowl, Mixing, Cherry, Blue, 9 1/4 In.	29.00
Stoneware, Bowl, Mixing, Western, Blue	5.00
Stoneware, Butter Crock, Lid, Bell, 19th Century, 5 1/2 In.High, 9 In.Diam.	350.00
Stoneware, Canister, Basket Weave & Blower	30.00
Stoneware, Canister, Marked Coffee, Blue & White, 6 In.	74.00
Stoneware, Canteen, Red Cross, Rochester, 1900, 3 X 3 In.	140.00
Stoneware, Chamber Pot, Flowers, Large	69.00
Stoneware, Churn, Earred, Cobalt Flower Front & Back, P.Hermann, 4 Gallon	105.00
Stoneware, Churn, Floral & Leaf, Cobalt, C.Hart Sherburne, 2 Gallon	95.00

Stoneware, Churn, Tan, Black Script, Applied Earred Handles, 12 In.	90.00
Stoneware, Churn, W.H. Farrar & Co., Geddes, N.Y., Bird & Flower, 5 Gallon	625.00
Stoneware, Cookie Jar, Embossed Rabbit, Green Glaze	12.00
Stoneware, Cooler, Water, Blue & White Banded, 3 Gallon	40.00
Stoneware, Cooler, Water, Blue Bands, 6 Gallon	50.00
Stoneware, Crock, Adam Caire, Poughkeepsie, Blue Bird On Stump, 4 Gallon	150.00
Stoneware, Crock, Bangor, Maine, 2-Gallon	30.00
Stoneware, Crock, Beige Glaze, Taper At Top, 16 In.	40.00
Stoneware, Crock, Blanton Cremo Butterine, Lid, 1914, 7 X 5 In.	48.00
Stoneware, Crock, Blue & White, Parrot Design, Norton, Worcester, Mass, 5 Gal.	160.00
Stoneware, Crock, Blue Cobalt, 1 Gallon	49.00
Stoneware, Crock, Blue Slip Design, Man, Bowler Hat, 5 Gal., 12 3/4 X 11 In.	1800.00
Stoneware, Crock, Butter, Amber Glaze, Embossed Eagle & 2 Stars, Wire Handle	82.50
Stoneware, Crock, Butter, Blue Leaf On Side, 5 Pound	100.00
Stoneware, Crock, Butter, Cover, Blue Circles, C.1880, 6 X 10 In.	85.00
Stoneware, Crock, Butter, Covered, Waffle Design, 5 X 7 1/2 In.Diameter	40.00
Stoneware, Crock, Butter, Daisy Pattern, Yellow & Green, Covered	25.00
Stoneware, Crock, Butter, Peerless Creamery, Cow's Head	47.00
Stoneware, Crock, Cobalt Bird, Gray Background, Earred, A.B.Wheeler & Co.	375.00
Stoneware, Crock, Cobalt Double Tulip, William E.Warner, 3 Gallon	85.00
Stoneware, Crock, Cobalt Floral, N.A.White & Son, Utica, N.Y., 3 Gallon	135.00
Stoneware, Crock, Cobalt Floral, Ottman Bros., Ft.Edward, N.Y., 4 Gallon	75.00
Stoneware, Crock, Cobalt Flower, P.Hermann, 4 Gallon	95.00
Stoneware, Crock, Cobalt Sunflower, Penn Yann, 2 Gallon	95.00
Stoneware, Crock, Double Cobalt Flower, J.Fisher, Lyons, N.Y., 3 Gallon	85.00
Stoneware, Crock, F.B. Norton & Co., Worcester, Massachusetts, 2 Gallon	75.00
Stoneware, Crock, Gardiner, Maine, Manufactory, 1 Gallon	22.50
Stoneware, Crock, Gray Glaze, Cobalt Blue, Sunburst Lines, 2 Gallon	24.00
Stoneware, Crock, Gray, Blue Cobalt, 3 Gallon	85.00
Stoneware, Crock, Hieroglyphic Decoration, 2 Gallon	35.00
Stoneware, Crock, Impressed Eagle, Gardiner, Maine, 2 Gallon	95.00
Stoneware, Crock, Parrot Standing On Stump, White, Utica, Signed, 2 Gallon	125.00
Stoneware, Crock, Two Impressed Eagles, 4 Gallon	175.00
Stoneware, Crock, White, Cobalt Flower, I Gallon, 7 1/2 X 7 1/2 In.	35.00
Stoneware, Crock, 3 Impressed Swans, 3 Gallon	145.00
Stoneware, Cup, Custard, Blue Blending To White	40.00
Stoneware, Cup, Loving, 3 Handle, Hallmarked Sterling Silver Rim, 6 In.	95.00
Stoneware, Cuspidor, Blue & Gray, 8 In.Diameter X 4 In.High	95.00
Stoneware, Dish, Butter, Covered, Blue	58.00
Stoneware, Dish, Butter, Daisy & Waffle, Blue & White	65.00
Stoneware, Dish, Butter, Lid, Blue & Cream, Scroll Pattern	50.00
Stoneware, Dish, Butter, Lid, Butterfly	50.00
Stoneware, Feeder & Waterer, Poultry, Directions In Blue Writing	60.00
Stoneware, Figurine, Pig, Amber Glaze, 5 3/8 In.	90.00
Stoneware, Flagon, Raised Figure, Impressed Crown & Scepter, 8 1/2 In.	95.00
Stoneware, Flask, Gin, Shape Of Fish, 1860, 8 1/2 In.	100.00
Stoneware, Foot Warmer, Henderson	18.00
Stoneware, Footwarmer, Lambeth Pottery, London	35.00
Stoneware, Footwarmer, Stevens	32.00
Stoneware, Holder, Umbrella, Blue & White, Straw Marks Inside, 21 In.	375.00
Stoneware, Inkwell, Blue Slip On Top & Bottom, 8 Sided	200.00
Stoneware, Inkwell, Chambered Edges. 3 1/2 In.Diameter	69.00
Stoneware, Jar, A.P. Donaghlo, 1/2 Gallon	28.50
Stoneware, Jar, Blue Decoration, Greensboro, Pennsylvania	35.00
Stoneware, Jar, Brushed Blue Leaf Design, 7 1/2 In.	45.00
Stoneware, Jar, Canning, Wax Sealer, 1 Gallon	50.00
Stoneware, Jar, Earred, Cobalt Flower, A.W.Smith & Sons, 3 Gallon	75.00
Stoneware, Jar, Open, Salt-Glazed, American, Inscribed May 3rd, 1855, 11 In.	175.00
Stoneware, Jar, Semi-Ovoid, Cobalt Floral, Haxton, Ottman, 2 Gallon	95.00
Stoneware, Jar, Storage, Salt-Glazed, S.Bell, Mid-19th Century, 16 In.	3250.00
Stoneware, Jar, Tobacco, Lidded, 5 1/2 In.	49.00
Stoneware, Jar, Tobacco, Raised Design Of Trees, Impressed Briar Root Front	38.00
Stoneware, Jug, Applied Leaves, Twig Handle, Ohio Harvest	475.00
Stoneware, Jug, Batter, Cobalt Flower	185.00
Stoneware, Jug, Batter, Gallon	59.00
Stoneware, Jug, Batter, Gray, Tulip, E.R.Jones, Pittston, Penn., 1 1/2 Gallon	300.00

Stoneware, Jug, Blue Decoration, A.B. Wheeler & Co., Boston, 1 Gallon 50.00
Stoneware, Jug, Blue Flower, Norton, Worcester, 1 Gallon 25.00
Stoneware, Jug, Blue Printing, Samual Felt Druggist, Watertown, N.Y. 40.00
Stoneware, Jug, Blue Splash, Julius Norton, Bennington, Vt., 2 Gallon 75.00
Stoneware, Jug, Blue, Froilich & Koehler, Mulberry, Newark, 1 Gallon 45.00
Stoneware, Jug, Brown Glaze, Handled, Ovoid, 1/2 Gallon 36.00
Stoneware, Jug, Cobalt Blue Floral Spray, Salt Glazed, Covered, 14 In. 150.00
Stoneware, Jug, Cobalt Blue, Double Ear Handles, 5 Gallon, 17 In. 45.00
Stoneware, Jug, Cobalt Blue, Flower, 3 Gallon, 14 3/4 In. 85.00
Stoneware, Jug, Cobalt Decoration, Impressed Albany New York, 2 Gallon 65.00
Stoneware, Jug, Cobalt Floral Design, Binghamton, N.Y., 2 Gallon 85.00
Stoneware, Jug, Cobalt Floral, Norton, Bennington, Vt., 3 Gallon 145.00
Stoneware, Jug, Cobalt Leaf Design, Norton, 2 Gallon 75.00
Stoneware, Jug, Corn Whiskey, McCormick Distilling, 1/2 Pint 18.50
Stoneware, Jug, E.Wentworth, Norwich, 1 Gallon 85.00
Stoneware, Jug, E.Woodworth, Bennington, Vermont, 3 Gallon 27.50
Stoneware, Jug, Gray, B.Bevan, Pittston, Penna., 2 Gallon 80.00
Stoneware, Jug, Impressed Signature, Craig, Vale, North Carolina, 19 In. 110.00
Stoneware, Jug, Liberty For Ever, Warne & Letts, 1807, 11 1/2 In. 2250.00
Stoneware, Jug, Neck & Handle Chocolate Brown, Lower In Cream, 4 Gallon 37.00
Stoneware, Jug, O'Keefe's Whiskey, Oswego, N.Y. 20.00
Stoneware, Jug, Puzzle, The Parson And Clerk, Fulham, 19th Century, 8 5/8 In. 190.00
Stoneware, Jug, Salt Glazed, Prancing Horse, N.Clark, Jr., 1843-92, 14 In. 1300.00
Stoneware, Jug, Salt-Glazed, Hamilton & Jones, 19th Century, 18 In. 225.00
Stoneware, Jug, Signed, F.B.Norton, Worcester, Massachusetts, 3 Gallon 80.00
Stoneware, Jug, Squat Neck, Beehive Shape, Pouring Lip & Handle, 1 Gallon 30.00
Stoneware, Jug, West Troy Pottery, 2 Gallon 170.00
Stoneware, Jug, Whiskey, Gold Lettering, Purple Flower, 1 Quart 20.00
Stoneware, Jug, Whiskey, Jack Daniel's, 1/2 Gallon 45.00
Stoneware, Jug, White, Brown Top, 1 Gallon 12.00
Stoneware, Kettle, Bail, Wooden Handle, Daisy Design, 10 In., Diameter 85.00
Stoneware, Mortar, Wood Handle, M On Base, 6 3/4 In. 35.00
Stoneware, Mug, Blue & White, Sleepy Eye, Tan, Green & Beige, Pair 380.00
Stoneware, Mug, Blue Bands, Gray, Burlington Vinegar & Pickle Works 30.00
Stoneware, Mug, Graf's Root Beer, The Best What Gives 12.50
Stoneware, Mug, Ode To The Farmer, Decorated, 4 In. 7.50
Stoneware, Mug, Ode To The Farmer, 4 In. 7.50
Stoneware, Mug, Raised Designs Of Golfer, Cobalt & Blue, Flemish 60.00
Stoneware, Oil Can, Twisted Handle, Amber Glaze, Rodenbaugh, 11 1/4 In. 910.00
Stoneware, Pitcher, Applied Handles, Attributed To New Paris, Pa., 4 1/2 In. 100.00
Stoneware, Pitcher, Apricot, Blue 65.00
Stoneware, Pitcher, Apricot, F.Brown, Pint 55.00
Stoneware, Pitcher, Barrel Type, Pint 40.00
Stoneware, Pitcher, Basket Weave, Green 40.00
Stoneware, Pitcher, Batter, Bail Handle, Yellow Glazing, Wood Grips 55.00
Stoneware, Pitcher, Batter, Handled, 8 In. 47.50
Stoneware, Pitcher, Blue & White, Large, Rose 80.00
Stoneware, Pitcher, Blue & White, Roses, Leaves, Oriental Figures, 9 In. 95.00
Stoneware, Pitcher, Blue & White, Windmill, Tulips, Bulbous Base, 7 1/2 In. 75.00
Stoneware, Pitcher, Blue Blending To White, 2 Quart 75.00
Stoneware, Pitcher, Butterfly, Blue & Gray 75.00
Stoneware, Pitcher, Buttermilk, Basketweave With Flower, Green 45.00
Stoneware, Pitcher, Buttermilk, Grapes, Green 45.00
Stoneware, Pitcher, Buttermilk, Indian Good Luck Symbol, Brown 38.00
Stoneware, Pitcher, Buttermilk, Rose Pattern, Blue & White 58.00
Stoneware, Pitcher, Buttermilk, Scene Of Hunter & Dog, 19th Century 68.00
Stoneware, Pitcher, Cow, Blue & White, 7 In. 75.00
Stoneware, Pitcher, Cow, Regular Size 110.00
Stoneware, Pitcher, Cow, White, Small 150.00
Stoneware, Pitcher, Deer With Fawn, Rust & Tan, Pint 80.00
Stoneware, Pitcher, Dutch Boy & Girl, Large 50.00
Stoneware, Pitcher, Embossed Chain, Blue Glaze, 5 1/4 In. 14.00
Stoneware, Pitcher, Gray, Cobalt Blue Flower Spray, Blue Sponge Top, 9 In. 80.00
Stoneware, Pitcher, Green & Tan, 8 In. 27.00
Stoneware, Pitcher, Green Glaze, Embossed Water Lilies, 5 In. 12.00
Stoneware, Pitcher, Green Glaze, 1/2 Gallon 29.50

Stoneware, Pitcher, Indian Head, Blue & White 150.00
Stoneware, Pitcher, Leaping Deer, E.Brown 65.00
Stoneware, Pitcher, Lid, Brown Glaze, 9 In. 35.00
Stoneware, Pitcher, Rose & Fishscale, Blue, 10 In. 79.00
Stoneware, Pitcher, Rose Trellis, Blue & Tan, Pint 65.00
Stoneware, Pitcher, Running Deer, Brown 45.00
Stoneware, Pitcher, Saddle Stitched, English Silver Banded, Hallmarked 175.00
Stoneware, Pitcher, Shaded Blue, Cows In Relief On Sides, 8 In. 75.00
Stoneware, Pitcher, White, Indian Boy & Girl 110.00
Stoneware, Pitcher, Windmill & Bush, Blue & White, 7 In. 40.00
Stoneware, Pitcher, Woman's Head, Blue, C.1860 .... 90.00
Stoneware, Plate, Fisherman Mending Nets, Captioned Border, 9 In. 20.00
Stoneware, Plate, Pie, Blue & Gray, Star On Bottom 60.00
Stoneware, Pot, Chamber, Blue & White, Basket Weave 30.00
Stoneware, Potty, Rose, Blue, 7 1/4 In. 38.00
Stoneware, Rolling Pin, Wildflower, Blue & White 65.00
Stoneware, Salt, Basket Weave, Blue & White 39.00
Stoneware, Spittoon, Basket Weave & Flower, Blue & White 48.00
Stoneware, Stein, Blue & Gray, Tavern Scene, Pewter Top, Germany, 6 1/2 In. 118.00
Stoneware, Stein, 2 Blue Incised Bands, Gray, Signed F.Heyde, N.Y. 50.00
Stoneware, Tankard, Raised People, Drinking Scene, Blue, 9 1/4 In. 65.00
Stoneware, Toothpick, Swan, 3 In. 65.00
Stoneware, Tub, Butter, Cover, Hunters & Deer 75.00
Stoneware, Urn, 4 Monster Heads, Stand, Korean, 30 In. 90.00
Stoneware, Vase, Blue & Gray, Signed, Indian, Cattails, Dragonfly 195.00
Stoneware, Wash Bowl Set, Rose & Fish Scale, Blue & White, 6 Piece 415.00
Stoneware, Water Cooler, Cylindrical, American, 19th Century, 16 1/2 In. 350.00
    Store, see also Card, Advertising; Coffee Grinder; Tool; Scale
Store, Almanac, Dr.Miles, C.1908 .... 15.00
Store, Ashtray & Match Holder, Green River Whiskey 25.00
Store, Ashtray, Goodrich Silvertown, Milk Glass Insert, 6 In. 10.00
Store, Ashtray, Impression Of Pack Of Lucky Strike, July 23, 1928, Signed 25.00
Store, Ashtray, Kelly Springfield Heavy Duty Tire 20.00
Store, Ashtray, Planters Peanuts, Ceramic 20.00
Store, Ashtray, Standing Terrier Dog In Center 10.00
Store, Ashtray, Tire, Goodrich Zipper Boots 10.00
Store, Ashtray, Weldit Company, Detroit, Bronze 10.00
Store, Back Bar & Base, Half Moon Mirror, Slag Lamp In Center, 22 X 12 Ft. 8900.00
Store, Barber Pole, Half Round, Look Better, Feel Better, Metal, 48 In. 40.00
Store, Barber Pole, Leaded Glass, Porcelain, C.1920 .... 450.00
Store, Barber Pole, Wood & Metal, 25 X 4 In. 55.00
Store, Barrel, Churn, Wooden 110.00
Store, Barrel, Flour, Red, Drawer On Bottom, Sifter, Round, Tin, 26 In. 70.00
Store, Barrel, Planters Peanut, Complete Label .... 165.00 To 175.00
Store, Basket, Covered, Green & Red Trim 185.00
Store, Beater, Rug, Wicker 24.00
Store, Beater, Rug, Wire 5.00
Store, Beer Tap, Ballantine Ale, Celluloid Ball 15.00
Store, Bin, Black Hawk Coffee, Tin 60.00
Store, Bin, Coffee, Glass Front, Scoop, Bean Dispenser, 24 X 10 X 10 In. 125.00
Store, Bin, Coffee, Johnson Peacemaker, Log Cabin 350.00
Store, Bin, Floor, But-A-Kiss, Bulk Display Container 125.00
Store, Bin, Flower Seeds, Oak, C.1880, 6 1/2 X 11 X 4 1/4 In. 35.00
Store, Bin, Grain, Poplar, Original Red, Slant Lid, Angled Front, 35 In. 139.00
Store, Bin, Japan Tea, Tin, 70 Pounds, Indian Portrait, 19 X 20 X 16 1/2 In. 55.00
Store, Bin, Polar Bear, Tin 100.00
Store, Bin, Tea, William Hills, Mirror Front 50.00
Store, Bin, Tiger Chewing Tobacco, Counter Top, 14 1/2 X 13 X 7 1/2 In. 17.50
Store, Bin, Tobacco, Maryland Club Mixture, 15 X 10 1/2 X 7 1/2 In. 155.00
Store, Bookmark, Mr.Peanut, 1940s, Cardboard 8.00
    Store, Bootjack, see also Iron, Bootjack
Store, Bootjack, Folding, Walnut 25.00
    Store, Bottle, see Bottle
Store, Bottle Carrier, Milkman's, Wire 5.00
Store, Bottle Opener, Frank Archer Invites You To Visit Moxiland, Sliding 20.00
Store, Bowl, Fish, Mr.Peanut, Small 145.00

Store, Box, American Fig Confection, Wooden, Round	12.00
Store, Box, Biscuit, Wood, Eagle, C.D.Boss & Sons, N.London, Connecticut	55.00
Store, Box, Cake, Schepp's, Scenes From Goethe, Black On White, 14 X 13 In.	185.00
Store, Box, Candy, Schrafft's, Gold Metal	12.00
Store, Box, Cardboard, Soap, C.P.C.	8.00
Store, Box, Cash, McCaskey Register	25.00
Store, Box, Chicklet's Gum, Glass Top, Spoon	38.00
Store, Box, Cigar, Blue Ribbon Special, Book Shape	8.00
Store, Box, Cigar, Book-Shaped, Buffalo Bill	25.00
Store, Box, Cigar, Rudolph Valentino, The Sheik Of 5 Cent Cigars	18.00
Store, Box, Clicquot Club Ginger Ale, Wooden, 12 X 18 X 10 1/2 In.	7.50
Store, Box, Coffin, Twin Oaks Mixture Tobacco, 8 1/2 X 4 1/2 X 4 1/4 In.	35.00
Store, Box, Coleman Lamp & Lantern Generator, Set Of 12	5.00
Store, Box, Collar Button, Art Deco	11.00
Store, Box, Document, Combination Lock, Gold Stenciling	17.50
Store, Box, Glove, Walnut, Fern Decoration	12.00
Store, Box, Gold Dust Twins, Cartooned, Wooden, 96 Pound Size	60.00
Store, Box, Handkerchief & Tie Holder, Brown Suede, 6 X 15 In.	8.00
Store, Box, Mail, Shield On Front, Belken & Griswold, 7 1/2 X 14 1/2 In.	22.50
Store, Box, Moore's 1855 Coffee, Iowa, Folds Up, 6 1/2 X 11 1/2 In. Unfolded	3.50
Store, Box, Opener & Hammer, Corn Bread Tobacco	45.00
Store, Box, Oswego Starch, Slotted, Wooden, 12 In.	35.00
Store, Box, Pencil, Wooden, Roll-Top	8.00
Store, Box, Sample, Bakers Educational Exhibit, Samples	150.00
Store, Box, Seed, A.H.Dunlap, Inlaid, Flowers On Inside Cover, Multicolor	25.00
Store, Box, Sen-Sen, Book Shape, Lid	8.00
Store, Box, Shoeshine, Dovetailed Bon Ami Box, C.I., Shoe Rest, 8 X 12 In.	25.00
Store, Box, Spool, Clark's, 4 3/4 In.	20.00
Store, Box, Tobacco, Dovetailed, Yankee Girl, 13 X 7 X 5 In.	17.50
Store, Box, Tobacco, Futurity Twist, Wooden	5.00
Store, Box, Tobacco, Havana Ribbon	8.00
Store, Box, Tobacco, Watchman, 10 For 50 Cents, 3 X 4 In.	10.00
Store, Box, Union Leader Cut Plug, Rectangular	8.00
Store, Box, World Navy, Tin	15.00
Store, Brush, Bull Dog, China Head	25.00
Store, Brush, Shaving, Made Rite, Amber Handle	3.50
Store, Bucket, Lid, Compliments Of Putz Bros., 1898-99, Tin	13.50
Store, Bucket, Poultry, Watkins Poultry, Tin, Holds 30 Pounds, 13 X 12 In.	28.50
Store, Bucket, Tea, Sears, Pink Striped, 5 Pound	28.00
Store, Bust, Teacher's Scotch, Professor, Papier-Mache, 12 In.	35.00
Store, Button, Pinback, Redshot Smokeless Powder, Bird Picture, 7/8 In.	25.00
Store, Button, 20 Grand A Winner, Head Of Horse, Celluloid, 1 1/4 In.	5.00
Store, Buttonhook, see also Art Nouveau, Buttonhook, Brass, Buttonhook	
Store, Buttonhook, Bloomington, Illinois	6.50
Store, Buttonhook, Child's, Pair	9.00
Store, Buttonhook, Shape Of Woman's Legs	29.00
Store, Buttonhook, Sterling Silver, 10 In.	9.75
Store, Buttonhook, Tortoise Shell, Celluloid Handle, Gold	6.00
Store, Buttonhook, Tortoise Shell, Celluloid Handle, Green	6.00
Store, Buttonhook, Walkover Shoe, Folding	4.00
Store, Cabinet, Bronco Remedies, Cardboard, Ten Cent Remedies, 16 X 19 In.	150.00
Store, Cabinet, Collar Display, Oak & Glass, 4 Sides, 13 X 25 X 7 In.Diam.	225.00
Store, Cabinet, De Laval Cream Separator, Tin Insert	240.00 To 325.00
Store, Cabinet, Dexter Braid, Oak, 2 Drawer	110.00
Store, Cabinet, Diamond Dye Mansion	375.00
Store, Cabinet, Diamond Dye, Children Jumping Rope	285.00
Store, Cabinet, Diamond Dye, Cycles Of Life, Tin & Cherry	625.00
Store, Cabinet, Diamond Dye, Wood, May Pole, 23 X 31 In.	385.00
Store, Cabinet, Display, Dated 1928, Yankee Tools, Tin & Wood	32.00
Store, Cabinet, Display, Feen-A-Mint, C.1920	110.00
Store, Cabinet, Douglas Capsicum Cough Drops, Tin	35.00
Store, Cabinet, Dr.Daniel's	500.00
Store, Cabinet, Dye-Ola Improved Home Dye, Wooden	65.00 To 115.00
Store, Cabinet, Flashlight & Battery, Tin, Yale	42.50
Store, Cabinet, Glass Door Front, Pine, 12 X 17 1/2 X 8 In.	45.00

Store, Cabinet, Hardware, 80 Drawers, Oak, 7 1/2 X 11 1/2 X 55 In.	425.00
Store, Cabinet, Humphries Remedies, Patent Medicine, Tin Front, 34 Drawers	400.00
Store, Cabinet, Jeweler, Swiss American Main Spring, 3 Drawer	85.00
Store, Cabinet, Mayo's Milk Pail, Paper Label, Tin	110.00
Store, Cabinet, Medicine, Oak, 17 1/2 X 20 In.	45.00
Store, Cabinet, Newport Park Coffee, 4 Pound	55.00
Store, Cabinet, Printer's, Oak, 24 Drawer, Hardware, No Paint, 32 In.Wide	350.00
Store, Cabinet, Printer's, Pine, Hardware, No Paint, 17 Drawer, 22 In.Wide	350.00
Store, Cabinet, Putnam Dye, Children With Balloon, Oak	475.00
Store, Cabinet, Putnam Fadeless Dye, Tin Front & Back	50.00
Store, Cabinet, Screw, Octagonal, 80 Drawer	800.00
Store, Cabinet, Seed, 3-Drawer, Red	245.00
Store, Cabinet, Spices, W.T.Delano, Tin	250.00
Store, Cabinet, Spool, Belding, 3 Drawer, Oak, 8 X 21 1/4 X 18 In.	145.00
Store, Cabinet, Spool, Brainerd & Armstrong Silk, 3 Drawer	59.00
Store, Cabinet, Spool, Clark's, 3 Drawer	145.00
Store, Cabinet, Spool, Drawers, Leonard Silk Co., 17 1/2 X 18 1/2 In.	187.50
Store, Cabinet, Spool, Goff & Braid, 2 Drawer	125.00
Store, Cabinet, Spool, J.P.Coats, Desk Type, Oak, 4 Drawer, 29 X 11 X 20 In.	315.00
Store, Cabinet, Spool, J.P.Coats, Looks Like Giant Spool Of Thread	375.00
Store, Cabinet, Spool, J.P.Coats, Spindle Front	250.00
Store, Cabinet, Spool, J.P.Coats, Walnut, 6 Drawer, Original Hardware	295.00
Store, Cabinet, Spool, J.P.Coats, 2 Drawer, 8 1/2 X 21 1/2 X 17 In.	97.50
Store, Cabinet, Spool, J.P.Coats, 2 Drawer, 18 X 21 X 9 In.	350.00
Store, Cabinet, Spool, J.P.Coats, 3 Drawers, Metal & Wood	55.00
Store, Cabinet, Spool, Merrick, Round, Revolving Center	625.00
Store, Cabinet, Spool, Richardson Silk Co., 3 Drawer	225.00
Store, Cabinet, Spool, Richardson Silk, 2 Drawer, Oak, 15 1/4 X 14 1/4 In.	125.00
Store, Cabinet, Spool, Star Mercerized, 4 Glass Front Drawers, Logo	85.00
Store, Cabinet, Spool, Star Thread Co., Oak, 5 Drawer	135.00 To 165.00
Store, Cabinet, Spool, 2 Drawer, Oak, Carved Design, 21 1/2 X 7 X 14 In.	135.00
Store, Cabinet, Spool, 3 Drawer, Corticelli, Oak	135.00
Store, Cabinet, Spool, 3 Drawer, Oak, Richardson Perfect Silk	135.00
Store, Cabinet, Spool, 3 Glass & 1 Wooden Drawer, Belding's Silk, Oak	135.00
Store, Cabinet, Spool, 4 Drawer, Porcelain Knobs, 20 X 13 X 9 1/2 In.	95.00
Store, Cabinet, Spool, 5 Drawer, Oak, 21 1/4 X 14 1/2 X 18 In.	165.00
Store, Cabinet, Spool, 6 Drawer, J. & P.Coats, Original Hardware	475.00
Store, Cabinet, Thread, Glass Front Opens, 30 Compartments, 6 X 15 In.	22.50
Store, Cabinet, Thread, Lily Mills Co., Blue, Sliding Glass Doors, Tin	22.00
Store, Cabinet, Veterinary, Wood, Tin Front, Advertising Pratts	350.00
Store, Cabinet, Washer Woman, Tin, Oak, Green Background	550.00
Store, Cage, Bank Teller, Ironwork Panels, 2 Case, 2 Doors, 24 X 8 Feet	3600.00
Store, Cage, Teller's, Bronze, 19 1/2 X 24 In.	195.00
Store, Cage, Teller's, Ironwork, Beveled Glass, 2 Cages, Dividers, 24 X 8 Feet	3600.00
Store, Calendar, see Calendar, Paper	
Store, Call Box, Western Union, Oval, Blue Enamel	65.00
Store, Camel, Arab Rider, Cairo Cigarettes, Papier-Mache, 38 X 38 In.	395.00
Store, Can, Coffee, Red Dot Coffee, Wire Handle, 3 Lb.	8.00
Store, Can, Cream, Lid, 1 Quart	19.00
Store, Can, Cream, 2 Gallon	12.50
Store, Can, Dupont Gun Powder, 1924	10.00
Store, Can, Eight Brothers, Yellow	18.00
Store, Can, Heine, Olive Oil	25.00
Store, Can, Kerosene, Black Tin Around Glass, 1 Gallon	45.00
Store, Can, Nabisco, Fruit Cake	10.00
Store, Can, Nabisco, Royal Wafer	25.00
Store, Can, Old Dutch Cleanser, Red & Black Bottom	8.00
Store, Can, Orcico Cigar, Indian	35.00
Store, Can, Planters Peanuts, Square, 1 Pound	50.00
Store, Candy Vendor, Blue Regal, 1935, 14 1/2 In.	34.95
Store, Canister, Red Tiger	70.00
Store, Canister, Tobacco, Briggs	6.00
Store, Canister, Union Leader, Picture Uncle Sam	50.00
Store, Capper, Bottle, Green, Cast Iron	12.00
Store, Card, see Card	
Store, Case, Bolt, Oak, Swivel Top, 98 Drawers, 5 Feet High	600.00

Store, Case, Boyd's Revolving Needle & Bobbin, Metal	65.00 To 75.00
Store, Case, Cigar, Pocket, Brass Clip, Holds 3 Cigars, Etched	14.00
Store, Case, Cigar, Pocket, Shaped Like 3 Cigars	8.00
Store, Case, Cigarette, Walnut, Burl, Gold Double Headed Eagle, Russian	150.00
Store, Case, Clark's Teaberry Gum, Amber Dish	22.00
Store, Case, Display, Case, Display, Parker's Lead & Erasers, Glass Front	35.00
Store, Case, Display, Clockwork Powered, Round Glass, Bevel Mirrors, Old Red	225.00
Store, Case, Display, Counter Top, Brod-Vana Cigar, 9 X 6 X 4 1/2 In.	30.00
Store, Case, Display, Diamond Dye, Court Jester	285.00
Store, Case, Display, Pen Tray	21.00
Store, Case, Display, Victorian, Curved Front, Mirrored Sliding Doors, 8 Ft.	1050.00
Store, Case, Eveready Battery	52.00
Store, Case, Knife, Remington, Holds 24 Pocket Knives, 20 X 14 In.	75.00
Store, Case, Map, Hanging, Oak Door, Dated Maps	125.00
Store, Case, Nash's Japan Tea, 40 Cartons, 1/2 Lb., Each, Tin Lined	175.00
Store, Case, Ribbon, Slant Top, Glass Front	49.00
Store, Case, Sarasota Potato Chip, Wood & Glass, 14 X 18 X 23 In.	75.00
Store, Cash Register, see Cash Register	
Store, Chain, Key, Planters Peanuts	5.00
Store, Chair, Barber, Child's, Red Seat, Metal	150.00
Store, Chair, Barber, Porcelain, Black Leather	200.00
Store, Change Receiver, Cigarette Box Under Glass, Raleigh's	55.00
Store, Cheese Safe, Lift Op, Oak, Board & Knife, Dials Compute Size Of Wedge	350.00
Store, Chopper, Nut, Planters Peanut, 1938	25.00
Store, Churn, Wooden, Wooden Bands, Red, C.1810	165.00
Store, Cigar Cutter, Guillotine Type, Circular Disc Blade	10.00
Store, Circus, Figural, Push-Out Cardboard, McCormick & Co., Set Of 4	5.00
Store, Clipper, Cigar, Tulip Shaped	14.00
Store, Clock, Alarm, Planters Peanuts, Original Box	24.00
Store, Clock, Beer Advertising, 1940s, 14 In.Diameter	38.00
Store, Clock, Carstairs White Seal	37.50
Store, Clock, Cuckoo, Keebler, Novelty, 3 1/2 X 3 1/2 In.	24.00
Store, Clock, Cuckoo, Lux, 6 X 4 In.	22.00
Store, Clock, Dr.Pepper, Diamond Shaped, Electric	55.00
Store, Clock, Edelweiss Rye, Keywind, Pendulum, Brass Letters	675.00
Store, Clock, Exide Battery, Wall, Electric	17.00
Store, Clock, Goodrich Rubber Tire, Clock In Center	15.00
Store, Clock, Ingraham, Coke In Bottles, 5 Cents On Glass	350.00
Store, Clock, Jackson Square Cigars, New Orleans, Figure 8, Baird	700.00
Store, Clock, Michelob Beer, Light, Anheuser-Busch Emblem	21.00
Store, Clock, Nu-Grape, Electric, 16 X 13 In.	25.00
Store, Clock, Our Uncle Sam, Die Cast, Back Lighted, 12 X 11 In.	85.00
Store, Clock, Pearl Beer, Lighted, Water Appears To Be Flowing Over Falls	25.00
Store, Clock, Pearl Beer, Octagonal, Metal, Plate Glass, Neon, 18 1/2 In.Diam.	100.00
Store, Clock, Premier Sweepers	37.50
Store, Clock, Ritz Watch, Nabisco Promotion	50.00
Store, Clock, Schmidts, Keystone Shape	15.00
Store, Clock, Squirt, Wall, Electric	14.00
Store, Clock, Tetley Tea, Tin, 14 X 14 In.	95.00
Store, Clock, Vantage Cigarettes, Battery Operated	35.00
Store, Coach Light, English, Walnut & Brass, Velvet Lined, 27 In., Pair	400.00
Store, Coat, Worker's, Mr.Peanut Embroidered On Back, Large	75.00
Store, Coffee Grinder, see Coffee Grinder	
Store, Collar, Horse	22.50
Store, Comb, Amber Mottling, 6 In.Reticulating, 4 Prongs, Rhinestones, 6 In.	35.00
Store, Comb, Hair, Long Pig Carved Of Horn	15.00
Store, Comb, Mustache, Sheffield Silver & Ivory, Hallmarked 1782	110.00
Store, Comb, Spanish, Black Hair, 3 1/2 In.	15.00
Store, Cooler, Soda, Drink Bogey Beverages, Floor Model, Early	375.00
Store, Corkscrew, Anheuser Busch, Beer Bottle	18.50
Store, Corkscrew, Bone Handle, Sterling Grapes, 6 In.	65.00
Store, Corkscrew, Bottle Shape, American Liquor Co., Brass	17.50
Store, Corkscrew, Bullet, Says Drink Lemp, St.Louis, Brass	12.50
Store, Corkscrew, Carter's Ink	5.00
Store, Corkscrew, Distillery Company, Wood Case	7.00
Store, Corkscrew, Figural, Waiter	35.00

Store, Corkscrew, Head Of German Shepherd	15.00
Store, Corkscrew, Lady's Legs, Morgan Distilling Co.	35.00
Store, Corkscrew, Metal, Germany	7.00
Store, Corkscrew, Wine, Burl Handle, 6 In.	20.00
Store, Counter, 15 Drawers, Oak	1700.00
Store, Creamer & Sugar, Lipton Tea	7.50
Store, Creamer, Salada Tea, Yellow	5.00
Store, Crusher, Ice, American Soda Fountain Co.	45.00
Store, Cuff Links, Planters Peanuts, Original Box	15.00
Store, Cup, Cyclist's, Brass, 1897	17.50
Store, Cup, Measure For Kenny's Coffee, Aluminum, 1 3/4 In.	10.00
Store, Cup, Measuring, Planters Peanuts	50.00
Store, Cup, Trophy, Quaker Oats Co., 1930	25.00
Store, Curler, Mustache, Decorated	10.00
Store, Cutter Cigar, Valet Auto, Strop Razor Knife	7.00
Store, Cutter, Cigar, Brass Cutter, Iron Saucer	4.00
Store, Cutter, Cigar, Bust Of Silk-Hatted Man, 19th Century, Mouth Cuts	225.00
Store, Cutter, Cigar, Clauss Warranted Cutlery	7.00
Store, Cutter, Cigar, Curtseying Ballet Dancer	95.00
Store, Cutter, Cigar, Dated May 17, 1877	35.00
Store, Cutter, Cigar, Desk, Wick Lighter	85.00
Store, Cutter, Cigar, Eclipse Novelty Corporation, Cutting Wheel	10.50
Store, Cutter, Cigar, Figural Pig, Counter, Cast Iron	235.00
Store, Cutter, Cigar, Finger Rest Type, Cast Iron Bowl, Advertising	125.00
Store, Cutter, Cigar, Fire Alarm Lighter, Ashtray, Fez To Put Out Fire	200.00
Store, Cutter, Cigar, Folding, Scissor Handled, Black & White 5 Cent	7.50
Store, Cutter, Cigar, Guillotine Type, Circular Disc Blade	10.00
Store, Cutter, Cigar, Judge Fair, Glass	135.00
Store, Cutter, Cigar, Lady's, Pearl Handled	15.00
Store, Cutter, Cigar, Moul Wines & Liquors, York, Pa.	12.00
Store, Cutter, Cigar, Pocket, Johnnie Walker Whiskey Bottle	75.00
Store, Cutter, Cigar, Pocket, Razor Type, B.P.O.E.	15.00
Store, Cutter, Cigar, Pocket, Shape Of Man	70.00
Store, Cutter, Cigar, Roi-Tan	15.00
Store, Cutter, Cigar, Ruled, Star Incised, Wood, 2 3/4 X 6 In.	20.00
Store, Cutter, Cigar, Slide Type, Dated 1910, 10K Gold, 2 In.	35.00
Store, Cutter, Cigar, Sliding Blade	8.50
Store, Cutter, Cigar, Smoke Havana Filled 108 5 Cent Cigars, Signed	35.00
Store, Cutter, Cigar, 10K Gold	55.00
Store, Cutter, Quill, Case	100.00
Store, Cutter, Tobaccco, Holmes, Walnut, Cast Iron	45.00
Store, Cutter, Tobacco Plug, P.J.Sorg & Co., Cast Iron	60.00
Store, Cutter, Tobacco, Arrow	35.00
Store, Cutter, Tobacco, Brown's Mule, Cast Iron	27.00
Store, Cutter, Tobacco, Cut Plug, Battle Ax	95.00 To 115.00
Store, Cutter, Tobacco, E.C.Simmon's Keen-Kutter	50.00
Store, Cutter, Tobacco, Great Slice Plug, Counter	95.00
Store, Cutter, Tobacco, Griswold Plug	28.00
Store, Cutter, Tobacco, Iron, Brighton, Red Devil	48.00
Store, Cutter, Tobacco, Iron, 16 X 7 In.	35.00
Store, Cutter, Tobacco, Plunkett & Jarrell Grocer Co., Little Rock, Ark.	65.00
Store, Cutter, Tobacco, Reading Hardware Co., Standard Tobacco Knife, 16 In.	35.00
Store, Cutter, Tobacco, Roger's Iron Co., Medieval Ax Shape, 17 In.	60.00
Store, Cutter, Tobacco, Spearhead, Original Paint	20.00
Store, Cutter, Tobacco, Standard, Reading Hardware Company	50.00
Store, Cutter, Tobacco, Star	50.00
Store, Cutter, Tobacco, The Champion Knife, Cast Iron, 18 In.	25.00
Store, Cutter, Tobacco, The Imp, Cast Iron	85.00
Store, Desk, Counter Top, Slant Top, Signed Baldwin, C.1830, 24 X 19 X 9 In.	125.00
Store, Dipper, The Nut House, Tin, Shape Of House	22.00
Store, Dish, Change, Rigoletto Cigars, Glass, 6 1/2 In.Diameter	28.00
Store, Dish, Clark's Teaberry Gum Display Dish, Amber, 2 Legs For Slant	22.00
Store, Dish, Soap, Hand, Watrous, Brass	10.00
Store, Dispenser, Anheuser Busch	175.00
Store, Dispenser, Buckeye Root Beer, Brown Log	160.00
Store, Dispenser, Buckeye Root Beer, Tan Log	140.00

Store, Dispenser, Carnation Malted Milk, Milk Glass, Tin Lid	50.00
Store, Dispenser, Cherri Bon	500.00
Store, Dispenser, Cherry Smash	325.00
Store, Dispenser, Cigarette Slot, 1 Cent, Cast Aluminum	225.00
Store, Dispenser, Cigarette, Mechanical Mule, 9 X 10 1/2 In.	50.00
Store, Dispenser, Coin Change, Brandt Automatic	95.00
Store, Dispenser, Diamond Matches, Coin Operated, One Book For One Cent	150.00
Store, Dispenser, Dixie Paper Cup, 1 Cent Coin Operated, 1913	500.00
Store, Dispenser, Dixie, Glass Etched Dome	150.00
Store, Dispenser, Fine Sherry, China	125.00
Store, Dispenser, Fry's Choice Chocolates, Etched Glass, 27 X 15 X 27 In.	250.00
Store, Dispenser, Grape Crush, Purple	250.00
Store, Dispenser, Gumball, Pistol Shoots Penny	150.00
Store, Dispenser, Heinz Vinegar Barrel On Glass Base, Advertising, C.1905	155.00
Store, Dispenser, Hires Root Beer	325.00
Store, Dispenser, Hot Water, Barber Shop, Copper, C.1860, 8 X 7 In.Diameter	100.00
Store, Dispenser, Hunter's Root Beer, Shaped Like Barrel, Dated 1917	125.00
Store, Dispenser, Ice Cream Sandwich, 1920	33.00
Store, Dispenser, Ice Cream, 20 Syrup Doors, Mahogany & Onyx	1000.00
Store, Dispenser, Malted Grape Nut	90.00
Store, Dispenser, Master's, Prophylactic	1050.00
Store, Dispenser, Matchbox, 1 Cent, Cast Iron	150.00
Store, Dispenser, Mission Fruit Juice, Green Glass Top, Chrome Base	75.00
Store, Dispenser, Mission Orange, Black Base, Barrel Top	95.00
Store, Dispenser, Orange Crush Syrup, Frosted Globe, Black Base	125.00
Store, Dispenser, Peanut, Double, Square Glass, Penny	275.00
Store, Dispenser, Planters, 2 Piece Glass Container	6.50
Store, Dispenser, Pool Chalk, Late 1800s, Uses Early American Penny	1200.00
Store, Dispenser, Right-Cut Chewing Tobacco, Tin, 4 1/2 X 2 1/2 X 11 In.	45.00
Store, Dispenser, Root Beer, Rochester, Barrel On Log	150.00
Store, Dispenser, Stamp, 10 Cent, Stampmaster	15.00
Store, Dispenser, Syrup, Pink Frosted Glass, Nesbitt's, 1920s	50.00
Store, Dispenser, Syrup, Ward's Lemon Crush	150.00 To 265.00
Store, Dispenser, Syrup, Ward's Lime Crush	350.00
Store, Dispenser, Syrup, Ward's Orange Crush	140.00 To 300.00
Store, Dispenser, Tape, Countertop, Footed, Nickel Plated, Cast Iron	95.00
Store, Dispenser, Tape, Victorian, Nickel Plated Iron	125.00
Store, Dispenser, Tobacco, Star Braid, 24 Pigeon Holes, Drawer	125.00
Store, Dispenser, Treu's Juices, Earthenware, Figural Cover, Red Teapot	325.00
Store, Dispenser, Twine, Old Nick Twine	45.00
Store, Dispenser, Vicks Cough Drops, Wall, Metal Front	25.00
Store, Dispenser, Vigoral, Copper Liner, 14 China Cups, Silver Pot, 2 1/2 Ft.	3000.00
Store, Dispenser, Welch-Ade	75.00
Store, Dispenser, 5 Cent Candy Bar, Wood, 6 Column, 1920s, 5 Feet	550.00
Store, Dispenser, 5 Column Cigarette, Counter Model	45.00
Store, Dispensor, 1 Cent, Hershey's Chocolate, 1940s	47.50
Store, Display Bin, Life Savers, 9 Flavors, Slant Top, 10 X 11 X 8 In.	45.00
Store, Display Cabinet, Venida Hair Net, Wood, 7 In.Square, 24 In.High	35.00
Store, Display Case, Candy, Oak & Glass, Mirror In Back, 36 X 24 Feet	95.00
Store, Display Case, Remington, Glass & Metal, 12 X 29 In.	45.00
Store, Display Case, Slant Front, 2 Shelves, 14 X 7 X 11 1/4 In.	100.00
Store, Display Case, Wrigley's Standard Brands, Tin, 16 X 6 1/2 In.	45.00
Store, Display Shelf, Baker's Vanilla, Tin	22.00
Store, Display, Canister, Sterling Finecut Tobacco, Hinged Lid	75.00
Store, Display, Regal Shoe Factory, Iron & Glass, Scale Model	750.00
Store, Display, Wrigley's 5 Cent Chewing Gum, 5 Section, 16 X 6 X 3 In.	35.00
Store, Door Bar, Orange Crush, 3 X 29 In., Pair	15.00
Store, Door Bar, Pepsi Cola, Porcelain, 3 X 20 In., Pair	30.00
Store, Door Latch, Bean Style, New Hampshire, C.1800, 10 In.	22.50
Store, Door Push, Canada Dry Hi Spot Lemon Soda, Tin, Pair	12.00
Store, Door Push, Dr.Pepper, 4 X 8 In.	24.00
Store, Door Push, Drink Eight Ball, Mirror In Tin, Pair	15.00
Store, Door Push, Fringe's Cigars, Tin, Pair	18.00
Store, Door Push, Palmolive, Porcelain	10.00
Store, Door Push, Sweet Heart Flour, Heart Shape, Porcelain, Pair	25.00
Store, Door, Post Office, Brass With Window & U.S. Front, 3 1/2 X 5 In.	6.00

Store, Drum, Tin, Lithograph, Used For Syrup, 10 Gallon	35.00
Store, Eyecup, Cobalt, Blue	22.00
Store, Eyecup, Elder Flower Lotion Company	12.00
Store, Fan, Ceiling, Electric, Adams Bagnell, Twin Powered	195.00
Store, Fan, Ceiling, Ornate Plate & Irons, Tulip Lights & Globes	135.00
Store, Fan, Ceiling, Subway, Light Globe	100.00
Store, Fan, Ceiling, 3-Speed, Perkins, Not Working	300.00
Store, Fan, Ceiling, 4 Blades, 48 In.	225.00
Store, Fan, Emerson Motor, Ice Cream Parlor, 4 Blades	225.00
Store, Fan, Hand, Missouri Farmers Association	2.00
Store, Fan, Putnam Dyes	8.00 To 9.00
Store, Fan, Royal Granite Ware, Shape Of Frying Pan	15.00
Store, Fan, Rush, Milton Standley Funeral Home	11.00
Store, Fan, Shoo-Fly	125.00
Store, Fan, Table, G.E., Brass Blades, 3 Speed Oscillates	65.00
Store, Fan, Westinghouse, Brass Blades & Frame, 8 1/2 In.Diameter	22.50
Store, Fan, Westinghouse, Brass Blades & Guards, 12 In.Blades	60.00
Store, Figure, Cigar Indian, DeMuth Zinc Casting Over Robb's Wood Figure	3500.00
Store, Figure, Nipper, Dog, Victor, Largest Size ... *Illus*	600.00
Store, Figure, Nipper, Dog, Victor, Papier-Mache, 14 In.	400.00
Store, Figure, Sappho Cigar	225.00
Store, Fire Extinguisher, Black & Gilt, Phoenix, Connecticut, 2 X 16 In.	22.00
Store, Fire Extinguisher, Kilfrye, N.Y.C., Black On Orange, 2 X 22 In.	22.00
Store, Flashlight, Winchester, 2 Cell, 1920, Nickel On Brass, 9 1/4 In.	30.00
Store, Flour Sack, Mother's Best, Printed On War Surplus Parachute Silk	8.00
Store, Foot Warmer, Carpet Covered, Drawer For Charcoal	16.00
Store, Foot Warmer, Pierced Tin Insert, Turned Wooden Frame, Red	67.00
Store, Fountain, Colored Tiles, Marble, Crock Jars With Dispensers	850.00

Store, Figure, Nipper, Dog, Victor, Largest Size

Store, Fountain, Soda, Double Sink, Crockery Dispensers, 6 Flavors, 1930s	1500.00
Store, Fountain, Stainless Steel, Soda, Double Sink & Freezer	500.00
Store, Frog, Compliments Of Michigan Stove Co., Cast Iron, 4 1/2 X 2 In.	100.00
Store, Funnel, Bryant & May's Wax Vesta, Glass	12.00
Store, Funnel, Hart's Delight Stove Polish	26.00
Store, Funnel, Shut Off Valve, Moonshine	35.00
Store, Glass, Beveled Ovals, 1919, 10 3/4 X 5 3/4 In.	5.00
Store, Glass, Magnifying, Elkhorn Handle, 10 1/2 In.	45.00
Store, Glass, Reverse On Glass, Hamm's Beer, 1905, 28 X 36 In.	850.00
Store, Glass, Shot, Benedict Rye, Purist Of Whiskies, Marked	4.00
Store, Glass, Shot, Everytime We Drink Things Look Different, Davis & Drake	4.50
Store, Globe, Apothecary, Amber Glass, 4 In.	4.75
Store, Globe, Budweiser Barley Malt Syrup	85.00
Store, Globe, Lamp, Elk's Lodge, Clock Between Antlers, 11 1/2 In.	85.00
Store, Globe, World, Schlitz Beer, Lighted, With Clock	60.00
Store, Gum Machine, see Store, Machine, Gum ball	
Store, Hamper, Clothes, Wicker, 20 In.	33.00
Store, Helmet, Signal Light, Cast Aluminum, Battery Lighted	90.00
Store, Holder, Broom	55.00
Store, Holder, Cigar, Peasant Woman, Sheaf Of Wheat, Match Holder & Strike	150.00
Store, Holder, Cigarettes, Camel, Lucky, Chesterfield, Hinged Lid, Wooden	20.00
Store, Holder, Paper Bag, Fan Shape, Red, Black Stenciling, 19th Century	125.00
Store, Holder, Pepsi-Cola, Carrying, Long Handle	25.00
Store, Holder, Straw, Soda Fountain, 11 3/4 In.	58.00

Store, Holder, String, Cast Iron, Beehive Shape	25.00
Store, Holder, String, Cat On Yarn, Ceramic	4.00
Store, Holder, String, Glass, Oblong Figures, Flint, 4 X 4 7/8 In., Diameter	83.00
Store, Holder, String, Italian Chef	10.00
Store, Holder, String, Shaped Like Ball Of String, Iron	87.50
Store, Holder, String, Sunbonnet Girls	7.00
Store, Hook, Bill, Hanging, Cast Iron	5.00
Store, Hook, Button, Foldaway	4.50
Store, Humidor, Figural, Dog With Cigar In Mouth, Glass Eyes, Wooden, 6 In.	65.00
Store, Humidor, Frog, Incised No. On Bottom	35.00
Store, Humidor, La Palina, Paper Label, Glass	45.00
Store, Humidor, Tobacco, Portrait, Girl With Guitar, Brown, Tan, Germany	75.00
Store, Jar, Apothecary, Ground Top, Graduated Sizes, Set Of 6	58.00
Store, Jar, Candy, 5 Section, Oak Lift On Each, 32 X 14 X 9 In.	165.00
Store, Jar, Counter Top, Kis-Me Gum	45.00
Store, Jar, Cracker, Lance, Tin Lid, 10 In.	15.00
Store, Jar, Drugstore, Butte County, Glass, 19 In.	55.00
Store, Jar, Franklin Caro Company, Square	60.00
Store, Jar, Gold Bloom Coffee, Original Top	5.00
Store, Jar, Horlick's Malted Milk, Drug Store	50.00
Store, Jar, Impressed Lion's Head, Monarch Finer Foods, Tin Screw Top	10.00
Store, Jar, Kis-Me Gum, Counter Top, Raised Letters	45.00
Store, Jar, Lance, Counter Top, Original Lid	35.00
Store, Jar, LaPalina Cigar, Glass, Top	10.00
Store, Jar, Peanut Finial, 9 In.Square, Set Of 4	175.00
Store, Jar, Peanut, Nut House, Picture Of Nut House On Jar	65.00
Store, Jar, Peanut, Squirrel Emblem, Lid	60.00
Store, Jar, Planters Peanut, Counter, Tin Lid	40.00
Store, Jar, Planters Peanut, Emblem With Large Peanut On Lid	110.00
Store, Jar, Planters Peanut, 4 Corner Blown Peanut Jar	135.00
Store, Jar, Planters Peanuts, Gold Fish	50.00
Store, Jar, Planters Peanuts, 6 Sided	42.00
Store, Jar, Planters, Tall Streamline, Tin Lid	45.00
Store, Jar, Power, Elephant Finial, Green Frosted, 5 1/4 X 4 1/2 In.	35.00
Store, Jar, Talcum, 1915 Violet, Colgate-Palmolive Company	50.00
Store, Jar, Tobacco, Boar Finial, Acid Finish, Blue Glass, 6 X 8 1/2 In.	67.50
Store, Jar, Tobacco, Figural, Full Figure Of Boy Scout	75.00
Store, Jar, Tobacco, Globe, Blown Pot, 1882, Lid & Bail Handle	110.00
Store, Jar, Tom's Peanut Butter Sandwiches & Sweet Sandwiches, 12 In.	20.00
Store, Jug, Old Judge Coffee, Glass, Embossed Owl, 1 Gallon	12.50
Store, Jug, Whiskey, Missouri Corn, McCormick	11.00
Store, Juicer, Lemon, Maple, Carved Edges, Lignum-Vitae Inserts	35.00
Store, Juicer, Sunkist, Milk Glass, Green	35.00
Store, Keg, Wine, Wooden Spigot, 20 X 15 In.	65.00
Store, Knife, see Knife	
Store, Knob & Spigot, Brass, Bartel, India Pale Ale, Syracuse, N.Y.	25.00
Store, Knob, Beer Tap, Enameled Type	15.00
Store, Knob, Beer Tap, Ortliebs Ale, Green, Celluloid Ball	15.00
Store, Lacer, Corset, Dated 1888, Case, 11 In.	42.00
Store, Lamp, Country Store	225.00
Store, Lamp, Grain Belt Beer Can	12.00
Store, Lamp, Hanging, Brass Font, 14 Inch Shade	119.50
Store, Lamp, Hanging, Oil, Tin Shades, Juneau, Made In U.S.A., Pair	500.00
Store, Lamp, Kerosene, Hanging, Prisms	325.00
Store, Lamp, Peanut Display, Bulb's Heat Revolves Top Circus Scene, 1950	17.50
Store, Leg Irons, Tubular Key, C.1870, Cast Steel, 26 In.	85.00
Store, Light, Bar, Coors, Scenic, Animated	55.00
Store, Light, Motorcycle, Carbide, Nickel Over Brass, 1899	39.00
Store, Lighter, Cigar, Counter, Keywound, Ruby Glass Shade, Mechanical, 3 In.	475.00
Store, Lighter, Cigar, Jump Spark, Midland	300.00
Store, Lighter, Cigar, Kerosene, Counter Model, Square Base, 26 In.	185.00
Store, Lighter, Cigarette, Glass Dome Ticker Tape	40.00
Store, Lighter, Cigarette, Oil Derrick	35.00
Store, Lighter, Cigarette, Planters Peanuts, Shape Of Peanut	100.00
Store, Lighter, Cigarette, R.C.Cola, Bottle Shape	10.00
Store, Lighter, Moxie, Horse & Car	38.00

Store, Lunch Box, Blue Tiger	30.00
Store, Lunch Box, Blue, Silver, Children Lithograph	12.50
Store, Lunch Box, Bonanza, 1963	10.00
Store, Lunch Box, Buccaneer	10.00
Store, Lunch Box, Children Playing In Sand Box	35.00
Store, Lunch Box, Dixie Queen, Picture Of Pretty Girl	65.00
Store, Lunch Box, Eutopia	125.00
Store, Lunch Box, Fashion Cut Plug Tobacco	95.00
Store, Lunch Box, H.O. Cut Plug	5.00
Store, Lunch Box, Hand Bag Shape, Cut Plug	65.00
Store, Lunch Box, Just Suits	25.00 To 40.00
Store, Lunch Box, Land Of The Giants	3.00
Store, Lunch Box, Mayo's Cut Plug, Deep Blue, 3 3/4 X 4 3/4 In.	35.00
Store, Lunch Box, Mayo's Fine Tobacco	8.50
Store, Lunch Box, Patterson Seal	9.00
Store, Lunch Box, Pedro	48.00 To 55.00
Store, Lunch Box, Red, Gold Eagle, Union Leader Cut Plug	20.00
Store, Lunch Box, Redicut	90.00
Store, Lunch Box, Tiger Chewing Tobacco, Red	35.00
Store, Lunch Box, Tiger Tobacco	16.00
Store, Lunch Box, Union Leader, Basketweave	15.00
Store, Lunch Box, Union Pacific Tea Co.	45.00
Store, Lunch Box, Warnick & Brown	35.00
Store, Lunch Box, Wild Fruit	55.00
Store, Lunch Box, Winner	65.00 To 115.00
Store, Lunch Box, Winney, Pictures Of Old Race Cars	100.00
Store, Lunch Pail, Corn Flake Girl	25.00
Store, Lunch Pail, Little Pig	10.00
Store, Lunch Pail, Patterson Tobacco	15.00
Store, Lunch Pail, Tiger Tobacco, 2 Handled, Red, 8 X 6 X 6 In.	25.00
Store, Lunch Pail, Warnick & Brown, Tobacco	25.00
Store, Machine, Arcade, Digger	675.00
Store, Machine, Arcade, Globe Ball Lift Grip Tester	2800.00
Store, Machine, Arcade, Peep Show	375.00
Store, Machine, Arcade, Solar Horoscope	575.00
Store, Machine, Automaton, Wood	675.00
Store, Machine, Ball Walk, 10 Cent	45.00
Store, Machine, Baseball, Penny Arcade, 18 1/2 In.	295.00
Store, Machine, Bear Gun, Seeburg	500.00
Store, Machine, Bennett, Peep Show, Drop Card	1495.00
Store, Machine, Brandt, Coin Changer	95.00
Store, Machine, Buckley, Slot, Pointmaker, Electronic	300.00
Store, Machine, Buffalo Bill Pistol Shooting Target	245.00
Store, Machine, Caille, Roulette, Counter Model, 25 Cent	4500.00
Store, Machine, Carbonator, Soda Fountain, Compressor Driven, 1899	175.00
Store, Machine, Coon Hunt, Seeburg	250.00
Store, Machine, Deputy Sheriff, Gun Game, Floor Model	275.00
Store, Machine, Dictaphone, Edison, Cylinder	45.00
Store, Machine, Digger, Gulf States, Light Up, Exhibit	950.00
Store, Machine, Drivemobile, Mutoscope	245.00
Store, Machine, Dunbar, Popcorn, Floor Model	775.00
Store, Machine, Empire, Wood Penny Drop	350.00
Store, Machine, Fortune, Miss Miami	85.00
Store, Machine, Game, Texas Ranger Gatling Gun, Chicago Coin	400.00
Store, Machine, Granny Fortune Teller	725.00
Store, Machine, Grip Test, Gottlieb	55.00
Store, Machine, Gum Ball, Atom, 3 Reel Trade Stimulator	100.00
Store, Machine, Gum Ball, Hart Bros.	24.00
Store, Machine, Gum Ball, 1 Cent, Floor Model, Titan	65.00
Store, Machine, Gum Ball, 5 Reel, Kounter King	155.00
Store, Machine, Gum, Pulver, Yellow Kid	175.00
Store, Machine, Gun Game, Challenger	110.00
Store, Machine, Hockey Game, 2 Player, Chicago	165.00
Store, Machine, Holcomb & Hoke, Popcorn, Floor Model, Quartered Oak	1200.00
Store, Machine, Holcomb & Hoke, Popcorn, Table Model	625.00
Store, Machine, Jenning's, Little Duke, 1 Cent	900.00

Store, Machine, Jenning's, Pays Out In Golf Balls, 25 Cent	1200.00
Store, Machine, Jenning's, Pinball, Sportsman, Cash Pay	550.00
Store, Machine, Jenning's, Slot, Deer Scene, 25 Cent	875.00
Store, Machine, Jenning's, Slot, Silver Chief, 5 Cent	775.00
Store, Machine, Kicker & Catcher	135.00
Store, Machine, Little Duke, Slot, 1 Cent	600.00
Store, Machine, Little-Pro Golf Game, Size Of Pinball	175.00
Store, Machine, Mansfield, Automatic Clerk	450.00
Store, Machine, Mills, Dewey, 5 Cent, Musical Front	8500.00
Store, Machine, Mills, Judge, Upright, 5 Cent	5900.00
Store, Machine, Mills, Panorama, Extra Fil & Parts	675.00
Store, Machine, Mills, Peep Show, Drop Card, Table Model	495.00
Store, Machine, Mills, Slot, Castle Front, 5 Cent	800.00
Store, Machine, Mills, Slot, Silver-King, Gooseneck	900.00
Store, Machine, Mills, Slot, Special Award	650.00
Store, Machine, Mutoscope, Candy Lifter, Monkey Climb	1500.00
Store, Machine, Mutoscope, Football Kick	750.00
Store, Machine, Mutoscope, Uses English Coin Size Of Quarter, Cast Iron	575.00
Store, Machine, Mystic Pen, Seeburg	750.00
Store, Machine, Pace, Bantam, 10 Cent	650.00
Store, Machine, Pace, Bantam, 25 Cent	550.00
Store, Machine, Pace, Slot, Upright, 25 Cent	2000.00
Store, Machine, Paycheck Writing, Todd Protectograph, 1915	39.00
Store, Machine, Peanut Vendor, Tin	65.00
Store, Machine, Peep Show, Counter Model, Oak Case, Wood Marque, 1 Cent	650.00
Store, Machine, Personality Meters	125.00
Store, Machine, Pinball, Chicago, Coin Band Box	650.00
Store, Machine, Pinball, Gottlieb, Dancing Dolls, Wood Rails, 1960	150.00
Store, Machine, Pinball, Lighthouse, Battery Operated	350.00
Store, Machine, Pinball, Mills, Cherry Front, 25 Cent	750.00
Store, Machine, Pinball, Pace Star, Early Gooseneck	1250.00
Store, Machine, Pinball, Pace Star, Twin Jackpot, Early Gooseneck	1450.00
Store, Machine, Pinball, Triple Your Money	75.00
Store, Machine, Pinball, William, Gun Club, Wood Rail, 1954	250.00
Store, Machine, Popcorn, Gas Model, Portable, Large	300.00
Store, Machine, Ribbon Candy Maker, Wooden Cog Wheels, Glass Handle, C.1870	165.00
Store, Machine, Scopitone, 36 Films, 16 Mm., Model 450, 25 Cent	1500.00
Store, Machine, Sky Fighter, Seeburg	550.00
Store, Machine, Slot, Blue Seal, 5 Cent, Watling	875.00
Store, Machine, Slot, Castle Front, 5 Cent, Mills	800.00
Store, Machine, Slot, Deer Scene, 25 Cent, Jenning	875.00
Store, Machine, Slot, Gold Ball Dispenser, Jennings Victoria	1375.00
Store, Machine, Slot, Gooseneck, 25 Cent, Pace	925.00
Store, Machine, Slot, Jennings Triplex	3000.00
Store, Machine, Slot, Little Duke, 1 Cent	600.00
Store, Machine, Slot, Pointmaker, Electronic, Buckley	300.00
Store, Machine, Slot, Silver Chief, 5 Cent, Jenning	775.00
Store, Machine, Slot, Silver-King Gooseneck, Mills	900.00
Store, Machine, Slot, Upright, White-Uno	9500.00
Store, Machine, Slot, Wall Mount, Novomat, German, 50 Cent	295.00
Store, Machine, Smilin Sam From Alabam, 1 Peanut, Aluminum	400.00
Store, Machine, Soccer, Chester Pollard, Small	850.00
Store, Machine, Solar Horoscope, Muto	450.00
Store, Machine, Stand Up Drivemobile, Muto	450.00
Store, Machine, Strength Tester, Floor Model, 1 Cent, 6 Way, Mercury	175.00
Store, Machine, Sweet Chocolate, One Cent, Dated 1915	175.00
Store, Machine, The Favorite, Jennings, Penny Flip	650.00
Store, Machine, Tol-A-Top, 25 Cent	1600.00
Store, Machine, Twin Tower Digger, Mutoscope, Counter Type	800.00
Store, Machine, Vending, Gum, Wood Case, Wood & Tin	500.00
Store, Machine, Vending, Match, 2 Chambers, C.1920s, Cast Iron, 12 X 4 1/2 In.	145.00
Store, Machine, Vending, 1 Cent Junior, United, Small	100.00
Store, Machine, Vendor, Automatic Clerk, Pepsin Gum, Mansfield	500.00
Store, Machine, Viewer, Cailescope, Drop Card, Oak, Crank	2000.00
Store, Machine, Washing, Copper	69.00
Store, Machine, Washing, Wringer, Wood	12.00

Store, Machine, Watling, Slot, Blue Seal, 5 Cent	875.00
Store, Machine, When Should You Marry	625.00
Store, Machine, Whirl-A-Ball, Wood Case, 1 Cent, Bally	250.00
Store, Machine, Wild Indian	875.00
Store, Machine, Williams, Pinch Hitter Baseball, Arcade, Wooden Rails	250.00
Store, Machine, Zeno, Gum	100.00
Store, Machine, 1 Cent Steeplechase	400.00
Store, Manicure Set, Ivory Handles, Original Case, 5 Pieces	9.00
Store, Mannequin, Boy In Sleepers With Dog, Hanes Merrichild Sleepers	140.00
Store, Map, U.S., 1834, School, Pull Roll, Vignette Engravings	75.00
Store, Match Safe, Dr.Pepper	12.00
Store, Match Safe, Schlitz	20.00
Store, Match Vendor, Ohio Match Box.1 Cent, The Only Ohio Worth Keeping	175.00
Store, Measure, Shoe Foot, Ivory Inlaid Ruler, Marked Kerby & Bros., 19 In.	50.00
Store, Measure, Syrup, Orange Crush, 6 Ounce	9.00
Store, Merry-Go-Round, 2 Horses, 10 Cent, Kiddie Ride	395.00
Store, Mirror, Acme Paints	10.00
Store, Mirror, Angelus Marshmallow, Horizontal Oval Mirror, Pocket	35.00
Store, Mirror, Barrel Shaped, Cudahay Refining Co., Oval	18.00
Store, Mirror, Beeman's Pepsin Gum	32.00
Store, Mirror, Beeman's Pepsin Gum, Oval	38.00
Store, Mirror, Boot & Shoe Worker's Union	18.00
Store, Mirror, Borden Co., Celluloid, 3 1/2 In.	17.00
Store, Mirror, Buster Brown, Brass	15.00
Store, Mirror, Camp John L.Thompson, 34th Annual Encampment, 1910, Pocket	16.00
Store, Mirror, Cascarets	20.00
Store, Mirror, Ceresota Flour	20.00
Store, Mirror, Cherub At Top, Lacy Edged, Cast Iron, Oval, 9 X 11 In.	38.00
Store, Mirror, Drewry's Extra Dry Beer, Mounted Policeman, 10 X 16 In.	20.00
Store, Mirror, Duffy's Pure Malt Whiskey	25.00
Store, Mirror, Elks, 1908	15.00
Store, Mirror, Erotica, 20s, Bobbed-Hair Girls	8.50
Store, Mirror, Ex-Lax, Round, 1912	15.00
Store, Mirror, Good Luck Bread, Celluloid Handle	15.00
Store, Mirror, Hand, Art Nouveau, Silver Plate, 1907 Jamestown Expo., 4 In.	16.75
Store, Mirror, Hand, Tin & Celluloid, Toledo Biscuit	30.00
Store, Mirror, Hired Man's, Wooden Frame, Original Glass, 13 1/2 X 18 In.	32.00
Store, Mirror, Horlick's Malted Milk	20.00
Store, Mirror, James Logan Cigar, Black Boy With Goose	28.00
Store, Mirror, Mascot Crushed Cut Tobacco, Dog Pictured, Round, Pocket, 2 In.	21.50
Store, Mirror, Mennen's Talcum Powder	15.00
Store, Mirror, New King Snuff, Rectangle	25.00
Store, Mirror, Old Taylor Whiskey	8.00
Store, Mirror, Palmer Cox Brownies, Policeman In Middle, 9 X 4 1/2 In.	55.00
Store, Mirror, Paperweight, Pickering Lumber, Kansas	20.00
Store, Mirror, Parry Manufacturing Co., Pocket	35.00
Store, Mirror, Paul Valetto Watches Of Quality, Bevelled Glass	10.00
Store, Mirror, Remington Standard Typewriter, Celluloid, 3 1/2 In.	22.00
Store, Mirror, Remington, Old Typewriter	20.00
Store, Mirror, Schaefer Pianos, Picture Of Piano	12.50
Store, Mirror, Somersworth Stoves & Ranges, Round, Pocket	4.00
Store, Mirror, Star Soap	10.00
Store, Mirror, The Franklin Portable Crane Hoist Company, 4 In.	35.00
Store, Mirror, The Tap-All Beers Drawn From The Wood, Round, Picture, Pocket	11.00
Store, Mirror, Thor, Bevelled Glass, Handle	18.00
Store, Mirror, University Theatre, Chicago	12.00
Store, Mirror, Victrola Record, Pocket	20.00
Store, Mirror, White House Coffee	18.00
Store, Mirror, White Swan Flour, Horoscope All Around, Pocket	20.00
Store, Mold, see also Pewter, Mold; Tin, Mold	
Store, Mold & Stamp, Sheep, Carved _Illus_	145.00
Store, Mold Chocolate, Tweetie Bird, 10 X 11 In.	35.00
Store, Mold, Cigar, Handforged Nails, Makes 20 Cigars	39.50
Store, Mold, Ice Cream, see Pewter, Mold, Ice Cream	
Store, Money Clip, Royal Crown _Illus_	15.50
Store, Moxie, Cutout Cardboard, Standup Boy Carrying Bag, C.1927	150.00

Store, Stamp: *(top)* Mold & Stamp, Sheep (see page 597);
(bottom, l. to r.) Butter, Partridge, Wafer Type (see page 603).

Store, Opener, Bottle, Pepsi-Cola Bottle Shaped

Store, Money Clip, Royal Crown
(See Page 597)

Store, Mug, Blatz Brown Beer	20.00
Store, Mug, Drink Hires Root Beer, Child In Color Under Glass, German	60.00
Store, Mug, Old Heidelberg	7.00
Store, Mug, Pabst	9.50
Store, Mug, Revere Romney Tapster Beer, Horse & Rider, Set Of 4	45.00
Store, Mug, Tivoli Copper	8.50
Store, Mug, Uncle Wiggily	25.00
Store, Nutcracker, Alligator, 7 1/2 In.	7.00
Store, Nutcracker, Elephant, Red Paint, Rope Tail, Cast Iron, 5 X 9 1/2 In.	45.00
Store, Nutcracker, Squirrel, C.1820	90.00
Store, Opener & Cork Stopper, Moxie	5.00
Store, Opener, Beck's Beer, Wooden	4.00
Store, Opener, Beer, Signal Beer, It Rings The Bell	10.00
Store, Opener, Bottle, Alligator Biting Black Boy, Cast Iron	20.00
Store, Opener, Bottle, Amber, Bohemian	6.50
Store, Opener, Bottle, Atlas Prager Beer, Flat Metal	4.00
Store, Opener, Bottle, Button Hook, Cigar Cutter, Shoe Shape	9.00
Store, Opener, Bottle, Dog, Wall	20.00
Store, Opener, Bottle, Drunk At Lamp Post, Leg Down	9.00
Store, Opener, Bottle, Drunk At Lamp Post, Leg Up	9.00
Store, Opener, Bottle, Embossed Handle, Dated 1894, Sterling, 5 1/2 In.	18.00
Store, Opener, Bottle, Fish, Opener Inside Mouth, Cast Iron	25.00
Store, Opener, Bottle, Fisherman With Net	25.00
Store, Opener, Bottle, Hand Shape, Falstaff	6.00
Store, Opener, Bottle, Horse On Handle	15.00
Store, Opener, Bottle, Horsehead, 4 3/4 In.	16.00
Store, Opener, Bottle, Kansas City Breweries Co., Stag Handle	22.50
Store, Opener, Bottle, Lizard, Brass	5.00
Store, Opener, Bottle, Lobster	5.00
Store, Opener, Bottle, Parrot	15.00
Store, Opener, Bottle, Pelican, Cast Iron	15.00
Store, Opener, Bottle, Pepsi-Cola Bottle Shaped *Illus*	31.00
Store, Opener, Bottle, Pink Elephant, Cast Iron	20.00
Store, Opener, Bottle, Seagull On Perch, Cast Iron	15.00
Store, Opener, Bottle, Shape Of Boot, Buffalo Brewing	25.00
Store, Opener, Bottle, St.Joseph Soda Seltzer, Bottle Shape, 1912	8.00
Store, Opener, Bottle, White Rock Water & Ginger Ale, Lady On Rock	5.00

Store, Opener, Box, Cigar, Little Chancello Cigar, 5 Cent Size	5.00
Store, Opener, Can, Fishtail, Iron	6.00
Store, Opener, Can, Shape Of Bull, Iron	35.00
Store, Opener, Cigar Box, Charles Denby, Hammer	12.50
Store, Opener, Fehr's Beer, Bottle Shaped, Wooden	10.00
Store, Opener, Letter, see Letter Opener	
Store, Orange Squeeze, Cardboard, Standup, 20 1/2 X 30 In.	110.00
Store, Overshoes, Rubber, Miniature, American Rubber Company	9.00
Store, Pail, Armour's Peanut Butter	40.00
Store, Pail, Armour's Veribest, Nursery Rhyme Characters	19.00
Store, Pail, Blue Sultana, Peanut Butter	45.00
Store, Pail, Boyle's Peanut Butter, 2 Ounces	12.95
Store, Pail, Buffalo Brand, Peanut Butter	19.00
Store, Pail, Candy, Rabbits.L. & C.Company	40.00
Store, Pail, Candy, Wooden, Cover	13.00
Store, Pail, Coffee, Big Chief, Indian Head, Turquoise Background, 1 Pound	16.00
Store, Pail, Mayfair Candy, Three Little Pigs	21.00
Store, Pail, Milk, DeLaval, Bronze, 5 Gallon, 13 In.	65.00
Store, Pail, Monarch Teeney Weeney, Peanut Butter	65.00
Store, Pail, Mosemann's Peanut Butter	38.00
Store, Pail, Mosemann's Peanut Butter, Circus Characters	45.00
Store, Pail, Pure Honey Pail, Lithograph, Tin, 5 3/4 In.Tall	20.00
Store, Pail, Rival Peanut Butter	40.00
Store, Pail, Squirrel, Peanut Butter, One Pound	55.00
Store, Pail, Tobacco, Plowboy	20.00
Store, Pail, Toyland, Peanut Butter	75.00
Store, Paper Dolls, Worcester Salt, Set Of 12	25.00
Store, Paperweight, see Paperweight	
Store, Pen, see Pen	
Store, Pencil, see Pencil	
Store, Pencil Sharpener, Atlas Holding World Globe	18.00
Store, Pencil Sharpener, Baker's Choclate Woman	18.00
Store, Pencil Sharpener, Minstrelman, Original Paint, Iron	12.50
Store, Pencil Sharpener, Shape Of Pistol, Red	9.50
Store, Pencil Sharpener, World Globe, Tin	4.50
Store, Pencil Sharpener, 2-Piece Graf Zeppelin, Germany, C.1930, 2 3/4 In.	25.00
Store, Pennant, Planters Peanut, 8-Sided	85.00
Store, Pickaninny, Peanut Butter, 1 Lb.	85.00
Store, Pig, Decker's Iowana Hams & Bacon, Papier-Mache, 7 X 14 In.	135.00
Store, Pin, Betty Boop, Roxy Theater	5.00
Store, Pin, Figural, Amtrak Train	4.00
Store, Pin, Quaker Oats, Celluloid, 1 1/4 In.Square	8.00
Store, Pitcher, Hiram Walker Ten High	10.00
Store, Pitcher, Measuring, Davis Baking Powder, Clear, 2 Quart	27.50
Store, Pitcher, Water, Johnnie Walker Black Label	12.00
Store, Pitcher, Water, Whiskey, 100 Pipers	10.00
Store, Plaque, Wieland's Brewery	130.00
Store, Plate, Chew Rose Leaf Fine Cut, 1882, 9 In.	45.00
Store, Plate, Push, Star Naphtha Washing Powder	12.00
Store, Plate, Sultana Peanut Butter, Tin	40.00
Store, Post Office, Brass Plates, General Delivery, Postal Mfg., 44 X 45 In.	1200.00
Store, Post Office, Storage Cabinet, 2 Raised Panel Doors, 42 X 6 Feet	250.00
Store, Poster, Anheuser Beer, The Two Bismarck's, 15 X 20 In.	50.00
Store, Poster, Baldwin The White Mahatma, Colorful, C.1920, 64 X 42 In.	200.00
Store, Poster, Barnum & Bailey Circus	10.00
Store, Poster, Carnival, Bump Cars, 1930s, 30 X 40 In.	45.00
Store, Poster, Cunard Line, Nathaniel Wales, Stoughton, Mass.	300.00
Store, Poster, Gene Autry, 1920s	18.00
Store, Poster, Hagenbeck Wallace Circus, Cowboys & Indians, 44 X 32 In.	89.00
Store, Poster, Hillsborough County Fair, 1918, 10 X 7 In.	15.00
Store, Poster, Mystic Odylicism, Colorful, C.1920, 64 X 56 In.	200.00
Store, Poster, Remington, Copyright 1923	125.00
Store, Poster, Sir Walter Raleigh, Light Canvas, Full Color, 1920s	40.00
Store, Poster, Smith & Wesson, Rider On Horse, 19 X 23 In.	150.00
Store, Poster, The Orpheum Show, Colorful, C.1905, 26 X 42 In.	35.00
Store, Press, Fruit, Dated 1865	55.00

Store, Press, Meat Juice, Iron 25.00
Store, Punch & Judy Theater, 10 Hand-Carved Puppets, 24 X 54 In. 400.00
Store, Push Plate, Vick's Va-Tro-Nol, Porcelain, 6 1/2 X 4 In. 25.00
Store, Puzzle, Heinz, C.1930 .... 20.00
Store, Rack, Clothes, T-Shape 40.00
Store, Razor, see Razor
Store, Reamer, Citrus, Juice Catcher, Ceramic, Grape & Leaf Design 12.00
Store, Reamer, Clown, Green, White, Yellow, 7 In. 45.00
Store, Reamer, Clown, Yellow, 6 In. 34.00
Store, Reamer, Figural Lemon, China, 2 Piece 35.00
Store, Reamer, Lemon, Monax, Glass, Insert 10.00
Store, Reamer, Opalescent, Signed Fry 30.00
Store, Reamer, Sunkist, Jadeite .... 12.50 To 18.50
Store, Reamer, Sunkist, Milk Glass .... 5.00 To 8.00
Store, Reamer, Sunkist, Opaque Green 14.00
Store, Reamer, Sunkist, Opaque White 14.00
Store, Receiver, Change, Old Port Cigars 4.00
Store, Ringer, Washing Machine, Salesman's Sample, Lovell Manufacturing Co. 95.00
Store, Roaster, Coffee, Arm Crank, Iron Handle, C.1870 .... 85.00
Store, Roaster, Peanut, Holcomb & Hoke 775.00
Store, Rug Beater 5.00
Store, Salt & Pepper, Aunt Jemima And Male Cook, Pottery 18.00
Store, Saltshaker, Mr.Peanut 8.50
Store, Saltshaker, R.C.Victor, His Master's Voice, China 15.00
Store, Scale, Apothecary, Brass Pans, Inlaid Mahogany, 1800s, 8 X 14 In. 275.00
Store, Scale, Household, Revonec 4.00
Store, Scissors, Garden, Pewter 9.00
Store, Scoop, Corn, Metal, Dated 1897 .... 12.00
Store, Scoop, Grain, Metal, Large, Wood Handle 12.00
Store, Scoop, Ice Cream, Brass Nickeled, Pint 40.00
Store, Scoop, Ice Cream, Gilchrist's No.31 .... 15.00
Store, Scoop, Ice Cream, Meyer's, Nickel Plated Brass 10.00
Store, Scoop, Ice Cream, Plated Brass 12.50
Store, Scoop, Planters Peanut, Tin 50.00
Store, Scraper, Beer, Pickwick Ale, Ivory, French, 1 X 9 In. 15.00
Store, Scraper, Foam, Knickerbocker 8.00
Store, Scraper, Foam, Krueger 12.00
Store, Sharpener, Pencil, Atlas Holding Globe, German 12.50
Store, Sharpener, Pencil, Baker's Chocolate Girl, 2 In. 14.00
Store, Sharpener, Pencil, Charlie McCarthy 12.00
Store, Sharpener, Pencil, Disney's Casey Junior, Train 9.00
Store, Sharpener, Pencil, Globe, Tin, 1 1/2 In. 7.50
Store, Sharpener, Pencil, Scottie Dog On Lid For Shavings 18.50
Store, Sign, Adrance Buckeye, Farm Girl With Hay, Paper, 1905, 24 X 32 In. 115.00
Store, Sign, All Charge Accounts Of Sun Oil Co., Honored Here, 1930s 65.00
Store, Sign, Amos 'n Andy Rexall, Tin, 1930, 34 X 16 In. 75.00
Store, Sign, Argo Salmon, Embossed Tin, C.1905, 9 3/4 X 13 3/4 In. 115.00
Store, Sign, Armour Co., Cardboard, Products On Shelves, 40 X 24 In. 38.00
Store, Sign, Arrow Shirts, Cardboard, Norman Rockwell, 9 1/4 X 12 1/4 In. 55.00
Store, Sign, Atlas Prager Beer, Chicago, Cardboard, 18 X 22 In. 8.00
Store, Sign, Babbitt's Soap, Little Lord Fauntleroy, Color, 15 X 2 In. 250.00
Store, Sign, Baby Ruth Gum, Embossed Tin, C.1930, 26 X 10 In. 40.00
Store, Sign, Baker's Cocoa, Etching Of Woman, 16 X 22 In. 100.00
Store, Sign, Baker's Cocoa, Tin, LaBelle, Original Frame, 36 X 48 In. 800.00
Store, Sign, Baltimore Rye, Pretty Girl, Lacy Blouse, C.1903, 22 X 28 In. 150.00
Store, Sign, Barber Trade, Wooden Hinged Straight Razor, 14 In. 53.00
Store, Sign, Barber, Look Better, Feel Better, Porcelain, 48 In. 45.00
Store, Sign, Bartholomay Brewing, Girl On Winged Wheel, 24 X 34 In. 750.00
Store, Sign, Bert Hopkins, Optician, Silver Letters, 9 X 36 In. 95.00
Store, Sign, Betsy Ross, Flag, 5 Cent Cigars, Tin, 1905, 20 X 25 In. 325.00
Store, Sign, Bire-Ley's, Embossed, Tin, 26 X 39 In. 11.00
Store, Sign, Black & Tan, Paper, Rat & Dog Fight, Barn, C.1884, 13 X 21 In. 300.00
Store, Sign, Black Mammy Syrup, Medicinal, Die-Cut, 16 In. 80.00
Store, Sign, Bo-Ko Cigars, Cardboard & Tin, C.1920 .... 28.00
Store, Sign, Braumeister Pilsener, Glass In Cardboard Frame, 6 1/2 X 12 In. 8.00
Store, Sign, Brownie Soda, Cardboard, Metal Edge, 21 X 60 In. 300.00

Store, Sign, Brunswick National Bowling Assn., 1909, 31 X 42 In.	600.00
Store, Sign, Buckeye Beer, Embossed, Tin, 3 X 13 1/2 In.	10.00
Store, Sign, Bull Durham, Cardboard, Red Bull By Fence, Black, 24 X 36 In.	450.00
Store, Sign, Bull Durham, Wood Frame, Cardboard Under Glass, 23 X 34 1/2 In.	750.00
Store, Sign, Burger Beer, River Front Scene, Tin, 8 X 14 In.	30.00
Store, Sign, Campbell's Soup, Expo., 1900, Porcelain, Shape Of Can, 22 In.	165.00
Store, Sign, Campfire Girl, Kellogg's Cornflakes, Paper, 1920, 29 X 23 In.	115.00
Store, Sign, Canadian Club Whiskey, Wooden, 36 X 7 1/2 In.	48.00
Store, Sign, Canvas Sickle Cut Plug, 17 X 35 In.	38.00
Store, Sign, Carling's Ale, 9 Pints Of The Law, Tin, 1940s	45.00
Store, Sign, Cascade Club Coffee, Tin, 14 X 30 In.	16.00
Store, Sign, Central Union Cut Plug, Cardboard, 13 1/2 X 10 1/2 In.	80.00
Store, Sign, Certified Mobil Lubrication, Porcelain, 8 1/2 X 3 Feet	125.00
Store, Sign, Chesterfield Cigarettes, Tin, 23 X 29 In.	20.00
Store, Sign, Chew Copenhagen, Tin, 14 X 25 In.	15.00
Store, Sign, Chief Two Moon, Bitter Oil, Cardboard Standup, 1930, 4 Feet High	75.00
Store, Sign, Chiropractor, Wood, 10 X 36 In.	85.00
Store, Sign, Cigar, Full Length Indian Princess, Wood Base, 62 1/2 In.	5750.00
Store, Sign, Circus, Giraffe Neck Women From Burma, 17 X 25 In.	45.00
Store, Sign, City Mutual, Embossed Tin.1930s	20.00
Store, Sign, Coach & Four Pocket, Tin	28.00
Store, Sign, Coca-Cola, Cardboard In Wood Frame, 1947, 20 X 36 In.	20.00
Store, Sign, Coca-Cola, Porcelain, 18 X 45 In.	65.00
Store, Sign, Colonial Ethyl Gasoline, Painted Glass, 10 X 14 In.	28.00
Store, Sign, Crosman Bros.Seeds, Family Holding Turnip, C.1873, 21 X 28 In.	350.00
Store, Sign, Crown Ice Cream, Embossed Tin, C.1920, 32 X 23 In.	90.00
Store, Sign, Dairy Made Ice Cream, Tin, Wood, Signed, C.1920, 34 X 25 In.	250.00
Store, Sign, De Laval Cream Separators, Tin, 30 X 41 In.	400.00
Store, Sign, De Witt's Pills, Cardboard, Stand-Up, 2 Sided, 30 X 18 In.	85.00
Store, Sign, De Witt's, Cardboard, 18 1/4 X 10 1/4 In.	38.00
Store, Sign, Dentist, Gold Leaf, Wood, 6 X 24 In.	95.00
Store, Sign, Devlish Good Cigar, 3 Kids Smoking, Tin, C.1910	50.00
Store, Sign, Dill's Tobacco, Cardboard, 20 X 26 In.	12.00
Store, Sign, Doctor, Gold Leaf, Wood, 6 X 24 In.	45.00
Store, Sign, Domino Cigarette, Fabric, 12 X 34 In.	30.00
Store, Sign, Don't Tell My Wife, Paper, C.1899, 21 X 28 In.	85.00
Store, Sign, Dr.Bigelow's Powders, Surrey & Trotter, C.1870, 23 X 20 In.	185.00
Store, Sign, Dr.E.L.Welbourn's, Metal Side Mount, 12 3/4 X 6 1/4 In.	50.00
Store, Sign, Dr.Flint's Quaker Bitters, Dr.Flint, Hat, Costume, Bottle, 48 In.	850.00
Store, Sign, Dr.J.Woodbury's Horse Remedies, Horse Pictures, 20 X 26 In.	100.00
Store, Sign, Dr.Mayer's 10-Foot Remedies, People & Package, 24 X 36 In.	85.00
Store, Sign, Dr.Pierce's, Cardboard, 10 3/4 X 13 1/4 In.	45.00
Store, Sign, Drink Granite Rock, Green On Yellow, Tin, 9 X 19 1/2 In.	16.50
Store, Sign, Drummond Tobacco, Girl Holding Flowers, 1895, Paper, 21 X 26 In.	95.00
Store, Sign, Du Bois Beer, Copper & Wood, C.1900, 22 X 15 In.	350.00
Store, Sign, Ebbinghouse Shoes, Tin, Wood Frame, 25 X 11 In.	45.00
Store, Sign, Edgeworth Tobacco, Fabric, 12 X 34 In.	30.00
Store, Sign, Egyptienne Straights, Red Background, Framed, 17 X 20 In.	110.00
Store, Sign, Elgin Watches, Grandfather Time Holding Watch, 18 X 25 In.	300.00
Store, Sign, Enjoy Bacardi Rum & Coca-Cola, Girl In Pool, Cardboard, 6 Ft.	60.00
Store, Sign, Fairy Soap, Cardboard, 21 X 11 In.	45.00
Store, Sign, Fairy Soap, Girl On Box & Soap, Ledge On Bottom, 40 X 7 In.	180.00
Store, Sign, Falstaff Hemp, Men & Women Around Table, Tin, 24 In.Diameter	110.00
Store, Sign, Fatima, Tin, Veiled Girl With Pack, Oval, 20 X 24 In.	425.00
Store, Sign, Feen-A-Mint, The Chewing Gum Laxative, 8 X 32 In.	45.00
Store, Sign, Ferry's Seeds, Cardboard, 20 X 2 In.	110.00
Store, Sign, Figural, Dutch Boy Paint, Papier-Mache, 30 In.	375.00
Store, Sign, Figural, Loose Wiles Chocolates, Tin, C.1900, 25 X 36 In.	600.00
Store, Sign, Flapper Drinking Hire's, Tin, 1920, 14 X 20 In.	175.00
Store, Sign, Ford, Porcelain, Blue & White, Oval, 36 X 72 In.	75.00
Store, Sign, Friends Smoking Tobacco, Tin, 21 1/2 X 10 1/4 In.	10.00
Store, Sign, Frostie Root Beer, Tin, Little Man Holding Bottle, 12 In.Round	25.00
Store, Sign, Gail & Ax Navy, Paper Mounted, 30 X 23 In.	325.00
Store, Sign, Gargoyle Mobil Oil, Both Sides, Porcelain, 15 1/2 X 23 3/4 In.	65.00
Store, Sign, Gem, Razor, Movable Hand, Cardboard, Early 1930s	125.00
Store, Sign, Gettelman Milwaukee Beer, Self-Framed, 10 3/8 X 16 1/2 In.	40.00

Store, Sign, Golden Virginia Tobacco, Porcelain, 12 X 18 In. 28.00
Store, Sign, Gollam's Ice Cream, Cartoon Type Boy, Metal, 1930s, 20 X 28 In. 125.00
Store, Sign, Green River Whiskey, Tin, Negro & Horse, 1899, 29x 26 In. 600.00
Store, Sign, Hamilton Brown Shoes, Porcelain Side Mount, 16 X 12 1/4 In. 75.00
Store, Sign, Harvester Cigars, Oval, Tin, C.1940, 7 X 13 In. 20.00
Store, Sign, Heart's Delight, Japan Tea, Lithograph, 18 X 11 X 9 1/2 In. 38.00
Store, Sign, Huebner Beer, 1900, Self-Frame, Tin, 38 X 25 In. 575.00
Store, Sign, Illinois Springfield Watches, Tin, 13 X 19 In. 350.00
Store, Sign, Imperial Club, Brass Hanging Chains, 10 X 14 In. 35.00
Store, Sign, Irving Ranges, Victorian Painting Portrait, 1900s, 23 X 17 In. 140.00
Store, Sign, Iver Johnson Bicycles, Cardboard, 21 X 11 In. 50.00
Store, Sign, Kayo, Chocolate Drink, Metal, 14 X 27 In. 38.00
Store, Sign, Kingan's, Cardboard, 15 X 21 In. 125.00
Store, Sign, Lamp Brewery, Metal Die Cut Sits On Shelf, 6 1/4 X 19 1/2 In. 225.00
Store, Sign, Lord Macaulay With 10 Cent Cigar, Round, Tin, 1910, 21 In. 185.00
Store, Sign, M-Up, Cardboard, C.1954, 12 X 23 In. 10.00
Store, Sign, Mayo, Girl In Woods, C.1884, 12 X 28 In. 125.00
Store, Sign, Mayo's Cut Plug, Rooster & Plugs, Canvas Banner, 18 X 58 In. 75.00
Store, Sign, Mayo's Plug, Yellow Background, Linen, 18 X 30 In. 75.00
Store, Sign, Missouri Pacific Lines, Tin, Calendar, C.1930, 20 X 16 In. 75.00
Store, Sign, Mobil Gas, Porcelain, 12 X 12 In. 20.00
Store, Sign, Mogul Cigarettes, Self-Framed, Tin, Arab Chieftain, 20 X 24 In. 350.00
Store, Sign, Morning After, Cardboard Hanger, Red, White, Blue, 10 X 23 In. 18.00
Store, Sign, Morrow Coaster Brakes, Paper, 1930, 21 X 28 In. 110.00
Store, Sign, Moxie, Pin Back, Metal .... *Illus* 29.00
Store, Sign, Nehi Curb Service, Sold Here Ice Cold, Tin, 19 X 28 In. 45.00
Store, Sign, Northern Seeds, Flowers, C.1912, 22 X 30 In. 150.00
Store, Sign, Northern Seeds, Girl With Corn, C.1912, 22 X 30 In. 175.00
Store, Sign, Old Virginia Cheroots, 2 Black Couples, C.1899, 17 X 16 In. 300.00
Store, Sign, Omar Cigarettes, Paperboard, Wood Frame, 1915, 25 X 18 In. 165.00
Store, Sign, Orange Squeeze, Embossed, Tin, 20 X 28 In. 20.00
Store, Sign, Overholt Whiskey, Canvas, Wood Frame, Dated 1913, 38 X 26 In. 200.00
Store, Sign, Pabst Blue Ribbon, Beer Wagon, 8 Horses & Dog, 16 X 33 In. 85.00

Store, Sign, Moxie, Pin Back, Metal

Store, Sign, Paw-Nee Oats, Cardboard, Wood Frame, 9 1/4 X 13 In. 35.00
Store, Sign, Peck's Bad Boy, Paper, C.1899, 21 X 28 In. 110.00
Store, Sign, Pepsi-Cola, Tin, C.1940, 28 In.Diameter 15.00
Store, Sign, Pepsinic, Cardboard, Metal Edge, 21 X 10 In. 60.00
Store, Sign, Perer's Cartridge Co., Oiled Paper, Self Frame, 30 X 26 In. 600.00
Store, Sign, Permit Cigars, Lady Striking Match, Cardboard, 24 X 30 In. 165.00
Store, Sign, Phillip Morris, Yellow & Red, With Boy, 10 X 20 In. 24.00
Store, Sign, Piper Heidsieck Tobacco, Tin, 14 1/2 X 17 1/2 In. 40.00
Store, Sign, Planet & Neptune Tobacco, Paper Banner, Victorian Lady, 29 In. 195.00
Store, Sign, Plaque, Owl Drug Store, 12 1/2 In.Diameter 100.00
Store, Sign, Pride Of Kentucky, Paper Under Glass, C.1896, 50 X 40 In. 550.00
Store, Sign, Prince Albert Tobacco, Fat Man's Face, Tin, 24 In.Diameter 225.00
Store, Sign, Railway Express Agency, Black & Yellow Letters, 72 X 12 In. 150.00
Store, Sign, RCA Victor Records, Shape Of Record, Double Faced, Tin, 20 In. 225.00
Store, Sign, Red Goose Shoes, Both Sides, Metal, 12 1/2 X 19 3/4 In. 55.00
Store, Sign, Redford's Navy Cut Tobacco, Sailor Climbing Mast, 20 X 30 In. 65.00
Store, Sign, Rhinelander Beer, Wisconsin, Porcelain, 30 X 48 In. 350.00
Store, Sign, Rosalind Cigars, Girl With Cherub, C.1880, 14 X 28 In. 150.00
Store, Sign, Russell's Ale, Lithograph, Tin, 23 X 30 In. 75.00
Store, Sign, Sar-A-Lee, Beauties, Paper, 1927, 24 X 9 In. 250.00

Store, Sign, Selz Shoes, Make Your Feet Glad, 2 Sided Wood, 10 X 22 In.	55.00
Store, Sign, Sensation Tobacco, Paperboard, Wood Frame, 1900, 27 X 20 In.	130.00
Store, Sign, Shield-Shaped, Spear's Pork Sausage, Tin, 9 In.	22.50
Store, Sign, Shoe Shop, Cut-Out Boot, Wood, Gray-White, 54 In.	500.00
Store, Sign, Shoot Remington Shur-Shot Shells, Cardboard, 20 X 15 In.	45.00
Store, Sign, Slade's Spice, Rows Of Jars With Contents, Oak, 15 X 23 In.	125.00
Store, Sign, South-Bend Watch, Pocket Watch In Cube, 10 X 27 In., Tin	22.50
Store, Sign, Springfield Brewery, Paperboard, Wood Frame, 1915, 31 X 24 In.	185.00
Store, Sign, Stag Beer, Girl Holding Flag, Paper, 1930, 16 X 15 In.	95.00
Store, Sign, Star Plug Tobacco, Round, Milk Glass, 9 3/4 In.Diameter	45.00
Store, Sign, Stetson Hat, 1934, Cardboard, 11 X 14 In.	6.00
Store, Sign, Steven's Pharmacy, Directional Arrow, Tin, 11 1/2 X 24 In.	17.50
Store, Sign, Stocktonia Flour, Baby In Wicker Basket, 19 X 15 In.	125.00
Store, Sign, Sunshine Cigarettes, Tin, 13 X 17 In.	55.00
Store, Sign, Swanee River, Paper, C.1899, 21 X 28 In.	85.00
Store, Sign, Sweet Caporal, Girl With Pack, Original Frame, 20 X 28 In.	225.00
Store, Sign, Sweet-Orr Co., Overalls, Curbed Porcelain, 1915, 18 X 14 In.	95.00
Store, Sign, Sweet-Orr Overalls, Yellow & Blue, 7 X 28 In.	50.00
Store, Sign, Sweetheart Flour, Porcelain, 5 In.Heart	20.00
Store, Sign, Take Lemon Chill Cure, Price 50 Cents, C.1870	95.00
Store, Sign, Tennessee White Rye Whiskey, On Mirror, 24 X 12 In.	70.00
Store, Sign, Texaco Sky Chief, 12 X 18 In.	25.00
Store, Sign, The Dazzler, Paper, C.1899, 21 X 28 In.	85.00
Store, Sign, Thermometer, Lash's Bitter, Wooden, 21 X 5 1/2 In.	65.00
Store, Sign, Thermometer, Standard Home Heating Oils, 11 1/2 In.	17.00
Store, Sign, Tower Root Beer, Tin, 13 X 19 In.	15.00
Store, Sign, Trade, Wood, Woman With Plaited Hair & Skirt, 1800s, 35 1/2 In.	550.00
Store, Sign, Trotter Whiskey, A Pair Of Fast Trotters, Tin, 1915, 36 X 36 In.	550.00
Store, Sign, Turnbull's Scotch, Lithograph, Tin, 12 X 18 In.	55.00
Store, Sign, Uneeda Biscuit, WW1 Bugler, 25 X 39 In.	125.00
Store, Sign, Victor Phonograph, Nipper, Canvas, Wood Frame, 1910, 20 X 23 In.	325.00
Store, Sign, Virginia Cigarettes, Girl In Swimsuit, Tin, 14 X 21 In.	45.00
Store, Sign, Wagon Lift, C.1880, Wood & Cast Iron, 48 Long	65.00
Store, Sign, Watchmaker's, Tin, 19th Century, 28 In.	800.00
Store, Sign, Waterman, Pen, Cardboard, 1930s	300.00
Store, Sign, Wells Fargo & Company Express, C.1900, Wood, 14 X 7 In.	575.00
Store, Sign, Westchester Fire Insurance Co., Aluminum, 12 X 27 In.	45.00
Store, Sign, Whistle, Embossed Tin, C.1940, 18x 48 In.	35.00
Store, Sign, White Label, Brass Hanging Chains, 10 X 14 In.	35.00
Store, Sign, Wildroot, Barber Shop, 13 X 40 In.	30.00
Store, Sign, Wilson & McCallay Tobacco Co., Paper Frame, 33 X 31 1/2 In.	195.00
Store, Sign, X-Ray Headache Tablets, Cardboard, 5 X 13 In.	5.00
Store, Sign, Ziegler Beer, Tin Over Cardboard, 8 1/2 X 11 1/2 In.	15.00
Store, Sign, 7-20-4, Embossed Cardboard, Girl & Scene Above, 10 X 15 In.	65.00
Store, Skates, Brinkman, 1920s, Rubber Tired Wheels	12.00
Store, Slate, School, Book Form, 1867	10.50
Store, Slate, School, Maple Frame, 10 X 16 In.	14.00
Store, Snuffer, Cigarette, Smokey Bear	4.00
Store, Spindle, Bill, National Cash Register, 6 In.	8.50
Store, Spittoon, Cast Brass	58.00
Store, Spoon, Mr.Peanut, Pierced Round Bowl, Silver & Gold Toned	17.00
Store, Stamp, Butter, Lollipop, Carved Flowers	*Illus* 160.00
Store, Stamp, Partridge, Carved, Miniature	*Illus* 125.00
Store, Stamp, Wafer Type, Cornucopia, Fruit Motif, Metal, 4 In.	*Illus* 60.00
Store, Stand, National Biscuit Display, Wood	145.00
Store, Stand, Shaving, Scalloped Beveled Mirror, Brush & Mug Holder	35.00
Store, Stand, Shoe Shine, Marble, 6 Oak Chairs, 12 Brass Rests	1950.00
Store, Stand, Umbrella, Jax Beer, Metal, 19 1/2 In.	27.00
Store, Stapler, National Cash Register Co., Dated 1890	23.00
Store, Statue, Soldier On Horse, El Principe De Gales Havana Cigars, 11 In.	53.00
Store, Stereoscope, see Stereoscope	
Store, Stool, Shoe Bench, Star Brand	225.00
Store, Stopper, Bung Hole, Cloisonne, Tip Top Lager	20.00
Store, Store, Display, Kaywoodie Pipe	95.00
Store, Tape Measure, see Sewing Tool, Tape Measure	
Store, Thermometer & Calendar, 1942, Fedora Oil Co., Reverse Painting	15.00

Store, Thermometer & Mirror, Royal Crown Cola, Framed, 9 X 1 In.	15.00
Store, Thermometer, Adam's Extract, Pictures Bottle, Wood, 3 X 11	25.00
Store, Thermometer, Carter Ink, Porcelain, 7 X 27 In.	55.00
Store, Thermometer, Clark Bar, Wood, 1920, Z5 1/2 X 19 In.	28.00
Store, Thermometer, Clark Bar, Wood, 5 1/2 X 19 In.	75.00
Store, Thermometer, Clark's, Wood, 5 1/4 X 19 In.	85.00
Store, Thermometer, Dairy, Cheese, Blown Glass, Mercury Tube, C.1880, 10 In.	10.00
Store, Thermometer, Dr. Pepper, 17 In.	26.00
Store, Thermometer, Dr.Simmon's Liver Regulator, Porcelain, 7 X 27 In.	195.00
Store, Thermometer, Erwin Diehl & Co., Philadelphia, Wood, 2 Feet High	50.00
Store, Thermometer, Ex-Lax, Porcelain, C.1930, 8 X 36 In.	50.00
Store, Thermometer, Ex-Lax, Porcelain, 8 X 36 In.	35.00
Store, Thermometer, Ford Automobile American, Tin, Gasoline, 24 In.	40.00
Store, Thermometer, Hill's Brothers Coffee, Porcelain, 8 X 20 1/2 In.	50.00
Store, Thermometer, Hills Bros., Coffee, Porcelain, 9 X 21 In.	75.00
Store, Thermometer, Kentucky Club Tobacco, 36 X 8 In.	45.00
Store, Thermometer, Kentucky Club, Horse & Rider, Pipe In Ashtray	75.00
Store, Thermometer, Landis Leaf Tobacco Co., Leaf Shape In Center, 24 In.	135.00
Store, Thermometer, Mail Pouch Tobacco, Porcelain, 38 In.	46.00
Store, Thermometer, Mail Pouch Tobacco, Porcelain, 8 X 39 In.	50.00
Store, Thermometer, Moxie, We Got Moxie A Great New Taste, 16 X 6 In.	45.00
Store, Thermometer, Nu-Grape, Bottle Shape, 17 In.	45.00
Store, Thermometer, Old Dutch Root Beer, 2 Windmills, 7 X 26 In.	25.00
Store, Thermometer, Pepsi Cola, Say Pepsi Please, Square, 9 In.	7.00
Store, Thermometer, Ramon's Backache, Wood, 9 X 21 In.	125.00
Store, Thermometer, Royal Crown Cola, Raised Bottle, 14 X 6 In.	25.00
Store, Thermometer, Royal Crown Cola, 25 In.	35.00
Store, Thermometer, Sauer's Extract, Shape Of Box, Wood, 8 X 22 In.	125.00
Store, Thermometer, Ship's Wheel, Missouri White Motor Co., Brass, 4 5/8 In.	12.50
Store, Thermometer, The World's News In The Daily News, 8 X 39 In.	95.00
Store, Thermometer, Tucker Oil Co., Glass & Metal Frame, 6 1/2 X 7 In.	30.00
Store, Thermos, Glass Lined, Brass, Dated 1909	35.00
Store, Thermos, Wild Bill Hickok	3.50
Store, Tin, Arco Peppermints, Red	3.00
Store, Tin, Arm & Hammer Baking Soda	15.00
Store, Tin, Auto, Pocket	45.00
Store, Tin, Baker's Breakfast Cocoa, Dated 1906, 5 Pound, 9 1/2 X 5 In.	89.50
Store, Tin, Belfast, Small	12.00
Store, Tin, Bell Shaped, Huntley & Palmer, 6 1/2 In.	96.00
Store, Tin, Biscuit, Dragon, Flower Border, 10 In.Diameter	20.00
Store, Tin, Biscuit, Loose-Wiles, Art Deco, Egyptian Design	10.00
Store, Tin, Biscuit, Loose-Wiles, Octagonal, Handled	15.00
Store, Tin, Biscuit, 8 Volume Shape, 6 1/4 In.	128.00
Store, Tin, Blanks, Saratoga Trunk	28.00
Store, Tin, Blue Boar	20.00
Store, Tin, Bokar Coffee	8.00
Store, Tin, Buckingham Cut Plug	18.00
Store, Tin, Bull Dog Candy, Brown	55.00
Store, Tin, California Perfection, Vernefleur	15.00
Store, Tin, Calumet Baking Powder, Indian Head	6.00
Store, Tin, Camel Cigarettes, Ashtray Emblem	3.00
Store, Tin, Camel Cigars	37.00
Store, Tin, Candy, Valentino	40.00
Store, Tin, Canister, Postmaster Tobacco	17.50
Store, Tin, Case, Phonograph Needles, Victor	7.50
Store, Tin, Central Union, Pocket	90.00
Store, Tin, Chicos Spanish Peanuts, Receptacle	40.00
Store, Tin, Cigar Box, Old Glory, Round, 50 Cigars, 3 For 5 Cents	50.00
Store, Tin, Cigar, Emerson	15.00
Store, Tin, Cigar, Good Cheer, Shape Of A Stein	85.00
Store, Tin, Climax Plug Tobacco	6.00
Store, Tin, Cocoa, Walter Baker Co., Label, 1 Pound	18.00
Store, Tin, Coffee, McLaughlin, Red, Glass Front, Lift Top, 38 X 21 In.	125.00
Store, Tin, Coffee, Monru Coffee, 1 Pound	12.00
Store, Tin, Coffee, Old Southern Coffee, 1 Pound	15.00
Store, Tin, Cold Cream	3.00

Store, Tin, Cremo Cigars, Store Bin	50.00
Store, Tin, Dan Patch, Cut Plug Tobacco	25.00
Store, Tin, De-Voes Sweet Smoke, Concave	42.00
Store, Tin, Dial, Pocket	15.00
Store, Tin, Dill's Best, Round	6.00
Store, Tin, Dill's Pocket	20.00
Store, Tin, Dixie Queen Plug Cut	70.00
Store, Tin, Dr.Hess	6.00
Store, Tin, Du Pont Gun Powder, 1920s	27.00
Store, Tin, Dupont Superfine FF Gun Powder, Paper Label	22.00
Store, Tin, Edgemont Crackers	8.00
Store, Tin, Edgeworth, Pocket	10.00
Store, Tin, El Capitan Coffee, Round	8.00
Store, Tin, El Trano Cigars	25.00
Store, Tin, Epicure, Pocket	95.00
Store, Tin, Famous Cake Box Mixture	18.00
Store, Tin, Fatima Flat Fifties	8.00
Store, Tin, Fireside Marshmallow, 5 Lb.	25.00
Store, Tin, Forest & Stream	30.00
Store, Tin, Fox Tobacco Mixture	20.00
Store, Tin, Fry Cocoa, Tole, Egyptian	27.00
Store, Tin, Gates Pioneer Coffee, Paper Label, Shows Lumberjack	15.00
Store, Tin, George Washington, Cut Plug	40.00
Store, Tin, Gold Dust	6.00
Store, Tin, Gold Label Baking Powder	3.50
Store, Tin, Guide, Pocket	85.00
Store, Tin, Handsome Dan	30.00
Store, Tin, Hanlon Baking	8.00
Store, Tin, Hershey, Brown, 10 Lb.	25.00
Store, Tin, Horlicks Malted Mile, 10 Pound	90.00
Store, Tin, Houde's Trunk	35.00
Store, Tin, Huntley & Palmer Biscuit, Bronze Bell Shape, 6 1/2 In.	96.00
Store, Tin, Huntley & Palmer Biscuit, Valise Shape, 6 1/2 In.	84.00
Store, Tin, Huntley & Palmer Windmill	65.00
Store, Tin, Huyler's Cocoa	15.00
Store, Tin, Ivory Starch	6.00
Store, Tin, Jenny Lind Talcum, Blue Birds	15.00
Store, Tin, Jolly Time Popcorn	15.00
Store, Tin, Jumbo, Wood Bucket, Lady With Child, 10 Pound Tobacco, 13 In.	150.00
Store, Tin, Just Suits	25.00
Store, Tin, Kemp Peanuts, Square	8.00
Store, Tin, Kemp's Step Ahead Nuts, 1931	6.00
Store, Tin, Kentucky Club, Blue With Jumping Horse	7.50
Store, Tin, Kickapoo Indian Salve, Buffalo Head	12.00
Store, Tin, King Pin Plug Tobacco, Leather Pouch	8.50
Store, Tin, Kisses, Bucket, Original Paper Label, 25 Lb.	40.00
Store, Tin, Lactate	8.00
Store, Tin, LaFendrich Tobacco, Picture	25.00
Store, Tin, Lion Coffee, 10 In.Diameter	17.00
Store, Tin, Lipton Tea, 1931	8.00
Store, Tin, Lorillard Rose Leaf, Flat, Nickel Plated, Compass In Lid	65.00
Store, Tin, Lucky Strike Green Flat 50	12.00
Store, Tin, Mammy's Favorite Coffee	125.00
Store, Tin, Mammy's, 4 Pound	55.00
Store, Tin, Maryland Club Tobacco	12.00
Store, Tin, Maryland Club, Pocket	325.00
Store, Tin, Match, Early Diamond, Black Family On Cover	85.00
Store, Tin, Mayfair Tea Balls, 1935	5.00
Store, Tin, McCormick Tea, 250 Bag Size, 10 In.Diameter	15.00
Store, Tin, Measure, Planters Peanut	35.00
Store, Tin, Mennen's Sen Yang	38.00
Store, Tin, Mother's Oats	20.00
Store, Tin, Mrs.Dinsmores Cough Drops, Somers Bros.	125.00
Store, Tin, Murad Cigarette	3.50
Store, Tin, Mustard, Colman's	4.00
Store, Tin, New Schultze Gun Powder	40.00

Store, Tin, Niggerhair 95.00
Store, Tin, Nueces Coffee, Pail With Bail, 5 Gallon 60.00
Store, Tin, Old English Tobacco, Curve Cut 5.00
Store, Tin, Old Gold Cigarettes 5.00
Store, Tin, Old Gold Yellow, Give-A-Way Package 20.00
Store, Tin, Old Time Aroma, Slant Top, Red, 20 X 20 In. 95.00
Store, Tin, Pall-Mall, Christmas 25.00
Store, Tin, Pastime, Hunting Scene 65.00
Store, Tin, Peachy, Pocket 30.00
Store, Tin, Peter Bilt Shoes, Pedestal, Pair Child's Shoes On Top 25.00
Store, Tin, Petro-Pine Tar Ointment For Man Or Beast 10.00
Store, Tin, Philip Morris Cigarettes, Pack Holder 15.00
Store, Tin, Philip Morris Cigarettes, Round, 100 .... 15.00
Store, Tin, Picobac 10.00
Store, Tin, Planters House, Picture Of Building, 1 Pound 35.00
Store, Tin, Plate, 1907 B.P.O. Elks, Philadelphia 38.00
Store, Tin, Popcorn, 10 Pounds 27.50
Store, Tin, Pride Of Virginia, Pocket 10.00
Store, Tin, Prince Albert, Round, 6 In. 12.00
Store, Tin, Purse, Handle, Women On Sides, Huntley & Palmer 65.00
Store, Tin, Rawleigh's Antiseptic Salve, 5 Ounce 5.00
Store, Tin, Rawleigh's Good Health Talc, Mother Goose Characters 35.00
Store, Tin, Red Turkey Coffee, Paper Label, Turkey 15.00
Store, Tin, Rex, Pocket 60.00
Store, Tin, Roly-Poly, Mammy, Mayo Cut Plug .... 250.00 To 425.00
Store, Tin, Roly-Poly, Mayo, Singing Waiter 189.00
Store, Tin, Royal Blend Coffee, Paper Label, Old Crown 8.00
Store, Tin, Rumpf Choice Roasted Coffee, Dubuque, Iowa, 18 X 17 In. 95.00
Store, Tin, Sailor's Pleasure, Pocket, Flat 125.00
Store, Tin, Sir Walter Raleigh Christmas 22.50
Store, Tin, Spice, Monarch, 5 Different 5.00
Store, Tin, Stag Tobacco, Pocket 10.00
Store, Tin, Sunset Trail Cigars 150.00
Store, Tin, Sweet Burley, Store Type, Yellow 95.00
Store, Tin, Sweet Clover, Pocket 65.00
Store, Tin, Sweet Cuba, Yellow, Store Bin 100.00
Store, Tin, Sweet Mist Tobacco, Store Type 135.00
Store, Tin, Sykes Comfort Powder, Two Girls 75.00
Store, Tin, Talc, Babcocks, Coreopsis 12.00
Store, Tin, Tall City Club, Pocket 60.00
Store, Tin, Tea, Breakfast 75.00
Store, Tin, Teenie Weenie Peanut Butter 95.00
Store, Tin, Times Square Tobacco 75.00
Store, Tin, Times Square, Pocket 110.00
Store, Tin, Towles Log Cabin Syrup, 1 1/2 Oz. 35.00
Store, Tin, Wagon Wheel, Pocket 195.00
Store, Tin, Windup, Mechanical, Soldier, Original Box 20.00
Store, Tobacco Jar, Head Of Black Boy, Pipe In Mouth 165.00
Store, Tongs, Ice Man's, City Ice Delivery 8.50
Store, Tongs, Ice, C.1920 .... 10.00
Store, Tray, Admiral Dewey & Ship, Tin, 6 In. 32.00
Store, Tray, American Brewery, Dutch Girl Holding Tray, 1814 ...... 75.00
Store, Tray, Artic Ice Cream, Polar Bear Floating On Ice 95.00
Store, Tray, Baker's Breakfast Cocoa, New England Homestead, 12 In.Diam. 200.00
Store, Tray, Ballantine, 1937, Wood Grain 22.00
Store, Tray, Bar, Johnnie Walker Whiskey, Copper, 13 1/2 In. 60.00
Store, Tray, Bartels, Syracuse, Viking With Tankard 65.00
Store, Tray, Belle Of Dauphin, Hanlen Bros., Girl Holding Jug 110.00
Store, Tray, Bevo Beer 45.00
Store, Tray, Billings Montana Old Fashion Beer, Red 60.00
Store, Tray, Blatz Beer, Students Drinking, Tin 65.00
Store, Tray, Broadway Brewing, Buffalo, New York, Hand Holding Bottle 150.00
Store, Tray, Budweiser Beer, 5 Gentlemen At Table Drinking 37.50
Store, Tray, Budweiser, Levi Scene, Rectangular 85.00
Store, Tray, Budweiser, St.Louis Levee In 1870s, 1914 ...... 95.00
Store, Tray, Buffalo Brewing, Sacramento, Dutch Girl, Rectangular 60.00

Store, Tray, C.A.Feisst Whiskey, The Dice Throwers	375.00
Store, Tray, Carlings, Bobbies Drinking Beer, Tin	25.00
Store, Tray, Change, Wm.Penn Cigars, Penn Bust, Celluloid, 6 1/2 X 7 3/4 In.	100.00
Store, Tray, Christian Feigenspan Brewing Co., 13 In.	85.00
Store, Tray, Country Club Brewery, St.Joseph, Montana	17.00
Store, Tray, Crown Premium By R. & H., 1940	30.00
Store, Tray, Dawes Brewery, Black Horse Ale & Porter, Porcelain	60.00
Store, Tray, Day, Night Tobacco, Pretty Girl, Low-Cut Dress, 1910	36.00
Store, Tray, DeLaval Cream Separator, Mother & Child, 1900	55.00
Store, Tray, Duesseldorfer Beer, 1905	85.00
Store, Tray, E.A.Robinson Beer, Pre-Prohibition, Oval, Girl With Rose	85.00
Store, Tray, Edelweiss Beer, Pre-Prohibition	85.00
Store, Tray, Enterprise Brewing Co., Yosemite Lager, Dated 1905	85.00
Store, Tray, Fan Fan Gum, Japanese Lady Holding Package, Basket Weave Edge	68.00
Store, Tray, Father Knickerbocker, 1950s	10.00
Store, Tray, Feckers, Danville, Illinois, Evangeline, Signed	65.00
Store, Tray, Feigenspan, Woman	30.00
Store, Tray, Fraternal Insurance, Philadelphia, , Brass, 5 1/4 X 3 1/4 In.	8.00
Store, Tray, Glennon's Porter Beer Ale, Bull Dog Standing, 13 In.	165.00
Store, Tray, Globe Brewing Co., Utica	95.00
Store, Tray, Gretz	15.00
Store, Tray, Gulf Beer, Utica	200.00
Store, Tray, Handsome Waiter	60.00
Store, Tray, Hires Root Beer, Ugly Kid Pointing Finger, 1910-20	225.00
Store, Tray, Holland Tunnel Commemorative, 1924, Copper, Oval, 10 In.	9.50
Store, Tray, Hyan Dry Ginger Ale	140.00 To 150.00
Store, Tray, Hyroier, Whiskey, 1900, Man In Top Hat	30.00
Store, Tray, Ice Cream, Rieck's, Dish Of Ice Cream, Flowers, Square, 13 In.	130.00
Store, Tray, Iroquois Beer, Gold, Indian Head	18.00
Store, Tray, Jax Beer, Alamo	55.00
Store, Tray, Johnny Walker, Name & Image, Copper, 13 In.Diameter	45.00
Store, Tray, Kentucky Whiskey	130.00
Store, Tray, Krueger, 1950s, 12 In.	10.00
Store, Tray, Krueger, 1950s, 13 In.	10.00
Store, Tray, Lawrence Welk, Entire Band, 1950	14.00
Store, Tray, Lawrence Welk, Lennon Sisters	14.00
Store, Tray, Lenhart's Beer, Dog Wearing Glasses, Smoking Cigar	75.00
Store, Tray, Littlemore Whiskey	110.00
Store, Tray, Louisiana Purchase Exposition, Oval	75.00
Store, Tray, Miller High Life, Oval, Girl On Moon	85.00
Store, Tray, Miller's, Oval, Girl On Moon, 1930s	60.00
Store, Tray, Monopolio Una San Luis, American Arts Works	85.00
Store, Tray, Mr. Peanut, 1930s, Bisque	35.00
Store, Tray, National Beer, St.Louis Factory	325.00
Store, Tray, Nu Grape Girl, 1920	35.00
Store, Tray, Old Faithful Beer, Bozeman, Montana, Old Faithful	70.00
Store, Tray, Old Seaton Rye, 2 Hunting Dogs, Pre-Prohibition	85.00
Store, Tray, Olympia Beer, Dashing Cavalier, 1910	115.00
Store, Tray, Pabst Blue Ribbon, Man Pouring Glass Of Beer	85.00
Store, Tray, Pepsi, Beach Scene	20.00
Store, Tray, Phoenix Brewery, Oval, Pre-Prohibition, Phoenix Bird	275.00
Store, Tray, Pickwick Beer	45.00
Store, Tray, Piels Beer, Elf Carrying Beer, Tin, 12 In.Diameter	15.00
Store, Tray, Red Raven Splits, Victorian Lady Hugging Red Raven, 1910	85.00
Store, Tray, Red Raven, Man & Raven, Round	110.00
Store, Tray, Rupert	12.00
Store, Tray, Ruthstaller's, Sacramento, California, Oval, Factory Scene	300.00
Store, Tray, S.S. Mexico Ward Liner, Porcelain Picture Of Ship, 4 In.	22.00
Store, Tray, Schaefer, 1950s, 13 In.	5.00
Store, Tray, Schlitz Beer, World Globe On Reverse Side	20.00
Store, Tray, Sen-Sen, Aluminum	14.00
Store, Tray, Sherican Export Beer, Yellow Background	55.00
Store, Tray, Simon Pure	12.00
Store, Tray, Stroh's, Pre-Prohibition, Waiter Carrying Tray	300.00
Store, Tray, Sunshine Biscuit, Mountain Scene	10.00
Store, Tray, Sweet Caporal, Victorian Lady Reading Letter, Cardboard, Oval	65.00

Store, Tray, Terre Haute Brewery, People, Cherubs, 1910	110.00
Store, Tray, Texas Brewing Co., Oval, 29 In.	100.00
Store, Tray, The Dice Throwers, Whiskey, C.1900	375.00
Store, Tray, Tieck's Ice Cream, Square	95.00
Store, Tray, Tin, Pan American Expo., Round, Buffalo Center, 5 In.Diameter	12.00
Store, Tray, Tip, Adolph Prince Grape Juice	65.00
Store, Tray, Tip, Aero Jenny Gasoline	34.00
Store, Tray, Tip, Aug Lang Co., Tivoli Lager, Lady	55.00
Store, Tray, Tip, Ballantine Keg, Tin	18.00
Store, Tray, Tip, Bartel's Beer & Ale, Bearded Man With Stein, Tin	55.00
Store, Tray, Tip, Bartholomay, Colored Picture	70.00
Store, Tray, Tip, Clysmic, King Of Table Waters, Bare-Breasted Lady	85.00
Store, Tray, Tip, Columbus Beer, Round	20.00
Store, Tray, Tip, Cottolene	38.00
Store, Tray, Tip, Cunard Line, Aquitania, 4 1/2 X 6 1/2 In.	55.00
Store, Tray, Tip, DeLaval Cream Separators	20.00
Store, Tray, Tip, E.Robinson's Sons, Pa.Pilsner Beer, Rold Red Black	45.00
Store, Tray, Tip, El Producto Cigars, Glass Triangular, 9 In.	14.00
Store, Tray, Tip, El Verso Havana Cigars	35.00
Store, Tray, Tip, Elroi-Tan, 6 1/8 In.Diameter	30.00
Store, Tray, Tip, Elverso Havana Cigars	20.00
Store, Tray, Tip, Export Beer, Cumberland Brewing Co., Gold On Black	35.00
Store, Tray, Tip, Fairy Soap	30.00 To 45.00
Store, Tray, Tip, Frank Jones Pale Ale	35.00
Store, Tray, Tip, Frank Jones Homestead Ale	24.00
Store, Tray, Tip, Fraternal Life Insurance, American Yeomen	12.00
Store, Tray, Tip, Harrington Ice Cream, Girl Eating Ice Cream	42.50
Store, Tray, Tip, Haupfel	25.00
Store, Tray, Tip, Home Lighting & Cooking Plant, Kitchen In Detail	45.00
Store, Tray, Tip, Huff Music Store, Bethlehem, Pa.	20.00
Store, Tray, Tip, Hupfel Brewing Company	30.00
Store, Tray, Tip, Hyroler	20.00
Store, Tray, Tip, Iroquois, Buffalo Brewery, Indian Head	65.00
Store, Tray, Tip, King's Maid	25.00 To 35.00
Store, Tray, Tip, King's Pure Malt, Panama Pacific Exposition, Unused, 1915	39.00
Store, Tray, Tip, King's Pure Malt, Waitress In White	45.00
Store, Tray, Tip, Kruger Beer, Celluloid Top Knob	12.00
Store, Tray, Tip, Kuebler Beer, Easton, Pa., Man Drinking Beer	18.50
Store, Tray, Tip, Lehnert's Beer, Dog Wearing Glasses, Smoking Cigar, 1910	110.00
Store, Tray, Tip, Maltosia	45.00 To 65.00
Store, Tray, Tip, Mercury Beer	35.00
Store, Tray, Tip, Miller High Life	9.00
Store, Tray, Tip, Miller, Ducks	10.00
Store, Tray, Tip, Moxie, Girl On Ground Of Violets	55.00
Store, Tray, Tip, National Cigar Stands Portrait	20.00
Store, Tray, Tip, Negro Woman & Child In Cotton Field	40.00
Store, Tray, Tip, North Hampton	75.00
Store, Tray, Tip, O'Keefe Brewing, 5 1/2 In.	125.00
Store, Tray, Tip, Occident Flour	18.00
Store, Tray, Tip, Oconto Brewing Company, 1907	27.00
Store, Tray, Tip, P.O.N.	28.00
Store, Tray, Tip, Pierce Wines, Spinner Type	25.00
Store, Tray, Tip, Popel, Giler	85.00
Store, Tray, Tip, Quandt	30.00
Store, Tray, Tip, Quick Meal Ranges	32.00
Store, Tray, Tip, Red Earl Cigars	40.00
Store, Tray, Tip, Red Raven, Girl With Bird & Bottle, 4 X 6 In.	60.00
Store, Tray, Tip, Resinol Soap, Girl With Pink Rose In Center	45.00
Store, Tray, Tip, Ruhstaller's Lager, Beer Maid With Steins	75.00
Store, Tray, Tip, Schlitz	65.00
Store, Tray, Tip, Schnecksville State Bank	25.00
Store, Tray, Tip, Seitz	30.00
Store, Tray, Tip, Stegmaier Brewing Co., Wilkes-Barre, Pa.	24.00
Store, Tray, Tip, Stegmaier Brewing, Picture Of Brewery	75.00
Store, Tray, Tip, Stollwerck's, 5 1/8 In.Diameter	12.00
Store, Tray, Tip, The Domestic Sewing Machine, Picture	55.00

Store, Tray, Tip, Tivoli	75.00
Store, Tray, Tip, Urbana Wine Co., Gold Seal Champagne	28.00
Store, Tray, Tip, Utica Gas Lamp Co., 1904	30.00
Store, Tray, Tip, White Rock, 6 5/8 X 3 3/4 In.	34.00
Store, Tray, Union Cascade, San Francisco, Rectangular	395.00
Store, Tray, Utica Club Beer, Round	10.00
Store, Tray, Utica Club Factory, 1930s	30.00
Store, Tray, Utica Club Pilsner, Hand & Bottle	12.00
Store, Tray, Utica Club Talking Steins	12.00
Store, Tray, Valley Forge	20.00 To 25.00
Store, Tray, Valley Forge Special, Waitress	85.00
Store, Tray, Van Nostrand	95.00
Store, Tray, Velvet Ice Cream, 1920s	95.00
Store, Tray, Virginia Dare, Round	95.00
Store, Tray, Washington At Valley Forge	25.00
Store, Tray, Welsbach	45.00
Store, Tray, West End Brewery, Semi-Nude Draped In Flag, 1900	125.00
Store, Tray, Wieland's Beer, Indian Maiden	275.00
Store, Tray, Wooden Shoe Beer, Children Carrying Basket, 1910	85.00
Store, Tray, 1903 Louisiana Purchase Exposition, Oval	75.00
Store, Tray, 1934, Weissmuller	150.00
Store, Tub, Straight Sides, 2 Iron Handles, Copper, 16 X 18 In.	75.00
Store, Tumbler, Measuring, Borden's Elsie, Glass, 4 5/8 In.	4.00
Store, Wagon, Goodwill Soap	195.00
Store, Wagon, Popcorn/peanut, Dunbar, 1908, Steam Engine, Whistle, Horse Drawn	5000.00
Store, Warmer, Hand, Oval, Pierced, Primitive, Steel, 4 1/4 In.	30.00
Store, Wash Boiler, Copper	35.00
Store, Washboard, Blue Enamel	15.00
Store, Washboard, Glass	15.00
Store, Washboard, Glass, National	8.00
Store, Washboard, Reasilk Hosiery, Wood & Brass, 4 X 7 In.	8.00
Store, Whip, Buggy, Braided Leather, 24 In.	18.00
Store, Whip, Horse, Gold & Silver Handle, Engraved Handle, 17 1/2 In.	16.00
Store, Whisk Broom, Ivory Handle	16.00
Store, Whistle, Brass, Large, Signed	100.00
Store, Window, Stained Glass, Yosemite Lager, 3 X 4 Feet	1200.00
Store, Wringer, Clothes, 1894	50.00
Store, Wristwatch, Planters Peanuts	40.00
Store, Yarn Winder, Turned Posts & Spindles, X Base, 24 1/2 In.	35.00
Stove, Acme Sunburst, Parlor	120.00
Stove, Cast Iron, Wood, Heat Catcher, William V.Many, Albany	300.00
Stove, Gem Starlight, Lion Heads, Oblong, Todd Stove, C.1889	995.00
Stove, Iron, Floral Design, Ten Plate, C.1800	250.00
Stove, Iron, Painted, Brass Finials, Paw Feet, Jones & Wardell, 18 1/4 In.	275.00
Stove, Lincoln, No.116, Burner Plate On Rear Duct, 5 Feet, 4 In.Tall	625.00
Stove, Monarch Malleable, Warming Ovens, Trivets, Side Shelves	1495.00
Stove, Potbelly, Iron, M & O	175.00
Stove, Potstove, Potbelly, 4 Lids, Montgomery Ward, Cast Iron, 35 In.	450.00
Stove, Radiant Home Baseburner, Tiles, Windows On 3 Sides Urn At Top	3995.00
Stove, Red Cross, Knight & Horse, Circular Tiles, New York, C.1889	6995.00
Stove, Round Oak, Dowagiac, Michigan	1095.00
Stove, Round Oak, From Firehouse, Dowell, Michigan, C.1900, 7 Ft.10 In.	3995.00
Stove, Superior Radiator No.213, Eisenglass Door, Cast Designs	675.00
Stove, Top, Round Oak Stove, Doe-Wah-Jack's Head, Wreaths Around	35.00
Stove, Wood Or Coal, Porcelain Door, Metal Shield, 24 In.	150.00
Stove, Wood, Philadelphia, Warnick & Leibrandt	265.00
Stove, 2 Column, Parlor, Evaporator Cup	750.00
Strawberry, see Soft Paste	
Streetcar, 2 Motors, 4 Wheeler, Windows, Seats, 1924	3000.00
Stretch Glass, Basket, Tray, 10 1/4 In.Diameter	100.00
Stretch Glass, Bowl, Amber, 4 X 12 In.Diameter	25.00
Stretch Glass, Bowl, Black Amethyst, 10 X 2 3/4 In.	90.00
Stretch Glass, Bowl, Blue Iridescent, 7 1/2 In.Diameter	15.00
Stretch Glass, Bowl, Blue Opaque, Azurite, 8 1/2 X 3 In.	40.00
Stretch Glass, Bowl, Clear, Orange Iridescence, 12 X 3 1/4 In.	35.00
Stretch Glass, Bowl, Flared, Black Amethyst Base, 3 1/2 X 6 3/4 In.	35.00

Stretch Glass, Bowl, Flared, Blue, 9 1/2 In. 20.00
Stretch Glass, Bowl, Flared, Green, 9 1/2 In. .... 19.00 To 20.00
Stretch Glass, Bowl, Flared, Yellow, 10 X 5 In. 35.00
Stretch Glass, Bowl, Footed, Gold Iridescent, 3 1/2 X 10 In.Diameter 45.00
Stretch Glass, Bowl, Footed, Iridescent, Flaring Rim, 3 1/2 X 10 In.Diam. 45.00
Stretch Glass, Bowl, Gold Rim, 12 X 4 In. 40.00
Stretch Glass, Bowl, Iridescent Blue, 9 3/4 In. 35.00
Stretch Glass, Bowl, Iridescent Peacock Blue, 10 In. 40.00
Stretch Glass, Bowl, Iridescent, Pastels, Gold, 10 In. 45.00
Stretch Glass, Bowl, Paneled, Blue, 8 1/4 In. 22.00
Stretch Glass, Bowl, Paneled, Smoke Blue, 8 1/4 In. 21.00
Stretch Glass, Bowl, Peacock Blue, Iridescent, 9 1/2 In. 27.50
Stretch Glass, Bowl, Ribbed, Rolled-In Edge, 6 1/2 X 2 1/2 In. 33.00
Stretch Glass, Bowl, Rolled-In Edge, 6 X 3 1/2 In. 30.00
Stretch Glass, Candlestick, Blue, 3 1/2 In., Pair 20.00
Stretch Glass, Candlestick, Blue, 8 3/4 In., Pair 60.00
Stretch Glass, Candlestick, Pair, 3 1/2 In. 23.00
Stretch Glass, Compote, Footed, White, 6 1/2 In. 18.00
Stretch Glass, Compote, Footed, 2 1/2 X 5 In.Diameter, Pair 25.00
Stretch Glass, Compote, Imperial Jewels, Gold Band, Flowers, 7 3/8 In. 55.00
Stretch Glass, Dish, Candy, Covered, Pedestal, Blue 27.50
Stretch Glass, Dish, Candy, Lid, White 25.00
Stretch Glass, Dish, Server, Center Handle, Blue 18.95
Stretch Glass, Goblet, Footed, Pink, 6 In. 16.50
Stretch Glass, Plate, Amber, 7 3/4 In. 7.00
Stretch Glass, Plate, Polished Pontil, Vaseline, Set Of 8 .... 100.00
Stretch Glass, Plate, Red, 14 Panel, 8 In. 135.00
Stretch Glass, Rose Bowl, Vaseline 35.00
Stretch Glass, Tray, Ring, Vaseline, 4 3/4 In. 14.00
Stretch Glass, Tray, Sandwich, Center Handle, Orange Iridescence, 10 1/2 In. 30.00
Stretch Glass, Vase & Candleholders, Green, 9 In., 3 Piece 20.00
Stretch Glass, Vase, Bottle Shape, Pinched Sides, 9 1/2 In. 20.00
Stretch Glass, Vase, Bud, Blue, 9 3/4 In. 19.00
Stretch Glass, Vase, Fan, Vaseline, 6 X 7 In. 32.50
Stretch Glass, Vase, Fluted, Hat Shape, Red, 5 X 8 In.Diameter 40.00
Stretch Glass, Vase, Iridescent, Marigold, 5 In. 35.00
Stretch Glass, Vase, Red, 7 1/2 In.Top Diameter 67.00
Stretch Glass, Water Set, Cobalt Handles, 5 Glasses & Coasters, 10 1/2 In. 325.00

*Sunbonnet Babies were first introduced in 1902 in the Sunbonnet Babies
Primer. The stories were by Eulalie Osgood Grover, illustrated by
Bertha Corbett. The children's faces were completely hidden by the
sunbonnets, and had been pictured in black and white before this time. The
color pictures in the book were immediately successful. The Royal
Bayreuth China Company made a full line of children's dishes decorated
with the Sunbonnet Babies.*

Sunbonnet Babies, Ashtray, Royal Bayreuth 100.00
Sunbonnet Babies, Book, ABC, Illustrated By B.C.Melcher, 1930 .... 25.00
Sunbonnet Babies, Book, At Work, At Play, 10 Pages, 9 1/2 X 11 1/2 In. 85.00
Sunbonnet Babies, Book, In Mother Goose Land, Grover 25.00
Sunbonnet Babies, Book, Record, Each Page Illustrated, B.L.Corbett, 1910 .... 75.00
Sunbonnet Babies, Book, The Sunbonnet Babies Primer, 1st Edition, 1902 .... 45.00
Sunbonnet Babies, Candlestick, Washing, Royal Bayreuth, 4 1/2 In. 175.00
Sunbonnet Babies, Creamer, Royal Bayreuth 135.00
Sunbonnet Babies, Cup & Saucer, Blue Mark 150.00
Sunbonnet Babies, Cup & Saucer, Let's Get Acquainted 47.00
Sunbonnet Babies, Cup & Saucer, Signed, Germany, Set Of 2 .... 18.50
Sunbonnet Babies, Dish, Feeding, Ironing, Black Mark 250.00
Sunbonnet Babies, Dish, Feeding, Roseville 35.00
Sunbonnet Babies, Dish, Relish, Girls Wash & Iron 185.00
Sunbonnet Babies, Dish, Relish, Sledding Down Hill 95.00
Sunbonnet Babies, Dishes, Child's, Signed, Germany 55.00
Sunbonnet Babies, Doll, Soap 5.00
Sunbonnet Babies, Hatpin Holder, Saucer, Royal Bayreuth 295.00
Sunbonnet Babies, High Chair, Open Center Tray For Bowl, 1912, Signed 255.00

Sunbonnet Babies, Nappy, Ring Handle, Blue Mark 135.00
Sunbonnet Babies, Pitcher, Child's, Signed 20.00
Sunbonnet Babies, Pitcher, Fishing, Royal Bayreuth, Blue Mark, 4 1/4 In. 160.00
Sunbonnet Babies, Pitcher, Mending, Royal Bayreuth, Blue Mark 135.00
Sunbonnet Babies, Pitcher, Washing & Hanging Clothes, Blue Mark, 5 3/4 In. 165.00
Sunbonnet Babies, Plate, Blue Mark, 6 1/4 In., Set Of 6 .... 85.00
Sunbonnet Babies, Plate, Cake, Open Handle 175.00
Sunbonnet Babies, Plate, Royal Bayreuth, Blue Mark, 4 1/2 X 4 1/2 In. 150.00
Sunbonnet Babies, Plate, Wash & Iron, 7 3/4 In. 95.00
Sunbonnet Babies, Plate, Washing & Hanging Out Clothes, Blue Mark, 8 In. 185.00
Sunbonnet Babies, Postcard, Days Of The Week, Set Of 7 .... 65.00 To 80.00
Sunbonnet Babies, Postcard, Sunday 10.00
Sunbonnet Babies, Quilt, Baby, Blue Gingham 28.00
Sunbonnet Babies, Quilt, Baby, Red Gingham 28.00
Sunbonnet Babies, Quilt, Hand Stitched 150.00
Sunbonnet Babies, Quilt, Print On White, Blue Stripes, Different Blocks 125.00
Sunbonnet Babies, Quilt, Top, Full 40.00
Sunbonnet Babies, Rose Bowl, Sweeping, Blue Mark, 3 In. 265.00
Sunbonnet Babies, Toothpick Holder, Dusting & Washing, Blue Mark 150.00
Sunbonnet Babies, Tray, Cleaning, Royal Bayreuth, 4 In.Square 165.00
Sunbonnet Babies, Tray, Ironing, Blue Mark, 7 1/4 X 10 In. 225.00
Sunbonnet Babies, Tray, Mending, Royal Bayreuth, Blue Mark, 5 1/2 In.Diam. 95.00
Sunbonnet Babies, Twins, A Story In Verse & Music For Little Tots, 1907 .... 35.00
Sunbonnet Babies, Washbowl, Miniature, Mending, Signed, 1 3/4 In. 135.00

Sunderland luster is a name given to a characteristic pink luster made by
Leeds, Newcastle, and other English firms during the nineteenth century.
The luster glaze is metallic and glossy and sometimes appears to have bubbles
as a decoration.

Sunderland, Jug, Pink Luster, 3 Reserves, C.1813, 8 3/4 In. 150.00
Sunderland, Pitcher, Melon Shaped, 4 In. 35.00
Sunderland, Plaque, Prepare To Meet Thy God, Luster, 6 1/2 In. .... 75.00 To 125.00
Sunderland, Plate, 6 3/4 In. 45.00
Superman, Booklet, Secret Code 15.00
Superman, Brush, 1940s 12.00
Superman, Button, Club, 3 1/2 In. 3.00
Superman, Gun, Water 3.50
Superman, Ring, Crusader 55.00
Sword, American Naval Officer's, Revolutionary War, 26 In. 450.00
Sword, American Officer's, C.1785, Eagle Pommel, Leather Sheath, 25 In. 2250.00
Sword, British Officer's, Silver Hilt, Lionhead Pommel, C.1750, 24 In. 950.00
Sword, Cadet, Iron Hilt, Single Guard, Leather Grips, 29 In. 97.50
Sword, Cavalry, Etched Steel Blade, Covered Scabbard, 18 In. 10.95
Sword, Cavalry, Etched Steel Blade, Covered Scabbard, 24 In. 13.95
Sword, Confederate Cavalry, Brass Hilt, Leather Grips, 31 In. 325.00
Sword, Dress, French Diplomat's, 1888, Leather Box, 32 In. 1295.00
Sword, Foot Officer's, Silver Hilt, Stirrup-Shaped Guard, C.1800, 26 In. 1450.00
Sword, French Officer's, Brass Hilt, Gilt Finish, Pearl Grips, 31 In. 125.00
Sword, French Officer's, Silver Hilt, 1760-70, 3-Cornered Blade, 34 In. 750.00
Sword, French, Iron Hilt, Chiseled Design, Silver Grip, 33 In. 850.00
Sword, Infantry, U.S. Army, Sheath, Brass Hilt, Sharkskin Grips, 32 1/2 In. 325.00
Sword, Inlaid Silver Hilt, Dutch, 17th Century, 35 In. 1250.00
Sword, Jade, Mounted Silver, Embossed Dragons, Wood Stand, Chinese, 40 In. 2000.00
Sword, Japanese, By Katsunaga 325.00
Sword, Knight's Head On Top, Skull, Crossbones, Ivory Handle, Incised 45.00
Sword, Made Of All Chinese Coins, 20 In. 50.00
Sword, Scabbard, Artillery Officer's, Carved Bone Grip, C.1820, 31 In. 450.00
Sword, Scabbard, Artillery Officer's, U.S., Pearl Grips, Gold Wash, 31 In. 550.00
Sword, Scabbard, British Officer's, C.1810, Tiger At Pommel, 29 In. 425.00
Sword, Scabbard, Cavalry, Etched Steel Blade, Covered, 36 In. 15.95
Sword, Scabbard, Civil War Officer's Infantary, Brass Hilt, 32 In. 295.00
Sword, Scabbard, Field Officer's, Civil War, Wire Wrapped, U.S. Flag, 29 In. 110.00
Sword, Scabbard, Figural, Armour, Knight's Head, K.Of C., 36 1/2 In. 29.50
Sword, Scabbard, Imperial Germany Officer, Lion Head Hilt, Ruby Eyes 100.00
Sword, Scabbard, Leather, Habana On Leather, , 1860 .... 65.00
Sword, Scabbard, Police, Japanese 42.00

Sword, Sergeant's, Brass Hilt & Grips, Marked Ames, U.S., 1864 .... 64.50
Sword, Swagger Stick, Webbed Sheath, Loop Ended, 22 In. 55.00
Sword, Wilkinson, Centennial Presentation 1500.00
Syracuse, Chamberstick, Ring Handle, Green Trim 16.50
Syracuse, Plate, Portrait, Indian Brave, 8 1/2 In. 16.50
Syracuse, Plate, Sherwood Pattern, 10 In. 75.00
Syracuse, Plate, Sherwood Pattern, 10 1/4 In. 75.00
Syracuse, Tureen, Soup, Oval, Onondaga Pottery Company, C.1880 .... 55.00
    Taffeta Glass, see Carnival Glass
    Tankard, see Stein
    Tapestry, Porcelain, see Rose Tapestry
Tarzan, Book, Coloring, 1952 .... 6.00
    Tea Caddy, see Furniture, Tea Caddy
    Tea Leaf, see Ironstone, Tea Leaf

Teco pottery is the art pottery line made by the Terra Cotta Tile Works of Terra Cotta, Illinois. The company was founded by William D.Gates in 1881. The Teco line was first made in 1902 and continued into the 1920s. It included over 500 designs, made in a variety of colors and glazes.

Teco, Mug, Tankard Shape, Green Matte, Molded Bamboo Decoration, 6 In. 135.00
Teco, Vase, Brown, Hourglass Shape, Signed, 6 1/2 In. 45.00
Teco, Vase, Bulbous Shape, Green Matte Finish, Signed, 9 X 10 In. 125.00
Teco, Vase, Green, 3 Handled, 8 X 5 In. .... 95.00 To 115.00
Teco, Vase, Squat, Matte Green, 4 X 5 In. 50.00
Teco, Vase, Three Vertical Handles, Coiled, Signed, 8 X 6 1/2 In. 95.00
Telephone, Candlestick, Black Paint Over Brass 65.00
Telephone, Candlestick, Buzzer Type, Brass 56.00
Telephone, Candlestick, Dispatcher's, Scissors Extension Arm, Desk Mount 175.00
Telephone, Candlestick, Stromberg Carlson, Ringer Box, Brass & Wood 62.50
Telephone, Candlestick, Western Electric, Brass, Dated 1915, Made Into Lamp 115.00
Telephone, Cradle, European 95.00
Telephone, Desk, Crank, 1930s 9.00
Telephone, Desk, Kellogg, Bakelite, 1937 .... 75.00
Telephone, Desk, Ringer Type, Leich 10.00
Telephone, Fiddleback, Julius Andre 175.00
Telephone, Kellogg, Cradle, Cloth Cord, 1941 .... 4.00
Telephone, Model WE325 LW, Union Railroad Terminal 37.50
Telephone, Sound Powered, Walnut Case, Brass Bell 300.00
Telephone, Switchboard, Hotel, Oak 135.00
Telephone, Switchboard, Kellogg, Magneto, Oak, 31 1/4 X 27 3/4 X 49 In. 375.00
Telephone, Wall, Hand-Carved, Oak, 23 In. 130.00
Telephone, Wall, Western Electric, Oak, Patented July 17, 1894 .... 250.00

Teplitz refers to art pottery manufactured by a number of companies in the Teplitz-Turn area of Bohemia during the late nineteenth and early twentieth centuries. The Amphora Porcelain Works and the Alexandra Works were two of these companies.

Teplitz, Bowl, 4-Handled, Iridescent Panels, Gold Outline, 4 In. 45.00
Teplitz, Dish, Amphora, Raised Acorns, Spider Webs, Gilding, 5 1/2 X 11 In. 165.00
Teplitz, Ewer, Amphora, Egyptian Design, Figural Medallions, 14 1/2 In. 175.00
Teplitz, Figurine, Amphora, Lioness On Rock, Czechoslovakia, 8 1/2 In. 125.00
Teplitz, Figurine, Girl In Victorian Attire, Marked, 10 In. 150.00
Teplitz, Figurine, Russian Wolfhound, 8 In.Long · 125.00
Teplitz, Jug, Amphora, Enameled Jewels, Minstrel Man, Crown Mark, 13 3/4 In. 195.00
Teplitz, Lamp, Mounted On Decorated Base, Royal Blue, Flowers, Finial 125.00
Teplitz, Lamp, Oil, Amphora, Applied Bud To Twig Base, Signed, 8 1/2 In. 175.00
Teplitz, Pitcher, Blues & Gold, Signed Turin-Teplitz R.ST.K., 15 In. 65.00
Teplitz, Vase, Amphora, Dutch Girl, Green & Beige, 15 In. 200.00
Teplitz, Vase, Amphora, Enameled, Raised Scroll Ribbing, C.1900 ....*Illus* 1500.00
Teplitz, Vase, Amphora, Flowers, Double Handles, Art Nouveau, 5 1/4 In. 55.00
Teplitz, Vase, Amphora, Gold Gilding, Jewel Work, Blooming Thistles, 6 In. 90.00
Teplitz, Vase, Amphora, Gourd Shape, 2 Golden Eagles Among Woods, 6 In. 125.00
Teplitz, Vase, Amphora, Iridescent Gold To Green, Signed, 11 In. 90.00
Teplitz, Vase, Amphora, Iris Design, 12 In. 130.00
Teplitz, Vase, Amphora, Jeweled Flowers, Blue, Scenic Top, 6 In. 75.00

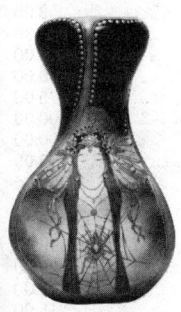

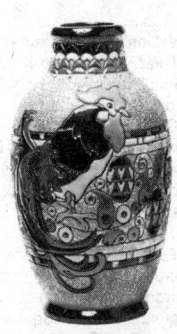

Teplitz, Vase, Amphora,
4 Stem Handles,
Molded Base, C.1905

Teplitz, Vase, Amphora, Enameled,
Raised Scroll Ribbing, C.1900

Teplitz, Vase, Amphora, Molded
With Palmettes, C.1915

Teplitz, **Vase,** Amphora, Man Fights Lion, Blue & White, Marked, 8 In., Pair	225.00
Teplitz, **Vase,** Amphora, Molded With Palmettes, C.1915 ....*Illus*	110.00
Teplitz, **Vase,** Amphora, Reticulated Top, Red & Beige With Gilt, 11 1/2 In.	365.00
Teplitz, **Vase,** Amphora, 4 Stem Handles, Molded Base, C.1905 ....*Illus*	300.00
Teplitz, **Vase,** Arab On Horse With Banner, Enameled, 3 Handled	160.00
Teplitz, **Vase,** Gibson Girl Surrounded By Violets, 5 In.Diameter	45.00
Teplitz, **Vase,** Reticulated Collar, Figural Toadstools, Luster Ground, 6 In.	150.00
Teplitz, **Vase,** Setting Sun, Gold, Enameled, Marked, 12 In.	225.00

Textile includes all types of table linens and household linens such as coverlets, quilts, fabrics, etc.

Textile, **Afghan,** Knit Cross Stitched, C.1860, Stripes, Animals, Double	200.00
Textile, **Afghan,** Wool, Handknit, Openwork Design, 72 X 102 In.	40.00
Textile, **Apron,** Eyelet & Lace	10.00
Textile, **Back Rest,** Crocheted, Colonial Gentlemen & Ladies Dancing, 28 In.	22.00
Textile, **Banner,** Embroidered, Over There	6.50
Textile, **Banner,** Silk, G.A.R.	28.00
Textile, **Bedspread,** Crewel, Hand-Worked, C.1800, Chinese	350.00
Textile, **Bedspread,** Crocheted, Cream Color, Queen Size	225.00
Textile, **Bedspread,** Crocheted, Ecru, Fringe, 87 X 87 In.	150.00
Textile, **Bedspread,** Crocheted, Fringed, White, Double	55.00
Textile, **Bedspread,** Crocheted, Off White & Satin, Large	75.00
Textile, **Bedspread,** Crocheted, Pearl Medallion Pattern, Cream, 94 X 111 In.	200.00
Textile, **Bedspread,** Crocheted, Rose Pattern, Large	75.00 To 95.00
Textile, **Bedspread,** Crocheted, Star With Popcorn	225.00
Textile, **Bedspread,** Hand Crocheted, Wheel Pattern, Off White, 94 X 102 In.	200.00
Textile, **Bedspread,** Hand Crocheted, 4 Inch Petal Pattern, 94 X 111 In.	175.00
Textile, **Bedspread,** Hand Embroidery, C.1880, Oriental	495.00
Textile, **Bedspread,** Lace Medallion Inserts, Figures, Lace Strips	42.00
Textile, **Bedspread,** Lace, 91 X 103 In.	67.50
Textile, **Bedspread,** Leaf Pattern, Scalloped Edge, Oyster White, Queen Size	200.00
Textile, **Bedspread,** Medallion Center, Diamond Border, C.1870, 74 X 80 In.	15.00
Textile, **Bedspread,** Patchwork, Lined, 75 X 85 In.	75.00
Textile, **Bedspread,** Popcorn Stitch, Lace, 84 X 100 In.	150.00
Textile, **Bedspread,** Popcorn Stitch, 78 X 90 In.	65.00
Textile, **Bedspread,** Satin, Pink, Long Fringe	49.00
Textile, **Bedspread,** Sham, Embroidered, White Linen	12.00
Textile, **Bedspread,** Star Pattern, Popcorn Effect, Fringed	125.00
Textile, **Blanket,** Lap, Red Border, 2 Foxes In Center, 63 X 46 In.	45.00
Textile, **Blanket,** Saddle, Red, Brown, Gray, Navajo, C.1900-20, 50 X 77 In.	1275.00
Textile, **Blanket,** Wool, British, World War II, 3/4 Size	20.00
Textile, **Blouse,** Middy, U.S.N., Wool, Blue	10.95
Textile, **Bonnet,** Lady's, Accordion Shaped Folds, Green Satin, Folds	25.00
Textile, **Bookmark,** Cloth, Lincoln's Picture, 10 In.	45.00
Textile, **Bookmark,** Woven Silk, Dated 1888, 1 1/2 X 6 1/2 In.	20.00
Textile, **Bunting,** Red, White & Blue Starred, 24 X 33 In.	45.00
Textile, **Calligraphic Specimen,** The Indian Osceola, J.Swank, 24 X 18 In.	1000.00
Textile, **Camisole,** Button On, Petticoat, Size 2	10.00

Textile, Cap, Army, Spanish, Insignia 8.00
Textile, Cape, British Bobby, Melton Wool, Lion's Head Closure 65.00
Textile, Carpet, Chinese, Birds, Flowers, Trees, Purple, 166 X 123 In. 1000.00
Textile, Carpet, Chinese, Blue, Flowers, Scrolling Foliage, 12 X 9 Feet 1200.00
Textile, Carpet, Chinese, Green & Ivory Tones, 12 X 9 Feet 175.00
Textile, Carpet, Chinese, Magenta Field, Green Border, 144 X 108 In. 400.00
Textile, Carpet, Chinese, Polychrome Flowering Tree, 364 X 116 In. 1400.00
Textile, Carpet, Indo-Chinese, Floral Medallion, Ivory Field, 14 X 10 Feet 600.00
Textile, Carpet, Kazak, Diamond, Blue, Ivory, 44 1/2 X 70 In. 1250.00
Textile, Carpet, Kirman, Ivory, Pink Palmettes, Vine Medallion, 148 X 103 In. .. 1100.00
Textile, Carpet, Sarouk, 11 Ft., 1 In. X 8 Ft., 5 In. 3500.00
Textile, Case, Comb, Embroidered, Chinese Silk, Hanging Tassel 15.00
Textile, Cloth, Banquet, Satin Damask, Scrolls, Lilies, 2 X 3 Yards 22.00
Textile, Cloth, Irish Linen, Cross-Stitch Borders, 52 X 54 In. 8.00
Textile, Cloth, Luncheon, Irish Linen, Embroidered, 36 In.Square 15.00
Textile, Coat, Bearskin, Globe Tanning Co., 4 Feet, 5 In.Long 295.00
Textile, Coat, Evening, Panne Velvet, Red, 1920s 15.00
Textile, Coat, Lady's, Long, Greta Garbo Look, Half Belt, All Sizes 50.00
Textile, Comforter, Quilted, Log Cabin, Dark Colors 50.00
Textile, Counterpane, Trapunto, Flowering Vine, Fringed, C.1820, 8 X 7 Ft. .. 500.00
Textile, Cover, Pillow, Felt, 1939 World's Fair, 12 In. 10.00
Textile, Cover, Pillow, Needlepoint, Roses & Violets, 9 X 9 In. 10.00
Textile, Cover, Quilt, Lone Star Pattern, Hand Made 28.00

Linen or wool coverlets were made during the nineteenth century. Most of
the coverlets date from 1800 to 1850. Four types were made, the double woven,
jacquard, summer and winter, and overshot.

Textile, Coverlet, Beige & White Natural Dye, Dated 1861 .... 235.00
Textile, Coverlet, Blue & Red On Natural, Fringe, 96 X 72 In. 60.00
Textile, Coverlet, Blue & White Overshot, Ohio, 66 X 84 In. 125.00
Textile, Coverlet, Blue & White, 64 X 76 In. 95.00
Textile, Coverlet, Centennial, Memorial Hall, 80 X 76 In. 275.00
Textile, Coverlet, Cream, Rose & Green, 2 Names, Dated 1848 .... 375.00
Textile, Coverlet, Double Woven, Blue, Natural, Applied Fringe, 91 X 98 In. .. 285.00
Textile, Coverlet, Double Woven, Pineapple & Tulip Bud Roundels, Stars, Birds .. 1100.00
Textile, Coverlet, Fliehr & Bottger, Pennsylvania, C.1850, 84 X 90 In. 275.00
Textile, Coverlet, Floral, Reversible, D.Beil, New Hamburg, C.1848, 91 In. .. 250.00
Textile, Coverlet, Florals & Geometric Design, C.1850, 84 X 90 In. 275.00
Textile, Coverlet, Indiana, W.Craig, Blue & White, C.1848 .... 325.00
Textile, Coverlet, Jacquard, Blue & White, Dated 1840, Double 350.00
Textile, Coverlet, Jacquard, Blue & White, Signed E.Davis, Dated 1832 ...... 375.00
Textile, Coverlet, Jacquard, Double Rows Of Boston Town, 70 X 80 In. 175.00
Textile, Coverlet, Jacquard, Floral & Leaf Design, Signed, 1837, 73 X 63 In. .. 285.00
Textile, Coverlet, Jacquard, Red, White & Blue, 1847, Anne Bartholomew 150.00
Textile, Coverlet, Jacquard, Red, White, Blue, Yellow, Star, Eagle, 72 X 76 In. .. 220.00
Textile, Coverlet, Jacquard, Signed Heleane Cooper 250.00
Textile, Coverlet, Jacquard, 2 Piece, Eagle Borders, C.1838, 77 1/2 X 93 In. .. 360.00
Textile, Coverlet, Linen & Wool, Geometric Design, C.1840, 72 X 90 In. 90.00
Textile, Coverlet, Multiple Shaft, Red, Blue & Natural, Fringe, 80 X 93 In. .. 300.00
Textile, Coverlet, Overshot, Blue, White, Geometric, Fringe 130.00
Textile, Coverlet, Red, Blue, Green, Hempfield Railroad, 1840s ...... *Illus* 5500.00
Textile, Coverlet, Rose, Blue & White, Block & Rosettes, 70 X 84 In. 110.00
Textile, Coverlet, Snowball, Flowerheads, Flower Filled Urns, Blue, White 150.00
Textile, Coverlet, Snowflake Pattern, Blue & White 235.00
Textile, Coverlet, Stenciled, Signed Sarah Mooers, C.1820 .... 2200.00
Textile, Coverlet, Woven, Grape Leaf Border, E.Ettinger, 1835 .... 450.00
Textile, Crewel Work, Girl Carrying Basket, Walking Down Path, 21 X 26 In. .. 30.00
Textile, Curtain, Lace, Panel, 90 X 42 In. 6.00
Textile, Cushion, Hatpin, Beaded, 11 X 9 In. 22.00
Textile, Doily, Cluny Lace, 31 In.Diameter 28.00
Textile, Doily, Punch Work 5.00
Textile, Dress, Brown Taffeta, C.1900 .... 8.50
Textile, Dress, Child's, Rose Silk Taffeta, C.1900 .... 30.00
Textile, Dress, Embroidered Broadcloth, White, 1900 .... 30.00
Textile, Dress, Embroidered, 1920s 12.00
Textile, Dress, Green Taffeta, Velvet & Lace Trim, Mid 1800s 50.00

Textile, Coverlet, Red, Blue, Green, Hempfield Railroad, 1840s

Textile, Dress, Green, Taffeta, Rose Buds, 1800s	50.00
Textile, Dress, Toddler, Matching Bonnet, Green, Late 1800s	35.00
Textile, Dress, Wedding, White, Cut Out & Eyelet Work, 1910	50.00
Textile, Embroidery Kit, Campbell Kids	9.00
Textile, Embroidery, Chinese, Flowers & Butterfly, 21 1/2 X 9 In.	375.00
Textile, Embroidery, Chinese, Metallic Threads, Framed, 18 1/4 X 24 In.	40.00
Textile, Embroidery, Chinese, Silk, Figures, Symbols, 24 X 9 1/2 In.	55.00
Textile, Embroidery, Silk, Eagle, Flags, E Pluribus Unum, Framed, 18 X 19 In.	125.00
Textile, Embroidery, Silk, Memorial, 19th Century, 15 X 17 In.	400.00
Textile, Flag, American, 45 Star, C.1910, 5 Feet X 6 Feet, 8 In.	85.00
Textile, Flag, Battleship, 48 Star, 15 X 8 Feet	75.00
Textile, Flag, Stars & Bars Confederate Flag, 1st Issue, 5 X 7 Feet	1000.00
Textile, Flag, 13 Star, Framed, 22 X 35 1/2 In.	1000.00
Textile, Flag, 44 Star, C.1893, 6 X 11 Feet	125.00
Textile, Gown, Wedding, Lace Yoke, Pointed Bodice, 8 Ft.Train, 1930s	25.00
Textile, Gown, Wedding, Veil, White Organdy, 1860s	35.00
Textile, Handerchief, Silk, St.Louis Exposition, Blue	25.00
Textile, Handkerchief, Admiral Dewey & 4 Boats, 20 In.Square	37.50
Textile, Handkerchief, Hand-Painted, Hemstitched Pongee, Satin Holder, 15	10.00
Textile, Handkerchief, Silk, Admiral Dewey, 20 In.Square	30.00
Textile, Handkerchief, Silk, Columbian Exposition, Machinery Hall	10.00
Textile, Handkerchief, Silk, View Of 1893 World's Fair, 16 In.Square	40.00
Textile, Handkerchief, Silk, 110th Infantry, 1921	5.00
Textile, Handkerchief, Silk, 1893 World's Fair	15.00
Textile, Hat, Australian Bush, WW II	12.95
Textile, Hat, British Slouch, WW II	6.00
Textile, Hat, Cadet, Parade, Staunton Military Academy	35.00
Textile, Hat, Derby, Deerskin Felt	22.50
Textile, Hat, Lady's, C.1940	3.00
Textile, Hat, Stetson, Black Pointed Tailcoat, C.1860	39.00
Textile, Hat, Straw, C.1920	25.00
Textile, Hat, Top, Folding, Original Box	20.00
Textile, Hat, Velvet, Boxed, C.1910	20.00
Textile, Hat, Woman's, Sequined, Feathered, Veiled, 1930s	4.00
Textile, Jacket, Battle, British, Dark Blue, Dated 1950	14.95
Textile, Kimono, Silk, 96 Embroidered Children, Chinese	300.00
Textile, Mantilla, Black Lace, 72 X 34 In.	35.00
Textile, Mat, Beaded, Flower & Bird, 9 X 11 In.	20.00
Textile, Mat, Tekke Turkoman, Brick Red, 4 Rows Of 6 Gulls, 38 X 38 In.	425.00
Textile, Mitts, Lace, Crochet	6.50
Textile, Muff, Child's, Neckpiece, White Fox	15.00
Textile, Muff, Monkey Fur	40.00
Textile, Muff, Muskrat, Large	17.50
Textile, Muff, Raccoon, Large	32.00
Textile, Napkin, Dinner, Damask, 19 In.Square, Set Of 10	15.00
Textile, Napkin, Double Damask, Rose Pattern, Irish Linen, 22 In., Set Of 12	60.00
Textile, Napkin, Hand-Made In China, 18 X 18 In., Set Of 12	36.00
Textile, Needlepoint, Picture, Biblical, 19th Century, Framed, 36 X 30 In.	250.00
Textile, Needlepoint, Shepherds, 17th Century Dress, 27 X 27 In.	155.00
Textile, Needlework, Framed, Oceanliner, United States, 33 X 24 In.	25.00
Textile, Needlework, Framed, Peace Be Unto This House, 10 X 22 In.	25.00
Textile, Nightgown, Lady's, Blue Satin, Lace Trim, 1940s	6.50
Textile, Obi, Wedding, Japanese, Gold & Silver Embroidery, Silk Brocade	85.00
Textile, Overcoat, West Point, Gray Melton Wool, Matching Cape	60.00
Textile, Overcoat, Wool Lining.Blue, WW II, British	75.00
Textile, Pants, Sailor, 13 Button	19.95
Textile, Petit Point, Flowers, Oval Frame, Victorian, Pair, 14 In.	45.00

Textile, Petticoat, White Cotton, Double Flounce, Embroidery	15.00
Textile, Pillow Cover, Lithograph, Gypsy Fortune Teller, 1907, 22 In.Square	55.00
Textile, Pillow Cover, Lithograph, The Angelus, 1907, 22 In.Square	37.50
Textile, Pillow Cover, Red Embroidered Lilies, Pair	19.50
Textile, Pillow Cover, Silk, World War II	25.00
Textile, Pillow, Crocheted, Ruffled, 11 X 17 In.	19.00
Textile, Pillow, Needlepoint, Beaded, Navy Ground, C.1890, 16 In.Square	65.00
Textile, Pillow, Needlepoint, Classic Landscape, Brown Border, 18 In.Square	40.00
Textile, Quilt, Appliqued Compass, Hand-Sewn, 76 X 77 1/4 In. *Illus*	450.00
Textile, Quilt, Arkansas Traveler, Hand-Stitching	70.00
Textile, Quilt, Basket, Red & White, Large	225.00
Textile, Quilt, Basket, 19th Century, Hand-Stitched, 72 X 77 In. *Illus*	600.00
Textile, Quilt, Bear's Paw, Red & Green, 74 In.	380.00
Textile, Quilt, Bethlehem Star, C.1900s, 75 1/2 X 75 1/2 In. *Illus*	375.00
Textile, Quilt, Blazing Star, Navy Blue & White, 78 X 9o In.	275.00
Textile, Quilt, Blue Stars, Amish, C.1900	475.00
Textile, Quilt, Blue, Red, Green, Amish Pieced, 19 X 20 In.	85.00
Textile, Quilt, Blue, 8 Pointed Appliqued Star, C.1920, 82 X 82 In.	90.00
Textile, Quilt, Bowtie Pattern, Pieced	435.00
Textile, Quilt, Bridal Wreath, Gold & White, Hand-Stitched	45.00
Textile, Quilt, Bride's, White Trapunto, 1820, 109 X 102 1/2 In. *Illus*	300.00
Textile, Quilt, Broken Star, Handmade, 1940, 74 X 76 In.	100.00
Textile, Quilt, Calico Patches, Chintz Appliques, Signed, C.1845	1000.00
Textile, Quilt, Calico, Variable Star, Orange, Maroon, Red, Pink, Green, White	125.00
Textile, Quilt, Carnation, Appliqued, 19th Century, 87 X 87 In. *Illus*	200.00
Textile, Quilt, Checkerboard, Reversible, Hand Knotted, Double	46.00
Textile, Quilt, Chimney Sweep, Indigo Prints, Amish, Hand Quilted, Double	115.00
Textile, Quilt, Cotton, Appliqued Wreaths, Flowers & Diamonds	225.00
Textile, Quilt, Crazy Quilt, Wool, 68 X 80 In.	40.00
Textile, Quilt, Crazy, Satin & Silk Pieces, 68 X 78 In.	35.00
Textile, Quilt, Crazy, Silk, Velvet, Satin, Embroidery, Victorian	80.00
Textile, Quilt, Crib, Amish, Sugarcreek, Ohio, C.1920, 54 X 46 In. *Illus*	375.00
Textile, Quilt, Crib, Appliqued Butterflies, White Ground, 52 In.Square	45.00
Textile, Quilt, Crib, Pennsylvania, Red & Green	60.00
Textile, Quilt, Crossed T Pattern, Blue & White, Pieced	365.00
Textile, Quilt, Diamond Cable, Amish, Flowerhead, Pink, Maroon, Green, Blue	300.00
Textile, Quilt, Double Irish Chain, Pink Squares, C.1870, 71 X 87 In.	60.00
Textile, Quilt, Double Wedding Ring, Double Border, Hand-Stitching	75.00
Textile, Quilt, Dresden Plate Pattern, Scalloped Sided, C.1870, 72 X 90 In.	145.00
Textile, Quilt, Dutch Britches, Hand-Quilted, 65 X 79 In.	150.00
Textile, Quilt, Eight-Point Star, C.1930, 83 1/2 X 75 1/2 In. *Illus*	375.00

Textile, Quilt, Appliqued Compass,
Hand-Sewn, 76 X 77 1/4 In.

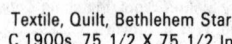

Textile, Quilt, Basket, 19th Century,
Hand-Stitched, 72 X 77 In.

(See Page 618)

Textile, Quilt, Bethlehem Star,
C.1900s, 75 1/2 X 75 1/2 In.

Textile, Quilt, Bride's, White Trapunto,
1820, 109 X 102 1/2 In.

Textile, Quilt, Carnation, Appliqued,
19th Century, 87 X 87 In.

Textile, Quilt, Crib, Amish,
Sugarcreek, Ohio, C.1920,
54 X 46 In.

Textile, Quilt, Eight-Point Star,
C.1930, 83 1/2 X 75 1/2 In.

Textile, Quilt, Hex, Calico,
19th Century, 80 X 79 In.

Textile, Quilt, Rose Wreath,
19th Century, 79 1/2 X 73 In.

(See Page 618)

Textile, Quilt, Embroidered Baskets Of Flowers & Butterflies, 63 X 79 In.	55.00
Textile, Quilt, Embroidered Pink Primroses, 78 X 80 In.	150.00
Textile, Quilt, Evening Star, Red & White, 81 X 92 In.	135.00
Textile, Quilt, Flannel, Tied Cigar Flag	55.00
Textile, Quilt, Flower Garden, Scalloped, Hand-Quilted, 1920, 62 X 70 In.	100.00
Textile, Quilt, Friendship, Amish, 1934, 90 X 91 In.	140.00
Textile, Quilt, Full Size Sunbonnet	110.00
Textile, Quilt, Hex, Calico, 19th Century, 80 X 79 In. ....*Illus*	375.00
Textile, Quilt, Hexagon Star One Side, Crazy Pattern Other	35.00
Textile, Quilt, Kate Greenaway Figures, Hand Quilted, C.1880, 61 X 72 In.	175.00
Textile, Quilt, King's Crown, Hand Pieced, 83 X 73 In.	90.00
Textile, Quilt, Little Red Calico Schoolhouse, White Muslin, 66 X 80 In.	200.00
Textile, Quilt, Log Cabin Pattern, Brown, Black, Red, 78 X 90 In.	95.00
Textile, Quilt, Lone Star, Pastels, Pink Border, 82 X 87 In.	200.00
Textile, Quilt, North Carolina Lily, 90 X 74 In.	195.00
Textile, Quilt, Ohio Star, Amish Prints, C.1880, 76 X 68 In.	145.00
Textile, Quilt, Patchwork, Butterfly Pattern, Handmade, 67 X 80 1/2 In.	125.00
Textile, Quilt, Patchwork, Irish Chain Pattern, 74 X 78 In.	60.00

Textile, Rug, Hooked & Shirred, Lion,
American, 53 X 73 3/4 In.

Textile, Rug, Hooked, American Flag,
Signed, 45 X 34 1/2 In.

Textile, Quilt, Patchwork, Velvet, Dated 1928	28.00
Textile, Quilt, Patchwork, Zigzag, 16 Patches, C.1870	60.00
Textile, Quilt, Pennsylvania Block Tulip, Pinwheel, Green, Pink, 1880, Double	165.00
Textile, Quilt, Pieced & Appliqued Sunflower, 68 X 76 In.	110.00
Textile, Quilt, Pine Tree, Pieced, C.1920, 87 X 61 1/2 In.	300.00
Textile, Quilt, Red & White Squares & Octagons, 80 X 68 In.	28.00
Textile, Quilt, Red Squares, Postage Stamp Squares, Pieced, 84 X 72 In.	105.00
Textile, Quilt, Red, Brown, Yellow & Black Calico Patches, Pinwheel	120.00
Textile, Quilt, Red, Green On White, Signed Little Winkler, 1932, Double	115.00
Textile, Quilt, Red, Yellow & Forest Green, Irish Chain, Mennonite	375.00
Textile, Quilt, Rocky Road, Navy, White & Red, 62 X 80 In.	105.00
Textile, Quilt, Rose Of Sharon, Scrolled Border, C.1840, 78 X 95 In.	100.00
Textile, Quilt, Rose Wreath, 19th Century, 79 1/2 X 73 In. *Illus*	550.00
Textile, Quilt, Rose Wreaths, Circles At Corners, 1910s	135.00
Textile, Quilt, Silk Patchwork, Embroidery, Red Lining, 43 X 67 In.	125.00
Textile, Quilt, Silk, Velvet, Punchwork Design, Feather Stitching, Double	130.00
Textile, Quilt, Trapunto, Fringed, C.1820, 8 X 7 1/2 Feet	500.00
Textile, Quilt, Triangle Baskets, Parallel Quilting, C.1875, 82 X 80 In.	110.00
Textile, Quilt, Tulip Pattern, C.1920, 64 X 85 In.	145.00
Textile, Quilt, Wandering Foot Pattern, Red On White, 74 X 90 In.	185.00
Textile, Quilt, Whig Rose Pattern, Appliqued, Extra Large	175.00
Textile, Quilt, White Cake Stand On Basket, Hand-Quilted, Double	90.00
Textile, Quilt, Wild Geese A Flying, 1878	125.00
Textile, Quilt, Wool, Feather Stitching, Embroidery, 76 X 88 In.	75.00
Textile, Quilt, Wreath, Green, Red, President's, Pennsylvania	250.00
Textile, Quilt, 9 Patch Center, Sawtooth Border, C.1860, 70 X 84 In.	120.00
Textile, Robe, Carriage, Horsehead With Glass Eye, Wine Ground	85.00
Textile, Robe, Carriage, Mohair, American Eagle, C.1900, 46 1/2 X 59 In.	125.00
Textile, Robe, Carriage, Mohair, Hand Screened, Concentrics, 40 X 26 In.	125.00
Textile, Robe, Carriage, Velvet, Roses, 60 X 47 In.	50.00
Textile, Robe, Chinese, Embroidered, Silk, Dragons, Red, Blue, White, Peach	750.00
Textile, Robe, Chinese, Symbols, Dragons, Flaming Pearls, Clouds, Bats	650.00
Textile, Robe, Imperial K'o-Ssu Dragon Robe, C.1800, 53 In. Long	1000.00
Textile, Robe, Lap, Red & Green Floral, 54 X 64 In.	65.00
Textile, Rug, Armenian Balkan, Purple, Crude Floral, 11 X 16 Feet	3000.00
Textile, Rug, Art Nouveau, European, Pre-Turn Of Century, 6 X 9 Ft.	300.00
Textile, Rug, Aubusson, Cocoa Field, Floral Sprays, 87 X 46 In.	250.00
Textile, Rug, Belouistan Oriental, Chinese Picture, 44 X 22 In.	600.00
Textile, Rug, Black Bear, Claws, Felt Lining, 45 In.	95.00
Textile, Rug, Chinese, Flower Filled Urns, Lotus Border, 112 X 84 In.	550.00
Textile, Rug, Chinese, Flowering Vines, Ivory Border, 116 X 93 In.	450.00
Textile, Rug, Hamadan, Oriental, 49 X 28 In.	340.00
Textile, Rug, Hand-Braided, Multicolored, 46 X 23 In.	35.00
Textile, Rug, Hooked & Shirred, Lion, American, 53 X 73 3/4 In. *Illus*	475.00
Textile, Rug, Hooked, American Flag, Signed, 45 X 34 1/2 In. *Illus*	600.00
Textile, Rug, Hooked, American Geometric, 2 Pieces, 51 3/4 X 50 1/2 In.	250.00
Textile, Rug, Hooked, American Pictorial, C.1920, 45 X 33 In.	750.00
Textile, Rug, Hooked, British Rose, 1800s, 51 1/2 X 30 1/2 In.	125.00
Textile, Rug, Hooked, Clown, 20th Century, 36 X 45 In.	395.00

Textile, Rug, Hooked, Houses Along Shore, C.1900, 24 X 36 In. 175.00
Textile, Rug, Hooked, Maine, 2 X 3 Feet 36.00
Textile, Rug, Hooked, Pots, Tulips, Pinwheels, American, 1800s, 93 X 38 In. 1500.00
Textile, Rug, Hooked, Prancing Horse, Flowering Vines, 19 X 39 3/4 In. 200.00
Textile, Rug, Hooked, Running Horse, 51 3/4 X 35 1/2 In. .... *Illus* 300.00
Textile, Rug, Hooked, Wool, Geometric With Fruit Design, 27 X 51 In. 59.00
Textile, Rug, Hooked, Wool, Rose Floral, Black Center, 25 1/2 X 41 1/2 In. 100.00
Textile, Rug, Hunt, Oriental, Red, Blue, Brown, Cream, 8 X 12 Feet 800.00
Textile, Rug, Indian Prayer, 21 X 22 In. 22.50
Textile, Rug, Indian, Diamond Design, Red, Grey, Black, 41 X 69 In. 55.00
Textile, Rug, Kazak, Caucasian, Geometrics, 4 X 6 Feet 1700.00
Textile, Rug, Large Flowers, 6 Ft., 4 In. X 30 In. 87.50
Textile, Rug, Lavar Kirman, Tree Of Life, Prayer, Calligraphy, 5 X 8 Feet 700.00
Textile, Rug, Navajo, Red, Brown, Yellow, Gray, C.1920, 52 X 36 In. 675.00
Textile, Rug, Navajo, Storm Pattern, Good Luck Symbols, C.1900, 87 X 60 In. 1500.00
Textile, Rug, Oriental, Bokhara, 38 X 64 In. 215.00
Textile, Rug, Oriental, Empress, Camel Label, Belgium, 9 X 1i Ft. 300.00
Textile, Rug, Oriental, Hand-Knotted Wool, Beige & Ivory, China, 9 X 12 Feet 950.00
Textile, Rug, Oriental, Heriz, Gold, Green, Red, Blue, 114 X 97 In. 1950.00
Textile, Rug, Oriental, Ispahan, Tree, Flowers, Birds, 35 X 55 In. 410.00
Textile, Rug, Oriental, Karastan, Kerman Pattern, 9 X 21 Feet 1500.00
Textile, Rug, Oriental, Meshed, Multicolored, Floral, 158 X 119 In. 1600.00
Textile, Rug, Oriental, Sarouk, Floral Spray Design, 142 X 100 In. 2750.00
Textile, Rug, Oriental, Sarouk, 52 X 89 In. 1450.00
Textile, Rug, Oriental, Tabriz, 1910, 6 X 9 Feet 1500.00
Textile, Rug, Prayer, Turkoman, 54 X 43 In. 60.00
Textile, Rug, Pulled, Black With Flowers, V.C.J. Initial, 64 X 30 In. 98.00
Textile, Rug, Sarouk, Floral Motif, Blue Field, Foliated Borders, 58 X 40 In. 1300.00
Textile, Rug, Sarouk, Flower Filled Vase, Birds, Red, 78 1/2 X 50 In. 1600.00
Textile, Rug, Tabriz, Ivory Medallion, Pomegranate Borders, 9 1/2 X 12 In. 0000.00
Textile, Rug, Tabriz, Prayer, Silk, Blue, Flowers, Latern, 77 X 56 In. 2600.00
Textile, Rug, Tekke Bokhara, Wide Aprons, 7 X 11 Feet 2000.00
Textile, Rug, Wool, Road Runner Design, Reversible, Mexico, 9 X 12 Feet 325.00
Textile, Rug, Yalameh, Ivory, India, 9 X 12 Feet 1690.00
Textile, Runner, Battenburg, 18 X 54 In. 35.00
Textile, Runner, Cutwork, Linen, 24 X 70 In. 10.00
Textile, Runner, Geometric Design, Rust, Red & Green, 7 X 3 Feet 100.00
Textile, Runner, Wheat Pattern, Satin Stripes, 27 X 44 In. 20.00

*Samplers were made in the United States during the early 1700s. The
best examples were made from 1790 to 1840. Long narrow samplers are usually
older than the square ones. Early samplers just had stitching or alphabets.
The later examples had numerals, borders, and pictorial decorations. Those
with mottoes are mid-Victorian.*

Textile, Sampler, ABC & Verse, Dated 1851 .... 75.00
Textile, Sampler, Ada Elizabeth Dalby, Age 10, 1863, 15 1/2 X 14 1/2 In. 160.00
Textile, Sampler, Adam & Eve, Dated 1841 .... 275.00
Textile, Sampler, Alphabet Theme, Linen, Blue, Natural Tones, 25 X 19 1/2 In. 125.00
Textile, Sampler, Alphabet, Birds, Baskets, Flowers, By F.L., C.1836 .... 155.00
Textile, Sampler, Alphabet, M.E.Wilcox, March 1880, Framed, 12 1/2 X 15 In. 75.00
Textile, Sampler, Alphabet, Numbers, Signed Jane Pullyn, C.1742, 16 X 11 In. 1200.00
Textile, Sampler, Ann Jennet Burgess, Chelsea, 1833, 9 X 18 In. 85.00
Textile, Sampler, Ann Thompson, 1803, Birds, Alphabet, Verse, 12 X 13 In. 150.00
Textile, Sampler, Bless This House, O Lord We Pray, Framed, 13 1/2 In.Sq. 17.00
Textile, Sampler, Dinah Riley, 1804, Alphabet, Acorn Border, 10 X 12 In. 225.00
Textile, Sampler, Home Sweet Home, 1888 .... 150.00
Textile, Sampler, In The Spring A Young Mans's Fancy, Dated 1931, Framed 13.00
Textile, Sampler, Jane Ford Sandford, Age 7, 1880, Earth Colors, Alphabet 110.00
Textile, Sampler, Levina Powell, 1815, Alphabets, Numbers, 9 X 10 In. 135.00
Textile, Sampler, Mary Carley, May 3, 1829, Verse, Figures, Framed, 13 X 17 In. ... 350.00
Textile, Sampler, Mourning, Sarah Jane Catterall, 1875, 26 X 28 In. 185.00
Textile, Sampler, Nancy Harrison, 8 Years, 1840, Framed, 8 1/2 X 11 1/2 In. 250.00
Textile, Sampler, Signed C.Lodbell, 19th Century, 17 3/4 X 17 1/2 In. 125.00
Textile, Sampler, Trees, Poem, Name & Parents Names, Framed, 17 X 17 In. 225.00
Textile, Sampler, Variety Of Stitches, Signed, C.1815, 13 3/4 X 11 3/4 In. 1200.00
Textile, Sampler, 6 Line Verse, Gold Leaf Frame, 1827, 19 1/2 X 17 1/2 In. 230.00

Textile, Scarf, Japanese Scene, Silk Embroidered, 20 X 14 In. 30.00
Textile, Scarf, Linen, Blue & White Mums, Chinese, 19 X 42 In. 15.00
Textile, Scarf, Neck, Pierpoint Lace, 1850s, 7 1/2 X 74 In. 45.00
Textile, Scarf, Piano, Silver Metallic Design On Ecru Lace, 80 X 25 In. 50.00
Textile, Scarf, Table, Linen, Hand Embroidery, C.1905, 66 1/2 X 16 In. 250.00
Textile, Scarf, 1876 Centennial Exhibition, Philadelphia, 21 In.Square 48.00
Textile, Scroll, Hand-Painted, Oriental, Hanging, Signed, 4 Feet Long 67.50
Textile, Shawl, Ecru, Silkalene, 46 In.Square 15.00
Textile, Shawl, Lacy Pattern, 3 In.Fringe, 60 In.Square 17.50
Textile, Shawl, Lavender, Embroidered Flowers, 20 In.Fringe 50.00
Textile, Shawl, Orange, Silk, Fringe, 58 In. 37.00
Textile, Shawl, Paisley Border, Rust, Signed Embroidery Work, 63 In.Square 85.00
Textile, Shawl, Paisley, Curvilinear Design, 140 X 62 In. 120.00
Textile, Spats, Lady's, Fur Trim 10.00
Textile, Spats, 4 Button, Gray, Strap Clasp 7.00
Textile, Stocking, Christmas, Printed, C.1900, 31 In. 35.00
Textile, Strap, Luggage Rack, Needlepoint, Black Ground, 3 X 19 In., Pair 15.00
Textile, Tablecloth, Art Nouveau, Blue & White, 35 In.Square 20.00
Textile, Tablecloth, Banquet, Hand Crocheted, Pinwheel Design, 72 X 103 In. 175.00
Textile, Tablecloth, Banquet, Linen, Satin Damask, 72 X 98 In. 22.00
Textile, Tablecloth, Battenberg Lace, 72 In.Diameter 88.00
Textile, Tablecloth, Battenberg Lace, 48 In.Diameter .... 40.00 To 85.00
Textile, Tablecloth, Crocheted Lace Edge, Medallion Center, 46 In.Diameter 10.00
Textile, Tablecloth, Crocheted, White, Bow Knots, 54 X 75 In. 35.00
Textile, Tablecloth, Cross-Stitch, Crochet Edging, 69 X 52 In. 18.50
Textile, Tablecloth, Cross-Stitch, Fruit Design, 48 X 60 In. 20.00
Textile, Tablecloth, Cut Work, Lace & Italian Filet Inserts, 72 In.Diam. 115.00
Textile, Tablecloth, Damask, Satin Stripe, Oval, 72 X 154 In. 50.00
Textile, Tablecloth, Hand Embroidered, Linen, 12 Napkins, 64 X 100 In. 200.00
Textile, Tablecloth, Handmade, Crewel, East Indian, C.1870, 72 X 105 In. 1250.00
Textile, Tablecloth, Lace, Art Nouveau, Angel Pattern Center 250.00
Textile, Tablecloth, Linen, Embroidered, Norway, 26 In.Square 22.00
Textile, Tablecloth, Organdy & Linen, Appliqued, 12 Napkins, 126 X 65 In. 47.00
Textile, Tablecloth, String Drawn Work, 72 X 84 In. 40.00
Textile, Tapestry, Courtiers, 18th Century, Belgian, 28 X 40 In. 27.00
Textile, Tapestry, Courtyard Scene, Belgium, 54 1/2 X 18 1/2 In. 65.00
Textile, Tapestry, Detailed Street Scene, Signed, 19th Century French, Pair 70.00
Textile, Tapestry, Dragons On Gold Silk, 19th Century, 24 X 39 In. 375.00
Textile, Tapestry, Flemish Style, Life At A Country Manor, 78 X 54 In. 2600.00
Textile, Tapestry, Greek War Scene, French, 20 X 60 In. 75.00
Textile, Tapestry, Oriental Ladies At Table, Signed, Belgium, 18 X 20 In. 30.00
Textile, Tapestry, Profile Bust, Wood Frame, Italian, 1700s, 20 In., Pair 425.00
Textile, Tapestry, Silk Embroidery, Early Chinese, 37 X 27 In. 100.00
Textile, Tapestry, Silk, Aubusson, Pastoral Scene, 76 X 61 In. 7000.00
Textile, Tapestry, 2 Women & Boy In Garden, 4 X 6 Feet 30.00
Textile, Top Hat, Beaver Fur, Leather Carrying Case, C.1900 .... 65.00
Textile, Towel, Queen Victoria Diamond Jubilee, Woven Inscription 45.00
Textile, Tunic, Double Breasted, Brass Buttons, West Point Cadet 19.95
Textile, Uniform, Russian Dress, C.1890, For Prince A.Dolgorouky 550.00
Textile, Wall Hanging, Chinese, Silk, Embroidery, C.1800, 20 X 9 1/2 In. 40.00
Textile, Wall Hanging, Chinese, 6 Vases Filled With Flowers, 13 X 16 In. 50.00
Textile, Wall Hanging, Japanese, Silk Embroidered, 1800s, 46 X 70 In. 350.00
Textile, Wall Hanging, Japanese, 3 Coiling Dragons, C.1800, 45 X 67 In. 700.00

Tiffany Bronze

Tiffany Bronze, Ashtray, Gold Dore Finish, Nest Of 4, Each Signed 300.00
Tiffany Bronze, Base, Lamp, American Indian Pattern, Signed 375.00
Tiffany Bronze, Blotter End, Grapevine, No.998, Signed, 2 1/8 X 12 In., Pair 75.00
Tiffany Bronze, Blotter End, Zodiac, Large, Pair 110.00
Tiffany Bronze, Blotter Rocker, Pine Needle Pattern 65.00
Tiffany Bronze, Bookends, Buddha, Signed & Numbered, 6 In., Pair 275.00
Tiffany Bronze, Bookends, Gold Finish, Leather Look, 4 3/4 X 5 1/2 In. 125.00
Tiffany Bronze, Bookends, Owl's Head, Signed, 5 1/2 In., Pair 275.00
Tiffany Bronze, Bookends, Zodiac Symbols, Signed, Patina Finish, 6 In., Pair 225.00
Tiffany Bronze, Bowl, Gold Dore, Ribs Form Scallop Top, Signed, 8 In.Diam. 150.00
Tiffany Bronze, Box, Cigarette, Acid Etched, Green Enamel, Stamped L.C.T. 150.00

Textile, Rug, Hooked, Running Horse,
51 3/4 X 35 1/2 In.
(See Page 619)

Tiffany Bronze, Candlestick,
4 Holders Applied On Base,
1900s

Tiffany Bronze, Box, Stamp, Pine Needle Pattern	85.00
Tiffany Bronze, Box, Zodiac, Circular Design, Signed, 6 1/4 X 6 X 2 1/4 In.	300.00
Tiffany Bronze, Bust, Shakespeare, Signed, 134 Oz.	485.00
Tiffany Bronze, Candlestick, 4 Holders Applied On Base, 1900s ....*Illus*	600.00
Tiffany Bronze, Clock, Desk, Gold Dore Finish, 4 1/4 X 4 1/4 X 2 3/4 In.	450.00
Tiffany Bronze, Clock, Enamel, Gold Dore, Hinged Cover, Signed, 6 X 4 1/2 In.	975.00
Tiffany Bronze, Compote, Abalone Shells Around Rim, 6 1/2 In.Diameter	55.00
Tiffany Bronze, Compote, Dore, Abalone, Signed, 3 1/2 X 6 3/4 In.	125.00
Tiffany Bronze, Compote, Footed, Enameled, Gold Dore, Signed, 10 In.Diameter	225.00
Tiffany Bronze, Desk Set, Dore, Zodiac, 9 Piece	750.00
Tiffany Bronze, Frame, Easel Style, Indian Pattern, Signed, 7 X 6 In.	150.00
Tiffany Bronze, Inkwell, Crab, Natural Shell Cover, Signed, 7 1/2 X 8 In.	2800.00
Tiffany Bronze, Inkwell, Dolphin With Shell Top, Marble & Bronze Base	350.00
Tiffany Bronze, Inkwell, Indian Pattern, Signed, 3 X 5 1/2 In.Diameter	225.00
Tiffany Bronze, Inkwell, Tray, Zodiac, Dore Finish, 10 3/4 X 10 3/4 X 5 In.	495.00
Tiffany Bronze, Jar, Covered, Glass Insert, Signed, 3 In.	95.00
Tiffany Bronze, Lighter, American Indian, Signed, 3 In.Bottom X 2 In.Top	150.00
Tiffany Bronze, Paperweight, Bulldog's Head, Tiffany Studios, New York	250.00
Tiffany Bronze, Paperweight, Bulldogs With Teddy Bear, 3 In.	125.00
Tiffany Bronze, Paperweight, Spaniel, Patina, Signed, No.889	285.00
Tiffany Bronze, Paperweight, Sphinx, Signed, Numbered	325.00
Tiffany Bronze, Platter, Gold Dore Finish, Footed, Signed, 9 3/4 X 4 In.	110.00
Tiffany Bronze, Scale, Letter, Bookmark Pattern, Gold Dore Finish, Signed	375.00
Tiffany Bronze, Ship's Candlestick On A Gimbal, No.143, Signed, 7 1/4 In.	1500.00
Tiffany Bronze, Toothpick, Signed	110.00
Tiffany Bronze, Tray, Art Deco, Abalone Inlay, 14 In.Diameter	300.00
Tiffany Bronze, Tray, Art Nouveau, Gold Dore, Raised Rim, Signed, 10 In.Diam.	250.00
Tiffany Bronze, Tray, Dore, Raised Geometric Border, Signed, Numbered, 9 In.	85.00
Tiffany Bronze, Tray, Footed, Serpent Handles, 10 1/2 In.Square	275.00
Tiffany Bronze, Tray, 3 Compartment, Adam Pattern, Signed, 9 1/2 X 2 3/4 In.	125.00
Tiffany Bronze, Urn, Match Holder, Pine Needle, Signed	110.00

Louis C. Tiffany

Tiffany glass was made by Louis Comfort Tiffany, the American glass designer who worked from about 1879 to 1933. His work included iridescent glass, art nouveau styles of design, and original contemporary styles. He was also noted for his stained glass windows, his unusual lamps, bronze work, pottery, and silver.

Tiffany Glass, Bobeche, Gold Iridescent, Stretch Edge, 5 7/8 In., Set Of 3	315.00
Tiffany Glass, Bonbon, Gold Iridescent, Signed & Numbered	300.00
Tiffany Glass, Bottle, Free Form, Iridescent Gold To Blue, Signed	300.00
Tiffany Glass, Bowl, Amber Iridescent, Signed L.C.Tiffany Favrile, 9 In.	350.00
Tiffany Glass, Bowl, Blue & Purple Iridescent, Signed, 3 In.Diameter	165.00
Tiffany Glass, Bowl, Blue Iridescent, Signed 1286, Favrile, 1905, 6 1/4 In.	375.00
Tiffany Glass, Bowl, Blue, Gold Iridescent, LCT Favrile, 9 X 2 X 2 In.	465.00
Tiffany Glass, Bowl, Crystal Stem, Green, White Base, Signed, 7 1/4 In.	200.00
Tiffany Glass, Bowl, Diamond Optic, Diamond Quilted, Signed, 6 In.Diameter	295.00
Tiffany Glass, Bowl, Finger, Underplates, Gold Iridescent, Signed	295.00
Tiffany Glass, Bowl, Flared Paneled Sides, Iridescence, 1 1/2 X 3 In.Diam.	115.00
Tiffany Glass, Bowl, Pink Pastel, 7 1/2 In.	165.00
Tiffany Glass, Bowl, 4 Footed, Flared Edge, Paper Label, 6 1/2 In.Diameter	500.00

Tiffany Glass, **Box**, Hexagon, Gold Iridescent, Gold Dore Finish, Signed 350.00
Tiffany Glass, **Candleholder**, Iridescent, Blue, Signed, 4 1/4 In. 350.00
Tiffany Glass, **Candleholder**, Oval Stretch Top, Iridescent, Signed, 3 X 4 In. 225.00
Tiffany Glass, **Centerpiece**, Stretched Edge, 3 1/4 In.High X 13 In. 210.00
Tiffany Glass, **Champagne**, Gold Iridescent, Amber Prism Cut Stem, Signed 165.00
Tiffany Glass, **Champagne**, Hollow Stem, Vintage Band, Blue & Amber, Signed 327.00
Tiffany Glass, **Champagne**, Pink, Opalescent Rim, Green Stem, Signed, 7 In. 325.00
Tiffany Glass, **Champagne**, Prince, Gold, Signed, 5 3/4 X 3 1/4 In.Diameter 135.00
Tiffany Glass, **Champagne**, Venetian Green Foot, Full Teardrop, 7 1/2 In. 275.00
Tiffany Glass, **Compote**, Blue Iridescent, Gold, Fluted, Signed, 6 X 6 In. 295.00
Tiffany Glass, **Compote**, Blue Iridescent, Scalloped Rim, Signed, 3 3/4 In. 535.00
Tiffany Glass, **Compote**, Diamond Quilted, Opalescent Butterscotch, Signed 550.00
Tiffany Glass, **Compote**, Gold Iridescence, Ten Colors, Signed, 8 In.Diameter 265.00
Tiffany Glass, **Compote**, Green Iridescent, C.1902, Signed, 8 X 2 5/8 In. 395.00
Tiffany Glass, **Compote**, Mirror Finish, Signed L.C.T.Favrile, 9 1/2 In. 450.00
Tiffany Glass, **Compote**, Queen, Gold Ruffled, Signed, 1 3/4 X 4 In.Diameter 180.00
Tiffany Glass, **Compote**, Quilted, Inverted Saucer Base, Signed, 19 In. 328.00
Tiffany Glass, **Compote**, Serpentine Rim, Blue Iridescent, Signed, 6 In. 535.00
Tiffany Glass, **Compote**, Wafer Stem, Gold, Signed, 4 X 7 1/4 In.Diameter 350.00
Tiffany Glass, **Compote**, Yellow Laurel Leaf, Signed, 3 1/2 X 5 In.Diameter 425.00
Tiffany Glass, **Corset Shape**, 8 Applied Lily Pads, Signed, Numbered, 4 In. 225.00
Tiffany Glass, **Cup**, Iridescent Gold, 3 Handled, Applied Design, Signed 675.00
Tiffany Glass, **Cup**, Nut, Gold Ribbed, Signed, 1 1/4 X 3 In.Diameter 130.00
Tiffany Glass, **Decanter**, Decorated, Signed, No.B2427, 10 In. .... *Illus* 4000.00
Tiffany Glass, **Dish**, Amber Inside, Opalescent Stripes Outside, 4 1/8 In. 115.00
Tiffany Glass, **Dish**, Blue Iridescent, Inscribed L.C.T.Favrile, 1892, 12 In. 450.00
Tiffany Glass, **Dish**, Nut, Gold Iridescent, Green, 3 Footed, Signed, 4 In. 395.00
Tiffany Glass, **Finger Bowl & Underplate**, Earl Pattern, Scalloped Rim 375.00
Tiffany Glass, **Finger Bowl & Underplate**, Victoria, Twisted Prunts, Signed 275.00
Tiffany Glass, **Finger Bowl**, Iridescent, C.1910, 4 3/4 In., Set Of 4 .... 500.00
Tiffany Glass, **Flower Frog**, Blue Iridescent, Signed 225.00
Tiffany Glass, **Flower Frog**, Gold Iridescent, Signed 225.00
Tiffany Glass, **Goblet & Champagne**, Pink Top, Green Stem, Teardrop In Each 250.00
Tiffany Glass, **Goblet**, Clear Cut.Top Edge Deep Cranberry, Signed 125.00
Tiffany Glass, **Goblet**, Hollow Stem, Ball Separating Wafers, Signed, 8 In. 375.00
Tiffany Glass, **Goblet**, Intaglio, Pedestal, Gold Iridescent, Signed, 6 In. 210.00
Tiffany Glass, **Goblet**, Opalescent, Opaque Base, Marked .... *Illus* 250.00
Tiffany Glass, **Goblet**, Pink, Opalescent Rim, Green Stem, Signed, 9 In. 325.00

Tiffany Glass, Decanter, Decorated,
Signed, No.B2427, 10 In.

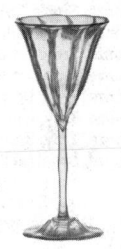

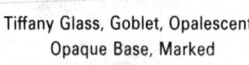

Tiffany Glass, Goblet, Opalescent,
Opaque Base, Marked

Tiffany Glass, **Goblet**, Stemmed, Purple Pastel 230.00
Tiffany Glass, **Goblet**, Venetian Yellow, Opalescent, Signed & Numbered 275.00
Tiffany Glass, **Juice**, Mitered Cut Panels, L.C.T.Favrile, Numbered 195.00
Tiffany Glass, **Juice**, Mitered Cut Panels, Signed & Numbered 195.00
Tiffany Glass, **Lamp**, Candle, Cobalt Blue Iridescent, Favrile 1800.00
Tiffany Glass, **Lamp**, Candle, Cobalt, Honeycomb Shade, Signed, 12 1/2 In. 1800.00
Tiffany Glass, **Mug**, Gold Iridescence, Green Pattern, Applied Handle, Signed 340.00
Tiffany Glass, **Mug**, Leaves, Vines, Applied Handle, 2 1/4 X 3 1/4 In. 350.00
Tiffany Glass, **Ornament**, Butterfly, Stained Glass, Jeweled Body, 11 X 7 In. 1500.00
Tiffany Glass, **Ornament**, Butterfly, Striated Glass, Multicolored, 11 X 7 In. 1500.00
Tiffany Glass, **Paperweight**, Apple, Numbered & Signed L.C.T.Favrile 295.00
Tiffany Glass, **Paperweight**, Dog, Signed, 2 1/2 In. 250.00
Tiffany Glass, **Paperweight**, Ladybug, Favrile 75.00
Tiffany Glass, **Pitcher**, Ice Tea, Wood Handle, Applied Leaves, 3 Pints 225.00
Tiffany Glass, **Plate**, Pink, Feathered, Signed, 10 1/2 In. 250.00

Tiffany Glass, Plate, Purple Iridescent, Gold, Signed, No.R4715, 6 1/2 In. 225.00
Tiffany Glass, Plate, Turquoise Edge, White Stripes Toward Center, Signed 475.00
Tiffany Glass, Plate, White Opalescent Feathering, Pink, Signed .... 195.00 To 225.00
Tiffany Glass, Rose Bowl, Millefiori, Gold Iridescent, Signed, 3 In. 1275.00
Tiffany Glass, Rose Bowl, Squat, Indented Mouth, Gold Design, Signed 400.00
Tiffany Glass, Salt, Allover Punts, Iridescent Silver, Signed, 2 X 1 1/4 In. 195.00
Tiffany Glass, Salt, Blue Iridescent, Ruffled Edge, Signed L.C.T., 2 3/4 In. 160.00
Tiffany Glass, Salt, Crimped Top Edge, Blue & Purple, Signed, 2 1/2 In.Diam. 135.00
Tiffany Glass, Salt, Flower Form, 4 Feet, Signed, L.C.T., 4 In.Wide 325.00
Tiffany Glass, Salt, Gold Iridescent, 3 Small Feet, Signed 145.00
Tiffany Glass, Salt, Pedestal, Paneled Body, Flared Rim, Signed, 1 3/4 In. 145.00
Tiffany Glass, Salt, Rainbow Iridescence, Ruffled, Signed .... 95.00 To 175.00
Tiffany Glass, Salt, Ruffled Edge, Blue Highlights, Gold, Signed L.C.T. 135.00
Tiffany Glass, Salt, Serpentine Rim, Blue, Signed 157.00
Tiffany Glass, Shade, Green Feather On Opalescent, Signed, 5 1/2 In. 325.00
Tiffany Glass, Sherbet, Colonial Pattern, Gold Iridescent, Signed, 3 1/2 In. 150.00
Tiffany Glass, Sherbet, Gold Iridescent, Signed, 4 In. 150.00
Tiffany Glass, Sherbet, Gold, Lily Pads, Signed 285.00
Tiffany Glass, Sherbet, Intaglio Cut, Vintage, Signed, 3 1/2 X 3 3/4 In. 200.00
Tiffany Glass, Sherbet, White Opalescent Feathering, Flared Foot, Signed 195.00
Tiffany Glass, Shot Glass, Iridescent, Pinched Side, Fitted Case, 12, Signed 2500.00
Tiffany Glass, Shot Glass, Prunted, Gold Iridescent, Signed 140.00
Tiffany Glass, Sugar & Creamer, Iridescent, Creamer Is Tankard Shape, 3 In. 595.00
Tiffany Glass, Sugar & Creamer, Miniature, Tankard Shape, Gold Iridescence 850.00
Tiffany Glass, Tile, Gold, White & Green, Marked, Set Of 3 .... 155.00
Tiffany Glass, Tile, Lobed Floret, Red Molded, 3 In.Square 95.00
Tiffany Glass, Toothpick, Gold Iridescent, Green Feathering, 3 In. 650.00
Tiffany Glass, Toothpick, Gold, Pinched, Signed, 2 In. 95.00
Tiffany Glass, Transom Window, Leaded Persian Design, Green, 10 1/2 Ft. 1500.00
Tiffany Glass, Tumbler, Clear With Green, Feather, 5 In. 175.00
Tiffany Glass, Tumbler, Paperweight Base, Amber, Signed & Numbered, 5 In. 550.00
Tiffany Glass, Vase, Alabaster, Gold Pulled Feathers, Signed, 10 1/4 In. 425.00
Tiffany Glass, Vase, Blue & Gold Iridescent, Ribbed, Bulbous, Signed, 6 In. 350.00
Tiffany Glass, Vase, Blue Iridescent, Long Thin Leaves, Signed, 8 1/4 In. 1375.00
Tiffany Glass, Vase, Blue Iridescent, Paneled Body, Signed & Numbered, 7 In. 475.00
Tiffany Glass, Vase, Blue Iridescent, Signed, Favrile, No.8530E, 5 3/4 In. 750.00
Tiffany Glass, Vase, Bowl Shape, Gold Iridescent, Signed, 3 In. 485.00
Tiffany Glass, Vase, Bud, Amber Iridescent, C.1913 .... Illus 1100.00
Tiffany Glass, Vase, Bud, Iridescent Marigold, Signed, No.Y3561, 3 1/2 In. 200.00
Tiffany Glass, Vase, Bud, Pulled Feather Over Clambroth, Green, Signed 395.00
Tiffany Glass, Vase, Cameo, Red, Yellow, Signed, 209B, 10 In. .... Illus 3750.00
Tiffany Glass, Vase, Cylindrical, Gold Iridescence, Signed, 9 1/2 In. 1350.00
Tiffany Glass, Vase, Cypriote, Signed L.C.T.K1371, 13 In. .... Illus 4600.00
Tiffany Glass, Vase, Flared Collared Mouth, Monogrammed, 7 1/2 In. 1600.00

Tiffany Glass, Vase, Bud, Amber Iridescent, C.1913

Tiffany Glass, Vase, Cypriote, Signed L.C.T.K1371, 13 In.

Tiffany Glass, Vase, Cameo, Red, Yellow, Signed, 209B, 10 In.

Tiffany Glass, Vase, Flower Form, Gold Iridescence, Signed, 5 In. 400.00
Tiffany Glass, Vase, Flower Form, Gold, L.C.Tiffany, Favrile, 7727d, 9 In. 1495.00
Tiffany Glass, Vase, Flower Form, Green & White Iridescence, Signed, 13 In. 1795.00
Tiffany Glass, Vase, Flower Form, Ribbed & Dimpled, Signed, 6 1/4 In. 400.00
Tiffany Glass, Vase, Flower Form, Striated Stems, Signed, 12 3/4 In. 2200.00
Tiffany Glass, Vase, Flower Form, Knob Stem, Ruffled Top, Label, 7 1/4 In. 400.00
Tiffany Glass, Vase, Footed, Iridescent Gold, 8 Panels, Signed, 3 3/4 In. 195.00
Tiffany Glass, Vase, Gold Iridescent, Damascene, Signed, 8 In. 775.00
Tiffany Glass, Vase, Gold Iridescent, Intaglio Cut, Signed, 5 1/8 In. 1250.00
Tiffany Glass, Vase, Gold Iridescent, Narrow Neck, Signed, 7 1/2 In. 900.00
Tiffany Glass, Vase, Gold Iridescent, Speckled Finish, Signed, 12 In. 300.00
Tiffany Glass, Vase, Gold Iridescent, 4 Legs, Signed, Numbered, 3 1/2 In. 395.00
Tiffany Glass, Vase, Gold, Embedded Leaves & Florettes, Signed, 9 1/2 In. 1650.00
Tiffany Glass, Vase, Gold, Signed, Curved Body, Inverted Lip, 2 In. 175.00
Tiffany Glass, Vase, Green Iridescent, Yellow, Silver Leaf Pulls, 3 1/2 In. 875.00
Tiffany Glass, Vase, Green, Amber, Floriform, Favrile, No.M7854, 12 7/8 In. 700.00
Tiffany Glass, Vase, Heart, Random Vines, Green Iridescent, Signed, Numbered 585.00
Tiffany Glass, Vase, Iridescent Red, Signed & Paper Label, 3 In. 1400.00
Tiffany Glass, Vase, Iridescent, Signed L.C.T.M7608, 13 1/2 In. ....*Illus* 2000.00
Tiffany Glass, Vase, Jack-In-The-Pulpit, Amber Iridescent, C.1905, 18 In. 3500.00
Tiffany Glass, Vase, King Tut, Turquoise, Gold, Yellow, Signed, Numbered, 4 In. 475.00
Tiffany Glass, Vase, Lily, Pulled Feathers, Signed L.C.Tiffany, 10 1/4 In. 475.00
Tiffany Glass, Vase, Ovoid, Egyptian Collar, Footed, Signed, 7 3/4 In. 4200.00
Tiffany Glass, Vase, Paperweight, Millefiori, Drilled, Signed, 10 1/2 In. 1450.00
Tiffany Glass, Vase, Pinched, Favrile, Gold, Pink & Blue, Signed, 2 In. 170.00
Tiffany Glass, Vase, Pink With White Opalescent Ribs, Signed, 6 In. 525.00
Tiffany Glass, Vase, Stick, Favrile, Enamel, Red, Amber, Green, 13 In. 300.00
Tiffany Glass, Vase, Translucent Red, Signed, 6658K, 6 1/2 In. ....*Illus* 4000.00
Tiffany Glass, Vase, Transparent Opalescent Amber, Signed, 2 7/8 In. 575.00
Tiffany Glass, Vase, Trumpet Shape, Blue & Opaque White, Signed, 10 In. 1075.00
Tiffany Glass, Vase, Trumpet, Gold Iridescent, Signed, No.1005g 685.00
Tiffany Glass, Vase, Trumpet, Leafage, Ribbed, Flaring Foot, 1918, 14 In. 650.00
Tiffany Glass, Vase, Trumpet, Ribbed & Footed, Signed & Numbered, 10 In. 500.00
Tiffany Glass, Vase, 2 Piece, Intaglio, Tiered Flower Holder, Signed, 11 In. 1350.00
Tiffany Glass, Wine, Blue Gold Iridescent, Citrine Stem, Signed, Set Of 6 .... 600.00
Tiffany Glass, Wine, Gold Iridescence, Amber Prism Cut Stem, Signed 185.00
Tiffany Glass, Wine, Green, Signed 145.00
Tiffany Glass, Wine, Opalescent White, Green Stem, Favrile ....*Illus* 150.00
Tiffany Glass, Wine, Venetian, Green Foot, Full Teardrop, Pink 265.00

Tiffany Pottery
Tiffany Pottery, Vase, Bisque Body, Relief Trumpet Vine, 12 In. 300.00
Tiffany Pottery, Vase, Gourd, Uneven Brown Striping, 5 In. 675.00
Tiffany Pottery, Vase, Tree Trunk, Signed, 5 1/4 In. 1050.00

Tiffany Silver
Tiffany Silver, Bonbon, Inverted Saucer Base, Heart Shape, 4 In. 35.00

Tiffany Glass, Vase, Iridescent, Signed L.C.T.M7608, 13 1/2 In.

Tiffany Glass, Vase, Translucent Red, Signed, 6658K, 6 1/2 In.

Tiffany Glass, Wine, Opalescent White,
Green Stem, Favrile

Tiffany, Candleholder, Iridescent Shade,
Signed, 14 5/8 In.

(See Page 627)

Tiffany Silver, Tea & Coffee Set, Oriental Movement, 7 Piece
(See Page 626)

Tiffany Silver, **Bowl,** Circular Form, Everted Rim, New York, C.1900, 13 In.	250.00
Tiffany Silver, **Bowl,** Heart Shape, Inverted Saucer Base, Marked, 4 In.	43.00
Tiffany Silver, **Bowl,** Low Pedestal, 3 1/4 X 6 1/4 In.Diameter	125.00
Tiffany Silver, **Bowl,** Pair, 6 1/4 In.Diameter, 1 In. High	175.00
Tiffany Silver, **Bowl,** Signed, 14 Ounces	125.00
Tiffany Silver, **Bowl,** 4 Paw Feet, Foliated Rolled Border, Troy, 82 Ounce	3000.00
Tiffany Silver, **Box,** Egg Shape	125.00
Tiffany Silver, **Box,** Match, Marked, Small	25.00
Tiffany Silver, **Box,** Powder, Gilt, 2 7/8 X 1 1/8 In.	125.00
Tiffany Silver, **Case,** Cigarette, 4 Oz.	75.00
Tiffany Silver, **Clock,** Travel, 8 Day, Art Nouveau Case	195.00
Tiffany Silver, **Cocktail Shaker,** 3 Pint, 11 1/2 In.	265.00
Tiffany Silver, **Cup,** Child's, Art Nouveau	85.00
Tiffany Silver, **Cup,** Loving, Double Handles, 1905, 25 Oz.	150.00
Tiffany Silver, **Dish,** Nut, Footed, Reticulated, Beaded Rim, Signed, Set Of 6	95.00
Tiffany Silver, **Dresser Set,** Signed, 10 Piece	235.00
Tiffany Silver, **Eggcup,** C.1895, 2 1/4 In.	24.00
Tiffany Silver, **Fish Set,** 6 Forks, 6 Knives, Marked	300.00
Tiffany Silver, **Flask,** Cologne	60.00
Tiffany Silver, **Holder,** Calendar, Perpetual, Grape Vine	75.00
Tiffany Silver, **Holder,** Dime Change	22.00
Tiffany Silver, **Holder,** Perpetual Calendar, Signed, 7 X 8 1/2 In.	75.00

Tiffany, Inkstand, Glass, Gilt Bronze,
Covered, Favrile

Tiffany, Lamp, 10 Light, Lily Pad Vase,
Signed, 20 1/2 In.
(See Page 628)

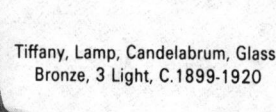

Tiffany, Lamp, Candelabrum, Glass,
Bronze, 3 Light, C.1899-1920

Tiffany Silver, Holder, Shaving Brush	50.00
Tiffany Silver, Inkwell, Grape Vine, Original Insert	195.00 To 250.00
Tiffany Silver, Knife, Fork & Spoon, Figural Nursery Rhyme	288.00
Tiffany Silver, Knife, Fruit & Fork, Woman's Full Figure On Handle	50.00
Tiffany Silver, Matchbox Holder, Book Design	22.00
Tiffany Silver, Nipper, Cigar Tip	80.00
Tiffany Silver, Nut Pick, Lightly Engraved, Marked, 5 In.	25.00
Tiffany Silver, Pincushion, Signed, 18 In.Diameter	78.50
Tiffany Silver, Pipe Tool	30.00
Tiffany Silver, Pitcher, Water, Scroll Handle, New York, C.1900, 10 1/4 In.	325.00
Tiffany Silver, Saltshaker, Vermeil Top, 2 1/2 In.	40.00
Tiffany Silver, Server, Cake & Pie, Lap Over Edge	110.00
Tiffany Silver, Serving Set, Coffee, Tea, Covered Creamer & Sugar, 1854-55	2250.00
Tiffany Silver, Skewer, Signed, 12 In.	40.00
Tiffany Silver, Spoon, Serving, Olympian, 9 5/8 In.	165.00
Tiffany Silver, Stirrer, Hot Toddy, End Is Pierced Snowflake, 11 1/2 In.	50.00
Tiffany Silver, Tea & Coffee Set, Oriental Movement, 7 Piece *Illus*	2200.00
Tiffany Silver, Tea Set, Teapot, Sugar, Creamer, Tray, Union Square Mark	750.00
Tiffany Silver, Teapot, 4 Feet, Bird Finial, 8 X 7 In.	250.00
Tiffany Silver, Tray, Flowers On Rim, Signed, 7 In.	56.00

Tiffany, Varied Materials

Tiffany, Bill Holder, Grape, Brown Patina, Signed	125.00
Tiffany, Blotter Corner, Brass	65.00
Tiffany, Blotter End, Abalone, Iridescent Discs, 19 X 2 1/4 In., Pair	150.00
Tiffany, Blotter Ends, Pine Needle, Carmel Slag	89.00
Tiffany, Blotter, Rocking, Venetian	130.00
Tiffany, Book Mark, Dore	195.00
Tiffany, Book Rack, Bronze & Glass, Adjustable Base, Signed, 14 X 6 1/2 In.	495.00
Tiffany, Bottle, Perfume, Signed, 5 1/2 In.	425.00
Tiffany, Bowl, Serpentine Rim, Gold Plated, Signed, 12 1/2 In.	254.00
Tiffany, Box, Abalone, Cedar Lined, Signed, Numbered, 7 X 5 X 3 In.	225.00
Tiffany, Box, Stamp, Dore, Etched Metal & Glass, Grapevine	95.00
Tiffany, Box, Stamp, Etched Metal & Glass, Pine Needle	120.00
Tiffany, Box, Trinket, Silver Plate, Repousse	45.00

Tiffany, Candle Lamp, Decorated Glass Riser, Signed Base & Shade, 11 In. 700.00
Tiffany, Candleholder, Iridescent Shade, Signed, 14 5/8 In. ....*Illus* 550.00
Tiffany, Candlestick, Cobra, Gold Dore Patina 385.00
Tiffany, Candlestick, Dore, 3 Ball Feet, Signed, No.1202, 9 In. 275.00
Tiffany, Candlestick, Jeweled, 2 Arm 750.00
Tiffany, Candlestick, Red & Pink Enamel, Gold Dore, Signed, 10 1/2 In., Pair 750.00
Tiffany, Chandelier, Slag, 8 Leaded Panels, Ruby Inserts, 38 In.Diameter 675.00
Tiffany, Charger, Brass Inlay, Oriental Style, Copper, 12 1/4 In. 55.00
Tiffany, Clip, Paper, Etched Metal, Grapevine 75.00
Tiffany, Clock Set, Marble & Bronze, Signed, 3 Piece 875.00
Tiffany, Clock, Blue Enameled Jewels, Signed 750.00
Tiffany, Clock, Brass & Onyx Decoration, Desk, 8 Day, Signed 75.00
Tiffany, Clock, Carriage, Brass & Crystal, Time & Alarm, Signed, 11 3/4 In. 600.00
Tiffany, Clock, Grandfather, Tubular Chimes, Moon Face, Signed, 8 Feet 2875.00
Tiffany, Clock, Regulator, Crystal, Porcelain Face, Brass, Marked, 11 In. 500.00
Tiffany, Clock, Shelf, Tambour, Chelsea Works, Mahogany 175.00
Tiffany, Compote, Blue & Gold, Signed & Numbered 623 & 624, Pair 1000.00
Tiffany, Compote, Gold Favrile, Bronze Base, 12 In.Diameter 750.00
Tiffany, Cuff Links, Gold & Red Enamel Striped, 18K Gold 250.00
Tiffany, Demitasse Set, 11 Cups, Holders & Saucers, Sterling & Lenox 595.00
Tiffany, Dish, Spun Brass, Multicolored Scalloped Border, 10 In. 160.00
Tiffany, Dresser Set, Trimmer, Buffer, Brush, Mirror, Tray, Signed 185.00
Tiffany, Egg Warmer, Silver Plate, Wooden Finial, Claw Feet, 8 1/2 In. 90.00
Tiffany, Fireplace Mantel & Shelf, Favrile Glass Decoration, 6 1/2 Ft. 5000.00
Tiffany, Flask, Scent, Gold & Lapis Lazuli, Marked, C.1893, 3 3/8 In. 650.00
Tiffany, Holder, Memo Pad, Signed 110.00
Tiffany, Holder, Pen, Easel Type, Bronze Over Amber Glass 145.00
Tiffany, Inkstand, Glass, Gilt Bronze, Covered, Favrile ....*Illus* 500.00
Tiffany, Inkwell, Abalone Pattern, Octagon, Cover, Signed, 3 1/2 X 3 1/2 In. 225.00
Tiffany, Inkwell, Blue & Gold, Signed, 6 X 5 3/4 In. 650.00
Tiffany, Inkwell, Chinese Pattern, 5 In. 210.00
Tiffany, Inkwell, Etched Metal & Glass, Pine Needle, Glass Well 145.00
Tiffany, Inkwell, Green Enamel, Signed, Numbered, Adams 140.00
Tiffany, Inkwell, Man With Flute Between Covered Wells, Signed & Numbered 600.00
Tiffany, Jewelry, Scarab, Iridescent Purple, 14K Gold 195.00
Tiffany, Lamp, Acorn & Oak Leaf, Signed, 18 In. 5900.00
Tiffany, Lamp, Aladdin, Silvered Pewter Base, Signed, Gorham Shade, 13 In. 550.00
Tiffany, Lamp, Bridge, Arms Curve, Bronze Base, Signed, 10 In.Diameter 2200.00
Tiffany, Lamp, Candelabrum, Glass, Bronze, 3 Light, C.1899-1920 ....*Illus* 1500.00
Tiffany, Lamp, Candle, Electric, Bibbed Swirled Base, Signed, 16 1/2 In. 675.00
Tiffany, Lamp, Candle, Glass Riser, Signed Shade & Base 725.00
Tiffany, Lamp, Candle, Turtleback Shade, Bronze Base, Signed, 19 In. 2500.00
Tiffany, Lamp, Desk, Adam Pattern, Signed 1350.00
Tiffany, Lamp, Desk, Adjustable, Quezal Shade, Signed, 13 1/2 In. 1200.00
Tiffany, Lamp, Desk, Bell Shaped, 2 Arms, Gold Leaf, Signed, 11 1/2 In. 1200.00
Tiffany, Lamp, Desk, Bronze Base & Feet, Arms Form Harp, Signed, 18 1/4 In. 850.00
Tiffany, Lamp, Desk, Bronze Base, Gold & Purple Shade, Signed 950.00
Tiffany, Lamp, Desk, Gold Dore, 2 Arms, Favrile Shade, Signed, 17 1/2 In. 750.00
Tiffany, Lamp, Desk, Harp Shape, Bronze Base, Iridescent Shade, Signed, 13 In. 950.00
Tiffany, Lamp, Desk, Striated Glass, Bronze Base, Signed, 16 In.Diameter 3100.00
Tiffany, Lamp, Desk, Turtleback, Leaded Shade, Bronze Base, Signed, 21 In. 4100.00
Tiffany, Lamp, Desk, Turtleback, Purple Glass Top, Bronze Base, Signed 2500.00
Tiffany, Lamp, Desk, Zodiac, Oval Base, Adjustable, Signed, 10 In. 900.00
Tiffany, Lamp, Fixture, Ceiling, Bucket Shape, Leaded Glass, Yellows, Greens 4500.00
Tiffany, Lamp, Floor, Bronze, Acorn Leaded Shade, Marked 2700.00
Tiffany, Lamp, Floor, Lily, Adjustable, 6 Shades, Signed 2750.00
Tiffany, Lamp, Floor, Metal & Glass, Counter-Balance, Signed, 53 In. 2200.00
Tiffany, Lamp, Floor, Pine Needle Over Green Glass Shade, 3 Legged, 10 In. 1325.00
Tiffany, Lamp, Gold Iridescent, Dore Shade, Bronze Root Base, Signed, 7 In. 1125.00
Tiffany, Lamp, Gooseneck Shape, Gold Ribbed Shade, Signed, 12 In. 650.00
Tiffany, Lamp, Green & Gold Shade, 4 Armed Bronze Base, Signed, 13 1/2 In. 900.00
Tiffany, Lamp, Green Lemon Leaf, Signed Base & Shade, 18 In. 6500.00
Tiffany, Lamp, Hanging Fixture, 25 Branches, Lily Shade, Lotton, 25 In. 7500.00
Tiffany, Lamp, Hanging, Bronze, Prisms, Beaded Chain, Signed, 24 In. 2500.00
Tiffany, Lamp, Leaded, Curved Glass, Orange & White, Matching Base & Shade 900.00

Tiffany, Lamp, Leaded, Nautilus, Bronze Base, Signed, 16 In.	8500.00
Tiffany, Lamp, Lily-Form, Bronze & Glass, 10 Branch, 1905, 21 In.	5500.00
Tiffany, Lamp, Low Harp, Decorated Shade, Signed	975.00
Tiffany, Lamp, Oil, Candlestick Type, Brass, Signed	650.00
Tiffany, Lamp, Piano, Bronze Base, Signed, 3 Lily Branch	320.00
Tiffany, Lamp, Raised Leaf Design, Gold Ribbed Shade, 13 In.	650.00
Tiffany, Lamp, Red Dragon Fly, Shade, 20 In.Across, 23 In.High	500.00
Tiffany, Lamp, Scarab, Bronze Beaded Edging, Pivot Shade, Signed, 9 In.	3700.00
Tiffany, Lamp, Table, Blown Glass Shade, Iridescent, Signed, 23 In.	2250.00
Tiffany, Lamp, Table, Jewelled Moth, Leaded Shade, Moths At Rim, 21 In.	4500.00
Tiffany, Lamp, Table, Nautilus, Iridescent Chambered Shell, No.403, 13 In.	1850.00
Tiffany, Lamp, 10 Light, Lily Pad Vase, Signed, 20 1/2 In. ....Illus	6500.00
Tiffany, Letter Opener, Enamel Pattern On Handle, Signed, 10 1/2 In.	150.00
Tiffany, Letter Opener, Green Glass & Bronze	35.00
Tiffany, Letter Opener, Venetian Pattern, Gold Dore, Signed, 10 In.	110.00
Tiffany, Magnifying Glass, Bronze, Zodiac Pattern, 4 In.Diameter, 9 In.	225.00
Tiffany, Magnifying Glass, Zodiac Pattern, Signed, 9 X 4 In.	225.00
Tiffany, Mirror, Enameled, 11 In.	350.00
Tiffany, Pad, Memo, American Indian, Handle Signed & Numbered	145.00
Tiffany, Paperweight, Dog, Signed, No.933	250.00
Tiffany, Pen Brush, Abalone Pattern, Octagon, Signed, 2 1/4 X 2 1/4 In.	110.00
Tiffany, Pendant, Art Deco, French Enamel & Diamond, 15K Gold, Signed	315.00
Tiffany, Pin, Leaf Design, 18K Gold Circlet, 1 3/8 In.	90.00
Tiffany, Planter, Bronze Over Opalescent Glass, Pine Needle, Signed, 11 In.	350.00
Tiffany, Planter, Mosaic, Favrile, Bronze, No.835, C.1900-20, 12 1/2 In.	5750.00
Tiffany, Pottery, Vase, Blue Glaze, Classic Shape, 7 1/2 In.	475.00
Tiffany, Purse, Chain Handle, Mesh, 6 X 6 In.	95.00
Tiffany, Shade, Candle Lamp, Grape Vine Pattern, Silvered Bronze, Signed	110.00
Tiffany, Shade, Foliate Shape, Iridescence, Signed, 7 1/4 In.Diameter	375.00
Tiffany, Shade, Hanging, Pyramid Shape, Green, 8 X 7 X 7 In., Pair	60.00
Tiffany, Shade, White Blown-Out Glass & Bronze, 3 1/4 In.	675.00
Tiffany, Stamp Box, Metal & Glass, Etched	110.00
Tiffany, Tile, Floral Design, Signed & Dated, 3 In.Square	37.50
Tiffany, Tray, Abalone Trimmed Border, 9 In.	100.00
Tiffany, Tray, Copper, Wedding Invitation, Dated 6/20/1911, 6 X 7 1/4 In.	40.00
Tiffany, Tray, Geometric Embossed Border, Signed, 9 In.Diameter	85.00
Tiffany, Tray, Pen, Green Glass Insert, Signed, 2 3/4 X 9 1/2 In.	90.00
Tiffany, Tray, Silvered Bronze, No.1672, 6 1/2 In.	95.00
Tiffany, Tray, 2 Piece Box, Ivory, 6 X 3 X 3/8 In.	135.00
Tiffany, Tureen, Soup, Band Of Gold, Pink & Blue Flowers, 18 X 10 In.	395.00
Tiffany, Vase, Triangular Shape, 6 Applied Lily Pads, Signed, 4 1/2 In.	600.00
Tiffany, Watch, Open Face, Gold, Leather Lined Case, 1878, Marked	1300.00

Tiffin Glass Company of Tiffin, Ohio, was a subsidiary of the United States Glass Co.of Pittsburgh, Pa. Black satin glass, made by the company between 1923 and 1926, is very popular among collectors. Other types were also made.

Tiffin, Basket, Black Satin, 11 In.	55.00
Tiffin, Compote, Yellow Satin, 8 In.	25.00
Tiffin, Mold, Butter, Cow	55.00
Tiffin, Rose Bowl, Black, Blown-Out Poppies, 5 X 6 In.	22.50
Tiffin, Vase, Claw Type Mouth, Green, 9 In.	55.00
Tiffin, Vase, Diamond Optic, Paper Label, 11 In.	45.00
Tiffin, Vase, Green, 9 In.	50.00
Tiffin, Vase, Iris, Raised Flowers, Black Satin, 6 1/2 In.	13.00 To 35.00
Tiffin, Vase, Molded Chrysanthemum, Ormolu Collar & Base, 8 In.	28.00
Tiffin, Vase, Silver Overlay Of Parrot On Branch, Green, 11 In.	135.00
Tiffin, Wine, Cherokee Rose, Etched, 6 1/4 In.	12.95
Tile, see listing by company name	
Tile, A Midnight's Dream, Minton, 6 In.Square	40.00
Tile, Aries, Moravian	20.00
Tile, Calendar, Jones, McDuffee & Stratton, 1891 Adams Birthplace	35.00
Tile, Chelsea, Low, 4 1/4 In.	42.00
Tile, Chinese Scene, Minton	10.00
Tile, Cobalt, Flowers, Wheeling, 6 In.Square	10.00
Tile, Delft, Goose In Center, Marked Belga	10.00

Tile, Dutch, Art Nouveau Design, 5 1/4 In.Square	6.00
Tile, Dutch, Butterflies, 5 1/4 In.Square	6.00
Tile, Dutch, Flowers, 5 1/4 In.Square	6.00
Tile, Farm Horses Scene, Minton, 6 In.	18.00
Tile, Fireplace, 3 Boys Among Roses, Robertson, Set Of 11	225.00
Tile, Grecian Woman Holding Jug, Hamilton Works Of Ohio, 13 X 7 1/2 In.	95.00
Tile, June, Wedgwood, 6 In.Square	49.00
Tile, Mosaic, Horse & Rider On Each, Marked	20.00
Tile, Musketeer Lying On Bench Gazing At Puppies, Green, English, 12 In.	90.00
Tile, Pisces, Moravian	20.00
Tile, Portrait Of Lady, Fur Trimmed Hat, Signed, 7 1/2 X 7 1/4 In.	24.00
Tile, Portrait, Profile Bust, Grecian Woman, Semi Relief, Olive, 10 X 16 In.	125.00
Tile, Round, Matte Finish, Green Wreath, Nippon	45.00
Tile, Scorpio, Moravian	20.00
Tile, Ship, Marked Wheeling, Columbus, Raised Design, 6 X 3 In., Set Of 3	45.00
Tile, Stoke-On-Kent, Minton, 7 X 15 In.	45.00
Tile, Tea, Hand-Painted, Raspberries & Flowers, Porcelain, Germany, 6 1/2 In.	10.00
Tile, Tea, New Lower School, St.Paul's School New Hampshire Center, Marked	15.00
Tile, Tea, Portrait In Center, Floral Border, 7 In.Square	25.00
Tile, Victorian Family Scene, Gold & Blue Design, Wheeling, 6 In.Square	25.00
Tile, Vivien, Sepia, 6 In.Square	38.00
Tin, see also Store	
Tin, Mold, Chocolate, see also Store, Mold, Chocolate	
Tin, Basket, Picnic, Basket Weave, Double Flip Top, Handle, Marked & Dated	25.00
Tin, Bathtub, Oak Rim	125.00
Tin, Boiler, Coffee, Hand-Punched, Tin Strainer In Spout, 10 Cup, 9 1/2 In.	45.00
Tin, Box, Cut Plug, Bagley Paper Label, Sun Cured	170.00
Tin, Box, Knife, Handled, 3 Compartments, 10 X 14 In.	25.00
Tin, Box, Spice, Rectangular, Set Of 6 Round Tins	35.00
Tin, Bucket, Magnolia Coffee, Covered, 4 Pound	15.00
Tin, Butter Churn, Bail Handle, Tin Dasher, Lap Seamed, Gray, C.1870, 25 In.	165.00
Tin, Cage, Squirrel, Schoolhouse Shape, 21 X 8 X 14 In.	145.00
Tin, Can, Texas Oil Company, 1918, 1 Pint	5.00
Tin, Candle Mold, 24 Candle	85.00
Tin, Candlestick, Hog Scraper, Finger Hold, 19th Century, 6 7/8 In., Pair	80.00
Tin, Case, Floral, Inlaid Abalone Shell, 3 Rogues, 3 1/4 X 3 3/4 In.	17.50
Tin, Chamberstick, Push-Up, Iron Ring Handle	30.00

Tole: *(top, l. to r.)* Basket and Canister; *(bottom, l. to r.)* Box, Document, 10 In.; Box, 11 1/2 x 11 In.; Box, Document, 7 5/8 In. *(See Page 631)*

Tole *(l. to r.):* Coffeepot, Gooseneck Spout (see page 631) and jug (see page 632)

Tin, Coffeepot, Conical Top, Strut Support Handle, C.1800, 12 In.	125.00
Tin, Coffeepot, Old Master, Slip Lid	10.00
Tin, Corer, Shredder, Peeler, Castello's All Purpose, In Box	7.50
Tin, Duck, Handcrafted, 7 1/4 X 14 1/4 In.	15.00
Tin, Flagman's Kit, Webbed Shoulder Strap, Front & Side Hinged Doors, Marked	38.00
Tin, Foot Warmer, Pierced Tin Hearts On Sides, Wooden Corner Posts	85.00
Tin, Footwarmer, Hex Sign In Middle, Hearts In Corners, Red	95.00
Tin, Freezer, Ice Cream, Receipts & Operating Instructions, Scoop	45.00
Tin, Funnel, Iron Handle, Screw In Tip, Removable Strainer, 4 1/2 In.	9.00
Tin, Grater, Nutmeg	5.00
Tin, Lamp, Betty, American	135.00
Tin, Lamp, Bracket, Reflector	35.00
Tin, Lantern, Arched Top, Pierced Smoke Chamber, Rectangular, 19th Century	150.00
Tin, Mold, Candle, Handle, 10 In.High, 7 In.Base Tapering To 4 In.	85.00
Tin, Mold, Candle, 3 Tube, Top Tray	35.00
Tin, Mold, Candle, 4 Tube, 1 Handle, Square Top	30.00
Tin, Mold, Candle, 4 Tube, 1 Handle, Square Top & Bottom	32.00
Tin, Mold, Candle, 6 Tube, Top & Bottom Tray, 10 In.	35.00
Tin, Mold, Candle, 9 Tube, 3 X 7 In.Diameter	19.00
Tin, Mold, Candle, 10 Tube, 1 Handle, Rectangle Top & Bottom	68.00
Tin, Mold, Candle, 12 Tube	45.00 To 65.00
Tin, Mold, Candle, 12 Tube, 1 Handle, Ring Hanger, Rectangle Top & Bottom	48.00
Tin, Mold, Candle, 16 Tube, Pewter In Wood Frame, 15 1/2 X 12 1/2 X 13 In.	400.00
Tin, Mold, Candle, 18 Tube, 2 Rows, Strap Handle, 10 X 3 1/4 X 15 In.	135.00
Tin, Mold, Candle, 32 Tube, Double Handle, Rectangle Top & Bottom	90.00
Tin, Mold, Candle, 36 Tube, 8 1/2 X 9 1/4 In.	75.00
Tin, Mold, Candle, 50 Tube, Wood Frame, 44 1/2 X 5 X 19 In.	300.00
Tin, Mold, Candy, Double Turkey	25.00
Tin, Mold, Candy, Jackie Coogan, The Kid, French, 4 1/2 In.	45.00
Tin, Mold, Candy, Large Double Santa	38.00
Tin, Mold, Chocolate, Figural Owl, 5 1/2 X 2 1/2 In.	25.00
Tin, Mold, Chocolate, Sitting Child With Coat & Bonnet	12.50
Tin, Mold, Heart-Shaped, Jello, 5 X 5 In.	5.00
Tin, Mold, Maple Sugar, Rabbit Design	8.00
Tin, Mold, Pudding, Melon Shaped	22.00
Tin, Mold, Turk's Head, Hexagonal	5.00
Tin, Pail, Milk	11.00
Tin, Pail, Sand, Red Riding Hood, Seaside	10.00
Tin, Pan, Strainer, Handled, 6 In.	8.00
Tin, Peel, 44 1/4 In.	35.00
Tin, Pitcher, Syrup, Flip Top Cover, Wire Finial, C.1860, 6 1/4 In.	35.00
Tin, Plate, ABC, Mosaic Design In Center, 2 1/4 In.	38.00
Tin, Plate, Hotel Rensselaer, Dresden, 9 1/2 In.	25.00
Tin, Plate, MacFarlane Lang & Co., Windmill & Skating Children	35.00
Tin, Plate, Peter Rabbit Easter Greeting	55.00
Tin, Plate, Union Pacific Tea Co., 1907	50.00
Tin, Plate, Union Pacific Tea Company, 1906, 8 In.Diameter	18.00
Tin, Rack, Blueberry	15.00
Tin, Rocking Horse, Diamond On Forehead, Poney-Bike Mfg., Co., 33 In.	300.00
Tin, Sander, Ink, Japanned, Yellow Line Design	35.00

Tole, Tray, Apple, Flowering Leaves, C.1820, 3 1/8 X 12 In.
Tole, Coffeepot, Red, Green, Yellow Flowers, Pennsylvania, 9 In.

(See Page 632)

Tin, Sconce, Candle, Curved Crimped Crest, 12 In.	85.00
Tin, Sconce, Wall, Mirrored, Electrified, Late 18th Century, Pair, 11 In.	500.00
Tin, Scoop, Ice Cream	12.50
Tin, Smoker, Bee, Leather Bellows, C.1860, 11 In.	20.00
Tin, Snuffer, Candle, Cone Shaped, Curved Wire Handle, Hook End, 7 In.	36.00
Tin, Splint Holder, Hanging, Punched, 19th Century, 10 1/2 In.	950.00
Tin, Stand, Noma Tree, Santa & Reindeer Decaled On Sides, Cone Shaped	55.00
Tin, Strainer, Milk, 12 In.Diameter	6.00
Tin, Strongbox, Wells Fargo, Red, Name Stamped Twice Into Steel Carcass	325.00
Tin, Stuffer, Sausage, Early	22.00
Tin, Syphon, Lemonade, Bond Woman Center, Twist Bail Handle, Brass Spigot	300.00
Tin, Tea Caddy, Divided Interior, Lock, Brass Finule, 4 X 3 1/2 X 4 In.	50.00
Tin, Tea Set, Red Riding Hood, 2 Cups & Saucers, Plate, Creamer, Blue	13.00
Tin, Teapot, Miniature, Original Japanning, 2 3/4 In.	125.00
Tin, Thermometer, Drink Frostie Root Beer, Tasty, Creamy Caption, 8 In.	12.50
Tin, Tobacco, Old English, Curve Cut	5.00
Tin, Tobacco, Round, Flat, The Twelve Best, Indian Head	8.00
Tin, Torch, Parade	18.00
Tin, Tray, James Hanley Peerless Ale, Bulldog, Round	25.00
Tin, Trumpet, Ear, Black Finish, Gilded Mesh	49.00
Tobacco, Tin, see Store, Tin	

Toby mugs have been made since the seventeenth century.
    Toby Mug, see also Royal Doulton, Toby Mug; Staffordshire,
    Toby Mug

Toby Mug, Polychrome Man Sittin On Barrel, 6 In.	195.00
Toby Mug, School Master, Wedgwood, 7 In.	62.00
Toilet Seat & Holding Tank, Copper Lined, Oak	125.00
Toilet Seat, Oak	12.00
Tole, Basket, Painted, Filled With Marble Fruit, American, 1800s *Illus*	2100.00
Tole, Box, Document, Floral Border, White Band, Yellow Brush Work	245.00
Tole, Box, Document, Original Paint, 10 X 6 X 7 1/2 In.	35.00
Tole, Box, Document, Red Flowers, Pennsylvania, C.1820, 7 5/8 In. *Illus*	750.00
Tole, Box, Document, Red, Yellow, Green Flowers & Leaves, 10 In. *Illus*	600.00
Tole, Box, Floral, Gold, Yellow, Red, 4 1/2 X 5 1/8 X 8 3/4 In.	18.00
Tole, Box, Hat, Brown Grained Finish	35.00
Tole, Box, Oliver Buckley Decoration, Maine, 8 3/4 X 5 1/2 In.	200.00
Tole, Box, Pink & Yellow Flowers, Swing Handle, 11 1/2 X 11 In. *Illus*	1600.00
Tole, Box, Pipe, Hanging, Drawer, Green Paint, 11 In.	325.00
Tole, Bucket, Coal, Painted, 24 In.	45.00
Tole, Canister, Tea, Red Flowers, Pennsylvania, C.1820, 8 1/4 In. *Illus*	375.00
Tole, Coffeepot, Red & Yellow Flowers, Gooseneck Spout, 12 In. *Illus*	1900.00
Tole, Coffeepot, Red, Green, Yellow Flowers, Pennsylvania, 9 In. *Illus*	1700.00
Tole, Coffeepot, Tin, Large Spout	35.00
Tole, Coffeepot, Tin, Small Spout	20.00
Tole, Container, Flour, 21 X 12 In.Diameter	45.00
Tole, Cookie Cutter, Double Tulip, 3 1/4 In.	85.00

Tole, Jug, Syrup, Red, Green, Yellow & Orange Flowers4 In. .... *Illus* 800.00
Tole, Lamp, Pig, Handle, 3 Burners, 9 In.Cylinder 295.00
Tole, Lantern, Skating .... 30.00 To 34.00
Tole, Match Holder, Wall, Kitchen 7.00
Tole, Scale, Desk, Inkstand With Drawers For Stamps, Dated 1904 .... 60.00
Tole, Tea Caddy, Casket, Keyhole, Scrolled Feet 30.00
Tole, Tea Caddy, Oval, Brushwork, C.1825 .... 155.00
Tole, Teapot, Painted, Domed Lid, Scrolled Handle, English, C.1800, 7 3/4 In. ... 80.00
Tole, Tray, Apple, Flowering Leaves, C.1820, 3 1/8 X 12 In. .... *Illus* 700.00
Tole, Tray, Bread, Oil-Painted Fruit, Oval 100.00
Tole, Tray, Floral Painting On A Black Ground, 16 X 22 In. 20.00
Tole, Tray, Red With Black & Yellow Striping, Octagonal, 8 1/4 X 12 In. ... 45.00
Tole, Tray, Red, Yellow Vines & Flowers, Pennsylvania, 4 In. 600.00
Tole, Tray, Red, Yellow, Green Flowers, Gold Base, 2 1/2 In. 850.00
Tole, Tray, Scene, Artist Signed, Large 187.00
Tole, Tray, Snuffer, Oil Painted 65.00
Tole, Urn, Chestnut, Loose Ring Handles, English, C.1800, Pair, 12 1/2 In. ... 600.00
Tole, Vase, Black, Gold Footed, Grecian Design 60.00
Tole, Vase, French, Claw Feet, Pedestal 40.00
Tole, Vase, Grecian Design 40.00
Tom Mix, Book, Paint, 96 Pages, 1935, 11 X 13 In. 15.00
Tom Mix, Buckle, Belt, Secret Compartment 25.00
Tom Mix, Button, Ralston Straight Shooters, Picture Of Horse, 1 In. 8.50
Tom Mix, Compass-Magnifier 21.00
Tom Mix, Compass, 1930s 22.00
Tom Mix, I.D.Bracelet 20.00
Tom Mix, Kit, Make-Up 30.00
Tom Mix, Manual, 1933 .... 40.00
Tom Mix, Medal, Sharpshooter, Glows In Dark 49.00
Tom Mix, Photograph, 8 X 10 In. 25.00
Tom Mix, Pocket Knife 16.00
Tom Mix, Ring, Ralston Straight Shooters 30.00
Tom Mix, Ring, Slide Whistle 35.00
Tom Mix, Six Gun Decoder 40.00
Tom Mix, Telescope, Decal 12.00
Tom Mix, Watch, Pocket, Ingersoll, Always Find Time For A Good Deed, Tom Mix ... 400.00
     Tool, see also Iron, Kitchen, Store, Tin, Wooden
Tool, Adze, Barrel Maker's 12.50
Tool, Adze, Bowl, C.Whitehouse & Sons, Cannock 60.00
Tool, Adze, Carpenter's, Marked 25.00
Tool, Adze, Carpenter's, Octagonal Pole 20.00
Tool, Adze, Foot, Carpenter, Handle 12.50
Tool, Adze, Gutter, 1 1/4 In. Deep 70.00
Tool, Adze, Shipwright's, Curved Blade, Edge 4 1/2 In. 35.00
Tool, Anvil, Blacksmith, Colonial 36.50
Tool, Anvil, Jeweler's, Hand-Forged, 5 1/2 X 12 1/2 In. 36.00
Tool, Auger, Barn 7.00
Tool, Auger, Handwrought Iron, Wooden Crossbar 10.00
Tool, Auger, Nose, 2 Inch, 26 1/2 In. 20.00
Tool, Auger, Wheelright's, Town & Chaffee, 3 In. 40.00
Tool, Ax, Broad, Curved Head, Narrow Blade, Dated 1887 .... 48.00
Tool, Ax, Broad, Myer's, Dayton, Original Handle 70.00
Tool, Ax, Cooper's, Greaves & Son 55.00
Tool, Ax, Goosewing 130.00
Tool, Ax, Meat, Sculptured, T.P.Moyer, 1891 .... 55.00
Tool, Ax, Shipwright's, Marked Hathaway, 6 Inch 50.00
Tool, Ax, Single Bit, Keen Kutter 12.00
Tool, Ax, Winchester 30.00
Tool, Basketry, Wooden Machine, Shaker, Pegged & Morticed 69.00
Tool, Beater, Rug, Wicker 25.00
Tool, Belt Slitter, Rosewood & Brass, Osborn, 1826 .... 50.00
Tool, Bench, Jeweler's, Oak 350.00
Tool, Bit Brace & Holder, Lignumvitae Breast Pad, Schoefield-Warranted ... 145.00
Tool, Bit Brace, Pewter Ferrule, 18th Century, Wooden 195.00
Tool, Bit, Auger, Russell Jennings, 3 Hinged Walnut Box, Brass Fittings ... 65.00
Tool, Bit, Coachmaker, Iron, C.1845 .... 55.00

Tool, Bit, Stock, Coachmaker's 18.00
Tool, Bit, Wood, Winchester 4.00
Tool, Blaster, Dynamite, From Gold Mine 45.00
Tool, Blower, Blacksmith, Hand Cranked, Cast Iron 40.00
Tool, Bootjack, Folding, Wooden, Brass Feet & Hinges, 11 In. 22.00
Tool, Box, International Harvester, With Oil Can Holder 10.00
Tool, Brace Bit, Wooden, Brass Inlay 120.00
Tool, Brace, Carpenter's 9.50
Tool, Brace, Chairmaker's, Wood 150.00
Tool, Brace, Maple, Ultimatum Framed Brace, Sheffield, Ebony & Brass 450.00
Tool, Brush, Stenciller's, Maple Handle, Tin Ferrule, Shaving Brush Shape 12.00
Tool, Caliper, Double Ended, Brass Rivets, Hand Wrought Iron, 3 1/2 X 5 In. 35.00
Tool, Caliper, Hand-Forged, 11 In. 55.00
Tool, Caliper, Log, Trimmed In Brass, Greenleaf 85.00
Tool, Chisel, Broad, Maple, Long Handle, 3 1/2 X 28 In. 50.00
Tool, Chisel, Gooseneck, Maple 50.00
Tool, Chiv, Saw, Cooper's, Maple, 8 1/2 X 15 In. 44.00
Tool, Chopper, Iron Blade, Tiger Maple Handle, 4 1/2 X 5 1/2 In. 52.00
Tool, Churn, Butter, F.Woodworth, Burlington, Vermont, C.1872-85, 4 Gallon 125.00
Tool, Clamp, Carpenter, Wooden 16.00
Tool, Clamp, Wood, Opens To 4 3/4 In., Double Wooden Screw Member, 12 1/2 In. 15.00
Tool, Cleaner, Clock Shop, Ultrasonic, 5 Gallon Tank 575.00
Tool, Coach Maker, Plow, Tiger Maple Handle, Brass 30.00
Tool, Coggle Wheel, Potter's, Brass Ferrule, Iron, C.1810, 6 1/2 In. 75.00
Tool, Comb, Carding, Ad In Wood On Top 18.00
Tool, Comb, Flax, Wooden Teeth, All Wood, 6 X 7 In. 65.00
Tool, Compass, Divider, Steel, Hand-Forged Wing Nut, Brass Hinges, 8 In. 18.00
Tool, Compass, Draftsman's, Beam, C.1880-1900 .... 15.00
Tool, Compass, Handwrought, Brass Hinge Rivet, Signed Sargent, 8 In. 15.00
Tool, Compass, Holds Pencil, Wooden, Legs, 17 In. 18.00
Tool, Cookie Cutter, Tinsmith's, Birds & Animals, Tin, Set Of 12 .... 75.00
Tool, Corker, Wood, 12 In. 18.00
Tool, Cowell, Cooper's, Cherry, 14 In. 55.00
Tool, Crimper, Shephard Hardware, Dated 1880, 3 Piece 25.00
Tool, Croze, Cooper's, Maple 44.00
Tool, Curler, Wig, Hand-Wrought Iron, Scissor Shaped, Ball End, 18th Century 32.00
Tool, Dispenser, Oil, For Watches, Shape Of Man's Watch, 1899 .... 7.50
Tool, Dispenser, Screen, Hardware Store, Wooden 75.00
    Tool, Doctor, see Doctor
Tool, Draw Shave, Open Handle, 2 In. Blade, Brass, 14 In. 58.00
Tool, Drill & Level, Miller's Falls, No.12 .... 17.50
Tool, Drill, Barn Beam 55.00
Tool, Drill, Hand, English 85.00
Tool, Dry Sink, Amish Pennsylvania, Blue 525.00
Tool, Duplicating Apparatus, Neostyle, 1894, Walnut Case 50.00
Tool, Finger, Spinning Wheel, Lignum Vitae 12.50
Tool, Flincher, Cooper's, Fixed Curved Blade, For Herring Barrel, Signed 44.00
Tool, Footwarmer, Copper, Hearts, Base, C.1757, 11 1/2 X 18 1/2 In. 275.00
Tool, Forge, Blacksmith's, With Bellows 250.00
Tool, Fork, Hay, Hand Carved, Wood Pegged, Tines Are Mortised, American 125.00
Tool, Fork, Tuning, Piano, Sheffield, England, Advertising, 4 1/4 In. 2.50
Tool, Froe, Curved, 11 1/2 In. 90.00
Tool, Froe, Shingle, Original Handle, 15 In. 18.00
Tool, Gauge, Clapboard, Dovetailed Splined Shaft 28.00
Tool, Gauge, Slitting, Cabinet Maker's, Tiger Maple 90.00
Tool, Gauge, Slitting, Roller With Wood Thread & Screw, Closed Handle 36.00
Tool, Gouge, Planemaker's, Handforged 7.00
Tool, Gourd Dipper, Vermont 20.00
Tool, Grinder, Herb, Cast Iron, Boat Shape 385.00
Tool, Hammer, Blacksmith, Claw End 8.50
Tool, Hammer, Caulking, Ship Builder's, Double Head, 6 In. 30.00
Tool, Hammer, Double Claw, Pat. November 1902 .... 150.00
Tool, Hammer, Horseshoeing, Farrier's 6.50
Tool, Harpoon, Hay, Cast Iron 10.00
Tool, Hatchel, Flax, Wood Cover 32.00
Tool, Hatchet, Crow Cigars F.M.K. & Co., Open Old Cigar Boxes 18.00

Tool, Hatchet, Winchester	25.00 To 45.00
Tool, Hetchel, Dovetailed, Aurelia Mace, Shaker, 19 In.	270.00
Tool, Hetchel, 1818-24	40.00
Tool, Hide Scraper & Flint Striker Combined	40.00
Tool, Horn Sander	55.00
Tool, Howel, Miniature, Beech, 3 1/2 X 5 In.	150.00
Tool, Iron, Branding, Iron	16.00
Tool, Iron, Branding, Loop Handle, Block Letters, 3/8 In., 18 1/2 In.Long	16.50
Tool, Iron, Branding, W.T., Iron, 11 1/2 In.	18.00
Tool, Jack, Wagon, Wood	20.00
Tool, Jigger, Hand Forged, Wooden Handle, 5 In.Haft, 13 1/2 In	47.50
Tool, Jointer, Cooper's, C.1700, 43 1/2 In.	165.00
Tool, Knife, Block, Bench Eye & Steps, James Booth, Manchester, 40 In.	160.00
Tool, Knife, Chamfering, Cooper's, Large	60.00
Tool, Knife, Draw, Cooper's, Curved Scraper, Wood Handle, 15 In.	20.00
Tool, Knife, Draw, Round Bladed, Carpenter's	16.00
Tool, Knife, Flax	20.00
Tool, Knife, Hay	9.00
Tool, Knife, Race, Rosewood, Folding, Camillus, N.Y.	35.00
Tool, Ladle & Strainer, Butcher's, Wrought Iron, Pennsylvania	49.00
Tool, Last Holder, Shoe, Cobbler, Carved Of 1 Piece Of Wood, C.1850, 21 In.	35.00
Tool, Level, Brass Top Plate & Base End Tips, Rosewood, 8 In.	60.00
Tool, Level, Brass Top Plate, Rosewood, Rectangular, 8 In.	38.00
Tool, Level, Brass Trim, Akron Rule & Level Company, 29 1/2 In.	40.00
Tool, Level, Carpenter's, Cast Iron, Brass, Davis Level & Tool Company	94.00
Tool, Level, Carpenter's, Wood, 1904	25.00
Tool, Level, Davis Patent, Iron	75.00
Tool, Level, Full Brass Plates, Rosewood, John Rabone & Sons, 10 In.	60.00
Tool, Level, Miniature, Brass Face, 3 1/4 In.	17.50
Tool, Level, Rosewood, Brass Plate Top & Bottom, Raone & Sons, 10 In.	60.00
Tool, Level, Rosewood, Brass Top Plate & Bottom Corner Plate, 8 In.	60.00
Tool, Level, Stanley, Cherry	8.00
Tool, Level, Stanley, Pat.28, 1896, 3 In.	12.00
Tool, Linen Press, Mahogany, 98 X 48 X 22 In.	1000.00
Tool, Logger's Board, 4-Hinged Panels, Numerical, Dark Wood, 52 X 17 In.	65.00
Tool, Mallet, Burl	15.00
Tool, Mallet, Carpenter's, Wooden, H.Benton Pavey	15.00
Tool, Marker, Tobacco, Brown's Mule, Metal, Mule Pictured	25.00
Tool, Meat Chopper, Over The Counter & On The Shelf, Plate 32, American	115.00
Tool, Meat Hanger, Iron, Decorative Brass, C.1860	48.00
Tool, Micrometer, Scales, 1903	160.00
Tool, Micrometer, Starrett, Dovetailed Wooden Case, 2 X 6 In.	65.00
Tool, Micrometer, 325-350 Mm.Chinese	20.00
Tool, Mold, Brick, Making Ingots, 2 Slots, 2 X 7 1/2 X 1 1/2 In.	25.00
Tool, Multiplane, Fulton, 24 Cutters	50.00
Tool, Nail, Picture, Brass With Porcelain Centers, C.1840, Pair	14.00
Tool, Needle, Fishnet Repair, Wood, 7 In.	5.00
Tool, Niddy Noddy	35.00
Tool, Opener, Cigar Box, Cutter, Hammer, Sterling Silver Handle	28.00
Tool, Pick, Miner's, Hand Forged Iron, 11 In.	20.00
Tool, Pitcher, Water, Hay Stack Shape, Tubular Handle, 2 Quart	95.00
Tool, Plane, Badger, Left & Right, Wooden, Scotland	235.00
Tool, Plane, Bull Horn, German	37.50
Tool, Plane, Chariot, Brass & Boxwood, 19th Century, 3 3/4 In.	225.00
Tool, Plane, Coachmaker's, England, Curve Of 1 1/4 To 1/4 In.	75.00
Tool, Plane, Compass, Birch Block, Curved Sole, 6 1/2 In.	12.00
Tool, Plane, Core, Pattern Maker's, V-Shaped Sole, 7 1/2 X 1 1/2 In.	35.00
Tool, Plane, Dated 1912, Original Box & Sales Catalogue	60.00
Tool, Plane, Flooring Jointer, Maple, 48 1/2 In.	175.00
Tool, Plane, Hollowing, Coachmaker's, 7 1/2 In.	25.00
Tool, Plane, Mahogany Infill, Norris Blade, Brass Lever Cap, Norris, London	185.00
Tool, Plane, Metal, Stanley Rule & Level Co, 3 1/2 In.	75.00
Tool, Plane, Molding, Cabinet Maker's, Set Of 16	8.00
Tool, Plane, Molding, English, 18th Century, John Cogdell	85.00
Tool, Plane, Molding, Round Sole, 9 1/2 In.	18.00
Tool, Plane, No.113, Curved Inside & Outside Work, Stanley	40.00

Tool, Plane, Patternmaker's, Wood, 4 Extra Soles, 14 1/2 In.	145.00
Tool, Plane, Plow, C.1860	135.00
Tool, Plane, Plow, Woodworking, Cherry & Boxwood, Brass Fittings	50.00
Tool, Plane, Rounding, Miniature, Carriage Maker's, 6 In.	30.00
Tool, Plane, Sash, Wooden, 2 Blades	20.00
Tool, Plane, Stanley, All Attachments & Book, Walnut Tool Box	97.50
Tool, Plane, Stanley, No.45, With Access	60.00
Tool, Plane, Stanley, 50 Cutters	170.00
Tool, Plane, Stanley, 51 Blades, Wooden Box	175.00
Tool, Plane, Sun, Cooper's, C.1884-1910, 3 X 2 1/4 In.	79.50
Tool, Plane, Sun, Maple, 2 In.Iron	110.00
Tool, Plane, Wood, Winchester, Metal	29.00
Tool, Plane, Wooden Base & Handle, Iron Blade & Fasteners, 10 In.	10.00
Tool, Pliers, Cutting, Winchester, 10 In.	16.00
Tool, Plumb Bob, Brass, Top Unscrews For Lead Line	16.50
Tool, Polisher, Button, For Railroad Buttons, C.1890s	18.50
Tool, Press, Printing, Peerless, Patent 1873, 10 X 15 In.	150.00
Tool, Press, Soap, Lemon Shaped, Butterfly Hinge, 18th Century, 12 1/2 In.	58.00
Tool, Puller, Boot, Ivory Handles	20.00
Tool, Pump, Cistern, Brass & Iron, 30 In.	33.00
Tool, Punch, Leather, Mother-Of-Pearl Handle, Nickle Plated, 3 1/2 In.	12.50
Tool, Rake, Cranberry, Cape Cod, 22 In.	85.00
Tool, Rake, Hay, Prong, Trip Type, 27 In.	70.00
Tool, Razor Strop, Leather, Paddle Handle, Red Case, Tremont, 13 1/2 In.	5.00
Tool, Reamer, Wheelwright's, Enlarge Hub Holes, 12 In.Bit, 16 In.	30.00
Tool, Riveter, Harness, Plymouth Rock, Cast Iron	5.00
Tool, Riveting Machine, Iron & Brass	6.50
Tool, Roasting Jack, Original Chain, Signed	100.00
Tool, Rounder, Spike, Wheelwright's, 5 1/2 In.	18.50
Tool, Router, Coachmaker's, Like Draw Knife, 1/2 In.Blade	35.00
Tool, Router, Coachmaker's, Old Woman's Tooth, Maple	60.00
Tool, Rule & Level, Stanley, Folding, Pocket, Ivory & Brass, 6 X 7/16 In.	40.00
Tool, Rule, Folding, Boxwood, Brass Joints, 4-Fold, 2 Feet	10.00
Tool, Rule, Folding, Stanley, Brass Edged, 24 In.	6.50
Tool, Rule, Lufkin, 4 Fold, 24 In., Set Of 3	10.00
Tool, Rule, 4 Fold, Ivory, Handcut Numbers, Brass Hinges, 12 In.	110.00
Tool, Ruler, Carpenter's, Folding, Brass Fittings	10.00
Tool, Ruler, Lufkin, Folding	3.00
Tool, Ruler, One-Foot, Ivory, Stanley No.92 1/2	90.00
Tool, Sander, Wood, 3 In.	32.00
Tool, Sausage Stuffer, Tin, Wooden Plunger, 20 1/4 In.	27.50
Tool, Saw, Circular, Cutting Soapstone, C.1890, 1/2 In.Diameter	10.00
Tool, Saw, Ice, Handle, Wooden	9.00
Tool, Saw, Jig	75.00
Tool, Saw, Pruning, Blade Folds Into Wooden Handle, Blade, 6 In.	18.00
Tool, Saw, Two-Hand, Keen Kutter	32.50
Tool, Scissors, Wick, Kerosene Lamp	12.50
Tool, Scraper, Hide	45.00
Tool, Scraper, Horse Sweat, Curved One Piece, Wooden	20.00
Tool, Screwdriver, Winchester, 4 In.	17.50
Tool, Scythe, Carley, Hand-Forged, 18th Century, Left Handed, Signed	28.00
Tool, Seeder, Wheelbarrow Mounted, Controls, Green, 3 X 3 1/2 X 145 In.	95.00
Tool, Shave, Draw, Cabinet Maker's, Curved Handle, Brass Plate, 9 1/2 In.	15.00
Tool, Shave, Jarvis, Brass Plated Sole, Ward Blade, Wheelwright	75.00
Tool, Shears, Sheep, 12 In.	10.00
Tool, Shears, Winchester, 7 In.	9.00
Tool, Shovel, Coal Scuttle, Openwork	45.00
Tool, Shovel, Grain, Made From One Piece Of Tree, Ware, Maine	170.00
Tool, Shovel, Grain, Wooden	95.00
Tool, Shovel, One Piece, Hickory, 17 In.Long, Scoop, 5 X 8 1/2 In.	85.00
Tool, Shovel, Snow, Wood & Tin	15.00
Tool, Shuttle, Tatting, Celluloid	4.00
Tool, Sieve, Winnowing, 2 Hoop, Splint Bound & Fastened, 24 In.Diameter	185.00
Tool, Skimmer, Brass, 6 In.	80.00
Tool, Slide Rule, Deuffel & Esser, 1908, Leather Case	20.00
Tool, Solder Iron, Blow Torch, Barthel No. 460, Brass, 17 In.	90.00

Tool, Sower, Seed, Cyclone	16.00
Tool, Spinning Jenny, 8 Spindles, Oak, Forged Iron, Dated 1813	700.00
Tool, Spinning Wheel, Flax, Brass, Ivory Trim, German	160.00
Tool, Spinning Wheel, Miniature, Walnut Wheel, C.1780, 38 X 21 In.	750.00
Tool, Spinning Wheel, Oak, Continental, C.1800s, 44 In.	275.00
Tool, Spinning Wheel, Oak, Medium Size	295.00
Tool, Spinning Wheel, Turned & Painted, Small, C.1800	175.00
Tool, Splint, Spring Action, Original Base, 18th Century	195.00
Tool, Square, American, Copper, 1 Foot	18.50
Tool, Stand, Cobbler's, Forged Iron Last, C.1800, 26 1/2 In.	25.00
Tool, Stave, 2 Mouths, Wedges & Irons, 1700s, 50 In.	165.00
Tool, Stretcher, Carpet, Wooden	3.50
Tool, Stretcher, Glove, Celluloid, German	10.00
Tool, Stretcher, Hat, Wooden	20.00
Tool, Tape Measure, Keen Kutter, 50 Foot	8.50
Tool, Tape, Mechanics Pal, Steel, 6 Foot	3.00
Tool, Tomahawk, Horst Company, Philadelphia	75.00
Tool, Trammel, Sawtooth, Wrought Iron, Adjustable, 43 In.	77.50
Tool, Transit, Surveyor's, Starrett, Dovetailed Wooden Box	75.00
Tool, Trap, Bear, Hand-Forged	125.00
Tool, Trap, F.C.Taylor Trap Setter	8.00
Tool, Trap, Fly, Clear Dome, Green Bottom, Glass	75.00
Tool, Trap, Fly, Glass, Beehive Shape, C.1860	210.00
Tool, Trap, Fly, Sur-Katchem, 1930s	4.00
Tool, Trap, Fly, Three Part Cone Shaped, Shur-Katch Bug & Fly Trap	30.00
Tool, Trap, Mouse, Bottle Type, Placed In Ground, 1918, Pair	15.00
Tool, Trap, Mouse, Steel Spring, Iron Jaws, 18th Century, 2 1/2 X 5 1/2 In.	95.00
Tool, Trap, Mouse, Wire With Wooden Base	15.00
Tool, Trap, Queen Bee	14.00
Tool, Trap, Triumph Trap Placer	8.00
Tool, Trencher, Wooden, Oval	58.00
Tool, Trivet, Steel, George III, Pad Feet, 1700s, 13 X 12 In.	90.00
Tool, Trivet, Wrought Iron, 18th Century	375.00
Tool, Vise, Harness Maker, Wood	10.00
Tool, Vise, Saw, Hargrave	10.00
Tool, Wheel, Buggy, Front 38 In., Back 45 In., Set Of 4	175.00
Tool, Wheelwright, With Hook, 27 In.	325.00
Tool, Wheelwright's, Traveler, Hand-Forged, Wood Handle	29.00
Tool, Whetstone, Knife, Sharpen Up, Buy Uncle Kim's Road Machine, 1 3/4 In.	18.50
Tool, Winder, Yarn, Gears & Counter, Original	95.00
Tool, Winder, Yarn, Ivory Trim, German	45.00
Tool, Winder, Yarn, Umbrella Swift, Folding, Clamp, 26 In.	85.00
Tool, Winder, Yarn, Wooden	20.00
Tool, Wire Cutter, Winchester, 5 In.	25.00
Tool, Wood Working, Brace, 24 Molding Plane, Saws, Boxed	550.00
Tool, Work Bench, Cabinet Maker's, Maple, One Vise, 6 Ft., 7 In.	225.00
Tool, Work Bench, Cabinet Maker's, Two Vises, Walnut, 8 Feet, 3 In.	425.00
Tool, Work Bench, 2 Vises, 8 Feet	175.00
Tool, Workbench, Oak, Tinsmith's, 70 X 34 X 38 In.	4500.00
Tool, Wrench, Bed, Wood, 18 In.	16.00
Tool, Wrench, Buggy	3.00
Tool, Wrench, Monkey, 18 In.	12.00
Tool, Wrench, Pipe, Keen Kutter, 10 Inch	17.50
Tool, Wrench, Stillson, G.T.D., Springfield, Massachusetts, 3 Feet	30.00
Tool, Wrench, Wagon, Steel Forged, Portland, Maine, 11 In.	10.00
Tool, Yarn Winder, Cross-Frame, Hand-Made, C.1810, 7 1/2 In.Square	155.00

Toothpick holders are sometimes called toothpicks by collectors. The variously shaped containers made to hold the small wooden toothpicks are of glass, china, or metal. Most of the toothpicks are Victorian.

Toothpick, see also other categories such as Bisque, Slag, etc.

Toothpick, Albert Pick, Silver	15.00
Toothpick, All Over Hobnail, Opalescent	13.00
Toothpick, Amber Frog On Round Melon, Ribbed Pedestal	60.00
Toothpick, Amberina, Daisy & Button	225.00
Toothpick, Austrian, Clear With Gold	40.00

Toothpick, Barred Hobnail	20.00
Toothpick, Barrel, Clear	15.00
Toothpick, Barrel, Green	25.00
Toothpick, Basket, Brown, Handles, Holding Opened Egg, China, 2 1/2 In.	30.00
Toothpick, Beaded Belt	20.00
Toothpick, Beatty, Opal Rib	22.00
Toothpick, Bird In Stump, Amber	32.50
Toothpick, Bisque, Art Nouveau, 4 1/2 In.	24.00
Toothpick, Bisque, Cobalt, Superimposed Lady's Bust	28.00
Toothpick, Bisque, Girl Beside Basket	9.00
Toothpick, Bisque, Hand-Painted, Signed, French	22.00
Toothpick, Blown Ruby Urn, Pedestal Base	25.00
Toothpick, Blue Iris, Meandor Gold Trim	45.00
Toothpick, Blue Opalescent, Honeycomb	50.00
Toothpick, Blue Opalescent, Ribbed	25.00
Toothpick, Boot, Purple Slag	30.00
Toothpick, Box In Box, Ruby Stained, Atlantic City 1897	30.00
Toothpick, Boy Sitting Beside Basket, Bisque, 3 1/2 In.	22.50
Toothpick, Brazilian, Fostoria	22.50
Toothpick, Bunny Pulling Cart	12.00
Toothpick, Button-Arches Pattern, Ruby Stained, Souvenir, 1906	30.00
Toothpick, Cactus	75.00
Toothpick, Carnival Glass, Flute, Marigold	35.00
Toothpick, Cat On Pillow, Amber	85.00
Toothpick, Champion	40.00
Toothpick, Cherub, Silver Plate	15.00
Toothpick, Cream, Pastel Flowers, Signed, Germany	10.00
Toothpick, Croesus, Green	85.00
Toothpick, Croesus, Purple	105.00
Toothpick, Crown Milano, Mt.Washington	75.00
Toothpick, Darwin, Well Detailed Monkey, Blue Glass	95.00
Toothpick, Diamond Spearhead, Vaseline Glass	50.00
Toothpick, Dog With Hat, Amber	29.50
Toothpick, Dog, Holding Top Hat, China	10.00
Toothpick, Domino	22.00
Toothpick, Double Dahlia	35.00
Toothpick, Elephant, Frosted	25.00
Toothpick, Emerald Green Shamrock	25.00
Toothpick, Enameled Berries, Leaves, Cameo Style, Signed Peynaud	165.00
Toothpick, Fancy Loop, Clear	28.00
Toothpick, Father, 1906, Button Arch	13.50
Toothpick, Feather	45.00
Toothpick, Figural Pig, Impressed Boston Bake Beans	28.00
Toothpick, Figural, Boys Climbing Into A Barrel, Silver Plate, Marked	85.00
Toothpick, Figural, Chick & Wishbone, Silver Plate	40.00
Toothpick, Figural, China Frog	30.00
Toothpick, Figural, Face, Satin Finish, 2 3/8 In.	12.00
Toothpick, Figural, Girl Ballerina, Silver Plate	45.00
Toothpick, Figural, Monkey Holding The Holder, Footed, Glass, 4 X 3 In.	25.00
Toothpick, Figural, Owl	7.50
Toothpick, Figural, Porcupine, Silver Plate	40.00
Toothpick, Figural, Swan	7.00
Toothpick, Fisherman, 3 Handles, Royal Bayreuth, Blue Mark	40.00
Toothpick, Francisware	52.00
Toothpick, Frog & Shell, Clear	45.00
Toothpick, Frosted Cranberry, Opaque Pull-Up, Northwood, 2 1/8 In.	165.00
Toothpick, Frosted Lion's Head, Square, 2 In.	48.00
Toothpick, Fuschia To Amber, Diamond-Quilted, Amberina, 2 1/8 In.	148.50
Toothpick, George Washington On Front, China, 2 3/4 In.	22.50
Toothpick, Georgia Gem, Custard Glass	35.00
Toothpick, Girl Doing Splits, Silver Plate	50.00
Toothpick, Glass Swans & Cattails, Swans Forming Handles, Blue Mark	15.00
Toothpick, Gold Columbian Coin	45.00
Toothpick, Gold Trim, Regal	22.50
Toothpick, Green Shamrock, Maine	28.00
Toothpick, Green, Gold Trim, Fancy Loop, Heisey	32.50

Toothpick, Green, Urn, 2 Rings, Brass Rim	40.00
Toothpick, Green, X-Ray	45.00
Toothpick, Hat, Cobalt, 2 1/4 In.	15.00
Toothpick, Hat, Green, Souvenir Of Omaha, Nebraska	15.00
Toothpick, Hobnail, Vaseline	22.00
Toothpick, Horseshoe, Clover, Milk Glass	33.00
Toothpick, Inverted Thumbprint, Electric Blue	18.00
Toothpick, Iris, Meander	60.00
Toothpick, Kansas, Clear	30.00
Toothpick, Kettle, Footed, Green, China	6.00
Toothpick, Kewpie, Clear, Manufacturer's Name & Pattern Number	125.00
Toothpick, King's Royal, 1905	15.00
Toothpick, Leaf Umbrella, Mauve	50.00
Toothpick, Little Lobe	125.00
Toothpick, Loving Cup, Green, Coney Island	18.00
Toothpick, Luster, Copper, Sanded Band	40.00
Toothpick, Maple Leaf, Custard Glass	450.00
Toothpick, Match Striker Ceramic Pig With Racket, Relief Around Bottom	65.00
Toothpick, Milk Glass	8.00
Toothpick, Minnesota, Clear	40.00
Toothpick, Minnesota, Clear With Gold	20.00
Toothpick, Monkey & Birds On Sides, Soapstone, 2 1/2 In.	12.00
Toothpick, Monkey & Tree Stump, Blue	22.00
Toothpick, National Eureka, Red	35.00
Toothpick, New Hampshire, Clear	20.00
Toothpick, One Thousand & One, Pink	53.00
Toothpick, Opal Beaded Swag, Heisey	48.00
Toothpick, Opalescent, Beatty Honeycomb	30.00
Toothpick, Opalescent, Diamond Spearhead	20.00
Toothpick, Opalescent, Iris With Meander	25.00
Toothpick, Opaque Powder Blue, Peking, Marked China	15.00
Toothpick, Open Beaked Bird	12.50
Toothpick, Owl On Branch, Quadruple Plate	70.00
Toothpick, Peachblow	575.00
Toothpick, Peacock, Bisque	25.00
Toothpick, Pedestal, Embossed Rim & Body, Hallmarked, Sterling	48.00
Toothpick, Pillar	55.00
Toothpick, Pink Pig, Green Purse Holder, Germany	18.00
Toothpick, Pomona	175.00
Toothpick, Porcupine, Meridan Silver Plate	75.00
Toothpick, Porcupine, Milk Glass	60.00
Toothpick, Portland	12.00
Toothpick, Preparedness, Sailor & Soldier	68.00
Toothpick, Priscilla	25.00
Toothpick, Purple Flute	65.00
Toothpick, Rabbit & Dog In Tree Stump	65.00
Toothpick, Ranson	53.00
Toothpick, Ribbed Base, Blue & White	20.00
Toothpick, Ribbed Spiral, Blue Opalescent	65.00
Toothpick, Roller Skate, Victorian	32.00
Toothpick, Royal Ivy, Frosted	75.00
Toothpick, Rubina Band	37.50
Toothpick, Ruby Thumbprint, Vine Etching	31.00
Toothpick, Saddle, Barrel, Blue	45.00
Toothpick, Satin Glass, Blue, Applied Cherry & Leaves	29.00
Toothpick, Saxon, Ruby Stained	20.00
Toothpick, Scalloped Swirl, Midwinter Fair 1894 Adele	20.00
Toothpick, Scoop Shape, Pedestal	22.00
Toothpick, Scrolled Shell, Gold Trim	18.00
Toothpick, Shoeshone	95.00
Toothpick, Slag, Marked Bogue Mercury	14.00
Toothpick, Slag, Purple, Footed	25.00
Toothpick, Slag, Ring Handled	22.00
Toothpick, Souvenir, Belle Plain, Iowa, 2 In.	9.50
Toothpick, Souvenir, Bertha, Nebraska	14.00
Toothpick, Souvenir, Chicago, Illinois, Custard Glass	25.00
Toothpick, Souvenir, Jasonville, Indiana, Pedestal, 2 Handled	12.50

Toothpick, Souvenir, Lincoln, Nebraska, 1918	14.00
Toothpick, Souvenir, Lohrville, Iowa, Enameled Rose, Clear	30.00
Toothpick, Souvenir, Lutheran Church, Wausa, Nebraska, Custard, Beaded Top	20.00
Toothpick, Souvenir, Mooreland, Oklahoma, Custard, Gold Beaded Edge	22.00
Toothpick, Souvenir, Omaha Exposition, 1899, Button Arches	14.00
Toothpick, Souvenir, Palco, Kansas, Custard Glass	35.00
Toothpick, Souvenir, Phillips, Maine, Georgia Gem, Green Custard	40.00
Toothpick, Souvenir, Uehling, Nebraska, Gold Beads, Pattern Bottom	30.00
Toothpick, Sprig, Pan-O-Pan	65.00
Toothpick, State, Connecticut	32.00
Toothpick, Stripe, Cranberry Opalescent	95.00
Toothpick, Swans, Milk Glass	18.00
Toothpick, Texas, Clear With Gold	20.00
Toothpick, Thimble Shape, Just A Thimble Full	8.00
Toothpick, Thompson's No.77, Ruby Stain	28.00
Toothpick, Top Hat, Emerald Green, Ribbed	18.00
Toothpick, Tramp Shoe, White Milk	15.00
Toothpick, Two Pigs With Hat, Germany	18.00
Toothpick, U.S.A., Crystal	12.00
Toothpick, Uncle Sam's Hat, Original Color	37.00
Toothpick, Utility Boot, Blue	35.00
Toothpick, Vase Shape, Daisy & Button, 2 5/8 In.High, 2 7/8 In.Diameter	22.50
Toothpick, Vermont, Green With Gold	50.00
Toothpick, Vermont, Opaque, Painted Flowers	75.00
Toothpick, Wagon Wheel Hub, Amber	8.00
Toothpick, Washington, Custard Glass	45.00
Toothpick, White & Gold Rim, Marked, Nippon	12.00
Toothpick, Winged Scroll, Green	125.00
Toothpick, Witch's Head, Green Slag	30.00
Toothpick, Wooden, Lignum Vitae, Pedestal, 3 1/4 In.	22.50
Toothpick, World's Fair, St.Louis, 1904, Metal	8.50
Tortoise, Comb, Pair	15.00

Tortoiseshell glass was made during the 1800s and after by the Sandwich Glass Works of Massachusetts and some firms in Germany. Tortoiseshell glass has been reproduced.

Tortoiseshell Glass, Basket, Gold Enamel Rim, 10 1/2 X 6 1/2 X 4 1/2 In.	165.00
Tortoiseshell Glass, Bowl, 8 X 3 1/4 In.	55.00
Tortoiseshell Glass, Box, Jewelry, Lever Lock, 3 Tiered, 5 3/4 X 4 X 4 1/4 In	175.00
Tortoiseshell Glass, Rose Bowl, Enameled Flowers, Gold Leaves	65.00
Tortoiseshell Glass, Vase, Sterling Top, 7 In.	50.00
Tortoiseshell, Box, Powder, Lid, Round	12.50
Tortoiseshell, Case, Calling Card, Mother-Of-Pearl Design	40.00
Tortoiseshell, Case, Cigarette, Rickshaws & Riders, 4 1/2 X 2 3/4 In.	65.00
Tortoiseshell, Comb, Openwork Top Bank	8.00
Tortoiseshell, Comb, Rhinestones	8.00
Tortoiseshell, Lorgnette, Black Necklace & Slide	85.00
Tortoiseshell, Scoop, Apothecary	7.00
Toy, Acrobat, Circus Lady, Wooden, Schoenhut	90.00
Toy, Acrobat, Male, Bisque Head, Schoenhut	195.00
Toy, Acrobats, 1910, Tin, Windup, 6 1/2 In.	87.50
Toy, Aircraft Carrier, Tootsietoy	12.00
Toy, Airplane, Bomber, Clockwork, Marx, Set Of 4	130.00
Toy, Airplane, Cessna, Friction	8.00
Toy, Airplane, Pan American World Airways, 24 In.Long X 27 In.Across	38.00
Toy, Airplane, Tootsietoy, Set Of 5, C.1953, Boxed	12.95
Toy, Alligator, Glass Eyes, Schoenhut	235.00
Toy, Ambulance, Wyandotte, Heavy Gauge Metal	12.00
Toy, Amusement Ride, Aerial, Children In Boats, German	135.00
Toy, Anvil, Brass, 4 In.	12.00
Toy, Army Tank, Flip Over, Tin, Wooden Wheels, Marx, 6 In.	17.50
Toy, Auto Express, Kenton	400.00
Toy, Auto, Mortimer Snerd Tricky Auto	225.00
Toy, Axe, Iron, 5 1/2 In.	10.00
Toy, B.O.Plenty, Windup, Tin	30.00

Toy, Baby, Crawling, Bobbing Head, Dressed, Papier Mache, Japanese, 8 In.	18.00
Toy, Baby, Crawling, Mechanical	5.00
Toy, Baking Set, Box Is Stove, Kiddycook	7.50
Toy, Balls, Carpet, Matched Set, 2 In.Diameter, Set Of 13	225.00
Toy, Band, Li'l Abner Dogpatch, Complete	150.00
Toy, Bandwagon Driver, Schoenhut	325.00
Toy, Bank, Ben Franklin, Marx	16.00
Toy, Barber Bear, Battery Operated	55.00
Toy, Barber Shop, Animal, Windup, Tin	25.00
Toy, Barnacle Bill, Walks, Windup, 1930s	95.00
Toy, Bartender, Battery Operated, C.Weaver	28.00
Toy, Baseball, Signed Charlie Keller, & 19 Others, September 14, 1937	25.00
Toy, Bassinette, Removable Push Handle, Mattress	135.00
Toy, Bathroom Set, Tootsietoy, White Paint, 5 Pieces	45.00
Toy, Batmobile, First Version	22.00
Toy, Battleship, Conqueror, Paper Covered, 1895, 20 In.	200.00
Toy, Battleship, 4 Guns, Original Paint, Friction, C.1919, 14 In.	125.00
Toy, Bear With Camera, Red China, Battery Operated	32.00
Toy, Bear, Boxing, Hits Punching Bag, Eyes Roll, Battery Operated, Japanese	105.00
Toy, Bear, Brown, Glass Eyes, Schoenhut	265.00
Toy, Bear, Riding Bicycle, Runs Along String, Tin	87.50
Toy, Bear, Tin, Wind Up, Chein	12.00
Toy, Bed, Doll, Iron, Embossed Birds, Children, Animals, 16 X 22 X 12 1/2 In.	155.00
Toy, Bed, Doll's, Metal Canopy, Victorian, 10 1/2 X 18 X 15 In.	30.00
Toy, Beetle, Crawling, Lehmann, Tin	50.00
Toy, Bell, Camel With Rider, Tin	600.00
Toy, Bicycle, see Bicycle	
Toy, Bird, In Gilded Cage, 4 Gilded Legs, Hanging Ring, 9 X 7 X 4 3/4 In.	225.00
Toy, Bird, Windup, Chein	10.00
Toy, Blocks, Anchor Stone, German, C.1900, Boxed	28.00
Toy, Blocks, Funny Face, Original Box, Schoenhut	40.00
Toy, Blocks, Interchangeable, Blondie & Dagwood, 1951, Gaston Co.	10.50
Toy, Blocks, Wooden Picture Puzzle, Greenaway Type Children, Set Of 30	80.00
Toy, Boat, Aluminum, Powered By Electric Evinrude Motor, 12 X 4 3/4 In.	18.00
Toy, Boat, Side-Wheeler, C.1915, Bing, 10 In.	175.00
Toy, Bobsled, Wooden, Red, Handmade, Tongue, Front Runners Swivel, 18 In.	10.50
Toy, Bonzo, Dog On Scooter, Windup, 1930s, Chein	325.00
Toy, Bowl, Punch, Pressed Glass, 5 Matching Cups, Bowl, 5 In.	65.00
Toy, Boxer, Black, In Ring, Wood Jointed, Mechanical	19.00
Toy, Boxing Teddy, Hits Bunching Bag, Cragston	105.00
Toy, Boy, Dancing & Whistling, Windup, Celluloid, 9 In.	8.00
Toy, Boy, The Atomic Robot, Windup, Tin	30.00
Toy, Buckboard, Cast Iron, Kenton, 14 3/4 In.	135.00
Toy, Buggy, Doll, Tin, 8 X 6 3/4 In.	12.50
Toy, Buggy, Doll, Wicker	45.00
Toy, Buggy, Doll, Wicker, Original	175.00
Toy, Buggy, Doll, Wicker, Rectangular Fringed Sun Shade	175.00
Toy, Buggy, Doll, Wooden, Original Red Paint	175.00
Toy, Building Set, Wood, Box & Litho Label, German	10.00
Toy, Bulldozer, Wood Wheels, Rubber Track, Hubley, 9 In.	15.00
Toy, Bunny, Pulling Cart, Tin, Chein	12.50
Toy, Bureau With Mirror, Tear Drop Pulls	35.00
Toy, Bus, Cast Iron, Stanley, 4 1/4 In.	35.00
Toy, Bus, Greyhound Fair, Chicago, 1933	55.00
Toy, Bus, Greyhound, Tootsietoy, 5 Piece, 1930s	68.00
Toy, Bus, Red, Cast Iron, 4 1/2 In.	34.00
Toy, Bus, Windup, Tin, German	7.00
Toy, Busy Miner, Marx	55.00
Toy, Cabinet, Kitchen, Oak, Signed Cass, 16 X 13 3/4 In.	55.00
Toy, Cable Car, Lehmann Rigi Dud, Battery Operated	45.00
Toy, Cable Car, Sunny Andy, Wolverine, 1920s	65.00
Toy, Cage, Circus, Cast Iron, Kenton, 14 1/8 In	190.00
Toy, Camel, Glass Eyes, Schoenhut	225.00
Toy, Cannon, Big-Bang, Iron, Rubber Wheels, Instructions, 9 In.	50.00
Toy, Cannon, Firecracker, Cast Iron, Kilgore	49.00
Toy, Car, Armoured, Battery Operated	25.00

Toy, Car, Circus, Wood With Lithograph, No.1911, 14 In.	100.00
Toy, Car, Driver, Tin, Windup, Lindstrom, 1920s	65.00
Toy, Car, Fire Chief, Friction, 7 In.	14.00
Toy, Car, Ford, Friction, Tin	7.50
Toy, Car, Milton Berle, Windup, Tin, C.1930	80.00
Toy, Car, Model T Coupe, Metal Wheels, Black, Cast Iron, 5 In.	60.00
Toy, Car, Model-S, Twin Switch Ford	35.00
Toy, Car, N.B.C., T.V., Tin, Friction	25.00
Toy, Car, Oho, Lehmann, 1903	85.00
Toy, Car, Open Touring, Tin, Penny Toys, German	40.00
Toy, Car, Pedal, Casey Jones Cannonball Express, C.1920	100.00
Toy, Car, Pepsi Cola, Friction, 1961	7.50
Toy, Car, Police, Battery Operated, 1950s, Linemar	10.00
Toy, Car, Racer, Windup, C.1920, Marx, 5 In.	18.00
Toy, Car, Railroad Switch, Pine, Wooden Track	125.00
Toy, Car, Railroad, Open, Electric Blue, 12 X 5 X 5 In.	150.00
Toy, Car, Schuco Dalli, Windup	15.00
Toy, Car, Sedan, Tin, Windup, 1930s, 4 In.	12.00
Toy, Car, T.V., Disney, Tin, Windup, Friction, Marx	65.00
Toy, Carpet Sweeper, Bissell, Child's, Wood, 27 In.	14.50
Toy, Carriage, Doll, Wooden, Canvas Top, Wire Wheels, C.1890, 22 X 14 In.	135.00
Toy, Cash Register, Secret Drawer	24.00
Toy, Cash Register, Tom Thumb, Aluminum Money	26.00
Toy, Cat, Rolls Ball, Turns Over & Rights Up, Key Wind, Tin	48.75
Toy, Cat, Windup, U.S. Zone, Germany	12.50
Toy, Cement Mixer, Horse Drawn, Kenton	650.00
Toy, Chad Valley Cat, Brown Velvet, Black Hair, 19 In.	75.00
Toy, Chair, Doll's, Red Velvet Cushion, Wicker, 9 In.	16.00
Toy, Champion Weight Lifter, Battery Operated	17.00
Toy, Charlie Chaplin, Ceramic, Hand-Painted, Revolving, Musical, 7 1/2 In.	13.00
Toy, Charlie Chaplin, Walks, Holding Cane, Windup, 9 In.	250.00 To 325.00
Toy, Chest, Cedar, Royal Oak, Michigan	5.00
Toy, Chimp, Guitar Playing, Battery Operated, Japan	30.00
Toy, Circus Cage, Overland, Cast Iron, Kenton	190.00
Toy, Circus Set, Humpty Dumpty, Schoenhut, 35-Pieces	1800.00
Toy, Circus Wagons, Arcade, Lion & Polar Bear, 9 In., Pair	650.00
Toy, Circus, Royal Circus, Hubley, Farmer Van, 1920	3250.00
Toy, Circus, Single Ring, Schoenhut, 13 Pieces	675.00
Toy, Clown Bell Ringer, 2 Clowns On Mule Illus	1800.00
Toy, Clown In Donkey Cart, Windup, Tin, Lehmann, Germany, 6 In.	55.00
Toy, Clown, Blows Whistle, Monkey Hits Cymbals, Battery Operated, Japanese	175.00
Toy, Clown, Hand-Painted, Tumbling	50.00
Toy, Clown, Mikuni, Japan, Windup	11.00
Toy, Clown, One Man Band, Battery Operated, Boxed	45.00

Toy, Clown Bell Ringer, 2 Clowns On Mule

Toy, Clown, Puppet Show, Moves Face Back & Forth, Battery Operated, Japanese	100.00
Toy, Clown, Riding Rocking Horse, Carved, Windup	195.00
Toy, Clown, Roly Poly, Mustached, Label, Schoenhut, 4 1/2 In.	75.00
Toy, Clown, Walking On Hands, Tin, Chein	7.00
Toy, Coach, Victorian, Iron, 2 7/8 X 1 7/8 In.	18.00
Toy, Coffee Grinder, Wood & Cast Iron	20.00
Toy, Coffee Mill, Daisy, Cast Iron	50.00
Toy, Cop On Motorcycle, Red, Cast Iron	24.00
Toy, Cop, Motorcycle, Windup, Tin, Siren, Marx	55.00
Toy, Coupe, Ford, Arcade, Iron, 5 In.	50.00
Toy, Coupe, Rumble Seat, Cast Iron, 6 In.	82.00
Toy, Cow, Moos While Moving Head, Tin, 1930s	55.00
Toy, Cradle, Doll, Hood, Wicker	22.00

Toy, Cradle, Doll, Large, Bentwood 45.00
Toy, Cradle, Swan Boat Style, Wrought Iron & Wire, White, 32 In.High 65.00
Toy, Crane, Friction, Tin, Red China 6.00
Toy, Crane, 3 Coal Cars, Beam, Wheel Turns Crane, German, 7 1/2 X 14 1/4 In. 95.00
Toy, Crapshooter, Battery Operated .... 18.00 To 21.00
Toy, Cribbage Board, Elephant Ivory, Hand Carved 500.00
Toy, Cupboard, 2 Doors On Bottom, Frosted Glass On Top, 40 X 24 In. 85.00
Toy, Dancer, Bojangles 15.00
Toy, Dancer, Jazzbo Jim, Plays Banjo, Windup, Unique Art 125.00
Toy, Dancer, Tombo, Alabama Coon Jigger, Windup, 1910, Strauss 145.00
Toy, Dancing Minstrel, Mechanical, LaGrove, Kemp & Webb Of New York 250.00
Toy, Dipsy Car, Mickey Mouse, Windup, Tin, C.1930, Disney 87.00
Toy, Dirigible, U.S.N., Tootsietoy 35.00
Toy, Dishes, Blue Windmill & Sailboats, China, 4 Plates, 5 Cups, Creamer, Sugar 14.00
Toy, Disneyland Express, Train Pictures Disney Characters, Windup 160.00
Toy, Dog, Astro, Battery Operated, Remote Control 22.00
Toy, Dog, Eating, Windup, Tin 7.00
Toy, Dog, Reclining Setter, Movable Head, Bronze 55.00
   Toy, Doll, see Doll
Toy, Dollhouse, Furnished, Schoenhut 550.00
Toy, Dollhouse, Green Trim, Porch, 2 1/2 Story, 29 1/2 X 22 X 25 1/2 In. 475.00
Toy, Dollhouse, Wood, Opens, 12 X 6 In. 47.50
Toy, Dollhouse, 2 Story, 1890 Cardboard, Original Box 185.00
Toy, Dollhouse, 3 Floors, 6 Rooms & Attic, Wood, 36 X 24 X 35 In. 165.00
Toy, Donald Duck Duet, Plays Drums, Pluto Dances, Windup, Tin .... 145.00 To 235.00
Toy, Donkey, Glass Eyes, Schoenhut, 8 X 10 In. 95.00
Toy, Dresser, Miniature, Victorian, Walnut, Swinging Mirror 300.00
Toy, Dresser, Wooden, Mirror, 4 Drawers, Brass Hardware 100.00
Toy, Driver & Sulky, Windup, 1950s, German 35.00
Toy, Driver, Clown, Lehmann 350.00
Toy, Drum, Uncle Wiggily's Parade, Character Drum, Dated 1924 .... 85.00
Toy, Drummer, Windup, Chein 35.00
Toy, Duck, Mechanical, Cloth, On Wheels, Bellows & Clockwork, 6 X 5 In. 55.00
Toy, Duck, Windup, Chein .... 12.00 To 16.00
Toy, Dump Truck, Original Sticker, 7 1/2 In. 125.00
Toy, Egg Laying Hen, Battery Operated 27.00
Toy, El Toro, Battery Operated 45.00
Toy, Elephant, Celluloid, Nodding 5.00
Toy, Elephant, Painted Eyes, Schoenhut, 7 X 10 In. 60.00
Toy, Encampment, Lead, 40 Soldiers, Bicyclist, Pigeon, German Shepherd, Group 200.00
Toy, Engine Robot, Battery Operated 27.00
Toy, Engine, Fire, Rubber, 8 In. 16.00
Toy, Engine, Lionel, No.1110 .... 15.00
Toy, Erector Set, Electric, Gilbert 20.00
Toy, Erector Set, Gilbert No.7, Wooden Case, Instruction Book 24.50
Toy, Erector Set, No.8 1/2, Gilbert, Metal Box 18.00
Toy, Erector Set, Pocket Size, Original Box 5.00
Toy, Erector Set, Wooden, Mysto 28.00
Toy, Erector Set, 1a, 1b, Meccano, Directions, 1913 .... 40.00
Toy, Ferdinand The Bull, Chases Bullfighter, Windup, 1938, Disney 95.00
Toy, Ferris Wheel, Mickey Mouse, Chein 100.00
Toy, Figurine, Bulldog, Metal, 2 1/2 In. 8.00
Toy, Figurine, Lead Whimsey, Rabbit On Branch Holding Hinged Walnut, 2 In. 25.00
Toy, Fire Chief, Bell, Pull, 9 In. 8.50
Toy, Fire Engine, Driver, 3 Horses, Cast Iron 350.00
Toy, Fire Engine, Horse Drawn, Ladder, 2 Men, 11 In. 145.00
Toy, Fire Engine, 3 Horses, Wilkins 415.00
Toy, Fireplace, Original Color & Stencil With Utensils 75.00
Toy, Firewagon & 3 Horses, Cast Iron, Kenton, 17 In. 155.00
Toy, Flatiron, Separate Handle 12.00
Toy, Ford, 1932, Tootsietoy 18.00
Toy, Foxy Grandpa, Roly Poly, Schoenhut 195.00
Toy, G.I.Joe & K-9 Pups, Windup, Unique Art 35.00
   Toy, Game, see Game
Toy, Girl On A Swing, Tin, Penny Toys, German 65.00
Toy, Girl On Trapeze, Key Wind, Celluloid, 9 In. 7.00

Toy, Goat, Glass Eyes, Schoenhut 125.00
Toy, Golfer, Ball Washer, Clubs & 6 Pieces Of Golf Greens, Schoenhut 265.00
Toy, Goose, Pulls Cart Of Baby Geese, Tin, Windup, Lehmann, 1924 .... 115.00
Toy, Gun, Cap, Bang, Cast Iron 18.00
Toy, Gun, Cap, Big Bill, Cast Iron 16.00
Toy, Gun, Cap, Big Horn, Kilgore 30.00
Toy, Gun, Cap, Buc A Roo, Kilgore 20.00
Toy, Gun, Cap, Buc-A-Roo, Iron, Kilgore 24.50
Toy, Gun, Cap, Buffalo Bill, Cast Iron .... 14.00 To 16.00
Toy, Gun, Cap, Cowboy King, Stevens .... 30.00 To 35.00
Toy, Gun, Cap, Eagle, 1890 .... 18.00
Toy, Gun, Cap, Kilgore, Invincible, Iron, 1914 .... 12.00
Toy, Gun, Cap, Kit Carson 3.50
Toy, Gun, Cap, Long Boy, Cast Iron, 11 In. 57.00
Toy, Gun, Cap, Long Tom, Kilgore 35.00
Toy, Gun, Cap, National, Dated 1909 .... 16.00
Toy, Gun, Cap, Pluck, Cast Iron .... 20.00 To 22.00
Toy, Gun, Cap, Ranger, Iron, Kilgore 27.00
Toy, Gun, Cap, Ranger, Kilgore 25.00
Toy, Gun, Cap, Ric-O-Shay, Hubley 6.00
Toy, Gun, Cap, 49er, Cast Iron 37.00
Toy, Gun, Clicker, Red Ranger 12.50
Toy, Gun, Cork, 6 1/2 In. 10.00
Toy, Gun, Daisy Rocket Dart, Metal 10.00
Toy, Gun, Floral Handle, Cast Iron, C.1890, 5 1/2 In. 12.00
Toy, Gun, G-Man, Windup, Box 24.00
Toy, Gun, Paper Popper 12.00
Toy, Gun, Pop, Daisy Zooka 32.00
Toy, Gun, Water, Daisy, Metal 40.00
Toy, Gun, Water, Dragnet 14.00
Toy, Gypsy, Marionette 12.00
Toy, Hand Clacker, Minstrel, Negro Happy Face, Papier Mache, 6 1/2 X 3 In. 15.00
Toy, Handcar, Railroad, Girard Toys, 1920, Windup, Tin, 6 X 5 1/2 In. 89.00
Toy, Hanger, Clothes, Wire, 4 Piece 6.50
Toy, Happy Ham, Pull, Wooden 35.00
Toy, Happy Hooligan, Acrobatic Stunts, Composition, Windup, 1905 .... 350.00
Toy, Happy Hooligan, Walking, Chein 105.00
Toy, Hatchet, Iron, 4 1/4 In. 12.00
Toy, Hen, Pulling Crate With Chicken On Top, German, 10 In. 175.00
Toy, Hi Jinks At The Circus, Blows Whistle & Plays Cymbals 175.00
Toy, Hippopotamus, Glass Eyes, Schoenhut .... 165.00 To 250.00
Toy, Hook & Ladder, Kenton, Cast Iron, 17 In. 125.00
Toy, Horn, 2 1/2 In Flared Porcelain Mouth Piece, Handle, Tin 19.00
Toy, Horse & Cart, Tin, Window Design 135.00
Toy, Horse & Jockey, Base, Tin, C.1870 .... 165.00
Toy, Horse, Glass Eyes, Schoenhut 75.00
Toy, Horse, Hobby, Glass Eyes, Original Paint, 72 X 46 In. 650.00
Toy, Horse, Hobby, Leather Saddle, Victorian 350.00
Toy, Horse, Pedals With Steering Bar In Front, Tin 95.00
Toy, Horse, Racing Jeu De Course, Mechanical, 1900 .... 135.00
Toy, Horse, Rubber, Pull, Rubber Wheel, 8 1/2 X 8 1/2 In. 12.50
Toy, House, Mechanical, Men Working, 1 In.To 1 Foot Scale 5000.00
Toy, Ice Skates, Cast Steel, Leather Straps, C.1890 .... 12.50
Toy, Ice Skates, Clamp-On, Winchester, American Club 15.00
Toy, Ice Skates, Keen Kutter 14.00
Toy, Ice Skates, On Shoes, Size 10 .... 35.00
Toy, Ice Skates, Winchester .... 15.00 To 25.00
Toy, Icebox, Metal 80.00
Toy, Indian Maiden, Carved, Wooden, Mason City, Illinois 1500.00
Toy, Indian, Drumming, Battery Operated 27.00
Toy, Jalopy, Marx, Tin 9.00
Toy, Jazzbo Kim, Wind-Up 235.00
Toy, Jeep, Movable Windshield, Friction, 12 In. 9.95
Toy, Joe Penner, Wanna Buy A Duck, Tin 165.00
Toy, Jumpin' Jeep, 4 Soldiers, Marx 25.00
Toy, Kangaroo, Stuffed, Windup, Plays Tune 40.00

Toy, Kettle, Iron, 3 Feet, 7/8 In.	7.00
Toy, Kid Flyer, Boy On Orange Crate Scooter, Tin, Windup, 1924	265.00
Toy, Kiddy Car, 3 Wheels, Wood, Original Yellow Paint, 35 In. X 17 In.	37.00
Toy, Leopard, Glass Eyes, Ball Jointed Neck, Schoenhut	225.00
Toy, Li'l Abner, The Dogpatch Turnip Time, Windup, Unique Art, 1945	155.00
Toy, Limousine, Driver, Hand Crank Flywheel Friction, German, 7 In.	110.00
Toy, Lion Tamer, Bisque Head, Schoenhut	195.00
Toy, Locomotive & Tender, Wood & Tin, Friction, Locomotive 14 In.	550.00
Toy, Lone Ranger, Windup, Tin, C.1930	145.00
Toy, Lunar Module, Windup, Tin & Plastic	12.50
Toy, Machine Gun, G-Man, Model 18-A50, Windup	13.00
Toy, Machine, Washing, Wringer, Wolverine	25.00
Toy, Maggie & Jiggs, Rolling Pin & Cabbage Pail, Schoenhut	850.00
Toy, Maharajah, Camel With Rider, Wheels, Brass, 4 1/2 In.	75.00
Toy, Mammy, Dances, Tin, Lindstrom, 8 In.	57.50
Toy, Man On Motorcycle, Daredevil, Windup, Tin, Lehmann	165.00
Toy, Man, Sam The Gardner, Marx, Windup	35.00
Toy, Marionette, Dancing Minstrel Man	26.00
Toy, McGregor, Battery Operated	32.00
Toy, Mechanical, Organ Grinder & Monkey	410.00
Toy, Mickey Mouse, see Disneyana	
Toy, Mighty Mouse, Squeeze	10.00
Toy, Minstrel Man, Negro, Beats Drum, Windup, German, 1900	250.00
Toy, Model-T, 4 Door, Windup, Gear Shaft Moves, German, Tin, 7 1/2 In.	175.00
Toy, Model, Ship, Made To Sail	215.00
Toy, Monkey Pouring Soda, Battery Operated	18.00
Toy, Monkey, Bubble Blowing	68.00
Toy, Monkey, Climbing, Original Box, Tin	95.00
Toy, Monkey, Fur, Red Hat, Windup, Tin	30.00
Toy, Monkey, Loop The Loop, Battery Operated	12.00
Toy, Monkey, See No Evil, Hands Move, Battery Operated, Japanese	200.00
Toy, Monkey, Stuffed, Windup, Eats Ice Cream	40.00
Toy, Mortimer Snerd & His Car	150.00
Toy, Mortimer Snerd's Home Town Band, Windup	155.00
Toy, Motorcycle & Side Car, Policeman Rider, Iron, 9 In.	80.00
Toy, Motorcycle Cop, Siren, Windup, Marx, 9 In.	22.00
Toy, Motorcycle Delivery, Battery Operated, Lights, Tin	85.00
Toy, Motorcycle, Cop, Windup, Marx, Tin, 8 In.	45.00
Toy, Motorcycle, Driver, White Rubber Tires, 5 X 3 1/4 In.	22.00
Toy, Motorcycle, Harley, Civilian Rider, Cast Iron, 6 In.	145.00
Toy, Motorcycle, Sidecar, Driver, Windup, Tipp, German, 9 3/4 In.	225.00
Toy, Motorcycle, Sidecar, Nickel Wheels, Cast Iron, 4 In.	72.00
Toy, Motorcycle, Tin, Windup, Portillo	21.00
Toy, Mule, Clown Driver, Lehmann, Windup, Tin	100.00
Toy, Mystery Pluto, Windup, Tin, Marx, 1938	95.00
Toy, Mystic, Motorcycle, Cop On Bike Rides In Circle, Windup, Marx	22.50
Toy, Noah's Ark, 15 Figures, Wood	65.00
Toy, Ostrich, Glass Eyes, Schoenhut	225.00 To 325.00
Toy, Overland Circus Wagon, 15 1/2 In.	325.00
Toy, Pail, Candy, 3 Little Pigs, Chein	16.00
Toy, Patrol Car, Jack Webb, Original Box, Dated 1954	20.00
Toy, Patty & The Pig, Lehmann, Tin	275.00
Toy, Pea Shooter, Posa-Matic, Steel	15.50
Toy, Peacock, Strutting, Wind Up, Tin	40.00
Toy, Peggy Parrot, Eyes Light, Head Turns, Wings Move, Squawks, Rosko	110.00
Toy, Pelican, Windup, Tin, Chein	10.00 To 15.00
Toy, Penny, Man With Spinner	50.00
Toy, Piano, Angel Keyboard, 6 Key, Schoenhut	35.00
Toy, Piano, Schoenhut, 21 X 13 X 9 In.	170.00
Toy, Piano, Upright, Schoenhut, 8 X 10 In.	60.00
Toy, Piano, 6 Key, Lithographed Panel, Schoenhut, 7 1/4 X 6 1/4 X 4 3/4 In.	58.00
Toy, Pig, Glass Eyes, Scheonhut	150.00 To 245.00
Toy, Pig, Pudgy, Pull, Wood, 1962	10.00
Toy, Pilot-House Eagle, From A Ferry Boat, 1800s, 28 In.Wingspan	1650.00
Toy, Pin, Zepplin, Child's	6.00
Toy, Pinocchio, Playing London Bridge On Xylophone	125.00

Toy, Pinocchio, Windup, Tin, Walt Disney	125.00
Toy, Plane, Single Engine, Army, Tootsietoy, 1940s	8.00
Toy, Playland Skybus, Tin, Windup	21.00
Toy, Plow, McCormick Deering, Cast Iron, 7 In.	55.00
Toy, Pluto, Pop Up, 1936, Kritter Toy	17.00
Toy, Pluto, Squeeze	2.00
Toy, Police Patrol, Mule Team, Driver, Wilkins	335.00
Toy, Policeman On Motorcycle, Barcley	8.00
Toy, Policeman, Police Patrol Wagon, Iron, 1895, 12 In.	115.00
Toy, Pony & Chariot, Paper On Wood, Walking Legs, Tin & Cast Iron, 7 In.	33.00
Toy, Poodle, Glass Eyes, Cloth Mane, Bell, Schoenhut	110.00
Toy, Pool Player, Table, Mechanical, Germany	75.00
Toy, Pool Players, Wind Up, Tin, 5 X 14 1/2 In.	42.50
Toy, Pop Gun, Kingtop, Markham Air Rifle Co.	25.00
Toy, Popeye & His Caged Parrots, Wind-Up, Tin	125.00
Toy, Popeye Express, Tin, Windup, Marx	305.00
Toy, Popeye, Celluloid, Driving Tin Cart, Marx	155.00
Toy, Popeye, Drives Crazy Truck, Celluloid, Tin, Windup, 1930s	260.00
Toy, Porky Pig, Talking, Tin, Original Box	75.00
Toy, Prancing Horse, Tonawanda Style, Glass Eyes, Hair Tail, 54 In.	1185.00
Toy, Projector, 8 Reels, C.1935, Electric	47.50
Toy, Pull Toy, Turtle, Painted	18.00
Toy, Punch & Judy Theatre, 10 Wooden Puppets	400.00
Toy, Puppet Show, Happy The Clown, Moves Strings To Wooden Pinocchio	100.00
Toy, Puppet, Finger, Red Riding Hood, 3 Piece	6.00
Toy, Puppet, Hand, Carved Wooden Heads, Hands & Feet, Wayang Golek, Java	85.00
Toy, Puppet, Hand, Khrushchev, Original Box	18.00
Toy, Puppet, Hand, Owl, Glass Eyes, 9 In.	12.50
Toy, Pushcart, Doll, 2-Wheel, Tole	95.00
Toy, Puzzle, Continental Object Lessons, 1890s, 10 X 12 X 2 3/4 In.	37.50
Toy, Puzzle, Flash Gordon, Inlaid, 10 X 15 In.	6.00
Toy, Puzzle, Horse Drawn Fire Engine, Train, Car, Set Of 3, 17 X 10 1/2 In.	60.00
Toy, Puzzle, Jigsaw, Buster Crabbe, King Of Jungle, 300 Pieces	12.50
Toy, Puzzle, Shape Of Automobile, Metal	15.00
Toy, Rabbit, Chein, Wind Up, Tin	17.50
Toy, Rabbit, Papier-Mache, 6 In.	5.00
Toy, Rabbit, Pulling Basket, Tin, Chein, 11 X 8 In.	10.00
Toy, Rabbit, Pulling Wagon, Papier-Mache	20.00
Toy, Rabbit, Windup, Chein	10.00
Toy, Race Car, Red, Metal, White Wheels, 6 In.	8.00
Toy, Race Car, Tin, Windup, Portillo	21.00
Toy, Race Car, Windup, Chein, 7 In.	9.00
Toy, Racer & Driver, Vinyl Head & Helmet, Modern	16.00
Toy, Racer, Blackbird, Tin, Windup, Lindstrom	18.00
Toy, Racer, Flywheel Friction, Driver, German, 5 1/4 In.	75.00
Toy, Racer, Silver Ghost, Tin, Windup, Lindstrom	18.00
Toy, Radio & T.V., Station, Tin, Marx, 28 X 10 In.	35.00
Toy, Railroad, Wolverine Streamline, Tin	35.00
Toy, Range Rider, Marx	90.00
Toy, Range Rider, Windup, Marx	24.00
Toy, Range, Top Shelf, Tall Legs, 11 1/2 In.	85.00
Toy, Rattle, Teetner, Sterling, 3 1/2 In.	15.00
Toy, Refrigerator, Tootsietoy	18.00
Toy, Rifle, Buffalo, Hubley	5.00
Toy, Rin-Tin-Tin, Fort Apache Set, Marx	42.00
Toy, Ringmaster, Two-Pointed Face, Schoenhut	155.00
Toy, Roadster, Red, Tootsietoy, 6 In.	8.00
Toy, Robot, Blink-A-Gear, Lights Up & Walks	110.00
Toy, Robot, Gears In Chest Turn, Light Blinks, Eyes Light, Walks, Japanese	110.00
Toy, Robot, Marvelous Mike, Electromatic Tractor	40.00
Toy, Robot, Windup, Tin, 1840s, Germany, 8 In.	50.00
Toy, Rocket Missile, C.1940, Tin, 13 1/2 In.	9.95
Toy, Rocking Horse, Dated 1848, Horse Hair, 33 X 24 In.	225.00
Toy, Rocking Horse, Padded Seat Between 2 Horses, Wicker Sides & Back	150.00
Toy, Rocking Horse, Wood, 34 1/2 X 29 In.High	225.00
Toy, Roller Coaster, Windup, Chein	20.00

Toy, Rolling Pin, Maple, 1-Piece Construction, 9 In. 15.00
Toy, Rooster, Spring Legs, Squeaks, 19th Century, Tin 175.00
Toy, Royal Circus, Chariot, Roman Driver, C.1906 .... 1000.00
Toy, Safe, Miniature, Floor Model, Working, 12 In. 65.00
Toy, Sandy-Andy, See-Saw, Tin, 1921 .... 55.00
Toy, Santa Claus, Red Velvet Suit, Papier-Mache, C.1920, 14 In. 170.00
Toy, Santa Scooter, Battery Operated 22.00
Toy, Saxophone, Spike Jones, Sax-O-Fun 20.00
Toy, Sea Captain, Down The Hatch, Drinks & Smokes, Battery Operated 10.00
Toy, Sewing Machine, Cat Sitting On Foot Pedal 20.00
Toy, Sewing Machine, Hand Operated, Singer, Original Case 25.00
Toy, Sewing Machine, Red Riding Hood 15.00
Toy, Sewing Machine, Singer 15.00
Toy, Shaving Sam, Face Reveals Whiskers, Shaves, Powders Face, Japanese 85.00
Toy, Shaving Sam, Man With Electric Razor, Powders Face With Smoke 85.00
Toy, Shotgun, Rocket, Tin & Wood 12.50
Toy, Shutter Bug, Photographer Raises Camera, Flash Goes Off, Tin, Japanese 110.00
Toy, Sifter, Flour, Little Miss Muffet, Tin 3.00
Toy, Sink, Kitchen, Tootsietoy 10.00
Toy, Skates, Ice, Clamp, Key, Pair 5.00
Toy, Skates, Ice, Hand-Wrought Iron Runners, Curved Front 35.00
Toy, Skates, Ice, Walnut, Iron Scroll Extending Over The Toe, Adult 22.50
Toy, Skillet, Iron, 3 Short Feet, Handled, 2 3/4 In. 8.00
Toy, Sled, Child's, Canadian 75.00
Toy, Sled, Child's, Push Type, Upholstered 225.00
Toy, Sled, Child's, Victorian, C.1876, 31 In. .... *Illus* 100.00
Toy, Sled, Front Steering Arms, Wood, 6 X 41 In. 50.00
Toy, Sled, Wooden, Runner Curled In Front, Steering Arms, Rear Rudder, 41 In. 45.00
Toy, Sleeping Bear, Battery Operated 65.00
Toy, Snake Charmer, Turbaned Man Blows Pipe, Snake Comes Out Of Basket 100.00
Toy, Snoopy, Metal, In Box 8.50
Toy, Snowshoes, Strung With Gut, 40 In. 50.00
Toy, Soldier, Beats Drum, Windup, Chien, 9 In. 22.00
Toy, Soldier, Crawling, Ohio Art, Tin, Windup 17.00
Toy, Soldier, Drummer, Celluloid, Windup 12.00
Toy, Soldier, Khaki Uniform & Overseas Cap, Flexy 68.00
Toy, Soldier, Lead, Britain, Boxed, Set Of 14 .... 29.00
Toy, Soldier, Lead, Mold, 2 Part, Wooden Handles, Cast Iron, Cadets, 3 1/4 In. 45.00
Toy, Space Ship, Flash Gordon, Plastic 8.00
Toy, Space Tank, Battery Operated, Red China 20.00
Toy, Sparkling Rocket Ship, Windup, Tin, C.1930 .... 90.00
Toy, Speedboat, Windup, Tin, Chein, 5 In. 6.00
Toy, Speedboat, Windup, Tin, Chein, 9 In. 6.00
Toy, Stage Coach, Lafayette, Wooden, C.1800, 13 X 6 X 7 1/4 In. 35.00
Toy, Steam Engine, Original Red Paint & Brass, Weeden Toy, 10 X 8 1/2 In. 69.00
Toy, Steam Shovel, General, Cast Iron, 10 In.Long 125.00
Toy, Steamship, Windup, Bing, 15 In. 595.00
Toy, Stove, Coal, Novelty, Tin & Iron, 8 1/2 X 5 1/2 X 7 In. 45.00
Toy, Stove, Eagle, Miniature, 16 X 14 X 7 In. 200.00
Toy, Stove, Electric, Empire, 1920s 30.00
Toy, Stove, Electric, Gauge On Door, 12 X 9 X 5 In. 25.00
Toy, Stove, Wood, Schoenhut 5.00
Toy, Stroller, Doll, Basket Weave 35.00
Toy, Stroller, Doll, Wicker 135.00
Toy, Submarine, Tin, C.1930 .... 17.50
Toy, Surrey, Original Cloth Roof, Cast Iron, Stanley, 13 In. 100.00
Toy, Surrey, Fringe On Top, Kenton 200.00
Toy, Swimmer, Celluloid, Windup 22.00
Toy, Tank Truck, Buddy L Toy 150.00
Toy, Tank, Animated, Windup, Marx 25.00
Toy, Tank, Cap Firing, Tin, 6 In. 10.00
Toy, Tank, Superman, Windup 95.00
Toy, Taxi, Amos & Andy 250.00
Toy, Taxi, Tricky Taxi, Windup 17.00
Toy, Taxi, Windup, Tin, Marx, 1940s 23.00
Toy, Tea Set, Hand-Painted Flowers, Porcelain, 4 Piece 65.00

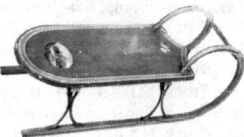

Toy, Sled, Child's, Victorian, C.1876, 31 In.

Toy, Tea Set, Tin, Ohio Art Co., 9 Piece	10.00
Toy, Teapot, Miniature, Tin, Original Japanning, C.1850, 2 3/4 In.	45.00
Toy, Teddy Bear, Brown Hair, Glass Eyes, 14 In.	150.00
Toy, Teddy Bear, Cloth, Riding Bicycle, Windup, C.1915	175.00
Toy, Teddy Bear, Glass Eyes, Swivel Head, Jointed Arms & Legs, 23 In.	125.00
Toy, Teddy Bear, Hump, Jointed	45.00
Toy, Teddy Bear, Picks Up Phone & Talks, Battery Operated, Cragstan	110.00
Toy, Teddy Bear, Roosevelt, Straw Filled, Jointed	120.00
Toy, Teddy The Artist, Bear At Desk, Draws, Battery Operated, Japanese	105.00
Toy, Telephone, Dial-A-Voice, Steel	12.00
Toy, Tent, Schoenhut, 25 X 35 In.	750.00
Toy, The Little King, Pull String Mechanism, Wood, Windup, 1930s	85.00
Toy, Thermos, Tom Corbett Space Cadet	17.00
Toy, Tiddley Winks, J.Pressman, Cobalt Blue Glass	3.50
Toy, Tiger, Glass Eyes, Schoenhut	225.00
Toy, Tony Tiger, Pull, Advertising	4.00
Toy, Tool Box, Child's, Hammer & Vise	15.00
Toy, Tool Chest, Miniature, Wood Box With Tools	12.00
Toy, Top, Spinning, Merry-Go-Round, Chein	7.00
Toy, Top, Wood, Ebony, Ivory On Bone Insets	8.50
Toy, Tractor, Deere, 1950s, 8 1/2 In.	6.00
Toy, Tractor, Fordster	250.00
Toy, Tractor, Olive, Cast Iron, 5 In.	53.00
Toy, Tractor, Wood Wheels, Rubber Track, Hubley, 14 In.	18.00
Toy, Train Passenger Set, Standard Gauge, 3 Cars, Signal, Lionel	215.00
Toy, Train Set, Engine, 6 Cars, Caboose, Track Transformer, Marx	70.00
Toy, Train Set, Standard Gauge, 7 Cars, Lionel	285.00
Toy, Train, American Flyer, 6 Units, Cast Iron Engine, No Track	85.00
Toy, Train, Battery Run, Whistles, Automatically Turns, Engineer, Tin	15.00
Toy, Train, Engine, Standard Gauge, Lionel, No.380	175.00
Toy, Train, Lionel, No.402, Double Freight Engine, Standard Gauge, 4 Cars	750.00
Toy, Train, Passenger, 4 Cars, Tootsietoy	25.00
Toy, Train, Windup, Tin, German	7.00
Toy, Traveler Bear, Battery Operated, Remote Control	25.00
Toy, Tricky Taxi, Windup, Marx	18.00
Toy, Trolley, Toonerville, Windup, Original Paint	225.00
Toy, Trolley, Universal, Wood, Chicago	10.00
Toy, Trolley, 5 Window, No.2 Gauge, Reverse Lever, Brass, 1903	385.00
Toy, Trolley, 8 Wheel, Lever Opens Doors, Ringing Bell, Friction, 19 In.	115.00
Toy, Truck, Army, Green, 6 Wheel, Buddy L, 12 In.	20.00
Toy, Truck, Baggage, Driver, Windup	24.00
Toy, Truck, Buddy L Fire & Chemical, 1930s, 23 In.	37.50
Toy, Truck, Cement Mixer, Structo, 21 In.	15.00
Toy, Truck, Cement Roller, Tootsietoy	6.50
Toy, Truck, Coca-Cola Bottle, Tin, 10 Clear Glass Coca-Cola Bottles	85.00
Toy, Truck, Dump, Buddy Lee Sand & Gravel, 13 In.	26.00
Toy, Truck, Dump, Iron, Arcade, 1928	130.00
Toy, Truck, Dump, Marx, 6 In.	12.00
Toy, Truck, Dump, Wyandotte, 13 In.	10.00
Toy, Truck, Fire Ladder, Ladder Extends To 46 In., Swivel Base, Tin	63.00
Toy, Truck, Firestone Tire Pickup, Red, With Tools	35.00
Toy, Truck, Gasoline, Cast Iron, 5 In.	40.00
Toy, Truck, Hubley, 3 1/2 In.	13.00
Toy, Truck, Iron, Advertising, Tootsietoy	200.00
Toy, Truck, Keystone, 1920s, 22 In.	32.50
Toy, Truck, Mack Cannon	15.00

Toy, Truck, Pepsi Cola, 1961	7.50
Toy, Truck, Pickup, Cast Iron, Green, 5 In.	37.50
Toy, Truck, Pickup, Firestone Tires, With Tools, 1940s, Marx	35.00
Toy, Truck, Pickup, Rubber Wheels, Tootsietoy, 6 In.	9.00
Toy, Truck, Sonny Long Distance Moving, 26 In.	125.00
Toy, Truck, Stake, Coca-Cola Coke Boy On Label, 20 In.	35.00
Toy, Truck, Sunshine Biscuits, Metalcraft Corp.	75.00
Toy, Truck, U.S.Army, Covered, Tootsietoy, 6 In.	22.50
Toy, Truck, Wyandotte Coal	8.00
Toy, Truck, Wyandotte Express, With Ladder, 17 In.	15.00
Toy, Trunk, see Trunk	
Toy, Turkey, Key Wind, U.S. German Zone	20.00
Toy, Turtle, Mechanical, Papier-Mache, C.1915, 6 In.	55.00
Toy, Typewriter, DeLuse Dial A Letter, Marx	12.50
Toy, Typewriter, Tin, Original Box, Simplex	12.00
Toy, Uncle Sam, Windup, Durham, Japan	18.00
Toy, Uncle Wiggily, Windup, Tin, Unused, C.1930	155.00
Toy, Vacuum Cleaner, Miniature, Hoover, Century Of Progress	50.00
Toy, Vibraphone, Electric, Battery Operated	15.00
Toy, Village, McLaughlin, Original Box & Houses	195.00
Toy, W. C. Fields, Does Splits, Holding Cane, Hand Painted, Windup, German	325.00
Toy, Wagon, Beer, Milwaukee, 2 Horses, 24 In.	295.00
Toy, Wagon, Borden's Milk, Wood & Tin	125.00
Toy, Wagon, Circus, Kenton, Boxed	175.00
Toy, Wagon, Contractor's, Black Driver, 15 1/2 In.	395.00
Toy, Wagon, Covered, Kenton, Boxed	200.00
Toy, Wagon, Dray, Kenton, Cast Iron, 15 3/8 In.	115.00
Toy, Wagon, Driver Pulled By Horse, Iron, 1910, 11 In.	95.00
Toy, Wagon, Flat Bed, Schoenhut	6.00
Toy, Wagon, Horse Drawn, Tin, Penny Toys, German	55.00
Toy, Wagon, Ice, Horse Drawn, Cast Iron, 8 In.	72.00
Toy, Wagon, Log, Single Horse, Kenton	275.00
Toy, Wagon, Milk, Kenton, Cast Iron, 12 3/4 In.	145.00
Toy, Wagon, Popcorn, Chassis, Hand Pushed, Steered Rubber Tires	165.00
Toy, Wagon, U.S.Mail, Single Horse, Postman Driver, 6 X 14 In.	250.00
Toy, Wagon, 2 Wheel, Donkey, Darkie Driver, Iron, 11 In.	175.00
Toy, Waiter, Celluloid, Windup	17.00
Toy, Washboard, Child's, Crystal	20.00
Toy, Washing Machine, Metal	18.00
Toy, Wheelbarrel, Tin, Penny Toys, German	15.00
Toy, Wheelbarrow, Child's, Wood, Paris Manufacturing Company	45.00
Toy, Whirligig, Lighthouse With Lobster Pot On Top, 22 In.High	36.00
Toy, Whistle, Metal, Bird	8.50
Toy, Wrecker, Red Baby, International	500.00
Toy, Wringer, Washing Machine, Lovell Mfg.Company, Erie, Pennsylvania	95.00
Toy, Yo-Yo, Sterling Silver	48.00
Toy, Yo-Yo, Tunbridge, C.1840	240.00
Toy, Zeppelin And Plane, Fly Around Tower, 1930s, Unique Art	110.00
Toy, Zeppelin, Cast Iron	15.00
Toy, Zeppelin, On Wheels, 1930s, 10 In.	85.00
Toy, Zeppelin, Tin, 26 In.	75.00

Tramp Art is a form of folk art made since the Civil War. It is usually made from chip-carved cigar boxes.

Tramp Art, Basket, Crown Of Thorns, Pagoda Shaped	65.00
Tramp Art, Box, Hinged, Flattened Pyramid Shape, 9 1/2 X 6 1/4 X 3 1/2 In.	75.00
Tramp Art, Box, Jewelry, Drawer For Handkerchiefs, Top Lid Opens	345.00
Tramp Art, Box, Jewelry, Geometric	50.00
Tramp Art, Box, Lining, 11 1/2 X 8 X 6 In.	55.00
Tramp Art, Box, Mahogany, Match Sticks, Maine, Inlaid On Lid, 10 X 5 X 4 In.	30.00
Tramp Art, Box, White Stars, Crescent Moons & Hearts, Lined, 7 X 13 X 9 In.	65.00
Tramp Art, Box, 6 X 8 In.	15.00
Tramp Art, Box, 7 In.	50.00
Tramp Art, Cabinet, Oak, Mirrored Panel & Door, American, C.1930, 27 In.	125.00
Tramp Art, Chest, Front Drawers	65.00

Tramp Art, Dresser, Child's, Chip Carved, 48 In.	350.00
Tramp Art, Dresser, 3 Drawers, Porcelain Knobs, 9 1/2 X 10 X 5 In.	95.00
Tramp Art, Frame, Old Photograph, 7 X 13 In.	35.00
Tramp Art, Frame, Picture, 10 1/2 X 13 1/4 In.	18.00
Tramp Art, Frame, 18 X 19 In.	55.00
Tramp Art, Mirror, Hanging, Shelf Pocket, 13 X 10 In.	25.00
Tramp Art, Shade, Lamp, Brass, C.1920, Pair, 3 1/2 X 4 In.	20.00
Tramp Art, Shade, Lamp, Pierced Brass, 3 1/2 X 4 In., Pair	29.50

Trap, see Tool, Trap

Treen are small wooden objects such as mugs, spoons, and bowls. The term is early English but is used in the United States in many areas.

Treen, Bowl, Covered, Small, 18th Century, 4 1/8 In.	125.00
Treen, Box, Blue, Footed, 4 3/8 In.	95.00
Treen, Box, Footed, Walnut & Maple, Walnut Lid, 6 1/2 X 6 In.	32.50
Treen, Dish, Butter, Covered, Hand-Turned	85.00
Treen, Jar, Acorn Finial, Squat Body, Domed Foot, 1800s, 8 3/4 In.	325.00
Treen, Mortar & Pestle, 5 1/2 X 9 In.	40.00

Trivets are now used to hold hot dishes. Most of the late nineteenth and early twentieth century trivets were made to hold hot irons. Iron or brass reproductions are being made of many of the old styles.

Trivet, Black Wood Handle, Cast Iron	28.00
Trivet, Brass, Form Of Horse Hoof, Peg Feet	18.00
Trivet, Colt, Cut Out Letters, C.1910-20	20.00
Trivet, Cutout Corners, Cherry	175.00
Trivet, Enterprise, Footed, Cast Iron	8.00
Trivet, Fireplace, 3 Legs, Hand Forged, 11 X 12 1/2 In.Diameter	35.00
Trivet, Fireplace, 3-5 In.Legs, Iron, 10 In.Handle, 7 In.Diameter	90.00
Trivet, Forged Iron, American, C.1820	110.00
Trivet, Good Luck Horseshoe	20.00
Trivet, Horseshoe, Cast Iron	25.00
Trivet, Horseshoe, Eagle On Top, Clasped Hands, Good Luck, Iron	30.00
Trivet, Horseshoe, New Bedford	29.00
Trivet, Iron, Crown & Cross, Cole Brookdale Iron Company	10.00
Trivet, Long Handled, American, 18th Century, American	155.00
Trivet, Lyre, Pineapple With Heart Handle, Cast Iron	28.00
Trivet, Ober, Chagrin Falls, Ohio, Footed	5.50
Trivet, Order Of Cincinnati, 19th Century, Iron	30.00
Trivet, Reunion, Richmond, Virginia, 1922	16.00
Trivet, Round Heart, Claw Feet	15.00
Trivet, Spade Shape, Lacy Center	16.00
Trivet, Tea, Lyndon B.Johnson	8.50
Trunk, Army, Doctor's, Leather, Dated 1880, 18 1/4 X 10 1/4 X 9 3/4 In.	80.00
Trunk, Brass Studded Leather, Domed Top, 1800s, 13 1/2 In.	225.00
Trunk, Camelback, Tray, Small	38.00
Trunk, Camelback, Tray, 1861	75.00
Trunk, Deerhide On Pine, C.1820, Small	17.50
Trunk, Doll, Camel Back, Clothing, Fabric, Key, 16 X 9 1/2 X 10 In.	85.00
Trunk, Doll, Covered, Brass Studded, Iron Lock, 9 X 14 X 6 1/2 In.	39.50
Trunk, Doll, Inner Tray, Tin	42.00
Trunk, Doll, Paper Covered, Tin Hinges, Dovetailed Tray, 5 X 7 X 5 In.	25.00
Trunk, Dome Topped, Hide Covered, Lined With 1792 Salem Gazette, 38 In.	65.00
Trunk, Embossed Cowhide, Brass Studs, Dated 1836	550.00
Trunk, Immigrant's, Hand-Made Hardware & Lock, Oak, 48 In.Long	440.00
Trunk, Norwegian, Orange-Red Background, Dated 1889	285.00
Trunk, Signed & Dated, 1888, Norwegian, Red	350.00
Trunk, Steamer, Cow Hide, Brass Studded, Leather Interior, Dated 1836	595.00
Trunk, Wood, Gilt, Black Lacquered, Butterflies Amidst Floral Sprays	385.00
Trunk, Wood, Gilt, Red Lacquered, Floral Sprays, Fruiting Vines	475.00
Tuthill, Compote, Cosmos, Signed, 4 In.	155.00
Tuthill, Dish, Candy, Sawtooth Rim, Intaglio Cut, Signed, 6 1/8 In.Diameter	160.00
Tuthill, Plate, Flower With Spruce Sprays, Signed, 5 1/8 In.	138.00
Tuthill, Vase, Primrose, Flared Trumpet Design, Signed, 10 In., Pair	395.00
Tuthill, Vase, Primrose, Signed, 10 In.	260.00
Typewriter, Blickenderfer, Portable, 1911, Wooden Case	95.00

Val St.Lambert, Vase, Cameo, Vines, Flowers, Signed, 9 3/4 In.

Typewriter, Corona, Dated 1917, 10 X 9 X 6 In.	40.00
Typewriter, Corona, Folding In Case	37.50
Typewriter, Corona, Portable, Original Case	40.00
Typewriter, L.C.Smith	18.00
Typewriter, Oliver, Model No.5, 1908	70.00
Typewriter, Rem-Blick, Original Oak Case	75.00
Typewriter, Remington, No. 6	18.00
Typewriter, Simplex, Original Carrying Case, 1892	125.00
Typewriter, Yost, Double Keyboard	75.00
Umbrella, Embroidered Linen, Ivory Tips, Gnarled Handle, 19th Century	35.00
Umbrella, Handle, Green, Red Flowers, Putty Scrolls	75.00
Umbrella, Handle, Ivory, Carved	85.00
Umbrella, Handle, Mother-Of-Pearl Panels, Gold Plated	40.00
Umbrella, Lady's, Beige Lace, Bamboo Handle	40.00
Umbrella, Parasol, Bamboo Handle, Beige Lace	25.00
Umbrella, Parasol, Carved Whalebone Band & Knob	65.00
Umbrella, Parasol, Lady's, Victorian, Carved Handle, Black	35.00
Umbrella, Parasol, Pierced, Carved Ivory	65.00
Umbrella, Parasol, Silk, Natural & Pink Ruffles	45.00
Umbrella, Scottie Dog Handle, Hand-Carved	5.00
Umbrella, Sterling Trim Handle, Man's	10.00
Union Porcelain Works, Oyster Plate, Scallop Shell Shape, 1888	25.00
Union Porcelain Works, Teacup, White, Greenpoint, New York, 1877-87	75.00
University City, Dish, Blue & Gray, 2 1/4 X 7 In.	37.50
University City, Vase, Crystalline, Signed, 6 1/2 X 4 1/2 In.	675.00
University No.Dakota School Of Mines, Vase, Blue Matte, 9 In.	75.00

Val St.Lambert Val St.Lambert Cristalleries of Belgium was founded by Messieurs Kemlin and Lelievre in 1825. The company is still in operation.

Val St.Lambert, Bottle, Perfume, Cameo Cut, Frosted Ground, Signed, 6 In.	145.00
Val St.Lambert, Bottle, Pink To Clear Cameo Stopper	145.00
Val St.Lambert, Box, Powder, Green Flowers, Square, Round Cover, Signed	285.00
Val St.Lambert, Candlestick, Signed, 9 1/2 In.	40.00
Val St.Lambert, Coaster, Zodiac, Intaglio Cut, 12 Signs, Set Of 12	150.00
Val St.Lambert, Decanter, Original Stopper, Ground Pontil, Flint, Signed	75.00
Val St.Lambert, Dish, Dresser, Cameo, Curved Gold Overlay, 2 X 9 In.	55.00
Val St.Lambert, Epergne, Belgium Cut Glass, Pewter Base, C.1860, 14 In., Pair	725.00
Val St.Lambert, Epergne, 5 Light, Lily Opening, C.1840, 14 1/2 In., Pair	725.00
Val St.Lambert, Glass, Wine, Green Top, Intaglio Cutting, Cut Stem, 6 3/4 In.	60.00
Val St.Lambert, Vase, Acid Cut Back, Gold Geese, Cattails, 6 X 4 1/2 In.	175.00
Val St.Lambert, Vase, Art Deco Stems & Prunts, Clear & Ruby, 12 In.	125.00
Val St.Lambert, Vase, Art Deco, Clear, Red Overlay, Footed, 10 In.	145.00
Val St.Lambert, Vase, Cameo, Vines, Flowers, Signed, 9 3/4 In. .... Illus	325.00
Val St.Lambert, Vase, Cranberry, Geometric, 6 In.	175.00
Val St.Lambert, Vase, Dutch Canal Scene, Green & Clear, Signed, 6 1/2 In.	850.00
Val St.Lambert, Vase, Overlaid With Metal Foil, Signed	150.00
Val St.Lambert, Wine Set, Etched, Clear, 7 Piece	85.00
Valentine, see Card, Valentine	
Valentine, Card, Hood's Sarsaparilla, Self-Folding, Comic, 7 1/2 X 10 In.	32.00
Valentine, Card, Lacy, 1913, German	4.00
Valentine, Card, Tuck, Set Of 3	6.00
Valentine, Pull-Outs, German	5.00
Vallerystahl, Dish, Dog On Floral Base Dish	37.50

Vallerystahl, Dish, Nested Hen	25.00
Vallerystahl, Jar, Jam, Covered, Blue, Grape & Leaf Pattern, 3 1/2 In.	50.00
Vallerystahl, Plate, Horseshoe, 10 In.	37.50
Vallerysthal, Box, Tea, Covered, Clocks Set For Tea Time, Signed	69.50
Vallerysthal, Compote, Square Rim, Blue Milk Glass, 6 1/4 In., Pair	145.00
Vallerysthal, Dish, Covered, Cobalt Blue, Signed, 4 3/4 X 4 In.	7.50
Vallerysthal, Dish, Rabbit Cover, Crouching, Clear, 6 In.	39.00
Vallerysthal, Dish, Relish, Covered, Cobalt Blue, 4 3/4 In.Diameter	15.00
Vallerysthal, Dish, Squirrel Finial, Blue, Milk Glass, 5 In.	55.00
Vallerysthal, Figurine, Setter, Embossed Dogwood Base	75.00
Vallerysthal, Goblet, Blue, 5 1/2 In.	22.00
Vallerysthal, Jar, Jam, Conical, Grape Pattern, 3 1/2 In.	40.00
Vallerysthal, Vase, Hand Finished, Fire Polish, Gilt, Signed, 9 1/2 In.	325.00

*Van Briggle Pottery was made by Artus Van Briggle in Colorado
Springs, Colorado, after 1901. Mr.Van Briggle had been a decorator at
the Rookwood Pottery of Cincinnati, Ohio, and he died in 1904. His
wares were original and had modeled relief decorations with a soft dull glaze.
It is still being made.*

Van Briggle, Ashtray, Dog & Doghouse, Turquoise Lining	80.00
Van Briggle, Base, Lamp, Blue & Green, Signed, 8 In.	135.00
Van Briggle, Basket, Turquoise, 3 In.	45.00
Van Briggle, Bowl, Butterscotch Brown Over Ocher, 08-II Marking, 7 In.	115.00
Van Briggle, Bowl, Dragonflies, Rose, PN903D, 8 3/4 X 2 3/4 In.	35.00
Van Briggle, Bowl, Duck Flower Frog, Rose, 7 1/2 X 2 5/8 In.	24.00
Van Briggle, Bowl, Duck Flower Frog, Turquoise, Dragonflies, 8 X 2 1/4 In.	43.00
Van Briggle, Bowl, Green, Acorns, Leaves, 5 1/2 In.	32.00
Van Briggle, Bowl, Oval, Scalloped, Matte Raspberry, 5 1/2 In.	11.50
Van Briggle, Bowl, Turquoise, No.903d, 9 3/4 In.	29.00
Van Briggle, Candleholder, Brown Leaf, Signed, 3 In.	25.00
Van Briggle, Candlestick, Handle, Rose & Purple Shades, Pair	25.00
Van Briggle, Candlestick, Handle, Turquoise, Dated 1915, 7 In.	135.00
Van Briggle, Candlestick, Holder, Double Tulip, Turquoise	100.00
Van Briggle, Candlestick, Leaf Base, Matte Brown, Signed, 2 3/4 In., Pair	36.00
Van Briggle, Conch Shell, Turquoise, 12 In.	15.00
Van Briggle, Conch Shell, Turquoise, 17 In.	80.00
Van Briggle, Ewer, Green Volcanic Ash, Signed, 12 In.	55.00
Van Briggle, Ewer, Mottled Turquoise, Signed, 12 In.	45.00
Van Briggle, Figurine, Elephant, Maroon, 7 1/2 X 4 1/8 In.	80.00
Van Briggle, Figurine, Elephant, Turquoise, 7 1/2 X 5 In.	35.00
Van Briggle, Figurine, Hopi Maiden, Turquoise Ming	97.50
Van Briggle, Figurine, Rabbit, Brown, Signed	30.00
Van Briggle, Lamp, Blue, Green Raised Flower, Marked	38.00
Van Briggle, Lamp, Lady Of Damascene, Blue	165.00
Van Briggle, Lamp, Table, Lass From Damascus, Blue, Shade	245.00
Van Briggle, Lamp, The Damsel, Blue	165.00
Van Briggle, Planter, Shell, Turquoise, 16 In.	25.00
Van Briggle, Rose Bowl, Dragonfly, Purple	25.00
Van Briggle, Rose Bowl, Turquoise, Raised Leaf & Vine	25.00
Van Briggle, Soap Dish, Girl Holds Shell, Turquoise, Ming, AA Mark, 8 In.	50.00
Van Briggle, Vase, Art Deco, Turquoise, 7 1/2 In.	45.00
Van Briggle, Vase, Brown, Green, No.520, C.1925, 6 1/2 In.	35.00
Van Briggle, Vase, Bud, Turquoise, Ming, 9 In.	20.00
Van Briggle, Vase, Bulbous, Turquoise, 4 1/2 In.	8.00
Van Briggle, Vase, Carafe Shape, Turquoise, Blue, 10 1/2 In.	28.00
Van Briggle, Vase, Embossed Leaves, Turquoise, 6 In.	29.00
Van Briggle, Vase, Goose Girl, Rose, 8 1/2 In.	45.00
Van Briggle, Vase, Honey Gold, Signed, 7 X 3 1/4 In.	45.00
Van Briggle, Vase, Lorelei, Turquoise, 12 In.	125.00
Van Briggle, Vase, Maroon & Blue, Art Nouveau, Trumpet Shape	95.00
Van Briggle, Vase, Molded Crocus, Turquoise, Ming, 5 In.	20.00
Van Briggle, Vase, Pedestal, Brown Glaze, Iris, 16 In.	110.00
Van Briggle, Vase, Persian Rose, Molded Butterflies, 4 X 4 In.	24.00
Van Briggle, Vase, Plum, Dated 1918, 6 1/2 In.	60.00
Van Briggle, Vase, Plum, Dated 1920, 6 In.	28.00
Van Briggle, Vase, Red Flowers, 1915, 6 In.	75.00

Van Briggle, Vase, Relief Molded Design, Green, 1902, Signed, 6 3/4 In.	195.00
Van Briggle, Vase, Rose, C.1908-11, 8 X 2 1/4 In.	35.00
Van Briggle, Vase, Shell, Turquoise, Ming, 9 In.	15.00
Van Briggle, Vase, Tulip, Leaves, Deep Red, 7 1/2 In.	20.00
Vance Pottery, Pitcher, Hound Handled, C.1900, 11 1/2 In., Pair	795.00

Vasa Murrhina is the name of a glassware made by the Vasa Murrhina Art Glass Company of Sandwich, Massachusetts, about 1884. The glassware was transparent and was embedded with small pieces of colored glass and metallic flakes. Some of the pieces were cased. The same type of glass was made in England. Collectors often confuse Vasa Murrhina glass with aventurine, spatter, or spangle glass. There is much confusion about what actually was made by the Vasa Murrhina Factory.

Vasa Murrhina, see also Spangle Glass

Vasa Murrhina, Box, Powder, Green Enameled	42.50
Vasa Murrhina, Match Holder, Cased Silver, Black Amethyst Handle, 6 1/2 In.	35.00
Vasa Murrhina, Pitcher, Pink & Custard Splotches, Gold Mica	275.00
Vasa Murrhina, Rose Bowl, Cased Glass, Mica Flecks, Crimped Rim, 3 1/2 In.	165.00
Vasa Murrhina, Rose Bowl, Gold, White Lining, 3 1/2 In.Diameter	80.00
Vasa Murrhina, Tumbler, Yellow, Silver Flecks	32.00
Vasa Murrhina, Vase, Bud, Green, 6 In.	25.00
Vasa Murrhina, Vase, Cranberry, Beige Bubbles & Swirls, Footed, 10 In.	50.00
Vasa Murrhina, Vase, Double, Gourd Shape, Mica Flakes, Cased, 7 3/4 In.	80.00
Vasa Murrhina, Vase, Footed, Cranberry, Gold Flecks, Amber Rigaree, 10 In.	50.00
Vasa Murrhina, Vase, Green, Gold Dust, Flower Form Opening, Dimples, 12 In.	125.00
Vasa Murrhina, Vase, Pink, White & Maroon Spatter, Ruffled Edge, 5 1/2 In.	48.00
Vasa Murrhina, Vase, Red With Silver Flecks	42.50
Vasa Murrhina, Vase, Uncased, Gold Mica Flakes, Bulbous, 9 1/4 In.	95.00

Vasart is the signature used on a late type of art glass made by the Streathearn Glass Company of Scotland.

Vasart, Bowl, Increases Diameter To Top, Orange To Black, Signed, 7 X 3 In.	45.00
Vasart, Bowl, Large Handles, Pink To Green, Signed, 4 X 6 X 2 1/2 In.	45.00
Vasart, Bowl, Mottled Black & Orange, Signed, 3 1/2 X 7 1/2 In.Diam.	35.00
Vasart, Bowl, Mottled Pink To Green, 4 X 6 X 2 1/2 In.	45.00
Vasart, Bowl, Mottled White To Green, Under Plate, 4 1/2 In.Deep, Set Of 3	100.00
Vasart, Bowl, Semi-Footed, Orange To Black, 3 X 7 In.Diameter	45.00
Vasart, Dish, Console, Purple Swirl, 14 In.	265.00
Vasart, Glass, Blossom Shaped Bowl, Mottled Blue, 1 1/2 X 5 In.	24.00
Vasart, Vase, Cylindrical, Flaring Rim, Mottled Blue, 2 1/4 In.	20.00

Vaseline glass is a greenish yellow glassware resembling petroleum jelly. Some vaseline glass is still being made in old and new styles. Pressed glass of the 1870s was often made of vaseline-colored glass. The old glass was made with uranium, but the reproductions are being colored in a different way. See Pressed Glass for more information about patterns that were also made of vaseline-colored glass.

Vaseline Glass, Basket, Bride's, Miniature, Blown, Silver Frame, 7 In.	75.00
Vaseline Glass, Basket, Hobnail, 7 X 5 In.	21.00
Vaseline Glass, Berry Bowl, Diamond Spearhead, Opalescent, 9 1/2 In.	49.75
Vaseline Glass, Berry Bowl, Fluted Scrolls	85.00
Vaseline Glass, Berry Bowl, Footed, Dewey, 8 1/2 In.Diameter	25.00
Vaseline Glass, Berry Bowl, Opalescent, Ruffled, 3 1/2 X 9 1/8 In.Diameter	135.00
Vaseline Glass, Berry Set, Daisy & Button, 6 Square Berries	95.00
Vaseline Glass, Berry Set, Petticoat, 7 Pieces	175.00
Vaseline Glass, Berry Set, Scalloped Opalescent Flange, Fluted Scroll	167.50
Vaseline Glass, Berry Set, Wild Flower, Clear, 7 Piece	55.00
Vaseline Glass, Boat, Daisy & Button, 7 1/4 In.	38.00
Vaseline Glass, Bottle, Perfume, Diamond Cut, Silver Hinged Lid, 3 3/4 In.	145.00
Vaseline Glass, Bowl, Blue Opalescent, 4 In.	20.00
Vaseline Glass, Bowl, Footed, Argonaut, Opalescent, 8 In.	32.50
Vaseline Glass, Bowl, Fruit, Quilted Diamond, Footed, 9 X 4 In.	35.00
Vaseline Glass, Bowl, Pedestal, Argonaut, Water Design, 8 X 6 3/4 In.	45.00
Vaseline Glass, Bride's Bowl, Bubble Lattice, Stand	125.00
Vaseline Glass, Candleholders, Twisted Stem, 10 In., Pair	48.00
Vaseline Glass, Candlestick, Canary, 6-Sided Wafer Joint, 7 1/2 In., Pair	220.00

Vaseline Glass, Candlestick, 7 In., Pair	38.00
Vaseline Glass, Canoe, Daisy & Button, 12 In.	40.00
Vaseline Glass, Compote, Daisy & Button, Scalloped Top, 10 In.	65.00
Vaseline Glass, Compote, Daisy & Button, 9 3/4 Diameter	75.00
Vaseline Glass, Compote, Dolphin, 5 1/2 In.	25.00
Vaseline Glass, Compote, Open, Anderson, 9 In.	25.00
Vaseline Glass, Compote, Open, Daisy & Button With Crossbar, 8 In.	40.00
Vaseline Glass, Compote, Open, Daisy & Button, 6 3/8 In.	30.00
Vaseline Glass, Compote, Rolled Rim, Clear, 6 In.	12.50
Vaseline Glass, Compote, Twisted Stem, 7 X 7 In.Diameter, Pair	48.00
Vaseline Glass, Creamer, Alaska	30.00 To 75.00
Vaseline Glass, Creamer, Finecut & Panel	35.00
Vaseline Glass, Creamer, Fluted Scroll	65.00
Vaseline Glass, Creamer, Hobnail With Thumbprint	25.00
Vaseline Glass, Creamer, Jackson	70.00
Vaseline Glass, Creamer, Leaf Mold, Spatter Satin	65.00
Vaseline Glass, Creamer, Maple Leaf, Log Feet	45.00
Vaseline Glass, Creamer, Mitered Diamond	35.00
Vaseline Glass, Creamer, Oaken Bucket	25.00 To 35.00
Vaseline Glass, Creamer, Red Block	45.00
Vaseline Glass, Creamer, Reverse Torpedo	60.00
Vaseline Glass, Creamer, Wedding Band	35.00
Vaseline Glass, Creamer, 3 Panel	32.00
Vaseline Glass, Cruet, Beaumont, Optic, Original Stopper	150.00
Vaseline Glass, Cruet, Gold Band, Original Stopper	145.00
Vaseline Glass, Cup & Saucer, Basket Weave	35.00
Vaseline Glass, Cup, Currier & Ives	18.00
Vaseline Glass, Cup, Punch, Applied Handle	15.00
Vaseline Glass, Cup, Punch, Inverted Baby Thumbprint, Reed Handle	45.00
Vaseline Glass, Dish, Butter, Wreath & Shell	175.00
Vaseline Glass, Dish, Candy, Covered	14.00
Vaseline Glass, Dish, Candy, Pointed Lid, Etched, Gold Trim, 9 In.	23.00
Vaseline Glass, Dish, Candy, Silver Plate Holder, 3 Section	25.00
Vaseline Glass, Dish, Dove On Basket Weave Nest, McKee, 4 1/2 In.	125.00
Vaseline Glass, Epergne, Cased, Ivory, 3 Branch, Frilled Rigaree, 20 In.	199.00
Vaseline Glass, Epergne, Hanging Baskets & Canes, 3 Cornucopia, 20 In.	365.00
Vaseline Glass, Epergne, Ivory, Cased Glass, 3-Branch, Fluted Bowl, 20 In.	199.00
Vaseline Glass, Epergne, Rib & Flute, 9 In.	55.00
Vaseline Glass, Goblet, Fishscale	20.00
Vaseline Glass, Goblet, Three Panel	35.00
Vaseline Glass, Mug, Child's, Stork Pattern	34.00
Vaseline Glass, Mug, V Bar	24.00
Vaseline Glass, Nappy, Handled, Hobnail, Opalescent	25.00
Vaseline Glass, Pitcher, Basket Weave	37.50
Vaseline Glass, Pitcher, Free Blown, Melon-Ribbed Body, C.1820	190.00
Vaseline Glass, Pitcher, Milk, Maple Leaf	60.00
Vaseline Glass, Pitcher, Water, Button With Crossbars	65.00
Vaseline Glass, Pitcher, Water, Iowa, Pedestal Base	65.00
Vaseline Glass, Plate, Cake, Footed, 10 In.Diameter	25.00
Vaseline Glass, Plate, Octagon, 8 In.	5.00
Vaseline Glass, Plate, Silver Plate Casing, Basket Handle, Signed & Dated	48.00
Vaseline Glass, Reamer, Juice, Sunkist	22.50
Vaseline Glass, Rose Bowl, Seaweed, Fiery Opalescent, 8 Crimps, 5 In.	50.00
Vaseline Glass, Salt & Pepper, Opalescent Swirl, Christmas, Dated 1877	140.00
Vaseline Glass, Salt, Open, 3 Legged, Wreath & Shell, Opalescent	45.00
Vaseline Glass, Saltshaker, Vertical Ribbon, Opalescent	35.00
Vaseline Glass, Sauce, Alaska, Opalescent	37.00
Vaseline Glass, Sauce, Daisy & Button, Set Of 3	25.00
Vaseline Glass, Sauce, Opalescent, Everglades	45.00
Vaseline Glass, Sauce, Opalescent, Wreath & Shell	45.00
Vaseline Glass, Sauce, Swag & Bracket	24.00
Vaseline Glass, Shade, Lamp, Opalescent, Set Of 5	80.00
Vaseline Glass, Slipper, Daisy & Button, 1886, 7 1/4 In.	68.00
Vaseline Glass, Spooner, Alaska	65.00
Vaseline Glass, Spooner, Red Block	30.00
Vaseline Glass, Spooner, 3 Panel	26.00

Vaseline Glass, **Stand**, Gum, Clark Teaberry	45.00
Vaseline Glass, **Sugar & Creamer**, Cherries, Opalescent Overlay	60.00
Vaseline Glass, **Sugar & Creamer**, Pedestal, Heart & Diamond, Opalescent	75.00
Vaseline Glass, **Sugar Shaker**, Reverse Swirl	79.00
Vaseline Glass, **Sugar**, Red Block	58.00
Vaseline Glass, **Sugar**, Three Panel	44.00
Vaseline Glass, **Syrup**, Rope & Thumbprint	95.00
Vaseline Glass, **Syrup**, Spatter Cased With Clear	265.00
Vaseline Glass, **Table Set**, Maple Leaf, 4 Piece	195.00
Vaseline Glass, **Table Set**, Pressed Diamond, 4 Piece	185.00
Vaseline Glass, **Toothpick Holder**, Opalescent, Ribbed Spiral	55.00
Vaseline Glass, **Toothpick**, Flat Base, Picket	95.00
Vaseline Glass, **Toothpick**, High Hat	25.00
Vaseline Glass, **Tray**, Teaberry Gum	37.00
Vaseline Glass, **Tumbler**, Daisy & Button, Duncan, 3 1/4 In.	22.50
Vaseline Glass, **Tumbler**, Hobnail, Opalescent	19.00
Vaseline Glass, **Tumbler**, Leaf Mold, Frosted	59.00
Vaseline Glass, **Tumbler**, Wreath & Shell	47.50
Vaseline Glass, **Vase**, Automobile, Pressed Floral	30.00
Vaseline Glass, **Vase**, Bud, 11 In.	12.00
Vaseline Glass, **Vase**, Bud, 13 In.	15.00
Vaseline Glass, **Vase**, Gold Enameled Flowers, Ground Top, 7 1/2 In.	35.00
Vaseline Glass, **Vase**, Hobnail Opalescent, Fluted Top, 5 3/4 In.	55.00
Vaseline Glass, **Vase**, Jefferson Spool, Opalescent	23.00
Vaseline Glass, **Vase**, Swirl, 5 In.	37.50
Vaseline Glass, **Water Set**, Daisy & Fern, Opalescent, Pitcher & 4 Tumblers	300.00
Vaseline Glass, **Water Set**, Ribbed, Spiral, Pitcher, 3 Tumblers	160.00

Venetian glass has been made near Venice, Italy, from the thirteenth to the twentieth century. Thin colored glass with applied decorations is favored although many other types have been made.

Venetian Glass, **Candlestick**, Dolphin, Gold Flecks, 5 1/4 In.	55.00
Venetian Glass, **Candlestick**, Pink, Full Figure Of Dolphin, 5 X 5 In.	65.00
Venetian Glass, **Candlestick**, Red, Speckled With Gold, Hand Blown, 10 In., Pr.	30.00
Venetian Glass, **Chalice**, Footed, 2 Dolphin Handles, 7 X 6 In.	85.00
Venetian Glass, **Compote**, Gold Flecked Swan Base, Goldstone, Latticinio, 6 In.	60.00
Venetian Glass, **Figurine**, Doves, Gold Dust, 9 X 7 In.	149.00
Venetian Glass, **Sconce**, Wall, Frosted White, Applied Lion Heads, 3 Lights	325.00
Venetian Glass, **Vase**, Applied Flowers & Leaves, Pedestal Base, 9 1/2 In.	65.00
Venetian Glass, **Vase**, Enameled Flowers, Applied Glass Shells, Green, 11 In.	85.00

Verlys

Verlys glass was made in France after 1931. Verlys was also made in the United States. The glass is either blown or molded. The American glass is signed with a diamond-point-scratched name, but the French pieces are marked with a molded signature.

Verlys, **Ashtray**, Doves, Flower Border, Script Signed	25.00
Verlys, **Ashtray**, Frosted Birds & Top Border, 3 1/2 X 4 In.	35.00
Verlys, **Ashtray**, Rectangular, Acid Etched Design, 3 1/2 X 4 In.	38.00
Verlys, **Ashtray**, Swallow, Clear, Acid Finished Birds, Top Border, 4 3/4 In.	35.00
Verlys, **Bowl**, Birds & Bees, 11 1/2 In.	140.00
Verlys, **Bowl**, Birds, Goldfish, Satin Glass, 14 In.	60.00
Verlys, **Bowl**, Blue, Thistle, 3 Footed, Signed	85.00
Verlys, **Bowl**, Covered With Water Scene & Fowl, Signed, 13 1/2 In.	135.00
Verlys, **Bowl**, Cupid With Bow & Arrow, Hearts In Center, Signed, 5 3/4 In.	100.00
Verlys, **Bowl**, Dragonflies, Flower In Relief, 13 3/4 In., Diameter	100.00
Verlys, **Bowl**, Footed, Pinecone & Needles, Signed, 2 X 7 In.	45.00
Verlys, **Bowl**, Footed, Pinecone, Blue, Signed, 6 In.Diameter	35.00 To 95.00
Verlys, **Bowl**, Frosted Roses In Relief, Signed, 5 1/4 In.	30.00
Verlys, **Bowl**, Frosted Roses In Relief, 5 In.	32.00
Verlys, **Bowl**, Orchids In Relief, 14 In.Diameter	115.00
Verlys, **Bowl**, Script, Poppies, Signed, 13 1/2 In.	85.00
Verlys, **Bowl**, Tassels, Frosted, Signed, 11 3/4 In.	75.00
Verlys, **Bowl**, Wild Ducks, Directoire Blue, Raised Signature	150.00
Verlys, **Bowl**, 3 Dragonflies, Flowers, Shallow, Script Signature, 13 1/2 In.	110.00
Verlys, **Box**, Relief Butterflies On Top, Amber, Signed, 6 1/4 In.Diameter	275.00
Verlys, **Box**, Violet, Raised Butterflies, Covered, Round, Signed, 6 1/2 In.	95.00

Verlys, Charger, Orchid Design, Frosted & Clear, Signed, 14 In.Diameter	95.00
Verlys, Dish, Oval, Goose Perched On End, Signed, 4 X 5 1/2 In.Diameter	42.00
Verlys, Figurine, Elephant, Topaz, Pair	275.00
Verlys, Jar, Powder, Art Nouveau, Nude Draped Around Lid	65.00
Verlys, Plate, Pine Cone, Green Frosted, 9 In.	30.00
Verlys, Vase Half-Moon Shape, Satin Frosted, Signed, 6 X 2 1/2 In.Diameter	50.00
Verlys, Vase, Blue Frosted Thistle, Signed, 10 In.	155.00
Verlys, Vase, Fan-Shaped, Lovebirds, Crystal, 4 1/2 X 3 In.	35.00 To 65.00
Verlys, Vase, Les Eglantines, Signed, Camphor Finish, 7 1/2 In.	85.00
Verlys, Vase, Lovebirds, Fan-Shaped, Frosted Birds & Base, 6 1/2 In.	35.00
Verlys, Vase, Thistle Pattern, Signed, 8 1/2 In.	125.00
Verlys, Vase, Trapped Air Bubles & Teardrop, Brown To Russet, Signed, 11 In.	200.00
Verona, Rose Bowl, Pansies & Leaves, Crimped Top, 4 In.	150.00
Verona, Vase, Jug, Lily-Of-The-Valley, Raised Gold & Black, 1900s, 8 1/2 In.	200.00
Verona, Vase, Ribbed, Purple Iris, Green Leaves, Mt. Washington, 9 3/4 In.	150.00

*Verre de soie glass was first made by Frederick Carder at the Steuben
Glass Works from about 1905 to 1930. It is an iridescent glass of soft
white or very, very pale green. The name means glass of silk, and it does
resemble silk. Other factories have made verre de soie, and some of the
English examples were made of different colors. Verre de soie is an art
glass and is not related to the iridescent pressed white carnival glass
mistakenly called by its name.*

Verre De Soie, see also Steuben

Verre De Soie, Atomizer, Perfume, Black, Signed Devilbiss, Paper Label, 5 In.	55.00
Verre De Soie, Bowl, Finger, Underplate, Dorflinger, Honesdale	38.00
Verre De Soie, Bowl, Iridescent Panels, Green Satin Glass Leaves, 4 1/2 In.	130.00
Verre De Soie, Bowl, Openwork, Scalloped Edge, 5 In.	22.50
Verre De Soie, Candlestick, Rose Edges, 10 In., Pair	395.00
Verre De Soie, Compote, Engraved Pattern, Iridescent, Hawkes, 5 1/4 In.	225.00
Verre De Soie, Compote, Hawkes, Engraved Garlands, Footed, 7 In.Diameter	175.00
Verre De Soie, Compote, Stemmed, Engraved Floral, Signed Hawkes, 5 1/4 In.	225.00
Verre De Soie, Compote, Steuben, 7 1/2 In.Diameter	45.00
Verre De Soie, Jar, Jam, Tapering Conical Body, Cover, Pear Finial	70.00
Verre De Soie, Plate, Ground Pontil, 8 In.	25.00
Verre De Soie, Plate, Steuben, 7 1/2 In.	24.00
Verre De Soie, Shade, Lamp, 2 1/4 In.Neck, 4 3/4 In.Base	65.00
Verre De Soie, Underplate, 6 In.Diameter, 3 In.Depression	22.50
Verre De Soie, Vase, Art Nouveau Stylized Design, Enameled & Gilt	60.00
Verre De Soie, Vase, Black Ribbon Effect, Bulbous Base, Ruffled Top, 10 In.	95.00
Verre De Soie, Vase, Fan, Air Trap Flower Form, Steuben, 6 X 3 1/4 In.	225.00
Verre De Soie, Vase, Three Handled, Polished Pontil, 7 1/8 In.	100.00

*Vienna Art plates were round metal serving trays produced around the turn
of the century. The designs, copied from Royal Vienna porcelain plates,
usually featured a portrait of a lady encircled by a wide, ornate border.
Many were used as advertising or promotional items and were produced in
Coshocton, Ohio, by J. F. Meek's Tuscarora Advertising Co., and
H. D. Beach's Standard Advertising Co.*

Vienna Art, Plate, Busch Malt Nutrine, 1905	90.00
Vienna Art, Plate, Full Figure Lady, 10 In.	16.50
Vienna Art, Plate, Grecian Lady In Garden	16.00
Vienna Art, Plate, Majestic Hotel, Philadelphia	20.00
Vienna Art, Plate, Portrait Bust Of Lady, Dated 1905, 10 In.	18.00
Vienna Art, Plate, Portrait, February 21st., 1905, 10 In.	35.00
Vienna Art, Plate, Pretty Girl, Reverse, Mathe Brewing	40.00
Vienna Art, Plate, Red Border, Lilies, Full Figure Woman	45.00
Vienna Art, Plate, Western Coca-Cola, 1905, Pair	375.00
Vienna, see Beehive, Royal Vienna	

*Villeroy & Boch Pottery of Mettlach, Germany, was founded in 1841.
The firm made many types of pottery, including the famous Mettlach steins.*

Villeroy & Boch, see also Mettlach

Villeroy & Boch, Bowl, Punch, Underplate, Raised Leaves	85.00
Villeroy & Boch, Compote, Creamware, 9 1/2 X 6 In.	55.00
Villeroy & Boch, Lemonade Set, 6 Glasses, Tray & Pitcher, Fruit Design	195.00

Villeroy & Boch, Pitcher, Field Hockey Player, Brown, 5 In. 75.00
Villeroy & Boch, Pitcher, No.2733, Blue & Black, 16 In. 189.00
Villeroy & Boch, Plate, Napoleonic, Titled & Dated, 9 1/2 In., Set Of 8 .... 200.00
Villeroy & Boch, Plate, Ship Scene, Mettlach 55.00
Villeroy & Boch, Plate, 6 Sided, Raised Leaves, 8 1/2 In., Set Of 6 .... 75.00
Villeroy & Boch, Vase, Cherubs, 9 In. 95.00
Villeroy & Boch, Vase, Pierced Top & Handles, Silver Luster Trim, 10 In. 44.00
Villeroy & Boch, Vase, Silver Luster Grapes On Brown, 4 In. 35.00

VOLKMAR
Corona N.Y.   *Volkmar pottery was made by Charles Volkmar from 1879 to about 1911.*
             He was part of several firms including the Volkmar Ceramic Company,
             Volkmar and Cory, and Charles Volkmar and Son.

Volkmar, Lamp, Oil, Crown Pointware, 22 In. 85.00
Volkmar, Plaque, Defender 1895, 11 In. 270.00
Volkmar, Vase, Yellow, 4 3/4 X 4 3/4 In. 60.00

Volkstadt was a soft paste porcelain manufactory started in 1760 by
Georg Heinrich Macheleid at Volkstadt, Thuringia.
Volkstadt-Rudolstadt was a porcelain factory started at
Volkstadt-Roudolstadt by Beyer and Bock in 1890.

Volkstadt, Vase & Cover, Blue, Spiral Bands, Marked, 1800s, 12 1/2 In., Pair 400.00
Wagon, Bakery 2000.00
Wagon, Depot, 4 Seats 2500.00
Wagon, Milk, Pevey Dairy Co., Horse-Drawn 2600.00
Wagon, 3 Seat, Yellowstone Park, Horse-Drawn 1500.00
    Wallace Nutting, see Print, Nutting
Wallenburg, Teapot, Cover Attached By Chain, Porcelain, C.1820 .... 70.00
Wallpaper, Morris & Co., Acorn, C.1890, Framed, 46 X 27 In. 250.00
Wallpaper, Morris & Co., Woodblock, C.1890, Norwich, Framed, 46 X 27 In. 350.00
    Walt Disney, see Disneyana
    Walter, see A. Walter

Warwick china was made in Wheeling, West Virginia, in a pottery factory
founded in 1887.

Warwick, Beverage Set, Pitcher, 10 1/2 In., 6 Handled Mugs, Colored Fruit 365.00
Warwick, Beverage Set, 4 Handled Mugs, Molded Trim, Pitcher, 10 1/2 In. 350.00
Warwick, Bookends, Horse Head 12.00
Warwick, Bowl, Cream Soup, Underplate, White, Gold Band, Green Helmet Mark 17.95
Warwick, Chocolate Pot, Floral, Signed 65.00
Warwick, Chocolate Pot, Scalloped Base & Brushed Gold Top, Signed, 11 In. 65.00
Warwick, Chocolate Set, Chocolate Pot, 8 Cups & Saucers 225.00
Warwick, Chocolate Set, Flowers, Browntone, 7 Piece 175.00
Warwick, Cracker Barrel, Brown, Flowers, Brass Lid 65.00
Warwick, Dish, Compote Shape, 8 In. 35.00
Warwick, Ewer, Floral, 12 In. 45.00
Warwick, Jar, Tobacco, Portrait Of Woman 75.00
Warwick, Jardiniere, Browntones Poppy, 4 X 6 In. 38.00
Warwick, Jug, Monk Holding Mug, Gray, IOGA Mark 68.00
Warwick, Mug, Doe Wah Jak, Indian, Souvenir Of Stove Company 95.00
Warwick, Mug, Elk 55.00
Warwick, Mug, Fat Man In Top Hat, Drink In Hand, IOGA 35.00
Warwick, Mug, Handled, Fruit Cluster On Brown To Ocher, Marked 27.50
Warwick, Mug, Indian, Full Headdress, IOGA 38.00
Warwick, Mug, Indian, Long Black Hair, IOGA 38.00
Warwick, Mug, Man With Guitar, IOGA 35.00
Warwick, Mug, Medieval Man, 3 Bathing Maidens, Ioga 35.00
Warwick, Mug, Monk, Chocolate Background .... 40.00 To 55.00
Warwick, Mug, Monk, Helmet Mark 50.00
Warwick, Mug, Monk, Red Frock, Set Of 6 .... 150.00
Warwick, Pitcher, Bulbous, Handle, Hibiscus Design, Signed, 8 1/4 In. 60.00
Warwick, Pitcher, Cardinal, Red & Brown, 8 5/8 In. 125.00
Warwick, Pitcher, Lemonade, Poppy Decoration, IOGA Mark, 6 1/2 In. 65.00
Warwick, Pitcher, Monk Holding Mug Picture, IOGA Gray 68.00
Warwick, Platter, Double Handled, B-6 Mark, 11 1/2 In.Round 35.00
Warwick, Pot, Bean, Acorn Decoration, Double Handle, IOGA 95.00
Warwick, Tankard, Cardinal, 10 1/2 In. 125.00

Warwick, Tankard, Chocolate Background, 13 In.	150.00
Warwick, Tankard, Green, 13 In.	150.00
Warwick, Tankard, Monk, Chocolate Background, 12 In.	150.00
Warwick, Tankard, 3 Mugs, Dickens Characters, IOGA, 4 Pieces	275.00
Warwick, Teapot, Scenic	125.00
Warwick, Vase, Brown, Rose, Bulbous, 9 In.	33.00
Warwick, Vase, Chocolate Brown, Ruby Red, Poinsettias, 15 1/4 In.	90.00
Warwick, Vase, Floral, Ring Handles, 11 3/4 In.	55.00
Warwick, Vase, Portrait Of Lady, Scalloped Top, Brown, Signed, 11 In.	85.00
Warwick, Vase, Portrait, Brown, IOGA, 8 In.	55.00
Warwick, Vase, Roses On Two Sides, Small Neck, 9 In.	65.00
Warwick, Vase, Twig Handled, Gypsy Woman, 10 1/2 In.	110.00
Warwick, Vase, Victorian Lady, Pink Ground, Signed, 10 In.	110.00
Warwick, Vase, Woman, Cylinder, Twig Handles, 10 1/4 In.	125.00
Warwick, Vase, Woman's Portrait, Twig Handles, IOGA, 10 1/2 In	75.00 To 85.00
Warwick, Water Set, Capped Cardinal, Red, Pitcher, 6 Mugs	395.00
Warwick, Water Set, Dog Portraits, Tankard & 6 Mugs	325.00 To 495.00

Watch fobs were worn on watch chains. They were popular during Victorian times and after.

Watch Fob, Adds Life Power To All Makes Motor Cars, Embossed Bear	35.00
Watch Fob, Airplane	20.00
Watch Fob, Alaska Yukon Pacific Expo., 1909	12.00
Watch Fob, Allis Chalmers, Shape Of Crawler Tractor	10.00
Watch Fob, American Bantam Assoc., Embossed Bantam Chicken	24.00
Watch Fob, American Legion, San Antonio, 1928	12.00
Watch Fob, American Legion, 14K Gold	125.00
Watch Fob, American Legion, 40th Convention, 1958, Evansville, Ind.	25.00
Watch Fob, American Red Cross Service Pin, Porcelain	17.50
Watch Fob, Apsley Rubber Co., Dry Shod, Porcelain	35.00
Watch Fob, Arrowhead, Shaped Indian Chief, Lead	5.00
Watch Fob, Ash Grove White Lime Assoc., Best On Earth, Ribbon Type	36.50
Watch Fob, Associated Western Yale Clubs, 1915, Bulldog	27.50
Watch Fob, Aultman-Taylor Machinery	40.00
Watch Fob, Austin Western Roadgrader	10.00
Watch Fob, Beechnut	10.00
Watch Fob, Bloomington, Indiana, 1930	10.00
Watch Fob, Boy Scout	35.00
Watch Fob, Bucyrus Erie Crane	8.00
Watch Fob, Buick, Enamel & Gilt, C.1926	18.00
Watch Fob, Bull Durham, Chain, 14K Gold Plate, Shape Of Bull	55.00
Watch Fob, Bull Durham, Gold Plated	35.00
Watch Fob, Bulldog Cut-Out, Reverse, Avery Co., 1 1/2 In.	37.50
Watch Fob, Bulldog, Watch Eyes, Hollow Head	37.50
Watch Fob, Careful Club, Northern Pacific, Porcelain, Leather Strap	28.50
Watch Fob, Carnelian, 14K Gold	55.00
Watch Fob, Carset Jack Bits, Brass	12.00
Watch Fob, Carved Ivory Monkey, Moves Up & Down	35.00
Watch Fob, Case Plow Works, Racine, Wis., Hand & Arm Holding Plow Shear	47.50
Watch Fob, Catalina Island	20.00
Watch Fob, Chero Cola, Bathtub Girl	22.00
Watch Fob, Cherry Smash	75.00
Watch Fob, Chicago, 1917	15.00
Watch Fob, Cigar Cutter, Sterling	20.00
Watch Fob, Cincinnati Horse & Mule Shoe Co., Brass	48.00
Watch Fob, Cleveland	15.00
Watch Fob, Cleveland Rock Drill	17.50
Watch Fob, Cloverleaf Life & Casualty Co., Cloverleaf	29.50
Watch Fob, Coca-Cola, Bulldog, 1 1/2 X 1 In.	135.00
Watch Fob, Collie Dog's Head Embossed	9.00
Watch Fob, Columbian Exposition, Chicago	35.00
Watch Fob, Crown Shaped, Gold Filled	12.50
Watch Fob, Cyrus Hall McCormick, Centennial Of Reaper, 1831-1931	27.50
Watch Fob, Denver, Colorado, Embossed Kit Carson On Horse	12.50
Watch Fob, Derrick Equipment Co., California & Texas	32.00
Watch Fob, Diamond Ring, O.C.Zinn, Established 1869, Hastings, Nebraska	30.00

Watch Fob, Duhamel Saddles Best On Earth, Leather 25.00
Watch Fob, Eagle 9.00
Watch Fob, East Buffalo Brewing Co., Embossed Buffalo 32.50
Watch Fob, Elk Head 8.00
Watch Fob, Elk's Locket, Gold 35.00
Watch Fob, Elk's Tooth, Charm 25.00
Watch Fob, Engaged To Wait, 1905 .... 2.00
Watch Fob, Euclid, Brass 8.00
Watch Fob, Fiber, Button Type, Jesse James's Picture 19.50
Watch Fob, Firebird, Metal 14.00
Watch Fob, Gay-Ola Co., Memphis, Little Boy With Pop Bottle 32.50
Watch Fob, Gold Shield In Center, English Hallmarked, Sterling 25.00
Watch Fob, Goldsmith League Ball, Sterling 32.00
Watch Fob, Green River Whiskey, Old Man & Mule 25.00
Watch Fob, Gutta Percha & Rubber Mfg.Co., Reverse, Good Luck Swastika 26.50
Watch Fob, Hamilton Brown Shoes, I Am A H-B Booster 25.00
Watch Fob, Harley 2.50
Watch Fob, Harley Davidson Motor Cycles 3.00
Watch Fob, Hauck's Red Monogram Beer 50.00
Watch Fob, Heinz 57 Girl In White Cap .... 22.50 To 30.00
Watch Fob, Herschel Oil Tempered, Cycle Blade 25.00
Watch Fob, I.O.O.F. 15.00
Watch Fob, Inauguration Of Taft & Sherman, March 4, 1909, Embossed Metal 65.00
Watch Fob, Indian On Arrowhead 8.00
Watch Fob, Ingersoll Rand 30.00
Watch Fob, Inspector, U.S. Revenue, Port Of New York 50.00
Watch Fob, Int'l.Brotherhood Of Blacksmiths & Helpers, Gold Filled 25.00
Watch Fob, International Harvester Co., Equipment Listed, Two Worlds 40.00
Watch Fob, International Stereotypers & Electrotypers, 1928 .... 27.50
Watch Fob, Iowa Dairy Association, 1911 .... 10.00
Watch Fob, Iowa Traveling Men's Assoc., Red, Blue, Slides Apart 10.00
Watch Fob, Jamestown Tercentennial Expo., 3 Segments 75.00
Watch Fob, John Deere, Leather, Reverse, Quality Farm Equipment 35.00
Watch Fob, John Deere, Mother-Of-Pearl, Gold 50.00
Watch Fob, John Deere, Mother-Of-Pearl, Silver, On Card Of Iowa Button Co. 55.00
Watch Fob, John Deere, Oxen One Side, Covered Wagon Other, Brass 47.50
Watch Fob, Joy Rock Drills 14.00
Watch Fob, Kellogg's Toasted Corn Flakes 29.50
Watch Fob, King Tut, Compass Embedded 20.00
Watch Fob, Knights Pythias, 1914 .... 10.00
Watch Fob, Lauson Gasoline Engines, Viking Holding Engine 20.00
Watch Fob, Liberty Lady, Embossed, Dated 929 .... 12.50
Watch Fob, Lynchburg Plow Works, Shape Of Plow, Red Enamel 18.00
Watch Fob, Mansfield Ohio Machinery 12.00
Watch Fob, Massachusetts Protective Assn., Metal 7.50
Watch Fob, Master Laminated Padlock, Milwaukee 60.00
Watch Fob, Memphis Furniture Manufacturing Company, Triangular 20.00
Watch Fob, Mickey Mouse 75.00
Watch Fob, Monarch Stoves, 1896 .... 5.00
Watch Fob, Moose Head, M In Medallion, Gold Mesh Star 25.00
Watch Fob, Moose Lodge 12.00
Watch Fob, Morgan Wright Tires 12.00
Watch Fob, National Letter Carriers Association, Set Of 7 .... 40.00
Watch Fob, National Sheriffs' Assoc., 1910, Springfield, Illinois 30.00
Watch Fob, National Stove & Range 25.00
Watch Fob, Nebraska Clothing Co., Omaha, Lion In Wreath, Celluloid 32.50
Watch Fob, Newark, Scenes Of Harbor 10.00
Watch Fob, Odd Fellows 17.50
Watch Fob, Old Reliable Coffee, Brass 40.00
Watch Fob, Our Next President William Howard Taft, Picture 18.50
Watch Fob, Pearl, Deer Jumping Over Plow 10.50
Watch Fob, Pennant Auto Oil, Auto On Top Serves As Strap 42.00
Watch Fob, Pepsi-Cola, New Bern, N.C., Hallmarked 47.50
Watch Fob, Perforated Pattern, Gold Overlaid Shield Each Side, Hallmarked 25.00
Watch Fob, Pharmaceutical Assn., Iowa City, Iowa, June 1916 .... 15.00
Watch Fob, Pontiac Chief Of The Sixes, Chain 20.00

Watch Fob, R.B.Rice Sausage Company, Cutout Silver Pit	36.50
Watch Fob, Red Diamond Overalls & Shirts, Union Made	30.00
Watch Fob, Reo	42.00
Watch Fob, Rochester Distilling	12.00
Watch Fob, Rock Island Railroad	35.00
Watch Fob, San Francisco Panama Pacific Expo., 1915, Brass & Porcelain	32.50
Watch Fob, San Francisco World's Fair, Brass	17.00
Watch Fob, Shape Of Hand Operated Adding Machine, Dalton Club, Brass	25.00
Watch Fob, Shape Of Wheel, Southwest Water Works, Assoc., Round	22.50
Watch Fob, Shield Shaped, Gold Filled	4.00
Watch Fob, Statue Of Liberty	12.50
Watch Fob, Sterling Clip, Grosgrain Ribbon, Chain	12.50
Watch Fob, Stirrup, Pigskin Strap, England	12.50
Watch Fob, Strap, Beaded, White Ground, 1 1/2 X 6 In.	9.00
Watch Fob, Swastika, Gold Filled	30.00
Watch Fob, Tiger Claw In Silver Filigree Mounting	28.00
Watch Fob, Trojan Dirt Mover	12.50
Watch Fob, Union Central Life, Ames	15.00
Watch Fob, University Of Michigan, 1837, Mesh	25.00
Watch Fob, Washburn Crosby Flour	24.50
Watch Fob, Western Electric Power, Power Generator	30.00
Watch Fob, Wings Over The Pole, Admiral Byrd, 2 Penguins, Tri-Motored Plant	60.00
Watch Fob, Witte Gasoline Engines	37.50
Watch Fob, Woodrow Wilson, Mirror Back	78.00
Watch Fob, Woodrow Wilson, Pen Is Mightier Than The Sword, Copper	8.50
Watch Fob, World Globe, Via Panama, Embossed, 1911, Copper	32.50
Watch Fob, Yellowstone Park, Stag With Stag's Head In Brass Ring	18.00
Watch Fob, 1910 Penny	12.00
Watch Fob, 1933 Century Of Progress, Porcelain	30.00
Watch, American Watch Co., S18, Key Wind, C.1875, Silverine Case	65.00
Watch, B.W.Raymond, Open Face, Railroad, 12 Size, Gold Filled	165.00
Watch, Babe Ruth	115.00
Watch, Ball, Railroad, Official Standard, Open Face, 16 Size	200.00
Watch, Bruin, 14K Gold, Gold Chain & 2 Blade Pen Knife, 17 Jewel	200.00
Watch, Cabinet, Watchmaker's, 20 Draw, Brass Hardware, 31 X 17 X 18 3/4 In.	250.00
Watch, Camerea Kuss & Co., London, Key Wind, Coin Silver, Porcelain Face	140.00
Watch, Chain, Gold & Woven Hair, Engraved Mounts, Set Of 3, 19th Century	90.00
Watch, Chain, 3/4 In.Gold Snap Shot Holder, Gold	39.00
Watch, Charlie, Starkist Tuna	30.00
Watch, Columbus, 16 Jewel, Railroad King	225.00
Watch, Commemorative, Dwight D.Eisenhower, Original Box	150.00
Watch, Commemorative, Franklin D.Roosevelt	150.00
Watch, Commemorative, John & Robert Kennedy	150.00
Watch, Dan Patch, Stop, 17 Jewel, Gold	1800.00
Watch, Derber Hampden, Ladhs, 15 Jewel, Chain, Slide, 2 Sapphires, 50 In.	200.00
Watch, Dueben, Hunting, 2 Ox.Gold, Dated 1893, 14K Gold	330.00
Watch, Elgin, Father Time Railroad, 18K Gold Filled Case, F.O.E.	195.00
Watch, Elgin, Father Time, Railroad Case	125.00
Watch, Elgin, Hunting Case, Gold Hands, O Size, 14K Gold	235.00
Watch, Elgin, Hunting Case, Porcelain Face, Gold Plated	52.00
Watch, Elgin, Hunting Case, Solid 14K Gold, 15 Jewel, Scroll Work	595.00
Watch, Elgin, Hunting Case, 6 Size, 14K Gold	265.00
Watch, Elgin, Key Wind, C.1885, Coin Silver, Size 18	60.00
Watch, Elgin, Key Wind, Railroad Grade 62, Yellow Gold Filled	140.00
Watch, Elgin, Lady's, 14K Gold Case, Rural Setting	275.00
Watch, Elgin, Locomotive Case, Lever Set, Silveroid Case, C.1890s	32.00
Watch, Elgin, Man's, Hunter, Gold Plate	125.00
Watch, Elgin, Multicolor Gold, Engine Turned, 1 3/4 In.Diameter	200.00
Watch, Elgin, Open Face, Yellow Gold Filled	115.00
Watch, Elgin, Open Face, 11 Jewel, Gold Engine Inlaid In Silver Case, 1904	95.00
Watch, Elgin, Open Face, 18 Size, White Metal	75.00
Watch, Elgin, Pocket, Chain, Knife & Masonic Medal, Gold Plated	85.00
Watch, Elgin, Pocket, Coin Silver Hunter Case, Lever Set	60.00
Watch, Elgin, Pocket, Coin Silver, 15 Jewels	55.00
Watch, Elgin, Pocket, Masonic, 17 Jewel	75.00
Watch, Elgin, Pocket, 18S, Doubleback, C.1890	45.00

Watch, Elgin, Railroad, Grade 280, Gold Center Wheel, Lever Set	125.00
Watch, Elgin, Railroad, Open Face, Father Time, Gold Filled	145.00
Watch, Elgin, Railroad, 7 Jewel, Size 18, Keywind, Silveroid Open Face Case	45.00
Watch, Elgin, Scrolled, Pop Open Face, Dated 1892, Gold	90.00
Watch, Elgin, Silverine, Open Face, Key Wind, 18 Size	75.00
Watch, Elgin, Size 0, Gold Filled Hunter Case, Scene On Back	90.00
Watch, Elgin, Steam Locomotive On Back Of Case, 1904	80.00
Watch, Elgin, 11 Jewel, Silver Hunting Case	115.00
Watch, Elgin, 15 Jewel, Gold Case, 1880s	55.00
Watch, Elgin, 18s, 15 Jewel, Double Sunk Dial	160.00
Watch, Elgin, 7 Jewel, Hunting, Yellow Gold Fill	130.00
Watch, Elgin, 7 Jewel, Silveroid, Train On Back	70.00
Watch, Exactus, Wrist, Ladies, 17 Jewel, 18K Gold Mesh Band	95.00
Watch, French, Lady's, Gold & Enamel, Open Face, Chatelaine, Paris, C.1780	1300.00
Watch, Fusee Movement, Keywind, Hunting Case, Coin Silver	90.00
Watch, Hamilton, Aircraft Navigational, Walnut Box, World War II	250.00
Watch, Hamilton, Model 956	69.00
Watch, Hamilton, Montgomery Dial, Railroad, Open Face, Gold Filled Case	215.00
Watch, Hamilton, Open Face, Railroad, 16 Size, Gold Filled	155.00
Watch, Hamilton, Open Face, 14K Gold	175.00
Watch, Hamilton, Pocket, Masonic	85.00
Watch, Hamilton, Railroad Case With Bar Over Crown, 21 Jewel	150.00
Watch, Hamilton, Railroad, Grade 972, Yellow Gold	90.00
Watch, Hamilton, Railroad, Pocket, 23 Jewels, 20 Year Case	145.00
Watch, Hamilton, Railroad, Size 16, 21 Jewel, Gold Filled Case, Engraved	95.00
Watch, Hamilton, Railroad, 16 Size, Open Face, 21 Jewel	175.00
Watch, Hamilton, Railroad, 21 Jewel, Model 999-B, Stainless Steel Case	135.00
Watch, Hamilton, Railroad, 6 Position, 10K Gold, Size 16	275.00
Watch, Hamilton, Railroad, 992, 14K Gold Filled Case, 5 Position, Size 16	195.00
Watch, Hamilton, Size 16, 17 Jewel, Signed Time King, Railroad Dial	75.00
Watch, Hamilton, Size 16, 21 Jewel, Bridge Model Pendent Set	200.00
Watch, Hamilton, U.S.Army, 22 Jewel, 6 Position, Sweep 2nd Hand	135.00
Watch, Hamilton, 14K Gold, White, Presentation Grade, 19 Jewel	225.00
Watch, Hamilton, 992-B, Electric Railway Special, 16 Size, White Metal	165.00
Watch, Hampden, Lady's, Pendant, Gold Filled, Hunter Case	125.00
Watch, Hampden, Pocket, Key Wind, Nickeled Silver, Hunting Case	50.00
Watch, Hampden, Pocket, 18s, New Railway	110.00
Watch, Hampden, Railroad, Open Face, Gold Filled Case, Dated 1889, 5 Position	185.00
Watch, Hampden, Silver Cased, Lever Set, Swing Out, Pocket	60.00
Watch, Hampden, 17 Jewel, William McKinley Model, Gold Plated	60.00
Watch, Hebdomas, 8 Day, Porcelain Open Face, Silveroid Case	265.00
Watch, Holder, Enamel Over Brass, Windmill, Pond, Trees & Birds	45.00
Watch, Howard, Key Wind & Set, Size 18, Dated 1860, Silver Hunting Case	850.00
Watch, Howard, No.700658, 4 Color Gold, Open Face, C.1900, 2 1/8 In.	1350.00
Watch, Howard, Open Face, White Case, 17 Jewel	125.00
Watch, Howard, Pocket, 21 Jewel, 14K Yellow Gold, Mahogany Box, Papers	550.00
Watch, Howard, Size 16, 21 Jewel, Open Case, 14K Gold	175.00
Watch, Howard, Size 18, Hunting Case, 14K Gold	850.00
Watch, Howard, Swingout 17 Jewel Movement, C.1912, 14K Gold	160.00
Watch, Howard, 21 Jewel, Chronometer, Howard Case	265.00
Watch, Humpty Dumpty	45.00
Watch, Illinois, Bunn Special, White Gold Fill, Railroad Case	250.00
Watch, Illinois, Bunn Special, 60 Hour, 21 Jewel, 10K Gold Filled	285.00
Watch, Illinois, Open Face, Octagonal, 12 Size, 14K White Gold	115.00
Watch, Illinois, Pocket, 17 Jewel, Model 167	45.00
Watch, Illinois, Railroad, 17 Jewel, Gold Damascened Plates, Gold Filled	60.00
Watch, Illinois, Railroad, 21 Jewel, 60 Hour Bunn Special, Double Sunk Dial	175.00
Watch, Illinois, 7 Jewel, Gold Hunting Case	155.00
Watch, Ingersoll Ltd., English, Festival Of Britain, 1951	95.00
Watch, Ingersoll, Chicago World's Fair, With Fob	175.00
Watch, Ingersoll, Dizzy Dean, 1933	175.00
Watch, Li'l Abner, Animated, Original Box	125.00
Watch, Lincoln, Open Case, Size 18, 14K White Gold, Advertising	250.00
Watch, M.J.Tobias, Liverpool Hunter Cased, Gold	1000.00
Watch, Manelli, Ivory, Open Face, Florence, Mother-Of-Pearl Dial, C.1790	5600.00
Watch, Patek Philippe, Size 16, 21 Jewel, 14K Gold, Open Face	650.00

Watch, Patek Philippe, 18 Jewels, Double-Sunk Dial, 18K Gold Hands & Dial	475.00
Watch, Planters Peanuts, Calendar	20.00
Watch, Plymouth, 15 Jewel, Size 0, Blank Shield & Scene On Back	85.00
Watch, Pocket, Elgin, Hunting Case, Key Wind, Silver Plate, 18 Size	95.00
Watch, Pocket, Elgin, 7 Jewel, Engraved Houses & Trees, 14K Yellow Gold	500.00
Watch, Pocket, Explorer's Sun Watch, Compass & Sundial, Brass	10.00
Watch, Pocket, Fusee Movement, Chain Operated, Key Wind, Roman Numerals	90.00
Watch, Pocket, Graff Zeppelin	110.00
Watch, Pocket, Kay's Keyless Challenge, Silver, Hallmarked	70.00
Watch, Pocket, Poll Parrot Shoes, For Boys & Girls	75.00
Watch, Pocket, Waltham, Silver Dial, Gold Arabic Numbers, 14K Gold Case	150.00
Watch, Rock Drill, International Aero Congress 1921	15.00
Watch, Rockford, Silveroid, Multi-Colored Dial, No.2, 18-15	85.00
Watch, Rockford, Winnebago, No.1, 16-17, Yellow Gold	165.00
Watch, Rockford, Wolf's Tooth Winding Movement, Kw-Sw-Ls-Ks	185.00
Watch, Rolex, Open Face, 17 Rubies, 14K Gold Chain	300.00
Watch, Sea Captain's, Open Face, Silver Case, Time Zones, Key Wind	325.00
Watch, Seiko, Jamn's, Automatic Day, Date	45.00
Watch, Seth Thomas, Gold Filled Hunter Case, Engraved, Porcelain Dial	110.00
Watch, Seth Thomas, Mantel, Lancet Case, Silver Dial, Westminster Chimes	150.00
Watch, Seth Thomas, Size 18, Railroad Grade 382, Silver Swing Case	125.00
Watch, Smokey Bear, Original Box	50.00
Watch, Snoopy, Original Box	25.00
Watch, South Bend, Open Face, Railroad, 16 Size, Gold Filled	155.00
Watch, South Bend, Railroad, 18 Lever Set, 15 Jewel, Gold Filled Case	45.00
Watch, Spiro Agnew	250.00
Watch, Swiss, Fleurier, Silver, Enamel, Open Face, Oriental Market, C.1830	3000.00
Watch, Swiss, Gold, Open Face, Musical, Erotic Automaton Scene, C.1820	4750.00
Watch, Swiss, Lady's, Round Case, Solid 14K Gold, Hunting Case	225.00
Watch, Swiss, 1/4 Hour Repeater, Slide Activated Enamel Deal	500.00
Watch, Tiffany & Co., Lady's, Open Face, 17 Jewel, Diamond Fleur-De-Lis	600.00
Watch, Tobias, Pocket, Key Wind, Coin Silver Case	100.00
Watch, U.S. Watch Co., 18s, Dueber Silverine Case, No.100875	75.00
Watch, Vanguard, Open Face, Yellow Gold Filled	110.00
Watch, W.C.Fields	45.00
Watch, Waltham, Close Case, 7 Jewel, Size 8, 14K Gold	325.00
Watch, Waltham, Coin Silver, Case, Closed Face, Mo.4230, 1 1/2 In.Diameter	85.00
Watch, Waltham, 18s, Key Wind, C.1883, Dueber, Coin Silver Case	65.00
Watch, Waltham, 18s, Sterling Silver Case, 24 Hour Dial, C.1899	60.00
Watch, Waltham, 18s, 17 Jewel, Yellow Gold Filled	125.00
Watch, Waltham, 11 Jewel, Gold Filled Hunter Case, Size 0, Scene On Back	95.00
Watch, Waltham, Engraved Locomotive On Back, Coin Silver, Signed	125.00
Watch, Waltham, Hunting Case, 18s, 13 Jewel, Engraved Deer, Gold Filled	95.00
Watch, Waltham, Indicator, Hairspring, 10K Gold Filled, Railroad Case	385.00
Watch, Waltham, Key Wind & Set From Back, Silver	175.00
Watch, Waltham, Lady's, Art Deco, 17 Jewel, 14K Gold	150.00
Watch, Waltham, Lady's, Hunting Case, Second Hand, To Elizabeth	145.00
Watch, Waltham, Lapel, Gold Filled Open Face, Original Box, 1 1/4 In.Diam.	60.00
Watch, Waltham, Masonic, Symbols On Dial For Numbers, 14K Gold	145.00
Watch, Waltham, Maximus, Open Face, 14K Gold	400.00
Watch, Waltham, Open Face, Engraved Movement, Deuber Sterling	95.00
Watch, Waltham, Open Face, Hercules Powder Company, 1917, Gold	250.00
Watch, Waltham, Pocket, Keywind, Beveled, Hair Braid	200.00
Watch, Waltham, Pocket, Model 645, Railroad	115.00
Watch, Waltham, Pocket, 7 Jewel, Solid 14K Gold Hunting Case	300.00
Watch, Waltham, Railroad, Size 16 Case, Porcelain Dial, Arabic Numbers	90.00
Watch, Waltham, Railroad, Vanguard, Yellow Gold Filled Case	145.00
Watch, Waltham, Railroad, 21 Jewel, White Metal Case, Locomotive, 645 Size	85.00
Watch, Waltham, Railroad, 7 Jewel, Size 18, Keywind, Silveroid Open Face	45.00
Watch, Waltham, Size 1819 Jewel, Cresent Street, Yellow Gold	75.00
Watch, Waltham, 21 Jewel, Up & Down Indicator	385.00
Watch, Walthma, LeHigh Valley, A.W.W. Co., 17 Jewel	125.00
Watchholder, Grandfather Clock, W.E.Brown, Nantucket, Mass.1894, 14 In.	72.00

*Waterford type glass resembles the famous glass made in the Waterford
Glass Works in Ireland. It is a clear glass that was often cut for*

decoration. Modern glass is still being made in Waterford, Ireland.

Waterford, Bowl, 16 Point Star, Star Overlay On Bottom, 2 1/4 X 10 In.Diam.	65.00
Waterford, Compote, Covered, Mushroom Top, Pokals, Georgian, 12 1/2 In., Pair	1500.00
Waterford, Decanter, Vertical Flutes & Diamond Band, Mushroom Stopper	85.00
Waterford, Decanter, 9 1/2 In., Pair	350.00
Waterford, Glass, Irish Coffee, Shamrock In Stem, Label	66.00
Waterford, Jar, Lid, Cut, Signed, 7 X 5 In.Diameter	145.00
Waterford, Salt, Boat Shaped, Pedestal, Diamond Cut, Rayed Base	27.50
Waterford, Shade, Crystal, 4 X 6 1/2 In.Diameter	55.00
Waterford, Toothpick, Cut Glass	22.50
Waterford, Vase, Fluted Rim, 14 In.	300.00
Waterford, Whiskey	15.00

Wave Crest glass is a white glassware manufactured by the Pairpoint Manufacturing Company of New Bedford, Massachusetts, and some French factories. It was then decorated by the C.F.Monroe Company of Meriden, Connecticut. The glass was painted in pastel colors and decorated with flowers. The name Wave Crest was used after 1898.

Wave Crest, Ashtray, White & Green, Metal Rim, Wavy Sides, Signed, 3 In.Diam.	120.00
Wave Crest, Biscuit Jar, Embossed, Floral	145.00
Wave Crest, Biscuit Jar, Hand-Painted Flowers, Silver Plated Cover & Bail	200.00
Wave Crest, Biscuit Jar, Wild Roses, Beige, White Ground, Signed, 7 In.	250.00
Wave Crest, Bottle, Cologne, Blue Flowers, Black Mark	55.00
Wave Crest, Box, Allover Tufted, Satin Finish, Original Gold Satin Lining	160.00
Wave Crest, Box, Blown-Out Florals & Scrolls, Black Mark, 5 X 4 In.	365.00
Wave Crest, Box, Blown-Out Shell Pattern, Blue, Signed, 7 1/2 In.	500.00
Wave Crest, Box, Blown-Out Shell, Yellow, Orange, Brown, Green Flowers, 7 In.	120.00
Wave Crest, Box, Blue Forget-Me-Nots, Puffy, Hinged Covered, Red Mark, 3 In.	150.00
Wave Crest, Box, Blue, Zinnia Cover, Signed, 4 1/2 In.	295.00
Wave Crest, Box, Boat Scene On Cover, Molded Swirls, Signed, 4 In.Diameter	200.00
Wave Crest, Box, Brass Ormolu All Over, Signed, 7 In.Square	550.00
Wave Crest, Box, Collar & Cuff ....*Illus*	1000.00
Wave Crest, Box, Collars & Cuffs, Signed	450.00
Wave Crest, Box, Covered, Bishop's Hat Mold, Footed, Signed, 4 X 4 In.	245.00
Wave Crest, Box, Covered, Hinged, Blue Flowers, 5 X 8 In.	850.00
Wave Crest, Box, Covered, Scenic Design, Signed, 3 1/2 X 2 1/2 In.	150.00
Wave Crest, Box, Covered, Shell Design Swirl, 3 In.Diameter	170.00
Wave Crest, Box, Covered, Shell Swirls, Pink Flowers, Signed, 3 In.Diameter	165.00
Wave Crest, Box, Covered, Square, Pink Blossoms, 3 1/4 In.	175.00
Wave Crest, Box, Creamy, Flowers, Signed, 26 In.	650.00
Wave Crest, Box, Footed, Hinged, Blown-Out Square Shape, 6 1/2 X 7 In.	650.00
Wave Crest, Box, Footed, Mirror Top, 8 In.Diameter	165.00
Wave Crest, Box, Handkerchief, White, Puffy, Signed, 8 1/2 In.Square	550.00
Wave Crest, Box, Handles, Yellow & Brown Flowers, 3 1/2 In.	60.00
Wave Crest, Box, Hinged Cover, Blue, Embossed Scrolls On Top, Marked, 3 In.	260.00
Wave Crest, Box, Hinged, Blue & White Flowers On Lid, 4 1/2 In.	160.00
Wave Crest, Box, Hinged, Blue Base, Enameling On Top, Swirls, 4 5/8 X 3 In.	140.00
Wave Crest, Box, Hinged, Hand-Painted Blue Daisies, Cover, 5 In.	122.00
Wave Crest, Box, Hinged, Swirled, Red Banner Mark, 3 1/2 In.	189.00
Wave Crest, Box, Jewel, Floral, Beads, Hinged Lid, 3 In.	119.00
Wave Crest, Box, Jewelry, Blue Flowers, 5 1/2 In.	160.00
Wave Crest, Box, Jewelry, Puffy, 6 In.	300.00
Wave Crest, Box, Large ....*Illus*	2200.00
Wave Crest, Box, Lattice & Swags, Blue, Decorated In Medallions, 7 1/2 In.	475.00
Wave Crest, Box, Lid, Brass Feet, Medallions, Scrolls, Banner Sign, 4 X 4 In.	220.00
Wave Crest, Box, Lid, Pink Ground, Enameled Flowers, Hat Shape, 4 In.Square	245.00
Wave Crest, Box, Open, Beige & Yellow Flowers, 3 1/4 In.	90.00
Wave Crest, Box, Open, Silver Rim, Black Block Signature, 5 1/2 X 3 1/2 In.	110.00
Wave Crest, Box, Orange & White Enamel Flowers, 3 X 3 In.	115.00
Wave Crest, Box, Pin, Blue, Red Banner Mark, 4 1/2 In.	95.00
Wave Crest, Box, Powder, Blue & White Floral, Hinged, 4 1/2 In.	160.00
Wave Crest, Box, Powder, Opalescent, Boy & Girl, Signed, 3 In.Diameter	200.00
Wave Crest, Box, Powder, Pink Rose On Lid, 3 1/4 X 4 1/2 In.	185.00
Wave Crest, Box, Rose & Blue, Original Lining, 7 1/2 In.	395.00
Wave Crest, Box, Shell Swirls, Pink Posies, Round, Covered, Signed, 3 In.	165.00

Wave Crest, Box, Swirl Pattern, Green Ground, Enameled Flowers, 3 In.Square	95.00
Wave Crest, Box, Trinket, Diamond Shaped Base, Blown-Out Lid, 3 X 4 1/2 In.	200.00
Wave Crest, Box, Trinket, Flowers, Blue, Round, Signed, 7 1/2 X 4 In.	395.00
Wave Crest, Box, Trinket, Hinged Lid, Keyhole, Signed, 5 X 4 In.	295.00
Wave Crest, Box, Trinket, Notched Corners, Keyhole, Signed, 4 X 5 In.	295.00
Wave Crest, Box, Trinket, Open, Ormolu Handles, Signed, 5 X 3 1/2 In.	139.00
Wave Crest, Box, Trinket, Open, Pink, Red Banner Mark, 3 In.Diameter	89.00
Wave Crest, Box, Trinket, Shell Design, Enameled Flowers, 4 X 7 1/2 In.	250.00
Wave Crest, Box, Violets, Pink, White, Brass Feet & Trim, Lid, Round, Signed	265.00
Wave Crest, Compote, Ormolu Footed, Flowers & Foliage, 3 1/4 In.	110.00
Wave Crest, Compote, Ormolu Footed, Flowers & Foliage, 3 3/4 In.	110.00
Wave Crest, Cookie Jar, Handles, Wild Rose Design, Signed	125.00
Wave Crest, Cracker Jar, Cream White, Gold & Brown In Florals	225.00
Wave Crest, Cracker Jar, Daisies, Green Leaves, Silver Lid & Bail	175.00
Wave Crest, Cracker Jar, Flowers On Front & Side, Square, 6 In.	275.00
Wave Crest, Cracker Jar, Pink Daisies, Green Leaves	135.00
Wave Crest, Cracker Jar, Pink Roses, Blue, White	175.00
Wave Crest, Cracker Jar, Puffy Panels, Silver Plate Bail & Lid, 8 1/2 In.	175.00
Wave Crest, Cracker Jar, Raised Trim, Silver Plate Cover, 8 1/2 X 16 In.	135.00
Wave Crest, Cracker Jar, Scroll Outlining Panel, Enameled Flowers, Signed	165.00
Wave Crest, Dish, Dresser, Gold Ormolu Rim, Banner Mark, 3 1/4 In.Diameter	65.00
Wave Crest, Dish, Dresser, Ormolu Rim, Hand-Painted Flowers, Marked	65.00
Wave Crest, Dish, Pin, Brass Collar, 3 In.Square	45.00
Wave Crest, Fernery, Blue, Scrolled Panels, Apple Blossom, Signed, 7 In.	210.00
Wave Crest, Fernery, Hand-Painted, Red Banner Mark, 8 In.Diameter	239.00
Wave Crest, Fernery, Ormolu Collar & Base, Marked, 5 1/2 X 8 1/2 In.Diam.	425.00
Wave Crest, Fernery, Ormolu Collar, Green & Pink Flowers, Black Mark, 7 In.	225.00
Wave Crest, Fernery, Red Banner, Blown-Out, Brass Collar, Signed	275.00
Wave Crest, Hair Receiver, Swirled, Brass Collar, Signed, 6 In.Diameter	210.00
Wave Crest, Holder, Cigarette, Brass Base & Insert	65.00
Wave Crest, Jar, Ormolu Rim, Blue To White, Pennant & Cfm Co., 3 1/4 In.	85.00
Wave Crest, Jar, Ormolu Rim, Pennant & CFM Co., 4 1/2 In.Diameter	110.00
Wave Crest, Jar, Pink Floral, Blue To White, Brass Rim, Signed, 3 1/4 In.	90.00
Wave Crest, Jar, Pink Floral, Blue To White, Brass Rim, Signed, 4 1/2 In.	120.00
Wave Crest, Jar, Pomade, Covered, Enameled Flowers, Red Banner Mark	135.00
Wave Crest, Jardiniere, Flowers On White, 8 X 9 In.	550.00
Wave Crest, Letter Holder, Enamel Pink Floral, Brass Rim, 3 X 5 1/2 X 4 In.	215.00
Wave Crest, Planter, Blue, Flowers, Square, 7 X 7 X 3 1/2 In.	155.00
Wave Crest, Rose Bowl, Floral Scrolls, Flower Sprays, Blown, Signed, 2 1/2 In.	98.00
Wave Crest, Salt & Pepper, On Silver Plated Stand, Pink Flowers	165.00
Wave Crest, Salt & Pepper, Pink Swirls, Blue Flowers, Pair	110.00
Wave Crest, Salt & Pepper, Swirl, Floral	125.00
Wave Crest, Saltshaker, Embossed Scrolls At Top & Base, Pink	35.00
Wave Crest, Saltshaker, Ribbed, Original Lid, Pair	45.00
Wave Crest, Spindle, Note, Hexagonal Base, Enameled Flowers	225.00
Wave Crest, Spooner, Flowers On Cream Swirls, 4 1/2 In.	195.00
Wave Crest, Spooner, Ribbed Shape, Ormolu Rim & Handles	145.00
Wave Crest, Sugar & Creamer, Covered, Blue Flowers, Enameling	210.00
Wave Crest, Sugar & Creamer, Covered, Swirl Design, Flowers	195.00
Wave Crest, Sugar & Creamer, Ivory, White & Yellow, Beaded Flowers	285.00
Wave Crest, Sugar & Creamer, Swirl, Flowers, Silver Top & Handle	185.00
Wave Crest, Syrup, Floral Decoration	185.00
Wave Crest, Syrup, Hand-Painted Flowers, Swirl Panels, Metal Top & Handle	125.00
Wave Crest, Tray, Pin, Red Banner Mark, Brass Rim, 3 1/2 In.	60.00
Wave Crest, Tray, Trinket, Red Banner, 5 In.	95.00
Wave Crest, Vase, Blue Strawflowers, Ormulu Rim, Feet, Handles, 14 In.	475.00
Wave Crest, Vase, Cartouche Of Relief Scrolls, Ormolu Rim, Handled, 6 In.	135.00
Wave Crest, Vase, Footed, Handled, Daisies On Dark Ground, 11 In.	795.00
Wave Crest, Vase, Green Design, Beading At Rim, Ormolu Feet, 9 In.	195.00
Wave Crest, Vase, Ormolu Brass Feet, Marked, 9 In.	95.00
Wave Crest, Vase, Shasta Daisy Enameling, Red Banner Mark, 5 1/2 In.	155.00
Weapon, Bayonet & Sheath, Dress, Nazi Wehrmacht, Nickeled Mounts, 7 1/2 In.	37.50
Weapon, Bayonet, British, 1750-70, Hand Forged, Colonial	185.00
Weapon, Bayonet, Chassepot, French, 1866	40.00
Weapon, Bayonet, French, One Piece Ivory Carved Handle, C.1700, 12 1/2 In.	450.00
Weapon, Bayonet, Scabbard & Frog, W.W.II, German	25.00

Weapon, Bayonet, Socket, U.S., C.1880, 4 Inspection Marks, 16 In. 39.50
Weapon, Bayonet, Tapered Blade, Fits Into Muzzle, C.1700, 11 In. 125.00
Weapon, Bayonet, U.S. Navy, Carbine, World War I 29.00
Weapon, Blunderbuss, British Naval, Boarding, C.1720, 25 In. 1450.00
Weapon, Blunderbuss, Dutch, C.1670, Octagon Barrel, Massive Butt, 37 1/2 In. 3250.00
Weapon, Blunderbuss, English, C.1780, Iron Barrel, Walnut Stock, 22 In. 795.00
Weapon, Box, Ammunition, Oak, Brass Fittings, 15 X 4 1/2 X 7 3/4 In. 18.00
Weapon, Cannon, Galbraith Lyle, Line Throwing, Brass, Pair 1800.00
Weapon, Cannon, Hand Fuse Ignited, Swivel Gun, 17th Century, 11 In. 155.00
Weapon, Cannon, Lantanka, Swivel, Flared, Relief Ring Muzzle & Breech, 47 In. 495.00
Weapon, Cannon, Muzzle Loading, Swivel, 17th Century, , Hand Forged, 29 In. 225.00
Weapon, Carbine, Cavalry, Joslyn, Inspection Marks 550.00
Weapon, Carbine, Cavalry, Ward-Burton, .50 Caliber, Springfield Armory 750.00
Weapon, Carbine, Cosmopolitan, 1st Model, Breech Block, Finger Loops 1450.00
Weapon, Carbine, Evans, Maine, Lever Action, Repeating, C.1876-77 .... 450.00
Weapon, Carbine, Gallager, Civil War, Lever Latch 295.00
Weapon, Carbine, Remington, Split Breech, Civil War, Saddle Ring 450.00
Weapon, Carbine, Repeating, Spencer, Stabler Cut-Off Device, 20 In. 450.00
Weapon, Carbine, Sharp's, Cavalry, Civil War, New Model 1863 .... 450.00 To 550.00
Weapon, Carbine, Springfield, Custer Type, High-Breech, Marked On Lock 795.00
Weapon, Crossbow, Ivory Inlay, European 450.00
Weapon, Cutlass & Sheath, U.S. Navy, C.1860, Anchor Mark, Brass 350.00
Weapon, Cutlass, American Naval, Forged Iron, Oak Grips, C.1740, 18 In. 325.00
Weapon, Cutlass, British Navy, 1858, Leather Carrying Case, 26 1/2 In. 295.00
Weapon, Dagger & Sheath, Russian Cossack, Leather Sheath, 17 1/2 In. 175.00
Weapon, Dagger, Dress, Russian Cossack, Silver Scabbard, 19th Century 800.00
Weapon, Dagger, Officer's, World War II 200.00
Weapon, Dagger, Sheath, Nazi Luftwaffe, 1937, Swastika Each Side 135.00
Weapon, Dagger, Voss, Stag Handle, German 45.00
Weapon, Gun, BB, Daisy, Military Model, Sling 75.00
Weapon, Gun, BB, Model H, Dated 1908 .... 25.00
Weapon, Gun, BB, Quackenbush 295.00
Weapon, Gun, BB, Red Ryder .... 15.00 To 25.00
Weapon, Gun, Camel, Flintlock, Middle Eastern, C.1800, Walnut Stock, 63 In. 145.00
Weapon, Gun, Elephant, Percussion, 12 Gauge, Marked Elge, 51 In. 110.00
Weapon, Gun, Mortimer, Percussion, 9 Gauge 90.00
Weapon, Gun, Range Finder, U.S., Dated 1917 .... 14.00
Weapon, Gun, Whale Darting, Brass Tips, Dated 1882, 15 1/2 In. 425.00
Weapon, Halbard, English Artillery, C.1740, Pierced Cross Blade, 6 Feet 850.00
Weapon, Harpoon, Whaling, Hand-Held, B.Flinn & Co., 1832, 37 In. 250.00
Weapon, Horn, Powder, Inscribed Jonathan Barns, His Horn, May 4, 1776, Concord 1600.00
Weapon, Knife, see Knife
Weapon, Holster, Police, Black Leather, Belt Attachment For 38 Caliber 6.50
Weapon, Loader & Extractor, Shell, Union Hardware, 12 Gauge, Original Box 30.00
Weapon, Measure, Shotgun Shell, Dated 1890, Brass & Wood 10.00
Weapon, Mold, Bullet, Colt 31 Caliber, 2 Cavity, Ball & Bullet 37.00
Weapon, Mold, Bullet, Enfield, 8 Mold, Civil War 20.00
Weapon, Mold, Bullet, Ideal Mfg., Co., Reloading & Bullet, Ladle 35.00
Weapon, Mold, Bullet, Winchester Repeating Arms Co., .38 Caliber 27.50
Weapon, Mold, Bullet, Winchester, Reloaders, 25-20 Bullet 50.00
Weapon, Musket & Fowling, Signed & Dated, 1757, Cherrywood Stock, 66 1/2 In. 6500.00
Weapon, Musket, British Brown Bess, Brass Trim, 45 3/4 In. 2500.00
Weapon, Musket, British, Banana Shaped Lock, C.1668-1700, 46 In. 2750.00
Weapon, Musket, Dutch, Stock Relief Carved, 20 In. 450.00
Weapon, Musket, Enfield, London Armoury Co., C.1862, Nipple Protector 495.00
Weapon, Musket, Flintlock Militia, New England, Walnut Stock, 39 In. 550.00
Weapon, Musket, Flintlock, Brass Hardware, Revolutionary War 650.00
Weapon, Musket, Flintlock, Harper's Ferry, , C.1811, U.S.Shield 895.00
Weapon, Musket, Flintlock, Marked Nipped, U.S., Mill Creek 1500.00
Weapon, Musket, Flintlock, Unaltered, Springfield, C.1842 .... 2500.00
Weapon, Musket, German, 7 In.Lock, Serpentine Sideplate, C.1680, 62 In. 1500.00
Weapon, Musket, Harper's Ferry, Ohio, Pointed Finial, C.1816, 44 3/4 In. 395.00
Weapon, Musket, Percussion Rifle, Civil War, Colt, 1864, N.J. State Marking 695.00
Weapon, Musket, Remington, Maynard, Percussion, Deep Bore, 1857, Initialed 425.00
Weapon, Musket, Scandinavian Military, Dog-Lock, C.1780, Sling Swivel, 43 In. 695.00
Weapon, Musket, U.S., Springfield, 1816, Cone-Type 425.00

Weapon, Musket, Whitney, Brass Flashpan, Marked New Haven, C.1808 .... 1250.00
Weapon, Musketoon, Enfield, British Artillery, Dated 1843, Brass Hardware 475.00
Weapon, Pistol, Acme Hammerless, 22 Caliber, 1898 .... 9.00
Weapon, Pistol, Boot, 40 Caliber, C.1840, Marked E.L.G. 124.00
Weapon, Pistol, Colt, Army, 1860 .... 175.00
Weapon, Pistol, Moore's Firearms Co., 1864, Cylinder Marked D.Williamson 67.50
Weapon, Pistol, Pearl Handle, C.1840s, Silver Barrel, Closed, 3 1/2 In. 850.00
Weapon, Pistol, Percussion, Box-Lock.69 .... 80.00
Weapon, Pistol, Smith & Wesson, 1898, 32 Caliber 135.00
Weapon, Pistol, Smith & Wesson, 32 Caliber 135.00
   Weapon, Rifle, see Rifle
Weapon, Pistol, The Southerner, Brown Mfg., Co., Patent 1897 .... 250.00 To 350.00
Weapon, Powder Flask, American Eagle, Union, Brass, C.1800, 9 1/4 In. 300.00
Weapon, Powder Flask, Copper, Fluted Upper Section, Hawksley, 8 1/2 In. 79.50
Weapon, Powder Flask, Horn, Ring & Fitting, Wood Base, 8 In. 22.50
Weapon, Powder Flask, Leather Covered, Brass Top & Spout, 8 In. 47.50
Weapon, Powder Flask, Leather, Metal Dispenser, Belt Loop, C.1860, 8 1/2 In. 45.00
Weapon, Powder Flask, Pewter & Brass, Shell Pattern 45.00
Weapon, Powder Flask, Pewter & Brass, 6 In. 20.00
Weapon, Powder Horn, Carved, 18th Century, Owner's Name, C.1760 .... 875.00
Weapon, Rifle, Winchester, 22 Caliber, Repeater, Model 1906 .... 100.00
Weapon, Saber, American Revolution, Brass Hilt, Maple Grips, 35 In. 550.00
Weapon, Saber, Cavalry, Confederate, 2 Branch Brass Hilt, 30 In. 325.00
Weapon, Saber, Civil War Cavalry, Marked Tiffany & Co. 135.00
Weapon, Saber, French Officer's, Shell Design, Leather Grip, C.1820, 35 In. 97.50
Weapon, Saber, German Officer's, C.1826-98, Iron Hilt, Leather Grips, 30 In. 69.50
Weapon, Scabbard, Silver Hilt, British Artillery, Hallmarked, 33 In. 650.00
Weapon, Shell Loader & Cap Extractor, 12 Gauge, Union Hardware, Boxed 20.00
Weapon, Shells, Winchester, Factory Primed, 16 Gauge, 1901, Box 150.00
Weapon, Shot Flask, Holds 5 Pounds Of Shot, Raised Dog On Side 75.00
Weapon, Shot Pouch & Powder Horn, Leather, Fold-Over Flap, 19th Century 325.00
Weapon, Shotgun Powder, Dogs On Label, Tin 29.50
Weapon, Shotgun, A.Baldwin & Co., Ltd., Single Barrel, 12 Gauge 250.00
Weapon, Shotgun, Cap & Ball, 20 Gauge, Engraved 110.00
Weapon, Shotgun, Colt, 6 Shot, 20 Gauge, Patent 1856 .... 1000.00
Weapon, Shotgun, E.Allen Co., Engraved Side Locks, Double Barrel, 12 Gauge 195.00
Weapon, Shotgun, Hyde Shaddock, Single Barrel, 12 Gauge, Double Trigger 80.00
Weapon, Shotgun, Manton, Breechloading, 12 Gauge 65.00
Weapon, Shotgun, Remington, Rolling Block, 20 Gauge 120.00
Weapon, Shotgun, Remington, Side Cock, 12 Gauge 72.00
Weapon, Shotgun, Remington, Side Lever, 12 Gauge 80.00
Weapon, Shotgun, 16 Gauge, Scheck, Damascus Twist Finish, Gold Inlay, 28 In. 475.00
Weapon, Siamese Mauser, Model 1887 .... 37.50
Weapon, Six Barrel Pepperbox, Allen & Thurber, Mahogany Handle 299.00
Weapon, Socket Bayonet, 69 Caliber Percussion Musket, American 24.50
Weapon, Spear, Trench, Revolutionary, Forged Iron Side Straps, Shaft, 6 Ft. 135.00
Weapon, Spear, Trench, Revolutionary, Hollow Haft, 8 In. 125.00
   Weapon, Sword, see Sword
Weather Vane, Angel Gabriel, Copper, 19th Century, 23 1/2 X 58 In. 2500.00
Weather Vane, Angel Gabriel, Sheet Metal, 31 In. 550.00
Weather Vane, Antique Car, Maxwell Touring, Iron Arrow 175.00
Weather Vane, Arrow, Copper & Iron, 41 In. 175.00
Weather Vane, Cow, 5 1/2 In., Vertical Rod, C.1850, Tin, 14 1/2 X 10 In. 175.00
Weather Vane, Dove, Outstretched Wings, Grasps Olive Branch In Beak, 35 In. 475.00
Weather Vane, Eagle, Copper & Brass Compass Indicator, 21 X 20 In. 125.00
Weather Vane, Eagle, N.E.S.W., 22 In.Wing Span, C.1890-1900, Copper, 16 In. 6000.00
Weather Vane, Eagle, Raised Wings, Perched On Orb, Directional, 29 In. 550.00
Weather Vane, Horse & Jockey, Molded Copper, Rod Standard, 19 In. 700.00
Weather Vane, Horse & Rider, Copper, Rod Standard, C.1840, 20 1/2 In. 1500.00
Weather Vane, Horse & Sulky, Everett & Sons, Boston 1200.00
Weather Vane, Horse, Brown, Directionals & Rod, Copper, 42 In. 1650.00
Weather Vane, Horse, Copper & Brass Compass Indicators, 15 X 30 In. 79.00
Weather Vane, Horse, Copper, Lead Head, C.1860, 17 X 31 In. 550.00
Weather Vane, Horse, Full Bodied, Dexter, Gold Gilt, 42 In. 1650.00
Weather Vane, Horse, Running, Copper, Directionals, 21 1/2 X 35 In. 1100.00
Weather Vane, Horse, Running, Molded Copper, Rod Standard, 20 In. 275.00

Weather Vane, Horse, Trotting, Copper, 28 In. .... *Illus*	180.00
Weather Vane, Jockey & Horse, Dexter, Molded Copper, Rod Standard, 24 In.	1200.00
Weather Vane, Lexington, Massachusetts, Iron, Gold, 19th Century, 22 X 20 In.	475.00
Weather Vane, Rooster, Brass Compass Indicator, 27 X 23 In.	75.00
Weather Vane, Rooster, Copper & Brass Compass Indicators, 19 X 26 In.	89.00
Weather Vane, Rooster, Sheet-Iron, Flat Silhouette, 19 1/2 In.	100.00
Weather Vane, Rooster, Tin, Original Paint, 13 In.	165.00
Weather Vane, Sailboat, Brass Arms & Arrow, Iron Bracket, 9 1/2 X 14 In	45.00
Weather Vane, Snow Eagle, Cast Iron, Wing Spread 6 1/2 In.	25.00
Weather Vane, Sulky & Horse, Copper & Brass Compass Indicators	135.00
Weather Vane, Tin Pig, 30 In.Rod, Tin Finial, 19 1/2 In.Iron Arrow	125.00
Weather Vane, Trotter Horse, Brass Compass Indicator, 32 In.	75.00
Weather Vane, Whale, Brass Compass Indicator, 26 In.	112.50
Weather Vane, Whale, Wood, Hump-Back, Eyes In Relief, 9 X 43 In.	575.00
Weather Vane, 3 Masted Warship In Copper, Directionals, 4 Ft.	1200.00

Webb glass was made by Thomas Webb & Sons of Stourbridge, England. Many types of art and cameo glass were made by them during the Victorian era. The factory is still producing glass.

Webb Burmese, Vase, Ruffled, Acid Finish, Ruffled Pedestal, 4 1/8 In.	225.00
Webb Burmese, Vase, Trumpet, Ten Colors, 11 In.	325.00
Webb, Base, Lamp, Three-Color, Cameo Border, 3 Feet, 4 X 5 1/4 In.Diameter	875.00
Webb, Basket, Overshot, Applied Rose & Leaves, Lemon Ground, 9 1/2 In.	65.00
Webb, Bottle, Perfume, Cameo, Blue, White, Floral, 3 1/4 In.	650.00
Webb, Bottle, Perfume, Ivory & Brown, Silver Cap, Signed, 5 In.	650.00
Webb, Bottle, Perfume, Ivory Cameo, Bulbous Base, Cut Flowers, Cover, 6 In.	950.00
Webb, Bottle, Scent, Ivory Rose Petal, Roman Gold, Silver Top, 5 1/2 In.	250.00
Webb, Bottle, Scent, Screw-On Lid, Silver Chain Guards, Cameo, 7 In.	950.00
Webb, Bowl, Cameo, Blue-White Overlay, Engraved Roses, Marked, 4 1/2 In.	2400.00
Webb, Bowl, Fluted Edge, Pink Inside & Out, Bottom White, 9 X 9 X 3 In.	225.00
Webb, Bowl, Purple, Lemon Yellow Ruffling, Gold Prunus Decoration, 13 In.	225.00
Webb, Bowl, Shell Shaped, Fluted, Frosted Edge, Signed, 10 1/2 X 9 1/2 In.	337.00
Webb, Bride's Basket, Cased Blue Satin, Meridan Silver Plate Holder, 8 In.	225.00
Webb, Bride's Bowl, Highly Decorated, Signed .... *Illus*	1500.00
Webb, Bride's Bowl, Pink To Red, Fluted, Enameled Inside, Silver Holder	500.00

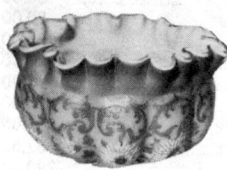

Webb, Vase, Cameo, 2 Color,
Flower, Unsigned, C.1900

Webb, Bride's Bowl, Highly Decorated, Signed

Webb, Bride's Bowl, Rose Inside, Enameled Flowers Outside, 9 1/2 In.	80.00
Webb, Bride's Dish, Enameled Flowers, Forbes Silver Holder	500.00
Webb, Burmese, Fairy Lamp, Dome Shade, 5 Petal Flowers, Clarke Base, 4 In.	225.00
Webb, Burmese, Pitcher, Yellow Applied Handle, 6-Sided, Pine Cones, 2 3/4 In.	450.00
Webb, Burmese, Rose Bowl, 5 Petal Flowers, 8-Crimp Top, 2 5/8 In.Diameter	275.00
Webb, Burmese, Vase, Petal Shaped Top, White Enameled Flowers, 3 In.	295.00
Webb, Burmese, Vase, Ruffled Pedestal Base, 4 3/8 X 2 3/4 In.Diameter	225.00
Webb, Burmese, Vase, 4 1/2 In.	275.00
Webb, Case, Cameo, Etched Crystal Ground, Art Nouveau, 8.3/4 In.	465.00
Webb, Centerpiece, Amethyst, Vaseline Ruffled Edges, Floral, 12 In.	250.00
Webb, Compote, Butterfly Wings On Underside, Signed, 4 1/2 X 6 In.Diam.	125.00
Webb, Compote, Intaglio, Prism Stem, 24 Point Star On Base, 7 X 8 In.	130.00
Webb, Cordial, Nudes In Center, Butterfly Signature, 3 1/4 In., Set Of 4	115.00
Webb, Ewer, Pink Satin Glass, Floral Enameling, Frosted Handle, Signed, 9 In.	145.00
Webb, Fairy Lamp, Burmese, Matching Ruffled Base, 11 1/8 X 5 1/4 In.Diam.	120.00
Webb, Fairy Lamp, Burmese, Ruffled Bowl Base, 5 1/8 X 3 7/8 In.	375.00

Webb, Glass, Champagne, Open Stem, Greek Key, Striped Bowl, Set Of 8	120.00
Webb, Jar, Cracker, Blue, Diamond Quilted, Mother-Of-Pearl, Signed, 4 1/2 In.	225.00
Webb, Jar, Jam, Mother-Of-Pearl, Pink, Silver Top, Signed, 4 1/4 X 2 1/2 In.	175.00
Webb, Jar, Scent, Butterscotch, Teardrop, Sterling Rim, Signed, 3 1/2 In.	225.00
Webb, Jar, Sweetmeat, Peachblow, Fluted Rim & Handle, 4 1/4 X 3 5/8 In.	495.00
Webb, Jar, Sweetmeat, Queen's Burmese, Grass Rim & Cover, Signed, 5 In.	750.00
Webb, Jug, Claret, Cameo, White Flowers, Frosted Blue Glass, 9 1/4 In.	165.00
Webb, Lamp, Fairy, Burmese, Epergne Mounted On Mirror, Marked, 7 1/4 In.	895.00
Webb, Lamp, Fairy, Burmese, Matching Footed Bowl Base, Marked, 6 1/2 In.	595.00
Webb, Peachblow, Basket, Rope Handles, Wild Rose, Signed	1250.00
Webb, Peachblow, Bowl, 8 Crimp Top, Cream Lining, 3 1/8 X 3 3/8 In.Diameter	295.00
Webb, Peachblow, Bride's Bowl, Gold Leaves, Signed, 5 5/8 In.Diameter	450.00
Webb, Peachblow, Gold Floral, Butterfly, Branches, Red To Grayish White	320.00
Webb, Peachblow, Jar, Sweetmeat, Off White Lining, 4 1/2 In.	395.00
Webb, Peachblow, Vase, Cased, Pink To Red, Raised Gilt Flowers & Butterfly	125.00
Webb, Peachblow, Vase, Cream Lining, Red Shaded To Pink Ground, 4 7/8 In.	295.00
Webb, Peachblow, Vase, Gold Elephant Head Handles, Gold Leaf, 6 1/2 In., Pair	600.00
Webb, Pitcher, Water, Pink Lining, Enameled Flowers, Signed Propeller Mark	225.00
Webb, Rose Bowl, Burmese, Flared Top, Pair	480.00
Webb, Rose Bowl, Diamond-Quilted Mother-Of-Pearl, 8-Crimp, 2 1/2 In.Diam.	275.00
Webb, Rose Bowl, Diamond-Quilted, Crimp Top, Amberina, 7 X 7 In.	1500.00
Webb, Rose Bowl, Gold Blossoms, Gold Butterfly On Back, 2 7/8 X 3 1/8 In.	695.00
Webb, Rose Bowl, Miniature, 8 Crimp Top, 2 1/4 X 2 5/8 In.Diameter	295.00
Webb, Toothpick, Satin Glass, Rose To White, Layered, Polished Pontil	175.00
Webb, Tumbler, Fan & Star, Signed, 3 1/2 In.	35.00
Webb, Tumbler, Fan & Star, 3 1/2 In.	35.00
Webb, Vase, Amber Applied Handles & Foot, Gold Trim, Peachblow, 7 1/2 In.	595.00
Webb, Vase, Barrel Shape, Enameled Flowers & Dots, Propeller Mark, 4 7/8 In.	178.00
Webb, Vase, Bulbous Base, Narrow Neck, Acid Finish, Burmese, 3 1/2 In.	200.00
Webb, Vase, Burmese, Pedestal Foot, Ruffled Top, 6 1/4 X 2 3/8 In.Diameter	295.00
Webb, Vase, Cameo, Blue, White Flowers, 3 1/2 In.	850.00
Webb, Vase, Cameo, 2 Color, Flower, Unsigned, C.1900 ....*Illus*	650.00
Webb, Vase, Carved Red & White Flowers, Signed, 4 1/2 In.	1950.00
Webb, Vase, Cased Glass, White Enamel Design, Signed, 9 3/4 X 5 1/4 In.	320.00
Webb, Vase, Citron Ground, Cameo White Flowers, Signed, 3 1/2 In.	525.00
Webb, Vase, Citron, Blooming Flowers On Vine, 4 In.	985.00
Webb, Vase, Cream Lining, Gold Butterfly, Satin Finish, 8 1/2 In.	495.00
Webb, Vase, Cream Lining, Scalloped Top, Berries, 10 In.	275.00
Webb, Vase, Cut Lily, Fish Scaled, Signed, 10 X 6 1/4 In.Diameter	330.00
Webb, Vase, Flared, Flowers, Pontil, White Lining, Blue, White, 10 In., Pair	300.00
Webb, Vase, Flowers & Leaves, Art Nouveau, Signed, 9 In.	600.00
Webb, Vase, Gilt Decoration With Butterfly, Yellow Stain, 6 1/2 In.	320.00
Webb, Vase, Gilt Decoration With Butterfly, Yellow Stain, 9 3/4 In.	385.00
Webb, Vase, Gold Bird & Bush, Blue On White, Propellor Mark, 9 5/8 In.	225.00
Webb, Vase, Gourd Shape, Ribbon Pattern, Signed, 10 In.	875.00
Webb, Vase, Hexagonal Pattern, Butterscotch Satin, Signed, 7 In.	145.00
Webb, Vase, Intaglio, Pink Overlay, Vines, Ivy & Foliage, 8 3/4 X 5 5/8 In.	850.00
Webb, Vase, Iridescent, Polished Pontil, Bronze Color, 7 In.	235.00
Webb, Vase, Maroon On White, Gold Flowers & Insects, 10 In.	225.00
Webb, Vase, Melon Ribbed, Mother-Of-Pearl, Salmon, Signed, 6 In.	185.00
Webb, Vase, Mother-Of-Pearl, Puff Coralene Flowers, Fluted Top, Apricot, 8 In.	450.00
Webb, Vase, Opal Interior, Ormolu Stand, 13 3/4 In.	1650.00
Webb, Vase, Peachblow, Foliage Design, Propellor Mark, 8 In.	365.00
Webb, Vase, Peachblow, Gold Butterfly & Flowers, Signed, 8 In.	395.00
Webb, Vase, Red, White Floral, Signed, Cameo, 4 1/2 In.	1150.00
Webb, Vase, Ruby Overlay, Gold Enamel Fronds, Decanter Shape, 6 1/2 In.	125.00
Webb, Vase, Ruffled Rim, Enamel, Blue, 10 In.	150.00
Webb, Vase, Ruffled Top, Bulbous Base, Enamel Design, 10 In.	55.00
Webb, Vase, Satin Glass, Cream Lining, Coin Gold Flowers, 6 1/4 In.	425.00
Webb, Vase, Satin Glass, Iridescent Beading, Thorn Handles, 5 In.	425.00
Webb, Vase, Stick, Peachblow, Cream Lining, Coin Gold Leaves, 9 1/2 In.	395.00
Webb, Vase, White Cameo Leaves On Citron Ground, Footed, Signed, 7 1/4 In.	2750.00
Webb, Vase, White, Flowers & Leaves, Double Cutting, Signed, 3 3/8 In.	395.00
Webb, Vase, Yellow Ground, Carved Flower, Signed, 4 1/2 In.	875.00
Webb, Vase, Yellow, Red & White, Floral, Butterfly, 4 1/2 In.	1350.00
Webb, Wine, Low Standard, Clear Crystal, Gold Trim, 1 Dozen	110.00

WEDGWOOD *Wedgwood pottery has been made at the famous Wedgwood Factory in England since 1759. A large variety of wares has been made, including the well-known jasperware, basalt, creamware, and even a limited amount of porcelain.*

Wedgwood, see also Gibson girl

Wedgwood, Ashtray, Spade & Clover, 1920, Pair	25.00
Wedgwood, Ashtray, Spade Shape, Lilac	35.00
Wedgwood, Ashtray, Terra Cotta	35.00
Wedgwood, Basket, Stand, Woven Lattice Work, Enamel & Gold Trim, 9 In.Oval	195.00
Wedgwood, Biscuit Barrel, Blue Jasper, Classical Figures, Edge Design	112.00
Wedgwood, Biscuit Barrel, Jasperware, Acorn Finial, C.1895, 7 In.	160.00
Wedgwood, Biscuit Barrel, Jasperware, Dark Blue, Silver Plate Lid & Handle	115.00
Wedgwood, Biscuit Barrel, Ladies & Cupids, Blue & White, Silver Top, Handle	135.00
Wedgwood, Biscuit Barrel, Silver Plated Bail, Lid & Rim, 5 X 4 1/2 In.	138.00
Wedgwood, Biscuit Barrel, Three Color, Cameo Figures, 10 In.	900.00
Wedgwood, Biscuit Barrel, White Classical Figure On Black Band, Tri-Color	600.00
Wedgwood, Biscuit Barrel, Yellow, Black & White, 10 In.	1050.00
Wedgwood, Biscuit Jar, Blue Jasperware, Cupids, Animal, Maiden, Lid & Bail	175.00
Wedgwood, Biscuit Jar, Jasperware, Classic Women & Cupids, 7 In.	135.00
Wedgwood, Biscuit Jar, Jasperware, Metal Handle & Cover, Classical Figures	120.00
Wedgwood, Biscuit Jar, Jasperware, Silver Plate Top, Rim & Handle, 6 In.	450.00
Wedgwood, Bottle, Green & White Jasper, England, 8 1/4 In., Pair	165.00
Wedgwood, Bottle, Scent, Cameos Both Sides, 18th Century, 2 1/2 In.	250.00
Wedgwood, Bowl, Basalt, White Harvest Figures, 7 5/8 In.Diameter	75.00
Wedgwood, Bowl, Bird Interior, Castle Exterior, 7 1/2 In.Diameter	1375.00
Wedgwood, Bowl, Black Basalt, Classic Scenes, 3 In.High X 7 1/4 In.Diameter	160.00
Wedgwood, Bowl, Blue, Octagon, Gilded, Dragon, Pearl Interior, 9 In.	500.00
Wedgwood, Bowl, Butterflies, Gold Border, Luster, Marked, 3 1/8 X 4 3/4 In.	295.00
Wedgwood, Bowl, Butterfly Luster, Portland Vase Mark, 3 1/2 In.	150.00
Wedgwood, Bowl, Butterfly Luster, Z4827, 1 3/4 X 2 3/4 In.Diameter	150.00
Wedgwood, Bowl, Butterfly Luster, Z4830 Portland Vase Mark, 2 3/8 In.	210.00
Wedgwood, Bowl, Butterfly Luster, Z4830 Portland Vase Mark, 5 In.	185.00
Wedgwood, Bowl, Covered, Caneware, Spaniel Finial, Arabesque	145.00
Wedgwood, Bowl, Crater Potpourri, White Jasper	575.00
Wedgwood, Bowl, Dragon Luster, Gold Foo Dogs, Marked, 2 1/2 In.	175.00
Wedgwood, Bowl, Dragon Luster, Portland Vase Mark Z4829, 5 1/2 In.	450.00
Wedgwood, Bowl, Dragon Luster, 3 Jewels Design, Marked, 3 1/4 X 6 In.Diam.	295.00
Wedgwood, Bowl, Dragon, Octagonal, Z4831 Portland Vase Mark, 6 1/4 In.	175.00
Wedgwood, Bowl, Fairyland Luster, Figures In Gold, Blue Inside, 4 X 2 In.	155.00
Wedgwood, Bowl, Fairyland Luster, Ghosts, Elves, 3 1/2 X 6 1/2 In.Diameter	1900.00
Wedgwood, Bowl, Fairyland Luster, 8 Sided, Portland Mark, No.25068, 4 1/4 In.	350.00
Wedgwood, Bowl, Fairyland, Fairies, Davenport, 8 X 4 In.	1975.00
Wedgwood, Bowl, Fairyland, Flame, Leaping Elves, 2 X 3 7/8 In.	850.00
Wedgwood, Bowl, Fairyland, Pedestal, Davenport, 10 X 4 1/2 In.	1940.00
Wedgwood, Bowl, Frog, Thumbelina, Firbolgs, Fairy Luster, 9 1/4 In.Diameter	1500.00
Wedgwood, Bowl, Hummingbird Luster, Mottled Blue Outside, 3 1/2 In.Diameter	175.00
Wedgwood, Bowl, Hummingbird Luster, Z5294 Portland Vase Mark, 5 In.	165.00
Wedgwood, Bowl, Hummingbird Luster, Z5360 Portland Vase Mark, 2 1/5 In.	650.00
Wedgwood, Bowl, Luster Ware, Miniature, Butterfly, Dragon & Bird, Set Of 3	635.00
Wedgwood, Bowl, Luster, Butterfly, Round Footed, C.1920, 4 1/4 X 2 1/2 In.	185.00
Wedgwood, Bowl, Luster, Geese In Flight, Blue & Orange, 2 3/8 In.	125.00
Wedgwood, Bowl, Luster, Hummingbird, Octagonal, C.1920, 4 1/4 X 2 1/2 In.	235.00
Wedgwood, Bowl, Octagonal, Fairyland Luster, Castle On Road, 7 In.	1175.00
Wedgwood, Bowl, Punch, Black Transfer Scenes Of Bowdoin College, Sesqui	1250.00
Wedgwood, Bowl, Punch, Woodland Bridge, Poplar Trees, 11 In.	2500.00
Wedgwood, Bowl, Salad, Jasperware, Silver Rim & Fork & Spoon, 8 In.Diameter	225.00
Wedgwood, Bowl, Scarab, Luster, 3 1/2 In.	140.00
Wedgwood, Bowl, Waste, Basalt, Impressed	50.00
Wedgwood, Bowl, Waste, Orange Ware, 5 1/4 In.Top Diameter	82.00
Wedgwood, Box, Basalt, Covered, Heart Shaped, Classic Figures	110.00
Wedgwood, Box, Blue Jasperware, Duke Of Edinburgh, 1953 Coronation	75.00
Wedgwood, Box, Classical Figures, Blue Jasper, Heart Shaped, C.1925	65.00
Wedgwood, Box, Dark Blue, Jasper Heart Shaped, Lidded, 3 X 2 In.	48.50
Wedgwood, Box, Fairyland Luster, Nizami, Pearl Interior, Covered, 5 1/2 In.	2150.00
Wedgwood, Box, Fairyland Luster, Widow Finial, No.Z4829 F, 6 1/2 X 5 1/4 In.	650.00
Wedgwood, Box, Heart Shape, Olive Green, Marked Made In England	140.00
Wedgwood, Box, Jasperware, Lilac, 2 1/2 X 2 In.	75.00

Wedgwood, Box, Jewel, Cover, Scenes Of Playful Children, 2 1/2 X 1 1/2 In.	95.00
Wedgwood, Box, Powder, Scalloped, Blue, White, Figures, Signed	45.00
Wedgwood, Box, Round, Cobalt, Lid, White Hunt Scene, Tunstall, England	65.00
Wedgwood, Box, Round, Terra Cotta, Spike Lid, 5 In.	105.00
Wedgwood, Box, Trinket, Jasperware, Shape Of Vanity Mirror, 4 1/4 In.	50.00
Wedgwood, Brooch, Pale Blue Jasper, Oval, Silver Mounting, Dated 1957	35.00
Wedgwood, Bulb Pot & Tray, Hedgehog, Green Glaze, Marked, 6 X 9 1/4 In.	625.00
Wedgwood, Bust, Basalt, John Bunyan, C.1860, 13 In.	1050.00
Wedgwood, Bust, Basalt, Mercury, C.1840, 18 In.	1050.00
Wedgwood, Bust, Basalt, Napoleon As First Consul, C.1850, Marked, 9 In.	850.00
Wedgwood, Bust, Black Basalt, God Mercury, Marked, 18 1/2 In.	875.00
Wedgwood, Bust, Hugo Grotius, Bentley, Black Basalt, 1779-80, 20 In.	1400.00
Wedgwood, Bust, Minerva, Silvered Helmet & Crown, C.1850, 17 1/2 In.	750.00
Wedgwood, Bust, Sir Isaac Newton, Black Basalt, 1768-80, 17 1/2 In.	1400.00
Wedgwood, Bust, Venus De Medici, Black Basalt, 1774-80, 17 1/2 In.	2000.00
Wedgwood, Bust, William Shakespeare, Black Basalt, 18th Century, 13 1/2 In.	800.00
Wedgwood, Cachepot, Jasperware, Ruffled, Fairies, 3 1/2 X 3 1/2 In.	40.00
Wedgwood, Cake Stand, Deer Pattern, Blue & White Urn Mark, 4 1/2 X 9 In.	37.00
Wedgwood, Candlestick, Classical Figures, Trees, Relief, Green, 10 In., Pair	190.00
Wedgwood, Candlestick, Jasperware, Blue, 1891, 6 1/2 In., Pair	125.00
Wedgwood, Candlestick, Jasperware, Classical Figures, Marked, 6 1/8 In., Pair	150.00
Wedgwood, Candlestick, Queensware, Grape Pillar, 8 In., Pair	45.00
Wedgwood, Chamberstick, Jasperware, Classical Figures, Blue	165.00
Wedgwood, Cheese Keeper, Tray, 9 1/4 In., Dome, 7 In., Blue, Marked	450.00
Wedgwood, Chocolate Pot, Jasperware, Top White & Blue, Bottom, Basket Weave	45.00
Wedgwood, Clock Case, Dancing Hours, Blue, 6 1/2 In.	390.00
Wedgwood, Clock, Urn, Dark Blue & White, 9 In.	520.00
Wedgwood, Coffeepot, Black Basalt, 6 3/4 In.	95.00
Wedgwood, Coffeepot, Charnwood	30.00
Wedgwood, Coffeepot, Peruvian, Mulberry, 9 1/2 In.	190.00
Wedgwood, Compote, Deer Pattern, Urn Mark, C.1900, 9 X 4 1/2 In.	38.00
Wedgwood, Cookie Jar, Blue, White Jasper, Raised Figures, 6 1/4 X 5 5/8 In.	135.00
Wedgwood, Cookie Jar, Classical Figures, White, C.1885, Blue	120.00
Wedgwood, Creamer, Basalt, Black, Enameled	195.00
Wedgwood, Creamer, Basalt, Canada Insignia	55.00
Wedgwood, Creamer, Basalt, Impressed	65.00
Wedgwood, Creamer, Black Basalt, Lion & Unicorn, Jasper, England, Signed	65.00
Wedgwood, Creamer, Blue With Figures, Rope Handle, 4 1/4 In.	35.00
Wedgwood, Creamer, Greek	70.00
Wedgwood, Creamer, Jasperware, Blue, White Classic Figures, Marked	45.00
Wedgwood, Creamer, Jasperware, Washington & Ben Franklin Bust	95.00
Wedgwood, Creamer, Salt Glaze, Caneware	150.00
Wedgwood, Crocus Pot & Stand, Hedgehog, Modern, 9 3/4 X 11 1/8 In.	100.00

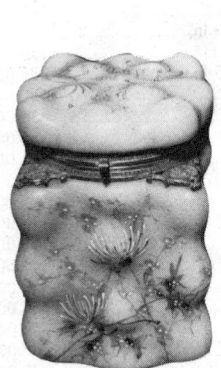

(See Page 662)
Wave Crest, Box, Large

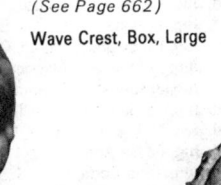

Wave Crest, Box, Collar & Cuff
(See Page 662)

(See Page 666)
Weather Vane, Horse, Trotting, Copper, 28 In.

Wedgwood, Cup & Saucer, Basalt	75.00
Wedgwood, Cup & Saucer, Cherub, Greek Figures, Horse, Blue Jasper	69.00
Wedgwood, Cup & Saucer, Demitasse, Medallion Of Courting Couple, Blue	95.00
Wedgwood, Cup & Saucer, Demitasse, Napoleon Ivy, Set Of 12	85.00
Wedgwood, Cup & Saucer, Hand-Painted Blue Flowers, 19th Century	45.00
Wedgwood, Cup & Saucer, Scalloped Cup, C.1878	45.00
Wedgwood, Cup & Saucer, White Classical Figures, Jasperware, Terra Cotta	75.00
Wedgwood, Cup, Child's, Peter Rabbit	20.00
Wedgwood, Decanter, Blue Overlay, Late 19th Century, Pair, 14 In.	320.00
Wedgwood, Dish, Butter, Caneware, Basket Weave, C.1830	135.00
Wedgwood, Dish, Condiment, Queensware, 8 1/2 In.	100.00
Wedgwood, Dish, Creamware, The Trio, Emile Lessore	795.00
Wedgwood, Dish, Feeding, Underplate, Mug, Peter Rabbit, 3 Piece	35.00
Wedgwood, Dish, Shape Of Shell, 3 Dolphin Feet, C.1872.9 In.Diameter	235.00
Wedgwood, Dish, Soup, California Pattern, Blue, 9 1/2 In.	28.00
Wedgwood, Ewer, Wine & Water, Black Basalt, 19th Century, 17 7/8 In., Pair	1300.00
Wedgwood, Figurine, Cupid & Psyche, Basalt, C.1795, 8 In., Pair	2200.00
Wedgwood, Figurine, Psyche, Pink Luster, 9 In.	850.00
Wedgwood, Figurine, Rabbit Sitting, Paperweight Eyes, Basalt, 3 X 2 1/2 In.	550.00
Wedgwood, Figurine, Sphinx, Black Basalt, 11 X 7 1/2 In., Pair	3250.00
Wedgwood, Game Plate, Caneware, Cauliflower Finial, Liner	195.00
Wedgwood, Hair Receiver, Jasperware, Heart Shaped, Nymphs, Marked	41.50
Wedgwood, Holder, Eggcup & 4 Eggcups, Twig Handle, Marked, 6 X 6 1/2 In.	125.00
Wedgwood, Holder, Place Card, Blue & White Jasper Cameo, Mounted In Silver	175.00
Wedgwood, Honey Pot, Beehive, Queensware	175.00
Wedgwood, Honey Pot, Salt Glaze, Caneware, 19th Century, 4 1/2 In.	220.00
Wedgwood, Honey Pot, Silver Plated Lid & Rim, Chinese Figures, 4 In.	97.00
Wedgwood, Humidor, Cover, Jasperware, Black, Classical Figures, 5 In.	220.00
Wedgwood, Inkstand, Two Ink Pots, Covers, 19th Century, 12 In.	1050.00
Wedgwood, Inkwell, Basalt, Round, Engine Turning, C.1800, 4 X 2 3/4 In.	275.00
Wedgwood, Inkwell, Saucer, 4 Vignettes, 8 Leaves Around Finial, 6 1/2 In.	175.00
Wedgwood, Jam Pot, Jasperware, Black, Sterling Rim, Dated 1904	75.00
Wedgwood, Jar, Biscuit, Cupids, Animal, Child, Blue Jasper, Lid & Bail	160.00
Wedgwood, Jar, Ginger, Fairy Luster, Black & Gilded Freen Fairies, 3 3/4 In.	1850.00
Wedgwood, Jar, Ginger, Gold Dragons, Blue Luster, 9 1/4 In.	450.00
Wedgwood, Jar, Ginger, Jasperware, Yellow & White, 7 In.	55.00
Wedgwood, Jar, Powder, Covered, Basalt	65.00
Wedgwood, Jar, Powder, Light Blue, Covered	42.00
Wedgwood, Jar, Tobacco, Jasperware, Washington & Franklin, 3 1/2 In.	205.00
Wedgwood, Jardiniere, Blue, 6 1/2 X 7 1/4 In.Diameter	285.00
Wedgwood, Jardiniere, Jasperware, Classical Figures, Green, 6 1/4 In.	135.00
Wedgwood, Jardiniere, Jasperware, Figures, Grape Garland, 7 1/2 X 8 1/2 In.	225.00
Wedgwood, Jardiniere, Jasperware, White Grape Design, 6 In.	85.00
Wedgwood, Jardiniere, Muses, Lion's Head & Garlands, Graduated Set Of 3	450.00
Wedgwood, Jardiniere, Olive Green, Marked	275.00
Wedgwood, Jug, Basalt, Rose, Thistle, Shamrock & Harp, 4 In.	100.00
Wedgwood, Jug, Creamware, Enamel Border, C.1790, 5 In.	140.00
Wedgwood, Jug, Drabware, Covered, C.1830, 11 In.	250.00
Wedgwood, Jug, Jasperware, Classical Ladies, White Bands, 7 X 5 1/4 In.	125.00
Wedgwood, Jug, Jasperware, Masque Spout, 1867, Ladies & Cupids, 8 1/2 In.	195.00
Wedgwood, Jug, Jasperware, Medallions Of Washington & Franklin, 4 1/2 In.	175.00
Wedgwood, Jug, Milk, Black Jasper, Multi-Color Enameled Flowers, 1840, 5 In.	365.00
Wedgwood, Jug, Rosso Antico, 5 1/4 In.	150.00
Wedgwood, Jug, Terra Cotta, 6 In.	80.00
Wedgwood, Jug, Water, Rope Handle, Dark Blue Jasper, 6 1/2 In.	120.00
Wedgwood, Lamp, Jasper, Cherubs, Silver Plated Base, 5 3/4 In., Pair	200.00
Wedgwood, Lamp, Oil, Zodiac, Blue & White, 18th Century, Cameo Top, 5 1/4 In.	650.00
Wedgwood, Letter Holder, Wall, Jasperware, Black, C.19th Century, 5 X 6 In.	125.00
Wedgwood, Lighter, Cigarette, Leaf Design, Signed	125.00
Wedgwood, Match Box Holder, Blue & White, 3 1/2 X 4 1/2 In.	185.00
Wedgwood, Match Box, Jasperware, Scratcher In Lid, Figures	49.00
Wedgwood, Match Holder, Striker Bottom, C.1900, Canadian Emblem	75.00
Wedgwood, Mug, Blue Transfer Printed, C.1811, 3 1/2 X 3 1/8 In.	40.00
Wedgwood, Mug, Creamware, Maroon Transfer, Slogans, 18th Century	125.00
Wedgwood, Mustard, Covered, Jasperware, England	75.00
Wedgwood, Pillbox, Lilac, Miniature	75.00

Wedgwood, Pitcher & Bowl, Porcelain, C.1880, Portland Vase Mark, 5 3/4 In.	115.00
Wedgwood, Pitcher, Blue & White, 3 3/4 In.	62.50
Wedgwood, Pitcher, Caneware, Rust Vintage Relief, C.1830, 3 In.	175.00
Wedgwood, Pitcher, Classical Figures, Drape, Scroll, Blue, Cream, England, 4 In.	60.00
Wedgwood, Pitcher, Classical Figures, Green, Signed, 5 1/2 In.	85.00
Wedgwood, Pitcher, Creamware, Polychrome Leaf Design, 3 Letter Mark	195.00
Wedgwood, Pitcher, Dark Blue, Grape Leaf Decoration, Marked, 6 1/4 In.	100.00
Wedgwood, Pitcher, G.Washington One Side, B.Franklin Other, 3 3/4 In.	135.00
Wedgwood, Pitcher, Garfield Born 1831-President 1881, Picture, 11 In.	650.00
Wedgwood, Pitcher, Hunting Scene, Hound Handle, Yellow & White, 6 1/2 In.	28.00
Wedgwood, Pitcher, Jasperware, Classical Figures, Blue & White, 4 In.	95.00
Wedgwood, Pitcher, Jasperware, Classical Figures, Blue, 5 3/4 In.	79.50
Wedgwood, Pitcher, Jasperware, Classical Figures, White & Blue, 6 1/4 In.	75.00
Wedgwood, Pitcher, Jasperware, Classical Figures, 3 7/8 In.	50.00
Wedgwood, Pitcher, Jasperware, Classical Ladies & Cupids, 5 1/4 X 4 1/2 In.	110.00
Wedgwood, Pitcher, Jasperware, Crimson, 4 In.	525.00
Wedgwood, Pitcher, Jasperware, Grecian Design, Blue, 5 In.	20.00
Wedgwood, Pitcher, Jasperware, Grecian Figures, Cupids, Roped Garlands, 6 In.	85.00
Wedgwood, Pitcher, Jasperware, Greek Classical Scene, Rope Handle, 6 3/4 In.	50.00
Wedgwood, Pitcher, Jasperware, Green, Rope Handle, 5 1/2 In.	65.00
Wedgwood, Pitcher, Jasperware, Green, 7 1/4 In.	125.00
Wedgwood, Pitcher, Jasperware, Yellow, White Classical Figures, 4 In.	350.00
Wedgwood, Pitcher, Metal Inset Top, Classical Figures, 7 3/8 X 4 1/2 In.	135.00
Wedgwood, Pitcher, Milk, Bulbous, Blue Classical Figures, 5 3/4 In.	110.00
Wedgwood, Pitcher, Milk, Classical Figures, Drape, Blue, 5 1/2 In.	95.00
Wedgwood, Pitcher, Milk, Jasperware, Classical Figures, Signed, 5 1/2 In.	750.00
Wedgwood, Pitcher, Milk, White Glazed Inside, Green, 4 1/2 In.	95.00
Wedgwood, Pitcher, Miniature, Dark Blue, 2 In.	45.00
Wedgwood, Pitcher, Olive Green, Classical Figures, 4 In.	125.00
Wedgwood, Pitcher, Queensware, White & Pink Figures, 6 1/2 In.	65.00
Wedgwood, Pitcher, Rope Handle, Brown & White, Adams, 6 1/4 In.	60.00
Wedgwood, Pitcher, Rope Handle, Olive Green, 4 1/2 In.	68.00 To 80.00
Wedgwood, Pitcher, Syrup, Ivory Finial, 6 1/2 X 3 1/2 In.	175.00
Wedgwood, Pitcher, Syrup, Rope Handle, Olive Green	98.00
Wedgwood, Planter, Cane, Bowed, Basket Weave, Enamel Stripe, C.1800, 7 In.	275.00
Wedgwood, Plaque, Bust Of Admiral Adam, Framed, C.1795, Oval, 3 1/2 X 3 In.	225.00
Wedgwood, Plaque, Jasper, Mounted In Gold Leaf Frame, 18 X 48 In.	650.00
Wedgwood, Plaque, Lady Decoration, Jasperware, Green, England, 6 X 4 In.	52.00
Wedgwood, Plaque, Sacrifice To Peace, Composition, Framed, 20 In.Long	900.00
Wedgwood, Plaque, Tri-Color Jubilee Of Queen, Limited Edition, 7 X 9 In.	235.00
Wedgwood, Plate, Adams, Manchester Royal Infirmary, 10 In.	12.50
Wedgwood, Plate, Battle Of Bennington, Rose & White, 9 3/4 In.	20.00
Wedgwood, Plate, Beatrice, Dated 16 June, 1880, 9 1/2 In.	25.00
Wedgwood, Plate, Bicentenary 1930, Josiah Wedgwood, Signed	25.00
Wedgwood, Plate, Braided Border, Pink Flowers, Cream Ground, Marked, 7 In.	28.00
Wedgwood, Plate, Christian Science & Mary Eddy House, 10 In.	32.50
Wedgwood, Plate, Commemorative, Ft.Ticonderoga, 10 In.	18.00
Wedgwood, Plate, Commemorative, Old South Church, Boston, Mass., 9 In.	22.00
Wedgwood, Plate, Creamware, Fortune And The Young Child, Signed, 9 1/4 In.	145.00
Wedgwood, Plate, Creamware, Mayflower In Plymouth Harbor, C.1900, 9 1/4 In.	37.50
Wedgwood, Plate, Creamware, Milkmaid With Broken Jug Of Milk, 9 1/2 In.	145.00
Wedgwood, Plate, Creamware, Washington, C.1900, 9 1/4 In.	37.50
Wedgwood, Plate, Dessert, Pink To Ivory, Shell, Set Of 6	270.00
Wedgwood, Plate, Dinner, Queensware, White, Blue Grape Leaf Border	15.00
Wedgwood, Plate, Elmira College, Rose & White, 10 1/2 In.	15.00
Wedgwood, Plate, Etruria Landscape, Blue, Green, 10 In.	20.00
Wedgwood, Plate, Fairbanks House, Dedham, Massachusetts, 9 1/4 In.	30.00
Wedgwood, Plate, Hand-Painted Fruit Center, Portland Vase Mark, 9 In.	195.00
Wedgwood, Plate, Ivanhoe, Rebecca Gives Purse Of Money To Garth, 8 In.	30.00
Wedgwood, Plate, January, Etruria, England, Polychrome Colors, 10 1/4 In.	65.00
Wedgwood, Plate, Kansas City, Missouri Centennial, 11 In., Pair	20.00
Wedgwood, Plate, Leaf Design, Caneware, Round	145.00
Wedgwood, Plate, McKinley's Home, Etruscan	37.50
Wedgwood, Plate, Monticello, Pink On White	30.00
Wedgwood, Plate, Mt.Vernon, Blue & White, 9 1/4 In.	30.00
Wedgwood, Plate, Mussel Shell, Moonlight Luster	425.00

Wedgwood, Plate, Old North Church, C.1899, Dark Blue	48.00
Wedgwood, Plate, Peruvian, Mulberry Ironstone, 9 1/4 In.	25.00
Wedgwood, Plate, St.Peter's Church, Albany, Blue & White, 9 1/4 In.	30.00
Wedgwood, Plate, State House Of Boston, Dated 1895, Blue & White	17.00
Wedgwood, Plate, Trophy, Jubilee, Five Color, Numbered Certificate	575.00
Wedgwood, Plate, Turkey, Polychrome, 10 In.	45.00
Wedgwood, Plate, Wadsworth House, 10 1/2 In.	25.00
Wedgwood, Plate, Whittier's Birthplace, C.1900	32.00
Wedgwood, Plate, 12 Signs Of Zodiac In White, Jasperware, Blue, 9 1/2 In.	65.00
Wedgwood, Platter, 8 Sided, Brown Splatter, C.1750, 13 X 10 In.	250.00
Wedgwood, Pot, Bough, Rosso Antico, Signed Base, C.1775, 4 1/4 In., Pair	600.00
Wedgwood, Potpourri, Basalt, Terra-Cotta Trim	1200.00
Wedgwood, Salad Bowl & Fork & Spoon, Blue Jasper, 1882, Signed, 10 1/4 In.	300.00
Wedgwood, Salt & Pepper, Terra Cotta	200.00
Wedgwood, Salt, Blue & White, Silver Rim, Marked, 1 1/4 X 2 1/2 In., Pair	100.00
Wedgwood, Sandshaker, Blue & White, Pierced Silver Top, Marked, 2 1/4 In.	58.00
Wedgwood, Spittoon, Basalt, Lady's, Engine Turned, Black	175.00
Wedgwood, Sucrier, Salt Glaze, Caneware	200.00
Wedgwood, Sucrier, Voer, Rosso Antico, Egyptian Design, Crocodile Finial	450.00
Wedgwood, Sugar & Creamer, Basalt, Wheat Pattern	135.00
Wedgwood, Sugar & Creamer, Jasperware, Grecian Design	160.00
Wedgwood, Sugar & Creamer, Open, Miniature, Classical Figures, 2 1/2 In.	65.00
Wedgwood, Sugar & Creamer, Red, Blue & Gold Trim, Portland Mark	75.00
Wedgwood, Sugar & Creamer, Sybil Finial, White	300.00
Wedgwood, Sugar Shaker, Blue, Classical Figures, Numbered In German, 6 In.	85.00
Wedgwood, Sugar Shaker, Jasperware, Blue, Silver Plated Top	115.00
Wedgwood, Sugar, Orange Ware, Footed, Oval, 6 X 3 3/4 In.	123.00
Wedgwood, Syrup, Pewter Top, Blue, C.1890	95.00
Wedgwood, Tankard, Jasperware, Classical Ladies, White Top, 5 3/8 In.	75.00
Wedgwood, Tea Caddie, Olive Green, 19th Century	85.00
Wedgwood, Tea Set, Light Blue & White, 3 Piece	600.00
Wedgwood, Teapot & Stand, Creamware, C.1790, Gold Handle, Spout & Finial	225.00
Wedgwood, Teapot, Basalt, Impressed	150.00
Wedgwood, Teapot, Basalt, Sunflower, C.1820	325.00
Wedgwood, Teapot, Basalt, Window Finish On Lid, C.1820	225.00
Wedgwood, Teapot, Blue Vintage Relief, Whiteware, C.1820	195.00
Wedgwood, Teapot, Caneware, Basketweave Wheat Finial, C.1820	265.00
Wedgwood, Teapot, Caneware, Blue Arabesque Relief, Flower Finial, C.1825	285.00
Wedgwood, Teapot, Caneware, Blue, Classical Relief, C.1820	325.00
Wedgwood, Teapot, Classic Figures, Green Jasperware	58.00
Wedgwood, Teapot, Classical Figures, Wreath On Lid, Blue, England	110.00
Wedgwood, Teapot, Commemorative Of Bermuda, Cobalt Blue, Shape No.30	75.00
Wedgwood, Teapot, Cornflower, Etruria, Ivory Background, England, 7 In.	55.00
Wedgwood, Teapot, Drabware, Bamboo Design, C.1820	275.00
Wedgwood, Teapot, Drabware, Basketweave Wheat Finial, C.1820	275.00
Wedgwood, Teapot, Drabware, White Smear Glaze, Spaniel Finial, C.1820, Marked	250.00
Wedgwood, Teapot, Jasperware, Black, Enamel Decoration, C.1850, 8 1/2 In.	320.00
Wedgwood, Teapot, Jasperware, Classical Figures, Marked, 4 1/4 In.	125.00
Wedgwood, Teapot, Rosso Antico, Plain, C.1820	175.00
Wedgwood, Teapot, White Smear Glaze, Wheat Finial, Basket Weave Body	185.00
Wedgwood, Teapot, Whiteware, Smear Glazed, Blue Border, C.1820	235.00
Wedgwood, Tile, Calendar, December, Sepia, 8 X 8 In.	75.00
Wedgwood, Tile, Calendar, 1895	65.00
Wedgwood, Tile, Calendar, 1896	65.00
Wedgwood, Tile, Calendar, 1897, Federal Street Theatre	110.00
Wedgwood, Tile, Calendar, 1898, King's Chapel, Boston	220.00
Wedgwood, Tile, Calendar, 1900, John Hancock House, Boston	48.00 To 56.00
Wedgwood, Tile, Calendar, 1901, Bunker Hill, Sepia, 4 1/2 X 3 1/2 In.	80.00
Wedgwood, Tile, Calendar, 1903	65.00
Wedgwood, Tile, Calendar, 1911, Frigate Constitution	62.00
Wedgwood, Tile, Calendar, 1914, Commonwealth Docks, Boston	65.00
Wedgwood, Tile, Calendar, 1917, U.S.Navy Yard, Boston	56.00
Wedgwood, Tile, Calendar, 1920, Mayflower In Plymouth Harbor	60.00
Wedgwood, Tile, Calendar, 1923 Minute Man, Concord, Massachusetts	55.00
Wedgwood, Tile, Lysander & Oberon, Sepia, 8 X 8 In.	75.00
Wedgwood, Tile, Memorial Hall, Harvard University, 1919	40.00

Wedgwood, Tile, Midsummer Night's Dream, Sepia, 8 X 8 In. 75.00
Wedgwood, Tile, November, Blue & White 65.00
Wedgwood, Tile, U.S.Navy Yard, Boston, 1917 .... 40.00
Wedgwood, Toby, Creamware, Coachman Holding Bell & Book 75.00
Wedgwood, Tray, Dresser, Classical Figures, Dark Blue 95.00
Wedgwood, Tray, Dresser, Jasperware, Blue, 10 1/4 X 7 1/2 In. 125.00
Wedgwood, Tray, Dresser, Oval, Basalt 85.00
Wedgwood, Tray, Jasperware, White, Blue, Closed Handles, 4 Scenes, 10 In.Diam. 110.00
Wedgwood, Tray, Pin, Jasperware, C.1780, 8 1/4 In. .... 100.00 To 120.00
Wedgwood, Tray, Pin, Lilac 40.00
Wedgwood, Tray, Pin, Olive Green 100.00
Wedgwood, Tray, Sprays Of Flowers, Brown, Blue, Pink, Green, 17 X 14 1/2 In. 135.00
Wedgwood, Tureen, Pearlware, Cover, Original Ladle, Black Rope Edge 350.00
Wedgwood, Tureen, Vegetable, Lid, White, Handled, 9 3/4 In. 65.00
Wedgwood, Urn, Black Jasper, Bronze, Gilding, 6 1/2 In. 1900.00
Wedgwood, Urn, Bulbous, 2 Handled, Acorn Finial, C.1820, 9 1/2 In. 550.00
Wedgwood, Urn, Cover, Mythological Panels, Green, Marked, 8 In. 585.00
Wedgwood, Urn, Jasperware, Campana Shape, C.1780, 3 3/4 In. 155.00
Wedgwood, Vase, Basalt, Engine Turned, C.1800, 5 1/2 In. 185.00
Wedgwood, Vase, Blue & White, Mythological Figures, Portland, 10 1/4 In. 1000.00
Wedgwood, Vase, Blue, White, Sage Green, 4 1/2 In. 750.00
Wedgwood, Vase, Butterfly Luster, Inside Border, 5 3/8 X 2 1/2 In.Diameter 195.00
Wedgwood, Vase, Butterfly Luster, Mottled Flame, Marked, 4 1/4 X 2 1/2 In. 195.00
Wedgwood, Vase, Cylindrical, Classical Scene, 6 In. 64.00
Wedgwood, Vase, Dark Blue, Portland, 2 1/2 In., Pair 350.00
Wedgwood, Vase, Dragon Luster, Mottled Green, 5 1/2 In. 125.00
Wedgwood, Vase, Dragon Luster, Trumpet Shape, Gold Dragons, Marked, 8 In. 350.00
Wedgwood, Vase, Dragon, Blue, Gilded, Luster, 9 In. 550.00
Wedgwood, Vase, Encaustic Decorated, C.1800, 8 In. 1750.00
Wedgwood, Vase, Fairyland Luster, Blue & Mauve, Dragon, 8 In. 340.00
Wedgwood, Vase, Fairyland Luster, Dragons In Gold, Blue, 9 In. 325.00
Wedgwood, Vase, Fairyland Luster, Flambe Color, 11 1/2 In. 1800.00
Wedgwood, Vase, Fairyland, Black Fairy, 9 3/4 In. 2000.00
Wedgwood, Vase, Fairyland, Flambe, 9 3/4 In. 2000.00
Wedgwood, Vase, Floral, Beading, Geometric Border, White On Blue, Marked, 8 In. 365.00
Wedgwood, Vase, Grapes & Vines, Double Handle, Brown, Gold, 1885, 11 In. 225.00
Wedgwood, Vase, Jasper, Portland, Drip Draped Figures, Marked, 10 1/2 In. 500.00
Wedgwood, Vase, Jasperware, Black & White, Classical Ladies, 10 1/4 In. 295.00
Wedgwood, Vase, Jasperware, Blue & White, C.1780, 5 In. 110.00
Wedgwood, Vase, Jasperware, Blue & White, 19th Century, 3 3/8 In. 100.00
Wedgwood, Vase, Jasperware, Off-White Ground, Oval Medallions, 5 In. 750.00
Wedgwood, Vase, Jasperware, Portland, Black, 4 In. 325.00
Wedgwood, Vase, Luster, Birds Of Paradise, Portland Mark, 10 1/2 In. 525.00
Wedgwood, Vase, Luster, Gold On Blue, 9 In. 350.00
Wedgwood, Vase, Original Pierced Holes, Flower Frog Top, 4 5/8 In. 165.00
Wedgwood, Vase, Pearlware, Fluting, White Swags, Black & White Diced Rim 395.00
Wedgwood, Vase, Portland, Blue & White, 5 In. 290.00
Wedgwood, Vase, Portland, Dark Blue, 6 In. 275.00
Wedgwood, Vase, Portland, Green, C.1896, 6 In. 275.00
Wedgwood, Vase, Scenes In Medallions 2 Sides, White Grapes & Leaves, Blue 350.00
Wedgwood, Vase, Sycamore Trees, 7 1/2 In. 1485.00
Wedgwood, Vase, Tapering Neck Ballooning Out, 9 X 2 1/2 In.Diameter, Pair 120.00
Wedgwood, Vase, Tortoise Shell, Tiger Luster, 5 1/2 In. 125.00
Wedgwood, Vase, Yellow Jasper-Dip, Ovoid Body, C.1900, England, 19 In. 700.00
Weis, Vase, Frosted Gold Ground, River Landscape, Signed, 5 7/8 In. 550.00

LOUWELSA
WELLER

Weller pottery was first made in 1873 in Fultonham, Ohio. The firm moved to Zanesville, Ohio, in 1882. Art wares were first made in 1893. Hundreds of lines of pottery were made including Louwelsa, Eocean, Dickens, and Sicardo before the pottery closed in 1948.

Weller, Basket, Louwelsa, Blue, 6 1/4 X 5 In. 60.00
Weller, Basket, Wood Rose, Handled, 5 3/4 X 2 3/4 In. 26.00
Weller, Basket, Woodcraft, 9 1/2 In. 72.50
Weller, Bowl, Burntwood, Mice, 3 1/4 X 1 7/8 In. 44.00
Weller, Bowl, Dogwood, 8 In. 11.00
Weller, Bowl, Forest, 3 In. 30.00

Weller, Bowl, Luster, 12 In. 175.00
Weller, Bowl, 4 Panels, Squirrel Eating Nut, 4 Footed, 7 X 3 1/2 In. 48.00
Weller, Bowl, 4 Raised Squirrels Around, 6 In. Diameter 50.00
Weller, Candlestick, Burntwood, 5 In., Pair 25.00
Weller, Dish, Feeding, Duckling In Center, Marked, 7 1/4 X 1 1/2 In. 17.50
Weller, Ewer, Louwelsa, Shiny Glaze, Squatty Form, Handle, 5 1/4 In. Diameter 165.00
Weller, Ewer, Roba, Label, Green, 6 In. 28.00
Weller, Flower Arranger, 3 Foxes, Log & Branch, Woodcraft, 7 1/2 In. 140.00
Weller, Flower Frog, Shape Of Lobster, 4 1/4 In. 12.00
Weller, Humidor, Lid, Roma 85.00
Weller, Humidor, Lid, Squirrel Finial, Muskota, 5 1/4 In. Diameter 40.00
Weller, Jar, Ginger, Cornish, Covered, Pair 92.50
Weller, Jar, Pedestal, Ivory Ground, Art Nouveau, 4 Nudes, 38 X 19 In. 650.00
Weller, Jardiniere, Aurelian, Brown, Green, Gold Tones, Bulbous, Signed, 9 In. 125.00
Weller, Jardiniere, Birdimal, Blue Trees, 8 1/2 X 10 In. Diameter 250.00
Weller, Jardiniere, Dancing Girl, Panpipe, Blueware, 6 1/2 X 7 1/8 In. 75.00
Weller, Jardiniere, Dickens Ware, 3 Footed, Yellow Flowers, 9 X 11 1/2 In. 160.00
Weller, Jardiniere, Fairfield, Brown, 7 In. 25.00
Weller, Jardiniere, Fruit & Flower Garlands, Roma, 7 3/4 X 6 1/4 In. 75.00
Weller, Jardiniere, Green, Brown, Art Nouveau Lily Pads, 7 3/4 In. 30.00
Weller, Jardiniere, Green, Pink Flowers, 3 Footed, 6 3/4 In. 59.00
Weller, Jardiniere, Knifewood, Squirrels & Birds, 9 X 8 In. 220.00
Weller, Jardiniere, Louwelsa, Signed, 8 1/2 X 10 In. Diameter 160.00
Weller, Jardiniere, Marvo, 7 3/4 In. 35.00
Weller, Jardiniere, Mythical Figures, Burntwood, Marked, 9 In. 135.00
Weller, Jardiniere, Red, Yellow, Blue, Green, Relief Forest, Signed, 5 1/2 In. 15.00
Weller, Jug, Louwelsa, Fruit Decoration, Handled, 5 3/4 In. 120.00
Weller, Lamp, Capiz-Shell Shade, Fern Design, Ciardo, Signed, 11 In. 350.00
Weller, Lamp, Louwelsa, Autumn Leaves, Electrified, Pull Chain Sockets 295.00
Weller, Light, Louwelsa, Leaves, Electric, 18 In. 150.00
Weller, Mug, Burntwood 45.00
Weller, Paperweight, Bug Eyed Dog 215.00
Weller, Pitcher, Kingfisher, Ink Stamp, Paper Sticker, 8 1/4 In. 125.00
Weller, Pitcher, Louwelsa, Footed, Bulbous, Under Glaze, Signed 220.00
Weller, Pitcher, Sabrinian, Sea Horse Handle, 11 3/4 In. 95.00
Weller, Pitcher, Syrup, Dickens Ware, Raised Corn Design, Pair 400.00
Weller, Planter, Cut Log, Woodcraft 42.50
Weller, Planter, Inner Liner, Roma 18.00
Weller, Planter, Sabrinian, Lavender, Pink, Blue, Scalloped Shells, 4 In. 60.00
Weller, Planter, Wood Rose, Round, 7 In. 35.00
Weller, Planter, 3 Foxes Peering From Knothole Of Tree, 5 1/2 X 6 1/2 In. 110.00
Weller, Pot, Bean, Brown, Embossed Mark, 5 1/2 In. 9.50
Weller, Spittoon, Flowered Panels, Glaze Drips, Burntwood, 6 3/4 X 4 1/2 In. 35.00
Weller, Stand, Umbrella, Cobalt Blue, Flower Design At Top 195.00
Weller, Stand, Umbrella, Louwelsa, Hand-Painted, Signed 495.00
Weller, Turtle, Muskota, 7 In. 38.00
Weller, Umbrella Stand, Ivory 105.00
Weller, Umbrella Stand, Relief Mythological Figures 250.00
Weller, Vase, Alvin, Double Bud, 7 1/2 X 8 1/4 In. 45.00
Weller, Vase, Alvin, 3 Trunks To Base, 9 X 4 1/4 In. 60.00
Weller, Vase, Aqua, 10 In. 15.00
Weller, Vase, Art Deco Lady Holding Out Skirt To Form Vase, Blues 35.00
Weller, Vase, Aurelian, Poppies, Signed Ferrell, 17 1/2 In. 350.00
Weller, Vase, Baldwin, Rust, 6 In. 21.00
Weller, Vase, Baldwin, 7 1/2 In. 26.00
Weller, Vase, Barcelona, 2 Handled, 6 1/2 In. 100.00
Weller, Vase, Bark Texture, Script Mark, 12 In. 30.00
Weller, Vase, Blown-Out Flowers, Detailed Molding, Art Nouveau, 13 1/2 In. 125.00
Weller, Vase, Blue, Man On Horse Jumping Fence, Dog Chasing, 5 1/2 In. 70.00
Weller, Vase, Blue, Turada, 3 In. 50.00
Weller, Vase, Bonita, Daisies, Tab Handles, Artist Signed, 7 1/2 In. 42.00
Weller, Vase, Bud, Alvin, 3 Trunk 29.00
Weller, Vase, Bud, Louwelsa, Signed, 6 1/4 X 2 1/2 In. 95.00
Weller, Vase, Bud, 3 Section, Roma, 7 In. 22.00
Weller, Vase, Bulbous, Baldwin, 7 1/2 In. 52.00
Weller, Vase, Cameo, Blue, White Flowers, Handled, 5 1/2 In. 20.00

Weller, Vase, Cameo, White Embossed Rose, Green, 2 Handles, Signed, 6 1/2 In.	25.00
Weller, Vase, Chalice Type, Open Vine Work, Pedestal, Baldwin, 9 1/4 In.	60.00
Weller, Vase, Coppertone, Flared, 8 5/8 X 5 1/4 In.	49.00
Weller, Vase, Cylinder, Sicardo, Sunflowers, Dimples, Signed, 10 1/2 In.	287.00
Weller, Vase, Dickens Ware, Cavalier, High Blue Glaze, 2nd Line, 13 1/2 In.	400.00
Weller, Vase, Dickens Ware, Curling Dragon, Blue, Marked, 13 In.	350.00
Weller, Vase, Dickens Ware, Lady Golfer, 2nd Line, Signed H, 10 X 3 7/8 In.	350.00
Weller, Vase, Dickens Ware, Sgraffito, Lady Golfer, 9 In.	350.00
Weller, Vase, Flemish, Rectangular, Pierced Flower Holder, 7 In.	38.00
Weller, Vase, Floral, Leaf, Burntwood, 5 In.	27.00
Weller, Vase, Florals, Long Stems, Fiery Splash Ground, Artist Signed, 7 In.	165.00
Weller, Vase, Floretta, Marked, 12 In.	65.00
Weller, Vase, Fluted Pink Top, Green, 14 In.	50.00
Weller, Vase, Forest, 8 1/2 In.	40.00
Weller, Vase, Hudson, Pink Roses, Dark Blue, 8 In.	65.00
Weller, Vase, Iridescent, Tropical Scene, Classical Shape, Lasa, 9 In.	165.00
Weller, Vase, Ivory, Leaf Design, Brown, Cylindrical, 10 In.	45.00
Weller, Vase, Ivory, 6 Oak Leaf Panels, Cylinder, 12 X 5 1/2 In.	24.00 To 26.00
Weller, Vase, Lasa, Iridescent, 10 In.	195.00
Weller, Vase, Lasa, Mountains, Water, Trees, Signed, 9 In.	235.00
Weller, Vase, Lasa, Scenic, Signed, 8 1/2 X 4 In.Diameter	120.00
Weller, Vase, Lasa, Sunset On Beach, Palm Trees, Artist Initial M, 9 In.	325.00
Weller, Vase, Louwelsa, Berries, 7 1/2 In.	60.00
Weller, Vase, Louwelsa, Pansies, Artist Signed, 8 1/4 In.	65.00
Weller, Vase, Louwelsa, Red Roses, Artist Signed, 7 1/4 In.	80.00
Weller, Vase, Marvo, 10 In.	35.00
Weller, Vase, Matte Finish, Hudson, Slip Painted, 6 1/2 In.	65.00
Weller, Vase, Mi-Flo, 6 In., Pair	30.00
Weller, Vase, Molded Flowers, 10 1/2 In.	15.00
Weller, Vase, Molded Leaves, 6 In., Pair	45.00
Weller, Vase, Oak Leaf, 9 In.	21.00
Weller, Vase, Owl, Woodcraft, 7 X 5 1/2 In.	130.00
Weller, Vase, Pansies On Gray, Weller In Block, 6 In.	65.00
Weller, Vase, Pansy Decoration, Glaze, 6 In.	85.00
Weller, Vase, Pillow, Aurelian, 6 1/2 X 5 1/2 In.	87.50
Weller, Vase, Pinecone, 10 X 5 1/2 In.	38.00
Weller, Vase, Purple Plums, Branches, Iridized Finish, Signed, 12 X 5 1/2 In.	75.00
Weller, Vase, Roma, Side Handled, 8 1/4 In.	27.00
Weller, Vase, Roma, 18 In.	65.00
Weller, Vase, Roses, Etna, Marked, 7 In.	60.00
Weller, Vase, Sabrinian, 2 Seahorses, 9 1/2 In.	68.00
Weller, Vase, Seneca, Lake & Sailboat Relief, Turquoise, Footed, 8 X 7 X 5 In.	24.00
Weller, Vase, Seneca, Turquoise, Lake & Sailboat, Footed, 8 X 7 1/4 In.	22.00
Weller, Vase, Sicardo, Flower & Leaf Design, Signed, 9 1/2 In.	325.00
Weller, Vase, Silvertone, Lavender, Green, Berries & Flowers, 7 X 5 In.	55.00
Weller, Vase, Swirl Handled, Signed Weller Sicardo, 5 X 6 In.	395.00
Weller, Vase, Tree Trunk Type, 9 In.	47.50
Weller, Vase, Tree Trunk, Double, Woodcraft, 7 1/2 X 8 1/2 In.	30.00
Weller, Vase, Vase, Weller, 9 3/4 In.	85.00
Weller, Vase, 3 Handled, Portrait, 6 1/2 In.	60.00
Weller, Wall Pocket, Drapery, Blue, 9 X 5 1/2 In.	42.00
Weller, Wall Pocket, Matte Turquoise, Lady In Center, Signed	27.00
Weller, Wall Pocket, Owl, Woodcraft, 11 In.	55.00
Weller, Wall Pocket, Panella, 8 In.	35.00
Weller, Wall Pocket, Roma, 8 1/2 In.	35.00
Weller, Wall Pocket, Semi-Nude Girl, Hobart, 8 1/4 X 5 3/8 In.	40.00
Weller, Wall Pocket, Tutone, 10 In.	45.00
Wemyss Ware, Vase, Hand Decorated, Red Roses & Green Leaves, 6 1/2 In.	45.00
Western Terra Cotta Co., Doorstop, Frog, Green	25.00
Whieldon Type, Figurine, Pug, Cream, Seated, Green Base, C.1765, 3 1/8 In.	500.00
Whieldon, Plate, Gadrooning, Cream Bodies, C.1765, Pair, 9 1/2 In.	1700.00
Willets, see Belleek	
Willow, see Blue Willow	
Window, Colored, Leaded, 28 Pieces Each Pane, 24 X 30 In., Pair	265.00
Window, Double Doors, Leaded Window, 460 Pieces In Each, 18 X 50 In.	550.00
Window, Leaded, Church, Non-Religious, 12 1/2 Ft. X 40 In.	775.00

Window, Stained Glass, Cottage Scene, 35 X 28 In.

Window, Leaded, Medallion & Bull's-Eye, 1800s, 77 X 20 In.	145.00
Window, Stained Glass, Annunciation, C.1898, 132 X 19 In.	2090.00
Window, Stained Glass, Arched, Hallway Trio	2500.00
Window, Stained Glass, Beveled, Baseball Theme	1250.00
Window, Stained Glass, Beveled, Victorian, 40 X 14 In.	200.00
Window, Stained Glass, Cottage Scene, 35 X 28 In. *Illus*	300.00
Window, Stained Glass, Detroit Glass Works, White Ground, 12 X 7 Feet	250.00
Window, Stained Glass, Dutch Windmill, Scenery In Circle, 6 X 6 Feet	550.00
Window, Stained Glass, Geometric Design, 26 X 34 In.	175.00
Window, Stained Glass, Nativity, C.1900, 132 X 19 In.	2090.00
Window, Stained Glass, Semicircle, Jewels, 19 1/2 In. *Illus*	250.00
Window, Stained Glass, Star Of David, Harlequin, 5 1/2 In. X 2 Ft., Pair	2000.00
Window, Stained Glass, Tennis Player, C.1875, 3 1/2 X 8 1/2 Feet	2400.00
Window, Stained Glass, Vase With Flowers, Jewels, 22 In. *Illus*	675.00
Window, Stained Glass, Windmill Scene, C.1900, 6 X 8 Feet	8900.00
Window, Stained Glass, 2 Horns Of Plenty	200.00
Window, Stained Glass, 5 Paneled, C.1900, 9 X 40 Feet	5720.00
Window, Transom, Ruby Red	40.00
Windowpane, Aqua Bull's Eye, C.1780, 7 X 8 1/2 In.	30.00
Windowpane, Bull's-Eye, Hand Blown, Rough Pontil, C.1800, 7 X 8 1/2 In.	30.00
Wood Carving, Alligator, Realistically Carved Figure, Open Jaws, 41 In.	325.00
Wood Carving, Angel, Spanish, Gesso, Red, Black & Gold, 20 X 12 1/2 In.	160.00
Wood Carving, Bird House, Form Of House, Porch, Shutters, Stand, 72 In.	350.00
Wood Carving, Black Woman Washing Clothes, C.1935, 14 X 20 In.	225.00
Wood Carving, Boot Jack, Lady's, Needlepoint Of Black Boy, Victorian, 40 In.	575.00
Wood Carving, Box, Oval, C.1766, 9 1/2 X 5 X 4 1/4 In.	300.00
Wood Carving, Buddha, Seated On Lotus Stand, Gilded, 6 In.	85.00
Wood Carving, Bust, Benjamin Franklin, Walnut, 19th Century, 11 3/4 In.	400.00
Wood Carving, Carousel Cresting, Deco Woman, 15 X 25 In.	185.00
Wood Carving, Carousel Cresting, Metal Heads, Indian, 15 X 25 In.	185.00
Wood Carving, Chopper Toy, Russia	75.00
Wood Carving, Deer, Head, Walnut, Done To Scale, Antlers, Mounted, 1800s	200.00
Wood Carving, Deity Seated On Fu Lion, Parcel-Gilt, 10 3/4 In.	300.00
Wood Carving, Eagle, American, On Orb, 19th Century, 44 1/2 X 30 In.	1100.00
Wood Carving, Eagle, American, Outstretched Wings, Painted, C.1800, 13 Feet	1600.00
Wood Carving, Eagle, C.1930, 10 In.	70.00
Wood Carving, Eagle, 7 1/2 In.	14.00
Wood Carving, Elephant, Circus Wagon, 5 1/2 In., Pair	45.00
Wood Carving, Elephant, Ivory Tusks & Eyes, Teakwood, 6 X 7 In.	55.00
Wood Carving, Elephant, Ivory Tusks, Tigerwood, 3 1/4 X 2 1/4 In.	22.50
Wood Carving, Elephant, Ivory Tusks, Toenail & Eyeballs, Teakwood, 14 In.	150.00
Wood Carving, Figure, For Band Organ, Pair	300.00
Wood Carving, Figurine, Bunny Rabbit, Sitting, 2 In.	3.50
Wood Carving, Figurine, Chinese, Gesso Kwan Yin Goddess, 1880-1925, 21 In.	275.00
Wood Carving, Figurine, Kannon Standing On Cloud Scrolls, 1800s, 22 1/2 In.	225.00
Wood Carving, Figurine, Princess, Pine, Wood Base, 40 1/2 In.	650.00
Wood Carving, Figurine, Uncle Sam, Red, White & Blue, 11 In.	750.00
Wood Carving, Figurine, Winged Monster, Balinese, C.1800, 13 In., Pair	300.00
Wood Carving, Garden Hose Holder, Black Boy Wearing Overalls, 33 1/2 In.	150.00
Wood Carving, Hand Truck, Fitted With Wood Pegs & Pins, 1800s, 42 In.	255.00
Wood Carving, Horse, Pine, 1870, 25 X 36 In.	295.00
Wood Carving, Leopard, Pine, 19th Century, 14 1/2 In.	550.00
Wood Carving, Monk, C.1880, 6 In.	75.00

Wood Carving, Muskie, Nails For Teeth, Painted, 1850-1950, 31 In.	250.00
Wood Carving, Noah's Ark, Hand-Carved, Painted, Pull Toy On Wheels, 90 Piece	500.00
Wood Carving, Pelican, Mounted As Umbrella Stand, 19th Century, 40 In.	550.00
Wood Carving, Pheasant, Painted In Red, Blue, Green, Yellow, 13 1/2 X 19 In.	325.00
Wood Carving, Plaque, Eagle, American, Late Federal, Black, 48 In., Pair	350.00
Wood Carving, Plaque, Wall, Depicting A Heron In Flight, 22 In.	250.00
Wood Carving, Prehistoric Reptile, Blue-Green, Glass Eyes, 1900s, 5 X 22 In.	250.00
Wood Carving, Pull Carriage, Child's, Chestnut & Walnut, 1700s, 28 1/2 In.	2100.00
Wood Carving, Rooster, Late 19th Century, 6 In.High	1000.00
Wood Carving, Seaman, Ship's Wheel, Signed & Dated, 6 Feet	5000.00
Wood Carving, Sheath, Needle, Hand, Heart, Tree, March 8, 1824, 8 In.	250.00
Wood Carving, Sheath, Needle, Remember Me, G.H., Bird, Fish, Musket, 7 In.	225.00
Wood Carving, Spoon, Bone, Fiddle Back Handle, C.1850, 5 1/2 In.	12.50
Wood Carving, Sternboard, Inscribed, May 1856, 20 1/2 X 50 In.	2000.00
Wood Carving, Teddy Bear, Standing, Outstretched Arms, Glass Eyes, 43 In.	1200.00
Wood Carving, Torchere, Gilded, Venetian, 6 Ft.	390.00
Wood Carving, Trout, 10 X 8 In., Pair	250.00
Wood Carving, Vase, Birds & Pinecones, Hand-Carved, 11 In.	59.00
Wood Carving, Wagon, Model, Howard's Special Delivery, Painted, 14 X 20 In.	300.00
Wood Carving, Whirligig, Man Sitting & Playing Violin, C.1920, 20 In.	195.00
Wood Carving, Whirligig, Man Washing Clothes, Wringer, C.1920, 29 In.	225.00
Wood Carving, Whistle, Shape Of Pistol	25.00
Wood Carving, Youth Playing Harp To A Maiden, Irish, 1600s, 13 X 14 1/2 In.	425.00
Wooden, see also Kitchen, Store, Tool	
Wooden, Abacus, 144 Beads	18.00
Wooden, Attachments, Swing, Oak, Wheeler & Wilson, 8 3/4 X 3 1/4 In.	17.50
Wooden, Ballot Box	15.00
Wooden, Barber Pole, Original Paint, 54 In.	245.00
Wooden, Board, Smoothing, With Roller	145.00
Wooden, Bookends, Hand-Carved, Expandable, Large Bear On Log	25.00
Wooden, Bookends, Mayan Gods, Mahogany	20.00
Wooden, Bootjack, Walnut, Folding	25.00
Wooden, Bottle, Maple, Hand-Turned	19.00
Wooden, Bowl, Burl, American, 12 In.	345.00
Wooden, Bowl, Dough, Hand-Hewn, Oval	50.00
Wooden, Bowl, Dough, 12 In.Diameter	17.50
Wooden, Bowl, Eating, 7 In.Diameter	38.00
Wooden, Bowl, Fruit Drying, Shallow, 17 1/2 In.Diameter	95.00
Wooden, Bowl, Green Paint, Oval, 11 1/2 X 20 1/2 In.	65.00
Wooden, Bowl, Original Gray, 17 In.	45.00
Wooden, Bowl, Oval, Red Paint, 13 3/4 X 20 In.	120.00
Wooden, Bowl, Pine, Oil Painted Farm Winter Scene, 5 In.Diameter	95.00
Wooden, Bowl, Redwood Burl, Panama Exposition, 3 X 2 1/2 In.	18.00
Wooden, Bowl, Sugar, Turned, Lid, Maple, 7 In.	310.00

Window, Stained Glass,
Semi-Circle, Jewels, 19 1/2 In.

Window, Stained Glass,
Vase With Flowers, Jewels, 22 In.

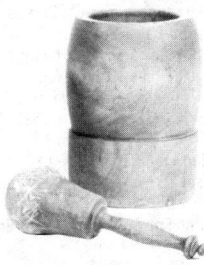

Wooden, Mortar & Pestle,
Maple, 8 In.

(See Page 679)

Wooden, Bowl, Tiger Maple 120.00
Wooden, Bowl, White & Yellow, Pond, Lilies On Matte Brown, 6 In. 28.00
Wooden, Box, Brook's Thread, Cover Shows Playing Cards, 4 X 5 X 2 In. 15.00
Wooden, Box, Butter, Button Hole Hoop, Green, 18th Century, 7 X 14 In. 90.00
Wooden, Box, Butter, Carrying, Lid & Wooden Bail, Red, 11 1/4 In.Diameter 68.00
Wooden, Box, Candle, Oak, Grooved Lift Lid Hanger 97.00
Wooden, Box, Candle, Slide Door, Black Oak, 16 In. 114.00
Wooden, Box, Cigar, Mahogany, Zinc Liner, Inlay Trim, 12 X 7 1/2 X 4 In. 50.00
Wooden, Box, Covered, Amish, Round, 19 In. 37.00
Wooden, Box, Decoupage, Dated 1837, 10 1/2 In. 175.00
Wooden, Box, Denim Cover, Brass Nail Studs & Handle, 10 1/4 X 4 X 6 In. 12.50
Wooden, Box, Document, Cherry, 18 X 11 X 6 3/4 In. 45.00
Wooden, Box, Dovetailed, Tiger Maple, Crotch Walnut 185.00
Wooden, Box, Inlay Design Of Bird, Bird's Eye Maple, 11 X 8 X 6 In. 50.00
Wooden, Box, Rosewood, English, Secret Drawer, 8 In.Long 110.00
Wooden, Box, Sailor's, Poplar, Hinged Lid, 19th Century, 6 1/2 X 11 In. 100.00
Wooden, Box, Salt, 2 Section 225.00
Wooden, Box, Slide Lid, Green Paint, 5 1/2 X 9 X 6 In. 38.00
Wooden, Box, Snuff, Boxwood, Covered, 2 In.Diameter 24.00
Wooden, Box, Tote, 12 X 7 1/2 In. 10.00
Wooden, Box, Wedding, Pigskin Cover, Painted Birds, Chinese, 25 X 11 X 15 In. 180.00
Wooden, Bucket, Banded, Old Red 22.00
Wooden, Bucket, Brass-Bound, George III, Mahogany, C.1800, 14 X 15 In. 350.00
Wooden, Bucket, Crubro Apple Butter, Paper Label 40.00
Wooden, Bucket, Grease, Conestoga, Covered 150.00
Wooden, Bucket, Paint, Bail, Label Dated 1870, Oak 45.00
Wooden, Bucket, Sap, Shoulder Yoke 20.00
Wooden, Bucket, Sugar, Green, Handle, Lid, 12 X 12 In. 27.50
Wooden, Bucket, Sugar, Lid & Handle, Staved, 6 X 6 In. 40.00
Wooden, Bucket, Sugar, Lid & Handle, Staved, 9 X 9 1/2 In. 50.00
Wooden, Bucket, Water, Child's, Staved, Brass Bands & Ears, 5 1/2 X 7 In. 30.00
Wooden, Butter Print, Stylized Plant Design, Handle, Round, 3 3/4 In. 70.00
Wooden, Candleholder Shelf, Wall, Inset Of Tiles, C.1840 .... 135.00
Wooden, Carrier, Center Handle, Slide-Lids, Cherry, G.Wilcox, 16 X 3 3/4 In. 345.00
   Wooden, Carousel Horse, see Carousel Horse
Wooden, Case, Salesman's, Carrying 18 Straight Edge Razors 25.00
Wooden, Checkerboard, Bird's-Eye Maple Frame, Oak Border, Square, 15 1/2 In. 45.00
Wooden, Chest, Bride's, 25 X 12 X 14 In. 225.00
Wooden, Chest, 3 Bottom Drawers, 2 Top, 1900 .... 22.00
Wooden, Complete Set Of Chessmen, Victorian, 1 3/4 In.To 2 3/4 In. 22.50
Wooden, Curd Breaker, Cheese, Wrought Iron Teeth, Mortised 89.00
Wooden, Decoy, Duck, Wood, Pacific Northwest 22.00
Wooden, Dipper, Burl, Chip Carved Handle, 18 In. 75.00
Wooden, Dispenser, Cigarette, Donkey, Handmade, 6 In.Long 4.50
Wooden, Elephant, Pulling Log, Carved, 5 In. 20.00
Wooden, Engraving, Max Webber, Signed, 1 In. 325.00
Wooden, Figurine, Bird With Fish 175.00
Wooden, Figurine, Cat Sitting On It's Haunches, Glass Eyes, 2 1/2 In. 25.00
Wooden, Figurine, Deity, Clothing Inset With Colored Glass, 59 In. 200.00
Wooden, Figurine, Eagle, Perched On Rockwood, Painted To Resemble Marble 2500.00
Wooden, Figurine, Oriental, Man Wearing Animal Skin, 5 3/4 In. 45.00
Wooden, Figurine, Saint, Polychrome Paint, 17 3/4 In. 265.00
Wooden, Figurine, Shorebird, Glass Eyes, 6 In. 205.00
Wooden, Figurines, Oriental, Dragon Costumes, Carved, 1 3/8 In., Pair 60.00
Wooden, Filler, Bag, Holds Burlap Bags Open For Filling, Pennsylvania 16.00
Wooden, Fishbait Carrier, Scandinavian, Dated October 6, 1867 .... 48.00
Wooden, Funnel, Sap, Maple, One Piece 65.00
Wooden, Holder, Spoon, One Piece Lignum Vitae, Round, 4 1/2 X 4 1/2 In. 65.00
Wooden, Holder, Washtub, Folding 20.00
Wooden, Indian, Dagger On Front, Carved, 11 3/4 In. 24.00
Wooden, Keg, Iron Banded, Handle & Tap, 17 X 11 In.Diameter 18.00
Wooden, Keg, Water, Lock, Lapped Hoops, Raised Bung Hole, 6 1/2 X 10 In. 125.00
Wooden, Letter, Original Gold & Blue Paint, C.1890, 11 3/4 X 7 In. 9.00
Wooden, Maiden's Yoke, Chains For Buckets At Each End, 35 1/2 In. 35.00
Wooden, Measure, Grain, Amish, 20 In.Diameter 34.00
Wooden, Model, Cabin Cruiser, Gypsy, 29 In. 85.00

Wooden, Model, Delivery Wagon, Moving Wheels, Brake, Harness, Cushion Seat 275.00
Wooden, Model, Fishing Boat, Lobster Pots, Anchor, Rope, Baskets, 14 1/4 In. 65.00
Wooden, Mold, Butter, Hexagonal Pewter Banded, Sheaf Of Wheat, 3 Piece 69.00
Wooden, Mortar & Pestle, Maple, 8 In. .... *Illus* 40.00
Wooden, Mortar & Pestle, 5 1/2 X 8 In. 49.00
Wooden, Mortar, Burl, 5 X 6 In. 150.00
Wooden, Mortar, Speckled Maple Burl, Scribed & Tooled Bands, 3 1/2 X 4 In. 175.00
Wooden, Needles, Knitting, Hand-Hewn, 18th Century 12.00
Wooden, Noisemaker, Noise Gear 17.00
Wooden, Nutcracker, Hand Carved, Bavarian Woodsman 49.00
Wooden, Nutcracker, With Gavel, 8 In.Diameter 6.00
Wooden, Ornament, Architectural, Crossed Trumpets, Urn Spouting Flame 115.00
Wooden, Paddle, Teacher's, Golden Pond, Kentucky, Oak 15.00
Wooden, Pickle Barrel, Bent Wood Lashings, 19th Century, 18 In. 175.00
Wooden, Pitcher, Noggin, One Piece Maple 175.00
Wooden, Plate, Money Collection, Carved, German 25.00
Wooden, Plate, 18th Century, 6 1/4 In. 95.00
Wooden, Print, Wallpaper, Cylinder, Maple, Brass Design, 1900s, 6 X 22 In. 25.00
Wooden, Rack, Clothes, Wall, Oak 12.00
Wooden, Reamer, Lemon, Hinged, Wood 28.00
Wooden, Rod Puppet, Cloth Costume, Java, Gold & Polychrome Paint, 24 In. 25.00
Wooden, Salt, Open, 18th Century, American, 3 1/4 In. 35.00
Wooden, Sander, Old Yellow, Bulbous Shape, 3 In. 47.00
Wooden, Schooner, 4 Masted, Hatches, Lifeboat, Red, White, 45 X 73 1/2 In. 500.00
Wooden, Scoop, Apple Butter, Open Handle 120.00
Wooden, Scoop, Cranberry, Handmade 65.00
Wooden, Scoop, Hard Wood, Hand-Carved, 4 1/2 X 13 In. 36.00
Wooden, Scoop, Tiger Maple, Long Handled, Narrow Bowl, Hand Hewn, 40 In. 150.00
Wooden, Scrub Stick, One Piece, Handled, Corrugated 140.00
Wooden, Shovel, Grain 110.00
Wooden, Sign, Gunsmith's, Link Chain, 19th Century, 36 In. 3500.00
Wooden, Sign, Shoe Shop, 19th Century, 16 3/4 X 51 5/8 In. 650.00
Wooden, Sign, Tavern, Pine, American Eagle, 19th Century, 28 1/4 X 40 3/4 In. 2750.00
Wooden, Skimmer, Tallow, Handled, All Wooden, 14 In. 95.00
Wooden, Smoother, Feather Bed 12.00
Wooden, Spoon, Tiger Maple 25.00
Wooden, Stopper, Bottle, Movable Mouth 8.00
Wooden, Tablespoon, Shaped Handle, Ball End, C.1830, Walnut, 12 In. 12.00
Wooden, Tea Caddies, William Crawford & Sons, Ltd., 5 1/2 In., Pair 110.00
Wooden, Till, Cash, Instructions, C.Gledhill & Sons, Ltd. 150.00
Wooden, Tray, Brass Handles, Fabric Under Glass, Oval, Mahogany, 13 1/4 In. 17.00
Wooden, Tray, Collection, Church 25.00
Wooden, Tray, Dough, 19 X 10 In. 50.00
Wooden, Trough, Dough, Oval, Large 50.00
Wooden, Washboard, C.1820, 10 X 18 In. 55.00
Wooden, Washboard, Child's 45.00
Wooden, Whirligig, Donkey Rider, Sheet Metal, 19th Century, 18 In. 1300.00
Wooden, Whirligig, Horse & Sulky, C.1890 .... 375.00
Wooden, Whirligig, Man Sawing Wood, 14 In. 115.00
Wooden, Whirligig, Naval Officer, Jacket, Brass Buttons, Wind Activated Arm 450.00
Wooden, Whirligig, Sailor Boy, Carved, Log Base, Metal Beret, 18 1/2 In. 100.00
Wooden, Yoke, Ox, Hand Hewn, Oak, Iron Hoops 75.00
     Worcester, see also Royal Worcester
Worcester, Bowl, Blue & Gold, 6 In. 85.00
Worcester, Bowl, Flight, Barr & Barr, Serpentine Rim, Gilt Edges, 9 In. 95.00
Worcester, Bowl, Gold Design, G.Grainger & Co., C.1812, 6 3/4 In. 85.00
Worcester, Butter Cooler & Cover, C.1758, 5 3/8 In. .... *Illus* 1900.00
Worcester, Cachepot, Roses On Beige Ground, Overlay Forms Rim, Pierced Lid 85.00
Worcester, Coffee Can & Saucer, Cracked Ice Panels 70.00
Worcester, Creamer, Double-Wall Reticulated, 4 In. 250.00
Worcester, Cup & Saucer, Handleless, Swirled Fluted & Gold, 18th Century 45.00
Worcester, Cup & Saucer, Handleless, White Body, Gold Flowers & Rims, C.1800 .... 48.00
Worcester, Cup, Tea Bowl & Saucer, Rose Madder Decoration, C.1700 .... 175.00
Worcester, Dish, Fluted, Gilt C-Scrolls, W Mark, First Period, 7 In. 150.00
Worcester, Figurine, Boy, Gold Trim, Hadley, 1897-1900, 7 5/8 In. 425.00
Worcester, Jug, Mask, Blue Scale, C.1765, 8 7/8 In. .... *Illus* 3400.00

Worcester, Muffineer, Pheasant, Signed	85.00
Worcester, Pitcher, Cobalt Band, Gilt, Blue Crescent Mark, 4 1/2 In.	155.00
Worcester, Plate, Blind Earl, C-Scrolls, First Period, Pair, 7 3/4 In.	400.00
Worcester, Plate, Cream Satin, Hand Painted Flowers, Purple Mark, 7 In.	29.00
Worcester, Plate, Dinner, Chamberlain's, Gold Edge, C.1811-40, Set Of 16	560.00
Worcester, Plate, Pine Cone, Crescent Mark, First Period, 8 5/8 In.Diameter	75.00
Worcester, Platter, Ming Tree Decoration, Embossed Rim, 22 3/4 X 19 In.	180.00
Worcester, Pot, Bough, Blue Scale, Pair ....Illus	8500.00
Worcester, Sauceboat, Leaf-Molded, First Period, Signed, 8 3/4 In.	475.00
Worcester, Teabowl & Saucer, Fruit & Gilding, First Period, Signed	900.00
Worcester, Teapot, Chinoiserie, Cover, Signed, First Period, 5 7/8 In.	200.00
Worcester, Teapot, Melon Shape, Dr.Wall, 18th Century, 5 1/2 In.	335.00
Worcester, Teapot, Queen Charlotte, 18th Century	230.00
Worcester, Teapot, Royal Lily Pattern, Barr Flight Barr, 7 1/2 In.	208.00
Worcester, Vase & Cover, Pierced, Grainger & Co., C.1892, Shield Mark, 17 In.	1000.00
Worcester, Vase, Cream, Gold Trim, Reticulated, 4 1/4 In.	75.00
Worcester, Vase, Gold Trim, Gold Handle, Bouquet On Front, Pair	95.00
Worcester, Vase, Hunting Horn Shape, Purple Mark, 9 X 11 1/2 In.	225.00
Worcester, Vase, Peacock, Miniature, C.1862	85.00
Worcester, Vase, Pen Holder, Reticulated, Six Sided, Marked, 1891, 4 5/8 In.	375.00
World War I, Bag, Horse's Feed, Marked, U.S.Q.M.C., Leather & Canvas	17.50
World War I, Bayonet, German, 1918, Set Of 3	100.00
World War I, Book, Song, Wilson Pictured On Cover	6.50
World War I, Buckle, Belt, German	6.25
World War I, Canteen, Cavalry	25.00
World War I, Card, German Propaganda	2.00
World War I, Case, Cigarette, For Rolled Cigarettes, Brass	20.00
World War I, Compass, Army, Brass, U.S. Stamped On Case	40.00
World War I, Cover, Pillow, Handkerchief Case, Pair	15.00
World War I, Flag, Signal, Kit	17.50
World War I, Hat, Officer's	10.00
World War I, Helmet, French	10.00 To 30.00
World War I, Helmet, German, Patent Leather, Spike, Iron Fittings	145.00
World War I, Helmet, Liner & Chin Strap	8.50
World War I, Helmet, Russian, Steel, Original Frontplate	195.00
World War I, Helmet, Spike, Brass Mounts, German	39.00
World War I, Helmet, Trench, U.S. Army, Lined, Steel	12.95
World War I, Lantern, Ship, Japanese, Brass	400.00
World War I, Leggings, Leather, Pair	25.00
World War I, Pinback, Captain Eddie Rickenbacker, America's War Ace	10.00
World War I, Poster, Fight Or Buy Bonds, Signed, 1917, 20 X 30 In.	55.00
World War I, Propeller, Plane, Jenny	450.00
World War I, Telephone, Signal Corps, Oak Box, Western Electric Co.	25.00
World War II, Banner, Nazi, 3 1/2 X 10 In.	59.00
World War II, Bayonet, Police, Eagle's Headdress, Bone Grip, Nazi	95.00
World War II, Binoculars, Anti-Aircraft, Sunshades, German, 10 X 80	1500.00
World War II, Blanket, Nazi S.S. Officer's, Wool, Insignia, 92 X 56 In.	275.00
World War II, Buckle, Brass, German	5.00
World War II, Buckle, U.S., General Patton, 2 Piece	15.00
World War II, Bugle, 7th Cavalry Cross Sabers & Letter A, Copper	40.00
World War II, Button, Keep Us Out Of War, 1939, Set Of 24	45.00
World War II, Compass, Airplane, Liquid Filled, Japanese	35.00
World War II, Compass, Army, Pouch	20.00
World War II, Cup, Feeder, Red Cross	22.00
World War II, Dagger, Fighting, 7 In.Blade	35.00
World War II, Dagger, Luftwaffe Officer's, 1937	195.00
World War II, Dagger, Nazi Officer's Dress, Luftwaffe	125.00
World War II, Flag, Nazi, Garrison Size, Swastika In Center, 24 X 8 Feet	400.00
World War II, Flag, Nazi, 17 1/2 X 31 In.	45.00
World War II, Flag, Nazi, 30 X 24 1/2 In.	28.50
World War II, Flag, Silk, Japanese, 38 X 27 In.	40.00
World War II, Frame, Crossed Guns At Bottom, Brass, Oval, 5 1/2 In.	12.00
World War II, Gas Mask, Canvas	5.00
World War II, Gun, Flare	35.00
World War II, Helmet, Outlined With Fur, R.A.F.	14.95
World War II, Helmet, Steel, German	20.00

World War II, Helmet, Tank, With Head-Phone	35.00
World War II, Helmet, Tanker's, Japanese, 5 Point Star, Fasteners	59.50
World War II, Helmet, Trench, Nazi Army, Leather Liner, Pair	29.50
World War II, Hotplate, Silver, Asbestos Insert, On Chain, Nazi, Set Of 3	200.00
World War II, Navy, Shirt, Eagle Insignia	3.50
World War II, Plate, Liberty Bell Center, 6 Pictures On Border, 10 In.	40.00
World War II, Poster, Keep Him Free, 36 X 24 In.	35.00
World War II, Receiver, Radio, U.S. Army Signal Corps, No.Bc-342-M	185.00
World War II, Ribbon, Picture Of Plane Downed In Flames, German, 16 In.	18.50
World War II, Ring, Skull, Cross Bones, Nazi S.S., Marked, 800 Silver	95.00
World War II, Sword & Scabbard, Japanese Police Officer's, Brass Hilt	74.50
World War II, Sword & Scabbard, Japanese Samurai, Navy, 27 In.	110.00
World War II, Uniform, Red Cross, 7 Piece	35.00
World's Fair, Bookmark, 1939, Figural, Planters Peanuts	6.00
World's Fair, Fan, Hand, 1876 International Exposition, Philadelphia	46.00
World's Fair, Teapot, 1939, New York	48.00
World's Fair, 1933, Truck, Metal, In Box, Tootsietoy	20.00
Yellowware, Bedpan	15.00
Yellowware, Bowl, Banded, Nest Of 3	75.00
Yellowware, Bowl, Irregular Shape, Blue Band, 9 1/2 In.Diameter	38.00
Yellowware, Bowl, Mixing, Brown & White Stripes, 6 X 12 1/2 In.Diameter	30.00
Yellowware, Bowl, Mocha Design, 9 In.	130.00
Yellowware, Bowl, Tan & White Stripes, 14 3/4 X 7 In.	40.00
Yellowware, Crock, Butter, Brown Bands	35.00
Yellowware, Dish, Cream, 10 In.Diameter	25.00
Yellowware, Jar, Covered, 6 X 7 In.Diameter	30.00
Yellowware, Jar, White Stripes, Covered, 4 3/4 X 6 3/8 In.	35.00
Yellowware, Mold, Vintage Pattern	25.00
Yellowware, Pitcher, White & Brown Stripes, 5 5/8 In.	30.00
Yellowware, Plate, Pie, 10 1/2 In.	24.00
Yellowware, Pot, Chamber, White Band, 8 X 2 1/4 In.	7.00
Yellowware, Sugar, White Bands, Large	60.00

Zane Pottery was founded in 1921 by Adam, Reed, and
McClelland in South Zanesville, Ohio. It was sold in 1941   ZANE WARE

Zane, see also Peters & Reed

Zane, Bowl, Land-Sun Glaze, 2 1/4 X 6 In.	15.00
Zane, Jug, 2 Handle, Brown Glaze, Cavalier Heads	70.00
Zane, Pitcher, Water, Brown Glaze, Cavalier Heads	70.00
Zane, Vase, Scenic, 9 In.	95.00

LA MORO   *Zanesville Art Pottery was founded in 1900 by David Schmidt in*
Zanesville, Ohio. The firm made faience, umbrella stands, jardinieres, and
pedestals. It worked until 1962.

Zanesville Pottery, Bowl, Bulb, 3 X 8 In.	20.00
ZS Bavaria, Hatpin Holder, Red Roses	30.00
ZS Bavaria, Relish, Flowers, 13 In.	15.50
ZS Bavaria, Vase, Portrait, Queen Louise, Brown Ground, 11 In.	95.00

Zsolnay pottery was made in Hungary after 1862, and was characterized
by Persian, Art Nouveau, or Hungarian motifs.

Zsolnay, Basket, Handled, 9 X 11 In.	65.00
Zsolnay, Bowl, Iridescent, Late 1800s, Impressed Zsolnay Pecs, 6 1/2 In.	350.00
Zsolnay, Bowl, Reticulated, Pink Roses, Pastel Leaves	50.00
Zsolnay, Box, Covered, Round, Warriors & Horses, Metallic Glaze, Steeple Mark	175.00
Zsolnay, Box, Warriors & Horses, Round, Covered, Old Steeple Mark	175.00
Zsolnay, Cup & Saucer, Reticulated Wall On Rim Of Cup & Saucer	60.00
Zsolnay, Figurine, Bird, 5 1/2 In.	125.00
Zsolnay, Figurine, Deer, Legs Tucked Under Stomach, Signed, 4 1/2 X 5 In.	150.00
Zsolnay, Figurine, Duck Sitting By Pond, Gold & Blue Iridescent, 3 X 6 In.	115.00
Zsolnay, Figurine, Fox, Metallic Green Luster, 5 1/2 X 4 1/2 In.	95.00
Zsolnay, Figurine, Frog, Iridescent, Signed	15.00
Zsolnay, Figurine, Girl Feeding Hen, Iridescent, Signed	15.00
Zsolnay, Figurine, Girl With Basket, Iridescent, Signed	15.00
Zsolnay, Figurine, Owl, Green Iridescent Luster Glaze, 3 In.	65.00
Zsolnay, Figurine, Owl, Iridescent, Signed	15.00

Worcester, Jug, Mask,
Blue Scale, C.1765, 8 7/8 In.

(See Page 679)

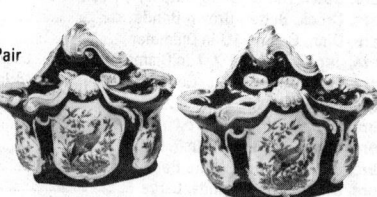

Worcester, Butter Cooler
& Cover, C.1758, 5 3/8 In.

(See Page 679)

Worcester, Pot, Bough, Blue Scale, Pair

(See Page 680)

Zsolnay, Vase, Matiyasousky, C.1900

Zsolnay, Figurine, Seated Girl, Iridescent, Signed	15.00
Zsolnay, Tumbler, Bacchanalian, Green Iridescence, 7 In.	59.00
Zsolnay, Vase, Art Deco, Signed, 13 3/4 In.	185.00
Zsolnay, Vase, Banjo, Double, Reticulated, Arabesque Design, 12 In.	250.00
Zsolnay, Vase, Female Figures, 1920s, 6 In.	85.00
Zsolnay, Vase, Gold Scrolling, Reticulated Medallions, 13 1/2 In.	185.00
Zsolnay, Vase, Iridescent Green, Dancing Nudes, 7 In.	59.00
Zsolnay, Vase, Leaf Decoration, Bulbous, Gold Rim, White, Small	97.50
Zsolnay, Vase, Matiyasousky, C.1900	Illus 800.00
Zsolnay, Vase, Polychrome, Reticulated & Applied Leaf Design, Signed, Pair	325.00
Zsolnay, Vase, Red Iridescent, Alligator Skin Texture, 5 3/4 In.	185.00
Zsolnay, Vase, 5 Semi-Nudes Holding Goblets, 7 In.	75.00